THE CANADIAN PRO FOOTBALL ENCYCLOPEDIA

BY

TOD MAHER AND BOB GILL

MSM

Published by Maher Sports Media

ISBN 978-0-9835136-3-6

Cover design by Mark Durr

Front cover photo: Game action from the 99th Grey Cup between the Winnipeg Blue Bombers and the BC Lions on November 27, 2011 at BC Place Stadium in Vancouver

2 4 6 8 10 9 7 5 3 1

www.profootballencyclopedia.com
www.profootballarchives.com
www.facebook.com/mahersportsmedia

Dedicated to Joe Cronin, without whose support
and enthusiasm this book would not have been undertaken.

OTHER BOOKS BY TOD MAHER AND BOB GILL

THE PRO FOOTBALL ENCYCLOPEDIA

THE PRO FOOTBALL PLAYOFF ENCYCLOPEDIA

OUTSIDERS

OUTSIDERS II
With Steve Brainerd

BY TOD MAHER

WORLD FOOTBALL LEAGUE ENCYCLOPEDIA
With Mark Speck

BY BOB GILL

PRO FOOTBALL TRIVIA

A MINOR MASTERPIECE

THE CANADIAN PRO FOOTBALL ENCYCLOPEDIA

INTRODUCTION

Welcome to the second edition of *The Canadian Pro Football Encyclopedia.* Like last year's groundbreaking first edition, this book represents nearly two decades of research.

What's new in this edition?

Not only has it been updated to include the 2011 season, but we have added a section on the annual college player draft and some 18 new statistical categories to the player and statistical registers.

The heart of the encyclopedia is the Player Register, which contains the biographical and main statistical record of every player to have stepped on the field since 1946 is being presented. New to this edition are forced fumbles, sack yards, interception yards, pass knowdowns (also known as passes defensed), plus average and long gains for rushing, receiving, punt return and kickoff returns.

Also, new to this edition is The Passing Register. Here you find all the stats presented in last year's edition, plus new ones such as completion percentage, average gain, long gain and times sacked.

The kicking and punting statistics are listed separately in The Kickers Register.

But there are other sections, which help round out the rich history of the Canadian Football League.

The Game Scores lists the dates, locations, score and attendance for every regular season and playoff game played since 1946.

The Grey Cup section records every Grey Cup matchup since the first game in 1907.

The Awards presents not only the annual all-star teams, but also all other annual player awards and the complete membership list of the Canadian Football Hall of Fame.

The Head Coaches presents the biographical and coaching records of every individual who has been given of the reins of a CFL team since 1946.

There is also a special section that is dedicated the Ontario Rugby Football Union (ORFU), which competed for the Grey Cup trophy through the 1954 season.

The yearly final standings, and team statistics are located in The Annual Record. The top career, single-season and single-game statistical performers are found in The Leaders.

ACKNOWLEDGEMENTS

A project of this size could not have been undertaken by the authors without the help of several of the several individuals. Much of the information found in these pages would simply not exist without their invaluable contributions.

Joe Cronin has assisted us on nearly every other book project and this volume is no exception. Without his vast collection of record manuals and media guides, the database which makes up this book would be severely lacking and we would have never have contemplated even an attempt at such a project. Our deepest thanks go out to Joe.

Steve Daniel, the head statistician of the Canadian Football League since 2008, is another person who made this book possible. Steve has not only undertaken the task in rectifying years of neglect to the league's records, but he has graciously allowed us to contribute to his efforts. He in turn has made his records available to us, for which we are very grateful.

Others from the Canadian Football League and its member teams that have been of assistance to us are Larry Robertson, former league statistician and currently head of research for the CFL; Eric Forest, public relations director of the Montreal Alouettes; Darryl Slade, head statistician of the Calgary Stampeders; and Mike Morreale of the Canadian Football League Players Association.

Other important contributions came from Michael Lemengello, Jerry Parker, Grant Lederhouse, Jeff Marcus, Brian Marshall, Steve Brainerd, Aaron Kramer and Don Logan.

The authors and many of this book's contributors are members of the Professional Football Association (PFRA), which is an invaluable source to anyone writing or researching the history of professional football. We would also like to thank the Canadian Football Research Society (CFRS) and its members.

The cover that graces this book was conceived and designed by Mark Durr.

And finally, a very special thank you to Marilyn for her support and patience.

1861 – The first known game is played at the University of Toronto.

1869 – The Hamilton Football Club is formed.

1872 – The Montreal Football Club is formed.

1873 – The Toronto Argonaut Rowing Club forms the Toronto Argonaut Football Club.

1876 – The Ottawa Football Club.

1879 – The Winnipeg Football Club is formed.

1883 – The Ontario Rugby Football Union (ORFU) and the Quebec Rugby Football Union (QRFU) are formed.

1891- The Canadian Rugby Union (CRU) is formed. ORFU rules are adopted by the CRU.

1892 – Manitoba Rugby Football Union is formed. Osgoode Hall defeats Montreal Football Club 45-5 on Thanksgiving Day in the first CRU championship game.

1896 – Size of field (110 yards by 65) is established by the CRU.

1903 – ORFU reduces size of teams from 15 to 12 players per side, institutes the center snap, requires teams to gain 10 yard in three downs, abolished the throw-in. CRU and QRFU reduces number of players on field to 14 per side.

1904 – Value of a touchdown increased from four to five points.

1907 – Interprovincial Rugby Football Union (IRFU, The Big Four) is formed. Members are the Hamilton Tigers, Toronto Argonauts, Ottawa Rough Riders and the Montreal Football Club. QRFU withdraws from senior competition. Calgary City Rugby Football Club and Edmonton City Rugby Football Club are formed.

1909 – The fourth Earl of Grey, Albert Henry George, donates a trophy for the rugby football championship of Canada. Only CRU members are eligible to compete for the Grey Cup. University of Toronto defeats the Toronto Parkdale Canoe Club 26-6 for the first Grey Cup title on December 4th. Hamilton Tigers defeat the Ottawa Rough Riders 16-6 on December 11th in New York in the first Canadian football game played in the United States.

1910 – The Regina Rugby Club.

1911 – The Alberta, Manitoba and Saskatchewan rugby football unions form the Western Canada Rugby Football Union on October 2st. Winnipeg realtor Higo Ross donates a trophy for the WCRFU championship. The Calgary Tigers win the first WCRFU championship and challenge for the Grey Cup. Challenge is declined by the CRU because WCRFU is not a full member of the CRU.

1916 – No games are played for the next three years due to the First World War.

1919 – Play resumes after the end of the First World War.

1921 – The WCRFU joins the CRU.

1926 – The British Columbia Rugby Football Union (BCRFU) is formed.

1929 – Use of the forward pass is allowed on WCRFU play and the Grey Cup.

1930 – Winnipegs Rugby Football Club is formed.

1936 – The Western Interprovincial Football Union (WIFU) is formed by Calgary, Regina and Winnipeg. Intercollegiate teams stop competing for the Grey Cup.

1937 – The QRFU stops challenging for the Grey Cup title.

1938 – The Edmonton Eskimos join the WIFU.

1939 – The Second World War begins.

1941 – The IRFU is temporarily dissolved. In its place the Eastern Canada Rugby Football Union (ECRFU) is formed. Calgary withdraws from the WIFU.

1942- The ECRFU and WIFU suspend operations due to the Second World War. Service teams take their place in competing for the Grey Cup.

1944 – Service teams are barred from challenging for the Grey Cup.

1945 – The Calgary Stampeders are formed. The IRFU resumes play. The WCRFU conducts a series of playoff games to determine the western championship.

1946 – The WIFU is reformed on Aprill 21 at a meeting in Calgary. The modern, post-war era begins. The Montreal Alouettes are formed. The Regina Roughriders are are renamed the Saskatchewan Roughriders on May 31.

1948 – The Hamilton Tigers of the IRFU and the Hamilton Wildcats of the ORFU switch leagues.

1949 – Edmonton rejoins the EIFU. The WCRFU is dissolved.

2 HISTORICAL HIGHLIGHTS

1950 – The Hamilton Tigers and the Hamilton Wildcats merge to form the Hamilton Tiger-Cats. The Tigers-Cats will compete in the IRFU. The WIFU keeps official statistics for the first time.

1952 – The IRFU conducts the first draft of Canadian intercollegiate players. Choices are the limited to players from, the four-team Intercollegiate Rugby Football Union (McGill, Ottawa, Toronto and Western Ontario). The CRU receives $7,500 from the CBC for the rights to broadcast the Grey Cup game.

1954 – The British Columbia Lions begin play in the WIFU. The ORFU challenge for the Grey Cup for the final time, with the Kitchener-Waterloo Dutchmen losing to Edmonton 38-6 in the semi-final on November 20. The IRFU keeps official statistics for the first time.

1956 – The Canadian Football Council (CFC) is formed. Negotiation lists are introduced. The value of a touchdown is increased from five to six points.

1958 – The CFC withdraws from the CRU. The CFC then renames itself the Canadian Football League, though the IRFU and WIFU will still play separate schedules of different lengths. The CFL does gain control of the Grey Cup.

1960 – The IRFU changes its name to the Eastern Football Conference.

1961 – The WIFU changes its name to the Western Football Conference. For the first time "interlocking" regular season games are played between EFC and WFC teams.

1965 – The Canadian Football League Players Association is formed.

1974 – The EFC and WFC both play a 16-game schedule.

1981 –The Eastern and Western conferences are renamed the Eastern and Western Divisions.

1982 – The Montreal Alouettes are renamed the Concordes.

1986 – The CFL adopts an 18-game schedule. The Montreal Concordes change their nickname back to the Alouettes. The depth of the end zones is reduced from 25 yards to 20.

1987 – The Montreal Alouettes fold on June 23, two days before their scheduled regular opener at Toronto. Winnipeg is moved to the Eastern Division.

1993- - The Sacramento Gold Miners are awarded a franchise on February 23 and become the first American-based franchise in CFL history. Sacramento will compete in the Western Division. They will not have any import restrictions and will not participate in the Canadian college draft.

1994 – Three additional American teams are formed. The Las Vegas Posse will compete in the Western Division and the Baltimore Football Club and the Shreveport Pirates will compete in the Eastern Division.

1995 – The Las Vegas Posse team folds. Two other American teams, the Birmingham Barracudas and the Memphis Mad Dogs join the CFL. The league is realigned into entirely new division – North and South. The North Division will have all eight Canadian teams and the South Division will be comprised of the five American teams.

1996 – Four of the five US-based teams fold. The lone survivor, the Baltimore Stallions are moved to Montreal and rechristened the Alouettes. The league is once again realigned into two new divisions – the East and West. The two divisions consist of their traditional members. The players from the four failed franchises are placed in a dispersal draft.

1997 - The Ottawa Rough Riders fold, once again leaving the CFL with only eight teams. The Ottawa players are placed in a dispersal draft and Winnipeg is moved into the East Division.

2002 – An expansion franchise is awarded to Ottawa. The Renegades will join the East Division and Winnipeg moves back to the West.

2006 – After just four seasons in operation, the Ottawa Renegades folded.

2008 – An expansion franchise is awarded to Jeff Hunt, on the condition a suitable stadium is built in Ottawa. The team is tentatively slated to officially join the league in 2013.

There are seven columns for each game.

The first column is the day of the week the game was played on.

The second column is the date of the game, expressed in the month/ day format.

The third column indicates whether it was an away game (A), a home game (H) or played at a neutral (N) site.

The fourth column gives the opponent for the game. The following abbreviations are used in this column:

BAL	Baltimore Stallions
BC	British Columbia Lions
BIR	Birmingham Barracudas
CAL	Calgary Stampeders
EDM	Edmonton Eskimos
HAM	Hamilton Tigers Hamilton Wildcats Hamilton Tiger-Cats (1950-)
HMT	Hamilton Tigers (ORFU)
KW	Kitchener-Waterloo Dutchmen (ORFU)
LV	Las Vegas Posse
MEM	Memphis Mad Dogs
MTL	Montreal Alouettes (1946-1981) Montreal Concordes (1982-1985) Montreal Alouettes (1986; 1996-)
OTR	Ottawa Trojans (ORFU)
OTT	Ottawa Rough Riders (1946-) Ottawa Renegades (2002-2005)
SA	San Antonio Texans
SAC	Sacramento Gold Miners
SAR	Sarnia Imperials (ORFU)
SAS	Saskatchewan Roughriders
SHR	Shreveport Pirates
TBB	Toronto Balmy Beach (ORFU)
TOR	Toronto Argonauts
WPG	Winnipeg Blue Bombers

The fifth column is the score of the game. An * indicates overtime.

The sixth column gives the result of the game for that team. A win is indicated by a W, a loss by an L and a tie by a T.

The seventh column gives the attendance for that game.

THE STADIUMS

Team	Years	Location	Stadium
Baltimore Stallions	1994-1995	Baltimore, MD	Memorial Stadium
British Columbia Lions	1954-1982/2010	Vancouver, BC	Empire Stadium
	1983-2009	Vancouver, BC	B.C. Place Stadium
	2011	Vancouver, BC	Empire Stadium
	2011	Vancouver, BC	B.C. Place Stadium (Sept. 30 to Nov. 5)
Birmingham Barracudas	1995	Birmingham, AL	Legion Field
Calgary Stampeders	1946-1959	Calgary, AB	Mewata Stadium
	1960-2011	Calgary, AB	McMahon Stadium
Edmonton Eskimos	1949-1978	Edmonton, AB	Joseph A. Clarke Memorial Stadium (to Aug. 1)
	1978-2011	Edmonton, AB	Commonwealth Stadium
Hamilton Tigers	1946-1947	Hamilton, ON	Ivor Wynne Stadium
	1947	Hamilton, ON	Civic Stadium (Nov. 8)
Hamilton Wildcats	1948-1949	Hamilton, ON	Ivor Wynne Stadium
Hamilton Tiger-Cats	1950	Hamilton, ON	Civic Stadium (Oct. 14 and Nov. 11)
	1950-2011	Hamilton, ON	Ivor Wynne Stadium
	2011	Moncton, NB	Stade Moncton Stadium (Sept. 25)
Las Vegas Posse	1994	Las Vegas, NV	Silver Bowl
Memphis Mad Dogs	1995	Memphis, TN	Liberty Bowl
Montreal Alouettes	1946-1955	Montreal, QC	Delorimer Downs
	1954	Montreal, QC	Molson Stadium (Nov. 20)
	1956-1967	Montreal, QC	McGill Stadium
	1968-1971/1973-1976	Montreal, QC	Autostade
	1972	Montreal, QC	Molson Stadium
	1977-1981/1986	Montreal, QC	Olympic Stadium
	1996-2011	Montreal, QC	Percival Molson Stadium
	2002-2011	Montreal, QC	Olympic Stadium (Oct. 23, 2004, Oct. 22, 2005, Nov. 21, and all playoff games)
Montreal Concordes	1982-1985	Montreal, QC	Olympic Stadium
Ottawa Rough Riders	1948-1992	Ottawa, ON	Landsdowne Park
	1993-1996	Ottawa, ON	Frank Clair Stadium
Ottawa Renegades	2002-2005	Ottawa, ON	Frank Clair Stadiun
San Antonio Texans	1995	San Antonio, TX	Alamodome
Sacramento Gold Miners	1993-1994	Sacramento, CA	Hornet Field
Saskatchewan Roughriders	1946	Regina, SK	Campion Grounds (Oct. 14)
	1946-2006	Regina, SK	Taylor Field
	2007-2011	Regina, SK	Mosaic Stadium
Shreveport Pirates	1994-1995	Shreveport, LA	Independence Stadium
Toronto Argonauts	1946	Toronto, ON	Oakwood Stadium (to Sept. 21)
	1946-1958	Toronto, ON	Varsity Stadium
	1959-1988	Toronto, ON	Exhibition Stadium
	1989-2005	Toronto, ON	SkyDome
	2006-2011	Toronto, ON	Rogers Centre
Winnipeg Blue Bombers	1946-1952	Winnipeg, MB	Osborne Stadium
	1953-2000	Winnipeg, MB	Winnipeg Stadium
	2001-2011	Winnipeg, MB	Canad Inns Stadium

4 THE GAME SCORES

1946 CALGARY STAMPEDERS

Sat	8/31	H	SAS	9- 0	W	4500
Sat	9/7	A	SAS	6- 0	W	3500
Mon	9/9	A	WPG	3- 1	W	5000
Mon	9/16	H	WPG	5- 13	L	5000
Sat	9/21	H	SAS	19- 7	W	
Sat	10/5	A	SAS	9- 10	L	2000
Mon	10/7	A	WPG	3- 6	L	3000
Sat	10/12	H	WPG	6- 0	W	3000
WIFU Final (21-30)						
Sat	10/26	H	WPG	21- 18	W	4000
Sat	11/2	A	WPG	0- 12	L	5600

1946 HAMILTON TIGERS

Sat	9/7	H	OTT	17- 34	L	7000
Sat	9/14	A	TOR	8- 31	L	7600
Sat	9/21	H	MTL	1- 24	L	5500
Wed	9/25	H	TOR	15- 15	T	6200
Sun	9/29	A	MTL	6- 21	L	13522
Sat	10/5	A	TOR	0- 22	L	15000
Sat	10/12	A	OTT	6- 6	T	4000
Mon	10/14	H	TOR	2- 7	L	7000
Fri	10/18	H	MTL	0- 19	L	3000
Sun	10/27	A	MTL	16- 21	L	13500
Sat	11/2	H	OTT	1- 11	L	
Sat	11/9	A	OTT	6- 23	L	8000

MONTREAL ALOUETTES

Sat	9/7	A	TOR	10- 10	T	9000
Sat	9/14	A	OTT	0- 4	L	10000
Sat	9/21	A	HAM	24- 1	W	5500
Sun	9/29	H	HAM	21- 6	W	13522
Sat	10/5	A	OTT	14- 24	L	10000
Sun	10/6	H	OTT	23- 23	T	12500
Sat	10/12	H	TOR	28- 6	W	8000
Fri	10/18	A	HAM	19- 0	W	3000
Sun	10/20	H	OTT	25- 15	W	17308
Sun	10/27	H	HAM	21- 16	W	13500
Sat	11/2	H	TOR	8- 9	L	12200
Sat	11/9	A	TOR	18- 4	W	19500
IRFU Final						
Sat	11/16	H	TOR	6- 12	L	21800

1946 OTTAWA ROUGH RIDERS

Sat	9/7	A	HAM	34- 17	W	7000
Sat	9/14	H	MTL	4- 0	W	10000
Sat	9/21	A	TOR	12- 13	L	8500
Sat	9/28	H	TOR	6- 12	L	12000
Sat	10/5	H	MTL	24- 14	W	10000
Sun	10/6	A	MTL	23- 23	T	12500
Sat	10/12	H	HAM	6- 6	T	4000
Sat	10/19	A	TOR	12- 3	W	17000
Sun	10/20	A	MTL	15- 25	L	17308
Sat	10/26	H	TOR	5- 8	L	12000
Sat	11/2	A	HAM	11- 1	W	
Sat	11/9	H	HAM	23- 6	W	8000

1946 SASKATCHEWAN ROUGHRIDERS

Sat	8/31	A	CAL	0- 9	L	4500
Sat	9/7	H	CAL	0- 6	L	3500
Sat	9/14	H	WPG	11- 17	L	3000
Sat	9/21	A	CAL	7- 19	L	
Sat	9/28	A	WPG	0- 6	L	5000
Sat	10/5	H	CAL	10- 9	W	2000
Mon	10/14	H	WPG	0- 9	L	200
Sat	10/19	A	WPG	18- 17	W	3000

1946 TORONTO ARGONAUTS

Sat	9/7	H	MTL	10- 10	T	9000
Sat	9/14	H	HAM	31- 8	W	7600
Sat	9/21	H	OTT	13- 12	W	8500
Wed	9/25	A	HAM	15- 15	T	6200
Sat	9/28	A	OTT	12- 6	W	12000
Sat	10/5	H	HAM	22- 0	W	15000
Sat	10/12	A	MTL	6- 28	L	8000
Mon	10/14	A	HAM	7- 2	W	7000
Sat	10/19	H	OTT	3- 12	L	17000
Sat	10/26	A	OTT	8- 5	W	12000
Sat	11/2	A	MTL	9- 8	W	12200
Sat	11/9	H	MTL	4- 18	L	19500
IRFU Final						
Sat	11/16	A	MTL	12- 6	W	21800
Eastern Final						
Sat	11/23	H	TORB	22- 12	W	19960
Grey Cup						
Sat	11/30	H	WPG	28- 6	W	19500

1946 WINNIPEG BLUE BOMBERS

Mon	9/9	H	CAL	1- 3	L	5000
Sat	9/14	A	SAS	17- 11	W	3000
Mon	9/16	A	CAL	13- 5	W	5000
Sat	9/28	H	SAS	6- 0	W	5000
Mon	10/7	H	CAL	6- 3	W	3000
Sat	10/12	A	CAL	0- 6	L	3000
Mon	10/14	A	SAS	9- 0	W	200
Sat	10/19	H	SAS	17- 18	L	3000
WIFU Final (30-21)						
Sat	10/26	A	CAL	18- 21	L	4000
Sat	11/2	H	CAL	12- 0	W	5600
Grey Cup						
Sat	11/30	A	TOR	6- 28	L	19500

1947 CALGARY STAMPEDERS

Mon	9/8	H	WPG	11- 13	L	4000
Sat	9/13	H	SAS	16- 11	W	3000
Sat	9/27	A	SAS	7- 12	L	4000
Mon	9/29	A	WPG	0- 16	L	5000
Mon	10/6	H	SAS	9- 8	W	3000
Sat	10/11	H	WPG	25- 13	W	3000
Sat	10/25	A	SAS	6- 5	W	5000
Mon	10/27	A	WPG	5- 15	L	4000
WIFU Final (22-29)						
Sat	11/1	A	WPG	4- 16	L	6200
Sat	11/11	H	WPG	15- 3	W	3500
Sat	11/15	A	WPG	3- 10	L	6000

1947 HAMILTON TIGERS

Sat	9/13	H	OTT	2- 8	L	12000
Wed	9/17	H	TOR	25- 34	L	12000
Sat	9/20	A	TOR	0- 2	L	13000
Sat	9/27	H	MTL	11- 7	W	8500
Sun	9/28	A	MTL	9- 20	L	14255
Sat	10/4	A	OTT	12- 33	L	10000
Sat	10/11	H	TOR	1- 13	L	8500
Mon	10/13	A	TOR	6- 6	T	15000
Sat	10/18	A	OTT	8- 13	L	9089
Sun	10/26	H	OTT	14- 8	W	7500
Sun	11/2	A	MTL	12- 33	L	10624
Sat	11/8	H	MTL	19- 27	L	5000

1947 MONTREAL ALOUETTES

Sat	9/13	A	TOR	15- 7	W	14000
Sat	9/20	A	OTT	23- 28	L	12000
Sun	9/21	H	OTT	3- 8	L	19102
Sat	9/27	A	HAM	7- 11	L	8500
Sun	9/28	H	HAM	20- 9	W	14255
Sat	10/4	H	TOR	6- 10	L	13400
Sat	10/11	A	OTT	7- 1	W	9586
Sun	10/12	H	OTT	3- 22	L	14000
Sat	10/18	A	TOR	3- 25	L	16000
Sat	10/25	H	TOR	17- 12	W	8600
Sun	11/2	H	HAM	33- 12	W	10624
Sat	11/8	A	HAM	27- 19	W	5000

1947 OTTAWA ROUGH RIDERS

Sat	9/6	H	TOR	23- 6	W	12000
Sat	9/13	A	HAM	8- 2	W	12000
Sat	9/20	H	MTL	28- 23	W	12000
Sun	9/21	A	MTL	8- 3	W	19102
Sat	9/27	A	TOR	0- 8	L	19000
Sat	10/4	H	HAM	33- 12	W	10000
Sat	10/11	H	MTL	1- 7	L	9586
Sun	10/12	A	MTL	22- 3	W	14000
Sat	10/18	H	HAM	13- 8	W	9089
Sun	10/26	A	HAM	8- 14	L	7500
Sat	11/1	A	TOR	15- 5	W	16000
Sat	11/8	H	TOR	11- 12	L	8500
IRFU Final (0-24)						
Tue	11/11	H	TOR	0- 3	L	10000
Sat	11/15	A	TOR	0- 21	L	19500

1947 SASKTACHEWAN ROUGHRIDERS

Sat	9/6	H	WPG	5- 6	L	4000
Sat	9/13	A	CAL	11- 16	L	3000
Sat	9/27	H	CAL	12- 7	W	4000
Sat	10/4	A	WPG	1- 13	L	4000
Mon	10/6	A	CAL	8- 9	L	3000
Mon	10/13	H	WPG	27- 6	W	4000
Sat	10/18	A	WPG	9- 1	W	4000
Sat	10/25	H	CAL	5- 6	L	5000

1947 TORONTO ARGONAUTS

Sat	9/6	A	OTT	6- 23	L	12000
Sat	9/13	H	MTL	7- 15	L	14000
Wed	9/17	A	HAM	34- 25	W	12000
Sat	9/20	H	HAM	2- 0	W	13000
Sat	9/27	H	OTT	8- 0	W	19000
Sat	10/4	A	MTL	10- 6	W	13400
Sat	10/11	A	HAM	13- 1	W	8500
Mon	10/13	H	HAM	6- 6	T	15000
Sat	10/18	H	MTL	25- 3	W	16000
Sat	10/25	A	MTL	12- 17	L	8600
Sat	11/1	H	OTT	5- 15	L	16000
Sat	11/8	A	OTT	12- 11	W	8500
IRFU Final (24-0)						
Tue	11/11	A	OTT	3- 0	W	10000
Sat	11/15	H	OTT	21- 0	W	19500
Eastern Final						
Sat	11/22	H	OTTT	22- 1	W	16000

1947 WINNIPEG BLUE BOMBERS

Sat	9/6	A	SAS	6- 5	W	4000
Mon	9/8	A	CAL	13- 11	W	4000
Mon	9/29	H	CAL	16- 0	W	5000
Sat	10/4	H	SAS	13- 1	W	4000
Sat	10/11	A	CAL	13- 25	L	3000
Mon	10/13	A	SAS	6- 27	L	4000
Sat	10/18	H	SAS	1- 9	L	4000
Mon	10/27	H	CAL	15- 5	W	4000
WIFU Final (29-22)						
Sat	11/1	H	CAL	16- 4	W	6200
Sat	11/11	A	CAL	3- 15	L	3500
Sat	11/15	H	CAL	10- 3	W	6000
Grey Cup						
Sat	11/29	A	TOR	9- 10	L	18885

1948 CALGARY STAMPEDERS

Wed	8/25	H	SAS	12- 1	W	4500
Mon	8/30	H	WPG	30- 0	W	5000
Fri	9/3	A	WPG	10- 5	W	6000
Mon	9/6	A	SAS	14- 8	W	6000
Mon	9/13	H	WPG	18- 0	W	7200
Sat	9/25	H	SAS	13- 12	W	7000
Sat	10/2	A	SAS	12- 11	W	5500
Mon	10/4	A	WPG	26- 6	W	7000
Sat	10/9	H	WPG	35- 3	W	7000
Sat	10/16	A	SAS	8- 7	W	5000
Mon	10/18	A	WPG	21- 8	W	4000
Sat	10/23	H	SAS	19- 0	W	7000
WIFU Final (21-10)						
Sat	11/6	A	SAS	4- 4	T	7000
Thu	11/11	H	SAS	17- 6	W	10000
Grey Cup						
Sat	11/27	N	OTT	12- 7	W	20013

1948 HAMILTON WILDCATS

Sat	9/4	A	OTT	5- 30	L	11000
Mon	9/6	H	TOR	7- 14	L	12000
Sat	9/11	A	TOR	13- 25	L	12000
Wed	9/15	H	MTL	13- 12	W	12000
Tue	9/28	A	MTL	6- 36	L	9000
Sat	10/2	H	OTT	6- 26	L	7000
Sat	10/9	A	TOR	7- 9	L	12000
Mon	10/11	H	TOR	8- 8	T	4500
Sun	10/17	A	MTL	1- 19	L	4500
Sat	10/23	H	OTT	8- 17	L	4000
Sat	10/30	A	OTT	5- 18	L	8704
Sat	11/6	H	MTL	9- 26	L	4000

1948 MONTREAL ALOUETTES

Tue	8/31	H	OTT	18- 36	L	11000
Sat	9/4	A	TOR	7- 20	L	12500
Sat	9/11	A	OTT	11- 8	W	11000
Wed	9/15	A	HAM	12- 13	L	12000
Tue	9/28	H	HAM	36- 6	W	9000
Sat	10/2	H	TOR	17- 8	W	10000
Sat	10/9	A	OTT	7- 17	L	11000
Sun	10/17	H	HAM	19- 1	W	4500
Sat	10/23	A	TOR	22- 17	W	14000
Sun	10/24	H	OTT	35- 13	W	16000
Sat	10/30	H	TOR	11- 24	L	13500
Sat	11/6	A	HAM	26- 9	W	4000
IRFU Final (28-34)						
Thu	11/11	H	OTT	21- 19	W	15000
Sat	11/13	A	OTT	7- 15	L	14000

1948 OTTAWA ROUGH RIDERS

Tue	8/31	A	MTL	36- 18	W	11000
Sat	9/4	H	HAM	30- 5	W	11000
Sat	9/11	H	MTL	8- 11	L	11000
Sat	9/18	A	TOR	32- 12	W	19500
Sat	9/25	H	TOR	12- 5	W	14158
Sat	10/2	A	HAM	26- 6	W	7000
Sat	10/9	H	MTL	17- 7	W	11000
Sat	10/16	H	TOR	41- 6	W	14000
Sat	10/23	A	HAM	17- 8	W	4000
Sun	10/24	A	MTL	13- 35	L	16000
Sat	10/30	H	HAM	18- 5	W	8704
Sat	11/6	A	TOR	14- 12	W	18000
IRFU Final (34-28)						
Thu	11/11	A	MTL	19- 21	L	15000
Sat	11/13	H	MTL	15- 7	W	14000
Eastern Final						
Sat	11/20	H	HAM	19- 0	W	15000
Grey Cup						
Sat	11/27	N	CAL	7- 12	L	20013

1948 SASKATCHEWAN ROUGHRIDERS

Sat	8/21	A	WPG	17- 6	W	4000
Wed	8/25	A	CAL	1- 12	L	4500
Sat	8/28	H	WPG	13- 14	L	5000
Mon	9/6	H	CAL	8- 14	L	6000
Sat	9/11	H	WPG	13- 16	L	5000
Sat	9/18	A	WPG	9- 15	L	5500
Sat	9/25	A	CAL	12- 13	L	7000
Sat	10/2	H	CAL	11- 12	L	5500
Mon	10/11	H	WPG	26- 1	W	6000
Sat	10/16	H	CAL	7- 8	L	5000
Sat	10/23	A	CAL	0- 19	L	7000
Sat	10/30	A	WPG	16- 7	W	5500
WIFU Final (10-21)						
Sat	11/6	H	CAL	4- 4	T	7000
Thu	11/11	A	CAL	6- 17	L	10000

1948 TORONTO ARGONAUTS

Sat	9/4	H	MTL	20- 7	W	12500
Mon	9/6	A	HAM	14- 7	W	12000
Sat	9/11	H	HAM	25- 13	W	12000
Sat	9/18	H	OTT	12- 32	L	19500
Sat	9/25	A	OTT	5- 12	L	14158
Sat	10/2	A	MTL	8- 17	L	10000
Sat	10/9	H	HAM	9- 7	W	12000
Mon	10/11	A	HAM	8- 8	T	4500
Sat	10/16	A	OTT	6- 41	L	14000
Sat	10/23	H	MTL	17- 22	L	14000
Sat	10/30	A	MTL	24- 1	W	13500
Sat	11/6	H	OTT	12- 14	L	18000

1948 WINNIPEG BLUE BOMBERS

Sat	8/21	H	SAS	6-17	L	4000
Sat	8/28	A	SAS	14-13	W	5000
Mon	8/30	A	CAL	0-30	L	5000
Fri	9/3	H	CAL	5-10	L	6000
Sat	9/11	A	SAS	16-13	W	5000
Mon	9/13	A	CAL	0-18	L	7200
Sat	9/18	H	SAS	15-9	W	5500
Mon	10/4	H	CAL	6-26	L	7000
Sat	10/9	A	CAL	3-35	L	7000
Mon	10/11	A	SAS	1-26	L	6000
Mon	10/18	H	CAL	8-21	L	4000
Sat	10/30	H	SAS	7-16	L	5500

1949 CALGARY STAMPEDERS

Mon	9/5	A	EDM	20-6	W	11123
Sat	9/10	H	SAS	22-19	W	6500
Mon	9/12	H	WPG	32-7	W	7500
Sat	9/17	A	WPG	20-1	W	6700
Mon	9/19	A	SAS	13-1	W	6700
Sat	9/24	H	EDM	41-5	W	9000
Sat	10/1	A	EDM	12-0	W	10000
Sat	10/8	A	SAS	10-3	W	7500
Mon	10/10	A	WPG	3-0	W	2000
Sat	10/15	H	EDM	31-6	W	8000
Sat	10/22	H	SAS	6-9	L	7000
Mon	10/24	H	WPG	22-11	W	5500
Sat	10/29	H	EDM	27-0	W	6700
Mon	10/31	A	EDM	11-1	W	
WIFU Final (22-21)						
Sat	11/5	A	SAS	18-12	W	8000
Fri	11/11	H	SAS	4-9	L	14500
Grey Cup						
Sat	11/26	N	MTL	15-28	L	20087

1949 EDMONTON ESKIMOS

Mon	9/5	H	CAL	6-20	L	11123
Sat	9/10	H	WPG	14-11	W	6500
Mon	9/12	H	SAS	0-12	L	6000
Sat	9/17	A	SAS	1-13	L	4000
Mon	9/19	A	WPG	10-3	W	4000
Sat	9/24	A	CAL	5-41	L	9000
Sat	10/1	H	CAL	8-12	L	10000
Sat	10/8	A	WPG	6-8	L	4000
Mon	10/10	A	SAS	12-11	W	3000
Sat	10/15	A	CAL	6-31	L	8000
Sat	10/22	H	WPG	13-6	W	7000
Mon	10/24	H	SAS	11-29	L	5000
Sat	10/29	A	CAL	0-27	L	6700
Mon	10/31	H	CAL	1-11	L	

1949 HAMILTON WILDCATS

Sat	9/3	A	TOR	18-26	L	12200
Mon	9/5	H	TOR	14-36	L	12000
Sat	9/10	H	MTL	16-38	L	7500
Sat	9/17	A	OTT	12-19	L	8000
Sat	9/24	H	OTT	11-14	L	7000
Sat	10/8	H	TOR	10-11	L	
Mon	10/10	A	TOR	8-29	L	16500
Sat	10/15	H	OTT	7-12	L	5000
Sun	10/16	A	MTL	16-29	L	14000
Sat	10/22	H	MTL	6-22	L	5000
Sun	10/30	A	MTL	18-29	L	15000
Sat	11/5	A	OTT	11-19	L	9000

1949 MONTREAL ALOUETTES

Sat	8/27	H	OTT	6-7	L	14958
Sat	9/3	A	OTT	21-22	L	16000
Sat	9/10	A	HAM	38-16	W	7500
Sat	9/17	A	TOR	24-11	W	19000
Sat	9/24	H	TOR	14-29	L	16000
Sat	10/8	A	OTT	20-19	W	14000
Sun	10/9	H	OTT	33-42	L	20000
Sat	10/15	A	TOR	24-16	W	19000
Sun	10/16	H	HAM	29-16	W	14000
Sat	10/22	A	HAM	22-6	W	5000
Sun	10/30	H	HAM	29-18	W	15000
Sat	11/5	H	TOR	35-2	W	6729
IRFU Final (36-20)						
Wed	11/9	H	OTT	22-7	W	15272
Sat	11/12	A	OTT	14-13	W	17000
Eastern Final						
Sat	11/19	H	HMT	40-0	W	15000
Grey Cup						
Sat	11/26	N	CAL	28-15	W	20087

1949 OTTAWA ROUGH RIDERS

Sat	8/27	A	MTL	7-6	W	14958
Sat	9/3	H	MTL	22-21	W	16000
Sat	9/10	A	TOR	19-1	W	19000
Sat	9/17	H	HAM	19-12	W	8000
Sat	9/24	A	HAM	14-11	W	7000
Sat	10/1	H	TOR	34-11	W	16424
Sat	10/8	H	MTL	19-20	L	14000
Sun	10/9	A	MTL	42-33	W	20000
Sat	10/15	A	HAM	12-7	W	5000
Sat	10/22	A	TOR	24-13	W	19000
Sat	10/29	H	TOR	30-24	W	15000
Sat	11/5	H	HAM	19-11	W	9000
IRFU Final (20-36)						
Wed	11/9	A	MTL	7-22	L	15272
Sat	11/12	H	MTL	13-14	L	17000

1949 SASKATCHEWAN ROUGHRIDERS

Sat	8/27	A	WPG	8-13	L	6500
Mon	9/5	H	WPG	20-0	W	7500
Sat	9/10	A	CAL	19-22	L	6500
Mon	9/12	A	EDM	12-0	W	6000
Sat	9/17	H	EDM	13-1	W	4000
Mon	9/19	H	CAL	1-13	L	6700
Sat	9/24	A	WPG	24-6	W	4200
Sat	10/1	H	WPG	24-7	W	4000
Sat	10/8	H	CAL	3-10	L	7500
Mon	10/10	H	EDM	11-12	L	3000
Sat	10/15	A	WPG	47-0	W	3500
Sat	10/22	A	CAL	9-6	W	7000
Mon	10/24	A	EDM	29-11	W	5000
Sat	10/29	H	WPG	15-1	W	3500
WIFU Final (21-22)						
Sat	11/5	H	CAL	12-18	L	8000
Fri	11/11	A	CAL	9-4	W	14500

1949 TORONTO ARGONAUTS

Sat	9/3	H	HAM	26-18	W	12200
Mon	9/5	A	HAM	36-14	W	12000
Sat	9/10	H	OTT	1-19	L	19000
Sat	9/17	H	MTL	11-24	L	19000
Sat	9/24	A	MTL	29-14	W	16000
Sat	10/1	A	OTT	11-34	L	16424
Sat	10/8	A	HAM	11-10	W	
Mon	10/10	H	HAM	29-8	W	16500
Sat	10/15	H	MTL	16-24	L	19000
Sat	10/22	H	OTT	13-24	L	19000
Sat	10/29	A	OTT	24-30	L	15000
Sat	11/5	A	MTL	2-35	L	6729

1949 WINNIPEG BLUE BOMBERS

Sat	8/27	H	SAS	13-8	W	6500
Mon	9/5	A	SAS	0-20	L	7500
Sat	9/10	A	EDM	11-14	L	6500
Mon	9/12	A	CAL	7-32	L	7500
Sat	9/17	H	CAL	1-20	L	6700
Mon	9/19	H	EDM	3-10	L	4000
Sat	9/24	H	SAS	6-24	L	4200
Sat	10/1	A	SAS	7-24	L	4000
Sat	10/8	H	EDM	8-6	W	4000
Mon	10/10	H	CAL	0-3	L	2000
Sat	10/15	H	SAS	0-47	L	3500
Sat	10/22	A	EDM	6-13	L	7000
Mon	10/24	A	CAL	11-22	L	5500
Sat	10/29	A	SAS	1-15	L	3500

1950 CALGARY STAMPEDERS

Sat	8/26	A	SAS	12-25	L	8000
Mon	8/28	A	WPG	4-7	L	7700
Sat	9/2	H	EDM	13-19	L	8500
Mon	9/4	A	EDM	8-18	L	10000
Sat	9/9	H	SAS	11-16	L	9500
Mon	9/11	H	WPG	13-6	W	8000
Sat	9/16	H	EDM	22-29	L	8500
Sat	9/23	A	EDM	8-33	L	10000
Sat	9/30	H	WPG	0-22	L	6500
Mon	10/2	H	SAS	16-13	W	7000
Sat	10/7	A	WPG	13-25	L	8000
Mon	10/9	A	SAS	0-21	L	8000
Sat	10/14	A	EDM	19-12	W	7500
Sat	10/21	H	EDM	13-7	W	2000

1950 EDMONTON ESKIMOS

Sat	8/26	A	WPG	7-18	L	8000
Mon	8/28	A	SAS	15-9	W	6000
Sat	9/2	A	CAL	19-13	W	8500
Mon	9/4	H	CAL	18-8	W	10000
Sat	9/9	H	WPG	6-20	L	8000
Mon	9/11	H	SAS	24-12	W	8000
Sat	9/16	A	CAL	29-22	W	8500
Sat	9/23	H	CAL	33-8	W	10000
Sat	9/30	H	SAS	6-9	L	6500
Mon	10/2	H	WPG	13-10	W	8000
Sat	10/7	A	SAS	6-8	L	6000
Mon	10/9	A	WPG	6-28	L	8000
Sat	10/14	H	CAL	12-19	L	7500
Sat	10/21	A	CAL	7-13	L	2000
WIFU Semi-Final						
Sat	10/28	A	SAS	24-1	W	8000
WIFU Final (1-2)						
Sat	11/4	H	WPG	17-16	W	14900
Sat	11/11	A	WPG	12-22	L	8300
Mon	11/13	A	WPG	6-29	L	8500

1950 HAMILTON TIGER-CATS

Sat	9/2	A	OTT	26-17	W	
Mon	9/4	H	TOR	13-6	W	13000
Sat	9/9	H	OTT	15-23	L	12000
Sat	9/16	A	TOR	8-48	L	21500
Sat	9/23	H	MTL	18-12	W	7000
Sun	10/1	A	MTL	18-31	L	15000
Sat	10/7	A	TOR	29-23	W	14957
Mon	10/9	H	TOR	19-20	L	11000
Sat	10/14	H	OTT	32-0	W	10000
Sun	10/22	A	MTL	13-16	L	16687
Sat	10/28	H	MTL	29-18	W	12000
Sat	11/4	A	OTT	11-3	W	10502
IRFU Final (19-35)						
Sat	11/11	H	TOR	13-11	W	14000
Wed	11/15	A	TOR	6-24	L	23349

1950 MONTREAL ALOUETTES

Sun	8/27	H	OTT	14-7	W	18000
Sat	9/2	A	TOR	6-26	L	16000
Sat	9/9	A	TOR	12-43	L	18000
Sat	9/16	A	OTT	15-42	L	15000
Sat	9/23	A	HAM	12-18	L	7000
Sun	10/1	H	HAM	31-18	W	15000
Sat	10/7	A	OTT	8-18	L	13000
Sun	10/8	H	OTT	18-14	W	18894
Sat	10/14	H	TOR	24-16	W	13424
Sun	10/22	H	HAM	16-13	W	16687
Sat	10/28	A	HAM	18-29	L	12000
Sat	11/4	A	TOR	18-17	W	11000

1950 OTTAWA ROUGH RIDERS

Sun	8/27	A	MTL	7-14	L	18000
Sat	9/2	H	HAM	17-26	L	
Sat	9/9	A	HAM	23-15	W	12000
Sat	9/16	H	MTL	42-15	W	15000
Sat	9/23	A	TOR	15-36	L	24938
Sat	9/30	H	TOR	15-5	W	16592
Sat	10/7	H	MTL	18-8	W	13000
Sun	10/8	A	MTL	14-18	L	18894
Sat	10/14	A	HAM	0-32	L	10000
Sat	10/21	H	TOR	21-21	T	15000
Sat	10/28	A	TOR	7-30	L	19995
Sat	11/4	H	HAM	3-11	L	10502

1950 SASKATCHEWAN ROUGHRIDERS

Sat	8/26	H	CAL	25-12	W	8000
Mon	8/28	H	EDM	9-15	L	6000
Mon	9/4	H	WPG	17-2	W	9000
Sat	9/9	A	CAL	16-11	W	9500
Mon	9/11	A	EDM	12-24	L	8000
Sat	9/16	H	WPG	13-26	L	7000
Sat	9/23	A	WPG	9-15	L	8000
Sat	9/30	A	EDM	9-6	W	6500
Mon	10/2	A	CAL	13-16	L	7000
Sat	10/7	H	EDM	8-6	W	6000
Mon	10/9	H	CAL	21-0	W	8000
Sat	10/14	H	WPG	0-23	L	7000
Mon	10/16	A	WPG	19-20	L	8000
Sat	10/21	A	WPG	36-1	W	7200
WIFU Semi-Final						
Sat	10/28	H	EDM	1-24	L	8000

1950 TORONTO ARGONAUTS

Sat	9/2	H	MTL	26-6	W	16000
Mon	9/4	A	HAM	6-13	L	13000
Sat	9/9	H	MTL	43-12	W	18000
Sat	9/16	H	HAM	48-8	W	21500
Sat	9/23	H	OTT	36-15	W	24938
Sat	9/30	A	OTT	5-15	L	16592
Sat	10/7	H	HAM	23-29	L	14957
Mon	10/9	A	HAM	20-19	W	11000
Sat	10/14	A	MTL	16-24	L	13424
Sat	10/21	A	OTT	21-21	T	15000
Sat	10/28	H	OTT	30-7	W	19995
Sat	11/4	H	MTL	17-18	L	11000
IRFU Final (35-19)						
Sat	11/11	A	HAM	11-13	L	14000
Wed	11/15	H	HAM	24-6	W	23349
Eastern Final						
Sat	11/18	H	TORB	43-13	W	13740
Grey Cup						
Sat	11/25	H	WPG	13-0	W	27101

1950 WINNIPEG BLUE BOMBERS

Sat	8/26	H	EDM	18-7	W	8000
Mon	8/28	H	CAL	7-4	W	7700
Mon	9/4	A	SAS	2-17	L	9000
Sat	9/9	A	EDM	20-6	W	8000
Mon	9/11	A	CAL	6-13	L	8000
Sat	9/16	A	SAS	26-13	W	7000
Sat	9/23	H	SAS	15-9	W	8000
Sat	9/30	A	CAL	22-0	W	6500
Mon	10/2	A	EDM	10-13	L	8000
Sat	10/7	H	CAL	25-13	W	8000
Mon	10/9	H	EDM	28-6	W	8000
Sat	10/14	A	SAS	23-0	W	7000
Mon	10/16	H	SAS	20-19	W	8000
Sat	10/21	H	SAS	1-36	L	7200
WIFU Final (2-1)						
Sat	11/4	A	EDM	16-17	L	14900
Sat	11/11	H	EDM	22-12	W	8300
Mon	11/13	H	EDM	29-6	W	8500
Grey Cup						
Sat	11/25	A	TOR	0-13	L	27101

1951 CALGARY STAMPEDERS

Sat	8/25	A	SAS	1-8	L	9000
Mon	8/27	A	WPG	24-34	L	9600
Sat	9/1	H	EDM	17-18	L	8000
Mon	9/3	A	EDM	0-5	L	12000
Sat	9/8	H	SAS	9-7	W	8000
Mon	9/10	H	WPG	18-12	W	9000
Sat	9/15	H	EDM	15-30	L	10000
Sat	9/22	A	EDM	11-30	L	10000
Sat	9/29	H	WPG	18-33	L	8000
Mon	10/1	H	SAS	12-22	L	6500
Sat	10/6	A	WPG	18-16	W	9500
Mon	10/8	A	SAS	18-28	L	10000
Sat	10/13	A	EDM	18-31	L	10000

Sat 10/20 H EDM 26- 25 W 4000

1951 EDMONTON ESKIMOS
Sat 8/25 A WPG 30- 24 W 9600
Mon 8/27 A SAS 0- 23 L 6000
Sat 9/1 A CAL 18- 17 W 8000
Mon 9/3 H CAL 5- 0 W 12000
Sat 9/8 H WPG 35- 19 W 11000
Mon 9/10 H SAS 31- 6 W 11000
Sat 9/15 A CAL 30- 15 W 10000
Sat 9/22 H CAL 30- 11 W 10000
Sat 9/29 H SAS 18- 25 L 10500
Mon 10/1 H WPG 8- 15 L 11000
Sat 10/6 A SAS 18- 25 L 7000
Mon 10/8 A WPG 27- 38 L 9500
Sat 10/13 H CAL 31- 18 W 10000
Sat 10/20 A CAL 25- 26 L 4000
WIFU Semi-Final
Sat 10/27 H WPG 4- 1 W 13000
WIFU Final (1-2)
Sat 11/3 H SAS 15- 11 W 13000
Sat 11/10 A SAS 5- 12 L 12000
Mon 11/12 A SAS 18- 19 L 12000

1951 HAMILTON TIGER-CATS
Wed 8/29 H MTL 37- 6 W 14000
Mon 9/3 H TOR 27- 6 W 15000
Sat 9/8 A TOR 21- 2 W 23375
Sat 9/15 H OTT 11- 6 W 15000
Sun 9/23 A MTL 16- 17 L 20000
Sat 9/29 A OTT 18- 20 L 18000
Sat 10/6 A TOR 22- 6 W 26000
Mon 10/8 H TOR 0- 10 L 14000
Sun 10/14 A MTL 21- 7 W 14687
Sat 10/20 H OTT 16- 32 L 14000
Sat 10/27 A OTT 9- 13 L 14794
Sat 11/3 H MTL 31- 6 W 8000
IRFU Semi-Final (31-28)
Wed 11/7 A TOR 24- 7 W 12200
Sat 11/10 H TOR 7- 21 L 15000
IRFU Final (16-28)
Wed 11/14 A OTT 7- 17 L 9000
Sat 11/17 H OTT 9- 11 L 17000

1951 MONTREAL ALOUETTES
Wed 8/29 A HAM 6- 37 L 14000
Sat 9/8 A OTT 9- 13 L 14166
Sun 9/9 H OTT 8- 33 L 21812
Sat 9/15 A TOR 8- 6 W 18200
Sun 9/23 H HAM 17- 16 W 20000
Sat 10/6 A OTT 13- 25 L
Mon 10/8 H OTT 9- 12 L 15322
Sun 10/14 H HAM 7- 21 L 14687
Sat 10/20 A TOR 11- 35 L 16623
Sun 10/21 H TOR 18- 35 L 12309
Sun 10/28 H TOR 34- 22 W 9215
Sat 11/3 A HAM 6- 31 L 8000

1951 OTTAWA ROUGH RIDERS
Sat 9/1 H TOR 17- 36 L 15000
Sat 9/8 H MTL 13- 9 W 14166
Sun 9/9 A MTL 33- 8 W 21812
Sat 9/15 A HAM 6- 11 L 15000
Sat 9/22 A TOR 10- 17 L 16250
Sat 9/29 H HAM 20- 18 W 18000
Sat 10/6 H MTL 25- 13 W
Mon 10/8 A MTL 12- 9 W 15322
Sat 10/13 H TOR 19- 28 L 15000
Sat 10/20 A HAM 32- 16 W 14000
Sat 10/27 H HAM 13- 9 W 14794
Sat 11/3 A TOR 18- 23 L 21844
IRFU Final (28-16)
Wed 11/14 H HAM 17- 7 W 9000
Sat 11/17 A HAM 11- 9 W 17000
Eastern Final
Wed 11/21 H SAR 43- 17 W 3000
Grey Cup
Sat 11/24 N SAS 21- 14 W 27341

1951 SASKATCHEWAN ROUGHRIDERS
Sat 8/25 H CAL 8- 1 W 9000
Mon 8/27 H EDM 23- 0 W 6000
Thu 8/30 A WPG 33- 1 W 9000
Mon 9/3 H WPG 22- 24 L 10000
Sat 9/8 A CAL 7- 9 L 8000
Mon 9/10 A EDM 6- 31 L 11000
Sat 9/15 H WPG 12- 21 L 10000
Sat 9/22 A WPG 30- 17 W 9600
Sat 9/29 A EDM 25- 18 W 10500
Mon 10/1 A CAL 22- 12 W 6500
Sat 10/6 H EDM 25- 18 W 7000
Mon 10/8 H CAL 28- 18 W 10000
Sat 10/13 H WPG 23- 30 L 7500
Sat 10/20 A WPG 13- 19 L 9000
WIFU Final (2-1)
Sat 11/3 A EDM 11- 15 L 13000
Sat 11/10 H EDM 12- 5 W 12000
Mon 11/12 H EDM 19- 18 W 12000
Grey Cup
Sat 11/24 N OTT 14- 21 L 27341

1951 TORONTO ARGONAUTS
Sat 9/1 A OTT 36- 17 W 15000
Mon 9/3 A HAM 6- 27 L 15000
Sat 9/8 H HAM 2- 21 L 23375
Sat 9/15 H MTL 6- 8 L 18200
Sat 9/22 H OTT 17- 10 W 16250
Sat 10/6 H HAM 6- 22 L 26000
Mon 10/8 A HAM 10- 0 W 14000
Sat 10/13 A OTT 28- 19 W 15000
Sat 10/20 H MTL 35- 11 W 16623
Sun 10/21 A MTL 35- 18 W 12309
Sun 10/28 A MTL 22- 34 L 9215
Sat 11/3 H OTT 23- 18 W 21844
IRFU Semi-Final (28-31)
Wed 11/7 H HAM 7- 24 L 12200
Sat 11/10 A HAM 21- 7 W 15000

1951 WINNIPEG BLUE BOMBERS
Sat 8/25 H EDM 24- 30 L 9600
Mon 8/27 H CAL 34- 24 W 9600
Thu 8/30 H SAS 1- 33 L 9000
Mon 9/3 A SAS 24- 22 W 10000
Sat 9/8 A EDM 19- 35 L 11000
Mon 9/10 A CAL 12- 18 L 9000
Sat 9/15 A SAS 21- 12 W 10000
Sat 9/22 H SAS 17- 30 L 9600
Sat 9/29 A CAL 33- 18 W 8000
Mon 10/1 A EDM 15- 8 W 11000
Sat 10/6 H CAL 16- 18 L 9500
Mon 10/8 H EDM 38- 27 W 9500
Sat 10/13 A SAS 30- 23 W 7500
Sat 10/20 H SAS 19- 13 W 9000
WIFU Semi-Final
Sat 10/27 A EDM 1- 4 L 13000

1952 CALGARY STAMPEDERS
Sat 8/23 A WPG 12- 8 W 10000
Mon 8/25 A SAS 21- 14 W 1000
Sat 8/30 H EDM 14- 7 W 12000
Mon 9/1 A EDM 10- 17 L 13172
Sat 9/6 H SAS 8- 18 L 12000
Mon 9/8 H WPG 6- 7 L 14000
Sat 9/13 A SAS 30- 20 W 10500
Sat 9/20 A EDM 18- 35 L 14922
Mon 9/22 H EDM 9- 10 L
Sat 9/27 A SAS 16- 9 W 12000
Mon 9/29 A WPG 28- 39 L 9600
Sat 10/4 H WPG 30- 41 L 12000
Mon 10/6 H SAS 30- 27 W 11000
Sat 10/11 A EDM 33- 30 W 13000
Mon 10/13 H EDM 10- 16 L 12000
Sat 10/18 H WPG 18- 42 L
WIFU Semi-Final (38-42)
Wed 10/22 H EDM 31- 12 W 12000
Sat 10/25 A EDM 7- 30 L 16000

1952 EDMONTON ESKIMOS
Sat 8/23 A SAS 5- 25 L 12000
Mon 8/25 A WPG 14- 14 T 10000
Sat 8/30 A CAL 7- 14 L 12000
Mon 9/1 H CAL 17- 10 W 13172
Sat 9/6 H WPG 18- 21 L 14000
Mon 9/8 H SAS 19- 15 W 13500
Sat 9/13 A WPG 11- 9 W 9600
Sat 9/20 H CAL 35- 18 W 14922
Mon 9/22 A CAL 10- 9 W
Sat 9/27 A WPG 18- 40 L 9600
Mon 9/29 A SAS 25- 13 W 10000
Sat 10/4 H SAS 20- 6 W 13000
Mon 10/6 H WPG 18- 12 W 15000
Sat 10/11 H CAL 30- 33 L 13000
Mon 10/13 A CAL 16- 10 W 12000
Sat 10/18 H SAS 28- 31 L 10000
WIFU Semi-Final (42-38)
Wed 10/22 A CAL 12- 31 L 12000
Sat 10/25 H CAL 30- 7 W 16000
WIFU Final (2-1)
Sat 11/1 H WPG 12- 28 L 16000
Sat 11/8 A WPG 18- 12 W 9600
Tue 11/11 A WPG 22- 11 W 9600
Grey Cup
Sat 11/29 A TOR 11- 21 L 27391

1952 HAMILTON TIGER-CATS
Mon 9/1 H TOR 13- 33 L 16000
Sat 9/6 A OTT 30- 8 W 14000
Sat 9/13 H MTL 30- 12 W 9000
Sat 9/20 A TOR 13- 13 T 26663
Sat 9/27 H OTT 27- 13 W 14000
Sun 10/5 A MTL 26- 0 W 14131
Sat 10/11 A TOR 27- 18 W 25974
Mon 10/13 H TOR 25- 16 W 17200
Sat 10/18 H MTL 21- 1 W 9200
Sun 10/26 A MTL 18- 21 L 10000
Sat 11/1 H OTT 25- 23 W 14000
Sat 11/8 A OTT 13- 4 W 12000
IRFU Final (40-45)
Sat 11/15 H TOR 6- 22 L 17312
Wed 11/19 A TOR 27- 11 W 25099
Sat 11/22 H TOR 7- 12 L 27242

1952 MONTREAL ALOUETTES
Wed 8/27 H OTT 28- 32 L 20586
Sat 9/6 A TOR 0- 43 L 18700
Sat 9/13 A HAM 12- 30 L 9000
Sat 9/20 A OTT 7- 8 L 16500
Sun 9/28 H TOR 6- 12 L 17472
Sun 10/5 H HAM 0- 26 L 14131
Sat 10/11 A OTT 12- 25 L
Sun 10/12 H OTT 6- 23 L 13000
Sat 10/18 A HAM 1- 21 L 9200
Sun 10/26 H HAM 21- 18 W 10000
Sun 11/2 H TOR 18- 29 L 13548
Sat 11/8 A TOR 25- 11 W 14664

1952 OTTAWA ROUGH RIDERS
Wed 8/27 A MTL 32- 28 W 20586
Sat 9/6 H HAM 8- 30 L 14000
Sat 9/13 A TOR 19- 24 L 19300
Sat 9/20 H MTL 8- 7 W 16500
Sat 9/27 A HAM 13- 27 L 14000
Sat 10/4 H TOR 25- 21 W 16500
Sat 10/11 H MTL 25- 12 W
Sun 10/12 A MTL 23- 6 W 13000
Sat 10/18 H TOR 6- 25 L 17000
Sat 10/25 A TOR 14- 20 L 24402
Sat 11/1 A HAM 23- 25 L 14000
Sat 11/8 H HAM 4- 13 L 12000

1952 SASKATCHEWAN ROUGHRIDERS
Sat 8/23 H EDM 25- 5 W 12000
Mon 8/25 H CAL 14- 21 L 10000
Fri 8/29 A WPG 9- 27 L 10000
Mon 9/1 H WPG 8- 16 L 13795
Sat 9/6 A CAL 18- 8 W 12000
Mon 9/8 A EDM 15- 19 L 13500
Sat 9/13 H CAL 20- 30 L 10500
Sat 9/20 H WPG 7- 18 L 11000
Mon 9/22 A WPG 6- 35 L 9600
Sat 9/27 H CAL 9- 16 L 12000
Mon 9/29 H EDM 13- 25 L 10000
Sat 10/4 A EDM 6- 20 L 13000
Mon 10/6 A CAL 27- 30 L 11000
Sat 10/11 A WPG 7- 28 L
Mon 10/13 H WPG 1- 37 L 11500
Sat 10/18 A EDM 31- 28 W 10000

1952 TORONTO ARGONAUTS
Mon 9/1 A HAM 33- 13 W 16000
Sat 9/6 H MTL 43- 0 W 18700
Sat 9/13 H OTT 24- 19 W 19300
Sat 9/20 H HAM 13- 13 T 26663
Sun 9/28 A MTL 12- 6 W 17472
Sat 10/4 A OTT 21- 25 L 16500
Sat 10/11 H HAM 18- 27 L 25974
Mon 10/13 A HAM 16- 25 L 17200
Sat 10/18 A OTT 25- 6 W 17000
Sat 10/25 H OTT 20- 14 W 24402
Sun 11/2 A MTL 29- 18 W 13548
Sat 11/8 H MTL 11- 25 L 14664
IRFU Final (45-40)
Sat 11/15 A HAM 22- 6 W 17312
Wed 11/19 H HAM 11- 27 L 25099
Sat 11/22 A HAM 12- 7 W 27242
Grey Cup Semi-Final
Wed 11/26 H SAR 34- 15 W 8900
Grey Cup
Sat 11/29 H EDM 21- 11 W 27391

1952 WINNIPEG BLUE BOMBERS
Sat 8/23 H CAL 8- 12 L 10000
Mon 8/25 H EDM 14- 14 T 10000
Fri 8/29 H SAS 27- 9 W 10000
Mon 9/1 A SAS 16- 8 W 13795
Sat 9/6 A EDM 21- 18 W 13500
Mon 9/8 A CAL 7- 6 W 14000
Sat 9/13 H EDM 9- 11 L 9600
Sat 9/20 A SAS 18- 7 W 11000
Mon 9/22 H SAS 35- 6 W 9600
Sat 9/27 H EDM 40- 18 W 9600
Mon 9/29 H CAL 39- 28 W 9600
Sat 10/4 A CAL 41- 30 W 12000
Mon 10/6 A EDM 12- 18 L 15000
Sat 10/11 H SAS 28- 7 W
Mon 10/13 A SAS 37- 1 W 11500
Sat 10/18 A CAL 42- 18 W
WIFU Final (1-2)
Sat 11/1 A EDM 28- 12 W 16000
Sat 11/8 H EDM 12- 18 L 9600
Tue 11/11 H EDM 11- 22 L 9600

1953 CALGARY STAMPEDERS
Sat 8/29 A SAS 29- 17 W 14000
Mon 8/31 A WPG 10- 16 L 16108
Sat 9/5 H EDM 6- 18 L 15000
Mon 9/7 A EDM 5- 19 L 15500
Sat 9/12 H WPG 23- 14 W 12000
Mon 9/14 H SAS 2- 34 L 13000
Sat 9/19 A WPG 15- 16 L 16578
Sat 9/26 A EDM 6- 15 L 15000
Mon 9/28 H EDM 12- 21 L 12000
Sat 10/3 A WPG 17- 24 L 16458
Mon 10/5 A SAS 9- 8 W 11116
Sat 10/10 H EDM 13- 34 L
Mon 10/12 A EDM 6- 22 L 15500
Sat 10/17 H SAS 18- 24 L 12000
Mon 10/19 H WPG 6- 18 L 10000
Sat 10/24 H SAS 13- 13 T 10000

1953 EDMONTON ESKIMOS

Sat 8/29 A WPG 6- 7 L 16108
Mon 8/31 A SAS 19- 17 W 11030
Sat 9/5 A CAL 18- 6 W 15000
Mon 9/7 H CAL 19- 5 W 15500
Sat 9/12 H SAS 13- 1 W 15300
Mon 9/14 H WPG 9- 7 W 16000
Sat 9/19 A SAS 12- 6 W 13024
Sat 9/26 H CAL 15- 6 W 15000
Mon 9/28 A CAL 21- 12 W 12000
Sat 10/3 A SAS 13- 19 L 12646
Mon 10/5 A WPG 16- 6 W 17014
Sat 10/10 A CAL 34- 13 W
Mon 10/12 H CAL 22- 6 W 15500
Sat 10/17 H WPG 32- 9 W
Mon 10/19 H SAS 19- 20 L 15000
Sat 10/24 H WPG 8- 17 L 15000
WIFU Final (1-2)
Sat 11/7 H WPG 25- 7 W 15500
Wed 11/11 A WPG 17- 21 L 17434
Sat 11/14 H WPG 24- 30 L 16000

1953 HAMILTON TIGER-CATS

Sat 8/29 H OTT 14- 10 W 12000
Mon 9/7 H TOR 14- 12 W 17000
Fri 9/11 A MTL 0- 17 L 13215
Wed 9/16 H TOR 20- 21 L
Sat 9/19 A TOR 12- 9 W 20382
Sat 9/26 H MTL 20- 15 W 16000
Sat 10/3 A OTT 6- 31 L 15500
Sat 10/10 A TOR 26- 0 W
Mon 10/12 H TOR 12- 30 L 19069
Sat 10/17 A OTT 33- 24 W 13500
Sat 10/24 A TOR 5- 17 L 19437
Sat 10/31 H MTL 31- 18 W 17000
Sun 11/8 A MTL 18- 31 L 12085
Sat 11/14 H OTT 18- 8 W 18000
IRFU Final (59-23)
Wed 11/18 H MTL 37- 12 W 16000
Sun 11/22 A MTL 22- 11 W 18070
Grey Cup
Sat 11/28 N WPG 12- 6 W 27313

1953 MONTREAL ALOUETTES

Wed 8/26 A TOR 9- 11 L 18000
Wed 9/2 H TOR 15- 7 W 13267
Sat 9/5 A OTT 6- 26 L 12000
Fri 9/11 H HAM 17- 0 W 13215
Wed 9/16 A OTT 13- 22 L
Sun 9/20 H OTT 37- 21 W 16902
Sat 9/26 A HAM 15- 20 L 16000
Sat 10/10 A OTT 24- 6 W 15482
Sun 10/11 H OTT 26- 18 W 15462
Sun 10/18 H TOR 39- 11 W 19603
Sun 10/25 H OTT 15- 30 L 16115
Sat 10/31 A HAM 18- 31 L 17000
Sun 11/8 H HAM 31- 18 W 12085
Sat 11/14 A TOR 27- 8 W 16153
IRFU Final (23-59)
Wed 11/18 A HAM 12- 37 L 16000
Sun 11/22 H HAM 11- 22 L 18070

1953 OTTAWA ROUGH RIDERS

Sat 8/29 A HAM 10- 14 L 12000
Sat 9/5 H MTL 26- 6 W 12000
Sat 9/12 A TOR 20- 16 W 17459
Wed 9/16 H MTL 22- 13 W
Sun 9/20 A MTL 21- 37 L 16902
Sat 9/26 H TOR 17- 18 L 16000
Sat 10/3 H HAM 31- 6 W 15500
Sat 10/10 H MTL 6- 24 L 15482
Sun 10/11 A MTL 18- 26 L 15462
Sat 10/17 H HAM 24- 33 L 13500
Sun 10/25 A MTL 30- 15 W 16115
Sat 10/31 A TOR 20- 8 W 20187
Sat 11/7 H TOR 13- 4 W 12688
Sat 11/14 A HAM 8- 18 L 18000

1953 SASKATCHEWAN ROUGHRIDERS

Sat 8/29 H CAL 17- 29 L 14000
Mon 8/31 H EDM 17- 19 L 11030
Fri 9/4 A WPG 6- 13 L 16000
Mon 9/7 H WPG 23- 19 W 14904
Sat 9/12 A EDM 1- 13 L 15300
Mon 9/14 A CAL 34- 2 W 13000
Sat 9/19 H EDM 6- 12 L 13024
Sat 9/26 H WPG 21- 15 W 12446
Mon 9/28 A WPG 2- 19 L 16400
Sat 10/3 H EDM 19- 13 W 12646
Mon 10/5 H CAL 8- 9 L 11116
Sat 10/10 A WPG 18- 13 W 16000
Mon 10/12 H WPG 14- 13 W 15565
Sat 10/17 A CAL 24- 18 W 12000
Mon 10/19 A EDM 20- 19 W 15000
Sat 10/24 A CAL 13- 13 T 10000
WIFU Semi-Final (23-60)
Wed 10/28 A WPG 5- 43 L 16827
Sat 10/31 H WPG 18- 17 W 14000

1953 TORONTO ARGONAUTS

Wed 8/26 H MTL 11- 9 W 18000
Wed 9/2 A MTL 7- 15 L 13267
Mon 9/7 A HAM 12- 14 L 17000
Sat 9/12 H OTT 16- 20 L 17459
Wed 9/16 A HAM 21- 20 W
Sat 9/19 H HAM 9- 12 L 20382
Sat 9/26 A OTT 18- 17 W 16000
Sat 10/10 H HAM 0- 26 L
Mon 10/12 A HAM 30- 12 W 19069
Sun 10/18 A MTL 11- 39 L 19603
Sat 10/24 H HAM 17- 5 W 19437
Sat 10/31 H OTT 8- 20 L 20187
Sat 11/7 A OTT 4- 13 L 12688
Sat 11/14 H MTL 8- 27 L 16153

1953 WINNIPEG BLUE BOMBERS

Sat 8/29 H EDM 7- 6 W 16108
Mon 8/31 H CAL 16- 10 W 16108
Fri 9/4 H SAS 13- 6 W 16000
Mon 9/7 A SAS 19- 23 L 14904
Sat 9/12 A CAL 14- 23 L 12000
Mon 9/14 A EDM 7- 9 L 16000
Sat 9/19 H CAL 16- 15 W 16578
Sat 9/26 A SAS 15- 21 L 12446
Mon 9/28 H SAS 19- 2 W 16400
Sat 10/3 H CAL 24- 17 W 16458
Mon 10/5 H EDM 6- 16 L 17014
Sat 10/10 H SAS 13- 18 L 16000
Mon 10/12 A SAS 13- 14 L 15565
Sat 10/17 A EDM 9- 32 L
Mon 10/19 A CAL 18- 6 W 10000
Sat 10/24 A EDM 17- 8 W 15000
WIFU Semi-Final (60-23)
Wed 10/28 H SAS 43- 5 W 16827
Sat 10/31 A SAS 17- 18 L 14000
WIFU Final (2-1)
Sat 11/7 A EDM 7- 25 L 15500
Wed 11/11 H EDM 21- 17 W 17434
Sat 11/14 A EDM 30- 24 W 16000
Grey Cup Semi-Final
Sat 11/21 H TORB 24- 4 W 16000
Grey Cup
Sat 11/28 N HAM 6- 12 L 27313

1954 BRITISH COLUMBIA LIONS

Sat 8/28 H WPG 6- 8 L 20606
Mon 8/30 H SAS 0- 17 L 14878
Sat 9/4 A CAL 0- 34 L 15000
Mon 9/6 A EDM 6- 12 L 18000
Sat 9/11 A SAS 7- 17 L 13000
Mon 9/13 A WPG 17- 22 L 16760
Sat 9/18 H CAL 9- 4 W 18786
Mon 9/20 H EDM 13- 23 L 21186
Sat 10/2 A SAS 12- 43 L 12000
Mon 10/4 A WPG 6- 24 L 15273
Sat 10/9 H CAL 6- 13 L 18555
Mon 10/11 A CAL 6- 42 L 12500
Sat 10/16 A EDM 3- 31 L 15000
Mon 10/18 H EDM 0- 22 L 13136
Sat 10/23 H WPG 0- 18 L 17061
Mon 10/25 H SAS 9- 15 L 10775

1954 CALGARY STAMPEDERS

Sat 8/21 A WPG 5- 17 L 17000
Mon 8/23 A SAS 7- 11 L 11469
Sat 8/28 H SAS 34- 0 W 14000
Mon 8/30 H WPG 41- 0 W 15000
Sat 9/4 H BC 34- 0 W 15000
Sat 9/11 A EDM 11- 30 L 18795
Mon 9/13 H EDM 20- 6 W 15090
Sat 9/18 A BC 4- 9 L 18786
Sat 9/25 H SAS 18- 10 W 15000
Mon 9/27 H WPG 4- 6 L 12000
Sat 10/2 H EDM 12- 13 L 10000
Mon 10/4 A EDM 6- 21 L 17000
Sat 10/9 A BC 13- 6 W 18555
Mon 10/11 H BC 42- 6 W 12500
Sat 10/16 A SAS 8- 19 L 14000
Mon 10/18 A WPG 12- 11 W 17240

1954 EDMONTON ESKIMOS

Sat 8/21 A SAS 13- 21 L 12000
Mon 8/23 A WPG 3- 7 L 17385
Mon 9/6 H BC 12- 6 W 18000
Sat 9/11 H CAL 30- 11 W 18795
Mon 9/13 A CAL 6- 20 L 15090
Mon 9/20 A BC 23- 13 W 21186
Sat 9/25 H WPG 12- 8 W 17841
Mon 9/27 H SAS 6- 8 L 15161
Sat 10/2 A CAL 13- 12 W 10000
Mon 10/4 H CAL 21- 6 W 17000
Sat 10/9 A WPG 16- 5 W 18538
Mon 10/11 A SAS 2- 12 L 14778
Sat 10/16 H BC 31- 3 W 15000
Mon 10/18 A BC 22- 0 W 13136
Sat 10/23 H SAS 24- 19 W 18236
Mon 10/25 H WPG 21- 12 W 19000
WIFU Final (2-1)
Sat 11/6 H WPG 9- 3 W 19817
Thu 11/11 A WPG 6- 12 L 20933
Sat 11/13 H WPG 10- 5 W 17000
Grey Cup Semi-Final
Sat 11/20 H KW 38- 6 W 8000
Grey Cup
Sat 11/27 N MTL 26- 25 W 27321

1954 HAMILTON TIGER-CATS

Sat 8/28 H MTL 6- 24 L 16000
Sat 9/4 A TOR 17- 6 W 14797
Mon 9/6 H TOR 7- 21 L 14000
Sat 9/11 A MTL 3- 21 L 17463
Sat 9/18 H MTL 7- 6 W 14000
Sat 9/25 A OTT 38- 12 W 9220
Sat 10/2 H OTT 45- 0 W 9300
Sat 10/9 H TOR 34- 6 W 15000
Mon 10/11 A TOR 22- 13 W 16050
Sat 10/16 A MTL 11- 46 L 21000
Sat 10/23 H OTT 25- 17 W 9300
Sat 10/30 A OTT 30- 9 W 8422
Sat 11/6 A MTL 15- 19 L 19127
Sat 11/13 H TOR 15- 7 W 9000
IRFU Final (28-38)
Wed 11/17 H MTL 9- 14 L 15000
Sat 11/20 A MTL 19- 24 L 21025

1954 MONTREAL ALOUETTES

Sat 8/28 A HAM 24- 6 W 16000
Sat 9/4 H OTT 21- 2 W 20563
Mon 9/6 A OTT 20- 11 W 13000
Sat 9/11 H HAM 21- 3 W 17463
Sat 9/18 A HAM 6- 7 L 14000
Sat 9/25 H TOR 28- 7 W 18104
Sat 10/2 A TOR 30- 12 W 20710
Sat 10/9 A OTT 25- 11 W 9155
Mon 10/11 H OTT 24- 6 W 12865
Sat 10/16 H HAM 46- 11 W 21000
Sat 10/23 A TOR 24- 30 L 16400
Sat 10/30 H TOR 41- 13 W 19125
Sat 11/6 H HAM 19- 15 W 19127
Sat 11/13 A OTT 12- 14 L 8370
IRFU Final (38-28)
Wed 11/17 A HAM 14- 9 W 15000
Sat 11/20 H HAM 24- 19 W 21025
Grey Cup
Sat 11/27 N EDM 25- 26 L 27321

1954 OTTAWA ROUGH RIDERS

Sat 8/28 A TOR 6- 13 L 16702
Sat 9/4 A MTL 2- 21 L 20563
Mon 9/6 H MTL 11- 20 L 13000
Sat 9/11 A TOR 12- 5 W 13910
Sat 9/18 H TOR 6- 34 L 11500
Sat 9/25 H HAM 12- 38 L 9220
Sat 10/2 A HAM 0- 45 L 9300
Sat 10/9 H MTL 11- 25 L 9155
Mon 10/11 A MTL 6- 24 L 12865
Sat 10/16 H TOR 11- 27 L 9000
Sat 10/23 A HAM 17- 25 L 9300
Sat 10/30 H HAM 9- 30 L 8422
Sat 11/6 A TOR 12- 18 L 11273
Sat 11/13 H MTL 14- 12 W 8370

1954 SASKATCHEWAN ROUGHRIDERS

Sat 8/21 H EDM 21- 13 W 12000
Mon 8/23 H CAL 11- 7 W 11469
Sat 8/28 A CAL 0- 34 L 14000
Mon 8/30 A BC 17- 0 W 14878
Fri 9/3 A WPG 12- 12 T 18090
Mon 9/6 H WPG 18- 14 W 14000
Sat 9/11 H BC 17- 7 W 13000
Sat 9/18 H WPG 10- 10 T 10663
Mon 9/20 A WPG 7- 28 L 16418
Sat 9/25 A CAL 10- 18 L 15000
Mon 9/27 A EDM 8- 6 W 15161
Sat 10/2 H BC 43- 12 W 12000
Mon 10/11 H EDM 12- 2 W 14778
Sat 10/16 H CAL 19- 8 W 14000
Sat 10/23 A EDM 19- 24 L 18236
Mon 10/25 A BC 15- 9 W 10775
WIFU Semi-Final (25-27)
Sat 10/30 H WPG 14- 14 T 15479
Mon 11/1 H WPG 11- 13 L 13700

1954 TORONTO ARGONAUTS

Sat 8/28 H OTT 13- 6 W 16702
Sat 9/4 H HAM 6- 17 L 14797
Mon 9/6 A HAM 21- 7 W 14000
Sat 9/11 H OTT 5- 12 L 13910
Sat 9/18 A OTT 34- 6 W 11500
Sat 9/25 A MTL 7- 28 L 18104
Sat 10/2 H MTL 12- 30 L 20710
Sat 10/9 A HAM 6- 34 L 15000
Mon 10/11 H HAM 13- 22 L 16050
Sat 10/16 A OTT 27- 11 W 9000
Sat 10/23 H MTL 30- 24 W 16400
Sat 10/30 A MTL 13- 41 L 19125
Sat 11/6 H OTT 18- 12 W 11273
Sat 11/13 A HAM 7- 15 L 9000

1954 WINNIPEG BLUE BOMBERS

Sat 8/21 H CAL 17- 5 W 17000
Mon 8/23 H EDM 7- 3 W 17385
Sat 8/28 A BC 8- 6 W 20606
Mon 8/30 A CAL 0- 41 L 15000
Fri 9/3 H SAS 12- 12 T 18090
Mon 9/6 A SAS 14- 18 L 14000
Mon 9/13 H BC 22- 17 W 16760
Sat 9/18 A SAS 10- 10 T 10663
Mon 9/20 H SAS 28- 7 W 16418

Sat	9/25	A	EDM	8- 12	L	17841
Mon	9/27	A	CAL	6- 4	W	12000
Mon	10/4	H	BC	24- 6	W	15273
Sat	10/9	H	EDM	5- 16	L	18538
Mon	10/18	H	CAL	11- 12	L	17240
Sat	10/23	A	BC	18- 0	W	17061
Mon	10/25	A	EDM	12- 21	L	19000
WIFU Semi-Final (27-25)						
Sat	10/30	A	SAS	14- 14	T	15749
Mon	11/1	A	SAS	13- 11	W	13700
WIFU Final (1-2)						
Sat	11/6	A	EDM	3- 9	L	19817
Thu	11/11	H	EDM	12- 6	W	20953
Sat	11/13	A	EDM	5- 10	L	17000

1955 BRITISH COLUMBIA LIONS

Mon	8/22	H	CAL	14- 8	W	28103
Sat	8/27	A	EDM	12- 29	L	17500
Mon	8/29	H	SAS	13- 19	L	27008
Sat	9/3	A	WPG	15- 7	W	16458
Mon	9/5	A	SAS	24- 23	W	16052
Sat	9/10	H	EDM	13- 18	L	29503
Sat	9/17	H	WPG	19- 20	L	27132
Mon	9/19	A	CAL	24- 18	W	11000
Mon	9/26	H	EDM	0- 15	L	24241
Sat	10/1	H	SAS	9- 24	L	23321
Mon	10/3	A	CAL	6- 18	L	12000
Sat	10/8	A	EDM	2- 38	L	16500
Mon	10/10	H	WPG	4- 18	L	21429
Sat	10/15	H	CAL	36- 18	W	16951
Sat	10/22	A	SAS	7- 33	L	10000
Mon	10/24	A	WPG	13- 24	L	14730

1955 CALGARY STAMPEDERS

Sat	8/20	H	EDM	10- 13	L	14000
Mon	8/22	A	BC	8- 14	L	28013
Sat	8/27	H	SAS	12- 29	L	17500
Mon	8/29	A	WPG	15- 13	W	15499
Mon	9/5	H	WPG	12- 9	W	13000
Sat	9/10	A	SAS	23- 24	L	12000
Mon	9/12	A	EDM	12- 24	L	15000
Mon	9/19	H	BC	18- 24	L	11000
Sat	9/24	H	EDM	0- 15	L	10000
Mon	9/26	A	WPG	6- 25	L	14724
Mon	10/3	H	BC	18- 6	W	12000
Sat	10/8	H	WPG	12- 13	L	12000
Mon	10/10	A	SAS	16- 18	L	13837
Sat	10/15	A	BC	18- 36	L	16951
Mon	10/24	H	SAS	24- 6	W	10000
Sat	10/29	A	EDM	5- 30	L	13000

1955 EDMONTON ESKIMOS

Sat	8/20	A	CAL	13- 10	W	14000
Mon	8/22	A	WPG	13- 9	W	16835
Sat	8/27	H	BC	29- 12	W	17500
Sat	9/3	H	SAS	19- 12	W	19500
Sat	9/10	A	BC	18- 13	W	29503
Mon	9/12	H	CAL	24- 12	W	15000
Sat	9/17	A	SAS	26- 9	W	14500
Mon	9/19	H	WPG	14- 8	W	12500
Sat	9/24	A	CAL	15- 0	W	10000
Mon	9/26	A	BC	15- 0	W	24241
Sat	10/1	A	WPG	0- 12	L	18884
Mon	10/3	H	SAS	17- 9	W	15000
Sat	10/8	H	BC	38- 2	W	16500
Sat	10/15	A	SAS	3- 4	L	11590
Sat	10/22	H	WPG	12- 0	W	16000
Sat	10/29	H	CAL	30- 5	W	13000
WIFU Final (2-0)						
Fri	11/11	A	WPG	29- 6	W	15553
Wed	11/16	H	WPG	26- 6	W	12000
Grey Cup						
Sat	11/26	N	MTL	34- 19	W	39417

1955 HAMILTON TIGER-CATS

Sat	9/3	A	TOR	6- 31	L	18261
Mon	9/5	H	TOR	37- 12	W	18628
Sat	9/10	H	OTT	23- 12	W	12491
Sat	9/17	A	MTL	20- 38	L	22940
Sat	9/24	H	MTL	22- 13	W	15396
Sat	10/1	A	OTT	40- 0	W	13000
Sat	10/8	H	TOR	15- 11	W	15000
Mon	10/10	A	TOR	15- 16	L	19060
Sat	10/15	H	OTT	28- 1	W	9300
Sat	10/22	A	OTT	21- 12	W	13000
Sat	10/29	A	MTL	16- 41	L	22849
Sat	11/5	H	MTL	28- 6	W	14800
IRFU Semi-Final						
Sat	11/12	H	TOR	28- 32	L	17600

1955 MONTREAL ALOUETTES

Sat	9/3	H	OTT	34- 22	W	21033
Mon	9/5	A	OTT	18- 19	L	16000
Sat	9/10	H	TOR	43- 11	W	22227
Sat	9/17	H	HAM	38- 20	W	22940
Sat	9/24	A	HAM	13- 22	L	15396
Sat	10/1	A	TOR	30- 28	W	19200
Sat	10/8	A	OTT	35- 7	W	12500
Mon	10/10	H	OTT	43- 6	W	22259
Sat	10/15	H	TOR	44- 23	W	21000
Sat	10/22	A	TOR	43- 12	W	18329
Sat	10/29	H	HAM	41- 16	W	22849
Sat	11/5	A	HAM	6- 28	L	14800
IRFU Final						
Sat	11/19	H	TOR	38- 36	W	21103
Grey Cup						
Sat	11/26	N	EDM	19- 34	L	39417

1955 OTTAWA ROUGH RIDERS

Sat	9/3	A	MTL	22- 34	L	21033
Mon	9/5	H	MTL	19- 18	W	16000
Sat	9/10	A	HAM	12- 23	L	12491
Sat	9/17	A	TOR	27- 12	W	16078
Sat	9/24	H	TOR	19- 30	L	14000
Sat	10/1	H	HAM	0- 40	L	13000
Sat	10/8	H	MTL	7- 35	L	12500
Mon	10/10	A	MTL	6- 43	L	22259
Sat	10/15	A	HAM	1- 28	L	9300
Sat	10/22	H	HAM	12- 21	L	13000
Sat	10/29	A	TOR	13- 29	L	12213
Sat	11/5	H	TOR	36- 24	W	8220

1955 SASKATCHEWAN ROUGHRIDERS

Sat	8/20	H	WPG	17- 7	W	14000
Sat	8/27	A	CAL	29- 12	W	12400
Mon	8/29	A	BC	19- 13	W	27008
Sat	9/3	A	EDM	12- 19	L	19500
Mon	9/5	H	BC	23- 24	L	16052
Sat	9/10	H	CAL	24- 23	W	12000
Mon	9/12	A	WPG	0- 25	L	16133
Sat	9/17	H	EDM	9- 26	L	14500
Sat	9/24	H	WPG	12- 7	W	10857
Sat	10/1	A	BC	24- 9	W	23321
Mon	10/3	A	EDM	9- 17	L	15000
Mon	10/10	H	CAL	18- 16	W	13837
Sat	10/15	H	EDM	4- 3	W	11590
Sat	10/22	H	BC	33- 7	W	10000
Mon	10/24	A	CAL	6- 24	L	10000
Sat	10/29	A	WPG	31- 13	W	14464
WIFU Semi-Final (16-24)						
Sat	11/5	H	WPG	7- 16	L	9000
Mon	11/7	A	WPG	9- 8	W	12768

1955 TORONTO ARGONAUTS

Sat	9/3	H	HAM	31- 6	W	18621
Mon	9/5	A	HAM	12- 37	L	18628
Sat	9/10	A	MTL	11- 43	L	22227
Sat	9/17	H	OTT	12- 27	L	16078
Sat	9/24	A	OTT	30- 19	W	14000
Sat	10/1	H	MTL	28- 30	L	19200
Sat	10/8	A	HAM	11- 15	L	15000
Mon	10/10	H	HAM	16- 15	W	19060
Sat	10/15	A	MTL	23- 44	L	21000
Sat	10/22	H	MTL	12- 43	L	18329
Sat	10/29	H	OTT	29- 13	W	12213
Sat	11/5	A	OTT	24- 36	L	8220
IRFU Semi-Final						
Sat	11/12	A	HAM	32- 28	W	17600
IRFU Final						
Sat	11/19	A	MTL	36- 38	L	21103

1955 WINNIPEG BLUE BOMBERS

Sat	8/20	A	SAS	7- 17	L	14000
Mon	8/22	H	EDM	9- 13	L	16835
Mon	8/29	H	CAL	13- 15	L	15499
Sat	9/3	H	BC	7- 15	L	16458
Mon	9/5	A	CAL	9- 12	L	13000
Mon	9/12	H	SAS	25- 0	W	16133
Sat	9/17	A	BC	20- 19	W	27132
Mon	9/19	A	EDM	8- 14	L	12500
Sat	9/24	A	SAS	7- 12	L	10857
Mon	9/26	H	CAL	25- 6	W	14724
Sat	10/1	H	EDM	12- 0	W	18884
Sat	10/8	A	CAL	13- 12	W	12000
Mon	10/10	A	BC	18- 4	W	21429
Sat	10/22	A	EDM	0- 12	L	16000
Mon	10/24	H	BC	24- 13	W	14730
Sat	10/29	H	SAS	13- 31	L	14464
WIFU Semi-Final (24-16)						
Sat	11/5	A	SAS	16- 7	W	9000
Mon	11/7	H	SAS	8- 9	L	12768
WIFU Final (0-2)						
Fri	11/11	H	EDM	6- 29	L	1555
Wed	11/16	A	EDM	6- 26	L	12000

1956 BRITISH COLUMBIA LIONS

Sat	8/18	A	CAL	17- 14	W	12889
Mon	8/20	H	SAS	20- 9	W	28825
Mon	8/27	H	EDM	0- 18	L	30374
Fri	8/31	A	WPG	1- 3	L	15727
Mon	9/3	A	SAS	10- 24	L	13000
Sat	9/8	H	CAL	45- 15	W	28737
Sat	9/15	A	EDM	8- 34	L	21737
Mon	9/17	H	WPG	15- 16	L	27502
Mon	9/24	H	EDM	11- 1	W	23066
Sat	9/29	A	SAS	28- 46	L	14000
Mon	10/1	A	WPG	7- 34	L	16467
Sat	10/6	H	CAL	24- 7	W	25663
Sat	10/13	H	WPG	8- 40	L	26300
Mon	10/15	A	CAL	22- 21	W	10000
Sat	10/20	H	SAS	22- 25	L	18239
Mon	10/22	A	EDM	13- 54	L	

1956 CALGARY STAMPEDERS

Sat	8/18	H	BC	17- 14	W	12889
Sat	8/25	A	EDM	22- 23	L	16500
Mon	8/27	A	WPG	15- 16	L	16687
Sat	9/1	H	SAS	27- 17	W	12000
Sat	9/8	A	BC	15- 45	L	28737
Mon	9/10	H	EDM	15- 28	L	12000
Sat	9/15	H	WPG	16- 6	W	12789
Mon	9/17	A	SAS	1- 18	L	14000
Sat	9/22	A	EDM	0- 52	L	20000
Sat	9/29	H	WPG	14- 37	L	12000
Sat	10/6	A	BC	7- 24	L	25663
Mon	10/8	H	EDM	8- 36	L	11261
Mon	10/15	H	BC	21- 22	L	10000
Sat	10/20	A	WPG	25- 17	W	15922
Mon	10/22	H	SAS	29- 19	W	9000
Sat	10/27	A	SAS	0- 33	L	8000

1956 EDMONTON ESKIMOS

Sat	8/18	H	SAS	15- 3	W	16500
Sat	8/25	H	CAL	23- 22	W	16500
Mon	8/27	A	BC	18- 0	W	30374
Mon	9/3	H	WPG	21- 20	W	15000
Sat	9/8	A	SAS	4- 31	L	13500
Mon	9/10	A	CAL	28- 15	W	12000
Sat	9/15	H	BC	34- 8	W	21737
Sat	9/22	H	CAL	52- 0	W	20000
Mon	9/24	A	BC	1- 11	L	23066
Mon	10/1	H	SAS	7- 33	L	20000
Sat	10/6	A	WPG	7- 10	L	18700
Mon	10/8	A	CAL	36- 8	W	11261
Sat	10/13	A	SAS	37- 17	W	14500
Mon	10/15	H	WPG	21- 11	W	20000
Mon	10/22	H	BC	54- 13	W	
Sat	10/27	A	WPG	0- 33	L	14409
WIFU Final (2-1)						
Sat	11/10	A	SAS	22- 23	L	13500
Mon	11/12	H	SAS	20- 12	W	19000
Sat	11/17	H	SAS	51- 7	W	22461
Grey Cup						
Sat	11/24	N	MTL	50- 27	W	27425

1956 HAMILTON TIGER-CATS

Wed	8/22	H	OTT	21- 29	L	19500
Wed	8/29	A	TOR	18- 0	W	23801
Mon	9/3	H	TOR	31- 21	W	20725
Sat	9/8	A	OTT	21- 0	W	14514
Wed	9/12	H	TOR	21- 22	L	19153
Fri	9/14	A	TOR	19- 41	L	24118
Sat	9/22	A	MTL	14- 56	L	22367
Sat	9/29	H	MTL	43- 44	L	18000
Sat	10/6	H	TOR	42- 6	W	15125
Mon	10/8	A	TOR	34- 29	W	19046
Sat	10/13	H	OTT	40- 24	W	16511
Sat	10/20	A	MTL	14- 82	L	22365
Sat	10/27	H	MTL	50- 14	W	20000
Sat	11/3	A	OTT	15- 17	L	14042
IRFU Semi-Final						
Wed	11/7	H	OTT	46- 21	W	12121
IRFU Final (62-78)						
Sat	11/10	H	MTL	21- 30	L	16000
Sat	11/17	A	MTL	41- 48	L	22280

1956 MONTREAL ALOUETTES

Sat	8/25	H	TOR	24- 20	W	22732
Fri	8/31	A	OTT	42- 10	W	17870
Mon	9/3	H	OTT	22- 20	W	23014
Sat	9/8	A	TOR	28- 51	L	20942
Wed	9/12	H	OTT	36- 21	W	19463
Sat	9/15	A	OTT	9- 20	L	15000
Sat	9/22	H	HAM	56- 14	W	22367
Sat	9/29	A	HAM	44- 43	W	18000
Sat	10/6	A	OTT	42- 35	W	17463
Mon	10/8	H	OTT	24- 9	W	22365
Sat	10/13	A	TOR	28- 13	W	18679
Sat	10/20	H	HAM	82- 14	W	22365
Sat	10/27	A	HAM	14- 50	L	20000
Sat	11/3	H	TOR	27- 41	L	20913
IRFU Final (78-62)						
Sat	11/10	A	HAM	30- 21	W	16000
Sat	11/17	H	HAM	48- 41	W	22280
Grey Cup						
Sat	11/24	N	EDM	27- 50	L	27425

1956 OTTAWA ROUGH RIDERS

Wed	8/22	A	HAM	29- 21	W	19500
Fri	8/31	H	MTL	10- 42	L	17870
Mon	9/3	A	MTL	20- 22	L	23014
Sat	9/8	H	HAM	0- 21	L	14514
Wed	9/12	A	MTL	21- 36	L	19463
Sat	9/15	H	MTL	20- 9	W	15000
Sat	9/22	A	TOR	31- 20	W	21825
Sat	9/29	H	TOR	43- 22	W	18791
Sat	10/6	H	MTL	35- 42	L	17643
Mon	10/8	A	MTL	9- 24	L	22365
Sat	10/13	A	HAM	24- 40	L	16511
Sat	10/20	H	TOR	37- 26	W	13770
Sat	10/27	A	TOR	30-19	W	15535
Sat	11/3	H	HAM	17- 15	W	14042
IRFU Semi-Final						
Wed	11/7	A	HAM	21- 46	L	12121

1956 SASKATCHEWAN ROUGHRIDERS

Sat	8/18	A	EDM	3- 15	L	16500
Mon	8/20	A	BC	9- 20	L	28825
Sat	8/25	H	WPG	28- 16	W	13000

Sat	9/1	A	CAL	17-27	L	12000
Mon	9/3	H	BC	24-10	W	13000
Sat	9/8	H	EDM	31-4	W	13500
Mon	9/10	A	WPG	0-35	L	17546
Mon	9/17	H	CAL	18-1	W	14000
Sat	9/22	A	WPG	24-7	W	19035
Sat	9/29	H	BC	46-28	W	14000
Mon	10/1	A	EDM	33-7	W	20000
Mon	10/8	H	WPG	26-14	W	15517
Sat	10/13	H	EDM	17-37	L	14500
Sat	10/20	A	BC	25-22	W	18239
Mon	10/22	A	CAL	19-29	L	9000
Sat	10/27	H	CAL	33-0	W	8000
WIFU Semi-Final (50-26)						
Sat	11/3	H	WPG	42-7	W	13000
Mon	11/5	A	WPG	8-19	L	13348
WIFU Final (1-2)						
Sat	11/10	H	EDM	23-22	W	13500
Mon	11/12	A	EDM	12-20	L	19000
Sat	11/17	A	EDM	7-51	L	22461

1956 TORONTO ARGONAUTS

Sat	8/25	A	MTL	20-24	L	22732
Wed	8/29	H	HAM	0-18	L	23801
Mon	9/3	A	HAM	21-31	L	20725
Sat	9/8	H	MTL	51-28	W	20942
Wed	9/12	A	HAM	22-21	W	19153
Fri	9/14	H	HAM	41-19	W	24118
Sat	9/22	H	OTT	20-31	L	21825
Sat	9/29	A	OTT	22-43	L	18791
Sat	10/6	A	HAM	6-42	L	15125
Mon	10/8	H	HAM	29-34	L	19046
Sat	10/13	H	MTL	13-28	L	18679
Sat	10/20	A	OTT	26-37	L	13770
Sat	10/27	H	OTT	19-30	L	15535
Sat	11/3	A	MTL	41-27	W	20913

1956 WINNIPEG BLUE BOMBERS

Sat	8/25	A	SAS	16-28	L	13000
Mon	8/27	H	CAL	16-15	W	16687
Fri	8/31	H	BC	3-1	W	15727
Mon	9/3	A	EDM	20-21	L	15000
Mon	9/10	H	SAS	35-0	W	17546
Sat	9/15	A	CAL	6-16	L	12789
Mon	9/17	A	BC	16-15	W	27502
Sat	9/22	H	SAS	7-24	L	19035
Sat	9/29	A	CAL	37-14	W	14000
Mon	10/1	H	BC	34-7	W	16467
Sat	10/6	H	EDM	10-7	W	18700
Mon	10/8	A	SAS	14-26	L	15517
Sat	10/13	A	BC	40-8	W	26300
Mon	10/15	A	EDM	11-21	L	20000
Sat	10/20	H	CAL	17-25	L	15922
Sat	10/27	H	EDM	33-0	W	14409
WIFU Semi-Final (26-50)						
Sat	11/3	A	SAS	7-42	L	13000
Mon	11/5	H	SAS	19-8	W	13348

1957 BRITISH COLUMBIA LIONS

Sat	8/17	H	SAS	44-20	W	26807
Mon	8/19	A	CAL	1-8	L	10000
Mon	8/26	H	CAL	20-22	L	28100
Fri	8/30	A	WPG	14-20	L	16442
Mon	9/2	A	SAS	13-28	L	14497
Sat	9/7	H	EDM	13-35	L	26121
Sat	9/14	A	EDM	6-25	L	17500
Mon	9/16	H	WPG	21-41	L	22218
Wed	9/25	A	CAL	21-22	L	11000
Mon	9/30	H	SAS	21-21	T	19398
Mon	10/7	H	CAL	27-1	W	16928
Sat	10/12	A	WPG	22-16	W	14700
Mon	10/14	A	SAS	30-10	W	10061
Sat	10/19	H	EDM	12-29	L	24619
Sat	10/26	A	EDM	0-29	L	14000
Sat	11/2	H	WPG	19-42	L	17695

1957 CALGARY STAMPEDERS

Mon	8/19	H	BC	8-1	W	10000
Sat	8/24	H	EDM	10-6	W	16000
Mon	8/26	A	BC	22-20	W	28100
Sat	8/31	H	SAS	26-22	W	16000
Mon	9/9	A	EDM	2-22	L	20000
Sat	9/14	H	WPG	13-40	L	16000
Mon	9/16	A	SAS	27-44	L	11500
Sat	9/21	A	WPG	7-30	L	18322
Wed	9/25	H	BC	22-21	W	11000
Sat	10/5	H	SAS	36-9	W	9500
Mon	10/7	A	BC	1-27	L	16928
Sat	10/12	A	EDM	7-46	L	17000
Mon	10/14	H	EDM	6-32	L	14000
Sat	10/19	H	WPG	7-31	L	10000
Sat	10/26	A	SAS	14-32	L	8500
Mon	10/28	A	WPG	13-30	L	12855
Western Semi-Final (16-28)						
Sat	11/9	A	WPG	13-13	T	12392
Mon	11/11	H	WPG	3-15	L	14000

1957 EDMONTON ESKIMOS

Thu	8/15	A	WPG	21-14	W	18029
Mon	8/19	H	SAS	37-7	W	20000
Sat	8/24	A	CAL	6-10	L	16000
Mon	9/2	H	WPG	41-8	W	17000
Sat	9/7	A	BC	35-13	W	26121
Mon	9/9	H	CAL	22-2	W	20000
Sat	9/14	H	BC	25-6	W	17500
Sat	9/21	A	SAS	24-17	W	13754
Sat	9/28	H	SAS	37-12	W	18000
Mon	9/30	A	WPG	27-28	L	20253
Sat	10/5	H	WPG	41-0	W	16000
Sat	10/12	H	CAL	46-7	W	17000
Mon	10/14	A	CAL	32-6	W	14000
Sat	10/19	A	BC	29-12	W	24619
Sat	10/26	H	BC	29-0	W	14000
Sat	11/2	A	SAS	23-0	W	8000
Western Final (1-2)						
Sat	11/16	A	WPG	7-19	L	13849
Wed	11/20	H	WPG	5-4	W	18000
Sat	11/23	H	WPG	2-17	L*	20000

1957 HAMILTON TIGER-CATS

Tue	8/20	A	OTT	7-20	L	18000
Sat	8/24	H	MTL	22-6	W	17000
Mon	9/2	H	TOR	35-8	W	21685
Fri	9/6	A	TOR	20-9	W	23194
Sat	9/14	H	OTT	18-14	W	22010
Sat	9/21	A	MTL	8-18	L	22984
Sat	9/28	H	MTL	8-14	L	21115
Sat	10/5	A	OTT	18-17	W	17240
Sat	10/12	H	TOR	38-14	W	16000
Mon	10/14	A	TOR	22-16	W	18604
Sat	10/19	H	MTL	18-15	W	19000
Sat	10/26	A	MTL	19-17	W	23000
Sat	11/2	A	OTT	4-9	L	16000
Sat	11/9	H	OTT	13-12	W	18000
IRFU Final (56-11)						
Sat	11/16	A	MTL	17-10	W	19609
Sat	11/23	H	MTL	39-1	W	17600
Grey Cup						
Sat	11/30	N	WPG	32-7	W	27051

1957 MONTREAL ALOUETTES

Tue	8/20	H	TOR	29-28	W	21632
Sat	8/24	A	HAM	6-22	L	17000
Fri	8/31	H	OTT	22-21	W	22984
Sat	9/7	A	OTT	16-17	L	19998
Sat	9/14	H	TOR	43-1	W	22712
Sat	9/21	H	HAM	18-8	W	22984
Sat	9/28	A	HAM	14-8	W	21115
Sat	10/5	A	TOR	31-41	L	14802
Sat	10/12	A	OTT	17-27	L	18356
Mon	10/14	H	OTT	32-24	W	22864
Sat	10/19	A	HAM	15-18	L	19000
Sat	10/26	H	HAM	17-19	L	23000
Sat	11/2	A	TOR	27-40	L	12971
Sat	11/9	H	TOR	0-27	L	20315
IRFU Semi-Final						
Wed	11/13	A	OTT	24-15	W	15000
IRFU Final (11-56)						
Sat	11/16	H	HAM	10-17	L	19609
Sat	11/23	A	HAM	1-39	L	17600

1957 OTTAWA ROUGH RIDERS

Tue	8/20	H	HAM	20-7	W	18000
Fri	8/23	A	TOR	22-17	W	21566
Fri	8/31	A	MTL	21-22	L	22984
Sat	9/7	H	MTL	17-16	W	19998
Sat	9/14	A	HAM	14-18	L	22010
Sat	9/21	A	TOR	55-14	W	15845
Sat	9/28	H	TOR	40-21	W	16506
Sat	10/5	H	HAM	17-18	L	17240
Sat	10/12	H	MTL	27-17	W	18356
Mon	10/14	A	MTL	24-32	L	22864
Sat	10/19	A	TOR	23-31	L	
Sat	10/26	H	TOR	25-7	W	12440
Sat	11/2	H	HAM	9-4	W	16000
Sat	11/9	A	HAM	12-13	L	18000
IRFU Semi-Final						
Wed	11/13	H	MTL	15-24	L	15000

1957 SASKATCHEWAN ROUGHRIDERS

Sat	8/17	A	BC	20-44	L	26807
Mon	8/19	A	EDM	7-37	L	20000
Sat	8/24	H	WPG	3-7	L	12500
Sat	8/31	A	CAL	22-26	L	16000
Mon	9/2	H	BC	28-13	W	14497
Sat	9/7	A	WPG	29-35	L	15975
Mon	9/16	H	CAL	44-27	W	11500
Sat	9/21	H	EDM	17-24	L	13754
Sat	9/28	A	EDM	12-37	L	18000
Mon	9/30	A	BC	21-21	T	19398
Sat	10/5	A	CAL	9-36	L	9500
Mon	10/7	H	WPG	3-37	L	8500
Mon	10/14	H	BC	10-30	L	10061
Mon	10/21	A	WPG	19-27	L	14186
Sat	10/26	H	CAL	32-14	W	8500
Sat	11/2	H	EDM	0-23	L	8000

1957 TORONTO ARGONAUTS

Tue	8/20	A	MTL	28-29	L	21632
Fri	8/23	H	OTT	17-22	L	21566
Mon	9/2	A	HAM	8-35	L	21685
Fri	9/6	H	HAM	9-20	L	23194
Sat	9/14	A	MTL	1-43	L	22712
Sat	9/21	H	OTT	14-55	L	15845
Sat	9/28	A	OTT	21-40	L	16506
Sat	10/5	H	MTL	41-31	W	14802
Sat	10/12	A	HAM	14-38	L	16000
Mon	10/14	H	HAM	16-22	L	18604
Sat	10/19	H	OTT	31-23	W	
Sat	10/26	A	OTT	7-25	L	12440
Sat	11/2	H	MTL	40-27	W	12971
Sat	11/9	A	MTL	27-0	W	20315

1957 WINNIPEG BLUE BOMBERS

Thu	8/15	H	EDM	14-21	L	18029
Sat	8/24	A	SAS	7-3	W	12500
Fri	8/30	H	BC	20-14	W	16442
Mon	9/2	A	EDM	8-41	L	17000
Sat	9/7	H	SAS	35-29	W	15975
Sat	9/14	A	CAL	40-13	W	16000
Mon	9/16	A	BC	41-21	W	22218
Sat	9/21	H	CAL	30-7	W	18322
Mon	9/30	H	EDM	28-27	W	20253
Sat	10/5	A	EDM	0-41	L	16000
Mon	10/7	A	SAS	37-3	W	8500
Sat	10/12	H	BC	16-22	L	14700
Sat	10/19	A	CAL	31-7	W	10000
Mon	10/21	H	SAS	27-19	W	14186
Mon	10/28	H	CAL	30-13	W	12855
Sat	11/2	A	BC	42-19	W	17695
Western Semi-Final (28-16)						
Sat	11/9	H	CAL	13-13	T	12392
Mon	11/11	A	CAL	15-3	W	14000
Western Final (2-1)						
Sat	11/16	H	EDM	19-7	W	13849
Wed	11/20	A	EDM	4-5	L	18000
Sat	11/23	A	EDM	17-2	W*	20000
Grey Cup						
Sat	11/30	N	HAM	7-32	L	27051

1958 BRITISH COLUMBIA LIONS

Fri	8/16	H	SAS	33-49	L	30408
Mon	8/18	A	CAL	0-42	L	15133
Mon	8/25	H	CAL	13-34	L	26358
Thu	8/28	A	WPG	1-31	L	16611
Mon	9/1	A	SAS	14-22	L	15595
Sat	9/6	H	EDM	7-26	L	26653
Sat	9/13	A	EDM	7-13	L	8000
Mon	9/15	H	WPG	8-19	L	20000
Sat	9/27	A	CAL	15-29	L	14500
Mon	9/29	H	SAS	6-22	L	20226
Mon	10/6	H	CAL	15-14	W	18574
Sat	10/11	A	WPG	10-8	W	14484
Mon	10/13	A	SAS	34-16	W	11909
Sat	10/18	H	EDM	22-25	L	24700
Sat	10/25	A	EDM	3-25	L	13000
Sat	11/1	H	WPG	14-24	L	18918

1958 CALGARY STAMPEDERS

Mon	8/18	H	BC	42-0	W	15133
Sat	8/23	H	EDM	35-7	W	17770
Mon	8/25	A	BC	34-13	W	26358
Mon	9/1	H	WPG	11-3	W	17750
Mon	9/8	A	EDM	28-32	L	20000
Sat	9/13	H	WPG	7-20	L	15700
Mon	9/15	A	SAS	7-30	L	13012
Sat	9/20	A	WPG	9-36	L	20059
Sat	9/27	H	BC	29-15	W	14500
Sat	10/4	H	SAS	14-22	L	18000
Mon	10/6	A	BC	14-15	L	18574
Sat	10/11	A	EDM	10-17	L	15000
Mon	10/13	H	EDM	14-19	L	10000
Sat	10/18	A	SAS	21-17	W	10148
Sat	10/25	H	SAS	29-29	T	13500
Mon	10/27	A	WPG	10-37	L	15564

1958 EDMONTON ESKIMOS

Thu	8/14	A	WPG	21-29	L	18166
Fri	8/18	H	SAS	40-6	W	18000
Sat	8/23	A	CAL	7-35	L	17770
Mon	8/25	H	WPG	8-15	L	17000
Sat	9/6	A	BC	26-7	W	26653
Mon	9/8	H	CAL	32-28	W	20000
Sat	9/13	H	BC	13-7	W	8000
Sat	9/20	A	SAS	26-13	W	12789
Sat	9/27	H	SAS	11-11	T	15000
Mon	9/29	A	WPG	13-43	L	18559
Sat	10/4	H	WPG	15-21	L	20000
Sat	10/11	H	CAL	17-10	W	15000
Mon	10/13	A	CAL	19-14	W	10000
Sat	10/18	A	BC	25-22	W	24700
Sat	10/25	H	BC	25-3	W	13000
Sat	11/1	A	SAS	14-28	L	9000
WIFU Semi-Final (58-12)						
Sat	11/8	A	SAS	27-11	W	12000
Tue	11/11	H	SAS	31-1	W	18000
WIFU Final (1-2)						
Sat	11/15	H	WPG	7-30	L	17000
Wed	11/19	A	WPG	30-7	W	16880
Sat	11/22	A	WPG	7-23	L	15671

1958 HAMILTON TIGER-CATS

Tue	8/19	A	MTL	27-14	W	22676
Sat	8/23	H	OTT	13-7	W	21297
Mon	9/1	H	TOR	31-24	W	20946
Sat	9/5	A	TOR	26-17	W	26781
Sun	9/14	N	OTT	24-18	W	15110
Sat	9/20	A	MTL	21-21	T	23641
Sat	9/27	H	MTL	35-29	W	20000

Sat 10/4 A OTT 14- 1 W 18000
Sat 10/11 H TOR 28- 15 W 16583
Mon 10/13 A TOR 0- 37 L 16583
Sat 10/18 H MTL 29- 10 W 17915
Sat 10/25 A MTL 12- 28 L 22391
Sat 11/1 A OTT 8- 14 L 13603
Sat 11/8 H OTT 23- 0 W 14874
IRFU Final (54-144)
Sat 11/15 A OTT 35- 7 W 10490
Sat 11/22 H OTT 19- 7 W 15671
Grey Cup
Sat 11/29 N WPG 28- 35 L 36567

1958 MONTREAL ALOUETTES
Tue 8/19 H HAM 14- 27 L 22676
Fri 8/22 A TOR 14- 15 L 19492
Sat 8/30 H OTT 11- 9 W 22943
Sat 9/6 A OTT 1- 17 L 17056
Sat 9/13 H TOR 24- 21 W 23000
Sat 9/20 H HAM 21- 21 T 23641
Sat 9/27 A HAM 29- 35 L 20000
Sat 10/4 A TOR 14- 10 W 16000
Sat 10/11 A OTT 7- 41 L 15000
Mon 10/13 H OTT 34- 13 W 24133
Sat 10/18 A HAM 10- 29 L 10148
Sat 10/25 H HAM 28- 12 W 22391
Sat 11/1 A TOR 44- 7 W 26813
Sat 11/8 H TOR 14- 12 W 22482
IRFU Semi-Final
Wed 11/12 H OTT 12- 26 L 18048

1958 OTTAWA ROUGH RIDERS
Tue 8/19 H TOR 44- 7 W 18470
Sat 8/23 A HAM 7- 13 L 21297
Sat 8/30 A MTL 9- 11 L 22943
Sat 9/6 H MTL 17- 1 W 17056
Sun 9/14 N HAM 18- 24 L 15110
Sat 9/20 A TOR 17- 14 W 20166
Sat 9/27 H TOR 28- 4 W 18500
Sat 10/4 H HAM 1- 14 L 18000
Sat 10/11 H MTL 41- 7 W 15000
Mon 10/13 A MTL 13- 34 L 24133
Sat 10/18 H TOR 0- 41 L 14313
Sat 10/25 A TOR 24- 42 L 23334
Sat 11/1 H HAM 14- 8 W 13603
Sat 11/8 A HAM 0- 23 L 14874
IRFU Semi-Final
Wed 11/12 A MTL 26- 12 W 18048
IRFU Final (14-54)
Sat 11/15 H HAM 7- 35 L 10490
Sat 11/22 A HAM 7- 19 L 15671

1958 SASKATCHEWAN ROUGHRIDERS
Fri 8/16 A BC 49- 33 W 30408
Fri 8/18 A EDM 6- 40 L 18000
Thu 8/21 H WPG 21- 13 W 13233
Mon 9/1 H BC 22- 14 W 15595
Sat 9/6 A WPG 6- 27 L 18336
Mon 9/15 H CAL 30- 7 W 13012
Sat 9/20 H EDM 13- 26 L 12789
Sat 9/27 A EDM 11- 11 T 15000
Mon 9/29 A BC 22- 6 W 20226
Sat 10/4 A CAL 22- 14 W 18000
Mon 10/6 H WPG 13- 14 L 11581
Mon 10/13 H BC 16- 34 L 11909
Sat 10/18 H CAL 17- 21 L 10148
Mon 10/20 A WPG 15- 21 L 16319
Sat 10/25 A CAL 29- 29 T 13500
Sat 11/1 H EDM 28- 14 W 9000
WIFU Semi-Final (12-58)
Sat 11/8 H EDM 11- 27 L 12000
Tue 11/11 A EDM 1- 31 L 18000

1958 TORONTO ARGONAUTS
Tue 8/19 A OTT 7- 44 L 18470
Fri 8/22 H MTL 15- 14 W 19492
Mon 9/1 A HAM 24- 31 L 20946
Fri 9/5 H HAM 17- 26 L 26781
Sat 9/13 A MTL 21- 24 L 23000
Sat 9/20 H OTT 14- 17 L 20166
Sat 9/27 A OTT 4- 28 L 18500
Sat 10/4 H MTL 10- 14 L 16000
Sat 10/11 A HAM 15- 28 L 16583
Mon 10/13 H HAM 10- 29 L 16583
Sat 10/18 A OTT 41- 0 W 14313
Sat 10/25 H OTT 42- 24 W 23334
Sat 11/1 H MTL 7- 44 L 26813
Sat 11/8 A MTL 12- 14 L 22482

1958 WINNIPEG BLUE BOMBERS
Thu 8/14 H EDM 29- 21 W 18166
Thu 8/21 A SAS 13- 21 L 13233
Mon 8/25 A EDM 15- 8 W 17000
Thu 8/28 H BC 31- 1 W 16611
Mon 9/1 A CAL 3- 11 L 17750
Sat 9/6 H SAS 27- 6 W 18336
Sat 9/13 A CAL 20- 7 W 15700
Mon 9/15 A BC 19- 8 W 20000
Sat 9/20 H CAL 36- 9 W 20059
Mon 9/29 H EDM 43- 13 W 18559
Sat 10/4 A EDM 21- 15 W 20000
Mon 10/6 A SAS 14- 13 W 11581
Sat 10/11 H BC 8- 10 L 14484
Mon 10/20 H SAS 21- 15 W 16319
Mon 10/27 H CAL 37- 10 W 15564
Sat 11/1 A BC 24- 14 W 18918
WIFU Final (2-1)
Sat 11/15 A EDM 30- 7 W 17000
Wed 11/19 H EDM 7- 30 L 16880
Sat 11/22 H EDM 23- 7 W 15671
Grey Cup
Sat 11/29 N HAM 35- 28 W 36567

1959 BRITISH COLUMBIA LIONS
Thu 8/13 H WPG 20- 42 L 29425
Mon 8/17 A EDM 12- 0 W 14000
Thu 8/20 H SAS 36- 21 W 29131
Mon 8/24 A CAL 17- 29 L
Mon 8/31 H EDM 8- 7 W 34273
Thu 9/3 A WPG 23- 34 L 18003
Mon 9/7 A SAS 35- 17 W 12566
Mon 9/14 H CAL 14- 8 W 32176
Sat 9/19 H WPG 17- 6 W 32061
Mon 9/21 A EDM 7- 29 L 18000
Sat 9/26 A CAL 28- 10 W 14800
Mon 10/5 H SAS 14- 15 L 25778
Sat 10/10 H EDM 14- 38 L 28679
Sat 10/17 A WPG 6- 31 L 18184
Mon 10/19 A SAS 45- 6 W 7500
Sat 10/24 H CAL 10- 8 W 31594
WIFU Semi-Final (15-61)
Sat 10/31 H EDM 8- 20 L 33993
Wed 11/4 A EDM 7- 41 L 16000

1959 CALGARY STAMPEDERS
Fri 8/14 A SAS 28- 8 W 13212
Mon 8/17 H WPG 21- 22 L 16200
Thu 8/20 A WPG 23- 21 W 18333
Mon 8/24 H BC 29- 17 W
Mon 8/31 H SAS 28- 10 W 10500
Mon 9/7 H EDM 10- 16 L 17200
Sat 9/12 A EDM 20- 27 L 20000
Mon 9/14 A BC 8- 14 L 32176
Mon 9/21 H WPG 10- 15 L 16000
Sat 9/26 H BC 10- 28 L 14800
Mon 9/28 A SAS 18- 15 W 6500
Mon 10/5 A WPG 24- 38 L 15813
Sat 10/10 H SAS 53- 13 W 8500
Mon 10/12 A EDM 41- 23 W 15500
Sat 10/17 H EDM 25- 24 W 17000
Sat 10/24 A BC 8- 10 L 31594

1959 EDMONTON ESKIMOS
Mon 8/17 H BC 0- 12 L 14000
Mon 8/24 H SAS 55- 0 W 14000
Thu 8/27 A WPG 16- 1 W 18928
Mon 8/31 A BC 7- 8 L 34273
Sat 9/5 H WPG 8- 16 L 17143
Mon 9/7 A CAL 16- 10 W 17200
Sat 9/12 H CAL 27- 20 W 20000
Sat 9/19 A SAS 32- 0 W 10000
Mon 9/21 H BC 29- 7 W 18000
Mon 9/28 A WPG 10- 13 L 17707
Sat 10/3 H SAS 44- 15 W 17500
Sat 10/10 A BC 38- 14 W 28679
Mon 10/12 H CAL 23- 41 L 15500
Sat 10/17 A CAL 24- 25 L 17000
Mon 10/19 H WPG 21- 20 W 15500
Sat 10/24 A SAS 20- 19 W 8000
WIFU Semi-Final (61-15)
Sat 10/31 A BC 20- 8 W 33993
Wed 11/4 H BC 41- 7 W 16000
WIFU Final (0-2)
Wed 11/11 H WPG 11- 19 L 16000
Sat 11/14 A WPG 8- 16 L 15872

1959 HAMILTON TIGER-CATS
Tue 8/18 H MTL 22- 16 W 22126
Fri 8/21 A TOR 16- 7 W 28000
Sat 8/29 H OTT 34- 10 W 17266
Mon 9/7 H TOR 37- 3 W 24425
Sat 9/12 A MTL 21- 27 L 26218
Wed 9/16 H MTL 25- 13 W 24759
Sun 9/20 A TOR 34- 17 W 27883
Sat 9/26 A OTT 23- 14 W 19837
Sat 10/3 H OTT 7- 9 L 20012
Sat 10/10 A TOR 13- 7 W 26223
Mon 10/12 H TOR 20- 7 W 22068
Sat 10/17 A OTT 16- 17 L 16000
Sat 10/24 H MTL 16- 0 W 15500
Sat 10/31 A MTL 14- 15 L 21817
IRFU Final (26-24)
Sat 11/14 A OTT 5- 17 L 18926
Sat 11/21 H OTT 21- 7 W 20000
Grey Cup
Sat 11/28 N WPG 7- 21 L 33133

1959 MONTREAL ALOUETTES
Tue 8/18 A HAM 16- 22 L 22126
Fri 8/21 H OTT 23- 8 W 22813
Fri 8/28 H TOR 24- 6 W 23927
Sat 9/5 A OTT 22- 7 W 16698
Sat 9/12 H HAM 27- 21 W 26218
Wed 9/16 A HAM 13- 25 L 24759
Sat 9/19 H OTT 6- 43 L 23811
Sat 9/26 A TOR 9- 39 L 20035
Sat 10/3 H TOR 14- 37 L 22152
Sat 10/10 A OTT 8- 36 L 17203
Mon 10/12 H OTT 12- 28 L 21817
Sat 10/17 A TOR 4- 3 W 19041
Sat 10/24 A HAM 0- 16 L 15500
Sat 10/31 H HAM 15- 14 W 21817
IRFU Semi-Final
Sat 11/7 A OTT 0- 43 L 19060

1959 OTTAWA ROUGH RIDERS
Tue 8/18 H TOR 20- 21 L 20675
Fri 8/21 A MTL 8- 23 L 22813
Sat 8/29 A HAM 10- 34 L 17266
Sat 9/5 H MTL 7- 22 L 16698
Sun 9/13 A TOR 6- 19 L 25849
Wed 9/16 H TOR 28- 1 W 13097
Sat 9/19 A MTL 43- 6 W 23811
Sat 9/26 H HAM 14- 23 L 19837
Sat 10/3 A HAM 9- 7 W 20012
Sat 10/10 H MTL 36- 8 W 17203
Mon 10/12 A MTL 28- 12 W 21817
Sat 10/17 H HAM 17- 16 W 16000
Sat 10/24 H TOR 18- 4 W 14698
Sat 10/31 A TOR 31- 21 W 19465
IRFU Semi-Final
Sat 11/7 H MTL 43- 0 W 19060
IRFU Final (24-26)
Sat 11/14 H HAM 17- 5 W 18926
Sat 11/21 A HAM 7- 21 L 20000

1959 SASKATCHEWAN ROUGHRIDERS
Fri 8/14 H CAL 8- 28 L 13212
Thu 8/20 A BC 21- 36 L 29131
Mon 8/24 A EDM 0- 55 L 14000
Sat 8/29 H WPG 8- 61 L 12000
Mon 8/31 A CAL 10- 28 L 10500
Mon 9/7 H BC 17- 35 L 12566
Sat 9/12 A WPG 14- 41 L 15962
Sat 9/19 H EDM 0- 32 L 10000
Mon 9/28 H CAL 15- 18 L 6500
Sat 10/3 A EDM 15- 44 L 17500
Mon 10/5 A BC 15- 14 W 25778
Sat 10/10 A CAL 13- 53 L 8500
Mon 10/12 H WPG 14- 27 L 8000
Mon 10/19 H BC 6- 45 L 7500
Sat 10/24 H EDM 19- 20 L 8000
Mon 10/26 A WPG 37-30 FL 14279

1959 TORONTO ARGONAUTS
Tue 8/18 A OTT 21- 20 W 20675
Fri 8/21 H HAM 7- 16 L 22813
Fri 8/28 A MTL 6- 24 L 23927
Mon 9/7 A HAM 3- 37 L 24425
Sun 9/13 H OTT 19- 6 W 25849
Wed 9/16 A OTT 1- 28 L 13097
Sun 9/20 H HAM 17- 34 L 27883
Sat 9/26 H MTL 39- 9 W 20035
Sat 10/3 A MTL 37- 14 W 22152
Sat 10/10 H HAM 7- 13 L 26223
Mon 10/12 A HAM 7- 20 L 22068
Sat 10/17 H MTL 3- 4 L 19041
Sat 10/24 A OTT 4- 18 L 14698
Sat 10/31 H OTT 21- 31 L 19465

1959 WINNIPEG BLUE BOMBERS
Thu 8/13 A BC 42- 20 W 29425
Mon 8/17 A CAL 22- 21 W 16200
Thu 8/20 H CAL 21- 23 L 18333
Thu 8/27 H EDM 1- 16 L 18928
Sat 8/29 A SAS 61- 8 W 12000
Thu 9/3 H BC 34- 23 W 18003
Sat 9/5 A EDM 16- 8 W 17143
Sat 9/12 H SAS 41- 14 W 15962
Sat 9/19 A BC 6- 17 L 32061
Mon 9/21 A CAL 15- 10 W 16000
Mon 9/28 H EDM 13- 10 W 17707
Mon 10/5 H CAL 38- 24 W 15813
Mon 10/12 A SAS 27- 14 W 8000
Sat 10/17 H BC 31- 6 W 18184
Mon 10/19 A EDM 20- 21 L 15500
Mon 10/26 H SAS 30- 37 FW 14279
WIFU Final (2-0)
Wed 11/11 A EDM 19- 11 W 16000
Sat 11/14 H EDM 16- 8 W 15872
Grey Cup
Sat 11/28 N HAM 21- 7 W 33133

1960 BRITISH COLUMBIA LIONS
Thu 8/11 H WPG 21- 35 L 31837
Mon 8/15 A EDM 14- 33 L 17500
Sat 8/20 H SAS 27- 12 W 29532
Mon 8/22 A CAL 26- 19 W 13000
Mon 8/29 H EDM 0- 26 L 28420
Thu 9/1 A WPG 14- 19 L 18300
Mon 9/5 A SAS 31- 21 W 14105
Mon 9/12 H CAL 21- 21 T 27759
Sat 9/17 H WPG 14- 26 L 30300
Mon 9/19 A EDM 10- 18 L
Sat 9/24 A CAL 14- 28 L 13000
Thu 10/6 H EDM 21- 13 W 21707
Thu 10/13 A WPG 21- 49 L 16750
Sat 10/15 A SAS 14- 14 T 7255
Sat 10/22 H CAL 10- 22 L 29599

Sat 10/29 H SAS 38- 0 W 21114

1960 CALGARY STAMPEDERS
Fri 8/12 A SAS 15- 15 T 13192
Mon 8/15 H WPG 23- 38 L 20450
Thu 8/18 A WPG 7- 50 L 18389
Mon 8/22 H BC 19- 26 L 13000
Mon 8/29 H SAS 23- 15 W 13500
Mon 9/5 H EDM 28- 29 L 19000
Sat 9/10 A EDM 10- 41 L 17993
Mon 9/12 A BC 21- 21 T 27759
Mon 9/19 H WPG 17- 19 L 14300
Sat 9/24 H BC 28- 14 W 13000
Mon 9/26 A SAS 35- 45 L 9512
Sat 10/1 A WPG 21- 31 L 15950
Wed 10/5 H SAS 39- 22 W 11000
Sat 10/8 A EDM 31- 11 W 13500
Sat 10/15 H EDM 35- 17 W 17000
Sat 10/22 A BC 22- 10 W 29599
WIFU Semi-Final (28-70)
Wed 11/2 A EDM 7- 30 L 16012
Sat 11/5 H EDM 21- 40 L 20000

1960 EDMONTON ESKIMOS
Mon 8/15 H BC 33- 14 W 17500
Mon 8/22 H SAS 19- 1 W 17000
Thu 8/25 A WPG 14- 18 L 17300
Mon 8/29 A BC 26- 0 W 28420
Sat 9/3 H WPG 14- 15 L 19550
Mon 9/5 A CAL 29- 28 W 19000
Sat 9/10 H CAL 41- 10 W 17993
Fri 9/16 A SAS 29- 6 W 10100
Mon 9/19 H BC 18- 10 W
Mon 9/26 A WPG 15- 2 W 20950
Fri 9/30 H SAS 9- 2 W 14997
Thu 10/6 A BC 13- 21 L 21707
Sat 10/8 H CAL 11- 31 L 13500
Sat 10/15 A CAL 17- 35 L 17000
Mon 10/17 H WPG 17- 21 L 15000
Sat 10/22 A SAS 13- 11 W 6600
WIFU Semi-Final (70-28)
Wed 11/2 H CAL 30- 7 W 16012
Sat 11/5 A CAL 40- 21 W 20000
WIFU Final (2-1)
Sat 11/12 H WPG 16- 22 L 17500
Mon 11/14 A WPG 10- 5 W 16708
Sat 11/19 A WPG 4- 2 W 18600
Grey Cup
Sat 11/26 N OTT 6- 16 L 38102

1960 HAMILTON TIGER-CATS
Tue 8/16 A MTL 10- 23 L 23531
Sat 8/20 H OTT 6- 35 L 18500
Mon 8/29 A OTT 21- 29 L 18344
Mon 9/5 H TOR 21- 32 L 26253
Sun 9/11 A TOR 12- 16 L 30863
Wed 9/14 A MTL 23- 22 W 22670
Sat 9/17 H MTL 29- 30 L 24000
Sat 9/24 H OTT 21- 35 L 19456
Sat 10/1 A OTT 27- 28 L 19264
Fri 10/7 A TOR 14- 24 L 27494
Mon 10/10 H TOR 20- 16 W 25000
Sat 10/15 A MTL 21- 43 L 19891
Sat 10/22 H MTL 22- 30 L 19199
Sat 10/29 H OTT 26- 24 W 12000

1960 MONTREAL ALOUETTES
Tue 8/16 H HAM 23- 10 W 23531
Fri 8/19 A TOR 14- 36 L 26524
Fri 8/26 H TOR 28- 29 L 24533
Sat 9/3 A OTT 16- 40 L 19343
Mon 9/5 H OTT 39- 22 W 23876
Wed 9/14 H HAM 22- 23 L 22670
Sat 9/17 A HAM 30- 29 W 24000
Sat 9/24 H TOR 9- 21 L 23452
Sat 10/1 A TOR 15- 50 L 24145
Sat 10/8 A OTT 23- 41 L 16721
Mon 10/10 H OTT 21- 51 L 22199
Sat 10/15 H HAM 43- 21 W 19891
Sat 10/22 A HAM 30- 22 W 19199
Sun 10/30 A TOR 27- 63 L 26069
IRFU Semi-Final
Sat 11/5 A OTT 14- 30 L 17987

1960 OTTAWA ROUGH RIDERS
Tue 8/16 H TOR 7- 21 L 20321
Sat 8/20 A HAM 35- 6 W 18500
Mon 8/29 H HAM 29- 21 W 18344
Sat 9/3 H MTL 40- 16 W 19343
Mon 9/5 A MTL 22- 39 L 23876
Wed 9/14 H TOR 21- 12 W 20477
Sun 9/18 A TOR 26- 12 W 30949
Sat 9/24 A HAM 35- 21 W 19456
Sat 10/1 H HAM 18- 27 L 19264
Sat 10/8 H MTL 41- 23 W 16721
Mon 10/10 A MTL 51- 21 W 22199
Sun 10/16 A TOR 13- 37 L 32896
Sat 10/22 H TOR 38- 1 W 19199
Sat 10/29 A HAM 24- 26 L 12000
IRFU Semi-Final
Sat 11/5 H MTL 30- 14 W 17987
IRFU Final (54-41)
Sat 11/12 H TOR 33- 21 W 18385
Sun 11/20 A TOR 21- 20 W 30529
Grey Cup
Sat 11/26 N EDM 16- 6 W 38102

1960 TORONTO ARGONAUTS
Tue 8/16 A OTT 21- 7 W 20321
Fri 8/19 H MTL 36- 14 W 26524
Fri 8/26 A MTL 29- 28 W 24533
Mon 9/5 A HAM 32- 21 W 26253
Sun 9/11 H HAM 16- 12 W 30863
Wed 9/14 A OTT 12- 21 L 20477
Sun 9/18 H OTT 12- 26 L 30949
Sat 9/24 A MTL 21- 9 W 23452
Sat 10/1 H MTL 50- 15 W 24145
Fri 10/7 H HAM 24- 14 W 27494
Mon 10/10 A HAM 16- 20 L 25000
Sun 10/16 H OTT 37- 13 W 32896
Sat 10/22 A OTT 1- 38 L 19199
Sun 10/30 H MTL 63- 27 W 26069
IRFU Final (41-54)
Sat 11/12 A OTT 21- 33 L 18385
Sun 11/20 H OTT 20- 21 L 30529

1960 WINNIPEG BLUE BOMBERS
Thu 8/11 A BC 35- 21 W 31837
Mon 8/15 A CAL 38- 23 W 20450
Thu 8/18 H CAL 50- 7 W 18389
Thu 8/25 H EDM 18- 14 W 17300
Sat 8/27 A SAS 27- 0 W 12150
Thu 9/1 H BC 19- 14 W 18300
Sat 9/3 A EDM 15- 14 W 19550
Mon 9/12 H SAS 38- 11 W 16530
Sat 9/17 A BC 26- 14 W 30300
Mon 9/19 A CAL 19- 17 W 14300
Mon 9/26 H EDM 2- 15 L 20950
Sat 10/1 H CAL 31- 21 W 15950
Mon 10/10 A SAS 48- 7 W 10350
Thu 10/13 H BC 49- 21 W 16750
Mon 10/17 A EDM 21- 17 W 15000
Mon 10/24 H SAS 17- 23 L 13900
WIFU Final (1-2)
Sat 11/12 A EDM 22- 16 W 17500
Mon 11/14 H EDM 5- 10 L 16708
Sat 11/19 H EDM 2- 4 L 18600

1961 BRITISH COLUMBIA LIONS
Mon 8/7 H EDM 19- 29 L 28617
Sat 8/12 A OTT 7- 41 L 17329
Tue 8/15 A HAM 21- 30 L 17103
Mon 8/21 H MTL 7- 7 T 26863
Thu 8/24 A SAS 6- 25 L 12341
Mon 8/28 A EDM 20- 21 L 13000
Sat 9/9 H CAL 17- 35 L 32066
Thu 9/14 A WPG 15- 36 L 16016
Mon 9/18 H TOR 7- 15 L 24428
Sat 9/23 A CAL 9- 28 L 16000
Sat 9/30 H EDM 21- 9 W 20210
Sat 10/7 A WPG 20- 24 L 13050
Mon 10/9 A SAS 7- 17 L 11529
Mon 10/16 H WPG 15- 16 L 20778
Sat 10/28 H SAS 17- 17 T 19836
Sun 11/5 H CAL 7- 43 L 19564

1961 CALGARY STAMPEDERS
Mon 8/7 H WPG 17- 18 L 13000
Thu 8/10 A SAS 20- 10 W 12700
Sat 8/19 H SAS 15- 22 L 15000
Sat 8/26 H OTT 1- 32 L 13928
Mon 9/4 H EDM 9- 10 L 15000
Sat 9/9 A BC 35- 17 W 32066
Sat 9/16 H HAM 36- 37 L 16707
Sat 9/23 H BC 28- 9 W 16000
Fri 9/29 A TOR 19- 22 L 23546
Mon 10/2 A MTL 6- 2 W 19028
Sat 10/7 A EDM 28- 21 W 15106
Sat 10/14 H WPG 6- 25 L 17225
Sat 10/21 A SAS 22- 17 W 10271
Mon 10/23 A WPG 7- 42 L 13777
Mon 10/30 H EDM 8- 20 L 10000
Sun 11/5 A BC 43- 7 W 19564
Western Semi-Final (27-26)
Sat 11/11 H EDM 10- 8 W 18000
Mon 11/13 A EDM 17- 18 L 14112
Western Final (0-2)
Sat 11/18 H WPG 1- 14 L 18500
Wed 11/22 A WPG 14- 43 L 16800

1961 EDMONTON ESKIMOS
Mon 8/7 A BC 29- 19 W 28617
Mon 8/14 H SAS 38- 8 W 16500
Sat 8/19 H MTL 33- 0 W 17000
Thu 8/24 A WPG 35- 20 W 19660
Mon 8/28 H BC 21- 20 W 13000
Mon 9/4 A CAL 10- 9 W 15000
Sat 9/9 A OTT 35- 26 W 22152
Mon 9/11 A HAM 15- 32 L 27646
Sat 9/16 H TOR 8- 8 T 21510
Sat 9/23 H WPG 10- 33 L 19198
Mon 9/25 A SAS 16- 1 W 10182
Sat 9/30 A BC 9- 21 L 20210
Sat 10/7 H CAL 21- 28 L 15106
Sat 10/14 H SAS 21- 10 W 12338
Mon 10/30 A CAL 20- 8 W 10000
Sat 11/4 H WPG 13- 14 L 10177
Western Semi-Final (26-27)
Sat 11/11 A CAL 8- 10 L 18000
Mon 11/13 H CAL 18- 17 W 14112

1961 HAMILTON TIGER-CATS
Tue 8/15 H BC 30- 21 W 17103
Sun 8/20 A TOR 28- 24 W 27809
Thu 8/31 A WPG 30- 9 W 18951
Mon 9/4 H TOR 21- 19 W 26533
Mon 9/11 H EDM 32- 15 W 27646
Sat 9/16 A CAL 37- 36 W 16707
Mon 9/18 A SAS 22- 15 W 10152
Sat 9/23 H MTL 7- 28 L 25291
Sat 9/30 A OTT 21- 47 L 22400
Mon 10/9 H OTT 10- 14 L 25273
Sun 10/15 A TOR 37- 10 W 29553
Sun 10/22 H MTL 15- 5 W 22723
Sat 10/28 H OTT 44- 29 W 20271
Sat 11/4 A MTL 6- 21 L 16199
Eastern Final (55-27)
Sat 11/18 A TOR 7- 25 L 33161
Sat 11/25 H TOR 48- 2 W 22671
Grey Cup
Sat 12/2 A WPG 14- 21 L* 32651

1961 MONTREAL ALOUETTES
Fri 8/11 H WPG 15- 21 L 18059
Sat 8/19 A EDM 0- 33 L 17000
Mon 8/21 A BC 7- 7 T 26863
Fri 8/25 H TOR 10- 15 L 18522
Sat 9/2 A OTT 24- 25 L 16009
Fri 9/8 H SAS 15- 16 L 18943
Sat 9/16 H OTT 26- 12 W 19190
Sat 9/23 A HAM 28- 7 W 25291
Mon 10/2 H CAL 2- 6 L 19028
Sat 10/7 H TOR 27- 33 L 19075
Sat 10/14 A OTT 24- 14 W 18589
Sun 10/22 A HAM 5- 15 L 22723
Sun 10/29 A TOR 9- 15 L 23316
Sat 11/4 H HAM 21- 6 W 16199

1961 OTTAWA ROUGH RIDERS
Sat 8/12 H BC 41- 7 W 17329
Thu 8/17 A WPG 19- 29 L 18517
Sat 8/26 A CAL 32- 1 W 13928
Mon 8/28 A SAS 29- 10 W 14291
Sat 9/2 H MTL 25- 24 W 16009
Sat 9/9 H EDM 26- 35 L 22152
Sat 9/16 A MTL 12- 26 L 19190
Sun 9/24 A TOR 29- 10 W 30648
Sat 9/30 H HAM 47- 21 W 22400
Mon 10/9 A HAM 14- 10 W 25273
Sat 10/14 H MTL 14- 24 L 18589
Sat 10/21 H TOR 7- 21 L 18821
Sat 10/28 A HAM 29- 44 L 20271
Sat 11/4 H TOR 35- 23 W 17144
Eastern Semi-Final
Sat 11/11 H TOR 19- 43 L 19151

1961 SASKATCHEWAN ROUGHRIDERS
Thu 8/10 H CAL 10- 20 L 12700
Mon 8/14 A EDM 8- 38 L 16500
Sat 8/19 A CAL 22- 15 W 15000
Thu 8/24 H BC 25- 6 W 12341
Mon 8/28 H OTT 10- 29 L 14291
Mon 9/4 H WPG 11- 17 L 15124
Fri 9/8 A MTL 16- 15 W 18943
Sun 9/10 A TOR 7- 27 L 24047
Mon 9/18 H HAM 15- 22 L 10152
Mon 9/25 H EDM 1- 16 L 10182
Sat 9/30 A WPG 6- 29 L 14354
Mon 10/9 H BC 17- 7 W 11529
Sat 10/14 A EDM 10- 21 L 12338
Sat 10/21 H CAL 17- 22 L 10271
Sat 10/28 A BC 17- 17 T 19836
Mon 10/30 A WPG 19- 13 W 15164

1961 TORONTO ARGONAUTS
Mon 8/14 H WPG 13- 14 L 27189
Sun 8/20 H HAM 24- 28 L 27809
Fri 8/25 A MTL 15- 10 W 18522
Mon 9/4 A HAM 19- 21 L 26533
Sun 9/10 H SAS 27- 7 W 24047
Sat 9/16 A EDM 8- 8 T 21510
Mon 9/18 A BC 15- 7 W 24428
Sun 9/24 H OTT 10- 29 L 30648
Fri 9/29 H CAL 22- 19 W 23546
Sat 10/7 A MTL 33- 27 W 19075
Sun 10/15 H HAM 10- 37 L 29553
Sat 10/21 A OTT 21- 7 W 18821
Sun 10/29 H MTL 15- 9 W 23316
Sat 11/4 A OTT 23- 35 L 17144
Eastern Semi-Final
Sat 11/11 A OTT 43- 19 W 19151
Eastern Final (27-55)
Sat 11/18 H HAM 25- 7 W 33161
Sat 11/25 A HAM 2- 48 L 22671

1961 WINNIPEG BLUE BOMBERS
Mon 8/7 A CAL 18- 17 W 13000
Fri 8/11 A MTL 21- 15 W 18059
Mon 8/14 A TOR 14- 13 W 27189

Thu	8/17	H	OTT	29- 19	W	18517
Thu	8/24	H	EDM	20- 35	L	19660
Thu	8/31	H	HAM	9- 30	L	18951
Mon	9/4	A	SAS	17- 11	W	15124
Thu	9/14	H	BC	36- 15	W	16016
Sat	9/23	A	EDM	33- 10	W	19198
Sat	9/30	H	SAS	29- 6	W	14354
Sat	10/7	H	BC	24- 20	W	13050
Sat	10/14	A	CAL	25- 6	W	17225
Mon	10/16	A	BC	16- 15	W	20778
Mon	10/23	H	CAL	42- 7	W	13777
Mon	10/30	H	SAS	13- 19	L	15164
Sat	11/4	A	EDM	14- 13	W	10177
Western Final (2-0)						
Sat	11/18	A	CAL	14- 1	W	18500
Wed	11/22	H	CAL	43- 14	W	16800
Grey Cup						
Sat	12/2	N	HAM	21- 14	W*	32651

1962 BRITISH COLUMBIA LIONS

Thu	8/9	H	SAS	33- 7	W	27684
Thu	8/16	H	CAL	20- 35	L	30135
Mon	8/20	A	CAL	12- 4	W	16200
Mon	8/27	H	OTT	7- 18	L	29423
Fri	8/31	A	EDM	10- 22	L	14500
Thu	9/6	A	MTL	19- 21	L	19350
Sun	9/9	A	TOR	37- 21	W	22254
Mon	9/17	H	HAM	6- 31	L	27051
Sat	9/22	A	SAS	14- 26	L	12283
Mon	9/24	H	WPG	27- 22	W	20143
Sat	9/29	A	EDM	46- 24	W	18322
Sat	10/6	A	WPG	18- 6	W	16060
Sat	10/13	H	EDM	7- 26	L	28058
Sat	10/20	A	CAL	28- 36	L	18800
Sat	10/27	H	WPG	34- 35	L	25419
Sun	11/4	H	SAS	28- 8	W	20498

1962 CALGARY STAMPEDERS

Mon	8/6	A	SAS	6- 17	L	12362
Mon	8/13	H	WPG	27- 45	L	14000
Thu	8/16	A	BC	35- 20	W	30135
Mon	8/20	H	BC	4- 12	L	16200
Mon	8/27	H	SAS	7- 7	T	11000
Thu	8/30	A	WPG	1- 26	L	16059
Mon	9/3	H	EDM	49- 17	W	18000
Sat	9/8	A	EDM	17- 12	W	15400
Sat	9/15	H	MTL	17- 7	W	18500
Fri	9/21	A	OTT	36- 32	W	16265
Mon	9/24	A	HAM	38- 21	W	22109
Mon	10/1	H	TOR	23- 38	L	16000
Sat	10/6	A	EDM	22- 15	W	15447
Sat	10/13	A	WPG	19- 15	W	15800
Sat	10/20	H	BC	36- 28	W	18800
Sat	10/27	H	SAS	15- 23	L	17780
Western Semi-Final (43-7)						
Sat	11/10	H	SAS	25- 0	W	17780
Mon	11/12	A	SAS	18- 7	W	9000
Western Final (1-2)						
Sat	11/17	H	WPG	20- 14	W	17230
Wed	11/21	A	WPG	11- 19	L	12500
Sat	11/24	A	WPG	7- 12	L	19175

1962 EDMONTON ESKIMOS

Thu	8/9	A	WPG	20- 16	W	16832
Tue	8/14	H	SAS	22- 7	W	13288
Mon	8/20	A	SAS	9- 17	L	12682
Fri	8/24	H	OTT	21- 29	L	15002
Fri	8/31	H	BC	22- 10	W	14500
Mon	9/3	A	CAL	17- 49	L	18000
Sat	9/8	H	CAL	12- 17	L	15400
Fri	9/14	H	HAM	15- 16	L	15667
Sat	9/22	A	MTL	18- 18	T	19129
Mon	9/24	A	TOR	31- 22	W	24117
Sat	9/29	H	BC	24- 46	L	18322
Sat	10/6	H	CAL	15- 22	L	15447
Mon	10/8	A	SAS	20- 28	L	12783
Sat	10/13	A	BC	26- 7	W	28058
Sat	10/20	H	WPG	20- 30	L	14000
Sat	11/3	A	WPG	18- 12	W	12500

1962 HAMILTON TIGER-CATS

Thu	8/9	A	OTT	28- 16	W	16259
Sat	8/18	H	TOR	29- 23	W	25316
Fri	8/24	A	MTL	31- 11	W	22393
Mon	9/3	H	MTL	25- 25	T	26411
Mon	9/10	H	WPG	10- 16	L	26363
Fri	9/14	A	EDM	16- 15	W	15667
Mon	9/17	A	BC	31- 6	W	27051
Mon	9/24	H	CAL	21- 38	L	22109
Sat	9/29	A	OTT	0- 27	L	17124
Sat	10/6	A	TOR	9- 10	L	25174
Mon	10/15	H	SAS	67- 21	W	19000
Sun	10/21	H	TOR	27- 24	W	24591
Sat	10/27	A	MTL	24- 20	W	20581
Sat	11/3	H	OTT	40- 34	W	20461
Eastern Final (58-38)						
Sat	11/17	A	MTL	28- 17	W	25675
Sun	11/25	H	MTL	30- 21	W	21000
Grey Cup						
Sat	12/1	N	WPG	27- 28	L	32655
(Resumed 12/2)						

1962 MONTREAL ALOUETTES

Fri	8/10	A	TOR	28- 15	W	26391
Thu	8/16	H	OTT	18- 29	L	23534
Fri	8/24	H	HAM	11- 31	L	22393
Mon	9/3	A	HAM	25- 25	T	26411
Thu	9/6	H	BC	21- 19	W	19350
Mon	9/10	A	SAS	10- 24	L	11006
Sat	9/15	A	CAL	7- 17	L	18500
Sat	9/22	H	EDM	18- 18	T	19129
Thu	9/27	A	WPG	23- 31	L	16528
Mon	10/8	H	OTT	24- 26	L	19288
Sun	10/14	A	TOR	50- 21	W	29521
Sat	10/20	A	OTT	21- 21	T	20559
Sat	10/27	H	HAM	20- 24	L	20581
Sat	11/3	H	TOR	32- 8	W	22933
Eastern Semi-Final						
Sat	11/10	A	OTT	18- 17	W	20252
Eastern Final (38-58)						
Sat	11/17	H	HAM	17- 28	L	25675
Sun	11/25	A	HAM	21- 30	L	21000

1962 OTTAWA ROUGH RIDERS

Thu	8/9	H	HAM	16- 28	L	16259
Thu	8/16	A	MTL	29- 18	W	23534
Fri	8/24	A	EDM	29- 21	W	15002
Mon	8/27	A	BC	18- 7	W	29423
Sat	9/1	H	TOR	26- 8	W	15799
Fri	9/7	H	WPG	28- 31	L	21050
Sun	9/16	A	TOR	10- 16	L	24721
Fri	9/21	H	CAL	32- 36	L	16265
Sat	9/29	H	HAM	27- 0	W	17124
Mon	10/8	A	MTL	26- 24	W	19288
Sat	10/13	H	SAS	21- 29	L	17246
Sat	10/20	H	MTL	21- 21	T	20559
Sun	10/28	A	TOR	22- 23	L	20862
Sat	11/3	A	HAM	34- 40	L	20461
Eastern Semi-Final						
Sat	11/10	H	MTL	17- 18	L	20252

1962 SASKATCHEWAN ROUGHRIDERS

Mon	8/6	H	CAL	17- 6	W	12362
Thu	8/9	A	BC	7- 33	L	27684
Tue	8/14	A	EDM	7- 22	L	13288
Mon	8/20	H	EDM	17- 9	W	12682
Mon	8/27	A	CAL	7- 7	T	11000
Mon	9/3	H	WPG	7- 30	L	16663
Mon	9/10	H	MTL	24- 10	W	11006
Mon	9/17	A	WPG	18- 20	L	16213
Sat	9/22	H	BC	26- 14	W	12283
Sat	9/29	H	TOR	21- 17	W	11758
Mon	10/8	H	EDM	28- 20	W	12783
Sat	10/13	A	OTT	29- 21	W	17246
Mon	10/15	A	HAM	21- 67	L	19000
Mon	10/22	H	WPG	8- 17	L	10339
Sat	10/27	A	CAL	23- 15	W	17780
Sun	11/4	A	BC	8- 28	L	20498
Western Semi-Final (7-43)						
Sat	11/10	A	CAL	0- 25	L	17780
Mon	11/12	H	CAL	7- 18	L	9000

1962 TORONTO ARGONAUTS

Fri	8/10	H	MTL	15- 28	L	26391
Sat	8/18	A	HAM	23- 29	L	25316
Thu	8/23	A	WPG	13- 33	L	16700
Sat	9/1	A	OTT	8- 26	L	15799
Sun	9/9	H	BC	21- 37	L	22254
Sun	9/16	H	OTT	16- 10	W	24721
Mon	9/24	H	EDM	22- 31	L	24117
Sat	9/29	A	SAS	17- 21	L	11758
Mon	10/1	A	CAL	38- 23	W	16000
Sat	10/6	H	HAM	10- 9	W	25174
Sun	10/14	H	MTL	21- 50	L	29521
Sun	10/21	A	HAM	24- 27	L	24591
Sun	10/28	H	OTT	23- 22	W	20862
Sat	11/3	A	MTL	8- 32	L	22933

1962 WINNIPEG BLUE BOMBERS

Thu	8/9	H	EDM	16- 20	L	16832
Mon	8/13	A	CAL	45- 27	W	14000
Thu	8/23	H	TOR	33- 13	W	16700
Thu	8/30	H	CAL	26- 1	W	16059
Mon	9/3	A	SAS	30- 7	W	16663
Fri	9/7	A	OTT	31- 28	W	21050
Mon	9/10	A	HAM	16- 10	W	26363
Mon	9/17	H	SAS	20- 18	W	16213
Mon	9/24	A	BC	22- 27	L	20143
Thu	9/27	H	MTL	31- 23	W	16528
Sat	10/6	H	BC	6- 18	L	16060
Sat	10/13	H	CAL	15- 19	L	15800
Sat	10/20	A	EDM	30- 20	W	14000
Mon	10/22	A	SAS	17- 8	W	10339
Sat	10/27	A	BC	35- 34	W	25419
Sat	11/3	H	EDM	12- 18	L	12500
Western Final (2-1)						
Sat	11/17	A	CAL	14- 20	L	17230
Wed	11/21	H	CAL	19- 11	W	12500
Sat	11/24	H	CAL	12- 7	W	19175
Grey Cup						
Sat	12/1	N	HAM	28- 27	W	32655
(Resumed 12/2)						

1963 BRITISH COLUMBIA LIONS

Thu	8/8	A	SAS	16- 7	W	12605
Mon	8/12	H	EDM	31- 12	W	27639
Mon	8/19	H	TOR	22- 14	W	31589
Mon	8/26	A	CAL	22- 19	W	22500
Thu	8/29	A	WPG	15- 16	L	19632
Sat	9/7	H	CAL	37- 21	W	36659
Mon	9/9	A	SAS	8- 2	W	15384
Mon	9/16	H	MTL	20- 9	W	31438
Sat	9/21	A	HAM	21- 38	L	26652
Mon	9/23	A	OTT	17- 23	L	20191
Mon	9/30	H	CAL	32- 14	W	32529
Sat	10/5	A	EDM	40- 1	W	14000
Sat	10/12	H	SAS	26- 6	W	30079
Sat	10/19	H	EDM	32- 6	W	29133
Sun	10/27	A	WPG	20- 34	L	16973
Sun	11/3	H	WPG	28- 10	W	32646
Western Final (2-1)						
Sat	11/16	A	SAS	19- 7	W	16262
Wed	11/20	H	SAS	8- 13	L	26738
Sat	11/23	H	SAS	36- 1	W	25603
Grey Cup						
Sat	11/30	H	HAM	10- 21	L	36461

1963 CALGARY STAMPEDERS

Tue	8/6	H	WPG	36- 27	W	18800
Mon	8/12	A	WPG	24- 8	W	19027
Mon	8/19	H	HAM	35- 31	W	21034
Fri	8/23	A	SAS	17- 16	W	12744
Mon	8/26	H	BC	19- 22	L	22500
Mon	9/2	H	EDM	13- 11	W	20600
Sat	9/7	A	BC	21- 37	L	36659
Sat	9/14	H	SAS	4- 4	T	18000
Sun	9/22	A	TOR	50- 0	W	31214
Tue	9/24	A	MTL	17- 25	L	23115
Mon	9/30	A	BC	14- 32	L	32529
Mon	10/7	H	OTT	47- 17	W	15125
Mon	10/14	H	WPG	14- 8	W	22000
Sat	10/19	A	SAS	33- 33	T	12600
Sat	10/26	A	EDM	45- 28	W	12000
Sat	11/2	H	EDM	38- 24	W	14000
Western Semi-Final (47-48)						
Sat	11/9	H	SAS	35- 9	W	19000
Mon	11/11	A	SAS	12- 39	L	12900

1963 EDMONTON ESKIMOS

Mon	8/5	H	SAS	16- 19	L	12117
Mon	8/12	A	BC	12- 31	L	27639
Fri	8/16	H	TOR	17- 16	W	20000
Fri	8/23	H	WPG	7- 36	L	15000
Mon	9/2	A	CAL	11- 13	L	20600
Sat	9/7	H	SAS	9- 22	L	15149
Sat	9/14	H	MTL	10- 1	W	13000
Sat	9/21	A	SAS	7- 8	L	15000
Mon	9/23	A	WPG	15- 24	L	13083
Sat	9/28	H	WPG	30- 38	L	13000
Sat	10/5	H	BC	1- 40	L	14000
Sat	10/12	A	OTT	10- 34	L	15682
Mon	10/14	A	HAM	17- 28	L	22642
Sat	10/19	A	BC	6- 32	L	29133
Sat	10/26	H	CAL	28- 45	L	12000
Sat	11/2	A	CAL	24- 38	L	14000

1963 HAMILTON TIGER-CATS

Sat	8/10	H	MTL	30- 7	W	25709
Thu	8/15	A	SAS	3- 5	L	12609
Mon	8/19	A	CAL	31- 35	L	21034
Sat	8/24	H	OTT	20- 16	W	24271
Mon	9/2	H	TOR	7- 1	W	26318
Sat	9/7	A	OTT	27- 28	L	19124
Sun	9/15	A	TOR	7- 15	L	30752
Sat	9/21	H	BC	38- 21	W	26652
Sun	9/29	H	MTL	24- 14	W	23614
Mon	10/7	A	WPG	26- 14	W	15340
Mon	10/14	H	EDM	28- 17	W	22642
Sun	10/20	A	TOR	11- 10	W	21196
Sat	10/26	H	OTT	11- 10	W	28007
Sun	11/3	A	MTL	49- 21	W	19337
Eastern Final (63-35)						
Sat	11/16	A	OTT	45- 0	W	20406
Sun	11/24	H	OTT	18- 35	L	23972
Grey Cup						
Sat	11/30	A	BC	21- 10	W	36461

1963 MONTREAL ALOUETTES

Sat	8/10	A	HAM	7- 30	L	25709
Thu	8/15	A	OTT	14- 31	L	20662
Fri	8/23	H	TOR	15- 8	W	19354
Mon	9/2	H	OTT	37- 15	W	24499
Sun	9/8	H	WPG	30- 1	W	24592
Sat	9/14	A	EDM	1- 10	L	13000
Mon	9/16	A	BC	9- 20	L	31438
Tue	9/24	H	CAL	25- 17	W	23115
Sun	9/29	A	HAM	14- 24	L	23614
Fri	10/4	A	TOR	29- 13	W	23587
Sun	10/13	H	TOR	34- 20	W	23277
Sat	10/19	A	OTT	21- 27	L	22763
Thu	10/24	H	SAS	20- 32	L	18509
Sun	11/3	H	HAM	21- 49	L	19337
Eastern Semi-Final						
Sat	11/9	A	OTT	5- 17	L	20358

1963 OTTAWA ROUGH RIDERS

Fri	8/9	A	TOR	5- 8	L	27557
Thu	8/15	H	MTL	31- 14	W	20662
Sat	8/24	A	HAM	16- 20	L	24271

Mon	9/2	A	MTL	15- 37	L	24499
Sat	9/7	H	HAM	28- 27	W	19124
Sat	9/14	A	WPG	32- 26	W	17645
Mon	9/23	H	BC	23- 17	W	20191
Sat	9/28	H	TOR	30- 12	W	18022
Sat	10/5	A	SAS	28- 13	W	14551
Mon	10/7	A	CAL	17- 47	L	15125
Sat	10/12	H	EDM	34- 10	W	15682
Sat	10/19	H	MTL	27- 21	W	22763
Sat	10/26	A	HAM	10- 11	L	28007
Sat	11/2	H	TOR	30- 21	W	13089
Eastern Semi-Final						
Sat	11/9	H	MTL	17- 5	W	20358
Eastern Final (35-63)						
Sat	11/16	H	HAM	0- 45	L	20406
Sun	11/24	A	HAM	35- 18	W	23972

1963 SASKATCHEWAN ROUGHRIDERS

Mon	8/5	A	EDM	19- 16	W	12117
Thu	8/8	H	BC	7- 16	L	12605
Thu	8/15	H	HAM	5- 3	W	12609
Mon	8/19	A	WPG	1- 16	L	16672
Fri	8/23	H	CAL	16- 17	L	12744
Mon	9/2	H	WPG	15- 9	W	16200
Sat	9/7	A	EDM	22- 9	W	15149
Mon	9/9	H	BC	2- 8	L	15384
Sat	9/14	A	CAL	4- 4	T	18000
Sat	9/21	H	EDM	8- 7	W	15000
Mon	9/30	A	WPG	12- 10	W	18216
Sat	10/5	H	OTT	13- 28	L	14551
Sat	10/12	A	BC	6- 26	L	30079
Sat	10/19	H	CAL	33- 33	T	12600
Thu	10/24	A	MTL	32- 20	W	18509
Sun	10/27	A	TOR	28- 44	L	19263
Western Semi-Final (48-47)						
Sat	11/9	A	CAL	9- 35	L	19000
Mon	11/11	H	CAL	39- 12	W	12900
Western Final (1-2)						
Sat	11/16	H	BC	7- 19	L	16262
Wed	11/20	A	BC	13- 8	W	26738
Sat	11/23	A	BC	1- 36	L	25603

1963 TORONTO ARGONAUTS

Fri	8/9	H	OTT	8- 5	W	27557
Fri	8/16	A	EDM	16- 17	L	20000
Mon	8/19	A	BC	14- 22	L	31589
Fri	8/23	A	MTL	8- 15	L	19354
Mon	9/2	A	HAM	1- 7	L	26318
Fri	9/6	H	WPG	20- 25	L	29902
Sun	9/15	H	HAM	15- 7	W	30752
Sun	9/22	H	CAL	0- 50	L	31214
Sat	9/28	A	OTT	12- 30	L	18022
Fri	10/4	H	MTL	13- 29	L	23587
Sun	10/13	A	MTL	20- 34	L	23277
Sun	10/20	H	HAM	10- 11	L	21196
Sun	10/27	H	SAS	44- 28	W	19263
Sat	11/2	A	OTT	21- 30	L	13089

1963 WINNIPEG BLUE BOMBERS

Tue	8/6	A	CAL	27- 36	L	18800
Mon	8/12	H	CAL	8- 24	L	19027
Mon	8/19	H	SAS	16- 1	W	16672
Fri	8/23	A	EDM	36- 7	W	15000
Thu	8/29	H	BC	16- 15	W	19632
Mon	9/2	A	SAS	9- 15	L	16200
Fri	9/6	A	TOR	25- 20	W	29902
Sun	9/8	A	MTL	1- 30	L	24592
Sat	9/14	H	OTT	26- 32	L	17645
Mon	9/23	H	EDM	24- 15	W	13083
Sat	9/28	A	EDM	38- 30	W	13000
Mon	9/30	H	SAS	10- 12	L	18216
Mon	10/7	H	HAM	14- 26	L	15340
Mon	10/14	A	CAL	8- 14	L	22000
Sun	10/27	H	BC	34- 20	W	16973
Sun	11/3	A	BC	10- 28	L	32646

1964 BRITISH COLUMBIA LIONS

Tue	8/4	A	WPG	10- 10	T	15125
Mon	8/10	H	CAL	22- 4	W	32664
Fri	8/14	A	SAS	17- 2	W	17787
Wed	8/19	H	SAS	27- 16	W	35618
Sun	8/30	H	WPG	21- 4	W	33607
Tue	9/8	H	OTT	17- 17	T	31355
Sat	9/19	A	EDM	49- 6	W	21000
Tue	9/22	A	CAL	12- 7	W	19546
Sat	9/26	H	HAM	16- 16	T	37008
Sat	10/3	A	TOR	20- 15	W	27249
Mon	10/5	A	MTL	7- 14	L	17084
Sat	10/10	H	EDM	26- 6	W	29277
Sat	10/17	A	EDM	24- 14	W	12000
Sat	10/24	H	SAS	20- 3	W	30856
Wed	10/28	A	CAL	14- 26	L	20000
Sun	11/1	H	WPG	26- 8	W	29614
Western Final (2-1)						
Sat	11/14	A	CAL	24- 10	W	21236
Wed	11/18	H	CAL	10- 14	L	28547
Sun	11/22	H	CAL	33- 14	W	32504
Grey Cup						
Sat	11/28	N	HAM	34- 24	W	32655

1964 CALGARY STAMPEDERS

Mon	8/3	H	SAS	4- 15	L	18500
Fri	8/7	A	EDM	52- 15	W	19689
Mon	8/10	A	BC	4- 22	L	32664
Mon	8/17	H	EDM	39- 6	W	14000
Mon	8/24	A	SAS	14- 13	W	16443
Thu	9/3	A	WPG	13- 10	W	15231
Mon	9/7	H	WPG	25- 8	W	18075
Sat	9/12	A	OTT	12- 52	L	19560
Tue	9/15	H	HAM	20- 18	W	25000
Tue	9/22	H	BC	7- 12	L	19546
Tue	9/29	H	TOR	30- 25	W	15000
Sun	10/4	A	WPG	24- 16	W	11300
Sat	10/10	H	MTL	23- 7	W	16000
Sat	10/17	H	SAS	42- 0	W	20000
Sat	10/24	A	EDM	17- 16	W	10000
Wed	10/28	H	BC	26- 14	W	20000
Western Semi-Final (76-40)						
Sat	11/7	A	SAS	25- 34	L	14462
Mon	11/9	H	SAS	51- 6	W	18455
Western Final (1-2)						
Sat	11/14	H	BC	10- 24	L	21236
Wed	11/18	A	BC	14- 10	W	28547
Sun	11/22	A	BC	14- 33	L	32504

1964 EDMONTON ESKIMOS

Fri	8/7	H	CAL	15- 52	L	19689
Wed	8/12	A	WPG	7- 37	L	13789
Mon	8/17	A	CAL	6- 39	L	14000
Fri	8/28	H	SAS	8- 56	L	12807
Fri	9/4	H	OTT	20- 1	W	12157
Fri	9/11	A	MTL	19- 10	W	22506
Sun	9/13	A	TOR	22- 35	L	21797
Sat	9/19	H	BC	6- 49	L	21000
Sat	9/26	A	SAS	11- 20	L	13600
Mon	9/28	H	HAM	14- 43	L	13000
Tue	10/6	H	WPG	25- 22	W	12403
Sat	10/10	A	BC	6- 26	L	29277
Sat	10/17	H	BC	14- 24	L	12000
Mon	10/19	A	WPG	13- 1	W	14882
Sat	10/24	H	CAL	16- 17	L	10000
Sat	10/31	A	SAS	20- 26	L	10300

1964 HAMILTON TIGER-CATS

Sat	8/8	H	MTL	5- 33	L	25000
Fri	8/14	A	OTT	10- 13	L	21665
Fri	8/21	H	WPG	32- 29	W	19485
Thu	8/27	A	MTL	32- 1	W	27477
Sun	9/7	H	TOR	24- 8	W	27156
Tue	9/15	A	CAL	18- 20	L	25000
Sun	9/20	A	TOR	27- 14	W	22447
Sat	9/26	A	BC	16- 16	T	37008
Mon	9/28	A	EDM	43- 14	W	13000
Sun	10/4	H	SAS	17- 15	W	25095
Mon	10/12	H	OTT	23- 1	W	27151
Sat	10/17	A	OTT	34- 16	W	23121
Sat	10/24	H	TOR	27- 7	W	30856
Sun	11/1	A	MTL	21- 14	W	16146
Eastern Final (39-38)						
Sat	11/14	A	OTT	13- 30	L	18388
Sat	11/21	H	OTT	26- 8	W	21100
Grey Cup						
Sat	11/28	N	BC	24- 34	L	32655

1964 MONTREAL ALOUETTES

Sat	8/8	A	HAM	33- 5	W	25000
Sat	8/15	A	TOR	21- 13	W	30769
Thu	8/20	H	TOR	16- 1	W	22436
Thu	8/27	H	HAM	1- 32	L	27477
Mon	9/7	A	SAS	0- 32	L	18187
Fri	9/11	H	EDM	10- 19	L	22506
Sat	9/19	H	OTT	8- 23	L	20462
Sat	9/26	A	OTT	14- 16	L	21296
Mon	10/5	H	BC	14- 7	W	17084
Sat	10/10	A	CAL	7- 23	L	16000
Mon	10/12	A	WPG	21- 20	W	11231
Sun	10/18	A	TOR	10- 31	L	21597
Sun	10/25	H	OTT	23- 21	W	18055
Sun	11/1	H	HAM	14- 21	L	16146
Eastern Semi-Final						
Sat	11/7	A	OTT	0- 27	L	18214

1964 OTTAWA ROUGH RIDERS

Fri	8/7	A	TOR	21- 23	L	29479
Fri	8/14	H	HAM	13- 10	W	21665
Tue	8/18	H	WPG	46- 20	W	17768
Tue	9/1	H	TOR	23- 21	W	20221
Fri	9/4	A	EDM	1- 20	L	12157
Tue	9/8	A	BC	17- 17	T	31355
Sat	9/12	H	CAL	52- 12	W	19560
Sat	9/19	A	MTL	23- 8	W	20462
Sat	9/26	H	MTL	16- 14	W	21296
Tue	10/6	H	SAS	27- 3	W	19710
Mon	10/12	A	HAM	1- 23	L	27151
Sat	10/17	H	HAM	16- 34	L	23121
Sun	10/25	A	MTL	21- 23	L	18055
Sat	10/31	A	TOR	36- 0	W	17701
Eastern Semi-Final						
Sat	11/7	H	MTL	27- 0	W	18214
Eastern Final (38-39)						
Sat	11/14	H	HAM	30- 13	W	18388
Sat	11/21	A	HAM	8- 26	L	21100

1964 SASKATCHEWAN ROUGHRIDERS

Mon	8/3	A	CAL	15- 4	W	18500
Fri	8/7	H	WPG	37- 29	W	16387
Fri	8/14	H	BC	2- 17	L	17787
Wed	8/19	A	BC	16- 27	L	35618
Mon	8/24	H	CAL	13- 14	L	16443
Fri	8/28	A	EDM	56- 8	W	12807
Mon	9/7	H	MTL	32- 0	W	18187
Sat	9/12	A	WPG	30- 2	W	17704
Sat	9/19	H	WPG	31- 30	W	16707
Sat	9/26	H	EDM	20- 11	W	13600
Sun	10/4	A	HAM	15- 17	L	25095
Tue	10/6	A	OTT	3- 27	L	19710
Mon	10/12	H	TOR	31- 14	W	16048
Sat	10/17	A	CAL	0- 42	L	20000
Sat	10/24	A	BC	3- 20	L	30856
Sat	10/31	H	EDM	26- 20	W	10300
Western Semi-Final (40-76)						
Sat	11/7	H	CAL	34- 25	W	14462
Mon	11/9	A	CAL	6- 51	L	18455

1964 TORONTO ARGONAUTS

Fri	8/7	H	OTT	23- 21	W	29479
Sat	8/15	H	MTL	13- 21	L	30769
Thu	8/20	A	MTL	1- 16	L	22436
Tue	9/1	A	OTT	21- 23	L	20221
Sun	9/7	A	HAM	8- 24	L	27156
Sun	9/13	H	EDM	35- 22	W	21797
Sun	9/20	H	HAM	14- 27	L	27447
Sun	9/27	A	WPG	36- 24	W	14342
Tue	9/29	A	CAL	25- 30	L	15000
Sat	10/3	H	BC	15- 20	L	27249
Mon	10/12	A	SAS	14- 31	L	16048
Sun	10/18	H	MTL	31- 10	W	21597
Sat	10/24	A	HAM	7- 27	L	30856
Sat	10/31	H	OTT	0- 36	L	17701

1964 WINNIPEG BLUE BOMBERS

Tue	8/4	H	BC	10- 10	T	15125
Fri	8/7	A	SAS	29- 37	L	16387
Wed	8/12	H	EDM	37- 7	W	13789
Tue	8/18	A	OTT	20- 46	L	17768
Fri	8/21	A	HAM	29- 32	L	19485
Sun	8/30	A	BC	4- 21	L	33607
Thu	9/3	H	CAL	10- 13	L	15231
Mon	9/7	A	CAL	8- 25	L	18075
Sat	9/12	H	SAS	2- 30	L	17704
Sat	9/19	A	SAS	30- 31	L	16707
Sun	9/27	H	TOR	24- 36	L	14342
Sun	10/4	H	CAL	16- 24	L	11360
Tue	10/6	A	EDM	22- 25	L	12403
Mon	10/12	H	MTL	20- 21	L	11231
Mon	10/19	H	EDM	1- 13	L	14882
Sun	11/1	A	BC	8- 26	L	29614

1965 BRITISH COLUMBIA LIONS

Sun	8/4	A	WPG	21- 23	L	17980
Sat	8/7	H	EDM	38- 13	W	32055
Mon	8/16	H	WPG	6- 12	L	36457
Fri	8/20	A	SAS	10- 10	T	16676
Sun	8/29	H	TOR	36- 1	W	20855
Thu	9/2	A	WPG	14- 7	W	21012
Sat	9/11	H	CAL	24- 10	W	36704
Sat	9/18	H	MTL	6- 11	L	
Sat	9/25	A	CAL	7- 21	L	19000
Mon	9/27	A	SAS	26- 14	W	12587
Sat	10/2	H	EDM	41- 27	W	31402
Sat	10/9	A	EDM	12- 14	L	18411
Sun	10/17	A	HAM	7- 25	L	26803
Tue	10/19	A	OTT	14- 35	L	18537
Sun	10/24	H	SAS	14- 30	L	37788
Sun	10/31	H	CAL	10- 20	L	24191

1965 CALGARY STAMPEDERS

Mon	8/2	H	SAS	37- 8	W	18000
Fri	8/6	A	SAS	18- 20	L	16000
Wed	8/11	A	WPG	8- 19	L	20100
Wed	8/18	H	EDM	16- 15	W	16000
Mon	8/23	A	EDM	20- 4	W	17739
Sat	8/28	H	HAM	18- 11	W	18800
Mon	9/6	H	WPG	35- 7	W	22711
Sat	9/11	A	BC	10- 24	L	36704
Sat	9/18	A	SAS	15- 12	W	15114
Sat	9/25	H	BC	21- 7	W	19000
Sat	10/2	H	OTT	31- 18	W	21476
Fri	10/8	A	TOR	27- 26	W	16711
Mon	10/11	A	MTL	36- 21	W	19838
Sat	10/16	H	EDM	28- 19	W	21476
Wed	10/27	H	WPG	0- 22	L	22226
Sun	10/31	A	BC	20- 10	W	24191
Western Final (1-2)						
Sat	11/13	H	WPG	27- 9	W	21226
Wed	11/17	A	WPG	11- 15	L	16100
Sat	11/20	H	WPG	12- 19	L	21361

1965 EDMONTON ESKIMOS

Fri	7/30	H	WPG	14- 21	L	16123
Sat	8/7	A	BC	13- 38	L	32055
Fri	8/13	H	SAS	15- 34	L	14297
Wed	8/18	A	CAL	15- 16	L	16000
Mon	8/23	H	CAL	4- 20	L	17739
Tue	8/31	H	TOR	23- 21	W	16745
Mon	9/6	A	SAS	24- 22	W	17501
Sat	9/11	H	WPG	30- 25	W	21955
Mon	9/20	H	MTL	13- 24	L	16000
Sat	9/25	A	OTT	1- 40	L	15360

Tue	9/28	A	HAM	9- 3	W	18575
Sat	10/2	A	BC	27- 41	L	31402
Sat	10/9	H	BC	14- 12	W	18411
Sat	10/16	A	CAL	19- 28	L	21476
Sat	10/23	A	WPG	24- 40	L	16104
Sat	10/30	H	SAS	12- 15	L	14000

1965 HAMILTON TIGER-CATS

Sat	8/7	H	MTL	18- 9	W	21735
Fri	8/13	A	TOR	17- 7	W	27190
Sat	8/21	H	OTT	27- 1	W	26000
Sat	8/28	A	CAL	11- 18	L	18800
Tue	8/31	A	SAS	30- 6	W	17530
Mon	9/6	H	MTL	17- 2	W	27000
Sat	9/11	A	OTT	13- 22	L	22491
Sun	9/19	A	TOR	33- 0	W	22854
Tue	9/28	H	EDM	3- 9	L	18575
Sun	10/3	A	WPG	21- 26	L	16542
Mon	10/11	H	OTT	25- 23	W	27755
Sun	10/17	H	BC	25- 7	W	26803
Sat	10/23	A	MTL	6- 2	W	17000
Sun	10/31	H	TOR	35- 21	W	17085
Eastern Final (35-20)						
Sun	11/14	A	OTT	18- 13	W	20271
Sat	11/20	H	OTT	17- 7	W	21530
Grey Cup						
Sat	11/27	A	WPG	22- 16	W	32655

1965 MONTREAL ALOUETTES

Sat	8/7	A	HAM	9- 18	L	21735
Thu	8/12	A	OTT	2- 23	L	18595
Wed	8/18	H	TOR	20- 0	W	20000
Thu	8/26	H	OTT	13- 31	L	18000
Mon	9/6	A	HAM	2- 17	L	27000
Sun	9/12	H	SAS	9- 11	L	19226
Sat	9/18	A	BC	11- 6	W	
Mon	9/20	A	EDM	24- 13	W	16000
Fri	9/24	H	WPG	8- 14	L	19600
Sun	10/3	H	TOR	25- 8	W	18000
Mon	10/11	H	CAL	21- 36	L	19838
Sat	10/16	A	TOR	21- 24	L	18693
Sat	10/23	H	HAM	2- 6	L	17000
Sat	10/30	A	OTT	16- 8	W	12697
Eastern Semi-Final						
Sat	11/6	A	OTT	7- 36	L	19171

1965 OTTAWA ROUGH RIDERS

Fri	8/6	A	TOR	17- 14	W	28041
Thu	8/12	H	MTL	23- 2	W	18595
Sat	8/21	A	HAM	1- 27	L	26000
Thu	8/26	A	MTL	31- 13	W	18000
Sun	9/5	H	TOR	41- 21	W	17303
Sat	9/11	H	HAM	22- 13	W	22491
Sun	9/19	A	WPG	12- 19	L	20658
Sat	9/25	H	EDM	40- 1	W	15360
Sat	10/2	A	CAL	18- 31	L	21476
Mon	10/4	A	SAS	14- 21	L	12500
Mon	10/11	A	HAM	23- 25	L	27755
Tue	10/19	H	BC	35- 14	W	18537
Sun	10/24	H	TOR	15- 17	L	13487
Sat	10/30	H	MTL	8- 16	L	12697
Eastern Semi-Final						
Sat	11/6	H	MTL	36- 7	W	19171
Eastern Final (20-35)						
Sun	11/14	H	HAM	13- 18	L	20271
Sat	11/20	A	HAM	7- 17	L	21520

1965 SASKATCHEWAN ROUGHRIDERS

Mon	8/2	A	CAL	8- 37	L	18000
Fri	8/6	H	CAL	20- 18	W	16000
Fri	8/13	A	EDM	34- 15	W	14297
Fri	8/20	H	BC	10- 10	T	16676
Wed	8/25	A	WPG	25- 6	W	22486
Tue	8/31	H	HAM	6- 30	L	17130
Mon	9/6	H	EDM	22- 24	L	17501
Fri	9/10	A	TOR	28- 9	W	20497
Sun	9/12	A	MTL	11- 9	W	19226
Sat	9/18	H	CAL	12- 15	L	15114
Mon	9/27	H	BC	14- 26	L	12587
Mon	10/4	H	OTT	21- 14	W	12500
Mon	10/11	A	WPG	20- 21	L	19285
Sun	10/17	H	WPG	0- 17	L	17919
Sun	10/24	A	BC	30- 14	W	37788
Sat	10/30	A	EDM	15- 12	W	14000
Western Semi-Final						
Sun	11/7	A	WPG	9- 15	L	21600

1965 TORONTO ARGONAUTS

Fri	8/6	H	OTT	14- 17	L	28041
Fri	8/13	H	HAM	7- 17	L	27190
Wed	8/18	A	MTL	0- 20	L	20000
Sun	8/29	A	BC	1- 36	L	20855
Tue	8/31	A	EDM	21- 23	L	16745
Sun	9/5	A	OTT	21- 41	L	17303
Fri	9/10	H	SAS	9- 28	L	20497
Sun	9/19	H	HAM	0- 33	L	22854
Sun	9/26	H	WPG	24- 22	W	17364
Sun	10/3	A	MTL	8- 25	L	18000
Fri	10/8	H	CAL	26- 27	W	16711
Sat	10/16	H	MTL	24- 21	W	18693
Sun	10/24	A	OTT	17- 15	W	13487
Sun	10/31	A	HAM	21- 35	L	17085

1965 WINNIPEG BLUE BOMBERS

Fri	7/30	A	EDM	21- 14	W	16123
Sun	8/4	H	BC	23- 21	W	17980
Wed	8/11	H	CAL	19- 8	W	20100
Mon	8/16	A	BC	12- 6	W	36457
Wed	8/25	H	SAS	6- 25	L	22486
Thu	9/2	H	BC	7- 14	L	21012
Mon	9/6	A	CAL	7- 35	L	22711
Sat	9/11	A	EDM	25- 30	L	21951
Sun	9/19	H	OTT	19- 12	W	20658
Fri	9/24	A	MTL	14- 8	W	19600
Sun	9/26	A	TOR	22- 24	L	17364
Sun	10/3	H	HAM	26- 21	W	16542
Mon	10/11	H	SAS	21- 20	W	19285
Sun	10/17	A	SAS	17- 0	W	17919
Sat	10/23	H	EDM	40- 24	W	16104
Wed	10/27	A	CAL	22- 0	W	22226
Western Semi-Final						
Sun	11/7	H	SAS	15- 9	W	21600
Western Final (2-1)						
Sat	11/13	A	CAL	9- 27	L	21226
Wed	11/17	H	CAL	15- 11	W	16100
Sat	11/20	A	CAL	19- 12	W	21361
Grey Cup						
Sat	11/27	H	HAM	16- 22	L	32655

1966 BRITISH COLUMBIA LIONS

Wed	8/3	A	CAL	21- 3	W	19536
Mon	8/8	H	EDM	7- 27	L	32284
Fri	8/12	A	SAS	14- 16	L	20379
Thu	8/18	H	WPG	7- 11	L	33697
Sun	8/28	H	SAS	29- 30	L	31560
Fri	9/2	A	EDM	6- 13	L	19930
Sat	9/10	H	CAL	14- 3	W	27147
Sat	9/17	H	OTT	16- 21	L	27264
Sun	9/25	A	TOR	27- 29	L	18926
Tue	9/27	A	MTL	23- 25	L	18000
Mon	10/3	H	HAM	17- 10	W	24107
Mon	10/10	A	EDM	19- 7	W	18003
Sat	10/15	H	SAS	21- 22	L	34163
Mon	10/17	A	CAL	13- 9	W	18000
Sun	10/23	A	WPG	7- 16	L	16772
Sun	10/30	H	WPG	13- 27	L	24103

1966 CALGARY STAMPEDERS

Wed	8/3	H	BC	3- 21	L	19536
Wed	8/10	A	OTT	6- 13	L	20375
Sat	8/13	A	HAM	3- 21	L	24765
Wed	8/17	H	SAS	26- 1	W	22119
Tue	8/23	A	WPG	9- 19	L	20817
Sat	8/27	A	EDM	5- 26	L	19800
Mon	9/5	H	TOR	13- 8	W	20000
Sat	9/10	A	BC	3- 14	L	27147
Sat	9/17	H	WPG	11- 8	W	18080
Sat	9/24	H	EDM	18- 18	T	19886
Tue	9/27	A	WPG	16- 9	W	15107
Sat	10/1	H	MTL	15- 26	L	17906
Sat	10/8	A	SAS	35- 28	W	16392
Mon	10/17	H	BC	9- 13	L	18000
Tue	10/25	H	SAS	26- 28	L	18435
Sat	10/29	A	EDM	29- 16	W	21000

1966 EDMONTON ESKIMOS

Fri	7/29	H	SAS	13- 40	L	16400
Tue	8/2	A	WPG	7- 26	L	15112
Mon	8/8	A	BC	27- 7	W	32284
Fri	8/12	H	WPG	9- 10	L	17557
Mon	8/22	A	SAS	18- 17	W	18052
Sat	8/27	H	CAL	26- 5	W	19800
Fri	9/2	H	BC	13- 6	W	19930
Fri	9/9	A	MTL	8- 3	W	18000
Sun	9/11	A	TOR	14- 34	L	21685
Mon	9/19	H	OTT	21- 49	L	18341
Sat	9/24	A	CAL	18- 18	T	19886
Sat	10/1	H	HAM	7- 28	L	18000
Mon	10/10	H	BC	7- 19	L	18003
Sun	10/16	A	WPG	14- 16	L	19020
Sat	10/22	A	SAS	33- 21	W	18000
Sat	10/29	H	CAL	16- 29	L	21000
Western Semi-Final						
Sun	11/6	A	WPG	8- 16	L	15463

1966 HAMILTON TIGER-CATS

Fri	8/5	A	TOR	18- 8	W	28594
Sat	8/13	H	CAL	21- 3	W	24765
Sat	8/20	H	TOR	23- 10	W	22261
Wed	8/24	A	MTL	8- 16	L	20000
Mon	9/5	H	OTT	16- 12	W	29903
Sat	9/10	A	OTT	16- 27	L	23664
Sat	9/17	H	MTL	33- 4	W	22512
Sat	9/24	H	SAS	29- 7	W	26057
Sat	10/1	A	EDM	28- 7	W	18000
Mon	10/3	A	BC	10- 17	L	24107
Mon	10/10	H	WPG	8- 7	W	23662
Sun	10/16	A	OTT	18- 20	L	24002
Sat	10/22	A	MTL	31- 14	W	17000
Sat	10/29	H	TOR	5- 8	L	15072
Eastern Semi-Final						
Sun	11/6	H	MTL	24- 14	W	20342
Eastern Final (17-72)						
Sun	11/13	H	OTT	1- 30	L	22387
Sat	11/19	N	OTT	16- 42	L	20000

1966 MONTREAL ALOUETTES

Wed	8/3	A	OTT	8- 10	L	19599
Fri	8/12	A	TOR	17- 6	W	24139
Wed	8/17	H	OTT	3- 15	L	22564
Wed	8/24	H	HAM	16- 8	W	20000
Wed	8/31	A	WPG	4- 2	W	20510
Mon	9/5	A	SAS	0- 44	L	19451
Fri	9/9	H	EDM	3- 8	L	18000
Sat	9/17	A	HAM	4- 33	L	22512
Tue	9/27	H	BC	25- 23	W	18000
Sat	10/1	A	CAL	26- 15	W	17906
Mon	10/10	H	TOR	8- 9	L	14000
Sat	10/15	A	TOR	27- 11	W	16000
Sat	10/22	H	HAM	14- 31	L	17000
Sun	10/30	H	OTT	1- 0	W	12000
Eastern Semi-Final ()						
Sun	11/6	A	HAM	14- 24	L	20342

1966 OTTAWA ROUGH RIDERS

Wed	8/3	H	MTL	10- 8	W	19599
Wed	8/10	H	CAL	13- 6	W	20375
Wed	8/17	A	MTL	15- 3	W	22564
Tue	8/30	H	TOR	24- 0	W	20137
Mon	9/5	A	HAM	12- 16	L	29903
Sat	9/10	H	HAM	27- 16	W	23664
Sat	9/17	A	BC	21- 16	W	27264
Mon	9/19	A	EDM	49- 21	W	18341
Mon	9/26	H	SAS	18- 8	W	22954
Sat	10/1	A	TOR	17- 8	W	20786
Sat	10/8	H	WPG	40- 21	W	19685
Sun	10/16	H	HAM	20- 18	W	24002
Sun	10/23	A	TOR	12- 35	L	16064
Sun	10/30	A	MTL	0- 1	L	12000
Eastern Final (72-17)						
Sun	11/13	A	HAM	30- 1	W	22387
Sat	11/19	N	HAM	42- 16	W	20000
Grey Cup						
Sat	11/26	H	SAS	14- 29	L	36553

1966 SASKATCHEWAN ROUGHRIDERS

Fri	7/29	A	EDM	40- 13	W	16400
Sun	8/7	H	WPG	38- 14	W	20009
Fri	8/12	H	BC	16- 14	W	20379
Wed	8/17	A	CAL	1- 26	L	22119
Mon	8/22	H	EDM	17- 18	L	18052
Sun	8/28	A	BC	30- 29	W	31560
Mon	9/5	H	MTL	44- 0	W	19451
Sun	9/11	A	WPG	27- 24	W	21655
Sun	9/18	H	TOR	23- 7	W	19339
Sat	9/24	A	HAM	7- 29	L	26057
Mon	9/26	A	OTT	8- 18	L	22954
Sun	10/2	H	WPG	11- 11	T	19045
Sat	10/8	H	CAL	18- 35	L	16392
Sat	10/15	A	BC	22- 21	W	34163
Sat	10/22	H	EDM	21- 33	L	18000
Tue	10/25	A	CAL	28- 26	W	18435
Western Final (2-0)						
Sun	11/13	H	WPG	14- 7	W	14013
Wed	11/16	A	WPG	21- 19	W	13624
Grey Cup						
Sat	11/26	A	OTT	29- 14	W	36553

1966 TORONTO ARGONAUTS

Fri	8/5	H	HAM	8- 18	L	28594
Fri	8/12	H	MTL	6- 17	L	24139
Sat	8/20	A	HAM	10- 23	L	22261
Tue	8/30	A	OTT	0- 24	L	20137
Mon	9/5	A	CAL	8- 13	L	20000
Sun	9/11	H	EDM	34- 14	W	21685
Sun	9/18	A	SAS	7- 23	L	19339
Wed	9/21	A	WPG	9- 43	L	17112
Sun	9/25	H	BC	29- 27	W	18926
Sat	10/1	H	OTT	8- 17	L	20786
Mon	10/10	A	MTL	9- 8	W	14000
Sat	10/15	H	MTL	11- 27	L	16000
Sun	10/23	H	OTT	35- 12	W	16064
Sat	10/29	A	HAM	8- 5	W	15072

1966 WINNIPEG BLUE BOMBERS

Tue	8/2	H	EDM	26- 7	W	15112
Sun	8/7	A	SAS	14- 38	L	20009
Fri	8/12	A	EDM	10- 9	W	17557
Thu	8/18	A	BC	11- 7	W	23697
Tue	8/23	H	CAL	19- 9	W	20812
Wed	8/31	H	MTL	2- 4	L	20510
Sun	9/11	H	SAS	24- 27	L	21655
Sat	9/17	A	CAL	8- 11	L	18080
Wed	9/21	H	TOR	43- 9	W	17112
Tue	9/27	H	CAL	9- 16	L	15107
Sun	10/2	A	SAS	11- 11	T	19045
Sat	10/8	A	OTT	21- 40	L	19685
Mon	10/10	A	HAM	7- 8	L	23662
Sun	10/16	H	EDM	16- 14	W	19020
Sun	10/23	H	BC	16- 7	W	16772
Sun	10/30	A	BC	27- 13	W	24103
Western Semi-Final						
Sun	11/6	H	EDM	16- 8	W	15463
Western Final (0-2)						
Sun	11/13	A	SAS	7- 14	L	14013
Wed	11/16	H	SAS	19- 21	L	13624

1967 BRITISH COLUMBIA LIONS

Tue	8/1	A	CAL	7- 20	L	19436

Mon	8/7	H	SAS	16- 24	L	28411
Fri	8/11	A	SAS	13- 36	L	19016
Wed	8/16	H	TOR	17- 18	L	27142
Sun	8/27	H	CAL	7- 16	L	28436
Thu	8/31	A	WPG	22- 13	W	17058
Sat	9/9	H	EDM	14- 14	T	28266
Sun	9/17	A	EDM	8- 19	L	20000
Wed	9/27	H	WPG	17- 1	W	25412
Sun	10/1	A	WPG	8- 19	L	13582
Sun	10/8	H	EDM	3- 19	L	23386
Sun	10/15	A	HAM	17- 22	L	19000
Wed	10/18	A	OTT	16- 19	L	19302
Mon	10/23	H	MTL	30- 20	W	24621
Sun	10/29	A	SAS	14- 24	L	13969
Sat	11/4	H	CAL	30- 35	L	23706

1967 CALGARY STAMPEDERS

Tue	8/1	H	BC	20- 7	W	19436
Wed	8/9	A	WPG	16- 27	L	19281
Tue	8/15	H	SAS	36- 10	W	22846
Wed	8/23	H	EDM	16- 0	W	24135
Sun	8/27	A	BC	16- 7	W	28436
Mon	9/4	H	WPG	39- 0	W	22561
Wed	9/12	H	OTT	20- 13	W	19886
Sat	9/16	A	MTL	4- 0	W	14000
Wed	9/20	A	TOR	13- 22	L	22092
Sun	9/24	A	SAS	27- 28	L	22028
Sat	9/30	A	EDM	25- 5	W	23604
Sat	10/7	H	HAM	34- 10	W	22096
Sun	10/15	H	WPG	51- 29	W	17710
Sun	10/22	A	SAS	19- 11	W	21865
Sat	10/28	H	EDM	11- 20	L	22164
Sat	11/4	A	BC	35- 30	W	23706
Western Final (1-2)						
Sat	11/18	H	SAS	15- 11	W	21031
Wed	11/22	A	SAS	9- 11	L	12456
Sun	11/26	H	SAS	13- 17	L	21036

1967 EDMONTON ESKIMOS

Wed	8/2	H	WPG	0- 20	L	15000
Wed	8/9	A	OTT	25- 28	L	21803
Sat	8/12	A	HAM	20- 14	W	22435
Sat	8/19	H	TOR	31- 10	W	21107
Wed	8/23	A	CAL	0- 16	L	21435
Wed	8/30	H	SAS	10- 21	L	22197
Mon	9/4	A	SAS	6- 18	L	21673
Sat	9/9	A	BC	14- 14	T	28266
Sun	9/17	H	BC	19- 8	W	20000
Sat	9/23	A	WPG	22- 9	W	17208
Sat	9/30	H	CAL	5- 25	L	22604
Sun	10/8	A	BC	19- 3	W	23386
Sun	10/15	H	SAS	21- 17	W	21000
Sat	10/21	H	MTL	30- 24	W	16000
Sat	10/28	A	CAL	20- 11	W	22164
Wed	11/1	H	WPG	24- 8	W	13000
Western Semi-Final						
Sat	11/11	A	SAS	5- 21	L	15999

1967 HAMILTON TIGER-CATS

Sat	8/12	H	EDM	14- 20	L	22435
Thu	8/17	A	MTL	17- 16	W	
Wed	8/23	H	OTT	22- 17	W	25482
Mon	9/4	H	TOR	12- 9	W	25357
Sun	9/10	A	TOR	23- 15	W	24343
Sun	9/17	A	OTT	16- 14	W	27058
Sat	9/23	H	MTL	19- 1	W	20435
Sun	10/1	H	OTT	8- 17	L	27125
Sat	10/7	A	CAL	10- 34	L	22096
Mon	10/9	A	SAS	21- 22	L	21405
Sun	10/15	H	BC	22- 17	W	19000
Sun	10/22	A	WPG	31- 4	W	13088
Sun	10/29	H	MTL	26- 4	W	16127
Sun	11/5	A	TOR	9- 5	W	24146
Eastern Final (37-3)						
Sun	11/19	A	OTT	11- 3	W	22287
Sat	11/25	H	OTT	26- 0	W	21254
Grey Cup						
Sat	12/2	N	SAS	24- 1	W	31358

1967 MONTREAL ALOUETTES

Fri	8/11	A	TOR	7- 14	L	29698
Thu	8/17	H	HAM	16- 17	L	
Sat	8/26	H	TOR	34- 22	W	15000
Mon	9/4	A	OTT	5- 17	L	24647
Sat	9/9	H	WPG	27- 26	W	16000
Sat	9/16	H	CAL	0- 4	L	14000
Sat	9/23	A	HAM	1- 19	L	20435
Wed	10/4	H	SAS	12- 22	L	13000
Mon	10/9	A	OTT	6- 40	L	21038
Sat	10/14	H	TOR	9- 20	L	10000
Sat	10/21	A	EDM	24- 30	L	16000
Mon	10/23	A	BC	20- 30	L	24621
Sun	10/29	A	HAM	4- 26	L	16127
Sat	11/4	H	OTT	1- 15	L	6000

1967 OTTAWA ROUGH RIDERS

Wed	8/9	H	EDM	28- 25	W	21803
Wed	8/16	A	WPG	40- 7	W	19502
Wed	8/23	A	HAM	17- 22	L	25482
Mon	9/4	H	MTL	17- 5	W	24647
Sun	9/10	A	SAS	23- 32	L	21696
Wed	9/12	A	CAL	13- 20	L	19886
Sun	9/17	H	HAM	14- 16	L	27058
Sun	9/24	H	TOR	38- 3	W	21081
Sun	10/1	A	HAM	17- 8	W	27125
Mon	10/9	H	MTL	40- 6	W	21078
Wed	10/18	H	BC	19- 16	W	19302
Sun	10/22	A	TOR	28- 28	T	27238
Sat	10/28	H	TOR	28- 18	W	21358
Sat	11/4	A	MTL	15- 1	W	6000
Eastern Semi-Final						
Sun	11/12	H	TOR	38- 22	W	20627
Eastern Final (3-37)						
Sun	11/19	H	HAM	3- 11	L	22287
Sat	11/25	A	HAM	0- 26	L	21259

1967 SASKATCHEWAN ROUGHRIDERS

Mon	8/7	A	BC	24- 16	W	28411
Fri	8/11	H	BC	36- 13	W	19016
Tue	8/15	A	CAL	10- 36	L	22846
Fri	8/25	H	WPG	24- 18	W	19292
Wed	8/30	A	EDM	21- 10	W	22197
Mon	9/4	H	EDM	18- 6	W	21673
Sun	9/10	H	OTT	32- 23	W	21696
Sun	9/17	A	WPG	16- 17	L	21681
Sun	9/24	H	CAL	28- 27	W	22028
Sat	9/30	A	TOR	17- 15	W	21271
Wed	10/4	A	MTL	22- 12	W	13000
Mon	10/9	H	HAM	22- 21	W	21405
Sun	10/15	A	EDM	17- 21	L	21000
Sun	10/22	H	CAL	11- 19	L	21865
Sun	10/29	H	BC	24- 14	W	13969
Sun	11/5	A	WPG	24- 14	W	11974
Western Semi-Final						
Sat	11/11	H	EDM	21- 5	W	15999
Western Final (2-1)						
Sat	11/18	A	CAL	11- 15	L	21031
Wed	11/22	H	CAL	11- 9	W	12456
Sun	11/26	A	CAL	17- 13	W	21036
Grey Cup						
Sat	12/2	N	HAM	1- 24	L	31358

1967 TORONTO ARGONAUTS

Fri	8/11	H	MTL	14- 7	W	29698
Wed	8/16	A	BC	18- 17	W	27142
Sat	8/19	A	EDM	10- 31	L	21107
Sat	8/26	A	MTL	22- 34	L	15000
Mon	9/4	A	HAM	9- 12	L	25357
Sun	9/10	H	HAM	15- 23	L	24343
Wed	9/20	H	CAL	22- 13	W	22092
Sun	9/24	A	OTT	3- 38	L	21081
Sat	9/30	H	SAS	15- 17	L	21271
Sun	10/8	H	WPG	53- 0	W	18575
Sat	10/14	A	MTL	20- 9	W	10000
Sun	10/22	H	OTT	16- 19	L	27238
Sat	10/28	A	OTT	18- 28	L	21358
Sun	11/5	H	HAM	5- 9	L	24146
Eastern Semi-Final						
Sun	11/12	A	OTT	22- 38	L	20627

1967 WINNIPEG BLUE BOMBERS

Wed	8/2	A	EDM	20- 0	W	15000
Wed	8/9	H	CAL	27- 16	W	19281
Wed	8/16	H	OTT	7- 40	L	19502
Fri	8/25	A	SAS	18- 24	L	15000
Thu	8/31	H	BC	13- 22	L	17058
Mon	9/4	A	CAL	0- 39	L	22561
Sat	9/9	A	MTL	26- 27	L	16000
Sun	9/17	H	SAS	17- 16	W	21681
Sat	9/23	H	EDM	9- 22	L	17208
Wed	9/27	A	BC	1- 17	L	25412
Sun	10/1	H	BC	19- 8	W	13582
Sun	10/8	A	TOR	0- 53	L	18575
Sun	10/15	A	CAL	29- 51	L	17710
Sun	10/22	H	HAM	4- 31	L	13088
Wed	11/1	A	EDM	8- 24	L	13000
Sun	11/5	H	SAS	14- 24	L	11974

1968 BRITISH COLUMBIA LIONS

Tue	7/30	A	WPG	18- 16	W	14395
Tue	8/6	H	CAL	7- 41	L	32765
Thu	8/15	H	EDM	17- 18	L	25722
Tue	8/20	A	EDM	12- 4	W	17305
Sun	8/25	H	WPG	10- 17	L	23638
Mon	9/2	A	CAL	6- 26	L	19436
Sat	9/7	H	SAS	8- 14	L	30432
Sat	9/14	H	OTT	22- 22	T	25352
Sun	9/22	A	SAS	12- 16	L	16151
Mon	9/30	H	HAM	13- 16	L	25165
Sat	10/5	A	EDM	5- 13	L	16551
Sat	10/12	A	TOR	29- 43	L	22373
Mon	10/14	A	MTL	13- 4	W	11000
Sat	10/19	H	WPG	16- 14	W	20040
Sat	10/26	A	CAL	23- 42	L	
Sat	11/2	H	SAS	6- 12	L	22645

1968 CALGARY STAMPEDERS

Tue	7/30	H	SAS	24- 25	L	21652
Tue	8/6	A	BC	41- 7	W	32765
Sun	8/11	H	WPG	43- 8	W	17027
Sun	8/18	A	WPG	31- 0	W	11248
Wed	8/21	H	TOR	7- 19	L	23186
Wed	8/28	A	EDM	12- 7	W	21691
Mon	9/2	H	BC	26- 6	W	19436
Sun	9/8	H	EDM	8- 10	L	17761
Wed	9/18	A	HAM	35- 14	W	25023
Sat	9/21	A	OTT	27- 24	W	24283
Sun	9/29	H	SAS	38- 35	W	23380
Wed	10/9	H	MTL	26- 10	W	18450
Mon	10/14	A	SAS	15- 19	L	22157
Sun	10/20	A	EDM	13- 14	L	19231
Sat	10/26	H	BC	42- 23	W	
Sun	11/3	A	WPG	24- 28	L	12000
Western Semi-Final						
Sun	11/10	H	EDM	29- 13	W	23380
Western Final (2-0)						
Sat	11/16	A	SAS	32- 0	W	18833
Wed	11/20	H	SAS	25- 12	W	23380
Grey Cup						
Sat	11/30	N	OTT	21- 24	L	32655

1968 EDMONTON ESKIMOS

Wed	7/31	A	MTL	27- 10	W	14500
Fri	8/2	A	TOR	4- 32	L	25991
Wed	8/7	H	SAS	10- 10	T	16960
Thu	8/15	A	BC	18- 17	W	25722
Tue	8/20	H	BC	4- 12	L	17305
Wed	8/28	H	CAL	7- 12	L	21691
Mon	9/2	A	SAS	2- 29	L	19763
Sun	9/8	A	CAL	10- 8	W	17761
Wed	9/11	H	OTT	25- 20	W	18600
Sun	9/22	A	WPG	13- 25	L	13000
Sat	9/28	H	HAM	7- 31	L	21500
Sat	10/5	H	BC	13- 5	W	16551
Sun	10/13	A	WPG	22- 8	W	12000
Sun	10/20	H	CAL	14- 13	W	19231
Sun	10/27	H	WPG	32- 22	W	15011
Wed	10/30	A	SAS	20- 34	L	17048
Western Semi-Final						
Sun	11/10	A	CAL	13- 29	L	23380

1968 HAMILTON TIGER-CATS

Thu	8/1	A	OTT	13- 53	L	23739
Sat	8/10	H	MTL	31- 25	W	19785
Sat	8/17	H	SAS	9- 3	W	24393
Wed	8/28	A	MTL	21- 23	L	23500
Mon	9/2	H	TOR	15- 18	L	27153
Sun	9/8	A	TOR	20- 6	W	33135
Wed	9/18	H	CAL	14- 35	L	25023
Sat	9/28	A	EDM	31- 7	W	21500
Mon	9/30	A	BC	16- 13	W	25165
Sat	10/5	H	WPG	23- 13	W	18123
Sun	10/13	H	OTT	23- 36	L	29960
Sat	10/19	A	OTT	24- 27	L	25411
Sun	10/27	H	TOR	1- 12	L	24206
Sat	11/2	A	MTL	21- 21	T	8000
Eastern Semi-Final						
Sat	11/9	A	TOR	21- 33	L	25723

1968 MONTREAL ALOUETTES

Wed	7/31	H	EDM	10- 27	L	14500
Sat	8/10	A	HAM	25- 31	L	19785
Thu	8/22	H	OTT	25- 24	W	16000
Wed	8/28	H	HAM	23- 21	W	23500
Sun	9/8	A	WPG	21- 15	W	21500
Sun	9/15	H	TOR	8- 23	L	27214
Sun	9/22	A	TOR	16- 37	L	30303
Sat	9/28	H	OTT	20- 30	L	15000
Sun	10/6	A	SAS	7- 11	L	14830
Wed	10/9	A	CAL	10- 26	L	18450
Mon	10/14	H	BC	4- 13	L	11000
Sun	10/20	A	TOR	25- 29	L	21142
Sat	10/26	A	OTT	19- 19	T	17747
Sat	11/2	H	HAM	21- 21	T	8000

1968 OTTAWA ROUGH RIDERS

Thu	8/1	H	HAM	53- 13	W	23739
Fri	8/9	A	TOR	38- 14	W	32810
Wed	8/14	H	SAS	37- 23	W	25254
Thu	8/22	A	MTL	24- 25	L	16000
Wed	9/4	H	WPG	24- 17	W	20151
Wed	9/11	A	EDM	20- 25	L	18600
Sat	9/14	A	BC	22- 22	T	25352
Sat	9/21	H	CAL	24- 27	L	24283
Sat	9/28	A	MTL	30- 20	W	15000
Sun	10/6	H	TOR	31- 10	W	23454
Sun	10/13	A	HAM	36- 23	W	29960
Sat	10/19	H	HAM	27- 24	W	25411
Sat	10/26	H	MTL	19- 19	T	17747
Sun	11/3	A	TOR	31- 9	W	33135
Eastern Final (47-27)						
Sun	11/17	A	TOR	11- 13	L	32304
Sun	11/24	H	TOR	36- 14	W	25085
Grey Cup						
Sat	11/30	N	CAL	24- 21	W	32655

1968 SASKATCHEWAN ROUGHRIDERS

Tue	7/30	A	CAL	25- 24	W	21652
Sun	8/4	H	WPG	27- 8	W	16465
Wed	8/7	A	EDM	10- 10	T	16960
Wed	8/14	A	OTT	23- 37	L	25254
Sat	8/17	A	HAM	3- 9	L	24393
Sun	8/25	H	TOR	32- 17	W	20390
Mon	9/2	H	EDM	29- 2	W	19763
Sat	9/7	A	BC	14- 8	W	30432
Sun	9/15	H	WPG	31- 3	W	16136
Sun	9/22	H	BC	16- 12	W	16151
Sun	9/29	A	CAL	35- 38	L	23380
Sun	10/6	H	MTL	11- 7	W	14830

Mon	10/14	H	CAL	19- 15	W	22157
Wed	10/23	A	WPG	24- 7	W	10000
Wed	10/30	H	EDM	34- 20	W	17048
Sat	11/2	A	BC	12- 6	W	22645
Western Final (0-2)						
Sat	11/16	H	CAL	0- 32	L	18833
Wed	11/20	A	CAL	12- 25	L	23380

1968 TORONTO ARGONAUTS

Fri	8/2	H	EDM	32- 4	W	25991
Fri	8/9	H	OTT	14- 38	L	32810
Wed	8/21	A	CAL	19- 7	W	23186
Sun	8/25	A	SAS	17- 32	L	20390
Mon	9/2	A	HAM	18- 15	W	27153
Sun	9/8	H	HAM	6- 20	L	33135
Sun	9/15	A	MTL	23- 8	W	27214
Sun	9/22	H	MTL	37- 16	W	30303
Sun	9/29	A	WPG	15- 9	W	17012
Sun	10/6	A	OTT	10- 31	L	23454
Sat	10/12	H	BC	43- 29	W	22373
Sun	10/20	H	MTL	29- 25	W	21142
Sun	10/27	A	HAM	12- 1	W	24206
Sun	11/3	H	OTT	9- 31	L	33135
Eastern Semi-Final						
Sat	11/9	H	HAM	33- 21	W	25723
Eastern Final (27-47)						
Sun	11/17	H	OTT	13- 11	W	32304
Sun	11/24	A	OTT	14- 36	L	25085

1968 WINNIPEG BLUE BOMBERS

Tue	7/30	H	BC	16- 18	L	14395
Sun	8/4	A	SAS	8- 27	L	16465
Sun	8/11	A	CAL	8- 43	L	17027
Sun	8/18	H	CAL	0- 31	L	11248
Sun	8/25	A	BC	17- 10	W	23638
Wed	9/4	A	OTT	17- 24	L	20151
Sun	9/8	H	MTL	15- 21	L	21500
Sun	9/15	A	SAS	3- 31	L	16136
Sun	9/22	H	EDM	25- 13	W	13000
Sun	9/29	H	TOR	9- 15	L	17012
Sat	10/5	A	HAM	13- 23	L	18123
Sun	10/13	H	EDM	8- 22	L	12000
Sat	10/19	A	BC	14- 16	L	20040
Wed	10/23	H	SAS	7- 24	L	10000
Sun	10/27	A	EDM	22- 32	L	15011
Sun	11/3	H	CAL	28- 24	W	12000

1969 BRITISH COLUMBIA LIONS

Wed	7/30	H	CAL	7- 32	L	28294
Sun	8/3	A	SAS	20- 22	L	13000
Wed	8/13	A	OTT	24- 41	L	20315
Sat	8/16	A	HAM	0- 25	L	18635
Sat	8/23	H	TOR	20- 42	L	27661
Mon	9/1	A	SAS	14- 32	L	16470
Sat	9/6	H	WPG	11- 7	W	25051
Sat	9/13	A	CAL	20- 28	L	18816
Wed	9/17	H	EDM	5- 13	L	22791
Sun	9/21	A	WPG	17- 19	L	18361
Sat	9/27	H	CAL	17- 22	L	21729
Sun	10/5	A	EDM	13- 5	W	16101
Sat	10/11	H	MTL	21- 12	W	22444
Sat	10/18	H	EDM	17- 14	W	31547
Sun	10/26	A	WPG	22- 3	W	15340
Thu	10/30	H	SAS	7- 18	L	32340
Western Semi-Final						
Sat	11/8	A	CAL	21- 35	L	22131

1969 CALGARY STAMPEDERS

Wed	7/30	A	BC	32- 7	W	28294
Wed	8/6	H	OTT	19- 35	L	23532
Fri	8/15	A	SAS	8- 24	L	18416
Wed	8/20	A	WPG	17- 10	W	19950
Mon	8/25	H	HAM	26- 27	L	22456
Mon	9/1	H	EDM	16- 14	W	23616
Sat	9/6	A	EDM	20- 10	W	20089
Sat	9/13	H	BC	28- 20	W	18816
Sat	9/20	H	SAS	12- 31	L	23616
Sat	9/27	A	BC	22- 17	W	21729
Sun	10/5	A	MTL	35- 29	W	10152
Wed	10/8	A	TOR	25- 31	L	33135
Sun	10/12	H	WPG	16- 15	W	18761
Sun	10/19	A	SAS	18- 24	L	20120
Sat	10/25	H	EDM	1- 11	L	17032
Sat	11/1	H	WPG	32- 9	W	14717
Western Semi-Final						
Sat	11/8	H	BC	35- 21	W	22131
Western Final (0-2)						
Sat	11/15	A	SAS	11- 17	L	15955
Wed	11/19	H	SAS	13- 36	L	23625

1969 EDMONTON ESKIMOS

Tue	7/29	A	WPG	33- 0	W	18106
Mon	8/4	H	WPG	13- 14	L	14000
Mon	8/11	H	SAS	20- 21	L	20370
Fri	8/22	A	SAS	9- 24	L	17055
Wed	8/27	H	TOR	12- 24	L	20800
Mon	9/1	A	CAL	14- 16	L	23616
Sat	9/6	H	CAL	10- 20	L	20089
Sun	9/14	H	WPG	30- 16	W	12600
Wed	9/17	A	BC	13- 5	W	22791
Sat	9/27	A	OTT	0- 17	L	16975
Tue	9/30	A	HAM	12- 17	L	20533
Sun	10/5	H	BC	5- 13	L	16101
Mon	10/13	H	MTL	20- 14	W	12500
Sat	10/18	A	BC	14- 17	L	31547
Sat	10/25	A	CAL	11- 1	W	17032
Sun	11/2	H	SAS	25- 27	L	20500

1969 HAMILTON TIGER-CATS

Thu	7/31	A	TOR	34- 28	W	33135
Sat	8/9	H	MTL	22- 22	T	23213
Sat	8/16	H	BC	25- 0	W	18635
Mon	8/25	A	CAL	27- 26	W	22456
Mon	9/1	H	OTT	27- 22	W	30298
Wed	9/10	A	WPG	17- 7	W	21310
Sun	9/14	A	SAS	31- 29	W	19556
Sun	9/21	H	MTL	35- 41	L	23338
Tue	9/30	H	EDM	17- 12	W	20533
Sat	10/4	A	OTT	20- 28	L	27003
Mon	10/13	H	TOR	7- 17	L	30314
Sun	10/19	A	TOR	8- 51	L	33135
Sun	10/26	A	MTL	9- 25	L	8590
Sat	11/1	H	OTT	28- 7	W	23012
Eastern Semi-Final						
Sun	11/9	A	TOR	9- 15	L	33135

1969 MONTREAL ALOUETTES

Wed	7/30	A	OTT	15- 47	L	18104
Tue	8/5	H	TOR	26- 33	L	9500
Sat	8/9	A	HAM	22- 22	T	23213
Wed	8/20	H	OTT	15- 17	L	18592
Mon	9/1	H	WPG	24- 24	T	15259
Sat	9/6	A	OTT	22- 47	L	19362
Wed	9/10	H	SAS	8- 27	L	9030
Sun	9/21	A	HAM	41- 35	W	23338
Sun	9/28	H	TOR	33- 36	L	14057
Sun	10/5	H	CAL	29- 35	L	10152
Sat	10/11	A	BC	12- 21	L	22444
Mon	10/13	A	EDM	14- 20	L	12500
Sun	10/26	H	HAM	25- 9	W	8590
Sun	11/2	A	TOR	18- 22	L	28916

1969 OTTAWA ROUGH RIDERS

Wed	7/30	H	MTL	47- 15	W	18104
Wed	8/6	A	CAL	35- 19	W	23532
Wed	8/13	H	BC	41- 24	W	20315
Wed	8/20	A	MTL	17- 15	W	18592
Mon	9/1	A	HAM	22- 27	L	30298
Sat	9/6	H	MTL	47- 22	W	19362
Sat	9/13	H	TOR	25- 23	W	26989
Sat	9/20	A	TOR	34- 27	W	33135
Sat	9/27	H	EDM	17- 0	W	16975
Sat	10/4	H	HAM	28- 20	W	27003
Sun	10/12	A	SAS	21- 38	L	21957
Wed	10/15	A	WPG	38- 31	W	12520
Sat	10/25	H	TOR	20- 9	W	27115
Sat	11/1	A	HAM	7- 28	L	23012
Eastern Final (46-25)						
Sun	11/16	A	TOR	14- 22	L	23135
Sat	11/22	H	TOR	32- 3	W	24354
Grey Cup						
Sun	11/30	N	SAS	29- 11	W	33172

1969 SASKATCHEWAN ROUGHRIDERS

Sun	8/3	H	BC	22- 20	W	13000
Mon	8/11	A	EDM	21- 20	W	20370
Fri	8/15	H	CAL	24- 8	W	18416
Fri	8/22	H	EDM	24- 9	W	17055
Wed	8/27	A	WPG	14- 16	L	21100
Mon	9/1	H	BC	32- 14	W	16470
Sun	9/7	A	TOR	15- 34	L	33135
Wed	9/10	A	MTL	27- 8	W	9030
Sun	9/14	H	HAM	29- 31	L	19556
Sat	9/20	A	CAL	31- 12	W	23616
Sun	9/28	H	WPG	24- 8	W	16828
Sun	10/5	A	WPG	22- 10	W	19334
Sun	10/12	H	OTT	38- 21	W	21957
Sun	10/19	H	CAL	24- 18	W	20120
Thu	10/30	A	BC	18- 7	W	32340
Sun	11/2	A	EDM	27- 25	W	20500
Western Final (2-0)						
Sat	11/15	H	CAL	17- 11	W	15955
Wed	11/19	A	CAL	36- 13	W	23625
Grey Cup						
Sun	11/30	N	OTT	11- 29	L	33172

1969 TORONTO ARGONAUTS

Thu	7/31	H	HAM	28- 34	L	33135
Tue	8/5	A	MTL	33- 26	W	9500
Thu	8/14	H	WPG	29- 3	W	32021
Sat	8/23	A	BC	42- 20	W	27661
Wed	8/27	A	EDM	24- 12	W	20850
Sun	9/7	H	SAS	34- 15	W	33135
Sat	9/13	A	OTT	23- 25	L	26989
Sat	9/20	H	OTT	27- 34	L	33135
Sun	9/28	A	MTL	36- 33	W	14057
Wed	10/8	H	CAL	31- 25	W	33135
Mon	10/13	A	HAM	17- 7	W	30314
Sun	10/19	H	HAM	51- 8	W	33135
Sat	10/25	A	OTT	9- 20	L	27115
Sun	11/2	H	MTL	22- 18	W	28916
Eastern Semi-Final						
Sun	11/9	H	HAM	15- 9	W	33135
Eastern Final (25-46)						
Sun	11/16	H	OTT	22- 14	W	33135
Sat	11/22	A	OTT	3- 32	L	24354

1969 WINNIPEG BLUE BOMBERS

Tue	7/29	H	EDM	0- 33	L	18106
Mon	8/4	A	EDM	14- 13	W	14000
Thu	8/14	A	TOR	3- 29	L	32021
Wed	8/20	H	CAL	10- 17	L	19950
Wed	8/27	H	SAS	16- 14	W	21100
Mon	9/1	A	MTL	24- 24	T	15259
Sat	9/6	A	BC	7- 11	L	25051
Wed	9/10	H	HAM	7- 17	L	21310
Sun	9/14	A	EDM	16- 30	L	12600
Sun	9/21	H	BC	19- 17	W	18361
Sun	9/28	A	SAS	8- 24	L	16828
Sun	10/5	H	SAS	10- 22	L	19334
Sun	10/12	A	CAL	15- 16	L	18761
Wed	10/15	H	OTT	31- 38	L	12520
Sun	10/26	H	BC	3- 22	L	15340
Sat	11/1	A	CAL	9- 32	L	14717

1970 BRITISH COLUMBIA LIONS

Tue	7/28	H	SAS	9- 42	L	29152
Tue	8/4	A	WPG	48- 21	W	17340
Mon	8/10	A	CAL	9- 16	L	20402
Thu	8/13	A	EDM	35- 7	W	18992
Thu	8/20	H	CAL	27- 13	W	35627
Thu	8/27	H	OTT	32- 30	W	35563
Tue	9/1	A	EDM	9- 20	L	18140
Sun	9/13	H	WPG	16- 13	W	36250
Fri	9/18	A	SAS	22- 23	L	17535
Wed	9/23	H	HAM	14- 26	L	29787
Sat	10/3	H	EDM	20- 32	L	35107
Sat	10/10	A	TOR	7- 50	L	33135
Wed	10/14	A	MTL	27- 28	L	18077
Wed	10/21	H	WPG	7- 1	W	22510
Sun	10/25	A	CAL	0- 29	L	20916
Sun	11/1	H	SAS	13- 33	L	23739

1970 CALGARY STAMPEDERS

Wed	7/29	H	WPG	34- 10	W	19436
Wed	8/5	A	EDM	2- 14	L	21267
Mon	8/10	H	BC	16- 9	W	20402
Mon	8/17	A	SAS	30- 0	W	18553
Thu	8/20	A	BC	13- 27	L	35627
Wed	8/26	H	SAS	17- 21	L	23616
Wed	9/2	A	WPG	29- 8	W	23553
Mon	9/7	H	EDM	28- 13	W	23310
Wed	9/16	A	HAM	18- 39	L	21100
Sat	9/19	A	OTT	1- 9	L	23013
Sun	9/27	H	TOR	27- 12	W	21292
Wed	10/7	H	MTL	11- 4	W	18970
Mon	10/12	A	EDM	13- 16	L	23846
Sun	10/18	H	SAS	14- 21	L	23616
Sun	10/25	H	BC	29- 0	W	20916
Sun	11/1	A	WPG	11- 6	W	10131
Western Semi-Final						
Sun	11/8	A	EDM	16- 9	W	23105
Western Final (2-1)						
Sat	11/14	A	SAS	28- 11	W	15510
Wed	11/18	H	SAS	3- 11	L	23616
Sun	11/22	A	SAS	15- 14	W	18385
Grey Cup						
Sat	11/28	N	MTL	10- 23	L	32669

1970 EDMONTON ESKIMOS

Fri	7/31	A	SAS	11- 23	L	13960
Wed	8/5	H	CAL	14- 2	W	21267
Thu	8/13	H	BC	7- 35	L	18992
Tue	8/18	A	MTL	10- 14	L	27046
Thu	8/20	A	TOR	14- 16	L	33135
Tue	8/25	H	OTT	23- 31	L	19221
Tue	9/1	H	BC	20- 9	W	18140
Mon	9/7	A	CAL	13- 28	L	23310
Sat	9/12	H	SAS	10- 6	W	19334
Sun	9/20	A	WPG	33- 15	W	16500
Sat	9/26	H	HAM	34- 13	W	23061
Sat	10/3	A	BC	32- 20	W	35109
Mon	10/12	H	CAL	16- 13	W	23846
Sat	10/17	A	WPG	20- 17	W	15717
Sat	10/24	H	WPG	15- 11	W	20157
Wed	10/28	A	SAS	10- 34	L	10969
Western Semi-Final						
Sun	11/8	H	CAL	9- 16	L	23105

1970 HAMILTON TIGER-CATS

Wed	7/29	A	OTT	17- 15	W	23094
Sat	8/8	H	SAS	22- 23	L	25135
Thu	8/13	A	TOR	3- 29	L	33135
Sat	8/22	H	WPG	27- 6	W	19723
Mon	9/7	H	MTL	17- 12	W	28702
Sat	9/12	A	MTL	23- 38	L	25721
Wed	9/16	H	CAL	39- 18	W	21100
Wed	9/23	A	BC	26- 14	W	29787
Sat	9/26	A	EDM	13- 34	L	23061
Sun	10/4	H	TOR	14- 33	L	29455
Mon	10/12	H	OTT	24- 17	W	21035
Sat	10/17	A	OTT	22- 15	W	21385
Sun	10/25	H	TOR	27- 7	W	29755
Sun	11/1	A	MTL	18- 18	T	25886
Eastern Final (26-43)						
Sun	11/15	A	MTL	22- 32	L	33212
Sat	11/21	H	MTL	4- 11	L	24270

1970 MONTREAL ALOUETTES

Tue	8/4	H	TOR	34- 27	W	26743

Wed 8/12 A WPG 16- 10 W 18992
Tue 8/18 H EDM 14- 10 W 27046
Wed 9/2 A OTT 7- 31 L 26996
Mon 9/7 A HAM 12- 17 L 28702
Sat 9/12 H HAM 38- 23 W 25721
Sun 9/20 A TOR 24- 17 W 33135
Sun 9/27 H OTT 16- 15 W 26677
Sun 10/4 A SAS 10- 29 L 21708
Wed 10/7 A CAL 4- 11 L 18970
Wed 10/14 H BC 28- 27 W 18077
Sun 10/18 A TOR 13- 16 L 33135
Sat 10/24 H OTT 12- 28 L 19758
Sun 11/1 H HAM 18- 18 T 25886
Eastern Semi-Final
Sat 11/7 A TOR 16- 7 W 31794
Eastern Final (43-26)
Sun 11/15 H HAM 32- 22 W 33212
Sat 11/21 A HAM 11- 4 W 24270
Grey Cup
Sat 11/28 N CAL 23- 10 W 32669

1970 OTTAWA ROUGH RIDERS
Wed 7/29 H HAM 15- 17 L 23094
Tue 8/11 H SAS 1- 24 L 25192
Tue 8/25 A EDM 31- 23 W 19221
Thu 8/27 A BC 30- 32 L 35563
Wed 9/2 H MTL 31- 7 W 26996
Mon 9/7 H TOR 21- 37 L 26000
Sun 9/13 A TOR 25- 30 L 33135
Sat 9/19 H CAL 9- 1 W 23013
Sun 9/27 A MTL 15- 16 L 26677
Sat 10/3 H WPG 0- 15 L 19575
Mon 10/12 A HAM 17- 24 L 21035
Sat 10/17 H HAM 15- 22 L 21385
Sat 10/24 A MTL 28- 12 W 19758
Sat 10/31 A TOR 17- 19 L 25886

1970 SASKATCHEWAN ROUGHRIDERS
Tue 7/28 A BC 42- 9 W 29152
Fri 7/31 H EDM 23- 11 W 13960
Sat 8/8 A HAM 23- 22 W 25135
Tue 8/11 A OTT 24- 1 W 25192
Mon 8/17 H CAL 0- 30 L 18553
Wed 8/26 A CAL 21- 17 W 23616
Sun 8/30 H TOR 36- 14 W 20179
Mon 9/7 H WPG 30- 11 W 15433
Sat 9/12 A EDM 6- 10 L 19334
Fri 9/18 H BC 23- 22 W 17535
Sun 9/27 A WPG 5- 2 W 16528
Sun 10/4 H MTL 29- 10 W 21708
Sun 10/11 H WPG 19- 10 W 15606
Sun 10/18 A CAL 21- 14 W 23616
Wed 10/28 H EDM 34- 10 W 10969
Sun 11/1 A BC 33- 13 W 23738
Western Final (1-2)
Sat 11/14 H CAL 11- 28 L 15510
Wed 11/18 A CAL 11- 3 W 23616
Sun 11/22 H CAL 14- 15 L 18385

1970 TORONTO ARGONAUTS
Tue 8/4 A MTL 27- 34 L 26743
Thu 8/13 H HAM 29- 3 W 33135
Thu 8/20 H EDM 16- 14 W 33135
Wed 8/26 A WPG 22- 28 L 19108
Sun 8/30 A SAS 14- 36 L 20179
Mon 9/7 A OTT 37- 21 W 26000
Sun 9/13 H OTT 30- 25 W 33135
Sun 9/20 H MTL 17- 24 L 33135
Sun 9/27 A CAL 12- 27 L 21292
Sun 10/4 A HAM 33- 14 W 29455
Sat 10/10 H BC 50- 7 W 33135
Sun 10/18 H MTL 16- 13 W 33135
Sun 10/25 A HAM 7- 27 L 29755
Sat 10/31 H OTT 19- 17 W 25886
Eastern Semi-Final
Sat 11/7 H MTL 7- 16 L 31794

1970 WINNIPEG BLUE BOMBERS
Wed 7/29 A CAL 10- 34 L 19436
Tue 8/4 H BC 21- 48 L 17340
Wed 8/12 H MTL 10- 16 L 17110
Sat 8/22 A HAM 6- 27 L 19723
Wed 8/26 H TOR 28- 22 W 19108
Wed 9/2 H CAL 8- 29 L 23553
Mon 9/7 A SAS 11- 30 L 15433
Sun 9/13 A BC 13- 16 L 36250
Sun 9/20 H EDM 15- 33 L 16500
Sun 9/27 H SAS 2- 5 L 16528
Sat 10/3 A OTT 15- 0 W 19575
Sun 10/11 A SAS 10- 19 L 15606
Sat 10/17 H EDM 17- 20 L 15717
Wed 10/21 A BC 1- 7 L 22510
Sat 10/24 A EDM 11- 15 L 20157
Sun 11/1 H CAL 6- 11 L 10131

1971 BRITISH COLUMBIA LIONS
Tue 7/27 H SAS 10- 14 L 30492
Wed 8/4 A EDM 19- 20 L 19816
Mon 8/9 A WPG 29- 16 W 19981
Wed 8/18 H EDM 11- 1 W 32454
Tue 8/24 A CAL 1- 32 L 23616
Sun 8/29 H TOR 27- 24 W 30242
Mon 9/6 A SAS 14- 35 L 21485
Sun 9/12 H CAL 10- 25 L 30660
Sun 9/19 A WPG 31- 31 T 22083
Sat 9/25 H WPG 25- 18 W 28063
Sat 10/2 H MTL 28- 0 W 25138
Sat 10/9 A OTT 21- 45 L 14788
Mon 10/11 A HAM 3- 36 L 25997
Sat 10/16 H EDM 4- 9 L 27207
Sun 10/24 A SAS 18- 50 L 13801
Sat 10/30 H CAL 31- 7 W 21489

1971 CALGARY STAMPEDERS
Fri 7/30 A SAS 21- 0 W 16000
Wed 8/4 H OTT 9- 8 W 22251
Wed 8/11 A EDM 31- 1 W 23049
Mon 8/16 H WPG 36- 12 W 23425
Tue 8/24 H BC 32- 1 W 23616
Wed 9/1 A WPG 15- 31 L 22553
Mon 9/6 H EDM 23- 7 W 23616
Sun 9/12 A BC 25- 10 W 30660
Wed 9/15 H WPG 20- 7 W 23616
Wed 9/22 A MTL 11- 26 L 20821
Sat 9/25 A TOR 7- 18 L 33135
Sun 10/3 H HAM 17- 1 W 23616
Mon 10/11 H SAS 17- 24 L 23616
Sun 10/17 A SAS 7- 7 T 21706
Sat 10/23 H EDM 12- 34 L 19549
Sat 10/30 A BC 7- 31 L 21489
Western Final (2-0)
Sat 11/13 H SAS 30- 21 W 23616
Wed 11/17 A SAS 23- 21 W 14583
Grey Cup
Sun 11/28 N TOR 14- 11 W 34484

1971 EDMONTON ESKIMOS
Tue 7/27 A OTT 11- 22 L 19959
Thu 7/29 A HAM 15- 17 L 22786
Wed 8/4 H BC 20- 19 W 19816
Wed 8/11 H CAL 1- 31 L 23049
Wed 8/18 A BC 1- 11 L 32454
Wed 8/25 H WPG 31- 40 L 20149
Wed 9/1 H TOR 15- 16 L 22261
Mon 9/6 A CAL 7- 23 L 23616
Sat 9/11 A WPG 14- 26 L 22553
Sat 9/18 H SAS 3- 19 L 22474
Sun 9/26 A SAS 14- 28 L 19018
Wed 9/29 H MTL 12- 11 W 13346
Sun 10/10 H WPG 22- 14 W 18762
Sat 10/16 A BC 9- 4 W 27207
Sat 10/23 A CAL 34- 12 W 19549
Sun 10/31 H SAS 28- 12 W 19549

1971 HAMILTON TIGER-CATS
Thu 7/29 H EDM 17- 15 W 22786
Wed 8/11 A OTT 20- 17 W 26385
Wed 8/25 H MTL 8- 12 L 33321
Tue 8/31 A MTL 24- 25 L 24401
Mon 9/6 H TOR 30- 17 W 34535
Sun 9/12 A TOR 14- 23 L 33135
Sat 9/18 H MTL 10- 9 W 28871
Sun 9/26 H OTT 19- 7 W 26953
Sun 10/3 A CAL 1- 17 L 23616
Wed 10/6 A SAS 20- 28 L 13914
Mon 10/11 H BC 36- 3 W 25997
Sun 10/17 A WPG 4- 18 L 20345
Sat 10/23 H OTT 16- 40 L 21700
Sun 10/31 A TOR 23- 15 W 33135
Eastern Semi-Final
Sun 11/7 H OTT 23- 4 W 26471
Eastern Final (25-40)
Sun 11/14 H TOR 8- 23 L 33392
Sat 11/20 A TOR 17- 17 T 33135

1971 MONTREAL ALOUETTES
Tue 8/3 H SAS 29- 16 W 18385
Thu 8/12 H TOR 14- 26 L 29609
Wed 8/25 A HAM 12- 8 W 33321
Tue 8/31 H HAM 25- 24 W 24401
Mon 9/6 A OTT 17- 40 L 24395
Sat 9/11 H OTT 25- 6 W 24374
Sat 9/18 A HAM 9- 10 L 28871
Wed 9/22 H CAL 26- 11 W 30821
Wed 9/29 A EDM 11- 12 L 13346
Sat 10/2 A BC 0- 28 L 25138
Sun 10/10 H TOR 5- 32 L 22470
Sun 10/17 A TOR 28- 7 W 33135
Sun 10/24 H WPG 18- 19 L 19312
Sat 10/30 A OTT 7- 9 L 27137

1971 OTTAWA ROUGH RIDERS
Tue 7/27 H EDM 22- 11 W 19959
Mon 8/2 A WPG 28- 22 W 21851
Wed 8/4 A CAL 8- 9 L 22251
Wed 8/11 H HAM 17- 20 L 26385
Thu 8/19 A TOR 28- 30 L 33135
Fri 8/27 A SAS 21- 42 L 16980
Mon 9/6 H MTL 40- 17 W 24395
Sat 9/11 A MTL 6- 25 L 24374
Sun 9/19 H TOR 17- 26 L 26063
Sun 9/26 A HAM 7- 19 L 26953
Sun 10/3 H TOR 3- 12 L 21868
Sat 10/9 H BC 45- 21 W 14758
Sat 10/23 A HAM 40- 16 W 21700
Sat 10/30 H MTL 9- 7 W 27137

Eastern Semi-Final
Sun 11/7 A HAM 4- 23 L 26471

1971 SASKATCHEWAN ROUGHRIDERS
Tue 7/27 A BC 14- 10 W 30492
Fri 7/30 H CAL 0- 21 L 16000
Tue 8/3 A MTL 16- 29 L 18385
Fri 8/6 A TOR 17- 22 L 33135
Fri 8/13 H WPG 22- 32 L 14358
Thu 8/19 A WPG 31- 25 W 20980
Fri 8/27 H OTT 42- 21 W 16980
Mon 9/6 H BC 35- 14 W 21485
Sat 9/18 A EDM 19- 3 W 22474
Sun 9/26 H EDM 28- 14 W 19018
Sat 10/2 A WPG 2- 35 L 20717
Wed 10/6 H HAM 28- 20 W 13914
Mon 10/11 A CAL 24- 17 W 23616
Sun 10/17 H CAL 7- 7 T 21706
Sun 10/24 H BC 50- 18 W 13801
Sun 10/31 A EDM 12- 28 L 19549
Western Semi-Final
Sat 11/6 H WPG 24- 23 W 14488
Western Final (0-2)
Sat 11/13 A CAL 21- 30 L 33616
Wed 11/17 H CAL 21- 23 L 14588

1971 TORONTO ARGONAUTS
Wed 7/28 H WPG 21- 20 W 33135
Fri 8/6 H SAS 22- 17 W 33135
Thu 8/12 A MTL 26- 14 W 29609
Thu 8/19 H OTT 30- 28 W 33135
Sun 8/29 A BC 24- 27 L 30242
Wed 9/1 A EDM 16- 15 W 22261
Mon 9/6 A HAM 17- 30 L 35435
Sun 9/12 H HAM 23- 14 W 33135
Sun 9/19 A OTT 26- 17 W 26063
Sat 9/25 H CAL 18- 7 W 33135
Sun 10/3 A OTT 12- 3 W 21868
Sun 10/10 A MTL 32- 5 W 22470
Sun 10/17 H MTL 7- 28 L 33135
Sun 10/31 H HAM 15- 23 L 33135
Eastern Final (40-25)
Sun 11/14 A HAM 23- 8 W 33392
Sat 11/20 H HAM 17- 17 T 33135
Grey Cup
Sun 11/28 N CAL 11- 14 L 34484

1971 WINNIPEG BLUE BOMBERS
Wed 7/28 A TOR 20- 21 L 33135
Mon 8/2 H OTT 22- 28 L 21851
Mon 8/9 H BC 16- 29 L 19981
Fri 8/13 A SAS 32- 22 W 14358
Mon 8/16 A CAL 12- 36 L 23425
Thu 8/19 H SAS 25- 31 L 20980
Wed 8/25 A EDM 40- 31 W 20149
Wed 9/1 H CAL 31- 15 W 22553
Sat 9/11 H EDM 26- 14 W 22553
Wed 9/15 A CAL 7- 20 L 23616
Sun 9/19 H BC 31- 31 T 22083
Sat 9/25 A BC 18- 25 L 28063
Sat 10/2 H SAS 35- 2 W 20717
Sun 10/10 A EDM 14- 22 L 18762
Sun 10/17 H HAM 18- 4 W 20345
Sun 10/24 A MTL 19- 18 W 19312
Western Semi-Final
Sat 11/6 A SAS 23- 24 L 14488

1972 BRITISH COLUMBIA LIONS
Tue 8/1 A EDM 22- 34 L 19844
Tue 8/8 H HAM 19- 17 W 26488
Mon 8/14 A CAL 14- 19 L 22615
Thu 8/17 H WPG 7- 39 L
Fri 8/25 H EDM 7- 29 L 22641
Thu 9/7 A WPG 7- 42 L 25210
Tue 9/12 H SAS 13- 24 L 21937
Sun 9/17 A MTL 17- 22 L 11872
Wed 9/20 A TOR 23- 9 W 33135
Tue 9/26 H OTT 17- 20 L 22108
Tue 10/3 H WPG 26- 24 W 20579
Sun 10/8 A SAS 14- 24 L 16500
Sat 10/14 H EDM 22- 16 W 22124
Sat 10/21 H CAL 17- 19 L 21284
Sat 10/28 A CAL 3- 28 L 17190
Sat 11/4 H SAS 26- 14 W 22597

1972 CALGARY STAMPEDERS
Wed 8/2 H WPG 31- 7 W 22386
Tue 8/8 A WPG 14- 41 L 25210
Mon 8/14 H BC 19- 14 W 22611
Tue 8/22 H SAS 10- 12 L 23616
Sun 8/27 A SAS 3- 35 L 18858
Mon 9/4 H EDM 19- 31 L 23616
Sun 9/10 A EDM 20- 27 L 22921
Sat 9/16 A WPG 8- 22 L 25210
Sun 9/24 H MTL 34- 15 W 18903
Sun 10/1 H SAS 31- 14 W 23616
Sat 10/7 A HAM 24- 50 L 27647
Mon 10/9 A OTT 30- 45 L 19606
Sun 10/15 H TOR 27- 33 L 18201
Sat 10/21 A BC 19- 17 W 21284
Sat 10/28 H BC 28- 3 W 17190
Sun 11/5 A EDM 14- 28 L 16107

1972 EDMONTON ESKIMOS

Tue	8/1	H	BC	34- 22	W	19844
Fri	8/11	H	HAM	30- 27	W	21363
Wed	8/16	A	SAS	31- 29	W	17516
Fri	8/25	H	BC	29- 7	W	22641
Wed	8/30	A	WPG	16- 49	L	25210
Mon	9/4	A	CAL	31- 19	W	23616
Sun	9/10	H	CAL	27- 20	W	22921
Sun	9/17	A	SAS	12- 14	L	21230
Sat	9/23	H	OTT	9- 10	L	21632
Sat	9/30	A	TOR	31- 30	W	33135
Tue	10/3	A	MTL	13- 29	L	11718
Mon	10/9	H	WPG	24- 15	W	20564
Sat	10/14	A	BC	16- 22	L	22124
Sun	10/22	H	SAS	25- 23	W	21426
Sun	10/29	A	WPG	24- 38	L	25210
Sun	11/5	H	CAL	28- 14	W	16107
Western Semi-Final						
Sun	11/12	H	SAS	6- 8	L	15773

1972 HAMILTON TIGER-CATS

Mon	7/31	H	SAS	20- 17	W	26497
Tue	8/8	A	BC	17- 19	L	26488
Fri	8/11	A	EDM	27- 30	L	21363
Sat	8/19	H	MTL	23- 25	L	32417
Thu	8/24	A	MTL	25- 12	W	18358
Mon	9/4	H	OTT	17- 16	W	34772
Sun	9/10	A	TOR	22- 18	W	33135
Sat	9/16	A	OTT	30- 22	W	25537
Sun	9/24	H	TOR	41- 14	W	34410
Sun	10/1	A	OTT	25- 20	W	25068
Sat	10/7	H	CAL	50- 24	W	27647
Sat	10/14	A	MTL	31- 26	W	12373
Sat	10/21	H	WPG	18- 3	W	33946
Sun	11/5	H	TOR	26- 16	W	35217
Eastern Final (30-27)						
Sat	11/18	A	OTT	7- 19	L	21800
Sun	11/26	H	OTT	23- 8	W	30721
Grey Cup						
Sun	12/3	H	SAS	13- 10	W	33993

1972 MONTREAL ALOUETTES

Thu	8/3	A	TOR	19- 8	W	33135
Thu	8/10	H	OTT	19- 28	L	16649
Sat	8/19	A	HAM	25- 23	W	32417
Thu	8/24	H	HAM	12- 25	L	18388
Mon	9/4	H	TOR	21- 43	L	14594
Sat	9/9	A	OTT	23- 38	L	22196
Sun	9/17	H	BC	22- 17	W	11872
Sun	9/24	A	CAL	15- 34	L	18903
Wed	9/27	A	WPG	22- 26	L	20826
Tue	10/3	H	EDM	29- 13	W	11718
Sun	10/8	A	TOR	3- 21	L	32571
Sat	10/14	H	HAM	26- 31	L	12373
Sun	10/22	H	OTT	7- 17	L	13972
Sun	10/29	A	SAS	3- 29	L	11958
Eastern Semi-Final						
Sat	11/11	A	OTT	11- 14	L	16548

1972 OTTAWA ROUGH RIDERS

Wed	8/2	H	SAS	22- 7	W	21662
Thu	8/10	A	MTL	28- 19	W	16649
Wed	8/16	A	TOR	14- 8	W	33135
Wed	8/30	H	TOR	14- 13	W	27472
Mon	9/4	A	HAM	16- 17	L	34772
Sat	9/9	H	MTL	38- 23	W	22196
Sat	9/16	H	HAM	22- 30	L	25537
Sat	9/23	A	EDM	10- 9	W	21632
Tue	9/26	A	BC	20- 17	W	22108
Sun	10/1	H	HAM	20- 25	L	25068
Mon	10/9	H	CAL	45- 30	W	19606
Sun	10/22	A	MTL	17- 7	W	13972
Sat	10/28	A	TOR	21- 16	W	33135
Sat	11/4	H	WPG	11- 7	W	22780
Eastern Semi-Final						
Sat	11/11	H	MTL	14- 11	W	16548
Eastern Final (27-30)						
Sat	11/18	H	HAM	19- 7	W	21800
Sun	11/26	A	HAM	8- 23	L	30721

1972 SASKATCHEWAN ROUGHRIDERS

Mon	7/31	A	HAM	17- 20	L	26497
Wed	8/2	A	OTT	7- 22	L	21662
Wed	8/9	H	TOR	15- 6	W	15771
Wed	8/16	H	EDM	29- 31	L	17516
Tue	8/22	A	CAL	12- 10	W	23616
Sun	8/27	H	CAL	35- 3	W	18858
Mon	9/4	H	WPG	32- 21	W	21531
Tue	9/12	A	BC	24- 13	W	21937
Sun	9/17	H	EDM	14- 12	W	21230
Sun	9/24	H	WPG	16- 18	L	19568
Sun	10/1	A	CAL	14- 31	L	23616
Sun	10/8	H	BC	24- 14	W	16500
Sun	10/15	A	WPG	25- 28	L	25210
Sun	10/22	A	EDM	23- 25	L	21426
Sun	10/29	H	MTL	29- 3	W	11958
Sat	11/4	A	BC	14- 26	L	22597
Western Semi-Final						
Sun	11/12	A	EDM	8- 6	W	15773
Western Final						
Sun	11/19	A	WPG	27- 24	W	19534
Grey Cup						
Sun	12/3	A	HAM	10- 13	L	33993

1972 TORONTO ARGONAUTS

Thu	8/3	H	MTL	8- 19	L	33135
Wed	8/9	A	SAS	6- 15	L	15571
Wed	8/16	H	OTT	8- 14	L	33135
Wed	8/23	A	WPG	19- 21	L	25210
Wed	8/30	A	OTT	13- 14	L	27472
Mon	9/4	A	MTL	43- 21	W	14594
Sun	9/10	H	HAM	18- 22	L	33135
Wed	9/20	H	BC	9- 23	L	33135
Sun	9/24	A	HAM	14- 41	L	34410
Sat	9/30	H	EDM	30- 31	L	33135
Sun	10/8	H	MTL	21- 3	W	32571
Sun	10/15	A	CAL	33- 27	W	18201
Sat	10/28	H	OTT	16- 21	L	33135
Sun	11/5	A	HAM	16- 26	L	35217

1972 WINNIPEG BLUE BOMBERS

Wed	8/2	A	CAL	7- 31	L	33135
Tue	8/8	H	CAL	41- 14	W	25210
Thu	8/17	A	BC	39- 7	W	
Wed	8/23	H	TOR	21- 19	W	25210
Wed	8/30	H	EDM	49- 16	W	25210
Mon	9/4	A	SAS	21- 32	L	21531
Thu	9/7	H	BC	42- 7	W	25210
Sat	9/16	H	CAL	22- 8	W	25210
Sun	9/24	A	SAS	18- 16	W	19568
Wed	9/27	H	MTL	26- 22	W	20826
Tue	10/3	A	BC	24- 26	L	20579
Mon	10/9	A	EDM	15- 24	L	20564
Sun	10/15	H	SAS	28- 25	W	25210
Sat	10/21	A	HAM	3- 18	L	33946
Sun	10/29	H	EDM	38- 24	W	25210
Sat	11/4	A	OTT	7- 11	L	22780
Western Final						
Sun	11/19	H	SAS	24- 27	L	19534

1973 BRITISH COLUMBIA LIONS

Tue	7/31	H	SAS	5- 21	L	27447
Wed	8/8	A	SAS	19- 38	L	17210
Tue	8/14	H	EDM	30- 11	W	23139
Wed	8/22	A	WPG	23- 19	W	24443
Tue	8/28	H	CAL	9- 2	W	29132
Mon	9/3	A	HAM	24- 44	L	32433
Wed	9/5	A	OTT	24- 26	L	18674
Tue	9/11	H	MTL	7- 10	L	30479
Tue	9/18	H	WPG	13- 33	L	21084
Sun	9/23	A	CAL	12- 13	L	26238
Sat	9/29	H	TOR	22- 22	T	23400
Sun	10/7	A	SAS	9- 24	L	22000
Sat	10/13	H	EDM	13- 27	L	21377
Sat	10/20	A	EDM	14- 14	T	20688
Sun	10/28	A	WPG	22- 17	W	22013
Sat	11/3	H	CAL	15- 7	W	28479
Western Semi-Final						
Sun	11/11	A	SAS	13- 33	L	9373

1973 CALGARY STAMPEDERS

Thu	8/2	H	SAS	23- 15	W	25328
Thu	8/9	A	WPG	7- 30	L	23338
Wed	8/15	H	WPG	18- 9	W	23287
Wed	8/22	H	EDM	4- 24	L	27188
Tue	8/28	A	BC	2- 9	L	29132
Mon	9/3	H	WPG	25- 24	W	21445
Sun	9/9	A	SAS	25- 8	W	21490
Sat	9/15	A	EDM	22- 33	L	22919
Sun	9/23	H	BC	13- 12	W	26238
Sun	9/30	H	HAM	29- 31	L	21258
Sat	10/6	A	TOR	10- 37	L	33135
Mon	10/8	A	MTL	0- 45	L	22137
Sun	10/14	H	OTT	8- 32	L	18450
Sun	10/21	A	SAS	7- 34	L	20379
Sat	10/27	H	EDM	14- 10	W	21055
Sat	11/3	A	BC	7- 15	L	28479

1973 EDMONTON ESKIMOS

Tue	7/31	A	WPG	33- 22	W	24526
Mon	8/6	H	WPG	10- 3	W	19801
Tue	8/14	A	BC	11- 30	L	23139
Wed	8/22	A	CAL	24- 4	W	27188
Wed	8/29	H	TOR	16- 24	L	22918
Mon	9/3	A	SAS	27- 28	L	22265
Sat	9/8	H	MTL	23- 18	W	22637
Sat	9/15	H	CAL	33- 22	W	22919
Sat	9/22	A	OTT	20- 32	L	20306
Mon	9/24	A	HAM	22- 17	W	27978
Sun	9/30	H	SAS	17- 13	W	21429
Mon	10/8	H	WPG	14- 14	T	21841
Sat	10/13	A	BC	27- 13	W	21377
Sat	10/20	H	BC	14- 14	T	20688
Sat	10/27	A	CAL	10- 14	L	21055
Sun	11/4	H	SAS	28- 16	W	21234
Western Final						
Sun	11/18	H	SAS	25- 23	W	20021
Grey Cup						
Sun	11/25	N	OTT	18- 22	L	36653

1973 HAMILTON TIGER-CATS

Wed	8/1	H	MTL	9- 18	L	29116
Tue	8/7	A	MTL	14- 21	L	23416
Mon	8/13	A	OTT	25- 16	W	22087
Wed	8/22	H	TOR	38- 4	W	36347
Mon	9/3	H	BC	44- 24	W	32433
Sun	9/9	A	TOR	7- 16	L	33135
Sat	9/15	H	OTT	19- 21	L	33254
Mon	9/24	H	EDM	17- 22	L	27978
Sun	9/30	A	CAL	31- 29	W	21258
Wed	10/3	A	WPG	21- 18	W	22688
Mon	10/8	H	OTT	13- 16	L	34050
Sun	10/14	A	TOR	16- 11	W	33135
Sun	10/28	A	SAS	25- 34	L	20782
Sun	11/4	H	MTL	25- 13	W	30240

1973 MONTREAL ALOUETTES

Wed	8/1	A	HAM	18- 9	W	29116
Tue	8/7	H	HAM	21- 14	W	23416
Wed	8/15	A	TOR	21- 22	L	33135
Sat	8/25	H	OTT	3- 30	L	27205
Mon	9/3	H	TOR	23- 23	T	22488
Sat	9/8	A	EDM	18- 23	L	22637
Tue	9/11	A	BC	10- 7	W	30479
Sun	9/16	H	SAS	20- 37	L	17142
Sun	9/23	H	TOR	19- 10	W	15494
Sun	9/30	A	OTT	28- 15	W	26316
Mon	10/8	H	CAL	45- 0	W	22137
Sat	10/20	H	WPG	34- 7	W	14505
Sun	10/28	A	OTT	0- 16	L	26734
Sun	11/4	A	HAM	13- 25	L	30240
Eastern Semi-Final						
Sun	11/11	A	TOR	32- 10	W*	33135
Eastern Final						
Sun	11/18	A	OTT	14- 23	L	19793

1973 OTTAWA ROUGH RIDERS

Tue	7/31	H	TOR	9- 25	L	23764
Wed	8/8	A	TOR	6- 19	L	33135
Mon	8/13	H	HAM	16- 25	L	22087
Mon	8/20	A	SAS	12- 18	L	21032
Sat	8/25	A	MTL	30- 3	W	27205
Wed	9/5	H	BC	26- 24	W	18674
Wed	9/12	A	WPG	24- 13	W	24385
Sat	9/15	A	HAM	21- 19	W	33254
Sat	9/22	H	EDM	32- 20	W	20306
Sun	9/30	H	MTL	15- 28	L	26316
Mon	10/8	A	HAM	16- 13	W	34050
Sun	10/14	A	CAL	32- 8	W	18450
Sun	10/21	H	TOR	20- 19	W	25328
Sun	10/28	H	MTL	16- 0	W	26734
Eastern Final						
Sun	11/18	H	MTL	23- 14	W	19793
Grey Cup						
Sun	11/25	N	EDM	22- 18	W	36653

1973 SASKATCHEWAN ROUGHRIDERS

Tue	7/31	A	BC	21- 5	W	27447
Thu	8/2	A	CAL	15- 23	L	25328
Wed	8/8	H	BC	38- 19	W	17210
Mon	8/20	H	OTT	18- 12	W	21032
Wed	8/29	A	WPG	13- 12	W	25210
Mon	9/3	H	EDM	28- 27	W	22265
Sun	9/9	H	CAL	8- 25	L	21490
Sun	9/16	A	MTL	37- 20	W	17142
Wed	9/19	A	TOR	21- 15	W	33135
Tue	9/25	H	WPG	23- 25	L	16310
Sun	9/30	A	EDM	13- 17	L	21429
Sun	10/7	H	BC	24- 9	W	22000
Sun	10/14	A	WPG	17- 18	L	24372
Sun	10/21	H	CAL	34- 7	W	20379
Sun	10/28	H	HAM	34- 25	W	20782
Sun	11/4	A	EDM	16- 28	L	21234
Western Semi-Final						
Sun	11/11	H	BC	33- 13	W	9373
Western Final						
Sun	11/18	A	EDM	23- 25	L	20021

1973 TORONTO ARGONAUTS

Tue	7/31	A	OTT	25- 9	W	23764
Wed	8/8	H	OTT	19- 6	W	33135
Wed	8/15	H	MTL	22- 21	W	33135
Wed	8/22	A	HAM	4- 38	L	36347
Wed	8/29	A	EDM	24- 16	W	22918
Mon	9/3	A	MTL	23- 23	T	22488
Sun	9/9	H	HAM	16- 7	W	33135
Wed	9/19	H	SAS	15- 21	L	33135
Sun	9/23	A	MTL	10- 19	L	15494
Sat	9/29	A	BC	22- 22	T	23400
Sat	10/6	H	CAL	37- 10	W	33135
Sun	10/14	H	HAM	11- 16	L	33135
Sun	10/21	A	OTT	19- 20	L	25328
Sat	11/3	H	WPG	18- 3	W	33135
Eastern Semi-Final						
Sun	11/11	H	MTL	10- 32	L*	33135

1973 WINNIPEG BLUE BOMBERS

Tue	7/31	H	EDM	22- 33	L	24526
Mon	8/6	A	EDM	3- 10	L	19801
Thu	8/9	H	CAL	30- 7	W	23338
Wed	8/15	A	CAL	9- 18	L	23287
Wed	8/22	H	BC	19- 23	L	24443
Wed	8/29	H	SAS	12- 13	L	25210
Mon	9/3	A	CAL	24- 25	L	21445
Wed	9/12	H	OTT	13- 24	L	24385
Tue	9/18	A	BC	33- 13	W	21084
Tue	9/25	A	SAS	25- 23	W	16310
Wed	10/3	H	HAM	18- 21	L	22688
Mon	10/8	A	EDM	14- 14	T	21841
Sun	10/14	H	SAS	18- 17	W	24372

Sat	10/20	A	MTL	7-34	L	14505
Sun	10/28	H	BC	17-22	L	22013
Sat	11/3	A	TOR	3-18	L	33135

1974 BRITISH COLUMBIA LIONS

Thu	7/25	H	CAL	23-20	W	22879
Wed	7/31	A	WPG	29-22	W	22478
Thu	8/8	H	WPG	26-6	W	24569
Wed	8/14	A	CAL	18-20	L	20100
Thu	8/22	H	OTT	4-9	L	26803
Tue	8/27	A	EDM	21-15	W	22446
Sat	9/7	H	SAS	16-38	L	30187
Thu	9/12	A	TOR	26-24	W	32782
Sun	9/15	A	MTL	12-31	L	17976
Sat	9/21	H	WPG	28-10	W	22793
Sun	9/29	H	HAM	32-10	W	23420
Sun	10/6	A	CAL	20-7	W	20508
Sun	10/13	A	SAS	15-17	L	16792
Sat	10/19	H	SAS	21-24	L	30348
Sat	10/26	A	EDM	8-31	L	25009
Sat	11/2	H	EDM	7-15	L	22730
Western Semi-Final						
Sun	11/10	H	SAS	14-24	L	20485

1974 CALGARY STAMPEDERS

Thu	7/25	A	BC	20-23	L	22879
Wed	7/31	H	SAS	18-24	L	22000
Mon	8/5	A	EDM	6-20	L	21696
Wed	8/14	H	BC	20-18	W	20100
Wed	8/21	H	SAS	8-10	L	26200
Wed	8/28	A	WPG	30-31	L	22644
Mon	9/2	H	EDM	16-20	L	25000
Wed	9/11	A	HAM	0-27	L	25110
Sat	9/14	A	OTT	16-9	W	14396
Mon	9/24	H	MTL	38-13	W	20000
Sun	9/29	A	SAS	10-34	L	17168
Sun	10/6	H	BC	7-20	L	20508
Mon	10/14	A	EDM	24-10	W	24214
Sun	10/20	H	TOR	21-18	W	18555
Sun	10/27	H	WPG	44-11	W	19323
Sun	11/3	A	WPG	9-19	L	16569

1974 EDMONTON ESKIMOS

Fri	7/26	H	SAS	31-7	W	21456
Mon	8/5	H	CAL	20-6	W	21696
Fri	8/9	A	SAS	23-24	W	19461
Mon	8/19	H	OTT	23-6	W	21966
Tue	8/27	H	BC	15-21	L	22446
Mon	9/2	A	CAL	20-16	W	25000
Sun	9/8	H	WPG	24-2	W	21346
Fri	9/13	A	SAS	24-18	W	21826
Wed	9/18	A	WPG	13-19	L	24921
Wed	9/25	H	HAM	31-29	W	23297
Sat	10/5	A	TOR	20-22	L	32614
Tue	10/8	A	MTL	28-28	T	17505
Mon	10/14	H	CAL	10-24	L	24214
Sun	10/20	A	WPG	17-10	W	24528
Sat	10/26	H	BC	31-8	W	25009
Sat	11/2	A	BC	15-7	W	22730
Western Final						
Sun	11/17	H	SAS	31-27	W	25026
Grey Cup						
Sun	11/24	N	MTL	7-20	L	34450

1974 HAMILTON TIGER-CATS

Wed	7/24	A	MTL	12-20	L	15246
Tue	7/30	H	TOR	29-22	W	28391
Tue	8/6	A	OTT	25-30	L	19133
Wed	8/14	A	TOR	6-17	L	33157
Tue	8/20	H	MTL	11-7	W	28732
Sun	8/25	A	MTL	10-29	L	16290
Mon	9/2	H	OTT	11-10	W	28050
Sat	9/7	A	OTT	16-10	W	18612
Wed	9/11	H	CAL	27-0	W	25110
Wed	9/18	H	SAS	23-10	W	30028
Wed	9/25	A	EDM	29-31	L	23297
Sun	9/29	A	BC	10-32	L	23420
Sun	10/6	H	OTT	21-33	L	26055
Mon	10/14	H	WPG	12-19	L	27491
Sun	10/27	A	TOR	11-19	L	35007
Sun	11/3	H	TOR	26-24	W	32790
Eastern Semi-Final						
Sun	11/10	A	OTT	19-21	L	14876

1974 MONTREAL ALOUETTES

Wed	7/24	H	HAM	20-12	W	15246
Wed	7/31	H	OTT	20-17	W	15732
Wed	8/7	A	TOR	42-25	W	33517
Tue	8/13	A	OTT	14-27	L	24649
Tue	8/20	A	HAM	7-11	L	28732
Sun	8/25	H	HAM	29-10	W	16290
Tue	9/3	A	TOR	12-11	W	34697
Sun	9/8	H	TOR	38-6	W	24525
Sun	9/15	H	BC	31-12	W	17976
Mon	9/24	A	CAL	13-38	L	20000
Sat	9/28	A	WPG	15-24	L	23126
Tue	10/8	H	EDM	28-28	T	17505
Sun	10/13	H	TOR	13-13	T	17136
Sun	10/20	A	OTT	28-0	W	24149
Sun	10/27	A	SAS	2-17	L	22394
Sat	11/2	H	OTT	27-20	W	16311
Eastern Final						
Sun	11/17	H	OTT	14-4	W	20531
Grey Cup						
Sun	11/24	N	EDM	20-7	W	34450

1974 OTTAWA ROUGH RIDERS

Thu	7/25	A	TOR	3-19	L	32485
Wed	7/31	A	MTL	17-20	L	15732
Tue	8/6	H	HAM	30-25	W	19133
Tue	8/13	H	MTL	27-14	W	24649
Mon	8/19	A	EDM	6-23	L	21966
Thu	8/22	A	BC	9-4	W	26803
Mon	9/2	A	HAM	10-11	L	28050
Sat	9/7	H	HAM	10-16	L	18612
Sat	9/14	H	CAL	9-16	L	14396
Thu	9/19	A	TOR	29-12	W	32081
Sun	9/22	H	SAS	24-6	W	16048
Sun	9/29	H	TOR	7-19	L	18902
Sun	10/6	A	HAM	33-21	W	26055
Sat	10/12	H	WPG	27-10	W	15500
Sun	10/20	H	MTL	0-28	L	24149
Sat	11/2	A	MTL	20-27	L	16311
Eastern Semi-Final						
Sun	11/10	H	HAM	21-19	W	14786
Eastern Final						
Sun	11/17	A	MTL	4-14	L	20531

1974 SASKATCHEWAN ROUGHRIDERS

Fri	7/26	A	EDM	7-31	L	21456
Wed	7/31	A	CAL	24-18	W	22000
Fri	8/9	H	EDM	24-23	L	19461
Fri	8/16	H	WPG	24-13	W	16552
Wed	8/21	A	CAL	10-8	W	26200
Sun	8/25	H	TOR	13-17	L	15688
Mon	9/2	H	WPG	18-20	L	19232
Sat	9/7	A	BC	38-16	W	30187
Fri	9/13	H	EDM	18-24	L	21826
Wed	9/18	A	HAM	10-23	L	30028
Sun	9/22	A	OTT	6-24	L	16048
Sun	9/29	H	CAL	34-10	W	17168
Sun	10/6	A	WPG	21-24	L	24535
Sun	10/13	H	BC	17-15	W	16792
Sat	10/19	A	BC	24-21	W	30348
Sun	10/27	H	MTL	17-2	W	22394
Western Semi-Final						
Sun	11/10	A	BC	24-14	W	20485
Western Final						
Sun	11/17	A	EDM	27-31	L	25026

1974 TORONTO ARGONAUTS

Thu	7/25	H	OTT	19-3	W	21456
Tue	7/30	A	HAM	22-29	L	28391
Wed	8/7	H	MTL	25-42	L	33517
Wed	8/14	H	HAM	17-6	W	33157
Wed	8/21	A	WPG	13-18	L	21139
Sun	8/25	A	SAS	17-13	W	15688
Tue	9/3	H	MTL	11-12	L	34697
Sun	9/8	A	MTL	6-38	L	24525
Thu	9/12	H	BC	24-26	L	32782
Thu	9/19	H	OTT	12-29	L	32081
Sun	9/29	A	OTT	19-7	W	18902
Sat	10/5	H	EDM	22-20	W	32614
Sun	10/13	A	MTL	13-13	T	17136
Sun	10/20	A	CAL	18-21	L	18555
Sun	10/27	H	HAM	19-11	W	35007
Sun	11/3	A	HAM	24-26	L	32790

1974 WINNIPEG BLUE BOMBERS

Wed	7/31	H	BC	22-29	L	22478
Thu	8/8	A	BC	6-26	L	24569
Fri	8/16	A	SAS	13-24	L	16552
Wed	8/21	H	TOR	18-13	W	21139
Wed	8/28	H	CAL	31-30	W	22644
Mon	9/2	A	SAS	20-18	W	19232
Sun	9/8	A	EDM	2-24	L	21346
Wed	9/18	H	EDM	19-13	W	24921
Sat	9/21	A	BC	10-28	L	22793
Sat	9/28	H	MTL	24-15	W	23126
Sun	10/6	H	SAS	24-21	W	24535
Sat	10/12	A	OTT	10-27	L	15500
Mon	10/14	A	HAM	19-12	W	27491
Sun	10/20	H	EDM	10-17	L	24528
Sun	10/27	A	CAL	11-44	L	19323
Sun	11/3	H	CAL	19-9	W	16569

1975 BRITISH COLUMBIA LIONS

Thu	7/24	A	WPG	9-17	L	22167
Wed	7/30	A	CAL	28-30	L	23010
Tue	8/5	H	CAL	13-28	L	18167
Sun	8/10	A	SAS	28-27	W	21834
Thu	8/14	H	EDM	24-27	L	18688
Wed	8/27	A	EDM	10-34	L	24843
Thu	9/4	H	WPG	29-17	W	17073
Tue	9/9	A	WPG	15-1	W	24105
Sat	9/13	H	TOR	32-10	W	24281
Sat	9/20	H	MTL	17-20	L	28172
Sun	9/28	A	SAS	6-33	L	19302
Sat	10/4	H	CAL	12-38	L	17213
Sun	10/12	A	HAM	8-14	L	20250
Wed	10/15	H	SAS	12-8	W	15691
Sat	10/25	A	OTT	25-15	W	19002
Sat	11/1	H	EDM	8-12	L	15765

1975 CALGARY STAMPEDERS

Wed	7/23	A	SAS	2-20	L	17273
Wed	7/30	H	BC	30-28	W	23010
Tue	8/5	A	BC	28-13	W	18167
Tue	8/12	H	WPG	15-18	L	27186
Thu	8/21	H	OTT	23-6	W	25878
Tue	8/26	A	WPG	22-25	L	25210
Mon	9/1	H	EDM	31-35	L	27188
Wed	9/10	A	SAS	17-31	L	17838
Tue	9/16	H	SAS	38-17	W	27188
Sun	9/21	A	TOR	17-23	L	36410
Sun	9/28	H	EDM	36-37	L	27188
Sat	10/4	A	BC	38-12	W	17213
Mon	10/13	A	EDM	12-21	L	26147
Sat	10/18	H	HAM	23-25	L	22897
Sun	10/26	A	MTL	20-26	L	21760
Sun	11/2	H	WPG	35-26	W	21106

1975 EDMONTON ESKIMOS

Tue	7/29	H	WPG	28-22	W	23926
Wed	8/6	A	WPG	16-17	L	25026
Thu	8/14	A	BC	27-24	W	18688
Wed	8/20	H	TOR	28-11	W	24636
Wed	8/27	H	BC	34-10	W	24843
Mon	9/1	A	CAL	35-31	W	27188
Sat	9/6	H	SAS	28-24	W	25201
Sun	9/14	A	HAM	17-3	W	22744
Wed	9/17	A	OTT	25-38	L	29063
Tue	9/23	H	MTL	31-29	W	26159
Sun	9/28	A	CAL	37-36	W	27188
Sun	10/5	H	SAS	18-28	L	26303
Mon	10/13	H	CAL	21-12	W	26147
Sun	10/19	A	SAS	27-36	L	22628
Sun	10/26	H	WPG	48-41	W	25367
Sat	11/1	A	BC	12-8	W	15765
Western Final						
Sun	11/16	H	SAS	30-18	W	25671
Grey Cup						
Sun	11/23	N	MTL	9-8	W	32454

1975 HAMILTON TIGER-CATS

Wed	7/23	H	MTL	23-33	L	23150
Wed	7/30	H	OTT	9-31	L	24249
Tue	8/5	A	MTL	15-8	W	22287
Wed	8/13	A	TOR	7-27	L	40474
Tue	8/19	H	MTL	13-35	L	22580
Mon	9/1	H	TOR	20-11	W	27104
Sun	9/7	A	OTT	31-56	L	27259
Sun	9/14	H	EDM	3-17	L	22144
Sun	9/21	A	SAS	28-28	T	18964
Wed	9/24	A	WPG	32-34	L	21397
Wed	10/1	H	OTT	11-16	L	20221
Wed	10/8	A	OTT	4-31	L	22467
Sun	10/12	H	BC	14-8	W	20250
Sat	10/18	A	CAL	25-23	W	22897
Sat	10/25	A	TOR	23-27	L	40284
Sat	11/1	H	TOR	26-10	W	35342
Eastern Semi-Final						
Sun	11/9	A	MTL	12-25	L	15378

1975 MONTREAL ALOUETTES

Wed	7/23	A	HAM	33-23	W	23150
Tue	7/29	H	SAS	20-24	L	25393
Tue	8/5	H	HAM	8-15	L	22287
Tue	8/12	A	OTT	34-31	W	31668
Tue	8/19	A	HAM	35-13	W	22580
Wed	8/27	H	TOR	33-17	W	24873
Wed	9/3	H	OTT	11-18	L	25225
Sun	9/7	A	TOR	23-20	W	39130
Sat	9/13	H	OTT	19-13	W	22879
Sat	9/20	A	BC	20-17	W	28172
Tue	9/23	A	EDM	29-31	L	26159
Sun	10/5	H	WPG	21-26	L	25145
Mon	10/13	A	TOR	24-13	W	37023
Sun	10/19	H	TOR	11-18	L	22323
Sun	10/26	H	CAL	26-20	W	21760
Sun	11/2	A	OTT	6-46	L	35342
Eastern Semi-Final						
Sun	11/9	H	HAM	25-12	W	15378
Eastern Final						
Sat	11/15	A	OTT	20-10	W	32699
Grey Cup						
Sun	11/23	N	EDM	8-9	L	32454

1975 OTTAWA ROUGH RIDERS

Thu	7/24	A	TOR	18-16	W	36912
Wed	7/30	A	HAM	31-9	W	24249
Wed	8/6	H	TOR	14-16	L	31023
Tue	8/12	H	MTL	31-34	L	31688
Thu	8/21	A	CAL	6-23	L	25878
Sun	8/24	A	SAS	23-16	W	20111
Wed	9/3	A	MTL	18-11	W	25225
Sun	9/7	H	HAM	56-31	W	27259
Sat	9/13	A	MTL	13-19	L	28879
Wed	9/17	H	EDM	38-25	W	29063
Sun	9/27	H	TOR	13-9	W	28810
Wed	10/1	A	HAM	16-11	W	20221
Wed	10/8	H	HAM	31-4	W	22647
Sun	10/19	A	WPG	25-25	T	23721
Sat	10/25	H	BC	15-25	L	19002
Sun	11/2	H	MTL	46-6	W	35342
Eastern Final						
Sat	11/15	H	MTL	10-20	L	32699

1975 SASKATCHEWAN ROUGHRIDERS

Wed 7/23 H CAL 20- 2 W 17273
Tue 7/29 A MTL 24- 20 W 25393
Fri 8/1 A TOR 14- 12 W 37305
Sun 8/10 H BC 27- 28 L 21834
Mon 8/18 A WPG 20- 13 W 25210
Sun 8/24 H OTT 16- 23 L 20111
Mon 9/1 H WPG 27- 23 W 21915
Sat 9/6 A EDM 24- 28 L 25201
Wed 9/10 H CAL 31- 17 W 17838
Tue 9/16 A CAL 17- 38 L 27188
Sun 9/21 H HAM 28- 28 T 18964
Sun 9/28 H BC 33- 6 W 19302
Sun 10/5 A EDM 28- 18 W 26303
Sun 10/12 A WPG 20- 14 W 25210
Wed 10/15 A BC 8- 12 L 15691
Sun 10/19 H EDM 36- 27 W 22628
Western Semi-Final
Sat 11/8 H WPG 42- 24 W 20357
Western Final
Sun 11/16 A EDM 18- 30 L 25671

1975 TORONTO ARGONAUTS

Thu 7/24 H OTT 16- 18 L 36912
Fri 8/1 H SAS 12- 14 L 37305
Wed 8/6 A OTT 16- 14 W 31023
Wed 8/13 H HAM 27- 7 W 40474
Wed 8/20 A EDM 11- 28 L 24636
Wed 8/27 A MTL 17- 33 L 24843
Mon 9/1 A HAM 11- 20 L 27104
Sun 9/7 H MTL 20- 23 L 39130
Sat 9/13 A BC 10- 32 L 24281
Sun 9/21 H CAL 23- 17 W 36410
Sun 9/27 A OTT 9- 13 L 28810
Thu 10/2 H WPG 21- 21 T 35510
Mon 10/13 H MTL 13- 24 L 37023
Sun 10/19 A MTL 18- 11 W 22323
Sat 10/25 H HAM 27- 23 W 40284
Sat 11/1 A HAM 10- 26 L 35342

1975 WINNIPEG BLUE BOMBERS

Thu 7/24 H BC 17- 9 W 22167
Tue 7/29 A EDM 22- 28 L 23926
Wed 8/6 H EDM 17- 16 W 25026
Tue 8/12 A CAL 18- 15 W 27186
Mon 8/18 H SAS 13- 20 L 25210
Tue 8/26 H CAL 25- 22 W 25210
Mon 9/1 A SAS 23- 27 L 21915
Thu 9/4 A BC 17- 29 L 17073
Tue 9/9 H BC 1- 15 L 24105
Wed 9/24 H HAM 34- 32 W 21397
Thu 10/2 A TOR 21- 21 T 35510
Sun 10/5 A MTL 26- 21 W 25145
Sun 10/12 H SAS 14- 20 L 25210
Sun 10/19 H OTT 25- 25 T 23721
Sun 10/26 A EDM 41- 48 L 25367
Sun 11/2 A CAL 26- 35 L 21106
Western Semi-Final
Sat 11/8 A SAS 24- 42 L 20357

1976 BRITISH COLUMBIA LIONS

Thu 7/22 H SAS 8- 35 L 21983
Thu 7/29 H HAM 39- 14 W 15731
Wed 8/4 A EDM 12- 19 L 25295
Wed 8/11 A CAL 13- 9 W 23606
Tue 8/17 H WPG 22- 14 W 21505
Tue 8/24 H OTT 23- 11 W 24797
Mon 8/30 A MTL 9- 30 L 20108
Mon 9/6 A SAS 14- 17 L 21726
Sun 9/12 H CAL 30- 15 W 18103
Sun 9/19 A WPG 20- 22 L 22809
Sat 10/2 H EDM 27- 27 T 21704
Mon 10/11 A EDM 12- 16 L 25982
Sun 10/17 H SAS 15- 28 L 21534
Sun 10/24 A CAL 31- 31 T 22717
Sat 10/30 A TOR 16- 25 L 45404
Sat 11/6 H WPG 17- 23 L 14469

1976 CALGARY STAMPEDERS

Tue 7/20 A EDM 22- 24 L 25269
Thu 7/29 H MTL 20- 20 T 22977
Tue 8/3 A WPG 3- 49 L 20438
Wed 8/11 H BC 9- 13 L 23606
Fri 8/20 H SAS 13- 38 L 26972
Wed 8/25 A HAM 11- 18 L 21332
Wed 9/1 A WPG 20- 29 L 22345
Mon 9/6 H EDM 17- 19 L 25282
Sun 9/12 A BC 15- 30 L 18103
Sat 9/18 H TOR 20- 28 L 22961
Sun 9/26 A SAS 10- 35 L 20534
Sat 10/9 H WPG 22- 10 W
Sat 10/16 A OTT 36- 37 L 21467
Sun 10/24 H BC 31- 31 T 22717
Sun 10/31 A EDM 36- 28 W 25783
Sun 11/7 H SAS 31- 33 L 26925

1976 EDMONTON ESKIMOS

Tue 7/20 H CAL 24- 22 W 25269
Wed 7/28 A TOR 25- 20 W 43002
Wed 8/4 H BC 19- 12 W 25295
Tue 8/10 A WPG 31- 30 W 25210
Sun 8/15 A SAS 0- 40 L 22235
Sat 8/21 H OTT 18- 20 L 25882
Tue 8/31 H HAM 5- 1 W 25461
Mon 9/6 A CAL 19- 17 W 25282
Sun 9/12 H SAS 7- 34 L 25978
Sun 9/19 A SAS 25- 22 W 22622
Sat 9/25 H WPG 17- 28 L 25936
Sat 10/2 A BC 27- 27 T 21704
Mon 10/11 H BC 16- 12 W 25982
Sun 10/17 A WPG 33- 36 L 24178
Sat 10/23 A MTL 17- 10 W 55337
Sun 10/31 H CAL 28- 36 L 25783
Western Semi-Final
Sun 11/14 H WPG 14- 12 W 24320
Western Final
Sat 11/20 A SAS 13- 23 L 21896

1976 HAMILTON TIGER-CATS

Wed 7/21 H OTT 16- 42 L 21269
Thu 7/29 A BC 14- 39 L 15731
Sat 8/7 H SAS 8- 24 L 18126
Thu 8/12 A MTL 12- 11 W 21285
Wed 8/18 A TOR 11- 14 L 49724
Wed 8/25 H CAL 18- 11 W 21332
Tue 8/31 A EDM 1- 5 L 25461
Mon 9/6 H WPG 17- 15 W 22162
Sun 9/12 A TOR 22- 31 L 48250
Sun 9/19 A OTT 28- 21 W 22466
Sat 9/25 H TOR 29- 14 W 31793
Sun 10/3 A MTL 26- 19 W 58730
Mon 10/11 H MTL 9- 34 L 32155
Sun 10/24 H OTT 10- 48 L 21568
Sun 10/31 A OTT 25- 6 W 20454
Sun 11/7 H TOR 23- 14 W 35394
Eastern Semi-Final
Sat 11/13 H MTL 23- 0 W 25107
Eastern Final
Sun 11/21 A OTT 15- 17 L 28246

1976 MONTREAL ALOUETTES

Mon 7/26 A SAS 26- 17 W 20136
Thu 7/29 A CAL 20- 20 T 22977
Wed 8/4 A TOR 10- 23 L 44920
Thu 8/12 H HAM 11- 12 L 21285
Mon 8/16 A OTT 9- 45 L 29779
Mon 8/23 H TOR 23- 3 W 25802
Mon 8/30 H BC 30- 9 W 20108
Sun 9/5 H TOR 28- 0 W 20444
Sat 9/11 A OTT 13- 21 L 25234
Sun 9/26 H OTT 23- 2 W 68505
Sun 10/3 H HAM 19- 26 L 58730
Mon 10/11 A HAM 34- 9 W 32155
Sun 10/17 A TOR 10- 29 L 49650
Sat 10/23 H EDM 10- 17 L 55337
Sun 10/31 A WPG 13- 23 L 24146
Sat 11/6 H OTT 26- 17 W 61950
Eastern Semi-Final
Sat 11/13 A HAM 0- 23 L 25107

1976 OTTAWA ROUGH RIDERS

Wed 7/21 A HAM 42- 16 W 21269
Tue 7/27 H WPG 38- 27 W 22541
Tue 8/3 H SAS 16- 29 L 24078
Wed 8/11 A TOR 27- 16 W 50212
Mon 8/16 H MTL 45- 9 W 29779
Sat 8/21 A EDM 20- 18 W 25882
Tue 8/24 A BC 11- 23 L 24797
Wed 9/1 H TOR 40- 27 W 28060
Sat 9/11 H MTL 21- 13 W 25234
Sun 9/19 H HAM 21- 28 L 22466
Sun 9/26 A MTL 2- 23 L 68505
Sat 10/2 A TOR 20- 20 T 47685
Sat 10/16 H CAL 37- 36 W 21467
Sun 10/24 A HAM 48- 10 W 21568
Sun 10/31 H HAM 6- 25 L 20454
Sat 11/6 A MTL 17- 26 L 61950
Eastern Final
Sun 11/21 H HAM 17- 15 W 28246
Grey Cup
Sun 11/28 N SAS 23- 20 W 53467

1976 SASKATCHEWAN ROUGHRIDERS

Thu 7/22 A BC 35- 8 W 21983
Mon 7/26 H MTL 17- 26 L 20136
Tue 8/3 A OTT 29- 16 W 24078
Sat 8/7 A HAM 24- 8 W 18126
Sun 8/15 H EDM 40- 0 W 22235
Fri 8/20 A CAL 38- 13 W 26972
Fri 8/27 H WPG 12- 13 L 21362
Mon 9/6 H BC 17- 14 W 21726
Sun 9/12 A EDM 34- 7 W 25978
Sun 9/19 H EDM 22- 25 L 22622
Sun 9/26 H CAL 35- 10 W 20534
Sat 10/2 A WPG 10- 28 L 25210
Sun 10/10 H TOR 34- 3 W 22140
Sun 10/17 A BC 28- 15 W 21534
Sun 10/24 H WPG 19- 21 L 22508
Sun 11/7 A CAL 33- 31 W 26925
Western Final
Sat 11/20 H EDM 23- 13 W 21896
Grey Cup
Sun 11/28 N OTT 20- 23 L 53467

1976 TORONTO ARGONAUTS

Thu 7/22 A WPG 22- 16 W 21433
Wed 7/28 H EDM 20- 25 L 43002
Wed 8/4 H MTL 23- 10 W 44920
Wed 8/11 H OTT 16- 27 L 50212
Wed 8/18 H HAM 14- 11 W 49724
Mon 8/23 A MTL 3- 23 L 25802
Wed 9/1 A OTT 27- 40 L 28060
Sun 9/5 A MTL 0- 28 L 20444
Sun 9/12 H HAM 31- 22 W 48250
Sat 9/18 A CAL 28- 20 W 22961
Sat 9/25 A HAM 14- 29 L 31793
Sat 10/2 H OTT 20- 20 T 47685
Sun 10/10 A SAS 3- 34 L 22140
Sun 10/17 H MTL 29- 10 W 49650
Sat 10/30 H BC 25- 16 W 45404
Sun 11/7 A HAM 14- 23 L 35394

1976 WINNIPEG BLUE BOMBERS

Thu 7/22 H TOR 16- 22 L 21433
Tue 7/27 A OTT 27- 38 L 22541
Tue 8/3 H CAL 49- 3 W 20438
Tue 8/10 H EDM 30- 31 L 25210
Tue 8/17 A BC 14- 22 L 21505
Fri 8/27 A SAS 13- 12 W 21362
Wed 9/1 H CAL 29- 20 W 22345
Mon 9/6 A HAM 15- 17 L 22162
Sun 9/19 H BC 22- 20 W 22809
Sat 9/25 A EDM 28- 17 W 25936
Sat 10/2 H SAS 28- 10 W 25210
Sat 10/9 A CAL 10- 22 L
Sun 10/17 H EDM 36- 33 W 24178
Sun 10/24 A SAS 21- 19 W 22508
Sun 10/31 H MTL 23- 13 W 24146
Sat 11/6 A BC 23- 17 W 14469
Western Semi-Final
Sun 11/14 A EDM 12- 14 L 24320

1977 BRITISH COLUMBIA LIONS

Tue 7/12 H CAL 14- 9 W 16903
Wed 7/20 A SAS 34- 14 W 18455
Tue 7/26 H SAS 5- 24 L 26459
Wed 8/3 A CAL 30- 26 W 25253
Tue 8/9 H EDM 18- 24 L 26131
Wed 8/17 A WPG 25- 17 W 25210
Tue 8/23 H TOR 30- 0 W 24873
Wed 8/31 A OTT 27- 24 W 27248
Sat 9/10 H CAL 33- 21 W 28213
Sat 9/17 A EDM 20- 18 W 25858
Sat 9/24 H EDM 30- 13 W 32419
Sun 10/2 A WPG 15- 19 L 25210
Sat 10/15 H MTL 18- 17 W 32719
Sun 10/23 A HAM 21- 31 L 19133
Sun 10/30 A SAS 28- 38 L 22173
Sat 11/5 H WPG 21- 31 L 30580
Western Semi-Final
Sat 11/12 H WPG 33- 32 W 27105
Western Final
Sun 11/20 A EDM 1- 38 L 25327

1977 CALGARY STAMPEDERS

Tue 7/12 A BC 9- 14 L 16903
Tue 7/19 H HAM 13- 11 W 24497
Tue 7/26 A MTL 6- 17 L 55085
Wed 8/3 H BC 26- 30 L 25253
Tue 8/16 A EDM 19- 32 L 25761
Tue 8/23 H WPG 12- 35 L 26836
Sun 8/28 A SAS 19- 30 L 21555
Mon 9/5 H EDM 8- 22 L 26657
Sat 9/10 A BC 21- 33 L 28213
Sat 9/17 H WPG 16- 10 W 26657
Sun 9/25 H SAS 11- 1 W 26484
Sun 10/2 A SAS 17- 19 L 21505
Sat 10/8 H OTT 20- 24 L 23512
Sun 10/23 A WPG 13- 19 L 23653
Sun 10/30 H EDM 21- 23 L 24890
Sat 11/5 A TOR 10- 7 W 40474

1977 EDMONTON ESKIMOS

Mon 7/18 H WPG 26- 29 L 25842
Wed 7/27 A WPG 43- 13 W 25210
Tue 8/2 H SAS 34- 9 W 25618
Tue 8/9 A BC 24- 18 W 26131
Tue 8/16 H CAL 32- 19 W 25761
Wed 8/24 A HAM 22- 27 L 23725
Tue 8/30 H MTL 20- 25 L 25875
Mon 9/5 A CAL 22- 8 W 26657
Sat 9/17 H BC 18- 20 L 25858
Sat 9/24 A BC 13- 30 L 32419
Sat 10/1 A OTT 17- 34 L 21312
Mon 10/10 H WPG 31- 24 W 26123
Sun 10/16 A SAS 33- 31 W 22452
Sun 10/23 H TOR 16- 12 W 25388
Sun 10/30 A CAL 23- 21 W 24890
Sun 11/6 H SAS 38- 0 W 25131
Western Final
Sun 11/20 H BC 38- 1 W 25327
Grey Cup
Sun 11/27 A MTL 6- 41 L 68205

1977 HAMILTON TIGER-CATS

Tue 7/12 H TOR 21- 20 W 27502
Tue 7/19 A CAL 11- 13 L 24497
Tue 8/2 H MTL 11- 21 L 25782
Wed 8/10 A TOR 1- 22 L 48120
Tue 8/16 A OTT 17- 31 L 23480

Wed	8/24	H	EDM	27-22	W	23725
Tue	8/30	A	WPG	19-20	L	25036
Mon	9/5	H	OTT	18-33	L	25677
Sat	9/10	A	TOR	25-12	W	47498
Sun	9/18	A	SAS	17-38	L	21307
Sun	9/25	H	MTL	20-19	W	21748
Mon	10/10	H	TOR	2-43	L	34390
Sat	10/15	A	OTT	28-36	L	24750
Sun	10/23	H	BC	31-21	W	19133
Sat	10/29	A	MTL	11-18	L	46620
Sun	11/6	H	OTT	24-25	L	17353

1977 MONTREAL ALOUETTES

Wed	7/13	A	OTT	27-17	W	25280
Wed	7/20	A	TOR	16-10	W	47320
Tue	7/26	H	CAL	17-6	W	55085
Tue	8/2	A	HAM	21-11	W	25782
Thu	8/11	H	WPG	27-10	W	63330
Tue	8/23	H	OTT	27-20	W	66544
Tue	8/30	A	EDM	25-20	W	25875
Tue	9/6	H	TOR	14-20	L	69093
Sun	9/11	A	OTT	16-11	W	33399
Sun	9/18	A	TOR	13-19	L	47138
Sun	9/25	A	HAM	19-20	L	21748
Sun	10/2	H	TOR	6-18	L	62832
Sun	10/9	H	SAS	20-18	W	50540
Sat	10/15	A	BC	17-18	L	32719
Sat	10/22	H	OTT	28-16	W	62157
Sat	10/29	H	HAM	18-11	W	46620
Eastern Final						
Sat	11/19	H	OTT	21-18	W	55400
Grey Cup						
Sun	11/27	H	EDM	41-6	W	68205

1977 OTTAWA ROUGH RIDERS

Wed	7/13	H	MTL	17-27	L	25280
Wed	7/27	A	TOR	1-17	L	45540
Wed	8/3	H	TOR	41-11	W	27643
Tue	8/9	A	SAS	17-27	L	19216
Tue	8/16	H	HAM	31-17	W	23480
Tue	8/23	A	MTL	20-27	L	66544
Wed	8/31	H	BC	24-27	L	27248
Mon	9/5	A	HAM	33-18	W	25677
Sun	9/11	H	MTL	11-16	L	33399
Sat	9/24	A	WPG	24-36	L	23211
Sat	10/1	H	EDM	34-17	W	21312
Sat	10/8	A	CAL	24-20	W	23512
Sat	10/15	H	HAM	36-28	W	24750
Sat	10/22	A	MTL	16-28	L	62157
Sun	10/30	H	TOR	14-4	W	31365
Sun	11/6	A	HAM	25-24	W	17353
Eastern Semi-Final						
Sun	11/13	H	TOR	21-16	W	24875
Eastern Final						
Sat	11/19	A	MTL	18-21	L	55400

1977 SASKATCHEWAN ROUGHRIDERS

Tue	7/12	A	WPG	11-33	L	24844
Wed	7/20	H	BC	14-34	L	18455
Tue	7/26	A	BC	24-5	W	26459
Tue	8/2	A	EDM	9-34	L	25618
Tue	8/9	H	OTT	27-17	W	19216
Wed	8/17	A	TOR	27-26	W	49714
Sun	8/28	H	CAL	30-19	W	21555
Mon	9/5	H	WPG	26-18	W	22616
Sun	9/11	A	WPG	17-39	L	25210
Sun	9/18	H	HAM	38-17	W	21307
Sun	9/25	A	CAL	1-11	L	26484
Sun	10/2	H	CAL	19-17	W	21505
Sun	10/9	A	MTL	18-20	L	50540
Sun	10/16	H	EDM	31-33	L	22452
Sun	10/30	H	BC	38-28	W	22173
Sun	11/6	A	EDM	0-38	L	25131

1977 TORONTO ARGONAUTS

Tue	7/12	A	HAM	20-21	L	27502
Wed	7/20	H	MTL	10-16	L	47320
Wed	7/27	H	OTT	17-1	W	45540
Wed	8/3	A	OTT	11-41	L	27643
Wed	8/10	H	HAM	22-1	W	48120
Wed	8/17	H	SAS	26-27	L	49714
Tue	8/23	A	BC	0-30	L	24873
Tue	9/6	A	MTL	20-14	W	69093
Sat	9/10	H	HAM	12-25	L	47498
Sun	9/18	H	MTL	19-13	W	47138
Sun	10/2	A	MTL	18-6	W	62832
Mon	10/10	A	HAM	43-2	W	34390
Sun	10/16	H	WPG	10-29	L	49242
Sun	10/23	A	EDM	12-16	L	25388
Sun	10/30	A	OTT	4-14	L	31365
Sat	11/5	H	CAL	7-10	L	40747
Eastern Semi-Final						
Sun	11/13	A	OTT	16-21	L	24875

1977 WINNIPEG BLUE BOMBERS

Tue	7/12	H	SAS	33-11	W	24844
Mon	7/18	A	EDM	29-26	W	25842
Wed	7/27	H	EDM	13-43	L	25210
Thu	8/11	A	MTL	10-27	L	63330
Wed	8/17	H	BC	17-25	L	25210
Tue	8/23	A	CAL	35-12	W	26836
Tue	8/30	H	HAM	20-19	W	25036
Mon	9/5	A	SAS	18-26	L	22616
Sun	9/11	H	SAS	39-17	W	25210
Sat	9/17	A	CAL	10-16	L	26657
Sat	9/24	H	OTT	36-24	W	23211
Sun	10/2	H	BC	19-15	W	25210
Mon	10/10	A	EDM	24-31	L	26123
Sun	10/16	A	TOR	29-10	W	49242
Sun	10/23	H	CAL	19-13	W	23653
Sat	11/5	A	BC	31-21	W	30580
Western Semi-Final						
Sat	11/12	A	BC	32-33	L	27105

1978 BRITISH COLUMBIA LIONS

Tue	7/11	H	WPG	30-14	W	25808
Wed	7/19	A	CAL	21-23	L	25606
Tue	7/25	H	CAL	19-19	T	26643
Tue	8/1	H	HAM	22-22	T	23662
Tue	8/8	A	SAS	43-14	W	19584
Tue	8/15	H	SAS	24-23	W	24860
Tue	8/22	A	MTL	26-30	L	65132
Wed	8/30	A	EDM	10-18	L	42768
Sat	9/9	H	SAS	9-15	L	23473
Sun	9/17	A	CAL	4-14	L	26885
Sun	9/24	A	WPG	25-32	L	27201
Sat	9/30	H	WPG	27-38	L	23345
Mon	10/9	A	EDM	15-3	W	42673
Sat	10/21	H	OTT	20-17	W	20971
Sun	10/29	A	TOR	31-15	W	40120
Sat	11/4	H	EDM	33-11	W	20822

1978 CALGARY STAMPEDERS

Thu	7/13	A	EDM	17-33	L	25277
Wed	7/19	H	BC	23-21	W	25606
Tue	7/25	A	BC	19-19	T	26643
Wed	8/9	H	MTL	14-28	L	26888
Wed	8/16	A	WPG	29-21	W	26259
Tue	8/22	H	SAS	43-22	W	26876
Wed	8/30	A	OTT	16-27	L	26665
Mon	9/4	H	EDM	28-28	T	26888
Sun	9/17	H	BC	14-4	W	26885
Sun	9/24	A	EDM	20-20	T	42778
Sun	10/1	A	SAS	19-20	L	20065
Sat	10/7	H	TOR	22-16	W	26190
Sun	10/15	H	SAS	32-13	W	26526
Sun	10/22	A	HAM	35-1	W	21178
Sun	10/29	A	WPG	28-24	W	26781
Sun	11/5	H	WPG	22-14	W	26888
Western Semi-Final						
Sun	11/12	H	WPG	38-4	W	26868
Western Final						
Sat	11/18	A	EDM	13-26	L	26888

1978 EDMONTON ESKIMOS

Thu	7/13	H	CAL	33-17	W	25277
Tue	7/18	A	WPG	29-28	W	25973
Wed	7/26	A	SAS	46-11	W	19587
Tue	8/1	H	OTT	23-24	L	
Wed	8/16	A	TOR	40-3	W	49168
Wed	8/23	H	WPG	14-8	W	24962
Wed	8/30	H	BC	18-10	W	42768
Mon	9/4	A	CAL	28-28	T	26888
Sun	9/10	H	HAM	56-16	W	26282
Sun	9/17	A	SAS	25-20	W	42778
Sun	9/24	H	CAL	20-20	T	42778
Sun	10/1	A	MTL	42-22	W	54652
Mon	10/9	H	BC	3-15	L	42673
Sun	10/15	A	WPG	38-10	W	28080
Sun	10/29	H	SAS	26-36	L	42000
Sat	11/4	A	BC	11-33	L	20822
Western Final						
Sat	11/18	H	CAL	26-13	W	42673
Grey Cup						
Sun	11/26	N	MTL	20-13	W	54386

1978 HAMILTON TIGER-CATS

Wed	7/12	A	TOR	22-34	L	49950
Wed	7/19	H	SAS	27-23	W	22746
Tue	7/25	A	MTL	12-24	L	52132
Tue	8/1	A	BC	22-22	T	23662
Wed	8/9	H	WPG	7-29	L	22647
Tue	8/15	A	OTT	6-32	L	25389
Wed	8/23	H	OTT	8-36	L	24314
Mon	9/4	H	TOR	19-16	W	31377
Sun	9/10	A	EDM	16-56	L	26282
Sun	9/17	A	MTL	4-14	L	50567
Sat	9/23	H	MTL	17-6	W	22794
Mon	10/9	H	OTT	25-5	W	25712
Sat	10/14	A	TOR	7-21	L	41250
Sun	10/22	H	CAL	1-35	L	21178
Sat	10/28	A	OTT	9-34	L	20775
Sun	11/5	H	TOR	23-16	W	310005
Eastern Semi-Final						
Sat	11/11	A	MTL	20-35	L	37017

1978 MONTREAL ALOUETTES

Tue	7/11	A	OTT	10-17	L	25391
Tue	7/18	H	TOR	30-23	W	51388
Tue	7/25	H	HAM	24-12	W	52132
Wed	8/2	A	TOR	11-16	L	52308
Wed	8/9	A	CAL	28-14	W	26888
Tue	8/22	H	BC	30-26	W	65132
Tue	8/29	A	WPG	10-36	L	27201
Tue	9/5	H	OTT	18-23	L	62197
Sun	9/10	A	TOR	27-2	W	46202
Sun	9/17	H	HAM	14-4	W	50567
Sat	9/23	A	HAM	6-17	L	22794
Sun	10/1	H	EDM	22-42	L	54652
Sun	10/8	A	SAS	35-35	T	20907
Sun	10/15	A	OTT	10-13	L	33976
Sat	10/21	H	TOR	30-7	W	45547
Sat	11/4	H	OTT	26-8	W	54159
Eastern Semi-Final						
Sat	11/11	H	HAM	35-20	W	37017
Eastern Final						
Sun	11/19	A	OTT	21-16	W	31960
Grey Cup						
Sun	11/26	N	EDM	13-20	L	54386

1978 OTTAWA ROUGH RIDERS

Tue	7/11	H	MTL	17-10	W	25391
Wed	7/26	A	TOR	16-20	L	48159
Tue	8/1	A	EDM	24-23	W	
Tue	8/8	H	TOR	37-18	W	30723
Tue	8/15	H	HAM	32-6	W	25389
Wed	8/23	A	HAM	36-8	W	24314
Wed	8/30	H	CAL	27-16	W	26665
Tue	9/5	A	MTL	23-18	W	62197
Sat	9/9	H	WPG	29-31	L	26282
Sun	9/24	H	SAS	53-18	W	24960
Sat	9/30	A	TOR	24-3	W	45210
Mon	10/9	A	HAM	5-25	L	25712
Sun	10/15	H	MTL	13-10	W	33976
Sat	10/21	A	BC	17-20	L	20971
Sat	10/28	H	HAM	34-9	W	20775
Sat	11/4	A	MTL	6-28	W	54159
Eastern Final						
Sun	11/19	H	MTL	16-21	L	31960

1978 SASKATCHEWAN ROUGHRIDERS

Wed	7/19	A	HAM	23-27	L	22746
Wed	7/26	H	EDM	11-46	L	19587
Wed	8/2	A	WPG	13-23	L	26619
Tue	8/8	H	BC	14-43	L	19584
Tue	8/15	A	BC	23-24	L	24860
Tue	8/22	A	CAL	22-43	L	26876
Sun	8/27	H	TOR	31-10	W	19341
Mon	9/4	H	WPG	29-31	L	22451
Sat	9/9	A	BC	15-9	W	23473
Sun	9/17	H	EDM	20-25	L	21149
Sun	9/24	A	OTT	18-53	L	24960
Sun	10/1	H	CAL	20-19	W	20065
Sun	10/8	H	MTL	35-35	T	20907
Sun	10/15	A	CAL	13-32	L	26526
Sun	10/22	H	WPG	7-13	L	19614
Sun	10/29	A	EDM	36-26	W	42000

1978 TORONTO ARGONAUTS

Wed	7/12	H	HAM	34-22	W	49950
Tue	7/18	A	MTL	23-30	L	51388
Wed	7/26	H	OTT	20-16	W	48159
Wed	8/2	H	MTL	16-11	W	52308
Tue	8/8	A	OTT	18-37	L	30723
Wed	8/16	H	EDM	3-40	L	49168
Sun	8/27	A	SAS	10-31	L	19341
Mon	9/4	A	HAM	16-19	L	31377
Sun	9/10	H	MTL	2-27	L	46202
Sat	9/16	A	WPG	14-19	L	27201
Sat	9/30	H	OTT	3-24	L	45210
Sat	10/7	A	CAL	16-22	L	26190
Sat	10/14	H	HAM	21-7	W	41250
Sat	10/21	A	MTL	7-30	L	45547
Sun	10/29	H	BC	15-31	L	40120
Sun	11/5	A	HAM	16-23	L	310005

1978 WINNIPEG BLUE BOMBERS

Tue	7/11	A	BC	14-30	L	25808
Tue	7/18	H	EDM	28-29	L	25973
Wed	8/2	H	SAS	23-13	W	26619
Wed	8/9	A	HAM	29-7	W	22647
Wed	8/16	H	CAL	21-29	L	26259
Wed	8/23	A	EDM	8-14	L	24962
Tue	8/29	H	MTL	36-10	W	27201
Mon	9/4	A	SAS	31-29	W	22451
Sat	9/9	A	OTT	31-29	W	26282
Sat	9/16	H	TOR	19-14	W	27201
Sun	9/24	H	BC	32-25	W	27201
Sat	9/30	A	BC	38-27	W	23345
Sun	10/15	H	EDM	10-38	L	28080
Sun	10/22	A	SAS	13-7	W	19614
Sun	10/29	H	CAL	24-28	L	26781
Sun	11/5	A	CAL	14-22	L	26868
Western Semi-Final						
Sun	11/12	A	CAL	4-38	L	26888

1979 BRITISH COLUMBIA LIONS

Wed	7/11	A	SAS	28-4	W	19030
Tue	7/17	H	MTL	25-10	W	51237
Tue	7/24	A	WPG	19-18	W	24727
Tue	7/31	H	SAS	24-15	W	23308
Tue	8/7	H	EDM	14-14	T	30137
Wed	8/15	A	CAL	10-22	L	34825
Tue	8/21	A	HAM	22-16	W	18420
Tue	8/28	H	CAL	18-17	W	30018
Sun	9/9	A	WPG	17-15	W	27203
Sun	9/16	A	EDM	8-40	L	42776
Sat	9/22	H	TOR	34-25	W	25819
Sat	9/29	H	WPG	22-21	W	23964

Sun 10/14 A OTT 26- 28 L 25708
Sat 10/20 H CAL 32- 37 L 25301
Sat 10/27 A SAS 12- 26 L 28012
Sat 11/3 H EDM 17- 25 L 26575
Western Semi-Final
Sat 11/10 A CAL 2- 37 L 31424

1979 CALGARY STAMPEDERS
Wed 7/18 H WPG 35- 7 W 33196
Wed 7/25 A MTL 19- 7 W 51237
Tue 7/31 A EDM 9- 44 L 42887
Wed 8/8 H OTT 27- 17 W 32780
Wed 8/15 H BC 22- 10 W 34825
Wed 8/22 A SAS 6- 5 W 20790
Tue 8/28 A BC 17- 18 L 30018
Mon 9/3 H EDM 1- 27 L 34825
Sun 9/16 A SAS 52- 10 W 20021
Sun 9/23 H WPG 28- 23 W 30125
Sun 9/30 H EDM 26- 19 W 33245
Mon 10/8 A WPG 18- 13 W 22429
Sun 10/14 H HAM 16- 26 L 30925
Sat 10/20 A BC 37- 32 W 25301
Sun 10/28 A TOR 28- 12 W 36226
Sun 11/4 H SAS 41- 8 W 30654
Western Semi-Final
Sat 11/10 H BC 37- 2 W 31424
Western Final
Sun 11/18 A EDM 7- 19 L 43033

1979 EDMONTON ESKIMOS
Tue 7/10 A WPG 28- 10 W 24024
Tue 7/17 H SAS 52- 20 W 43321
Tue 7/31 H CAL 44- 9 W 42887
Tue 8/7 A BC 14- 14 T 30137
Tue 8/14 A OTT 24- 24 T 27050
Tue 8/21 H WPG 41- 13 W 42778
Tue 8/28 H TOR 28- 13 W 42778
Mon 9/3 A CAL 27- 1 W 34825
Sun 9/9 H SAS 40- 0 W 40231
Sun 9/16 H BC 40- 8 W 42776
Sun 9/23 A HAM 22- 21 W 18186
Sun 9/30 A CAL 19- 26 L 33245
Mon 10/8 H MTL 47- 6 W 42778
Sun 10/14 A SAS 25- 26 L 20042
Sun 10/28 H WPG 19- 11 W 42778
Sat 11/3 A BC 25- 17 W 26575
Western Final
Sun 11/18 H CAL 19- 7 W 43033
Grey Cup
Sun 11/25 A MTL 17- 9 W 65113

1979 HAMILTON TIGER-CATS
Wed 7/11 A OTT 19- 30 L 21674
Wed 7/18 H TOR 11- 18 L 25104
Wed 7/25 A SAS 24- 20 W 19759
Wed 8/1 H MTL 8- 21 L 41232
Wed 8/8 A TOR 0- 25 L 41282
Tue 8/14 A WPG 21- 27 L 24660
Tue 8/21 H BC 16- 22 L 18420
Mon 9/3 H OTT 16- 9 W 19246
Sat 9/8 A OTT 4- 44 L 23589
Sun 9/16 H MTL 14- 21 L 18511
Sun 9/23 H EDM 21- 22 L 18186
Sat 9/29 A TOR 17- 16 W 37023
Mon 10/8 H TOR 42- 3 W 27293
Sun 10/14 A CAL 26- 16 W 30925
Sun 10/21 H OTT 21- 3 W 27211
Sun 11/4 A MTL 20- 41 L 41382
Eastern Semi-Final
Sun 11/11 A OTT 26- 29 L 25540

1979 MONTREAL ALOUETTES
Tue 7/10 A TOR 11- 9 W 42108
Tue 7/17 A BC 10- 25 L 51237
Wed 7/25 H CAL 7- 19 L 51237
Wed 8/1 A HAM 21- 8 W 41232
Tue 8/7 H WPG 25- 10 W 41232
Mon 8/20 H OTT 32- 14 W 51487
Wed 8/29 A OTT 29- 31 L 31672
Tue 9/4 A TOR 28- 25 W 45202
Sun 9/9 H TOR 31- 11 W 51203
Sun 9/16 A HAM 21- 14 W 18511
Sun 9/23 H SAS 11- 3 W 35240
Sun 9/30 A OTT 29- 29 T 32669
Mon 10/8 A EDM 6- 47 L 42778
Sat 10/20 H TOR 25- 11 W 37690
Sat 10/27 H OTT 24- 8 W 47368
Sun 11/4 H HAM 41- 20 W 41382
Eastern Final
Sat 11/17 H OTT 17- 6 W 35103
Grey Cup
Sun 11/25 H EDM 9- 17 L 65113

1979 OTTAWA ROUGH RIDERS
Wed 7/11 H HAM 30- 19 W 21674
Tue 7/24 A TOR 31- 2 W 42160
Tue 7/31 H TOR 16- 18 L 27034
Wed 8/8 A CAL 17- 27 L 32780
Tue 8/14 H EDM 24- 24 T 27050
Mon 8/20 A MTL 14- 32 L 51487
Wed 8/29 H MTL 31- 29 W 31672
Mon 9/3 A HAM 9- 16 L 19246
Sat 9/8 H HAM 44- 4 W 23589
Sat 9/15 A WPG 22- 19 W 25644
Sun 9/30 H MTL 29- 29 T 32669
Sun 10/7 A SAS 20- 19 W 19300
Sun 10/14 H BC 28- 26 W 25708
Sun 10/21 A HAM 3- 21 L 27211
Sat 10/27 A MTL 8- 24 L 47368
Sat 11/3 H TOR 23- 6 W 21490
Eastern Semi-Final
Sun 11/11 H HAM 29- 26 W 25540
Eastern Final
Sat 11/17 A MTL 6- 17 L 35103

1979 SASKATCHEWAN ROUGHRIDERS
Wed 7/11 H BC 4- 28 L 19030
Tue 7/17 A EDM 20- 52 L 43321
Wed 7/25 H HAM 20- 24 L 19759
Tue 7/31 A BC 15- 24 L 23308
Wed 8/15 A TOR 12- 21 L 41251
Wed 8/22 H CAL 5- 6 L 20790
Tue 8/28 A WPG 1- 30 L 25159
Mon 9/3 H WPG 11- 28 L 22190
Sun 9/9 A EDM 0- 40 L 40231
Sun 9/16 H CAL 10- 52 L 20021
Sun 9/23 A MTL 3- 11 L 35240
Sun 10/7 H OTT 19- 20 L 19300
Sun 10/14 H EDM 26- 25 W 20042
Sun 10/21 A WPG 14- 23 L 23032
Sat 10/27 H BC 26- 12 W 29012
Sun 11/4 A CAL 8- 41 L 306554

1979 TORONTO ARGONAUTS
Tue 7/10 H MTL 9- 11 L 42108
Wed 7/18 A HAM 18- 11 W 25104
Tue 7/24 H OTT 2- 31 L 42160
Tue 7/31 A OTT 18- 16 W 27034
Wed 8/8 H HAM 25- 0 W 41282
Wed 8/15 H SAS 21- 12 W 41251
Tue 8/28 A EDM 13- 28 L 42778
Tue 9/4 H MTL 25- 28 L 45202
Sun 9/9 A MTL 11- 31 L 51203
Sat 9/22 A BC 25- 34 L 25819
Sat 9/29 H HAM 16- 17 L 37023
Mon 10/8 A HAM 3- 42 L 27293
Sat 10/13 H WPG 19- 15 W 35106
Sat 10/20 A MTL 11- 25 L 37690
Sun 10/28 H CAL 12- 28 L 36226
Sat 11/3 A OTT 6- 23 L 21490

1979 WINNIPEG BLUE BOMBERS
Tue 7/10 H EDM 10- 28 L 24024
Wed 7/18 A CAL 7- 35 L 33196
Tue 7/24 H BC 18- 19 L 24727
Tue 8/7 A MTL 10- 25 L 41232
Tue 8/14 H HAM 27- 21 W 24660
Tue 8/21 A EDM 13- 41 L 42778
Tue 8/28 H SAS 30- 1 W 25159
Mon 9/3 A SAS 28- 11 W 22190
Sun 9/9 H BC 15- 17 L 27203
Sat 9/15 H OTT 19- 22 L 25644
Sun 9/23 A CAL 23- 28 L 30125
Sat 9/29 A BC 21- 22 L 23964
Mon 10/8 H CAL 13- 18 L 22429
Sat 10/13 A TOR 15- 19 L 35106
Sun 10/21 H SAS 23- 14 W 23032
Sun 10/28 A EDM 11- 19 L 42778

1980 BRITISH COLUMBIA LIONS
Tue 7/8 H SAS 39- 24 W 19536
Tue 7/22 H WPG 26- 6 W 23214
Wed 7/30 A EDM 21- 33 L 42887
Tue 8/5 H CAL 31- 23 W 25465
Tue 8/12 A CAL 7- 24 L 34134
Wed 8/20 A SAS 31- 21 W 25124
Tue 8/26 H HAM 17- 17 T 21312
Mon 9/1 A MTL 14- 6 W 29827
Sat 9/13 H EDM 14- 42 L 30793
Sat 9/20 A CAL 16- 24 L 32749
Sun 9/28 A WPG 22- 28 L 29622
Sat 10/4 H SAS 44- 8 W 17247
Mon 10/13 A EDM 9- 33 L 43346
Sat 10/18 H OTT 27- 7 W 17399
Sun 10/26 A TOR 20- 38 L 30175
Sun 11/2 H WPG 43- 17 W 16676

1980 CALGARY STAMPEDERS
Tue 7/8 A OTT 20- 26 L 21064
Tue 7/15 H MTL 19- 8 W 32663
Wed 7/23 H SAS 40- 24 W 30524
Tue 7/29 A WPG 18- 35 L 20774
Tue 8/5 A BC 23- 31 L 25465
Tue 8/12 H BC 24- 7 W 34134
Tue 8/19 A EDM 16- 15 W 42778
Mon 9/1 H EDM 23- 38 L 34562
Sun 9/7 A WPG 29- 30 L 25784
Sat 9/20 H BC 24- 16 W 32749
Sun 9/28 A SAS 14- 18 L 24607
Sun 10/5 H TOR 27- 14 W 29914
Mon 10/13 A HAM 28- 30 L 19989
Sun 10/19 H WPG 31- 28 W 31132
Sun 10/26 A EDM 34- 25 W 43346
Sun 11/2 H SAS 37- 10 W 31979
Western Semi-Final
Sun 11/9 A WPG 14- 32 L 31622

1980 EDMONTON ESKIMOS
Wed 7/9 H WPG 36- 13 W 42778
Wed 7/16 A SAS 21- 6 W 22145
Wed 7/30 H BC 33- 21 W 42887
Wed 8/6 A TOR 23- 3 W 48595
Wed 8/13 A WPG 30- 17 W 26422
Tue 8/19 H CAL 15- 16 L 42778
Tue 8/26 H OTT 45- 20 W 42728
Mon 9/1 A CAL 38- 23 W 34562
Sun 9/7 H HAM 53- 18 W 43460
Sat 9/13 A BC 42- 14 W 30793
Sun 9/21 H SAS 24- 17 W 35328
Sun 10/5 A WPG 14- 28 L 28238
Mon 10/13 H BC 33- 9 W 43346
Sun 10/19 A SAS 29- 28 W 23744
Sun 10/26 H CAL 25- 34 L 43346
Sat 11/1 A MTL 44- 14 W 42234
Western Final
Sat 11/15 H WPG 34- 24 W 43346
Grey Cup
Sun 11/23 N HAM 48- 10 W 54661

1980 HAMILTON TIGER-CATS
Tue 7/15 H OTT 41- 23 W 23100
Tue 7/22 A MTL 14- 17 L 32048
Wed 7/30 H SAS 18- 19 L 22398
Tue 8/5 A OTT 13- 3 W 24181
Wed 8/13 A TOR 18- 16 W 45201
Wed 8/20 H WPG 13- 34 L 24152
Tue 8/26 A BC 17- 17 T 21312
Mon 9/1 H TOR 23- 2 W 30229
Sun 9/7 A EDM 18- 53 L 43460
Sat 9/13 H MTL 14- 25 L 19619
Sun 9/21 A MTL 10- 49 L 28185
Sun 9/28 H OTT 29- 24 W 18383
Mon 10/13 H CAL 30- 28 W 19989
Sun 10/19 A TOR 25- 24 W 34150
Sat 10/25 A OTT 26- 27 L 21788
Sun 11/2 H TOR 23- 16 W 30479
Eastern Final
Sun 11/16 H MTL 24- 13 W 30898
Grey Cup
Sun 11/23 N EDM 10- 48 L 54661

1980 MONTREAL ALOUETTES
Wed 7/9 A TOR 11- 18 L 34250
Tue 7/15 A CAL 8- 19 L 32663
Tue 7/22 H HAM 17- 14 W 32048
Wed 8/6 A SAS 18- 10 W 25947
Tue 8/12 H OTT 17- 27 L 34426
Mon 8/18 A OTT 11- 33 L 29994
Tue 8/26 H TOR 43- 33 W 29256
Mon 9/1 H BC 6- 14 L 29827
Sat 9/6 A TOR 35- 24 W 37214
Sat 9/13 A HAM 25- 14 W 19619
Sun 9/21 H HAM 49- 10 W 28185
Sat 9/27 H TOR 29- 23 W 31633
Sun 10/5 A OTT 14- 49 L 24971
Sun 10/12 H OTT 34- 17 W 31919
Sun 10/26 A WPG 25- 26 L 26352
Sat 11/1 H EDM 14- 44 L 42234
Eastern Semi-Final
Sat 11/8 H OTT 25- 21 W 17420
Eastern Final
Sun 11/16 A HAM 13- 24 L 30898

1980 OTTAWA ROUGH RIDERS
Tue 7/8 H CAL 26- 20 W 21064
Tue 7/15 A HAM 23- 41 L 23100
Wed 7/23 A TOR 20- 16 W 40112
Tue 7/29 H TOR 10- 18 L 28742
Tue 8/5 H HAM 3- 13 L 24181
Tue 8/12 A MTL 27- 17 W 34426
Mon 8/18 H MTL 33- 11 W 29994
Tue 8/26 A EDM 20- 45 L 42728
Sun 9/7 H SAS 31- 21 W 20681
Sun 9/14 H WPG 19- 20 L 21241
Sun 9/21 A TOR 17- 41 L 33156
Sun 9/28 A HAM 24- 29 L 18383
Sun 10/5 H MTL 49- 14 W 24971
Sun 10/12 A MTL 17- 34 L 31919
Sat 10/18 A BC 7- 27 L 17399
Sat 10/25 H HAM 27- 26 W 21788
Eastern Semi-Final
Sat 11/8 A MTL 21- 25 L 17420

1980 SASKATCHEWAN ROUGHRIDERS
Tue 7/8 A BC 24- 39 L 19536
Wed 7/16 H EDM 6- 21 L 22145
Wed 7/23 A CAL 24- 40 L 30524
Wed 7/30 A HAM 19- 18 W 22398
Wed 8/6 H MTL 10- 18 L 25947
Wed 8/20 H BC 21- 31 L 25124
Wed 8/27 A WPG 16- 24 L 22154
Mon 9/1 H WPG 29- 32 L 25699
Sun 9/7 A OTT 21- 31 L 20681
Sun 9/14 H TOR 17- 28 L 25448
Sun 9/21 A EDM 17- 24 L 35328
Sun 9/28 H CAL 18- 14 W 24607
Sat 10/4 A BC 8- 44 L 17247
Sun 10/12 H WPG 16- 39 L 23938
Sun 10/19 H EDM 28- 29 L 23744
Sun 11/2 A CAL 10- 37 L 31979

1980 TORONTO ARGONAUTS

Wed	7/9	H	MTL	18- 11	W	34250
Wed	7/16	A	WPG	20- 17	W	20980
Wed	7/23	H	OTT	16- 20	L	40112
Tue	7/29	A	OTT	18- 10	W	28742
Wed	8/6	H	EDM	3- 23	L	48595
Wed	8/13	H	HAM	16- 18	L	45201
Tue	8/26	A	MTL	33- 43	L	29256
Mon	9/1	A	HAM	2- 23	L	30229
Sat	9/6	H	MTL	24- 35	L	37214
Sun	9/14	A	SAS	28- 17	W	25448
Sun	9/21	H	OTT	41- 17	W	33156
Sat	9/27	A	MTL	23- 29	L	31633
Sun	10/5	A	CAL	14- 27	L	29914
Sun	10/19	H	HAM	24- 25	L	34150
Sun	10/26	H	BC	38- 20	W	30175
Sun	11/2	A	HAM	16- 23	L	30479

1980 WINNIPEG BLUE BOMBERS

Wed	7/9	A	EDM	13- 36	L	42778
Wed	7/16	H	TOR	17- 20	L	20900
Tue	7/22	A	BC	6- 26	L	23214
Tue	7/29	H	CAL	35- 18	W	20774
Wed	8/13	H	EDM	17- 30	L	26422
Wed	8/20	A	HAM	34- 13	W	24152
Wed	8/27	H	SAS	24-16	W	22154
Mon	9/1	A	SAS	32- 29	W	25699
Sun	9/7	H	CAL	30- 29	W	25784
Sun	9/14	A	OTT	20- 19	W	21241
Sun	9/28	H	BC	28- 22	W	29622
Sun	10/5	H	EDM	28- 14	W	28238
Sun	10/12	A	SAS	39- 16	W	23938
Sun	10/19	A	CAL	28- 31	L	31132
Sun	10/26	H	MTL	26- 25	W	26352
Sun	11/2	A	BC	17- 43	L	16676
Western Semi-Final						
Sun	11/9	H	CAL	32- 14	W	31622
Western Final						
Sat	11/15	A	EDM	24- 34	L	43346

1981 BRITISH COLUMBIA LIONS

Sat	7/4	H	MTL	48- 8	W	26627
Thu	7/16	A	TOR	32- 29	W	37116
Sat	7/25	H	OTT	31- 17	W	26661
Fri	7/31	A	CAL	52- 29	W	32135
Sun	8/9	A	SAS	28- 24	W	28168
Sun	8/16	H	HAM	23- 37	L	30616
Sun	8/23	A	MTL	29- 14	W	28932
Sat	8/29	H	CAL	31- 21	W	28932
Fri	9/4	A	OTT	7- 17	L	18393
Sun	9/13	A	EDM	21- 38	L	45346
Sat	9/19	H	TOR	45- 14	W	20196
Sun	9/27	A	WPG	10- 46	L	27930
Sat	10/3	H	EDM	12- 22	L	30296
Sat	10/17	H	WPG	22- 49	L	23826
Sun	10/25	A	HAM	34- 7	W	20113
Sat	10/31	H	SAS	13- 5	W	21183
Western Semi-Final						
Sun	11/8	A	WPG	15- 11	W	32936
Western Final						
Sun	11/15	H	EDM	16- 22	L	52861

1981 CALGARY STAMPEDERS

Sat	7/11	A	EDM	10- 30	L	43346
Fri	7/17	H	HAM	26- 6	W	30812
Fri	7/24	A	SAS	25- 16	W	26992
Fri	7/31	H	BC	29- 52	L	32135
Sat	8/8	A	HAM	16- 28	L	20270
Fri	8/14	H	WPG	18- 17	W	32349
Fri	8/21	H	OTT	30- 18	W	30276
Sat	8/29	A	BC	21- 31	L	28932
Mon	9/7	H	TOR	23- 5	W	30381
Sat	9/19	H	EDM	10- 21	L	34657
Sun	9/27	A	TOR	26- 29	L	28664
Sun	10/4	A	MTL	16- 22	L	22222
Sat	10/10	H	MTL	29- 3	W	29986
Sun	10/18	A	OTT	10- 21	L	15002
Sun	10/25	H	SAS	11- 24	L	33279
Sun	11/1	A	WPG	6- 44	L	27489

1981 EDMONTON ESKIMOS

Fri	7/3	A	OTT	47- 21	W	22023
Sat	7/11	H	CAL	30- 10	W	43346
Sun	7/19	A	WPG	28- 38	L	25745
Sun	7/26	A	MTL	33- 17	W	45385
Sat	8/1	H	HAM	41- 5	W	43346
Thu	8/13	A	TOR	22- 12	W	38268
Sat	8/22	H	WPG	28- 10	W	43346
Sun	8/30	H	SAS	44- 34	W	43346
Mon	9/7	A	HAM	34- 34	T	30121
Sun	9/13	H	BC	38- 21	W	45346
Sat	9/19	A	CAL	21- 10	W	34657
Sat	9/26	H	MTL	62- 11	W	48422
Sat	10/3	A	BC	22- 12	W	30296
Mon	10/12	H	OTT	24- 6	W	45805
Sun	10/18	A	SAS	41- 29	W	30312
Sat	10/24	H	TOR	61- 7	W	46146
Western Final						
Sun	11/15	A	BC	22- 16	W	52861
Grey Cup						
Sun	11/22	N	OTT	26- 23	W	53307

1981 HAMILTON TIGER-CATS

Sun	7/5	A	WPG	33- 23	W	21219
Sat	7/11	H	OTT	47- 10	W	22345
Fri	7/17	A	CAL	6- 26	L	30812
Sat	7/25	H	TOR	57- 13	W	30022
Sat	8/1	A	EDM	5- 41	L	43346
Sat	8/8	H	CAL	28- 16	W	20270
Sun	8/16	A	BC	37- 23	W	30616
Sat	8/29	H	MTL	16- 11	W	27180
Mon	9/7	H	EDM	34- 34	T	30121
Sat	9/12	A	MTL	26- 10	W	27720
Sun	9/20	H	WPG	25- 13	W	24130
Sat	9/26	A	OTT	30- 16	W	20451
Sun	10/4	A	SAS	30- 26	W	29458
Mon	10/12	H	SAS	12- 28	L	27149
Sun	10/25	H	BC	7- 34	L	20113
Sat	10/31	A	TOR	21- 11	W	30615
Eastern Final						
Sun	11/15	H	OTT	13- 17	L	28104

1981 MONTREAL ALOUETTES

Sat	7/4	A	BC	8- 48	L	26627
Fri	7/10	H	TOR	23- 22	W	35281
Fri	7/17	A	OTT	31- 33	L	24827
Sun	7/26	H	EDM	17- 33	L	45385
Sun	8/2	H	SAS	23- 43	L	33209
Sat	8/8	A	WPG	2- 58	L	32896
Sun	8/23	H	BC	14- 29	L	28932
Sat	8/29	A	HAM	11- 16	L	27180
Sun	9/6	A	SAS	26- 35	L	28526
Sat	9/12	H	HAM	10- 26	L	27720
Sat	9/26	A	EDM	11- 62	L	48422
Sun	10/4	H	CAL	22- 16	W	22222
Sat	10/10	A	CAL	3- 29	L	29986
Sat	10/17	A	TOR	14- 20	L	31038
Sat	10/24	H	WPG	13- 33	L	20487
Sun	11/1	H	OTT	39- 15	W	20867
Eastern Semi-Final						
Sun	11/8	A	OTT	16- 20	L	17554

1981 OTTAWA ROUGH RIDERS

Fri	7/3	H	EDM	21- 47	L	22023
Sat	7/11	A	HAM	10- 47	L	22345
Fri	7/17	H	MTL	33- 31	W	24827
Sat	7/25	A	BC	17- 31	L	26661
Fri	8/7	H	TOR	38- 11	W	22658
Sat	8/15	H	SAS	16- 32	L	18408
Fri	8/21	A	CAL	18- 30	L	30276
Fri	8/28	A	WPG	8- 31	L	26031
Fri	9/4	H	BC	17- 7	W	18393
Sun	9/13	A	TOR	23- 6	W	30340
Sun	9/20	A	SAS	23- 26	L	28335
Sat	9/26	H	HAM	16- 30	L	20451
Sat	10/3	H	WPG	24- 44	L	15523
Mon	10/12	A	EDM	6- 24	L	45805
Sun	10/18	H	CAL	21- 10	W	15002
Sun	11/1	A	MTL	15- 39	L	20867
Eastern Semi-Final						
Sun	11/8	H	MTL	20- 16	W	17554
Eastern Final						
Sun	11/15	A	HAM	17- 13	W	28104
Grey Cup						
Sun	11/22	N	EDM	23- 26	L	53307

1981 SASKATCHEWAN ROUGHRIDERS

Thu	7/2	A	TOR	19- 18	W	28168
Sun	7/12	H	WPG	20- 22	L	24740
Fri	7/24	H	CAL	16- 25	L	26991
Sun	8/2	A	MTL	43- 23	W	33209
Sun	8/9	H	BC	24- 28	L	28168
Sat	8/15	A	OTT	32- 16	W	18408
Sun	8/23	H	TOR	38- 14	W	26100
Sun	8/30	A	EDM	34- 44	L	43346
Sun	9/6	H	MTL	35- 26	W	28526
Sat	9/12	A	WPG	32- 25	W	31773
Sun	9/20	H	OTT	26- 23	W	28335
Sun	10/4	H	HAM	26- 30	L	29458
Mon	10/12	A	HAM	28- 12	W	27149
Sun	10/18	H	EDM	29- 41	L	30312
Sun	10/25	A	CAL	24- 11	W	33279
Sat	10/31	A	BC	5- 13	L	21183

1981 TORONTO ARGONAUTS

Thu	7/2	H	SAS	18- 19	L	28168
Fri	7/10	A	MTL	22- 23	L	35281
Thu	7/16	H	BC	29- 32	L	37116
Sat	7/25	A	HAM	13- 57	L	30022
Thu	7/30	H	WPG	18- 21	L	36102
Fri	8/7	A	OTT	11- 38	L	22658
Thu	8/13	H	EDM	12- 22	L	38268
Sun	8/23	A	SAS	14- 38	L	26100
Mon	9/7	A	CAL	5- 23	L	30381
Sun	9/13	H	OTT	6- 23	L	30340
Sat	9/19	A	BC	14- 45	L	20196
Sun	9/27	H	CAL	29- 26	W	28664
Sun	10/11	A	WPG	12- 43	L	22717
Sat	10/17	H	MTL	20- 14	W	31038
Sat	10/24	A	EDM	7- 61	L	46146
Sat	10/31	H	HAM	11- 21	L	30615

1981 WINNIPEG BLUE BOMBERS

Sun	7/5	H	HAM	23- 33	L	21219
Sun	7/12	A	SAS	22- 20	W	24740
Sun	7/19	H	EDM	38- 28	W	25745
Thu	7/30	A	TOR	21- 18	W	36102
Sat	8/8	H	MTL	58- 2	W	32896
Fri	8/14	A	CAL	17- 18	L	32349
Sat	8/22	A	EDM	10- 28	L	43346
Fri	8/28	H	OTT	31- 8	W	26031
Sat	9/12	H	SAS	25- 32	L	31773
Sun	9/20	A	HAM	13- 25	L	24130
Sun	9/27	H	BC	46- 10	W	27930
Sat	10/3	A	OTT	44- 24	W	15523
Sun	10/11	H	TOR	43- 12	W	22717
Sat	10/17	A	BC	49- 22	W	23826
Sat	10/24	A	MTL	33- 13	W	20487
Sun	11/1	H	CAL	44- 6	W	27489
Western Semi-Final						
Sun	11/8	H	BC	11- 15	L	32936

1982 BRITISH COLUMBIA LIONS

Sat	7/10	H	HAM	51- 34	W	23389
Sun	7/18	A	SAS	26- 24	W	27534
Sun	7/25	H	EDM	38- 28	W	28329
Sun	8/8	A	WPG	16- 29	L	32946
Sat	8/14	H	CAL	8- 30	L	26184
Sun	8/22	A	MTL	45- 9	W	15208
Sat	8/28	H	TOR	19- 20	L	27285
Fri	9/3	A	OTT	45- 13	W	20609
Sat	9/18	H	SAS	36- 32	W	28523
Sun	9/26	A	TOR	46- 14	W	40250
Sat	10/2	H	WPG	17- 29	L	31867
Sun	10/10	A	EDM	1- 30	L	59979
Sat	10/16	H	OTT	28- 22	W	20068
Sun	10/24	A	HAM	22- 35	L	16275
Sun	10/31	A	CAL	19- 25	L	31980
Sat	11/6	H	MTL	32- 16	W	15071

1982 CALGARY STAMPEDERS

Thu	7/8	A	TOR	24- 24	T	32760
Sat	7/24	H	SAS	19- 25	L	31061
Sat	7/31	A	HAM	30- 12	W	18350
Fri	8/6	H	OTT	30- 19	W	29038
Sat	8/14	A	BC	30- 8	W	26184
Fri	8/20	H	WPG	4- 35	L	34951
Fri	8/27	A	MTL	31- 30	W	12268
Mon	9/6	H	EDM	32- 20	W	33577
Sat	9/11	A	WPG	15- 11	W	30119
Fri	9/17	H	TOR	30- 34	L	34271
Sun	9/26	A	EDM	17- 36	L	59836
Sun	10/3	A	SAS	8- 53	L	28245
Sat	10/9	H	MTL	34- 24	W	24599
Sun	10/17	H	HAM	55- 48	W	25720
Sat	10/23	A	OTT	19- 42	L	18748
Sun	10/31	H	BC	25- 19	W	31980
Western Semi-Final						
Sun	11/14	A	WPG	3- 24	L	20894

1982 EDMONTON ESKIMOS

Sun	7/11	A	OTT	55- 7	W	21435
Sat	7/17	H	TOR	31- 12	W	55974
Sun	7/25	A	BC	28- 38	L	28329
Sun	8/1	H	WPG	26- 32	L	57596
Sat	8/7	A	TOR	22- 30	L	37985
Sun	8/15	H	MTL	46- 8	W	56354
Sun	8/29	H	SAS	25- 32	L	59723
Mon	9/6	A	CAL	20- 32	L	33577
Sun	9/12	H	OTT	47- 11	W	54622
Sun	9/19	A	HAM	32- 14	W	21625
Sun	9/26	H	CAL	36- 17	W	59836
Sun	10/10	H	BC	30- 1	W	59979
Sat	10/16	A	MTL	53- 39	W	16375
Sat	10/23	A	WPG	33- 17	W	32946
Sat	10/30	H	HAM	14- 11	W	59104
Sun	11/7	A	SAS	46- 22	W	27830
Western Final						
Sun	11/21	H	WPG	24- 21	W	51111
Grey Cup						
Sun	11/28	A	TOR	32- 16	W	54741

1982 HAMILTON TIGER-CATS

Sat	7/10	A	BC	34- 51	L	23389
Sat	7/17	H	OTT	20- 14	W	15860
Sat	7/24	A	WPG	36- 25	W	27919
Sat	7/31	H	CAL	12- 30	L	18350
Fri	8/6	A	MTL	10- 21	L	17762
Fri	8/13	H	TOR	37- 27	W	28799
Sat	8/21	A	SAS	15- 18	L	28457
Mon	9/6	H	MTL	28- 9	W	17370
Fri	9/10	A	TOR	30- 25	W	52521
Sun	9/19	H	EDM	14- 32	L	21625
Sun	10/3	A	OTT	18- 13	W	23670
Mon	10/11	H	SAS	24- 24	T	17987
Sun	10/17	A	CAL	48- 55	L	25720
Sun	10/24	H	BC	35- 22	W	16275
Sat	10/30	A	EDM	11- 14	L	59104
Sun	11/7	H	WPG	24- 21	W	18162
Eastern Semi-Final						
Sun	11/14	H	OTT	20- 30	L	20087

1982 MONTREAL CONCORDES

Fri	7/16	H	WPG	0- 36	L	14700
Fri	7/23	A	TOR	13- 16	L	31875
Thu	7/29	A	OTT	5- 55	L	18991
Fri	8/6	H	HAM	21- 10	W	17762
Sun	8/15	A	EDM	8- 46	L	56354
Sun	8/22	H	BC	9- 45	L	15208

Fri	8/27	H	CAL	30- 31	L	12268
Mon	9/6	A	HAM	9- 28	L	17370
Sun	9/12	H	SAS	16- 13	W	14111
Sat	9/25	A	WPG	16- 19	L	24462
Sat	10/2	H	TOR	9- 25	L	15622
Sat	10/9	A	CAL	24- 34	L	24599
Sat	10/16	H	EDM	39- 53	L	16375
Sun	10/24	A	SAS	20- 25	L	26470
Sun	10/31	H	OTT	32- 34	L	17179
Sat	11/6	A	BC	16- 32	L	15071

1982 OTTAWA ROUGH RIDERS

Sun	7/11	H	EDM	7- 55	L	21435
Sat	7/17	A	HAM	14- 20	L	15860
Thu	7/29	H	MTL	55- 5	W	18991
Fri	8/6	A	CAL	19- 30	L	29038
Thu	8/12	H	SAS	19- 26	L	21455
Thu	8/19	A	TOR	25- 35	L	38258
Sat	8/28	A	WPG	20- 27	L	25904
Fri	9/3	H	BC	13- 45	L	20609
Sun	9/12	A	EDM	11- 47	L	54622
Sat	9/18	H	WPG	38- 28	W	17227
Fri	9/24	A	SAS	30- 19	W	27601
Sun	10/3	H	HAM	13- 18	L	23670
Sat	10/16	A	BC	22- 28	L	20068
Sat	10/23	H	CAL	42- 19	W	18748
Sun	10/31	A	MTL	34- 32	W	17179
Sat	11/6	H	TOR	14- 28	L	25868
Eastern Semi-Final						
Sun	11/14	A	HAM	30- 20	W	20087
Eastern Final						
Sun	11/21	A	TOR	7- 44	L	43432

1982 SASKATCHEWAN ROUGHRIDERS

Fri	7/9	A	WPG	21- 31	L	28342
Sun	7/18	H	BC	24- 26	L	27534
Sat	7/24	A	CAL	25- 19	W	31061
Fri	7/30	H	TOR	22- 44	L	26076
Thu	8/12	A	OTT	26- 19	W	21455
Sat	8/21	H	HAM	18- 15	W	28457
Sun	8/29	A	EDM	32- 25	W	59723
Sun	9/5	H	WPG	35- 36	L	30621
Sun	9/12	A	MTL	13- 16	L	14111
Sat	9/18	A	BC	32- 36	L	28523
Fri	9/24	H	OTT	19- 30	L	27601
Sun	10/3	H	CAL	53- 8	W	28245
Mon	10/11	A	HAM	24- 24	T	17987
Sun	10/24	H	MTL	25- 20	W	26470
Sat	10/30	A	TOR	36- 41	L	30927
Sun	11/7	H	EDM	22- 46	L	27830

1982 TORONTO ARGONAUTS

Thu	7/8	H	CAL	24- 24	T	32760
Sat	7/17	A	EDM	12- 31	L	55974
Fri	7/23	H	MTL	16- 13	W	31875
Fri	7/30	A	SAS	44- 22	W	26076
Sat	8/7	H	EDM	30- 22	W	37985
Fri	8/13	A	HAM	27- 37	L	28799
Thu	8/19	H	OTT	35- 25	W	38258
Sat	8/28	A	BC	20- 19	W	27285
Fri	9/10	H	HAM	25- 30	L	52521
Fri	9/17	A	CAL	34- 30	W	34271
Sun	9/26	H	BC	14- 46	L	40250
Sat	10/2	A	MTL	25- 9	W	15622
Mon	10/11	A	WPG	35- 39	L	26129
Sun	10/17	H	WPG	16- 29	L	42830
Sat	10/30	H	SAS	41- 36	W	30927
Sat	11/6	A	OTT	28- 14	W	25868
Eastern Final						
Sun	11/21	H	OTT	44- 7	W	43432
Grey Cup						
Sun	11/28	H	EDM	16- 32	L	54741

1982 WINNIPEG BLUE BOMBERS

Fri	7/9	H	SAS	31- 21	W	28342
Fri	7/16	A	MTL	36- 0	W	14700
Sat	7/24	H	HAM	25- 36	L	27919
Sun	8/1	A	EDM	32- 26	W	57596
Sun	8/8	H	BC	29- 16	W	32946
Fri	8/20	A	CAL	35- 4	W	34951
Sat	8/28	H	OTT	27- 20	W	25904
Sun	9/5	A	SAS	36- 35	W	30621
Sat	9/11	H	CAL	11- 15	L	30119
Sat	9/18	A	OTT	28- 38	L	17227
Sat	9/25	H	MTL	19- 16	W	24462
Sat	10/2	A	BC	29- 17	W	31867
Mon	10/11	H	TOR	39- 35	W	26129
Sun	10/17	A	TOR	29- 16	W	42830
Sat	10/23	H	EDM	17- 33	L	32946
Sun	11/7	A	HAM	21- 24	L	18162
Western Semi-Final						
Sun	11/14	H	CAL	24- 3	W	20894
Western Final						
Sun	11/21	A	EDM	21- 24	L	51111

1983 BRITISH COLUMBIA LIONS

Thu	7/14	A	TOR	14- 17	L	39437
Sun	7/24	H	SAS	44- 28	W	41801
Sat	7/30	A	HAM	34- 20	W	16101
Sun	8/7	H	CAL	32- 16	W	37496
Fri	8/12	A	EDM	43- 13	W	52765
Sat	8/20	H	WPG	44- 6	W	56852
Sat	8/27	H	MTL	28- 6	W	36743
Fri	9/2	A	OTT	19- 49	L	22234
Sat	9/10	H	TOR	14- 32	L	52656
Sat	9/17	A	MTL	42- 26	W	17161
Sun	9/25	H	EDM	31- 30	W	52430
Mon	10/10	A	WPG	30- 18	W	31508
Sun	10/16	A	CAL	16- 25	L	24013
Sat	10/22	H	HAM	41- 16	W	43513
Sun	10/30	A	SAS	5- 11	L	23471
Sat	11/5	H	OTT	40- 13	W	42901
Western Final						
Sun	11/20	H	WPG	39- 21	W	59409
Grey Cup						
Sun	11/27	H	TOR	17- 18	L	59345

1983 CALGARY STAMPEDERS

Thu	7/7	H	TOR	30- 45	L	25124
Thu	7/21	A	OTT	27- 16	W	18621
Sun	7/31	H	MTL	42- 10	W	22665
Sun	8/7	A	BC	16- 32	L	37496
Sun	8/14	A	SAS	36- 28	W	25533
Sun	8/21	H	HAM	29- 15	W	24565
Sun	8/28	A	WPG	21- 36	L	23032
Mon	9/5	H	EDM	18- 15	W	30481
Fri	9/16	H	WPG	14- 19	L	26198
Sat	9/24	A	TOR	49- 20	W	35679
Sun	10/2	A	EDM	28- 31	L	52255
Sat	10/8	H	OTT	24- 29	L	24167
Sun	10/16	H	BC	25- 16	W	24013
Sat	10/22	A	MTL	8- 27	L	27573
Sun	10/30	A	HAM	35- 12	W	14010
Sun	11/6	H	SAS	23- 27	L	28250

1983 EDMONTON ESKIMOS

Sat	7/9	A	HAM	35- 32	W	17211
Fri	7/15	H	WPG	18- 20	L	39472
Thu	7/28	A	OTT	44- 4	W	18622
Fri	8/5	H	SAS	36- 21	W	51448
Fri	8/12	H	BC	13- 43	L	52765
Sat	8/20	A	MTL	28- 15	W	20126
Fri	8/26	H	OTT	14- 17	L	49880
Mon	9/5	A	CAL	15- 18	L	30481
Sun	9/11	H	HAM	50- 21	W	51428
Sun	9/18	A	SAS	46- 21	W	28237
Sun	9/25	A	BC	30- 31	L	52430
Sun	10/2	H	CAL	31- 28	W	52255
Sun	10/9	A	TOR	15- 19	L	37746
Sat	10/15	H	MTL	45- 32	W	49074
Sun	10/23	A	WPG	15- 33	L	24206
Sat	10/29	H	TOR	15- 22	L	53577
Western Semi-Final						
Sun	11/13	A	WPG	22- 49	L	31379

1983 HAMILTON TIGER-CATS

Sat	7/9	H	EDM	32- 35	L	17211
Sat	7/16	A	SAS	50- 19	W	25569
Fri	7/22	A	WPG	18- 29	L	24052
Sat	7/30	H	BC	20- 34	L	16101
Sat	8/6	A	TOR	31- 18	W	43568
Sat	8/13	H	OTT	24- 22	W	14729
Sun	8/21	A	CAL	15- 29	L	24565
Mon	9/5	H	MTL	35- 30	W	18547
Sun	9/11	A	EDM	21- 50	L	51428
Sun	9/18	H	TOR	16- 50	L	25128
Sun	9/25	A	OTT	25- 29	L	26014
Sat	10/1	H	WPG	19- 34	L	19266
Sat	10/15	H	SAS	34- 22	W	11000
Sat	10/22	A	BC	16- 41	L	43513
Sun	10/30	H	CAL	12- 35	L	14010
Sun	11/6	A	MTL	21- 21	T	41157
Eastern Semi-Final						
Sun	11/13	A	OTT	33- 31	W	28524
Eastern Final						
Sun	11/20	A	TOR	36- 41	L	54530

1983 MONTREAL CONCORDES

Thu	7/7	H	SAS	14- 21	L	26643
Sat	7/16	H	OTT	36- 28	W	15621
Sat	7/23	A	TOR	13- 28	L	35490
Sun	7/31	A	CAL	10- 42	L	22665
Sun	8/7	H	WPG	25- 30	L	20774
Sat	8/20	H	EDM	15- 28	L	20126
Sat	8/27	A	BC	6- 28	L	36743
Mon	9/5	A	HAM	30- 35	L	18547
Sat	9/10	A	WPG	30- 18	W	21189
Sat	9/17	H	BC	26- 42	L	17161
Sun	10/2	H	TOR	17- 30	L	20046
Sun	10/9	A	SAS	40- 23	W	23498
Sat	10/15	A	EDM	32- 45	L	49074
Sat	10/22	H	CAL	27- 8	W	27573
Sat	10/29	A	OTT	25- 20	W	20959
Sun	11/6	H	HAM	21- 21	T	41157

1983 OTTAWA ROUGH RIDERS

Fri	7/8	A	WPG	26- 25	W	18995
Sat	7/16	A	MTL	28- 36	L	15621
Thu	7/21	H	CAL	16- 27	L	18621
Thu	7/28	H	EDM	4- 44	L	18622
Sat	8/13	A	HAM	22- 24	L	14729
Fri	8/19	H	TOR	17- 27	L	30006
Fri	8/26	A	EDM	17- 14	W	49880
Fri	9/2	H	BC	49- 19	W	22234
Fri	9/9	H	SAS	28- 29	L	23475
Sun	9/25	H	HAM	29- 25	W	26014
Sat	10/1	A	SAS	24- 23	W	24404
Sat	10/8	A	CAL	29- 24	W	24167
Sun	10/16	H	WPG	42- 23	W	25642
Sun	10/23	A	TOR	20- 19	W	36526
Sat	10/29	H	MTL	20- 25	L	20959
Sat	11/5	A	BC	13- 40	L	42901
Eastern Semi-Final						
Sun	11/13	H	HAM	31- 33	L	28524

1983 SASKATCHEWAN ROUGHRIDERS

Thu	7/7	A	MTL	21- 14	W	26643
Sat	7/16	H	HAM	19- 50	L	25569
Sun	7/24	A	BC	28- 44	L	41801
Fri	7/29	H	TOR	21- 40	L	25541
Fri	8/5	A	EDM	21- 36	L	51448
Sun	8/14	H	CAL	28- 36	L	25533
Fri	8/26	A	TOR	15- 36	L	35414
Sun	9/4	H	WPG	32- 30	W	28237
Fri	9/9	A	OTT	29- 28	W	23475
Sun	9/18	H	EDM	21- 46	L	28237
Sat	9/24	A	WPG	19- 50	L	26132
Sat	10/1	H	OTT	23- 24	L	24404
Sun	10/9	H	MTL	23- 40	L	23498
Sat	10/15	A	HAM	22- 34	L	11000
Sun	10/30	H	BC	11- 5	W	23471
Sun	11/6	A	CAL	27- 23	W	28250

1983 TORONTO ARGONAUTS

Thu	7/7	A	CAL	45- 30	W	25124
Thu	7/14	H	BC	17- 14	W	39437
Sat	7/23	H	MTL	28- 13	W	35490
Fri	7/29	A	SAS	40- 21	W	25541
Sat	8/6	H	HAM	18- 31	L	43568
Sat	8/13	A	WPG	16- 32	L	27796
Fri	8/19	A	OTT	27- 17	W	30006
Fri	8/26	H	SAS	36- 15	W	35414
Sat	9/10	A	BC	32- 14	W	52656
Sun	9/18	A	HAM	50- 16	W	25128
Sat	9/24	H	CAL	20- 49	L	35679
Sun	10/2	A	MTL	30- 17	W	20046
Sun	10/9	H	EDM	19- 15	W	37746
Sun	10/23	H	OTT	19- 20	L	36526
Sat	10/29	A	EDM	22- 15	W	53577
Sat	11/5	H	WPG	33- 9	W	32921
Eastern Final						
Sun	11/20	H	HAM	41- 36	W	54530
Grey Cup						
Sun	11/27	A	BC	18- 17	W	59345

1983 WINNIPEG BLUE BOMBERS

Fri	7/8	H	OTT	25- 26	L	18995
Fri	7/15	A	EDM	20- 18	W	39472
Fri	7/22	H	HAM	29- 18	W	24052
Sun	8/7	A	MTL	30- 25	W	20774
Sat	8/13	H	TOR	32- 16	W	27796
Sat	8/20	A	BC	6- 44	L	56852
Sun	8/28	H	CAL	36- 21	W	23032
Sun	9/4	A	SAS	30- 32	L	28237
Sat	9/10	H	MTL	18- 30	L	21189
Fri	9/16	A	CAL	19- 14	W	26198
Sat	9/24	H	SAS	50- 19	W	26132
Sat	10/1	A	HAM	34- 19	W	19266
Mon	10/10	H	BC	18- 30	L	31508
Sun	10/16	A	OTT	23- 42	L	25642
Sun	10/23	H	EDM	33- 15	W	24206
Sat	11/5	A	TOR	9- 33	L	32921
Western Semi-Final						
Sun	11/13	H	EDM	49- 22	W	31379
Western Final						
Sun	11/20	A	BC	21- 39	L	59409

1984 BRITISH COLUMBIA LIONS

Fri	7/6	H	EDM	44- 10	W	43501
Sun	7/15	A	TOR	39- 29	W	34092
Sun	7/22	A	WPG	3- 25	L	31113
Sat	7/28	H	MTL	22- 7	W	39991
Sun	8/5	A	SAS	29- 7	W	24558
Sat	8/11	H	OTT	34- 21	W	37560
Sun	8/19	A	HAM	19- 11	W	14101
Sat	8/25	H	CAL	15- 4	W	38419
Sun	9/9	H	HAM	46- 11	W	34630
Sat	9/15	A	MTL	17- 33	L	15085
Sat	9/22	H	SAS	28- 37	L	35955
Fri	9/28	A	EDM	34- 32	W	47015
Sat	10/6	H	TOR	21- 21	T	49358
Sat	10/13	A	OTT	33- 17	W	21280
Sat	10/20	A	CAL	41- 13	W	23230
Sat	10/27	H	WPG	20- 3	W	59421
Western Final						
Sun	11/11	H	WPG	14- 31	L	59421

1984 CALGARY STAMPEDERS

Fri	6/29	H	WPG	24- 17	W	21812
Sat	7/7	A	OTT	16- 17	L	20042
Fri	7/13	A	EDM	13- 40	L	40215
Fri	7/20	H	HAM	23- 18	W	20769
Fri	7/27	H	TOR	17- 43	L	22761
Sat	8/4	A	MTL	14- 28	L	15363
Sun	8/19	H	SAS	32- 11	W	23422
Sat	8/25	A	BC	4- 15	L	38419
Mon	9/3	H	EDM	28- 30	L	26046
Sun	9/9	A	SAS	32- 18	W	23042
Fri	9/14	H	OTT	23- 21	W	20120

Sun 9/23 A HAM 26- 29 L 12501
Sat 9/29 H MTL 13- 27 L 20229
Mon 10/8 A WPG 8- 46 L 28025
Sun 10/14 A TOR 28- 24 W 30406
Sat 10/20 H BC 13- 41 L 23230

1984 EDMONTON ESKIMOS

Sat 6/30 H OTT 32- 31 W 32441
Fri 7/6 A BC 10- 44 L 43501
Fri 7/13 H CAL 40- 13 W 40215
Sun 7/22 A TOR 26- 43 L 31132
Fri 8/3 H WPG 21- 22 L 40470
Sun 8/12 A SAS 37- 21 W 22321
Sat 8/18 A MTL 24- 44 L 16187
Fri 8/24 H HAM 35- 14 W 42750
Mon 9/3 A CAL 30- 28 W 26046
Sat 9/8 H TOR 34- 33 W 39517
Fri 9/21 A OTT 23- 32 L 19387
Fri 9/28 H BC 32- 34 L 47015
Sun 10/7 A HAM 28- 21 W 13452
Sat 10/13 A WPG 11- 30 L 29135
Sat 10/13 H MTL 29- 26 W 42766
Sun 10/28 H SAS 52- 7 W 42664
Western Semi-Final
Sun 11/4 H WPG 20- 55 L 27711

1984 HAMILTON TIGER-CATS

Sat 6/30 A MTL 49- 31 W 16569
Sun 7/8 H SAS 27- 27 T 16530
Sat 7/14 A OTT 9- 31 L 22405
Fri 7/20 A CAL 18- 23 L 20769
Sat 7/28 H WPG 20- 42 L 17301
Sun 8/12 H TOR 22- 30 L 22201
Sun 8/19 H BC 11- 19 L 14101
Fri 8/24 A EDM 14- 35 L 42750
Mon 9/3 H MTL 30- 11 W 12888
Sun 9/9 A BC 11- 46 L 34630
Sat 9/15 A WPG 16- 48 L 32946
Sun 9/23 H CAL 29- 26 W 12501
Sun 10/7 H EDM 21- 28 L 13452
Sun 10/14 A SAS 31- 8 W 28414
Sat 10/20 H OTT 20- 14 W 18101
Sat 10/27 A TOR 25- 20 W 32578
Eastern Semi-Final
Sun 11/4 A MTL 17- 11 W 20756
Eastern Final
Sun 11/11 A TOR 14- 13 W* 48414
Grey Cup
Sun 11/18 N WPG 17- 47 L 60081

1984 MONTREAL CONCORDES

Sat 6/30 H HAM 31- 49 L 16569
Sun 7/15 A SAS 32- 16 W 23006
Sat 7/21 H OTT 28- 31 L 19758
Sat 7/28 A BC 7- 22 L 39991
Sat 8/4 H CAL 28- 14 W 15363
Fri 8/10 A WPG 15- 45 L 26716
Sat 8/18 H EDM 44- 24 W 16187
Sun 8/26 A TOR 23- 29 L 35319
Mon 9/3 A HAM 11- 30 L 12888
Sat 9/15 H BC 33- 17 W 15085
Sat 9/22 H WPG 14- 14 T 17854
Sat 9/29 A CAL 27- 13 W 20229
Sat 10/6 H SAS 24- 30 L 18296
Sat 10/13 A EDM 26- 29 L 42766
Sun 10/21 H TOR 14- 17 L 19652
Sun 10/28 A OTT 29- 24 W 17162
Eastern Semi-Final
Sun 11/4 H HAM 11- 17 L 20756

1984 OTTAWA ROUGH RIDERS

Sat 6/30 A EDM 31- 32 L 32441
Sat 7/7 H CAL 17- 16 W 20042
Sat 7/14 H HAM 31- 9 W 22405
Sat 7/21 A MTL 31- 28 W 19758
Sun 7/29 H SAS 24- 46 L 23575
Sun 8/5 A TOR 14- 49 L 33077
Sat 8/11 A BC 21- 34 L 37560
Fri 8/17 H WPG 17- 46 L 24204
Fri 8/31 H TOR 20- 23 L 25708
Fri 9/7 A WPG 25- 65 L 26187
Fri 9/14 A CAL 21- 23 L 20120
Fri 9/21 H EDM 32- 23 W 19387
Sun 9/30 A SAS 15- 31 L 24747
Sat 10/13 H BC 17- 33 L 21280
Sat 10/20 A HAM 14- 20 L 18101
Sun 10/28 H MTL 24- 29 L 17162

1984 SASKATCHEWAN ROUGHRIDERS

Sun 7/1 H TOR 10- 25 L 23381
Sun 7/8 A HAM 27- 27 T 16530
Sun 7/15 H MTL 16- 32 L 23006
Sun 7/29 A OTT 46- 24 W 23575
Sun 8/5 H BC 7- 29 L 24558
Sun 8/12 H EDM 21- 37 L 22321
Sun 8/19 A CAL 11- 32 L 23422
Sun 8/26 A WPG 28- 48 L 27213
Sun 9/2 H WPG 30- 25 W 25204
Sun 9/9 H CAL 18- 32 L 23042
Sun 9/16 A TOR 21- 18 W 30025
Sat 9/22 A BC 37- 28 W 35955
Sun 9/30 H OTT 31- 15 W 24747
Sat 10/6 A MTL 30- 24 W 18296

Sun 10/14 H HAM 8- 31 L 28414
Sun 10/28 A EDM 7- 52 L 42664

1984 TORONTO ARGONAUTS

Sun 7/1 A SAS 25- 10 W 23381
Sun 7/8 A WPG 26- 28 L 25235
Sun 7/15 H BC 29- 39 L 34092
Sun 7/22 H EDM 43- 26 W 31132
Fri 7/27 A CAL 43- 17 W 22761
Sun 8/5 H OTT 49- 14 W 33077
Sun 8/12 A HAM 30- 22 W 22201
Sun 8/26 H MTL 29- 23 W 35319
Fri 8/31 A OTT 23- 20 W 25708
Sat 9/8 A EDM 33- 34 L 39517
Sun 9/16 H SAS 18- 21 L 30025
Sun 9/30 H WPG 31- 19 W 35401
Sat 10/6 A BC 21- 21 T 49358
Sun 10/14 H CAL 24- 28 L 30406
Sun 10/21 A MTL 17- 14 W 19652
Sat 10/27 H HAM 20- 25 L 32578
Eastern Final
Sun 11/11 H HAM 13- 14 L* 48414

1984 WINNIPEG BLUE BOMBERS

Fri 6/29 A CAL 17- 24 L 21812
Sun 7/8 H TOR 28- 26 W 25235
Sun 7/22 H BC 25- 3 W 31113
Sat 7/28 A HAM 42- 20 W 17301
Fri 8/3 A EDM 22- 21 W 40470
Fri 8/10 H MTL 45- 15 W 26716
Fri 8/17 A OTT 46- 17 W 24204
Sun 8/26 H SAS 48- 28 W 27213
Sun 9/2 A SAS 25- 30 L 25204
Fri 9/7 H OTT 65- 25 W 26187
Sat 9/15 H HAM 48- 16 W 32946
Sat 9/22 A MTL 14- 14 T 17854
Sun 9/30 A TOR 19- 31 L 35401
Mon 10/8 H CAL 46- 8 W 28025
Sat 10/13 H EDM 30- 11 W 29135
Sat 10/27 A BC 3- 20 L 59421
Western Semi-Final
Sun 11/4 A EDM 55- 20 W 27711
Western Final
Sun 11/11 A BC 31- 14 W 59421
Grey Cup
Sun 11/18 N HAM 47- 17 W 60081

1985 BRITISH COLUMBIA LIONS

Sat 7/6 A HAM 42- 8 W 13101
Sat 7/13 H EDM 25- 10 W 38055
Sun 7/21 A CAL 39- 14 W 15769
Sat 7/27 H MTL 28- 15 W 48281
Thu 8/1 A TOR 43- 18 W 31276
Sat 8/17 H CAL 32- 35 L 37462
Sat 8/24 H HAM 21- 11 W 34351
Fri 8/30 A OTT 18- 13 W 23611
Fri 9/6 H TOR 32- 23 W 40782
Fri 9/20 A MTL 31- 20 W 24363
Sat 9/28 H SAS 33- 9 W 41618
Sun 10/6 A WPG 26- 33 L 32946
Fri 10/11 H WPG 10- 31 L 59478
Sun 10/20 A SAS 42- 18 W 19940
Sun 10/27 A EDM 42- 29 W 48193
Fri 11/1 H OTT 17- 10 W 38661
Western Final
Sun 11/17 H WPG 42- 22 W 59478
Grey Cup
Sun 11/24 N HAM 37- 24 W 56723

1985 CALGARY STAMPEDERS

Wed 7/10 A MTL 18- 22 L 22946
Sun 7/21 H BC 14- 39 L 15769
Sun 7/28 A OTT 12- 14 L 20153
Sat 8/3 H SAS 17- 30 L 16089
Sun 8/11 H MTL 6- 29 L 13153
Sat 8/17 A BC 35- 32 W 37462
Sun 8/25 A WPG 6- 43 L 28166
Mon 9/2 H EDM 28- 34 L 18253
Sat 9/14 H OTT 32- 7 W 12076
Sat 9/21 A EDM 6- 17 L 39327
Sun 9/29 H HAM 13- 30 L 14121
Fri 10/4 A SAS 10- 21 L 19700
Mon 10/14 H TOR 28- 17 W 18303
Sun 10/20 A TOR 10- 26 L 26352
Fri 10/25 H WPG 4- 47 L 11184
Sat 11/2 A HAM 17- 21 L 14052

1985 EDMONTON ESKIMOS

Fri 7/5 H TOR 25- 23 W 40373
Sat 7/13 A BC 10- 25 L 38055
Thu 7/18 A OTT 19- 41 L 20425
Thu 7/25 H WPG 25- 23 W 41173
Fri 8/2 H OTT 49- 14 W 41493
Fri 8/9 A TOR 23- 43 L 29056
Fri 8/23 H SAS 34- 42 L 45894
Mon 9/2 A CAL 34- 28 W 18253
Sun 9/8 H HAM 27- 17 W 39144
Sun 9/15 A SAS 27- 15 W 26205
Sat 9/21 H CAL 17- 6 W 39327
Sat 10/5 A HAM 17- 12 W 15512
Sat 10/12 H MTL 39- 1 W 39822
Fri 10/18 A WPG 37- 18 W 29743
Sun 10/27 H BC 29- 42 L 48193

Sun 11/3 A MTL 20- 23 L 15765
Western Semi-Final
Sun 11/10 A WPG 15- 22 L 29191

1985 HAMILTON TIGER-CATS

Sat 7/6 H BC 8- 42 L 13101
Thu 7/11 A WPG 11- 16 L 25428
Fri 7/26 H TOR 10- 35 L 17566
Fri 8/2 A MTL 39- 11 W 25318
Sat 8/10 A SAS 29- 33 L 24697
Sun 8/18 H WPG 10- 28 L 14206
Sat 8/24 A BC 11- 21 L 34351
Mon 9/2 H MTL 19- 16 W 15549
Sun 9/8 A EDM 17- 27 L 39144
Sun 9/15 A TOR 41- 10 W 28824
Sun 9/22 H OTT 32- 11 W 16101
Sun 9/29 A CAL 30- 13 W 14121
Sat 10/5 H EDM 12- 17 L 15512
Mon 10/14 H SAS 51- 14 W 15026
Sat 10/26 A OTT 36- 4 W 23692
Sat 11/2 H CAL 21- 17 W 14052
Eastern Final
Sun 11/17 H MTL 50- 26 W 24423
Grey Cup
Sun 11/24 N BC 24- 37 L 56723

1985 MONTREAL CONCORDES

Thu 7/4 H WPG 34- 18 W 23627
Wed 7/10 H CAL 22- 18 W 22946
Fri 7/19 A SAS 21- 12 W 24806
Sat 7/27 A BC 15- 28 L 48281
Fri 8/2 H HAM 11- 39 L 25318
Sun 8/11 A CAL 29- 6 W 13153
Fri 8/16 H TOR 28- 10 W 26747
Mon 9/2 A HAM 16- 19 L 15549
Sun 9/8 H SAS 33- 12 W 19238
Fri 9/13 A WPG 0- 24 L 30593
Fri 9/20 H BC 20- 31 L 24363
Sun 9/29 A OTT 7- 23 L 24909
Sat 10/12 A EDM 1- 39 L 39822
Sat 10/19 H OTT 7- 30 L 15951
Sun 10/27 A TOR 17- 3 W 28837
Sun 11/3 H EDM 23- 20 W 15765
Eastern Semi-Final
Sun 11/10 H OTT 30- 20 W 11372
Eastern Final
Sun 11/17 A HAM 26- 50 L 24423

1985 OTTAWA ROUGH RIDERS

Sun 7/7 A SAS 22- 46 L 20785
Thu 7/18 H EDM 41- 19 W 20425
Sun 7/28 H CAL 14- 12 W 20153
Fri 8/2 A EDM 14- 49 L 41493
Thu 8/8 A WPG 15- 58 L 27709
Thu 8/15 H SAS 17- 4 W 20348
Thu 8/22 A TOR 18- 8 W 29637
Fri 8/30 H BC 13- 18 L 23611
Sat 9/7 H WPG 14- 42 L 19165
Sat 9/14 A CAL 7- 32 L 12076
Sun 9/22 A HAM 11- 32 L 16101
Sun 9/29 H MTL 23- 7 W 24909
Sun 10/6 H TOR 19- 15 W 18363
Sat 10/19 A MTL 30- 7 W 15951
Sat 10/26 H HAM 4- 36 L 23692
Fri 11/1 A BC 10- 17 L 38661
Eastern Semi-Final
Sun 11/10 A MTL 20- 30 L 11372

1985 SASKATCHEWAN ROUGHRIDERS

Sun 7/7 H OTT 46- 22 W 20785
Fri 7/12 A TOR 25- 29 L 30421
Fri 7/19 H MTL 12- 21 L 24806
Sat 8/3 A CAL 30- 17 W 16089
Sat 8/10 H HAM 33- 29 W 24697
Thu 8/15 A OTT 4- 17 L 20348
Fri 8/23 A EDM 42- 34 W 45894
Sun 9/1 H WPG 10- 18 L 29588
Sun 9/8 A MTL 12- 33 L 19238
Sun 9/15 H EDM 15- 27 L 26205
Sun 9/22 A WPG 3- 49 L 27684
Sat 9/28 A BC 9- 33 L 41618
Fri 10/4 H CAL 21- 10 W 19700
Mon 10/14 A HAM 14- 51 L 15026
Sun 10/20 H BC 18- 42 L 19940
Sun 11/3 H TOR 26- 30 L 19212

1985 TORONTO ARGONAUTS

Fri 7/5 A EDM 23- 25 L 40373
Fri 7/12 H SAS 29- 25 W 30421
Sat 7/20 A WPG 27- 28 L 27641
Fri 7/26 A HAM 35- 10 W 17566
Thu 8/1 H BC 18- 43 L 31276
Fri 8/9 H EDM 43- 23 W 29056
Fri 8/16 A MTL 10- 28 L 26747
Thu 8/22 H OTT 8- 18 L 29637
Fri 9/6 A BC 23- 32 L 40782
Sun 9/15 H HAM 10- 41 L 28824
Fri 9/27 H WPG 27- 24 W 28052
Sun 10/6 A OTT 15- 19 L 18363
Mon 10/14 A CAL 17- 28 L 18303
Sun 10/20 H CAL 26- 10 W 26352
Sun 10/27 H MTL 3- 17 L 28837
Sun 11/3 A SAS 30- 26 W 19212

1985 WINNIPEG BLUE BOMBERS

Thu	7/4	A	MTL	18-34	L	23627
Thu	7/11	H	HAM	16-11	W	25428
Sat	7/20	H	TOR	28-27	W	27641
Thu	7/25	A	EDM	23-25	L	41173
Thu	8/8	H	OTT	58-15	W	27709
Sun	8/18	A	HAM	28-10	W	14206
Sun	8/25	H	CAL	43-6	W	28166
Sun	9/1	A	SAS	18-10	W	29588
Sat	9/7	A	OTT	42-14	W	19165
Fri	9/13	H	MTL	24-0	W	30593
Sun	9/22	H	SAS	49-3	W	27684
Fri	9/27	A	TOR	24-27	L	28052
Sun	10/6	H	BC	33-26	W	32946
Fri	10/11	A	BC	31-10	W	59478
Fri	10/18	H	EDM	18-37	L	29743
Fri	10/25	A	CAL	47-4	W	11184
Western Semi-Final						
Sun	11/10	H	EDM	22-15	W	29191
Western Final						
Sun	11/17	A	BC	22-42	L	59478

1986 BRITISH COLUMBIA LIONS

Thu	6/26	H	WPG	28-17	W	41704
Thu	7/3	A	EDM	13-36	L	32757
Fri	7/11	H	TOR	28-17	W	42326
Sat	7/19	H	MTL	27-20	W	42158
Fri	7/25	A	HAM	36-21	W	16462
Thu	7/31	A	CAL	18-17	W	27659
Sat	8/9	H	SAS	39-24	W	48984
Fri	8/15	A	OTT	25-19	W	23177
Thu	8/21	H	CAL	14-30	L	49147
Thu	9/4	H	OTT	40-10	W	40091
Sun	9/14	A	TOR	34-24	W	29714
Fri	9/19	H	EDM	3-32	L	59478
Fri	9/26	A	EDM	13-31	L	41570
Sun	10/5	A	MTL	15-28	L	10826
Sat	10/18	H	HAM	17-23	L	40127
Sun	10/26	A	SAS	29-17	W	16388
Sun	11/2	A	WPG	26-20	W	31817
Sat	11/8	H	WPG	36-24	W	54723
Western Semi-Final						
Sat	11/15	H	WPG	21-14	W	40381
Western Final						
Sun	11/23	A	EDM	5-41	L	32490

1986 CALGARY STAMPEDERS

Tue	6/24	H	EDM	20-21	L	27120
Sun	6/29	A	SAS	14-28	L	16937
Thu	7/10	A	OTT	31-15	W	21266
Fri	7/18	H	HAM	23-21	W	26201
Thu	7/24	A	WPG	20-25	L	25197
Thu	7/31	H	BC	17-18	L	27659
Fri	8/8	A	TOR	31-26	W	25752
Thu	8/14	H	MTL	21-10	W	28063
Thu	8/21	A	BC	30-14	W	49147
Mon	9/1	H	EDM	19-42	L	33626
Thu	9/11	H	WPG	28-27	W	26184
Sun	9/21	A	HAM	15-20	L	15105
Sun	9/28	A	SAS	39-24	W	25078
Fri	10/3	H	OTT	41-21	W	26074
Mon	10/13	H	TOR	37-14	W	25939
Sun	10/19	A	EDM	30-38	L	53504
Fri	10/24	A	MTL	32-12	W	9665
Fri	10/31	H	SAS	36-4	W	24704
Western Semi-Final						
Sun	11/16	A	EDM	18-27	L	24064

1986 EDMONTON ESKIMOS

Tue	6/24	A	CAL	21-20	W	27120
Thu	7/3	H	BC	36-13	W	32757
Sat	7/12	A	SAS	31-19	W	16494
Thu	7/17	H	OTT	49-39	W	33922
Fri	8/1	H	TOR	34-35	L	38672
Thu	8/7	A	MTL	6-17	L	11203
Fri	8/15	H	WPG	33-5	W	40617
Sat	8/23	A	TOR	20-26	L	28833
Mon	9/1	A	CAL	42-19	W	33626
Sun	9/7	H	MTL	37-22	W	37332
Fri	9/19	A	BC	32-3	W	59478
Fri	9/26	H	BC	31-13	W	41570
Sat	10/4	A	HAM	24-23	W	17352
Fri	10/10	H	HAM	28-9	W	38385
Sun	10/19	H	CAL	38-30	W	53504
Sat	10/25	A	WPG	20-42	L	32946
Sat	11/1	A	OTT	16-16	T*	13936
Sun	11/9	H	SAS	42-14	W	44121
Western Semi-Final						
Sun	11/16	H	CAL	27-18	W	24064
Western Final						
Sun	11/23	H	BC	41-5	W	32490
Grey Cup						
Sun	11/30	N	HAM	15-39	L	59621

1986 HAMILTON TIGER-CATS

Thu	6/26	A	TOR	20-21	L	23100
Thu	7/3	H	OTT	2-18	L	15877
Sat	7/12	H	WPG	28-11	W	13664
Fri	7/18	A	CAL	21-23	L	26201
Fri	7/25	H	BC	21-36	L	16462
Thu	8/7	A	WPG	30-36	L	25982
Sat	8/16	H	SAS	23-21	W	14907
Thu	8/21	A	MTL	28-23	W	12158
Mon	9/1	H	MTL	42-7	W	23185
Sun	9/7	A	TOR	23-25	L	28531
Sun	9/14	A	SAS	21-21	T*	18565
Sun	9/21	H	CAL	20-15	W	15105
Sat	9/27	A	OTT	31-11	W	17192
Sat	10/4	H	EDM	23-24	L	17352
Fri	10/10	A	EDM	9-28	L	38385
Sat	10/18	A	BC	23-17	W	40127
Sun	10/26	H	TOR	20-10	W	24430
Fri	11/7	H	OTT	20-19	W	14101
Eastern Final ()						
Sun	11/16	H	TOR	17-31	L	23126
Sun	11/23	A	TOR	42-25	W	32041
Grey Cup						
Sun	11/30	N	EDM	39-15	W	59621

1986 MONTREAL ALOUETTES

Fri	6/27	A	OTT	11-20	L	17409
Fri	7/4	H	TOR	12-20	L	13281
Sat	7/19	A	BC	20-27	L	42158
Thu	7/24	A	OTT	29-28	W	20156
Fri	8/1	H	WPG	10-37	L	14127
Thu	8/7	H	EDM	17-6	W	11203
Thu	8/14	A	CAL	10-21	L	28063
Thu	8/21	H	HAM	23-28	L	12158
Mon	9/1	A	HAM	7-42	L	23185
Sun	9/7	A	EDM	22-37	L	37332
Fri	9/12	H	OTT	28-29	L	11399
Thu	9/18	A	WPG	14-39	L	21899
Sun	10/5	H	BC	28-15	W	10826
Sun	10/12	A	SAS	11-29	L	17422
Fri	10/17	H	SAS	29-28	W	9204
Fri	10/24	H	CAL	12-32	L	9665
Sun	11/2	A	TOR	21-25	L	23488
Sun	11/9	H	TOR	16-37	L	9045

1986 OTTAWA ROUGH RIDERS

Fri	6/27	H	MTL	20-11	W	17409
Thu	7/3	A	HAM	18-2	W	15877
Thu	7/10	H	CAL	15-31	L	21266
Thu	7/17	A	EDM	39-49	L	33922
Thu	7/24	H	MTL	28-29	L	20156
Mon	8/4	A	SAS	14-33	L	18024
Fri	8/15	H	BC	19-25	L	23177
Fri	8/22	A	WPG	14-46	L	23918
Fri	8/29	H	TOR	12-25	L	22347
Thu	9/4	A	BC	10-40	L	40091
Fri	9/12	A	MTL	29-28	W	11399
Sat	9/20	H	SAS	24-34	L	15390
Sat	9/27	H	HAM	11-31	L	17192
Fri	10/3	A	CAL	21-41	L	26074
Mon	10/13	H	WPG	16-18	L	13572
Sun	10/19	A	TOR	21-35	L	27320
Sat	11/1	H	EDM	16-16	T*	13936
Fri	11/7	A	HAM	19-20	L	14101

1986 SASKATCHEWAN ROUGHRIDERS

Sun	6/29	H	CAL	28-14	W	16937
Sat	7/5	A	WPG	0-56	L	26746
Sat	7/12	H	EDM	19-31	L	16494
Thu	7/17	A	TOR	21-14	W	23500
Sat	7/26	H	TOR	17-27	L	18307
Mon	8/4	H	OTT	33-14	W	18024
Sat	8/9	A	BC	24-39	L	48984
Sat	8/16	A	HAM	21-23	L	14907
Sun	8/31	H	WPG	34-30	W	25274
Fri	9/5	A	WPG	14-38	L	24996
Sun	9/14	H	HAM	21-21	T*	18565
Sat	9/20	A	OTT	34-24	W	15390
Sun	9/28	H	CAL	24-39	L	25078
Sun	10/12	H	MTL	29-11	W	17422
Fri	10/17	A	MTL	28-29	L	9204
Sun	10/26	H	BC	17-29	L	16388
Fri	10/31	A	CAL	4-36	L	24704
Sun	11/9	A	EDM	14-42	L	44121

1986 TORONTO ARGONAUTS

Thu	6/26	H	HAM	21-20	W	23100
Fri	7/4	A	MTL	20-12	W	13281
Fri	7/11	A	BC	17-28	L	42326
Thu	7/17	H	SAS	14-21	L	23500
Sat	7/26	A	SAS	27-17	W	18307
Fri	8/1	A	EDM	35-34	W	38672
Fri	8/8	H	CAL	26-31	L	25752
Sat	8/23	H	EDM	26-20	W	28833
Fri	8/29	A	OTT	25-12	W	22347
Sun	9/7	H	HAM	25-23	W	28531
Sun	9/14	H	BC	24-34	L	29714
Sun	9/28	H	WPG	16-26	L	25300
Sun	10/5	A	WPG	20-48	L	28356
Mon	10/13	A	CAL	14-37	L	25939
Sun	10/19	H	OTT	35-21	W	27320
Sun	10/26	A	HAM	10-20	L	24430
Sun	11/2	H	MTL	25-21	W	23488
Sun	11/9	A	MTL	37-16	W	9045
Eastern Final ()						
Sun	11/16	A	HAM	31-17	W	23126
Sun	11/23	H	HAM	25-42	L	32041

1986 WINNIPEG BLUE BOMBERS

Thu	6/26	A	BC	17-28	L	41704
Sat	7/5	H	SAS	56-0	W	26746
Sat	7/12	A	HAM	11-28	L	13664
Thu	7/24	H	CAL	25-20	W	25197
Fri	8/1	A	MTL	37-10	W	14127
Thu	8/7	H	HAM	36-30	W	25982
Fri	8/15	A	EDM	5-33	L	40617
Fri	8/22	H	OTT	46-14	W	23918
Sun	8/31	A	SAS	30-34	L	25274
Fri	9/5	H	SAS	38-14	W	24996
Thu	9/11	A	CAL	27-28	L	26184
Thu	9/18	H	MTL	39-14	W	21899
Sun	9/28	A	TOR	26-16	W	25300
Sun	10/5	H	TOR	48-20	W	28356
Mon	10/13	A	OTT	18-16	W	13572
Sat	10/25	H	EDM	42-20	W	32946
Sun	11/2	H	BC	20-26	L	31817
Sat	11/8	A	BC	24-36	L	54723
Western Semi-Final						
Sat	11/15	A	BC	14-21	L	40381

1987 BRITISH COLUMBIA LIONS

Sun	6/28	H	SAS	44-1	W	30157
Wed	7/1	A	CAL	40-15	W	22239
Sat	7/18	H	EDM	26-18	W	43772
Sat	7/25	H	OTT	21-1	W	33771
Fri	7/31	A	HAM	20-21	L	18088
Sat	8/8	A	WPG	22-30	L	29296
Thu	8/13	H	TOR	30-23	W	37843
Thu	8/20	A	CAL	26-31	L	24377
Sun	8/30	H	WPG	24-23	W	38338
Fri	9/11	A	OTT	55-16	W	19201
Sun	9/20	H	WPG	30-20	W	39859
Sun	9/27	A	SAS	20-35	L	24682
Sun	10/4	A	TOR	14-33	L	26232
Sun	10/11	H	CAL	6-34	L	31244
Sat	10/17	H	HAM	25-11	W	34909
Sun	10/25	A	CAL	32-12	W	25233
Sun	11/1	A	EDM	33-32	W	40414
Sun	11/8	H	SAS	34-14	W	38370
Western Final						
Sun	11/22	H	EDM	7-31	L	44385

1987 CALGARY STAMPEDERS

Sun	6/21	A	SAS	29-28	W	21340
Sat	6/27	A	EDM	16-54	L	29930
Wed	7/1	H	BC	15-40	L	22239
Fri	7/10	A	WPG	22-38	L	22808
Thu	7/16	H	WPG	14-21	L	20553
Wed	7/22	A	TOR	16-26	L	31524
Sun	8/2	H	TOR	13-32	L	21125
Sat	8/9	A	OTT	39-38	W	21036
Thu	8/20	H	BC	31-26	W	24377
Mon	9/7	H	EDM	29-20	W	33842
Sun	9/13	A	WPG	5-40	L	25549
Fri	9/18	H	OTT	41-19	W	21483
Sun	9/27	A	HAM	33-17	W	14189
Sat	10/3	H	SAS	28-11	W	23052
Sun	10/11	A	BC	34-6	W	31244
Sun	10/25	H	BC	12-32	L	25233
Sun	11/1	A	HAM	34-33	W	13520
Fri	11/6	H	HAM	42-36	W	25944
Western Semi-Final						
Sun	11/15	A	EDM	16-30	L	26809

1987 EDMONTON ESKIMOS

Sat	6/27	H	CAL	54-16	W	29930
Sun	7/5	A	HAM	36-33	W	15720
Sun	7/12	H	HAM	30-40	L	32265
Sat	7/18	A	BC	18-26	L	43772
Fri	7/24	A	WPG	42-28	W	29260
Sat	8/1	H	SAS	38-28	W	30399
Fri	8/7	A	TOR	20-23	L	30264
Sun	8/23	H	OTT	45-24	W	32167
Fri	8/28	A	SAS	39-13	W	24000
Mon	9/7	A	CAL	20-29	L	33842
Sat	9/12	H	TOR	42-20	W	40486
Sat	9/19	H	SAS	34-13	W	31862
Fri	10/2	H	OTT	34-19	W	31331
Mon	10/12	A	WPG	20-38	L	24999
Sun	10/18	A	SAS	25-34	L	24282
Sun	10/25	H	WPG	49-24	W	33376
Sun	11/1	H	BC	32-33	L	40414
Sat	11/7	A	OTT	39-21	W	15107
Western Semi-Final						
Sun	11/15	H	CAL	30-16	W	26809
Western Final						
Sun	11/22	A	BC	31-7	W	44385
Grey Cup						
Sun	11/29	N	TOR	38-36	W	59478

1987 HAMILTON TIGER-CATS

Fri	6/26	A	OTT	32-36	L	20129
Sun	7/5	H	EDM	33-36	L	15720
Sun	7/12	A	EDM	40-30	W	32265
Fri	7/17	H	TOR	27-30	L	18214
Sun	7/26	A	SAS	28-25	W	24820
Fri	7/31	H	BC	21-20	W	18088
Fri	8/14	H	WPG	26-14	W	18503
Fri	8/21	A	TOR	28-25	W	33648
Sat	8/29	H	OTT	28-23	W	17447
Mon	9/7	H	TOR	19-25	L	24770
Sun	9/20	A	TOR	29-39	L	26619
Sun	9/27	H	CAL	17-33	L	14189
Sun	10/4	A	WPG	14-47	L	31655
Sun	10/11	H	SAS	20-23	L	12541

Sat	10/17	A	BC	11-25	L	34909
Sat	10/24	A	OTT	28-2	W	16370
Sun	11/1	H	CAL	33-34	L	13520
Fri	11/6	A	CAL	36-42	L	25944
Eastern Semi-Final						
Sun	11/15	A	TOR	13-29	L	21339

1987 OTTAWA ROUGH RIDERS

Fri	6/26	H	HAM	36-32	W	20129
Fri	7/3	A	WPG	24-51	L	23121
Sat	7/11	H	TOR	34-27	W	19699
Sun	7/19	H	SAS	23-27	L	20006
Sat	7/25	A	BC	1-21	L	33771
Sat	8/9	H	CAL	38-39	L	21036
Sun	8/16	A	SAS	33-36	L	24346
Sun	8/23	A	EDM	24-45	L	32167
Sat	8/29	A	HAM	23-28	L	17447
Fri	9/11	H	BC	16-55	L	19201
Fri	9/18	A	CAL	19-41	L	21483
Sat	9/26	H	WPG	13-36	L	17101
Fri	10/2	A	EDM	19-34	L	31331
Fri	10/9	H	TOR	22-30	L	16541
Fri	10/16	A	TOR	17-20	L	21127
Sat	10/24	H	HAM	2-28	L	16370
Fri	10/30	A	SAS	12-9	W	21773
Sat	11/7	H	EDM	21-39	L	15107

1987 SASKATCHEWAN ROUGHRIDERS

Sun	6/21	H	CAL	28-29	L	21340
Sun	6/28	A	BC	1-44	L	30157
Sat	7/4	H	TOR	33-33	T*	23927
Sun	7/19	A	OTT	27-23	W	20006
Sun	7/26	H	HAM	25-28	L	24820
Sat	8/1	A	EDM	28-38	L	30399
Sun	8/16	H	OTT	36-33	W	24346
Sat	8/22	A	WPG	6-35	L	28591
Fri	8/28	H	EDM	13-39	L	24000
Sun	9/6	H	WPG	25-29	L	27457
Sat	9/19	A	EDM	13-34	L	31862
Sun	9/27	H	BC	35-20	W	24682
Sat	10/3	A	CAL	11-28	L	23052
Sun	10/11	A	HAM	23-20	W	12541
Sun	10/18	H	EDM	34-25	W	24282
Fri	10/23	A	TOR	3-25	L	22329
Fri	10/30	H	OTT	9-12	L	21773
Sun	11/8	A	BC	14-34	L	38370

1987 TORONTO ARGONAUTS

Fri	6/25	H	WPG	30-38	L	33412
Sat	7/4	A	SAS	33-33	T*	23927
Sat	7/11	A	OTT	27-34	L	19699
Fri	7/17	A	HAM	30-27	W	18214
Wed	7/22	H	CAL	26-16	W	31524
Sun	8/2	A	CAL	32-13	W	21125
Fri	8/7	H	EDM	23-20	W	30264
Thu	8/13	A	BC	23-30	L	37843
Fri	8/21	H	HAM	25-28	L	33648
Mon	9/7	A	HAM	25-19	W	24770
Sat	9/12	A	EDM	20-42	L	40486
Sun	9/20	H	HAM	39-29	W	26619
Sun	10/4	H	BC	33-14	W	26232
Fri	10/9	A	OTT	30-22	W	16541
Fri	10/16	H	OTT	20-17	W	21127
Fri	10/23	H	SAS	25-3	W	22329
Sun	11/1	A	WPG	23-24	L	26288
Sun	11/8	H	WPG	20-18	W	21042
Eastern Semi-Final						
Sun	11/15	H	HAM	29-13	W	21339
Eastern Final						
Sun	11/22	A	WPG	19-3	W	32946
Grey Cup						
Sun	11/29	N	EDM	36-38	L	59478

1987 WINNIPEG BLUE BOMBERS

Fri	6/25	A	TOR	38-30	W	33412
Fri	7/3	H	OTT	51-24	W	23121
Fri	7/10	H	CAL	38-22	W	22808
Thu	7/16	A	CAL	21-14	W	20553
Fri	7/24	H	EDM	28-42	L	29260
Sat	8/8	H	BC	30-22	W	29296
Fri	8/14	A	HAM	14-26	L	18503
Sat	8/22	H	SAS	35-6	W	28591
Sun	8/30	A	BC	23-24	L	38338
Sun	9/6	A	SAS	29-25	W	27457
Sun	9/13	H	CAL	40-5	W	25549
Sun	9/20	A	BC	20-30	L	39859
Sat	9/26	A	OTT	36-13	W	17101
Sun	10/4	H	HAM	47-14	W	31655
Mon	10/12	H	EDM	38-20	W	24999
Sun	10/25	A	EDM	24-49	L	33376
Sun	11/1	H	TOR	24-23	W	26288
Sun	11/8	A	TOR	18-20	L	21042
Eastern Final						
Sun	11/22	H	TOR	3-19	L	32946

1988 BRITISH COLUMBIA LIONS

Tue	7/12	H	WPG	36-3	W	38347
Fri	7/22	H	CAL	44-31	W	33147
Thu	7/28	A	TOR	21-26	L	21846
Sat	8/6	A	WPG	21-38	L	24854
Thu	8/11	H	TOR	12-24	L	29621
Thu	8/18	A	OTT	27-20	W	24598
Thu	8/25	H	EDM	28-10	W	33825
Thu	9/1	A	EDM	9-17	L	34157
Tue	9/6	H	OTT	24-11	W	25504
Sun	9/11	A	WPG	8-34	L	23281
Fri	9/16	H	SAS	32-36	L	33088
Fri	9/23	A	CAL	22-40	L	17578
Sat	10/1	A	HAM	24-23	W	14207
Fri	10/7	H	HAM	25-21	W	28019
Sun	10/16	A	SAS	25-28	L	27649
Sun	10/23	A	EDM	35-15	W	30030
Sat	10/29	H	EDM	51-16	W	32234
Sat	11/5	H	WPG	45-24	W	35063
Western Semi-Final						
Sun	11/13	A	SAS	42-18	W	26229
Western Final						
Sun	11/20	A	EDM	37-19	W	26091
Grey Cup						
Sun	11/27	N	WPG	21-22	L	50604

1988 CALGARY STAMPEDERS

Thu	7/14	A	EDM	0-33	L	27889
Fri	7/22	A	BC	31-44	L	33147
Sat	7/30	H	HAM	20-45	L	24437
Fri	8/5	A	HAM	38-14	W	18112
Wed	8/10	H	SAS	48-10	W	23437
Sat	8/20	A	SAS	21-24	L	24265
Wed	8/24	H	WPG	11-12	L	21012
Wed	8/31	A	TOR	17-33	L	24210
Mon	9/5	H	EDM	11-27	L	27768
Sat	9/10	H	OTT	17-16	W	16969
Sat	9/17	A	WPG	20-14	W	25587
Fri	9/23	H	BC	40-22	W	17578
Fri	9/30	H	TOR	25-42	L	18281
Sun	10/9	A	SAS	17-47	L	23224
Sun	10/16	H	EDM	29-32	L	29430
Sat	10/22	A	OTT	3-19	L	16237
Sun	10/30	H	SAS	28-22	W	18863
Sun	11/6	A	EDM	19-20	L	27499

1988 EDMONTON ESKIMOS

Thu	7/14	H	CAL	33-0	W	27889
Sat	7/23	A	SAS	15-26	L	22682
Wed	7/27	A	OTT	35-28	W	19947
Thu	8/4	H	SAS	43-27	W	35383
Fri	8/12	A	HAM	14-22	L	13127
Fri	8/19	H	WPG	46-21	W	30172
Thu	8/25	A	BC	10-28	L	33825
Thu	9/1	H	BC	17-9	W	34157
Mon	9/5	A	CAL	27-11	W	27768
Sun	9/11	H	HAM	37-13	W	29984
Sun	9/18	H	TOR	38-21	W	33549
Sun	9/25	A	TOR	22-35	L	24104
Sun	10/2	H	OTT	40-12	W	28052
Mon	10/10	A	WPG	17-21	L	26298
Sun	10/16	A	CAL	32-29	W	29430
Sun	10/23	H	BC	15-35	L	30030
Sat	10/29	A	BC	16-51	L	32234
Sun	11/6	H	CAL	20-19	W	27499
Western Final						
Sun	11/20	H	BC	19-37	L	26091

1988 HAMILTON TIGER-CATS

Sat	7/16	H	TOR	29-24	W	13157
Thu	7/21	A	WPG	9-21	L	23316
Sat	7/30	A	CAL	45-20	W	24437
Fri	8/5	H	CAL	14-38	L	18112
Fri	8/12	H	EDM	22-14	W	13127
Tue	8/16	A	TOR	5-19	L	25103
Sat	8/27	H	OTT	51-24	W	15067
Thu	9/1	A	OTT	46-20	W	22535
Mon	9/5	H	TOR	56-28	W	18300
Sun	9/11	A	EDM	13-37	L	29984
Sun	9/18	H	OTT	35-25	W	13024
Sun	9/25	A	SAS	24-26	L	28171
Sat	10/1	H	BC	23-24	L	14207
Fri	10/7	A	BC	21-25	L	28019
Sun	10/16	H	WPG	29-35	L	14106
Fri	10/21	H	SAS	24-21	W	13702
Sat	10/29	A	OTT	23-15	W	16402
Sun	11/6	A	TOR	9-49	L	24503
Eastern Semi-Final						
Sun	11/13	A	WPG	28-35	L	12210

1988 OTTAWA ROUGH RIDERS

Fri	7/15	H	SAS	21-48	L	22565
Wed	7/20	A	TOR	11-34	L	20114
Wed	7/27	H	EDM	28-35	L	19947
Tue	8/2	H	TOR	7-41	L	24322
Sat	8/13	A	WPG	28-17	W	23293
Thu	8/18	H	BC	20-27	L	24598
Sat	8/27	A	HAM	24-51	L	15067
Thu	9/1	H	HAM	20-46	L	22535
Tue	9/6	A	BC	11-24	L	25504
Sat	9/10	A	CAL	16-17	L	16969
Sun	9/18	A	HAM	25-35	L	13024
Sat	9/24	H	WPG	0-31	L	18523
Sun	10/2	A	EDM	12-40	L	28052
Sat	10/8	H	TOR	3-52	L	18527
Fri	10/14	A	TOR	7-49	L	21513
Sat	10/22	H	CAL	19-3	W	16237
Sat	10/29	H	HAM	15-23	L	16402
Sun	11/6	A	SAS	11-45	L	25615

1988 SASKATCHEWAN ROUGHRIDERS

Fri	7/15	A	OTT	48-21	W	22565
Sat	7/23	H	EDM	26-15	W	22682
Fri	7/29	H	WPG	46-18	W	24301
Thu	8/4	A	EDM	27-43	L	35383
Wed	8/10	A	CAL	10-48	L	23437
Sat	8/20	H	CAL	24-21	W	24265
Fri	8/26	H	TOR	21-23	L	24662
Wed	8/31	A	WPG	35-38	L	26177
Sun	9/4	H	WPG	29-19	W	29438
Fri	9/9	A	TOR	14-13	W	23498
Fri	9/16	A	BC	36-32	W	33088
Sun	9/25	H	HAM	26-24	W	28171
Sun	10/2	A	WPG	20-32	L	27356
Sun	10/9	H	CAL	47-17	W	23224
Sun	10/16	H	BC	28-25	W	27649
Fri	10/21	A	HAM	21-24	L	13702
Sun	10/30	A	CAL	22-28	L	18863
Sun	11/6	H	OTT	45-11	W	25615
Western Semi-Final						
Sun	11/13	H	BC	18-42	L	26229

1988 TORONTO ARGONAUTS

Sat	7/16	A	HAM	24-29	L	13157
Wed	7/20	H	OTT	34-11	W	20114
Thu	7/28	H	BC	26-21	W	21846
Tue	8/2	A	OTT	41-7	W	24322
Thu	8/11	A	BC	24-12	W	29621
Tue	8/16	H	HAM	19-5	W	25103
Fri	8/26	A	SAS	23-21	W	24662
Wed	8/31	H	CAL	33-17	W	24210
Mon	9/5	A	HAM	28-56	L	18300
Fri	9/9	H	SAS	13-14	L	23498
Sun	9/18	A	EDM	21-38	L	33549
Sun	9/25	H	EDM	35-22	W	24104
Fri	9/30	A	CAL	42-25	W	18281
Sat	10/8	A	OTT	52-3	W	18527
Fri	10/14	H	OTT	49-7	W	21513
Sun	10/23	H	WPG	36-13	W	23324
Sun	10/30	A	WPG	22-16	W	23557
Sun	11/6	H	HAM	49-9	W	24503
Eastern Final						
Sun	11/20	H	WPG	11-27	L	26091

1988 WINNIPEG BLUE BOMBERS

Tue	7/12	A	BC	3-36	L	38347
Thu	7/21	H	HAM	21-9	W	23316
Fri	7/29	A	SAS	18-46	L	24301
Sat	8/6	H	BC	38-21	W	24854
Sat	8/13	H	OTT	17-28	L	23293
Fri	8/19	A	EDM	21-46	L	30172
Wed	8/24	A	CAL	12-11	W	21012
Wed	8/31	H	SAS	38-35	W	26177
Sun	9/4	A	SAS	19-29	L	29438
Sun	9/11	H	BC	34-8	W	23281
Sat	9/17	H	CAL	14-20	L	25587
Sat	9/24	A	OTT	31-0	W	18523
Sun	10/2	H	SAS	32-20	W	27356
Mon	10/10	H	EDM	21-17	W	26298
Sun	10/16	A	HAM	35-29	W	14106
Sun	10/23	A	TOR	13-36	L	23324
Sun	10/30	H	TOR	16-22	L	23557
Sat	11/5	A	BC	24-45	L	35063
Eastern Semi-Final						
Sun	11/13	H	HAM	35-28	W	12210
Eastern Final						
Sun	11/20	A	TOR	27-11	W	26091
Grey Cup						
Sun	11/27	N	BC	22-21	W	50604

1989 BRITISH COLUMBIA LIONS

Thu	7/13	A	EDM	15-20	L	30041
Tue	7/18	H	SAS	37-42	L	41472
Wed	7/26	H	CAL	26-28	L	27342
Fri	8/4	A	HAM	38-44	L	17433
Wed	8/9	H	EDM	13-33	L	32158
Tue	8/15	H	TOR	16-11	W	27436
Thu	8/24	A	SAS	37-25	W	23544
Thu	8/31	A	OTT	39-30	W	18576
Tue	9/5	H	OTT	49-32	W	31069
Sun	9/10	A	WPG	34-53	L	26689
Sat	9/16	H	WPG	20-24	L	49093
Sun	9/24	A	EDM	25-32	L	30173
Sat	9/30	A	SAS	32-30	W	25013
Fri	10/6	H	HAM	46-27	W	27021
Sat	10/14	A	CAL	11-51	L	16355
Sat	10/21	A	TOR	18-29	L	34267
Sat	10/28	H	EDM	19-25	L	27116
Sat	11/4	H	CAL	46-21	W	23452

1989 CALGARY STAMPEDERS

Wed	7/12	A	SAS	29-32	L	21595
Fri	7/21	H	EDM	4-54	L	21235
Wed	7/26	A	BC	28-26	W	27342
Tue	8/1	H	OTT	35-29	W	18853
Thu	8/10	H	HAM	40-8	W	19031
Wed	8/16	A	WPG	24-27	L	23582
Tue	8/22	H	WPG	31-10	W	19631
Mon	8/28	A	HAM	34-22	W	14291
Mon	9/4	H	EDM	14-31	L	33139
Fri	9/8	A	EDM	27-38	L	44327
Fri	9/15	H	TOR	36-16	W	19131
Sat	9/23	A	TOR	20-13	W	35776
Sun	10/1	A	OTT	33-13	W	21643

Sun	10/8	H	SAS	26- 39	L	30174
Sat	10/14	H	BC	15- 11	W	16355
Sun	10/22	A	SAS	23- 17	W	25200
Sun	10/29	H	SAS	19- 34	L	20754
Sat	11/4	A	BC	21- 46	L	23452
Western Semi-Final						
Sun	11/12	H	SAS	26- 33	L	16286

1989 EDMONTON ESKIMOS

Thu	7/13	H	BC	20- 15	W	30041
Fri	7/21	A	CAL	54- 4	W	21235
Thu	7/27	A	TOR	17- 21	L	34840
Thu	8/3	H	TOR	22- 21	W	28238
Wed	8/9	A	BC	33- 13	W	32158
Thu	8/17	A	OTT	39- 4	W	21413
Wed	8/23	H	HAM	37- 14	W	28861
Wed	8/30	H	SAS	45- 19	W	31667
Mon	9/4	A	CAL	31- 14	W	33139
Fri	9/8	H	CAL	38- 27	W	44327
Sun	9/17	A	SAS	35- 48	L	24776
Sun	9/24	H	BC	32- 25	W	30173
Fri	9/29	A	HAM	33- 12	W	16387
Mon	10/9	H	WPG	45- 7	W	28869
Sun	10/15	H	OTT	55- 11	W	30920
Sun	10/22	A	WPG	34- 11	W	23590
Sat	10/28	A	BC	25- 19	W	27116
Sun	11/5	H	SAS	49- 17	W	27471
Western Final						
Sun	11/19	H	SAS	21- 32	L	35112

1989 HAMILTON TIGER-CATS

Wed	7/12	A	TOR	24- 15	W	32527
Thu	7/20	H	WPG	28- 22	W	15525
Fri	7/28	A	SAS	34- 17	W	25996
Fri	8/4	H	BC	44- 38	W	17433
Thu	8/10	A	CAL	8- 40	L	19031
Fri	8/18	H	SAS	46- 40	W	19336
Wed	8/23	A	EDM	14- 37	L	28861
Mon	8/28	H	CAL	22- 34	L	14291
Mon	9/4	H	TOR	23- 18	W	25968
Sun	9/10	A	OTT	23- 40	L	16942
Sun	9/17	H	OTT	52- 34	W	14327
Fri	9/22	A	WPG	20- 19	W	28449
Fri	9/29	H	EDM	12- 33	L	16387
Fri	10/6	A	BC	27- 46	L	27021
Sun	10/15	H	WPG	29- 21	W	14399
Sun	10/22	A	OTT	32- 22	W	14416
Sun	10/29	H	TOR	45- 14	W	17428
Sat	11/4	A	TOR	36- 27	W	42209
Eastern Final						
Sun	11/19	H	WPG	14- 10	W	20389
Grey Cup						
Sun	11/26	N	SAS	40- 43	L	54088

1989 OTTAWA ROUGH RIDERS

Fri	7/14	A	WPG	24- 29	L	22332
Wed	7/19	H	TOR	17- 21	L	23016
Tue	7/25	H	WPG	32- 43	L	23695
Tue	8/1	A	CAL	29- 35	L	18853
Mon	8/7	A	SAS	22- 58	L	22194
Thu	8/17	H	EDM	4- 39	L	21413
Mon	8/21	A	TOR	17- 22	L	33060
Thu	8/31	H	BC	30- 39	L	18576
Tue	9/5	A	BC	32- 49	L	31069
Sun	9/10	H	HAM	40- 23	W	16942
Sun	9/17	A	HAM	34- 52	L	14327
Sun	9/24	H	SAS	36- 27	W	17284
Sun	10/1	H	CAL	13- 33	L	21643
Mon	10/9	A	TOR	21- 49	L	31116
Sun	10/15	A	EDM	11- 55	L	30920
Sun	10/22	H	HAM	22- 32	L	14416
Sun	10/29	A	WPG	18- 14	W	20541
Sun	11/5	H	WPG	24- 10	W	13757

1989 SASKATCHEWAN ROUGHRIDERS

Wed	7/12	H	CAL	32- 29	W	21595
Tue	7/18	A	BC	42- 37	W	41472
Fri	7/28	H	HAM	17- 34	L	25996
Wed	8/2	A	WPG	29- 27	W	25612
Mon	8/7	H	OTT	58- 22	W	22194
Fri	8/18	A	HAM	40- 46	L	19336
Thu	8/24	H	BC	25- 37	L	23544
Wed	8/30	A	EDM	19- 45	L	31667
Sun	9/3	H	WPG	20- 28	L	28315
Sat	9/9	A	TOR	29- 24	W	35281
Sun	9/17	H	EDM	48- 35	W	24776
Sun	9/24	A	OTT	27- 36	L	17284
Sat	9/30	H	BC	30- 32	L	25013
Sun	10/8	A	CAL	39- 26	W	30174
Sun	10/15	H	TOR	24- 18	W	20953
Sun	10/22	H	CAL	17- 23	L	25200
Sun	10/29	A	CAL	34- 19	W	20754
Sun	11/5	A	EDM	17- 49	L	27471
Western Semi-Final						
Sun	11/12	A	CAL	33- 26	W	16286
Western Final						
Sun	11/19	A	EDM	32- 21	W	35112
Grey Cup						
Sun	11/26	N	HAM	43- 40	W	54088

1989 TORONTO ARGONAUTS

Wed	7/12	H	HAM	15- 24	L	32527
Wed	7/19	A	OTT	21- 17	W	23016
Thu	7/27	H	EDM	21- 17	W	34840
Thu	8/3	A	EDM	21- 22	L	28238
Thu	8/10	H	WPG	20- 12	W	34549
Tue	8/15	A	BC	11- 16	L	27436
Mon	8/21	H	OTT	22- 17	W	33060
Tue	8/29	A	WPG	6- 34	L	24459
Mon	9/4	A	HAM	18- 23	L	25968
Sat	9/9	H	SAS	24- 29	L	35281
Fri	9/15	A	CAL	16- 36	L	19131
Sat	9/23	H	CAL	13- 20	L	35776
Sun	10/1	A	WPG	24- 17	W	22189
Mon	10/9	H	OTT	49- 21	W	31116
Sun	10/15	A	SAS	18- 24	L	20953
Sat	10/21	H	BC	29- 18	W	34267
Sun	10/29	A	HAM	14- 45	L	17428
Sat	11/4	H	HAM	27- 36	L	42209
Eastern Semi-Final						
Sun	11/12	H	WPG	7- 30	L	22758

1989 WINNIPEG BLUE BOMBERS

Fri	7/14	H	OTT	29- 24	W	22332
Thu	7/20	A	HAM	22- 28	L	15525
Tue	7/25	A	OTT	43- 32	W	23695
Wed	8/2	H	SAS	27- 29	L	25612
Thu	8/10	A	TOR	12- 20	L	34549
Wed	8/16	H	CAL	27- 24	W	23582
Tue	8/22	A	CAL	10- 31	L	19631
Tue	8/29	H	TOR	34- 6	W	24459
Sun	9/3	A	SAS	28- 20	W	28315
Sun	9/10	H	BC	53- 34	W	26689
Sat	9/16	A	BC	24- 20	W	49093
Fri	9/22	H	HAM	19- 20	L	28449
Sun	10/1	H	TOR	17- 24	L	22189
Mon	10/9	A	EDM	7- 45	L	28869
Sun	10/15	A	HAM	21- 29	L	14399
Sun	10/22	H	EDM	11- 34	L	23590
Sun	10/29	H	OTT	14- 18	L	20541
Sun	11/5	A	OTT	10- 24	L	13757
Eastern Semi-Final						
Sun	11/12	A	TOR	30- 7	W	22758
Eastern Final						
Sun	11/19	A	HAM	10- 14	L	20389

1990 BRITISH COLUMBIA LIONS

Fri	7/13	H	CAL	38- 38	T*	34233
Wed	7/18	A	EDM	23- 41	L	38401
Fri	7/27	H	WPG	24- 23	W	34622
Thu	8/2	H	SAS	25- 36	L	33068
Wed	8/8	A	WPG	14- 28	L	25952
Tue	8/14	A	SAS	32- 20	W	22976
Mon	8/20	H	HAM	34- 36	L	32699
Tue	8/28	A	OTT	34- 41	L	22450
Sat	9/1	A	TOR	43- 68	L	31003
Thu	9/6	H	TOR	19- 49	L	36330
Thu	9/13	H	EDM	13- 32	L	26830
Sat	9/22	A	HAM	34- 4	W	10270
Sun	9/30	A	SAS	34- 37	L	26176
Sat	10/6	H	OTT	26- 42	L	27905
Sun	10/14	A	CAL	33- 25	W	18154
Sun	10/21	A	EDM	30- 8	W	31176
Sat	10/27	H	CAL	29- 54	L	29536
Sat	11/3	H	SAS	35- 28	W	26342

1990 CALGARY STAMPEDERS

Fri	7/13	A	BC	38- 38	T*	34233
Thu	7/19	H	SAS	30- 25	W	24818
Fri	7/27	A	SAS	54- 16	W	26713
Fri	8/3	H	HAM	40- 35	W	23667
Thu	8/9	H	TOR	42- 17	W	22241
Tue	8/14	A	EDM	20- 46	L	35104
Wed	8/22	H	OTT	34- 31	W	20311
Wed	8/28	A	WPG	37- 39	L*	28480
Mon	9/3	H	EDM	4- 38	L	36107
Fri	9/7	A	EDM	17- 34	L	57444
Fri	9/14	H	WPG	18- 17	W	22588
Thu	9/20	A	TOR	18- 70	L	27868
Sun	9/30	A	OTT	52- 8	W	20035
Sun	10/7	H	SAS	23- 16	W	27964
Sun	10/14	H	BC	25- 33	L	18154
Sun	10/21	A	HAM	48- 42	W	20076
Sat	10/27	A	BC	54- 29	W	29536
Sun	11/4	H	EDM	34- 32	W	26676
Western Final						
Sun	11/18	H	EDM	23- 43	L	31923

1990 EDMONTON ESKIMOS

Sat	7/14	A	TOR	40- 34	W	26815
Wed	7/18	H	BC	41- 23	W	38401
Thu	7/26	A	OTT	46- 50	L	26411
Thu	8/2	A	WPG	20- 23	L	24320
Tue	8/7	H	SAS	57- 31	W	39060
Tue	8/14	H	CAL	46- 20	W	35104
Sun	8/19	A	SAS	24- 49	L	24109
Mon	8/27	H	TOR	56- 36	W	28151
Mon	9/3	A	CAL	38- 4	W	36107
Fri	9/7	H	CAL	34- 17	W	57444
Thu	9/13	A	BC	32- 13	W	26830
Fri	9/21	H	OTT	41- 29	W	30109
Fri	9/28	H	WPG	25- 48	L	28950
Mon	10/8	A	HAM	23- 25	L	11121
Sun	10/14	A	SAS	24- 29	L	27423
Sun	10/21	H	BC	8- 30	L	31176
Sun	10/28	H	HAM	25- 15	W	27434
Sun	11/4	A	CAL	32- 34	L	26676
Sun	11/11	H	SAS	43- 27	W	23006
Western Final						
Sun	11/18	A	CAL	43- 23	W	31923
Grey Cup						
Sun	11/25	N	WPG	11- 50	L	46968

1990 HAMILTON TIGER-CATS

Thu	7/12	A	SAS	35- 38	L	24362
Thu	7/19	H	OTT	29- 26	W	13087
Sat	7/28	H	TOR	29- 41	L	20387
Fri	8/3	A	CAL	35- 40	L	23667
Thu	8/9	A	OTT	31- 30	W	26684
Wed	8/15	H	WPG	20- 10	W	14887
Mon	8/20	A	BC	36- 34	W	32699
Sat	8/25	H	SAS	33- 46	L	16717
Mon	9/3	H	OTT	17- 40	L	20330
Sun	9/9	A	WPG	18- 29	L	23805
Sat	9/15	H	TOR	16- 39	L	14025
Sat	9/22	H	BC	4- 34	L	10270
Sat	9/29	A	TOR	39- 60	L	30793
Mon	10/8	H	EDM	25- 23	W	11121
Sun	10/14	A	OTT	37- 33	W	23139
Sun	10/21	H	CAL	42- 48	L	20076
Sun	10/28	A	EDM	15- 25	L	27434
Sun	11/4	A	WPG	15- 32	L	26528

1990 OTTAWA ROUGH RIDERS

Thu	7/12	H	WPG	26- 31	L*	22911
Thu	7/19	A	HAM	26- 29	L	13087
Thu	7/26	H	EDM	50- 46	W	26411
Sat	8/4	A	TOR	26- 30	L	28333
Thu	8/9	H	HAM	30- 31	L	26684
Thu	8/16	H	TOR	25- 41	L	27591
Wed	8/22	A	CAL	31- 34	L	20311
Tue	8/28	H	BC	41- 34	W	22450
Mon	9/3	A	HAM	40- 17	W	20330
Sun	9/9	H	SAS	30- 21	W	25384
Sun	9/16	A	SAS	19- 45	L	27822
Fri	9/21	A	EDM	29- 41	L	30109
Sun	9/30	H	CAL	8- 52	L	20035
Sat	10/6	A	BC	42- 26	W	27905
Sun	10/14	H	HAM	33- 37	L	23139
Sun	10/21	A	WPG	27- 20	W	27323
Sun	10/28	H	WPG	27- 18	W	18216
Sat	11/3	A	TOR	30- 49	L	36321
Eastern Semi-Final						
Sun	11/11	A	TOR	25- 34	L	24427

1990 SASKATCHEWAN ROUGHRIDERS

Thu	7/12	H	HAM	38- 35	W	24362
Thu	7/19	A	CAL	25- 30	L	24818
Fri	7/27	H	CAL	16- 54	L	26713
Thu	8/2	A	BC	36- 25	W	33068
Tue	8/7	A	EDM	31- 57	L	39060
Tue	8/14	H	BC	30- 32	L	22976
Sun	8/19	H	EDM	49- 24	W	24109
Sat	8/25	A	HAM	46- 33	W	16717
Sun	9/2	H	WPG	55- 11	W	31121
Sun	9/9	A	OTT	21- 30	L	25384
Sun	9/16	H	OTT	45- 19	W	27822
Sun	9/23	A	WPG	7- 36	L	32177
Sun	9/30	H	BC	37- 34	W	26176
Sun	10/7	A	CAL	16- 23	L	27964
Sun	10/14	H	EDM	29- 24	W	27423
Sat	10/20	A	TOR	15- 59	L	40429
Sun	10/28	H	TOR	33- 31	W	26139
Sat	11/3	A	BC	28- 35	L	26342
Sun	11/11	A	EDM	27- 43	L	23006

1990 TORONTO ARGONAUTS

Sat	7/14	H	EDM	34- 40	L	26815
Fri	7/20	A	WPG	17- 34	L	25691
Sat	7/28	A	HAM	41- 29	W	20387
Sat	8/4	H	OTT	30- 26	W	28333
Thu	8/9	A	CAL	17- 42	L	22241
Thu	8/16	A	OTT	41- 25	W	27591
Wed	8/22	H	WPG	23- 27	L	30249
Mon	8/27	A	EDM	36- 56	L	28151
Sat	9/1	H	BC	68- 43	W	31003
Thu	9/6	A	BC	49- 19	W	36330
Sat	9/15	A	HAM	39- 16	W	14025
Thu	9/20	H	CAL	70- 18	W	27868
Sat	9/29	H	HAM	60- 39	W	30793
Fri	10/5	A	WPG	9- 25	L	14025
Sat	10/13	H	WPG	16- 21	L	33269
Sat	10/20	H	SAS	59- 15	W	40429
Sun	10/28	A	SAS	31- 33	L	26139
Sat	11/3	H	OTT	49- 30	W	36321
Eastern Semi-Final						
Sun	11/11	H	OTT	34- 25	W	24427
Eastern Final						
Sun	11/18	A	WPG	17- 20	L	29192

1990 WINNIPEG BLUE BOMBERS

Thu	7/12	A	OTT	31- 26	W*	22911
Fri	7/20	H	TOR	34- 17	W	25691
Fri	7/27	A	BC	23- 24	L	34622
Thu	8/2	H	EDM	23- 20	W	24320
Wed	8/8	H	BC	28- 14	W	25952
Wed	8/15	A	HAM	10- 20	L	14887
Wed	8/22	A	TOR	27- 23	W	30249
Wed	8/28	H	CAL	39- 37	W*	28480

Sun	9/2	A	SAS	11- 55	L	31121
Sun	9/9	H	HAM	29- 18	W	23805
Fri	9/14	A	CAL	17- 18	L	22588
Sun	9/23	H	SAS	36- 7	W	32177
Fri	9/28	A	EDM	48- 25	W	28950
Fri	10/5	H	TOR	25- 9	W	14025
Sat	10/13	A	TOR	21- 16	W	33269
Sun	10/21	H	OTT	20- 27	L	27323
Sun	10/28	A	OTT	18- 27	L	18216
Sun	11/4	H	HAM	32- 15	W	26528
Eastern Final						
Sun	11/18	H	TOR	20- 17	W	29192
Grey Cup						
Sun	11/25	N	EDM	50- 11	W	46968

1991 BRITISH COLUMBIA LIONS

Thu	7/11	H	CAL	34- 39	L	24722
Fri	7/19	A	WPG	26- 23	W*	26862
Thu	7/25	H	EDM	37- 36	W	31747
Thu	8/1	H	TOR	52- 41	W*	53527
Thu	8/8	A	CAL	30- 34	L*	31159
Thu	8/15	H	CAL	28- 37	L*	45485
Wed	8/21	A	SAS	50- 47	W	21434
Tue	8/27	A	TOR	25- 34	L	39508
Wed	9/4	H	OTT	24- 20	W	28107
Sun	9/8	A	OTT	56- 29	W	24171
Sat	9/14	H	WPG	36- 23	W	41285
Sat	9/21	H	SAS	47- 49	L	41192
Sat	9/28	A	HAM	37- 27	W	13626
Sun	10/6	A	CAL	49- 34	W	21146
Sat	10/12	H	EDM	38- 45	L*	54108
Sun	10/20	A	EDM	39- 38	W*	39472
Sun	10/27	A	SAS	36- 5	W	18192
Sat	11/2	H	HAM	17- 26	L	47823
Western Semi-Final						
Sun	11/10	A	CAL	41- 43	L	14026

1991 CALGARY STAMPEDERS

Thu	7/11	A	BC	39- 34	W	24722
Thu	7/18	H	SAS	48- 28	W	22055
Wed	7/24	A	OTT	42- 28	W	18788
Fri	8/2	A	HAM	21- 11	W	11802
Thu	8/8	H	BC	34- 30	W*	31159
Thu	8/15	A	BC	37- 28	W*	45485
Thu	8/22	H	WPG	26- 39	L	27011
Tue	8/27	A	WPG	15- 28	L	29102
Mon	9/2	H	EDM	48- 36	W	32511
Fri	9/6	A	EDM	37- 51	L	57843
Sun	9/15	H	TOR	33- 24	W	26122
Sun	9/22	H	HAM	28- 17	W	21512
Sun	9/29	A	SAS	21- 40	L	22736
Sun	10/6	H	BC	34- 49	L	21146
Sun	10/13	H	OTT	44- 24	W	18761
Sun	10/20	A	TOR	27- 34	L	33590
Sun	10/27	A	EDM	23- 24	L	23391
Sun	11/3	H	SAS	39- 27	W	18488
Western Semi-Final						
Sun	11/10	H	BC	43- 41	W	14026
Western Final						
Sun	11/17	A	EDM	38- 36	W	30142
Grey Cup						
Sun	11/24	N	TOR	21- 36	L	51985

1991 EDMONTON ESKIMOS

Fri	7/12	A	SAS	34- 25	W	20582
Wed	7/17	H	OTT	40- 33	W	35511
Thu	7/25	A	BC	36- 27	W	31747
Wed	7/31	H	SAS	54- 24	W	28138
Sat	8/10	A	HAM	38- 13	W	15107
Thu	8/15	A	OTT	35- 36	L	25884
Wed	8/21	H	TOR	53- 39	W	43826
Wed	8/28	H	SAS	41- 44	L	26825
Mon	9/2	A	CAL	36- 48	L	32511
Fri	9/6	H	CAL	51- 37	W	57843
Sun	9/15	A	SAS	41- 36	W	24166
Sat	9/21	A	TOR	28- 47	L	34985
Fri	9/27	H	WPG	31- 15	W	30212
Fri	10/4	H	HAM	18- 17	W	23128
Sat	10/12	A	BC	45- 38	W*	54108
Sun	10/20	H	BC	38- 39	L*	39472
Sun	10/27	H	CAL	24- 23	W	23391
Sun	11/3	A	WPG	28- 18	W	24240
Western Final						
Sun	11/17	H	CAL	36- 38	L	30142

1991 HAMILTON TIGER-CATS

Sat	7/13	H	WPG	9- 23	L	13945
Thu	7/18	A	TOR	18- 41	L	41178
Fri	7/26	A	SAS	16- 52	L	19381
Fri	8/2	H	CAL	11- 21	L	11802
Sat	8/10	H	EDM	13- 38	L	15107
Fri	8/16	A	WPG	24- 25	L	25985
Sat	8/24	H	OTT	19- 24	L	11027
Thu	8/29	A	OTT	14- 38	L	24532
Mon	9/2	H	TOR	48- 24	W	18461
Sat	9/7	A	TOR	25- 52	L	36102
Sat	9/14	H	OTT	26- 33	L	10402
Sun	9/22	A	CAL	17- 28	L	21512
Sat	9/28	H	BC	27- 37	L	13626
Fri	10/4	A	EDM	17- 18	L	23128
Mon	10/14	H	SAS	42- 21	W	12682
Sat	10/19	A	WPG	14- 68	L	27127
Sun	10/27	H	TOR	34- 39	L	17453
Sat	11/2	A	BC	26- 17	W	47823

1991 OTTAWA ROUGH RIDERS

Thu	7/11	H	TOR	18- 35	L	23254
Wed	7/17	A	EDM	33- 40	L	35511
Wed	7/24	H	CAL	28- 42	L	18788
Fri	8/2	A	WPG	19- 26	L	24743
Thu	8/8	H	WPG	41- 31	W	23414
Thu	8/15	H	EDM	36- 35	W	25884
Sat	8/24	A	HAM	24- 19	W	11027
Thu	8/29	H	HAM	38- 14	W	24532
Wed	9/4	A	BC	20- 24	L	28107
Sun	9/8	H	BC	29- 56	L	24171
Sat	9/14	A	HAM	33- 26	W	10402
Sun	9/22	A	WPG	8- 40	L	32675
Sun	9/29	H	TOR	24- 25	L	26172
Sun	10/6	H	SAS	42- 25	W	22038
Sun	10/13	A	CAL	24- 44	L	18761
Sun	10/20	A	SAS	28- 41	L	19478
Sat	10/26	H	WPG	46- 20	W	23060
Sun	11/3	A	TOR	31- 34	L	36001
Eastern Semi-Final						
Sun	11/10	A	WPG	8- 26	L	22799

1991 SASKATCHEWAN ROUGHRIDERS

Fri	7/12	H	EDM	25- 34	L	20582
Thu	7/18	A	CAL	28- 48	L	22055
Fri	7/26	H	HAM	52- 16	W	19381
Wed	7/31	A	EDM	24- 54	L	28138
Fri	8/9	H	TOR	35- 37	L	27093
Thu	8/15	A	TOR	10- 62	L	35786
Wed	8/21	H	BC	47- 50	L	21434
Wed	8/28	A	EDM	44- 41	W	26825
Sun	9/1	H	WPG	56- 23	W	30314
Sun	9/8	A	WPG	41- 49	L*	28323
Sun	9/15	H	EDM	36- 41	L	24166
Sat	9/21	A	BC	49- 47	W	41192
Sun	9/29	H	CAL	40- 21	W	22736
Sun	10/6	A	OTT	25- 42	L	22038
Mon	10/14	A	HAM	21- 42	L	12682
Sun	10/20	H	OTT	41- 28	W	19478
Sun	10/27	H	BC	5- 36	L	18192
Sun	11/3	A	CAL	27- 39	L	18488

1991 TORONTO ARGONAUTS

Thu	7/11	A	OTT	35- 18	W	23254
Thu	7/18	H	HAM	41- 18	W	41178
Thu	7/25	H	WPG	30- 16	W	37486
Thu	8/1	A	BC	41- 52	L*	53527
Fri	8/9	A	SAS	37- 35	W	27093
Thu	8/15	H	SAS	62- 10	W	35786
Wed	8/21	A	EDM	39- 53	L	43826
Tue	8/27	H	BC	34- 25	W	39508
Mon	9/2	A	HAM	24- 48	L	18461
Sat	9/7	H	HAM	52- 25	W	36102
Sun	9/15	A	CAL	24- 33	L	26122
Sat	9/21	H	EDM	47- 28	W	34985
Sun	9/29	A	OTT	25- 24	W	26172
Sat	10/5	H	WPG	22- 21	W	32194
Fri	10/11	A	WPG	27- 28	L	30760
Sun	10/20	H	CAL	34- 27	W	33590
Sun	10/27	A	HAM	39- 34	W	17453
Sun	11/3	H	OTT	34- 31	W	36001
Eastern Final						
Sun	11/17	H	WPG	42- 3	W	50380
Grey Cup						
Sun	11/24	N	CAL	36- 21	W	51985

1991 WINNIPEG BLUE BOMBERS

Sat	7/13	A	HAM	23- 9	W	13945
Fri	7/19	H	BC	23- 26	L*	26862
Thu	7/25	A	TOR	16- 30	L	37486
Fri	8/2	H	OTT	26- 19	W	24743
Thu	8/8	A	OTT	31- 41	L	23414
Fri	8/16	H	HAM	25- 24	W	25985
Thu	8/22	A	CAL	39- 26	W	27011
Tue	8/27	H	CAL	28- 15	W	29102
Sun	9/1	A	SAS	23- 56	L	30314
Sun	9/8	H	SAS	49- 41	W*	28323
Sat	9/14	A	BC	23- 36	L	41285
Sun	9/22	H	OTT	40- 8	W	32675
Fri	9/27	A	EDM	15- 31	L	30212
Sat	10/5	A	TOR	21- 22	L	32194
Fri	10/11	H	TOR	28- 27	W	30760
Sat	10/19	H	HAM	68- 14	W	27127
Sat	10/26	A	OTT	20- 46	L	23060
Sun	11/3	H	EDM	18- 28	L	24240
Eastern Semi-Final						
Sun	11/10	H	OTT	26- 8	W	22799
Eastern Final						
Sun	11/17	A	TOR	3- 42	L	50380

1992 BRITISH COLUMBIA LIONS

Thu	7/9	H	EDM	26- 37	L	23917
Thu	7/16	A	TOR	20- 61	L	36682
Thu	7/23	H	CAL	19- 37	L	31053
Thu	7/30	A	WPG	15- 41	L	23293
Thu	8/6	H	HAM	25- 27	L	24606
Thu	8/13	H	SAS	43- 46	L*	25653
Fri	8/21	A	CAL	23- 44	L	21508
Sat	8/29	A	SAS	36- 47	L	19345
Thu	9/3	H	OTT	33- 27	W	20997
Fri	9/11	A	EDM	34- 20	W	48793
Sat	9/19	H	TOR	36- 29	W	34646
Sun	9/27	A	OTT	23- 27	L	24938
Sat	10/3	A	HAM	20- 34	L	13628
Sat	10/10	H	CAL	21- 40	L	26618
Fri	10/16	A	EDM	17- 43	L	21164
Sun	10/25	A	SAS	22- 41	L	19788
Sat	10/31	H	WPG	26- 29	L	18183
Sat	11/7	H	EDM	33- 37	L	22200

1992 CALGARY STAMPEDERS

Wed	7/8	A	SAS	44- 26	W	20416
Thu	7/16	H	HAM	34- 22	W	25144
Thu	7/23	A	BC	37- 19	W	31053
Thu	7/30	H	TOR	28- 26	W	31504
Fri	8/7	A	SAS	21- 30	L	21100
Thu	8/13	A	OTT	11- 32	L	24752
Fri	8/21	H	BC	44- 23	W	21508
Fri	8/28	A	EDM	45- 38	W*	31812
Mon	9/7	H	EDM	21- 34	L	38205
Sun	9/13	A	TOR	31- 0	W	29044
Sun	9/20	H	WPG	57- 29	W	22320
Sun	9/27	A	WPG	16- 17	L	24964
Sun	10/4	H	OTT	47- 11	W	20207
Sat	10/10	A	BC	40- 21	W	26618
Sun	10/18	H	SAS	34- 30	W	24451
Sat	10/24	H	EDM	40- 23	W	22884
Sun	11/1	A	HAM	17- 32	L	12227
Sun	11/8	H	SAS	40- 17	W	22740
Western Final						
Sun	11/22	H	EDM	23- 22	W	28100
Grey Cup						
Sun	11/29	N	WPG	24- 10	W	45863

1992 EDMONTON ESKIMOS

Thu	7/9	A	BC	37- 26	W	23917
Wed	7/15	H	SAS	34- 31	W*	26764
Wed	7/22	A	WPG	32- 51	L	24265
Thu	7/30	A	OTT	30- 25	W	25625
Thu	8/6	H	OTT	29- 14	W	25113
Wed	8/12	A	HAM	30- 28	W	21327
Thu	8/20	H	TOR	39- 16	W	30186
Fri	8/28	H	CAL	38- 45	L*	31812
Mon	9/7	A	CAL	34- 21	W	38205
Fri	9/11	H	BC	20- 34	L	48793
Sun	9/20	A	SAS	18- 22	L	22256
Fri	9/25	H	HAM	25- 26	L	21537
Fri	10/2	H	WPG	45- 25	W	26680
Sat	10/10	A	TOR	14- 31	L	33189
Fri	10/16	H	BC	43- 17	W	21164
Sat	10/24	A	CAL	23- 40	L	22884
Sun	11/1	H	SAS	24- 30	L	26329
Sat	11/7	A	BC	37- 33	W	22200
Sun	11/15	H	SAS	22- 20	W	25565
Western Final						
Sun	11/22	A	CAL	22- 23	L	28100

1992 HAMILTON TIGER-CATS

Thu	7/9	H	WPG	33- 36	L*	20641
Thu	7/16	A	CAL	22- 34	L	25144
Thu	7/23	A	TOR	39- 30	W	30899
Thu	7/30	H	SAS	38- 24	W	21023
Thu	8/6	A	BC	27- 25	W	24606
Wed	8/12	H	EDM	28- 30	L	21327
Wed	8/19	H	WPG	21- 20	W	20932
Thu	8/27	A	WPG	37- 35	W*	26215
Mon	9/7	H	TOR	27- 24	W	30003
Sun	9/13	A	OTT	31- 44	L	24364
Sat	9/19	H	OTT	25- 54	L	17682
Fri	9/25	A	EDM	26- 25	W	21537
Sat	10/3	H	BC	34- 20	W	13628
Sun	10/11	A	SAS	44- 6	W	20025
Sun	10/18	A	WPG	15- 24	L	25543
Sun	10/25	H	OTT	9- 31	L	16742
Sun	11/1	H	CAL	32- 17	W	12227
Sun	11/8	A	TOR	48- 35	W	29075
Eastern Semi-Final						
Sun	11/15	H	OTT	29- 28	W	21412
Eastern Final						
Sun	11/22	A	WPG	11- 59	L	27033

1992 OTTAWA ROUGH RIDERS

Thu	7/9	H	TOR	53- 42	W*	23222
Thu	7/16	H	WPG	29- 14	W	23594
Fri	7/24	A	SAS	13- 23	L	20117
Thu	7/30	H	EDM	25- 30	L	25625
Thu	8/6	A	EDM	14- 29	L	25113
Thu	8/13	H	CAL	32- 11	W	24752
Thu	8/20	H	SAS	20- 9	W	24020
Wed	8/26	A	TOR	16- 24	L	44922
Thu	9/3	A	BC	27- 33	L	20997
Sun	9/13	H	HAM	44- 31	W	24364
Sat	9/19	A	HAM	54- 25	W	17682
Sun	9/27	H	BC	27- 23	W	24938
Sun	10/4	A	CAL	11- 47	L	20207
Mon	10/12	H	WPG	47- 49	L	23898
Sun	10/18	A	TOR	4- 10	L	26337
Sun	10/25	A	HAM	31- 9	W	16742
Sat	10/31	H	TOR	31- 12	W	24694
Sun	11/8	A	WPG	6- 18	L*	27589
Eastern Semi-Final						
Sun	11/15	A	HAM	28- 29	L	21412

1992 SASKATCHEWAN ROUGHRIDERS

Wed	7/8	H	CAL	26- 44	L	20416
Wed	7/15	A	EDM	31- 34	L*	26764
Fri	7/24	H	OTT	23- 13	W	20117
Thu	7/30	A	HAM	24- 38	L	21023
Fri	8/7	H	CAL	30- 21	W	21100
Thu	8/13	A	BC	46- 43	W*	25653
Thu	8/20	A	OTT	9- 20	L	24020
Sat	8/29	H	BC	47- 36	W	19345
Sun	9/6	H	WPG	32- 20	W	29298
Sun	9/13	A	WPG	16- 37	L	26242
Sun	9/20	H	EDM	22- 18	W	22256
Sat	9/26	A	TOR	32- 39	L	26132
Sun	10/4	H	TOR	43- 18	W	22991
Sun	10/11	H	HAM	6- 44	L	20025
Sun	10/18	A	CAL	30- 34	L	24451
Sun	10/25	H	BC	41- 22	W	19788
Sun	11/1	A	EDM	30- 24	W	26329
Sun	11/8	A	CAL	17- 40	L	22740
Sun	11/15	A	EDM	20- 22	L	25565

1992 TORONTO ARGONAUTS

Thu	7/9	A	OTT	42- 53	L*	23222
Thu	7/16	H	BC	61- 20	W	36682
Thu	7/23	H	HAM	30- 39	L	30899
Thu	7/30	A	CAL	26- 28	L	31504
Thu	8/6	H	WPG	32- 6	W	32201
Thu	8/13	A	WPG	17- 32	L	26714
Thu	8/20	A	EDM	16- 39	L	30186
Wed	8/26	H	OTT	24- 16	W	44922
Mon	9/7	A	HAM	24- 27	L	30003
Sun	9/13	H	CAL	0- 31	L	29044
Sat	9/19	A	BC	29- 36	L	34646
Sat	9/26	H	SAS	39- 32	W	26132
Sun	10/4	A	SAS	18- 43	L	22991
Sat	10/10	H	EDM	31- 14	W	33189
Sun	10/18	H	OTT	10- 4	W	26337
Sun	10/25	A	WPG	23- 24	L*	30193
Sat	10/31	A	OTT	12- 31	L	24694
Sun	11/8	H	HAM	35- 48	L	29075

1992 WINNIPEG BLUE BOMBERS

Thu	7/9	A	HAM	36- 33	W*	20641
Thu	7/16	A	OTT	14- 29	L	23594
Wed	7/22	H	EDM	51- 32	W	24265
Thu	7/30	H	BC	41- 15	W	23293
Thu	8/6	A	TOR	6- 32	L	32201
Thu	8/13	H	TOR	32- 17	W	26714
Wed	8/19	A	HAM	20- 21	L	20932
Thu	8/27	H	HAM	35- 37	L*	26215
Sun	9/6	A	SAS	20- 32	L	29298
Sun	9/13	H	SAS	37- 16	W	26242
Sun	9/20	A	CAL	29- 57	L	22320
Sun	9/27	H	CAL	17- 16	W	24964
Fri	10/2	A	EDM	25- 45	L	26680
Mon	10/12	A	OTT	49- 47	W	23898
Sun	10/18	H	HAM	24- 15	W	25543
Sun	10/25	H	TOR	24- 23	W*	30193
Sat	10/31	A	BC	29- 26	W	18183
Sun	11/8	H	OTT	18- 6	W*	27589
Eastern Final						
Sun	11/22	H	HAM	59- 11	W	27033
Grey Cup						
Sun	11/29	N	CAL	10- 24	L	45863

1993 BRITISH COLUMBIA LIONS

Fri	7/9	H	SAS	33- 26	W*	25849
Wed	7/14	A	TOR	40- 27	W	26759
Sat	7/17	A	WPG	14- 36	L	20665
Sat	7/24	H	CAL	20- 34	L	31199
Fri	7/30	H	OTT	28- 24	W	22667
Sat	8/7	A	EDM	39- 23	W	25236
Thu	8/12	H	TOR	55- 38	W	24691
Wed	8/18	H	WPG	48- 28	W	28541
Fri	8/27	A	CAL	30- 35	L	27011
Sat	9/4	A	OTT	25- 24	W	21567
Sat	9/11	H	HAM	55- 25	W	24789
Sat	9/18	A	CAL	21- 40	L	29110
Sat	9/25	H	SAS	16- 31	L	31888
Fri	10/1	A	SAS	50- 28	W	22103
Fri	10/8	H	SAC	23- 27	L	30615
Sun	10/24	A	HAM	36- 19	W	11574
Fri	10/29	H	EDM	14- 54	L	35674
Sat	11/6	A	SAC	27- 64	L	18748
Western Semi-Final						
Sun	11/14	A	CAL	9- 17	L	15407

1993 CALGARY STAMPEDERS

Tue	7/6	H	WPG	54- 34	W	25486
Sat	7/17	A	SAC	38- 36	W	20082
Sat	7/24	A	BC	34- 20	W	31199
Wed	7/28	H	TOR	39- 36	W	25510
Tue	8/3	A	WPG	40- 35	W	23869
Fri	8/6	A	OTT	47- 22	W	27341
Sat	8/14	H	OTT	21- 7	W	24153
Fri	8/20	A	HAM	31- 12	W	19402
Fri	8/27	H	BC	35- 30	W	27011
Mon	9/6	H	EDM	33- 13	W	38205
Fri	9/10	A	EDM	16- 29	L	54324
Sat	9/18	H	BC	40- 21	W	29110
Fri	9/24	H	HAM	26- 3	W	29817
Sun	10/10	H	SAS	34- 18	W	28210
Sun	10/17	A	TOR	51- 7	W	21023
Sat	10/23	A	SAS	45- 48	L	26137
Sat	10/30	H	SAC	41- 8	W	26105
Sun	11/7	A	EDM	21- 39	L	23536
Western Semi-Final						
Sun	11/14	H	BC	17- 9	W	15407
Western Final						
Sun	11/21	H	EDM	15- 29	L	20218

1993 EDMONTON ESKIMOS

Sat	7/10	H	TOR	38- 8	W	26336
Thu	7/15	A	SAS	22- 23	L	17566
Wed	7/21	H	SAS	35- 3	W	27894
Sat	7/31	A	SAC	43- 11	W	17827
Sat	8/7	H	BC	23- 39	L	25236
Fri	8/13	A	WPG	11- 53	L	25786
Wed	8/18	A	TOR	45- 14	W	20563
Wed	8/25	H	HAM	46- 8	W	24356
Thu	9/2	H	SAC	13- 12	W	37042
Mon	9/6	A	CAL	13- 33	L	38205
Fri	9/10	H	CAL	29- 16	W	54324
Fri	9/17	A	HAM	10- 34	L	17102
Sun	9/26	H	WPG	14- 52	L	30972
Sat	10/2	A	SAC	34- 13	W	15914
Sat	10/16	H	OTT	19- 1	W	25140
Fri	10/22	A	OTT	19- 17	W	19580
Fri	10/29	A	BC	54- 14	W	35674
Sun	11/7	H	CAL	39- 21	W	23536
Western Semi-Final						
Sun	11/7	H	SAS	51- 13	W	26397
Western Final						
Sun	11/21	A	CAL	29- 15	W	20218
Grey Cup						
Sun	11/28	N	WPG	33- 23	W	50035

1993 HAMILTON TIGER-CATS

Sat	7/10	H	SAC	30- 14	W	20307
Fri	7/16	A	TOR	21- 20	W	20016
Thu	7/22	A	TOR	25- 9	W	27373
Thu	7/29	H	WPG	11- 40	L	16198
Fri	8/6	H	SAS	10- 37	L	16061
Sat	8/14	A	SAC	10- 46	L	14656
Fri	8/20	H	CAL	12- 31	L	19402
Wed	8/25	A	EDM	8- 46	L	24356
Sat	8/28	A	WPG	11- 35	L	24475
Mon	9/6	H	TOR	23- 21	W	21762
Sat	9/11	A	BC	25- 55	L	24789
Fri	9/17	H	EDM	34- 10	W	17102
Fri	9/24	A	CAL	3- 26	L	29817
Sat	10/2	A	WPG	10- 61	L	26386
Mon	10/11	H	TOR	28- 20	W	18425
Sun	10/17	A	SAS	10- 33	L	21772
Sun	10/24	H	BC	19- 36	L	11574
Sun	11/7	H	OTT	26- 27	L	17032
Eastern Semi-Final						
Sun	11/14	H	OTT	21- 10	W	18781
Eastern Final						
Sun	11/21	A	WPG	19- 20	L	23332

1993 OTTAWA ROUGH RIDERS

Wed	7/7	H	SAC	32- 23	W	23916
Fri	7/16	H	HAM	20- 21	L	20016
Fri	7/23	A	WPG	18- 21	L	19030
Fri	7/30	A	BC	24- 28	L	22667
Fri	8/6	H	CAL	22- 47	L	27341
Wed	8/11	A	SAS	28- 45	L	20254
Sat	8/14	A	CAL	7- 21	L	24153
Thu	8/19	H	SAS	26- 27	L	23463
Wed	8/25	A	TOR	26- 25	W	21327
Sat	9/4	H	BC	24- 25	L	21567
Sat	9/11	A	SAC	15- 47	L	16510
Sat	9/25	H	TOR	30- 22	W	24631
Sun	10/3	A	TOR	16- 17	L	24087
Sat	10/9	H	WPG	38- 48	L	18486
Sat	10/16	A	EDM	1- 19	L	25140
Fri	10/22	H	EDM	17- 19	L	19580
Sat	10/30	H	WPG	16- 36	L	19240
Sun	11/7	A	HAM	27- 26	W	17032
Eastern Semi-Final						
Sun	11/14	A	HAM	10- 21	L	18781

1993 SACRAMENTO GOLD MINERS

Wed	7/7	A	OTT	23- 32	L	23916
Sat	7/10	A	HAM	14- 30	L	20307
Sat	7/17	H	CAL	36- 38	L	20082
Sat	7/24	H	SAS	37- 26	W	17319
Sat	7/31	H	EDM	11- 43	L	17827
Thu	8/5	A	TOR	35- 37	L	28612
Sat	8/14	H	HAM	46- 10	W	14656
Sat	8/21	H	WPG	18- 30	L	15509
Fri	8/27	A	SAS	23- 26	L	33032
Thu	9/2	A	EDM	12- 13	L	37042
Sat	9/11	H	OTT	47- 15	W	16510
Sun	9/19	A	SAS	20- 27	L	25367
Sat	10/2	H	EDM	13- 34	L	15914
Fri	10/8	A	BC	27- 23	W	30615
Fri	10/15	A	WPG	26- 33	L	27541
Sat	10/23	H	TOR	38- 24	W	16242
Sat	10/30	A	CAL	8- 41	L	26105
Sat	11/6	H	BC	64- 27	W	18748

1993 SASKATCHEWAN ROUGHRIDERS

Fri	7/9	A	BC	26- 33	L*	25849
Thu	7/15	H	EDM	23- 22	W	17566
Wed	7/21	A	EDM	3- 35	L	27894
Sat	7/24	A	SAC	26- 37	L	17319
Sat	7/31	H	TOR	36- 17	W	18212
Fri	8/6	A	HAM	37- 10	W	16061
Wed	8/11	H	OTT	45- 28	W	20254
Thu	8/19	A	OTT	27- 26	W	23463
Fri	8/27	H	SAC	26- 23	W	33032
Sun	9/5	H	WPG	24- 25	L	30216
Sun	9/12	A	WPG	23- 41	L	35959
Sun	9/19	H	SAC	27- 20	W	25367
Sat	9/25	A	BC	31- 16	W	31888
Fri	10/1	H	BC	28- 50	L	22103
Sun	10/10	A	CAL	18- 34	L	28210
Sun	10/17	H	HAM	33- 10	W	21772
Sat	10/23	H	CAL	48- 45	W	26137
Sun	10/31	A	TOR	30- 23	W	29348
Western Semi-Final						
Sun	11/7	A	EDM	13- 51	L	26397

1993 TORONTO ARGONAUTS

Sat	7/10	A	EDM	8- 38	L	26336
Wed	7/14	H	BC	27- 40	L	26759
Thu	7/22	H	HAM	9- 25	L	27373
Wed	7/28	A	CAL	36- 39	L	25510
Sat	7/31	A	SAS	17- 36	L	18212
Thu	8/5	H	SAC	37- 35	W	28612
Thu	8/12	A	BC	38- 55	L	24691
Wed	8/18	H	EDM	14- 45	L	20563
Wed	8/25	H	OTT	25- 26	L	21327
Mon	9/6	A	HAM	21- 23	L	21762
Sun	9/19	H	WPG	35- 26	W	29915
Sat	9/25	A	OTT	22- 30	L	24631
Sun	10/3	H	OTT	17- 16	W	24087
Mon	10/11	A	HAM	20- 28	L	18425
Sun	10/17	H	CAL	7- 51	L	21023
Sat	10/23	A	SAC	24- 38	L	16242
Sun	10/31	H	SAS	23- 30	L	29348
Sun	11/7	A	WPG	10- 12	L	22287

1993 WINNIPEG BLUE BOMBERS

Tue	7/6	A	CAL	34- 54	L	25486
Sat	7/17	H	BC	36- 14	L	20665
Fri	7/23	H	OTT	21- 18	W	19030
Thu	7/29	A	HAM	40- 11	W	16198
Tue	8/3	H	CAL	35- 40	L	23869
Fri	8/13	H	EDM	53- 11	W	25786
Wed	8/18	A	BC	28- 48	L	28541
Sat	8/21	A	SAC	30- 18	W	15509
Sat	8/28	H	HAM	35- 11	W	24475
Sun	9/5	A	SAS	25- 24	W	30216
Sun	9/12	H	SAS	41- 23	W	35959
Sun	9/19	A	TOR	26- 35	L	29915
Sun	9/26	A	EDM	52- 14	W	30972
Sat	10/2	H	HAM	61- 10	W	26386
Sat	10/9	A	OTT	48- 38	W	18486
Fri	10/15	H	SAC	33- 26	W	27541
Sat	10/30	A	OTT	36- 16	W	19240
Sun	11/7	H	TOR	12- 10	W	22287
Eastern Final						
Sun	11/21	H	HAM	20- 19	W	23332
Grey Cup						
Sun	11/28	N	EDM	23- 33	L	50035

1994 BALTIMORE

Thu	7/7	A	TOR	28- 20	W	13101
Sat	7/16	H	CAL	16- 42	L	39247
Sat	7/23	H	SHR	40- 24	W	31172
Thu	7/28	A	WPG	32- 39	L	22398
Sat	8/6	A	LV	38- 33	W	10122
Wed	8/10	H	HAM	30- 15	W	37231
Sat	8/20	H	TOR	24- 31	L	41155
Sat	8/27	A	HAM	28- 17	W	15227
Sat	9/3	A	SHR	28- 16	W	16332
Sat	9/10	H	SAC	29- 30	L	42116
Sun	9/18	A	SAS	35- 18	W	28035
Sun	9/25	A	OTT	42- 27	W	20764
Sat	10/1	H	OTT	40- 13	W	36187
Fri	10/7	H	LV	22- 16	W	34186
Sun	10/16	A	EDM	24- 31	L	31198
Sat	10/22	H	BC	48- 31	W	35416
Sat	10/29	H	WPG	57- 10	W	39417
Sat	11/5	A	SAC	0- 18	L	14056
Division Semi-Final						
Sat	11/12	H	TOR	34- 15	W	35223
Division Final						
Sun	11/20	A	WPG	14- 12	W	25067
Grey Cup						
Sun	11/27	A	BC	23- 26	L	55097

1994 BRITISH COLUMBIA LIONS

Fri	7/8	H	WPG	24- 20	W	20069
Fri	7/15	A	OTT	57- 18	W	20069
Thu	7/21	H	HAM	42- 25	W*	18976
Fri	7/29	A	CAL	21- 62	L	23963
Thu	8/4	H	SAC	46- 10	W	18459
Thu	8/11	H	TOR	54- 39	W	19424
Sat	8/20	A	LV	39- 16	W	14432
Sat	8/27	H	SHR	67- 15	W	20398
Fri	9/2	A	SAC	15- 15	T*	12633
Sun	9/11	A	TOR	28- 18	W	15259
Sat	9/17	H	EDM	18- 25	L	34929
Fri	9/23	A	WPG	18- 30	L	30134
Fri	9/30	A	EDM	26- 24	W	23189
Fri	10/8	H	SAS	23- 22	W	31955

Sat	10/15	A	SAS	27-38	L	27008
Sat	10/22	A	BAL	31-48	L	35416
Sat	10/29	H	LV	45-7	W	22701
Sat	11/5	H	CAL	23-24	L	40556
Division Semi-Final						
Sat	11/12	A	EDM	24-23	W	23156
Division Final						
Sun	11/20	A	CAL	37-36	W	18260
Grey Cup						
Sun	11/27	H	BAL	26-23	W	55097

1994 CALGARY STAMPEDERS

Fri	7/8	A	SAS	21-22	L	23342
Sat	7/16	A	BAL	42-16	W	39247
Sat	7/23	H	WPG	58-19	W	26243
Fri	7/29	H	BC	62-21	W	23963
Wed	8/3	A	OTT	30-27	W	17163
Wed	8/10	H	SAC	25-11	W	21110
Fri	8/19	H	SAS	54-15	W	29044
Thu	8/25	A	TOR	52-3	W	19158
Mon	9/5	H	EDM	48-15	W	37317
Fri	9/9	A	EDM	12-38	L	51180
Fri	9/16	H	LV	35-25	W	24852
Sat	9/24	A	SAC	39-25	W	17192
Sun	10/2	A	LV	45-26	W	7438
Mon	10/10	H	OTT	28-24	W	22615
Sun	10/16	A	HAM	24-27	L	19516
Fri	10/21	H	SHR	52-8	W	21317
Sun	10/30	H	HAM	47-10	W	20029
Sat	11/5	A	BC	24-23	W	40556
Division Semi-Final						
Sun	11/13	H	SAS	36-3	W	25633
Division Final						
Sun	11/20	H	BC	36-37	L	18260

1994 EDMONTON ESKIMOS

Sat	7/9	H	HAM	26-11	W	25687
Thu	7/14	A	WPG	35-50	L	21686
Wed	7/20	H	OTT	23-21	W	27188
Sat	7/30	A	SHR	24-10	W	17434
Thu	8/4	H	SAS	42-23	W	27633
Fri	8/12	A	SAS	7-20	L	24548
Thu	8/18	A	SAC	44-15	W	13959
Thu	8/25	H	LV	44-17	W	28559
Mon	9/5	A	CAL	15-48	L	37317
Fri	9/9	H	CAL	38-12	W	51180
Sat	9/17	A	BC	25-18	W	34929
Sun	9/25	H	TOR	28-25	W	24132
Fri	9/30	H	BC	24-26	L	23189
Sun	10/9	A	HAM	33-32	W	14402
Sun	10/16	H	BAL	31-24	W	31198
Sun	10/23	A	TOR	6-23	L	22210
Sat	10/29	H	SAC	22-16	W	29332
Sat	11/5	H	LV	51-10	W	14228
Division Semi-Final						
Sat	11/12	H	BC	23-24	L	23156

1994 HAMILTON TIGER-CATS

Sat	7/9	A	EDM	11-26	L	25687
Thu	7/14	H	SAC	22-25	L	19291
Thu	7/21	A	BC	25-42	L*	18976
Thu	7/28	H	OTT	25-53	L	12339
Fri	8/5	H	SHR	38-15	W	12612
Wed	8/10	A	BAL	15-30	L	37231
Sat	8/20	A	SHR	30-26	W	14364
Sat	8/27	H	BAL	17-28	L	15227
Mon	9/5	H	TOR	19-31	L	20687
Sat	9/10	A	OTT	28-18	W	17321
Sat	9/17	H	WPG	21-38	L	11248
Sat	9/24	A	LV	21-25	L	4761
Sun	10/2	A	TOR	36-39	L	18709
Sun	10/9	H	EDM	32-33	L	14402
Sun	10/16	H	CAL	27-24	W	19516
Sat	10/22	A	WPG	44-46	L	24357
Sun	10/30	A	CAL	10-47	L	20029
Sun	11/6	H	SAS	14-16	L	24242

1994 LAS VEGAS POSSE

Fri	7/8	A	SAC	32-26	W	14816
Sat	7/16	H	SAS	32-22	W*	12213
Sat	7/23	H	SAC	20-22	L	10740
Fri	7/29	A	TOR	20-39	L	14296
Sat	8/6	H	BAL	33-38	L	10122
Sat	8/13	A	SHR	49-13	W	18011
Sat	8/20	H	BC	16-39	L	14432
Thu	8/25	A	EDM	17-44	L	28559
Sat	9/3	A	OTT	50-54	L*	17732
Sat	9/10	H	SHR	34-21	W	9467
Fri	9/16	A	CAL	25-35	L	24852
Sat	9/24	H	HAM	25-21	W	4761
Sun	10/2	H	CAL	26-45	L	7438
Fri	10/7	A	BAL	16-22	L	34186
Sat	10/15	H	WPG	17-48	L	2350
Sun	10/23	A	SAS	18-37	L	28583
Sat	10/29	A	BC	7-45	L	22701
Sat	11/5	A	EDM	10-51	L	14228

1994 OTTAWA ROUGH RIDERS

Wed	7/6	H	SHR	40-10	W	18134
Fri	7/15	H	BC	18-57	L	20069
Wed	7/20	A	EDM	21-23	L	27188
Thu	7/28	A	HAM	53-25	W	12339
Wed	8/3	H	CAL	27-30	L	17163
Thu	8/11	H	WPG	41-59	L	19173
Wed	8/17	A	WPG	1-46	L	21308
Fri	8/26	A	SAS	19-35	L	21738
Sat	9/3	H	LV	54-50	W*	17732
Sat	9/10	H	HAM	18-28	L	17321
Sun	9/18	A	TOR	40-32	W	15102
Sun	9/25	H	BAL	27-42	L	20764
Sat	10/1	A	BAL	13-40	L	36187
Mon	10/10	A	CAL	24-28	L	22615
Sun	10/16	H	TOR	22-24	L	21029
Sat	10/22	A	SAC	9-44	L	13760
Sat	10/29	H	SAS	29-46	L	23292
Fri	11/4	A	SHR	24-28	L	32011
Division Semi-Final						
Sun	11/13	A	WPG	16-26	L	18888

1994 SACRAMENTO GOLD MINERS

Fri	7/8	H	LV	26-32	L	14816
Thu	7/14	A	HAM	25-22	W	19291
Sat	7/23	A	LV	22-20	W	10740
Sat	7/30	H	SAS	30-27	W	14848
Thu	8/4	A	BC	10-46	L	18459
Wed	8/10	A	CAL	11-25	L	21110
Thu	8/18	H	EDM	15-44	L	13959
Wed	8/24	A	WPG	28-31	L	21804
Fri	9/2	H	BC	15-15	T*	12633
Sat	9/10	A	BAL	30-29	W	42116
Sat	9/17	H	SHR	56-3	W	13741
Sat	9/24	H	CAL	25-39	L	17192
Fri	9/30	A	SAS	19-16	W	23669
Sat	10/8	H	TOR	34-32	W	13050
Sun	10/16	A	SHR	12-24	L	12465
Sat	10/22	H	OTT	44-9	W	13760
Sat	10/29	A	EDM	16-22	L	29332
Sat	11/5	H	BAL	18-0	W	14056

1994 SASKATCHEWAN ROUGHRIDERS

Fri	7/8	H	CAL	22-21	W	23342
Sat	7/16	A	LV	22-32	L*	12213
Fri	7/22	H	TOR	35-24	W	23433
Sat	7/30	A	SAC	27-30	L	14848
Thu	8/4	A	EDM	23-42	L	27633
Fri	8/12	H	EDM	20-7	W	24548
Fri	8/19	A	CAL	15-54	L	29044
Fri	8/26	H	OTT	35-19	W	21738
Sun	9/4	H	WPG	42-31	W	28738
Sun	9/11	A	WPG	49-18	W	29618
Sun	9/18	H	BAL	18-35	L	28035
Sat	9/24	A	SHR	29-11	W	15502
Fri	9/30	H	SAC	16-19	L	23669
Fri	10/8	A	BC	22-23	L	31955
Sat	10/15	H	BC	38-27	W	27008
Sun	10/23	H	LV	37-18	W	28583
Sat	10/29	A	OTT	46-29	W	23292
Sun	11/6	A	HAM	16-14	W	24242
Division Semi-Final						
Sun	11/13	A	CAL	3-36	L	25633

1994 SHREVEPORT PIRATES

Wed	7/6	A	OTT	10-40	L	18134
Sat	7/16	H	TOR	34-35	L	20634
Sat	7/23	A	BAL	24-40	L	31172
Sat	7/30	H	EDM	10-24	L	17434
Fri	8/5	A	HAM	15-38	L	12612
Sat	8/13	H	LV	13-49	L	18011
Sat	8/20	H	HAM	26-30	L	14364
Sat	8/27	A	BC	15-67	L	20398
Sat	9/3	H	BAL	16-28	L	16332
Sat	9/10	A	LV	21-34	L	9467
Sat	9/17	A	SAC	3-56	L	13741
Sat	9/24	H	SAS	11-29	L	15502
Sat	10/1	A	WPG	21-39	L	20426
Sat	10/8	H	WPG	22-38	L	14088
Sun	10/16	H	SAC	24-12	W	12465
Fri	10/21	A	CAL	8-52	L	21317
Fri	10/28	A	TOR	29-27	W	20328
Fri	11/4	H	OTT	28-24	W	32011

1994 TORONTO ARGONAUTS

Thu	7/7	H	BAL	20-28	L	13101
Sat	7/16	A	SHR	35-34	W	20634
Fri	7/22	A	SAS	24-35	L	23433
Fri	7/29	H	LV	39-20	W	14296
Thu	8/4	H	WPG	34-54	L	13407
Thu	8/11	A	BC	39-54	L	19424
Sat	8/20	A	BAL	31-24	W	41155
Thu	8/25	H	CAL	3-52	L	19158
Mon	9/5	A	HAM	31-19	W	20687
Sun	9/11	H	BC	18-28	L	15259
Sun	9/18	H	OTT	32-40	L	15102
Sun	9/25	A	EDM	25-28	L	24132
Sun	10/2	H	HAM	39-36	W	18709
Sat	10/8	A	SAC	32-34	L	13050
Sun	10/16	A	OTT	24-22	W	21029
Sun	10/23	H	EDM	23-6	W	22210
Fri	10/28	H	SHR	27-29	L	20328
Sun	11/6	A	WPG	28-35	L	20720
Division Semi-Final						
Sat	11/12	A	BAL	15-34	L	35223

1994 WINNIPEG BLUE BOMBERS

Fri	7/8	A	BC	20-24	L	20069
Thu	7/14	H	EDM	50-35	W	21686
Sat	7/23	A	CAL	19-58	L	26243
Thu	7/28	H	BAL	39-32	W	22398
Thu	8/4	A	TOR	54-34	W	13407
Thu	8/11	A	OTT	59-41	W	19173
Wed	8/17	H	OTT	46-1	W	21308
Wed	8/24	H	SAC	31-28	W	21804
Sun	9/4	A	SAS	31-42	L	28738
Sun	9/11	H	SAS	18-49	L	29618
Sat	9/17	A	HAM	38-21	W	11248
Fri	9/23	H	BC	30-18	W	30134
Sat	10/1	H	SHR	39-21	W	20426
Sat	10/8	A	SHR	38-22	W	14088
Sat	10/15	A	LV	48-17	W	2350
Sat	10/22	H	HAM	46-44	W	24357
Sat	10/29	A	BAL	10-57	L	39417
Sun	11/6	H	TOR	35-28	W	20720
Division Semi-Final						
Sun	11/13	H	OTT	26-16	W	18888
Division Final						
Sun	11/20	H	BAL	12-14	L	25067

1995 BALTIMORE STALLIONS

Fri	6/30	A	BC	34-37	L	23999
Sat	7/8	H	SA	50-24	W	31016
Sat	7/15	A	SA	28-23	W	18112
Sat	7/22	H	WPG	43-7	W	30641
Sat	7/29	A	BIR	36-8	W	30729
Wed	8/2	A	EDM	19-12	W	30698
Sun	8/6	A	CAL	15-29	L	24463
Sat	8/12	H	MEM	15-25	L	31221
Sat	8/19	A	MEM	16-13	W	20012
Sat	8/26	H	TOR	41-14	W	27853
Sat	9/2	A	HAM	41-14	W	23120
Sat	9/9	H	BIR	28-20	W	29013
Fri	9/15	A	SHR	24-17	W	12455
Sat	9/23	H	SHR	42-32	W	27321
Sun	10/1	A	SAS	28-24	W	30738
Sat	10/7	H	SAS	29-27	W	31421
Sat	10/21	H	BC	28-26	W	33208
Sun	10/29	H	HAM	24-17	W	29310
Division Semi-Final						
Sat	11/4	H	WPG	36-21	W	21040
Division Final						
Sun	11/12	H	SA	21-11	W	30217
Grey Cup						
Sun	11/19	N	CAL	37-20	W	52564

1995 BRITISH COLUMBIA LIONS

Fri	6/30	H	BAL	37-34	W	23999
Fri	7/7	A	MEM	31-13	W	14278
Thu	7/13	H	TOR	35-34	W	24276
Fri	7/21	A	CAL	24-46	L	30012
Thu	7/27	H	OTT	48-11	W	22226
Thu	8/3	H	BIR	30-23	W*	21948
Wed	8/9	A	SAS	43-25	W	20421
Mon	8/14	A	TOR	19-6	W	17084
Fri	8/18	A	WPG	6-11	L	22769
Sat	8/26	H	SHR	19-20	L	24535
Sat	9/9	A	OTT	43-24	W	22564
Sat	9/16	H	HAM	49-14	W	25432
Fri	9/22	H	EDM	18-33	L	32837
Sun	10/1	A	EDM	36-39	L	30046
Mon	10/9	H	CAL	27-41	L	32907
Sun	10/15	A	HAM	14-43	L	23112
Sat	10/21	A	BAL	26-28	L	33208
Sat	10/28	H	SAS	30-25	L	27464
Division Semi-Final						
Sun	11/5	A	EDM	15-26	L	28817

1995 BIRMINGHAM BARRACUDAS

Tue	7/4	A	WPG	38-10	W	22208
Sat	7/8	A	HAM	13-31	L	23042
Sat	7/15	H	HAM	51-28	W	31185
Sat	7/22	H	SAS	24-14	W	25321
Sat	7/29	H	BAL	8-36	L	30729
Thu	8/3	A	BC	23-30	L*	21948
Sat	8/12	H	WPG	50-24	W	17328
Fri	8/18	A	CAL	31-28	W	25129
Sat	8/26	H	CAL	14-37	L	19652
Fri	9/1	A	OTT	56-46	W	20062
Sat	9/9	A	BAL	20-28	L	29013
Sun	9/17	H	OTT	40-9	W	5289
Sun	9/24	A	MEM	19-28	L	13797
Sun	10/1	H	SHR	34-20	W	6314
Sun	10/8	H	SA	38-28	W	6859
Fri	10/13	A	SHR	29-28	W	21117
Thu	10/19	H	EDM	18-45	L	8910
Sun	10/29	A	SA	42-48	L	19025
Division Semi-Final						
Sun	11/5	A	SA	9-52	L	13031

1995 CALGARY STAMPEDERS

Thu	6/29	H	MEM	24-18	W	25071
Sat	7/8	A	SHR	48-17	W	14026
Thu	7/13	A	OTT	57-7	W	24861
Fri	7/21	H	BC	46-24	W	30012
Fri	7/28	H	SHR	27-19	W	21098
Sun	8/6	H	BAL	29-15	W	24463
Sat	8/12	A	SA	38-32	W	22043
Fri	8/18	H	BIR	28-31	L	25129
Sat	8/26	A	BIR	37-14	W	19652
Mon	9/4	H	EDM	51-26	W	37317
Fri	9/8	A	EDM	33-17	W	49434

Tue	9/19	H	WPG	43-28	W	21738
Sun	9/24	A	WPG	43-39	W	24598
Sat	9/30	H	TOR	26-19	W	22570
Mon	10/9	A	BC	41-27	W	32907
Sat	10/14	A	SAS	20-25	L	55438
Sun	10/22	H	SAS	18-15	W	33258
Fri	10/27	A	TOR	22-31	L	23196
Division Semi-Final						
Sat	11/4	H	HAM	31-13	W	16026
Division Final						
Sun	11/12	H	EDM	37-4	W	30871
Grey Cup						
Sun	11/19	N	BAL	20-37	L	52564

1995 EDMONTON ESKIMOS

Sat	7/1	H	TOR	45-23	W	27465
Fri	7/7	A	SAS	26-19	W*	23584
Mon	7/17	H	SHR	37-7	W	29463
Sat	7/22	A	SA	27-32	L	12856
Fri	7/28	A	HAM	26-18	W	20104
Wed	8/2	H	BAL	12-19	L	30698
Wed	8/9	A	TOR	31-10	W	14192
Sun	8/13	A	OTT	17-18	L	20012
Fri	8/18	H	SAS	32-13	W	30204
Sun	8/27	H	OTT	63-3	W	28135
Mon	9/4	A	CAL	26-51	L	37317
Fri	9/8	H	CAL	17-33	L	49434
Fri	9/15	H	WPG	64-10	W	27718
Fri	9/22	A	BC	33-18	W	32837
Sun	10/1	H	BC	39-36	W	30046
Fri	10/13	H	MEM	34-17	W	30111
Thu	10/19	A	BIR	45-18	W	8910
Thu	10/26	A	MEM	25-14	W	12078
Division Semi-Final						
Sun	11/5	H	BC	26-15	W	28817
Division Final						
Sun	11/12	A	CAL	4-37	L	30871

1995 HAMILTON TIGER-CATS

Fri	6/30	A	SAS	37-16	W	23396
Sat	7/8	H	BIR	31-13	W	23042
Sat	7/15	A	BIR	28-51	L	31185
Mon	7/24	H	MEM	21-23	L	20324
Fri	7/28	H	EDM	18-26	L	20104
Thu	8/3	A	TOR	20-16	W*	19174
Fri	8/11	H	SHR	30-20	W	20182
Sat	8/19	H	SA	35-31	W	20520
Fri	8/25	A	WPG	36-33	W*	22211
Sat	9/2	H	BAL	14-41	L	23120
Sat	9/9	H	TOR	33-27	W	24820
Sat	9/16	A	BC	14-49	L	25432
Sat	9/23	A	SA	7-45	L	14614
Fri	9/29	H	WPG	20-24	L	20727
Sat	10/7	A	SHR	14-26	L	12619
Sun	10/15	H	BC	43-14	W	23112
Sat	10/21	A	OTT	9-30	L	17160
Sun	10/29	A	BAL	17-24	L	29310
Division Semi-Final						
Sat	11/4	A	CAL	13-31	L	16026

1995 MEMPHIS MAD DOGS

Thu	6/29	A	CAL	18-24	L	25071
Fri	7/7	H	BC	13-31	L	14278
Fri	7/14	H	SAS	11-5	W	11748
Wed	7/19	A	OTT	23-20	W	21221
Mon	7/24	A	HAM	23-21	W	20324
Sat	7/29	H	TOR	7-10	L*	20183
Sat	8/5	A	SA	9-24	L	15557
Sat	8/12	A	BAL	25-15	W	31221
Sat	8/19	H	BAL	13-16	L	20012
Sat	8/26	H	SA	6-26	L	16223
Sun	9/3	A	SHR	31-22	W	17593
Sun	9/10	H	SHR	22-21	W	10198
Sun	9/17	A	SAS	32-34	L	27787
Sun	9/24	H	BIR	28-19	W	13797
Sun	10/8	H	OTT	26-7	W	12437
Fri	10/13	A	EDM	17-34	L	30111
Fri	10/20	A	TOR	28-10	W	14122
Thu	10/26	H	EDM	14-25	L	12078

1995 OTTAWA ROUGH RIDERS

Wed	6/28	H	WPG	25-15	W	23241
Thu	7/6	A	TOR	24-37	L	18404
Thu	7/13	H	CAL	7-57	L	24861
Wed	7/19	H	MEM	20-23	L	21221
Thu	7/27	A	BC	11-48	L	22226
Fri	8/4	H	SAS	20-31	L	20830
Sun	8/13	H	EDM	18-17	W	20012
Fri	8/18	A	SHR	11-61	L	11554
Wed	8/23	A	SAS	16-31	L	21615
Sun	8/27	A	EDM	3-63	L	28135
Fri	9/1	H	BIR	46-56	L	20062
Sat	9/9	H	BC	24-43	L	22564
Sun	9/17	A	BIR	9-40	L	5289
Sat	9/30	H	SA	14-49	L	19957
Sun	10/8	A	MEM	7-26	L	12437
Thu	10/12	A	SA	30-43	L	10027
Sat	10/21	H	HAM	30-9	W	17160
Sun	10/29	A	WPG	33-36	L	27022

1995 SAN ANTONIO TEXANS

Sat	7/1	A	SHR	47-24	W	15133
Sat	7/8	A	BAL	24-50	L	31016
Sat	7/15	H	BAL	23-28	L	18112
Sat	7/22	H	EDM	32-27	W	12856
Wed	7/26	A	WPG	17-20	L	20961
Sun	7/30	A	SAS	36-15	W	22215
Sat	8/5	H	MEM	24-9	W	15557
Sat	8/12	H	CAL	32-38	L	22043
Sat	8/19	A	HAM	31-35	L	20520
Sat	8/26	A	MEM	26-6	W	16223
Mon	9/4	A	TOR	48-27	W	14593
Sat	9/16	H	TOR	42-21	W	16028
Sat	9/23	H	HAM	45-7	W	14614
Sat	9/30	A	OTT	49-14	W	19957
Sun	10/8	A	BIR	28-38	L	6859
Thu	10/12	H	OTT	43-30	W	10027
Thu	10/19	H	SHR	35-26	W	14437
Sun	10/29	H	BIR	48-42	W	19025
Division Semi-Final						
Sun	11/5	H	BIR	52-9	W	13031
Division Final						
Sun	11/12	A	BAL	11-21	L	30217

1995 SASKATCHEWAN ROUGHRIDERS

Fri	6/30	H	HAM	16-37	L	23396
Fri	7/7	H	EDM	19-26	L*	23584
Fri	7/14	A	MEM	5-11	L	11748
Sat	7/22	A	BIR	14-24	L	25321
Sun	7/30	H	SA	15-36	L	22215
Fri	8/4	A	OTT	31-20	W	20830
Wed	8/9	H	BC	25-43	L	20421
Fri	8/18	A	EDM	13-32	L	30204
Wed	8/23	H	OTT	31-16	W	21615
Sun	9/3	H	WPG	56-4	W	31308
Sun	9/10	A	WPG	24-25	L	24698
Sun	9/17	H	MEM	34-32	W	27787
Sat	9/23	A	TOR	23-20	W	14655
Sun	10/1	H	BAL	24-28	L	30738
Sat	10/7	A	BAL	27-29	L	31421
Sat	10/14	H	CAL	25-20	W	55438
Sun	10/22	A	CAL	15-18	L	33258
Sat	10/28	A	BC	25-30	W	27464

1995 SHREVEPORT PIRATES

Sat	7/1	H	SA	24-47	L	15133
Sat	7/8	H	CAL	17-48	L	14026
Thu	7/13	A	WPG	29-37	L	20449
Mon	7/17	A	EDM	7-37	L	29463
Sat	7/22	H	TOR	11-10	W	13184
Fri	7/28	A	CAL	19-27	L	21098
Sat	8/5	H	WPG	65-17	W	11554
Fri	8/11	A	HAM	20-30	L	20182
Fri	8/18	H	OTT	61-11	W	11554
Sat	8/26	A	BC	20-19	W	24535
Sun	9/3	H	MEM	22-31	L	17593
Sun	9/10	A	MEM	21-22	L	10198
Fri	9/15	H	BAL	17-24	L	12455
Sat	9/23	A	BAL	32-42	L	27321
Sun	10/1	A	BIR	20-34	L	6314
Sat	10/7	H	HAM	26-14	W	12619
Fri	10/13	H	BIR	28-29	L	21117
Thu	10/19	A	SA	26-35	L	14437

1995 TORONTO ARGONAUTS

Sat	7/1	A	EDM	23-45	L	27465
Thu	7/6	H	OTT	37-24	W	18404
Thu	7/13	A	BC	34-35	L	24276
Sat	7/22	A	SHR	10-11	L	13184
Sat	7/29	A	MEM	10-7	W*	20183
Thu	8/3	H	HAM	16-20	L*	19174
Wed	8/9	H	EDM	10-31	L	14192
Mon	8/14	H	BC	6-19	L	17084
Sat	8/26	A	BAL	14-41	L	27853
Mon	9/4	H	SA	27-48	L	14593
Sat	9/9	A	HAM	27-33	L	24820
Sat	9/16	A	SA	21-42	L	16028
Sat	9/23	H	SAS	20-23	L	14655
Sat	9/30	A	CAL	19-26	L	22570
Mon	10/9	H	WPG	31-20	W	14507
Sat	10/14	A	WPG	30-44	L	21076
Fri	10/20	H	MEM	10-28	L	14122
Fri	10/27	H	CAL	31-22	W	23196

1995 WINNIPEG BLUE BOMBERS

Wed	6/28	A	OTT	15-25	L	23241
Tue	7/4	H	BIR	10-38	L	22208
Thu	7/13	H	SHR	37-29	W	20449
Sat	7/22	A	BAL	7-43	L	30641
Wed	7/26	H	SA	20-17	W	20961
Sat	8/5	A	SHR	17-65	L	11554
Sat	8/12	A	BIR	24-50	L	17328
Fri	8/18	H	BC	11-6	W	22769
Fri	8/25	H	HAM	33-36	L*	22211
Sun	9/3	A	SAS	4-56	L	31308
Sun	9/10	H	SAS	25-24	W	24698
Fri	9/15	A	EDM	10-64	L	27718
Tue	9/19	A	CAL	28-43	L	21738
Sun	9/24	H	CAL	39-43	L	24598
Fri	9/29	A	HAM	24-20	W	20727
Mon	10/9	A	TOR	20-31	L	14507
Sat	10/14	H	TOR	44-30	W	21076
Sun	10/29	H	OTT	36-33	W	27022
Division Semi-Final						
Sat	11/4	A	BAL	21-36	L	21040

1996 BRITISH COLUMBIA LIONS

Thu	6/27	H	EDM	14-28	L	29425
Sat	7/6	A	WPG	22-25	L	25416
Fri	7/12	A	OTT	31-32	L	13489
Fri	7/19	H	MTL	24-44	L	21855
Sat	7/27	H	HAM	24-28	L	12761
Fri	8/2	A	HAM	30-25	W	20551
Sat	8/10	H	CAL	7-32	L	15101
Thu	8/15	H	WPG	13-38	L	15531
Wed	8/21	A	CAL	21-23	L	17271
Mon	8/26	A	WPG	22-20	W	25209
Sat	9/7	A	MTL	27-28	L	15961
Sat	9/14	H	TOR	35-11	W	15323
Sat	9/21	H	SAS	22-10	W	21221
Sun	9/29	A	EDM	12-32	L	28784
Sat	10/12	H	EDM	31-34	L	18031
Sat	10/19	A	SAS	19-27	L	25155
Sun	10/27	A	TOR	21-25	L	20657
Sat	11/2	H	OTT	35-24	W	18306

1996 CALGARY STAMPEDERS

Sun	6/23	A	SAS	33-13	W	20311
Sat	6/29	H	WPG	39-12	W	23081
Wed	7/10	A	MTL	62-22	W	19362
Sat	7/20	H	HAM	40-22	W	22721
Mon	7/29	A	WPG	36-38	L	24900
Mon	8/5	H	SAS	38-11	W	26110
Sat	8/10	A	BC	32-7	W	15101
Fri	8/16	A	HAM	47-10	W	20072
Wed	8/21	H	BC	23-21	W	17271
Mon	9/2	H	EDM	31-13	W	35314
Fri	9/6	A	EDM	19-20	W	40727
Fri	9/13	H	MTL	23-25	L	19196
Sat	9/21	A	TOR	22-23	L	27209
Fri	9/27	H	OTT	24-17	W	21607
Sat	10/5	A	OTT	31-24	W	15025
Mon	10/14	H	TOR	30-23	W	27436
Sun	10/27	A	EDM	32-41	W	27332
Sun	11/3	H	SAS	46-23	W	19747
Western Final						
Sun	11/17	H	EDM	12-15	L	17693

1996 EDMONTON ESKIMOS

Thu	6/27	A	BC	28-14	W	29425
Fri	7/5	H	MTL	16-13	W	26211
Wed	7/10	A	SAS	24-27	L	21014
Wed	7/17	H	WPG	16-27	L	28751
Thu	7/25	A	OTT	34-18	W	13323
Sat	8/3	H	OTT	30-2	W	25733
Thu	8/8	A	TOR	21-24	L	20030
Sat	8/17	H	SAS	25-8	W	36011
Fri	8/23	H	HAM	35-8	W	27202
Mon	9/2	A	CAL	13-31	L	35314
Fri	9/6	H	CAL	20-19	W	70727
Sun	9/15	A	HAM	14-20	L	17301
Fri	9/20	A	WPG	41-12	W	28744
Sun	9/29	H	BC	32-12	W	28784
Fri	10/4	A	MTL	18-32	L	17886
Sat	10/12	A	BC	34-31	W	18031
Sun	10/20	H	TOR	17-24	L	27567
Sun	10/27	H	CAL	41-32	W	27332
Western Semi-Final						
Sun	11/10	H	WPG	68-7	W	13472
Western Final						
Sun	11/17	A	CAL	15-12	W	17963
Grey Cup						
Sun	11/24	N	TOR	37-43	L	38595

1996 HAMILTON TIGER-CATS

Fri	6/28	H	OTT	35-23	W	19179
Thu	7/4	A	TOR	38-36	W	26333
Sun	7/14	H	SAS	27-24	W	20542
Sat	7/20	A	CAL	22-40	L	22721
Sat	7/27	A	BC	28-24	W	12761
Fri	8/2	H	BC	25-30	L	20551
Wed	8/7	A	MTL	22-29	L	25210
Fri	8/16	H	CAL	10-47	L	20072
Fri	8/23	A	EDM	8-35	L	27202
Mon	9/2	H	TOR	7-38	L	27517
Sun	9/8	A	WPG	15-33	L	25690
Sun	9/15	H	EDM	20-14	W	17301
Sun	9/22	A	OTT	24-21	W	26813
Sun	9/29	H	MTL	39-38	W	17740
Sun	10/6	A	SAS	26-37	L	22682
Fri	10/18	H	WPG	25-15	W	17567
Fri	10/25	A	MTL	41-45	L	20231
Sat	11/2	H	TOR	14-47	L	23001
Eastern Semi-Final						
Sun	11/10	A	MTL	11-22	L	20036

1996 MONTREAL ALOUETTES

Thu	6/27	H	TOR	24-27	L	24653
Fri	7/5	A	EDM	13-16	L	26211
Wed	7/10	H	CAL	22-62	L	19362
Fri	7/19	A	BC	44-24	W	21855
Wed	7/24	H	WPG	36-10	W	20302
Thu	8/1	A	TOR	31-40	L	20302
Wed	8/7	H	HAM	29-22	W	25210
Sun	8/11	A	SAS	32-20	W	21997
Fri	8/23	H	SAS	23-16	W	26511
Fri	8/30	A	OTT	6-17	L	28451
Sat	9/7	H	BC	28-27	W	15961
Fri	9/13	A	CAL	25-23	W	19196

Sun	9/29	A	HAM	38- 39	L	17740
Fri	10/4	H	EDM	32- 18	W	17886
Mon	10/14	A	OTT	25- 18	W	14080
Sat	10/19	H	OTT	39- 25	W	18671
Fri	10/25	H	HAM	45- 41	W	20231
Fri	11/1	A	WPG	42- 24	W	25968
Eastern Semi-Final						
Sun	11/10	H	HAM	22- 11	W	20036
Eastern Final						
Sun	11/17	A	TOR	7- 43	L	28390

1996 OTTAWA ROUGH RIDERS

Fri	6/28	A	HAM	23- 35	L	19179
Wed	7/3	H	SAS	14- 29	L	10125
Fri	7/12	H	BC	32- 31	W	13489
Wed	7/17	A	TOR	4- 34	L	17288
Thu	7/25	H	EDM	18- 34	L	13323
Sat	8/3	A	EDM	2- 30	L	25773
Fri	8/9	A	WPG	27- 31	L	25219
Thu	8/15	H	TOR	19- 42	L	15220
Sat	8/24	A	TOR	21- 28	L	17186
Fri	8/30	H	MTL	17- 6	W	28451
Sun	9/15	A	SAS	18- 16	W	19567
Sun	9/22	H	HAM	21- 24	L	26813
Fri	9/27	A	CAL	17- 24	L	21607
Sat	10/5	H	CAL	24- 31	L	15025
Mon	10/14	H	MTL	18- 25	L	14080
Sat	10/19	A	MTL	25- 39	L	18671
Sat	10/26	H	WPG	29- 30	L	15095
Sat	11/2	A	BC	24- 35	L	18306

1996 SASKATCHEWAN ROUGHRIDERS

Sun	6/23	H	CAL	13- 33	L	20311
Wed	7/3	A	OTT	29- 14	W	10125
Wed	7/10	H	EDM	27- 24	W	21014
Sun	7/14	A	HAM	24- 27	L	20542
Fri	7/26	H	TOR	16- 40	L	24902
Mon	8/5	A	CAL	11- 38	L	26110
Sun	8/11	H	MTL	20- 32	L	21997
Sat	8/17	A	EDM	8- 25	L	36011
Fri	8/23	A	MTL	16- 23	L	26511
Sun	9/1	H	WPG	41- 23	W	25876
Sun	9/8	A	TOR	13- 31	L	17576
Sun	9/15	H	OTT	16- 18	L	19567
Sat	9/21	A	BC	10- 22	L	21221
Sat	9/28	H	WPG	15- 37	L	19861
Sun	10/6	H	HAM	37- 26	W	22682
Sun	10/13	A	WPG	14- 20	L	26161
Sat	10/19	H	BC	27- 19	W	25155
Sun	11/3	A	CAL	23- 46	L	19747

1996 TORONTO ARGONAUTS

Thu	6/27	A	MTL	27- 24	W	24653
Thu	7/4	H	HAM	36- 38	L	26333
Thu	7/11	A	WPG	35- 14	W	24882
Wed	7/17	H	OTT	34- 4	W	17288
Fri	7/26	A	SAS	40- 16	W	24902
Thu	8/1	H	MTL	40- 31	L	20302
Thu	8/8	H	EDM	24- 21	W	20030
Thu	8/15	A	OTT	42- 19	W	15220
Sat	8/24	H	OTT	28- 21	W	17186
Mon	9/2	A	HAM	38- 7	W	27517
Sun	9/8	H	SAS	31- 13	W	17576
Sat	9/14	A	BC	11- 35	L	15323
Sat	9/21	H	CAL	23- 22	W	27209
Sat	10/5	H	WPG	28- 12	W	17310
Mon	10/14	A	CAL	23- 30	L	27436
Sun	10/20	A	EDM	24- 17	W	27567
Sun	10/27	H	BC	25- 21	W	20657
Sat	11/2	A	HAM	47- 14	W	23001
Eastern Final						
Sun	11/17	H	MTL	43- 7	W	28390
Grey Cup						
Sun	11/24	N	EDM	43- 37	W	38595

1996 WINNIPEG BLUE BOMBERS

Sat	6/29	A	CAL	12- 39	L	23081
Sat	7/6	H	BC	25- 22	W	25416
Thu	7/11	H	TOR	14- 35	L	24882
Wed	7/17	A	EDM	27- 16	W	28751
Wed	7/24	A	MTL	10- 36	L	20302
Mon	7/29	H	CAL	38- 36	W	24900
Fri	8/9	H	OTT	31- 27	L	25219
Thu	8/15	A	BC	38- 13	W	15531
Mon	8/26	H	BC	20- 22	L	25209
Sun	9/1	A	SAS	23- 41	L	25876
Sun	9/8	H	HAM	33- 15	W	25690
Fri	9/20	H	EDM	12- 41	L	28744
Sat	9/28	A	SAS	37- 15	W	19861
Sat	10/5	A	TOR	12- 28	L	17310
Sun	10/13	H	SAS	20- 14	W	26161
Fri	10/18	A	HAM	15- 25	L	17567
Sat	10/26	A	OTT	30- 29	W	15095
Fri	11/1	H	MTL	24- 42	L	25968
Western Semi-Final						
Sun	11/10	A	EDM	7- 68	L	13472

1997 BRITISH COLUMBIA LIONS

Thu	6/26	H	SAS	23- 24	L	18881
Thu	7/3	H	CAL	17- 16	W	17206
Thu	7/10	A	EDM	41 -31	W	26010
Sat	7/19	H	WPG	21- 17	W	22312
Thu	7/24	H	TOR	20- 34	L	23330
Sat	8/2	A	HAM	42- 24	W	12032
Sat	8/9	H	MTL	31- 45	L	19106
Fri	8/15	A	SAS	39- 26	W	28556
Fri	8/22	H	CAL	37- 23	W	20303
Sat	8/30	A	MTL	33- 34	L	11050
Sun	9/7	A	SAS	12- 46	L	22966
Sat	9/13	H	EDM	27- 1	W	25088
Fri	9/19	A	WPG	14- 26	L	21732
Fri	9/26	H	HAM	34- 33	W	18258
Sat	10/4	A	TOR	3- 46	L	17019
Fri	10/10	H	SAS	19- 26	L	22399
Sun	10/19	A	EDM	7- 41	L	31958
Sun	10/26	A	CAL	9- 43	L	24690
Eastern Semi-Final						
Sun	11/2	A	MTL	35- 45	L	16257

1997 CALGARY STAMPEDERS

Wed	6/25	H	EDM	22- 23	L	24868
Thu	7/3	A	BC	16- 17	L	17206
Wed	7/9	A	MTL	28- 34	L	7669
Fri	7/18	H	SAS	22- 13	W	30366
Sat	7/26	A	SAS	19- 21	L	26483
Fri	8/1	H	WPG	43- 22	W	22752
Thu	8/7	H	TOR	45- 35	W	25311
Thu	8/14	A	WPG	35- 24	W	19674
Fri	8/22	A	BC	23- 37	L	20303
Mon	9/1	H	EDM	27- 14	W	37611
Fri	9/5	A	EDM	20- 24	L	43913
Sun	9/14	H	SAS	28- 24	W	28414
Sun	9/21	A	HAM	25- 21	W	13010
Sun	9/28	H	MTL	43- 22	W	27153
Sun	10/5	A	EDM	32- 42	L	31572
Mon	10/13	H	HAM	31- 13	W	29298
Sat	10/18	A	TOR	17- 48	L	24083
Sun	10/26	H	BC	43- 9	W	24690
Western Semi-Final						
Sun	11/2	H	SAS	30- 33	L	20369

1997 EDMONTON ESKIMOS

Wed	6/25	A	CAL	23- 22	W	24868
Fri	7/4	A	SAS	24- 18	W	25751
Thu	7/10	H	BC	31- 41	L	26010
Thu	7/17	H	MTL	32- 0	W	27811
Thu	7/24	A	MTL	34- 24	W	10025
Thu	7/31	H	SAS	37- 34	W	30917
Thu	8/7	H	WPG	45- 11	W	29293
Thu	8/14	A	TOR	14- 38	L	18301
Thu	8/21	H	HAM	28- 24	W	27960
Mon	9/1	A	CAL	14- 27	L	37611
Fri	9/5	H	CAL	24- 20	W	43913
Sat	9/13	A	BC	1- 27	L	25088
Sat	9/20	H	TOR	24- 25	L	38619
Sun	9/28	A	SAS	15- 29	L	29361
Sun	10/5	H	CAL	42- 32	W	31572
Sun	10/12	A	WPG	20- 2	W	18524
Sun	10/19	H	BC	41- 7	W	31958
Sat	10/25	A	HAM	30-19	W	16110
Western Final						
Sun	11/9	H	SAS	30- 31	L	38258

1997 HAMILTON TIGER-CATS

Fri	6/27	A	MTL	17- 27	L	7380
Sun	7/6	H	TOR	15- 20	L	14033
Fri	7/11	H	WPG	18- 33	L	12136
Thu	7/17	A	TOR	20- 27	L	17222
Fri	7/25	A	WPG	36- 21	W	20863
Sat	8/2	H	BC	24- 42	L	12032
Fri	8/8	H	SAS	20- 30	L	12582
Sat	8/16	A	MTL	26- 36	L	10039
Thu	8/21	A	EDM	24- 28	L	27960
Mon	9/1	H	TOR	3-46	L	18377
Sat	9/6	H	MTL	18- 38	L	9253
Sun	9/14	A	TOR	9- 34	L	20234
Sun	9/21	H	CAL	21- 25	L	13010
Fri	9/26	A	BC	33- 34	L	18258
Sun	10/5	H	WPG	27- 25	W	14987
Mon	10/13	A	CAL	13- 31	L	29298
Sun	10/19	A	SAS	19- 22	L	31909
Sat	10/25	H	EDM	19- 30	L	16110

1997 MONTREAL ALOUETTES

Fri	6/27	H	HAM	27- 17	W	7380
Thu	7/3	A	WPG	27- 24	W	20497
Wed	7/9	H	CAL	34- 28	W	7669
Thu	7/17	A	EDM	0- 32	L	27811
Thu	7/24	H	EDM	24- 34	L	10025
Thu	7/31	A	TOR	8- 46	L	16213
Sat	8/9	A	BC	45- 31	W	19106
Sat	8/16	H	HAM	36- 26	W	10039
Fri	8/22	A	WPG	26- 21	W	19930
Sat	8/30	H	BC	34- 33	W	11050
Sat	9/6	A	HAM	38- 18	W	9253
Fri	9/12	H	WPG	29- 28	W	10259
Sun	9/21	A	SAS	24- 22	W	25570
Sun	9/28	A	CAL	22- 43	L	27153
Fri	10/3	H	SAS	30- 29	W	12322
Sat	10/11	A	TOR	21- 28	L	17355
Sun	10/19	H	WPG	41- 34	W	6721
Sun	10/26	H	TOR	43- 38	W	10801
Eastern Semi-Final						
Sun	11/2	H	BC	45- 35	W	16257
Eastern Final						
Sun	11/9	A	TOR	30- 37	L	30085

1997 SASKATCHEWAN ROUGHRIDERS

Thu	6/26	A	BC	24- 23	W	18881
Fri	7/4	H	EDM	18- 24	L	25751
Sat	7/12	H	TOR	27- 23	W	22956
Fri	7/18	A	CAL	13- 22	L	30366
Sat	7/26	H	CAL	21- 19	W	26483
Thu	7/31	A	EDM	34- 37	L	30917
Fri	8/8	A	HAM	30- 20	W	12582
Fri	8/15	H	BC	26- 39	L	28556
Thu	8/21	A	TOR	1- 27	L	17330
Sun	8/31	H	WPG	12- 43	L	29788
Sun	9/7	H	BC	46- 12	W	22966
Sun	9/14	A	CAL	24- 28	L	28414
Sun	9/21	H	MTL	22- 24	L	25570
Sun	9/28	H	EDM	29- 15	W	29361
Fri	10/3	A	MTL	29- 30	L	12322
Fri	10/10	A	BC	26- 19	W	22399
Sun	10/19	H	HAM	22- 19	W	31909
Fri	10/24	A	WPG	9- 55	L	30222
Western Semi-Final						
Sun	11/2	A	CAL	33- 30	W	20369
Western Final						
Sun	11/9	A	EDM	31- 30	W	38258
Grey Cup						
Sun	11/16	N	TOR	23- 47	L	60431

1997 TORONTO ARGONAUTS

Fri	6/27	H	WPG	38- 23	W	16551
Sun	7/6	A	HAM	20- 15	W	14033
Sat	7/12	A	SAS	23- 27	L	22956
Thu	7/17	H	HAM	27- 20	W	17222
Thu	7/24	A	BC	34- 20	W	23330
Thu	7/31	H	MTL	46- 8	W	16213
Thu	8/7	A	CAL	35- 45	L	25311
Thu	8/14	H	EDM	38- 14	W	18031
Thu	8/21	H	SAS	27- 1	W	17330
Mon	9/1	A	HAM	46- 3	W	18377
Sun	9/7	A	WPG	66- 25	W	21080
Sun	9/14	H	HAM	34- 9	W	20234
Sat	9/20	A	EDM	25- 24	W	38619
Sun	9/28	A	WPG	41- 9	W	20004
Sat	10/4	H	BC	46- 3	W	17019
Sat	10/11	H	MTL	28- 21	W	17355
Sat	10/18	H	CAL	48- 17	W	24083
Sun	10/26	A	MTL	38- 43	L	10801
Eastern Final						
Sun	11/9	H	MTL	37- 30	W	30085
Grey Cup						
Sun	11/16	N	SAS	47- 23	W	60431

1997 WINNIPEG BLUE BOMBERS

Fri	6/27	A	TOR	23- 38	L	16551
Thu	7/3	H	MTL	24- 27	L	20497
Fri	7/11	A	HAM	33- 18	W	12136
Sat	7/19	A	BC	17- 21	L	22312
Fri	7/25	H	HAM	21- 36	L	20863
Fri	8/1	A	CAL	22- 43	L	22752
Thu	8/7	A	EDM	11- 45	L	29293
Thu	8/14	H	CAL	24- 35	L	19674
Fri	8/22	H	MTL	21- 26	L	19930
Sun	8/31	A	SAS	43- 12	W	29788
Sun	9/7	H	TOR	25- 66	L	21080
Fri	9/12	A	MTL	28-29	L	10259
Fri	9/19	H	BC	26- 14	W	21732
Sun	9/28	H	TOR	9- 41	L	20004
Sun	10/5	A	HAM	25- 27	L	14987
Sun	10/12	H	EDM	2- 20	L	18524
Sun	10/19	A	MTL	34- 41	L	6721
Fri	10/24	H	SAS	55- 9	W	30222

1998 BRITISH COLUMBIA LIONS

Thu	7/2	H	EDM	12- 20	L	16212
Fri	7/10	A	EDM	10- 15	L	31582
Thu	7/16	H	TOR	15- 30	L	15725
Fri	7/24	A	SAS	25- 20	W	25055
Thu	7/30	H	WPG	20- 13	W	15726
Thu	8/6	A	MTL	16- 22	L	14050
Fri	8/14	A	WPG	24- 22	W	20293
Thu	8/20	H	CAL	9- 55	L	15008
Thu	8/27	A	HAM	8- 18	L	17063
Sat	9/5	H	MTL	15- 26	L	14408
Sat	9/12	A	TOR	28- 37	L	14218
Sat	9/19	H	EDM	21- 27	L	13380
Sat	9/26	H	HAM	34- 31	W	12256
Sun	10/4	A	CAL	22- 11	W	33179
Fri	10/9	H	SAS	31- 14	W	22465
Sun	10/18	A	EDM	31- 7	W	30362
Sun	10/25	A	SAS	42- 37	W	26537
Sat	10/31	H	CAL	31- 22	W	20770
Western Semi-Final						
Sun	11/8	A	EDM	33- 40	L	26102

1998 CALGARY STAMPEDERS

Wed	7/1	H	HAM	21- 20	W	29145
Thu	7/9	A	TOR	22- 19	W	15672
Thu	7/16	H	MTL	26- 29	L	27515
Fri	7/24	A	WPG	44- 25	W	21399
Thu	7/30	H	TOR	14- 15	L	26061
Fri	8/7	A	SAS	46-27	W	22588
Thu	8/13	H	SAS	47-24	W	31507
Thu	8/20	A	BC	55- 9	W	15008
Fri	8/28	A	MTL	32- 40	L	17501
Mon	9/7	H	EDM	26- 8	W	37611

Fri 9/11 A EDM 30- 23 W 50856
Fri 9/18 H SAS 35- 18 W 30633
Sun 9/27 A SAS 22- 27 L 26145
Sun 10/4 H BC 11- 22 L 33179
Sun 10/11 A HAM 35- 18 W 17854
Sun 10/18 H WPG 39- 23 W 26727
Sun 10/25 H EDM 31- 19 W 27984
Sat 10/31 A BC 22- 31 L 20770
Western Final
Sun 11/15 H EDM 33- 10 W 31121
Grey Cup
Sun 11/22 N HAM 26- 24 W 34157

1998 EDMONTON ESKIMOS
Thu 7/2 A BC 20- 12 W 16212
Fri 7/10 H BC 15- 10 W 31582
Thu 7/16 A SAS 14- 28 L 21686
Thu 7/23 A TOR 30- 27 W 15106
Fri 7/31 H MTL 22- 10 W 30813
Fri 8/7 H HAM 10- 39 L 33058
Thu 8/13 A HAM 23- 48 L 21175
Fri 8/21 H WPG 25- 16 W 29123
Thu 8/27 H SAS 35- 13 W 31894
Mon 9/7 A CAL 8- 26 L 37611
Fri 9/11 H CAL 23- 30 L 50856
Sat 9/19 A BC 27- 21 W 13380
Sat 9/26 H TOR 29- 30 L 31923
Sun 10/4 A MTL 3- 34 L 16152
Mon 10/12 A WPG 40- 20 W 19448
Sun 10/18 H BC 7- 31 L 30362
Sun 10/25 A CAL 19- 31 L 27984
Sun 11/1 H SAS 46- 24 W 28470
Western Semi-Final
Sun 11/8 H BC 40- 33 W 26102
Western Final
Sun 11/15 A CAL 10- 33 L 31121

1998 HAMILTON TIGER-CATS
Wed 7/1 A CAL 20- 21 L 29145
Wed 7/8 H WPG 33- 13 W 17104
Fri 7/17 A WPG 29- 7 W 20817
Thu 7/23 A MTL 23- 21 W 16149
Thu 7/30 H SAS 26- 8 W 18726
Fri 8/7 A EDM 39- 10 W 33058
Thu 8/13 H EDM 48- 23 W 21175
Thu 8/20 A TOR 6- 42 L 23368
Thu 8/27 H BC 18- 8 W 17063
Mon 9/7 H TOR 26- 7 W 30065
Sun 9/13 A MTL 30- 9 W 18262
Sun 9/20 H MTL 31- 31 T 18509
Sat 9/26 A BC 31- 34 L 12256
Sun 10/4 H WPG 35- 21 W 14879
Sun 10/11 H CAL 18- 35 L 17854
Fri 10/16 A SAS 34- 31 W 21893
Fri 10/23 A TOR 45- 8 W 32717
Sun 11/1 H MTL 11- 22 L 20025
Eastern Final
Sun 11/15 H MTL 22- 20 W 20025
Grey Cup
Sun 11/22 N CAL 24- 26 L 31457

1998 MONTREAL ALOUETTES
Wed 7/1 A WPG 27- 24 W 22013
Thu 7/9 H SAS 30- 24 W 14388
Thu 7/16 A CAL 29- 26 W 27515
Thu 7/23 H HAM 21- 23 L 16149
Fri 7/31 A EDM 10- 22 L 30813
Thu 8/6 H BC 22- 16 W 14050
Thu 8/13 H TOR 24- 20 W 16399
Fri 8/21 A SAS 13- 12 W 22042
Fri 8/28 H CAL 40- 32 W 17501
Sat 9/5 A BC 26- 15 W 14408
Sun 9/13 H HAM 9- 30 L 18262
Sun 9/20 A HAM 31- 31 T 18509
Fri 9/25 A WPG 23- 34 L 16152
Sun 10/4 H EDM 34- 3 W 16152
Mon 10/12 H TOR 13- 40 L 16268
Sat 10/17 A TOR 38- 28 W 24230
Sun 10/25 H WPG 58- 44 W 16205
Sun 11/1 A HAM 22- 11 W 20025
Eastern Semi-Final
Sun 11/8 H TOR 41- 28 W 17495
Eastern Final
Sun 11/15 A HAM 20- 22 L 25739

1998 SASKATCHEWAN ROUGHRIDERS
Fri 7/3 H TOR 19- 10 W 21714
Thu 7/9 A MTL 24- 30 L 14388
Thu 7/16 H EDM 28- 14 W 21686
Fri 7/24 H BC 20- 25 L 25055
Thu 7/30 A HAM 8- 26 L 18276
Fri 8/7 H CAL 27- 46 L 22588
Thu 8/13 A CAL 24- 47 L 31507
Fri 8/21 H MTL 12- 13 L 22042
Thu 8/27 A EDM 13- 35 L 31894
Sun 9/6 H WPG 32- 18 W 30152
Sun 9/13 A WPG 35- 36 L 23726
Fri 9/18 A CAL 18- 35 L 30633
Sun 9/27 H CAL 27- 22 W 26145
Sat 10/3 A TOR 18- 15 W 15272
Fri 10/9 A BC 14- 31 L 22465
Fri 10/16 H HAM 31- 34 L 21893
Sun 10/25 H BC 37- 42 L 26537
Sun 11/1 A EDM 24- 46 L 28470

1998 TORONTO ARGONAUTS
Fri 7/3 A SAS 10- 19 L 21714
Thu 7/9 H CAL 19- 22 L 15672
Thu 7/16 A BC 30-15 W 15725
Thu 7/23 H EDM 27- 30 L 15106
Thu 7/30 A CAL 15-14 W 26061
Thu 8/6 H WPG 29- 14 W 15712
Thu 8/13 A MTL 20- 24 L 16399
Thu 8/20 H HAM 42- 6 W 23368
Thu 8/27 A WPG 37- 16 W 20102
Mon 9/7 A HAM 7- 26 L 30065
Sat 9/12 H BC 37- 28 W 14218
Sat 9/19 H WPG 46- 22 W 13894
Sat 9/26 A EDM 30- 29 W 31923
Sat 10/3 H SAS 15- 18 L 15272
Mon 10/12 A MTL 40- 13 W 16268
Sat 10/17 H MTL 28- 38 L 24230
Fri 10/23 H HAM 8- 45 L 32717
Fri 10/30 A WPG 12- 31 L 33810
Eastern Semi-Final
Sun 11/8 A MTL 28- 41 L 17495

1998 WINNIPEG BLUE BOMBERS
Wed 7/1 H MTL 24- 27 L 22013
Wed 7/8 A HAM 13- 33 L 17104
Fri 7/17 H HAM 7- 29 L 20817
Fri 7/24 H CAL 25- 44 L 21399
Thu 7/30 A BC 13- 20 L 15726
Thu 8/6 A TOR 14- 29 L 15712
Fri 8/14 H BC 22- 24 L 20293
Fri 8/21 A EDM 16- 25 L 29123
Thu 8/27 H TOR 16- 37 L 20102
Sun 9/6 A SAS 18- 32 L 30152
Sun 9/13 H SAS 36- 35 W 23726
Sat 9/19 A TOR 22- 46 L 13894
Fri 9/25 H MTL 34- 23 W 16152
Sun 10/4 A HAM 21- 35 L 14879
Mon 10/12 H EDM 20- 40 L 19448
Sun 10/18 A CAL 23- 39 L 26727
Sun 10/25 A MTL 44- 58 L 16205
Fri 10/30 H TOR 31- 12 W 33810

1999 BRITISH COLUMBIA LIONS
Fri 7/9 A EDM 25- 13 W 33404
Thu 7/15 H CAL 37- 27 W 22683
Fri 7/23 A SAS 32-21 W 19785
Thu 7/29 H WPG 18- 30 L 24441
Thu 8/5 A CAL 13- 9 W 30699
Thu 8/12 H TOR 26- 28 L 20586
Thu 8/19 A HAM 38- 33 W 18875
Thu 8/26 H SAS 28- 21 W 21617
Thu 9/2 H MTL 44- 23 W 19724
Sun 9/12 A WPG 20- 16 W 19471
Sun 9/19 A MTL 12- 21 L 19461
Sat 9/25 H CAL 21- 20 W 28431
Sat 10/2 A TOR 28- 19 W 21084
Mon 10/11 H EDM 20- 26 L 26177
Sun 10/17 A EDM 21- 13 W 30713
Sun 10/24 A CAL 1- 14 L 31258
Sat 10/30 H HAM 26- 21 W 18817
Fri 11/5 H SAS 19- 18 W 19378
Western Final
Sun 11/21 H CAL 24- 26 L 28236

1999 CALGARY STAMPEDERS
Wed 7/7 H SAS 28- 18 W 31878
Thu 7/15 A BC 27- 37 L 22683
Thu 7/22 H EDM 41- 37 W 31246
Thu 7/29 A MTL 38- 17 W 19443
Thu 8/5 H BC 9- 13 L 30699
Fri 8/13 A SAS 37- 22 W 19545
Thu 8/19 H WPG 29- 17 W 34466
Thu 8/26 A WPG 36- 11 W 23343
Mon 9/6 H EDM 30- 33 L 37611
Fri 9/10 A EDM 38- 13 W 52458
Sat 9/18 H TOR 29- 26 W 32883
Sat 9/25 A BC 20- 21 L 28431
Fri 10/1 H HAM 21- 17 W 26062
Sat 10/9 A TOR 13- 24 L 20036
Sun 10/17 A SAS 34- 31 W 16448
Sun 10/24 H BC 14- 1 W 31258
Sun 10/31 H MTL 31- 24 W 28250
Sat 11/6 A HAM 28- 31 L 19460
Western Semi-Final
Sun 11/14 H EDM 30- 17 W 25305
Western Final
Sun 11/21 A BC 26- 24 W 28236
Grey Cup
Sun 11/28 N HAM 21- 32 L 45118

1999 EDMONTON ESKIMOS
Fri 7/9 H BC 13- 25 L 33404
Fri 7/16 H SAS 39- 6 W 32113
Thu 7/22 A CAL 37- 41 L 31246
Thu 7/29 A HAM 8- 54 L 16815
Fri 8/6 H MTL 13- 20 L 33154
Fri 8/13 A WPG 56- 26 W 22454
Fri 8/20 A SAS 27- 29 L 16554
Fri 8/27 H HAM 23- 30 L 34180
Mon 9/6 A CAL 33- 30 W 37611
Fri 9/10 H CAL 13- 38 L 52458
Fri 9/17 A SAS 41- 38 W 18231
Sun 9/26 H TOR 16- 20 L 31085
Sun 10/3 H WPG 19- 27 L 27211
Mon 10/11 A BC 26- 20 W 26177
Sun 10/17 H BC 13- 21 L 30713
Sat 10/23 A MTL 33- 36 L 19461
Sat 10/30 H SAS 34- 21 W 33850
Sat 11/6 A TOR 15- 20 L 28387
Western Semi-Final
Sun 11/14 A CAL 17- 30 L 25305

1999 HAMILTON TIGER-CATS
Thu 7/8 A WPG 39- 9 W 29681
Fri 7/16 H MTL 16- 22 L 18352
Fri 7/23 A TOR 21- 24 L 25558
Thu 7/29 H EDM 54- 8 W 16815
Thu 8/5 H SAS 63- 17 W 16423
Thu 8/12 A MTL 17- 24 L 19461
Thu 8/19 H BC 33- 38 L 18875
Fri 8/27 A EDM 30- 23 W 34180
Mon 9/6 H TOR 35- 28 W 28895
Sun 9/12 A MTL 19- 52 L 19461
Sat 9/18 H WPG 65- 15 W 17157
Sat 9/25 H MTL 39- 13 W 20648
Fri 10/1 A CAL 17- 21 L 26062
Sun 10/10 A WPG 43- 16 W 21915
Sat 10/16 H TOR 18- 2 W 23832
Sun 10/24 A SAS 42- 12 W 18166
Sat 10/30 A BC 21- 26 L 18817
Sat 11/6 H CAL 31- 28 W 19460
Eastern Semi-Final
Sun 11/14 H TOR 27- 6 W 21873
Eastern Final
Sun 11/21 A MTL 27- 26 W 19461
Grey Cup
Sun 11/28 N CAL 32- 21 W 45118

1999 MONTREAL ALOUETTES
Sat 7/10 A TOR 15- 12 L 21028
Fri 7/16 A HAM 22- 16 W 18352
Thu 7/22 H WPG 30- 18 W 18199
Thu 7/29 H CAL 17- 38 L 19443
Fri 8/6 A EDM 20- 13 W 33154
Thu 8/12 H HAM 24- 17 W 19461
Fri 8/20 A TOR 20- 23 L 20152
Fri 8/27 H TOR 20- 5 W 19461
Thu 9/2 A BC 23- 44 L 19724
Sun 9/12 H HAM 52- 19 W 19461
Sun 9/19 H BC 21- 12 W 19461
Sat 9/25 A HAM 13- 39 L 20648
Sun 10/3 A SAS 41- 26 W 17715
Mon 10/11 H SAS 43- 7 W 19461
Sun 10/17 A WPG 29- 32 L 15602
Sat 10/23 H EDM 36- 33 W 19461
Sun 10/31 A CAL 24- 31 L 28250
Sun 11/7 H WPG 45- 10 W 19461
Eastern Final
Sun 11/21 H HAM 26- 27 L 19461

1999 SASKATCHEWAN ROUGHRIDERS
Wed 7/7 A CAL 18- 28 L 31878
Fri 7/16 A EDM 6- 39 L 32113
Fri 7/23 H BC 21- 32 L 19785
Fri 7/30 H TOR 20- 15 W 18256
Thu 8/5 A HAM 17- 63 L 16423
Fri 8/13 H CAL 22- 37 L 19545
Fri 8/20 H EDM 29- 27 W 16554
Thu 8/26 A BC 21- 28 L 21617
Sun 9/5 H WPG 42- 17 W 29249
Sat 9/11 A TOR 3- 28 L 17216
Fri 9/17 H EDM 38- 41 L 18231
Fri 9/24 A WPG 18- 24 L 18727
Sun 10/3 H MTL 26- 41 L 17715
Mon 10/11 A MTL 7- 43 L 19461
Sun 10/17 H CAL 31- 34 L 16448
Sun 10/24 H HAM 12- 42 L 18166
Sat 10/30 A EDM 21- 34 L 33850
Fri 11/5 A BC 18- 19 L 19378

1999 TORONTO ARGONAUTS
Sat 7/10 H MTL 12- 15 W 21028
Thu 7/15 A WPG 27- 47 L 18025
Fri 7/23 H HAM 24- 21 W 25558
Fri 7/30 A SAS 15- 20 L 18256
Fri 8/6 H WPG 40- 7 W 21308
Thu 8/12 A BC 28- 26 W 20586
Fri 8/20 H MTL 23- 20 W 20152
Fri 8/27 A MTL 5- 20 L 19461
Mon 9/6 A HAM 28- 35 L 28895
Sat 9/11 H SAS 28- 3 W 17216
Sat 9/18 A CAL 26- 29 L 32883
Sun 9/26 A EDM 20- 16 W 31085
Sat 10/2 H BC 19- 28 L 21084
Sat 10/9 H CAL 24- 13 W 20036
Sat 10/16 A HAM 2- 18 L 23832
Fri 10/22 H WPG 32- 22 W 23632
Fri 10/29 A WPG 13- 18 L 27043
Sat 11/6 H EDM 20- 15 W 28387
Eastern Semi-Final
Sun 11/14 A HAM 6- 27 L 21873

1999 WINNIPEG BLUE BOMBERS
Thu 7/8 H HAM 9- 39 L 29681

Thu	7/15	H	TOR	47-27	W	18025
Thu	7/22	A	MTL	18- 30	L	18199
Thu	7/29	A	BC	30- 18	W	24441
Fri	8/6	A	TOR	7- 40	L	21308
Fri	8/13	H	EDM	26- 56	L	22454
Thu	8/19	A	CAL	17- 29	L	34466
Thu	8/26	H	CAL	11- 36	L	23343
Sun	9/5	A	SAS	17- 42	L	29249
Sun	9/12	H	BC	16- 20	L	19471
Sat	9/18	A	HAM	15- 65	L	17157
Fri	9/24	H	SAS	24- 18	W	18727
Sun	10/3	A	EDM	27- 19	W	27211
Sun	10/10	H	HAM	16- 43	L	21915
Sun	10/17	H	MTL	32- 29	W	15602
Fri	10/22	A	TOR	22- 32	L	23632
Fri	10/29	H	TOR	18- 13	W	27043
Sun	11/7	A	MTL	10- 45	L	19461

2000 BRITISH COLUMBIA LIONS

Fri	7/7	A	HAM	33- 26	W*	18411
Thu	7/13	H	SAS	30- 28	W	28736
Thu	7/20	A	CAL	2- 35	L	34081
Thu	7/27	H	EDM	13- 29	L	23714
Fri	8/4	A	WPG	16- 31	L	25840
Thu	8/10	H	CAL	26- 47	L	20103
Thu	8/17	H	TOR	36- 26	W	19858
Thu	8/24	A	TOR	51- 4	W	11350
Thu	8/31	H	MTL	25- 35	L	19621
Sat	9/9	A	SAS	20- 28	L	24416
Sat	9/16	H	EDM	26- 14	W	20234
Sun	9/24	A	MTL	28- 29	L	19461
Sun	10/1	A	EDM	42- 49	L*	28865
Mon	10/9	H	WPG	33- 40	L	18453
Sat	10/14	A	SAS	39- 15	W	24776
Sun	10/22	A	CAL	38- 45	L	33890
Sat	10/28	H	HAM	28- 22	W	21303
Sat	11/4	H	SAS	27- 26	W	33232
Western Semi-Final						
Sun	11/12	A	EDM	34- 32	W	25103
Western Final						
Sun	11/19	A	CAL	37- 23	W	30829
Grey Cup						
Sun	11/26	N	MTL	28- 26	W	43822

2000 CALGARY STAMPEDERS

Wed	7/5	H	EDM	44- 22	W	34383
Fri	7/14	A	WPG	42- 38	W*	24571
Thu	7/20	H	BC	35- 2	W	34081
Fri	7/28	A	SAS	52- 52	T*	25061
Fri	8/4	H	TOR	37- 17	W	33783
Thu	8/10	A	BC	47- 26	W	20103
Wed	8/16	H	WPG	37- 16	W	35494
Fri	8/25	A	MTL	13- 48	L	19481
Mon	9/4	H	EDM	18- 30	L	35967
Fri	9/8	A	EDM	10- 31	L	53248
Sat	9/16	H	HAM	41- 38	W*	35187
Fri	9/22	A	SAS	40- 17	W	27141
Thu	9/28	A	TOR	31- 14	W	11343
Fri	10/6	H	SAS	28- 18	W	35967
Sun	10/15	A	EDM	30- 33	L	34318
Sun	10/22	H	BC	45- 38	W	33890
Sun	10/29	H	MTL	32- 31	W	45010
Sun	11/5	A	HAM	22- 24	L	20795
Western Final						
Sun	11/19	H	BC	23- 37	L	30829

2000 EDMONTON ESKIMOS

Wed	7/5	A	CAL	22- 44	L	34383
Fri	7/14	H	HAM	21- 28	L	30033
Fri	7/21	H	WPG	51- 49	L	27596
Thu	7/27	A	BC	29- 13	W	23714
Fri	8/4	A	HAM	16- 10	W	21333
Fri	8/11	H	MTL	29- 7	W	31472
Fri	8/18	A	SAS	28- 22	W	21707
Fri	8/25	H	SAS	20- 30	L	36813
Mon	9/4	A	CAL	30- 18	W	35967
Fri	9/8	H	CAL	31- 10	W	53248
Sat	9/16	A	BC	14- 26	L	20234
Fri	9/22	H	TOR	21- 34	L	28649
Sun	10/1	H	BC	49- 42	W*	28865
Mon	10/9	A	MTL	15- 45	L	19461
Sun	10/15	H	CAL	33- 30	W	34318
Sat	10/21	A	TOR	48- 28	W	18129
Sat	10/28	H	SAS	52- 54	L*	34218
Fri	11/3	A	WPG	18- 30	L	26537
Western Semi-Final						
Sun	11/12	H	BC	32- 34	L	25103

2000 HAMILTON TIGER-CATS

Fri	7/7	H	BC	26- 33	L*	18411
Fri	7/14	A	EDM	28- 21	W	30033
Fri	7/21	H	SAS	40- 34	W	16480
Fri	7/28	A	TOR	23- 17	W	15385
Fri	8/4	H	EDM	10- 16	L	21333
Fri	8/11	A	SAS	29- 23	W	21116
Fri	8/18	H	MTL	37- 26	W	20720
Fri	8/25	A	WPG	33- 38	L	29082
Mon	9/4	H	TOR	42- 12	W	28830
Sun	9/10	A	MTL	15- 9	W	19461
Sat	9/16	A	CAL	38- 41	L*	35187
Sat	9/23	H	WPG	43- 6	W	13100
Sat	9/30	H	MTL	16- 32	L	21212
Sat	10/7	A	TOR	12- 29	L	20729
Fri	10/13	H	TOR	8- 32	L	19632
Fri	10/20	A	WPG	24- 27	L	25582
Sat	10/28	A	BC	22- 28	L	21303
Sun	11/5	H	CAL	24- 22	W	20795
Eastern Semi-Final						
Sun	11/12	H	WPG	20- 22	L	15105

2000 MONTREAL ALOUETTES

Wed	7/5	H	WPG	38- 22	W	19461
Tue	7/11	A	TOR	45- 6	W	20612
Thu	7/20	H	TOR	41- 4	W	19461
Fri	7/28	A	WPG	33- 31	W	24111
Thu	8/3	H	SAS	62- 7	W	14461
Fri	8/11	A	EDM	7- 29	L	31472
Fri	8/18	A	HAM	26- 37	L	20720
Fri	8/25	H	CAL	48- 13	W	19481
Thu	8/31	A	BC	35- 25	W	19621
Sun	9/10	H	HAM	9- 15	L	19461
Sat	9/16	A	WPG	27- 30	L	22917
Sun	9/24	H	BC	29- 28	W	19461
Sat	9/30	A	HAM	32- 16	W	21212
Mon	10/9	H	EDM	45- 15	W	19461
Sun	10/15	H	WPG	36- 30	W	19461
Sun	10/22	A	SAS	39- 22	W	27138
Sun	10/29	A	CAL	31- 32	L	45010
Sun	11/5	H	TOR	11- 17	L	19461
Eastern Final						
Sun	11/19	H	WPG	35- 24	W	19461
Grey Cup						
Sun	11/26	N	BC	26- 28	L	43822

2000 SASKATCHEWAN ROUGHRIDERS

Thu	7/6	H	TOR	28- 36	L	20995
Thu	7/13	A	BC	28- 30	L	28736
Fri	7/21	A	HAM	34- 40	L	16480
Fri	7/28	H	CAL	52- 52	T*	25061
Thu	8/3	A	MTL	7- 62	L	19461
Fri	8/11	H	HAM	23- 29	L	21116
Fri	8/18	H	EDM	22- 28	L	21707
Fri	8/25	A	EDM	30- 20	W	36813
Sun	9/3	H	WPG	38- 29	W	30088
Sat	9/9	H	BC	28- 20	W	24416
Fri	9/15	A	TOR	44- 17	W	28724
Fri	9/22	H	CAL	17- 40	L	27141
Fri	9/29	A	WPG	30- 38	L	26041
Fri	10/6	A	CAL	18- 28	L	35967
Sat	10/14	H	BC	15- 39	L	24776
Sun	10/22	H	MTL	22- 39	L	27138
Sat	10/28	A	EDM	54- 52	W*	34218
Sat	11/4	A	BC	26- 27	L	33232

2000 TORONTO ARGONAUTS

Thu	7/6	A	SAS	36- 28	W	20995
Tue	7/11	H	MTL	6- 45	L	20612
Thu	7/20	A	MTL	4- 41	L	19461
Fri	7/28	H	HAM	17- 23	L	15385
Fri	8/4	A	CAL	17- 37	L	33783
Thu	8/10	H	WPG	41- 41	T*	11723
Thu	8/17	A	BC	26- 36	L	19858
Thu	8/24	H	BC	4- 51	L	11350
Mon	9/4	A	HAM	12- 42	L	28830
Sat	9/9	A	WPG	24- 12	W	24021
Fri	9/15	H	SAS	17- 44	L	28724
Fri	9/22	A	EDM	34- 21	W	28649
Thu	9/28	H	CAL	14- 31	L	11343
Sat	10/7	H	HAM	29- 12	W	20729
Fri	10/13	A	HAM	32- 8	W	19632
Sat	10/21	H	EDM	28- 48	L	18129
Fri	10/27	H	WPG	32- 31	W	18473
Sun	11/5	A	MTL	17- 11	W	19461

2000 WINNIPEG BLUE BOMBERS

Wed	7/5	A	MTL	22- 38	L	19461
Fri	7/14	H	CAL	38- 42	L*	24571
Fri	7/21	A	EDM	49- 51	W	27596
Fri	7/28	H	MTL	31- 33	L	24111
Fri	8/4	H	BC	31- 16	W	25840
Thu	8/10	A	TOR	41- 41	T*	11723
Wed	8/16	A	CAL	16- 37	L	35494
Fri	8/25	H	HAM	38- 33	W	29082
Sun	9/3	A	SAS	29- 38	L	30088
Sat	9/9	H	TOR	12- 24	L	24021
Sat	9/16	H	MTL	30- 27	W	22917
Sat	9/23	A	HAM	6- 43	L	13100
Fri	9/29	H	SAS	38- 30	W	26041
Mon	10/9	A	BC	40- 33	W	18453
Sun	10/15	A	MTL	30- 36	L	19461
Fri	10/20	H	HAM	27- 24	W	25582
Fri	10/27	A	TOR	31- 32	L	18473
Fri	11/3	H	EDM	30- 18	W	26537
Eastern Semi-Final						
Sun	11/12	A	HAM	22- 20	W	15105
Eastern Final						
Sun	11/19	A	MTL	24- 35	L	19461

2001 BRITISH COLUMBIA LIONS

Sat	7/7	H	EDM	35- 28	W*	18125
Thu	7/12	A	HAM	5- 26	L	19350
Sat	7/21	H	SAS	7- 12	L	19409
Fri	7/27	A	CAL	22- 28	L	32210
Sat	8/4	H	MTL	44- 31	W	18185
Sat	8/11	H	EDM	42- 39	W	18171
Fri	8/17	A	EDM	35- 17	W	35394
Sat	8/25	H	CAL	27- 13	W	23642
Fri	8/31	A	MTL	19- 23	L	19541
Sat	9/8	A	TOR	17- 32	L	17642
Sat	9/22	A	SAS	17- 15	W	19777
Fri	9/28	A	WPG	22- 23	L	29503
Sat	10/6	H	TOR	17- 34	L	17822
Fri	10/12	A	EDM	22- 28	L	30518
Sat	10/20	H	WPG	18- 26	L	23510
Sun	10/28	A	CAL	34- 16	W	33144
Sat	11/3	H	SAS	10- 42	L	20684
Tue	11/6	H	HAM	24- 12	W	19769
Western Semi-Final						
Sun	11/11	A	CAL	19- 28	L	23642

2001 CALGARY STAMPEDERS

Wed	7/4	H	WPG	20- 48	L	33678
Thu	7/12	A	MTL	14- 32	L	19544
Fri	7/20	A	EDM	23- 33	L	33524
Fri	7/27	H	BC	28- 22	W	32210
Fri	8/3	H	TOR	35- 36	L	32605
Sat	8/11	A	SAS	33- 4	W	22436
Fri	8/17	H	SAS	37- 13	W	35967
Sat	8/25	A	BC	13- 27	L	23642
Mon	9/3	H	EDM	32- 33	L	35967
Fri	9/7	A	EDM	34- 33	W	48279
Mon	9/17	H	SAS	21- 14	W	32548
Sat	9/22	A	HAM	26- 29	L*	15500
Fri	9/28	A	TOR	31- 33	L	15387
Mon	10/8	H	HAM	33- 35	L	31794
Sun	10/14	A	SAS	29- 26	W	18496
Sat	10/20	H	MTL	29- 9	W	33144
Sun	10/28	H	BC	16- 34	L	27678
Fri	11/2	A	WPG	22- 15	W	27678
Western Semi-Final						
Sun	11/11	H	BC	28- 19	W	23642
Western Final						
Sun	11/18	A	EDM	34- 16	W	42156
Grey Cup						
Sun	11/25	N	WPG	27- 19	W	65255

2001 EDMONTON ESKIMOS

Sat	7/7	A	BC	28- 35	L*	18125
Fri	7/13	H	SAS	13- 11	W	32722
Fri	7/20	H	CAL	33- 23	W	33524
Thu	7/26	A	MTL	6- 34	L	19541
Thu	8/2	A	HAM	24- 14	W	17107
Sat	8/11	A	BC	39- 42	L	18171
Fri	8/17	H	BC	17- 35	L	35394
Fri	8/24	H	HAM	12- 20	L	37666
Mon	9/3	A	CAL	33- 32	W	35967
Fri	9/7	H	CAL	33- 34	L	48279
Mon	9/17	A	WPG	22- 23	L	26144
Fri	9/21	H	TOR	23- 22	W	28687
Sat	9/29	A	SAS	35- 19	W	18086
Fri	10/5	H	WPG	33- 37	L	29659
Fri	10/12	H	BC	28- 22	W	30518
Fri	10/19	A	TOR	25- 22	W*	15438
Sat	10/27	A	SAS	3- 12	L	20917
Sun	11/4	H	MTL	32- 26	W	43123
Western Final						
Sun	11/18	H	CAL	16- 34	L	42156

2001 HAMILTON TIGER-CATS

Fri	7/6	A	SAS	28- 30	L	23421
Thu	7/12	H	BC	26- 5	W	19350
Fri	7/20	A	TOR	24- 18	W	16252
Thu	7/26	H	WPG	24- 19	W	17140
Thu	8/2	H	EDM	14- 24	L	17107
Fri	8/10	A	MTL	17- 27	L	19541
Thu	8/16	H	WPG	17- 20	L	14415
Fri	8/24	A	EDM	20- 12	W	37666
Mon	9/3	H	TOR	26- 13	W	20456
Sat	9/8	A	WPG	31- 63	L	29005
Sat	9/22	H	CAL	29- 26	W*	15500
Sun	9/30	H	MTL	21- 20	W	19300
Mon	10/8	A	CAL	35- 33	W	31794
Sun	10/14	A	WPG	17- 24	L	28558
Sun	10/21	H	SAS	30- 24	W	17266
Sun	10/28	A	MTL	38- 18	W	19601
Sat	11/3	H	TOR	31- 20	W	21019
Tue	11/6	A	BC	12- 24	L	19769
Eastern Semi-Final						
Sun	11/11	H	MTL	24- 12	W	18500
Eastern Final						
Sun	11/18	A	WPG	13- 28	L	29503

2001 MONTREAL ALOUETTES

Wed	7/4	A	TOR	27- 3	W	14065
Thu	7/12	H	CAL	32- 14	W	19544
Fri	7/20	A	WPG	37- 34	W	29503
Thu	7/26	H	EDM	34- 6	W	19541
Sat	8/4	A	BC	31- 44	L	18185
Fri	8/10	H	HAM	27- 17	W	19541
Thu	8/16	H	TOR	40- 25	W	19541
Fri	8/24	A	WPG	19- 24	L	29503
Fri	8/31	H	BC	23- 19	W	19541
Sun	9/9	A	SAS	31- 3	W	18358
Mon	9/17	H	TOR	24- 18	W	19544
Sun	9/23	H	WPG	25- 28	L	19601
Sun	9/30	A	HAM	20- 21	L	19300
Mon	10/8	H	SAS	7- 13	L	19601
Sat	10/13	A	TOR	24- 51	L	17258
Sat	10/20	A	CAL	9- 29	L	34029

Sun 10/28 H HAM 18-38 L 19601
Sun 11/4 A EDM 26-32 L 43123
Eastern Semi-Final
Sun 11/11 A HAM 12-24 L 18500

2001 SASKATCHEWAN ROUGHRIDERS
Fri 7/6 H HAM 30-28 W 23421
Fri 7/13 A EDM 11-13 L 32722
Sat 7/21 A BC 12-7 W 19409
Sat 7/28 H TOR 24-50 L 27255
Fri 8/3 A WPG 14-32 L 27310
Sat 8/11 H CAL 4-35 L 22438
Fri 8/17 A CAL 13-37 L 35967
Sat 8/25 A TOR 14-11 W 18378
Sun 9/2 H WPG 18-20 L 30127
Sun 9/9 H MTL 3-31 L 18358
Mon 9/17 A CAL 14-21 L 32548
Sat 9/22 H BC 15-17 L 1977
Sat 9/29 H EDM 19-35 L 18086
Mon 10/8 A MTL 13-7 W 19601
Sun 10/14 H CAL 26-29 L 18496
Sun 10/21 A HAM 24-30 L 17266
Sat 10/27 H EDM 12-3 W 20917
Sat 11/3 A BC 42-10 W 20684

2001 TORONTO ARGONAUTS
Wed 7/4 H MTL 3-27 L 14065
Fri 7/13 H WPG 16-30 L 11041
Fri 7/20 H HAM 18-24 L 16252
Sat 7/28 A SAS 50-24 W 27255
Fri 8/3 A CAL 36-35 W 32605
Fri 8/10 A WPG 16-36 L 25598
Thu 8/16 A MTL 25-40 L 19541
Sat 8/25 H SAS 11-14 L 18378
Mon 9/3 A HAM 13-26 L 20456
Sat 9/8 H BC 32-17 W 17642
Mon 9/17 A MTL 18-24 L 19544
Fri 9/21 A EDM 22-23 L 28687
Fri 9/28 H CAL 33-31 W 15387
Sat 10/6 A BC 34-17 W 17822
Sat 10/13 H MTL 51-24 W 17258
Fri 10/19 H EDM 22-25 L* 15438
Fri 10/26 H WPG 12-7 W 16782
Sat 11/3 A HAM 20-31 L 21019

2001 WINNIPEG BLUE BOMBERS
Wed 7/4 A CAL 48-20 W 33678
Fri 7/13 A TOR 30-16 W 11041
Fri 7/20 H MTL 34-37 L 29503
Thu 7/26 A HAM 19-24 L 17140
Fri 8/3 H SAS 32-14 W 27310
Fri 8/10 H TOR 36-16 W 25598
Thu 8/16 A HAM 20-17 W 14415
Fri 8/24 H MTL 24-19 W 29503
Sun 9/2 A SAS 20-18 W 30127
Sat 9/8 H HAM 63-31 W 29005
Mon 9/17 H EDM 23-22 W 26144
Sun 9/23 A MTL 28-25 W 19601
Fri 9/28 H BC 23-22 W 29503
Fri 10/5 A EDM 37-33 W 29659
Sun 10/14 H HAM 24-17 W 28558
Sat 10/20 A BC 26-18 W 23510
Fri 10/26 A TOR 7-12 L 16782
Fri 11/2 H CAL 15-22 L 27678
Eastern Final
Sun 11/18 H HAM 28-13 W 29503
Grey Cup
Sun 11/25 N CAL 19-27 L 65255

2002 BRITISH COLUMBIA LIONS
Tue 6/25 A MTL 20-27 L 19628
Sat 6/29 A HAM 15-27 L 16032
Tue 7/9 H TOR 22-30 L 15796
Thu 7/18 H HAM 51-21 W 14218
Fri 7/26 A EDM 27-37 L 32844
Thu 8/1 H CAL 15-23 L 15117
Fri 8/9 A WPG 29-21 W 28734
Thu 8/15 H OTT 22-18 W 15258
Wed 8/21 H MTL 48-37 W 17221
Fri 8/30 A OTT 28-4 W 22343
Sun 9/8 A WPG 28-44 L 27298
Fri 9/13 H EDM 23-18 W 21886
Fri 9/27 H WPG 38-28 W 20191
Sat 10/5 A TOR 23-18 W 16827
Fri 10/11 H CAL 37-14 W 20950
Sat 10/19 A SAS 11-13 L 24957
Sun 10/27 A CAL 15-16 L 31698
Fri 11/1 H SAS 28-3 W 25929
Western Semi-Final
Sun 11/10 A WPG 3-30 L 22508

2002 CALGARY STAMPEDERS
Fri 6/28 H EDM 21-27 L 33584
Fri 7/5 A SAS 21-32 L 21968
Fri 7/12 A HAM 31-34 L* 17140
Thu 7/18 H MTL 20-37 L 32018
Thu 7/25 H SAS 26-21 W 35967
Thu 8/1 A BC 23-15 W 15117
Thu 8/8 H TOR 31-11 W 31920
Thu 8/15 A MTL 23-38 L 20002
Fri 8/23 A WPG 48-51 L* 27876
Mon 9/2 H EDM 20-28 L 35967
Fri 9/6 A EDM 11-45 L 61481
Sat 9/14 H OTT 12-26 L 31891
Sun 9/22 A OTT 26-22 W* 23136
Fri 10/4 H HAM 43-5 W 30575
Fri 10/11 A BC 14-37 L 20950
Fri 10/18 H WPG 20-35 L 30776
Sun 10/27 H BC 16-15 W 31698
Sun 11/3 A TOR 32-33 L 19232

2002 EDMONTON ESKIMOS
Fri 6/28 A CAL 27-21 W 33584
Thu 7/4 H OTT 40-24 W 30152
Sat 7/13 H TOR 31-17 W 33108
Fri 7/19 A SAS 11-45 L 25149
Fri 7/26 H BC 37-27 W 32844
Fri 8/2 A MTL 14-37 L 20002
Wed 8/7 H HAM 33-5 W 38852
Thu 8/15 H WPG 35-32 W 32174
Fri 8/23 A TOR 30-7 W 23642
Mon 9/2 A CAL 28-20 W 35967
Fri 9/6 H CAL 45-11 W 61481
Fri 9/13 A BC 18-23 L 21886
Sat 9/21 H SAS 31-25 W 44480
Sun 9/29 A HAM 34-33 W 16054
Mon 10/6 A OTT 37-34 W 20576
Sun 10/14 H MTL 30-48 L 36255
Fri 10/25 H SAS 27-21 W 34101
Sat 11/2 A WPG 8-20 L 27830
Western Final
Sun 11/17 H WPG 33-30 W 34322
Grey Cup
Sun 11/24 H MTL 16-25 L 62531

2002 HAMILTON TIGER-CATS
Sat 6/29 H BC 27-15 W 16032
Fri 7/5 A WPG 15-24 L 25609
Fri 7/12 H CAL 34-31 W* 17140
Thu 7/18 A BC 21-51 L 14218
Thu 7/25 A OTT 37-38 L 24335
Thu 8/1 H SAS 34-31 W* 15369
Wed 8/7 A EDM 5-33 L 38852
Sun 8/11 A SAS 14-30 L 23889
Thu 8/22 H OTT 30-9 W 15249
Mon 9/2 H TOR 22-14 W 25327
Sun 9/8 A MTL 30-32 L 20002
Sun 9/15 H MTL 35-28 W* 15061
Sun 9/22 A TOR 21-28 L 18932
Sun 9/29 H EDM 33-34 L 16054
Fri 10/4 A CAL 5-43 L 30575
Sun 10/14 H TOR 28-29 L* 20216
Sun 10/20 A MTL 29-26 W 20002
Sun 10/27 H WPG 7-28 L 18349

2002 MONTREAL ALOUETTES
Tue 6/25 H BC 27-20 W 19628
Wed 7/3 A TOR 28-12 W 21175
Thu 7/11 H SAS 26-20 W 20002
Thu 7/18 A CAL 37-20 W 32018
Sat 7/27 H WPG 31-22 W 20002
Fri 8/2 H EDM 37-14 W 20002
Thu 8/8 A OTT 29-6 W 26221
Thu 8/15 H CAL 38-23 W 20002
Wed 8/21 A BC 37-48 L 17221
Sat 8/25 A SAS 23-9 W 23212
Sun 9/8 H HAM 32-30 W 20002
Sun 9/15 A HAM 28-35 L* 15061
Fri 9/20 A WPG 24-27 L 29503
Sun 9/29 H TOR 38-3 W 20002
Sun 10/14 A EDM 48-30 W 36255
Sun 10/20 H HAM 26-29 L 20002
Sat 10/26 A OTT 43-34 W 26411
Sun 11/3 H OTT 25-26 L 20002
Eastern Final
Sun 11/17 H TOR 35-18 W 57125
Grey Cup
Sun 11/24 A EDM 25-16 W 62531

2002 OTTAWA RENEGADES
Fri 6/28 H SAS 27-30 L* 26898
Thu 7/4 A EDM 24-40 L 30152
Thu 7/11 H WPG 25-24 W 22436
Wed 7/17 A WPG 7-55 L 26671
Thu 7/25 H HAM 38-37 W 24335
Thu 8/1 A TOR 8-24 L 18734
Thu 8/8 H MTL 6-29 L 26221
Thu 8/15 A BC 18-22 L 15258
Thu 8/22 A HAM 9-30 L 15249
Fri 8/30 H BC 4-28 L 22343
Sat 9/7 H TOR 25-30 L 21604
Sat 9/14 A CAL 26-12 W 31891
Sun 9/22 H CAL 22-26 L* 23136
Sat 9/28 A SAS 11-29 L 20098
Mon 10/6 H EDM 34-37 L 20576
Sun 10/20 A TOR 12-29 L 24932
Sat 10/26 H MTL 34-43 L 26411
Sun 11/3 A MTL 26-25 W 20002

2002 SASKATCHEWAN ROUGHRIDERS
Fri 6/28 A OTT 30-27 W* 26898
Fri 7/5 H CAL 32-21 W 21968
Thu 7/11 A MTL 20-26 L 20002
Fri 7/19 H EDM 45-11 W 25149
Thu 7/25 A CAL 21-26 L 35967
Thu 8/1 A HAM 31-34 L* 15369
Sun 8/11 H HAM 30-14 W 23889
Fri 8/16 A TOR 10-18 L 19652
Sat 8/25 H MTL 9-23 L 23212
Sun 9/1 H WPG 33-19 W 30220
Sun 9/15 H TOR 40-11 W 24387
Sat 9/21 A EDM 25-31 L 44480
Sat 9/28 H OTT 29-11 W 20098
Mon 10/6 H WPG 32-35 L* 24157
Sat 10/12 A WPG 11-20 L 29503
Sat 10/19 H BC 13-11 W 24957
Fri 10/25 A EDM 21-27 L 34101
Fri 11/1 A BC 3-28 L 25929
Eastern Semi-Final
Sun 11/10 A TOR 14-24 L 23124

2002 TORONTO ARGONAUTS
Fri 6/28 A WPG 15-39 L 24063
Wed 7/3 H MTL 12-28 L 21175
Tue 7/9 A BC 30-22 W 15796
Sat 7/13 A EDM 17-31 L 33108
Tue 7/23 H WPG 15-42 L 21724
Thu 8/1 H OTT 24-8 W 18734
Thu 8/8 A CAL 11-31 L 31920
Fri 8/16 H SAS 18-10 W 19652
Fri 8/23 H EDM 7-30 L 23642
Mon 9/2 A HAM 14-22 L 25327
Sat 9/7 A OTT 30-25 W 21604
Sun 9/15 A SAS 11-40 L 24387
Sun 9/22 H HAM 28-21 W 18932
Sun 9/29 A MTL 3-38 L 20002
Sat 10/5 H BC 18-23 L 16827
Sun 10/14 A HAM 29-28 W* 20216
Sun 10/20 H OTT 29-12 W 24932
Sun 11/3 H CAL 33-32 W 19232
Eastern Semi-Final
Sun 11/10 H SAS 24-14 W 23124
Eastern Final
Sun 11/17 A MTL 18-35 L 57125

2002 WINNIPEG BLUE BOMBERS
Fri 6/28 H TOR 39-15 W 24063
Fri 7/5 H HAM 24-15 W 25609
Thu 7/11 A OTT 24-25 L 22436
Wed 7/17 H OTT 55-7 W 26671
Tue 7/23 A TOR 42-15 W 21724
Sat 7/27 A MTL 22-31 L 20002
Fri 8/9 H BC 21-29 L 28734
Thu 8/15 A EDM 32-35 L 32174
Fri 8/23 H CAL 51-48 W* 27876
Sun 9/1 A SAS 19-33 L 30220
Sun 9/8 H BC 44-28 W 27298
Fri 9/20 H MTL 27-24 W 29503
Fri 9/27 A BC 28-38 L 20191
Mon 10/6 A SAS 35-32 W* 24157
Sat 10/12 H SAS 20-11 W 29503
Fri 10/18 A CAL 35-20 W 30776
Sun 10/27 A HAM 28-7 W 18349
Sat 11/2 H EDM 20-8 W 27830
Western Semi-Final
Sun 11/10 H BC 30-3 W 22508
Western Final
Sun 11/17 A EDM 30-33 L 34322

2003 BRITISH COLUMBIA LIONS
Fri 6/20 H WPG 27-34 L 20191
Sat 6/28 A SAS 30-32 L 22155
Fri 7/4 H TOR 30-27 W* 20131
Sat 7/12 A MTL 28-27 W 20202
Fri 7/18 A OTT 48-14 W 23800
Thu 7/24 H OTT 37-19 W 21554
Fri 8/1 A TOR 26-28 L* 15623
Fri 8/8 H CAL 48-4 W 24222
Sat 8/16 A CAL 30-7 W 30217
Fri 8/22 H HAM 47-25 L 23010
Sat 9/6 A SAS 2-28 L 27495
Sat 9/13 H EDM 30-34 L 27070
Sat 9/20 A WPG 26-20 W 27605
Fri 9/26 A EDM 7-27 L 44432
Sat 10/4 H WPG 35-31 W 25591
Sat 10/11 H MTL 28-24 W 21046
Sat 10/18 A HAM 29-23 W 13106
Sat 10/25 H SAS 23-26 L 29706
Eastern Semi-Final
Sun 11/2 A TOR 7-28 L 21029

2003 CALGARY STAMPEDERS
Tue 6/17 H MTL 20-23 L* 30102
Thu 6/26 A EDM 24-34 L 30568
Tue 7/1 H OTT 32-12 W 32028
Fri 7/11 A HAM 17-11 W 15193
Sat 7/19 A MTL 25-36 W 20202
Sat 7/26 H TOR 24-41 L 30976
Fri 8/1 H SAS 11-27 L 34260
Fri 8/8 A BC 4-48 L 24222
Sat 8/16 H BC 7-30 L 30217
Fri 8/22 A WPG 17-52 L 28240
Mon 9/1 H EDM 28-22 W 36251
Fri 9/5 A EDM 0-38 L 62444
Sun 9/14 H WPG 21-19 W 29432
Fri 9/26 A OTT 21-26 L 23212
Fri 10/3 H HAM 32-12 W 32052
Mon 10/13 A SAS 22-24 L 43613
Sun 10/19 H SAS 6-34 L 34287

Fri	10/24	A	TOR	12-13	L	18223

2003 EDMONTON ESKIMOS

Sat	6/21	H	MTL	16-34	L	30109
Thu	6/26	H	CAL	34-24	W	30568
Tue	7/1	A	WPG	12-14	L	28495
Sat	7/5	A	HAM	37-20	W	12492
Wed	7/16	H	HAM	52-15	W	33785
Fri	7/25	A	SAS	14-32	L	26767
Thu	7/31	A	OTT	31-26	W	21200
Sat	8/9	H	TOR	49-20	W	44189
Sun	8/17	A	TOR	18-15	W	11021
Sat	8/23	H	SAS	49-31	W	45083
Mon	9/1	A	CAL	22-28	L	36251
Fri	9/5	H	CAL	38-0	W	62444
Sat	9/13	A	BC	34-30	W	27070
Fri	9/19	H	OTT	45-33	W	35264
Fri	9/26	H	BC	27-7	W	44432
Sun	10/5	A	MTL	20-19	W	20202
Fri	10/17	H	WPG	41-32	W	45164
Sat	10/25	A	WPG	30-34	L	26601
Western Final						
Sun	11/9	H	SAS	30-23	W	40081
Grey Cup						
Sun	11/16	N	MTL	34-22	W	50909

2003 HAMILTON TIGER-CATS

Fri	6/20	H	OTT	17-27	L	15318
Mon	6/30	A	TOR	8-49	L	14842
Sat	7/5	H	EDM	20-37	L	12492
Fri	7/11	H	CAL	11-17	L	15193
Wed	7/16	A	EDM	15-52	L	33785
Sun	7/20	A	SAS	9-42	L	23510
Sat	8/2	H	WPG	20-37	L	13809
Fri	8/8	A	MTL	17-30	L	20202
Sat	8/16	H	MTL	10-28	L	14169
Fri	8/22	A	BC	25-47	W	23010
Mon	9/1	H	TOR	11-19	L	21323
Sat	9/6	A	OTT	28-45	L	26588
Fri	9/12	H	SAS	27-24	W*	14313
Tue	9/16	A	TOR	14-24	L	15472
Sat	9/27	H	MTL	17-30	L	14048
Fri	10/3	A	CAL	12-32	L	32052
Fri	10/10	A	WPG	9-14	L	25526
Sat	10/18	H	BC	23-29	L	13106

2003 MONTREAL ALOUETTES

Tue	6/17	A	CAL	23-20	W*	30102
Sat	6/21	A	EDM	34-16	W	30109
Fri	7/4	A	SAS	32-31	W	23295
Sat	7/12	H	BC	27-28	L	20202
Sat	7/19	H	CAL	36-25	L	20202
Thu	7/24	A	WPG	50-19	W	28484
Tue	7/29	H	WPG	37-27	W	20202
Fri	8/8	H	HAM	30-17	W	20202
Sat	8/16	A	HAM	28-10	W	14169
Thu	8/21	H	TOR	46-22	W	20202
Fri	8/29	A	OTT	38-43	L	24583
Sun	9/14	H	OTT	30-10	W	20202
Sun	9/21	H	SAS	28-23	W	20202
Sat	9/27	A	HAM	30-17	W	14048
Sun	10/5	H	EDM	19-20	L	20202
Sat	10/11	A	BC	24-28	L	21046
Fri	10/17	A	TOR	13-45	L	14921
Sun	10/26	H	OTT	37-8	W	20202
Eastern Final						
Sun	11/9	H	TOR	30-26	W	60007
Grey Cup						
Sun	11/16	N	EDM	22-34	L	50909

2003 OTTAWA RENEGADES

Fri	6/20	A	HAM	27-17	W	15318
Fri	6/27	H	WPG	32-34	L	21823
Tue	7/1	A	CAL	12-32	L	32028
Thu	7/10	H	TOR	34-32	W	22242
Fri	7/18	H	BC	14-48	L	23800
Thu	7/24	A	BC	19-37	L	21554
Thu	7/31	H	EDM	26-31	L	21200
Thu	8/7	H	SAS	29-24	W	21817
Tue	8/12	A	WPG	29-34	L	26232
Sun	8/17	A	SAS	41-51	L	26772
Fri	8/29	H	MTL	43-38	W	24583
Sat	9/6	H	HAM	45-28	W	2658
Sun	9/14	A	MTL	10-30	L	20202
Fri	9/19	A	EDM	33-45	L	35264
Fri	9/26	H	CAL	26-21	W	23212
Sat	10/4	A	TOR	18-27	L	16431
Mon	10/13	H	TOR	21-15	W	25133
Sun	10/26	A	MTL	8-37	L	20202

2003 SASKATCHEWAN ROUGHRIDERS

Thu	6/19	A	TOR	20-18	W	15318
Sat	6/28	H	BC	32-30	W	22155
Fri	7/4	H	MTL	31-32	L	23295
Thu	7/10	A	WPG	27-29	L	27374
Sun	7/20	H	HAM	42-9	W	23510
Fri	7/25	H	EDM	32-14	W	26767
Fri	8/1	A	CAL	27-11	W	34260
Thu	8/7	A	OTT	24-29	L	21817
Sun	8/17	H	OTT	51-41	W	26772
Sat	8/23	A	EDM	31-49	L	45083
Sun	8/31	H	WPG	18-36	L	40320
Sat	9/6	H	BC	28-2	W	27495
Fri	9/12	A	HAM	24-27	L*	14313
Sun	9/21	A	MTL	23-28	L	20202
Sun	9/28	H	TOR	41-24	W	30249
Mon	10/13	H	CAL	24-22	W	43613
Sun	10/19	A	CAL	34-6	W	34287
Sat	10/25	A	BC	26-23	W	29706
Western Semi-Final						
Sun	11/2	A	WPG	27-21	W	22110
Western Final						
Sun	11/9	A	EDM	23-30	L	40081

2003 TORONTO ARGONAUTS

Thu	6/19	H	SAS	18-20	L	15318
Mon	6/30	H	HAM	49-8	W	14842
Fri	7/4	A	BC	27-30	L*	20131
Thu	7/10	A	OTT	32-34	L	22242
Tue	7/15	H	WPG	24-14	W	14089
Sat	7/26	A	CAL	41-24	W	30976
Fri	8/1	H	BC	28-26	W*	15623
Sat	8/9	A	EDM	20-49	L	44189
Sun	8/17	H	EDM	15-18	L	11021
Thu	8/21	A	MTL	22-46	L	20202
Mon	9/1	A	HAM	19-11	W	21323
Sun	9/7	A	WPG	30-34	L	26468
Tue	9/16	H	HAM	24-14	W	15472
Sun	9/28	A	SAS	24-41	L	30249
Sat	10/4	H	OTT	27-18	W	16431
Mon	10/13	A	OTT	15-21	L	25133
Fri	10/17	H	MTL	45-13	W	14921
Fri	10/24	H	CAL	13-12	W	18223
Eastern Semi-Final						
Sun	11/2	H	BC	28-7	W	21029
Eastern Final						
Sun	11/9	A	MTL	26-30	L	60007

2003 WINNIPEG BLUE BOMBERS

Fri	6/20	A	BC	34-27	W	20191
Fri	6/27	A	OTT	34-32	W	21823
Tue	7/1	H	EDM	14-12	W	28945
Thu	7/10	H	SAS	29-27	W	27374
Tue	7/15	A	TOR	14-24	L	14089
Thu	7/24	H	MTL	19-50	L	28484
Tue	7/29	A	MTL	27-37	L	20202
Sat	8/2	A	HAM	37-20	W	13809
Tue	8/12	H	OTT	34-29	W	26232
Fri	8/22	H	CAL	52-17	W	28240
Sun	8/31	A	SAS	36-18	W	40320
Sun	9/7	H	TOR	34-30	W	26468
Sun	9/14	A	CAL	19-21	L	29432
Sat	9/20	H	BC	20-26	L	27605
Sat	10/4	A	BC	31-35	L	25951
Fri	10/10	H	HAM	14-9	W	25526
Fri	10/17	A	EDM	32-41	L	45164
Sat	10/25	H	EDM	34-30	W	26601
Western Semi-Final						
Sun	11/2	H	SAS	21-27	L	22110

2004 BRITISH COLUMBIA LIONS

Fri	6/18	H	HAM	36-38	L	20950
Sat	6/26	A	EDM	41-34	W	35367
Fri	7/2	A	SAS	29-42	L	21605
Fri	7/9	H	EDM	9-25	L	22227
Thu	7/22	A	WPG	48-17	W	25567
Thu	7/29	H	MTL	32-9	W	23788
Fri	8/6	H	OTT	47-27	W	25255
Fri	8/13	A	HAM	49-11	W	27891
Sat	8/21	A	CAL	25-18	W*	28351
Fri	8/27	H	TOR	31-10	W	29484
Sat	9/11	A	OTT	31-13	W	22380
Sat	9/18	H	EDM	36-33	W*	29704
Fri	9/24	A	CAL	21-22	L	28524
Sat	10/2	H	WPG	42-31	W	29170
Mon	10/11	A	TOR	16-22	L	25212
Thu	10/17	A	MTL	32-29	W	20202
Fri	10/22	H	CAL	19-17	W	27295
Sat	10/30	H	SAS	40-38	W	32402
Western Final						
Sun	11/14	H	SAS	27-25	L*	55227
Grey Cup						
Sun	11/21	N	TOR	19-27	L	51242

2004 CALGARY STAMPEDERS

Sun	6/20	A	SAS	33-10	W	21119
Sun	6/27	H	MTL	14-32	L	30207
Sun	7/4	H	HAM	34-41	L	26884
Thu	7/15	A	MTL	23-42	L	20202
Sat	7/24	H	SAS	21-40	L	35651
Thu	7/29	A	OTT	30-31	L	22509
Sat	8/7	H	WPG	49-27	W	30144
Sat	8/14	A	SAS	16-46	L	26228
Sat	8/21	H	BC	18-25	L*	28351
Fri	8/27	A	HAM	7-26	L	28850
Mon	9/6	H	EDM	7-25	L	35651
Fri	9/10	A	EDM	12-44	L	50366
Fri	9/17	H	OTT	24-26	L	28114
Fri	9/24	H	BC	22-21	W	28524
Wed	9/29	A	TOR	24-49	L	22429
Sat	10/16	H	TOR	29-11	W	30082
Fri	10/22	A	BC	17-19	L	27925
Fri	10/29	A	WPG	16-37	L	23119

2004 EDMONTON ESKIMOS

Sat	6/19	A	MTL	9-33	L	20202
Sat	6/26	H	BC	34-41	L	35637
Fri	7/2	A	OTT	15-44	L	22843
Fri	7/9	A	BC	25-9	W	22227
Sat	7/17	H	HAM	51-30	W	35728
Fri	7/30	H	WPG	41-24	W	38363
Sun	8/8	A	TOR	14-39	L	23897
Thu	8/12	A	WPG	14-25	L	23998
Fri	8/20	H	SAS	31-7	W	42399
Sun	8/29	H	OTT	57-16	W	37109
Mon	9/6	A	CAL	25-7	W	35651
Fri	9/10	H	CAL	44-12	W	50366
Sat	9/18	A	BC	33-36	L*	29704
Sat	9/25	H	TOR	17-26	L	41113
Fri	10/1	A	HAM	27-30	L	27805
Mon	10/11	H	MTL	39-19	W	37708
Sun	10/17	A	SAS	16-40	L	30087
Sun	10/24	H	WPG	40-34	W	33131
Western Semi-Final						
Sun	11/7	H	SAS	6-14	L	37359

2004 HAMILTON TIGER-CATS

Fri	6/18	A	BC	38-36	W	20950
Fri	6/25	H	WPG	32-22	W	25712
Sun	7/4	A	CAL	41-34	W	26884
Sat	7/10	H	TOR	6-34	L	27664
Sat	7/17	A	EDM	30-51	L	35728
Fri	7/23	H	MTL	13-34	L	26301
Sat	7/31	A	SAS	24-33	L	23348
Fri	8/13	H	BC	11-49	L	27891
Thu	8/19	A	OTT	31-19	W	23754
Fri	8/27	H	CAL	26-7	W	28850
Mon	9/6	H	TOR	30-30	T*	29170
Sun	9/12	A	MTL	18-47	L	20202
Sun	9/19	H	SAS	30-32	L	27893
Fri	10/1	H	EDM	30-27	W	27805
Fri	10/8	A	WPG	20-13	W	26323
Fri	10/15	H	OTT	20-17	W*	29220
Thu	10/21	A	TOR	31-38	L	30369
Sat	10/30	A	OTT	24-19	W	25839
Eastern Semi-Final						
Fri	11/5	A	TOR	6-24	L	37835

2004 MONTREAL ALOUETTES

Sat	6/19	H	EDM	33-9	W	20202
Sun	6/27	A	CAL	32-14	W	30207
Sat	7/3	A	TOR	19-9	W	23923
Fri	7/9	H	OTT	46-22	W	20202
Thu	7/15	H	CAL	42-23	W	20202
Fri	7/23	A	HAM	34-13	W	26301
Thu	7/29	A	BC	9-32	L	23788
Thu	8/5	H	SAS	24-20	W	20202
Thu	8/12	H	TOR	22-10	W	20202
Thu	8/26	A	WPG	29-13	W	22826
Fri	9/3	A	OTT	23-16	W	24639
Sun	9/12	H	HAM	47-18	W	20202
Sat	9/25	H	WPG	47-25	L	20202
Sat	10/2	A	SAS	19-35	L	23692
Mon	10/11	A	EDM	19-39	L	37708
Thu	10/17	H	BC	29-32	L	20202
Sat	10/23	H	OTT	52-21	W	53302
Thu	10/28	A	TOR	58-20	W	31212
Eastern Final						
Sun	11/14	H	TOR	18-26	L	51296

2004 OTTAWA RENEGADES

Thu	6/17	A	WPG	37-25	W	22059
Thu	6/24	H	TOR	20-10	W	20241
Fri	7/2	H	EDM	44-15	W	22843
Fri	7/9	A	MTL	22-46	L	20202
Fri	7/16	H	WPG	1-29	L	21114
Wed	7/21	A	TOR	25-28	W	24209
Thu	7/29	H	CAL	31-30	W	22509
Fri	8/6	A	BC	27-47	L	25255
Thu	8/19	H	HAM	19-31	L	23754
Sun	8/29	A	EDM	16-57	L	37109
Fri	9/3	H	MTL	16-23	L	24639
Sat	9/11	H	BC	13-31	L	22380
Fri	9/17	A	CAL	26-24	W	28114
Sun	9/26	A	SAS	22-36	L	24410
Sat	10/9	H	SAS	25-32	L	23833
Fri	10/15	A	HAM	17-20	L*	29220
Sat	10/23	A	MTL	21-52	L	53302
Sat	10/30	H	HAM	19-24	L	25839

2004 SASKATCHEWAN ROUGHRIDERS

Tue	6/15	A	TOR	10-21	L	26821
Sun	6/20	H	CAL	10-33	L	21119
Fri	7/2	H	BC	42-29	W	21605
Thu	7/8	A	WPG	15-32	L	22059
Fri	7/16	H	TOR	12-17	L	22340
Sat	7/24	A	CAL	40-21	W	35651
Sat	7/31	H	HAM	33-24	W	23348
Thu	8/5	A	MTL	20-24	L	20202
Sat	8/14	H	CAL	46-16	W	26228
Fri	8/20	A	EDM	7-31	L	42399
Sun	9/5	H	WPG	4-17	L	30220
Sun	9/12	A	WPG	24-27	L	27160
Sun	9/19	A	HAM	32-30	W	27893
Sun	9/26	H	OTT	36-22	W	24410
Sat	10/2	H	MTL	35-19	W	23692
Sat	10/9	A	OTT	32-25	W	23833
Sun	10/17	H	EDM	40-16	W	30087
Sat	10/30	A	BC	38-40	L	32402

Western Semi-Final
Sun 11/7 A EDM 14-6 W 37359
Western Final
Sun 11/14 A BC 25-27 W* 55227

2004 TORONTO ARGONAUTS
Tue 6/15 H SAS 21-10 W 26821
Thu 6/24 A OTT 10-20 L 20241
Sat 7/3 H MTL 9-19 L 23923
Sat 7/10 A HAM 34-6 W 27664
Fri 7/16 A SAS 17-12 W 22340
Wed 7/21 H OTT 28-25 L 24209
Sun 8/8 H EDM 39-14 W 23897
Thu 8/12 A MTL 10-22 L 20202
Tue 8/17 H WPG 14-6 W 24246
Fri 8/27 A BC 10-31 L 29484
Mon 9/6 A HAM 30-30 T* 29170
Sat 9/18 A WPG 34-44 L 24855
Sat 9/25 A EDM 26-17 W 41113
Wed 9/29 H CAL 49-24 W 22429
Mon 10/11 H BC 22-16 W 25212
Sat 10/16 A CAL 11-29 L 30082
Thu 10/21 H HAM 38-31 W 30369
Thu 10/28 H MTL 20-58 L 31212
Eastern Semi-Final
Fri 11/5 H HAM 24-6 W 37835
Eastern Final
Sun 11/14 A MTL 26-18 W 51296
Grey Cup
Sun 11/21 N BC 27-19 W 51242

2004 WINNIPEG BLUE BOMBERS
Thu 6/17 H OTT 25-37 L 22059
Fri 6/25 A HAM 22-32 L 25712
Thu 7/8 H SAS 32-15 W 22059
Fri 7/16 A OTT 29-1 W 21114
Thu 7/22 H BC 17-48 L 25567
Fri 7/30 A EDM 24-41 L 38363
Sat 8/7 A CAL 27-49 L 30144
Thu 8/12 H EDM 25-14 W 23998
Tue 8/17 A TOR 6-14 L 24246
Thu 8/26 H MTL 13-29 L 22826
Sun 9/5 A SAS 17-4 W 30220
Sun 9/12 H SAS 27-24 W 27160
Sat 9/18 H TOR 44-34 W 24855
Sat 9/25 A MTL 25-47 W 20202
Sat 10/2 A BC 31-42 L 29170
Fri 10/8 H HAM 13-20 L 26323
Sun 10/24 A EDM 34-40 L 33131
Fri 10/29 H CAL 37-16 W 23119

2005 BRITISH COLUMBIA LIONS
Sat 6/25 A TOR 27-20 W 30712
Fri 7/8 H OTT 37-29 W 27506
Fri 7/15 H TOR 30-22 W 29217
Sat 7/23 A HAM 28-22 W 27692
Fri 7/29 H CAL 40-27 W 28714
Fri 8/5 A EDM 25-19 W 35568
Fri 8/12 A CAL 39-31 W 31847
Fri 8/19 H HAM 39-15 W 33119
Sat 8/27 A SAS 19-15 W 24899
Thu 9/8 A OTT 61-27 W 19013
Sat 9/17 H MTL 27-26 W 36066
Sat 9/24 A EDM 20-37 L 48048
Sat 10/1 H SAS 19-28 L 34711
Mon 10/10 A WPG 23-44 L 22630
Sun 10/16 A MTL 44-46 L 20202
Sat 10/22 H WPG 41-1 W 29780
Fri 10/28 A EDM 19-22 L 37544
Sat 11/5 H SAS 12-13 L 38847
Western Final
Sun 11/20 H EDM 23-28 L 37337

2005 CALGARY STAMPEDERS
Fri 7/1 A TOR 16-22 L 34102
Thu 7/7 A WPG 21-15 W 23236
Sat 7/16 A OTT 18-33 L 16303
Sat 7/23 H SAS 44-18 W 35652
Fri 7/29 A BC 27-40 L 28714
Sat 8/6 H WPG 30-21 W 30128
Fri 8/12 H BC 31-39 L 31847
Thu 8/18 A MTL 40-37 W 20202
Wed 8/24 A TOR 16-25 L 26437
Mon 9/5 H EDM 23-25 L 35652
Fri 9/9 A EDM 16-11 W 42654
Sat 9/17 A HAM 39-17 W 27821
Thu 9/22 H OTT 45-23 W 25234
Sat 10/1 H MTL 11-32 L 28304
Fri 10/14 H HAM 34-17 W 29490
Sun 10/23 A SAS 29-21 W 28800
Sun 10/30 A WPG 46-24 W 23455
Sun 11/6 H EDM 43-23 W 31017
Western Semi-Final
Sun 11/13 H EDM 26-33 L 26799

2005 EDMONTON ESKIMOS
Fri 6/24 H OTT 41-16 W 36912
Thu 6/30 A WPG 27-8 W 22087
Fri 7/8 A MTL 29-32 L 20202
Fri 7/15 H WPG 14-12 W 37455
Thu 7/21 A OTT 29-21 W 17607
Sat 7/30 H HAM 36-30 W 38018
Fri 8/5 H BC 19-25 L 35568
Sat 8/20 H TOR 18-22 L 38927
Fri 8/26 H MTL 36-26 W 44624
Mon 9/5 A CAL 25-23 W 35652
Fri 9/9 H CAL 11-16 L 42654
Sun 9/18 A SAS 36-37 L 25226
Sat 9/24 H BC 37-20 W 48048
Fri 9/30 A HAM 14-40 L 27582
Mon 10/10 A TOR 17-13 W 34116
Sat 10/15 H SAS 19-18 W 53216
Fri 10/28 H BC 22-19 W 37544
Sun 11/6 A CAL 23-43 L 31017
Western Semi-Final
Sun 11/13 A CAL 33-26 W 26799
Western Final
Sun 11/20 A BC 28-23 W 37337
Grey Cup
Sun 11/27 A MTL 38-35 W* 59157

2005 HAMILTON TIGER-CATS
Wed 6/22 A MTL 21-31 L 20202
Sat 7/2 H SAS 21-23 L 29032
Sun 7/17 A SAS 13-32 L 23421
Sat 7/23 H BC 22-28 L 27692
Sat 7/30 A EDM 30-36 L 38018
Sat 8/6 H OTT 12-28 L 28822
Sat 8/13 A WPG 14-44 L 24326
Fri 8/19 A BC 15-39 L 33119
Fri 8/26 H WPG 41-39 W 27443
Mon 9/5 H TOR 33-30 W 29600
Sat 9/10 A TOR 0-48 L 32274
Sat 9/17 H CAL 17-39 L 27821
Fri 9/30 H EDM 40-14 W 27582
Fri 10/7 A OTT 21-43 L 19069
Fri 10/14 A CAL 17-34 L 29490
Fri 10/21 H OTT 40-32 W 26912
Thu 10/27 A TOR 11-34 L 40085
Sat 11/4 H MTL 15-9 W 27114

2005 MONTREAL ALOUETTES
Wed 6/22 H HAM 31-21 W 20202
Fri 7/1 A OTT 36-39 L* 18899
Fri 7/8 H EDM 32-29 W 20202
Fri 7/22 A WPG 46-51 L 24550
Thu 7/28 H TOR 24-36 L 20202
Thu 8/4 H SAS 42-13 W 20202
Fri 8/12 A TOR 18-10 W 31621
Thu 8/18 H CAL 37-40 L 20202
Fri 8/26 A EDM 26-36 L 44624
Fri 9/2 H OTT 41-18 W 20202
Sat 9/17 A BC 26-27 L 36066
Sun 9/25 H WPG 42-23 W 20202
Sat 10/1 A CAL 32-11 W 28304
Sat 10/8 A SAS 38-34 W 26900
Sun 10/16 H BC 46-44 W 20202
Sat 10/22 H TOR 23-49 L 51269
Sat 10/29 A OTT 43-23 W 20833
Sat 11/4 A HAM 9-15 L 27114
Eastern Semi-Final
Sun 11/13 H SAS 30-14 W 31199
Eastern Final
Sun 11/20 A TOR 33-17 W 44211
Grey Cup
Sun 11/27 H EDM 35-38 L* 59157

2005 OTTAWA RENEGADES
Fri 6/24 A EDM 16-41 L 36912
Fri 7/1 H MTL 39-36 W* 18899
Fri 7/8 A BC 29-37 L 27506
Sat 7/16 H CAL 33-18 W 16303
Thu 7/21 H EDM 21-29 L 17607
Fri 7/29 A SAS 21-16 W 25198
Sat 8/6 A HAM 28-12 W 28822
Thu 8/11 H SAS 22-17 W 20607
Fri 8/19 A WPG 17-38 L 26595
Fri 9/2 A MTL 18-41 L 20202
Thu 9/8 H BC 27-61 L 19013
Fri 9/16 H WPG 21-37 L 17567
Thu 9/22 A CAL 23-45 L 25234
Wed 9/28 A TOR 18-29 L 24886
Fri 10/7 H HAM 43-21 W 19069
Fri 10/21 A HAM 32-40 L 26912
Sat 10/29 H MTL 23-43 L 20833
Sat 11/5 H TOR 27-17 W 16504

2005 SASKATCHEWAN ROUGHRIDERS
Sat 6/25 H WPG 42-15 W 23067
Sat 7/2 A HAM 23-21 W 29032
Sat 7/9 A TOR 26-27 L 26218
Sun 7/17 H HAM 32-13 W 23421
Sat 7/23 A CAL 18-44 L 35652
Fri 7/29 H OTT 16-21 L 25198
Thu 8/4 A MTL 13-42 L 20202
Thu 8/11 A OTT 17-22 L 20607
Sat 8/27 H BC 15-19 L 24899
Sun 9/4 H WPG 45-26 W 28800
Sat 9/10 A WPG 19-17 W 29653
Sun 9/18 H EDM 37-36 W 25226
Fri 9/23 H TOR 24-13 W 22779
Sat 10/1 A BC 28-19 W 34711
Sat 10/8 H MTL 34-38 L 26900
Sat 10/15 A EDM 18-19 L 53216
Sun 10/23 H CAL 21-29 L 28800
Sat 11/5 A BC 13-12 W 38847
Eastern Semi-Final
Sun 11/13 A MTL 14-30 L 31199

2005 TORONTO ARGONAUTS
Sat 6/25 H BC 20-27 L 30712
Fri 7/1 H CAL 22-16 W 34102
Sat 7/9 H SAS 27-26 W 26218
Fri 7/15 A BC 22-30 L 29217
Thu 7/28 A MTL 36-24 W 20202
Mon 8/1 H WPG 34-27 W 27214
Fri 8/12 H MTL 10-18 L 31621
Sat 8/20 A EDM 22-18 W 38927
Wed 8/24 H CAL 25-16 W 26437
Mon 9/5 A HAM 30-33 L 29600
Sat 9/10 H HAM 48-0 W 32274
Fri 9/23 A SAS 13-24 L 22779
Wed 9/28 H OTT 29-18 W 24886
Mon 10/10 H EDM 13-17 L 34116
Sun 10/16 A WPG 35-32 W 22323
Sat 10/22 A MTL 49-23 W 51269
Thu 10/27 H HAM 34-11 W 40085
Sat 11/5 A OTT 17-27 L 16504
Eastern Final
Sun 11/20 H MTL 17-33 L 44211

2005 WINNIPEG BLUE BOMBERS
Sat 6/25 A SAS 15-42 L 23067
Thu 6/30 H EDM 8-27 L 22087
Thu 7/7 H CAL 15-21 L 23236
Fri 7/15 A EDM 12-14 L 37455
Fri 7/22 H MTL 51-46 W 24550
Mon 8/1 A TOR 27-34 L 27214
Sat 8/6 A CAL 21-30 L 30128
Sat 8/13 H HAM 44-14 W 24326
Fri 8/19 H OTT 38-17 W 26595
Fri 8/26 A HAM 39-41 L 27443
Sun 9/4 A SAS 26-45 L 28800
Sat 9/10 H SAS 17-19 L 29653
Fri 9/16 A OTT 37-21 W 17567
Sun 9/25 A MTL 23-42 L 20202
Mon 10/10 H BC 44-23 W 22630
Sun 10/16 H TOR 32-35 L 22323
Sat 10/22 A BC 1-41 L 29780
Sun 10/30 H CAL 24-46 L 23455

2006 BRITISH COLUMBIA LIONS
Fri 6/16 H SAS 45-28 W 27539
Sun 6/25 A SAS 24-32 L 21082
Fri 6/30 H TOR 26-19 W 30514
Fri 7/7 A EDM 20-27 L 35035
Fri 7/14 H SAS 28-29 L 28513
Fri 7/21 A CAL 43-20 W 31210
Sat 7/29 A TOR 28-8 W 28356
Fri 8/4 H EDM 34-17 W 27312
Thu 8/10 A WPG 32-5 W 25033
Fri 8/18 H EDM 30-28 W 33589
Fri 9/1 A MTL 48-13 W 20202
Sat 9/16 H MTL 36-20 W 35971
Sun 9/24 A SAS 20-23 L* 27592
Sat 9/30 A HAM 28-8 W 24163
Fri 10/6 H CAL 39-13 W 32232
Sun 10/15 A CAL 25-32 L 33546
Sat 10/21 H HAM 23-17 W 31294
Sat 10/28 H WPG 26-16 W 33744
Western Final
Sun 11/12 H SAS 45-18 W 50084

2006 CALGARY STAMPEDERS
Sat 6/17 H EDM 24-14 W 25895
Sat 6/24 A EDM 14-18 L 40491
Thu 6/29 H HAM 23-22 W 28396
Sat 7/8 A SAS 53-36 W 23942
Fri 7/14 A HAM 17-20 L 26944
Fri 7/21 H BC 20-43 L 31210
Sat 7/29 A SAS 9-19 L 23107
Sat 8/5 H SAS 23-7 W 34319
Sat 8/12 H MTL 27-24 W 29452
Thu 8/24 A MTL 41-23 W 20202
Mon 9/4 H EDM 44-23 W 35744
Fri 9/8 A EDM 26-35 L 47965
Fri 9/15 H WPG 43-9 W 26843
Sat 9/23 H TOR 39-18 W 31539
Sat 9/30 A TOR 16-23 L 32410
Fri 10/6 A BC 13-39 L 32232
Sun 10/15 H BC 32-25 W 33546
Sat 10/21 A WPG 13-28 L 30092
Western Semi-Final
Sun 11/5 H SAS 21-30 L 35650

2006 EDMONTON ESKIMOS
Sat 6/17 A CAL 14-24 L 25895
Sat 6/24 H CAL 18-14 W 40491
Sat 7/1 A WPG 10-46 L 23521
Fri 7/7 H BC 27-20 W 35035
Thu 7/20 H WPG 22-25 L 37611
Fri 7/28 H MTL 13-21 L 32411
Fri 8/4 A BC 17-34 L 27312
Fri 8/11 H SAS 24-18 W 39599
Fri 8/18 A BC 28-30 L 33589
Mon 9/4 A CAL 23-44 L 35744
Fri 9/8 H CAL 35-26 W 47965
Sat 9/16 A HAM 22-27 L 25107
Fri 9/22 H HAM 18-20 L 36406

Sat	9/30	A	SAS	30- 25	W	27894
Mon	10/9	A	TOR	23- 28	L	26891
Sat	10/14	H	TOR	25- 28	L	39533
Sat	10/21	A	MTL	30- 20	W	45607
Fri	10/27	H	SAS	20- 18	W	31779

2006 HAMILTON TIGER-CATS

Sat	6/17	A	TOR	17- 27	L	27689
Sat	6/24	H	MTL	14- 32	L	27911
Thu	6/29	A	CAL	22- 23	L	28396
Thu	7/6	A	MTL	21- 27	L	20202
Fri	7/14	H	CAL	20- 17	W	26944
Thu	7/20	A	MTL	38- 41	L	20202
Fri	7/28	H	WPG	0- 29	L	27027
Fri	8/4	A	WPG	26- 11	W	26521
Sat	8/12	H	TOR	2- 20	L	29010
Sat	8/19	A	SAS	15- 46	L	22820
Sat	8/26	H	SAS	8- 51	L	26564
Mon	9/4	H	TOR	6- 40	L	28891
Sat	9/9	A	TOR	9- 11	L	26212
Sat	9/16	H	EDM	27- 22	W	35107
Fri	9/22	A	EDM	20- 18	W	36406
Sat	9/30	H	BC	8- 28	L	24163
Sun	10/15	H	WPG	22- 29	L	24955
Sat	10/21	A	BC	17- 23	L	31294

2006 MONTREAL ALOUETTES

Fri	6/16	H	WPG	27- 17	W	20202
Sat	6/24	A	HAM	32- 14	W	27911
Thu	7/6	H	HAM	27- 21	W	20202
Sat	7/15	A	WPG	44- 16	W	28131
Thu	7/20	H	HAM	41- 38	W	20202
Fri	7/28	A	EDM	21- 13	W	32411
Thu	8/3	H	TOR	31- 7	W	20202
Sat	8/12	A	CAL	24- 27	L	29452
Sat	8/19	A	TOR	6- 31	L	30786
Thu	8/24	H	CAL	23- 41	L	20202
Fri	9/1	H	BC	13- 48	L	20202
Sat	9/16	A	BC	20- 36	L	35971
Sun	9/24	H	WPG	14- 17	L	20202
Fri	9/29	A	WPG	23- 20	W	28028
Mon	10/9	H	SAS	35- 8	W	20202
Fri	10/13	A	SAS	26- 27	L	25329
Sat	10/21	H	EDM	20- 30	L	45607
Sat	10/28	A	TOR	24- 20	W	38123
Eastern Final						
Sun	11/12	H	TOR	33- 24	W	35607

2006 SASKATCHEWAN ROUGHRIDERS

Fri	6/16	A	BC	28- 45	L	27539
Sun	6/25	H	BC	32- 24	W	21082
Sat	7/8	H	CAL	36- 53	L	23942
Fri	7/14	A	BC	29- 28	W	28513
Sat	7/22	H	TOR	23- 26	L	24967
Sat	7/29	H	CAL	19- 9	W	23107
Sat	8/5	A	CAL	7- 23	L	34319
Fri	8/11	A	EDM	18- 24	L	39599
Sat	8/19	H	HAM	46- 15	W	22820
Sat	8/26	A	HAM	51- 8	W	26564
Sun	9/3	H	WPG	39- 12	W	30900
Sun	9/10	A	WPG	23- 27	L	30026
Sun	9/24	H	BC	23- 20	W*	27592
Sat	9/30	H	EDM	25- 30	L	27894
Mon	10/9	A	MTL	8- 35	L	20202
Fri	10/13	H	MTL	27- 26	W	25329
Fri	10/20	A	TOR	13- 9	W	30323
Fri	10/27	A	EDM	18- 20	L	31779
Western Semi-Final						
Sun	11/5	A	CAL	30- 21	W	35650
Western Final						
Sun	11/12	A	BC	18- 45	L	50084

2006 TORONTO ARGONAUTS

Sat	6/17	H	HAM	27- 17	W	27689
Fri	6/23	A	WPG	9- 16	L	26524
Fri	6/30	A	BC	19- 26	L	30514
Sat	7/8	H	WPG	17- 24	L	26304
Sat	7/22	A	SAS	26- 23	W	24967
Sat	7/29	H	BC	8- 28	L	28356
Thu	8/3	A	MTL	7- 31	L	20202
Sat	8/12	A	HAM	20- 2	W	29010
Sat	8/19	H	MTL	31- 6	W	30786
Fri	8/25	A	WPG	18- 15	W	25014
Mon	9/4	A	HAM	40- 6	W	28891
Sat	9/9	H	HAM	11- 9	W	26212
Sat	9/23	A	CAL	18- 39	L	31539
Sat	9/30	H	CAL	23- 16	W	32410
Mon	10/9	H	EDM	28- 23	W	26891
Sat	10/14	A	EDM	28- 25	W	39533
Fri	10/20	H	SAS	9- 13	L	30323
Sat	10/28	H	MTL	20- 24	L	38123
Eastern Semi-Final						
Sun	11/5	H	WPG	31- 27	W	26214
Eastern Final						
Sun	11/12	A	MTL	24- 33	L	35607

2006 WINNIPEG BLUE BOMBERS

Fri	6/16	A	MTL	17- 27	L	20202
Fri	6/23	H	TOR	16- 9	W	26524
Sat	7/1	H	EDM	46- 10	W	23521
Sat	7/8	A	TOR	24- 17	W	26304
Sat	7/15	H	MTL	16- 44	L	28131
Thu	7/20	A	EDM	25- 22	W	37611
Fri	7/28	A	HAM	29- 0	W	27027
Fri	8/4	H	HAM	11- 26	L	26521
Thu	8/10	H	BC	5- 32	L	25033
Fri	8/25	H	TOR	15- 18	L	25014
Sun	9/3	A	SAS	12- 39	L	30900
Sun	9/10	H	SAS	27- 23	W	30026
Fri	9/15	A	CAL	9- 43	L	26843
Sun	9/24	A	MTL	17- 14	W	20202
Fri	9/29	H	MTL	20- 23	L	28028
Sun	10/15	A	HAM	29- 22	W	24955
Sat	10/21	H	CAL	28- 13	W	30092
Sat	10/28	A	BC	16- 26	L	33744
Eastern Semi-Final						
Sun	11/5	A	TOR	27- 31	L	26214

2007 BRITISH COLUMBIA LIONS

Thu	6/28	A	TOR	24- 22	W	29157
Fri	7/6	H	EDM	29- 9	W	32893
Fri	7/13	A	SAS	42- 12	W	26981
Thu	7/19	H	HAM	22- 18	W	29045
Sat	7/28	A	CAL	32- 27	W	[illegible]
Thu	8/2	H	SAS	9- 21	L	31858
Fri	8/10	H	WPG	21- 22	L	31525
Fri	8/17	A	CAL	45- 45	T*	30826
Fri	8/31	H	MTL	46- 14	W	32115
Sun	9/9	A	MTL	14- 32	L	20202
Sat	9/15	H	TOR	40- 7	W	31156
Sat	9/22	A	SAS	37- 34	W	28800
Sat	9/29	H	CAL	42- 9	W	32263
Fri	10/5	A	WPG	26- 20	W	26593
Sat	10/13	A	EDM	24- 18	W	33663
Sat	10/20	H	EDM	37- 26	W	37011
Fri	10/26	A	HAM	27- 19	W	19322
Sat	11/3	H	CAL	25- 24	W	34242
Western Final						
Sun	11/18	H	SAS	17- 26	L	54712

2007 CALGARY STAMPEDERS

Sat	6/30	H	HAM	37- 9	W	29103
Sun	7/8	A	SAS	8- 49	L	25862
Thu	7/12	A	TOR	15- 48	L	29304
Sat	7/21	H	TOR	33- 10	W	28202
Sat	7/28	H	BC	27-32	L	28564
Sat	8/4	A	EDM	34- 32	W	32644
Thu	8/9	A	MTL	18- 30	L	20202
Fri	8/17	H	BC	45- 45	T*	30826
Mon	9/3	H	EDM	35- 24	W	35650
Fri	9/7	A	EDM	20- 17	W	42329
Sat	9/15	H	SAS	44- 22	W	35650
Fri	9/21	A	HAM	20- 24	L	23115
Sat	9/29	A	BC	9- 42	L	32263
Mon	10/8	H	SAS	21- 33	L	33075
Sun	10/14	H	WPG	38- 25	W	30897
Fri	10/19	A	WPG	13- 27	L	23955
Sat	10/27	H	MTL	32- 33	L	29247
Sat	11/3	A	BC	24- 25	L	34242
Western Semi-Final						
Sun	11/11	A	SAS	24- 26	L	28800

2007 EDMONTON ESKIMOS

Thu	6/28	H	WPG	39- 39	T*	33038
Fri	7/6	A	BC	9- 29	L	32893
Fri	7/13	A	WPG	19- 15	W	29533
Fri	7/20	H	SAS	21- 20	W	46704
Sat	7/28	A	SAS	14- 54	L	26840
Sat	8/4	H	CAL	32- 34	L	32644
Sat	8/11	H	HAM	19- 17	W	35750
Sat	8/18	A	SAS	32- 39	L	28800
Mon	9/3	A	CAL	24- 35	L	35650
Fri	9/7	H	CAL	17- 20	L	42329
Fri	9/14	H	MTL	47- 28	W	36280
Sun	9/23	A	MTL	16- 10	W	20202
Fri	9/28	H	TOR	11- 18	L	31056
Sat	10/6	A	TOR	8- 33	L	28354
Sat	10/13	H	BC	18- 24	L	33663
Sat	10/20	A	BC	26- 37	L	37011
Fri	10/26	H	SAS	29- 36	L*	40127
Sat	11/3	A	HAM	19- 21	L	20411

2007 HAMILTON TIGER-CATS

Sat	6/30	A	CAL	9- 37	L	29103
Sat	7/7	H	TOR	5- 30	L	28198
Sat	7/14	H	MTL	20- 29	L	21542
Thu	7/19	A	BC	18- 22	L	29045
Fri	7/27	A	WPG	18- 36	L	29533
Fri	8/3	H	WPG	43- 22	W	24201
Sat	8/11	A	EDM	17- 19	L	35750
Sat	8/25	A	MTL	9- 27	L	20202
Mon	9/3	H	TOR	14- 32	L	28644
Sat	9/8	A	TOR	22- 35	L	28279
Sat	9/15	H	WPG	4- 34	L	21205
Fri	9/21	H	CAL	24- 20	W	23115
Sat	9/29	A	WPG	19- 21	L	27102
Mon	10/8	A	MTL	19- 27	L	20202
Sun	10/14	H	SAS	23- 40	L	22167
Sun	10/21	A	SAS	11- 38	L	28800
Fri	10/26	H	BC	19- 27	L	19322
Sat	11/3	H	EDM	21- 19	W	20411

2007 MONTREAL ALOUETTES

Fri	6/29	H	SAS	7- 16	L	20202
Thu	7/5	A	WPG	23- 32	L	29533
Sat	7/14	A	HAM	29- 20	W	21542
Thu	7/19	H	WPG	18- 20	L	20202
Thu	7/26	A	TOR	26- 13	W	31097
Thu	8/2	H	TOR	29- 27	W*	20202
Thu	8/9	H	CAL	30- 18	W	20202
Sat	8/25	H	HAM	27- 9	W	20202
Fri	8/31	A	BC	14- 46	L	32115
Sun	9/9	H	BC	32- 14	W	20202
Fri	9/14	A	EDM	28- 47	L	36280
Sun	9/23	H	EDM	10- 16	L	20202
Sat	9/29	A	SAS	22- 33	L	28800
Mon	10/8	H	HAM	27- 19	W	20202
Fri	10/12	A	TOR	17- 35	L	31416
Sat	10/20	H	TOR	9- 16	L	44510
Sat	10/27	A	CAL	33- 32	W	29247
Fri	11/2	A	WPG	17- 20	L	23744
Eastern Semi-Final						
Sun	11/11	A	WPG	22- 24	L	22843

2007 SASKATCHEWAN ROUGHRIDERS

Fri	6/29	A	MTL	16- 7	W	20202
Sun	7/8	H	CAL	49- 8	W	[illegible]
Fri	7/13	H	BC	12- 42	L	26981
Fri	7/20	A	EDM	20- 21	L	46704
Sat	7/28	H	EDM	54- 14	W	26840
Thu	8/2	A	BC	21- 9	W	31858
Fri	8/10	A	TOR	24- 13	W	34234
Sat	8/18	H	EDM	39- 32	W	28800
Sun	9/2	H	WPG	31- 26	W	28800
Sun	9/9	A	WPG	15- 34	L	29783
Sat	9/15	A	CAL	22- 44	L	35650
Sat	9/22	H	BC	34- 37	L	28800
Sat	9/29	H	MTL	33- 22	W	28800
Mon	10/8	A	CAL	33- 21	W	33075
Sun	10/14	A	HAM	40- 23	W	22167
Sun	10/21	H	HAM	38- 11	W*	28800
Fri	10/26	A	EDM	36- 29	W	40127
Sat	11/3	H	TOR	13- 41	L	28800
Western Semi-Final						
Sun	11/11	H	CAL	26- 24	W	28800
Western Final						
Sun	11/18	A	BC	26- 17	W	54712
Grey Cup						
Sun	11/25	N	WPG	23- 19	W	52230

2007 TORONTO ARGONAUTS

Thu	6/28	H	BC	22- 24	L	29157
Sat	7/7	A	HAM	30- 5	W	28198
Thu	7/12	H	CAL	48- 15	W	29304
Sat	7/21	A	CAL	10- 33	L	28202
Thu	7/26	H	MTL	13- 26	L	31097
Thu	8/2	A	MTL	27-29	L*	20202
Fri	8/10	H	SAS	13- 24	L	34234
Fri	8/24	A	WPG	13- 15	L	29533
Mon	9/3	A	HAM	32- 14	W	28644
Sat	9/8	H	HAM	35- 22	W	28279
Sat	9/15	A	BC	7- 40	L	31156
Sun	9/23	H	WPG	31- 23	W	26423
Fri	9/28	A	EDM	18- 11	W	31056
Sat	10/6	H	EDM	33- 8	W	28354
Fri	10/12	H	MTL	35- 17	W	31416
Sat	10/20	A	MTL	16- 9	W	44510
Sat	10/27	H	WPG	16- 8	W	40116
Sat	11/3	A	SAS	41- 13	W	28800
Eastern Final						
Sun	11/18	H	WPG	9- 19	L	33467

2007 WINNIPEG BLUE BOMBERS

Thu	6/28	A	EDM	39- 39	T*	33038
Thu	7/5	H	MTL	32- 23	W	29533
Fri	7/13	H	EDM	15- 19	L	29533
Thu	7/19	A	MTL	20- 18	W	20202
Fri	7/27	H	HAM	36- 18	W	29533
Fri	8/3	A	HAM	22- 43	L	24201
Fri	8/10	A	BC	22- 21	W	31525
Fri	8/24	H	TOR	15- 13	W	29533
Sun	9/2	A	SAS	26- 31	L	28800
Sun	9/9	H	SAS	34- 15	W	29783
Sat	9/15	A	HAM	34- 4	W	21205
Sun	9/23	A	TOR	23- 31	L	26423
Sat	9/29	H	HAM	21- 19	W	27102
Fri	10/5	H	BC	20- 26	L	26593
Sun	10/14	A	CAL	25- 38	L	30897
Fri	10/19	H	CAL	27- 13	W	23955
Sat	10/27	A	TOR	8- 16	L	40116
Fri	11/2	H	MTL	20- 17	W	23744
Eastern Semi-Final						
Sun	11/11	H	MTL	24- 22	W	22843
Eastern Final						
Sun	11/18	A	TOR	19- 9	W	33467
Grey Cup						
Sun	11/25	N	SAS	19- 23	L	52230

2008 BRITISH COLUMBIA LIONS

Thu	6/26	A	CAL	18- 28	L	30159
Fri	7/4	H	SAS	16- 26	L	33813
Fri	7/11	A	WPG	42- 24	W	26735
Fri	7/18	H	WPG	27- 18	W	37174
Fri	7/25	H	MTL	36- 34	W	30132
Thu	7/31	A	EDM	24- 35	L	35008
Fri	8/8	H	EDM	40- 34	W	30863
Fri	8/22	H	CAL	29- 36	L	34221
Fri	8/29	A	MTL	25- 30	L	20202
Sat	9/6	A	HAM	35- 12	W	18723

Sat 9/13 H SAS 28- 23 W 38608
Sat 9/20 A SAS 27- 21 W 30945
Sat 9/27 H HAM 40- 10 W 31161
Fri 10/3 A TOR 24- 20 W 28273
Fri 10/10 H EDM 20- 27 L 34778
Fri 10/17 A EDM 43- 28 W 34342
Sat 10/25 H TOR 55- 32 W 35994
Sat 11/1 A CAL 30- 41 L 30275
Western Semi-Final
Sat 11/8 A SAS 33- 12 W 30945
Western Final
Sat 11/15 A CAL 18- 22 L 35650

2008 CALGARY STAMPEDERS
Thu 6/26 H BC 28- 18 W 30159
Thu 7/3 A EDM 31- 34 L 32706
Thu 7/10 A MTL 23- 19 W 20202
Thu 7/17 H HAM 43- 16 W 31116
Thu 7/24 A WPG 28- 32 L 26882
Sat 8/2 H SAS 21- 22 L 35650
Thu 8/7 A SAS 30- 25 W 28800
Fri 8/22 A BC 36- 29 W 34221
Mon 9/1 H EDM 16- 37 L 35650
Fri 9/5 A EDM 38- 33 W 46014
Fri 9/12 H MTL 41- 30 W 30960
Sat 9/20 H TOR 34- 4 W 33135
Sat 9/27 A TOR 44- 16 W 28672
Fri 10/3 A SAS 34- 37 L 30945
Mon 10/13 H SAS 42- 5 W 35650
Sat 10/18 H WPG 37- 16 W 30110
Fri 10/24 A HAM 28- 17 W 20614
Sat 11/1 H BC 41- 30 W 30275
Western Final
Sat 11/15 H BC 22- 18 W 35650
Grey Cup
Sun 11/23 A MTL 22- 14 W 66308

2008 EDMONTON ESKIMOS
Sat 6/28 A SAS 13- 34 L 28800
Thu 7/3 H CAL 34- 31 W 32706
Thu 7/10 H TOR 47- 28 W 31707
Sun 7/20 A TOR 31- 35 L 28522
Fri 7/25 A HAM 19- 13 W 21402
Thu 7/31 H BC 35- 24 W 35008
Fri 8/8 A BC 34- 40 L 30863
Thu 8/21 H SAS 27- 10 W 48808
Mon 9/1 A CAL 37- 16 W 35650
Fri 9/5 H CAL 33- 38 L 46014
Sat 9/13 H HAM 38- 33 W 37500
Sun 9/21 A MTL 4- 40 L 20202
Fri 9/26 A WPG 23- 30 L 29794
Sat 10/4 H WPG 36- 22 W 40453
Fri 10/10 A BC 27- 20 W 34778
Fri 10/17 H BC 28- 43 L 34342
Sat 10/25 A SAS 9- 55 L 30945
Fri 10/31 H MTL 37- 14 W 29911
Eastern Semi-Final
Sat 11/8 A WPG 29- 21 W 27493
Eastern Final
Sat 11/15 A MTL 26- 36 L 38132

2008 HAMILTON TIGER-CATS
Thu 6/26 H MTL 10- 33 L 20589
Thu 7/3 A TOR 32- 13 W 30822
Sat 7/12 H SAS 28- 33 W 20874
Thu 7/17 A CAL 16- 43 L 31116
Fri 7/25 H EDM 13- 19 L 21402
Thu 7/31 A MTL 33- 40 L 20202
Thu 8/7 H TOR 45- 21 W 19423
Thu 8/14 A WPG 24- 37 L 25484
Mon 9/1 H TOR 31- 34 L 25911
Sat 9/6 H BC 12- 35 L 18723
Sat 9/13 A EDM 33- 38 L 37500
Fri 9/19 H WPG 23- 25 L 19102
Sat 9/27 A BC 10- 40 L 31161
Sat 10/4 H MTL 44- 38 W 20423
Mon 10/13 A MTL 11- 42 L 20202
Sun 10/19 A SAS 29-30 L 30945
Fri 10/24 H CAL 17- 28 L 20614
Sat 11/1 A WPG 30-44 L 24595

2008 MONTREAL ALOUETTES
Thu 6/26 A HAM 33- 10 W 20589
Fri 7/4 H WPG 38- 24 W 20202
Thu 7/10 H CAL 19- 23 L 20202
Sat 7/19 A SAS 33- 41 L 28800
Fri 7/25 A BC 34- 36 L 30132
Thu 7/31 H HAM 40- 33 W 20202
Fri 8/8 A WPG 39- 11 W 27674
Fri 8/15 A TOR 32- 14 W 30521
Fri 8/29 H BC 30- 25 W 20202
Sun 9/7 H TOR 45- 19 W 20202
Fri 9/12 A CAL 30- 41 L 30960
Sun 9/21 H EDM 40- 4 W 20202
Sun 9/28 H SAS 37- 12 W 20202
Sat 10/4 A HAM 38- 44 L 20423
Mon 10/13 H HAM 42- 11 W 20202
Sat 10/18 A TOR 43- 34 W 30262
Sun 10/26 H WPG 23- 24 L 20202
Fri 10/31 A EDM 14- 37 L 29911
Eastern Final
Sat 11/15 H EDM 36- 26 W 38132
Grey Cup
Sun 11/23 H CAL 14- 22 L 66308

2008 SASKATCHEWAN ROUGHRIDERS
Sat 6/28 H EDM 34- 13 W 28800
Fri 7/4 A BC 26- 16 W 33813
Sat 7/12 A HAM 33- 28 W 20874
Sat 7/19 H MTL 41- 33 W 28800
Sun 7/27 H TOR 28- 22 W 28800
Sat 8/2 A CAL 22- 21 W 35650
Thu 8/7 H CAL 25- 30 L 28800
Thu 8/21 A EDM 10- 27 L 48808
Sun 8/31 H WPG 19- 6 W 30985
Sun 9/7 A WPG 34- 31 W 29770
Sat 9/13 A BC 23- 28 L 38608
Sat 9/20 H BC 21- 27 L 30945
Sun 9/28 A MTL 12- 37 L 20202
Fri 10/3 H CAL 37- 34 W 30945
Mon 10/13 A CAL 5- 42 L 35650
Sun 10/19 H HAM 30- 29 W 30945
Sat 10/25 H EDM 55- 9 W 30945
Thu 10/30 A TOR 45- 38 W 28654
Western Semi-Final
Sat 11/8 H BC 12- 33 L 30945

2008 TORONTO ARGONAUTS
Fri 6/27 A WPG 23- 16 W 26155
Thu 7/3 H HAM 13- 32 L 30822
Thu 7/10 A EDM 28- 47 L 31707
Sun 7/20 H EDM 35- 31 W 28522
Sun 7/27 A SAS 22- 28 L 28800
Fri 8/1 H WPG 19- 11 W 28523
Thu 8/7 A HAM 21- 45 L 19423
Fri 8/15 H MTL 14- 32 L 30521
Mon 9/1 A HAM 34- 31 W 25911
Sun 9/7 A MTL 19- 45 L 20202
Fri 9/12 H WPG 9- 39 L 28543
Sat 9/20 A CAL 4- 34 L 33135
Sat 9/27 H CAL 16- 44 L 28672
Fri 10/3 H BC 20- 24 L 28273
Fri 10/10 A WPG 16- 25 L 27268
Sat 10/18 H MTL 34- 43 W 30262
Sat 10/25 A BC 32- 55 L 35994
Thu 10/30 H SAS 38- 45 W 28654

2008 WINNIPEG BLUE BOMBERS
Fri 6/27 H TOR 16- 23 L 26155
Fri 7/4 A MTL 24- 38 L 20202
Fri 7/11 H BC 24- 42 L 26735
Fri 7/18 A BC 18- 27 L 37174
Thu 7/24 H CAL 32- 28 W 26882
Fri 8/1 A TOR 11- 19 L 28523
Fri 8/8 H MTL 11- 39 L 27674
Thu 8/14 H HAM 37- 24 W 25484
Sun 8/31 A SAS 6- 19 L 30985
Sun 9/7 H SAS 31- 34 L 29770
Fri 9/12 A TOR 39- 9 W 28543
Fri 9/19 A HAM 25- 23 W 19102
Fri 9/26 H EDM 30- 23 W 29794
Sat 10/4 A EDM 22- 36 L 40453
Fri 10/10 H TOR 25- 16 W 27268
Sat 10/18 A CAL 16- 37 L 30110
Sun 10/26 A MTL 24- 23 W 20202
Sat 11/1 H HAM 44- 30 W 24595
Eastern Semi-Final
Sat 11/8 H EDM 21- 29 L 27493

2009 BRITISH COLUMBIA LIONS
Fri 7/3 A SAS 24- 28 L 30062
Fri 7/10 H HAM 28- 31 L 26885
Thu 7/16 A EDM 40- 22 W 33661
Fri 7/24 H CAL 10- 48 L 27191
Fri 7/31 A HAM 18- 30 L 20103
Fri 8/7 H SAS 35- 20 W 30117
Fri 8/14 A TOR 36- 28 W 24754
Fri 8/21 H WPG 10- 37 L 27983
Fri 9/4 H MTL 19- 12 W 27199
Sun 9/13 A MTL 24- 28 L 20202
Sat 9/19 H TOR 23- 17 W 27515
Fri 9/25 A CAL 18- 27 L 36702
Fri 10/2 H SAS 19- 16 W 31958
Fri 10/9 A EDM 34- 31 W 30120
Sun 10/18 A WPG 24-21 W 24048
Sat 10/24 A SAS 30- 33 L* 30945
Sat 10/31 H CAL 26- 28 L 27131
Fri 11/6 H EDM 13- 45 L 31515
Eastern Semi-Final
Sun 11/15 A HAM 34- 27 W 27430
Eastern Final
Sun 11/22 A MTL 18- 56 L 53792

2009 CALGARY STAMPEDERS
Wed 7/1 H MTL 27- 40 L 35650
Fri 7/10 A WPG 30- 42 L 29533
Fri 7/17 H TOR 44- 9 W 33109
Fri 7/24 A BC 48- 10 W 27191
Sat 8/1 H SAS 23- 24 L 35650
Sat 8/8 H WPG 31- 23 W 35650
Thu 8/13 A EDM 35- 38 L 33065
Fri 8/28 A TOR 23- 20 W 25329
Mon 9/7 H EDM 32- 8 W 40729
Fri 9/11 A EDM 35- 34 W 46212
Fri 9/18 A HAM 17- 24 L 19448
Fri 9/25 H BC 27- 18 W 36702
Sat 10/3 H HAM 15- 14 W 36753
Mon 10/12 A MTL 11- 32 L 20202
Sat 10/17 H SAS 44- 44 T* 36823
Fri 10/23 H EDM 30- 7 W 35650
Sat 10/31 A BC 28- 26 W 27131
Sat 11/7 A SAS 14- 30 L 30945
Western Semi-Final
Sun 11/15 H EDM 24- 21 W 31356
Western Final
Sun 11/22 A SAS 17- 27 L 30945

2009 EDMONTON ESKIMOS
Thu 7/2 H WPG 19- 17 W 30650
Thu 7/9 A MTL 16- 50 L 20202
Thu 7/16 H BC 22- 40 L 33661
Sat 7/25 A SAS 38- 33 W 30945
Thu 7/30 H MTL 33- 19 W 33206
Sat 8/8 A HAM 21- 28 L 19206
Thu 8/13 H CAL 38- 25 W 33065
Sat 8/29 H HAM 31- 30 W 35036
Mon 9/7 A CAL 8- 32 L 40729
Fri 9/11 H CAL 34- 35 L 46212
Sun 9/20 A SAS 31- 27 W 30945
Sat 9/26 H SAS 20- 23 L 62517
Fri 10/2 A WPG 17- 27 L 21965
Fri 10/9 H BC 31- 34 L 30120
Fri 10/16 A TOR 22- 19 W 26515
Fri 10/23 A CAL 7- 30 L 35650
Fri 10/30 H TOR 36- 10 W 30012
Fri 11/6 A BC 45- 13 W 31515
Western Semi-Final
Sun 11/15 A CAL 21- 24 L 31356

2009 HAMILTON TIGER-CATS
Wed 7/1 H TOR 17- 30 L 23211
Fri 7/10 A BC 31- 28 W 26885
Sat 7/18 H WPG 25- 13 W 24292
Thu 7/23 A MTL 8- 21 L 20202
Fri 7/31 H BC 30-18 W 20103
Sat 8/8 H EDM 28- 21 W 19206
Sun 8/16 A SAS 23- 33 L 30360
Sat 8/29 A EDM 30- 31 L 35036
Mon 9/7 H TOR 34- 15 W 30293
Fri 9/11 A TOR 22- 25 L* 26421
Fri 9/18 H CAL 24- 17 W 19448
Fri 9/25 H MTL 8- 42 L 22083
Sat 10/3 A CAL 14- 15 L 36753
Mon 10/12 H WPG 28- 38 L 19562
Sun 10/18 A MTL 38-41 L 20202
Fri 10/23 A TOR 26-1 7 W 25352
Sat 10/31 H SAS 24- 6 W 24586
Sun 11/8 A WPG 39- 17 W 29038
Eastern Semi-Final
Sun 11/15 H BC 27- 34 L 27430

2009 MONTREAL ALOUETTES
Wed 7/1 A CAL 40- 27 W 35650
Thu 7/9 H EDM 50- 16 W 20202
Sat 7/18 A SAS 43-10 W 30945
Thu 7/23 H HAM 21- 8 W 20202
Thu 7/30 A EDM 19- 33 L 33206
Fri 8/7 H TOR 25- 0 W 20202
Sat 8/15 A WPG 39- 12 W 25053
Fri 8/21 H SAS 34- 25 W 20202
Fri 9/4 A BC 12- 19 L 27199
Sun 9/13 H BC 28- 24 W 20202
Sun 9/20 H WPG 33- 14 W 20202
Fri 9/25 A HAM 42- 8 W 22083
Sat 10/3 A TOR 27- 8 W 26828
Mon 10/12 H CAL 32- 11 W 20202
Sun 10/18 H HAM 41- 38 W 20202
Sat 10/24 A WPG 24- 41 L 21378
Mon 11/1 H WPG 48- 13 W 20202
Sat 11/7 A TOR 42- 17 W 28293
Division Final
Sun 11/22 H BC 56- 18 W 53792
Grey Cup
Sun 11/29 N SAS 28- 27 W 46020

2009 SASKATCHEWAN ROUGHRIDERS
Fri 7/3 H BC 28- 24 W 30062
Sat 7/11 A TOR 46- 36 W 30055
Sat 7/18 H MTL 10- 43 L 30945
Sat 7/25 H EDM 33- 38 L 30945
Sat 8/1 A CAL 24- 23 W 35650
Fri 8/7 A BC 20- 35 L 30117
Sat 8/16 H SAS 33- 23 W 30360
Fri 8/21 A MTL 25- 34 L 20202
Sun 9/6 H WPG 29- 14 W 30945
Sun 9/13 A WPG 55- 10 W 29553
Sun 9/20 H EDM 27- 31 L 30945
Sat 9/26 A EDM 23- 20 W 62517
Fri 10/2 A BC 16- 19 L 31958
Sat 10/10 H TOR 32- 22 W 29361
Sat 10/17 A CAL 44- 44 T* 38623
Sat 10/24 H BC 33- 30 W* 30945
Sat 10/31 A HAM 6- 24 L 24586
Sat 11/7 H CAL 30-14 W 30945
Western Final
Sun 11/22 H CAL 27- 17 W 30945
Grey Cup
Sun 11/29 N MTL 27- 28 L 46020

2009 TORONTO ARGONAUTS

Wed	7/1	A	HAM	30-17	W	23211
Sat	7/11	H	SAS	36-46	L	30055
Fri	7/17	A	CAL	9-44	L	33109
Fri	7/24	A	WPG	19-5	W	28466
Sat	8/1	H	WPG	12-13	L	23821
Fri	8/7	A	MTL	0-25	L	20202
Fri	8/14	H	BC	28-36	L	24754
Fri	8/28	H	CAL	20-23	L	25329
Mon	9/7	A	HAM	15-34	L	30293
Fri	9/11	H	HAM	25-22	W*	26421
Sat	9/19	A	BC	17-23	L	27515
Sat	9/26	A	WPG	24-29	W	22446
Sat	10/3	H	MTL	8-27	L	26828
Sat	10/10	A	SAS	22-33	L	29361
Fri	10/16	H	EDM	19-22	L	26515
Fri	10/23	H	HAM	17-26	L	25352
Fri	10/30	A	EDM	10-36	L	30012
Sat	11/7	H	MTL	17-42	L	28293

2009 WINNIPEG BLUE BOMBERS

Thu	7/2	A	EDM	17-19	L	30650
Fri	7/10	H	CAL	42-30	W	29533
Sat	7/18	A	HAM	13-25	L	24292
Fri	7/24	H	TOR	5-19	L	28466
Sat	8/1	A	TOR	13-12	W	23821
Sat	8/8	A	CAL	23-31	L	35650
Sat	8/15	H	MTL	12-39	L	25063
Fri	8/21	A	BC	37-10	W	27983
Sun	9/6	A	SAS	14-29	L	30945
Sun	9/13	H	SAS	10-55	L	29553
Sun	9/20	A	MTL	14-33	L	20202
Sat	9/26	H	TOR	29-24	W	22446
Fri	10/2	H	EDM	27-17	W	21965
Mon	10/12	A	HAM	38-28	W	19562
Sun	10/18	H	BC	21-24	L	24048
Sat	10/24	H	MTL	41-24	W	21378
Sun	11/1	A	MTL	13-48	L	20202
Sun	11/8	H	HAM	17-39	L	29038

2010 BRITISH COLUMBIA LIONS

Sun	7/4	A	EDM	25-10	W	32439
Sat	7/10	H	SAS	18-37	L	29517
Fri	7/16	H	MTL	12-16	L	25162
Fri	7/23	A	TOR	20-24	L	19709
Fri	7/30	A	EDM	25-28	L	32281
Thu	8/12	A	SAS	13-37	L	30045
Fri	8/27	H	CAL	35-48	L	25127
Fri	9/3	A	MTL	38-17	W	25012
Sat	9/11	H	TOR	37-16	W	22703
Sat	9/18	H	HAM	31-35	L	21481
Sat	9/25	A	CAL	29-10	W	29637
Sat	10/2	H	WPG	16-14	W	23186
Mon	10/11	A	WPG	35-47	L	25016
Sat	10/16	H	EDM	28-31	L	21414
Fri	10/22	A	CAL	36-31	W	28054
Sun	10/31	H	SAS	17-23	L	25479
Sat	11/6	A	HAM	23-21	W	23913
Western Semi-Final						
Sun	11/14	A	SAS	38-41	L	29215

2010 CALGARY STAMPEDERS

Thu	7/1	H	TOR	30-16	W	29333
Sat	7/10	A	HAM	23-22	W	25248
Wed	7/14	A	TOR	24-27	L	20242
Sat	7/24	H	SAS	40-20	W	35650
Sat	7/31	H	WPG	23-20	W	30150
Sun	8/15	H	EDM	56-15	W	30242
Fri	8/27	A	BC	48-35	W	25127
Mon	9/6	H	EDM	52-5	W	34559
Fri	9/10	A	EDM	36-20	W	35349
Fri	9/17	A	SAS	37-43	L	30048
Sat	9/25	H	BC	10-29	L	29637
Fri	10/1	H	MTL	46-21	W	31167
Mon	10/11	A	MTL	19-46	L	25012
Sun	10/17	A	SAS	34-26	W	30048
Fri	10/22	H	BC	31-36	L	28054
Fri	10/29	H	HAM	24-55	L	27644
Fri	11/5	A	WPG	35-32	W	22056
Western Final						
Sun	11/21	H	SAS	16-20	L	35650

2010 EDMONTON ESKIMOS

Sun	7/4	H	BC	10-25	L	32439
Sun	7/11	H	MTL	23-33	L	30442
Sat	7/17	A	SAS	20-24	L	30048
Sat	7/24	A	WPG	21-47	L	26041
Fri	7/30	H	BC	28-25	W	32281
Fri	8/6	H	TOR	28-29	L	31888
Sun	8/15	A	CAL	15-56	L	30242
Sat	8/28	H	SAS	17-14	W	47829
Mon	9/6	A	CAL	5-52	L	34559
Fri	9/10	H	CAL	20-36	L	35349
Sun	9/19	A	MTL	14-31	L	25012
Sun	9/26	A	TOR	24-6	W	20725
Sun	10/3	H	HAM	27-35	L	34479
Fri	10/8	A	HAM	11-36	L	20791
Sat	10/16	A	BC	31-28	W	21414
Sat	10/23	H	SAS	39-24	W	38325
Sat	10/30	H	WPG	13-16	L	32192
Sat	11/6	A	SAS	23-31	L	30048

2010 HAMILTON TIGER-CATS

Fri	7/2	A	WPG	29-49	W	26302
Sat	7/10	H	CAL	22-23	L	25248
Fri	7/16	H	WPG	28-7	W	21408
Thu	7/22	A	MTL	14-37	L	25012
Sat	7/31	A	SAS	24-37	L	30048
Sat	8/7	H	WPG	29-22	W	23653
Fri	8/13	A	WPG	39-28	W	27892
Fri	8/20	A	TOR	16-12	W	24493
Mon	9/6	H	TOR	28-13	W	30319
Sat	9/11	H	MTL	6-27	L	23452
Sat	9/18	A	BC	35-31	W	21481
Sat	9/25	H	SAS	25-32	L	23108
Sun	10/3	A	EDM	35-27	W	34479
Fri	10/8	H	EDM	36-11	W	20791
Fri	10/15	A	TOR	30-3	W	25181
Fri	10/22	H	MTL	40-3	W	23118
Fri	10/29	A	CAL	55-24	W	27644
Sat	11/6	H	BC	21-23	L	23913
Eastern Semi-Final						
Sun	11/14	H	TOR	13-16	L	27828

2010 MONTREAL ALOUETTES

Thu	7/1	A	SAS	51-54	W	30048
Sun	7/11	A	EDM	33-23	W	30442
Fri	7/16	A	BC	16-12	W	25162
Thu	7/22	H	HAM	37-14	W	25012
Thu	7/29	H	TOR	41-10	W	25012
Fri	8/6	H	SAS	30-26	W	25012
Sat	8/14	A	TOR	22-37	L	22311
Thu	8/19	H	WPG	39-17	W	25012
Fri	9/3	H	BC	17-38	L	25012
Sat	9/11	A	HAM	27-6	W	23452
Sun	9/19	H	EDM	31-14	W	25012
Fri	9/24	A	WPG	44-40	W	26154
Fri	10/1	A	CAL	21-46	L	31167
Mon	10/11	H	CAL	46-19	W	25012
Sun	10/17	H	WPG	22-19	W	25012
Fri	10/22	A	HAM	3-40	L	23118
Fri	10/29	A	TOR	37-30	W	22427
Sun	11/7	H	TOR	4-30	L	25012
Eastern Final						
Sun	11/21	H	TOR	48-17	W	58021
Grey Cup						
Sun	11/28	N	SAS	21-18	W	63317

2010 SASKATCHEWAN ROUGHRIDERS

Thu	7/1	H	MTL	54-51	L	30048
Sat	7/10	A	BC	37-18	W	29517
Sat	7/17	H	EDM	24-20	W	30048
Sat	7/24	A	CAL	20-40	L	35650
Sat	7/31	H	HAM	37-24	W	30048
Fri	8/6	A	MTL	26-30	L	25012
Thu	8/12	H	BC	37-13	W	30045
Sat	8/28	A	EDM	14-17	L	47829
Sun	9/5	H	WPG	27-23	W	30048
Sun	9/12	A	WPG	2-31	L	29833
Fri	9/17	H	CAL	43-37	W	30048
Sat	9/25	A	HAM	32-25	W	23108
Sat	10/2	A	TOR	27-16	W	23873
Sat	10/9	H	TOR	19-24	L	30048
Sun	10/17	H	CAL	26-34	L	30048
Sat	10/23	A	EDM	24-39	L	38325
Sun	10/31	A	BC	23-17	W	25479
Sat	11/6	H	EDM	31-23	W	30048
Western Semi-Final						
Sun	11/14	H	BC	41-38	W	29215
Western Final						
Sun	11/21	A	CAL	20-16	W	35650
Grey Cup						
Sun	11/28	N	MTL	18-21	L	63317

2010 TORONTO ARGONAUTS

Thu	7/1	A	CAL	16-30	L	29333
Fri	7/9	A	WPG	36-34	W	28009
Wed	7/14	H	CAL	27-24	W	20242
Fri	7/23	H	BC	24-20	W	19709
Thu	7/29	A	MTL	10-41	L	25012
Fri	8/6	A	EDM	29-28	W	31888
Sat	8/14	H	MTL	37-22	W	22311
Fri	8/20	H	HAM	12-16	L	24493
Mon	9/6	A	HAM	13-28	L	30319
Sat	9/11	A	BC	16-37	L	22703
Sun	9/19	H	WPG	17-13	W	19662
Sun	9/26	H	EDM	6-24	L	20725
Sat	10/2	H	SAS	16-27	L	23873
Sat	10/9	A	SAS	24-19	W	30048
Fri	10/15	H	HAM	3-30	L	25181
Sat	10/23	A	WPG	27-8	W	23446
Fri	10/29	H	MTL	30-37	L	22427
Sun	11/7	A	MTL	30-4	W	25012
Eastern Semi-Final						
Sun	11/14	A	HAM	16-13	W	27828
Eastern Final						
Sun	11/21	A	MTL	17-48	L	58021

2010 WINNIPEG BLUE BOMBERS

Fri	7/2	H	HAM	49-29	L	26302
Fri	7/9	H	TOR	34-36	L	28009
Fri	7/16	A	HAM	7-28	L	21408
Sat	7/24	H	EDM	47-21	W	26041
Sat	7/31	A	CAL	20-23	L	30150
Sat	8/7	A	HAM	22-29	L	23653
Fri	8/13	H	HAM	28-39	L	27892
Thu	8/19	A	MTL	17-39	L	25012
Sun	9/5	A	SAS	23-27	L	30048
Sun	9/12	H	SAS	31-2	W	29833
Sun	9/19	A	TOR	13-17	L	19662
Fri	9/24	H	MTL	40-44	L	26154
Sat	10/2	A	BC	14-16	L	23186
Mon	10/11	H	BC	47-35	W	25016
Sun	10/17	A	MTL	19-22	L	25012
Sat	10/23	H	TOR	8-27	L	23446
Sat	10/30	A	EDM	16-13	W	32192
Fri	11/5	H	CAL	32-35	L	22056

2011 BRITISH COLUMBIA LIONS

Thu	6/30	A	MTL	26-30	L	22317
Fri	7/8	H	CAL	32-34	L	22738
Sat	7/16	A	EDM	17-33	L	32297
Fri	7/22	H	HAM	31-39	L	24117
Thu	7/28	A	WPG	20-25	L	29553
Fri	8/5	H	SAS	24-11	W	25238
Sat	8/13	H	WPG	17-30	L	24131
Fri	8/19	A	EDM	36-1	W	35216
Fri	9/2	A	TOR	29-16	W	19593
Sat	9/10	H	TOR	28-6	W	25263
Sat	9/17	A	CAL	32-19	W	29929
Sat	9/24	A	SAS	42-5	W	30048
Fri	9/30	H	EDM	33-24	W	50213
Sat	10/8	H	CAL	33-31	W	30622
Sun	10/16	A	SAS	29-18	W	30048
Sat	10/22	A	HAM	10-42	L	25536
Sat	10/29	H	EDM	29-20	W	29749
Sat	11/5	H	MTL	43-1	W	35454
Western Final						
Sun	11/20	H	EDM	40-23	W	41313
Grey Cup						
Sun	11/27	N	WPG	34-23	W	54313

2011 CALGARY STAMPEDERS

Fri	7/1	H	TOR	21-23	L	27428
Fri	7/8	A	BC	34-32	W	22738
Thu	7/14	A	WPG	21-20	W	27890
Sat	7/23	H	EDM	19-24	L	29910
Sat	7/30	A	SAS	22-18	W	30048
Sat	8/6	H	HAM	32-20	W	29307
Fri	8/12	A	SAS	45-35	W	30048
Sat	8/27	H	MTL	38-31	W	30386
Mon	9/5	H	EDM	7-35	L	35650
Fri	9/9	A	EDM	30-20	W	45672
Sat	9/17	H	BC	19-32	L	29929
Sun	9/25	A	HAM	36-55	L	20153
Sat	10/1	H	SAS	40-3	W	33469
Sat	10/8	A	BC	31-33	L	30622
Fri	10/14	A	TOR	29-31	L	18720
Fri	10/21	H	SAS	25-13	W	29698
Sun	10/30	A	MTL	32-27	W	24051
Sat	11/5	H	WPG	30-24	W	29076
Western Semi-Final						
Sun	11/13	A	EDM	19-33	L	30183

2011 EDMONTON ESKIMOS

Sun	7/3	A	SAS	42-28	W	30048
Sat	7/9	H	HAM	28-10	W	26059
Sat	7/16	H	BC	33-17	W	32297
Sat	7/23	A	CAL	24-19	W	29910
Fri	7/29	H	TOR	26-25	W	32478
Fri	8/5	A	WPG	16-28	L	29533
Thu	8/11	A	MTL	4-27	L	24448
Fri	8/19	H	BC	1-36	L	35216
Mon	9/5	A	CAL	35-7	W	35650
Fri	9/9	H	CAL	20-30	L	45672
Fri	9/16	A	HAM	38-23	W	22654
Fri	9/23	H	MTL	21-34	L	40274
Fri	9/30	A	BC	24-33	L	50213
Mon	10/10	H	SAS	17-1	W	38054
Sat	10/15	H	WPG	24-10	W	30734
Fri	10/21	A	TOR	31-24	W	19176
Sat	10/29	A	BC	20-29	L	29749
Fri	11/4	H	SAS	23-20	W	30845
Western Semi-Final						
Sun	11/13	H	CAL	33-19	W	30183
Western Final						
Sun	11/20	A	BC	23-40	L	41313

2011 HAMILTON TIGER-CATS

Fri	7/1	H	WPG	16-24	L	23852
Sat	7/9	A	EDM	10-28	L	26059
Sat	7/16	H	SAS	33-3	W	22245
Fri	7/22	A	BC	39-31	W	24117
Fri	7/29	H	MTL	34-26	W	24068
Sat	8/6	A	CAL	20-32	L	29307
Sat	8/13	H	TOR	37-32	W	24347
Fri	8/26	A	WPG	27-30	L	30338
Mon	9/5	H	MTL	44-21	W	26964
Sun	9/11	A	MTL	13-43	L	24304
Fri	9/16	H	EDM	23-38	L	22654
Sun	9/25	H	CAL	55-36	W	20153
Sat	10/1	A	TOR	27-12	W	21853
Fri	10/7	H	WPG	17-33	L	23268
Sun	10/16	A	MTL	25-27	L	23668
Sat	10/22	H	BC	42-10	W	25536
Sat	10/29	A	SAS	3-19	L	29813
Thu	11/3	A	TOR	16-33	L	20833
Eastern Semi-Final						
Sun	11/13	A	MTL	52-44	W*	33051

Eastern Final

Sun	11/20	A	WPG	3-19	L	30051

2011 MONTREAL ALOUETTES

Thu	6/30	H	BC	30-26	W	22317
Sat	7/9	A	SAS	39-25	W	30045
Fri	7/15	H	TOR	40-17	W	24698
Sun	7/24	H	SAS	24-27	L	24434
Fri	7/29	A	HAM	26-34	L	24068
Thu	8/4	A	TOR	36-23	W	19204
Thu	8/11	H	EDM	27- 4	W	24448
Sat	8/27	A	CAL	31-38	L	30386
Mon	9/5	A	HAM	21-44	L	26964
Sun	9/11	H	HAM	43-13	W	24304
Sun	9/18	H	WPG	23-25	L	24642
Fri	9/23	A	EDM	34-21	W	40274
Fri	9/30	A	WPG	32-26	W	30447
Mon	10/10	H	TOR	29-19	W	23960
Sun	10/16	H	HAM	27-25	W	23668
Sat	10/22	A	WPG	25-26	L	30360
Sun	10/30	H	CAL	27-32	L	24051
Sat	11/5	A	BC	1-43	L	35454
Eastern Semi-Final						
Sun	11/13	H	HAM	44-52	L*	33051

2011 SASKATCHEWAN ROUGHRIDERS

Sun	7/3	H	EDM	28-42	L	30048
Sat	7/9	H	MTL	25-39	L	30045
Sat	7/16	A	HAM	3-33	L	22245
Sun	7/24	A	MTL	27-24	W	24434
Sat	7/30	H	CAL	18-22	L	30048
Fri	8/5	A	BC	11-24	L	25238
Fri	8/12	H	CAL	35-45	L	30048
Thu	8/18	A	TOR	18-24	L	20482
Sun	9/4	H	WPG	27- 7	W	30048
Sun	9/11	A	WPG	45-23	W	30518
Sat	9/17	H	TOR	30-20	W	30048
Sat	9/24	H	BC	5-42	W	30048
Sat	10/1	A	CAL	3-40	L	33469
Mon	10/10	A	EDM	1-17	L	38054
Sun	10/16	H	BC	18-29	L	30048
Fri	10/21	A	CAL	13-25	L	29698
Sat	10/29	H	HAM	19- 3	W	29813
Fri	11/4	A	EDM	20-23	L	30845

2011 TORONTO ARGONAUTS

Fri	7/1	A	CAL	23-21	W	27428
Fri	7/8	A	WPG	16-22	L	27638
Fri	7/15	A	MTL	17-40	L	24698
Sat	7/23	H	WPG	24-33	L	21189
Fri	7/29	A	EDM	25-26	L	32478
Thu	8/4	H	MTL	23-36	L	19204
Sat	8/13	A	HAM	32-37	L	24347
Thu	8/18	H	SAS	24-18	W	20482
Fri	9/2	H	BC	16-29	L	19593
Sat	9/10	A	BC	6-28	L	25263
Sat	9/17	A	SAS	20-30	L	30048
Sat	9/24	H	WPG	25-24	W	19108
Sat	10/1	H	HAM	12-27	L	21853
Mon	10/10	A	MTL	19-29	L	23960
Fri	10/14	H	CAL	31-29	W	18720
Fri	10/21	H	EDM	24-31	L	19176
Fri	10/28	A	WPG	27-22	W	29751
Thu	11/3	H	HAM	33-16	W	20833

2011 WINNIPEG BLUE BOMBERS

Fri	7/1	A	HAM	24-16	W	23852
Fri	7/8	H	TOR	22-16	W	27638
Thu	7/14	H	CAL	20-21	L	27890
Sat	7/23	A	TOR	33-24	W	21189
Thu	7/28	H	BC	25-20	W	29553
Fri	8/5	H	EDM	28-16	W	29533
Sat	8/13	A	BC	30-17	W	24131
Fri	8/26	H	HAM	30-27	W	30338
Sun	9/4	A	SAS	7-27	L	30048
Sun	9/11	H	SAS	23-45	L	30518
Sun	9/18	A	MTL	25-23	W	24642
Sat	9/24	A	TOR	24-25	L	19108
Fri	9/30	H	MTL	26-32	W	30447
Fri	10/7	A	HAM	33-17	W	23268
Sat	10/15	A	EDM	10-24	L	30734
Sat	10/22	H	MTL	26-25	W	30360
Fri	10/28	H	TOR	22-27	L	29751
Sat	11/5	A	CAL	24-30	L	29076
Eastern Final						
Sun	11/20	H	HAM	19- 3	W	30051
Grey Cup						
Sun	11/27	N	BC	23-34	L	54313

Today the Grey Cup represents the championship of the Canadian Football League, but that was not always the case.

Like the history of the CFL, the history of the Grey Cup is full of twists and turns from its amateur origins to today's full-fledged professionalism. In fact, the Grey Cup itself still bears the inscription "for the amateur football championship of Canada."

Originally only teams whose unions (leagues) were members of the Canadian Rugby Union (CRU) were allowed to compete for the trophy. Those unions were the Intercollegiate Rugby Football Union, Interprovincial Rugby Football Union (IRFU) and Ontario Rugby Football Union (ORFU). In 1921 the Western Canada Rugby Football Union (WCRFU) joined the CRU and was allowed to challenge for the cup. Since the title game was always played in an eastern city, there were three years (1924, 1926 and 1927) when the WCRFU champion declined to challenge for the title.

In 1934 the intercollegiate union withdrew from Grey Cup competition.

The ORFU continued to challenge for the title after the Second World War, despite its obvious inferiority to the more professional IRFU and WIFU. 1954 was the final year the ORFU competed in the Grey Cup playoffs.

From 1955 on it has been strictly a game between the two unions that ultimately formed today's CFL.

1st Grey Cup
December 4, 1909 at Toronto (3,807)

University of Toronto	6	0	10	10	-26
Toronto Parkdale	0	5	1	0	- 6

UT Gall single
UT Gall fumble recovery (Ricthie failed)
PAR Meigham fumble recovery (failed)
UT Thomson fumble recovery (Ritchie)
UT Gall single
UT Lawson single
PAR Killaly single
UT Gall single
UT Gall single
UT Gall single
UT Gall single
UT Gall single
UT Lawson single
UT Gall single
UT Lawson 50 run (failed)

2nd Grey Cup
November 26, 1910 at Hamilton (12,000)

University of Toronto	5	6	0	5	-16
Hamilton Tigers	0	0	2	5	- 7

UT Dixon fumble recovery (Maynard failed)
UT Maynard run (Maynard)
HAM ? single
HAM Simpson single
HAM ? single
HAM ? single
HAM Smith FG
UT Gall single
UT Dixon single
UT Gall single
UT Gall single
UT Maynard single

Simopson scored three singles and Smith scored one single for Hamilton.

3rd Grey Cup
November 25, 1911 at Toronto (13,687)

University of Toronto	0	6	7	1	-14
Toronto Argonauts	1	0	2	4	- 7

TOR Binkley single
UT Ramsey 5 run (Maynard)
TOR Binkley single
TOR Binkley single
UT Maynard singleUT Knight fumble recovery (Maynard)
TOR Binkley FG
TOR Mallett single
UT Maynard single

4th Grey Cup
November 30, 1912 at Hamilton (5,337)

Toronto Argonauts	0	2	0	2	- 4
Hamilton Alerts	2	2	7	0	-11

HAM Leckie single
HAM Leckie single
TOR Safety
HAM Leckie single
HAM Leckie single
HAM Harper run (Craig)
HAM Leckie single
TOR Clarke single
TOR Clarke single

5th Grey Cup
November 29, 1913 at Hamilton (2,100)

Toronto Parkdale	2	0	0	0	- 2
Hamilton Tigers	7	14	0	23	-44

HAM Craig run (Manson)
TOR Gall single
TOR Gall single
HAM Mallett single
HAM Wilson run (Manson)
HAM Mallett single
HAM Wilson run (Manson)
HAM Mallett single
HAM Manson single
HAM Manson single
HAM Manson single
HAM Wilson run (Manson failed)
HAM Glassford fumble recovery (Manson failed)
HAM Wilson own punt recovery (Manson failed)
HAM Craig run (failed)

6th Grey Cup
December 5, 1914 at Toronto (10,500)

Toronto Argonauts	6	8	0	0	-14
University of Toronto	0	0	1	1	- 2

TOR Murphy fumble recovery (O'Connor)
TOR Mills fumble recovery (O'Connor failed)
TOR O'Connor 35 FG
UT McKenzie single
UT Saunders single

7th Grey Cup
November 20, 1915 at Toronto (2,808)

Hamilton Tigers	0	1	6	6	-13
Toronto Rugby and Athletic Club	4	0	2	1	- 7

TOR ? single
TOR Bickle FG
HAM Manson single
HAM Erskine TD (Manson)
TOR ? single
TOR ? single
HAM Lutz TD (Manson failed)
TOR ? single
HAM Manson single

DeGruchy scored two singles and Bickle scored two singles for Toronto.

1916-1919 no games played.

8th Grey Cup
December 4, 1920 at Toronto (10,088)

University of Toronto	0	6	5	5	-16
Toronto Argonauts	1	0	1	1	- 3

TOR Munro single
UT Snyder 25 run (McKenzie)
TOR Munro single
UT G. Stirrett fumble recovery (failed)
UT McKenzie TD (failed)
TOR Munro single

9th Grey Cup
December 3, 1921 at Toronto (9,558)

Edmonton Eskimos	0	0	0	0	- 0
Toronto Argonauts	10	4	7	2	-23

TOR Cochrane 3 run (Batstone failed)
TOR Cochrane run (Batstone failed)
TOR Conacher single
TOR Conacher FG
TOR Conacher run (Batstone)
TOR Conacher single
TOR Sullivan single
TOR Sullivan single

10th Grey Cup
December 2, 1922 at Kingston (4,700)

Edmonton Eskimos	0	1	0	0	- 1
Queen's University	0	0	8	5	-13

EDM Fraser single
QUE Leadlay single
QUE Leadlay single
QUE Mundell 4 run (Leadley)
QUE Harding runs (failed)

11th Grey Cup
December 1, 1923 at Toronto (8,629)

Regina Roughriders	0	0	0	0	- 0
Queen's University	7	13	23	11	-54

QUE Leadlay single
QUE Batstone run (Leadley)
QUE Campbell run (Leadley)
QUE Leadlay single
QUE Campbell fumble recovery (Leadley)
QUE Leadlay single
QUE Evans punt return (failed)
QUE Batstone run (Batstone)
QUE Walker 50 interception return (Batstone)
QUE Evans run (failed)
QUE Reynolds run (Leadley)
QUE Quinn run (failed)

12th Grey Cup
November 29, 1924 at Toronto (5,978)

Team					
Queen's University	2	3	6	0	-11
Toronto Balmy Beach	0	1	0	2	-3

QUE	Safety, Britton tackled
QUE	Leadlay single
TOR	Hughes single
QUE	Leadlay single
QUE	Wright blocked punt recovery (Leadley)
TOR	Britton single
TOR	Hughes single

December 6, 1924 game between the Winnipeg Victorias and Queen's University was cancelled by Winnipeg.

13th Grey Cup
December 5, 1925 at Ottawa (6,900)

Team					
Winnipeg Tammany Tigers	0	0	1	0	- 1
Ottawa Senators	5	8	0	11	-24

OTT	Connell own punt recovery (Lynch failed)
OTT	Lynch single
OTT	Mulroney 20 run (not attempted)
OTT	Lynch single
OTT	Lynch single
WPG	Grant single
OTT	Connell 5 run (Lynch failed)
OTT	Young fumble recovery (Connell failed)
OTT	Lynch single

14th Grey Cup
December 4, 1926 at Toronto (8,276)

Team					
Ottawa Senators	7	0	3	0	-10
University of Toronto	2	4	0	1	- 7

OTT	Miller single
OTT	Lynch single
UT	Irwin single
UT	Trimble single
OTT	Lynch 3 run (failed)
UT	Trimble single
UT	Roos single
UT	Trimble single
UT	Trimble single
OTT	Miller single
OTT	Miller single
OTT	Bruce single
UT	Snyder single

Regina Roughriders declined to travel east to challenge for the cup.

15th Grey Cup
November 26, 1927 at Toronto (13,676)

Team					
Hamilton Tigers	0	0	6	0	- 6
Toronto Balmy Beach	7	2	0	0	- 9

TOR	Cowhurst single
TOR	Ponton run (failed)
TOR	Foster single
TOR	Foster single
TOR	Foster single
HAM	Leadley single
HAM	McKelvey own punt recovery (failed)

Regina Roughriders declined to travel east to challenge for the cup.

16th Grey Cup
December 1, 1928 at Hamilton (4,767)

Team					
Regina Roughriders	0	0	0	0	- 0
Hamilton Tigers	6	0	19	5	-30

HAM	Timmis 10 run (Veale failed)
HAM	Welch single
HAM	Simpson fumble recovery (Leadley)
HAM	Walker 1 run (Leadley)
HAM	Simpson 20 run (Leadley)
HAM	Timmis TD (Leadley failed)

17th Grey Cup
November 30, 1929 at Hamilton (1,906)

Team					
Regina Roughriders	1	0	1	1	- 3
Hamilton Tigers	1	1	7	5	-14

HAM	? single
REG	Bloomfield single
HAM	? single
HAM	Welch single
REG	Bloomfield single
HAM	Simpson fumble recovery (Simpson failed)
HAM	? single
REG	Erskine single
HAM	Leadlay single
HAM	Welch single
HAM	Welch single
HAM	Leadley single
HAM	Welch single

Welch scored six singles and Leadley three singles for Hamilton.

18th Grey Cup
December 6, 1930 at Toronto (3,914)

Team					
Regina Roughriders	0	0	6	0	- 6
Toronto Balmy Beach	3	7	0	1	-11

TOR	Box single
TOR	Box single
TOR	Harris single
TOR	Box single
TOR	Harris single
TOR	Harris 1 run (failed)
REG	Bloomfield single
REG	Brown onside punt recovery (failed)
TOR	Harris single

19th Grey Cup
December 5, 1931 at Montreal (5,112)

Team					
Regina Roughriders	0	0	0	0	- 0
Montreal Winged Wheelers	7	0	6	9	-22

MTL	Welch single
MTL	Jotkus fumble recovery (Welch)
MTL	Welch single
MTL	Grant 24 pass from Stevens (Welch failed)
MTL	Welch FG
MTL	Whitty 6 pass from Stevens (Stevens)

20th Grey Cup
December 3, 1932 at Hamilton (4,806)

Team					
Regina Roughriders	0	0	0	6	- 6
Hamilton Tigers	9	7	9	0	-25

HAM	Gardner 13 run (Turville)
HAM	Turvile single
HAM	Safety conceded by Harrison
HAM	Boadway single
HAM	Wright 20 interception return (Gardner)
HAM	Simpson 20 fumble recovery (Gardner)
REG	DeFrate 1 run (Schave)

21st Grey Cup
December 9, 1933 at Sarnia (2,751)

Team					
Toronto Argonauts	0	0	3	1	- 4
Sarnia Imperials	0	1	1	1	- 3

SAR	Stirling single
SAR	Stirling single
TOR	Burns FG
SAR	Stirling single
TOR	Box single

The Winnipeg Winnipegs lost to the Argonuats in the semi-final game.

22nd Grey Cup
November 24, 1934 at Toronto (8,900)

Team					
Regina Roughriders	0	5	1	6	-12
Sarnia Imperials	5	6	6	3	-20

SAR	Stirling single
SAR	Hayes FG
SAR	Stirling single
SAR	Paterson 13 run (Hayes)
REG	Olson 1 run (Kirk failed)
SAR	Manore fumble recovery in end zone (Hayes)
REG	Kirk single
REG	Adkins pass from Olson (Kirk)
SAR	Hayes single
SAR	Stirling single
SAR	Stirling single

23rd Grey Cup
December 7, 1935 at Hamilton (6,405)

Team					
Winnipeg Winnipegs	5	7	6	0	-18
Hamilton Tigers	3	1	6	2	-12

WPG	Marquardt pass from Rebholz (Kabat failed)
HAM	Turville 23 FG
WPG	Kabat 33 pass from Rebholz (Hanson)
HAM	Turville single
WPG	Kabat single
HAM	Paterson run (Turville failed)
HAM	Turville single
WPG	Hanson 75 punt return (Rebholz)
HAM	Safety conceded by Kabat

24th Grey Cup
December 5, 1936 at Toronto (5,883)

Team					
Sarnia Imperials	12	12	2	0	-26
Ottawa Rough Riders	5	7	0	8	-20

SAR	Beach 9 run (Hayes)
SAR	Hedgewick lateral from Parsaca lateral from ? run (Hayes)
OTT	Tommy lateral from Daley run (Herman failed)
OTT	Morrison single
OTT	Wadsworth 2 run (Herman)
SAR	Beach 3 run (Hayes)
SAR	Hedgewick lateral from Parsaca pass from Hedgweick (Hayes)
SAR	Stirling single
SAR	Stirling single
OTT	Morrison single
OTT	Leore single
OTT	Morrison 1 run (Herman)

25th Grey Cup
December 11, 1937 at Toronto (11,522)

Team					
Winnipeg Blue Bombers	1	1	1	0	- 3

Toronto Argonauts	3	1	0	0	- 4

WPG Olander single
TOR Selkirk 31 FG
WPG Olander single
TOR Isbister single
WPG Kabat single

26th Grey Cup
December 10, 1938 at Toronto (18,778)

Winnipeg Blue Bombers	1	6	0	0	- 7
Toronto Argonauts	0	5	1	24	-30

WPG Stevenson single
WPG Kabat 15 FG
TOR West 52 pass from B. Stukus (A. Stukus failed)
WPG Kabat 20 FG
TOR A. Stukus single
TOR Storey 27 run (A. Stukus)
TOR Storey 2 lateral from Storey 10 run (A. Stukus)
TOR Morris 5 pass from B. Stukus (A. Stukus) Thornton catch?
TOR Storey 4 run (A. Stukus)

27th Grey Cup
December 9, 1939 at Ottawa (11,738)

Winnipeg Blue Bombres	5	1	0	3	- 8
Ottawa Rough Riders	6	0	0	1	- 7

OTT Tommy 40 lateral from Perley 25 pass from Burke (Herman)
WPG Boeber 5 run (Kabat failed)
WPG Kabat single
WPG Kabat single
OTT Herman single
WPG Stevenson single

28th Grey Cup (two-game series: Ottawa 20, Toronto 7)
November 30, 1940 at Toronto (4,998)

Ottawa Rough Riders	0	1	1	6	- 8
Toronto Balmy Beach	0	1	1	0	- 2

OTT Sward single
TOR Porter single
OTT Sward single
TOR Porter single
OTT Sprague 4 run (Perley pass from Burke)

December 7, 1940 at Ottawa (1,700)

Toronto Balmy Beach	5	0	0	0	- 5
Ottawa Rough Riders	1	0	7	4	-12

TOR Porter 3 run (Crowe failed)
OTT Sward single
OTT Sward single
OTT Daley run (Herman)
OTT Sward single
OTT Sward single
OTT Herman single
OTT Sward single

29th Grey Cup
November 29, 1941 at Toronto (19,065)

Winnipeg Blue Bombers	3	6	9	0	-18
Ottawa Rough Riders	6	3	6	1	-16

WPG McCance FG
OTT Golab 42 own punt recovery (Fraser)
OTT Fraser 16 FG
WPG Wilson lateral from Marquardt pass from Sheley (McCance)
WPG Marquardt interception return (McCance)
OTT Fraser 26 FG
OTT Fraser 19 FG
WPG McCance FG
OTT Fraser single

30th Grey Cup
December 5, 1942 at Toronto (12,455)

Toronto RCAF Hurricanes	0	2	5	1	- 8
Winnipeg RCAF Bombers	0	0	5	0	- 5

TOR Kijek single
TOR Kijek single
WPG Boivin pass from Sheley (failed)
TOR Poplwsky 2 run (Crowe failed)
TOR Crowe single

31st Grey Cup
November 27, 1943 at Toronto (16,423)

Hamilton Flying Wildcats	18	0	3	2	-23
Winnipeg RCAF Bombers	7	0	6	1	-14

HAM D. Smith 30 pass from Krol (Krol)
WPG Quinn single
WPG G. Smith 17 run (McCance)
HAM Fumio blocked punt recovery (Krol)
HAM Lawson 1 run (Krol)
HAM Krol FG
WPG Berry 42 pass from Qyuinn (McCance)
WPG Quinn single
HAM Krol single
HAM D. Smith single

32nd Grey Cup
November 25, 1944 at Hamilton (3,871)

St. Hyacinthe-Donnacona Navy	1	5	0	1	- 7
Hamilton Wildcats	0	0	0	6	- 6

STH Davey single
STH Taylor pass from Crncich (Davey failed)
HAM Miocinovich 3 run (Krol)
STH Davey single

33rd Grey Cup
December 1, 1945 at Toronto (18,660)

Winnipeg Blue Bombers	0	0	0	0	- 0
Toronto Argonauts	12	0	12	11	-35

TOR Smylie run (Smylie)
TOR Myers pass from Krol (Krol)
TOR Copeland 13 run (failed)
TOR Skidmore single
TOR Smylie pass from Krol (Krol)
TOR Krol 60 interception return (Hickey)
TOR Myers 70 run (run failed)

34th Grey Cup
November 30, 1946 at Toronto (18,960)

Winnipeg Blue Bombers	0	0	0	6	- 6
Toronto Argonauts	0	16	6	6	-28

TOR Copeland 25 pass from Krol (Krol failed)
TOR Krol pass from Copeland (Krol)
TOR Smylie pass from Krol (pass failed)
TOR B. Karrys 2 run (Krol)
TOR Tipoff pass from Krol (Krol)
WPG Dobler 2 run (Dobler)

35th Grey Cup
November 29, 1947 at Toronto (18,885)

Winnipeg Blue Bombers	6	3	0	0	- 9
Toronto Argonauts	0	1	6	3	-10

WPG Sandberg 3 run (Hiney)
WPG Hiney 30 FG
TOR Krol single
TOR Copeland 10 pass from Krol (Krol)
TOR Krol single
TOR Krol single
TOR Krol single

TEAM STATISTICS	WPG	TOR
First Downs	15	15
Yards Rushing	210	172
Passes	6-3-1	8-4-1
Yards Passing	39	91
Punts-Average	11-38	11-35
Punt Return Yards	43	137
Fumbles-Lost	-2	-4
Penalties-Yards	-25	-20

36th Grey Cup
November 27, 1948 at Toronto (20,013)

Calgary Stampeders	0	6	0	6	-12
Ottawa Rough Riders	1	0	6	0	- 7

OTT Golab single
CAL Hill 15 pass from Spaith (Wilmot)
OTT Paffrath 1 run (Chipper)
CAL Thodos 10 run (Wilmot)

TEAM STATISTICS	CAL	OTT
First Downs	16	20
Ruashes-Yards	39-190	44-297
Passes	18-10-0	18-3-2
Yards Passing	144	49
Punts-Average	16-39.7	10-43.5
Punt Returns-Yards	4-31	14-119
Kickoff Returns-Yards	2-19	2-45
Fumbles-Lost	1-0	5-5
Penalties-Yards	8-75	5-35

RUSHING: CAL-Thodos, 5/54; Rowe, 11/52; Gyles, 8/32; Pantages, 5/28; Spaith, 5/14; Hood, 5/10.

PASSING: CAL-Spaith, 18-10-0, 144.

RECEIVING: CAL-Strode, 5/87; Thodos, 2/25; Hill, 2/16; Hood, 1/16.

37th Grey Cup
November 26, 1949 at Toronto (20,087)

Calgary Stampeders	0	7	0	8	-15
Montreal Alouettes	11	6	6	5	-28

MTL Wagner 5 run (McCance)
MTL Cunningham 34 pass from Filchock (penalty against MTL)
CAL Spaith single
CAL Hood 2 run (Graham)
MTL Trawick 25 fumble recovery (McCance)
MTL Wagner 2 run (McCance)
MTL McCance 29 FG
CAL Safety, Cunningham tackled by Aguirre
CAL E. Anderson 21 fumble recovery (Graham)
MTL McCance single
MTL Kijek single

TEAM STATISTICS	CAL	MTL

First Downs	16	22
Rushes-Yards	43-181	49-176
Passes	32-19-4	20-11-1
Yards Passing	180	204
Punts-Average	12-40.8	13-39.1
Punt Returns-Yards	9-48	11-91
Kickoff Returns-Yards	5-118	3-21
Fumbles-Lost	2-2	4-4
Penalties-Yards	6-40	3-15

RUSHING: CAL-Rowe, 14/53; Hood, 12/50; Thodos, 5/37; Kwong, 4/23; Pantages, 6/15; Spaith, 2/3.

PASSING: CAL-Spaith, 32-19-4, 180.

RECEIVING: CAL-Anderson, 6/57; Rowe, 2/41; Thodos, 5/36; Hood, 3/31; Strode, 3/15.

38th Grey Cup
November 25, 1950 at Toronto (27,101)

Winnipeg Blue Bombers	0	0	0	0	- 0
Toronto Argonauts	1	6	6	0	-13

TOR	Krol single
TOR	Volpe 21 FG
TOR	Volpe 23 FG
TOR	Dekdebrun 1 run (Volpe failed)
TOR	Krol single

TEAM STATISTICS	WPG	TOR
First Downs	3	11
Yards Rushing	111	220
Passes	15-3-2	3-1-0
Yards Passing	48	/
Punts-Average	16-39	18-37
Punt Return Yards	79	65
Fumbles-Lost	4-2	3-1
Penalties-Yards	-15	-15

RUSHING: TOR-Toogood, /79; Bass, /47; Westlake, /31.

PASSING: TOR-Dekdebrun, -1-0, 7.

RECEIVING: TOR-Curtis, 1/7.

39th Grey Cup
November 24, 1951 at Toronto (27,341)

Saskatchewan Roughriders	2	0	0	12	-14
Ottawa Rough Riders	6	6	7	2	-21

SAS	Dobbs single
SAS	Dobbs single
OTT	MacDonnell 3 run (Gain)
OTT	Baldwin pass from O'Malley (Gain)
OTT	Cummings single
OTT	Karpuk 63 pass from O'Malley (Gain)
OTT	Cummings single
SAS	Nix 30 pass from Dobbs (Ettinger)
SAS	Glasser 10 run (Ettinger)
OTT	O'Malley single

TEAM STATISTICS	SAS	OTT
First Downs	17	17
Rushes-Yards	-179	-194
Passes	18-6-2	21-5-1
Yards Passing	138	140
Punts-Average	17-45	16-42
Punt Return Yards	154	183
Fumbles-Lost	-3	-3
Penalties-Yards	-70	-30

RUSHING: SAS-Charlton, /54. OTT-Turner, /107; Karpuk, /18.

PASSING: SAS-Dobbs, 18-6-2, 138.

RECEIVING: SAS-Charlton, 1/8. OTT-Turner, 1/4.

40th Grey Cup
November 29, 1952 at Toronto (27,391)

Edmonton Eskimos	5	0	6	0	-11
Toronto Argonauts	0	15	0	6	-21

EDM	Kwong 5 run (Snyder failed)
TOR	Wirkowski 1 run (Ettinger)
TOR	Ettinger 14 FG
TOR	Bass 1 run (Ettinger)
EDM	Kwong 3 run (Snyder)
TOR	O'Connor 37 pass from Wirkowski (Ettinger)

TEAM STATISTICS	EDM	TOR
First Downs	20	15
Rushes-Yards	22-133	33-149
Passes	36-17-2	19-8-0
Yards Passing	271	232
Punts-Average	9-42.1	11-43.9
Punt Returns-Yards	8-60	8-44
Kickoff Returns-Yards	4-34	3-42
Fumbles-Lost	5-1	1-1
Penalties-Yards	2-30	0-0

RUSHING: EDM-Chambers, 3/43; Miles, 7/42; Pantages, 5/19; King, 2/11; Arnold, 1/0. TOR-Bass, 11/69; Pyzer, 11/56; Curtis, 7/11; Wirkowski, 3/10; Toogood, 1/3.

PASSING: EDM-Arnold, 36-17-2, 271. TOR-Wirkowski, 19-8-0, 232.

RECEIVING: EDM-Miles, 5/63; Pantages, 4/111; Prather, 4/49; Chmabers, 2/5; Bendiak, 1/33; Anderson, 1/10.

41st Grey Cup
November 28, 1953 at Toronto (27,313)

Winnipeg Blue Bombers	0	0	6	0	- 6
Hamilton Tiger-Cats	6	0	6	0	-12

HAM	Songin 1 run (Logan)
WPG	James 1 run (Korchak)
HAM	Ragazzo 55 pass from Songin (Logan)

TEAM STATISTICS	WPG	HAM
First Downs	25	19
Rushes-Yards	20-99	29-152
Passes	48-31-2	23-11-1
Yards Passing	354	183
Punts-Average	8.36.5	10-39.9
Punt Returns-Yards	10-69	7-40
Kickoff Returns-Yards	3-64	2-39
Fumbles-Lost	4-1	3-1
Penalties-Yards	3-20	1-5

RUSHING: WPG: James, 12/49; Casey, 4/29; Meltzer, 2/14; Sokol, 2/7. HAM-Hapes, 12/53; Custis, 7/50; Bailey, 5/31; Kusserow, 2/13; Brown, 2/4; Songin, 1/1.

PASSING: WPG-Jacobs, 48-31-1, 354. HAM-Songin, 22-10-1, 163; Kusserow, 1-1-0, 20.

RECEIVING: WPG-Armstrong, 10, 140; Sokol, 4/41; Casey, 4/37; Meltzer, 3/37; Grant, 3/19; Pearce, 2/45; James, 2/15; Huffman, 1/11; Korchak, 1/8; McAllister, 1/1.

42nd Grey Cup
November 27, 1954 at Toronto (27,321)

Edmonton Eskimos	11	3	0	12	-26
Montreal Alouettes	6	12	1	6	-25

EDM	Lindley 3 pass from Miles (Dean)
MTL	O'Quinn 90 pass from Etcheverry (Poole)
EDM	Faloney 1 run (Faloney run failed)
EDM	Dean 37 FG
MTL	O'Quinn 14 pass from Etcheverry (Poole)
MTL	Hunsinger 7 run (Poole)
MTL	Poole single
MTL	Pal 14 pass from Etcheverry (Poole)
EDM	Lippman 14 run (Dean)
EDM	Parker 90 fumble recovery (Dean)

TEAM STATISTICS	EDM	MTL
First Downs	25	34
Rushes-Yards	264	284
Passes	23-10-2	32-22-2
Yards Passing	161	393
Punts-Average	9-38.8	3-45.3
Punt Returns-Yards	3-19	9-55
Kickoff Returns-Yards	6-88	4-85
Fumbles-Lost	6-2	8-6
Penalties-Yards	4-53	1-15

RUSHING: EDM-Kwong, 16/79; Parker, 9/62; Lippman, 7/55; Miles, 5/28; Faloney 11/21; Kruger, 3/19. MTL-Webster, 16/114; Hunsinger, 15/66; Etcheverry, 5/44; Bewley, 3/34; Wagner, 4/9; Belec, 1/1.

PASSING: EDM-Faloney, 16-6-2, 101; Miles 4-4-0, 60; Parker, 3-0-0, 0. MTL-Etcheverry, 32-22-2, 393.

RECEIVING: EDM-Bendiak, 4/77; Parker, 3/57; Lindley, 2/12; McWhinney, 1/15, MTL-O'Quinn, 12/290; Pal, 3/52; Poole, 3/50; Hunsinger, 2/5; Webster, 1/17; Wagner, 1/-1.

43rd Grey Cup
November 26, 1955 at Vancouver (39,417)

Edmonton Eskimos	6	12	12	4	-34
Montreal Alouettes	13	6	0	0	-19

MTL	Korchak single
EDM	Kwong 1 run (Dean)
MTL	Abbruzzi 1 run (Blaicher)
MTL	Patterson 42 pass from Etcheverry (Blaicher)
EDM	Bright 42 run (Dean)
MTL	Patterson 15 pass from Etcheverry (Korchak)
EDM	Heydenfeldt 15 pass from Parker (Dean)
EDM	Kwong 1 run (Dean)
EDM	Bright 3 run (Dean)
EDM	Dean single
EDM	Dean 19 FG

TEAM STATISTICS	EDM	MTL
First Downs	36	30
Rushes-Yards	62-438	20-69
Passes	16-8-1	40-29-2
Yards Passing	128	508
Punts-Average	6-41.5	6-37.0
Punt Returns-Yards	6-32	6-3
Kickoff Returns-Yards	4-91	5-58
Fumbles-Lost	2-2	4-3
Penalties-Yards	6-42	3-25

RUSHING: EDM-Kwong, 30/145; Bright, 7/77; Parker, 8/75; Miles, 7/71; Lindley, 6/50; Kelly, 1/7; Kimoff, 1/7; Getty, 2/6. MTL-Belec, 4/22; Caroline, 5/18; Abbruzzi, 7/17; Etcheverry, 4/12.

PASSING: EDM-Parker, 16-8-1, 128. MTL-Etcheverry, 41-30-2, 508.

RECEIVING: EDM-Kwong, 3/20; Miles, 1/30; Lindley, 1/25; Bright, 1/23; Bendiak, 1/15; Heydenfelt, 1/15. MTL-O'Quinn, 8/134; Patterson, 5/99; Pal, 4/62; Bewley, 3/38; Moran, 3/37; Belec, 3/29; Abbruzzi, 2/55; Caroline, 1/42; Miller, 1/12.

44th Grey Cup
November 24, 1956 at Toronto (27,425)

Edmonton Eskimos	6	13	18	13	-50
Montreal Alouettes	7	7	6	7	-27

MTL	Patterson 9 run (Bewley)
EDM	Bright 4 run (Mobra failed)
EDM	Getty 1 run (Mobra failed)
MTL	Patterson 37 pass from Etcheverry (Bewley)
EDM	Parker 10 pass from Getty (Mobra)
MTL	Etcheverry 1 run (Bewley failed)
EDM	Parker single
EDM	Bright 36 run (Mobra)
EDM	Mobra 25 FG
EDM	Getty 1 run (Mobra)
EDM	Parker 5 run (Mobra)
MTL	Abbruzzi 2 run (Bewley)
EDM	Parker 8 run (no attempt)

TEAM STATISTICS	EDM	MTL
First Downs	38	25
Rushes-Yards	82-457	34-186
Passes	17-7-2	38-16-4
Yards Passing	105	329
Punts-Average	14-35.0	11-35.6
Punt Returns-Yards	10-61	11-33
Kickoff Returns-Yards	5-54	7-117
Fumbles-Lost	4-1	4-4
Penalties-Yards	6-40	7-50

RUSHING: EDM-Bright, 27/169; Parker, 19/116; Kwong, 19/81; Miles, 11/66; Getty, 3/14; Kruger, 3/11. MTL-Abruzzi, 13/76; James, 7/46; Pascal, 9/40; Etcheverry, 4/15; Patterson, 1/9.

PASSING: EDM-Getty 15-7-1, 105; Getty, 1-0-0, 0; Parker, 1-0-1, 0. MTL-Etcheverry, 38-16-4, 329.

RECEIVING: EDM-Bright, 3/40; Parker, 2/27; Miles, 1/19; Walker 1/19. MTL-Patterson, 6/139; James, 3/89; O'Quinn, 3/36; Pascal, 2/21; Abbruzzi, 1/24; Pal, 1/20.

45th Grey Cup
November 30, 1957 at Toronto (27,051)

Winnipeg Blue Bombers	0	0	0	7	- 7
Hamilton Tiger-Cats	13	0	0	19	-32

HAM	Bawel 50 fumble recovery (Oneschuk)
HAM	Faloney 6 run (run failed)
HAM	McDougall 27 run (run failed)
HAM	Gilchrist 5 run (Oneschuk failed)
HAM	Gilchrist 16 run (Oneschuk)
WPG	Mendyk 15 pass from Roseborough (Ploen)

TEAM STATISTICS	WPG	HAM
First Downs	21	10
Rushes-Yards	47-199	32-160
Passes	28-15-2	15-5-0
Yards Passing	183	67
Punts-Average	10-38.6	14-43.9
Punt Returns-Yards	14-56	9-45
Kickoff Returns-Yards	6-89	2-26
Fumbles-Lost	8-6	4-2
Penalties-Yards	4-55	8-64

RUSHING: WPG-James, 16/62; Ploen, 9/54; Lewis, 11/38; Mendyk. 5/19; Miller, 5/19; Roseborough, 1/0. HAM-McDougall, 11/86; Gilchrist, 17/48; Faloney, 2/13; Grant, 2/13.

PASSING: WPG-Ploen, 19-11-1, 103; Roseborough, 6-4-0, 80; Mendyk, 2-0-0, 0; Vincent, 1-0-1, 0. HAM-Faloney, 15-5-0. 67.

RECEIVING: WPG-Pitts, 8/93; Mendyk, 4/42; Gilliam, 3/33; James, 0/8; Canakes, 0/1. HAM-Gilchrist, 2/30; Dekker, 1/19; Grant, 1/13; McDougall, 1/5.

46th Grey Cup
November 29, 1958 at Vancouver (36,567)

Hamilton Tiger-Cats	14	0	14	0	-28
Winnipeg Blue Bombers	7	13	7	8	-25

HAM	McDougall 10 run (Oneschuk)
HAM	Goldston 70 fumble return (Oneschuk)
WPG	Van Pelt 20 pass from Lewis (Van Pelt)
WPG	Van Pelt 22 FG
WPG	Van Pelt 27 FG
WPG	Rauhaus blocked punt recovery in end zone (Van Pelt)
HAM	Howell 12 pass from Faloney (Oneschuk)
WPG	Shepard 3 run (Van Pelt)
HAM	Howell 34 pass from Faloney (Oneschuk)
WPG	Van Pelt 1 run (Van Pelt)
WPG	Shepard single

TEAM STATISTICS	HAM	WPG
First Downs	23	27
Rushes-Yards	29-175	41-252
Passes	25-16-2	19-11-0
Yards Passing	233	195
Punts-Average	7-43.3	6-42.3
Punt Returns-Yards	5-7	6-39
Kickoff Returns-Yards	5-66	4-49
Fumbles-Lost	4-2	3-3
Penalties-Yards	12-112	6-36

RUSHING: HAM-McDougall, 11/57; Faloney, 8/56; Campbell, 7/43; Sutherin, 3/19. WPG-Shepard, 14/120; Lewis, 13/66; Varone, 8/33; Van Pelt, 5/29; Ploen, 1/1.

PASSING: HAM-Faloney, 25-16-2, 233. WPG-Van Pelt, 15-8-0, 140; Ploen, 2-2-0, 35; Lewis, 2-1-0, 20.

RECEIVING: HAM-Dekker, 5/75; McDougall, 5/53; Howell, 4/76; Macon, 1/22; Lampman, 1/7. WPG-Ploen, 2/54; Pitts, 2/36; Pitts, 2/36; Shepard, 2/35; Gilliam, 2/26; Lewis, 2/24; Van Pelt, 1/20.

47th Grey Cup
November 28, 1959 at Toronto (33,133)

Winnipeg Blue Bombers	3	0	0	18	-21
Hamilton Tiger-Cats	0	1	6	0	- 7

WPG	James 21 FG
HAM	Scott single
HAM	Oneschuk 10 FG
HAM	Oneschuk 28 FG
WPG	Shepard single
WPG	Shepard 2 run (James)
WPG	Shepard single
WPG	Shepard single
WPG	Shepard single
WPG	Pitts 33 pass from Ploen (James)

TEAM STATISTICS	WPG	HAM
First Downs	13	11
Rushes-Yards	42-150	35-113
Passes	12-5-0	21-9-0
Yards Passing	123	97
Punts-Average	17-45.3	16-40.6
Punt Return Yards	16-82	14-67
Kickoff Returns-Yards	1-8	3-31
Fumbles-Lost	5-2	2-1
Penalties-Yards	4-37	2-5

RUSHING: WPG-Shepard, 16/45; James, 10/32; :Lewis, 9/31; Shannon, 4/29; Ploen, 3/13. HAM-McDougall, 21/68; Goldston, 9/39; Wood, 4/4; Faloney, 1/2.

PASSING: WPG-Ploen, 11-4-0, 115; Lewis, 1-1-0, 8. HAM-Faloney, 20-8-0, 89; Fraser, 1-1-0, 8.

RECEIVING: WPG-Pitts, 2/56; Funston, 1/41; Shannon, 1/18; James, 1/8. HAM-Howell, 3/36; McDougall, 3/34; Lampman, 1/11; Chandler, 1/8; Godlston, 1/8.

48th Grey Cup
November 26, 1960 at Vancouver (38,102)

Ottawa Rough Riders	3	6	0	7	-16
Edmonton Eskimos	0	6	0	0	- 6

OTT	Schreider 15 FG
EDM	Letcavits 63 pass from Parker (Parker)
OTT	Sowalksi 31 pass from Jackson (Schreider failed)
OTT	Vaughn fumble recovery in end zone (Schreider)

TEAM STATISTICS	OTT	EDM
First Downs	19	14
Rushes-Yards	48-276	21-66
Passes	15-6-1	26-12-1
Yards Passing	102	197
Punts-Average	11-43.7	13-42.8
Punt Returns-Yards	12-67	10-60
Kickoff Returns-Yards	2-38	3-126
Fumbles-Lost	4-2	2-2
Penalties-Yards	5-5	3-20

RUSHING: OTT: Thelen, 21/118; Stewart, 18/99; Jackson, 4/41; Kelly, 4/14; Lancaster, 1/4. EDM-Parker, 4/22; Shipka, 5/22; Bright, 5/15; Kwong, 7/7.

PASSING: OTT-Jackson, 11-5-1, 100; Lancaster, 4-1-0, 2. EDM-Parker, 23-10-1, 179; Getty, 3-2-1, 18.

RECEIVING: OTT-Kelly, 2/27; Sowalski, 1/31; Simpson, 1/17; Graham, 1/16; Thelen, 1/11. EDM-Letcavits, 6/132; Smith, 3/35; Schumm, 1/12; Parker, 1/11; Coffey, 1/7.

49th Grey Cup
December 2, 1961 at Toronto (32,651)

Winnipeg Blue Bombers	0	1	3	10	7	-21
Hamilton Tiger-Cats	7	0	7	0	0	-14

HAM	Dekker 90 pass from Faloney (Sutherin)
WPG	Delveaux single
WPG	James 18 FG
HAM	Goldston 23 pass from Faloney (Sutherin)
WPG	James 28 FG
WPG	James 1 run (James)
WPG	Ploen 18 run (James)

TEAM STATISTICS	WPG	HAM
First Downs	26	19
Rushes-Yards	57-284	29-85
Passes	22-12-1	34-19-0
Yards Passing	222	330
Punts-Average	14-43.5	19-39.4
Punt Returns-Yards	19-111	14-73
Kickoff Returns-Yards	4-90	4-71

Fumbles-Lost	5-2	2-0
Penalties-Yards	5-45	4-18

RUSHING: WPG-Lewis, 16/98; Hagberg, 18/81; James, 13/47; Jauch, 1/-13. HAM-Hickman, 3/21; Shannon, 6/21; Faloney, 8/17; McDougall, 9/17; Henley, 2/13; Goldston, 1/-4.

PASSING: WPG-Ploen, 17-9-0, 174; Ledyard, 5-3-1, 46. HAM-Faloney, 34-19-0, 330.

RECEIVING: WPG-Pitts, 4/85; Latourelle, 3/56; James, 3/22; Funston, 2/59. HAM-Patterson, 7/103; Goldston, 4/55; Dekker, 3/114; Grant, 3/26; McDougall, 2/32.

50th Grey Cup
December 1/2, 1962 at Toronto (32,655)

Winnipeg Blue Bombers	0	21	7	0	-28
Hamilton Tiger-Cats	6	13	8	0	-27

HAM	Henley 74 run (Sutherin failed)
WPG	Lewis 6 run (James)
WPG	Shepard 15 pass from Lewis (James)
HAM	Kuntz 1 run (Sutherin failed)
HAM	Henley 18 run (Sutherin)
WPG	Lewis 36 pass from Ledyard (James)
HAM	Viti 36 pass from Zuger (Sutherin)
WPG	Shepard 4 run (James)
HAM	Sutherin single

TEAM STATISTICS	WPG	HAM
First Downs	21	21
Rushes-Yards	21-96	32-248
Passes	30-18-1	30-12-0
Yards Passing	272	249
Punts-Average	12-41.3	9-43.0
Punt Returns-Yards	7-36	11-72
Kickoff Returns-Yards	5-165	5-82
Fumbles-Lost	1-1	2-1
Penalties-Yards	5-40	9-105

RUSHING: WPG-Ploen, 3/41; Lewis, 12/35; James, 3/14; Latourelle, 2/2. HAM-Henley, 4/100; Kuntz, 19/55; Zuger, 5/51; Cosentino, 2/34; Caleb, 2/8.

PASSING: WPG-Ledyard, 18-14-1, 223; Ploen, 11-3-0, 34; Lewis, 1-1-0, 15. HAM-Zuger, 23-8-0, 187; Cosentino, 7-4-0, 62.

RECEIVING: WPG-Funston, 6/66; Lewis, 5/83; Pitts, 4/91; Shepard, 2/24; Latourelle, 1/8. HAM-Henley, 5/118; Patterson, 3/60; Viti, 1/36; Easterly, 1/17; Dekker, 1/11; Caleb, 1/7.

51st Grey Cup
November 30, 1963 at Vancouver (36,545)

Hamilton Tiger-Cats	0	14	7	0	-21
British Columbia Lions	0	3	0	7	-10

HAM	Bethea 4 pass from Faloney (Sutherin)
BC	Kempf 29 FG
HAM	Baker 1 run (Sutherin)
HAM	Patterson 70 pass from Faloney (Sutherin)
BC	Burton 5 pass from Kapp (Kempf)

TEAM STATISTICS	HAM	BC
First Downs	19	21
Rushes-Yards	32-182	26-124
Passes	20-13-1	33-17-1
Yards Passing	261	243
Punts-Average	9-40.3	9-42.0
Punt Returns-Yards	9-40	9-20
Kickoff Returns-Yards	2-43	4-85
Fumbles-Lost	0-0	3-1
Penalties-Yards	7-70	3-17

RUSHING: HAM-Faloney, 7/59; Baker, 10/50; Bethea, 4/41; Pace, 11/32. BC-Beamer, 11/56; Kapp, 6/37; Lasseter, 3/15; Fleming, 5/12; Morris, 1/4.

PASSING: HAM-Faloney. 20-13-1, 261. BC-Kempf, 33-17-1.243.

RECEIVING: HAM-Grant, 6/100; Patterson, 3/95; Henley, 1/40; Bethea, 2/14; Viti, 1/12. BC-Burton, 4/49; Janes, 3/72; Claridge, 3/44; Findlay, 2/45; Morris, 2/14; Homer, 1/8; Beamer, 1/7.

52nd Grey Cup
November 28, 1964 at Toronto (32,655)

British Columbia Lions	7	13	14	0	-34
Hamilton Tiger-Cats	0	1	7	16	-24

BC	Swift 1 run (Kempf)
BC	Carphin 8 paas from Ohler (Kempf failed)
HAM	Zuger single
BC	Fleming 46 run (Kempf)
HAM	Counts 58 run (Sutherin)
BC	Munsey 18 run (Kempf)
BC	Munsey 65 fumble recovery (Kempf)
HAM	Grant 11 pass from Faloney (Sutherin)
HAM	Safety conceded by Beaumont
HAM	Crisson 8 pass from Faloney (Sutherin)

TEAM STATISTICS	BC	HAM
First Downs	16	24
Rushes-Yards	25-161	35-211
Passes	22-10-1	34-18-1
Yards Passing	153	224
Punts-Average	9-33.7	11-41.3
Punt Returns-Yards	9-40	8-44
Kickoff Returns-Yards	2-5	8-146
Fumbles-Lost	2-1	4-2
Penalties-Yards	6-40	3-35

RUSHING: BC-Fleming, 6/68; Munsey, 8/56; Kapp, 3/17; Swift, 7/17; Morris, 1/3. HAM-Counts, 6/65; Faloney 10/52; Baker, 7/42; Bethea, 8/42; Kuntz, 4/10.

PASSING: BC-Kapp, 21-9-1, 145; Ohler, 1-1-0, 8. HAM-Faloney, 33-18-0, 224; Sutherin, 1-0-1, 0.

RECEIVING: BC-Morris, 4/63; Homer, 3/46; Fleming, 2/36; Carphin, 1/8. HAM-Grant, 7/102; Patterson, 5/79; Crisson, 3/29; Counts, 3/14.

53rd Grey Cup
November 27, 1965 at Toronto (32,655)

Hamilton Tiger-Cats	10	0	12	0	-22
Winnipeg Blue Bombers	0	13	0	3	-16

HAM	Sutherin single
HAM	Cohee 7 run (Sutherin)
HAM	Safety conceded by Ploen
WPG	Perkins 8 run (Winton failed)
WPG	Lewis 6 run (Winton)
HAM	Bethea 69 pass from Zuger (Sutherin)
HAM	Safety conceded by Ulmer
HAM	Safety conceded by Ploen
HAM	Zuger single
WPG	Winton FG

TEAM STATISTICS	HAM	WPG
First Downs	6	18
Rushes-Yards	31-149	49-185
Passes	5-2-0	12-7-1
Yards Passing	71	65
Punts-Average	8-32.4	8-27.5
Punt Returns-Yards	7-22	6-25
Kickoff Returns-Yards	2-28	4-87
Fumbles-Lost	7-5	1-1
Penalties-Yards	5-40	5-15

RUSHING: HAM-Bethea, 12/68; Cohee, 4/44; Zuger, 5/32; Kuntz, 3/7; McDougall, 2/4; Anthony 1/3. WPG-Lewis, 13/85; Ploen, 9/40; Raimey. 10/38; Thornton, 2/6; Cooper, 1/-13.

PASSING: HAM-Zuger, 4-2-0, 71; Cosentino, 1-0-0, 0. WPG-Ploen, 11-6-1, 51; Lewis, 1-1-0, 14.

RECEIVING: HAM-Bethea, 2/71. WPG-Perkins, 3/11; Raimey, 2/37; Funston, 1/9; Nielsen, 1/8.

54th Grey Cup
November 26, 1966 at Vancouver (36,553)

Saskatchewan Roughriders	7	7	0	15	-29
Ottawa Rough Riders	6	8	0	0	-14

OTT	Tucker 61 pass from Jackson (Racine failed)
SAS	Worden 6 pass from Lancaster (Abendschan)
SAS	Ford 19 pass from Lancaster (Abendschan)
OTT	Tucker 85 pass from Jackson (Racine)
OTT	Cline single
SAS	Campbell 5 pass from Lancaster (Abendschan)
SAS	Reed 31 run (Abendschan)
SAS	Ford single

TEAM STATISTICS	SAS	OTT
First Downs	18	12
Rushes-Yards	36-196	29-92
Passes	20-10-0	16-6-2
Yards Passing	160	195
Punts-Average	8-35.1	9-39.2
Punt Returns-Yards	8-37	7-19
Kickoff Returns-Yards	3-78	5-130
Fumbles-Lost	0-0	3-1
Penalties-Yards	6-35	5-63

RUSHING: SAS-Reed, 23/133; Buchanan, 10/54; Ford, 2/5; Lancaster, 1/4. OTT-Dillard, 9/29; Jackson, 4/25; Stewart, 8/23; Scott, 8/15.

PASSING; SAS-Lancaster, 20-10-0, 160. OTT-Jacskon, 15-6-1, 195; Stewart, 1-0-1, 0.

RECEIVING: SAS-Worden, 3/48; Campbell, 3/28; Buchanan, 2/19; Barwell, 1/46. OTT-Tucker, 4/174; Roberts, 2/21.

55th Grey Cup
December 2, 1967 at Ottawa (31,358)

Hamilton Tiger-Cats	7	10	0	7	-24
Saskatchewan Roughriders	1	0	0	0	- 1

HAM	Zuger 3 run (Coffey)
SAS	Ford single
HAM	Watkins 72 pass from Zuger (Coffey)
HAM	Coffey single
HAM	Zuger single
HAM	Zuger single
HAM	Zuger single
HAM	Locklin 44 fumble recovery (Coffey failed)

TEAM STATISTICS	HAM	SAS
First Downs	11	11
Rushes-Yards	26-70	33-97
Passes	21-8-1	20-8-3
Yards Passing	164	119

Punts-Average	17-44.7	13-37.8
Punt Returns-Yards	12-59	15-50
Kickoff Returns-Yards	2-40	3-49
Fumbles-Lost	1-0	2-2
Penalties-Yards	10-85	4-38

RUSHING: HAM-Bethea, 7/30; Smith, 10/22; Fleming, 3/10; Zuger, 5/9; Turek,1/-1. SAS-Reed, 23/73; Dorsch, 2/10; Buchanan, 5/9; Ford, 2/3; Lancaster, 1/2.

PASSING: HAM-Zuger, 20-8-1, 164; Turek, 1-0-0, 0. SAS-Lancaster, 20-8-3, 119.

RECEIVING: HAM-Bethea, 5/65; Watkins, 2/86; Coffey, 1/13. SAS-Buchanan 4/99; Reed, 1/9; Campbell, 1/7; Worden, 1/4; Ford, 1/0.

56th Grey Cup
November 30, 1968 at Toronto (32,655)

Ottawa Rough Riders	1	3	7	15	-24
Calgary Stampeders	0	14	0	7	-21

OTT Giardino single
OTT Sutherin 20 FG
CAL Liske 1 run (Robinson)
CAL Evanshen 21 pass from Liske (Robinson)
OTT Jackson 1 run (Sutherin)
OTT Washington 80 run (Sutherin failed)
OTT Adkins 70 pass from Jackson (Sutherin)
CAL Evanshen 2 pass from Liske (Robinson)

TEAM STATISTICS	OTT	CAL
First Downs	14	24
Rushes-Yards	33-202	21-80
Passes	17-8-0	36-21-1
Yards Passing	185	258
Punts-Average	9-43.8	9-39.4
Punt Returns-Yards	9-19	9-27
Kickoff Returns-Yards	4-48	4-107
Fumbles-Lost	3-2	3-2
Penalties-Yards	6-44	2-24

RUSHING: OTT-Washington, 13/128; Jackson, 4/43; Scott, 14/26; Stewart, 1/3; Coleman, 1/2. CAL-Woods, 5/27; Liske, 5/21; Linterman, 4/16; Watson, 5/13; Evanshen, 1/3.

PASSING: OTT-Jackson, 17-8-0, 185. CAL-Liske, 36-21-1, 258.

RECEIVING: OTT-Washingtion, 3/25; Adkins, 2/93; Roberts, 2/43; Stewart, 1/24. CAL-Shaw, 7/75; McCarthy, 5/86; Evanshen, 5/68; Harrison, 2/16; Watson, 2/13.

57th Grey Cup
November 30, 1969 at Montreal (33,172)

Ottawa Rough Riders	0	14	7	8	-29
Saskatchewan Roughriders	9	0	2	0	-11

SAS Ford 28 pass from Lancaster (Abendschan)
SAS Safety conceded by Van Burkleo
OTT Roberts 11 pass from Jackson (Sutherin)
OTT Stewart 80 pass from Jackson (Sutherin)
SAS Abendschan single
SAS Ford single
OTT Mankins 12 pass from Jackson (Sutherin)
OTT Stewart 32 pass from Jackson (Sutherin)
OTT Sutherin single

TEAM STATISTICS	OTT	SAS
First Downs	17	13
Rushes-Yards	31-171	19-63
Passes	22-13-0	30-15-1
Yards Passing	254	239
Punts-Average	11-41.5	9-39.8
Punt Returns-Yards	8-28	11-47
Kickoff Returns-Yards	3-65	4-139
Fumbles-Lost	3-2	4-3
Penalties-Yards	5-55	5-10

RUSHING: OTT-Mankins, 10/72; Stewart, 5/41; Jackson, 5/31; Giardino, 11/27. SAS-Reed, 11/28; Molnar, 2/21; Thompson, 5/19; Lancaster, 1/-5.

PASSING: OTT-Jackson, 22-13-0, 254. SAS-Lancaster, 30-15-1, 239.

RECEIVING: OTT-Mankons, 5/56; Roberts, 3/36; Stewart, 2/112; Tucker, 1/34; Giardino, 1/11; Cooper, 1/5. SAS-Campbell, 4/57; Molnar, 4/43; Ford, 2/44; Thompson, 2/22; Fletcher, 2/18; Reed, 1/55.

58th Grey Cup
November 28, 1970 at Toronto (32,669)

Montreal Alouettes	6	3	7	7	-23
Calgary Stampeders	7	0	3	0	-10

CAL McKinnis 5 run (Robinson)
MTL Alfin 10 pass from Denson (Springate failed)
MTL Springate 21 FG
CAL Robinson 33 FG
MTL Pullen 7 run (Springate)
MTL Lefebrve 10 pass from Wade (Springate)

TEAM STATISTICS	MTL	CAL
First Downs	18	9
Rushes-Yards	25-103	22-64
Passes	38-19-3	39-16-2
Yards Passing	215	119
Punts-Average	12-36.7	15-37.6
Punt Returns-Yards	15-81	11-70
Kickoff Returns-Yards	1-25	4-68
Fumbles-Lost	2-2	2-2
Penalties-Yards	1-0	2-15

RUSHING: MTL-Denson, 16/66; Van Ness, 8/30; Pullen, 1/7. CAL-McKinnis, 12/46; Cranmer, 4/16; Lintermanm 5/5; Holm, 1/-3.

PASSING: MTL-Wade, 35-16-3, 159; Van Ness, 2-2-0, 46; Denson, 1-1-0, 10. CAL-Keeling, 37-16-2, 119; Lawrence, 2-0-0, 0.

RECEIVING: MTL-Evanshen, 6/95; Pullen, 4/38; Van Ness, 3/25; Dalla Riva, 2/23; Lefebvre, 2/20; Denson, 1/4. CAL-Linterman, 3/23; Harrison, 3/22; McKinnis, 3/15; Shaw, 2/18; Cranmer, 2/14; Johnson, 2/11; Sillye, 1/6.

59th Grey Cup
November 28, 1971 at Vancouver (34,484)

Calgary Stampeders	7	7	0	0	-14
Toronto Argonauts	0	3	8	0	-11

CAL Harrison 14 pass from Keeling (Robinson)
TOR MacMillan 18 FG
CAL Mims 0 run (Robinson)
TOR Scales 34 lateral from Vikuk 2 fumble recovery (MacMillan)
TOR MacMillan single

TEAM STATISTICS	CAL	TOR
First Downs	8	13
Rushes-Yards	33-111	28-108
Passes	16-6-3	20-10-0
Yards Passing	111	192
Punts-Average	14-38.0	12-43.1
Punt Returns-Yards	12-38	0-0
Kickoff Returns-Yards	2-30	3-54
Fumbles-Lost	4-1	7-4
Penalties-Yards	6-40	6-52

RUSHING: CAL-McKinnis, 12/50; Mims, 12/42; Keeling, 3/12; Linterman, 5/7; Henderson, 1/0. TOR-McQuay, 12/39; Theismann, 5/36; Symons, 11/33.

PASSING: CAL-Keeling, 16-6-3, 111. TOR-Theismann, 14-8-0, 189; Barton, 5-2-0, 3; Symons, 1-0-0, 0.

RECEIVING: CAL-Linterman, 2/68; Shaw, 1/15; Harrison, 1/14; McKinnis, 1/8; Henderson, 1/6. TOR-Eben, 3/44; Profit, 2/67; McQuay, 2/24; Henderson, 1/43; Thornton, 1/14; Symons, 1/0.

60th Grey Cup
December 3, 1972 at Hamilton (33,993)

Hamilton Tiger-Cats	10	0	0	3	-13
Saskatchewan Roughriders	0	10	0	0	-10

HAM Fleming 16 pass from Ealey (Sunter)
HAM Sunter 27 FG
SAS Campana 8 pass from Lancaster (Abendschan)
SAS Abendschan 19 FG
HAM Sunter 34 FG

TEAM STATISTICS	HAM	SAS
First Downs	23	23
Rushes-Yards	30-101	30-111
Passes	29-18-2	29-20-2
Yards Passing	291	243
Punts-Average	9-39.0	7-35.9
Punt Returns-Yards	5-10	9-21
Kickoff Returns-Yards	2-30	2-34
Fumbles-Lost	0-0	1-1
Penalties-Yards	6-35	6-67

RUSHING: HAM-Ealey, 9/63; Buchanan, 16/22; Fleming, 5/16. SAS-Reed, 22/93; Thompson, 6/14; Molnar, 1/4; Campana, 1/0.

PASSING: HAM-Ealey, 29-18-2, 291. SAS-Lancaster, 29-20-2, 243.

RECEIVING: HAM-Henley, 7/98; Coffey, 3/61; Gabriel, 3/54; Fleming, 2/28; Porter, 1/23; Buchanan, 1/15; Richardson, 1/12. SAS-Campana, 9/87; Barwell, 5/43; Ford, 3/41; Pearce, 2/66; Reed, 1/6.

61st Grey Cup
November 25, 1973 at Toronto (36,653)

Ottawa Rough Riders	7	5	7	3	-22
Edmonton Eskimos	10	0	0	8	-18

EDM Bell 39 run (Cutler)
OTT Nixon 38 pass from Cassata (Organ)
EDM Cutler 11 FG
OTT Safety, Lefebvre tackled by Tosh
OTT Organ 46 FG
OTT Evenson 18 run (Organ)
OTT Organ 39 FG
EDM Lefebvre single
EDM Lefebvre 4 pass from Wilkinson (Cutler)

TEAM STATISTICS	OTT	EDM
First Downs	12	18
Rushes-Yards	25-119	22-92
Passes	23-11-2	42-20-0
Yards Passing	161	208
Punts-Average	8-41.9	11-36.9
Punt Returns-Yards	10-35	8-20
Kickoff Returns-Yards	3-49	3-43
Fumbles-Lost	2-1	8-3
Penalties-Yards	10-101	4-29

RUSHING: OTT-Evenson, 11/53; Cassata, 5/29; Green, 6/25; Foley, 2/7; Adams, 1/5. EDM-Bell-12/46; Harrell, 7/43; Wilkinson, 3/3.

PASSING: OTT-Cassata, 23-11-2, 161. EDM-Lemmerman, 22-10-0, 101; Wilkinson, 20-10-0, 107.

RECEIVING: OTT-Nixon, 4/72; Green, 4/56; Pullen, 3/26; Wellesley, 0/7. EDM-Walls, 7/61; McGowan, 5/58; Harrell, 4/51;
Lefebvre, 2/16; Bell, 1/14; Highbaugh, 1/8.

62nd Grey Cup
November 24, 1974 at Vancouver (34,450)

Montreal Alouettes	0	11	3	6	-20
Edmonton Eskimos	7	0	0	0	- 7

EDM Harrell 8 pass from Wilkinson (Cutler)
MTL Sweet single
MTL Sherrer 5 run (Sweet)
MTL Sweet 18 FG
MTL Sweet 27 FG
MTL Sweet 28 FG
MTL Sweet 25 FG

TEAM STATISTICS	MTL	EDM
First Downs	16	9
Rushes-Yards	29-115	20-44
Passes	28-12-0	25-11-2
Yards Passing	151	126
Punts-Average	9-50.9	12-31.3
Punt Returns-Yards	12-40	8-36
Kickoff Returns-Yards	3-56	1-10
Fumbles-Lost	7-1	4-2
Penalties-Yards	8-54	7-72

RUSHING: MTL-Ferrughelli, 13/59; Sherrer, 11/50; Smith, 2/6; Wade, 1/3; Rodgers, 2/-3. EDM-Bell, 13/17; Warrington, 1/15; Harrell, 4/10; Wilkinson, 2/2.

PASSING: MTL-Wade, 24-10-0, 139; Jones, 4-2-0, 12. EDM-Wilkinson, 16-7-1, 64; Lemmerman, 8-4-1.62; Lefebvre, 1-0-0, 0.

RECEIVING: MTL-Rodgers, 4/67; Sherrer, 3/41; Ferrughelli, 2/5; Dalla Riva, 1/14; Smith, 1/14; Eaman, 1/10. EDM-McGowan, 5/85; Harrell, 4/22; Warrington, 1/13; Lefebvre, 1/6.

63rd Grey Cup
November 23, 1975 at Calgary (32,454)

Edmonton Eskimos	0	3	6	9	- 9
Montreal Alouettes	6	1	0	1	- 8

MTL Sweet 35 FG
MTL Sweet 47 FG
EDM Cutler 40 FG
EDM Sweet single
EDM Cutler 25 FG
EDM Cutler 52 FG
MTL Sweet single

TEAM STATISTICS	EDM	MTL
First Downs	13	14
Rushes-Yards	22-70	28-183
Passes	29-15-1	21-15-1
Yards Passing	165	183
Punts-Average	9-34.9	6-39.5
Punt Returns-Yards	5-41	8-79
Kickoff Returns-Yards	2-20	1-0
Fumbles-Lost	1-1	2-1
Penalties-Yards	3-25	11-75

RUSHING: EDM-Bell, 11/46; Harrell, 6/17; Wilkinson 4/10; Lemmerman, 1/-3. MTL-Ferrughellli, 14/85; Rodgers, 9/34; Jones, 2/15; Smith, 3/4.

PASSING: EDM-Wilkinson, 18-10-0, 105; Lemmerman, 11-5-1, 60. MTL-Jones, 18-12-1, 115; Wade, 3-3-0, 68.

RECEIVING: EDM-McGowan, 9/98; Konihowski, 3/26; Lang, 2/27; Walls, 1/14. MTL-Smith, 8/55; Petty, 3/88; Ferrughelli, 2/20; Dalla River, 1/14l Eaman, 1/6.

64th Grey Cup
November 26, 1976 at Toronto (53,467)

Ottawa Rough Riders	10	0	3	10	-23
Saskatchewan Roughriders	0	17	3	0	-20

OTT Organ 31 FG
OTT Hatanaka 79 punt return (Organ)
SAS Macoritti 31 FG
SAS Mazurak 14 pass from Lancaster (Macoritti)
SAS Richardson 25 pass from Lancaster (Macoritti)
OTT Organ 40 FG
OTT Organ 32 FG
OTT Gabriel 24 pass from Clements (Organ)

TEAM STATISTICS	OTT	SAS
First Downs	14	18
Rushes-Yards	29-173	20-61
Passes	25-11-3	36-22-0
Yards Passing	174	263
Punts-Average	6-39.0	8-33.5
Punt Returns-Yards	7-114	4-30
Kickoff Returns-Yards	3-52	3-57
Fumbles-Lost	1-0	2-1
Penalties-Yards	14-80	5-22

RUSHING: OTT-Green, 19/75; Organ, 1/52; Clements, 5/37; Palazetti, 3/7; Foley, 1/2. SAS-Molnar, 12/43; McGee, 3/11; Campana. 5/7.

PASSING: OTT-Clements,, 25-11-3, 174. SAS-Lancaster, 36-22-0, 263.

RECEIVING: OTT-Gabriel, 7/124; Green, 1/15; Avery, 1/14; Foley, 1/14; Kuzyk,1/7. SAS-Pettersen, 7/80; Richardson, 5/78; McGee, 5/48; Mazurak, 2/31; Dawson, 2/25; Campana, 1/1.

65th Grey Cup
November 27, 1977 at Montreal (68,318)

Montreal Alouettes	3	7	20	11	-41
Edmonton Eskimos	0	3	3	0	- 6

MTL Sweet 17 FG
MTL Sweet 38 FG
MTL Sweet 33 FG
MTL Sweet single
EDM Cutler 38 FG
MTL Sweet 30 FG
EDM Cutler 44 FG
MTL Sweet 23 FG
MTL Dalla Riva 6 pass from Wade (Sweet)
MTL O'Leary 10 pass from Wade (Sweet)
MTL Gaddis 7 pass from Wade (Sweet)
MTL Sweet single
MTL Sweet 21 FG

TEAM STATISTICS	MTL	EDM
First Downs	20	11
Rushes-Yards	25-99	20-69
Passes	41-22-1	29-8-4
Yards Passing	340	92
Punts-Average	8-40.3	9-42.1
Punt Returns-Yards	8-117	5-22
Kickoff Returns-Yards	2-46	7-178
Fumbles-Lost	6-3	7-4
Penalties-Yards	19-157	8-15

RUSHING: MTL-O'Leary, 9/40; Belton, 12/36; Wade, 2/16; Mofford, 1/4; Smith, 1/3. EDM-Strickland, 8/39; Santucci, 6/20; Germany, 3/6; Lemmerman, 1/2; Wilkinson, 2/2.

PASSING: MTL-Wade, 40-22-1, 340; Smith, 1-0-0, 0. EDM-Lemmerman, 22-5-4, 77; Wilkinson, 7-3-0, 15.

RECEIVING: MTL-O'Leary, 6/90; Gaddis, 4/108; Belton, 4/30; Dalla Riva, 3/42; Dattilio, 2/39; Mofford, 2/19; Smith, 1/12. EDM-Lang, 4/65; Konihowski, 1/11; McGowan, 1/9; Strickland, 1/7; Germany, 1/0.

66th Grey Cup
November 26, 1978 at Toronto (54,695)

Edmonton Eskimos	10	4	3	3	-20
Montreal Alouettes	3	0	0	0	-13

EDM Cutler 37 FG
EDM Germany 2 run (Cutler)
MTL Sweet 33 FG
EDM Cutler single
EDM Cutler 35 FG
EDM Cutler 42 FG
MTL Barnes 10 run (Sweet)
MTL Sweet 38 FG
EDM Cutler 25 FG

TEAM STATISTICS	EDM	MTL
First Downs	15	10
Rushes-Yards	31-93	25-78
Passes	26-16-1	26-13-0
Yards Passing	119	147
Punts-Average	10-41.4	12-39.4
Punt Returns-Yards	11-72	9-77
Kickoff Returns-Yards	4-83	2-35
Fumbles-Lost	4-2	2-2
Penalties-Yards	7-30	6-62

RUSHING: EDM-Germany, 18/47; Santucci, 7/31; Wilkinson, 3/9; Moon, 1/3; Warrington, 2/3. MTL-Barnes, 4/31; O'Leary, 7/31; Green, 12/22; Watrin, 0/4; Wade, 2/-10.

PASSING: EDM-Wilkinson, 26-16-1, 119. MTL-Wade, 17-7-0, 74; Barnes, 9-6-0, 73.

RECEIVING: EDM-Scott, 6/53; Santucci, 5/25; Germany, 3/26; Smith, 1/11; McGowan, 1/4. MTL-O'Leary, 5/37; Gaddis, 4/78; Green, 2/6; Dalla Riva, 1/17; Smith, 1/9.

67th Grey Cup
November 25, 1979 at Montreal (65,113)

Edmonton Eskimos	7	0	10	0	-17
Montreal Alouettes	3	3	3	0	- 9

EDM Smith 43 pass from Wilkinson (Cutler)
MTL Sweet 38 FG
MTL Sweet 45 FG
MTL Sweet 29 FG
EDM Scott 33 pass from Moon (Cutler)
EDM Cutler 38 FG

TEAM STATISTICS	EDM	MTL
First Downs	16	21
Rushes-Yards	22-94	30-213
Passes	21-11-1	24-13-1
Yards Passing	205	151

Punts-Average	8-40.4	8-45.5
Punt Returns-Yards	8-51	6-42
Kickoff Returns-Yards	1-16	3-58
Fumbles-Lost	0-0	3-0
Penalties-Yards	5-25	15-145

RUSHING: EDM-Germany, 15/70; Moon, 5/18; Santucci, 2/6. MTL-Green, 21/147; Barnes, 6/55; O'Leary, 3/11.

PASSING: EDM-Moon, 11-5-0, 96; Wilkinson, 10-6-1, 107. MTL-Barnes, 23-13-1, 151; Baker, 1-0-0, 0.

RECEIVING: EDM-W. Smith, 4/90; Scott, 3/72; Kelly, 2/27; Lang, 1/9; Santucci, 1/7. MTL-Green, 4/30; Gaddis, 3/53; O'Leary, 3/44; Baker, 2/14; Smith, 1/10.

68th Grey Cup
November 23, 1980 at Toronto (54,661)

Edmonton Eskimos	10	14	10	14	-48
Hamilton Tiger-Cats	3	6	1	0	-10

EDM	Cutler 25 FG
EDM	Germany 1 run (Cutler)
HAM	Ruoff 48 FG
HAM	Ruoff 37 FG
EDM	Germany 1 run (Cutler)
EDM	Kelly 75 pass from Moon (Cutler)
HAM	Ruoff 42 FG
HAM	Ruoff single
EDM	Scott 19 pass from Moon (Cutler)
EDM	Cutler 9 FG
EDM	Scott 8 pass from Moon (Cutler)
EDM	Scott 17 pass from Wilkinson (Cutler)

TEAM STATISTICS	EDM	HAM
First Downs	30	12
Rushes-Yards	27-205	16-112
Passes	39-23-1	29-9-4
Yards Passing	428	151
Punts-Average	2-42.0	7-43.7
Punt Returns-Yards	7-25	1-8
Kickoff Returns-Yards	1-18	7-132
Fumbles-Lost	3-3	1-1
Penalties-Yards	4-30	9-90

RUSHING: EDM-Lumsden, 8/85; Moon, 7/71; Wilkinson, 2/27; Germany, 7/15; Santucci, 3/7. HAM-Graves, 12/67; Marler, 4/45.

PASSING: EDM-Moon, 33-21-1, 398; Wilkinson, 6-2-0, 30. HAM-Marler, 24-9-3, 151; Rozantz, 5-0-1, 0.

RECEIVING: EDM-Scott, 12/174; Kelly, 4/104; Fryer, 4/77; Buggs, 3.73. HAM-Pettersen, 3/47; Holland, 2/43; Cyncar, 2/37; Paterson, 2/47.

69th Grey Cup
November 22, 1981 at Montreal (52,478)

Edmonton Eskimos	0	1	14	11	-26
Ottawa Rough Riders	11	7	0	3	-23

OTT	Organ 34 FG
OTT	Organ 31 FG
OTT	Reid 1 run (Organ)
OTT	Platt 14 run (Organ)
EDM	Cutler single
EDM	Germany 2 run (Cutler)
EDM	Moon 1 run (Cutler)
OTT	Organ 28 FG
EDM	Moon 1 run (Cyncar pass from Moon)
EDM	Cutler 27 FG

TEAM STATISTICS	EDM	OTT
First Downs	22	14
Rushes-Yards	25-88	18-83
Passes	40-23-3	29-16-3
Yards Passing	261	204
Punts-Average	9-49.1	9-43.1
Punt Returns-Yards	9-49	9-80
Kickoff Returns-Yards	3-59	4-96
Fumbles-Lost	1-1	1-1
Penalties-Yards	7-57	8-53

RUSHING: EDM-Germany, 13/56; Moon, 11/30; Lumsden, 1/2. OTT-Platt, 12/48; Watts, 5/29; Reid 1/1, Stoqua, 0/5.

PASSING: EDM-Moon, 27-13-3, 181; Wilkinson, 13-10-0, 80. OTT-Watts, 29-16-3, 204.

RECEIVING: EDM-Lumsden, 8/91; Cyncar, 7/61; Kelly, 4/46; Scott, 2/44; Germany, 1/14; Smith, 1/5. OTT-Gabfriel, 6/76; Platt, 4/29; Kirk, 2/32; Reid, 2/29; Stoqua,1/34; Avery, 1/4.

70th Grey Cup
November 28, 1982 at Toronto (54,741)

Edmonton Eskimos	3	17	6	6	-32
Toronto Argonauts	7	7	0	2	-16

EDM	Cutler 38 FG
TOR	Tolbert 84 pass from Holloway (Dorsey)
EDM	Kelly 14 pass from Moon (Cutler)
TOR	Greer 10 pass from Holloway (Dorsey)
EDM	Kelly 41 pass from Moon (Cutler)
EDM	Cutler 29 FG
EDM	Lumsden 1 run (Cutler failed)
EDM	Cutler 44 FG
EDM	Cutler 33 FG
TOR	Safety

TEAM STATISTICS	EDM	TOR
First Downs	33	16
Rushes-Yards	28-200	8-53
Passes	33-21-1	36-17-1
Yards Passing	319	319
Punts-Average	3-46.0	8-37.8
Punt Returns-Yards	7-31	3-24
Kickoff Returns-Yards	2-30	5-86
Fumbles-Lost	7-1	2-1
Penalties-Yards	4-10	6-40

RUSHING: EDM-Moon, 9/91; Germany, 12/70; Lumsden, 7/39. TOR-Holloway, 7/54; Minter, 1/-1.

PASSING: EDM-Moon, 33-21-1, 319. OTT-Holloway, 34-17-0, 319; Greer, 2-0-1, 0.

RECEIVING: EDM-Kelly, 6/111; Fryer, 4/55; Smith, 4/47; Scott, 3/59; Lumsden, 2/29; Germany, 1/18; Kehoe, 1/0. OTT-Greer, 7/105; Minter, 7/105; Tolbert, 1/84; Bronk, 1/13; Pearson, 1/12.

71st Grey Cup
November 27, 1983 at Vancouver (59,345)

Toronto Argonauts	0	7	2	9	-18
British Columbia Lions	7	10	0	0	-17

BC	Fernandez 45 pass from Dewalt (Passaglia)
TOR	Carinci 14 pass from Holloway (Ilesic)
BC	White 20 pass from Dewalt (Passaglia)
BC	Passaglie 31 FG
TOR	Ilesic single
TOR	Ilesic single
TOR	Ilesic 43 FG
TOR	Minter 1 pass from Barnes (Barnes pass failed)

TEAM STATISTICS	TOR	BC
First Downs	20	19
Rushes-Yards	13-96	10-46
Passes	39-21-1	47-28-1
Yards Passing	270	325
Punts-Average	8-47.0	11-41.9
Punt Returns-Yards	10-68	8-31
Kickoff Returns-Yards	3-82	2-41
Fumbles-Lost	2-1	1-1
Penalties-Yards	2-10	4-25

RUSHING: TOR-Barnes, 3/36; Minter, 8/36; Holloway, 2/24. BC-Strong, 6/35; White, 3/10; Dewalt, 1/1.

PASSING: TOR-Barnes, 24-14-0, 175; Holloway, 15-7-1, 95. BC-Dewalt, 47-28-1, 325.

RECEIVING: TOR-Minter, 6/68; Greer, 4/73; Tolbert, 3/45; Pearson, 2/34; Townsend, 2/20; Carinci, 2/16. BC-White, 8/92; Fernandez, 7/130; Strong, 6/33; Armour, 4/42; Pankratz, 1/12; Chapdelaine, 1/8; Debrueys, 1/8.

72nd Grey Cup
November 18, 1984 at Edmonton (60,081)

Winnipeg Blue Bombers	3	27	3	14	-47
Hamilton Tiger-Cats	14	3	0	0	-17

HAM	Brock 15 run (Ruoff)
HAM	DiPietro 7 pass from Brock (Ruoff)
WPG	Kennerd 25 FG
HAM	Ruoff 20 FG
WPG	Kennerd 46 FG
WPG	Reaves 3 run (Kennerd)
WPG	Poplawski 12 pass from Clements (Kennerd)
WPG	Mikawos 24 fumble recovery (Kennerd)
WPG	Kennerd 19 FG
WPG	Kennerd 16 FG
WPG	Reaves 3 run (Kennerd)
WPG	Boyd 4 pass from Hufnagel (Kennerd)

TEAM STATISTICS	WPG	HAM
First Downs	27	14
Rushes-Yards	32-177	9-24
Passes	32-23-2	43-23-1
Yards Passing	311	209
Punts-Average	4-43.0	12-39.9
Punt Returns-Yards	12-92	4-41
Kickoff Returns-Yards	3-36	10-141
Fumbles-Lost	2-1	2-1
Penalties-Yards	9-63	7-20

RUSHING: WPG-Kehoe, 12/89; Reaves, 15/64; Cantner, 1/16; Clements, 4/8. HAM-Brock, 2/17; Bragagnolo, 2/4; Shepherd, 2/4; Graffi, 1/1; Tedford, 1/1; Crawford, 1/-3.

PASSING: WPG-Clements, 29-20-2, 281; Hufnagel, 3-3-0 30. HAM-Brock, 42-22-1, 200.

RECEIVING: WPG-Poplawski, 5/101; Kehoe, 5/47; Murphy, 3/53; Boyd, 3/28; Reaves, 3/21; Cantner, 2/35; House, 2/26. HAM-Bragagnolo, 7/48; Jett, 6/45; DiPietro, 4/64; Shepherd, 3/27; Johnson, 2/23; Francis, 1/2.

73rd Grey Cup
November 24, 1985 at Montreal (56,723)

British Columbia Lions	10	13	3	11	-37
Hamilton Tiger-Cats	0	14	0	10	-24

BC	Armour 84 pass from Dewalt (Passaglia)

BC	Passaglia 44 FG
BC	Passaglia 20 FG
HAM	Ingram 35 pass from Hobart (Ruoff)
HAM	Shepherd 1 run (Ruoff)
BC	Armour 59 pass from Dewalt (Passglia)
BC	Passaglia 24 FG
BC	Passaglia 37 FG
BC	Passaglia 27 FG
HAM	Ruoff 21 FG
BC	Sandusky 66 pass from Dewalt (Passaglia)
HAM	Stapler 12 pass from Hobart (Ruoff)
BC	Passaglia single

TEAM STATISTICS	BC	HAM
First Downs	15	17
Rushes-Yards	28-121	24-213
Passes	28-14-0	35-11-2
Yards Passing	394	184
Punts-Average	11-41.5	12-46.3
Punt Returns-Yards	12-105	10-45
Kickoff Returns-Yards	3-66	5-101
Fumbles-Lost	2-1	1-1
Penalties-Yards	9-41	5-5

RUSHING: BC-Sims, 19/98; Passaglia, 1/13; Dewalt, 4/5; White, 4/5. HAM-Hobart 10/125; Shepherd, 14/88.

PASSING: BC-Dewalt, 28-14-0, 394. HAM-Hobart, 32-10-1, 174; Porras, 3-1-1, 10.

RECEIVING: BC-Sandusky, 6/135; Armour, 3/151; Pankratz, 3/79; White, 2/29. HAM-Stapler, 5/55; Ingram, 3/107; Crawford, 2/12; DiPietro, 1/10.

74th Grey Cup

November 30, 1986 at Vancouver (59,621)

Hamilton Tiger-Cats	17	12	7	3	-39
Edmonton Eskimos	0	0	7	8	-15

HAM	Stapler 35 pass from Kerrigan (Osbaldiston)
HAM	Rockford 1 blocked punt recovery (Osbaldiston)
HAM	Osbaldiston 39 FG
HAM	Osbaldiston 30 FG
HAM	Osbaldiston 26 FG
HAM	Osbaldiston 40 FG
HAM	Osbaldiston 40 FG
HAM	Ingram 44 pass from Kerrigan (Osbaldiston)
EDM	Da. Allen 6 run (Dixon)
EDM	Kelly 11 pass from Da. Allen (Da. Allen run)
HAM	Osbaldiston 47 FG

TEAM STATISTICS	HAM	EDM
First Downs	16	18
Rushes-Yards	23-80	19-76
Passes	35-16-3	38-18-2
Yards Passing	309	286
Punts-Average	7-35.9	7-43.7
Punt Returns-Yards	7-48	6-31
Kickoff Returns-Yards	3-39	6-135
Fumbles-Lost	2-2	8-7
Penalties-Yards	6-61	9-54

RUSHING: HAM-Huclack, 10/48; Hobart, 3/9; Bender, 4/9; Kerrigan, 2/7; Tommy, 4/7. EDM-Dunigan, 7/27; Da. Allen, 4.20; Johnstone, 3/14; Jones, 3/13; Skinner, 2/2.

PASSING: HAM-Kerrigan, 32-15-2, 304; Hobart, 3-1-1, 5. EDM-Dunigan, 26-11-1, 158; Da. Allen, 12-7-1, 128.

RECEIVING: HAM-Stapler, 4/130; Ingram, 4/100; Champion, 3/49; DiPietro, 3/14; Huclack, 2/16. EDM-Jones, 5/84;l Kelly, 3/47; Do. Allen, 3/38; House, 2/51; Skinner, 2/31; Johnstone, 1/20; Richards, 1/9; Cyncar, 1/6,

75th Grey Cup

November 29, 1987 at Vancouver (59,478)

Edmonton Eskimos	7	10	4	17	-38
Toronto Argonauts	3	21	3	9	-36

EDM	Williams 155 missed field goal return (Kauric)
TOR	Chomyc 34 FG
EDM	Kauric 34 FG
TOR	Fenerty 61 pass from Renfroe (Chomyc)
TOR	Fenerty 4 run (Chomyc)
TOR	Landry 54 fumble recovery (Chomyc)
EDM	Cyncar 6 pass from Allen (Kauric)
EDM	Kauric 22 FG
TOR	Chomyc 50 FG
EDM	Kauric single
EDM	Kelly 15 pass from Allen (Kauric)
TOR	Chomyc 32 FG
EDM	Allen 17 run (Kauric)
TOR	Barrett 25 run (? failed two-point conversion)
EDM	Kauric 49 FG

TEAM STATISTICS	EDM	TOR
First Downs	25	20
Rushes-Yards	19-138	25-171
Passes	32-23-1	31-13-0
Yards Passing	359	213
Punts-Average	4-44.8	4-44.0
Punt Returns-Yards	4-18	4-29
Kickoff Returns-Yards	7-123	8-140
Fumbles-Lost	3-2	1-0
Penalties-Yards	7-25	5-35

RUSHING: EDM-M. Jones, 9/76; Allen, 6/46; Dunigan, 3/18; Johnstone, 1/-2. TOR-Fenerty, 17/106; Barrett, 1/25; Hudson, 5/25; Renfroe, 2/15.

PASSING: EDM-Allen 20-15-0, 255; Dunigan, 12-8-1, 204. TOR-Renfroe, 19-9-0, 153; Barrett, 12-4-0, 60.

RECEIVING: EDM-House, 7/134; M. Jones, 4/52; Kelly, 3/59; S. Jones, 3/41; Skinner, 3/28; Johnstone, 2/39; Cyncar, 1/6. TOR-Pearson, 4/38; D. Smith, 3/51; J. Smith, 2/33; Thomas, 2/29; Fenerty, 1/61; Johns, 1/1.

76th Grey Cup

November 27, 1988 at Ottawa (50,604)

Winnipeg Blue Bombers	4	10	5	3	-22
British Columbia Lions	7	8	4	2	-21

WPG	Cameron single
BC	Cherry 14 run (Passaglia)
WPG	Kennerd 22 FG
WPG	Kennerd 43 FG
BC	Williams 26 pass from Dunigan (Passaglia)
WPG	Murphy 35 pass from Salisbury (Kennerd)
BC	Passaglia single
BC	Passaglia 28 FG
WPG	Kennerd 20 FG
WPG	Kennerd single
BC	Passaglia single
WPG	Cameron single
WPG	Kennerd 30 FG
BC	Safety conceded by Cameron

TEAM STATISTICS	WPG	BC
First Downs	12	24
Rushes-Yards	17-58	37-218
Passes	32-12-0	32-14-2
Yards Passing	246	198
Punts-Average	12-47.3	9-45.7
Punt Returns-Yards	7-44	12-28
Kickoff Returns-Yards	3-54	6-163
Fumbles-Lost	0-0	2-1
Penalties-Yards	12-86	11-95

RUSHING: WPG-Jessie, 8/35; Johns, 9/23. BC-Cherry, 23/133; Dunigan, 7/49; Parker, 7/36.

PASSING: WPG-Salisbury, 32-12-0, 246. BC-Dunigan, 32-14-2, 196.

RECEIVING: WPG-Murphy, 5/165; Johns, 3/38; Winey,1/16; Fabi, 1/12; Rhymes, 1/9; Jessie, 1/6. BC-Carinci, 4/59; Williams, 3/78; Lecky, 3/34; Cherry, 3/24; Parker, 1/1,

77th Grey Cup

November 26, 1989 at Toronto (54,088)

Saskatchewan Roughriders	1	21	19	9	-43
Hamilton Tiger-Cats	13	14	3	10	-40

HAM	Osbaldiston 42 FG
HAM	Osbaldiston 38 FG
SAS	Baker single
HAM	Champion 13 pass from Kerrigan (Osbaldiston)
SAS	Elgaard 5 pass from Austin (Ridgway)
HAM	McAdoo 30 pass from Kerrigan (Osbaldiston)
SAS	Fairholm 75 pass from Austin (Ridgway)
HAM	McAdoo 1 run (Osbaldiston)
SAS	Narcisse 5 pass from Austin (Ridgway)
SAS	Ridgway 34 FG
HAM	Osbaldiston 40 FG
SAS	Safety conceded by Osbaldiston
SAS	McCray 1 run (Ridgway)
SAS	Ridgway 25 FG
HAM	Osbaldiston 47 FG
SAS	Ridgway 20 FG
HAM	Champion 9 pass from Kerrigan (Osbaldiston)
SAS	Ridgway 35 FG

TEAM STATISTICS	SAS	HAM
First Downs	28	24
Rushes-Yards	14-41	23-89
Passes	44-26-2	37-23-1
Yards Passing	474	303
Punts-Average	6-46.5	6-46.7
Punt Returns-Yards	6-42	3-67
Kickoff Returns-Yards	10-296	8-143
Fumbles-Lost	0-0	2-1
Penalties-Yards	3-36	4-28

RUSHING: SAS-McCray, 8/22; Jones, 4/11; Austin, 2/8. HAM-McAdoo, 21/83; Tommy, 2/6.

PASSING: SAS-Austin, 43-26-1, 474; Elgaard, 1-0-0, 0. HAM-Kerrigan, 37-23-1, 303.

RECEIVING: SAS-Elgaard, 6/73; Narcisse, 5/98; Ellingson, 5/64; Guy, 4/100; McCray, 4/42; Fairholm, 2/97. HAM-Champion, 8/106; DiPietro, 5/54; Estell, 3/33; Knight, 3/34; Winfield, 2/43; McAdoo, 3/29; Zatylny, 1/13.

78th Grey Cup

November 25, 1990 at Vancouver (46,968)

Winnipeg Blue Bombers	10	0	28	12	-50
Edmonton Eskimos	0	4	0	7	-11

WPG	Kennerd 13 FG
WPG	Hull 1 pass from Burgess (Kennerd)
EDM	Macoritti single

EDM	Macoritti 37 FG
WPG	Battle 32 interception return (Kennerd)
WPG	Tuttle 5 pass from Burgess (Kennerd)
WPG	Hudson 18 pass from Burgess (Kennerd)
WPG	Hudson 2 run (Kennerd)
EDM	Willis 20 pass from Ham (Macoritti)
WPG	Safety Ham tackled by West
WPG	Kennerd 14 FG
WPG	House 56 pass from McManus (Kennerd)

TEAM STATISTICS	WPG	EDM
First Downs	23	23
Rushes-Yards	22-88	27-156
Passes	37-21-1	37-20-3
Yards Passing	367	253
Punts-Average	7-42.3	7-44.9
Punt Returns-Yards	6-100	7-26
Kickoff Returns-Yards	3-65	7-117
Fumbles-Lost	3-1	6-4
Penalties-Yards	7-45	11-88

RUSHING: WPG-Mimbs, 11/55; Burgess, 7/26; Hudson, 4/7. EDM-Ham, 11/84; Marshall, 13/54; Johnstone, 1/11; Soles, 1/8; Walling, 1/-1.

PASSING: WPG-Burgess, 31-18-0, 286; Garza, 4-1-1, 15; McManus, 2-2-0, 66. EDM-Ham, 37-20-3, 253.

RECEIVING: WPG-House, 6/107; Hudson, 4/66; Tuttle, 3/70; Winey, 3/67; Hull, 2/26; Steater, 2/17; Mimbs, 1/14. EDM-Ellis, 7/102; Willis, 5/75; Cyncar, 2/24; Soles, 2/17; Wright, 1/11; Smith, 1/8; Marshall, 1/6.

79th Grey Cup
November 24, 1991 at Winnipeg (51,895)

Toronto Argonauts	8	3	8	17	-36
Calgary Stampeders	7	3	4	7	-21

TOR	Berry 50 interception return (Chomyc)
TOR	Chomyc single
CAL	Barrett 8 run (McLoughlin)
CAL	McLoughlin 34 FG
TOR	Chomyc 27 FG
CAL	McLoughlin single
CAL	McLoughlin 27 FG
TOR	Chomyc single
TOR	Smith 48 pass from Dunigan (Chomyc)
TOR	Chomyc FG
CAL	Pitts 13 pas from Barrett (McLoughlin)
TOR	Ismail 87 kickoff return (Chomyc)
TOR	Masotti 36 pass from Dunigan (Chomyc)

TEAM STATISTICS	TOR	CAL
First Downs	7	28
Rushes-Yards	15-53	18-87
Passes	29-12-0	58-34-3
Yards Passing	142	376
Punts-Average	11-36.2	9-28.3
Punt Returns-Yards	7-82	10-48
Kickoff Returns-Yards	6-244	5-65
Fumbles-Lost	5-3	3-2
Penalties-Yards	4-54	1-15

RUSHING: TOR-Dunigan, 7/44; Smellie, 5/11; Clemons,3/-2. CAL-Jenkins, 7/28; Sapunjis, 2.27; Smith, 1/16; Barrett, 8/16.

PASSING: TOR-Dunigan, 29-12-0, 142. CAL-Barrett, 58-34-3, 376.

RECEIVING: TOR-Smith, 3/62; Williams, 3/14; Masotti, 2/45; Ismail, 2/7; Clemons, 1/7; Smellie, 1/7. CAL-Bland, 10/117; Beals, 7/67; Sapunjis, 5/64; Pitts, 4/66; Smith, 4/39; Simien, 2/13; Jenkins, 2/10.

80th Grey Cup
November 29, 1992 at Toronto (45,863)

Calgary Stampeders	11	6	0	7	-24
Winnipeg Blue Bombers	0	0	0	0	-10

CAL	McLoughlin 37 FG
CAL	McLoughlin single
CAL	Sapunjis 35 pass from Flutie (McLoughlin)
CAL	McLoughlin 17 FG
CAL	McLoughlin 17 FG
CAL	Pitts 15 pass from Flutie (McLoughlin)
WPG	Westwood 46 FG
WPG	Alphin 27 pass from McManus (Westwood)

TEAM STATISTICS	CAL	WPG
First Downs	25	12
Rushes-Yards	15-48	10-36
Passes	49-33-0	37-13-1
Yards Passing	480	202
Punts-Average	8-34.4	10-43.7
Punt Returns-Yards	10-72	5-28
Kickoff Returns-Yards	2-19	3-49
Fumbles-Lost	1-1	2-1
Penalties-Yards	11-116	7-40

RUSHING: CAL-Flutie, 4/20; Jenkins, 9/25; McVey, 2/3. WPG-Richardson, 8/27; Dunigan, 2/9.

PASSING: CAL-Flutie, 49-33-0, 480. WPG-Dunigan, 19-6-0, 47; McManus, 18-7-1, 155.

RECEIVING: CAL-Bland, 8/116; Sapunjis, 7/85; Pitts, 7/75; Crawford, 6/162; Smith, 3/33; Jenkins, 2/9. WPG-Alphin, 5-103; Richardson, 3/18; Crifo, 2/14; Pillow, 1/42; Thompson, 1/15; Hudson,1/0.10

81st Grey Cup
November 28, 1993 at Calgary (50,035)

Edmonton Eskimos	17	7	0	9	-33
Winnipeg Blue Bombers	0	10	7	6	-23

EDM	Floyd 4 run (Fleming)
EDM	Sandusky 2 pass from Allen (Fleming)
EDM	Fleming 41 FG
EDM	Fleming single
EDM	Fleming 26 FG
WPG	Richardson 2 run (Westwood)
EDM	Fleming 45 FG
WPG	Westwood 48 FG
WPG	Garza 1 run (Westwood)
WPG	Westwood 32 FG
EDM	Fleming 36 FG
EDM	Fleming 15 FG
WPG	Westwood 32 FG
EDM	Fleming 19 FG

TEAM STATISTICS	EDM	WPG
First Downs	20	23
Rushes-Yards	33-138	16-42
Passes	27-17-1	40-23-2
Yards Passing	283	322
Punts-Average	6-48.7	7-45.3
Punt Returns-Yards	5-4	5-16
Kickoff Returns-Yards	4-94	3-31
Fumbles-Lost	3-2	7-5
Penalties-Yards	7-37	11-85

RUSHING: EDM-Allen, 13/93; Floyd, 15/41; Soles, 5/4. WPG-Richardson, 10/26; Garza, 5/10; Johnstone, 1/6.

PASSING: EDM-Allen, 27-16-1, 238. WPG-Garza, 40-23-2, 322.

RECEIVING: EDM-Brown, 4/114; Soles, 4/46; Sabdusky, 3/36; Floyd, 3/17; Christensen, 2/25. WPG-Williams, 7/118; Jackson, 4/57; Richardson, 4/44; Wilcox, 4/39; Alphin, 3/55; Johnstone, 1/9.

82nd Grey Cup
November 27, 1994 at Vancouver (55,097)

British Columbia Lions	3	7	10	6	-26
Baltimore	0	17	3	3	-23

BC	Passaglia 47 FG
BAL	Ham 1 run (Igwebuike)
BAL	Anthony 36 interception return (Igwbuike)
BC	Gordon 17 interception return (Passaglia)
BAL	Igwebuike 17 FG
BAL	Igwebuike 26 FG
BC	McManus 1 run (Passaglia)
BC	Passaglia 42 FG
BC	Passaglia 27 FG
BAL	Igwebuike 29 FG
BC	Passaglia 38 FG

TEAM STATISTICS	BC	BAL
First Downs	16	15
Rushes-Yards	33-213	28-171
Passes	23-9-3	24-9-2
Yards Passing	162	193
Punts-Average	7-38.1	8-39.0
Punt Returns-Yards	8-36	5-39
Kickoff Returns-Yards	3-54	5-95
Fumbles-Lost	1-0	1-1
Penalties-Yards	6-35	5-42

RUSHING: BC-Philpot, 17/109; Millington, 13/85; Flutie, 2/18; McManus, 1/1. BAL-Ham, 9/88; Pringle, 18/71; Drummond, 1/12.

PASSING: BC-Austin, 16-6-3, 60; McManus, 7-3-0, 93. BAL-Ham, 24-9-2, 193.

RECEIVING: BC-Alexander, 5/119; Flutie, 2/25; Clark, 1/9; Murphy, 1/0. BAL-Washington, 2/72; Wilson, 2/52; Drummond, 2/38; Pringle, 2/18; Armstrong, 1/13.

83rd Grey Cup
November 19, 1995 at Regina (52,064)

Baltimore Stallions	7	16	8	6	-37
Calgary Stampeders	6	7	7	0	-20

BAL	Wright 82 punt return (Huerta)
CAL	McLoughlin 35 FG
CAL	McLoughlin 32 FG
CAL	Pope 2 pass fron Flutie (McLoughlin)
BAL	Huerta 30 FG
BAL	Walton 5 fumble recovery (Huerta)
BAL	Huerta 45 FG
BAL	Huerta 53 FG
BAL	Miller single
CAL	Flutie 1 run (Mcloughlin)
BAL	Ham 13 run (Huerta)
BAL	Huerta 41 FG
BAL	Huerta 18 FG

TEAM STATISTICS	BAL	CAL
First Downs	18	22
Rushes-Yards	29-148	20-78
Passes	29-17-0	48-23-1

Yards Passing	214	286
Punts-Average	6-49.5	7-33.7
Punt Returns-Yards	4-93	2-6
Kickoff Returns-Yards	3-37	4-79
Fumbles-Lost	2-1	2-2
Penalties-Yards	6-60	5-40

RUSHING: BAL-Pringle, 21/135; Ham, 7/24; Alphin, 1/-11. CAL-Flutie, 10/45; Stewart, 10/33.

PASSING: BAL-Ham, 29-17-0, 214. CAL-Flutie, 48-23-1, 286.

RECEIVING: BAL-Drummond, 3/47; Clark, 3/43; Armstrong, 3/29; Alphin, 2.40; Tuippuoltu, 2/21; Culver, 2/18; Pringle, 2/16. CAL-Sapunjis, 8/113; Stewart, 7/58; Pitts, 3/54; Vaughn, 3/46; Williams, 1/13; Pope, 1/2.

84th Grey Cup
November 24, 1996 at Hamilton (38,595)

Toronto Argonauts	0	27	3	13	-43
Edmonton Eskimos	9	14	0	14	-37

EDM	Safety, Flutie tackled by Blugh
EDM	Brown 64 pass from McManus (Fleming)
TOR	Vanderjagt 38 FG
TOR	Cunningham 80 punt return (Vanderjagt)
TOR	Vanderjagt 33 FG
EDM	Sanduksy 75 pass from McManus (Fleming)
TOR	Drummond 2 run (Vanderjagt)
EDM	Williams 91 kickoff return (Fleming)
TOR	Flutie 10 run (Vanderjagt)
TOR	Vanderjagt 17 FG
TOR	Vanderjagt 29 FG
EDM	Blount 5 run (Fleming)
TOR	Vanderjagt 27 FG
TOR	Smith 49 interception return (Vanderjagt)
EDM	Tolbert 6 pass from McManus (Fleming)

TEAM STATISTICS	TOR	EDM
First Downs	20	21
Rushes-Yards	24-153	13-48
Passes	35-22-0	38-25-1
Yards Passing	302	413
Punts-Average	3-41.3	4-32.8
Punt Returns-Yards	2-81	3-38
Kickoff Returns-Yards	7-111	6-136
Fumbles-Lost	2-0	0-0
Penalties-Yards	3-30	4-30

RUSHING: TOR-Flutie, 12/103; Drummond, 12/50. EDM-Blount, 8/29; Burse, 4/14; Tobert, 1/5.

PASSING: TOR-Flutie, 35-22-0, 302. EDM-McManus, 38-25-1, 413.

RECEIVING: TOR-Masotti, 6/100; Drummond, 6/77; Cunningham, 4/58; Clemons, 4/49; Izquierdo, 2/18. EDM-Flutie, 7/84; Brown, 5/125; Tobert, 4/58; Sandusky, 3/120; Blount, 3/7; Burse, 2/11; Mazzoli, 1/8.

85th Grey Cup
November 16, 1997 at Edmonton (60,431)

Toronto Argonauts	7	13	21	6	-47
Saskatchewan Roughriders	3	6	0	14	-23

SAS	McCallum 28 FG
TOR	Mitchell 14 pass from Flutie (Vanderjagt)
TOR	Drummond 6 pass from Flutie (Vanderjagt)
TOR	Vanderjagt 22 FG
SAS	Daniels 3 run (failed)
TOR	Vanderjagt 12 FG
TOR	Smith 95 kickoff return
TOR	Flutie 10 run (Vanderjagt)
TOR	Clemons 5 pass from Flutie (Vanderjagt)
TOR	Vanderjagt 22 FG
SAS	Saunders 51 pass from Slack (McCallum)
TOR	Vanderjagt 31 FG
SAS	Slack 1 run (McCallum)

TEAM STATISTICS	TOR	SAS
First Downs	34	22
Rushes-Yards	27-208	17-62
Passes	38-30-1	38-22-2
Yards Passing	352	279
Punts-Average	2-45.5	5-31.8
Punt Returns-Yards	4-39	2-7
Kickoff Returns-Yards	5-136	8-169
Fumbles-Lost	0-0	1-0
Penalties-Yards	10-71	7-40

RUSHING: TOR-Drummond, 16/128; Clemons, 6/45; Flutie, 5/35. SAS-Daniels, 9/35; Saunders, 7/26; Slack, 1/1.

PASSING: TOR-Flutie, 38-30-1, 352. SAS-Slack, 37-22-2, 279; Mason, 1-0-0. 0.

RECEIVING: TOR-Masotti, 6/102; Drummond, 6/59; Dmytryshyn, 6/56; Mitchell, 5/58; Clemons, 5/53; Casola, 1/13; Kirwan, 1/11. SAS-Narcisse, 7/67; Saunders, 7/103; Mayfield, 4/59; Farthing, 4/42; Walters, 1/8.

86th Grey Cup
November 22, 1998 at Winnipeg (34,157)

Calgary Stampeders	4	6	7	9	-26
Hamilton Tiger-Cats	3	13	2	6	-24

CAL	McLoughlin single
HAM	Osbaldiston 24 FG
CAL	McLoughlin 34 FG
CAL	Anderson 3 run (run failed)
HAM	Osbaldiston 20 FG
HAM	Williams 35 pass from McManus (Osbaldiston)
HAM	Osbaldiston 40 FG
HAM	Osbaldiston single
HAM	Osbaldiston single
CAL	Garcia 1 run (McLoughlin)
CAL	McLoughlin 22 FG
CAL	McLoughlin 33 FG
HAM	Williams 1 run (McManus pass failed)
CAL	McLoughlin 35 FG

TEAM STATISTICS	CAL	HAM
First Downs	29	22
Rushes-Yards	29-152	19-78
Passes	34-22-0	40-20-1
Yards Passing	259	288
Punts-Average	3-33.7	5-46.6
Punt Returns-Yards	3-21	2-12
Kickoff Returns-Yards	3-58	4-83
Fumbles-Lost	1-0	1-0
Penalties-Yards	3-37	2-8

RUSHING: CAL-Anderson, 18/105; Garcia, 11/47, HAM-Williams, 12/42; Smith, 1/20; McManus, 3/14; Amerson, 3/2.

PASSING: CAL-Garcia, 33-22-0, 259; Dickerson, 1-0-0, 0. HAM-McManus, 40-20-1, 288.

RECEIVING: CAL-Danielsen, 6/82; Pitts, 5/74; Moore, 3/34; Anderson, 3/27; Vaughn, 3/24; Cummings, 2/18. HAM-Williams, 5/78; Morreale, 4/62; Flutie, 4.50; Grigg, 4/43; Amerson, 2/56; Olive, 1/-1.

87th Grey Cup
November 27, 1999 at Vancouver (45,118)

Hamilton Tiger-Cats	10	11	4	7	-32
Calgary Stampeders	0	0	14	7	-21

HAM	Williams 1 run (Osbaldiston)
HAM	Osbaldiston 46 FG
HAM	Osbaldiston single
HAM	Flutie 9 pass from McManus (Osbaldiston)
HAM	Osbaldiston single
CAL	Danielson 71 pass from Dickenson (McLoughlin)
CAL	Pitts 18 pass from Dickenson (McLoughlin)
HAM	Osbaldiston 20 FG
HAM	Flutie 7 pass from McManus (Osbaldiston)
CAL	Forde 1 run (McLoughlin)

TEAM STATISTICS	HAM	CAL
First Downs	22	18
Rushes-Yards	27-80	13-57
Passes	34-22-0	38-24-1
Yards Passing	347	320
Punts-Average	8-44.5	10-38.0
Punt Returns-Yards	8-39	5-38
Kickoff Returns-Yards	4-53	6-92
Fumbles-Lost	1-0	1-1
Penalties-Yards	5-25	3-25

RUSHING: HAM-Lapointe, 9/40; Williams, 13/25; McManus, 5/15. CAL-Anderson, 7/28; Dickenson, 4/26; McCoy, 1/2; Forde, 1/1.

PASSING: HAM-McManus, 34-22-0, 347. CAL-Dickenson, 38-24-1, 321.

RECEIVING: HAM-Flutie, 6/109; Akins, 4/43; Williams, 3/77; Amerson, 3/52; Grigg, 2/11; Grant, 1/4. CAL-Pitts, 6/95; Danielsen, 40; Dowdell, 5/40; Moore, 3/101; Anderson, 3/26; Cummings, 2/8; Arlain, 1/14.

88th Grey Cup
November 26, 2000 at Calgary (43,822)

British Columbia Lions	8	4	0	16	-28
Montreal Alouettes	3	0	7	16	-26

BC	Passaglia single
BC	Allen 1 run (Passaglia)
MTL	Baker 19 FG
BC	Passaglia single
BC	Passaglia 23 FG
MTL	Climie 1 pass from Calvillo (Baker)
BC	Drummond 44 run (Passaglia)
MTL	Baker 51 FG
BC	Allen 1 run (failed)
MTL	Pringle 5 run (Baker)
BC	Passaglia 29 FG
MTL	Cahoon 59 pass from Calvillo (Calvillo pass failed)

TEAM STATISTICS	BC	MTL
First Downs	27	21
Rushes-Yards	36-260	25-131
Passes	31-18-0	26-13-2
Yards Passing	234	242
Punts-Average	3-43.0	6-42.2
Punt Returns-Yards	5-23	3-18
Kickoff Returns-Yards	4-78	6-98
Fumbles-Lost	1-1	0-0
Penalties-Yards	5-55	6-54

RUSHING: BC-Drummond, 10/122; Millington, 17/99; Allen, 9/39. MTL-Pringle, 20/115; Calvillo, 4/16; Haskins, 1/0.

PASSING: BC-Allen, 31-18-0, 234. MTL-Calvillo, 26-13-2, 242.

RECEIVING: BC-Blair, 6/87; Drummond, 3/41; Millington, 3/38; Jackson, 3/33; Oliver, 2/24; Graham, 1/11. MTL-Climie, 6/97; Cahoon, 2/73; Alexander, 2/39; Heppell, 1/16; Haskins, 1/10; Pringle, 1/7.

89th Grey Cup
November 25, 2001 at Montreal (65,255)

Calgary Stampeders	0	17	0	10	-27
Winnipeg Blue Bombers	4	0	8	7	-19

WPG	Westwood 29 FG
WPG	Westwood single
CAL	McLoughlin 37 FG
CAL	Boergiter 68 pass from Crandell (McLoughlin)
CAL	Moore 9 pass from Crandell (McLoughlin)
WPG	Bruce 23 pass from Jones (Westwood)
WPG	Westwood single
CAL	Fells 11 blocked punt recovery (McLoughlin)
WPG	Stegall 23 pass from Jones (Westwood)
CAL	McLoughlin 24 FG

TEAM STATISTICS	CAL	WPG
First Downs	19	20
Rushes-Yards	18-75	17-110
Passes	35-18-0	41-19-0
Yards Passing	308	286
Punts-Average	9-40.6	9-42.2
Punt Returns-Yards	7-71	5-66
Kickoff Returns-Yards	4-73	5-120
Fumbles-Lost	1-1	1-1
Penalties-Yards	9-60	9-98

RUSHING: CAL-Crandell, 5/23; Anderson, 8/22; Warren, 3/21; Deibert, 2/9. WPG-Roberts, 8/70; Jones, 5/28; Mills, 3/11; Blount,1/1.

PASSING: CAL-Crandell, 35-18-0, 308. WPG-Jones, 40-19-0, 286; Roberts, 1-0-0, 0.

RECEIVING: CAL-Danielsen, 5/73; Boergister, 4/114; Moore, 3/29; Anderson, 2/57; Regimbald, 1/15; Cummings, 1/10; Peterson, 1/5; Warren, 1/5. WPG-Stegall, 7/118; Bruce, 5/81; Gordon, 5/75; Mills, 1/7; Bllount, 1/5.

90th Grey Cup
November 24, 2002 at Edmonton (62,531)

Montreal Alouettes	1	10	0	14	-25
Edmonton Eskimos	0	0	10	6	-16

MTL	Baker single
MTL	Woodcock 99 pass from Calvillo (Baker)
MTL	Baker 42 FG
EDM	Walters 17 pass from Ray (Fleming)
MTL	Copeland 47 pass from Calvillo (Baker)
EDM	Hervey 17 pass from Ray (failed)
MTL	Copeland 47 kickoff return (Baker)

TEAM STATISTICS	MTL	EDM
First Downs	7	25
Rushes-Yards	13-56	27-118
Passes	31-11-0	47-24-1
Yards Passing	260	324
Punts-Average	13-38.3	13-44.7
Punt Returns-Yards	7-82	9-96
Kickoff Returns-Yards	4-94	4-66
Fumbles-Lost	2-2	4-2
Penalties-Yards	7-70	9-108

RUSHING: MTL-Phillips, 11/40; Calvillo, 1/12; Heppell,1/4. EDM-Mills, 12/87; Ray, 7/25; Avery, 1/6.

PASSING: MTL-Calvillo, 31-11-0, 260. EDM-Ray, 47-24-1, 324.

RECEIVING: MTL-Copeland, 3/101; Woodcock, 2/119; Cahoon, 2/20; Phillips, 2/19; Haskins, 1/2; Hall, 1/-1. EDM-Tucker, 8/127; Vaughn, 4/30; Bazzell, 3/65; Mills, 3/41; Hervey, 2/31; Waletrs, 2/29; Avery, 2/1.

91st Grey Cup
November 16, 2003 at Regina (50,909)

Edmonton Eskimos	7	17	0	10	-34
Montreal Alouettes	0	21	1	0	-22

EDM	Pringle 4 run (Fleming)
EDM	Tucker 41 pass from Ray (Fleming)
MTL	Woodcock 4 pass from Whitaker (Kellett)
MTL	Girard 32 pass from Calvillo (Kellett)
EDM	Tucker 15 pass from Ray (Fleming)
MTL	Cahoon 27 pass from Calvillo (Kellett)
EDM	Fleming 27 FG
MTL	Kellett single
EDM	Ray 1 run (Fleming)
EDM	Fleming 17 FG

TEAM STATISTICS	EDM	MTL
First Downs	24	19
Rushes-Yards	25-98	9-44
Passes	31-22-0	40-23-0
Yards Passing	301	375
Punts-Average	10-39.6	10-41.2
Punt Returns-Yards	5-22	7-21
Kickoff Returns-Yards	4-66	7-93
Fumbles-Lost	3-1	3-3
Penalties-Yards	14-67	13-122

RUSHING: EDM-Pringle, 17/70; Ray, 5/21; Mills, 3/7. MTL-Lapointe, 5/23; Woodcock, 1/9; Whitaker, 2/8; Calvillo, 1/4.

PASSING: EDM-Ray, 31-22-0, 301. MTL-Calvillo, 38-22-0, 371; Whitaker, 1-1-0, 4; Kellett, 1-0-0, 0.

RECEIVING: EDM-Tucker, 7/132; Vaughn, 4/33; Hervey, 3/48; Robinson, 3/27; Walters, 2/19; Mills, 1/29; October, 1/10; Pringle, 1/3. MTL-Copeland, 8/102; Cahoon, 6/148; Girard, 4/86; Woodcock, 4/26; Whitaker, 1/13.

92nd Grey Cup
November 21, 2004 at Ottawa (51,242)

Toronto Argonauts	0	17	7	3	-27
British Columbia Lions	7	3	3	6	-19

BC	Clermont 11 pass from Dickenson (O'Mahony)
TOR	Prefontaine 27 FG
TOR	Allen 1 run (Prefontaine)
BC	O'Mahony 42 FG
TOR	Baker 23 pass from Allen (Prefontaine)
TOR	Allen 1 run (Prefontaine)
BC	O'Mahony 37 FG
BC	Dickenson 7 run (failed)
TOR	Prefontaine 16 FG

TEAM STATISTICS	TOR	BC
First Downs	24	24
Rushes-Yards	18-92	29-165
Passes	38-26-0	27-18-0
Yards Passing	337	201
Punts-Average	6-40.0	7-27.9
Punt Returns-Yards	4-24	4-60
Kickoff Returns-Yards	5-81	6-102
Fumbles-Lost	1-0	3-1
Penalties-Yards	7-40	7-62

RUSHING: TOR-Avery, 11/75; Allen, 5/10; Bishop, 2/7. BC-Warren, 18/159; Dickenson, 8/36.

PASSING: TOR-Allen, 34-23-0, 299; Bishop, 4-3-0, 38. BC-Dickenson, 27-18-0, 201.

RECEIVING: TOR-Baker, 6/101; Mills, 6/75; Bruce, 5/79; Avery, 4/24; Soward, 3/31; Talbot, 2/27. BC-Clermont, 4/71; Thelwell, 3/39; Green, 3/35; Simon, 3/31; Warren, 3/18; Brazzell, 2/.7.

93rd Grey Cup
November 27, 2005 at Vancouver (59157)

Edmonton Eskimos	3	7	10	8	10	-38
Montreal Alouettes	1	0	17	10	7	-35

EDM	Fleming 18 FG
MTL	Duval single
EDM	Hervey 9 pass from Ray (Fleming)
MTL	Lapointe 1 run (Duval)
EDM	Fleming 35 FG
MTL	Lapointe 1 run (Duval)
MTL	Duval 13 FG
EDM	Tompkins 96 kickoff return (Fleming)
MTL	Calvillo 1 run (Duval)
EDM	Ray 1 run (Tucker pass from Ray)
MTL	Duval 27 FG
MTL	Stala 30 pass from Calvillo (Duval)
EDM	Tucker 11 pass from Ray (Fleming)
EDM	Fleming 36 FG

TEAM STATISTICS	EDM	MTL
First Downs	30	22
Rushes-Yards	18-100	16-69
Passes	45-35-0	43-29-1
Yards Passing	359	361
Punt Returns-Yards	5-32	4-50
Kickoff Returns-Yards	5-143	6-112
Fumbles-Lost	2-2	1-1
Penalties-Yards	12-75	11-45

RUSHING: EDM-Davis, 11/68; Ray, 4/18; Mitchell, 2/12; Maurer, 1/2. MTL-Lapointe, 11/46; Calvillo, 4/21; Watkins, 1/2.

PASSING: EDM-Ray, 45-35-0, 359. MTL-Calvillo, 43-29-1, 361.

RECEIVING: EDM-Mitchell, 8/117; Gaylor, 7/59; Hervey, 6/49; Tucker, 5/46; Maurer, 4/41; Nowacki, 2/29; Davis, 2/5; Dubuc, 1/13. MTL-Cahoon, 9/94; Watkins, 7/62; Stala, 4/48; Vaughn, 3/53; Anderson, 3/30; Girard, 2/69; Lapointe, 1/5.

94th Grey Cup
November 19, 2006 at Winnipeg (44,786)

British Columbia Lions	9	10	0	6	-25
Montreal Alouettes	0	3	9	2	-14

BC	McCallum 34 FG
BC	McCallum 35 FG
BC	McCallum 24 FG
BC	Smart 25 run (McCallum)
MTL	Duval 43 FG
BC	McCallum 30 FG
MTL	Safety conceded by McCallum
MTL	Edwards 2 run (Duval)
BC	McCallum 21 FG
BC	McCaalum 47 FG
MTL	Safety conceded by McCallum

TEAM STATISTICS	BC	MTL
First Downs	21	20

Rushes-Yards	27-161	19-101
Passes	29-18-0	41-20-0
Yards Passing	184	234
Punt Returns-Yards	6-51	3-14
Kickoff Returns-Yards	1-18	5-71
Fumbles-Lost	2-1	2-2
Penalties-Yards	5-23	9-90

RUSHING: BC-Smith, 16/72; Dickenson, 6/53; Smart 2/32; Jackson, 2/4; Pierce, 1/0. MTL-Edwards, 15/85; Calvillo, 2/12; Brady, 2/4.

PASSING: BC-Dickenson, 29-18-0, 184. MTL-Calvillo, 41-20-0, 234.

RECEIVING: BC-Jackson, 5/65; Thelwell, 5/45; Simon, 4/41; Jones, 2/12; Smith, 1/12; Green, 1/9. MTL-Cahoon, 11/137; Stala, 3/33; Vilimek, 2/22; Watkins, 2/18; Anderson, 1/13; Edwards 1/11.

95th Grey Cup
November 25, 2007 at Toronto (52,230)

Saskatchewan Roughriders	0	10	6	7	-23
Winnipeg Blue Bombers	3	4	7	5	-19

WPG	Westwood 16 FG
WPG	Safety conceded by Boreham
WPG	Safety coneeded by Boreham
SAS	J. Johnson 30 interception return (Congi)
SAS	Congi 45 FG
SAS	Congi 17 FG
WPG	Armstrong 50 pass from Dinwiddie (Westwood)
SAS	Congi 12 FG
SAS	Fantuz 29 pass from Joseph (Congi)
WPG	Safety conceded by Boreham
WPG	Westwood 42 FG

TEAM STATISTICS	SAS	WPG
First Downs	18	12
Rushes-Yards	23-159	15-52
Passes	34-13-1	33-15-3
Yards Passing	181	225
Punts-Average	7-41.9	11-46.0
Punt Returns-Yards	9-63	7-39
Kickoff Returns-Yards	2-43	5-127
Fumbles-Lost	1-1	1-1
Penalties-Yards	7-71	6-65

RUSHING: SAS-Joseph, 10/101; Cates, 13/58. WPG-Roberts, 13/47; Dinwiddie, 2/5.

PASSING: SAS-Joseph, 34-13-1, 181. WPG-Dinwiddie, 33-15-3, 225.

RECEIVING: SAS-Fantuz, 4/70; Flicl, 4/38; Grant, 2/20; Cates, 1/24; Murphy, 1/21; Palmer, 1/8. WPG-Stegall, 5/85; Edwards, 4/30; Franklin, 2/38; Roberts, 2/8; Armstrong, 1/50; Stoddard, 1/14.

96th Grey Cup
November 23, 2008 at Montreal (66,308)

Calgary Stampeders	0	10	6	6	-22
Montreal Alouettes	3	10	1	0	-14

MTL	Duval 14 FG
CAL	DeAngelis 44 FG
MTL	Cobourne 16 run (Duval)
MTL	Duval 19 FG
CAL	Ralph 20 pass from Burris (DeAngelis)
MTL	Duval single
CAL	DeAngelis 21 FG'
CAL	DeAngelis 30 FG
CAL	DeAngelis 50 FG

TEAM STATISTICS	CAL	MTL
First Downs	25	19
Rushes-Yards	21-117	8-40
Passes	37-28-1	38-29-2
Yards Passing	328	352
Punts-Average	5-46.8	6-44.2
Punt Returns-Yards	2-8	5-86
Kickoff Returns-Yards	4-90	3-52
Fumbles-Lost	0-0	0-0
Penalties-Yards	5-40	4-30

RUSHING: CAL-Burris, 9/79; Reynolds, 11/29; Summers, 1/9. MTL-Cobourne, 8/40.

PASSING: CAL-Burris, 37-28-1, 328. MTL-Calvillo, 38-29-2, 352.

RECEIVING: CAL-Lewis, 11/122; Copeland, 7/53; Rambo, 5/84; Reynolds, 4/49; Ralph, 1/20. MTL-Cahoon, 8/95; Richardson, 6/123; Bratton, 5/49; Watkins, 4/51; Carter, 3/19; Cobourne, 3/15.

97th Grey Cup
November 29, 2009 at Calgary (46,020)

Montreal Alouettes	0	3	7	18	-28
Saskatchewan Roughriders	10	7	3	7	-27

SAS	Congi 40 FG
SAS	Fantuz 8 pass from Durant (Congi)
MTL	Duval 28 FG
SAS	Congi 44 FG
SAS	Sakoda single
SAS	Congi 9 FG
MTL	Richardson 8 pass from Calvillo (Durant)
SAS	Congi 23 FG
MTL	Duval single
SAS	Durant 16 run (Congi)
MTL	Cobourne 3 run (Carter pass from Calvillo)
MTL	Cahoon 11 pss from Calvillo (Calvillo pass failed)
MTL	Duval 33 FG

TEAM STATISTICS	MTL	SAS
First Downs	25	20
Rushes-Yards	21-110	22-191
Passes	39-26-0	29-17-2
Yards Passing	314	201
Punts-Average	8-39.8	6-48.2
Punt Returns-Yards	4-9	5-59
Kickoff Returns-Yards	4-97	5-89
Fumbles-Lost	3-2	0-0
Penalties-Yards	4-10	4-47

RUSHING: MTL-Cobourne, 16/85; Calvillo, /423; McPherson, 1/2. SAS-Cates, 13/91; Durant, 4/57; Walker, 1/18; Bagg, 1/13; Szarka, 3/12.

PASSING: MTL-Calvillo, 39-26-0, 314. SAS-Durant, 29-17-2, 201.

RECEIVING: MTL-Richardson, 8/113; Cobourne, 6/64; Cahoon, 5/57; Carter, 3/22; Bratton, 2/39; Watkins, 2/19. SAS-Fantuz, 5/67; Clermont, 3/46; Bagg, 3/27; Getzlaf, 2/15; Walker, 2/12.

98th Grey Cup
November 28, 2010 at Edmonton (63,317)

Montreal Alouettes	8	0	3	10	-21
Saskatchewan Roughriders	7	4	0	7	-18

MTL	Cobourne 3 run (Duval)
MTL	Duval single
SAS	Cates 1 run (Kean)
SAS	Kean 27 FG
SAS	Johnson single
MTL	Duval 22 FG
MTL	Duval 42 FG
MTL	Cobourne 2 run (Duval)
SAS	Parenteau 1 pass from Durant (Kean)

TEAM STATISTICS	MTL	SAS
First Downs	27	16
Rushes-Yards	23-116	12-90
Passes	42-29-0	31-18-1
Yards Passing	336	215
Punts-Average	7-32.4	10-42.1
Punt Returns-Yards	5-28	3-28
Kickoff Returns-Yards	4-94	2-28
Fumbles-Lost	0-0	0-0
Penalties-Yards	8-90	8-80

RUSHING: MTL-Cobourne, 15/67; McPherson, 3/7; Calvillo, 2/26; Deslauriers, 1/10; Bratton, 1/9; Watkins, 1/7; McPherson, 3/7. SAS-Cates, 10/83; Durant, 1/8; Dressler, 1/-1.

PASSING: MTL-Calvillo, 42-29-0, 336. SAS-Durant, 31-18-1, 215.

RECEIVING: MTL-Green, 9/102; Richardson, 8/109; Cahoon, 3/34; Cobourne, 3/15; Watkins, 2/19; Bratton, 2/15. SAS-Fantuz, 4/66; Koch, 4/57; Getzlaf, 3/22; Clermont, 2/40; Cates, 2/18; Dressler, 2/11; Parentau, 1/1.

CANADIAN FOOTBALL HALL OF FAME

Induction into the Hall of Fame is the ultimate award not only for players, but also for coaches, team owners and others involved in the game. The 19-member charter class was selected on June 19, 1963. The hall itself, located in Hamilton, did not officially open until November 28, 1972. The members of the hall are selected by a panel of 15 voters. They are selected are from one of two categories: players and builders. Players must be retired for at least three years to be eligible.

Name	Category	Year
Jack Abendschan	Player	2012
Bob Ackles	Builder	2002
Junior Ah You	Player	1997
Roger Aldag	Player	2002
Danon Allen	Player	2012
Tony Anselmo	Builder	2009
Ron Atchison	Player	1978
Leonard Back	Builder	1971
Byron Bailey	Player	1975
Harold Bailey	Builder**	1965
Bill Baker	Player	1994
Harold Ballard	Builder	1987
Donald Barker	Builder	1999
John Barrow	Player	1976
Danny Bass	Player	2000
Harry Batstone	Player	1963
Greg Battle	Player	2007
Ormond Beach	Player**	1963
Al Benecick	Player	1996
Paul Bennett	Player	2002
Samuel Berger	Builder	1993
John Bonk	Player	2008
Ab Box	Player**	1965
David Braley	Builder	2012
Joseph Breen	Player**	1963
Johnny Bright	Player	1970
Dieter Brock	Player	1995
Tom Brook	Builder	1975
Tom Brown	Player	1984
Wes Brown	Builder	1963
Less Browne	Player	2002
Willie Burden	Player	2001
Bob Cameron	Player	2010
Hugh Campbell	Builder	2000
Jerry Campbell	Player	1996
Tom Casey	Player	1964
Ken Charlton	Player	1992
Arthur Chipman	Builder	1969
Frank Clair	Builder	1981
Bill Clarke	Player	1996
Tom Clements	Player	1994
Michael Clemons	Player	2008
Tommy Joe Coffey	Player	1977
Lionel Conacher	Player	1963
Pete Connellan*	Builder	2012
Rod Connop	Player	2005
Ralph Cooper	Builder	1992
Royal Copeland	Player	1988
Jim Corrigall	Player	1990
Bruce Coulter	Builder**	1997
Grover Covington	Player	2000
Ernest Cox	Player**	1963
Ross Craig	Player**	1964
Hec Crighton	Builder	1985
Carl Cronin	Player**	1967
Andrew Currie	Builder	1974
Gord Currie	Builder*	2005
Bernie Custis	Builder*	1998
Dave Cutler	Player	1998
Wes Cutler	Player**	1968
Peter Dalla Riva	Player	1993
Andrew Davies	Builder**	1969
John DeGruchy	Builder	1963
Rocky DiPietro	Player	1997
George Dixon	Player	1974
Paul Dojack	Builder	1978
Eck Duggan	Builder	1981
Seppi DuMoulin	Builder	1963
Matt Dunigan	Player	2006
Ray Elgaard	Player	2002
Abe Eliowitz	Player	1969
Eddie Emerson	Player	1963
Ron Estay	Player	2003
Sam Etcheverry	Player	1969
Terry Evanshen	Player	1984
Bernie Faloney	Player	1974
Cap Fear	Player	1967
Dave Fennell	Player	1990
John Ferraro	Player	1966
Norm Fieldgate	Player	1979
Willie Fleming	Player	1982
Darren Flutie	Player	2007
Doug Flutie	Player	2008
Chris Flynn	Player*	2011
Sid Forster	Builder	2001
William Foulds	Builder	1963
Gino Fracas	Builder	2011
Bill Frank	Player	2001
Gregory Fulton	Builder	1995
Tony Gabriel	Player	1984
Gene Gaines	Player	1994
Hugh Gall	Player	1963
Jake Gaudaur	Builder	1984
Ed George	Player	2005
Frank Gibson	Builder	1996
Tony Golab	Player	1964
Bud Grant	Builder	1983
Tommy Grant	Player	1995
Herb Gray	Player	1983
Earl Albert Grey	Builder	1963
Dean Griffing	Player	1965
Harry Griffith	Builder	1963
Sydney Halter	Builder	1966
Tracy Ham	Player	2010
Frank Hannibal	Builder	1963
Fritz Hanson	Player	1963
Dickie Harris	Player	1999
Wayne Harris	Player	1976
Herman Harrison	Player	1993
Lew Hayman	Builder	1975
John Helton	Player	1985
Ed Henick	Builder	2003
Garney Henley	Player	1979
Larry Highbaugh	Player	2004
Tom Hinton	Player	1991
Condredge Holloway	Player	1999
Dick Huffman	Player	1987
Billy Hughes	Builder	1974
Bob Isbister Sr.	Player	1965
Russ Jackson	Player	1973
Jack Jacobs	Player	1963
Eddie James	Player	1963
Gerry James	Player	1981
Alondra Johnson	Player	2009
Tyrone Jones	Player	2012
Bobby Jurasin	Player	2006
Greg Kabat	Player	1966
Joe Kapp	Player	1984
Jerry Keeling	Player	1989
Brian Kelly	Player	1991
Ellison Kelly	Player	1992
Danny Kepley	Player	1996
Eagle Keys	Builder	1990
Norman Kimball	Builder	1991
Dave Knight	Builder	2007
Bob Kramer	Builder	1987
Joe Krol	Player	1963
Normie Kwong	Player	1969
Ron Lancaster	Player	1982
Eric Lapointe*	Player	2012
Smirle Lawson	Player	1963
Frank Leadlay	Player	1963
Les Lear	Player	1974
Ken Lehmann	Player	2011
Leo Lewis	Player	1973
Moe Lieberman	Builder	1973
Earl Lunsford	Player	1983
Marv Luster	Player	1990
Don Luzzi	Player	1985
Don Matthews	Builder	2011
Harry McBrien	Builder	1978
Jimmy McCaffrey	Builder	1967
Ches McCance	Player	1976
Dave McCann	Builder	1966
Frank McGill	Player	1965
George McGowan	Player	2003
Danny McManus	Player	2011
Donald McNaughton	Builder	1994
Don McPherson	Builder	1983
Ed McQuarters	Player	1988
Johnny Metras Sr.	Builder	1980
Rollie Miles	Player	1980
James Mills	Player	2009
Percy Molson	Player	1963
Joe Montford	Player	2011
Kenneth Montgomery	Builder	1970
Warren Moon	Player	2001
Frank Morris	Player	1983
Ted Morris	Player	1964
Angelo Mosca	Player	1967
Cal Murphy	Builder	2004
James Murphy	Player	2000
Don Narcisse	Player	2010
Roger Nelson	Player	1985
Ray Nettles	Player	2005
Peter Neumann	Player	1979
Jack Newton	Builder	1964
Red O'Quinn	Player	1981
Tony Pajaczkowski	Player	1988
Jackie Parker	Player	1971
James Parker	Player	2001
Lui Passaglia	Player	2004
Hal Patterson	Player	1971
Elfrid Payton	Player	2010
Gordon Perry	Player	1970
Norman Perry	Player	1963
Rudy Phillips	Player	2009
Joe Pistilli	Builder*	2010

Allen Pitts	Player	2006
Willie Pless	Player	2005
Ken Ploen	Player	1975
Joe Poplawski	Player	1998
Ken Preston	Builder	1990
Mike Pringle	Player	2008
Silver Quilty	Player	1966
Dave Raimey	Player	2000
Russ Rebholz	Player	1963
George Reed	Player	1979
Ted Reeve	Player	1963
Dave Ridgway	Player	2003
Frank Rigney	Player	1984
Alvin Ritchie	Builder	1963
Larry Robinson	Player	1998
Michael Rodden	Builder	1964
Rocco Romano	Player	2007
Paul Rowe	Player	1964
Martin Ruby	Player	1974
Jeff Russell	Player	1963
Joseph Ryan	Builder	1968
Ralph Sazio	Builder	1988
Tom Scott	Player	1998
Vince Scott	Player	1982
Dick Shatto	Player	1975
Shag Shaughnessy	Builder	1963
Tom Sheperd	Builder	2008
Hap Shouldice	Builder	1977
Benjamin Simpson	Player	1963
Bob Simpson	Player	1976
Jimmy Simpson	Builder	1985
Karl Slocomb	Builder	1989
Victor Spencer	Builder	2006
David Sprague	Player	1963
Harry Spring	Builder	1976
Milt Stegall	Player	2012
Art Stevenson	Player	1969
Ron Stewart	Player	1977
Hugh Stirling	Player	1966
Annis Stukus	Builder	1974
Don Sutherin	Player	1992
Bill Symons	Player	1997
Piffles Taylor	Builder	1963
Dave Thelen	Player	1989
Brian Timmis	Player	1963
Frank Tindall	Builder	1984
Buddy Tinsley	Player	1982
Andy Tommy	Player	1989
Herb Trawick	Player	1975
Joe Tubman	Player	1968
Whit Tucker	Player	1993
Ted Urness	Player	1989
Kaye Vaughan	Player	1978
Terry Vaughn	Player	2011
Pierre Vercheval	Player	2007
Virgil Wagner	Player	1980
Chris Walby	Player	2003
Clair Warner	Builder	1965
Bert Warwick	Builder	1964
Glen Weir	Player	2009
Huck Welch	Player	1964
Tom Wilkinson	Player	1987
Henry Williams	Player	2006
Al Wilson	Player	1997
Seymour Wilson	Builder	1984
Harvey Wylie	Player	1980
Dan Yochum	Player	2004
Jim Young	Player	1991
Ben Zambiasi	Player	2004
Bill Zock	Player	1984

The following abbreviations are used throughout this section.

Teams

BAL Baltimore
BC British Columbia
BIR Birmingham
CAL Calgary
EDM Edmonton
HAM Hamilton
LV Las Vegas
MEM Memphis
MTL Montreal
OTT Ottawa
SA San Antonio
SAC Sacramento
SAS Saskatchewan
TOR Toronto
WPG Winnipeg

Positions

C Centre
CB Cornerback
E End
FB Fullback
FL Flanker
FW Flying Wing
G Guard
HB Halfback
ILB Inside Linebacker
K Kicker
LB Linebacker
MG Middle Guard
MLB Middle Linebacker
OLB Outside Linebacker
P Punter
QB Quarterback
REC Receiver
S Safety
SB Slot Back
SE Split End
ST Special Teams
T Tackle
TE Tight End
WR Wide Receiver

COACH OF THE YEAR
(Annis Stukus Trophy)

2011 Wally Buono, BC
2010 Jim Barker, TOR
2009 Marc Trestman, MTL
2008 John Hufnagel, CAL
2007 Kent Austin, SAS
2006 Wally Buono, BC
2005 Tom Higgins, CAL
2004 Greg Marshall, HAM
2003 Tom Higgins, EDM
2002 Don Matthews, MTL
2001 Dave Ritchie, WPG
2000 Charlie Taaffe, MTL
1999 Charlie Taaffe, MTL
1998 Ron Lancaster, HAM
1997 Don Matthews, TOR
1996 Ron Lancaster, EDM
1995 Don Matthews, BAL
1994 Don Matthews, BAL
1993 Wally Buono, CAL
1992 Wally Buono, CAL
1991 Adam Rita, TOR
1990 Mike Riley, WPG
1989 John Gregory, SAS
1988 Mike Riley, WPG
1987 Bob O'Billovich, TOR
1986 Al Bruno, HAM
1985 Don Matthews, BC
1984 Cal Murphy, WPG
1983 Cal Murphy, WPG
1982 Bob O'Billovich, TOR
1981 Joe Faragalli, SAS
1980 Ray Jauch, WPG
1979 Hugh Campbell, EDM
1978 Jack Gotta, CAL
1977 Vic Rapp, BC
1976 Bob Shaw, HAM
1975 George Brancato, OTT
1974 Marv Levy, MTL
1973 Jack Gotta, OTT
1972 Jack Gotta, OTT
1971 Leo Cahill, TOR
1970 Ray Jauch, EDM
1969 Frank Clair, OTT
1968 Eagle Keys, SAS
1967 Jerry Williams, CAL
1966 Frank Clair, OTT
1965 Bud Grant, WPG
1964 Ralph Sazio, HAM
1963 Dave Skrien, BC
1962 Steve Owen, SAS
1961 Jim Trimble, HAM

PLAYER OF THE YEAR
(Schenley Award, 1953-1988)

2011 Travis Lulay, BC
2010 Henry Burris, CAL
2009 Anthony Calvillo, MTL
2008 Anthony Calvillo, MTL
2007 Kerry Joseph, SAS
2006 Geroy Simon, BC
2005 Damon Allen, TOR
2004 Casey Printers, BC
2003 Anthony Calvillo, MTL
2002 Milt Stegall, WPG
2001 Khari Jones, WPG
2000 Dave Dickenson, CAL
1999 Danny McManus, HAM
1998 Mike Pringle, MTL
1997 Doug Flutie, TOR
1996 Doug Flutie, TOR
1995 Mike Pringle, BAL
1994 Doug Flutie, CAL
1993 Doug Flutie, CAL
1992 Doug Flutie, CAL
1991 Doug Flutie, BC
1990 Mike Clemons, TOR
1989 Tracy Ham, EDM
1988 David Williams, BC
1987 Tom Clements, WPG
1986 James Murphy, WPG
1985 Merv Fernandez, BC
1984 Willard Reaves, WPG
1983 Warren Moon, EDM
1982 Condredge Holloway, TOR
1981 Dieter Brock, WPG
1980 Dieter Brock, WPG
1979 David Green, MTL
1978 Tony Gabriel, OTT
1977 Jimmy Edwards, HAM
1976 Ron Lancaster, SAS
1975 Willie Burden, CAL
1974 Tom Wilkinson, EDM
1973 George McGowan, EDM
1972 Garney Henley, HAM
1971 Don Jonas, WPG
1970 Ron Lancaster, SAS
1969 Russ Jackson, OTT
1968 Bill Symons, TOR
1967 Peter Liske, CAL
1966 Russ Jackson, OTT
1965 George Reed, SAS
1964 Lovell Coleman, CAL
1963 Russ Jackson, OTT
1962 George Dixon, MTL
1961 Bernie Faloney, HAM
1960 Jackie Parker, EDM
1959 Johnny Bright, EDM
1958 Jackie Parker, EDM
1957 Jackie Parker, EDM
1956 Hal Patterson, MTL
1955 Pat Abbruzzi, MTL
1954 Sam Etcheverry, MTL
1953 Billy Vessels, EDM

LINEMAN OF THE YEAR

In 1974 this award was broken into two categories: Outstanding Offensive Lineman and Outstanding Defensive Player.

1973 Ray Nettles, BC
1972 John Helton, CAL
1971 Wayne Harris, CAL
1970 Wayne Harris, CAL
1969 John Lagrone, EDM
1968 Ken Lehmann, OTT
1967 Ed McQuarters, SAS
1966 Wayne Harris, CAL
1965 Wayne Harris, CAL
1964 Tom Brown, BC
1963 Tom Brown, BC
1962 John Barrow, HAM
1961 Frank Rigney, WPG
1960 Herb Gray, WPG
1959 Roger Nelson, EDM
1958 Don Luzzi, CAL
1957 Kaye Vaughan, OTT
1956 Kaye Vaughan, OTT
1955 Tex Coulter, MTL

OFFENSIVE LINEMAN OF THE YEAR

2011 Josh Bourke, MTL
2010 Ben Archibald, CAL
2009 Scott Flory, MTL
2008 Scott Flory, MTL
2007 Rob Murphy, BC
2006 Rob Murphy, BC
2005 Gene Makowsky, SAS
2004 Gene Makowsky, SAS
2003 Andrew Greene, SAS
2002 Bryan Chiu, MTL
2001 Dave Mudge, WPG
2000 Pierre Vercheval, MTL
1999 Uzooma Okeke, MTL
1998 Fred Childress, CAL
1997 Mike Kiselak, TOR
1996 Mike Kiselak, TOR
1995 Mike Withycombe, BAL
1994 Shar Pourdanesh, BAL
1993 Chris Walby, WPG
1992 Robert Smith, OTT
1991 Jim Mills, BC
1990 Jim Mills, BC
1989 Rod Connop, EDM
1988 Roger Aldag, SAS
1987 Chris Walby, WPG
1986 Roger Aldag, SAS
1985 Nick Bastaja, WPG
1984 John Bonk, WPG
1983 Rudy Phillips, OTT
1982 Rudy Phillips, OTT
1981 Larry Butler, WPG
1980 Mike Wilson, EDM
1979 Mike Wilson, EDM
1978 Jim Coode, OTT
1977 Al Wilson, BC
1976 Dan Yochum, MTL
1975 Charlie Turner, EDM
1974 Ed George, MTL

DEFENSIVE PLAYER OF THE YEAR

2011 Jovon Johnson, WPG
2010 Markeith Knowlton, HAM
2009 John Chick, SAS
2008 Cam Wake, BC
2007 Cam Wake, BC
2006 Brent Johnson, BC
2005 John Grace, CAL
2004 Anwar Stewart, MTL
2003 Joe Fleming, CAL
2002 Elfrid Payton, EDM
2001 Joe Montford, HAM
2000 Joe Montford, HAM
1999 Calvin Tiggle, HAM
1998 Joe Montford, HAM
1997 Willie Pless, EDM
1996 Willie Pless, EDM
1995 Willie Pless, EDM
1994 Willie Pless, EDM
1993 Jearld Baylis, SAS
1992 Willie Pless, EDM
1991 Greg Battle, WPG
1990 Greg Battle, WPG
1989 Danny Bass, EDM
1988 Grover Covington, HAM
1987 Greg Stumon, BC
1986 James Parker, BC
1985 Tyrone Jones, WPG
1984 James Parker, BC
1983 Greg Marshall, OTT
1982 James Parker, EDM
1981 Dan Kepley, EDM
1980 Dan Kepley, EDM
1979 Ben Zambiasi, HAM
1978 Dave Fennell, EDM
1977 Dan Kepley, EDM
1976 Bill Baker, BC
1975 Jim Corrigall, TOR
1974 John Helton, CAL

ROOKIE OF THE YEAR

2011 Chris Williams, HAM
2010 Solomon Elimimian, BC
2009 Martell Mallett, BC
2008 Weston Dressler, SAS
2007 Cam Wake, BC
2006 Aaron Hunt, BC
2005 Gavin Walls, WPG
2004 Nikolas Lewis, CAL
2003 Frank Cutolo, BC
2002 Jason Clermont, BC
2001 Barrin Simpson, BC
2000 Albert Johnson III, WPG
1999 Paul Lacoste, BC
1998 Steve Muhammad, BC
1997 Derrell Mitchell, TOR
1996 Kelvin Anderson, CAL
1995 Shalon Baker, EDM
1994 Matt Goodwin, BAL
1993 Michael O'Shea, HAM
1992 Michael Richardson, WPG
1991 Jon Volpe, BC
1990 Reggie Barnes, OTT
1989 Stephen Jordan, HAM
1988 Orville Lee, OTT
1987 Gill Fenerty, TOR
1986 Harold Hallman, CAL
1985 Michael Gray, BC
1984 Dwaine Wilson, MTL
1983 Johnny Shepherd, HAM
1982 Chris Isaac, OTT
1981 Vince Goldsmith, SAS
1980 William Miller, WPG
1979 Brian Kelly, EDM
1978 Joe Poplawski, WPG
1977 Leon Bright, BC
1976 John Sciarra, BC
1975 Tom Clements, OTT
1974 Sam Cvijanovich, TOR
1973 Johnny Rodgers, MTL
1972 Chuck Ealey, HAM

CANADIAN PLAYER OF THE YEAR

2011 Jerome Messam, EDM
2010 Andy Fantuz, SAS
2009 Ricky Foley, BC
2008 Kamau Peterson, EDM
2007 Jason Clermont, BC
2006 Brent Johnson, BC
2005 Brent Johnson, BC
2004 Jason Clermont, BC
2003 Ben Cahoon, MTL
2002 Ben Cahoon, MTL
2001 Doug Brown, WPG
2000 Sean Millington, BC
1999 Michael O'Shea, TOR
1998 Mike Morreale, HAM
1997 Sean Millington, BC
1996 Leroy Blugh, EDM
1995 David Sapunjis, CAL
1994 Gerald Wilcox, WPG
1993 David Sapunjis, CAL
1992 Ray Elgaard, SAS
1991 Blake Marshall, EDM
1990 Ray Elgaard, SAS
1989 Rocky DiPietro, HAM
1988 Ray Elgaard, SAS
1987 Scott Flagel, WPG
1986 Joe Poplawski, WPG
1985 Paul Bennett, HAM
1984 Nick Arakgi, MTL
1983 Paul Bennett, MTL
1982 Rocky DiPietro, HAM
1981 Joe Poplawski, WPG
1980 Gerry Dattillio, MTL
1979 Dave Fennell, EDM
1978 Tony Gabriel, OTT
1977 Tony Gabriel, OTT
1976 Tony Gabriel, OTT
1975 Jim Foley, OTT
1974 Tony Gabriel, HAM
1973 Gerry Organ, OTT
1972 Jim Young, BC
1971 Terry Evanshen, MTL
1970 Jim Young, BC
1969 Russ Jackson, OTT
1968 Ken Nielsen, WPG
1967 Terry Evanshen, CAL
1966 Russ Jackson, OTT
1965 Zeno Karcz, HAM
1964 Tommy Grant, HAM
1963 Russ Jackson, OTT
1962 Harvey Wylie, CAL
1961 Tony Pajaczkowski, CAL
1960 Ron Stewart, OTT
1959 Russ Jackson, OTT
1958 Ron Howell, HAM
1957 Gerry James, WPG
1956 Normie Kwong, EDM
1955 Normie Kwong, EDM
1954 Gerry James, WPG

WESTERN PLAYER OF THE YEAR
(Jeff Nicklin Memorial Trophy)

In 1995 this trophy went to the outstanding player in the North Division.

2011 Travis Lulay, BC
2010 Henry Burris, CAL
2009 Joffrey Reynolds, CAL
2008 Henry Burris, CAL
2007 Kerry Joseph, SAS
2006 Geroy Simon, BC
2005 Corey Holmes, SAS
2004 Casey Printers, BC
2003 Dave Dickenson, BC
2002 Milt Stegall, WPG
2001 Kelvin Anderson, CAL
2000 Dave Dickenson, CAL
1999 Allen Pitts, CAL
1998 Kelvin Anderson, CAL
1997 Jeff Garcia, CAL

1996 Robert Mimbs, SAS
1995 Dave Sapunjis, CAL
1994 Doug Flutie, CAL
1993 Doug Flutie, CAL
1992 Doug Flutie, CAL
1991 Doug Flutie, BC
1990 Craig Ellis, EDM
1989 Tracy Ham, EDM
1988 David Williams, BC
1987 Brian Kelly, EDM
1986 James Murphy, WPG
1985 Mervyn Fernandez, BC
1984 Willard Reaves, WPG
1983 Warren Moon, EDM
1982 Tom Scott, EDM
1981 Dieter Brock, WPG
1980 Dieter Brock, WPG
1979 Waddell Smith, EDM
1978 Tom Wilkinson, EDM
1977 Jerry Tagge, BC
1976 Ron Lancaster, SAS
1975 Willie Burden, CAL
1974 Tom Wilkinson, EDM
1973 George McGowan, EDM
1972 Mack Herron, WPG
1971 Don Jonas, WPG
1970 Ron Lancaster, SAS
1969 Ron Lancaster, SAS
1968 Ron Lancaster, SAS
1967 Peter Liske, CAL
1966 Ron Lancaster, SAS
1965 George Reed, SAS
1964 Tom Brown, BC
1963 Joe Kapp, BC
1962 Eagle Day, CAL
1961 Jackie Parker, EDM
1960 Jackie Parker, EDM
1959 Jackie Parker, EDM
1958 Jackie Parker, EDM
1957 Jackie Parker, EDM
1956 Jackie Parker, EDM
1955 Ken Carpenter, SAS
1954 Jackie Parker, EDM
1953 John Henry Johnson, CAL
1952 Jack Jacobs, WPG
1951 Glen Dobbs, SAS
1950 Lindy Berry, EDM
1949 Keith Spaith, CAL
1948 Keith Spaith, CAL
1947 Bob Sandberg, WPG
1946 Bill Wusyk, CAL

EASTERN PLAYER OF THE YEAR
(Jeff Russel Memorial Trophy through 1993; Terry Evanshen Trophy from 1994)

In 1995 the award went to the outstanding player in the South Division.

2011 Anthony Calvillo, MTL
2010 Anthony Calvillo, MTL
2009 Anthony Calvillo, MTL
2008 Anthony Calvillo, MTL
2007 Kevin Glenn, WPG
2006 Charles Roberts, WPG
2005 Damon Allen, TOR
2004 Anthony Calvillo, MTL
2003 Anthony Calvillo, MTL
2002 Anthony Calvillo, MTL
2001 Khari Jones, WPG
2000 Mike Pringle, MTL
1999 Danny McManus, HAM
1998 Mike Pringle, MTL
1997 Doug Flutie, TOR
1996 Doug Flutie, TOR
1995 Mike Pringle, BAL
1994 Mike Pringle, BAL
1993 Matt Dunigan, WPG
1992 Angelo Snipes, OTT
1991 Robert Mimbs, WPG
1990 Michael Clemons, TOR
1989 Tony Champion, HAM
1988 Earl Winfield, HAM
1987 Tom Clements, WPG
1986 James Hood, MTL
1985 Ken Hobart, HAM
1984 Rufus Crawford, HAM
1983 Terry Greer, TOR
1982 Condredge Holloway, TOR
1981 Tom Clements, HAM
1980 Gerry Dattilio, MTL
1979 David Green, MTL
1978 Tony Gabriel, OTT
1977 Jimmy Edwards, HAM
1976 Jimmy Edwards, HAM
1975 Johnny Rodgers, MTL
1974 Johnny Rodgers, MTL
1973 John Harvey, MTL
1972 Garney Henley, HAM
1971 Mel Profit, TOR
1970 Bill Symons, TOR
1969 Russ Jackson, OTT
1968 Larry Fairholm, MTL
1967 Ron Stewart, OTT
1966 Gene Gaines, OTT
1965 Bernie Faloney, HAM
1964 Dick Shatto, TOR
1963 Garney Henley, HAM
1962 George Dixon, MTL
1961 Bob-Jack Oliver, MTL
1960 Ron Stewart, OTT
1959 Russ Jackson, OTT
1958 Sam Etcheverry, MTL
1957 Dick Shatto, TOR
1956 Hal Patterson, MTL
1955 Avatus Stone, OTT
1954 Sam Etcheverry, MTL
1953 Bob Cunningham, OTT
1952 Vince Mazza, HAM
1951 Bruce Cummings, OTT
1950 Don Loney, OTT
1949 Royal Copeland, TOR
1948 Eric Chipper, OTT
1947 Virgil Wagner, MTL
1946 Joe Krol, TOR

WESTERN DEFENSIVE PLAYER OF THE YEAR
(Norm Fieldgate Trophy since 1978)

In 1995 the award went to the outstanding defensive player in the North Division.

2011 Jerrell Freeman, SAS
2010 Juwan Simpson, CAL
2009 John Chick, SAS
2008 Cameron Wake, BC
2007 Cameron Wake, BC
2006 Brent Johnson, BC
2005 John Grace, CAL
2004 John Grace, CAL
2003 Joe Fleming, CAL
2002 Elfrid Payton, EDM
2001 Barrin Simpson, BC
2000 Terry Ray, EDM
1999 Daved Benefield, BC
1998 Alondra Johnson, CAL
1997 Willie Pless, EDM
1996 Willie Pless, EDM
1995 Willie Pless, EDM
1994 Willie Pless, EDM
1993 Jearld Baylis, SAS
1992 Willie Pless, EDM
1991 Will Johnson, CAL
1990 Stewart Hill, EDM
1989 Danny Bass, EDM
1988 Danny Bass, EDM
1987 Greg Stumon, BC
1986 James Parker, BC
1985 Tyrone Jones, WPG
1984 James Parker, BC
1983 Danny Bass, CAL
1982 James Parker, EDM
1981 Dan Kepley, EDM
1980 Dan Kepley, EDM
1979 John Helton, WPG
1978 Dave Fennell, EDM
1977 Dan Kepley, EDM
1976 Bill Baker, BC
1975 Bill Baker, BC
1974 John Helton, CAL

EASTERN DEFENSIVE PLAYER OF THE YEAR
(James P. McCaffrey Trophy)

In 1995 the award went to the outstanding player in the South Division.

2011 Jovon Johnson, WPG
2010 Markeith Knowlton, HAM
2009 Anwar Stewart, MTL
2008 Doug Brown, WPG
2007 Jonathan Brown, TOR
2006 Barrin Simpson, WPG
2005 Michael Fletcher, TOR
2004 Anwar Stewart, MTL
2003 Kevin Johnson, MTL
2002 Barron Miles, MTL
2001 Joe Montford, HAM
2000 Joe Montford, HAM
1999 Calvin Tiggle, HAM
1998 Joe Montford, HAM
1997 Shonte Peoples, WPG
1996 Tracy Gravely, MTL
1995 Tim Cofield, MEM
1994 Tim Cofield, HAM
1993 Elfrid Payton, WPG
1992 Angelo Snipes, OTT
1991 Greg Battle, WPG
1990 Greg Battle, WPG
1989 Greg Battle, WPG
1988 Grover Covington, HAM
1987 James West, WPG
1986 Brett Williams, MTL
1985 Paul Bennett, HAM
1984 Harry Skipper, MTL
1983 Greg Marshall, OTT
1982 Zac Henderson, TOR
1981 Ben Zambiasi, HAM
1980 Tom Cousineau, MTL
1979 Ben Zambiasi, HAM
1978 Randy Rhino, MTL
1977 Glen Weir, MTL
1976 Granville Liggins, TOR
1975 Jim Corrigall, TOR

WESTERN ROOKIE OF THE YEAR
(Dr. Beattie Martin Trophy through 1973; Jackie Parker Trophy from 1974 on)

In 1995 the award went to the outstanding rookie in the North Division.

2011 J.C. Sherritt, EDM
2010 Solomon Eliminian, BC
2009 Martell Mallett, BC
2008 Weston Dressler, SAS
2007 Cameron Wake, BC
2006 Aaron Hunt, BC
2005 Gavin Walls, WPG
2004 Nikolas Lewis, CAL
2003 Frank Cutolo, BC
2002 Jason Clermont, BC
2001 Barrin Simpson, BC
2000 George White, SAS
1999 Paul Lacoste, BC
1998 Steve Muhammad, BC
1997 B.J. Gallis, BC
1996 Kelvin Anderson, CAL
1995 Shalon Baker, EDM
1994 Carlos Huerta, LV
1993 Brian Wiggins, CAL
1992 Bruce Covernton, CAL
1991 Jon Volpe, BC
1990 Lucius Floyd, SAS
1989 Darrell Wallace, BC
1988 Jeff Fairholm, SAS
1987 Stanley Blair, EDM
1986 Harold Hallman, CAL
1985 Michael Gray, BC
1984 Stewart Hill, EDM
1983 Willard Reaves, WPG
1982 Mervyn Fernandez, BC
1981 Vince Goldsmith, SAS
1980 William Miller, WPG
1979 Brian Kelly, EDM
1978 Joe Poplawski, WPG
1977 Leon Bright, BC
1976 John Sciarra, BC
1975 Larry Cameron, BC
1974 Tom Scott, WPG

EASTERN ROOKIE OF THE YEAR
(Frank M. Gibson Trophy)

In 1995 the award went to the outstanding rookie in the South Division.

2011 Chris Williams, HAM
2010 Marcus Thigpen, HAM
2009 Jonathan Hefney, WPG
2008 Prechae Rodriques, HAM
2007 Nick Setta, HAM
2006 Etienne Boulay, MTL
2005 Matthieu Proulx, MTL
2004 Almondo Curry, MTL
2003 Julian Radlein, HAM
2002 Keith Stokes, MTL
2001 Charles Roberts, WPG
2000 Albert Johnson III, WPG
1999 Corey Grant, HAM
1998 Barron Miles, MTL
1997 Derrell Mitchell, TOR
1996 Joseph Rogers, OTT
1995 Chris Wright, BAL
1994 Matt Goodwin, BAL
1993 Michael O'Shea, HAM
1992 Michael Richardson, WPG
1991 Raghib Ismail, TOR
1990 Reggie Barnes, OTT
1989 Stephen Jordan, HAM
1988 Orville Lee, OTT
1987 Gill Fenerty, TOR
1986 Willie Pless, TOR
1985 Nick Benjamin, OTT
1984 Dwaine Wilson, MTL
1983 Johnny Shepherd, HAM
1982 Chris Isaac, OTT
1981 Cedric Minter, TOR
1980 Dave Newman, TOR
1979 Martin Cox, OTT
1978 Ben Zambiasi, HAM
1977 Mike Murphy, OTT
1976 Neil Lumsden, TOR
1975 Tom Clements, OTT

WESTERN OFFENSIVE LINEMAN OF THE YEAR
(DeMarco-Becket Memorial Trophy)

Originally awarded simply to the outstanding lineman in the West Division; changed to offensive lineman in 1974. In 1995 the award went to the top offensive lineman in the North Division.

2011 Jovan Olafioye, BC
2010 Ben Archibald, CAL
2009 Ben Archibald, CAL
2008 Gene Makowsky, SAS
2007 Rob Murphy, BC
2006 Rob Murphy, BC
2005 Gene Makowsky, SAS
2004 Gene Makowsky, SAS
2003 Andrew Greene, SAS
2002 Bruce Beaton, EDM
2001 Jay McNeil, CAL
2000 Andrew Greene, SAS
1999 Jamie Taras, BC
1998 Fred Childress, CAL
1997 Fred Childress, CAL
1996 Rocco Romano, CAL
1995 Jamie Taras, BC
1994 Rocco Romano, CAL
1993 Bruce Covernton, CAL
1992 Vic Stevenson, SAS
1991 Jim Mills, BC
1990 Jim Mills, BC
1989 Rod Connop, EDM
1988 Roger Aldag, SAS
1987 Bob Poley, CAL
1986 Roger Aldag, SAS
1985 Nick Bastaja, WPG
1984 John Bonk, WPG
1983 John Bonk, WPG
1982 Lloyd Fairbanks, CAL
1981 Larry Butler, WPG
1980 Mike Wilson, EDM
1979 Mike Wilson, EDM
1978 Al Wilson, BC
1977 Al Wilson, BC
1976 Al Wilson, BC
1975 Charlie Turner, EDM
1974 Curtis Wester, BC
1973 Ray Nettles, BC
1972 John Helton, CAL
1971 Wayne Harris, CAL
1970 Greg Pipes, EDM
1969 Ed McQuarters, SAS
1968 Ed McQuarters, SAS
1967 John LaGrone, EDM
1966 Wayne Harris, CAL
1965 Dick Fouts, BC
1964 Tom Brown, BC
1963 Tom Brown, BC
1962 Tom Brown, BC
1961 Frank Rigney, WPG
1960 Frank Rigney, WPG
1959 Art Walker, EDM
1958 Don Luzzi, CAL
1957 Art Walker, EDM

EASTERN OFFENSIVE LINEMAN OF THE YEAR
(Leo Dandurand Trophy)

In 1995 the award went to the outstanding offensive lineman in the South Division.

2011 Josh Bourke, MTL
2010 Marwan Hage, HAM
2009 Scott Flory, MTL
2008 Scott Flory, MTL
2007 Dan Goodspeed, WPG
2006 Scott Flory, MTL
2005 Scott Flory, MTL
2004 Uzooma Okeke, MTL
2003 Scott Flory, MTL
2002 Bryan Chiu, MTL
2001 Dave Mudge, WPG
2000 Pierre Vercheval, MTL
1999 Uzooma Okeke, MTL
1998 Uzooma Okeke, MTL
1997 Mike Kiselak, TOR
1996 Mike Kiselak, TOR
1995 Mike Withycombe, BAL
1994 Shar Pourdanesh, BAL
1993 Chris Walby, WPG
1992 Rob Smith, OTT
1991 Chris Walby, WPG
1990 Chris Walby, WPG
1989 Miles Gorrell, HAM
1988 Ian Beckstead, TOR
1987 Chris Walby, WPG
1986 Miles Gorrell, HAM

1985 Dan Ferrone, TOR
1984 Dan Ferrone, TOR
1983 Rudy Phillips, OTT
1982 Rudy Phillips, OTT
1981 Val Belcher, OTT
1980 Val Belcher, OTT
1979 Ray Watrin, MTL
1978 Jim Coode, OTT
1977 Mike Wilson, TOR
1976 Dan Yochum, MTL
1975 Dave Braggins, MTL

WESTERN CANADIAN PLAYER OF THE YEAR
(Dr. Beattie Martin Trophy)

In 1995 the award went to the outstanding Canadian in the North Division.

2011 Jerome Messam, EDM
2010 Andy Fantuz, SAS
2009 Rick Foley, BC
2008 Kamau Peterson, EDM
2007 Jason Clermont, BC
2006 Brent Johnson, BC
2005 Brent Johnson, BC
2004 Jason Clermont, BC
2003 Chris Szarka, SAS
2002 Sean Millington, BC
2001 Cameron Legault, BC
2000 Sean Millington, BC
1999 Jamie Taras, BC
1998 Vince Danielsen, CAL
1997 Sean Millington, BC
1996 Leroy Blugh, EDM
1995 Larry Wruck, EDM
1994 Larry Wruck, EDM
1993 David Sapunjis, CAL
1992 Ray Elgaard, SAS
1991 Blake Marshall, EDM
1990 Ray Elgaard, SAS
1989 Jeff Fairholm, SAS
1988 Ray Elgaard, SAS
1987 Nelson Martin, BC
1986 Joe Poplawski, WPG
1985 Joe Poplawski, WPG
1984 Joe Poplawski, WPG
1983 Paul Bennett, WPG
1982 Rick House, WPG
1981 Joe Poplawski, WPG
1980 Dave Fennell, EDM
1979 Dave Fennell, EDM
1978 Joe Poplawski, WPG
1977 Gordon Paterson, WPG
1976 Bill Baker, BC
1975 Tom Forzani, CAL
1974 Rudy Linterman, CAL
1973 Lorne Richardson, SAS
1972 Walt McKee, WPG
1971 Bob Kraemer, WPG
1970 John Senst, WPG
1969 Dave Easley, BC
1968 Dave Cranmer, CAL
1967 Ted Gerela, BC
1966 Garry Lefebvre, EDM
1965 Ron Forwick, EDM
1964 Billy Cooper, WPG
1963 Peter Kempf, BC
1962 Ted Frechette, EDM
1961 Larry Robinson, CAL
1960 Neal Beaumont, BC
1959 Henry Janzen, WPG
1958 Walt Radzick, CAL
1957 Mike Lashuk, EDM
1956 Norm Rauhaus, WPG
1955 Harry Lunn, SAS
1954 Lynn Bottoms, CAL
1953 Gordon Sturtridge, SAS
1952 Lorne Benson, WPG
1951 Jim Chambers, EDM
1950 Gordon Brown, CAL

EASTERN CANADIAN PLAYER OF THE YEAR
(Lew Hayman Trophy)

In 1995 the award went to the outstanding Canadian player in the South Division.

2011 Sean Whyte, MTL
2010 Dave Stala, HAM
2009 Ben Cahoon, MTL
2008 Ben Cahoon, MTL
2007 Doug Brown, WPG
2006 Doug Brown, WPG
2005 Kevin Eiben, TOR
2004 Kevin Eiben, TOR
2003 Ben Cahoon, MTL
2002 Ben Cahoon, MTL
2001 Doug Brown, WPG
2000 Davis Sanchez, MTL
1999 Mike O'Shea, TOR
1998 Mike Morreale, HAM
1997 Jock Climie, MTL
1996 Michael Soles, MTL
1995 Dave Sapunjis, CAL
1994 Gerald Wilcox, WPG
1993 Gerald Wilcox, WPG
1992 Ken Evraire, HAM
1991 Lance Chomyc, TOR
1990 Paul Osbaldiston, HAM
1989 Rocky DiPietro, HAM
1988 Orville Lee, OTT
1987 Scott Flagel, WPG
1986 Rocky DiPietro, HAM
1985 Paul Bennett, HAM
1984 Nick Arakgi, MTL
1983 Denny Ferdinand, MTL
1982 Rocky DiPietro, HAM
1981 Tony Gabriel, OTT
1980 Gerry Dattilio, MTL
1979 Leif Pettersen, HAM
1978 Tony Gabriel, OTT
1977 Tony Gabriel, OTT
1976 Tony Gabriel, OTT

SPECIAL TEAMS PLAYER OF THE YEAR

2011 Paul McCallum, BC
2010 Chad Owens, TOR
2009 Larry Taylor, MTL
2008 Dominique Dorsey, TOR
2007 Ian Smart, BC
2006 Sandro DeAngelis, CAL
2005 Corey Holmes, SAS
2004 Keith Stokes, WPG
2003 Bashir Levingston, TOR
2002 Corey Holmes, SAS
2001 Albert Johnson, WPG
2000 James Cunningham, BC

OFFICIAL ALL-STAR TEAMS

The IRFU/Eastern Conference and WIFU/Western Conference teams from 1946 to 1961 were selected for the Canadian Press by the coaches, sportswriters and broadcasters. Starting in 1962 voting was done by the Football Reporters of Canada, and today it also includes coaches and fans.

1946 IRFU
FW Ken Charlton, OTT
HB Joe Krol, TOR
HB Royal Copeland, TOR
HB Virgil Wagner, MTL
QB Frank Dunlap, OTT
C Don Loney, TOR
G Benny Steck, MTL
G Bill Zock, TOR
T Herb Trawick, MTL
T Hank Christman, OTT
E Dick Groom, HAM
E Bert Haigh, OTT

1946 WIFU
FW Bill Wusyk, CAL
FB Paul Rowe, CAL
HB Sully Glasser, SAS
HB Bill Ordway, WPG
QB Wally Dobler, WPG
C Mel Wilson, WPG
G Bill Ceretti, WPG
G Dave (Steaky) Adams, CAL
T Andy Nagy, SAS
T Martin Gainor, WPG
E Johnny Bell, SAS
E Nate Shore, WPG

1947 IRFU
FW Tony Golab, OTT
HB Virgil Wagner, MTL
HB Royal Copeland, TOR
HB Joe Krol, TOR
QB Frank Filchock, HAM
C Don Loney, OTT
G Eddie Remegis, HAM
G Bill Zock, TOR
T Hank Christman, OTT
T Herb Trawick, MTL
E Bert Haigh, OTT
E Matt Anthony, OTT

1947 WIFU
FB Bob Sandberg, WPG
HB Gabe Patterson, SAS
HB Paul Rowe, CAL
HB Del Wardien, SAS
QB Stan Stasica, SAS
C Mel Wilson, WPG
G Doug Drew, SAS
G Dave (Steaky) Adams, CAL
G Bert Iannone, WPG
T Bob Smith, WPG
T Bill Puller, CAL
E Johnny Bell, SAS
E Red Noel, SAS
E Ken Sluman, CAL

1948 IRFU
FW Tony Golab, OTT
HB Virgil Wagner, MTL
HB Joe Krol, TOR
HB Howie Turner, OTT
QB Bob Paffrath, OTT
C Don Loney, OTT
G Eddie Michaels, OTT
G Lloyd Reese, MTL
T John Wagoner, OTT
T Herb Trawick, MTL
E Ralph Toohy, MTL
E Bert Haigh, OTT

1948 WIFU
FB Paul Rowe, CAL
HB Gabe Patterson, SAS
HB Ken Charlton, SAS
HB Don Hiney, WPG
QB Keith Spaith, CAL
C Chuck Anderson, CAL
G Dave Tomlinson, CAL
G Bert Iannone, CAL
G Bud Irving, WPG
T John Aguirre, CAL
T Mike Cassidy, SAS
E Woody Strode, CAL
E Johnny Bell, SAS

1949 IRFU
FW Bob Paffrath, OTT
HB Howie Turner, OTT
HB Royal Copeland, TOR
HB Virgil Wagner, MTL
QB Frank Filchock, MTL
QB Andy Gordon, OTT
C Don Loney, OTT
G Vince Scott, HAM
G Eddie Michaels, OTT
T Herb Trawick, MTL
T John Wagoner, OTT
E Ralph Toohy, MTL
E Robert Hood, HAM

1949-WIFU
FB Sammy Pierce, SAS
HB Del Wardien, SAS
HB Ken Charlton, SAS
HB Vern Graham, CAL
QB Keith Spaith, CAL
C Mel Wilson, CAL
G Riley Matheson, CAL
G Mike Kissell, WPG
T John Aguirre, CAL
T Mike Cassidy, SAS
E Ezzrett Anderson, CAL
E Woody Strode, CAL
Coach Les Lear, CAL

1950 IRFU
FW Rod Pantages, MTL
HB Bill Gregus, HAM
HB Ulysses Curtis, TOR
HB Edgar Jones, HAM
QB Frank Filchock, MTL
C Ed Hirsch, TOR
G Ray Cicia, MTL
G Vince Scott, HAM
T Herb Trawick, MTL
T Ralph Sazio, HAM
E Vince Mazza, HAM
E Bill Stanton, OTT

1950 WIFU
FB Mike King, EDM
HB Tom Casey, WPG
HB Al Bodine, SAS
HB Bob Paffrath, EDM
QB Jack Jacobs, WPG
C John Brown, WPG
G Max Druen, SAS
G Riley Matheson, CAL
T Glen Johnson, WPG
T Buddy Tinsley, WPG
E Joe Aguirre, WPG
E Morris Bailey, EDM
Coach Frank Larson, WPG

1951 IRFU
FW Bruce Cummings, OTT
HB Hal Waggoner, HAM
HB Ulysses Curtis, TOR
HB Billy Bass, TOR
QB Bernie Custis, HAM
C Ed Hirsch, TOR
G Ray Cicia, MTL
G Eddie Bevan, HAM
T Bob Gain, OTT
T Jack Carpenter, HAM
E Vince Mazza, HAM
E Bob Simpson, OTT

1951 WIFU
FB Mike King, EDM
FW Bob Paffrath, EDM
HB Tom Casey, WPG
HB Normie Kwong, EDM
QB Glenn Dobbs, SAS
C Red Ettinger, SAS
G Mario DeMarco, EDM
G Bert Iannone, SAS
T Martin Ruby, SAS
T Buddy Tinsley, WPG
E Jack Russell, SAS
E Neill Armstrong, WPG
Coach Harry Smith, SAS

Second Team
FB Jim Spavital, WPG
FW Bud Korchak, WPG
HB Rollie Miles, EDM
HB Ken Charlton, SAS
QB Jack Jacobs, WPG
C Bill Blackburn, CAL
G Jim Quandamatteo, EDM
G Gerry DeLeeuw, WPG
T Chuck Quilter, EDM
T Dick Huffman, WPG
E Rollin Prather, EDM
E Jack Nix, SAS
Coach Annis Stukus, EDM

1952 IRFU
FW Bob Simpson, OTT
HB Ulysses Curtis, TOR
HB Hal Waggoner, HAM
HB Gene Roberts, OTT
QB Bill Mackrides, HAM
C Red Ettinger, TOR
G Eddie Bevan, HAM
G Vince Scott, HAM
T Vince Mazza, HAM
T Jim Staton, MTL
E Al Bruno, TOR
E Red O'Quinn, MTL

1952 WIFU
FW Bud Korchak, WPG
HB Tom Casey, WPG
HB Johnny Bright, CAL
HB Rollie Miles, EDM
QB Jack Jacobs, WPG
C Bill Blackburn, CAL
G Mario DeMarco, EDM
G Jim McPherson, WPG
T Buddy Tinsley, WPG
T Dick Huffman, WPG
E Bob Shaw, CAL
E Rollin Prather, EDM
Coach George Trafton, WPG

Second Team
FW Butch Avinger, SAS
HB Normie Kwong, EDM
HB Pete Thodos, CAL
HB Ralph McAllister, WPG
QB Frank Filchock, EDM
QB Claude Arnold, EDM
C Eagle Keys, EDM
G Dean Bandiera, WPG
G Harry Langford, CAL
T Martin Ruby, SAS
T Bob Bryant, CAL
E Paul Salata, CAL
E Hollin Aplin, SAS;
E Joe Aguirre, EDM
Coach Frank Filchock, EDM

1953 IRFU
Offence
FW Bob Simpson, OTT
HB Gene Roberts, OTT
HB Avatus Stone, OTT
HB Joe Scudero, TOR
QB Sam Etcheverry, MTL
C Tom Hugo, MTL
G Ed Bradley, MTL
G Kaye Vaughan, OTT
T Tex Coulter, MTL
T Vince Mazza, HAM
E Bernie Flowers, OTT
E Red O'Quinn, MTL

Defence
S Ted Toogood, TOR
HB Lou Kusserow, HAM
HB Dick Brown, HAM

HB Howie Turner, OTT
LB Red Ettinger, TOR
LB Ralph Toohy, HAM
G Vince Scott, HAM
G Eddie Bevan, HAM
T Vince Mazza, HAM
T Tex Coulter, MTL
E Pete Neumann, HAM
E Doug McNichol, MTL

1953 WIFU
Offence
FB Normie Kwong, EDM
FW Bud Korchak, WPG
HB Billy Vessels, EDM
HB Rollie Miles, EDM
QB Claude Arnold, EDM
C Eagle Keys, EDM
G Jim Quondamatteo, EDM
G Mike Cassidy, SAS
T Martin Ruby, SAS
T Willie Manley, EDM
E Bud Grant, WPG
E Mac Speedie, SAS
Coach Darrell Royal, EDM

Defence
HB Tom Casey, WPG
HB Neill Armstrong, WPG
HB Ray Willsey, EDM
HB Bobby Marlow, SAS
LB John Wozniak, SAS
LB Tony Momsen, CAL
G Porky Brown, CAL
G Dean Bandiera, WPG
T Martin Ruby, SAS
T Dick Huffman, WPG
E Frankie Anderson, EDM
E Ezzrett Anderson, CAL

1954 IRFU
Offence
FW Joey Pal, MTL
HB Alex Webster, MTL
HB Bernie Custis, HAM
HB Gene Wilson, TOR
QB Sam Etcheverry, MTL
C Tom Hugo, MTL
G Ray Cicia, MTL
G Herb Trawick, MTL
T Tex Coulter, MTL
T Vince Mazza, HAM
E Red O'Quinn, MTL
E Ray Ramsey, HAM

Defence
S Billy Cross, TOR
HB Hal Patterson, MTL
HB Bill McFarlane, TOR
HB Lou Kusserow, HAM
LB Tom Hugo, MTL
LB Red Ettinger, HAM
G Vince Scott, HAM
G Eddie Bevan, HAM
T Tex Coulter, MTL
T Jim Staton, MTL
E Doug McNichol, MTL
E Pete Neumann, HAM

1954 WIFU
Offence
FB Howie Waugh, CAL
HB Rollie Miles, EDM
HB Jackie Parker, EDM
HB Eddie Macon, CAL
QB Frank Tripucka, SAS
C Eagle Keys, EDM
G Mario DeMarco, SAS
G Roy Jenson, CAL
T Martin Ruby, SAS
T Dick Huffman, WPG
E Bud Grant, WPG
E Mac Speedie, SAS

Defence
HB Tom Casey, WPG
HB Bobby Marlow, SAS
HB Rollie Miles, EDM
HB Stan Williams, SAS
LB Ed Henke, CAL
LB John Wozniak, SAS
G Bob Levenhagen, BC
G Mike Cassidy, SAS
T Martin Ruby, SAS
T Dick Huffman, WPG
E Frankie Anderson, EDM
E Gene Brito, CAL
Coach Frank Filchock, SAS

1955 IRFU
Offence
FW Joey Pal, MTL
HB Pat Abbruzzi, MTL
HB Lou Kusserow, HAM
HB Tom Tracy, OTT
QB Sam Etcheverry, MTL
C Tom Hugo, MTL
G Bill Albright, TOR
G Herb Trawick, MTL
T Tex Coulter, MTL
T Billy Shipp, TOR
E Red O'Quinn, MTL
E Al Pfeifer, TOR

Defence
S Johnny Fedosoff, HAM
HB Hal Patterson, MTL
HB Avatus Stone, OTT
HB Lou Kusserow, HAM
LB Tom Hugo, MTL
LB Frank Dempsey, HAM/OTT
G Vince Scott, HAM
G Eddie Bevan, HAM
T Tex Coulter, MTL
T Billy Shipp, TOR
E Doug McNichol, MTL
E Pete Neumann, HAM

1955 WIFU
Offence
FB Normie Kwong, EDM
HB Ken Carpenter, SAS
HB Leo Lewis, WPG
HB Gerry James, WPG
QB Jackie Parker, EDM
C Kurt Burris, EDM
G Art Walker, EDM
G Harry Langford, CAL
T Buddy Tinsley, WPG
T Dale Meinert, EDM
E Willie Roberts, CAL
E Stan Williams, SAS

Defence
S Rupe Andrews, EDM
HB Bobby Marlow, SAS
HB Tom Casey, WPG
HB Rollie Miles, EDM
LB Ted Tully, EDM
LB Kurt Burris, EDM
G Bob Levenhagen, BC
G Floyd Harrawood, WPG
T Dale Meinert, EDM
T Dick Huffman, WPG
E Frankie Anderson, EDM
E Gordie Sturtridge, SAS
Coach Pop Ivy, EDM

1956 IRFU
Offence
FW Joey Pal, MTL
FB Pat Abbruzzi, MTL
HB Cookie Gilchrist, HAM
HB Dick Shatto, TOR
QB Sam Etcheverry, MTL
C Tom Hugo, MTL
G Larry Hayes, OTT
G Fran Machinsky, TOR
T Kaye Vaughan, OTT
T Bill Albright, TOR
E Hal Patterson, MTL
E Bob Simpson, OTT

Defence
S Don Pinhey, OTT
HB Hal Patterson, MTL
HB Ralph Goldston, HAM
HB Ray Truant, HAM
LB Ken Vargo, OTT
LB Tom Hugo, MTL
G Vince Scott, HAM
G Hardiman Cureton, TOR
T Kaye Vaughan, OTT
T Bill Albright, TOR
E Pete Neumann, HAM
E Jim Miller, MTL

1956 WIFU
Offence
FB Normie Kwong, EDM
HB Bob McNamara, WPG
HB Ed Vereb, BC
HB Ken Carpenter, SAS
QB Jackie Parker, EDM
C George Druxman, WPG (tie)
C Mel Becket, SAS (tie)
G Buddy Alliston, WPG
G Harry Langford, CAL
T Buddy Tinsley, WPG
T Martin Ruby, SAS
E Bud Grant, WPG
E Danny Edwards, BC

Defence
S Paul Cameron, BC
HB Rollie Miles, EDM
HB Larry Isbell, SAS
LB Bobby Marlow, SAS
LB Earl Lindley, EDM
LB Ted Tully, EDM
LB John Wozniak, SAS
MG Ron Atchison, SAS
T Dick Huffman, CAL
T Martin Ruby, SAS
E Gordie Sturtridge, SAS
E Frankie Anderson, EDM
Coach Pop Ivy, EDM

1957 IRFU
Offence
FW Bob Simpson, OTT
FB Cookie Gilchrist, HAM
HB Gerry McDougall, HAM
HB Dick Shatto, TOR
QB Sam Etcheverry, MTL
C Tom Hugo, MTL
G Larry Hayes, OTT
G Dave Suminski, HAM
T Kaye Vaughan, OTT
T John Barrow, HAM
E Hal Patterson, MTL
E Tex Schriewer, TOR

Defence
S Bob Simpson, OTT
HB Hal Patterson, MTL
HB Ralph Goldston, HAM
HB Bobby Kuntz, TOR
LB Tony Curcillo, HAM
LB Tom Hugo, MTL
G Vince Scott, HAM
G Larry Hayes, OTT
T Kaye Vaughan, OTT
T John Barrow, HAM
E Pete Neumann, HAM
E John Welton, TOR

1957 WIFU
Offence
FB Johnny Bright, EDM
HB Jackie Parker, EDM
HB Gerry James, WPG
HB By Bailey, BC
QB Kenny Ploen, WPG
C Galen Wahlmeier, SAS
G Harry Langford, CAL
G Ed Sharkey, BC
T Roger Nelson, EDM
T Dick Huffman, CAL
E Ernie Pitts, WPG
E Jack Gotta, CAL

Defence
S Oscar Kruger, EDM
HB Larry Isbell, SAS
HB Jack Gotta, CAL
LB Bobby Marlow, SAS
LB Ed Sharkey, BC
LB Ted Tully, EDM
LB Gordie Rowland, WPG
MG Art Walker, EDM
T Buddy Tinsley, WPG
T Dick Huffman, CAL
E Frankie Anderson, EDM
E Herb Gray, WPG
Coach Pop Ivy, EDM

1958 IRFU
Offence
FW Ron Howell, HAM
FB Gerry McDougall, HAM
HB Dick Shatto, TOR
HB Joel Wells, MTL
QB Bernie Faloney, HAM
C Tom Hugo, MTL (tie)
C Norm Stoneburgh, TOR (tie)
G Hardiman Cureton, OTT
G Jacki Simpson, MTL
T Dick Fouts, TOR
T John Barrow, HAM
E Paul Dekker, HAM
E Red O'Quinn, MTL

Defence
S Bob Simpson, OTT
HB Ralph Goldston, HAM
HB Eddie Macon, HAM
HB Hal Patterson, HAM
LB Tom Hugo, MTL
LB Tony Curcillo, HAM
G Vince Scott, HAM
G Jacki Simpson, MTL
T John Barrow, HAM
T Milt Graham, OTT
E Doug McNichol, MTL
E Pete Neumann, HAM

1958 WIFU
Offence
HB Johnny Bright, EDM
HB Cookie Gilchrist, SAS
HB Leo Lewis, WPG
HB Jack Hill, SAS
QB Jackie Parker, EDM
C Jim Furey, CAL
G Harry Langford, CAL
G Tim Hinton, BC
T Roger Nelson, EDM
T Don Luzzi, CAL
E Ken Carpenter, SAS
E Ernie Warlick, CAL

Defence
S Oscar Kruger, EDM
HB Larry Isbell, SAS
HB Jack Gotta, CAL
LB Gordie Rowland, WPG
LB Dave Burkholder, WPG
LB Ted Tully, EDM
LB Rollie Miles, EDM
MG Steve Patrick, WPG
T Don Luzzi, CAL
T Buddy Tinsley, WPG
E Herb Gray, WPG
E Art Walker, EDM
Coach Bud Grant, WPG

1959 IRFU
Offence
FW Ron Howell, HAM
HB Dave Thelen, OTT
HB Dick Shatto, TOR
HB Cookie Gilchrist, TOR
QB Bernie Faloney, HAM
C Tom Hugo, MTL
G Dave Suminski, HAM
G Kaye Vaughan, OTT
T Billy Shipp, MTL
T John Barrow, HAM
E Paul Dekker, HAM
E Bob Simpson, OTT

Defence
S Duane Wood, HAM
HB Ralph Goldston, HAM
HB Jim Rountree, TOR
OLB Bill Sowalski, OTT
OLB Eddie Bell, HAM
ILB Ernie Danjean, HAM
ILB Larry Hayes, OTT
MG Vince Scott, HAM
T Kaye Vaughan, OTT
T John Barrow, HAM
E Doug McNichol, MTL
E Pete Neumann, HAM

1959 WIFU
Offence
FB Johnny Bright, EDM
FB Charlie Shepard, WPG
HB Gene Filipski, CAL
HB Jackie Parker, EDM
QB Jim Van Pelt, WPG
C Neil Habig, SAS
G Tom Hinton, BC
G Ed Kotowich, WPG
T Roger Nelson, EDM
T Frank Rigney, WPG
E Ernie Pitts, WPG
E Ernie Warlick, CAL

Defence
S Harvey Wylie, CAL
HB Kenny Ploen, WPG
HB Billy Jessup, BC
OLB Rollie Miles, EDM
OLB Norm Fieldgate, BC
ILB Garland Warren, WPG
ILB Al Ecuyer, EDM
MG Steve Patrick, WPG
T Art Walker, EDM
T Urban Henry, BC
E Herb Gray, WPG
E Ed Gray, EDM

1960 Eastern Conference
Offence
HB Dave Mann, TOR
HB Cookie Gilchrist, TOR
HB Dave Thelen, OTT
HB Ron Stewart, OTT
QB Sam Etcheverry, MTL
C Norm Stoneburgh, TOR
G Kaye Vaughan, OTT
G Jacki Simpson, MTL
T Bill Hudson, MTL
T John Barrow, HAM
E Hal Patterson, MTL
E Paul Dekker, HAM

Defence

S Stan Wallace, TOR
HB Jim Rountree, TOR
HB Joe Poirier, OTT
OLB Gerry Nesbitt, OTT
OLB Garry Schreider, OTT
ILB Jim Andreotti, TOR
ILB Cookie Gilchrist, TOR
MG Marty Martinello, TOR
T Angelo Mosca, HAM
T John Barrow, HAM
E Dick Fouts, TOR
E Lou Bruce, OTT

1960 WIFU
Offence
FB Johnny Bright, EDM
FB Earl Lunsford, CAL
HB Leo Lewis, WPG
HB Willie Fleming, BC
QB Jackie Parker, EDM
C Neil Habig, SAS
G Cornel Piper, WPG
G Tony Pajaczkowski, CAL
T Roger Nelson, EDM
T Frank Rigney, WPG
E Ernie Pitts, WPG
E Ernie Warlick, CAL

Defence
S Harvey Wylie, CAL
HB Bill Smith, EDM
HB Clare Exelby, CAL
OLB Gord Rowland, WPG
OLB Norm Fieldgate, BC
ILB Bill Burrell, SAS
ILB Dave Burkholder, WPG
MG Ron Atchison, SAS
T Urban Henry, BC
T Don Luzzi, CAL
E Herb Gray, WPG
E Ed Gray, EDM

1961 Eastern Conference
Offence
FL Dave Mann, TOR
HB Don Clark, MTL
HB Ron Stewart, OTT
HB Dick Shatto, TOR
QB Bernie Faloney, HAM
C Norm Stoneburgh, TOR
G Kaye Vaughan, OTT
G Ellison Kelly, HAM
T Milt Crain, MTL
T Tom Jones, OTT
E Paul Dekker, HAM
E Marv Luster, MTL

Defence
S Jim Rountree, TOR
HB Don Sutherin, HAM
HB George Brancato, OTT
OLB Gerry Nesbitt, OTT
OLB Ron Brewer, MTL
ILB Jim Andreotti, TOR
ILB Hardiman Cureton, HAM
MG Marty Martinello, TOR
T John Barrow, HAM
T Bobby Jack Oliver, MTL
E Pete Neumann, HAM
E Billy Ray Locklin, MTL

1961 Western Conference
Offence
FB Johnny Bright, EDM
FB Earl Lunsford, CAL
HB Leo Lewis, WPG
HB Willie Fleming, BC
QB Jackie Parker, EDM
C Neil Habig, SAS
G Cornel Piper, WPG
G Mike Kmech, EDM
T Don Luzzi, CAL
T Frank Rigney, WPG
E Farrell Funston, WPG
E Jack Gotta, SAS

Defence
S Harvey Wylie, CAL
HB Norm Rauhaus, WPG
HB Oscar Kruger, EDM
OLB Gordie Rowland, WPG
OLB Bob Ptacek, SAS
ILB Wayne Harris, CAL
ILB Dave Burkholder, WPG
MG Ron Atchison, SAS
T Bill Clarke, SAS
T Mike Wright, WPG
E Herb Gray, WPG
E Tony Pajaczkowski, CAL

1962 Eastern Conference
Offence
HB George Dixon, MTL
HB Ernie White, OTT
HB Dick Shatto, TOR
HB Bobby Kuntz, HAM
QB Russ Jackson, OTT
C Ron Watton, HAM
G Hardiman Cureton, HAM
G Ellison Kelly, HAM
T Bronko Nagurski, HAM
T Moe Racine, OTT
E Hal Patterson, HAM
E Marv Luster, MTL

Defence
DB Don Sutherin, HAM
DB Jim Rountree, TOR
DB Joe Poirier, OTT
OLB Jim Conroy, OTT
OLB Zeno Karcz, HAM
ILB Jim Andreotti, TOR
ILB Ed Nickla, MTL
MG Kaye Vaughan, OTT
T John Barrow, HAM
T Bobby Jack Oliver, MTL
E Billy Ray Locklin, MTL
E Mel Semenko, OTT

1962 Western Conference
Offence
HB Earl Lunsford, CAL
HB Ray Purdin, SAS
HB Leo Lewis, WPG
HB Nub Beamer, BC
QB Eagle Day, CAL
C Neil Habig, SAS
G Tony Pajaczkowski, CAL
G Sherwyn Thorson, WPG
T Frank Rigney, WPG
T Lonnie Dennis, BC
E Tommy Joe Coffey, EDM
E Pete Manning, CAL

Defence
DB Harvey Wylie, CAL
DB Dick Thornton, WPG
DB Oscar Kruger, EDM
OLB Gordie Rowland, WPG
OLB Bill Burrell, SAS
ILB Tom Brown, BC
ILB Wayne Harris, CAL
MG Ron Atchison, SAS
T Don Luzzi, CAL
T Roger Savoie, WPG
E Herb Gray, WPG
E Garner Ekstran, SAS

1963 Eastern Conference
Offence
HB George Dixon, MTL
HB Dick Shatto, TOR
HB Dave Thelen, OTT
HB Tommy Grant, HAM
QB Russ Jackson, OTT
C Milt Crain, MTL
G Chuck Walton, MTL
G Ellison Kelly, HAM
T Roger Kramer, OTT
T Hardiman Cureton, HAM
E Hal Patterson, HAM
E Ted Watkins, OTT

Defence
DB Garney Henley, HAM
DB Joe Poirier, OTT
DB Jim Rountree, TOR
OLB Jim Reynolds, MTL
OLB Jim Conroy, OTT
ILB Gene Gaines, OTT
ILB Jim Andreotti, MTL
MG John Barrow, HAM
T Angelo Mosca, HAM
T Ed Nickla, MTL
E John Autry, TOR
E Billy Joe Booth, OTT

1963 Western Conference
Offence
HB Willie Fleming, BC
HB Lovell Coleman, CAL
HB Nub Beamer, BC
HB Jim Dillard, CAL
QB Joe Kapp, BC
C Neil Habig, SAS
G Tom Hinton, BC
G Tony Pajaczkowski, CAL
T Lonnie Dennis,BCr
T Al Benecick, SAS
E Pete Manning, CAL
E Farrell Funston, WPG

Defence
DB Harvey Wylie, CAL
DB Dick Thornton, WPG
DB Dale West, SAS
OLB Wayne Shaw, SAS
OLB Norm Fieldgate, BC
ILB Tom Brown, BC
ILB Wayne Harris, CAL
MG Ron Atchison, SAS
T Don Luzzi, CAL
T Bill Clarke, SAS
E Garner Ekstran, SAS
E Dick Fouts, BC

1964 Eastern Conference
Offence
FB Dave Thelen, OTT
HB Dick Shatto, TOR
HB Ron Stewart, OTT
FL Tommy Grant, HAM
QB Bernie Faloney, HAM
C Chet Miksza, HAM
G Ellison Kelly, HAM
G Ed Harrington, TOR
T Roger Kramer, OTT
T Bronco Nagurski, HAM
E Hal Patterson, HAM
E Ted Watkins, OTT

Defence
DB Garney Henley, HAM
DB Don Sutherin, HAM
DB Ed Learn, MTL
DB Jim Rountree, TOR
DB Joe Poirier, OTT
LB Ron Brewer, TOR
LB Bobby Kuntz, HAM
MG John Barrow, HAM
T Billy Shipp, TOR
T Ted Elsby, MTL
E Pete Neumann, HAM
E Billy Joe Booth, OTT

1964 Western Conference
Offence
FB Lovell Coleman, CAL
HB Ed Buchanan, SAS
HB Leo Lewis, WPG
FL Hugh Campbell, SAS
QB Joe Kapp, BC
C Neil Habig, SAS
G Al Benecick, SAS
G Tom Hinton, BC
T Lonnie Dennis, BC
T Frank Rigney, WPG
E Tommy Joe Coffey, EDM
E Pat Claridge, BC
E Pete Manning, CAL

Defence
DB Bill Munsey, BC
DB Jerry Keeling, CAL
DB Bob Ptacek, SAS
DB Neal Beaumont, BC
DB Dale West, SAS
LB Wayne Harris, CAL
LB Wayne Shaw, SAS
MG Tom Brown, BC
T Mike Cacic, BC
T Ron Atchison, SAS
E Dick Fouts, BC
E Bill Whisler, WPG

1965 Eastern Conference
Offence
HB Dave Thelen, TOR
HB Jim Dillard, OTT
HB Bo Scott, OTT
FL Terry Evanshen, MTL
QB Bernie Faloney, MTL
C Norm Stoneburgh, TOR
G John Pentecost, OTT
G Chuck Walton, OTT
T Moe Racine, OTT
T Bronco Nagurski, HAM
E Stan Crisson, HAM
E Ted Watkins, OTT

Defence
DB Garney Henley, HAM
DB Billy Wayte, HAM
DB Don Sutherin, HAM
DB Bob O'Billovich, OTT
DB Gene Gaines, OTT
LB Ron Brewer, TOR
LB Zeno Karcz, HAM
LB Ken Lehmann, OTT
T John Barrow, HAM
T Angelo Mosca, HAM
E Billy Ray Locklin, HAM
E John Baker, MTL

1965 Western Conference
Offence
HB George Reed, SAS
HB Lovell Coleman, CAL
HB Dave Raimey, WPG
HB Jim Thomas, EDM
FL Hugh Campbell, SAS
QB Kenny Ploen, WPG
C Ted Urness, SAS
G Al Benecick, SAS
G Herb Gray, WPG
T Clyde Brock, SAS
T Frank Rigney, WPG
E Tommy Joe Coffey, EDM
E Herman Harrison, CAL

Defence
DB Dale West, SAS
DB Larry Robinson, CAL
DB Dick Thornton, WPG
DB Jerry Keeling, CAL
DB Henry Janzen, WPG
LB Wayne Harris, CAL
LB Al Miller, WPG
LB Jim Furlong, CAL
T Mike Cacic, BC
T Pat Holmes, CAL
E E.A. Sims, EDM
E Dick Fouts, BC

1966 Eastern Conference
Offence
FB Dave Thelen, TOR
HB Don Lisbon, MTL
HB Bo Scott, OTT
FL Whit Tucker, OTT
QB Russ Jackson, OTT
C Doug Specht, OTT
G Tony Pajaczkowski, MTL
G Chuck Walton, HAM
T Bill Frank, TOR
T Moe Racine, OTT
E Hal Patterson, HAM
E Ted Watkins, OTT

Defence
DB Gene Gaines, OTT
DB Garney Henley, HAM
DB Joe Poirier, OTT
DB Marv Luster, TOR
DB Ed Learn, MTL
LB Ken Lehmann, OTT
LB Wilbur Scott, MTL
LB Jim Conroy, OTT
T John Barrow, HAM
T Angelo Mosca, HAM
E Billy Ray Locklin, HAM
E Billy Joe Booth, OTT

1966 Western Conference
Offence
FB George Reed, SAS
HB Dave Raimey, WPG
HB Jim Thomas, EDM
FL Hugh Campbell, SAS
QB Ron Lancaster, SAS
C Ted Urness, SAS
G Al Benecick, SAS
G Jack Abendschan, SAS
G Tom Hinton, BC
T Clyde Brock, SAS
T Frank Rigney, WPG
E Jim Worden, SAS
E Terry Evanshen, CAL

Defence
DB Jerry Keeling, CAL
DB Ernie Pitts, WPG
DB Bob Kosid, SAS
DB Bill Redell, EDM
DB Ed Ulmer, WPG
LB Wayne Harris, CAL
LB Phil Minnick, WPG
LB Wayne Shaw, SAS
T Don Luzzi, CAL
T Mike Cacic, BC
E E.A. Sims, EDM
E Garner Ekstran, SAS

1967 Eastern Conference
Offence
FB Bo Scott, OTT
HB Willie Bethea, HAM
HB Jim Dillard, TOR
FL Whit Tucker, OTT
QB Russ Jackson, OTT
C Gene Ceppetelli, HAM
G Bill Danychuk, HAM
G Roger Perdrix, OTT
T Bill Frank, TOR
T Danny Nykoluk, TOR
E Tommy Joe Coffey, HAM
E Margene Adkins, OTT

Defence
DB Garney Henley, HAM
DB Phil Brady, MTL
DB Marv Luster, TOR

DB Jim Rountree, TOR
DB Gene Gaines, OTT
MLB Ken Lehmann, OTT
OLB Bob Krouse, HAM
OLB Mike Blum, OTT
T John Barrow, HAM
T Bob Minihane, MTL
E John Baker, MTL
E Bob Brown, OTT

1967 Western Conference
Offence
FB George Reed, SAS
HB Jim Thomas, EDM
HB Dave Raimey, WPG
FL Ken Nielsen, WPG
QB Pete Liske, CAL
C Ted Urness, SAS
G Jack Abendschan, SAS
G Bob Lueck, CAL
T Clyde Brock, SAS
T Roger Kramer, CAL
E Terry Evanshen, CAL
E Herman Harrison, CAL

Defence
DB Frank Andruski, CAL
DB Jerry Keeling, CAL
DB Joe Hernandez, EDM
DB John Wydareny, EDM
DB Bruce Bennett, SAS
MLB Wayne Harris, CAL
OLB Wayne Shaw, SAS
OLB Garner Ekstran, SAS
T Ed McQuarters, SAS
T John LaGrone, EDM
E Dick Suderman, CAL
E Bill Whisler, WPG

1968 Eastern Conference
Offence
RB Bo Scott, OTT
RB Bill Symons, TOR
RB Vic Washington, OTT
FL Whit Tucker, OTT
QB Russ Jackson, OTT
C Basil Bark, MTL
G Charlie Parker, MTL
G Bill Danychuk, HAM
T Bill Frank, TOR
T Ellison Kelly, HAM
E Tommy Joe Coffey, HAM
E Mel Profit, TOR

Defence
DB Don Sutherin, OTT
DB Larry Fairholm, MTL
DB Garney Henley, HAM
DB Ed Learn, TOR
DB Marv Luster, TOR
LB Allen Ray Aldridge, TOR
LB Jerry Campbell, OTT
LB Ken Lehmann, OTT
T Mike Wadsworth, TOR
T Marshall Shirk, OTT
E Billy Ray Locklin, HAM
E Ed Harrington, TOR

1968 Western Conference
Offence
RB George Reed, SAS
RB Dave Raimey, WPG
RB Jim Evenson, BC
FL Ken Nielsen, WPG
QB Ron Lancaster, SAS
C Ted Urness, SAS
G Bob Lueck, CAL
G John Atamian, SAS
T Ken Sugarman, BC
T Clyde Brock, SAS
E Terry Evanshen, CAL
E Herman Harrison, CAL

Defence
DB Frank Andruski, CAL
DB Bob Kosid, SAS
DB Bruce Bennett, SAS
DB Jerry Keeling, CAL
DB Ernie Pitts, WPG
LB Wayne Harris, CAL
LB Wally Dempsey, SAS
LB Phil Minnick, WPG
LB Greg Findlay, BC
T Ed McQuarters, SAS
T John LaGrone, EDM
E Dick Suderman, CAL
E Bill Whisler, WPG

1969 Eastern Conference
Offence
RB Dennis Duncan, MTL
RB Vic Washington, OTT
RB Dave Raimey, TOR
FL Bobby Taylor, TOR
QB Russ Jackson, OTT
C Basil Bark, MTL
G Charlie Bray, TOR
G Charlie Parker, MTL
T Danny Nykoluk, TOR
T Ellison Kelly, HAM
SE Margene Adkins, OTT
SE Tommy Joe Coffey, HAM
TE Mel Profit, TOR

Defence
DB Don Sutherin, OTT
DB Dick Thornton, TOR
DB Marv Luster, TOR
DB Garney Henley, HAM
DB Ed Learn, TOR
MLB Ken Lehmann, OTT
OLB Jerry Campbell, OTT
OLB Henry Sorrell, HAM
T Marshall Shirk, OTT
T John Barrow, HAM
E Billy Joe Booth, OTT
E Ed Harrington, TOR

1969 Western Conference
Offence
RB George Reed, SAS
RB Jim Evenson, BC
RB Jim Young, BC
FL Ken Nielsen, WPG
QB Ron Lancaster, SAS
C Ted Urness, SAS
G Ken Sugarman, BC
G Jack Abendschan, SAS
T Clyde Brock, SAS
T Lanny Boleski, CAL
SE Terry Evanshen, CAL
TE Herman Harrison, CAL

Defence
DB John Wydareny, EDM
DB Bruce Bennett, SAS
DB Rick Robinson, BC
DB Frank Andruski, CAL
DB Jerry Bradley, BC
MLB Wayne Harris, CAL
OLB Wayne Shaw, SAS
OLB Wally Dempsey, SAS
T Ed McQuarters, SAS
T John LaGrone, EDM
E Bill Whisler, WPG
E Ken Reed, SAS
E John Helton, CAL

1970 Eastern Conference
Offence
RB Moses Denson, MTL
RB Bill Symons, TOR
RB DaveFLeming, HAM
FL Jim Thorpe, TOR
QB Gary Wood, OTT
C Gene Ceppetelli, MTL
G Charlie Bray, TOR
G Bill Danychuk, HAM
T Ed George, MTL
T Ellison Kelly, HAM
SE Tommy Joe Coffey, HAM
TE Mel Profit, TOR

Defence
DB Al Phaneuf, MTL
DB Garney Henley, HAM
DB Al Marcelin, OTT
DB Jim Tomlin, TOR
DB Marv Luster, TOR
LB Charlie Collins, MTL
LB Jerry Campbell, OTT
LB Mike Widger, MTL
T Angelo Mosca, HAM
T Marshall Shirk, OTT
E Steve Booras, MTL
E Steve Smear, MTL

1970 Western Conference
Offence
RB Hugh McKinnis, CAL
RB Jim Evenson, BC
RB Silas McKinnie, SAS
FL Mike Eben, EDM
QB Ron Lancaster, SAS
C Ted Urness, SAS
G Ken Sugarman, BC
G Jack Abendschan, SAS
T Bill Frank, WPG
T Lanny Boleski, CAL
SE Rich Shaw, WPG
TE Herman Harrison, CAL

Defence
DB John Wydareny, EDM
DB Ted Dushinski, SAS
DB Joe Hernandez, EDM
DB Bruce Bennett, SAS
DB Paul Brule, WPG
LB Wayne Harris, CAL
LB Dave Gasser, EDM
LB Greg Findlay, BC
T John Helton, CAL
T Greg Pipes, EDM
E Ken Frith, SAS
E Ron Forwick, EDM

1971 Eastern Conference
Offence
RB Bruce Van Ness, MTL
RB Dennis Duncan, OTT
RB Leon McQuay, TOR
FL Mike Eben, TOR
QB Joe Theismann, TOR
C Paul Desjardins, TOR
G Justin Canale, MTL
G Charlie Bray, TOR
T Ellison Kelly, TOR
T Ed George, MTL
SE Terry Evanshen, MTL
TE Mel Profit, TOR

Defence
DB John Williams, HAM
DB Gene Gaines, MTL
DB Garney Henley, HAM
DB Marv Luster, TOR
DB Dick Thornton, TOR
LB Steve Smear, MTL
LB Mark Kosmos, MTL
LB Mike Blum, HAM
T Rudy Sims, OTT
T Jim Stillwagon, TOR
E Jim Corrigall, TOR
E Tom Laputka, OTT

1971 Western Conference
Offence
RB Jim Evenson, BC
RB George Reed, SAS
RB Mack Herron, WPG
FL Bob LaRose, WPG
QB Don Jonas, WPG
C Bob Swift, WPG (tie)
C Basil Bark, CAL (tie)
G Jack Abendschan, SAS
G Bob Lueck, WPG
T Bill Frank, WPG
T Ken Sugarman, BC
SE Jim Thorpe, WPG
TE Herman Harrison, CAL

Defence
DB Dick Dupuis, EDM
DB Frank Andruski, CAL
DB Larry Robinson, CAL
DB Bruce Bennett, SAS
DB Howard Starks, CAL
LB Wayne Harris, CAL
LB Wayne Shaw, SAS
LB Dave Gasser, EDM
LB Rob McLaren, WPG
T John Helton, CAL
T John LaGrone, EDM
E Bill Baker, SAS
E Craig Koinzan, CAL
E Dick Suderman, CAL

1972 Eastern Conference
Offence
RB Dave Buchanan, HAM
RB Ike Brown, MTL
RB Moses Denson, MTL
QB Chuck Ealey, HAM
C Paul Desjardins, TOR
G John Hohman, HAM
G Ed Chalupka, HAM
T Bill Danychuk, HAM
T Ed George, MTL
WR Garney Henley, HAM
WR Eric Allen, TOR
TE Peter Dalla Riva, MTL
TE Tony Gabriel, HAM

Defence
S Marv Luster, TOR
HB Al Brenner, HAM
HB John Williams, HAM
HB Dickie Adams, OTT
HB Rod Woodward, OTT
LB Mike Widger, MTL
LB Gene Mack, TOR
LB Jerry Campbell, OTT
T Jim Stillwagon, TOR
T Rudy Sims, OTT
E Wayne Smith, OTT
E Jim Corrigall, TOR
E George Wells, HAM

1972 Western Conference
Offence
RB Mack Herron, WPG
RB George Reed, SAS
RB Tom Campana, SAS
QB Don Jonas, WPG
C Bob Swift, WPG
G Bob Lueck, WPG
G Granville Liggins, CAL
G Larry Watkins, EDM
T Bill Frank, WPG
T Charlie Turner, EDM
WR Jim Thorpe, WPG
WR Jim Young, BC
WR Gerry Shaw, CAL
TE Tyrone Walls, EDM

Defence
S Larry Robinson, CAL
HB Grady Cavness, WPG
HB Bruce Bennett, SAS
HB Dick Dupuis, EDM
HB Gene Lakusiak, WPG
HB Frank Andruski, CAL
LB Dave Gasser, EDM
LB Ray Nettles, BC
LB Mickey Doyle, WPG
T John Helton, CAL
T John LaGrone, EDM
E Bill Baker, SAS
E Jim Heighton, WPG

1973 Eastern Conference
Offence
RB John Harvey, MTL
RB Andy Hopkins, HAM
RB Jim Evenson, OTT
QB Joe Theismann, TOR
C Paul Desjardins, TOR
G Ed George, MTL
G Ed Chalupka, HAM
T Dan Yochum, MTL
T Bill Danychuk, HAM
WR Johnny Rodgers, MTL
WR Eric Allen, TOR
TE Tony Gabriel, HAM

Defence
DB Dickie Harris, MTL
DB Dickie Adams, OTT
DB Al Marcelin, OTT
DB Tim Anderson, TOR
DB Lewis Porter, HAM
LB Jerry Campbell, OTT
LB Mike Widger, MTL
LB Gene Mack, TOR
T Gordon Judges, MTL
T Rudy Sims, OTT
E Carl Crennel, MTL
E Jim Corrigall, TOR

1973 Western Conference
Offence
RB Roy Bell, EDM
RB George Reed, SAS
RB Johnny Musso, BC
QB Ron Lancaster, SAS
C Bob Swift, WPG (tie)
C Basil Bark, CAL (tie)
C Bob Howes, EDM (tie)
G Ralph Galloway, SAS
G Jack Abendschan, SAS
T Bill Frank, WPG
T Charlie Turner, EDM
WR George McGowan, EDM
WR Tom Forzani, CAL
TE Lynn Hendrickson, BC

Defence
DB Lorne Richardson, SAS
DB Ted Provost, SAS
DB Frank Andruski, CAL
DB Gene Lakusiak, WPG
DB Larry Highbaugh, EDM
LB Ray Nettles, BC
LB Sam Britts, EDM
LB Roger Goree, CAL
T John Helton, CAL
T John LaGrone, EDM
E Bill Baker, SAS
E Ron Estay, EDM

1974 Eastern Conference
Offence
RB Steve Ferrughelli, MTL
RB Andy Hopkins, HAM
RB Art Green, OTT
QB Jimmy Jones, MTL
C Bob McKeown, OTT
G Ed Chalupka, HAM
G Ed George, MTL
T Noah Jackson, TOR
T Dan Yochum, MTL
WR Johnny Rodgers, MTL

WR Rhome Nixon, OTT
TE Tony Gabriel, HAM

Defence
DB Al Marcelin, OTT
DB Dickie Harris, MTL
DB Dickie Adams, OTT
DB Phil Price, MTL
DB Al Brenner, HAM
DB Ron Woodward, OTT
MLB Jerry Campbell, OTT
OLB Mike Widger, MTL
OLB Chuck Zapiec, MTL
T Jim Stillwagon, TOR
T Rudy Sims, OTT
E Wayne Smith, OTT
E Junior Ah You, MTL

1974 Western Conference
Offence
RB George Reed, SAS
RB Lou Harris, BC
RB Roy Bell, EDM
QB Tom Wilkinson, EDM
C Bob Swift, WPG
G Curtis Wester, BC
G Ralph Galloway, SAS
T Charlie Turner, EDM
T Larry Watkins, EDM
WR Tom Forzani, CAL
WR Rudy Linterman, CAL
TE Tyrone Walls, EDM

Defence
DB Lorne Richardson, SAS
DB Paul Williams, WPG
DB Larry Highbaugh, EDM
DB Ted Provost, SAS
DB Howard Starks, CAL
MLB Ray Nettles, BC
OLB Pete Wysocki, SAS
OLB Roger Goree, CAL
T John Helton, CAL
T Garrett Hunsperger, BC
E George Wells, SAS
E Jim Heighton, WPG

1975 Eastern Conference
Offence
RB Art Green, OTT
RB Doyle Orange, TOR
RB Johnny Rodgers, MTL
QB Tom Clements, OTT
C Wayne Conrad, MTL
G Dave Braggins, MTL
G Tom Schuette, OTT
T Dan Yochum, MTL
T Jeff Turcotte, OTT
WR Tony Gabriel, OTT
WR Terry Evanshen, HAM
TE Peter Dalla Riva, MTL

Defence
DB Rod Woodward, OTT
DB Dickie Adams, OTT
DB Dickie Harris, MTL
DB Larry Uteck, TOR
DB Wayne Tosh, OTT
MLB Jerry Campbell, OTT
OLB Mike Widger, MTL
OLB Mark Kosmos, OTT
T Glen Weir, MTL
T Granville Liggins, TOR
E Jim Corrigall, TOR
E Junior Ah You, MTL

1975 Western Conference
Offence
RB George Reed, SAS
RB Willie Burden, CAL
RB Lou Harris, BC
QB Ron Lancaster, SAS
C Al Wilson, BC
G Ralph Galloway, SAS
G Willie Martin, EDM
T Charlie Turner, EDM
T Layne McDowell, BC
WR George McGowan, EDM
WR Rhett Dawson, SAS
TE Tyrone Walls, EDM

Defence
DB Lorne Richardson, SAS
DB Vern Roberson, CAL
DB Brian Herosian, WPG
DB Ted Dushinski, SAS
DB Jim Marshall, SAS
DB Larry Highbaugh, EDM
MLB Harry Walters, WPG
OLB Larry Cameron, BC
OLB Joe Forzani, CAL
T John Helton, CAL
T Tim Roth, SAS

E Bill Baker, BC
E George Wells, SAS

1976 Eastern Conference
Offence
RB Jimmy Edwards, HAM
RB Art Green, OTT
RB Andy Hopkins, MTL
QB Tom Clements, OTT
C Donn Smith, OTT
G Dave Braggins, MTL
G Larry Butler, HAM
T Dan Yochum, MTL
T Jim Coode, OTT
WR Johnny Rodgers, MTL
WR Mike Eben, TOR
TE Tony Gabriel, OTT

Defence
DB Dickie Harris, MTL
DB Phil Price, MTL
DB Steve Dennis, TOR
DB David Shaw, HAM
DB Larry Uteck, TOR
DB Lewis Porter, HAM
MLB Larry Cameron, OTT
OLB Chuck Zapiec, MTL
OLB Mark Kosmos, OTT
T Granville Liggins, TOR
T Glen Weir, MTL
E Junior Ah You, MTL
E Mike Samples, HAM

1976 Western Conference
Offence
RB Jim Washington, WPG
RB Mike Strickland, BC
RB Steve Beaird, WPG
QB Ron Lancaster, SAS
C Al Wilson, BC
G Ralph Galloway, SAS
G Buddy Brown, WPG
T Butch Norman, WPG
T Layne McDowell, BC
WR Rhett Dawson, SAS
WR George McGowan, EDM
TE Bob Richardson, SAS

Defence
DB Brian Herosian, WPG
DB Lorne Richardson, SAS
DB Paul Williams, SAS
DB Joe Hollimon, EDM
DB Ken McEachern, SAS
MLB Harry Walters, WPG
OLB Roger Goree, SAS
OLB Bill Manchuk, SAS
T John Helton, CAL
T Tim Roth, SAS
E Bill Baker, BC
E George Wells, SAS

1977 Eastern Conference
Offence
RB Jimmy Edwards, HAM
RB Richard Holmes, OTT
SB Peter Dalla Riva, MTL
QB Tom Clements, OTT
C Donn Smith, OTT
G Jeff Turcotte, OTT
G Larry Butler, HAM
T Mike Wilson, TOR
T Dan Yochum, MTL
WR Brock Aynsley, MTL
WR Jeff Avery, OTT
TE Tony Gabriel, OTT
P Ken Clark, HAM
K Don Sweet, MTL

Defence
S Randy Rhino, MTL
HB Paul Bennett, TOR
HB Tony Proudfoot, MTL
CB Dickie Harris, MTL
CB Eric Harris, TOR
MLB Ray Nettles, TOR
OLB Mike Widger, OTT
OLB Chuck Zapiec, MTL
T Glen Weir, MTL
T Ecomet Burley, TOR
E Jim Corrigall, TOR
E Jim Piaskoski, OTT

1977 Western Conference
Offence
RB Jim Washington, WPG
RB Willie Burden, CAL
SB Tom Scott, WPG
QB Jerry Tagge, BC
C Al Wilson, BC
G Ralph Galloway, SAS
G Buddy Brown, WPG
T Layne McDowell, BC

T Charlie Turner, EDM
WR Tom Forzani, CAL
WR Leon Bright, BC
TE Gord Paterson, WPG
P Lui Passaglia, BC
K Dave Cutler, EDM

Defence
S Grady Cavness, BC
HB Pete Laborato, EDM
HB Chuck Wills, WPG
CB Larry Highbaugh, EDM
CB Paul Williams, SAS
CB Joe Fourqurean, BC
CB Rocky Long, BC
MLB Dan Kepley, EDM
OLB Roger Goree, SAS
OLB Glen Jackson, BC
T Dave Fennell, EDM
T Frank Landy, BC
E Ron Estay, EDM
E David Boone, EDM

1978 Eastern Conference
Offence
RB Jimmy Edwards, HAM
RB Mike Murphy, OTT
SB Art Green, OTT
QB Condredge Holloway, OTT
C Donn Smith, OTT
G Larry Butler, HAM
G Charlie Brandon, OTT
T Jim Coode, OTT
T Dan Yochum, MTL
WR Jeff Avery, OTT
WR Bob Gaddis, MTL
TE Tony Gabriel, OTT
P Ken Clark, TOR
K Don Sweet, MTL

Defence
S Randy Rhino, MTL
HB Larry Brune, OTT
HB Jim Burrow, MTL
CB Dickie Harris, MTL
CB Eric Harris, TOR
MLB Carl Crennel, MTL
OLB Chuck Zapiec, MTL
OLB Ben Zambiasi, HAM
T Mike Raines, OTT
T Glen Weir, MTL
E Mike Fanucci, OTT
E Jim Corrigall, TOR

1978 Western Conference
Offence
RB James Sykes, CAL
RB Mike Strickland, SAS
SB Tom Scott, EDM
QB Tom Wilkinson, EDM
C Al Wilson, BC
G Harold Holton, CAL
G Bill Stevenson, EDM
T Lloyd Fairbanks, CAL
T Butch Norman, WPG
WR Joe Poplawski, WPG
WR Mike Holmes, WPG
TE Willie Armstead, CAL
P Hank Ilesic, EDM
K Dave Cutler, EDM

Defence
S Al Burleson, CAL
HB Greg Butler, EDM
HB Ed Jones, EDM
CB Joe Hollimon, EDM
CB Terry Irvin, CAL
MLB Dan Kepley, EDM
OLB Tom Towns, EDM
OLB Glen Jackson, BC
T Dave Fennell, EDM
T John Helton, CAL
E Reggie Lewis, CAL
E Ron Estay, EDM

1979 Eastern Conference
Offence
RB David Green, MTL
RB Terry Metcalf, TOR
SB Leif Pettersen, HAM
QB Tom Clements, HAM
C Doug Smith, MTL
G Ray Watrin, MTL
G Larry Butler, HAM
T Dan Yochum, MTL
T Nick Bastaja, TOR
WR Bob Gaddis, MTL
WR Martin Cox, OTT
TE Tony Gabriel, OTT
P Ian Sunter, TOR
K Don Sweet, MTL

Defence
S Billy Hardee, TOR
HB Jim Burrow, MTL
HB Tony Proudfoot, MTL
CB Dickie Harris, MTL
CB Mike Nelms, OTT
MLB Carl Crennel, MTL
OLB Ben Zambiasi, HAM
OLB Ron Foxx, OTT
T Glen Weir, MTL
T Mike Raines, OTT
E Junior Ah You, MTL
E Jim Corrigall, TOR

1979 Western Conference
Offence
RB Jim Germany, EDM
RB Larry Key, BC
SB Willie Armstead, CAL
QB Tom Wilkinson, EDM
C Al Wilson, BC
G Bill Stevenson, EDM
G Eric Upton, EDM
T Mike Wilson, EDM
T Lloyd Fairbanks, CAL
WR Waddell Smith, EDM
WR Brian Kelly, EDM
TE Harry Holt, BC
P Hank Ilesic, EDM
K Lui Passaglia, BC

Defence
S Al Burleson, CAL
HB Gregg Butler, EDM
HB Ed Jones, EDM
CB Ray Odums, CAL
CB Terry Irvin, CAL
MLB Dan Kepley, EDM
OLB Glen Jackson, BC
OLB Tom Towns, EDM
T Dave Fennell, EDM
T John Helton, WPG
E David Boone, EDM
E Reggie Lewis, CAL

1980 Eastern Conference
Offence
RB Richard Crump, OTT
RB Skip Walker, MTL
SB David Newman, TOR
QB Gerry Dattilio, MTL
C Henry Waszczuk, HAM
G Val Belcher, OTT
G Alan Moffatt, HAM
T Doug Payton, MTL
T Willie Martin, HAM
WR Bob Gaddis, TOR
WR Keith Baker, MTL
TE Tony Gabriel, OTT
P Zenon Andrusyshyn, TOR
K Bernie Ruoff, HAM

Defence
S Billy Hardee, TOR
HB Jerry Anderson, HAM
HB Harold Woods, HAM
CB Dickie Harris, MTL
CB David Shaw, HAM
MLB Tom Cousineau, MTL
OLB Ben Zambiasi, HAM
OLB Ron Foxx, OTT
OLB Rick Sowieta, OTT
T Bruce Clark, TOR
T Mike Raines, OTT
E Jim Corrigall, TOR
E Junior Ah You, MTL

1980 Western Conference
Offence
RB James Sykes, CAL
RB William Miller, WPG
SB Tom Scott, EDM
QB Dieter Brock, WPG
C Al Wilson, BC
G Larry Butler, WPG
G Mike Horton, CAL
T Mike Wilson, EDM
T Butch Norman, WPG
WR Mike Holmes, WPG
WR Brian Kelly, EDM
TE Harry Holt, BC
P Hank Ilesic, EDM
K Lui Passaglia, BC (tie)
K Dave Cutler, EDM (tie)

Defence
S Ken McEachern, SAS
HB Ed Jones, EDM
HB Greg Butler, EDM
CB Ray Odums, CAL
CB Charley Williams, WPG
MLB Dan Kepley, EDM
OLB Tom Towns, EDM
OLB Dale Potter, EDM

T Dave Fennell, EDM
T Ed McAleney, CAL
E Ron Estay, EDM
E Reggie Lewis, CAL

1981 Eastern Division
Offence
RB Cedric Minter, TOR
RB Rufus Crawford, HAM
SB Rocky DiPietro, HAM
QB Tom Clements, HAM
C Henry Waszczuk, HAM
G Val Belcher, OTT
G Bill Norton, MTL
T Ed Fulton, HAM
T Doug Payton, MTL
WR Keith Baker, HAM
WR James Scott, MTL
TE Tony Gabriel, OTT
P Zenon Andrusyshyn, TOR
K Bernie Ruoff, HAM

Defence
S Randy Rhino, OTT
DB Harold Woods, HAM
DB Larry Brune, OTT
CB Leroy Paul, HAM
CB David Shaw, HAM
MLB John Priestner, HAM
OLB Ben Zambiasi, HAM
OLB Carmelo Carteri, HAM
T Ecomet Burley, HAM
T Mike Raines, OTT
E Grover Covington, HAM
E Greg Marshall, OTT

1981 Western Division
Offence
RB Larry Key, BC
RB Jim Germany, EDM
SB Joe Poplawski, WPG
QB Dieter Brock, WPG
C Al Wilson, BC
G Nick Bastaja, WPG
G Larry Butler, WPG
T Bill Stevenson, EDM
T Hector Pothier, EDM
WR Brian Kelly, EDM
WR Tyron Gray, BC
WR Eugene Goodlow, WPG
TE Joey Walters, SAS
P Hank Ilesic, EDM
K Trevor Kennerd, WPG

Defence
S Ken McEachern, SAS
HB Merv Walker, CAL
HB Ed Jones, EDM
CB Ray Odums, CAL
CB Charley Williams, WPG
MLB Dan Kepley, EDM
OLB Vince Goldsmith, SAS
OLB James Parker, EDM
T Dave Fennell, EDM
T Mike Samples, SAS
T John Helton, WPG
E David Boone, EDM
E Lyall Woznesensky, SAS

1982 Eastern Division
Offence
RB Skip Walker, OTT
RB Cedric Minter, TOR
SB Nick Arakgi, MTL
SB Rocky DiPietro, HAM
QB Condredge Holloway, TOR
C Henry Waszczuk, HAM
G Val Belcher, OTT
G Rudy Phillips, OTT
T Ed Fulton, HAM
T Doug Payton, MTL
WR Terry Greer, TOR
WR Keith Baker, HAM
P Bernie Ruoff, HAM
K Gerry Organ, OTT

Defence
S Zac Henderson, TOR
HB Howard Fields, HAM
HB Mark Young, MTL
CB David Shaw, HAM
CB Carl Brazley, OTT
MLB John Pointer, TOR
OLB Bill Hampton, MTL
OLB Ben Zambiasi, HAM
T Gary Dulin, OTT
T Glen Weir, MTL
E Doug Scott, MTL
E Gregory Marshall, OTT

1982 Western Division
Offence
RB James Sykes, CAL
RB William Miller, WPG
SB Tom Scott, EDM
SB Joey Walters, SAS
QB Dieter Brock, WPG
C John Bonk, WPG
G Nick Bastaja, WPG
G Roger Aldag, SAS
G Leo Blanchard, EDM
T Bobby Thompson, WPG
T Lloyd Fairbanks, CAL
WR Mervyn Fernandez, BC
WR Willie Armstead, CAL
P Ken Clark, SAS
K Dave Ridgway, SAS

Defence
S Paul Bennett, WPG
HB Vince Phason, WPG
HB Fran McDermott, SAS
CB Joe Hollimon, EDM
CB Ray Odums, CAL
MLB Dan Bass, CAL
OLB James Parker, EDM
OLB Glen Jackson, BC
T Mike Samples, SAS
T John Helton, WPG
E Nick Hebeler, BC
E Pete Catan, WPG

1983 Eastern Division
Offence
RB Alvin Walker, OTT
RB Johnny Shepherd, HAM
SB Emanuel Tolbert, TOR
SB Ron Robinson, MTL
QB Condredge Holloway, TOR
C Larry Tittley, OTT
G Dan Ferrone, TOR
G Rudy Phillips, OTT
T Miles Gorrell, MTL
T Kevin Powell, OTT
WR Keith Baker, HAM
WR Terry Greer, TOR
P/K Bernie Ruoff, HAM

Defence
S Ken McEachern, TOR
HB Howard Fields, HAM
HB Darrell Wilson, TOR
HB Carl Brazley, TOR
CB Harry Skipper, MTL
CB Leroy Paul, TOR
MLB Darrell Nicholson, TOR
OLB Delbert Fowler, MTL
OLB Rick Sowieta, OTT
OLB William Mitchell, TOR
T Franklin King, TOR
T Gary Dulin, OTT
E Greg Marshall, OTT
E Rick Mohr, TOR

1983 Western Division
Offence
RB Willard Reaves, WPG
RB Ray Crouse, CAL
SB Tom Scott, EDM
SB Chris DeFrance, SAS
QB Warren Moon, EDM
C John Bonk, WPG
G Leo Blanchard, EDM
G Roger Aldag, SAS
T John Blain, BC
T Dave Kirzinger, CAL
WR Brian Kelly, EDM
WR Mervyn Fernandez, BC
P/K Lui Passaglia, BC
P/K Trevor Kennerd, WPG

Defence
S Paul Bennett, WPG
HB Larry Crawford, BC
HB Richie Hall, CAL
CB David Shaw, WPG
CB Kerry Parker, BC
MLB Dan Bass, CAL
OLB James West, CAL
OLB Vince Goldsmith, SAS
T Mack Moore, BC
T Randy Trautman, CAL
E Tony Norman, WPG
E James Parker, EDM

1984 Eastern Division
Offence
RB Lester Brown, TOR
RB Dwaine Wilson, MTL
SB Paul Pearson, TOR
QB Joe Barnes, TOR
C Henry Waszczuk, HAM
G Dan Ferrone, TOR
G Lloyd Fairbanks, MTL
T John Malinosky, TOR
T Miles Gorrell, MTL
WR Terry Greer, TOR
WR Ron Johnson, HAM
TE Nick Arakgi, MTL
P/K Bernie Ruoff, HAM

Defence
DB Carl Brazley, TOR
DB Harry Skipper, MTL
DB Ricky Barden, OTT
DB FelixWRight, HAM
DB Phil Jones, MTL
MLB William Mitchell, TOR
OLB Ben Zambiasi, HAM
OLB Al Washington, OTT
T James Curry, TOR
T Doug Scott, MTL
E Steve Raquet, MTL
E Greg Marshall, OTT

1984 Western Division
Offence
RB Willard Reaves, WPG
RB Craig Ellis, SAS
SB Chris DeFrance, SAS
SB Joe Poplawski, WPG
QB Tom Clements, WPG
C John Bonk, WPG
G Leo Blanchard, EDM
G Nick Bastaja, WPG
T Chris Walby, WPG
T John Blain, BC
WR Brian Kelly, EDM
WR Mervyn Fernandez, BC
P Bob Cameron, WPG
K Lui Passaglia, BC

Defence
DB David Shaw, WPG
DB Terry Irvin, SAS
DB Ken Hailey, WPG
DB Larry Crawford, BC
DB Laurent DesLauriers, EDM
MLB Aaron Brown, WPG
OLB Tyrone Jones, WPG
OLB Stewart Hill, EDM
T Randy Trautman, CAL
T Mack Moore, BC
E Tony Norman, WPG
E James Parker, BC

1985 Eastern Division
Offence
RB Lester Brown, OTT
RB Bob Bronk, TOR
SB Nick Arakgi, MTL
SB Mike McTague, MTL
QB Ken Hobart, HAM
C Marv Allemang, HAM
G Lloyd Fairbanks, MTL
G Dan Ferrone, TOR
T Kevin Powell, OTT
T Roger Cattelan, OTT
WR Steve Stapler, HAM
WR Terry Greer, TOR
P Ken Clark, OTT
K Bernie Ruoff, HAM (tie)
K Dean Dorsey, OTT (tie)

Defence
S Paul Bennett, HAM
HB Howard Fields, HAM
HB Ricky Barden, OTT
CB Less Browne, HAM
CB Carl Brazley, TOR
MLB Ben Zambiasi, HAM
OLB William Mitchell, TOR
OLB Rick Sowieta, OTT
T James Curry, TOR
T Doug Scott, MTL
E Grover Covington, HAM
E Loyd Lewis, OTT

1985 Western Division
Offence
RB Willard Reaves, WPG
RB Keyvan Jenkins, BC
SB Joe Poplawski, WPG
SB Ray Elgaard, SAS
QB Matt Dunigan, EDM
C John Bonk, WPG
G Leo Blanchard, EDM
G Nick Bastaja, WPG
T John Blain, BC
T Chris Walby, WPG
WR Mervyn Fernandez, BC
WR Jeff Boyd, WPG
P Tom Dixon, EDM
K Trevor Kennerd, WPG

Defence
S ScottFLagel, WPG
HB Ken Hailey, WPG
HB Wylie Turner, WPG (tie)
HB Melvin Byrd, BC (tie)
CB Darnell Clash, BC
CB David Shaw, WPG
MLB Dan Bass, EDM
OLB Tyrone Jones, WPG
OLB Kevin Konar, BC (tie)
OLB Glen Jackson, BC (tie)
T Mike Gray, BC
T Rick Klassen, BC
E James Parker, BC
E Tony Norman, WPG

1986 Eastern Division
Offence
RB Walter Bender, HAM
RB Jim Reid, OTT
SB Mark Barousse, OTT
SB Rocky DiPietro, HAM
QB Mike Kerrigan, HAM
C Marv Allemang, HAM
G Dan Ferrone, TOR
G Jason Riley, HAM
T Lloyd Fairbanks, MTL
T Miles Gorrell, HAM
WR James Hood, MTL
WR Tony Champion, HAM
P Hank Ilesic, TOR
K Lance Chomyc, TOR

Defence
S Rick Ryan, MTL
HB Carl Brazley, TOR
HB Mark Streeter, HAM
CB Less Browne, HAM
CB Terry Irvin, MTL
MLB Ben Zambiasi, HAM
OLB Leo Ezerins, HAM
OLB Willie Pless, TOR
T Brett Williams, MTL
T Mike Walker, HAM
E Grover Covington, HAM
E Rodney Harding, TOR
ST Jeff Trefflin, MTL

1986 Western Division
Offence
RB Gary Allen, CAL
RB Bobby Johnson, SAS
SB Joe Poplawski, WPG
SB Emanuel Tolbert, CAL
QB Rick Johnson, CAL
C Bob Poley, CAL
G Roger Aldag, SAS
G Leo Blanchard, EDM
T Chris Walby, WPG
T Rudy Phillips, EDM
WR James Murphy, WPG
WR Ray Alexander, CAL
P Tom Dixon, EDM
K J.T. Hay, CAL

Defence
S ScottFLagel, WPG
HB Larry Crawford, BC
HB Richie Hall, CAL
CB Roy Bennett, WPG
CB Mel Jenkins, CAL
MLB Dan Bass, EDM
OLB Tyrone Jones, WPG
OLB Billy Jackson, SAS
T Harold Hallman, CAL
T James Zachery, EDM
E James Parker, BC
E Stewart Hill, EDM
ST Gary Allen, CAL

1987 Eastern Division
Offence
RB Willard Reaves, WPG
RB Gill Fenerty, TOR
SB Darrell Smith, TOR
SB Perry Tuttle, WPG
QB Tom Clements, WPG
C Ian Beckstead, TOR
G Nick Bastaja, WPG
G Dan Ferrone, TOR
T Chris Walby, WPG
T Chris Schultz, TOR
WR Steve Stapler, HAM
WR James Murphy, WPG
P Hank Ilesic, TOR
K Dean Dorsey, OTT

Defence
S ScottFLagel, WPG
DB Howard Fields, HAM
DB Ken Hailey, WPG
CB Roy Bennett, WPG
CB James Jefferson, WPG
MLB James West, WPG
OLB Tyrone Jones, WPG
OLB Frank Robinson, HAM
T Mike Walker, HAM

T Jearld Baylis, TOR
E Grover Covington, HAM
E Rodney Harding, TOR
ST Darnell Clash, TOR

1987 Western Division
Offence
RB Gary Allen, CAL
RB Walter Bender, SAS
SB Emanuel Tolbert, CAL
SB Ray Elgaard, SAS
QB Roy Dewalt, BC
C Rod Connop, EDM
G Roger Aldag, SAS
G Gerald Roper, BC
T Hector Pothier, EDM
T John Blain, BC
WR Brian Kelly, EDM
WR Jim Sandusky, BC
P Glenn Harper, CAL
K Dave Ridgway, SAS

Defence
S Nelson Martin, BC
DB Larry Crawford, BC
DB Melvin Byrd, BC
CB Harry Skipper, SAS
CB Keith Gooch, BC
MLB Dan Bass, EDM
OLB Glen Jackson, BC
OLB Kevin Konar, BC
T James Curry, SAS
T Harold Hallman, CAL
E Gregg Stumon, BC
E Bobby Jurasin, SAS
ST Henry Williams, EDM

1988 Eastern Division
Offence
RB Orville Lee, OTT
RB Gill Fenerty, TOR
SB Gerald Alphin, OTT
SB Darrell Smith, TOR
QB Gilbert Renfroe, TOR
C Ian Beckstead, TOR
G Jason Riley, HAM
G Nick Bastaja, WPG
T Chris Schultz, TOR
T Miles Gorrell, HAM
WR James Murphy, WPG
WR Earl Winfield, HAM
P Bob Cameron, WPG
K Lance Chomyc, TOR

Defence
S Bennie Thompson, WPG
HB Howard Fields, HAM
HB Selwyn Drain, TOR
CB Reggie Pleasant, TOR
CB James Jefferson, WPG
MLB James West, WPG
OLB Willie Pless, TOR
OLB Don Moen, TOR
T Mike Walker, HAM
T Rodney Harding, TOR
E Grover Covington, HAM
E Glen Kulka, TOR
ST Earl Winfield, HAM

1988 Western Division
Offence
RB Anthony Cherry, BC
RB Anthony Parker, BC
SB Ray Elgaard, SAS
SB Emanuel Tolbert, CAL
QB Matt Dunigan, BC
C Mike Anderson, SAS
G Roger Aldag, SAS
G Gerald Roper, BC
T Hector Pothier, EDM
T Jim Mills, BC
WR David Williams, BC
WR Larry Willis, CAL
P Jerry Kauric, EDM
K Dave Ridgway, SAS

Defence
S Don Wilson, EDM
HB Larry Crawford, BC
HB Richie Hall, SAS
CB Stanley Blair, EDM
CB Chris Major, CAL
MLB Dan Bass, EDM
OLB Ken Ford, CAL
OLB Gregg Stumon, BC
T Gary Lewis, SAS
T Brett Williams, EDM
E Vince Goldsmith, SAS
E Bobby Jurasin, SAS
ST Henry Williams, EDM

1989 Eastern Division
Offence
RB Gill Fenerty, TOR
RB Derrick McAdoo, HAM
SB Rocky DiPietro, HAM
SB Darrell Smith, TOR
QB Mike Kerrigan, HAM
C Dale Sanderson, HAM
G Jason Riley, HAM
G David Black, WPG
T Miles Gorrell, HAM
T Chris Walby, WPG
WR Tony Champion, HAM
WR James Murphy, WPG
P Bob Cameron, WPG
K Paul Osbaldiston, HAM

Defence
S ScottFLagel, OTT
HB Stephen Jordan, HAM
HB Ed Berry, TOR
CB Rod Hill, WPG
CB Reggie Pleasant, TOR
MLB Greg Battle, WPG
OLB Frank Robinson, HAM
OLB James West, WPG
T Harold Hallman, TOR
T Mike Walker, HAM
E Grover Covington, HAM
E Mike Gray, WPG
ST Wally Zatylny, HAM

1989 Western Division
Offence
RB Reggie Taylor, EDM
RB Tim McCray, SAS
SB Jeff Fairholm, SAS
SB Craig Ellis, EDM
QB Tracy Ham, EDM
C Rod Connop, EDM
G Roger Aldag, SAS
G Dan Ferrone, CAL
T Hector Pothier, EDM
T Blake Dermott, EDM
WR David Williams, BC
WR Don Narcisse, SAS
P Brent Matich, CAL
K Dave Ridgway, SAS

Defence
S Glen Suitor, SAS
HB Don Wilson, EDM
HB Enis Jackson, EDM
CB Stanley Blair, EDM
CB Andre Francis, EDM
MLB Dan Bass, EDM
OLB Eddie Lowe, SAS
OLB LarryWRuck, EDM
T James Curry, SAS
T Brett Williams, EDM
E Stewart Hill, EDM
E Bobby Jurasin, SAS
ST Tony Hunter, EDM

1990 Eastern Division
Offence
FB Warren Hudson, WPG
RB Robert Mimbs, WPG
SB Darrell Smith, TOR
SB Rick House, WPG
QB Tom Burgess, WPG
C Lyle Bauer, WPG
G Gerald Roper, OTT
G Dan Ferrone, TOR
T Chris Walby, WPG
T Rob Smith, OTT
WR Stephen Jones, OTT
WR Earl Winfield, HAM
P Bob Cameron, WPG
K Paul Osbaldiston, HAM

Defence
S ScottFLagel, OTT
HB Troy Wilson, OTT
HB Don Wilson, TOR
CB Less Browne, WPG
CB Rod Hill, WPG
MLB Bruce Holmes, OTT
OLB Greg Battle, WPG
OLB Tyrone Jones, WPG
T Loyd Lewis, OTT
T Harold Hallman, TOR
E Greg Stumon, OTT
E Grover Covington, HAM
ST Mike Clemons, TOR

1990 Western Division
Offence
FB Blake Marshall, EDM
RB Reggie Taylor, EDM
SB Craig Ellis, EDM
SB Ray Elgaard, SAS
QB Kent Austin, SAS
C Rod Connop, EDM
G Roger Aldag, SAS
G Leo Blanchard, CAL
T Jim Mills, BC
T Lloyd Fairbanks, CAL
WR Ray Alexander, BC
WR Don Narcisse, SAS
P Brent Matich, CAL
K Dave Ridgway, SAS

Defence
S Greg Peterson, CAL
HB Richie Hall, SAS
HB David McCrary, CAL
CB Andre Francis, EDM
CB Keith Gooch, EDM
MLB Dan Bass, EDM
OLB Dan Rashovich, SAS
OLB Willie Pless, BC
T Kent Warnock, CAL
T Brett Williams, EDM
E Stewart Hill, EDM
E Will Johnson, CAL
ST Derrick Crawford, CAL

1991 Eastern Division
Offence
FB David Conrad, OTT
RB Robert Mimbs, WPG
SB Darrell Smith, TOR
SB Rob Crifo, WPG
QB Damon Allen, OTT
C Irv Daymond, OTT
G Dan Ferrone, TOR
G Gerald Roper, OTT
T Chris Walby, WPG
T Chris Schultz, TOR
WR Raghib Ismail, TOR
WR David Williams, TOR
P Hank Ilesic, TOR
K Lance Chomyc, TOR

Defence
S Scott,FLagel, OTT
HB Don Wilson, TOR
HB Anthony Drawhorn, OTT
CB Less Browne, WPG
CB Reggie Pleasant, TOR
MLB Greg Battle, WPG
OLB Brian Bonner, OTT
OLB Darryl Ford, TOR
T Harold Hallman, TOR
T Loyd Lewis, OTT
E Brian Warren, TOR
E Mike Campbell, TOR
ST Raghib Ismail, TOR

1991 Western Division
Offence
FB Blake Marshall, EDM
RB Jon Volpe, BC
SB Matt Clark, BC
SB Allen Pitts, CAL
QB DougFLutie, BC
C Rod Connop, EDM
G Leo Groenewegen, BC
G Roger Aldag, SAS
T Jim Mills, BC
T Vic Stevenson, SAS
WR Ray Alexander, BC
WR Jim Sandusky, EDM
P Brent Matich, CAL
K Dave Ridgway, SAS

Defence
S Glen Suitor, SAS
HB Darryl Hall, CAL
HB Enis Jackson, EDM
CB Eddie Thomas, EDM
CB Junior Thurman, CAL
MLB Alondra Johnson, CAL
OLB Willie Pless, EDM
OLB O.J. Brigance, BC
T Brett Williams, EDM
T Gary Lewis, SAS
E Will Johnson, CAL
E Stewart Hill, BC
ST Henry Williams, EDM

1992 Eastern Division
Offence
FB Warren Hudson, WPG
RB Mike Richardson, WPG
SB Ken Evraire, HAM
SB Rob Crifo, WPG
QB Tom Burgess, OTT
C Irv Daymond, OTT
G Dan Ferrone, TOR
G Jason Riley, HAM
T Rob Smith, OTT
T Chris Walby, WPG
WR Stephen Jones, OTT
WR Larry Thompson, WPG
P Hank Ilesic, TOR
K Troy Westwood, WPG

Defence
S Todd Wiseman, HAM
HB Anthony Drawhorn, OTT
HB Don Wilson, TOR
CB Less Browne, OTT
CB Rod Hill, WPG
MLB John Motton, HAM
OLB Angelo Snipes, OTT
OLB Gregg Stumon, OTT
T Rodney Harding, TOR
T Jeff Fields, HAM
E John Kropke, OTT
E Mike Campbell, TOR
ST Raghib Ismail, TOR

1992 Western Division
Offence
FB Blake Marshall, EDM
RB Jon Volpe, BC
SB Ray Elgaard, SAS
SB Allen Pitts, CAL
QB DougFLutie, CAL
C Rod Connop, EDM
G Pierre Vercheval, EDM
G Rocco Romano, CAL
T Vic Stevenson, SAS
T Jim Mills, BC
WR DarrenFLutie, BC
WR Jim Sandusky, EDM
P Lui Passaglia, BC
K Mark McLoughlin, CAL

Defence
S Glen Suitor, SAS
HB Enis Jackson, EDM
HB Darryl Hall, CAL
CB Junior Thurman, CAL
CB Damion Lyons, EDM
MLB Alondra Johnson, CAL
OLB Willie Pless, EDM
OLB Matt Finlay, CAL
T Jearld Baylis, SAS
T Loyd Lewis, EDM
E Will Johnson, CAL
E Bobby Jurasin, SAS
ST Henry Williams, EDM

1993 Eastern Division
Offence
FB Chris Johnstone, WPG
RB Mike Richardson, WPG
SB Gerald Wilcox, WPG
SB Jock Climie, OTT
QB Matt Dunigan, WPG
C Dave Vankoughnett, WPG
G Denny Chronopoulos, OTT
G David Black, WPG
T Mike Graybill, OTT
T Chris Walby, WPG
WR Stephen Jones, OTT
WR David Williams, WPG
P Bob Cameron, WPG
K Troy Westwood, WPG

Defence
S Remi Trudel, OTT
HB Bobby Evans, WPG
HB Darryl Sampson, WPG
CB Donald Smith, WPG
CB Kim Phillips, WPG
MLB John Motton, HAM
OLB Angelo Snipes, OTT
OLB Elfrid Payton, WPG
T Stan Mikawos, WPG
T John Kropke, OTT
E Tim Cofield, HAM
E Loyd Lewis, WPG
ST Mike Clemons, TOR

1993 Western Division
Offence
FB Sean Millington, BC
RB Mike Oliphant, SAC
SB Ray Elgaard, SAS
SB David Sapunjis, CAL
QB DougFLutie, CAL
C Rod Connop, EDM
G Rocco Romano, CAL
G Rob Smith, BC
T Bruce Covernton, CAL
T Jim Mills, BC
WR Don Narcisse, SAS
WR Rod Harris, SAC
P Glenn Harper, EDM
K Dave Ridgway, SAS

Defence
S Glen Suitor, SAS
HB Don Wilson, EDM
HB Glenn Rogers, EDM
CB Karl Anthony, CAL
CB Barry Wilburn, SAS

MLB Marvin Pope, CAL
OLB O.J. Brigance, BC
OLB Willie Pless, EDM
T Jearld Baylis, SAS
T Harald Hasselbach, CAL
E Will Johnson, CAL
E Bennie Goods, EDM
ST Henry Williams, EDM

1994 Eastern Division
Offence
FB Peter Tuipulotu, BAL
RB Mike Pringle, BAL
SB Gerald Wilcox, WPG
SB Chris Armstrong, BAL
QB Matt Dunigan, WPG
C Nick Subis, BAL
G Pierre Vercheval, TOR
G David Black, WPG
T Shar Pourdanesh, BAL
T Chris Walby, WPG
WR Paul Masotti, TOR
WR Earl Winfield, HAM
P Josh Miller, BAL
K Troy Westwood, WPG

Defence
S Michael Brooks, BAL
HB Joe Fuller, SHR
HB Bobby Evans, WPG
CB Donald Smith, WPG
CB Irvin Smith, BAL
LB Daved Benefield, OTT
LB Mike O'Shea, HAM
LB Calvin Tiggle, TOR
T Rodney Harding, TOR
T Ben Williams, SHR
E Tim Cofield, HAM
E John Kropke, OTT
ST Mike Clemons, TOR

1994 Western Division
Offence
FB Sean Millington, BC
RB Mike Saunders, SAS
SB Allen Pitts, CAL
SB DarrenFLutie, BC
QB DougFLutie, CAL
C Mike Anderson, SAS
G Rocco Romano, CAL
G Rob Smith, BC
T Bruce Covernton, CAL
T Blake Dermott, EDM
WR Ray Alexander, BC
WR Rod Harris, SAC
P Tony Martino, CAL
K Mark McLoughlin, CAL

Defence
S Greg Knox, CAL
HB Robert Holland, EDM
HB Charles Gordon, BC
CB Less Browne, BC
CB Albert Brown, SAS
LB Willie Pless, EDM
LB Ron Goetz, SAS
LB Marvin Pope, CAL
T Bennie Goods, EDM
T Stu Laird, CAL
E Bobby Jurasin, SAS
E Will Johnson, CAL
ST Henry Williams, EDM

1995 North Division
Offence
FB Michael Soles, EDM
RB Cory Philpot, BC
SB Dave Sapunjis, CAL
SB Allen Pitts, CAL
QB Jeff Garcia, CAL
C Rod Connop, EDM
G Jamie Taras, BC
G Pierre Vercheval, TOR
T Rocco Romano, CAL
T Vic Stevenson, BC
WR Earl Winfield, HAM
WR Don Narcisse, SAS
P Bob Cameron, WPG
K Mark McLoughlin, CAL

Defence
S Tom Europe, BC
DB Brett Young, OTT
DB Glenn Rogers, EDM
CB Marvin Coleman, CAL
CB Eric Carter, HAM
LB Alondra Johnson, CAL
LB Willie Pless, EDM
LB Mike O'Shea, HAM
T Benny Goods, EDM
T John Kropke, OTT
E Will Johnson, CAL
E Andrew Stewart, BC
ST Sam Rogers, HAM

1995 South Division
Offence
FB Mike Saunders, SA
RB Mike Pringle, BAL
SB Chris Armstrong, BAL
SB Jason Phillips, BIR
QB Matt Dunigan, BIR
C Mike Kiselak, SA
G Mike Withycombe, BAL
G Fred Childress, SHR
T Shar Pourdanesh, BAL
T Neal Fort, BAL
WR Marcus Grant, BIR
WR Joe Horn, Memphis
P Josh Miller, BAL
K Roman Anderson, SA

Defence
S Anthony Drawhorn, BIR
DB Charles Anthony, BAL
DB Andre Strode, BIR
CB Irvin Smith, BAL
CB Donald Smith, MEM
LB O.J. Brigance, BAL
LB Tracy Gravely, BAL
LB David Harper, SA
T Jearld Baylis, BAL
T Rodney Harding, MEM
E Tim Cofield, MEM
E Elfrid Payton, BAL
ST ChrisWRight, BAL

1996 East Division
Offence
FB Robert Drummond, TOR
RB Mike Pringle, MTL
SB Mac Cody, HAM
SB Jock Climie, MTL
QB DougFLutie, TOR
C Mike Kiselak, TOR
G Blaine Schmidt, HAM
G Bruce Beaton, MTL
T Chris Perez, TOR
T Neal Fort, MTL
WR Joseph Rogers, OTT
WR Paul Masotti, TOR
P Paul Osbaldiston, HAM
K Terry Baker, MTL

Defence
S Spencer McLennan, MTL
DB Kenny Wilhite, OTT
DB Charles Gordon, MTL
CB Irvin Smith, MTL
CB Adrion Smith, TOR
LB Lamar McGriggs, OTT
LB Tracy Gravely, MTL
LB Paul Randolph, MTL
T Rob Waldrop, TOR
T Mike Philbrick, HAM
E Grant Carter, MTL
E Reggie Givens, TOR
ST Jimmy Cunningham, TOR

1996 West Division
Offence
FB Sean Millington, BC
RB Robert Mimbs, SAS
SB DarrenFLutie, EDM
SB Allen Pitts, CAL
QB Jeff Garcia, CAL
C Rod Connop, EDM
G Rocco Romano, CAL
G Leo Groenewegen, EDM
T Chris Walby, WPG
T Fred Childress, CAL
WR Eddie Brown, EDM
WR Terry Vaughn, CAL
P Tony Martino, CAL
K Mark McLoughlin, CAL

Defence
S Trent Brown, EDM
DB Andre Strode, BC
DB Glenn Rogers, EDM
CB Marvin Coleman, CAL
CB Al Jordan, CAL
LB Angelo Snipes, WPG
LB Willie Pless, EDM
LB K.D. Williams, WPG
T Benny Goods, EDM
T Rodney Harding, CAL
E Leroy Blugh, EDM
E Malvin Hunter, EDM
ST Marvin Coleman, CAL

1997 East Division
Offence
RB Robert Drummond, TOR
RB Mike Pringle, MTL
SB Derrell Mitchell, TOR
SB Jock Climie, MTL
QB DougFLutie, TOR
C Mike Kiselak, TOR
G Pierre Vercheval, TOR
G Bruce Beaton, MTL
T Uzooma Okeke, MTL
T Neal Fort, MTL
WR Milt Stegall, WPG
WR Paul Masotti, TOR
P Mike Vanderjagt, TOR
K Mike Vanderjagt, TOR

Defence
S Lester Smith, TOR
DB Johnnie Harris, TOR
DB Harold Nash, MTL
CB Orlondo Steinauer, HAM
CB Adrion Smith, TOR
LB Ken Benson, TOR
LB Mike O'Shea, TOR
LB Shonte Peoples, WPG
T Rob Waldrop, TOR
T Doug Petersen, MTL
E Elfrid Payton, MTL
E Willie Whitehead, HAM
ST Mike Clemons, TOR

1997 West Division
Offence
RB Sean Millington, BC
RB Kelvin Anderson, CAL
SB DarrenFLutie, EDM
SB Vince Danielsen, CAL
QB Jeff Garcia, CAL
C Mike Withycombe, BC
G Fred Childress, CAL
G Leo Groenewegen, EDM
T Thomas Rayam, EDM
T John Terry, SAS
WR Alfred Jackson, BC
WR Terry Vaughn, CAL
P Tony Martino, CAL
K Mark McLoughlin, CAL

Defence
S Trent Brown, EDM
DB Dale Joseph, SAS
DB Glenn Rogers, EDM
CB Marvin Coleman, CAL
CB Kavis Reed, EDM
LB Alondra Johnson, CAL
LB Willie Pless, EDM
LB Maurice Kelly, BC
T Benny Goods, EDM
T JoeFLeming, BC
E Bobby Jurasin, SAS
E Malvin Hunter, EDM
ST Henry Williams, EDM

1998 East Division
Offence
RB Ronald Williams, HAM
RB Mike Pringle, MTL
SB Derrell Mitchell, TOR
SB DarrenFLutie, HAM
QB Kerwin Bell, TOR
C Carl Coulter, HAM
G Pierre Vercheval, TOR
G Val St. Germain, HAM
T Uzooma Okeke, MTL
T Chris Perez, WPG
WR Andrew Grigg, HAM
WR Paul Masotti, TOR
P Noel Prefontaine, TOR
K Paul Osbaldiston, HAM

Defence
S Lester Smith, TOR
DB Gerald Vaughn, HAM
DB Orlondo Steinauer, HAM
CB Donald Smith, TOR
CB Eric Carter, HAM
LB Calvin Tiggle, HAM
LB Kelly Wiltshire, TOR
LB Grant Carter, WPG
T JoeFLeming, WPG
T Doug Petersen, MTL
E Elfrid Payton, MTL
E Joe Montford, HAM
ST Eric Blount, WPG

1998 West Division
Offence
RB Juan Johnson, BC
RB Kelvin Anderson, CAL
SB Allen Pitts, CAL
SB Vince Danielsen, CAL
QB Jeff Garcia, CAL
C Jamie Crysdale, CAL
G Fred Childress, CAL
G Bruce Beaton, EDM
T Moe Elewonibi, BC
T John Terry, SAS
WR Don Narcisse, SAS
WR Terry Vaughn, CAL
P Tony Martino, CAL
K Lui Passaglia, BC

Defence
S Dale Joseph, BC
DB Jackie Kellogg, CAL
DB Glenn Rogers, EDM
CB Marvin Coleman, CAL
CB Steve Muhammad, BC
LB Alondra Johnson, CAL
LB Willie Pless, EDM
LB Darryl Hall, CAL
T Dave Chaytors, BC
T Johnny Scott, BC
E Leroy Blugh, EDM
E Malvin Hunter, EDM
ST Marvin Coleman, CAL

1999 East Division
Offence
RB Ronald Williams, HAM
RB Mike Pringle, MTL
SB Milt Stegall, WPG
SB DarrenFLutie, HAM
QB Danny McManus, HAM
C Carl Coulter, HAM
G Pierre Vercheval, TOR
G Chris Burns, HAM
T Uzooma Okeke, MTL
T Dave Hack, HAM
WR Robert Gordon, WPG
WR Ben Cahoon, MTL
P Noel Prefontaine, TOR
K Paul Osbaldiston, HAM

Defence
S Rob Hitchcock, HAM
DB Gerald Vaughn, HAM
DB Barron Miles, MTL
CB Adrion Smith, TOR
CB Irvin Smith, MTL
LB Calvin Tiggle, HAM
LB Mike O'Shea, TOR
LB Maurice Kelly, WPG
T Demetrious Maxie, TOR
T Jason Richards, MTL
E Elfrid Payton, MTL
E Joe Montford, HAM
ST Wade Miller, WPG

1999 West Division
Offence
RB Robert Drummond, BC
RB Kelvin Anderson, CAL
SB Allen Pitts, CAL
SB Terry Vaughn, EDM
QB Damon Allen, BC
C Jamie Taras, BC
G Val St. Germain, EDM
G Leo Groenwegen, EDM
T Rocco Romano, CAL
T John Terry, SAS
WR Travis Moore, CAL
WR Eddie Brown, BC
P Lui Passaglia, BC
K Mark McLoughlin, CAL

Defence
S Greg Frers, CAL
DB Jackie Kellogg, CAL
DB Dale Joseph, BC
CB William Hampton, CAL
CB Eric Carter, BC
LB Terry Ray, EDM
LB Willie Pless, SAS
LB Paul Lacoste, BC
T Doug Petersen, EDM
T Johnny Scott, BC
E Daved Benefield, BC
E Neal Smith, SAS
ST Jimmy Cunningham, BC

2000 East Division
Offence
RB Mike Pringle, MTL
RB Ronald Williams, HAM
SB Derrell Mitchell, TOR
SB Milt Stegall, WPG
QB Anthony Calvillo, MTL
C Bryan Chiu, MTL
G Chris Burns, HAM
G Pierre Vercheval, MTL
T Moe Elewonibi, WPG
T Dave Hack, HAM
WR Ben Cahoon, MTL
WR Robert Gordon, WPG
P Noel Prefontaine, TOR
K Paul Osbaldiston, HAM

Defence
S Lester Smith, MTL

DB Barron Miles, MTL
DB Chris Shelling, HAM
CB Davis Sanchez, MTL
CB Irvin Smith, MTL
LB Antonio Armstrong, WPG
LB Mike O'Shea, HAM
LB Calvin Tiggle, TOR
T Mike Philbrick, HAM
T Johnny Scott, TOR
E Swift Burch, MTL
E Joe Montford, HAM
ST Albert Johnson, WPG

2000 West Division
Offence
RB Kelvin Anderson, CAL
RB Sean Millington, BC
SB Alfred Jackson, BC
SB Terry Vaughn, EDM
QB Dave Dickenson, CAL
C Leo Groenewegen, EDM
G Fred Childress, CAL
G Andrew Greene, SAS
T Bruce Beaton, EDM
T Chris Perez, BC
WR Curtis Marsh, SAS
WR Travis Moore, CAL
P Tony Martino, CAL
K Lui Passaglia, BC

Defence
S Greg Frers, CAL
DB Eddie Davis, CAL
DB Ralph Staten, EDM
CB Eric Carter, BC
CB Marvin Coleman, CAL
LB Alondra Johnson, CAL
LB Terry Ray, EDM
LB George White, SAS
T JoeFLeming, CAL
T Demetrious Maxie, SAS
E Shonte Peoples, CAL
E Herman Smith, BC
ST Marvin Coleman, CAL

2001 East Division
Offence
RB Michael Jenkins, TOR
RB Mike Pringle, MTL
SB Derrell Mitchell, TOR
SB Milt Stegall, WPG
QB Khari Jones, WPG
C Bryan Chiu, MTL
G Brett MacNeil, WPG
G Jude St. John, TOR
T Dave Hack, HAM
T Dave Mudge, WPG
WR Ted Alford, TOR
WR Andrew Grigg, HAM
P Terry Baker, MT
K Paul Osbaldiston, HAM

Defence
S Rob Hitchcock, HAM
DB Juran Bolden, WPG
DB Harold Nash, WPG
CB Marvin Coleman, WPG
CB Wayne Shaw, TOR
LB Jason Lamar, HAM
LB Chris Shelling, HAM
LB Sean Woodson, HAM
T Doug Brown, WPG
T Mike Philbrick, HAM
E Joe Montford, HAM
E Elfrid Payton, TOR
ST Charles Roberts, WPG

2001 West Division
Offence
RB Kelvin Anderson, CAL
RB Darren Davis, SAS
SB Marc Boerigter, CAL
SB Terry Vaughn, EDM
QB Jason Maas, EDM
C Jamie Taras, BC
G Andrew Greene, SAS
G Jay McNeil, CAL
T Bruce Beaton, EDM
T Fred Childress, CAL
WR Ed Hervey, EDM
WR Travis Moore, CAL
P SeanFLeming, EDM
K SeanFLeming, EDM

Defence
S Greg Frers, CAL
DB Eddie Davis, SAS
DB Shannon Garrett, EDM
CB Eric Carter, BC
CB Omarr Morgan, SAS
LB Terry Ray, EDM
LB Barrin Simpson, BC
LB George White, SAS

T JoeFLeming, CAL
T Doug Petersen, EDM
E Shonte Peoples, SAS
E Herman Smith, BC
ST Antonio Warren, CAL

2002 East Division
Offence
RB Troy Davis, HAM
RB Lawrence Phillips, MTL
SB Ben Cahoon, MTL
SB Derrell Mitchell, TOR
QB Anthony Calvillo, MTL
C Bryan Chiu, MTL
G Sandy Annunziata, TOR
G ScottFLory, MTL
T Dave Hack, HAM
T Uzooma Okeke, MTL
WR Jimmy Oliver, OTT
WR Pat Woodcock, MTL
P Noel Prefontaine, TOR
K Noel Prefontaine, TOR

Defence
S Rob Hitchcock, HAM
DB Clifford Ivory, TOR
DB Barron Miles, MTL
CB Wayne Shaw, MTL
CB Adrion Smith, TOR
LB John Grace, OTT
LB Kevin Johnson, MTL
LB Stefen Reid, MTL
T Robert Brown, MTL
T Johnny Scott, TOR
E Marc Megna, MTL
E Joe Montford, TOR
ST Keith Stokes, MTL

2002 West Division
Offence
RB John Avery, EDM
RB Charles Roberts, WPG
SB Milt Stegall, WPG
SB Terry Vaughn, EDM
QB Khari Jones, WPG
C Jamie Taras, BC
G Steve Hardin, BC
G Jay McNeil, CAL
T Bruce Beaton, EDM
T Dave Mudge, WPG
WR Derick Armstrong, SAS
WR Jason Tucker, EDM
P Duncan O'Mahony, CAL
K SeanFLeming, EDM

Defence
S Tom Europe, WPG
DB Derrick Lewis, BC
DB Harold Nash, WPG
CB Eric Carter, BC
CB Omarr Morgan, SAS
LB Brendan Ayanbadejo, BC
LB Carl Kidd, BC
LB Barrin Simpson, BC
T Doug Brown, WPG
T Denny Fortney, WPG
E Elfrid Payton, EDM
E Herman Smith, BC
ST Corey Holmes, SAS

2003 East Division
Offence
RB Troy Davis, HAM
RB Josh Ranek, OTT
SB Ben Cahoon, MTL
SB Jeremaine Copeland, MTL
QB Anthony Calvillo, MTL
C Bryan Chiu, MTL
G ScottFLory, MTL
G Val St. Germain, OTT
T Neal Fort, MTL
T Uzooma Okeke, MTL
WR D.J.FLick, OTT
WR Tony Miles, TOR
P Noel Prefontaine, TOR
K Lawrence Tynes, OTT

Defence
S Orlondo Steinauer, TOR
DB Clifford Ivory, TOR
DB Barron Miles, MTL
CB Brandon Hamilton, HAM
CB Adrion Smith, TOR
LB Kevin Johnson, MTL
LB Timothy Strickland, MTL
LB Kelly Wiltshire, OTT
T Eric England, TOR
T Ed Philion, MTL
E Tim Cheatwood, HAM
E Anwar Stewart, MTL
ST Bashir Levingston, TOR

2003 West Division
Offence
RB Mike Pringle, EDM
RB Charles Roberts, WPG
SB Geroy Simon, BC
SB Terry Vaughn, EDM
QB Dave Dickenson, BC
C Jeremy O'Day, SAS
G Dan Comiskey, EDM
G Andrew Greene, SAS
T Bruce Beaton, EDM
T Cory Mantyka, BC
WR Ed Hervey, EDM
WR Darnell McDonald, CAL
P SeanFLeming, EDM
K Paul McCallum, SAS

Defence
S Mark Washington, BC
DB Donny Brady, EDM
DB Shannon Garrett, EDM
CB Eric Carter, BC
CB Omarr Morgan, SAS
LB Reggie Hunt, SAS
LB Jackie Mitchell, SAS
LB Barrin Simpson, BC
T Nathan Davis, SAS
T JoeFLeming, CAL
E Daved Benefield, WPG
E Ray Jacobs, BC
ST Wane McGarity, CAL

2004 East Division
Offence
RB Troy Davis, HAM
RB Josh Ranek, OTT
SB Ben Cahoon, MTL
SB Jeremaine Copeland, MTL
QB Anthony Calvillo, MTL
C Bryan Chiu, MTL
G ScottFLory, MTL
G Paul Lambert, MTL
T Dave Hack, HAM
T Uzooma Okeke, MTL
WR Kwame Cavil, MTL
WR D.J.FLick, HAM
P Noel Prefontaine, TOR
K Noel Prefontaine, TOR

Defence
S Orlondo Steinauer, TOR
DB Clifford Ivory, TOR
DB Kelly Malveaux, MTL
CB Almondo Curry, MTL
CB Davis Sanchez, MTL
LB Kevin Eiben, TOR
LB Kevin Johnson, MTL
LB Timothy Strickland, MTL
T Noah Cantor, TOR
T Ed Philion, MTL
E Tim Cheatwood, HAM
E Anwar Stewart, MTL
ST Bashir Levingston, TOR

2004 West Division
Offence
RB Kenton Keith, SAS
RB Charles Roberts, WPG
SB Jason Clermont, BC
SB Geroy Simon, BC
QB Casey Printers, BC
C Angus Reid, BC
G Andrew Greene, SAS
G Jay McNeil, CAL
T Seth Dittman, CAL
T Gene Makowsky, SAS
WR Ryan Thelwell, BC
WR Jason Tucker, EDM
P SeanFLeming, EDM
K SeanFLeming, EDM

Defence
S Wes Lysack, WPG
DB Joey Boese, CAL
DB Eddie Davis, SAS
CB Malcolm Frank, EDM
CB Sam Young, BC
LB John Grace, CAL
LB Reggie Hunt, SAS
LB Barrin Simpson, BC
T Nathan Davis, SAS
T JoeFLeming, CAL
E Tom Canada, WPG
E Brent Johnson, BC
ST Keith Stokes, WPG

2005 East Division
Offence
RB Robert Edwards, MTL
RB Josh Ranek, OTT
SB Arland Bruce, TOR
SB Ben Cahoon, MTL
QB Damon Allen, TOR
C Bryan Chiu, MTL
G ScottFLory, MTL
G Jude St. John, TOR
T Uzooma Okeke, MTL
T Bernard Williams, TOR
WR Jason Armstead, OTT
WR Kerry Watkins, MTL
P Noel Prefontaine, TOR
K Noel Prefontaine, TOR

Defence
S Richard Karikari, MTL
DB Korey Banks, OTT
DB Kenny Wheaton, TOR
CB Adrion Smith, TOR
CB Jordan Younger, TOR
LB Duane Butler, MTL
LB Kevin Eiben, TOR
LB MichaelFLetcher, TOR
T Adriano Belli, HAM
T Ed Philion, MTL
E Jonathan Brown, TOR
E Anthony Collier, OTT
ST Jason Armstead, OTT

2005 West Division
Offence
RB Joffrey Reynolds, CAL
RB Charles Roberts, WPG
SB Milt Stegall, WPG
SB Jason Tucker, EDM
QB Henry Burris, CAL
C Jeremy O'Day, SAS
G Andrew Greene, SAS
G Jay McNeil, CAL
T Gene Makowsky, SAS
T Jeff Pilon, CAL
WR Ryan Thelwell, BC
WR Elijah Thurmon, SAS
P Jon Ryan, WPG
K Sandro DeAngelis, CAL

Defence
S Barron Miles, BC
DB Donny Brady, EDM
DB Eddie Davis, SAS
CB Malcolm Frank, EDM
CB Omarr Morgan, SAS
LB OtisFLoyd, BC
LB John Grace, CAL
LB George White, CAL
T Sheldon Napastuk, CAL
T Scott Schultz, SAS
E Brent Johnson, BC
E Gavin Walls, WPG
ST Corey Holmes, SAS

2006 East Division
Offence
RB Robert Edwards, MTL
RB Charles Roberts, WPG
REC Arland Bruce, TOR
REC Ben Cahoon, MTL
REC Milt Stegall, WPG
REC Kerry Watkins, MTL
QB Anthony Calvillo, MTL
C Bryan Chiu, MTL
G ScottFLory, MTL
G Jude St. John, TOR
T Jerome Davis, TOR
T Bernard Williams, TOR
P Noel Prefontaine, TOR
K Damon Duval, MTL

Defence
S Orlondo Steinauer, TOR
DB Tay Cody, HAM
DB Kenny Wheaton, TOR
CB Byron Parker, TOR
CB Jordan Younger, TOR
LB Kevin Eiben, TOR
LB Barrin Simpson, WPG
LB Timothy Strickland, MTL
T Doug Brown, WPG
T Ed Philion, MTL
E Jonathan Brown, TOR
E Gavin Walls, WPG
ST Albert Johnson, WPG

2006 West Division
Offence
RB Kenton Keith, SAS
RB Joffrey Reynolds, CAL
REC Matt Dominguez, SAS
REC Nik Lewis, CAL
REC Geroy Simon, BC
REC Jason Tucker, EDM
QB Ricky Ray, EDM
C Jeremy O'Day, SAS
G Dan Comiskey, EDM
G Jay McNeil, CAL
T Gene Makowsky, SAS

T Rob Murphy, BC
P Burke Dales, CAL
K Sandro DeAngelis, CAL

Defence
S Barron Miles, BC
DB Korey Banks, BC
DB Eddie Davis, SAS
CB Dante Marsh, BC
CB Coby Rhinehart, CAL
LB Brian Clark, CAL
LB OtisFLoyd, BC
LB Reggie Hunt, SAS
T Aaron Hunt, B
T Tyrone Williams, BC
E Brent Johnson, BC
E Fred Perry, SAS
ST Carl Kidd, BC

2007 East Division
Offence
RB Jesse Lumsden, HAM
RB Charles Roberts, WPG
REC Derick Armstrong, WPG
REC Ben Cahoon, MTL
REC Terrence Edwards, WPG
REC Milt Stegall, WPG
QB Kevin Glenn, WPG
C Marwan Hage, HAM
G ScottFLory, MTL
G Taylor Robertson, TOR
T Alexandre Gauthier, WPG
T Dan Goodspeed, WPG
P Damon Duval, MTL
K Nick Setta, HAM

Defence
S Orlondo Steinauer, TOR
DB Randee Drew, MTL
DB Kenny Wheaton, TOR
CB Byron Parker, TOR
CB Jordan Younger, TOR
LB Kevin Eiben, TOR
LB Zeke Moreno, HAM
LB Barrin Simpson, WPG
T Adriano Belli, TOR
T Doug Brown, WPG
E Jonathan Brown, TOR
E Tom Canada, WPG
ST Dominique Dorsey, TOR

2007 West Division
Offence
RB Joffrey Reynolds, CAL
RB Joe Smith, BC
REC Jason Clermont, BC
REC D.J.FLick, SAS
REC Nik Lewis, CAL
REC Geroy Simon, BC
QB Kerry Joseph, SAS
C Jeremy O'Day, SAS
G Kelly Bates, BC
G Jay McNeil, CAL
T Gene Makowsky, SAS
T Rob Murphy, BC
P Paul McCallum, BC
K Sandro DeAngelis, CAL

Defence
S Barron Miles, BC
DB Korey Banks, BC
DB Ryan Phillips, BC
CB Lavar Glover, BC
CB James Johnson, SAS
LB OtisFLoyd, BC
LB Reggie Hunt, SAS
LB Maurice Lloyd, SAS
T Aaron Hunt, BC
T Tyrone Williams, BC
E Fred Perry, SAS
E Cameron Wake, BC
ST Ian Smart, BC

2008 East Division
Offence
RB Avon Cobourne, MTL
RB Fred Reid, WPG
REC Arland Bruce, TOR
REC Ben Cahoon, MTL
REC Jamel Richardson, MTL
REC Kerry Watkins, MTL
QB Anthony Calvillo, MTL
C Bryan Chiu, MTL
G ScottFLory, MTL
G Paul Lambert, MTL
T Josh Bourke, MTL
T Dan Goodspeed, WPG
P Nick Setta, HAM
K Damon Duval, MTL

Defence
S Kenny Wheaton, TOR
DB Kelly Malveaux, WPG
DB Chris Thompson, HAM
CB Mark Estelle, MTL
CB Davis Sanchez, MTL
LB T.J. Hill, MTL
LB Markeith Knowlton, HAM
LB Zeke Moreno, WPG
T Doug Brown, WPG
T Keron Williams, MTL
E Jonathan Brown, TOR
E Gavin Walls, WPG
ST Dominique Dorsey, TOR

2008 West Division
Offence
RB Wes Cates, SAS
RB Joffrey Reynolds, CAL
REC Paris Jackson, BC
REC Kamau Peterson, EDM
REC Ken-Yon Rambo, CAL
REC Geroy Simon, BC
QB Henry Burris, CAL
C Rob Lazeo, CAL
G Patrick Kabongo, EDM
G Gene Makowsky, SAS
T Jason Jiminez, BC
T Rob Murphy, BC
P Paul McCallum, BC
K Sandro DeAngelis, CAL

Defence
S Barron Miles, BC
DB Korey Banks, BC
DB Jason Goss, EDM
CB Brandon Browner, CAL
CB Dante Marsh, BC
LB Javier Glatt, BC
LB Maurice Lloyd, SAS
LB Anton McKenzie, SAS
T Aaron Hunt, BC
T Dario Romero, EDM
E Cameron Wake, BC
E Brent Johnson, BC
ST Ian Smart, BC

2009 East Division
Offence
RB Avon Cobourne, MTL
RB Fred Reid, WPG
REC Arland Bruce, HAM
REC Ben Cahoon, MTL
REC Jamel Richardson, MTL
REC Kerry Watkins, MTL
QB Anthony Calvillo, MTL
C Bryan Chiu, MTL
G ScottFLory, MTL
G Brendon LaBatte, WPG
T Josh Bourke, MTL
T Dan Goodspeed, HAM
P Damon Duval, MTL
K Damon Duval, MTL

Defence
S Mathieu Proulx, MTL
DB Jonathon Hefney, WPG
DB Lenny Walls, WPG
CB Mark Estelle, MTL
CB Jovon Johnson, WPG
LB Chip Cox, MTL
LB Markeith Knowlton, HAM
LB Jamall Johnson, HAM
T Doug Brown, WPG
T Keron Williams, MTL
E Anwar Stewart, MTL
E John Bowman, MTL
ST Larry Taylor, MTL

2009 West Division
Offence
RB Martell Mallett, BC
RB Joffrey Reynolds, CAL
REC Jeremaine Copeland, CAL
REC Weston Dressler, SAS
REC Fred Stamps, EDM
REC Geroy Simon, BC
QB Darian Durant, SAS
C Jeremy O'Day, SAS
G Dimitri Tsoumpas, CAL
G Gene Makowsky, SAS
T Ben Archibald, CAL
T Calvin Armstrong, EDM
P Burke Dales, CAL
K Sandro DeAngelis, CAL

Defence
S Barron Miles, BC
DB Korey Banks, BC
DB Lance Frazier, SAS
CB Dwight Anderson, CAL
CB Brandon Browner, CAL
LB Tad Kornegay, SAS
LB Sean Lucas, SAS
LB Anton McKenzie, BC
T Aaron Hunt, BC
T Dario Romero, EDM
E Steve Baggs, SAS
E John Chick, SAS
ST Jason Arakgi, BC

2010 East Division
Offence
RB Cory Boyd, TOR
RB Fred Reid, WPG
REC Arland Bruce, HAM
REC Terrence Edwards, WPG
REC Jamel Richardson, MTL
REC Dave Stala, HAM
QB Anthony Calvillo, MTL
C Marwan Hage, HAM
G ScottFLory, MTL
G Brendon LaBatte, WPG
T Josh Bourke, MTL
T Rob Murphy, TOR
P Mike Renaud, WPG
K Damon Duval, MTL

Defence
S Willie Pile, TOR
DB Jerald Brown, MTL
DB Lin-J Shell, TOR
CB Mark Estelle, MTL
CB Jovon Johnson, WPG
LB Chip Cox, MTL
LB Kevin Eiben, TOR
LB Markeith Knowlton, HAM
T Doug Brown, WPG
T Kevin Huntley, TOR
E John Bowman, MTL
E Phillip Hunt, WPG
ST Chad Owens, TOR

2010 West Division
Offence
RB Wes Cates, SAS
RB Joffrey Reynolds, CAL
REC Romby Bryant, CAL
REC Andy Fantuz, SAS
REC Nik Lewis, CAL
REC Fred Stamps, EDM
QB Henry Burris, CAL
C Jeremy O'Day, SAS
G Jovan Olafioye, BC
G Dimitri Tsoumpas, CAL
T Ben Archibald, CAL
T Gene Makowsky, SAS
P Burke Dales, CAL
K Paul McCallum, BC

Defence
S James Patrick, SAS
DB Ryan Phillips, BC
DB Chris Thompson, EDM
CB Dwight Anderson, CAL
CB Brandon Browner, CAL
LB Korey Banks, BC
LB Barrin Simpson, SAS
LB Juwan Simpson, CAL
T DeVone Claybrooks, CAL
T Tom Johnson, CAL
E Charleston Hughes, CAL
E Brent Johnson, BC
ST Yonus Davis, BC

2011 East Division
Offence
QB Anthony Calvillo, MTL
RB Cory Boyd, TOR
RB Brandon Whitaker, MTL
REC Terrence Edwards, WPG
REC S.J. Green, MTL
REC Jamel Richardson, MTL
REC Chris Williams, HAM
T Josh Bourke, MTL
T Glenn January, WPG
G Scott Flory, MTL
G Brendon LaBatte, WPG
C Dominic Picard, TOR

Defence
T Doug Brown, WPG
T Kevin Huntley, TOR
E Justin Hickman, HAM
E Odell Willis, WPG
LB Chip Cox, MTL
LB Jamall Johnson, WPG
LB Renauld Williams, HAM
CB Jovon Johnson, WPG
CB Byron Parker, TOR
DB Johnathan Hefney, WPG
DB Lin-J Shell, TOR
S Ian Logan, WPG

Special Teams
K Justin Medlock, HAM
P Noel Prefontaine, TOR
ST Chad Owens, TOR

2011 West Division
Offence
QB Travis Lulay, BC
RB Jon Cornish, CAL
RB Jerome Messam, EDM
REC Weston Dressler, SAS
REC Nik Lewis, CAL
REC Geroy Simon, BC
REC Fred Stamps, EDM
T Ben Archibald, BC
T Jovan Olafioye, BC
G Dimitri Tsoumpas, CAL
G Greg Wojt, EDM
C Angus Reid, BC

Defence
T Aaron Hunt, BC
T Khalif Mitchell, BC
E Marcus Howard, EDM
E Keron Williams, BC
LB Rod Davis, EDM
LB Solomon Elimimian, BC
LB Jerrell Freeman, SAS
CB Dante Marsh, BC
CB Roderick Williams, EDM
DB Korey Banks, BC
DB Keon Raymond, CAL
S Carig Butler, SAS

Special Teams
K Paul McCallum, BC
P Burke Dales, CAL
ST Larry Taylor, CAL

CFL ALL-STARS

Selected by the Football Reporters of Canada. Today the voting also includes coaches and fans.

1962
Offence
RB Earl Lunsford, CAL
RB George Dixon, MTL
RB Leo Lewis, WPG
RB Ray Purdin, SAS
QB Eagle Day, CAL
E Hal Patterson, HAM
E Tommy Joe Coffey, EDM
C Neil Habig, SAS
G Tony Pajaczkowski, CAL
G Gerry Patrick, TOR
T Frank Rigney, WPG
T Bronko Nagurski, HAM

Defence
DB Harvey Wylie, CAL
DB Jim Rountree, TOR
DB Don Sutherin, HAM
LB Wayne Harris, CAL
LB Tom Brown, BC
LB Gord Rowland, WPG
LB Jim Conroy, OTT
MG Kaye Vaughan, OTT
T Don Luzzi, CAL
T John Barrow, HAM
E Garner Ekstran, SAS
E Herb Gray, WPG

1963
Offence
RB Dick Shatto, TOR
RB WillieFLeming, BC
RB George Dixon, MTL
RB Lovell Coleman, CAL
QB Joe Kapp, BC
E Hal Patterson, HAM
E Pete Manning, CAL
C Milt Crain, MTL
G Tony Pajaczkowski, CAL
G Tom Hinton, BC
T Roger Kramer, OTT
T Lonnie Dennis, BC

Defence
DB Garney Henley, HAM
DB Harvey Wylie, CAL
DB Dick Thornton, WPG
LB Tom Brown, BC
LB Jim Andreotti, MTL
LB Jim Conroy, OTT
LB Norm Fieldgate, BC
MG John Barrow, HAM
T Don Luzzi, CAL
T Angelo Mosca, HAM
E Garner Ekstran, SAS
E Dick Fouts, BC

1964
Offence
RB Lovell Coleman, CAL
RB Dick Shatto, TOR
RB Ed Buchanan, SAS

FL Tommy Grant, HAM
QB Joe Kapp, BC
E Tommy Joe Coffey, EDM
E Hal Patterson, HAM
C Chet Miksza, HAM
G Tony Pajaczkowski, CAL
G Ellison Kelly, HAM
G Al Benecick, SAS
T Roger Kramer, OTT
T Lonnie Dennis, BC

Defence
DB Garney Henley, HAM
DB Don Sutherin, HAM
DB Bill Munsey, BC
DB Jerry Keeling, CAL
DB Bob Ptacek, SAS
LB Wayne Harris, CAL
LB Ron Brewer, TOR
LB Bobby Kuntz, HAM
MG Tom Brown, BC
T John Barrow, HAM
T Mike Cacic, BC
E Dick Fouts, BC
E Peter Neumann, HAM

1965
Offence
RB George Reed, SAS
RB Bo Scott, OTT
RB Lovell Coleman, CAL
FL Hugh Campbell, SAS
QB Kenny Ploen, WPG
E Tommy Joe Coffey, EDM
E Ted Watkins, OTT
C Ted Urness, SAS
G Al Benecick, SAS
G Tony Pajaczkowski, CAL
T Frank Rigney, WPG
T Bronko Nagurski, HAM

Defence
DB Garney Henley, HAM
DB Billy Wayte, HAM
DB Dick Thornton, WPG
DB Jerry Keeling, CAL
DB Gene Gaines, OTT
LB Wayne Harris, CAL
LB Ken Lehmann, OTT
LB Zeno Karcz, HAM
T John Barrow, HAM
T Pat Holmes, CAL
E Billy Ray Locklin, HAM
E Dick Fouts, BC

1966
Offence
RB George Reed, SAS
RB Jim Thomas, EDM
RB Dave Raimey, WPG
FL Hugh Campbell, SAS
QB Russ Jackson, OTT
E Jim Worden, SAS
E Tommy Joe Coffey, EDM
C Ted Urness, SAS
G Al Benecick, SAS
G Chuck Walton, HAM
T Bill Frank, TOR
T Frank Rigney, WPG
T Clyde Brock, SAS

Defence
DB Gene Gaines, OTT
DB Garney Henley, HAM
DB Marv Luster, TOR
DB Ed Ulmer, WPG
DB Joe Poirier, OTT
LB Wayne Harris, CAL
LB Phil Minnick, WPG
LB Ken Lehmann, OTT
LB Jim Conroy, OTT
T John Barrow, HAM
T Don Luzzi, CAL
E Billy Ray Locklin, HAM
E E.A. Sims, EDM

1967
Offence
RB George Reed, SAS
RB Bo Scott, OTT
RB Jim Thomas, EDM
FL Whit Tucker, OTT
QB Pete Liske, CAL
E Terry Evanshen, CAL
E Tommy Joe Coffey, HAM
C Ted Urness, SAS
G Jack Abendschan, SAS
G Roger Perdrix, OTT
T Clyde Brock, SAS
T Bill Frank, WPG

Defence
DB Jerry Keeling, CAL
DB Phil Brady, MTL
DB Gene Gaines, OTT
DB Garney Henley, HAM
DB Frank Andruski, CAL
LB Wayne Harris, CAL
LB Garner Ekstran, SAS
LB Wayne Shaw, SAS
T John Barrow, HAM
T Ed McQuarters, SAS
E E.A. Sims, EDM
E John Baker, MTL

1968
Offence
RB George Reed, SAS
RB Bill Symons, TOR
RB Vic Washington, OTT
FL Ken Nielsen, WPG
QB Russ Jackson, OTT
E Tommy Joe Coffey, HAM
E Herman Harrison, CAL
C Ted Urness, SAS
G Charlie Parker, MTL
G Bill Danychuk, HAM
T Bill Frank, TOR
T Clyde Brock, SAS

Defence
DB Frank Andruski, CAL
DB Bob Kosid, SAS
DB Garney Henley, HAM
DB Ed Learn, TOR
DB Marv Luster, TOR
LB Wayne Harris, CAL
LB Wally Dempsey, SAS
LB Ken Lehmann, OTT
T Ed McQuarters, SAS
T John LaGrone, EDM
E Billy Ray Locklin, HAM
E Ed Harrington, TOR

1969
Offence
RB George Reed, SAS
RB Vic Washington, OTT
RB Dave Raimey, TOR
FL Ken Nielsen, WPG
QB Russ Jackson, OTT
TE Herman Harrison, CAL
SE Margene Adkins, OTT
C Ted Urness, SAS
G Jack Abendschan, SAS
G Charlie Bray, TOR
T Clyde Brock, SAS
T Ellison Kelly, HAM

Defence
DB John Wydareny, EDM
DB Marv Luster, TOR
DB Bruce Bennett, SAS
DB Don Sutherin, OTT
DB Garney Henley, HAM
DB Larry Fairholm, MTL
LB Ken Lehmann, OTT
LB Jerry Campbell, OTT
LB Phil Minnick, WPG
T John LaGrone, EDM
T Ed McQuarters, SAS
E Billy Joe Booth, OTT
E Ed Harrington, TOR

1970
Offence
RB Bill Symons, TOR
RB Hugh McKinnis, CAL
RB Jim Evenson, BC
FL Jim Thorpe, TOR
QB Ron Lancaster, SAS
TE Herman Harrison, CAL
SE Tommy Joe Coffey, HAM
C Ted Urness, SAS
G Charlie Bray, TOR
G Bill Danychuk, HAM
G Ken Sugarman, BC
T Bill Frank, WPG
T Ellison Kelly, HAM

Defence
DB John Wydareny, EDM
DB Garney Henley, HAM
DB Al Phaneuf, MTL
DB Al Marcelin, OTT
DB Marv Luster, TOR
LB Wayne Harris, CAL
LB Jerry Campbell, OTT
LB Greg Findlay, BC
T Angelo Mosca, HAM
T Greg Pipes, EDM
E Steve Smear, MTL
E Ed Harrington, TOR

1971
Offence
RB George Reed, SAS
RB Jim Evenson, BC
RB Leon McQuay, TOR
QB Don Jonas, WPG
TE Mel Profit, TOR
SE Jim Thorpe, WPG
WR Bob LaRose, WPG
C Bob Swift, WPG
G Jack Abendschan, SAS
G Granville Liggins, CAL
T Bill Frank, WPG
T Ed George, MTL

Defence
DB Dick Dupuis, EDM
DB Frank Andruski, CAL
DB Garney Henley, HAM
DB Marv Luster, TOR
DB Dick Thornton, TOR
LB Wayne Harris, CAL
LB Mark Kosmos, MTL
LB Jerry Campbell, OTT
T John Helton, CAL
T Jim Stillwagon, TOR
E Jim Corrigall, TOR
E Craig Koinzan, CAL

1972
Offence
RB George Reed, SAS
RB Mack Herron, WPG
RB Dave Buchanan, HAM
QB Don Jonas, WPG
TE Peter Dalla Riva, MTL
TE Tony Gabriel, HAM
WR Garney Henley, HAM
WR Jim Young, BC
C Bob Swift, WPG
G Bob Lueck, WPG
G Jack Abendschan, SAS
T Bill Frank, WPG
T Ed George, MTL

Defence
DB Al Brenner, HAM
DB John Williams, HAM
DB Grady Cavness, WPG
DB Dick Adams, OTT
DB Marv Luster, TOR
LB Dave Gasser, EDM
LB Ray Nettles, BC
LB Jerry Campbell, OTT
T Jim Stillwagon, TOR
T John Helton, CAL
E Bill Baker, SAS
E Wayne Smith, OTT

1973
Offence
RB George Reed, SAS
RB Roy Bell, EDM
RB John Harvey, MTL
QB Ron Lancaster, SAS
TE Peter Dalla Riva, MTL
WR George McGowan, EDM
WR Johnny Rodgers, MTL
C Paul Desjardins, TOR
G Jack Abendschan, SAS
G Ed George, MTL
T Bill Frank, WPG
T Charlie Turner, EDM

Defence
DB Lorne Richardson, SAS
DB Larry Highbaugh, EDM
DB Al Marcelin, OTT
DB Lewis Porter, HAM
DB Dick Adams, OTT
LB Jerry Campbell, OTT
LB Ray Nettles, BC
LB Mike Widger, MTL
T John Helton, CAL
T Rudy Sims, OTT
E Bill Baker, SAS
E Jim Corrigall, TOR

1974
Offence
RB George Reed, SAS
RB Lou Harris, BC
RB Roy Bell, EDM
QB Tom Wilkinson, EDM
TE Tony Gabriel, HAM
WR Johnny Rodgers, MTL
WR Rhome Nixon, Omaha
C Bob Swift, WPG
G Ed George, MTL
G Curtis Wester, BC
T Charlie Turner, EDM
T Larry Watkins, EDM

Defence
DB Al Marcelin, OTT
DB Dick Adams, OTT
DB Larry Highbaugh, EDM
DB Paul Williams, WPG
DB Lorne Richardson, SAS (tie)
DB Dickie Harris, MTL (tie)
MLB Jerry Campbell, OTT
OLB Mike Widger, MTL
OLB Roger Goree, CAL
T John Helton, CAL
T Jim Stillwagon, TOR
E Wayne Smith, OTT
E George Wells, SAS

1975
Offence
RB Willie Burden, CAL
RB Art Green, OTT
RB Johnny Rodgers, MTL
QB Ron Lancaster, SAS
TE Peter Dalla Riva, MTL
TE Tony Gabriel, OTT
WR George McGowan, EDM
C Wayne Conrad, MTL (tie)
C Al Wilson, BC (tie)
G Dave Braggins, MTL
G Willie Martin, EDM
T Charlie Turner, EDM
T Dan Yochum, MTL

Defence
DB Rod Woodward, OTT
DB Dick Adams, OTT
DB Lorne Richardson, SAS
DB Vern Roberson, CAL
DB Dickie Harris, MTL
MLB Jerry Campbell, OTT
OLB Larry Cameron, BC
OLB Mike Widger, MTL
T John Helton, CAL
T Glen Weir, MTL
E Jim Corrigall, TOR
E Bill Baker, BC

1976
Offence
RB Jimmy Edwards, HAM
RB Jim Washington, WPG
RB Art Green, OTT
QB Ron Lancaster, SAS
TE Tony Gabriel, OTT
WR Rhett Dawson, SAS
WR George McGowan, EDM
C Al Wilson, BC
G Ralph Galloway, SAS
G Dave Braggins, MTL
T Dan Yochum, MTL
T Butch Norman, WPG

Defence
DB Lorne Richardson, SAS
DB Brian Herosian, WPG
DB Dickie Harris, MTL
DB David Shaw, HAM
DB Paul Williams, SAS (tie)
DB Lewis Porter, HAM (tie)
MLB Harry Walters, WPG
OLB Mark Kosmos, OTT
OLB Roger Goree, SAS
T Granville Liggins, TOR
T John Helton, CAL
E Bill Baker, BC
E Junior Ah You, MTL

1977
Offence
RB Jimmy Edwards, HAM
RB Jim Washington, WPG
SB Tom Scott, WPG
QB Jerry Tagge, BC
TE Tony Gabriel, OTT
WR Tom Forzani, CAL
WR Leon Bright, BC
C Al Wilson, BC
G Jeff Turcotte, OTT
G Ralph Galloway, SAS
T Mike Wilson, TOR
T Dan Yochum, MTL
K Dave Cutler, EDM
P Ken Clark, HAM

Defence
DB Dickie Harris, MTL
DB Larry Highbaugh, EDM
DB Paul Bennett, TOR
DB Pete Lavorato, EDM
DB Randy Rhino, MTL
MLB Dan Kepley, EDM
OLB Mike Widger, OTT
OLB Chuck Zapiec, MTL
T Glen Weir, MTL
T Dave Fennell, EDM
E Jim Corrigall, TOR
E Ron Estay, EDM

1978
Offence
RB James Sykes, CAL
RB Mike Strickland, SAS
SB Tom Scott, EDM
QB Tom Wilkinson, EDM
TE Tony Gabriel, OTT
WR Joe Poplawski, WPG
WR Bob Gaddis, MTL
C Al Wilson, BC
G Harold Holton, CAL
G Bill Stevenson, EDM
T Jim Coode, OTT
T Dan Yochum, MTL
K Dave Cutler, EDM
P Hank Ilesic, EDM

Defence
DB Joe Hollimon, EDM
DB Dickie Harris, MTL
DB Larry Brune, OTT
DB Greg Butler, EDM
DB Randy Rhino, MTL
MLB Dan Kepley, EDM
OLB Ben Zambiasi, HAM
OLB Chuck Zapiec, MTL
T Dave Fennell, EDM
T John Helton, CAL
E Mike Fanucci, OTT
E Reggie Lewis, CAL

1979 CFL
Offence
RB David Green, MTL
RB Larry Key, BC
SB Willie Armstead, CAL
QB Tom Wilkinson, EDM
TE Tony Gabriel, OTT
WR Waddell Smith, EDM
WR Brian Kelly, EDM
C Al Wilson, BC
G Ray Watrin, MTL
G Larry Butler, HAM
T Mike Wilson, EDM
T Lloyd Fairbanks, CAL
K Lui Passaglia, BC
P Hank Ilesic, EDM

Defence
DB Dickie Harris, MTL
DB Mike Nelms, OTT
DB Greg Butler, EDM
DB Ed Jones, EDM
DB Al Burleson, CAL
MLB Dan Kepley, EDM
OLB Ben Zambiasi, HAM
OLB Ron Foxx, OTT
T Dave Fennell, EDM
T John Helton, WPG
E Junior Ah You, MTL
E Reggie Lewis, CAL

1980
Offence
RB James Sykes, CAL
RB William Miller, WPG
SB Tom Scott, EDM
QB Dieter Brock, WPG
TE Tony Gabriel, OTT
WR Brian Kelly, EDM
WR Mike Holmes, WPG
C Al Wilson, BC
G Larry Butler, WPG
G Val Belcher, OTT
T Mike Wilson, EDM
T Butch Norman, WPG
K Bernie Ruoff, HAM
P Hank Ilesic, EDM

Defence
DB Ray Odums, CAL
DB Ed Jones, EDM
DB Greg Butler, EDM
DB Ken McEachern, SAS
DB Dickie Harris, MTL (tie)
DB David Shaw, HAM (tie)
MLB Dan Kepley, EDM
OLB Ben Zambiasi, HAM
OLB Dale Potter, EDM
T Dave Fennell, EDM
T Bruce Clark, TOR
E Ron Estay, EDM
E Reggie Lewis, CAL

1981
Offence
RB Larry Key, BC
RB Jim Germany, EDM
SB Joe Poplawski, WPG
SB Joey Walters, SAS
QB Dieter Brock, WPG
WR Brian Kelly, EDM
WR James Scott, MTL
C Al Wilson, BC
G Val Belcher, OTT
G Larry Butler, WPG
T Bill Stevenson, EDM
T Hector Pothier, EDM
K Trevor Kennerd, WPG
P Hank Ilesic, EDM

Defence
DB Ray Odums, CAL
DB David Shaw, HAM
DB Harold Woods, HAM
DB Ed Jones, EDM
DB Randy Rhino, OTT
MLB Dan Kepley, EDM
OLB Ben Zambiasi, HAM
OLB James Parker, EDM
T Dave Fennell, EDM
T Mike Raines, OTT
E David Boone, EDM
E Greg Marshall, OTT

1982
Offence
RB Alvin Walker, OTT
RB William Miller, WPG
SB Tom Scott, EDM
SB Joey Walters, SAS
QB Condredge Holloway, TOR
C John Bonk, WPG
G Val Belcher, OTT
G Rudy Phillips, OTT
T Bobby Thompson, WPG
T Lloyd Fairbanks, CAL
WR Terry Greer, TOR
WR Keith Baker, HAM
P Ken Clark, SAS
K Dave Ridgway, SAS

Defence
DB David Shaw, HAM
DB Ray Odums, CAL
DB Vince Phason, WPG
DB Fran McDermott, SAS
DB Zac Henderson, TOR
MLB Dan Bass, CAL
OLB James Parker, EDM
OLB Ben Zambiasi, HAM
T Mike Samples, SAS
T John Helton, WPG
E Nick Hebeler, BC
E Pete Catan, WPG

1983
Offence
RB Alvin Walker, OTT
RB Johnny Shepherd, HAM
SB Tom Scott, EDM
SB Ron Robinson, MTL
QB Warren Moon, EDM
C John Bonk, WPG
G Leo Blanchard, EDM
G Rudy Phillips, OTT
T John Blain, BC
T Kevin Powell, OTT
WR Brian Kelly, EDM
WR Terry Greer, TOR
P Lui Passaglia, BC
K Lui Passaglia, BC

Defence
DB Harry Skipper, MTL
DB Kerry Parker, BC
DB Larry Crawford, BC
DB Richie Hall, CAL (tie)
DB Carl Brazley, TOR (tie)
DB Paul Bennett, WPG
MLB Dan Bass, CAL
OLB James Parker, EDM
OLB Ben Zambiasi, HAM
T Mack Moore, BC
T Garry Dulin, OTT
E Greg Marshall, OTT
E Rick Mohr, TOR

1984
Offence
RB Willard Reaves, WPG
RB Dwaine Wilson, MTL
SB Nick Arakgi, MTL
SB Joe Poplawski, WPG
QB Tom Clements, WPG
C John Bonk, WPG
G Nick Bastaja, WPG
G Dan Ferrone, TOR
T Chris Walby, WPG
T John Blain, BC
WR Brian Kelly, EDM
WR Mervyn Fernandez, BC
P Bernie Ruoff, HAM
K Lui Passaglia, BC

Defence
DB David Shaw, WPG
DB Harry Skipper, MTL
DB Ken Hailey, WPG
DB Larry Crawford, BC
DB Laurent DesLauriers, EDM
MLB Aaron Brown, WPG
OLB Tyrone Jones, WPG
OLB Stewart Hill, EDM
T James Curry, TOR
T Mack Moore, BC
E Steve Raquet, MTL
E James Parker, BC

1985
Offence
RB Willard Reaves, WPG
RB Keyvan Jenkins, BC
SB Joe Poplawski, WPG
SB Ray Elgaard, SAS
QB Matt Dunigan, EDM
C John Bonk, WPG
G Dan Ferrone, TOR
G Nick Bastaja, WPG
T John Blain, BC
T Chris Walby, WPG
WR Mervyn Fernandez, BC
WR Jeff Boyd, WPG
P Ken Clark, OTT
K Trevor Kennerd, WPG

Defence
DB Darnell Clash, BC
DB Less Browne, HAM
DB Ken Hailey, WPG
DB Howard Fields, HAM
DB Paul Bennett, HAM
MLB Ben Zambiasi, HAM
OLB Tyrone Jones, WPG
OLB Kevin Konar, BC
T Mike Gray, BC
T James Curry, TOR
E Grover Covington, HAM
E James Parker, BC

1986
Offence
RB Gary Allen, CAL
RB Bobby Johnson, SAS
SB Joe Poplawski, WPG
SB Rocky DiPietro, HAM
QB Rick Johnson, CAL
C Bob Poley, CAL
G Roger Aldag, SAS
G Leo Blanchard, EDM
T Chris Walby, WPG
T Rudy Phillips, EDM
WR James Murphy, WPG
WR James Hood, MTL
P Hank Ilesic, TOR
K Lance Chomyc, TOR

Defence
S ScottFLagel, WPG
DB Larry Crawford, BC
DB Mark Streeter, HAM
CB Roy Bennett, WPG
CB Less Browne, HAM
MLB Dan Bass, EDM
OLB Tyrone Jones, WPG
OLB Willie Pless, TOR
T Harold Hallman, CAL
T Brett Williams, MTL
E James Parker, BC
E Grover Covington, HAM
ST Gary Allen, CAL

1987
Offence
RB Willard Reaves, WPG
RB Gill Fenerty, TOR
SB Darrell Smith, TOR
SB Perry Tuttle, WPG
QB Tom Clements, WPG
C Rod Connop, EDM
G Roger Aldag, SAS
G Dan Ferrone, TOR
T Chris Walby, WPG
T Chris Schultz, TOR
WR Brian Kelly, EDM
WR Jim Sandusky, BC
P Hank Ilesic, TOR
K Dave Ridgway, SAS

Defence
S ScottFLagel, WPG
DB Larry Crawford, BC
DB Ken Hailey, WPG
CB Roy Bennett, WPG
CB James Jefferson, WPG
MLB James West, WPG
OLB Tyrone Jones, WPG
OLB Kevin Konar, BC
T Mike Walker, HAM
T Jearld Baylis, TOR
E Greg Stumon, BC
E Bobby Jurasin, SAS
ST Henry Williams, EDM

1988
Offence
RB Anthony Cherry, BC
RB Gill Fenerty, TOR
SB Ray Elgaard, SAS
SB Emanuel Tolbert, CAL
QB Matt Dunigan, BC
C Ian Beckstead, TOR
G Roger Aldag, SAS
G Gerald Roper, BC
T Chris Schultz, TOR
T Jim Mills, BC
WR David Williams, BC
WR James Murphy, WPG
P Bob Cameron, WPG
K Dave Ridgway, SAS

Defence
S Bennie Thompson, WPG
HB Selwyn Drain, TOR
HB Howard Fields, HAM
CB Stanley Blair, EDM
CB Reggie Pleasant, TOR
MLB Dan Bass, EDM
OLB Greg Stumon, BC
OLB Willie Pless, TOR
T Mike Walker, HAM
T Brett Williams, EDM
E Grover Covington, HAM
E Bobby Jurasin, SAS
ST Earl Winfield, HAM

1989
Offence
RB Tim McCray, SAS
RB Reggie Taylor, EDM
SB Rocky DiPietro, HAM
SB Craig Ellis, EDM
QB Tracy Ham, EDM
C Rod Connop, EDM
G Jason Riley, HAM
G Roger Aldag, SAS
T Miles Gorrell, HAM
T Chris Walby, WPG
WR Tony Champion, HAM
WR Don Narcisse, SAS
P Bob Cameron, WPG
K Dave Ridgeway, SAS

Defence
S ScottFLagel, OTT
HB Don Wilson, EDM
HB Enis Jackson, EDM
CB Stanley Blair, EDM
CB Rod Hill, WPG
MLB Dan Bass, EDM
OLB Eddie Lowe, SAS
OLB James West, HAM
T Harold Hallman, TOR
T Mike Walker, HAM
E Grover Covington, HAM
E Stewart Hill, EDM
ST Tony Hunter, EDM

1990
Offence
FB Blake Marshall, EDM
RB Robert Mimbs, WPG
SB Darrell Smith, TOR
SB Craig Ellis, EDM
QB Kent Austin, SAS
C Rod Connop, EDM
G Dan Ferrone, TOR
G Roger Aldag, SAS
T Jim Mills, BC
T Chris Walby, WPG
WR Stephen Jones, OTT
WR Don Narcisse, SAS
P Bob Cameron, WPG
K Dave Ridgway, SAS

Defence
S Greg Peterson, CAL
HB Troy Wilson, OTT
HB Don Wilson, TOR
CB Less Browne, WPG
CB Rod Hill, WPG
MLB Dan Bass, EDM
OLB Willie Pless, BC
OLB Greg Battle, WPG
T Kent Warnock, CAL
T Harold Hallman, TOR
E Stewart Hill, EDM
E Greg Stumon, OTT
ST Mike Clemons, TOR

1991
Offence

FB Blake Marshall, EDM
RB Robert Mimbs, WPG
SB Matt Clark, BC
SB Allen Ptts, CAL
QB DougFLutie, BC
C Rod Connop, EDM
G Leo Groenewegen, BC
G Dan Ferrone, TOR
T Jim Mills, BC
T Chris Walby, WPG
WR Ray Alexander, BC
WR Raghib Ismail, TOR
P Hank Ilesic, TOR
K Lance Chomyc, TOR

Defence
S Glen Suitor, SAS
HB Darryl Hall, CAL
HB Don Wilson, TOR
CB Less Browne, WPG
CB Junior Thurman, CAL
LB Willie Pless, EDM
LB Darryl Ford, TOR
LB Greg Battle, WPG
T Harold Hallman, TOR
T Brett Williams, EDM
E Will Johnson, CAL
E Mike Campbell, TOR
ST Henry Williams, EDM

1992
Offence
FB Blake Marshall, EDM
RB Mike Richardson, WPG
SB Ray Elgaard, SAS
SB Allen Pitts, CAL
QB DougFLutie, CAL
C Rod Connop, EDM
G Pierre Vercheval, EDM
G Rocco Romano, CAL
T Rob Smith, OTT
T Vic Stevenson, SAS
WR Stephen Jones, OTT
WR Jim Sandusky, EDM
P Hank Ilesic, TOR
K Troy Westwood, WPG

Defence
S Glen Suitor, SAS
HB Anthony Drawhorn, OTT
HB Darryl Hall, CAL
CB Less Browne, OTT
CB Junior Thurman, CAL
LB Angelo Snipes, OTT
LB Willie Pless, EDM
LB John Motton, HAM
T Rodney Harding, TOR
T Jearld Baylis, SAS
E Will Johnson, CAL
E Bobby Jurasin, SAS
ST Henry Williams, EDM

1993
Offence
FB Sean Millington, BC
RB Mike Richardson, WPG
SB Ray Elgaard, SAS
SB David Sapunjis, CAL
QB DougFLutie, CAL
C Rod Connop, EDM
G David Black, WPG
G Rob Smith, BC
T Bruce Covernton, CAL
T Chris Walby, WPG
WR David Williams, WPG
WR Rod Harris, SAC
P Bob Cameron, WPG
K Dave Ridgway, SAS

Defence
S Glen Suitor, SAS
HB Don Wilson, EDM
HB Darryl Sampson, WPG
CB Karl Anthony, CAL
CB Barry Wilburn, SAS
LB Elfrid Payton, WPG
LB Willie Pless, EDM
LB John Motton, HAM
T Jearld Baylis, SAS
T Harald Hasselbach, CAL
E Will Johnson, CAL
E Tim Cofield, HAM
ST Henry Williams, EDM

1994
Offence
FB Sean Millington, BC
RB Mike Pringle, BAL
SB Allen Pitts, CAL
SB Gerald Wilcox, WPG
QB DougFLutie, CAL
C Mike Anderson, SAS
G Pierre Vercheval, TOR
G Rocco Romano, CAL
T Shar Pourdanesh, BAL
T Chris Walby, WPG
WR Paul Masotti, TOR
WR Rod Harris, SAC
P Josh Miller, BAL
K Mark McLoughlin, CAL

Defence
S Greg Knox, CAL
HB Charles Gordon, BC
HB Robert Holland, EDM
CB Less Browne, BC
CB Irvin Smith, BAL
LB Ron Goetz, SAS
LB Willie Pless, EDM
LB Calvin Tiggle, TOR
T Bennie Goods, EDM
T Rodney Harding, TOR
E Will Johnson, CAL
E Tim Cofield, HAM
ST Henry Williams, EDM

1995
Offence
FB Mike Saunders, SA
RB Mike Pringle, BAL
SB Dave Sapunjis, CAL
SB Allen Pitts, CAL
QB Matt Dunigan, BIR
C Mike Kiselak, SA
G Jamie Taras, BC
G Mike Withycombe, BAL
T Rocco Romano, CAL
T Neal Fort, BAL
WR Don Narcisse, SAS
WR Earl Winfield, HAM
P Josh Miller, BAL
K Roman Anderson, SA

Defence
S Anthony Drawhorn, BIR
HB Glenn Rogers, EDM
HB Charles Anthony, BAL
CB Eric Carter, HAM
CB Irvin Smith, BAL
LB Alondra Johnson, CAL
LB O.J. Brigance, BAL
LB Willie Pless, EDM
T Bennie Goods, EDM
T Jearld Baylis, BAL
E Tim Cofield, MEM
E Will Johnson, CAL
ST ChrisWRight, BAL

1996
Offence
FB Robert Drummond, TOR
RB Robert Mimbs, SAS
SB Mac Cody, HAM
SB DarrenFLutie, EDM
QB DougFLutie, TOR
C Mike Kiselak, TOR
G Rocco Romano, CAL
G Leo Groenewegen, EDM
T Chris Perez, TOR
T Fred Childress, CAL
WR Joseph Rogers, OTT
WR Eddie Brown, EDM
P Paul Osbaldiston, HAM
K Mark McLoughlin, CAL

Defence
S Trent Brown, EDM
HB Glenn Rogers, MTL
HB Charles Gordon, MTL
CB Al Jordan, CAL
CB Marvin Coleman, CAL
LB Tracy Gravely, MTL
LB Willie Pless, EDM
LB K.D. Williams, WPG
T Rob Waldrop, TOR
T Bennie Goods, EDM
E Malvin Hunter, EDM
E Grant Carter, MTL
ST Jimmy Cunningham, TOR

1997
Offence
FB Robert Drummond, TOR
RB Mike Pringle, MTL
SB Derrell Mitchell, TOR
SB DarrenFLutie, HAM
QB DougFLutie, TOR
C Mike Kiselak, TOR
G Fred Childress, CAL
G Pierre Vercheval, MTL
T Uzooma Okeke, MTL
T Neal Fort, MTL
WR Alfred Jackson, BC
WR Milt Stegall, WPG
P Mike Vanderjagt, TOR
K Mike Vanderjagt, TOR

Defence
S Lester Smith, TOR
HB Glenn Rogers, EDM
HB Johnnie Harris, TOR
CB Kavis Reed, EDM
CB Marvin Coleman, CAL
LB Maurice Kelly, BC
LB Willie Pless, EDM
LB Shonte Peoples, WPG
T Rob Waldrop, TOR
T Doug Petersen, MTL
E Elfrid Payton, MTL
E Bobby Jurasin, SAS
ST Mike Clemons, TOR

1998
Offence
RB Kelvin Anderson, CAL
RB Mike Pringle, MTL
SB Derrell Mitchell, TOR
SB Allen Pitts, CAL
QB Jeff Garcia, CAL
C Carl Coulter, HAM
G Fred Childress, CAL
G Pierre Vercheval, MTL
T Uzooma Okeke, MTL
T Moe Elewonibi, BC
WR Don Narcisse, SAS
WR Terry Vaughn, CAL
P Tony Martino, CAL
K Paul Osbaldiston, HAM

Defence
S Dale Joseph, BC
HB Gerald Vaughn, HAM
HB Orlando Steinauer, HAM
CB Eric Carter, HAM
CB Steve Muhammad, BC
LB Calvin Tiggle, HAM
LB Willie Pless, EDM
LB Alondra Johnson, CAL
T JoeFLeming, WPG
T Johnny Scott, BC
E Elfrid Payton, MTL
E Joe Montford, HAM
ST Eric Blount, WPG

1999
Offence
RB Kelvin Anderson, CAL
RB Mike Pringle, MTL
SB DarrenFLutie, HAM
SB Allen Pitts, CAL
QB Danny McManus, HAM
C Jamie Taras, BC
G Leo Groenewegen, EDM
G Pierre Vercheval, MTL
T Uzooma Okeke, MTL
T Rocco Romano, CAL
WR Ben Cahoon, MTL
WR Travis Moore, CAL
P Noel Prefontaine, TOR
K Mark McLoughlin, CAL

Defence
S Rob Hitchcock, HAM
HB Gerald Vaughn, HAM
HB Barron Miles, MTL
CB William Hampton, CAL
CB Adrion Smith, TOR
LB Calvin Tiggle, HAM
LB Mike O'Shea, TOR
LB Maurice Kelly, WPG
T Demetrious Maxie, TOR
T Johnny Scott, BC
E Daved Benefield, MTL
E Joe Montford, HAM
ST Jimmy Cunningham, BC

2000
Offence
RB Sean Millington, BC
RB Mike Pringle, MTL
SB Derrell Mitchell, TOR
SB Milt Stegall, WPG
QB Dave Dickenson, CAL
C Bryan Chiu, MTL
G Andrew Greene, SAS
G Pierre Vercheval, MTL
T Bruce Beaton, EDM
T Chris Perez, BC
WR Curtis Marsh, SAS
WR Travis Moore, CAL
P Noel Prefontaine, TOR
K Lui Passaglia, BC

Defence
S Greg Frers, CAL
DB Eddie Davis, CAL
DB Barron Miles, MTL
CB Marvin Coleman, CAL
CB Davis Sanchez, MTL
LB Alondra Johnson, CAL
LB Terry Ray, EDM
LB George White, SAS
T JoeFLeming, CAL
T Demetrious Maxie, SAS
E Joe Montford, HAM
E Shonte Peoples, CAL
ST Albert Johnson, WPG

2001
Offence
RB Kelvin Anderson, CAL
RB Michael Jenkins, TOR
SB Milt Stegall, WPG
SB Terry Vaughn, EDM
QB Khari Jones, WPG
C Bryan Chiu, MTL
G Brett MacNeil, WPG
G Jay McNeil, CAL
T Bruce Beaton, EDM
T Dave Mudge, WPG
WR Ed Hervey, EDM
WR Travis Moore, CAL
P Terry Baker, MTL
K Paul Osbaldiston, HAM

Defence
S Rob Hitchcock, HAM
DB Juran Bolden, WPG
DB Harold Nash, WPG
CB Eric Carter, BC
CB Wayne Shaw, TOR
LB Terry Ray, EDM
LB Chris Shelling, HAM
LB Barrin Simpson, BC
T Doug Brown, WPG
T JoeFLeming, CAL
E Joe Montford, HAM
E Elfrid Payton, TOR
ST Charles Roberts, WPG

2002
Offence
RB John Avery, EDM
RB Charles Roberts, WPG
SB Milt Stegall, WPG
SB Terry Vaughn, EDM
QB Anthony Calvillo, MTL
C Bryan Chiu, MTL
G ScottFLory, MTL
G Jay McNeil, CAL
T Dave Mudge, WPG
T Uzooma Okeke, MTL
WR Derick Armstrong, SAS
WR Jason Tucker, EDM
P Noel Prefontaine, TOR
K SeanFLeming, EDM

Defence
S Orlondo Steinauer, TOR
DB Clifford Ivory, TOR
DB Barron Miles, MTL
CB Eric Carter, BC
CB Omarr Morgan, SAS
LB Brendan Ayanbadejo, BC
LB John Grace, OTT
LB Barrin Simpson, BC
T Doug Brown, WPG
T Denny Fortney, WPG
E Joe Montford, TOR
E Elfrid Payton, EDM
ST Corey Holmes, SAS

2003
Offence
RB Mike Pringle, EDM
RB Charles Roberts, WPG
SB Jeremaine Copeland, MTL
SB Geroy Simon, BC
QB Anthony Calvillo, MTL
C Bryan Chiu, MTL
G ScottFLory, MTL
G Andrew Greene, SAS
T Bruce Beaton, EDM
T Uzooma Okeke, MTL
WR Ed Hervey, EDM
WR Tony Miles, TOR
P Noel Prefontaine, TOR
K Lawrence Tynes, OTT

Defence
S Orlondo Steinauer, TOR
DB Donny Brady, EDM
DB Clifford Ivory, TOR
CB Omarr Morgan, SAS
CB Adrion Smith, TOR
LB Reggie Hunt, SAS
LB Jackie Mitchell, SAS
LB Barrin Simpson, BC
T Eric England, TOR
T JoeFLeming, CAL
E Daved Benefield, WPG

E Ray Jacobs, BC
ST Bashir Levingston, TOR

2004
Offence
RB Troy Davis, HAM
RB Charles Roberts, WPG
SB Ben Cahoon, MTL
SB Geroy Simon, BC
QB Casey Printers, BC
C Bryan Chiu, MTL
G Andrew Greene, SAS
G Paul Lambert, MTL
T Gene Makowsky, SAS
T Uzooma Okeke, MTL
WR D.J.FLick, HAM
WR Jason Tucker, EDM
P Noel Prefontaine, TOR
K SeanFLeming, EDM

Defence
S Orlondo Steinauer, TOR
DB Eddie Davis, SAS
DB Clifford Ivory, TOR
CB Almondo Curry, MTL
CB Malcolm Frank, EDM
LB Kevin Eiben, TOR
LB John Grace, CAL
LB Barrin Simpson, BC
T Noah Cantor, TOR
T Nathan Davis, SAS
E Tim Cheatwood, HAM
E Anwar Stewart, MTL
ST Keith Stokes, WPG

2005
Offence
RB Joffrey Reynolds, CAL
RB Charles Roberts, WPG
SB Milt Stegall, WPG
SB Jason Tucker, EDM
QB Damon Allen, TOR
C Bryan Chiu, MTL
G ScottFLory, MTL
G Andrew Greene, SAS
T Gene Makowsky, SAS
T Uzooma Okeke, MTL
WR Jason Armstead, OTT
WR Kerry Watkins, MTL
P Jon Ryan, WPG
K Sandro DeAngelis, CAL

Defence
S Richard Karikari, MTL
DB Korey Banks, OTT
DB Eddie Davis, SAS
CB Omarr Morgan, SAS
CB Jordan Younger, TOR
LB Kevin Eiben, TOR
LB MichaelFLetcher, TOR
LB John Grace, CAL
T Adriano Belli, HAM
T Scott Schultz, SAS
E Jonathan Brown, TOR
E Brent Johnson, BC
ST Corey Holmes, SAS

2006
Offence
RB Joffrey Reynolds, CAL
RB Charles Roberts, WPG
REC Arland Bruce, TOR
REC Geroy Simon, BC
REC Milt Stegall, WPG
REC Jason Tucker, EDM
QB Ricky Ray, EDM
C Jeremy O'Day, SAS
G ScottFLory, MTL
G Jay McNeil, CAL
T Gene Makowsky, SAS
T Rob Murphy, BC
P Noel Prefontaine, TOR
K Sandro DeAngelis, CAL

Defence
S Barron Miles, BC
DB Korey Banks, BC
DB Eddie Davis, SAS
CB Byron Parker, TOR
CB Coby Rhinehart, CAL
LB Brian Clark, CAL
LB OtisFLoyd, BC
LB Barrin Simpson, WPG
T Doug Brown, WPG
T Tyrone Williams, BC
E Brent Johnson, BC
E Fred Perry, SAS
ST Albert Johnson, WPG

2007
Offence
RB Charles Roberts, WPG
RB Joe Smith, BC
REC Derick Armstrong, WPG
REC Jason Clermont, BC
REC Terrence Edwards, WPG
REC Geroy Simon, BC
QB Kerry Joseph, SAS
C Jeremy O'Day, SAS
G Kelly Bates, B
G ScottFLory, MTL
T Dan Goodspeed, WPG
T Rob Murphy, BC
P Damon Duval, MTL
K Nick Setta, HAM

Defence
S Orlondo Steinauer, TOR
DB Ryan Phillips, BC
DB Kenny Wheaton, TOR
CB Byron Parker, TOR
CB Jordan Younger, TOR
LB Kevin Eiben, TOR
LB Zeke Moreno, HAM
LB Barrin Simpson, WPG
T Doug Brown, WPG
T Tyrone Williams, BC
E Jonathan Brown, TOR
E Cameron Wake, BC
ST Ian Smart, BC

2008
Offence
RB Wes Cates, SAS
RB Joffrey Reynolds, CAL
REC Ben Cahoon, MTL
REC Ken-Yon Rambo, CAL
REC Jamel Richardson, MTL
REC Geroy Simon, BC
QB Anthony Calvillo, MTL
C Bryan Chiu, MTL
G ScottFLory, MTL
G Gene Makowsky, SAS
T Dan Goodspeed, WPG
T Jason Jiminez, BC
P Nick Setta, HAM
K Sandro DeAngelis, CAL

Defence
S Barron Miles, BC
DB Jason Goss, EDM
DB Chris Thompson, HAM
CB Brandon Browner, CAL
CB Dante Marsh, BC
LB Maurice Lloyd, SAS
LB Anton McKenzie, SAS
LB Zeke Moreno, WPG
T Doug Brown, WPG
T Aaron Hunt, BC
E Brent Johnson, BC
E Cameron Wake, BC
ST Dominique Dorsey, TOR

2009
Offence
RB Avon Cobourne, MTL
RB Joffrey Reynolds, CAL
REC Arland Bruce, HAM
REC Jeremaine Copeland, CAL
REC Fred Stamps, EDM
REC Kerry Watkins, MTL
QB Anthony Calvillo, MTL
C Jeremy O'Day, SAS
G ScottFLory, MTL
G Gene Makowsky, SAS
T Dan Goodspeed, WPG
T Ben Archibald, CAL
P Damon Duval, MTL
K Damon Duval, MTL

Defence
S Barron Miles, BC
DB Korey Banks, BC
DB Jonathan Hefney, WPG
CB Brandon Browner, CAL
CB Jovon Johnson, WPG
LB Chip Cox, MTL
LB Markeith Knowlton, HAM
LB Jamall Johnson, HAM
T Doug Brown, WPG
T Keron Williams, MTL
E John Chick, SAS
E Anwar Stewart, MTL
ST Larry Taylor, MTL

2010
Offence
RB Cory Boyd, TOR
RB Fred Reid, WPG
REC Arland Bruce, HAM
REC Andy Fantuz, SAS
REC Nik Lewis, CAL
REC Terrence Edwards, WPG
QB Henry Burris, CAL
C Marwan Hage, HAM
G ScottFLory, MTL
G Dimitri Tsoumpas, CAL
T Ben Archibald, CAL
T Rob Murphy, TOR
P Burke Dales, CAL
K Paul McCallum, BC

Defence
S James Patrick, SAS
DB Ryan Phillips, BC
DB Chris Thompson, EDM
CB Dwight Anderson, CAL
CB Brandon Browner, CAL
LB Chip Cox, MTL
LB Markeith Knowlton, HAM
LB Juwan Simpson, CAL
T Doug Brown, WPG
T Kevin Huntley, TOR
E Phillip Hunt, WPG
E John Bowman, MTL
ST Chad Owens, TOR

2011
Offence
QB Travis Lulay, BC
RB Jerome Messam, EDM
RB Brandon Whitaker, MTL
C Angus Reid, BC
G Brendon LaBatte, WPG
G Dimitri Tsoumpas, CAL
T Josh Bourke, MTL
T Jovan Olafioye, BC
REC Nik Lewis, CAL
REC Jamel Richardson, MTL
REC Geroy Simon, BC
REC Fred Stamps, EDM

Defence
E Justin Hickman, HAM
E Odell Willis, WPG
T Aaron Hunt, BC
T Khalif Mitchell, BC
LB Chip Cox, MTL
LB Solomon Elimimian, BC
LB Jerrell Freeman, SAS
DB Korey Banks, BC
DB Jonathan Hefney, WPG
CB Jovon Johnson, WPG
CB Byron Parker, TOR
S Ian Logan, WPG

Special Teams
P Burke Dales, CAL
K Paul McCallum, BC
ST Chad Owens, TOR

CFLPA ALL-STAR TEAMS

Chosen by the Canadian Football League Players Association.

1996
Offence
QB Doug Flutie, TOR
T Chris Perez, TOR
T Mark Dixon, MTL
G Rocco Romano, CAL
G Jamie Taras, BC
C Mike Kiselak, TOR
RB Rob Mimbs, SAS
FB Tony Burse, EDM
SB Maclin Cody, HAM
SB Darren Flutie, EDM
WR Curtis Mayfield, SAS
WR Terry Vaughn, CAL

Defence
T Grant Carter, MTL
T Leroy Blugh, EDM
E John Kropke, WPG
E Rob Waldrop, TOR
OLB Angelo Snipes, WPG
OLB K.D. Williams, WPG
ILB Willie Pless, EDM
CB Donald Smith, TOR
CB Marvin Coleman, CAL
HB Glenn Rogers, EDM
HB Charles Gordon, MTL
S Greg Knox, CAL

Special Teams
K Mark McLoughlin, CAL
P Paul Osbaldiston, HAM
ST Jimmy Cunningham, TOR

Coach Don Matthews, TOR

1997
Offence
QB Doug Flutie, TOR
E John Terry, SAS
E Rocco Romano, CAL
G Fred Childress, CAL
G Bruce Beaton, MTL
C Mike Kiselak, TOR
RB Robert Drummond, TOR
FB Sean Millington, BC
SB MiltSTegall, WPG
SB Darren Flutie, EDM
WR Alfred Jackson, BC
WR Terry Vaughn, CAL

Defence
T Elfrid Payton, MTL
T Leroy Blugh, EDM
E John Kropke, SAS
E Rob Waldrop, TOR
OLB Darryl Hall, CAL
OLB Shonte Peoples, WPG
ILB Calvin Tiggle, HAM
CB Donald Smith, TOR
CB Marvin Coleman, CAL
HB Glenn Rogers, EDM
HB Johnnie Harris, TOR
S Trent Brown, EDM

Special Teams
K Mark McLoughlin, CAL
P Tony Martino, CAL
ST Mike Clemons, TOR

Coach Adam Rita, BC

1998
Offence
QB Jeff Garcia, CAL
E John Terry, SAS
E Uzooma Okeke, MTL
G Fred Childress, CAL
G Jamie Taras, BC
C Jamie Crysdale, CAL
RB Mike Pringle, MTL
FB Michael Soles, MTL
SB Derrell Mitchell, TOR
SB Darren Flutie, EDM
WR Donald Narcisse, SAS
WR Terry Vaughn, CAL

Defence
T Elfrid Payton, MTL
T Joe Montford, HAM
E Doug Petersen, MTL
E Joe Fleming, CAL
LB Alondra Johnson, CAL
LB Willie Pless, EDM
LB Calvin Tiggle, HAM
CB Donald Smith, TOR
CB Marvin Coleman, CAL
HB Gerald Vaughn, HAM
HB Kelly Wiltshire, TOR
S Maurice Kelly, WPG

Special Teams
K Sean Fleming, EDM
P Tony Martino, CAL
ST Eric Blount, WPG

Coach Ron Lancaster, HAM

1999
Offence
QB Damon Allen, BC
E Uzooma Okeke, MTL
E Chris Perez, WPG
G Fred Childress, CAL
G Val St. Germain, EDM
C Jamie Taras, BC
RB Mike Pringle, MTL
FB Michael Soles, MTL
SB Allen Pitts, CAL
SB Darren Flutie, HAM
WR Milt Stegall, WPG
WR Travis Moore, CAL

Defence
T Joe Montford, HAM
T Elfrid Payton, MTL
E Johnny Scott, BC
E Ed Philion, MTL
LB Alondra Johnson, CAL
LB Darryl Hall, CAL
LB Mike O'Shea, TOR
CB Adrion Smith, TOR
CB Eric Carter, BC
HB Gerald Vaughn, HAM
HB Barron Miles, MTL
S Lester Smith, MTL

Special teams
K Mark McLoughlin, CAL
P Terry Baker, MTL
ST Jimmy Cunningham, BC

Coach Charlie Taaffe, MTL

2000

Offence
QB Dave Dickenson, CAL
E Moe Elewonibi, WPG
E Chris Perez, BC
G Fred Childress, CAL
G Andrew Greene, SAS
C Carl Coulter, HAM
RB Mike Pringle, MTL
FB Sean Millington, BC
SB Kez McCorvey, EDM
SB Derrell Mitchell, TOR
WR Curtis Marsh, SAS
WR Milt Stegall, WPG

Defence
T Joe Montford, HAM
T Herman Smith, BC
E Johnny Scott, TOR
E Joe Fleming, CAL
LB Darryl Hall, CAL
LB Alondra Johnson, CAL
LB Terry Ray, EDM
CB Juran Bolden, WPG
CB Davis Sanchez, MTL
HB Jackie Kellogg, CAL
HB Barron Miles, MTL
S Greg Frers, CAL

Special Teams
K Lui Passaglia, BC
P Noel Prefontaine, TOR
ST Albert Johnson III, WPG

Coach Charlie Taaffe, MTL

2001
Offence
QB Khari Jones, WPG
T Uzooma Okeke, MTL
T Bruce Beaton, EDM
G Andrew Greene, SAS
G Steve Hardin, BC
C Bryan Chiu, MTL
RB Kelvin Anderson, CAL
FB Sean Millington, BC
SB Derrell Mitchell, TOR
SB Terry Vaughn, EDM
WR Milt Stegall, WPG
WR Travis Moore, CAL

Defence
T Joe Montford, HAM
T Elfrid Payton, TOR
E Joe Fleming, CAL
E Doug Petersen, EDM
LB Terry Ray, EDM
LB Alondra Johnson, CAL
LB Lamar McGriggs, WPG
CB Juran Bolden, WPG
CB Omarr Morgan, SAS
HB Harold Nash, WPG
HB Ricky Bell, CAL
S Greg Frers, CAL

Special Teams
K Paul Osbaldiston, HAM
P Terry Baker, MTL
ST Charles Roberts, WPG

Coach Dave Ritchie, WPG

2002
Offence
QB Anthony Calvillo, MTL
T Uzooma Okeke, MTL
T Dave Mudge, WPG
G Andrew Greene, SAS
G Steve Hardin, BC
C Bryan Chiu, MTL
RB John Avery, EDM
FB Mike Sellers, WPG
SB Milt Stegall, WPG
SB Terry Vaughn, EDM
WR Arland Bruce III, WPG
WR Ben Cahoon, MTL

Defence
T Herman Smith, BC
T Elfrid Payton, EDM
E Robert Brown, MTL
E Johnny Scott, TOR
LB Barrin Simpson, BC
LB Alondra Johnson, CAL
LB Kevin Johnson, MTL
CB Omarr Morgan, SAS
CB Marvin Coleman, WPG
HB Gerald Vaughn, OTT
HB Barron Miles, MTL
S Rob Hitchcock, HAM

Special Teams
K Sean Fleming, EDM
P Noel Prefontaine, TOR
ST Keith Stokes, MTL

Coach Don Matthews, MTL

2003
Offence
QB Anthony Calvillo, MTL
T Uzooma Okeke, MTL
T Bruce Beaton, EDM
G Andrew Greene, SAS
G Dan Comiskey, EDM
C Bryan Chiu, MTL
RB Charles Roberts, WPG
FB Mike Sellers, WPG
SB Geroy Simon, BC
SB Terry Vaughn, EDM
WR Jeremaine Copeland, MTL
WR Ed Hervey, EDM

Defence
T Tim Cheatwood, HAM
T Eric England, TOR
E Joe Fleming, CAL
E Demetrious Maxie, CAL
LB Barrin Simpson, BC
LB Reggie Hunt, SAS
LB Brian Clark, WPG
CB Omarr Morgan, SAS
CB Davis Sanchez, CAL
HB Clifford Ivory, TOR
HB Barron Miles, MTL
S Donovan Carter, OTT

Special Teams
K Lawrence Tynes, OTT
P Noel Prefontaine, TOR
ST Bashir Levingston, TOR

Coach Joe Paopao, OTT

2004
Offence
QB Casey Printers, BC
T Uzooma Okeke, MTL
T Cory Mantyka, BC
G Andrew Greene, SAS
G Dan Comiskey, EDM
C Jamie Crysdale, CAL
RB Troy Davis, HAM
FB Julian Radlein, HAM
SB Geroy Simon, BC
SB Derrell Mitchell, EDM
WR Jason Tucker, EDM
WR David Flick, HAM

Defence
T Joe Montford, HAM
T Timothy Cheatwood, HAM
E Joe Fleming, WPG
E Nate Davis, SAS
LB Barrin Simpson, BC
LB John Grace, CAL
LB Kevin Johnson, MTL
CB Malcolm Frank, EDM
CB Omarr Morgan, SAS
HB Clifford Ivory, TOR
HB Eddie Davis, SAS
S Orlondo Steinauer, TOR

Special Teams
K Paul McCallum, SAS
P Noel Prefontaine, TOR
ST Keith Stokes, WPG

Coach Greg Marshall, HAM

2005
Offence
QB Damon Allen, TOR
E Uzooma Okeke, MTL
E Gene Makowsky, SAS
G Dan Comiskey, EDM
G Scott Flory, MTL
C Bryan Chiu, MTL
RB Charles Roberts, WPG
FB Chris Szarka, SAS
SB Milt Stegall, WPG
SB Jason Tucker, EDM
WR Arland Bruce III, TOR
WR Kerry Watkins, MTL

Defence
T Joe Montford, EDM
T Brent Johnson, BC
E Adriano Belli, HAM
E Scott Schultz, SAS
LB Barrin Simpson, BC
LB Reggie Hunt, SAS
LB John Grace, CAL
CB Omarr Morgan, SAS
CB Malcolm Frank, EDM
HB Korey Banks, OTT
HB Eddie Davis, SAS
S Richard Karikari, MTL

Special Teams
K Damon Duval, MTL
P Jonathan Ryan, WPG
ST Corey Holmes, SAS

Coach Michael Clemons, TOR

2006
Offence
QB Henry Burris, CAL
T Gene Makowsky, SAS
T Bernard Williams, TOR
G Dan Comiskey, EDM
G Scott Flory, MTL
C Bryan Chiu, MTL
RB Joffrey Reynolds, CAL
FB Chris Szarka, SAS
SB Geroy Simon, BC
SB Milton Stegall, WPG
WR Arland Bruce III, TOR
WR Kerry Watkins, MTL

Defence
T Brent Johnson, BC
T Fred Perry, SAS
E Doug Brown, WPG
E Tyrone Williams, BC
LB Barrin Simpson, WPG
LB Otis Floyd, BC
LB Brian Clark, CAL
CB Tay Cody, HAM
CB Omarr Morgan, SAS
HB Korey Banks, BC
HB Eddie Davis, SAS
S Barron Miles, BC

Special Teams
K Sandro DeAngelis, CAL
P Damon Duval, MTL
ST Sandro DeAngelis, CAL

Coach Wally Buono, BC

2007
Offence
QB Kevin Glenn, WPG
T Dan Goodspeed, WPG
T Patrick Kabongo, EDM
G Andrew Greene, WPG
G Scott Flory, MTL
C Marwan Hage, HAM
RB Charles Roberts, WPG
FB Chris Szarka, SAS
SB Terrence Edwards, WPG
SB Milt Stegall, WPG
WR Derick Armstrong, WPG
WR Kamau Peterson, EDM

Defence
T Jonathan Brown, TOR
T Cameron Wake, BC
E Doug Brown, WPG
E Adriano Belli, TOR
LB Barrin Simpson, WPG
LB Zeke Moreno, HAM
LB JoJuan Armour, HAM
CB Byron Parker, TOR
CB Jordan Younger, TOR
HB Korey Banks, BC
HB Ryan Phillips, BC
S Barron Miles, BC

Special Teams
K Nick Setta, HAM
P Damon Duval, MTL
ST Dominique Dorsey, TOR

Coach Kent Austin, SAS

2008
Offence
QB Anthony Calvillo, MTL
T Wayne Smith, SAS
T Patrick Kabongo, EDM
G Gene Makowsky, SAS
G Scott Flory, MTL
C Marwan Hage, HAM
RB Wes Cates, SAS
FB Mathieu Bertrand, EDM
SB Geroy Simon, BC
SB Jamel Richardson, MTL
WR Ken-Yon Rambo, CAL
WR Kerry Watkins, MTL

Defence
T Cameron Wake. BC
T Brent Johnson. BC
E Keron Williams. MTL
E Doug Brown. WPG
LB Maurice Lloyd. SAS
LB Jojuan Armour. CAL
LB Zeke Moreno. WPG
CB Brandon Browner. CAL
CB Dante Marsh. BC
HB Jason Goss. EDM
HB Korey Banks. BC
S Barron Miles. BC

Special Teams
K Sandro DeAngelis, CAL
P Damon Duval, MTL (tie)
P Nick Setta, HAM (tie)
ST Dominique Dorsey, TOR

Coach Marc Trestman, MTL

2009
Offence
QB Anthony Calvillo, MTL
T Ben Archibald, CAL
T Dan Goodspeed, HAM
G Dmitri Tsoumpas, CAL
G Scott Flory, MTL
C Marwan Hage, HAM
RB Joffrey Reynolds, CAL
RB Mathieu Bertrand, EDM
WR Maurice Mann, EDM
WR Arland Bruce III, HAM
WR Kerry Watkins, MTL
WR Fred Stamps, EDM

Defence
T Doug Brown, WPG
T Keron Williams, MTL
E Anwar Stewart, MTL
E John Chick, SAS
LB Maurice Lloyd, EDM
LB Otis Floyd, HAM
LB Jamall Johnson, HAM
CB Brandon Browner, CAL
CB Jovon Johnson, WPG
DB Jonathan Hefney, WPG
DB Korey Banks, BC
S Barron Miles, BC

Special Teams
K Damon Duval, MTL
P Burke Dales, CAL
ST Larry Taylor, MTL

Coach Marc Trestman, MTL

2010
Offence
QB Anthony Calvillo, MTL
T Ben Archibald, CAL
T Dan Goodspeed, SAS
G Patrick Kabongo, EDM
G Cedric Gagne-Marcoux, TOR
C Marwan Hage, HAM
RB Cory Boyd, TOR
RB Fred Reid, WPG
SB Arland Bruce III, HAM
SB Fred Stamps, EDM
WR Romby Bryant, CAL
WR Jamel Richardson, MTL

Defence
T Doug Brown, WPG
T Dario Romero, EDM
E Phillip Hunt, WPG
E Odel Willis, WPG
LB Chip Cox, MTL
LB Barrin Simpson, SAS
LB Solomon Elimmian, BC
CB Brandon Browner, CAL
CB Dwight Anderson, CAL
DB Korey Banks, BC
DB Chris Thompson, EDM
S James Patrick, SAS

Special Teams
K Paul McCallum, BC
P Burke Dales, CAL
ST Chad Owens, TOR

Coach Jim Barker, TOR

2011
Offence
QB Anthony Calvillo, MTL
T Ben Archibald, BC
T Josh Boruke, MTL
G Dimitry Tsoumpas, CAL
G Brendon LaBatte, WPG
C Angus Reid, BC
RB Brandon Whitaker, MTL
RB Avon Cobourne, HAM
SB Jamel Richardson, MTL
SB Fred Stamps, EDM
WR Chris Williams, HAM
WR Adarius Bowman, EDM

Defence

E	Keron Williams, BC
E	John Bowman, MTL
T	Khalif Mitchell, BC
T	Doug Brown, WPG
LB	Solomon Elimimian, BC
LB	Jerrell Freeman, LB
LB	Chip Cox, LB
CB	Jovon Johnson, WPG
CB	Byron Parker, TOR
DH	Korey Banks, BC
DH	Jonathan Hefney, DB
S	Ian Logan, WPG

Special Teams

K	Paul McCallum, NC
P	Damon Duval, EDM
ST	Chad Owens, TOR

Coach Wally Buono, BC

The Head Coaches contains the coaching records of everyone who has held the position of head coach in the post-Second World War era of the Canadian Football League.

Each entry consists of two parts.

The first is the biographical line, which provides detailed biographical and roster information. This line includes (when available), the following information:

The name the coach is most commonly known by, in upper-case letters.
The coach's first and middle names.
Any common nicknames associated with that coach, given in parenthesis.
A B: entry lists a coach's birth date (in the month/day/year format) and place of birth.
A D: entry lists a coach's death date (in the month/day/year format) and place of death.

The following state and provincial abbreviations are used in these two entries:

AB Alberta
AK Alaska
AL Alabama
AR Arkansas
AZ Arizona
BC British Columbia
CA California
CO Colorado
CT Connecticut
DC District of Columbia
DE Delaware
FL Florida
GA Georgia
HI Hawaii
IA Iowa
ID Idaho
IL Illinois
IN Indiana
KS Kansas
KY Kentucky
LA Louisiana
MA Massachusetts
MB Manitoba
MD Maryland
ME Maine
MI Michigan
MN Minnesota
MO Missouri
MS Mississippi
MT Montana
NB New Brunswick
NC North Carolina
ND North Dakota
NE Nebraska
NH New Hampshire
NJ New Jersey
NL Newfoundland
NM New Mexico
NS Nova Scotia
NV Nevada
NY New York
OH Ohio
OK Oklahoma
ON Ontario
OR Oregon
PA Pennsylvania
QC Quebec
RI Rhode Island
SC South Carolina
SD South Dakota
SK Saskatchewan
TN Tennessee
TX Texas
UT Utah
VA Virginia
VT Vermont
WA Washington
WI Wisconsin
WV West Virginia
WY Wyoming

The post-high school amateur teams played for and universities attended when eligible to play.

After each coach's biographical data is his year-by-year and career coaching record.

The following column headings are used:

FIN The place in which a team finished. If a coach was replaced during the season, the first number indicates which place the team was in at the time of the coaching change and the second number is where the team finished at the end of the regular season.

G Regular season games coached

L Regular season games lost

LCD League, conference or division

- E East or Eastern
- I IRFU
- N North
- S South
- W West, Western or WIFU

PCT Regular season winning percentage

PG Playoff games coached

PL Playoff games lost

PPCT Playoff winning percentage

PT Playoff games tied

PW Playoff games won

SEQ If a team made a coaching change during the season, the sequence will be indicated in this column.

- 1/2 indicates the first of two head coaches during the season
- 2/2 indicates the second of two head coaches during the season
- 2/3 indicates the second of three head coaches during the season
- 3/3 indicates the third of three head coaches during the season

T Regular season games tied

TEAM The following abbreviations are used:

- BAL Baltimore (1994)
  Baltimore Stallions (1995)
- BC British Columbia Lions (1954-)
- BIR Birmingham Barracudas (1995)
- CAL Calgary Stampeders (1946-)
- EDM Edmonton Eskimos (1949-)
- HAM Hamilton Tigers (1946-1947)
  Hamilton Wildcats (1948-1949)
  Hamilton Tiger-Cats (1950-)
- LV Las Vegas Posse (1994)
- MEM Memphis Mad Dogs (1995)
- MTL Montreal Alouettes (1946-1981)
  Montreal Concordes (1982-1985)
  Montreal Alouettes (1986; 1996-)
- OTT Ottawa Rough Riders (1946-1996)
  Ottawa Renegades (2002-2005)
- SA San Antonio Texans (1995)
- SAC Sacramento Gold Miners (1993-1994)
- SAS Saskatchewan Roughriders (1946-)
- SHR Shreveport Pirates (1994-1995)
- TOR Toronto Argonauts (1946-)
- WPG Winnipeg Blue Bombers (1946-)

W Regular season games won

YEAR If a coach coached for more than one year, the total number of years is listed on his career total line.

YEAR	TEAM	LCD	FIN	SEQ	G	W	L	T	PCT	PG	PW	PL	PT	PPCT
LOU AGASE Agase, Louis B: 8/2/1924 Evanston, IL D: 6/26/2006 East Lansing, MI Illinois														
1960	TOR	I	1		14	10	4	0	.714	2	0	2	0	.000
1961	TOR	E	3		14	7	6	1	.536	3	2	1	0	.667
1962	TOR	E	4/4	1/2	3	0	3	0	.000					
3	Years				31	17	13	1	.565	5	2	3	0	.400
BART ANDRUS Bart B: 3/30/1958Los Angeles Valley JC; Montana														
2009	TOR	E	4		18	3	15	0	.167					
NEILL ARMSTRONG Neill Ford B: 3/9/1926 Tishomingo, OK Oklahoma State														
1964	EDM	W	4		16	4	12	0	.250					
1965	EDM	W	5		16	5	11	0	.313					
1966	EDM	W	3		16	6	9	1	.406	1	0	1	0	.000
1967	EDM	W	3		16	9	6	1	.594	1	0	1	0	.000
1968	EDM	W	3		16	8	7	1	.531	1	0	1	0	.000
1969	EDM	W	4		16	5	11	0	.313					
6	Years				96	37	56	3	.401	3	0	3	0	.000
KENT AUSTIN Austin, Richard Kent B: 6/25/1963 Natick, MA Mississippi														
2007	SAS	W	2		18	12	6	0	.667	3	3	0	0	1.000
BOB BAKER Baker, Bob B: 11/28/1927 Lima, OH Ball State														
1975	CAL	W	5/4	2/2	6	2	4	0	.333					
1976	CAL	W	5/5	1/2	10	0	9	1	.050					
2	Years				16	2	13	1	.156					
JIM BARKER James T. B: 8/25/1956 Pasadena, CA Southern California														
1999	TOR	E	3		18	9	9	0	.500	1	0	1	0	.000
2003	CAL	W	5		18	5	13	0	.278					
2010	TOR	E	3		18	9	9	0	.500	2	1	1	0	.500
2011	TOR	E	4		18	6	12	0	.333					
3	Years				72	29	43	0	.403	3	1	2		.333
DANNY BARRETT Danny Lee B: 12/18/1961 Boynton Beach, FL Cincinnati														
2000	SAS	W	4		18	5	12	1	.306					
2001	SAS	W	4		18	6	12	0	.333					
2002	SAS	W	4		18	8	10	0	.444	1	0	1	0	.000
2003	SAS	W	3		18	11	7	0	.611	2	1	1	0	.500
2004	SAS	W	3		18	9	9	0	.500	2	1	1	0	.500
2005	SAS	W	4		18	9	9	0	.500	1	0	1	0	.000
2006	SAS	W	3		18	9	9	0	.500	2	1	1	0	.500
7	Years				126	57	68	1	.456	8	3	5	0	.375
DAVE BECKMAN David R. B: 6/8/1938 Baldwin-Wallace														
1990	HAM	E	3/4	2/2	6	2	4	0	.333					
1991	HAM	E	4/4	1/2	7	0	7	0	.000					
2	Years				13	2	11	0	.154					
MARCEL BELLEFUEILLE Marcel B: 3/19/1966 Ottawa, ON Ottawa														
2008	HAM	E	3/4	2/2	8	1	7	0	.125					
2009	HAM	E	2		18	9	9	0	.500	1	0	1	0	.000
2010	HAM	E	2		18	9	9	0	.500	1	0	1	0	.000
2011	HAM	E	3		18	8	10	0	.444	2	1	1	0	.500
4	Years				62	27	35	0	.435	4	1	3	0	.250
DOUG BERRY Doug B: 7/17/1958 Claremont, NH New Hampshire														
2006	WPG	E	3		18	9	9	0	.500	1	0	1	0	.000
2007	WPG	E	2		18	10	7	1	.583	3	2	1	0	.667
2008	WPG	E	2		18	8	10	0	.444	1	0	1	0	.000
3	Years				54	27	26	1	.509	5	2	3	0	.400
REUBEN BERRY Rueben L. 7/3/1934 OK D: 4/7/1998 Welch, OK Southwest Missouri State														
1983	SAS	W	5/5	2/2	10	4	6	0	.400					
1984	SAS	W	4		16	6	9	1	.406					
2	Years				26	10	15	1	.404					
URBAN BOWMAN Urban M., Jr. B: 11/16/1937 Westminster, MD Delaware														
1992	WPG	E	1		18	11	7	0	.611	2	1	1	0	.500
1997	HAM	E	3/4	2/2	11	1	10	0	.091					
2	Years				29	12	17	0	.414	2	1	1	0	.500
GEORGE BRANCATO George B: 5/27/1931 New York, NY Santa Ana JC; Louisiana State														
1974	OTT	E	2		16	7	9	0	.438	2	1	1	0	.500
1975	OTT	E	1		16	10	5	1	.656	1	0	1	0	.000
1976	OTT	E	1		16	9	6	1	.594	2	2	0	0	1.000
1977	OTT	E	2		16	8	8	0	.500	2	1	1	0	.500
1978	OTT	E	1		16	11	5	0	.688	1	0	1	0	.000
1979	OTT	E	2		16	8	6	2	.563	2	1	1	0	.500
1980	OTT	E	3		16	7	9	0	.438	1	0	1	0	.000
1981	OTT	E	2		16	5	11	0	.313	2	1	1	0	.500
1982	OTT	E	3		16	5	11	0	.313	2	1	1	0	.500
1983	OTT	E	2		16	8	8	0	.500	1	0	1	0	.000
1984	OTT	E	4		16	4	12	0	.250					
11	Years				176	82	90	4	.477	16	7	9	0	.438
AL BRUNO Albert P. B: 3/28/1927 West Chester, PA Kentucky														
1983	HAM	E	3/3	2/2	4	1	2	1	.375	2	1	1	0	.500
1984	HAM	E	3		16	6	9	1	.406	3	2	1	0	.667
1985	HAM	E	2		16	8	8	0	.500	2	1	1	0	.500
1986	HAM	E	2		18	9	8	1	.528	3	2	1	0	.667
1987	HAM	E	3		18	7	11	0	.389	1	0	1	0	.000
1988	HAM	E	3		18	9	9	0	.500	1	0	1	0	.000
1989	HAM	E	1		18	12	6	0	.667	2	1	1	0	.500
1990	HAM	E	3/4	1/2	12	4	8	0	.333					
8	Years				120	56	61	3	.479	14	7	7	0	.500
WALLY BUONO Pasquale B: 7/2/1950 Potenza, Italy Montreal Jrs.; Idaho State														
1990	CAL	W	1		18	11	6	1	.639	1	0	1	0	.000
1991	CAL	W	2		18	11	7	0	.611	3	2	1	0	.667
1992	CAL	W	1		18	13	5	0	.722	2	2	0	0	1.000
1993	CAL	W	1		18	15	3	0	.833	2	1	1	0	.500
1994	CAL	W	1		18	15	3	0	.833	2	1	1	0	.500
1995	CAL	N	1		18	15	3	0	.833	3	2	1	0	.667
1996	CAL	W	1		18	13	5	0	.722	1	0	1	0	.000
1997	CAL	W	2		18	10	8	0	.556	1	0	1	0	.000
1998	CAL	W	1		18	12	6	0	.667	2	2	0	0	1.000
1999	CAL	W	2		18	12	6	0	.667	3	2	1	0	.667
2000	CAL	W	1		18	12	5	1	.694	1	0	1	0	.000
2001	CAL	W	2		18	8	10	0	.444	3	3	0	0	1.000
2002	CAL	W	5		18	6	12	0	.333					
2003	BC	W	4		18	11	7	0	.611	1	0	1	0	.000
2004	BC	W	1		18	13	5	0	.722	2	1	1	0	.500
2005	BC	W	1		18	12	6	0	.667	1	0	1	0	.000
2006	BC	W	1		18	13	5	0	.722	2	2	0	0	1.000
2007	BC	W	1		18	14	3	1	.806	1	0	1	0	.000
2008	BC	W	3		18	11	7	0	.611	2	1	1	0	.500

YEAR	TEAM	LCD	FIN	SEQ	G	W	L	T	PCT	PG	PW	PL	PT	PPCT
2009	BC	W	4		18	8	10	0	.444	2	1	1	0	.500
2010	BC	W	3		18	8	10	0	.444	1	0	1	0	.000
2011	BC	W	1		18	11	7	0	.611	2	2	0	0	1.000
22	Years				396	254	139	3	.645	38	22	16	0	.579
STEVE BURATTO Buratto, Steven Arthur B: 9/29/1943 Seattle, WA Idaho														
1984	CAL	W	5		16	6	10	0	.375					
1985	CAL	W	5/5	1/2	5	0	5	0	.000					
2000	BC	W	3/3	2/2	11	5	6	0	.455	3	3	0	0	1.000
2001	BC	W	3		18	8	10	0	.444	1	0	1	0	.000
2002	BC	W	4/3	1/2	6	1	5	0	.167					
5	Years				56	20	36	0	.357	4	3	1	0	.750
LEO CAHILL Cahill, Leo H. B: 7/30/1928 LaSalle, IL Illinois														
1967	TOR	E	3		14	5	8	1	.393	1	0	1	0	.000
1968	TOR	E	2		14	9	5	0	.643	3	2	1	0	.667
1969	TOR	E	2		14	10	4	0	.714	3	2	1	0	.667
1970	TOR	E	2		14	8	6	0	.571	1	0	1	0	.000
1971	TOR	E	1		14	10	4	0	.714	3	1	1	1	.500
1972	TOR	E	4		14	3	11	0	.214					
1977	TOR	E	3		16	6	10	0	.375	1	0	1	0	.000
1978	TOR	E	3/4	1/2	9	3	6	0	.333					
8	Years				109	54	54	1	.500	12	5	6	1	.458
CHAN CALDWELL Caldwell, Charles A. B: 1/6/1920 D: 6/14/2000 Knoxville, TN Tennessee														
1955	OTT	I	4		12	3	9	0	.250					
HUGH CAMPBELL Campbell, Hugh Thomas B: 5/21/1941 San Jose, CA Washington State														
1977	EDM	W	1		16	10	6	0	.625	2	1	1	0	.500
1978	EDM	W	1		16	10	4	2	.688	2	2	0	0	1.000
1979	EDM	W	1		16	12	2	2	.813	2	2	0	0	1.000
1980	EDM	W	1		16	13	3	0	.813	2	2	0	0	1.000
1981	EDM	W	1		16	14	1	1	.906	3	3	0	0	1.000
1982	EDM	W	1		16	11	5	0	.688	2	2	0	0	1.000
6	Years				96	70	21	5	.755	13	12	1	0	.923
KEN CARPENTER Carpenter, Kenneth Leroy B: 2/26/1926 Carlisle, WA D: 1/28/2011 OR Oregon State														
1960	SAS	W	5		16	2	12	2	.188					
JIM CHAMPION Champion, Jim Henry B: 1/11/1926 Tillatoba, MS Mississippi State														
1967	BC	W	5/5	2/2	13	3	9	1	.269					
1968	BC	W	4		16	4	11	1	.281					
1969	BC	W	5/3	1/2	10	1	9	0	.100					
3	Years				39	8	29	2	.231					
FRANK CLAIR Clair, Frank James (The Professor) B: 5/12/1917 Hamilton, OH D: 4/3/2005 Sarasota, FL Ohio State														
1950	TOR	I	2		12	6	5	1	.542	4	3	1	0	.750
1951	TOR	I	2		12	7	5	0	.583	2	1	1	0	.500
1952	TOR	I	2		12	7	4	1	.625	5	4	1	0	.800
1953	TOR	I	4		14	5	9	0	.357					
1954	TOR	I	3		14	6	8	0	.429					
1956	OTT	I	3		14	7	7	0	.500	1	0	1	0	.000
1957	OTT	I	2		14	8	6	0	.571	1	0	1	0	.000
1958	OTT	I	3		14	6	8	0	.429	3	1	2	0	.333
1959	OTT	I	2		14	8	6	0	.571	3	2	1	0	.667
1960	OTT	I	2		14	9	5	0	.643	4	4	0	0	1.000
1961	OTT	E	2		14	8	6	0	.571	1	0	1	0	.000
1962	OTT	E	2		14	6	7	1	.464	1	0	1	0	.000
1963	OTT	E	2		14	9	5	0	.643	3	2	1	0	.667
1964	OTT	E	2		14	8	5	1	.607	3	2	1	0	.667
1965	OTT	E	2		14	7	7	0	.500	3	1	2	0	.333
1966	OTT	E	1		14	11	3	0	.786	3	2	1	0	.667
1967	OTT	E	2		14	9	4	1	.679	3	1	2	0	.333
1968	OTT	E	1		14	9	3	2	.714	3	2	1	0	.667
1969	OTT	E	1		14	11	3	0	.786	3	2	1	0	.667
19	Years				260	147	106	7	.579	46	27	19	0	.587
MICHAEL CLEMONS Clemons, Michael Lutrell (Pinball) B: 1/15/1965 Clearwater, FL William & Mary														
2000	TOR	E	4/4	2/2	10	6	4	0	.600					
2001	TOR	E	4		18	7	11	0	.389					
2002	TOR	E	3/2	2/2	6	4	2	0	.667	2	1	1	0	.500
2003	TOR	E	2		18	9	9	0	.500	2	1	1	0	.500
2004	TOR	E	2		18	10	7	1	.583	3	3	0	0	1.000
2005	TOR	E	1		18	11	7	0	.611					
2006	TOR	E	2		18	10	8	0	.556	2	1	1	0	.500
2007	TOR	E	1		18	11	7	0	.611	1	0	1	0	.000
8	Years				124	68	55	1	.552	10	6	4	0	.600
CLEM CROWE Crowe, Clem Frederick B: 10/18/1903 Lafeyette, IN D: 4/13/1983 Rochester, NY Notre Dame														
1951	OTT	I	2		12	7	5	0	.583	4	4	0	0	1.000
1952	OTT	I	3		12	5	7	0	.417					
1953	OTT	I	3		14	7	7	0	.500					
1954	OTT	I	4		14	2	12	0	.143					
1956	BC	W	4		16	6	10	0	.375					
1957	BC	W	4		16	4	11	1	.281					
1958	BC	W	5/5	1/3	3	0	3	0	.000					
7	Years				87	31	55	1	.362	4	4	0	0	1.000
JIM DALEY Daley, Jim B: 7/15/1955 Ottawa, ON														
1996	SAS	W	4		18	5	13	0	.278					
1997	SAS	W	3		18	8	10	0	.444	3	2	1	0	.667
1998	SAS	W	4		18	5	13	0	.278					
2004	WPG	W	4/4	2/2	11	5	6	0	.455					
2005	WPG	W	5		18	5	13	0	.278					
5	Years				83	28	55	0	.337	3	2	1	0	.667
KAY DALTON Dalton, Orris Kay B: 5/4/1932 Moab, UT Colorado State														
1967	MTL	E	4		14	2	12	0	.143					
1968	MTL	E	4		14	3	9	2	.286					
1969	MTL	E	4		14	2	10	2	.214					
3	Years				42	7	31	4	.214					
GEORGE DICKSON Dickson, George Charles B: 9/27/1921 Boston, MA Notre Dame														
1976	HAM	E	4/2	1/2	2	0	2	0	.000					
TOM DIMITROFF Dimitroff, Thomas George B: 6/6/1935 Akron, OH D: 1/20/1996 Strongsville, OH Miami (Ohio)														
1978	HAM	E	4/3	1/2	5	1	3	1	.300					
1986	OTT	E	3/4	2/2	5	0	4	1	.100					
2	Years				10	1	7	2	.150					
BOBBY DOBBS Dobbs, Robert Lee B: 10/13/1922 Munday, TX D: 4/2/1986 Altus, OK Tulsa; Army														
1961	CAL	W	3		16	7	9	0	.438	4	1	3	0	.250
1962	CAL	W	2		16	9	6	1	.594	5	3	2	0	.600
1963	CAL	W	2		16	10	4	2	.688	2	1	1	0	.500
1964	CAL	W	2		16	12	4	0	.750	5	2	3	0	.400
4	Years				64	38	23	3	.617	16	7	9	0	.438

YEAR	TEAM	LCD	FIN	SEQ	G	W	L	T	PCT	PG	PW	PL	PT	PPCT
GLENN DOBBS Dobbs, Glenn, Jr. B: 7/12/1920 McKinney, TX D: 11/12/2002 Tulsa, OK Tulsa														
1952	SAS	W	4		16	3	13	0	.188					
LARRY DONOVAN Donovan, Larry B: 3/31/1941 Scottsbluff, NE Nebraska														
1987	BC	W	1/1	2/2	4	4	0	0	1.000	1	0	1	0	.000
1988	BC	W	3		18	10	8	0	.556	3	2	1	0	.667
1989	BC	W	4/4	1/2	4	0	4	0	.000					
3	Years				26	14	12	0	.538	4	2	2	0	.500
AL DOROW Dorow, Albert Richard B: 11/15/1929 Imlay City, MI D: 12/7/2009 Okemos, MI Michigan State														
1971	HAM	E	2		14	7	7	0	.500	3	1	1	1	.500
OTIS DOUGLAS Douglas, Otis Whitfield, Jr. B: 7/25/1911 Reedville, VA D: 3/21/1989 Kilmarnock, VA William & Mary														
1956	CAL	W	4/5	2/2	8	1	7	0	.125					
1957	CAL	W	3		16	6	10	0	.375	2	0	1	1	.250
1958	CAL	W	4		16	6	9	1	.406					
1959	CAL	W	4		16	8	8	0	.500					
1960	CAL	W	5/3	1/3	3	0	2	1	.167					
5	Years				59	21	36	2	.373	2	0	1	1	.250
JIM DUNCAN Duncan, James Hampton B: 5/2/1925 Reidsville, NC D: Sunset Beach, NC Wake Forest														
1969	CAL	W	2		16	9	7	0	.563	3	1	2	0	.333
1970	CAL	W	3		16	9	7	0	.563	5	3	2	0	.600
1971	CAL	W	1		16	9	6	1	.594	3	3	0	0	1.000
1972	CAL	W	4		16	6	10	0	.375					
1973	CAL	W	3/4	1/2	13	5	8	0	.385					
5	Years				77	38	38	1	.500	11	7	4	0	.636
MATT DUNIGAN Dunigan, Mathew A. B: 12/6/1960 Lakewood, OH Louisiana Tech														
2004	CAL	W	5		18	4	14	0	.222					
GARY DURCHIK Durchik, Gary B: 5/30/1944 Martinsville, VA Miami (Ohio)														
1985	MTL	E	2/1	2/2	2	2	0	0	1.000	2	1	1	0	.500
1986	MTL	E	3		18	4	14	0	.222					
2	Years				20	6	14	0	.300	2	1	1	0	.500
JIM EDDY Eddy, Jim F. B: 5/2/1936 Checotah, OK New Mexico State														
1977	SAS	W	4		16	8	8	0	.500					
1978	SAS	W	5/5	1/2	5	0	5	0	.000					
1981	MTL	E	3/3	2/2	6	2	4	0	.333	1	0	1	0	.000
3	Years				27	10	17	0	.370	1	0	1	0	.000
DANNY EDWARDS Edwards, Daniel Moody B: 7/18/1926 Osage, TX D: 8/7/2001 Gatesville, TX Georgia														
1958	BC	W	5/5	3/3	11	3	8	0	.273					
GARY ETCHEVERRY Etcheverry, Gary J. B: 11/17/1956 Lynwood, CA Southern California														
2002	TOR	E	3/2	1/2	12	4	8	0	.333					
SAM ETCHEVERRY Etcheverry, Samuel (The Rifle) B: 5/20/1930 Carlsbad, NM D: 8/29/2009 Canada Denver														
1970	MTL	E	3		14	7	6	1	.536	4	4	0	0	1.000
1971	MTL	E	4		14	6	8	0	.429					
1972	MTL	E	3		14	4	10	0	.286	1	0	1	0	.000
3	Years				42	17	24	1	.417	5	4	1	0	.800
JOE FARAGALLI Faragalli, Joseph A. B: 4/18/1929 Philadelphia, PA D: 4/10/2006 Villanova														
1981	SAS	W	4		16	9	7	0	.563					
1982	SAS	W	5		16	6	9	1	.406					
1983	SAS	W	5/5	1/2	6	1	5	0	.167					
1987	EDM	W	1/2	2/2	16	9	7	0	.563	3	3	0	0	1.000
1988	EDM	W	1		18	11	7	0	.611	1	0	1	0	.000
1989	EDM	W	1		18	16	2	0	.889	1	0	1	0	.000
1990	EDM	W	2		18	10	8	0	.556	3	2	1	0	.667
1991	OTT	E	3/3	2/2	14	7	7	0	.500	1	0	1	0	.000
8	Years				122	69	52	1	.570	9	5	4	0	.556
MIKE FARAGALLI Faragalli, Mike B: 11/5/1956 Philadelphia, PA Rhode Island														
1995	TOR	N	6/7	1/2	9	2	7	0	.222					
FRANK FILCHOCK Filchock, Frank Joseph B: 10/8/1916 Crucible, PA D: 6/20/1994 Washington County, OR Indiana														
1947	HAM	I	4/4	2/2	6	1	4	1	.250					
1952	EDM	W	2		16	9	6	1	.594	6	3	3	0	.500
1953	SAS	W	2		16	8	7	1	.531	2	1	1	0	.500
1954	SAS	W	2		16	10	4	2	.688	2	0	1	1	.250
1955	SAS	W	2		16	10	6	0	.625	2	1	1	0	.500
1956	SAS	W	2		16	10	6	0	.625	5	2	3	0	.400
1957	SAS	W	5		16	3	12	1	.219					
7	Years				102	51	45	6	.505	17	7	9	1	.441
JIM FINKS Finks, James Edward B: 8/31/1927 St. Louis, MO D: 5/8/1994 New Orleans, LA Tulsa														
1960	CAL	W	5/3	2/3	1	0	1	0	.000					
SAM FOX Fox, Samuel S. B: 5/14/1918 Washington, DC D: 4/11/2004 Kendall, FL Ohio State														
1947	OTT	I	1		12	8	4	0	.667	2	0	2	0	.000
GEORGE FRASER Fraser, George Henry B: 2/2/1911 Stanley, Scotland D: 12/9/1992 Ottawa Gladstone Jrs.														
1946	OTT	I	3		12	6	4	2	.583					
JOE GALAT Galat, Joseph J. B: 4/22/1939 Gresson, PA Miami (Ohio)														
1982	MTL	E	4		16	2	14	0	.125					
1983	MTL	E	4		16	5	10	1	.344					
1984	MTL	E	2		16	6	9	1	.406	1	0	1	0	.000
1985	MTL	E	2/1	1/2	14	6	8	0	.429					
1989	BC	W	4/4	2/2	14	7	7	0	.500					
5	Years				76	26	48	2	.355	1	0	1	0	.000
JIM GILSTRAP Gilstrap, James Patrick B: 5/11/1942 South Bend, IN D: 7/19/2007 Corvallis, OR Western Michigan														
1995	OTT	N	8		18	3	15	0	.167					
1996	OTT	E	3/4	1/2	2	0	2	0	.000					
2	Years				20	3	17	0	.150					
FREDDY GLICK Glick, Freddy Couture B: 2/25/1937 Aurora, CO Colorado State														
1987	OTT	E	4		18	3	15	0	.167					
1988	OTT	E	4/4	1/2	3	0	3	0	.000					
2	Years				21	3	18	0	.143					
FRANK GNUP Gnup, Frank Theodore B: 1917 Aliquippa, PA D: 9/27/1976 Vancouver, BC Manhattan														
1948	HAM	I	4		12	1	10	1	.125					
1949	HAM	I	4		12	0	12	0	.000					
2	Years				24	1	22	1	.063					
STEVE GOLDMAN Goldman, Steven B: 2/8/1945 Colorado State														
1989	OTT	E	4		18	4	14	0	.222					
1990	OTT	E	3		18	7	11	0	.389	1	0	1	0	.000
1991	OTT	E	3/3	1/2	4	0	4	0	.000					
3	Years				40	11	29	0	.275	1	0	1	0	.000
JACK GOTTA Gotta, John C. B: 11/14/1930 Bessemer, MI Minnesota State-Moorhead; Oregon State														
1970	OTT	E	4		14	4	10	0	.286					
1971	OTT	E	3		14	6	8	0	.429	1	0	1	0	.000
1972	OTT	E	1		14	11	3	0	.786	3	2	1	0	.667
1973	OTT	E	1		14	9	5	0	.643	2	2	0	0	1.000
1977	CAL	W	5		16	4	12	0	.250					
1978	CAL	W	2		16	9	4	3	.656	2	1	1	0	.500
1979	CAL	W	2		16	12	4	0	.750	2	1	1	0	.500

YEAR	TEAM	LCD	FIN	SEQ	G	W	L	T	PCT	PG	PW	PL	PT	PPCT
1982	CAL	W	3		16	9	6	1	.594	1	0	1	0	.000
1983	CAL	W	4		16	8	8	0	.500					
1985	SAS	W	4		16	5	11	0	.313					
1986	SAS	W	5		18	6	11	1	.361					
11	Years				170	83	82	5	.503	11	6	5	0	.545
BUD GRANT Grant, Harold Peter B: 5/20/1927 Superior, WI Minnesota														
1957	WPG	W	2		16	12	4	0	.750	6	3	2	1	.583
1958	WPG	W	1		16	13	3	0	.813	4	3	1	0	.750
1959	WPG	W	1		16	12	4	0	.750	3	3	0	0	1.000
1960	WPG	W	1		16	14	2	0	.875	3	1	2	0	.333
1961	WPG	W	1		16	13	3	0	.813	3	3	0	0	1.000
1962	WPG	W	1		16	11	5	0	.688	4	3	1	0	.750
1963	WPG	W	4		16	7	9	0	.438					
1964	WPG	W	5		16	1	14	1	.094					
1965	WPG	W	2		16	11	5	0	.688	5	3	2	0	.600
1966	WPG	W	2		16	8	7	1	.531	3	1	2	0	.333
10	Years				160	102	56	2	.644	31	20	10	1	.661
FRED GRANT Grant, Fred W. B: 1/20/1925 Christiansburg, VA D: 8/3/1993 Atlanta, GA Wake Forrest; Alabama														
1947	REG	W	3/3	2/2	3	2	1	0	.667					
1948	SAS	W	2		12	3	9	0	.250	2	0	1	1	.250
1949	SAS	W	2		14	9	5	0	.643	3	1	2	0	.333
1950	SAS	W	2		14	7	7	0	.500	1	0	1	0	.000
4	Years				43	21	22	0	.488	6	1	4	1	.250
FORREST GREGG Gregg, Alvis Forrest B: 10/18/1933 Birthright, TX Southern Methodist														
1979	TOR	E	4		16	5	11	0	.313					
1994	SHR	E	6		18	3	15	0	.167					
1995	SHR	S	5		18	5	13	0	.278					
3	Years				52	13	39	0	.250					
JOHN GREGORY Gregory, John B: 11/22/1938 Webster City, IA Northern Iowa														
1987	SAS	W	4		18	5	12	1	.306					
1988	SAS	W	2		18	11	7	0	.611	1	0	1	0	.000
1989	SAS	W	3		18	9	9	0	.500	3	3	0	0	1.000
1990	SAS	W	3		18	9	9	0	.500	1	0	1	0	.000
1991	SAS	W	4/4	1/2	7	1	6	0	.143					
1991	HAM	E	4/4	2/2	11	3	8	0	.273					
1992	HAM	E	2		18	11	7	0	.611	2	1	1	0	.500
1993	HAM	E	2		18	6	12	0	.333	2	1	1	0	.500
1994	HAM	E	5		18	4	14	0	.222					
9	Years				144	59	84	1	.413	9	5	4	0	.556
DEAN GRIFFING Griffing, O. Dean B: 5/17/1913 St. George, KS D: 2/9/1998 Sarasota County, FL Kansas State														
1946	CAL	W	1		8	5	3	0	.625	2	1	1	0	.500
1947	CAL	W	2		8	4	4	0	.500	3	1	2	0	.333
2	Years				16	9	7	0	.563	5	2	3	0	.400
RICHIE HALL Hall, Richard Harold, Jr. B: 10/4/1960 San Antonio, TX Colorado State														
2009	EDM	W	3		18	9	9	0	.500	1	0	1	0	.000
2010	EDM	W	4		18	7	11	0	.389					
2	Years				36	16	20	0	.444	1	0	1	0	.000
LEW HAYMAN Hayman, Louis Edward B: 9/30/1908 Paterson, NJ D: 6/29/1984 Toronto, ON Syracuse														
1946	MTL	I	1		12	7	3	2	.667	1	0	1	0	.000
1947	MTL	I	3		12	6	6	0	.500					
1948	MTL	I	2		12	7	5	0	.583	2	1	1	0	.500
1949	MTL	I	2		12	8	4	0	.667	4	4	0	0	1.000
1950	MTL	I	3		12	6	6	0	.500					
1951	MTL	I	4		12	3	9	0	.250					
6	Years				72	37	33	2	.528	7	5	2	0	.714
JACK HENNEMIER Hennemier, John M. B: 2/13/1913 Savannah, GA D: 11/4/1993 Rock Hill, SC Duke														
1955	CAL	W	5		16	4	12	0	.250					
1956	CAL	W	4/5	1/2	8	3	5	0	.375					
2	Years				24	7	17	0	.292					
TOM HIGGINS Higgins, Thomas Joseph John, Jr. B: 7/13/1954 Newark, NJ North Carolina State														
2001	EDM	W	1		18	9	9	0	.500	1	0	1	0	.000
2002	EDM	W	1		18	13	5	0	.722	2	1	1	0	.500
2003	EDM	W	1		18	13	5	0	.722	2	2	0	0	1.000
2004	EDM	W	2		18	9	9	0	.500	1	0	1	0	.000
2005	CAL	W	2		18	11	7	0	.611	1	0	1	0	.000
2006	CAL	W	2		18	10	8	0	.556	1	0	1	0	.000
2007	CAL	W	3		18	7	10	1	.417	1	0	1	0	.000
7	Years				126	72	53	1	.575	9	3	6	0	.333
GARY HOFFMAN Hoffman, Gary B: 2/22/1944 Olivia, MN Westmar														
1998	WPG	E	4/4	2/2	4	1	3	0	.250					
JOHN HUARD Huard, John Roland B: 3/9/1944 Waterville, ME Maine														
2000	TOR	E	4/4	1/2	8	1	6	1	.188					
TOMMY HUDSPETH Hudspeth, Tommy Joe B: 9/14/1931 Cherryvale, KS Tulsa														
1981	TOR	E	4/4	2/2	6	2	4	0	.333					
JOHN HUFNAGEL Hufnagel, John Coleman B: 9/13/1951 Coraopolis, PA Penn State														
2008	CAL	W	1		18	13	5	0	.722	2	2	0	0	1.000
2009	CAL	W	2		18	10	7	1	.583	2	1	1	0	.500
2010	CAL	W	1		18	13	5	0	.722	1	0	1	0	.000
2011	CAL	W	3		18	11	7	0	.611	1	0	1	0	.000
4	Years				72	47	24	1	.660	6	3	3	0	.500
POP IVY Ivy, Lee Frank B: 1/25/1916 Skiatook, OK D: 5/17/2003 Norman, OK Oklahoma														
1954	EDM	W	1		16	11	5	0	.688	5	4	1	0	.800
1955	EDM	W	1		16	14	2	0	.875	3	3	0	0	1.000
1956	EDM	W	1		16	11	5	0	.688	4	3	1	0	.750
1957	EDM	W	1		16	14	2	0	.875	3	1	2	0	.333
4	Years				64	50	14	0	.781	15	11	4	0	.733
RUSS JACKSON Jackson, Russ B: 7/28/1936 Hamilton, ON McMaster														
1975	TOR	E	4		16	5	10	1	.344					
1976	TOR	E	4		16	7	8	1	.469					
2	Years				32	12	18	2	.406					
RAY JAUCH Jauch, Raymond Andrew B: 2/11/1938 Sublette, IL Iowa														
1970	EDM	W	2		16	9	7	0	.563	1	0	1	0	.000
1971	EDM	W	5		16	6	10	0	.375					
1972	EDM	W	2		16	10	6	0	.625	1	0	1	0	.000
1973	EDM	W	1		16	9	5	2	.625	2	1	1	0	.500
1974	EDM	W	1		16	10	5	1	.656	2	1	1	0	.500
1975	EDM	W	1		16	12	4	0	.750	2	2	0	0	1.000
1976	EDM	W	3		16	9	6	1	.594	2	1	1	0	.500
1978	WPG	W	3		16	9	7	0	.563	1	0	1	0	.000
1979	WPG	W	4		16	4	12	0	.250					
1980	WPG	W	2		16	10	6	0	.625	2	1	1	0	.500
1981	WPG	W	2		16	11	5	0	.688	1	0	1	0	.000

YEAR	TEAM	LCD	FIN	SEQ	G	W	L	T	PCT	PG	PW	PL	PT	PPCT
1982	WPG	W	2		16	11	5	0	.688	2	1	1	0	.500
1994	SAS	W	4		18	11	7	0	.611	1	0	1	0	.000
1995	SAS	N	6		18	6	12	0	.333					
14	Years				228	127	97	4	.566	17	7	10	0	.412
MIKE KELLY Kelly, Mike B: 2/11/1958 Waterbury, CT Bluffton														
2009	WPG	E	3		18	7	11	0	.389					
PETE KETTELA Kettela, Peter P. B: 5/28/1938 Buffalo, NY UC Riverside														
1983	EDM	W	4/3	1/2	8	4	4	0	.500					
EAGLE KEYS Keys, Eagle (Buddy) B: 12/4/1923 Western Kentucky														
1959	EDM	W	2		16	10	6	0	.625	4	2	2	0	.500
1960	EDM	W	2		16	10	6	0	.625	6	4	2	0	.667
1961	EDM	W	2		16	10	5	1	.656	2	1	1	0	.500
1962	EDM	W	5		16	6	9	1	.406					
1963	EDM	W	5		16	2	14	0	.125					
1965	SAS	W	3		16	8	7	1	.531	1	0	1	0	.000
1966	SAS	W	1		16	9	6	1	.594	3	3	0	0	1.000
1967	SAS	W	1		16	12	4	0	.750	5	3	2	0	.600
1968	SAS	W	1		16	12	3	1	.781	2	0	2	0	.000
1969	SAS	W	1		16	13	3	0	.813	3	2	1	0	.667
1970	SAS	W	1		16	14	2	0	.875	3	1	2	0	.333
1971	BC	W	4		16	6	9	1	.406					
1972	BC	W	5		16	5	11	0	.313					
1973	BC	W	3		16	5	9	2	.375	1	0	1	0	.000
1974	BC	W	3		16	8	8	0	.500	1	0	1	0	.000
1975	BC	W	5/4	1/2	6	1	5	0	.167					
16	Years				246	131	107	8	.549	31	16	15	0	.516
LARY KUHARICH Kuharich, Joseph Lawrence, Jr. B: 12/20/1945 Middletown, NY Boston College														
1987	CAL	W	4/3	2/2	10	8	2	0	.800	1	0	1	0	.000
1988	CAL	W	4		18	6	12	0	.333					
1989	CAL	W	2		18	10	8	0	.556	1	0	1	0	.000
1990	BC	W	4/4	1/2	10	2	7	1	.250					
4	Years				56	26	29	1	.473	2	0	2	0	.000
FRANK KUSH Frank Jospeh B: 1/20/1929 Winber, PA Michigan State														
1981	HAM	E	1		16	11	4	1	.719	1	0	1	0	.000
RON LANCASTER Ronald B: 10/14/1938 Fairchance, PA D: 9/18/2008 Hamilton, ON Wittenberg														
1979	SAS	W	5		16	2	14	0	.125					
1980	SAS	W	5		16	2	14	0	.125					
1991	EDM	W	1		18	12	6	0	.667	1	0	1	0	.000
1992	EDM	W	2		18	10	8	0	.556	2	1	1	0	.500
1993	EDM	W	2		18	12	6	0	.667	3	3	0	0	1.000
1994	EDM	W	2		18	13	5	0	.722	1	0	1	0	.000
1995	EDM	N	2		18	13	5	0	.722	2	1	1	0	.500
1996	EDM	W	2		18	11	7	0	.611	3	2	1	0	.667
1997	EDM	W	1		18	12	6	0	.667	1	0	1	0	.000
1998	HAM	E	1		18	12	5	1	.694	2	1	1	0	.500
1999	HAM	E	2		18	11	7	0	.611	3	3	0	0	1.000
2000	HAM	E	2		18	9	9	0	.500	1	0	1	0	.000
2001	HAM	E	2		18	11	7	0	.611	2	1	1	0	.500
2002	HAM	E	3		18	7	11	0	.389					
2003	HAM	E	4		18	1	17	0	.056					
15	Years				266	138	127	1	.521	21	12	9	0	.571
PAUL LaPOLICE Paul J. B: 6/12/1970 Plymouth State														
2010	WPG	E	4		18	4	14	0	.222					
2011	WPG	E	1		18	10	8	0	.556	2	1	1	0	.500
2	Years				36	14	22	0	.389	2	1	1	0	.500
FRANK LARSON Frank G. (Butch) B: 5/30/1912 D: 9/1/1983 International Falls, MN Minnesota														
1949	WPG	W	4		14	2	12	0	.143					
1950	WPG	W	1		14	10	4	0	.714	4	2	2	0	.500
2	Years				28	12	16	0	.429	4	2	2	0	.500
LES LEAR Leslie (Butch) B: 8/22/1918 Grafton, ND D: 1/5/1979 Dade County, FL Winnipeg Victorias Jrs.; Manitoba														
1948	CAL	W	1		12	12	0	0	1.000	3	2	0	1	.833
1949	CAL	W	1		14	13	1	0	.929	4	2	2	0	.500
1950	CAL	W	4		14	4	10	0	.286					
1951	CAL	W	4		14	4	10	0	.286					
1952	CAL	W	3		16	7	9	0	.438	2	1	1	0	.500
5	Years				70	40	30	0	.571	9	5	3	1	.611
MARV LEVY Marvin Daniel B: 8/3/1925 Chicago, IL Coe														
1973	MTL	E	3		14	7	6	1	.536	2	1	1	0	.500
1974	MTL	E	1		16	9	5	2	.625	2	2	0	0	1.000
1975	MTL	E	2		16	9	7	0	.563	3	2	1	0	.667
1976	MTL	E	3		16	7	8	1	.469	1	0	1	0	.000
1977	MTL	E	1		16	11	5	0	.688	2	2	0	0	1.000
5	Years				78	43	31	4	.577	10	7	3	0	.700
SAM LYLE Melvin E. B: 6/18/1924 D: 5/30/2007 Atlanta, GA Louisiana State														
1958	EDM	W	2		16	9	6	1	.594	5	3	2	0	.600
DANNY MACIOCIA Dan B: 5/26/1967 Montreal, QC Texas Christian														
2005	EDM	W	3		18	11	7	0	.611	3	3	0	0	1.000
2006	EDM	W	4		18	7	11	0	.389					
2007	EDM	W	4		18	5	12	1	.306					
2008	EDM	W	4		18	10	8	0	.556	2	1	1	0	.500
4	Years				72	33	38	1	.465	5	4	1	0	.800
GREG MARSHALL Gregory D. B: 4/16/1959 Guelph, ON Western Ontario														
2004	HAM	E	3		18	9	8	1	.528	1	0	1	0	.000
2005	HAM	E	4		18	5	13	0	.278					
2006	HAM	E	4		18	4	14	0	.222					
2011	SAS	W	4/4	1/2	8	1	7	0	.125					
4	Years				62	19	42	1	.315	1	0	1	0	.000
ART MASSUCCI Arthur Joseph B: 2/9/1905 D: 12/3/1995 Detroit, MI Detroit Mercy														
1946	HAM	I	4		12	0	10	2	.083					
WALT MASTERS Walter Thomas B: 3/28/1907 Pen Argyl, PA D: 7/10/1992 Ottawa, ON Pennsylvania														
1948	OTT	I	1		12	10	2	0	.833	4	2	2	0	.500
1949	OTT	I	1		12	11	1	0	.917	2	0	2	0	.000
1950	OTT	I	4		12	4	7	1	.375					
4	Years				36	25	10	1	.708	6	2	4	0	.333
DON MATTHEWS Donald John B: 6/22/1939 Amesbury, MA Idaho														
1983	BC	W	1		16	11	5	0	.688	2	1	1	0	.500
1984	BC	W	1		16	12	3	1	.781	1	0	1	0	.000
1985	BC	W	1		16	13	3	0	.813	2	2	0	0	1.000
1986	BC	W	2		18	12	6	0	.667	2	1	1	0	.500
1987	BC	W	1/1	1/2	14	8	6	0	.571					
1990	TOR	E	2		18	10	8	0	.556	2	1	1	0	.500
1991	SAS	W	4/4	2/2	11	5	6	0	.455					

YEAR	TEAM	LCD	FIN	SEQ	G	W	L	T	PCT	PG	PW	PL	PT	PPCT
1992	SAS	W	3		18	9	9	0	.500	1	0	1	0	.000
1993	SAS	W	3		18	11	7	0	.611	1	0	1	0	.000
1994	BAL	E	2		18	12	6	0	.667	3	2	1	0	.667
1995	BAL	S	1		18	15	3	0	.833	3	3	0	0	1.000
1996	TOR	E	1		18	15	3	0	.833	2	2	0	0	1.000
1997	TOR	E	1		18	15	3	0	.833	2	2	0	0	1.000
1998	TOR	E	3		18	9	9	0	.500	1	0	1	0	.000
1999	EDM	W	3		18	6	12	0	.333	1	0	1	0	.000
2000	EDM	W	2		18	10	8	0	.556					
2002	MTL	E	1		18	13	5	0	.722	2	2	0	0	1.000
2003	MTL	E	1		18	13	5	0	.722	2	1	1	0	.500
2004	MTL	E	1		18	14	4	0	.778	1	0	1	0	.000
2005	MTL	E	2		18	10	8	0	.556	3	2	1	0	.667
2006	MTL	E	1/1	1/2	14	8	6	0	.571					
2008	TOR	E	2/3	2/2	8	0	8	0	.000					
22	Years				365	231	133	1	.634	31	19	12	0	.613
DENNIS MEYER Meyer, John Dennis B: 4/8/1950 Jefferson City, MO Arkansas State														
1992	TOR	E	/4	2/2	8	3	5	0	.375					
1993	TOR	E	4		18	3	15	0	.167					
2	Years				26	6	20	0	.231					
RON MEYER Meyer, Ronald Shaw B: 2/17/1941 Columbus, OH Purdue														
1994	LV	W	6		18	5	13	0	.278					
KEN MILLER Miller, Ken B: 10/15/1941														
2008	SAS	W	2		18	12	6	0	.667	1	0	1	0	.000
2009	SAS	W	1		18	10	7	1	.583	2	1	1	0	.500
2010	SAS	W	2		18	10	8	0	.556	3	2	1	0	.667
2011	SAS	W	4/4	2/2	10	4	6	0	.400					
3	Years				64	36	27	1	.570	6	3	3	0	.500
GREG MOHNS Mohns, Gregory Ross B: 5/1/1950 Pasadena, CA Bradley; Baker														
1998	BC	W	3/3	2/2	9	6	3	0	.667	1	0	1	0	.000
1999	BC	W	1		18	13	5	0	.722	1	0	1	0	.000
2000	BC	W	3/3	1/2	7	3	4	0	.429	1	0	1	0	.000
3	Years				34	22	12	0	.647	3	0	3	0	.000
TED MORRIS Morris, Allan Byron B: 3//1910 Toronto, ON D: 9/5/1965 Malton, ON Winnipeg Native Sons Jrs.														
1946	TOR	I	2		12	7	3	2	.667	3	3	0	0	1.000
1947	TOR	I	2		12	7	4	1	.625	4	4	0	0	1.000
1948	TOR	I	3		12	5	6	1	.458					
1949	TOR	I	3		12	5	7	0	.417					
4	Years				48	24	20	4	.542	7	7	0	0	1.000
JOE MOSS Moss, Joseph Charles B: 4/9/1930 Elkins, WV Maryland														
1974	TOR	E	2/4	2/2	9	3	5	1	.389					
1985	OTT	E	3		16	7	9	0	.438	1	0	1	0	.000
1986	OTT	E	3/4	1/2	13	3	10	0	.231					
3	Years				38	13	24	1	.355	1	0	1	0	.000
PERRY MOSS Moss, Perry Lee B: 8/4/1926 Tulsa, OK Tulsa; Illinois														
1960	MTL	I	3		14	5	9	0	.357	1	0	1	0	.000
1961	MTL	E	4		14	4	9	1	.321					
1962	MTL	E	3		14	4	7	3	.393	3	1	2	0	.333
3	Years				42	13	25	4	.357	4	1	3	0	.250
DARRELL MUDRA Mudra, Darrell E. B: 1/4/1929 Omaha, NE Peru State														
1966	MTL	E	3		14	7	7	0	.500	1	0	1	0	.000
ANDY MULLAN Mullan, Andy (Moon) B: 1908 Syracuse														
1947	HAM	E	4/4	1/2	6	1	5	0	.167					
CAL MURPHY Murphy, Clarence B: 3/12/1932 Winnipeg, MB D: 2/18/2012 Regina, SK Vancouver CYO Red Raiders Jrs.; British Columbia														
1975	BC	W	5/4	2/2	10	5	5	0	.500					
1976	BC	W	4		16	5	9	2	.375					
1983	WPG	W	2		16	9	7	0	.563	2	1	1	0	.500
1984	WPG	W	2		16	11	4	1	.719	3	3	0	0	1.000
1985	WPG	W	2		16	12	4	0	.750	2	1	1	0	.500
1986	WPG	W	3		18	11	7	0	.611	1	0	1	0	.000
1993	WPG	E	1		18	14	4	0	.778	2	1	1	0	.500
1994	WPG	E	1		18	13	5	0	.722	2	1	1	0	.500
1995	WPG	N	5		18	7	11	0	.389	1	0	1	0	.000
1996	WPG	W	3		18	9	9	0	.500	1	0	1	0	.000
1999	SAS	W	4		18	3	15	0	.167					
11	Years				182	99	80	3	.552	14	7	7	0	.500
BOB O'BILLOVICH O'Billovich, Robert B: 6/30/1940 Butte, MT Montana														
1982	TOR	E	1		16	9	6	1	.594	2	1	1	0	.500
1983	TOR	E	1		16	12	4	0	.750	2	2	0	0	1.000
1984	TOR	E	1		16	9	6	1	.594	1	0	1	0	.000
1985	TOR	E	4		16	6	10	0	.375					
1986	TOR	E	1		18	10	8	0	.556	2	1	1	0	.500
1987	TOR	E	2		18	11	6	1	.639	3	2	1	0	.667
1988	TOR	E	1		18	14	4	0	.778	1	0	1	0	.000
1989	TOR	E	2		18	7	11	0	.389	1	0	1	0	.000
1990	BC	W	4/4	2/2	8	4	4	0	.500					
1991	BC	W	3		18	11	7	0	.611	1	0	1	0	.000
1992	BC	W	4		18	3	15	0	.167					
1994	TOR	E	3		18	7	11	0	.389	1	0	1	0	.000
1995	TOR	N	6/7	2/2	9	2	7	0	.222					
13	Years				207	105	99	3	.514	14	6	8	0	.429
STEVE OWEN Owen, Stephen Joseph (Stout Steve) B: 4/21/1898 Cleo Springs, OK D: 5/17/1964 Onedia, NY Phillips														
1959	TOR	I	3/4	2/2	7	2	5	0	.286					
1960	CAL	W	5/3	3/3	12	6	5	1	.542	2	0	2	0	.000
1961	SAS	W	4		16	5	10	1	.344					
1962	SAS	W	3		16	8	7	1	.531	2	0	2	0	.000
3	Years				51	21	27	3	.441	4	0	4	0	.000
JOE PAOPAO Paopao, Joseph B: 6/30/1955 Honolulu, HI Mira Costa JC; Long Beach State														
1996	BC	W	4		18	5	13	0	.278					
2002	OTT	E	4		18	4	14	0	.222					
2003	OTT	E	3		18	7	11	0	.389					
2004	OTT	E	4		18	5	13	0	.278					
2005	OTT	E	3		18	7	11	0	.389	1	0	1	0	.000
5	Years				90	28	62	0	.311	1	0	1	0	.000
JACK PARDEE John Perry B: 4/19/1936 Exira, IA Texas A&M														
1995	BIR	S	3		18	10	8	0	.556	1	0	1	0	.000
JACKIE PARKER Jack Dickenson B: 8/3/1932 Knoxville, TN D: 11/7/2006 Edmoton, AB Jones County JC; Mississippi State														
1969	BC	W	5/3	2/2	6	4	2	0	.667	1	0	1	0	.000
1970	BC	W	4		16	6	10	0	.375					
1983	EDM	W	4/3	2/2	8	4	4	0	.500	1	0	1	0	.000
1984	EDM	W	3		16	9	7	0	.563	1	0	1	0	.000
1985	EDM	W	3		16	10	6	0	.625	1	0	1	0	.000

YEAR	TEAM	LCD	FIN	SEQ	G	W	L	T	PCT	PG	PW	PL	PT	PPCT
1986	EDM	W	1		18	13	4	1	.750	3	2	1	0	.667
1987	EDM	W	1/2	1/2	2	2	0	0	1.000					
7	Years				82	48	33	1	.591	8	2	6	0	.250
JOHN PAYNE John D. B: 5/15/1933 Schoolton, OK Oklahoma State														
1973	SAS	W	2		16	10	6	0	.625	2	1	1	0	.500
1974	SAS	W	2		16	9	7	0	.563	2	1	1	0	.500
1975	SAS	W	2		16	10	5	1	.656	2	1	1	0	.500
1976	SAS	W	1		16	11	5	0	.688	2	1	1	0	.500
1978	HAM	E	4/3	2/2	11	4	7	0	.364	1	0	1	0	.000
1979	HAM	E	3		16	6	10	0	.375	1	0	1	0	.000
1980	HAM	E	1		16	8	7	1	.531	2	1	1	0	.500
1996	OTT	E	3/4	2/2	16	3	13	0	.188					
8	Years				123	61	60	2	.504	12	5	7	0	.417
HAMP POOL John Hampton B: 3/11/1915 D: 5/26/2000 Mariposa, CA California; Army; Stanford														
1957	TOR	I	4		14	4	10	0	.286					
1958	TOR	I	4		14	4	10	0	.286					
1959	TOR	I	3/4	1/2	7	2	5	0	.286					
3	Years				35	10	25	0	.286					
JIM POPP James Thomas B: 12/21/1964 Elkin, NC Michigan State														
2001	MTL	E	3/3	2/2	1	0	1	0	.000	1	0	1	0	.000
2006	MTL	E	1/1	2/2	4	2	2	0	.500	2	1	1	0	.500
2007	MTL	E	3		18	8	10	0	.444	1	0	1	0	.000
3	Years				23	10	13	0	.434	4	1	3	0	.250
WALT POSADOWSKI Posadowski, Walter J. B: 11/17/1937 Villanova														
1978	SAS	W	5/5	2/2	11	4	6	1	.409					
KEN PRESTON Preston, Kenneth Joseph B: 10/19/1917 Portland, ON Smith Falls, ON D: 8/2/1991 Queen's														
1946	REG	W	3		8	2	6	0	.250					
1947	REG	W	3/3	1/2	5	1	4	0	.200					
2	Years				13	3	10	0	.231					
BOB PRICE Bob B: 7/24/1955 New York, NY Idaho State; Cal Poly (Pomona)														
1996	MTL	E	2		18	12	6	0	.667	2	1	1	0	.500
VIC RAPP Victor M. B: 12/23/1935 Marionville, MO Missouri State														
1977	BC	W	2		16	10	6	0	.625	2	1	1	0	.500
1978	BC	W	4		16	7	7	2	.500					
1979	BC	W	3		16	9	6	1	.594	1	0	1	0	.000
1980	BC	W	4		16	8	7	1	.531					
1981	BC	W	3		16	10	6	0	.625	2	1	1	0	.500
1982	BC	W	4		16	9	7	0	.563					
6	Years				96	53	39	4	.573	5	2	3	0	.400
JOHN RAUCH John M. B: 8/20/1927 Philadelphia, PA D: 6/10/2008 Oldsmar, FL Georgia														
1973	TOR	E	2		14	7	5	2	.571	1	0	1	0	.000
1974	TOR	E	2/4	1/2	7	3	4	0	.429					
2	Years				21	10	9	2	.524	1	0	1	0	.000
KAVIS REED Kavis Darick B: 2/24/1973 Georgetown, SC Furman														
2011	EDM	W	2		18	11	7	0	.611	2	1	1	0	.500
JEFF REINEBOLD Jeffrey D. B: 11/19/1957 South Bend, IN Maine														
1997	WPG	E	3		18	4	14	0	.222					
1998	WPG	E	4/4	1/2	14	2	12	0	.143					
2	Years				32	6	26	0	.188					
JOE RESTIC Restic, Joseph William B: 7/21/1927 Hastings, PA St. Francis; Villanova														
1968	HAM	E	3		14	6	7	1	.464	1	0	1	0	.000
1969	HAM	E	3		14	8	5	1	.607	1	0	1	0	.000
1970	HAM	E	1		14	8	5	1	.607	2	0	2	0	.000
3	Years				42	22	17	3	.560	4	0	4	0	.000
BUD RILEY Riley, Edward J., Jr. B: 111/30/1925 Guin, AL Idaho														
1974	WPG	W	4		16	8	8	0	.500					
1975	WPG	W	3		16	6	8	2	.438	1	0	1	0	.000
1976	WPG	W	2		16	10	6	0	.625	1	0	1	0	.000
1977	WPG	W	3		16	10	6	0	.625	1	0	1	0	.000
1978	TOR	E	3/4	2/2	7	1	6	0	.143					
1982	HAM	E	2		16	8	7	1	.531	1	0	1	0	.000
1983	HAM	E	3/3	1/2	12	4	8	0	.333					
1985	CAL	W	5/5	2/2	11	3	8	0	.273					
8	Years				110	50	57	3	.468	4	0	4	0	.000
MIKE RILEY Riley, Michael Joseph B: 7/6/1953 Wallace, ID Alabama														
1987	WPG	E	1		18	12	6	0	.667	1	0	1	0	.000
1988	WPG	E	2		18	9	9	0	.500	3	3	0	0	1.000
1989	WPG	E	3		18	7	11	0	.389	2	1	1	0	.500
1990	WPG	E	1		18	12	6	0	.667	2	2	0	0	1.000
4	Years				72	40	32	0	.556	8	6	2	0	.750
ADAM RITA Rita, Adam B: 9/21/1947 Honolulu, HI Boise State														
1991	TOR	E	1		18	13	5	0	.722	2	2	0	0	1.000
1992	TOR	E	/4	1/2	10	3	7	0	.300					
1994	OTT	E	4		18	4	14	0	.222	1	0	1	0	.000
1997	BC	W	3		18	8	10	0	.444	1	0	1	0	.000
1998	BC	W	3/3	1/2	9	3	6	0	.333					
2002	BC	W	4/3	2/2	12	9	3	0	.750	1	0	1	0	.000
6	Years				85	40	45	0	.471	5	2	3	0	.400
DAVE RITCHIE Ritchie, David F., II B: 9/3/1938 New Bedford, MA Cincinnati														
1993	BC	W	4		18	10	8	0	.556	1	0	1	0	.000
1994	BC	W	3		18	11	6	1	.639	3	3	0	0	1.000
1995	BC	N	3		18	10	8	0	.556	1	0	1	0	.000
1997	MTL	E	2		18	13	5	0	.722	2	1	1	0	.500
1998	MTL	E	2		18	12	5	1	.694	2	1	1	0	.500
1999	WPG	E	4		18	6	12	0	.333					
2000	WPG	E	3		18	7	10	1	.417	2	1	1	0	.500
2001	WPG	E	1		18	14	4	0	.778	2	1	1	0	.500
2002	WPG	W	2		18	12	6	0	.667	2	1	1	0	.500
2003	WPG	W	2		18	11	7	0	.611	1	0	1	0	.000
2004	WPG	W	4/4	1/2	7	2	5	0	.286					
11	Years				187	108	76	3	.586	16	8	8	0	.500
WAYNE ROBINSON Robinson, Wayne Lavern B: 1/14/1930 Minneapolis, MN Minnesota														
1959	BC	W	3		16	9	7	0	.563	2	0	2	0	.000
1960	BC	W	4		16	5	9	2	.375					
1961	BC	W	5/5	1/2	7	0	6	1	.071					
3	Years				39	14	22	3	.397	2	0	2	0	.000
PEPPER RODGERS Rodgers, Franklin Cullen B: 10/8/1931 Atlanta, GA Georgia Tech														
1995	MEM	S	4		18	9	9	0	.500					
DARRYL ROGERS Rogers, Darryl Dale B: 5/28/1934 Los Angeles, CA Long Beach CC; Fresno State														
1991	WPG	E	2		18	9	9	0	.500	2	1	1	0	.500
DARRELL ROYAL Royal, Darrell K. B: 7/6/1924 Hollis, OK Oklahoma														
1953	EDM	W	1		16	12	4	0	.750	3	1	2	0	.333

YEAR	TEAM	LCD	FIN	SEQ	G	W	L	T	PCT	PG	PW	PL	PT	PPCT
ROD RUST Rust, Rodney A. B: 8/2/1928 Webster City, IA Iowa State														
2001	MTL	E	3/3	1/2	17	9	8	0	.529					
RALPH SAZIO Sazio, Ralph Joseph B: 7/22/1922 Avellino, Italy D: 9/26/2008 Burlington, ON William & Mary														
1963	HAM	E	1		14	10	4	0	.714	3	2	1	0	.667
1964	HAM	E	1		14	10	3	1	.750	3	1	2	0	.333
1965	HAM	E	1		14	10	4	0	.714	3	3	0	0	1.000
1966	HAM	E	2		14	9	5	0	.643	3	1	2	0	.333
1967	HAM	E	1		14	10	4	0	.714	3	3	0	0	1.000
5	Years				70	49	20	1	.707	15	10	5	0	.667
JOE SCANNELLA Joseph L. B: 5/22/1928 Passaic, NJ Lehigh														
1978	MTL	E	2		16	8	7	1	.531	3	2	1	0	.667
1979	MTL	E	1		16	11	4	1	.719	2	1	1	0	.500
1980	MTL	E	2		16	8	8	0	.500	2	1	1	0	.500
1981	MTL	E	3/3	1/2	10	1	9	0	.100					
4	Years				58	28	28	2	.500	7	4	3	0	.571
BOB SHAW Robert B: 5/22/1921 Richwood, OH Ohio State														
1963	SAS	W	3		16	7	7	2	.500	5	2	3	0	.400
1964	SAS	W	3		16	9	7	0	.563	2	1	1	0	.500
1965	TOR	E	4		14	3	11	0	.214					
1966	TOR	E	4		14	5	9	0	.357					
1976	HAM	E	4/2	2/2	14	8	6	0	.571	2	1	1	0	.500
1977	HAM	E	4		16	5	11	0	.313					
6	Years				90	37	51	2	.422	9	4	5	0	.444
ALLIE SHERMAN Alexander (Lefty) B: 2/10/1923 New York, NY Brooklyn														
1954	WPG	W	3		16	8	6	2	.563	5	2	2	1	.500
1955	WPG	W	3		16	7	9	0	.438	4	1	3	0	.250
1956	WPG	W	3		16	9	7	0	.563	2	1	1	0	.500
3	Years				48	24	22	2	.521	11	4	6	1	.409
LARRY SIEMERING Laurence Edwin B: 11/24/1910 San Francisco, CA D: 7/27/2009 Watsonville, CA San Francisco														
1954	CAL	W	4		16	8	8	0	.500					
DAVE SKRIEN David Albert B: 4/4/1929 Brooten, MN D: 11/30/2010 Mound, MN Minnesota														
1961	BC	W	5/5	2/2	9	1	7	1	.167					
1962	BC	W	4		16	7	9	0	.438					
1963	BC	W	1		16	12	4	0	.750	4	2	2	0	.500
1964	BC	W	1		16	11	2	3	.781	4	3	1	0	.750
1965	BC	W	4		16	6	9	1	.406					
1966	BC	W	5		16	5	11	0	.313					
1967	BC	W	5/5	1/2	3	0	3	0	.000					
1971	SAS	W	1		16	9	6	1	.594	3	1	2	0	.333
1972	SAS	W	3		16	8	8	0	.500	3	2	1	0	.667
9	Years				124	59	59	6	.500	14	8	6	0	.571
RON SMELTZER Ronald A. B: 10/29/1941 York, PA West Chester														
1992	OTT	E	3		18	9	9	0	.500	1	0	1	0	.000
1993	OTT	E	3		18	4	14	0	.222	1	0	1	0	.000
2	Years				36	13	23	0	.361	2	0	2	0	.000
HARRY SMITH Harry Elliott B: 8/26/1918 Russellville, MO Southern California														
1951	SAS	W	1		14	8	6	0	.571	4	2	2	0	.500
BOB SNYDER Robert A. B: 2/6/1913 Fremont, OH D: 1/4/2001 Sylvania, OH Ohio University														
1953	CAL	W	4		16	3	12	1	.219					
JIM SPAVITAL James J. B: 9/15/1926 Oklahoma City, OK D: 3/7/1993 Stillwater, OK Oklahoma State														
1970	WPG	W	5		16	2	14	0	.125					
1971	WPG	W	3		16	7	8	1	.469	1	0	1	0	.000
1972	WPG	W	1		16	10	6	0	.625	1	0	1	0	.000
1973	WPG	W	5		16	4	11	1	.281					
4	Years				64	23	39	2	.375	2	0	2	0	.000
KAY STEPHENSON George Kay B: 12/17/1944 DeFuniak Springs, FL Florida														
1993	SAC	W	5		18	6	12	0	.333					
1994	SAC	W	5		18	9	8	1	.528					
1995	SA	S	2		18	12	6	0	.667	2	1	1	0	.500
1998	EDM	W	2		18	9	9	0	.500	2	1	1	0	.500
4	Years				72	36	35	1	.507	4	2	2	0	.500
RICH STUBLER Richard D. B: 8/4/1949 Northern Colorado														
2008	TOR	E	2/3	1/2	10	4	6	0	.400					
ANNIS STUKUS Anicautus Paul B: 10/25/1914 Toronto, ON D: 5/20/2006 Canmore, AB Argos Jrs.														
1949	EDM	W	3		14	4	10	0	.286					
1950	EDM	W	3		14	7	7	0	.500	4	2	2	0	.500
1951	EDM	W	2		14	8	6	0	.571	4	2	2	0	.500
1954	BC	W	5		16	1	15	0	.063					
1955	BC	W	4		16	5	11	0	.313					
5	Years				74	25	49	0	.338	8	4	4	0	.500
DON SUTHERIN Donald Paul B: 2/29/1936 Empire, OH Ohio State														
1995	HAM	N	4		18	8	10	0	.444	1	0	1	0	.000
1996	HAM	E	3		18	8	10	0	.444	1	0	1	0	.000
1997	HAM	E	3/4	1/2	7	1	6	0	.143					
3	Years				43	17	26	0	.395	2	0	2	0	.000
BILL SWIACKI William Adam B: 10/2/1922 Southbridge, MA D: 7/6/1976 Sturbridge, MA Holy Cross; Columbia														
1955	TOR	I	3		12	4	8	0	.333	2	1	1	0	.500
1956	TOR	I	4		14	4	10	0	.286					
2	Years				26	8	18	0	.308	2	1	1	0	.500
CHARLIE TAAFFE Charles P. B: 4/20/1950 Albany, NY Clemson; Siena														
1999	MTL	E	1		18	12	6	0	.667	1	0	1	0	.000
2000	MTL	E	1		18	12	6	0	.667	2	1	1	0	.500
2007	HAM	E	4		18	3	15	0	.167					
2008	HAM	E	3/4	1/2	10	2	8	0	.200					
4	Years				64	29	35	0	.453	3	1	2	9	1.833
GEORGE TERLEP George Rudolph (Duke) B: 4/12/1923 Elkhart, IN D: 5/17/2010 Springhill, FL Notre Dame														
1958	SAS	W	3		16	7	7	2	.500	2	0	2	0	.000
1959	SAS	W	5/5	1/2	9	0	9	0	.000					
2	Years				25	7	16	2	.320	2	0	2	0	.000
JOE TILLER Joseph H. B: 7/12/1942 Toledo, OH Montana State														
1976	CAL	W	5/5	2/2	6	2	3	1	.417					
GEORGE TRAFTON George Edward (Beast) B: 12/6/1896 Chicago, IL D: 9/5/1971 Los Angeles, CA Notre Dame														
1951	WPG	W	3		14	8	6	0	.571	1	0	1	0	.000
1952	WPG	W	1		16	12	3	1	.781	3	1	2	0	.333
1953	WPG	W	3		16	8	8	0	.500	7	4	3	0	.571
3	Years				46	28	17	1	.620	11	5	6	0	.455
MARC TRESTMAN Marc Marlyn B: 1/15/1956 Minneapolis, MN Minnesota; Minnesota State-Moorhead														
2008	MTL	E	1		18	11	7	0	.611	2	1	1	0	.500
2009	MTL	E	1		18	15	3	0	.833	2	2	0	0	1.000
2010	MTL	E	1		18	12	6	0	.667	2	2	0	0	1.000
2011	MTL	E	2		18	10	8	0	.556	1	0	1	0	.000
4	Years				72	48	24	0	.667	7	5	2	0	.714

YEAR	TEAM	LCD	FIN	SEQ	G	W	L	T	PCT	PG	PW	PL	PT	PPCT
JIM TRIMBLE James William B: 5/29/1918 McKeesport, PA D: 5/23/2006 Indianapolis, IN Indiana														
1956	HAM	I	2		14	7	7	0	.500	3	1	2	0	.333
1957	HAM	I	1		14	10	4	0	.714	3	3	0	0	1.000
1958	HAM	I	1		14	10	3	1	.750	3	2	1	0	.667
1959	HAM	I	1		14	10	4	0	.714	3	1	2	0	.333
1960	HAM	I	4		14	4	10	0	.286					
1961	HAM	E	1		14	10	4	0	.714	3	1	2	0	.333
1962	HAM	E	1		14	9	4	1	.679	3	2	1	0	.667
1963	MTL	E	3		14	6	8	0	.429	1	0	1	0	.000
1964	MTL	E	3		14	6	8	0	.429	1	0	1	0	.000
1965	MTL	E	3		14	5	9	0	.357	1	0	1	0	.000
10	Years				140	77	61	2	.557	21	10	11	0	.476
FRANK TRIPUCKA Tripucka, Francis Joseph B: 12/8/1927 Bloomfield, NJ Notre Dame														
1959	SAS	W	5/5	2/2	7	1	6	0	.143					
BOB VESPAZIANI Vespaziani, Bob B: 6/15/1935 Mount Vernon, NY														
1986	CAL	W	3		18	11	7	0	.611	1	0	1	0	.000
1987	CAL	W	4/3	1/2	8	2	6	0	.250					
2	Years				26	13	13	0	.500	1	0	1	0	.000
CARL VOYLES Voyles, Carl Marvin B: 8/11/1898 McLoud, OK D: 1/11/1982 Fort Myers, FL Oklahoma State														
1950	HAM	I	1		12	7	5	0	.583	2	1	1	0	.500
1951	HAM	I	1		12	7	5	0	.583	4	1	3	0	.250
1952	HAM	I	1		12	9	2	1	.792	3	1	2	0	.333
1953	HAM	I	1		14	8	6	0	.571	3	3	0	0	1.000
1954	HAM	I	2		14	9	5	0	.643	2	0	2	0	.000
1955	HAM	I	2		12	8	4	0	.667	1	0	1	0	.000
6	Years				76	48	27	1	.638	15	6	9	0	.400
DOUGLAS WALKER Walker, Douglas Clyde (Peahead) B: 2/17/1899 Ensley, AL D: 7/16/1970 Charlotte, NC														
1952	MTL	I	4		12	2	10	0	.167					
1953	MTL	I	1		14	8	6	0	.571	2	0	2	0	.000
1954	MTL	I	1		14	11	3	0	.786	3	2	1	0	.667
1955	MTL	I	1		12	9	3	0	.750	2	1	1	0	.500
1956	MTL	I	1		14	10	4	0	.714	3	2	1	0	.667
1957	MTL	I	3		14	6	8	0	.429	3	1	2	0	.333
1958	MTL	I	2		14	7	6	1	.536	1	0	1	0	.000
1959	MTL	I	3		14	6	8	0	.429	1	0	1	0	.000
8	Years				108	59	48	1	.551	15	6	9	0	.400
BOB WEBER Weber, Robert Wayne B: 4/21/1933 Fort Collins, CO D: 11/1/2008 Tuscon, AZ Colorado State														
1988	OTT	E	4/4	2/2	15	2	13	0	.133					
JACK WEST West, Charles A. B: 3/13/1890 IA D: 10/30/1957 Grand Forks, ND Coe														
1946	WPG	W	1		8	5	3	0	.625	3	1	2	0	.333
1947	WPG	W	1		8	5	3	0	.625	4	2	2	0	.500
1948	WPG	W	3		12	3	9	0	.250					
3	Years				28	13	15	0	.464	7	3	4	0	.429
ARDELL WIEGANDT Wiegandt, Ardell M. B: 6/28/1940 Lakota, ND North Dakota State														
1980	CAL	W	3		16	9	7	0	.563	1	0	1	0	.000
1981	CAL	W	5/5	1/2	12	5	7	0	.417					
2	Years				28	14	14	0	.500					
JERRY WILLIAMS Williams, Jerome Ralph B: 11/1/1923 Spokane, WA D: 12/31/1998 Chandler, AZ Idaho; Washington State														
1965	CAL	W	1		16	12	4	0	.750	3	1	2	0	.333
1966	CAL	W	4		16	6	9	1	.406					
1967	CAL	W	1		16	12	4	0	.750	3	1	2	0	.333
1968	CAL	W	2		16	10	6	0	.625	4	3	1	0	.750
1972	HAM	E	1		14	11	3	0	.786	3	2	1	0	.667
1973	HAM	E	4		14	7	7	0	.500					
1974	HAM	E	3		16	7	9	0	.438	1	0	1	0	.000
1975	HAM	E	3		16	5	10	1	.344	1	0	1	0	.000
1981	CAL	W	5/5	2/2	4	1	3	0	.250					
9	Years				128	71	55	2	.563	15	7	8	0	.467
NOBBY WIRKOWSKI Wirkowski, Norbert B: 8/20/1926 Chicago, IL Miami (Ohio)														
1962	TOR	E	4/4	2/2	11	4	7	0	.364					
1963	TOR	E	4		14	3	11	0	.214					
1964	TOR	E	4		14	4	10	0	.286					
3	Years				39	11	28	0	.282					
JIM WOOD Wood, Jim D. B: 1938 Oklahoma State														
1973	CAL	W	3/4	2/2	3	1	2	0	.333					
1974	CAL	W	5		16	6	10	0	.375					
1975	CAL	W	5/4	1/2	10	4	6	0	.400					
3	Years				29	11	18	0	.379					
WILLIE WOOD Wood, William Vernell B: 12/23/1936 Washington, DC Coalinga JC; Southern California														
1980	TOR	E	4		16	6	10	0	.375					
1981	TOR	E	4/4	1/2	10	0	10	0	.000					
2	Years				26	6	20	0	.231					
JOE ZALESKI Zaleski, Joseph John B: 3/19/1930 New Kensington, PA Dayton														
1967	WPG	W	4		16	4	12	0	.250					
1968	WPG	W	5		16	3	13	0	.188					
1969	WPG	W	5		16	3	12	1	.219					
3	Years				48	10	37	1	.219					

The annual draft of Canadian college players has drastically changed since the first draft held in April 1952. Today all members of the CFL participate and can select from any Canadians playing college football on either side of border. This is in stark contrast to that first draft. That year only the four members of the IRFU selected players from five eastern schools (McGill, McMaster, Queen's, Toronto and Western Ontario).

Over the years the draft has undergone several changes. In 1956, the five teams from the WIFU began what would be an on-again, off-again participation in the draft. Also that year, the University of British Columbia was added to the list of colleges that teams could select players from.

Starting in 1963, players from all Canadian university teams were eligible for the draft. In 1973, the list of eligible players was expanded to include Canadians playing for American colleges. Also that year, each team was allowed to select two players from its territory, but in 1985 the territorial exemptions were dropped.

What follows is a listing of each year's draft of college players, the 2002 Ottawa expansion draft, the two dispersal drafts and all known supplemental drafts.

With the exception of the 1952, 1958, 1962, 1965, 1967, 1968 and 1969 drafts, the players are listed in the overall order they were drafted. The first number indicates the round they were drafted, followed by the overall order, the team they were selected by, the position they were drafted at and the college they were selected from. Also, if a choice was acquired from another team (or teams), those teams will be shown in brackets [ ] after the college.

With no detailed information for the 1952 and 1958 drafts, players from those years are listed under the teams they were drafted by, in alphabetical order. The teams are listed in the order they drafted. Also, each team was scheduled to select seven players in the 1952 draft, so those results could be incomplete.

For the remaining draft lists, players are listed in the order of their selection by each team.

If a pick originally belonged to another team (or teams) then those teams are listed in brackets.

The following abbreviations are used throughout this section.

Teams

BAL	Baltimore
BC	British Columbia
BIR	Birmingham
CAL	Calgary
EDM	Edmonton
HAM	Hamilton
LV	Las Vegas
MEM	Memphis
MTL	Montreal
OTT	Ottawa
SA	San Antonio
SAC	Sacramento
SAS	Saskatchewan
TOR	Toronto
WPG	Winnipeg

Positions

C	Centre
CB	Cornerback
E	End
FB	Fullback
FL	Flanker
FW	Flying Wing
G	Guard
HB	Halfback
ILB	Inside Linebacker
K	Kicker
LB	Linebacker
MG	Middle Guard
MLB	Middle Linebacker
OLB	Outside Linebacker
P	Punter
QB	Quarterback
REC	Receiver
S	Safety
SB	Slot Back
SE	Split End
ST	Special Teams
T	Tackle
TE	Tight End
WR	Wide Receiver

1952
April 6, 1952, Ottawa

Montreal
1 1 Lampman, Harry E Queen's
McClelland, Bob LM McGill
Robillard, Gene HB McGill
Tilley, Dawson LM McGill
Wagner, Ken HB McGill

Toronto
Dancy, Al C Toronto
Hames, Marsh T Toronto
Roberts, Jack E Toronto
McKelvey, Ross HB Queen's

Hamilton
Beatty, Don E Western Ontario
Berezowski, Bill C McMaster
Hawkrigg, Mel HB McMaster
McMonogle, Bob HB Western Ontario
Fitzgerald, Gerry E Western Ontario

Ottawa
Bashak, Walt T McMaster
Brown, Al E Toronto
Garside, Bob HB Toronto
Lawson, Alex QB Toronto
5 Rumball, Bob HB Toronto

1953
January 23, 1953, Toronto

1 1 MTL McNichol, Doug E Western Ontario
1 2 OTT Harris, Joe T Toronto
1 3 TOR Crain, Geoff QB McGill
1 4 HAM Truant, Ray HB Western Ontario
2 5 MTL Bewley, Bill HB Toronto
2 6 OTT Kennedy, Stu T Queen's
2 7 TOR Munn, Lee T McMaster
2 8 HAM Ellis, Dunc T Toronto
3 9 MTL Miller, Jim E McGill
3 10 OTT Arnoldi, Tony E Queen's
3 11 TOR Griffin, Don HB Queen's
3 12 HAM Wrigglesworth, Lorne HB McMaster
4 13 MTL Gallow, Millar C Western Ontario
4 14 OTT 5Tamowski, Hank E Toronto
4 15 TOR Feaster, Gerry T Western Ontario
4 16 HAM McTaggart, Gerry E McMaster
5 17 MTL Varcoe, John G Queen's
5 18 OTT Atwood, Ken HB Queen's
5 19 TOR Haig, Al HB Toronto
5 20 HAM Carroll, Jim HB Western Ontario
6 21 MTL McCracken, Jim T McMaster
6 22 OTT Kenney, Cameron HB McGil
6 23 TOR Shannon, Paul FB McMaster
6 24 HAM Sisson, Jack HB Queen's
7 25 MTL Bertrand, Garnet G McGill
7 26 OTT Bynoe, Clive G McMaster
7 27 TOR Williams, Don QB McGill
7 28 HAM Sutherland, Gerry HB Toronto
8 29 MTL Menard, Don HB McGill
8 30 OTT Johnston, Pete G Queen's
8 31 TOR Foster, Bud G McGill
8 32 HAM Thomson, Blair HB Western Ontario
9 33 MTL Ball, Don HB Queen's
9 34 OTT Gatfield, Bill HB Queen's
9 35 TOR Foster, Ian T Queen's
9 36 HAM McMurdo, Bob QB Western Ontario
10 37 MTL Burley, Bill FB Toronto
10 38 OTT Waddell, W. G Queen's
10 39 TOR Hyde, Harry G Toronto
10 40 HAM Forrester, Jim E McMaster

1954
January 15, 1954, Toronto

1 1 TOR McFarlane, Bill HB Toronto
1 2 OTT Klein, George HB McGill
1 3 MTL Mattason Don G Toronto
1 4 HAM Oneschuk, Steve HB Toronto
2 5 TOR Belec, Jacques FB Western Ontario
2 6 OTT Shaw, Len FB McGill
2 7 MTL Wilmot, Fred WB McGill
2 8 HAM Dodds, Jimmy FB McMaster
3 9 TOR Crawford, Wilmer HB McMaster
3 10 OTT Capogreco, Vince G McGill
3 11 MTL McMurty, Ray T Toronto
3 12 HAM Thompson, Jack HB Western Ontario
4 13 TOR Higgins, Dennis T Western Ontario
4 14 OTT Wyatt, Jack HB Western Ontario
4 15 MTL McGill, John C McGill
4 16 HAM Moulton, Bill G McGill
5 17 TOR Koski, Bill G Queen's
5 18 OTT McCombe, John G Queen's
5 19 MTL Leeming, Bob HB Toronto
5 20 HAM Bertrand, George G McGill
6 21 TOR Fitzhenry, Bob G McMaster
6 22 OTT Hadlow, Murray HB Toronto
6 23 MTL Mandryk, Ollie QB Toronto
6 24 HAM Pugliese, Dan T McMaster
7 25 TOR Dale, Bob HB Toronto
7 26 OTT Mark Hatt, Mark G McGill
7 27 MTL Geckie, Doug QB Toronto
7 28 HAM Sterling, Don E McGill
8 29 TOR Bernoit, Joe C McGill
8 30 OTT Roberts, Jack QB Queen's
8 31 MTL Fraser, Dave HB McMaster
8 32 HAM Cranson, Pete QB Queen's

1955
November 28, 1954, Toronto

1 1 OTT Fracas, Gino HB Western Ontario
1 2 TOR Macklin, Alex T Toronto
1 3 HAM Getty, Don QB Western Ontario
1 4 MTL Darragh, Ernie FB McMaster
2 5 OTT Pinkney, Bob Toronto
2 6 TOR Kimoff, Bob Toronto
2 7 HAM Prowse, Don Western Ontario
2 8 MTL Quinn, Lionel McGill
3 9 OTT Nicholson, Pete Queen's
3 10 TOR Mackie, Baz Toronto
3 11 HAM Hank Zuzek, Hank Queen's
3 12 MTL Stevenson, Bill Toronto
4 13 OTT Stulac, George Toronto
4 14 TOR Horton, Bill Toronto
4 15 HAM Cook, Jack Queen's
4 16 MTL English, Herb McGill
5 17 OTT Henderson, Larry Western Ontario
5 18 TOR Prendergast, John Toronto
5 19 HAM Pelec, Jack McMaster
5 20 MTL Olszeski, Ed McGill
6 21 OTT Turner, Bob Western Ontario
6 22 TOR Sopinka, John HB Toronto
6 23 HAM Day, Bruce Toronto
6 24 MTL Dyson, Norm Queen's
7 25 OTT Palerno, Fred Toronto
7 26 TOR Strapp, Jack T Toronto
7 27 HAM Howell, Murray McMaster
7 28 MTL Levine, Norm McGill
8 29 OTT O'Brien, Joe Queen's
8 30 TOR Yednorez, Mike McMaster
8 31 HAM Wismer, John Toronto
8 32 MTL Woods, Ross Toronto
9 33 OTT Rogers, Jack Toronto
9 34 TOR Johnson, Doug McMaster
9 35 HAM Mellor, Wally Queen's
9 36 MTL Ksiazek, Ray Toronto
10 37 OTT Marston, Don Queen's
10 38 TOR Biewald, Hal McGill
10 39 HAM Miller, Tony McGill
10 40 MTL Woods, Don McGill
11 41 OTT Hilz, John McGill
11 42 TOR Baikie, Roger McGill
11 43 HAM Merling, Earl McGill
11 44 MTL ?

1956
January 22, 1956, Winnipeg

1 1 OTT Bruce, Loy DE Queen's
1 2 CAL Muntz, Phil FB Toronto
1 3 HAM Cheeseman, Don FB Toronto
1 4 BC Kochman, Al HB Queen's
1 5 TOR Smale, Fred E Toronto
1 6 SAS Drew, Doug C Western Ontario
1 7 MTL Collins, Ted G Western Ontario
1 8 WPG Bodrug, John G Toronto
1 9 EDM Waugh, Bobby G Toronto
2 10 OTT Simmons, Ralph FB Western Ontario
2 11 CAL Roman, Ted T Western Ontario
2 12 HAM Sellens, Clare G Queen's
2 13 BC Johnson, Don G Toronto
2 14 TOR Risk, Dick HB Toronto
2 15 SAS Cresswell, Dave HB Toronto
2 16 MTL Hutchison, Bill HB Queen's
2 17 WPG Tuchon, Bill G Western Ontario
2 18 EDM Ford, Earl G Toronto
3 19 OTT Uzbalis, Vic G Queen's
3 20 CAL Taporowski, Ted T-E McGill
3 21 HAM Smith, Don E Toronto
3 22 BC Milliken, John E Queen's
3 23 TOR O'Flanagan, Gerry T British Columbia
3 24 SAS Stewart, Jim E McMaster
3 25 MTL Lansky, Gerry HB Toronto
3 26 WPG Wilson, Harry QB Toronto
3 27 EDM Geard, Frank HB Queen's
4 28 OTT Rome, Jack HB McMaster
4 29 CAL Bell, Bill T McMaster
4 30 HAM Bosacki, Emil QB McGill
4 BC passed
4 31 TOR Bulchak, Walt HB Toronto
4 32 SAS Cruikshank, Jim HB Queen's
4 MTL passed
4 33 WPG Rowney, Jim G Toronto
4 34 EDM Martin, Peter G McMaster

1957
January 20, 1957, Winnipeg

1 1 BC Hughes, Jim T Queen's [TOR]
1 2 BC Skrzypek, Ed QB Toronto [CAL]
1 3 OTT Radchuk, Russ G Queen's
1 4 BC Rawlyk, George C McMaster
1 5 HAM Larsen, John T McGill
1 6 WPG Armstrong, Murdy HB McGill
1 7 CAL Williams, Norm HB Toronto [MTL]
1 8 CAL Martini, Santo T Toronto [SAS]
1 9 EDM McIntyre, David C Toronto
2 10 TOR McIntyre, Bill HB Toronto
2 11 CAL Stewart, Ron E British Columbia
2 12 OTT Mitchell, Pete E McMaster
2 13 BC Stewart, Ian E British Columbia
2 14 EDM Maik, Peter HB Toronto [HAM]
2 15 WPG Thomas, Russ T Queen's
2 16 MTL McVey, Vaughn C McGill
2 17 SAS Watt, Allen T Toronto
2 18 EDM Desimone, Livio G McGill
3 19 TOR Riva, Aldo HB Toronto
3 20 CAL Schimda, Walt T Toronto
3 21 OTT Polecrone, Pete C Toronto
3 22 BC Holland, Bob HB McGill
3 23 HAM Adrian, Rick HB McGill
3 24 WPG Killinger, Don E Western Ontario
3 25 MTL Yakutchik, Tony G McMaster
3 SAS passed
3 26 EDM Copeland, Peter G Toronto
4 27 TOR Howe, Peter HB Queen's
4 28 CAL Eyton, Trevor G Toronto
4 OTT passed
4 BC passed
4 29 HAM Gleeson, Al E Western Ontario
4 30 WPG Dingle, Paul E McGill
4 31 MTL Picard, Bill HB McGill
4 SAS passed
4 32 EDM Wong, Alan HB Queen's
5 TOR passed
5 33 CAL Winter, Stewart HB Toronto
5 OTT passed
5 BC passed
5 34 HAM Rogers, Bob HB McGill
5 WPG, MTL, SAS, EDM passed
6 TOR passed
6 35 CAL Russell, Curtis G Toronto
6 OTT, BC, HAM, WPG, MTL, SAS, EDM passed

1958
January 19, 1958, Winnipeg

Saskatchewan
1 1 Sigurdson, Len T McGill
Bertrand, Garnet C McGill
Konyk, Leo G McGill
Pulford, Chuck G Western Ontario
Redfern, John E Queen's
Shaw, Merv G McGill
Zarry, Peter E Western Ontario

Toronto
1 2 Fedor, Paul E Queen's
Casey, John T Toronto
Desborough, Neil HB Western Ontario
Rogers, Buth HB McMaster
Stulac, George E Toronto

British Columbia
1 3 Britton, Bill HB Western Ontario
Cummings, George T McMaster
Jokanovitch, Art T UBC

Ottawa
1 4 Jackson, Russ HB McMaster
Ashton, Brian QB Toronto
Bennett, John E McGill
Chisholm, John C Toronto
Kelloch, Burt E Toronto
Nelson, Dan E Toronto

Calgary
1 5 Casanova, Willie HB Western Ontario
2 14 Harrison, Graydon G Queen's

Montreal
1 6 Murphy, Ron E McGill
Loftus, Frank HB Western Ontario
Ward, Bruce G Western Ontario
Yuska, Ham E McGill

Edmonton
Halverson, Bill G Queen's
Johnston, Ray T Western Ontario
Miller, Bill T Toronto
Tattle, John HB Toronto

Winnipeg
1 8 Sandzelius, Jan HB McGill
2 17 White, Tom T Western Ontario

Hamilton
Brown, Ray T McGill
Cronin, John HB McGill

1959
January 18, 1959, Winnipeg

1 1 TOR Stacey, Larry DE Toronto
1 2 HAM Reid, Tim HB Toronto [BC]
1 3 MTL Miller, Bob HB Western Ontario

1 4 OTT Thompson, Jocko HB Queen's [BC/CAL]
1 5 HAM Bates, Dave T McMaster [OTT]
1 6 SAS MacKenzie, Doug FB McMaster
1 7 EDM Porter, Julian T Toronto
1 8 HAM Atchison, Bob C McMaster
1 9 WPG Brodie, Duncan HB Toronto
2 10 TOR Lougheed, Doug E Toronto
2 11 BC Aitken, Wayne HB UBC
2 12 MTL Cioran, Nick HB McMaster
2 13 HAM Wasek, Mitch T Queen's [CAL]
2 14 OTT Dann, Bob HB Toronto
2 15 SAS Stuart, Don E Western Ontario
2 16 EDM Delisle, Ron C Queen's
2 17 HAM Kutas, Jerry T McMaster
2 18 WPG Drever, Morgan G Toronto
3 TOR passed
3 BC passed
3 19 MTL Hunter, Bill G Toronto
3 CAL passed
3 20 OTT O'Farroll, Stovo HB MoCill
3 SAS passed
3 21 EDM Aston, Brian QB Toronto
3 22 HAM Sopinka, Nick QB Toronto
3 WPG passed
4all teams passed

1960
February 11, 1960, Winnipeg

1 1 TOR Mitchell, Bill T Western Ontario
1 2 CAL Poliziani, Miko FB Western Ontario
1 3 MTL Conacher, Jr., Lionel FB Western Ontario
1 4 OTT Chisholm, Steve HB Toronto
1 5 HAM Cosentino, Frank QB Western Ontario
2 6 TOR Jackson, Bruce T Toronto
2 7 CAL Humphrey, John T Western Ontario
2 8 MTL Sopinka, Walt E Toronto
2 9 OTT Jack, Doug E Toronto
2 10 HAM Bradley, Dennis T Western Ontario
3 11 TOR Meyers, Ken HB Toronto
3 12 CAL Merritt, Gordon E McGill
3 13 MTL Hargraves, Doug G Queen's
3 14 OTT Bradstock, Brian T Toronto
3 15 HAM Tucker, Bob E McGill
4 TOR passed
4 16 CAL Bulicon, William G Toronto
4 17 MTL Johnson, Gordon QB Queen's
4 18 OTT Irvin, Joe HB McGill
4 19 HAM Plumley, Kent QB Queen's
5 TOR passed
5 CAL passed
5 20 MTL Pearson, Bob E Western Ontario
5 21 OTT Edgar, Jim E Western Ontario
5 22 HAM Wilson, Dave G Queen's
6 TOR passed
6 CAL passed
6 23 MTL Richards, Dave HB Queen's
6 24 OTT Arborg, Foss G Queen's
6 HAM passed

1961
February 10, 1961, Winnipeg

1 1 HAM Wood, Casey T Toronto [TOR]
1 2 CAL Harding, Glen C Toronto
1 3 HAM Ware, John C Queen's [MTL]
1 4 TOR Wicklum, Mike HB Queen's
1 5 OTT Burroughs, Paul HB Toronto
2 6 HAM Barrie, Wallie LB McGill
2 7 CAL Robb, Don E Queen's
2 8 MTL Neal, Wayne G Western Ontario
2 9 TOR Muir, Mike E Toronto
2 10 OTT Moore, John HB McGill
3 11 HAM Thorburn, Weldon T Toronto
3 12 CAL Hoisak, Peter DE NcGill
3 13 MTL Jewell, Milt G Toronto
3 14 TOR Milligan, Bob FB McGill
3 15 OTT Pearce, Dick HB Queen's
4 16 HAM House, Bob E Toronto
4 CAL passed
4 17 MTL McAleese, Bob HB Queen's
4 18 TOR Poaps, Sam G Queen's
4 19 OTT Loftus, Frank HB Western Ontario
5 20 HAM Godley, Bob G Toronto
5 CAL passed
5 21 MTL Braekvelt, Al G McGill
5 22 TOR Chykaliuk, Mike G Toronto
5 23 OTT Evan, John T Toronto
6 HAM passed
6 CAL passed
6 24 MTL Rush, Ed HB Toronto
6 TOR passed
6 OTT passed

1962
February 16, 1962, Vancouver

Montreal
Crawford, Ron C Toronto
Lucenti, Gary T Queen's
Samwaya, Clem HB Western Ontario
Kelly, Mike HB Toronto
McMurray, Neil T Western Ontario
Dolicki, Larry T Queen's
Connor, Cal QB Queen's
Ewart, Gary HB Western Ontario
Raukkais, Hary HB McGill

Ottawa
Wood, Chuck G/HB McHill
Tucker, Whitman HB Western Ontario
Windsor, Bob E/HB McGill
Shaw, Larry E/HB Western Ontario
Cook, Hugh E Toronto
Niklas, Doug T Queen's

Toronto
Gary Strickler LB Queen's
John Erickson G Queen's
Gordon Semester HB Queen's
Tony Blair G McGill
John Cleghorn C McGill
Murray Rowan T Toronto

Calgary
Scott, Harvey LB/G Western Ontario
Boyd, Doug DB Toronto
Pettit, Mike B Queen's
Turner, Norm QB/DB Toronto
Muchi, Jim FB Toronto

Hamilton
Cooper, Brian HB Toronto
Whityk, Pete T Queen's
McGill, Wayne HB Queen's
Bethune, George G Queen's
Roberts, John QB/HB McGill
Dunstan, Norm HB Queen's
Kay, Bill T Toronto
Konyk, Leo T McGill
Hutzel, Ben HB Toronto
Kennel, Bob T McGill
Russell, Colin T McGill
Clements, Don G Toronto

1963
February 16, 1963, Hamilton

1 1 TOR Wydareny, John HB Western Ontario
1 2 HAM Rysdale, Ken HB-QB Western Ontario [EDM]
1 3 OTT Black, Rick HB Mount Allison [BC]
1 4 OTT Miklas, Bill G Queen's
1 5 SAS Hogan, Jim T Western Ontario
1 6 EDM Howlett, Pete FB Loyola [MTL]
1 7 CAL Shatzko, Ray G British Columbia
1 8 OTT Quinn, Peter HB Queen's [HAM]
1 9 WPG Monteith, Ian FB McGill
2 10 TOR Metras, John C Western Ontario
2 11 EDM Endley, Fred LB Queen's
2 12 BC Bates, Noal G Toronto
2 13 OTT Benoit, Paul HB Carleton
2 14 SAS Cranmer, Gary HB Western Ontario
2 15 MTL German, Ray C Ottawa
2 16 CAL Neilsen, Ken HB Alberta
2 17 HAM Chris, George HB McMaster
2 18 WPG Shanksi, John HB Manitoba
3 19 TOR Reeder, Wayne HB Royal Military College
3 20 EDM Kostin, Mike QB Loyola
3 21 BC Kemp, Peter C British Columbia
3 22 OTT Robinson, Len T Ottawa
3 23 SAS Sirman, Bill HB Queen's
3 24 MTL Boug, Gary QB Western Ontario
3 25 CAL Carron, Bert HB Alberta
3 26 HAM Brereton, Al HB Toronto
3 27 WPG Wickland, Ray FB British Columbia
4 28 TOR Blackladder, Len HB Ottawa
4 29 EDM Smith, Gary QB Alberta
4 30 OTT Bourgalt, Bob G Loyola [BC]
4 31 OTT Moore, Ted C St. Mary's
4 32 SAS Williams, Don G Sasktachewan
4 33 MTL Desjardins, Paul C Ottawa
4 34 CAL de la Vergne, John E Queen's
4 35 HAM Dever, Jack B Carleton
4 36 WPG Near, Ron E Toronto
5 37 TOR Weber, Neil HB St. Francis Xavier
5 38 EDM Millken, John QB Bishop's
5 39 OTT Sevigny, John HB Carleton [BC]
5 OTT passed?
5 SAS passed
5 40 MTL Trudell, Peter HB Loyola
5 41 CAL Quinn, John HB Queen's
5 42 HAM Cottrell, Dave HB New Brunswick
5 WPG passed
6 43 TOR Farrow, Ted T Western Ontario
6 44 EDM Martinux, Ed G Alberta
6 BC passed
6 45 OTT Nash, John HB Western Ontario
6 SAS passed
6 46 MTL Futa, John E Queen's
6 47 CAL West, Gary HB Queen's
6 48 HAM Duncan, Bill T Alberta
6 WPG passed
7 49 TOR Kristenbrun, Tom T Toronto
7 50 EDM Boilan, Maynard C Alberta
7 BC passed
7 51 OTT Greben, John T McMaster
7 SAS passed
7 52 MTL St. John, Len HB Carleton
7 CAL, HAM, WPG passed
8 53 TOR Corkmer, Barry QB British Columbia
8 EDM, BC, OTT, SAS passed
8 54 MTL Cullen, Larry HB McMaster
8 55 CAL Strathdee, Graeme HB McGill
8 56 HAM Skypeck, Tom QB McGill [ineligible]
8 WPG passed
9 57 TOR, EDM, BC, OTT, SAS passed
9 58 MTL Allen, Jim E Ottawa
9 59 CAL Budgell, Ewart HB McGill
9 60 HAM, WPG passed

All teams passed in the following rounds except for those teams that made the following choices:

10 61 MTL Dineen, Jake E St. Francis Xavier
11 62 MTL Jazbac, Fred C McMaster
12 63 MTL Narvey, Irv E Loyola
13 61 MTL Thomas, Murray HB McGill
14 65 MTL Allen, Fraser HB McGill
15 66 MTL Halmay, Peter T McGill
16 67 MTL Osborne, Wayne T British Columbia
17 68 MTL Smith, Arnie C British Columbia
18 69 MTL Shetter, Rick E Mount Allison
19 70 EDM Allen, Les C Manitoba
19 71 MTL Christoff, Jim G Alberta
20 72 MTL Messier, Vic HB Alberta

1964
February 7, 1964, Edmonton

1 1 EDM Mitchelson, Barry E Western Ontario
1 2 TOR Watters, Phil FB Toronto
1 3 WPG Cowin, Jack T Western Ontario
1 4 CAL Edwards, Bill HB Queen's
1 5 MTL Irwin, Al E McMaster
1 6 CAL Hollett, Mike E Toronto [SAS]
1 7 OTT Martin, Pete FB Western Ontario
1 8 BC Aldridge, Dick HB Waterloo
1 9 HAM Desjardins, Paul C Ottawa
2 10 EDM Thomson, Tom FL British Columbia
2 11 TOR Shaw, John E St. Francis Xavier
2 12 WPG Hamerton, Brian FB Saskatchewan
2 13 CAL Brady, Ian C Queen's
2 14 MTL Carkner, Barry QB British Columbia
2 15 SAS Rens, Bob T Saskatchewan
2 16 OTT Shaw, Andy T Queen's
2 17 BC Randall, Jim QB Wilfrid Laurier
2 18 HAM Jackson, Bill W Toronto
3 19 EDM Fisher, Jim T Toronto
3 20 TOR Thompson, Vince HB Ottawa
3 21 WPG Wintermute, Dick C Alberta
3 22 CAL Suderman, Dick E Western Ontario
3 23 MTL Gilbert, John G Western Ontario
3 24 SAS Bauk, Gerry T Saskatchewan
3 25 OTT Poirier, George HB Loyola
3 26 BC Hanley, Bob G British Columbia
3 27 HAM Weber, Jim HB Western Ontario
4 28 EDM Budds, Ray T Carleton
4 29 TOR Vormittag, Frank G Western Ontario
4 30 WPG Henderson, Mike T Manitoba
4 31 CAL Short, George HB Alberta
4 32 MTL Dainty, Ross E Toronto
4 33 SAS Girard, Proctor E Saskatchewan
4 34 OTT Leggatt, Bruce HB McMaster
4 35 OTT LaMorre, Joel E St. Francis Xavier [BC]
4 36 HAM Fabbott, Ted FB Wilfrid Laurier
5 37 EDM Van Vliet, Maury E Alberta
5 38 TOR Young, Bernie QB Loyola
5 WPG passed
5 39 CAL Latham, Bob LB Queen's
5 40 MTL Eger, Al E British Columbia
5 41 SAS McIntyre, John HB Western Ontario
5 42 OTT Burke, Jim T St. Francis Xavier
5 BC, HAM passed
6 43 EDM Cicotte, Rene HB Ottawa
6 44 TOR Crich, Peter HB McMaster
6 WPG, CAL passed
6 45 MTL Lewis, Peter T British Columbia
6 46 SAS Marisi, Dan G Saskatchewan
6 47 OTT Rose, Harold HB Queen's
6 BC, HAM passed
7 48 EDM Puchniak, John HB Manitoba
7 49 TOR Hall, Harold QB Toronto
7 WPG, CAL passed
7 50 MTL Johanson, Bruce HB McGill
7 SAS passed
7 51 OTT McLennan, John QB McMaster
7 BC, HAM passed
8 52 EDM Gowa, Bill E Alberta
8 53 TOR Grodzinski, Andrew T Toronto
8 WPG, CAL passed
8 54 MTL O'Donnell, Denny E Alberta
8 SAS, OTT, HAM passed
9 EDM passed
9 55 TOR Odway, Bob QB Royal Military College
9 WPG, CAL passed
9 56 MTL Coussion, Jean HB St. Marie
9 SAS, OTT, BC, HAM passed
10 EDM passed
10 57 TOR Genova, Bill FB Ryerson
10 WPG, CAL passed

10 58 MTL Thomas, Norman HB British Columbia
10 SAS, OTT, BC, HAM passed

1965
February 12, 1965, Ottawa

Toronto
1 1 Jim Young HB Queen's
3 Jim Ware FL Queen's
Jim Reid HB Western Ontario
Ian Bruce HB McGill
Ken McCuaig E Carleton
Bill Ball LB Western Ontario

Winnipeg
1 2 Desjardins, Paul, T Ottawa
Crouchman, John LB Queen's
Potvin, Guy HB Queen's
Hammerton, Brian HB Saskatchewan
Poutie, John HB Manitoba
Rekrutiak, Ken FB Manitoba
Kachman, Clarence HB Alberta

Edmonton
Sternberg, Gerry HB Toronto
St. George, Paul FB Loyola
Greenwood, Jim T Queen's
Heinbacker, Bill LM Wilfrid Laurier
McLaughlin, Charles LM British Columbia

Montreal
2 10? Jenner, Al T McGill
Jamieson, Norm C Queen's
8 Shaw, Andy T Queen's
Sommerville, Mike FB Bishop's
Cullen, Roger C Bishop's
Walker, Pete FB Royal Military College
6 Lorrie, Brian HB McMaster
Sicotte, Rene QB Ottawa
James, Paul FB Mount Allison

Saskatchewan
Simonson, Vern E Alberta
Rosevich, Demtro FB Alberta
Hale, Jim HB Alberta
Saunders, Ken G Carleton
Clarke, Don E Saskatchewan

Calgary
1 7 Conacher, Brian HB Western Ontario
Keenan, Mike T Western Ontario
Strifler, Irvin HB Alberta
Korchinsky, Nestor E Alberta
Semotiuk, Darwin E Alberta
Walter, Eric HB McGill

Hamilton
1 3 Neilsen, Ken HB Alberta [EDM]
1 4 Buckman, Doug E Toronto [MTL]
1 5 Apps, Bob HB McMaster [SAS]
1 8 Beynon, Tom T Queen's
Kerfoot, Arnie T Toronto
Hollett, Paul LM Toronto
Wooznick, Vic QB Toronto
Chappele, Clem E Bishop's
Davis, Lloyd T British Columbia

Ottawa
Bentley, Brian C Mount Allison
Campbell, Don HB Mount Allison
Ferguson, Peter LM Mount Allison
Norcott, Mike QB Mount Allison
O'Brien, Stu E St. Mary's
Canning, Rich T Bishop's
Mills, Keith HB Bishop's
Lafferty, Pat T Bishop's
Hofeman, Eric HB Queen's

British Columbia
1 9 Norrie, Bayne HB Queen's
Boston, Dave LB Mount Allison
Hardy, Roger HB British Columbia
6 Reykdal, John C British Columbia

1966
February 24, 1966, Calgary

1 1 EDM Turek, Ed HB Wilfrid Laurier
1 2 TOR Nicholson, Ross T Western Ontario
1 3 CAL James, Fred T Alberta [BC]
1 4 SAS Simonson, Vern E Alberta
1 5 MTL Greenwood, Jim T Queen's
1 6 CAL Williams, Mike HB Loyola
1 7 OTT Markle, Glen DB Toronto
1 8 WPG Feasby, Tom HB Manitoba
1 9 HAM Ostapchuk, Steve HB McMaster
2 10 EDM Bennett, Bob T Alberta
2 11 TOR Szandiner, Andy HB Toronto
2 12 BC Lillies, Heino FB Queen's
2 13 SAS Goodman, Bob LB Wilfrid Laurier
2 14 MTL Norrie, Bayne HB Queen's
2 15 OTT Keltcher, Doug LB St. Patrick's [CAL]
2 16 OTT Dickie, Jim E McGill
2 17 WPG Schmidt, Kris HB Alberta
2 18 HAM O'Brien, Wayne C St. Mary's
3 19 EDM Froese, Art HB Western Ontario
3 20 TOR Parker, Ranny LB Toronto
3 21 OTT Lightfoot, Norm LB Mount Allison [BC]
3 22 SAS Bukonen, Erkie FB Toronto
3 23 MTL Marisi, Dan G Saskatchewan
3 24 CAL Howes, Bob C Queen's
3 25 OTT Scott, Tod FL St. Francis Xavier
3 26 WPG Green, Jack E McMaster
3 27 HAM Jobe, Gary T McMaster
4 28 EDM Seymour, Gary DE Saskatchewan
4 29 TOR Mason, Bob E Royal Military College
4 30 BC Barrazuol, Bob LB British Columbia
4 31 SAS Emory, Bill T Western Ontario
4 32 MTL Quinney, Art T Saskatchewan
4 33 CAL Gray, Mike HB Toronto
4 34 OTT Keith, Al DB McMaster
4 35 WPG Akman, Bob FL Manitoba
4 36 HAM White, Gordon HB Toronto
5 EDM passed
5 37 TOR McKenzie, George T St. Patrick's
5 38 OTT Grachina, Allan LB Toronto [from BC]
5 39 SAS Ripstein, Rip QB McGill
5 40 MTL Pfaff, Jim G Royal Military College
5 41 CAL Spurr, Peter T Carleton
5 42 OTT Bradley, Terry HB McDonald
5 43 WPG Thompson, Vince HB Ottawa
5 44 HAM Richardson, Tom E Wilfrid Laurier
6 EDM passed
6 45 TOR Daub, Merv G Queen's
6 46 OTT Houston, Wayne LB Wilfrid Laurier [BC]
6 47 SAS Knoll, Blaine HB Saskatchewan
6 48 MTL Mitchell, Mike HB Wilfrid Laurier
6 CAL passed
6 49 OTT Hermitage, Harold E McDonald
6 50 WPG Howlett, Pete FB McGill
6 51 HAM Mitchell, Doug LM Western Ontario
7 EDM passed
7 52 TOR Smith, Al E Western Ontario
7 53 TOR Dalton, David HB Carleton [BC]
7 54 SAS Tyler, Peter HB Alberta
7 55 MTL Cote, Ben HB Montreal
7 CAL passed
7 56 OTT Hughes, Phil G St. Francis Xavier
7 WPG passed
7 57 HAM Johnston, Bob E St. Mary's
8 EDM, TOR, BC passed
8 58 SAS Parnega, Brian LB Queen's
8 MTL, CAL passed
8 59 OTT Holmes, Donald LB Toronto
8 WPG passed
8 60 HAM Tynedale, Jack LB Waterloo
9 EDM, TOR, BC passed
9 61 SAS Connelly, Steve T St. Francis Xavier
9 MTL, CAL passed
9 62 OTT Ball, John B Mount Allison
9 WPG, HAM passed
10 EDM, TOR, BC, SAS, MTL passed
10 63 OTT Fielder, Dick G McGill
10 WPG, HAM passed

1967
February 23, 1967, Montreal

Toronto
1 1 Barrett, Chip HB/FL British Columbia
2 Shvio, Mike HB/LB Manitoba
3 Adams, George FL McMaster

British Columbia
1 2 Kohler, Dick E/FL Manitoba
2? Braicich, George G/T British Columbia
3? Tellier, Ross T Loyola
4 Rohan, Mike C British Columbia

Calgary
1 3 Froese, Art HB Western Ontario
Clipperton, Gary T Toronto
Burridge, Larry FB Western Ontario
Wynn, Brian E Loyola
Redmond, Gerry E/G St. Mary's
Green, Don DB Calgary

Montreal
Amer, Bob QB Carleton
Sorensen, Leo HB Alberta
Latham, John HB Queen's
Quinn, Cass HB Loyola
Carter, Phil DB Bishop's

Edmonton
1 5 Campbell, Robbie HB Alberta
Mather, Gil HB Alberta

Hamilton
1 4 Scanlon, Al HB Ottawa
1 6 Elliott, Laird C Toronto
1 7 Kellam, Jim T Toronto
Wilson, John C Alberta
Bailey, Chris HB Waterloo
Allen, Tom E Waterloo
Rose, Brian T McGill
Law, Bob LM Ottawa
Armstrong, Mike E Western Ontario
Biggs, Bret LM Western Ontario

Winnipeg
2 Molstad, Ed E Alberta
2 Howard, Bob E McMaster
Lilles, Heino FB Queen's
Cara, Steve HB Manitoba
Ferguson, Larry E Queen's

Ottawa
1 8 McQueen, Greg HB Waterloo
2 Wearing, Robert HB/E Western Ontario
3 Bayne, Don QB Queen's
4 Rodrigue, Moe HB McMaster

Saskatchewan
1 9 Parsons, Wayne E Toronto
Knechtel, Dave E Wilfrid Laurier
Fletcher, Lance HB British Columbia
Wilton, Bob HB Bishop's
Zvbtniuk, Gerry HB Saskatchewab

1968
February 8, 1968, Vancouver

British Columbia
1 1 Eben, Mike FL Toronto
Gee, David Toronto
Monteith, Brian Wilfried Laurier
Strudwick, Wayne LB Saskatchewan
Richmond, George New Brunswick
Kravinchuk, Sam British Columbia

Montreal
2 Scanlon, Willie DB Ottawa
3 Cowan, Douglas HB Queen's
Weenk, John C Saskatchewan
Andrews, Garry FL Saskatchewan
Mitchell, Will Bishop's
Lamourie, Gary Carleton
McKillop, John Western Ontario
Murphy, Brian St. Mary's
Israel, Bill Western Ontario

Winnipeg
1 3 Guindon, Pierre T Ottawa
Francis, John Peter HB Saskatchewan
Bitchok, John Manitoba
Sutton, John Loyola
Payne, Phil Western Ontario
Ilves, Rivo Toronto
Desontis, Eon McGill
Shields, Larry Manitoba

Edmonton
1 4 Plancke, Larry FL Queen's
Dersch, Doug OG/DT Calgary
Reinson, Jim OG Calgary
Lobay, Gene Alberta

Toronto
1 5 Liebrock, Chuck OG St. Mary's
Purcell, Jon TE St. Francis Xavier
Markle, Paul TE Wilfrid Laurier
4 McGregor, Bruce DE Carleton
McKillop, Bob DB Waterloo
Chown, Tom DE Queen's
Gorman, Terry DB St. Francis Xavier
Gallop, Wayne LB Saskatchewan
Frost, John TE McGill
Dunkley, Lyle TE Saskatchewan
Grant, Jim McMaster

Calgary
2 10 Johnston, Bob DE McMaster [BC]
2 Raham, Mike Toronto
Johnson, Jamie Queen's
Milne, John Manitoba
Irvine, Brian Waterloo
Ironside, Dave Dalhousie
Best, Skip T Saskatchewan
Johnson, Earl Bishop's
9 Lucyk, Vern HB McMaster

Ottawa
1 2 Brule, Paul HB St. Francis Xavier [MTL]
1 6 Burgess, Darryl LB St. Mary's [CAL]
1 8 Wakelin, Ron G Toronto
1 9 Cooper, Dan C Bishop's [HAM]
2 Wilson, John Alberta
3 Craig, Theron Queen's
4 Fryer, Brian LB McMaster
5 Shuh, Don Waterloo
6 Tait, Jim Queen's
7 Abercrombie, Ted St. Mary's
8 Wyatt, Neill Ottawa

Saskatchewan
1 8 Gilbert, Pete C Alberta
Derocher, Larry Toronto
Quackenbush, Doug Dalhousie

Ingalls, Winston McDonald
Moyle, Bob Laurentian
Lampert, Terry Alberta
Garvie, Gord Saskatchewan
Lowes, Norm Saskatchewan

Hamilton
2 Reynolds, Tod HB McMaster
3 Timpany, Mark HB McMaster
Korgemagi, Yori Toronto
Potvin, Guy Queen's
Bell, Ronald Western Ontario
Martin, Bill Western Ontario
8 Chiarelli, Jim HB McMaster
Springate, George McGill

1969
February 13, 1969, Ottawa

Winnipeg
1 1 Strong, Doug HB Wilfrid Laurier
1 2 McLaren, Bob LB Simon Fraser [MTL]
Robinson, Gary E Simon Fraser
Jardine, Jim LB Simon Fraser
McGovern, Terry C Ottawa
Walker, Jim FL Saskatchewan
McKie, Ian LB-TE Carleton
Donnelly, Terry QB St. Francis Xavier
Bell, Bryce T St. Francis Xavier

Montreal
Robinson, John DE Windsor
Kruspe, John HB Wilfrid Laurier
Bukovac, Mike LB Toronto
Sheffield, Doug G Simon Fraser
Haggerty, Terry T Queen's
Smith, Rod E British Columbia
Chaorneyko, Matt HB Windsor
Langley, Walter HB New Brunswick
Debbis, Eric DHB St. Mary's
Balfo, Bill T, Laurentian

British Columbia
1 7 Warkentin, Ted E Simon Fraser [TOR]
Wray, Dave LB Alberta
Corcoran, Dave LB British Columbia
Flewelling, Roger LB Simon Fraser
Dumas, Paul DHB Simon Fraser
Beaton, Chris T Simon Fraser
8 Holm, Wayne QB Simon Fraser

Edmonton
1 4 Culter, Dave LB Simon Fraser
Miner, Norm DB Calgary
Daubner, Ludwig HB Alberta
Craig, Theron LB Queen's

Hamilton
1 5 Krawczyk, John DB McMaster
2 Krawczyk, Tom T McMaster
Johnston, Terry E St. Mary's
Will, Ken TE Wilfrid Laurier
Turek, Ernie QB St. Mary's
Lawl, Ken DB Mount Allison
Rommoldi, Bob DB Windsor
Alcock, Rick HB St. Francis Xavier
Pranshke, Gord FL Ottawa

Saskatchewan
1 3 Eamon, Skip HB Queen's [BC]
1 6 Squires, Alex DE Toronto
Haugh, Bruce DB Western Ontario
McKeen, Jim DB Queen's
Gainer, Bruce OG/LB Alberta
Orange, Bill T Laurentian
Ricker, John T Laurentian
7 Burgess, Daryll LB St. Mary's
Fleiszer, Dave HB McGill
McCarthy, Dan HB Queen's
Keabeney, John T St. Francis Xavier

Toronto
3 Trainor, Norm T Toronto
4 diGiuseppe, Nick LB Toronot

Calagry
1 8 Gilbert, Brent T Wilfrid Laurier
2 Walker, Dennis E Western Ontario
2 Main, Bob T British Columbia
3 Walker, Doug T Queen's
3 Silye, Jim HB Ottawa
4? Collett, Ross DE-T Calgary
5? Sweetland, John E Calgary
6 Coyle, Tom G Manitoba
7 Culham, Lyle E Alberta

Ottawa
1 9 Foley, Jim QB St. Dunstan's
2 Lukey, Norm QB St. Mary's
3 Donnelly, Brian FL Queen's
4? Powell, Wayne G Ottawa
5 Croteau, Dan HB Laurentian
6 McGregor, Bruce FL Carleton

1970
February 11, 1970, Toronto

1 1 CAL Holm, Wayne QB Simon Fraser [WPG]
1 2 HAM Fahrner, Dave FB Western Ontario [MTL]
1 3 EDM Timusk, Evald T Wilfrid Laurier
1 4 BC McManus, John E Alberta
1 5 HAM Bennett, Jim T Toronto
1 6 CAL Jamieson, Barry DT Wilfrid Laurier
1 7 WPG LaRose, Bob DE Western Ontario [TOR]
1 8 SAS Schmidt, Bob T Alberta
1 9 OTT Sharp, Mike HB Carleton
2 10 WPG Senst, John FL Simon Fraser
2 11 MTL McPherson, Burns DB St. Francis Xavier
2 12 EDM Hensall, Jim DB Western Ontario
2 13 BC D'Aloisio, Tony DB Windsor
2 14 WPG Sugden, Rick DB Simon Fraser [HAM]
2 15 CAL Lumb, Don T British Columbia
2 16 TOR Brown, Paul T Wilfrid Laurier
2 17 SAS Rancourt, Andre DE Ottawa
2 18 OTT Kwapisz, Gerald T Windsor
3 19 WPG Powell, Wayne DE Ottawa
3 20 MTL Smith, Andy LB Mount Allison
3 21 EDM Hendershot, Paul DB Wilfrid Laurier
3 22 BC Raham, Peter DB Toronto
3 23 HAM McKay, Paul DB Toronto
3 24 CAL Schultz, Tom DB Ottawa
3 25 TOR Candiotto, John E Dalhousie
3 26 SAS McCulla, Bob T Ottawa
3 27 HAM Hilton, Jeff FB Western Ontario
4 28 WPG Storey, John DB Saskatchewan
4 29 MTL Porter, John DT St. Mary's
4 30 EDM Lindros, Carl E Western Ontario
4 31 BC Warrington, Don DB Simon Fraser
4 32 HAM Graydon, Jay DB McMaster
4 33 CAL Sterritt, Dave T Waterloo
4 34 TOR Lyons, Vince DB McMaster
4 35 SAS Hunter, Greg DB Alberta
4 36 OTT Doherty, Dave DB McGill
5 37 WPG Prokopy, Lorne DB Calgary
5 38 MTL Foley, James QB Prince Edward Island
5 39 EDM McIntyre, Don E Queen's
5 40 BC Gray, Paul QB Wilfrid Laurier
5 41 HAM Clarke, Dave DB Guelph
5 42 CAL Kinley, Alan T Manitoba
5 43 SAS Scorgie, Ed DE Waterloo
5 44 OTT Whalen, Ken DB Guelph
6 45 WPG Stockton, Laurence LB Manitoba
6 46 MTL McLean, Fred C New Brunswick
6 47 EDM Promoli, Fred E Guelph
6 48 BC Moffat, Bob C Simon Fraser
6 49 HAM DiFruscia, Bob FL Guelph
6 50 CAL Stein, Dick G British Columbia
6 51 TOR Brown, Bear T Royal Military College
6 52 SAS Kunyckyj, George QB Brandon
7 53 WPG Moss, Terry DB Manitoba
7 54 MTL Arnason, Terry FL St. Francis Xavier
7 55 EDM Hawkes, Chris QB Simon Fraser
7 56 BC Currie, Brian T Royal Military College
7 57 HAM Quinlan, Peter QB McMaster
7 58 CAL McLeod, Craig G Calgary
7 59 TOR Simmons, Bill DB Royal Military College
7 60 SAS Turnbull, Jim DB Queen's
7 61 OTT Clarke, Ron G Queen's
8 62 WPG Sitter, Len C Brandon
8 63 MTL Abercrombie, Ted LB St. Mary's
8 64 EDM McGregor, Bob FB Wilfrid Laurier
8 65 BC Taylor, Robert T McGill
8 66 HAM Hinan, Doug FB Laurentian
8 67 CAL Batting, Brent DB Saskatchewan
8 TOR passed
8 68 SAS Werry, Pete DB Western Ontario
8 69 OTT Climie, Bob G Queen's
9 WPG passed
9 70 MTL Lavers, Don T New Brunswick
9 EDM passed
9 71 BC Conley, Gary DB Simon Fraser
9 72 HAM Harvey, Terry DE Wilfrid Laurier
9 CAL, TOR passed
9 73 SAS Passmore, Roger DB Wilfrid Laurier
9 OTT passed
10 WPG passed
10 74 MTL Brierley, Mike DE McMaster
10 EDM passed
10 75 BC Reid, Barry DB Saskatchewan
10 HAM, CAL, TOR passed
10 76 SAS Thomson, Eric G Dalhousie
10 OTT passed

1971
February 9, 1971, Winnipeg

1 1 SAS Donnelly, Brian DB Simon Fraser [WPG]
1 2 OTT Eccles, Bob LB Carleton
1 3 BC McCord, Archie T Simon Fraser
1 4 EDM Smith, Mel E Alberta
1 5 WPG Ribbins, Peter DB Ottawa [TOR]
1 6 SAS Manchuk, Bill DB Alberta
1 7 WPG Kraemer, Bob QB Manitoba [HAM]
1 8 EDM Innes, Cam C Queen's [CAL]
1 9 WPG Gauthier, John T Ottawa [MTL]
2 10 CAL Petrone, Joe K Calgary [WPG]
2 11 OTT Folusewych, Bob FB Guelph [HAM]
2 12 BC Leveille, Mike FL Ottawa
2 13 EDM Lett, Pat T Guelph
2 14 TOR Hamilton, Bob E Wilfrid Laurier
2 15 SAS Steele, John LB Simon Fraser
2 16 HAM Sehr, Walter HB Toronto
2 17 CAL Dulmage, Dan T McGill
2 18 CAL Gibson, Greg DB Calgary [MTL]
3 19 WPG McEvoy, Clay RB Simon Fraser
3 20 OTT Padfield, Bob T Waterloo
3 21 BC Lodewyks, Henry F Manitoba
3 22 EDM Wolkowski, Gene E Guelph
3 23 TOR Faulkner, Ron T Queen's
3 24 SAS Lazaruk, Jim C Alberta
3 25 HAM Zarek, Paul F McMaster
3 26 CAL Bond, Jim DT Simon Fraser
3 27 CAL Dudgeon, Dwayne E Loyola [MTL]
4 28 WPG McKee, Walt K Manitoba
4 29 OTT Lord, Art DB Saskatchewan
4 30 BC Chapman, John E Toronto
4 31 EDM Flynn, Dick G New Brunswick
4 32 TOR Morrison, Bill DE Guelph
4 33 SAS Clarke, Bob DE Alberta
4 34 HAM Wakefield, Chuck E Waterloo
4 35 CAL Cote, Ross G Calgary
4 36 MTL Proudfoot, Tony LB New Brunswick
5 37 WPG Howell, Steve E Windsor
5 38 OTT Derbyshire, Steve T Western Ontario
5 39 BC Begg, Mike WR Simon Fraser
5 40 EDM Tallas, Don DB Alberta
5 41 TOR Dresser, Allan G Windsor
5 42 SAS Pazarena, Fred LB Simon Fraser
5 43 HAM Dimitroff, Jim FB St. Mary's
5 44 CAL Murray, Bryden C Bishop's
5 45 MTL Galbraith, Jack T Manitoba
6 46 WPG Paddon, Paul DB Ottawa
6 47 OTT Hoffman, Steve DE Windsor
6 48 BC Fowler, Ron RB British Columbia
6 49 EDM Rowe, Bob LB Calgary
6 50 TOR Hartley, Bill G St. Francis Xavier
6 51 WPG Parker, Roy FL Manitoba [SAS]
6 52 HAM Hunter, Rodger DB Guelph
6 53 CAL Macrae, Bruce HB Western Ontario
6 54 MTL Keating, Bob T Manitoba
7 55 WPG Labovich, Ben E Carleton
7 56 OTT Hill, George LB Western Ontario
7 57 BC Farlinger, John DB Calgary
7 58 EDM Buchan, Jack E Toronto
7 TOR passed
7 59 WPG Rochette, Art QB Queen's [SAS]
7 60 HAM Chevers, Mike E Waterloo
7 61 CAL Hickey, Don E Alberta
7 62 MTL Schneider, Jack LB Bishop's
8 63 WPG Jukes, Ian G British Columbia
8 64 OTT Caplan, Marshall LB McMaster
8 65 BC Ansley, Bryan DT Simon Fraser
8 EDM, TOR, SAS passed
8 66 HAM Fox, Wayne F Waterloo
8 CAL passed
8 67 MTL Merrill, Peter QB New Brunswick
9 68 WPG Hrychiko, Dennis HB Manitoba
9 OTT passed
9 69 BC Fraser, Gerald G Manitoba
9 EDM, TOR, SAS, HAM, CAL passed
9 70 MTL Strothart, Art DB New Brunswick

1972
February 8, 1972, Montreal

1 1 MTL Smith, Larry RB Bishop's
1 2 EDM Lambros, Mike LB Queen's
1 3 BC Szapka, Steve G Simon Fraser
1 4 HAM Walker, Tom FB Wilfrid Laurier [OTT]
1 5 MTL Paliotti, Pete WR Loyola [WPG]
1 6 HAM Harris, John T York
1 7 HAM O'Shaugnessy, Mike DE McMaster [SAS]
1 8 TOR Chevers, Rick LB Waterloo
1 9 CAL Moulton, Don DB Calgary
2 10 MTL Baptist, Alexander LB Bishop's
2 11 WPG Miatello, Bruce T McMaster [EDM]
2 12 TOR Francis, Stewart LB Simon Fraser [BC]
2 13 CAL Konihowski, John WR Saskatchewan [OTT]
2 14 CAL Hogan, Bill WR Wilfrid Laurier]WPG]
2 15 WPG Dellandrea, Jon T Toronto [HAM]
2 16 SAS Toogood, Bob DE Manitoba
2 17 TOR Turnbull, Bill DB Wilfrid Laurier
2 18 CAL Bayter, Bob DB McMaster
3 19 MTL Kaupp, Rick DB New Brunswick
3 20 EDM Colwill, Glen RB Simon Fraser
3 21 BC Friend, Bob DB Simon Fraser
3 22 OTT Cihocki, Doug E Western Ontario
3 23 WPG Enno, Rein C Toronto
3 24 HAM Chalkley, Jim FB McMaster
3 25 SAS Watt, Joe T McMaster
3 26 TOR Buda, John T Waterloo
3 27 CAL Owen, Jeff T Windsor
4 28 MTL Leone, Jim G St. Francis Xavier
4 29 EDM Beechey, Roy WR Alberta
4 30 BC Lestins, Art T Wilfrid Laurier
4 31 OTT MacSween, Stew DB Toronto
4 32 WPG Morash, John DT Windsor
4 33 HAM Mays, Jerry WR McMaster

4 34 SAS Cooper, Jim DB Wilfrid Laurier
4 35 TOR Urban, Mike QB Windsor
4 36 CAL Westlake, Don HB Guelph
5 37 MTL Tanner, Mike DB Dalhousie
5 38 EDM St. George, Barry WR Ottawa
5 39 BC MacDonald, Bill QB Bishop's
5 40 OTT Perowne, Ron RB Bishop's
5 41 WPG Horne, Jamie LB Manitoba
5 42 HAM Smith, Dan QB Ottawa
5 SAS passed
5 43 TOR Jefferies, Gary DB Waterloo
5 44 CAL Knill, Paul DB Western Ontario
6 45 MTL Scharman, Dave G Wilfrid Laurier
6 46 EDM Syme, Dave QB Simon Fraser
6 47 BC Gouin, Jean T Ottawa
6 48 OTT Ladbrook, Gordon LB Dalhousie
6 49 WPG Nardone, Mario DT Carleton
6 50 HAM Drexler, Mark DE Western Ontario
6 SAS passed?
6 51 HAM Baldosoro, Mark HB McMaster
6 52 TOR Henderson, Rick G Wilfrid Laurier
6 53 CAL Lockington, Alec QB McMaster
7 54 MTL Danaher, John DE New Brunswick
7 55 EDM Coupland, Bud WR Calgary
7 56 BC Terry, Wayne DB Ottawa
7 57 OTT Tokaryk, Fred DT Dalhousie
7 58 WPG Millen, Mark DE Manitoba
7 59 HAM Wiedenhoeft, Rick DB Waterloo
7 SAS passed
7 60 TOR Ball, Doug HB Toronto
7 61 CAL Belvedere, Frank HB Loyola
8 62 MTL Purcell, Ian DB Simon Fraser
8 63 EDM Simpson, Jerry DB Dalhousie
8 64 BC Warner, Ron G British Columbia
8 OTT passed
8 65 WPG Thompson, Bill DE Queen's
8 HAM, SAS, TOR passed
8 66 CAL Henderson, Scott C Calgary
9 67 MTL Rodenbush, Larry C Brandon
9 EDM passed
9 68 MTL Beaton, William G Carleton [BC]
9 OTT passed
9 69 WPG Cozac, Doug HB Queen's
9 HAM, SAS, TOR passed
9 70 CAL Coleman, Rick DT Calgary

1973
February 6, 1973, Toronto

Territorial Exemptions:
BC Grozdanich, Harold G Boise State
BC Clarkson, Ross WR Simon Fraser
BC Allen, Robbie T Bishop's
TOR Clare, Lou RB Minnesota
TOR Muller, Peter TE Western Illinois
CAL Forzani, Tom WR Utah State
CAL Lamoureux, Blaine LB Washington State
EDM Worobec, Joe T Drake
EDM Adam, Gary DT Alberta
EDM McKay, Rick LB North Dakota State
MTL Bonnett, Pat T Idaho State
WPG Albertson, Roy T Simon Fraser
WPG Ducharme, Wayne RB Bowling Green State
OTT Smith, Donn T Purdue
SAS Bolych, Terry LB Weber State
SAS McLeod, Andy LB Alberta
HAM Milosevic, George E Cornell
HAM Macoritti, Bob K Wooster

1 1 BC Sopatyk, Brian G Boise State
1 2 TOR Finlay, Barry QB McMaster
1 3 CAL Logan, Mike QB Eastern Michigan
1 4 MTL Le Febvre, Pierre DB St. Mary's [EDM]
1 5 MTL Schwartzberg, Jacob K Alberta
1 6 BC Willis, Slade WR Drake [WPG]
1 7 EDM McGillis, Dave HB Calgary [OTT]
1 8 SAS Edgson, Art DB Idaho State
1 9 EDM Allison, Wayne QB Wilfrid Laurier [HAM]
2 10 BC Giroday, Paul LB California
2 11 TOR Higson, Greg HB McMaster
2 12 CAL Perras, Paul G McMaster
2 13 BC Helman, Bob RB North Dakota State [EDM]
2 14 HAM Hass, Ken LB Moorhead [MTL]
2 15 WPG Potter, Dale LB Ottawa
2 16 OTT McMillan, Bruce RB Mount Allison
2 17 SAS Passmore, Ted RB Wilfrid Laurier
2 18 BC Doret, Cor HB Toronto [HAM]
3 19 BC Fabiani, Joe QB Western Ontario
3 20 TOR Skopelianos, Chris DB Western Ontario
3 21 CAL Thompson, Doug RB Otterbein
3 22 EDM Sherwood, Bill G Ottawa
3 23 MTL Coray, Stacey DB Wilfrid Laurier
3 24 WPG Kanakos, Nick DB Simon Fraser
3 25 OTT Comartin, Roger DB Alberta
3 26 SAS Harris, Gerry TE Saskatchewan
3 27 HAM McColeman, Gord DT Wilfrid Laurier
4 28 BC McGregor, Bill WR Simon Fraser
4 29 TOR Cuncic, Wayne G Utah State
4 30 CAL Dunkley, Wayne QB Toronto
4 31 EDM Blacker, Gerry RB Wilfrid Laurier
4 32 MTL Mair, Dave TE Youngstown State
4 33 WPG Warrender, Brian HB Queen's
4 34 OTT Budge, Jim DB Western Ontario
4 35 SAS Ewachniuk, Mike DT Alberta
4 36 HAM Kerr, Dave RB Western Ontario
5 37 BC Florio, Rudy RB Youngstown State
5 38 TOR Wetsell, Brian DE British Columbia
5 39 CAL Kane, Roan WR Wilfrid Laurier
5 40 EDM Syratuik, Dan T McMaster
5 41 MTL Whitfield, Bob T Guelph
5 42 WPG Hilborn, Paul T Simon Fraser
5 OTT passed
5 43 SAS Benard, Lee DB Manitoba
5 44 HAM Spears, Jamie RB McMaster
6 45 BC Sharpe, Terry G Simon Fraser
6 46 TOR Ross, Bill DE Western Ontario
6 47 CAL Young, Allan G Montana State
6 48 EDM Duffy, Gary QB La Crosse State
6 49 MTL Cater, John DB Wilfrid Laurier
6 50 WPG Clarke, Fred G Western Ontario
6 OTT passed
6 51 SAS Savich, Don TE Alberta
6 52 HAM Telepchuk, Mike QB Guelph
7 53 BC Flynn, Mike DT Waterloo
7 54 TOR Jack, Larry DT New Brunswick
7 55 CAL Watters, Lorne LB Calgary
7 56 EDM Jones, Brian DE Alberta
7 57 MTL Drummond, Jim G Alberta
7 58 WPG Crowe, Tim T Windsor
7 OTT passed
7 59 SAS Drakich, Nick T Windsor
7 60 HAM Dunn, Brian DB Northwood
8 61 BC Quinlan, John HB McMaster
8 62 TOR Hunter, Bill DB Western Ontario
8 63 CAL Fownes, Brock G Carleton
8 64 EDM Keene, Doug RB Eastern Michigan
8 65 MTL Oulton, Mike DB Mount Allison
8 66 WPG Evans, Bart G Manitoba
8 OTT passed
8 67 SAS Janzen, Merv DB Saskatchewan
8 68 HAM de Montigny, Peter C Ottawa
9 69 BC Thomas, Al DB Simon Fraser
9 TOR passed
9 70 CAL Kelly, Denis QB Simon Fraser
9 71 EDM Campbell, Dave DB Queen's
9 72 MTL McEachern, Ed LB Guelph
9 73 WPG Samson, Dean DB Manitoba
9 OTT passed
9 74 HAM Bunting, Bill LB Ottawa [SAS]
9 75 HAM Wakeman, Jim RB Windsor

1974
February 19, 1974, Toronto

Territorial Exemptions:
WPG Paterson, Gord RB Manitoba
WPG Perrin, Glen RB Bemidji State
HAM Greaves, Ted WB Ithaca
HAM Mueller, Gary LB Wilfrid Laurier
CAL Anderson, Murray C Calgary
CAL Yeomans, Gordon RB Washington State
BC Bailey, Terry RB Simon Fraser
BC Sherbina, Lorne DT Idaho
TOR Uteck, Larry DB Wilfrid Laurier
TOR Zubkewych, Morris DT Simon Fraser
SAS McEachern, Ken DB Weber State
SAS Skolrood, Lawrie T North Dakota
MTL Chown, Gary LB Bishop's
MTL Knowlton, Gordie RB Jacksonville State
EDM Fennell, Dave DT North Dakota
EDM Stevenson, Bill DT Drake
OTT Arnold, Perry DB Western Ontario
OTT Craig, Darryl T North Carolina

1 1 TOR Halsall, Randy T Wake Forest [HAM/WPG]
1 2 HAM Clark, Ken WR St. Mary's
1 3 CAL Janssen, Henry TE Western Ontario
1 4 BC Hornes, Bob DB Idaho State
1 5 TOR Simpson, Larry TE Wilfrid Laurier
1 6 SAS McLeod, Vic E Western Ontario
1 7 CAL Macdonald, Fraser LB St. Mary's [MTL]
1 8 OTT Hadden, Dave HB Queen's [EDM]
1 9 OTT Rushton, Bob LB Otterbein
2 10 TOR Konopka, Rick LB Wilfrid Laurier [OTT/HAM/WPG]
2 11 HAM Dufault, Tom HB Wisconsin-LaCrosse
2 12 CAL Cousineau, Morris LB Windsor
2 13 BC Stevenson, Mark DT Simon Fraser
2 14 EDM Shemanchuk, Al DT Alberta [TOR]
2 15 SAS Pettersen, Leif WR Otterbein
2 16 MTL Levesque, Phil G Guelph
2 17 HAM Currie, Andy DE Acadia [EDM]
2 18 MTL Petrie, Bob WR Western Ontario [OTT]
3 19 WPG Forbes, Derek LB McMaster
3 20 HAM Yakimchuk, Frank T St. Mary's
3 21 CAL Hedges, Brian T Carleton
3 22 BC Jonassen, Andy DE Calgary
3 23 TOR Baker, Bill DB British Columbia
3 24 SAS Findlay, Duncan RB Whitworth
3 25 MTL Fenner, Micheal DT Fordham
3 26 EDM Heiland, Brian TE Simon Fraser
3 27 OTT Robinson, Billy QB St. Mary's
4 28 WPG Semple, David C Simon Fraser
4 29 HAM McNabb, Peter DB Queen's
4 30 CAL Sommerfeldt, Donn LB Whitworth
4 31 BC Kaduhr, Dave WR Simon Fraser
4 32 TOR Sudsbury, Wayne LB Mount Allison
4 33 SAS Berg, Brian G Augsburg
4 34 MTL Smith, Doug G Wilfrid Laurier
4 35 EDM Quigley, Peter RB Ottawa
4 36 BC Kilger, Paul LB Ottawa [OTT]
5 37 WPG Sutherland, Geoff FB Waterloo
5 38 HAM McLean, Fred HB Wilfrid Laurier
5 39 CAL Bzdel, Len E Saskatchewan
5 40 BC Pal, Joe DB Queen's
5 41 TOR Brademan, Heinz DT Alberta
5 42 SAS Pazarena, Bruce DB Puget Sound
5 43 MTL Allen, Jim DT Western Ontario
5 44 EDM Ellert, Rich WR Minot State
5 45 OTT Balfe, Tom DT Wilfrid Laurier
6 46 WPG Chapman, Jay DE Western Ontario
6 47 HAM Corvino, Ralph DB McMaster
6 48 CAL Fudge, Steve E Mount Allison
6 49 BC Page, Herb K Kent State
6 50 TOR Dionisi, John WR Acadia
6 51 SAS Curtis, Vance TE Alberta
6 52 MTL Griffiths, Rick C Wilfrid Laurier
6 53 EDM Lang, Stuart WR Queen's
6 54 OTT Cope, Jeff DB Simon Fraser
7 55 WPG Howse, Rick FB Waterloo
7 56 HAM Lane, Dave DB Guelph
7 57 CAL Southwick, Ron DE McMaster
7 58 BC Campbell, Charlie DE Simon Fraser
7 59 TOR Spree, Bob QB Waterloo
7 60 HAM Ward, Doug DB York [SAS]
7 61 MTL Boltin, Jim LB Otterbein
7 62 EDM Falkeid, Neil T Alberta
7 63 OTT Ridding, Doug LB Otterbein
8 64 WPG Knovac, Carl DE Bridgeport
8 65 HAM Porteous, Jamie DB New Brunswick
8 66 CAL Morris, Bruce HB Guelph
8 67 BC Osness, Bob E Augsburg
8 68 TOR Wintermeyer, John RB Queen's
8 69 HAM Lawson, Dave QB McMaster [SAS]
8 70 MTL Hills, Howard WR Acadia
8 71 EDM Pugliese, Tony LB Alberta
8 OTT passed
9 72 WPG Malus, John DE Manitoba
9 73 HAM Hutton, Dave LB Guelph
9 74 CAL Carefoote, Art T Guelph
9 75 BC Lapensee, Mike K Loyola
9 76 TOR Graham, Tom C Guelph
9 77 HAM Holt, Craig WR Guelph [SAS]
9 78 MTL Clement, Terry LB Eastern Washington
9 79 EDM Walker, Blake G Saskatchewan
9 OTT passed

1975
January 8, 1975, Washington, D.C.

Territorial Exemptions:
CAL Carlson, Doug DB Colorado
CAL Fairbanks, Lloyd G Brigham Young
TOR Gilson, Paul DT Guelph
TOR Mairs, Neil RB Otterbein
WPG Barclay, Mel DE Manitoba
WPG MacIver, Doug DT Manitoba
BC Houlihan, Barry RB Simon Fraser
BC McDonald, Mark WR Washington State
HAM Bastaja, Nick G Simon Fraser
HAM Santucci, Angelo RB St. Mary's
SAS Moen, Ron LB Saskatchewan
SAS Remmen, Larry RB Saskatchewan
OTT Stenerson, Pete QB Carleton
OTT Turcotte, Jeff DT Colorado
EDM Lavorato, Pete DB Utah State
EDM Towns, Tom LB Alberta
MTL Dattilio, Gerry QB Northern Colorado
MTL Gelinas, Pierre DT Iowa State

February 19, 1975, Toronto

1 1 WPG Scully, Steve T Syracuse [CAL]
1 2 TOR Charuk, Al WR Acadia
1 3 HAM Kunyk, Gerald QB Alberta [WPG]
1 4 WPG Bowman, Don DB Western Ontario [BC]
1 5 HAM Sullivan, Sean RB Simon Fraser
1 6 HAM Kasprzyk, Krys DT Wooster [SAS]
1 7 OTT Allemang, Marv LB Acadia
1 8 WPG Ruoff, Bernie K Syracuse [EDM]
1 9 MTL Simmons, Bill DB New Brunswick
2 10 CAL Charbonneau, Maurice T McMaster
2 11 EDM Martin, John DE Carleton [TOR]
2 12 SAS Monckton, Phil TE Western Ontario [WPG]
2 13 OTT Patterson, Dave LB Simon Fraser [BC]
2 14 CAL Warkentin, Greg E Simon Fraser [HAM]
2 15 SAS Clare, Wade RB Loyola
2 16 OTT Baker, Jim C Alberta
2 17 EDM Gillies, Bob G Bishop's
2 18 SAS Evans, Bill LB Alberta [MTL]
3 19 CAL Crowle, Don RB McGill
3 20 BC Harrington, Mike DB Saskatchewan [TOR]
3 21 WPG Munzar, Mike QB Bishop's
3 22 SAS Bryans, Ian LB Western Ontario [BC]
3 23 BC Walker, Peter T Wilfrid Laurier [HAM]
3 24 SAS Woloschuk, Bob RB McMaster

3 25 OTT Summers, Cliff LB Western Ontario
3 26 EDM Rush, Curt WR Western Ontario
3 27 WPG Morris, Alex DB Queen's [MTL]
4 28 CAL Finseth, Rick QB Pacific Lutheran
4 29 TOR Brandt, Doug DB Winona State
4 30 WPG Spink, Kevin C Western Ontario
4 31 BC Ragon, Randy K U.S. International
4 32 HAM Castillo, Libert RB Toronto
4 33 SAS Thoma, Carl G Saskatchewan
4 34 OTT Stephenson, Grant LB St. Mary's
4 35 EDM Latter, John T Bishop's
4 36 MTL Brooks, Ross WR McGill
5 37 CAL Pederson, Rick T Wilfrid Laurier
5 38 TOR Cornwell, Don LB Guelph
5 39 WPG Peters, Jim DE Guelph
5 40 BC Cook, Martin DT Wildrid Laurier
5 41 HAM Plenderleith, Brian WR Windsor
5 42 SAS Schwartz, Brent LB Manitoba
5 43 OTT Gibson, Scott G Manitoba
5 44 EDM Fraser, Barrie QB Saskatchewan
6 MTL passed
6 45 CAL Krahn, Rick LB Delta State
6 46 TOR Dietrich, Ed DE Wilfrid Laurier
6 47 WPG Wagner, Wayne FB Manitoba
6 48 BC Barchiesi, Paul DT Western Ontario
6 49 HAM Anderson, Ian LB Queen's
6 50 SAS Cameron, Alan T Colorado
6 51 OTT Pleckaitis, Arunas TE Carleton
6 52 EDM Kiland, Warren T Hawaii
6 53 EDM Luchkow, Ken DE Alberta [MTL]
7 54 CAL Seniuk, Doug DB Alberta
7 TOR passed
7 55 WPG Pearson, Dave DB Manitoba
7 56 BC McLellan, Don LB Simon Fraser
7 57 HAM Howe, Warren FL Wilfrid Laurier
7 58 SAS Messner, Marv DE North Dakota
7 59 OTT Biljetina, Roy TE Wooster
7 60 EDM Doyle, Marty T Carleton
7 61 EDM Anderson, Greg TE Queen's [MTL]
8 62 CAL Niederbuhl, Art DB Loyola
8 TOR passed
8 63 WPG Sabistan, Peter G Queen's
8 64 BC Murray, Doug T Bishop's
8 65 HAM Heartwell, Bob HB Western Ontario
8 66 HAM Chalupka, Richard RB Wilfrid Laurier [SAS]
8 OTT, EDM, MTL passed

1976
January 21, 1976, Edmonton

Terrirorial Exemptions:
TOR Lumsden, Neil RB Ottawa
TOR Telfer, Steve TE St. Mary's
TOR Wasilenko, Vic DB British Columbia [CAL]
BC Norton, Bill DT Weber State
BC Jackson, Glen LB Simon Fraser
BC Davies, Mitch E Calgary [CAL]
HAM Harrison, Bill RB Ottawa
HAM Kelley, John DB Guelph
WPG Milian, Ted G Manitoba
WPG Koswin, Rick WR Manitoba
OTT Avery, Jeff WR Ottawa
OTT Palazeti, John RB Richmond
SAS Cherkas, Ron DT Utah
SAS O'Hara, Brian RB Whitworth
MTL Thibeault, Yvon T McGill
MTL Ward, Rodney LB Bishop's
EDM Fryer, Brian WR Alberta
EDM Bauer, Walt TE Drake

February 18, 1976, Toronto

1 1 EDM Berryman, Tim LB Ottawa [TOR]
1 2 BC Graham, Randy DB Simon Fraser
1 3 EDM Moffat, Alan DT Ottawa [CAL]
1 4 OTT Gelley, Steve DB Simon Fraser [HAM]
1 5 BC Passaglia, Lui K Simon Fraser [WPG]
1 6 OTT Hatanaka, Bill WR York
1 7 SAS Pickett, Tim DB Waterloo
1 8 EDM Kudaba, Tom G Simon Fraser [MTL]
1 9 EDM MacPherson, Ian DE Ottawa
2 10 BC Platt, Len WR Tulsa [TOR]
2 11 BC Turecki, John DE British Columbia
2 12 CAL Parry, Jay WR Western Ontario
2 13 HAM Cozack, Barry RB Mount Allison
2 14 WPG Taylor, Gordon QB Wilfrid Laurier
2 15 EDM Andryjowicz, Steve RB Toronto [OTT]
2 16 SAS Gibbons, Bob DT Saskatchewan
2 17 WPG Mironuck, Ron LB Whitworth [MTL]
2 18 EDM Upton, Eric G Ottawa
3 19 TOR Allison, Rodney LB St. Mary's
3 20 BC Parkhouse, Dale TE Western Ontario
3 21 CAL McMillan, Dave WR Concordia
3 22 HAM Whaley, Paul DB Guelph
3 23 WPG Maitre, Tim WR Memphis State
3 24 MTL McMann, Charles RB Wilfrid Laurier [OTT]
3 25 SAS Glassford, John LB Wilfrid Laurier
3 26 MTL Moen, Errol DT Alberta
3 27 EDM Penner, Darrell DB Queen's
4 28 TOR Utley, Brian TE Saskatchewan
4 29 BC Inglis, Gerry LB Alberta
4 30 CAL Haswell, Richard FB Wilfrid Laurier
4 31 HAM Genovese, Paul G McMaster
4 32 WPG Booy, Henry E British Columbia
4 33 OTT Allan, Drew G Carleton
4 34 SAS West, Terry DB Ottawa
4 35 MTL Leach, Glen DB Wilfrid Laurier
4 36 EDM Scarborough, Rick RB Western Ontario
5 37 TOR Palmer, Bob RB York
5 38 BC Cimba, Jim DB Western Ontario
5 39 CAL Titley, Larry LB Concordia
5 40 HAM Slipetz, Rick LB York
5 41 WPG Churchill, Wayne DE Windsor
5 42 OTT Kitts, Doug QB York
5 43 SAS Wood, Greg DB Windsor
5 44 MTL McIver, Bill DB Queen's
5 45 EDM Ackley, Mark WR Toronto
6 46 TOR Falcoer, Doug DB York
6 47 BC Gardner, Greg QB British Columbia
6 48 CAL Grittani, Nick DT Toronto
6 49 HAM Sokonvin, Mike DT Toronto
6 50 WPG Anderson, Gary DE Concordia
6 51 OTT Anderson, Jim T Alberta
6 52 SAS Gallagher, Hugh DB Carleton
6 53 MTL Szlichta, Paul QB Purdue
6 54 EDM Kemp, Jim T Saskatchewan
7 55 TOR Montelepare, John LB Concordia
7 56 TOR Sorenson, Peter DT Bishop's [BC]
7 57 CAL Walukavich, Mike DT Concordia
7 58 HAM Jeysman, Rick DB Toronto
7 59 WPG Riopelle, Claude DE Western Ontario
7 60 OTT Brown, Fred LB Wilfrid Laurier
7 61 SAS Smarsh, Dalton RB Alberta
7 62 MTL Millard, Rod DB McMaster
7 63 EDM Nelms, Rob DT Carleton
8 64 TOR Trimm, Jim TE Toronto
8 65 BC Wallace, Glen RB Simon Fraser
8 66 CAL Lockhart, Bill C Guelph
8 67 HAM McKay, Frank DB Western Ontario
8 68 WPG Young, Bruce RB Manitoba
8 69 OTT Lojewski, Paul G Windsor
8 70 SAS Platz, Ken RB Saskatchewan
8 71 MTL Baines, Larry RB McMaster
8 72 CAL Hagarty, Norm WR Wilfrid Laurier [EDM]
9 73 TOR McCann, Gary RB Windsor
9 74 BC Coll, Peter DB Dalhousie
9 75 CAL Weiler, Mike WR Wilfrid Laurier
9 76 HAM Dixon, Marty E Western Ontario
9 77 WPG Wagner, Brian DE Manitoba
9 78 OTT Forbes, Robert WR New Brunswick
9 SAS passed
9 79 TOR Beattie, George DB Acadia [MTL]
9 80 CAL Penn, Gordon RB British Columbia [EDM]
10 81 TOR Martin, Maurice St. T Queen's
10 82 BC Ricci, Tony G British Columbia
10 83 CAL Ransome, Doug WR Dalhousie
10 84 HAM Jewell, Jon LB Western Ontario
10 85 WPG Kashty, Mike TE Manitoba
10 86 OTT Kziezopoloski, Chris WR Waterloo
10 SAS passed
10 87 TOR Muldoon, Bernie RB Windsor [MTL]
10 88 BC Janzen, Bob T British Columbia [EDM]

Supplementary Draft #1
Unknown date

1 BC Pegg, Dave K Windsor
2 CAL McFadden, Lee WR Concordia
3 HAM McFadden, Ross DB Guelph
4 HAM Rasmussen, Bo TE South Dakota State

Supplementary Draft #2
May 26, 1976

1 TOR Lorimer, Craig DT York
2 HAM Perri, Joe QB Concordia
3 MTL Trepanier, Michel WR Trois Rivers

1977
January 19, 1977, Edmonton

Territorial Exemptions:
CAL Harrison, Lawrence G Calgary
CAL Leathem, Larry WR Calgary
CAL Malinosky, John OT Michigan State [BC]
TOR Bennett, Paul DB Wilfrid Laurier
TOR Bragagnolo, Mark RB Toronto
BC Blain, John OT San Jose State
WPG Rosolowich, Gary DB Boise State
WPG Woznesensky, Lyall DE Simon Fraser
EDM Lyszkiewicz, Leon DT Alberta
EDM Salloum, Dave OT Alberta
HAM Kinch, John RB Youngstown State
HAM Bovair, Dan DB Wilfrid Laurier
SAS Hubick, Lorne RB Eastern Illinois
SAS Younge, Preston DB Simon Fraser
OTT Murphy, Mike RB Ottawa
OTT McGee, Doug G Richmond
OTT Fournier, Dan WR Princeton [MTL]
OTT McLaughlin, Brian OT Simon Fraser [MTL]

February 16, 1977, Toronto

1 1 OTT Riley, Mike DT Dalhousie [CAL]
1 2 TOR Sowieta, Rick LB Richmond
1 3 SAS Nielsen, Emil DB Simon Fraser [BC]
1 4 WPG Honey, Ray OT Drake
1 5 MTL Thomson, Craig LB Ottawa
1 6 EDM Cameron, Bob QB Acadia
1 7 EDM Chad, Tom DB Saskatchewan [HAM]
1 8 HAM Martini, John LB Toronto [SAS]
1 9 OTT DeFazio, Kirk DB Waterloo
2 10 BC Adair, Robin WR Saskatchewan [CAL]
2 11 TOR Pelham, Cliff DB Dalhousie
2 12 BC Seymour, Doug DT Missouri
2 13 SAS Nelson, John FB Manitoba [WPG]
2 14 MTL Pothier, Hector DT St. Mary's
2 15 EDM Brescacin, J.P. TE North Dakota
2 16 HAM Rothwell, John DB Waterloo
2 17 SAS Adams, Roger TE Windsor
2 18 OTT Lynn, Jim T Windsor
3 19 CAL Harber, Robin DB Ottawa
3 20 TOR MacLean, Alan G Bishop's
3 21 BC Moore, Mike DE British Columbia
3 22 WPG MacKinlay, Duncan LB Western Ontario
3 23 CAL Cotta, Jim WR Guelph [MTL]
3 24 EDM Beaton, Dave DT Simon Fraser
3 25 HAM Sheridan, Paul DE York
3 26 SAS Murphy, Mike LB Wilfrid Laurier
3 27 OTT McCaffrey, Jim DB Richmond
4 28 CAL Thompson, Cam LB Ottawa
4 29 TOR Anderson, Brian C Guelph
4 30 BC Leonhard, Glenn DT Manitoba
4 31 WPG Bone, Jamie QB Western Ontario
4 32 MTL Kotsopoulos, Chris WR Toronto
4 33 EDM Clark, Ray DB Simon Fraser
4 34 HAM Giordani, Julio LB Toronto
4 35 SAS Gaska, Gary DB Manitoba
4 36 OTT Bell, Rod TE New Brunswick
5 37 CAL Ogilvy, Colin DB Simon Fraser
5 38 TOR Bossey, David LB Notre Dame
5 39 BC Hogan, Bob HB Windsor
5 40 WPG McCorquindale, John RB Brigham Young
5 41 MTL Treleaven, Rocky K Minot State
5 42 EDM Sandre, Larry WR Windsor
5 43 HAM Dawson, Glen K Marshall
5 44 SAS Kruger, Harry DB Calgary
5 45 OTT Wheller, Roger WR Acadia
6 46 CAL Reimer, Tom WR British Columbia
6 47 TOR Fraser, Hugh WR Ottawa
6 48 BC Wilson, Nigel WR Western Ontario
6 49 WPG Bowness, Al RB Manitoba
6 50 MTL Hagerty, Grant G Wilfrid Laurier
6 51 EDM Duncan, Jim RB Queen's
6 52 HAM Morin, Andre DT Ottawa
6 53 SAS Steele, Mike OG Toronto
6 54 OTT Sartor, Dan C Ottawa
7 55 CAL Stinton, Rick LB Calgary
7 56 TOR Mosher, Greg DB Dalhousie
7 57 BC Davis, Terris G Western Ontario
7 58 WPG Matheson, Doyle DB Calgary
7 59 MTL Johnston, Brian DT Mount Allison
7 60 EDM Warbick, Mike WR Wilfrid Laurier
7 61 HAM Rozalowsky, Bill RB Western Ontario
7 62 HAM Tapak, Terry DE Acadia [SAS]
7 63 OTT Tripp, Ross RB McMaster
8 64 CAL Langley, Dave QB Toronto
8 65 TOR Arnott, Tom DT Guelph
8 66 BC Shaw, Dennis G Ottawa
8 67 WPG Capobianco, Peter LB Livingston
8 68 MTL Wilkins, Bruce RB Bishop's
8 69 EDM Gullekson, Dale RB Alberta
8 70 HAM Dumont, Mark LB St. Francis Xavier
8 71 HAM Chemeris, Pat T Waterloo [SAS]
8 72 OTT Harrison, John DB McMaster
9 73 CAL Zvonkin, Vince RB Waterloo
9 74 TOR Sinopoli, Sam TE Toronto
9 75 BC Sheenan, Paul WR Western Kentucky
9 76 WPG Krahn, Gary LB North Dakota
9 77 MTL Brescacin, Dave C Windsor
9 78 EDM Alexov, Lubomir DE Toronto
9 79 HAM D'Andrea, Jim DB Queen's
9 80 HAM Lees, Dean LB St. Mary's [SAS]
9 81 OTT Ridley, Phil FB St. Francis Xavier
10 82 CAL Pedersen, Roger DT Calgary
10 83 TOR Vernon, John LB Toronto
10 84 BC Dupuis, Dan RB Windsor
10 85 WPG Parizeau, Wayne QB Wilfrid Laurier
10 86 MTL Bohan, Mark WR Mount Allison
10 87 HAM Logan, Peter WR Western Ontario
10 88 HAM Howard, James T McMaster [SAS]
10OTT passed

1978
January 26, 1978, Edmonton

Territorial Exemptions:
CAL Gorrell, Miles DT Ottawa
CAL Lubig, Bob G Montana State
HAM DiPietro, Rocky RB Ottawa
HAM Holland, Bruce DT Wilfrid Laurier
HAM Kogler, Ted LB Waterloo [TOR]
SAS Besler, Rodney T Utah
SAS Redl, Doug G Saskatchewan
WPG Ezerins, Leo TE Whitworth
WPG Morrison, Bernie LB Manitoba
WPG Allan, Tim G Toronto [TOR]

BC Blake, John G San Jose State
BC Luke, Phil DE Simon Fraser
OTT Bakker, Dick T Queen's
OTT Walker, Bruce WR Windsor
EDM Poplawski, Joe WR Alberta
EDM Willox, Dave DE Alberta
MTL Deschamps, Rene DT Calgary
MTL Labbett, Craig TE Western Ontario

February 15, 1978, Toronto

1 1 CAL Kirzinger, Dave OT Ottawa
1 2 HAM O'Doherty, Bob WR Queen's
1 3 BC Goltz, Rick DT Simon Fraser [SAS]
1 4 WPG Jones, Evan TE British Columbia
1 5 TOR Brown, Mark RB Guelph
1 6 MTL Quilter, Neil OT British Columbia [BC]
1 7 OTT Taylor, Dan RB Central (Iowa)
1 8 EDM Dundas, Rick LB Whitworth
1 9 MTL Noble, Phil LB Western Ontario
2 10 CAL Kochel, Rob DB Western Ontario
2 11 HAM Colbey, Larry T Simon Fraser
2 12 MTL Boecheler, Gary G Saskatchewan [SAS]
2 13 WPG Stracina, Bob WR Acadia
2 14 MTL Friesen, Jerry LB Saskatchewan [TOR]
2 15 BC Schultz, Tom LB Simon Fraser
2 16 MTL Hultgren, Bob WR McMaster [OTT]
2 17 EDM Bellamy, Rick G Wilfrid Laurier
2 18 MTL Morris, Ty WR Puget Sound
3 19 CAL Allen, Dave DE Bishop's
3 20 HAM Castellan, Angelo DT Toronto
3 21 SAS McFarlane, Les DB Saskatchewan
3 22 WPG Wright, Vaughn RB Guelph
3 23 TOR Gulyes, Jerry K Wilfrid Laurier
3 24 EDM Palmer, Gerry DB Carleton [BC]
3 25 MTL O'Bryan, Bill C Oregon State [OTT]
3 26 EDM Watson, Paul K Washington State
3 27 CAL Tom, Gary WR McMaster [MTL]
4 28 CAL Karpow, Mike K Waterloo
4 29 HAM Stumpf, Dave T Toronto
4 30 SAS Butler, Maurice WR Simon Fraser
4 31 WPG Hanlon, Julian G Ottawa
4 32 TOR Greenough, John DT McMaster
4 33 BC Roberts, Phil LB McGill
4 34 OTT Battaglia, Phil LB New Brunswick
4 35 EDM Hole, Jim G Alberta
4 36 MTL Gray, Sandy DB Ottawa
5 37 CAL Moors, Mark G Acadia
5 38 HAM Levine, Bill DT Toronto
5 39 SAS Hume, Mike RB Concordia
5 40 WPG Neber, Dave DE British Columbia
5 41 TOR Jones, Tim WR Simon Fraser
5 42 BC Dobson, Barry TE McGill
5 43 OTT Davidson, Linden T Ottawa
5 44 EDM Foggo, Richard DB Calgary
5 45 MTL Powell, Kerry HB Queen's
6 46 CAL Dear, Bob G Calgary
6 47 HAM Leclerc, Yves QB Ottawa
6 48 SAS Lamborn, Mike DB Saskatchewan
6 49 WPG Davis, Steve DT Bishop's
6 50 TOR Jones, Tim C Simon Fraser
6 51 BC Tietzen, John WR Alberta
6 52 OTT Yurincich, Dave DT Wilfrid Laurier
6 53 EDM Coflin, Mark G Alberta
6 54 MTL Svec, Henry DT Western Ontario
7 55 CAL Mossop, Jim DB Toronto
7 56 HAM Katarincic, Mike DB Wilfrid Laurier
7 57 SAS Graham, Daniel LB McGill
7 58 WPG Bone, Gord TE Manitoba
7 59 TOR Johnson, Clark WR Concordia
7 60 BC Hole, Bill DT Alberta
7 61 OTT Barbeau, Tom RB McGill
7 62 EDM Zacharko, Dave LB Alberta
7 63 MTL Coleman, Clarence RB Ottawa
8 64 CAL Prange, Cam C Waterloo
8 65 HAM Medwin, Dan TE Ottawa
8 66 SAS Molnar, Tim RB Saskatchewan
8 67 WPG Hysop, Duane QB Manitoba
8 68 TOR Strecker, Stan DB Guelph
8 69 BC Guy, Don DB Alberta
8 70 OTT Lyriotokis, Mike DT Prince Edward Island
8 71 EDM McHarg, Wes DB Alberta
8 72 MTL Salvatori, Eris RB McGill

1979
January 25, 1979, Edmonton

Territorial Exemptions:
TOR McTague, Mike WR North Dakota State
SAS Johns, Al DT Pacific
SAS Hook, Tim OG Montana
BC Hebeler, Nick DT Simon Fraser
BC Morehouse, Ron LB San Diego State
HAM Priestner, John LB Western Ontario
HAM Reid, Jim RB Wilfrid Laurier
WPG Chernoff, Rick TE Manitoba
WPG Yaworsky, Bill DE Manitoba
OTT Inglis, Malcolm OT Carleton
OTT Stoqua, Pat DB Carleton
CAL Krebs, Tom G Utah
CAL Battershill, Doug DB Weber State
CAL Forbes, Rob FB Drake [TOR]
MTL Arakgi, Nick TE Bishop's
MTL Colwell, Phil RB Wilfrid Laurier
EDM Cyncar, Marco DB Alberta
EDM O'Connor, Kerry RB Alberta

February 14, 1979, Toronto

1 1 TOR Powell, Kevin OT Utah State
1 2 SAS Chorney, Al DB British Columbia
1 3 BC Houghton, Mark RB California State
1 4 SAS Hornett, Gerry OT Simon Fraser [HAM]
1 5 WPG House, Rick RB Simon Fraser
1 6 OTT Cartieri, Carm LB Montana
1 7 CAL Moir, Darrell WR Calgary
1 8 CAL Burko, Daryl LB Saskatchewan [MTL]
1 9 EDM Brown, Dan TE Calgary
2 10 TOR Huclack, Dan RB Simon Fraser
2 11 SAS Crump, Bernie DB British Columbia
2 12 BC Curran, Chris DB Western Ontario
2 13 HAM O'Keefe, Jim DB Wilfrid Laurier
2 14 WPG Dziedzina, Jim TE Simon Fraser
2 15 OTT Dosant, Al DB Windsor
2 16 CAL Thomas, Ed DB Boise State
2 17 HAM Payerl, Walt WR Western Ontario [MTL]
2 18 EDM Davies, Chris TE British Columbia
3 19 MTL Szpytma, Ed DE McMaster [TOR]
3 20 BC Aver, Kevin DB St. Francis Xavier [SAS]
3 21 BC Watson, Murray DE Western Ontario
3 22 WPG Passaglia, Walt WR Simon Fraser [HAM]
3 23 WPG Biggerstaff, Doug DE British Columbia
3 24 MTL Polesel, Adrian T McMaster [OTT]
3 25 CAL Inglis, Jeff OT Guelph
3 26 MTL Rutka, Jim WR Queen's
3 27 EDM Roberts, Dave LB Queen's
4 28 TOR Racette, Brent DE British Columbia
4 29 SAS Sturby, Joe LB Saskatchewan
4 30 BC Panetta, Torinado LB Carleton
4 31 WPG Brewer, Chris DE Acadia [HAM]
4 32 WPG McHugh, Jim LB McMaster
4 33 OTT Green, David RB Carleton
4 34 CAL Richards, Clay DB Gavilan JC
4 35 MTL Mangold, Roland OG Northeast Missouri
4 36 EDM Shier, Blair T Bishop's
5 37 TOR Forsyth, Mark DB Wilfrid Laurier
5 38 SAS Bauer, Lyle OG Weber State
5 39 BC MacKay, John RB British Columbia
5 40 HAM Heidebrecht, Mark DT Springfield
5 41 WPG McEachern, Bob LB Weber State
5 42 OTT Shore, Blaine K Queen's
5 43 CAL Hagen, Dan TE Seneca
5 44 MTL Webster, Harry OT Bishop's
5 45 EDM Simpson, Gary DB Calgary
6 46 TOR Racey, Peter OT Simon Fraser
6 47 SAS Krepinski, Paul DT Utah State
6 48 BC Muis, Berry WR British Columbia
6 49 HAM Davis, Jack DT Wilfrid Laurier
6 50 WPG Hatherly, Gerry LB Manitoba
6 51 OTT Spurgeon, Scott DB St. Francis Xavier
6 52 CAL Wilson, Ossie DB McMaster
6 53 MTL Payne, Rich LB Wilfrid Laurier
6 54 EDM Colak, Bob LB Windsor
7 55 TOR Goodrow, John RB Toronto
7 56 SAS DeGroot, Lorne DT Alberta
7 57 BC Jaffe, Paul G Carleton
7 58 HAM Hepburn, Peter DT Wilfrid Laurier
7 59 WPG Safiniuk, Barry RB Manitoba
7 60 OTT Behm, Dave RB Ottawa
7 61 CAL Fieber, George C Manitoba
7 62 MTL Cutler, Keir WR McGill
7 63 EDM Shugart, Paul TE Queen's

1980
January 23, 1980, Edmonton

Territorial Exemptions:
TOR Jones, Phil DB Simon Fraser
SAS Wall, Gene RB Saskatchewan
SAS Manz, Jim RB Saskatchewan
WPG Seidel, George OT Manitoba
HAM Ross, Don WR Acadia
HAM Ward, Ian DT Western Ontario
BC Innes, Derek LB Simon Fraser
BC Pankratz, John WR Simon Fraser
OTT Cook, Gary SB Carleton
OTT Cook, Glenn CB Richmond
CAL Nelson, Mark LB East Central
CAL Threlfall, Elwood LB Utah State
CAL Kearns, Steve TE Liberty [TOR]
MTL Scott, Doug DT Boise State
MTL Gair, Bruce WR Bishop's
MTL Kist, Tim DE Manitoba [WPG]
EDM Toth, Pat CB Alberta
EDM Getty, Dale DB Weber State

Februuary 20, 1980, Toronto

1 1 TOR Barrow, Greg OL Florida
1 2 SAS Hirose, Jack DB British Columbia
1 3 WPG Ciancone, Ken LB Utah State
1 4 SAS Fletcher, Bob P Northeast Missouri [HAM]
1 5 BC Konar, Kevin LB British Columbia
1 6 OTT McBride, Pat C North Dakota State
1 7 CAL Paris, Sheldon QB Kansas State
1 8 MTL Hawco, Joe QB Toronto
1 9 EDM Francis, Ross DE Queen's
2 10 CAL Vallevand, Ken WR U.S. International [TOR]
2 11 OTT Philp, Mark RB Richmond [SAS]
2 12 EDM Donaldson, Derry RB Tulane [WPG]
2 13 OTT Edwards, Neville RB Western Ontario [HAM]
2 14 BC Gohier, Paul OT McGill
2 15 TOR Stevenson, Tom TE Valley City State [OTT]
2 16 CAL Hackney, Cam LB Simon Fraser
2 17 SAS Fraser, Stewart FL New Brunswick [MTL]
2 18 EDM Kearns, Dan DE Simon Fraser
3 19 WPG Bunce, Rob DE Saskatchewan [TOR]
3 20 SAS Toth, Charles DB U.S. International
3 21 WPG Pahl, Vernon OG Prince Edward Island
3 22 MTL Kutasiewich, Jack OG Moorhead State [HAM]
3 23 MTL Belliveau, Gene DE St. Francis Xavier [BC]
3 24 MTL McMillan, Ed DB Carleton [OTT]
3 25 CAL Krogh, Darcy WR Calgary
3 26 HAM Murray, Eddie K Tulane [MTL]
3 27 EDM Gataveckas, Ed LB Acadia
4 28 TOR Kiviranta, Robert DE Emporia State
4 29 SAS Hamilton, Pat DB U.S. International
4 30 WPG Perkins, Brian OT Saskatchewan
4 31 HAM Yarmoluk, David DE Toronto
4 32 BC Deslauriers, Michel QB British Columbia
4 33 OTT Woof, Wesley WR Wilfrid Laurier
4 34 CAL MacDonald, Barry C Montana Tech
4 35 MTL Normand, J.P. WR Royal Military College
4 36 EDM Bridgeman, Bob DT Windsor
5 37 TOR Kalvaitis, Rick DT Wilfrid Laurier
5 38 SAS Harbord, Larry OL British Columbia
5 39 WPG Mamer, Peter DE Saskatchewan
5 40 HAM Muller, Jim DE Queen's
5 41 BC Bellinger, Ted WR Queen's
5 42 OTT Shubat, Steve OT York
5 43 CAL Mayes, Jud DB Boise State
5 44 MTL Washburn, Mike WR New Brunswick
5 45 EDM Sheridan, Francis OE Queen's
6 46 TOR Marinucci, Dave FB Queen's
6 47 SAS Mackie, Ron LB Youngstown State
6 48 WPG Danese, Mike LB Toronto
6 49 HAM Sprague, Mark LB Wilfrid Laurier
6 50 BC Wilson, Peter C Simon Fraser
6 51 OTT Szemeredy, Mike TE Toronto
6 52 CAL Vasiladis, George DE Waterloo
6 53 MTL Pooler, Mike WR New Brunswick
6 54 EDM Dippolito, Richard DB Western Ontario
7 55 TOR Krohn, Todd OT Southern Oregon
7 56 SAS Neal, Jeff WR St. Mary's
7 57 WPG Topolovec, Mike DE Ottawa
7 58 HAM Giftopoulos, Mike HB Ottawa
7 59 BC Advocat, Reg LB Simon Fraser
7 60 OTT Worobec, Elwin OG Utah
7 61 CAL Meagher, Brian LB/FB Mount Allison
7 MTL passed
7 62 EDM Dippolito, Anthony DE McMaster

1981
January 21, 1981, Edmonton

Territorial Exemptions:
SAS Larocque, Eugene DT Utah
TOR Carinci, Jan WR Maryland
TOR Ferrone, Dan OG Simon Fraser
TOR Bronk, Bob RB Queen's [WPG]
TOR Pickett, Bernie RB Wilfrid Laurier [MTL]
OTT Park, John TE Bowling Green State
OTT Beckstead, Ian TE Richmond
MTL Lacelle, Mark RB McGill
BC Smith, Rob OG Utah State
BC Klassen, Rick OG Simon Fraser
CAL MacArthur, Scott DE Calgary
CAL Beaton, Shawn DL Boise State
CAL Fournier, Randy DT Cincinnati [HAM]
CAL Besler, Randy OG Northeast Missouri [SAS]
WPG Kuras, Perry OG North Dakota
HAM Howard, Bill C Western Ontario
EDM Kehoe, Sean RB Alberta
EDM Borger, Josh WR Calgary

February 18, 1981, Toronto

1 1 CAL Kosec, Fank LB Waterloo [SAS]
1 2 TOR Trifaux, Tom OT Calgary
1 3 OTT Doyle, Maurice RB Toronto
1 4 MTL Walby, Chris DT Dickinson State
1 5 BC Martin, Nelson WR Seneca
1 6 CAL Wolfram, Mike TE Alberta
1 7 TOR Bray, Tom DT Bishop's [WPG]
1 8 TOR Engleson, Ron DT Simon Fraser [HAM]
1 9 EDM Logan, Rob DE Waterloo
2 10 SAS Henderson, Hazen DB Simon Fraser
2 11 TOR Elser, Gord LB Calgary
2 12 OTT Burns, Don WR Ottawa
2 13 MTL Marshall, Samuel DB Simon Fraser
2 14 TOR Miles, Warner OL Ottawa [BC]
2 15 MTL Prinzen, Fred LB Queen's [CAL]
2 16 WPG Brown, Dave WR Alberta
2 17 CAL Lehne, Terry DB Saskatchewan [HAM]

2 18 EDM Reid, Mike OC Ottawa
3 19 SAS Busto, Dom FLB Simon Fraser
3 20 TOR Dominico, Dan WR Western Ontario
3 21 BC Armstead, Jamie DB Calgary [OTT]
3 22 MTL Kuklo, Joe DB Simon Fraser
3 23 BC Priestnall, Larry RB Acadia
3 24 CAL Suutari, Kari LB Wisconsin
3 25 WPG Walsh, Hubert RB Acadia
3 26 HAM Arp, Jeff OG Western Ontario
3 27 EDM Essery, Scott TE Windsor
4 28 SAS Pearson, David DT Western Ontario
4 29 TOR Lowe, John RB Guelph
4 30 OTT Boss, Eric DT Toronto
4 31 MTL Claridge, Dean DE British Columbia
4 32 BC Jones, Ed DB Simon Fraser
4 33 CAL Kozik, Ted DE St. Mary's
4 34 WPG Rigelhof, Dick LB North Dakota
4 35 HAM Sommerville, Rob DB Waterloo
4 36 EDM Lammer, Ron DL Alberta
5 37 SAS Stevenson, Vic TE Calgary
5 38 TOR Goodwin, Gord RB Calgary
5 39 OTT Ring, Larry DB Bishop's
5 40 MTL Wenhardt, Murray TE Saskatchewan
5 41 BC Roberto, Frank RB Simon Fraser
5 42 CAL Pavlicik, Dan TE Concordia
5 43 WPG Pardell, Martin RB Alberta
5 44 HAM Maloney, Rick TE Western Ontario
5 45 EDM Lawrence, Robin DB Alberta
6 46 SAS Celestino, John DT Windsor
6 47 TOR Hale, Jeff OT Guelph
6 48 OTT Refosso, Anthony OT Toronto
6 49 MTL Vetro, Dom WR Wilfrid Laurier
6 50 BC Thornhill, David WR Bishop's
6 51 CAL Troiano, Jav DB Simon Fraser
6 52 WPG Goodman, Hugh DL Acadia
6 53 HAM Troop, Ian OG Wilfrid Laurier
6 54 EDM Wisharts, Wyatt DT Concordia
7 55 SAS Stremel, Wayne LB Simon Fraser
7 56 TOR Malone, Kevin DB Queen's
7 57 OTT Ball, Rob DL Queen's
7 58 MTL Ridgeway, Dave K Toledo
7 59 BC Hole, Ed OT Alberta
7 60 CAL Harris, Wayne LB Calgary
7 61 WPG Martell, Pete RB St. Francis Xavier
7 62 HAM Paul, Bill RB Sheridan
7 63 EDM Mallender, Craig RB Windsor

1982
January 20, 1982, Edmonton

Territorial Exemptions:
TOR Townsend, Geoff RB Boston College
TOR Del Col, Steve DT Simon Fraser
MTL Tousignant, Luc QB Fairmont State
CAL Moore, Ken TE Hawaii
CAL Peterson, Greg DB Brigham Young
CAL Molle, Kevin OL Fresno State [SAS]
SAS Molnar, Brent OL Minot State
BC Guevin, Dennis OT Simon Fraser
BC Roper, Gerald OG Arizona
WPG Jones, Milson RB North Dakota
WPG Mikawos, Stan DT North Dakota
HAM Yli-Renko, Kari OT Cincinnati
OTT Seale, Mark DT Richmond
OTT Dalliday, Kevin OG/DT Carleton
OTT Poulton, Ron St. DB McGill [MTL]
EDM Bolzon, Nereo LB Alberta
EDM Eshenko, Peter WR Alberta
EDM Marshall, Greg RB Western Ontario [HAM]

February 16, 1982, Toronto

1 1 TOR Kirkley, Mike RB Western Ontario
1 2 TOR Holmes, Greg WR Carroll (Wisconsin) [MTL]
1 3 CAL Evans, Neil RB Toronto
1 4 SAS Soper, Trent DB Eastern Oregon
1 5 BC Glier, Bernie DB British Columbia
1 6 TOR Antunovic, Tony OT Simon Fraser [WPG]
1 7 TOR Schultz, Chris DT Arizona [HAM]
1 8 BC Ciochetti, Troy WR Alberta [OTT]
1 9 EDM Connop, Rod OT Wilfrid Laurier
2 10 EDM Doering, Harry DE Guelph [TOR]
2 11 MTL Van Ostrand, Clint OL Whitworth
2 12 CAL Waite, Rob DL British Columbia
2 13 SAS Prud'homme, Gerald WR Concordia
2 14 BC Moen, Don DB British Columbia
2 15 WPG Faggiani, Derek DT Simon Fraser
2 16 HAM Zilli, Dave LB Toronto
2 17 HAM Langford, Peter DE Guelph [OTT]
2 18 EDM DeBrueys, Mark TE Western Ontario
3 19 CAL Charron, Phil WR Bishop's [TOR]
3 20 TOR Lemery, Marc LB McGill [MTL]
3 21 CAL Amer, Dave SB Bishop's
3 22 SAS Hughes, Mike T Sheridan
3 23 BC Potter, Ryan RB Western Ontario
3 24 WPG Bowes, Dan DE McMaster
3 25 BC Jolette, Bernie LB Ottawa [HAM]
3 26 OTT Cahill, Terry DB East Stroudsburg
3 27 EDM Janiuk, Peter OG York
4 28 BC Sidoo, Dave RB British Columbia [HAM/TOR]
4 29 MTL Stewart, Larry OT St. Mary's
4 30 CAL Amborse, Rod OG Manitoba
4 31 SAS Lord, Pierre WR Fairmont State
4 32 BC Leuty, Dave WR Western Ontario
4 33 WPG Boivin, Darrin DL Manitoba
4 34 HAM McCann, David WR Western Ontario
4 35 OTT Milks, Bruce DB Southern Arkansas
4 36 EDM Sauve, Dave DE Harvard
5 37 SAS Williams, James DE Acadia [TOR]
5 38 MTL Salvatore, Carmen DB Wilfrid Laurier
5 39 CAL Tardif, Denis LB McGill
5 40 SAS Rydeard, Kevin DB Western Ontario
5 41 BC Prencipe, Tony LB Manitoba
5 42 WPG Papaconstantinou, Sam LB Toronto
5 43 HAM Purves, Dave TE Simon Fraser
5 44 OTT Elik, Terry LB Simon Fraser
5 45 EDM Quarrel, Barry DB Wilfrid Laurier
6 46 SAS Starkey, Paul C East Oregon [TOR]
6 47 MTL West, Fred DE Wilfrid Laurier
6 48 CAL Maclean, Stuart LB Acadia
6 49 SAS Joncas, Mark DT McGill
6 50 BC Kavanaugh, Matt C Simon Fraser
6 51 WPG Kiesman, Mitch DE Manitoba
6 52 HAM Waggoner, Scott RB Florida
6 53 OTT Clarke, Greg QB British Columbia
6 54 EDM Paulitsch, Rick RB Alberta

1983
January 20, 1983, Edmonton

Territorial Exemptions:
OTT Mike Hudson TE Guelph
OTT Cattelan, Roger OT Boston College [MTL]
SAS Redl, Scott DE Saskatchewan
HAM Pendergast, Jim WR Queen's
BC Mills, Jim OT Hawaii
CAL Vavra, Greg QB Calgary
WPG Oliver, Scott LB Moorhead State
TOR Pruenster, Kelvin OT Cal Poly (Pomona)
EDM Derrmott, Blake DE Alberta

February 13, 1983, Toronto

1 1 CAL Dobrovolny, Jeff OT British Columbia [MTL]
1 2 OTT Harrison, Steve LB British Columbia
1 3 SAS Emery, Mike LB British Columbia
1 4 EDM Vanden Bos, Pieter OG British Columbia [HAM]
1 5 BC Chapdelaine, Jacquues WR Simon Fraser
1 6 CAL Byrne, Chris RB Western Ontario
1 7 WPG Riley, Jason DE British Columbia
1 8 BC Buis, Jamie OT Simon Fraser [TOR]
1 9 EDM Lawson, Tony DE McGill
2 10 MTL Hopkins, Mark LB York
2 11 OTT Robinson, Junior DB Guelph
2 12 SAS Elgaard, Ray TE Utah
2 13 HAM Palma, Paul OT Concordia
2 14 BC Lapa, Kevin LB Weber State
2 15 CAL Lynch, John DB Western Ontario
2 16 EDM Kinney, Dale DE St. Francis Xavier [WPG]
2 17 BC Leclaire, Peter FB British Columbia [TOR]
2 18 EDM McAndrews, Stew LB Alberta
3 19 MTL Nill, Blake DL Calgary
3 20 OTT Benincasa, Sam LB Guelph
3 21 SAS White, Richard LB Simon Fraser
3 22 HAM Lapa, Carey LB British Columbia
3 23 BC Bickowski, William FB Wilfrid Laurier
3 24 CAL Mintsoulis, Bill WR Toronto
3 25 WPG Pitts, John LB Western Ontario
3 26 TOR Adams, Kevin DB Waterloo
3 27 EDM Makos, Rick OG Toronto
4 28 MTL Kardash, Jim TE Western Ontario
4 29 OTT Kane, John OL Michigan State
4 30 SAS Heier, Art WR Waterloo
4 31 HAM Radford, Rory LB Guelph
4 32 BC Erdman, Jerome WR Simon Fraser
4 33 CAL Strong, Brian OL Montana Tech
4 34 WPG Cantner, Pat TE British Columbia
4 35 TOR Young, Boyd DL Ottawa
4 36 EDM Hall, Steve WR Guelph
5 37 MTL Nagel, Steve DE Wilfrid Laurier
5 38 OTT Taylor, Courtney DB Wilfrid Laurier
5 39 SAS Johnston, Joel FB Simon Fraser
5 40 HAM Piva, George OT British Columbia
5 41 BC Jackmann, Harold OT Minnesota State-Moorhead
5 42 CAL Petros, Tim RB Calgary
5 43 WPG Turnbull, Todd OG Wilfrid Laurier
5 44 TOR Black, Bryan OG Guelph
5 45 EDM Philip, Jerry DB York
6 46 MTL Slabikowski, Ed DB Windsor
6 47 OTT Payer, Francois DE Bishop's
6 48 SAS McGauley, Todd TE Western Ontario
6 49 HAM Brace, David TE West Conneticut
6 50 BC Barrow, Kyle LB Western Ontario
6 51 CAL Janes, Matt LB Western Ontario
6 52 WPG Lyseyko, Fred LB Manitoba
6 53 TOR Tynes, Joey RB St. Francis Xavier
6 54 EDM Hickie, Paul K Saskatchewan
7 55 MTL Ross, Ken DE Carleton
7 56 OTT Rhora, Chris DE Acadia
7 57 SAS Groleau, Alain DB Ottawa
7 58 HAM Zivolak, Mike C Western Ontario
7 59 BC Brown, Mike DB Toronto
7 60 CAL Kurchak, Mike K Nevada-Las Vegas
7 61 WPG Bowness, Dave TE Manitoba
7 62 TOR Waud, Dave LB Wilfrid Laurier
7 63 EDM Reinich, Gord SB Alberta
8 64 MTL Leckie, Scott DB Toronto
8 65 OTT Clow, Don WR Acadia
8 66 SAS Dundas, Reiny DT Minot State
8 67 HAM Kalthof, Jack LB Saskatchewan
8 68 BC Munroe, Ken WR British Columbia
8 69 CAL Gromer, Yorg TE Montana Western
8 70 WPG Jakobs, Danny DB Manitoba
8 71 TOR Van Maanen, Rick DL Western Ontario
8 72 EDM Crawford, Jaimie QB Alberta

1984
January 19, 1984, Edmonton

Territorial Exemptions:
SAS Anderson, Mike OG San Diego State
HAM Scholz, Ralph DT Cornell
OTT Bourgeau, Michel DT Boise State [MTL]
OTT DeSilva, Jim C Carleton
CAL Palumbo, Mike OL Washington State
EDM Bolstad, Gordon WR Alberta
WPG Ethier, Mike WR South Dakota State
BC DesLauriers, Laurent DB British Columbia
TOR Hinds, Sterling TB Washington

February 14, 1984, Toronto

1 1 BC Balkovec, Frank LB Toronto [SAS]
1 2 MTL Sinclair, Ian C Miami (Florida)
1 3 WPG Williams, Trevor DB York [HAM]
1 4 OTT Martin, Maurice DB Toronto
1 5 CAL McKeown, Sean DL Western Ontario
1 6 EDM Robinson, Mike LB Utah State
1 7 EDM Skinner, Chris RB Bishop's [WPG]
1 8 EDM Mandarich, John OT Kent State [BC]
1 9 SAS Reid, Robert RB Simon Fraser [TOR]
2 10 SAS Suitor, Glen DB Simon Fraser
2 11 MTL Bowles, Trevor OT San Jose State
2 12 HAM Marrone, Tony C Concordia
2 13 OTT Rashovich, Dan LB Simon Fraser
2 14 EDM Chapman, Kurt OL Simon Fraser [CAL]
2 15 EDM Shadrach, David DB Simon Fraser
2 16 WPG Nemeth, Richard WR Western Ontario
2 17 BC Kurtz, Roy K Wilfrid Laurier
2 18 TOR Lovegrove, Dave DB Wilfrid Laurier
3 19 SAS Stansbury, Todd LB Georgia Institute
3 20 MTL Tiffin, Paul DL Simon Fraser
3 21 HAM Disabatino, Martin OT Concordia
3 22 OTT Dupin, Damir DL Nevada-Las Vegas
3 23 CAL Williams, Nord RB York
3 24 EDM Godry, John RB Guelph
3 25 WPG Black, David OL Wilfrid Laurier
3 26 BC McKay, Murry C Alberta
3 27 CAL Ceci, Parri RB Guelph [TOR]
4 28 SAS Thomas, Greg RB Concordia
4 29 SAS McQuarters, Eddie G Minot State [MTL]
4 30 HAM Kaminski, Les RB Montana State
4 31 SAS Simpson, Peter OL Guelph [OTT]
4 32 CAL Lohin, Roman LB Alberta
4 33 EDM Runge, Dan TE Guelph
4 34 SA Visentin, Angelo OT St. Mary's [WPG]
4 35 BC Brouwers, Joe DE Wilfrid Laurier
4 36 SAS Sparenberg, Dave DL Western Ontario [TOR]
5 37 SAS Cornwall, Wendell LB British Columbia
5 38 MTL Lawrence, Bill DL Simon Fraser
5 39 HAM Wiens, Tim DB Saskatchewan
5 40 SAS Ryan, Mike OT McMaster [OTT]
5 41 CAL Filice, Corrado RB Alberta
5 42 EDM Mohr, Larry FB Queen's
5 43 WPG Hrechkosy, Tom DT Manitoba
5 44 BC Timlin, Tom DB Carleton
5 45 TOR Pearson, David SB Toronto
6 46 SAS Kopp, Darcy DB Calgary
6 47 MTL Voelk, George DE Saskatchewan
6 48 HAM Derks, Mike C Cincinnati
6 49 OTT Maganja, Dave OL York
6 50 CAL Leers, Derk DL York
6 51 EDM Chisotti, Gio DB Alberta
6 52 WPG Ploen, Doug DB North Dakota
6 53 BC Daymond, Irv OG Western Ontario
6 54 TOR Joyce, Mike SB York
7 55 SAS Wheatley, Ray OT Oregon
7 56 MTL Lalonde, Steve WR Bishop's
7 57 HAM Steele, Leroy LB South Dakota State
7 58 OTT White, Mike DB Waterloo
7 59 CAL Harvie, John LB Calgary
7 60 EDM Clark, Brad WR Alberta
7 61 WPG Rybachuk, James DL British Columbia
7 62 BC Kitchen, Greg LB British Columbia
7 63 TOR Papadakos, Adam TE Toronto
8 64 SAS Slipetz, Carl DT Illinois
8 65 MTL Baker, Terry K/P Mount Allison
8 66 HAM Fotopoulos, George OG Mount Allison
8 67 OTT Armstrong, Barry DB Ottawa
8 68 CAL Butteau, Wade LB Calgary
8 69 EDM Treftlin, Jeff DB McMaster
8 70 WPG Stevens, Jim DB Manitoba
8 71 BC Peperdy, Brad CB Saskatchewan

8 72 TOR Fraser, Neil DE York

1985
February 19, 1985, Toronto

1 1 OTT Benjamin, Nick OL Concordia
1 2 CAL Ambroise, Randy OL Manitoba
1 3 BC Ulmer, John DE North Dakota [SAS]
1 4 MTL Johns, Tony TB Henderson State
1 5 EDM Emsky, Peter OL Washington State
1 6 WPG Langdon, Pat TE Tennessee [TOR]
1 7 BC Ryan, Rick DB Weber State
1 8 HAM Tommy, Jed RB Guelph
1 9 WPG Molle, Bob DE Simon Fraser
2 10 OTT Munroe, Tom WR British Columbia
2 11 CAL Doll, Garrett LB Alberta
2 12 SAS Conrad, David TE Acadia
2 13 MTL Robson, Scott C North Dakota
2 14 BC Barnett, Bruce DB British Columbia [EDM]
2 15 CAL Spoletini, Tom OT Calgary [TOR]
2 16 BC Pariselli, Joe RB York
2 17 HAM Thompson, Lance LB Carleton
2 18 WPG Vernon, Derron RB Eastern Michigan
3 19 OTT Fratin, Neri RB Ottawa
3 20 CAL Cooper, Wes RB Weber State
3 21 SAS Lashyn, Gerald LB Saskatchewan
3 22 BC Jedicke, Bob DL Western Ontario [MTL]
3 23 EDM Horvath, Mark DB McMaster
3 24 TOR Adamic, Don OL British Columbia
3 25 EDM Passaretti, Renzo LB St. Mary's [BC]
3 26 BC Spence, Chris RB Simon Fraser [HAM]
3 27 WPG Prodanovic, Rob DL Calgary
4 28 SAS Dennis, Tony WR Simon Fraser [OTT]
4 29 CAL Bissessar, Scott WR Queen's
4 30 SAS Clefstad, Lloyd DT Simon Fraser
4 31 MTL O'Donnell, Mike QB Manitoba
4 32 EDM Grilli, Clorindo RB McMaster
4 33 TOR Keillor, Kris OT Wilfrid Laurier
4 34 BC Wilchuck, Kurt LB Oregon
4 35 OTT Palazeti, Marty DE Marshall [HAM]
4 36 HAM Sanderson, Dale C Tennessee [WPG]
5 37 SAS Crane, Steve DB Acadia [OTT]
5 38 CAL Cochrane, Terry RB British Columbia
5 39 SAS Bresciani, Rob WR Saskatchewan
5 40 MTL Bulman, Bloyce DE Mount Allison
5 41 EDM Richards, Tom RB Alberta
5 42 TOR Petschenig, Dan OL Carleton
5 43 BC Moffat, John WR Western Ontario
5 44 HAM Miller, Glen SB McGill
5 45 WPG Steele, Glenn RB British Columbia
6 46 OTT Chomyc, Lance K/P Toronto
6 47 CAL Mahnic, Joe RB Saskatchewan
6 48 SAS Nash, Jerry DB Alberta
6 49 MTL Clatney, Mark DT Moorhead State
6 50 EDM Riemer, Harold OL Alberta
6 51 TOR Troop, Alex LB Wilfrid Laurier
6 52 BC Krala, Chester LB Calgary
6 53 HAM Harry, Lance G Concordia
6 54 WPG Miller, Greg LB Concordia
7 55 OTT Ganas, George RB York
7 56 CAL DesLauriers, Roger DB British Columbia
7 57 SAS Urness, Mark G Boise State
7 58 MTL Brown, Donovan DB York
7 59 EDM Starke, Bill WR Western Ontario
7 60 TOR Filipiuk, Andy WR Toronto
7 61 WPG Campbell, Doug LB Alberta [BC]
7 62 HAM Lepore, John RB Guelph
7 63 WPG Saunders, Randy TE Simon Fraser
8 64 OTT Elfenbaum, Morris OL Minot State
8 65 CAL White, James WR Simon Fraser
8 66 SAS Mayer, Roger DL Concordia
8 67 MTL Binkle, David LB Panhandle State
8 68 EDM Donald, Dana DB Alberta
8 69 TOR Duke, Nolan C Wilfrid Laurier
8 70 BC Melvin, John DL British Columbia
8 71 HAM Bone, Brian WR Western Ontario
8 72 WPG Fabi, Randy WR Western Ontario
9 73 OTT Keenan, Craig QB Colorado
9 74 CAL Simpson, Robin OL Calgary
9 75 SAS Armstrong, Colum K Acadia
9 76 MTL Boisclair, Denis K/P Illinois
9 77 EDM McLean, Mike LB Alberta
9 78 TOR Reaume, Kevin TE St. Francis Xavier
9 79 BC Ros, Bob TE British Columbia
9 80 HAM McKenna, Sean LB McMaster
9 81 WPG Mars, Ron St. LB Manitoba

1986
February 22, 1986, Toronto

1 1 CAL Warnock, Kent DE Calgary
1 2 SAS Mayes, Rueben RB Washington State
1 3 TOR Koch, Markus DE Boise State
1 4 OTT Schad, Mike OT Queen's
1 5 MTL Finlay, Matt LB Eastern Michigan
1 6 EDM Coflinn, John OL Simon Fraser
1 7 WPG Belway, Brian DL Calgary
1 8 HAM Watson, Jeff OT St. Mary's
1 9 BC Nastasiuk, Paul RB Wilfrid Laurier
2 10 TOR Grant, Donohue DB Simon Fraser [CAL]
2 11 SAS Ellingson, James WR British Columbia
2 12 TOR Derban, Dwayne LB British Columbia
2 13 OTT Harding, Bob TE York
2 14 CAL Stubbert, Andy RB/FB Queen's [MTL]
2 15 EDM Volpe, Jeff DB Guelph
2 16 WPG Sampson, Darryl DB York
2 17 EDM Schmidt, Blaine DE Guelph [TOR/HAM]
2 18 BC Turner, Mark DL Miami (Ohio)
3 19 CAL Torresan, Mike OG British Columbia
3 20 SAS McEachern, Dave DB Princeton [MTL/SAS]
3 21 CAL Pappin, Dave LB McMaster [TOR]
3 22 TOR Siroishka, Mike WR Calgary [OTT]
3 23 OTT Wust, Chuck DB Acadia [MTL]
3 24 EDM McCormack, Greg DL Simon Fraser
3 25 BC Crick, Ron LB Idaho [MTL/WPG]
3 26 HAM Reynard, Greg DL Western Montana
3 27 BC Skemp, Bob OC British Columbia
4 28 CAL Hudson, Steve OT/OG Queen's
4 29 OTT Taylor, Rob DE/OL Toronto [SAS]
4 30 SAS Brown, Tony K San Jose State [TOR]
4 31 OTT Donnelly, Angus DE Carleton
4 32 MTL Hess, Peter TE Mount Allison
4 33 EDM Pauls, Mike RB/FB Simon Fraser
4 34 WPG Taylor, David TE Simon Fraser
4 35 HAM Lococo, Rick C York
4 36 BC Lecky, Scott WR Guelph
5 37 CAL Robinson, Tyler DB Calgary
5 38 SAS Henry, Bill DL British Columbia
5 39 TOR Cluff, Brian OG Guelph
5 40 WPG McLellan, Ian TE/FB Simon Fraser [HAM/OTT]
5 41 MTL Spradbrow, Jim DE Windsor
5 42 EDM Stephan, Andrew OG Alberta
5 43 SAS Harper, Glenn P Washington State [WPG]
5 44 HAM Curwin, Peter DE St. Mary's
5 45 BC Jeffrey, Peter OT Simon Fraser
6 46 CAL Calaguiro, Albert RB Concordia
6 47 SAS Geremia, Elio RB Calgary
6 48 TOR Elliott, Bruce LB Western Ontario
6 49 OTT Storey, Richard DL McMaster
6 50 MTL Touchette, Dennis DB McGill
6 51 EDM Mounzer, Dale DL Alberta
6 52 WPG Hoillett, Trevor DB Manitoba
6 53 HAM Jellema, Mike LB Simon Fraser
6 54 BC Mingo, Floyd DB Simon Fraser
7 55 CAL Holliday, Keith LB Calgary
7 56 SAS Ostertag, Dave DB Saskatchewan
7 57 TOR Jensen, Eric OT York
7 58 OTT Hanson, Devon DB York
7 59 MTL Johnson, Paul WR Mount Allison
7 60 EDM Bundy, Stuart OL/NT Western Kentucky
7 61 WPG Watson, Craig OG Calgary
7 62 HAM Pozzobon, Steve DE/LB Cornell
7 63 BC Osbaldiston, Paul K/P Western Montana
8 64 CAL Smith, John LB Calgary
8 65 SAS Sikorski, Calvin LB Minot State
8 66 TOR Delzotto, Steve WR York
8 67 OTT Van Vugt, Andre OT Windsor
8 68 MTL Salazar, Vince CB Toronto
8 69 EDM Telidetski, Gerald LB Alberta
8 70 WPG Minarivic, Jadran K St. Francis Xavier
8 71 HAM Clatney, Paul DB McMaster
8 72 BC Bernstein, Steve DB Simon Fraser

1987
February 21, 1987, Ottawa

1 1 OTT Groenewegen, Leo OL British Columbia
1 2 EDM Marshall, Blake FB Western Ontario [MTL]
1 3 EDM Storme, Todd OL Utah State [SAS]
1 4 BC Visco, Tony DL Purdue [TOR]
1 5 CAL Romano, Rocco OL Concordia
1 6 WPG McConnell, Andrew DL St. Francis Xavier
1 7 BC Clarkson, Larry OL Montana
1 8 MTL Salo, Matthew OL Bishop's [WPG]
1 9 HAM Germain, Joe WR Simon Fraser
2 10 OTT Hall, Kyle DB Western Ontario
2 11 MTL Davies, Doug OL Simon Fraser
2 12 OTT Wayne, Patrick LB Simon Fraser [SAS]
2 13 BC Wiseman, Todd DB Simon Fraser [TOR]
2 14 CAL McVey, Andy FB Toronto
2 15 WPG Orr, Sean OL British Columbia
2 16 BC Gerritsen, Luc FB Wilfrid Laurier
2 17 EDM Vercheval, Pierre OC Western Ontario
2 18 BC Shorten, Paul WR Toronto
3 19 WPG Johnson, Jeff FB Cornell
3 20 EDM Brathwaite, David DL Toronto [MTL]
3 21 TOR Vaughan, Jake DB Bishop's [SAS]
3 22 WPG Rodehutskors, Steve OL Calgary [TOR]
3 23 BC Jovanovic, Karl OL Simon Fraser [CAL]
3 24 WPG MacLeod, Matt K Oregon
3 25 BC Taras, Jamie OG Western Ontario
3 26 EDM Norman, Mark DB British Columbia
3 27 HAM Godry, Lou OL Guelph
4 28 OTT Robirtis, Rae OC British Columbia
4 29 MTL Stroud, David DB Minot State [BC/MTL]
4 30 SAS Sybblis, Oral OL Acadia
4 31 TOR Lesperance, Scott OL Colgate
4 32 CAL Geremia, Bruno DB Calgary
4 33 WPG Pavan, Rob LB Guelph
4 34 BC Murray, Andrew WR Carleton
4 35 EDM Funtasz, Jeff RB Alberta
4 36 BC Belanger, Robin DB McGill [HAM]
5 37 OTT Lewis, Brent LB Western Ontario
5 38 MTL Schad, Andre LB Carleton
5 39 SAS Lowe, Bruce NT Wilfrid Laurier
5 40 TOR Stiliadis, Veron DL/LB Wilfrid Laurier
5 41 CAL Kerber, Paul OL Calgary
5 42 WPG Alevizos, Gus OL Guelph
5 43 BC Ljubistic, Ray OL Hawaii
5 44 EDM Spriel, Tim TE Western Ontario
5 45 HAM McIntyre, Bill WR St. Francis Xavier
6 46 OTT Lehmberg, Gary DL Simon Fraser
6 47 MTL Barnabe, Joe WR Carleton
6 48 SAS Marchildon, Joe LB York
6 49 TOR Klein, Ron DB Wilfrid Laurier
6 50 CAL Pierson, Tony WR Alberta
6 51 WPG Sutton, John RB/FB McMaster
6 52 BC Kovacik, Roald LB British Columbia
6 53 EDM Skuse, Darrell RB Guelph
6 54 HAM Fortune, Joe OL McMaster
7 55 OTT Wolkensperg, Rick WR Western Ontario
7 56 MTL Bertone, Mike OL Concordia
7 57 SAS Stroud, Kevin OL Minot State
7 58 TOR Raycroft, Rob OL Toronto
7 59 CAL Robson, Craig OL North Dakota
7 60 WPG Lekun, Allan OC McGill
7 61 BC Moretto, Rob DB British Columbia
7 62 EDM Spoletini, Tony RB Calgary
7 63 HAM Guy, Sean DL Purdue
8 64 OTT Waterhouse, David RB Ottawa
8 65 MTL Leith, Jordan DB British Columbia
8 66 SAS McCorkell, Byron DT Saskatchewan
8 67 TOR Kohler, Dave LB Wilfrid Laurier
8 68 CAL Lapa, Kent DL Murray State
8 69 WPG Riley, Pete QB Livingston
8 70 BC Murphy, Mike DB Central Washington
8 71 EDM Hoppus, Ken OL Whitworth
8 72 HAM Doren, Greg OL Nevada Reno

Montreal Alouettes Dispersal Draft
June 26, 1987

1 1 OTT Hood, James WR
1 2 SAS Williams, Brett DL
1 3 TOR Finlay, Matt LB
1 4 CAL Ryan, Rick DB
1 5 WPG Arakgi, Nick TE
1 6 BC Kulka, Glen DL
1 7 EDM Benjamin, Steve DB
1 8 HAM Chapdelaine, Jacques WR
2 9 OTT Mohr, Larry RB
2 10 SAS Ridgway, David K
2 11 TOR Skemp, Bob OL
2 12 CAL Palumbo, Mike OL
2 13 WPG Treftlin, Jeff DB
2 14 SAS Rashovich, Dan LB [BC]
2 15 EDM Mitchell, William LB
2 16 HAM Fairbanks, Lloyd OL
3 17 OTT Scott, Doug DL
3 18 SAS Taylor, Brad QB
3 19 TOR Turner, Calvin DL
3 CAL passed
3 20 WPG Wilson, Don DB
3 BC, EDM passed
3 21 HAM McKeown, Sean OL
4 OTT passed
4 22 SAS Gordon, Jeremy WR
4 TOR, CAL passed
4 23 WPG Emery, Eric LB
4 BC, EDM, HAM passed

1988
March 5, 1988, Hamilton

1 1 OTT Lee, Orville RB Simon Fraser
1 2 SAS Fairholm, Jeff WR Arizona
1 3 WPG Wicklum, Dan LB Guelph [HAM]
1 4 CAL Georganos, Poly OT Bishop's
1 5 WPG Hanson, Ryan RB Slippery Rock
1 6 SAS Giftopoulos, Pete LB Penn State [BC]
1 7 BC Martino, Tony P Kent State [TOR]
1 8 EDM Forde, Brian LB Washington State
2 9 SAS Evraire, Ken WR Wilfrid Laurier [OTT]
2 10 SAS Mangold, Peter FB Western Kentucky
2 11 HAM Lorenz, Tim DE Santa Barbara State
2 12 CAL Bleue, Chris TE Washburn
2 13 CAL Yearwood, Wayne WR West Virginia [TOR/WPG]
2 14 BC Vankoughnett, Dave C Boise State
2 15 TOR Masotti, Paul WR Acadia
2 16 EDM Vincic, Branko DE/DT Eastern Michigan
3 17 WPG Wise, Brian DE Utah [OTT]
3 18 SAS Jauch, Jim DB North Carolina
3 19 HAM Daniels, Shawn FB Bowling Green State
3 20 CAL McLouglin, Mark K South Dakota
3 21 WPG Crifo, Rob WR Toronto
3 22 OTT Hatziioannou, Leon DL Simon Fraser [BC]
3 23 TOR Kane, Tommy WR Syracuse
3 24 EDM Nyte, Greg S Simon Fraser
4 25 WPG Tierney, Brad OL Acadia [OTT]
4 26 OTT Baptiste, Sheridon WR/HB Queen's [SAS]
4 27 HAM Cummings, Burt WR/CB North Dakota
4 28 CAL Zatylny, Wally WR Bishop's
4 29 WPG Allen, Micheal CB/RB Carleton
4 30 BC Robinson, Warren OT York
4 31 TOR Salazar, Floyd CB/HB McGill

4 32 EDM Middleton, Todd LB Dickinson State
5 33 OTT Will, Sieg OTE Guelph
5 34 OTT Rick, Chris LB Queen's [SAS]
5 35 HAM MacDonald, Jeff S New Mexico State
5 36 CAL Yausie, Jeff HB Saskatchewan
5 37 SAS Hoffman, John HB/P Saskatchewan [WPG]
5 38 BC Ljungberg, Carl P/K Guelph
5 39 TOR Munford, Chris S Simon Fraser
5 40 EDM Kratzer, Greg WR Dickinson State
6 41 OTT Matich, Brent P/K Calgary
6 42 SAS Harle, Darrell OT Eastern Michigan
6 43 HAM Yach, John LB Queen's
6 44 CAL Watts, Steve CB Toronto
6 45 WPG Fitzpatrick, Matt DE British Columbia
6 46 BC Johnson, Dave LB Simon Fraser
6 47 TOR Karbonik, Tim SB/TE Calgary
6 48 EDM Ainge, Terry HB British Columbia
7 49 OTT Warr, Scott OT McGill
7 50 SAS Alexander, Hugh OT Utah
7 51 HAM Frenkel, Bob NG Arizona State
7 52 CAL Gagner, Jordan QB British Columbia
7 53 WPG Deluca, Rob P/K McMaster
7 54 BC Mandarich, Tony OT Michigan State
7 55 TOR Paradiso, Frank LB York
7 56 EDM Kasowski, Steve P/K/WR Alberta
8 57 OTT Goerke, Ray OT Weber State
8 58 SAS Collins, Floyd RB Boise State
8 59 HAM Carrier, Michael RB Western Kentucky
8 60 CAL James, Ian LB Calgary
8 61 WPG Taplin, Jim FB Acadia
8 62 BC Vlasic, Tom TE British Columbia
8 63 TOR Williamson, Jamie HB York
8 64 EDM Ferguson, Neil DB Alberta

1989
February 25, 1989, Hamilton

1 1 OTT Wilcox, Gerald TE Weber State
1 2 SAS Smellie, Kevin RB Massachusetts [CAL]
1 3 SAS Thomas, Andrew CB Massachusetts [HAM]
1 4 SAS Wright, Donovan CB Slippery Rock
1 5 EDM Soles, Micheal RB McGill
1 6 BC MacCready, Derek DE Ohio State [TOR]
1 7 EDM Blugh, Leroy LB Bishop's [BC]
1 8 WPG O'Brien, John LB York
2 9 SAS Payne, Dan DT Simon Fraser [OTT]
2 10 TOR Campbell, Mike DT Slippery Rock [CAL]
2 11 HAM Bell, Curtis WR Washington
2 12 HAM Schramayr, Ernie FB Purdue [SAS]
2 13 EDM Bec, Randy SB Calgary
2 14 TOR Keller, Craig SB British Columbia
2 15 BC Wetmore, Paul LB Acadia
2 16 WPG Ali, Moustafa CB Carleton
3 17 OTT Foudy, Sean HB York
3 18 CAL Cafazzo, Lou DE Western Ontario
3 19 HAM Drinkwalter, Wayne LB Thunder Bay Giants Jr.
3 20 CAL McCroy, Richard T Concordia [SAS]
3 21 EDM Schumann, Derek S Bishop's
3 22 TOR Kinzie, Dave DE Bowling Green State
3 23 BC Choma, Mike T Wilfrid Laurier
3 24 WPG Joyal, Bertrand TE Bishop's
4 25 OTT Schimmer, Tom P Boise State
4 26 CAL Zizakovic, Srecko LB Ohio State
4 27 HAM Brus, Mark RB Tulsa
4 28 CAL Pollock, Brent T Fresno State [SAS]
4 29 EDM Olsacher, Lou G St. Mary's
4 30 TOR Cote, Mike T Colgate
4 31 BC Dove, Rohan CB Wilfrid Laurier
4 32 WPG Pearce, Matt FB British Columbia
5 33 OTT Radulovich, Nenad T Western Ontario
5 34 CAL Hasselbach, Harald DT Washington
5 35 HAM Blyth, Steve DT San Diego State
5 36 SAS Zimmerman, Rob FB Calgary
5 37 EDM Korte, Brent DE Alberta
5 38 TOR Joseph, Derrick DT Bishop's
5 39 BC Nield, Pat LB Guelph
5 40 WPG Croonen, Jeff LB Western Ontario
6 41 OTT Brown, Trent DB Alberta
6 42 CAL Mossman, Dave S Hawaii
6 43 HAM Loucks, Sam RB McMaster
6 44 SAS Gardiner, Shaun LB Saskatchewan
6 45 EDM Davidson, Rob DT Toronto
6 46 TOR Dietrich, Roger DT Simon Fraser
6 47 BC England, Wayne LB Guelph
6 48 WPG Scranton, Lance OT Dickinson State
7 49 OTT Weber, Gord LB Ottawa
7 50 CAL Dunkle, Travis DB Calgary
7 51 HAM Buchanan, Pete LB Nebraska
7 52 SAS Trithart, Kelly LB Saskatchewan
7 53 EDM Hildebrand, Mike DB Calgary
7 54 TOR Beckles, Brian C Wilfrid Laurier
7 55 BC Shaw, Dave LB Waterloo
7 56 WPG Hitchcock, Paul SB Acadia
8 57 OTT Forest, Bob LB Carleton
8 58 CAL Steidle, Brian T Simon Fraser
8 59 HAM Scollard, Bill P St. Mary's
8 60 SAS Galan, Greg QB Saskatchewan
8 61 EDM McDonald, Bruce S British Columbia
8 62 TOR Hjarr, Dave LB Carleton
8 63 BC Nykolaichuk, Mark HB British Columbia
8 64 WPG Bresch, Ron T Manitoba

1990
February 23, 1990, Hamilton

1 1 EDM Millington, Sean RB Simon Fraser [OTT]
1 2 BC Beckles, Ian OG/DT Indiana
1 3 SAS Scrivener, Glen DE/DT William Jewell [WPG]
1 4 TOR Climie, Jock WR Queen's
1 5 CAL Sapunjis, Dave SB Western Ontario
1 6 EDM Christie, Steve P/K William & Mary
1 7 HAM Dennis, Mark LB Central Michigan
1 8 SAS McArthur, Dane DB/RB Hawaii
2 9 SAS Boyko, Bruce SB/TE Western Michigan [OTT]
2 10 BC Whitney, Ken OG/TE California Lutheran
2 11 WPG Bovell, David CB/S Colgate
2 12 BC Kelly, Keith RB Bishop's [TOR]
2 13 CAL Singer, Mark LB/FB Alberta
2 14 EDM MacDonald, Bob OT McMaster
2 15 SAS Gioskos, Chris OT/OG Ottawa [HAM]
2 16 SAS Chuhaniuk, Brent P/K Weber State
3 17 TOR Kerr, Paul DE/DT McGill [OTT]
3 18 CAL Hinds, Pat OT/OG San Jose State [BC]
3 19 WPG Boyko, Allan WR Western Michigan
3 20 TOR Yule, John LB Manitoba
3 21 SAS Henderson, Craig OT Minnesota [CAL]
3 22 EDM Trumble, Lance FB/DE McMaster
3 23 HAM Nurse, Richard WR/DB Canisius
3 24 SAS Hitchcock, Bill OT/DT Purdue
4 25 OTT Philbrick, Mike DE Carleton
4 26 BC Coulter, Carl OG/LB Carleton
4 27 CAL Sang, Derek OT San Diego State [WPG]
4 28 TOR Van Belleghem, Dave DB Calgary
4 29 CAL Chen, Richard S Waterloo
4 30 EDM Steeves, Gordon DB Manitoba
4 31 HAM King, Kevin DB/LB Simon Fraser
4 32 SAS Bushley, Paul FB Colgate
5 33 OTT Neufeld, Alan OG Saskatchewan
5 34 BC Elenowibi, Moe OG/OT Brigham Young
5 35 WPG Vandersloot, Dave OG/OT Henderson State
5 36 TOR Madden, Bill DB Wilfrid Laurier
5 37 CAL Godley, Rob S Western Ontario
5 38 EDM Gaertner, Jordan WR Saskatchewan
5 39 HAM Douglas, Scott OT/OG Western Ontario
5 40 SAS Chapman, Paul FB/RB Dickinson State
6 41 OTT Sackschewsky, Cam OG/OT Calgary
6 42 BC Shorman, Doug LB British Columbia
6 43 WPG Zatylny, Steve WR Bishop's
6 44 TOR Ilfill, Gerry RB McGill
6 45 CAL Kazan, Kevin WR/K Calgary
6 46 EDM Porter, Chris RB Windsor
6 47 HAM Monaco, John TE Canisius
6 48 OTT Wilson, Brett WR Ottawa [SAS]
7 49 OTT Coombs, Jamie DL/OG Carleton
7 50 BC Poirier, Phil DT/DE Cincinnati
7 51 WPG McCasin, Lorne DE/DT North Dakota
7 52 TOR MacLean, Richard OT St. Mary's
7 53 CAL Power, Randy LB Mount Allison
7 54 EDM Katsube, Maki SB/RB St. Francis Xavier
7 55 HAM Martens, Jeff OL/DT Alberta
7 56 OTT Mehnert, Hagen LB McGill [SAS]
8 57 OTT Forde, Darryl CB Western Ontario
8 58 BC Kitchener, Richard OT Simon Fraser
8 59 WPG Wiens, Ray OL Saskatchewan
8 60 TOR Arbour, Marco LB Ottawa
8 61 CAL Furlong, Sean WR Calgary
8 62 EDM Webert, Ron P/K Washington State
8 63 HAM Raymond, Mike FB York
8 64 OTT Koladich, Mike LB Western Ontario [SAS]

Supplemental Draft
TOR Zajdel,John LB Vancouver Meralomas Jrs.

1991
February 24, 1991, Hamilton

1 1 HAM Mazzoli, Nick WR Simon Fraser
1 2 SAS Farthing, Dan SB Saskatchewan [BC]
1 3 EDM Murphy, Dan DB Acadia [OTT]
1 4 BC Hull, Bart FB Boise State [SAS]
1 5 SAS Vajda, Paul OG Concordia [TOR]
1 6 CAL Forde, Duane RB Western Ontario
1 7 OTT MacNeil, Brett OT Boston [EDM]
1 8 BC Beaton, Bruce DE Acadia [SAS/WPG]
2 9 HAM Jovanovich, Mike OT Boston College
2 10 TOR Izquierdo, J.P. RB Calgary [BC]
2 11 HAM Schnepf, Phil DB Carleton [OTT]
2 12 SAS Hannem, Anthony LB Acadia
2 13 TOR Green, Chris OT Ottawa
2 14 CAL Douglas, Don TE Western Ontario
2 15 EDM Masotti, Christian SB McGill
2 16 WPG Battaglini, Guy FB Ottawa
3 17 HAM Zizakovic, Lubo DL Maryland
3 18 TOR Dickson, Bruce DB Simon Fraser [BC]
3 19 OTT Mitchell, Geoff RB Weber State
3 20 SAS Maines, Paul OT Concordia
3 21 TOR Giacomazzo, Dave OG Boise State
3 22 CAL Torrance, Bob QB Calgary
3 23 EDM Davis, John LB Western Ontario
3 24 WPG Grant, Steve DE Simon Fraser
4 25 EDM Walker, Gordon DB Manitoba [HAM]
4 26 BC Patterson, Andrew DB Simon Fraser
4 27 OTT Hlady, Gerald OG/DE Windsor
4 28 SAS Rowe, Peter QB Wyoming
4 29 TOR Brown, Mitch RB Eastern Michigan
4 30 EDM Herman, Ron OG Queen's [CAL]
4 31 EDM Brosseau, Cam LB Eastern Illinois
4 32 WPG Rogers, Brendan LB Eastern Washington
5 33 HAM Duncan, Cal OL British Columbia
5 34 TOR Clarke, Tony LB Ottawa [BC]
5 35 OTT Flynn, Chris QB St. Mary's
5 36 SAS Stewart, Jim RB British Columbia
5 37 TOR Lindley, Mike LB Western Ontario
5 38 CAL Knight, Earl CB New Mexico State
5 39 EDM Purcell, Mike DL Calgary
5 40 TOR Nealon, Matthew WR St. Mary's [WPG]
6 41 HAM Tatton, Clark DE Akron
6 42 BC Joseph, Lloyd DL Valley City State
6 43 OTT Turrin, Sylvano OG Bishop's
6 44 SAS Wright, Dan TE Queen's
6 45 TOR Roest, Steve DL Toronto
6 46 CAL Smith, Nigel SB Concordia
6 47 EDM Houlder, Mark LB York
6 48 WPG Westwood, Troy P/K Augustana (South Dakota)
7 49 HAM Hennig, Roger DB British Columbia
7 50 BC Serieska, David OL Simon Fraser
7 51 OTT Baillargeon, Steven WR McGill
7 52 SAS Dopud, Michel RB Southern Illinois
7 53 TOR Soulieres, Stefan OG New Haven
7 54 CAL Zerr, Blair FB San Jose State
7 55 EDM Herget, Todd LB Brigham Young
7 56 WPG Dzikowicz, Jason DB Manitoba
8 57 HAM Belanger, Francois T McGill
8 58 BC Van Vliet, Troy LB British Columbia
8 59 OTT Mahon, Pat G Western Ontario
8 60 SAS Dutton, Rob DL Saskatchewan
8 61 TOR Hanson, Rocky FS Dickinson State
8 62 CAL Ferner, Darren WR Northern State
8 63 EDM Gardner, James WR Simon Fraser
8 WPG Forfeited choice

Supplemental Draft
April 15, 1991

1 1 HAM Pavelec, Mike OT Calgary
1 2 BC Clark, Matt WR Montana
1 3 OTT Raby, Michel DT Ottawa
1 4 SAS Baird, Todd WR Fullerton State
1 5 TOR Lammle, Wayne K Utah
1 CAL, EDM, WPG passed

1992
February 29, 1992, Hamilton

1 1 CAL Covernton, Bruce OT Weber State [HAM]
1 2 SAS Scott, Mark LB Virginia Tech
1 3 OTT Chronopoulos, Denny OG Purdue
1 4 BC King, Lorne RB Toronto [WPG]
1 5 BC Furdyk, Todd OL Rocky Mountain
1 6 EDM Fleming, Sean K/P Wyoming
1 7 CAL Williams, Tyrone WR Western Ontario
1 8 EDM Morris, Chris OL Toronto [TOR]
2 9 HAM Jauch, Joey WR North Carolina
2 10 SAS Bernard, Ray LB Bishop's
2 11 OTT Walcott, Ken DB St. Mary's
2 12 WPG Tsangaris, Chris LB Long Beach State
2 13 BC Peterson, Doug OL/DL Simon Fraser
2 14 EDM Martin, Errol LB Louisville
2 15 SAS Hendrickson, Scott C Minnesota [CAL]
2 16 OTT Sardo, Joe DB Hawaii [OTT]
3 17 HAM Santorelli, Frank LB Simon Fraser
3 18 EDM Taylor, Simon OT Concordia [SAS]
3 19 OTT Chaytors, Dave DL Utah
3 20 WPG Pimiskern, Konrad OL Washington State
3 21 WPG Stackaruk, Tom OL Weber State [BC]
3 22 HAM Young, Glen LB Syracuse [EDM]
3 23 CAL Pandelidis, Bobby OT/OG Eastern Michigan
3 24 TOR Dube, Marc LB Maine
4 25 HAM Bynoe, Rawle DB Louisville
4 26 EDM Chorney, Terris C Nebraska [SAS]
4 27 CAL Marof, Frank RB/SB Guelph [OTT]
4 28 WPG Martin, Andrew WR Cornell
4 29 BC Crysdale, Jamie C Cincinnati
4 30 EDM Elsaghir, Mohammed WR Calgary
4 31 CAL Stiverne, Jean DB Miami (Florida)
4 32 TOR Hughes, Chris DL Hayward State
5 33 HAM Gianakopoulos, Jim DE Colgate
5 34 SAS Wilmsmeyer, Klaus K/P Louisville
5 35 OTT Trebllcock, Rob WR Weber State
5 36 WPG Bary, Ousmane DB Syracuse
5 37 BC Ikonikov, Alex LB Tiffin
5 38 EDM Boyer, Darren RB Illinois
5 39 CAL Annuziata, Sandy DT Western Ontario
5 40 TOR Wilson, Chris LB Bishop's
6 41 HAM Johnson, Brian LB St. Mary's
6 42 SAS MacCallum, Tom OL Minot State
6 43 OTT Boone, Mike LB Queen's
6 44 TOR Partchenko, Peter OT Michigan State [WPG]
6 45 BC Thompson, Steve RB Rocky Mountain
6 46 EDM Dorn, Bruce CB Manitoba

6 47 CAL Knox, Greg DB Wilfrid Laurier
6 48 TOR Bisci, Tim DB Wilfrid Laurier
7 49 HAM Henderson, Rickey OT Manitoba
7 50 SAS Miller, Peter LB Pacific
7 51 OTT Doucette, Mike CB Ottawa
7 52 WPG Rayner, Chris DB Western Ontario
7 53 BC Rend, Mike DB Simon Fraser
7 54 EDM Jongejean, Grant LB Alberta
7 55 CAL Kittleson, Craig RB Calgary
7 56 TOR Schwabe, Jason WR Mayville State
8 57 HAM Fairbairn, Andrew WR Carleton
8 58 SAS Vanderjagt, Mike WR/P West Virginia
8 59 OTT Ployart, Ian DB Concordia
8 60 WPG Goodwin, Shane NG Tulsa
8 61 BC Farquharson, Rod WR Simon Fraser
8 62 EDM Woodward, Todd LB Idaho State
8 63 CAL Buchanan, James WR Calgar
8 64 TOR Lawson, Hugh DL Wilfrid Laurier

1993
March 6, 1993, Calgary

1 1 BC Burke, Patrick DB Fresno CC
1 TOR Forfeited choice [exceeded salary cap]
1 2 SAS Elberg, Brad RB Queen's
1 3 OTT Yatkowski, Paul DT Tennessee
1 4 EDM O'Shea, Mike LB Guelph
1 HAM Forfeited choice [exceeded salary cap]
1 5 WPG Wetmore, Alan LB Acadia
1 6 CAL Pearce, Mark DL Cape Breton
2 7 BC Europe, Tom DB Bishop's
2 8 TOR McCurdy, Brian DB Northern Arizona
2 9 SAS Findlay, Brooks LB Portland State
2 10 OTT Richards, Dwight RB Weber State
2 11 EDM Stucke, Brent SB Wilfrid Laurier
2 12 HAM Martin, P.J. FB Wilfrid Laurier
2 13 WPG McLaughlin, Dave LB British Columbia
2 14 CAL Frers, Greg DB Simon Fraser
3 15 SAS Hickey, Kevin OT Ottawa [BC]
3 16 TOR Johnson, Jerrold FB Azusa Pacific
3 17 SAS Brown, Errol DB Saskatchewan
3 18 OTT Levy, Nigel WR Western Ontario
3 19 EDM Frederick, Albert LB Livingston
3 20 HAM Ishkanian, Ara DE Fullerton State
3 21 CAL Dmytryshyn, Duane SB Saskatchewan [WPG]
3 22 CAL McNeil, Scott OL Boise State
4 23 HAM Yeboah-Kodie, Frank CB Penn State [BC]
4 24 TOR Nimako, George DB Liberty
4 25 SAS Cranmer, Paul DB Grand Valley State
4 26 OTT Noel, Dean RB Delaware State
4 27 EDM McKenzie, Scott K Alberta
4 28 HAM Palmer, Gavin LB Boston University
4 29 HAM Grayson, Sean TE Virginia Tech [WPG]
4 30 CAL Reid, Bruce RB Simon Fraser
5 31 BC Pakulak, Paul SB Simon Fraser
5 32 TOR Stewart, Dean RB Mansfield
5 33 SAS Daigle, Christian DL Bishop's
5 34 OTT Moller, Jason OL Queen's
5 35 EDM Cutler, John K Alberta
5 36 HAM Fischer, Richard DE Toronto
5 37 WPG Burke, Trevor DB St. Mary's
5 38 CAL Williams, Mark DL Houston
6 39 BC Keller, Reinhart DL Wilfrid Laurier
6 40 TOR Jagas, Frank P/K Western Ontario
6 41 SAS Rowe, Kent DE Bishop's
6 42 OTT Marquette, Fred OL Concordia
6 43 EDM Tolbert, Mark SB Alberta
6 44 HAM D'Agostino, Tony RB McMaster
6 45 WPG Magnuson, Quinn OG Washington State
6 46 CAL Sterkenburg, Tom DB Rocky Mountain
7 47 BC Gerela, Ted LB Rocky Mountain
7 48 TOR Scandiffio, Dave OL Toronto
7 49 SAS Watkins, Thane C Delaware State
7 50 OTT Monroe, James C Syracuse
7 51 EDM Benoit, Jeff RB Mansfield
7 52 HAM Dell, Eric DT Queen's
7 53 WPG Johnson, Jay SB Carleton
7 54 CAL Freiter, Mike SB Calgary

Supplemental Draft
4 BC Mantyka, Cory OL Jamestown
5 OTT ?
6 OTT ?
6 EDM ?
? OTT Oxley, Anthony RB St. Mary's

1994
March 5, 1994, Vancouver

Bonus 1 HAM St. German, Val OL McGill
Bonus 2 SAS Burns, Chris OT Portland State
Bonus 3 CAL Danielsen, Vince WR British Columbia
Bonus 4 WPG Carey, Ryan DB Acadia
1 5 OTT Bailey, Tony DE St. Mary's [League]
1 6 BC Shaw, Trevor WR Weber State [TOR]
1 7 OTT Murphy, Rod LB Idaho State
1 8 CAL Kalin, John DB/QB Calgary [HAM]
1 9 BC Ptasek, Stefan WR Wilfrid Laurier
1 10 SAS Quiviger, Matthiew OT McGill
1 11 CAL Philion, Ed DL Ferris State
1 12 WPG Berger, Mitch P/K Colorado
1 13 EDM Wessling, Rob OT Guelph
2 14 TOR Bertone, Claudio FB Lehigh
2 15 OTT Malott, Mike RB Waterloo
2 16 HAM Braitenback, Jeremy WR Saskatchewan
2 17 BC Morreale, Mike WR McMaster
2 18 SAS Greene, Andrew OL Indiana
2 19 CAL Yeboah-Kodie, Phil LB Penn State
2 20 WPG Browne, Kenny OL Colorado
2 21 EDM McNerney, Pat TE/OL Weber State
3 22 TOR Campbell, Mike OL Idaho State
3 23 OTT McCausland, Glenn WR Toronto
3 24 HAM Morgan, Ainsworth WR Toledo
3 25 BC Bromilow, Mike DT Simon Fraser
3 26 CAL Rayner, Ken OL Weber State [SAS]
3 27 CAL Brenner, Craig SB/FB Wilfrid Laurier
3 28 HAM Tindale, Tim FB Western Ontario [WPG]
3 29 EDM Fridd, Darryl DL Alberta
4 30 TOR Irwin, Dave WR Guelph
4 31 OTT Spanic, Obie DT Weber State
4 32 HAM Harris, Chris CB Simon Fraser
4 BC Forfeited choice
4 33 SAS Walters, Andrew DB British Columbia
4 34 CAL McNeil, Jay OL Kent State
4 35 WPG Kucy, Ed OG Arizona
4 36 EDM Zacharias, Brad RB Acadia
5 37 TOR Bennett, Jamie DT Fresno State
5 OTT Forfeited choice
5 38 HAM Cheevers, Mike LB Wilfrid Laurier
5 39 BC Blackwood, Paul FB Cincinnati
5 40 SAS Tighe, Tony OL Edinboro
5 41 CAL Reinson, Roger LB Calgary
5 42 WPG Robson, Kevin OL North Dakota
5 43 EDM Day, Stephen LB Alberta
6 44 TOR Casola, Norm WR Windsor
6 OTT Forfeited choice
6 45 HAM Nichol, Jeff LB Colgate
6 46 BC Zuccato, Paul LB Simon Fraser
6 47 SAS Kozan, Paul RB Queen's
6 48 CAL Harris, Cooper LB Pittsburg State
6 49 WPG Mitchell, Scott QB Toronto
6 EDM Forfeited choice

Supplemental Draft
3 HAM ?

1995
March 11, 1995, Saskatoon

Bonus 1 HAM Nutten, Tom OL Western Michigan
Bonus 2 OTT Reid, Stefen LB Boise State
Bonus 3 TOR Montreuil, Mark DB Concordia
Bonus 4 SAS Alexander, Troy LB Eastern Washington
Bonus 5 EDM El-Mashtoub, Hicham C Arizona
Bonus 6 WPG Graham, Sean SB British Columbia
Bonus 7 CAL Reid, Kevin WR Guelph
Bonus 8 BC Hatfield, Mark OL Bishop's
1 9 HAM Murphy, John OL Morningside
1 10 SAS Provo, Dwayne DB St. Mary's [OTT]
1 11 TOR Benoit, Sheldon LB Western Kentucky
1 12 SAS Lazeo, Rob OT Western Illinois
1 13 EDM Lawson, Mark DB/LB Western Ontario
1 14 WPG Mallett, Jason DB Carleton
1 15 CAL Mattison, Steve FB Illinois
1 16 BC Conlan, Brian T British Columbia
2 17 HAM Hitchcock, Rob LB Weber State
2 18 OTT Masi, Stewart G Western Michigan
2 19 TOR Jones, Frank WR Missouri
2 20 HAM St. John, Jude OL Western Ontario [SAS]
2 21 EDM Sholdice, Derrick OT Northern Illinois
2 22 WPG Skorput, Ante G Michigan
2 23 SAS Makowsky, Gene OL Saskatchewan [CAL]
2 24 SAS Yorston, Brian DT Middle Tennessee State [OTT/BC]
3 HAM Forfeited choice
3 25 OTT Hiscock, Keith G Simon Fraser
3 26 TOR Ralph, Sean RB Ottawa
3 27 OTT Tait, Heron DB Guelph
3 28 EDM Bunting, Blake TE Evangel
3 29 WPG Pejovic, Peter OT Simon Fraser
3 30 CAL Hudecki, Ryan RB McMaster
3 31 OTT Sarty, Steve WR St. Mary's [BC]
4 32 HAM Assmann, Charles DB Guelph
4 33 OTT Fowles, Glen OT Willamette
4 34 OTT Dorenlien, Pierre-Paul OT Ottawa [TOR]
4 35 CAL Warawa, Sheldon OT Minot State [SAS]
4 36 EDM Algajer, Kevin LB Alberta
4 37 WPG Miller, Wade LB Manitoba
4 38 SAS Smith, Gerry LB Wilfrid Laurier [CAL]
4 39 OTT Marriott, Sean LB St. Mary's [BC]
5 40 HAM Wigmore, Kip WR Guelph
5 41 OTT Konno, Massaki SB Bishop's
5 42 TOR Raposo, John DE Toronto
5 43 OTT Lavallee, Danny DL Concordia [SAS]
5 44 EDM Dallison, Steve DL Alberta
5 45 WPG Graham, Todd NG Glenville State
5 46 CAL Clarke, Mark WR Simon Fraser
5 47 BC Jusdanis, Larry QB Acadia
6 48 HAM Kuntz, Micheal TE McMaster
6 49 OTT Simoncic, Micheal OL Concordia
6 50 TOR Carruthers, Micheal DT Princeton
6 51 SAS Schneider, Brent QB Saskatchewan
6 52 EDM Beak, Stewart TE Western Ontario
6 53 WPG Newman, Chris LB Utah
6 54 CAL Fielding, Brad DT St. Francis Xavier
6 55 BC Crawford, Ian WR Bishop's

Las Vegas Dispersal Draft
April 18, 1995, via conference call

1 1 HAM Calvillo, Anthony QB [MEM]
1 2 BIR Peoples, Shont'e LB
1 3 SHR Mayfield, Curtis WR
1 4 HAM Hall, Kalin RB
1 5 OTT Stephens, Michael WR
1 6 TOR Kelly, Maurice CB
1 7 SA Sawyer, Jeff DE
1 8 SAS Wembley, Prince SB
1 9 EDM Hagan, Darian RB
1 10 WPG Vanover, Tamarick WR
1 11 CAL Jordan, Al CB
1 12 BAL Huerta, Carlos K
1 13 BC Shipley, Ron OL
2 14 BIR Anderson, Steve DE
2 15 HAM Robinson, Don DB [MEM]
2 16 SHR Jefferson, Ben OT
2 17 HAM Nicholson, Calvin DB
2 18 OTT Geter, Eric DB
2 19 TOR Kronenberg, Bob OL
2 20 SA Claiborne, Robert WR
2 21 SAS Broady, Tim LB
2 22 EDM Whiting, Al SB
2 23 WPG Johnson, Leonard DT
2 24 CAL Medlock, Jason DE
2 25 BAL Bullock, James CB
2 26 BC Clark, Michael DB
3 27 MEM Maeva, David DB
3 28 BIR Hart, Roy DT
3 29 SHR Keen, Robbie K
3 30 HAM Crawford, Cedric DB
3 31 OTT Burch, Alfie DB
3 32 TOR Cummins, Jeff DT
3 33 SA Garten, Joe OL
3 34 SAS Allen, Zock LB
3 35 EDM Sheppard, Derrick WR
3 WPG passed
3 36 CAL Hollis, David DB
3 37 BAL Tucker, Greg LB
3 38 BC Leach, John RB
4 BIR passed
4 39 MEM Gibson, Craig OT
4 40 SHR Houston, Brandon OL
4 41 HAM Embray, Keith DE
4 42 OTT Steele, Norman DL
4 TOR passed
4 43 SA Richards, James OL
4 44 SAS Cook, Lance DE
4 EDM, WPG, CAL, BAL passed
4 45 BC Gomes, Lenny DL
5 MEM passed
5 46 BIR Haynes, Hayward OL
5 SHR passed
5 47 HAM Becton, Jesse LB
5 48 OTT Robertson, Derrell DE
5 TOR, SA, SAS, EDM, WPG, CAL, BAL, BC passed

1996

Dispersal Draft
March 7, 1996, via conference call

1 1 OTT Archer, David QB SA
1 2 TOR Gordon, Alex DE MEM
1 3 SAS Mayfield, Chris WR SHR
1 4 WPG Snipes, Angelo LB BIR
1 5 HAM Grant, Marcus WR BIR
1 6 BC Hamilton, Brandon CB SHR
1 7 EDM Shipman, Al RB MEM
1 8 CAL Harding, Rodney DT MEM
1 9 MTL Saunders, Mike RB SA
2 10 HAM Phillips, Jason WR BIR [OTT]
2 11 TOR Dawson, Bobby DB MEM
2 12 SAS Harris, Rod WR SHR
2 13 WPG Lyons, Damion CB MEM
2 14 HAM Gans, Donovan DE BIR
2 15 BC Strode, Andre DB BIR
2 16 EDM Cavness, Grady DB SA
2 17 CAL Anderson, Steve DE BIR
2 18 MTL Battle, Greg LB MEM
3 19 OTT Britton, Eddie WR BIR
3 20 TOR Smith, Donald CB MEM
3 21 SAS Peoples, Shont'e DE BIR
3 22 WPG Armstrong, Mike DT MEM
3 23 HAM Phillips, Kim CB SHR
3 24 BC Maeve, David LB MEM
3 25 EDM Miller, Maurice LB SA
3 26 CAL Davis, Eddie DB BIR
3 27 MTL Kemp, Jim QB SA
4 28 OTT Wallace, Jason CB SA
4 29 TOR Berry, Ed CB MEM
4 30 SAS Ford, Darryl LB MEM
4 31 WPG Stock, Mark WR SA
4 32 HAM Cody, Mac WR BIR
4 33 BC Moore, Delius WR BIR
4 34 EDM Rayam, Tom OL BIR
4 35 CAL Cozart, Travis RB SHR
4 36 MTL Bradford, Norman RB SHR

5 37 OTT Zingo, Chris LB SHR
5 38 TOR Perez, Chris OT MEM
5 39 SAS Collins, Shawn WR MEM
5 40 WPG Baysinger, Freeman WR SHR
5 41 HAM Reed, Jimmy LB BIR
5 42 BC Thomas, Fernando CB BIR
5 43 EDM Keen, Robbie K SHR
5 44 CAL Peoples, Sam CB BIR
5 45 MTL Karlick, Joe WR SA
6 46 OTT Mash, Alex DE SHR
6 47 TOR Muilenburg, Darrin OL SA
6 48 SAS Dyko, Chris OT BIR
6 49 WPG Jordan, Anthony RB MEM
6 50 HAM Patterson, Roosevelt OL BIR
6 51 BC Scott, Johnny DL SHR
6 52 EDM Harris, Johnny DB SA
6 53 CAL Austin, Schredrick WR BIR
6 54 MTL Perry, Mario LB SHR
7 55 OTT Hess, Billy WR SA
7 56 TOR Anderson, Jami LB MEM
7 57 SAS Ledbetter, Mark DL BIR
7 58 WPG Fuller, Eddie RB SA
7 59 HAM King, Quenton DB SHR
7 60 BC Montgomery, Fred WR SHR
7 61 EDM Franks, Charles DB SA
7 62 CAL Hammond, Vance OL MEM
7 63 MTL Brown, Hurlie DB SA
8 64 OTT Gates, Marcus DB SA
8 65 TOR Player, Scott P BIR
8 66 SAS Drawhorn, Anthony DB BIR
8 67 WPG Evans, Bobby DB SHR
8 68 HAM Long, Ted WR BIR
8 69 BC Jones, Mike LB BIR
8 70 EDM Delaney, Akaba DL BIR
8 71 CAL Simmons, Kelvin QB BIR
8 72 MTL Zendejas, Luis K BIR
9 73 OTT Garrett, Judd RB SA
9 74 TOR Dingle, Mike RB MEM
9 75 SAS Faulkner, Kyle DE BIR
9 76 WPG Smith, Daryle OT SA
9 77 HAM Montford, Joe LB SHR
9 78 BC Oates, Tommy DB BIR
9 79 EDM Roland, Bobby DB BIR
9 80 CAL Mills, Troy RB SA
9 81 MTL Foggie, Rickey QB MEM
10 82 OTT Dausin, Chris C SHR
10 83 TOR Giles, Oscar DL SA
10 84 SAS Kiselak, Mike C SA
10 85 WPG Pearson, Matt DE SHR
10 86 HAM Ward, Jim DT MEM
10 87 BC Carthon, Reggie DB SHR
10 88 EDM Henley, Steve LB BIR
10 89 CAL Ragsdale, Kenyon LB BIR
10 90 MTL Walton, Tim LB SA
11 91 OTT Covington, Will WR SHR
11 92 TOR Lee, Jimmy WR SA
11 93 SAS Morris, Gary SB MEM
11 94 WPG Redmond, Jamie DB MEM
11 95 Smith, Junior RB SHR
11 96 BC Mystrom, Nick K MEM
11 EDM passed
11 97 CAL Lucas, David WR SA
11 98 MTL Bates, Steve DE MEM
12 99 OTT Neal, Jeff OL BIR
12100 TOR Jones, Todd G MEM
12101 SAS Anderson, Gary RB MEM
12102 WPG Brown, Phil RB SA
12103 HAM Barto, Danton LB MEM
12 BC, EDM, CAL passed
12104 MTL Sherman, Heath RB SA
13105 OTT Bech, Brett SB SA
13106 TOR Paige, Todd WR MEM
13107 SAS Perkins, Bruce RB MEM
13108 WPG Brantley, Sean DE BIR
13109 HAM Jefferson, Ben OT SHR
13 BC, EDM, CAL passed
13110 MTL Kirksey, William LB BIR
14111 OTT Teichelman, Lance DL SA
14112 TOR Nee, John OL MEM
14113 SAS Wilson, Walter WR MEM
14114 WPG Tolliver, Billy Joe QB SHR
14115 HAM Sheldon, Anthony DB SHR
14 BC, EDM, CAL passed
14116 MTL David, Drew RB BIR
15117 OTT Wembley, Prince SB BIR
15 TOR passed
15118 SAS Stoell, Mike OL SHR
15 WPG passed
15119 Martin, John RB MEM
15 BC, EDM, CAL, MTL passed
16 OTT, TOR passed
16120 SAS Woodside, Keith RB BIR
16 WPG passed
16121 HAM White, Will DB SHR
16 BC, EDM, CAL, MTL passed

March 14, 1996, Toronto

1 1 EDM Blair, Don SB Calgary [OTT]
1 2 TOR Wiltshire, Kelly CB James Madison
1 3 SAS Sutherland, Mike OL Northern Illinois
1 4 WPG Henry, Andrew DB C.W. Post
1 5 HAM Ring, Justin LB Simon Fraser
1 6 BC Pimiskern, Mark LB Washington State
1 7 EDM Arrindell, Duane OL Nothern Illinois
1 8 CAL Duclair, Farell LB Concordia
1 9 MTL Montana, Denis WR Concordia
2 10 HAM Walters, Kyle RB Guelph [OTT]
2 11 WPG Van Hofwegen, Harry DL Carleton [TOR]
2 12 SAS Monois, Tom WR Northeastern
2 13 WPG Reade, Sean RB Western Ontario
2 14 HAM Mihelic, Mike OT Indiana
2 15 BC English, Andrew WR British Columbia
2 16 EDM Hamilton, Jay RB Alberta
2 17 CAL Robinson, Robert DT Cincinnati
2 18 MTL Chiu, Bryan DT Washington State
3 19 OTT Brennan, Sammie DB Bishop's
3 20 TOR Eiben, L.J. WR Humboldt State
3 21 CAL Charles, Jean-Agnes DB Michigan [SAS]
3 22 WPG Speena, Shane LB Henderson State
3 23 SAS Francis, Alton RB/K Northern Illinois [HAM]
3 24 BC Yamaoka, Brad RB British Columbia
3 25 EDM Napastuk, Sheldon DT Iowa State
3 26 CAL Stevens, Cory P/K Minot State
3 27 MTL Cassidy, Adam OL Alberta
4 28 OTT Shillingford, Grayson SB British Columbia
4 29 SAS Frlan, Paul LB St. Francis Xavier [TOR]
4 30 SAS Ell, Dwayne DL North Dakota
4 31 WPG Jean-Pierre, Leonard RB York
4 32 HAM Brown, Dan FB/RB Bemidji State
4 33 BC Ho-Young, Kevin RB St. Francis Xavier
4 34 EDM Cunningham, Murray DL Alberta
4 35 CAL Greco, Vito LB/FB Carleton
4 36 MTL Hipsz, Tom DE Toronto
5 37 OTT Curtis, Darcy DT/OL Simon Fraser
5 38 OTT Savard, George OL Ottawa [TOR]
5 39 SAS Van Waes, Nelson SB/LB Tulsa
5 40 WPG MacKenzie, Stuart OT Western Kentucky
5 41 HAM Kent, Paul OL Kuztown
5 42 BC Bryan, Victor DB Simon Fraser
5 43 EDM Saul, Joe DE Saskatchewan
5 44 CAL Kim, Jung-Yul OT Toronto
5 MTL Forfeited choice
6 45 OTT McElwain, Robert DB Windsor
6 46 TOR Biakabutuka, Tim RB Michigan
6 47 SAS Flory, Christopher OL Saskatchewan
6 48 WPG Holmstrom, Mark LB Manitoba
6 49 HAM Russel, Troy DB Bishop's
6 50 BC Bourne, Bryan OL British Columbia
6 51 EDM Park, Darcy FB Alberta
6 52 CAL Lane, David OL Simon Fraser
6 53 MTL Rainbow, Adrian QB British Columbia
7 54 OTT Hendricks, Micheal LB Ottawa
7 55 TOR Poole, Craig WR Windsor
7 56 SAS Moe, Greg K Saskatchewan
7 57 WPG Lewis, Gerald LB Eastern Michigan
7 58 HAM Burnie, David DE Western Ontario
7 59 BC Greenhow, Paul CB Queen's
7 60 EDM Shwetz, Troy DB Jamestown
7 61 CAL passed
7 62 MTL Charles, Marc DT Morgan State

1997

Ottawa Rough Riders Dispersal Draft
March 12, 1997, via conference call

Bonus 1 SAS Archer, David QB
1 2 SAS McGriggs, Lamar LB
1 3 BC Humphries, Leonard CB
1 4 HAM Wilhite, Kenny CB
1 5 EDM Bolduc, Andre SB [WPG]
1 6 MTL Okeke, Uzooma OG
1 7 CAL Rogers, Joseph WR
1 8 EDM Gordon, Bob WR
1 9 TOR Brennan, Sammie DB
2 10 SAS Daniels, Shawn FB
2 11 BC Arrindell, Duane OL
2 12 HAM Steinauer, Orlondo S
2 13 WPG Spanic, Obie DL
2 14 MTL Burch, Swift DT
2 15 CAL Bernard, Ray LB
2 16 EDM Henry, Tommy DB
2 17 TOR Anderson, Travis WR
3 18 SAS Dinnall, Dave RB
3 19 BC Gillock, Mike DB
3 20 HAM West, Frank DB
3 21 WPG Evans, Stacy DE
3 22 MTL Hendricks, Michael LB
3 23 CAL Mills, Troy RB
3 24 EDM Reade, Sean RB
3 25 TOR Mero, Joe CB
4 26 SAS Grier, Profail RB
4 BC passed
4 27 HAM Younger, Jermaine LB
4 28 WPG Zizakovic, Lubo DT
4 29 MTL Stevenson, Robert OG
4 30 CAL Esty, Chuck OG
4 EDM, TOR passed
5 SAS, BC, HAM passed
5 31 WPG Dzikowicz, Jayson DB
5 32 MTL Harper, David LB
5 CAL, EDM, TOR passed

April 7, 1997, Toronto

1 1 TOR Folk, Chad OL Utah [OTT]
1 2 SAS Fairbrother, Ben OL Calgary
1 3 EDM Franklin, Ian CB Weber State [BC]
1 4 HAM Prinsen, Tim OG North Dakota
1 5 CAL Brown, Doug DL Simon Fraser [WPG]
1 6 MTL Charbonneau, Steve DL New Hampshire
1 7 CAL Clemett, Jason LB Simon Fraser
1 8 EDM Verbeek, Mark OL St. Francis Xavier
1 9 TOR DuBuc, Matt SB Texas Tech
2 10 BC Beveridge, Bob OL British Columbia [SAS]
2 11 MTL Pathon, Jerome WR Washington [BC]
2 12 HAM Rumolo, Joe DL Akron
2 13 SAS Szarka, Chris FB Eastern Illinois [BC/WPG]
2 14 MTL Coughlin, Ryan OL McGill
2 15 CAL Traversy, Jeff DT Edinboro
2 16 EDM Denis, Patrice LB Western Ontario
2 17 TOR Salter, Steve OL Ottawa
3 18 TOR Henry, Aldi CB Michigan State [WPG/SAS]
3 19 BC Stoilen, Paul LB Simon Fraser
3 HAM Choice traded to OTT
3 20 BC Partchenko, John OT Michigan [WPG]
3 21 MTL Heppell, Bruno RB Western Michigan
3 22 CAL Rocca, Frank OL Eastern Michigan
3 23 WPG Henriques, Marice S Colorado [EDM]
3 24 TOR Mudge, Dave OT Michigan State
4 25 BC Anderson, Bret P Simon Fraser [OTT]
4 26 SAS Raphael, Mark CB Ottawa
4 27 BC Miller, Martin CB Manitoba
4 28 HAM Nohra, Mark RB British Columbia
4 29 MTL Krete, Derek LB Western Ontario [WPG]
4 30 MTL Carruthers, Ryan SB Calgary
4 31 CAL Ubani, Uzo SB Concordia
4 32 EDM Heasman, David OL Northern Arizona
4 33 TOR Hansen, Jayson OL Texas Tech
5 34 SAS Batson, Andre WR York
5 35 BC MacDonald, Jamie OT Northern Illinois
5 36 HAM Normand, Luc WR Bishop's
5 37 WPG Swift, Jonathan LB Tennessee-Martin
5 38 MTL Brereton, Andy SB Western Michigan
5 39 CAL Bagnail, Trent DB Saskatchewan
5 40 EDM Santiago, O.J. TE Kent State
5 41 TOR Giardetti, Mark DE Evangel
6 42 SAS Comisky, Dan OL Windsor
6 43 BC Lochbaum, Kelly LB Northern Arizona
6 HAM Choice forfeited
6 44 WPG Weathers, Wayne DE Manitoba
6 45 MTL Bellefroid, Francis LB Bishop's
6 46 CAL Donkersley, Paul RB Acadia
6 47 EDM Hardy, Chris QB Manitoba
6 48 TOR Kershaw, Kris QB Salisbury State

Supplmental Draft
May, 1997
TOR Kirwan, Andre WR Stanford
TOR O'Day, Jeremy OL Edinboro

1998

April 7, 1998, via conference call

1 1 HAM Fleiszer, Tim DL Harvard
1 2 TOR Miller-Johnston, Dave P/K Concordia [WPG]
1 3 BC Hardin, Steve T Oregon
1 4 CAL Pilon, Marc LB Syracuse
1 5 EDM Girard, Phillippe DB Mount Allison
1 6 MTL Cahoon, Ben WR Brigham Young
1 7 SAS Galick, Curtis S British Columbia
1 TOR Forfeited choice
2 8 SAS Tounkara, Ousmane WR Ottawa [HAM]
2 WPG Forfeited choice
2 9 BC Thelwell, Ryan WR Minnesota
2 10 CAL Arlain, Andre SB St. Francis Xavier
2 11 EDM Chahine, Samir G McGill
2 MTL Forfeited choce
2 12 TOR Dunbrack, Roger DL Western Ontario [SAS]
2 TOR ?
3 13 HAM Grant, Devin OL Utah
3 14 BC Kellett, Matt K Saskatchewan [WPG]
3 15 MTL Flory, Scott OL Saskatchewan [WPG/BC]
3 16 CAL Ah You, Harland DL Brigham Young
3 17 EDM Deibert, Scott RB Minot State
3 18 MTL Loftus, William DB Manitoba
3 19 SAS Pressburger, Kevin LB Waterloo
3 20 TOR Brown, Jermaine RB Winona State
4 21 HAM Jayoussi, Tarek WR Calgary
4 22 WPG Sutherland, Garrett LB Northern Illinois
4 23 WPG Roy, Jean-Daniel DL Ottawa [BC]
4 24 CAL Cummings, Aubrey WR Acadia
4 25 EDM Evraire, Chris SB Ottawa
4 26 WPG Williams, Eddie WR Southwest State [MTL]
4 27 SAS Van Geel, Jason LB Waterloo
4 28 TOR Mlachak, Brian K Calgary
5 29 HAM Brown, Jeff CB Acadia
5 30 BC Gravel, Bernard DB Laval [WPG]
5 31 BC Pepe-Esposito, Francesco LB Laval
5 32 CAL Stahl, Gene RB Calgary
5 33 EDM Cooper, Jim OL British Columbia

5 34 MTL Lafontaine, Daniel OL McGill
5 35 TOR Shilts, Eric WR Toronto
6 36 HAM Hutchison, Benjie DL British Columbia
6 37 WPG Baunemann, John K Manitoba
6 38 WPG Vath, Chad LB Manitoba [BC]
6 39 CAL Bednarek, Jodi LB Calgary
6 40 EDM Kossack, Adam OL Hastings
6 41 MTL Ireland, Kelly OL St. Mary's
6 42 SAS Rapesse, James LB Saskatchewan
6 43 TOR Mitoulas, Bill LB Notre Dame

Supplemental Draft
May, 1998
TOR Prefontaine.Noel K San Diego State

1999
April 13, 1999, via conference call

1 1 BC Meier, Rob DE Washington State [WPG]
1 2 TOR DeLaPeralle, David OL Kentucky [SAS]
1 3 BC Lotysz, Greg OL North Dakota
1 4 EDM Bollers, Tervor FB Iowa
1 5 MTL Girard, Sylvain WR Concordia [TOR]
1 6 MTL Sanchez, Davis DB Oregon
1 7 HAM Grant, Corey WR Wilfrid Laurier
1 8 CAL Singh, Bobby OL Portland State
2 9 EDM Williams, Aaron DE Indiana [WPG]
2 10 SAS Fortin, Stephane S Indianapolis
2 11 BC Beaudoin, Mathieu OL Syracuse
2 12 MTL Hoople, Chris DB British Columbia [EDM]
2 13 TOR Shaw, Wayne CB Kent State
2 14 BC Pol, David OT British Columbia [MTL]
2 15 BC Mercier, Richard OL Miami (Florida) [HAM]
2 16 CAL Legault, Cameron DT Carleton
3 17 WPG Pilon, Jeff OL Syracuse
3 18 SAS Nkeyasen, Kennedy RB Idaho State
3 19 BC Kralt, Jason DB Carleton
3 20 EDM LaPointe, Eric RB Mount Allison
3 21 TOR Darche, J.P. LB McGill
3 22 MTL Semanou, Yannick DL Howard
3 23 HAM Bryce, Morty DB Bowling Green
3 24 CAL Davis, Evan RB Concordia
4 25 MTL Chalmers, Brad OL St. Mary's [WPG]
4 26 SAS Hammer, Matthew DB Guelph
4 27 BC Higgins, Craig RB Western Ontario
4 28 EDM Walker, Brent WR Mary
4 29 TOR Trudel, Andre OL Laval
4 30 MTL Anderson, Jeffrey DT Concordia
4 31 HAM Tibbits, Jason DB Waterloo
5 CAL Forfeited choice
5 32 WPG Abou-Mechrek, Mike OL Western Ontario
5 33 SAS Sanderson, Eric OT York
5 34 BC Crumb, Jason QB Saskatchewan
5 35 EDM Clarkson, Frantz CB Manitoba
5 36 TOR Hall, Glynn WR St. Mary's
5 37 MTL Lefsrud, Kevin OL Saskatchewan
5 38 HAM MacKenzie, Michael RB Eastern Washington
5 39 CAL Disley, Dan WR Western Ontario
6 40 WPG Wilkinson, Ryan QB Waterloo
6 41 SAS Panaro, Carlo OL Alberta
6 42 BC Singh, Akbal RB British Columbia
6 43 EDM Bowen, Orlando DB Nothern Illinois
6 TOR Forfeited choice
6 44 MTL Landry, Pierre DB Ottawa
6 45 HAM Cheron, Pascal OL Laval
6 46 CAL Kolaczek, Andy OL Calgary

Supplemental Draft
May 14, 1999
CAL Blair, Wayne LB Tulane

2000
April 18, 2000, via conference call

1 1 SAS St. James, Tyson LB British Columbia
1 2 WPG McField, Daaron DL British Columbia
1 3 EDM Bakker, Tim C Western Ontario
1 4 TOR Carter, Donnavan S Northern Illinois
1 5 CAL Tounkara, Ibrahim SB Ottawa [MTL]
1 6 BC Belli, Adriano DE Houston
1 7 CAL Regimbald, Scott TE Houston
1 HAM Forfeited choice
2 8 SAS Gallant, Shawn DB Eastern Kentucky
2 9 EDM Harrod, Rob WR Ottawa [WPG]
2 10 EDM Carr, Craig RB Manitoba
2 11 TOR Clarke, Richard WR Weber State
2 12 MTL Petz, Mat DE Wake Forest
2 BC Forfeited choice
2 13 CAL Ward, Ryan OT New Hampshire
2 14 HAM Juhasz, Mike WR North Dakota
3 15 SAS Ching, Dylan WR San Diego
3 16 MTL Kane, Morgan RB Wake Forest [BC/WPG]
3 17 EDM Hudson, George G New Mexico State
3 18 TOR Souter, Carson K Montana State
3 19 MTL Gavadza, Jason TE Kent State
3 20 BC Johnson, Brent DL Ohio State
3 21 CAL Wayne, Clinton DE Ohio State
3 22 HAM Lambert, Paul G Western Michigan
4 23 SAS O'Brien, Mike QB/P Western Ontario
4 24 TOR Meloche, Benoit LB Laval [WPG]
4 25 WPG Howell, Markus WR Texas Southern [BC/EDM]
4 26 TOR Millington, Kojo DE Wilfrid Laurier
4 27 MTL Stables, Harvey WR Wilfrid Laurier
4 28 BC Padelford, Loren OL Guelph
4 29 CAL Ring, Kent LB Simon Fraser
4 30 HAM McCullum, Joe OL Utah
5 31 SAS Clarke, Hudson TE Western Ontario
5 32 WPG Schwab, Eric DE Wilfrid Laurier
5 33 EDM Vickers, Rob OT Wilfrid Laurier
5 34 TOR Coutts, Brad WR British Columbia
5 35 MTL Hewitt, Ian K Minot State
5 36 WPG Everett, Grant G North Dakota [BC]
5 37 CAL Blenkhorn, Paul OL Western Ontario
5 38 HAM MacLean, James SB Queen's
6 39 SAS Forsythe, Jamie OL Western Ontario
6 40 WPG Sheridan, Matthew DL Manitoba
6 41 EDM Dossous, Yves LB Kent State
6 42 TOR Posy-Audette, Jean-Vincent DB Laval
6 43 MTL Clarke, Andre DB Southeast Missouri State
6 44 BC Rayne, Fabian RB Western Ontario
6 45 CAL Balog, Brock DB Calgary
6 46 HAM Moorsed, Doug Van OL California (Pennsylvania)

2001
April 26, 2001, via conference call

1 1 SAS Schultz, Scott DL North Dakota
1 2 BC Williams, Ian LB Memphis [TOR]
1 3 BC Green, Lyle FB Toledo [WPG]
1 4 TOR Reid, Angus G Simon Fraser [HAM]
1 5 EDM Chevrier, Randy DT McGill
1 6 CAL Peterson, Kamau WR New Hampshire
1 7 MTL Fritz, Luke OL Eastern Washington
1 8 BC Thorsen, Leif G Montana
2 9 SAS French, Jason WR Murray State
2 10 CAL Deck, Lawrence DB Fresno State [TOR]
2 11 MTL Woodock, Pat WR Syracuse [WPG]
2 12 HAM Grant, Karim LB Acadia
2 13 EDM Burke, Fabian CB Toledo
2 14 CAL O'Mahony, Duncan K British Columbia
2 15 MTL Palmer, Jesse QB Florida
2 16 BC Boreham, Jamie K/WR Saskatchewan
3 17 SAS Neptune, Teddy LB Ottawa
3 18 MTL Gibson, Phil DL Toledo [TOR]
3 19 WPG Wearing, Ben WR McGill
3 20 HAM Bowles, Randy TE Simon Fraser
3 21 EDM Carson, Glen OL Saskatchewan
3 22 CAL Zubedi, Farwan WR Washington State
3 23 CAL Shaver, Luke S Ottawa [MTL]
3 24 BC Robinson, Scott WR Simon Fraser
4 25 MTL Gifford, Shawn OT Charleston Southern [SAS]
4 26 TOR Eiben, Kevin S Bucknell
4 27 WPG Tsatsaronis, Nick RB Memphis
4 28 HAM Donnelly, Ryan OL McMaster
4 29 MTL Moore, Peter DL Syracuse [EDM]
4 30 CAL Carter, Andrew DB Bishop's
4 31 MTL Maheu, Steven WRB Simon Fraser
4 32 BC Bates, Kelly OL Saskatchewan
5 33 SAS DiBattista, Mike WR Ottawa
5 34 TOR Talbot, Andre WR Wilfrid Laurier
5 35 WPG Dryden, Howie DB Manitob
5 36 HAM Waszczuk, Mike LB Slippery Rock
5 37 EDM Petit, Guillaume DL Alberta
5 38 CAL Simmer, Jeffrey LB Regina
5 39 TOR Romans, Jermaine DB Acadia [MTL]
5 40 BC Tucker, Dave LB Manitoba
6 41 SAS Frenette, Jocelyn G Ottawa
6 42 TOR McKnight, Matt S Waterloo
6 43 WPG Fabiani, Darryl DB Western Ontario
6 44 HAM Grant, Will QB Acadia
6 45 EDM Wright, William DB Bishop's
6 46 CAL D'Onofrio, David LB York
6 47 MTL Cote, Phil QB Ottawa
6 48 BC Collings, Eric OL British Columbia

2002

Ottawa Renegades Expansion Draft
January 17, 2002, via conference call

Asbell, Troy LB SAS
Bell, Ricky CB CAL
Coulter, Carl C HAM
Dittman, Seth OL HAM
Gallant, Shawn DB EDM
Giancola, Dan K TOR
Grace, John LB MTL
Henry, Andrew DB EDM
Hudson, George G EDM
Lochbaum, Kelly LB CAL
Mauer, Mike RB BC
O'Reilly, Joseph DL WPG
Oliver, Jimmy WR BC
Perry, Fred DL EDM
Robichaud, Matt LB HAM
Ruiz, Donald S WPG
Scott, Earl C Toronto
Wayne, Clinton DL CAL
Wiltshire, Kelly LB MTL

April 25, 2002, via conference call

1 1 OTT Gauthier, Alexandre OL Laval
1 2 OTT Vilmek, Mike RB Simon Fraser
1 SAS Forfeited choice
1 3 TOR Annett, Cory OL Eastern Michigan
1 4 BC Clermont, Jason SB Regina
1 5 MTL Dorvelus, Patrick LB Hofstra
1 6 BC Cheng, Patrick DL Simon Fraser [HAM/EDM?]
1 7 HAM Macdonald, John DL McGill
1 8 CAL Oosterhuis, Jon DE New Hampshire [WPG]
1 9 CAL Nugen, Brian WR York
2 10 OTT Owchar, D.J. DL Bowling Green State
2 11 OTT Fleming, Pat P Bowling Green State [SAS]
2 12 MTL Haji-Rasouli, Sherko OL Miami (Florida) [TOR]
2 13 OTT Ralph, Brock WR Wyoming [BC]
2 14 CAL Dubuc, Deitan TE Michigan [OTT/TOR/MTL]
2 15 SAS Boulianne, Francois OL Laval [EDM]
2 16 HAM Robertson, Jake OL Simon Fraser
2 17 BC Romberg, Brett OL Miami (Florida) [WPG]
2 18 CAL Gordon, Scott DB Ottawa
3 19 OTT Lawrence, Kevin RB Northwestern
3 20 SAS Thibeault, Patrick SB St. Mary's
3 21 TOR Tremblay, Robin DE Houston
3 22 BC Gayton, Chris LB Kentucky
3 23 MTL Jansen, Josh LB Occidental
3 24 EDM Diedrick, Dahrran RB Nebraska
3 25 HAM Borden, Doug DL St. Mary's
3 26 WPG Shaver, Micheal FB Ottawa
3 27 CAL Seitz, Reid WR Northern Iowa
4 28 TOR Stewart, Rob DT Manitoba [SAS/OTT]
4 29 SAS Edwards, Darnell CB Manitoba
4 30 TOR Sanschagrin, Alexis DB Western Ontario
4 31 BC Williams, John RB Edinboro
4 32 MTL Fiacconi, Aaron OL Mansfield
4 33 MTL Landon, Jonathan DL Queen's [EDM]
4 34 HAM Elliott, Jamie WR Calgary
4 35 WPG Faisthuber, Mike SB Manitoba
4 36 CAL Almon, Jeff FB Calgary
5 37 OTT Marcellus, Youdlain DB Buffalo
5 38 SAS Segovia, Gonzalo DT Eastern Illinois
5 39 TOR Brereton, Marvin RB Buffalo
5 40 WPG Orris, Lloyd RB Simon Fraser [BC]
5 41 BC Maeko, Atnas WR St. Mary's [MTL]
5 42 EDM Jarrett, Olanzo DE Toledo
5 43 HAM Coe, Scott LB Manitoba
5 44 WPG Mikawoz, Joey LB Manitoba
5 45 TOR Walsh, Chuck LB Waterloo [CAL]
6 46 OTT Paopao, Tyler QB Occidental
6 47 SAS Nash, Curtis DB St. Mary's
6 48 TOR Spender, Sean LB Guelph
6 49 TOR Cockburn, Jarel WR Columbia [BC]
6 50 MTL Sutherland, Mitch DL Alberta
6 51 EDM Dubiellak, Andrew WR Nevada-Las Vegas
6 52 HAM Vermette, Kenneth RB Manitoba
6 53 BC Orel, Joe WR Manitoba [WPG]
6 54 TOR Ray, Darryl WR Ottawa [CAL]

2003
April 30, 2003, via conference call

1 1 CAL Morley, Steve OL St. Mary's [EDM/OTT]
1 2 CAL McGrath, Joe OT Miami (Florida)
1 3 HAM Radlein, Julian RB British Columbia
1 4 EDM Casseus, Emmanuel LB Michigan [CAL/TOR]
1 5 CAL Lysack, Wes DB Manitoba [SAS]
1 6 BC Jackson, Paris WR Utah
1 7 CAL Calixte, Marc LB Tennessee-Martin [WPG]
1 8 EDM Spencer, Randy DT Weber State
1 9 MTL Noel, Andrew WR Acadia
2 10 EDM Aidoo, Kojo FB McMaster [OTT]
2 11 CAL Robertson, Taylor OL Central Florida
2 12 CAL Sciortino, Sandro K Boston College [HAM]
2 13 OTT Kine, Trevor OT New Mexico State [TOR]
2 14 MTL Karikari, Richard CB St. Francis Xavier [SAS]
2 15 BC Glatt, Javier LB British Columbia
2 16 OTT Hobson, Louis DL Stanford [WPG]
2 17 OTT Idonije, Israel DE Manitoba [EDM]
2 18 MTL Carter, Kerry RB Stanford
3 19 OTT Kabongo, Patrick DT Nebraska
3 20 EDM Whitehouse, Dounia CB Charleston Southern [CAL]
3 21 HAM Scott, Kevin LB California (Pennsylvania)
3 22 WPG Krenbrink, Todd OL Regina [TOR]
3 23 SAS McCullough, Mike LB St. Francis Xavier
3 24 BC Gourgues, Carl OL Laval
3 25 CAL Labinjo, Mike DL Michigan State [WPG]
3 26 EDM Bonaventura, Joseph LB St. Mary's
3 27 MTL Brandt, Mat TE Miami (Ohio)
4 28 TOR Mariuz, Ray LB McMaster [OTT]
4 29 CAL Probherbs, Hassan WR Portland State
4 30 HAM Barrenechea, Agustin LB Calgary
4 TOR Forfeited choice
4 31 SAS Merrick, Jim OG McGill

4 32 WPG Roy, Sebastian LB Mount Allison [OTT/BC]
4 33 WPG Shelswell, Ian DL Stanford
4 34 EDM Ram, Larry OL Florida A&M
4 35 MTL Archer, Paul OL St. Mary's
5 36 OTT Parenteau, Marc OG Boston College
5 37 CAL Machan, Blake SB Calgary
5 38 HAM Kasouf, Davod WR Holy Cross
5 39 TOR Fury, Derik LB Mount Allison
5 40 SAS Thomas, Mike WR Regina
5 41 BC Hoffman, Nicholas FB McGill
5 42 WPG Olynick, Cory WR Regina
5 43 CAL Arnold, Travis OL Manitoba [EDM]
5 44 MTL Bertrand, Mathieu WB McGill
6 45 OTT Seely, Todd LB Ottawa
6 46 CAL Schaefer, Greg OT British Columbia
6 47 HAM Hakim, Erico-Olivier FB St. Mary's
6 48 TOR Palmer, Micheal WR Guelph
6 49 SAS Olenick, Adrian OL Saskatchewan
6 50 MTL Stala, Dave WR St. Mary's [BC]
6 51 MTL Botterill, Mike LB McMaster [BC/WPG]
6 52 EDM Ormejuste, Didier DL Toledo
6 53 MTL Becker, Ed K Wilfrid Laurier

2004
April 28, 2004, via conference call

1 1 HAM Smith, Wayne OL Appalachian State
1 2 OTT Khan, Obby OL Simon Fraser [CAL]
1 3 OTT Azzi, David WR Ottawa
1 4 TOR Moroz, Mark OL Wake Forest
1 5 BC Atogwe, O.J. S Stanford
1 6 SAS Augustin, Ducarmel FB Villanova
1 7 TOR Tremblay, J.F. WR Laval [WPG]
1 8 MTL Kashama, Alain DL Michigan
1 9 EDM Sanghera, Amar OL British Columbia
2 10 EDM Lezi, Gilles FB Northwestern [HAM]
2 11 CAL Lymem, Tyler DL Calgary
2 12 OTT Leibl-Cote, Christian OL New Hampsphire
2 13 BC McKay-Loescher, Nautyn DE Alabama [TOR]
2 14 HAM Hage, Marwan OL Colorado [EDM/BC]
2 15 MTL Jeffrey, Ryan OL Wilfrid Laurier [SAS]
2 WPG Forfeited choice
2 16 CAL Masson, Pascal DB Laval [MTL]
2 17 EDM McLane, Rhett OL Saskatchewan
3 18 HAM Kent, Sean OL Regina
3 19 CAL Taylor, Jason DE British Columbia
3 20 OTT Suisham, Shaun K Bowling Green State
3 21 MTL Bourke, Josh OL Grand Valley State [WPG/TOR]
3 22 BC Plummer, Scott DB Simon Fraser
3 23 SAS Spencer, Walter DB Indianapolis
3 24 WPG Ryan, Jon WR/K Regina
3 25 MTL Wilson, O'Neil WR Connecticut
3 26 EDM Nowacki, Andrew WR Murray State
4 27 HAM Healey, Connor DB Wilfrid Laurier
4 28 CAL Forgione, Anthony OL York
4 29 OTT LaDouceur, L.P. DT California
4 30 TOR Hoffman, Frank DL York
4 31 SAS Mullinder, Luc DE Michigan State [BC]
4 32 SAS Strong, Ryan OL Wayne State
4 33 WPG McKinlay, Neil LB Simon Fraser
4 34 MTL Hage, Rudy DE Concordia
4 35 EDM Rempel, Chad WR Saskatchewan
5 36 HAM Mason, Anthony OL Guelph
5 37 CAL Simmerling, Christian DB St. Mary's
5 38 OTT Kirk, Matt DL Queen's
5 39 TOR Mahoney, Mike LB McGill
5 40 BC Cunningham, Troy DE Concordia
5 41 SAS Zimmer, Craig LB Regina
5 42 CAL Mitchell, Marc LB Queen's [WPG]
5 43 WPG Folk, Ryan LB CAL [MTL]
5 44 EDM Gagnon, Martin DB Laval
6 45 HAM Shakell, Justin DL Wilfrid Laurier
6 46 CAL Gallant, Andrew SB St. Francis Xavier
6 47 OTT Heffernan, Christian SB Western Ontario
6 48 TOR Mahoney, Brandan WR Simon Fraser
6 49 BC Palmer, Billy TE Notre Dame
6 50 MTL White, Landon DB Alberta [SAS]
6 51 WPG Sullivan, John S Waterloo
6 52 MTL Frake, Steven DB Wilfrid Laurier
6 53 EDM Thorne, David OL Mount Allison

2005
April 28, 2005, via conference call

1 1 CAL Robede, Miguel DE Laval
1 2 OTT Yeow, Cam LB Akron
1 3 SAS O'Meara, Matt OT McMaster [TOR/WPG]
1 4 SAS Best, Chris OL Duke
1 5 MTL Proulx, Matthieu DB Laval [OTT/EDM]
1 6 HAM Lumsden, Jesse RB McMaster
1 7 SAS Hoffart, Nathan SB Saskatchewan [MTL]
1 8 BC Bwenge, Alexis RB Kentucky
1 9 TOR Kaczur, Nick OL Toledo
2 10 CAL Ellis, Godfrey OL Acadia
2 11 TOR Fontaine, Raymond LB Kentucky [CAL/OTT]
2 12 MTL Piercy, Jeff RB Saskatchewan [WPG]
2 13 MTL Whitfield, Thomas DB Syracuse [SAS]
2 14 TOR Audet, Philippe DL Laval [HAM/OTT/EDM]
2 15 HAM Filice, Fabio OL McMaster
2 16 MTL Gauthier, Phillip DB Laval
2 17 BC Tremblay, Pierre OL Laval
2 18 TOR Keeping, Jeff OT Western Ontario
3 19 CAL Comiskey, John OT Windsor
3 20 OTT Mullings, Les RB St. Mary's
3 21 SAS Kudu, Matt DL Eastern Michigan
3 22 EDM O'Neill, Tim OL Calgary
3 23 HAM Brochu, Francois ST Boston College
3 24 MTL Cabral, Victor DT Georgia Southern
3 25 BC Lowry, David LB Alberta
3 26 BC Pierre-Louis, Patrick LB UCLA [TOR]
4 27 CAL Jukes, Kyler OL Regina
4 28 OTT Hathaway, Cory TE/FB Tulsa
4 29 WPG Mennie, Scott LB Manitoba
4 30 SAS Gagnon-Gordillo, J.O. DL Eastern Michigan
4 31 EDM Posteraro, Anthony K/P Graceland
4 32 HAM Steeves, Jeremy S St. Francis Xavier
4 33 MTL Ray, Mike K/P McMaster
4 34 BC Clovis, Sebastian DB St. Mary's
4 35 TOR Smith, Tye OL Manitoba
5 36 CAL Hewson, David DB Manitoba
5 37 OTT Baird, Adrian DE Ottawa
5 38 WPG Lapostolle, Martin DL Indiana
5 39 SAS Cherniawski, Dustin DB British Columbia
5 40 EDM LeBlanc, Robert SB McGill
5 41 HAM Fleming, Iain SB Queen's
5 42 MTL Hundeby, Curt OL Saskatchewan
5 43 BC Bassi, Nuvraj DT Oregon
5 44 TOR Crawford, Bryan RB Queen's
6 45 CAL Ralph, Brett WR Alberta
6 46 OTT Semajuste, Lenard FB Adams State
6 47 WPG Bisson, Ryan OL Northwood
6 48 SAS Gottselig, Ryan DL Saskatchewan
6 49 MTL Eckert, Adam WR Dickinson State [EDM]
6 50 HAM Paopao, Andrew DL San Jose State
6 51 MTL Manigat, Olivier OL Columbia
6 52 BC Ortmanns, Karl OL Acadia
6 53 TOR Forde, Ian RB Waterloo

2006

Ottawa Renegades Dispersal Draft
April 12, 2006, via conference call

1 1 SAS Joseph, Kerry QB [HAM]
1 2 WPG Khan, Obby OL
1 3 SAS Armstead, Jason WR
1 4 CAL Yeow, Cam LB
1 5 WPG St. Germain, Val OL [TOR]
1 6 BC Banks, Korey DB
1 7 MTL Ellis, Kai DB
1 8 EDM Collier, Anthony DE
2 9 HAM Fleming, Pat P
2 10 TOR Pilon, Marc DL [WPG]
2 11 SAS Hathaway, Cory FB
2 12 CAL Howell, Markus WR
2 13 WPG Banks, Brad QB [TOR]
2 14 BC Kirk, Matt DL
2 15 MTL Moss, Greg DB
2 16 EDM Suisham, Shaun K
3 17 HAM Lezi, Gilles FB
3 18 WPG Kashama, Hakeem DL
3 19 SAS Howard, Charles DT
3 20 CAL Clemons, Crance DB
3 21 TOR Azzi, David WR
3 22 BC Weston, Sean DB
3 23 Taylor, D'Wayne LB
3 24 EDM LaDouceur, L.P. LS
4 25 HAM Bearman, Greg DB
4 26 WPG Legault, Cameron DL
4 27 SAS Ruiz, Donald DB
4 28 CAL Thomas, Jason QB
4 29 TOR Poole, Sean OL
4 30 BC Sciortino, Sandro K
4 31 MTL Evans, Brandon OL
4 32 EDM Woodcock, Pat SB
5 33 HAM Smith, Steve CB
5 34 WPG Semajuste, Lenard FB
5 SAS passed
5 35 CAL Cole, Greg LB
5 36 TOR Bennett, Sean RB
5 37 BC Jones, Anthony WR
5 38 MTL Levels, Dwayne LB
5 39 EDM Idonije, Israel DL
6 HAM passed
6 40 WPG Childs, Henri RB
6 41 SAS Kine, Trevor OL
6 42 CAL Knight, Canary DL
6 43 TOR Riley, Sean WR
6 BC passed
6 44 MTL Smith, Kenny DL
6 EDM passed
7 HAM passed
7 45 WPG Grant, Robert DB/RB
7 46 SAS Burrell, Allen WR
7 47 CAL Perry, Jamaal WR
7 48 TOR Warren, Roderick WR
7 BC passed
7 49 MTL Ashkinaz, David OL
7 EDM passed
8 HAM, WPG, SAS, CAL, TOR, BC passed
8 50 MTL Pearl, Jeremy DB
8 EDM passed
9 HAM, WPG, SAS, CAL, TOR, BC passed
9 51 MTL Duncan, Chris WR
9 EDM passed

April 20, 2006, via conference call

1 1 EDM Braidwood, Adam DE Washington State [HAM]
1 2 BC Pottinger, Jay LB McMaster [WPG]
1 3 SAS Fantuz, Andrew WR Western Ontario
1 4 BC Foley, Ricky LB York [CAL]
1 5 TOR Federkeil, Daniel DL Calgary
1 6 BC Valli, Steven OL Simon Fraser
1 7 MTL Deslauriers, Eric WR Eastern Michigan
1 8 HAM Gagne-Marcoux, Cedric OL Central Florida [EDM]
2 9 HAM Reid, Jermaine DL Akron
2 10 TOR Mitchell, Leron DB Western Ontario [WPG]
2 11 HAM Dyakowski, Peter OL Louisiana State [OTT]
2 12 SAS Congi, Luca K Simon Fraser
2 13 CAL Cornish, Jon RB Kansas
2 14 TOR Wagner, Aaron LB Brigham Young
2 15 BC Hameister-Ries, Jon OL Tulsa
2 16 MTL Boulay, Etienne DB New Hampshire
2 17 EDM Nugent, Jason DB Rutgers
3 18 HAM Mayne, Shawn DE Connecticut
3 19 WPG Franklin, Arjei WR Windsor
3 20 SAS Cowan, Chris OL St. Mary's
3 21 EDM Mundle, Dwayne LB West Virginia [CAL]
3 22 SAS Clovis, Tristan LB McMaster [TOR]
3 23 WPG Picard, Dominic OL Laval [BC]
3 24 MTL Perrett, Jeff OT Tulsa
3 25 EDM Williams, Mike DE Boise State
4 26 EDM Brown, Andrew LB Lafayette [HAM]
4 27 CAL Clayton, Riley OL Manitoba [WPG]
4 28 HAM Sutherland, Chris OL Saskatchewan [OTT]
4 29 SAS Hogarth, Peter OL McMaster
4 30 CAL Commissiong, Gerald RB Stanford
4 31 TOR Cetoute, Obed WR Central Florida
4 32 MTL Birungi, Ivan WR Acadia [BC]
4 33 MTL Davis, Adrian DL Marshall
4 34 EDM Abraham, Jean Philippe LB Laval
5 35 HAM Roberts, Michael CB Ohio State
5 36 WPG Stevens, David RB Saskatchewan
5 37 SAS Alexander, Jesse LB Wilfrid Laurier
5 38 CAL Armstrong, Derek OL St. Francis Xavier
5 39 TOR Ramsay, Brian OL New Mexico
5 40 BC Lions Lindstrom, Mike SB British Columbia
5 41 MTL Wright, Joel DB Wilfrid Laurier
5 42 EDM Bisaillon, Nicolas RB Laval
6 43 MTL Desriveaux, Danny WR Richmond [WPG/HAM]
6 44 CAL Knights, Andre DB St. Mary's [WPG]
6 45 SAS Hughes, Stephen RB Calgary
6 46 CAL Trepanier, Marc LB Montreal
6 47 TOR Dawson, Clifton RB Harvard
6 48 BC Ward, Jason DL Connecticut
6 49 WPG Ross, Dexter DE Minot State [MTL]
6 50 EDM Longchamps, Greig OL Montreal

Supplemental Draft
June 12, 2006
6 EDM Lee, Jermaine DE Albany

2007
May 2, 2007, via conference call

1 1 HAM Bauman, Chris WR Regina
1 2 EDM Kean, Warren K Concordia
1 3 CAL Gyetvai, Mike OL Michigan State [WPG]
1 4 HAM Bekasiak, J.P. DL Toledo [SAS]
1 5 CAL Phillips, Justin LB Wilfrid Laurier [TOR]
1 6 CAL Arthur, Jabari WR Akron
1 7 MTL Yalowsky, Richard OL Calgary
1 8 BC Nicolson, Adam WR Ottawa
2 9 SAS McKoy, Dave WR Guelph [HAM]
2 10 EDM Nedd, Jason DB Akron
2 11 WPG Mace, Corey DT Wyoming
2 12 HAM Rempel, Jordan OL Saskatchewan [SAS]
2 13 HAM Ince, Eric OL St. Mary's [EDM/TOR]
2 14 CAL Challenger, Kevin WR Boston College
2 15 MTL Conrad, Darryl T Manitoba
2 16 BC Bean, Josh LB Boise State
3 17 BC Crawford, Tad S Columbia [HAM]
3 18 MTL Van Zeyl, Chris DL McMaster [EDM]
3 19 MTL Jones, Brian OL Windsor [HAM/WPG]
3 20 SAS Carter, Yannick LB Wilfrid Laurier
3 21 CAL MacDonald, Pat DL Alberta [TOR]
3 22 WPG Boakye, Eugene LB McMaster [CAL]
3 23 MTL Alexander, Donovan DB North Dakota
3 24 BC Sadeghian, Andre RB McMaster
4 25 HAM Pavlovic, Robert TE South Carolina [MTL/HAM]
4 26 EDM Jean-Louis, Michael DL Laval
4 27 EDM McCarty, Calvin RB Western Washington [WPG]
4 28 SAS Ackerman, Ryan OL Regina
4 29 TOR Maranda, Eric LB Laval

4 30 TOR Schmidt, Steve TE San Diego State [CAL]
4 31 MTL Judges, James DE Buffalo
4 32 BC Jones, Andrew DL McMaster
5 33 HAM Getzlaf, Chris SB Regina
5 34 SAS Bradshaw, Reggie RB Montana [WPG/EDM]
5 35 CAL Bekkering, Henry K Eastern Washington [WPG]
5 36 HAM Kordic, Nick DB Western Ontario [SAS]
5 37 TOR Simms, Sean DL York
5 38 CAL Hazlett, Ian LB Queen's
5 39 SAS Karhut, Ryan OL Manitoba [MTL]
5 40 BC Kirkwood, Kyle OL Ottawa
6 41 HAM Goncalves, Michael DL Toronto
6 EDM Forfeited Choice
6 42 WPG Noel, Travis DB St. Francis Xavier
6 43 HAM Kania, Adam DE St. Francis Xavier [SAS]
6 44 TOR Smith, Brad WR Queen's
6 45 CAL Hetherington, Greg SB McGill
6 46 MTL Smith, Braden QB UBC
6 47 BC Edgson, Nic DB Idaho State

2008
April 30, 2008, via conference call

1 1 HAM Barker, Dylan DB Saskatchewan
1 2 CAL Tsoumpas, Dimitri OL Weber State [EDM]
1 3 CAL Newman, Jesse OL Louisiana-Lafayette
1 4 SAS Shologan, Keith DL Central Florida [TOR]
1 5 BC Sorensen, Justin OL South Carolina
1 6 WPG LaBatte, Brendon OL Regina
1 7 MTL Emry, Shea LB British Columbia [SAS]
1 8 HAM Giguere, Sam REC Sherbrooke [MTL] [forfeited]
2 9 BC Lumbala, Rolly RB/FB Idaho [HAM]
2 10 SAS St. Pierre, Jonathan OL Illinois State [EDM/TOR/EDM]
2 11 EDM Wojt, Greg OL Central Michigan [CAL]
2 12 MTL Woodruff, Andrew OL Boise State
2 13 TOR Bradwell, Mike REC McMaster
2 14 SAS Stadnyk, Michael DL Montana [BC]
2 15 WPG Hargreaves, Aaron REC Simon Fraser
2 16 CAL Kashama, Fernand DL Western Michigan [EDM/SAS]
3 17 HAM Giffin, Michael RB/FB Queen's
3 18 BC Shaw, Justin DL Manitoba [EDM]
3 19 EDM St. Pierre, Tim LB St. Mary's [CAL]
3 20 BC Arakgi, Jason LB McMaster [SAS/MTL]
3 21 TOR Carriere, Jean-Nicolas LB McGill
3 22 BC McEachern, Mike LB Western Illinois
3 23 EDM Cooper, Justin DL Manitoba [BC/WPG]
3 24 WPG Stephenson, Daryl RB Windsor [EDM/SAS)
4 25 EDM Okpro, Sammy DB Concordia [HAM]
4 26 EDM Hood, Jonathan DB St. Francis Xavier
4 27 CAL Hilaire, Ronald DL Buffalo
4 28 MTL Firr, Terence REC Manitoba
4 29 TOR Clarke, Delroy DB Ottawa
4 30 SAS Morin-Roberge, Jean-Francois OL Montreal [BC]
4 31 WPG Beswick, Marc DB St. Mary's
4 32 MTL Thind, Gurminder OL South Carolina [SAS]
5 33 HAM Lavigne Masse, Lauren REC Laval
5 34 EDM Luciani, Dante REC Wilfrid Laurier
5 35 CAL Gott, Jon OL Boise State
5 36 MTL Woldu, Paul DB Saskatchewan
5 37 TOR Zulys, Richard OL Western Ontario
5 38 BC Browne, Brady DB Manitoba
5 39 WPG Oramasionwu, Don DL Manitoba
5 40 SAS Zelinski, Jeff DB St. Mary's
6 41 SAS Orban, Teale QB Regina [HAM]
6 42 TOR Dewit, Mark OL Calgary [EDM]
6 43 CAL Lapointe, Jonathan FB Montreal
6 44 TOR Scott, Tyler REC Western Ontario [MTL]
6 45 TOR Black, Matt DB Saginaw Valley State
6 46 BC Buydens, Hubert OL Saskatchewan
6 47 WPG Labbe, Pierre-Luc LB Sherbrooke
6 48 MTL Brodeur-Jourdain, Luc OL Laval [SAS]

2009
May 2, 2009, via conference call

1 1 HAM Rottier, Simeon OL Alberta
1 2 TOR Legare, Etienne DL Laval
1 3 BC Lee, Jamall RB Bishop's [HAM]
1 4 BC Yurichuk, James LB Bishop's [TOR/EDM]
1 5 BC Carter, Matt WR Acadia
1 6 HAM Brown, Darcy WR St. Mary's [BC]
1 7 MTL Steenbergen, Dylan OL Calgary
1 8 CAL Fraser, Eric DB Central Michigan
2 9 SAS George, Tamon DB Regina [HAM]
2 10 TOR Lambros, Matt WR Liberty
2 11 EDM Hinse, Gord OL Alberta [WPG]
2 12 EDM Sterling, Dee DL Queen's
2 13 HAM Hinds, Ryan DB New Hampshire [BC]
2 14 MTL Bedard, Martin TE Connecticut [SAS]
2 15 MTL Singer, Matt OL Manitoba
2 16 CAL Black, Tristan LB Wayne State (Michigan)
3 17 SAS Hutchins, Nick OL Regina [HAM]
3 18 TOR Green, James DB Calgary
3 19 WPG Morris, Mike OL British Columbia
3 20 EDM Bonaventura, Andrea LB Calgary
3 21 BC Morencie, Matt OL Windsor
3 22 HAM McCuaig, Scott DE British Ciolumbia [SAS]
3 23 MTL Morin-Soucy, Nickolas DL Montreal
3 24 CAL Hashem, John OT Regina
4 25 MTL Van Sichem, Stan DL Regina [HAM]
4 26 TOR Pollari, Zachary OT Western Ontario
4 27 WPG Bestard, Adam OL Wilfrid Laurier
4 28 CAL Armstrong, Spencer WR Air Force [EDM]
4 29 BC Bacheyie, Tang DB Kansas
4 30 CAL Myddelton, Steve DE St. Francis Xavier [SAS]
4 31 MTL Brown, Ivan DL Saskatchewan
4 32 CAL McHenry, Scott SB Saskatchewan
5 33 HAM Allard-Cameus, Guillaume RB Laval
5 34 TOR Sawler, Gordon DL St. Francis Xavier
5 35 WPG Quinney, Peter FB Wilfrid Laurier
5 36 EDM Lee, Eric RB Weber State
5 37 BC Pierre-Etienne, Jonathan DE Montreal
5 38 HAM Wladichuk, Raymond DB Simon Fraser [SAS]
5 39 MTL Boulanger, Benoit RB Sherbrooke
5 40 CAL Ukwuoma, Osie DL Queen's
6 41 HAM Doneff, Cassidy WR Washburn
6 42 TOR Deslauriers, Anthony DB Simon Fraser
6 43 TOR Crawford, Brad DB Guelph [WPG]
6 44 EDM Kosec, Jason LB Western Ontario
6 45 WPG Carter, Thaine LB Queen's [BC]
6 46 HAM McGrath, Bill OL Indiana State [SAS]
6 47 MTL Mousseau, Ryan OL Ottawa
6 48 CAL Kanaroski, John WR Regina

Supplemental Draft
1HAM Carlson, Zac OL Weber State

2010
May 2, 2010, via conference call

1 1 SAS Williams, Shomari LB Queen's [TOR]
1 2 TOR Eppele, Joe OT Washington State [SAS/WPG]
1 3 TOR Greenwood, Cory LB Concordia [BC]
1 4 BC Watkins, Danny OT Baylor [TOR/SAS]
1 HAM Forfeited choice
1 5 CAL Maver, Rob K/P Guelph
1 6 EDM Bulcke, Brian DL Stanford [WPG]
1 7 MTL Matte, Kristian OL Concordia
2 8 SAS Sisco, Jordan WR Regina [TOR/SAS/TOR]
2 9 WPG Watson, Cory WR Concordia [EDM/WPG]
2 10 BC Gore, Shawn WR Bishop's
2 11 TOR Shaw, Grant DB/K Saskatchewan [EDM]
2 12 EDM Borhot, Saleem DB St. Mary's [HAM]
2 13 CAL Allen, Taurean DB Wilfrid Laurier
2 14 MTL Ihekwoaba, Chima DE Wilfrid Laurier [SAS]
2 15 MTL Dublanko, Curtis LB North Dakota
3 16 BC Gesse, Joash LB Montreal ([TOR]
3 17 CAL Bender, John OL Nevada-Reno [WPG]
3 18 TOR Watt, Spencer WR Simon Fraser [BC]
3 19 HAM Fournier, Samuel RB Laval [EDM]
3 20 BC Mahmoudi, Hamid DB Montreal [TOR/HAM]
3 21 CAL Deane, J'Michael OL Michigan State
3 22 HAM Steele, Eddie DT Manitoba [WPG /EDM/TOR/SAS]
3 23 MTL Brouillette, Marc-Olivier QB Montreal
4 24 BC Binder, Nate WR Tusculum [TOR]
4 25 BC Foster, Akeem WR St. Francis Xavier [TOR/EDM/WPG]
4 26 TOR Reinders, Joel OT Waterloo [BC]
4 27 HAM Rwabukamba, Chris DB Duke [EDM]
4 28 WPG Smith, Chris LB Queen's [HAM]
4 29 WPG Woodson, Anthony RB Calgary [CAL]
4 30 TOR Turner, Steven WR Bishop's [BC/SAS]
4 31 MTL Bomben, Ryan OL Guelph
5 32 TOR Warner, Michael OL Waterloo
5 33 SAS Neufeld, Patrick OL Saskatchewan [WPG]
5 34 BC Muamba, Cauchy DB St. Francis Xavier
5 35 EDM Ferguson, Scott OL St. Cloud State
5 36 HAM Palardy, Justin K/P St. Mary's
5 37 CAL McCartney, Karl LB St. Mary's
5 38 SAS LaPointe, Bruno DL Buffalo [TOR/SAS]
5 39 MTL Ridgeway, Brian LB Simon Fraser
6 40 TOR Jamal, Nasser OL Louisiana-Lafayette
6 41 BC Baboulas, Adam OL St. Mary's [WPG]
6 42 BC Chapdelaine, Matthew WR Simon Fraser
6 43 EDM Sharun, Corbin DB St. Francis Xavier
6 44 TOR Elliott, Conor LB Western Ontario [HAM]
6 45 WPG Greaves, Chris DL Western Ontario [CAL]
6 46 CAL Culbreath, Oamu OL British Columbia [WPG/SAS)
6 47 MTL Conn, Justin LB Bishop's

Supplemental Draft
May 21, 2010
3 CAL Forzani, Johnny WR Washington State

2011
May 8, 2011 via conference call

1 1 WPG Muamba, Henoc LB St. Francis Xavier
1 2 EDM Mitchell, Scott OL Rice
1 3 CAL Parker, Anthony WR Calgary [BC]
1 4 WPG Etienne, Jade WR Saskatchewan [TOR]
1 5 EDM Coehoorn, Nathan WR Calgary [HAM]
1 6 BC Iannuzzi, Marco WR Harvard [CAL]
1 7 TOR Holmes, Tyler OL Tulsa [SAS]
1 8 MTL McKnight, Brody K Montana
2 9 CAL Turner, Junior DL Bishop's [WPG]
2 10 HAM Petrus, Moe OL Connecticut [EDM]
2 11 BC O'Neill, Hugh P Alberta [CAL/BC]
2 12 SAS Butler, Craig DB Western Ontario [TOR]
2 13 HAM Forbes, Maurice DT Concordia [EDM/HAM]
2 14 EDM Lopez, Hugo DB Toronto [CAL]
2 15 SAS O'Donnell, Matt OL Queen's
2 16 MTL Barrette, Anthony OL Concordia
3 17 WPG Dunn, Brendan DL Western Ontario
3 18 TOR Kouame, Djems WR Montreal [HAM/EDM]
3 19 BC Carter, Michael DB Maryland
3 20 HAM Fortin, Marc-Antoine DL Laval [SAS/TOR]
3 21 HAM Baillargeon, Pascal OL Laval
3 CAL Choice forfeited
3 22 TOR Robinson, Alexander DE Western Ontario [SAS]
3 23 MTL Blake, Philip OL Baylor
4 24 WPG Swiston, Paul OL Calgary
4 25 MTL Sagesse, Renaldo DL Michigan [TOR/EDM]
4 26 CAL Antwi, Akwasi DL Mount Allison [BC]
4 27 SAS Krausnick-Groh, Alexander OL Calgary [TOR]
4 28 TOR Gardner, Jedd WR Guelph [HAM]
4 29 CAL Sinopoli, Brad QB Ottawa
4 30 SAS Milo, Christopher K Laval
4 31 MTL Alexander, Reed OL Calgary
5 32 WPG Volny, Carl RB Central Michigan [EDM/WPG]
5 33 HAM Jean-Mary, Patrick LB Howard [EDM]
5 34 CAL Walter, Matt RB Calgary [BC]
5 35 TOR Alexandre, Gregory DL Montreal
5 36 HAM Francisco, Tyrell TE Weber State
5 37 BC Sage, Yannick OL Sherbrooke [CAL]
5 38 TOR Feoli Gudino, Julian WR Laval [SAS]
5 39 MTL Martin, Vaughn DL Western Ontario
6 40 SAS Exume, Kyle RB Bishop's [WPG]
6 41 WPG Mahoney, Liam WR Concordia [EDM]
6 42 BC Hodgson, Chris DL St. Mary's
6 43 TOR Knill, Michael OL Wilfrid Laurier
6 44 HAM Wagner, Jadon LB Brigham Young
6 45 CAL Manchelenko, Jared TE Concordia
6 46 EDM Pierre, Youssy WR Montreal [SAS]
6 47 MTL Ruttan, Blaine LB Carson-Newman

The Ontario Rugby Football Union was founded in 1883. The league included college teams, and the rules it used followed the evolution of the Canadian game from its rugby origins to its current form.

The most significant year in terms of rule changes was 1903, when the ORFU adopted the "Burnside Rules." These included twelve players per team, the snapback and the requirement of gaining ten yards in three downs. Four years later the ORFU saw its ranks shrink when the two of its top teams — the Hamilton Tigers and the Toronto Argonauts — bolted to form the Interprovincial Football Union (IRFU).

Thus overnight the ORFU was replaced as the top league in Canada. The ORFU still challenged for the supremacy of Canadian football, winning the Grey Cup in 1912, 1927, 1930, 1934 and 1936.

Presented here are the nine post-World War II years in which the league still competed against the IRFU and WIFU for the Grey Cup. During these years the ORFU was at a disadvantage in comparison to the better financed teams of the IRFU and WIFU.

Finally, after the 1954 season the ORFU withdrew from Grey Cup competition. But the league continued to operate, until it finally folded in June 1973.

The following abbreviations are used in this section:

Standings

L	Games lost
PA	Points against
PCT	Winning percentage
PF	Points for
PTS	Championship points
T	Games tied
W	Games won

Teams

BRA	Brantford
HAM	Hamilton
KW	Kitchener-Waterloo
MCM	McMaster
OTT	Ottawa
SAR	Sarnia
TORI	Toronto Indians
TORB	Toronto Balmy Beaches/Beaches-Indians
WIN	Windsor

Scoring Leaders

C	Converts
FG	Field goals
PTS	Points
S	Singles
TD	Touchdowns

Positions

C	Centre
E	End
FW	Flying Wing
G	Guard
HB	Halfback
QB	Quarterback
T	Tackle

1946 Standings	W	L	T	PTS	PCT	PF	PA
Hamilton Wildcats	8	1	1	17	.889	166	66
Toronto Indians	8	1	1	17	.889	176	66
Toronto Balmy Beaches	6	4	0	12	.600	112	84
Sarnia Imperials	4	6	0	8	.400	88	158
Windsor Rockets	3	7	0	6	.300	61	138
Ottawa Trojans	0	10	0	0	.000	36	127

Semi-Final
11/ 8 Toronto Indians 7 at Toronto Balmy Beaches 12
Final
11/16 Toronto Balmy Beach 13 at Hamilton Wildcats 6
Grey Cup Semi-Final
11/23 Toronto Balmy Beach 12 at Toronto Argonauts 22

Team Scoring	TD	FG	C	SI	ST	PTS
TORI	24	7	14	15	1	176
HAM	26	0	15	17	2	166
TORB	16	1	16	13	2	112
SAR	13	3	9	5	0	88
WIN	6	5	4	12	0	61
OTT	4	2	3	7	0	36

Scoring	TD	FG	C	SI	PTS
Don Toms, HAM	12	0	0	0	60
Johnny Lake, TORB	3	1	9	8	35
Doug Pyzer, TORI	7	0	1	0	36
Annis Stukus, TORI	0	7	9	4	34
Bob Cunningham, TORB	6	0	0	0	30
Norm Millen, TORB	6	0	0	0	30
Jack Stewart, HAM	4	0	1	7	28
Gordon Miller, HAM	3	0	0	10	25
Mike Meikle, SAR	1	3	4	2	20
Rocky Robillard, OTT	1	2	3	6	20
Ross McKelvey, TORI	3	0	2	1	18
Alton Reid, WIN	1	2	3	3	17
Jack Gray, TORI	3	0	0	2	17
Gerry Dawson, WIN	1	2	1	1	13
Don Crowe, TORI	2	0	1	2	13
Fred Kijek, TORI	1	0	0	6	11
Ken Moore, SAR	2	0	1	0	11
Frank Moroz, HAM	2	0	1	0	11
Dutch Davey, SAR	2	0	0	0	10
Miller Harper, OTT	2	0	0	0	10
Mike Hedgewick, WIN	2	0	0	0	10
Benny Dyack, HAM	2	0	0	0	10
Gus Scheiers, SAR	2	0	0	0	10
Joe Woodcock, SAR	2	0	0	0	10
Ike Norris, SAR	2	0	0	0	10
Johnny Farmer, TORI	2	0	0	0	10
Jack Gray, TORI	2	0	0	0	10
Fred Brown, TORI	2	0	0	0	10
Bill Wylupek, WIN	2	0	0	0	10
Frank Gnup, HAM	1	0	3	0	8
Bill Murmylyk, HAM	0	0	8	0	8
Andy Withers, SAR	1	0	0	1	6
Harry Booth, TORI	1	0	0	0	5
Murray Bulger, TORI	1	0	0	0	5
Jimmy Cumming, TORI	1	0	0	0	5
Chuck Harrison, HAM	1	0	0	0	5
Martin, HAM	1	0	0	0	5
Bruce Mattingley, SAR	1	0	0	0	5
Frankie Seymour, TORB	1	0	0	0	5
Ron Sharpe, OTT	1	0	0	0	5
Del Willick, WIN	0	1	0	2	5
Len Camlis, WIN	0	0	0	2	2
Ralph Larue, TORB	0	0	0	2	2
Bobby Porter, TORB	0	0	1	1	2
Joe Scislowski, WIN	0	0	0	2	2
Lorne Barkley, OTT	0	0	0	1	1
Don Durno, TORI	0	0	1	0	1
Bob McKay. HAM	0	0	1	0	1
Bob McMillan, WIN	0	0	0	1	1
Buck Reaume, WIN	0	0	0	1	1
Don Sinclair, TORB	0	0	0	1	1
Don Smythe, TORB	0	0	1	0	1
Sammy Sward, TORB	0	0	1	0	1

Player of the Year: Frank Gnup, HAM

All-Star Team

E	Len Wright, HAM
E	Johnny Farmer, TORI
T	Don Durno, TORI
T	Vic Ghetti, WIN
G	Don McKenzie, TORB
G	Trip Trepanier, SAR
C	Doug Turner, TORB
QB	Frank Gnup, HAM
HB	Don Toms, HAM
HB	Ross McKelvey, TORI
HB	Johnny Lake, TORB
FW	Fred Kijek, TORI

1947 Standings	W	L	T	PTS	PCT	PF	PA
Hamilton Wildcats	9	1	0	18	.900	245	84
Toronto Balmy Beaches	7	3	0	14	.700	103	100
Ottawa Trojans	5	4	1	11	.556	148	133
Toronto Indians	4	5	1	9	.444	99	120
Windsor Rockets	4	6	0	8	.400	86	138
Sarnia Imperials	0	10	0	0	.000	60	166

Semi-Finals
11/ 7 Toronto Indians 0 at Hamilton Wildcats 14
11/ 8 Ottawa Trojans 16 at Toronto Balmy Beach 7
Final
11/15 Ottawa Trojans 15 at Hamilton Wildcats 3
Grey Cup Semi-Final
11/22 Ottawa Trojans 1 at Toronto Argonauts 22

Team Scoring	TD	FG	C	SI	ST	PTS
HAM	40	3	31	7	0	245
TORB	16	1	11	8	0	103
OTT	23	2	18	5	2	148
TORI	15	3	10	4	0	99

WIN	12	3	3	12	1	86
SAR	8	4	4	7	0	60

Scoring	TD	FG	C	SI	PTS
Joe Farley, OTT	5	2	7	0	38
Gordon Miller, HAM	6	0	0	3	33
Gord Lawson, HAM	6	0	0	0	30
Doug Smylie, OTT	4	0	7	0	27
Tony Labarbera, HAM	2	0	15	2	27
Don Crowe, TORI	4	1	3	1	27
Bill Murmylyk, HAM	1	3	13	0	26
Benny Dyack, HAM	5	0	0	0	25
Bill Addis, WIN	4	0	0	4	24
Bruce Coulter, TORB	3	0	5	1	21
Don Toms, HAM	4	0	0	0	20
Don Knowles, SAR	4	0	0	0	20
Arnie McWatters, OTT	3	0	0	2	17
Al Anderson, OTT	3	0	0	1	16
Bob Paffrath, TORI	3	0	1	0	16
Bob Westlake, HAM	3	0	0	0	15
Frank Moroz, HAM	3	0	0	0	15
Bill Petrilas, OTT	3	0	0	0	15
Walt Masters, OTT	2	0	0	2	12
Billy Myers, TORB	2	0	2	0	12
Gerry Dawson, WIN	1	0	4	3	12
Hank Galloway, SAR	0	2	1	4	11
Rud Rudinski, HAM	2	0	0	0	10
Ray Jones, HAM	2	0	0	0	10
Vic Schmidt, WIN	2	0	0	0	10
Ted McLarty, OTT	2	0	0	0	10
Norm Millen, TORB	2	0	0	0	10
Bill Stockman, TORB	2	0	0	0	10
Johnny Lake, TORB	1	0	2	1	8
Leo Bucheski, WIN	1	1	0	0	8
Jack Renna, WIN	1	0	0	3	8
Tommy Ford, TORB	1	0	0	2	7
Bill Douglas, TORI	0	1	2	2	7
Gary Smith, TORI	1	0	2	0	7
Skeets Harrison, WIN	0	2	0	1	7
Norm Marratto, HAM	1	0	0	1	6
Dutch Davey, SAR	1	0	1	0	6
Bob Cunningham, TORB	0	1	1	2	6
Ken Hollingsworth, TORI	1	0	1	0	6
Art Cousins, HAM	1	0	0	0	5
Ross Hemingway, HAM	1	0	0	0	5
George Kopulos, HAM	1	0	0	0	5
Jimmy Stewart, HAM	1	0	0	0	5
Rod Smylie, OTT	1	0	0	0	5
Frank Hugett, SAR	1	0	0	0	5
Harry Turner, SAR	1	0	0	0	5
Joe Woodcock, SAR	1	0	0	0	5
Billy Leuty, TORB	1	0	0	0	5
Don MacKenzie, TORB	1	0	0	0	5
Eddie Powers, TORB	1	0	0	0	5
Dick Tuckey, TORB	1	0	0	0	5
Stan Vrabec, TORB	1	0	0	0	5
Kenny Booker, TORI	1	0	0	0	5
Johnny Farmer, TORI	1	0	0	0	5
Bud Fowler, TORI	1	0	0	0	5
Vern Picard, TORI	1	0	0	0	5
Bill Sheridan, TORI	1	0	0	0	5
Don Sinclair, TORI	1	0	0	0	5
Boris Tipoff, TORI	1	0	0	0	5
Joe Lesinsky, WIN	1	0	0	0	5
Bob McMillan, WIN	1	0	0	0	5
Buck Reaume, WIN	1	0	0	0	5
Spud Daley, OTT	0	0	2	0	2
Bill Weiss, SAR	0	0	0	2	2
Stu Scott, TORB	0	0	1	1	2
Sammy Sward, TORB	0	0	0	2	2
Nilo Ciotti, TORI	0	0	1	1	2
Frank Gnup, HAM	0	0	1	0	1
George Gilmour, OTT	0	0	1	0	1
Mike Meikle, SAR	0	0	1	0	1
Ike Norris, SAR	0	0	0	1	1
Gus Scheiers, SAR	0	0	0	1	1
Hamm, SAR	0	0	0	1	1
Ralph Larue, TORI	0	0	0	1	1

Player of the Year: Bob Paffrath, TORI

All-Star Team

E	Joe Farley, OTT
E	Gord Lawson, HAM
T	Vic Ghetti, WIN
T	Steve Chamko, WIN
G	Don McKenzie, TORB
G	Bud Donald, HAM
C	Basil Petry, TORB (tie)
	Fred Gabriel, HAM (tie)
QB	Mel Lawson, HAM
HB	Bob Cunningham, TORB
HB	Bill Petrilas, OTT
HB	Bob Paffrath, TORI
FW	Bill Murmylyk, HAM

1948 Standings	W	L	T	PTS	PCT	PF	PA
Hamilton Tigers	9	0	0	18	1.000	279	53
Toronto Beaches-Indians	5	4	0	10	.556	124	86
Sarnia Imperials	3	5	1	7	.375	71	130
Windsor Rockets	0	8	1	1	.000	40	245

Final (Hamilton 39-1)
11/ 5 Hamilton Tigers 8 at Toronto Beaches-Indians 0
11/13 Toronto Beaches-Indians 1 at Hamilton Tigers 31
Grey Cup Semi-Final
11/20 Hamilton Tigers 0 at Ottawa Rough Riders 19

Team Scoring	TD	FG	C	SI	ST	PTS
HAM	44	5	40	5	0	279
TORBI	20	1	20	13	0	124
SAR	8	6	8	7	1	71
WIN	4	3	4	10	0	40

Scoring	TD	FG	C	SI	PTS
Jack Harper, HAM	12	0	0	0	60
Gerry Walsh, HAM	7	0	0	1	36
Doug Pyzer, TORBI	6	0	1	0	31
Jack Stewart, HAM	6	0	0	0	30
Pat Santucci, HAM	0	1	25	0	28
Garry Smith, TORBI	5	0	1	1	27
Potsy Parr, SAR	0	4	3	1	16
Boris Tipoff, HAM	3	0	0	0	15
Doug Smith, HAM	2	0	0	4	14
Joe Capriotti, HAM	0	1	10	0	13
Ralph Bartolini, HAM	2	0	2	0	12
Delmar Willick, WIN	1	2	1	0	12
Tommy Ford, TORBI	2	0	1	1	12
Mike King, TORBI	2	0	0	1	11
Frank Filchock, HAM	2	0	1	0	11
Skeets Harrison, WIN	1	1	0	3	11
Stan Wolkowski, HAM	2	0	0	0	10
Bob Dunlop, TORBI	2	0	0	0	10
Danny Difrancisco, HAM	2	0	0	0	10
Joe Koskie, SAR	2	0	0	0	10
Eric McKeever, SAR	2	0	0	0	10
Joe Cihocki, HAM	1	1	0	0	8
Bill Douglas, TORBI	0	0	2	6	8
Eric McKeever, SAR	1	0	1	0	6
Don Crowe, TORBI	0	1	3	0	6
Tom Hickey, HAM	1	0	0	0	5
Ray Jones, HAM	1	0	0	0	5
Bruce Maxwell, HAM	1	0	0	0	5
Alex Muzyka, HAM	1	0	0	0	5
Steve Repei, HAM	1	0	0	0	5
Jack Bell, SAR	1	0	0	0	5
Dutch Davey, SAR	0	1	1	1	5
Hank Galloway, SAR	0	1	0	2	5
Bill Miller, SAR	1	0	0	0	5
Gus Scheiers, SAR	1	0	0	0	5
Bill Weiss, SAR	1	0	0	0	5
Ernie Becker, TORBI	1	0	0	0	5
Harry Bunting, TORBI	1	0	0	0	5
Johnny Lake, TORBI	1	0	0	0	5
Leo Gusba, WIN	1	0	0	0	5
Bob Wylupek, WIN	1	0	0	0	5
Joe Bloomingdale, HAM	0	1	0	0	3
Andy Sokol, SAR	0	0	0	3	3
Bobby Porter, TORBI	0	0	0	2	2
Bill Addis, WIN	0	0	0	2	2
Jack Brown, WIN	0	0	0	2	2
Johnny Dengel, WIN	0	0	0	2	2
Alex Aitken, HAM	0	0	1	0	1
Bob Hazel, TORBI	0	0	0	1	1
Sam Hollingsworth, TORBI	0	0	1	0	1
Len Camisl, WIN	0	0	0	1	1

Player of the Year: Frank Filchock, HAM

All-Star Team

E	Verne Picard, TORBI
E	Danny Difrancisco, HAM
T	Pat Santucci, HAM
T	Lorne Parkin, TORBI
G	Don McKenzie, TORBI
G	Eddie Remigis, HAM
C	Jake Gaudaur, HAM
QB	Frank Filchock, HAM
HB	Jack Harper, HAM
HB	Jack Stewart, HAM
HB	Doug Pyzer, TORBI
FW	Gerry Walsh, HAM

1949 Standings	W	L	T	PTS	PCT	PF	PA
Hamilton Tigers	10	2	0	20	.833	228	68
Sarnia Imperials	8	4	0	16	.667	142	101
Windsor Rockets	5	7	0	10	.417	141	108
Toronto Balmy Beaches	1	11	0	2	.083	55	289

Final (Hamilton 26-18)
11/11 Hamilton Tigers 6 at Sarnia Imperials 15
11/12 Sarnia Imperials 3 at Hamilton Tigers 20
Grey Cup Semi-Final
11/19 Hamilton Tigers 0 at Montreal Alouettes 40

Team Scoring	TD	FG	C	SI	ST	PTS
HAM	32	9	26	16	0	228
SAR	21	1	21	18	1	142
WIN	23	1	11	12	0	141
TORB	8	1	3	9	0	55

Scoring Leaders	TD	FG	C	SI	PTS
Joe Capriotti, HAM	0	7	20	6	47
Jack Stewart, HAM	9	0	0	0	45

Merle Hapes, HAM	7	0	0	1	36
Jim Caine, HAM	5	2	2	0	33
Eric McKeever, SAR	6	0	1	0	31
Jack Murphy, WIN	6	0	0	0	30
Don Knowles, SAR	5	0	0	0	25
Doug Smith, HAM	3	0	0	9	24
Ed Krause, WIN	4	0	0	0	20
Boris Tipoff, HAM	3	0	0	0	15
Bob Simpson, WIN	3	0	0	0	15
Sylvester Mike, WIN	3	0	0	0	15
Bill Douglas, TORB	1	0	2	8	15
Skeets Harrison, WIN	0	1	8	2	13
Bill Weiss, SAR	0	0	0	13	13
Harry Kaloogian, WIN	2	0	0	1	11
Stan Wolkowski, HAM	2	0	0	0	10
Keith Fisher, SAR	2	0	0	0	10
Johnny Crincich, SAR	2	0	0	0	10
Gus Scheiers, SAR	2	0	0	0	10
Dutch Davey, SAR	0	0	8	2	10
Bob Hollup, WIN	2	0	0	0	10
Dave West, TORB	2	0	0	0	10

Player of the Year: Don Knowles, SAR

All-Star Team

E Keith Fisher, SAR
E Bill Damiano, HAM (tie)
Rube Ainsworth, HAM (tie)
T Dutch Davey, SAR
T Len Wright, WIN
G Jack Morneau, WIN
G Don McKenzie, TORB
C Jake Gaudaur, HAM
QB Stan Wolkowski, HAM
HB Don Knowles, SAR
HB Jack Stewart, HAM
HB Sylvester Mike, WIN
FW Joe Capriotti, HAM

1950 Standings	W	L	T	PTS	PCT	PF	PA
Toronto Balmy Beaches	6	2	0	12	.750	162	100
Sarnia Imperials	4	4	0	8	.500	164	102
Windsor Rockets	2	6	0	4	.250	52	176

Final (Toronto 35-21)
11/ 5 Sarnia Imperials 11 at Toronto Balmy Beaches 17
11/11 Toronto Balmy Beaches 18 at Sarnia Imperials 10
Grey Cup Semi-Final
11/18 Toronto Balmy Beaches 13 at Toronto Argonauts 43

Team Scoring	TD	FG	C	SI	ST	PTS
TORB	27					162
SAR	25	5	17	7	0	164
WIN	8	0	2	4	2	52

Scoring Leaders	TD	FG	C	SI	PTS
Johnny Chorostecki, SAR	10	5	6	4	88
Carl Galbreath, TOR	10	0	4	0	54
Billy Haddleton, TOR	7	0	0	0	35
Lyle Ross, WIN	4	0	1	0	21
Eric McKeever, SAR	4	0	0	0	20
George Watson, TOR	0	0	17	2	19
Gerry Tuttle, TOR	3	0	0	0	15
Tom Harpley, TOR	3	0	0	0	15
Bill Weiss, SAR	2	0	0	3	13
Art Scullion, TOR	2	0	0	0	10
Gus Scheiers, SAR	2	0	0	0	10
George Curtis, SAR	2	0	0	0	10

Player of the Year: Carl Galbreath, TORB

All-Star Team

E Keith Fisher, SAR
E Art Scullion, TORB
T Oatten Fisher, TORB
T George Gilchrist, TORB
G Bruce Mattingly, SAR
G Ross Taylor, TORB
C Dwight Follin, TORB
QB Gerry Tuttle, TORB
HB Carl Galbreath, TORB
HB Johnny Chorostecki, SAR
HB Jim Caine, WIN
FW Billy Haddleton, TORB

1951 Standings	W	L	T	PTS	PCT	PF	PA
Sarnia Imperials	9	1	0	22	.900	268	60
Toronto Balmy Beaches	7	3	0	18	.700	173	124
McMaster University	2	4	0	8	.333	114	114
Windsor Rockets	0	10	0	0	.000	29	286

McMaster games worth four points.

Final (Sarnia 56-53)
11/ 3 Sarnia Imperials 15 at Toronto Balmy Beaches 23
11/10 Toronto Balmy Beaches 30 at Sarnia Imperials 41
Grey Cup Semi-Final
11/21 Sarnia Imperials 17 at Ottawa Rough Riders 43

Team Scoring	TD	FG	C	SI	ST	PTS
SAR	44	4	31	5	0	268
TORB	26	2	21	10	0	173
MCM	20	0	11	3	0	114
WIN	5	0	2	2	0	29

Scoring Leaders	TD	FG	C	SI	PTS
Mel Hawkrigg, MCM	3	0	5	0	70
Johnny Chorostecki, SAR	2	4	30	3	55
Corky Duchene, SAR	7	0	0	0	35
Al Farris, SAR	7	0	0	0	35
Ralph Pulley, TOR	6	0	0	0	30
Murray Johnston, SAR	5	0	0	0	25
Eric McKeever, SAR	5	0	0	0	25
Andy Gilmour, TOR	5	0	0	0	25
Bobby Lee, TOR	5	0	0	0	25
George Watson, TOR	1	0	19	0	24
Bill Miller, SAR	3	0	0	0	15
Jack Glendenning, SAR	3	0	0	0	15
Archie McAffer, SAR	3	0	0	0	15
Bob Hendry, TOR	3	0	0	0	15
Howie French, TOR	1	0	1	6	12
Lorne Wigglesworth, MCM	2	0	0	0	10
Ed Fisher, TOR	2	0	0	0	10
George Curtis, SAR	2	0	0	0	10
Jack McKelvie, SAR	2	0	0	0	10
Jim Thomas, TOR	0	2	3	1	10

Player of the Year: Bruce Mattingly, SAR

All-Star Team

E Andy Gilmour, TOR
E Keith Fisher, SAR
T Walt Bashuk, HAM
T Dutch Davey, SAR
G Jim Thomas, TOR
G Matt Ferrentino, TOR
C Bruce Mattingly, SAR
QB George Curtis, SAR
HB Mel Hawkrigg, HAM
HB Johnny Chorestecki, SAR
HB Ralph Pulley, TOR (tie)
HB Al Farris, SAR (tie)
HB Corky Duchene, SAR (tie)
FW Jon Florence, SAR

1952 Standings	W	L	T	PTS	PCT	PF	PA
Sarnia Imperials	11	1	0	22	.917	312	68
Toronto Balmy Beaches	8	3	0	16	.727	215	156
Brantford Redskins	2	8	0	4	.200	100	189
Windsor Rockets	0	9	0	0	.000	60	274

Final (Sarnia 65-19)
11/ 9 Sarnia Imperials 24 at Toronto Balmy Beaches 7
11/15 Toronto Balmy Beaches 7 at Sarnia Imperials 24
Grey Cup Semi-Final
11/26 Sarnia Imperials 15 at Toronto Argonauts 34

Team Scoring	TD	FG	C	SI	ST	PTS
SAR	49	3	40	16	1	312
TORB	37	0	23	7	0	215
BRA	16	0	13	2	0	100
WIN	10	0	8	2	0	60

Scoring Leaders	TD	FG	C	SI	PTS
Corky Duchene, SAR	14	0	0	0	70
Johnny Pont, TORB	13	0	0	0	65
Archie McAffer, SAR	9	0	0	1	46
Fred Smale, TORB	8	0	0	0	40
Johnny Chorostecki, SAR	5	0	11	1	37
Jack McKelvie, SAR	2	2	11	4	31
Tom Moran, BRA	5	0	0	0	25
Dale Doland, TORB	0	0	23	1	24
Dutch Davey, SAR	0	1	18	2	23
Scotty Bissett, WIN	3	0	6	2	23
Bobby Lee, WIN	4	0	0	0	20
Marty Carrington, TORB	4	0	0	0	20
Bill Weiss, SAR	2	0	0	7	17
Ken Wagner, TORB	3	0	0	0	15
Freddie Street, TORB	3	0	0	0	15
Glenn Dawson, BRA	1	0	10	0	15
Jack Glendenning, SAR	3	0	0	0	15
Jon Florence, SAR	3	0	0	0	15
Al Dekdebrun, BRA	2	0	0	1	11
Johnny Sells, SAR	2	0	0	0	10
Bill Brady, BRA	2	0	0	0	10
Dutch Holland, BRA	2	0	0	0	10
Eric McKeever, SAR	2	0	0	0	10
Slough Bolton, TORB	2	0	0	0	10

Player of the Year: Johnny Pont, TORB

All-Star Team

E Fred Smale, TORB
E Jack Glendenning, SAR
T Oatten Fisher, TORB
T Dutch Davey, SAR (tie)
Maurice Dorocke, SAR (tie)
G Bob O'Ree, TORB
G Wally McIntosh, SAR
C Bruce Mattingly, SAR
QB Jack McKelvie, SAR
HB Johnny Pont, TORB
HB Corky Duchene, SAR
HB Archie McAffer, SAR

FW Jon Florence, SAR

1953 Standings	W	L	T	PTS	PCT	PF	PA
Kitchener-Waterloo Dutchmen	8	4	0	16	.667	219	178
Toronto Balmy Beaches	8	4	0	16	.667	250	145
Sarnia Imperials	8	4	0	16	.667	231	101
Brantford Redskins	0	12	0	0	.000	73	349

Semi-Final (Toronto 18-12)
11/ 7 Toronto Balmy Beaches 0 at Sarnia Imperials 2
11/ 8 Sarnia Imperials 10 at Toronto Balmy Beaches 18
Final (Toronto 30-21)
11/11 Toronto Balmy Beaches 6 at Kitchener-Waterloo Dutchmen 9
11/15 Kitchener-Waterloo Dutchmen 12 at Toronto Balmy Beaches 24
Grey Cup Semi-Final
11/21 Toronto Balmy Beaches 4 at Winnipeg Blue Bombers 24

Team Scoring	TD	FG	C	SI	ST	PTS
KW	35	2	26	7	1	219
TORB	41	2	29	8	2	250
SAR	35	3	23	15	4	231
BRA	12	1	6	4	0	73

Scoring Leaders	TD	FG	C	SI	PTS
Dick Gregory, TORB	13	2	23	1	95
Jack Mancos, KW	13	0	0	7	72
Bobby Lee, SAR	9	0	0	1	46
Jack McKelvie, SAR	0	4	22	2	36
Harvey Singleton, TORB	6	0	0	0	30
Corky Duchene, SAR	6	0	0	0	30
Eric McKeever, SAR	6	0	0	0	30
Ron Tracey, KW	0	2	22	0	28
Johnny Bell, TORB	4	0	0	0	20
Bob Schneidenbach, TORB	4	0	0	0	20
Sully Ford, KW	4	0	0	0	20
Paul Amodio, KW	4	0	0	0	20
Jack Barry, TORB	3	0	2	0	17
Jim Burr, SAR	1	0	0	11	16
Nayland Moll, TORB	3	0	0	0	15
Art Faguy, BRA	3	0	0	0	15
Jon Florence, SAR	3	0	0	0	15
Don Siemon, KW	3	0	0	0	15
Nat Pagnan, KW	2	0	0	0	10
Johnny Chorostecki, SAR	2	0	0	0	10
Johnny Sells, SAR	2	0	0	0	10
Bill Sowalski, BRA	2	0	0	0	10
Boris Kotoff, BRA	2	0	0	0	10
Sam Laverty, TOR	2	0	0	0	10
Gerry Tuttle, KW	2	0	0	0	10
Stan Terejko, BRA	2	0	0	0	10

Player of the Year: Dick Gregory, TORB

All-Star Team
E Harvey Singleton, TORB
E Keith Fisher, SAR
T Oatten Fisher, TORB
T Maurice Dorocke, SAR
G Jay Fry, KW
G Dutch Davey, SAR
C Bruce Mattingly, SAR
QB Bob Schneidenbach, TOR
HB Dick Gregory, TOR
HB Jack Mancos, KW
HB Corky Duchene, SAR
FW Johnny Chorostecki, SAR

1954 Standings	W	L	T	PTS	PCT	PF	PA
Kitchener-Waterloo Dutchmen	9	2	1	19	.818	279	183
Sarnia Imperials	7	4	1	15	.636	218	193
Toronto Balmy Beaches	1	11	0	2	.083	169	290

Final (Kitchener-Waterloo 29-20)
11/ 3 Sarnia Imperials 12 at Kitchener-Waterloo 13
11/11 Kitchener-Waterloo 16 at Sarnia Imperials 8
Grey Cup Semi-Final
Sat 11/20 Kitchener-Waterloo 6 at Edmonton Eskimos 38

Player of the Year: Bob Celeri, Kitchener-Waterloo

All-Star Team
E Harvey Singleton, TORB
E Gerry MacTaggart, KW
T Keith Carpenter, TORB
T Dan Nykoluk, TORB
G Dutch Davey, SAR
G Jay Fry, KW
C Bruce Mattingly, SAR
QB Bob Celeri, KW
HB Paul Amodio, KW
HB Cookie Gilchrist, SAR
HB Nayland Moll, TORB (tie)
Blake Taylor, KW (tie)
FW Carl Totzke, KW

Team Scoring	TD	FG	C	SI	ST	PTS
KW	45	4	35	7	0	279
SAR	31	8	27	10	1	218
TORB	28	1	15	8	2	169

Scoring Leaders	TD	FG	C	SI	PTS
Paul Amodio, KW	8	3	28	0	77
Cookie Gilchrist, SAR	8	8	3	6	73
Gerry McTaggart, KW	8	0	0	0	40
Nayland Moll, TOR	8	0	0	0	40
Vince Drake, TOR	7	0	1	0	35
Bob Celeri, KW	5	0	0	5	30
Ralph Hunter, KW	6	0	0	0	30
Jim Lambert, SAR	1	0	16	8	29
Al Richmond, SAR	5	0	0	0	25
Blake Taylor, KW	5	0	0	0	25
Bill Tonnegusso, KW	4	0	1	0	21
Maurice O'Callaghan, TOR	4	0	0	0	20
Johnny Chorostecki, SAR	3	0	0	0	15
Billy Lowe, TOR	3	0	0	0	15
Eric McKeever, SAR	3	0	0	0	15
Greg McKelvey, TOR	0	1	12	0	15
Bobby Lee, SAR	2	0	0	0	10
Bobby Kuntz, KW	2	0	0	0	10
Don Siemon, KW	2	0	0	0	10
Jon Florence, SAR\	2	0	0	0	10

Rushing Leaders	ATT	YDS	AVG
Cookie Gilchrist, SAR	118	845	7.1
Nayland Moll, TOR	116	782	6.8
Blake Taylor, KW	135	772	5.7
Elbert Richmond, SAR	75	530	7.1
Johnny Chorostecki, SAR	72	448	6.2
Billy Lowe, TOR	82	407	5.0
Sam Laverty, TOR	47	352	7.5
Ralph Hunter, KW	72	343	4.8
Bill Tonnegusso, KW	46	288	6.3
Bob Celeri, KW	62	273	4.4
Eric McKeever, SAR	40	254	6.4
Ross Dowswell, SAR	30	103	3.4

Passing Leaders	ATT	COM	YDS
Jim Lambert, SAR	193	76	1525
Bob Celeri, KW	225	120	1969
Vince Drake, TOR	182	88	1436

Receiving Leaders	NO	YDS	AVG
Gerry MacTaggart, KW	25	513	20.5
Nayland Moll, TOR	25	474	19.0
Paul Amodio, KW	21	449	21.4
Perk Johnson, SAR	16	299	18.7
Elbert Richmond, SAR	14	221	15.8
Cookie Gilchrist, SAR	9	185	20.6
Johnny Chorostecki, SAR	11	162	14.7
Jack Glendenning, SAR	10	133	13.3

Punting Leaders	NO	YDS	AVG
Jim Burr, SAR	75	2922	39.0
Bob Celeri, KW	83	3216	38.7
Don Guest, TOR	65	1992	30.6

SCORING	TEAM	INDIVIDUAL
Touchdowns	1946-date	1946-date
Converts	1946-date	1946-date
Convert Attempts	1946-date	1946-date
Two-point Converts	1974-date	1974-date
Two-point Convert Attempts	1974-date	2010
Field Goals	1946-date	1946-date
Field Goal Attempts	1950-date West	1950-date West
	1954-date East	1954-date East
Safeties	1946-date	not credited
Singles	1946-date	1946-date
Points	1946-date	1946-date

Two-point converts began in 1974.

RUSHING	TEAM	INDIVIDUAL
Attempts	1950-date West	1950-date West
	1954-date East	1954-date East
Yards	1950-date West	1950-date West
	1954-date East	1954-date East
Long Gain	1999-date	1952 West; 1954-date
Touchdowns	1946-date	1946-date

PASSING	TEAM	INDIVIDUAL
Attempts	1950-date West	1950-date West
	1954-date East	1954-date East
Completions	1950-date West	1950-date West
	1954-date East	1954-date East
Interceptions	1950-date West	1950-date West
	1954-date East	1954-date East
Yards	1950-date West	1950-date West
	1954-date East	1954-date East
Long Gain	1999-date	1952,1955-date West
		1954-date East
Touchdowns	1946-date	1946-date
Times Sacked	1994-date	1995-date
		1960, 1963-1964, 1966 West
		1959, 1961, 1963-1966 East
Yards Lost	1963-66 West	1959-1966 West
	1954-1957, 1959-1966 East	1959, 1961, 1963-1966 East

PASS RECEIVING	TEAM	INDIVIDUAL
Receptions	1950-date West	1950-date West
	1954-date East	1954-date East
Yards	1950-date West	1950-date West
	1954-date East	1954-date East
Long Gain	1999-date	1952 West; 1954-date
Touchdowns	1946-date	1946-date

INTERCEPTIONS	TEAM	INDIVIDUAL
Returns	1950-date West	1952-date West
	1954-date East	1954-date East
Yards	1952-date West	1952-date West*
	1954-date East	1954-date East
Long Gain	1999-date	1952, 1965-date
		1954-date East
Touchdowns	1946-date	1946-date
Knock Downs	1999-date	1994-date

**Yards for players with only one interception is unknown from 1953 to 1965.*

PUNTING	TEAM	INDIVIDUAL
Punts	1950-date West	1950-date West
	1954-date East	1954-date East
Yards	1950-date West	1950-date West
	1954-date East	1954-date East
Long Kick	1999-date	1952 West; 1954-date
Blocked	1996-2010	1996-2010
	1950-1957, 1960 West	1950-1957, 1961 West
	1960 East	1955-1957, 1959-1961 East
Singles	1999-date	1952, 1963-date West
		1959-date East

PUNT RETURNS	TEAM	INDIVIDUAL
Returns	1951-date West	1951-date West
	1954-date East	1954-date East
Yards	1951-date West	1951-date West
	1954-date East	1954-date East
Long Gain	1999-date	1952 West, 1954-date
Touchdowns	1946-date	1946-date

KICKOFFS	**TEAM**	**INDIVIDUAL**
Kickoffs	1952-date West 1958-date East	1952-date West 1958-1959, 1961, 1963-date East
Yards	1952-date West 1958-1961, 1963-date East	1952-date West 1958-1959, 1961, 1963-date East
Long Kick	1999-date	1952, 1955-date West 1959, 1961, 1936-date East
Singles	1999-date	1952 West 1967-date

KICKOFF RETURNS	**TEAM**	**INDIVIDUAL**
Returns	1951-date West 1954-date East	1951-date West 1954-date East
Yards	1951-date West 1954-date East	1951-date West 1954-date East
Long Gain	1999-date	1952 West; 1954-date
Touchdowns	1946-date	1946-date

FUMBLES	**TEAM**	**INDIVIDUAL**
Fumbles	1950-date West 1954-date East	1954-date West 1964-date East
Lost	1950-date West 1954-date East	1967-date
Own Recoveries	1950-date West 1954-date East	1967-date
Opponents Recoveries	1950-date West 1954-date East	1952 West; 1967-date
Total Recoveries	1950-date West 1954-date East	1950-date West 1964-date East
Yards	1952-date West 1967-date East	1967-date
Touchdowns	1946-date	1946-date
Forced Fumbles		

SACKS	**TEAM**	**INDIVIDUAL**
Sacks	1980-date	1981-date
Yards	not kept	1992-date

TACKLES	**TEAM**	**INDIVIDUAL**
Defensive	1999-date	1992-date
Special Teams	1999-date	1992-date
Total	1999-date	1987-date

FIRST DOWNS	**TEAM**	**INDIVIDUAL**
	1950-date West 1954-date East	not kept

PENALTIES	**TEAM**	**INDIVIDUAL**
Penalties	1950-date West 1954-date East	2008-date
Yards	1950-date West 1954-date East	2008-date

The Annual Record covers every season since the modern era of Canadian football began in 1946. It includes the final regular season standings and team statistics for each season.

The following column headings are used in this section:

AVG	Average	
C1	One-point converts	
C2	Two-point converts	
COM	Pass completions	
FDP	First downs by passing	
FDR	First downs by rushing	
FDX	First downs by penalty	
FDT	Total first downs	
FG	Field goals made	
FGA	Field goals attempted	
FL	Fumbles lost	
FUM	Fumbles	
G	Games played	
KO	Kickoffs	
KOR	Kickoff returns	
L	Games lost	
OPP	Opponents' points allowed	
PASS	Passing attempts	
PCT	Pass completion percentage	
PEN	Penalties	
PF	Points scored	
PI	Passes Intercepted	
PR	Punt returns	
PTS	Championship points (awarded on a basis of two per win and one per tie, with the exceptions of the 1949 WIFU when four games were worth only one point and from 2000 to 2002 when teams were awarded one point per overtime loss).	
PUNT	Punts	
RUSH	Rushing attempts	
SI	Singles	
ST	Safety touches	
T	Games tied	
TD	Touchdowns	
TDO	Touchdowns other than by rushing or passing	
TDP	Touchdowns passing	
TDR	Touchdowns rushing	
TEAM	BAL	Baltimore (1994)
		Baltimore Stallions (1995)
	BC	British Columbia Lions (1954-)
	BIR	Birmingham Barracudas (1995)
	CAL	Calgary Stampeders (1946-)
	EDM	Edmonton Eskimos (1949-)
	HAM	Hamilton Tigers (1946-1947)
		Hamilton Wildcats (1948-1949)
		Hamilton Tiger-Cats (1950-)
	LV	Las Vegas Posse (1994)
	MEM	Memphis Mad Dogs (1995)
	MTL	Montreal Alouettes (1946-1981)
		Montreal Concordes (1982-1985)
		Montreal Alouettes (1986; 1996-)
	OTT	Ottawa Rough Riders (1946-1996)
		Ottawa Renegades (2002-2005)
	SA	San Antonio Texans (1995)
	SAC	Sacramento Gold Miners (1993-1994)
	SAS	Saskatchewan Roughriders (1946-)
	SHR	Shreveport Pirates (1994-1995)
	TOR	Toronto Argonauts (1946-)
	WPG	Winnipeg Blue Bombers (1946-)
TS	Times sacked	
W	Games won	
YDS	Yards	

1946 IRFU

TEAM	G	W	L	T	PTS	PCT	PF	OPP	TD	TDR	TDP	TDO	C1	C2	FG	FGA	ST	SI	FDT	FDR	FDP	FDX	PEN	YDS	FUM	FL
MTL	12	7	3	2	16	.667	211	118	30	16	8	6	23		10		0	8								
TOR	12	7	3	2	16	.667	140	124	17	10	4	3	11		8		2	16								
OTT	12	6	4	2	14	.583	175	128	26	9	10	7	19		3		0	17								
HAM	12	0	10	2	2	.083	78	234	10	7	0	3	7		3		0	12								

1946 WIFU

TEAM	G	W	L	T	PTS	PCT	PF	OPP	TD	TDR	TDP	TDO	C1	C2	FG	FGA	ST	SI	FDT	FDR	FDP	FDX	PEN	YDS	FUM	FL
CAL	8	5	3	0	10	.625	60	37	5	2	0	3	4		8		1	5								
WPG	8	5	3	0	10	.625	69	46	9	2	5	2	7		5		0	2								
SAS	8	2	6	0	4	.250	46	92	7	2	5	0	4		1		1	2								

1947 IRFU

TEAM	G	W	L	T	PTS	PCT	PF	OPP	TD	TDR	TDP	TDO	C1	C2	FG	FGA	ST	SI	FDT	FDR	FDP	FDX	PEN	YDS	FUM	FL
OTT	12	8	4	0	16	.667	170	103	25	9	11	5	18		6		0	9								
TOR	12	7	4	1	15	.625	140	122	21	10	7	4	17		2		1	10								
MTL	12	6	6	0	12	.500	164	164	24	13	7	4	16		6		0	10								
HAM	12	2	9	1	5	.208	119	204	16	10	3	3	12		4		2	11								

1947 WIFU

TEAM	G	W	L	T	PTS	PCT	PF	OPP	TD	TDR	TDP	TDO	C1	C2	FG	FGA	ST	SI	FDT	FDR	FDP	FDX	PEN	YDS	FUM	FL
WPG	8	5	3	0	10	.625	83	83	12	8	3	1	10		1		0	10								
CAL	8	4	4	0	8	.500	79	93	11	8	0	3	9		4		0	3								
SAS	8	3	5	0	6	.375	78	64	10	3	4	3	5		5		0	8								

1948 IRFU

TEAM	G	W	L	T	PTS	PCT	PF	OPP	TD	TDR	TDP	TDO	C1	C2	FG	FGA	ST	SI	FDT	FDR	FDP	FDX	PEN	YDS	FUM	FL
OTT	12	10	2	0	20	.833	264	130	42	22	13	7	32		3		1	11								
MTL	12	7	5	0	14	.583	221	172	35	15	13	7	26		2		2	10								
TOR	12	5	6	1	11	.458	160	191	23	16	4	3	15		5		1	13								
HAM	12	1	10	1	3	.125	88	240	11	9	2	0	8		4		1	11								

1948 WIFU

TEAM	G	W	L	T	PTS	PCT	PF	OPP	TD	TDR	TDP	TDO	C1	C2	FG	FGA	ST	SI	FDT	FDR	FDP	FDX	PEN	YDS	FUM	FL
CAL	12	12	0	0	24	1.000	218	61	31	13	14	4	29		6		0	16								
SAS	12	3	9	0	6	.250	133	137	19	11	4	4	16		2		0	16								
WPG	12	3	9	0	6	.250	81	234	11	7	3	1	4		5		0	7								

1949 IRFU

TEAM	G	W	L	T	PTS	PCT	PF	OPP	TD	TDR	TDP	TDO	C1	C2	FG	FGA	ST	SI	FDT	FDR	FDP	FDX	PEN	YDS	FUM	FL
OTT	12	11	1	0	22	.917	261	170	42	22	18	2	34		1		0	14								
MTL	12	8	4	0	16	.667	295	204	47	18	22	7	37		3		0	14								
TOR	12	5	7	0	10	.417	209	254	31	20	7	4	25		4		1	15								
HAM	12	0	12	0	0	.000	147	284	24	17	5	2	13		1		0	11								

1949 WIFU

TEAM	G	W	L	T	PTS	PCT	PF	OPP	TD	TDR	TDP	TDO	C1	C2	FG	FGA	ST	SI	FDT	FDR	FDP	FDX	PEN	YDS	FUM	FL
CAL	14	13	1	0	26	.929	270	77	41	19	15	7	33		7		1	9								
SAS	14	9	5	0	18	.643	235	102	35	24	10	1	30		4		1	16								
EDM	14	4	10	0	8	.286	93	235	14	7	4	3	8		2		0	9								
WPG	14	2	12	0	2	.143	74	258	11	3	5	3	8		1		0	8								

1950 IRFU

TEAM	G	W	L	T	PTS	PCT	PF	OPP	TD	TDR	TDP	TDO	C1	C2	FG	FGA	ST	SI	FDT	FDR	FDP	FDX	PEN	YDS	FUM	FL
HAM	12	7	5	0	14	.583	231	217	35	27	7	1	25		4		0	19								
TOR	12	6	5	1	13	.542	291	187	47	20	15	12	41		2		1	7								
MTL	12	6	6	0	12	.500	192	261	30	14	15	1	23		3		0	10								
OTT	12	4	7	1	9	.375	182	231	27	14	9	4	18		4		2	13								

1950 WIFU

TEAM	G	W	L	T	PTS	PCT	PF	OPP	TD	TDR	TDP	TDO	C1	C2	FG	FGA	ST	SI	FDT	FDR	FDP	FDX	PEN	YDS	FUM	FL
WPG	14	10	4	0	20	.714	223	156	30	10	17	3	25		6	21	0	30	159	78	72	9	60	498	42	21
SAS	14	7	7	0	14	.500	207	177	29	16	10	3	27		7	15	0	14	209	128	77	4	38	347	43	24
EDM	14	7	7	0	14	.500	201	197	31	16	14	1	28		3	10	0	9	182	72	101	9	48	500	36	17
CAL	14	4	10	0	8	.286	152	253	22	13	9	0	17		5	12	0	10	181	88	83	10	44	333	28	19

TEAM	RUSH	YDS	AVG	PASS	COM	PCT	PI	YDS	AVG	TS	INT	PUNT	YDS	AVG	PR	YDS	AVG	KO	AVG	KOR	YDS	AVG
WPG	394	1599	4.1	246	104	42.3	16	1904	7.7		34	123	4919	40.0								
SAS	458	2226	4.9	228	102	44.7	23	1742	7.6		16	127	4711	37.1								
EDM	338	1364	4.0	304	156	51.3	24	2609	8.6		14	103	3870	37.6								
CAL	426	1575	3.7	282	132	46.8	16	2027	7.2		15	116	4842	41.7								

1951 IRFU

TEAM	G	W	L	T	PTS	PCT	PF	OPP	TD	TDR	TDP	TDO	C1	C2	FG	FGA	ST	SI	FDT	FDR	FDP	FDX	PEN	YDS	FUM	FL
HAM	12	7	5	0	14	.583	229	131	36	20	10	6	26		5		0	8								
OTT	12	7	5	0	14	.583	218	197	33	5	21	7	28		2		0	19								
TOR	12	7	5	0	14	.583	226	205	35	20	15	0	26		4		0	13								
MTL	12	3	9	0	6	.250	146	286	22	11	11	0	18		3		1	7								

1951 WIFU

TEAM	G	W	L	T	PTS	PCT	PF	OPP	TD	TDR	TDP	TDO	C1	C2	FG	FGA	ST	SI	FDT	FDR	FDP	FDX	PEN	YDS	FUM	FL
SAS	14	8	6	0	16	.571	277	219	41	13	28	0	34		4	11	1	24	174	78	80	16	55	465	37	23
EDM	14	8	6	0	16	.571	306	262	49	30	14	5	42		3	14	0	10	252	164	73	15	56	566	33	15
WPG	14	8	6	0	16	.571	303	311	47	9	36	2	39		3	10	2	16	214	72	123	19	73	543	32	25
CAL	14	4	10	0	8	.286	205	299	32	12	15	5	30		3	10	1	4	204	68	116	20	62	554	27	20

TEAM	RUSH	YDS	AVG	PASS	COM	PCT	PI	YDS	AVG	TS	INT	PUNT	YDS	AVG	PR	YDS	AVG	KO	AVG	KOR	YDS	AVG
SAS	380	1456	3.8	291	152	52.2	15	2433	8.4		28	138	5786	41.9	101	773	7.7			36	642	17.8
EDM	579	3082	5.3	228	114	50.0	12	2113	9.3		25	121	4588	37.9	100	824	8.2			61	859	14.1
WPG	347	1408	4.1	415	221	53.3	17	3520	8.5		12	131	5101	38.9	103	874	8.5			59	880	14.9
CAL	342	1158	3.4	393	197	50.1	32	2916	7.4		11	122	4601	37.7	111	933	8.4			57	1081	19.0

1952 IRFU

TEAM	G	W	L	T	PTS	PCT	PF	OPP	TD	TDR	TDP	TDO	C1	C2	FG	FGA	ST	SI	FDT	FDR	FDP	FDX	PEN	YDS	FUM	FL
HAM	12	9	2	1	19	.792	268	162	42	19	18	5	38		0		1	18								
TOR	12	7	4	1	15	.625	265	191	43	21	21	1	37		1		1	21								
OTT	12	5	7	0	10	.417	200	238	30	9	19	2	24		3		1	19								
MTL	12	2	10	0	2	.167	136	278	21	10	9	2	17		3		0	9								

1952 WIFU

TEAM	G	W	L	T	PTS	PCT	PF	OPP	TD	TDR	TDP	TDO	C1	C2	FG	FGA	ST	SI	FDT	FDR	FDP	FDX	PEN	YDS	FUM	FL
WPG	16	12	3	1	25	.781	394	211	63	18	40	5	48		4	6	1	17	193	85	93	15	85	788	39	23
EDM	16	9	6	1	19	.594	291	280	46	21	22	3	36		1	11	3	16	231	115	104	12	71	723	47	28
CAL	16	7	9	0	14	.438	293	340	43	9	28	6	38		8	15	1	14	258	113	120	25	102	925	32	21
SAS	16	3	13	0	6	.188	216	363	32	8	19	4	29		1	4	1	22	201	84	85	32	96	843	47	28

TEAM	RUSH	YDS	AVG	PASS	COM	PCT	PI	YDS	AVG	TS	INT	PUNT	YDS	AVG	PR	YDS	AVG	KO	AVG	KOR	YDS	AVG
WPG	362	2036	5.6	366	182	49.7	19	3347	9.1		28	112	4892	43.7	124	1311	10.6	78	52.2	46	1096	23.8
EDM	448	2042	4.6	352	189	53.7	17	2930	8.3		21	117	5027	43.0	114	913	8.0	53	54.2	56	1334	23.8
CAL	399	1777	4.5	426	192	45.1	31	3453	8.1		10	112	4244	37.9	96	654	6.8	51	48.8	68	1735	25.5
SAS	379	1452	3.8	347	151	43.5	17	2571	7.4		25	132	5898	44.7	104	668	6.4	50	49.6	62	1553	25.0

1953 IRFU

TEAM	G	W	L	T	PTS	PCT	PF	OPP	TD	TDR	TDP	TDO	C1	C2	FG	FGA	ST	SI	FDT	FDR	FDP	FDX	PEN	YDS	FUM	FL
HAM	14	8	6	0	16	.571	229	243	32	12	13	7	32		4		4	17								
MTL	14	8	6	0	16	.571	292	229	42	15	23	4	38		11		3	5								
OTT	14	7	7	0	14	.500	266	238	39	13	23	3	36		5		1	18								
TOR	14	5	9	0	10	.357	172	249	26	7	16	3	17		2		5	9								

1953 WIFU

TEAM	G	W	L	T	PTS	PCT	PF	OPP	TD	TDR	TDP	TDO	C1	C2	FG	FGA	ST	SI	FDT	FDR	FDP	FDX	PEN	YDS	FUM	FL
EDM	16	12	4	0	24	.750	276	157	40	23	14	3	38		6	17	1	18	234	153	73	8	59	537	34	20
SAS	16	8	7	1	17	.531	243	239	35	13	20	2	30		5	14	5	13	207	96	93	18	49	438	33	20
WPG	16	8	8	0	16	.500	226	226	31	11	20	0	29		9	20	2	11	238	98	126	12	69	639	36	23
CAL	16	3	12	1	7	.219	190	313	32	11	17	4	23		1	6	1	2	186	87	87	12	56	392	26	21

TEAM	RUSH	YDS	AVG	PASS	COM	PCT	PI	YDS	AVG	TS	INT	PUNT	YDS	AVG	PR	YDS	AVG	KO	AVG	KOR	YDS	AVG
EDM	519	3095	6.0	241	128	53.1	17	2217	9.2		29	119	5280	44.4	109	915	8.4	58	51.5	36	740	20.6
SAS	481	1827	3.8	339	192	56.6	20	2604	7.7		22	137	6101	44.5	128	1233	9.6	44	42.1	56	1048	18.7
WPG	399	1583	4.0	408	230	56.4	23	3104	7.6		23	112	4440	39.6	115	932	8.1	52	52.0	40	786	19.7
CAL	375	1180	3.1	392	187	47.7	30	2786	7.1		16	150	5872	39.1	120	1213	10.1	46	44.8	63	1213	19.3

1954 IRFU

TEAM	G	W	L	T	PTS	PCT	PF	OPP	TD	TDR	TDP	TDO	C1	C2	FG	FGA	ST	SI	FDT	FDR	FDP	FDX	PEN	YDS	FUM	FL
MTL	14	11	3	0	22	.786	341	148	53	26	25	2	48		6	14	0	10	323	155	161	7	72	658	43	21
HAM	14	9	5	0	18	.643	275	207	40	14	21	5	38		3	9	3	22	239	107	117	15	62	535	35	21
TOR	14	6	8	0	12	.429	212	265	33	16	14	3	31		2	3	1	8	254	108	137	9	72	562	47	27
OTT	14	2	12	0	4	.143	129	337	21	12	8	1	14		2	5	0	4	200	107	88	5	52	536	39	17

TEAM	RUSH	YDS	AVG	PASS	COM	PCT	PI	YDS	AVG	TS	INT	PUNT	YDS	AVG	PR	YDS	AVG	KO	AVG	KOR	YDS	AVG
MTL	512	2757	5.4	379	209	55.1	31	3659	9.7		34	153	6272	41.0	151	945	6.3			41	918	22.4
HAM	407	1822	4.5	362	198	54.7	30	2679	7.4		32	153	6596	43.1	142	940	6.6			36	808	22.4
TOR	370	1921	5.2	379	212	55.9	24	3143	8.3		36	143	5325	37.2	125	988	7.9			52	981	18.9
OTT	393	1796	4.6	307	143	46.6	35	2062	6.7		18	165	6987	42.3	133	807	6.1			63	1228	19.5

1954 WIFU

TEAM	G	W	L	T	PTS	PCT	PF	OPP	TD	TDR	TDP	TDO	C1	C2	FG	FGA	ST	SI	FDT	FDR	FDP	FDX	PEN	YDS	FUM	FL
EDM	16	11	5	0	22	.688	255	163	37	26	8	3	37		8	18	0	9	251	169	69	13	62	604	31	23
SAS	16	10	4	2	22	.688	239	204	28	12	16	0	25		19	30	1	15	230	130	85	15	68	714	25	19
WPG	16	8	6	2	18	.563	202	190	30	13	14	3	21		4	14	2	15	178	88	76	14	65	627	36	25
CAL	16	8	8	0	16	.500	271	165	37	21	10	6	34		14	30	0	10	241	139	88	14	72	639	27	20
BC	16	1	15	0	2	.063	100	345	14	6	6	2	11		6	11	0	1	151	66	79	6	64	596	26	18

TEAM	RUSH	YDS	AVG	PASS	COM	PCT	PI	YDS	AVG	TS	INT	PUNT	YDS	AVG	PR	YDS	AVG	KO	AVG	KOR	YDS	AVG
EDM	575	3118	5.4	211	104	49.3	14	1708	8.1		37	126	5173	41.1	121	742	6.1	56	50.5	35	686	19.6
SAS	522	2234	4.3	290	165	56.9	18	2265	7.8		20	127	5790	45.6	123	969	7.9	42	52.9	45	1099	24.4
WPG	441	1722	3.9	298	154	51.7	18	2079	7.0		17	139	5602	40.3	123	969	7.9	45	49.2	41	873	21.3
CAL	492	2689	5.5	311	145	46.6	29	2440	7.8		26	124	4872	39.3	140	1079	7.7	52	53.9	39	798	20.5
BC	391	1002	2.6	333	146	43.8	33	1933	5.8		12	160	6038	37.7	136	988	7.3	31	54.2	64	1256	19.6

1955 IRFU

TEAM	G	W	L	T	PTS	PCT	PF	OPP	TD	TDR	TDP	TDO	C1	C2	FG	FGA	ST	SI	FDT	FDR	FDP	FDX	PEN	YDS	FUM	FL
MTL	12	9	3	0	18	.750	388	214	60	26	31	3	56		6	11	1	12	370	181	181	8	47	350	44	21
HAM	12	8	4	0	16	.667	271	193	39	28	6	5	36		8	11	2	12	241	142	86	13	40	315	47	21
TOR	12	4	8	0	8	.333	239	328	41	9	31	1	33		0	2	0	1	312	128	176	8	53	493	40	19
OTT	12	3	9	0	6	.250	174	337	27	8	14	5	23		4	7	0	4	184	100	76	8	49	392	46	19

TEAM	RUSH	YDS	AVG	PASS	COM	PCT	PI	YDS	AVG	TS	INT	PUNT	YDS	AVG	PR	YDS	AVG	KO	AVG	KOR	YDS	AVG
MTL	476	2799	5.9	410	231	56.3	24	3733	9.1		25	109	4346	39.9	128	899	7.0			44	912	20.7
HAM	508	2871	5.7	226	113	50.0	12	1652	7.3		30	125	5920	47.4	98	1090	11.1			42	882	21.0
TOR	407	2057	5.1	412	234	56.8	37	3710	9.0		19	111	3830	34.5	105	820	7.8			59	1161	19.7
OTT	349	1838	5.3	253	104	41.1	28	2029	8.0		27	119	5203	43.7	75	604	8.1			61	1297	21.3

1955 WIFU

TEAM	G	W	L	T	PTS	PCT	PF	OPP	TD	TDR	TDP	TDO	C1	C2	FG	FGA	ST	SI	FDT	FDR	FDP	FDX	PEN	YDS	FUM	FL
EDM	16	14	2	0	28	.875	286	117	39	21	13	5	36		14	28	1	11	283	212	64	7	69	515	42	26
SAS	16	10	6	0	20	.625	270	245	38	21	14	3	32		14	24	0	6	291	166	115	10	50	367	27	18
WPG	16	7	9	0	14	.438	210	195	30	24	5	1	28		7	19	0	11	271	193	72	6	78	583	39	31
BC	16	5	11	0	10	.313	211	330	32	15	13	4	31		3	8	0	11	275	133	132	10	61	477	29	20
CAL	16	4	12	0	8	.250	209	299	32	12	17	3	29		2	13	1	12	246	99	127	20	60	492	39	33

TEAM	RUSH	YDS	AVG	PASS	COM	PCT	PI	YDS	AVG	TS	INT	PUNT	YDS	AVG	PR	YDS	AVG	KO	AVG	KOR	YDS	AVG
EDM	655	3392	5.2	192	85	44.3	12	1398	7.3		34	126	5398	42.8	130	717	5.5	58	49.7	29	593	20.4
SAS	618	3311	5.4	281	169	60.1	18	2595	9.2		21	137	5551	40.5	117	864	7.4	52	55.4	47	1032	22.0
WPG	610	2487	4.1	248	109	44.0	24	1708	6.9		20	117	4926	42.1	130	940	7.2	40	51.1	50	1054	21.1
BC	459	2063	4.5	357	192	53.8	24	2850	8.0		13	122	5083	41.7	114	759	6.7	50	54.0	60	1085	18.1
CAL	416	1496	3.6	385	201	52.2	29	3147	8.2		19	119	4967	41.7	114	884	7.8	51	46.2	54	1107	20.5

1956 IRFU

TEAM	G	W	L	T	PTS	PCT	PF	OPP	TD	TDR	TDP	TDO	C1	C2	FG	FGA	ST	SI	FDT	FDR	FDP	FDX	PEN	YDS	FUM	FL
MTL	14	10	4	0	20	.714	478	361	67	31	33	3	54		2	6	1	14	420	181	227	12	83	765	52	29
HAM	14	7	7	0	14	.500	383	385	54	15	35	4	42		1	5	0	14	290	123	152	15	103	959	55	31
OTT	14	7	7	0	14	.500	326	359	44	25	17	2	35		4	7	1	13	299	158	128	13	54	412	37	18
TOR	14	4	10	0	8	.286	331	413	48	13	33	2	33		1	3	2	3	360	123	212	25	85	748	46	20

TEAM	RUSH	YDS	AVG	PASS	COM	PCT	PI	YDS	AVG	TS	INT	PUNT	YDS	AVG	PR	YDS	AVG	KO	AVG	KOR	YDS	AVG
MTL	507	2765	5.5	499	306	61.3	30	5067	10.2		34	95	3913	41.2	97	701	7.2			65	1408	21.7
HAM	457	2466	5.4	368	203	55.2	32	3451	9.4		24	123	5644	45.9	110	875	8.0			66	1266	19.2
OTT	465	2538	5.5	377	178	47.2	29	3214	8.5		37	124	5427	43.8	95	767	8.1			60	1313	21.9
TOR	432	2136	4.9	510	290	56.9	28	4167	8.2		24	118	4415	37.4	105	806	7.7			67	1301	19.4

1956 WIFU

TEAM	G	W	L	T	PTS	PCT	PF	OPP	TD	TDR	TDP	TDO	C1	C2	FG	FGA	ST	SI	FDT	FDR	FDP	FDX	PEN	YDS	FUM	FL
EDM	16	11	5	0	22	.688	358	235	48	27	15	6	36		7	17	1	11	318	205	104	9	70	462	42	30
SAS	16	10	6	0	20	.625	353	272	42	24	18	0	35		13	17	2	23	313	152	148	13	66	466	26	26
WPG	16	9	7	0	18	.563	315	228	40	25	12	3	32		12	20	0	7	338	194	125	19	77	591	35	29
BC	16	6	10	0	12	.375	251	361	34	13	17	4	23		4	8	0	12	255	141	102	12	81	618	47	36
CAL	16	4	12	0	8	.250	229	410	32	23	7	2	23		1	10	0	11	283	163	103	17	79	577	42	33

TEAM	RUSH	YDS	AVG	PASS	COM	PCT	PI	YDS	AVG	TS	INT	PUNT	YDS	AVG	PR	YDS	AVG	KO	AVG	KOR	YDS	AVG
EDM	612	3482	5.7	281	138	49.1	21	2192	7.8		30	117	4728	40.4	128	703	5.5	67	54.0	42	904	21.5
SAS	547	2357	4.3	419	232	55.4	25	3663	8.7		23	136	6211	45.7	126	730	5.8	52	53.1	59	1105	18.7
WPG	664	3034	4.6	356	186	52.2	23	2709	7.6		29	132	4965	37.6	130	710	5.5	57	51.5	44	949	21.6
BC	573	2463	4.3	317	140	44.2	34	2202	6.9		25	132	5692	43.1	129	577	4.5	52	55.7	61	1363	22.3
CAL	570	2733	4.8	339	167	49.3	26	2283	6.7		22	127	4860	38.3	103	675	6.6	48	47.8	70	1355	19.4

1957 IRFU

TEAM	G	W	L	T	PTS	PCT	PF	OPP	TD	TDR	TDP	TDO	C1	C2	FG	FGA	ST	SI	FDT	FDR	FDP	FDX	PEN	YDS	FUM	FL
HAM	14	10	4	0	20	.714	250	189	30	18	6	6	23		9	18	0	20	254	152	88	14	94	744	62	33
OTT	14	8	6	0	16	.571	326	237	44	19	18	7	33		7	12	0	8	290	174	103	13	66	570	56	21
MTL	14	6	8	0	12	.429	287	301	38	17	16	5	34		5	10	0	10	324	154	160	10	53	435	53	21
TOR	14	4	10	0	8	.286	274	410	36	17	18	1	27		8	18	0	7	277	132	124	21	79	735	55	30

TEAM	RUSH	YDS	AVG	PASS	COM	PCT	PI	YDS	AVG	TS	INT	PUNT	YDS	AVG	PR	YDS	AVG	KO	AVG	KOR	YDS	AVG
HAM	579	2937	5.1	279	118	42.3	20	1879	6.7		28	160	7354	46.0	147	748	5.1					
OTT	608	2809	4.6	308	155	50.3	23	2759	9.0		38	154	5563	36.1	134	997	7.4					
MTL	512	2486	4.9	438	231	52.7	26	3591	8.2		18	142	5757	40.5	126	770	6.1					
TOR	514	2520	4.9	384	181	47.1	37	2621	6.8		22	146	5817	39.8	130	976	7.5					

1957 WIFU

TEAM	G	W	L	T	PTS	PCT	PF	OPP	TD	TDR	TDP	TDO	C1	C2	FG	FGA	ST	SI	FDT	FDR	FDP	FDX	PEN	YDS	FUM	FL
EDM	16	14	2	0	28	.875	475	142	63	46	14	3	50		10	18	0	17	403	272	117	14	57	537	33	25
WPG	16	12	4	0	24	.750	406	300	56	38	14	4	43		4	8	0	15	306	216	82	8	108	932	23	18
CAL	16	6	10	0	12	.375	221	413	31	13	16	2	19		2	6	0	10	255	140	110	5	56	429	33	26
BC	16	4	11	1	9	.281	284	369	40	19	20	1	29		2	5	1	7	270	139	123	8	98	867	24	16
SAS	16	3	12	1	7	.219	276	438	37	20	13	4	29		4	7	3	7	282	135	133	14	60	483	15	13

TEAM	RUSH	YDS	AVG	PASS	COM	PCT	PI	YDS	AVG	TS	INT	PUNT	YDS	AVG	PR	YDS	AVG	KO	AVG	KOR	YDS	AVG
EDM	722	4345	6.0	270	149	55.2	21	2730	10.1		30	101	4194	41.5	138	851	6.2	75	54.1	35	767	21.9
WPG	685	3744	5.5	204	108	52.9	15	1814	8.9		20	131	5232	39.9	119	858	7.2	71	53.0	56	1501	26.8
CAL	500	1983	4.0	335	172	51.3	23	2765	8.3		25	121	5034	41.6	100	671	6.7	47	51.6	67	1466	21.9
BC	539	2347	4.4	332	169	50.9	24	2561	7.7		23	136	5735	42.2	125	766	6.1	57	50.1	62	1266	20.4
SAS	526	2243	4.3	367	182	49.6	32	2819	7.7		17	137	5475	40.0	109	585	5.4	50	51.3	79	1529	19.4

1958 IRFU

TEAM	G	W	L	T	PTS	PCT	PF	OPP	TD	TDR	TDP	TDO	C1	C2	FG	FGA	ST	SI	FDT	FDR	FDP	FDX	PEN	YDS	FUM	FL
HAM	14	10	3	1	21	.750	291	235	39	15	21	3	27		2	12	1	22	247	101	126	20	115	1028	36	24
MTL	14	7	6	1	15	.536	265	269	35	15	18	2	28		6	13	1	7	307	137	151	19	92	750	36	27
OTT	14	6	8	0	12	.429	233	243	32	18	10	4	18		4	16	0	11	270	164	93	13	72	697	34	25
TOR	14	4	10	0	8	.286	266	308	34	18	13	3	32		8	23	0	6	261	134	112	15	88	867	33	27

TEAM	RUSH	YDS	AVG	PASS	COM	PCT	PI	YDS	AVG	TS	INT	PUNT	YDS	AVG	PR	YDS	AVG	KO	AVG	KOR	YDS	AVG
HAM	525	2080	4.0	322	172	53.4	28	3019	9.4		20	157	7193	45.8	144	889	6.2	53	53.2	43	1027	23.9
MTL	525	1799	3.4	426	248	58.2	26	3573	8.4		29	145	5668	39.1	139	825	5.9	51	51.5	48	1043	21.7
OTT	597	2760	4.6	269	135	50.2	23	2160	8.0		23	150	5548	37.0	143	978	6.8	45	54.8	46	917	19.9
TOR	489	2492	5.1	324	183	56.5	25	2508	7.7		30	128	5305	41.4	116	917	7.9	47	55.5	57	1167	20.5

1958 WIFU

TEAM	G	W	L	T	PTS	PCT	PF	OPP	TD	TDR	TDP	TDO	C1	C2	FG	FGA	ST	SI	FDT	FDR	FDP	FDX	PEN	YDS	FUM	FL
WPG	16	13	3	0	26	.813	361	182	46	28	17	1	35		12	19	0	14	344	219	116	9	89	778	25	16
EDM	16	9	6	1	19	.594	312	292	38	29	9	0	25		14	29	1	15	337	214	111	12	67	489	43	31
SAS	16	7	7	2	16	.500	320	324	41	11	23	7	36		7	16	0	17	302	147	144	11	78	669	32	26
CAL	16	6	9	1	13	.406	314	312	43	22	19	2	36		4	10	0	8	294	135	151	8	72	467	28	19
BC	16	3	13	0	6	.188	202	399	28	12	14	2	20		2	8	1	6	268	115	147	6	90	725	39	25

TEAM	RUSH	YDS	AVG	PASS	COM	PCT	PI	YDS	AVG	TS	INT	PUNT	YDS	AVG	PR	YDS	AVG	KO	AVG	KOR	YDS	AVG
WPG	726	3957	5.5	284	146	51.4	19	2560	9.0		25	148	6557	44.3	144	1000	6.9	61	52.4	39	1059	27.2
EDM	738	3722	5.0	314	155	49.4	19	2409	7.7		34	138	5073	36.8	142	851	6.0	54	54.7	53	1185	22.4
SAS	593	2768	4.7	385	204	53.0	34	2981	7.7		20	155	6437	41.5	143	1471	10.3	52	52.5	58	1457	25.1
CAL	543	2160	4.0	402	223	55.5	22	3301	8.2		30	148	6180	41.8	129	845	6.6	59	56.2	54	1240	23.0
BC	526	1899	3.6	407	200	49.1	36	2939	7.2		21	148	6143	41.5	136	939	6.9	45	46.6	65	1315	20.2

1959 IRFU

TEAM	G	W	L	T	PTS	PCT	PF	OPP	TD	TDR	TDP	TDO	C1	C2	FG	FGA	ST	SI	FDT	FDR	FDP	FDX	PEN	YDS	FUM	FL
HAM	14	10	4	0	20	.714	298	162	38	12	21	5	28		5	13	4	19	241	90	130	21	111	989	22	15
OTT	14	8	6	0	16	.571	275	217	37	20	16	1	28		4	8	2	9	286	155	111	20	85	711	26	18
MTL	14	6	8	0	12	.429	193	305	25	12	10	3	20		4	17	1	9	289	116	150	23	61	538	33	21
TOR	14	4	10	0	8	.286	192	274	24	9	15	0	16		9	14	0	5	250	119	118	13	91	802	26	18

TEAM	RUSH	YDS	AVG	PASS	COM	PCT	PI	YDS	AVG	TS	INT	PUNT	YDS	AVG	PR	YDS	AVG	KO	AVG	KOR	YDS	AVG
HAM	451	2004	4.4	321	179	55.8	18	2817	8.8		32	141	6542	46.4	128	1025	8.0	51	48.6	38	632	16.6
OTT	537	2841	5.3	289	149	51.6	25	2563	8.9		11	142	5510	38.8	144	883	6.1	50	49.2	43	845	19.7
MTL	412	2001	4.9	419	237	56.6	21	3212	7.7		26	131	4937	37.7	129	763	5.9	41	50.4	54	923	17.1
TOR	439	2288	5.2	353	175	49.6	34	2406	6.8		29	126	4853	38.5	115	863	7.5	40	52.6	46	942	20.5

1959 WIFU

TEAM	G	W	L	T	PTS	PCT	PF	OPP	TD	TDR	TDP	TDO	C1	C2	FG	FGA	ST	SI	FDT	FDR	FDP	FDX	PEN	YDS	FUM	FL
WPG	16	12	4	0	24	.750	418	272	57	19	36	2	40		9	16	0	9	340	162	167	11	69	615	25	16
EDM	16	10	6	0	20	.625	370	221	46	27	18	1	34		16	26	2	8	337	190	139	8	63	497	33	26
BC	16	9	7	0	18	.563	306	301	39	15	20	4	31		12	26	0	5	286	139	130	17	101	848	31	25
CAL	16	8	8	0	16	.500	356	301	45	20	23	2	38		14	25	0	6	352	187	155	10	91	714	30	23
SAS	16	1	15	0	2	.063	212	567	27	10	11	6	24		6	10	0	8	240	111	118	11	58	476	30	20

TEAM	RUSH	YDS	AVG	PASS	COM	PCT	PI	YDS	AVG	TS	INT	PUNT	YDS	AVG	PR	YDS	AVG	KO	AVG	KOR	YDS	AVG
WPG	575	3157	5.5	374	197	52.7	22	3282	8.8		29	136	5785	42.5	134	799	6.0	70	54.2	53	1166	22.0
EDM	618	3094	5.0	343	196	57.1	20	3287	9.6		36	135	5504	40.8	142	893	6.3	63	51.4	40	899	22.5
BC	573	2908	5.1	360	174	48.3	35	3072	8.5		22	113	4402	39.0	143	854	6.0	55	52.6	52	1156	22.2
CAL	603	3197	5.3	371	214	57.7	21	3207	8.6		31	128	4856	37.9	132	721	5.5	61	52.3	54	1163	21.5
SAS	499	2087	4.2	386	177	45.9	45	2301	6.0		25	149	5842	39.2	112	694	6.2	43	52.5	93	1849	19.9

1960 EASTERN CONFERENCE

TEAM	G	W	L	T	PTS	PCT	PF	OPP	TD	TDR	TDP	TDO	C1	C2	FG	FGA	ST	SI	FDT	FDR	FDP	FDX	PEN	YDS	FUM	FL
TOR	14	10	4	0	20	.714	370	265	49	9	39	1	43		5	18	1	16	306	101	191	14	111	1005	28	16
OTT	14	9	5	0	18	.643	400	283	55	32	19	4	42		5	10	1	11	311	196	101	14	89	818	21	12
MTL	14	5	9	0	10	.357	340	458	45	17	24	4	41		4	15	0	17	328	148	159	21	69	458	26	12
HAM	14	4	10	0	8	.286	273	377	37	9	24	4	30		6	12	1	1	256	95	149	12	77	693	30	21

TEAM	RUSH	YDS	AVG	PASS	COM	PCT	PI	YDS	AVG	TS	INT	PUNT	YDS	AVG	PR	YDS	AVG	KO	AVG	KOR	YDS	AVG
TOR	295	1770	6.0	474	269	56.8	26	4548	9.6		28	98	4305	43.9	117	634	5.4	64	58.2	48	1030	21.5
OTT	587	3678	6.3	261	124	47.5	23	2243	8.6		30	129	4976	38.6	98	458	4.7	65	52.4	52	1107	21.3
MTL	468	2530	5.4	378	229	60.6	19	3571	9.4		28	102	4196	41.1	84	302	3.6	59	50.4	75	1655	22.1
HAM	373	1959	5.3	391	199	50.9	32	3149	8.1		14	112	4769	42.6	110	598	5.4	51	51.6	61	1330	21.8

1960 WIFU

TEAM	G	W	L	T	PTS	PCT	PF	OPP	TD	TDR	TDP	TDO	C1	C2	FG	FGA	ST	SI	FDT	FDR	FDP	FDX	PEN	YDS	FUM	FL
WPG	16	14	2	0	28	.875	453	239	61	34	20	7	44		6	11	1	23	347	223	110	14	87	587	29	23
EDM	16	10	6	0	20	.625	318	225	41	28	9	4	25		12	23	0	11	392	179	99	14	87	603	32	19
CAL	16	6	8	2	14	.438	374	404	47	24	18	5	40		11	24	2	15	328	176	137	15	97	740	36	29
BC	16	5	9	2	12	.375	296	356	40	22	17	1	32		5	12	2	5	260	173	79	8	117	924	48	34
SAS	16	2	12	2	6	.188	205	422	25	8	16	1	23		6	14	2	10	291	130	142	9	78	631	25	23

TEAM	RUSH	YDS	AVG	PASS	COM	PCT	PI	YDS	AVG	TS	INT	PUNT	YDS	AVG	PR	YDS	AVG	KO	AVG	KOR	YDS	AVG
WPG	657	3972	6.0	269	136	50.6	18	2299	8.5		32	119	5214	43.8	120	589	4.9	75	52.0	48	1140	23.8
EDM	593	2718	4.6	267	133	49.8	16	2301	8.6		25	128	5137	40.1	124	660	5.3	58	51.5	42	778	18.5
CAL	534	3010	5.6	353	189	53.5	18	3153	8.9		23	104	4202	40.4	101	505	5.0	66	54.8	65	1611	24.8
BC	482	3248	6.7	241	103	42.7	26	1775	7.4		15	116	4588	39.6	111	543	4.9	54	57.0	64	1548	24.2
SAS	448	1669	3.7	402	200	49.8	28	3016	7.5		11	140	5705	40.8	118	569	4.8	40	53.3	71	1483	20.9

1961 EASTERN CONFERENCE

TEAM	G	W	L	T	PTS	PCT	PF	OPP	TD	TDR	TDP	TDO	C1	C2	FG	FGA	ST	SI	FDT	FDR	FDP	FDX	PEN	YDS	FUM	FL
HAM	14	10	4	0	20	.714	340	293	44	12	28	4	36		10	25	1	8	286	108	156	22	78	601	27	18
OTT	14	8	6	0	16	.571	359	285	49	27	17	5	44		4	10	0	9	288	190	87	11	90	651	28	21
TOR	14	7	6	1	15	.536	255	258	32	13	16	3	20		9	16	1	14	269	106	1444	19	93	781	30	23
MTL	14	4	9	1	9	.321	213	225	26	17	8	2	20		9	16	0	10	230	142	73	15	79	502	25	17

TEAM	RUSH	YDS	AVG	PASS	COM	PCT	PI	YDS	AVG	TS	INT	PUNT	YDS	AVG	PR	YDS	AVG	KO	AVG	KOR	YDS	AVG
HAM	398	2213	5.6	363	194	53.4	20	3198	8.8		20	119	5318	44.7	116	525	4.5	58	58.9	47	997	21.2
OTT	543	3564	6.6	222	108	48.6	15	2014	9.1		20	116	4870	42.0	115	622	5.4	63	49.2	51	1125	22.1
TOR	359	1997	5.6	402	223	55.5	19	3137	7.8		31	109	5206	47.8	104	555	5.3	44	57.5	47	1163	24.7
MTL	504	2749	5.5	241	115	47.7	24	1785	7.4		15	131	5234	40.0	121	783	6.5	41	52.9	39	776	19.9

1961 WESTERN CONFERENCE

TEAM	G	W	L	T	PTS	PCT	PF	OPP	TD	TDR	TDP	TDO	C1	C2	FG	FGA	ST	SI	FDT	FDR	FDP	FDX	PEN	YDS	FUM	FL
WPG	16	13	3	0	26	.813	360	251	45	24	17	4	33		11	22	1	22	334	197	114	23	86	620	22	18
EDM	16	10	5	1	21	.656	334	257	40	20	19	1	35		14	21	0	17	329	187	133	9	85	486	22	16
CAL	16	7	9	0	14	.438	300	311	38	21	13	4	32		9	19	1	11	295	171	116	8	99	775	32	23
SAS	16	5	10	1	11	.344	211	314	23	12	8	3	20		12	27	0	17	209	117	73	14	74	405	22	16
BC	16	1	13	2	4	.125	215	393	27	12	14	1	22		8	21	0	7	233	120	97	16	115	716	24	18

TEAM	RUSH	YDS	AVG	PASS	COM	PCT	PI	YDS	AVG	TS	INT	PUNT	YDS	AVG	PR	YDS	AVG	KO	AVG	KOR	YDS	AVG
WPG	628	3360	5.4	285	152	53.3	14	2510	8.8		13	123	5235	42.6	116	666	5.7	55	42.8	49	1127	23.0
EDM	565	3264	5.8	312	162	51.9	21	2694	8.6		18	112	5060	45.2	124	671	5.4	55	47.0	50	1199	24.0
CAL	594	3183	5.4	318	154	48.4	14	2454	7.7		20	144	5830	40.5	143	876	6.1	55	53.7	47	1052	22.4
SAS	527	2276	4.3	266	120	45.1	26	1658	6.2		17	142	6361	44.8	132	773	5.9	39	34.3	54	1270	23.5
BC	504	2215	4.4	315	137	43.5	22	2329	7.4		21	135	5647	41.8	123	587	4.8	45	51.4	62	1140	18.4

1962 EASTERN CONFERENCE

TEAM	G	W	L	T	PTS	PCT	PF	OPP	TD	TDR	TDP	TDO	C1	C2	FG	FGA	ST	SI	FDT	FDR	FDP	FDX	PEN	YDS	FUM	FL
HAM	14	9	4	1	19	.679	358	286	46	17	26	3	37		12	27	0	9	254	109	127	18	98	912	17	14
OTT	14	6	7	1	13	.464	339	302	43	20	19	4	36		12	24	0	9	271	155	103	13	77	771	15	9
MTL	14	4	7	3	11	.393	308	309	38	25	11	2	36		11	18	0	11	252	155	78	19	72	660	18	12
TOR	14	4	10	0	8	.286	259	378	32	14	17	1	28		9	19	2	8	242	103	126	13	89	773	27	15

TEAM	RUSH	YDS	AVG	PASS	COM	PCT	PI	YDS	AVG	TS	INT	PUNT	YDS	AVG	PR	YDS	AVG	KO	AVG	KOR	YDS	AVG
HAM	418	2156	5.2	350	178	50.9	20	2995	8.6		27	123	5327	43.3	117	600	5.1			45	1074	23.9
OTT	487	2830	5.8	260	128	49.2	26	2445	9.4		21	107	3870	36.2	103	506	4.9			50	1175	23.5
MTL	454	2949	6.5	263	129	49.0	25	1897	7.2		20	116	4456	38.4	108	538	5.0			50	1025	20.5
TOR	345	1722	5.0	397	214	53.9	24	2830	7.1		14	105	4592	43.7	106	554	5.2			60	1259	21.0

1962 WESTERN CONFERENCE

TEAM	G	W	L	T	PTS	PCT	PF	OPP	TD	TDR	TDP	TDO	C1	C2	FG	FGA	ST	SI	FDT	FDR	FDP	FDX	PEN	YDS	FUM	FL
WPG	16	11	5	0	22	.688	385	291	47	15	23	9	41		12	27	1	24	296	156	132	8	85	499	25	19
CAL	16	9	6	1	19	.594	352	335	46	29	16	1	39		8	13	0	13	331	185	138	8	102	625	18	13
SAS	16	8	7	1	17	.531	268	336	32	15	16	1	27		9	24	0	22	228	114	99	15	69	370	25	18
BC	16	7	9	0	14	.438	346	342	47	18	28	1	31		8	18	0	9	321	154	156	11	81	546	19	10
EDM	16	6	9	1	13	.406	310	346	38	10	24	4	31		11	19	0	18	289	121	158	10	73	633	24	16

TEAM	RUSH	YDS	AVG	PASS	COM	PCT	PI	YDS	AVG	TS	INT	PUNT	YDS	AVG	PR	YDS	AVG	KO	AVG	KOR	YDS	AVG
WPG	548	2899	5.3	301	183	60.8	9	2845	9.5		22	136	5560	40.9	110	633	5.8	60	44.2	55	1357	24.7
CAL	582	3301	5.7	362	194	53.6	18	3083	8.5		19	144	5644	39.2	127	765	6.0	62	46.8	54	1324	24.5
SAS	470	2327	5.0	256	143	55.9	15	2567	10.0		20	150	6641	44.3	118	604	5.1	49	48.7	59	1122	19.0
BC	520	2987	5.7	376	205	54.5	18	3431	9.1		17	122	4755	39.0	121	441	3.6	60	50.8	58	1057	18.2
EDM	454	2069	4.6	389	214	55.0	22	3220	8.3		18	133	5804	43.6	117	607	5.2	54	50.1	63	1279	20.3

1963 EASTERN CONFERENCE

TEAM	G	W	L	T	PTS	PCT	PF	OPP	TD	TDR	TDP	TDO	C1	C2	FG	FGA	ST	SI	FDT	FDR	FDP	FDX	PEN	YDS	FUM	FL
HAM	14	10	4	0	20	.714	312	214	40	20	18	2	28		11	22	1	9	237	91	126	20	93	1021	21	16
OTT	14	9	5	0	18	.643	326	284	42	22	19	1	32		10	21	0	12	267	123	126	18	81	795	18	14
MTL	14	6	8	0	12	.429	277	297	35	23	9	2	29		8	14	1	12	218	127	69	22	100	899	17	9
TOR	14	3	11	0	6	.214	202	310	28	4	19	5	16		3	11	0	9	256	91	143	22	84	690	22	16

TEAM	RUSH	YDS	AVG	PASS	COM	PCT	PI	YDS	AVG	TS	INT	PUNT	YDS	AVG	PR	YDS	AVG	KO	AVG	KOR	YDS	AVG
HAM	438	2043	4.7	313	161	51.4	20	2726	8.7		22	113	4721	41.8	109	737	6.8	58	56.2	35	697	19.9
OTT	422	2369	5.6	272	159	58.5	10	3002	11.0		19	86	3209	37.3	80	382	4.8	55	53.1	48	1280	26.7
MTL	477	2641	5.5	250	102	40.8	20	1376	5.5		14	123	5119	41.6	97	562	5.8	47	56.7	54	1012	18.7
TOR	354	1685	4.8	400	200	50.0	23	2901	7.3		14	116	4748	40.9	109	578	5.3	39	48.2	52	1062	20.4

1963 WESTERN CONFERENCE

TEAM	G	W	L	T	PTS	PCT	PF	OPP	TD	TDR	TDP	TDO	C1	C2	FG	FGA	ST	SI	FDT	FDR	FDP	FDX	PEN	YDS	FUM	FL
BC	16	12	4	0	24	.750	387	232	45	22	20	3	39		22	33	1	10	305	146	140	19	92	679	12	8
CAL	16	10	4	2	22	.688	427	323	53	33	19	1	45		15	25	1	17	378	176	181	21	113	918	24	19
SAS	16	7	7	2	16	.500	223	266	28	8	15	5	15		7	14	0	19	234	110	106	18	86	574	20	12
WPG	16	7	9	0	14	.438	302	325	35	11	18	6	28		15	30	1	17	269	119	135	15	75	620	17	13
EDM	16	2	14	0	4	.125	220	425	25	7	17	1	20		13	20	1	9	262	115	133	14	95	569	27	17

TEAM	RUSH	YDS	AVG	PASS	COM	PCT	PI	YDS	AVG	TS	INT	PUNT	YDS	AVG	PR	YDS	AVG	KO	AVG	KOR	YDS	AVG
BC	489	2877	5.9	356	190	53.4	15	3100	8.7		26	116	4854	41.8	112	449	4.0	62	53.5	43	808	18.8
CAL	564	3113	5.5	418	253	60.5	11	3612	8.6		23	134	5564	41.5	130	720	5.5	67	54.4	55	1106	20.1
SAS	482	1956	4.1	338	162	47.9	27	2362	7.0		34	155	6804	43.9	122	723	5.9	44	43.7	46	1040	22.6
WPG	495	2211	4.5	331	185	55.9	20	2848	8.6		15	132	5505	41.7	132	674	5.1	49	48.8	59	1547	26.2
EDM	433	1850	4.3	431	206	47.8	37	2932	6.8		16	130	4999	38.5	115	656	5.7	42	50.7	57	1424	25.0

1964 EASTERN CONFERENCE

TEAM	G	W	L	T	PTS	PCT	PF	OPP	TD	TDR	TDP	TDO	C1	C2	FG	FGA	ST	SI	FDT	FDR	FDP	FDX	PEN	YDS	FUM	FL
HAM	14	10	3	1	21	.750	329	201	38	15	21	2	34		15	35	2	18	252	131	99	22	88	896	20	14
OTT	14	8	5	1	17	.607	313	228	40	17	20	3	33		11	21	0	7	246	150	86	10	68	725	21	19
MTL	14	6	8	0	12	.429	192	264	26	11	12	3	19		1	14	3	8	184	78	85	21	92	880	18	14
TOR	14	4	10	0	8	.286	243	332	33	9	20	4	26		3	8	1	8	262	108	137	17	95	1014	21	13

TEAM	RUSH	YDS	AVG	PASS	COM	PCT	PI	YDS	AVG	TS	INT	PUNT	YDS	AVG	PR	YDS	AVG	KO	AVG	KOR	YDS	AVG
HAM	483	2429	5.0	252	123	48.8	18	2386	9.5		23	109	4720	43.3	116	685	5.9	48	57.1	43	968	22.5
OTT	475	2679	5.6	241	121	50.2	17	2250	9.3		20	106	4367	41.2	110	559	5.1	54	56.9	42	842	20.0
MTL	341	1607	4.7	289	131	45.3	19	1540	5.3		15	132	5562	42.1	110	693	6.3	42	51.4	42	923	22.0
TOR	365	1846	5.1	378	207	54.8	24	2904	7.7		18	112	4626	41.3	93	448	4.8	48	52.4	55	1209	22.0

1964 WESTERN CONFERENCE

TEAM	G	W	L	T	PTS	PCT	PF	OPP	TD	TDR	TDP	TDO	C1	C2	FG	FGA	ST	SI	FDT	FDR	FDP	FDX	PEN	YDS	FUM	FL
BC	16	11	2	3	25	.781	328	168	40	26	14	0	32		15	25	1	9	327	175	125	27	92	850	25	20
CAL	16	12	4	0	24	.750	352	249	40	21	16	3	31		22	37	0	15	308	165	124	19	86	848	17	12
SAS	16	9	7	0	18	.563	330	282	43	22	19	2	34		8	19	2	10	291	151	121	19	90	808	21	16
EDM	16	4	12	0	8	.250	222	458	27	17	10	0	17		10	29	1	11	221	115	90	16	93	682	19	16
WPG	16	1	14	1	3	.094	270	397	33	15	16	2	27		8	26	3	15	262	124	120	18	101	930	22	17

TEAM	RUSH	YDS	AVG	PASS	COM	PCT	PI	YDS	AVG	TS	INT	PUNT	YDS	AVG	PR	YDS	AVG	KO	AVG	KOR	YDS	AVG
BC	566	2646	4.7	342	202	59.1	15	2941	8.6		26	123	5097	41.4	134	679	5.1	57	53.6	33	734	22.2
CAL	554	3095	5.6	328	197	60.1	19	2621	8.0		19	125	5110	40.9	133	841	6.3	54	55.4	46	1061	23.1
SAS	497	3021	6.1	332	181	54.5	22	2699	8.1		20	111	4501	40.5	130	712	5.5	60	54.4	48	1185	24.7
EDM	469	2090	4.5	305	152	49.8	18	2143	7.0		17	129	4820	37.4	98	487	5.0	43	59.3	74	1727	23.3
WPG	469	2359	5.0	356	183	51.4	23	2691	7.6		17	127	4764	37.5	120	484	4.0	49	49.9	66	1707	25.9

1965 EASTERN CONFERENCE

TEAM	G	W	L	T	PTS	PCT	PF	OPP	TD	TDR	TDP	TDO	C1	C2	FG	FGA	ST	SI	FDT	FDR	FDP	FDX	PEN	YDS	FUM	FL
HAM	14	10	4	0	20	.714	281	153	29	13	8	8	19		19	36	6	19	178	96	67	15	90	883	18	9
OTT	14	7	7	0	14	.500	300	234	36	13	18	5	34		12	21	1	12	242	119	103	20	107	1046	19	17
MTL	14	5	9	0	10	.357	183	215	24	13	8	3	15		3	15	2	11	215	86	97	32	80	741	28	18
TOR	14	3	11	0	6	.214	193	360	23	8	12	3	21		7	16	1	11	222	105	103	14	84	676	29	18

TEAM	RUSH	YDS	AVG	PASS	COM	PCT	PI	YDS	AVG	TS	INT	PUNT	YDS	AVG	PR	YDS	AVG	KO	AVG	KOR	YDS	AVG
HAM	453	2015	4.4	230	92	40.0	20	1545	6.7		30	134	5990	44.7	130	916	7.0	41	57.1	34	737	21.7
OTT	449	2419	5.4	270	135	50.0	15	2414	8.9		26	116	4701	40.5	105	524	5.0	51	53.0	40	798	20.0
MTL	393	1533	3.9	285	148	51.9	30	2253	7.9		18	114	4431	38.9	107	641	6.0	40	55.9	34	615	18.1
TOR	380	1986	5.2	339	150	44.2	23	2230	6.6		18	125	5320	42.6	103	689	6.7	37	48.8	60	1231	20.5

1965 WESTERN CONFERENCE

TEAM	G	W	L	T	PTS	PCT	PF	OPP	TD	TDR	TDP	TDO	C1	C2	FG	FGA	ST	SI	FDT	FDR	FDP	FDX	PEN	YDS	FUM	FL
CAL	16	12	4	0	24	.750	340	243	40	18	19	3	36		15	28	2	15	264	118	122	24	99	798	24	15
WPG	16	11	5	0	22	.688	301	262	40	18	18	4	26		6	18	1	15	279	154	105	20	82	651	23	15
SAS	16	8	7	1	17	.531	276	277	34	17	17	0	28		11	19	1	9	301	151	126	24	82	751	32	20
BC	16	6	9	1	13	.406	286	273	36	20	15	1	32		10	24	1	6	293	134	138	21	86	666	16	12
EDM	16	5	11	0	10	.313	257	400	31	20	10	1	20		12	24	2	11	267	134	119	14	83	659	29	16

TEAM	RUSH	YDS	AVG	PASS	COM	PCT	PI	YDS	AVG	TS	INT	PUNT	YDS	AVG	PR	YDS	AVG	KO	AVG	KOR	YDS	AVG
CAL	477	2537	5.3	326	175	53.7	13	2566	7.9		29	137	5578	40.7	129	744	5.8	58	60.5	38	922	24.3
WPG	555	3005	5.4	278	143	51.4	23	2118	7.6		21	136	5578	41.0	128	734	5.7	54	49.7	52	1345	25.9
SAS	515	2814	5.5	343	171	49.9	29	2722	7.9		12	118	4813	40.8	110	661	6.0	52	48.7	50	1114	22.3
BC	445	2180	4.9	438	227	51.8	19	3070	7.0		30	139	5773	41.5	127	576	4.5	52	55.5	50	1069	21.4
EDM	442	2241	5.1	350	201	57.4	25	2815	8.0		13	117	4977	42.5	105	407	3.9	46	57.1	65	1300	20.0

1966 EASTERN CONFERENCE

TEAM	G	W	L	T	PTS	PCT	PF	OPP	TD	TDR	TDP	TDO	C1	C2	FG	FGA	ST	SI	FDT	FDR	FDP	FDX	PEN	YDS	FUM	FL
OTT	14	11	3	0	22	.786	278	177	34	16	17	1	29		12	27	1	7	267	123	119	25	82	782	17	10
HAM	14	9	5	0	18	.643	264	160	31	11	17	3	25		10	25	1	21	223	103	99	21	113	942	17	13
MTL	14	7	7	0	14	.500	156	215	16	11	3	2	15		12	24	0	9	213	130	69	14	73	654	20	15
TOR	14	5	9	0	10	.357	182	271	22	9	12	1	15		6	16	0	17	240	106	107	27	80	823	20	13

TEAM	RUSH	YDS	AVG	PASS	COM	PCT	PI	YDS	AVG	TS	INT	PUNT	YDS	AVG	PR	YDS	AVG	KO	AVG	KOR	YDS	AVG
OTT	473	2430	5.1	293	147	50.2	16	2473	8.4		34	119	4435	37.3	109	444	4.1	49	56.3	34	806	23.7
HAM	429	2136	5.0	284	128	45.1	24	2214	7.8		23	131	5694	43.5	138	691	5.0	43	59.9	33	869	26.3
MTL	484	2370	4.9	232	120	51.7	21	1506	6.5		24	129	4909	38.1	113	610	5.4	30	59.3	40	820	20.5
TOR	421	1893	4.5	330	161	48.8	18	2476	7.5		26	130	5667	43.6	95	440	4.6	36	51.9	47	990	21.1

1966 WESTERN CONFERENCE

TEAM	G	W	L	T	PTS	PCT	PF	OPP	TD	TDR	TDP	TDO	C1	C2	FG	FGA	ST	SI	FDT	FDR	FDP	FDX	PEN	YDS	FUM	FL
SAS	16	9	6	1	19	.594	351	318	42	10	30	2	37		13	31	6	11	290	126	150	14	79	714	31	20
WPG	16	8	7	1	17	.531	264	230	31	9	19	3	26		11	21	3	13	275	128	130	17	85	794	21	13
EDM	16	6	9	1	13	.406	251	328	31	17	10	4	24		5	15	4	18	238	131	93	14	96	815	27	19
CAL	16	6	9	1	13	.406	227	259	26	5	19	2	19		13	42	0	13	235	72	142	21	114	764	20	11
BC	16	5	11	0	10	.313	254	269	30	19	11	0	24		11	25	2	13	308	145	144	19	88	682	10	8

TEAM	RUSH	YDS	AVG	PASS	COM	PCT	PI	YDS	AVG	TS	INT	PUNT	YDS	AVG	PR	YDS	AVG	KO	AVG	KOR	YDS	AVG
SAS	529	2638	5.0	334	196	58.7	22	3159	9.5		17	121	4670	38.6	118	685	5.8	56	53.6	58	1238	21.3
WPG	468	2658	5.7	349	188	53.9	21	2773	7.9		16	132	5618	42.6	123	662	5.4	47	58.7	37	834	22.5
EDM	495	2457	5.0	296	138	46.6	23	2037	6.9		16	136	5832	42.9	112	603	5.4	45	53.4	56	1363	24.3
CAL	358	1477	4.1	427	211	49.4	34	3155	7.4		20	124	4695	37.9	132	656	5.0	44	60.4	40	850	21.3
BC	506	2454	4.8	373	213	57.1	20	2971	8.0		23	119	4621	38.8	98	501	5.1	45	57.2	48	1095	22.8

1967 EASTERN CONFERENCE

TEAM	G	W	L	T	PTS	PCT	PF	OPP	TD	TDR	TDP	TDO	C1	C2	FG	FGA	ST	SI	FDT	FDR	FDP	FDX	PEN	YDS	FUM	FL
HAM	14	10	4	0	20	.714	250	195	26	12	12	2	20		18	27	0	20	188	75	99	14	97	688	19	17
OTT	14	9	4	1	19	.679	337	207	43	16	26	1	38		9	20	2	10	226	95	118	13	84	628	18	15
TOR	14	5	8	1	11	.393	252	266	28	13	12	3	23		12	31	3	19	207	92	93	22	84	716	14	10
MTL	14	2	12	0	4	.143	166	302	20	7	10	3	14		6	18	0	14	165	67	87	11	73	485	22	16

TEAM	RUSH	YDS	AVG	PASS	COM	PCT	PI	YDS	AVG	TS	INT	PUNT	YDS	AVG	PR	YDS	AVG	KO	AVG	KOR	YDS	AVG
HAM	373	1690	4.5	322	165	51.2	17	2829	8.8		20	134	6039	45.1	131	706	5.4	40	57.0	35	805	23.0
OTT	371	2016	5.4	333	193	58.0	11	3452	10.4		21	120	4644	38.7	104	596	5.7	55	57.1	38	749	19.7
TOR	410	2171	5.3	305	149	48.9	18	2314	7.6		16	152	6862	45.1	119	750	6.3	41	51.2	49	1154	23.6
MTL	321	1377	4.3	304	139	45.7	23	2392	7.9		11	133	5596	42.1	117	705	6.0	37	56.6	47	994	21.1

1967 WESTERN CONFERENCE

TEAM	G	W	L	T	PTS	PCT	PF	OPP	TD	TDR	TDP	TDO	C1	C2	FG	FGA	ST	SI	FDT	FDR	FDP	FDX	PEN	YDS	FUM	FL
CAL	16	12	4	0	24	.750	382	219	49	4	41	4	42		8	33	2	18	255	64	170	21	71	587	18	10
SAS	16	12	4	0	24	.750	346	282	41	23	16	2	33		17	28	3	10	261	125	115	21	79	617	27	22
EDM	16	9	6	1	19	.594	266	246	29	14	10	5	29		17	30	2	8	204	100	88	16	73	516	19	14
WPG	16	4	12	0	8	.250	212	414	28	7	17	4	16		5	16	1	11	213	80	116	17	82	675	29	23
BC	16	3	12	1	7	.219	239	319	27	6	18	3	21		16	35	0	8	200	77	120	12	90	801	20	10

TEAM	RUSH	YDS	AVG	PASS	COM	PCT	PI	YDS	AVG	TS	INT	PUNT	YDS	AVG	PR	YDS	AVG	KO	AVG	KOR	YDS	AVG
CAL	304	1361	4.5	514	306	59.5	26	4536	8.8		31	138	5750	41.7	141	754	5.3	69	61.0	36	726	20.2
SAS	528	2712	5.1	361	177	49.0	26	2961	8.2		22	131	5161	39.4	114	530	4.6	53	53.0	51	1208	23.7
EDM	481	2316	4.8	289	162	56.1	19	2288	7.9		27	147	5981	40.7	129	786	6.1	44	57.1	47	1007	21.4
WPG	348	1821	5.2	396	213	53.8	30	2692	6.8		20	138	5654	41.0	110	669	6.1	44	50.9	68	1576	23.2
BC	351	1498	4.3	415	227	54.7	26	3729	9.0		28	135	5429	40.2	117	603	5.2	44	56.9	54	1079	20.0

1968 EASTERN CONFERENCE

TEAM	G	W	L	T	PTS	PCT	PF	OPP	TD	TDR	TDP	TDO	C1	C2	FG	FGA	ST	SI	FDT	FDR	FDP	FDX	PEN	YDS	FUM	FL
OTT	14	9	3	2	20	.714	416	271	51	21	25	5	44		17	37	1	13	285	138	129	18	67	503	22	16
TOR	14	9	5	0	18	.643	284	266	35	15	19	1	33		7	22	1	18	269	108	145	16	95	920	20	16
HAM	14	6	7	1	13	.464	262	292	28	11	15	2	23		18	33	0	17	210	90	110	10	103	828	13	10
MTL	14	3	9	2	8	.286	234	327	26	5	20	1	23		16	31	0	7	226	67	144	15	66	451	13	11

TEAM	RUSH	YDS	AVG	PASS	COM	PCT	PI	YDS	AVG	TS	INT	PUNT	YDS	AVG	PR	YDS	AVG	KO	AVG	KOR	YDS	AVG
OTT	409	2528	6.2	321	175	54.5	19	3257	10.1		30	114	4781	41.9	112	644	5.8	63	59.5	44	1125	25.6
TOR	379	2257	6.0	383	215	56.1	22	3376	8.8		25	129	5742	44.5	108	818	7.6	50	59.4	41	991	24.2
HAM	379	1865	4.9	331	170	51.4	20	2702	8.2		32	145	6888	47.5	117	723	6.2	42	51.1	48	1142	23.8
MTL	325	1570	4.8	369	193	52.3	34	3015	8.2		12	127	5803	45.7	102	569	5.6	41	55.9	49	894	18.2

1968 WESTERN CONFERENCE

TEAM	G	W	L	T	PTS	PCT	PF	OPP	TD	TDR	TDP	TDO	C1	C2	FG	FGA	ST	SI	FDT	FDR	FDP	FDX	PEN	YDS	FUM	FL
SAS	16	12	3	1	25	.781	345	223	38	24	12	2	36		19	48	2	20	292	137	136	19	78	643	23	15
CAL	16	10	6	0	20	.625	412	249	52	12	34	6	45		12	28	2	15	291	68	213	10	92	833	16	13
EDM	16	8	7	1	17	.531	228	288	24	16	7	1	21		16	31	0	15	227	123	80	24	77	566	16	11
BC	16	4	11	1	9	.281	217	318	16	8	8	9	16		30	59	3	9	267	124	125	18	72	637	22	15
WPG	16	3	13	0	6	.188	210	374	22	13	8	1	19		15	34	1	12	209	89	101	19	60	447	31	23

TEAM	RUSH	YDS	AVG	PASS	COM	PCT	PI	YDS	AVG	TS	INT	PUNT	YDS	AVG	PR	YDS	AVG	KO	AVG	KOR	YDS	AVG
SAS	519	2590	5.0	401	191	47.6	17	3181	7.9		28	162	6688	41.3	141	865	6.1	50	59.0	42	1021	24.3
CAL	355	1309	3.7	524	317	60.5	33	4899	9.3		24	143	5950	41.6	154	882	5.7	71	61.9	37	833	22.5
EDM	460	2178	4.7	301	148	49.2	16	1909	6.3		26	170	6795	40.0	118	898	7.6	40	57.1	43	937	21.8
BC	478	2178	4.6	397	224	56.4	26	2764	7.0		19	139	5526	39.8	138	646	4.7	32	57.4	53	1117	21.1
WPG	371	1580	4.3	384	169	44.0	36	2329	6.1		27	158	6850	43.4	131	956	7.3	36	53.4	60	1444	24.1

1969 EASTERN CONFERENCE

TEAM	G	W	L	T	PTS	PCT	PF	OPP	TD	TDR	TDP	TDO	C1	C2	FG	FGA	ST	SI	FDT	FDR	FDP	FDX	PEN	YDS	FUM	FL
OTT	14	11	3	0	22	.786	399	298	48	9	34	5	43		18	42	0	14	292	118	160	14	74	527	25	15
TOR	14	10	4	0	20	.714	406	280	53	19	28	6	48		9	23	0	13	280	124	138	18	106	749	17	14
HAM	14	8	5	1	17	.607	307	315	36	10	21	5	30		13	31	4	14	256	106	140	10	124	843	17	10
MTL	14	2	10	2	6	.214	304	395	39	19	16	4	32		8	20	1	12	240	95	132	13	71	691	26	19

TEAM	RUSH	YDS	AVG	PASS	COM	PCT	PI	YDS	AVG	TS	INT	PUNT	YDS	AVG	PR	YDS	AVG	KO	AVG	KOR	YDS	AVG
OTT	364	2283	6.3	384	204	53.1	14	3824	10.0		31	124	4982	40.2	114	673	5.9	65	56.7	49	1079	22.0
TOR	410	2376	5.8	352	186	52.8	24	3393	9.6		31	124	5269	42.5	119	813	6.8	66	57.2	46	1134	24.7
HAM	404	1981	4.9	372	202	54.3	26	2963	8.0		19	135	6122	45.3	126	838	6.7	47	48.7	57	1261	22.1
MTL	384	1928	5.0	406	196	48.3	32	3252	8.0		21	136	5543	40.8	112	538	4.8	53	51.7	61	1335	21.9

1969 WESTERN CONFERENCE

TEAM	G	W	L	T	PTS	PCT	PF	OPP	TD	TDR	TDP	TDO	C1	C2	FG	FGA	ST	SI	FDT	FDR	FDP	FDX	PEN	YDS	FUM	FL
SAS	16	13	3	0	26	.813	392	261	45	17	26	2	42		21	42	1	15	280	133	136	11	75	478	19	14
CAL	16	9	7	0	18	.563	327	314	38	16	22	0	30		18	37	1	13	292	108	173	11	80	550	27	21
BC	16	5	11	0	10	.313	235	335	22	8	14	0	17		22	54	2	16	252	119	119	14	62	474	16	12
EDM	16	5	11	0	10	.313	241	246	26	14	11	1	15		17	41	1	17	267	122	130	15	78	527	18	13
WPG	16	3	12	1	7	.219	192	359	20	11	8	1	17		15	34	1	8	268	110	136	22	64	473	32	21

TEAM	RUSH	YDS	AVG	PASS	COM	PCT	PI	YDS	AVG	TS	INT	PUNT	YDS	AVG	PR	YDS	AVG	KO	AVG	KOR	YDS	AVG
SAS	484	2478	5.1	380	197	51.8	31	3335	8.8		35	144	5572	38.7	110	813	7.4	60	52.7	45	1074	23.9
CAL	418	1927	4.6	481	270	56.1	34	3740	7.8		28	142	5225	36.8	138	866	6.3	54	58.6	43	1010	23.5
BC	473	2308	4.9	431	210	48.7	37	2789	6.5		38	161	6495	40.3	123	789	6.4	38	61.6	52	1258	24.2
EDM	472	2138	4.5	400	203	50.8	29	2600	6.5		32	165	6303	38.2	145	958	6.6	42	53.2	42	983	23.4
WPG	415	1955	4.7	411	203	49.4	29	2626	6.4		21	146	5914	40.5	131	911	7.0	35	53.6	58	1329	22.9

1970 EASTERN CONFERENCE

TEAM	G	W	L	T	PTS	PCT	PF	OPP	TD	TDR	TDP	TDO	C1	C2	FG	FGA	ST	SI	FDT	FDR	FDP	FDX	PEN	YDS	FUM	FL
HAM	14	8	5	1	17	.607	292	279	34	16	14	4	29		15	30	1	12	241	101	127	13	90	674	21	17
TOR	14	8	6	0	16	.571	329	290	38	12	24	2	33		15	27	3	17	282	115	151	16	102	841	11	6
MTL	14	7	6	1	15	.536	246	279	31	13	18	0	21		9	21	2	8	288	118	154	16	87	634	25	21
OTT	14	4	10	0	8	.286	255	279	29	8	18	3	25		14	29	2	10	219	86	117	16	64	534	23	18

TEAM	RUSH	YDS	AVG	PASS	COM	PCT	PI	YDS	AVG	TS	INT	PUNT	YDS	AVG	PR	YDS	AVG	KO	AVG	KOR	YDS	AVG
HAM	409	1935	4.7	314	177	56.4	24	2533	8.1		31	129	5655	43.8	108	651	6.0	49	58.3	46	1113	24.2
TOR	391	2114	5.4	404	210	52.0	37	3499	8.7		29	131	5801	44.3	119	641	5.4	50	56.3	51	1104	21.6
MTL	387	2191	5.7	438	221	50.5	37	3105	7.1		28	116	4627	39.9	117	687	5.9	47	54.7	40	945	23.6
OTT	376	1646	4.4	350	175	50.0	28	2800	8.0		34	134	5455	40.7	122	634	5.2	43	57.9	45	1075	23.9

1970 WESTERN CONFERENCE

TEAM	G	W	L	T	PTS	PCT	PF	OPP	TD	TDR	TDP	TDO	C1	C2	FG	FGA	ST	SI	FDT	FDR	FDP	FDX	PEN	YDS	FUM	FL
SAS	16	14	2	0	28	.875	369	206	42	22	17	3	36		24	38	0	9	305	152	139	14	53	384	19	15
EDM	16	9	7	0	18	.563	282	287	29	8	16	5	28		22	42	1	12	230	66	151	13	62	474	21	17
CAL	16	9	7	0	18	.563	293	209	35	10	23	2	31		12	36	1	14	268	100	158	10	64	471	22	17
BC	16	6	10	0	12	.375	295	384	30	14	15	1	30		22	43	2	15	257	119	133	5	64	570	23	15
WPG	16	2	14	0	4	.125	184	332	23	13	10	0	15		5	28	2	12	247	112	117	18	62	470	25	17

TEAM	RUSH	YDS	AVG	PASS	COM	PCT	PI	YDS	AVG	TS	INT	PUNT	YDS	AVG	PR	YDS	AVG	KO	AVG	KOR	YDS	AVG
SAS	534	2671	5.0	374	198	52.9	28	3158	8.4		30	146	5942	40.7	140	1139	8.1	57	53.6	35	836	23.9
EDM	318	1165	3.7	493	247	50.1	40	3316	6.7		30	148	6218	42.0	135	834	6.2	45	60.4	44	1181	26.8
CAL	429	2238	5.2	449	220	49.0	29	3132	7.0		31	175	7099	40.6	168	1104	6.6	51	59.7	35	828	23.7
BC	456	2263	5.0	389	200	51.4	28	3120	8.0		36	147	6560	44.6	121	765	6.3	46	60.2	64	1486	23.2
WPG	469	1915	4.1	383	185	48.3	30	2554	6.7		32	165	6938	42.0	129	959	7.4	39	49.4	54	1272	23.6

1971 EASTERN CONFERENCE

TEAM	G	W	L	T	PTS	PCT	PF	OPP	TD	TDR	TDP	TDO	C1	C2	FG	FGA	ST	SI	FDT	FDR	FDP	FDX	PEN	YDS	FUM	FL
TOR	14	10	4	0	20	.714	289	248	34	9	21	4	28		12	21	4	13	240	89	131	20	115	843	19	15
HAM	14	7	7	0	14	.500	242	246	27	6	11	10	26		11	27	2	17	164	68	79	17	101	840	21	14
OTT	14	6	8	0	12	.429	291	277	33	9	17	7	32		17	26	1	8	220	94	107	19	98	762	34	29
MTL	14	6	8	0	12	.429	226	248	22	6	13	3	17		20	43	2	13	264	98	146	20	124	949	30	22

TEAM	RUSH	YDS	AVG	PASS	COM	PCT	PI	YDS	AVG	TS	INT	PUNT	YDS	AVG	PR	YDS	AVG	KO	AVG	KOR	YDS	AVG
TOR	367	2124	5.8	375	204	54.4	28	3168	8.4		30	134	5872	43.8	129	682	5.3	49	56.3	40	786	19.7
HAM	377	1282	3.4	319	152	47.6	25	1994	6.3		31	162	7700	47.5	116	702	6.1	40	57.6	40	853	21.3
OTT	417	1982	4.8	338	155	45.9	24	2167	6.4		24	145	6170	42.6	133	1072	8.1	45	56.1	43	1029	23.9
MTL	370	1955	5.3	460	212	46.1	34	2885	6.3		21	145	5449	37.6	144	1028	7.1	38	53.7	36	893	24.8

1971 WESTERN CONFERENCE

TEAM	G	W	L	T	PTS	PCT	PF	OPP	TD	TDR	TDP	TDO	C1	C2	FG	FGA	ST	SI	FDT	FDR	FDP	FDX	PEN	YDS	FUM	FL
CAL	16	9	6	1	19	.594	290	218	32	14	16	2	30		11	26	8	19	270	113	143	14	79	542	33	25
SAS	16	9	6	1	19	.594	347	316	40	18	18	4	38		17	37	1	16	292	126	141	25	75	581	21	17
WPG	16	7	8	1	15	.469	366	349	44	13	30	1	40		15	36	1	15	309	93	196	20	85	615	23	14
BC	16	6	9	1	13	.406	282	363	30	14	12	4	25		19	46	0	20	260	135	109	16	87	582	29	20
EDM	16	6	10	0	12	.375	237	305	25	11	12	2	23		16	47	0	16	262	106	136	20	59	354	24	15

TEAM	RUSH	YDS	AVG	PASS	COM	PCT	PI	YDS	AVG	TS	INT	PUNT	YDS	AVG	PR	YDS	AVG	KO	AVG	KOR	YDS	AVG
CAL	436	2237	5.1	449	242	53.9	33	3093	6.9		35	165	6982	42.3	147	923	6.3	49	58.6	35	788	22.5
SAS	457	2437	5.3	437	218	49.9	25	3140	7.2		32	143	5839	40.8	121	1028	8.5	54	55.4	53	1325	25.0
WPG	391	1940	5.0	531	270	50.8	34	4332	8.2		28	144	5589	38.8	128	751	5.9	61	50.7	53	1284	24.2
BC	490	2588	5.3	334	176	52.7	26	2513	7.5		29	144	6159	42.8	122	757	6.2	46	60.0	60	1556	25.9
EDM	410	1887	4.6	447	223	49.9	36	2849	6.4		35	157	6483	41.3	113	599	5.3	39	61.9	44	955	21.7

1972 EASTERN CONFERENCE

TEAM	G	W	L	T	PTS	PCT	PF	OPP	TD	TDR	TDP	TDO	C1	C2	FG	FGA	ST	SI	FDT	FDR	FDP	FDX	PEN	YDS	FUM	FL
HAM	14	11	3	0	22	.786	372	262	46	15	24	7	44		14	38	0	10	250	103	130	17	85	686	26	15
OTT	14	11	3	0	22	.786	298	228	28	8	14	6	28		29	50	1	13	230	85	125	20	99	721	20	17
MTL	14	4	10	0	8	.286	246	353	31	11	17	3	22		9	21	0	11	241	106	122	13	114	894	25	16
TOR	14	3	11	0	6	.214	254	298	27	7	20	0	25		14	33	2	21	241	79	144	18	96	743	19	12

TEAM	RUSH	YDS	AVG	PASS	COM	PCT	PI	YDS	AVG	TS	INT	PUNT	YDS	AVG	PR	YDS	AVG	KO	AVG	KOR	YDS	AVG
HAM	449	2132	4.7	295	169	57.3	12	2952	10.0		39	140	5312	37.9	106	586	5.5	58	52.6	44	1125	25.6
OTT	414	1734	4.2	388	189	48.7	24	2718	7.0		40	149	5838	39.2	126	640	5.1	41	41.1	40	827	20.7
MTL	386	2010	5.2	382	184	48.2	41	2476	6.5		32	132	5089	38.6	95	426	4.5	44	52.7	42	1011	24.1
TOR	339	1600	4.7	424	211	49.8	40	3101	7.3		21	146	6457	44.2	131	643	4.9	40	56.9	48	957	19.9

1972 WESTERN CONFERENCE

TEAM	G	W	L	T	PTS	PCT	PF	OPP	TD	TDR	TDP	TDO	C1	C2	FG	FGA	ST	SI	FDT	FDR	FDP	FDX	PEN	YDS	FUM	FL
WPG	16	10	6	0	20	.625	401	300	49	18	29	2	45		17	33	1	9	326	114	191	21	101	698	23	15
EDM	16	10	6	0	20	.625	380	368	42	12	26	4	38		25	48	1	13	319	108	175	36	89	692	26	12
SAS	16	8	8	0	16	.500	330	283	41	14	25	2	38		10	25	3	10	293	119	147	27	77	489	23	16
CAL	16	6	10	0	12	.375	331	394	39	11	25	3	33		19	29	0	7	316	109	194	13	69	516	24	20
BC	16	5	11	0	10	.313	254	380	27	11	16	0	25		19	33	1	8	298	135	146	17	96	670	29	20

TEAM	RUSH	YDS	AVG	PASS	COM	PCT	PI	YDS	AVG	TS	INT	PUNT	YDS	AVG	PR	YDS	AVG	KO	AVG	KOR	YDS	AVG
WPG	443	2505	5.7	480	265	55.2	29	3929	8.2		35	124	5163	41.6	124	601	4.8	66	56.4	48	1091	22.7
EDM	438	2144	4.9	424	261	61.6	29	3792	8.9		33	127	5084	40.0	100	464	4.6	55	58.3	63	1504	23.9
SAS	436	2028	4.7	434	241	55.5	26	3514	8.1		21	131	5363	40.9	118	806	6.8	59	55.9	36	988	27.4
CAL	400	2090	5.2	503	263	52.3	45	3864	7.7		29	142	5564	39.2	147	830	5.6	63	58.2	52	1175	22.6
BC	465	2301	4.9	432	205	47.5	30	3446	8.0		26	142	5956	41.9	121	697	5.8	40	57.3	66	1688	25.6

1973 EASTERN CONFERENCE

TEAM	G	W	L	T	PTS	PCT	PF	OPP	TD	TDR	TDP	TDO	C1	C2	FG	FGA	ST	SI	FDT	FDR	FDP	FDX	PEN	YDS	FUM	FL
OTT	14	9	5	0	18	.643	275	234	25	7	15	3	25		31	48	1	5	218	83	113	22	104	815	15	14
TOR	14	7	5	2	16	.571	265	231	26	7	16	3	25		19	37	4	19	223	78	125	19	108	846	33	22
MTL	14	7	6	1	15	.536	273	238	30	8	18	4	29		19	29	1	5	238	117	106	15	105	871	35	30
HAM	14	7	7	0	14	.500	304	263	33	12	15	6	32		21	35	1	9	253	118	117	18	79	641	11	9

TEAM	RUSH	YDS	AVG	PASS	COM	PCT	PI	YDS	AVG	TS	INT	PUNT	YDS	AVG	PR	YDS	AVG	KO	AVG	KOR	YDS	AVG
OTT	397	1724	4.3	353	182	51.6	12	2472	7.0		28	139	5568	40.1	118	650	5.5	37	53.2	40	818	20.5
TOR	380	1666	4.4	309	175	56.6	16	2833	9.2		22	139	6293	45.3	120	643	5.4	40	56.3	34	796	23.4
MTL	450	2567	5.7	292	168	57.5	15	2367	8.1		20	116	4531	39.1	121	614	5.1	45	56.1	36	864	24.0
HAM	432	2289	5.3	317	185	58.4	14	2360	7.4		15	126	4929	39.1	113	682	6.0	46	50.6	39	957	24.5

1973 WESTERN CONFERENCE

TEAM	G	W	L	T	PTS	PCT	PF	OPP	TD	TDR	TDP	TDO	C1	C2	FG	FGA	ST	SI	FDT	FDR	FDP	FDX	PEN	YDS	FUM	FL
EDM	16	9	5	2	20	.625	329	284	31	6	24	1	29		32	54	4	10	301	112	172	17	99	686	21	17
SAS	16	10	6	0	20	.625	360	287	41	18	22	1	37		22	35	1	9	320	125	171	24	82	727	24	16
BC	16	5	9	2	12	.375	261	328	27	18	8	1	23		20	46	2	12	303	132	155	16	116	914	19	9
CAL	16	6	10	0	12	.375	214	368	20	5	14	1	18		19	30	3	13	256	66	172	18	97	687	18	12
WPG	16	4	11	1	9	.281	267	315	28	10	15	3	23		18	39	2	18	282	101	159	22	70	449	24	15

TEAM	RUSH	YDS	AVG	PASS	COM	PCT	PI	YDS	AVG	TS	INT	PUNT	YDS	AVG	PR	YDS	AVG	KO	AVG	KOR	YDS	AVG
EDM	475	2417	5.1	433	257	59.4	23	3037	7.0		19	124	5252	42.4	120	644	5.4	48	55.7	43	1207	28.1
SAS	444	2074	4.7	473	264	55.8	27	3778	8.0		29	126	5113	40.6	125	830	6.6	59	54.7	39	883	22.6
BC	472	2333	4.9	418	227	54.3	23	3159	7.6		18	143	5945	41.6	113	620	5.5	42	55.2	50	1152	23.0
CAL	303	1201	4.0	518	276	53.3	33	3508	6.8		21	164	6334	38.6	126	564	4.5	34	64.6	52	1042	20.0
WPG	464	2116	4.6	463	228	49.2	31	3376	7.3		22	150	6611	44.1	138	448	3.2	45	56.9	39	823	21.1

1974 EASTERN CONFERENCE

TEAM	G	W	L	T	PTS	PCT	PF	OPP	TD	TDR	TDP	TDO	C1	C2	FG	FGA	ST	SI	FDT	FDR	FDP	FDX	PEN	YDS	FUM	FL
MTL	16	9	5	2	20	.625	339	271	38	12	23	3	32		24	41	1	5	288	142	134	12	103	871	20	16
OTT	16	7	9	0	14	.438	261	271	21	7	11	3	19		36	56	0	8	250	82	137	31	121	1005	13	10
HAM	16	7	9	0	14	.438	279	313	23	12	10	1	22		35	53	0	14	267	94	164	9	97	733	18	11
TOR	16	6	9	1	13	.406	281	314	24	8	15	1	22		32	54	1	17	230	95	117	18	107	711	20	14

TEAM	RUSH	YDS	AVG	PASS	COM	PCT	PI	YDS	AVG	TS	INT	PUNT	YDS	AVG	PR	YDS	AVG	KO	AVG	KOR	YDS	AVG
MTL	495	2629	5.3	378	200	52.9	28	2902	7.7		23	150	5978	39.9	148	663	4.5	54	53.6	42	1035	24.6
OTT	401	1633	4.1	462	218	47.2	28	3085	6.7		29	157	6301	40.1	151	887	5.9	36	55.8	41	927	22.6
HAM	431	1816	4.2	435	232	53.3	27	3190	7.3		24	170	6656	39.2	143	793	5.5	38	54.8	42	956	22.8
TOR	430	1979	4.6	375	182	48.5	22	2614	7.0		26	164	7714	47.0	139	711	5.1	42	55.0	41	930	22.7

1974 WESTERN CONFERENCE

TEAM	G	W	L	T	PTS	PCT	PF	OPP	TD	TDR	TDP	TDO	C1	C2	FG	FGA	ST	SI	FDT	FDR	FDP	FDX	PEN	YDS	FUM	FL
EDM	16	10	5	1	21	.656	345	247	33	15	17	1	32		34	54	1	11	295	129	145	21	102	755	16	12
SAS	16	9	7	0	18	.563	305	289	37	9	24	4	35		15	27	0	3	321	148	157	16	96	720	24	19
BC	16	8	8	0	16	.500	306	299	33	14	18	1	28		18	42	2	22	298	159	125	14	121	833	19	12
WPG	16	8	8	0	16	.500	258	350	29	8	16	5	20		15	35	2	15	252	120	121	11	90	541	20	14
CAL	16	6	10	0	12	.375	287	307	30	11	14	5	25		24	46	1	8	282	82	173	27	84	494	22	21

TEAM	RUSH	YDS	AVG	PASS	COM	PCT	PI	YDS	AVG	TS	INT	PUNT	YDS	AVG	PR	YDS	AVG	KO	AVG	KOR	YDS	AVG
EDM	521	2256	4.3	403	242	60.0	17	3058	7.6		17	131	5208	39.8	132	766	5.8	49	57.9	38	916	24.1
SAS	469	2329	5.0	462	258	55.8	26	3468	7.5		22	127	5171	40.7	124	668	5.4	57	49.6	45	1025	22.8
BC	536	2880	5.4	383	194	50.7	21	2943	7.7		24	157	6404	40.8	139	678	4.9	48	59.8	50	1164	23.3
WPG	513	2326	4.5	343	176	51.3	17	2460	7.2		17	163	6857	42.1	128	758	5.9	44	52.0	56	1524	27.2
CAL	323	1548	4.8	513	292	56.9	16	4073	7.9		20	141	5572	39.5	121	557	4.6	49	63.9	45	1089	24.2

1975 EASTERN CONFERENCE

TEAM	G	W	L	T	PTS	PCT	PF	OPP	TD	TDR	TDP	TDO	C1	C2	FG	FGA	ST	SI	FDT	FDR	FDP	FDX	PEN	YDS	FUM	FL
OTT	16	10	5	1	21	.656	394	280	44	18	23	3	38	2	27	44	0	7	287	114	160	13	143	1203	15	10
MTL	16	9	7	0	18	.563	353	345	38	11	22	5	25	7	25	38	0	11	273	107	149	17	113	996	19	11
HAM	16	5	10	1	11	.344	284	395	27	6	18	3	17	4	28	43	1	11	246	98	130	18	118	940	29	18
TOR	16	5	10	1	11	.344	261	324	22	10	10	2	20	2	30	56	2	11	251	99	120	32	130	1049	26	15

TEAM	RUSH	YDS	AVG	PASS	COM	PCT	PI	YDS	AVG	TS	INT	PUNT	YDS	AVG	PR	YDS	AVG	KO	AVG	KOR	YDS	AVG
OTT	457	2367	5.2	432	220	50.9	24	3326	7.7		38	139	5533	39.8	123	1169	9.5	86	51.0	60	1339	22.3
MTL	439	1933	4.4	436	223	51.1	24	3280	7.5		16	144	5999	41.7	106	1606	15.2	75	55.1	77	1794	23.3
HAM	452	1968	4.4	421	211	50.1	29	2736	6.5		18	149	6527	43.8	127	1412	11.1	61	57.0	67	1470	21.9
TOR	421	2118	5.0	384	207	53.9	20	2433	6.3		26	152	6513	42.8	109	1057	9.7	59	62.8	68	1547	22.8

1975 WESTERN CONFERENCE

TEAM	G	W	L	T	PTS	PCT	PF	OPP	TD	TDR	TDP	TDO	C1	C2	FG	FGA	ST	SI	FDT	FDR	FDP	FDX	PEN	YDS	FUM	FL
EDM	16	12	4	0	24	.750	432	370	42	10	27	5	36	5	40	69	0	14	321	99	196	26	131	1000	15	12
SAS	16	10	5	1	21	.656	373	309	42	15	23	4	39	2	24	38	1	4	306	111	170	25	126	933	18	16
WPG	16	6	8	2	14	.438	340	383	36	17	17	2	27	3	26	48	0	13	290	138	125	27	111	803	15	9
BC	16	6	10	0	12	.375	276	331	32	11	20	1	29	2	12	34	0	15	271	117	140	14	142	1144	25	11
CAL	16	6	10	0	12	.375	387	363	44	14	25	5	41	2	21	41	0	15	292	141	137	14	111	828	16	12

TEAM	RUSH	YDS	AVG	PASS	COM	PCT	PI	YDS	AVG	TS	INT	PUNT	YDS	AVG	PR	YDS	AVG	KO	AVG	KOR	YDS	AVG
EDM	447	1818	4.1	476	291	61.1	18	4261	9.0		22	128	5206	40.7	114	1278	11.2	86	54.1	68	1443	21.2
SAS	431	1895	4.4	465	247	53.1	31	3627	7.8		18	127	4782	37.7	116	1182	10.2	80	47.7	67	1365	20.4
WPG	521	2539	4.9	373	183	49.1	14	2939	7.9		15	144	6334	44.0	117	901	7.7	71	53.0	71	1507	21.2
BC	427	2021	4.7	408	216	52.9	19	3232	7.9		24	149	6037	40.5	110	1021	9.3	58	50.4	77	1950	25.3
CAL	454	2261	5.0	405	214	52.8	25	2733	6.7		27	134	6038	45.1	95	648	6.8	72	60.7	70	1549	22.1

1976 EASTERN CONFERENCE

TEAM	G	W	L	T	PTS	PCT	PF	OPP	TD	TDR	TDP	TDO	C1	C2	FG	FGA	ST	SI	FDT	FDR	FDP	FDX	PEN	YDS	FUM	FL
OTT	16	9	6	1	19	.594	411	346	49	19	29	1	45	2	19	38	0	11	336	123	191	22	165	1236	30	25
HAM	16	8	8	0	16	.500	269	348	31	11	17	3	29	0	9	25	0	27	246	97	122	27	112	883	27	18
MTL	16	7	8	1	15	.469	305	273	26	5	19	2	23	2	38	50	1	6	296	104	140	25	155	1240	27	21
TOR	16	7	8	1	15	.469	289	354	31	10	20	1	29	0	22	38	0	8	274	117	142	15	144	1087	29	26

TEAM	RUSH	YDS	AVG	PASS	COM	PCT	PI	YDS	AVG	TS	INT	PUNT	YDS	AVG	PR	YDS	AVG	KO	AVG	KOR	YDS	AVG
OTT	424	2332	5.5	451	262	58.1	21	3894	8.6		27	116	4637	40.0	100	996	10.0	83	48.7	73	1692	23.2
HAM	367	1745	4.8	427	211	49.4	17	2538	5.9		26	154	7187	46.7	109	1070	9.8	52	54.8	66	1607	24.3
MTL	455	2061	4.5	445	237	53.3	35	2935	6.6		18	148	6294	42.5	133	1568	11.8	77	53.3	59	1239	21.0
TOR	411	2176	5.3	408	206	50.5	20	2977	7.3		20	154	6713	43.6	102	1030	10.1	63	55.7	75	1583	21.1

1976 WESTERN CONFERENCE

TEAM	G	W	L	T	PTS	PCT	PF	OPP	TD	TDR	TDP	TDO	C1	C2	FG	FGA	ST	SI	FDT	FDR	FDP	FDX	PEN	YDS	FUM	FL
SAS	16	11	5	0	22	.688	427	238	49	14	26	9	48	0	23	35	0	16	331	113	187	31	137	1138	28	19
WPG	16	10	6	0	20	.625	384	316	40	21	18	1	37	1	31	50	0	12	300	131	149	20	143	1140	24	18
EDM	16	9	6	1	19	.594	311	367	30	9	17	4	28	1	28	48	1	15	279	81	168	30	147	1009	18	15
BC	16	5	9	2	12	.375	308	336	30	19	9	2	28	0	28	49	2	12	259	122	117	20	135	1058	17	14
CAL	16	2	12	2	6	.188	316	442	31	11	19	1	26	3	29	46	0	11	275	98	158	19	154	1143	17	11

TEAM	RUSH	YDS	AVG	PASS	COM	PCT	PI	YDS	AVG	TS	INT	PUNT	YDS	AVG	PR	YDS	AVG	KO	AVG	KOR	YDS	AVG
SAS	446	1893	4.2	524	309	59.0	27	4089	7.8		36	138	5751	41.7	125	1193	9.5	82	52.9	43	849	19.7
WPG	498	2457	4.9	431	238	55.2	20	3292	7.6		31	149	6628	44.5	119	888	7.5	79	62.9	67	1494	22.3
EDM	375	1302	3.5	540	299	55.4	28	3543	6.6		15	147	5951	40.5	107	1011	9.4	58	58.2	75	2044	27.3
BC	464	2386	5.1	425	195	45.9	20	2476	5.8		24	163	6758	41.5	114	1301	11.4	70	49.1	71	1711	24.1
CAL	390	1929	4.9	457	249	54.5	23	3215	7.0		14	150	6313	42.1	107	1131	10.6	72	54.5	88	2163	24.6

1977 EASTERN CONFERENCE

TEAM	G	W	L	T	PTS	PCT	PF	OPP	TD	TDR	TDP	TDO	C1	C2	FG	FGA	ST	SI	FDT	FDR	FDP	FDX	PEN	YDS	FUM	FL
MTL	16	11	5	0	22	.688	311	245	28	10	17	1	27	1	35	46	1	7	283	115	130	38	166	1564	27	22
OTT	16	8	8	0	16	.500	368	344	39	16	21	2	36	0	30	45	1	6	323	114	177	32	162	1453	28	20
TOR	16	6	10	0	12	.375	251	266	23	9	10	4	22	1	23	37	2	16	269	145	102	22	198	1529	46	31
HAM	16	5	11	0	10	.313	283	394	26	15	10	1	24	2	27	37	0	18	276	129	122	25	126	1084	28	20

TEAM	RUSH	YDS	AVG	PASS	COM	PCT	PI	YDS	AVG	TS	INT	PUNT	YDS	AVG	PR	YDS	AVG	KO	AVG	KOR	YDS	AVG
MTL	493	2239	4.5	366	205	56.0	13	2630	7.2		32	149	6369	42.7	104	1172	11.3	64	53.6	41	794	19.4
OTT	456	2477	5.4	403	245	60.8	21	3809	9.5		11	124	5057	40.8	103	926	9.0	64	46.0	61	1344	22.0
TOR	515	2552	5.0	340	177	52.1	22	2162	6.4		23	150	6908	46.1	121	1260	10.4	43	54.9	47	926	19.7
HAM	430	2502	5.8	376	202	53.7	19	2472	6.6		14	146	6797	46.6	108	1099	10.2	56	52.7	64	1324	20.7

1977 WESTERN CONFERENCE

TEAM	G	W	L	T	PTS	PCT	PF	OPP	TD	TDR	TDP	TDO	C1	C2	FG	FGA	ST	SI	FDT	FDR	FDP	FDX	PEN	YDS	FUM	FL
EDM	16	10	6	0	20	.625	412	320	35	11	19	5	34	1	50	73	1	14	270	91	160	19	167	1387	28	16
BC	16	10	6	0	20	.625	369	326	34	12	18	4	30	3	40	53	1	7	259	69	144	46	115	989	21	14
WPG	16	10	6	0	20	.625	382	336	41	16	24	1	38	0	25	57	1	21	297	122	158	17	125	1161	37	24
SAS	16	8	8	0	16	.500	330	389	36	16	15	5	31	2	22	36	1	11	285	101	155	29	130	1114	24	20
CAL	16	4	12	0	8	.250	241	327	20	7	12	1	11	5	30	51	1	8	281	111	143	27	148	1241	17	14

TEAM	RUSH	YDS	AVG	PASS	COM	PCT	PI	YDS	AVG	TS	INT	PUNT	YDS	AVG	PR	YDS	AVG	KO	AVG	KOR	YDS	AVG
EDM	435	1784	4.1	486	278	57.2	17	3436	7.1		26	140	6281	44.9	124	1175	9.5	76	58.7	58	1138	19.6
BC	370	1391	3.8	491	273	55.6	19	3333	6.8		17	136	6023	44.3	116	1340	11.6	70	60.4	67	1632	24.4
WPG	464	2178	4.7	498	283	56.8	24	3552	7.1		27	161	7085	44.0	130	1242	9.6	69	54.7	65	1370	21.1
SAS	385	1675	4.4	547	291	53.2	29	3600	6.6		20	158	6642	42.0	126	1223	9.7	60	49.4	68	1458	21.4
CAL	432	2080	4.8	444	233	52.5	19	3014	6.8		12	149	6083	40.8	105	911	8.7	52	55.2	53	1210	22.8

1978 EASTERN CONFERENCE

TEAM	G	W	L	T	PTS	PCT	PF	OPP	TD	TDR	TDP	TDO	C1	C2	FG	FGA	ST	SI	FDT	FDR	FDP	FDX	PEN	YDS	FUM	FL
OTT	16	11	5	0	22	.688	395	261	43	7	30	6	43	0	26	43	0	16	319	93	199	27	142	1301	39	22
MTL	16	8	7	1	17	.531	331	295	33	11	18	4	31	1	30	35	0	10	255	86	146	23	158	1327	25	19
HAM	16	5	10	1	11	.344	225	403	24	4	14	6	15	7	11	26	1	17	239	95	121	23	140	1089	32	23
TOR	16	4	12	0	8	.250	234	389	23	10	12	1	22	0	16	33	4	18	264	109	120	35	185	1455	30	22

TEAM	RUSH	YDS	AVG	PASS	COM	PCT	PI	YDS	AVG	TS	INT	PUNT	YDS	AVG	PR	YDS	AVG	KO	AVG	KOR	YDS	AVG
OTT	421	1866	4.4	456	287	62.9	14	4039	8.9		30	127	5078	40.0	105	800	7.6	73	52.4	49	1044	21.3
MTL	410	1817	4.4	390	205	52.6	23	3112	8.0		21	132	5706	43.2	110	1158	10.5	56	56.3	46	921	20.0
HAM	357	1581	4.4	404	217	53.7	19	2864	7.1		13	144	6273	43.6	93	749	8.1	46	54.8	64	1175	18.4
TOR	407	1806	4.4	447	230	51.5	24	2897	6.5		13	158	6776	42.9	110	884	8.0	43	53.9	70	1562	22.3

1978 WESTERN CONFERENCE

TEAM	G	W	L	T	PTS	PCT	PF	OPP	TD	TDR	TDP	TDO	C1	C2	FG	FGA	ST	SI	FDT	FDR	FDP	FDX	PEN	YDS	FUM	FL
EDM	16	10	4	2	22	.688	452	301	46	13	26	7	45	0	36	49	0	23	291	84	182	25	110	750	18	14
CAL	16	9	4	3	21	.656	381	311	36	16	17	3	36	0	37	53	1	16	287	123	152	12	144	1158	15	11
WPG	16	9	7	0	18	.563	371	351	37	12	24	1	33	0	31	43	0	23	287	104	158	25	136	1248	20	15
BC	16	7	7	2	16	.500	359	308	33	17	16	0	30	0	37	44	1	18	287	103	148	36	159	1381	20	12
SAS	16	4	11	1	9	.281	330	459	32	10	19	3	27	1	32	41	2	10	284	107	156	21	137	1173	18	12

TEAM	RUSH	YDS	AVG	PASS	COM	PCT	PI	YDS	AVG	TS	INT	PUNT	YDS	AVG	PR	YDS	AVG	KO	AVG	KOR	YDS	AVG
EDM	381	1627	4.3	506	291	57.5	18	3826	7.6		28	145	6889	47.5	136	1110	8.2	72	60.3	58	1261	21.7
CAL	460	2159	4.7	407	224	55.0	20	3517	8.6		28	146	6500	44.5	95	843	8.9	66	59.1	52	1136	21.8
WPG	317	1601	5.1	536	317	59.1	19	4052	7.6		23	144	6781	47.1	112	1046	9.3	69	60.1	66	1684	25.5
BC	423	1980	4.7	483	273	56.5	22	3542	7.3		18	135	6298	46.7	129	1175	9.1	68	61.0	62	1559	25.1
SAS	398	1686	4.2	505	261	51.7	31	3595	7.1		16	133	5930	44.6	105	890	8.5	68	52.3	69	1644	23.8

1979 EASTERN CONFERENCE

TEAM	G	W	L	T	PTS	PCT	PF	OPP	TD	TDR	TDP	TDO	C1	C2	FG	FGA	ST	SI	FDT	FDR	FDP	FDX	PEN	YDS	FUM	FL
MTL	16	11	4	1	23	.719	351	284	39	19	14	6	38	0	22	32	1	11	293	146	134	13	160	1366	21	13
OTT	16	8	6	2	18	.563	349	315	41	12	26	3	38	1	17	38	0	12	274	92	162	20	130	1162	29	18
HAM	16	6	10	0	12	.375	280	338	29	10	17	2	25	1	18	36	2	21	288	93	171	24	150	1221	28	19
TOR	16	5	11	0	10	.313	234	352	22	7	13	2	18	1	21	32	1	17	262	95	137	30	152	1280	30	18

TEAM	RUSH	YDS	AVG	PASS	COM	PCT	PI	YDS	AVG	TS	INT	PUNT	YDS	AVG	PR	YDS	AVG	KO	AVG	KOR	YDS	AVG
MTL	505	2752	5.4	344	180	52.3	20	2698	7.8		21	148	5876	39.7	113	1266	11.2	63	58.2	45	926	20.6
OTT	401	1807	4.5	443	249	56.2	20	3361	7.6		30	165	6609	40.1	139	1372	9.9	62	53.5	47	1102	23.4
HAM	394	1851	4.7	466	239	51.3	31	3352	7.2		18	145	6001	41.4	111	794	7.2	47	59.6	60	1237	20.6
TOR	411	1798	4.4	435	259	59.5	22	2907	6.7		31	159	6615	41.6	110	861	7.8	44	57.5	55	1244	22.6

1979 WESTERN CONFERENCE

TEAM	G	W	L	T	PTS	PCT	PF	OPP	TD	TDR	TDP	TDO	C1	C2	FG	FGA	ST	SI	FDT	FDR	FDP	FDX	PEN	YDS	FUM	FL
EDM	16	12	2	2	26	.813	495	219	57	14	38	5	54	1	25	46	1	20	313	100	186	27	110	917	20	17
CAL	16	12	4	0	24	.750	382	278	42	13	24	5	38	2	21	32	0	25	284	108	150	26	154	1249	30	17
BC	16	9	6	1	19	.594	328	333	30	13	14	3	27	0	32	45	2	21	268	106	139	23	165	1313	36	22
WPG	16	4	12	0	8	.250	283	340	22	4	18	0	18	0	39	52	0	16	256	83	146	27	125	1047	12	9
SAS	16	2	14	0	4	.125	194	437	17	6	9	2	14	0	19	35	2	17	264	81	146	37	150	1478	20	13

TEAM	RUSH	YDS	AVG	PASS	COM	PCT	PI	YDS	AVG	TS	INT	PUNT	YDS	AVG	PR	YDS	AVG	KO	AVG	KOR	YDS	AVG
EDM	394	1961	5.0	482	271	56.2	23	4559	9.5		31	140	6607	47.2	140	1183	8.5	75	59.3	44	990	22.5
CAL	418	1759	4.2	434	248	57.1	13	3161	7.3		28	158	6905	43.7	113	1044	9.2	63	59.2	39	808	20.7
BC	420	2021	4.8	427	238	55.7	20	3115	7.3		17	146	6864	47.0	128	1272	9.9	52	59.0	62	1591	25.7
WPG	337	1381	4.1	502	275	54.8	20	3346	6.7		16	145	6600	45.5	103	753	7.3	50	59.5	50	1179	23.6
SAS	336	1441	4.3	493	233	47.3	38	3265	6.6		15	147	6340	43.1	98	888	9.1	43	55.4	61	1278	21.0

1980 EASTERN CONFERENCE

TEAM	G	W	L	T	PTS	PCT	PF	OPP	TD	TDR	TDP	TDO	C1	C2	FG	FGA	ST	SI	FDT	FDR	FDP	FDX	PEN	YDS	FUM	FL
HAM	16	8	7	1	17	.531	332	377	31	11	16	4	28	0	32	46	4	14	285	105	155	25	179	1530	29	18
MTL	16	8	8	0	16	.500	356	375	41	19	19	3	40	0	19	31	0	13	314	123	166	25	131	1253	28	20
OTT	16	7	9	0	14	.438	353	393	37	13	23	1	32	3	26	41	1	13	288	116	141	31	144	1139	29	18
TOR	16	6	10	0	12	.375	334	358	32	11	18	3	31	1	30	42	2	15	296	104	166	26	152	1272	28	22

TEAM	RUSH	YDS	AVG	PASS	COM	PCT	PI	YDS	AVG	TS	INT	PUNT	YDS	AVG	PR	YDS	AVG	KO	AVG	KOR	YDS	AVG
HAM	429	1929	4.5	444	234	52.7	37	3196	7.2	41	23	142	5956	41.9	112	893	8.0	58	57.4	58	1150	19.8
MTL	439	2114	4.8	408	226	55.4	30	3440	8.4	42	21	136	5505	40.5	101	1035	10.2	60	58.8	56	1247	22.3
OTT	413	1983	4.8	399	229	57.4	22	3006	7.5	57	20	139	5936	42.7	100	963	9.6	61	51.8	70	1608	23.0
TOR	354	1598	4.5	503	280	55.7	25	3718	7.4	57	30	134	6039	45.1	98	833	8.5	55	57.0	53	1183	22.3

1980 WESTERN CONFERENCE

TEAM	G	W	L	T	PTS	PCT	PF	OPP	TD	TDR	TDP	TDO	C1	C2	FG	FGA	ST	SI	FDT	FDR	FDP	FDX	PEN	YDS	FUM	FL
EDM	16	13	3	0	26	.813	505	281	56	19	32	5	55	0	28	49	2	26	306	108	181	17	98	771	17	10
WPG	16	10	6	0	20	.625	394	387	41	11	29	1	38	2	31	47	0	13	322	103	200	19	125	977	19	11
CAL	16	9	7	0	18	.563	407	355	43	15	26	2	40	1	27	36	2	22	297	109	171	17	155	1145	21	11
BC	16	8	7	1	17	.531	381	351	38	12	22	4	38	0	31	46	3	16	258	117	125	16	149	1474	25	12
SAS	16	2	14	0	4	.125	284	469	27	7	17	3	24	1	27	47	1	13	281	86	158	37	126	1150	26	17

TEAM	RUSH	YDS	AVG	PASS	COM	PCT	PI	YDS	AVG	TS	INT	PUNT	YDS	AVG	PR	YDS	AVG	KO	AVG	KOR	YDS	AVG
EDM	395	2130	5.4	479	265	55.3	20	4198	8.8	40	33	142	6566	46.2	131	1014	7.7	79	59.3	40	877	21.9
WPG	352	1478	4.2	531	314	59.1	16	4392	8.3	41	31	128	5356	41.8	79	726	9.2	70	56.2	52	1026	19.7
CAL	376	2127	5.7	490	259	52.9	27	3604	7.4	13	26	134	6005	44.8	102	870	8.5	65	60.6	61	1347	22.1
BC	428	2226	5.2	395	221	55.9	20	3016	7.6	33	21	142	6135	43.2	111	1583	14.3	56	61.4	70	1837	26.2
SAS	325	1499	4.6	544	280	51.5	32	3424	6.3	48	24	142	5737	40.4	100	876	8.8	58	53.1	59	1220	20.7

1981 EASTERN DIVISION

TEAM	G	W	L	T	PTS	PCT	PF	OPP	TD	TDR	TDP	TDO	C1	C2	FG	FGA	ST	SI	FDT	FDR	FDP	FDX	PEN	YDS	FUM	FL
HAM	16	11	4	1	23	.719	414	335	43	10	29	4	40	2	29	46	0	25	309	62	232	15	146	1224	20	13
OTT	16	5	11	0	10	.313	306	446	30	8	18	4	28	1	28	38	1	10	286	93	160	33	124	903	23	12
MTL	16	3	13	0	6	.188	267	518	29	10	17	2	22	2	18	31	0	13	291	93	172	26	150	1079	42	26
TOR	16	2	14	0	4	.125	241	506	24	6	15	3	21	2	18	25	1	16	275	98	146	31	120	976	24	16

TEAM	RUSH	YDS	AVG	PASS	COM	PCT	PI	YDS	AVG	TS	INT	PUNT	YDS	AVG	PR	YDS	AVG	KO	AVG	KOR	YDS	AVG
HAM	308	1162	3.8	558	316	56.6	25	4732	8.5	36	26	146	6621	45.3	114	1021	9.0	69	61.2	46	869	18.9
OTT	341	1751	5.1	498	283	56.8	33	3613	7.3	73	23	133	5594	42.1	108	1338	12.4	55	54.0	70	1588	22.7
MTL	300	1317	4.4	576	309	53.6	36	4224	7.3	34	15	148	6186	41.8	116	1140	9.8	45	52.8	70	1438	20.5
TOR	370	1724	4.7	459	229	49.9	23	3134	6.8	73	15	156	7321	46.9	106	1119	10.6	44	54.7	71	1598	22.5

1981 WESTERN DIVISION

TEAM	G	W	L	T	PTS	PCT	PF	OPP	TD	TDR	TDP	TDO	C1	C2	FG	FGA	ST	SI	FDT	FDR	FDP	FDX	PEN	YDS	FUM	FL
EDM	16	14	1	1	29	.906	576	277	65	26	35	4	62	1	33	48	1	21	366	105	242	19	110	995	20	11
WPG	16	11	5	0	22	.688	517	299	55	14	36	5	55	0	39	58	0	15	391	115	245	31	116	1013	16	11
BC	16	10	6	0	20	.625	438	377	48	17	29	2	42	1	27	40	2	21	283	93	170	20	155	1467	25	13
SAS	16	9	7	0	18	.563	431	371	47	11	33	3	41	4	22	41	5	24	321	78	216	27	122	1009	23	16
CAL	16	6	10	0	12	.375	306	367	26	6	19	1	22	0	36	48	2	16	322	103	190	29	162	1373	37	21

TEAM	RUSH	YDS	AVG	PASS	COM	PCT	PI	YDS	AVG	TS	INT	PUNT	YDS	AVG	PR	YDS	AVG	KO	AVG	KOR	YDS	AVG
EDM	347	1802	5.2	538	328	61.0	18	5289	9.8	46	39	131	5998	45.8	132	1083	8.2	89	58.5	37	625	16.9
WPG	361	1685	4.7	618	391	63.3	15	5231	8.5	35	28	115	5118	44.5	102	1067	10.5	86	56.8	49	1213	24.8
BC	346	1782	5.2	479	256	53.4	24	4120	8.6	48	29	154	7071	45.9	112	1227	11.0	66	60.5	62	1385	22.3
SAS	283	1238	4.4	591	321	54.3	27	4888	8.3	29	25	152	6867	45.2	122	893	7.3	64	60.4	63	1321	21.0
CAL	371	1679	4.5	565	319	56.5	28	4202	7.4	41	29	136	5830	42.9	109	937	8.6	50	56.3	57	1243	21.8

1982 EASTERN DIVISION

TEAM	G	W	L	T	PTS	PCT	PF	OPP	TD	TDR	TDP	TDO	C1	C2	FG	FGA	ST	SI	FDT	FDR	FDP	FDX	PEN	YDS	FUM	FL
TOR	16	9	6	1	19	.594	426	426	48	13	34	1	41	4	24	39	2	13	303	74	209	20	144	1214	13	10
HAM	16	8	7	1	17	.531	396	401	41	9	30	2	34	3	30	50	1	18	343	85	233	25	121	782	20	12
OTT	16	5	11	0	10	.313	376	462	40	17	21	2	37	3	28	33	0	9	326	125	174	27	160	1230	28	19
MTL	16	2	14	0	4	.125	267	502	25	4	18	3	16	4	27	38	0	12	275	84	168	23	144	1126	31	21

TEAM	RUSH	YDS	AVG	PASS	COM	PCT	PI	YDS	AVG	TS	INT	PUNT	YDS	AVG	PR	YDS	AVG	KO	AVG	KOR	YDS	AVG
TOR	257	1377	5.4	575	328	57.0	17	5039	8.8	45	25	160	6955	43.5	106	974	9.2	69	55.0	74	1539	20.8
HAM	296	1217	4.1	598	381	63.7	26	5116	8.6	39	24	135	6205	46.0	108	972	9.0	62	57.4	63	1249	19.8
OTT	388	2014	5.2	496	260	52.4	23	4169	8.4	52	22	134	5395	40.3	109	858	7.9	70	55.8	67	1411	21.1
MTL	298	1385	4.6	569	285	50.1	28	3630	6.4	38	22	156	6387	40.9	109	1243	11.4	50	53.2	77	1777	23.1

1982 WESTERN DIVISION

TEAM	G	W	L	T	PTS	PCT	PF	OPP	TD	TDR	TDP	TDO	C1	C2	FG	FGA	ST	SI	FDT	FDR	FDP	FDX	PEN	YDS	FUM	FL
EDM	16	11	5	0	22	.688	544	323	61	16	40	5	59	0	31	48	0	26	390	89	276	25	120	800	18	10
WPG	16	11	5	0	22	.688	444	352	48	19	28	1	46	0	27	52	1	27	332	96	210	26	145	1193	21	10
CAL	16	9	6	1	19	.594	403	440	43	18	18	7	37	5	29	39	0	11	301	107	173	21	141	1116	28	17
BC	16	9	7	0	18	.563	449	390	51	20	28	3	45	3	26	35	1	12	316	115	173	28	139	1089	27	18
SAS	16	6	9	1	13	.406	427	436	42	14	25	3	34	2	38	51	1	21	347	103	229	15	151	1096	26	19

TEAM	RUSH	YDS	AVG	PASS	COM	PCT	PI	YDS	AVG	TS	INT	PUNT	YDS	AVG	PR	YDS	AVG	KO	AVG	KOR	YDS	AVG
EDM	325	1617	5.0	602	356	59.1	19	5384	8.9	64	26	148	6753	45.6	148	1211	8.2	86	62.2	45	996	22.1
WPG	310	1443	4.7	587	336	57.2	17	4560	7.8	34	28	155	6800	43.9	111	1069	9.6	74	58.4	54	1285	23.8
CAL	318	1737	5.5	565	275	48.7	33	3851	6.8	51	21	158	6789	43.0	122	862	7.1	61	61.1	63	1262	20.0
BC	357	2049	5.7	512	293	57.2	21	3971	7.8	46	19	151	6178	40.9	128	1203	9.4	75	53.1	62	1475	23.8
SAS	284	1515	5.3	666	354	53.2	26	4846	7.3	28	23	138	6445	46.7	128	1288	10.1	65	58.6	70	1624	23.2

1983 EASTERN DIVISION

TEAM	G	W	L	T	PTS	PCT	PF	OPP	TD	TDR	TDP	TDO	C1	C2	FG	FGA	ST	SI	FDT	FDR	FDP	FDX	PEN	YDS	FUM	FL
TOR	16	12	4	0	24	.750	452	328	49	14	30	5	42	4	26	39	0	30	345	97	230	18	124	952	25	14
OTT	16	8	8	0	16	.500	384	424	40	15	23	2	34	1	30	45	1	16	328	137	178	13	141	878	27	19
HAM	16	5	10	1	11	.344	389	498	39	8	27	4	35	2	31	42	1	21	286	82	181	23	119	952	27	19
MTL	16	5	10	1	11	.344	367	447	38	16	20	2	36	0	31	46	0	10	305	105	173	27	123	1112	24	18

TEAM	RUSH	YDS	AVG	PASS	COM	PCT	PI	YDS	AVG	TS	INT	PUNT	YDS	AVG	PR	YDS	AVG	KO	AVG	KOR	YDS	AVG
TOR	255	1369	5.4	646	380	58.8	14	5497	8.5	63	25	152	6812	44.8	120	846	7.1	70	62.6	51	1033	20.3
OTT	395	2598	6.6	494	241	48.8	36	4014	8.1	64	23	146	6250	42.8	135	1409	10.4	64	55.0	66	1533	23.2
HAM	318	1498	4.7	569	328	57.6	27	3950	6.9	39	25	161	7617	47.3	118	1053	8.9	64	57.6	66	1423	21.6
MTL	358	1829	5.1	536	282	52.6	30	3760	7.0	44	30	155	6628	42.8	105	1164	11.1	59	57.9	71	1948	27.4

1983 WESTERN DIVISION

TEAM	G	W	L	T	PTS	PCT	PF	OPP	TD	TDR	TDP	TDO	C1	C2	FG	FGA	ST	SI	FDT	FDR	FDP	FDX	PEN	YDS	FUM	FL
BC	16	11	5	0	22	.688	477	326	47	14	24	9	45	1	43	59	1	17	340	109	197	34	111	889	33	16
WPG	16	9	7	0	18	.563	412	402	39	17	21	1	34	1	40	50	1	20	322	105	191	26	128	1072	27	21
EDM	16	8	8	0	16	.500	450	377	48	15	32	1	44	1	27	45	2	31	407	101	292	14	116	995	22	13
CAL	16	8	8	0	16	.500	425	378	45	12	29	4	41	3	27	41	1	25	306	96	202	8	106	975	34	22
SAS	16	5	11	0	10	.313	360	536	38	7	28	3	32	2	23	36	1	25	320	93	205	22	122	1052	17	9

TEAM	RUSH	YDS	AVG	PASS	COM	PCT	PI	YDS	AVG	TS	INT	PUNT	YDS	AVG	PR	YDS	AVG	KO	AVG	KOR	YDS	AVG
BC	292	1464	5.0	612	365	59.6	28	4568	7.5	55	42	133	6578	49.5	120	1205	10.0	69	55.3	57	1419	24.9
WPG	342	1608	4.7	571	285	49.9	21	4668	8.2	49	18	145	6814	47.0	128	1242	9.7	60	58.2	52	1184	22.8
EDM	296	1588	5.4	691	394	57.0	21	5887	8.5	49	19	142	6382	44.9	121	822	6.8	63	62.5	52	1144	22.0
CAL	323	1885	5.8	531	292	55.0	29	4278	8.1	41	30	143	6732	47.1	113	1211	10.7	70	59.7	44	1027	23.3
SAS	306	1383	4.5	619	315	50.9	22	4533	7.3	39	16	166	7708	46.4	113	1049	9.3	61	56.9	67	1567	23.4

1984 EASTERN DIVISION

TEAM	G	W	L	T	PTS	PCT	PF	OPP	TD	TDR	TDP	TDO	C1	C2	FG	FGA	ST	SI	FDT	FDR	FDP	FDX	PEN	YDS	FUM	FL
TOR	16	9	6	1	19	.594	461	361	49	13	35	1	44	2	30	46	2	25	358	88	248	22	152	1108	28	17
MTL	16	6	9	1	13	.406	386	404	39	12	21	6	27	8	33	46	1	8	302	126	154	22	116	920	31	18
HAM	16	6	9	1	13	.406	353	439	34	16	16	2	29	1	34	44	1	14	304	83	196	25	147	1047	25	17
OTT	16	4	12	0	8	.250	354	507	38	8	27	3	37	0	26	32	0	11	270	88	162	20	152	1161	28	17

TEAM	RUSH	YDS	AVG	PASS	COM	PCT	PI	YDS	AVG	TS	INT	PUNT	YDS	AVG	PR	YDS	AVG	KO	AVG	KOR	YDS	AVG
TOR	290	1337	4.6	635	378	59.5	20	5401	8.5	58	30	141	6231	44.2	126	1176	9.3	69	66.7	56	1147	20.5
MTL	466	2226	4.8	496	267	53.8	29	3504	7.1	53	29	129	5644	43.8	119	1116	9.4	67	53.9	66	1521	23.0
HAM	301	1061	3.5	608	345	56.7	24	4342	7.1	60	34	156	7302	46.8	124	1284	10.4	55	61.1	62	1339	21.6
OTT	336	1668	5.0	509	261	51.3	41	3947	7.8	58	19	150	7023	46.8	118	1075	9.1	63	55.9	78	1683	21.6

1984 WESTERN DIVISION

TEAM	G	W	L	T	PTS	PCT	PF	OPP	TD	TDR	TDP	TDO	C1	C2	FG	FGA	ST	SI	FDT	FDR	FDP	FDX	PEN	YDS	FUM	FL
BC	16	12	3	1	25	.781	445	281	46	8	34	4	46	0	35	48	1	16	321	90	212	19	152	1200	38	27
WPG	16	11	4	1	23	.719	523	309	61	19	36	6	61	0	26	44	0	18	349	126	207	16	126	1020	28	19
EDM	16	9	7	0	18	.563	464	443	55	23	26	6	47	2	20	35	1	21	353	150	181	22	148	1225	34	22
SAS	16	6	9	1	13	.406	348	479	35	9	19	7	30	3	28	42	0	18	315	92	202	21	170	1385	39	29
CAL	16	6	10	0	12	.375	314	425	28	4	19	5	25	0	33	45	0	22	273	93	163	17	123	793	29	19

TEAM	RUSH	YDS	AVG	PASS	COM	PCT	PI	YDS	AVG	TS	INT	PUNT	YDS	AVG	PR	YDS	AVG	KO	AVG	KOR	YDS	AVG
BC	284	1252	4.4	630	359	57.0	26	5118	8.1	68	32	125	5803	46.4	139	1491	10.7	70	54.8	52	1226	23.6
WPG	372	1996	5.4	562	340	60.5	30	4895	8.7	75	35	114	5233	45.9	126	1270	10.1	82	54.8	38	771	20.3
EDM	398	2471	6.2	523	275	52.6	27	4200	8.0	59	28	131	5774	44.1	121	1083	9.0	78	58.2	65	1393	21.4
SAS	305	1308	4.3	648	357	55.1	31	4639	7.2	58	33	141	6085	43.2	116	1067	9.2	60	56.9	70	1527	21.8
CAL	287	1535	5.3	582	289	49.7	33	3595	6.2	58	21	154	6839	44.4	138	1133	8.2	53	58.4	55	1110	20.2

1985 EASTERN DIVISION

TEAM	G	W	L	T	PTS	PCT	PF	OPP	TD	TDR	TDP	TDO	C1	C2	FG	FGA	ST	SI	FDT	FDR	FDP	FDX	PEN	YDS	FUM	FL
MTL	16	8	8	0	16	.500	284	332	27	14	11	2	26	1	28	39	0	10	297	129	150	18	103	803	22	15
HAM	16	8	8	0	16	.500	377	315	35	10	20	5	35	0	34	56	2	26	269	113	140	16	129	811	33	21
OTT	16	7	9	0	14	.438	272	402	24	7	13	4	24	0	28	38	0	20	284	105	155	24	134	992	31	22
TOR	16	6	10	0	12	.375	344	397	37	9	22	6	34	1	17	34	1	33	292	92	182	18	115	911	32	25

TEAM	RUSH	YDS	AVG	PASS	COM	PCT	PI	YDS	AVG	TS	INT	PUNT	YDS	AVG	PR	YDS	AVG	KO	AVG	KOR	YDS	AVG
MTL	387	1605	4.1	524	306	58.4	27	3327	6.3	38	18	141	5986	42.5	120	1192	9.9	58	54.2	51	1193	23.4
HAM	381	1832	4.8	544	275	50.6	21	3168	5.8	46	46	151	6729	44.6	114	1036	9.1	59	58.7	60	1259	21.0
OTT	303	1772	5.8	553	292	52.8	33	3657	6.6	70	27	140	6573	47.0	115	1048	9.1	50	56.1	61	1225	20.1
TOR	303	1404	4.6	592	342	57.8	26	4177	7.1	47	26	166	7253	43.7	112	849	7.6	54	58.6	63	1171	18.6

1985 WESTERN DIVISION

TEAM	G	W	L	T	PTS	PCT	PF	OPP	TD	TDR	TDP	TDO	C1	C2	FG	FGA	ST	SI	FDT	FDR	FDP	FDX	PEN	YDS	FUM	FL
BC	16	13	3	0	26	.813	481	297	49	14	33	2	49	0	37	55	1	25	322	115	195	12	153	1173	34	21
WPG	16	12	4	0	24	.750	500	259	48	14	29	5	47	0	43	64	3	30	353	101	235	17	111	861	27	19
EDM	16	10	6	0	20	.625	432	373	49	23	22	4	49	0	25	36	0	14	350	157	181	12	125	885	33	16
SAS	16	5	11	0	10	.313	320	462	33	16	14	3	26	2	24	39	1	18	359	101	231	27	180	1323	35	22
CAL	16	3	13	0	6	.188	256	429	22	4	15	3	21	1	27	42	1	18	262	65	172	25	103	822	36	21

TEAM	RUSH	YDS	AVG	PASS	COM	PCT	PI	YDS	AVG	TS	INT	PUNT	YDS	AVG	PR	YDS	AVG	KO	AVG	KOR	YDS	AVG
BC	368	1747	4.7	560	348	62.1	18	4944	8.8	62	34	140	6287	44.9	137	1408	10.3	76	57.6	57	1137	19.9
WPG	351	1631	4.6	589	354	60.1	27	5203	8.8	39	28	118	5256	44.5	134	1157	8.6	79	52.7	41	689	16.8
EDM	422	2484	5.9	509	293	57.6	25	4097	8.0	52	26	134	6096	45.5	113	965	8.5	69	59.0	60	1160	19.3
SAS	296	1141	3.9	685	406	59.3	32	5238	7.6	54	24	126	5097	40.5	100	708	7.1	54	53.0	60	1355	22.6
CAL	245	1020	4.2	605	317	52.4	35	4224	7.0	75	15	163	6682	41.0	134	972	7.3	48	57.0	49	818	16.7

1986 EASTERN DIVISION

TEAM	G	W	L	T	PTS	PCT	PF	OPP	TD	TDR	TDP	TDO	C1	C2	FG	FGA	ST	SI	FDT	FDR	FDP	FDX	PEN	YDS	FUM	FL
TOR	18	10	8	0	20	.556	417	441	39	14	22	3	38	1	37	48	0	32	308	89	188	31	166	1301	32	19
HAM	18	9	8	1	19	.528	405	366	38	16	18	4	37	0	40	58	0	20	344	122	194	28	149	1230	29	21
MTL	18	4	14	0	8	.222	320	500	25	11	13	1	22	2	42	58	1	16	353	106	221	26	164	1379	32	21
OTT	18	3	14	1	7	.194	346	514	33	8	22	3	28	3	33	42	0	15	313	103	189	21	157	1169	25	19

TEAM	RUSH	YDS	AVG	PASS	COM	PCT	PI	YDS	AVG	TS	INT	PUNT	YDS	AVG	PR	YDS	AVG	KO	AVG	KOR	YDS	AVG
TOR	309	1231	4.0	607	334	55.0	31	4454	7.3	103	29	165	8004	48.5	129	1020	7.9	66	63.1	81	1593	19.7
HAM	400	1789	4.5	645	348	54.0	26	4263	6.6	58	43	174	7187	41.3	139	1221	8.8	77	55.3	74	1615	21.8
MTL	383	1667	4.4	735	367	49.9	42	4608	6.3	75	34	168	6766	40.3	136	963	7.1	61	55.6	85	1741	20.5
OTT	321	1686	5.3	651	335	51.5	42	4393	6.7	69	21	158	7307	46.2	123	1021	8.3	67	55.4	96	1843	19.2

1986 WESTERN DIVISION

TEAM	G	W	L	T	PTS	PCT	PF	OPP	TD	TDR	TDP	TDO	C1	C2	FG	FGA	ST	SI	FDT	FDR	FDP	FDX	PEN	YDS	FUM	FL
EDM	18	13	4	1	27	.750	540	365	58	17	33	8	55	0	34	60	1	33	396	145	214	37	168	1306	36	26
BC	18	12	6	0	24	.667	441	410	41	16	18	7	40	1	44	65	1	19	340	112	204	24	185	1425	30	16
CAL	18	11	7	0	22	.611	484	380	49	10	36	3	47	1	40	57	1	19	332	103	198	31	162	1161	30	19
WPG	18	11	7	0	22	.611	545	387	56	11	39	6	54	1	41	65	2	26	399	126	245	28	182	1390	28	17
SAS	18	6	11	1	13	.361	382	517	37	17	19	1	34	0	37	60	2	11	344	119	194	31	200	1650	24	17

TEAM	RUSH	YDS	AVG	PASS	COM	PCT	PI	YDS	AVG	TS	INT	PUNT	YDS	AVG	PR	YDS	AVG	KO	AVG	KOR	YDS	AVG
EDM	457	2192	4.8	587	333	56.7	18	4747	8.1	79	30	144	6523	45.3	128	1431	11.2	87	60.4	63	1405	22.3
BC	377	1566	4.2	665	362	54.4	27	4796	7.2	75	44	168	6809	40.5	145	1557	10.7	81	55.5	73	1542	21.1
CAL	375	1966	5.2	642	323	50.3	30	4774	7.4	43	28	156	6487	41.6	145	1447	10.0	84	53.9	64	1312	20.5
WPG	373	1641	4.4	699	427	61.1	31	5958	8.5	62	26	136	5771	42.4	139	1233	8.9	90	54.2	68	1540	22.6
SAS	418	2045	4.9	616	333	54.1	33	4523	7.3	54	25	154	6153	40.0	112	671	6.0	77	60.1	76	1322	17.4

1987 EASTERN DIVISION

TEAM	G	W	L	T	PTS	PCT	PF	OPP	TD	TDR	TDP	TDO	C1	C2	FG	FGA	ST	SI	FDT	FDR	FDP	FDX	PEN	YDS	FUM	FL
WPG	18	12	6	0	24	.667	554	409	61	12	38	11	59	0	35	57	2	20	348	99	222	27	211	1577	26	14
TOR	18	11	6	1	23	.639	484	427	46	20	22	4	44	2	47	64	0	19	345	113	208	24	191	1459	28	20
HAM	18	7	11	0	14	.389	470	509	47	12	28	7	43	3	37	58	3	22	370	115	231	24	165	1350	38	29
OTT	18	3	15	0	6	.167	377	598	34	9	23	2	31	2	39	60	2	17	351	102	215	34	164	1304	28	19

TEAM	RUSH	YDS	AVG	PASS	COM	PCT	PI	YDS	AVG	TS	INT	PUNT	YDS	AVG	PR	YDS	AVG	KO	AVG	KOR	YDS	AVG
WPG	385	1787	4.6	630	357	56.7	33	4916	7.8	41	39	165	6904	41.8	126	870	6.9	91	53.3	61	1141	18.7
TOR	367	1735	4.7	647	335	51.8	19	4395	6.8	58	31	148	6313	42.7	119	940	7.9	79	59.0	78	1397	17.9
HAM	409	1876	4.6	703	394	56.0	35	5296	7.5	52	39	153	5779	37.8	140	1028	7.3	76	58.2	93	1496	16.1
OTT	306	1446	4.7	766	402	52.5	39	5032	6.6	79	17	168	7033	41.9	129	1017	7.9	69	52.9	97	1770	18.2

1987 WESTERN DIVISION

TEAM	G	W	L	T	PTS	PCT	PF	OPP	TD	TDR	TDP	TDO	C1	C2	FG	FGA	ST	SI	FDT	FDR	FDP	FDX	PEN	YDS	FUM	FL
BC	18	12	6	0	24	.667	502	370	48	8	25	15	47	0	52	66	0	11	343	108	203	32	187	1393	34	19
EDM	18	11	7	0	22	.611	617	462	70	20	39	11	69	0	35	52	2	19	390	134	228	28	164	1189	37	22
CAL	18	10	8	0	20	.556	453	517	46	21	23	2	42	1	39	55	0	16	358	131	195	32	143	1119	38	22
SAS	18	5	12	1	11	.306	364	529	28	12	13	3	25	1	51	60	3	10	310	105	182	23	143	1221	37	23

TEAM	RUSH	YDS	AVG	PASS	COM	PCT	PI	YDS	AVG	TS	INT	PUNT	YDS	AVG	PR	YDS	AVG	KO	AVG	KOR	YDS	AVG
BC	373	1663	4.5	659	367	55.7	21	4918	7.5	72	38	162	6649	41.0	130	1224	9.4	95	54.0	69	1410	20.4
EDM	373	2055	5.5	650	341	52.5	35	5776	8.9	62	28	135	5327	39.5	124	1339	10.8	105	56.8	89	1711	19.2
CAL	426	2245	5.3	611	297	48.6	38	4548	7.4	73	27	140	5986	42.8	120	1182	9.9	79	50.6	91	1862	20.5
SAS	386	1824	4.7	618	324	52.4	38	4034	6.5	68	39	170	6762	39.8	120	810	6.8	72	52.6	81	1679	20.7

1988 EASTERN DIVISION

TEAM	G	W	L	T	PTS	PCT	PF	OPP	TD	TDR	TDP	TDO	C1	C2	FG	FGA	ST	SI	FDT	FDR	FDP	FDX	PEN	YDS	FUM	FL
TOR	18	14	4	0	28	.778	571	326	58	19	33	6	58	0	48	59	3	15	391	131	232	28	181	1482	30	24
WPG	18	9	9	0	18	.500	407	458	42	10	25	7	39	0	34	47	0	14	292	81	186	25	201	1802	43	25
HAM	18	9	9	0	18	.500	478	465	49	10	29	10	49	0	36	56	3	21	337	81	228	28	151	1225	27	17
OTT	18	2	16	0	4	.111	278	618	25	9	14	2	24	1	26	51	0	24	306	111	161	34	113	791	31	17

TEAM	RUSH	YDS	AVG	PASS	COM	PCT	PI	YDS	AVG	TS	INT	PUNT	YDS	AVG	PR	YDS	AVG	KO	AVG	KOR	YDS	AVG
TOR	442	2061	4.7	642	355	55.3	34	5063	7.9	43	39	142	6246	44.0	141	1300	9.2	87	60.0	65	1298	20.0
WPG	343	1364	4.0	609	293	48.1	24	4334	7.1	67	25	188	8214	43.7	134	900	6.7	74	63.4	76	1513	19.9
HAM	377	1450	3.8	681	362	53.2	31	4969	7.3	33	40	159	6017	37.8	122	1123	9.2	87	59.0	80	1645	20.6
OTT	394	1986	5.0	608	277	45.6	36	3940	6.5	82	22	168	6726	40.0	113	691	6.1	58	57.8	95	1868	19.7

1988 WESTERN DIVISION

TEAM	G	W	L	T	PTS	PCT	PF	OPP	TD	TDR	TDP	TDO	C1	C2	FG	FGA	ST	SI	FDT	FDR	FDP	FDX	PEN	YDS	FUM	FL
EDM	18	11	7	0	22	.611	477	408	49	20	20	9	46	1	39	56	0	18	369	140	202	27	144	1156	40	26
SAS	18	11	7	0	22	.611	525	452	49	17	28	4	45	2	55	66	4	9	371	137	204	30	120	1019	48	31
BC	18	10	8	0	20	.556	489	417	58	23	30	5	52	1	21	41	1	22	388	181	174	33	201	1622	46	27
CAL	18	6	12	0	12	.333	395	476	40	15	23	2	36	2	32	51	2	15	309	89	189	31	160	1335	37	18

TEAM	RUSH	YDS	AVG	PASS	COM	PCT	PI	YDS	AVG	TS	INT	PUNT	YDS	AVG	PR	YDS	AVG	KO	AVG	KOR	YDS	AVG
EDM	465	2310	5.0	603	294	48.8	31	4342	7.2	60	29	154	6718	43.6	145	1206	8.3	81	54.0	70	1262	18.0
SAS	478	2477	5.2	613	322	52.5	27	4672	7.6	66	30	154	6118	39.7	144	1190	8.3	87	53.1	79	1568	19.8
BC	517	2953	5.7	554	297	53.6	28	4214	7.6	52	33	139	5411	38.9	117	1084	9.3	86	52.1	86	1808	21.0
CAL	366	1727	4.7	629	287	45.6	39	4391	7.0	63	32	165	6684	40.5	128	1276	10.0	79	55.2	72	1412	19.6

1989 EASTERN DIVISION

TEAM	G	W	L	T	PTS	PCT	PF	OPP	TD	TDR	TDP	TDO	C1	C2	FG	FGA	ST	SI	FDT	FDR	FDP	FDX	PEN	YDS	FUM	FL
HAM	18	12	6	0	24	.667	519	517	47	14	26	7	47	0	54	74	2	24	363	93	233	37	175	1430	41	26
TOR	18	7	11	0	14	.389	369	428	36	15	15	6	35	0	33	50	0	19	299	114	153	32	189	1471	33	19
WPG	18	7	11	0	14	.389	408	462	41	10	28	3	41	0	31	47	2	24	309	87	198	34	187	1517	29	22
OTT	18	4	14	0	8	.222	426	630	44	8	31	3	36	3	35	50	1	13	336	99	205	32	156	1214	34	29

TEAM	RUSH	YDS	AVG	PASS	COM	PCT	PI	YDS	AVG	TS	INT	PUNT	YDS	AVG	PR	YDS	AVG	KO	AVG	KOR	YDS	AVG
HAM	407	1643	4.0	681	355	52.1	31	5099	7.5	35	33	151	6056	40.1	123	1072	8.7	96	58.6	94	1799	19.1
TOR	409	1991	4.9	601	287	47.8	34	3537	5.9	36	30	170	6928	40.8	118	940	8.0	67	57.5	75	1574	21.0
WPG	337	1476	4.4	687	328	47.7	33	4498	6.5	36	34	175	7425	42.4	110	711	6.5	79	54.6	75	1267	16.9
OTT	381	1649	4.3	635	291	45.8	26	4610	7.3	68	15	156	5908	37.9	106	1172	11.1	87	52.1	97	1719	17.7

1989 WESTERN DIVISION

TEAM	G	W	L	T	PTS	PCT	PF	OPP	TD	TDR	TDP	TDO	C1	C2	FG	FGA	ST	SI	FDT	FDR	FDP	FDX	PEN	YDS	FUM	FL
EDM	18	16	2	0	32	.889	644	302	70	32	37	1	70	0	45	66	0	19	478	210	238	30	196	1697	26	15
CAL	18	10	8	0	20	.556	495	466	47	21	23	3	43	0	48	67	2	22	338	134	184	20	153	1341	41	25
SAS	18	9	9	0	18	.500	547	567	53	12	38	3	49	2	54	68	1	12	402	146	220	36	161	1285	35	27
BC	18	7	11	0	14	.389	521	557	57	18	33	6	52	2	37	51	0	12	393	141	218	34	195	1572	30	18

TEAM	RUSH	YDS	AVG	PASS	COM	PCT	PI	YDS	AVG	TS	INT	PUNT	YDS	AVG	PR	YDS	AVG	KO	AVG	KOR	YDS	AVG
EDM	560	3364	6.0	619	312	50.4	24	4999	8.1	55	37	141	5623	39.9	142	1409	9.9	113	54.1	59	1060	18.0
CAL	462	2433	5.3	579	272	47.0	28	4435	7.7	52	27	145	6155	42.4	133	1147	8.6	91	60.1	84	1866	22.2
SAS	466	2329	5.0	667	345	51.7	30	5190	7.8	55	28	142	5699	40.1	141	1372	9.7	90	52.6	100	2122	21.2
BC	386	2061	5.3	655	361	55.1	23	5094	7.8	53	25	154	6345	41.2	105	896	8.5	100	52.0	118	2529	21.4

1990 EASTERN DIVISION

TEAM	G	W	L	T	PTS	PCT	PF	OPP	TD	TDR	TDP	TDO	C1	C2	FG	FGA	ST	SI	FDT	FDR	FDP	FDX	PEN	YDS	FUM	FL
WPG	18	12	6	0	24	.667	472	398	46	10	32	4	43	1	43	58	1	20	372	119	231	22	189	1457	38	29
TOR	18	10	8	0	20	.556	689	538	81	21	50	10	76	1	38	52	0	11	417	148	241	28	179	1519	41	23
OTT	18	7	11	0	14	.389	540	602	59	19	36	4	55	0	38	53	3	11	411	167	203	41	185	1353	41	22
HAM	18	6	12	0	12	.333	476	628	43	8	31	4	41	1	52	62	2	15	349	79	235	35	176	1373	33	25

TEAM	RUSH	YDS	AVG	PASS	COM	PCT	PI	YDS	AVG	TS	INT	PUNT	YDS	AVG	PR	YDS	AVG	KO	AVG	KOR	YDS	AVG
WPG	424	1936	4.6	707	386	54.6	31	4936	7.0	26	48	160	6724	42.0	106	846	8.0	81	57.1	79	1409	17.8
TOR	367	2173	5.9	678	366	54.0	33	5774	8.5	48	42	123	4917	40.0	99	1197	12.1	124	53.3	91	1804	19.8
OTT	489	2677	5.5	608	310	51.0	31	4393	7.2	42	41	149	5935	39.8	92	702	7.6	106	54.3	112	2295	20.5
HAM	329	1193	3.6	709	379	53.5	45	5251	7.4	41	23	130	5058	38.9	99	675	6.8	91	58.5	108	1975	18.3

1990 WESTERN DIVISION

TEAM	G	W	L	T	PTS	PCT	PF	OPP	TD	TDR	TDP	TDO	C1	C2	FG	FGA	ST	SI	FDT	FDR	FDP	FDX	PEN	YDS	FUM	FL
CAL	18	11	6	1	23	.639	588	566	61	23	29	9	56	3	45	69	1	23	355	108	216	31	174	1480	45	31
EDM	18	10	8	0	20	.556	612	510	70	22	43	5	64	1	36	53	2	14	455	193	231	31	171	1339	45	31
SAS	18	9	9	0	18	.500	557	592	53	19	33	1	47	2	59	72	0	11	454	138	268	48	161	1207	22	17
BC	18	6	11	1	13	.361	520	620	56	17	36	3	48	3	39	61	0	13	432	143	259	30	194	1554	44	26

TEAM	RUSH	YDS	AVG	PASS	COM	PCT	PI	YDS	AVG	TS	INT	PUNT	YDS	AVG	PR	YDS	AVG	KO	AVG	KOR	YDS	AVG
CAL	407	1903	4.7	606	318	52.5	30	4913	8.1	45	30	133	5728	43.1	121	1443	11.9	112	57.8	113	2761	24.4
EDM	494	3226	6.5	663	347	52.3	30	5043	7.6	66	36	134	5765	43.0	114	1120	9.8	121	52.6	92	1642	17.8
SAS	400	1935	4.8	793	450	56.7	43	5793	7.3	40	28	112	4213	37.6	114	1015	8.9	99	52.7	115	2147	18.7
BC	419	2423	5.8	704	386	54.8	32	5446	7.7	38	27	120	4531	37.8	91	746	8.2	103	50.6	109	2209	20.3

1991 EASTERN DIVISION

TEAM	G	W	L	T	PTS	PCT	PF	OPP	TD	TDR	TDP	TDO	C1	C2	FG	FGA	ST	SI	FDT	FDR	FDP	FDX	PEN	YDS	FUM	FL
TOR	18	13	5	0	26	.722	647	526	67	21	37	9	64	1	55	65	1	12	373	134	214	25	188	1428	42	26
WPG	18	9	9	0	18	.500	516	499	55	15	32	8	48	2	37	50	3	17	396	127	233	36	216	1822	35	22
OTT	18	7	11	0	14	.389	522	577	51	23	25	3	45	3	46	60	4	19	396	178	194	24	169	1434	36	20
HAM	18	3	15	0	6	.167	400	599	37	8	23	6	33	2	40	61	1	19	310	101	192	17	192	1501	30	20

TEAM	RUSH	YDS	AVG	PASS	COM	PCT	PI	YDS	AVG	TS	INT	PUNT	YDS	AVG	PR	YDS	AVG	KO	AVG	KOR	YDS	AVG
TOR	366	2141	5.8	605	315	52.1	32	5425	9.0	49	36	123	5314	43.2	90	1095	12.2	114	56.7	97	1618	16.7
WPG	450	2322	5.2	668	325	48.7	40	5389	8.1	34	36	147	5902	40.1	108	746	6.9	98	54.8	82	1447	17.6
OTT	548	3196	5.8	580	296	51.0	33	4481	7.7	41	17	126	5476	43.5	118	994	8.4	94	56.8	99	1862	18.8
HAM	372	1711	4.6	614	305	49.7	31	4159	6.8	48	30	147	6141	41.8	94	1035	11.0	83	58.0	99	1952	19.7

1991 WESTERN DIVISION

TEAM	G	W	L	T	PTS	PCT	PF	OPP	TD	TDR	TDP	TDO	C1	C2	FG	FGA	ST	SI	FDT	FDR	FDP	FDX	PEN	YDS	FUM	FL
EDM	18	12	6	0	24	.667	671	569	77	28	42	7	75	0	40	62	0	14	482	215	232	35	198	1738	46	34
CAL	18	11	7	0	22	.611	596	552	63	19	32	12	57	1	46	64	1	19	390	113	245	32	213	1711	48	27
BC	18	11	7	0	22	.611	661	587	74	34	38	2	67	3	44	59	0	12	508	174	318	16	184	1485	41	28
SAS	18	6	12	0	12	.333	606	710	62	16	41	5	56	1	52	61	5	10	404	116	237	51	201	1549	33	21

TEAM	RUSH	YDS	AVG	PASS	COM	PCT	PI	YDS	AVG	TS	INT	PUNT	YDS	AVG	PR	YDS	AVG	KO	AVG	KOR	YDS	AVG
EDM	526	3335	6.3	631	341	54.0	21	5176	8.2	51	30	122	4639	38.0	103	1461	14.2	117	52.5	106	2028	19.1
CAL	333	1669	5.0	707	385	54.5	18	5453	7.7	73	26	149	6122	41.1	115	1446	12.6	111	57.6	108	2297	21.3
BC	454	2634	5.8	739	470	63.6	25	6714	9.1	30	22	112	4634	41.4	96	776	8.1	126	51.6	126	2591	20.6
SAS	318	1732	5.4	782	414	52.9	23	5577	7.1	35	26	142	5540	39.0	95	1165	12.3	108	51.9	110	2172	19.7

1992 EASTERN DIVISION

TEAM	G	W	L	T	PTS	PCT	PF	OPP	TD	TDR	TDP	TDO	C1	C2	FG	FGA	ST	SI	FDT	FDR	FDP	FDX	PEN	YDS	FUM	FL
WPG	18	11	7	0	22	.611	507	499	50	16	29	5	47	0	47	62	1	17	348	125	189	34	212	1884	50	32
HAM	18	11	7	0	22	.611	536	514	55	18	27	10	52	1	41	64	4	21	340	106	198	36	211	1613	48	27
OTT	18	9	9	0	18	.500	484	439	49	11	33	5	48	1	40	57	2	16	376	117	214	45	208	1709	38	23
TOR	18	6	12	0	12	.333	469	523	50	17	24	9	41	4	35	49	1	13	347	115	200	32	192	1602	39	25

TEAM	RUSH	YDS	AVG	PASS	COM	PCT	PI	YDS	AVG	TS	INT	PUNT	YDS	AVG	PR	YDS	AVG	KO	AVG	KOR	YDS	AVG
WPG	407	2243	5.5	627	301	48.0	23	4580	7.3	43	31	161	6780	42.1	114	755	6.6	89	58.2	71	1131	15.9
HAM	365	1857	5.1	647	323	49.9	22	4909	7.6	54	26	150	6080	40.5	105	1082	10.3	91	55.4	79	1333	16.9
OTT	431	2145	5.0	610	330	54.1	28	4726	7.7	65	35	155	6547	42.2	126	1113	8.8	82	55.1	78	1405	18.0
TOR	355	1662	4.7	669	301	45.0	36	4756	7.1	38	28	150	6575	43.8	112	912	8.1	83	56.0	93	1947	20.9

1992 WESTERN DIVISION

TEAM	G	W	L	T	PTS	PCT	PF	OPP	TD	TDR	TDP	TDO	C1	C2	FG	FGA	ST	SI	FDT	FDR	FDP	FDX	PEN	YDS	FUM	FL
CAL	18	13	5	0	26	.722	607	430	64	27	34	3	63	0	44	64	4	20	436	125	285	26	209	1673	36	21
EDM	18	10	8	0	20	.556	552	515	63	17	41	5	60	2	30	49	2	16	417	155	221	41	209	1881	27	19
SAS	18	9	9	0	18	.500	505	545	55	16	36	3	50	3	36	47	1	9	431	110	278	43	230	1974	27	19
BC	18	3	15	0	6	.167	472	667	50	22	22	6	46	2	34	49	4	12	413	130	244	39	216	1853	48	32

TEAM	RUSH	YDS	AVG	PASS	COM	PCT	PI	YDS	AVG	TS	INT	PUNT	YDS	AVG	PR	YDS	AVG	KO	AVG	KOR	YDS	AVG
CAL	352	1970	5.6	728	422	58.0	30	6263	8.6	34	20	111	4347	39.2	104	779	7.5	102	56.4	82	1759	21.5
EDM	437	2517	5.8	598	304	50.8	22	4975	8.3	52	29	131	5286	40.4	111	1247	11.2	102	56.2	87	1534	17.6
SAS	319	1192	3.7	792	465	58.7	32	6346	8.0	33	29	145	5666	39.1	102	754	7.4	97	51.1	85	1528	18.0
BC	406	1956	4.8	743	373	50.2	26	5076	6.8	47	21	142	5573	39.2	96	882	9.2	85	49.2	127	2259	17.8

1993 EASTERN DIVISION

TEAM	G	W	L	T	PTS	PCT	PF	OPP	TD	TDR	TDP	TDO	C1	C2	FG	FGA	ST	SI	FDT	FDR	FDP	FDX	PEN	YDS	FUM	FL
WPG	18	14	4	0	28	.778	646	421	71	20	43	8	68	1	45	56	2	11	417	151	229	37	198	1530	37	22
HAM	18	6	12	0	12	.333	316	567	29	9	12	8	28	0	31	48	3	15	305	103	169	33	165	1257	35	18
OTT	18	4	14	0	8	.222	387	517	41	6	32	3	38	0	29	44	1	14	363	97	228	38	214	1770	37	20
TOR	18	3	15	0	6	.16	390	593	41	15	24	2	35	2	30	44	1	13	358	97	232	29	198	1561	33	24

TEAM	RUSH	YDS	AVG	PASS	COM	PCT	PI	YDS	AVG	TS	INT	PUNT	YDS	AVG	PR	YDS	AVG	KO	AVG	KOR	YDS	AVG
WPG	395	2118	5.4	708	396	55.9	21	5666	8.0	20	37	141	5916	42.0	135	769	5.7	105	57.0	65	1223	18.8
HAM	363	1751	4.8	620	281	45.3	37	3857	6.2	59	16	166	6745	40.6	102	1000	9.8	57	54.3	85	1409	16.6
OTT	340	1436	4.2	671	362	53.9	32	5596	8.3	77	27	165	6680	40.5	109	717	6.6	72	54.8	80	1110	13.9
TOR	285	1706	6.0	648	340	52.5	24	4914	7.6	93	14	143	5717	40.0	106	963	9.1	71	57.3	97	1702	17.5

1993 WESTERN DIVISION

TEAM	G	W	L	T	PTS	PCT	PF	OPP	TD	TDR	TDP	TDO	C1	C2	FG	FGA	ST	SI	FDT	FDR	FDP	FDX	PEN	YDS	FUM	FL
CAL	18	15	3	0	30	.833	646	418	70	16	49	5	63	3	47	62	1	14	421	103	289	29	188	1646	28	18
EDM	18	12	6	0	24	.667	507	372	55	15	31	9	54	0	34	48	2	17	326	120	172	34	202	1592	28	20
SAS	18	11	7	0	22	.611	511	495	51	15	32	4	51	0	48	53	1	8	402	108	257	37	230	1780	31	22
BC	18	10	8	0	20	.556	574	583	64	25	34	5	63	0	38	51	2	9	404	89	274	41	223	1740	34	22
SAC	18	6	12	0	12	.333	498	509	56	15	37	4	56	0	28	45	0	22	407	98	269	40	193	1497	33	20

TEAM	RUSH	YDS	AVG	PASS	COM	PCT	PI	YDS	AVG	TS	INT	PUNT	YDS	AVG	PR	YDS	AVG	KO	AVG	KOR	YDS	AVG
CAL	296	1421	4.8	759	444	58.5	18	6494	8.6	29	27	121	4939	40.8	114	1128	9.9	109	58.5	73	1377	18.9
EDM	366	2006	5.5	552	284	51.4	17	4376	7.9	44	34	154	6385	41.5	105	1315	12.5	82	59.9	64	1209	18.9
SAS	278	1200	4.3	773	441	57.1	27	6164	8.0	22	19	140	5724	40.9	101	669	6.6	88	51.8	68	1138	16.7
BC	268	1360	5.1	740	409	55.3	26	5764	7.8	27	24	124	4947	39.9	88	585	6.6	90	44.7	109	2331	21.4
SAC	258	1479	5.7	737	425	57.7	24	6319	8.6	73	28	138	5449	39.5	95	778	8.2	78	56.9	89	1720	19.3

1994 EASTERN DIVISION

TEAM	G	W	L	T	PTS	PCT	PF	OPP	TD	TDR	TDP	TDO	C1	C2	FG	FGA	ST	SI	FDT	FDR	FDP	FDX	PEN	YDS	FUM	FL
WPG	18	13	5	0	26	.722	651	572	72	18	47	7	72	0	42	58	1	19	436	133	261	42	184	1699	33	19
BAL	18	12	6	0	24	.667	561	431	56	18	33	5	55	0	49	63	3	17	410	154	234	22	166	1427	47	20
TOR	18	7	11	0	14	.389	504	578	54	17	32	5	51	0	37	57	0	18	356	105	221	30	186	1590	31	15
OTT	18	4	14	0	8	.222	480	647	46	20	24	2	41	2	46	64	6	9	395	137	221	37	231	1893	38	22
HAM	18	4	14	0	8	.222	435	562	41	13	21	7	40	0	43	56	4	12	311	99	177	35	167	1399	33	19
SHR	18	3	15	0	6	.167	330	662	33	15	16	2	29	0	28	38	3	13	281	95	157	29	154	1237	45	25

TEAM	RUSH	YDS	AVG	PASS	COM	PCT	PI	YDS	AVG	TS	INT	PUNT	YDS	AVG	PR	YDS	AVG	KO	AVG	KOR	YDS	AVG
WPG	373	2019	5.4	671	394	58.7	32	5853	8.7	31	32	129	5377	41.7	104	621	6.0	101	58.3	78	1535	19.7
BAL	435	2823	6.5	603	316	52.4	22	5100	8.5	22	24	117	5024	42.9	118	1179	10.0	91	57.2	70	1383	19.8
TOR	359	1834	5.1	629	335	53.3	32	5012	8.0	40	23	134	4928	36.8	98	902	9.2	90	56.9	97	1780	18.4
OTT	457	2300	5.0	623	328	52.6	18	4559	7.3	36	16	129	5373	41.7	97	589	6.1	73	56.7	102	1739	17.0
HAM	365	1645	4.5	645	343	53.2	25	4393	6.8	41	32	167	6716	40.2	111	722	6.5	68	56.5	84	1611	19.2
SHR	332	1602	4.8	587	258	44.0	37	3559	6.1	45	21	149	6331	42.5	106	884	8.3	63	57.7	92	1814	19.7

1994 WESTERN DIVISION

TEAM	G	W	L	T	PTS	PCT	PF	OPP	TD	TDR	TDP	TDO	C1	C2	FG	FGA	ST	SI	FDT	FDR	FDP	FDX	PEN	YDS	FUM	FL
CAL	18	15	3	0	30	.833	698	355	82	24	52	6	80	0	37	44	1	13	461	145	282	34	152	1378	31	22
EDM	18	13	5	0	26	.722	518	401	51	15	27	9	48	0	48	61	3	17	366	123	219	24	143	1253	35	19
BC	18	11	6	1	23	.639	604	456	68	29	33	6	65	1	39	52	0	12	426	148	244	34	239	2121	31	17
SAS	18	11	7	0	22	.611	512	454	53	18	30	5	51	0	41	53	3	14	368	115	215	38	219	1626	31	17
SAC	18	9	8	1	19	.528	436	436	42	13	27	2	40	0	39	55	2	23	380	116	233	31	170	1331	32	27
LV	18	5	13	0	10	.278	447	622	46	15	25	6	37	4	38	46	2	8	294	94	166	34	184	1430	40	17

TEAM	RUSH	YDS	AVG	PASS	COM	PCT	PI	YDS	AVG	TS	INT	PUNT	YDS	AVG	PR	YDS	AVG	KO	AVG	KOR	YDS	AVG
CAL	350	2059	5.9	703	430	61.2	20	6204	8.8	20	30	107	4550	42.5	107	1161	10.9	108	60.2	67	1419	21.2
EDM	361	1727	4.8	670	347	51.8	25	4836	7.2	31	29	139	5628	40.5	121	1307	10.8	79	58.7	66	1425	21.6
BC	370	2220	6.0	714	399	55.9	31	5789	8.1	31	32	126	4847	38.5	114	842	7.4	97	53.3	81	1413	17.4
SAS	361	1678	4.6	632	353	55.9	21	4755	7.5	35	30	132	5570	42.2	87	621	7.1	86	55.3	72	1205	16.7
SAC	341	1973	5.8	671	358	53.4	24	5206	7.8	55	25	136	5793	42.6	105	961	9.2	75	56.5	65	1244	19.1
LV	357	1639	4.6	546	263	48.2	26	4252	7.8	49	19	142	5893	41.5	93	731	7.9	72	57.1	97	2133	22.0

1995 NORTH DIVISION

TEAM	G	W	L	T	PTS	PCT	PF	OPP	TD	TDR	TDP	TDO	C1	C2	FG	FGA	ST	SI	FDT	FDR	FDP	FDX	PEN	YDS	FUM	FL
CAL	18	15	3	0	30	.833	631	404	67	18	43	6	63	1	50	60	0	14	475	114	319	42	209	1761	27	18
EDM	18	13	5	0	26	.722	599	359	63	21	36	6	61	1	44	63	3	20	388	126	229	33	192	1649	30	14
BC	18	10	8	0	20	.556	535	470	55	31	20	4	50	2	45	62	2	12	373	124	223	26	238	2008	44	32
HAM	18	8	10	0	16	.444	427	509	45	9	34	2	37	4	31	49	0	19	353	83	238	32	153	1283	42	27
WPG	18	7	11	0	14	.389	404	653	40	19	18	3	34	0	36	49	5	12	323	107	190	26	193	1836	46	29
SAS	18	6	12	0	12	.333	422	451	35	11	21	3	32	3	51	66	5	11	365	117	216	32	216	1788	30	23
TOR	18	4	14	0	8	.222	376	519	41	14	21	6	39	0	23	37	5	12	334	109	198	27	191	1636	28	16
OTT	18	3	15	0	6	.167	348	685	34	8	19	7	28	1	31	42	5	11	308	85	198	25	196	1728	40	29

TEAM	RUSH	YDS	AVG	PASS	COM	PCT	PI	YDS	AVG	TS	INT	PUNT	YDS	AVG	PR	YDS	AVG	KO	AVG	KOR	YDS	AVG
CAL	341	1766	5.2	724	469	64.8	12	6398	8.8	33	21	108	4531	42.0	118	1189	10.1	105	58.3	64	1276	19.9
EDM	374	1794	4.8	701	408	58.2	24	5479	7.8	45	35	148	6162	41.6	110	1114	10.1	95	59.1	84	1686	20.1
BC	410	2103	5.1	650	332	51.1	27	5058	7.8	18	29	133	5129	38.6	112	898	8.0	90	55.8	86	1782	20.7
HAM	266	1300	4.9	771	434	56.3	39	5608	7.3	42	31	145	6168	42.5	109	951	8.7	73	55.9	80	1462	18.3
WPG	344	1689	4.9	632	328	51.9	28	4177	6.6	64	20	166	7070	42.6	101	765	7.6	75	55.1	86	1728	20.1
SAS	366	1684	4.6	703	391	55.6	23	4638	6.6	39	25	148	6127	41.4	116	1133	9.8	71	53.9	74	1406	19.0
TOR	314	1307	4.2	646	363	56.2	32	4405	6.8	53	21	146	5906	40.5	90	1085	12.1	75	56.8	98	2032	20.7
OTT	293	1292	4.4	664	348	52.4	32	4552	6.9	55	21	153	6311	41.2	104	921	8.9	66	53.5	105	1977	18.8

1995 SOUTH DIVISION

TEAM	G	W	L	T	PTS	PCT	PF	OPP	TD	TDR	TDP	TDO	C1	C2	FG	FGA	ST	SI	FDT	FDR	FDP	FDX	PEN	YDS	FUM	FL
BAL	18	15	3	0	30	.833	541	369	50	19	24	7	50	0	57	72	4	12	361	162	175	24	186	1597	26	17
SA	18	12	6	0	24	.667	630	457	65	21	34	10	62	0	56	65	2	6	363	113	216	34	151	1410	35	18
BIR	18	10	8	0	20	.556	548	518	59	12	41	6	55	2	40	55	2	11	358	77	239	42	168	1604	25	13
MEM	18	9	9	0	18	.500	346	364	26	9	14	3	24	1	45	67	2	25	317	101	190	26	156	1321	42	30
SHR	18	5	13	0	10	.278	465	514	45	22	17	6	43	0	46	53	3	8	305	100	178	27	155	1369	31	26

TEAM	RUSH	YDS	AVG	PASS	COM	PCT	PI	YDS	AVG	TS	INT	PUNT	YDS	AVG	PR	YDS	AVG	KO	AVG	KOR	YDS	AVG
BAL	477	2754	5.8	470	271	57.7	18	3848	8.2	51	20	118	5629	47.7	105	1291	12.3	92	57.0	78	1512	19.4
SA	428	2052	4.8	559	335	59.9	17	5284	9.5	39	26	107	4459	41.7	112	873	7.8	103	55.9	78	1672	21.4
BIR	169	1141	6.8	814	454	55.8	25	6085	7.5	39	21	143	6247	43.7	111	929	8.4	96	56.9	76	1436	18.9
MEM	381	1855	4.9	566	305	53.9	21	4505	8.0	40	27	137	5812	42.4	128	1178	9.2	74	57.8	65	1439	22.1
SHR	370	1823	4.9	536	307	57.3	15	4192	7.8	48	18	129	5645	43.8	91	743	8.2	76	57.5	84	1589	18.9

1996 EAST DIVISION

TEAM	G	W	L	T	PTS	PCT	PF	OPP	TD	TDR	TDP	TDO	C1	C2	FG	FGA	ST	SI	FDT	FDR	FDP	FDX	PEN	YDS	FUM	FL
TOR	18	15	3	0	30	.833	556	359	59	26	29	4	59	0	40	56	2	19	439	149	262	28	166	1369	21	10
MTL	18	12	6	0	24	.667	534	469	58	19	32	7	55	2	37	46	2	12	348	148	174	26	214	1809	20	13
HAM	18	8	10	0	16	.444	426	576	40	6	33	1	37	2	43	57	2	12	359	75	254	30	188	1388	32	21
OTT	18	3	15	0	6	.167	353	524	40	9	26	5	35	1	18	31	2	18	330	90	212	28	193	1512	19	10

TEAM	RUSH	YDS	AVG	PASS	COM	PCT	PI	YDS	AVG	TS	INT	PUNT	YDS	AVG	PR	YDS	AVG	KO	AVG	KOR	YDS	AVG
TOR	333	2075	6.2	691	440	63.7	20	5764	8.3	18	22	103	4459	43.3	96	1121	11.7	85	58.0	79	1635	20.7
MTL	460	2719	5.9	502	283	56.4	14	4008	8.0	34	31	134	5847	43.6	104	984	9.5	99	60.8	100	2018	20.2
HAM	226	1261	5.6	711	391	55.0	34	5743	8.1	58	24	124	5446	43.9	90	765	8.5	77	59.0	80	1395	17.4
OTT	301	1464	4.9	657	362	55.1	30	4954	7.5	60	20	154	6484	42.1	99	839	8.5	69	56.2	86	1624	18.9

1996 WEST DIVISION

TEAM	G	W	L	T	PTS	PCT	PF	OPP	TD	TDR	TDP	TDO	C1	C2	FG	FGA	ST	SI	FDT	FDR	FDP	FDX	PEN	YDS	FUM	FL
CAL	18	13	5	0	26	.722	608	365	61	19	36	6	58	2	55	68	3	9	388	125	230	33	155	1229	25	15
EDM	18	11	7	0	22	.611	459	354	44	17	22	5	43	0	44	56	3	14	342	87	220	35	180	1502	23	10
WPG	18	9	9	0	18	.500	421	496	40	12	19	9	36	2	37	51	7	16	332	94	205	33	214	1977	30	21
BC	18	5	13	0	10	.278	410	486	41	13	23	5	40	1	36	53	3	8	366	150	185	31	222	1850	24	12
SAS	18	5	13	0	10	.278	360	498	33	16	11	6	32	0	38	53	2	12	302	119	159	24	184	1492	35	22

TEAM	RUSH	YDS	AVG	PASS	COM	PCT	PI	YDS	AVG	TS	INT	PUNT	YDS	AVG	PR	YDS	AVG	KO	AVG	KOR	YDS	AVG
CAL	359	1796	5.0	657	386	58.8	18	5288	8.0	27	32	120	5221	43.5	112	1267	11.3	95	60.0	66	1433	21.7
EDM	347	1467	4.2	665	340	51.1	30	4847	7.3	26	23	157	6594	42.0	144	1449	10.1	68	58.8	65	1329	20.4
WPG	324	1478	4.6	657	352	53.6	28	4571	7.0	55	23	163	6919	42.4	120	1138	9.5	70	62.5	70	1348	19.3
BC	412	2528	6.1	568	315	55.5	15	4296	7.6	50	16	133	5574	41.9	113	659	5.8	79	53.6	78	1600	20.5
SAS	401	1889	4.7	550	303	55.1	24	4005	7.3	63	22	155	6441	41.6	106	1163	11.0	71	56.0	69	1234	17.9

1997 EAST DIVISION

TEAM	G	W	L	T	PTS	PCT	PF	OPP	TD	TDR	TDP	TDO	C1	C2	FG	FGA	ST	SI	FDT	FDR	FDP	FDX	PEN	YDS	FUM	FL
TOR	18	15	3	0	30	.833	660	327	78	22	49	7	77	1	33	43	0	14	433	147	260	26	160	1183	17	15
MTL	18	13	5	0	26	.722	509	532	55	20	26	9	50	1	34	52	4	17	383	150	197	36	211	1597	31	22
WPG	18	4	14	0	8	.222	443	548	44	17	24	3	40	1	39	54	6	9	305	110	171	24	185	1519	21	12
HAM	18	2	16	0	4	.111	362	549	39	12	24	3	31	2	24	42	3	15	310	89	194	27	187	1493	39	24

TEAM	RUSH	YDS	AVG	PASS	COM	PCT	PI	YDS	AVG	TS	INT	PUNT	YDS	AVG	PR	YDS	AVG	KO	AVG	KOR	YDS	AVG
TOR	335	2088	6.2	703	447	63.6	24	5708	8.1	19	29	118	5303	44.9	119	1126	9.5	113	58.8	65	1410	21.7
MTL	451	2675	5.9	532	304	57.1	17	4255	8.0	44	24	111	4932	44.4	92	810	8.8	80	60.5	92	1862	20.2
WPG	395	1982	5.0	570	314	55.1	29	4098	7.2	40	20	143	6192	43.3	101	907	9.0	79	59.6	98	2145	21.9
HAM	328	1547	4.7	601	332	55.2	26	4523	7.5	54	30	148	6248	42.2	100	545	5.5	79	56.9	80	1522	19.0

1997 WEST DIVISION

TEAM	G	W	L	T	PTS	PCT	PF	OPP	TD	TDR	TDP	TDO	C1	C2	FG	FGA	ST	SI	FDT	FDR	FDP	FDX	PEN	YDS	FUM	FL
EDM	18	12	6	0	24	.667	479	400	46	16	27	3	41	4	41	56	4	23	365	88	241	36	142	1170	32	20
CAL	18	10	8	0	20	.556	519	443	55	17	36	2	50	3	39	51	1	14	405	132	247	26	178	1572	18	10
BC	18	8	10	0	16	.444	429	536	45	18	21	6	43	0	35	45	2	7	345	130	198	17	213	1507	31	19
SAS	18	8	10	0	16	.444	413	479	39	17	17	5	34	3	40	57	4	11	321	124	170	27	157	1310	29	20

TEAM	RUSH	YDS	AVG	PASS	COM	PCT	PI	YDS	AVG	TS	INT	PUNT	YDS	AVG	PR	YDS	AVG	KO	AVG	KOR	YDS	AVG
EDM	352	1344	3.8	655	381	58.2	29	5383	8.2	34	27	115	4667	40.6	105	1064	10.1	78	60.9	72	1374	19.1
CAL	394	1924	4.9	617	391	63.4	16	4981	8.1	37	16	121	5396	44.6	93	832	8.9	88	60.1	79	1711	21.7
BC	352	2109	6.0	598	386	64.5	13	4714	7.9	49	25	146	5950	40.8	91	984	10.8	79	51.1	87	1700	19.5
SAS	400	2054	5.1	554	287	51.8	31	4221	7.6	49	16	135	5568	41.2	106	944	8.9	69	56.1	68	1368	20.1

1998 EAST DIVISION

TEAM	G	W	L	T	PTS	PCT	PF	OPP	TD	TDR	TDP	TDO	C1	C2	FG	FGA	ST	SI	FDT	FDR	FDP	FDX	PEN	YDS	FUM	FL
HAM	18	12	5	1	25	.694	503	351	52	21	26	5	50	1	41	50	1	14	356	109	221	26	158	1182	28	16
MTL	18	12	5	1	25	.694	470	435	44	14	27	3	43	1	47	66	2	16	367	161	183	23	185	1425	23	17
TOR	18	9	9	0	18	.500	452	410	45	8	30	7	44	0	33	59	5	29	394	87	274	33	176	1327	27	15
WPG	18	3	15	0	6	.167	399	588	40	11	16	13	30	3	36	54	2	11	287	109	156	22	166	1402	33	26

TEAM	RUSH	YDS	AVG	PASS	COM	PCT	PI	YDS	AVG	TS	INT	PUNT	YDS	AVG	PR	YDS	AVG	KO	AVG	KOR	YDS	AVG
HAM	382	1833	4.8	646	364	56.3	22	5178	8.0	15	37	141	6091	43.2	111	985	8.9	92	57.2	56	1244	22.2
MTL	497	2888	5.8	503	279	55.5	23	4105	8.2	43	20	125	5718	45.7	109	1063	9.8	73	63.0	80	1501	18.8
TOR	257	1050	4.1	756	495	65.5	22	6390	8.5	65	19	132	6169	46.7	110	1132	10.3	79	55.8	67	1422	21.2
WPG	380	1714	4.5	582	315	54.1	27	3701	6.4	37	19	139	6266	45.1	100	1292	12.9	61	56.0	102	2349	23.0

1998 WEST DIVISION

TEAM	G	W	L	T	PTS	PCT	PF	OPP	TD	TDR	TDP	TDO	C1	C2	FG	FGA	ST	SI	FDT	FDR	FDP	FDX	PEN	YDS	FUM	FL
CAL	18	12	6	0	24	.667	558	397	61	21	38	2	57	1	35	54	2	24	450	128	282	40	205	1504	25	13
EDM	18	9	9	0	18	.500	396	450	40	11	23	6	37	1	34	40	3	9	321	92	206	23	173	1303	26	19
BC	18	9	9	0	18	.500	394	427	32	12	17	3	30	1	52	66	1	12	346	139	174	33	193	1422	18	12
SAS	18	5	13	0	10	.278	411	525	45	17	24	4	42	0	28	39	1	13	368	128	206	34	151	1103	19	12

TEAM	RUSH	YDS	AVG	PASS	COM	PCT	PI	YDS	AVG	TS	INT	PUNT	YDS	AVG	PR	YDS	AVG	KO	AVG	KOR	YDS	AVG
CAL	353	1967	5.6	678	433	63.9	20	5529	8.2	45	33	113	5451	48.2	120	1211	10.1	97	60.9	61	1540	25.2
EDM	369	1675	4.5	573	315	55.0	21	4575	8.0	55	18	147	6004	40.8	102	753	7.4	72	59.7	60	1422	23.7
BC	424	2470	5.8	547	319	58.3	20	3910	7.1	43	32	131	5793	44.2	82	775	9.5	76	55.8	71	1532	21.6
SAS	350	1989	5.7	604	360	59.6	22	4640	7.7	49	12	139	5683	40.9	85	704	8.3	71	57.6	76	1600	21.1

1999 EAST DIVISION

TEAM	G	W	L	T	PTS	PCT	PF	OPP	TD	TDR	TDP	TDO	C1	C2	FG	FGA	ST	SI	FDT	FDR	FDP	FDX	PEN	YDS	FUM	FL
MTL	18	12	6	0	24	.667	495	395	51	21	24	6	51	0	40	52	1	16	378	151	193	34	182	1476	29	24
HAM	18	11	7	0	22	.611	603	378	65	26	29	10	63	1	43	53	4	11	373	118	239	25	175	1641	25	17
TOR	18	9	9	0	18	.500	386	373	30	12	17	1	28	1	48	66	5	22	312	124	169	19	157	1143	37	20
WPG	18	6	12	0	12	.333	362	601	34	12	17	5	27	2	34	49	4	17	335	95	204	36	195	1724	39	29

TEAM	RUSH	YDS	AVG	PASS	COM	PCT	PI	YDS	AVG	TS	INT	PUNT	YDS	AVG	PR	YDS	AVG	KO	AVG	KOR	YDS	AVG
MTL	498	2436	4.9	481	303	63.0	9	4604	9.6	37	27	124	5878	47.4	102	824	8.1	86	60.3	71	1325	18.7
HAM	371	2055	5.5	646	377	58.4	18	5493	8.5	7	25	125	5334	42.7	113	1089	9.6	100	58.1	64	1208	18.9
TOR	447	2311	5.2	526	300	57.0	20	3926	7.5	45	18	142	6775	47.7	137	1078	7.9	62	57.3	68	1405	20.7
WPG	314	1350	4.3	665	387	58.2	26	4913	7.4	39	15	133	5690	42.8	87	767	8.8	60	51.2	95	1721	18.1

1999 WEST DIVISION

TEAM	G	W	L	T	PTS	PCT	PF	OPP	TD	TDR	TDP	TDO	C1	C2	FG	FGA	ST	SI	FDT	FDR	FDP	FDX	PEN	YDS	FUM	FL
BC	18	13	5	0	26	.722	429	373	45	17	22	6	39	4	30	47	3	16	374	154	194	26	196	1522	35	20
CAL	18	12	6	0	24	.667	503	393	49	13	30	6	44	2	48	59	2	13	389	121	234	34	229	1891	18	8
EDM	18	6	12	0	12	.333	459	502	44	18	20	6	41	0	45	68	4	11	356	177	149	30	202	1593	25	13
SAS	18	3	15	0	6	.167	370	592	41	13	24	4	36	3	23	29	2	9	331	127	173	31	163	1192	33	21

TEAM	RUSH	YDS	AVG	PASS	COM	PCT	PI	YDS	AVG	TS	INT	PUNT	YDS	AVG	PR	YDS	AVG	KO	AVG	KOR	YDS	AVG
BC	483	2550	5.3	548	328	59.9	13	4379	8.0	35	25	140	5882	42.0	95	678	7.1	75	54.9	72	1416	19.7
CAL	388	1967	5.1	588	373	63.4	17	5256	8.9	59	21	117	4958	42.4	90	878	9.8	94	57.8	54	1151	21.3
EDM	463	3043	6.6	529	277	52.4	25	3469	6.6	47	20	117	4869	41.6	82	762	9.3	79	57.7	82	1886	23.0
SAS	376	1681	4.5	552	304	55.1	35	4037	7.3	50	12	152	6044	39.8	86	816	9.5	59	55.3	85	1408	16.6

2000 EAST DIVISION

TEAM	G	W	L	T	PTS	PCT	PF	OPP	TD	TDR	TDP	TDO	C1	C2	FG	FGA	ST	SI	FDT	FDR	FDP	FDX	PEN	YDS	FUM	FL
MTL	18	12	6	0	24	.667	594	379	61	23	28	10	60	0	46	60	4	22	392	143	214	35	144	1195	30	21
HAM	18	9	9	0	20	.500	470	446	46	15	24	7	42	1	43	53	7	7	340	94	216	30	179	1609	22	15
WPG	18	7	10	1	16	.417	539	596	55	13	34	8	52	1	45	58	5	10	328	80	220	28	201	1706	22	10
TOR	18	7	10	1	15	.417	390	562	42	9	24	9	36	3	27	43	0	15	311	113	175	23	163	1236	31	15

TEAM	RUSH	YDS	AVG	PASS	COM	PCT	PI	YDS	AVG	TS	INT	PUNT	YDS	AVG	PR	YDS	AVG	KO	AVG	KOR	YDS	AVG
MTL	469	2440	5.2	522	320	61.3	8	4926	9.4	40	31	119	5504	46.3	103	1197	11.6	93	60.8	69	1370	19.9
HAM	336	1534	4.6	649	332	51.2	41	5003	7.7	15	18	125	5454	43.6	111	914	8.2	76	57.1	67	1212	18.1
WPG	296	1392	4.7	663	349	52.6	27	5123	7.7	36	23	131	5617	42.9	94	801	8.5	85	59.7	97	2258	23.3
TOR	393	1997	5.1	583	333	57.1	27	3970	6.8	41	20	136	6334	46.6	96	767	8.0	75	56.1	77	1448	18.8

2000 WEST DIVISION

TEAM	G	W	L	T	PTS	PCT	PF	OPP	TD	TDR	TDP	TDO	C1	C2	FG	FGA	ST	SI	FDT	FDR	FDP	FDX	PEN	YDS	FUM	FL
CAL	18	12	5	1	25	.694	604	495	64	17	39	8	63	1	43	55	6	14	391	111	243	37	194	1520	27	22
EDM	18	10	8	0	21	.556	527	520	55	15	34	6	53	0	37	55	6	21	386	144	216	26	186	1451	23	16
BC	18	8	10	0	17	.444	513	529	54	22	30	2	51	1	43	50	1	5	412	145	248	19	211	1627	21	15
SAS	18	5	12	1	11	.306	516	626	57	16	36	5	54	2	34	45	3	8	409	117	249	43	187	1527	26	17

TEAM	RUSH	YDS	AVG	PASS	COM	PCT	PI	YDS	AVG	TS	INT	PUNT	YDS	AVG	PR	YDS	AVG	KO	AVG	KOR	YDS	AVG
CAL	359	1926	5.4	621	384	61.8	17	5627	9.1	55	24	138	5952	43.1	118	1114	9.4	94	58.8	74	1696	22.9
EDM	416	2340	5.6	602	359	59.6	20	4635	7.7	59	26	126	5334	42.3	87	857	9.9	73	62.9	86	1800	20.9
BC	446	2506	5.6	627	382	60.9	13	5699	9.1	36	24	124	4807	38.8	96	722	7.5	84	54.2	80	1575	19.7
SAS	335	1847	5.5	662	355	53.6	27	5351	8.1	29	14	114	4596	40.3	78	874	11.2	85	58.6	78	1575	20.2

2001 EAST DIVISION

TEAM	G	W	L	T	PTS	PCT	PF	OPP	TD	TDR	TDP	TDO	C1	C2	FG	FGA	ST	SI	FDT	FDR	FDP	FDX	PEN	YDS	FUM	FL
WPG	18	14	4	0	28	.778	509	383	56	16	32	8	54	1	31	51	5	14	381	111	225	45	197	1914	20	12
HAM	18	11	7	0	22	.611	440	420	40	16	20	4	35	2	47	58	6	8	340	95	214	31	173	1608	29	16
MTL	18	9	9	0	18	.500	454	419	44	21	18	5	43	0	42	43	4	13	317	145	202	30	160	1250	35	22
TOR	18	7	11	0	15	.389	432	455	45	10	28	7	42	1	32	50	3	16	345	128	192	23	170	1300	28	20

TEAM	RUSH	YDS	AVG	PASS	COM	PCT	PI	YDS	AVG	TS	INT	PUNT	YDS	AVG	PR	YDS	AVG	KO	AVG	KOR	YDS	AVG
WPG	387	1993	5.1	582	346	59.5	25	4763	8.2	40	24	121	5121	42.3	105	949	9.0	79	60.8	78	1603	20.6
HAM	323	1536	4.8	622	350	56.3	12	4773	7.7	14	17	126	5407	42.9	87	545	6.3	79	55.5	64	1270	19.8
MTL	456	2284	5.0	531	315	59.3	17	4428	8.3	31	17	110	5010	45.5	89	975	11.0	70	60.2	79	1527	19.3
TOR	372	2032	5.5	555	328	59.1	26	4535	8.2	51	25	116	5020	43.3	94	910	9.7	80	58.0	70	1322	18.9

2001 WEST DIVISION

TEAM	G	W	L	T	PTS	PCT	PF	OPP	TD	TDR	TDP	TDO	C1	C2	FG	FGA	ST	SI	FDT	FDR	FDP	FDX	PEN	YDS	FUM	FL
EDM	18	9	9	0	19	.500	439	463	41	11	24	6	37	1	45	60	3	13	339	114	202	23	192	1583	25	17
CAL	18	8	10	0	17	.444	478	476	47	17	28	2	44	3	42	57	4	12	366	128	205	33	155	1258	25	14
BC	18	8	10	0	16	.444	417	445	46	23	22	1	43	2	25	38	3	13	365	152	187	26	190	1381	38	18
SAS	18	6	12	0	12	.333	308	416	28	12	14	2	26	0	33	47	3	9	310	124	154	32	152	1241	29	17

TEAM	RUSH	YDS	AVG	PASS	COM	PCT	PI	YDS	AVG	TS	INT	PUNT	YDS	AVG	PR	YDS	AVG	KO	AVG	KOR	YDS	AVG
EDM	393	1877	4.8	595	339	57.0	19	5054	8.5	49	19	136	5819	42.8	101	971	9.6	70	58.1	77	1476	19.2
CAL	436	2464	5.7	546	334	61.2	15	4687	8.6	47	16	122	5169	42.4	100	927	9.3	87	56.4	74	1819	24.6
BC	449	2284	5.1	572	305	53.3	21	4430	7.7	24	23	142	5750	40.5	112	1017	9.1	79	54.1	73	1406	19.3
SAS	404	2069	5.1	510	254	49.8	26	3480	6.8	32	20	140	5830	41.6	102	856	8.4	62	62.1	55	1125	20.5

2002 EAST DIVISION

TEAM	G	W	L	T	PTS	PCT	PF	OPP	TD	TDR	TDP	TDO	C1	C2	FG	FGA	ST	SI	FDT	FDR	FDP	FDX	PEN	YDS	FUM	FL
MTL	18	13	5	0	27	.722	577	408	63	21	29	13	63	0	36	54	6	16	401	141	226	34	220	1701	31	23
TOR	18	8	10	0	16	.444	344	482	35	10	19	6	32	2	27	32	3	11	266	94	137	35	176	1338	28	18
HAM	18	7	11	0	15	.389	427	524	40	12	25	3	35	1	43	55	2	17	347	102	211	34	170	1434	32	21
OTT	18	4	14	0	10	.222	356	550	36	12	18	6	32	2	28	40	5	10	308	106	170	32	223	1895	31	21

TEAM	RUSH	YDS	AVG	PASS	COM	PCT	PI	YDS	AVG	TS	INT	PUNT	YDS	AVG	PR	YDS	AVG	KO	AVG	KOR	YDS	AVG
MTL	403	2342	5.8	606	353	58.3	11	5242	8.7	25	29	104	4590	44.1	76	896	11.8	89	62.1	59	1226	20.8
TOR	384	1834	4.8	469	262	55.9	21	3352	7.1	47	29	156	7197	46.1	85	957	11.3	64	61.6	76	1612	21.2
HAM	339	1558	4.6	649	338	52.1	31	4807	7.4	15	21	125	5389	43.1	88	1061	12.1	66	55.0	80	1699	21.2
OTT	301	1488	4.9	652	334	51.2	25	3933	6.0	25	18	146	5850	40.1	94	1021	10.9	65	58.3	75	1405	18.7

2002 WEST DIVISION

TEAM	G	W	L	T	PTS	PCT	PF	OPP	TD	TDR	TDP	TDO	C1	C2	FG	FGA	ST	SI	FDT	FDR	FDP	FDX	PEN	YDS	FUM	FL
EDM	18	13	5	0	26	.722	516	450	57	17	33	7	54	0	34	42	2	14	385	153	201	31	199	1512	37	29
WPG	18	12	6	0	24	.667	566	421	58	9	47	2	56	1	45	62	5	15	399	108	249	42	214	1891	28	18
BC	18	10	8	0	20	.556	480	399	54	24	24	6	49	0	31	47	2	10	355	130	188	37	192	1596	26	15
SAS	18	8	10	0	18	.444	435	393	41	21	16	4	39	1	41	54	3	19	341	152	156	33	168	1206	26	14
CAL	18	6	12	0	14	.333	438	512	45	12	29	4	42	2	34	52	4	12	364	111	225	28	196	1714	15	7

TEAM	RUSH	YDS	AVG	PASS	COM	PCT	PI	YDS	AVG	TS	INT	PUNT	YDS	AVG	PR	YDS	AVG	KO	AVG	KOR	YDS	AVG
EDM	412	2250	5.5	573	343	59.9	15	4881	8.5	37	19	126	5362	42.6	111	1050	9.5	75	65.7	75	1604	21.4
WPG	360	1850	5.1	646	399	61.8	29	5544	8.6	35	18	107	4379	40.9	106	1114	10.5	93	60.5	61	1133	18.6
BC	428	2183	5.1	519	285	54.9	14	4357	8.4	42	25	139	5696	41.0	101	878	8.7	82	55.9	59	1158	19.6
SAS	493	2518	5.1	498	285	57.2	13	3600	7.2	52	14	137	5853	42.7	97	1240	12.8	62	62.8	60	1310	21.8
CAL	368	1930	5.2	604	320	53.0	25	4766	7.9	35	11	126	5732	45.5	93	786	8.5	69	56.0	79	2137	27.1

2003 EAST DIVISION

TEAM	G	W	L	T	PTS	PCT	PF	OPP	TD	TDR	TDP	TDO	C1	C2	FG	FGA	ST	SI	FDT	FDR	FDP	FDX	PEN	YDS	FUM	FL
MTL	18	13	5	0	26	.722	562	409	60	14	39	7	58	2	43	55	3	7	418	117	273	28	252	1859	35	19
TOR	18	9	9	0	18	.500	473	433	49	13	23	13	45	0	40	56	2	10	302	93	179	30	189	1413	27	22
OTT	18	7	11	0	14	.389	467	581	43	14	25	4	36	2	51	62	2	12	349	143	182	24	214	1697	22	13
HAM	18	1	17	0	2	.056	293	583	31	16	13	2	25	3	22	38	0	10	325	109	175	41	176	1466	26	21

TEAM	RUSH	YDS	AVG	PASS	COM	PCT	PI	YDS	AVG	TS	INT	PUNT	YDS	AVG	PR	YDS	AVG	KO	AVG	KOR	YDS	AVG
MTL	354	1602	4.5	724	433	59.8	18	6191	8.6	28	20	104	4334	41.7	92	1029	11.2	104	53.9	69	1263	18.3
TOR	318	1728	5.4	562	309	55.0	18	4182	7.4	40	26	126	5828	46.3	84	1055	12.6	81	58.3	83	1992	24.0
OTT	362	2364	6.5	606	338	55.8	23	4455	7.4	43	18	123	5091	41.4	91	616	6.8	83	59.5	90	1824	20.3
HAM	337	1525	4.5	621	318	51.2	25	4045	6.5	31	14	137	5343	39.0	78	770	9.9	62	51.6	95	1739	18.3

2003 WEST DIVISION

TEAM	G	W	L	T	PTS	PCT	PF	OPP	TD	TDR	TDP	TDO	C1	C2	FG	FGA	ST	SI	FDT	FDR	FDP	FDX	PEN	YDS	FUM	FL
EDM	18	13	5	0	26	.722	569	414	64	23	37	4	61	1	32	39	10	6	393	136	223	34	204	1819	34	19
WPG	18	11	7	0	22	.611	514	485	51	18	28	5	48	0	47	61	5	9	375	128	201	46	209	1818	22	12
SAS	18	11	7	0	22	.611	535	430	56	26	22	8	53	1	41	48	8	5	388	151	202	35	193	1569	29	17
BC	18	11	7	0	22	.611	531	430	56	11	42	3	54	1	44	56	1	5	393	95	263	35	174	1504	28	15
CAL	18	5	13	0	10	.278	323	502	30	5	19	6	26	0	30	45	8	11	315	93	192	30	213	1676	23	14

TEAM	RUSH	YDS	AVG	PASS	COM	PCT	PI	YDS	AVG	TS	INT	PUNT	YDS	AVG	PR	YDS	AVG	KO	AVG	KOR	YDS	AVG
EDM	396	2081	5.3	580	388	66.9	17	5188	8.9	25	24	125	5229	41.8	81	752	9.3	98	57.6	70	1523	21.8
WPG	416	2347	5.6	571	302	52.9	17	4410	7.7	55	22	136	5661	41.6	82	690	8.4	84	53.2	73	1375	18.8
SAS	454	2605	5.7	553	330	59.7	13	4054	7.3	27	22	124	5119	41.3	81	834	10.3	92	57.3	63	1381	21.9
BC	325	1894	5.8	618	418	67.6	13	6178	10.0	53	17	103	4015	39.0	97	790	8.1	92	56.3	80	1432	17.9
CAL	345	1693	4.9	584	319	54.6	28	4160	7.1	37	9	153	6330	41.4	84	888	10.6	64	56.5	79	1630	20.6

2004 EAST DIVISION

TEAM	G	W	L	T	PTS	PCT	PF	OPP	TD	TDR	TDP	TDO	C1	C2	FG	FGA	ST	SI	FDT	FDR	FDP	FDX	PEN	YDS	FUM	FL
MTL	18	14	4	0	28	.778	584	371	62	21	32	9	61	0	40	56	7	17	411	125	260	26	252	1864	21	9
TOR	18	10	7	1	21	.583	422	414	43	14	18	11	42	0	34	46	5	10	295	106	151	38	225	1783	27	21
HAM	18	9	8	1	19	.528	455	542	50	16	29	5	45	2	28	53	5	12	367	116	212	39	262	2096	29	18
OTT	18	5	13	0	10	.278	401	560	47	15	25	7	45	0	20	38	2	10	311	113	176	22	229	1955	33	22

TEAM	RUSH	YDS	AVG	PASS	COM	PCT	PI	YDS	AVG	TS	INT	PUNT	YDS	AVG	PR	YDS	AVG	KO	AVG	KOR	YDS	AVG
MTL	331	1716	5.2	717	451	62.9	18	6326	8.8	39	30	123	5048	41.0	105	1038	9.9	103	58.3	59	1059	17.9
TOR	329	1761	5.4	546	299	54.8	19	4000	7.3	54	22	139	6228	44.8	86	992	11.5	73	56.5	83	1675	20.2
HAM	396	1907	4.8	678	379	55.9	32	5516	8.1	10	16	111	4337	39.1	79	610	7.7	79	56.6	78	1475	18.9
OTT	340	1834	5.4	557	334	60.0	17	4505	8.1	57	13	136	5397	39.7	74	914	12.4	67	53.0	93	1862	20.0

2004 WEST DIVISION

TEAM	G	W	L	T	PTS	PCT	PF	OPP	TD	TDR	TDP	TDO	C1	C2	FG	FGA	ST	SI	FDT	FDR	FDP	FDX	PEN	YDS	FUM	FL
BC	18	13	5	0	26	.722	584	436	68	17	45	6	64	0	33	45	2	9	429	124	262	43	223	1748	31	18
EDM	18	9	9	0	18	.500	532	472	57	17	31	9	57	0	37	47	5	12	355	94	222	39	220	1754	41	23
SAS	18	9	9	0	18	.500	476	444	48	22	23	3	47	1	39	53	7	8	398	148	211	39	176	1448	26	16
WPG	18	7	11	0	14	.389	448	507	44	14	21	9	41	1	39	50	5	14	372	96	229	47	217	1641	33	19
CAL	18	4	14	0	8	.222	396	552	38	12	20	6	36	1	33	44	7	17	318	76	209	33	242	1883	33	17

TEAM	RUSH	YDS	AVG	PASS	COM	PCT	PI	YDS	AVG	TS	INT	PUNT	YDS	AVG	PR	YDS	AVG	KO	AVG	KOR	YDS	AVG
BC	379	1985	5.2	628	409	65.1	12	6335	10.1	54	17	117	4854	41.5	96	854	8.9	109	53.4	85	1732	20.4
EDM	352	1486	4.2	581	379	65.2	15	5567	9.6	36	24	119	5069	42.6	83	923	11.1	86	55.2	85	1734	20.4
SAS	444	2504	5.6	615	356	57.9	24	4619	7.5	28	20	122	4855	39.8	94	848	9.0	78	59.0	69	1276	18.5
WPG	380	1928	5.1	587	338	57.6	16	4534	7.7	40	18	120	5169	43.1	87	990	11.4	78	54.3	75	1425	19.0
CAL	268	1224	4.6	689	378	54.9	31	4651	6.8	22	24	135	5746	42.6	73	747	10.2	75	53.6	88	1629	18.5

2005 EAST DIVISION

TEAM	G	W	L	T	PTS	PCT	PF	OPP	TD	TDR	TDP	TDO	C1	C2	FG	FGA	ST	SI	FDT	FDR	FDP	FDX	PEN	YDS	FUM	FL
TOR	18	11	7	0	22	.611	486	387	51	9	37	5	50	0	34	45	8	12	378	107	243	28	195	1683	28	21
MTL	18	10	8	0	20	.556	592	519	64	22	35	7	60	2	38	52	6	18	454	156	274	24	221	1663	23	18
OTT	18	7	11	0	14	.389	458	578	49	16	26	7	42	2	32	48	5	12	350	140	176	34	199	1554	28	14
HAM	18	5	13	0	10	.278	383	583	42	13	21	8	39	1	23	32	6	9	336	105	195	36	192	1571	35	18

TEAM	RUSH	YDS	AVG	PASS	COM	PCT	PI	YDS	AVG	TS	INT	PUNT	YDS	AVG	PR	YDS	AVG	KO	AVG	KOR	YDS	AVG
TOR	286	1494	5.2	636	397	62.4	22	5678	8.9	47	19	102	4599	45.1	79	795	10.1	82	61.1	80	1601	20.0
MTL	370	2147	5.8	713	460	64.5	23	5824	8.2	32	27	99	4417	44.6	59	625	10.6	101	63.8	87	1751	20.1
OTT	398	2366	5.9	562	343	61.0	25	4570	8.1	65	25	127	5150	40.6	76	761	10.0	86	53.5	82	1549	18.9
HAM	342	1543	4.5	632	357	56.5	25	4483	7.1	38	23	118	4646	39.4	61	505	8.3	77	58.3	90	1886	21.0

2005 WEST DIVISION

TEAM	G	W	L	T	PTS	PCT	PF	OPP	TD	TDR	TDP	TDO	C1	C2	FG	FGA	ST	SI	FDT	FDR	FDP	FDX	PEN	YDS	FUM	FL
BC	18	12	6	0	24	.667	550	444	58	20	33	5	51	3	35	54	11	18	406	116	256	34	171	1444	21	13
CAL	18	11	7	0	22	.611	529	443	56	20	29	7	54	0	40	52	5	9	372	119	226	27	182	1409	35	21
EDM	18	11	7	0	22	.611	453	421	47	15	26	6	47	0	33	49	6	13	397	113	250	34	202	1761	31	12
SAS	18	9	9	0	18	.500	441	433	47	20	19	8	41	2	31	42	4	13	410	154	219	37	150	1273	39	21
WPG	18	5	13	0	10	.278	474	558	52	14	31	7	46	3	28	40	3	20	314	112	173	29	169	1233	25	17

TEAM	RUSH	YDS	AVG	PASS	COM	PCT	PI	YDS	AVG	TS	INT	PUNT	YDS	AVG	PR	YDS	AVG	KO	AVG	KOR	YDS	AVG
BC	325	1821	5.6	636	430	67.6	12	5723	9.0	74	24	117	4975	42.5	76	905	11.9	96	55.6	90	1770	19.7
CAL	391	2295	5.9	534	312	58.4	20	4959	9.3	27	24	115	5094	44.3	79	814	10.3	84	58.9	85	1530	18.0
EDM	288	1360	4.7	718	482	67.1	24	5585	7.8	38	15	126	5076	40.3	86	995	11.6	80	56.1	75	1578	21.0
SAS	439	2436	5.5	651	383	58.8	19	4229	6.5	23	19	112	4517	40.3	82	1074	13.1	84	53.9	71	1635	23.0
WPG	359	1856	5.2	554	300	54.2	24	4427	8.0	31	18	123	6166	50.1	84	704	8.4	82	54.3	85	1617	19.0

2006 EAST DIVISION

TEAM	G	W	L	T	PTS	PCT	PF	OPP	TD	TDR	TDP	TDO	C1	C2	FG	FGA	ST	SI	FDT	FDR	FDP	FDX	PEN	YDS	FUM	FL
MTL	18	10	8	0	20	.556	451	431	40	17	20	3	40	0	51	59	5	8	397	129	233	35	224	1790	27	17
TOR	18	10	8	0	20	.556	359	343	35	8	19	8	32	1	31	42	5	12	280	92	165	23	192	1493	21	11
WPG	18	9	9	0	18	.500	362	408	35	12	22	1	32	1	30	43	6	16	341	124	187	30	204	1720	26	18
HAM	18	4	14	0	8	.222	292	495	25	8	12	5	24	1	31	42	6	11	303	87	173	43	206	1537	32	19

TEAM	RUSH	YDS	AVG	PASS	COM	PCT	PI	YDS	AVG	TS	INT	PUNT	YDS	AVG	PR	YDS	AVG	KO	AVG	KOR	YDS	AVG
MTL	354	1760	5.0	665	416	62.6	20	4866	7.3	43	21	114	5164	45.3	80	609	7.6	72	60.5	76	1527	20.1
TOR	343	1600	4.7	508	303	59.6	17	3886	7.6	46	30	137	6345	46.3	97	970	10.0	69	60.2	68	1363	20.0
WPG	389	2022	5.2	571	316	55.3	24	4112	7.2	35	13	143	5999	42.0	99	871	8.8	64	58.4	70	1277	18.2
HAM	294	1382	4.7	607	353	58.2	29	3906	6.4	36	18	131	5665	43.2	82	613	7.5	62	60.5	86	1631	19.0

2006 WEST DIVISION

TEAM	G	W	L	T	PTS	PCT	PF	OPP	TD	TDR	TDP	TDO	C1	C2	FG	FGA	ST	SI	FDT	FDR	FDP	FDX	PEN	YDS	FUM	FL
BC	18	13	5	0	26	.722	555	355	58	13	36	9	55	1	43	51	7	7	380	120	227	33	185	1521	14	11
CAL	18	10	8	0	20	.556	477	426	42	16	24	2	42	0	56	65	3	9	372	124	220	28	194	1463	23	12
SAS	18	9	9	0	18	.500	465	434	47	16	28	3	42	2	38	44	8	7	364	137	193	34	163	1267	36	16
EDM	18	7	11	0	14	.389	399	468	40	16	21	3	35	1	33	43	7	9	389	141	219	24	194	1598	20	11

TEAM	RUSH	YDS	AVG	PASS	COM	PCT	PI	YDS	AVG	TS	INT	PUNT	YDS	AVG	PR	YDS	AVG	KO	AVG	KOR	YDS	AVG
BC	339	1802	5.3	603	412	68.3	15	5261	8.7	56	36	126	5222	41.4	95	715	7.5	109	56.0	67	1161	17.3
CAL	378	2407	6.4	566	322	56.9	21	4744	8.4	27	19	109	4902	45.0	74	590	8.0	84	56.7	75	1629	21.7
SAS	382	2362	6.2	570	327	57.4	19	4351	7.6	50	16	137	5213	38.1	99	1029	10.4	83	49.3	65	1127	17.3
EDM	346	1845	5.3	646	423	65.5	18	5183	8.0	42	10	121	4910	40.6	89	627	7.0	70	55.8	81	1503	18.6

2007 EAST DIVISION

TEAM	G	W	L	T	PTS	PCT	PF	OPP	TD	TDR	TDP	TDO	C1	C2	FG	FGA	ST	SI	FDT	FDR	FDP	FDX	PEN	YDS	FUM	FL
TOR	18	11	7	0	22	.611	440	336	48	9	29	10	46	0	29	44	4	11	309	80	196	33	204	1589	26	14
WPG	18	10	7	1	21	.583	439	404	46	18	25	3	44	1	30	49	2	23	391	111	241	39	178	1346	23	16
MTL	18	8	10	0	16	.444	398	433	38	14	21	3	35	1	33	47	9	16	381	125	234	22	218	1959	26	14
HAM	18	3	15	0	6	.167	315	515	23	5	15	3	19	1	45	53	4	13	315	110	175	30	212	1909	26	15

TEAM	RUSH	YDS	AVG	PASS	COM	PCT	PI	YDS	AVG	TS	INT	PUNT	YDS	AVG	PR	YDS	AVG	KO	AVG	KOR	YDS	AVG
TOR	347	1654	4.8	547	296	54.1	20	4299	7.9	40	25	137	6148	44.9	106	993	9.4	79	59.7	59	1153	19.5
WPG	352	1864	5.3	645	405	62.8	13	5289	8.2	27	10	130	5587	43.0	91	629	6.9	72	60.2	62	1295	20.9
MTL	383	1791	4.7	626	399	63.7	15	5044	8.1	68	20	132	6162	46.7	95	769	8.1	69	63.2	63	1322	21.0
HAM	351	2180	6.2	583	327	56.1	20	3842	6.6	49	13	130	5725	44.0	88	575	6.5	53	59.7	86	1613	18.8

2007 WEST DIVISION

TEAM	G	W	L	T	PTS	PCT	PF	OPP	TD	TDR	TDP	TDO	C1	C2	FG	FGA	ST	SI	FDT	FDR	FDP	FDX	PEN	YDS	FUM	FL
BC	18	14	3	1	29	.806	542	379	58	25	27	6	56	1	37	45	8	9	366	139	184	43	169	1547	24	11
SAS	18	12	6	0	24	.667	530	434	59	25	29	5	58	1	31	45	4	15	379	124	223	32	161	1491	20	11
CAL	18	7	10	1	15	.417	473	527	52	8	40	4	51	0	30	36	5	10	406	126	260	20	231	1978	31	24
EDM	18	5	12	1	11	.306	400	509	36	6	28	2	36	0	37	54	7	22	368	102	236	30	170	1460	27	16

TEAM	RUSH	YDS	AVG	PASS	COM	PCT	PI	YDS	AVG	TS	INT	PUNT	YDS	AVG	PR	YDS	AVG	KO	AVG	KOR	YDS	AVG
BC	401	2174	5.4	530	310	58.5	17	4444	8.4	32	24	116	5138	44.3	97	927	9.6	84	57.4	70	1474	21.1
SAS	338	2012	6.0	591	345	58.4	13	4984	8.4	44	21	118	4954	42.0	84	815	9.7	86	62.9	64	1082	16.9
CAL	364	2212	6.1	629	375	59.6	21	5446	8.7	52	13	123	5376	43.7	87	775	8.9	76	60.3	78	1571	20.1
EDM	315	1577	5.0	666	440	66.1	21	5059	7.6	52	14	123	5351	43.5	89	716	8.0	69	58.4	70	1184	16.9

2008 EAST DIVISION

TEAM	G	W	L	T	PTS	PCT	PF	OPP	TD	TDR	TDP	TDO	C1	C2	FG	FGA	ST	SI	FDT	FDR	FDP	FDX	PEN	YDS	FUM	FL
MTL	18	11	7	0	22	.611	610	443	65	17	46	2	62	1	44	53	5	14	444	139	274	31	124	1162	19	15
WPG	18	8	10	0	16	.444	435	490	43	11	25	7	40	1	34	51	8	17	360	117	217	26	138	1145	18	9
TOR	18	4	14	0	8	.222	397	627	38	15	21	2	35	1	39	51	3	9	358	110	224	24	178	1504	25	17
HAM	18	3	15	0	6	.167	441	593	48	23	21	4	45	1	28	36	4	14	360	144	193	23	152	1173	33	20

TEAM	RUSH	YDS	AVG	PASS	COM	PCT	PI	YDS	AVG	TS	INT	PUNT	YDS	AVG	PR	YDS	AVG	KO	AVG	KOR	YDS	AVG
MTL	316	2048	6.5	712	495	69.5	15	5829	8.2	22	18	87	3980	45.7	69	719	10.4	95	61.5	64	1166	18.2
WPG	362	1952	5.4	639	396	62.0	28	5073	7.9	29	15	124	5215	42.1	100	1015	10.2	73	58.8	80	1655	20.7
TOR	292	1680	5.8	684	389	56.9	17	5110	7.5	48	18	132	5839	44.2	97	1111	11.5	80	56.3	102	2280	22.4
HAM	391	2532	6.5	541	324	59.9	20	4474	8.3	67	23	114	5401	47.4	66	593	9.0	78	60.4	95	2012	21.2

2008 WEST DIVISION

TEAM	G	W	L	T	PTS	PCT	PF	OPP	TD	TDR	TDP	TDO	C1	C2	FG	FGA	ST	SI	FDT	FDR	FDP	FDX	PEN	YDS	FUM	FL
CAL	18	13	5	0	26	.722	595	420	61	19	39	3	61	0	50	58	3	12	417	140	252	25	165	1322	25	13
SAS	18	12	6	0	24	.667	500	471	52	23	25	4	50	0	38	44	7	10	368	133	206	29	154	1092	25	11
BC	18	11	7	0	22	.611	559	479	59	14	37	8	55	2	40	48	7	12	410	135	246	29	146	1286	21	15
EDM	18	10	8	0	20	.556	512	526	53	20	26	7	52	0	38	49	5	18	394	113	253	28	137	1194	37	26

TEAM	RUSH	YDS	AVG	PASS	COM	PCT	PI	YDS	AVG	TS	INT	PUNT	YDS	AVG	PR	YDS	AVG	KO	AVG	KOR	YDS	AVG
CAL	380	2422	6.4	614	393	64.0	14	5270	8.6	30	19	110	5076	46.1	83	718	8.7	98	60.1	63	1406	22.3
SAS	392	2242	5.7	552	327	59.2	28	4805	8.7	36	17	116	4794	41.3	98	787	8.0	84	63.6	70	1375	19.6
BC	358	2129	5.9	656	394	60.1	19	5246	8.0	33	27	127	5621	44.3	102	940	9.2	92	59.3	92	2155	23.4
EDM	314	1533	4.9	654	450	68.8	19	6031	9.2	37	23	106	4940	46.6	87	847	9.7	82	59.7	82	1712	20.9

2009 EAST DIVISION

TEAM	G	W	L	T	PTS	PCT	PF	OPP	TD	TDR	TDP	TDO	C1	C2	FG	FGA	ST	SI	FDT	FDR	FDP	FDX	PEN	YDS	FUM	FL
MTL	18	15	3	0	30	.833	600	324	58	17	33	8	56	0	55	63	5	21	406	140	239	27	164	1451	23	13
HAM	18	9	9	0	18	.500	449	428	44	14	25	5	43	0	41	53	3	13	374	120	225	29	151	1326	23	14
WPG	18	7	11	0	14	.389	386	506	35	10	17	8	34	0	40	49	5	12	285	99	155	31	184	1672	32	17
TOR	18	3	15	0	6	.167	328	502	28	12	14	2	25	1	41	47	2	6	315	95	182	38	215	1889	35	22

TEAM	RUSH	YDS	AVG	PASS	COM	PCT	PI	YDS	AVG	TS	INT	PUNT	YDS	AVG	PR	YDS	AVG	KO	AVG	KOR	YDS	AVG
MTL	392	2159	5.5	633	453	71.6	6	5191	8.2	35	24	105	4706	44.8	95	818	8.6	130	63.6	80	1536	19.2
HAM	332	1885	5.7	659	411	62.4	15	4886	7.4	42	17	121	5196	42.9	97	752	7.8	104	57.2	87	1623	18.7
WPG	381	2150	5.6	536	256	47.8	28	3600	6.7	26	31	143	5830	40.8	101	809	8.0	101	57.4	109	2262	20.8
TOR	300	1485	5.0	628	363	57.8	25	4128	6.6	55	11	131	5571	42.5	93	576	6.2	85	60.2	115	2371	20.6

2009 WEST DIVISION

TEAM	G	W	L	T	PTS	PCT	PF	OPP	TD	TDR	TDP	TDO	C1	C2	FG	FGA	ST	SI	FDT	FDR	FDP	FDX	PEN	YDS	FUM	FL
SAS	18	10	7	1	21	.583	514	484	54	23	26	5	47	6	33	43	8	16	377	128	207	42	154	1208	25	15
CAL	18	10	7	1	21	.583	514	443	53	24	24	5	48	2	42	49	3	12	403	141	236	26	179	1584	28	13
EDM	18	9	9	0	18	.500	469	502	50	24	22	4	47	1	33	42	7	7	363	113	224	26	156	1262	29	20
BC	18	8	10	0	16	.444	431	502	45	13	27	5	41	0	36	46	3	6	350	108	212	30	164	1330	26	19

TEAM	RUSH	YDS	AVG	PASS	COM	PCT	PI	YDS	AVG	TS	INT	PUNT	YDS	AVG	PR	YDS	AVG	KO	AVG	KOR	YDS	AVG
SAS	370	1973	5.3	604	365	60.4	23	4672	7.7	41	18	118	4938	41.8	81	630	7.8	105	62.7	103	1917	18.6
CAL	390	2334	6.0	592	354	59.8	16	4981	8.4	35	13	118	5397	45.7	85	624	7.3	109	61.6	90	1922	21.4
EDM	341	1934	5.7	626	419	66.9	15	5151	8.2	39	19	116	5115	44.1	100	935	9.4	107	56.7	104	2118	20.4
BC	366	2079	5.7	589	358	60.8	26	4569	7.8	40	21	121	5067	41.9	96	879	9.2	97	58.9	109	2270	20.8

2010 EAST DIVISION

TEAM	G	W	L	T	PTS	PCT	PF	OPP	TD	TDR	TDP	TDO	C1	C2	FG	FGA	ST	SI	FDT	FDR	FDP	FDX	PEN	YDS	FUM	FL
MTL	18	12	6	0	24	.667	521	475	52	9	36	7	49	3	43	59	5	15	415	114	262	39	195	1952	18	9
HAM	18	9	9	0	18	.500	481	450	53	12	34	7	45	3	32	42	3	10	390	102	247	41	169	1378	24	15
TOR	18	9	9	0	18	.500	373	442	36	13	16	7	32	1	35	50	5	8	327	120	179	28	138	1058	44	25
WPG	18	4	14	0	8	.222	464	485	48	14	27	7	44	1	34	44	7	14	329	137	163	29	194	1729	26	16

TEAM	RUSH	YDS	AVG	PASS	COM	PCT	PI	YDS	AVG	TS	INT	PUNT	YDS	AVG	PR	YDS	AVG	KO	AVG	KOR	YDS	AVG
MTL	335	1865	5.6	718	467	65.0	13	5675	7.9	34	25	113	4949	43.8	76	469	6.2	88	61.9	91	2032	22.3
HAM	317	1715	5.4	636	406	63.8	19	5329	8.4	26	18	114	4867	42.7	70	602	8.6	92	56.9	62	1185	19.1
TOR	350	2174	6.2	533	327	61.4	23	3980	7.5	48	19	120	4953	41.3	94	1116	11.9	66	65.5	91	1899	20.9
WPG	373	2456	6.6	556	328	59.0	16	4487	8.1	47	17	140	6029	43.1	95	989	10.4	82	54.1	78	1406	18.0

2010 WEST DIVISION

TEAM	G	W	L	T	PTS	PCT	PF	OPP	TD	TDR	TDP	TDO	C1	C2	FG	FGA	ST	SI	FDT	FDR	FDP	FDX	PEN	YDS	FUM	FL
CAL	18	13	5	0	26	.722	626	459	70	18	45	7	70	0	37	47	8	9	445	162	253	30	181	1633	28	19
SAS	18	10	8	0	20	.556	497	488	54	25	27	2	50	2	31	42	5	16	405	135	240	30	136	1179	30	16
BC	18	8	10	0	16	.444	466	466	42	17	19	6	39	1	52	58	4	9	339	97	205	37	196	1618	39	17
EDM	18	7	11	0	14	.389	382	545	37	16	15	7	35	0	36	43	3	11	362	132	191	39	178	1651	31	16

TEAM	RUSH	YDS	AVG	PASS	COM	PCT	PI	YDS	AVG	TS	INT	PUNT	YDS	AVG	PR	YDS	AVG	KO	AVG	KOR	YDS	AVG
CAL	429	2618	6.1	621	414	66.7	20	5466	8.8	30	24	119	5418	45.5	94	606	6.4	110	59.2	78	1546	19.8
SAS	312	1923	6.2	658	397	60.3	23	5645	8.6	43	15	118	4977	42.2	82	537	6.5	84	63.4	81	1557	19.2
BC	317	1849	5.8	604	361	59.8	20	4640	7.7	65	23	139	5767	41.5	103	1183	11.5	91	57.7	80	1711	21.4
EDM	369	2304	6.2	577	352	61.0	28	4307	7.5	41	21	112	4755	42.5	85	682	8.0	72	55.3	88	1724	19.6

2011 EAST DIVISION

TEAM	G	W	L	T	PTS	PCT	PF	OPP	TD	TDR	TDP	TDO	C1	C2	FG	FGA	ST	SI	FDT	FDR	FDP	FDX	PEN	YDS	FUM	FL
WPG	18	10	8	0	20	.556	432	432	42	17	20	5		0	40	52	3	15	342	123	178	41	191	1717	31	14
MTL	18	10	8	T	20	.556	515	468	52	16	33	3		0	45	52	3	12	429	129	270	30	162	1507	25	13
HAM	18	8	10	0	16	.444	481	478	47	21	23	3		0	49	55	1	4	371	113	213	45	163	1448	16	10
TOR	18	6	12	0	12	.333	397	498	38	15	17	6		0	41	50	1	6	322	125	173	24	168	1394	32	19

TEAM	RUSH	YDS	AVG	PASS	COM	PCT	PI	YDS	AVG	TS	INT	PUNT	YDS	AVG	PR	YDS	AVG	KO	AVG	KOR	YDS	AVG
WPG	390	1988	5.1	575	363	63.1	22	4494	7.8	46	25	143	5991	41.9	93	834	9.0	86	57.4	80	1411	17.6
MTL	354	2006	5.7	697	432	62.0	10	5562	8.0	34	13	115	4746	41.3	67	513	7.7	91	56.4	86	1648	19.2
HAM	342	1620	4.7	607	377	62.1	21	4736	7.8	35	10	119	4948	41.6	70	629	9.0	93	59.2	76	1432	18.8
TOR	359	2275	6.3	545	342	59.4	27	3770	6.9	40	16	118	5016	42.5	82	973	11.9	78	61.1	109	2404	22.1

2011 WEST DIVISION

TEAM	G	W	L	T	PTS	PCT	PF	OPP	TD	TDR	TDP	TDO	C1	C2	FG	FGA	ST	SI	FDT	FDR	FDP	FDX	PEN	YDS	FUM	FL
BC	18	11	7	0	22	.611	511	385	50	13	33	4		0	50	53	3	5	372	109	230	33	127	1016	18	11
EDM	18	11	7	0	22	.611	427	401	40	15	24	1		1	39	53	4	22	346	115	207	24	175	1554	29	9
CAL	18	11	7	0	22	.611	511	476	55	23	28	4		2	36	49	1	18	366	132	193	41	167	1524	33	20
SAS	18	5	13	0	10	.278	346	482	34	11	21	2		0	32	40	1	10	356	137	189	30	158	1439	19	**11**

TEAM	RUSH	YDS	AVG	PASS	COM	PCT	PI	YDS	AVG	TS	INT	PUNT	YDS	AVG	PR	YDS	AVG	KO	AVG	KOR	YDS	AVG
BC	329	1795	5.5	626	361	57.7	15	5090	8.1	29	17	123	5183	42.1	97	900	9.3	102	57.6	78	1540	19.7
EDM	384	1872	4.9	558	362	64.9	12	4721	8.6	46	24	137	6434	46.7	97	769	7.9	80	61.0	67	1159	17.3
CAL	364	2244	6.2	601	382	63.6	17	5033	8.3	34	16	111	5243	47.2	86	643	7.5	91	60.0	80	1730	21.6
SAS	321	1740	5.4	607	357	58.8	18	4526	7.5	41	21	120	5116	42.6	72	639	8.9	70	55.7	91	1957	21.5

THE CAREER LEADERS

	SERVICE	YEARS
1	Lui Passaglia	25
2	Damon Allen	23
	Bob Cameron	23
4	Hank Ilesic	20
5	Miles Gorrell	19
	Ron Lancaster	19
	Paul McCallum	19
8	Anthony Calvillo	18
	Paul Osbaldiston	18
	Troy Westwood	18

		GP
1	Lui Passaglia	408
2	Bob Cameron	394
3	Damon Allen	370
4	Miles Gorrell	311
5	Anthony Calvillo	301
6	Danny McManus	298
7	Paul Osbaldiston	296
8	Troy Westwood	293
9	Ron Lancaster	287
10	Gene Makowsky	286

	SCORING	PTS
1	Lui Passaglia	3991
2	Mark McLoughlin	2995
3	Paul Osbaldiston	2931
4	Troy Westwood	2748
5	Sean Fleming	2572
6	Paul McCallum	2546
7	David Ridgway	2374
8	Dave Cutler	2237
9	Terry Baker	2123
10	Trevor Kennerd	1840

		TD
1	Milt Stegall	147
2	Mike Pringle	137
	George Reed	137
4	Allen Pitts	117
5	Geroy Simon	99
6	Brian Kelly	97
7	Derrell Mitchell	95
8	Damon Allen	93
9	Tom Scott	91
	Dick Shatto	91

		FG
1	Lui Passaglia	875
2	Mark McLoughlin	673
3	Paul Osbaldiston	669
4	Troy Westwood	617
5	Paul McCallum	579
6	David Ridgway	574
7	Sean Fleming	554
8	Dave Cutler	464
9	Terry Baker	455
10	Trevor Kennerd	394

		C1
1	Lui Passgalia	1045
2	Mark McLoughlin	827
3	Troy Westwood	732
4	Sean Fleming	713
5	Paul Osbaldiston	675
6	Paul McCallum	665
7	Dave Cutler	627
8	Terry Baker	557
9	David Ridgway	541
10	Trevor Kennerd	509

		S
1	Lui Passaglia	309
2	Paul Osbaldiston	249
3	Bernie Ruoff	219
4	Dave Cutler	218
5	Terry Baker	202
6	Sean Fleming	197
7	Hank Ilesic	185
8	Troy Westwood	159
9	Trevor Kennerd	149
	Mark McLoughlin	149

	RUSHING	YDS
1	Mike Pringle	16424
2	George Reed	16116
3	Damon Allen	11920
4	Johnny Bright	10909
5	Charles Roberts	10285
6	Kelvin Anderson	9340
7	Joffrey Reynolds	9213
8	Normie Kwong	9022
9	Leo Lewis	8861
10	Dave Thelen	8463

		ATT
1	George Reed	3243
2	Mike Pringle	2962
3	Johnny Bright	1969
4	Charles Roberts	1918
5	Kelvin Anderson	1858
6	Damon Allen	1766
7	Normie Kwong	1745
8	Joffrey Reynolds	1590
9	Dave Thelen	1530
10	Jim Evenson	1460

		TD
1	George Reed	134
2	Mike Pringle	125
3	Damon Allen	93
4	Matt Dunigan	77
5	Normie Kwong	76
6	Sean Millington	75
7	Ronald Williams	71
8	Johnny Bright	70
9	Charles Roberts	69
10	Jackie Parker	67

		AVG
1	Tracy Ham	7.595
2	Willie Fleming	7.056
3	Russ Jackson	6.836
4	Damon Allen	6.750
5	Kerry Joseph	6.728
6	Doug Flutie	6.619
7	Nealon Greene	6.565
8	Leo Lewis	6.559
9	Reggie Taylor	6.381
10	Corey Holmes	6.352

400 attempts to qualify

	PASSING	YDS
1	Anthony Calvillo	73412
2	Damon Allen	72381
3	Danny McManus	53255
4	Ron Lancaster	50535
5	Matt Dunigan	43857
6	Doug Flutie	41355
7	Henry Burris	41235
8	Tracy Ham	40534
9	Ricky Ray	40531
10	Tom Clements	39041

		ATT
1	Damon Allen	9138
2	Anthony Calvillo	8686
3	Danny McManus	6689
4	Ron Lancaster	6233
5	Matt Dunigan	5476
6	Tracy Ham	4943
7	Doug Flutie	4854
8	Ricky Ray	4827
9	Henry Burris	4821
10	Kent Austin	4700

		COM
1	Anthony Calvillo	5444
2	Damon Allen	5158
3	Danny McManus	3640
4	Ron Lancaster	3384
5	Ricky Ray	3225
6	Matt Dunigan	3057
7	Doug Flutie	2975
8	Henry Burris	2908
9	Tom Clements	2807
10	Kent Austin	2709

		TD
1	Anthony Calvillo	418
2	Damon Allen	394
3	Ron Lancaster	333
4	Matt Dunigan	303
5	Tracy Ham	284
6	Doug Flutie	270
7	Danny McManus	259
8	Henry Burris	257
9	Tom Clements	252
10	Dieter Brock	210
	Ricky Ray	210

		INT
1	Ron Lancaster	396
2	Danny McManus	281
3	Damon Allen	278
4	Tom Clements	214
5	Matt Dunigan	211
6	Anthony Calvillo	205
7	Bernie Faloney	201
8	Kent Austin	191
	Tom Burgess	191
10	Sonny Wade	169

		COM%
1	Dave Dickenson	67.53
2	Ricky Ray	66.81
3	Buck Pierce	64.89
4	Anthony Calvillo	62.68
5	Jeff Garcia	61.76
6	Doug Flutie	61.29
7	Jason Maas	61.12
8	Kevin Glenn	61.09
9	Kerwin Bell	60.99
10	Darian Durant	60.66

1000 attempts to qualify

		AVG
1	Russ Jackson	9.721
2	Dave Dickenson	9.464
3	Sam Etcheverry	9.043
4	Warren Moon	8.912
5	Kenny Ploen	8.596
6	Henry Burris	8.553
7	Doug Flutie	8.520
8	David Archer	8.493
9	Tom Wilkinson	8.485
10	Casey Printers	8.483

1000 attempts to qualify

	RECEIVING	YDS
1	Milt Stegall	15153
2	Geroy Simon	15087
3	Allen Pitts	14891
4	Darren Flutie	14341
5	Terry Vaughn	13746
6	Ben Cahoon	13294
7	Ray Elgaard	13198
8	Don Narcisse	12366
9	Derrell Mitchell	12014
10	Brian Kelley	11169

		NO
1	Ben Cahoon	1017
2	Terry Vaughn	1006
3	Darren Flutie	971
4	Allen Pitts	966
5	Geroy Simon	935
6	Don Narcisse	919
7	Milt Stegall	854
8	Ray Elgaard	830
9	Derrell Mitchell	821
10	Rocky DiPietro	706

		TD
1	Milt Stegall	144
2	Allen Pitts	117
3	Geroy Simon	98
4	Brian Kelley	97
5	Derrell Mitchell	90
6	Tom Scott	88
7	Arland Bruce	84
8	Terry Evanshen	80
9	Travis Moore	79
10	Ray Elgaard	78
	David Williams	78

		AVG
1	Whit Tucker	22.397
2	Bob Simpson	22.022
3	Hal Patterson	20.593
4	Tommy Grant	19.884
5	Jim Thorpe	19.574
6	Brian Kelly	19.424
7	Willie Fleming	19.394
8	Garney Henley	19.165
9	Stephan Jones	18.838
10	Willie Armstead	18.579

200 receptions to qualify

	INTERCEPTIONS	NO
1	Less Browne	87
2	Larry Highbaugh	66
	Barron Miles	66
4	Terry Irvin	62
5	Don Wilson	61
6	Garney Henley	60
7	Don Sutherin	58
8	Larry Crawford	52
	John Wydareny	52
10	four tied with	51

		YDS
1	Less Browne	1508
2	Orlondo Steinauer	1178
3	Harry Skipper	1067
4	Don Wilson	1046
5	Paul Bennett	1004
6	Barron Miles	985
7	Andre Francis	951
8	Garney Henley	916
9	Adrion Smith	852
10	Dick Thornton	847

	PUNTING	AVG
1	Noel Prefontaine	45.899
2	Ken Clark	45.553
3	Joe Zuger	45.516
4	Bernie Ruoff	44.876
5	Zenon Andrusyshyn	44.873
6	Hank Ilesic	44.753
7	Dave Mann	44.207
8	Mike McTague	43.159
9	Terry Baker	43.097
10	Bob Cameron	42.921

1000 punts to qualify

		NO
1	Lui Passaglia	3142
2	Bob Cameron	3129
3	Paul Osbaldiston	2143
4	Hank Ilesic	2062
5	Terry Baker	2031
6	Paul McCallum	1792
7	Noel Prefontaine	1662
8	Bernie Ruoff	1600
9	Ken Clark	1592
10	Glenn Harper	1569

		YDS
1	Bob Cameron	134301
2	Lui Passaglia	133832
3	Hank Ilesic	92281
4	Paul Osbaldiiston	89103
5	Terry Baker	87529
6	Noel Prefontaine	76284
7	Paul McCallum	74375
8	Ken Clark	72520
9	Bernie Ruoff	71801
10	Glenn Harper	64319

	PUNT RETURNS	YDS
1	Henry Williams	11227
2	Paul Bennett	6358
3	Michael Clemons	6025
4	Marvin Coleman	5211
5	Winston October	4417
6	Jason Armstead	4234
7	Larry Crawford	4159
8	Keith Stokes	3734
9	Corey Holmes	3639
10	Darnell Clash	3407

		NO
1	Henry Williams	1003
2	Paul Bennett	659
3	Michael Clemons	610
4	Gene Wlasiuk	545
5	Marvin Coleman	516
6	Ed Learn	496
7	Ron Latourelle	471
8	Ron Howell	449
9	Jason Armstead	448
10	Billy Cooper	436

		AVG
1	Chad Owens	11.768
2	Dickie Harris	11.465
3	Randy Rhino	11.375
4	Corey Holmes	11.266
5	Henry Williams	11.193
6	David Shaw	10.860
7	Bashir Levingston	10.779
8	Larry Highbaugh	10.716
9	Aaron Lockett	10.679
10	Demetrius Smith	10.610

150 returns to qualify

	KICKOFFS	AVG
1	Damon Duval	62.274
2	Hank Ilesic	61.796
3	Terry Baker	59.152
4	Sandro DeAngelis	59.064
5	Sean Fleming	59.014
6	Noel Prefontaine	58.733
7	Mark McLoughlin	58.682
8	Dave Cutler	58.678
9	Bernie Ruoff	58.334
10	Larry Robinson	58.230

500 kickoffs to qualify

		NO
1	Mark McLoughlin	1370
2	Troy Westwood	1291
3	Paul Osbaldiston	1253
4	Lui Passaglia	1199
5	Sean Fleming	1186
6	David Ridgway	1068
7	Paul McCallum	1031
8	Dave Cutler	1030
9	Terry Baker	960
10	Trevor Kennerd	867

		YDS
1	Mark McLoughlin	80394
2	Troy Westwood	74093
3	Paul Osbaldiston	71423
4	Sean Fleming	69991
5	Lui Passaglia	64131
6	Dave Cutler	60438
7	Paul McCallum	59537
8	David Ridgway	58020
9	Terry Baker	56786
10	Noel Prefontaine	50452

	KICKOFF RETURNS	YDS
1	Henry Williams	7354
2	Michael Clemons	6349
3	Marvin Coleman	5565
4	Jason Armstead	5494
5	Leo Lewis	5443
6	Dwight Edwards	5384
7	Ron Hopkins	5238
8	Corey Holmes	4973
9	Larry Highbaugh	4966
10	Harvey Wylie	4293

		NO
1	Henry Williams	335
2	Michael Clemons	300
3	Jason Armstead	275
4	Dwight Edwards	247
5	Marvin Coleman	234
6	Corey Holmes	229
7	Ron Hopkins	226
8	Keith Stokes	203
9	Winston October	192
10	Leo Lewis	187

		AVG
1	Larry Highbaugh	35.220
2	Leo Lewis	29.107
3	Harvey Wylie	28.430
4	Rocky Long	27.590
5	Hal Patterson	27.343
6	Lewis Porter	26.835
7	Dave Raimey	26.586
8	Vince Phason	25.799
9	Joe Hollimon	25.254
10	Al Marcelin	25.154

100 returns to qualify

	SACKS	NO
1	Grover Covington	157.0
2	Elfrid Payton	153.0
3	Bobby Jurasin	140.0
4	James Parker	139.5
5	Joe Montford	135.0
6	Vince Goldsmith	130.5
7	Stewart Hill	126.0
8	Tyrone Jones	110.0
9	Rodney Harding	105.0
10	Will Johnson	99.0

	TACKLES	NO
1	Mike O'Shea	1320
2	Willie Pless	1277
3	Alondra Johnson	1254
4	Barrin Simpson	1006
5	Eddie Davis	913
6	Greg Battle	813
7	Kevin Eiben	783
8	Shannon Garrett	699
9	Don Wilson	697
10	Calvin Tiggle	688

	FUMBLES	NO
1	Damon Allen	161
2	Henry Burris	91
3	Anthony Calvillo	88
4	Matt Dunigan	84
5	Ricky Ray	83
6	Tracy Ham	80
7	Roy Dewalt	73
8	George Reed	70
9	Mike Pringle	66
10	Kerry Joseph	61

	TOTAL FUMBLE RECOVERIES	NO
1	Willie Pless	41
2	Damon Allen	39
3	Greg Battle	29
4	Glen Jackson	26
	Bobby Jurasin	26
6	Danny Bass	25
	Elfrid Payton	25
8	Norm Fieldgate	23
	Singor Mobley	23
	Mike Widger	23

THE ANNUAL LEADERS

YEAR		SCORING	PTS
1946	IRFU	Joe Krol, TOR	65
		Virgil Wagner, MTL	65
	WIFU	Bill Wusyk, CAL	32
1947	IRFU	Virgil Wagner, MTL	71
	WIFU	Gabe Patterson, SAS	38
1948	IRFU	Virgil Wagner, MTL	60
	WIFU	Paul Rowe, CAL	35
1949	IRFU	Virgil Wagner, MTL	77
	WIFU	Vern Graham, CAL	58
1950	IRFU	Edgar Jones, HAM	108
	WIFU	Joe Aguirre, WPG	57
1951	IRFU	Tip Logan, HAM	51
	WIFU	Bob Shaw, CAL	61
1952	IRFU	Ulysses Curtis, TOR	80
	WIFU	Bob Shaw, CAL	110
1953	IRFU	Gene Roberts, OTT	88
	WIFU	Bud Korchak, WPG	66
1954	IRFU	Alex Webster, MTL	80
	WIFU	Joe Aguirre, SAS	85
1955	IRFU	Al Pfeifer, TOR	98
	WIFU	Ken Carpenter, SAS	90
1956	IRFU	Pat Abbruzzi, MTL	120
	WIFU	Buddy Leake, WPG	103
1957	IRFU	Hal Patterson, MTL	78
	WIFU	Gerry James, WPG	131
1958	IRFU	Bill Bewley, MTL	62
	WIFU	Jack Hill, SAS	145
1959	IRFU	Cookie Gilchrist, TOR	75
	WIFU	Jackie Parker, EDM	109
1960	EFC	Cookie Gilchrist, TOR	115
	WIFU	Gerry James, WPG	114
1961	EFC	Don Sutherin, HAM	69
	WFC	Jackie Parker, WPG	104
1962	EFC	George Dixon, MTL	90
	WFC	Tommy Joe Coffey, EDM	129
1963	EFC	Dick Shatto, TOR	81
	WFC	George Fleming, WPG	135
1964	EFC	Don Sutherin, HAM	94
	WFC	Larry Robinson, CAL	106
1965	EFC	Don Sutherin, HAM	82
	WFC	Larry Robinson, CAL	95
1966	EFC	Moe Racine, OTT	71
	WFC	Hugh Campbell, SAS	102
1967	EFC	Tommy Joe Coffey, HAM	107
	WFC	Terry Evanshen, CAL	102
1968	EFC	Don Sutherin, OTT	112
	WFC	Ted Gerela, BC	115
1969	EFC	Tommy Joe Coffey, HAM	148
	EFC	Jack Abendschan, SAS	116
1970	EFC	Tommy Joe Coffey, HAM	113
	WFC	Jack Abendchan, SAS	116
1971	EFC	Gerry Organ, OTT	92
	WFC	Don Jonas, WPG	121
1972	EFC	Gerry Organ, OTT	131
	WFC	Dave Cutler, EDM	126
1973	EFC	Gerry Organm OTT	133
	WFC	Dave Cutler, EDM	123
1974	EFC	Ian Sunter, HAM	141
	WFC	Dave Cutler, EDM	144
1975	EFC	Gerry Organ, OTT	124
	WFC	Dave Cutler, EDM	169
1976	EFC	Don Sweet, MTL	141
	WFC	Bernie Ruoff, WPG	142
1977	EFC	Don Sweet, MTL	136
	WFC	Dave Cutler, EDM	195
1978	EFC	J.T. Hay, OTT	136
	WFC	Dave Cutler, EDM	167
1979	EFC	Don Sweet, MTL	111
	WFC	Bernie Ruoff, WPG	151
1980	EFC	Zenon Andrusyshyn, TOR	136
	WFC	Dave Cutler, EDM	158
1981	Eastern	Bernie Ruoff, HAM	152
	Western	Trevor Kennerd, WPG	185
1982	Eastern	Bernie Ruoff, WPG	142
	Western	Dave Cutler, EDM	170
1983	Eastern	Bernie Ruoff, WPG	191
	Western	Lui Passaglia, BC	191
1984	Eastern	Hank Ilesic, TOR	159
	Western	Lui Passaglia, BC	167
1985	Eastern	Bernie Ruoff, HAM	154
	Western	Trevor Kennerd, WPG	198
1986	Eastern	Lance Chomyc, TOR	157
	Western	Tom Dixon, EDM	190
1987	Eastern	Lance Chomyc, TOR	193
	Western	Lui Passaglia, BC	214
1988	Eastern	Lance Chomyc, TOR	207
	Western	David Ridgway, SAS	215
1989	Eastern	Paul Osbaldiston, HAM	233
	Western	Jerry Kauric, EDM	224
1990	Eastern	Paul Osvaldiston, HAM	212
	Western	David Ridgway, SAS	233
1991	Eastern	Lance Chomyc, TOR	236
	Western	David Ridgway, SAS	216
1992	Eastern	Troy Westwoood, WPG	199
	Western	Mark McLoughlin, CAL	208
1993	Eastern	Troy Westwood, WPG	209
	Western	Mark McLouglin, CAL	215
1994	Eastern	Troy Westwood, WPG	213
	Western	Sean Fleming, EDM	207
1995	North	Mark McLoughlin, CAL	220
	South	Roman Anderson, SA	235
1996	East	Mike Vanderjagt, TOR	198
	West	Mark McLoughlin, CAL	221
1997	East	Mike Vanderjagt, TOR	190
	West	Sean Fleming, EDM	187
1998	East	Terry Baker, MTL	200
	West	Lui Passaglia, BC	197
1999	East	Paul Osbaldiston, HAM	203
	West	Mark McLoughlin, CAL	192
2000	East	Terry Baker, MTL	220
	West	Mark McLoughlin, CAL	199
2001	East	Paul Osbaldiston, HAM	183
	West	Sean Fleming, EDM	183
2002	East	Terry Baker, MTL	184
	West	Troy Westwood, WPG	203
2003	East	Lawrence Tynes, OTT	198
	West	Troy Westwood, WPG	198
2004	East	Matt Kellett, MTL	174
	West	Sean Fleming, EDM	180
2005	East	Damon Duval, MTL	191
	West	Sandro DeAngelis, CAL	179
2006	East	Damon Duval, MTL	201
	West	Sandro DeAngelis, CAL	214
2007	East	Nick Setta, HAM	167
	West	Paul McCallum, BC	166
2008	East	Damon Duval, MTL	206
	West	Sandro DeAngelis, CAL	217
2009	East	Damon Duval, MTL	242
	West	Sandro DeAngelis, CAL	176
2010	East	Damon Duval, MTL	156
	West	Rob Maver, CAL	185
2011	East	Justin Medlock, HAM	197
	West	Paul McCallym, BC	203

		SCORING	TD
1946	IRFU	Virgil Wagner, MTL	13
	WIFU	Roy Wright, SAS	3
1947	IRFU	Virgil Wagner, MTL	14
	WIFU	Bob Sandberg, WPG	5
1948	IRFU	Virgil Wagner, MTL	12
	WIFU	Paul Rowe, CAL	7
1949	IRFU	Virgil Wagner, MTL	15
	WIFU	Sammy Pierce, SAS	9
1950	IRFU	Ulysses Curtis, TOR	14
	WIFU	Tom Casey, WPG	9
		Mike King, EDM	9
1951	IRFU	Howie Turner, OTT	10
		Hal Waggoner, HAM	10
	WIFU	Neill Armstrong, WPG	11
		Jimmy Chamners, EDM	11
1952	IRFU	Ulysses Curtis, TOR	16
	WIFU	Tom Casey, WPG	16
1953	IRFU	Chuck Hunsinger, MTL	11
		Avatus Stone, OTT	11
	WIFU	Rollie Miles, EDM	11
1954	IRFU	Alex Webster, MTL	16
	WIFU	Jackie Parker, EDM	13
1955	IRFU	Pat Abbruzzi, MTL	19
	WIFU	Ken Carpenter, SAS	18
1956	IRFU	Pat Abbruzzi, MTL	20
	WIFU	Bob McNamara, WPG	17
1957	IRFU	Hal Patterson, MTL	13
	WIFU	Gerry James, WPG	19
1958	IRFU	Dick Shatto, TOR	9
	WIFU	Jack Hill, SAS	16
1959	IRFU	Dave Thelen, OTT	11
	WIFU	Ernie Pitts, WPG	16
1960	EFC	George Dixon, MTL	18
	WIFU	Willie Fleming, BC	18
1961	EFC	Gerry McDougall, HAM	11
	WFC	Johnny Bright, EDM	11
1962	EFC	George Dixon, MTL	15
	WFC	Willie Fleming, BC	14
		Ray Purdin, SAS	14
1963	EFC	Dick Shatto, TOR	13
	WFC	Lovell Coleman, CAl	15
1964	EFC	Dick Shatto, TOR	11
	WFC	Hugh Campbell, SAS	11
		Bob Swift, BC	11
1965	EFC	J.W. Lockett, MTL	8
		Ted Watkins, OTT	8
	WFC	Lovell Coleman, CAL	12
		George Reed, SAS	12
1966	EFC	Tommy Grant, HAM	8
	WFC	Hugh Campbell, SAS	17
1967	EFC	Bo Scott, OTT	10
	WFC	Terry Evanshen, CAL	17
1968	EFC	Whit Tucker, OTT	13
	WFC	George Reed, SAS	16
1969	EFC	Vic Washington, OTT	14
	WFC	George Reed, SAS	12
1970	EFC	Hugh Oldham, OTT	13
	WFC	Herm Harrison, CAL	12
1971	EFC	Leon McQuay, TOR	9
	WFC	George Reed, SAS	12
1972	EFC	three tied with	8
	WFC	Mack Heron, WPG	16
1973	EFC	Garney Henley, HAM	8
	WFC	George Reed, SAS	14
1974	EFC	Johnny Rodgers, MTL	11
	WFC	Lou Harris, BC	12
1975	EFC	Art Green, OTT	14
	WFC	Willie Burden, CAL	15

1976	EFC	Art Green, OTT	15
	WFC	Jim Washington, WPG	14
1977	EFC	Richard Holmes, TOR-OTT	11
	WFC	Jim Germany, EDM	10
		Tom Scott, EDM	10
1978	EFC	Tony Gabriel, OTT	11
	WFC	James Sykes, CAL	15
1979	EFC	David Green, MTL	11
	WFC	Waddell Smith, EDM	14
1980	EFC	Richard Crump., OTT	12
	WFC	Tom Scott, EDM	14
1981	Eastern	Keith Baker, HAM	11
	Western	Jim Germany, EDM	19
		Larry Key, BC	19
1982	Eastern	Skip Walker, OTT	18
	Western	Tom Scott, EDM	13
1983	CFL	Ron Robinson, SAS-MTL	14
	Eastern	Skip Walker, OTT	12
	Western	Ray Crouse, CAL	11
		Brian Kelly, EDM	11
1984	Eastern	Lester Brown, TOR	18
	Western	Brian Kelly, EDM	18
		Willard Reaves, WPG	18
1985	Eastern	Terry Greer, TOR	9
		Steve Stapler, HAM	9
	Western	Craig Ellis, SAS	17
1986	Eastern	Craig Ellis, TOR	10
	Western	Bobby Johnson, SAS	13
1987	Eastern	Gill Fenerty, TOR	15
	Western	three tied with	13
1988	Eastern	Earl Winfield, HAM	13
	Western	David Williams, BC	18
1989	Eastern	Tony Champion, HAM	15
	Western	Blake Marshall, EDM	14
		David Williams, BC	14
1990	Eastern	Darrell Smith, TOR	20
	Western	Craig Ellis, EDM	17
1991	Eastern	Robert Mimbs, WPG	16
		Blake Marshall, EDM	20
		Jon Volpe, BC	20
1992	Eastern	Earl Winfield, HAM	11
	Western	Jim Sandusky, EDM	15
		Jon Volpe, BC	15
1993	Eastern	David Williams, WPG	15
	Western	Eddie Brown, EDM	15
		Dave Sapunjis, CAL	15
1994	Eastern	Chris Armstrong, BAL	18
		Gerald Alphin, WPG	18
	Western	Allen Pitts, CAL	21
1995	North	Cory Philpot, BC	22
	South	Mike Saundes, SA	16
1996	East	Robert Drummond, TOR	17
	West	Kelvin Anderson, CAL	14
1997	East	Robert Drummond, TOR	18
	West	Tony Burse, EDM	13
1998	East	Ronald Williams, HAM	13
	West	Kelvin Anderson, CAl	16
1999	East	Ronald Williams, HAM	15
	West	Curtis Mayfield, SAS	12
2000	East	Mike Pringle, MTL	19
	West	Kez McCorvey, EDM	15
		Travis Moore, CAL	15
2001	East	Mike Pringle, MTL	17
	West	Ed Hervey, EDM	12
		Sean Millington, BC	12
2002	East	Derrell Mitchell, TOR	14
	West	Milt Stegall, WPG	23
2003	East	Ben Cahoon, MTL	14
		Jermaine Copeland, MTL	14
	West	Mike Pringle, EDM	15
		Milt Stegall, WPG	15
2004	East	Autry Denson, MTl	12
	West	Geroy Simon, BC	14
2005	East	Arland Bruce, TOR	11
	West	Milt Stegall, WPG	17
2006	East	Robert Edwards, MTL	17
	West	Geroy Simon, BC	15
2007	East	Charles Roberts, WPG	16
	West	Joe Smith, BC	19
2008	East	Jamel Richardson, MTL	16
	West	Wes Cates, SAS	14
2009	East	Avon Cobourne, MTL	15
	West	Joffrey Reynolds, CAL	13
		Arkee Whitlock, EDM	13
2010	East	Terrence Edwards, WPG	12
	West	Wes Cates, SAS	16
2011	East	Jamel Richardson, MTL	11
	West	Jon Cornish, CAL	11

YEAR		RUSHING	YDS
1950	WIFU	Tom Casey, WPG	637
1951	WIFU	Normie Kwong, EDM	933
1952	WIFU	Johnny Bright, CAL	815
1953	WIFU	Billy Vessels	926
1954	IRFU	Alex Webster, MTL	984
	WIFU	Howie Waugh, CAL	1043
1955	IRFU	Pat Abbruzzi, MTL	1248
	WIFU	Normie Kwong, EDM	1250
1956	IRFU	Pat Abbruzzi, MTL	1062
	WIFU	Normie Kwong, EDM	1437
1957	IRFU	Gerry McDougall, HAM	1053
	WIFU	Johnny Bright, EDM	1679
1958	IRFU	Gerry McDougall, HAM	1109
	WIFU	Johnny Bright, EDM	1722
1959	IRFU	Dave Thelen, OTT	1339
	WIFU	Johnny Bright, EDM	1340
1960	EFC	Dave Thelen, ITT	1407
	WIFU	Earl Lunsford, CAL	1343
1961	EFC	Don Clark, MTL	1143
	WFC	Earl Lunsford, CAL	1794
1962	EFC	George Dixon, MTL	1520
	WFC	Nub Beamer, BC	1161
1963	EFC	George Dixon, MTL	1270
	WFC	Lovell Coleman, CAL	1343
1964	EFC	Ron Stewart, OTT	867
	WFC	Lovell Coleman, CAL	1629
1965	EFC	Dave Thelen, TOR	801
	WFC	George Reed, SAS	1768
1966	EFC	Don Lisbon, MTL	1007
	WFC	George Reed, SAS	1409
1967	EFC	Bo Scott, OTT	762
	WFC	George Reed, SAS	1471
1968	EFC	Bill Symons, TOR	1107
	WFC	George Reed, SAS	1222
1969	EFC	Dennis Duncan, MTL	1037
	WFC	George Reed, SAS	1353
1970	EFC	Bill Symons, TOR	908
	WFC	Hugh NcKinnis, CAL	1135
1971	EFC	Leon McQuay, TOR	977
	WFC	Jim Evenson, BC	1237
1972	EFC	Dave Buchanan, WPG	1163
	WFC	Mack Herron, WPG	1527
1973	EFC	Andy Hopkins, HAM	1223
	WFC	Roy Bell, EDM	1455
1974	EFC	Steve Ferrughelli, MTL	1134
	WFC	George Reed., SAS	1447
1975	EFC	Art Green, OTT	1188
	WFC	Willie Burden, CAL	1896
1976	EFC	Art Green, OTT	1257
	WFC	Jim Washington, WPG	1277
1977	EFC	Jimmy Edwards, HAM	1581
	WFC	Jim Washington, WPG	1262
1978	EFC	Jimmy Edwards, HAM	840
	WFC	Mike Strickland, SAS	1306
1979	EFC	David Green, MTL	1678
	WFC	Jim Germany, EDM	1324
1980	EFC	Richard Crump, OTT	1074
	WFC	James Sykes, CAL	1263
1981	Eestern	David Overstreet, MTL	952
	Western	James Sykes, CAL	1107
1982	Eastern	Skip Walker, OTT	1141
	Western	William Miller, WPG	1076
1983	Eastern	Skip Walker, OTT	1431
	Western	Willard Reaves, WPG	898
1984	Eastern	Dwaine Wilson, MTL	1083
	Western	Willard Reaves, WPG	1733
1985	Eastern	Ken Hobart, HAM	928
	Western	Willard Reaves, WPG	1323
1986	Eastern	Walter Benderm Ham	618
	Western	Gary Allen, CAL	1153
1987	Eastern	Willard Reaves, WPG	1471
	Western	Gary Allen, CAL	857
1988	Eastern	Orville Lee, OTT	1075
	Western	Tony Cherry, BC	889
1989	Eastern	Gill Fenerty, TOR	1247
	Western	Reggie Taylor, EDM	1503
1990	Eastern	Robert Mimbs, WPG	1341
	Western	Tracy Ham, EDM	1096
1991	Eastern	Robert Mimbs, WPG	1769
	Western	Jon Volpe, BC	1395
1992	Eastern	Mike Richardson, WPG	1153
	Western	Jon Volpe, BC	941
1993	Eastern	Mike Richardson, WPG	925
	Western	Damon Allen, EDM	920
1994	Eastern	Mike Pringle, BAL	1972
	Western	Cory Philpot, BC	1451
1995	North	Cory Philpot, BC	1308
	South	Mike Pringle, BAL	1791
1996	East	Robert Drummond, TOR	935
	West	Robert Mimbs, SAS	1403
1997	East	Mike Pringle, MTL	1775
	West	Kelvin Anderson, CAL	1088
1998	East	Mike Pringle, MTL	2065
	West	Kelvin Anderson, CAL	1325
1999	East	Mike Pringle, MTL	1656
	West	Robert Drummond, BC	1309
2000	East	Mike Pringle, MTL	1778
	West	Kelvin Anderson, CAL	1048
2001	East	Mike Jenkins, TOR	1484
	West	Kelvin Anderson, CAL	1383
2002	East	Troy Davis, HAM	1143
	West	John Avery, EDM	1448
2003	East	Troy Davis, HAM	1206
	West	Charles Roberts, WPG	1554
2004	East	Troy Davis, HAM	1628
	West	Charles Roberts, WPG	1522
2005	East	Robert Edwards, MTL	1199
	West	Charles Roberts, WPG	1624
2006	East	Charles Roberts, WPG	1609
	West	Joffrey Reynolds, CAL	1541
2007	East	Charles Roberts, WPG	1379
	West	Joe Smith, BC	1510
2008	East	Avon Cobourne, MTL	1310
	West	Joffrey Reynolds, CAL	1310
2009	East	Fred Reid, WPG	1317

	West	Joffrey Reynolds, CAL	1504
2010	East	Fred Reid, WPG	1396
	West	Joffrey Reynolds, CAL	1200
2011	East	Brandon Whitaker, MTL	1381
	West	Jerome Messam, EDM	1057

YEAR		RUSHING	TD
1946	IRFU	Virgil Wagner, MTL	11
	WIFU	Harry Hood, WPG	2
1947	IRFU	Virgil Wagner, MTL	10
	WIFU	Bob Sandberg, WPG	4
1948	IRFU	Virgil Wagner, MTL	10
	WIFU	Paul Rowe, CAL	7
1949	IRFU	Virgil Wagner, MTL	12
	WIFU	Sammy Pierce, SAS	9
1950	IRFU	Bill Gregus, HAM	10
		Edgar Jones, HAM	10
	WIFU	Mike King, EDM	9
1951	IRFU	Hal Waggoner, HAM	8
	WIFU	four tied with	7
1952	IRFU	Hal Waggoner, HAM	7
	WIFU	Normie Kwong, EDM	8
1953	IRFU	Chuck Hunsinger, MTL	6
	WIFU	Rollie Miles, EDM	8
1954	IRFU	Alex Webster, MTL	10
	WIFU	Jackie Parker, EDM	10
1955	IRFU	Pat Abbruzzi, MTL	17
	WIFU	Ken Carpenter, SAS	12
1956	IRFU	Pat Abbruzzi, MTL	17
	WIFU	Bob McNamara, WPG	13
1957	IRFU	Gerry McDougall, HAM	8
	WIFU	Gerry James, WPG	18
1958	IRFU	Gerry McDougall, HAM	7
	WIFU	Charlie Shepard, WPG	11
1959	IRFU	Dave Thelen, OTT	10
	WIFU	Johnny Bright, EDM	11
1960	EFC	Ron Stewart, OTT	15
	WFC	Johnny Bright, EDM	14
1961	EFC	George Dixon, MTL	7
	WFC	Johnny Bright, EDM	11
1962	EFC	George Dixon, MTL	11
	WFC	Earl Lunsford, CAL	8
		Ray Purdin, SAS	8
1963	EFC	George Dixon, MTL	10
	WFC	Lovell Coleman, CAL	13
1964	EFC	Dave Thelen, OTT	8
	WFC	Bob Swift, BC	11
1965	EFC	J.W.Lockett, MTL	8
	WFC	George, Reed, SAS	12
1966	EFC	Jim Dillard, OTT	7
	WFC	Bill Munsey, BVC	7
1967	EFC	Jim Dillard, TOR	7
	WFC	George Reed, SAS	15
1968	EFC	Bill Symons, TOR	9
	WFC	George Reed< SAS	16
1969	EFC	Dennis Duncan, MTL	9
	WFC	George Reed, SAS	12
1970	EFC	Dennis Duncan, MTL	6
		Bill Symons, TOR	6
	WFC	Hugh McKinnis, CAL	9
1971	EFC	Leon McQuay, TOR	5
		Bruce Van Ness, MTL	5
	WFC	George Reed, SAS	12
1972	EFC	four tied with	4
	WFC	George Reed, SAS	13
1973	EFC	Andy Hopkins,HAM	5
		Bill Symons, TOR	5
	WFC	George Reed, SAS	12
1974	EFC	three tied with	5
	WFC	Calvin Harrell, EDM	9
1975	EFC	Art Green, OTT	11
	WFC	George Reed, SS	11
1976	EFC	Art Green, OTT	13
	WFC	Jim Washington, WPG	12
1977	EFC	Richard Holmes, TOR-OTT	10
	WFC	Jim Germany, EDM	8
1978	EFC	John O'Leary, MTL	4
	WFC	James Sykes, CAL	13
1979	EFC	David Green, MTL	11
	WFC	JimGermany, EDM	9
		Larry Key, BC	9
1980	EFC	Richard Crump, OTT	9
		Skip Walker, MTL	9
	WFC	Jim Germany, EDM	10
		James Sykes, CAL	10
1981	Eastern	David Overstreet, MTL	8
	Western	Jim Germany, EDM	18
1982	Eastern	Skip Walker, OTT	13
	Western	James Sykes	11
1983	Eastern	Skip Walker, OTT	10
	Western	Ray Crouse, CAL	9
		Willard Reaves, WPG	9
1984	Eastern	Lester Brown, TOR	10
	Western	Willard Reaves, WPG	14
1985	Eastern	Ken Hobart, HAM	6
	Western	Craig Ellis, SAS	14
1986	Eastern	Walter Bender, HAM	8
	Western	Bobby Johnson, SAS	12
1987	Eastern	Gill Fenerty, TOR	12
	Western	Milson Jones, EDM	7
1988	Eastern	Gill Fenerty, TOR	10
	Western	Milson Jones, SAS	11
1989	Eastern	Derrick McAdoo, HAM	11
	Western	Blake Marshall, EDM	11
1990	Eastern	Damon Allen, TOR	7
		Matt Dunigan, TOR	7
	Western	Blake Marshall, EDM	12
1991	Eastern	Robert Mimbs, WPG	15
	Western	Blake Marshall, EDM	16
		Jon Volpe, BC	16
1992	Eastern	Rickey Foggie, TOR	8
	Western	Jon Volpe, BC	13
1993	Eastern	Matt Dunigan, WPG	11
	Western	Doug Flutie, CAL	11
1994	Eastern	Blaise Bryant, WPG	10
	Western	Tony Stewart, CAL	14
1995	North	Cory Philpot, BC	17
	South	Mike Pringle,	13
1996	East	Robert Drummond, TOR	11
	West	Kelvin Anderson, CAL	10
1997	East	Ronald Williams, WPG	16
	West	Tony Burse, EDM	13
1998	East	Ronald Williams, HAM	13
	West	Kelvin Anderson, CAL	9
		Reggie Slack, SAS	9
1999	East	Ronald Williams, HAM	14
	West	three tied with	8
2000	East	Mike Pringle, MTL	19
	West	Robert Drummond, BC	10
2001	East	Mike Prinhle, MTL	16
	West	Sean Millington, BC	11
2002	East	Lawrence Phillips, MTL	13
	West	Sean Millington, BC	14
2003	East	Josh Ranek, OTT	8
	West	Mike Pringle, EDM	13
2004	East	Troy Davis, HAM	10
	West	Kenton Keith, SAS	9
		Casey Printers, BC	9
2005	East	Kerry Joseph, OTT	9
	West	Antonio Warren, BC	13
2006	East	Robert Edwards, MTL	14
	West	three tied with	9
2007	East	Charles Roberts, WPG	16
	West	Joe Smith, BC	18
2008	East	five tied with	6
	West	Wes Cates, SAS	12
2009	East	Avon Cobourne, MTL	13
	West	Arkee Whitlock, EDM	12
2010	East	DeAndra Cobb, HAM	8
	West	Wes Cates, SAS	15
2011	East	Quinton Porter, HAM	9
	West	Jon Cornish, CAL	9

YEAR		PASSING	YDS
1950	WIFU	Lindy Berry, EDM	2201
1951	WIFU	Jack Jacobs, WPG	3248
1952	WIFU	Jack Jacobs, WPG	2586
1953	WIFU	Jack Jacobs, WPG	1924
1954	IRFU	Sam Etcheverry, MTL	3610
	WIFU	Frank Tripucka, SAS	2003
1955	IRFU	Sam Etcheverry, MTL	3657
	WIFU	Don Klosterman, CAL	2405
1956	IRFU	Sam Etcheverry, MTL	4723
	WIFU	Frank Tripucka, SAS	3274
1957	IRFU	Sam Etcheverry, MTL	3341
	WIFU	Frank Tripucka, SAS	2589
1958	IRFU	Sam Etcheverry, MTL	3548
	WIFU	Frank Tripucka, SAS	2766
1959	IRFU	Sam Etcheverry, MTL	3133
	WIFU	Joe Kapp, CAL	2990
1960	EFC	Tobin Rote, TOR	4247
	WIFU	Joe Kapp, CAL	3060
1961	EFC	Tobin Rote, TOR	3093
	WFC	Eagle Day, CAL	1800
1962	EFC	Tobin Rote, TOR	2532
	WFC	Joe Kapp, BC	3279
1963	EFC	Russ Jackson, OTT	2910
	WFC	Eagle Day, CAL	3126
1964	EFC	Russ Jackson, OTT	2156
	WFC	Joe Kapp, BC	2816
1965	EFC	Russ Jackson, OTT	2303
	WFC	Joe Kapp, BC	2961
1966	EFC	Russ Jackson, OTT	2400
	WFC	Ron Lancaster, SAS	2976
1967	EFC	Russ Jackson, OTT	3332
	WFC	Pete Liske, CAL	4479
1968	EFC	Wally Gabler, TOR	3242
	WFC	Pete Liske, CAL	4333
1969	EFC	Russ Jacskon, OTT	3641
	WFC	Jerry Keeling, CAL	3179
1970	EFC	Gary Wood, OTT	2759
	WFC	Ron Lancaster, SAS	2779
1971	EFC	Joe Theismann, TOR	2440
	WFC	Don Jonas, WPG	4036
1972	EFC	Chuck Ealey, HAM	2573
	WFC	Don Jonas, WPG	3583
1973	EFC	Joe Theismann, TOR	2496
	WFC	Ron Lancaster, SAS	3767
1974	EFC	Mike Rae, TOR	2501
	WFC	Pete Liske, CAL-BC	3259
1975	EFC	Tom Clements, OTT	2013
	WFC	Ron Lancaster, SAS	3545
1976	EFC	Tom Clements, OTT	2856
	WFC	Ron Lancaster, SAS	3869
1977	EFC	Tom Clements, OTT	2804
	WFC	Ron Lancaster, SAS	3072

1978	EFC	Jimmy Jones, HAM	2060
	WFC	Dieter Brock, WPG	3755
1979	CFL	Tom Clements, SAS-HAM	2803
	EFC	Tony Adams, TOR	2692
	WFC	Dieter Brock, WPG	2383
1980	EFC	Mark Jackson, TOR	3041
	WFC	Warren Moon, EDM	3127
1981	Eastern	Tom Clements, HAM	4536
	Western	Dieter Brock, WPG	4796
1982	Eastern	Tom Clements, HAM	4706
	Western	Warren Moon, EDM	5000
1983	Eastern	Condredge Holloway, TOR	3814
	Western	Warren Moon, EDM	5648
1984	Eastern	Dieter Brock, HAM	3966
	Western	Tom Clements, WPG	3845
1985	Eastern	J,C. Watts, OTT	2975
	Western	Roy Dewalt, BC	4237
1986	Eastern	Brian Ransom, MTL	3204
	Western	Rick Johnson, CAL	4379
1987	Eastern	Tom Clements, WPG	4686
	Western	Roy Dewalt, BC	3855
1988	Eastern	Gilbert Renfroe, TOR	4113
	Western	Matt Dunigan, BC	3776
1989	Eastern	Sean Salisbury, WPG	4049
	Western	Matt Dunigan, BC	4509
1990	Eastern	Tom Burgess, WPG	3958
	Western	Kent Austin, SAS	4604
1991	Eastern	Damon Allen, OTT	4275
	Western	Doug Flutie, BC	6619
1992	Eastern	Tom Burgess, OTT	4026
	Western	Kent Austin, SAS	6225
1993	Eastern	Tom Burgess, OTT	5063
	Western	Doug Flutie, CAL	6092
1994	Eastern	Tracy Ham, BAL	4348
	Western	Doug Flutie, CAL	5726
1995	North	Danny McManus, BC	4655
	South	Matt Dunigan, BIR	4911
1996	East	Doug Flutie, TOR	5720
	West	Danny McManus, EDM	4425
1997	East	Doug Flutie, TOR	5505
	West	Damon Allen, BC	4653
1998	East	Kerwin Bell, TOR	4991
	West	Jeff Garcia, CAL	4276
1999	East	Danny McManus,, HAM	5318
	West	Damon Allen, BC	4219
2000	East	Anthony Calvillo, MTL	4277
	West	Damon Allen, BC	4840
2001	East	Khari Jones, WPG	4545
	West	Jason Maas, EDM	3646
2002	East	Anthony Calvillo, MTL	5013
	West	Khari Jones, WPG	5334
2003	East	Anthony Calvillo, MTL	5891
	West	Dave Dickenson, BC	5496
2004	East	Anthony Calvillo, MTL	6041
	West	Jason Maas, EDM	5270
2005	East	Anthony Calvillo, MTL	5556
	West	Ricky Ray, EDM	5510
2006	East	Anthony Calvillo, MTL	4714
	West	Ricky Ray, EDM	5000
2007	East	Kevin Glenn, WPG	5117
	West	Henry Burris, CAL	4279
2008	East	Anthony Calvillo, MTL	5633
	West	Ricky Ray, EDM	5663
2009	East	Anthony Calvillo, MTL	4639
	West	Ricky Ray, EDM	4916
2010	East	Kevin Glenn, HAM	5106
	West	Darian Durant, SAS	5542
2011	East	Anthony Calvillo, MTL	5251
	West	Travis Lulay, BC	4815

YEAR		PASSING	TD
1946	IRFU	Frank Dunlap, OTT	7
	WIFU	Walt Dobler, WPG	4
1947	IRFU	Tommy Cates, MTL	6
		Frank Dunlap, OTT	6
	WIFU	Stan Stasica, SAS	3
1948	IRFU	Bruce Coulter, MTL	8
		Bob Paffrath, OTT	8
	WIFU	Keith Spaith, CAL	13
1949	IRFU	Frank Filchock, MTL	18
	WIFU	Keith Spaith, CAL	14
1950	IRFU	Al Dekdrebun, TOR	13
		Frank Filchock, MTL	13
	WIFU	Jack Jacobs, WPG	14
1951	IRFU	Tom O'Malley, OTT	20
	WIFU	Jack Jacobs, WPG	33
1952	IRFU	Nobby Wirkowski, TOR	21
	WIFU	Jack Jacobs, WPG	34
1953	IRFU	Sam Etcheverry, MTL	23
	WIFU	Frankie Albert, CAL	12
1954	IRFU	Sam Etcheverry, MTL	25
	WIFU	Frank Tripucka, SAS	14
1955	IRFU	Sam Etcheverry, MTL	30
		Tom Dublinski, TOR	30
	WIFU	Don Klosterman, CAL	13
1956	IRFU	Sam Etcheverry, MTL	32
		Arnie Galiffa, TOR	32
	WIFU	Frank Tripucka, SAS	18
1957	IRFU	Sam Etcheverry, MTL	14
	WIFU	Maury Duncan, BC	12
		Frank Tripucka, SAS	12
1958	IRFU	Sam Etcheverry, MTl	18
		Bernie Faloney, HAM	18
	WIFU	Frank Tripucka, SAS	20
1959	IRFU	Bernie Faloney, HAM	15
	WIFU	Jim Van Pelt, WPG	31
1960	EFC	Tobin Rote, TOR	38
	WIFU	Joe Kapp, CAL	18
1961	EFC	Bernie Faloney, HAM	23
	WFC	Jackie Parker, EDM	11
1962	EFC	Joe Zuger, HAm	15
	WFC	Joe Kapp, BC	28
1963	EFC	Russ Jackson, OTT	19
	WFC	Joe Kapp, BC	20
1964	EFC	Russ Jackson, OTT	18
	WFC	Ron Lancaster, SAS	16
1965	EFC	Russ Jackson, OTT	18
	WFC	Ron Lancaster, SAS	17
1966	EFC	Russ Jackson, OTT	17
	WFC	Ron Lancaster, SAS	28
1967	EFC	Russ Jackson, OTT	25
	WFC	Pete Liske, CAL	40
1968	EFC	Russ Jackson, OTT	25
	WFC	Pete Liske, CAL	31
1969	EFC	Russ Jackson, OTT	33
	WFC	Ron Lancaster, SAS	25
1970	EFC	Gary Wood, OTT	18
	WFC	Jerry Keeling, CAL	18
1971	EFC	Joe Theismann, TOR	17
	WFC	Don Jonas, WPG	27
1972	EFC	Chuck Ealey, HAM	22
	WFC	Don Jonas, WPG	27
1973	EFC	Chuck Ealey, HAM	14
	WFC	Ron Lancaster, SAS	22
1974	EFC	Jimmy Jones, MTL	18
	WFC	Ron Lancaster, SAS	20
1975	EFC	Tom Clements, OTT	13
	WFC	Ron Lancaster, SAS	23
1976	EFC	Tom Clements, OTT	20
	WFC	Ron Lancaster, SAS	25
1977	EFC	Tom Clements, OTT	16
	WFC	Dieter Brock, WPG	23
1978	EFC	Tom Clements, OTT	18
	WFC	Dieter Brock, WPOG	23
1979	EFC	Condredge Holloway, OTT	17
	WFC	Warren Moon, EDM	20
1980	EFC	Gerry Dattilio, MTL	19
	WFC	Dieter Brock, WPG	28
1981	Eastern	Tom Clements, HAM	27
	Western	Dieter Brock, WPG	32
1982	Eastern	Condredge Holloway, OTT	31
	Western	Warren Moon, EDM	36
1983	Eastern	Kevin Starkey, OTT-MTL	40
	Western	Warren Moonm, EDM	31
1984	Eastern	J.C. Watts, OTT	21
	Western	Tom Clements, WPG	29
1985	Eastern	Ken Hobart, HAM	19
	Western	Roy Dewalt, BC	27
1986	Eastern	Mike Kerrigan, HAM	16
	Western	Rick Johnson, CAL	31
1987	Eastern	Tom Clements, WPG	35
	Western	Matt Dunigan, EDM	21
1988	Eastern	Gilbert Renfroe, TOR	26
	Western	Matt Dunigan, BC	26
1989	Eastern	Sean Salisbury, WPG	26
	Western	Tracy Ham, EDM	30
1990	Eastern	Damon Allen, OTT	34
	Western	Tracy Ham, EDM	36
1991	Eastern	Damon Allen, OTT	24
	Western	Doug Flutie, BC	38
1992	Eastern	Tom Burgess, OTT	29
	Western	Kent Austin, SAS	35
1993	Eastern	Matt Dunigan, WPG	36
	Western	Doug Flutie, CAL	44
1994	Eastern	Matt Dunigan, WPG	31
	Western	Doug Flutie, CAL	48
1995	North	Jeff Garcia, CAL	25
	South	Matt Dunigan, BIR	34
1996	East	Doug Flutie, TOR	29
	West	Jeff Garcia, CAL	25
1997	East	Doug Flutie, TOR	47
	West	Jeff Garcia, CAL	33
1998	East	Kerwin Bell, TOR	27
	West	Jeff Garcia, CAl	28
1999	East	Danny McManus, HAM	28
	West	Damon Allen, BC	22
2000	East	Khari Jones, WPG	31
	West	Dave Dickenson, CAL	36
2001	East	Danny McManus, HAM	19
	West	Khari Jones, WPG	30
2002	East	Anthony Calvillo, MTL	27
	West	Kahri Jones, WPG	46
2003	East	Anthony Calvillo, MTL	37
	West	Dave Dickenson, BC	36
2004	East	Anthony Calvillo, MTL	31
	West	Casey Printers, BC	35
2005	East	Anthony Calvillo, MTL	34
	West	Kevin Glenn, WPG	27
2006	East	Anthony Calvillo, MTL	20
	West	Henry Burris, CAL	23
2007	East	Kevin Glenn, WPG	25
	West	Henry Burris, CAL	34
2008	East	Anthony Calvillo, MTL	43
	West	Henry Burris, CAL	39
2009	East	Anthony Calvillo, MTL	26
	West	Darian Durant, SAS	24

2010	East	Kevin Glenn, HAM	33
	West	Henry Burris, CAL	38
2011	East	Anthony Calvillo, MTL	32
	West	Travis Lulay, BC	32

YEAR		RECEIVING	YDS
1950	WIFU	Ezzrett Anderson, CAL	673
1951	WIFU	Neill Armstrong, WPG	1024
1952	WIFU	Bob Shaw, CAL	1094
1953	WIFU	Bud Grant, WPG	922
1954	IRFU	AL Pfeifer, TOR	1142
	WIFU	Rupe Andrews, CAL	904
1955	IRFU	Al Pfeifer, TOR	1342
	WIFU	Willie Roberts, CAL	1091
1956	IRFU	Hal Patterson, MTL	1914
	WIFU	Bud Grant, WPG	970
1957	IRFU	Red O'Quinn	1006
	WIFU	Ernie Pitts, WPG	683
1958	IRFU	Red O'Quinn, MTL	962
	WIFU	Jack Hill, SAS	1065
1959	IRFU	Bob Simpson, OTT	787
	WIFU	Ernie Pitts, WPG	1126
1960	EFC	Dave Mann, TOR	1380
	WIFU	Gene Filipski, CAL	875
1961	EFC	Dave Mann, TOR	659
	WFC	Farrell Funston, WPG	892
1962	EFC	Hal Patterson, HAM	881
	WFC	Tommy Joe Coffey, EDM	951
1963	EFC	Whit Tucker, OTT	967
	WFC	Tommy Joe Coffey, EDM	1104
1964	EFC	Tommy Grant, HAM	1029
	WFC	Tommy Joe Coffey, EDM	1142
1965	EFC	Ted Watkins, OTT	724
	WFC	Hugh Campbell, SAS	1329
1966	EFC	Bobby Taylor, TOR	827
	WFC	Terry Evanshen, CAL	1200
1967	EFC	Whit Tucker, OTT	1171
	WFC	Terry Evanshen, CAL	1662
1968	EFC	Bobby Taylor, TOR	985
	WFC	Herm Harriosn, CAL	1306
1969	EFC	Margene Adkins, OTT	1402
	WFC	Herm Harrison, CAL	1043
1970	EFC	Hugh Oldham, OTT	1043
	WFC	Jim Young, BC	1041
1971	EFC	Terry Evanshen, MTL	852
	WFC	Jim Thorpe, WPG	1436
1972	EFC	Eric Allen, TOR	1067
	WFC	Jim Young, BC	1362
1973	EFC	Johnny Rodgers, MTL	841
	WFC	George McGowan, EDM	1123
1974	EFC	Johnny Rodgers, MTL	1024
	WFC	Rudy Linterman, CAL	951
1975	EFC	Tony Gabriel, OTT	1115
	WFC	George McGowan, EDM	1472
1976	EFC	Tony Gabriel, OTT	1320
	WFC	Rhett Dawson, SAS	996
1977	EFC	Tony Gabriel, OTT	1362
	WFC	Tom Scott, WPG	1079
1978	EFC	Tony Gabriel, OTT	1091
	WFC	Tom Scott, EDM	1091
1979	EFC	Leif Pattersen, HAM	838
	WFC	Waddell Smith, EDM	1214
1980	EFC	Bob Gaddis, TOR	1112
	WFC	Tom Scott, EDM	1245
1981	Eastern	James Scott, MTL	1422
	Western	Joe Walters, SAS	1715
1982	Eastern	Terry Greer, TOR	1466
	Western	Joey Walters, SAS	1692
1983	Eastern	Terry Greer, TOR	2003
	Western	Brian Kelly, EDM	1812
1984	Eastern	Terry Greer, TOR	1189
	Western	Mervyn Fernandez, BC	1486
1985	Eastern	Terry Greer, TOR	1323
	Western	Mervyn Fernandez, BC	1727
1986	Eastern	James Hood, MTL	1411
	Western	James Murphy, WPG	1746
1987	Eastern	Steve Stapler, HAM	1516
	Western	Brian Kelly, EDM	1626
1988	Eastern	James Murphy, WPG	1409
	Western	David Williams, BC	1468
1989	Eastern	Tony Champion, HAM	1656
	Western	Larry Willis, CAL	1451
1990	Eastern	Darrell Smith, TOR	1826
	Western	Craig Ellis, EDM	1654
1991	Eastern	Darrell Smith, TOR	1399
	Western	Allen Pitts, CAL	1764
1992	Eastern	Stephan Jones, OTT	1400
	Western	Allen Pitts, CAL	1591
1993	Eastern	Gerald Wilcox, WPG	1340
	Western	Dave Sapunjis, CAL	1484
1994	Eastern	Gerald Wilcox, WPG	1624
	Western	Allen Pitts, CAL	2036
1995	North	Marcus Grant, BIR	1559
	South	Dave Sapunjis, CAL	1655
1996	East	Mac Cody, HAM	1426
	West	Darren Flutie, EDM	1362
1997	East	Milt Stegall, WPG	1616
	West	Alfred Jackson, BC	1322
1998	East	Darrell Mitchell, TOR	2000
	West	Allen Pitts, CAL	1372
1999	East	Milt Stegall, WPG	1193
	West	Allen Pitts, CAL	1449
2000	East	Milt Stegall, WPG	1499
	West	Curtis Marsh	1560
2001	East	Milt Stegall, WPG	1214
	West	Terry Vaughn, EDM	1497
2002	East	Ben Cahoon, MTL	1060
	West	Milt Stegall, WPG	1896
2003	East	Jeremaine Copeland, MTL	1757
	West	Geroy Simon, BC	1687
2004	East	Craig Yeast, HAM	1184
	West	Geroy Simon, BC	1750
2005	East	Kerry Watkins, MTL	1364
	West	Jason Tucker, EDM	1411
2006	East	Arland Bruce, TOR	1370
	West	Geroy Simon, BC	1856
2007	East	Terrence Edwards, WPG	1280
	West	Geroy Simon, BC	1293
2008	East	Jamel Richardson, MTL	1287
	West	Ken-Yon Rambo, CAL	1473
2009	East	Kerry Watkins, MTL	1243
	West	Fred Stamps, EDM	1402
2010	East	Terrence Edwards, WPG	1372
	West	Andrew Fantuz, SAS	1380
2011	East	Jamel Richardson, MTL	1777
	West	Geroy Simon, BC	1350

YEAR		RECEIVING	TD
1946	IRFU	Ken Charlton, OTT	3
	WIFU	four tied with	2
1947	IRFU	Ken Charlton, OTT	3
		Virgil Wagner, MTL	3
	WIFU	Sully Glasser, SAS	2
1948	IRFU	Bob Cunningham MTL	5
	WIFU	Woody Strode, CAL	5
1949	IRFU	Bob Cunningham, MTL	6
	WIFU	Ezzrett Anderson, CAL	5
		Matt Anthony, SAS	5
1950	IRFU	Ulysses Curtis, TOR	7
	WIFU	Tommy Ford, WPG	5
1951	IRFU	Al Pfeifer, TOR	8
	WIFU	Neill Armstrong, WPG	10
1952	IRFU	Ulysses Curtis, TOR	10
	WIFU	Paul Salata, CAL	11
1953	IRFU	Bernie Flowers, OTT	9
	WIFU	three tied withy	7
1954	IRFU	Ray Ramsey, HA	8
	WIFU	Ken Carpenter, SAS	6
1955	IRFU	Al Pfeifer, TOR	15
	WIFU	Ken Carpenter, SAS	6
1956	IRFU	Hal Patterson, MTL	12
	WIFU	Ed Vereb, BC	7
1957	IRFU	three tied with	7
	WIFU	Jerry Janes, BC	6
1958	IRFU	Tommy Grant, HAM	7
	WIFU	Ernie Pitts, WPG	6
1959	IRFU	Ron Howell, HAM	8
		Bob Simpson, OTT	8
	WIFU	Ernie Pitts, WPG	16
1960	EFC	Dave Mann, TOR	13
	WIFU	three tied with	8
1961	EFC	Paul Dekker, HAM	7
		Gerry McDougall, HAM	7
	WFC	Farrell Funston, WPG	8
1962	EFC	Garney Henley, HAM	10
	WFC	Tommy Joe Coffey, EDM	11
1963	EFC	Dick Shatto, TOR	10
	WFC	Farrel Funston, WPG	9
1964	EFC	Dick Shatto, TOR	9
	WFC	Hugh Campbell, SAS	11
1965	EFC	Ted Watkins, OTT	8
	WFC	Hugh Campbell, SAS	10
1966	EFC	Tommy Grant, HAM	8
	WFC	Hugh Campbell, SAS	17
1967	EFC	Whit Tucker, OTT	9
	WFC	Terry Evanshen, CAL	17
1968	EFC	Whit Tucker, OTT	13
	WFC	Terry Evanshen, CAL	9
1969	EFC	Tommy Joe Coffey, HAM	11
	WFC	Hugh Campbell,SAS	11
1970	EFC	Hugh Oldham, OTT	13
	WFC	Herm Harrison, CAL	12
1971	EFC	Hugh Oldham, OTT	6
	WFC	Jim Thorpe, WPG	9
1972	EFC	Eric Allen, TOR	8
		Tommy Joe Coffey, HAM	8
	WFC	Gerry Shaw, CAL	12
1973	EFC	Garney Henley, HAM	8
	WFC	George McGowan, EDM	9
1974	EFC	Peter Dalla Riva, MTL	8
	WFC	Tom Scott, WOPG	5
1975	EFC	Terry Evanshen, HAM	13
	WFC	Rhett Dawson, SAS	10
1976	EFC	Tony Gabriel, OTT	14
	WFC	Rhett Dawson, SAS	10
1977	EFC	Peter Dalla Riva, MTL	8
		Tony Gabriel, OTT	8
	WFC	Tom Scott, WPG	10
1978	EFC	Tony Gabriel, OTT	11
	WFC	Tom Scott, WPG	10
1979	EFC	Tony Gabriel, OTT	8
	WFC	Waddel Smith, EDM	13
1980	EFC	Dave Newman, TOR	10
	WFC	Tom Scott, EDM	13
1981	Eastern	Keith Baker, HAM	11
	Western	Eugene Goodlow, WPG	14

		Joey Walters, SAS	14
1982	Eastern	Terry Greer, TOR	11
	Western	Tom Scott, EDM	13
1983	CFL	Ron Robinson, SAS-MTL	14
	Eastern	Emanuel Tolbert, TOR	11
	Western	Brian Kelly, EDM	11
1984	Eastern	Terry Greer, TOR	14
	Western	Brian Kelly, EDM	18
1985	Eastern	Terry Greer, TOR	9
		Steve Stapler, HAM	9
	Western	Mervyn Fernandez, BC	15
1986	Eastern	Mark Barousse, OTT	8
	Western	James Murphy, WPG	12
1987	Eastern	Steve Stapler, HAM	13
	Western	Brian Kelly, EDM	13
1988	Eastern	Jeff Boyd, TOR	11
	Western	David Williams, BC	18
1989	Eastern	Tony Champion, HAM	15
	Western	David Williams, BC	14
1990	Eastern	Darrell Smith, TIR	20
	Western	Craig Ellis, EDM	17
1991	CFL	David Williams, EDM-TOR	15
	Eastern	Rocket Ismail, TOR	9
		Darrell Smith, TOR	9
	Western/CFL	Allen Pitts, CAL	15
1992	Eastern	Stephan Jones, OTT	10
		Larry Thompson, WPG	10
	Western	Jim Sandusky, EDM	15
1993	Eastern	David Williams, WPG	15
	Western	Eddie Brown, EDM	15
		Dave Sapunjis, CAL	15
1994	Eastern	Chris Armstrong, BAL	18
		Gerald Alphin, WPG	18
	Western	Allen Pitts, CAL	21
1995	North	Earl Winfield, HAM	13
	South	Chris Armstrong, BAL	11
		Marcus Grant, BIR	11
1996	East	Mac Cody, HAM	11
	West	Allen Pitts, CAL	11
1997	East	Darrell Mitchell, TOR	17
	West	Alfred Jackson, BC	10
1998	East	Darrell Mitchell, TOR	10
	West	Allen Pitts, CAL	11
1999	East	three tied with	7
	West	Terry Vaughn, EDM	11
2000	East	Milt Stegall, WPG	15
	West	Kez McCorvey, EDM	15
		Travis Moore, CAL	15
2001	East	Milt Stegall, WPG	14
	West	Ed Hervey, EDM	12
2002	East	Darrell Mitchell, TOR	13
	West	Milt Stegall, WPG	23
2003	East	Jermaine Copeland, MTL	14
	West	Milt Stegall, WPG	15
2004	East	Jermaine Copeland, MTL	10
	West	Geroy Simon, NC	14
2005	East	Arland Bruce, TOR	11
	West	Milt Stegall, WPG	17
2006	East	Arland Bruce, TOR	11
	West	Geroy Simon, BC	15
2007	East	Terrence Edwards, WPG	9
	West	Jermaine Copeland, CAL	10
		D.J. Flick, SAS	10
		Ken-Yon Rambo, CAL	10
2008	East	Jamel Richardson, MTL	16
	West	Nik Lewis, CAL	10
		Geroy Simon, BC	10
2009	East	Arland Bruce, TOR-HAM	10
	West	Jermaine Copeland, CAL	12
2010	East	Terrence Edwards, WPG	12
	West	Romby Bryant, CAL	15
2011	East	Jamel Richardson, MTL	11
	West	Chris Getzlaf, SAS	10

YEAR		**INTERCEPTIONS**	**NO**
1952	WIFU	Butch Avinger, SAS	8
1953	WIFU	Tom Casey, WPG	7
		Ray Willsey, EDM	7
1954	IRFU	Bill McFarlane, TOR	10
	WIFU	Stan Williams, SAS	8
1955	IRFU	Hal Patterson, MTL	7
	WIFU	Rupe Andrews, EDM	8
1956	IRFU	Tirel Burton, OTT	8
		Ray Truant, HAM	8
	WIFU	Oscar Kruger, EDM	7
1957	IRFU	George Brancato, OTT	7
		Ralph Goldston, HAM	7
	WIFU	Oscar Kruger, EDM	7
1958	IRFU	Tom Hugo, MTL	9
	WIFU	Rollie Miles, EDM	10
1959	IRFU	Ralph Goldston, HAM	9
	WIFU	Kenny Ploen, WPG	10
		Harvey Wylie, CAL	10
1960	EFC	Jim Rountree, TOR	10
	WIFU	Clare Exelby, CAL	8
1961	EFC	Don Sutherin, HAM	11
	WFC	Oscar Kruger, EDM	6
1962	EFC	Don Sutherin, HAM	8
	WFC	Gene Wlasiuk, SAS	5
		Harvey Wylie, CAL	5
1963	EFC	Garney Henley, HAM	6
	WFC	Dale West, SAS	10
1964	EFC	three tied with	6
	WFC	Bill Munsey, BC	9
1965	EFC	Billy Wayte, HAM	9
	WFC	Henry Janzen, WPG	7
1966	EFC	Joe Poirier, OTT	9
	WFC	Norm Fieldgate, BC	6
		Bill Redell, EDM	6
1967	EFC	Bob O'Billovich, OTT	7
	WFC	Joe Hernandez, EDM	6
		John Wydareny, EDM	6
1968	EFC	Ed Learn, TOR	7
	WFC	Bob Kosid, SAS	8
1969	EFC	Don Sutherin, OTT	10
	WFC	John Wydareny, EDM	11
1970	EFC	Garney Henley, HAM	10
	WFC	John Wyadreny, EDM	11
1971	EFC	Al Brenner, HAM	9
	WFC	Bruce Bennett, SAS	8
1972	EFC	Al Brenner, HAM	15
	WFC	Pete Ribbins, WPG	9
1973	EFC	Al Marcelin, OTT	8
	WFC	Lorne Richardson, SAS	7
		Mike Wilson, SAS	7
1974	EFC	Al Marcelin, OTT	8
	WFC	five tied with	5
1975	EFC	Wayne Tosh, OTT	9
	WFC	Vern Roberson, CAL	10
1976	EFC	Lewis Porter, HAM	6
	WFC	Grady Cavness, BC	7
		Lorne Richardson, SAS	7
		Merv Walker, WPG	7
		Chuck Wills, WPG	7
1977	EFC	Vernon Perry, MTL	9
	WFC	Merv Walker, WPG	6
1978	EFC	Kenny Downing, OTT	7
	WFC	Joe Hollimon, EDM	8
1979	EFC	Mike Nelms, OTT	10
	WFC	Larry Highbaugh, EDM	10
1980	EFC	Billy Hardee, TOR	7
	WFC	Ed Jones, EDM	10
		Ken McEachern, SAS	10
1981	Eastern	Harold Woods, HAM	6
	Western	Larry Crawford, BC	8
1982	Eastern	Mark Young, MTL	7
	Western	Joe Hollimon, EDM	9
1983	Eastern	Harry Skipper, MTL	10
	Western	Larry Crawford, BC	12
1984	Eastern	Gerald Bess, HAM	12
	Western	Darryl Hall, EDM	11
		Terry Irvin, SAS	11
1985	Eastern	Paul Bennett, HAM	12
		Less Browne, HAM	12
	Western	Darnell Clash, BC	9
		Laurent Des Lauriers, EDM	9
1986	Eastern	Terry Irvin, MTL	12
	Western	Larry Crawford, BC	9
1987	Eastern	Roy Bennett, WPG	13
	Western	Keith Gooch, BC	9
1988	Eastern	Troy Wilson, OTT	10
	Western	Chris Major, CAL	10
1989	Eastern	Rod Hill, WPG	12
	Western	Albert Brown, SAS	8
1990	Eastern	Less Browne, WPG	14
	Western	Andre Francis, EDM	7
		Keith Gooch, EDM	7
1991	Eastern	Less Browne, WPG	10
	Western	Glen Suitor, SAS	8
1992	Eastern	Less Browne, OTT	11
	Western	Damion Lyons, EDM	8
1993	Eastern	Darryl Sampson, WPG	6
		Remi Trudel, OTT	6
	Western	Andre Francis, NC	8
1994	Eastern	Joe Fuller, SHR	8
	Western	Less Browne, BC	11
1995	North	Eric Carter, HAM	10
	South	Andre Strode, BIR	7
1996	East	Charles Gordon, MTL	7
	West	Al Jordan, CAL	8
1997	East	Orlondo Steinauer, HAM	7
	West	Kavis Reed, EDM	7
1998	East	Orlondo Steinauer, HAM	8
	West	Mustafah Muhammad, BC	10
1999	East	Gerald Vaughn, HAM	9
	West	William Hampton, CAL	8
2000	East	Davis Sanchez, MTL	9
	West	Greg Frers, CAL	7
2001	East	Juran Bolden, WPG	6
		Rob Hitchcock, HAM	6
		Wayne Shaw, TOR	6
	West	William Fields, CAL	5
		Michael Fletcher, BC	5
		Jackie Kellogg, CAL-EDM	5
2002	East	Rob Hitchcock, HAM	8
		Clifford Ivory, TOR	8
	West	four tied with	5
2003	East	Adrion Smith, TOR	8
	West	Brian Clark, WPG	7
		Jackie Mitchell, SAS	7
2004	East	Almondo Curry, MTL	5
	West	Malcolm Frank, EDM	7
2005	East	Korey Banks, OTT	10
	West	Barron Miles, BC	6
2006	East	Byron Parker, TOR	8
	West	Barron Miles, BC	10

2007	East	Orlondo Steinauer, TOR	7
	West	Rudy Phillips, BC	12
2008	East	Chris Thompson, HAM	9
	West	Barron Miles, BC	9
2009	East	Lenny Walls, WPG	7
	West	Barron Miles, BC	8
2010	East	Jerald Brown, MTL	5
	West	James Patrick, SAS	9
2011	East	Jovon Johnson, WPG	8
	West	Rod Williams, EDM	6

YEAR		PUNTING	AVG
1950	WIFU	Keith Spaith, CAL	41.5
1951	WIFU	Glenn Dobbs, SAS	44.2
1952	WIFU	Butch Avinger, SAS	44.7
1953	WIFU	Rod Pantages, EDM	44.4
1954	IRFU	Cam Fraser, HAM	43.1
	WIFU	Larry Isbell, SAS	46.3
1955	IRFU	Cam Fraser, HAM	47.4
	WIFU	Bob Heydenfeldt, EDM	43.3
1956	IRFU	Cam Fraser, HAM	46.0
	WIFU	Larry Isbell, SAS	44.2
1957	IRFU	Cam Fraser, HAM	46.0
	WIFU	Vic Chapman, BC	42.4
1958	IRFU	Cam Fraser, HAM	45.6
	WIFU	Charlie Shepard, WPG	44.2
1959	IRFU	Cam Fraser, HAM	45.1
	WIFU	Charlie Shepard, WPG	43.1
1960	EFC	Dave Mann, TOR	43.9
	WIFU	Chralie Shepard, WPG	44.7
1961	EFC	Dave Mann, TOR	48.0
	WFC	Bobby Walden, EDM	46.9
1962	EFC	Dave Mann, TOR	43.7
	WFC	Ferdie Burket, SAS	45.3
1963	EFC	Dave Mann, TOR	41.7
	WFC	Martin Fabi, SAS	44.0
1964	EFC	Joe Zuger, HAM	42.8
	WFC	Neal Beaumont, BC	42.2
1965	EFC	Joe Zuger, HAM	44.7
	WFC	Martin Fabi, SAS	42.5
1966	EFC	Joe Zuger, HAM	44.0
	WFC	Randy Kerbow, EDM	42.9
1967	EFC	Dave Mann, TOR	46.8
	WFC	Randy Kerbow, EDM	41.7
1968	EFC	Joe Zuger, HAM	48.4
	WFC	Ed Ulmer, WPG	43.0
1969	EFC	Joe Zuger, HAM	48.2
	WFC	Ed Ulmer, WPG	40.8
1970	EFC	Dave Mann, TOR	44.8
	WFC	Ken Phillips, BC	44.6
1971	EFC	Joe Zuger, HAM	48.5
	WFC	Bill Van Burkleo, CAL	41.8
1972	EFC	Zenon Andrusyshyn, TOR	45.0
	WFC	Eric Guthrie, BC	42.2
1973	EFC	Zenon Andrusyshyn, TOR	45.6
	WFC	Walt McKee, WPG	44.2
1974	EFC	Zenon Andrusyshyn, TOR	46.9
	WFC	Walt McKee, WPG	41.8
1975	EFC	Ken Clark, HAM	43.8
	WFC	Gerald Kunyk, CAL	45.9
1976	EFC	Ken Clark, HAM	47.0
	WFC	Bernie Ruoff, WPG	45.1
1977	EFC	Ken Clark, HAM	46.8
	WFC	Hank Ilesic, EDM	45.1
1978	EFC	Ken Clark, HAM-TOR	45.1
	WFC	Hank Ilesic, EDM	47.3
1979	EFC	Zenon Andrusyshyn, HAM	43.2
	WFC	Lui Passaglia, BC	47.3
1980	EFC	Zenon Andrusyshyn, TOR	45.3
	WFC	Hank Ilesic, EDM	45.6
1981	Eastern	Zenon Andrusyshyn, TOR	47.2
	Western	Lui Passaglia, BC	46.0
1982	Eastern	Zenon Andrusyshyhn, TOR	45.8
	Western	Hank Ilesic, EDM	46.1
1983	Eastern	Bernie Ruoff, HAM	47.4
	Western	Lui Passaglia, BC	50.2
1984	Eastern	Ken Clark, OTT	46.8
	Western	Lui Passaglia, BC	46.4
1985	Eastern	Ken Clark, OTT	47.0
	Western	Tom Dixon, EDM	45.5
1986	Eastern	Hank Ilesic, TOR	48.5
	Western	Tom Dixon, EDM	45.3
1987	Eastern	Hank Ilesic, TOR	42.6
	Western	Glenn Harper, CAL	42.8
1988	Eastern	Hank Ilesic, TOR	44.0
	Western	Jerry Kauric, EDM	43.6
1989	Eastern	Hank Ilesic, TOR	42.6
	Western	Lui Passaglia, BC	41.2
1990	Eastern	Bob Cameron, WPG	42.0
	Western	Brent Matich, CAL	43.1
1991	Eastern	Hank Ilesic, TOR	44.4
	Western	Brent Matich, CAL	42.7
1992	Eastern	Hank Ilesic, TOR	45.0
	Western	Glenn Harper, EDM	40.5
1993	Eastern	Bob Cameron, WPG	42.0
	Western	Glenn Harper, EDM	41.5
1994	Eastern	Josh Miller, BAL	42.9
	Western	Tony Martino, CAL	42.6
1995	North	Bob Cameron, WPG	42.6
	South	Josh Miller, BAL	47.7
1996	East	Paul Osbaldiston, HAM	43.9
	West	Tony Martino, CAL	43.5
1997	East	Mike Vanderjagt, TOR	44.9
	West	Tony Martino, CAL	44.6
1998	East	Noel Prefontaine, TOR	46.7
	West	Tony Martino, CAL	48.2
1999	East	Noel Prefontaine, TOR	47.7
	West	Lui Passaglia, BC	42.0
2000	East	Noel Prefontaine, TOR	46.8
	West	Tony Martino, CAL	43.1
2001	East	Paul Osbaldiston, HAM	43.01
	West	Sean Fleming, EDM	43.02
2002	East	Noel Prefontaine, TOR	46.1
	West	Duncan O'Mahony, CAL	45.5
2003	East	Noel Prefontaine, TOR	46.9
	West	Sean Fleming, EDM	41.7
2004	East	Noel Prefontaine, TOR	45.9
	West	Jon Ryan, WPG	43.2
2005	East	Noel Prefontaine, TOR	45.2
	West	Burke Dales, CAL	44.3
2006	East	Noel Prefontaine, TOR	46.3
	West	Burke Dales, CAL	45.0
2007	East	Damon Duval, MTL	47.0
	West	Paul McCallum, BC	44.3
2008	East	Nick Setta, HAM	47.4
	West	Noel Prefontaine, EDM	46.9
2009	East	Damon Duval, MTL	44.8
	West	Burke Dales, CAL	46.0
2010	East	Mike Renaud, WPG	42.9
	West	Burke Dales, CAL	45.5
2011	East	Noel Prefontaine, TOR	43.3
	West	Burke Dales, CAL	47.2

YEAR		PUNT RETURNS	YDS
1951	WIFU	Ken Charlton, SAS	388
1952	WIFU	Gerry James, WPG	517
1953	WIFU	Herb Johnson, SAS	634
1954	IRFU	Johnny Fedosoff, TOR	605
	WIFU	Gordie Rowland, WPG	435
1955	IRFU	Dick Brown, TOR	614
	WIFU	Harry Lunn, SAS	486
1956	IRFU	Don Pinhey, OTT	416
	WIFU	Pete Thodos, SAS	363
1957	IRFU	Davey West, TOR	479
	WIFU	Gordie Rowland, WPG	428
1958	IRFU	Don Pinhey, OTT	563
	WIFU	Mike Hagler, SAS	768
1959	IRFU	Ron Howell, HAM	478
	WIFU	Henry Janzen, WPG	499
1960	EFC	Harry Lunn, HAM	262
	WIFU	Gene Wlasiuk, SAS	322
1961	EFC	Len Chandler, OTT	372
	WFC	Henry Janzen, WPG	394
1962	EFC	Ed Learn, MTL	379
	WFC	Gene Wlasiuk, SAS	407
1963	EFC	Ted Page, MTL	307
	WFC	Jim Copeland, SAS	352
1964	EFC	Ted Page, MTL	428
	WFC	Ron Morris, BC	407
1965	EFC	Garney Henley, HAM	657
	WFC	Gene Wlasiuk,, SAS	528
1966	EFC	Garney Henley, HAM	438
	WFC	Gene Wlaskiuk, SAS	486
1967	EFC	Ed Learn, TOR	460
	WFC	Trent Walters, EDM	403
1968	EFC	Jim Copeland, TOR	514
	WFC	Rudy Linterman, CAL	668
1969	EFC	Mike Eben, TOR	487
	WFC	Jim Silye, CAL	566
1970	EFC	Ed Turek, HAM	339
	WFC	Jim Silye, Cal	729
1971	EFC	Brad Upshaw, MTL	483
	WFC	Steve Molnar, SAS	541
1972	EFC	Elmer Sprogis, TOR	458
	WFC	Jim Walter, SAS	406
1973	EFC	Dickie Adams, OTT	327
	WFC	Jim Walter, SA	451
1974	EFC	Dickie Adams, OTT	608
	WFC	Dave Campbell, EDM	380
1975	EFC	Johnny Rodgers, MTL	912
	WFC	Larry Highbaugh, EDM	705
1976	EFC	Johnny Rodgers, MTL	931
	WFC	Rocky Long, BC	688
1977	EFC	Paul Bennett, TOR	965
	WFC	Rocky Long BC	774
1978	EFC	Randy Rhino, MTL	868
	WFC	Leon Bright, BC	498
1979	EFC	Mike Nelms, OTT	1155
	WFC	Gregg Butler, EDM	623
1980	EFC	Dickie Harris, MTL	472
	WFC	Leon Bright, BC	790
1981	Eastern	Randy Rhino, OTT	918
	Western	Paul Bennett, WPG	892
1982	Eastern	Preston Young, MTL	672
	Western	Paul Bennett, WPG	845
1983	Eastern	Jeff Patterson, MTL	503
	Western	Paul Bennett, WPG	890
1984	Eastern	Rufus Crawford, HAM	1107
	Western	Fran McDermott, SAS	724
1985	Eastern	Daric Zeno, OTT	590
	Western	Darnell Clash, BC	1148
1986	Eastern	Paul Bennett, HAM	728
	Western	Gary Allen, CAL	768
1987	Eastern	Darnell Clash, TOR	853
	Western	Henry Williams, EDM	951
1988	Eastern	Earl Winfield, HAM	865

	Western	Henry Williamns, EDM	964
1989	Eastern	Tyrone Thurman, OTT	678
	Western	Tony Hunter, EDM	1181
1990	Eastern	Michael Clemons, TOR	1045
	Western	Henry Williams, EDM	987
1991	Eastern	Anthony Drawhorn, OTT	677
	Western	Henry Williams, EDM	1440
1992	Eastern	Treamelle Taylor, OTT	936
	Western	Henry Williams, EDM	1124
1993	Eastern	Michael Clemons, TOR	716
	Western	Henry Williams, EDM	1157
1994	Eastern	Michael Clemons, TOR	671
	Western	Rod Harris, SAC	869
1995	North	Henry Williams, EDM	871
	South	Chris Wright, BAL	1236
1996	East	Jimmy Cunningham, TOR	976
	West	Marvin Coleman, CAL	714
1997	East	Michael Clemons, TOR	1070
	West	Henry Williams, EDM	821
1998	East	Eric Blount, WPG	1051
	West	Marvin Coleman, CAL	635
1999	East	Winston October, MTL	724
	West	Jimmy Cunningham, BC	662
2000	East	Winston October, MTL	898
	West	Marvin Coleman, CAL	946
2001	East	Charles Roberts, WPG	782
	West	Antonio Warren, CAL	764
2002	East	Keith Stokes, MTL	896
	West	Corey Holmes, SAS	1023
2003	East	Bashir Levinsgton, TOR	811
	West	Winston October, EDM	719
2004	East	Jason Armstead, OTT	821
	West	Keith Stokes, WPG	949
2005	East	Jason Armstead, OTT	699
	West	Tony Tompkins, EDM	931
2006	East	Albert Johnson, WPG	810
	West	Dominique Dorsey, SAS	591
2007	East	Dominique Dorsey, TOR	703
	West	Ian Smart, BC	912
2008	East	Dominique Dorsey, TOR	782
	West	Tristan Jackson, EDM	809
2009	East	Larry Taylor, MTL	788
	West	Tristan Jackson, EDM	761
2010	East	Chad Owens, TOR	1060
	West	Yonus Davis, BC	761
2011	East	Chad Owens, TOR	754
	West	Larry Taylor, CAL	538

YEAR		KICKOFFS	AVG
1952	WIFU	Bud Korchak, WPG	52.4
1953	WIFU	Bud Korchak, WPG	52.1
1954	WIFU	Tom Miner, CAL	53.7
1955	WIFU	Joe Aguirre, SAS	54.8
1956	WIFU	Al Pollard, BC	56.5
1957	WIFU	Joe Mobra, EDM	54.2
1958	IRFU	Vic Kristopaitis, TOR	55.7
	WIFU	Jim Bakhtiar, CAL	57.1
1959	IRFU	Cookie Gilchrist, TOR	52.6
	WIFU	Gerry James, WPG	56.5
1960	EFC	*unavailable*	
	WIFU	George Grant, BC	57.3
1961	EFC	Don Sutherin, HAM	58.9
	WFC	Tony Pajaczkowski, CAL	55.8
1962	EFC	*unavailable*	
	WFC	Tommy Joe Coffey, EDM	52.4
1963	EFC	Don Sutherin, HAM	59.1
	WFC	Larry Robinson, CAL	54.4
1964	EFC	Don Sutherin, HAM	57.9
	WFC	Bill Mitchell, EDM	61.6
1965	EFC	Don Sutherin, HAM	57.5
	WFC	Bill Mitchell, EDM	62.1
1966	EFC	John Baker, MTL	60.45
	WFC	Larry Robinson, CAL	60.43
1967	EFC	Don Sutherin, HAM	57.1
	WFC	Larry Robinson, CAL	61.6
1968	EFC	Don Sutherin, OTT	59.5
	WFC	Larry Robinson, CAL	61.9
1969	EFC	Doug Mitchell, HAM	62.0
	WFC	Ted Gerela, BC	61.6
1970	EFC	Doug Mitchell, HAM	59.1
	WFC	Dave Cutler, EDM	60.4
1971	EFC	Doug Mitchell, HAM	57.6
	WFC	Dave Cutler, EDM	61.9
1972	EFC	Zenon Andrusyshyn, TOR	56.9
	WFC	Dave Cutler, EDM	58.3
1973	EFC	Zenon Andrusyshyn, TOR	56.3
	WFC	Walt McKee, WPG	57.1
1974	EFC	Gerry Organ, OTT	55.8
	WFC	Rudy Linterman, CAL	65.3
1975	EFC	Zenon Andrusyshyn, TOR	62.8
	WFC	Rudy Linterman, CAL	57.4
1976	EFC	Ken Clark, HAM	57.1
	WFC	Bernie Ruoff, WPG	62.9
1977	EFC	Zenon Andrusyshyn, TOR	54.9
	WFC	Lui Passaglia, BC	60.4
1978	EFC	Don Sweet, MTL	56.3
	WFC	Lui Passaglia, BC	61.0
1979	EFC	Don Sweet, MTL	58.2
	WFC	Bernie Ruoff, WPG	59.5
1980	EFC	Gerry McGrath, MTL	58.2
	WFC	J.T. Hay, CAL	60.8
1981	Eastern	Bernie Ruoff, HAM	61.2
	Western	Lui Passaglia, BC	60.5
1982	Eastern	Zenon Andrusyshyn, TOR	58.6
	Western	Dave Cutler, EDM	62.2
1983	Eastern	Hank Ilesic, TOR	62.8
	Western	Dave Cutler, EDM	62.5
1984	Eastern	Hank Ilesic, TOR	66.7
	Western	J.T. Hay, CAL	58.4
1985	Eastern	Hank Ilesic, TOR	60.1
	Western	David Ridgway, SAS	59.4
1986	Eastern	Hank Ilesic, TOR	66.1
	Western	Tom Dixon, EDN=M	60.4
1987	Eastern	Lance Chomyc, TOR	58.6
	Western	Jerry Kauric, EDM	56.5
1988	Eastern	Hank Ilesic, TOR	60.0
	Western	Mark McLoughlin, CAL	56.8
1989	Eastern	Paul Osbaldiston, HAM	58.6
	Western	Nark McLoughlin, CAL	60.1
1990	Eastern	Trevor Kennerd, WPG	57.1
	Western	Mark McLoughlin, CAL	60.2
1991	Eastern	Hank Ilesic, TOR	60.8
	Western	Mark McLoughlin, CAL	57.6
1992	Eastern	Hank Ilesic, TOR	59.9
	Western	Mark McLoughlin, CAL	56.4
1993	Eastern	Troy Westwood, WPG	57.0
	Western	Sean Fleming, EDM	59.9
1994	Eastern	Bjorn Nittmo, SHR	57.7
	Western	Mark McLoughlin, CAL	60.2
1995	North	Sean Fleming, EDM	59.1
	South	Josh Miller, BAL	58.1
1996	East	Terry Baker, MTL	60.8
	West	Troy Westwood, WPG	62.5
1997	East	Terry Baker, MTL	60.5
	West	Sean Fleming, EDM	60.9
1998	East	Terry Baker, MTL	63.0
	West	Mark McLoughlin, CAL	60.9
1999	East	Terry Baker, MTL	60.3
	West	Mark McLoughlin, CAL	57.8
2000	East	Terry Baker, MTL	60.8
	West	Sean Fleming, EDM	63.0
2001	East	Troy Westwood, WPG	60.8
	West	Paul McCallum, SAS	62.2
2002	East	Terry Baker, MTL	62.1
	West	Sean Fleming, EDM	66.5
2003	East	Lawrence Tynes, OTT	59.5
	West	Sean Fleming, EDM	57.6
2004	East	Jamie Boreham, HAM	58.3
	West	Paul McCallum, SAS	59.0
2005	East	Damon Duval, MTL	63.8
	West	Sandro DeAngelis, CAL	58.9
2006	East	Jamie Boreham, HAM	61.1
	West	Sandro DeAngelis, CAL	56.7
2007	East	Damon Duval, MTL	64.1
	West	Jamie Boreham, SAS	62.9
2008	East	Damon Duval, MTL	61.9
	West	Jamie Boreham, SAS	64.6
2009	East	Damon Duval, MTL	63.7
	West	Jamie Boreham, SAS	63.6
2010	East	Jame Boreham, TOR	67.9
	West	Eddie Johnson, SAS	66.1
2011	East	Grant Shaw, TOR	62.2
	West	Damon Duval, EDM	61.0

YEAR		KICKOFF RETURNS	YDS
1951	WIFU	George McPhail, WPG	454
1952	WIFU	Pete Thodos, CAL	816
1953	WIFU	John Henry Johnson, CAL	578
1954	IRFU	Alex Webster, MTL	393
	WIFU	Ken Carpenter, SAS	630
1955	IRFU	Don Pinhey, OTT	632
	WIFU	Harry Lunn, SAS	557
1956	IRFU	Hal Patterson, MTL	771
	WIFU	By Bailey, BC	680
1957	IRFU	Hal Patterson, MTL	648
	WIFU	Leo Lewis, WPG	854
1958	IRFU	Bobby Judd, OTT	439
	WIFU	Mike Hagler, SAS	744
1959	IRFU	Jim Rountree, TOR	433
	WIFU	Willie Fleming, BC	545
1960	EFC	Don Clark, MTL	660
	WIFU	Harvey Wylie, CAL	670
1961	EFC	Art Johnson, TOR	436
	WFC	Harvey Wylie, CAL	622
1962	EFC	Tommy Grant, HAM	615
	WFC	Harvey Wylie, CAL	876
1963	EFC	Ernie White, OTT	665
	WFC	Leo Lewis, WPG	796
1964	EFC	George Hughley, TOR	602
	WFC	Leo Lewis, WPG	768
1965	EFC	Dick Shatto, TOR	374
	WFC	Dave Raimey, WPG	635
1966	EFC	Bo Scott, OTT	434
	WFC	Trent Walters, EDM	557
1967	EFC	Charley Scales, MTL	541
	WFC	Dave Raimey, WPG	744
1968	EFC	Vic Washington, OTT	853
	WFC	Dave Raimey, WPG	930
1969	EFC	Mike D'Amato, MTL	556
	WFC	Bobby Thompson, SAS	600
1970	EFC	Al Marcelin, OTT	659
	WFC	Joe Hernandez, EDM	636
1971	EFC	Al Marcelin, OTT	384
	WFC	Mack Herron, WPG	1019
1972	EFC	Lewis Porter, HAM	614
	WFC	Monroe Eley,, BC	1033

1973	EFC	Lewis Porter, HAM	539
	WFC	Larry Highbaugh, EDM	873
1974	EFC	Tommy Campbell, HAM	425
	WFC	Tom Scott, WPG	752
1975	EFC	Dickie Harris, MTL	727
	WFC	Rocky Long, BC	944
1976	EFC	David Shaw, HAM	726
	WFC	Rocky Long, BC	979
1977	EFC	Bill Hatanaka, OTT	576
	WFC	Paul Williams, SAS	812
1978	EFC	Paul Bennett, TOR	757
	WFC	Vince Phason, WPG	796
1979	EFC	Ian Mofford, MTL-OTT	701
	WFC	Leon Bright, BC	820
1980	EFC	Martin Cox, OTT	793
	WFC	James Sykes, CAL	715
1981	Eastern	Carl Brazley, MTL-OTT	475
	Western	Devon Ford, BC	888
1982	Eastern	Denny Ferdinand, MTL	757
	Western	Dwight Edwards, SAS	869
1983	Eastern	Denny Ferdinand, MTL	749
	Western	Joe Hollimon, EDM	765
1984	Eastern	Dwight Edwards, OTT	983
	Western	Craig Ellis, SAS	1040
1985	Eastern	Vince Phason, MTL	586
	Western	Keyvan Jenkins, BC	720
1986	Eastern	Jeff Treftlin, MTL	984
	Western	Stephan Jones, EDM	750
1987	Eastern	Dwight Edwards, TOR	678
	Western	Ron Hopkins, CAL	1098
1988	Eastern	Orville Lee, OTT	940
	Western	Anthony Drawhorn, BC	691
1989	Eastern	Wally Zatylny, HAM	793
	Western	Darrell Wallace, BC	1225
1990	Eastern	Stacey Dawsey, OTT	1307
	Western	Ron Hopkins, CAL	1287
1991	Eastern	Anthony Drawhorn, OTT	1095
	Western	Willis Jacox, SAS	1231
1992	Eastern	Rocket Ismail, TOR	1139
	Western	Demetrius Smith, CAL	924
1993	Eastern	Michael Clemons, TOR	604
	Western	Cory Philpot, BC	1008
1994	Eastern	David Lucas, SHR	832
	Western	Lucius Floyd, EDM	845
1995	North	Aaron Ruffin, SAS	989
	South	Freeman Baysinger, SHR	1023
1996	East	Kenny Wilhite, OTT	1167
	West	Marvin Coleman, CAL	1039
1997	East	Michael Clemons, CAL	1117
	West	Marvin Coleman, CAL	1297
1998	East	Eric Blount, WPG	1695
	West	Marvin Coleman, CAL	1115
1999	East	Thomas Haskins, MTL	815
	West	Jimmy Cunningham, BC	1032
2000	East	Albert Johnson, WPG	1506
	West	Jimmy Cunningham, BC	1090
2001	East	Charles Roberts, WPG	981
	West	Antonio Warren, CAL	1501
2002	East	Steve Fisher, HAM	1208
	West	Corey Holmes, SAS	1015
2003	East	Bashir Levingston, EDM	881
	West	Winston October, EDM	1018
2004	East	Craig Yeast, HAM	805
	West	Keith Stokes, WPG	1112
2005	East	Jason Armstead, OTT	1082
	West	Aaron Lockett, BC	1249
2006	East	Avon Cobourne, MTL	1122
	West	J.R. Ruffin, CAL	1461
2007	East	Albert Johnson, WPG	776
	West	Ian Smart, BC	1228
2008	East	Dominique Dorsey, TOR	1257
	West	Ian Smart, BC	1805
2009	East	Marquay McDaniel, HAM	1153
	West	Titus Ryan, CAL-WPG	1198
2010	East	Chad Owens, TOR	1216
	West	Deon Murphy	911
2011	East	Chad Owens, TOR	1750
	West	Larry Taylor, CAL	1008

YEAR		SACKS	NO
1981	Eastern	Grover Covington, HAM	16
	Western	James Parker, EDM	18.5
1982	Eastern	Grover Covington, HAM	12.5
	Western	James Parker, EDM	17.5
1983	Eastern	Greg Marshall, OTT	15.5
	Western	Vince Goldsmith, SAS	20
1984	Eastern	James Curry, TOR	22
	Western	James Parker, BC	26.5
1985	Eastern	Grover Covington, HAM	16
	Western	Tony Norman, WPG	14
1986	Eastern	Mike Walker, HAM	21
		Brett Williams, MTL	21
	Western	James Parker, BC	22
1987	Eastern	Grover Covington, HAM	17
		Mike Walker, HAM	17
	Western	Gregg Stumon, BC	23
1988	Eastern	Grover Covington, HAM	25
	Western	Bobby Jurasin, SAS	16
1989	Eastern	Grover Covington, HAM	15
	Western	James Curry, SAS	16
		Bobby Jurasin, SAS	16
1990	Eastern	Gregg Stumon, OTT	13
	Western	Stewart Hill, EDM	17
1991	Eastern	Mike Campbell, TOR	13
	Western	Will Johnson, CAL	15
1992	Eastern	Angelo Snipes, OTT	20
	Western	Bennie Goods, EDM	10
		Will Johnson, CAL	10
		Bobby Jurasin, SAS	10
1993	Eastern	Elfrid Payton, WPG	22
	Western	O.J. Brigance, BC	20
1994	Eastern	Timmy Cofield, HAM	16
		Rodney Harding, TOR	16
	Western	Will Johnson, CAL	17
1995	North	Bennie Goods, EDM	14
	South	Timmy Cofield, MEM	24
1996	East	Grant Carter, MTL	15
	West	Angelo Snipes, WPG	15
1997	East	Elfrid Payton, MTL	14
	West	Troy Alexander, SAS	10
		Bobby Jurasin, SAS	10
1998	East	Joe Montford, HAM	21
	West	Malvin Hunter, EDM	13
		Johnny Scott, BC	13
1999	East	Joe Montford, HAM	26
	West	Johnny Scott, BC	10
2000	East	Joe Montford, HAM	20
	West	Shont'e Peoples, CAL	12
2001	East	Joe Montford, HAM	19
	West	Shont'e Peoples, SAS	12
2002	East	Joe Montford, TOR	9
	West	Elfrid Payton, EDM	16
2003	East	Eric England, TOR	14
	West	Joe Fleming, CAL	11
2004	East	Tim Cheatwood, HAM	14
	West	Brent Johnson, BC	10
2005	East	Jonathan Brown, TOR	13
	West	Brent Johnson, BC	17
2006	East	Gavin Walls, WPG	11
	West	Brent Johnson, BC	16
2007	East	Jonathan Brown, TOR	13
	West	Cameron Wake, BC	16
2008	East	Gavin Walls, WPG	10
		Keron Williams, MTL	10
	West	Cameron Wake	23
2009	East	John Bowman, MTL	12
	West	Stevie Baggs, SAS	12
		Ricky Foley, BC	12
2010	East	Phillip Hunt, WPG	16
	West	six tied witrh	7
2011	East	Justin Hickman, HAM	13
		Odell Willis, WPG	13
	West	Keron Williams, BC	11
		Marcus Howard, BC	11

YEAR		TOTAL FUMBLE RECOVERIES	NO
1954	WIFU	four tied with	4
1955	WIFU	Norm Fieldgate, BC	6
		Gord Sturtridge, SAS	6
1956	WIFU	Oscar Kruger, EDM	7
1957	WIFU	Don Lord, BC	4
1958	WIFU	Paul Cameron, BC	5
1959	WIFU	George Hansen, CAL	4
1960	WIFU	Garland Warren, WPG	5
1961	WFC	three tied with	4
1962	WFC	Ernie Danjean, CAL	4
		Ron Latourelle, WPG	4
1963	WFC	Wayne Shaw, SAS	6
1964	EFC	four tied with	3
	WFC	eight tied with	3
1965	EFC	John Baker, MTL	6
	WFC	Mario Mariani, WPG	5
1966	EFC	five tied with	3
	WFC	three tied with	4
1967	EFC	Marv Luster, TOR	4
		Dave Viti, HAM	4
	WFC	Frank Andruski, CAL	6
1968	EFC	Bob Trygstad, MT:	5
	WFC	Larry Robinson, CAL	5
1969	EFC	Larry Fairholm, MTL	4
		Ed Joyner, OTT	4
	WFC	John LaGrone, EDM	6
1970	EFC	Paul Schmidlin, HAM	4
		Marshall Shirk, OTT	4
	WFC	Craig Koinzan, CAL	5
		Ken Frith, SAS	5
1971	EFC	Mike Blum, HAM	5
	WFC	Ron Forwick, EDM	4
1972	EFC	three tied with	4
	WFC	seven tied with	3
1973	EFC	Jerry Campbell, OTT	5
	WFC	Sam Britts, EDM	4
1974	EFC	Mike Widger, MTL	6
	WFC	Pete Palmer, BC	4
		Lorne Richardson	4
1975	EFC	three tied with	3
	WFC	Larry Carr, CAL	5
1976	CFL	Elton Brown, HAM-WPG	6
	EFC	Mark Kosmos	6
	WFC	Glen Jackson, BC	4
		Dennis Meyer, CAL	4
1977	EFC	Eric Harris, TOR	4
		Chuck Zapiec, MTL	4
	WFC	Angelo Santuccim EDM	5
		Brian Herosian, WPG	5
1978	EFC	Rick Sowieta, TOR	6

	WFC	Louie Richardson, BC	4
1979	EFC	Ben Zambiasi, HAM	4
	WFC	three tied with	4
1980	EFC	Lou Clare, HAM	5
	WFC	three tied with	4
1981	Eastern	Jim Corigall, TOR	3
		John Priestner, HAM	3
	Western	Larry Key, BC	4
		Tony Norman, WPG	4
1982	Eastern	three tied with	3
	Western	seven tied with	3
1983	Eastern	Howard Fields, HAM	5
	Western	JoJo Heath, BC	5
1984	Eastern	Howard Fields, HAM	5
	Western	three tied with	4
1985	Eastern	Ricky Barden, OTT	5
	Western	three tied with	4
1986	Eastern	David Marshall, TOR	5
	Western	Glen Suitor, SAS	5
1987	Eastern	Tony Johns, TOR	4
		Ben Zambiasi, HAM	4
	Western	Vince Goldsmith, CAL	5
		Keith Gooch, BC	5
1988	Eastern	five tied with	4
	Western	Anthony Parker, BC	6
1989	Eastern	four tied with	4
	Western	Danny Bass, EDM	6
1990	Eastern	Troy Wilson, OTT	8
	Western	Willie Pless, BC	5
1991	Eastern	Greg Battle, WPG	4
		Clark Gaines, TOR	4
	Western	three tied with	5
1992	Eastern	Damon Allen, HAM	7
	Western	Willie Plessm EDM	8
1993	Eastern	Tom Burgess, OTT	6
	Western	Charles Anthony, SAS	6
		Keilan Matthews, SAC	6
1994	Eastern	Matt Goodwin, BAL	8
		Keilly Rush, WPG	8
	Western	Willie Pless, EDM	8
1995	North	three tied with	5
	South	four tied with	4
1996	East	Robert Drummond, TOR	5
	West	seven tied with	3
1997	East	Rickey Foggie, HAM	4
	West	Damon Allen, BC	4
		Jeff Garcia, CAL	4
1998	East	Antonious Bonner, TOR	5
	West	Jeff Garcia, CAL	4
1999	East	Maurice Kelly, WPG	8
	West	three tied with	4
2000	East	Harold Nash, WPG	4
	West	six tied with	3
2001	East	Joe Montford, HAM	4
		Elfrid Payton, TOR	4
	West	Robert Drummond, BC	4
		Shont'e Peoples, SAS	4
2002	East	John Grace, OTT	5
	West	Brendon Ayanbadejo, CAL	7
2003	East	Anthony Calvillo, MTL	4
		Terence Melton, MTL	4
	West	Dave Dickenson, BC	5
2004	East	Gerald Vaughn, OTT	5
	West	Jason Maas, EDM	9
2005	East	Duane Butler, MTL	6
	West	Ricky Ray, EDM	6
2006	East	four tied with	3
	West	Jason Armstead, SAS	4
		Sheldon Napastuk	4
2007	East	four tied with	3
	West	Brent Johnson, BC	4
		Stefan LeFors, EDM	4
2008	East	Kerry Joseph, TOR	4
	West	Jason Goss, EDM	4
		Kitwana Jones, SAS	4
2009	East	Markeith Knowlton, HAM	4
	West	Dwight Anderson, CAL	4
		Dwaine Carpenter, CAL	4
2010	East	Markeith Knowlton, HAM	6
	West	Darian Durant, SAS	5
2011	East	Lin-J Shell, TOR	5
	West	Henry Burris, CAL	5
		Ricky Ray, EDM	5

YEAR		TACKLES	NO
1987	Eastern	Willie Pless, TOR	93
	Western	David Albright, SAS	118
1988	Eastern	Willie Pless, TOR	96
	Western	Danny Bass, EDM	116
1989	Eastern	Greg Battle, WPG	108
	Western	Doug Landry, CAL	122
1990	Eastern	Bruce Holmes, OTT	127
	Western	Willie Pless, BC	107
1991	Eastern	Darryl Ford, TOR	117
	Western	O.J, Brigance, BC	112
1992	Eastern	John Motton, HAM	98
	Western	Willie Pless, EDM	121
1993	Eastern	Ken Benson, TOR	98
	Western	Ray Bernard, SAS	98
1994	Eastern	Calvin Tiggle, TOR	135
	Western	Ron Goetz, SAS	115
1995	North	Willie Pless, EDM	101
	South	Mike James, BIR	95
1996	East	Tracy Gravely, MTL	116
	West	K.D. Williams, WPG	112
1997	East	Calvin Tiggle,HAM	85
	West	Willie Pless, EDM	116
1998	East	Calvin Tiggle, HAM	99
	West	Willie Pless, EDM	117
1999	East	Calvin Tiggle, HAM	108
	West	Willie Pless, SAS	102
		Terry Ray, EDM	102
2000	East	Mile O'Shea, HAM	103
	West	George White, SAS	127
2001	East	Jason Lamar, HAM	108
	West	George White, SAS	128
2002	East	Mike O'Shea, TOR	95
	West	Brendon Ayandbadejo, BC	104
2003	East	Mike O'Shea, TOR	98
	West	George White, CAL	100
2004	East	Kevin Eiben, TOR	114
	West	Joey Boese, CAL	105
2005	East	Kevin Eiben, TOR	118
	West	George White, CAL	136
2006	East	Barrin Simpson, WPG	118
	West	Javier Glatt, BC	91
2007	East	Zeke Moreno, HAM	126
	West	Sideeq Shabazz, EDM	95
2008	East	Zeke Moreno, Ham-WPG	98
	West	Sean Lucas, SAS	98
2009	East	Jamall Johnson, HAM	117
	West	Anton McKenzie, BC	99
2010	East	Jamall Johnson, HAM	111
	West	Barrin Simpson, SAS	107
2011	East	Lin-J Shell, TOR	102
	West	Jerrell Freeman, SAS	108

INDIVIDUAL SINGLE-GAME RECORDS

SCORING

Points
36 Bob McNamara, WPG 10/13/1956 vs BC

Touchdowns
6 Bob McNamara, WPG 10/13/1956 vs BC

Converts (One-point)
9 Eight players
Last time: Paul Osbaldiston, HAM 9/18/1999 vs WPG

Converts (Two-point)
2 Seven players
Last time: Jay Christensen, BC 1990

Field Goals
0 Four players
Last time: Paul Osbaldiston, HAM 9/22/1996

Field Goal Attempts
13 Paul McCallum, SAS 9/28/1997 vs EDM

Long Field Goal
62 Paul McCallum, SAS 10/27/2001 vs EDM

Singles

RUSHING

Attempts
37 Doyle Orange, TOR 8/13/1975 vs HAM

Yards
287 Ron Stewart, OTT 10/10/1960 vs MTL

Touchdowns
5 Earl Lunsford, CAL 9/2/1962 vs EDM
Martin Patton, SHR 8/5/1995 vs WPG

Long Gain
109 George Dixon, MTL 9/2/1853 vs OTT

PASSING

Attempts
65 Kent Austin, SAS 9/15/1991 vs EDM

Completions
44 Anthony Calvillo, MTL 10/4/2008 vs HAM

Yards
713 Matt Dunigan, WPG 7/14/1994 vs EDM

Touchdowns
8 Joe Zuger, HAm 10/15/1962 vs SAS

Interceptions
7 Three players
Last time: Sonny Wade, MTL 9/24/1972 vs CAL

Long Gain
109 Sam Etcheverry, MTL 9/22/1956 vs HAM

RECEIVING

Receptions
16 Four players
Last time: Arland Bruce, HAM 7/31/2110 vs SAS

Yards
338 Hal Patterson, MTL 9/29/1956 vs HAM

Touchdowns
5 Ernie Pitts, 5 8/29/1959 vs SAS

Long Gain
109 Hal Patterson, MTL 9/22/1956 vs HAM

INTERCEPTIONS

Returns
5 Rod Hill, WPG 9/9/1990 vs HAM

Yards
172 Barry Ardern, OTT 11/1/1969 vs HAM

Touchdowns
3 Vernon Mitchell, TOR 10/7/2000 vs HAM

Long Gain
120 Neal Beaumont, BC 10/12/1963 vs SAS

Knockdowns
5 Three players
Last time: Davis Sanchez, CAL 9/14/2003 vs WPG

PUNTING

Punts
18 Martin Fabi, SAS 9/14/1963 vs CAL

Yards
814 Martin Fabi, SAS 9/14/1963 CAL

Average (minimum 4 punts)
64.7 Nick Setta, GAM 7/17/2008 vs CAL

Long Kick
108 Zenon Andrusyshyn, TOR 9/14/1977 vs CAL
Chris Milo, SAS 10/29/2011 vs HAM

PUNT RETURNS

Returns
14 Rudy Linterman, CAL 10/15/1968 vs EDM
Will Lewis, OTT 8/29/1987 vs HAM

Yards
232 Henry Williams, EDM 7/17/1991 vs OTT

Touchdowns
2 Seven players
Last time: Keith Stokes, MTL 8/2/2002 vs EDM

Long Return
116 Larry Highbaugh, EDM 10/26/1975 vs WPG

KICKOFF RETURNS

Returns Ten players
9 Last time: Brandon West, SAS 9/24/2011 vs BC

Yards
257 Anthony Cherry, BC 8/4/1989 vs HAM

Touchdowns
1?

Long Return
120 Mack Herron, WPG 8/30/1972 VS EDM

SACKS

Sacks
5.0 Eleven players
Last time: Anthony Collier 7/8/2005 vs OTT

TACKLES

Defensive
16 Reggie Hunt, SAS 7/10/2003 vs WPG

Special Teams
7 Six players
Last time: Darren Joseph, OTT 10/13/2003 vs TOR

Tackles for Loss
6 K.D. Williams, WPG 10/9/1995 vs TOR

The Player Register is the listing of every player who have played in the post-World War II, professional era of Canadian football. Much of information in this register has never been published before and is the result of a painstaking reconstruction of the records of the Canadian Football League.

There are two parts to each player's record.

The first is the biographical line which provides detailed biographical and roster information.

This line will include the following information:

The name that player is most commonly known under is in boldfaced capital letters.

The player's name full name.

Any common nicknames associated with that player are in parenthesis.

The positions that player performed at, using the following abbreviations:

B	Back
C	Centre
CB	Cornerback
DB	Defensive Back
DE	Defensive End
DG	Defensive Guard
DH	Defensive Halfback
DL	Defensive Line
DT	Defensive Tackle
E	End
FB	Fullback
FL	Flanker
FW	Flying Wing
G	Guard
HB	Halfback
K	Kicker
LB	Linebacker
MG	Middle Guard
NG	Nose Guard
NT	Nose Tackle
OE	Offensive End
OG	Offensive Guard
OHB	Offensive Halfback
OL	Offensive Line
OT	Offensive Tackle
P	Punter
QB	Quarterback
S	Safety
SB	Slot Back
SE	Spit End
T	Tackle
TE	Tight End
WR	Wide Receiver

The player's average career height and weight.

The post-high school amateur teams played for and universities/colleges attended when eligible to play. Junior teams are abbreviated Jrs. And Intermediate teams are abbreviated Ints.

B: indicates a player's birth date (in the month/day/year format) and place of birth.

D: indicates a player's death date (in the month/day/year format) and place of death.

The following state and provincial abbreviations are used in these two entries:

AB	Alberta
AK	Alaska
AL	Alabama
AR	Arkansas
AZ	Arizona
BC	British Columbia
CA	California
CO	Colorado
CT	Connecticut
DC	District of Columbia
DE	Delaware
FL	Florida
GA	Georgia
HI	Hawaii
IA	Iowa
ID	Idaho
IL	Illinois
IN	Indiana
KS	Kansas
KY	Kentucky
LA	Louisiana
MA	Massachusetts
MB	Manitoba
MD	Maryland
ME	Maine
MI	Michigan
MN	Minnesota
MO	Missouri
MS	Mississippi
MT	Montana
NB	New Brunswick
NC	North Carolina
ND	North Dakota
NE	Nebraska
NH	New Hampshire
NJ	New Jersey
NL	Newfoundland
NM	New Mexico
NS	Nova Scotia
NV	Nevada
NY	New York
OH	Ohio
OK	Oklahoma
ON	Ontario
OR	Oregon
PA	Pennsylvania
QC	Quebec
RI	Rhode Island
SC	South Carolina
SD	South Dakota
SK	Saskatchewan
TN	Tennessee
TX	Texas
UT	Utah
VA	Virginia
VT	Vermont
WA	Washington
WI	Wisconsin
WV	West Virginia
WY	Wyoming

Draft: indicates any college entry draft the player was selected by a CFL, NFL, AAFC, AFL (1960-69), WFL or USFL team. Each entry is in the following format:

Round-Overall Year Team

In the round portion of each entry, TE indicated a territorial exempt pick in the CFL draft, TD a territorial pick in a USFL draft, FS a "first selection in the 1960 AFL draft and SS a "second selection" in the 1960 AFL draft. An "rs" indicates a selection in one of the AFL's redshirt drafts.

-AA refers to an All-American Conference team

-USFL to an United States Football League team

-WFL to a World Football League team

The following abbreviations are used to indicate the teams a player was drafted by:

ARI	Arizona
ATL	Atlanta
BAL	Baltimore

BC	British Columbia
BIR	Birmingham
BKN	Brooklyn
BOS	Boston
BUF	Buffalo
CAL	Calgary
CAR	Carolina
CHI	Chicago
CHIB	Chicago Bears
CHIC	Chicago Cardinals
DAL	Dallas
DALT	Dallas Texans
DEN	Denver
DET	Detroit
EDM	Edmonton
FLA	Florida
GB	Green Bay
HAM	Hamilton
HOU	Houston
IND	Indianapolis
JAC	Jacksonville
KC	Kansas City
LA	Los Angeles
LAC	Los Angeles Chargers
LARI	Los Angeles Raiders
LARM	Los Angeles Rams
MEM	Memphis
MIA	Miami
MIC	Michigan
MIN	Minnesota
MTL	Montreal
NE	New England
NO	New Orleans
NY	New York
NYG	New York Giants
NYJ	New York Jets
NYT	New York Titans
NYY	New York Yankees/Yanks
OAK	Oakland
ORL	Orlando
OTT	Ottawa
PHI	Philadelphia
PHX	Phoenix
POR	Portland
PIT	Pittsburgh
SAS	Saskatchewan
SC	Southern California
SD	San Diego
SEA	Seattle
SF	San Francisco
TB	Tampa Bay
TEN	Tennessee
TOR	Toronto
WAS	Washington
WPG	Winnipeg

Pro: indicates if a player also played in one of the following leagues:

A	All-America Football Conference
E	World League of American Football/NFL Europe
N	National Football League
	American Football League (1960-69)
U	United States Football League (1983-1985)
	United Football League (2009-2011)
W	World Football League
X	XFL

After each player's biographical data is his year-by-year and career playing record.

The following column headings are used:

COM	Pass completions
FF	Forced fumbles
FR	Fumble Recoveries
FUM	Fumbles
GP	Games played
IR	Interception returns
KOR	Kickoff returns
PASS	Pass attempts
PD	Pass knockdowns (passes defensed)
PI	Passes intercepted
PR	Punt returns
PTS	Points
REC	Pass receptions
RA	Rushing Attempts
SK	Sacks
TD	Touchdowns
TEAM	The following abbreviations are used:

BAL	Baltimore (1994)
	Baltimore Stallions (1995)
BC	British Columbia Lions (1954-)
BIR	Birmingham Barracudas (1995)
CAL	Calgary Stampeders (1946-)
EDM	Edmonton Eskimos (1949-)
HAM	Hamilton Tigers (1946-1947)
	Hamilton Wildcats (1948-1949)
	Hamilton Tiger-Cats (1950-)
LV	Las Vegas Posse (1994)
MEM	Memphis Mad Dogs (1995)
MTL	Montreal Alouettes (1946-1981)
	Montreal Concordes (1982-1985)
	Montreal Alouettes (1986; 1996-)
OTT	Ottawa Rough Riders (1946-1996)
	Ottawa Renegades (2002-2005)
SA	San Antonio Texans (1995)
SAC	Sacramento Gold Miners (1993-1994)
SAS	Saskatchewan Roughriders (1946-)
SHR	Shreveport Pirates (1994-1995)
TOR	Toronto Argonauts (1946-)
WPG	Winnipeg Blue Bombers (1946-)

Year The cumulative totals for a player that played for more than one team in a given season.

Years The career totals for a player that played two or more seasons.

\+ Indicates that a player was selected to an eastern or western (north or south in 1995) all-star team.

* Indicates that a player was an All-Canadian selection that year.

TKL	Tackles
YDS	Yards
YEAR	Year (if a player played in more than one season, than the final line will list the total number of years played, followed by his career totals).

Year	Team	GP	FM	FF	FR	TK	SK	YDS	IR	YDS	PD	PTS	TD	RA	YDS	AVG	LG	TD	REC	YDS	AVG	LG	TD	PR	YDS	AVG	LG	KOR	YDS	AVG	LG
PAT ABBRUZZI Pasquale J. FB-OHB 5'9 205 Rhode Island B: 8/29/1932 Warren, RI D: 6/3/1998 Boston, MA Draft: 30-352 1954 BAL; 13-147 1955 BAL																															
1955	MTL+	12										95	19	182	1248	6.9	63	17	20	277	13.9	42	2					6	85	14.2	38
1956	MTL+	14										120	20	207	1062	5.1	30	17	32	306	9.6	24	3					3	32	10.7	24
1957	MTL	14										42	7	178	809	4.5	28	7	23	190	8.3	40	0					1	11	11.0	11
1958	MTL	9										24	4	133	630	4.7	28	4	9	111	12.3	32	0					1	1	1.0	1
4	Years	49										281	50	700	3749	5.4	63	45	84	884	10.5	42	5					11	129	11.7	38
KHALID ABDULLAH Khalid U. LB 6'2 227 Mars Hill B: 3/6/1979 Jacksonville, FL Draft: 5-136 2003 CIN Pro: N																															
2006	CAL	12				60	1.0	3.0			2																				
2007	MTL	4				6																									
2	Years	16				66	1.0	3.0			2																				
RAHIM ABDULLAH Rahim Fahim DE 6'5 233 Clemson B: 3/22/1976 Jacksonville, FL Draft: 2B-45 1999 CLE Pro: N																															
2002	EDM	2	0	1	0	7	1.0	7.0																							
2003	EDM	18				31	8.0	67.0	1	0	6																				
2004	EDM	18	0	0	1	32	5.0	42.0	1	1	6																				
2005	CAL	18	0	2	1	28	8.0	58.0			5																	1	0	0.0	0
2006	CAL	17	0	3	0	29	9.0	38.0			1																				
2007	EDM	10	0	0	1	19	5.0	20.0			4																				
6	Years	83	0	6	3	146	36.0	232.0	2	1	22																	1	0	0.0	0
JACK ABENDSCHAN John Jacob, Jr. OG-K-LB 6'2 245 New Mexico B: 12/18/1942 San Francisco, CA																															
1965	SAS	16	0		2							65	0																		
1966	SAS+	16	0		1							86	0																		
1967	SAS*	16	2		1							89	0						1	0	0.0	0	0								
1968	SAS	7										31	0																		
1969	SAS*	16										116	0																		
1970	SAS+	16	1		0							116	0																		
1971	SAS*	16	1		0							94	0																		
1972	SAS*	16										74	0																		
1973	SAS*	16										110	0																		
1975	SAS	15										82	0																		
10	Years	150	4		4							863	0						1	0	0.0	0	0								
HARRY ABOFS Harry OHB-DB 6'1 207 Tennessee Tech B: 4/14/1948 Germany D: 1993																															
1971	TOR	14	1		0							12	2	22	106	4.8	26	1	10	67	6.7	34	1	57	227	4.0	15	4	71	17.8	25
1972	TOR	6																	1	4	4.0	4	0								
1972	EDM	7							1	1																		8	152	19.0	23
1972	Year	13							1	1									1	4	4.0	4	0					8	152	19.0	23
1973	EDM	8	1		1				3	37														1	0	0.0	0				
1973	BC	1																										3	58	19.3	24
1973	Year	9	1		1				3	37														1	0	0.0	0	3	58	19.3	24
1974	HAM	9	2		3																			31	108	3.5	13				
4	Years	37	4		4				4	38		12	2	22	106	4.8	26	1	11	71	6.5	34	1	89	335	3.8	15	15	281	18.7	25
DICK ABOUD Richard LB-OG 6'0 208 Mount Royal Lions Jrs.; Tulsa B: 7/24/1941 Montreal, QC																															
1963	MTL	14																													
1966	TOR	6																													
1967	TOR	14	0		1																										
3	Years	34	0		1																										
MIKE ABOU-MECHREK Mike OT-OG 6'5 285 Western Ontario B: 10/14/1975 Toronto, ON Draft: 5-32 1999 WPG																															
1999	WPG	1				0																									
2000	WPG	10				3																									
2001	WPG	18	0	0	2	1																									
2002	OTT	18				3																									
2003	OTT	17	0	0	1	3																									
2004	OTT	9				3																									
2005	WPG	17				1																									
2006	WPG	13				1																									
2007	SAS	18				1																									
2008	SAS	17				0																									
10	Years	138	0	0	3	16																									
CLIFTON ABRAHAM Cliffton Eugene, Jr. CB 5'9 184 Florida State B: 12/9/1971 Dallas, TX Draft: 5-143 1995 TB Pro: NX																															
1998	TOR	10				35					4																				
1999	TOR	8	0	0	1	15					9																				
2001	TOR	3				8			2	48																					
3	Years	21	0	0	1	58			2	48	13																				
JEAN PHILIPPE ABRAHAM Jean Philippe LB 6'0 216 Laval B: 6/21/1982 St. Augustin, QC Draft: 4B-34 2006 EDM																															
2006	EDM	9				1																									
JOSH ABRAMS Joshua CB-DH-LB 5'11 196 Ohio University B: 1/18/1986 Dunwoody, GA																															
2010	TOR	5				7			0	0	2																				
ALLI ABREW Alfred C. QB 6'0 195 San Jose State; Cal Poly (San Luis Obispo) B: 7/3/1974 Alameda County, CA																															
1999	SAS	2				0																									
JIMMY ABSON James Donald FW-HB Ottawa Gladstones Jrs. B: 1920 Ottawa, ON D: 11/21/2008																															
1946	OTT	10																													
D.D. ACHOLONU Dilibe Chisamaga DE 6'2 239 Washington State B: 10/17/1980 Seattle, WA																															
2006	MTL	12				26	2.0	10.0	0	0	1																				
ROD ACHTER Rodney Lee WR 6'1 196 Toledo B: 2/14/1961 Oregon, OH Draft: 9-239 1983 MIN																															
1984	OTT	2																	3	10	3.3	6	0								
T.J. ACKERMAN T.J. OT 6'6 315 Eastern Washington B: 8/20/1975 Bellingham, WA																															
1999	TOR	5				0																									
AL ACKLAND Al OE 6'3 195 Weston Wildcats Jrs. B: 1940 Winnipeg, MB																															
1961	WPG	2																													
STEVE ACKROYD Steven S-WR 6'1 175 Sheridan B: 6/5/1956																															
1978	TOR	2																													
1978	HAM	2																						7	52	7.4	13	1	10	10.0	10
1978	Year	4																						7	52	7.4	13	1	10	10.0	10
1979	HAM	5																	1	9	9.0	9	0								
1979	TOR	5							1	18																					
1979	Year	10							1	18									1	9	9.0	9	0								
1980	TOR	3																													
1981	TOR	12	0		1																										
1982	TOR	16	0		1				3	38		6	1											1	3	3.0	3				
1983	TOR	16	0		1				2	0														3	16	5.3	21				
1984	TOR	16	0		1																			1	15	15.0	15				
7	Years	70	0		4				6	56		6	1						1	9	9.0	9	0	12	86	7.2	21	1	10	10.0	10
T.J. ACREE T.J. WR 6'0 180 Boise State B: 7/21/1982 Pocatello, ID																															
2005	BC	1				0																									
2006	BC	8	1	0	0	0													28	266	9.5	25	0	5	28	5.6	13	1	17	17.0	0
2007	EDM	11	1	0	0	1						18	3						32	478	14.9	75	3	2	11	5.5	8	2	26	13.0	26
2008	TOR	1				0													2	11	5.5	6	0								
2008	SAS	1				0																									
2008	Year	2				0													2	11	5.5	6	0								
4	Years	21	2	0	0	1						18	3						62	755	12.2	75	3	7	39	5.6	13	3	43	14.3	26
GARRY ADAM Garry DT 6'4 240 Alberta B: 5/29/1947 Draft: TE 1973 EDM																															
1973	EDM	4																													
RON ADAM Ron S-QB 6'1 195 Saskatoon Hilltops Jrs. B: 1933																															

Year	Team	GP	FM	FF	FR	TK	SK	YDS	IR	YDS	PD	PTS	TD	RA	YDS	AVG	LG	TD	REC	YDS	AVG	LG	TD	PR	YDS	AVG	LG	KOR	YDS	AVG	LG
1954	SAS	15	2		0				3	2				3	-5	-1.7	5	0						41	221	5.4	16	8	152	19.0	49
1955	SAS	16	2		3				2	30		5	1	15	45	3.0	14	0						20	96	4.8	15	11	208	18.9	54
1956	SAS	16	0		5				2	14		6	1	4	3	0.8	15	0	2	29	14.5	15	1	2	0	0.0	0				
1957	SAS	14							1	0				7	21	3.0	20	0	1	39	39.0	39	0	15	82	5.5	13	12	225	18.8	42
1958	SAS	16	1						2	74				11	23	2.1	12	0						1	11	11.0	11				
1959	SAS	5												5	19	3.8	12	0													
1960	SAS	16												7	6	0.9	14	0													
7	Years	98	5		8				10	120		11	2	52	112	2.2	20	0	3	68	22.7	39	1	79	410	5.2	16	31	585	18.9	54
CALVIN ADAMS Calvin A. CB 5'9 170 East Carolina B: 1/4/1962 Guilford County, NC																															
1986	HAM	4	1		0				2	34																					
DARRELL ADAMS Darrell DT 6'0 282 Villanova B: 9/16/1983 New York, NY																															
2007	HAM	2				2																									
2008	HAM	16	0	1	0	41	9.0	29.0																							
2009	HAM	9				17	2.0	13.0			3																				
3	Years	27	0	1	0	60	11.0	42.0			3																				
DAVE ADAMS David (Steaky) G 170 none B: 1919																															
1946	CAL+	8																													
1947	CAL+	8																													
1948	CAL	11																													
3	Years	27																													
DAVID ADAMS David Delaney RB 5'6 170 Arizona B: 6/24/1964 Tucson, AZ Draft: 12-309 1987 IND Pro: N																															
1989	HAM	1				0								3	2	0.7	3	0	1	0	0.0	0	0					2	43	21.5	25
1990	HAM	3	3		0	1						6	1	19	65	3.4	14	1	8	67	8.4	24	0	2	13	6.5	10	5	52	10.4	18
2	Years	4	3		0	1						6	1	22	67	3.0	14	1	9	67	7.4	24	0	2	13	6.5	10	7	95	13.6	25
DEMOINE ADAMS Demoine R. DE 6'2 235 Nebraska B: 8/17/1980																															
2004	EDM	1				1																									
DICKIE ADAMS Richard DB 6'0 195 Miami (Ohio) B: 2/13/1948 Athens, OH Draft: 14-343 1971 HOU																															
1972	OTT*	14	2		1				7	150		9	1											79	425	5.4	22	1	25	25.0	25
1973	OTT*	14	2		3				4	78		12	2	1	-3	-3.0	-3	0						57	327	5.7	30	3	38	12.7	19
1974	OTT*	16	0		1				3	37		1	0	1	0	0.0	0	0						92	608	6.6	27	2	24	12.0	24
1975	OTT*	16	0		1				5	94		8	1	4	73	18.3	36	0						15	182	12.1	37	1	16	16.0	16
1976	OTT	3			1				1	11																					
5	Years	63	4		7				20	370		30	4	6	70	11.7	36	0						243	1542	6.3	37	7	103	14.7	25
FRANK ADAMS Harold Frank, Jr. CB 5'8 175 South Carolina B: 11/7/1970 Gatsonia, NC																															
1995	TOR	3				16					2																	3	42	14.0	16
JOE ADAMS Joe QB 6'3 190 Tennessee State B: 4/5/1948 Gulfport, MS Draft: 12B-322 1981 SF																															
1982	SAS	16	4		0							12	2	22	148	6.7	33	2													
1983	SAS	6	2		1							6	1	11	33	3.0	11	1													
1983	TOR	1																													
1983	Year	7	2		1									11	33	3.0	11	1													
1984	OTT	7												1	8	8.0	8	0													
3	Years	29	6		1							18	3	34	189	5.6	33	3													
MARCUS ADAMS Marcus DT-DE 5'11 285 Eastern Kentucky B: 7/20/1979 Indianapolis, IN																															
2003	SAS	9	0	1	0	13					1																				
2005	SAS	5				4	2.0	14.0																							
2006	SAS	5				7	1.0	8.0																							
2007	SAS	16				35	6.0	36.0			1																				
2008	SAS	14	0	0	2	11																									
2009	SAS	18				33	1.0	8.0			1																				
2010	SAS	16	0	0	1	27	2.0	2.0																							
7	Years	83	0	1	3	130	12.0	68.0			3																				
MIKE ADAMS Michael Christopher WR 5'11 184 Texas B: 3/25/1974 Dallas, TX Draft: 7-223 1997 PIT Pro: N																															
2000	BC	8				0						12	2						23	355	15.4	67	2	1	10	10.0	10	1	16	16.0	16
RAYMONN ADAMS Raymonn Doniciansher (Goldie) RB 6'0 206 Doane B: 10/23/1978 Long Beach, CA Pro: E																															
2002	CAL	6				0								2	5	2.5	3	0						21	172	8.2	30	23	777	33.8	87
2003	OTT	4	1	0	0	0													1	29	29.0	29	0	16	109	6.8	21	12	221	18.4	24
2004	OTT	14	1	0	1	9								3	0	0.0	2	0	1	2	2.0	2	0	6	42	7.0	14	17	388	22.8	46
3	Years	24	2	0	1	9								5	5	1.0	3	0	2	31	15.5	29	0	43	323	7.5	30	52	1386	26.7	87
SAM ADAMS Samuel OE 6'3 198 Whitworth B: 1930 Fort Worth, TX																															
1954	BC	13	1																23	259	11.3	28	0								
1955	BC	15										15	3						30	575	19.2	52	3								
2	Years	28	1		0							15	3						53	834	15.7	52	3								
STEFON ADAMS Stefon Lee DB 5'10 185 East Carolina B: 8/11/1963 High Point, NC Draft: 3B-80 1985 LARI; 4-58 1985 BAL-USFL Pro: EN																															
1995	HAM	3				10					2													1	9	9.0	9				
TOM ADAMS Tom E 6'2 218 UCLA B: 1934 Draft: 17-202 1956 CHIB																															
1956	OTT	12										18	3						17	350	20.6	69	3					4	41	10.3	14
TONY ADAMS Anthony Lee QB 6'0 190 Texas; Riverside CC; Utah State B: 3/19/1950 San Antonio, TX Draft: 14-343 1973 SD Pro: NW																															
1979	TOR	16	4		0							6	1	59	205	3.5	20	1													
1980	TOR	4	1		0									5	12	2.4	4	0													
2	Years	20	5		0							6	1	64	217	3.4	20	1													
WILLIE ADAMS Willie James DE 6'2 245 New Mexico State B: 12/12/1941 Corpus Christi, TX Draft: 11-146 1965 WAS Pro: N																															
1968	MTL	9																													
1969	MTL	14	0		2																										
2	Years	23	0		2																										
MARGENE ADKINS Margene SE 5'10 183 Trinity Valley CC B: 4/30/1947 Smith County, TX Draft: 2B-49 1970 DAL Pro: NW																															
1967	OTT+	14	2		0							48	8	1	8	8.0	8	0	46	985	21.4	71	8	1	1	1.0	1	16	347	21.7	34
1968	OTT	14										48	8	1	-21	-21.0	-21	0	32	821	25.7	57	8								
1969	OTT*	14										54	9						56	1402	25.0	74	9					14	307	21.9	41
3	Years	42	2		0							150	25	2	-13	-6.5	8	0	134	3208	23.9	74	25	1	1	1.0	1	30	654	21.8	41
TOMMY ADKINS Thomas J., Jr. C-LB 6'1 210 Kentucky B: 5/7/1932 Draft: 17-197 1954 BAL																															
1954	TOR	12							2	20																					
PHIL ADRIAN Phil HB-FB-FW-LB 6'0 190 none B: 1933																															
1951	MTL	8																													
1952	MTL	3																													
1953	MTL	14										10	2					1					1								
1954	MTL	14							1	5				8	26	3.3	10	0	1	14	14.0	14	0					1	16	16.0	16
4	Years	39							1	5		10	2	8	26	3.3	10	1	1	14	14.0	14	1					1	16	16.0	16
KESI AFALAVA Kesi K. DT-DE 6'4 250 Hawaii B: 9/26/1961																															
1984	WPG	2					0.5																								
1984	BC	1																													
1984	Year	3					0.5																								
PATRICK AFIF Patrick Simon OT 6'7 320 Orange Coast JC; Washington State B: 3/20/1983 Los Angeles, CA Pro: U																															
2010	EDM	2				1																									
BOB AGLER Robert J. FB 6'1 210 Otterbein B: 3/13/1924 Columbus, OH D: 9/16/2005 Westerville, OH Pro: N																															
1951	CAL	13										11	2	34	109	3.2	29	2	2	26	13.0		0	1	8	8.0	8	8	141	17.6	
JOE AGUIRRE Joseph A. E 6'3 225 St. Mary's (California) B: 1/1918 Rock Springs, WY D: 7/13/1985 Grass Valley, CA Draft: 11-100 1941 WAS Pro: AN																															
1950	WPG+	11										57	2						17	292	17.2		2								
1951	WPG	7										23	0						2	12	6.0		0								
1952	EDM	9										57	5						38	549	14.4	53	5								
1953	SAS	1										1	0						3	43	14.3		0								
1954	SAS	16										85	0	1	-2	-2.0	-2	0	2	32	16.0	0	0								
1955	SAS	14										73	0																		

Year	Team	GP	FM	FF	FR	TK	SK	YDS	IR	YDS	PD	PTS	TD	RA	YDS	AVG	LG	TD	REC	YDS	AVG	LG	TD	PR	YDS	AVG	LG	KOR	YDS	AVG	LG
6	Years	58										296	7	1	-2	-2.0	-2	0	62	928	15.0	53	7								
JOHNNY AGUIRRE Juanito T 6'2 225 Southern California B: 8/22/1919 San Francisco, CA Draft: 16-163 1944 CLE																															
1948	CAL	12																													
1949	CAL	14																													
1950	CAL	1																													
3	Years	27																													
JERRY AHLIN Jerry F. LB 6'4 225 Idaho B: 8/12/1945																															
1969	HAM	1																													
ERNIE AHOFF Ernest G-T 5'10 230 Winnipeg YMHA Jrs. B: 1923 D: 11/23/1985																															
1946	WPG	8																													
1947	WPG	8																													
1948	WPG	7																													
1949	WPG	13																													
4	Years	36																													
BRIAN AH YAT Brian QB 6'0 190 Montana B: 11/21/1975 Honolulu, HI																															
1999	WPG	18				0																									
2000	WPG	9				0																									
2001	WPG	18				0								2	8	4.0	6	0													
3	Years	45				0								2	8	4.0	6	0													
HARLAND AH YOU Harland K. DE 6'2 280 Brigham Young B: 2/26/1972 Kailua, HI Draft: 3-16 1998 CAL																															
1998	CAL	10				1																									
JUNIOR AH YOU Miki DE 6'2 233 Arizona State B: 12/30/1948 Honolulu, HI Draft: 17-425 1972 NE Pro: U																															
1972	MTL	14	0		1																										
1973	MTL	8	1		0				1	14																					
1974	MTL+	9			1																										
1975	MTL+	16																													
1976	MTL*	16	0		1																										
1977	MTL	9																													
1978	MTL	10	0		1							6	1																		
1979	MTL*	16	0		1							6	1																		
1980	MTL	16																													
1981	MTL+	15	0		2		5.5					6	1															1	0	0.0	0
10	Years	129	1		7		5.5		1	14		18	3															1	0	0.0	0
KOJO AIDOO Kojo FB 6'0 240 McMaster B: 11/27/1978 Ashtown Kumasi, Ghana Draft: 2-10 2003 EDM																															
2003	EDM	10				6								1	2	2.0	2	0													
2003	WPG	2				0																									
2003	Year	12				6								1	2	2.0	2	0													
2004	HAM	12				2								6	11	1.8	3	0	1	11	11.0	11	0								
2005	HAM	18				5								18	116	6.4	33	0	2	19	9.5	12	0								
2006	HAM	17	1	0	0	7								2	4	2.0	2	0	1	15	15.0	15	0								
2007	TOR	1				0																									
5	Years	58	1	0	0	20								27	133	4.9	33	0	4	45	11.3	15	0								
KRIS AIKEN Kristopher S 5'9 186 Western Ontario B: 8/24/1978 Montreal, QC																															
2004	TOR	7				4																						1	4	4.0	4
2005	TOR	7				4																									
2	Years	14				8																						1	4	4.0	4
WAYNE AIKEN Wayne HB-LB 6'1 190 British Columbia B: 1936																															
1959	CAL	8							2	20				3	3	1.0	2	0						12	58	4.8	9				
1960	CAL	6	0		2				1																						
2	Years	14	0		2				3	20				3	3	1.0	2	0						12	58	4.8	9				
TONY AKINS Anthony Royell WR 5'9 181 East Mississippi JC; Northeastern Louisiana B: 5/10/1977 Starkville, MS																															
1999	HAM	9				0						24	4	1	7	7.0	7	0	17	375	22.1	70	4	18	151	8.4	38	18	381	21.2	45
2000	HAM	9	1	0	0	4						12	2	1	-1	-1.0	-1	0	7	88	12.6	20	0	38	393	10.3	67	2	48	24.0	43
2001	HAM	16	1	0	1	0						6	1	1	7	7.0	7	0	29	461	15.9	55	1	35	178	5.1	16	4	62	15.5	23
2002	HAM	13	1	0	1	1						42	7						38	732	19.3	84	7	5	31	6.2	12				
2003	HAM	14				0						12	2						30	482	16.1	56	2								
5	Years	61	3	0	2	5						96	16	3	13	4.3	7	0	121	2138	17.7	84	14	96	753	7.8	67	24	491	20.5	45
CLIFTON ALAPA Clifton Farrell DE 6'2 238 Arizona State B: 12/14/1954 Kahuku, HI Pro: U																															
1977	MTL	12	0		1																										
1978	MTL	10	0		1																										
1978	HAM	4																													
1978	Year	14	0		1																										
2	Years	22	0		2																										
STEVE ALATORRE Steven M. QB 6'0 175 Cypress JC; Tennessee B: 9/3/1959 Los Angeles County, CA																															
1982	MTL	3	1		0									4	20	5.0	11	0													
FRANKIE ALBERT Frank Cullen QB 5'9 160 Stanford B: 1/27/1920 Chicago, IL D: 9/4/2002 Palo Alto, CA Draft: 1-10 1942 CHIB Pro: AN																															
1953	CAL	14										10	2	53	-26	-0.5	31	2	1	9	9.0	9	0								
NICK ALBERT Nick G 5'9 210 Tulsa B: 1918																															
1949	EDM	4																													
BILL ALBRIGHT William Charles OG-OT-DT 6'1 245 Wisconsin B: 4/4/1929 Racine, WI Draft: 20-242 1951 NYG Pro: N																															
1955	TOR+	8							1	3																					
1956	TOR+	12																													
1957	TOR	14																										7	33	4.7	12
1958	MTL	1																													
4	Years	35							1	3																		7	33	4.7	12
DAVID ALBRIGHT David J. LB 6'2 235 Chabot JC; San Jose State B: 1/25/1960 Oakland, CA Pro: U																															
1986	SAS	8	0		2		2.0																					3	28	9.3	19
1987	SAS	18	0		2	118	2.0																								
1988	SAS	18			2	92	5.0		1	2																					
1989	SAS	12	0		2	79	1.0																								
1990	SAS	11				44																									
1991	SAS	9				44	2.0																								
6	Years	76	0		8	377	12.0		1	2																		3	28	9.3	19
IRA ALBRIGHT Ira Ladol RB 5'11 260 Tyler JC; Northeastern State B: 1/2/1959 Dallas, TX Pro: NU																															
1986	MTL	1												1	2	2.0	2	0													
BARRY ALDAG Barry OG-OT-DT 6'0 240 Regina Rams Jrs. B: 1945																															
1968	SAS	3																													
1969	SAS	16	0		2																										
1970	SAS	16	0		1																										
1971	SAS	16																													
4	Years	51	0		3																										
ROGER ALDAG Roger OG-C 6'0 245 Regina Rams Jrs. B: 10/6/1953 Gull Lake, SK																															
1976	SAS	3																													
1977	SAS	16																										1	0	0.0	0
1978	SAS	16																													
1979	SAS	16	0		1																										
1980	SAS	16	0		1																										
1981	SAS	16	0		1																										
1982	SAS+	16																													
1983	SAS+	16																													
1984	SAS	16	0		1																										
1985	SAS	16																													

Year	Team	GP	FM	FF	FR	TK	SK	YDS	IR	YDS	PD	PTS	TD	RA	YDS	AVG	LG	TD	REC	YDS	AVG	LG	TD	PR	YDS	AVG	LG	KOR	YDS	AVG	LG
1986	SAS*	18																													
1987	SAS*	18				4																									
1988	SAS*	18			1	1																									
1989	SAS*	18				0																									
1990	SAS*	18				3																									
1991	SAS+	16				1																									
1992	SAS	18				1																									
17	Years	271	0		5	10																						1	0	0.0	0
JOHN ALDERTON John Reber DE 6'1 200 Maryland B: 9/5/1931 Draft: 7-78 1953 PIT Pro: N																															
1956	CAL	3																	3	33	11.0	14	0								
ALLEN RAY ALDRIDGE Allen Ray LB 6'6 240 Prairie View A&M B: 4/27/1945 Pro: NW																															
1967	TOR	4	0		1																										
1968	TOR+	14							2	6		6	1																		
1969	TOR	14			1				2	33		6	1																		
1970	HAM	10	2		1				2	53		6	1																		
4	Years	42	2		3				6	92		18	3																		
DICK ALDRIDGE Dick LB-HDB 6'0 198 Lakeshore Jrs.; Waterloo B: 1/19/1941 Toronto, ON Draft: 1-8 1964 BC																															
1965	TOR	14	0		2				2	42		6	1											35	218	6.2	22	4	9	2.3	6
1966	TOR	14	2		0				3	94														24	123	5.1	13	2	22	11.0	20
1967	TOR	14	2		0																			30	171	5.7	19	1	10	10.0	10
1968	TOR	5	0		1				1	0																					
1969	TOR	14			2																										
1970	TOR	14	2		2				7	33														16	53	3.3	9	1	22	22.0	22
1971	TOR	14	0		2				3	26																					
1972	TOR	14	0		1				1	1																					
1973	TOR	14	0		3				1	6																					
1974	HAM	10							1	11																					
10	Years	127	6		13				19	213		6	1											105	565	5.4	22	8	63	7.9	22
MELVIN ALDRIDGE Melvin Keith LB-DB 6'2 195 Tyler JC; Murray State B: 7/22/1970 Mount Pleasant, TX Pro: EN																															
1996	OTT	4				21					1																				
1997	HAM	7				24	1.0	7.0			1																				
2	Years	11				45	1.0	7.0			2																				
INK ALEAGA Ink A. LB 6'1 241 Washington B: 4/27/1973 Honolulu, HI Pro: N																															
2002	BC	2	0	1	1	9																									
GEORGE ALEVISATOS George DG 5'11 225 Concordia (Quebec); Lakeshore Alouette Flyers Ints. B: 8/25/1938 Montreal, QC																															
1960	MTL	3																													
1962	HAM	4																													
2	Years	7																													
ANDRE ALEXANDER Henry Alex WR 5'6 165 Fresno State B: 4/15/1967 San Francisco, CA Pro: E																															
1989	CAL	7	1		0	1						12	2	2	2	1.0	2	0	19	311	16.4	51	2	16	78	4.9	15	4	111	27.8	33
BILL ALEXANDER William HB B: 6/12/1924 Calgary, AB																															
1946	CAL	5																													
1947	CAL	4																													
2	Years	9																													
CURTIS ALEXANDER James Curtis RB 6'0 204 Alabama B: 6/11/1974 Memphis, TN Draft: 4-122 1998 DEN Pro: EX																															
2002	HAM	1	2	0	0	0								13	58	4.5	12	0	1	6	6.0	6	0								
DONOVAN ALEXANDER Donovan CB-S 5'11 181 North Dakota B: 4/30/1985 Winnpeg, MB Draft: 3C-23 2007 MTL																															
2008	MTL	4				0																									
2009	SAS	16	0	0	2	36					3																				
2010	SAS	15				14																									
2011	EDM	18	0	1	0	41			2	0	5																				
4	Years	53	0	1	2	91			2	0	8																				
GEORGE ALEXANDER George HB 180 East Calgary Jrs. B: 1918																															
1946	CAL	8										1	0																		
1947	CAL	8																													
2	Years	16										1	0																		
JESSE ALEXANDER Jesse LB 6'1 226 Wilfrid Laurier B: 5/8/1991 Kitchener, ON Draft: 5-37 2006 SAS																															
2007	TOR	2				1																									
KEVIN ALEXANDER Kevin John WR 5'9 185 Glendale CC; Utah State B: 1/23/1975 Baton Rouge, LA Pro: N																															
2000	MTL	9				0						18	3	1	6	6.0	6	0	18	272	15.1	38	3					0	23		23
2001	MTL	13				2						18	3						26	343	13.2	31	3								
2002	OTT	6	0	0	1	0													10	73	7.3	20	0								
3	Years	28	0	0	1	2						36	6	1	6	6.0	6	0	54	688	12.7	38	6					0	23		23
MIKE ALEXANDER Michael Fitzgerald SB 6'3 205 Nassau CC; Penn State B: 3/19/1965 New York, NY Draft: 8-199 1988 LARI Pro: N																															
1994	BAL	7	0		1	3						6	1						3	71	23.7	49	1								
1995	BAL	3				1																									
2	Years	10	0		1	4						6	1						3	71	23.7	49	1								
RAY ALEXANDER Vernest Raynard WR 6'4 195 Florida A&M B: 1/8/1962 Miami, FL Draft: TD 1984 TB-USFL Pro: N																															
1985	CAL	8	1		0							6	1						22	361	16.4	44	1								
1986	CAL+	18	3		0							62	10						88	1590	18.1	59	10								
1990	BC+	15	1		0	2						54	9						65	1120	17.2	44	9								
1991	BC*	16	1		0	1						18	3						104	1605	15.4	31	3								
1992	BC	10	3		0	1						12	2	1	-5	-5.0	-5	0	56	786	14.0	44	2								
1993	BC	15	0		1	0						24	4						77	1300	16.9	43	4								
1994	BC+	18	1		0	8						36	6	1	3	3.0	3	0	85	1234	14.5	40	6								
1995	OTT	14				4						36	6						59	801	13.6	47	5	18	174	9.7	76				
8	Years	114	10		1	16						248	41	2	-2	-1.0	3	0	556	8797	15.8	59	40	18	174	9.7	76				
TROY ALEXANDER Troy NT 6'0 245 Eastern Washington B: 8/16/1971 Edmonton, AB Draft: Bonus-4 1995 SAS																															
1995	SAS	16				24	1.0	2.0																							
1996	SAS	10	0		1	13	1.0	6.0																							
1997	SAS	18				28	10.0	73.0			1																				
1998	BC	4	0	0	1	3																									
4	Years	48	0	0	2	68	12.0	81.0			1																				
STEVE ALEXANDRE Steve DE 6'0 238 Ottawa B: 9/20/1978 Montreal, QC																															
2002	HAM	16				10	1.0																								
2003	HAM	6				0																									
2	Years	22				10	1.0																								
ALTON ALEXIS Alton WR 6'0 184 Tulane B: 11/16/1957 New Iberia, LA Draft: 11-281 1980 CIN Pro: NU																															
1981	CAL	2																	5	95	19.0	39	0								
1982	CAL	16	2		0							30	5	1	9	9.0	9	0	25	440	17.6	41	5	18	96	5.3	20	15	380	25.3	71
2	Years	18	2		0							30	5	1	9	9.0	9	0	30	535	17.8	41	5	18	96	5.3	20	15	380	25.3	71
PAUL ALFORD Paul G-HB 5'11 210 Hamilton Wildcats Jrs; Hamilton Tiger Jrs. B: 1928																															
1950	EDM	6																													
1951	CAL	3																													
1952	CAL	15																													
3	Years	24																													
TED ALFORD Ted WR 5'9 165 Langston B: 2/2/1971 Columbia, MS																															
1996	BC	14	0		1	2					1	12	2						47	721	15.3	49	2	28	167	6.0	46	3	76	25.3	33
1997	HAM	3				0													9	112	12.4	18	0								
1997	WPG	5	1	0	0	1													19	247	13.0	65	0					2	60	30.0	40
1997	Year	8	1	0	0	1													28	359	12.8	65	0					2	60	30.0	40
2001	TOR+	17				0						26	4						75	1172	15.6	75	4	1	8	8.0	8	1	6	6.0	6

Year	Team	GP	FM	FF	FR	TK	SK	YDS	IR	YDS	PD	PTS	TD	RA	YDS	AVG	LG	TD	REC	YDS	AVG	LG	TD	PR	YDS	AVG	LG	KOR	YDS	AVG	LG
2002	TOR	9				1						6	1						34	322	9.5	35	1								
2004	CAL	2				0						6	1						7	74	10.6	25	1								
5	Years	45	1	0	1	4					1	50	8						191	2648	13.9	75	8	29	175	6.0	46	6	142	23.7	40
BAMIDELE ALI Bamidele DE 6'3 218 Kentucky B: 11/1/1976 Cheverly, MD																															
1999	SAS	13	0	0	1	46	5.0	31.0	1	9	0																				
2000	SAS	11	0	0	1	27	2.0	11.0	2	58	1																				
2	Years	24	0	0	2	73	7.0	42.0	3	67	1																				
MOUSTAFA ALI Moustafa DB 6'3 200 Carleton B: 12/30/1965 Alexandria, Egypt Draft: 2-16 1989 WPG																															
1989	WPG	17				21			2	25																					
1990	CAL	8				0																		1	4	4.0	4				
2	Years	25				21			2	25														1	4	4.0	4				
TUINEAU ALIPATE Tuineau A. LB 6'1 245 Washington State B: 8/21/1967 Tonga Pro: EN																															
1989	SAS	17	0		3	31			1	12																		7	70	10.0	19
1990	SAS	18	1		0	35								1	3	3.0	3	0										3	33	11.0	16
1991	HAM	7	0		1	25	3.0																								
3	Years	42	1		4	91	3.0		1	12				1	3	3.0	3	0										10	103	10.3	19
TIM ALLAN Tim OT 6'2 240 Toronto B: 5/29/1955 Draft: TE 1978 WPG																															
1978	WPG	1																													
1978	TOR	5	0		1							6	1																		
1978	Year	6	0		1							6	1																		
DON ALLARD Donald J. QB-HB-DB 6'0 189 Boston College B: 4/21/1936 D: 5/4/2002 Winchester, MA Draft: 1-4 1959 WAS Pro: N																															
1959	SAS	12										6	1	59	287	4.9	17	1													
1960	SAS	7	5		0									45	232	5.2	29	0													
1961	MTL	2												8	46	5.8	19	0													
3	Years	21	5		0							6	1	112	565	5.0	29	1													
GUILLAUME ALLARD-CAMEUS Guillaume FB 6'0 215 Laval B: 2/11/1984 Laval, QC Draft: 5A-33 2009 HAM																															
2009	HAM	4				2																									
2009	MTL	3				0																									
2009	Year	7				2																									
RON ALLBRIGHT Ron OG-OT-DE-LB 6'0 220 Calgary Bronks Jrs. B: 1934																															
1956	CAL	14	1		2				1	0																					
1957	CAL	16	0		3				1	0																					
1958	CAL	16	0		2																										
1959	CAL	16							1																						
1960	CAL	16	0		2																										
1961	CAL	14																													
1962	CAL	16																													
1963	CAL	16	0		1														1	-4	-4.0	-4	0								
1964	CAL	16																													
1965	CAL	16																													
1966	CAL	16																													
1967	CAL	16																													
12	Years	188	1		10				3	0									1	-4	-4.0	-4	0								
MARV ALLEMANG Marvin DE-C-G-DT 6'3 255 Burlington Braves Jrs.; Acadia B: 12/3/1953 Ancaster, ON Draft: 1-7 1975 OTT																															
1975	OTT	16																													
1976	OTT	16			1																										
1977	HAM	15	0		1																										
1978	HAM	16	0		1																										
1979	WPG	16																													
1980	WPG	16																													
1981	WPG	4																													
1982	HAM	16																													
1983	HAM	16																													
1984	HAM	15																													
1985	HAM+	16	0		2																										
1986	HAM+	18																													
1987	OTT	11				0																									
1988	OTT	18	0		2																										
14	Years	209	0		7	0																									
AMOS ALLEN Albert RB 5'8 185 Dixie State; South Dakota B: 7/20/1983 Miami, FL																															
2009	TOR	5				1																		18	98	5.4	12	9	236	26.2	84
ANDRE ALLEN Andre OL 6'0 320 Jacksonville State B: 2/28/1971 Anniston, AL																															
1994	LV	5																													
ANDRE ALLEN Andre DE 6'3 245 Northern Iowa B: 6/24/1973 Itta Bene, MS Pro: E																															
1995	WPG	1				1																									
BARCLAY ALLEN Barclay QB-DH-WR 6'2 200 NDG Maple Leafs Jrs.; Southern Illinois B: 6/23/1945																															
1970	MTL	3																													
1970	OTT	9												2	2	1.0	7	0													
1970	Year	12												2	2	1.0	7	0													
1971	OTT	14							2	48		6	1																		
1972	CAL	14							2	11																					
1973	MTL	8							1	0														4	3	0.8	6				
1974	MTL	1																													
5	Years	40							5	59		6	1	2	2	1.0	7	0						4	3	0.8	6				
BRIAN ALLEN Brian G. WR 6'0 184 Hutchinson CC; Idaho B: 8/6/1962 San Bernardino, CA Draft: 15B-314 1984 OKL-USFL																															
1984	EDM	1																	2	10	5.0	7	0								
DALVA ALLEN Dalva Ray T 6'5 224 Houston B: 1/13/1935 Gonzales, TX Draft: 23-267 1957 LARM Pro: N																															
1957	TOR	3																													
DAMON ALLEN Damon L. QB 6'1 170 Fullerton State B: 7/29/1963 San Diego, CA Draft: TD 1985 LA-USFL																															
1985	EDM	16	3		3							30	5	36	190	5.3	18	5													
1986	EDM	18	2		0							36	6	31	245	7.9	39	6													
1987	EDM	18	8		3	1						36	6	66	562	8.5	40	6													
1988	EDM	10	5		0	0						6	1	33	130	3.9	13	1													
1989	OTT	13	7		1	4						8	1	75	532	7.1	51	1													
1990	OTT	17	9		3	2						42	7	124	776	6.3	41	7													
1991	OTT+	18	6		1	2						50	8	129	1036	8.0	42	8													
1992	HAM	18	18		7	1						42	7	111	850	7.7	37	7													
1993	EDM	18	8		1	1						36	6	120	920	7.7	43	6													
1994	EDM	18	11		0	1						42	7	120	707	5.9	43	7													
1995	MEM	15	5		3	2								63	427	6.8	25	0													
1996	BC	14	7		3	1						12	2	52	400	7.7	31	2													
1997	BC	18	9	0	4	2						48	8	111	837	7.5	28	8													
1998	BC	18	5	0	1	0						12	2	115	782	6.8	29	2													
1999	BC+	18	13	0	1	1						54	8	136	785	5.8	30	8													
2000	BC	18	7	0	1	1						12	2	58	284	4.9	34	2													
2001	BC	16	10	0	3	0						12	2	86	580	6.7	45	2													
2002	BC	18	7	0	1	2						24	4	70	479	6.8	22	4													
2003	TOR	18	9	0	0	2						24	4	76	507	6.7	26	4													
2004	TOR	12				0						18	3	40	212	5.3	32	3													
2005	TOR*	18	9	0	0	1						24	4	85	467	5.5	26	4													
2006	TOR	14	1	4	1	1								25	197	7.9	22	0													
2007	TOR	9	2	0	2	0								4	15	3.8	6	0													

Year	Team	GP	FM	FF	FR	TK	SK	YDS	IR	YDS	PD	PTS	TD	RA	YDS	AVG	LG	TD	REC	YDS	AVG	LG	TD	PR	YDS	AVG	LG	KOR	YDS	AVG	LG
23	Years	370	161	4	39	25						568	93	1766	11920	6.7	51	93													
DAVID ALLEN David Lee RB 5'9 195 Kansas State B: 2/9/1978 Euless, TX Pro: EN																															
2005	CAL	4	1	0	0	0						12	2	13	86	6.6	22	1	5	84	16.8	25	1	10	73	7.3	36	11	203	18.5	27
2006	CAL	3				0						6	1	1	2	2.0	2	0	2	11	5.5	6	1	12	75	6.3	16	1	13	13.0	13
2	Years	7	1	0	0	0						18	3	14	88	6.3	22	1	7	95	13.6	25	2	22	148	6.7	36	12	216	18.0	27
ELMER ALLEN Elmer Dale LB 6'2 237 Mississippi B: 11/3/1949 Delhi, LA Draft: 6B-136 1972 HOU																															
1972	MTL	1																													
ERIC ALLEN Eric Benjamin HB-SE 5'10 162 Michigan State B: 5/18/1949 Georgetown, SC Draft: 4-104 1972 BAL																															
1972	TOR+	14	1		0							48	8	50	220	4.4	14	0	53	1067	20.1	62	8	3	15	5.0	8	18	405	22.5	46
1973	TOR+	14	4		1							24	4	19	52	2.7	14	0	40	797	19.9	100	4	6	56	9.3	18	16	442	27.6	78
1974	TOR	7	1		0							18	3						18	281	15.6	48	3					2	39	19.5	20
1975	TOR	9	1		1							6	1	14	51	3.6	9	0	19	256	13.5	46	1	1	24	24.0	24	24	565	23.5	44
4	Years	44	7		2							96	16	83	323	3.9	14	0	130	2401	18.5	100	16	10	95	9.5	24	60	1451	24.2	78
ERNIE ALLEN Ernest Duncan, Jr. (Pokey) CB-DH 6'1 191 Utah B: 1/29/1943 Superior, MT D: 12/30/1996 Missoula, MT																															
1965	BC	15	0		1				4	27														55	262	4.8	14	4	90	22.5	34
1966	BC	16	0		1				2	15		6	1	3	43	14.3	33	1						6	53	8.8	18	2	46	23.0	24
1967	BC	5							1	0														18	97	5.4	13				
1967	EDM	2							1	3																					
1967	Year	7							2	3														18	97	5.4	13				
3	Years	36	0		2				8	45		6	1	3	43	14.3	33	1						79	412	5.2	18	6	136	22.7	34
GARY ALLEN Gary Eugene RB 5'10 183 Hawaii B: 4/23/1960 Draft: 6-148 1982 HOU Pro: N																															
1986	CAL*	15	8		0							30	5	205	1153	5.6	38	4	27	226	8.4	32	1	61	768	12.6	72	5	79	15.8	22
1987	CAL+	15	5		0	3						42	7	165	857	5.2	34	5	43	449	10.4	42	2	35	321	9.2	39	1	9	9.0	9
1988	CAL	3				0						6	1	20	100	5.0	17	1	9	68	7.6	15	0	12	67	5.6	13				
1988	WPG	3	1		0	0								8	53	6.6	20	0						8	25	3.1	8	7	170	24.3	47
1988	Year	6	1		0	0						6	1	28	153	5.5	20	1	9	68	7.6	15	0	20	92	4.6	13	7	170	24.3	47
3	Years	33	14		0	3						78	13	398	2163	5.4	38	10	79	743	9.4	42	3	116	1181	10.2	72	13	258	19.8	47
IAN ALLEN Ian Ramon OT 6'4 313 Purdue B: 7/22/1978 Newark, NJ Pro: EN																															
2006	MTL	6				0																									
JEFF ALLEN Jeffrey DB 5'11 185 California-Davis B: 7/1/1958 Richmond, IN Draft: 8A-212 1980 MIA Pro: N																															
1981	TOR	1																													
KEVIN ALLEN Kevin DB 5'10 170 Virginia State B: 5/14/1972																															
1995	CAL	4				5																									
LOU ALLEN Louis Eugene T 6'3 220 Duke B: 7/12/1924 Gadsden, AL D: 4/16/2008 Greensboro, NC Draft: 5B-60 1950 PIT Pro: N																															
1952	MTL	1																													
MICHAEL ALLEN Michael DB 5'11 165 Thunder Bay Giants Jrs.; Carleton B: 8/1/1964 Clarendon, Jamaica Draft: 4B-29 1988 WPG																															
1988	WPG	17	1		4	0						18	3											1	3	3.0	3	13	241	18.5	37
1989	WPG	16	0		2	27			2	25		6	1																		
1990	WPG	18				4																		1	20	20.0	20				
1991	WPG	12	0		2	38	1.0		1	37		6	1															2	44	22.0	24
1992	OTT	18				19																						1	5	5.0	5
1993	OTT	5				9																									
1993	BC	9				8																									
1993	Year	14				19																									
1994	BC	9	0		2	9																									
7	Years	95	1		10	114	1.0		3	62		30	5											2	23	11.5	20	16	290	18.1	37
TAUREAN ALLEN Taurean DB 5'10 195 Wilfrid Laurier B: 2/15/1987 Etobicoke, ON Draft: 2-13 2010 CAL																															
2010	CAL	6				7																									
VINCE ALLEN Vincent HB 5'8 180 Indiana State B: 5/13/1955 Richmond, IN																															
1978	HAM	3	1		0							6	1	34	145	4.3	12	1	6	78	13.0	52	0	10	151	15.1	35	4	81	20.3	27
ZOCK ALLEN Zock Alexander LB 6'1 220 Texas A&M-Kingsville B: 6/12/1968 Madisonville, TX																															
1991	BC	6	0		1	31	2.0																								
1992	BC	3				13																									
1993	BC	15	0		1	67	2.0	11.0																							
1994	BC	2				8																									
1994	LV	1				0																									
1994	Year	3				8																									
4	Years	26	0		2	119	4.0	11.0																							
BUTCH ALLISON Buford Needham OG 6'3 245 Missouri B: 10/29/1944 Fort Worth, TX Draft: 7A-57 1966 OAK; 2-31 1966 BAL																															
1967	EDM	1																													
JOE ALLISON Joe K 6'0 200 Memphis B: 1/20/1970																															
1995	MEM	1				0						5	0																		
RODNEY ALLISON Rodney Gene QB 5'11 188 Texas Tech B: 1/29/1956 Odessa, TX																															
1978	TOR	15												13	49	3.8	23	0													
WAYNE ALLISON Wayne DB 5'11 185 Waterloo; Wilfrid Laurier B: 12/17/1949 Toronto, ON Draft: 1B-9 1973 EDM																															
1973	TOR	14	2		1				1	15														4	35	8.8	13	8	175	21.9	27
1974	TOR	16	1		1				2	65														62	318	5.1	19				
1975	TOR	16	0		1				1	24														24	222	9.3	30				
1976	TOR	16							2	40																					
1977	TOR	5																	1	14	14.0	14	0								
1977	CAL	4							1	5														10	94	9.4	24				
1977	Year	9							1	5									1	14	14.0	14	0	10	94	9.4	24				
1978	TOR	5	0		1																							1	15	15.0	15
1978	WPG	9	0		1																										
1978	Year	14	0		2																							1	15	15.0	15
6	Years	72	3		5				7	149									1	14	14.0	14	0	100	669	6.7	30	9	190	21.1	27
BUDDY ALLISTON Vaughn Samuel, Jr. OG-LB 6'0 218 Mississippi B: 12/14/1933 Jackson, MS Draft: 15-176 1956 GB Pro: N																															
1956	WPG+	16							2	15																		1	0	0.0	0
1959	WPG	1																													
2	Years	17							2	15																		1	0	0.0	0
JEFF ALMON Jeff FB 6'3 225 Calgary B: 5/20/1978 Draft: 4-36 2002 CAL																															
2003	BC	1				0																									
GERALD ALPHIN Gerald Alan WR-SB 6'3 220 Kansas State B: 5/21/1964 Portland, OR Pro: N																															
1986	MTL	6	1		0							12	2						20	409	20.5	55	2								
1987	OTT	14	4		0	2						48	8	4	12	3.0	9	0	67	1029	15.4	57	8					10	189	18.9	32
1988	OTT+	15	2		0							32	5	1	-2	-2.0	-2	0	64	1307	20.4	61	5								
1989	OTT	17				4						60	10	3	9	3.0	14	0	68	1471	21.6	78	10								
1992	WPG	9				3						12	2						26	507	19.5	73	2								
1993	WPG	16	2		0	2						24	4						55	1052	19.1	54	4					1	0	0.0	0
1994	WPG	18	2		0	4						108	18						73	994	13.6	50	18								
1995	WPG	9				1													32	417	13.0	33	0								
1995	BAL	4				1						12	2						9	129	14.3	26	2								
1995	Year	13				2						12	2						41	546	13.3	33	2								
8	Years	104	11		0	17						308	51	8	19	2.4	14	0	414	7315	17.7	78	51					11	189	17.2	32
ANTHONY ALRIDGE Anthony Eugene RB 5'9 175 Houston B: 11/24/1983 Tarrant County, TX																															
2010	TOR	3	1	0	0	1								13	47	3.6	8	0	2	3	1.5	4	0					2	41	20.5	24
WAYMON ALRIDGE Waymon Lee WR-SB 5'10 180 Nevada-Las Vegas B: 3/30/1960																															
1983	CAL	2										6	1						8	152	19.0	34	1					1	35	35.0	35
1984	OTT	13	2		2							30	5						36	700	19.4	90	5	4	29	7.3	10	5	83	16.6	25
1985	OTT	13	2		0							24	4						49	797	16.3	53	4					0	14		14
1986	EDM	1																	2	25	12.5	15	0					1	35	35.0	35
4	Years	29	4		2							60	10						95	1674	17.6	90	10	4	29	7.3	10	7	167	23.9	35

Year	Team	GP	FM	FF	FR	TK	SK	YDS	IR	YDS	PD	PTS	TD	RA	YDS	AVG	LG	TD	REC	YDS	AVG	LG	TD	PR	YDS	AVG	LG	KOR	YDS	AVG	LG
CHARLES ALSTON Charles DE 6'5 272 Marshall*; Independence CC; Bowie State B: 6/8/1978 Washington, DC Pro: E																															
2005	EDM	3	0	1	0	5																									
2006	EDM	13	0	2	1	21	4.0	20.0				6	1																		
2007	EDM	6	0	1	0	11	1.0	2.0																							
3	Years	22	0	4	1	37	5.0	22.0				6	1																		
RICHARD ALSTON Richard WR 5'11 215 East Carolina B: 11/20/1980 Newark, NJ Pro: EN																															
2006	EDM	7	1	0	0	0						2	0						23	261	11.3	55	0	3	19	6.3	8	1	9	9.0	9
2007	HAM	1				0													1	12	12.0	12	0					1	30	30.0	30
2	Years	8	1	0	0	0						2	0						24	273	11.4	55	0	3	19	6.3	8	2	39	19.5	30
RONNIE AMADI Ronnie DH 6'0 185 Kansas B: 10/6/1981																															
2009	CAL	11				28	1.0		0	0	3																				
JIM AMBROSE Jim T 6'2 232 NDG Maple Leafs Jrs. B: 1930 D: 9/10/1953 Ottawa, ON																															
1950	MTL	10																													
1951	MTL	10										8	0																		
1952	MTL	10																													
3	Years	30										8	0																		
RANDY AMBROSIE Randy OG 6'4 250 Manitoba B: 3/16/1963 Winnipeg, MB Draft: 1-2 1985 CAL																															
1985	CAL	13																	1	0	0.0	0	0					1	0	0.0	0
1986	CAL	17																													
1987	CAL	4				0																									
1987	TOR	13				0																									
1987	Year	17				0																									
1988	TOR	15				2																									
1989	EDM	18	0		1	1																									
1990	EDM	13				3																						1	0	0.0	0
1991	EDM	18				1																									
1992	EDM	18				1																									
1993	EDM	13	0		1	0																									
9	Years	129	0		2	8													1	0	0.0	0	0					2	0	0.0	0
LYNN AMEDEE Lynn QB 5'9 185 Louisiana State B: 8/3/1941 Baton Rouge, LA																															
1963	EDM	10	2		0							6	1	28	143	5.1	17	0	1	32	32.0	32	1								
1964	EDM	6												6	-16	-2.7	2	0	1	7	7.0	7	0								
2	Years	16	2		0							6	1	34	127	3.7	17	0	2	39	19.5	32	1								
DAVE AMER David TE 6'4 220 Simon Fraser B: 9/22/1957 Draft: 3B-21 1982 CAL																															
1982	CAL	5																	2	37	18.5	23	0								
ARCHIE AMERSON Archie J. RB-SB 5'8 175 Northern Arizona B: 8/24/1974 San Diego, CA																															
1997	HAM	15	6	0	0	3						30	5	144	630	4.4	64	4	40	414	10.4	46	1					2	34	17.0	17
1998	HAM	18	4	0	0	3						48	8	160	703	4.4	69	3	65	750	11.5	89	5					24	594	24.8	54
1999	HAM	13	2	0	0	0						36	6	4	67	16.8	70	1	47	700	14.9	60	5	25	183	7.3	42	18	393	21.8	57
2000	HAM	18	2	0	0	5						36	6	6	16	2.7	10	0	70	1198	17.1	75	6	51	351	6.9	38	51	948	18.6	40
2001	TOR	1				0													5	32	6.4	15	0					2	42	21.0	28
2001	HAM	9	4	0	0	2						30	5	21	120	5.7	25	0	26	380	14.6	41	5	29	231	8.0	25	3	67	22.3	32
2001	Year	10	4	0	0	2						30	5	21	120	5.7	25	0	31	402	13.0	41	5	29	231	8.0	25	5	109	21.8	32
2002	HAM	17	3	0	0	4						36	6	11	53	4.8	13	0	61	970	15.9	53	6	8	105	13.1	68	1	7	7.0	7
2003	HAM	18				7						26	4	9	41	4.6	9	0	75	960	12.8	45	4	4	51	12.8	23				
2004	HAM	14				3						32	5	1	24	24.0	24	0	47	894	19.0	68	5								
8	Years	114	21	0	0	27						274	45	356	1654	4.6	70	8	436	6298	14.4	89	37	117	921	7.9	68	101	2085	20.6	57
OTIS AMEY Fred Otis Holmes WR 5'10 197 Sacramento State B: 12/4/1981 Alameda County, CA Pro: NU																															
2009	WPG	5				3													13	188	14.5	47	0	2	8	4.0	7				
WILLIE AMOS Willie CB 6'0 190 Nebraska B: 7/28/1982 Nolan County, TX Pro: E																															
2008	WPG	11	0	1	1	52			1	46	7																				
JON ANABO Johanes S. QB 6'3 210 Los Angeles Valley JC; Fresno State B: 8/24/1939 Los Angeles, CA Draft: 19-263(f) 1962 CLE; 3-177 1963 OAK																															
1964	EDM	6												17	65	3.8	21	0													
1965	EDM	5	1		0									1	-12	-12.0	-12	0													
2	Years	11	1		0									18	53	2.9	21	0													
ROY ANANNY Roy Fredrick FW-E B: 10/11/1924 D: 4/12/2011																															
1946	OTT	7																													
1947	OTT	3																													
2	Years	10																													
ANDRE ANDERSON Andre Deshon DT 6'5 259 New Mexico State B: 12/6/1955 Garland, TX Draft: 9-246 1978 LARM																															
1978	BC	4	0		1																										
BRET ANDERSON Bret SB-K 6'3 210 Simon Fraser B: 4/23/1975 New Westminster, BC Draft: 4-25 1997 BC																															
1997	BC	13				7																									
1998	BC	13				12													1	12	12.0	12	0								
1999	BC	18				21						2	0						1	9	9.0	9	0								
2000	BC	7				10													5	49	9.8	13	0								
2001	BC	15	1	0	0	7						7	1						18	189	10.5	16	1								
2002	BC	18	1	0	0	7						7	1						28	409	14.6	33	1								
2003	BC	18	0	0	1	5						14	2	1	-3	-3.0	-3	0	20	237	11.9	36	2								
2004	BC	5				0																									
2005	BC	18	1	0	0	11						1	0						3	25	8.3	11	0					1	7	7.0	7
2006	BC	18	1	0	0	8													7	75	10.7	15	0					1	0	0.0	0
2007	BC	18				5						10	0						1	14	14.0	14	0								
2008	BC	15	1	0	0	3						6	1						9	118	13.1	28	1								
2009	BC	5				0																									
13	Years	181	5	0	1	96						47	5	1	-3	-3.0	-3	0	93	1137	12.2	36	5					2	7	3.5	7
CHUCK ANDERSON Charles C. C-G-E 6'0 225 Ohio State B: 1919 Montgomery, AL																															
1948	CAL+	11																													
1949	MTL	12										15	3										3								
1950	MTL	12																													
1952	MTL	12																													
1953	OTT	14																													
5	Years	61										15	3										3								
CURTIS ANDERSON Jerome Curtis CB 6'0 196 Pittsburgh B: 9/29/1973 Lynchburg, VA Pro: N																															
2001	BC	9	0	1	1	18	1.0	9.0	1	2	1																				
DAMIEN ANDERSON Damien Ramone RB 5'11 209 Northwestern B: 7/17/1979 Wilmington, IL Pro: N																															
2007	EDM	5				1								43	225	5.2	14	0	7	62	8.9	38	0					14	213	15.2	27
2008	EDM	2	1	0	1	0								17	57	3.4	16	0	7	57	8.1	15	0					3	56	18.7	20
2	Years	7	1	0	1	1								60	282	4.7	16	0	14	119	8.5	38	0					17	269	15.8	27
DAVE ANDERSON David QB 6'0 178 Arkansas-Monticello B: 1930 Monticello, AR																															
1952	CAL	10												38	108	2.8	40	0													
DUNSTAN ANDERSON Dunstan Everett DE 6'5 270 Tulsa B: 12/31/1970 Fort Worth, TX D: 5/31/2004 Fort Myers, FL Pro: ENX																															
1996	WPG	5				4	1.0	6.0			1																				
DWIGHT ANDERSON Dwight Orlando CB-DH 5'10 172 Arizona Western JC; South Dakota B: 7/5/1981 Spanish Town, Jamaica Pro: N																															
2007	HAM	15	0	0	2	54			1	0	8																				
2008	CAL	18	0	1	2	54			2	14	11																				
2009	CAL+	18	0	2	4	56			3	53	6	6	1																		
2010	CAL*	18	0	2	2	49			5	246	7	12	2																		
2011	MTL	10				40	1.0	3.0	1	50	5	6	1																		
5	Years	79	0	5	10	253	1.0	3.0	12	363	37	24	4																		
EZZRETT ANDERSON Ezzrett, Jr. (Sugarfoot) DE-OE 6'4 215 Kentucky State B: 2/10/1920 Nashville, AR Pro: A																															
1949	CAL+	14										25	5										5								

Year	Team	GP	FM	FF	FR	TK	SK	YDS	IR	YDS	PD	PTS	TD	RA	YDS	AVG	LG	TD	REC	YDS	AVG	LG	TD	PR	YDS	AVG	LG	KOR	YDS	AVG	LG
1950	CAL	14										15	3						46	673	14.6	28	3								
1951	CAL	7										10	2						34	370	10.9	76	1								
1952	CAL	16			6							10	2						13	147	11.3	27	1					0	8		8
1953	CAL+	16										12	2						19	291	15.3	47	0								
1954	CAL	16	0		1									1	0	0.0	0	0	4	85	21.3	31	0					1	11	11.0	11
6	Years	83	0		7							72	14	1	0	0.0	0	0	116	1566	13.5	76	10					1	19	19.0	11
FRANKIE ANDERSON Frank G. DE-OG 6'1 210 Oklahoma B: 5/24/1928 Oklahoma City, OK D: 9/28/1983 Edmonton, AB Draft: 11-128 1951 DET																															
1952	EDM	12			2							13	1						16	269	16.8	79	1								
1953	EDM+	16										15	3						22	430	19.5		3					1	6	6.0	6
1954	EDM+	12																	2	18	9.0	9	0	1	25	25.0	25	1	4	4.0	4
1955	EDM+	15	2		0														4	39	9.8	14	0								
1956	EDM+	15	0		4																										
1957	EDM+	16	0		2				1	11																					
6	Years	86	2		8				1	11		28	4						44	756	17.2	79	4	1	25	25.0	25	2	10	5.0	6
GARY ANDERSON Gary DL 6'5 235 Concordia B: 7/1/1954 Draft: 6-50 1976 WPG																															
1979	TOR	4																													
GARY ANDERSON Gary Wayne HB 6'0 181 Arkansas B: 4/18/1961 Columbia, MO Draft: 1B-20 1983 SD; 1-5 1983 NJ-USFL Pro: NU																															
1995	MEM	14	1		1	13	2.0	25.0				24	4	66	250	3.8	17	3	28	273	9.8	27	1								
GEORGE ANDERSON George LB 6'3 230 North Shore Cougars Jrs.; Simon Fraser B: 12/30/1948																															
1971	BC	16			1				2	92		6	1															1	8	8.0	8
1972	BC	16	0		1																										
1973	BC	16							2	12																		1	7	7.0	7
1974	TOR	16																										2	28	14.0	18
1975	TOR	16	1		1				2	18																					
1976	TOR	16	0		2																							1	16	16.0	16
6	Years	96	1		5				6	122		6	1															5	59	11.8	18
GREG ANDERSON Gregory CB-DH 5'8 177 Montana B: 9/16/1953 D: 1/8/2000 IL Pro: U																															
1979	MTL	3																										4	111	27.8	38
1979	SAS	1																										4	78	19.5	26
1979	Year	4																										8	189	23.6	38
HARRY ANDERSON Harry (Auby) C-T-G-HB 6'0 185 East Calgary Jrs. B: 1927 Calgary, AB																															
1946	CAL	7										5	1																		
1947	CAL	8																													
1948	CAL	10																													
1949	CAL	14																													
1954	CAL	14																													
5	Years	53										5	1																		
JAMI ANDERSON Jami LB 6'1 220 Pacific B: 7/29/1972 Riverside, CA																															
1995	MEM	17	0		2	43	1.0	6.0																							
JERRY ANDERSON Jerry O. DB 5'11 196 Northeastern Oklahoma A&M JC; Oklahoma B: 10/27/1953 Murfreesboro, TN D: 5/27/1989 Murfreesboro, TN Draft: 4C-105 1977 CIN Pro: N																															
1980	HAM+	16	0		1				3	120		6	1											1	0	0.0	0				
1981	HAM	1	0		1																										
2	Years	17	0		2				3	120		6	1											1	0	0.0	0				
JOHN ANDERSON John DE 6'3 239 Alcorn State B: 3/30/1956																															
1978	OTT	2																													
1979	WPG	1																													
2	Years	3																													
JOHN ANDERSON John HB 6'3 210 Kansas B: 9/28/1933 Draft: 21-249 1955 PHI																															
1955	MTL	2												13	84	6.5	16	0	1	2	2.0	2	0								
KELVIN ANDERSON Kelvin SB-RB 5'8 205 Southeast Missouri State B: 2/4/1972 South Bend, IN Pro: X																															
1996	CAL	18	7		2	1						84	14	240	1068	4.5	49	10	45	409	9.1	51	4					6	116	19.3	28
1997	CAL+	18	3	0	0	1						66	11	246	1088	4.4	34	9	31	227	7.3	23	2					11	184	16.7	27
1998	CAL*	18	6	0	3	7						98	16	236	1325	5.6	44	9	64	605	9.5	29	7					6	132	22.0	38
1999	CAL*	18	3	0	1	5	2.0	14.0				66	11	262	1306	5.0	39	8	48	572	11.9	76	3					20	438	21.9	70
2000	CAL+	15	2	0	2	1						48	8	203	1048	5.2	49	6	34	283	8.3	25	2					12	283	23.6	41
2001	CAL+	17	3	0	1	3						54	9	262	1383	5.3	46	6	48	433	9.0	39	3					6	71	11.8	22
2002	CAL	18	1	0	1	4					1	42	7	221	1074	4.9	40	4	24	272	11.3	50	3					9	145	16.1	28
2003	BC	17	1	0	0	2						36	6	188	1048	5.6	52	6	43	365	8.5	32	0					6	75	12.5	19
8		139	26	0	10	24	2.0	14.0			1	494	82	1858	9340	5.0	52	58	337	3166	9.4	76	24					76	1444	19.0	70
LARRY ANDERSON Larry Kent DT-MG-OT-OG 6'2 235 Calgary Bronks Jrs.; Boise JC; Brigham Young B: 8/15/1936 Taber, AB D: 6/6/1994 Provo, UT																															
1961	CAL	16							1	6																					
1962	CAL	16																													
1963	CAL	16																													
1964	CAL	16																													
1965	CAL	15																													
1966	CAL	16	0		1																										
1967	CAL	16			3																										
7	Years	111	0		4				1	6																					
MAX ANDERSON Max Arthur HB Trinity Valley CC; Arizona State B: 6/6/1955 Draft: 5C-132 BUF Pro: N																															
1971	HAM	6	1		0							12	2	72	267	3.7	27	2	4	-7	-1.8	8	0					5	96	19.2	29
MIKE ANDERSON Michael C-OG 6'3 260 Saskatoon Hilltops Jrs.; San Diego State B: 8/15/1961 Regina, SK Draft: TE 1984 SAS																															
1984	SAS	9																													
1985	SAS	16	0		1																										
1986	SAS	18																													
1987	SAS	18				1																									
1988	SAS+	18	0		1	0																									
1989	SAS	18				0																									
1990	SAS	18				1																									
1991	SAS	18				0																									
1992	SAS	18				0																									
1993	SAS	18	0		1	1																									
1994	SAS*	18	1		0	1																									
1995	SAS	18	0		1	2																									
12	Years	205	1		4	6																									
PAUL ANDERSON Paul DE-OT-DT 6'5 245 Saskatoon Hilltops Jrs. B: 10/31/1932 Vancouver, BC D: 7/17/2005 Saskatoon, SK																															
1953	SAS	16																													
1954	SAS	15																	1	9	9.0	9	0								
1955	SAS	16	1		2																			1	14	14.0	14				
1956	SAS	15																													
1957	SAS	15							1	6																					
1958	SAS	16	0		2																										
6	Years	93	1		4				1	6									1	9	9.0	9	0	1	14	14.0	14				
RALPH ANDERSON Ralph M. OE 6'4 223 Santa Monica JC; Los Angeles State B: 1/1/1937 D: 11/26/1960 Los Angeles, CA Draft: 9-101 1958 CHIB Pro: N																															
1959	WPG	1																	3	33	11.0	18	0								
REGGIE ANDERSON Reggie LB 6'1 235 Texas Christian B: 5/17/1972																															
1995	SHR	8	0		1	19																									
ROGER ANDERSON Roger Cole DT 6'5 263 Virginia Union B: 11/11/1942 Bedford, VA Draft: 7A-51 1964 SD; 7-96 1964 NYG Pro: NW																															
1966	MTL	7																													
ROMAN ANDERSON Roman K 5'10 190 Houston B: 4/19/1969 London, England																															
1994	SAC	18				4						174	0																		
1995	SA*	18				1						235	0																		

Year	Team	GP	FM	FF	FR	TK	SK	YDS	IR	YDS	PD	PTS	TD	RA	YDS	AVG	LG	TD	REC	YDS	AVG	LG	TD	PR	YDS	AVG	LG	KOR	YDS	AVG	LG
2	Years	36				5						409	0																		
SCOTTY ANDERSON Scott WR 6'2 189 Grambling State B: 11/24/1979 Monroe, LA Draft: 5A-148 2001 DET Pro: N																															
2006	WPG	1				0																									
2006	CAL	3				0													2	20	10.0	11	0								
2006	Year	4				0													2	20	10.0	11	0								
STEVE ANDERSON Stephen Lamont DE-LB 6'3 270 Tyler JC; Nevada-Las Vegas B: 3/26/1972 Tyler, TX																															
1994	LV	18	0		1	31	3.0	20.0			2																				
1995	BIR	15	0		1	21	3.0	42.0			1																				
1996	CAL	11				10	4.0	20.0			3																				
1997	CAL	10				13	2.0	20.0	1	1	1																				
1998	CAL	18	0	3	3	27	5.0	27.0			2																				
1999	CAL	18	0	1	1	33	2.0	11.0			3																				
2000	BC	8				9																									
2000	EDM	9				15																									
2000	Year	17				24																									
2001	EDM	6	0	0	1	13	1.0	8.0				6	1																		
2002	EDM	1				4																									
2002	CAL	12	0	1	0	18	2.0	12.0																							
2002	Year	13	0	1	0	22	2.0	12.0																							
9	Years	105	0	5	7	194	22.0	160.0	1	1	12	6	1																		
THYRON ANDERSON Thyron WR 6'4 202 Grambling State B: 8/28/1979 Jonesboro, LA																															
2003	MTL	6				0						6	1						11	193	17.5	62	1								
2004	MTL	18				1						18	3						76	1147	15.1	81	3								
2005	MTL	9	1	0	0	1						6	1						27	408	15.1	49	1								
2006	MTL	18	1	0	0	2						24	4						60	686	11.4	45	4								
2007	HAM	2				0													3	31	10.3	13	0								
5	Years	53	2	0	0	4						54	9						177	2465	13.9	81	9								
TIM ANDERSON William Tim DB 6'0 193 Ohio State B: 8/1/1949 Colliers, WV Draft: 1-23 1971 SF Pro: N																															
1971	TOR	10	0		1				3	77																					
1972	TOR	1																													
1973	TOR+	14							4	27		6	1																		
1974	TOR	16	1		2				3	38																					
4	Years	41	1		3				10	142		6	1																		
TRAVIS ANDERSON Travis WR 5'10 185 Iowa Central CC B: 2/18/1973 Toronto, ON																															
1996	OTT	5				3													7	73	10.4	38	0					1	10	10.0	10
1998	WPG	5				0													3	26	8.7	12	0								
2	Years	10				3													10	99	9.9	38	0					1	10	10.0	10
TYLER ANDERSON Tyler WR 6'2 180 Brigham Young																															
1994	LV	1																													
VICKEY RAY ANDERSON Vickey Ray RB 6'0 205 Oklahoma B: 5/3/1956 Oklahoma City, OK Pro: NU																															
1979	SAS	1												4	17	4.3	6	0													
WAYNE ANDERSON Wayne HB 5'11 160 Saskatoon Hilltops Jrs.																															
1952	SAS	10										5	1	7	26	3.7	16	1	3	74	24.7	45	0	9	52	5.8	15	5	101	20.2	35
ZACH ANDERSON Zachary DL 6'4 267 East Mississippi JC; Louisville B: 10/23/1982 Scooba, MS																															
2007	EDM	1				2																									
JIM ANDREOTTI James P. LB-C 6'1 205 Northwestern B: 3/27/1938 Chicago, IL Draft: FS 1960 OAK; 4A-39 1960 DET																															
1960	TOR+	14							1	10																					
1961	TOR+	14							2	75																					
1962	TOR+	13																													
1963	MTL*	14							2	2																					
1964	MTL	12	0		2																										
1965	MTL	10																													
1966	MTL	14	0		2				1	11																					
1967	TOR	10							1	15																					
8	Years	101	0		4				7	113																					
RICKY ANDREWS Richard Guy DE 6'2 236 Washington B: 4/14/1966 Western Samoa Draft: 10-260 1989 SD Pro: EN																															
1994	BAL	7				19																									
ROMEL ANDREWS Romel DT-DE 6'5 255 Tennessee-Martin B: 7/4/1963 Ripley, TN																															
1986	HAM	4	0		1		2.0		0	6																					
1988	WPG	8				2	2.0																								
1989	WPG	18	0		1	31	9.0																								
1990	HAM	10				18	7.0																								
1991	HAM	12				24	5.0																								
1992	HAM	4	0		1	4	1.0	2.0																							
1993	HAM	11				11	4.0	30.0																							
1994	HAM	2				1	1.0																								
8	Years	69	0		3	91	31.0	32.0	0	6																					
RUPE ANDREWS Rupert Burke, Jr. S 6'0 197 Menlo JC; Stanford B: 10/23/1926 La Jolla, CA D: 1/15/2008 San Diego, CA Draft: 18-232 1950 CHIB																															
1954	CAL	15	2		2				3	37		35	7						32	904	28.3	95	5	18	205	11.4	95				
1955	EDM+	16	2		3				8	93		10	2	1	0	0.0	0	0	6	122	20.3	28	2	5	41	8.2	17				
2	Years	31	4		5				11	130		45	9	1	0	0.0	0	0	38	1026	27.0	95	7	23	246	10.7	95				
CONRAD ANDREYCHUK Conrad (Andy) OHB-DB 6'1 190 Hamilton Tiger-Cats B B: 1935																															
1957	HAM	1																													
LOU ANDRUS Louis John T 6'6 230 Brigham Young B: 7/10/1943 Murray, UT Draft: 11-269 1967 DEN Pro: N																															
1970	WPG	13										12	2						26	319	12.3	45	2								
1971	WPG	2																													
2	Years	15										12	2						26	319	12.3	45	2								
FRANK ANDRUSKI Frank E. CB 6'1 190 San Ana JC; Utah B: 7/14/1943 Draft: 14-184 1965 SF Pro: W																															
1966	CAL	9	0		2																										
1967	CAL*	16			6				5	84		12	2						1	10	10.0	10	0					1	15	15.0	11
1968	CAL*	15	0		1				1	56		12	2																		
1969	CAL+	16							3	43														1	0	0.0	0				
1970	CAL	16	1		1				4	36																					
1971	CAL*	16	0		2				7	178		6	1																		
1972	CAL+	12							6	75																					
1973	CAL+	16	1		0				4	204		6	1																		
8	Years	116	2		12				30	676		36	6						1	10	10.0	10	0	1	0	0.0	0	1	15	15.0	11
ZENON ANDRUSYSHYN Zenon K-P 6'2 210 UCLA B: 2/25/1948 Gunzburg, Germany Draft: 9-231 1970 DAL Pro: NU																															
1971	TOR	14										9	0	1	4	4.0	4	0													
1972	TOR	14	2		2							35	0	1	66	66.0	66	0													
1973	TOR	14										100	0																		
1974	TOR	16										134	0																		
1975	TOR	16	4		1							121	0	3	13	4.3	19	0													
1976	TOR	16	1		0							102	0																		
1977	TOR	16	2		0							106	0																		
1979	HAM	8	3		0							55	0																		
1980	TOR+	16	3		1							136	0	2	20	10.0	13	0													
1981	TOR+	16	1		0							91	0	1	8	8.0	8	0													
1982	TOR	9										1	0	1	-11	-11.0	-11	0						1	11	11.0	11				
1982	EDM	2										65	0																		
1982	Year	11										66	0	1	-11	-11.0	-11	0						1	11	11.0	11				
1986	MTL	6	1		0							55	0																		

Year	Team	GP	FM	FF	FR	TK	SK	YDS	IR	YDS	PD	PTS	TD	RA	YDS	AVG	LG	TD	REC	YDS	AVG	LG	TD	PR	YDS	AVG	LG	KOR	YDS	AVG	LG
12	Years	161	17		4							1010	0	9	100	11.1	66	0						1	11	11.0	11				
TERRY ANDRYSIAK Terrence J. QB 6'1 185 Notre Dame B: 12/4/1965 Trenton, MI																															
1988	HAM	5				0																									
1989	HAM	2	1		0	0								2	7	3.5	5	0													
1990	HAM	8	1		1	0						6	1	5	11	2.2	9	1													
1991	OTT	7				0																									
4	Years	22	2		1	0						6	1	7	18	2.6	9	1													
GIL ANE Gilbert Paul G 6'1 250 Compton JC; Southern California B: 3/4/1936 Honolulu, HI D: 4/26/2006 Honolulu, HI																															
1959	MTL	1																													
EMIL ANGI Emil F. HB Dayton B: 12/30/1920 IN D: 9/11/1974 Dayton, OH																															
1946	SAS	4																													
TONY ANGLIN Anthony Leroy LB-DE 6'2 205 Texas Southern B: 12/18/1961 Tampa, FL																															
1983	MTL	1																													
1984	EDM	12	0		1		2.0		1	7														1	3	3.0	3				
2	Years	13	0		1		2.0		1	7														1	3	3.0	3				
DOUG ANNAN Doug T Queen's																															
1946	HAM	2																													
COREY ANNETT Corey C 6'3 308 Eastern Michigan B: 7/2/1979 Niagara Falls, ON Draft: 1-3 2002 TOR																															
2002	TOR	18	0	1	0	1																									
2003	TOR	18				0																									
2004	WPG	18				0																									
2005	WPG	5				0																									
4	Years	59	0	1	0	1																									
SANDY ANNUNZIATA Sandy OG 6'2 275 Western Ontario B: 10/11/1969 Fort Erie, ON Draft: 5-39 1992 CAL																															
1995	EDM	7				0																									
1997	WPG	1				0																									
1998	WPG	17	1	0	0	2																									
1999	WPG	3				1																									
1999	TOR	5				0																									
1999	Year	8				1																									
2000	TOR	18	2	0	0	4																									
2001	TOR	18	0	0	1	0																									
2002	TOR+	18	0	0	1	1																									
2003	TOR	17				0																									
2004	TOR	15				1																									
2005	EDM	17				0																									
10	Years	131	3	0	2	9																									
JOE ANOAI Leati Joseph DT 6'3 280 Georgia Tech B: 5/25/1985 Pensacola, FL																															
2008	EDM	5	0	1	0	9																									
VIC ANONSEN Victor WR 5'10 178 Manitoba B: 5/19/1954 Moose Jaw, SK																															
1978	CAL	3																	1	45	45.0	45	0								
1978	MTL	2																	1	38	38.0	38	0								
1978	Year	5																	2	83	41.5	45	0								
1979	TOR	12	0		1														6	32	5.3	10	0								
1979	WPG	2																													
1979	Year	14	0		1																										
2	Years	15	0		1														8	115	14.4	45	0								
CHARLES ANTHONY Charles DH 6'2 195 Nevada-Las Vegas B: 10/16/1968 Las Vegas, NV																															
1991	CAL	2				8																									
1992	SAS	16	1		1	47			3	17																					
1993	SAS	18	0		6	56			5	10		6	1																		
1994	BAL	18	0		5	41			4	29	5													3	32	10.7	32				
1995	BAL*	18	0		2	48			5	156	4	6	1																		
1997	TOR	9	0	0	1	21			2	41	1																				
1999	EDM	15	0	1	1	52					5																				
7	Years	96	1	1	16	273			19	253	15	12	2											3	32	10.7	32				
CHARLES ANTHONY Charles Raymond LB 6'0 220 Southern California B: 7/10/1952 Draft: 15A-366 1974 SD; 27-316 1974 MEM-WFL Pro: N																															
1977	BC	11																													
1978	OTT	5	1		2				3	41																					
1978	SAS	2																													
1978	Year	7	1		2				3	41																					
2	Years	16	1		2				3	41																					
CORNELIUS ANTHONY Cornelius Armand LB 6'0 235 Texas A&M B: 7/7/1978 Pinesville, LA Pro: EN																															
2005	CAL	5	0	1	0	6																									
2006	CAL	9	0	0	1	42	6.0	31.0	1	2	0																				
2007	CAL	13	0	2	1	60	8.0	57.0			5																				
2008	HAM	14	0	0	1	53	2.0	7.0			1																				
4	Years	41	0	3	3	161	16.0	95.0	1	2	6																				
KARL ANTHONY Karl CB 5'9 175 Blinn JC; Missouri State B: 3/14/1967 New Iberia, LA																															
1990	CAL	1				3																									
1991	CAL	15	0		1	43			3	83																					
1992	CAL	18	0		1	54			5	110		6	1																		
1993	CAL*	18	0		2	69			6	145		6	1																		
1994	BAL	18				43			3	3	6													6	65	10.8	18				
1995	BAL	1				11					1																				
6	Years	71	0		4	223			17	341	7	12	2											6	65	10.8	18				
MATT ANTHONY Matt (Mike) E 5'11 185 B: 1921 D: 7/13/2000 Ottawa, ON																															
1946	MTL	11										10	2										1								
1947	OTT+	12										10	2										2								
1948	OTT	6																													
1949	SAS	14										25	5										5								
1950	SAS	14										5	1						27	390	14.4		1								
1951	OTT	12																													
1952	OTT	12																													
1953	OTT	12										5	1										1								
8	Years	93										55	11						27	390	14.4		10								
MEL ANTHONY Melvin FB 6'0 210 Michigan B: 1/30/1943 Cincinnati, OH Draft: 16-223 1965 CLE																															
1965	HAM	4	1											44	227	5.2	35	0	1	-5	-5.0	-5	0								
ANDY ANTOINE Andy WR 5'7 170 Northern Illinois B: 8/5/1970 Montreal, QC																															
1996	MTL	3				1																									
1997	MTL	10				4													1	17	17.0	17	0					1	5	5.0	5
2	Years	13				5													1	17	17.0	17	0					1	5	5.0	5
TONY ANTUNOVIC Tony C-OG 6'2 245 Simon Fraser B: 7/24/1961 Vancouver, BC Draft: 1C-6 1982 TOR																															
1982	TOR	6																													
1983	TOR	13																													
1984	TOR	13																													
1985	TOR	16																													
1986	TOR	1																													
5	Years	49																													
AKWASI ANTWI Akwasi LB 6'2 250 Mount Allison B: 5/9/1985 Toronto, ON Draft: 4-26 2011 CAL																															
2011	CAL	18	0	0	1	23																						1	8	8.0	8
TABUGBO ANYANSI Tabugbo LB 6'1 225 Georgia Tech B: 10/4/1981 Nigeria																															

Year	Team	GP	FM	FF	FR	TK	SK	YDS	IR	YDS	PD	PTS	TD	RA	YDS	AVG	LG	TD	REC	YDS	AVG	LG	TD	PR	YDS	AVG	LG	KOR	YDS	AVG	LG
2005	MTL	1				0																									
STEVE ANZALONE Stephen P. DE 6'2 250 Northeastern B: 8/18/1979																														
2004	WPG	2	0	1	0	7																									
NEO AOGA Patoto Neo QB 6'4 265 Long Beach CC; Missouri Western; Azusa Pacific B: 6/19/1973 Leore, American Samoa Pro: E																														
2001	SAS	2				0																									
HOLLY APLIN Holland E. (Luke) OE 6'4 220 Tampa B: 5/19/1926 D: 6/23/1998 Tampa, FL Draft: 15-180 1952 CLE																														
1952	SAS	12			1							35	7						41	801	19.5	79	6					1	12	12.0	12
GERRY APOSTOLATOS Gerry HB 5'11 190 none B: 9/24/1935 Montreal, QC																														
1956	MTL	4												4	15	3.8	6	0	1	11	11.0	11	0								
1957	MTL	10												4	13	3.3	7	0	1	1	1.0	1	0					2	46	23.0	25
1958	MTL	5																												
3	Years	19												8	28	3.5	7	0	2	12	6.0	11	0					2	46	23.0	25
RICK APPLEBY Richard TE 6'3 215 Georgia B: 12/25/1952 Athens, GA Draft: 4A-121 1976 TB																														
1977	BC	7										6	1						12	225	18.8	68	1								
1978	BC	3										6	1						2	14	7.0	9	1								
2	Years	10										12	2						14	239	17.1	68	2								
BOB APPS Bob FL-DB 5'11 180 McMaster B: 1942 Draft: 1C-5 1965 HAM																														
1966	BC	2																	4	112	28.0	63	0								
BEN APUNA Ben Calvin LB 6'1 222 Mesa CC; Arizona State B: 6/26/1957 Honolulu, HI Draft: 7-171 1980 STL Pro: NU																														
1981	TOR	5					4.0																							
ANDY ARACRI Andrew T. DT 6'1 280 Miami (Ohio) B: 4/16/1978 Dayton, OH																														
2001	BC	2				0																									
OBI ARAH Obiajulu DE 6'3 251 Howard B: 7/4/1980 Jos, Nigeria																														
2003	MTL	8				3	1.0	11.0			1																			
JASON ARAKGI Jason S-LB 6'2 220 McMaster B: 5/12/1985 Montreal, QC Draft: 3B-20 2008 BC																														
2008	BC	18				32																									
2009	BC+	17	0	0	2	35																									
2010	BC	17	0	0	2	21																									
2011	BC	16				15																									
4	Years	68	0	0	4	103																									
NICK ARAKGI Nick TE 6'6 250 Bishop's B: 8/9/1955 Cairo, Egypt Draft: TE 1979 MTL																														
1979	MTL	16	0		2							6	1						5	73	14.6	26	1								
1980	MTL	14	0		1							12	2						22	427	19.4	39	2					1	12	12.0	12
1981	MTL	16	1		1							6	1						25	368	14.7	30	1								
1982	MTL+	16	2		0							38	6						89	1062	11.9	46	6								
1983	MTL	16	1		1							12	2	1	-5	-5.0	-5	0	61	582	9.5	31	2								
1984	MTL*	16	1		2							68	10						67	1078	16.1	82	10					1	0	0.0	0
1985	MTL+	16	1		0							18	3						58	741	12.8	57	3								
1987	WPG	17	0		0	1						12	2						43	534	12.4	44	2	1	0	0.0	0	1	2	2.0	2
8	Years	127	6		7	1						172	27	1	-5	-5.0	-5	0	370	4865	13.1	82	27	1	0	0.0	0	3	14	4.7	12
HASSON ARBUBAKRR Hasson DE 6'4 250 Pasadena CC; Texas Tech B: 12/9/1960 Newark, NJ Draft: 9-238 1983 TB; TD 1983 DEN-USFL Pro: N																														
1985	WPG	2	0		1		1.0																							
1986	WPG	12	0		1		4.0																							
1987	WPG	6				6	1.0																							
1987	OTT	10	0		1	20	9.0																							
1987	Year	16	0		1	26	10.0																							
1988	OTT	6				19	1.0																							
4	Years	26	0		3	45	16.0																							
JOE ARCARO Joseph FB 6'1 217 Montreal NDG Maple Leafs Jrs.; Arizona B: 3/5/1944 Montreal, QC																														
1965	MTL	1												6	6	1.0	3	0	1	4	4.0	4	0					1	16	16.0	16
ANTHONY ARCENEAUX Anthony WR 5'10 180 Utah B: 8/19/1981 Portland, OR																														
2007	HAM	2				0												5	22	4.4	5	0								
EMMANUEL ARCENEAUX Emmanuel WR 6'2 211 Alcorn State B: 9/17/1987 Alexandria, LA Pro: N																														
2009	BC	18				1						42	7						63	858	13.6	60	7								
2010	BC	18	1	0	1	4						30	5	8	29	3.6	14	0	67	1114	16.6	74	5								
2	Years	36	1	0	1	5						72	12	8	29	3.6	14	0	130	1972	15.2	74	12								
GILLES ARCHAMBAULT Gilles DT 6'2 245 Ottawa; Verdun Bulldogs B: 3/9/1934 Richelieu, QC D: 10/25/2009 Gatineau, QC																														
1954	CAL	15																												
1955	CAL	12																												
1957	OTT	14																												
1958	OTT	14																										1	9	9.0	9
1959	OTT	14																												
1960	OTT	14																												
1961	OTT	14										12	2																	
1962	OTT	14																												
1963	OTT	1																												
9	Years	112										12	2																1	9	9.0	9
DEMECO ARCHANGEL Demeco J. WR 5'7 175 Fayetteville State B: 6/24/1975 Kinston, NC																														
2001	MTL	4	1	0	0	0																		12	122	10.2	49	6	98	16.3	44
DAVID ARCHER David Mark QB 6'2 208 Snow JC; Iowa State B: 2/15/1962 Fayetteville, NC Draft: 9-172 1984 DEN-USFL Pro: EN																														
1993	SAC	18	8		2	0						12	2	60	287	4.8	18	2													
1994	SAC	11	6		2	3						6	1	20	99	5.0	13	1													
1995	SA	17	6		3	0						18	3	21	57	2.7	15	3													
1996	OTT	18	3		0	1								38	143	3.8	14	0													
1998	EDM	18	5	0	2	2						12	2	25	109	4.4	28	2													
5	Years	82	28	0	9	6						48	8	164	695	4.2	28	8													
PAUL ARCHER Paul C 6'4 280 St. Mary's (Nova Scotia) B: 3/16/1979 Montreal, QC Draft: 4-35 2003 MTL																														
2005	MTL	6				0																									
2006	MTL	8				0																									
2007	MTL	2				0																									
2007	WPG	2				0																									
2007	Year	4				0																									
3	Years	16				0																									
BEN ARCHIBALD Benjamin Thomas OT 6'3 320 Brigham Young B: 8/26/1978 Tacoma, WA Pro: EN																														
2008	CAL	12				0																									
2009	CAL*	18	0	0	1	2																									
2010	CAL*	18				2																									
2011	BC+	18				0																									
4	Years	66	0	0	1	4																									
ADRIAN ARCHIE Adrian LB 5'11 215 Richmond B: 7/30/1980 Alexandria, VA																														
2003	MTL	12	0	1	2	16	1.0	6.0			1																			
ALLEN ARCHIE Allen J. CB 6'1 190 Morris Brown B: 11/18/1954 Mobile, AL																														
1980	OTT	6							2	25																					
BARRY ARDERN Barry CB 5'10 181 Ottawa Sooners Jrs B: 5/12/1946																														
1968	OTT	14	2		0																				59	318	5.4	26				
1969	OTT	14	1		0				4	236		6	1											58	304	5.2	19	2	37	18.5	32
1970	OTT	14	1		1				3	76														56	231	4.1	22				
1971	OTT	14	5		1				4	38		6	1											62	387	6.2	26	1	0	0.0	0
1972	OTT	14	0		1				3	1		6	1																	
1973	BC	16	0		1				1	41														2	6	3.0	4				
1974	BC	16	0		1				5	47																					
1975	BC	16	1		0				5	136														4	19	4.8	10				

Year	Team	GP	FM	FF	FR	TK	SK	YDS	IR	YDS	PD	PTS	TD	RA	YDS	AVG	LG	TD	REC	YDS	AVG	LG	TD	PR	YDS	AVG	LG	KOR	YDS	AVG	LG
1976	BC	16							3	42																					
1977	SAS	4																													
1977	MTL	7																													
1977	Year	11																													
10	Years	138	10		5				28	617		18	3											241	1265	5.2	26	3	37	12.3	32
RON ARENDS Ronald George DH 6'1 167 Weston Invictus Redmen Jrs. B: 3/11/1945 Toronto, ON																															
1966	TOR	8																										2	33	16.5	17
1967	TOR	14							2	5														4	9	2.3	6				
1968	TOR	14	1		0				4	74																					
1969	TOR	14							1	30		6	1																		
1970	TOR	14	0		1				1	0																					
5	Years	64	1		1				8	109		6	1											4	9	2.3	6	2	33	16.5	17
KEN ARKELL Ken (King) DT 6'4 233 Western Ontario B: 1932 Calgary, AB																															
1956	BC	13																													
1957	BC	7																													
2	Years	20																													
ANDRE ARLAIN Andre SB-WR 6'2 215 St. Francis Xavier B: 11/3/1975 Grimsby, ON Draft: 2-10 1998 CAL																															
1998	CAL	16				14													2	36	18.0	26	0								
1999	CAL	18	0	0	1	16																									
2000	CAL	18				16						6	1						5	63	12.6	19	1								
2001	WPG	18				16													6	60	10.0	13	0								
2002	WPG	18				12	1.0																								
2003	CAL	18				16													8	123	15.4	51	0	1	8	8.0	8				
2004	CAL	17	0	0	1	19													9	112	12.4	26	0	1	0	0.0	0				
7	Years	123	0	0	2	109	1.0					6	1						30	394	13.1	51	1	2	8	4.0	8				
CARLOS ARMOUR Carlos LB 6'3 210 Miami (Florida) B: 1/31/1986 Memphis, TN																															
2009	SAS	2				2																									
JoJUAN ARMOUR JoJuan L. LB 5'11 215 Miami (Ohio) B: 7/10/1976 Toledo, OH Draft: 7-224 1999 OAK Pro: EN																															
2004	BC	4				16																									
2005	BC	14				17																									
2006	HAM	18	0	1	0	78	5.0	36.0			1																				
2007	HAM	16	0	2	2	88	3.0	22.0			4	6	1																		
2008	CAL	16	0	0	1	68	4.0	46.0	1	21	1																				
2009	BC	13				64	4.0	19.0			1																				
6	Years	81	0	3	3	331	16.0	123.0	1	21	7	6	1																		
NED ARMOUR Talmadge A. WR 6'1 185 Mesa JC; San Diego State* B: 3/6/1957 Indianapolis, IN																															
1983	BC	3	2		0														6	62	10.3	27	0					2	36	18.0	21
1984	BC	12										36	6						50	788	15.8	57	6								
1985	BC	1																	1	44	44.0	44	0								
1986	BC	10										14	2	1	5	5.0	5	0	45	709	15.8	86	2	1	5	5.0	5	4	82	20.5	22
1987	BC	6	1		0	1						12	2	1	32	32.0	32	0	25	305	12.2	51	2								
5	Years	32	3		0	1						62	10	2	37	18.5	32	0	127	1908	15.0	86	10	1	5	5.0	5	6	118	19.7	22
JASON ARMSTEAD Jason WR-SB 5'9 165 Mississippi Gulf Coast CC; Mississippi B: 9/18/1979 Pascagoula, MS																															
2004	OTT	16	3	0	1	5						30	5	3	17	5.7	14	0	41	608	14.8	83	4	64	821	12.8	91	37	700	18.9	38
2005	OTT*	18	7	0	0	4						36	6	6	44	7.3	16	0	89	1307	14.7	75	5	70	699	10.0	87	51	1082	21.2	46
2006	SAS	15	1	1	4	0						42	7	19	80	4.2	11	1	47	651	13.9	56	6	42	412	9.8	40	20	267	13.4	29
2007	SAS	8	1	0	0	0						12	2						15	226	15.1	35	1	43	371	8.6	90	12	211	17.6	31
2007	HAM	10	1	0	0	3						2	0						31	392	12.6	48	0	36	181	5.0	21	35	645	18.4	38
2007	Year	18	2	0	0	3						14	2						46	618	13.4	48	1	79	552	7.0	90	47	856	18.2	38
2008	MTL	4	1	0	0	0								2	13	6.5	11	0	3	38	12.7	22	0	16	104	6.5	20	10	165	16.5	26
2008	WPG	10	3	0	0	1						6	1											60	624	10.4	84	34	795	23.4	46
2008	Year	14	4	0	0	1						6	1	2	13	6.5	11	0	3	38	12.7	22	0	76	728	9.6	84	44	960	21.8	46
2009	SAS	10				0					1			1	2	2.0	2	0	3	28	9.3	14	0	42	387	9.2	54	33	806	24.4	54
2010	EDM	3				0						6	1						1	6	6.0	6	0	13	149	11.5	58	8	139	17.4	34
2011	EDM	12	1	0	1	1						6	1	6	17	2.8	10	0	11	104	9.5	35	0	62	486	7.8	72	35	684	19.5	49
8	Years	86	18	1	6	14					1	140	23	37	173	4.7	16	1	241	3360	13.9	83	16	448	4234	9.5	91	275	5494	20.0	54
WILLIE ARMSTEAD Willie Earl WR 6'2 215 Utah B: 4/10/1952 Hampton, VA Draft: 13-317 1975 CLE																															
1976	CAL	4										12	2	1	21	21.0	21	0	6	172	28.7	78	2					1	21	21.0	21
1978	CAL+	16										54	9	1	10	10.0	10	0	39	881	22.6	101	9								
1979	CAL*	16	1		1							50	8	2	42	21.0	37	0	48	968	20.2	105	8					0	-4		-4
1980	CAL	16										54	9	2	6	3.0	6	0	35	712	20.3	78	9	1	14	14.0	14				
1981	CAL	16	3		1							60	10	3	21	7.0	19	0	57	861	15.1	75	10								
1982	CAL+	16	1		2							34	5	2	13	6.5	8	0	61	1081	17.7	74	5								
1983	CAL	14	1		0							44	7						46	750	16.3	50	7								
7	Years	98	6		4							308	50	11	113	10.3	37	0	292	5425	18.6	105	50	1	14	14.0	14	1	17	17.0	21
ANTONIO ARMSTRONG Antonio Donnell LB 6'1 234 Texas A&M B: 10/15/1973 Houston, TX Draft: 6-201 1995 SF Pro: N																															
1998	SAS	1				2	1.0	11.0																							
1998	BC	5	0	0	1	25																						1	12	12.0	12
1998	Year	6	0	0	1	26	1.0	11.0																				1	12	12.0	12
1999	BC	16	0	1	0	76	5.0	29.0			4																				
2000	WPG+	15	0	2	3	71	8.0	58.0	1	21	0	6	1																		
2001	WPG	10				31	3.0	10.0																							
4	Years	42	0	3	4	205	17.0	108.0	1	21	4	6	1															1	12	12.0	12
BILL ARMSTRONG Bill DB 6'3 202 Wake Forest B: 6/24/1955 Dover, NJ Draft: 8-213 1977 CLE																															
1977	HAM	1																													
1978	HAM	4							2	19																					
2	Years	5							2	19																					
CALVIN ARMSTRONG Calvin OT-OG 6'7 325 Washington State B: 3/31/1982 Seattle, WA Draft: 6-211 2005 PHI																															
2008	EDM	17				4																									
2009	EDM+	18				0																									
2010	EDM	9	0	0	1	1																									
2010	TOR	1				1																									
2010	Year	10				2																									
3	Years	44	0	0	1	6																									
CHRIS ARMSTRONG Christopher SB-WR 6'2 200 Fayetteville State B: 8/28/1967 Fayetteville, NC																															
1991	EDM	8				4						30	5	2	3	1.5	9	0	23	534	23.2	66	5					16	418	26.1	58
1992	EDM	12				1						36	6						31	580	18.7	59	6					4	88	22.0	27
1992	OTT	2				0													2	34	17.0	25	0								
1992	Year	14				1						36	6						33	614	18.6	59	6					4	88	22.0	27
1994	BAL+	18	1		0	7						108	18	1	4	4.0	4	0	72	1586	22.0	83	18					1	0	0.0	0
1995	BAL+	18	2		0	3						66	11						64	1111	17.4	47	11					1	11	11.0	11
1996	MTL	18				0						44	7						63	979	15.5	45	7	2	15	7.5	18	9	202	22.4	67
1997	MTL	18	3	0	0	3						72	12						80	1411	17.6	65	12					3	7	2.3	6
1998	WPG	5	1	0	0	1						6	1	1	7	7.0	7	0	23	312	13.6	46	1								
1998	MTL	13				1						30	5						44	850	19.3	97	5					2	0	0.0	0
1998	Year	18	1	0	0	2						36	6	1	7	7.0	7	0	67	1162	17.3	97	6					2	0	0.0	0
1999	MTL	7				0						6	1						20	351	17.6	76	1								
1999	WPG	10				1						18	3						27	356	13.2	37	3					1	8	8.0	8
1999	Year	17				1						24	4						47	707	15.0	76	4					1	8	8.0	8
8	Years	104	7	0	0	21						416	69	4	14	3.5	9	0	449	8104	18.0	97	69	2	15	7.5	18	37	734	19.8	67
DEREK ARMSTRONG Derek OG 6'2 292 St. Francis Xavier B: 6/19/1981 Perth, ON Draft: 5-38 2006 CAL																															
2006	CAL	7				0																									

Year	Team	GP	FM	FF	FR	TK	SK	YDS	IR	YDS	PD	PTS	TD	RA	YDS	AVG	LG	TD	REC	YDS	AVG	LG	TD	PR	YDS	AVG	LG	KOR	YDS	AVG	LG
2007	CAL	6				0																									
2008	CAL	11				0																									
3	Years	24				0																									
DERICK ARMSTRONG Derick D, WR 6'2 203 Tyler JC; Arkansas-Monticello B: 4/2/1979 Pro: N																															
2001	SAS	10				0						6	1						30	436	14.5	46	1					0	13		13
2002	SAS*	18				1						30	5						70	1104	15.8	100	5								
2006	WPG	5				0						20	3						25	302	12.1	34	3								
2007	WPG*	17	1	1	0	1						36	6						83	1142	13.8	52	6								
2008	WPG	17				0						30	5						81	1010	12.5	63	5								
2009	WPG	1				0																									
2010	BC	6				1													22	316	14.4	58	0								
2010	EDM	4				1						6	1						11	121	11.0	28	1								
2010	Year	10				2						6	1						33	437	13.2	58	1								
7	Years	74	1	1	0	4						128	21						322	4431	13.8	100	21					0	13		13
MIKE ARMSTRONG Michael DT 6'3 265 Central Missouri B: 6/4/1972 Bethesda, MD																															
1995	MEM	14				27	3.0	25.0																							
NEILL ARMSTRONG Neill Ford DB-OE 6'2 189 Oklahoma State B: 3/9/1926 Tishomingo, OK Draft: 1-3 1947 BKN-AAFC; 1-8 1947 PHI Pro: N																															
1951	WPG+	14										55	11	1	2	2.0	2	0	56	1024	18.3	100	10								
1953	WPG+	14							2	38		35	7	1	-15	-15.0	-15	0	38	668	17.6		7								
1954	WPG	10	1		0							10	2						28	416	14.9	46	2	1	5	5.0	5				
3	Years	44	1		0				2	38		100	20	2	-13	-6.5	2	0	122	2108	17.3	100	19	1	5	5.0	5				
QUINCY ARMSTRONG Carl Quince, Jr. C-LB 6'3 231 North Texas B: 11/22/1928 Clyde, TX Draft: 26-314 1951 NYG Pro: N																															
1952	HAM	8										5	1																		
1953	HAM	8										5	1																		
2	Years	16										10	2																		
SANDY ARMSTRONG Sandy DE 6'2 230 Colorado B: 10/18/1961 Miami, FL Draft: TD 1984 DEN-USFL																															
1984	MTL	10			2		5.5																					1	16	16.0	16
1985	MTL	14					5.0																								
1986	MTL	17	0		1		11.0																					3	31	10.3	14
1987	CAL	2				4	1.0																								
4	Years	43	0		3	4	22.5																					4	47	11.8	16
TRON ARMSTRONG Tron Ortega WR 6'1 195 Eastern Kentucky B: 8/18/1961 St. Petersburg, FL Draft: 5-122 1984 NYJ; 3B-49 1984 CHI-USFL																															
1986	SAS	1										12	2						5	144	28.8	44	2								
1987	SAS	9	1		0	0						18	3						31	411	13.3	36	3					8	151	18.9	29
2	Years	10	1		0	0						30	5						36	555	15.4	44	5					8	151	18.9	29
GEORGE ARNETT George OT 6'2 240 Toronto Argonauts Jrs.; McMaster B: 1928																															
1951	TOR	3																													
1952	TOR	11																													
1953	TOR	14																													
1954	HAM	14																													
1955	HAM	12																													
1956	HAM	14																													
1957	HAM	3																													
1957	OTT	3																													
1957	Year	6																													
1958	OTT	14																													
8	Years	85																													
CLAUDE ARNOLD Claude QB 6'0 175 Oklahoma B: 11/1/1925 Okmulgee, OK																															
1952	EDM	15												31	-157	-5.1	25	0													
1953	EDM+	12										10	2	48	98	2.0		2	1	16	16.0	16	0								
1954	EDM	2	1		0									6	-36	-6.0	2	0													
3	Years	29	1		0							10	2	85	-95	-1.1	25	2	1	16	16.0	16	0								
DAVID ARNOLD David Paul LB 6'2 194 Michigan B: 11/21/1966 Warren, OH Draft: 5-118 1989 PIT Pro: N																															
1992	HAM	3				13	1.0																								
PERRY ARNOLD Perry LB 6'3 207 Western Ontario B: 11/23/1951 Sarnia, ON Draft: TE 1974 OTT																															
1974	OTT	7																													
TRAVIS ARNOLD Travis OL 6'2 295 Calgary Colts Jrs.; Manitoba B: 3/17/1977 Draft: 5B-43 2003 CAL																															
2004	CAL	6				0																									
GEORGE ARNOTT George QB 5'9 155 Western Ontario B: 1926 D: 12/15/2008 Kincardine, ON																															
1951	TOR	10																													
JEFF ARP Jeff OG-LB 6'3 225 Western Ontario B: 7/19/1959 Kitchener, ON Draft: 3-26 1981 HAM																															
1982	HAM	16	0		1																										
1983	HAM	16																													
1984	HAM	8																													
1985	HAM	8																													
1986	TOR	6																													
5	Years	54	0		1																										
DUANE ARRINDELL Duane OL 6'2 280 Northern Illinois B: 9/8/1972 Mississauga, ON Draft: 1B-7 1996 EDM																															
1996	MTL	3				0																									
1996	OTT	8				0																									
1996	Year	11				0																									
RICK ARRINGTON Richard Cameron QB 6'2 187 Georgia; Tulsa B: 2/26/1947 Charlotte, NC Pro: N																															
1974	TOR	5												2	12	6.0	11	0													
JABARI ARTHUR Jabari SB-WR 6'4 225 Akron B: 8/28/1982 Montreal, QC Draft: 1C-6 2007 CAL; SS 1947 BUF-AAFC																															
2008	CAL	4				6																									
2010	CAL	14				5													11	97	8.8	20	0								
2011	CAL	14	1	0	0	2						6	1						28	372	13.3	32	1								
3	Years	32	1	0	0	13						6	1						39	469	12.0	32	1								
TROY ASBELL Troy LB 5'9 220 Tyler JC; Texas A&M-Kingsville B: 9/3/1974 Tyler, TX																															
2000	SAS	1				0																									
2001	SAS	18	0	0	1	51	3.0	25.0			1																				
2002	OTT	6				32	1.0																								
3	Years	25	0	0	1	83	4.0	25.0			1																				
DARREL ASCHBACHER Darrel Godsil OG 6'1 223 Oregon B: 6/2/1935 Pineville, OR Pro: N																															
1962	SAS	12																													
FRANK ASCHENBRENNER Francis Xavier HB 5'10 188 Marquette; North Carolina*; Northwestern B: 7/12/1925 Heibuehl, Germany D: 1/30/2012 Draft: 6-38 1947 PIT Pro: A																															
1951	MTL	4										1	0																		
LES ASCOTT Leslie T-G 6'0 235 B: 1921 Peterborough, ON																															
1946	TOR	12																													
1947	TOR	12										2	0																		
1948	TOR	12																													
1949	TOR	9																													
1950	TOR	12																													
1951	TOR	12																													
1952	TOR	11																													
1953	TOR	13																													
8	Years	93										2	0																		
RAY ASH Ray OG-LB 5'11 225 Winnipeg Rods Jrs.; St. Vital Bulldogs Ints. B: 11/11/1936 Timmins, ON																															
1959	SAS	10																													
1961	WPG	13																													
1962	WPG	5																													
1963	WPG	16	0		1																										

Year	Team	GP	FM	FF	FR	TK	SK	YDS	IR	YDS	PD	PTS	TD	RA	YDS	AVG	LG	TD	REC	YDS	AVG	LG	TD	PR	YDS	AVG	LG	KOR	YDS	AVG	LG
1964	WPG	9
1964	EDM	7
1964	Year	16
1965	EDM	14
6	Years	67	0		1
DONNIE ASHLEY Donnie Ray WR 5'7 175 McNeese State B: 3/6/1976 McComb, MS
1999	EDM	17	2	0	0	0						12	2	3	18	6.0	8	0	25	400	16.0	59	1	17	191	11.2	47	30	776	25.9	92
2000	EDM	13				0						12	2						8	49	6.1	22	1	4	19	4.8	13	36	769	21.4	57
2001	EDM	8				1													4	64	16.0	29	0	32	198	6.2	19	17	341	20.1	34
2002	OTT	8	1	0	0	0						6	1	1	3	3.0	3	0	16	181	11.3	27	1	21	196	9.3	48	16	290	18.1	30
4	Years	46	3	0	0	1						30	5	4	21	5.3	8	0	53	694	13.1	59	3	74	604	8.2	48	99	2176	22.0	92
JOSH ASHTON Josh, Jr. RB 6'1 204 Tulsa B: 8/24/1949 Eagle Lake, TX D: 10/4/1993 Harris County, TX Draft: 9-209 1971 NE Pro: N
1971	BC	6	2		0							12	2	25	162	6.5	54	2	9	112	12.4	28	0					10	291	29.1	47
BERT ASKSON Bert H. TE 6'3 223 Texas Southern B: 12/16/1945 Draft: 14-340 1970 PIT Pro: NW
1972	OTT	1
JOE ASQUINI Joe HB-FW 6'0 190 none B: 1925
1947	OTT	5
1948	OTT	11
1949	OTT	8
1950	OTT	12										5	1										1
1951	OTT	12
5	Years	48										5	1										1
CHARLES ASSMANN Charles LB 6'2 221 Guelph B: 2/27/1972 Richmond Hill, ON Draft: 4-32 1995 HAM
1998	TOR	6	0	0	0	2
1998	EDM	10				6
1998	Year	16	0	0	1	8
1999	EDM	16	0	1	0	50	1.0	1.0	1	2	1
2000	EDM	18				13																						4	8	2.0	7
2002	TOR	18	0	1	0	8
2003	CAL	18	1	0	0	14																		1	2	2.0	2
2004	CAL	4	1	0	1	2
2004	OTT	3				1
2004	Year	7	1	0	1	3
6	Years	80	2	2	1	96	1.0	1.0	1	2	1													1	2	2.0	2	4	8	2.0	7
BRIAN ASTON Brian OHB-DB 5'11 186 Toronto B: 1936 Draft: 3-21 1959 OTT
1959	TOR	5																						18	130	7.2	15
1960	TOR	5											4	22	5.5	14	0	2	26	13.0	15	0	5	18	3.6	5
1961	TOR	13							1	55				1	-3	-3.0	-3	0						8	38	4.8	7	2	28	14.0	17
1962	TOR	5																						1	0	0.0	0
1962	MTL	6
1962	Year	11																						1	0	0.0	0
4	Years	28							1	55				5	19	3.8	14	0	2	26	13.0	15	0	32	186	5.8	15	2	28	14.0	17
JOHN ATAMIAN John OG-DG 6'1 245 Notre Dame B: 9/7/1942 Canada
1965	HAM	2
1965	TOR	5
1965	Year	7
1966	TOR	14
1967	TOR	4
1967	SAS	9
1967	Year	13
1968	SAS+	16
1969	WPG	16			1									1	9	9.0	9	0
1970	CAL	7
1971	CAL	14
1972	CAL	6
8	Years	79			1									1	9	9.0	9	0
JEFF ATCHESON Jeff OHB-DB-FL 5'11 195 Nebraska; Scarborough Rams Jrs. B: 1932
1963	TOR	14												10	27	2.7	7	0	6	47	7.8	15	0					17	319	18.8	25
1964	TOR	14												3	26	8.7	14	0	1	5	5.0	5	0	1	8	8.0	8	7	89	12.7	19
1965	CAL	14												2	1	0.5	4	0
1966	CAL	16	2		0							6	1	55	230	4.2	18	0	25	228	9.1	22	1					6	120	20.0	31
1967	CAL	11	1		0									7	22	3.1	13	0	4	53	13.3	24	0					5	111	22.2	29
1968	CAL	8												2	1	0.5	6	0	11	106	9.6	23	0
1970	EDM	1																	1	30	30.0	30	0					1	5	5.0	5
7	Years	78	3		0							6	1	79	307	3.9	18	0	48	469	9.8	30	1	1	8	8.0	8	36	644	17.9	31
RON ATCHISON Ron MG-DT 6'3 235 Saskatoon Hilltops Jrs. B: 4/21/1930 Central Butte, SK D: 6/23/2010 Saskatoon, SK
1952	SAS	7
1953	SAS	12
1954	SAS	16	1		4
1955	SAS	15	0		4
1956	SAS+	10
1957	SAS	16
1958	SAS	16
1959	SAS	13
1960	SAS+	16	0		1
1961	SAS+	12			3
1962	SAS+	16
1963	SAS+	16	0		1
1964	SAS+	16
1965	SAS	7							1
1966	SAS	15
1967	SAS	16	0		1
1968	SAS	16	0		1
17	Years	235	1		15				1	0
ARNIE ATKINS Arnold Truman E 5'10 185 B: 11/21/1923 Muscatine, IA D: 6/11/2010 Ashford, AL
1946	HAM	11										5	1
BLAIR ATKINSON Blair WR 6'4 220 South Fraser Ramns Jrs.; Manitoba B: 8/29/1980 Langley, BC
2007	WPG	1				0
IMOKHAI ATOGWE Imokhai DB 5'10 185 Windsor AKO Fratmen Jrs.; St. Francis Xavier B: 7/15/1977 Windsor, ON
2004	EDM	15				4
2005	HAM	8				8																		1	1	1.0	1
2006	HAM	1				2
2006	SAS	6				0
2006	Year	7				2
2007	SAS	2				0
4	Years	26				14																		1	1	1.0	1
DERRICK ATTERBERRY Derrick D. CB 5'1125 187 Vanderbilt B: 11/1/1972 Dayton, OH
1995	MEM	6				4
TED AUCREMAN Ted L. OE 180 Indiana B: 6/6/1937 Draft: FS 1960 LAC; 11-123 1960 DET
1961	SAS	1
EARLE AUDET Earle Toussaint T-G 6'2 251 Georgetown (DC); Southern California B: 5/14/1921 D: 12/18/2002 Los Angeles, CA Draft: 3-23 1944 WAS Pro: AN
1950	CAL	14

Year	Team	GP	FM	FF	FR	TK	SK	YDS	IR	YDS	PD	PTS	TD	RA	YDS	AVG	LG	TD	REC	YDS	AVG	LG	TD	PR	YDS	AVG	LG	KOR	YDS	AVG	LG
PHILIPPE AUDET Philippe DL 6'2 231 Laval B: 9/17/1981 Sainte-Justine, QC Draft: 2A-14 2005 TOR																															
2005	TOR	4				0																									
DUCARMEL AUGUSTIN Ducarmel S. RB 5'11 223 Villanova B: 10/24/1978 Draft: 1-6 2004 SAS																															
2004	SAS	10				10								1	0	0.0	0	0													
IRBY AUGUSTINE Irby, Jr. LB 6'0 212 California B: 3/5/1948 Port Arthur, TX																															
1970	OTT	10							2	47																		2	11	5.5	11
MEL AULL Mel G-E-T 5'11 210 Hamilton Tigers Jrs. B: 1928																															
1950	HAM	10																													
1951	OTT	7																													
1952	OTT	9																													
1953	SAS	9																													
4	Years	35																													
DA'SHANN AUSTIN Da'Shann CB-DH 5'10 182 Purdue; Northwestern Oklahoma State B: 12/1/1977 Cleveland, OH																															
2001	CAL	2				3																		1	7	7.0	7				
2002	CAL	16				45					9													3	31	10.3	19	11	264	24.0	46
2003	BC	13				48	2.0	15.0	2	42	10																				
2004	BC	17	0	1	1	51					6																				
2005	OTT	10				27			1	18	2																				
5	Years	58	0	1	1	174	2.0	15.0	3	60	27													4	38	9.5	19	11	264	24.0	46
KENT AUSTIN Richard Kent QB 6'1 195 Mississippi B: 6/25/1963 Natick, MA Draft: 12-312 1986 STL Pro: N																															
1987	SAS	5	6		1	0								24	138	5.8	31	0													
1988	SAS	14	7		2	0						12	2	51	258	5.1	34	2													
1989	SAS	18	4		1	0						18	3	42	168	4.0	18	3													
1990	SAS*	16	4		1	1						30	5	50	158	3.2	17	5													
1991	SAS	13	2		1	0						36	6	21	10	0.5	-9	6													
1992	SAS	18	4		1	0						66	11	71	200	2.8	17	11													
1993	SAS	17	3		0	1						42	7	32	88	2.8	21	7													
1994	BC	16	4		0	2						18	3	29	102	3.5	16	3													
1995	TOR	16	4		3	2						6	1	17	35	2.1	12	1													
1996	WPG	15	4		0	0								21	100	4.8	16	0													
10	Years	148	42		10	6						228	38	358	1257	3.5	34	38													
LARRY AUSTIN Larry Darrell DB 5'8 187 Virginia Tech B: 5/17/1979 Norfolk, VA Pro: E																															
2003	CAL	1				1																									
SCHREDRICK AUSTIN Schredrick B. WR 5'10 172 Clark Atlanta B: 7/30/1972 Atlanta, GA																															
1995	BIR	7				4						18	3						8	197	24.6	42	3	1	10	10.0	10				
JOHN AUTRY John L. DE 6'1 232 Prairie View A&M B: 2/17/1938 Quinlan, TX D: 3/11/2001 Port Arthur, TX																															
1963	TOR+	14																													
1964	HAM	1																													
2	Years	15																													
DON AVERY Donald Lee T-G 6'4 254 Alabama; Southern California B: 2/10/1921 Los Angeles, CA D: 8/8/2006 Long Beach, CA Pro: AN																															
1950	CAL	14																													
JEFF AVERY Jeff FL-P 6'2 185 Ottawa B: 3/28/1953 Draft: TE 1976 OTT																															
1976	OTT	16										12	2						21	338	16.1	62	2	6	34	5.7	13				
1977	OTT+	12	1		0							24	4						34	625	18.4	82	4								
1978	OTT+	16	0		1							18	3						50	767	15.3	68	3								
1979	OTT	15										24	4						27	402	14.9	53	4								
1980	OTT	11																	8	93	11.6	16	0								
1981	OTT	16										6	1						14	151	10.8	21	1								
1982	OTT	16										8	1						15	243	16.2	39	1								
7	Years	102	1		1							92	15						169	2619	15.5	82	15	6	34	5.7	13				
JIM AVERY James Richard DE 6'2 235 North Central B: 7/11/1944 Grand Rapids, MI Pro: N																															
1968	WPG	14	0		1														1	15	15.0	15	0								
JOHN AVERY John Edward, III RB 5'9 190 Northwest Mississippi CC; Mississippi B: 1/11/1976 Richmond, VA Draft: 1-29 1998 MIA Pro: NX																															
2002	EDM*	18	10	0	0	4						66	11	229	1448	6.3	61	9	45	387	8.6	31	2	6	34	5.7	13	26	661	25.4	75
2004	TOR	17	5	0	0	1						30	5	202	974	4.8	74	4	48	364	7.6	27	1					4	77	19.3	29
2005	TOR	13	4	0	0	0						30	5	109	526	4.8	26	2	36	393	10.9	46	3					2	42	21.0	28
2006	TOR	7	1	0	0	0						12	2	82	432	5.3	23	2	8	41	5.1	17	0								
2007	TOR	5	1	0	1	0						18	3	75	327	4.4	22	3	7	66	9.4	18	0								
5	Years	60	21	0	1	5						156	26	697	3707	5.3	74	20	144	1251	8.7	46	6	6	34	5.7	13	32	780	24.4	75
BUTCH AVINGER Clarence Edmund FW-HB 6'1 215 Alabama B: 12/15/1928 Beatrice, AL D: 8/20/2008 AL Draft: 1-9 1951 PIT Pro: N																															
1952	SAS	14			2				8	34		34	3	13	60	4.6	12	1	16	172	10.8	45	2								
BRENDON AYANBADEJO Oladele Brendon DE 6'1 227 Cabrillo JC; UCLA B: 9/6/1976 Chicago, IL Pro: EN																															
2000	WPG	12				25	1.0	4.0																				1	0	0.0	0
2000	TOR	2	1	0	0	3																						1	6	6.0	6
2000	Year	14	1	0	0	28	1.0	4.0																				2	6	3.0	6
2002	BC*	14	2	2	7	104	3.0	12.0	3	28	3																				
2	Years	26	3	2	7	132	4.0	16.0	3	28	3																	2	6	3.0	6
BROCK AYNSLEY Brock FL-RB 6'2 190 Washington State B: 1/18/1950 Vancouver, BC																															
1973	BC	12	0		1									1	3	3.0	3	0	7	88	12.6	41	0	11	48	4.4	14	3	78	26.0	38
1974	BC	9																	25	453	18.1	85	0					12	288	24.0	33
1975	BC	10										6	1						18	243	13.5	20	1					5	85	17.0	33
1976	MTL	13	1		0							18	3	2	5	2.5	15	0	20	474	23.7	62	3								
1977	MTL+	16										18	3	2	9	4.5	11	0	39	739	18.9	105	3								
1978	MTL	12										18	3						20	375	18.8	82	3								
1978	HAM	3																	3	35	11.7	18	0								
1978	Year	15										18	3						23	410	17.8	82	3								
1979	HAM	12	1		0							24	4	1	-3	-3.0	-3	0	22	382	17.4	59	4								
1980	HAM	4																	5	75	15.0	18	0								
1980	WPG	9																	5	57	11.4	24	0								
1980	Year	13																	10	132	13.2	24	0								
8	Years	88	2		1							84	14	6	14	2.3	15	0	164	2921	17.8	105	14	11	48	4.4	14	20	451	22.6	38
DAVID AZZI David WR 6'2 205 Ottawa B: 1/25/1981 Lebanon Draft: 1B-3 2004 OTT																															
2004	OTT	8				0						6	1						9	88	9.8	18	1								
2005	OTT	8				1						6	1						5	67	13.4	40	1								
2006	TOR	9	0	1	0	1													9	124	13.8	25	0					1	11	11.0	11
2007	SAS	6				0																									
4	Years	31	0	1	0	2						12	2						23	279	12.1	40	2					1	11	11.0	11
MIKE BABB Michael O. DB 6'2 200 Weber State B: 5/22/1967 Fullerton, CA																															
1991	EDM	2				5			1	20																					
JOHNNY BABINEAU John Edward G Saskatoon Collegians Jrs. B: // Rouleau, SK D: 1/8/2008 Mile House, BC																															
1946	SAS	5																													
JOHN BABINECZ John Michael LB 6'1 222 Villanova B: 7/27/1950 Pittsburgh, PA Draft: 2B-39 1972 DAL Pro: N																															
1976	WPG	8							1	0																					
1977	WPG	6																													
2	Years	14							1	0																					
ADAM BABOULAS Adam OG 6'4 300 St. Mary's (Noiva Scotia) B: 4/5/1987 Oshawa, ON Draft: 6A-41 2010 BC																															
2011	BC	5				0																									
TANG BACHEYIE Godfrey Tang LB 6'1 207 Kansas B: 3/3/1985 Windsor, ON Draft: 4-29 2009 BC																															
2010	TOR	10				15																						3	36	12.0	17
RYAN BACHMAN Ryan OT 6'6 304 Nebraska-Kearney B: 7/28/1980 Ponca, NE																															
2005	WPG	1				0																									
TED BACHMAN Theodore Lewis DB 6'0 190 Porterville JC; New Mexico State B: 1/19/1952 Pensacola, FL Pro: N																															

Year	Team	GP	FM	FF	FR	TK	SK	YDS	IR	YDS	PD	PTS	TD	RA	YDS	AVG	LG	TD	REC	YDS	AVG	LG	TD	PR	YDS	AVG	LG	KOR	YDS	AVG	LG
1973	CAL	5																													
1974	CAL	12							5	65																		10	254	25.4	37
2	Years	17							5	65																		10	254	25.4	37
TOM BACKES Thomas Jeffery, Jr. OT 6'4 273 Oklahoma B: 3/19/1968 El Paso, TX Draft: 10-272 1991 CHIB Pro: E																															
1994	LV	8																													
KAREEM BACON Kareem A. CB 5'10 185 Clark Atlanta B: 7/19/1972 Hinesville, GA																															
1995	BAL	3				5			0	0	1																				
RICH BADAR Richard Chester QB 6'1 190 Indiana B: 3/8/1943 Cleveland, OH Pro: N																															
1966	WPG	8										6	1	11	83	7.5	23	1													
1967	WPG	2												1	0	0.0	0	0													
2	Years	10										6	1	12	83	6.9	23	1													
HARRY BADGER Harry HB Deer Lodge Jrs.																															
1947	WPG	6																													
DAVE BADOWICH Dave P-K 6'2 195 Regina Rams Jrs. B: 4/2/1959																															
1983	SAS	4	2		0							1	0																		
1984	SAS	3										1	0																		
2	Years	7	2		0							2	0																		
JIM BAFFICO James Angelo OG 6'2 262 San Francisco; Marquette; San Francisco CC; Nebraska B: 1/1/1942 San Francisco, CA																															
1965	TOR	8																													
SIMON BAFFOE Simon RB 5'11 224 Alberta B: 3/2/1975 Ghana																															
1998	BC	12				10																						1	23	23.0	23
1999	BC	18	0	0	1	15																									
2000	BC	18	0	1	0	6						6	1	22	144	6.5	21	0	4	46	11.5	23	1					1	1	1.0	1
2001	BC	2	0	0	1	2																									
2001	EDM	11				12						6	1	4	20	5.0	18	0	3	49	16.3	29	1								
2001	Year	13				14						6	1	4	20	5.0	18	0	3	49	16.3	29	1								
2002	SAS	18				11								5	47	9.4	13	0													
2003	SAS	17	1	0	0	8								15	64	4.3	26	0										1	0	0.0	0
6	Years	85	1	1	2	64						12	2	46	275	6.0	26	0	7	95	13.6	29	2					3	24	8.0	23
ROB BAGG Rob WR-SB 6'0 192 Queen's B: 2/3/1985 Kingston, ON																															
2008	SAS	16				2													22	371	16.9	72	0								
2009	SAS	18	0	1	0	8						32	5	2	16	8.0	10	0	59	807	13.7	60	5								
2010	SAS	15				0						18	3	2	43	21.5	46	0	44	688	15.6	87	3								
3	Years	49	0	1	0	10						50	8	4	59	14.8	46	0	125	1866	14.9	87	8								
STEVIE BAGGS Stevie, Jr. DE-LB 6'0 235 Bethune-Cookman B: 12/30/1981 Pompano Beach, FL																															
2006	WPG	5				4																									
2007	WPG	2	0	0	0	8	2.0	14.0			1																				
2007	EDM	7				12	1.0	5.0			1																				
2007	Year	9	0	0	0	20	3.0	19.0			2																				
2008	SAS	5	0	1	0	9	1.0	19.0			2																				
2009	SAS+	18	0	4	2	60	12.0	92.0	1	0	5																				
2010	HAM	7	0	1	3	24	5.0	24.0	1	4	2	12	2																		
2011	HAM	18	0	1	2	50	5.0	23.0			1																				
6	Years	55	0	7	7	167	26.0	177.0	2	4	12	12	2																		
ANTOINE BAGWELL Antoine RB 5'11 186 Joliet JC; California (Pennsylvania) B: 9/13/1984 Lansing, MI																															
2007	HAM	2				0								3	2	0.7	5	0	1	8	8.0	8	0								
DON BAHNUIK Don DT-DE-LB 6'3 245 Regina Rams Jrs. B: 1935																															
1967	SAS	16																													
1968	SAS	16																													
1969	SAS	16	0		1																										
1970	SAS	16	0		4																										
1971	SAS	14																													
1972	SAS	16	0		1																										
1973	SAS	16	0		2																										
1974	SAS	16	0		1																										
8	Years	126	0		9																										
ALVIN BAILEY Alvin CB 5'10 183 Alcorn State B: 8/8/1958 Port Gibson, MS Pro: U																															
1987	HAM	5	1		0	11	1.0		2	40		6	1											8	71	8.9	28	4	66	16.5	22
1988	HAM	2				2																		4	33	8.3	18	4	87	21.8	28
2	Years	7	1		0	13	1.0		2	40		6	1											12	104	8.7	28	8	153	19.1	28
BY BAILEY Byron Ledare FB-DB-OHB 5'10 192 Washington State B: 10/12/1930 Omaha, NE D: 1/18/1998 Winfield, BC Draft: 25-298 1952 DET Pro: N																															
1954	BC	14										15	3	102	376	3.7	25	3	3	15	5.0	8	0					4	44	11.0	19
1955	BC	14	2		0							10	2	79	384	4.9	18	2	12	158	13.2	63	0					3	71	23.7	44
1956	BC	16	8		0							24	4	134	620	4.6	19	1	14	294	21.0	72	2					24	680	28.3	96
1957	BC+	15	1		0							66	11	184	885	4.8	30	11	24	188	7.8	22	0					22	585	26.6	51
1958	BC	11	3									24	4	99	489	4.9	45	4	16	131	8.2	29	0					24	569	23.7	68
1959	BC	7										6	1	33	142	4.3	16	1	4	39	9.8	14	0					13	336	25.8	35
1960	BC	16	2		1							18	3	68	342	5.0	33	3	14	156	11.1	31	0					12	332	27.7	59
1961	BC	14										6	1	76	386	5.1	36	1	12	125	10.4	24	0					16	312	19.5	32
1962	BC	16	1						3	59				8	19	2.4	5	0	2	55	27.5	47	0					10	185	18.5	30
1963	BC	14							8	85																					
1964	BC	16							1															1	2	2.0	2				
11	Years	153	17		1				12	144		169	29	783	3643	4.7	45	26	101	1161	11.5	72	2	1	2	2.0	2	128	3114	24.3	96
C.J. BAILEY C.J. CB 5'10 188 Southern Mississippi B: 9/7/1987 Moss Point, MS																															
2011	EDM	2				7					1																				
DAVID BAILEY David WR 6'1 190 Alabama B: 2/23/1950 Bailey, MS Draft: 11-266 1972 GB Pro: W																															
1974	WPG	15										12	2						35	550	15.7	40	2								
DAVID BAILEY David DE 6'4 240 Oklahoma State B: 9/3/1965 Coatesville, PA Pro: EN																															
1991	HAM	9	0		2	21	6.0																								
1992	HAM	18	0		1	33	6.0	44.0	1	3																					
1993	HAM	13	0		2	16	8.0	53.0																							
1994	SHR	2				1																									
1994	EDM	9				7																									
1994	Year	11				8																									
1995	EDM	7	0		1	13	1.0	5.0																							
5	Years	49	0		6	91	21.0	102.0	1	3																					
DAVID BAILEY David OT 6'5 280 James Madison B: 5/18/1973 Pro: E																															
1997	HAM	1				0																									
DON BAILEY Donald Patrick (Duke) QB 6'0 190 Penn State B: 4/13/1933 Pittsburgh, PA Draft: 18-207 1955 WAS																															
1955	OTT	5												35	104	3.0	13	0													
1956	CAL	1	1		0									9	-12	-1.3	11	0													
2	Years	6	1		0									44	92	2.1	13	0													
FRED BAILEY Fredrick L. WR 5'8 185 Southern University B: 5/28/1974 Torrance, CA																															
1997	CAL	6				2						12	2						13	130	10.0	35	2	1	25	25.0	25	3	63	21.0	33
1999	SAS	2	0	0	1	0						6	1	2	10	5.0	8	0	6	67	11.2	23	1	3	12	4.0	9	5	115	23.0	35
1999	EDM	5				0						6	1	2	2	1.0	2	0	17	244	14.4	57	1					13	365	28.1	72
1999	Year	7				0						12	2	4	12	3.0	8	0	23	311	13.5	57	2	3	12	4.0	9	18	480	26.7	72
2000	EDM	3				0													5	61	12.2	31	0								
2000	SAS	2				0													2	23	11.5	14	0	6	37	6.2	13	1	11	11.0	11
2000	Year	5				0													7	84	12.0	31	0	6	37	6.2	13	1	11	11.0	11
2001	EDM	1				0																									
4	Years	12	0	0	1	2						24	4	4	12	3.0	8	0	43	525	12.2	57	4	10	74	7.4	25	22	554	25.2	72

Year	Team	GP	FM	FF	FR	TK	SK	YDS	IR	YDS	PD	PTS	TD	RA	YDS	AVG	LG	TD	REC	YDS	AVG	LG	TD	PR	YDS	AVG	LG	KOR	YDS	AVG	LG
HAROLD BAILEY Harold Craig SB 6'2 197 Oklahoma State B: 4/12/1957 Houston, TX Draft: 8-217 1980 HOU Pro: N																															
1984	MTL	6										6	1						17	276	16.2	77	1								
HASSAN BAILEY Hassan M. LB 6'0 205 Kansas B: 1/28/1971 Detroit, MI																															
1994	HAM	14	0		3	66	3.0	24.0	1	9	1																	1	27	27.0	27
1995	HAM	17				90	1.0	7.0			2																				
2	Years	31	0		3	156	4.0	31.0	1	9	3																	1	27	27.0	27
KARSTEN BAILEY Karsten Mario WR 6'0 203 Auburn B: 4/26/1977 Newnan, GA Draft: 3B-82 1999 SEA Pro: N																															
2004	SAS	8				0						6	1						24	305	12.7	70	1								
2005	SAS	11				0						6	1						31	300	9.7	22	1					9	146	16.2	26
2	Years	19				0						12	2						55	605	11.0	70	2					9	146	16.2	26
KECALF BAILEY Kecalf DB 5'9 175 Alabama B: 12/30/1978 Tuscaloosa, AL																															
2001	MTL	1				5																									
KORY BAILEY Kory WR 6'1 195 North Carolina B: 3/31/1979 Durham, NC																															
2003	EDM	6	0	0	1	2						12	2						12	153	12.8	26	2	1	9	9.0	9	1	7	7.0	7
LARRY BAILEY Larry DE-DT 6'4 238 Pacific B: 5/10/1952 San Mateo, CA Draft: 9-225 1974 ATL; 9-105 1974 HAW-WFL Pro: NW																															
1976	HAM	2			1																										
MARIO BAILEY Mario Demetrious WR 5'9 162 Washington B: 11/30/1970 Oakland, CA Draft: 6-162 1992 HOU Pro: EX																															
1996	BC	2				0						6	1						4	24	6.0	10	1								
1998	WPG	2				0						6	1						12	118	9.8	47	1								
2	Years	4				0						12	2						16	142	8.9	47	2								
MONK BAILEY Claron Everett HB 6'0 178 Utah B: 4/22/1938 Moab, UT Pro: N																															
1966	TOR	2												15	43	2.9	6	0	1	43	43.0	43	0								
MORRIS BAILEY Morris E. E 6'3 210 Texas Christian B: 5/26/1925 D: 7/17/2002 Amarillo, TX Draft: 4-49 1950 SF																															
1950	EDM+	12										20	4						67	1060	15.8		4								
NOLAN BAILEY Nolan TE 6'2 240 Prairie View A&M B: 1945																															
1970	SAS	16	2		0							6	1	3	35	11.7	24	0	30	475	15.8	31	1								
1971	SAS	16										12	2	11	90	8.2	31	0	36	597	16.6	61	2								
1972	SAS	2																	1	9	9.0	9	0								
3	Years	34	2		0							18	3	14	125	8.9	31	0	67	1081	16.1	61	3								
ROY BAILEY E. Royal HB 5'8 200 Tulane B: 1930 VA Draft: 14-165 1953 PHI																															
1953	HAM	10										15	3					3													
SID BAILEY Sidney Johnson DE 6'4 221 Texas-Arlington B: 12/14/1948 Marlin, TX Draft: 16-401 1971 CHIB																															
1971	WPG	3																													
TERRY BAILEY Terry FB-WB 6'0 205 Simon Fraser B: 1/2/1951 Draft: TE 1974 BC																															
1974	BC	16												30	146	4.9	14	0	10	146	14.6	47	0					2	27	13.5	16
1975	BC	16	1		2							30	5	60	252	4.2	16	1	19	308	16.2	63	4					2	17	8.5	9
1976	BC	16										6	1	18	84	4.7	37	1	22	249	11.3	38	0					1	0	0.0	0
1977	BC	16	1		0							20	3	12	54	4.5	8	0	50	558	11.2	76	3					1	0	0.0	0
1978	BC	16										12	2	11	39	3.5	8	0	34	391	11.5	32	2								
1979	BC	16	1		2							6	1	1	8	8.0	8	0	23	232	10.1	25	1								
1980	BC	16	1		1							12	2	1	3	3.0	3	0	17	141	8.3	12	2								
1981	BC	16												7	26	3.7	8	0	11	177	16.1	65	0								
1982	BC	16	0		1														11	111	10.1	31	0					1	3	3.0	3
9	Years	144	4		6							86	14	140	612	4.4	37	2	197	2313	11.7	76	12					7	47	6.7	16
TOM BAILEY Thomas Alvin T 6'5 249 Alcorn State B: 7/16/1940 Delco, LA Pro: W																															
1971	EDM	1																													
TONY BAILEY Anthony DE 6'4 260 St. Mary's (Nova Scotia) B: 12/1/1970 Winnipeg, MB Draft: 1A-5 1994 OTT																															
1994	OTT	12	0		1	6																									
1995	HAM	4	0		1	7	1.0	7.0																							
1996	HAM	4				5																									
1996	MTL	2				0																									
1996	BC	6				3					2																				
1996	Year	12				8					2																				
3	Years	20	0		2	21	1.0	7.0			2																				
TROY BAILEY Troy C. DT 6'3 288 Oregon B: 3/9/1973 Modesto, CA Pro: E																															
1998	BC	7	0	1	0	14	1.0	0.0																							
2000	WPG	6				11	3.0	15.0			1																				
2	Years	13	0	1	0	25	4.0	15.0			1																				
WALTER BAILEY Walter DB 5'11 190 Washington B: 3/16/1970 Portland, OR																															
1993	SAC	15	1		2	29	2.0	25.0	2	29																		1	37	37.0	37
CHARLIE BAILLIE Charles HB-C-LB-K 6'0 208 Lakeshore Flyers Ints. B: 12/14/1935 Montreal, QC																															
1954	MTL	2																													
1956	MTL	1																													
1957	MTL	10												7	37	5.3	13	0	1	10	10.0	10	0								
1960	MTL	14							2	2																					
1961	MTL	3																													
1965	MTL	6										6	0																		
6	Years	36							2	2		6	0	7	37	5.3	13	0	1	10	10.0	10	0								
RAY BAILLIE Raymond DT-MG 6'0 275 B: 12/14/1935 Montreal, QC																															
1954	CAL	16							1	0																					
1955	CAL	16																													
1956	MTL	9																													
1957	MTL	2																													
1957	HAM	2																													
1957	Year	4																													
1960	MTL	7																													
1961	MTL	5																													
1962	EDM	16																													
1963	EDM	16	0		1																										
1965	MTL	2																													
9	Years	89	0		1				1	0																					
BRIAN BAIMA Brian Scott Michael WR 6'0 190 Los Angeles Valley JC; The Citadel B: 4/14/1949 Los Angeles, CA																															
1974	MTL	8										6	1						10	219	21.9	70	1								
LU BAIN Lucious, Jr. OHB 5'11 193 Oregon B: 9/2/1942 Paint Rock, AL D: 2/4/2011 Portland, OR																															
1964	CAL	9	3		0							12	2	49	225	4.6	31	2	5	112	22.4	46	0	17	110	6.5	15	8	150	18.8	31
1965	CAL	16	1		1				3	47				22	95	4.3	20	0	20	231	11.6	22	0	57	343	6.0	44	2	26	13.0	21
1966	CAL	6	0		1									23	101	4.4	23	0	3	40	13.3		0	6	38	6.3		4	55	13.8	
1966	EDM	6	2		0									23	109	4.7		0	4	40	10.0		0	14	69	4.9		5	132	26.4	
1966	Year	12	2		1									46	210	4.6	23	0	7	80	11.4	25	0	20	107	5.4	14	9	187	20.8	36
3	Years	31	6		2				3	47		12	2	117	530	4.5	31	2	32	423	13.2	46	0	94	560	6.0	44	19	363	19.1	31
ADRIAN BAIRD Adrian DE 6'4 245 Ottawa B: 7/15/1979 Scarsborough, ON Draft: 5-37 2005 OTT																															
2005	OTT	2				1																									
2006	WPG	17				12																									
2007	WPG	18				20																									
2008	EDM	2	0	2	0	14																									
2009	HAM	4				2																									
5	Years	43	0	2	0	49																									
DEK BAKE Donald DE 6'5 272 Fresno CC; Texas Tech B: 2/6/1984																															
2008	SAS	3				12	1.0																								
ART BAKER Arthur L. FB 6'0 220 Syracuse B: 12/31/1937 Erie, PA Draft: 3A-17 1961 BUF; 1-14 1961 PHI Pro: N																															
1963	HAM	7							1	-18		12	2	18	154	8.6	60	2										2	36	18.0	27
1964	HAM	14	1		2							24	4	150	726	4.8	55	3	5	11	2.2	7	1					4	51	12.8	19

Year	Team	GP	FM	FF	FR	TK	SK	YDS	IR	YDS	PD	PTS	TD	RA	YDS	AVG	LG	TD	REC	YDS	AVG	LG	TD	PR	YDS	AVG	LG	KOR	YDS	AVG	LG
1965	HAM	10	1									18	3	114	555	4.9	90	3													
1966	HAM	1										6	1	11	43	3.9	10	1													
1966	CAL	3												35	123	3.5	12	0	8	28	3.5	9	0								
1966	Year	4												46	166	3.6	12	1	8	28	3.5	9	0								
4	Years	32	2		2				1	-18		60	10	374	1767	4.7	90	10	13	39	3.0	9	1					6	87	14.5	27
BILL BAKER William DE-DT 6'4 250 Regina Rams Jrs.; Otterbein B: 8/29/1944																															
1968	SAS	16	0		1																										
1969	SAS	16	0		1																										
1970	SAS	16																													
1971	SAS+	16																													
1972	SAS*	16	0		1																										
1973	SAS*	16																													
1974	BC	14	0		1																										
1975	BC*	16																													
1976	BC*	16	0		2				1	0																					
1977	SAS	16	0		2																										
1978	SAS	16																													
11	Years	174	0		8				1	0																					
DALLAS BAKER Dallas WR 6'3 206 Florida B: 11/20/1982 New Smyrna Beach, FL Draft: 7-227 2007 PIT Pro: N																															
2011	MTL	3				0													3	29	9.7	13	0								
2011	SAS	7				1													20	271	13.6	72	0								
2011	Year	10				1																									
JIM BAKER James LB 5'11 225 Arizona State B: 6/13/1950 Smithfield, VA Draft: 36-433 1974 SC-WFL Pro: W																															
1976	BC	4	0		1																										
1976	CAL	1																													
1976	Year	5	0		1																										
1977	CAL	11	0		4														1	14	14.0	14	0					3	100	33.3	58
1978	CAL	3																													
3	Years	18	0		5														1	14	14.0	14	0					3	100	33.3	58
JOHN BAKER John Willey Alexander DE 6'5 260 Virginia Union; Norfolk State B: 8/15/1942 Detroit, MI Draft: 19-265 1964 GB Pro: NW																															
1964	MTL	10										1	0																		
1965	MTL+	14	0		6							1	0																		
1966	MTL	14	0		2																							1	0	0.0	0
1967	MTL*	14	0		1				1	0																					
1968	MTL	14										27	0																		
1969	MTL	14	1		3				2	58		31	1																		
1971	HAM	7	0		2							6	1																		
1972	HAM	4																													
8	Years	91	1		14				3	58		66	2															1	0	0.0	0
JON BAKER Jon DT 6'7 275 Pittsburgh B: 2/6/1968 Pro: E																															
1991	HAM	2				4																									
JON BAKER Jonathan David K 6'1 170 Bakersfield CC; Arizona State B: 8/13/1972 Orange, CA Pro: EN																															
1999	EDM	8				1						83	0																		
2000	BC	5				1						10	0																		
2001	EDM	1				0						1	0																		
3	Years	14				2						94	0																		
KEITH BAKER Keith Leonard WR 5'10 185 Texas A&M; Texas Southern B: 6/4/1957 Dallas, TX Pro: N																															
1979	MTL	12	0		1							30	5	3	42	14.0	24	0	29	571	19.7	72	5	12	134	11.2	38	5	95	19.0	39
1980	MTL+	15										48	8	4	-20	-5.0		0	51	891	17.5	58	8	11	85	7.7	14	3	48	16.0	30
1981	HAM+	16										66	11	3	2	0.7	7	0	68	1218	17.9	81	11	9	80	8.9	50				
1982	HAM*	16										48	8	5	19	3.8	15	0	80	1282	16.0	75	8	10	69	6.9	29	1	26	26.0	26
1983	HAM+	15										62	10	2	10	5.0	16	0	66	911	13.8	52	10	5	21	4.2	11				
1984	HAM	8										12	2						24	352	14.7	70	2					2	32	16.0	23
1984	OTT	4	1		0							18	3	2	27	13.5	15	0	15	271	18.1		3	5	18	3.6	14				
1984	Year	12	1		0							30	5	2	27	13.5	15	0	39	623	16.0	70	5	5	18	3.6	14	2	32	16.0	23
1986	TOR	2	1		0									2	9	4.5	10	0	3	33	11.0	17	0								
7	Years	84	2		1							284	47	21	89	4.2	24	0	336	5529	16.5	81	47	52	407	7.8	50	11	201	18.3	39
LORENZA BAKER Lorenza J. LB 5'11 220 Louisiana Tech B: 2/7/1969 Shreveport, LA																															
1992	WPG	11	0		1	35	2.0																					6	134	22.3	28
ROBERT BAKER Robert Cedrick, III WR 5'11 200 Auburn B: 5/14/1976 Miami, FL Pro: EN																															
2004	TOR	18	4	0	0	3						24	4						62	1086	17.5	65	4					4	61	15.3	29
2005	TOR	17	2	1	1	3						24	4						70	1065	15.2	90	4					1	0	0.0	0
2006	TOR	7				1													22	217	9.9	31	0								
2006	WPG	1				0																									
2006	Year	8				1													22	217	9.9	31	0								
3	Years	42	6	1	1	7						48	8						154	2368	15.4	90	8					5	61	12.2	29
RON BAKER Ronald Leroy C 6'2 238 Ottawa Seconds Jrs. B: 7/11/1932 Ottawa, ON D: 3/7/2009																															
1953	OTT	9																													
1954	OTT	14										1	0																		
1955	BC	16										19	0						0	3		3	0								
1956	BC	16										20	0																		
4	Years	55										40	0						0	3		3	0								
SHALON BAKER Shalon Jermaine WR 5'6 170 Montana B: 8/22/1973 Seattle, WA																															
1995	EDM	18				5						30	5	1	-6	-6.0	-6	0	79	1156	14.6	62	5	6	62	10.3	17	3	68	22.7	30
1996	EDM	13	2		1	4						30	5						31	428	13.8	56	4	56	580	10.4	86				
1997	WPG	5				0								1	2	2.0	2	0	13	119	9.2	26	0	18	86	4.8	12	8	134	16.8	27
1997	BC	2				0								1	5	5.0	5	0	10	72	7.2	16	0	2	12	6.0	7	1	21	21.0	21
1997	Year	7				0								2	7	3.5	5	0	23	191	8.3	26	0	20	98	4.9	12	9	155	17.2	27
3	Years	36	2		1	9						60	10	3	1	0.3	5	0	133	1775	13.3	62	9	82	740	9.0	86	12	223	18.6	30
SHANNON BAKER Shannon Maurice WR 5'9 185 Florida State B: 7/20/1970 Bartow, FL Draft: 8-205 1993 ATL Pro: N																															
1995	WPG	5	1		0	2						6	1	1	5	5.0	5	0	19	214	11.3	29	0	12	172	14.3	51	18	440	24.4	84
1996	WPG	12	1		0	2								3	65	21.7	32	0	38	390	10.3	27	0	40	315	7.9	46	17	364	21.4	46
1997	SAS	4				0													1	8	8.0	8	0	7	43	6.1	12	10	237	23.7	48
1998	SAS	4				0						6	1						6	101	16.8	67	1	4	22	5.5	7	5	93	18.6	24
4	Years	25	2		0	4						12	2	4	70	17.5	32	0	64	713	11.1	67	1	63	552	8.8	51	50	1134	22.7	84
STEVE BAKER Steve P 5'11 205 Arizona State; Southern Oregon B: 12/28/1977 Pro: E																															
2004	HAM	1				1						10	0																		
TERRY BAKER Terry Wayne OHB 6'3 198 Oregon State B: 5/5/1941 Pine River, MN Draft: 12-90 1963 SD; 1A-1 1963 LARM Pro: N																															
1967	EDM	14	2		0							6	1	36	120	3.3	15	1	9	103	11.4	18	0								
TERRY BAKER Terry P-K 6'1 200 Mount Allison; Acadia B: 5/8/1962 Bridgewater, NS Draft: 8-65 1984 MTL																															
1987	SAS	15	2		0	0						6	0	1	-2	-2.0	-2	0													
1988	SAS	18	4		0	0						4	0	2	1	0.5	1	0													
1989	SAS	18	5		1	0						7	0	3	-9	-3.0	-13	0													
1990	OTT	18	2		1	0						4	0																		
1991	OTT	18	4		1	7						202	0	2	35	17.5	34	0	1	-1	-1.0	-1	0	1	0	0.0	0				
1992	OTT	18	2		1	5						184	0																		
1993	OTT	11	1		0	7						89	0	1	7	7.0	7	0													
1994	OTT	18	8		0	6						188	0	2	20	10.0	17	0													
1995	OTT	6	1		1	0						43	0																		
1995	TOR	12	2		1	7						76	0																		
1995	Year	18	3		2	7						119	0																		
1996	MTL+	18	5		0	3						178	0																		

Year	Team	GP	FM	FF	FR	TK	SK	YDS	IR	YDS	PD	PTS	TD	RA	YDS	AVG	LG	TD	REC	YDS	AVG	LG	TD	PR	YDS	AVG	LG	KOR	YDS	AVG	LG
1997	MTL	18	2	0	0	6						169	0	2	35	17.5	24	0													
1998	MTL	18	2	0	0	6						200	0	3	29	9.7	15	0													
1999	MTL	18	1	0	0	12						188	0																		
2000	MTL	18	6	1	0	5						220	0	2	23	11.5	12	0													
2001	MTL*	18	1	0	0	2						181	0																		
2002	MTL	18	4	0	0	6						184	0	1	8	8.0	8	0													
16	Years	266	52	1	6	72						2123	0	19	147	7.7	34	0	1	-1	-1.0	-1	0	1	0	0.0	0				
JIM BAKHTIAR James A. FB 6'1 198 Virginia B: 1/8/1934																															
1958	CAL	15	4		0				0	9		25	4	192	971	5.1	24	4	10	60	6.0	14	0					4	67	16.8	25
OLLIE BAKKEN Oliver James LB 6'2 224 Minnesota B: 1/30/1953 St. Paul, MN Draft: 15-388 1975 MIN																															
1976	WPG	2																													
1976	CAL	13							2	31																		4	34	8.5	14
1976	Year	15							2	31																		4	34	8.5	14
1977	CAL	16	0		4				1	2																		1	13	13.0	13
1978	CAL	14	0		2				2	26																					
1979	CAL	13							1	1																					
1980	BC	10	0		1				1	19																					
5	Years	55	0		7				7	79																		5	47	9.4	14
TIM BAKKER Tim C-OG 6'4 300 Western Ontario B: 11/23/1977 Oakville, ON Draft: 1-3 2000 EDM																															
2000	EDM	11				0																									
2001	EDM	18				0																									
2002	EDM	18	0	0	1	0																									
2003	BC	18				0																									
2004	HAM	17				1																									
2005	HAM	18	1	0	0	0																									
2006	EDM	18				2																									
2007	EDM	18				1																									
2008	EDM	18				0																									
9	Years	154	1	0	1	4																									
WALT BALASIUK Walter DT 6'2 260 B: 10/19/1939 Benito, MB																															
1965	TOR	9																													
1966	TOR	1																													
1967	TOR	14																													
1968	TOR	5																													
1969	TOR	14																													
1970	TOR	14																													
1971	MTL	14	0		1																										
7	Years	71	0		1																										
AL BALDWIN Alton E-QB-FW 6'2 205 Arkansas B: 2/21/1923 Hot Springs, AR D: 5/23/1994 Hot Springs, AR Draft: 29-271 1946 CHIC; 1-2 1947 BUF-AAFC; 4-25 1947 BOS Pro: AN																															
1951	OTT	12										30	6										6								
1952	OTT	12										35	7										7								
1953	HAM	5																													
3	Years	29										65	13										13								
DON BALDWIN Donald Wayne DE 6'3 263 Purdue B: 7/9/1964 St. Charles, MO Pro: N																															
1988	TOR	5	0		2	5	5.0		1	0																					
1989	TOR	2																													
1989	OTT	3																													
1989	Year	5				10																									
2	Years	7	0		2	5	5.0		1	0																					
JACK BALDWIN John David T 6'3 223 Centenary B: 7/31/1921 Clyde, TX D: 9/13/1989 Kerrville, TX Draft: 24-243 1944 BKN Pro: A																															
1949	EDM	10																													
MIKE BALENKO Mike OT 6'3 250 Bridgeport B: 2/17/1949 Montreal, QC																															
1971	MTL	14																													
FRANK BALKOVEC Frank LB 6'0 235 Toronto B: 11/26/1959 Novo Mesto, Yugoslavia Draft: 1-1 1984 BC																															
1984	EDM	16	0		3																										
1985	EDM	12					1.0																								
1986	EDM	16					2.0		1	19																					
1987	EDM	15			1	7																									
1988	CAL	12				1																									
1989	CAL	5				4																									
1990	OTT	2				0																									
1991	OTT	1																													
8	Years	79	0		4	12	3.0		1	19																					
CHRIS BALL Chris LB 6'3 220 Mount San Antonio JC; California B: 12/27/1977 Pro: E																															
2003	BC	1				0																									
2005	HAM	7				10																									
2	Years	8				10																									
RAPHAEL BALL Raphael DB 5'11 185 Ball State B: 12/9/1974 Cincinnati, OH																															
2000	BC	16				35			1	54	3	6	1																		
RAPHAOL BALL Raphaol CB 5'10 182 Ball State B: 12/9/1974 Cincinnati, OH																															
1999	BC	10	0	1	1	24			1	0	4																				
2000	BC	16	0	1	0	47			2	26	14																				
2001	WPG	12	0	1	1	36			1	0	6																				
2002	WPG	7	0	0	1	23					2	1	0																		
2003	TOR	12				35			1	0	3																				
2004	TOR	3				6																									
6	Years	60	0	3	3	171			5	26	29	1	0																		
HOWARD BALLAGE Howard Louis WR 6'0 183 Colorado B: 7/13/1957 Fort Polk, LA Draft: 10B-252 1979 SF Pro: U																															
1982	MTL	10										8	1						17	280	16.5	36	1					14	360	25.7	43
DEMARIO BALLARD Demario SB 6'5 219 Siskiyous CC; Western Oregon B: 1/17/1984 Thomson, GA																															
2011	TOR	1				0																									
GREG BALLARD Greg WR 6'3 190 Kansas B: 5/5/1971																															
1994	SHR	2				0													3	61	20.3	27	0								
1995	SHR	2				0													1	15	15.0	15	0								
2	Years	4				0													4	76	19.0	27	0								
JIM BALLARD James R. QB 6'3 223 Wilmington; Mount Union B: 4/16/1972 Akron, OH Pro: EX																															
1999	TOR	18				0								3	13	4.3	9	0													
2000	SAS	4				0																									
2002	TOR	9	2	0	0	1						2	0	11	10	0.9	4	0													
3	Years	31	2	0	0	1						2	0	14	23	1.6	9	0													
KEITH BALLARD Keith OG-OT 6'4 300 Minnesota B: 2/16/1970 Detroit, MI																															
1994	BAL	16				1																									
WALTER BALLARD Walter J. DE-DT-LB 6'2 235 Texas-El Paso B: 8/8/1961 Pascagoula, MS																															
1983	CAL	1					2.0																								
1984	CAL	14	0		2				1	31		6	1																		
1985	TOR	14					9.0																								
1986	BC	18	0		2		10.0																								
1987	BC	18	0		2	25	13.0																								
1988	BC	18	0		2	38	6.0																								
1989	BC	3				6																									
1990	CAL	18	0		1	51	3.0		1	0																		1	16	16.0	16

Year	Team	GP	FM	FF	FR	TK	SK	YDS	IR	YDS	PD	PTS	TD	RA	YDS	AVG	LG	TD	REC	YDS	AVG	LG	TD	PR	YDS	AVG	LG	KOR	YDS	AVG	LG
1991	CAL	14	0		2	25	3.0																								
9	Years	118	0		11	145	46.0		2	31		6	1															1	16	16.0	16
BROCK BALOG Brock DB 6'1 195 Calgary B: 8/8/1977 Calgary, AB Draft: 6-45 2000 CAL																															
2001	CAL	2				0																									
2003	EDM	11				4																									
2003	BC	1				0																									
2003	Year	12				4																									
2	Years	13				4																									
PAUL BALONICK Paul L. C 6'2 225 North Carolina State B: 1/24/1938 D: 5/15/1992 Monroeville, PA Draft: 20-240 1959 BAL																															
1960	HAM	3																													
BILL BANCROFT Bill E-G 5'11 216																															
1946	MTL	3																													
DANNY BANDA Danny DB-LB 5'9 155 Regina Rams Jrs. B: 1938																															
1958	SAS	15	0		2				3	44				2	3	1.5	7	0						2	30	15.0	11				
1959	SAS	16							3	30				1	-10	-10.0	-10	0						37	102	2.8	10	19	351	18.5	37
1960	SAS	16	5		1				1					1	3	3.0	3	0						60	210	3.5	13	8	184	23.0	33
1961	SAS	16																						3	28	9.3	26				
1962	SAS	16																						6	8	1.3	2				
5	Years	79	5		3				7	74				4	-4	-1.0	7	0						108	378	3.5	26	27	535	19.8	37
DEAN BANDIERA Dean (Dino) DG 5'11 201 Queen's B: 1/1/1926																															
1946	MTL	1																													
1947	MTL	11																													
1949	SAS	11										5	1					1													
1950	SAS	14																													
1951	WPG	13																													
1952	WPG	16			2																										
1953	WPG+	16																													
1954	CAL	16																													
1955	CAL	12	0		1																										
9	Years	110	0		3							5	1					1													
BRUNO BANDUCCI Bruno G-T 5'11 216 Stanford B: 11/11/1921 Tsignano, Italy D: 9/15/1985 Sonoma, CA Draft: 6-42 1943 PHI Pro: AN																															
1955	TOR	9																													
OPIE BANDY Opie Anderson OT-MG 6'2 231 Tulsa B: 1937 deceased Draft: 18-216 1959 BAL																															
1959	CAL	16	0		2				1										1	16	16.0	16	0								
1960	CAL	10	0		1																										
1961	CAL	12																										1	-2	-2.0	-2
3	Years	38	0		3				1	0									1	16	16.0	16	0					1	-2	-2.0	-2
JOHN BANKHEAD John DE 6'6 235 Snow JC B: 1/15/1968																															
1991	SAS	4				10	2.0																								
TODD BANKHEAD Todd A. QB 6'2 215 Massachusetts B: 6/6/1977 San Diego, CA																															
2000	HAM	16	2	0	1	1								8	45	5.6	17	0													
ANTONIO BANKS Antonio Dontral DH-S 5'10 195 Virginia Tech B: 3/12/1973 Ivor, VA Draft: 4-113 1997 MIN Pro: EN																															
1998	WPG	4	0	0	1	7			1	0	0	6	1																		
2002	MTL	1				0																									
2003	WPG	4				4			1	0	1																				
3	Years	9	0	0	1	11			2	0	1	6	1																		
BILL BANKS Bill LB 6'1 225 Penn State B: 6/29/1955 Camden, NJ																															
1979	HAM	9	0		1																										
1980	OTT	16	0		4				1	5																					
1981	MTL	2																													
3	Years	27	0		5				1	5																					
BRAD BANKS Brad QB 5'11 204 Iowa B: 4/22/1980 Belle Glades, FL																															
2004	OTT	12	2	0	1	0						12	2	20	138	6.9	20	2													
2005	OTT	11				0								1	3	3.0	3	0													
2006	WPG	18	1	0	0	0								6	36	6.0	23	0													
2007	MTL	11				0								1	5	5.0	5	0													
2008	MTL	4				0								2	20	10.0	11	0													
5	Years	56	3	0	1	0						12	2	30	202	6.7	23	2													
FRED BANKS Fredrick Ray WR 5'10 177 Chowan JC; Liberty B: 5/26/1962 Columbus, GA Draft: 8-203 1985 CLE; 8A-107 1985 DEN-USFL Pro: N																															
1994	SAC	3				1						0	1						6	85	14.2	27	1								
JON BANKS Jon LB 6'2 232 Iowa Centra CC; Iowa State B: 4/11/1984 East Moline, IL																															
2009	MTL	2				8			1	15	0																				
2010	MTL	9				14	1.0	7.0																							
2	Years	11				22	1.0	7.0	1	15	0																				
KEN BANKS Kenneth Duane LB 6'4 215 Eastern Michigan B: 10/14/1959 Flint, MI																															
1982	OTT	3					3.5																								
KOREY BANKS Korey Lamar DH-S-LB 5'10 188 Garden City CC; Mississippi State B: 8/15/1979 Camden, NJ																															
2004	OTT	3				7			0	0	2																				
2005	OTT*	18	0	2	1	44			10	190	12	12	2																		
2006	BC*	18	0	1	1	55			7	106	6	6	1																		
2007	BC+	17	0	1	1	38	3.0	26.0	4	38	8																				
2008	BC+	18	0	1	2	57	4.0	27.0	6	134	5	12	2																		
2009	BC*	18	0	2	1	57	5.0	54.0	4	47	6																				
2010	BC+	18	0	3	4	55	7.0	53.0	2	1	10	6	1																		
2011	BC*	18	0	0	2	42	3.0	17.0	1	0	6	6	1																		
8	Years	128	0	10	12	355	22.0	177.0	34	516	55	42	7																		
ROBERT BANKS Robert Nathan DE 6'5 255 Notre Dame B: 12/10/1963 Williamsburg, VA Draft: 7-176 1987 HOU Pro: N																															
1992	SAS	14	0		1	30	3.0																								
CALVIN BANNISTER Calvin DH 5'8 180 Hampton B: 2/17/1984 Roanoke, VA																															
2007	CAL	10				19			2	51	3																	17	360	21.2	36
2008	CAL	11	0	1	0	39			1	0	4																				
2	Years	21	0	1	0	58			3	51	7																	17	360	21.2	36
BILL BARBER William OE 6'3 209 Florida A&M B: 5/3/1936																															
1960	CAL	2										6	1						3	21	7.0	15	1								
1961	CAL	1																	2	45	22.5	29	0					1	0	0.0	0
2	Years	3										6	1						5	66	13.2	29	1					1	0	0.0	0
BOB BARBER Robert J. DE 6'3 240 Grambling State B: 12/26/1951 Ferriday, LA Draft: 2-51 1975 PIT Pro: NUW																															
1980	EDM	2																													
1981	TOR	7	0		2		3.5																								
2	Years	9	0		2		3.5																								
CHRIS BARBER Christopher Edgar DB 6'0 187 North Carolina A&T State B: 1/15/1964 Fort Bragg, NC Pro: EN																															
1991	TOR	3				7																									
WOLF BARBER Wolf DB 6'0 185 Pasadena JC; California B: 4/20/1970																															
1994	LV	1												1	6	6.0	6	0						3	22	7.3					
1994	SAS	1				1																		4	25	6.3	17				
1994	Year	2												1	6	6.0	6	0						7	47	6.7					
1995	SAS	1	1		0	1								9	44	4.9	19	0	5	31	6.2	9	0								
2	Years	2	1		0	2								10	50	5.0	19	0	5	31	6.2	9	0	7	47	6.7	17				
BILL BARBISH William J. (Moose) FB 5'11 205 Tennessee B: 7/14/1931 Cleveland, OH D: 7/23/2002 Lenoir City, TN Draft: 8A-95 1954 CLE																															
1954	TOR	1																													
RICKY BARDEN Ricky CB 5'9 185 North Carolina B: 6/6/1958 Norfolk, VA																															
1981	OTT	8	2		1				1	36																		18	416	23.1	41

Year	Team	GP	FM	FF	FR	TK	SK	YDS	IR	YDS	PD	PTS	TD	RA	YDS	AVG	LG	TD	REC	YDS	AVG	LG	TD	PR	YDS	AVG	LG	KOR	YDS	AVG	LG
1982	OTT	10	0		2		0.5		2	5		6	1																		
1983	OTT	14	1		0		0.5		3	27														7	43	6.1	17	18	410	22.8	40
1984	OTT+	16	0		4		0.5		4	70														9	116	12.9	74	2	34	17.0	34
1985	OTT+	16	0		5				4	37		6	1											2	19	9.5	7				
1986	OTT	8	0		1				1	61																					
6	Years	72	3		13		1.5		15	236		12	2											18	178	9.9	74	38	860	22.6	41
JACK BARGER Floyd Joseph T 6'1 210 Nevada-Reno; New Mexico B: 5/5/1925 nr Perkins, OK D: 5/13/1997 Jacksonville, AR Draft: 14-170 1953 DET																															
1953	MTL	3																													
BASIL BARK Basil C 6'2 235 NDG Maple Leafs Jrs. B: 7/21/1945 Montreal, QC																															
1965	MTL	11																													
1966	MTL	14																													
1967	MTL	14																													
1968	MTL+	14																													
1969	MTL+	14																													
1970	CAL	16	1		0																										
1971	CAL+	16	1		0																										
1972	CAL	16																													
1973	CAL+	16																													
1974	CAL	16																													
1975	CAL	16	0		1																							2	7	3.5	7
1976	CAL	16																													
1977	CAL	16																													
13	Years	195	2		1																							2	7	3.5	7
DYLAN BARKER Dylan S 6'3 206 Saskatchewan B: 8/21/1986 Moose Jaw, SK Draft: 1A-1 2008 HAM																															
2009	HAM	18	0	2	1	43			1	0	0																				
2010	HAM	17	0	2	0	48	1.0	16.	3	22	6																				
2	Years	35	0	4	1	91	1.0	16.0	4	22	6																				
JAY BARKER Jay, Jr. QB 6'3 220 Alabama B: 7/20/1972 Birmingham, AL Draft: 5A-160 1995 GB Pro: X																															
1998	TOR	18	3	0	2	1						18	3	34	176	5.2	17	3													
1999	TOR	18	7	0	5	2						12	2	52	371	7.1	27	2													
2000	TOR	10	1	0	0	0								7	29	4.1	14	0													
3	Years	46	11	0	7	3						30	5	93	576	6.2	27	5													
LARRY BARKER Larry LB 5'11 215 Idaho B: 8/3/1958 Medford, OR																															
1982	CAL	16	0		3		1.0		4	120		6	1											0	2		2	3	40	13.3	18
MIKE BARKER Michael Anthony DT 6'4 280 Grambling State B: 12/3/1959 Bogalusa, LA Draft: 10-250 1981 NYG																															
1983	HAM	9	0		1		3.5																								
1984	HAM	4					1.0																								
2	Years	13	0		1		4.5																								
CHARLES BARNES Charles DE 6'6 253 Jackson State																															
1996	OTT	1				0																									
EMERY BARNES Emery Oakland DT 6'6 230 Oregon B: 12/15/1929 New Orleans, LA D: 7/1/1998 Port Moody, BC Draft: 18-207 1954 GB Pro: N																															
1962	BC	5																													
1963	BC	13																													
1964	BC	12																													
3	Years	30																													
FREDDIE BARNES Freddie Lee SB 6'0 215 Bowling Green State B: 12/6/1986 Chicago, IL																															
2011	SAS	1				1																									
JASON BARNES Jason Henry SB-WR 6'3 185 Sierra JC; Sacramento State B: 4/11/1984 San Jose, CA																															
2009	EDM	4				0						6	1						14	156	11.1	41	1								
2010	EDM	12	0	1	2	4						18	3						35	608	17.4	70	3								
2011	EDM	14	1	0	1	2						42	7						50	869	17.4	61	7								
3	Years	30	1	1	3	6						66	11						99	1633	16.5	70	11								
JOE BARNES Joseph William QB 5'11 196 Texas Tech B: 12/18/1951 Fort Worth, TX Draft: 13-316 1974 CHIB; 11-129 1974 HAW-WFL Pro: N																															
1976	MTL	13	2		0							6	1	18	127	7.1	16	1													
1977	MTL	8	1		0							18	3	61	485	8.0	79	3													
1978	MTL	12	1		0							6	1	32	147	4.6	18	1													
1979	MTL	16	3		1							18	3	63	269	4.3	18	3													
1980	MTL	6	0		1									15	74	4.9	25	0													
1980	SAS	10	2		1							6	1	20	137	6.9	29	1													
1980	Year	16	2		2							6	1	35	211	6.0	29	1													
1981	SAS	16	4		0							14	2	24	140	5.8	21	2													
1982	TOR	10	2		0									7	36	5.1	13	0													
1983	TOR	16	2		0							22	3	38	231	6.1	24	3													
1984	TOR+	16	5		2							18	3	52	278	5.3	26	3													
1985	CAL	11	8		1									42	198	4.7	14	0													
1985	MTL	4	4		2									16	65	4.1	33	0													
1985	Year	15	12		2									58	263	4.5	33	0													
1986	MTL	7												6	14	2.3	6	0													
11	Years	131	34		8							108	17	394	2201	5.6	79	17													
JOE BARNES Joe DH 5'11 190 Idaho State B: 3/12/1975 Aurora, CO																															
2001	CAL	18	0	1	1	42			1	4	2																				
2002	CAL	11	0	2	0	38					3																				
2	Years	29	0	3	1	80			1	4	5																				
PAT BARNES Patrick M. QB 6'3 215 California B: 2/23/1975 Arlington Heights, IL Draft: 4-110 1997 KC Pro: ENX																															
2001	CAL	8	1	0	0	0																									
2002	WPG	18				0								6	29	4.8	12	0													
2003	WPG	13	2	0	0	0								4	8	2.0	12	0													
3	Years	39	3	0	0	0								10	37	3.7	12	0													
REGGIE BARNES Reginald R. RB 5'9 210 Delaware State B: 10/19/1967 Philadelphia, PA																															
1990	OTT	14	12		5	2						36	6	211	1260	6.0	58	5	29	360	12.4	74	1					16	359	22.4	42
1991	OTT	18	7		2	3						80	13	291	1486	5.1	57	10	33	246	7.5	26	3					7	135	19.3	38
1992	OTT	17	5		1	1						18	3	204	926	4.5	38	2	22	168	7.6	22	1	1	6	6.0	6				
1993	OTT	4				0								45	233	5.2	28	0	11	128	11.6	40	0								
1994	SHR	9	1		0	2						12	2	22	150	6.8	64	2	13	110	8.5	21	0	2	36	18.0	20	1	20	20.0	20
1994	HAM	4	1		0	0						24	4	69	372	5.4	51	4	20	197	9.9	45	0								
1994	Year	13	1		0	2						36	6	91	522	5.7	64	6						2	36	18.0	20	1	20	20.0	20
1995	TOR	8	1		0	0						30	5	74	248	3.4	18	4	11	76	6.9	16	1					0	24		24
1996	OTT	3				1								26	96	3.7	13	0	16	101	6.3	15	0								
7	Years	73	27		8	9						200	33	942	4771	5.1	64	27	155	1386	8.9	74	6	3	42	14.0	20	24	538	22.4	42
BRUCE BARNETT Bruce DB 6'1 190 British Columbia B: 4/14/1963 Montreal, QC Draft: 2A-14 1985 BC																															
1985	BC	16																													
1986	BC	10																													
2	Years	26																													
JAMIE BARNETTE Jamie Lamarte QB 6'0 196 North Carolina State B: 12/2/1976 Roxboro, NC																															
2000	MTL	8				0								2	20	10.0	11	0													
2001	MTL	18	2	0	0	0								8	58	7.3	25	0													
2	Years	26	2	0	0	0								10	78	7.8	25	0													
KEITH BARNETTE Keith E. FB-HB 6'2 209 Boston College B: 5/30/1952 Stoneham, MA Draft: 5B-150 1976 MIN																															
1976	EDM	6			0							12	2	104	380	3.7	16	2	11	69	6.3	15	0					3	30	10.0	16
1976	SAS	4			0							12	2	17	68	4.0	11	1	4	27	6.8	13	1								
1976	Year	10	3		0							24	4	121	448	3.7	16	3	15	96	6.4	15	1					3	30	10.0	16
MARK BAROUSSE Mark Darrell WR 5'9 180 McNeese State B: 1/28/1961 Lake Charles, LA Pro: U																															

Year	Team	GP	FM	FF	FR	TK	SK	YDS	IR	YDS	PD	PTS	TD	RA	YDS	AVG	LG	TD	REC	YDS	AVG	LG	TD	PR	YDS	AVG	LG	KOR	YDS	AVG	LG
1985	OTT	8	2		0							6	1						27	371	13.7	49	1								
1986	OTT+	14	1		0							48	8	4	36	9.0	19	0	71	893	12.6	68	8								
2	Years	22	3		0							54	9	4	36	9.0	19	0	98	1264	12.9	68	9								
AGUSTIN BARRENECHEA Agustin LB-FB 6'2 235 Calgary B: 5/20/1979 Mar del Plata, Argentina Draft: 4-30 2003 HAM																															
2004	HAM	17				42																									
2005	HAM	17	1	2	3	98	3.0	21.0	2	81	0																				
2006	HAM	15	0	0	1	46	1.0	8.0			1																				
2007	HAM	10				16			1	16	0																				
2007	EDM	5				4																									
2007	Year	15				20			1	16	0																				
2008	EDM	18				70	3.0	21.0	2	16	1																				
2009	HAM	7				5					1																				
2010	HAM	13				7																									
2011	HAM	18				6													1	38	38.0	38	0								
8	Years	115	1	2	4	294	7.0	50.0	5	113	3								1	38	38.0	38	0								
BOYD BARRETT Boyd CB 5'9 180 Manitoba B: 2/4/1977 Manchester, Jamaica																															
2003	WPG	1				0																									
2004	WPG	2				2																									
2005	WPG	14	0	0	2	19																									
3	Years	17	0	0	2	21																									
CHIP BARRETT Lawrence DH-S 6'2 200 British Columbia B: 8/10/1944 Toronto, ON Draft: 1-1 1967 TOR																															
1967	WPG	16							4	66														2	10	5.0	7				
1968	WPG	16	0		3				4	93																		1	5	5.0	5
1970	TOR	14							2	47		6	1											6	46	7.7	17				
1971	TOR	14	0		1				3	55														1	-2	-2.0	-2				
1972	TOR	14	1		2				4	48														2	2	1.0	4				
5	Years	74	1		6				17	309		6	1											11	56	5.1	17	1	5	5.0	5
DANNY BARRETT Danny Lee QB 5'11 195 Cincinnati B: 12/18/1961 Boynton Beach, FL																															
1983	CAL	2												6	26	4.3	10	0													
1984	CAL	10	1		0									14	90	6.4	22	0													
1985	CAL	8	2		1							12	2	1	2	2.0	2	0	32	455	14.2	35	2								
1985	TOR	4	2		1							6	1	9	29	3.2	8	1	2	46	23.0	59	0								
1985	Year	12	4		0							18	3	10	31	3.1	8	1	34	501	14.7	59	2								
1987	TOR	13	4		0	0						6	1	65	345	5.3	24	1													
1988	TOR	4				0								3	22	7.3	13	0													
1989	CAL	13	7		2	0						30	5	64	421	6.6	29	5													
1990	CAL	13	5		1	1						42	7	57	295	5.2	46	7													
1991	CAL	13	7		2	0						36	6	50	263	5.3	18	6													
1992	BC	10	3		1	2						18	3	37	125	3.4	12	3													
1993	BC	18	5		2	1						24	4	42	162	3.9	15	4													
1994	OTT	18	6		0	0						18	3	96	550	5.7	22	3													
1995	OTT	4				1						6	1	15	97	6.5	17	1													
1996	CAL	18				1								4	-1	-0.3	2	0													
1998	BC	15	1	0	0	0								4	10	2.5	7	0													
14	Years	159	43	0	10	6						198	33	467	2436	5.2	46	31	34	501	14.7	59	2								
GREG BARROW Gregory John OG-OT 6'4 265 Florida B: 1/6/1957 Draft: 1-1 1980 TOR																															
1981	HAM	5																													
JOHN BARROW John B. DT-OT-MG 6'2 255 Florida B: 10/31/1935 Delray Beach, FL Draft: 5-59 1957 DET																															
1957	HAM+	14							1	10																					
1958	HAM+	14																													
1959	HAM+	13							1	10																					
1960	HAM+	14							1	17		12	2	0	36		36	0	1	31	31.0	31	1					1	12	12.0	12
1961	HAM+	13																													
1962	HAM*	14							1	8																		2	8	4.0	8
1963	HAM*	13							1	21																					
1964	HAM*	14																													
1965	HAM*	14	0		2																										
1966	HAM*	14																													
1967	HAM*	14			2																										
1968	HAM	14							2	24																					
1969	HAM+	14																													
1970	HAM	13	0		1																										
14	Years	192	0		5				7	90		12	2	0	36		36	0	1	31	31.0	31	1					3	20	6.7	12
DAVE BARRUS David Earl OT-DE 6'2 233 Brigham Young B: 7/21/1938 El Cajon, CA																															
1960	BC	15	0		3																										
DON BARRY Don C-MG 5'11 215 Edmonton Maple Leafs Jrs. B: 1931																															
1952	EDM	15																													
1953	EDM	15																													
1954	EDM	11																													
1955	EDM	16																													
1956	EDM	15																													
1957	EDM	12																													
1958	EDM	16																													
1959	EDM	16																													
1960	EDM	16																													
1961	EDM	16																													
1962	EDM	8																													
11	Years	156																													
ED BARRY Ed G-T 6'2 200 Vancouver Blue Bombers Jrs. B: 1927 D: //2008																															
1951	CAL	4																													
1954	BC	3																													
2	Years	7																													
JACK BARRY Jack HB 5'10 165 Midwestern State B: 1928																															
1953	OTT	1																													
1953	TOR	2										6	0																		
1953	Year	3										6	0																		
BOB BARTHOLOMEW Robert Thomas T 6'2 225 Wake Forest B: 4/20/1932 Rocky Mount, NC Draft: 30-360 1956 CLE																															
1956	MTL	2																													
EPHESIANS BARTLEY Ephesians Alexander, Jr. LB 6'2 213 Florida B: 8/9/1969 Jacksonville, FL Draft: 9-241 1992 PHI Pro: N																															
1995	SA	3				0																									
DANTON BARTO Danton L. LB 6'0 245 Memphis B: 3/30/1971																															
1995	MEM	18	0		2	37	1.0	7.0	0	0	1	6	1																		
RALPH BARTOLINI Ralph HB-FW 5'9 184 Hamilton Jrs. B: 1927																															
1949	OTT	9																													
1950	HAM	10																													
1951	HAM	12										15	3					3													
3	Years	31										15	3					3													
GREG BARTON Greg Lee QB 6'2 195 Long Beach CC; Tulsa B: 7/14/1946 Denver, CO Draft: 9-229 1968 DET Pro: NW																															
1971	TOR	12	1		0									7	-1	-0.1	2	0													
1972	TOR	4	3		2									7	-13	-1.9	2	0													
2	Years	16	4		2									14	-14	-1.0	2	0													
HANK BARTON Hank DE 6'7 230 Portland State B: 3/18/1948 Bend, OR																															

Year	Team	GP	FM	FF	FR	TK	SK	YDS	IR	YDS	PD	PTS	TD	RA	YDS	AVG	LG	TD	REC	YDS	AVG	LG	TD	PR	YDS	AVG	LG	KOR	YDS	AVG	LG
1972	BC	1																													
GIL BARTOSH Gilbert Charles HB 5'9 175 Texas Christian B: 5/1930 Draft: 27-314 1952 DAL																															
1955	BC	15	2		0				1	0		25	5	66	350	5.3	52	1	33	428	13.0	52	4	15	57	3.8	20	8	146	18.3	24
DICK BARWEGEN Richard James G 6'1 227 Purdue B: 12/25/1922 Chicago, IL D: 9/3/1966 Baltimore, MD Draft: 6-44 1945 BKN Pro: AN																															
1955	OTT	5							1	5																					
GORD BARWELL Gordon SE-FL 6'0 190 Saskatoon Hilltops Jrs. B: 1945 Saskatoon, SK D: 4/21/1988 Toronto, ON																															
1964	SAS	6																	1	12	12.0	12	0	1	7	7.0	7	2	40	20.0	26
1965	SAS	16										12	2						8	186	23.3	102	2								
1966	SAS	16										18	3						27	488	18.1	43	3								
1967	SAS	16	1		0							30	5						30	753	25.1	88	5								
1968	SAS	16	0		2							24	4	2	1	0.5	3	0	40	783	19.6	83	4								
1969	SAS	16										24	4						28	490	17.5	53	4					1	2	2.0	2
1970	SAS	16	1		0							36	6						37	618	16.7	67	6								
1971	SAS	16										12	2						30	429	14.3	48	2								
1972	SAS	16										36	6						25	340	13.6	78	6								
1973	SAS	16																	16	215	13.4	52	0								
10	Years	150	2		2							192	32	2	1	0.5	3	0	242	4314	17.8	102	32	1	7	7.0	7	3	42	14.0	26
OUSMANE BARY Ousmane S. S 6'0 195 Syracuse B: 1/22/1968 Bordeaux, France Draft: 5-36 1992 WPG Pro: E																															
1993	WPG	12				13			1	-7																					
1994	TOR	2				0																									
1996	TOR	4				1																									
3	Years	18				14			1	-7																					
WALT BASHAK Walter T-G 6'1 223 McMaster B: 1929 Draft: 1952 OTT																															
1952	OTT	12																													
1953	OTT	8																													
1954	OTT	14																													
3	Years	34																													
CLIFF BASKERVILLE Clifton T. CB 5'11 180 North Carolina B: 8/27/1971																															
1994	SHR	7				22					2																				
BILLY BASS William T. HB-FB 5'10 180 Tennessee State; Nevada-Reno B: 1922 Greensboro, NC D: 9/28/1967 Tillsonburg, ON Pro: A																															
1948	MTL	11																													
1950	TOR	9										35	7					6													
1951	TOR+	12										10	2					2													
1952	TOR	11										10	2					2													
1953	TOR	13										5	1					1													
1954	OTT	14										5	1	57	297	5.2	28	1	8	67	8.4	22	0					2	24	12.0	20
6	Years	70										65	13	57	297	5.2	28	12	8	67	8.4	22	0					2	24	12.0	20
DANNY BASS Danny OG-DL 6'2 265 Elon B: 10/17/1954 Draft: 7B-193 1978 CIN																															
1978	HAM	16	0		1																										
1979	HAM	8																													
2	Years	24	0		1																										
DANNY BASS Daniel E. LB 6'1 220 Michigan State B: 3/31/1958 Lansing, MI																															
1980	TOR	13	0		1				1	15																					
1981	TOR	12					1.0																								
1981	CAL	3					3.0																								
1981	Year	15					4.0																								
1982	CAL	16	0		1		5.5					6	1																		
1983	CAL	16	0		1		3.5		3	17														1	0	0.0	0				
1984	EDM	16	0		1		6.0																	2	11	5.5	11				
1985	EDM	14	0		3		2.0		4	29																					
1986	EDM	18	0		2		6.0		2	52		6	1																		
1987	EDM	17				90	4.0		2	31		6	1																		
1988	EDM	18	1		2	116	4.0		2	25																					
1989	EDM	18	0		6	79	8.0		4	42																					
1990	EDM	18	0		4	105	4.0		4	19																		1	0	0.0	0
1991	EDM	18	0		4	79	5.0		1	13																					
12	Years	194	1		25	469	52.0		23	243		18	3											3	11	3.7	11	1	0	0.0	0
NICK BASTAJA Nick OT 6'2 255 Simon Fraser B: 2/4/1953 Grantham, England Draft: TE 1975 HAM																															
1975	HAM	12	0		1																										
1976	HAM	16																													
1977	TOR	13	0		1																										
1978	TOR	16	0		1																										
1979	TOR+	12	0		2																										
1980	WPG	16																													
1981	WPG+	15																													
1982	WPG+	16	0		1																										
1983	WPG	12	0		1																										
1984	WPG*	16																													
1985	WPG*	16																													
1986	WPG	18																													
1987	WPG+	16			1	1																									
1988	WPG+	18																													
14	Years	212	0		8	1																									
BOB BATEMAN Bob QB 6'5 195 Vermont; Brown B: 2/15/1954 Darien, CT Draft: 7A-187 1976 CIN																															
1976	MTL	1																													
DAVID BATES David QB 6'0 190 Texas-Arlington B: 11/7/1960																															
1986	TOR	4												1	4	4.0	4	0													
KELLY BATES Kelly OG 6'3 290 Saskatchewan B: 7/27/1975 Humboldt, SK Draft: 4-32 2001 BC																															
2002	BC	14				1																									
2003	BC	18				0																									
2004	BC	11				0																									
2005	BC	18				1																									
2006	BC	18				0																									
2007	BC*	18				1																									
2008	BC	18	0	0	1	0																									
2009	WPG	6				0																									
2010	EDM	9				0																									
2011	BC	4				0																									
10	Years	134	0	0	1	3																									
STEVE BATES Stephen DE 6'4 249 James Madison B: 6/28/1966 Pittsburgh, PA Draft: 10-272 1990 LARM Pro: E																															
1992	HAM	3				10	3.0	30.0																							
1993	HAM	2				7	1.0	4.0																							
1994	HAM	2				5	2.0	10.0																							
1995	MEM	15				27	4.0	24.0			1																				
4	Years	22				49	10.0	68.0			1																				
ANDRE BATSON Andre WR 5'10 180 York B: 6/28/1974 Toronto, ON Draft: 5-34 1997 SAS																															
1998	TOR	16	0	0	1	1						12	2						2	23	11.5	15	2								
1999	EDM	18	0	0	1	3													3	32	10.7	16	0								
2	Years	34	0	0	2	4						12	2						5	55	11.0	16	2								
ROY BATTAGELLO Roy Alessandro E 5'7 187 Windsor AKO Jrs.; Assumption (Canada) B: 9/29/1927 Windsor, ON D: 10/29/2005																															
1951	OTT	5																													
MATT BATTAGLIA Matthew Martin LB 6'2 225 Louisville B: 9/25/1965 Tallahassee, FL Pro: N																															

Year	Team	GP	FM	FF	FR	TK	SK	YDS	IR	YDS	PD	PTS	TD	RA	YDS	AVG	LG	TD	REC	YDS	AVG	LG	TD	PR	YDS	AVG	LG	KOR	YDS	AVG	LG
1987	OTT	2				13
PAT BATTEN Patrick Ward FB 6'2 225 Drake; Fort Scott JC; Hardin-Simmons B: 12/5/1941 Indianola, IA Draft: 7B-56 1964 SD; 3A-30 1964 DET Pro: N
1965	MTL	8	1		0							42	4	69	349	5.1	47	2	9	102	11.3	47	2					1	23	23.0	23
DOUG BATTERSHILL Doug LB-DB 6'2 200 Weber State B: 11/11/1957 Draft: TE 1979 CAL
1979	CAL	16	0		2				1	35		6	1
1980	CAL	16																										1	-1	-1.0	-1
1981	CAL	16	0		1		7.5		3	5
1982	CAL	16	0		3		7.0
1983	CAL	16	0		1		1.0
1984	CAL	7
1984	TOR	6	0		1
1984	Year	13	0		1
6	Years	87	0		8		15.5		4	40		6	1															1	-1	-1.0	-1
CHARLIE BATTLE Charles Edward LB 6'4 237 Colorado; Grambling State B: 8/26/1953 Shreveport, LA Draft: 5B-124 1974 NE Pro: W
1975	HAM	1
GREG BATTLE Gregory D. LB 6'1 225 Arizona State B: 4/14/1964 Long Beach, CA
1987	WPG	6	0		1	20	3.0		1	25
1988	WPG	18	1		4	54	5.0		1	12		6	1
1989	WPG+	18	1		2	108	2.0		3	15									2	52	26.0	30	0					1	25	25.0	25
1990	WPG*	18	0		6	100	4.0		3	14																		0	5		5
1991	WPG*	17	0		4	100			3	31																		1	13	13.0	13
1992	WPG	17	2		4	81	3.0		4	59		6	1											1	18	18.0	18
1993	WPG	16	1		2	47	2.0	8.0	4	53		12	2															3	36	12.0	19
1994	LV	11	0		1	50	1.0		1	11	5			1	16	16.0	16	0
1994	OTT	5				13	1.0		1	2	1
1994	Year	16	0		1	63	2.0		2	13	6			1	16	16.0	16	0
1995	MEM	16	0		1	71	3.0	20.0	6	100	5
1996	SAS	12	0		3	62			1	25	4
1997	WPG	18	0	1	0	82	1.0	5.0	3	32	1								1	17	17.0	17	0
1998	WPG	8	0	1	1	25	1.0	17.0			1
12	Years	175	5	2	29	813	26.0	50.0	31	379	17	24	4	1	16	16.0	16	0	3	69	23.0	30	0	1	18	18.0	18	5	79	15.8	25
JEMONTE BATTLE Jemonte Cecil CB 6'0 196 Catawba B: 12/8/1981 Rocky Mount, NC
2004	HAM	10	1	0	1	30			1	0	1
JIM BATTLE James OG 6'0 240 Southern Illinois B: 2/20/1938 Bartow, FL Pro: N
1964	EDM	9	0		1
1965	EDM	12	0		4
2	Years	21	0		5
JULIAN BATTLE Julian DH 6'2 205 Los Angeles Valley JC; Tennessee B: 7/11/1981 Royal Palm Beach, FL Draft: 3-92 2003 KC Pro: N
2007	CAL	7	1	0	0	20	1.0	10.0	1	33	1
2008	CAL	6	0	1	0	8					5
2	Years	13	1	1	0	28	1.0	10.0	1	33	6
LYLE BAUER Lyle OG-C 6'2 235 Saskatoon Hilltops Jrs.; Calgary Colts Jrs.; Weber State B: 8/22/1958 Saskatoon, SK Draft: 5-38 1979 SAS
1982	WPG	15																	1	28	28.0	28	0
1983	WPG	14
1984	WPG	13
1985	WPG	14
1986	WPG	18
1987	WPG	18			1	1
1988	WPG	18	0		2	2													0	2		2	0
1989	WPG	15				1													0	5		5	0
1990	WPG+	18				0
1991	WPG	18				1
10	Years	161	0		3	5													1	35	35.0	28	0
WALT BAUER Walter TE 6'4 220 Drake B: 8/21/1952 Draft: TE 1976 EDM
1976	HAM	16			1							4	0						8	91	11.4	17	0					1	0	0.0	0
CHRIS BAUMAN Chris WR-SB 6'4 212 Regina; Winnipeg Rifles Jrs.; Regina B: 9/5/1984 Brandon, MB Draft: 1A-1 2007 HAM
2007	HAM	14	1	0	1	2								1	-11	-11.0	-11	0	30	370	12.3	36	0
2008	HAM	15				2						20	3						48	588	12.3	63	3
2009	HAM	17				1													19	255	13.4	38	0
2010	HAM	17				1						20	3						17	298	17.5	43	3
2011	EDM	7				1													11	132	12.0	27	0
5	Years	70	1	0	1	7						40	6	1	-11	-11.0	-11	0	125	1643	13.1	63	6
CHARLIE BAUMANN Bruce Charles K 6'1 203 West Virginia B: 8/25/1967 Erie, PA Pro: EN
1994	BAL	2				0						29	0
BIBBLES BAWEL Edward Raymond DB 6'1 185 Evansville B: 11/21/1930 Boonville, IN Pro: N
1957	HAM	8							2	23		6	1						11	129	11.7	26	0					5	135	27.0	51
GAR BAXTER Garth C-T 6'2 212 Winnipeg Rods Jrs. B: 1929
1951	WPG	9
1952	WPG	15
1953	WPG	6
1954	WPG	11
4	Years	41
JEARLD BAYLIS Jearld Pernell DT-NT 6'0 230 Southern Mississippi B: 8/12/1962 Jackson, MS Draft: TD 1984 NO-USFL Pro: U
1986	TOR	9					5.0
1987	TOR*	16	0		3	47	7.0
1988	TOR	10				22	4.0
1989	TOR	16	0		1	65
1991	BC	7	0		1	16	1.0
1992	SAS*	18	0		1	53	8.0	58.0
1993	SAS*	18	0		4	57	11.0	79.0
1994	BAL	17	0		1	44	3.0	15.0
1995	BAL*	18				43	3.0	18.0			1
9	Years	129	0		11	347	42.0	170.0			1
RAYMOND BAYLOR Raymond, II DT 6'2 285 Minnesota B: 8/16/1974 Houston, TX
2001	SAS	3				5
CHRIS BAYNE Christopher Oliver LB 6'0 205 San Bernardino Valley JC; Fresno State B: 3/22/1975 Draft: 7B-222 1997 ATL Pro: ENX
2003	HAM	10	0	0	1	29					2
FREEMAN BAYSINGER Freeman Lee, Jr. WR-SB 5'9 175 Humboldt State B: 12/22/1969 Oklahoma City, OK Draft: 12-333 1992 NE
1993	SAC	13	1		0	1						24	4						48	736	15.3	83	3	52	405	7.8	59
1993	BC	3	2		0	1						0	0						5	97	19.4	42	0	12	99	8.3	20	18	385	21.4	47
1993	Year	16	3		0	2						24	4						53	833	15.7	83	3	64	504	7.9	59	18	385	21.4	47
1994	BC	6	4		0	2						18	3	1	10	10.0	10	0	15	165	11.0	36	2	28	247	8.8	36	21	376	17.9	29
1995	SHR	17	3		0	1						18	3	3	16	5.3	14	0	35	490	14.0	50	1	45	384	8.5	47	50	1023	20.5	86
1996	WPG	5	1		0	1								2	-4	-2.0	2	0	19	230	12.1	28	0	14	146	10.4	52	16	278	17.4	28
1996	BC	5	1		0	0													12	106	8.8	12	0	28	133	4.8	16	16	356	22.3	47
1996	Year	10	2		0	1								2	-4	-2.0	2	0	31	336	10.8	28	0	42	279	6.6	52	32	634	19.8	47
4	Years	41	15		0	6						60	10	6	22	3.7	14	0	134	1824	13.6	83	6	179	1414	7.9	59	121	2418	20.0	86
JERRY BEABOUT Jerry DE-OT 6'3 240 Purdue B: 1940 Draft: SS-(f) 1960 LAC; 7-82 1960 BAL
1961	BC	2
WALTER BEACH Walter, III OHB 6'0 184 Central Michigan B: 1/31/1935 Pontiac, MI Draft: SS 1960 OAK; 15-180 1960 NYG Pro: N
1960	HAM	1
STEVE BEAIRD Steve RB 5'8 190 Blinn JC; Baylor B: 7/22/1952 Draft: 7-177 1975 STL

Year	Team	GP	FM	FF	FR	TK	SK	YDS	IR	YDS	PD	PTS	TD	RA	YDS	AVG	LG	TD	REC	YDS	AVG	LG	TD	PR	YDS	AVG	LG	KOR	YDS	AVG	LG
1975	WPG	14	1		0							60	10	123	533	4.3	59	8	16	254	15.9	59	2	24	226	9.4	30	14	406	29.0	66
1976	WPG+	13	4		0							36	6	184	834	4.5	35	5	35	330	9.4	33	1	35	201	5.7	19	21	539	25.7	71
2	Years	27	5		0							96	16	307	1367	4.5	59	13	51	584	11.5	59	3	59	427	7.2	30	35	945	27.0	71
ROY BEALE Roy G Regina Dales Jrs.																															
1946	SAS	3																														
SHAWN BEALS Shawn E. WR-SB 5'10 178 Idaho State B: 8/16/1966 Walnut Creek, CA Pro: N																															
1990	CAL	10	0		1	1								1	17	17.0	17	0	28	448	16.0	43	0								
1991	CAL	17	1		0	4						44	7						64	943	14.7	83	7	1	0	0.0	0	1	13	13.0	13
1992	CAL	6	1		0														16	192	12.0	32	0								
1994	BAL	16	1		0	2						12	2						28	488	17.4	52	2								
4	Years	49	3		1	7						56	9	1	17	17.0	17	0	136	2071	15.2	83	9	1	0	0.0	0	1	13	13.0	13
NUB BEAMER Clarence, Jr. FB 5'11 210 Oregon State B: 2/14/1936																															
1960	BC	11	6		1							18	3	118	709	6.0	55	3	2	51	25.5	29	0					5	91	18.2	26
1961	BC	16	2									54	9	169	878	5.2	53	9	7	108	15.4	39	0					8	114	14.3	24
1962	BC+	16	3									42	7	208	1161	5.6	40	7	11	190	17.3	28	0					9	120	13.3	23
1963	BC+	15	2		0							72	12	204	914	4.5	20	11	12	128	10.7	30	1					9	172	19.1	35
4	Years	58	13		1							186	31	699	3662	5.2	55	30	32	477	14.9	39	1					31	497	16.0	35
TIM BEAMER Timothy Carl RB-DB 5'11 185 Illinois; Johnson C. Smith B: 4/6/1948 Galax, VA Draft: 5B-113 1971 BUF Pro: NW																															
1973	HAM	8							1	31		6	1	1	42	42.0	42	0						1	84	84.0	84	12	302	25.2	51
1973	WPG	4	2		0				2	27														12	25	2.1	7	3	38	12.7	21
1973	Year	12	2		0				3	58				1	42	42.0	42	0						13	109	8.4	84	15	340	22.7	51
DWAIN BEAN Dwain Aldine FB 6'0 205 Tyler JC; North Texas B: 10/22/1941 Jefferson County, TX Draft: 12-167 1964 GB																															
1964	HAM	1												2	9	4.5	6	0													
ROBERT BEAN Robert D., Jr. CB 5'11 177 Georgia Military JC; Mississippi State B: 1/6/1978 Atlanta, GA Draft: 5-133 2000 CIN Pro: N																															
2006	WPG	14	0	1	0	24			4	35	4																				
2007	WPG	12	0	2	0	45					7																				
2008	WPG	8	0	0	1	33					2																				
3	Years	34	0	3	1	102			4	35	13																				
GENE BEARD Eugene DB 6'0 190 Virginia Union B: 1946 Draft: 16-400 1967 MIN																															
1969	CAL	9																										5	116	23.2	28
GREG BEARMAN Greg S 5'7 180 New Mexico State B: 8/2/1975 Richmond, BC																															
1999	BC	6				4																								
2000	BC	3				0																								
2003	OTT	9				10																								
2004	OTT	12				4																						1	11	11.0	11
2005	OTT	18				13																								
2006	WPG	14				5																								
2007	WPG	18	0	0	1	15						6	1																		
2008	WPG	15	0	1	0	6																								
8	Years	95	0	1	1	57						6	1															1	11	11.0	11
DEON BEASLEY Kenneth Deon CB 5'10 180 Texas B: 9/19/1987 Orange, TX																															
2010	WPG	12	2	0	1	27			2	72	0	6	1															31	607	19.6	38
2011	WPG	17	1	2	0	33					1																		35	711	20.3	50
2	Years	29	3	2	1	60			2	72	1	6	1															66	1318	20.0	50
JERRY BEASLEY Jerry W. LB 6'3 245 Arizona B: 2/13/1965 Tucson, AZ																															
1989	BC	15	1		1	61	2.0		2	15																					
1990	BC	2				6																								
2	Years	17	1		1	67	2.0		2	15																					
JIM BEASLEY Jim C 6'4 220 Tulsa B: 1930 Draft: 6-70 1952 SF																															
1952	SAS	4																														
JONATHAN BEASLEY Jonathan QB 6'0 220 Kansas State B: 4/20/1978 Bloomington, IN																															
2001	SAS	10				0								1	13	13.0	13	0													
2002	SAS	14	0	0	1	0								5	33	6.6	12	0													
2	Years	24	0	0	1	0								6	46	7.7	13	0													
SCOTT BEASLEY Winfield Scott E 6'1 205 Upper Iowa; Nevada-Reno B: 11/13/1924 Sullivan, IN D: 12/27/2004 Reno, NV Draft: 16-105 1948 CLE-AAFC; 9-72 1948 PHI																															
1950	HAM	1																														
BRUCE BEATON Bruce OT-OG 6'5 285 Acadia B: 6/13/1968 Port Hood, NS Draft: 1B-8 1991 BC Pro: X																															
1993	OTT	16				0																								
1994	OTT	16				0																								
1995	CAL	18	0		1	1																								
1996	MTL+	18				0																								
1997	MTL+	18				0																								
1998	EDM+	18				1																								
1999	EDM	18				0																								
2000	EDM*	18				0																								
2001	EDM*	18	0	0	1	1																								
2002	EDM+	18				1																								
2003	EDM*	18				2																								
2005	EDM	18				1																								
12	Years	212	0	0	2	7																								
JOHN BEATON John DB-LB 6'2 190 Tulsa; Simon Fraser B: 3/2/1950																															
1973	EDM	10							1	0																		1	5	5.0	5
1974	EDM	16							5	33														3	20	6.7	15	1	3	3.0	3
1975	EDM	16							4	6														1	0	0.0	0				
1976	EDM	5	0		1																										
1976	MTL	8	0		1																										
1976	Year	13	0		2																										
1977	MTL	9							4	11																				
1978	BC	16	0		1				1	16																		1	0	0.0	0
1979	BC	16	0		2				4	20																				
1980	BC	8							1	2																				
8	Years	96	0		5				20	88														4	20	5.0	15	3	8	2.7	5
BEATTY																															
1948	HAM	3																														
DERRICK BEATTY Derrick DB 5'8 175 Weber State B: 10/21/1973																															
1996	EDM	14				25			3	57	3																				
1997	EDM	16	0	1	1	61	1.0	3.0	1	4	5																				
2	Years	30	0	1	1	86	1.0	3.0	4	61	8																				
DON BEATTY Don DE 6'3 197 Western Ontario																															
1952	CAL	15			3							10	2						1	11	11.0	11	0								
1953	HAM	14										7	1																		
2	Years	29	0		3							17	3						1	11	11.0	11	0								
HAROLD BEATY Harold (Clyde) DE 6'1 240 Oklahoma State B: 3/10/1938 Pauls Valley, OK Draft: 8-61 1961 NYT; 3A-32 1961 LARM																															
1961	CAL	5																														
1962	CAL	2																														
1962	OTT	7																														
1962	Year	9																														
2	Years	7																														
TIM BEAUCHAMP Timothy Ryan DE 6'2 271 Florida B: 3/18/1977 Oak Hill, FL Pro: EX																															
2001	HAM	1				2																								
MATHIEU BEAUDOIN Mathieu OL 6'3 277 Syracuse B: 11/9/1974 Montreal, QC Draft: 2-11 1999 BC																															
1999	BC	10				1																								

Year	Team	GP	FM	FF	FR	TK	SK	YDS	IR	YDS	PD	PTS	TD	RA	YDS	AVG	LG	TD	REC	YDS	AVG	LG	TD	PR	YDS	AVG	LG	KOR	YDS	AVG	LG
TERRY BEAUFORD Terry Jerone OG 6'1 300 Florida A&M B: 3/27/1968 Fort Pierce, FL Draft: 7B-192 1991 SD																															
1994	SHR	10																													
1995	SHR	15				1																									
2	Years	25				1																									
NEAL BEAUMONT Neal S-DH-FB-OHB 6'1 225 Vancouver Meralomas Jrs B: 1941																															
1960	BC	16	1		1																			53	226	4.3	13				
1961	BC	16	2						2	40		2	0	7	19	2.7	7	0	3	47	15.7	21	0	37	157	4.2	16	3	54	18.0	27
1962	BC	16	2						4	47														45	224	5.0	16				
1963	BC	16	1		1				4	164		12	1	2	7	3.5		0						50	230	4.6	27				
1964	BC+	14	1		1				5	64		3	0	2	-5	-2.5	6	0						51	229	4.5	22	19	445	23.4	33
1965	BC	16	1		3				6	62		3	0											5	19	3.8	7				
1966	BC	14										3	0	12	53	4.4	8	0													
1967	BC	16							1	22																					
8	Years	124	8		6				22	399		23	1	23	74	3.2	8	0	3	47	15.7	21	0	241	1085	4.5	27	22	499	22.7	33
DARRELL BEAVERS Darrell LB 6'3 230 Morehead State B: 11/24/1967 Joliet, IL Draft: 12-327 1991 PHI																															
1993	HAM	7	0		1	10																									
RANDY BEC Randall SB 6'1 215 Calgary B: 10/17/1967 Calgary, AB Draft: 2-13 1989 EDM																															
1989	EDM	1				1																									
BRETT BECH Brett Lamar SB 6'1 184 Louisiana State B: 8/20/1971 Slidell, LA Pro: NX																															
1995	SA	5				1																									
KEN BECK Kenneth L. OG-DT 6'2 245 Texas A&M B: 9/3/1935 Minden, LA Draft: 4-38 1959 CHIC Pro: N																															
1961	TOR	2																													
1962	TOR	13																													
1963	SAS	6																													
3	Years	21																													
ERNIE BECKER Ernie DB-FB 5'10 188 none B: 4/27/1925																															
1951	SAS	13												28	143	5.1		0	3	161	53.7		0					4	89	22.3	
1952	WPG	14			2				1	0									1	7	7.0	7	0					1	13	13.0	13
1953	WPG	10																	1	18	18.0	18	0								
3	Years	37			2				1	0				28	143	5.1	0	0	5	186	37.2	18	0					5	102	20.4	13
JOEL BECKER Joel DE 6'2 268 Southeast Missouri B: 12/10/1976 Park Falls, WI																															
2000	HAM	6				1	1.0	4.0																							
MEL BECKET Melvin Howard C-LB 6'3 225 Indiana B: 1929 D: 12/9/1956 Mount Slesse, BC Draft: 8-87 1952 GB																															
1953	SAS	5							1	1																					
1954	SAS	8																						1	10	10.0	10				
1955	SAS	16	0		3																										
1956	SAS+	16																													
4	Years	45	0		3				1	1														1	10	10.0	10				
EMERY BECKLES Emery Rudolph WR 5'9 175 Compton JC; Idaho State B: 8/23/1980 Los Angeles County, CA																															
2004	SAS	3				0																		8	72	9.0	22	3	55	18.3	22
IAN BECKSTEAD Ian C-OG 6'4 245 Ottawa Sooners Jrs.; Richmond B: 9/7/1957 Ottawa, ON Draft: TE 1981 OTT																															
1981	OTT	16																													
1982	OTT	14																										1	11	11.0	11
1983	OTT	9																													
1983	TOR	2																													
1983	Year	11																										1	11	11.0	11
1984	TOR	16	0		1																										
1985	TOR	16	0		2																										
1987	TOR+	18				0																									
1988	TOR*	16				1																									
1989	TOR	18				0																									
1990	TOR	12	1		1	2																									
1991	TOR	17				1																									
1992	TOR	15	0		1	2																									
11	Years	167	1		5	6																						1	11	11.0	11
JESSE BECTON Jesse LB 6'0 200 Western New Mexico; New Mexico B: 6/3/1969 Detroit, MI																															
1994	BAL	2	0		2	6																									
1994	LV	8	0		1	14	1.0	8.0											1	20	20.0	20	0								
1994	Year	10	0		3	20	1.0	8.0											1	20	20.0	20	0								
1995	HAM	3				7																									
2	Years	5	0		3	27	1.0	8.0											1	20	20.0	20	0								
MARTIN BEDARD Martin FB 6'3 239 Connecticut B: 3/23/1984 Laval, QC Draft: 2B-14 2009 MTL																															
2009	MTL	18	0	0	1	11																									
2010	MTL	18				9																									
2011	MTL	18				6																									
3	Years	54	0	0	1	26																									
BRIAN BEDFORD Brian Allen WR 6'4 205 California B: 6/29/1965 Milwaukee, WI Draft: 9-232 1988 DAL																															
1989	TOR	4				0						12	2	1	9	9.0	9	0	10	171	17.1	73	2								
1990	BC	2				0													4	54	13.5	20	0								
2	Years	6				0						12	2	1	9	9.0	9	0	14	225	16.1	73	2								
ROY BEECHEY Roy SE-FL-DB 6'1 180 Edmonton Huskies Jrs.; Alberta B: 8/26/1949 Draft: 4-29 1972 EDM																															
1974	TOR	9																	2	83	41.5	45	0	2	10	5.0	8				
1975	TOR	16																										5	109	21.8	26
1976	TOR	11																													
3	Years	36																	2	83	41.5	45	0	2	10	5.0	8	5	109	21.8	26
J.P. BEKASIAK J.P. DT-DE 6'6 299 Windsor AKO Fratmen Jrs.; Toledo B: 1/1/1982 Edmonton, AB Draft: 1B-7 2007 HAM																															
2007	HAM	17				5																									
2008	HAM	2				0																									
2009	MTL	3	0	0	1	2	1.0	0.0																							
2010	MTL	17	0	0	1	15	4.0	15.0																							
2011	MTL	16	0	1	0	21	1.0	14.0																							
5	Years	55	0	1	2	43	6.0	29.0																							
BOB BELAK Robert OHB 6'0 185 Saskatoon Hilltops Jrs. B: 9/5/1939																															
1961	BC	16	2																2	29	14.5	20	0	40	191	4.8	17				
1962	BC	16	1																					37	92	2.5	5				
2	Years	32	3		0														2	29	14.5	20	0	77	283	3.7	17				
FRANCOIS BELANGER Francois OT 6'6 290 McGill B: 2/21/1968 Ste. Foy, QC Draft: 8-57 1991 HAM																															
1991	HAM	1				0																									
1992	HAM	12	0		1	0																									
1993	TOR	12				0																									
1994	TOR	11				1																									
4	Years	36	0		1	1																									
ROBIN BELANGER Robin S 5'9 180 McGill B: 9/25/1964 Quebec City, QC Draft: 4B-36 1987 BC																															
1989	BC	18	0		1	38			1	54														1	-3	-3.0	-3				
1990	BC	18	0		2	4			1	0									1	17	17.0	17	0								
1991	BC	18				58			2	48																					
1992	BC	6				3																									
1992	TOR	2				0																									
1992	Year	8				3																									
4	Years	60	0		3	103			4	102									1	17	17.0	17	0	1	-3	-3.0	-3				
VAL BELCHER Val Joseph OG 6'3 255 Houston B: 7/6/1954 Houston, TX D: 9/12/2010 Ottawa, ON Draft: 3B-81 1977 DAL																															
1979	OTT	16																													

Year	Team	GP	FM	FF	FR	TK	SK	YDS	IR	YDS	PD	PTS	TD	RA	YDS	AVG	LG	TD	REC	YDS	AVG	LG	TD	PR	YDS	AVG	LG	KOR	YDS	AVG	LG
1980	OTT*	16																													
1981	OTT*	16	0		1																										
1982	OTT*	13	0		2																										
1983	OTT	1																													
1983	WPG	4																													
1983	Year	5																													
1984	WPG	3	0		1																										
6	Years	65	0		4																										
DOUG BELDEN Douglas Ray QB-DB 6'0 197 Florida B: 4/24/1927 D: 7/8/1972 Hillsborough County, FL Draft: 27-255 1948 CHIC																															
1949	SAS	14										5	1					1													
1952	SAS	12			2				3	12		5	1	15	-21	-1.4	14	1										4	73	18.3	23
2	Years	26			2				3	12		10	2	15	-21	-1.4	14	2										4	73	18.3	23
JACQUES BELEC Jacques FB-HB 5'10 183 Western Ontario B: 9/13/1931 Draft: 2-5 1954 TOR																															
1954	MTL	14										5	1	38	147	3.9	17	1	1	11	11.0	11	0	20	87	4.4	12				
1955	MTL	10										15	3	51	340	6.7	22	2	10	107	10.7	18	1								
1956	MTL	6										6	1	4	25	6.3	11	1	1	6	6.0	6	0								
3	Years	30										26	5	93	512	5.5	22	4	12	124	10.3	18	1	20	87	4.4	12				
BILL BELK William Arthur DE 6'3 248 Maryland-Eastern Shore B: 2/19/1946 Lancaster, SC Draft: 6B-153 1968 SF Pro: N																															
1975	TOR	5	0		1																										
1976	TOR	1																													
2	Years	6	0		1																										
ANTHONY BELL Anthony Dewitt LB 6'3 231 Michigan State B: 7/2/1964 Miami, FL Draft: 1-5 1986 STL Pro: N																															
1995	OTT	6	0		1	11	1.0	9.0	0	0	1																				
BILL BELL Bill DB North York Knights Jrs.; East York Ints.																															
1960	CAL																														
BILLY BELL W.E.N. QB-HB																															
1946	TOR	7																													
1947	TOR	7										1	0																		
2	Years	14										1	0																		
BILLY BELL Billy Ray CB 5'10 170 Lamar B: 1/16/1961 Dayton, TX Pro: N																															
1990	BC	4				10			1	16																					
BOB BELL Bob WR 6'0 185 Hamilton Jrs. B: 1953																															
1975	HAM	3																													
1975	WPG	1																													
1975	Year	4																													
CURTIS BELL Curtis WR 6'2 170 Burlington Braves Jrs.; Washington B: 8/18/1966 Hamilton, ON Draft: 2A-11 1989 HAM																															
1989	TOR	7				0													6	55	9.2	19	0								
DALTON BELL Dalton Jay QB 6'2 206 West Texas A&M B: 3/9/1983 Canyon, TX																															
2009	SAS	18				0																									
2010	TOR	2	2	0	1	0						6	1	4	26	6.5	12	1													
2011	TOR	18	2	0	0	0								4	20	5.0	12	0													
3	Years	38	4	0	1	0						6	1	8	46	5.8	12	1													
EDDIE BELL Edward Boaz LB 6'1 212 Pennsylvania B: 3/25/1931 Philadelphia, PA D: 11/16/2009 Philadelphia, PA Draft: 5A-57 1953 PHI Pro: N																															
1959	HAM+	14							5	26		6	1																		
EDGAR BELL Edgar OG 6'1 236 New Mexico B: 3/31/1953																															
1976	BC	14																													
GRAEME BELL Graeme FB 5'11 220 Saskatoon Hilltops Jrs.; Saskatchewan B: 10/15/1980 Regina, SK																															
2005	WPG	7				3																						1	0	0.0	0
2006	WPG	18	0	1	0	19						6	1	14	59	4.2	14	0	1	3	3.0	3	1								
2008	WPG	18				25						6	1	3	1	0.3	2	1	2	11	5.5	8	0								
2009	EDM	18	0	0	1	7								1	6	6.0	6	0	3	13	4.3	6	0					7	60	8.6	16
2010	EDM	3				2																									
2011	SAS	18				7																						1	12	12.0	12
6	Years	82	0	1	1	63						12	2	18	66	3.7	14	1	6	27	4.5	8	1					9	72	8.0	16
JAMES BELL James CB 5'10 175 New Mexico B: 3/2/1959 Albuquerque, NM																															
1985	EDM	12	0		1		2.0		1	0																					
1986	EDM	11	0		1		1.0		1	6																					
2	Years	23	0		2		3.0		2	6																					
JOE BELL Joseph DE 6'3 250 Norfolk State B: 4/20/1956 Pro: N																															
1980	WPG	2																													
JOEL BELL Joel Richard OT 6'7 315 Furman B: 7/29/1985 Cleveland, OH Pro: U																															
2009	SAS	15				1																									
2010	SAS	8	0	1	0	1																									
2	Years	23	0	1	0	2																									
JOHN BELL John H. DE 6'0 195 Oklahoma B: 10/14/1934																															
1957	EDM	14	0		2							6	1						3	81	27.0	45	1					1	14	14.0	14
1958	EDM	11										0	0						1	12	12.0	12	0	1	5	5.0	5				
2	Years	25	0		2							6	1						4	93	23.3	45	1	1	5	5.0	5	1	14	14.0	14
JOHNNY BELL Johnny (Red) E-HB 6'4 188 none B: 1922 Toronto, ON																															
1946	SAS+	7										11	2										2								
1947	SAS+	8										3	0																		
1948	SAS+	8										5	1																		
1949	SAS	14										12	2										2								
1950	SAS	4																	9	92	10.2		0								
1951	SAS	14																	5	35	7.0		0								
1952	SAS	11			1									1	2	2.0	2	0	14	147	10.5	22	0								
7	Years	66			1							31	5	1	2	2.0	2	0	28	274	9.8	22	4								
KERWIN BELL Kerwin Douglas QB 6'2 205 Florida B: 6/15/1965 Live Oak, FL Draft: 7-180 1988 MIA Pro: EN																															
1993	SAC	18				0								4	13	3.3	8	0													
1994	SAC	18	4		0	1								15	58	3.9	11	0													
1995	EDM	18	11		0	0						24	4	25	89	3.6	22	4													
1998	TOR*	18	6	0	2	0								19	70	3.7	10	0													
1999	WPG	18	13	0	0	2						6	1	33	85	2.6	16	1													
2000	WPG	8	1	0	0	0								6	16	2.7	6	0													
2000	TOR	10	5	0	1	0						6	1	5	8	1.6	9	1													
2000	Year	18	6	0	0	0						6	1	11	24	2.2	9	1													
2001	TOR	18	1	0	0	1								3	10	3.3	7	0													
7	Years	116	41	0	3	4						36	6	110	349	3.2	22	6													
RICKY BELL Richard, Jr. DH-CB 5'10 192 North Carolina State B: 10/2/1974 Columbia, SC D: 2/17/2011 Columbia, SC Pro: ENX																															
2001	CAL	18				46	2.0	14.0	1	16	7																				
2002	OTT	15				31			1	0	1																				
2002	WPG	3				10			1	0	1																				
2002	Year	18				41			2	0	2																				
2003	WPG	18				50			1	10	6													1	6	6.0	6				
2004	WPG	18	0	1	1	47			1	39	4	6	1																		
2005	MTL	4				17	1.0	7.0			3																				
2006	MTL	17	0	1	1	52	1.0	4.0			3																				
6	Years	90	0	2	2	253	4.0	25.0	5	65	25	6	1											1	6	6.0	6				
ROY BELL Roy Lemount OHB-FB 6'0 208 Oklahoma B: 7/29/1949 Draft: 9-234 1972 DAL																															
1972	EDM	10	2		1							18	3	140	690	4.9	53	2	25	283	11.3	46	1					7	197	28.1	30
1973	EDM+	16	5		0							30	5	254	1455	5.7	76	5	29	200	6.9	22	0					7	165	23.6	64
1974	EDM+	15	5		1							24	4	286	1341	4.7	70	4	19	190	10.0	28	0					7	197	28.1	32

Year	Team	GP	FM	FF	FR	TK	SK	YDS	IR	YDS	PD	PTS	TD	RA	YDS	AVG	LG	TD	REC	YDS	AVG	LG	TD	PR	YDS	AVG	LG	KOR	YDS	AVG	LG
1975	EDM	16	5		0							42	7	232	1006	4.3	33	5	26	324	12.5	47	2					11	122	11.1	31
1976	EDM	5	1		0							12	2	50	175	3.5	12	2	8	52	6.5	11	0								
5	Years	62	18		2							126	21	962	4667	4.9	76	18	107	1049	9.8	47	3					32	681	21.3	64
TYRONE BELL Tyrone Edward DB 6'2 210 North Alabama B: 10/20/1974 West Point, MS Draft: 5C-178 1999 SD Pro: NX																															
2001	BC	12	0	0	2	38			1	18	4																				
2002	BC	5				14					2																				
2002	WPG	6	0	1	0	12					4																				
2002	Year	11				26					6																				
2	Years	17	0	1	2	64			1	18	10																				
WHITNEY BELL Whitney Hale DT 6'2 284 Ferris State B: 1/5/1979 Sault Sainte Marie, MI																															
2006	BC	1				0																									
MIKE BELLAMY Michael Sinclair, II WR 6'0 195 DuPage JC; Illinois B: 6/28/1966 New York, NY Draft: 2-50 1990 PHI Pro: EN																															
1993	WPG	7				0													12	104	8.7	17	0	3	13	4.3	8	1	32	32.0	32
1960	CAL	5																													
MIKE BELLEFONTAINE Mike SB 5'10 185 Vancouver Meralomas Jrs.; British Columbia B: 7/16/1962 Vancouver, BC																															
1989	BC	11				0						12	2						14	211	15.1	33	2								
ADRIANO BELLI Adriano DT-NT 6'4 273 Houston B: 8/25/1977 Toronto, ON Draft: 1-6 2000 BC Pro: X																															
2001	BC	2				0																									
2001	MTL	4	0	1	0	7																									
2001	Year	6	0	1	0	7																									
2002	MTL	18	0	1	0	14	4.0	17.0																							
2003	MTL	7	1	1	1	9																									
2004	HAM	15				23	3.0	19.0																							
2005	HAM*	18	0	0	1	27	7.0	46.0			1																				
2006	HAM	11	0	1	1	12	3.0	13.0																							
2006	MTL	8				7	2.0	12.0																							
2006	Year	19	0	1	1	19	5.0	25.0																							
2007	TOR+	18	0	1	0	44	2.0	16.0			1																				
2008	TOR	18				40	2.0	8.0																							
2009	TOR	17				21	5.0	22.0			1																				
2010	TOR	2	0	1	0	8																									
10	Years	126	1	6	3	212	28.0	153.0			3																				
GENE BELLIVEAU Eugene DT-DE 6'4 235 St. Francis Xavier B: 5/30/1958 Clark City, QC Draft: 3B-23 1980 MTL																															
1980	MTL	12	0		1							6	1																		
1981	MTL	8																													
1982	MTL	16					4.5																								
1983	MTL	16					6.5																								
1984	MTL	8					2.0																								
1985	CAL	14					4.0		1	0																					
1986	CAL	15					3.0		1	0																					
1987	CAL	18	0		2	17	5.0																								
1988	CAL	18				32	6.0																								
1989	CAL	18	0		1	30	10.0																								
10	Years	143	0		4	79	41.0		2	0		6	1																		
GEORGE BELOTTI George Daniel T 6'3 253 Southern California B: 11/29/1934 D: 6/15/2009 Arcadia, CA Draft: 8-87 1957 GB Pro: N																															
1958	SAS	16																													
CEASAR BELSER Ceasar Edward DB 6'0 212 Arkansas-Pine Bluff B: 9/13/1944 Montgomery, AL Draft: 10-145 1966 WAS Pro: N																															
1972	EDM	7																													
1973	EDM	12							1	2																		1	17	17.0	17
2	Years	19							1	2																		1	17	17.0	17
HORACE BELTON Horace J. RB 5'8 200 Southeastern Louisiana B: 7/16/1955 Baton Rouge, LA Pro: N																															
1977	MTL	2	1		0							12	2	27	126	4.7	13	0	9	93	10.3	21	2					1	19	19.0	19
GEORGE BELU George A. OE-DB 6'1 200 Ohio University B: 6/11/1939 Lorain, OH																															
1963	OTT	14										9	1						15	228	15.2	50	1					1	1	1.0	1
1964	OTT	1																	1	9	9.0	9	0								
1964	SAS	3							1			6	1						1	6	6.0	6	0								
1964	Year	4							1			6	1						2	15	7.5	9	0								
2	Years	15							1	0		15	2						17	243	14.3	50	1					1	1	1.0	1
BRIAN BELWAY Brian P. OT-NT 6'6 265 Calgary B: 5/28/1963 Ottawa, ON Draft: 1-7 1986 WPG Pro: N																															
1986	CAL	2																													
1987	CAL	1	1		2	0																									
1988	BC	17				26	2.0																								
1989	BC	7	0		1	1																									
1990	TOR	4				3	1.0																								
5	Years	31	1		3	30	3.0																								
LEE BENARD Lee DB 6'1 185 Manitoba B: 11/6/1950 Draft: 5-43 1973 SAS																															
1974	SAS	10	1		0																			29	153	5.3	13				
1975	SAS	15							1	63		6	1											17	190	11.2	22				
1976	WPG	11	0		2				1	37														2	27	13.5	20				
1977	WPG	16	0		1				3	68																					
4	Years	52	1		3				5	168		6	1											48	370	7.7	22				
WALTER BENDER Walter L. RB 5'11 195 Kent State B: 9/8/1961 Detroit, MI																															
1984	TOR	1	1		1							6	1	6	19	3.2	13	0	6	78	13.0	27	1								
1985	TOR	5	2		0							6	1	52	182	3.5	19	0	19	183	9.6	23	1					5	104	20.8	25
1986	HAM+	12	4		1							48	8	162	618	3.8	32	8	26	167	6.4	23	0					11	259	23.5	32
1987	SAS+	11	4		2	3						42	7	148	525	3.5	37	6	30	301	10.0	30	1					15	265	17.7	38
1988	WPG	9	4		1	0						18	3	77	384	5.0	41	3	9	82	9.1	22	0					3	29	9.7	15
5	Years	38	15		5	3						120	20	445	1728	3.9	41	17	90	811	9.0	30	3					34	657	19.3	38
STEVE BENDIAK Steve OE-DB 6'4 210 Edmonton Wildcats Jrs. B: 1931 Edmonton, AB D: 5/17/2004 Edmonton, AB																															
1952	EDM	16																													
1953	EDM	12																													
1954	EDM	15																	15	239	15.9	67	0								
1955	EDM	14																	5	86	17.2	21	0								
1956	EDM	16										6	1						7	118	16.9	26	1								
1957	EDM	15	2		0				2	27														1	28	28.0	16				
1958	EDM	12	0		2				1	2									5	90	18.0	33	0								
1959	EDM	16							5	61				0	17		17	0						1	14	14.0	14				
1960	EDM	14																													
9	Years	130	2		2				8	90		6	1	0	17		17	0	32	533	16.7	67	1	2	42	21.0	16				
DEMETRIS BENDROSS Demetris W. RB-WR 5'8 180 Florida A&M B: 12/22/1976 Miami, FL																															
2000	SAS	14	2	0	0	0						42	7	1	10	10.0	10	0	39	699	17.9	54	5	10	118	11.8	44	36	814	22.6	96
2001	SAS	16	1	0	0	3						24	4	6	18	3.0	12	0	47	674	14.3	71	4	21	88	4.2	23	9	169	18.8	38
2002	SAS	7				0						12	2	1	7	7.0	7	0	18	232	12.9	46	2								
2002	TOR	5	1	0	0	0						12	2						22	431	19.6	74	2	3	49	16.3	22	1	10	10.0	10
2002	Year	12	1	0	0	0						24	4	1	7	7.0	7	0	40	663	16.6	74	4	3	49	16.3	22	1	10	10.0	10
2003	OTT	16	3	0	1	1						36	6	8	92	11.5	26	0	51	734	14.4	61	5	46	335	7.3	50	32	746	23.3	82
2004	OTT	15	3	0	0	3						48	8	3	-6	-2.0	0	0	37	519	14.0	71	8	4	51	12.8	43	14	301	21.5	53
5	Years	68	10	0	1	7						174	29	19	121	6.4	26	0	214	3289	15.4	74	26	84	641	7.6	50	92	2040	22.2	96
AL BENECICK Alexander G. OG-OT 6'2 245 Syracuse B: 3/20/1937 Draft: 6-62 1959 PHI																															
1959	SAS	7																	1	6	6.0	6	0								
1960	SAS	16	0		1																										
1961	SAS	16																													

Year	Team	GP	FM	FF	FR	TK	SK	YDS	IR	YDS	PD	PTS	TD	RA	YDS	AVG	LG	TD	REC	YDS	AVG	LG	TD	PR	YDS	AVG	LG	KOR	YDS	AVG	LG
1962	SAS	16																													
1963	SAS+	16																													
1964	SAS*	16																													
1965	SAS*	16																													
1966	SAS*	15	0		1							6	1																		
1967	SAS	5																													
1968	SAS	16																													
1969	EDM	4																													
11	Years	143	0		2							6	1						1	6	6.0	6	0								
DAVED BENEFIELD Daved C. LB 6'4 231 Glendale JC; Northridge State B: 2/16/1968 Pro: N																															
1992	OTT	2				9	2.0	13.0																							
1993	OTT	11				14	6.0	63.0																							
1994	OTT+	17	0		3	43	10.0	95.0			1																				
1995	BC	17	0		2	40	12.0	74.0			3																				
1997	BC	7	0	1	1	16	2.0	13.0			1																	1	10	10.0	10
1998	BC	18	0	1	2	44	9.0	57.0																				1	0	0.0	0
1999	BC*	18	1	5	2	56	9.0	60.0	2	14	6																				
2000	BC	17	0	4	2	54	3.0	16.0			5	6	1																		
2001	BC	18	0	4	2	54	4.0	41.0			4																				
2002	WPG	14	0	1	1	16	6.0	32.0			2																				
2003	WPG*	17	0	5	2	31	9.0	52.0	1	29	2	12	2																		
2004	SAS	18	0	2	1	39	4.0	23.0	2	39	6	12	2																		
2005	SAS	10	0	3	0	15	1.0	7.0			1																				
13	Years	184	1	26	18	431	77.0	546.0	5	82	31	30	5															2	10	5.0	10
NICK BENJAMIN Nicholas Dexter OG 6'2 270 Oshawa Hawkeyes Jrs.; Concordia (Canada) B: 5/29/1961 Trinidad,Trinidad & Tobago D: 8/20/2007 Winnipeg, MB Draft: 1-1 1985 OTT																															
1985	OTT	16																													
1986	OTT	10																													
1987	OTT	17				1																									
1988	OTT	18	0		3	4																									
1989	OTT	2	0		1	0																									
1989	WPG	6				0																									
1989	Year	8	0		1	0																									
1990	WPG	17				4																									
1991	WPG	18	1		2	10						6	1																		
1992	WPG	11	2		0	6																									
1993	WPG	12	2		0	7																									
1994	OTT	5				1																									
10	Years	126	5		6	33						6	1																		
RYAN BENJAMIN Ryan Lamont RB 5'7 183 Sequoias JC; Pacific B: 4/23/1970 Santa Clara County, CA Pro: N																															
1994	SHR	11	2		0	3						12	2	62	392	6.3	43	2	9	138	15.3	59	0					14	294	21.0	47
STEVE BENJAMIN Steve CB 5'10 185 Northridge State B: 8/17/1964 Los Angeles, CA																															
1986	MTL	18							2	15														0	-12		-12				
1987	EDM	9				34			1	0														1	1	1.0	1				
1988	EDM	18				55			1	89		6	1											1	0	0.0	0				
3	Years	45				89			4	104		6	1											2	-11	-5.5	1				
BRUCE BENNETT Bruce S 5'10 175 Florida B: 1944																															
1966	SAS	16	4		4				1			6	1	19	60	3.2	31	1													
1967	SAS+	16	1		0				5	31				1	21	21.0	21	0													
1968	SAS+	16	0		1				6	115																					
1969	SAS*	16	0		2				8	48																					
1970	SAS+	16	0		1				4	39														1	0	0.0	0				
1971	SAS+	16	0		1				8	189		6	1																		
1972	SAS+	16	0		1				3	170		6	1																		
7	Years	112	5		10				35	592		18	3	20	81	4.1	31	1						1	0	0.0	0				
CHARLES BENNETT Charles Anthony DT 6'5 257 Mississippi Delta JC; Louisiana-Lafayette B: 2/9/1963 Alligator, MS Draft: 7-190 1985 CHIB; 5-65 1985 POR-USFL Pro: N																															
1985	SAS	1																													
CLYDE BENNETT Clyde E 6'2 215 South Carolina B: 1932 Draft: 3-28 1954 NYG																															
1954	OTT	13																	26	321	12.3	25	0								
JOHN BENNETT John E 6'1 187 McGill B: 1931 Draft: 1958 OTT																															
1958	CAL	8																													
1959	CAL	1																													
2	Years	9																													
KEITH BENNETT Keith HB-FB-LB 6'0 186 Vancouver Blue Bombers Jrs. B: 1931																															
1950	CAL	14												4	4	1.0		0	2	35	17.5		0								
1951	CAL	14												10	49	4.9		0						4	46	11.5		7	119	17.0	
1952	CAL	15			1				2	30				4	24	6.0	11	0						3	17	5.7	10				
1953	CAL	16							1	0				6	36	6.0		0	2	25	12.5		0					1	3	3.0	3
1954	BC	16			3				1	40		5	1											2	7	3.5	7				
1955	BC	10																						1	0	0.0	0				
6	Years	85	0		4				4	70		5	1	24	113	4.7	11	0	4	60	15.0		0	10	70	7.0	10	8	122	15.3	3
PAUL BENNETT Paul DB 5'10 195 Wilfrid Laurier B: 3/27/1954 Scarborough, ON Draft: TE 1977 TOR																															
1977	TOR*	16	4		0				4	82														75	965	12.9	59	14	375	26.8	49
1978	TOR	16	2		1				2	72														46	365	7.9	28	32	757	23.7	47
1979	TOR	14	3		2				1	2				1	0	0.0	0	0						54	465	8.6	43	18	429	23.8	32
1980	WPG	14	1		0				7	181														10	96	9.6	35	1	19	19.0	19
1981	WPG	15	1		1		1.0		1	0														72	892	12.4	49	9	223	24.8	31
1982	WPG+	16	3		0		2.5		6	163														85	845	9.9	51	3	36	12.0	16
1983	WPG*	16	1		0		1.0		4	93														97	890	9.2	52	2	32	16.0	11
1984	TOR	11	1		0				6	87														35	286	8.2	21				
1984	HAM	4																						8	54	6.8	14				
1984	Year	15	1		0				6	87														43	340	7.9	21				
1985	HAM*	16	3		2				12	246		12	2											44	487	11.1	99				
1986	HAM	18	2		3				2	10														91	728	8.0	32				
1987	HAM	18	5		1	54			6	68														42	285	6.8	21				
11	Years	170	26		10	54	4.5		51	1004		12	2	1	0	0.0	0	0						659	6358	9.6	99	79	1871	23.7	49
PETE BENNETT Peter T 6'3 240 Toronto Balmy Beach Jrs.; Toronto B: 1927																															
1948	TOR	7																													
1950	TOR	12																													
1951	TOR	12																													
1952	TOR	12																													
1953	TOR	14																													
1954	TOR	14																													
1955	TOR	11																													
1956	TOR	14																													
1957	TOR	14																										1	0	0.0	0
1958	TOR	14																													
1959	TOR	14																													
1960	TOR	1																													
1960	HAM	10																													
1960	Year	11																													
12	Years	139																										1	0	0.0	0

Year	Team	GP	FM	FF	FR	TK	SK	YDS	IR	YDS	PD	PTS	TD	RA	YDS	AVG	LG	TD	REC	YDS	AVG	LG	TD	PR	YDS	AVG	LG	KOR	YDS	AVG	LG
ROY BENNETT Roy Mitchell CB 6'2 195 Jackson State B: 7/5/1961 Birmingham, AL Draft: 15B-318 1984 JAC-USFL Pro: N																															
1985	WPG	16	0		1				5	105														1	10	10.0	10				
1986	WPG*	17	1		0				8	204		12	2											2	-4	-2.0	6				
1987	WPG*	18	0		2	67			13	146																					
1991	EDM	9	1		1	40																									
4	Years	60	2		4	107			26	455		12	2											3	6	2.0	10				
SEAN BENNETT William Sean RB 6'1 230 Illinois*; Evansville; Northwestern B: 11/9/1975 Wurzburg, West Germany Draft: 4-112 1999 NYG Pro: N																															
2004	OTT	3				2						6	1						4	74	18.5	42	1								
2005	OTT	5				0								1	12	12.0	12	0	4	76	19.0	46	0								
2006	TOR	3				3													2	49	24.5	41	0								
3	Years	11				5						6	1	1	12	12.0	12	0	10	199	19.9	46	1								
SHELDON BENOIT Sheldon LB 6'2 235 Western Kentucky B: 8/23/1972 Toronto, ON Draft: 1-11 1995 TOR																															
1995	TOR	14				20																									
1996	SAS	9				5																									
1997	BC	1				0																									
1999	MTL	15	0	1	0	19																									
2000	MTL	18	0	1	1	47																						1	8	8.0	8
2001	EDM	4				5			1	15	0																				
2002	EDM	18	0	0	2	22	1.0																					1	0	0.0	0
2003	EDM	14				9																									
2004	EDM	3				4																									
9	Years	96	0	2	3	131	1.0		1	15	0																	2	8	4.0	8
KEN BENSON Kenneth LB-DE 6'2 220 Butler JC; Arkansas B: 3/4/1969 Kansas City, KS																															
1992	TOR	18	0		1	92	2.0	10.0																				1	0	0.0	0
1993	TOR	18	0		2	98	5.0	30.0	1	2																					
1994	BAL	5				20	1.0																								
1995	BAL	2				3																									
1996	MTL	1				1																									
1996	TOR	16				77	2.0	21.0	2	23	3																				
1996	Year	17				78	2.0	21.0	2	23	3																				
1997	TOR+	18	0	1	0	73	4.0	23.0	1	0	3																				
1998	SAS	16	0	1	0	77					1																				
1999	SAS	8				36	2.0	7.0																							
8	Years	86	0	2	3	477	16.0	91.0	4	25	7																	1	0	0.0	0
LESLIE BENSON Leslie DE 6'3 266 Baylor B: 3/29/1953 Draft: 6A-164 1976 BUF																															
1976	EDM	1																													
LORNE BENSON Lorne FB-LB 6'0 188 Weston Wildcats Jrs. B: 1930																															
1951	WPG	1												3	9	3.0		0													
1952	WPG	16										15	3	83	491	5.9	31	2	6	52	8.7	14	1					1	18	15.0	18
1953	WPG	14										20	4	124	563	4.5		3	20	225	11.3		1					4	49	12.3	
1954	WPG	15	1		1							10	2	31	150	4.8	14	1	1	4	4.0	4	0								
1955	WPG	15	3		0				1	40		10	2	85	460	5.4	18	1	4	64	16.0	37	1	1	0	0.0	0	2	35	17.5	20
5	Years	61	4		1				1	40		55	11	326	1673	5.1	31	7	31	345	11.1	37	3	1	0	0.0	0	7	102	14.6	20
HOWARD BENTON Howard T 6'2 250 Mississippi State B: 1940																															
1963	EDM	2																													
KEITH BENTON Keith QB 5'10 180 Sequoias JC; Memphis B: 3/1/1968 Miami, FL																															
1995	MEM	7	1		0	4								4	24	6.0	11	0	3	48	16.0	17	0								
JEFF BENTRIM Jeffrey David QB 6'0 205 North Dakota State B: 6/21/1965 St. Paul, MN																															
1987	SAS	17	3		0	1						6	1	29	228	7.9	26	1													
1988	SAS	4				0																									
1989	SAS	3				0													4	89	22.3	32	0					10	217	21.7	35
1990	SAS	18	1		1	1						6	1	31	180	5.8	23	1													
4	Years	42	4		1	2						12	2	60	408	6.8	26	2	4	89	22.3	32	0					10	217	21.7	35
BILL BEREZOWSKI Williams C-LB 6'2 215 McMaster B: 1928 Draft: 1952 HAM																															
1952	HAM	11																													
1953	HAM	14																													
1954	TOR	14																													
3	Years	39																													
BRIAN BERG Brian OG-K-T 6'1 240 Augsburg B: 1952 Draft: 4-33 1974 SAS																															
1974	SAS	16	3		0							82	0																		
1975	SAS	3										22	0																		
1975	BC	3										11	0																		
1975	Year	6										33	0																		
2	Years	19	3		0							115	0																		
DON BERGER Donald C 6'1 225 Michigan State B: 1933																															
1958	SAS	11																													
BRUCE BERGEY Bruce Gene DE 6'4 240 Glendale JC; UCLA B: 8/8/1946 South Dayton, NY Draft: 14-354 1971 KC Pro: NW																															
1972	TOR	4										6	1						1	10	10.0	10	1								
1973	TOR	14	0		2																										
2	Years	18	0		2							6	1						1	10	10.0	10	1								
COLE BERGQUIST Cole Reed QB 6'2 205 Montana B: 1/16/1985 San Clemente, CA																															
2010	SAS	18				0																									
2011	SAS	18				0								3	2	0.7	1	0													
2	Years	36				0								3	2	0.7	1	0													
MARV BERGSON Marvin HB none B: 1928																															
1947	WPG	8										5	1					1													
1948	WPG	12										5	1					1													
2	Years	20										10	2					2													
RICK BERGSON Rick HB 6'0 185 Norwood-St. Boniface Ints.																															
1948	WPG	10																													
CARL BERMAN Carl William SB 5'9 166 Indiana State B: 4/5/1985 St. Petersburg, FL																															
2008	SAS	4	2	0	0	0								1	14	14.0	14	0	1	13	13.0	13	0	15	89	5.9	12	7	133	19.0	25
RAY BERNARD Ray LB 6'1 220 Bishop's B: 5/29/1967 Laval, QC Draft: 2A-10 1992 SAS																															
1992	SAS	16				48																									
1993	SAS	18	0		3	98	1.0	10.0																							
1994	SAS	7	0		4	27	2.0	6.0	1	17	1	6	1																		
1995	OTT	13				64	2.0	10.0	2	40	0																				
1996	OTT	18	0		1	41	3.0	13.0																							
1997	CAL	5	0	2	0	11																									
1997	MTL	13	0	1	1	15	1.0	5.0				6	1																		
1997	Year	18	0	3	1	26	1.0	5.0				6	1																		
6	Years	77	0	3	9	304	9.0	44.0	3	57	1	12	2																		
YVENSON BERNARD Yvenson RB 5'9 201 Oregon State B: 10/25/1984 Boynton Beach, FL																															
2009	WPG	14	4	0	0	8								53	336	6.3	27	0	17	153	9.0	29	0					2	27	13.5	18
2010	WPG	3				1						6	1	5	22	4.4	13	1	1	7	7.0	7	0								
2011	SAS	2				0																									
3	Years	19	4	0	0	9						6	1	58	358	6.2	27	1	18	160	8.9	29	0					2	27	13.5	18
GINO BERRETTA Giovanni P-K-E 6'1 208 NDG Maple Leafs Jrs. B: 10/5/1942																															
1961	MTL	8										3	0											1	0	0.0	0				
1963	MTL	13										47	1						4	61	15.3	28	1								
1964	MTL	14										24	0															2	32	16.0	20
1965	MTL	4	0		1							1	0															1	13	13.0	13

Year	Team	GP	FM	FF	FR	TK	SK	YDS	IR	YDS	PD	PTS	TD	RA	YDS	AVG	LG	TD	REC	YDS	AVG	LG	TD	PR	YDS	AVG	LG	KOR	YDS	AVG	LG
1966	MTL	14	1		0							4	0																		
1968	OTT	3																													
1969	MTL	7										33	0																		
7	Years	63	1		1							112	1						4	61	15.3	28	1	1	0	0.0	0	3	45	15.0	20
BERT BERRY Bertrand Demond DL 6'3 258 Notre Dame B: 8/15/1975 Houston, TX Draft: 3-86 1997 IND Pro: N																															
2000	EDM	2				1																									
BRENT BERRY Brent OT 6'4 248 Foothill JC; San Jose State B: 12/14/1940 Draft: RS-10-75 1965 OAK; 13-177(f) 1965 LARM																															
1967	EDM	4																													
DAVE BERRY David E-T 6'3 220 Winnipeg Jrs. B: 1921 Birkenhead, England D: 4/16/2007 Westbank, BC																															
1946	CAL	8																													
1947	CAL	8																													
1948	CAL	12										5	1										1								
1949	CAL	14																													
1950	CAL	14																	1	3	3.0	3	0								
1951	CAL	14																													
6	Years	70										5	1						1	3	3.0	3	1								
ED BERRY Edward J., Jr. CB 5'10 183 Utah State B: 9/28/1963 San Francisco, CA Draft: 7-183 1986 GB Pro: N																															
1988	TOR	6	0		1	16			2	115		6	1																		
1989	TOR+	14	0		3	66			5	147		6	1																		
1990	TOR	18				72			7	153		6	1																		
1991	TOR	16	0		1	69			4	78		6	1																		
1992	TOR	17				50			9	97		6	1											1	1	1.0	1	6	64	10.7	21
1993	EDM	14	0		1	47			2	26																					
1994	EDM	9				26			2	14	5																				
1995	MEM	16				56			2	54	7	6	1																		
1996	TOR	14				33			1	51	9																				
9	Years	124	0		6	435			34	735	21	36	6											1	1	1.0	1	6	64	10.7	21
LINDY BERRY Lindy QB 5'10 173 Texas Christian B: 1928 Draft: 7-89 1950 SF																															
1950	EDM	13										10	2	55	209	3.8		2													
1951	EDM	1																													
2	Years	14										10	2	55	209	3.8	0	2													
REGGIE BERRY Reginald CB 5'11 185 Wyoming B: 9/6/1966 Chicago, IL Pro: E																															
1989	TOR	13	0		4	43			1	6																					
KERRY BERRYMAN Kerry C-LB 6'0 225 Regina Rams Jrs. B: 10/4/1957 Yorkton, SK																															
1980	SAS	2																													
1981	SAS	5																													
1982	SAS	2																													
1984	CAL	16																													
1985	CAL	4																													
5	Years	29																													
TIM BERRYMAN Tim LB 6'0 220 Ottawa B: 12/21/1954 Draft: 1A-1 1976 EDM																															
1976	EDM	14																												1	0	0.0	0
1977	HAM	1																													
1977	OTT	9	1		0																							3	30	10.0	17
1977	Year	10	1		0																							3	30	10.0	17
1978	OTT	13	0		1				1	6																					
1979	OTT	16							1	3																					
1980	OTT	5																													
1981	OTT	4																													
1982	TOR	16	0		1		1.0		1	7																		1	15	15.0	15
7		69	1		2		1.0		3	16																		5	45	9.0	17
CLAUDIO BERTONE Claudio FB 5'11 240 Lehigh B: 3/10/1970 Montreal, QC Draft: 2-14 1994 TOR																															
1994	TOR	3				2																									
MATHIEU BERTRAND Mathieu FB 6'3 228 Laval B: 12/28/1977 Chambly, QC Draft: 5-44 2003 MTL																															
2004	EDM	15				13								2	4	2.0	3	0	5	21	4.2	9	0								
2005	EDM	18				16						6	1	13	32	2.5	15	0	21	169	8.0	19	1					2	16	8.0	10
2006	EDM	14	0	0	1	12						6	1	4	5	1.3	3	0	15	106	7.1	19	1					1	6	6.0	6
2007	EDM	13	0	1	2	21						6	1						11	111	10.1	23	1								
2008	EDM	18				22						24	4	13	28	2.2	4	4	22	161	7.3	29	0					3	34	11.3	16
2009	EDM	15	0	1	0	15						6	1	7	22	3.1	6	1	22	207	9.4	35	0					4	36	9.0	16
2010	EDM	16	2	0	0	10						12	2	6	17	2.8	10	2	15	114	7.6	14	0					5	42	8.4	19
2011	EDM	18	1	1	1	13								4	10	2.5	5	7	4	17	4.3	12	0					1	0		0
8	Years	127	3	3	4	122						60	10	49	118	2.4	15	14	115	906	7.9	35	3					16	134	8.4	19
WILLIE BERZINSKI Willis John Paul HB 6'2 195 Wisconsin-LaCrosse B: 7/18/1934 Arcadia, WI D: 3/4/1994 Rochester, MN Draft: 4A-46 1956 LARM Pro: N																															
1957	TOR	1												6	8	1.3	3	0	1	4	4.0	4	0								
RANDY BESLER Randy OG 6'2 240 Truman State B: 4/1/1958 Draft: TE 1981 CAL																															
1981	CAL	1																													
GERALD BESS Gerald D. DB 6'0 188 Tuskegee B: 5/24/1958 Pensacola, FL Pro: N																															
1981	HAM	3							1	0																					
1982	HAM	12	0		2				2	45		6	1																		
1983	HAM	15							4	145		12	2																		
1984	HAM	16	0		4		1.0		12	123		6	1																		
1985	HAM	4							2	18																					
1986	HAM	2																													
1986	OTT	1																													
1986	Year	3																													
6	Years	52	0		6		1.0		21	331		24	4																		
CHRIS BEST Chris OG 6'5 295 Duke; Waterloo B: 4/3/1983 Calgary, AB Draft: 1B-4 2005 SAS																															
2007	SAS	3				0																									
2008	SAS	7				0																									
2009	SAS	18				0																									
2010	SAS	18				7																									
2011	SAS	18	0	0	1	1																									
5	Years	64	0	0	1	8																									
ADAM BESTARD Adam C 6'4 295 Wilfrid Laurier B: 11/30/1986 Sarnia, ON Draft: 4-27 2009 WPG																															
2010	WPG	1				0																									
MARC BESWICK Marc CB-S-DH 6'1 198 Butte JC; St. Mary's (Nova Scotia) B: 1/23/1983 Vancouver, BC Draft: 4-31 2008 WPG																															
2008	WPG	6				6																									
2009	HAM	13	0	0	1	20																									
2010	HAM	18				22					1																				
2011	HAM	18	0	0	1	27																									
4	Years	55	0	0	2	75					1																				
JAMES BETHEA James W., Jr. DB 5'10 190 California B: 9/24/1982 Honolulu, HI Pro: E																															
2007	BC	5				10																									
WILLIE BETHEA Willie FB 6'0 190 Rider B: 1939																															
1963	HAM	9										24	4	89	435	4.9	51	3	11	105	9.5	26	1					5	99	19.8	22
1964	HAM	7	3		1							18	3	83	408	4.9	33	1	6	129	21.5	34	2					11	356	32.4	59
1965	HAM	14	3									30	5	117	598	5.1	45	4	8	77	9.6	21	0					10	176	17.6	43
1966	HAM	14	1		0							13	2	95	531	5.6	55	0	20	238	11.9	49	2					12	327	27.3	36
1967	HAM+	14	5		0							36	6	147	737	5.0	39	5	40	520	13.0	42	1					13	320	24.6	43
1968	HAM	14	3		1							30	5	127	607	4.8	17	3	32	381	11.9	51	2					6	120	20.0	23
1969	HAM	14	3		0							24	4	109	543	5.0	19	3	26	305	11.7	28	1								

Year	Team	GP	FM	FF	FR	TK	SK	YDS	IR	YDS	PD	PTS	TD	RA	YDS	AVG	LG	TD	REC	YDS	AVG	LG	TD	PR	YDS	AVG	LG	KOR	YDS	AVG	LG
1970	HAM	4	1		1							6	1	14	60	4.3	11	1	2	45	22.5	35	0								
8	Years	90	19		3							181	30	781	3919	5.0	55	20	145	1800	12.4	51	9					57	1398	24.5	59
GEORGE BETHUNE George Edward DE-DT 6'4 240 Alabama B: 3/30/1967 Fort Walton Beach, FL Draft: 7-188 1989 LARM Pro: EN																														
1993	WPG	1				0																										
1994	SAC	15	0		1	30	2.0	7.			3																				
1995	SA	18				21	8.0	61.0			1																				
3	Years	34	0		1	51	10.0	68.0			4																				
ED BETTRIDGE Edward Neil LB 6'1 235 Bowling Green State B: 9/16/1940 Sandusky, OH Pro: N																														
1965	EDM	2																												
JON BEUTJER Jon QB 6'5 217 Iowa; Illinois B: 8/15/1980 Wheaton, IL																														
2005	HAM	8				0																										
EDDIE BEVAN Ed DG 5'9 220 none B: 1926 Hamilton, ON D: 6//1988 Hamilton, ON																														
1946	HAM	8																												
1947	HAM	10																												
1949	HAM	11																												
1950	HAM	12										5	1																			
1951	HAM+	12																												
1952	HAM+	12																												
1953	HAM+	14																												
1954	HAM+	14							1	3																					
1955	HAM+	12																												
1956	HAM	14																												
1957	HAM	14																												
1958	HAM	14																												
1959	HAM	13																												
13	Years	160							1	3		5	1																			
MARV BEVAN Marvin OG-DE 6'0 225 Hamilton Tiger-Cats Jrs. B: 1935																														
1956	OTT	2																												
1958	OTT	8																												
1960	OTT	11																												
1961	OTT	1																												
1962	OTT	7																												
1963	OTT	13																												
1964	OTT	9																									1	0	0.0	0
7	Years	51																									1	0	0.0	0
BOB BEVERIDGE Bob OT 6'6 290 British Columbia B: 6/1/1973 Toronto, ON Draft: 2-10 1997 BC																														
1998	MTL	4				0																										
1999	HAM	18				0																										
2000	HAM	13				0																										
2000	BC	3				0																										
2000	Year	16				0																										
3	Years	35				0																										
SANDY BEVERIDGE Sandy S 6'2 214 British Columbia B: 12/9/1981 Port Coquiltam, BC																														
2003	HAM	18				39			3	37	1																	1	7	7.0	7
2004	HAM	13	0	0	2	22					1	6	1																		
2005	HAM	11	0	0	1	13																										
2006	HAM	10	0	0	1	19																										
2007	HAM	17	0	1	2	31					2																				
2008	HAM	17				20																										
2009	HAM	15	0	0	1	45	1.0	6.0	2	38	0																				
2010	HAM	4				12																										
8	Years	105	0	1	7	201	1.0	6.0	5	75	4	6	1															1	7	7.0	7
DWIGHT BEVERLY Dwight Anthony RB 5'11 205 Illinois B: 12/5/1961 Los Angeles, CA Draft: 6-147 1984 IND; TD 1984 CHI-USFL Pro: NU																														
1985	CAL	4	5		1							20	3	56	238	4.3	18	3	14	128	9.1	38	0								
1986	CAL	2												22	85	3.9	12	0	8	39	4.9	18	0								
1988	CAL	2																												
3	Years	8	5		1							20	3	78	323	4.1	18	3	22	167	7.6	38	0								
BRYCE BEVILL Bryce K. DH 5'9 180 Syracuse B: 7/27/1972 Hyattsville, MD																														
1996	SAS	16	0		2	50			2	63	11	12	2																		
1997	SAS	18	0	2	1	30			4	115	5													1	6	6.0	6				
1998	SAS	7				20					1																				
1998	WPG	1				2	1.0	9.0																							
1998	Year	8				22	1.0	9.0			1																				
3	Years	41	0	2	3	102	1.0	9.0	6	178	17	12	2											1	6	6.0	6				
BILL BEWLEY William OHB-LB-S-K 5'11 190 Toronto B: 8/11/1931 Hamilton, ON Draft: 2-5 1953 MTL																														
1954	MTL	14										5	1	20	123	6.2	34	1	6	98	16.3	29	0	33	241	7.3	32				
1955	MTL	5										14	0	16	67	4.2	11	0	3	42	14.0	20	0	5	42	8.4	17				
1956	MTL	11										57	1	28	166	5.9	29	1	8	130	16.3	29	0								
1957	MTL	14							6	88		53	1	23	155	6.7	16	0	10	65	6.5	14	1					2	21	10.5	16
1958	MTL	14							2	25		62	2	30	166	5.5	14	0	33	395	12.0	87	1	1	10	10.0	10	1	9	9.0	9
1959	MTL	13							1	0		34	0	19	105	5.5	14	0	36	404	11.2	41	0					2	27	13.5	18
1960	MTL	14							2	25		78	3	8	-1	-0.1	6	1	27	394	14.6	64	1	1	13	13.0	13	1	13	13.0	13
1961	MTL	14										36	0	11	33	3.0	7	0	12	112	9.3	17	0	2	27	13.5	25				
1965	MTL	6										6	0															3	49	16.3	26
9	Years	105							11	138		345	8	155	814	5.3	34	3	135	1640	12.1	87	3	42	333	7.9	32	9	119	13.2	26
TOM BEYNON Tom OT 6'2 242 Queen's; Western Ontario B: 1941 Draft: 1D-8 1965 HAM																														
1966	SAS	9																												
1967	SAS	16	0		1																						1	1	1.0	1
1968	OTT	14	0		1																									
1969	OTT	14																												
1970	OTT	7																												
5	Years	60	0		2																						1	1	1.0	1
STEVE BEYRLE Steve Joseph OT 6'4 255 Kansas State B: 6/15/1950 Hutchinson, KS Draft: 8-195 1972 NE																														
1973	BC	1																												
YUDONN BIASSOU Yudonn DH 5'10 205 West Hills CC; Alabama-Birmingham B: 8/11/1976 Miami, FL																														
2000	SAS	2				16																										
2000	CAL	7	0	0	1	16					1																				
2000	Year	9	0	0	1	32					1																				
EZIL BIBBS Ezil D., Jr. DE-DT 6'3 252 Grambling State B: 6/30/1952 Harvey, LA Draft: 8-184 1974 NYG; 8-89 1974 PHI-WFL																														
1974	HAM	16	0		3																									
1975	HAM	14																												
2	Years	30	0		3																									
BOB BICKEL Robert Arthur HB 6'1 195 Duke B: 4/15/1928 Reading, PA Draft: 23-275 1952 NYG																														
1952	HAM	1																												
DON BICKLE Don FB																														
1947	CAL	6																												
LEO BIEDERMANN Leo George OT 6'7 254 Diablo Valley JC; California B: 10/19/1955 Omaha, NE Draft: 12-317 1978 CLE Pro: NU																														
1982	MTL	8																												
WILBERT BIGGENS Wilbert Lee RB 5'8 187 Texas A&M B: 12/24/1972 Houston, TX																														
1995	WPG	1				0																		3	6	2.0	8				
BOB BIGGS George Robert QB 6'0 180 Solano CC; California-Davis B: 2/21/1951 San Diego County, CA																														
1973	WPG	2																												

Year	Team	GP	FM	FF	FR	TK	SK	YDS	IR	YDS	PD	PTS	TD	RA	YDS	AVG	LG	TD	REC	YDS	AVG	LG	TD	PR	YDS	AVG	LG	KOR	YDS	AVG	LG
RAY BIGGS Raymond LB 6'1 220 New Mexico State B: 10/20/1968 Toronto, ON																															
1993	CAL	18	0		3	28			1	26																					
1994	CAL	18				29																									
1995	CAL	18				26																									
1996	CAL	18				37					1																				
1997	CAL	18	0	2	2	47	1.0	6.0			1																				
1998	CAL	8	0	0	1	13																									
1999	CAL	17				14																									
2000	CAL	18				35					2																				
8	Years	133	0	2	6	229	1.0	6.0	1	26	4																				
JACK BIGHEAD John OE 6'3 215 Pepperdine B: 4/23/1930 Beggs, OK D: 4/28/1993 Parker, AZ Draft: 23-274(di) 1951 PHI; 15-170 1952 DAL Pro: N																															
1956	HAM	8										6	1						16	228	14.3	26	1								
ADAM BIGHILL Adam LB 5'10 230 Central Washington B: 10/16/1988																															
2011	BC	12				28																									
AREK BIGOS Arek K 5'9 178 Waterloo B: 7/25/1973 Rumia, Poland																															
1998	TOR	12				2						111	0																		
MIKE BILAN Michael G-T 6'0 237 Calgary East End Golden Arrows Jrs. B: 1930																															
1950	CAL	14																													
1951	CAL	14																													
1952	CAL	6																										1	13	13.0	13
1954	CAL	12																													
4	Years	46																										1	13	13.0	13
FRED BILETNIKOFF Frederick S. WR 6'1 190 Florida State B: 2/23/1943 Erie, PA Draft: 2- 1965 OAK; 3-39 1965 DET Pro: N																															
1980	MTL	16	0		1							24	4						38	470	12.4	22	4								
WALT BILICKI Walter LB-C-OG 5'10 205 Manitoba; Winnipeg Rods Jrs. B: 5/1/1936 Montreal, QC																															
1956	WPG	16	0		3																										
1957	WPG	13																													
1958	WPG	14							1	0																					
1959	WPG	15							1																						
1960	WPG	6																													
1961	BC	14																													
1962	BC	16																													
1963	BC	16	0		1				1																						
1964	BC	16							1																						
1965	BC	16																													
10	Years	142	0		4				4	0																					
TERRY BILLUPS Terry Michael DH 5'9 179 North Carolina B: 2/9/1975 Weisbaden, West Germany Pro: ENX																															
2001	HAM	10				13			1	0	3																				
ED BILSKI Ed T 6'0 200 Winnipeg Roamers Jrs. B: 1923																															
1948	WPG	3																													
NATE BINDER Nate WR 6'2 200 Missouri Tech; Tusculum B: 9/20/1985 Windsor, ON Draft: 4A-24 2010 BC																															
2010	EDM	1				0																									
CODY BINKLEY Charles Cody C 6'2 215 Vanderbilt B: 12/23/1939 Benton, KY Draft: 15-207(f) 1961 NYG; 30-236(f) 1962 BUF																															
1964	MTL	10																													
DENNY BIODROWSKI Dennis James OT 6'1 253 Memphis B: 6/27/1940 Gary, IN Draft: 18-144(f) 1962 SD; 16-221(f) 1962 CLE Pro: N																															
1968	HAM	9																													
LARRY BIRD Larry C-OG 6'1 230 Edmonton Huskies Jrs.; Western Ontario B: 10/17/1945																															
1967	EDM	1																													
1971	SAS	16																													
1972	SAS	16																													
1973	SAS	16	0		1																										
1974	SAS	16																													
1975	SAS	16																													
1976	SAS	10																													
1977	SAS	16																													
1978	SAS	16	1		0																										
9	Years	123	1		1																										
STEVE BIRD Steven L. WR 5'11 171 Eastern Kentucky B: 10/20/1960 Indianapolis, IN Draft: 5-130 1983 STL; 11B-130 1983 WAS-USFL Pro: N																															
1985	EDM	2																	3	33	11.0	12	0	10	87	8.7	16	4	62	15.5	21
1986	MTL	5																	17	228	13.4	25	0								
2	Years	7																	20	261	13.1	25	0	10	87	8.7	16	4	62	15.5	21
LARRY BIRDINE Larry, Jr. DE 6'4 265 Oklahoma B: 10/6/1983 Altus, OK																															
2010	EDM	10	0	0	1	14																									
BOB BISACRE Robert C., Jr. C 5'11 192 Wyoming B: 4/11/1937																															
1962	OTT	14							1	5				3	5	1.7	5	0										3	35	11.7	17
PAT BISCEGLIA Pasquale G., Jr. G 5'10 192 Notre Dame B: 6/23/1931 Worcester, MA D: 2/7/2009 Shrewsbury, MA Draft: 29-347 1956 WAS																															
1956	MTL	4																													
PAUL BISCHOFF Paul Lawrence E 6'1 189 West Virginia B: 3/24/1930 Draft: 15-179 1952 NYG																															
1955	HAM	10							3	66		5	1						6	63	10.5	20	1	1	5	5.0	5	1	15	15.0	15
MICHAEL BISHOP Michael Paul QB 6'2 215 Blinn JC; Kansas State B: 5/15/1976 Galveston, TX Draft: 7A-227 1999 NE Pro: EN																															
2002	TOR	14	9	0	4	3						12	2	45	225	5.0	24	2													
2003	TOR	18				1								3	33	11.0	14	0													
2004	TOR	18	7	0	1	3						30	5	60	408	6.8	38	5													
2005	TOR	18				0								13	102	7.8	21	0													
2006	TOR	11				0						6	1	21	31	1.5	3	1													
2007	TOR	13	6	0	1	2								38	260	6.8	20	0													
2008	TOR	8	1	0	0	1								5	42	8.4	19	0													
2008	SAS	10	5	0	1	2						24	4	41	202	4.9	20	4													
2008	Year	18	6	0	1	3						24	4	46	244	5.3	20	4													
2009	WPG	14	9	0	0	3								19	84	4.4	10	0													
2011	CAL	5				0						6	1	6	17	2.8	10	1													
9	Years	119	37	0	7	15						78	13	251	1404	5.6	38	13													
RICHARD BISHOP Richard Allen DT-DE 6'1 265 Marshalltown CC; Louisville B: 3/23/1950 Cleveland, OH Draft: 5B-127 1974 CIN; 8-91 1974 POR-WFL Pro: N																															
1974	HAM	5																													
1975	HAM	2																													
1975	OTT	4																													
1975	Year	6																													
2	Years	7																													
SCOTT BISSESSAR Scott WR 5'9 154 Queen's B: 5/24/1962 Montreal, QC Draft: 4-29 1985 CAL																															
1985	CAL	9	0		1														1	22	22.0	22	0	1	0	0.0	0				
SCOTTY BISSETT Robert HB 5'9 181 Windsor AKO Jrs. B: 1931																															
1953	SAS	10												23	28	1.2		0	4	-1	-0.3		0								
JOHN BITCHOK John OHB-DB 5'11 195 Weston Wildcats Jrs.; Manitoba B: 4/22/1943 Draft: 1968 WPG																															
1968	WPG	13																						11	104	9.5	28				
BRUNO BITKOWSKI Bruno C-DE 6'2 220 Ottawa B: 1930																															
1951	OTT	8																													
1952	OTT	12																													
1953	OTT	14																													
1954	OTT	14																													
1955	OTT	12																													
1956	OTT	14							1	0																					
1958	OTT	14																													

Year	Team	GP	FM	FF	FR	TK	SK	YDS	IR	YDS	PD	PTS	TD	RA	YDS	AVG	LG	TD	REC	YDS	AVG	LG	TD	PR	YDS	AVG	LG	KOR	YDS	AVG	LG
1959	OTT	14																													
1960	OTT	14																													
1961	OTT	14																													
1962	OTT	10																													
11	Years	140							1	0																					
MICKEY BITSKO Michael LB 6'1 235 Notre Dame; Dayton B: 12/15/1942 Van Voorhis, PA Draft: 24-185(f) 1964 DEN; 9-124(f) 1964 NYG																															
1966	EDM	11	0		1																										
BARNEY BJARNSON William FW-HB 5'11 180 North Shore Jrs. B: 1929 Elfros, SK																															
1949	CAL	14																													
1950	CAL	14												4	9	2.3		0	3	72	24.0	28	0								
1951	CAL	12												1	3	3.0	3	0	1	39	39.0	39	0					1	11	11.0	11
1952	CAL	4																													
4	Years	44												5	12	2.4	3	0	4	111	27.8	39	0					1	11	11.0	11
KAI BJORN Kai OT 6'5 290 Bishop's B: 7/13/1968 Montreal, QC																															
1995	OTT	17				1																									
1996	OTT	4				0																									
1997	WPG	7				0																									
1997	MTL	3				0																									
1997	Year	10				0																									
3	Years	28				1																									
DAVID BLACK David OT-OG-DL 6'3 245 Oshawa Hawkeyes Jrs.; Wilfrid Laurier B: 4/13/1962 Oshawa, ON Draft: 3-25 1984 WPG																															
1985	WPG	10																													
1986	WPG	11																													
1987	WPG	18				1																									
1988	WPG	18				0																									
1989	WPG+	17				0																									
1990	WPG	18				2																									
1991	WPG	17				2																									
1992	WPG	18	0		1	1																									
1993	WPG*	18				2																									
1994	WPG+	16				1																									
1995	WPG	5				0																									
1995	OTT	12				1																									
1995	Year	17				1																									
11	Years	166	0		1	10																									
FRED BLACK Fred OG-C-MG 6'0 220 Toronto Argonauts Jrs. B: 1930																															
1949	TOR	7																													
1950	TOR	12																													
1951	TOR	11																													
1952	TOR	9																													
1953	TOR	11																													
1954	TOR	14																													
1955	TOR	12							1	8																					
1956	TOR	14										2	0																		
1957	TOR	14																													
1959	TOR	14																													
1960	TOR	14																	1	34	34.0	34	0					2	1	0.5	4
11		132							1	8		2	0						1	34	34.0	34	0					2	1	0.5	4
GREG BLACK Gregory OG-OT 6'5 310 North Carolina B: 9/14/1973 Pro: E																															
1996	HAM	1				0																									
LEONARD BLACK Leonard E 6'1 200 Duke B: 1935																															
1957	TOR	3																	3	54	18.0	36	0								
MATT BLACK Matt CB-DH 5'9 187 Saginaw Valley State B: 3/1/1985 Toronto, ON Draft: 6C-45 2008 TOR																															
2009	TOR	6				5																		3	20	6.7	13	1	19	19.0	19
2010	TOR	13	1	0	0	20					1													1	1	1.0	0				
2011	TOR	18	0	0	1	17					1	6	1															1	7	7.0	7
3	Years	37	1	0	1	42					2	6	1											4	21	5.3	13	2	26	13.0	19
RICK BLACK Rick FB 6'0 210 Mount Allison B: 1943 Draft: 1A-3 1963 OTT																															
1963	OTT	14										20	1	7	17	2.4	5	0	1	10	10.0	10	1	14	84	6.0	11				
1964	OTT	14	1									12	2	30	180	6.0	20	1	5	66	13.2	27	1	39	191	4.9	14				
1965	OTT	14	2		1							18	3	84	480	5.7	73	3	8	123	15.4	47	0	58	354	6.1	19				
1966	OTT	12										13	2	39	300	7.7	40	1	8	93	11.6	25	1	28	146	5.2	18				
1967	OTT	6	1		0							18	3	51	223	4.4	15	1	3	70	23.3	45	2								
1968	OTT	9										6	1	28	109	3.9	11	1	3	13	4.3	7	0								
6	Years	69	4		1							87	12	239	1309	5.5	73	7	28	375	13.4	47	5	139	775	5.6	19				
STEVEN BLACK Steven Lynn WR-SB 6'3 213 East Mississippi CC; Memphis B: 12/11/1986 Birmingham, AL																															
2010	BC	10				1						30	5	1	13	13.0	13	0	22	370	16.8	65	5								
2011	BC	1				0								1	5	5.0	5	0	2	17	8.5	9	0								
2	Years	11				1						30	5	2	18	9.0	13	0	24	387	16.1	65	5								
TERRY BLACK Terry HB Ottawa Sooners Jrs.																															
1969	OTT	14	2		0									3	6	2.0	6	0						8	71	8.9	11				
TRISTAN BLACK Tristan J. LB 6'3 243 Wayne State (Michigan) B: 4/8/1984 Toronto, ON Draft: 2-16 2009 CAL																															
2009	CAL	5				12																									
2010	TOR	9				14																						2	15	7.5	8
2011	TOR	18				25			1	5	0													3	87	29.0	81	3	5	1.7	3
3	Years	32				51			1	5	0													3	87	29.0	81	5	20	4.0	8
BILL BLACKBURN William Whitford, Jr. C 6'5 228 Southwestern Louisiana JC; Rice B: 2/5/1923 Welutka, OK D: 4/17/2007 Draft: 5-33 1944 CHIC Pro: N																															
1951	CAL	14										10	2																		
1952	CAL+	15			2																										
2	Years	29			2							10	2																		
TRAY BLACKMON Tray LB 6'0 220 Auburn B: 10/20/1985 LaGrange, GA																															
2009	CAL	7	0	1	0	31					1																				
PAUL BLACKWOOD Paul FB 6'1 225 Cincinnati B: 6/8/1972 Scarborough, ON Draft: 5-39 1994 BC																															
1995	BC	18	2		0	14						12	2	24	67	2.8	8	1	7	85	12.1	42	1								
1996	BC	18				15								2	6	3.0	4	0	3	52	17.3	38	0					1	2	2.0	2
1998	BC	1				1																									
1998	SAS	1				0																									
1998	Year	2				1																									
1999	WPG	18	1	0	1	7								3	20	6.7	14	0	7	56	8.0	16	0					1	3	3.0	3
2000	TOR	3				0																									
5	Years	58	3	0	1	37						12	2	29	93	3.2	14	1	17	193	11.4	42	1					2	5	2.5	3
JOHNNY BLAICHER John LB-FB-FW 5'11 190 none B: 3/5/1930 Hamilton, ON D: 3/13/2006																															
1953	MTL	14																													
1954	MTL	12							4	25																					
1955	MTL	12							2	20		1	0															5	60	12.0	21
1956	MTL	11							2	70		2	0	3	17	5.7	10	0	1	3	3.0	3	0								
1957	MTL	14							1	5				5	28	5.6	14	0													
1958	MTL	14							1	10				8	31	3.9	7	0													
1959	MTL	7										1	0															1	6	6.0	6
7	Years	84							10	130		4	0	16	76	4.8	14	0	1	3	3.0	3	0					6	66	11.0	21
JOHN BLAIN John OG-OT 6'6 265 San Jose State B: 2/1/1955 North Vancouver, BC Draft: TE 1977 BC; 11-285 1977 NO																															
1977	BC	11	0		1																										

Year	Team	GP	FM	FF	FR	TK	SK	YDS	IR	YDS	PD	PTS	TD	RA	YDS	AVG	LG	TD	REC	YDS	AVG	LG	TD	PR	YDS	AVG	LG	KOR	YDS	AVG	LG
1978	BC	16	0		1																										
1979	BC	16																													
1980	BC	16	0		1																										
1981	BC	16																													
1982	BC	16																													
1983	BC*	16	0		1																										
1984	BC*	16	0		1																										
1985	BC*	16																													
1986	BC	18																													
1987	BC+	17	0		1	0																									
11	Years	174	0		6	0																									
BILL BLAIR Bill OE 6'3 220 Mount Allison; East York Argos Jrs. B: 1941																															
1965	TOR	4	1		0														3	30	10.0	16	0								
DON BLAIR Donald SB 6'0 195 Calgary B: 4/6/1972 Ottawa, ON Draft: 1A-1 1996 EDM																															
1996	EDM	8				6						6	1						1	35	35.0	35	0	12	181	15.1	85				
1997	EDM	17	2	0	1	4						20	3						36	623	17.3	47	3	18	221	12.3	56				
1998	EDM	18	2	0	1	6						38	6						64	1091	17.0	51	6	24	214	8.9	35				
1999	BC	18	2	0	0	1						32	5						61	785	12.9	47	5								
2000	BC	15	0	0	1	0						24	4						46	631	13.7	50	4	1	14	14.0	14				
2001	BC	5				0													10	147	14.7	29	0								
2002	CAL	17				2						24	4						46	751	16.3	55	4	3	14	4.7	10				
2003	CAL	18				3						24	4						46	579	12.6	45	4								
8	Years	116	6	0	3	22						168	27						310	4642	15.0	55	26	58	644	11.1	85				
EARL BLAIR Earl E. HB 5'10 175 Mississippi B: 1/10/1934 Pascagoula, MS D: 12/25/2004 Overland Park, KS																															
1956	TOR	6							2	29		12	2	6	24	4.0	10	0	3	47	15.7	21	2	4	14	3.5	9	3	48	16.0	20
JACK BLAIR Jack LB 6'1 192 Hamilton Hurricanes Jrs. B: 10/19/1956																															
1978	HAM	15																													
1979	HAM	16	0		2							6	1											1	0	0.0	0				
1980	HAM	5	0		1																										
1980	TOR	1																													
1980	Year	6	0		1																										
1981	HAM	13																													
4	Years	49	0		3							6	1											1	0	0.0	0				
STANLEY BLAIR Stanley R. CB 6'0 192 Oklahoma State; Southeastern Oklahoma State B: 7/4/1964 Pine Bluff, AR Pro: N																															
1987	EDM	18				57			4	118		6	1											0	17		17	1	1	1.0	1
1988	EDM*	18			4	42			4	3														1	3	3.0	3				
1989	EDM*	18	0		2	38			7	23																					
3	Years	54	0		6	137			15	144		6	1											1	20	20.0	17	1	1	1.0	1
WAYNE BLAIR Wayne LB 6'1 227 Tulane B: 8/12/1975 Toronto, ON																															
1999	CAL	1				1																									
1999	MTL	3				2																									
1999	Year	4				3																									
2000	TOR	4	0	0	1	3																									
2	Years	5	0	0	1	6																									
EDDIE BLAKE Robert Edward OT-OG 6'4 300 Northwest Mississippi JC; Auburn B: 12/18/1969 Fayetteville, TN Draft: 2-43 1992 MIA																															
1996	WPG	9				0																									
2000	WPG	2				0																									
2	Years	11				0																									
EMORY BLAKE Emory SB-RB 6'1 225 Bethune-Cookman B: 10/11/1950																															
1974	TOR	1																	1	16	16.0	16	0								
JAMES BLAKE James DB 6'0 200 Tulsa B: 7/4/1971 San Springs, OK																															
1994	LV	4			1	10																									
JOE BLAKE Joe DE 6'2 280 Northwestern; Bakersfield JC; Tulsa B: 8/31/1944 East Chicago, IN Draft: 9-223 1968 NO																															
1971	MTL	14							1	18																					
JOHN BLAKE John OG 6'6 260 San Jose State B: 9/1/1952 Vancouver, BC Draft: TE 1978 BC																															
1978	BC	12																													
1979	BC	16	0		2																										
1980	BC	4																													
1981	HAM	16	0		1																										
4	Years	48	0		3																										
P.L. BLAKE Pressley Larcus DE 6'1 212 Mississippi State B: 8/18/1936																															
1960	EDM	1																													
1961	SAS	2																	3	84	28.0	52	0								
1962	SAS	5																	1	10	10.0	10	0								
3	Years	8																	4	94	23.5	52	0								
RICKY BLAKE Ricky Darnell RB 6'2 244 Northwest Mississippi JC; Alabama A&M* B: 7/15/1967 Fayetteville, TN Pro: EN																															
1989	WPG	6	2		0	4						12	2	81	354	4.4	20	1	8	46	5.8	15	1								
BOB BLAKELY Robert Irvin HB 5'11 197 Minnesota B: 12/30/1935 St. Paul, MN																															
1968	TOR	1																	1	5	5.0	5	0								
JEFF BLANCHARD Jeff LB 6'2 230 Rutgers B: 6/15/1959																															
1982	HAM	11					3.0																								
JOE BLANCHARD Joseph E. T 6'2 220 Kansas State B: 12/7/1928 Haskell, OK																															
1951	EDM	11																													
1952	EDM	13			1							5	1						1	13	13.0	13	1	1	24	24.0	24				
1953	EDM	13																										1	0	0.0	0
1954	CAL	1																													
4	Years	38			1							5	1						1	13	13.0	13	1	1	24	24.0	24	1	0	0.0	0
LEO BLANCHARD Leo OG 6'4 260 Edmonton Huskies Jrs.; Alberta B: 3/12/1955 Edmonton, AB																															
1979	EDM	2																													
1980	EDM	16																													
1981	EDM	16																													
1982	EDM+	16	0		3																										
1983	EDM*	16	0		1																										
1984	EDM+	16	0		1																										
1985	EDM+	16	0		3									1	37	37.0	26	0													
1986	EDM*	18																													
1987	EDM	18				5																									
1988	BC	6				0																									
1988	CAL	10				2																									
1988	Year	16				2																									
1989	CAL	18	0		1	1													0	25		25	0								
1990	CAL+	16				2																									
1991	CAL	18	0		1	0																									
13	Years	192	0		10	10								1	37	37.0	26	0	0	25		25	0								
CARL BLAND Carl Nathaniel WR 5'11 182 Virginia Union B: 8/17/1961 Fluvanna County, VA Pro: N																															
1991	CAL	14	1		1	4						18	3						56	903	16.1	47	3	8	94	11.8	47	3	47	15.7	29
1992	CAL	18	1		0	4						24	4						72	1052	14.6	79	4	1	2	2.0	2				
2	Years	32	2		1	8						42	7						128	1955	15.3	79	7	9	96	10.7	47	3	47	15.7	29
TOM BLAND Tom FL 5'11 170 Oklahoma; West Liberty State B: 7/2/1940 Wheeling, WV																															
1970	TOR	13										30	5						29	480	16.6	45	5	22	174	7.9	23	1	7	7.0	7
JERRY BLANTON Gerald DE-LB 6'1 225 Kentucky B: 12/20/1956 Toledo, OH Draft: 11-282 1978 BUF Pro: N																															
1978	HAM	1																													

Year	Team	GP	FM	FF	FR	TK	SK	YDS	IR	YDS	PD	PTS	TD	RA	YDS	AVG	LG	TD	REC	YDS	AVG	LG	TD	PR	YDS	AVG	LG	KOR	YDS	AVG	LG
MIKE BLANTON Michael J. DE-DT 6'5 246 Georgia Tech B: 2/19/1957 Fort Riley, KS Draft: 11-299 1979 MIA																															
1979	BC	1																													
1980	BC	1																													
1980	SAS	7																													
1980	Year	8																													
2	Years	2																													
JOHN BLEDSOE John A. FB 6'1 224 Ohio State B: 6/15/1951 Cleveland, OH D: 6/30/2002 North Olmsted, OH Draft: 8B-203 1973 DET																															
1973	WPG	9	3		0							18	3	158	811	5.1	34	3	25	262	10.5	21	0					2	29	14.5	16
1974	WPG	9	2		0							30	5	134	623	4.6	33	4	16	155	9.7	26	1								
1974	OTT	1																	1	9	9.0	9	0								
1974	Year	10	2		0							30	5	134	623	4.6	33	4	17	164	9.6	26	1								
1975	OTT	5	1		0							18	3	30	142	4.7	38	2	3	28	9.3	23	1								
3	Years	23	6		0							66	11	322	1576	4.9	38	9	45	454	10.1	26	2					2	29	14.5	16
PAUL BLENKHORN Paul OL 6'3 290 Western Ontario B: 6/9/1976 Sarnia, ON Draft: 5-37 2000 CAL																															
2000	CAL	1				0																									
2001	CAL	3				0																									
2	Years	4				0																									
CHRIS BLEUE Chris TE 6'4 240 Washburn B: 7/24/1965 Toronto, ON Draft: 2A-12 1988 CAL																															
1988	CAL	6				1																									
CARROLL BLOOM Carroll (Red) HB-E-C 6'0 175 none B: 3/11/1928 Ottawa, ON																															
1946	OTT	5																													
1947	SAS	8																													
2	Years	13																													
AL BLOOMINGDALE Alan RB 6'2 210 Maryland B: 3/1/1953																															
1975	OTT	2												8	23	2.9	14	0										1	18	18.0	18
1975	TOR	3												18	102	5.7	26	0	2	55	27.5	51	0					2	26	13.0	14
1975	Year	5												26	125	4.8	26	0	2	55	27.5	51	0					3	44	14.7	18
1976	TOR	5										6	1	33	116	3.5	9	0	4	38	9.5	22	1					1	19	19.0	19
2	Years	7										6	1	59	241	4.1	26	0	6	93	15.5	51	1					4	63	15.8	19
ERIC BLOUNT Eric Lamont RB 5'9 192 North Carolina B: 9/22/1970 Ayden, NC Draft: 8-202 1992 PHX Pro: N																															
1995	EDM	9	4		1	4						72	12	98	677	6.9	51	6	40	543	13.6	98	5	15	173	11.5	60	29	645	22.2	70
1996	EDM	18	4		1	1						24	4	246	1091	4.4	55	4	43	275	6.4	24	0	10	48	4.8	12	16	277	17.3	41
1997	EDM	17	3	0	1	2								177	672	3.8	24	0	44	365	8.3	31	0	1	9	9.0	9	13	200	15.4	36
1998	WPG*	18	5	0	0	5						38	6	123	544	4.4	28	3	45	339	7.5	55	0	78	1051	13.5	92	64	1695	26.5	96
1999	TOR	4	4	0	0	1						6	1	26	65	2.5	32	1	9	116	12.9	33	0	24	175	7.3	33	4	54	13.5	18
1999	MTL	3				0								4	2	0.5	2	0						9	33	3.7	9	9	111	12.3	21
1999	Year	7	4	0	0	1						6	1	30	67	2.2	32	1	9	116	12.9	33	0	9	33	3.7	9	13	165	12.7	21
2001	WPG	18	1	0	0	2						42	7	122	586	4.8	57	5	34	379	11.1	40	2	1	2	2.0	2	20	417	20.9	43
2002	WPG	1				0								6	15	2.5	7	0	5	22	4.4	8	0	1	2	2.0	2				
7	Years	85	21	0	3	15						182	30	802	3652	4.6	57	19	220	2039	9.3	98	7	139	1493	10.7	92	155	3399	21.9	96
ERIC BLOUNT Eric C. LB 6'0 240 Houston B: 4/20/1970																															
1994	TOR	3				8																									
1995	TOR	5				14	1.0	3.0																							
2	Years	8				22	1.0	3.0																							
ANTHONY BLUE Anthony Allen DB 5'9 185 Nevada-Las Vegas B: 9/19/1964 Inglewood, CA Pro: N																															
1994	LV	14	0		2	23																									
LUTHER BLUE Luther J. WR 5'11 180 Iowa State B: 10/21/1954 Valdosta, GA Draft: 4-96 1977 DET Pro: N																															
1981	TOR	1																	2	23	11.5	16	0								
LEROY BLUGH Leroy LB 6'2 230 Bishop's B: 5/14/1966 St. Vincent Draft: 1B-7 1989 EDM																															
1989	EDM	18	0		2	8																									
1990	EDM	14				28	3.0		1	3																		1	9	9.0	9
1991	EDM	18				34	7.0												2	30	15.0	16	0								
1992	EDM	18	0		2	44	7.0	41.0				6	1															1	12	12.0	12
1993	EDM	18	0		2	47	7.0	41.0																							
1994	EDM	18	0		1	24	9.0	63.0				6	1																		
1995	EDM	18	0		1	28	10.0	77.0			1																				
1996	EDM+	14				19	11.0	82.0																							
1997	EDM	18	0	1	0	26	7.0	64.0																							
1998	EDM+	15	0	1	1	32	8.0	56.0				6	1																		
1999	EDM	16				16	5.0	32.0																							
2000	TOR	9	0	2	0	4	2.0	10.0																				3	29	9.7	12
2001	TOR	12				13																									
2002	TOR	10	0	0	1	10	1.0																								
14	Years	216	0	4	10	333	77.0	466.0	1	3	1	18	3						2	30	15.0	16	0					5	50	10.0	12
MIKE BLUM Michael LB-FB 6'0 225 Northern Michigan B: 10/24/1943 Ottawa, ON D: 12/15/2008																															
1964	OTT	14	0		2																										
1965	OTT	7																										1	7	7.0	7
1966	OTT	14	0		3				1	0																					
1967	OTT+	14																													
1968	TOR	8																													
1969	TOR	14																													
1970	TOR	14	0		2				2	18																					
1971	HAM+	14	0		5				2	0																					
1972	HAM	14							1	0																					
1973	TOR	14	0		1				2	11																					
1974	TOR	3																													
11	Years	130	0		13				8	29																		1	7	7.0	7
NICK BLUM Nick HB Regina Eastend Bombers Jrs.																															
1947	SAS	1																													
1948	SAS	11																													
2	Years	12																													
JOHN BLYTH John LB 6'2 230 Marquette B: 1939																															
1960	CAL	9	0		1																										
BRUCE BOA Bruce T Western Ontario B: 7/10/1930 Calgary, AB D: 4/17/2004 London, England																															
1952	CAL	7																													
SHANNON BOATMAN Shannon D'Ville OT 6'6 342 Tyler JC; Florida State B: 11/24/1984 Beaumont, TX																															
2010	TOR	5				0																									
HUBERT BOBO Hubert Lee FB-HB 6'1 217 Ohio State B: 7/2/1934 Athens, OH Draft: 13-146(f) 1957 PHI Pro: N																															
1958	HAM	3												38	110	2.9	12	0	6	66	11.0	19	0								
ORLANDO BOBO Orlando Lamont OG 6'3 306 East Mississippi CC; Louisiana-Monroe B: 2/9/1974 West Point, MS D: 5/14/2007 Dallas, TX Pro: N																															
2004	WPG	16				0																									
PHILLIP BOBO Phillip L. WR 5'11 186 Washington State B: 12/6/1971 Pro: E																															
1999	EDM	2				0													2	40	20.0	28	0	2	9	4.5	5				
KEN BOCHEN Ken OT-DT 6'3 235 Winnipeg Rods Jrs.; St. Vital Bulldogs Ints. B: 1939 Winnipeg, MB																															
1959	WPG	2																													
JOSH BODEN Josh WR 6'1 205 South Fraser Rams Jrs. B: 7/17/1986 Vancouver, BC																															
2007	BC	18	1	0	0	8													14	237	16.9	49	0	2	7	3.5	4				
AL BODINE Alvin DB-OHB 5'10 197 Georgia B: 1928 Draft: 17-216 1950 PIT																															
1950	SAS+	13										36	7	71	296	4.2		3	5	99	19.8		3								
1951	SAS	11										10	2	52	189	3.6		1	2	17	8.5		1					7	117	16.7	
2	Years	24										46	9	123	485	3.9	0	4	7	116	16.6		4					7	117	16.7	
TROY BODINE Troy M. QB 6'1 215 Cincinnati B: 6/21/1963 Westminster, CA Draft: 11A-149 1985 BAL-USFL																															

Year	Team	GP	FM	FF	FR	TK	SK	YDS	IR	YDS	PD	PTS	TD	RA	YDS	AVG	LG	TD	REC	YDS	AVG	LG	TD	PR	YDS	AVG	LG	KOR	YDS	AVG	LG
1985	OTT	4	1		0									1	-2	-2.0	-2	0													
MEL BOEHLAND Melvin George DE-DT 6'3 250 North Dakota B: 4/21/1943 Bertha, MN																															
1966	CAL	1																													
MARC BOERIGTER Marc Robert WR 6'3 220 Hastings B: 5/4/1978 Sioux Center, IA Pro: N																															
2000	CAL	18	1	0	1	1						56	9						63	1092	17.3	63	8								
2001	CAL+	18				1						68	11	3	25	8.3	17	0	48	931	19.4	72	11	1	0	0.0	0	0	41		41
2007	CAL	6	1	0	0	2						6	1						16	246	15.4	70	1								
2007	TOR	7				1													6	77	12.8	19	0								
2007	Year	13	1	0	0	3						6	1						22	323	14.7	70	1								
3	Years	42	2	0	1	5						130	21	3	25	8.3	17	0	133	2346	17.6	72	20	1	0	0.0	0	0	41		41
JOEY BOESE Joey DH 5'11 185 Wisconsin B: 2/8/1980																															
2003	CAL	12	0	0	1	40			2	2	3													1	11	11.0	11	1	11	11.0	11
2004	CAL+	18	0	1	0	105			3	4	3																				
2005	CAL	11	0	0	1	42			2	17	3																				
2006	CAL	2				4																									
4	Years	43	0	1	2	191			7	23	9													1	11	11.0	11	1	11	11.0	11
ARMAND BOGLIN Armand T. LB 6'1 215 Utah B: 6/25/1973 Ontario, CA																															
2001	SAS	3				0																									
2002	SAS	1				0																									
2	Years	4				0																									
STEVE BOHUNICKI Steve FL none																															
1946	WPG	1																													
ROSS BOICE Henry Ross DT 6'2 245 Pacific Lutheran B: 7/31/1949 Bellingham, WA Draft: 16-409 1971 LARM																															
1971	BC	3																													
1972	BC	3																													
2	Years	6																													
JOHN BOICH John G 6'0 243 McMaster; Hamilton Panthers Ints. B: 1933																															
1954	OTT	9																													
1955	OTT	11																													
1956	OTT	5																													
3	Years	25																													
MICHAEL BOIREAU Michael Innocent DE 6'4 274 Northeast Mississippi CC; Miami (Florida) B: 7/24/1978 Miami, FL Draft: 2B-56 2000 MIN																															
2002	OTT	13				22	3.0				2																				
DEMONTE' BOLDEN Demonte' DT 6'5 290 Tennessee B: 11/17/1985 Chattanooga, TN																															
2009	HAM	13				21	1.0	2.0			1																				
2010	HAM	17	0	0	2	39	2.0	13.0			1																				
2	Years	30	0	0	2	60	3.0	15.0			2																				
JURAN BOLDEN Juran T. CB-DH 6'2 205 Mississippi Delta CC B: 6/27/1974 Washington, DC Draft: 4B-127 1996 ATL Pro: N																															
1995	WPG	9	1		1	18			6	28	4																	1	2	2.0	2
2000	WPG	14	0	1	1	40			4	66	4																				
2001	WPG*	18	0	1	1	61			6	142	10	6	1																		
2007	WPG	5				11			1	7	0																				
4	Years	46	1	2	3	130			17	243	18	6	1															1	2	2.0	2
TAVARES BOLDEN Tavares QB 6'1 250 Toledo B: 6/8/1979 Cleveland, OH																															
2002	MTL	18				0					1			7	46	6.6	19	0													
2003	MTL	18	1	0	0	0								9	47	5.2	14	0													
2004	MTL	18				0																									
3	Years	54	1	0	0	0					1			16	93	5.8	19	0													
D.J. BOLDIN Demir Javon WR 6'0 220 Wake Forest B: 6/20/1986 Pahokee, FL																															
2011	TOR	2				0													3	35	11.7	27	0								
ANDRE BOLDUC Andre SB 6'0 200 Concordia (Quebec) B: 3/25/1971 Alma, QC																															
1996	OTT	18	2		0	12						8	1	32	121	3.8	15	0	32	287	9.0	24	1								
1997	EDM	9	2	0	1	7								6	17	2.8	9	0	2	52	26.0	41	0								
1998	MTL	12	0	0	1	8																									
1999	MTL	18				8													3	38	12.7	23	0								
2000	MTL	16				11													1	16	16.0	16	0								
2001	MTL	12	0	0	1	9						6	1	2	11	5.5	9	0													
6	Years	85	4	0	3	55						14	2	40	149	3.7	15	0	38	393	10.3	41	1								
LANNY BOLESKI Anthony L. OT-OG-LB 6'4 250 Mount Royal College; Wyoming B: 1941 Red Deer, AB																															
1965	CAL	16																													
1966	CAL	16																													
1967	CAL	16																													
1968	CAL	16																													
1969	CAL+	16																													
1970	CAL+	16																													
1971	CAL	16																										1	0	0.0	0
1972	CAL	16	0		1																										
1973	CAL	16																													
1974	BC	16	1		0																							1	0	0.0	0
10	Years	160	1		1																							2	0	0.0	0
GUY BOLIAUX Guy Joseph LB 6'0 200 Wisconsin B: 9/21/1959 Chicago, IL Draft: 11-283 1982 CHIB																															
1983	WPG	1																													
BO BOLINGER Virgil Lee G 5'10 206 Oklahoma B: 1933 Draft: 13-149 1956 CHIC																															
1956	EDM	2																													
GRADY BOLTON Grady DT 6'2 250 Mississippi State B: 1943 Draft: 5-34 1966 MIA; 15-228 1966 GB																															
1966	SAS	1	0		1																										
NATHANIEL BOLTON Nathaniel L. WR 5'11 200 Mississippi College B: 7/1/1968 Mobile, AL Pro: E																															
1993	WPG	12	1		0	3						36	6	2	6	3.0	17	0	42	730	17.4	57	5	49	325	6.6	71	20	494	24.7	55
1994	WPG	3				0													6	76	12.7	27	0	3	15	5.0	8	1	24	24.0	24
2	Years	15	1		0	3						36	6	2	6	3.0	17	0	48	806	16.8	57	5	52	340	6.5	71	21	518	24.7	55
JASON BOLTUS Jason C 6'4 225 Hartwick B: 8/21/1986 Baldwinsville, NY																															
2011	HAM	18				0								2	16	8.0	12	0													
NEREO BOLZON Nereo LB 6'1 210 Alberta B: 7/27/1960 Draft: TE 1982 EDM																															
1982	EDM	7																										1	16	16.0	16
RYAN BOMBEN Ryan OG 6'4 299 Guelph B: 5/16/1987 Burlington, ON Draft: 4-31 2010 MTL																															
2011	MTL	18	0	0	1	1																									
JOSEPH BONAVENTURA Joseph LB 5'10 235 St. Mary's (Nova Scotia) B: 8/9/1977 Draft: 3B-26 2003 EDM																															
2004	CAL	15	0	1	0	12																						3	39	13.0	25
JIM BOND James DE-DT 6'3 245 Simon Fraser B: 4/24/1949 Draft: 3A-26 1971 CAL																															
1971	CAL	16																													
1972	CAL	16																													
1973	CAL	16																													
1974	CAL	16																													
1975	CAL	9																													
5	Years	73																													
BRACY BONHAM Bracy Herman, Jr. OG 6'2 242 North Carolina Central B: 4/10/1950 Winston-Salem, NC D: 10/10/2003 Winston-Salem, NC Draft: 9-232 1973 PIT Pro: W																															
1973	TOR	5																													
JOHN BONK John C-LB-DE-OG 6'2 245 Burlington Braves Jrs. B: 8/27/1950 Hamilton, ON																															
1972	HAM	1																													
1973	HAM	10																													
1973	WPG	5																													
1973	Year	15																													

Year	Team	GP	FM	FF	FR	TK	SK	YDS	IR	YDS	PD	PTS	TD	RA	YDS	AVG	LG	TD	REC	YDS	AVG	LG	TD	PR	YDS	AVG	LG	KOR	YDS	AVG	LG
1974	WPG	16	0		1																							1	6	6.0	6
1975	WPG	16										1	0																		
1976	WPG	16																													
1977	WPG	16																										1	4	4.0	4
1978	WPG	16	0		1																										
1979	WPG	16	0		1																							1	0	0.0	0
1980	WPG	16	1		0																										
1981	WPG	16																													
1982	WPG*	16	0		1																										
1983	WPG*	16																													
1984	WPG*	16																													
1985	WPG*	14	1		0																										
14	Years	201	2		4							1	0															3	10	3.3	6
ROGER BONK Roger Franklin LB 5'11 230 North Dakota B: 6/9/1944 Chippewa County, MN																															
1967	WPG	15	0		1				1	14																		2	29	14.5	15
ANTONIOUS BONNER Antonious DB-LB 6'1 200 Mississippi Delta CC; Mississippi B: 9/3/1972 Chicago, IL																															
1995	OTT	9	2		1	24			2	44	3																	10	201	20.1	36
1997	TOR	8	0	1	2	25	1.0	8.0	2	0	3																				
1998	TOR	17	0	0	5	53	1.0	7.0	3	76	6	6	1																		
1999	TOR	18	0	1	1	51			3	88	3																				
2000	TOR	12	0	0	2	36			4	15	2																				
2001	TOR	2				7	1.0	15.0	1	36		6	1																		
2002	TOR	17	0	2	1	51			1	75	7	6	1																		
2003	TOR	18	0	3	0	79	1.0	7.0	2	19	4																				
2004	TOR	18	0	3	2	81	5.0	31.0	1	9	4																				
2005	TOR	8	0	1	1	28	1.0	2.0	0	0	3																				
2006	TOR	15	0	0	1	64	1.0		0	0	4																				
11	Years	142	2	11	16	499	11.0	70.0	19	362	39	18	3															10	201	20.1	36
BRIAN BONNER Brian K. LB 6'1 225 Wisconsin; Minnesota B: 10/9/1965 Mount Vernon, NY Draft: 9-247 1988 SF Pro: N																															
1991	OTT+	15	0		3	84	9.0																								
1992	OTT	15	0		1	49	4.0	24.0																							
1993	SAS	10	0		1	40	1.0	8.0																							
1993	OTT	7				27	3.0	12.0																							
1993	Year	17				67	4.0	20.0																							
1994	OTT	16	0		1	63	2.0	6.0	0	0	1																				
1995	SHR	4				15																									
5	Years	60	0		6	278	19.0	50.0																							
BRIAN BONNER Brian Michael CB-LB 5'11 195 Texas Christian B: 4/13/1984 San Patricio County, TX Pro: U																															
2011	EDM	4	2	0	1	1																		3	3	1.0	3	6	101	16.8	27
PAT BONNETT Pat OG-DE 6'3 239 Idaho State B: 9/11/1951 Draft: TE 1973 MTL																															
1973	MTL	14																										2	26	13.0	19
1974	MTL	12																													
1975	MTL	16	0		1																										
1976	MTL	16	1		0																										
1977	MTL	12																													
1978	MTL	16																													
1979	MTL	5																													
7	Years	91	1		1																							2	26	13.0	19
DANTE BOOKER Dante L. DT 6'3 275 Auburn B: 10/9/1977 Akron, OH																															
2004	BC	18	0	1	1	24	3.0																								
2006	WPG	1				1			0	0	1																				
2	Years	19	0	1	1	25	3.0																								
DARRELL BOOKER Darrell L. LB 5'11 230 Delaware B: 12/19/1964																															
1989	OTT	2				10																									
FRED BOOKER Fred DB 5'9 199 Louisiana State B: 6/4/1978 Independence, LA Pro: EN																															
2004	MTL	1				0																									
VAUGHN BOOKER Vaughn Jamel DE 6'5 298 Cincinnati B: 2/24/1968 Cincinnati, OH Pro: N																															
1992	WPG	15	0		4	36	2.0	7.0																				1	3	3.0	3
1993	WPG	9				18	4.0	16.0																							
2	Years	24	0		4	54	6.0	23.0																				1	3	3.0	3
ANTHONY BOOKMAN Anthony Rashad RB 5'7 190 Stanford B: 1/11/1976 Dallas, TX																															
1998	TOR	3	1	0	1	1								6	41	6.8	26	0						17	122	7.2	22	7	187	26.7	35
ADAM BOOMER Adam S. LB 6'1 235 Montana B: 11/22/1977 Kamiah, ID																															
2001	WPG	4	0	2	0	5																									
DAVE BOONE Humphrey David, Jr. DE 6'3 248 Eastern Michigan B: 10/30/1951 Detroit, MI D: 3/19/2005 Point Roberts, WA Draft: 11-285 1974 MIN; 24-277 1974 DET-WFL Pro: N																															
1975	BC	6																													
1976	HAM	16			2																							1	1	1.0	1
1977	EDM+	16	0		1																										
1978	EDM	16																													
1979	EDM+	16																													
1980	EDM	16	0		3																										
1981	EDM*	16	0		2		14.5																								
1982	EDM	14	0		2		6.0		1	38		6	1																		
1983	EDM	16	0		1		6.0																								
1984	TOR	15	0		1		2.5																								
10	Years	147	0		12		29.0		1	38		6	1															1	1	1.0	1
STEVE BOORAS Steve DE 6'4 250 Mesa JC B: 4/29/1948 Draft: 12-298 1971 CHIB; 12-296 1972 NE Pro: W																															
1970	MTL+	8																													
1976	MTL	1																													
2	Years	9																													
DORIAN BOOSE Dorian Alexander DE 6'5 292 Walla Walla CC; Washington State B: 1/29/1974 Frankfurt, West Germany Draft: 2-56 1998 NYJ Pro: N																															
2003	EDM	16	0	1	0	44	7.0		0	0	3																				
2004	EDM	3				3																									
2	Years	19	0	1	0	47	7.0																								
BILLY JOE BOOTH Billy Joe DE-OT 6'0 230 Louisiana State B: 4/7/1940 D: 6/30/1972 London, ON Draft: 13-181 1962 NYG																															
1962	OTT	14																													
1963	OTT+	14																													
1964	OTT+	14	0		3																										
1965	OTT	14																													
1966	OTT+	14	0		1																										
1967	OTT	11	0		1																										
1968	OTT	14							1	-4																					
1969	OTT*	14	0		2																										
1970	OTT	14																													
9	Years	123	0		7				1	-4																					
BERT BORDER Bert T-G 230 Saskatchewan																															
1946	CAL	8																													
1948	CAL	2																													
2	Years	10																													
JAMIE BOREHAM Jamie K-P 5'11 202 British Columbia; Saskatchewan; Manitoba B: 3/29/1978 Vancouver, BC Draft: 2-16 2001 BC																															
2004	HAM	12	2	0	2	5						99	0	1	4	4.0	4	0													

Year	Team	GP	FM	FF	FR	TK	SK	YDS	IR	YDS	PD	PTS	TD	RA	YDS	AVG	LG	TD	REC	YDS	AVG	LG	TD	PR	YDS	AVG	LG	KOR	YDS	AVG	LG
2005	HAM	18	3	0	1	7						117	0																		
2006	HAM	15				2						100	0																		
2007	SAS	18	2	0	0	7						10	0																		
2008	SAS	18				7						8	0																		
2009	SAS	13	5	0	1	4						9	0	2	8	4.0	5	0													
2010	TOR	14	1	0	0	5								1	4	4.0	4	0													
2011	WPG	3	1	0	0	1						2	0																		
8	Years	111	14	0	4	38						345	0	4	16	4.0	5	0													
JOCELYN BORGELLA Jocelyn Kenza CB 5'10 180 Cincinnati B: 8/26/1971 Nassau, Bahamas Draft: 6-183 1994 DET Pro: EN																															
1997	WPG	5				31			1	112	4																				
1998	BC	8	0	0	1	51			1	35	3																				
2	Years	13	0	0	1	82			2	147	7																				
JOHN BORGER John LB 6'0 195 Edmonton Huskies Jrs. B: 1935 Lynburn, AB																															
1956	CAL	3																													
1957	CAL	16							1	34																					
2	Years	19							1	34																					
JOSH BORGER Joshua SB-TE 6'3 207 Edmonton Wildcats Jrs.; Calgary B: 7/5/1958 Draft: TE 1981 EDM																															
1981	EDM	2																													
1981	TOR	4																													
1981	Year	6																													
SALEEM BORHOT Saleem S 6'2 195 Okanagan Suns Jrs.; St. Mary's (Nova Scotia) B: 6/28/1985 Calgary, AB Draft: 2-12 2010 EDM																															
2010	EDM	5	0	0	1	9																									
TOM BORIS Tom HB 6'1 186 Purdue B: 1942 Draft: 10-128 1964 PHI																															
1964	HAM	1												4	11	2.8	5	0	1	12	12.0	12	0								
GEORGE BORK George P. QB 6'1 177 Northern Illinois B: 2/8/1942 Mount Prospect, IL																															
1964	MTL	11	2		0									16	63	3.9	18	0													
1966	MTL	11	1		0									13	51	3.9	17	0													
1967	MTL	6												6	23	3.8	11	0													
3	Years	28	3		0									35	137	3.9	18	0													
DAVE BOSSON Dave T 6'1 245 Duke B: 1940																															
1961	BC	1																													
GEORGE BOSSY George Walter E 6'1 190 McGill; Lakeshore Flyers Ints. B: 5/21/1927																															
1952	MTL	1																													
DAVID BOSTON David Byron WR 6'2 224 Ohio State B: 8/19/1978 Humble, TX Draft: 1A-8 1999 ARI Pro: N																															
2008	TOR	1				0													2	16	8.0	12	0								
MIKE BOTTERILL Michael LB 6'2 225 McMaster B: 11/9/1980 Belleville, ON Draft: 6B-51 2003 MTL																															
2003	MTL	18	0	1	0	36																									
2004	MTL	18				34	2.0	8.0	0	0	3																				
2005	MTL	15				40	1.0	6.0																							
2006	MTL	1				3																									
2006	EDM	14				5																									
2006	Year	15				8																									
2007	EDM	18				18	1.0	7.0																							
2008	HAM	16				11																									
2009	CAL	1				1																									
7	Years	87	0	1	0	148	4.0	21.0																							
LYNN BOTTOMS Lynn FL-LB-DB 5'10 185 Washington; Calgary Bronks Jrs. B: 1933																															
1954	CAL	16	3		0				1	19		20	4	81	379	4.7	19	2	30	368	12.3	22	1	25	142	5.7	16	5	93	18.6	21
1955	CAL	16	7		4				1	17		10	2	85	402	4.7	20	1	19	312	16.4	57	1	23	175	7.6	28	12	252	21.0	28
1956	CAL	16	2		1				3	25		33	5	61	332	5.4	23	5	9	100	11.1	24	0	19	113	5.9	18	11	248	22.5	40
1957	CAL	15	5		2				1	0				70	326	4.7	21	0	21	249	11.9	35	0	56	330	5.9	16	7	113	16.1	35
1958	CAL	16	2		1				2	5		6	1	16	90	5.6	16	0	1	5	5.0	5	1	70	507	7.2	21	1	16	16.0	16
1959	CAL	16	1		3				2	22		12	2	1	11	11.0	11	0	4	74	18.5	37	1	79	441	5.6	17				
1960	CAL	5	1		0				2	26														15	80	5.3	11	1	28	28.0	28
1960	TOR	3																	1	11	11.0	11	0	7	52	7.4	16	3	75	25.0	31
1960	Year	8	1		0				2	26									1	11	11.0	11	0	22	132	6.0	16	4	103	25.8	31
1961	TOR	13												7	20	2.9	10	0	9	142	15.8	37	0	48	251	5.2	14				
1962	TOR	14																	2	21	10.5	14	0	53	319	6.0	15	7	107	15.3	21
1963	TOR	10																						31	156	5.0	14	1	13	13.0	13
10	Years	137	21		11				12	114		81	14	321	1560	4.9	23	8	96	1282	13.4	57	4	426	2566	6.0	28	52	1048	20.2	40
JACK BOUCHARD Jack T 6'1 195 Weston Wildcats Jrs. B: 1930																															
1950	WPG	9																													
REG BOUDREAU Reg OHB-P 5'10 180 Saskatoon Hilltops Jrs. B: 5/13/1956																															
1979	SAS	10										15	0	6	30	5.0	12	0	3	20	6.7	12	0								
1979	HAM	3																													
1979	Year	13												6	30	5.0	12	0	3	20	6.7	12	0								
ETIENNE BOULAY Etienne S-LB-CB 5'9 189 New Hampshire B: 3/10/1983 Montreal, QC Draft: 2-16 2006 MTL																															
2006	MTL	18	0	0	1	33			2	14	3																				
2007	MTL	15	0	0	1	32			3	39	7																				
2008	MTL	8	1	0	0	22			1	2	1																				
2009	MTL	18				30			1	0	2																				
2010	MTL	17	0	1	1	40			4	70	2																				
2011	MTL	4				13					1																				
6	Years	80	1	1	3	170			11	125	16																				
MATHIEU BOULAY Mathieu DE 6'2 250 Bishop's B: 11/23/1987 Montreal, QC																															
2011	SAS	10	0	1	0	1																									
MICHEL BOURGEAU Michel DT-NT-LB 6'5 275 Boise State B: 6/28/1961 Montreal, QC Draft: TE 1984 OTT; 11-291 1984 NO; 11-220 1984 CHI-USFL																															
1984	OTT	6	0		1																										
1985	OTT	16	0		1		4.0		1	0																					
1986	OTT	17					4.0																								
1987	OTT	14	0		2	40	4.0																								
1988	OTT	13	0		1	24	3.0																								
1989	EDM	16				8																									
1990	EDM	12	0		3	13	2.0																								
1991	EDM	13				19	4.0																								
1992	EDM	18				15	1.0	8.0																							
1993	EDM	17	0		1	14																									
10	Years	142	0		9	133	22.0	8.0	1	0																					
JOSH BOURKE Josh OT 6'7 310 Grand Valley State B: 10/16/1982 Tecumseh, ON Draft: 3A-21 2004 MTL																															
2007	MTL	8				0																									
2008	MTL+	16				1																									
2009	MTL+	14				0																									
2010	MTL+	18	0	0	1	2																									
2011	MTL*	16	0	0	2	0																									
5	Years	72	0	0	3	3																									
WILLIE BOUYER Willie Louis WR 6'3 200 Michigan State B: 9/24/1966 Detroit, MI Pro: EN																															
1993	SAC	6	1		0	2						12	2						15	175	11.7	31	2								
1994	SAC	8	1		0	0													6	101	16.8	26	0								
2	Years	14	2		0	2						12	2						21	276	13.1	31	2								
DAN BOVAIR Daniel DB 6'1 185 Wilfrid Laurier B: 5/13/1953 Draft: TE 1977 HAM																															
1977	HAM	16	1		0									1	0	0.0	0	0	2	15	7.5	9	0	9	101	11.2	44	4	52	13.0	24
1978	HAM	3																													

Year	Team	GP	FM	FF	FR	TK	SK	YDS	IR	YDS	PD	PTS	TD	RA	YDS	AVG	LG	TD	REC	YDS	AVG	LG	TD	PR	YDS	AVG	LG	KOR	YDS	AVG	LG
1978	TOR	3																													
1978	Year	6																													
2	Years	19	1		0									1	0	0.0	0	0	2	15	7.5	9	0	9	101	11.2	44	4	52	13.0	24
REG BOVAIRD Reg T 6'1 230 B: 1922 D: 3//2001																															
1948	HAM	8																													
1949	HAM	4																													
2	Years	12																													
JOHN BOVE John Louis T-G 6'0 225 Sampson; West Virginia B: 4/14/1924 Auburn, NY Draft: 19-224 1951 PHI																															
1951	OTT	9																													
1952	OTT	10																													
1953	OTT	4																													
1955	OTT	4																													
1959	OTT	13																													
5	Years	40																													
DAVID BOVELL David W. DB 6'0 210 Colgate B: 1/24/1966 London, England Draft: 2-11 1990 WPG																															
1990	WPG	18	0		2	48	2.0		2	17														1	8	8.0	8				
1991	WPG	7				13																									
1991	TOR	2				6			1	38																					
1991	Year	9				19			1	38																					
1992	TOR	3				9																									
1992	SAS	5				6			2	3																					
1992	Year	8				15			2	3																					
3	Years	28	0		2	82	2.0		5	58														1	8	8.0	8				
DAVE BOWEN Dave HB-FL 6'0 184 NDG Maple Leafs Jrs. B: 11/11/1942 Montreal, Q																															
1964	MTL	14												4	23	5.8	16	0	10	106	10.6	18	0								
1966	MTL	3																													
2	Years	17												4	23	5.8	16	0	10	106	10.6	18	0								
ORLANDO BOWEN Orlando DB 6'2 238 Northern Illinois B: 6/25/1975 Montego Bay, Jamaica Draft: 6-43 1999 EDM																															
2000	TOR	9				2																									
2001	TOR	18	0	0	2	17																									
2002	TOR	18	0	1	0	14																									
2003	HAM	16	0	0	2	15																									
4	Years	61	0	1	4	48																									
CECIL BOWENS Cecil Bernard RB 6'3 235 Kentucky B: 12/24/1950 Bloomfield, KY Draft: 14-346 1974 NE; 23-272 1974 PHI-WFL Pro: W																															
1973	MTL	4	2		0									16	53	3.3	21	0	2	15	7.5	12	0					1	20	20.0	20
BILL BOWERMAN Bill QB 6'2 200 New Mexico State B: 6/27/1953 Rochester, NY Draft: 10-279 1976 DET																															
1977	CAL	3																													
SAM BOWERS Sam Tyrone TE 6'4 250 Westchester CC*; Tennessee State*; Fordham B: 12/22/1957 White Plains, NY Pro: NU																															
1981	TOR	1	1		1																										
RANDY BOWLES Randy FB 6'1 226 Simon Fraser B: 2/23/1978 Fort St. John, BC Draft: 3-20 2001 HAM																															
2001	HAM	16				6						6	1	2	7	3.5	5	1	3	27	9.0	18	0								
2002	HAM	18				24													1	9	9.0	9	0					1	12	12.0	12
2003	TOR	15	2	1	0	4						12	2	21	120	5.7	31	1	11	81	7.4	23	1								
2004	WPG	11	1	0	1	3								1	-4	-4.0	-4	0													
2004	CAL	4	1	0	0	0								5	7	1.4	5	0	1	5	5.0	5	0					4	35	8.8	10
2004	Year	15	2	0	1	3								6	3	0.5	5	0	1	5	5.0	5	0					4	35	8.8	10
4	Years	60	4	1	1	37						18	3	29	130	4.5	31	2	16	122	7.6	23	1					5	47	9.4	12
TREVOR BOWLES Trevor OT 6'5 280 San Jose State B: 5/30/1961 North Vancouver, BC Draft: 2-11 1984 MTL																															
1984	MTL	5																													
1985	MTL	11																													
1986	MTL	17																													
1987	EDM	10				0																									
1988	EDM	17			2	1																									
1989	EDM	11				0																									
1990	EDM	18	0		2	1																									
1991	EDM	18	0		1	1																									
8	Years	107	0		5	3																									
BO BOWLING Bo WR 5'9 183 Northeastern Oklahoma A&M JC; Oklahoma State B: 11/1/1987 Ponca City, OK																															
2011	MTL	1	1	0	0	1													1	21	21.0	21	0	3	28	9.3	14	1	14	14.0	14
ADARIUS BOWMAN Adarius SB-WR 6'4 219 North Carolina; Oklahoma State B: 7/10/1985 Chattanooga, TN																															
2008	SAS	9				0						18	3						23	358	15.6	73	3								
2009	WPG	15	2	0	0	2						42	6						55	925	16.8	55	6								
2010	WPG	12	2	0	1	1						18	3	2	9	4.5	8	0	50	691	13.8	63	3								
2011	EDM	14	2	0	3	0						24	4						62	1153	18.6	74	4	0	44		44	0	5		5
4	Years	50	6	0	4	3						102	16	2	9	4.5	8	0	190	3127	16.5	74	16	0	44		44	0	5		5
DON BOWMAN Don DB-WR 6'0 185 Western Ontario B: 7/27/1952 Draft: 1B-4 1975 WPG																															
1975	WPG	13	0		1				1	18														15	186	12.4	37				
1976	WPG	16	0		1																										
1977	HAM	12	0		1				1	0																		3	58	19.3	25
1977	WPG	1																													
1977	Year	13	0		1				1	0																		3	58	19.3	25
1978	HAM	16																													
4	Years	57	0		3				2	18														15	186	12.4	37	3	58	19.3	25
JOHN BOWMAN John DE 6'3 253 Wingate B: 7/19/1982 New York, NY																															
2006	MTL	11	0	2	0	14	2.0	19.0																							
2007	MTL	14	0	1	2	26	7.0	57.0																							
2008	MTL	18	0	1	2	38	8.0	57.0																							
2009	MTL+	18	0	5	1	35	12.0	95.0																				1	0	0.0	0
2010	MTL*	18	0	4	0	32	12.0	54.0			3																				
2011	MTL	18	0	2	1	33	12.0	82.0			2																				
6	Years	97	0	15	6	178	53.	364.0			5																	1	0	0.0	0
KEVIN BOWMAN Kevin J. WR 6'3 205 Sacramento JC; San Jose State B: 2/23/1962 Sacramento, CA Draft: TD 1985 OAK-USFL Pro: N																															
1987	BC	2				0													4	43	10.8	13	0								
MARCELLUS BOWMAN Marcellus R. LB 6'3 231 Boston College B: 10/12/1986																															
2010	WPG	14	0	0	2	59	3.0	11.0	1	11	3																				
2011	WPG	16	0	4	0	60	4.0	25.0			2																				
2	Years	30	0	4	2	119	7.0	36.0	1	11	5																				
WALT BOWYER Walter Nathaniel, Jr. DE 6'4 260 Arizona State B: 9/8/1960 Pittsburgh, PA Draft: 10-254 1983 DEN Pro: N																															
1985	EDM	1					2.0																								
AB BOX Albert George P Malvern Grads Jrs. B: 3/8/1909 Toronto, ON D: 7/29/2000																															
1950	MTL	1																													
PHIL BOYCE Phil WR 5'11 176 Azusa Pacific B: 3/16/1955																															
1977	MTL	2																	1	6	6.0	6	0								
CORY BOYD Cory J. RB 6'1 218 South Carolina B: 8/6/1985 Orange, NJ Draft: 7-238 2008 TB Pro: N																															
2010	TOR*	15	5	0	2	1						48	8	226	1359	6.0	49	6	38	363	9.6	66	2								
2011	TOR+	14	2	0	0	3						36	6	187	1141	6.1	64	6	22	118	5.4	18	0								
2	Years	29	7	0	2	4						84	14	413	2500	6.1	64	12	60	481	8.0	66	2								
JEFF BOYD Jeffrey Santee WR 6'2 180 Los Angeles Southwest JC; Colorado; Chapman B: 4/17/1958 Los Angeles, CA																															
1983	WPG	14	1		1							42	7	2	9	4.5	6	0	50	974	19.5	75	7								
1984	WPG	16										66	11	1	0	0.0	0	0	65	1106	17.0	79	11								
1985	WPG*	15	2		1							90	15	5	57	11.4	20	1	76	1372	18.1	105	14								
1986	WPG	7	2		1							30	5						35	619	17.7	80	5								

Year	Team	GP	FM	FF	FR	TK	SK	YDS	IR	YDS	PD	PTS	TD	RA	YDS	AVG	LG	TD	REC	YDS	AVG	LG	TD	PR	YDS	AVG	LG	KOR	YDS	AVG	LG
1987	WPG	16				3						54	9						57	1039	18.2	67	9								
1988	TOR	16	1		1	1						66	11	1	-8	-8.0	-8	0	65	1159	17.8	78	11								
1989	TOR	9	1		0	1						6	1						35	540	15.4	48	1								
1990	TOR	17	1		0	4						50	8						59	1053	17.8	76	8								
1991	TOR	9				1						18	3						22	460	20.9	85	3								
9	Years	119	8		4	10						422	70	9	58	6.4	20	1	464	8322	17.9	105	69								
THOMAS BOYD Thomas Taylor LB 6'2 210 Alabama B: 11/24/1959 Huntsville, AL Draft: 8-210 1982 GB Pro: NU																															
1982	SAS	5					1.0		1	2																					
1983	SAS	3																													
2	Years	8					1.0		1	2																					
TRACY BOYD Tracy Jerome OG-OT 6'4 296 Pearl River CC; Southern University*; Arkansas-Pine Bluff; Elizabeth City State B: 8/27/1967 Lake Charles, LA Draft: 6-165 1992 NE																															
1995	MEM	4				1																									
1995	WPG	3				1																									
1995	Year	7				2																									
MAX BOYDSTON Max Ray OE 6'2 210 Oklahoma B: 1/22/1932 Ardmore, OK D: 12/12/1998 Muskogee, OK Draft: 1-2 1955 CHIC Pro: N																															
1959	HAM	2																	2	26	13.0	15	0								
GARLAND BOYETTE Garland Dean LB 6'1 237 Grambling State B: 3/22/1940 Rayville, LA Pro: NW																															
1964	MTL	9	0		2																										
1965	MTL	14	0		1																										
2	Years	23	0		3																										
ALLAN BOYKO Allan SB-WR 6'2 175 Western Michigan B: 3/2/1967 Hamilton, ON Draft: 3-19 1990 WPG																															
1991	SAS	13	1		0	2																		5	82	16.4	37	4	53	13.3	26
1993	WPG	17				10			1	30		18	3						7	108	15.4	27	3	63	299	4.7	20	27	446	16.5	43
1994	WPG	18	1		0	3						6	1						5	115	23.0	47	1	73	415	5.7	27	5	91	18.2	24
1995	WPG	18	2		1	1						12	2						23	258	11.2	30	2	35	182	5.2	21				
1996	WPG	17				4						6	1						27	370	13.7	49	1	6	18	3.0	8				
1997	WPG	16	0	0	1	7						12	2						30	280	9.3	29	2								
6	Years	99	4	0	2	27			1	30		54	9						92	1131	12.3	49	9	182	996	5.5	37	36	590	16.4	43
BRUCE BOYKO Bruce SB 6'3 210 Western Michigan B: 3/2/1967 Hamilton, ON Draft: 2A-9 1990 SAS																															
1990	SAS	18	0		1	0								1	2	2.0	2	0	18	259	14.4	24	0								
1991	SAS	18	0		1	28													5	44	8.8	12	0					2	-7	-3.5	6
1992	SAS	17	0		1	26													1	19	19.0	19	0					2	0	0.0	0
1993	SAS	18	2		3	13						12	2	20	72	3.6	10	0	30	299	10.0	28	2					2	1	0.5	1
1994	SAS	18	1		0	12													11	143	13.0	51	0	1	-11	-11.0	-11				
1995	SAS	18	3		2	10								2	5	2.5	3	0	25	274	11.0	31	0					2	14	7.0	14
1996	SAS	17	0		1	13						6	1	1	4	4.0	4	0	17	206	12.1	78	1								
1997	WPG	18	0	0	1	15						6	1	6	19	3.2	5	0	29	247	8.5	25	1	1	6	6.0	6				
1998	BC	3				1																									
1998	WPG	11				10													2	8	4.0	6	0								
1998	Year	14				11													2	8	4.0	6	0								
1999	WPG	12				4						6	1	1	3	3.0	3	0	16	125	7.8	17	1								
10	Years	157	6	0	10	132						30	5	31	105	3.4	10	0	154	1624	10.5	78	5	2	-5	-2.5	6	8	8	1.0	14
SHERMAR BRACEY Shermar RB 6'2 225 Coffeyville JC; Arkansas State B: 7/11/1982 Chicago, IL																															
2006	SAS	10	0	0	1	1						18	3	38	233	6.1	63	3	10	85	8.5	17	0								
KEN BRADEN Kenneth R. LB 6'0 230 Missouri State B: 5/28/1965 Memphis, TN																															
1988	OTT	16	0		3	70	4.0																								
1989	OTT	2				5																									
2	Years	18	0		3	75	4.0																								
TOMMY BRADEN Tommie Ray DB 5'11 175 Northwestern State (Louisiana) B: 11/14/1955 Shreveport, LA																															
1979	SAS	7																													
NORMAN BRADFORD Norman RB 6'3 200 Grambling State B: 10/10/1971 Jonesboro, LA																															
1995	SHR	18	3		2	32						30	5	40	213	5.3	28	2	46	586	12.7	80	3								
1996	MTL	5	4		0	0						38	6	77	465	6.0	34	6	17	205	12.1	41	0								
2	Years	23	7		2	32						68	11	117	678	5.8	34	8	63	791	12.6	80	3								
PATRICK BRADFORD Patrick DT 6'2 290 Georgia Tech B: 11/20/1975 New York, NY Pro: E																															
2002	BC	2	0	1	1	5																									
CHUCK BRADLEY Charles Warren, II OT 6'5 296 Kentucky B: 4/9/1970 Covington, KY Draft: 6-158 1993 HOU Pro: EN																															
1995	MEM	7	0		1	1																									
1996	TOR	12				3																									
1997	BC	14	1	0	1	1																									
3	Years	33	1	0	2	5																									
DICK BRADLEY Richard G 6'0 215 Louisiana State																															
1952	CAL	1																													
ED BRADLEY Edward William, II OG 6'0 212 Wake Forest B: 9/16/1926 Stratford, CT Draft: 16-206 1950 CHIB Pro: N																															
1953	MTL+	13										5	1																		
1954	TOR	12																													
2	Years	25										5	1																		
GERALD BRADLEY Gerald WR 6'1 180 Weber State B: 1/16/1961 Pro: U																															
1983	BC	1																	2	12	6.0	7	0								
1986	MTL	2																	3	35	11.7	23	0								
2	Years	3																	5	47	9.4	23	0								
JERRY BRADLEY Jerrold David CB-S 5'10 170 California B: 6/6/1945 San Francisco, CA																															
1967	TOR	3												1	-5	-5.0	-5	0	1	4	4.0	4	0	1	7	7.0	7	7	183	26.1	26
1968	BC	16	2		0				4	144				2	1	0.5	2	0	3	31	10.3	14	0	102	471	4.6	36	14	329	23.5	44
1969	BC+	16							9	179									1	52	52.0	52	0	20	160	8.0	27				
1970	BC	16	0		1				9	188		6	1						1	27	27.0	27	0	102	566	5.5	29				
4	Years	51	2		1				22	511		6	1	3	-4	-1.3	2	0	6	114	19.0	52	0	225	1204	5.4	36	21	512	24.4	44
JYKINE BRADLEY Jykine CB-DH 5'9 188 Middle Tennessee State B: 6/5/1980 Knoxville, TN Pro: E																															
2005	HAM	4				3			3	78	2	6	1																		
2006	HAM	14	0	0	2	47			1	13	3																				
2007	HAM	2				3			2	6	0																				
2008	HAM	15	0	1	0	39			3	42	2	6	1																		
2009	HAM	17	0	0	1	40			2	59	3	6	1																		
2010	HAM	6	0	1	0	15					1																				
2011	EDM	17	0	0	2	31			2	0	8																				
7	Years	75	0	2	5	178			13	198	19	18	3																		
MARCUS BRADLEY Marcus DH 6'0 200 Western Carolina B: 10/20/1976 Gaffney, SC																															
2000	CAL	4				9			1	5																					
2003	CAL	2				0																									
2		6				9			1	5																					
MELVIN BRADLEY Melvin DT 6'2 271 Arkansas B: 8/15/1976 Helena, AR Draft: 6B-202 1999 ARI Pro: N																															
2002	CAL	16	1	1	2	54	5.0	29.0			1																				
2004	WPG	12	0	1	0	30	2.0																								
2	Years	28	1	2	2	84	7.0	29.0			1																				
MIKE BRADLEY Mike RB 5'8 205 Waterloo B: 9/16/1979 Haliburton, ON																															
2002	EDM	18	1	0	1	12								12	35	2.9	7	0	1	18	18.0	18	0								
2003	EDM	17	0	0	1	10	1.0	12.0				6	1	6	59	9.8	42	0	2	15	7.5	12	0	1	3	3.0	3	10	352	35.2	92
2004	EDM	18				12								2	40	20.0	39	0	3	32	10.7	20	0					25	609	24.4	67
2005	EDM	13	1	0	2	6						12	2	17	87	5.1	60	1	3	11	3.7	7	0	1	0	0.0	0	18	410	22.8	65
2006	EDM	16				6								2	4	2.0	2	0										3	50	16.7	22
2007	EDM	18	2	0	0	7																						6	88	14.7	32
6	Years	100	4	0	4	53	1.0	12.0				18	3	39	225	5.8	60	1	9	76	8.4	20	0	2	3	1.5	3	62	1509	24.3	92

Year	Team	GP	FM	FF	FR	TK	SK	YDS	IR	YDS	PD	PTS	TD	RA	YDS	AVG	LG	TD	REC	YDS	AVG	LG	TD	PR	YDS	AVG	LG	KOR	YDS	AVG	LG
OTHA BRADLEY Otha M. DT 6'2 260 Los Angeles CC; Southern California B: 1/18/1952 St. Joseph, LA Draft: 10-242 1975 SD																															
1975	BC	3																													
ROYLIN BRADLEY Roylin T. LB 6'2 232 Texas A&M B: 7/15/1978 Galveston, TX																															
2003	WPG	1	0	1	0	1																									
MIKE BRADWELL Michael SB-WR 6'3 199 McMaster B: 7/11/1986 Toronto, ON Draft: 2-13 2008 TOR																															
2009	TOR	18	0	0	1	2						6	1						25	350	14.0	40	1								
2010	TOR	18	1	0	0	1						6	1						10	108	10.8	18	1					1	3	3.0	3
2011	TOR	17	1	0	1	2						6	1						24	298	12.4	44	1								
3	Years	53	2	0	2	5						18	3						59	756	12.8	44	3					1	3	3.0	3
BOB BRADY Robert OG-LB 6'0 220 British Columbia B: 1932 Sault Ste. Marie, ON																															
1956	BC	16																													
1957	BC	14																													
1958	BC	16							1	22		6	1																		
1959	BC	13																										1	0	0.0	0
1960	BC	1																													
1961	TOR	7																													
6	Years	67							1	22		6	1															1	0	0.0	0
DALE BRADY Dale OHB-DB 6'0 210 Memphis B: 1947 Draft: 7-186 1968 CLE																															
1968	BC	13	1		0							6	1	46	226	4.9	21	1	24	224	9.3	32	0					2	46	23.0	31
1969	BC	4	2		0									23	99	4.3	12	0	9	81	9.0	15	0					2	41	20.5	24
2	Years	17	3		0							6	1	69	325	4.7	21	1	33	305	9.2	32	0					4	87	21.8	31
DONNY BRADY Donny Maynard DH 6'2 195 Nassau CC; Wisconsin B: 11/24/1973 North Bellmore, NY Pro: N																															
1995	SAS	2				3			1	2	0																				
2002	EDM	16	0	3	0	43					5			5	27	5.4	11	0													
2003	EDM*	16	0	7	1	51			6	43	4	6	1																		
2004	EDM	18	0	0	1	68			5	16	8																				
2005	EDM+	18	0	0	1	51			1	20	2																				
2006	EDM	6				14			1	6	0																				
6	Years	76	0	10	3	230			14	87	19	6	1	5	27	5.4	11	0													
JIM BRADY James T., Jr. E St. Mary's (California); Buffalo B: 2/3/1926 Niagara Falls, NY D: 8/27/2008 Wilson, NY																															
1948	HAM	12																													
JIM BRADY Jim QB 6'3 215 Arizona State B: 8/29/1951 Scottsdale, AZ																															
1973	MTL	5												4	14	3.5	8	0	2	23	11.5	13	0								
MARCUS BRADY Marcus Lorenzo QB 6'0 195 Northridge State B: 9/24/1979 San Diego, CA																															
2002	TOR	5				0								4	23	5.8	10	0													
2003	TOR	18	4	0	1	0						12	2	18	149	8.3	26	2													
2004	HAM	18	3	0	1	1						6	1	19	120	6.3	19	1													
2005	HAM	16	5	0	2	2						6	1	16	109	6.8	16	1													
2006	MTL	18	2	0	0	0								13	45	3.5	12	0													
2007	MTL	17	2	0	0	0						12	2	48	223	4.6	25	2													
2008	MTL	15	2	0	1	1								4	10	2.5	4	0													
7	Years	107	18	0	5	4						36	6	122	679	5.6	26	6													
PAT BRADY Patrick Thomas QB 6'1 195 Nevada-Reno; Bradley B: 9/7/1926 Seattle, WA D: 7/14/2009 Reno, NV Draft: 13-155 1952 NYG Pro: N																															
1952	HAM	1										1	0																		
PAT BRADY Pat OG 6'1 240 London Beefeaters Jrs.; Western Ontario B: 4/17/1960 Toronto, ON																															
1983	HAM	16	1		0																							1	8	8.0	8
1984	HAM	16	0		1																										
1985	HAM	16	0		1																										
1986	HAM	18	1		0																										
1987	HAM	18				0																									
5	Years	84	2		2	0																						1	8	8.0	8
PHIL BRADY Philip Alonzo CB-OHB 6'3 210 Brigham Young B: 4/22/1943 Mesa, AZ Pro: N																															
1966	MTL	14	0		1				2	36				29	202	7.0	33	0	13	117	9.0	23	0					5	81	16.2	24
1967	MTL+	14	1		2				2	61		18	3	13	72	5.5	13	1	11	236	21.5	57	1	38	298	7.8	70	5	131	26.2	31
1968	MTL	10																						8	73	9.1	18	2	29	14.5	15
3	Years	38	1		3				4	97		18	3	42	274	6.5	33	1	24	353	14.7	57	1	46	371	8.1	70	12	241	20.1	31
MARK BRAGAGNOLO Mark RB 6'1 215 Toronto B: 10/20/1955 Timmins, ON Draft: TE 1977 TOR																															
1977	TOR	18	1		1							6	1	52	261	5.0	23	0	3	49	16.3	21	1					1	38	38.0	38
1978	TOR	14	5		0							30	5	82	377	4.6	19	3	25	160	6.4	30	2								
1979	TOR	14	2		0							6	1	48	118	2.5	15	1	9	64	7.1	18	0								
1980	WPG	16	3		1							6	1	62	239	3.9	15	1	34	324	9.5	36	0								
1981	HAM	13	1		2							12	2	73	278	3.8	16	2	22	242	11.0	34	0								
1982	HAM	16	1		0							44	7	99	384	3.9	19	3	38	470	12.4	60	4								
1983	HAM	15	3		0							12	2	40	197	4.9	12	0	33	257	7.8	20	2								
1984	HAM	14	1		1							18	3	54	223	4.1	19	3	32	256	8.0	19	0								
8	Years	120	17		5							134	22	510	2077	4.1	23	13	196	1822	9.3	60	9					1	38	38.0	38
DAVE BRAGGINS David M., Jr. OG-DE 6'2 245 Florida State B: 1/9/1945 D: 7/19/2004 Tampa, FL																															
1968	OTT	14	0		1																										
1969	OTT	10	0		1																										
1970	OTT	14	0		2																										
1971	OTT	14																													
1972	MTL	12																	1	1	1.0	1	0								
1973	MTL	14																													
1974	MTL	13																													
1975	MTL*	16																													
1976	MTL*	11																													
9	Years	118	0		4														1	1	1.0	1	0								
ADAM BRAIDWOOD Adam DE-DT 6'4 274 Washington State B: 6/1/1984 Delta, BC Draft: 1-1 2006 EDM																															
2006	EDM	15	0	5	2	20	4.0	22.0				6	1																		
2007	EDM	17	0	2	1	34	7.0	72.0																							
2010	EDM	14				13	1.0	10.0			1																				
3	Years	46	0	7	3	67	12.0	104.0			1	6	1																		
GEORGE BRAJCIK George LB 6'2 222 British Columbia B: 1945																															
1967	BC	7																													
LARRY BRAME Lawrence Ray LB-DT 6'1 215 Western Kentucky B: 7/20/1948 Hopkinsville, KY Draft: 16-407 1971 STL Pro: W																															
1971	TOR	10	0		1																										
1972	TOR	1																													
1973	HAM	12	0		3																										
1974	HAM	14	0		1																										
1977	HAM	4																													
1977	TOR	6							1	0																					
1977	Year	10							1	0																					
1978	TOR	5							1	14																					
6	Years	46	0		5				2	14																					
CASEY BRAMLET Casey QB 6'4 225 Wyoming B: 4/2/1981 Casper, WY Draft: 7-218 2004 CIN Pro: E																															
2009	WPG	9				0																									
GEORGE BRANCATO George CB-FL 5'9 177 Santa Ana JC; Louisiana State B: 5/27/1931 New York, NY Pro: N																															
1956	MTL	8							1	9		12	2	46	213	4.6	17	0	30	459	15.3	54	2	14	97	6.9	15	5	91	18.2	31
1957	OTT	14							7	61		30	5	16	40	2.5	16	0	25	776	31.0	84	5					3	58	19.3	27
1958	OTT	14							7	58		24	4						21	405	19.3	46	4								
1959	OTT	14							1	32				1	8	8.0	8	0													
1960	OTT	14							6	24		12	2	1	1	1.0	1	0	6	115	19.2	27	2	2	6	3.0	3				

Year	Team	GP	FM	FF	FR	TK	SK	YDS	IR	YDS	PD	PTS	TD	RA	YDS	AVG	LG	TD	REC	YDS	AVG	LG	TD	PR	YDS	AVG	LG	KOR	YDS	AVG	LG
1961	OTT+	13							4	51		6	1						12	209	17.4	21	1								
1962	OTT	9							3	11																					
7	Years	86							29	246		84	14	64	262	4.1	17	0	94	1964	20.9	84	14	16	103	6.4	15	8	149	18.6	31
CLAIR BRANCH Clair M. FB-LB 6'1 207 Texas B: 1938 Draft: SS 1960 HOU																															
1960	SAS	15	3		2							30	5	107	514	4.8	28	4	18	192	10.7	35	1					1	12	12.0	12
1961	SAS	8										6	1	26	149	5.7	28	1	2	39	19.5	28	0	1	0	0.0	0				
1962	SAS	10												10	52	5.2	12	0													
1963	SAS	4																	1	8	8.0	8	0								
1963	EDM	4												24	75	3.1	7	0													
1963	Year	8												24	75	3.1	7	0	1	8	8.0	8	0								
1964	EDM	1																													
5	Years	38	3		2							36	6	167	790	4.7	28	5	21	239	11.4	35	1	1	0	0.0	0	1	12	12.0	12
DARRICK BRANCH Darrick Dion WR 5'11 195 Hawaii B: 2/10/1970 Dallas, TX Draft: 8A-220 1993 TB Pro: E																															
1993	TOR	2				0																						2	41	20.5	31
1994	TOR	5				0						6	1						10	127	12.7	25	1	8	123	15.4	39	13	264	20.3	33
1995	TOR	8	0		1	6						18	3	1	14	14.0	14	0	20	367	18.4	61	2	2	30	15.0	24	15	339	22.6	95
2002	BC	2				1													4	54	13.5	25	0	2	31	15.5	18	1	15	15.0	15
4	Years	17	0		1	7						24	4	1	14	14.0	14	0	34	548	16.1	61	3	12	184	15.3	39	31	659	21.3	95
JESSE BRANCH Jesse O. DB 5'11 186 Arkansas B: 2/1/1941 Pine Bluff, AR																															
1963	CAL	1																													
1964	CAL	15	1		1				3	24		18	3	2	-8	-4.0	2	0	1	33	33.0	33	1	29	306	10.6	105	2	48	24.0	26
1965	EDM	1	1		0									1	-2	-2.0	-2	0	3	46	15.3	19	0					2	43	21.5	27
3	Years	17	2		1				3	24		18	3	3	-10	-3.3	2	0	4	79	19.8	33	1	29	306	10.6	105	4	91	22.8	27
PHIL BRANCH Joseph Philip G 6'0 205 Texas B: 1931 Draft: 9-105 1954 PHI																															
1956	SAS	13	0		2				1	6																					
CHARLIE BRANDON Charles OG-OT-DE 6'3 255 Shaw B: 9/13/1943 Norfolk, VA																															
1967	WPG	1																													
1972	OTT	14	0		1																										
1973	OTT	14																													
1974	OTT	16	0		2																										
1975	OTT	1																													
1976	OTT	15																													
1977	OTT	16																													
1978	OTT+	11	0		1																										
8	Years	88	0		4																										
DWAN BRANDON Dwan LB 6'1 214 Northern Arizona B: 1/26/1969 Portland, OR																															
1991	CAL	12	0		1	39	2.0					6	1																		
GARY BRANDT Gary OG-OT-C-LB 6'1 220 Washington B: 4/11/1943																															
1967	SAS	11																													
1968	SAS	16																													
1969	SAS	16	1		0																							1	0	0.0	0
1970	SAS	16	0		2																										
1971	SAS	16	1		0																							0	4		4
1972	SAS	16																													
1973	SAS	16	0		1																										
1974	SAS	16	1		0																										
1975	SAS	16	0		1																										
1976	SAS	16																													
1977	SAS	16	0		1																										
11	Years	171	3		5																							1	4	4.0	4
JACK BRANDT Jack QB 5'10 185 Bemidji State B: 1940																															
1963	SAS	4																													
JIM BRANDT James Richard HB 6'1 200 St. Thomas (Minnesota) B: 5/19/1929 Fargo, ND Draft: 12-140 1951 PIT Pro: N																															
1955	MTL	1												9	37	4.1	11	0													
DANNY BRANNAGAN Danny QB 6'0 195 Queen's B: 7/4/1986 Burlington, ON																															
2010	TOR	2				0								1	2	2.0	2	0													
STEVE BRANNON Steve DT 6'4 280 Hampton B: 11/27/1968 Hampton, VA Pro: E																															
1995	TOR	6	0		1	17	3.0	20.0	0	0	1																				
SEAN BRANTLEY Sean J. DT-DE 6'1 285 Florida A&M B: 6/30/1969 Washington, DC																															
1993	SAS	3				7	1.0	7.0																							
1994	SAS	18	0		1	41	5.0	27.0	1	21	0																				
1995	SAS	3				5																									
1995	BIR	6				1																									
1995	Year	9				6																									
3	Years	24	0		1	54	6.0	34.0	1	21	0																				
BOB BRANYON Robert T 6'1 220 Toledo																															
1953	CAL	2																													
JEFF BRASWELL Jeffrey E., Jr. LB 6'1 225 Iowa State B: 11/23/1964 Lake Worth, FL																															
1988	BC	16	0		5	109	4.0		2	26																					
1989	EDM	16	0		3	63	2.0																								
1990	EDM	17	1		1	53	2.0		2	50																					
1991	OTT	3				13	1.0																								
1991	TOR	2	0		1	16																									
1991	Year	5	0		1	29	1.0																								
1992	TOR	11	0		2	70	3.0		2	47		6	1																		
1994	OTT	2				5																									
6	Years	65	1		12	329	12.0		6	123		6	1																		
BRIAN BRATTON Brian Cornell WR-SB 5'10 186 Furman B: 7/31/1982 Wheeling, WV Pro: E																															
2007	MTL	12	4	0	1	2						6	1						20	199	10.0	17	0	52	511	9.8	79	19	438	23.1	35
2008	MTL	18	2	0	0	3						42	7	1	7	7.0	7	0	54	636	11.8	75	7	4	34	8.5	26	14	261	18.6	39
2009	MTL	18				0						12	2	1	4	4.0	4	0	58	613	10.6	47	2	3	20	6.7	12	10	155	15.5	28
2010	MTL	17	1	0	1	0						30	5	15	133	8.9	25	0	48	530	11.0	48	5	8	54	6.8	14	8	142	17.8	31
2011	MTL	18				0						30	5	4	15	3.8	5	0	55	675	12.3	46	5					1	10		10
5	Years	83	7	0	2	5						120	20	21	159	7.6	25	0	235	2653	11.3	75	19	67	619	9.2	79	52	1006	19.3	39
KARL BRAUN Karl DB 6'0 185 Simon Fraser; Richmond Raiders Jrs. B: 11/21/1963																															
1986	CAL	1																													
ALEX BRAVO Alex DB 6'0 190 Cal Poly (San Luis Obispo) B: 7/27/1930 Tucson, AZ Draft: 9-106 1954 LARM Pro: N																															
1956	SAS	13	2		0							18	3	72	399	5.5	98	2	8	209	26.1	43	1								
CHARLIE BRAY Charles OG-OT 6'0 255 Pratt JC; Central Oklahoma B: 9/25/1945 Pittsburgh, PA Pro: W																															
1968	TOR	9	1		1																										
1969	TOR*	14			1																										
1970	TOR*	14																	1	7	7.0	7	0								
1971	TOR+	14	0		1																										
1972	TOR	14																													
1973	TOR	9	0		1														1	9	9.0	9	0								
1976	HAM	1																													
7	Years	75	1		4														2	16	8.0	9	0								
JAYSON BRAY Jayson Deshun DH-CB 5'9 190 Auburn B: 3/7/1976 LaGrange, GA Pro: EX																															
2002	CAL	18	0	1	3	58			2	31	9	6	1																		
2003	CAL	11	0	1	0	30			2	1	3																				
2003	BC	5				13			1	0	1																				
2003	Year	16	0	1	0	43			3	1	4																				

Year	Team	GP	FM	FF	FR	TK	SK	YDS	IR	YDS	PD	PTS	TD	RA	YDS	AVG	LG	TD	REC	YDS	AVG	LG	TD	PR	YDS	AVG	LG	KOR	YDS	AVG	LG
2004	WPG	7				16																								
3	Years	36	0	2	3	117			5	32	13	6	1																		
SAM BRAZINSKY Samuel Jospeh E 6'1 215 Villanova B: 1/9/1921 Kulpmont, PA D: 5/12/2003 Manville, NJ Pro: A																															
1947	HAM	3																												
CARL BRAZLEY Carl Eugene CB 6'0 180 Western Kentucky B: 9/5/1957 Louisville, KY Pro: N																															
1980	MTL	3	0		2				1	0																				
1981	MTL	10	3		0																			40	266	6.7	29	17	379	22.3	44
1981	OTT	4					1.0		1	0														2	7	3.5	10	5	96	19.2	28
1981	Year	14	3		0		1.0		1	0														42	273	6.5	29	22	475	21.6	44
1982	OTT+	16	1		1				4	55														23	148	6.4	23	10	192	19.2	26
1983	TOR*	7							1	63		6	1											26	165	6.3	23	8	177	22.1	41
1984	TOR+	16	1		2				6	75														22	198	9.0	42	18	420	23.3	50
1985	TOR+	16	1		1				8	68		6	1											9	64	7.1	19	1	11	11.0	11
1986	TOR+	18	1		2				6	83														23	205	8.9	31				
1988	TOR	12	0		1	32			3	43														29	242	8.3	45	1	0	0.0	0
1989	TOR	18	1		3	52			4	42														33	190	5.8	21	8	106	13.3	29
1990	TOR	18	0		3	57			3	7		6	1											1	1	1.0	1	1	17	17.0	17
1991	TOR	16	0		1	48			5	90		6	1											2	-12	-6.0	-12	15	268	17.9	34
1992	TOR	17	1		3	64	1.0	5.0	1	-4														2	0	0.0	7				
12	Years	167	9		19	253	2.0	5.	43	522		24	4											212	1474	7.0	45	84	1666	19.8	50
CHRIS BRAZZELL Christopher Edward WR 6'2 193 Blinn JC; Angelo State B: 5/22/1976 Fort Worth, TX Draft: 6B-174 1998 NYJ Pro: N																															
2001	EDM	1				2													3	76	25.3	45	0								
2002	EDM	11				1						18	3						30	546	18.2	101	3								
2003	BC	17	2	0	0	1						36	6	1	0	0.0	0	0	68	1111	16.3	74	6								
2004	BC	16				0						48	8						49	906	18.5	73	8								
2005	HAM	6				0						12	2						22	252	11.5	25	2								
2005	WPG	10				1						26	4						24	456	19.0	75	4					1	28	28.0	28
2005	Year	16				1						38	6						46	708	15.4	75	6					1	28	28.0	28
2006	WPG	17				1						42	7	3	-3	-1.0	2	0	43	604	14.0	79	7								
2007	WPG	7				0						6	1	2	40	20.0	34	0	17	182	10.7	27	1								
7	Years	75	2	0	0	6						188	31	6	37	6.2	34	0	256	4133	16.1	101	31					1	28	28.0	28
TYRON BRECKENRIDGE Tyron Lyle DH 6'0 189 Chaffey JC; Washington State B: 6/30/1984 Pasadena, CA																															
2011	SAS	5				7			1	0	1																				
INOKE BRECKTERFIELD Inoke E. DE 5'9 244 Oregon State B: 4/25/1977 Honolulu, HI																															
1999	TOR	15	0	1	0	29	1.0																								
2001	WPG	13	0	1	2	17	2.0	17.0																							
2002	WPG	17				23	6.0																					3	5	1.7	5
2003	WPG	13	0	1	1	17	3.0																								
4	Years	58	0	3	3	86	12.0	17.0																				3	5	1.7	5
ED BREDING Edward Vincent LB 6'4 235 Texas A&M B: 11/3/1944 Billings, MT Draft: 15-378 1967 WAS Pro: N																															
1969	WPG	8			2				1	9																				
1970	WPG	8							1	3		6	1						1	2	2.0	2	1								
1971	WPG	3																												
3	Years	19			2				2	12		6	1						1	2	2.0	2	1								
SAM BREEDEN Samuel Lee WR 6'4 208 Butler CC; Arkansas; Northwestern Oklahoma State B: 7/12/1979 Hamlet, NC Pro: E																															
2006	SAS	2				0																								
BRAD BREEDLOVE William Bradley WR 5'11 170 Duke B: 10/30/1969 Chicago, IL																															
1995	MEM	10				1						6	1						17	233	13.7	30	1	5	23	4.6	13	2	33	16.5	29
DIMITRIUS BREEDLOVE Dimitrius WR 6'4 210 Evangel B: 6/9/1978 Apopka, FL Pro: E																															
2004	HAM	10	1	0	0	3						12	2						25	380	15.2	54	2								
ED BREHM Ed HB Regina Eastend Bombers Jrs.																															
1947	SAS	3																												
MOE BREMNER Maurice C-LB 6'1 220 Montreal Orfuns Ints. B: 6/26/1930 Montreal, QC D: 8/29/2002																															
1955	MTL	2																												
1957	MTL	10																												
1958	MTL	10																												
1959	MTL	4																												
4	Years	26																												
BERNIE BRENNAN Bernie HB-FW-E 5'10 185 Guelph B: 1928																															
1946	OTT	12										10	2										2								
1947	OTT	5																												
1951	OTT	2																												
3	Years	19										10	2										2								
SAMMIE BRENNAN Sammie S 6'3 200 Bishop's B: 3/11/1973 Pembroke, ON Draft: 3-19 1996 OTT																															
1996	OTT	17				31			1	3	2																				
1997	BC	6				5																								
1997	WPG	7				7																								
1997	Year	13				12																								
2		23				43			1	3	2																				
AL BRENNER Allen Ray DB 6'1 200 Michigan State B: 11/13/1947 Benton Harbour, MI D: 2/13/2012 Clinton, NC Draft: 7-170 1969 NYG Pro: N																															
1971	HAM	14	0		2				9	178		12	2															1	0	0.0	0
1972	HAM*	14	0		2				15	167														1	-1	-1.0	-1				
1973	HAM	14	0		2				4	61																				
1974	HAM+	16							7	79														2	3	1.5	2				
1975	WPG	9							2	43																				
1975	OTT	1																												
1975	Year	10							2	43																				
1976	OTT	13			2				1	15																				
1977	OTT	9	0		1																			1	8	8.0	8				
7	Years	89	0		9				38	543		12	2											4	10	2.5	8	1	0	0.0	0
CRAIG BRENNER Craig FB 6'4 230 Wilfrid Laurier B: 5/29/1970 Calgary, AB Draft: 3B-27 1994 CAL																															
1994	CAL	1																												
1995	CAL	18	1		1	14								2	6	3.0	4	0	4	74	18.5	22	0								
2	Years	19	1		1	14								2	6	3.0	4	0	4	74	18.5	22	0								
ROB BRESCIANI Rob WR 6'1 205 Saskatchewan; Regina Rams Jrs. B: 6/16/1964 Regina, SK Draft: 5B-39 1985 SAS																															
1985	CAL	8	2		1																			3	16	5.3	17	2	21	10.5	21
1986	CAL	5																	2	27	13.5	17	0					1	23	23.0	23
1988	SAS	7				0													2	41	20.5	24	0								
1989	SAS	17				1						6	1	3	6	2.0	3	0	10	243	24.3	59	1								
1990	OTT	1				0													1	9	9.0	9	0								
5	Years	38	2		1	1						6	1	3	6	2.0	3	0	15	320	21.3	59	1	3	16	5.3	17	3	44	14.7	23
BILLY BREWER Homer Ervin HB 6'0 190 Mississippi B: 10/8/1934 Columbus, MS Draft: 20-233(f) 1959 WAS; SS 1960 BOS Pro: N																															
1961	BC	1																												
RON BREWER Ron LB-OHB 6'1 230 Parkdale Lions Jrs. B: 1937																															
1958	TOR	14							1	5																				
1959	TOR	13																	2	20	10.0	12	0								
1960	TOR	14																									2	29	14.5	17
1961	MTL+	13																												
1962	MTL	7																									1	4	4.0	4
1963	TOR	14							1	7																	1	0	0.0	0
1964	TOR*	14	0		1				1	11																				
1965	TOR+	11	0		2				1	33																				

Year	Team	GP	FM	FF	FR	TK	SK	YDS	IR	YDS	PD	PTS	TD	RA	YDS	AVG	LG	TD	REC	YDS	AVG	LG	TD	PR	YDS	AVG	LG	KOR	YDS	AVG	LG
1966	EDM	16	0		3																										
1967	HAM	8			1				1	14																					
10	Years	124	0		7				5	70									2	20	10.0	12	0					4	33	8.3	17
DOUG BREWSTER Doug LB 6'1 220 Clemson B: 10/11/1969 Athens, GA																															
1991	SAS	8	0		5	24																									
1992	CAL	2				2																									
2	Years	10	0		5	26																									
ALUNDIS BRICE Alundis Marcell CB 5'10 178 Mississippi B: 5/1/1970 Brookhaven, MA Draft: 4B-129 1995 DAL Pro: N																															
1999	TOR	18	0	0	2	37	2.0	19.0	2	0	8																				
2000	SAS	4				14			0	0	1																				
2	Years	22	0	0	2	51	2.0	19.0	2	0	9																				
BUBBA BRIDGES Harold DE-DT 6'6 245 Colorado* B: 11/7/1950 Houston, TX Draft: 16-409 1975 DEN Pro: W																															
1973	EDM	3																													
1974	HAM	2																													
1974	EDM	3																													
1974	Year	5																													
1975	OTT	2																						1	0	0.0	0				
1975	CAL	1																													
1975	Year	3																						1	0	0.0	0				
3	Years	7																						1	0	0.0	0				
COREY BRIDGES Corey WR 5'7 170 South Carolina B: 6/30/1974 Newnan, GA Pro: E																															
1998	HAM	5				0													1	12	12.0	12	0	20	252	12.6	62	9	124	13.8	26
O.J. BRIGANCE Orenthial James LB-DE 6'0 236 Rice B: 9/29/1969 Houston, TX Pro: N																															
1991	BC+	18				112	2.0		1	7																					
1992	BC	18	0		3	94																						5	40	8.0	13
1993	BC+	18	0		1	59	20.0	131.0																							
1994	BAL	18	0		2	44	6.0	51.0																							
1995	BAL*	18	0		3	66	7.	41.0	1	13	4																				
5	Years	90	0		9	375	35.0	223.0	2	20	4																	5	40	8.0	13
BILL BRIGGS Bill C-OE-LB 6'4 208 B: 4/6/1925 Toronto, ON deceased																															
1947	TOR	12										1	0																		
1948	TOR	12																													
1949	TOR	4																													
1950	EDM	14										13	2	1	14	14.0	14	0	5	100	20.0		2								
1951	EDM	14																	1	2	2.0	2	0								
1952	EDM	16			2				1	1		1	0						6	78	13.0	21	0								
1953	EDM	16							2	2									1	1	1.0	1	0								
1954	EDM	15			4				6	39		5	1																		
1955	EDM	16	0		2							5	1																		
1956	EDM	16	0		2				2	10																					
1957	EDM	16	0		1				1	8		6	1																		
11	Years	151	0		11				12	60		31	5	1	14	14.0	14	0	13	181	13.9	21	2								
BOB BRIGGS Robert DT 6'2 220 Montreal Alouettes Jrs. B: 6/26/1961 Montreal, QC																															
1983	MTL	1																													
JOHNNY BRIGHT John D. FB-LB 6'1 215 Drake B: 6/11/1930 Fort Wayne, IN D: 12/14/1983 Edmonton, AB Draft: 1-5 1952 PHI																															
1952	CAL+	13										10	2	144	815	5.7	75	2	7	74	10.6	15	0	2	7	3.5	7	5	117	23.4	34
1953	CAL	9							3	35				38	128	3.4	32	0	1	7	7.0	7	0	5	60	12.0	35	2	23	11.5	
1954	CAL	1	1		0									8	30	3.8		0	3	50	16.7	30	0					1	24	24.0	24
1954	EDM	11	1		2				3	43				37	184	5.0		0	2	39	19.5		0								
1954	Year	12	2		2									45	214	4.8	14	0	5	89	17.8	30	0					1	24	24.0	24
1955	EDM	12	4		0				1	8		10	2	107	643	6.0	34	2	5	110	22.0	38	0					1	13	13.0	13
1956	EDM	9	3		0				0	9		30	5	93	573	6.2	22	4	9	151	16.8	28	1					1	15	15.0	15
1957	EDM+	16	5		0							96	16	259	1679	6.5	27	16	18	300	16.7	29	0					2	32	16.0	23
1958	EDM+	16	11									48	8	296	1722	5.8	90	8	19	265	13.9	37	0					7	83	11.9	23
1959	EDM+	16										66	11	231	1340	5.8	53	11	23	274	11.9	28	0					3	40	13.3	20
1960	EDM+	16	4		1							84	14	251	1268	5.1	28	14	10	139	13.9	26	0								
1961	EDM+	16	5									66	11	236	1350	5.7	81	11	13	219	16.8	34	0					3	26	8.7	15
1962	EDM	11	1									12	2	142	650	4.6	23	2	7	70	10.0	21	0					3	41	13.7	17
1963	EDM	13	5		1									83	324	3.9	15	0	11	111	10.1	32	0								
1964	EDM	16	1		0									44	203	4.6	16	0	4	17	4.3	6	0					1	10	10.0	10
13	Years	164	41		4				7	95		422	71	1969	10909	5.5	90	70	132	1826	13.8	38	1	7	67	9.6	35	29	424	14.6	34
LEON BRIGHT Leon, Jr. WR-OHB 5'9 192 Florida State B: 5/19/1955 Starke, FL Pro: N																															
1977	BC*	15	4		0							54	9	6	43	7.2	24	0	45	816	18.1	78	7	29	419	14.4	108	18	596	33.1	100
1978	BC	15										18	3	4	90	22.5	63	1	52	781	15.0	89	2	40	498	12.5	51	18	425	23.6	35
1979	BC	11	5		2							30	5	2	7	3.5	13	0	36	569	15.8	106	3	21	319	15.2	101	27	820	30.4	79
1980	BC	15	3		3				1	94		18	3	1	1	1.0	1	0	13	204	15.7	57	1	47	790	16.8	93	25	635	25.4	48
4	Years	56	12		5				1	94		120	20	13	141	10.8	63	1	146	2370	16.2	106	13	137	2026	14.8	108	88	2476	28.1	100
LAMONT BRIGHTFUL Lamont Eugene CB 5'10 165 Eastern Washington B: 1/29/1979 Oak Harbor, WA Draft: 6A-195 2002 BAL Pro: EN																															
2006	MTL	9	1	0	1	23			2	26	5													10	53	5.3	23	7	147	21.0	32
2007	CAL	2				1																									
2	Years	11	1	0	1	24			2	26	5													10	53	5.3	23	7	147	21.0	32
DOUG BRIGHTWELL Douglas C 6'0 220 Texas Christian B: 1929 Draft: 6-56 1949 PIT																															
1949	SAS	14																													
1950	EDM	14																													
2	Years	28																													
LOWRY BRILEY Lowry Bernard DB 5'11 180 Texas A&M-Commerce B: 6/22/1949 Bowie County, TX																															
1974	EDM	4	1		1				1	0																		1	20	20.0	20
LaMARK BRIM LaMark E. RB 5'9 170 Langston B: 4/3/1971 New Orleans, LA																															
1996	BC	1				0								2	5	2.5	6	0										1	18	18.0	18
ALEX BRINK Alex QB 6'3 216 Washington State B: 6/2/1985 Eugene, OR Draft: 7-223 2008 HOU																															
2010	WPG	16	1	0	0	0						6	1	23	73	3.2	12	1													
2011	WPG	18	4	0	0							36	6	43	148	3.4	21	6													
2	Years	34	5	0	0	0						42	7	66	221	3.3	21	7													
LESTER BRINKLEY Lester Lamar DE 6'6 270 Mississippi B: 5/13/1965 Ruleville, MS D: 7/11/2002 Houston, TX Pro: N																															
1992	WPG	1				0																									
LORENZO BRINKLEY Lorenzo HB 6'0 180 Missouri B: 8/5/1949 St. Louis, MO Draft: 4A-80 1972 PIT Pro: W																															
1972	EDM	3							2	23																		3	46	15.3	29
CHUCK BRISLIN Charles W. OT 6'3 238 Mississippi State B: 4/23/1954 Columbus, MS Draft: 11-302 1976 ATL																															
1976	CAL	1																													
GENE BRITO Genaro E. DE 6'1 226 Loyola Marymount B: 10/23/1925 Los Angeles, CA D: 6/8/1965 Duarte, CA Draft: 17-196 1951 WAS Pro: N																															
1954	CAL+	15																	5	60	12.0	33	0					1	16	16.0	16
BILL BRITTON Bill LB-FB 5'11 190 Western Ontario B: 1935 Draft: 1-3 1958 BC																															
1958	BC	13	1		2				1	13				48	210	4.4	39	0	3	19	6.3	14	0					5	100	20.0	25
1959	BC	16							1			12	2	51	242	4.7	19	2	12	108	9.0	28	0	6	32	5.3	20	2	27	13.5	20
1960	BC	11	2		2				1															5	14	2.8	10				
1961	BC	16	4		2																			35	147	4.2	10				
1962	CAL	16							1															3	6	2.0	2	1	16	16.0	16
1963	CAL	15	0		3				1			6	1	2	20	10.0	14	0													
1964	CAL	16										6	1	4	33	8.3	18	1										1	8	8.0	8
7	Years	103	7		9				5	13		24	4	105	505	4.8	39	3	15	127	8.5	28	0	49	199	4.1	20	9	151	16.8	25
EDDIE BRITTON Eddie Maurell WR 5'9 160 Central State (Ohio) B: 12/1/1968 Chicago, IL Pro: E																															
1993	CAL	2				0													1	27	27.0	27	0								

Year	Team	GP	FM	FF	FR	TK	SK	YDS	IR	YDS	PD	PTS	TD	RA	YDS	AVG	LG	TD	REC	YDS	AVG	LG	TD	PR	YDS	AVG	LG	KOR	YDS	AVG	LG
1994	BAL	5				0						6	1						13	125	9.6	24	1					2	30	15.0	16
1995	BIR	15				2						24	4						49	681	13.9	71	4	40	292	7.3	33	24	401	16.7	29
1996	OTT	2	2		0	1													6	36	6.0	14	0	4	9	2.3	5				
1996	HAM	1				0																		1	0	0.0	0	4	56	14.0	21
1996	Year	3	2		0	1													6	36	6.0	14	0	5	9	1.8	5	4	56	14.0	21
4	Years	24	2		0	3						30	5						69	869	12.6	71	5	45	301	6.7	33	30	487	16.2	29
SAM BRITTS Samuel Alfred LB 6'0 215 Missouri B: 2/23/1950 Pro: W																															
1973	EDM+	16	0		4				2	11																		5	44	8.8	19
1975	EDM	12	0		1																			1	12	12.0	12				
1976	HAM	16	1		2																							1	-2	-2.0	-2
1977	HAM	16	0		3																										
1978	BC	16	0		1				1	0																		2	46	23.0	28
1979	BC	11	0		2																										
1980	BC	6																													
1981	BC	15	0		2		3.0																								
8	Years	108	1		15		3.0		3	11														1	12	12.0	12	8	88	11.0	28
ROD BROADWAY Roderick Craig DE 6'4 250 North Carolina B: 4/9/1955 Oakboro, NC																															
1978	HAM	1																													
TIM BROADY Timothy Wayne LB 6'0 215 Murray State B: 2/20/1966 Madisonville, KY Pro: E																															
1994	LV	16				54	4.0	30.0	1	5	5	6	1						1	39	39.0	39	1								
1995	SAS	6				11																									
2	Years	22				65	4.0	30.0	1	5	5	6	1						1	39	39.0	39	1								
CLYDE BROCK Clyde Vern OT-DT 6'5 268 Utah State B: 8/30/1940 Los Angeles, CA Draft: 8-63 1962 HOU; 2A-20 1962 CHIB Pro: N																															
1964	SAS	9																													
1965	SAS+	16	0		1																										
1966	SAS*	16	0		2																										
1967	SAS*	16																													
1968	SAS*	16	0		1																										
1969	SAS*	16																										1	0	0.0	0
1970	SAS	16																										1	6	6.0	6
1971	SAS	16																													
1972	SAS	16																													
1973	SAS	11																													
1974	SAS	5																													
1975	SAS	16	0		1																										
12	Years	169	0		5																							2	6	3.0	6
DIETER BROCK Ralph Dieter QB 6'0 195 Auburn; Jacksonville State B: 2/12/1951 Birmingham, AL Pro: N																															
1974	WPG	16	1		0									2	6	3.0	7	0													
1975	WPG	16	8		0							12	2	36	173	4.8	31	2													
1976	WPG	16	7		0							12	2	46	72	1.6	11	2	1	-9	-9.0	-9	0								
1977	WPG	16	7		1							36	6	62	220	3.5	26	6													
1978	WPG	16	4		0							18	3	28	47	1.7	12	3													
1979	WPG	15	2		0							6	1	30	97	3.2	17	1													
1980	WPG*	16	4		0							24	4	43	87	2.0	14	4													
1981	WPG*	16	1		0									35	116	3.3	18	0													
1982	WPG+	16	5		1							24	4	33	123	3.7	13	4													
1983	WPG	6	5		0							12	2	13	38	2.9	11	2													
1983	HAM	6	5		0							12	2	14	24	1.7	6	2													
1983	Year	12	10		0							24	4	27	62	2.3	11	4													
1984	HAM	15	7		0							36	6	48	134	2.8	18	6													
11	Years	164	56		2							192	32	390	1137	2.9	31	32	1	-9	-9.0	-9	0								
PAUL BROCK Paul T 6'3 250 Tulane B: 1/18/1955 Mobile, AL																															
1976	BC	9	0		2							6	1																		
LUC BRODEUR-JOURDAIN Luc C-OG 6'2 318 Laval B: 3/17/1983 Sainte-Hyacinthe, QC Draft: 6-48 2008 MTL																															
2009	MTL	17				0																									
2010	MTL	18				1													1	10	10.0	10	0								
2011	MTL	18	1	0	0	2																									
3	Years	53	1	0	0	3													1	10	10.0	10	0								
BOB BRODHEAD Robert Edgar QB 6'2 207 Duke B: 12/20/1936 Kittanning, PA D: 2/11/1996 Baton Rouge, LA Draft: 12-144 1958 CLE Pro: N																															
1959	SAS	8												30	121	4.0	23	0													
BOB BRONK Bob FB 6'0 215 Winnipeg Rods Jrs.; Queen's B: 11/18/1959 Winnipeg, MB Draft: TE 1981 TOR																															
1982	TOR	16										36	6	42	150	3.6	16	3	39	452	11.6	52	3								
1983	TOR	5	1		0							12	2	14	62	4.4	27	0	14	144	10.3	27	2								
1984	TOR	15	2		1							12	2	20	96	4.8	14	0	22	195	8.9	21	2					1	0	0.0	0
1985	TOR+	16	1		0							8	1	21	79	3.8	14	0	41	325	7.9	29	1					3	30	10.0	12
1986	TOR	18	0		1									11	32	2.9	8	0	18	163	9.1	20	0					1	11	11.0	11
5	Years	70	4		2							68	11	108	419	3.9	27	3	134	1279	9.5	52	8					5	41	8.2	12
BOBBY BROOKS Robert L. LB 6'2 238 Fresno State B: 3/3/1976 Vallejo, CA Pro: EN																															
2006	HAM	10	0	0	3	36			1	29	1	6	1																		
DONNY BROOKS Donny Lynn DB 5'11 188 Texas Tech B: 1/26/1970 Dallas County, TX																															
1994	SHR	4				7					2																				
HORACE BROOKS Horace WR 5'9 170 Alabama State B: 2/12/1970 Montgomery, AL																															
1994	OTT	17	2		3	20			1	15	4	12	2	4	51	12.8	37	1	21	246	11.7	53	1	11	54	4.9	15	22	300	13.6	26
1995	OTT	9	2		1	18																		22	179	8.1	21	17	306	18.0	49
2	Years	26	4		4	38			1	15	4	12	2	4	51	12.8	37	1	21	246	11.7	53	1	33	233	7.1	21	39	606	15.5	49
KEVIN BROOKS Kevin CB 5'8 174 Garden City CC; South Carolina B: 12/20/1973 Jacksonville, FL Pro: E																															
2000	HAM	10	0	0	1	26																									
MICHAEL BROOKS Michael Antonio S 6'0 192 North Carolina State B: 3/12/1967 Greensboro, NC Pro: N																															
1994	BAL+	18	0		1	56			4	20	5																				
1995	MEM	4				8																									
2	Years	22	0		1	64			4	20	5																				
RICHARD BROOKS Richard DB 5'8 175 Florida A&M B: 6/6/1973 Honduras																															
2000	TOR	4	0	0	1	7																		1	0	0.0	0				
RON BROOKS Ron OG 5'11 230 Parkdale Jrs.; Miami (Ohio) B: 1937 Toronto, ON																															
1961	MTL	7																													
1962	MTL	14																													
1963	SAS	16	0		1																										
3	Years	37	0		1																										
BRIAN BROOMELL Brian Keith QB 6'1 190 Temple B: 6/26/1958 Somerdale, NJ																															
1981	EDM	1												2	7	3.5	6	0													
PAT BROSNAN Patrick Harry FL 5'10 185 Long Beach State B: 4/30/1942 Culver City, CA																															
1965	TOR	10							1	3		24	4						24	452	18.8	58	4								
PAUL BROTHERS Paul QB 6'1 191 Oregon State B: 4/18/1945 Rock Springs, WY Draft: 16-416 1967 DAL																															
1968	BC	16	0		1							6	1	26	96	3.7	12	1													
1969	BC	16	4		0							6	1	43	139	3.2	16	1	1	5	5.0	5	0								
1970	BC	16										18	3	38	227	6.0	22	3													
1971	BC	7			0							6	1	27	119	4.4	25	1													
1971	OTT	4			0									2	12	6.0		0													
1971	Year	11	1		0							6	1	29	131	4.5	25	1													
1972	OTT	14												1	-1	-1.0	-1	0													
5	Years	69	4		1							36	6	137	592	4.3	25	6	1	5	5.0	5	0								
RICHARD BROTHERS Richard Leon DB 5'10 201 Arkansas B: 4/5/1965 Houston, TX Draft: 7A-189 1989 CHIB																															

Year	Team	GP	FM	FF	FR	TK	SK	YDS	IR	YDS	PD	PTS	TD	RA	YDS	AVG	LG	TD	REC	YDS	AVG	LG	TD	PR	YDS	AVG	LG	KOR	YDS	AVG	LG
1989	TOR	2	0		1	10																									
MARC-OLIVIER BROUILLETTE Marc-Olivier LB-S 6'0 230 Montreal B: 9/4/1986 Draft: 3-23 2010 MTL																															
2010	MTL	9				9			1	0	0																				
2011	MTL	9	0	1	0	26						6	1	1	72	72.0	72	1													
2	Years	18	0	1	0	35			1	0	0	6	1	1	72	72.0	72	1													
GERALD BROUSSARD Gerald CB 6'1 170 Tulane B: 4/3/1962																															
1985	OTT	1																													
JAMALL BROUSSARD Phillip Jamall WR 5'9 172 Texas Tech; Canyons JC; San Jose State B: 8/19/1981 Nederland, TX Pro: EN																															
2007	TOR	4				0						6	1	1	7	7.0	7	0	11	169	15.4	70	1					1	15	15.0	15
JOE BROUWERS Joseph OG 6'4 260 Wilfrid Laurier B: 7/18/1961 Waterloo, ON Draft: 4-35 1984 BC																															
1985	BC	5																													
AARON BROWN Aaron Cedric LB 6'2 238 Ohio State B: 1/13/1956 Warren, OH Draft: 10-252 1978 TB Pro: N																															
1982	WPG	3																													
1983	WPG	16	0		1		6.0																								
1984	WPG*	16	0		1		7.0		4	65		6	1															1	9	9.0	9
1988	WPG	17	0		1	79	3.0		3	26																		1	9	9.0	9
4	Years	52	0		3	79	16.0		7	91		6	1															2	18	9.0	9
AL BROWN Al, Jr. E Toronto Draft: 1952 OTT																															
1952	OTT	1																													
ALBERT BROWN Albert CB-WR 6'0 180 Western Illinois B: 12/19/1963 Omaha, NE																															
1987	SAS	2				0								1	1	1.0	1	0	1	4	4.0	4	0					3	69	23.0	23
1988	SAS	11	3		0	0			1	58														14	208	14.9	54	18	395	21.9	51
1989	SAS	17				50			8	176		18	3											73	849	11.6	87	21	600	28.6	65
1990	SAS	17	1		1	59			5	42														45	416	9.2	33	33	589	17.8	43
1991	SAS	15	2		1	29			4	30		6	1											3	15	5.0	9	30	675	22.5	97
1992	SAS	16	0		2	32			6	150		6	1											19	68	3.6	21	17	290	17.1	44
1993	SAS	18				41			3	20		6	1											5	23	4.6	8				
1994	SAS+	18	0		1	40			4	78	5													5	20	4.0	15	5	69	13.8	24
1995	SAS	8				25			1	4	3																				
1995	WPG	2				1																		1	5	5.0	5	2	30	15.0	16
1995	Year	10				26			1	4	3													1	5	5.0	5	2	30	15.0	16
9	Years	122	6		5	277			32	558	8	36	6	1	1	1.0	1	0	1	4	4.0	4	0	165	1604	9.7	87	129	2717	21.1	97
ANDRE BROWN Andre Lamont SB 6'3 210 Miami (Florida) B: 8/21/1966 Chicago, IL Pro: EN																															
1993	OTT	8	0		1	2						0	0						19	287	15.1	31	0								
1993	TOR	2				0						6	1						5	84	16.8	35	1								
1993	Year	10	0		1	2						6	1						24	371	15.5	35	1								
ANDRE BROWN Andre DE 6'1 230 Delta State B: 7/27/1979 Clarksdale, MS																															
2001	SAS	2				3																									
2002	SAS	2				0																									
2003	SAS	9				20					1																				
3	Years	13				23					1																				
ANTONIO BROWN Antonio Duval WR 5'10 175 West Virginia B: 3/3/1978 Miami, FL Pro: N																															
2002	WPG	5	0	1	0	1						12	2						14	208	14.9	45	2	2	18	9.0	17				
BILL BROWN William H. HB 6'1 200 New Mexico; Oklahoma																															
1958	EDM	1												1	0	0.0	0	0										1	11	11.0	11
BOB BROWN Robert DE 6'2 239 Miami (Florida) B: 1944																															
1965	OTT	13																													
1966	OTT	14																													
1967	OTT+	14																													
1968	OTT	4	0		1																										
1968	BC	10	0		1																										
1968	Year	14	0		2																										
1969	BC	16	2		0							6	1	75	448	6.0	46	1	11	52	4.7	18	0					6	195	32.5	51
1970	BC	1												5	27	5.4	4	0	1	1	1.0	1	0					3	75	25.0	26
6	Years	62	2		2							6	1	80	475	5.9	46	1	12	53	4.4	18	0					9	270	30.0	51
BOB BROWN Robert Eddie T 6'5 268 Arkansas-Pine Bluff B: 2/23/1939 Bonita, LA D: 1/10/1998 Memphis, TN Draft: 13-169 1964 SF Pro: N																															
1965	TOR	5																													
BRANDON BROWN Brandon LB 6'1 255 Howard Payne B: 4/17/1979																															
2004	SAS	2				3	1.0																								
BUDDY BROWN Halver, Jr. OG 6'1 255 Alabama B: 6/9/1950 Florala, AL Draft: 16-392 1974 NYG; 14-164 1974 BIR-WFL Pro: W																															
1975	WPG	8																													
1976	WPG+	16																													
1977	WPG+	13																													
1978	WPG	16	0		1																										
4	Years	53	0		1																										
BUSTER BROWN James OG-OT 6'0 210 McGill B: 1930																															
1951	HAM	10																													
1952	HAM	12																													
1953	HAM	12																													
3	Years	34																													
CARLOS BROWN Carlos Allen QB 6'3 210 Pacific B: 7/31/1952 Shreveport, LA Draft: 12-296 1975 GB Pro: N																															
1979	BC	6	1		1									4	-10	-2.5	1	0													
CHARLIE BROWN Charles Edwin OT 6'4 245 Houston B: 8/1/1936 Pro: N																															
1964	EDM	12																													
1965	EDM	16	0		1																										
2	Years	28	0		1																										
CHARLIE BROWN Charles Edward DB 6'1 194 Syracuse B: 9/13/1942 Heflin, AL Draft: 4-32 1966 SD; 2-28 1966 CHIB Pro: N																															
1969	HAM	7	0		2				2	127		6	1											1	5	5.0	5	13	284	21.8	36
CHARLIE BROWN Charles Robert RB 5'10 187 Missouri B: 10/16/1945 Jefferson City, MO Draft: 10A-238 1967 NO Pro: N																															
1969	BC	8																													
1970	BC	1																													
2	Years	9																													
DARCY BROWN Darcy FB 6'4 251 Missisauga Warriors Jrs.; St. Mary's (Nova Scotia) B: 5/29/1986 Mississauga, ON Draft: 1B-6 2009 HAM																															
2009	HAM	13				2																						1	2	2.0	2
2010	HAM	18				3													4	30	7.5	13	0								
2011	HAM	18				3													8	110	13.8	30	0								
3	Years	49				8													12	140	11.7	30	0					1	2	2.0	2
DEREK BROWN Derek OT 6'8 295 Hampden-Sydney; Kansas B: 3/26/1971																															
1995	MEM	10				1																									
DICK BROWN Richard DB-FW-E 5'10 170 Toronto B: 5/9/1926 D: 5/20/2000																															
1950	HAM	9										16	3					3													
1951	HAM	11										5	1					1													
1952	HAM	12										15	3					1					2								
1953	HAM+	14										5	1																		
1954	HAM	13							2	53		10	2	16	99	6.2	16	1						58	340	5.9	33	2	52	26.0	35
1955	TOR	12							2	35				1	6	6.0	6	0						74	614	8.3	21	1	20	20.0	20
1956	TOR	13							2	11														44	379	8.6	18	1	7	7.0	7
1957	TOR	2																						8	55	6.9	12				
1957	MTL	7																						41	310	7.6	16				
1957	Year	9																						49	365	7.4	16				
8	Years	86							6	99		51	10	17	105	6.2	16	6					2	225	1698	7.5	33	4	79	19.8	35
DONALD BROWN Donald DH 5'9 195 Wingate B: 7/8/1985 Bostic, NC																															

Year	Team	GP	FM	FF	FR	TK	SK	YDS	IR	YDS	PD	PTS	TD	RA	YDS	AVG	LG	TD	REC	YDS	AVG	LG	TD	PR	YDS	AVG	LG	KOR	YDS	AVG	LG
2008	BC	1				1																									
2010	WPG	3				5																									
2	Years	4				6																									
DOUG BROWN Doug LB-K 6'0 230 Surrey Rams Ints. B: 1934																															
1958	CAL	16										51	0																		
1959	CAL	16	1		0				3	13		83	0																		
1960	CAL	16	1		1							81	0	1	-31	-31.0	-31	0													
3	Years	48	2		1				3	13		215	0	1	-31	-31.0	-31	0													
DOUG BROWN Douglas Gordon DT 6'7 290 Simon Fraser B: 9/29/1974 Coquitam, BC Draft: 1A-5 1997 CAL Pro: N																															
2001	WPG*	18	0	1	2	32	7.0	44.0			1	6	1																		
2002	WPG*	18	0	3	0	29	3.0	6.0			1																				
2003	WPG	18	0	0	1	34	4.0	23.0			1																				
2004	WPG	18	0	4	4	40	3.0	8.0																							
2005	WPG	13	0	0	1	31	5.0	32.0																							
2006	WPG*	18				52	3.0	27.0																							
2007	WPG*	17	0	0	1	40	7.0	48.0																							
2008	WPG*	18	0	1	1	43	6.0	56.0			2																				
2009	WPG*	17	0	0	1	50	6.0	39.0																							
2010	WPG*	18	0	1	1	49	5.0	31.0																					6	128	21.3	27
2011	WPG+	15				29	3.0	8.0																							
11	Years	188	0	10	12	429	52.0	322.0			5	6	1																6	128	21.3	27
EDDIE BROWN Eddie WR-SB 5'11 175 Iowa State B: 8/6/1966 Topeka, KS Pro: E																															
1990	CAL	10	2		0	0						6	1	1	-12	-12.0	-12	0	23	357	15.5	56	1	19	166	8.7	29	7	104	14.9	27
1991	OTT	11	3		0	0						24	4	2	9	4.5	7	0	21	458	21.8	70	4	22	171	7.8	51	1	14	14.0	14
1992	TOR	10	1		1	1						30	5	1	12	12.0	12	0	31	571	18.4	72	5	7	-11	-1.6	29	8	149	18.6	25
1993	EDM	18	3		0	3						90	15	3	19	6.3	21	0	67	1378	20.6	75	15	15	119	7.9	49				
1994	EDM	18	2		1	4						90	15	4	31	7.8	14	0	79	1126	14.3	68	12	27	394	14.6	92	2	37	18.5	25
1995	MEM	9	1		0	0						12	2	1	-1	-1.0	-1	0	28	435	15.5	73	2	15	80	5.3	12	1	18	18.0	18
1995	EDM	4				0						6	1	1	-7	-7.0	-7	0	9	113	12.6	32	1								
1995	Year	13	1		0	0						18	3	2	-8	-4.0	-1	0	37	548	14.8	73	3	15	80	5.3	12	1	18	18.0	18
1996	EDM*	18	3		0	3						42	7	7	18	2.6	11	0	70	1325	18.9	46	7	22	178	8.1	30	2	31	15.5	19
1997	EDM	13	2	0	0	2						24	4						54	822	15.2	71	4								
1998	MTL	5				1						18	3						14	197	14.1	33	3								
1998	BC	12	1	0	0	3						18	3						43	572	13.3	54	3	4	18	4.5	8				
1998	Year	17				4						36	6						57	769	13.5	54	6	4	18	4.5	8				
1999	BC+	18				1						12	2	3	-10	-3.3	3	0	59	850	14.4	78	2								
2000	TOR	4				1													9	143	15.9	47	0								
2002	OTT	10	1	0	0	0						6	1	3	9	3.0	24	0	25	316	12.6	78	1	8	29	3.6	11	3	44	14.7	18
12	Years	144	19	0	2	19						378	63	26	68	2.6	24	0	532	8663	16.3	78	60	139	1144	8.2	92	24	397	16.5	27
ELTON BROWN Elton DE-DT 6'2 254 San Diego CC; Utah State B: 9/17/1951 Charleston, SC Draft: 11-269 1973 DEN																															
1974	BC	16	0		2				1	6																					
1975	BC	16	0		1																										
1976	HAM	9	0		4																										
1976	WPG	8	0		2				1	0																					
1976	Year	17	0		6				1	0																					
1977	WPG	16																													
1978	WPG	6																													
1978	TOR	2																													
1978	BC	1																													
1978	Year	9																													
5	Years	63	0		9				2	6																					
ERNIE BROWN Ernest Davis DT 6'3 295 Syracuse B: 3/14/1971 Pittsburgh, PA Pro: N																															
1996	SAS	3				10																									
1996	CAL	6				9	1.0	1.0																							
1996	Year	9				19	1.0	1.0																							
1997	CAL	14	0	0	1	30	2.0	10.0																							
1998	SAS	14	0	1	1	22	7.0	65.0																							
3	Years	31	0	1	2	71	10.0	76.0																							
ERROL BROWN Errol S 5'8 170 Saskatchewan B: 1/4/1971 Wolverhampton, England Draft: 3B-17 1993 SAS																															
1993	SAS	14				8																		22	158	7.2	26	8	144	18.0	26
1993	WPG	2				2																		5	23	4.6	16	1	12	12.0	12
1993	Year	16				10																		27	181	6.7	26	9	156	17.3	26
1994	WPG	18	0		1	44			1	0	2																				
1995	SAS	14				17			1	0	0																				
1996	SAS	14				31	1.0	7.0	2	46	0																				
1997	WPG	4	0	0	1	16					1																				
5	Years	64	0	0	2	118	1.0	7.0	4	46	3													27	181	6.7	26	9	156	17.3	26
FAKHIR BROWN Fakhir Hamin DB 5'11 193 Grambling State B: 9/21/1977 Detroit, MI Pro: NU																															
1998	TOR	6	0	1	0	17			1	0	0																				
FRED BROWN Fred HB-FW																															
1947	TOR	11										5	1					1													
1948	TOR	12										10	2					2													
1949	HAM	9																													
3	Years	32										15	3					3													
GARY BROWN Gary Lee OT-OG 6'4 320 Nassau CC; Georgia Tech B: 6/25/1971 Amityville, NY Draft: 5B-148 1994 PIT Pro: EN																															
2000	HAM	13				0																									
2001	HAM	9				0																									
2002	HAM	12				1																									
3	Years	34				1																									
GEORGE BROWN George William T-G 6'2 222 Texas Christian B: 9/23/1923 Boyd, TX Draft: 8-76 1949 PIT Pro: AN																															
1951	EDM	12										5	1																		
1954	BC	2																													
2	Years	14										5	1																		
GORD BROWN Gordon E. LB 6'3 238 Oklahoma B: 6/4/1944																															
1966	WPG	13																	2	24	12.0	15	0								
1967	WPG	15										6	1						3	56	18.7	22	1								
1968	WPG	16	0		1				1	7									2	53	26.5	30	0					1	9	9.0	9
1969	WPG	16																													
4	Years	60	0		1				1	7		6	1						7	133	19.0	30	1					1	9	9.0	9
GORDON BROWN Gordon T 6'2 245 Louisiana Tech B: 6/24/1932 Hughes, AR Draft: 14-158 1955 CHIC																															
1955	CAL+	13																													
HARDY BROWN Hardy (Thumper) LB 6'0 193 Southern Methodist; Tulsa B: 5/8/1924 D: 11/8/1991 Stockton, CA Draft: 12-104(di) 1947 NYG; 21-245 1951 SF Pro: AN																															
1956	HAM	7																													
HURLIE BROWN Hurlie LB-DB 6'1 200 Miami (Florida) B: 6/21/1969 Rockledge, FL																															
1993	SAC	1				4	1.0	6.0																							
1994	SAC	13				55			1	10	4													1	6	6.0	6				
1995	SA	8	0		1	10					1																				
1996	MTL	3				2																									
4	Years	25	0		1	71	1.0	6.0	1	10	5													1	6	6.0	6				
IKE BROWN Isaac Monroe, Jr. RB 6'0 205 Western Kentucky B: 1/9/1951 Owensboro, KY Draft: 8-186 1973 NE																															
1972	MTL+	14	3		1							36	6	140	817	5.8	73	3	24	269	11.2	28	3					7	132	18.9	34
ISAAC BROWN Isaac LB 5'11 206 Central Michigan B: 4/29/1985 Saginaw, MI																															

Year	Team	GP	FM	FF	FR	TK	SK	YDS	IR	YDS	PD	PTS	TD	RA	YDS	AVG	LG	TD	REC	YDS	AVG	LG	TD	PR	YDS	AVG	LG	KOR	YDS	AVG	LG
2009	HAM	3				2																									
2010	HAM	9	0	1	0	13	1.0	6.0																							
2	Years	12	0	1	0	20	1.0	6.0																							
IVAN BROWN Ivan DE 6'2 240 Saskatchewan B: 7/18/1985 Regina, SK Draft: 4B-31 2009 MTL																															
2009	MTL	6				0																									
2010	MTL	2				2																									
2011	HAM	16				0																									
3	Years	24				2																									
JEFF BROWN Jeff S 5'9 190 Acadia B: 5/30/1972 Hamilton, ON Draft: 5-29 1998 HAM																															
1998	HAM	4				5																									
JERALD BROWN Jerald DH 5'11 185 Glenville State B: 12/3/1980 Washington, DC																															
2009	MTL	17	0	0	1	45			4	109	3																				
2010	MTL+	18	0	2	1	57			5	63	5	6	1																		
2011	MTL	1				0																									
3	Years	36	0	2	2	102			9	172	8	6	1																		
JOHN BROWN John Edward (The Body) C 6'4 230 North Carolina Central B: 4/9/1922 Belen, MS D: 6/1/2009 Baton Rouge, LA Pro: A																															
1950	WPG+	13										5	1																		
1952	WPG	5																													
1953	WPG	3							1	0									0	7		7	0								
1954	WPG	2																													
1954	BC	13							2	12														1	33	33.0	33				
1954	Year	15																						1	33	33.0	33				
4	Years	23							3	12		5	1						0	7		7	0	1	33	33.0	33				
JONATHAN BROWN Jonathan Bernard (J.B.) DE-DT-NT 6'4 265 Tennessee B: 11/28/1975 Chickasha, OK Draft: 3-90 1998 GB Pro: EN																															
2004	TOR	16	0	1	2	39	8.0	56.0																							
2005	TOR*	18	1	1	3	36	13.0	89.0			1	6	1																		
2006	TOR+	18	0	0	1	35	6.0	29.0	1	29	1																				
2007	TOR*	18	0	0	1	49	13.0	94.0																							
2008	TOR+	18	0	0	1	44	7.0	34.0			6																				
2009	TOR	9				13	4.0	18.0			1																				
2010	BC	11				16	4.0	27.0			1																				
7	Years	108	1	2	8	232	55.0	347.0	1	29	10	6	1																		
JUSTIN BROWN Justin O'Mara DT 6'2 260 East Central B: 4/16/1982 Fletcher, OK Pro: E																															
2009	CAL	3	0	0	1	7																									
2009	EDM	1				2	1.0	7.0																							
2009	Year	4	0	0	1	9	1.0	7.0																							
2010	EDM	4				6			0	0	1																				
2	Years	7	0	0	1	15	1.0	7.0																							
KEN BROWN Ken DE 6'4 235 Kent State																															
1982	SAS	2					3.5																								
KERRY BROWN Kerry M. DB 6'4 200 Pacific B: 2/12/1972 Boynton Beach, FL D: 7/30/2007 Kaukauna, WI Pro: E																															
1995	OTT	16	2		0	2						6	1	2	21	10.5	11	0	26	427	16.4	72	1								
1996	OTT	1				0													2	14	7.0	7	0								
2	Years	17	2		0	2						6	1	2	21	10.5	11	0	28	441	15.8	72	1								
KEVIN BROWN Kevin DH 6'0 190 Glenville State B: 10/27/1974 Jacksonville, FL																															
2000	WPG	1				3																									
LEON BROWN Leon RB 5'10 190 Eastern Kentucky B: 5/16/1970																															
1994	LV	1				2								8	17	2.1	4	0													
LESTER BROWN Lester RB 5'11 180 Clemson B: 1/5/1957 Georgetown, SC Draft: 7-189 1980 DAL																															
1980	SAS	7	3		0							24	4	114	590	5.2	39	4	23	185	8.0	24	0					1	3	3.0	3
1981	SAS	16	4		1							36	6	189	804	4.3	34	6	32	211	6.6	20	0								
1982	MTL	14	6		0							14	2	87	388	4.5	33	0	61	684	11.2	60	2					11	231	21.0	36
1983	MTL	16	2		0							36	6	148	792	5.4	29	6	37	327	8.8	55	0					15	459	30.6	48
1984	TOR+	15	4		1							108	18	140	594	4.2	24	10	53	780	14.7	71	8					7	151	21.6	28
1985	TOR	3										6	1	15	47	3.1	7	1	10	125	12.5	35	0					1	25	25.0	25
1985	OTT	8										18	3	95	497	5.2	38	3	21	155	7.4	25	0								
1985	Year+	11										24	4	110	544	4.9	38	4	31	280	9.0	35	0					1	25	25.0	25
1986	WPG	5	1		3							20	3	56	302	5.4	47	2	15	120	8.0		1					4	97	24.3	52
1986	OTT	9	0		1							20	3	83	411	5.0	62	3	12	128	10.7	42	0					26	511	19.7	37
1986	Year	14	3		3							40	6	139	713	5.1	62	5	27	248	9.2	42	1					30	608	20.3	52
1987	WPG	4				0						12	2	54	161	3.0	17	1	11	146	13.3	45	1					5	99	19.8	35
8	Years	80	22		6	0						294	48	981	4586	4.7	62	36	275	2861	10.4	71	12					70	1576	22.5	52
MARK BROWN Mark DB 5'10 185 Guelph B: 3/29/1955 Draft: 1-5 1978 TOR																															
1978	WPG	1																													
MARLON BROWN Marlon Dante LB 6'3 233 Memphis B: 6/30/1962 Memphis, TN Draft: 12-328 1989 CLE Pro: E																															
1990	BC	5				7	3.0																								
NORM BROWN Norman Paul WR 6'0 180 Compton CC; Fullerton State B: 2/17/1960 New Orleans, LA																															
1983	TOR	3																	9	74	8.2	18	0								
1984	TOR	2										2	0						7	61	8.7	13	0								
2	Years	5										2	0						16	135	8.4	18	0								
PATRICK BROWN Patrick WR 6'1 178 B: 5/26/1988 New Brunswick, NJ LaSalle; Rutgers; Bethune-Cookman																															
2011	SAS	3				0																									
PETE BROWN Samuel Moris C 6'2 210 Georgia Tech B: 12/19/1930 Rossville, GA D: 9/4/2001 Atlanta, GA Draft: 10-119 1953 SF Pro: N																															
1958	BC	5																													
PHIL BROWN Phil RB 5'11 215 Texas B: 12/20/1970 Austin, TX																															
1995	SA	2	1		0	0						6	1	11	81	7.4	23	1													
PORKY BROWN Gordon DG-DT-OG 6'0 255 St. Martin's B: 1928 Victoria, BC																															
1950	CAL	14																													
1951	CAL	14																													
1953	CAL	15																													
1954	CAL	16	0		2																										
1955	CAL	16																													
1956	CAL	16	0		3																										
1957	CAL	16	0		1																										
1958	CAL	16																													
1959	CAL	16	0		1																										
1960	CAL	16																													
10	Years	155	0		7																										
REGGIE BROWN Reggie RB 5'11 175 Mesa State B: 6/1/1968																															
1992	SAS	4	1		0	1						6	1						6	76	12.7	27	1					10	219	21.9	34
ROBERT BROWN Robert DE 6'1 264 Southern Mississippi B: 12/5/1974 Taiwan																															
1998	EDM	15				15	3.0	24.0																							
1999	EDM	18	0	3	0	31	2.0	15.0																							
2000	EDM	15	0	1	1	21	2.0	10.0	1	-11	1																				
2001	EDM	18	0	0	1	28	6.0	41.0																				1	9	9.0	9
2002	MTL+	18	0	0	2	19	8.0	41.0			5	6	1																		
2003	MTL	12	0	1	0	17	5.0	42.0			1																				
2004	MTL	17	0	0	1	13	5.0	29.0			2																				
2005	MTL	15	0	0	1	7	2.0	6.0			1																				
2006	EDM	18	0	1	1	21	12.0	62.0			2																				
2007	EDM	17	0	1	0	23	3.0	20.0				6	1						1	5	5.0	5	1					1	1	1.0	1
10	Years	163	0	7	7	195	48.0	290.0	1	-11	12	12	2						1	5	5.0	5	1					2	10	5.0	9

Year	Team	GP	FM	FF	FR	TK	SK	YDS	IR	YDS	PD	PTS	TD	RA	YDS	AVG	LG	TD	REC	YDS	AVG	LG	TD	PR	YDS	AVG	LG	KOR	YDS	AVG	LG
ROD BROWN Roderick CB 6'1 188 Oklahoma State B: 6/10/1962																															
1987	OTT	14	0		1	40			2	7														1	0	0.0	0				
1988	OTT	18	0		1	49			4	38		6	1																		
2	Years	32	0		2	89			6	45		6	1											1	0	0.0	0				
RON BROWN Ronald William WR 5'10 186 Colorado; Pasadena CC; Colorado B: 1/11/1963 Long Island, NY Draft: 6A-139 1986 NYG Pro: N																															
1986	SAS	4										6	1						7	121	17.3	40	1					1	25	25.0	25
RUSTY BROWN Rusty OG-OT 6'5 245 Seneca B: 10/30/1956																															
1980	TOR	7																													
1981	TOR	6																													
1982	TOR	2																													
1982	MTL	1																													
1982	Year	3																													
3	Years	15																													
STAN BROWN Byron Stanley WR 5'9 184 Purdue B: 8/4/1949 Martinez, CA Draft: 5-118 1971 CLE Pro: NW																															
1973	WPG	10	1		0							30	5	104	449	4.3	78	4	19	272	14.3	52	1					13	293	22.5	35
STEVE BROWN Wesley Stephen LB 6'3 230 Oregon State B: 6/28/1951 Sikeston, MO Draft: 7A-161 1973 LARM Pro: W																															
1973	CAL	16	0		2				3	13																					
STEVE BROWN Steve WR 6'1 190 Wake Forest B: 1/6/1969 Washington, DC																															
1991	HAM	6	1		0	2						6	1						16	183	11.4	22	1								
TIM BROWN Tim LB 5'11 225 West Virginia B: 1/1/1971 McKeesport, PA Pro: E																															
1995	HAM	10				36	1.0	5.0																							
1996	HAM	3				16	1.0	6.0																							
2	Years	13				52	2.0	11.0																							
TIM BROWN Tim RB 5'8 190 San Francisco CC; Temple B: 10/25/1984 Stockton, CA																															
2011	BC	15	4	0	2	2						36	6	64	376	5.9	43	5	11	72	6.5	13	0	52	521	10.0	97	48	994	20.7	44
TIM BROWN Timothy SB 5'8 165 Rutgers B: 11/9/1987 Miami, FL																															
2011	WPG	3	2	0	1	0								1	9	9.0	9	0	1	8	8.0	8	0	11	82	7.5	21	16	258	16.1	35
TODD BROWN Todd WR-SB 6'0 180 Nebraska B: 7/16/1960 Holdredge, NE Draft: 6-154 1983 DET; TD 1983 BOS-USFL																															
1983	MTL	16	2		0							12	2						50	731	14.6	82	2	1	6	6.0	6	1	10	10.0	13
1984	MTL	10			1							10	1						29	334	11.5	20	1								
1985	MTL	10	1		0							2	0						23	247	10.7	23	0	0	85		45	0	14		14
1987	SAS	10				1						12	2						27	495	18.3	62	2					0	30		30
1988	SAS	1																													
1988	WPG	5										6	1						10	121	12.1	27	1								
1988	Year	6										6	1						10	121	12.1	27	1								
5	Years	47	3		1	1						42	6						139	1928	13.9	82	6	1	91	91.0	45	1	54	54.0	30
TOM BROWN Thomas E. LB-DT-DE-K 6'0 251 Minnesota B: 1937 Draft: 9-108 1959 BAL; 1-3 1961 NYT																															
1961	BC	13			2																										
1962	BC*	16							1																						
1963	BC*	16	0		1				1																						
1964	BC*	16	0		1				4	63																					
1965	BC	16							1																						
1966	BC	16							3	31																					
1967	BC	4																													
7	Years	97	0		4				10	94																					
TRENT BROWN Trent DB 5'11 190 Alberta B: 10/7/1966 Edmonton, AB Draft: 6-41 1989 OTT																															
1991	EDM	12	0		2	19																						0	-6		-6
1992	EDM	18	0		1	52			2	38																					
1993	EDM	16				28	1.0	7.0																							
1994	EDM	17				36					2																				
1995	EDM	13	0		2	46	1.0	9.0	5	28	1																				
1996	EDM*	18				61			1	0	2																				
1997	EDM+	17	0	1	2	47			1	31	2																				
1998	EDM	18	0	0	1	61			1	5	2	6	1																		
8	Years	129	0	1	8	350	2.0	16.0	10	102	9	6	1															0	-6		-6
TYRONE BROWN Tyrone Berry WR 5'11 164 Toledo B: 1/3/1973 Cincinnati, OH Pro: N																															
1999	TOR	15	1	0	0	1						30	5						57	911	16.0	68	5					15	339	22.6	49
2000	TOR	12	2	0	0	4						18	3						36	463	12.9	49	3	26	249	9.6	40	14	260	18.6	45
2001	TOR	8				0						12	2						9	110	12.2	28	2	23	198	8.6	42	17	317	18.6	42
3	Years	35	3	0	0	5						60	10						102	1484	14.5	68	10	49	447	9.1	42	46	916	19.9	49
WELDON BROWN Weldon CB-DH 5'10 185 Louisiana Tech B: 5/12/1987 Shreveport, LA																															
2010	EDM	16	0	0	1	39			0	0	2																	16	362	22.6	41
2011	EDM	18	1	2	1	82	2.0	14.0	5	22	11													14	114	8.1	37	3	52	17.3	27
2	Years	34	1	2	2	121	2.0	14.0	5	22	13													14	114	8.1	37	19	414	21.8	41
WILLIE BROWN Willie Lorenzo RB 5'11 193 Southwestern Oklahoma State B: 6/30/1971 Houston, TX																															
1997	HAM	3	2	0	0	0								8	24	3.0	12	0	2	35	17.5	33	0					5	50	10.0	20
BRADY BROWNE Brady S 5'10 200 Manitoba B: 4/24/1983 Burnaby, BC Draft: 5-38 2008 BC																															
2008	BC	1				0																									
2009	WPG	14				10																									
2010	WPG	13	0	0	1	17			1	60	0																				
2011	WPG	2				0																									
4	Years	30	0	0	1	27			1	60	0																				
KENNY BROWNE Ken OL 6'6 275 Colorado B: 1/24/1962 Scarborough, ON Draft: 2-20 1994 WPG																															
1995	WPG	9				0																									
LESS BROWNE Less CB 5'11 170 Colorado State B: 12/7/1959 East Liverpool, OH Draft: 13B-276 1984 PIT-USFL Pro: U																															
1984	HAM	8	2		0																							2	72	36.0	31
1985	HAM*	15	0		1		1.0		12	165														5	42	8.4	25	2	13	6.5	10
1986	HAM*	17	1		1		1.0		8	128		6	1											1	111	111.0	47	20	520	26.0	61
1987	HAM	16				45			5	32		6	1											1	82	82.0	75	1	26	26.0	26
1988	HAM	15	0		2	42			8	90																		1	62	62.0	62
1989	WPG	17				32			3	31														5	-8	-1.6	6	1	5	5.0	5
1990	WPG*	18	0		3	42			14	273		6	1											1	2	2.0	2				
1991	WPG*	16	1		2	38			10	267									1	19	19.0	19	0	2	15	7.5	9	3	57	19.0	25
1992	OTT*	17	0		2	48			11	259																		1	15	15.0	15
1993	BC	18	0		1	49			5	140		12	2											1	0	0.0	0				
1994	BC*	17				50			11	123	9	6	1											2	0	0.0	0				
11	Years	174	4		12	346	2.0		87	1508	9	36	6						1	19	19.0	19	0	18	244	13.6	75	31	770	24.8	62
BRANDON BROWNER Brandon Kemar CB 6'4 221 Oregon State B: 8/2/1984 Sylmar, CA Pro: N																															
2007	CAL	17	0	4	0	71	1.0	8.0	1	20	5	6	1																		
2008	CAL*	18	0	3	2	75	1.0	1.0	3	7	8																				
2009	CAL*	15				43			3	25	8	6	1																		
2010	CAL*	18	0	1	0	53			5	51	9																				
4	Years	68	0	8	2	242	2.0	9.0	12	103	30	12	2																		
KEITH BROWNER Keith Tellus DE-DT 6'6 245 Southern California B: 1/24/1962 Warren, OH Draft: 2-30 1984 TB; TD 1984 LA-USFL Pro: N																															
1990	TOR	7	0		3	19																									
1994	SHR	11	0		2	9			1	16	4																				
2	Years	18	0		5	28			1	16	4																				
ALFONZO BROWNING Alfonzo WR 6'2 200 Kentucky B: 7/27/1972 Montreal, QC Pro: E																															
1999	MTL	14	1	0	0	2						42	7						33	750	22.7	73	7								
2000	MTL	11	2	0	0	0						48	8						27	528	19.6	55	8								
2001	TOR	10				2						24	4						24	378	15.8	52	4					1	27	27.0	27
3	Years	35	3	0	0	4						114	19						84	1656	19.7	73	19					1	27	27.0	27

Year	Team	GP	FM	FF	FR	TK	SK	YDS	IR	YDS	PD	PTS	TD	RA	YDS	AVG	LG	TD	REC	YDS	AVG	LG	TD	PR	YDS	AVG	LG	KOR	YDS	AVG	LG
VINCENT BROWNLEE Vincent B. WR 6'0 188 Itawamba JC; Mississippi B: 12/20/1969 Amory, MS Draft: 8-219 1992 NYJ																															
1993	BC	2	1		0	0													2	41	20.5	36	0	5	29	5.8	21	9	160	17.8	36
ARLAND BRUCE Arland R., III SB-WR 5'10 193 Hutchinson CC; Minnesota B: 11/23/1977 Kansas City, KS Pro: N																															
2001	WPG	18				4						42	7						48	818	17.0	62	7	3	17	5.7	6	1	3	3.0	3
2002	WPG	17	2	0	1	6						78	13	3	18	6.0	12	1	67	1062	15.9	55	12	20	277	13.9	38	20	410	20.5	36
2004	TOR	7	1	0	1	0						18	3	2	-9	-4.5	4	0	16	247	15.4	34	1	17	332	19.5	81	29	696	24.0	55
2005	TOR+	16	1	0	0	4						66	11	2	-21	-10.5	-5	0	67	1205	18.0	89	11	17	171	10.1	33	27	525	19.4	56
2006	TOR*	18				2						66	11	5	1	0.2	8	0	77	1370	17.8	94	11	5	64	12.8	29	6	154	25.7	43
2007	TOR	14	0	0	1	5						42	7	1	-3	-3.0	-3	0	61	855	14.0	49	7	10	116	11.6	47	6	109	18.2	37
2008	TOR+	18	2	0	0	4						56	9	4	-3	-0.8	9	0	92	1210	13.2	51	9	17	201	11.8	59	8	138	17.3	30
2009	TOR	3				0						6	1						14	199	14.2	38	1	6	25	4.2	9				
2009	HAM	14	1	0	0	1						54	9	2	13	6.5	11	0	74	1043	14.1	49	9	1	5	5.0	5	6	119	19.8	33
2009	Year*	17	1	0	0	1						60	10	2	13	6.5	11	0	88	1242	14.1	49	10	7	32	4.6	9	6	119	19.8	33
2010	HAM*	16				3						48	8						86	1303	15.2	58	8								
2011	HAM	4				0													9	104	11.6	33	0								
2011	BC	12	1	0	0	3						48	8	2	-6	-3.0	0	0	49	755	15.4	100	8								
2011	Year	16	1	0	0	3						48	8	2	-6	-3..0	0	0	58	859	24.8	100	8								
10	Years	131	8	0	3	32						524	87	21	-10	-0.5	12	1	660	10171	15.4	100	84	96	1208	12.6	81	103	2154	20.9	56
LOU BRUCE Lou DE 6'0 205 Queen's B: 1934 Draft: 1-1 1956 OTT																															
1956	OTT	14							1	7		6	1						5	70	14.0	24	1					1	0	0.0	0
1957	OTT	13							1	9																		5	42	8.4	11
1958	OTT	14							1	58																					
1959	OTT	11																													
1960	OTT+	12																													
5	Years	64							3	74		6	1						5	70	14.0	24	1					6	42	7.0	11
HANK BRUCKNER Henry T 6'2 235 Hamilton Panthers Ints. B: 1934																															
1955	SAS	1																													
BOB BRUER Robert Anthony TE 6'5 234 Minnesota State B: 5/22/1953 Madison, WI Draft: 9-221 1975 HOU Pro: N																															
1977	SAS	4										2	0						8	80	10.0	18	0								
1978	SAS	12										12	2						34	491	14.4	52	2								
2	Years	16										14	2						42	571	13.6	52	2								
PAUL BRULE Paul CB-OHB 5'11 205 St. Francis Xavier B: 1945 Draft: 1A-2 1968 OTT																															
1968	WPG	15	2		0				1	7		6	1	13	32	2.5	9	1	5	43	8.6	12	0	40	304	7.6	25				
1969	WPG	16	1		1									1	6	6.0	6	0						63	498	7.9	23	3	39	13.0	15
1970	WPG+	16							9	139				6	11	1.8	14	0						67	496	7.4	16	12	367	30.6	86
1971	WPG	16	2		3				4	92														63	385	6.1	40	2	0	0.0	0
1972	MTL	4							2	59														7	73	10.4	15				
5	Years	67	5		4				16	297		6	1	20	49	2.5	14	1	5	43	8.6	12	0	240	1756	7.3	40	17	406	23.9	86
CLAUDE BRUMFIELD Claude, Jr. OG 6'4 240 Tennessee State B: 2/18/1947 New Orleans, LA Draft: 5-117 1970 NYG																															
1971	HAM	2																													
LARRY BRUNE Larry Dee S 6'2 202 Rice B: 5/4/1953 San Diego, CA Draft: 7-206 1976 MIN Pro: N																															
1976	HAM	7							5	67																		5	53	10.6	22
1977	HAM	4							1	10																		1	46	46.0	46
1977	OTT	7																						2	9	4.5	5				
1977	Year	11							1	10																		1	46	46.0	46
1978	OTT	16	0		2				3	51		6	1																		
1979	OTT	16	0		2				4	35				1	10	10.0	10	0	1	23	23.0	23	0								
1981	OTT	10	0		1		2.0		3	8																					
1982	OTT	3																													
6	Years	56	0		5		2.0		16	171		6	1	1	10	10.0	10	0	1	23	23.0	23	0	2	9	4.5	5	6	99	16.5	46
ANDY BRUNET Andy HB 5'9 160 Ottawa																															
1952	MTL	2																													
AL BRUNO Albert P. E 6'3 195 Kentucky B: 3/28/1927 West Chester, PA Draft: 3-32 1951 PHI																															
1952	TOR+	11										40	8										8								
1953	TOR	10										20	4										4								
1954	OTT	1																	2	23	11.5	16	0								
1955	WPG	14										5	1						19	282	14.8	56	1								
1956	WPG	13							2	2		6	1						32	579	18.1	49	1	2	13	6.5	13				
5	Years	49							2	2		71	14						53	884	16.7	56	14	2	13	6.5	13				
JOHNNY BRUNSON John HB 5'10 195 Benedict B: 2/16/1944 Draft: 8A-189 1967 HOU																															
1968	MTL	1	1		0									3	4	1.3	9	0													
MARK BRUS Mark FB 6'1 215 Tulsa B: 5/13/1967 Edmonton, AB Draft: 4-27 1989 HAM																															
1991	HAM	2				0								1	0	0.0	0	0													
1991	TOR	1				0																									
1991	Year	3				1								1	0	0.0	0	0													
JACK BRUZELL Jack C-DE-LB 6'3 230 Winnipeg Rods Jrs. B: 1938 Winnipeg, MB																															
1959	WPG	7																													
1960	WPG	1																													
1961	WPG	2																													
1962	WPG	12																													
1963	WPG	16																													
1964	WPG	14	1		0																										
6	Years	52	1		0																										
VICTOR BRYAN Victor S 6'2 196 Simon Fraser B: 6/22/1972 Trinidad & Tobago Draft: 5-42 1996 BC																															
1997	BC	2				0																									
1998	WPG	4				1																									
1999	WPG	4				0																									
3	Years	10				1																									
IAN BRYANS Ian LB 6'2 220 Western Ontario B: 2/2/1953 Draft: 3A-22 1975 SAS																															
1975	TOR	16																													
1976	HAM	7							1	7																					
1976	EDM	2			1																										
1976	Year	9			1				1	7																					
1977	EDM	16																													
1978	EDM	16	0		1														1	-2	-2.0	-2	0								
4	Years	55	0		2				1	7									1	-2	-2.0	-2	0								
AL BRYANT Al HB 6'0 170 Edmonton Maple Leafs Jrs.																															
1952	EDM	5			1							5	1	1	12	12.0	12	0	2	37	18.5	23	1								
1953	EDM	8												1	5	5.0	5	0													
1954	EDM	13																													
3	Years	26			1							5	1	2	17	8.5	12	0	2	37	18.5	23	1								
BENO BRYANT Wilson G. RB 5'9 170 Washington B: 1/1/1971 Los Angeles, CA Pro: EN																															
1995	OTT	6	1		0	1								8	24	3.0	6	0	6	61	10.2	16	0	20	91	4.6	15	5	131	26.2	42
BLAISE BRYANT Blaze X. RB 5'11 203 Iowa State B: 11/23/1969 Huntington Beach, CA Draft: 6A-148 1991 NYJ																															
1993	WPG	8	3		0	1						6	1	62	313	5.0	68	1	31	252	8.1	31	0					1	31	31.0	31
1993	SAS	2	2		0	0								24	100	4.2	25	0	16	132	8.3	35	0					4	88	22.0	28
1993	Year	10	5		0	1						6	1	86	413	4.8	68	1	47	384	8.2	35	0					5	119	23.8	31
1994	WPG	16	8		2	8						66	11	232	1289	5.6	65	10	45	541	12.0	46	0	3	15	5.0	10	26	473	18.2	92
1995	WPG	14	6		1	6						48	8	159	664	4.2	25	7	33	268	8.1	32	1								
1996	WPG	7	3		0	3						12	2	69	278	4.0	32	1	23	212	9.2	24	1								
4	Years	45	22		3	18						132	22	546	2644	4.8	68	19	148	1405	9.5	46	2	3	15	5.0	10	31	592	19.1	92
BOB BRYANT Robert R. T 6'3 226 Santa Ana JC; Texas Tech B: 6/14/1918 Frederick, OK D: 11/3/2000 Oklahoma City, OK Pro: A																															

Year	Team	GP	FM	FF	FR	TK	SK	YDS	IR	YDS	PD	PTS	TD	RA	YDS	AVG	LG	TD	REC	YDS	AVG	LG	TD	PR	YDS	AVG	LG	KOR	YDS	AVG	LG
1952	CAL	12			3																							1	9	9.0	9
1953	CAL	14																													
2	Years	26	0		3																							1	9	9.0	9
CHARLIE BRYANT Charles Limar RB 6'1 207 Allen B: 3/7/1941 Wampee, SC D: 10/19/2001 Florence, SC Draft: 9-135 1966 STL Pro: N																															
1970	WPG	6										12	2	46	246	5.3	41	1	6	39	6.5	25	1					6	157	26.2	36
1971	WPG	3												29	107	3.7	19	0	5	94	18.8	67	0					3	50	16.7	21
1971	EDM	6	1		0							12	2	38	228	6.0	44	2	11	140	12.7	31	0					3	83	27.7	37
1971	Year	9	1		0							12	2	67	335	5.0	44	2	16	234	14.6	67	0					6	133	22.2	37
2	Years	9	1		0							24	4	113	581	5.1	44	3	22	273	12.4	67	1					12	290	24.2	37
JASON BRYANT Jason LB-DB 6'2 200 Morehead State B: 12/9/1970 Steelton, PA																															
1995	BAL	14	0		1	39			1	-1	4																				
1996	MTL	16	0		2	80			2	102	5	6	1															1	12	12.0	12
1998	BC	9				46	3.0	23.0																							
3	Years	39	0		3	165	3.0	23.0	3	101	9	6	1															1	12	12.0	12
LaDRELLE BRYANT LaDrelle M. DL 6'1 235 Purdue; Garden City CC; Indiana State B: 4/3/1983 Muncie, IN																															
2006	CAL	1				0																									
LAMONT BRYANT Lamont Demond DE 6'3 260 Notre Dame B: 10/11/1976 Pro: X																															
2002	HAM	17	0	3	2	52	7.0				3	6	1																		
2003	HAM	7				6																									
2004	SAS	15	0	0	1	39	4.0				1																				
3	Years	39	0	3	3	97	11.0				4	6	1																		
ROMBY BRYANT Romby WR-SB 6'1 181 Northeastern Oklahoma A&M JC; Tulsa B: 12/21/1979 Oklahoma City, OK Pro: EN																															
2008	WPG	18	1	0	0	1						54	9	2	4	2.0	3	0	65	1206	18.6	85	9								
2009	WPG	11	2	1	0	7								4	12	3.0	7	0	20	232	11.6	36	0					2	-5	-2.5	0
2009	CAL	7	1	0	0	2								1	11	11.0	11	0	27	548	20.3	53	0								
2009	Year	18	3	1	0	9								5	23	4.6	11	0	47	780	16.6	53	0					2	-5	-2.5	0
2010	CAL+	18	1	0	1	7						90	15	5	13	2.6	6	0	77	1167	15.2	68	15					1	0	0.0	0
2011	CAL	18	2	0	1	4						36	6	2	5	2.5	4	1	51	632	12.4	39	5					2	4	2.0	2
4	Years	65	7	1	2	21						180	30	14	45	3.2	11	1	240	3785	15.8	85	29					5	-1	-0.2	2
STANLEY BRYANT Stanley Myron OT 6'5 282 Elizabeth City State; East Carolina B: 5/7/1985 Goldsboro, NC																															
2010	CAL	3				0																									
2011	CAL	17				3																									
2	Years	20				3																									
TIM BRYANT Timothy Craig LB 6'1 217 Vanderbilt; Southern Mississippi B: 5/5/1962 Nashville, TN Pro: N																															
1984	TOR	2																													
TRENT BRYANT Trent Baron CB 5'9 180 Arkansas B: 8/14/1959 Arkadelphia, AR Draft: 10B-259 1981 BAL Pro: NU																															
1986	SAS	18	0		1				6	56																					
1987	SAS	3				5																									
2	Years	21	0		1	5			6	56																					
WES BRYANT Wesley Taylor T 6'2 225 Arkansas B: 5/2/1942 Texarkana, AR D: 2/11/2010 Missouri City, TX Draft: 16-126 1963 BOS; 7-90 1964 MIN																															
1965	TOR	3																													
TONY BUA Tony J. LB 5'11 218 Arkansas B: 2/11/1980 New Orleans, LA Draft: 5-160 2004 MIA Pro: N																															
2007	CAL	5				10																									
DAVE BUCHANAN David HB 5'9 200 Arizona State B: 4/23/1948 Los Angeles, CA Pro: W																															
1971	HAM	9	1		0							6	1	62	213	3.4	23	0	8	56	7.0	20	1					5	94	18.8	26
1972	HAM*	14	11		2							42	7	263	1163	4.4	52	4	25	275	11.0	68	3								
1974	WPG	9	1		1									95	328	3.5	18	0	10	92	9.2	21	0								
3	Years	32	13		3							48	8	420	1704	4.1	52	4	43	423	9.8	68	4					5	94	18.8	26
ED BUCHANAN Edwin Earl OHB 6'1 186 San Diego JC B: 7/31/1939 D: 8/31/1991 San Diego, CA																															
1961	CAL	9	2									24	4	45	348	7.7	40	1	10	264	26.4	63	3					4	78	19.5	36
1962	CAL	16	2									60	10	136	824	6.1	86	7	30	450	15.0	75	3					4	111	27.8	37
1963	CAL	11	3		0							12	2	63	343	5.4	19	2	17	203	11.9	35	0					9	206	22.9	52
1963	SAS	3	3		0							6	1	23	104	4.5	20	0	5	88	17.6		1					3	96	32.0	
1963	Year	14	6		0							18	3	86	447	5.2	30	2	22	291	13.2	36	1					12	302	25.2	52
1964	SAS*	16	5		2							54	9	179	1390	7.8	93	7	36	681	18.9	48	2					13	352	27.1	55
1965	SAS	4												24	86	3.6	15	0	4	87	21.8	28	0					7	232	33.1	45
1966	SAS	6	1		1							18	3	32	181	5.7	43	0	14	296	21.1	80	3					6	138	23.0	33
1967	SAS	16	2		1							24	4	120	695	5.8	85	2	33	477	14.5	53	2					20	506	25.3	36
1969	HAM	14	1		1							36	6	62	281	4.5	20	1	31	555	17.9	83	5					16	480	30.0	62
1970	HAM	14	5		0							36	6	112	605	5.4	78	4	35	500	14.3	42	2					16	396	24.8	40
9	Years	106	24		5							270	45	796	4857	6.1	93	24	215	3601	16.7	83	21					98	2595	26.5	62
PETE BUCHANAN Peter LB 6'0 230 Nebraska B: 9/29/1964 Winnipeg, MB Draft: 7-51 1989 HAM																															
1989	TOR	7	0		1	0																									
1989	HAM	1				0																									
1989	V	8	0		1	0																									
1990	HAM	13				13																						2	21	10.5	16
2	Years	20	0		1	13																						2	21	10.5	16
STEVE BUCHKO Steve T none B: 7/27/1925																															
1946	WPG	6																													
BERNIE BUCHOLTZ Bernard LB 6'1 190 North Bay Roughriders Ints. B: 1934																															
1955	SAS	2												1	1	1.0	1	0						1	7	7.0	7				
ED BUCKINGHAM Edwin E. T 6'4 255 Minnesota B: 7/16/1934 Terre Haute, IN Draft: 16-183 1957 GB Pro: N																															
1959	EDM	1																													
ROSS BUCKLE Ross FL-DE-LB 6'0 200 none B: 2/26/1936 London, ON																															
1959	MTL	11																													
1960	MTL	11																	1	33	33.0	33	0								
1961	MTL	10										12	2						5	197	39.4	94	2								
1962	MTL	14																	7	73	10.4	25	0								
1963	MTL	13																	6	104	17.3	22	0								
1964	MTL	1																													
6	Years	60										12	2						19	407	21.4	94	2								
FRANK BUDD Francis Joseph FL-OHB 5'10 187 Villanova* B: 7/20/1939 Long Branch, NJ Draft: 7B-96 1962 PHI Pro: N																															
1965	CAL	16										24	4	1	3	3.0	3	0	20	468	23.4	90	4					1	32	32.0	32
1966	CAL	16	2		1							12	2	2	16	8.0	14	0	18	423	23.5	69	2					1	13	13.0	13
2	Years	32	2		1							36	6	3	19	6.3	14	0	38	891	23.4	90	6					2	45	22.5	32
JOHN BUDDENBERG John Edward, Jr. OG-OT 6'6 270 Akron B: 10/9/1965 Wheeling, WV Draft: 10-274 1989 CLE Pro: E																															
1994	SAC	18				2																									
1995	SA	17				0																									
2	Years	35				2																									
MYRO BUDZAN Myro E 6'1 165 Winnipeg Rods Jrs.; Norwood-St. Boniface Ints. B: 1930																															
1952	WPG	2																													
BART BUETOW Barton Max (The Mad Scientist) OG 6'5 250 Minnesota B: 10/28/1950 Minneapolis, MN Draft: 3-59 1972 MIN Pro: N																															
1974	TOR	6																													
1975	TOR	9																													
2	Years	15																													
BILL BUFTON Bill DT-DE 6'3 220 Idaho B: 1946																															
1967	BC	16	0		1														1	22	22.0	22	0								
1968	BC	16																													
2	Years	32	0		1														1	22	22.0	22	0								
DANNY BUGGS Daniel WR 6'2 185 West Virginia B: 4/22/1953 Duluth, GA Draft: 3-62 1975 NYG Pro: NU																															
1980	EDM	4										18	3						11	134	12.2	35	3								
JONTE' BUHL Jonte' Lamon DH 5'9 170 Texas A&M B: 4/4/1982 San Antonio, TX																															

Year	Team	GP	FM	FF	FR	TK	SK	YDS	IR	YDS	PD	PTS	TD	RA	YDS	AVG	LG	TD	REC	YDS	AVG	LG	TD	PR	YDS	AVG	LG	KOR	YDS	AVG	LG
2006	EDM	15	0	2	2	39			1	0	6																				
2007	EDM	3	0	1	0	9			1	19	0																				
2008	EDM	18				53	1.0	4.0	4	46	4																				
2009	EDM	8				29			1	0	2																				
4	Years	44	0	3	2	130	1.0	4.0	7	65	12																				
JARRIETT BUIE Jarriett C. DE 6'3 255 South Florida B: 9/7/1985 Tampa, FL																															
2010	MTL	1	0	1	0	1			1	3	0																				
JAMIE BUIS Jamie OT-C 6'4 265 Simon Fraser B: 4/12/1962 New Westminster, BCDraft: 1B-8 1983 BC																															
1983	BC	1																													
1984	BC	16	0		2																										
1985	BC	16	0		1																										
1986	BC	18																													
1987	BC	14				0																						1	7	7.0	7
1988	BC	18				0																									
1989	BC	18	0		1	2																									
7	Years	101	0		4	2																						1	7	7.0	7
BRIAN BULCKE Brian DT 6'4 285 Stanford B: 4/27/1987 Windsor, ON Draft: 1-6 2010 EDM																															
2011	CAL	8				11	1.0	3.0			2																				
BYRON BULLOCK Byron Carl LB 6'0 218 Canyons JC; South Dakota B: 3/4/1987 Inglewood, CA																															
2010	SAS	3	0	1	0	5																									
JAMES BULLOCK James D. CB 5'10 190 Odessa JC; Arizona B: 10/22/1968 Dallas, TX																															
1994	LV	10	2		2	13						12	2															19	572	30.1	94
AMOS BULLOCKS Amos Lee OHB 6'0 201 Southern Illinois B: 2/7/1939 Chicago, IL Draft: 10-76 1962 BUF; 20-270 1962 DAL Pro: N																															
1965	BC	9	1									7	1	44	215	4.9	14	1	17	194	11.4	34	0					7	156	22.3	38
TERRY BULYCH Terry RB 6'0 208 Weber State B: 1941 Draft: TE 1973 SAS																															
1973	SAS	16										18	3	8	24	3.0	5	3	2	18	9.0	19	0								
1974	SAS	3												5	22	4.4	19	0													
1975	SAS	16										1	0	2	0	0.0	0	0						2	12	6.0	12				
3	Years	35										19	3	15	46	3.1	19	3	2	18	9.0	19	0	2	12	6.0	12				
MATT BUMGARDNER James Matthew WR 6'2 200 Texas A&M B: 4/2/1977 Piedo Negras, New Mexico																															
2001	BC	1				0													3	41	13.7	23	0								
MICHAEL BUMPUS Michael Leron WR 5'11 194 Washington State B: 12/13/1985 Honolulu, HI Pro: N																															
2009	BC	4				0						6	1						5	36	7.2	29	1	16	203	12.7	40	1	17	17.0	17
DON BUNCE Donald R. QB 6'1 196 Stanford B: 1/17/1949 D: 4/15/2003 Palo Alto, CA Draft: 12-307 1972 WAS																															
1972	BC	15	3		0									8	58	7.3	16	0													
KEN BUNGARDA Kestutis John OT 6'6 270 Arizona Western JC; Missouri B: 1/25/1957 Hartford, CT Draft: 11-278 1979 CIN Pro: N																															
1979	TOR	4																													
HARRY BUNTING Harry E 6'0 188 Toronto Jrs. B: 1928																															
1949	EDM	11																													
1950	EDM	14																	9	97	10.8		0								
1951	EDM	13										5	1						2	68	34.0		1								
3	Years	38										5	1						11	165	15.0		1								
TERRY BUNTING Terry G 6'2 225 Port Arthur Mustangs Ints. B: 1935																															
1960	SAS	16																													
1961	SAS	16																													
2	Years	32																													
ARVYD BUNTINS Arvyd DE 6'5 217 none B: 1937 Lithuania																															
1957	TOR	13																													
1958	TOR	14																													
1959	TOR	2																													
3	Years	29																													
WALLY BUONO Pasquale LB 5'11 214 Montreal Jrs.; Idaho State B: 7/2/1950 Potenza, Italy																															
1972	MTL	14																													
1973	MTL	14	2		2				2	19		3	0																		
1974	MTL	16							1	27																					
1975	MTL	16																										3	44	14.7	17
1976	MTL	16	0		1																							1	0	0.0	0
1977	MTL	16	0		2				2	7				1	18	18.0	18	0										1	0	0.0	0
1978	MTL	16	0		2				4	61		8	0															1	6	6.0	6
1979	MTL	16	0		2				2	-5		4	0																		
1980	MTL	16																													
1981	MTL	16					1.0					1	0															0	2		2
10	Years	156	2		9		1.0		11	109		16	0	1	18	18.0	18	0										6	52	8.7	17
CORNELL BURBAGE Cornell Rodney WR 5'10 181 Kentucky B: 2/22/1965 Lexington, KY Pro: EN																															
1993	HAM	12	1		1	6						18	3						31	367	11.8	31	3	16	126	7.9	45	35	597	17.1	43
1994	HAM	5	1		0	1						6	1						15	199	13.3	37	0	10	69	6.9	14	10	246	24.6	93
2	Years	17	2		1	7						24	4						46	566	12.3	37	3	26	195	7.5	45	45	843	18.7	93
ALFIE BURCH Alfie DB 6'0 196 Michigan B: 3/24/1971																															
1994	LV	6				9																									
JOE BURCH Joe OG 6'2 280 Texas Southern B: 8/8/1971 Dallas, TX Draft: 3B-90 1994 NE																															
2000	TOR	1				0																									
SWIFT BURCH Swift DT 6'4 265 Temple B: 5/8/1969 Washington, DC																															
1994	TOR	16	0		2	31	9.0	40.0	1	0														1	3	3.0	3				
1995	TOR	18	0		1	62	8.0	47.			2																				
1996	OTT	16				45	6.0	44.0			3																	2	8	4.0	8
1997	MTL	18	0	3	2	49	7.0	24.0			1																				
1998	MTL	16	0	1	0	33	9.0	65.0			2																				
1999	MTL	14	0	1	0	33	5.0	33.0			1																				
2000	MTL+	17	0	0	1	32	9.0	55.0			5	6	1																		
2001	MTL	18	0	5	1	41	7.0	33.0			2																				
8	Years	133	0	10	7	326	60.0	341.0	1	0	16	6	1											1	3	3.0	3	2	8	4.0	8
WILLIE BURDEN Willie James RB 5'11 205 North Carolina State B: 7/21/1951 Longwood, NC Draft: 6A-139 1974 DET; 17-198 1974 POR-WFL																															
1974	CAL	6	1		0							18	3	94	541	5.8	71	3	13	106	8.2	25	0					1	37	37.0	37
1975	CAL*	16	5		0							90	15	332	1896	5.7	40	10	36	231	6.4	52	5					16	360	22.5	33
1976	CAL	13	2		1							54	9	181	962	5.3	35	7	43	363	8.4	51	2								
1977	CAL+	16	4		0							30	5	220	1032	4.7	47	3	63	611	9.7	42	2								
1978	CAL	15	4		1							18	3	160	627	3.9	23	2	31	307	9.9	54	1								
1979	CAL	13	1		3							50	8	145	658	4.5	19	5	42	373	8.9	33	3								
1980	CAL	16	3		0							30	5	87	423	4.9	23	2	49	495	10.1	51	3								
1981	CAL	8												23	95	4.1	28	0	22	183	8.3	19	0								
8	Years	103	20		5							290	48	1242	6234	5.0	71	32	299	2669	8.9	54	16					17	397	23.4	37
GORD BURDICK Gordon, Jr. G-T 5'11 190 B: 1927																															
1946	TOR	1																													
JAMES BURGESS James Paul LB 5'11 230 Miami (Florida) B: 3/31/1974 Miami, FL Pro: NX																															
2002	CAL	10				29	2.0	12.0	1	16	1																				
TOM BURGESS Thomas A. QB 6'0 195 Colgate B: 3/6/1964 Newark, NJ																															
1986	OTT	18	1		0									26	113	4.3	14	0													
1987	SAS	10	4		1	0						6	1	26	114	4.4	14	1													
1988	SAS	18	2		1	1						18	3	61	249	4.1	25	3													
1989	SAS	18	2		0	1								48	209	4.4	28	0													
1990	WPG+	18	6		2	2								70	260	3.7	26	0													
1991	WPG	18	8		2	0								73	326	4.5	19	0													

Year	Team	GP	FM	FF	FR	TK	SK	YDS	IR	YDS	PD	PTS	TD	RA	YDS	AVG	LG	TD	REC	YDS	AVG	LG	TD	PR	YDS	AVG	LG	KOR	YDS	AVG	LG
1992	OTT+	18	10		2	3						30	5	68	348	5.1	19	5													
1993	OTT	18	11		6	2						18	3	75	347	4.6	18	3													
1994	SAS	18	4		1	0						36	6	51	188	3.7	16	6													
1995	SAS	18	4		1	0						6	1	30	86	2.9	12	1													
10	Years	172	52		16	9						114	19	528	2240	4.2	28	19													
JOE BURGOS Joe OT 6'3 290 Temple B: 3/12/1971 New York, NY																															
1994	TOR	17				1																									
1995	TOR	10	0		1	2																									
1996	TOR	6				0																									
1997	HAM	7				0																									
4		40	0		1	3																									
FABIAN BURKE Fabian S 6'0 190 Toledo B: 5/5/1978 Kitchener, ON Draft: 2-13 2001 EDM																															
2001	EDM	9				9					2																				
2002	EDM	15				10			1	35	0																				
2003	EDM	18				16					2																				
2004	EDM	6	1	0	0	7																						2	2	1.0	2
2004	BC	11				3																									
2004	Year	17	1	0	0	10																						2	2	1.0	2
4	Years	48	1	0	0	45			1	35	4																	2	2	1.0	2
ORVILLE BURKE Orville QB 5'10 160 none B: 1917																															
1946	OTT	1										4	0																		
PATRICK BURKE Patrick S 5'11 180 Fresno CC B: 11/6/1968 Willowdale, ON Draft: 1-1 1993 BC																															
1993	OTT	18				44			1	0																		27	415	15.4	30
1994	OTT	12				34			1	0	6																	8	123	15.4	36
1995	OTT	1				4																						2	36	18.0	22
1995	TOR	4				7																									
1995	Year	5				11																						2	36	18.0	22
1997	SAS	13	0	3	1	31			1	33	3													1	4	4.0	4				
1998	SAS	5				3																									
1998	WPG	4	0	0	1	17																									
1998	Year	9	0	0	1	20																									
5	Years	49	0	3	2	140			3	33	9													1	4	4.0	4	37	574	15.5	36
TOMMY BURKE Tommy T Regina Dales Jrs.																															
1947	SAS	1																													
FERDIE BURKET Fred FB 6'1 220 Southeastern Oklahoma State B: 1/9/1934 Draft: 14-168 1959 BAL																															
1959	SAS	9										40	6	105	423	4.0	16	5	10	68	6.8	25	1	1	16	16.0	16	5	129	25.8	29
1960	SAS	10	2		0							17	2	127	544	4.3	15	2	8	66	8.3	24	0					1	10	10.0	10
1961	SAS	16	6									31	3	142	583	4.1	37	3	17	166	9.8	23	0					1	17	17.0	17
1962	SAS	16	2									37	4	114	531	4.7	18	3	12	96	8.0	27	1					1	10	10.0	10
1963	MTL	7										13	2	62	340	5.5	61	1	4	57	14.3	38	1					8	106	13.3	21
5	Years	58	10		0							138	17	550	2421	4.4	61	14	51	453	8.9	38	3	1	16	16.0	16	16	272	17.0	29
DAVE BURKHOLDER David Alan LB-OT 6'1 225 Minnesota B: 10/21/1936 Minneapolis, MN D: 10/12/1999 Minnetonka, MN Draft: 26-310 1958 NYG																															
1958	WPG+	15							3	26																					
1959	WPG	16																													
1960	WPG+	14	0		1				3	14																					
1961	WPG+	12			2							6	1																		
1962	WPG	16	0		3				2	3		6	1																		
1963	WPG	10																													
1964	WPG	15							1																						
7	Years	98	0		6				9	43		12	2																		
DARRELL BURKO Darrell LB 6'2 224 Saskatchewan B: 7/8/1957 Draft: 1B-8 1979 CAL																															
1980	TOR	2																													
AL BURLESON Alvin Bernard DB 6'2 185 Washington B: 9/24/1954 San Francisco, CA Draft: 14-400 1976 LARM Pro: U																															
1976	CAL	7																										7	150	21.4	46
1977	CAL	16	1		2				4	24									2	15	7.5	8	0	13	85	6.5	18	12	299	24.9	42
1978	CAL+	16	1		1				7	72																					
1979	CAL*	16	0		3				9	130														1	0	0.0	0				
1980	CAL	8	0		1				3	4																					
1981	CAL	16	0		1				3	17																					
6	Years	79	2		8				26	247									2	15	7.5	8	0	14	85	6.1	18	19	449	23.6	46
PAUL BURLESON Paul OE 6'2 190 Oregon B: 1942																															
1967	BC	7										6	1						17	222	13.1	40	1								
ECOMET BURLEY Ecomet, Jr. DT 5'10 240 Texas Tech B: 6/6/1954 Anderson County, TX																															
1976	TOR	7	0		1																										
1977	TOR+	16	0		1																										
1978	TOR	1																													
1979	TOR	16	0		1							6	1																		
1980	WPG	16	0		1																										
1981	HAM+	14	0		2		7.5																								
6	Years	70	0		6		7.5					6	1																		
KEITH BURNELL Keith Tyrone RB 5'11 205 Virginia Tech; Delaware B: 1/8/1979 Northfolk, VA																															
2005	HAM	1				0								1	3	3.0	3	0										1	13	13.0	13
LEM BURNHAM Lem L. DE 6'4 236 Santa Ana JC; U.S. International B: 8/30/1947 Winter Haven, FL Draft: 15-378 1974 KC; 17-201 1974 HAW-WFL Pro: NW																															
1976	WPG	1																													
TIM BURNHAM Timothy Scott OT 6'5 280 Washington B: 5/6/1963 Redding, CA Pro: N																															
1987	BC	3				0																									
CHRIS BURNS Chris OT 6'4 295 Portland State B: 12/2/1972 Greenwich, CT Draft: Bonus-2 1994 SAS																															
1994	SAS	18	0		1	3																									
1995	OTT	17				4																									
1996	OTT	18				2																									
1997	CAL	18				2																									
1998	HAM	18				2																									
1999	HAM+	18				3																									
2000	HAM+	18				1																									
2001	HAM	5				0																									
2002	OTT	18				2																									
2003	OTT	18				1																									
2004	OTT	18				2																									
11	Years	184	0		1	22																									
DOYLE BURNS Doyle Ray WR 6'3 200 Stephen F. Austin State B: 8/17/1973 Harris County, TX																															
1996	WPG	1				0													1	7	7.0	7	0								
BRYAN BURNTHORNE Bryan E. T 6'1 220 Tulane B: 1933 Draft: 27-314 1956 DET																															
1956	CAL	10																						0	16		16				
BILL BURRELL William G. OG-LB 6'0 215 Illinois B: 1938 Draft: FS 1960 BUF; 5A-50 1960 STL																															
1960	SAS+	16																													
1961	SAS	13							3	37																					
1962	SAS+	16	0		2				3	57																					
1963	SAS	14	0		1																										
1964	SAS	14	0		1									1	3	3.0	3	0													
5	Years	73	0		4				6	94				1	3	3.0	3	0													
DON BURRELL Donald K. DB 6'0 195 Indiana; Mississippi State B: 8/2/1956 Birmingham, AL Pro: U																															
1981	WPG	11							3	23		6	1											1	5	5.0	5	5	206	41.2	110

Year	Team	GP	FM	FF	FR	TK	SK	YDS	IR	YDS	PD	PTS	TD	RA	YDS	AVG	LG	TD	REC	YDS	AVG	LG	TD	PR	YDS	AVG	LG	KOR	YDS	AVG	LG
1982	WPG	2																										1	43	43.0	43
2	Years	13							3	23		6	1											1	5	5.0	5	6	249	41.5	110
KEN BURRESS Ken CB 5'11 180 Bowling Green State B: 2/16/1970 Middletown, OH																															
1994	WPG	11	1		0	25			1	0	5													7	10	1.4	6	5	107	21.4	28
1995	WPG	16	3		4	37			3	3	10													7	52	7.4	17	20	411	20.6	31
1996	BC	2				7																									
3	Years	29	4		4	69			4	3	15													14	62	4.4	17	25	518	20.7	31
HENRY BURRIS Henry Armand QB 6'0 195 Temple B: 6/4/1975 Fort Smith, AR Pro: EN																															
1997	CAL	1				0																									
1998	CAL	18				0								2	4	2.0	2	0													
1999	CAL	3	1	0	0	0								13	81	6.2	16	0													
2000	SAS	18	12	0	1	0						48	8	68	188	2.8	17	8													
2003	SAS	9				0								2	16	8.0	9	0													
2004	SAS	18	14	1	4	5						42	7	84	464	5.5	34	7													
2005	CAL+	16	15	0	5	3						54	9	82	513	6.3	31	9													
2006	CAL	18	7	0	2	0						30	5	70	480	6.9	21	5													
2007	CAL	16	6	0	1	1						30	5	85	623	7.3	39	5													
2008	CAL+	18	9	0	3	1						18	3	87	595	6.8	35	3													
2009	CAL	18	8	0	0	0						66	11	106	552	5.2	30	11													
2010	CAL*	18	6	0	1	2						10	0	70	401	7.0	27	3													
2011	CAL	18	13	0	5	1						24	4	51	385	7.5	34	4													
13	Years	189	91	1	22	13						330	55	720	4392	6.1	39	55													
KURT BURRIS Kurt B. C-LB 6'1 205 Oklahoma B: 6/27/1932 Nowata, OK D: 7/21/1999 Billings, MT Draft: 1-13 1955 CLE																															
1955	EDM+	15	0		2				5	57																					
1957	EDM	11							1	32																					
1958	SAS	13	0		3																										
1960	CAL	8																													
4	Years	47	0		5				6	89																					
JIM BURROW James Arthur, Jr. DB 5'11 181 Nebraska B: 11/29/1953 Hampton, VA Draft: 8-218 1976 GB Pro: N																															
1977	MTL	4							2	4																					
1978	MTL+	16	0		1				5	34		6	1											6	59	9.8	22				
1979	MTL+	16	1		2				6	133		6	1																		
1980	MTL	9	0		2				1	21																					
1980	CAL	6							1	16																					
1980	Year	15							2	37																					
1981	OTT	3							2	31																					
5	Years	48	1		5				17	239		12	2											6	59	9.8	22				
TONY BURSE Tony Lee FB 6'0 220 Middle Tennessee State B: 4/4/1965 Lafayette, GA Draft: 12B-324 1987 SEA Pro: EN																															
1994	SAC	6				8						6	1	13	41	3.2	12	1	10	74	7.4	16	0								
1995	SA	17	2		0	26						12	2	60	304	5.1	40	2	30	291	9.7	43	0								
1996	EDM	10	0	0	1	12						48	8	50	213	4.3	59	6	18	168	9.3	18	2								
1997	EDM	13	5	0	2	10						78	13	80	254	3.2	26	13	29	309	10.7	27	0								
1998	EDM	4				2						12	2	22	96	4.4	20	2	7	68	9.7	20	0								
1999	TOR	11	2	1	0	11						18	3	92	431	4.7	46	3	14	176	12.6	52	0					5	52	10.4	22
2000	TOR	8	1	0	0	4						14	2	27	94	3.5	11	2	6	52	8.7	20	0								
7	Years	69	10	1	3	73						188	31	344	1433	4.2	59	29	114	1138	10.0	52	2					5	52	10.4	22
MACK BURTON Mack SE-FL-DH 6'2 195 San Francisco CC; San Jose State B: 1939 San Francisco, CA Draft: 4B-32 1962 SD; 5A-57 1962 CHIB																															
1962	BC	12	1									36	6						52	818	15.7	73	6					7	121	17.3	37
1963	BC	11										18	3						23	352	15.3	45	3								
1964	BC	16							2	43		18	3						30	536	17.9	78	3					1	4	4.0	4
1965	BC	16							3	22		18	3						44	501	11.4	25	3								
1966	BC	5																													
5	Years	60	1						5	65		90	15						149	2207	14.8	78	15					8	125	15.6	37
MAURICE BURTON Maurice CB 5'10 170 Morgan State B: 3/9/1958 Benton Harbor, MI																															
1981	MTL	3																													
1981	HAM	1																													
1981	Year	4																													
TIRREL BURTON Tirrel E. (The Turtle) HB 5'11 165 Miami (Ohio) B: 11/19/1929 Draft: 6-65 1956 PHI																															
1956	OTT	12							8	64		24	4	29	155	5.3	18	3	14	319	22.8	68	1					11	175	15.9	27
TOM BUSCH Thomas LeRoy OE 6'0 190 Iowa State B: 7/8/1946 Garner, IA D: 12/5/2006 Cedar Rapids, IA Draft: 10-259 1968 STL																															
1969	WPG	6				1													14	188	13.4	18	0								
LOREN BUSER Loren E. LB 5'11 215 Northern Iowa B: 8/26/1944																															
1966	MTL	6							1	9																		2	28	14.0	19
CHRIS BUSH Christopher WR 6'1 193 Tulane B: 7/22/1981 Metairie, LA																															
2006	BC	4				2													5	65	13.0	30	0								
DAVIN BUSH Davin S. DH-CB 5'8 165 Central Florida B: 10/5/1977 Miami, FL																															
2001	SAS	1				1																									
2002	SAS	9				26			1	20	4													2	17	8.5	15	2	50	25.0	32
2003	SAS	17	1	1	1	43			4	58	12	6	1											4	36	9.0	16				
2004	SAS	18				49			2	0	7																				
2005	SAS	16	0	1	0	43			3	111	13	6	1																		
2006	SAS	17				33			5	28	7																				
2007	WPG	11				35					3																				
7	Years	89	1	2	1	230			15	217	46	12	2											6	53	8.8	16	2	50	25.0	32
JOHN BUSH John C 6'5 295 Rhode Island B: 6/17/1977 Sunbury, PA																															
2000	TOR	6				0																									
PAUL BUSHEY Paul F. FB 6'1 220 Colgate B: 4/9/1966 Hamilton, ON Draft: 4-32 1990 SAS																															
1990	SAS	14				1								5	28	5.6	18	0										7	95	13.6	23
1991	SAS	9	1		0	10						6	1	13	81	6.2	25	1	3	21	7.0	9	0					1	11	11.0	11
1991	HAM	6				21						2	0	2	8	4.0	6	0	1	5	5.0	5	0					3	45	15.0	20
1991	Year	15	1		0	31						8	1	15	89	5.9	25	1	4	26	6.5	9	0					4	56	14.0	20
1992	HAM	8	0		1	17								5	48	9.6	23	0	12	163	13.6	22	0					2	22	11.0	15
1993	HAM	15	1		0	20						6	1	15	60	4.0	12	1	18	135	7.5	30	0					2	23	11.5	13
1994	HAM	12	0		2	15								2	7	3.5	4	0	7	70	10.0	25	0					2	4	2.0	7
1995	OTT	5	1		0	1								5	7	1.4	5	0	3	27	9.0	18	0								
6	Years	63	3		3	85						14	2	47	239	5.1	25	2	44	421	9.6	30	0					17	200	11.8	23
DAN BUTCHER Dan OG 6'2 260 Edmonton Huskies Jrs. B: 12/11/1959																															
1982	EDM	1																													
1983	EDM	2																													
2	Years	3																													
AL BUTLER Al CB 6'3 220 Compton CC B: 10/16/1945																															
1972	MTL	8	0		1				7	78		6	1																		
1973	MTL	1																													
1973	EDM	1																													
1973	Year	2																													
2	Years	9	0		1				7	78		6	1																		
BILL BUTLER William R. OHB 5'10 189 Tennessee-Chattanooga B: 7/10/1937 Berlin, WI Draft: 19-217 1959 GB Pro: N																															
1965	SAS	12	2		2							6	1	44	138	3.1	13	0	16	139	8.7	29	1	1	2	2.0	2	9	206	22.9	40
CRAIG BUTLER Craig S 6'2 196 Western Ontario B: 12/19/1988 London, ON Draft: 2-12 2011 SAS																															
2011	SAS+	17	0	0	1	59	1.0	7.0	5	67	6																				
DARIA BUTLER Daria D. LB 6'2 215 Oklahoma State B: 9/15/1956 Metairie, LA Draft: 12-320 1978 ATL																															
1979	SAS	5																													

Year	Team	GP	FM	FF	FR	TK	SK	YDS	IR	YDS	PD	PTS	TD	RA	YDS	AVG	LG	TD	REC	YDS	AVG	LG	TD	PR	YDS	AVG	LG	KOR	YDS	AVG	LG
DUANE BUTLER Duane M. DH-LB 6'1 203 Eastern Michigan; Illinois State B: 11/29/1973 Dayton, OH Pro: ENX																															
2001	HAM	16	0	2	0	48	1.0	10.0	1	53	4													1	3	3.0	3	1	0	0.0	0
2002	HAM	17	0	0	1	59					5	6	1																		
2003	MTL	12	0	3	1	45	6.0	48.0	2	104	5	6	1																		
2004	MTL	15	0	6	1	57	8.0	84.0	1	44	6													1	0	0.0	0				
2005	MTL+	15	0	3	6	76	3.0	12.0	2	7	1	6	1															2	12	6.0	8
2006	MTL	18	0	0	3	75	1.0				5																				
6	Years	93	0	14	12	360	19.0	154.0	6	208	26	18	3											2	3	1.5	3	3	12	4.0	8
GARY BUTLER Gary DE 6'1 235 California (Pennsylvania) B: 11/13/1984 Pittsburgh, PA																															
2009	BC	8				11			0	0	1																	3	27	9.0	18
GREGG BUTLER Gregory Tyrone DB 5'10 175 Howard B: 12/26/1952 Washington, DC Pro: UW																															
1977	EDM	7	2		1				1	46														15	220	14.7	42	3	33	11.0	15
1978	EDM*	16	2		1				2	27		6	1						1	28	28.0	28	0	54	442	8.2	46	26	653	25.1	59
1979	EDM*	16	3		2				7	60		6	1											71	623	8.8	47	2	53	26.5	41
1980	EDM*	16	2		1																			41	338	8.2	42				
1981	MTL	7	1		0		0.5																	8	158	19.8	41				
1982	WPG	7							1	18														6	35	5.8	11	2	43	21.5	30
6	Years	69	10		5		0.5		11	151		12	2						1	28	28.0	28	0	195	1816	9.3	47	33	782	23.7	59
HOMER BUTLER Homer Bowen, III DB 6'2 190 Los Angeles CC; UCLA B: 1/26/1957 Washington, DC Draft: 8-222 1978 DAL																															
1978	SAS	2	0		1				1	0																		8	142	17.8	31
1979	SAS	6	0		1				2	41														1	25	25.0	25				
2	Years	8	0		2				3	41														1	25	25.0	25	8	142	17.8	31
IAN BUTLER Ian R. (Rocky) QB 6'0 190 Hofstra B: 8/7/1979 Allentown, PA																															
2002	SAS	11				0						18	3	12	68	5.7	32	3													
2003	SAS	8				0								2	29	14.5	16	0													
2004	SAS	18				0						6	1	26	107	4.1	19	1													
2005	SAS	18	2	0	2	0																									
2006	SAS	16	3	0	1	0						6	1	16	115	7.2	17	1													
2007	TOR	15	3	0	0	2						0	0	10	59	5.9	16	0													
6	Years	86	8	0	3	2						30	5	66	378	5.7	32	5													
JIM BUTLER Jim G-T 5'11 185 B: 1930																															
1952	OTT	6																													
KELLY BUTLER Kelly Don OT 6'7 327 Purdue B: 7/24/1982 Grand Rapids, MI Draft: 6-172 2004 DET Pro: N																															
2010	WPG	18				1																									
LARRY BUTLER Larry Dean OG 6'3 250 Appalachian State B: 7/10/1952 Johnson City, TN Pro: W																															
1976	HAM+	8	1		0																										
1977	HAM+	16																										1	2	2.0	2
1978	HAM+	16	0		1																							1	0	0.0	0
1979	HAM*	16	0		1																							2	34	17.0	18
1980	WPG*	16	0		1																										
1981	WPG*	16																													
6	Years	88	1		3																							4	36	9.0	18
MAURICE BUTLER Maurice WR 5'11 170 Simon Fraser; Regina Rams Jrs. B: 2/18/1956 Draft: 4-30 1978 SAS																															
1978	SAS	8	2		0																			28	293	10.5	31				
QUINCY BUTLER Quincy Devone DH 6'1 190 Tyler JC; Texas Christian B: 11/25/1981 San Antonio, TX Pro: N																															
2011	CAL	2				0																									
THERMUS BUTLER Thermus FB 6'1 190 Kansas B: 3/20/1947																															
1968	EDM	6	0		1							24	4	63	281	4.5	23	4	9	90	10.0	28	0								
1969	EDM	16	4		0							24	4	153	706	4.6	47	4	25	195	7.8	30	0					19	472	24.8	44
2	Years	22	4		1							48	8	216	987	4.6	47	8	34	285	8.4	30	0					19	472	24.8	44
WAYDE BUTLER Wayde Douglas, Jr. WR 6'0 180 Southwestern Louisiana B: 12/25/1969 Beaumont, TX																															
1993	EDM	3				1													1	7	7.0	7	0								
REGGIE BUTTS Reginald L. WR 5'9 175 Tulane B: 10/23/1961 Jacksonville, FL Pro: U																															
1986	OTT	11	1		0							36	6	1	3	3.0	3	0	21	294	14.0	41	5	31	301	9.7	57	21	362	17.2	30
ALEX BUZBEE Alex DT-DE-TE 6'3 262 Georgetown (DC) B: 11/27/1985 Memphis, TN																															
2010	TOR	18				34	6.0	30.0	1	2	0																				
2011	TOR	18	1	0	0	25	3.0	19.0											1	6	6.0	6	0					3	19	6.3	15
2	Years	36	1	0	0	59	9.0	49.0	1	2	0								1	6	6.0	6	0					3	19	6.3	15
ALEXIS BWENGE Alexis FB-RB 6'1 217 Kentucky B: 10/19/1981 Sainte Apollinaire, QC Draft: 1-8 2005 BC																															
2006	BC	18				5						6	1						1	4	4.0	4	1								
2007	BC	18				7													1	3	3.0	3	0								
2008	BC	18				3													1	41	41.0	41	0								
2009	BC	9				2																									
4	Years	63				17						6	1						3	48	16.0	41	1								
BILLY BYE William D. HB 5'8 182 Minnesota B: 6/19/1927 Thief River Falls, MN D: 6/12/2009 Bay Lake, MN Draft: 19-244 1950 CHIB																															
1953	WPG	1												1	13	13.0	13	0	3	18	6.0		0	1	15	15.0	15	1	34	34.0	34
1954	WPG	12	3		2							10	2	32	133	4.2	18	1	8	74	9.3	68	1	9	60	6.7	12	2	19	9.5	15
2	Years	13	3		2							10	2	33	146	4.4	18	1	11	92	8.4	68	1	10	75	7.5	15	3	53	17.7	34
MARK BYERS Mark S. LB Nevada-Las Vegas B: 12/17/1971 San Jose, CA Pro: E																															
1995	BC	3				4																									
BILL BYNUM Billie Gene QB 6'2 205 Western New Mexico B: 7/11/1949 Torrance, CA Draft: 14-349 1971 WAS																															
1975	TOR	13	0		1									24	143	6.0	19	0													
REGGIE BYNUM Reginald Deshain WR 6'1 185 Oregon State B: 2/10/1964 Greenville, MS Draft: 9-222 1986 BUF Pro: EN																															
1989	HAM	1				1																									
DAVID BYRD David Lewis, Jr. DB 6'1 250 Syracuse B: 11/15/1977 Schenectady, NY																															
2002	BC	7	0	0	1	13					2																				
2003	BC	4				3	1.0																								
2	Years	11	0	0	1	16	1.0				2																				
EUGENE BYRD Eugene Wayne WR 6'0 180 Michigan State B: 6/7/1957 East St. Louis, IL Draft: 6-158 1980 MIA																															
1980	SAS	2										6	1						6	63	10.5	18	1	3	26	8.7	10	4	80	20.0	29
MELENDEZ BYRD Melendez O. LB 6'1 226 Virginia Tech B: 3/11/1971 Hampton, VA																															
1994	BAL	7				12																									
MELVIN BYRD Melvin DB 5'9 160 UC Davis B: 12/17/1958 Hampton, VA																															
1982	BC	2																						2	18	9.0	11				
1983	BC	15					3.0		4	140		6	1											5	61	12.2	20				
1984	BC	16	2		1				4	159		6	1											16	151	9.4	66				
1985	BC+	14	0		2		1.0		6	49																					
1986	BC	18	1		3		1.0		6	135		12	2											0	5		5	24	551	23.0	49
1987	BC+	17	1		2	42	1.0		4	97		6	1											4	37	9.3	19	32	822	25.7	65
6	Years	82	4		8	42	6.0		24	580		30	5											27	272	10.1	66	56	1373	24.5	65
WILLIE BYRD Willie CB-DH 6'3 198 Miles B: 7/19/1983 Boynton Beach, FL																															
2008	CAL	4				3																									
2008	WPG	1				1																									
2008	Year	5				4																									
2010	SAS	3	0	1	0	1																									
2	Years	7	0	1	0	5																									
MIKE CACIC Michael Nicholas DT-MG-DG 6'5 265 Vancouver CYO Red Raiders Jrs. B: 1/4/1937 Vancouver, BC D: 1/22/2008 Surrey, BC																															
1957	BC	10																													
1958	BC	4																													
1960	BC	16	0		1																										
1961	BC	16																													
1962	BC	16																													

Year	Team	GP	FM	FF	FR	TK	SK	YDS	IR	YDS	PD	PTS	TD	RA	YDS	AVG	LG	TD	REC	YDS	AVG	LG	TD	PR	YDS	AVG	LG	KOR	YDS	AVG	LG
1963	BC	5																													
1964	BC*	16	0		2																										
1965	BC+	16	0		1																										
1966	BC+	13	0		1																										
1967	BC	7																													
10	Years	119	0		5																										
GERALD CADOGAN Gerald Anthony OT 6'3 280 Penn State B: 1/16/1986 Oakland, CA																															
2011	CAL	5				1																									
WAYNE CADOGAN Wayne DB 6'1 185 Manitoba B: 2/22/1963 Bridgetown, Jamaica																															
1986	MTL	8																													
LOU CAFAZZO Luigi DE-OG 6'3 250 London Beefeaters Jrs.; Eastern Michigan B: 6/14/1966 Hamilton, ON Draft: 3A-18 1989 CAL																															
1989	CAL	6				1																									
1990	CAL	1				0																									
1991	CAL	5				5																									
1992	CAL	18				1																									
1993	CAL	12	0		1	1																									
1994	HAM	17				9	1.0	10.0			1																				
1995	HAM	11				7	2.0	6.0	1	7	0																				
1996	HAM	18				8																									
8	Years	88	0		1	32	3.0	16.0	1	7	1																				
FRAN CAHILL Francis J. E 6'1 190 Northern Illinois B: 12/9/1926 Draft: 19-227 1952 NYG																															
1952	HAM	1																													
BEN CAHOON Benjamin G. WR-SB 5'9 185 Brigham Young B: 7/16/1972 Orem, UT Draft: 1-6 1998 MTL																															
1998	MTL	18				3						18	3						33	471	14.3	36	3	1	6	6.0	6				
1999	MTL*	18	2	0	1	0						12	2						51	823	16.1	48	2								
2000	MTL+	18	2	0	1	1						30	5	1	-5	-5.0	-5	0	71	1022	14.4	73	5								
2001	MTL	18	2	0	1	4						6	1						56	809	14.4	68	1								
2002	MTL+	18	1	0	0	1						36	6	2	49	24.5	28	0	76	1076	14.2	52	6								
2003	MTL+	18	2	0	2	6						84	14	4	18	4.5	17	1	112	1561	13.9	66	13	1	0	0.0	0	1	0	0.0	0
2004	MTL*	16	2	0	1	4						36	6	1	4	4.0	4	0	93	1183	12.7	60	6								
2005	MTL+	14	1	0	0	4						56	9						73	1067	14.6	73	9								
2006	MTL+	17				1						24	4	1	1	1.0	1	0	99	1190	12.0	51	4								
2007	MTL+	17	1	0	1	2						34	5						90	1127	12.5	97	5								
2008	MTL*	17	3	0	0	6						42	7						107	1231	11.5	29	7								
2009	MTL+	18	1	0	0	0						12	2						89	1031	11.6	30	2								
2010	MTL	17	1	0	1	1						14	2						67	703	10.5	29	2								
13	Years	224	18	0	8	33						404	66	9	67	7.4	28	1	1017	13294	13.1	97	65	2	6	3.0	6	1	0		0
JIM CAIN James Edgar, Jr. E 6'1 202 Alabama B: 10/1/1927 Eudora, AR D: 10/5/2001 Draft: 8-54 1949 CHI-AAFC; 7B-70 1949 CHIC Pro: N																															
1956	CAL	4																													
JIM CAIN Jim G-T 6'4 240 Detroit Mercy B: 1939																															
1961	OTT	14																													
1962	OTT	14																													
1963	OTT	14																													
1964	OTT	14	0		1																										
1965	OTT	14																													
1966	OTT	14																													
1967	OTT	14																													
1968	OTT	14																													
1969	OTT	14	0		1																										
9	Years	126	0		2																										
RAY CAISSIE Raymond WR 5'11 180 Montreal Concorde Jrs.; Ottawa B: 11/12/1963 Montreal, QC																															
1986	MTL	12										2	0						11	83	7.5	13	0								
STEVE CALABRIA Steve M. QB 6'4 210 Colgate B: 6/20/1963 Carle Place, NY Draft: TD 1985 NJ-USFL; 9-232 1985 TB																															
1986	MTL	10																													
RON CALCAGNI Ronald M. QB 6'0 190 Arkansas B: 2/6/1957 Youngstown, OH																															
1979	MTL	16												6	30	5.0	11	0													
1980	OTT	3												3	40	13.3	21	0													
1981	OTT	6	1		0									9	87	9.7	20	0													
3	Years	25	1		0									18	157	8.7	21	0													
RON CALCAGNO Ronald George QB 6'0 190 Santa Clara B: 6/30/1942 San Francisco, CA Draft: 18-143 1964 OAK																															
1965	TOR	1																													
JIM CALDWELL James T 6'3 Tennessee State Draft: 28-330 1953 CHIB																															
1954	CAL	1																													
JAMIE CALEB Jamie J. FB 6'1 210 Grambling State B: 10/29/1936 Calhoun, LA Draft: 16-191 1959 CLE Pro: N																															
1962	HAM	1												12	70	5.8	17	0										2	40	20.0	30
1963	HAM	5										24	4	50	192	3.8	23	3	2	1	0.5	6	0					5	83	16.6	20
2	Years	6										24	4	62	262	4.2	23	3	2	1	0.5	6	0					7	123	17.6	30
CHARLIE CALHOUN Charles HB 5'10 174 Florida State B: 1943																															
1964	HAM	1	1		0																			5	39	7.8	11	1	43	43.0	43
MIKE CALHOUN Michael Edward DE 6'4 260 Notre Dame B: 5/6/1957 Youngstown, OH Draft: 10-274 1979 DAL Pro: N																															
1981	WPG	1																													
MIKE CALHOUN Michael QB 6'1 185 Rice B: 3/4/1961																															
1983	MTL	4																	1	8	8.0	8	0								
BRAD CALIP Calip. Brad SB 5'9 173 East Central B: 12/12/1962 Hobart, OK Draft: 2-23 1985 DEN-USFL Pro: U																															
1986	OTT	9	1		1							6	1	8	32	4.0	22	0	43	457	10.6	44	1					12	238	19.8	35
JIMMIE CALIP James RB 5'10 185 Southwestern Oklahoma State B: 1/30/1950 Pro: W																															
1973	WPG	5	2		0							6	1	64	233	3.6	20	1	6	105	17.5	36	0					2	85	42.5	50
MARC CALIXTE Marc LB 6'0 203 Tennessee-Martin B: 9/26/1978 Montreal, QC Draft: 1D-7 2003 CAL																															
2003	CAL	17	0	0	1	2																						0	3		3
2004	CAL	10				7																									
2005	CAL	15				25					1																				
2006	CAL	18	0	0	1	13																									
2007	CAL	18	0	1	0	17																									
2008	CAL	16				7																									
2009	CAL	13	0	1	1	17																									
2010	CAL	18				17																									
2011	CAL	7				6																									
9	Years	132	0	2	3	111					1																	0	3		3
ROD CALLOWAY Roderick Wayne LB 6'1 225 Bishop B: 2/13/1964 Dallas, TX																															
1988	WPG	5	0		1	10	2.0																								
ANTHONY CALVILLO Anthony QB 6'2 197 Mount San Antonio JC; Utah State B: 8/23/1972																															
1994	LV	17	9		2	1						12	2	42	195	4.6	21	2													
1995	HAM	18	5		1	0						12	2	24	51	2.1	13	2													
1996	HAM	13	2		0	0						6	1	40	311	7.8	53	1													
1997	HAM	12	12	0	1	1						12	2	53	242	4.6	29	2													
1998	MTL	18	1	0	1	1						6	1	31	121	3.9	11	1													
1999	MTL	18	3	0	0	0						18	3	56	211	3.8	27	3													
2000	MTL+	18	6	0	0	0						12	2	58	230	4.0	26	2													
2001	MTL*	18	2	0	2	2						6	1	40	253	6.3	29	1													
2002	MTL*	18	5	0	0	3						18	3	45	327	7.3	24	3													
2003	MTL+	18	12	0	4	0						6	1	45	169	3.8	46	1													
2004	MTL	18	2	0	3	1						6	1	44	237	5.4	18	1													

Year	Team	GP	FM	FF	FR	TK	SK	YDS	IR	YDS	PD	PTS	TD	RA	YDS	AVG	LG	TD	REC	YDS	AVG	LG	TD	PR	YDS	AVG	LG	KOR	YDS	AVG	LG
2005	MTL	18	4	0	0	1						36	6	35	189	5.4	15	6													
2006	MTL+	18	3	0	1	0						12	2	28	185	6.6	21	2													
2007	MTL	13	3	0	1	0						2	0	21	137	6.5	17	0													
2008	MTL*	17	1	0	1	0						12	2	26	189	7.3	29	2													
2009	MTL*	18	3	0	0	0						12	2	32	198	6.2	30	2													
2010	MTL+	16	6	0	1	1								16	107	6.7	16	0													
2011	MTL+	18	9	0	1	0						6	1	21	155	7.4	20	1													
18	Years	304	88	0	19	11						194	32	657	3507	5.3	53	32													
BOB CAMERON Robert P-QB 6'0 185 Acadia B: 7/18/1954 Hamilton, ON Draft: 1A-6 1977 EDM																															
1980	WPG	15	2		1							2	0																		
1981	WPG	16	1		0							2	0																		
1982	WPG	16	1		0							5	0																		
1983	WPG	16	1		0							8	0																		
1984	WPG+	16										5	0											1	-3	-3.0	-3				
1985	WPG	16	2		0							8	0																		
1986	WPG	18	2		0							11	0																		
1987	WPG	18	1		1	0						7	0																		
1988	WPG*	18	1		1	1						6	0																		
1989	WPG*	18	2		0	1						12	0																		
1990	WPG*	18	3		2	0						10	0																		
1991	WPG	18	1		1	1						12	0																		
1992	WPG	18	4		2	0						6	0	1	8	8.0	8	0													
1993	WPG*	18	3		4	2						5	0																		
1994	WPG	18				1						4	0																		
1995	WPG*	18	1		0	1						7	0																		
1996	WPG	18	0		1	0						7	0																		
1997	WPG	18				0						1	0																		
1998	WPG	18	2	0	0	1						5	0																		
1999	WPG	18				0						5	0																		
2000	WPG	11	1	0	0	0						2	0																		
2001	WPG	18				1						2	0																		
2002	WPG	18	1	0	0	1						2	0																		
23	Years	394	29	0	13	10						134	0	1	8	8.0	8	0						1	-3	-3.0	-3				
DeCHANE CAMERON DeChane L. QB 6'1 190 Clemson B: 3/7/1969 LeGrange, GA																															
1992	EDM	18				0								1	-3	-3.0	-3	0													
LARRY CAMERON Larry LB 6'0 225 Alcorn State B: 11/4/1952 Adams County, MO Draft: 12-301 1974 DEN																															
1975	BC*	16	0		2				3	50																		1	-1	-1.0	-1
1976	OTT+	16	1		1				5	53		6	1															3	63	21.0	26
1977	OTT	10	0		2																										
3	Years	42	1		5				8	103		6	1															4	62	15.5	26
PAUL CAMERON Paul Leslie OHB-S 6'0 190 UCLA B: 8/17/1932 Burbank, CA Draft: 8-91 1954 PIT Pro: N																															
1956	BC+	15	4		3				4	142		20	3	82	430	5.2	47	0	24	428	17.8	68	3	10	62	6.2	11	14	264	18.9	46
1957	BC	16	1		0				6	63		42	7	78	514	6.6	31	2	36	593	16.5	70	5	2	22	11.0	12				
1958	BC	15	1		5				5	137		18	3	54	304	5.6	25	0	58	834	14.4	61	2	5	17	3.4	5	3	64	21.3	25
1959	BC	1																	4	48	12.0	15	0								
4	Years	47	6		8				15	342		80	13	214	1248	5.8	47	2	122	1903	15.6	70	10	17	101	5.9	12	17	328	19.3	46
ROY CAMERON Roy (Rocky) FB-DB 6'0 200 Wenatchee Valley CC B: 1941 Winnipeg, MB D: 9/11/2009																															
1960	BC	2	1		0																			7	42	6.0	12				
1961	EDM	10												4	15	3.8	5	0						3	11	3.7	5	1	19	19.0	19
1962	SAS	16																										5	83	16.6	29
1963	SAS	15	3		0							3	0	23	84	3.7	8	0	1	-3	-3.0	-3	0	3	16	5.3	13	14	347	24.8	48
1965	SAS	7																0						8	33	4.1	11	1	12	12.0	
1965	BC	4	1		1													0										9	181	20.1	
1965	Year	11	1		1									6	20	3.3	5	0						8	33	4.1	11	10	193	19.3	34
1966	BC	16	0		1									2	9	4.5	5	0	1	7	7.0	7	0	50	231	4.6	14	2	19	9.5	14
6	Years	66	5		2							3	0	29	108	3.7	8	0	2	4	2.0	7	0	71	333	4.7	14	32	661	20.7	48
CHICK CAMILERI Chick (Red) QB 145																															
1946	TOR	7																													
1947	TOR	2																													
1948	TOR	1																													
3	Years	10																													
TOM CAMPANA Thomas WB-DB 5'10 185 Ohio State B: 11/18/1950 Draft: 13-316 1972 STL																															
1972	SAS+	16	1		0							18	3	74	365	4.9	27	1	45	719	16.0	57	2					23	676	29.4	49
1973	SAS	16										48	8	20	53	2.7	9	0	57	910	16.0	68	8					14	274	19.6	40
1974	SAS	16	1		0							30	5						37	505	13.6	71	5					2	12	6.0	10
1975	SAS	16	1		0							48	8	32	136	4.3	24	1	52	818	15.7	59	6	47	584	12.4	78	21	425	20.2	52
1976	SAS	16	2		2							30	5	6	0	0.0	5	0	51	771	15.1	72	4	53	629	11.9	80	16	307	19.2	35
1977	SAS	9										18	3						27	317	11.7	23	3	23	181	7.9	24	11	269	24.5	35
6	Years	89	5		2							192	32	132	554	4.2	27	2	269	4040	15.0	72	28	123	1394	11.3	80	87	1963	22.6	52
ARNOLD CAMPBELL Arnold Rene DE 6'3 260 Alcorn State B: 11/13/1962 Charleston, MS Pro: N																															
1989	OTT	2				8																									
BILLY CAMPBELL William Roscoe C 6'0 195 Oklahoma B: 8/6/1920 Pawhuska, OK D: 10//1974 Draft: 17-153 1943 CHIC Pro: N																															
1951	WPG	10																													
DARRELL CAMPBELL Darrell DT 6'4 290 Notre Dame B: 7/6/1981 South Holland, IL																															
2009	MTL	12				8	1.0	11.0																							
DAVE CAMPBELL Dave DB 6'0 190 Queen's B: 1951 Draft: 9-71 1973 EDM																															
1974	EDM	16			1																			70	380	5.4	26	3	12	4.0	12
1975	EDM	4																										3	43	14.3	21
1975	WPG	4																													
1975	CAL	3																													
1975	Year	11																										3	43	14.3	21
2	Years	20	0		1																			70	380	5.4	26	6	55	9.2	21
DOUG CAMPBELL Doug DL 6'3 250 Rosemount Bombers Jrs. B: 1939																															
1962	TOR	14																													
1963	EDM	5																													
1963	WPG	1																													
1963	SAS	1																													
1963	Year	7																													
2	Years	19																													
GARY CAMPBELL Gary Kalani LB 6'1 219 Colorado B: 3/4/1952 Honolulu, HI Draft: 10-291 1976 PIT Pro: N																															
1976	CAL	3																													
HARVEY CAMPBELL Harvey G 5'11 215 Regina Rams Jrs. B: 1940																															
1961	SAS	11																													
HUGH CAMPBELL Hugh Thomas FL-OE 6'0 185 Washington State B: 5/21/1941 San Jose, CA Draft: 22-169 1963 OAK; 4B-50 1963 SF																															
1963	SAS	7										18	3						30	426	14.2	27	3								
1964	SAS+	16	1		0							66	11						65	1000	15.4	35	11								
1965	SAS*	16	4		2							60	10	0	16		16	0	73	1329	18.2	53	10	1	0	0.0	0				
1966	SAS*	16										102	17						66	1109	16.8	73	17								
1967	SAS	16										48	8						42	710	16.9	59	8								
1969	SAS	16	2		0							66	11						45	851	18.9	57	11								
6	Years	87	7		2							360	60	0	16		16	0	321	5425	16.9	73	60	1	0	0.0	0				
JACK CAMPBELL Jack Carter OT 6'5 277 Southern California; Utah B: 12/16/1958 Los Angeles, CA Draft: 6-144 1982 SEA Pro: N																															

Year	Team	GP	FM	FF	FR	TK	SK	YDS	IR	YDS	PD	PTS	TD	RA	YDS	AVG	LG	TD	REC	YDS	AVG	LG	TD	PR	YDS	AVG	LG	KOR	YDS	AVG	LG
1987	CAL	1				0																									
JERRY CAMPBELL Jerry Bruce LB 5'11 210 Idaho B: 7/14/1944 Binghamton, NY																														
1966	CAL	14	0		3				1	13																						
1967	CAL	15							1	5																						
1968	CAL	8																													
1968	OTT	7	0		2				5	37		6	1															2	20	10.0	13
1968	Year+	15	0		2				5	37		6	1															2	20	10.0	13
1969	OTT*	14	0		1				2	41																						
1970	OTT*	14	0		3				4	39																						
1971	OTT*	14			3				1	2		6	1																		
1972	OTT*	14	1		1				8	52																						
1973	OTT*	14	0		5				5	116																						
1974	OTT*	16							3	67																			2	19	9.5	14
1975	OTT*	16	0		1				4	38																						
1976	CAL	2																													
11	Years	141	1		19				34	410		12	2															4	39	9.8	14
JIMMY CAMPBELL Jim Ray LB 6'2 226 West Texas A&M B: 1/16/1946 Draft: 14-371 1968 SD Pro: N																														
1970	WPG	1																													
JOE CAMPBELL Joseph, Jr. DE 6'3 245 New Mexico State B: 12/28/1966 Chandler, AZ Draft: 4A-91 1988 SD Pro: EN																														
1991	BC	1				3																									
1991	HAM	13	0		1	26	3.0																								
1991	Year	14	0		1	29	3.0																								
JOE CAMPBELL Joe RB 5'9 180 Middle Tennessee State B: 1/14/1970 Nashville, TN Draft: 6-144 1992 LARM																														
1994	OTT	5	3		0	2						18	3	45	231	5.1	22	3	6	70	11.7	22	0	8	37	4.6	12	24	487	20.3	39
1994	HAM	2				0								29	114	3.9	11	0	11	51	4.6	15	0					3	62	20.7	29
1994	Year	7				2						18	3	74	345	4.7	22	3	17	121	7.1	22	0	8	37	4.6	12	27	549	20.3	39
KELLY CAMPBELL Kelly SB 5'10 172 Georgia Tech B: 7/23/1980 Atlanta, GA Pro: N																														
2008	EDM	17	3	0	2	2						42	7	1	6	6.0	6	0	54	1223	22.6	53	7	1	0	0.0	0	13	291	22.4	51
2010	EDM	14	1	0	0	1						12	2	5	37	7.4	13	0	63	801	12.7	46	1	13	191	14.7	95	10	264	26.4	47
2	Years	31	4	0	2	3						54	9	6	43	7.2	13	0	117	2024	17.3	53	8	14	191	13.6	95	23	555	24.1	51
LeROY CAMPBELL LeRoy C. WR 6'1 180 Los Angeles Harbor JC; Texas Christian; Sonoma State B: 10/18/1958 Los Angeles, CA Pro: U																														
1983	SAS	7	1		0							12	2					21	380	18.1	71	2	21	177	8.4	19				
MIKE CAMPBELL Michael DT 6'1 260 Slippery Rock B: 9/19/1965 North York, ON Draft: 2A-10 1989 TOR																														
1989	TOR	13				2	1.0																								
1990	TOR	12				11	1.0					6	1					1	41	41.0	41	1								
1991	TOR*	18	0		2	28	13.0					6	1																		
1992	TOR+	17	0		1	40	6.0	44.0																							
1993	TOR	17				21	5.0	21.0																							
1994	TOR	18	0		1	26	4.0	25.0																							
1995	HAM	16	0		1	32	2.0	14.0			1																			
1996	HAM	15	0		1	23	9.0	64.0			2																			
1997	HAM	12	0	1	0	23	3.0	19.0	1	2	0																			
1999	HAM	18	0	0	1	26	1.0	1.0			3																			
10	Years	156	0	1	7	232	45.0	188.0	1	2	6	12	2					1	41	41.0	41	1								
MILT CAMPBELL Milton Gray DB-OHB-LB 6'3 217 Indiana B: 12/9/1933 Plainfield, NJ Draft: 5B-53 1957 CLE Pro: N																														
1958	HAM	8											24	4	98	468	4.8	73	3	11	157	14.3	53	1								
1959	MTL	3							1	0				2	11	5.5	10	0											4	91	22.8	40
1961	TOR	1																													
1964	TOR	8							1	0																						
4	Years	20							2	0		24	4	100	479	4.8	73	3	11	157	14.3	53	1					4	91	22.8	40
ROBBIE CAMPBELL Robert S-FB 5'11 200 Western Ontario B: 1944 Draft: 1-5 1967 EDM																														
1967	EDM	4	1		0																							4	63	15.8	23
1968	EDM	16	0		1				3	26									1	10	10.0	10	0	1	2	2.0	2	4	76	19.0	21
1970	BC	1																													
3	Years	21	1		1				3	26									1	10	10.0	10	0	1	2	2.0	2	8	139	17.4	23
SAM CAMPBELL Samuel Cornelius T 6'5 225 Iowa State B: 1/7/1947 Lorain, OH Draft: 11-275 1969 CHIB																														
1970	EDM	5	1		0							6	1					7	118	16.9	37	1								
SCOTT CAMPBELL Robert Scott QB 6'0 195 Purdue B: 4/15/1962 Hershey, PA Draft: 7-191 1984 PIT; 4-77 1984 PHI-USFL Pro: N																														
1992	OTT	18	1		0	1						6	1	6	18	3.0	5	1														
TOMMY CAMPBELL George Thomas CB 6'0 188 Rochester JC; Iowa State B: 12/30/1949 New York, NY Draft: 7-170 1973 ATL Pro: NW																														
1974	HAM	16	0		1				2	47															5	87	17.4	25	18	425	23.6	45
1975	HAM	10	0		1				4	39																			22	498	22.6	33
1978	SAS	4																													
3	Years	30	0		2				6	86															5	87	17.4	25	40	923	23.1	45
DON CAMPORA Don Carlo T 6'3 268 Pacific B: 8/30/1927 Trenton, UT D: 6/5/1978 San Bernardino, CA Draft: 2-23 1950 SF Pro: N																														
1954	CAL	10																													
TOM CANADA Tom DE 6'3 255 Allan Hancock JC; California B: 1/8/1980 Iowa City, IA																														
2004	WPG+	18	0	2	1	43	7.0	49.0			1																			
2005	WPG	18	0	1	3	44	9.0	52.0			1																			
2006	WPG	18	0	1	1	35	10.0	41.0			3																			
2007	WPG+	17	0	2	0	32	12.0	78.0			1																			
2008	WPG	10	0	2	1	18	3.0	2.0	1	45	1	6	1																		
5	Years	81	0	8	6	172	41.0	222.0	1	45	7	6	1																		
STAV CANAKES Stavros Paul OT 6'0 225 Minnesota B: 9/19/1930 Minneapolis, MN D: 10/25/2008 Shakopee, MN Draft: 30-357 1953 NYG																														
1954	WPG	14																											1	11	11.0	11
1955	WPG	16	0		2				1	0																						
1956	WPG	5																							1	0	0.0	0				
1956	SAS	3																													
1956	Year	8																							1	0	0.0	0				
1957	WPG	9																													
1958	WPG	1																													
5	Years	45	0		2				1	0															1	0	0.0	0	1	11		11
JUSTIN CANALE Dominic Justin OG 6'2 242 Mississippi State B: 4/11/1943 Memphis, TN D: 10/11/2011 Memphis, TN Draft: 6- 1965 BOS; 12-167 1965 CLE Pro: NW																														
1970	MTL	6											3	0																		
1971	MTL+	14	0		1							77	0																		
1972	MTL	4																													
1973	CAL	13	0		1																										
1976	TOR	3																													
5	Years	40	0		2							80	0																		
LEN CANAVAN Leonard E. T 6'1 222 San Francisco State B: 4/1/1918 D: 1/19/1977 Alameda County, CA																														
1948	OTT	10																													
SHELDON CANLEY Sheldon Lavell [born Dartagna P.] RB 5'9 195 Allan Hancock JC; San Jose State B: 4/19/1968 Santa Barbara, CA Draft: 7-193 1991 SF Pro: N																														
1994	BAL	18	2		0	13						6	1	31	143	4.6	15	1	6	37	6.2	18	0	15	115	7.7	18	8	154	19.3	31
PAT CANNAMELA Patterson N. G 5'10 205 Ventura JC; Southern California B: 4/27/1929 New London, CT D: 1/28/1973 Los Angeles, CA Draft: 11-122 1952 DAL Pro: N																														
1956	OTT	7							1	0																						
JOE CANNAVINO Joseph Patrick LB 5'11 186 Ohio State B: 1/20/1935 Cleveland, OH Draft: 16A-185 1957 BAL Pro: N																														
1963	HAM	12							2	37															1	1	1.0	1	2	18	9.0	18
ANTHONY CANNON Anthony Devon LB 6'0 227 Tulane B: 12/31/1984 Pensacola, FL Draft: 7-247 2006 DET Pro: N																														
2011	TOR	14	0	1	0	56				5																			1	4		4
WILLIE CANNON Willie James RB 6'1 206 Murray State B: 9/28/1964 Sarasota, FL																														
1988	WPG	2												18	48	2.7	12	0	2	19	9.5	13	0								
PAT CANTNER Pat FB 5'11 210 Richmond Raiders Jrs.; British Columbia B: 10/5/1959 Vancouver, BC Draft: 4-34 1983 WPG																														

Year	Team	GP	FM	FF	FR	TK	SK	YDS	IR	YDS	PD	PTS	TD	RA	YDS	AVG	LG	TD	REC	YDS	AVG	LG	TD	PR	YDS	AVG	LG	KOR	YDS	AVG	LG
1983	WPG	16												4	10	2.5	4	0	7	72	10.3	25	0					1	0	0.0	0
1984	WPG	13												2	7	3.5	5	0	2	50	25.0	26	0								
1985	WPG	16	1		2							30	5	24	103	4.3	10	2	10	71	7.1	16	2					1	3	3.0	3
1986	WPG	17	1		0							12	2	24	64	2.7	8	2	9	58	6.4	17	0								
1987	WPG	18			1	1						12	2	17	56	3.3	13	0	33	220	6.7	21	2					1	0	0.0	0
5	Years	80	2		3	1						54	9	71	240	3.4	13	4	61	471	7.7	26	4					3	3	1.0	3
NOAH CANTOR Noah DT 6'3 210 St. Mary's (Nova Scotia) B: 1/11/1971 Ottawa, ON																															
1995	TOR	18	0		1	33	2.0	13.0																							
1996	TOR	18				7	2.0	25.0																							
1997	TOR	18	0	2	0	21	1.0	3.0																							
1998	BC	18				16																						1	-2	-2.0	-2
1999	BC	18	0	1	1	29	3.0	19.0			1																				
2000	BC	17	0	1	0	36	4.0	22.0	1	0	1																				
2001	BC	18	0	0	1	30					2																				
2002	BC	18	0	0	2	16	3.0	25.0			1																				
2003	TOR	18	0	2	2	24	3.0	23.0			2																				
2004	TOR*	18	0	0	1	32	10.0	50.0			8																				
2005	TOR	17	0	1	2	15	2.0	14.0			2																				
2006	TOR	11				5					1																				
12	Years	207	0	7	10	264	30.0	194.0	1	0	18																	1	-2		-2
ART CANTRELLE Arthur RB 6'0 203 Louisiana State B: 7/25/1948 Thibodaux, LA Pro: W																															
1972	OTT	14	2		0							12	2	160	652	4.1	55	2	44	407	9.3	27	0								
1973	OTT	7												35	127	3.6	18	0	12	93	7.8	12	0								
2	Years	21	2		0							12	2	195	779	4.0	55	2	56	500	8.9	27	0								
DON CAPAROTTI Donald CB 5'9 180 Massachusetts B: 1/10/1970 Damascus, MD																															
1994	SHR	9	0		1	19					2																				
BYRON CAPERS Byron Maurice CB 6'1 194 Florida State B: 3/21/1974 Washington, DC Draft: 7B-225 1997 PHI																															
1998	TOR	16	0	3	0	42					10																				
1999	TOR	12	0	0	1	26					4																				
2000	TOR	14				32			3	67	4																				
2001	TOR	2				7																									
2001	BC	3	0	0	1	11					3																				
2001	WPG	7	1	0	0	22			4	34	3																				
2001	Year	9	1	0	1	40			4	34	6																				
2002	WPG	9	0	1	1	16					3																				
2002	OTT	3	0	1	0	7					4																				
2002	Year	12	0	2	1	23					7																				
2003	OTT	5	0	1	1	11					4																				
2004	OTT	10	0	0	1	19					2																				
7	Years	68	1	6	5	193			7	101	37																				
JAMES CAPERS James O. DE-LB 6'4 232 Central Michigan B: 6/14/1959 Kalamazoo, MI Pro: N																															
1985	SAS	4	0		1							6	1																		
RON CAPHAM Ron C-LB 6'2 240 Edmonton Huskies Jrs.; Edmonton Prospectors Srs. B: 12/2/1943 Flin Flon, MB																															
1965	EDM	14																													
1966	EDM	16																													
1967	EDM	16																													
1968	TOR	14	0		1																										
1969	CAL	16																													
1970	TOR	14																													
1971	SAS	4																													
7	Years	94	0		1																										
HERB CAPOZZI Herbert Peter T 6'1 227 British Columbia B: 4/24/1925 Kalowna, BC D: 11/21/2011 Vancouver, BC																															
1952	CAL	15																													
1953	MTL	13										1	0																		
1954	MTL	12																													
1955	MTL	12																													
4	Years	52										1	0																		
JOE CAPRIOTTI Joe FW-HB 5'7 190 B: 1918																															
1946	HAM	12										5	1					1													
1947	HAM	10										2	0																		
2	Years	22										7	1					1													
AL CARAPELLA Alfred Richard T 6'0 235 Miami (Florida) B: 4/26/1927 Tuckahoe, NY Draft: 5B-54 1951 SF Pro: N																															
1956	HAM	5																													
GIULIO CARAVATTA Giulio QB-P-K 6'0 220 Simon Fraser B: 3/20/1966 Toronto, ON Pro: E																															
1991	BC	18				3						1	0																		
1992	BC	15	1		0	2								2	5	2.5	5	0													
1993	BC	6				0																									
1994	BC	18				0						20	1	2	23	11.5	21	1													
1995	BC	18	1		0	3						11	1	3	1	0.3	1	1													
1996	BC	18				2						6	1	4	7	1.8	4	1													
1997	BC	18				2								2	26	13.0	19	0													
1998	BC	3	1	0	0	0																									
8	Years	114	3	0	0	12						38	3	13	62	4.8	21	3													
DONNIE CARAWAY Don Manuel OG-LB 6'1 230 Hinds JC; Houston B: 3/1/1934 Draft: 7-83 1956 WAS; 29-348 1957 CHIB; 4-47 1958 NYG																															
1957	CAL	4	0		1				1	8		12	1	19	79	4.2	12	1	1	5	5.0	5	0								
1958	TOR	9										2	0																		
1959	TOR	9							3	18																					
1960	TOR	2																													
1961	TOR	3																													
1961	HAM	5																													
1961	Year	8																													
5	Years	27	0		1				4	26		14	1	19	79	4.2	12	1	1	5	5.0	5	0								
RYAN CAREY Ryan S 5'11 185 Acadia B: 6/21/1971 Carleton Place, ON Draft: Bonus-4 1994 WPG																															
1994	WPG	13				8																									
1995	WPG	16	0		2	9																									
1996	SAS	6				4																									
1997	SAS	18	0	1	1	21			3	36	0																				
1998	SAS	11	0	0	1	15			1	8	0																				
5	Years	64	0	1	4	57			4	44	0																				
JAN CARINCI Jan SB-WR-FB-DB 6'2 200 Maryland B: 2/2/1959 London, England Draft: TE 1981 TOR																															
1981	TOR	16	5		0							6	1	1	3	3.0	3	0	22	297	13.5	31	1	63	653	10.4	35	2	40	20.0	21
1982	TOR	16	3		0							6	0	4	22	5.5	14	0	14	152	10.9	24	0	64	634	9.9	46	1	2	2.0	2
1983	TOR	14	4		0							16	2	11	40	3.6	15	1	32	357	11.2	29	1	46	380	8.3	39	1	0	0.0	0
1984	TOR	16	6		0							12	2	8	52	6.5	14	0	44	644	14.6	45	2	57	575	10.1	36	1	0	0.0	0
1985	TOR	13	5		0				1	4		6	1	14	64	4.6	21	0	19	148	7.8	20	1	62	510	8.2	24				
1986	BC	17	2		2							36	6	6	11	1.8	5	0	50	634	12.7	30	5								
1987	BC	12	1		0	0						24	4	1	0	0.0	0	0	36	532	14.8	34	4					1	0	0.0	0
1988	BC	9	2		2	3						6	1						20	262	13.1	42	1					1	0	0.0	0
1989	BC	11	2		1	1			2	5		24	4						37	545	14.7	35	4								
1990	BC	8				0						6	1	2	19	9.5	20	0	11	171	15.5	27	1								
10	Years	132	30		5	4			3	9		142	22	47	211	4.5	21	1	285	3742	13.1	45	20	292	2752	9.4	46	7	42	6.0	21
VIDAL CARLIN Vidal Carlos QB 6'2 195 Tyler JC; North Texas B: 4/6/1945 Tucson, AZ Draft: 3-69 1967 STL																															

Year	Team	GP	FM	FF	FR	TK	SK	YDS	IR	YDS	PD	PTS	TD	RA	YDS	AVG	LG	TD	REC	YDS	AVG	LG	TD	PR	YDS	AVG	LG	KOR	YDS	AVG	LG
1970	BC	9												1	2	2.0	2	0													
JOHN CARLOS John Wesley WR 6'3 200 Texas A&M-Commerce*; San Jose State* B: 3/6/1947 New York, NY Draft: 15-371 1970 PHI																															
1971	MTL	9																	5	44	8.8	20	0					5	117	23.4	35
DOUG CARLSON Doug DB 6'1 195 Calgary Colts Jrs.; Colorado B: 4/10/1952 Draft: TE 1975 CAL																															
1975	BC	1																													
1976	BC	16																										1	4	4.0	4
1977	BC	16	0		2				3	56		6	1											1	4	4.0	4				
1978	BC	8							1	12														6	37	6.2	15				
1979	BC	16							1	0																					
1983	WPG	2																													
6	Years	59	0		2				5	68		6	1											7	41	5.9	15	1	4		4
ZAC CARLSON Zachary Robbin Leroy OG 6'4 300 Weber State B: 8/8/1987 Winnipeg, MB																															
2010	CAL	1				0																									
WRAY CARLTON Linwood Wray HB 6'2 218 Duke B: 6/18/1937 Wallace, NC Draft: 3-26 1959 PHI Pro: N																															
1959	TOR	1										1	0	9	5	0.6	9	0	2	19	9.5	11	0								
GIOVANNI CARMAZZI Giovanni Daniel QB 6'3 224 Pacific*; Hofstra B: 4/14/1977 Sacramento, CA Draft: 3A-65 2000 SF Pro: E																															
2004	BC	13				0																									
AL CARMICHAEL Albert Reinhold T 6'1 192 Santa Ana JC; Southern California B: 11/10/1928 Boston, MA Draft: 1-7 1953 GB Pro: N																															
1959	CAL	2																													
ERNIE CARNEGIE Ernie RB 5'11 205 Seneca B: 1952																															
1974	TOR	13																													
J.C. CAROLINE James C. HB 6'1 190 Illinois B: 1/17/1933 Warrenton, GA Draft: 7-82 1956 CHIB Pro: N																															
1955	TOR	4										5	1	43	190	4.4	15	1	7	23	3.3	9	0					13	336	25.8	39
1955	MTL	6							1	21		15	3	64	385	6.0	19	2	6	62	10.3	32	1	25	154	6.2	16	5	110	22.0	30
1955	Year	10										20	4	107	575	5.4	19	3	13	85	6.5	32	1	25	154	6.2	16	18	446	24.8	39
DWAINE CARPENTER Dwaine Lamont LB-DB 6'1 204 North Carolina A&T State B: 11/4/1976 Pinehurst, NC Pro: N																															
2007	CAL	15	0	1	2	58			0	0	4																				
2008	CAL	18	0	0	2	52	1.0	11.0	2	49	5																				
2009	CAL	17	0	3	4	53	1.0	25.0	0	0	7	6	1																		
3	Years	50	0	4	8	163	2.0	36.0	2	49	16	6	1																		
JACK CARPENTER Jack Chrisman T 6'0 235 Columbia; Missouri; Michigan B: 7/29/1923 Kansas City, MO D: 10/16/2005 Honolulu, HI Draft: 15-143 1944 CHIC; 3-24 1947 CLE-AAFC Pro: A																															
1950	HAM	12																													
1951	HAM+	12																													
1952	TOR	12										2	0																		
1953	TOR	14																													
1954	TOR	14							1	2																					
5	Years	64							1	2		2	0																		
JOHNNY CARPENTER John HB 5'8 180 Manitoba B: 1926																															
1949	WPG	14										10	2					1					1								
KEITH CARPENTER Keith T 6'2 225 Bakersfield JC; San Jose State B: 1930 Draft: 26-306 1951 SF																															
1952	EDM	2																													
1953	WPG	3																													
2	Years	5																													
KEN CARPENTER Kenneth Leroy OHB-S-OE 6'0 195 Oregon State B: 2/26/1926 Carlisle, WA D: 1/28/2011 OR Draft: 1-13 1950 CLE Pro: N																															
1954	SAS	14	2		0							45	9	110	545	5.0	18	3	37	523	14.1	42	6	19	93	4.9	17	17	630	37.1	62
1955	SAS+	16	2		0				1	7		90	18	131	586	4.5	29	12	39	678	17.4	53	6	26	191	7.3	27				
1956	SAS+	14	2		0							84	14	148	727	4.9	25	8	43	784	18.2	67	6								
1957	SAS	7	1									36	6	66	284	4.3	13	2	24	376	15.7	76	4								
1958	SAS+	14	1						4	88		30	5						33	576	17.5	48	4					5	74	14.8	24
1959	SAS	10							1			18	3	58	270	4.7	18	2	19	220	11.6	23	1	1	2	2.0	2				
6	Years	75	8		0				6	95		303	55	513	2412	4.7	29	27	195	3157	16.2	76	27	46	286	6.2	27	22	704	32.0	62
ROB CARPENTER Robert Gordon WR 6'2 190 Notre Dame; Syracuse B: 8/1/1968 Amityville, NY Draft: 4B-109 1991 CIN Pro: N																															
1995	WPG	1				1													7	88	12.6	20	0					1	17	17.0	17
STEVE CARPENTER Steven LB 6'2 195 Western Illinois B: 1/22/1958 Staunton, IL Pro: N																															
1984	CAL	12	0		2		5.0					6	1						1	12	12.0	12	1								
1985	CAL	7	0		1		1.0																								
2	Years	19	0		3		6.0					6	1						1	12	12.0	12	1								
JIM CARPHIN Jim TE 6'3 210 Vancouver Meralomas Jrs.; Washington B: 1939 Vancouver, BC																															
1960	BC	16	1		2							12	2						10	159	15.9	43	2					3	23	7.7	10
1961	BC	13																	4	53	13.3	13	0								
1962	BC	16										12	2						27	390	14.4	40	2					2	12	6.0	10
1964	BC	14																	7	110	15.7	23	0								
1965	BC	12										6	1						9	143	15.9	26	1								
1966	BC	13	0		1														2	22	11.0	14	0								
1967	SAS	12																	6	85	14.2	26	0								
1968	BC	11																	22	292	13.3	54	0								
8	Years	107	1		3							30	5						87	1254	14.4	54	5					5	35	7.0	10
BRAD CARR Brad LB 6'1 224 Maryland B: 2/4/1956 Harrisburg, PA Draft: 12-327 1978 PIT																															
1978	OTT	8							2	21																					
1979	OTT	12	0		2				1	0																					
1980	HAM	2																													
3	Years	22	0		2				3	21																					
CRAIG CARR Craig RB 6'0 205 Manitoba B: 1/4/1975 St. John's, NB Draft: 2B-10 2000 EDM																															
2000	EDM	15	1	1	0	3						12	2	40	162	4.1	13	2	1	15	15.0	15	0					6	125	20.8	24
2002	MTL	4				1								2	-8	-4.0	0	0													
2005	CAL	5				0								6	16	2.7	7	0	1	1	1.0	1	0								
3	Years	24	1	1	0	4						12	2	48	170	3.5	13	2	2	16	8.0	15	0					6	125	20.8	24
GEORGE CARR George LB 6'2 218 Oregon State B: 1944																															
1966	CAL	1																													
GREG CARR Greg SB-WR 6'6 214 Florida State B: 10/8/1985 Reddick, FL																															
2010	WPG	7				1						24	4						32	579	18.1	74	4								
2011	WPG	11	1	0	1	2						24	4						46	648	14.1	59	4								
2	Years	18	1	0	1	3						48	8						78	1227	15.7	74	8								
JIMMY CARR James Henry DB 6'1 206 Charleston B: 3/25/1933 Kayford, WV Pro: N																															
1958	MTL	6							2	21				2	7	3.5	6	0	2	18	9.0	9	0								
LARRY CARR Larry LB 6'0 225 Brigham Young B: 1/24/1952																															
1975	CAL	16	0		5				3	51																					
PHIL CARR-HARRIS Phil G-T-E-FW 5'11 195																															
1946	TOR	1																													
1947	TOR	10																													
1949	TOR	1																													
3	Years	12																													
JEAN-NICOLAS CARRIERE Jean-Nicolas LB 6'2 228 McGill B: 10/3/1985 Rockland, ON Draft: 3-21 2008 TOR																															
2008	TOR	8				3																									
RUSS CARROCCIO Russell B. T 6'1 235 Virginia B: 4/28/1931 D: 6/28/1994 Wayne, NJ Pro: N																															
1956	HAM	1																													
BILL CARROLL Bill OE 6'5 230 Texas A&M-Commerce B: 8/23/1953 Draft: 12-347 1976 PIT																															
1978	WPG	2																	5	57	11.4	20	0								
KEVIN CARROLL Kevin Laray DE 6'3 265 Hampton; Prairie View A&M; Knoxville B: 6/17/1969 Hempstead, TX																															
1994	TOR	6				11	4.0	34.0																							
TERRENCE CARROLL Terrence D. LB 6'0 215 Oregon State B: 8/18/1978 Houston, TX																															

Year	Team	GP	FM	FF	FR	TK	SK	YDS	IR	YDS	PD	PTS	TD	RA	YDS	AVG	LG	TD	REC	YDS	AVG	LG	TD	PR	YDS	AVG	LG	KOR	YDS	AVG	LG
2003	CAL	12	0	0	1	13																									
JIM CARRUTHERS Jim																															
1947	TOR	1																													
JOE CARRUTHERS Joseph D. OG-DE 6'1 215 Michigan State B: 1935 Detroit, MI																															
1960	BC	16																													
1961	CAL	16																													
1962	MTL	3																													
1962	HAM	10																													
1962	Year	13																													
3	Years	35																													
RYAN CARRUTHERS Ryan SB 6'2 212 Calgary B: 2/23/1976 Red Deer, AB Draft: 4B-30 1997 MTL																															
1999	HAM	4				0																									
ALEX CARSON Alexander C 6'0 210 B: 1924																															
1949	OTT	12																													
1950	OTT	10																													
1951	OTT	9																													
3	Years	31																													
GLEN CARSON Glen OG 6'4 293 Saskatchewan B: 8/19/1978 Melfort, SK Draft: 3-21 2001 EDM																															
2001	EDM	3				0																									
2002	EDM	17				0																									
2004	EDM	18	0	0	1	2																									
2005	EDM	3				1																									
2006	EDM	11				0																									
5	Years	52	0	0	1	3																									
KERN CARSON Kern Clay HB 6'0 202 San Diego State B: 1/29/1941 Hope, AR Draft: 29-229(f) 1963 DEN; 17-229(f) 1963 BAL Pro: N																															
1966	TOR	1												5	18	3.6	6	0	2	25	12.5	21	0					1	32	32.0	32
ALEX CARTER Alexander DE 6'3 255 Tennessee State B: 9/6/1963 Miami, FL Pro: N																															
1988	EDM	16				38	6.0																								
1989	OTT	13	0		1	38	5.0																								
2	Years	29	0		1	76	11.0																								
ANDREW CARTER Andrew CB 6'10 320 Bishop's B: 2/13/1977 Draft: 4-30 2001 CAL																															
2002	CAL	1				0																									
2003	CAL	2				0																									
2003	WPG	16				0																									
2003	Year	18				0																									
2	Years	3				0																									
BOYD CARTER Boyd [born Cole] OE-DB 6'0 192 Santa Monica CC B: 1935 Winnipeg, MB D: 8//2007																															
1957	TOR	13							5	120		6	1						9	139	15.4	43	1	2	9	4.5	7	25	530	21.2	70
1958	TOR	14							6	36		24	4						32	473	14.8	40	4	29	187	6.4	15	6	127	21.2	32
1959	TOR	13										24	4	0	-3		-3	0	31	510	16.5	38	4								
1960	TOR	11										24	4	1	6	6.0	6	0	23	339	14.7	50	4								
1961	TOR	7							1	0									1	5	5.0	5	0					1	11	11.0	11
1962	TOR	5																	1	13	13.0	13	0								
1962	MTL	7																	1	11	11.0	11	0					1	16	16.0	16
1962	Year	12																	2	24	12.0	13	0					1	16	16.0	16
6	Years	63							12	156		78	13	1	3	3.0	6	0	98	1490	15.2	50	13	31	196	6.3	15	33	684	20.7	70
DON CARTER Don T 6'2 240 Tulsa B: 1934																															
1954	OTT	9																													
DONNAVAN CARTER Donnavan LB-S 6'1 183 Northern Illinois B: 4/20/1975 Toronto, ON Draft: 1-4 2000 TOR																															
2000	TOR	18	0	0	2	46	2.0	14.0	2	30	0	6	1																		
2001	TOR	18	0	1	2	27	1.0	7.0																							
2002	OTT	16	0	3	3	78			1	0	0																				
2003	OTT	18	0	1	1	67			1	36	1	6	1																		
2004	HAM	17	0	2	2	59	4.0	29.0			2																				
2005	HAM	10	0	0	1	23			1	1	0	6	1																		
2005	OTT	5	0	0	1	1	1.0	7.0																							
2005	Year	15	0	0	1	24	1.0	7.0	1	1	0	6	1																		
2006	WPG	16	0	1	0	57			2	7	3																				
7	Years	113	0	8	12	358	8.0	57.0	7	74	6	18	3																		
ERIC CARTER Eric CB 6'1 185 Knoxville B: 1/23/1969 Wayne, GA																															
1994	HAM	13	0		2	26			2	45	1																				
1995	HAM*	18	0		1	64			10	117	12	6	1																		
1997	HAM	17	0	1	1	35			4	4	6																				
1998	HAM*	14	0	1	2	39			5	85	8	12	2																		
1999	BC+	18	0	0	1	49			7	65	1																	1	0	0.0	0
2000	BC+	17	0	1	1	40			6	39	6																				
2001	BC*	16				34			4	108	5																				
2002	BC*	17	0	2	0	46			4	47	12	6	1																		
2003	BC+	18	0	1	1	46	1.0	6.0	4	70	9																	1	0	0.0	0
2004	WPG	12	0	1	0	40			3	81	8	6	1																		
10	Years	160	0	7	9	419	1.0	6.0	49	661	68	30	5															2	0	0.0	0
GRANT CARTER Grant Matthew DE 6'2 230 Pacific B: 12/30/1970 Lake Oswego, OR																															
1994	BAL	1				1																									
1995	BAL	17	0		2	40	6.0	81.0	1	6	8																				
1996	MTL*	18	0		2	39	15.0	130.0			3																				
1997	WPG	9	0	1	2	22	4.0	57.0			2																				
1998	WPG+	18	0	1	4	58	8.0	61.0	2	40	3	6	1																		
1999	WPG	6	0	0	1	15					2																				
1999	EDM	9				31	4.0	28.0	3	8	3																				
1999	Year	15	0	0	1	46	4.0	28.0	3	8	5																				
2000	EDM	18	0	1	1	80	6.0	35.0	1	75	3	12	2																		
7	Years	87	0	3	12	286	43.0	392.0	7	129	24	18	3																		
JASON CARTER Jason Edward WR 6'0 205 Texas A&M B: 9/15/1982 Caldwell, TX Pro: N																															
2009	TOR	9	3	0	0	6						6	1	1	5	5.0	5	0	43	535	12.4	95	1	8	54	6.8	20	1	32	32.0	32
JODIE CARTER Jodie T. CB 5'11 180 Henderson State B: 8/17/1951 Scott, AR																															
1974	EDM	4																													
KAHLIL CARTER Kahlil R. DH 6'0 185 Arkansas; Southern Arkansas; Arkansas-Little Rock* B: 3/13/1976 Washington, DC Pro: E																															
2005	TOR	1				3																									
2006	TOR	12				34			5	184	0	6	1																		
2007	TOR	18	0	2	0	40	1.0	1.0	3	86	4	12	2																		
2008	MTL	4				8			2	74	1	6	1																		
4	Years	35	0	2	0	85	1.0	1.0	10	344	5	24	4																		
KENT CARTER Kent Alexander LB 6'3 235 Los Angeles CC; Southern California B: 5/25/1950 Los Angeles, CA Draft: 17-422 1972 STL Pro: N																															
1975	OTT	10																													
1976	EDM	4																													
1976	HAM	3																													
1976	Year	7																													
1977	HAM	7																													
1978	TOR	2																													
4	Years	23																													
KERRY CARTER Kerry FB 6'1 238 Stanford B: 12/19/1980 Port of Spain, Trinidad & Tobago Draft: 2B-18 2003 MTL Pro: N																															
2007	MTL	9				3						12	2	21	123	5.9	22	1	2	55	27.5	32	1								

Year	Team	GP	FM	FF	FR	TK	SK	YDS	IR	YDS	PD	PTS	TD	RA	YDS	AVG	LG	TD	REC	YDS	AVG	LG	TD	PR	YDS	AVG	LG	KOR	YDS	AVG	LG
2008	MTL	18				10						12	2	12	79	6.6	20	1	23	270	11.7	55	1					1	12	12.0	12
2009	MTL	18				6						12	2	21	90	4.3	11	0	29	239	8.2	25	2					2	25	12.5	17
2010	MTL	18	0	0	1	10						6	1	1	3	3.0	3	0	21	189	9.0	17	1					1	12	12.0	12
2011	MTL	18	1	0	0	5													20	220	11.0	26	0					1	17	17.0	17
5	Years	81	1	0	1	34						42	7	55	295	5.4	22	2	95	973	10.2	55	5					5	66	13.2	17
MATT CARTER Matt WR 6'1 199 Acadia B: 8/8/1986 Kelowna, BC Draft: 1C-5 2009 BC																															
2009	HAM	3				1																									
2010	HAM	16				4						12	2						10	137	13.7	34	2								
2011	HAM	11				3																									
3	Years	30				8						12	2						10	137	13.7	34	2								
MICHAEL CARTER Michael CB-DH 5'10 175 Erie CC; Maryland B: 4/28/1986 Draft: 3-19 2011 BC																															
2011	HAM	5				1													20	209	10.5	29	0								
M.L. CARTER Milton Louis CB 5'9 173 Monterey Peninsula JC; Fullerton State; San Jose State* B: 12/9/1955 Beaufort, SC Pro: NU																															
1982	HAM	1																													
NORM CARTER Norm G 5'11 192 North Hill Blizzard Jrs. B: 1928 Calgary, AB																															
1948	CAL	11																													
1949	CAL	14																													
1950	CAL	14																													
3	Years	39																													
PERRY CARTER Perry Lynn CB 6'0 190 Southern Mississippi B: 8/5/1971 McComb, MS Draft: 4A-107 1994 ARI Pro: N																															
2000	EDM	9				18			2	0	2																				
2001	EDM	18	0	0	1	24					4																				
2002	MTL	15				35			1	1	3																				
3	Years	42	0	0	1	77			3	1	9																				
PHIL CARTER Phillip RB 5'10 190 Notre Dame B: 8/31/1959 Tacoma, WA Draft: TD 1983 CHI-USFL																															
1984	CAL	5	1			1								23	116	5.0	16	0	12	114	9.5	31	0								
TIM CARTER Timothy Jerome CB 6'0 183 Tulane B: 7/15/1978 Tallahassee, FL Pro: EN																															
2003	WPG	7				15			1	0	7																				
2005	WPG	2	0	1	0	7																									
2	Years	9	0	1	0	22			1	0	7																				
YANNICK CARTER Yannick LB 6'1 205 Wilfrid Laurier B: 5/2/1984 Pickering, ON Draft: 3-20 2007 SAS																															
2007	SAS	16				22																									
2008	SAS	15	0	0	1	16																									
2009	HAM	18	0	1	0	24																									
2010	HAM	18				16																									
2011	HAM	4				2																									
5	Years	71	0	1	1	80																									
CARM CARTERI Carmelo LB 6'2 216 Montana B: 7/17/1956 Regina, SK Draft: 1-6 1979 OTT																															
1979	SAS	12																													
1980	SAS	16																						1	0	0.0	0	1	18	18.0	18
1981	HAM+	16	0		2																										
1982	HAM	16	0		2		3.0																					2	0	0.0	0
1983	MTL	9					1.0		1	0																					
1985	SAS	3																													
6	Years	72	0		4		4.0	0.0	1	0														1	0	0.0	0	3	18	6.0	18
REGGIE CARTHON Reginald W. DH-CB 5'11 175 Montana State B: 7/26/1971 Carson, CA																															
1995	SHR	18				35					4																				
1996	BC	13	0		2	36			1	0	7	6	1																		
1997	WPG	17	0	3	1	41	1.0	9.0	3	28	3													1	0	0.0	0				
1998	WPG	12	0	1	1	29	1.0	6.0	2	58	5	12	2																		
1999	BC	13	0	0	1	43			3	46	8																				
5	Years	73	0	4	5	184	2.0	15.0	9	132	27	18	3											1	0	0.0	0				
RICO CARTWRIGHT Ricardo CB 5'10 180 Florida A&M* B: 5/17/1965 Nassau, Bahamas Pro: E																															
1991	HAM	6	1		0	0						6	1	2	13	6.5	11	0	1	0	0.0	0	0	7	125	17.9	90	8	242	30.3	47
1992	HAM	7	0		1	17																									
1992	BC	5	3		0	5						6	1											16	169	10.6	85	6	90	15.0	24
1992	Year	12	3		1	22						6	1											16	169	10.6	85	6	90	15.0	24
1993	SAS	2				5																		4	18	4.5	10	3	36	12.0	20
3	Years	15	4		1	27						12	2	2	13	6.5	11	0	1	0	0.0	0	0	27	312	11.6	90	17	368	21.6	47
MARK CASALE Mark Joseph QB 6'3 230 Montclair State B: 9/17/1962 Union, NJ Draft: 9-244 1984 CHIB; 10A-195 1984 NJ-USFL																															
1985	TOR	8	2		0							6	1	20	28	1.4	12	1	1	-1	-1.0	-1	0								
JORDAN CASE Jordan Lee QB 6'1 190 North Texas B: 1/6/1957 Seagoville, TX																															
1980	OTT	11	3		1							6	1	39	249	6.4	23	1													
1981	OTT	10	1		0									32	175	5.5	21	0													
1982	OTT	9	5		1							12	2	27	174	6.4	20	2													
3	Years	30	9		2							18	3	98	598	6.1	23	3													
JOHN CASEY John G-T 6'1 210 Toronto B: 1935 Draft: 2-11 1958 TOR																															
1958	TOR	14																													
1959	TOR	13																													
1960	TOR	12																													
1961	TOR	13																													
4	Years	52																													
TOM CASEY Thomas Ray DB-OHB 5'11 175 Hampton B: 7/30/1924 Wellsville, OH D: 10/10/2002 Pro: A																															
1949	HAM	12										61	9					8													
1950	WPG+	13										46	9	111	637	5.7		5	17	318	18.7		3								
1951	WPG+	13										36	7	80	645	8.1		3	30	601	20.0		4	36	293	8.1		12	202	16.8	
1952	WPG+	11			2				7	205		80	16	39	317	8.1	100	4	30	549	18.3	56	10	32	324	10.1	30	9	343	38.1	85
1953	WPG+	14							7	75		10	2	34	250	7.4		0	10	105	10.5		2	51	427	8.4		7	160	22.9	
1954	WPG+	16	0		2				6	102		5	1	8	32	4.0	11	1	2	34	17.0	17	0	20	163	8.2	22				
1955	WPG+	16	0		2				3	44		14	2	37	223	6.0	20	1	2	14	7.0	11	0	8	46	5.8	19				
7	Years	95	0		6				23	426		252	46	309	2104	6.8	100	22	91	1621	17.8	56	19	147	1253	8.5	30	28	705	25.2	85
KEN CASNER Kenneth Wayne T 6'2 245 Baylor B: 1/23/1930 Fort Scott, KS D: 8/19/2009 Waco, TX Draft: 4A-40 1952 LARM Pro: N																															
1956	SAS	1																													
NORM CASOLA Norman WR 6'3 225 Windsor B: 8/4/1969 Sault Ste. Marie, ON D: 9/20/1998 Draft: 6-44 1994 TOR																															
1994	TOR	18				11								1	31	31.0	31	0	3	51	17.0	25	0	1	1	1.0	1	10	69	6.9	20
1995	TOR	15				6								1	4	4.0	4	0	1	7	7.0	7	0					3	24	8.0	15
1996	TOR	18				5													2	71	35.5	36	0								
1997	TOR	18	0	0	1	13													2	17	8.5	10	0					1	13	13.0	13
4	Years	69	0	0	1	35								2	35	17.5	31	0	8	146	18.3	36	0	1	1	1.0	1	14	106	7.6	20
JIM CASON James Allnut, Jr. DB 6'0 171 Louisiana State B: 7/25/1927 Sondheimer, LA Draft: 3-15 1948 SF-AAFC; 7-55 1948 CHIC Pro: AN																															
1953	SAS	5							2	15				11	26	2.4		0	9	77	8.6		0	18	182	10.1		7	152	21.7	
RICK CASSATA James Richard QB-DH 6'1 205 Syracuse B: 11/17/1947 Buffalo, NY Pro: W																															
1968	SAS	16	1		0									16	100	6.3	16	0	1	40	40.0	40	0								
1969	WPG	6							2	24		1	0	3	27	9.0	10	0						2	1	0.5	1				
1971	OTT	14	4		0							6	1	65	393	6.0	58	1													
1972	OTT	14	4		0							12	2	85	442	5.2	43	2													
1973	OTT	14	1		0							6	1	34	128	3.8	14	1													
1974	OTT	16	1		0							6	1	35	143	4.1	25	1													
1976	HAM	7												4	0	0.0	5	0													
1976	BC	7	1		0							12	2	25	116	4.6	29	2													
1976	Year	14	1		0							12	2	29	116	4.0	29	2													
7	Years	87	12		0				2	24		43	7	267	1349	5.1	58	7	1	40	40.0	40	0	2	1	0.5	1				

Year	Team	GP	FM	FF	FR	TK	SK	YDS	IR	YDS	PD	PTS	TD	RA	YDS	AVG	LG	TD	REC	YDS	AVG	LG	TD	PR	YDS	AVG	LG	KOR	YDS	AVG	LG
TOM CASSESE Thomas Lee FL-DB 6'1 198 C.W. Post B: 4/7/1946 New York, NY Draft: 8-191 1967 DEN Pro: N																															
1969	MTL	14	0		1							42	7						32	712	22.3	68	7					1	20	20.0	20
LEN CASSIDY Leonard E 5'10 160 B: 1919 D: 1/30/2007																															
1946	TOR	4																													
1947	TOR	6										5	1																		
1948	TOR	4																													
3	Years	14										5	1																		
MIKE CASSIDY Francis OT-OG-DG 6'2 210 Alabama B: 1923																															
1948	SAS+	12																													
1949	SAS+	14																													
1950	SAS	14																													
1951	SAS	12																													
1952	SAS	12																													
1953	SAS+	16																													
1954	SAS+	16			2				1	9																					
1955	SAS	14							1	8														1	14	14.0	14				
8	Years	110	0		2				2	17														1	14	14.0	14				
PAT CASSIDY Pat QB 160 Calgary Navy Jrs; East Calgary Stampeders Jrs. B: 1924																															
1946	CAL	7																													
KEITH CASTELLO Keith LB 6'2 215 Oshawa Hawkeyes Jrs. B: 3/31/1964 Toronto, ON																															
1988	HAM	1				0																									
1989	HAM	13				1																									
1990	TOR	16	0		2	12	1.0					6	1																		
1991	TOR	15				28																									
1992	TOR	17	0		2	30	1.0	5.0				6	1																		
1993	TOR	18				30													1	5	5.0	5	0								
1994	TOR	15				34	1.0	7.0	1	20	1																				
1995	BC	8				11																									
1996	BC	5				13																									
9	Years	108	0		4	159	3.0	12.0	1	20	1	12	2						1	5	5.0	5	0								
WILLIE CASTON Willie RB 5'10 190 Idaho State B: 3/6/1966 Little Rock, AR																															
1989	CAL	1				0																						1	26	26.0	26
CAYETANO CASTRO Cayetano R. OL 6'6 324 Wisconsin B: 11/27/1974 Dominican Republic Pro: E																															
1998	BC	1																													
PETE CATAN Pete M. DE 6'2 240 Eastern Illinois B: 11/12/1957 Rochester, NY Pro: U																															
1981	WPG	14	0		3		10.0																								
1982	WPG*	16	1		2		12.5					6	1						1	2	2.0	2	1								
1983	WPG	11	0		1		4.0																								
1987	HAM	1				0																									
4	Years	42	1		6	0	26.5					6	1						1	2	2.0	2	1								
TONEY CATCHINGS Toney Bruce LB 6'3 236 Copiah-Lincoln JC; Cincinnati B: 8/11/1965 Jackson, MS Pro: N																															
1988	HAM	4				7	2.0																								
MIKE CATERBONE Michael Thomas WR 5'11 175 Franklin & Marshall B: 2/17/1962 Lancaster, PA Draft: 17B-359 1984 OKL-USFL Pro: N																															
1985	OTT	14	2		0							30	5						43	654	15.2	70	5	37	328	8.9	25	21	436	20.8	45
1986	OTT	1																	2	33	16.5	21	0								
2	Years	15	2		0							30	5						45	687	15.3	70	5	37	328	8.9	25	21	436	20.8	45
LARRY CATES Larry DB 5'11 185 Western Michigan B: 9/25/1950 Columbus, OH Draft: 15-390 1974 MIA; 31-372 1974 DET-WFL																															
1974	CAL	4							1	2				10	46	4.6	17	0	1	0	0.0	0	0					4	125	31.3	35
1975	CAL	16	4		1				3	136		12	2	22	89	4.0	30	0						1	0	0.0	0	26	748	28.8	67
1976	CAL	16	4		1				1	35		20	3	81	458	5.7	38	3	18	141	7.8	15	0	42	489	11.6	53	32	901	28.2	73
1977	OTT	16	5		1				2	7		24	4	34	125	3.7	11	1	13	130	10.0	20	2	46	364	7.9	53	23	525	22.8	44
1978	OTT	8	2		0				2	12		6	1											19	145	7.6	62	4	49	12.3	21
5	Years	60	15		3				9	192		62	10	147	718	4.9	38	4	32	271	8.5	20	2	108	998	9.2	62	89	2348	26.4	73
TOBY CATES Toby G. WR 6'1 195 South Carolina B: 3/3/1972 Greer, SC																															
1995	BAL	5				2													8	113	14.1	49	0								
TOMMY CATES Thomas V. HB 5'10 170 Minnesota B: 7/19/1925 D: 9/19/2005																															
1947	MTL	12										11	2					2													
WES CATES Wesley A. RB 6'0 215 California (Pennsylvania) B: 10/3/1979 Columbus, OH																															
2006	CAL	17				19						18	3	25	181	7.2	64	2	21	286	13.6	74	1					6	90	15.0	25
2007	SAS	14	2	0	0	4						32	5	152	866	5.7	49	5	45	452	10.0	40	0					3	54	18.0	30
2008	SAS*	15	4	0	3	2						84	14	216	1229	5.7	36	12	39	451	11.6	40	2								
2009	SAS	16	2	0	0	0						42	7	195	932	4.8	37	5	33	336	10.2	32	2								
2010	SAS+	18	3	0	1	4						96	16	203	1054	5.2	83	15	42	355	8.5	33	1								
2011	SAS	13	1	0	0	3						24	4	138	680	4.9	32	4	24	185	7.7	16	0								
6	Years	93	12	0	4	32						296	49	929	4942	5.3	83	43	204	2065	10.1	74	6					9	144	16.0	30
DERHAM CATO Derham DT 6'4 291 Dartmouth B: 7/28/1982																															
2007	TOR	2				1																									
ROGER CATTELAN Roger OT-DT 6'5 270 Boston College B: 7/3/1961 Jolliete, QC Draft: TE 1983 OTT; 24-285 1983 WAS-USFL																															
1983	OTT	16	0		1																										
1984	OTT	16																													
1985	OTT+	16																													
1986	OTT	18																													
1987	OTT	7				1																									
5	Years	73	0		1	1																									
TERRY CAULLEY Terry J. RB 5'7 185 Connecticut B: 6/22/1984 Honolulu, HI																															
2007	HAM	8	2	0	2	2						18	3	76	466	6.1	44	1	13	130	10.0	24	2								
2008	HAM	7				2						42	7	66	448	6.8	47	6	9	65	7.2	16	1					4	100	25.0	55
2009	HAM	2				1						6	1	8	38	4.8	12	0	2	16	8.0	13	1	2	10	5.0	12	8	139	17.4	27
3	Years	17	2	0	2	5						66	11	150	952	6.3	47	7	24	211	8.8	24	4	2	10	5.0	12	12	239	19.9	55
TOM CAVALLO Thomas J. LB 6'2 245 Louisville B: 4/21/1971 Pro: E																															
1995	BC	1				0																									
GLEN CAVANAUGH Glen DL 6'7 295 Stanford																															
1994	LV	1																													
QUINTON CAVER Quinton Tyrone DE 6'4 237 Arkansas B: 8/22/1978 Anniston, AL Draft: 2-55 2001 PHI Pro: N																															
2007	HAM	1				3																									
JOE CAVIGLIA Joseph A. CB 5'11 200 California-Davis B: 12/24/1976 Mountain View, CA																															
2001	MTL	1				1																									
KWAME CAVIL Kwame Sekou WR-SB 6'2 203 Texas B: 5/3/1979 Waco, TX Pro: EN																															
2002	MTL	1				0						6	1						1	19	19.0	14	1								
2003	MTL	12	3	0	2	5						12	2						57	686	12.0	52	2								
2004	MTL+	18	1	0	0	1						48	8	6	38	6.3	23	1	78	1090	14.0	60	7								
2005	MTL	3				0													11	118	10.7	20	0								
2005	EDM	7	1	0	0	2						6	1						31	259	8.4	27	1								
2005	Year	10	1	0	0	2						6	1						42	377	9.0	27	1								
2006	HAM	4				0													8	49	6.1	14	0								
2006	WPG	2				0						12	2	1	0	0.0	0	0	7	107	15.3	72	2								
2006	Year	6				0						12	2	1	0	0.0	0	0	15	156	10.4	72	2								
5	Years	38	5	0	2	8						84	14	7	38	5.4	23	1	193	2328	12.1	72	13								
HOMER CAVITTE Homer DB 6'2 205 Lincoln (Missouri) B: 1947																															
1971	SAS	3																										3	51	17.0	21
MARKO CAVKA Marko OG 6'7 294 Sacramento State B: 4/4/1981 Burbank, CA Draft: 6-178 2004 NYJ Pro: E																															
2007	HAM	5				0																									

Year	Team	GP	FM	FF	FR	TK	SK	YDS	IR	YDS	PD	PTS	TD	RA	YDS	AVG	LG	TD	REC	YDS	AVG	LG	TD	PR	YDS	AVG	LG	KOR	YDS	AVG	LG
2008	HAM	10	0	0	1	0						6	1	0	1		1	1													
2	Years	15	0		1	0						6	1	0	1		1	1													
GRADY CAVNESS Grady Crayton S 5'11 186 Texas-El Paso B: 3/1/1947 Houston, TX Draft: 2-36 1969 DEN Pro: N																															
1972	WPG*	16	0		2				8	146																					
1973	WPG	12	0		2				3	57																					
1974	BC	16	0		2				4	53																		1	3	3.0	3
1975	BC	16	0		1				4	59		6	1																		
1976	BC	16	0		3				7	58														2	-1	-0.5	0				
1977	BC+	16	0						4	32																					
1978	BC	16							3	26																					
7	Years	108	0		10				33	431		6	1											2	-1	-0.5	0	1	3	3.0	3
GRADY CAVNESS Grady Crayton, Jr. DB 5'10 187 Texas B: 9/13/1971 Houston, TX																															
1995	SA	18	1		2	42			3	52	8													4	17	4.3	7	3	14	4.7	13
1996	EDM	5				6					1																				
2	Years	23	1		2	48			3	52	9													4	17	4.3	7	3	14	4.7	13
MIKE CAWLEY Michael Rodney QB 6'1 200 Syracuse; James Madison B: 8/28/1972 Mount Lebanon, PA Draft: 6B-205 1996 IND Pro: EX																															
1997	HAM	8				0								20	181	9.1	25	0													
1998	HAM	16				0						6	1	2	10	5.0	8	1													
1999	SAS	2				0																									
2000	OAL	7	1	0	0	0								4	11	2.0	12	0													
4	Years	33	1	0	0	0						6	1	26	202	7.8	25	1													
PARRI CECI Parri Anthony WR 6'0 200 Guelph B: 9/3/1961 Draft: 3B-27 1984 CAL																															
1985	CAL	7																	2	14	7.0	14	0								
BOB CELERI Robert Laverne QB 5'10 180 California B: 6/1/1927 Fort Bragg, CA D: 3/9/1975 Buffalo, NY Draft: 10-127 1950 SF Pro: N																															
1953	HAM	1																													
J.J. CELESTINE Jonathan J. WR 5'9 195 Fullerton State B: 9/30/1968																															
1992	EDM	8	2		0	1													8	135	16.9	44	0					11	206	18.7	39
GENE CEPPETELLI Eugene C. C 6'2 247 Villanova B: 7/28/1942 Sudbury, ON Pro: N																															
1963	HAM	14																													
1964	HAM	14																													
1965	HAM	14	0		1																										
1966	HAM	14												1	0	0.0	0	0													
1967	HAM+	14																													
1970	MTL+	14	1		0																										
1971	MTL	14																													
7	Years	98	1		1									1	0	0.0	0	0													
BILL CERETTI Willie (Red Dog) G 206 Winnipeg Native Sons Jrs.; St. John Srs. B: 3/10/1912 MB D: 5/5/1974																															
1946	WPG+	7																													
1947	WPG	7																													
1948	WPG	11																													
1949	WPG	1																													
4	Years	26																													
OBED CETOUTE Obed WR-SB 6'2 214 Central Michigan B: 1/7/1983 Montreal, QC Draft: 4-31 2006 TOR																															
2007	TOR	15				2						18	3						22	367	16.7	46	3								
2008	TOR	8				0													9	94	10.4	16	0								
2010	SAS	4				0																									
3	Years	27				2						18	3						31	461	14.9	46	3								
WALT CHADWICK Walter OHB 6'0 205 Tennessee B: 3/30/1946 Draft: 6-164 1968 GB																															
1968	WPG	9										6	1	35	126	3.6	33	1	3	0	0.0	5	0					1	31	31.0	31
SAMIR CHAHINE Samir OG 6'1 295 McGill B: 3/9/1974 Beirut, Lebanon Draft: 2-11 1998 EDM																															
1998	EDM	18				1																									
1999	EDM	8				0																									
2000	EDM	14				0																									
2000	TOR	2				0																									
2000	Year	16				0																									
2001	TOR	17				0																									
2002	HAM	5				0																									
2003	CAL	6				0																									
2004	OTT	7				0																									
7	Years	75				1																									
WALT CHAHLEY Walt HB 5'9 165 Vancouver Blue Bombers Jrs. B: 1929																															
1949	CAL	14										6	0																		
1950	CAL	3										4	0																		
2		17										10	0																		
KEVIN CHALLENGER Kevin WR-SB 5'8 179 Boston College B: 5/4/1982 Montreal, QC Draft: 2-14 2007 CAL																															
2008	EDM	18				1													8	166	20.8	80	0								
2009	EDM	18				1																									
2	Years	36				2													8	166	20.8	80	0								
MARK CHALMERS Richard Mark DE-DT 6'4 250 Texas B: 4/2/1952 Austin, TX																															
1975	HAM	9	0		1																										
1977	BC	1																													
2	Years	10	0	0	1																										
ED CHALUPKA Edward S. OG 6'0 225 North Carolina B: 2/23/1947																															
1970	HAM	14																										1	12	12.0	12
1971	HAM	10	0		1							6	1																		
1972	HAM+	14																													
1973	HAM+	14	0		1																										
1974	HAM+	16	0		3																										
1975	HAM	16																													
1976	HAM	16																										1	0	0.0	0
7	Years	100	0		5							6	1															2	12	6.0	12
BILL CHAMBERLAIN Bill SB 6'2 230 British Columbia B: 6/19/1977 Victoria, BC																															
2003	BC	18				4																									
2004	CAL	5	0	0	1	1																									
2007	SAS	1				0																									
3	Years	24	0	0	1	5																									
BILL CHAMBERS William Joseph G-T 6'2 230 Georgia Tech; Alabama; UCLA B: 1923 Draft: 13-129 1945 PHI Pro: A																															
1951	MTL	12																													
1952	OTT	5																													
2		17																													
JACKIE CHAMBERS Jackie SB 5'11 180 South Florida; Lane B: 9/8/1984 Miami, FL																															
2009	CAL	2	1	0	0	0													2	4	2.0	10	0								
JIMMY CHAMBERS Jimmy HB 6'1 195 Montreal Ints. B: 3/16/1927 Montreal, QC																															
1951	EDM	14										55	11	52	513	9.9		7	18	378	21.0		4	1	21	21.0	21	13	192	14.8	
1952	EDM	14			1							20	4	61	400	6.6	75	2	17	290	17.1	69	2					1	103	103.0	70
1953	EDM	7												2	8	4.0	15	0										3	40	13.3	
1954	BC	10												8	27	3.4	12	0	4	67	16.8	35	0	1	0	0.0	0	6	84	14.0	28
4	Years	45	0		1							75	15	123	948	7.7	75	9	39	735	18.8	69	6	2	21	10.5	21	23	419	18.2	70
STEVE CHAMKO Steve T-G 6'1 210																															
1946	HAM	10																													
1948	MTL	10																													
2	Years	20																													

Year	Team	GP	FM	FF	FR	TK	SK	YDS	IR	YDS	PD	PTS	TD	RA	YDS	AVG	LG	TD	REC	YDS	AVG	LG	TD	PR	YDS	AVG	LG	KOR	YDS	AVG	LG
ED CHAMPAGNE Edward J. T 6'3 236 Louisiana State B: 12/4/1922 New Orleans, LA D: 6/15/2003 Raleigh, NC Draft: 18-163 1947 LARM Pro: N																															
1951	CAL	5																													
TONY CHAMPION Tony WR 6'3 240 Tennessee-Martin B: 3/19/1963 Humbold, TN																															
1985	HAM	6	1		1							6	1	1	2	2.0	2	0	13	203	15.6	67	1					3	86	28.7	33
1986	HAM+	18	2		0							36	6	1	8	8.0	8	0	74	1216	16.4	75	6	1	5	5.0	5	10	233	23.3	43
1987	HAM	11				4						36	6						53	851	16.1	75	6	1	6	6.0	6	5	78	15.6	18
1988	HAM	9				3						6	1						16	270	16.9	42	1								
1989	HAM*	17				2						90	15						95	1656	17.4	83	15								
1990	HAM	9				4						30	5						37	581	15.7	75	5								
1991	HAM	12				7						14	2						45	545	12.1	26	2								
1992	HAM	3				1						6	1						7	176	25.1	75	1								
8	Years	85	3		1	21						224	37	2	10	5.0	8	0	340	5498	16.2	83	37	2	11	5.5	6	18	397	22.1	43
ZAC CHAMPION Zac QB 6'0 200 Louisiana Tech B: 6/29/1984 Birmingham, AL																															
2008	BC	18				0								1	19	19.0	19	0													
2009	BC	7				0																									
2010	WPG	2				0																									
3	Years	27				0								1	19	19.0	19	0													
CAMERON CHANCE Cameron F. DT 5'11 280 San Diego State B: 1/27/1976 Orlando, FL																															
1999	TOR	12	0	1	0	16	1.0	6.0			1																				
2000	TOR	3	0	1	0	7	1.0	0.0																							
2	Years	15	0	2	0	23	2.0	6.0			1																				
KEN CHANCELLOR James Kenneth LB 6'2 240 Baylor; Houston B: 7/2/1940 Lufkin, TX																															
1965	EDM	1																													
LEN CHANDLER Len DB-FL 5'8 165 Hamilton Tiger-Cats B B: 1/28/1937																															
1958	HAM	10																						40	197	4.9	20	2	40	20.0	26
1959	HAM	14							2	17														2	20	10.0	8				
1960	HAM	13							2	14				2	9	4.5	8	0						7	35	5.0	12				
1961	OTT	14										12	2						12	220	18.3	46	2	68	372	5.5	23				
1962	OTT	14										24	4						9	143	15.9	29	4	46	130	2.8	11				
1964	TOR	14	3		2				1	0									8	114	14.3	23	0	47	252	5.4	24	1	12	12.0	12
6	Years	79	3		2				5	31		36	6	2	9	4.5	8	0	29	477	16.4	46	6	210	1006	4.8	24	3	52	17.3	26
TOM CHANDLER Thomas Hiram, II LB 6'2 224 Minnesota B: 6/12/1950 Pasadena, TX Draft: 14-354 1972 ATL Pro: W																															
1976	TOR	8	0		1				1	27																					
1977	CAL	5																													
2	Years	13	0		1				1	27																					
DON CHANEY Don TE 6'5 262 Sequoias CC; South Carolina B: 7/14/1971																															
1994	SHR	2				2																		1	3	3.0	3				
JERMAINE CHANEY Jermaine T. DB-RB 6'1 210 Indiana B: 4/6/1973 Athens, GA Pro: E																															
1995	OTT	4	0		1	1						6	1	12	39	3.3	11	1	8	81	10.1	25	0					5	100	20.0	24
1996	OTT	1	1		0	0								4	10	2.5	6	0	7	39	5.6	14	0								
2	Years	5	1		1	1						6	1	16	49	3.1	11	1	15	120	8.0	25	0					5	100	20.0	24
TIMMY CHANG Tim QB 6'1 207 Hawaii B: 10/9/1981 Honolulu, HI Pro: E																															
2007	HAM	18	0	0	1	0								5	24	4.8	11	0													
2008	WPG	1				0																									
2	Years	19	0	0	1	0								5	24	4.8	11	0													
JACQUES CHAPDELAINE Jacques SB-WR 6'0 185 Simon Fraser B: 8/24/1961 Sherbrooke, QC Draft: 1A-5 1983 BC																															
1983	BC	16																	22	258	11.7	34	0					1	18	18.0	18
1984	BC	16																	7	74	10.6	20	0								
1985	MTL	7																	3	19	6.3	9	0								
1986	MTL	18	0		1							6	1						53	668	12.6	44	1	1	1	1.0	1				
1987	HAM	13				0						8	1						37	438	11.8	40	1								
1988	HAM	18				1						24	4						43	542	12.6	61	4					1	0	0.0	0
1989	HAM	5				0													1	7	7.0	7	0								
1989	CAL	1				0																									
1989	Year	6				0													1	7	7.0	7	0								
7	Years	93	0		1	1						38	6						166	2006	12.1	61	6	1	1	1.0	1	2	18	9.0	18
KURT CHAPMAN Kurt OG-C 6'4 245 Simon Fraser B: 10/14/1962 Vancouver, BC Draft: 2A-14 1984 EDM																															
1985	EDM	16	0		1																										
1986	EDM	16																										1	0	0.0	0
2	Years	32	0		1																							1	0	0.0	0
LAMAR CHAPMAN Lamar A. CB 6'0 176 Kansas State B: 11/6/1976 Liberal, KS Draft: 5B-146 2000 CLE Pro: N																															
2005	MTL	4				12			2	38	1																				
VIC CHAPMAN Victor Garbutt OE-DE-K-P-FW 6'0 200 Vancouver Meralomas Jrs.; British Columbia B: 1930 Vancouver, BC D: 12/21/1987 Ottawa, ON																															
1952	CAL	1										1	0																		
1954	BC	12										1	0						3	97	32.3	65	0								
1955	BC	14										7	0						6	90	15.0	19	0								
1956	BC	16	2		0							6	0	2	-24	-12.0	-10	0	12	188	15.7	29	0								
1957	BC	16							4	31		31	4						10	197	19.7	58	3	3	7	2.3	3				
1958	BC	14										7	1						20	368	18.4	67	1								
1959	EDM	16										11	1						4	57	14.3	22	1								
1960	EDM	15	1		1							12	1	1	-9	-9.0	-9	0	5	86	17.2	24	0								
1961	EDM	15										5	0						17	299	17.6	50	0								
1962	EDM	10	2									7	0	1	-13	-13.0	-13	0	2	21	10.5	11	0								
1962	MTL	1										2	0											1	0	0.0	0				
1962	Year	11	2									9	0	1	-13	-13.0	-13	0	2	21	10.5	11	0	1	0	0.0	0				
10	Years	129	5		1				4	31		90	7	4	-46	-11.5	-9	0	79	1403	17.8	67	5	4	7	1.8	3				
RAY CHARAMBURA Ray OE 6'2 184 Winnipeg Light Infantry Jrs. B: 11/29/1928																															
1950	WPG	12																													
STEVE CHARBONNEAU Steve DT 6'5 260 New Hampshire B: 5/30/1973 Cowansville, QC Draft: 1-6 1997 MTL																															
1997	MTL	18				24					1																				
1998	MTL	16	0	1	2	32	2.0	27.0				6	0															1	11	11.0	11
1999	MTL	15				28					1																				
2000	MTL	16				34	8.0	56.0			2																				
2001	MTL	14	0	1	1	29	4.0	23.0			2																				
2002	EDM	17	0	1	2	28	4.0	26.0																							
2003	EDM	15	0	0	2	25	2.0	14.0			2																				
2004	EDM	8				19	1.0	11.0																							
2005	EDM	15	0	0	1	16	3.0	17.0			1																				
2006	EDM	17				29	4.0	25.0			1																				
10	Years	151	0	3	8	264	28.0	199.0			10	6	0															1	11	11.0	11
HENCY CHARLES Hency S-LB 5'10 200 Laval Scorpions Jrs. B: 10/4/1970 St. Marc, Haiti Pro: E																															
1994	TOR	7				6					1																				
1995	SAS	2				3																									
1995	EDM	6	0		1	18																									
1995	Year	8	0		1	21																									
1996	MTL	18				16																									
1997	MTL	18				13																									
1998	MTL	18	0	0	1	41																									
1999	MTL	15	0	1	0	23																									
2000	EDM	14				16																									
2001	SAS	1				1																									
2001	EDM	5				3																									

Year	Team	GP	FM	FF	FR	TK	SK	YDS	IR	YDS	PD	PTS	TD	RA	YDS	AVG	LG	TD	REC	YDS	AVG	LG	TD	PR	YDS	AVG	LG	KOR	YDS	AVG	LG
2001	Year	6				4																										
8	Years	93	0	1	2	140					1																				
HUGH CHARLES Hugh RB 5'8 185 Colorado B: 1/7/1986 Tulsa, OK																														
2008	SAS	2				0								12	64	5.3	21	0	1	7	7.0	7	0					2	17	8.5	12
2009	SAS	4	3	0	1	0						24	4	35	136	3.9	20	3	4	80	20.0	45	1					1	23	23.0	23
2010	SAS	8				0						12	2	13	115	8.8	30	2	3	39	13.0	17	0					17	376	22.1	46
2011	SAS	7	1	0	0	1						18	3	38	242	6.4	35	1	15	94	6.3	15	2	4	65	16.3	22	14	296	21.1	53
2011	EDM	2				0								8	35	4.4	13	0	3	51	17.0	40	0					1	9	9.0	9
2011	Year	9				1						18	3	46	277	6.0	35	1	18	145	8.1	40	2	4	65	16.3	22	15	305	20.3	53
4	Years	21	4	0	1	1						54	9	106	592	5.6	35	6	26	271	10.4	45	3	4	65	16.3	22	35	721	20.6	53
JEAN-AGNES CHARLES Jean-Agnes DB 5'11 195 Michigan B: 10/9/1971 Montreal, QC Draft: 3A-21 1996 CAL																														
1996	CAL	11				9																										
LES CHARLETON Les HB Regina Jrs.																														
1946	SAS	7																												
IKE CHARLTON Isaiah C., IV LB-DB 5'11 204 Virginia Tech B: 10/6/1977 Orlando, FL Draft: 2-52 2000 SEA Pro: N																														
2005	WPG	2	0	1	0	7																										
2006	WPG	15	0	0	2	62	1.0	9.0				6	1																		
2007	WPG	8	0	1	0	29	2.0	12.0			3																			
2008	WPG	11	0	0	1	38	1.0	7.0			4																			
2009	WPG	18	0	2	3	80			1	20	5																			
2010	WPG	5	0	2	0	23					3																			
2010	MTL	1				4																										
2010	Year	14	0	2	0	27					3																			
6	Years	59	0	6	6	243	4.0	28.0	1	29	15	6	1																		
KEN CHARLTON Ken HB-FW-FB-QB 6'0 171 Regina West Enders Jrs.; Regina Dales Jrs. B: 1921																														
1946	OTT+	9										54	10					6					3								
1947	OTT	11										25	5					2					3								
1948	SAS+	11										33	4					3					1								
1949	SAS+	14										38	6					4					1								
1950	SAS	14										27	4	76	498	6.6		2	24	458	19.1		2								
1951	SAS	11										37	7	80	356	4.5		1	24	348	14.5		6	41	388	9.5		8	136	17.0	
1952	SAS	14							4	25		15	3	43	152	3.5	43	2	18	345	19.2	77	1	3	42	14.0	28	2	74	37.0	32
1953	SAS	16							3	0		4	0	1	3	3.0	3	0						34	414	12.2					
1954	SAS	3							1	13														3	38	12.7	17				
9	Years	103							8	38		233	39	200	1009	5.0	43	20	66	1151	17.4	77	17	81	882	10.9	28	10	210	21.0	32
PHIL CHARRON Philip SB-WR 6'0 185 Bishop's B: 3/21/1960 Montreal, QC Draft: 3A-19 1982 CAL																														
1983	OTT	12																		6	108	18.0	26	0								
1984	CAL	6																		6	70	11.7	27	0								
2	Years	18																		12	178	14.8	27	0								
AL CHARUK Alan WR-FL 5'11 185 Acadia B: 6/21/1954 Draft: 1-2 1975 TOR																														
1975	TOR	16										6	1						11	183	16.6	46	1					2	42	21.0	27
1976	TOR	16	1		0							12	2						25	486	19.4	82	2								
1977	BC	16	0		1							18	3						27	317	11.7	42	3	1	-1	-1.0	-1				
1978	BC	16										24	4						51	790	15.5	53	4								
1979	BC	16	1		0							18	3						33	515	15.6	43	3								
1980	BC	16										42	7						32	674	21.1	50	7								
1981	BC	16	0		1							30	5						35	582	16.6	84	5								
1982	BC	8										6	1						11	114	10.4	20	1								
8	Years	120	2		2							156	26						225	3661	16.3	84	26	1	-1	-1.0	-1	2	42	21.0	27
JIM CHASEY Jim QB 6'1 185 Dartmouth B: 1949																														
1971	MTL	13	3		0									16	89	5.6	28	0													
1972	MTL	1												1	11	11.0	11	0													
1972	TOR	6										6	1	12	54	4.5	12	1													
1972	Year	7										6	1	13	65	5.0	12	1													
2	Years	14	3		0							6	1	29	154	5.3	28	1													
JERMAINE CHATMAN Jermaine LaMont CB-DH 5'11 182 Pasadena CC; Arizona B: 2/15/1980 Compton, CA Pro: E																														
2005	CAL	13				52			3	105	6	6	1											8	81	10.1	15				
2006	CAL	17	0	0	2	52					1																			
2007	CAL	3	0	0	1	11					1	6	1																		
2007	SAS	5	0	0	1	12			1	21	2																			
2007	Year	8	0	0	2	23			1	21	3	6	1																		
3	Years	33	0	0	4	127			4	126	10	12	2											8	81	10.1	15				
TYRONE CHATMAN Tyrone LB 5'8 220 Arkansas B: 4/12/1971 Dumas, AR																														
1994	BC	16	0		1	59	1.0	8.0			2																			
1995	BC	15	0		1	62	2.0	9.0																				1	14	14.0	14
1996	BC	15	0		1	75	2.0	12.0	2	15	0																			
1997	BC	10	0	1	1	42	2.0	7.0			1																			
4	Years	56	0	1	4	238	7.0	36.0	2	15	3																	1	14	14.0	14
DAVE CHAYTORS David DT 6'2 258 Calgary Colts Jrs.; Utah B: 10/12/1969 Calgary, AB Draft: 3-19 1992 OTT																														
1993	OTT	13	0		1	9																										
1994	BC	17	0		2	30	2.0	11.0			5																			
1995	BC	16	0		1	35	2.0	12.0			1																			
1996	BC	16				20	3.0	9.0																								
1997	BC	12	0	0	1	26	8.0	47.0			2																			
1998	BC+	18	0	1	2	41	10.0	71.0																								
1999	BC	18	0	0	1	33	1.0	8.0			2																			
7	Years	110	0	1	8	194	26.0	158.0			10																			
RAY CHEATHAM Ray Charles LB 6'0 197 Independence JC; Kansas State B: 8/6/1986 El Dorado, AR																														
2010	CAL	1				0																										
TIM CHEATWOOD Tim DE 6'4 258 Ohio State B: 11/8/1978 East Cleveland, OH																														
2002	HAM	17	0	2	1	51	5.0	30.0																								
2003	HAM+	17	0	2	1	63	10.0	79.0			3																			
2004	HAM*	18	0	0	1	40	14.0	84.0			1																	1	8	8.0	8
2005	HAM	11	0	1	2	34	6.0	43.0				6	1															1	9	9.0	9
2006	HAM	13	0	2	0	37	6.0	32.0			2																			
2007	EDM	7				11	3.0	23.0																								
6	Years	83	0	7	5	236	44.0	291.0			6	6	1															2	17	8.5	9
PAUL CHENG Paul DL 6'3 280 Simon Fraser B: 8/4/1978 Draft: 1B-6 2002 BC																														
2002	BC	4				4																										
2002	CAL	3				0																										
2002	Year	7				4																										
RON CHERKAS Ronald J. DT 6'4 240 Regina Rams Jrs.; Utah B: 12/30/1953 Kamsack, SK Draft: TE 1976 SAS																														
1976	SAS	16			1																									
1977	SAS	16	0		1																									
1978	SAS	16	0		1																									
1980	WPG	11																												
1981	WPG	16					1.0																					1	0	0.0	0
1982	WPG	8							1	6																					
1982	SAS	2	0		1																									
1982	Year	10	0		1				1	6																					
1983	MTL	3																												
1983	WPG	5																												

Year	Team	GP	FM	FF	FR	TK	SK	YDS	IR	YDS	PD	PTS	TD	RA	YDS	AVG	LG	TD	REC	YDS	AVG	LG	TD	PR	YDS	AVG	LG	KOR	YDS	AVG	LG
1983	BC	5					1.0																								
1983	Year	8					1.0																								
1984	BC	16	0		1																										
1985	SAS	2																													
9	Years	104	0		5		2.0		1	6																		1	0	0.0	0
DUSTIN CHERNIAWSKI Dustin DB 6'0 202 British Columbia B: 9/22/1981 Edmonton, AB Draft: 5-39 2005 SAS																															
2005	SAS	17				19																									
2006	SAS	17	0	0	1	18																									
2007	SAS	7	0	0	1	3																									
3	Years	41	0	0	2	40																									
PASCAL CHERON Pascal OG 6'4 280 Laval B: 6/22/1974 Charlesbourg, QC Draft: 6-45 1999 HAM																															
2000	HAM	14				0																									
2001	HAM	10				1																									
2002	HAM	17				2																									
2003	HAM	18	0	0	1	0																									
2004	HAM	18				2																									
2005	OTT	18				6																									
2006	HAM	4				0																									
2007	HAM	7				0																									
8	Years	106	0	0	1	11																									
TONY CHERRY Anthony Earl RB 5'7 187 Riverside CC; Oregon B: 2/8/1963 Tripoli, Libya Draft: 9-240 1986 SF Pro: N																															
1988	BC*	12	4		2	1						54	9	149	889	6.0	70	6	16	164	10.3	45	3					12	373	31.1	85
1989	BC	12	2		1	2						24	4	111	521	4.7	68	2	36	380	10.6	50	2	1	2	2.0	2	29	696	24.0	56
1990	OTT	4	2		0	0						12	2	53	228	4.3	28	2	9	61	6.8	11	0					1	20	20.0	20
1990	CAL	6	2		0	1						42	7	88	391	4.4	28	6	7	53	7.6	23	1					4	96	24.0	34
1990	Year	10	4		0	1						54	9	141	619	4.4	28	8	16	114	7.1	23	1					5	116	23.2	34
1991	EDM	1				0								2	0	0.0	2	0										1	18	18.0	18
4	Years	29	10		3	4						132	22	403	2029	5.0	70	16	68	658	9.7	50	6	1	2	2.0	2	47	1203	25.6	85
AL CHESTER Albert DB 6'1 195 Florida A&M B: 2/19/1958																															
1979	TOR	2												1	-2	-2.0	-2	0	3	19	6.3	13	0								
RANDY CHEVRIER Randy Robert DT-OG-C 6'2 281 McGill B: 6/6/1976 St. Leonard, QC Draft: 1-5 2001 EDM; 7D-241 2001 JAC Pro: EN																															
2002	EDM	5				4																									
2003	EDM	18	0	1	0	21	1.0	1.0			3																	1	0	0.0	0
2005	CAL	18				14	2.0	7.0	1	2	2																				
2006	CAL	18				17	1.0	10.0																							
2007	CAL	17	0	1	1	27	2.0	24.0			1	6	1						1	1	1.0	1	1								
2008	CAL	18				14					1																				
2009	CAL	18	0	1	0	7																									
2010	CAL	18	0	0	1	5						6	1						1	1	1.0	1	1								
2011	CAL	18				8																									
9	Years	148	0	3	2	117	6.0	42.0	1	2	7	12	2						2	2	1.0	1	2					1	0	0.0	0
GORDON CHIAROT Gordon T-G 6'0 235 McMaster B: 1937																															
1958	BC	4																													
JOHN CHICK John, Jr. DE 6'4 248 Utah State B: 11/20/1982 St. Joseph, MO Pro: N																															
2007	SAS	13	0	0	1	23	5.0	40.0			2	6	1																		
2008	SAS	8	0	2	0	13	3.0	45.0																							
2009	SAS+	16	0	4	2	34	11.0	71.0			5																				
3	Years	37	0	6	3	70	19.0	156.0			7	6	1																		
CHIC CHICKOWSKI Walter E 6'0 190 Winnipeg YMHA Jrs. B: 1919 Winnipeg, MB D: 1999																															
1946	WPG	7																													
1948	CAL	12										5	1										1								
2	Years	19										5	1										1								
FREDDIE CHILDRESS Freddie Lee OG-OT 6'4 333 Arkansas B: 9/17/1965 Little Rock, AR Draft: 2B-55 1989 CIN Pro: N																															
1994	SHR	12				2																									
1995	BIR+	16				0																									
1996	CAL*	18				1																									
1997	CAL*	18				0																									
1998	CAL*	18				3																									
1999	CAL	8				0																									
2000	CAL+	18				0																									
2001	CAL+	18				0																									
2002	CAL	17				1																									
2003	CAL	8				2																									
2004	SAS	6				0																									
2005	SAS	13				0																									
2006	SAS	15	0	0	1	1																									
13	Years	185	0	0	1	10																									
JOHN CHILDRESS John DE 6'2 220 Arkansas B: 4/24/1940 Forrest City, AR Draft: 10-127 1962 WAS																															
1962	CAL	12							1																						
CLARENCE CHILDS Clarence Norris HB 6'0 180 Florida A&M B: 1/13/1938 Lakeland, FL Draft: 20- 1961 BOS Pro: N																															
1961	CAL	1												7	14	2.0	4	0	3	32	10.7	20	0								
HENRI CHILDS Henri Keenan RB 6'1 217 Kansas; Colorado State B: 1/15/1980 Kansas City, MO Pro: E																															
2006	WPG	3	1	0	0	0								5	24	4.8	8	0	3	43	14.3	21	0								
2007	SAS	11	1	0	0	0						18	3	38	143	3.8	16	2	9	94	10.4	34	1					3	37	12.3	14
2008	SAS	5				0													7	69	9.9	16	0	1	6	6.0	6				
3	Years	19	2	0	0	0						18	3	43	167	3.9	16	2	19	206	10.8	34	1	1	6	6.0	6	3	37	12.3	14
DYLAN CHING Dylan SB-WR 5'10 210 San Diego B: 4/16/1978 Honolulu, HI Draft: 3-15 2000 SAS																															
2000	SAS	18	1	0	0	4						6	1						19	302	15.9	80	1								
2001	SAS	17	3	0	1	3													5	66	13.2	35	0								
2002	SAS	18				0						8	1	1	5	5.0	5	0	13	139	10.7	29	1								
3	Years	53	4	0	1	7						14	2	1	5	5.0	5	0	37	507	13.7	80	2								
ERIC CHIPPER Eric T-G-E 5'11 197 Strathconas Jrs. B: 1915																															
1946	OTT	11										7	0																		
1947	OTT	12										25	0																		
1948	OTT	12										37	1																		
1949	OTT	12										37	0																		
1950	OTT	10										26	0																		
5	Years	57										132	1																		
BRYAN CHIU Bryan C 6'2 287 Pacific; Washington State B: 8/16/1974 Vancouver, BC Draft: 2-18 1996 MTL																															
1997	MTL	12				2																									
1998	MTL	18				1																									
1999	MTL	18				1																									
2000	MTL*	18				0																									
2001	MTL*	18	1	0	1	1																									
2002	MTL*	17	1	0	1	0																									
2003	MTL*	18				1																									
2004	MTL*	15	2	0	0	1																									
2005	MTL+	15				0																									
2006	MTL	18				0																									
2007	MTL	16	0	0	1	1																									
2008	MTL*	18				0																									
2009	MTL+	17	1	0	0	0																									

Year	Team	GP	FM	FF	FR	TK	SK	YDS	IR	YDS	PD	PTS	TD	RA	YDS	AVG	LG	TD	REC	YDS	AVG	LG	TD	PR	YDS	AVG	LG	KOR	YDS	AVG	LG
13	Years	218	5	0	3	8																									
HARRY CHOLAKIS Harry A. G-T B: 12/16/1926 Winnipeg, MB D: 7/16/2007 Toronto, ON																															
1949	WPG	4																													
PAUL CHOLAKIS Paul HB 5'8 160 Manitoba B: 6/23/1928																															
1949	WPG	10										6	1																		
1950	WPG	3																													
2	Years	13										6	1																		
LANCE CHOMYC Lance K-P 6'0 195 Edmonton Wildcats Jrs.; Toronto B: 3/2/1963 Edmonton, AB Draft: 6-46 1985 OTT																															
1985	TOR	12										72	0																		
1986	TOR*	18										157	0																		
1987	TOR	18	1		0	0						193	0																		
1988	TOR+	18				0						207	0																		
1989	TOR	18				0						144	0																		
1990	TOR	18	1		1	0						200	0						1	22	22.0	22	0								
1991	TOR*	18				2						236	0																		
1992	TOR	18	3		1	1						154	0																		
1993	TOR	18	3		1	0						135	0																		
9	Years	156	8		3	3						1498	0						1	22	22.0	22	0								
AL CHORNEY Alan DB 6'0 186 British Columbia B: 9/20/1957 Draft: 1A-2 1979 SAS																															
1070	ƐΛƐ	15	2		2							7	0											48	425	8.9	38	15	352	23.5	33
1980	SAS	6																													
1980	MTL	10	1		1							6	1															13	430	33.1	99
1980	Year	16	1		1																							13	430	33.1	99
2	Years	21	3		3							13	1											48	425	8.9	38	28	782	27.9	99
TERRIS CHORNEY Terris OL 6'1 240 Nebraska B: 11/11/1969 Ituna, SK Draft: 4A-26 1992 EDM																															
1993	EDM	9				0																									
1994	EDM	2																													
2	Years	11				0																									
ERNIE CHOUKALIS Ernie (Chick) G-T-E 6'1 205 Vancouver Blue Bombers Jrs. B: 1929																															
1946	CAL	2																													
1949	CAL	11																													
1951	SAS	3																													
1952	SAS	9			1							5	1																		
1953	SAS	9																													
1954	BC	6																													
1955	BC	5																													
7	Years	45	0		1							5	1																		
GARY CHOWN Gary LB 5'11 235 Bishop's B: 11/4/1951 Draft: TE 1974 MTL																															
1974	MTL	9																													
1975	MTL	16																													
1976	MTL	3																													
1977	MTL	12	1		0				1	0																		2	32	16.0	20
4	Years	40	1		0				1	0																		2	32	16.0	20
TOM CHOWN Tom FL 6'2 197 Queen's B: 12/26/1945 Brantford, ON Draft: 1968 TOR																															
1973	EDM	3																						2	2	1.0	4				
ERIK CHRISTENSEN Erik Robert, Jr. DT-E 6'3 235 Richmond B: 10/30/1931 Elizabeth, NJ Draft: 7A-76 1955 WAS Pro: N																															
1956	CAL	3																													
1957	CAL	11																													
2	Years	14																													
JAY CHRISTENSEN Jay SB-WR 6'3 190 Okanagan Sun Jrs. B: 11/19/1963 Vancouver, BC																															
1986	CAL	4																	3	29	9.7	21	0								
1987	CAL	13	0		1	1						6	1						13	178	13.7	37	1								
1988	CAL	18			2	1						12	2						14	179	12.8	27	2					1	0	0.0	0
1989	CAL	16	0		1	0													5	59	11.8	19	0					1	0	0.0	0
1990	BC	18	2		1	2						52	8						62	1036	16.7	48	8					2	1	0.5	1
1991	BC	16	1		1	1						56	9	1	10	10.0	10	1	45	630	14.0	53	8					1	0	0.0	0
1992	EDM	8				1						6	1						14	238	17.0	50	1								
1993	EDM	9				4													16	273	17.1	38	0								
1994	EDM	14	1		0	2													32	435	13.6	30	0								
1995	OTT	17	3		0	3						8	1						44	574	13.0	36	1								
10	Years	133	7		6	15						140	22	1	10	10.0	10	1	248	3631	14.6	53	21					5	1	0.2	1
KEITH CHRISTENSEN Keith Elmore OT 6'4 265 Kansas B: 5/10/1947 Concordia, KS Draft: 5B-117 1969 NO																															
1970	EDM	8																													
1971	EDM	4																													
2	Years	12																													
GLEN CHRISTIAN Glen HB-FB 5'9 185 Idaho B: 1929 Calgary, AB Draft: 9-105 1952 SF																															
1953	CAL	16										18	0	18	104	5.8		0	5	140	28.0	65	0	14	145	10.4	21	12	257	21.4	56
1954	CAL	11	0		3				2	62		11	2	2	4	2.0	3	0	1	2	2.0	2	0	39	415	10.6	93	1	16	16.0	16
1955	CAL	5	0		2																										
1955	BC	5	1		0				2	11				2	20	10.0	20	0						5	34	6.8	12	3	32	10.7	19
1955	Year	10	1		2									2	20	10.0	20	0						5	34	6.8	12	3	32	10.7	19
1956	BC	12	2		0				1	41		6	1	10	86	8.6	52	1	1	2	2.0	2	0	29	143	4.9	34	1	20	20.0	20
1957	CAL	13	3		0							5	0											28	179	6.4	24	13	255	19.6	35
5	Years	57	6		5				5	114		40	3	32	214	6.7	52	1	7	144	20.6	65	0	115	916	8.0	93	30	580	19.3	56
GORD CHRISTIAN Gord OE 6'4 228 Hamilton Hurricanes Jrs. B: 3/3/1946 D: 9/23/2008																															
1967	HAM	14										6	1						5	120	24.0	41	1								
1968	HAM	14																	1	6	6.0	6	0					1	8	8.0	8
1969	HAM	13	0		1							6	1	3	22	7.3	15	0	17	313	18.4	38	1								
1970	HAM	14	1		3									2	6	3.0	4	0	16	300	18.8	47	0					4	38	9.5	14
1971	HAM	14										6	1						11	146	13.3	21	1								
1972	HAM	14																	4	70	17.5	24	0					1	0	0.0	0
6	Years	83	1		4							18	3	5	28	5.6	15	0	54	955	17.7	47	3					6	46	7.7	14
J.B. CHRISTIAN J.B. OT-OG 6'1 235 Oklahoma State B: 5/22/1945 Watonga, OK Draft: 12B-307 1967 BAL																															
1968	EDM	16																													
1969	EDM	7	0		1																										
2	Years	23	0		1																										
RYAN CHRISTIAN Ryan Cain RB-SB-WR 5'11 180 Texas Christian B: 1/7/1986 Tarrant County, TX																															
2010	TOR	10	1	0	0	6						6	1	1	3	3.0	3	0	9	103	11.4	37	0					19	458	24.1	110
DICK CHRISTIANSEN Richard A. E 6'3 233 Arizona B: 7/1/1932 Draft: 20-239 1953 NYG																															
1954	BC	14																	41	545	13.3	45	0					2	11	5.5	11
STEVE CHRISTIE Geoffrey Stephen K 6'0 191 William & Mary B: 11/13/1967 Hamilton, ON Draft: 1B-6 1990 EDM Pro: N																															
2007	TOR	1				0						10	0																		
HANK CHRISTMAN Henry T 6'3 195 Villanova																															
1946	OTT+	12										5	1																		
1947	OTT+	11																													
2	Years	23										5	1																		
ERNIE CHRISTMAS Ernest M. S 5'11 189 San Francisco State B: 10/28/1960 Los Angeles County, CA																															
1983	WPG	1																													
JIM CHRISTOFF Jim OG-LB 5'11 225 Toronto Jrs.; Miami (Ohio) B: 1938																															
1960	CAL	2																													
JIM CHRISTOPHERSON James Monroe LB 6'0 215 Concordia (Moorhead) B: 2/17/1938 Wadena, MN Pro: N																															
1964	TOR	3	0		1							4	0																		

Year	Team	GP	FM	FF	FR	TK	SK	YDS	IR	YDS	PD	PTS	TD	RA	YDS	AVG	LG	TD	REC	YDS	AVG	LG	TD	PR	YDS	AVG	LG	KOR	YDS	AVG	LG
DICK CHROBAK Dick OG 5'11 215 Vancouver Blue Bombers Jrs. B: 1941 Winnipeg, MB																														
1959	BC	1																												
1962	EDM	2																												
1963	EDM	5	0		1																									
1964	EDM	4																												
4	Years	12	0		1																									
DENNY CHRONOPOULOS Denny OG 6'4 289 Purdue B: 6/12/1968 Montreal, QC D: 8/27/2000 Montreal, QC Draft: 1-3 1992 OTT																														
1992	OTT	18				0																								
1993	OTT+	18	0		2	1																								
1994	BC	17				0																								
1995	CAL	18				0																								
4	Years	71	0		2	1																								
DON CHUMLEY Donald W. DL 6'4 265 Georgia B: 3/14/1962 Heidelberg, West Germany Draft: 12-336 1985 SF																														
1985	CAL	6					2.0																							
KEN CIANCONE Ken LB 6'4 210 Utah State B: 11/18/1958 Kamloops, BC Draft: 1-3 1980 WPG																														
1981	WPG	16	0		2		2.0					6	1																	
1982	WPG	16	0		2		3.5		1	0																				
1983	WPG	16					1.0																							
1984	MTL	16			1		3.5		4	64		6	1																	
1985	MTL	11	0		1		1.0		3	49																				
1986	MTL	18	0		2		4.0																							
6	Years	93	0		8		15.0		8	113		12	2																	
GENE CICHOWSKI Eugene Walker QB-LB 6'0 195 Indiana B: 5/20/1934 Chicago, IL Draft: 21-246 1957 PIT Pro: N																														
1960	CAL	8											11	93	8.5	20	0	2	23	11.5	12	0	1	6	6.0	6				
1961	CAL	4							2	0				7	17	2.4	8	0						1	3	3.0	3				
2	Years	12							2	0				18	110	6.1	20	0	2	23	11.5	12	0	2	9	4.5	6				
RAY CICIA Raymond J. OG 5'10 212 Wake Forest B: 7/9/1928 Ansonia, CT D: 8/22/1996 Fort Lauderdale, FL																														
1950	MTL+	12																												
1951	MTL+	12																												
1952	MTL	11										5	1																	
1953	MTL	7																												
1954	MTL+	14																												
1955	MTL	5																												
6	Years	61										5	1																	
CHRIS CIEZKI Chris FB 5'11 220 British Columbia B: 1/6/1981 Edmonton, AB																														
2008	EDM	16	0	1	2	24																								
2009	EDM	18				23													1	3	3.0	3	0								
2010	EDM	8				2																						1	0	0.0	0
3	Years	42	0	1	2	49													1	3	3.0	3	0					1	0	0.0	0
JOE CIHOCKI Joe HB-FW 5'10 175 B: 1919 D: 8/14/1993																														
1947	HAM	4																												
JOHN CIMBA John E. LB-HB 6'0 210 Buffalo B: 1942																														
1964	HAM	14							1	0																		2	20	10.0	13
1965	HAM	14											3	14	4.7	11	0													
1966	HAM	14	0		1								7	30	4.3	8	0													
1967	HAM	14											2	9	4.5	6	0										1	8	8.0	8
4	Years	56	0		1				1	0				12	53	4.4	11	0										3	28	9.3	13
TROY CIOCHETTI Troy WR 5'11 175 Alberta B: 4/16/1960 Draft: 1B-8 1982 BC																														
1983	SAS	4																1	41	41.0	41	0					5	111	22.2	28
NICK CIORAN Nick LB-DB 5'10 180 McMaster B: 2/6/1937 Hamilton, ON																														
1960	MTL	4																												
NILO CIOTTI Nilo QB																														
1948	TOR	4																												
HOWIE CISSELL Howard L. DB-FB-OE 6'1 185 Arkansas State B: 8/21/1936																														
1960	MTL	14							6	16				7	42	6.0	12	0	19	244	12.8	48	0	6	28	4.7	9	5	82	16.4	21
1961	MTL	12							2	30				3	17	5.7	11	0	2	20	10.0	11	0	21	144	6.9	19				
1962	MTL	3																					6	11	1.8	7	1	11	11.0	11
3	Years	29							8	46				10	59	5.9	12	0	21	264	12.6	48	0	33	183	5.5	19	6	93	15.5	21
BILL CIZ Bill QB Regina Jrs. deceased																														
1948	SAS	1																												
DARRYL CLACK Darryl Earl RB 5'10 219 Arizona State B: 10/29/1963 San Antonio, TX Draft: 2-33 1986 DAL Pro: EN																														
1991	TOR	4	0		1							6	1	22	24	1.1	-19	0	4	113	28.3	56	1					2	13	6.5	10
ROBERT CLAIBORNE Robert Cardell WR 5'10 175 Grossmont JC; Los Angeles Southwest JC; San Diego State B: 7/10/1967 New Orleans, LA Draft: 12-313 1990 DET Pro: N																														
1994	LV	15				3						12	2						31	570	18.4	59	2	7	34	4.9	18	5	101	20.2	25
LOU CLARE Louis W. LB-DB 6'1 225 Minnesota B: 3/13/1950 Draft: TE 1973 TOR																														
1973	HAM	14	1		2				3	73		6	1											36	177	4.9	15				
1974	HAM	16	0		2				3	51		6	1											1	4	4.0	4				
1975	HAM	16	1		1							6	1											9	121	13.4	25				
1976	SAS	16	1		0				1	1									1	31	31.0	31	0	1	0	0.0	0				
1977	SAS	16	0		1																									
1978	SAS	12																										2	34	17.0	17
1979	SAS	4																												
1979	HAM	8	0		2																									
1979	Year	12	0		2																									
1980	HAM	15	0		5																									
1981	HAM	3																												
1981	MTL	12	0		1				1	0																				
1981	Year	15	0		1				1	0																				
9	Years	112	3		14				8	125		18	3						1	31	31.0	31	0	47	302	6.4	25	2	34	17.0	17
BRUCE CLARIDGE Bruce SE-DE 6'4 215 Vancouver Blue Bombers Jrs.; Washington B: 1934 D: 4/17/1999																														
1959	BC	14										24	4						32	519	16.2	53	4					1	13	13.0	13
1960	BC	14	0		2							6	1						6	75	12.5	19	1								
1961	CAL	11											0	3		3	0	16	223	13.9	19	0								
1962	TOR	9																8	83	10.4	15	0								
1963	EDM	11										6	1						19	230	12.1		1								
1963	CAL	4										12	2						6	94	15.7	25	2					1	4	4.0	4
1963	Year	15										18	3						25	324	13.0	25	3					1	4	4.0	4
1964	CAL	11	0		1							18	3						16	247	15.4	41	3								
6	Years	70	0		3							66	11	0	3		3	0	103	1471	14.3	53	11					2	17	8.5	13
PAT CLARIDGE Pat TE 6'2 212 Vancouver Blue Bombers Jrs.; Washington B: 7/12/1938 Vancouver, BC D: 3//2012																														
1961	BC	14																28	327	11.7	19	0								
1962	BC	16										6	1						23	263	11.4	35	1					2	20	10.0	18
1963	BC	15										12	2						37	377	10.2	25	2					1	5	5.0	5
1964	BC+	16	1		1							6	1						39	577	14.8	39	1								
1965	BC	16											2	4	2.0	3	0	41	554	13.5	36	0					3	2	0.7	2
1966	BC	16										6	1						30	399	13.3	27	1					2	12	6.0	10
1968	CAL	1																												
7	Years	94	1		1							30	5	2	4	2.0	3	0	198	2497	12.6	39	5					8	39	4.9	18
TRAVIS CLARIDGE Travis A. OG 6'5 302 Southern California B: 3/23/1978 Altmont, MI D: 2/28/2006 Las Vegas, NV Draft: 2-37 2000 ATL Pro: N																														
2005	HAM	2	0	0	1	0													1	2	2.0	2	0								
BERT CLARK Robert Bertrand, Jr. C 6'0 210 Oklahoma B: 2/12/1930 Wichita Falls, TX D: 12/13/2004 Katy, TX																														
1953	CAL	5																												

Year	Team	GP	FM	FF	FR	TK	SK	YDS	IR	YDS	PD	PTS	TD	RA	YDS	AVG	LG	TD	REC	YDS	AVG	LG	TD	PR	YDS	AVG	LG	KOR	YDS	AVG	LG
BILL CLARK Bill FB 6'0 209 Prairie View A&M																															
1955	TOR	1																										2	24	12.0	13
BRIAN CLARK Brian LB 6'3 205 Hofstra B: 5/5/1974 Quincy, IL																															
1997	MTL	1				0																									
1998	MTL	13	0	1	1	46	3.0	20.0																							
2000	WPG	16	0	0	1	67	1.0	5.0	1	2	2																				
2001	WPG	18	1	0	1	76	2.0	9.0	1	38	2	6	1															2	8	4.0	8
2002	WPG	18	1	1	3	72	3.0	21.0	1	26	7																				
2003	WPG	18	0	2	2	55	2.0	13.0	7	52	3	6	1																		
2004	CAL	18	0	1	2	62	4.0	22.0	2	72	7	6	1																		
2005	CAL	18	0	1	0	77	5.0	33.0	2	122	8	6	1	1	-1	-1.0	-1	0													
2006	CAL*	16	0	6	3	63	2.0	7.0	2	13	3	6	1	2	42	21.0	29	0													
2007	CAL	16	0	0	1	48	1.0	13.0	1	0	2																				
10	Years	152	2	12	14	566	23.0	143.0	17	325	34	30	5	3	41	13.7	29	0										2	8	4.0	8
BRUCE CLARK Bruce M. DT 6'3 270 Penn State B: 3/31/1958 New Castle, PA Draft: 1A-4 1980 GB Pro: EN																															
1980	TOR*	16	0		4				1	0																					
1981	TOR	16	0		1		7.5							1	4	4.0	4	0													
2	Years	32	0		5		7.5		1	0				1	4	4.0	4	0													
DARYLL CLARK Daryll Lawrence QB 6'3 232 Penn State B: 2/5/1986 Youngstown, OH																															
2010	CAL	13	1	0	0	0								1	0	0.0	0	0													
DICK CLARK Richard Lee LB 6'2 205 Baylor B: 1937 Draft: 8A-92 1959 CHIB																															
1959	TOR	3																						1	14	14.0	14				
1960	CAL	1																													
2	Years	4																						1	14	14.0	14				
DON CLARK Donald OHB-FB 6'0 190 Ohio State B: 12/27/1936 Draft: 1-7 1959 CHIB																															
1959	OTT	8										12	2	75	343	4.6	55	2	16	229	14.3	57	0	1	15	15.0	15	13	289	22.2	46
1960	MTL	13							2	39		42	7	170	902	5.3	55	5	22	312	14.2	73	2					28	660	23.6	37
1961	MTL+	14										42	7	200	1143	5.7	106	5	22	378	17.2	85	2					8	181	22.6	38
1962	MTL	4										24	4	60	435	7.3	85	4	5	70	14.0	38	0					3	44	14.7	22
1963	MTL	8										36	6	74	447	6.0	73	4	11	192	17.5	52	2					5	126	25.2	29
5	Years	47							2	39		156	26	579	3270	5.6	106	20	76	1181	15.5	85	6	1	15	15.0	15	57	1300	22.8	46
ERNIE CLARK Ernest Robert LB 6'1 222 Michigan State B: 8/11/1937 Arcadia, FL Draft: 13-180 1963 DET Pro: N																															
1969	HAM	1																													
GAIL CLARK Gail Allen LB 6'1 223 Michigan State B: 4/14/1951 Bellefontaine, OH Draft: 4-102 1973 PIT Pro: N																															
1976	TOR	5																													
1976	HAM	2																													
1976	Year	7																													
GENE CLARK Eugene Anthony OG-OT 6'3 250 UCLA B: 12/3/1951 Tampa, FL Draft: 9A-222 1975 PIT Pro: W																															
1977	TOR	13																													
1978	TOR	7																													
2	Years	20																													
GREG CLARK Gregory Klondike LB 6'0 230 Arizona State B: 3/5/1965 Los Angeles, CA Draft: 12-329 1988 CHIB Pro: N																															
1993	WPG	4				12	1.0	2.0																							
1994	WPG	16	0		4	79	3.0	14.0			3	12	2																		
1995	WPG	17	0		1	84	4.0	32.0			1																				
1996	WPG	17				69	7.0	41.0	3	42	1	6	1																		
1997	SAS	8				42					1																				
5	Years	62	0		5	286	15.0	89.0	3	42	6	18	3																		
HOWARD CLARK Howard (Rusty) QB 6'0 215 Houston																															
1970	EDM	16	2		0							6	1	11	33	3.0	14	1													
1971	EDM	3			0									1	12	12.0	12	0													
1971	BC	7			0									1	-2	-2.0	-2	0													
1971	Year	10	2		0									2	10	5.0	12	0													
2	Years	19	2		0							6	1	13	43	3.3	14	1													
KEN CLARK Kenneth Lawrence P-K-WR 6'2 197 St. Mary's (Nova Scotia) B: 5/26/1948 Southampton, England Draft: 1-2 1974 HAM Pro: NW																															
1975	HAM	16										3	0	5	37	7.4	22	0	1	11	11.0	11	0								
1976	HAM	16	1		1							85	2	3	27	9.0	19	0	2	33	16.5	27	2								
1977	HAM*	16	1		0							11	0	2	-1	-0.5	2	0	14	229	16.4	71	0								
1978	HAM+	5										1	0																		
1978	TOR	11	1		0							5	0	1	7	7.0	7	0	1	80	80.0	80	0								
1978	Year	16	1		0							6	0	1	7	7.0	7	0	1	80	80.0	80	0								
1980	SAS	3										1	0																		
1981	SAS	16										5	0	1	-1	-1.0	-1	0													
1982	SAS*	16										6	0																		
1983	SAS	12										14	0																		
1983	OTT	5	1		0							1	0																		
1983	Year	17										15	0																		
1984	OTT	16	0		2							4	0																		
1985	OTT*	16	2		0							8	0																		
1986	OTT	18	1		0							8	0						1	-6	-6.0	-6	0								
1987	OTT	18	3		1							11	0																		
12	Years	168	10		4							163	2	12	69	5.8	22	0	19	347	18.3	80	2								
KEVIN CLARK Kevin Randall (K.C.) DB 5'10 185 San Jose State B: 6/8/1964 Sacramento, CA Pro: N																															
1990	EDM	7	0		3	20			2	48														0	0		0	1	25	25.0	25
1990	BC	3				10																		0	32		32				
1990	Year	10	0		3	30																									
MATT CLARK Matt WR 6'0 180 Montana B: 5/14/1968 Calgary, AB Draft: SD-1-2 1991 BC																															
1991	BC*	18	3		1	1						62	10	4	28	7.0	12	0	79	1530	19.4	89	10					1	13	13.0	13
1992	BC	18	2		0	12						30	5						49	718	14.7	37	5								
1993	BC	16	2		0	1						24	4						74	970	13.1	55	4								
1994	BC	13	2		1	2													26	311	12.0	26	0								
1995	BC	18	1		0	2						12	2						51	813	15.9	75	2								
1996	BC	17	2		0	3						24	4	3	8	2.7	12	0	57	730	12.8	38	4								
1998	EDM	1				1													2	27	13.5	18	0								
7	Years	101	12		2	22						152	25	7	36	5.1	12	0	338	5099	15.1	89	25					1	13	13.0	13
MATT CLARK Matthew Terrell DB 5'8 180 UCLA B: 1/18/1983 Los Angeles, CA Pro: E																															
2006	HAM	1				1			1	27	0																				
2007	HAM	2				5																									
2	Years	3				6			1	27	0																				
MIKE CLARK Michael CB 5'9 190 Oklahoma State B: 5/7/1970 St. Louis, MO																															
1994	LV	6	1		0							6	1															9	165	18.3	28
MORGAN CLARK Morgan DE 6'0 230 Windsor AKO Jrs.; Western Ontario B: 1936																															
1959	TOR	7																													
1960	CAL	3																										1	22	22.0	22
2	Years	10																										1	22	22.0	22
RAY CLARK Ray DB 5'11 183 Simon Fraser B: 1/3/1945 Draft: 4-33 1977 EDM																															
1977	EDM	6																													
1977	WPG	9	0		1																							1	5	5.0	5
1977	Year	15	0		1																							1	5	5.0	5
1978	WPG	1																													
1979	HAM	16																										1	6	6.0	6
3	Years	23	0		1																							2	11	5.5	6

Year	Team	GP	FM	FF	FR	TK	SK	YDS	IR	YDS	PD	PTS	TD	RA	YDS	AVG	LG	TD	REC	YDS	AVG	LG	TD	PR	YDS	AVG	LG	KOR	YDS	AVG	LG
REGGIE CLARK Reggie Boice LB 6'2 240 North Carolina B: 10/17/1967 Charlotte, NC Pro: EN																															
1993	TOR	2				4																									
ROBERT CLARK Robert James WR 5'11 176 North Carolina Central B: 8/6/1965 New York, NY Draft: 10-263 1987 NO Pro: N																															
1993	TOR	14				3						18	3						50	900	18.0	64	3								
1994	BAL	14	1		0	4													16	294	18.4	35	0								
1995	BAL	15				1						12	2						23	397	17.3	43	2								
3	Years	43	1		0	8						30	5						89	1591	17.9	64	5								
SEDRIC CLARK Sedric Coppock DE 6'1 248 Tulsa B: 1/28/1973 Missouri City, TX Draft: 7A-220 1996 OAK Pro: ENX																															
2002	HAM	2	0	0	1	1	1.0																								
BILL CLARKE Norman Edwin William DT-C 6'4 235 Regina Dales Jrs. B: 11/25/1932 Regina, SK D: 12/20/2000 Regina, SK																															
1951	SAS	3																													
1952	SAS	15																													
1953	SAS	16																													
1954	SAS	16																													
1955	SAS	14	0		2				1	18																					
1956	SAS	16																													
1957	SAS	16																													
1958	SAS	16																													
1959	SAS	16																													
1960	SAS	16																													
1961	SAS+	14																													
1962	SAS	16																													
1963	SAS+	16							1																						
1964	SAS	15	0		1																										
14	Years	205	0		3				2	18																					
BOB CLARKE Bob LB 6'4 225 Alberta B: 8/17/1949 Draft: 4-33 1971 SAS																															
1973	EDM	16	0		3				1	12																					
1975	SAS	5	0		1														1	13	13.0	13	0	1	0	0.0	0				
2	Years	21	0		4				1	12									1	13	13.0	13	0	1	0	0.0	0				
DAVE CLARKE Dave DB 5'11 175 Guelph; Western Ontario B: 2/14/1950 Draft: 5-41 1970 HAM																															
1972	HAM	14	2		0							6	1											55	258	4.7	13	15	477	31.8	102
DAVID CLARKE David T. C 6'3 250 Maine; Nevada-Las Vegas B: 10/19/1967 New York, NY																															
1994	LV	3																										1	20	20.0	20
DELROY CLARKE Delroy CB-S-DH 6'1 187 Ottawa B: 12/29/1982 Kingston, Jamaica Draft: 4-29 2008 TOR																															
2008	TOR	8				2																									
2009	TOR	13	1	1	0	12																						1	5	5.0	5
2010	TOR	7				4																									
2011	EDM	17	0	0	2	14																									
4	Years	45	1	1	2	32																						1	5	5.0	5
GREG CLARKE Greg SB 6'1 190 British Columbia B: 4/29/1960 Draft: 6-53 1982 OTT																															
1982	OTT	7	0		1									1	8	8.0	8	0	3	48	16.0	30	0								
MATT CLARKE Matt LB 6'0 225 British Columbia B: 4/6/1968 Vancouver, BC																															
1991	BC	18				7																									
1992	BC	18				9																									
1993	BC	18				3																									
1994	BC	18	1		1	3																									
1995	BC	18	0		1	10													1	8	8.0	8	0								
5	Years	90	1		2	32													1	8	8.0	8	0								
RICHARD CLARKE Richard WR 6'3 231 Weber State B: 4/4/1975 Toronto, ON Draft: 2-11 2000 TOR																															
2000	TOR	9				2													2	42	21.0	35	0					1	6	6.0	6
RICKY CLARKE Ricky SB 6'0 210 Manitoba B: 10/6/1984 Toronto, ON																															
2011	WPG	1				0																									
FRANTZ CLARKSON Frantz CB 6'2 185 Manitoba B: 6/12/1973 Toronto, ON Draft: 5-35 1999 EDM																															
1999	EDM	10				10			1	18	0																				
2000	EDM	14				10			1	0	2																				
2001	EDM	11				5					1																	1	1	1.0	1
2001	MTL	1				0																									
2001	Year	12				5					1																	1	1	1.0	1
2002	OTT	2				1																									
2003	HAM	14				24	1.0				4																				
2004	HAM	6	1	0	1	4																		1	0	0.0	0				
6	Years	57	1	0	1	54	1.0		2	18	7													1	0	0.0	0	1	1	1.0	1
LARRY CLARKSON Larry OT 6'7 305 Montana B: 3/11/1965 Abbotsford, BC Draft: 1B-7 1987 BC; 8-219 1988 SF																															
1988	BC	10				0																									
1989	BC	5				0																									
1990	BC	18				2																									
1991	BC	8				0																									
4	Years	41				2																									
REG CLARKSON Reginald L. HB 5'9 177 British Columbia B: 1925 Victoria, BC																															
1949	EDM	9																													
1951	CAL	7										11	2	27	90	3.3		2	11	140	12.7	23	0	7	47	6.7		1	25	25.0	25
2	Years	16										11	2	27	90	3.3	0	2	11	140	12.7	23	0	7	47	6.7	0	1	25		25
ROSS CLARKSON Ross FL-DB 5'10 175 Simon Fraser B: 10/26/1951 Draft: TE 1973 BC																															
1973	BC	12												2	26	13.0	20	0	18	240	13.3	50	0	31	179	5.8	53	10	243	24.3	39
1975	BC	14										30	5						29	497	17.1	70	5	9	54	6.0	22	1	28	28.0	28
1976	BC	16	0		1														26	273	10.5	26	0	1	2	2.0	2				
1977	OTT	15																	20	287	14.4	54	0	2	-6	-3.0		1	19	19.0	19
1978	OTT	12	2		0							18	3	0	26		18	0	19	434	22.8	74	3								
1979	OTT	16	1		1							6	1						20	265	13.3	27	1								
1980	OTT	5																	5	60	12.0	16	0								
1980	HAM	11										18	3						21	346	16.5	44	3								
1980	Year	16										18	3						26	406	15.6	44	3								
7	Years	90	3		2							72	12	2	52	26.0	20	0	158	2402	15.2	74	12	43	229	5.3	53	12	290	24.2	39
STEVE CLARKSON Steven L. QB 6'0 205 San Jose State B: 10/31/1961 Los Angeles, CA Draft: TD 1983 OAK-USFL																															
1983	SAS	3																													
STU CLARKSON Stuart Lenox C 6'2 217 Texas A&M-Kingsville B: 7/4/1919 Corpus Christi, TX D: 10/25/1957 Brazoria County, TX Draft: 22-200 1942 CHIB Pro: N																															
1952	WPG	11							5	97		5	1																		
1953	WPG	2																													
2	Years	13							5	97		5	1																		
DARNELL CLASH Emory Darnell DB 5'9 170 Wyoming B: 6/18/1962 Cambridge, MD																															
1984	BC	14	4		3				2	0		6	1											62	664	10.7	83	22	506	23.0	41
1985	BC*	16	4		4				9	69		6	1											111	1148	10.3	53	10	210	21.0	41
1986	BC	9							4	77		12	2											63	742	11.8	66	2	31	15.5	20
1987	TOR+	16	4		2	73			5	153		12	2											104	853	8.2	76	1	0	0.0	0
4	Years	55	12		9	73			20	299		36	6											340	3407	10.0	83	35	747	21.3	41
PAUL CLATNEY Paul S-LB 6'2 205 McMaster B: 12/5/1963 Toronto, ON Draft: 8-71 1986 HAM																															
1988	WPG	18	0		4	6																									
1989	WPG	18	0		1	11			1	-2		6	1															1	5	5.0	5
1990	CAL	7				2																						1	0	0.0	0
1991	CAL	14	0		3	28						12	2																		
1992	CAL	8				14																									
1994	OTT	9				12																						1	2	2.0	2

Year	Team	GP	FM	FF	FR	TK	SK	YDS	IR	YDS	PD	PTS	TD	RA	YDS	AVG	LG	TD	REC	YDS	AVG	LG	TD	PR	YDS	AVG	LG	KOR	YDS	AVG	LG
1994	TOR	4				4					1																				
1994	Year	13				16					1																	1	2	2.0	2
6	Years	74	0		8	77			1	-2	1	18	3															3	7	2.3	5
JOE CLAUSI Joe DE 6'2 235 Utah B: 3/28/1968 New York, NY																															
1990	CAL	18	0		3	84	1.0		5	72																					
TOM CLAVIN Thomas FB 5'11 210 Villanova B: 1926																															
1950	OTT	2										5	1					1													
BILL CLAWSON Bill E 6'1 200 Montana State B: 1924																															
1949	WPG	14										5	1										1								
DENNIS CLAY Dennis R. DB 5'10 180 Oregon B: 2/5/1960 Los Angeles, CA																															
1984	TOR	13	0		3		0.5		3	56																		1	31	31.0	31
1985	TOR	16	0		3				3	81		6	1						1	19	19.0	19	0								
1986	TOR	7	0		1																			2	5	2.5	5				
1986	OTT	9							1	66		6	1											1	-1	-1.0	-1				
1986	Year	16	0		1				1	66		6	1											3	4	1.3	5				
3	Years	36	0		7		0.5		7	203		12	2						1	19	19.0	19	0	3	4	1.3	5	1	31	31.0	31
STEVE CLAY Steve WR 5'5 160 Eastern Michigan B: 2/3/1974 Cincinnati, OH																															
1996	OTT	2				0													6	64	10.7	21	0	7	29	4.1	12	1	24	24.0	24
BRIAN CLAYBOURN Brian Kent P 6'1 185 Western Kentucky B: 10/21/1981 Evansville, IN																															
2000	WPG	2				0																									
DeVONE CLAYBROOKS Natravis DeVone DT 6'3 306 East Carolina B: 9/15/1977 Martinsville, VA Pro: EN																															
2007	MTL	16	0	1	1	42	5.0	35.0			4																				
2008	MTL	18				39	4.0	18.0																							
2009	CAL	11	0	1	0	17					2																				
2010	CAL+	15				26	4.0	25.0																							
2011	CAL	15	0	0	1	36	1.0	6.0			3																				
5	Years	75	0	2	2	160	14.0	84.0			9																				
FELIPE CLAYBROOKS Felipe A. DE 6'5 275 Georgia Tech B: 1/22/1978 Decatur, GA Pro: EN																															
2005	MTL	5				8	3.0	17.0			1																				
L.J. CLAYTON L.J., Jr. WR-DB 6'3 181 Howard Payne B: 12/27/1950 Fort Worth, TX																															
1975	TOR	13	0		2				2	67									10	119	11.9	38	0	42	506	12.0	48	18	451	25.1	40
1976	TOR	5	1		0																			17	149	8.8	31	3	73	24.3	25
2	Years	18	1		2				2	67									10	119	11.9	38	0	59	655	11.1	48	21	524	25.0	40
RILEY CLAYTON Riley OL 6'5 300 Manitoba B: 6/11/1983 Winnipeg, MB Draft: 4A-27 2006 CAL																															
2006	CAL	1				0																									
TOM CLEARY Tom LB 6'3 230 Pennsylvania B: 1923																															
1950	EDM	13																													
ED CLEMENS Ed T 6'1 230 Dayton B: 1930 Draft: 25-301 1953 LARM																															
1955	HAM	2							1	16																					
NICK CLEMENT Nick LB-DH 6'0 196 North Carolina A&T State B: 3/23/1988 Arden, NC																															
2011	TOR	5				13	1.0	9.0			1																				
CHUCK CLEMENTS Chuck QB 6'3 214 Houston B: 8/29/1973 Draft: 6B-191 1997 NYJ Pro: ENX																															
2002	OTT	18	2	0	1	0								8	64	8.0	19	0													
JIMMY CLEMENTS Jimmy LB 6'3 225 Georgia Tech B: 12/28/1973 Marietta, GA Pro: EX																															
1999	TOR	5				8																									
TOM CLEMENTS Thomas Albert QB 5'10 183 Notre Dame B: 6/18/1953 McKees Rocks, PA Pro: N																															
1975	OTT+	16	1		0									28	87	3.1	13	0													
1976	OTT+	16	6		1							24	4	37	260	7.0	30	4													
1977	OTT+	16	8		0							6	1	59	356	6.0	39	1													
1978	OTT	16	8		3									32	159	5.0	20	0						1	0	0.0	0				
1979	SAS	7	3		1									22	101	4.6	18	0													
1979	HAM	8	1		2							6	1	22	145	6.6	21	1													
1979	Year+	15	4		3							6	1	44	246	5.6	21	1													
1981	HAM+	16	5		1							6	1	32	178	5.6	26	1													
1982	HAM	16	5		1							14	2	34	137	4.0	42	2													
1983	HAM	10	2		2									12	18	1.5	8	0													
1983	WPG	3												8	13	1.6	7	0													
1983	Year	13	2		2									20	31	1.6	8	0													
1984	WPG*	16	6		0							6	1	27	101	3.7	15	1													
1985	WPG	15	1		0							6	1	11	16	1.5	17	1													
1986	WPG	9	2		0							6	1	19	48	2.5	12	1													
1987	WPG*	18	5		0							12	2	31	44	1.4	8	2													
12	Years	171	53		11							86	14	374	1663	4.4	42	14						1	0	0.0	0				
JASON CLEMETT Jason LB 6'1 225 Simon Fraser B: 8/23/1973 Edmonton, AB Draft: 1B-7 1997 CAL																															
1997	CAL	18				11																									
1998	CAL	18				35																									
1999	CAL	16	0	1	0	18	3.0	21.0			2																				
2000	CAL	17	0	0	1	34	2.0	16.0			2																				
2001	EDM	4				2																									
2003	CAL	2				0																									
6	Years	75	0	1	1	100	5.0	37.0			2																				
CHARLIE CLEMONS Charlie Fitzgerald LB 6'2 252 Northeast Oklahoma JC; Georgia B: 7/4/1972 Griffin, GA Pro: N																															
1994	WPG	7	0		1	17					2																				
1995	WPG	6				17	3.0	32.0																							
1995	OTT	7				27	3.0	26.0			2																	1	10	10.0	10
1995	Year	13				44	6.0	58.0			2																	1	10	10.0	10
1996	WPG	14				37	6.0	46.0			4																				
3	Years	27	0		1	98	12.0	104.0			8																	1	10	10.0	10
CRANCE CLEMONS Crance Osric CB 5'9 175 Texas-El Paso B: 12/20/1979 Mission Viejo, CA																															
2003	OTT	8	0	0	2	19			3	23	5													4	40	10.0	25				
2005	OTT	7	0	1	1	26			3	12	1																				
2006	CAL	6				6	1.0	5.0	1	9	1																				
2007	CAL	17	0	3	0	30			1	11	5																				
4	Years	38	0	4	3	81	1.0	5.0	8	55	12													4	40	10.0	25				
MICHAEL CLEMONS Michael Lutrell (Pinball) RB 5'5 166 William & Mary B: 1/15/1965 Clearwater, FL Draft: 8-218 1987 KC Pro: N																															
1989	TOR	10	5		2	1						12	2	28	134	4.8	23	1	1	2	2.0	2	0	50	507	10.1	48	13	356	27.4	45
1990	TOR*	16	8		2	4						84	14	105	519	4.9	62	4	72	905	12.6	65	8	74	1045	14.1	92	39	831	21.3	51
1991	TOR	11	4		0	0						36	6	64	443	6.9	64	3	38	417	11.0	28	2	32	440	13.8	94	19	216	11.4	23
1992	TOR	18	5		1	5						32	5	148	572	3.9	20	0	46	559	12.2	52	5	34	279	8.2	32	15	295	19.7	38
1993	TOR+	18	6		4	3						38	6	89	481	5.4	32	1	32	313	9.8	31	3	77	716	9.3	79	30	604	20.1	41
1994	TOR+	16	7		0	3						36	6	149	787	5.3	60	3	51	577	11.3	69	2	76	671	8.8	90	16	317	19.8	40
1995	TOR	18	2		0	2						66	11	181	836	4.6	29	7	59	433	7.3	30	4	56	470	8.4	44	35	706	20.2	63
1996	TOR	18	6		1	5						54	9	61	286	4.7	23	5	116	1268	10.9	52	4	11	145	13.2	49	33	883	26.8	72
1997	TOR*	18	6	0	0	4						92	15	50	315	6.3	47	4	122	1085	8.9	56	10	111	1070	9.6	65	49	1117	22.8	62
1998	TOR	16	0	0	1	0						54	9	148	610	4.1	25	3	93	995	10.7	41	6	10	67	6.7	15	8	149	18.6	34
1999	TOR	16	2	0	0	3								58	249	4.3	17	0	30	249	8.3	29	0	61	473	7.8	58	22	496	22.5	47
2000	TOR	10	2	0	0	1						12	2	26	109	4.2	23	0	22	212	9.6	33	2	18	142	7.9	25	21	379	18.0	49
12	Years	185	53	0	11	31						516	85	1107	5341	4.8	64	31	682	7015	10.3	69	46	610	6025	9.9	94	300	6349	21.2	72
JASON CLERMONT Jason SB 6'3 229 Regina Rams Jrs.; Regina B: 5/24/1978 Regina, SK Draft: 1A-4 2002 BC																															
2002	BC	18	2	0	1	9						36	6						46	735	16.0	41	6	1	0	0.0	0	1	3	3.0	3
2003	BC	15				6						42	7	1	10	10.0	10	0	41	615	15.0	39	7					1	1	1.0	1
2004	BC+	18				7						42	7						83	1220	14.7	80	7								

Year	Team	GP	FM	FF	FR	TK	SK	YDS	IR	YDS	PD	PTS	TD	RA	YDS	AVG	LG	TD	REC	YDS	AVG	LG	TD	PR	YDS	AVG	LG	KOR	YDS	AVG	LG
2005	BC	18	2	0	0	3						24	4						78	1042	13.4	69	4								
2006	BC	11	2	0	0	0						18	3						44	507	11.5	26	3								
2007	BC*	18				5						42	7						86	1158	13.5	93	7								
2008	BC	15	0	0	2	2						18	3						50	640	12.8	36	3								
2009	SAS	16	2	0	0	2													23	317	13.8	65	0					1	9	9.0	9
2010	SAS	18				0													27	300	11.1	35	0								
2011	SAS	18				2						6	1						23	232	10.1	25	1					1	14	14.0	14
10	Years	165	8	0	3	36						228	38	1	10	10.0	10	0	501	6766	13.5	93	38	1	0	0.0	0	4	27	6.8	14
JOCK CLIMIE Jock SB-WR 6'1 185 Queen's B: 9/28/1968 Toronto, ON Draft: 1-4 1990 TOR																															
1990	TOR	2				1													2	20	10.0	16	0								
1991	OTT	16	1		1	14						6	1	2	2	1.0	4	0	32	599	18.7	62	1	8	42	5.3	18	1	0	0.0	0
1992	OTT	18	1		0	4						38	6	0	21		16	0	57	901	15.8	50	6								
1993	OTT+	18	2		1	7						67	11						67	1281	19.1	89	11								
1994	OTT	10				1						30	5						46	622	13.5	39	5								
1995	TOR	13				0						18	3						48	563	11.7	49	3								
1996	MTL+	18				0						54	9						68	1209	17.8	62	9								
1997	MTL+	18	1	1	0	1						36	6						89	1214	13.6	43	6								
1998	MTL	18				1						36	6						55	783	14.2	75	6					1	0	0.0	0
1999	MTL	11	1	0	0	1						18	3						50	581	11.6	29	3								
2000	MTL	17				0						30	5						67	1002	15.0	80	5								
2001	MTL	15	4	0	0	2						6	1						46	844	18.3	68	1								
12	Years	174	10	1	2	32						339	56	2	23	11.5	16	0	627	9619	15.3	89	56	8	42	5.3	18	2	0	0.0	0
BILL CLINE William Jerome QB-OHB-DH 6'0 190 East Carolina B: 9/2/1943 Valdese, NC																															
1965	OTT	14							2	1		7	0	7	20	2.9	10	0													
1966	OTT	14	1		2				5	26				2	-12	-6.0	2	0						18	49	2.7	12				
1967	OTT	14	1		0				2	52		3	0											50	243	4.9	14				
1968	SAS	5							2	17																					
4	Years	47	2		2				11	96		10	0	9	8	0.9	10	0						68	292	4.3	14				
MICHAEL CLINE Michael DE 6'3 256 Arkansas State B: 7/27/1963 Pine Bluff, AR Draft: 8-210 1986 GB																															
1986	OTT	4					3.0																								
1987	OTT	8				1	1.0																								
1988	OTT	14				41	7.0																								
3	Years	26				42	11.0																								
RON CLINKSCALE Ronald William HB-QB 6'0 185 Texas Christian B: 10/22/1933 Amarillo, TX																															
1955	BC	16							1	0		20	4	92	376	4.1	52	4	15	188	12.5	30	0	18	114	6.3	24	6	114	19.0	22
1956	BC	1												3	26	8.7		0	1	16	16.0	16	0	2	12	6.0	12	1	39	39.0	39
1956	CAL	12	4		2				2	15		6	1	52	210	4.0	23	0	15	182	12.1	44	1	1	9	9.0	9	4	88	22.0	
1956	Year	13	4		2							6	1	55	236	4.3	23	0	16	198	12.4	44	1	3	21	7.0	12	5	127	25.4	39
1957	CAL	15							3	6		24	4	21	105	5.0	17	4	2	38	19.0	27	0					5	119	23.8	38
1958	CAL	15	2		1				2	28		12	2	57	155	2.7	27	1	12	145	12.1	29	1	3	12	4.0	8	5	110	22.0	30
4	Years	47	6		3				8	49		62	11	225	872	3.9	52	9	45	569	12.6	44	2	24	147	6.1	24	21	470	22.4	39
MATT CLIZBE Matthew J. DB 5'11 185 California B: 11/19/1971 San Francisco, CA																															
1995	BIR	11	0		1	11																									
SCOTT CLOMAN Scott Jason WR 6'2 205 Southern University B: 11/6/1975 Compton, CA Pro: EX																															
2004	EDM	1				0																									
2005	WPG	2				0													2	30	15.0	25	0								
2	Years	3				0													2	30	15.0	25	0								
TOM CLOUTIER Thomas James OE 6'3 215 California B: 10/13/1939 Albany, CA																															
1962	MTL	14										6	1						12	199	16.6	34	1								
1963	TOR	11																	20	254	12.7	30	0					1	2	2.0	2
2	Years	25										6	1						32	453	14.2	34	1					1	2	2.0	2
SEBASTIAN CLOVIS Sebastian S 6'0 202 St. Mary's (Nova Scotia) B: 9/1/1979 Toronto, ON Draft: 4-34 2005 BC																															
2006	BC	18				10					1																	1	3	3.0	3
2007	BC	5				4																									
2008	SAS	10				8																									
3	Years	33				22					1																	1	3	3.0	3
TRISTAN CLOVIS Tristan S 6'0 197 McMaster B: 8/25/1982 St. John's, NL Draft: 3B-22 2006 SAS																															
2006	SAS	17				36	1.0	4.0	1	14	0																				
2007	SAS	18	0	0	1	35	3.0	21.0	3	19	3																				
2008	SAS	7				6																									
3	Years	42	0	0	1	77	4.0	25.0	4	33	3																				
TYLER CLUTTS Tyler Ross DE 6'2 245 Fresno State B: 11/9/1984 Vallejo, CA Pro: NU																															
2008	EDM	18	1	0	1	37					2																	6	37	6.2	12
SHERROD COATES Sherrod L. LB 6'2 233 Western Kentucky B: 12/22/1978 Boynton Beach, FL Pro: N																															
2006	EDM	4				5					2																				
ANDY COBAUGH Andrew P. DE 6'2 244 Villanova B: 5/14/1972 Wynnewood, PA																															
1995	SA	7				5																									
CHRIS COBB Christopher (Poke) RB 5'7 198 Eastern Illinois B: 10/17/1958																															
1980	HAM	1												12	61	5.1	11	0	1	8	8.0	8	0								
DeANDRA COBB DeAndra D. RB 5'10 196 Antelope Valley JC; Michigan State B: 5/18/1981 Las Vegas, NV Draft: 6-201 2005 ATL Pro: N																															
2009	HAM	17	5	0	0	3						48	8	216	1217	5.6	40	5	60	542	9.0	48	3								
2010	HAM	18	4	0	0	3						62	10	227	1173	5.2	52	8	38	334	8.8	31	2					1	13	13.0	13
2	Years	35	9	0	0	6						110	18	443	2390	5.4	52	13	98	876	8.9	48	5					1	13	13.0	13
GLENN COBB Glenn LB 6'0 206 Pasadena CC; Illinois B: 10/14/1966 Pro: E																															
1990	TOR	2				5																									
KEITH COBB Keith CB 5'8 175 Memphis B: 3/4/1975 Cleveland, TN																															
1999	HAM	3	0	0	1	8																									
ROBERT COBB Robert Winford QB 6'3 220 Louisiana-Monroe B: 2/7/1971 Bossier City, LA D: 6/6/1999 Baton Rouge, LA																															
1994	SHR	10	1		0	0								3	9	3.0	7	0													
1995	SHR	9				0						12	2	3	7	2.3	5	2													
2	Years	19	1		0	0						12	2	6	16	2.7	7	2													
AVON COBOURNE Avon R. RB 5'8 205 West Virginia B: 3/6/1979 Camden, NJ Pro: EN																															
2006	MTL	16	3	0	1	22								7	21	3.0	5	0	2	14	7.0	8	0	59	477	8.1	27	54	1122	20.8	43
2007	MTL	12				15						12	2	33	160	4.8	14	2	8	79	9.9	16	0	11	70	6.4	10	10	210	21.0	31
2008	MTL+	12	4	1	0	4						50	8	145	950	6.6	42	6	66	616	9.3	60	2								
2009	MTL*	16	3	0	0	3						90	15	224	1214	5.4	43	13	56	458	8.2	20	2								
2010	MTL	15	4	0	0	4						42	7	184	956	5.2	27	6	64	556	8.7	47	1								
2011	HAM	17	3	0	1	1						48	8	202	961	4.8	46	8	50	459	9.2	38	0	2	17	8.5	15				
6	Years	88	17	1	2	49						242	40	795	4262	5.4	46	35	246	2182	8.9	60	5	72	564	7.8	27	64	1332	20.8	43
JOSH COCHRAN Josh OT 6'6 310 Utah B: 12/21/1974 Park City, UT																															
2000	MTL	1				0																									
2001	MTL	8	0	0	1	0																									
2	Years	9	0	0	1	0																									
TERRY COCHRANE Terry RB 5'11 190 Regina Rams Jrs.; British Columbia B: 1/22/1963 Regina, SK Draft: 5-38 1985 CAL																															
1987	SAS	18	1		0	2								17	115	6.8	48	0	11	84	7.6	27	0					3	37	12.3	13
1988	WPG	15				2								10	43	4.3	12	0	4	25	6.3	9	0	1	2	2.0	2	1	9	9.0	9
1989	WPG	18	2		1	2						12	2	13	47	3.6	14	0	43	390	9.1	34	2	1	13	13.0	13	3	21	7.0	13
1990	WPG	4																	1	5	5.0	5	0								
4	Years	55	3		1	6						12	2	40	205	5.1	48	0	59	504	8.5	34	2	2	15	7.5	13	7	67	9.6	13
STEVE COCKERHAM Steven, M. LB 5'11 210 Akron B: 6/22/1956																															
1978	HAM	1	0		1																										
GENE COCKRELL Gene Oliver (Bud) T 6'3 247 Oklahoma; Hardin-Simmons B: 6/10/1934 Pampa, TX Draft: 28-330 1957 CLE Pro: N																															

Year	Team	GP	FM	FF	FR	TK	SK	YDS	IR	YDS	PD	PTS	TD	RA	YDS	AVG	LG	TD	REC	YDS	AVG	LG	TD	PR	YDS	AVG	LG	KOR	YDS	AVG	LG
1957	SAS	12																												
MERL CODE Merl F. CB 6'0 195 North Carolina A&T State B: 9/8/1948 Seneca, SC Pro: W																														
1970	MTL	14	1		1																							7	195	27.9	31
1971	MTL	11							4	11																		2	42	21.0	26
1972	MTL	4																												
1973	MTL	1																												
1976	OTT	5							2	21																					
5	Years	35	1		1				6	32																		9	237	26.3	31
NIGEL CODRINGTON Nigel C. WR 6'2 189 Rice B: 8/20/1968 Pro: E																														
1991	BC	1	1		0														2	20	10.0	15	0					3	50	16.7	19
ED CODY Edward Joseph (Catfoot) FW-HB 5'9 190 Boston College; Purdue B: 2/27/1923 Newington, CT D: 10/16/1994 Orange County, CA Draft: 5-36 1946 GB; 16-125 1947 LA-AAFC Pro: N																														
1951	TOR	2																												
MAC CODY Maclin SB-WR 5'9 182 Memphis B: 8/7/1972 St. Louis, MO Pro: N																														
1994	OTT	2																	1	9	9.0	9	0	13	100	7.7	20	13	276	21.2	33
1995	BIR	15	1		0	0						18	3						31	452	14.6	41	3	26	278	10.7	25	18	334	18.6	35
1996	HAM*	17	2		0	3						70	11	1	1	1.0	1	0	80	1426	17.8	74	11	17	123	7.2	45	20	333	16.7	47
1998	MTL	12	1	0	0	1						30	5						33	479	14.5	50	5	7	30	4.3	10	6	115	19.2	28
2002	TOR	1				0																		3	35	11.7	20	5	133	26.6	38
5	Years	47	4	0	0	4						118	19	1	1	1.0	1	0	145	2366	16.3	74	19	66	566	8.6	45	62	1191	19.2	47
TAY CODY Tay DB 5'9 180 Florida State B: 10/6/1977 Colquitt, GA Draft: 3-67 2001 SD Pro: N																														
2005	EDM	3				6			1	0	0																				
2005	HAM	5	0	3	1	9					1																				
2005	Year	8	0	3	1	15			2	0	1																				
2006	HAM+	15	0	3	3	71			3	37	4																				
2007	HAM	12	0	0	1	50			1	39	1																				
3	Years	30	0	6	5	136			5	76	6																				
SCOTT COE Scot LB 6'2 220 Manitoba B: 3/16/1980 Winnipeg, MB Draft: 5-43 2002 HAM																														
2002	HAM	18	0	1	2	18																						0	4		4
2003	HAM	15				39	1.0	1.0	2	11	2																				
2004	CAL	18	0	2	4	77	4.0	24.0	2	43	3	6	1																		
2005	CAL	18	0	2	1	75	3.0	25.0	1	10	4																	1	0	0.0	0
2006	CAL	18	1	0	1	61	1.0	1.0			3																	2	9	4.5	9
2007	CAL	15	0	3	3	60	1.0	14.0			3																				
2008	EDM	12				7					1																				
7	Years	114	1	8	11	337	10.0	65.0	5	64	16	6	1															3	13	4.3	9
NATE COEHOORN Nate WR-SB 6'2 220 Calgary B: 9/17/1986 Medicine Hat, AB Draft: 1-5 2011 EDM																														
2011	EDM	10				4													2	29	14.5	20	0								
TOMMY JOE COFFEY Tommy Joe SE-K 6'0 195 West Texas A&M B: 11/18/1936 Polk County, TX Draft: 8-96 1959 BAL																														
1959	EDM	9							3	28		24	1						14	277	19.8	57	1	1	5	5.0	5				
1960	EDM	16	1		1				1			19	1	1	-18	-18.0	-18	0	27	532	19.7	65	1								
1962	EDM*	14										129	12	17	90	5.3	13	1	65	951	14.6	59	11								
1963	EDM	16	1		1							37	5	2	-16	-8.0	-4	0	61	1104	18.1	79	5					1	0	0.0	0
1964	EDM*	16	0		1							36	6	1	-9	-9.0	-9	0	81	1142	14.1	72	6								
1965	EDM*	16	2		0							65	2						81	1286	15.9	65	2	2	0	0.0	0				
1966	EDM*	16	2		0							58	2						60	902	15.0	45	2								
1967	HAM*	14										107	5						42	683	16.3	45	5								
1968	HAM*	14										111	4	1	2	2.0	2	0	47	800	17.0	83	4	0	-10		-10				
1969	HAM+	14	1		2							148	12	2	-5	-2.5	0	0	71	1110	15.6	68	11	1	0	0.0	0				
1970	HAM*	14	2		0							113	5						46	678	14.7	44	5								
1971	HAM	14	5		0							76	2						28	423	15.1	49	2								
1972	HAM	14										48	8	1	-3	-3.0	-3	0	27	432	16.0	37	8								
1973	TOR	13	3		1																		58	256	4.4	17				
14	Years	200	17		6				4	28		971	65	25	41	1.6	13	1	650	10320	15.9	83	63	62	251	4.0	17	1	0	0.0	0
TIMMY COFIELD Timmy Lee DE 6'2 243 Elizabeth City State B: 5/18/1963 Murfreesboro, NC Pro: N																														
1991	CAL	4	0		2	17	2.0																								
1992	CAL	14				24	6.0	30.0																							
1993	HAM*	18	0		2	30	18.0	148.0																							
1994	HAM*	18	0		6	31	16.0	112.0				18	3																		
1995	MEM*	18	0		1	36	24.0	150.0																							
1996	TOR	13	0		1	16	9.0	61.0																							
6	Years	85	0		12	154	75.0	501.0				18	3																		
JOHN COFLIN John C-OG 6'1 250 Simon Fraser B: 6/26/1964 Tsawwassen, BC Draft: 1-6 1986 EDM																														
1986	CAL	17					1.0							1	8	8.0	8	0												
1987	CAL	9				0																								
1987	BC	5				0																								
1987	Year	14				0																								
1988	BC	18				1																								
1989	BC	8				0																								
1990	TOR	12	0		1	1																								
1991	TOR	9				2																								
1992	OTT	2				0																								
7	Years	75	0		1	4	1.0							1	8	8.0	8	0												
MARK COFLIN Mark C-OG 6'0 242 Alberta B: 5/8/1956 Draft: 6-53 1978 EDM																														
1979	HAM	9																												
1979	EDM	6																												
1979	Year	15																												
1980	TOR	13	1		0																									
1982	HAM	11																												
3	Years	33	1		0																									
DAMON COGDELL Damon LB 6'2 250 West Virginia B: 6/3/1975 Miami, FL																														
2000	BC	2				3																								
DICK COHEE Richard OHB-DB-TE-FB-LB 6'1 190 New Mexico State; Reedley JC B: 11/26/1939 Wichita Falls, TX																														
1960	MTL	11							1	43		18	3	31	193	6.2	24	0	22	450	20.5	82	1	1	0	0.0	0	14	390	27.9	102
1961	MTL	8												29	203	7.0	39	0	3	25	8.3	13	0					5	64	12.8	22
1962	MTL	3												12	73	6.1	28	0	3	12	4.0	5	0					5	70	14.0	23
1962	OTT	5							1	8		6	1																		
1962	Year	8							1	8		6	1	12	73	6.1	28	0	3	12	4.0	5	0					5	70	14.0	23
1963	SAS	16	1		0				1			18	3						11	192	17.5	35	2	2	3	1.5	3	3	35	11.7	13
1964	SAS	8										12	2	8	38	4.8	14	0	7	128	18.3	44	1	1	3	3.0	3	3	131	43.7	58
1964	HAM	4	0		1				1	4																				
1964	Year	12	0		1				1	4		12	2	8	38	4.8	14	0	7	128	18.3	44	1	1	3	3.0	3	3	131	43.7	58
1965	HAM	14	0							3	63		6	1	1	4	4.0	4	0											13	331	25.5	35
1966	HAM	14	2		0							12	2	104	635	6.1	81	2	9	174	19.3	44	0					14	398	28.4	52
1967	HAM	6	1		0							18	3	53	238	4.5	33	3	5	98	19.6	22	0					5	143	28.6	50
1968	HAM	1												3	6	2.0	3	0													
9	Years	81	4		1				7	118		90	15	241	1390	5.8	81	5	60	1079	18.0	82	4	4	6	1.5	3	62	1562	25.2	102
EDDIE COHEN Eddie WR 5'11 200 Western Carolina B: 3/13/1985 Hilton Head, SC																														
2008	HAM	5				0						6	1						15	197	13.1	67	1	3	9	3.0	10	5	130	26.0	37
WILL COKELEY Will Harlin LB 6'2 220 Coffeyville JC; Kansas State B: 12/6/1960 Topeka, KS Draft: 18-207 1983 MIC-USFL Pro: NU																														
1986	MTL	3					1.0																								
LaMARCUS COKER LaMarcus Darnell RB 5'11 195 Tennessee; Hampton B: 6/26/1986																														

Year	Team	GP	FM	FF	FR	TK	SK	YDS	IR	YDS	PD	PTS	TD	RA	YDS	AVG	LG	TD	REC	YDS	AVG	LG	TD	PR	YDS	AVG	LG	KOR	YDS	AVG	LG
2011	CAL	5	2	0	0	1						6	1	24	234	9.8	75	1	5	31	6.2	8	0					10	182	18.2	33
HESHIMU COLAR Heshimu Kululekile DB 5'10 195 San Jose State B: 10/15/1970 Shreveport, LA																															
1993	SAC	6				14																									
DARRELL COLBERT Darrell Ray WR 5'10 174 Texas Southern B: 11/16/1964 Pro: EN																															
1990	EDM	14	4		2	5			1	0		30	5						40	616	15.4	43	5	10	63	6.3	19	35	611	17.5	34
1990	BC	3	0		1	1													7	122	17.4	36	0					2	36	18.0	19
1990	Year	17	4		3	6			1	0		30	5						47	738	15.7	43	5	10	63	6.3	19	37	647	17.5	34
1992	EDM	3																	2	27	13.5	15	0	5	40	8.0	23	7	174	24.9	38
2	Years	17	4		3	6			1	0		30	5						49	765	15.6	43	5	15	103	6.9	23	44	821	18.7	38
JIM COLCLOUGH James Michael DB-OHB 6'0 185 Boston College B: 3/31/1936 Medford, MA D: 5/16/2004 Boston, MA Draft: 30-353 1959 WAS Pro: N																															
1959	MTL	11							3	24				7	32	4.6	14	0	9	67	7.4	21	0	45	238	5.3	16	9	129	14.3	18
FRED COLE Frederick Michael OT-DT 5'11 226 Maryland B: 6/14/1937 Newark, NJ Draft: 6-68 1959 CHIB Pro: N																															
1959	WPG	5																													
KEVIN COLE Kevin Jeffrey RB 6'1 210 Los Angeles Harbor JC; San Jose State B: 1/27/1956 Benton Harbor, MI																															
1982	EDM	7	1		0							30	5	73	390	5.3	38	4	24	252	10.5	31	1					5	124	24.8	34
1982	WPG	1										6	1	13	33	2.5	7	0	4	74	18.5	35	1								
1982	Year	8	1		0							36	6	86	423	4.9	38	4	28	326	11.6	35	2								
VERNON COLE Vernon QB 6'0 190 North Texas B: 5/26/1938 Draft: SS 1960 DAL																															
1960	WPG	6	1		1				1			7	1	8	66	8.3	22	1													
1964	MTL	8	4		0							24	4	35	163	4.7	23	3	5	62	12.4	26	1								
2	Years	14	5		1				1	0		31	5	43	229	5.3	23	4	5	62	12.4	26	1								
COREY COLEHOUR Corey Alan QB 6'3 210 North Dakota B: 9/2/1945 Minneapolis, MN Draft: 7-162 1967 ATL																															
1968	EDM	7												4	-13	-3.3	2	0													
1969	EDM	16	3		1							36	6	32	95	3.0	18	6													
2	Years	23	3		1							36	6	36	82	2.3	18	6													
ANDRE COLEMAN Andre Oton DT 6'3 290 Albany B: 7/26/1984 Inglewood, CA Pro: N																															
2010	EDM	4				5	1.0	7.0																							
CHRIS COLEMAN Christopher Tyrone WR 6'0 203 North Carolina State B: 5/8/1977 Shelby, NC Pro: EN																															
2003	MTL	5				0								1	3	3.0	3	0	9	120	13.3	37	0								
CLARENCE COLEMAN Clarence, Jr. WR 5'10 193 Ferris State B: 6/4/1980 Miami, FL Pro: N																															
2008	BC	14	1	0	0	2						18	3						34	389	11.4	39	3								
DENNIS COLEMAN Dennis Franklin LN-DE 6'3 225 Mississippi B: 12/19/1948 Aberdeen, MS Draft: 6-151 1971 MIA Pro: N																															
1972	CAL	8	0		2							6	1																		
1973	CAL	5																													
2	Years	13	0		2							6	1																		
HERB COLEMAN Herbert G. DT 6'4 295 Trinity International B: 9/4/1971 Chicago, IL Draft: 7-238 1995 SF Pro: E																															
1998	SAS	2				3																									
JUSTIN COLEMAN Ronald Justin CB 5'10 185 Mississippi B: 10/24/1976 Columbus, GA																															
2004	WPG	13	0	2	3	35					2																				
2005	WPG	10	0	1	0	29	1.0	4.0	3	26	2																				
2	Years	23	0	3	3	64	1.0	4.0	3	26	4																				
KaRON COLEMAN KaRon Rashad RB 5'7 198 Stephen F. Austin State B: 5/22/1978 Missouri City, TX Pro: N																															
2005	OTT	9	1	0	1	1						6	1	6	15	2.5	6	1	5	40	8.0	17	0	3	32	10.7	17	4	72	18.0	22
LOVELL COLEMAN Lovell FB-OHB 5'10 195 Western Michigan B: 1938 Draft: SS 1960 DEN; 17-199 1960 CLE																															
1960	CAL	5	2		1							6	1	30	249	8.3	57	1	6	154	25.7	45	0	5	49	9.8	16	2	68	34.0	45
1961	CAL	16	5						2	40		36	6	42	227	5.4	21	0	16	367	22.9	100	5	13	64	4.9	20	8	217	27.1	36
1962	CAL	13	3									42	7	111	661	6.0	59	6	6	100	16.7	39	1	2	8	4.0	8	1	6	6.0	6
1963	CAL*	16	6		0							90	15	237	1343	5.7	51	13	32	443	13.8	47	2					7	173	24.7	70
1964	CAL*	16	4		3							60	10	260	1629	6.3	85	10	27	247	9.1	29	0					18	545	30.3	105
1965	CAL*	16	9		1							72	12	249	1509	6.1	69	8	27	302	11.2	46	4					8	185	23.1	40
1966	CAL	3												35	183	5.2	43	0	3	15	5.0	19	0					2	74	37.0	39
1967	CAL	16	3		1							60	10	120	594	5.0	49	3	51	646	12.7	84	7					1	39	39.0	39
1968	OTT	14	1		0									39	136	3.5	19	0	10	205	20.5	54	0								
1970	BC	16										6	1	12	35	2.9	9	1	3	41	13.7	29	0					5	111	22.2	27
10	Years	131	33		6				2	40		372	62	1135	6566	5.8	85	42	181	2520	13.9	100	19	20	121	6.1	20	52	1418	27.3	105
MARVIN COLEMAN Marvin CB-DH 5'9 170 Central State (Ohio) B: 1/31/1972 Ocala, FL Pro: X																															
1994	CAL	15	3		1	25			1	35	0	12	2											42	479	11.4	38	22	501	22.8	77
1995	CAL+	18				71			6	92	12	18	3											69	793	11.5	83	20	443	22.2	57
1996	CAL*	18	1		1	70			7	135	7	12	2											62	714	11.5	55	42	1039	24.7	51
1997	CAL*	18	1	0	2	81			1	36	7													56	481	8.6	39	52	1297	24.9	72
1998	CAL+	17	1	0	1	66			1	19	11													64	635	9.9	58	43	1115	25.9	50
1999	CAL	18	2	1	3	66			2	4	4	12	2											65	647	10.0	81	9	170	18.9	30
2000	CAL*	18	3	1	0	62			2	48	4	6	1											95	946	10.0	71	35	766	21.9	51
2001	WPG+	15	0	0	1	62			3	88	5	12	2											10	64	6.4	11	4	99	24.8	48
2002	WPG	18	0	0	1	43			5	95	7	6	1											36	321	8.9	34	4	77	19.3	27
2003	WPG	11	1	0	2	22			0	0	4													17	131	7.7	28	3	58	19.3	26
10	Years	166	12	2	12	568			28	552	61	78	13											516	5211	10.1	83	234	5565	23.8	77
MILL COLEMAN Millard WR 5'9 175 Michigan State B: 6/19/1972 Albion, MI																															
1997	MTL	11				1						24	4						31	427	13.8	35	4	3	23	7.7	12	2	44	22.0	27
1998	MTL	9				0						12	2						16	182	11.4	23	2								
2	Years	20				1						36	6						47	609	13.0	35	6	3	23	7.7	12	2	44	22.0	27
PAT COLEMAN Patrick Darryl WR 5'7 173 Mississippi Delta JC; Mississippi B: 4/8/1967 Cleveland, MS Draft: 9-237 1990 HOU Pro: N																															
1995	TOR	3	0		1	0								2	12	6.0	20	0	5	50	10.0	16	0					8	250	31.3	83
QUINCY COLEMAN Quincy DH 5'10 182 Jackson State B: 7/23/1975 Macon, MS Pro: EX																															
2002	EDM	12	0	1	1	32			1	0	5																				
2003	EDM	15	0	0	2	39			3	0	7																				
2004	EDM	13	0	0	1	30			3	89	7																				
2005	OTT	16	0	0	1	46			1	0	5																	2	46	23.0	25
4	Years	56	0	1	5	147			8	89	24																	2	46	23.0	25
WAYNE COLEMAN Wayne DE 6'3 275 none B: 9/10/1943																															
1968	MTL	5																													
VINCE COLIZZA Vince T 5'10 207 McGill B: 1928																															
1952	HAM	1																													
SCOTT COLLIE Scott Alan SB 6'1 190 Brigham Young B: 4/21/1960 Jewel, KS Draft: 6-64 1983 DEN-USFL																															
1983	HAM	5										12	2						11	152	13.8	30	2								
1985	HAM	9	0		1														23	333	14.5	37	0								
2	Years	14	0		1							12	2						34	485	14.3	37	2								
ANTHONY COLLIER Anthony Dewayne Bernard DE 6'4 260 Baylor B: 11/11/1979 Dallas, TX																															
2004	OTT	3	0	2	0	6																									
2005	OTT+	13	0	0	2	23	12.0	71.0	3	55	3																				
2006	HAM	11	0	2	1	8	5.0	26.0			2																				
2007	HAM	3	0	0	1	5	2.0	7.0																							
4	Years	30	0	4	4	42	19.0	104.0	3	55	5																				
OZELL COLLIER Ozell DB 5'10 185 Arizona Western JC; Colorado B: 4/27/1951 Marianna, AR Draft: 4-92 1974 DEN																															
1974	CAL	7	1		1																							8	222	27.8	42
1977	CAL	7																													
2	Years	14	1		1																							8	222	27.8	42
REGGIE COLLIER Reginald C. QB 6'3 207 Southern Mississippi B: 5/14/1961 Biloxi, MS Draft: 6-162 1983 DAL; 1-3 1983 BIR-USFL Pro: NU																															
1987	OTT	2				0								6	51	8.5	18	0													
TONY COLLIER Antonio CB 5'9 180 Mississippi B: 10/16/1970 Tupelo, MS																															
1994	BC	11	0		1	13			1	71	1	6	1											1	0	0.0	0	1	19	19.0	19
1995	BC	8	0		1	17					1																				

Year	Team	GP	FM	FF	FR	TK	SK	YDS	IR	YDS	PD	PTS	TD	RA	YDS	AVG	LG	TD	REC	YDS	AVG	LG	TD	PR	YDS	AVG	LG	KOR	YDS	AVG	LG
1996	BC	4				7					3																				
3	Years	23	0		2	37			1	71	5	6	1											1	0	0.0	0	1	19	19.0	19
AARON COLLINS Aaron LB 5'11 233 Penn State B: 7/19/1975 Mount Holly, NJ																															
1998	SAS	2				11																									
1998	WPG	2	0	0	1	6	1.0	4.0				6	1																		
1998	Year	4	0	0	1	17	1.0	4.0				6	1																		
2000	SAS	18	1	4	3	88	1.0	10.0																							
2001	SAS	4				11	2.0	20.0			1																				
2001	EDM	4				8	1.0																								
2001	Year	8				19	3.0				1																				
3	Years	24	1	4	4	124	5.0	34.0			1	6	1																		
BRETT COLLINS Brett William LB 6'1 226 Washington B: 10/8/1968 Sheridan, WY Draft: 12-314 1992 GB Pro: N																															
1995	TOR	5				17																									
CHARLIE COLLINS Charles Herman LB 6'1 220 Auburn B: 1/24/1946 Marietta, GA D: 2/23/2012 Smyrna, GA																															
1968	MTL	10	0		2				1	55																					
1969	MTL	7																													
1970	MTL+	14							2	18																					
1971	SAS	16	0		2				3	6																		1	3	3.0	3
1972	SAS	16	1		0				4	61														1	5	5.0	5				
1973	SAS	10							1	0																					
1974	SAS	7	0		1				1	4																					
1975	SAS	7																													
8	Years	93	1		5				12	144														1	5	5.0	5	1	3	3.0	3
DOBSON COLLINS Dobson WR-SB 6'2 178 Gardner-Webb B: 7/12/1987 Stone Mountain, GA																															
2011	BC	5												3	22	7.3	12	0	14	217	15.5	49	0								
2011	EDM	1																	3	36	12.0	18	0								
2011	Year	6												3	22	7.3	12	0	17	243	14.3	49	0								
DOUG COLLINS Doug OT-DT-OG 6'4 240 Cincinnati B: 2/18/1945 Windsor, ON																															
1968	OTT	6																													
1969	OTT	14	0		2																										
1970	OTT	14	0		2																										
1971	OTT	14																													
1972	OTT	14																													
1973	OTT	14	0		2																										
1974	OTT	16																													
1975	HAM	8																													
8	Years	100	0		6																										
GERRY COLLINS Gerald Scott RB 5'7 190 Colorado State; Penn State B: 6/4/1969 Riverside, NJ																															
1994	OTT	9	2		0	1						12	2	105	526	5.0	24	2	31	328	10.6	27	0					2	29	14.5	19
1995	OTT	6				1						2	0	34	123	3.6	25	0	11	80	7.3	27	0					14	251	17.9	31
1995	EDM	1				0								12	54	4.5	18	0	4	11	2.8	7	0					3	37	12.3	15
1995	Year	7				1						2	0	46	177	3.8	25	0	15	91	6.1	27	0					17	288	16.9	31
1996	EDM	8				7								7	11	1.6	5	0	17	129	7.6	20	0					11	214	19.5	37
3	Years	23	2		0	9						14	2	158	714	4.5	25	2	63	548	8.7	27	0					30	531	17.7	37
MERV COLLINS Merve OG-OT-DE-LB-K 6'1 220 none B: 1933																															
1953	TOR	13																													
1954	TOR	10																													
1955	HAM	5																													
1956	OTT	14							1	7																					
1957	OTT	14							1	4																		1	26	26.0	26
1958	OTT	14																													
1959	OTT	14																													
1960	OTT	5																													
1961	OTT	14																													
1962	OTT	14																													
1963	OTT	14																													
1964	OTT	13																													
1965	OTT	14																													
1966	EDM	12																													
14	Years	170							2	11																		1	26	26.0	26
MILT COLLINS Milton DH-S 6'1 187 Jones County JC; Mississippi B: 3/9/1985 New Orleans, LA																															
2008	CAL	10	0	0	1	11	1.0	9.0	3	40	1																				
2009	CAL	18	0	0	1	43			2	2	1	6	1																		
2010	CAL	17	0	3	0	37	2.0	15.0	3	102	4	6	1																		
2011	CAL	2				1					1																				
2011	HAM	1				2																									
2011	Year	3				3					1																				
4	Years	47	0	3	2	94	3.0	24.0	8	144	7	12	2																		
ODELL COLLINS Odell, Jr. FB 6'2 245 Merced JC; Georgia B: 11/4/1973																															
1999	MTL	1				1																									
PHIL COLLINS Phillip RB 5'9 175 Missouri State B: 7/27/1968																															
1991	CAL	2				1																		2	10	5.0	10	2	74	37.0	54
RAY COLLINS Alvin Ray DT 5'11 238 Louisiana State B: 8/4/1927 Wilbarger County, TX D: 11/3/1991 Bexar County, TX Draft: 3-37 1950 SF Pro: N																															
1953	SAS	13																													
1955	HAM	8																										1	0	0.0	0
2	Years	21																										1	0	0.0	0
ROOSEVELT COLLINS Roosevelt, Jr. DE 6'4 235 Texas Christian B: 1/25/1968 Shreveport, LA Draft: 6-155 1992 MIA Pro: EN																															
1994	SAC	4				3																									
1995	SA	18	0		2	44	6.0	43.0	1	27	2	6	1																		
2	Years	22	0		2	47	6.0	43.0	1	27	2	6	1																		
SHAWN COLLINS Shawn L. WR 6'2 207 Northern Arizona B: 2/20/1967 Los Angeles County, CA Draft: 1B-27 1989 ATL Pro: EN																															
1995	WPG	2	1		0	2													7	106	15.1	20	0								
1995	MEM	9	2		0	0						12	2						22	430	19.5	58	2								
1995	Year	11	3		0	2						12	2						29	536	18.5	58	2								
TED COLLINS Ted DT-OT 6'0 255 Detroit Mercy B: 1943																															
1965	OTT	14																													
1966	OTT	14							1	0																					
1967	OTT	14	0		1							6	1																		
1968	WPG	16																													
1969	WPG	16																										1	2	2.0	2
1970	MTL	14																													
1971	MTL	14	0		1																										
1972	MTL	4																													
8	Years	106	0		2				1	0		6	1															1	2	2.0	2
THUNDER COLLINS Thunder Gmerio, Jr. RB 6'1 205 East Los Angeles CC; Nebraska B: 9/17/1979 Los Angeles, CA																															
2003	MTL	1				0								2	7	3.5	7	0													
TORY COLLINS Tory DT 6'2 285 Louisiana State; Northwestern State (Louisiana) B: 12/29/1982 New Orleans, LA																															
2008	HAM	4				4																									
BRAD COLLINSON Brad C 6'2 290 Concordia (Canada) B: 3/28/ Montreal, QC																															
2003	MTL	17	1	0	0	12																									
MICHAEL COLLYMORE Michael WR 6'1 185 Etobicoke Argos Jrs. B: 9/24/1958 Toronto, ON																															
1981	WPG	5																	3	33	11.0	14	0								

Year	Team	GP	FM	FF	FR	TK	SK	YDS	IR	YDS	PD	PTS	TD	RA	YDS	AVG	LG	TD	REC	YDS	AVG	LG	TD	PR	YDS	AVG	LG	KOR	YDS	AVG	LG
1982	WPG	7																	4	39	9.8	15	0					1	0	0.0	0
1982	OTT	6										6	1						8	109	13.6	34	1								
1982	Year	13										6	1						12	148	12.3	34	1								
1983	OTT	15										6	1	1	18	18.0	18	0	25	434	17.4	59	1								
1984	OTT	5																	4	42	10.5	27	0								
1984	SAS	7																	20	277	13.9	33	0								
1984	Year	12																	24	319	13.3	33	0								
1985	SAS	3																	11	133	12.1	22	0								
5	Years	35										12	2	1	18	18.0	18	0	75	1067	14.2	59	2					1	0	0.0	0
GILLES COLON Gilles WR 6'0 200 Bishop's B: 7/25/1981 Port-au-Prince, Haiti																															
2004	WPG	11				4													3	54	18.0	23	0								
2005	WPG	8	1	0	1	2						6	1						18	232	12.9	43	1	2	15	7.5	17	13	265	20.4	43
2006	BC	7				1						6	1						7	79	11.3	17	1	6	14	2.3	10				
3	Years	26	1	0	1	7						12	2						28	365	13.0	43	2	8	29	3.6	17	13	265	20.4	43
CLEVELAND COLTER Cleveland DB 6'4 245 Southern California B: 7/15/1968 Tuscon, AZ																															
1995	BIR	6	0		1	14			0	0	1																				
JOE COLVEY Joseph RB 5'11 194 Verdun Invcitus Jrs.; Carleton (Ontario) B: 1/19/1950																															
1975	OTT	10	0		1									8	14	1.8	5	0													
1976	OTT	10												6	32	5.3	8	0										2	30	15.0	17
1976	MTL	1																													
1976	Year	11												6	32	5.3	8	0										2	30	15.0	17
1977	OTT	6												2	18	9.0	14	0	2	21	10.5	16	0								
1977	CAL	5										6	1	1	5	5.0	5	1													
1977	Year	11												3	23	7.7	14	1	2	21	10.5	16	0								
3	Years	26	0		1							6	1	17	69	4.1	14	1	2	21	10.5	16	0					2	30	15.0	17
SONNY COLVIN Sonny HB-FB B: 1929																															
1946	HAM	4										5	1					1													
1948	TOR	2										2	0																		
2	Years	6										7	1					1													
PHIL COLWELL Phil RB 6'1 195 Wilfrid Laurier B: 9/19/1956 Draft: TE 1979 MTL																															
1980	HAM	16	1		2									13	29	2.2	6	0	2	15	7.5	13	0								
1981	HAM	2												1	0	0.0	0	0													
1981	TOR	3																													
1981	Year	5												1	0	0.0	0	0													
2	Years	18	1		2									14	29	2.1	6	0	2	15	7.5	13	0								
DAN COMISKEY Dan OG 6'4 301 Windsor B: 6/30/1972 Windsor, ON Draft: 6-42 1997 SAS																															
1997	SAS	5				0																									
1998	SAS	17				0																									
1999	SAS	12				1																									
2000	SAS	16				0																									
2001	SAS	18	0	0	1	1																									
2002	EDM	17				5																									
2003	EDM+	18	0	0	1	1																									
2004	EDM	18	0	0	1	1																									
2005	HAM	13				0																									
2005	EDM	4				0																									
2005	Year	17				0																									
2006	EDM+	16				0																									
2007	EDM	4				0																									
2008	EDM	8				1																									
2010	CAL	12				0																									
13	Years	174	0	0	3	10																									
JOHN COMISKEY John C-OG 6'4 297 Windsor AKO Fratmen Jrs.; Rutgers; Windsor B: 11/11/1980 Prince Albert, SK Draft: 3-19 2005 CAL																															
2005	CAL	7				0																									
2006	CAL	18				2																									
2007	CAL	13				2																									
2008	EDM	18				2																									
2009	EDM	12				0																									
5	Years	68				6																									
GERALD COMMISSIONG Gerald RB 6'0 230 Stanford B: 4/6/1982 Montreal, QC Draft: 4B-30 2006 CAL																															
2007	CAL	16	1	0	0	4								18	64	3.6	16	0	2	2	1.0	5	0								
JERRY COMPTON Jerry Len WR 5'11 180 East Central B: 5/31/1958 Shawnee, OK																															
1981	TOR	3																	3	46	15.3	26	0					7	143	20.4	30
LIONEL CONACHER, JR. Lionel, Jr. FB 6'2 202 Western Ontario B: 1936 Draft: 1-3 1960 MTL																															
1960	MTL	6																													
LOU CONFESSORI Louis A., Jr. QB 6'1 195 Wichita State B: 10/19/1941 New York, NY																															
1967	WPG	4	1		0									1	9	9.0	9	0													
JASON CONGDON Jason LB 6'2 235 Western Ontario B: 9/25/1975 St. Thomas, ON																															
2002	WPG	18				3																									
2003	WPG	18				9																									
2004	MTL	18	1	0	1	11																									
2005	HAM	5				1																									
4	Years	59	1	0	1	24																									
JOHN CONGEMI John M. QB 6'0 185 Pittsburgh B: 6/19/1964 Youngstown, OH																															
1987	TOR	14	1		0	0						2	0	5	17	3.4	9	0													
1988	TOR	14	2		0	1								9	30	3.3	9	0													
1989	TOR	14	4		1	1						6	1	13	35	2.7	15	1													
1990	TOR	15	3		1	2						6	1	11	63	5.7	13	1													
1991	OTT	11	1		0	1								1	9	9.0	9	0													
1992	TOR	15	2		0	0						6	1	13	26	2.0	10	1													
1994	BAL	18	1		0	0								1	2	2.0	2	0													
7	Years	101	14		2	5						20	3	53	182	3.4	15	3													
LUCA CONGI Luca K-P 5'10 190 Simon Fraser B: 6/15/1983 Waterloo, ON Draft: 2-12 2006 SAS																															
2006	SAS	18	3	0	0	2						163	0																		
2007	SAS	18				0						156	0																		
2008	SAS	18				0						166	0																		
2009	SAS	18	1	0	0	4						151	0																		
2010	SAS	15				0						121	0																		
5	Years	87	4	0	0	6						757	0																		
BRIAN CONLAN Brian OL 6'5 295 British Columbia B: 5/7/1972 Kamloops, BC Draft: 1-16 1995 BC																															
2002	SAS	1				0																									
STEVE CONLEY Stephen Craig LB 6'2 225 Arizona Western JC; Kansas B: 9/3/1949 Chicago, IL Draft: 7-158 1972 CIN Pro: NW																															
1973	HAM	5										6	1	3	5	1.7	5	0	5	47	9.4	15	1								
STEVE CONLEY Donald Steven DE 6'5 237 Arkansas B: 1/18/1972 Chicago, IL Draft: 3A-72 1996 PIT Pro: NX																															
1999	SAS	6	0	0	3	23	2.0	15.0	0	0	1																				
KEITH CONLIN Keith Arthur OL 6'7 305 Penn State B: 11/9/1972 Glenside, PA Draft: 61A-191 1996 IND																															
1996	SAS	2				0																									
JUSTIN CONN Justin LB 6'3 230 Bishop's B: 8/29/1988 Draft: 6-47 2010 MTL																															
2011	MTL	1				0																									
2011	CAL	10	0	0	1	4																									
2011	Year	11	0	0	1	4																									
ALBERT CONNELL Albert Gene Anthony WR 6'0 181 Trinity Valley CC; Texas A&M B: 5/13/1974 Fort Lauderdale, FL Draft: 4-115 1997 WAS Pro: N																															

Year	Team	GP	FM	FF	FR	TK	SK	YDS	IR	YDS	PD	PTS	TD	RA	YDS	AVG	LG	TD	REC	YDS	AVG	LG	TD	PR	YDS	AVG	LG	KOR	YDS	AVG	LG
2003	CAL	4				2						6	1						10	163	16.3	65	1								
2004	CAL	10				1						12	2						37	631	17.1	70	2								
2	Years	14				3						18	3						47	794	16.9	70	3								
BOB CONNELL Bob FB Saskatoon Hilltops Jrs.																															
1949	SAS	1																													
ROD CONNOP Rod C-OT-OG 6'6 245 Wilfrid Laurier B: 6/4/1959 Burnaby, BC Draft: 1-9 1982 EDM																															
1982	EDM	16	0		1																										
1983	EDM	14																													
1984	EDM	16												1	-4	-4.0	-4	0										1	7	7.0	7
1985	EDM	16																													
1986	EDM	18	0		1																										
1987	EDM*	18	1		1	0																						1	20	20.0	20
1988	EDM	18				0																									
1989	EDM*	18	1		0	0																									
1990	EDM*	18				3																									
1991	EDM*	18	0		1	6																									
1992	EDM*	18				3																									
1993	EDM*	18				2																									
1994	EDM	16				2																									
1995	EDM+	18	1		0	2																									
1996	EDM+	16	0		1	0																									
1997	EDM	18				1																									
16	Years	274	3		5	19								1	-4	-4.0	-4	0										2	27	13.5	20
TED CONNOR Ted T 6'4 218 Nebraska B: 1931 Draft: 3-33 1954 PHI																															
1954	TOR	1																													
DARRYL CONRAD Darryl OL 6'3 312 Winnipeg Rifles Jrs.; Manitoba B: 7/8/1984 Winnipeg, MB Draft: 2-15 2007 MTL																															
2008	WPG	4				0																									
DAVID CONRAD David FB 6'1 225 Acadia B: 4/1/1963 Halifax, NS Draft: 2-12 1985 SAS																															
1985	SAS	10	2		0									10	48	4.8	16	0	26	257	9.9	26	0								
1986	SAS	17	3		0									30	139	4.6	13	0	26	240	9.2	20	0					2	17	8.5	16
1987	SAS	17	2		1	0						18	3	36	156	4.3	21	2	47	532	11.3	52	1								
1988	SAS	15	3		0	1						6	1	9	31	3.4	8	0	22	255	11.6	39	1					2	22	11.0	20
1989	OTT	10	2		0	0						24	4	28	138	4.9	15	1	8	92	11.5	32	3								
1990	OTT	16	1		1	0						30	5	60	247	4.1	15	3	40	434	10.9	30	2					1	13	13.0	13
1991	OTT+	17	0		1	0						12	2	56	325	5.8	59	0	51	589	11.5	30	2								
1992	OTT	18				6						18	3	15	48	3.2	10	0	27	239	8.9	25	3								
8	Years	120	13		3	7						108	18	244	1132	4.6	59	6	247	2638	10.7	52	12					5	52	10.4	20
WAYNE CONRAD Wayne C-OG 6'0 222 Mount Royal College Jrs.; Calgary B: 4/18/1946 Edmonton, AB																															
1972	MTL	14																													
1973	MTL	14																													
1974	MTL	13	1		1																										
1975	MTL*	16	2		1																										
1976	MTL	11																													
1977	MTL	12	1		0																										
6	Years	80	4		2																										
JIM CONROY James Joseph LB-FB-P 6'0 190 Southern California B: 10/18/1937 Vancouver, BC D: 10/3/2011 Ottawa, ON Draft: FS 1960 BUF																															
1960	OTT	14							2	23		5	0	8	15	1.9	21	0													
1961	OTT	14							1	26		3	0																		
1962	OTT*	14							3	53		8	1											4	21	5.3	9	6	87	14.5	30
1963	OTT*	14							1	0																		7	68	9.7	18
1964	OTT	14	1		0				1	59				7	28	4.0	7	0										1	0	0.0	0
1965	OTT	1																													
1966	OTT+	14							1	0																					
1967	OTT	12												12	53	4.4	9	0	5	41	8.2	12	0					1	5	5.0	5
1968	WPG	13	1		1				1	-4																					
9	Years	110	2		1				10	157		16	1	27	96	3.6	21	0	5	41	8.2	12	0	4	21	5.3	9	15	160	10.7	30
JOHN CONROY John HB-LB 6'1 190 Mount San Antonio JC B: 12/6/1939 Vancouver, BC																															
1961	MTL	14							3	7														13	56	4.3	10				
1962	MTL	1																													
1963	MTL	11																													
3	Years	26							3	7														13	56	4.3	10				
JIM COODE James Edward IT 6'4 260 Michigan B: 10/22/1951 Mayfield Heights, OH Draft: 7-173 1974 ATL; 11-132 1974 DET-WFL Pro: W																															
1974	OTT	1																													
1975	OTT	11																													
1976	OTT+	16																													
1977	OTT	16																													
1978	OTT*	16																													
1979	OTT	16																													
1980	OTT	4																													
7	Years	80																													
JERRY COODY Jerry FB 5'11 185 Baylor B: 10/3/1931 Draft: 17-200 1954 WAS																															
1954	CAL	1												10	45	4.5	9	0	1	9	9.0	9	0								
DAMION COOK Damion Lamar OT 6'5 330 Bethune-Cookman B: 4/16/1979 Nashville, TN Pro: ENU																															
2006	HAM	10				0																									
2007	HAM	3				0																									
2	Years	13				0																									
DON COOK Don T 6'2 235 Hamilton Tiger-Cats B B: 1938																															
1961	HAM	2																													
DOUG COOK Doug C Western Ontario																															
1947	SAS	8										1	0																		
1948	TOR	11																													
2	Years	19										1	0																		
DUANE COOK James Duane DE 6'1 220 Oklahoma B: 1942 Draft: 8-101 1963 STL																															
1964	EDM	3	0		1																										
GARY COOK Gary FL-DB 6'1 180 Carleton B: 6/15/1957 Draft: TE 1980 OTT																															
1980	OTT	16							1	1		6	1	1	1	1.0	1	0	2	36	18.0	19	1	20	231	11.6	62	3	60	20.0	25
1981	OTT	10																													
1982	OTT	4												1	41	41.0	41	0													
3	Years	30							1	1		6	1	2	42	21.0	41	0	2	36	18.0	19	1	20	231	11.6	62	3	60	20.0	25
GLENN COOK Glenn DB 6'1 190 Richmond B: 6/15/1957 Draft: TE 1980 OTT																															
1980	OTT	15							1	10																					
1981	OTT	15					1.0																								
1982	OTT	9							1	52									1	6	6.0	6	0								
3	Years	39					1.0	0.0	2	62									1	6	6.0	6	0								
HUBERT COOK Hubert K. (Duke) C 6'2 220 Oklahoma State; Trinity (Texas) B: 1933																															
1956	CAL	8																													
JACK COOK Jack WB 5'10 190 Queen's B: 1930 Draft: 4-15 1955 HAM																															
1955	BC	10																	3	25	8.3	9	0					1	25	25.0	25
JOHNNY COOK John Homer, Jr. QB 5'8 152 Georgia B: 12/18/1925 Lenox, GA D: 9/17/1986 Rome. GA Draft: 23-233(di) 1945 CHIC; 29-274 1946 CHIB																															
1948	SAS	11																													
LANCE COOK Lance DE 6'2 225 The Citadel B: 10/2/1970 Atlanta, GA																															
1992	SAS	8	0		1	17	5.0	41.0	1	10																					

Year	Team	GP	FM	FF	FR	TK	SK	YDS	IR	YDS	PD	PTS	TD	RA	YDS	AVG	LG	TD	REC	YDS	AVG	LG	TD	PR	YDS	AVG	LG	KOR	YDS	AVG	LG
1993	SAS	1				0																									
2	Years	9	0		1	17	5.0	41.0	1	10																					
LEWIS COOK Lewis E. CB-LB 5'11 180 Arizona Western JC; Idaho State B: 12/5/1946 Tucson, AZ Pro: W																															
1970	MTL	3							1	-3																		5	134	26.8	37
1972	SAS	14							6	195		6	1															1	24	24.0	24
1973	SAS	11							2	33																					
1975	MTL	14	1		1				1	17		6	1	1	-2	-2.0	-2	0						2	107	53.5	98	8	214	26.8	86
1976	HAM	16			1				4	11														1	0	0.0	0				
1977	SAS	2																										1	25	25.0	25
1977	MTL	4	1		0																							3	50	16.7	22
1977	TOR	2																													
1977	Year	8	1		0																							4	75	18.8	25
6	Years	60	2		2				14	253		12	2	1	-2	-2.0	-2	0						3	107	35.7	98	18	447	24.8	86
MIKE COOK Mike WR 6'4 205 Stanford B: 3/20/1971																															
1995	BAL	3				0													3	46	15.3	27	0								
ROLLIE COOK Rollie T-G 6'1 192 B: 1935 Edmonton, AB																															
1955	EDM	16	0		2																										
1956	EDM	11																													
2	Years	27	0		2																										
TERRENCE COOK Terrence DL 6'2 288 Tulane B: 7/28/1976																															
1998	TOR	1				0																									
GEORGE COOKE George HB 5'8 196 B: 1928																															
1950	TOR	2																													
RAYFORD COOKS Rayford Earl, Jr. DT-DE 6'3 245 North Texas B: 8/25/1962 Draft: 15C-317 1984 HOU-USFL Pro: NU																															
1986	MTL	6	0		1																										
1989	BC	5				10	1.0																								
2	Years	11	0		1	10	1.0																								
ANTHONY COOLEY Anthony WR 5'9 180 North Carolina Central B: 8/19/1965 Rocky Mount, NC																															
1992	TOR	2				0						6	1						6	127	21.2	47	1								
HAROLD COOLEY Harold A. G 5'11 220 Jackson State B: 5/22/1940 Erie, PA																															
1964	MTL	14																													
BILLY COOPER William FL-DB 5'10 180 St. James Rods Jrs. B: 1/1/1945 Winnipeg, MB																															
1964	WPG	16	2		1				1			24	4	6	51	8.5	16	1	24	409	17.0	59	3	26	105	4.0	15	5	149	29.8	53
1965	WPG	16	1		0							30	5	9	8	0.9	35	0	25	382	15.3	53	5	52	238	4.6	29	1	8	8.0	8
1966	WPG	15	4		0							12	2	7	101	14.4	68	0	32	534	16.7	50	2	35	96	2.7	23	1	15	15.0	15
1967	WPG	16	3		0				3	29		6	1	11	55	5.0	41	0	8	91	11.4	25	0	51	301	5.9	75	14	311	22.2	35
1968	OTT	14	2		2				1	19									1	20	20.0	20	0	44	196	4.5	31	9	211	23.4	53
1969	OTT	14	0		1																			38	190	5.0	31	5	113	22.6	35
1970	OTT	14										12	2						35	613	17.5	55	2	34	145	4.3	35				
1971	OTT	14	1		1							30	5						25	422	16.9	45	5	51	315	6.2	24	5	139	27.8	37
1972	OTT	14	1		0							6	1						17	356	20.9	63	1	32	82	2.6	14				
1973	OTT	6	1		0														2	32	16.0	19	0	18	52	2.9	11				
1973	EDM	9	0		1														1	6	6.0	6	0	18	83	4.6	12				
1973	Year	15	1		1																			36	135	3.8	12				
1974	TOR	13	2		2				1	0														37	157	4.2	16	4	81	20.3	32
11	Years	152	17		8				6	48		120	20	33	215	6.5	68	1	170	2865	16.9	63	18	436	1960	4.5	75	44	1027	23.3	53
FLOYD COOPER Floyd HB 5'11 175 Hamilton Wildcats Jrs. B: 1930																															
1950	HAM	5																													
1951	HAM	9																													
1952	HAM	7																													
3		21																													
FRED COOPER Fred DB 5'1025 178 Purdue B: 11/14/1951 Chicago, IL Draft: 6A-138 1975 DET																															
1975	HAM	3																													
GWEN COOPER Gwen OE 6'2 208 UCLA B: 12/13/1948 Wichita, KS																															
1970	OTT	1																													
JIM COOPER James OL 6'1 215 British Columbia B: 11/29/1973 Toronto, ON Draft: 5-33 1998 EDM																															
1998	EDM	18	1	0	0	17																		1	0	0.0	0				
1999	EDM	2				1																									
1999	SAS	5	1	0	1	3																						1	14	14.0	14
1999	Year	7	1	0	1	4																						1	14	14.0	14
2000	TOR	9	1	0	0	6						2	0						1	5	5.0	5	0								
3	Years	29	3	0	1	27						2	0						1	5	5.0	5	0	1	0	0.0	0	1	14	14.0	14
JOE COOPER Joe LB 6'0 240 Ohio State B: 1/22/1979 Columbus, OH																															
2002	CAL	3				10																									
JUSTIN COOPER Justin DE 6'0 250 Edmonton Huskies Jrs.; Manitoba B: 7/7/1982 Red Deer, AB Draft: 3B-23 2008 EDM																															
2008	EDM	18				13																									
2009	EDM	17				9																									
2010	EDM	18				8																						1	0	0.0	0
3	Years	53				30																						1	0	0.0	0
LARRY COOPER Larry HB																															
1952	CAL	3																													
MARKEITH COOPER Markeith A. WR 5'7 175 Auburn B: 1/15/1977 Miami, FL																															
2002	TOR	4				0																		16	155	9.7	63	12	262	21.8	48
SHELDON COOPER Sheldon FB 5'10 210 Calgary B: 4/26/1967																															
1991	HAM	1																													
WES COOPER Wes RB 5'10 185 Weber State B: 9/25/1962 Vernon, BC Draft: 3-20 1985 CAL																															
1986	MTL	18	0		2							12	2	9	42	4.7	9	1	4	17	4.3	7	0					2	3	1.5	3
1988	BC	14	1		1	0								8	38	4.8	14	0	2	3	1.5	5	0					2	26	13.0	14
1989	BC	17	0		2	1						6	1	5	20	4.0	12	0	6	58	9.7	33	1								
3	Years	49	1		5	1						18	3	22	100	4.5	14	1	12	78	6.5	33	1					4	29	7.3	14
JIM COPE James Charles OG 6'1 235 Ohio State B: 6/23/1953 Oil City, PA Draft: 5B-119 1975 CLE Pro: N																															
1975	MTL	4																													
HENRY COPELAND Henry HB 6'2 220 Parsons B: 8/11/1948 Portsmouth, VA Pro: W																															
1973	CAL	1												7	23	3.3	6	0										1	0	0.0	0
JEREMAINE COPELAND Jeremaine WR-SB 6'2 200 Tennessee B: 2/19/1977 Harriman, TN Pro: EX																															
2001	MTL	7				2						6	1	1	5	5.0	5	0	13	182	14.0	26	1								
2002	MTL	5	1	0	0	0						24	4						18	352	19.6	41	4								
2003	MTL*	18	2	0	0	1						84	14						99	1757	17.7	57	14					2	19	9.5	12
2004	MTL+	16	1	0	0	3						60	10						83	1154	13.9	42	10								
2005	CAL	18				3						48	8						64	1211	18.9	70	8					2	13	6.5	13
2006	CAL	18	1	0	0	1						36	6	2	14	7.0	9	0	54	978	18.1	70	6								
2007	CAL	18	1	0	0	4						60	10	1	-5	-5.0	-5	0	67	1110	16.6	84	10								
2008	CAL	18	1	0	0	1						42	7						52	764	14.7	60	7					1	0	0.0	0
2009	CAL*	18	2	0	0	1						72	12						81	1235	15.2	57	12								
2010	TOR	14	2	0	1	2						18	3						48	639	13.3	50	3								
2011	TOR	18	0	0	1	2													43	633	14.7	45	0								
11	Years	168	11	0	2	20						450	75	4	14	3.5	9	0	622	10015	16.1	84	75					5	32	6.4	13
JIM COPELAND James Richard DB-FL 5'9 180 none B: 1/2/1939 Windsor, ON																															
1960	MTL	13							2	12														43	148	3.4	15				
1961	SAS	16	2						3	37														59	384	6.5	28	1	3	3.0	3
1962	SAS	13							3	49														37	185	5.0	25				
1963	SAS	16							2	33		6	1						1	9	9.0	9	0	59	352	6.0	22				

Year	Team	GP	FM	FF	FR	TK	SK	YDS	IR	YDS	PD	PTS	TD	RA	YDS	AVG	LG	TD	REC	YDS	AVG	LG	TD	PR	YDS	AVG	LG	KOR	YDS	AVG	LG
1964	SAS	16	2		0																			72	381	5.3	28	1	12	12.0	12
1965	TOR	5																						25	172	6.9	15	5	88	17.6	29
1966	TOR	14	2		1									4	14	3.5	5	0						61	246	4.0	15	17	393	23.1	36
1967	TOR	2																						15	82	5.5	15	1	24	24.0	24
1968	TOR	13												4	30	7.5	14	0						64	514	8.0	34	5	141	28.2	32
9	Years	108	6		1				10	131		6	1	8	44	5.5	14	0	1	9	9.0	9	0	435	2464	5.7	34	30	661	22.0	36
ROYAL COPELAND Royal HB-FW-DE-OE-K 6'0 190 none B: 10/12/1924 North Bay, ON D: 8/8/2011 Toronto, ON																															
1946	TOR+	12										30	6					3					1								
1947	TOR+	12										10	2					1					1								
1948	TOR	10										26	5					3					1								
1949	TOR+	12										40	8					6					2								
1950	CAL	14										30	6	94	412	4.4	52	5	20	236	11.8	36	1								
1951	CAL	11										10	2	55	152	2.8	12	1	19	248	13.1	18	1	5	6	1.2		10	187	18.7	
1952	TOR	12																													
1953	TOR	14										2	0																		
1954	TOR	13							4	39																					
1955	TOR	9							1	2		20	4	0	10		10	1	17	301	17.7	42	3	1	7	7.0	7	1	15	15.0	15
1956	TOR	11										8	1						10	138	13.8	32	1					1	5	5.0	5
11	Years	130							5	41		176	34	149	574	3.9	52	20	66	923	14.0	42	11	6	13	2.2	7	12	207	17.3	15
RUSSELL COPELAND Russell Samoan WR 6'0 200 Memphis B: 11/4/1971 Tupelo, MS Draft: 4-111 1993 BUF Pro: N																															
2001	TOR	1				0													1	5	5.0	5	0								
RON COPPENBARGER Ronnie DB 6'1 195 Kansas State B: 10/6/1951 Stuttgart, Germany Pro: W																															
1973	WPG	1																													
BILLY CORBETT Billy Joseph OT 6'4 275 Johnson C. Smith B: 7/9/1952 Hillsboro, NC D: 2/23/2010 Roxboro, GA Draft: 2-40 1974 CLE; 28-333 1974 MEM-WFL																															
1974	TOR	4																													
DARRELL CORBIN Darrell LB 6'2 225 South Carolina State B: 9/13/1964 Columbia, SC																															
1988	HAM	12	0		3	44	3.0																								
1989	HAM	11				33	3.0		2	29																					
1990	HAM	15	0		2	64	2.0		2	9																					
1991	EDM	1				4																									
1992	WPG	8	0		1	22	1.0					6	1																		
1994	LV	3				3	2.0																								
6	Years	50	0		6	170	11.0	0.0	4	38		6	1																		
KEN CORBIN Ken G 6'1 225 Miami (Florida) B: 6/8/1945 Draft: 15-388 1968 MIA																															
1968	TOR	4																													
TONY CORBIN Anton Christian QB 6'4 215 Sacramento State B: 3/21/1974 Phoenix, AZ Draft: 7B-237 1997 SD																															
2001	BC	18	2	0	0	0								4	0	0.0	4	0													
DAVE CORLEY David FB 5'11 210 Louisiana College B: 1943																															
1965	TOR	3																										1	30	30.0	30
DAVID CORLEY David, Jr. QB 5'11 203 William & Mary B: 4/12/1980 Salisbury, NC																															
2003	HAM	18	1	0	0	0						12	2	8	32	4.0	12	2													
JERRY CORNELISON Jerry Gale T 6'3 250 Southern Methodist B: 9/13/1936 Dallas, TX Draft: 16-192 1958 CLE Pro: N																															
1958	SAS	12	0		2																										
CHARLES CORNELIUS Charles Edward CB 5'9 178 Bethune-Cookman B: 7/27/1952 Boynton Beach, FL Pro: N																															
1981	MTL	8							4	45																					
1982	MTL	16							2	22																					
1983	OTT	14	0		1				2	67																					
1984	OTT	8	1		0				3	22																					
4	Years	46	1		1				11	156																					
SHANNON CORNELIUS Shannon Lamon DE 6'1 282 Louisiana State; Louisiana Tech B: 4/30/1970 Houston, TX																															
1994	SHR	8				5	1.0	8.0																							
MIKE CORNELL Mike LB-RB 6'0 221 Ottawa B: 12/5/1986 Hamilton, ON																															
2010	CAL	6				4																									
2011	EDM	18				19																									
2	Years	24				23																									
JON CORNISH Jon HB 6'0 205 Kansas B: 11/5/1984 New Westminster, BC Draft: 2-13 2006 CAL																															
2007	CAL	18				15								1	30	30.0	18	0						1	10	10.0	10	8	141	17.6	32
2008	CAL	18				21						6	1	30	254	8.5	48	1	5	67	13.4	22	0								
2009	CAL	15	0	0	1	18						18	3	20	105	5.3	28	2	8	76	9.5	19	1								
2010	CAL	18	3	0	1	13						6	1	85	618	7.3	52	0	14	226	16.1	37	1					12	224	18.7	28
2011	CAL+	18	1	0	0	15						66	11	119	863	7.3	57	9	26	385	14.8	62	2					8	167	20.9	26
5	Years	87	4	0	2	82						96	16	255	1870	7.3	57	12	53	754	14.2	62	4	1	10	10.0	10	28	532	19.0	32
DOUG CORREA Doug WR Simon Fraser																															
1988	BC	1																													
JIM CORRIGALL James DE-LB-DT 6'3 235 Kent State B: 5/7/1946 Barrie, ON Draft: 2A-33 1970 STL																															
1970	TOR	14	0		2				1	5																					
1971	TOR*	14	0		2																										
1972	TOR+	13	0		2																										
1973	TOR*	12	0		1																										
1974	TOR	16	0		1																										
1975	TOR*	16																													
1976	TOR	3	0		1																										
1977	TOR*	15	0		1																										
1978	TOR+	12																													
1979	TOR+	16	0		1																										
1980	TOR+	6	0		2																										
1981	TOR	9	0		3		4.0					6	1																		
12	Years	146	0		16		4.0		1	5		6	1																		
KEITH CORRIGAN Keith QB Illinois																															
1946	WPG	7																													
FRANK COSENTINO Frank QB 6'3 195 Western Ontario B: 5/22/1937 Hamilton, ON Draft: 1-5 1960 HAM																															
1960	HAM	11												1	4	4.0	4	0													
1961	HAM	14												16	77	4.8	13	0													
1962	HAM	14										24	4	49	364	7.4	33	4													
1963	HAM	14										12	2	28	231	8.3	33	2													
1964	HAM	14	2		0							6	1	22	127	5.8	24	1													
1965	HAM	14	2		2							12	2	29	76	2.6	18	2													
1966	HAM	14	2		0									19	75	3.9	22	0													
1967	EDM	16	3		0							12	2	35	151	4.3	22	2													
1968	EDM	16	3		1									23	89	3.9	17	0													
1969	TOR	14	1		0							6	1	19	99	5.2	25	1													
10	Years	141	13		3							72	12	241	1293	5.4	33	12													
BOB COSGROVE Robert T Montana B: CA																															
1949	TOR	7																													
DAVE COSTA David C. OT 6'5 304 Wisconsin B: 9/8/1978 Erie, PA Pro: EN																															
2004	TOR	12				0																									
2005	TOR	11				1																									
2006	TOR	18				1																									
2007	TOR	9				0																									
2007	CAL	1				0																									
2007	Year	10				0																									
4	Years	50				2																									

Year	Team	GP	FM	FF	FR	TK	SK	YDS	IR	YDS	PD	PTS	TD	RA	YDS	AVG	LG	TD	REC	YDS	AVG	LG	TD	PR	YDS	AVG	LG	KOR	YDS	AVG	LG
JOE COSTELLO Joseph Patrick, Jr. DE 6'3 245 Central Connecticut State B: 6/1/1960 New York, NY Pro: NU																															
1982	MTL	2	0		1																										
JUNIUS COSTON Junius Emanuel OT-OG 6'3 316 North Carolina A&T B: 11/5/1983 Framingham, MA Draft: 5A-143 2005 GB Pro: N																															
2011	EDM	3																													
ROB COTE Robin FB-SB 6'1 220 Calgary; Victoria Rebels Jrs. B: 7/5/1986 Calgary, AB																															
2007	CAL	18				9						12	2	2	3	1.5	3	0	11	112	10.2	21	2								
2008	CAL	10				4													2	23	11.5	19	0					1	15	15.0	15
2009	CAL	17				19						12	2	4	20	5.0	10	0	7	99	14.1	28	2					1	0	0.0	0
2010	CAL	18	1	1	0	11						12	2	3	11	3.7	6	0	11	111	10.1	20	2								
2011	CAL	14	1	0	1	5						2	0						15	171	11.4	41	0					1	7	7.0	7
5	Years	77	2	1	1	48						38	6	9	34	3.8	10	0	46	516	11.2	41	6					3	22	7.3	15
STEVE COTTER Steve OG 6'3 225 Vancouver Jrs.; Wenatchee Valley CC B: 1941																															
1960	BC	14																													
1961	BC	16																													
1962	BC	16																													
1963	BC	16	0		1							6	1	0	5		5	0													
1964	BC	16																													
1965	BC	16												1	1	1.0	1	0													
1966	EDM	16																													
1967	EDM	16																													
1969	EDM	4																													
9	Years	130	0		1							6	1	1	6	6.0	5	0													
CURTIS COTTON Curtis DB 6'0 210 Nebraska B: 10/15/1969 Draft: 7A-173 1992 LARI Pro: E																															
1995	WPG	1				0																									
JAMES COTTON James Antwane DE-LB 6'2 249 Cuyahoga CC; San Francisco CC; Ohio State B: 11/7/1976 Cleveland, OH Draft: 7-223 2000 CHIB Pro: X																															
2001	CAL	17	0	4	1	52	9.0	62.0			1	6	1																		
2002	CAL	6	0	1	1	20	1.0	7.0			2																				
2005	HAM	17	0	1	2	38	10.0	72.0	1	15	1	6	1																		
2006	HAM	15	0	1	0	34																									
4	Years	55	0	7	4	144	20.0	141.0	1	15	4	12	2																		
KOTTO COTTON Kotto WR 6'0 180 Arkansas B: 4/17/1973 North Little Rock, AR Pro: E																															
1998	WPG	7				1						6	1						18	237	13.2	39	1					1	12	12.0	12
1998	SAS	3				1													5	46	9.2	20	0					3	45	15.0	17
1998	Year	10				2						6	1						23	283	12.3	39	1					4	57	14.3	17
MARCUS COTTON Marcus Glenn DE 6'3 237 Southern California B: 8/11/1966 Los Angeles, CA Draft: 2-28 1988 ATL Pro: N																															
1994	HAM	5				11	1.0	3.0			3																				
1995	HAM	6				9	3.0	35.0			1																				
2	Years	11				20	4.0	38.0			4																				
TED COTTRELL Theodore John LB 6'1 233 Delaware Valley B: 6/13/1947 Chester, PA Draft: 7B-164 1969 ATL Pro: N																															
1971	WPG	2																													
THERMAN COUCH Therman Lee LB 6'2 220 Iowa State B: 3/18/1949 Chapel Hill, NC Draft: 9-231 1971 SF																															
1972	EDM	8	0		1				2	41																					
RYAN COUGHLIN Ryan OG 6'6 295 McGill B: 4/4/1973 Renfrew, ON Draft: 2B-14 1997 MTL																															
1997	MTL	17	1	0	1	3																									
1998	MTL	17				3																									
1999	MTL	14				1																									
3	Years	48	1	0	1	7																									
EDAWN COUGHMAN Edawn OT 6'4 309 Shaw B: 7/21/1988 Riverdale, GA																															
2011	TOR	9																													
BRUCE COULTER Bruce QB-S 6'0 170 none B: 11/19/1927																															
1948	MTL	12										5	1					1													
1949	MTL	12																													
1950	MTL	12																													
1951	MTL	12																													
1952	MTL	12																													
1953	MTL	14																													
1954	MTL	14							3	47														27	105	3.9	11				
1955	MTL	11							3	12				1	3	3.0	3	0													
1956	MTL	14							3	6				3	5	1.7	5	0													
1957	MTL	14							1	6																					
10	Years	127							10	71		5	1	4	8	2.0	5	1						27	105	3.9	11				
CARL COULTER Carl C-OG 6'0 270 Carleton B: 11/14/1966 Lindsay, ON Draft: 4-26 1990 BC																															
1990	BC	18	1		0	1																						1	18	18.0	18
1991	BC	18				1																						2	13	6.5	8
1992	BC	18	0		1	23						6	1						1	3	3.0	3	1					3	30	10.0	13
1993	OTT	1				1																									
1994	TOR	15				10																									
1995	TOR	16	0		2	0						6	1						0	0		0	1								
1996	BC	18				1																									
1997	SAS	18				1																									
1998	HAM	18	3	0	0	3																									
1999	HAM	18	2	0	1	3																									
2000	HAM	18	3	0	0	1																									
2001	HAM	18	0	0	1	1																									
2002	OTT	16	1	0	0	0																									
2003	HAM	18	1	0	0	0																									
2004	HAM	17	0	0	2	1																									
15	Years	245	11	0	7	47						12	2						1	3	3.0	3	2					6	61	10.2	18
TEX COULTER Dewitt Echoles OT-DT 6'4 250 Army B: 10/2/1924 D: 10/2/2007 Austin, TX Draft: 1-7 1947 CHIC Pro: N																															
1953	MTL+	11										3	0																		
1954	MTL+	14										7	0																		
1955	MTL+	12										8	0																		
1956	MTL	14										7	0															1	1	1.0	1
4	Years	51										25	0															1	1	1.0	1
JOHNNY COUNTS John E., Jr. HB 5'10 170 Illinois B: 2/28/1939 Mount Pleasant, NY D: 2/21/2004 Newburgh, NY Draft: 24-189 1962 NYT Pro: N																															
1964	HAM	11	4		0							18	3	85	508	6.0	60	2	17	148	8.7	23	1					5	124	24.8	31
1965	HAM	10	1									6	1	49	219	4.5	23	1	8	74	9.3	39	0					5	110	22.0	32
1966	TOR	2	1		0									8	-7	-0.9	4	0	1	9	9.0	9	0					1	25	25.0	25
3	Years	23	6		0							24	4	142	720	5.1	60	3	26	231	8.9	39	1					11	259	23.5	32
TED COURTNEY Ted G																															
1946	TOR	8																													
1947	TOR	3																													
1948	TOR	5																													
3	Years	16																													
STEVE COURY Steven J. SE 5'9 170 Oregon State B: 7/3/1957 Santa Ana, CA																															
1980	OTT	3										6	1						7	94	13.4	21	1	6	54	9.0	20				
TOM COUSINEAU Thomas Michael LB 6'3 225 Ohio State B: 5/6/1957 Fairview Park, OH Draft: 1A-1 1979 BUF Pro: N																															
1979	MTL	14	0		2																										
1980	MTL	16	0		1				1	33																					
1981	MTL	4					3.0																								
3	Years	34	0		3		3.0		1	33																					
BRAD COUSINO Bradley Gene LB 6'0 215 Miami (Ohio) B: 4/5/1953 Toledo, OH Pro: N																															

Year	Team	GP	FM	FF	FR	TK	SK	YDS	IR	YDS	PD	PTS	TD	RA	YDS	AVG	LG	TD	REC	YDS	AVG	LG	TD	PR	YDS	AVG	LG	KOR	YDS	AVG	LG
1978	TOR	4	0		2																										
ART COUSINS Art G-T 5'9 200 B: 1918																															
1948	HAM	12										2	0																		
1949	HAM	1																													
2	Years	13										2	0																		
JOHN COUTURE John S 5'8 170 Hamilton Hurricanes Jrs. B: 1948																															
1970	MTL	13	0		1																			44	336	7.6	17	2	20	10.0	11
BRUCE COVERNTON Bruce OT 6'5 292 St. Vital Mustangs Jrs.; Weber State B: 8/12/1966 Morris, MB Draft: 1A-1 1992 CAL																															
1992	CAL	18				1																									
1993	CAL	18	0		1	0													0	5		5	0								
1994	CAL	17				0																									
1995	CAL	1				0																									
1996	CAL	18				1																									
5	Years	72	0		1	2													0	5		5	0								
GROVER COVINGTON Grover DE 6'2 235 Johnson C. Smith B: 3/25/1956 Monroe, NC																															
1981	HAM	16	0		1		16.0																								
1982	HAM	16					12.5																								
1983	HAM	16					10.0																								
1984	HAM	16	0		1		18.5																								
1985	HAM	15	0		1		16.0																								
1986	HAM	15	0		2		18.0																								
1987	HAM	18				25	17.0																								
1988	HAM	18				21	25.0																								
1989	HAM	18	0		1	22	15.0																								
1990	HAM	15	0		1	34	7.0																								
1991	HAM	5				9	2.0																								
11	Years	168	0		7	111	157.0																								
RAHEEM COVINGTON Raheem Holmes CB 5'9 183 Northwestern B: 12/27/1979																															
2003	WPG	5				17					5																				
2004	WPG	14				38			2	15	6																				
2	Years	19				55			2	15	11																				
WILL COVINGTON William, Jr. WR 5'9 175 Troy B: 12/2/1969 Brady, TX																															
1995	SHR	15	1		0	8						12	2						22	224	10.2	24	2	35	278	7.9	35	8	109	13.6	19
LARRY COWAN Larry Donnell RB 5'11 190 Jackson State B: 7/11/1960 Mobile, AL Draft: 7B-192 1982 MIA Pro: N																															
1983	EDM	2	2		0									17	120	7.1	26	0	2	17	8.5	9	0								
1984	EDM	15	4		0							8	1	130	759	5.8	65	1	55	508	9.2	29	0								
1985	EDM	15	2		1							6	1	96	451	4.7	20	0	44	463	10.5	35	1								
3	Years	32	8		1							14	2	243	1330	5.5	65	1	101	988	9.8	35	1								
TIM COWAN Timothy John QB 6'0 190 Washington B: 8/17/1960 Lynwood, CA Draft: 16-182 1983 BOS-USFL																															
1983	BC	3																													
1984	BC	16	6		0									28	53	1.9	10	0													
1985	BC	14												5	6	1.2	8	0													
1986	TOR	9	1		0									3	9	3.0	5	0													
1986	BC	9	1		0							12	2	4	9	2.3	4	2													
1986	Year	18	2		0							12	2	7	18	2.6	5	2													
4	Years	42	8		0							12	2	40	77	1.9	10	2													
LARRY COWART Larry Joe C 6'4 235 Baylor B: 8/10/1936 Cameron County, TX Draft: 3-26 1958 CHIC																															
1958	TOR	8																													
1959	TOR	8																													
2	Years	16																													
DON COWIE Don DB 6'1 210 McGill B: 3/3/1952																															
1975	CAL	16																													
BEN COWINS Ben Henderson RB 6'0 192 Arkansas B: 4/7/1956 St. Louis, MO Draft: 4-94 1979 PHI																															
1980	TOR	3										6	1	28	144	5.1	14	1	5	33	6.6	18	0								
AL COWLINGS Allen G. (A.C.) DE-LB 6'5 247 San Francisco CC; Southern California B: 6/16/1947 Draft: 1-5 1970 BUF Pro: N																															
1978	MTL	4	0		1							6	1																		
CHIP COX Chip LB-DH 5'9 185 Ohio University B: 6/24/1983 Tacoma, WA																															
2006	MTL	18	0	3	1	55			3	95	5																				
2007	MTL	18	0	0	1	66			3	115	10	6	1																		
2008	MTL	18	0	1	0	75					2																				
2009	MTL*	18	0	5	2	90	3.0	13.0	1	21	2	12	2																		
2010	MTL*	17	0	4	2	91	3.0	27.0	2	9	6	6	1											1	6	6.0	6	0	49		49
2011	MTL*	18	0	4	1	93	3.0	26.0	3	99	6	6	1																		
6	Years	107	0	17	7	470	9.0	66.0	12	339	31	30	5											1	6	6.0	6	0	49		49
KEN COX Ken HB																															
1949	CAL	2																													
MARTIN COX James Martin WR 6'0 180 Vanderbilt B: 8/12/1956 Mullins, SC Draft: 10A-270 1979 NE Pro: U																															
1979	OTT+	8	0		1							42	7						32	546	17.1	66	7								
1980	OTT	14	1		0							36	6						29	386	13.3	45	6	27	312	11.6	64	33	793	24.0	39
1981	OTT	1																	3	26	8.7	11	0								
1981	TOR	7	1		0							24	4						16	370	23.1	58	4					1	25	25.0	25
1981	Year	8	1		0														19	396	20.8	58	4					1	25	25.0	25
1982	TOR	8										18	3	2	-13	-6.5	4	0	15	333	22.2	68	3	6	51	8.5	19				
1982	WPG	3										6	1						14	203	14.5	29	1								
1982	Year	11										24	4	2	-13	-6.5	4	0	29	536	18.5	68	4	6	51	8.5	19				
4	Years	31	2		1							126	21	2	-13	-6.5	4	0	109	1864	17.1	68	21	33	363	11.0	64	34	818	24.1	39
NORM COX Norman Lawrence HB-FB 6'2 210 Texas Christian B: 9/22/1925 Stamford, TX D: 4/28/2008 Draft: 31-291 1948 CHIB Pro: A																															
1948	MTL	11																													
RENARD COX Renard CB 5'11 188 Lackawanna CC; Maryland B: 3/3/1978 Richmond, VA Pro: EN																															
2004	HAM	15	0	1	1	65	1.0	5.0	1	18	8																				
2005	HAM	16	0	1	0	49	3.0	21.0			2																				
2006	HAM	15	0	1	0	43			1	18	1																				
2007	HAM	3	0	1	1	7																									
4	Years	49	0	4	2	164	4.0	26.0	2	36	11																				
RON COX Ron E 6'1 185 Parkdale Lions Jrs.; Western Ontario B: 1934																															
1955	TOR	5																										1	10	10.0	10
RUFUS COX Rufus, Jr. WR 5'9 170 Troy B: 4/12/1963 Gadsden, AL Draft: TD 1985 BIR-USFL																															
1985	CAL	6																	16	228	14.3	33	0	14	88	6.3	13	3	37	12.3	21
STEVE COX Steven SB-WR 5'9 175 Utah B: 5/3/1960 Providence, RI																															
1984	TOR	11	1		2							6	1	1	1	1.0	1	0	35	587	16.8	58	1	4	11	2.8	6				
1985	TOR	1																	2	7	3.5	6	0								
1986	TOR	8										6	1						16	229	14.3	44	1								
3	Years	20	1		2							12	2	1	1	1.0	1	0	53	823	15.5	58	2	4	11	2.8	6				
CONRAD COYE Conrad DL 6'4 235 Northeastern B: 9/1/1961 Kingston, Jamaica																															
1984	EDM	3					1.0																								
ROSS COYLE Charles Ross OE-DB-LB 6'2 195 Oklahoma B: 3/23/1937 Marlow, OK Draft: 20-237 1959 LARM Pro: N																															
1959	TOR	13							5	8		24	4						12	176	14.7	63	4	1	0	0.0	0				
1960	CAL	10							2	0									7	89	12.7	30	0								
2	Years	23							7	8		24	4						19	265	13.9	63	4	1	0	0.0	0				
TRAVIS COZART Travis RB 6'1 215 Tennessee* B: 9/9/1974																															
1995	SHR	7				5						12	2	24	150	6.3	31	2	3	70	23.3	37	0					8	145	18.1	30
DAVE CRABBE David LB-FB-HB 6'2 210 Kent State B: 1947																															

Year	Team	GP	FM	FF	FR	TK	SK	YDS	IR	YDS	PD	PTS	TD	RA	YDS	AVG	LG	TD	REC	YDS	AVG	LG	TD	PR	YDS	AVG	LG	KOR	YDS	AVG	LG
1969	CAL	16																										1	18	18.0	18
1970	CAL	16																										4	84	21.0	24
1971	CAL	16							2	8																					
1972	CAL	14																													
4	Years	62							2	8																		5	102	20.4	24
DICK CRADDOCK Dick T-C 6'0 230 Edmonton Jrs. B: 1938																															
1958	EDM	3																													
1959	EDM	5																													
1960	EDM	15																													
3	Years	23																													
NAT CRADDOCK Nathaniel (Crash) OHB-FB 6'0 220 Parsons B: 12/3/1940 Des Moines, IA Draft: 22-174 1963 BOS Pro: N																															
1964	MTL	8	3		0							24	4	106	486	4.6	73	3	8	127	15.9	44	1					3	63	21.0	31
1965	MTL	1												3	-3	-1.0	2	0	1	16	16.0	16	0								
2	Years	9	3		0							24	4	109	483	4.4	73	3	9	143	15.9	44	1					3	63	21.0	31
DONNIE CRAFT Donald Joseph RB 6'0 209 Louisville B: 11/19/1959 Panama City, FL Draft: 12-314 1982 HOU Pro: N																															
1984	HAM	2												10	27	2.7	7	0	8	56	7.0	12	0					1	37	37.0	37
DOUG CRAFT Douglas CB 6'0 195 Southern University B: 7/23/1968 Houghton, LA																															
1993	CAL	8	0		1	36			2	104		6	1																		
1994	CAL	18	0		3	71			7	82	13																				
1995	BAL	6	0		1	18					1																				
1996	MTL	18	0		1	41			2	38	3																				
1997	MTL	18	0	0	1	42			5	2	4													1	0	0.0	0				
1998	MTL	17	0	1	1	49	1.0	3.0	3	59	8																				
1999	SAS	14	0	0	1	45			1	3	4	6	1																		
7	Years	99	0	1	9	302	1.0	3.0	20	288	33	12	2											1	0	0.0	0				
HERB CRAFT Herb DB 5'8 163 Weber State B: 12/28/1978 Phoenix, AZ																															
2003	OTT	3				4					1																	1	16	16.0	16
MONTRELL CRAFT Montrell DT 6'3 280 North Alabama B: 8/14/1987 Memphis, TN																															
2010	BC	5				11					1																				
JERRY CRAFTS Jerry Wayne S 6'5 334 Oklahoma; Louisville B: 1/6/1968 Tulsa, OK Draft: 11-292 1991 IND Pro: ENX																															
2000	TOR	15				1																									
2001	TOR	2				0																									
2002	MTL	5				0																									
2002	HAM	3				0																									
2002	Year	8				0																									
2003	HAM	3				0																									
4	Years	25				1																									
WILLIE CRAFTS Willie (Cowboy) T 6'3 230 Texas A&M-Kingsville B: 1939 Draft: 15-113 1961 DEN																															
1961	EDM	1																													
ANGELO CRAIG Angelo Demturis DE 6'5 242 Cincinnati B: 9/5/1985 Cleveland, OH Draft: 7A-244 2008 CIN																															
2010	BC	1				1																									
2011	HAM	1				2																									
2	Years	2				3																									
DARRYL CRAIG Darryl OG 6'3 250 Queen's B: 2/12/1952																															
1977	HAM	9																													
PACO CRAIG Francisco Luis WR 5'10 170 UCLA B: 2/2/1965 Santa Maria, CA Draft: 10-254 1988 DET Pro: EN																															
1989	TOR	1				1													2	9	4.5	6	0								
TYSON CRAIGGS Tyson LB 6'0 220 Tri-City Bulldogs Jrs.; Saskatchewan B: 8/8/1981 Kamloops, BC																															
2005	BC	18				9																									
2006	BC	18				18																									
2007	BC	18	1	0	0	16																									
2008	HAM	3	1	0	0	1																									
4	Years	57	2	0	0	44																									
GEOFF CRAIN Geoffrey QB-DB-C 6'0 173 McGill B: 1931 Draft: 1-3 1953 TOR																															
1953	WPG	12							2	13		10	2	18	50	2.8		2	1	20	20.0	20	0								
1954	WPG	10												6	11	1.8	9	0						1	2	2.0	2				
1955	OTT	12												3	-4	-1.3		0													
3	Years	34							2	13		10	2	27	57	2.1	9	2	1	20	20.0	20	0	1	2	2.0	2				
MILT CRAIN Milton C-OT-DE-MG 6'5 245 Mississippi B: 12/27/1937 New Albany, MS Draft: 19-228 1959 BAL																															
1960	MTL	11																										1	0	0.0	0
1961	MTL+	12																													
1962	MTL	7																													
1963	MTL*	13																													
1964	MTL	4																													
1964	SAS	1																													
1964	Year	5																													
5	Years	47																										1	0	0.0	0
MARCUS CRANDELL Marcus Cornelius QB 5'11 200 East Carolina B: 1/6/1974 Pro: EX																															
1997	EDM	4	2	0	0	0								2	18	9.0	25	0													
1998	EDM	18				0																									
1999	EDM	13				0						6	1	17	75	4.4	15	1													
2001	CAL	15	3	0	0	1						42	7	58	295	5.1	61	7													
2002	CAL	18	1	0	0	2						12	2	80	503	6.3	28	2													
2003	CAL	15	3	0	2	0								17	57	3.4	10	0													
2004	CAL	14	1	0	0	0						20	3	20	72	3.6	14	3													
2005	SAS	18	1	1	1	2						30	5	39	160	4.1	16	5													
2006	SAS	12				0						12	2	6	22	3.7	11	2													
2007	SAS	18				1								10	47	4.7	12	0													
2008	SAS	8				0								7	54	7.7	14	0													
11	Years	153	11	1	3	6						122	20	256	1303	5.1	61	20													
STEVE CRANE Stephen LB 6'2 205 Acadia B: 8/15/1963 Halifax, NS Draft: 5A-37 1985 SAS																															
1986	SAS	10	0		1		1.0																								
1987	SAS	17	0		1	31	1.0																								
1988	SAS	13			1	34	4.0		2	5																					
1989	SAS	6				23			1	32																					
4	Years	46	0		3	88	6.0		3	37																					
DAVE CRANMER David OHB 6'1 205 Bowling Green State B: 9/18/1944																															
1968	CAL	16	2		1							36	6	140	572	4.1	23	3	34	492	14.5	54	3	30	179	6.0	16	12	318	26.5	49
1969	CAL	8	1		0							13	2	64	228	3.6	15	1	13	94	7.2	20	1					1	25	25.0	25
1970	CAL	16										37	6	73	328	4.5	22	0	32	518	16.2	39	6								
1971	TOR	14	1		0							12	2	12	46	3.8	9	0	27	506	18.7	94	2					1	12	12.0	12
1972	TOR	8	0		1							6	1	10	44	4.4	15	0	17	310	18.2	48	1								
1973	BC	3																													
1973	HAM	4										6	1	21	80	3.8	8	0	11	141	12.8	25	1								
1973	Year	7										6	1	21	80	3.8	8	0	11	141	12.8	25	1								
6	Years	65	4		2							110	18	320	1298	4.1	23	4	134	2061	15.4	94	14	30	179	6.0	16	14	355	25.4	49
PAUL CRANMER Paul SB-DB 6'1 195 Grand Valley State B: 11/27/1969 Calgary, AB Draft: 4-25 1993 SAS																															
1993	SAS	1				1																									
1994	TOR	2				0																									
2	Years	3				1																									
JON CRAVER Jonathan D. DT 6'3 240 James Madison B: 3/24/1961 York, PA																															
1983	BC	2					2.0																								

Year	Team	GP	FM	FF	FR	TK	SK	YDS	IR	YDS	PD	PTS	TD	RA	YDS	AVG	LG	TD	REC	YDS	AVG	LG	TD	PR	YDS	AVG	LG	KOR	YDS	AVG	LG
KEYUO CRAVER Keyou Boderek CB 5'10 195 Nebraska B: 8/22/1980 Dallas, TX Draft: 4-125 2002 NO Pro: N																															
2005	EDM	6	1	0	0	11					1													7	57	8.1	13	3	61	20.3	22
2006	EDM	13	0	1	0	51			3	81	2																	4	80	20.0	23
2009	WPG	18	1	0	1	45			2	52	5													6	33	5.5	11				
2010	WPG	1				0																									
4	Years	38	2	1	1	107			5	133	8													13	90	6.9	13	7	141	20.1	23
BILL CRAWFORD William OG-C 6'1 235 British Columbia B: 7/17/1937 New Westminster, BC Pro: N																															
1961	CAL	11																													
1962	CAL	16																													
1963	CAL	16	0		1																										
1964	CAL	16																													
1966	BC	16																													
5	Years	75	0		1																										
BRYAN CRAWFORD Bryan RB-FB 5'10 201 Queen's B: 2/18/1982 Hamilton, ON Draft: 5-44 2005 TOR																															
2005	TOR	8	0	0	1	7								3	14	4.7	6	0													
2006	TOR	16	1	0	0	16								7	35	5.0	11	0	2	25	12.5	19	0								
2007	TOR	18	0	0	2	28													2	18	9.0	15	0								
2008	TOR	17	1	0	1	25						12	2	5	24	4.8	10	2	1	5	5.0	5	0								
2009	TOR	18	1	0	0	21								5	23	4.6	16	0	10	70	7.0	25	0								
2010	TOR	17				28								6	121	20.2	42	0	2	22	11.0	15	0								
2011	TOR	18				16																									
7	Years	112	3	0	4	141						12	2	26	217	8.3	42	2	17	140	8.2	25	0								
CEDRIC CRAWFORD Cedric Renard DB 5'10 205 Utah B: 1/18/1971 Dallas, TX																															
1994	LV	16	0		1	51																						1	19	19.0	19
DERRICK CRAWFORD Derrick Lorenzo WR 5'10 185 Memphis B: 9/3/1960 Memphis, TN Draft: TD 1984 MEM-USFL Pro: NU																															
1990	CAL+	18	4		1	0						90	15						57	1096	19.2	58	11	56	796	14.2	82	23	734	31.9	88
1991	CAL	5	1		0	0						6	1						13	209	16.1	50	1	8	52	6.5	21	6	81	13.5	19
1992	CAL	17	1		1	3						30	5						47	714	15.2	68	5	7	24	3.4	8	18	392	21.8	52
1993	CAL	18	3		1	1						70	11	4	19	4.8	7	0	57	1007	17.7	75	10	65	589	9.1	70	24	462	19.3	40
1995	BIR	3				1						6	1						5	24	4.8	10	1								
5	Years	61	9		3	5						202	33	4	19	4.8	7	0	179	3050	17.0	75	28	136	1461	10.7	82	71	1669	23.5	88
LARRY CRAWFORD Larry DB 5'11 175 Iowa State B: 12/18/1959 Miami, FL																															
1981	BC	16	2		2		1.0		8	133		6	1											50	551	11.0	62	5	149	29.8	62
1982	BC	16	6		1		1.0		4	41														70	691	9.9	53	27	720	26.7	60
1983	BC*	16	2		1				12	172		12	2											74	766	10.4	50	6	150	25.0	32
1984	BC*	16	1		3		1.0		5	165		6	1											23	221	9.6	21	5	127	25.4	36
1985	BC	10	0		1		3.0		5	15														3	29	9.7	22	5	121	24.2	33
1986	BC*	18	2		3		6.0		9	170		6	1											32	318	9.9	55	8	197	24.6	38
1987	BC*	17	1		0	38	4.0		3	66		18	3											65	682	10.5	82	17	325	19.1	39
1988	BC+	18	1		2	34			5	28														69	810	11.7	66	5	101	20.2	30
1989	BC	3	1		0	9																		2	-10	-5.0	2				
1989	TOR	4				8			1	20														17	101	5.9	16	3	54	18.0	22
1989	Year	7	1		0	17			1	20														19	91	4.8	16	3	54	18.0	22
9	Years	130	16		13	89	16.0	0.0	52	810		48	8											405	4159	10.3	82	81	1944	24.0	62
MELVIN CRAWFORD Melvin DB 6'1 185 Hampton B: 2/15/1973																															
1995	BAL	5				10																									
RUFUS CRAWFORD Rufus, Jr. RB 5'10 180 Virginia State B: 5/21/1955 Gastonia, NC Pro: N																															
1979	HAM	1	2		0							12	2	8	65	8.1	21	1	5	54	10.8	31	1	4	40	10.0	13	3	69	23.0	24
1980	HAM	8	6		1							30	5	125	470	3.8	30	4	13	79	6.1	17	0	38	273	7.2	94	8	176	22.0	33
1981	HAM+	13	3		0							24	4	109	400	3.7	35	4	49	607	12.4	36	0	8	33	4.1	15	8	127	15.9	29
1982	HAM	8										18	3	56	290	5.2	47	2	33	452	13.7	62	1	28	197	7.0	14	14	272	19.4	29
1983	HAM	12	4		1							36	6	35	114	3.3	17	5	44	350	8.0	46	1	51	478	9.4	32	21	493	23.5	46
1984	HAM	16	6		1							30	5	43	136	3.2	14	2	66	864	13.1	47	3	100	1107	11.1	63	36	788	21.9	39
1985	HAM	10	5		0							18	3	12	69	5.8	29	0	43	441	10.3	26	2	48	333	6.9	75	11	259	23.5	44
7	Years	68	26		3							168	28	388	1544	4.0	47	18	253	2847	11.3	62	8	277	2461	8.9	94	101	2184	21.6	46
SCOTT CRAWFORD Scott RB 5'11 180 Lenoir-Rhyne B: 12/28/1953																															
1977	CAL	3	3		0									1	2	2.0	2	0	1	7	7.0	7	0	7	48	6.9	22	7	209	29.9	49
TAD CRAWFORD Tad S 6'2 181 Columbia B: 4/16/1984 Burlington, ON Draft: 3A-17 2007 BC																															
2007	BC	18	0	0	1	21	1.0	12.0			1																				
2008	BC	18	0	0	2	23	1.0	5.0	1	10	1																				
2009	BC	18	0	0	1	20						2	0															1	1	1.0	1
2010	BC	15	0	1	0	58			2	41	4																				
2011	MTL	9				5																									
5	Years	78	0	1	4	127	2.0	17.0	3	51	6	2	0															1	1	1.0	1
KEITH CREDIT Keith WR 6'3 200 Kent State B: 8/24/1956 Washington, DC																															
1980	MTL	1																	2	18	9.0	12	0								
1981	MTL	7	0		2														13	198	15.2	29	0								
2	Years	8	0		2														15	216	14.4	29	0								
CARL CRENNEL Carl Lee LB 6'1 230 West Virginia B: 9/14/1948 Lynchburg, VA Draft: 9-209 1970 PIT Pro: N																															
1971	WPG	5	0		1																										
1972	MTL	14	0		3				3	34																					
1973	MTL+	14	0		3							6	1															2	22	11.0	12
1974	MTL	16			1																										
1975	MTL	16	1		1				1	0																		5	58	11.6	15
1976	MTL	7	0		1																							3	14	4.7	14
1977	MTL	16	0		1				3	45																		1	5	5.0	5
1978	MTL+	16	0		3				2	30														1	-1	-1.0	-1	1	6	6.0	6
1979	MTL	13							1	15																					
1979	EDM	2							1	18		6	1																		
1979	Year+	15							2	33		6	1																		
1980	HAM	16	0		2				2	15																					
1981	SAS	15	0		2		2.0		1	7																					
11	Years	148	1		18		2.0		14	164		12	2											1	-1	-1.0	-1	12	105	8.8	15
PETER CREPIN Peter S-WR 6'0 180 Ottawa Sooners Jrs. B: 11/5/1952 Ottawa, ON																															
1974	OTT	16	1		0														1	14	14.0	14	0	11	40	3.6	8	5	116	23.2	27
1975	OTT	16							4	45														2	5	2.5	4	2	47	23.5	26
1977	OTT	13							1	22																					
1978	OTT	8							3	13																					
1979	OTT	16	0		3				1	6		6	1																		
1980	OTT	10	1		1				1	2														5	50	10.0	19				
1981	WPG	8							1	26																					
7	Years	87	2		4				11	114		6	1						1	14	14.0	14	0	18	95	5.3	19	7	163	23.3	27
KEITA CRESPINA Keita CB 5'8 183 Temple B: 2/25/1971 Philadelphia, PA Pro: E																															
1994	TOR	16	1		6	70			5	105	11																	0	1		1
1995	HAM	1				0																									
2	Years	17	1		6	70			5	105	11																	0	1		1
TYRONE CREWS Tyrone LB 6'2 230 Kansas State B: 6/17/1956 New York, NY																															
1981	BC	2																													
1982	BC	16	0		2		2.0		1	8																					
1983	BC	16	1		0		3.0		3	62														0	5		5				
1984	BC	14	0		3		2.5		3	49																					
1985	BC	15	0		3		3.0		1	3														0	5		5				

Year	Team	GP	FM	FF	FR	TK	SK	YDS	IR	YDS	PD	PTS	TD	RA	YDS	AVG	LG	TD	REC	YDS	AVG	LG	TD	PR	YDS	AVG	LG	KOR	YDS	AVG	LG
1986	BC	18	0		2		4.0		3	83																					
1987	BC	3				14																									
7	Years	84	1		10	14	14.5		11	205														0	10		5				
RON CRICK Ron LB 6'2 215 Vancouver Meralomas Jrs; Wenatchee Valley JC; Idaho; British Columbia B: 7/21/1963 Draft: 3-25 1986 BC																															
1987	WPG	4				3																									
ROB CRIFO Robert WR 6'6 225 Toronto B: 11/10/1965 Toronto, ON Draft: 3B-21 1988 WPG																															
1989	WPG	3				0													2	17	8.5	14	0								
1990	WPG	11				0													5	147	29.4	51	0								
1991	WPG+	18	1		1	1						24	4						39	775	19.9	47	4					1	0	0.0	0
1992	WPG+	18	2		0	5						30	5						53	798	15.1	55	5								
1993	WPG	4				0						2	0						2	21	10.5	11	0								
1993	OTT	7				2						12	2						15	252	16.8	39	2								
1993	Year	11				2						14	2						17	273	16.1	39	2								
1994	SAS	4				0													1	18	18.0	18	0								
1994	TOR	4				0						6	1						17	300	17.6	36	1								
1994	Year	8				0						6	1						18	318	17.7	36	1								
1995	TOR	14				3						18	3	1	-9	-9.0	-9	0	35	475	13.6	56	3								
1996	HAM	8				1						6	1						4	103	25.8	70	1								
8	Years	80	3		1	12						98	16	1	-9	-9.0	-9	0	173	2906	16.8	70	16					1	0	0.0	0
SHAD CRISS Shadwick Leon DH 5'10 185 Missouri B: 1/11/1976 Sherman, TX Pro: N																															
1999	CAL	18	0	0	1	65	1.0	1.0	2	5	4																				
2003	BC	18	0	0	1	57			3	51	3																				
2	Years	36	0	0	2	122	1.0	1.0	5	56	7																				
STAN CRISSON Stan OE 6'1 205 Duke B: 1942																															
1964	HAM	13	0		1							6	1						8	187	23.4	46	1					1	-2	-2.0	-2
1965	HAM+	13	0		1							6	1						28	431	15.4	30	1								
2	Years	26	0		2							12	2						36	618	17.2	46	2					1	-2	-2.0	-2
JOE CRITCHLOW Joseph W. DT-LB 6'2 240 Southeast Missouri State B: 7/4/1943 Sikeston, MO Pro: W																															
1969	WPG	16			1																										
1970	WPG	16																													
1971	WPG	16	0		1																										
1972	WPG	16							1	2																					
1973	WPG	16	0		1																										
1974	MTL	16			1																										
1975	MTL	4																													
7	Years	100	0		4				1	2																					
RAY CRITTENDEN Raymond C. WR 6'1 188 Virginia Tech B: 3/1/1970 Washington, DC Pro: N																															
1999	MTL	1				0																									
JOHNNY CRNCICH John E 5'11 172 McGill B: 2/8/1925 Krk, Yugoslavia																															
1946	TOR	1																													
DON CROFT Donald Thomas DT 6'3 256 Texas-El Paso B: 1/7/1949 Temple, TX Draft: 5-115 1972 BAL Pro: N																															
1977	SAS	7																													
KEATON CROMARTIE Keaton Akfred DE-LB 6'2 240 Tulane B: 4/19/1976 Bradenton, FL Pro: E																															
1999	HAM	2				2																									
2000	HAM	4				3																									
2002	OTT	14				28	5.0	33.0																							
2003	OTT	17	0	1	2	39	7.0	41.0	1	5	0																				
2004	OTT	14	0	0	2	30					2																				
2005	OTT	4	0	0	1	3																									
6	Years	55	0	1	5	105	12.0	74.0	1	5	2																				
MARC CROMBEEN Marc K McMaster																															
1996	HAM	1				0																									
TIM CRONK Tim FB 6'0 245 Bishop's B: 6/22/1987 Kingston, ON																															
2011	BC	12	0	1	2	6						6	1																		
ALFIE CROOKER Alf HB-FW 5'9 182 B: 1926																															
1950	HAM	12										10	2										2								
1951	HAM	1																													
1952	HAM	1																													
3	Years	14										10	2										2								
JEFF CROONEN Jeff LB-DT 6'3 240 London Beefeaters Jrs.; Western Ontario B: 9/2/1966 Hamilton, ON Draft: 5-40 1989 WPG																															
1989	WPG	8				0																									
1990	WPG	16				6			0	39																					
1991	HAM	4				4																									
1992	TOR	4				5																									
1993	TOR	3				3								1	2	2.0	2	0													
5	Years	35				18			0	39				1	2	2.0	2	0													
BILLY CROSS Billie Jerrel S 5'6 151 West Texas A&M B: 5/3/1929 Fry, TX Draft: 24-283 1951 CHIC Pro: N																															
1954	TOR+	13							3	43		15	3	38	181	4.8	25	1	11	191	17.4	62	1	13	147	11.3	55	16	373	23.3	38
BOBBY CROSS Robert Joe T 6'4 248 Kilgore JC; Stephen F. Austin State B: 7/4/1931 Ranger, TX D: 6/18/1989 Kilgore, TX Draft: 9-104 1952 CHIB Pro: N																															
1953	HAM	11																													
JIM CROTTY James Richard HB 5'10 192 Notre Dame B: 3/3/1938 Storm Lake, IA Draft: FS 1960 DAL; 12-136 1960 WAS Pro: N																															
1963	CAL	7							1															7	48	6.9	10				
ERIC CROUCH Eric Eugene QB 6'0 195 Nebraska B: 11/16/1978 Omaha, NE Draft: 3B-95 2002 STL Pro: EU																															
2006	TOR	7				0								6	36	6.0	20	0													
JIM CROUCH James Edward K-P 6'4 175 Foothill JC*; Shasta JC; Sacramento State B: 9/13/1968 Sacramento, CA																															
1993	SAC	18	3		2	1						156	0																		
RAY CROUSE Marlon Ray RB 5'11 214 Laney JC; Nevada-Las Vegas B: 3/16/1959 Oakland, CA Pro: N																															
1983	CAL+	16	6		1							68	11	124	703	5.7	67	9	47	444	9.4	39	2								
1986	BC	2										6	1	18	84	4.7	14	1	3	33	11.0	17	0					2	54	27.0	32
1987	BC	14	2		0	3						36	6	108	531	4.9	22	5	49	480	9.8	49	1					2	53	26.5	29
3	Years	32	8		1	3						110	18	250	1318	5.3	67	15	99	957	9.7	49	3					4	107	26.8	32
EDDIE CROWDER Eddie QB 6'0 170 Oklahoma B: 8/26/1931 Draft: 2-22 1953 NYG																															
1953	EDM	4							2	25				23	106	4.6		0						4	26	6.5					
DON CROWE Don HB-FB 5'11 190 none B: 1921																															
1949	TOR	4										3	0																		
1951	OTT	2																													
2	Years	6										3	0																		
MURRAY CROWE Murray E																															
1946	HAM	2																													
1947	HAM	1																													
2	Years	3																													
DAN CROWLEY Dan QB 6'2 190 Towson State B: 3/14/1973 Washington, DC																															
1995	BAL	18				1																									
1996	MTL	8	1		0	0																									
1999	EDM	18	1	0	0	0								6	36	6.0	9	0													
2000	EDM	18				1						6	1	19	143	7.5	20	1	1	0	0.0	0	0								
2001	EDM	18	1	0	1	0								1	19	19.0	19	0													
2002	OTT	18	4	0	0	2						24	4	41	275	6.7	35	4													
2003	OTT	3				1								9	57	6.3	17	0													
7	Years	101	7	0	1	5						30	5	76	530	7.0	35	5	1	0	0.0	0	0								
DWAYNE CROZIER Dwayne G 6'0 230 Morningside B: 3/30/1943																															
1967	WPG	9	0		1																										

Year	Team	GP	FM	FF	FR	TK	SK	YDS	IR	YDS	PD	PTS	TD	RA	YDS	AVG	LG	TD	REC	YDS	AVG	LG	TD	PR	YDS	AVG	LG	KOR	YDS	AVG	LG
MAURICE CRUM Maurice LB 6'0 220 Miami (Florida) B: 4/19/1969 Tampa, FL Pro: E																															
1993	SAS	18	0		1	87	1.0	9.0	1	0																		1	1	1.0	1
JASON CRUMB Jason CB-S-DH-WR 6'0 185 Okanagan Sun Jrs.; Saskatchewan B: 4/26/1973 Vancouver, BC Draft: 5-34 1999 BC																															
2000	BC	17	0	1	1	9													6	114	19.0	45	0								
2001	BC	13	0	0	1	17			1	33	0																	1	4	4.0	4
2002	BC	18	0	1	1	18																		1	0	0.0	0	1	3	3.0	3
2003	BC	8				11	1.0	12.0																				1	0	0.0	0
2004	BC	18	1	2	1	47	1.0	5.0	1	14	7			1	-9	-9.0	-9	0													
2005	BC	15	2	0	1	13			1	35	0																				
6	Years	89	3	4	5	115	2.0	17.0	3	82	7			1	-9	-9.0	-9	0	6	114	19.0	45	0	1	0	0.0	0	3	7	2.3	4
MIKE CRUMB Mike S 6'0 195 Okanagan Sun Jrs.; Saskatchewan B: 11/24/1970 Kelowna, BC																															
1998	BC	17				25																									
1999	BC	17				18													1	20	20.0	20	0								
2000	BC	15	0	0	1	31			1	1	1																				
2001	BC	16				15			1	3	0																				
2002	BC	14				16					1																				
2003	TOR	18				23																									
2004	TOR	15	0	1	0	23																									
2005	TOR	14	0	0	1	8																									
8	Years	126	0	1	2	159			2	4	2								1	20	20.0	20	0								
DWAYNE CRUMP Dwayne Anthony DB 5'11 180 Fresno CC; Pasadena CC; Fresno State B: 8/9/1950 Madera, CA Draft: 6A-137 1973 STL Pro: N																															
1977	MTL	8							1	5																					
1978	MTL	8	0		1																										
2	Years	16	0		1				1	5																					
RICHARD CRUMP Richard RB 6'0 205 Miami-Dade JC; Jacksonville State B: 2/28/1955 Cairo, GA Draft: 12-308 1978 BUF Pro: U																															
1975	WPG	10	0		2							12	2	101	425	4.2	27	2	16	166	10.4	42	0	6	57	9.5	27	9	168	18.7	64
1976	WPG	3	1		0							12	2	36	211	5.9	43	2	8	104	13.0	33	0	6	34	5.7	10				
1977	WPG	16	0		1							42	7	138	675	4.9	71	4	48	386	8.0	46	3	31	329	10.6	42	13	341	26.2	71
1978	WPG	16	9		2							36	6	80	471	5.9	103	3	48	585	12.2	78	3	42	363	8.6	40	27	773	28.6	65
1979	CAL	8	4		0							12	2	65	250	3.8	24	2	20	167	8.4	29	0	21	149	7.1	28	4	88	22.0	29
1979	OTT	6	4		2							18	3	71	331	4.7	21	3	17	149	8.8	30	0	11	101	9.2	20	6	112	18.7	33
1979	Year	14	8		2							30	5	136	581	4.3	24	5	37	316	8.5	30	0	32	250	7.8	28	10	200	20.0	33
1980	OTT+	16	8		2							74	12	228	1074	4.7	54	9	21	170	8.1	34	3	10	104	10.4	18	25	568	22.7	47
1981	OTT	8	3		0							18	3	97	440	4.5	23	3	20	166	8.3	42	0					2	46	23.0	27
7	Years	77	37		9							224	37	816	3877	4.8	103	28	198	1893	9.6	78	9	127	1137	9.0	42	86	2096	24.4	71
DARREL CRUTCHFIELD Darrel Akili DB 6'0 177 Clemson B: 2/26/1979 San Diego, CA Pro: N																															
2002	EDM	5				10					2																				
2003	EDM	17				30			1	8	8																				
2004	EDM	10	0	1	0	30					1																				
2005	MTL	12				32			1	0	4																				
2006	MTL	15				43			1	0	3																				
5	Years	59	0	1	0	145			3	8	18																				
JAMIE CRYSDALE Jamie C 6'4 289 Cincinnati B: 12/14/1968 Toronto, ON Draft: 4-29 1992 BC																															
1993	CAL	7				0																									
1994	CAL	18	0		1	1																									
1995	CAL	18	1		1	1													1	11	11.0	11	0								
1996	CAL	18	1		0	1																									
1997	CAL	18	1	0	0	1													1	10	10.0	10	0								
1998	CAL+	18	3	0	0	3																									
1999	CAL	18				2																									
2000	CAL	18	0	0	2	1						6	1																		
2001	CAL	18				0																									
2002	CAL	18	1	0	0	0																									
2003	CAL	18	2	0	1	1																									
2004	CAL	18	0	0	1	1																									
2005	CAL	11				0																									
13	Years	216	9	0	6	12						6	1						2	21	10.5	11	0								
TOM CUDNEY Thomas George WR 6'0 180 London Beefeaters Jrs. B: 5/7/1957 London, ON																															
1980	WPG	2																													
1981	TOR	1																													
2	Years	3																													
GEORGE CULLEN George HB Regina Dales Jrs. B: 1920																															
1946	SAS	4																													
CALVIN CULLIVER Calvin RB 6'1 210 Alabama B: 4/11/1955 Escambia, AL Draft: 8-212 1977 DEN																															
1978	BC	5	2		0							18	3	41	207	5.0	58	3	8	60	7.5	20	0					2	39	19.5	26
KNOX CULPEPPER W. Knox LB 6'0 220 Georgia B: 4/13/1963 Atlanta, GA Draft: TD 1985 JAC-USFL																															
1985	CAL	9	0		2							6	1	1	-1	-1.0	-1	0													
WILLIE CULPEPPER Willie James WR 5'11 155 Louisiana-Lafayette B: 3/27/1967 Jacksonville, FL Pro: N																															
1993	SAS	3	1		0	0						6	1						6	95	15.8	34	1	2	16	8.0	14	2	42	21.0	24
SHANNON CULVER Shannon D. WR 5'11 170 Los Angeles Pierce JC; Oklahoma State B: 5/10/1970 San Bernardino County, CA Pro: X																															
1994	BAL	1																	1	4	4.0	4	0	3	12	4.0	7				
1995	BAL	16	0		1	2						30	5	0	0		0	1	41	532	13.0	46	4	1	34	34.0	34	1	-8	-8.0	-8
2	Years	17	0		1	2						30	5					1	42	536	12.8	46	4	4	46	11.5	34	1	-8	-8.0	-8
AUBREY CUMMINGS Aubrey WR 5'11 170 Acadia B: 3/28/1970 Hamilton, ON Draft: 4-24 1998 CAL																															
1998	CAL	18	1	0	0	10						6	1						24	354	14.8	67	1								
1999	CAL	18				7						12	2						32	355	11.1	43	2								
2000	CAL	18	1	0	1	8						12	2						53	578	10.9	38	2	3	13	4.3	6				
2001	CAL	18	0	0	1	5						6	1	1	14	14.0	14	0	30	399	13.3	30	1								
2002	OTT	16	0	0	3	7						6	1						15	201	13.4	30	1								
2003	OTT	15	2	0	0	6								2	16	8.0	12	0	20	289	14.5	42	0								
2004	OTT	3				0													2	27	13.5	15	0								
7	Years	106	4	0	5	43						42	7	3	30	10.0	14	0	176	2203	12.5	67	7	3	13	4.3	6				
BRUCE CUMMINGS Bruce HB-FW 5'11 172 Toronto B: 1927																															
1950	OTT	12										16	1					1													
1951	OTT+	12										23	2					1													
1952	OTT	10										8	0																		
1953	OTT	10										1	0																		
4	Years	44										48	3					2													
BURT CUMMINGS Burtland S 5'8 175 North Dakota B: 11/19/1965 London, England Draft: 4-27 1988 HAM																															
1989	WPG	4	0		1	12																									
1990	WPG	3				2																									
1991	WPG	12				10																		6	16	2.7	12	5	71	14.2	24
1993	BC	3				0																									
1993	OTT	6	0		1	8			1	6																					
1993	Year	9	0		1	8			1	6																					
4	Years	22	0		2	32			1	6														6	16	2.7	12	5	71	14.2	24
JOE CUMMINGS Joe E 6'1 190 Alabama B: 1933																															
1956	OTT	2																													
KEVIN CUMMINGS Kevin RB 5'11 175 Central State (Ohio) B: 9/12/1964																															
1987	TOR	2				0						6	1	13	46	3.5	17	1	2	10	5.0	7	0					4	80	20.0	46
1988	TOR	8	2		0							18	3	43	200	4.7	14	2	15	205	13.7	42	1					1	20	20.0	20
2	Years	10	2		0	0						24	4	56	246	4.4	17	3	17	215	12.6	42	1					5	100	20.0	46

Year	Team	GP	FM	FF	FR	TK	SK	YDS	IR	YDS	PD	PTS	TD	RA	YDS	AVG	LG	TD	REC	YDS	AVG	LG	TD	PR	YDS	AVG	LG	KOR	YDS	AVG	LG
JEFF CUMMINS Jeffrey M. DT 6'6 270 El Camino JC; Oregon B: 5/25/1969 Pro: X																															
1994	LV	9				15	1.0	0.0			3																	2	15	7.5	
1995	TOR	17	0		1	43	7.0	33.0			6	6	1																		
1996	OTT	18	0		3	48	8.0	62.0			5																	3	46	15.3	21
1998	HAM	14	0	1	1	23	6.0	43.0			2																				
1999	HAM	18	0	1	0	18	5.0	20.0			5								1	14	14.0	14	0								
2000	HAM	18				34	7.0	33.0			4																				
6	Years	94	0	2	5	181	34.0	191.0				6	1						1	14	14.0	14	0					5	61	12.2	21
WAYNE CUNCIC Wayne OG-OT 6'0 235 Utah State B: 6/14/1950 Draft: 4-29 1973 TOR																															
1974	TOR	16																													
1975	TOR	15																													
1976	CAL	16	0		1																										
3	Years	47	0		1																										
BOB CUNNINGHAM Bob HB-FB 6'0 193 B: 9/26/1927 D: 10/8/2006																															
1948	MTL	9										35	7					2					5								
1949	MTL	11										53	10					4					6								
1950	MTL	2																													
1951	MTL	7																													
1953	OTT	12										20	4					4													
1955	OTT	9										5	1	8	47	5.9	13	0	4	47	11.8	15	0					2	47	23.5	30
6	Years	50										113	22	8	47	5.9	13	10	4	47	11.8	15	11					2	47	23.5	30
CHRIS CUNNINGHAM Chris WR 5'7 174 Southern Methodist B: 8/9/1981																															
2004	TOR	7				0								1	-5	-5.0	-5	0	10	149	14.9	51	0	7	55	7.9	12	4	59	14.8	28
JIMMY CUNNINGHAM James Douglas (The Jet) WR 5'7 160 Howard B: 1/1/1973 Houston, TX Pro: X																															
1995	TOR	6	1		0	3						18	3	1	2	2.0	2	0	15	147	9.8	20	0	28	581	20.8	108	19	436	22.9	39
1996	TOR*	18	2		0	2						18	3	1	9	9.0	9	0	62	800	12.9	37	1	85	976	11.5	93	38	693	18.2	49
1997	BC	1				0						6	1						8	85	10.6	39	1	1	9	9.0	9	4	118	29.5	38
1998	BC	4	0	0	1	0						12	2						15	202	13.5	28	1	7	150	21.4	89	8	144	18.0	28
1999	BC*	18	6	0	3	1			1	3	0	36	6	2	10	5.0	6	0	41	564	13.8	58	3	89	662	7.4	81	47	1032	22.0	98
2000	BC	16	3	0	0	0						18	3						54	726	13.4	52	3	58	344	5.9	24	56	1090	19.5	47
2002	TOR	4				0													9	106	11.8	30	0	7	61	8.7	18	14	315	22.5	51
7	Years	67	12	0	4	6			1	3	0	108	18	4	21	5.3	9	0	204	2630	12.9	58	9	275	2783	10.1	108	186	3828	20.6	98
RICK CUNNINGHAM Patrick Dante Ross OG-OT 6'7 315 Oregon State; Sacramento CC; Texas A&M B: 1/4/1967 Draft: 4D-106 1990 IND Pro: EN																															
2000	MTL	7				2																									
2000	EDM	9				0																									
2000	Year	16				2																									
2001	EDM	5				0																									
2002	MTL	12				1																									
3	Years	24				3																									
TROY CUNNINGHAM Troy DL 6'3 260 Concordia (Quebec) B: 10/29/1981 Kingston, ON Draft: 5-40 2004 BC																															
2005	HAM	3				2																									
2006	HAM	5				3																									
2	Years	8				5																									
TONY CURCILLO Anthony, Jr. LB-QB 6'1 200 Ohio State B: 5/27/1931 Long Branch, NJ Draft: 6A-64 1953 CHIC Pro: N																															
1956	HAM	7										24	4	39	335	8.6	34	4													
1957	HAM+	13							3	19				3	13	4.3	7	0													
1958	HAM+	12							3	7				1	7	7.0	7	0													
1960	HAM	2																	1	1	1.0	1	0								
4	Years	34							6	26		24	4	43	355	8.3	34	4	1	1	1.0	1	0								
HARDIMAN CURETON Hardiman Dunn OG-DG-LB-OT 5'11 235 Los Angeles Valley JC; UCLA B: 12/8/1933 D: 10/1/2003 Draft: 26-312 1956 LARM																															
1956	TOR+	14							4	16																					
1957	OTT	12																						1	0	0.0	0				
1958	OTT+	13							3	2																					
1959	OTT	14							1	7																					
1960	HAM	12																										1	10	10.0	10
1961	HAM+	13																													
1962	HAM+	14																													
1963	HAM+	14																													
1964	HAM	3																													
9	Years	109							8	25														1	0	0.0	0	1	10	10.0	10
RON CURL Ronald C. OG 6'2 250 Michigan State B: 7/6/1949 Chicago, IL Draft: 12-298 1972 PIT Pro: W																															
1973	TOR	3	0		1																										
1974	TOR	1																													
2	Years	4	0		1																										
CURRIE HB-E																															
1949	HAM	1																													
AIRESE CURRIE Airese K. WR 5'10 186 Clemson B: 11/16/1982 Columbia, SC Draft: 5-140 2005 CHIB Pro: N																															
2009	HAM	6	2	0	0	2													12	171	14.3	39	0	7	40	5.7	15	2	31	15.5	22
ANDY CURRIE Andrew OT 6'4 240 Acadia B: 5/10/1951 Draft: 2B-17 1974 HAM																															
1974	HAM	13																													
1975	WPG	1																													
2	Years	14																													
BILL CURRIE Bill FW McMaster																															
1954	BC	1																													
BOB CURRIE Bob OT-DT 6'3 250 Hawaii B: 5/9/1948																															
1972	BC	3																													
1973	BC	7																													
2	Years	10																													
HERSCHEL CURRIE Herschel Lamont DB 6'1 190 Chabot JC; Oregon State B: 9/8/1965 Chicago, IL Pro: N																															
1994	SAC	3				4																									
JASON CURRIE Jason K-P 6'3 208 Nelson Lords Jrs.; St. Mary's (Nova Scotia) B: 4/10/1978 Hamilton, ON																															
2003	HAM	15	1	0	0	5						14	0																		
2004	HAM	10				1						32	0																		
2	Years	25	1	0	0	6						46	0																		
BOBBY CURRINGTON Bob HB 6'0 205 North Carolina Central B: 8/16/1941 Durham, NC Draft: 8-107 1964 PIT																															
1965	TOR	2												4	18	4.5	14	0	1	7	7.0	7	0					5	58	11.6	21
ALMONDO CURRY Almondo Alfonzo CB 5'8 177 Virginia B: 8/18/1980 Hampton, VA																															
2004	MTL*	18	0	3	0	56	1.0	3.0	5	140	8	6	1																		
2005	MTL	10				32			4	53	1																				
2006	SAS	8	0	1	0	17			1	11	6																				
3	Years	36	0	4	0	105	1.0	3.0	10	204	15	6	1																		
IVORY CURRY Ivory DB 5'11 185 Florida B: 2/6/1961 Miami, FL D: 8/23/1989 Brandon, FL Draft: TD 1983 TB-USFL Pro: N																															
1983	OTT	2																										4	101	25.3	35
JAMES CURRY James E. DT-DE 6'2 245 Nevada-Reno B: 10/26/1957 Chowchilla, CA																															
1983	BC	9	1		1		6.0																					1	0	0.0	0
1983	TOR	2					1.5																								
1983	Year	11	1		1		7.5																					1	0	0.0	0
1984	TOR*	13	0		3		22.0																								
1985	TOR*	16					12.0																								
1986	OTT	8					10.0																								
1987	SAS+	17	0		2	31	11.0																								
1988	SAS	14	0		2	15	7.0																								

Year	Team	GP	FM	FF	FR	TK	SK	YDS	IR	YDS	PD	PTS	TD	RA	YDS	AVG	LG	TD	REC	YDS	AVG	LG	TD	PR	YDS	AVG	LG	KOR	YDS	AVG	LG
1989	SAS+	14	0		1	25	16.0		1	0																					
7	Years	91	1		9	71	85.5		1	0																		1	0	0.0	0
NATE CURRY Nathaniel Tyrone, Jr. WR 5'10 196 Georgia Tech B: 3/11/1982 Miami, FL Pro: E																															
2007	HAM	18	1	1	1	0						6	1						30	320	10.7	39	1	3	28	9.3	15	15	350	23.3	60
2008	CAL	2	1	0	0	0																		9	68	7.6	15	1	16	16.0	16
2	Years	20	2	1	1	0						6	1						30	320	10.7	39	1	12	96	8.0	15	16	366	22.9	60
PHIL CURRY Phillip LB 6'1 240 Cincinnati B: 1/3/1976 Pontiac, MI																															
1999	WPG	10				43	2.0	23.0																							
2000	WPG	5				12	1.0	2.0																							
2	Years	15				55	3.0	25.0																							
SEDRICK CURRY Sedrick Demon DB 6'1 197 Texas A&M B: 11/23/1976 Houston, TX Pro: X																															
2001	BC	15	0	0	1	25					2																				
2002	BC	8				22			1	7	1																				
2	Years	23	0	0	1	47			1	7	3																				
WALTER CURRY Walter Morrell DT 6'4 284 Albany State B: 6/18/1981 Daytona Beach, FL Pro: E																															
2008	TOR	8				17	2.0	13.0																							
2009	TOR	5				3					1																	1	7	7.0	7
2	Years	13				20	2.0	13.0			1																	1	7	7.0	7
BUCKY CURTIS Ernoot Jaokoon E 6'3 212 Vondorbilt B: 1020 Draft: 2 26 1061 CLE																															
1955	TOR	11							2	27		30	6						39	642	16.5	40	6					2	20	10.0	12
1956	TOR	14										49	8						48	927	19.3	50	8					5	48	9.6	29
2	Years	25							2	27		79	14						87	1569	18.0	50	14					7	68	9.7	29
BUD CURTIS Bud HB 6'0 175 Saskatoon Hilltops Jrs. B: 1938																															
1959	SAS	12												5	7	1.4	2	0													
1960	SAS	8	0		1																			2	10	5.0	9	1	20	20.0	20
2	Years	20	0		1									5	7	1.4	2	0						2	10	5.0	9	1	20	20.0	20
CHUCK CURTIS Charles QB 6'4 205 Texas Christian B: 1936 Draft: 7-85 1957 NYG																															
1957	WPG	2	2											3	-14	-4.7	0	0													
ULYSSES CURTIS Ulysses (Crazy Legs) HB 5'10 176 Florida A&M B: 5/10/1926 Albion, MI																															
1950	TOR+	11										70	14					7					7								
1951	TOR+	10										35	7					5					2								
1952	TOR+	12										80	16					6					10								
1953	TOR	12										30	6					3					3								
1954	TOR	13										20	4	73	303	4.2	31	3	17	268	15.8	48	1								
5	Years	58										235	47	73	303	4.2	31	24	17	268	15.8	48	23								
BRENT CURVEY Brent Akeef DT 6'0 295 Iowa State B: 3/15/1985 Houston, TX																															
2007	SAS	1				1																									
2008	SAS	1				1																									
2	Years	2				2																									
BERNIE CUSTIS Bernard E. OHB-QB-FW 6'0 183 Syracuse B: 1928 Draft: 11-135 1951 CLE																															
1951	HAM+	12										35	7					7													
1952	HAM	12										25	5					5													
1953	HAM	13										27	5					3					2								
1954	HAM+	13							1	35		40	8	104	472	4.5	38	4	37	399	10.8	60	4	3	18	6.0	11	13	364	28.0	51
1955	OTT	8							3	46		10	2	17	66	3.9	10	0	4	52	13.0	24	1					3	69	23.0	27
5	Years	58							4	81		137	27	121	538	4.4	38	19	41	451	11.0	60	7	3	18	6.0	11	16	433	27.1	51
DAVE CUTLER Dave K-P 5'10 200 Simon Fraser B: 10/17/1945 Biggar, SK Draft: 1-4 1969 EDM																															
1969	EDM	14	1		0							77	0																		
1970	EDM	16										106	0	1	0	0.0	0	0													
1971	EDM	16	2		0							85	0																		
1972	EDM	16										126	0																		
1973	EDM	16	2		0							133	0																		
1974	EDM	16	1		0							144	0																		
1975	EDM	16	1		0							169	0																		
1976	EDM	16	1		1							126	0																		
1977	EDM*	16										195	0																		
1978	EDM*	16										167	0																		
1979	EDM	16	1		0							140	0	1	13	13.0	13	0													
1980	EDM+	16	0		1							158	0																		
1981	EDM	16										175	0																		
1982	EDM	16										170	0																		
1983	EDM	16										143	0																		
1984	EDM	16										123	0																		
16	Years	254	9		2							2237	0	2	13	6.5	13	0													
PERCY CUTLER Percy C 6'0 195 none																															
1950	WPG	2																													
FRANK CUTOLO Frank J. WR 5'10 181 Mississippi*; Palm Beach CC*; Eastern Illinois B: 1/8/1978 Fort Lauderdale, FL																															
2003	BC	18	4	0	0	2						54	9	1	7	7.0	7	0	64	908	14.2	70	8	60	553	9.2	81	33	693	21.0	42
2004	BC	18	4	0	2	3						54	9						47	786	16.7	102	9	42	302	7.2	46				
2005	OTT	9				0						6	1	1	8	8.0	8	0	21	222	10.6	26	1	1	9	9.0	9	3	35	11.7	15
3	Years	45	8	0	2	5						114	19	2	15	7.5	8	0	132	1916	14.5	102	18	103	864	8.4	81	36	728	20.2	42
CHRIS CVETKOVIC Chris FB 6'2 235 Concordia (Quebec) B: 6/28/1977 Hamilton, ON																															
2002	SAS	18	1	0	0	3																									
2003	SAS	3				0																									
2004	WPG	18	1	0	0	16																						2	9	4.5	9
2005	WPG	18				11																									
2006	WPG	18				4																									
2007	WPG	9				3																									
2008	WPG	18				11																									
2009	WPG	18	1	1	0	12																									
2011	WPG	18				3																									
9	Years	138	3	1	0	63																						2	9	4.5	9
SAM CVIJANOVICH Sam LB 6'1 220 California Lutheran B: 5/26/1950																															
1974	TOR	16	0		2				7	53																					
1975	TOR	16	0		2				2	10																					
1976	TOR	11							1	2																					
1977	BC	5																													
1977	OTT	3																													
1977	Year	8																													
4	Years	48	0		4				10	65																					
GRANT CVITANICH Grant Peter DT 6'3 252 San Francisco State B: 3/21/1950 San Francisco, CA Pro: W																															
1972	CAL	1																													
JOHN CVITANOVICH John OG 6'1 222 Vancouver Blue Bombers Jrs.																															
1954	BC	6																													
1955	BC	8																													
2	Years	14																													
MARCO CYNCAR Marco SB0WR 6'0 175 Edmonton Wildcats Jrs.; Alberta B: 4/13/1958 Edmonton, AB Draft: TE 1979 EDM																															
1980	HAM	16	0		1							2	0						13	180	13.8	27	0	20	95	4.8	9	7	139	19.9	24
1981	EDM	16										6	1						40	541	13.5	28	1	6	64	10.7	18	2	2	1.0	1
1982	EDM	8																	6	87	14.5	38	0								
1983	EDM	15	0		1							6	1	1	1	1.0	1	0	16	298	18.6	30	1					1	0	0.0	0
1984	EDM	16	1		0							6	1						26	460	17.7	48	1								

Year	Team	GP	FM	FF	FR	TK	SK	YDS	IR	YDS	PD	PTS	TD	RA	YDS	AVG	LG	TD	REC	YDS	AVG	LG	TD	PR	YDS	AVG	LG	KOR	YDS	AVG	LG
1985	EDM	16	1		0							6	1						27	372	13.8	41	1					3	5	1.7	3
1986	EDM	18	1		0							18	3						37	522	14.1	34	3					2	9	4.5	9
1987	EDM	18	1		1	3						18	3						43	710	16.5	58	3					5	17	3.4	12
1988	EDM	18	0		1	0						2	0						31	419	13.5	32	0								
1989	EDM	17				0						6	1						11	193	17.5	46	1					1	0	0.0	0
1990	EDM	18				2													26	385	14.8	34	0					1	-1	-1.0	-1
1991	EDM	14				0													13	178	13.7	35	0					1	0	0.0	0
12	Years	190	4		4	5						70	11	1	1	1.0	1	0	289	4345	15.0	58	11	26	159	6.1	18	23	171	7.4	24
ZAC CYPERT Zachary N. LB 6'2 210 North Texas B: 5/17/1958																															
1983	MTL	7	0		1		1.5																								
1984	MTL	9					0.5																								
2	Years	16	0		1		2.0																								
BARRIE CYR Barrie OHB-DB 5'10 180 Calgary Bronks Jrs. B: 1935																															
1958	CAL	11										6	1	4	13	3.3	9	0	5	58	11.6	17	1								
1959	CAL	9																	1	2	2.0	2	0								
1960	CAL	4																	1	11	11.0	11	0	1	0	0.0	0				
1961	CAL	12																	1	10	10.0	10	0	1	0	0.0	0				
4	Years	36										6	1	4	13	3.3	9	0	8	81	10.1	17	1	2	0	0.0	0				
CLIFF CYR Cliff T 6'2 210																															
1952	CAL	15			1																							1	25	25.0	25
WARREN CYRUS Warren E Kentucky State; Tennessee State																															
1948	MTL	1																													
WALT CYZ Walter T-G-HB 6'0 232 Regina Bombers Jrs. B: 1931																															
1952	SAS	1																													
1954	BC	13																													
1955	BC	2																													
3	Years	16																													
DICK CZAP Richard DE 6'2 250 Nebraska B: 12/7/1943 Bay City, MI Draft: RS-5-45 1966 BUF; 12-183 1966 CLE																															
1968	WPG	2																													
ED CZAPLAK Edmund T-G 6'0 215 Arizona State B: 2/9/1927 NY																															
1949	HAM	12																													
JOE CZECZEK Joe E Syracuse																															
1947	HAM	11										5	1										1								
DEWEY CZUPKA Dwaine LB 5'10 215 Utah State B: 3/1/1942 Rock Island, IL																															
1967	BC	16	0		1				5	32																					
WALE DADA Omowale DB 5'11 194 Eastern Illinois; Saddleback JC; Washington State B: 5/31/1983 Chicago, IL Pro: EU																															
2008	EDM	3				5																									
TED DAFFER Terrell Edwin G-T 6'0 200 Tennessee B: 9/24/1929 Norfolk, VA D: 3/1/2006 Atlanta, GA Draft: 21-248 1952 CHIB Pro: N																															
1955	OTT	6							1	0																					
FRANK D'AGOSTINO Francis Joseph T 6'1 245 Auburn B: 3/11/1934 Philadelphia, PA D: 9/28/1997 Tampa, FL Draft: 2-16 1956 PHI Pro: N																															
1957	HAM	2																													
DARCY DAHLEM Darcy L-P 5'11 185 North Dakota B: 3/30/1970 Westlock, AB																															
1994	SAS	1				0						4	0																		
1996	SAS	1				0						7	0																		
2	Years	2				0						11	0																		
DOUG DAIGNEAULT Douglas OHB-DB 6'2 192 Clemson B: 8/4/1936 Valleyfield, QC																															
1960	OTT	14							1	23				1	2	2.0	2	0	3	66	22.0	32	0	7	18	2.6	12	12	327	27.3	48
1961	OTT	10							5	42		6	1	14	48	3.4	6	1	4	65	16.3	23	0	8	37	4.6	9	6	81	13.5	23
1962	OTT	6																													
1963	OTT	4												1	4	4.0	4	0						1	4	4.0	4				
1963	WPG	9							1																						
1963	Year	13							1					1	4	4.0	4	0						1	4	4.0	4				
1964	MTL	14												2	7	3.5	4	0	2	13	6.5	10	0								
1965	MTL	14	0		1				1	46				1	3	3.0	3	0						1	0	0.0	0	3	38	12.7	19
6	Years	62	0		1				8	111		6	1	19	64	3.4	6	1	9	144	16.0	32	0	17	59	3.5	12	21	446	21.2	48
JOHN DAILEY John LB 6'3 232 Auburn B: 10/5/1962 Birmingham, AL																															
1985	EDM	9	0		1				1	5		6	1																		
DICK DALATRI Dick OT-C-DT 6'1 236 North Carolina State B: 1933																															
1962	MTL	14																													
1963	MTL	14																													
1965	MTL	8	1		0																										
3	Years	36	1		0																										
BURKE DALES Burke P 6'2 208 Concordia (Ontario) B: 2/16/1977 Collingwood, ON																															
2005	CAL	18	2	0	1	3						4	0																		
2006	CAL+	18	1	0	0	0						5	0						1	11	11.0	11	0								
2007	CAL	10	1	0	0	1						4	0																		
2008	CAL	18	1	0	0	3						6	0																		
2009	CAL+	18	1	0	0	2						10	0																		
2010	CAL*	18	2	0	0	4						5	0																		
2011	CAL*	18	1	0	0	2						11	0																		
7	Years	118	9	0	1	15						45	0						1	11	11.0	11	0								
PETER DALLA RIVA Peter TE 6'3 222 Burlington Braves Jrs. B: 12/11/1946 Teviso, Italy																															
1968	MTL	14										12	2						8	129	16.1	30	2								
1969	MTL	14	0		1							18	3						30	492	16.4	47	2					1	1	1.0	1
1970	MTL	14	1		0							6	1						43	609	14.2	38	1					1	17	17.0	17
1971	MTL	9																	18	212	11.8	24	0								
1972	MTL*	14										30	5						44	607	13.8	44	5								
1973	MTL*	14	1		0							18	3						29	415	14.3	28	3								
1974	MTL	16			1							48	8						37	549	14.8	38	8								
1975	MTL*	16	1		1							50	7						56	743	13.3	43	7								
1976	MTL	16										60	10						56	763	13.6	36	10								
1977	MTL+	16										48	8	2	4	2.0	5	0	50	676	13.5	30	8								
1978	MTL	12										26	4						33	557	16.9	42	4								
1979	MTL	14																	10	210	21.0	57	0					1	10	10.0	10
1980	MTL	12										6	1						11	174	15.8	27	1					1	0	0.0	0
1981	MTL	16										18	3						25	277	11.1	22	3								
14	Years	197	3		3							340	55	2	4	2.0	5	0	450	6413	14.3	57	54					4	28	7.0	17
KEVIN DALLIDAY Kevin OT 6'3 250 Carleton B: 5/30/1959 Peterborough, ON Draft: TE 1982 OTT																															
1983	OTT	7	0		1																										
1984	OTT	14																													
2	Years	21	0		1																										
ANTICO DALTON Antico Lamont LB 6'1 242 Hampton B: 12/31/1975 Eden, NC Draft: 6B-199 1999 MIN Pro: EN																															
2005	EDM	12	0	1	0	13																									
2006	EDM	16	0	3	1	32	4.0	8.0																							
2007	EDM	6				12																									
3	Years	34	0	4	1	57	4.0	8.0																							
BEAVER DALTON William E-G																															
1947	OTT	2										5	1										1								
1948	OTT	1																													
1949	OTT	1																													
3	Years	4										5	1										1								
MIKE D'AMATO Michael Anthony HB 6'2 205 Hofstra B: 3/3/1943 New York, NY Draft: 10-264 1968 NYJ Pro: N																															

Year	Team	GP	FM	FF	FR	TK	SK	YDS	IR	YDS	PD	PTS	TD	RA	YDS	AVG	LG	TD	REC	YDS	AVG	LG	TD	PR	YDS	AVG	LG	KOR	YDS	AVG	LG
1969	MTL	8							2	20																		22	556	25.3	37
BILL DAMIANO William R. E Niagara B: 3/29/1925 Niagara Falls, NY D: 7/26/1997 Boca Raton, FL																															
1948	HAM	12										5	1					1													
KEN DANCHUK Kenneth HB-FB 5'11 193 British Columbia B: 3/6/1942 Edmonton, AB																															
1965	CAL	8																													
1966	WPG	14	0		2				1			0	0																		
2	Years	22	0		2				1			0	0																		
AL DANCY Al C 5'11 204 Toronto Draft: 1952 TOR																															
1952	TOR	1																													
LUKI DANELIUK Luki T-G 6'4 220 Windsor AKO Jrs. B: 1934																															
1955	OTT	9																													
1956	OTT	14																													
2	Years	23																													
TIM DANIEL Tim WR 5'11 184 Florida A&M B: 9/14/1969 Atlanta, GA Draft: 11-302 1992 DAL																															
1994	WPG	4										18	3						9	168	18.7	40	2	3	91	30.3	85	6	111	18.5	
1995	WPG	10	2		1	3						6	1						30	342	11.4	52	1	25	175	7.0	35	10	191	19.1	35
2	Years	14	2		1	3						24	4						39	510	13.1	52	3	28	266	9.5	85	16	302	18.9	35
BILL DANIELS Bill C Southern University																															
1948	WPG	12																													
DAN DANIELS Dan E 5'9 168																															
1946	MTL	7																													
DAVE DANIELS David CB 5'11 175 Tennessee State B: 8/16/1962 Albany, GA																															
1986	MTL	15	1		3				4	37																					
1987	TOR	5				22	1.0		0	2																					
2	Years	20	1		3	22	1.0		4	39																					
HARRY DANIELS Harry G-HB 6'0 210 Manitoba B: 1924																															
1946	WPG	2																													
1948	TOR	1																													
1950	TOR	6																													
1951	TOR	6																													
1951	MTL	2																													
1951	Year	8																													
4	Years	15																													
JIM DANIELS James DB 6'1 185 Texas A&M B: 11/11/1951 Draft: 7-180 1975 OAK																															
1975	WPG	7							1	81		6	1																		
SHAWN DANIELS Shawn FB 5'11 240 Snow JC; Bowling Green State B: 9/3/1966 Montreal, QC Draft: 3-19 1988 HAM																															
1989	SAS	10	3		0	0								20	48	2.4	7	0	10	100	10.0	19	0					2	41	20.5	33
1990	OTT	2				0								4	23	5.8	8	0	1	8	8.0	8	0								
1991	OTT	16	1		0	8						36	6	52	229	4.4	26	5	4	38	9.5	25	1					1	0	0.0	0
1992	OTT	14	0		1	6								9	49	5.4	31	0	10	41	4.1	12	0								
1993	OTT	18	2		0	5						18	3	52	238	4.6	20	2	43	326	7.6	28	1								
1994	SAS	12				3						12	2	18	67	3.7	9	1	8	40	5.0	14	1								
1994	CAL	6	1		0	2						6	1	15	55	3.7	9	1	1	6	6.0	6	0								
1994	Year	18	1		0	5						18	3	33	122	3.7	9	2	9	46	5.1	14	1								
1995	CAL	18	2		0	3						30	5	61	251	4.1	17	4	6	28	4.7	13	1								
1996	OTT	12				3								18	37	2.1	6	0	11	75	6.8	12	0								
1997	SAS	8	0	0	1	2						20	3	13	31	2.4	7	3	14	110	7.9	31	0								
1998	SAS	18	1	0	1	2						24	4	45	156	3.5	16	3	24	241	10.0	33	1								
1999	SAS	17	0	0	2	4						6	1	41	140	3.4	10	1	16	139	8.7	22	0								
2000	EDM	18				1						36	6	29	79	2.7	6	4	10	165	16.5	39	2								
2001	EDM	15	0	0	3	4						12	2	18	64	3.6	13	2	5	29	5.8	10	0								
2002	TOR	17	2	0	0	2						12	2	29	111	3.8	15	2	4	23	5.8	11	0					1	21	21.0	21
14	Years	195	12	0	8	45						212	35	424	1578	3.7	31	28	167	1369	8.2	39	7					4	62	15.5	33
WILLIAM DANIELS William DE 6'3 250 Alabama State B: 2/13/1958 Chicago, IL Draft: 6-158 1981 LARM																															
1981	CAL	2					1.0																								
VINCE DANIELSEN Vince SB 6'4 210 British Columbia B: 11/26/1971 Vancouver, BC Draft: Bonus-3 1994 CAL																															
1994	CAL	18				9						6	1						21	274	13.0	23	1								
1995	CAL	18	1		0	3						36	6						55	683	12.4	32	6								
1996	CAL	18	1		1	7						24	4	0	0		0	1	43	506	11.8	44	3					1	0	0.0	0
1997	CAL+	17	0	0	2	0						36	6						91	1174	12.9	52	6					2	1	0.5	1
1998	CAL+	15	1	0	0	0						36	6						83	1039	12.5	49	6					1	0	0.0	0
1999	CAL	18	1	0	0	1						42	7						71	923	13.0	42	7								
2000	CAL	18	1	0	0	0						12	2						58	892	15.4	54	2								
2001	CAL	13	1	0	0	0						12	2						46	577	12.5	40	2								
8	Years	135	6	0	3	20						204	34					1	468	6068	13.0	54	33					4	1	0.3	1
ERNIE DANJEAN Ernest Joseph LB 6'0 230 Auburn B: 3/5/1934 New Orleans, LA D: 6/19/1995 Draft: 19-220 1957 GB Pro: N																															
1959	HAM+	13							3	10																					
1960	HAM	3																										1	5	5.0	5
1960	CAL	3																													
1960	Year	6																										1	5	5.0	5
1961	CAL	14																													
1962	CAL	16	0		4				1																						
1963	CAL	11																													
5	Years	57	0		4				4	10																		1	5	5.0	5
STEVE DANKEWICH Steve FB 5'10 189 Winnipeg Rods Jrs.; Winnipeg Rams Ints.																															
1957	CAL	7							1	0																					
BILL DANYCHUK Bill OG-OT 6'3 240 Tennessee B: 8/29/1940																															
1965	HAM	14	0		1																										
1966	HAM	14	0		1																										
1967	HAM+	14			2																										
1968	HAM*	14																													
1969	HAM	14	0		1																										
1970	HAM*	13	0		1																										
1971	HAM	14																													
1972	HAM+	14	0		1																										
1973	HAM+	14																													
1974	HAM	7																													
1975	HAM	13																													
11	Years	145	0		7																										
ART DARCH Arthur Clifford OG-DG 6'1 222 none B: 1932 Niagara Falls, ON																															
1953	HAM	14																													
1954	HAM	14																													
1955	HAM	12																													
1956	HAM	1																													
1957	HAM	9																	0	7		7	0								
1960	TOR	14																													
6	Years	64																	0	7		7	0								
J.P. DARCHE Jean-Philippe C 6'0 245 McGill B: 2/28/1975 Montreal, QC Draft: 3-21 1999 TOR Pro: N																															
1999	TOR	17				16																									
MARIO DaRE Mario Selveo T 6'2 225 Southern California B: 5/21/1933 Crockett, CA Draft: 5-50 1955 CHIC																															
1955	WPG	2																													
TREY DARILEK Trey Keith OL 6'5 310 Texas-El Paso B: 4/23/1981 San Antonio, TX Draft: 4B-131 2004 PHI Pro: N																															

Year	Team	GP	FM	FF	FR	TK	SK	YDS	IR	YDS	PD	PTS	TD	RA	YDS	AVG	LG	TD	REC	YDS	AVG	LG	TD	PR	YDS	AVG	LG	KOR	YDS	AVG	LG
2007	EDM	5	3	0	1	2																									
FRANK DARK Frank Leon DB 6'0 180 Ferrum JC; Virginia Union B: 12/20/1953 Richmond, VA																															
1979	WPG	2							2	4																				
1979	SAS	6	2		1				3	128		6	1											7	33	4.7	14				
1979	Year	8	2		1				5	132		6	1											7	33	4.7	14				
MYLES DARLING Myles DB 6'3 200 South Carolina State B: 1/3/1962 Waynesboro, GA Draft: TD 1985 ORL-USFL																															
1985	MTL	7							1	36																				
1986	MTL	1							1	0																				
2	Years	8							2	36																				
SAM DARRAGH Sam DB 5'10 178 McMaster B: 10/17/1931 Toronto, ON D: 3/8/1997																															
1955	MTL	12							3	35				4	8	2.0	5	0						5	23	4.6	6				
JIM DATRICE James RB 5'9 190 St. Mary's (California) B: 1942																															
1975	HAM	4	1		1									44	123	2.8	18	0	5	7	1.4	10	0								
GERRY DATTILIO Gerry QB 6'1 200 Verdun Maple Leafs Jrs.; Northern Colorado B: 6/11/1953 Montreal, QC Draft: TE 1975 MTL																															
1975	TOR	1																													
1976	MTL	16	1		4							6	1	4	15	3.8	19	0	2	19	9.5	12	0								
1977	MTL	16	0		1																			1	9	9.0	9				
1978	MTL	16	3		0							6	1	31	212	6.8	27	1	1	14	14.0	14	0								
1979	MTL	16	1		0									6	18	3.0	15	0	4	80	20.0	38	0								
1980	MTL+	16	4		1							12	2	61	324	5.3	24	2													
1981	MTL	16	2		0									12	49	4.1	19	0													
1982	CAL	16	4		0							24	4	46	254	5.5	60	4													
1983	CAL	16													13	65	5.0	30	0													
1984	MTL	16											6	1	14	59	4.2	10	1													
1985	MTL	16													2	-3	-1.5	0	0	1	13	13.0	13	0								
11	Years	161	15		6							54	9	189	993	5.3	60	8	8	126	15.8	38	0	1	9	9.0	9				
CHRIS DAUSIN Chris C 6'4 285 Texas A&M B: 12/18/1969 Pro: E																															
1995	SHR	1				0																									
BOB DAVENPORT Bob Woodrow FB 6'0 210 UCLA B: 4/30/1933 Draft: 25-301 1956 CLE																															
1956	WPG	16	5		0							24	4	140	677	4.8	24	2	12	105	8.8	15	2					3	62	20.7	24
1957	WPG	2													20	91	4.6	14	0	1	-9	-9.0	-9	0								
2	Years	18	5		0							24	4	160	768	4.8	24	2	13	96	7.4	15	2					3	62	20.7	24
DUTCH DAVEY Lloyd HB 5'10 229 B: 1923 Stratford, ON																															
1946	OTT	2																													
COLT DAVID Colt Justin K-P 5'10 175 Louisiana State B: 11/26/1985 Bedford, TX																															
2010	MTL	3				0						35	0																		
DREW DAVID Drew Daniel RB 6'1 215 Georgia B: 12/3/1971 Cairo, GA																															
1995	BIR	15				12																									
COTTON DAVIDSON Francis Marion QB 6'0 182 Baylor B: 11/30/1931 Gatesville, TX Draft: 1-5 1954 BAL Pro: N																															
1958	CAL	4													3	5	1.7	14	0													
LINDEN DAVIDSON Linden DT-DE 6'4 253 Ottawa B: 9/24/1955 Draft: 5-43 1978 OTT																															
1979	WPG	7																													
1979	HAM	6																													
1979	Year	13																													
1980	HAM	12																									1	-8	-8.0	-8
2	Years	19																									1	-8	-8.0	-8
ROB DAVIDSON Rob DT 6'4 275 Toronto B: 5/10/1967 Montreal, QC Draft: 6-45 1989 EDM																															
1990	EDM	15				6																									
1991	EDM	11	0		1	15	3.0																							
1992	EDM	18				33	5.0	21.0																						
1993	WPG	6	1		0	3																						1	0	0.0	0
1994	WPG	16				18	2.0	16.0																						
1995	WPG	5				6																									
6	Years	71	1		1	81	10.0	37.0																				1	0	0.0	0
QUENTIN DAVIE Quentin R. DE 6'4 230 Northwestern B: 2/15/1988 St. Louis, MO																															
2011	WPG	1				1																									
BILL DAVIES Bill T 6'0 188 B: 1/25/1916 Montreal, QC D: 5/28/1990																															
1946	MTL	4																													
DOUG DAVIES Doug C 6'4 270 Simon Fraser B: 12/2/1964 Toronto, ON Draft: 2-11 1987 MTL																															
1988	HAM	17	0		1	0																									
1990	CAL	18	1		0	1																									
1991	CAL	18	1		0	4																									
1992	CAL	18	0		2	3																									
1993	CAL	18				2													0	5		5	0								
1994	CAL	17				0																									
1995	HAM	17	0		1	2																									
1996	HAM	18				5																									
1997	HAM	8				0																									
1997	BC	8				1			1	7	0																				
1997	Year	16				1			1	7	0																				
1998	BC	13				6																									
1999	BC	18	1	0	0	8																									
11	Years	180	3	0	4	32			1	7	0								0	5		5	0								
MIKE DAVIES Michael QB 6'0 180 Parkdale Lions Jrs. B: 2/28/1937 Toronto, ON																															
1958	BC	16	1		2				4	56				1	-4	-4.0	-4	0													
1960	WPG	10													4	-2	-0.5	2	0													
2	Years	26	1		2				4	56				5	-6	-1.2	2	0													
ADRIAN DAVIS Adrian Frederick DT-DE 6'3 265 Marshall; Concordia (Quebec) B: 12/17/1981 Greenfield Park, QC Draft: 4B-33 2006 MTL																															
2008	TOR	3				0																									
2009	TOR	11				2	1.0	9.0																						
2010	TOR	7				4	1.0	8.0																						
2011	CAL	7				4					1																			
4	Years	28				10	2.0	17.0																						
ANTHONY DAVIS Anthony RB 5'10 190 Southern California B: 9/8/1952 Huntsville, TX Draft: 2-37 1975 NYJ Pro: NUW																															
1976	TOR	13	3		0							24	4	104	417	4.0	48	2	37	408	11.0	41	2	5	96	19.2	28	27	701	26.0	62
ANTHONY DAVIS Anthony RB 5'7 200 Wisconsin B: 5/21/1982 Plainfied, NJ Draft: 7-243 2005 IND																															
2006	HAM	4	0	0	2	0						6	1	25	97	3.9	14	1	4	29	7.3	11	0								
2007	HAM	9	2	0	0	0								61	360	5.9	51	0	8	63	7.9	17	0								
2	Years	13	2	0	2	0						6	1	86	457	5.3	51	1	12	92	7.7	17	0								
ASHLAN DAVIS Ashlan Jamon WR 5'8 179 Tyler JC; Tulsa B: 2/15/1983 Mesquite, TX																															
2006	MTL	1				0																		5	39	7.8	15	4	46	11.5	13
2007	MTL	12	2	0	1	1						18	3	3	12	4.0	10	0	40	476	11.9	59	3	28	179	6.4	16	30	632	21.1	54
2	Years	13	2	0	1	1						18	3	3	12	4.0	10	0	40	476	11.9	59	3	33	218	6.6	16	34	678	19.9	54
BRETT DAVIS Brett RB 5'11 205 Nevada-Las Vegas B: 2/3/1957 Draft: 10B-275 1980 TB																															
1982	CAL	4											6	1	16	75	4.7	16	0	11	96	8.7	31	1								
BURR DAVIS Harold C-LB 6'0 222 Houston B: 1937 Draft: 9-103 1959 PIT																															
1959	WPG	1																													
1960	WPG	4																													
2	Years	5																													
CHARLES DAVIS Charles RB 6'0 202 Alcorn State B: 8/20/1950 Hollandale, MS Draft: 3B-73 1973 NE																															
1975	BC	1																													
CHARLES DAVIS Charles J. (C.J.) WR 6'0 185 Washington State B: 5/7/1969 Clark Air Force Base, The Philippines																															

Year	Team	GP	FM	FF	FR	TK	SK	YDS	IR	YDS	PD	PTS	TD	RA	YDS	AVG	LG	TD	REC	YDS	AVG	LG	TD	PR	YDS	AVG	LG	KOR	YDS	AVG	LG
1995	EDM	12	0		1	1						14	2	3	15	5.0	11	0	28	481	17.2	48	2								
1996	EDM	1				1																									
2	Years	13	0		1	2						14	2	3	15	5.0	11	0	28	481	17.2	48	2								
CHRIS DAVIS Christopher Taj WR-SB 5'10 180 Wake Forest B: 12/1/1983 Atlanta, GA Pro: N																															
2006	MTL	3				0													5	40	8.0	19	0								
2007	MTL	1	1	0	0	1													4	43	10.8	14	0								
2008	HAM	4	1	0	1	0						18	3	1	-9	-9.0	-9	0	20	228	11.4	52	3								
2009	HAM	9				1						12	2						34	440	12.9	37	2								
2010	WPG	7				0						6	1	1	4	4.0	4	0	16	184	11.5	40	1					1	24	24.0	24
5	Years	24	2	0	1	2						36	6	2	-5	-2.5	4	0	79	935	11.8	52	6					1	24	24.0	24
CHUCKY DAVIS Chucky Alan RB 6'1 200 Wisconsin B: 4/21/1961 Macon, GA																															
1984	OTT	3	2		0							6	1	26	135	5.2	19	0	7	54	7.7	19	1					2	39	19.5	21
DARREN DAVIS Darren RB 5'8 190 Iowa State B: 3/1/1977 Miami, FL																															
2000	SAS	12	3	0	2	1						36	6	161	1024	6.4	59	4	22	258	11.7	42	2								
2001	SAS+	16	2	0	1	2						24	4	217	1243	5.7	52	4	34	301	8.9	30	0					10	179	17.9	29
2002	OTT	5	2	0	0	0						18	3	60	247	4.1	18	2	12	95	7.9	21	1								
2003	OTT	6	1	0	0	0								60	298	5.0	33	0	15	183	12.2	38	0								
4	Years	39	8	0	3	3						78	13	498	2812	5.6	59	10	83	837	10.1	42	3					10	179	17.9	29
DARRICK DAVIS Darrick CB 5'8 165 Santa Monica JC; Long Beach State; Idaho B: 9/29/1969 Chicago, IL Pro: E																															
1993	SAC	9				28																									
1995	BC	2	1		0	7																		10	45	4.5	35				
2	Years	11	1		0	35																		10	45	4.5	35				
DONNIE DAVIS Donnie Ray TE-OE 6'4 220 Southern University B: 9/18/1940 Opelousas, LA D: 1/19/2004 Houston, TX Draft: 6A-74 1962 DAL Pro: NW																															
1965	MTL	9	0		2				1	0		6	1	5	31	6.2	22	0	26	411	15.8	50	1								
1966	MTL	12	1		0				1	20				27	196	7.3	28	0	23	365	15.9	50	0					1	23	23.0	23
1967	MTL	12	0		2							12	2	6	25	4.2	11	0	31	656	21.2	50	2					2	16	8.0	16
1968	MTL	13										12	2						26	401	15.4	41	2								
4	Years	46	1		4				2	20		30	5	38	252	6.6	28	0	106	1833	17.3	50	5					3	39	13.0	23
EDDIE DAVIS Eddie DH-CB 5'10 175 Northern Illinois B: 1/27/1973 St. Louis, MO																															
1995	BIR	17				93			1	11	8																				
1996	CAL	18	0		3	74			2	66	8	6	1																		
1997	CAL	17	1	0	1	78	1.0	6.0	4	94	11																				
1998	CAL	18	0	0	1	77	3.0	16.0	4	127	14																				
1999	CAL	3				11					2																				
2000	CAL*	18				54	2.0	14.0	4	5	13																				
2001	SAS+	18	0	0	1	67			4	0	4																				
2002	SAS	14				45	1.0	11.0	1	0	5																				
2003	SAS	18				53			1	1	8																				
2004	SAS*	18	0	0	0	65	2.0	14.0	6	83	5																				
2005	SAS*	18	0	0	2	60			3	8	9	6	1																		
2006	SAS*	17	0	0	3	66	2.0	6.0	2	34	7	12	2																		
2007	SAS	9	0	1	0	45	2.0	18.0	1	4	6																				
2008	SAS	18				63	1.0	9.0	1	3	7																				
2009	SAS	16	0	1	1	62	2.0	29.0			4																				
15	Years	237	1	2	12	913	16.0	123.0	34	436	111	24	4																		
GERALD DAVIS Gerald OT 6'4 300 Valdosta State B: 12/12/1985 Greensboro, GA																															
2008	HAM	6				1																									
GLENN DAVIS Glenn CB 5'11 185 South Florida B: 8/17/1978 St. Petersburg, FL																															
2002	WPG	6				12			0	0	1																				
JACK DAVIS John James G-DE 6'0 226 Maryland B: 3/12/1932 Braddock, PA Pro: N																															
1957	HAM	6																													
1958	HAM	2																													
2	Years	8																													
JEROME DAVIS Jerome Devon OT-DE 6'5 300 Minnesota B: 2/4/1974 Detroit, MI Pro: EN																															
2000	CAL	2				3					2																				
2005	TOR	15	0	0	1	1																									
2006	TOR+	15				1																									
2007	HAM	11	0	0	1	2								1	3	3.0	3	0													
2008	TOR	13				2																									
5	Years	56	0	0	2	9					2			1	3	3.0	3	0													
JIM DAVIS James Edward, Jr. DT 6'3 270 Virginia Tech B: 10/4/1981 Richmond, VA Pro: N																															
2008	EDM	14	0	1	0	26	6.0	42.0			3																				
2009	CAL	10	0	1	1	19	6.0	57.0			1																				
2	Years	24	0	2	1	45	12.0	99.0			4																				
JOHN DAVIS John LB 6'4 215 Western Ontario B: 5/10/1968 Campbellton, NB Draft: 3-23 1991 EDM																															
1992	EDM	5				2																									
JOSE DAVIS Jose QB 6'1 195 Kent State B: 7/29/1978 Bellaire, ON																															
2000	WPG	18	1	0	0	0																									
2001	WPG	18				0																									
2	Years	36	1	0	0	0																									
KENT DAVIS Kenneth D. DB 5'11 172 Southeast Missouri State B: 4/22/1957 Nettleton, MS Draft: 9-231 1980 BUF																															
1980	SAS	14	2		0				1	22														5	30	6.0	14	5	98	19.6	25
LARRY DAVIS Larry Dewayne Gardner WR 5'9 195 Blinn JC; Illinois; New Mexico B: 11/5/1977 Houston, TX																															
2003	HAM	6	4	0	0	1													5	61	12.2	27	0	25	194	7.8	30	19	383	20.2	36
MARVIN DAVIS Marvin Eugene DE-LB 6'4 235 Southern University B: 5/25/1952 Shreveport, LA Pro: NW																															
1976	MTL	11	0		2																										
1977	MTL	16	1		2																										
1978	WPG	2	0		1																							4	21	5.3	14
1978	HAM	1	0		1																										
1978	Year	3	0		2																										
3	Years	29	1		6																							4	21	5.3	14
MIKE DAVIS Michael E. DB 6'1 213 Colorado B: 12/1/1957 Draft: 6-146 1980 ATL																															
1980	OTT	5	0		1																			1	10	10.0	10	5	132	26.4	49
1981	OTT	4	0		1				1	30		6	1											4	36	9.0	15	7	170	24.3	35
2	Years	9	0		2				1	30		6	1											5	46	9.2	15	12	302	25.2	49
MONDOE DAVIS Mondoe Ramone LB 6'1 225 Delaware B: 3/19/1982																															
2007	MTL	1				2																									
NATHAN DAVIS Nathan Michael DT 6'5 312 Indiana B: 2/6/1974 Hartford, CT Draft: 2A-32 1997 ATL Pro: NX																															
2001	SAS	13	0	2	2	40	3.0	11.0	1	1	2																				
2002	SAS	15	0	0	1	38	3.0	22.0			4																				
2003	SAS+	17				32	10.0	54.0																							
2004	SAS*	18	0	1	2	20	8.0	54.0			1																				
2005	SAS	12				15	4.0	29.0			2																				
2006	SAS	16				20	4.0	29.0																							
2007	WPG	1				1																									
7	Years	92	0	3	5	166	32.0	199.0	1	1	9																				
PASCHALL DAVIS Paschal Tederall LB 6'2 234 Trinity Valley CC; Texas A&M-Kingsville B: 6/5/1969 Bryan, TX Pro: EN																															
1993	SAC	18	0		1	28			2	46		6	1															1	13	13.0	13
1994	SHR	18				36																									
2	Years	36	0		1	64			2	46		6	1															1	13	13.0	13
RICHIE DAVIS Richard Curtis CB 5'11 195 Upsala B: 12/24/1945 Plainfield, NJ Draft: 14-364 1968 DET																															
1970	MTL	11							6	112														1	5	5.0	5	6	88	14.7	24

Year	Team	GP	FM	FF	FR	TK	SK	YDS	IR	YDS	PD	PTS	TD	RA	YDS	AVG	LG	TD	REC	YDS	AVG	LG	TD	PR	YDS	AVG	LG	KOR	YDS	AVG	LG
ROB DAVIS Robert Emmett OL 6'3 284 Shippensburg B: 12/10/1968 Washington, DC Pro: N																															
1995	BAL	18				13																									
ROBERT DAVIS Robert Earl, II DH 5'9 195 Vanderbilt B: 8/6/1972 Nashville, TN Pro: E																															
1995	BC	17	1		1	54	1.0	15.0	4	69	3																				
1996	BC	12				39	2.0	16.0			4													10	42	4.2	15	0	24		24
1997	WPG	7				24	2.0	11.0	1	58	0													14	144	10.3	27	1	21	21.0	21
3	Years	36	1		1	117	5.0	42.0	5	127	7													24	186	7.8	27	1	45		24
ROD DAVIS Rod LB 6'2 239 Southern Mississippi B: 4/2/1981 Gulfport, MS Draft: 5-155 2004 MIN Pro: N																															
2009	EDM	9	0	1	0	26			2	32	2																				
2010	EDM	18	0	0	1	66			2	96	5	12	2																		
2011	EDM+	14	0	3	2	79	5.0	26.0	1	0	4																	2	18	9.0	10
3	Years	41	0	4	3	171	5.0	26.0	5	128	11	12	2															2	18	9.0	10
RON DAVIS Ronald Rozelle DB 5'10 190 Tennessee B: 2/24/1972 Bartlett, TN Draft: 2-41 1995 ATL Pro: N																															
1999	BC	3				4																						1	11	11.0	11
ROY DAVIS Roy Lee LB 6'2 230 Prairie View A&M B: 5/29/1945 Galveston, TX																															
1968	HAM	2																													
1969	HAM	4							1	17																					
2	Years	6							1	17																					
SHOCKMAIN DAVIS Shockmain Nastase WR 6'0 205 Blinn JC; Angelo State B: 8/20/1977 Port Arthur, TX Pro: EN																															
2006	WPG	2				0													2	33	16.5	30	0					2	45	22.5	29
2006	TOR	3				2													3	28	9.3	10	0								
2006	Year	5				2													5	61	12.2	30	0					2	45	22.5	29
TANARD DAVIS Tanard J. DB 6'0 186 Miami (Florida) B: 1/27/1983 Miami, FL																															
2010	MTL	1				0																									
TOM DAVIS Thomas Lloyd OG-E 6'2 260 Nebraska B: 7/31/1955 Omaha, NE Draft: 6A-143 1978 OAK Pro: U																															
1978	TOR	4																													
1979	TOR	4	1		0																										
1979	OTT	7																													
1979	Year	11	1		0																										
2	Years	8	1		0																										
TONY DAVIS Tony RB 5'11 211 Florida B: 4/26/1973																															
1994	LV	1																													
TORREY DAVIS Torrey DT 6'3 310 Florida; Jacksonville State B: 9/24/1988 Tampa, FL																															
2011	CAL	10				12					1																				
TROY DAVIS Troy RB 5'7 191 Iowa State B: 9/14/1975 Miami, FL Draft: 3-62 1997 NO Pro: N																															
2001	HAM	12	4	0	0	0						36	6	96	527	5.5	75	6	14	122	8.7	17	0					36	790	21.9	42
2002	HAM+	14	4	0	1	4						42	7	230	1143	5.0	74	6	27	221	8.2	31	1								
2003	HAM+	18	6	0	1	4						30	5	227	1206	5.3	34	5	31	230	7.4	24	0					13	275	21.2	34
2004	HAM*	18	6	0	0	4						62	10	324	1628	5.0	58	10	40	250	6.3	15	0					2	44	22.0	26
2005	HAM	13	5	0	1	0						18	3	176	792	4.5	54	3	25	142	5.7	15	0					4	75	18.8	22
2005	EDM	4				1						12	2	64	359	5.6	30	2	17	157	9.2	17	0								
2005	Year	17	5	0	1	1						30	5	240	1151	4.8	54	5	42	299	7.1	17	0					4	75	18.8	22
2006	EDM	16	4	0	0	3						24	4	190	1060	5.6	44	4	67	546	8.1	27	0								
2007	TOR	2				0								6	24	4.0	10	0													
7	Years	93	29	0	3	16						224	37	1313	6739	5.1	75	36	221	1668	7.5	31	1					55	1184	21.5	42
TYREE DAVIS Tyree Bernard WR 5'9 175 Central Arkansas B: 9/23/1970 Altheimer, AR Draft: 7-176 1993 TB Pro: EN																															
1998	MTL	3				0						6	1						6	157	26.2	57	0	9	135	15.0	76	5	87	17.4	28
1999	MTL	17	1	0	0	1						18	3						43	832	19.3	73	3	3	-3	-1.0	5	1	28	28.0	28
2000	MTL	18	2	0	0	2						12	2						48	872	18.2	52	1	20	271	13.6	61	3	60	20.0	25
2001	MTL	17	3	0	2	4						30	5						56	874	15.6	61	5	18	152	8.4	31	2	23	11.5	12
2002	TOR	2	1	0	1	0													9	65	7.2	13	0	3	8	2.7	5				
2002	CAL	3				0													6	69	11.5	18	0	13	124	9.5	41				
2002	Year	5	1	0	0	0													15	134	8.9	18	0	16	132	8.3	41				
2003	HAM	10				1													40	458	11.5	32	0								
6	Years	67	7	0	3	8						66	11						208	3327	16.0	73	9	66	687	10.4	76	11	198	18.0	28
WENDELL DAVIS Wendell FB 6'3 224 Mississippi Gulf Coast CC; Temple B: 10/24/1975 Escatawapa, MS Pro: N																															
2002	EDM	11	1	0	0	6						12	2	23	97	4.2	11	2	9	64	7.1	16	0					3	32	10.7	24
WILLIAM DAVIS William WR 5'10 170 Angelo State B: 1961 Pro: U																															
1984	SAS	3	2		0														4	113	28.3	94	0					1	12	12.0	12
YONUS DAVIS Yonus Ramon RB 5'7 185 San Jose State B: 7/21/1984 Oakland, CA																															
2010	BC+	14	7	0	3	2						42	7	34	213	6.3	51	3	7	42	6.0	17	1	64	761	11.9	88	32	815	25.5	88
JERONE DAVISON Jerone Lamar RB 6'1 225 Solano CC; Arizona State B: 9/16/1970 Picayune, MS Pro: EN																															
1994	SAC	3				0								3	1	0.3	2	0													
STACEY DAWSEY Stacey L. WR 5'9 154 Indiana B: 10/24/1965 Bradenton, FL Pro: N																															
1988	CAL	4				2						6	1						5	82	16.4	27	1					3	65	21.7	32
1989	CAL	3	1		1	0						6	1						3	32	10.7	15	0	13	205	15.8	85	5	60	12.0	16
1989	OTT	4	1		0	2								1	10	10.0	10	0	1	13	13.0	13	0	20	233	11.7	64	13	280	21.5	61
1989	Year	7	2		0	2						6	1	1	10	10.0	10	0	4	45	11.3	15	0	33	438	13.3	85	18	340	18.9	61
1990	OTT	18	5		2	0						6	1						8	110	13.8	20	1	70	608	8.7	40	59	1307	22.2	56
1991	BC	1																						3	31	10.3	22	7	150	21.4	28
4	Years	26	7		3	4						18	3	1	10	10.0	10	0	17	237	13.9	27	2	106	1077	10.2	85	87	1862	21.4	61
BOBBY DAWSON Bob QB-DB 5'10 161 Windsor AKO Fratmen Jrs. B: 2/4/1932 Windsor																															
1953	HAM	9																													
1954	HAM	14																						2	8	4.0	4				
1955	HAM	9																													
1956	HAM	14							2	52				6	-9	-1.5		0						11	77	7.0	17				
1957	HAM	2																													
1958	HAM	14							2	31														5	63	12.6	15				
1959	HAM	14							1	8				2	8	4.0	8	0													
7	Years	76							5	91				8	-1	-0.1	8	0						18	148	8.2	17				
BOBBY DAWSON Bobby J. DB 5'11 210 Sacramento JC; Illinois B: 2/18/1966 Sacramento, CA Draft: 11-295 1988 PIT																															
1990	HAM	15				51			3	8																					
1991	HAM	15	0		2	74			5	34																					
1992	HAM	18	0		1	77	1.0	17.0	4	52		6	1															1	18	18.0	18
1993	HAM	11				34			2	35		6	1																		
1994	HAM	8				38			3	8	2																				
1995	MEM	13	0		1	58	1.0	4.0	1	17	2																				
1996	OTT	1				0																									
7	Years	81	0		4	332	2.0	21.0	18	154	4	12	2															1	18	18.0	18
DEXTER DAWSON Dexter CB-WR 5'9 185 Georgia Southern B: 9/2/1974 Camilla, GA																															
1996	MTL	8				0						6	1	16	32	2.0	11	1	7	57	8.1	17	0	48	410	8.5	46	12	260	21.7	31
1997	WPG	16	3	0	0	17			1	35	1	18	3	23	46	2.0	8	0	37	339	9.2	21	1	59	525	8.9	92	27	667	24.7	86
1998	SAS	4				1						6	1	1	-4	-4.0	-4	0	13	179	13.8	26	1	8	37	4.6	8	11	262	23.8	50
3	Years	28	3	0	0	18			1	35	1	30	5	40	74	1.9	11	1	57	575	10.1	26	2	115	972	8.5	92	50	1189	23.8	86
GERRY DAWSON Gerry QB 5'11 167 B: 1924																															
1948	OTT	4																													
RHETT DAWSON Rhett Motte WR 6'1 180 Florida State B: 12/22/1948 Valdosta, GA Draft: 10A-240 1972 HOU Pro: N																															
1974	SAS	5										18	3						14	232	16.6	58	3								
1975	SAS+	16	1		0							62	10						69	1191	17.3	85	10								
1976	SAS*	16										60	10						65	996	15.3	57	10								
3	Years	37	1		0							140	23						148	2419	16.3	85	23								
BOB DAY Bob E 6'2 218 Parkdale Jrs.; East York Ints. B: 1937																															

Year	Team	GP	FM	FF	FR	TK	SK	YDS	IR	YDS	PD	PTS	TD	RA	YDS	AVG	LG	TD	REC	YDS	AVG	LG	TD	PR	YDS	AVG	LG	KOR	YDS	AVG	LG
1959	TOR	10																													
EAGLE DAY Herman Sidney QB 6'0 183 Mississippi B: 10/2/1932 Columbia, MS D: 2/23/2008 Nashville, TN Draft: 17-203(f) 1956 WAS Pro: N																															
1956	WPG	16	13		2							25	4	164	477	2.9	53	4	2	21	10.5	13	0								
1961	CAL	12	4									31	5	93	322	3.5	20	5													
1962	CAL*	12	3									12	2	27	88	3.3	9	2													
1963	CAL	14	0		1							19	3	24	91	3.8	11	3													
1964	CAL	16	4		0							24	4	64	306	4.8	51	4	1	-1	-1.0	-1	0								
1965	CAL	13	4		0									12	30	2.5	10	0													
1966	CAL	3												2	-7	-3.5	-1	0													
1966	TOR	9	1		1									6	14	2.3	5	0													
1966	Year	12	1		1									8	7	0.9	5	0													
7	Years	86	29		4							111	18	392	1321	3.4	53	18	3	20	6.7	13	0								
IRV DAYMOND Irv C-OT 6'5 255 Western Ontario B: 10/9/1962 St. Thomas, ON Draft: 6-53 1984 BC																															
1986	OTT	3																													
1987	OTT	16	0		1	1																									
1988	OTT	12				1																									
1989	OTT	18	1		0	4																									
1990	OTT	18				8																									
1991	OTT+	17				4																									
1992	OTT+	17	1		0	3																									
1993	OTT	12				4																									
1994	OTT	18				1																									
1995	OTT	12	1		0	2																									
10	Years	143	3		1	28																									
TOM DEACON Tom DB 6'1 195 Wake Forest B: 3/18/1946																															
1970	OTT	4																													
1970	WPG	9										1	0																		
1970	Year	13										1	0																		
LEO DEADEY Leo E																															
1946	TOR	7																													
1947	HAM	6										5	1										1								
2	Years		13										5	1										1							
BOB DEAN Robert Wadsworth OT-K 6'1 245 Maryland B: 12/17/1929 Pittsburgh, PA D: 5/10/2007																															
1954	EDM	15										62	0																		
1955	EDM	16	0		2							78	0																		
1956	EDM	9										37	0																		
1957	MTL	1										3	0																		
4	Years	41	0		2							180	0																		
TERRY DEAN Terry QB 6'2 210 Florida B: 11/1/1971 Pro: E																															
1995	WPG	9	2		0	1						6	1	4	30	7.5	17	1													
WALTER DEAN Walter Kevin RB 5'10 216 Grambling State B: 6/ /1968 Ruston, LA Draft: 6A-149 1991 GB Pro: N																															
1994	SHR	4	3		0	5								13	37	2.8	14	0	1	7	7.0	7	0					1	7	7.0	7
J'MICHAEL DEANE J'Michael OG-DT 6'5 320 Metro Toronto Wildcats Jrs.; Michigan State B: 5/4/1986 Draft: 3B-21 2010 CAL																															
2011	CAL	9				7																									
NED DEANE Edward C 6'3 240 Massachusetts B: 2/7/1954 Westfield, MA																															
1976	TOR	4																													
SANDRO DeANGELIS Sandro K 5'8 195 Nebraska B: 5/1/1981 Niagara Falls, ON																															
2005	CAL*	18	0	1	0	1						179	0																		
2006	CAL*	18				3						214	0																		
2007	CAL+	18	1	0	0	2						144	0																		
2008	CAL*	18				7						217	0																		
2009	CAL+	18				6						176	0																		
2010	HAM	18	1	0	0	6						144	0																		
6	Years	108	2	1	0	25						1074	0																		
MARK DeBRUEYS Mark TE-SB 6'2 210 Western Ontario B: 8/8/1958 London, ON Draft: 2B-18 1982 EDM																															
1982	EDM	15										12	2						5	51	10.2	19	2								
1983	BC	12	2		1														14	170	12.1	32	0								
1984	BC	1																													
1985	BC	16																	1	15	15.0	15	0					1	-1	-1.0	-1
4	Years	44	2		1							12	2						20	236	11.8	32	2					1	-1	-1.0	-1
LAWRENCE DECK Lawrence CB 5'10 190 Fresno State B: 6/5/1977 Saskatoon, SK Draft: 2A-10 2001 CAL																															
2001	CAL	16				15																									
2002	CAL	18	0	0	1	19			1	0	1																				
2003	CAL	3				7					1																				
2003	SAS	6				0																									
2003	Year	9				7					1																				
2004	SAS	8				3																									
2005	CAL	12	0	0	1	4			1	0	0																				
5	Years	57	0	0	2	48			2	0	2																				
BILL deCOLIGNY Bill OT-DT 6'3 248 Trinity (Connecticut) B: 5/17/1937 Hartford, CT																															
1960	SAS	3																													
BOB DEEGAN Robert H. DE 6'3 228 Minnesota B: 1938																															
1962	WPG	5										6	1						10	121	12.1	39	1								
1963	SAS	2																													
2	Years	7										6	1						10	121	12.1	39	1								
TOBY DEESE Marion Drew OT 6'2 230 Georgia Tech B: 7/10/1937 Talladega, AL D: 11/24/2002 Talladega, AL Draft: 20-234(f) 1959 SF; SS 1960 DAL																															
1960	EDM	15																													
1961	EDM	7																													
1962	EDM	11																													
3	Years	33																													
JOE DeFOREST Joseph John LB 6'1 240 Louisiana-Lafayette B: 4/17/1965 Teaneck, NJ Pro: N																															
1988	CAL	4			1																										
CHRIS DeFRANCE Chris Anthony SE-SB 6'1 205 Bakersfield JC; Arizona State B: 9/13/1956 Waldo, AR Draft: 6C-164 1979 DAL Pro: N																															
1981	SAS	16										32	5						64	1195	18.7	100	5								
1982	SAS	15	2		0							14	2						78	1062	13.6	44	2								
1983	SAS+	14	1		0							54	9	1	16	16.0	16	0	71	1165	16.4	88	9								
1984	SAS+	14	1		0							30	5						59	917	15.5	42	5								
1985	SAS	12	1		0									1	3	3.0	3	0	56	3	0.1	34	0								
5	Years	71	5		0							130	21	2	19	9.5	16	0	328	4342	13.2	100	21								
ALLEN DeGRAFFENREID Allen Justice WR 6'3 200 Ohio State B: 5/1/1970 Cincinnati, OH Pro: EN																															
1996	WPG	4				0													8	132	16.5	30	0					1	5	5.0	5
LARRY DeGRAW Larry DH 5'11 180 Mount San Antonio JC; Utah B: 1941																															
1963	OTT	13							5	53																					
1964	OTT	11	0		1				2	34																					
1965	OTT	14	0		1				3	28														2	1	0.5	3				
1966	OTT	14	0		1				1	18																					
1967	OTT	13																						1	0	0.0	0				
1968	SAS	16	2		0				4	51														80	509	6.4	23	2	53	26.5	27
1969	SAS	16	1		1				5	54		6	1											59	391	6.6	75				
1970	SAS	1																						1	2	2.0	2				
8	Years	98	3		4				20	238		6	1											143	903	6.3	75	2	53	26.5	27
BOB DEHLINGER Robert DB-OHB 6'0 185 Idaho B: 1937																															

Year	Team	GP	FM	FF	FR	TK	SK	YDS	IR	YDS	PD	PTS	TD	RA	YDS	AVG	LG	TD	REC	YDS	AVG	LG	TD	PR	YDS	AVG	LG	KOR	YDS	AVG	LG
1959	TOR	12							6	81														9	67	7.4	36	15	327	21.8	46
1960	TOR	12							8	124		6	1											48	256	5.3	21	6	143	23.8	33
2	Years	24							14	205		6	1											57	323	5.7	36	21	470	22.4	46
SCOTT DEIBERT Scott SB-FB 6'0 210 Minot State B: 10/2/1970 Moose Jaw, SK Draft: 3-17 1998 EDM																															
1998	EDM	16				8								6	16	2.7	8	0	5	59	11.8	26	0								
1999	EDM	18	1	0	1	7						6	1	19	83	4.4	26	1	12	125	10.4	29	0								
2000	WPG	17	0	1	0	5													1	-5	-5.0	-5	0								
2001	CAL	18				9						12	2	10	77	7.7	38	1	1	19	19.0	19	1								
2002	CAL	18	0	0	1	9						24	4	20	94	4.7	29	4	1	7	7.0	7	0								
2003	CAL	18	1	0	0	8						6	1	34	173	5.1	25	1	6	89	14.8	35	0					8	122	15.3	33
2004	CAL	11	0	0	1	6								14	60	4.3	16	0	2	9	4.5	7	0					2	42	21.0	23
2005	CAL	15	0	0	1	2								8	21	2.6	7	0													
8	Years	131	2	1	4	54						48	8	111	524	4.7	38	7	28	303	10.8	35	1					10	164	16.4	33
GEORGE DEIDERICH George Ronald OG-LB 6'1 213 Vanderbilt B: 3/19/1936 Pittsburgh, PA D: 7/2/1999 Gallatin, TN Draft: 23-272 1959 LARM																															
1959	MTL	2																													
1960	MTL	8							1	52		6	1																		
1961	MTL	3																													
1961	OTT	6																													
1961	Year	9																													
3	Years	13							1	52		6	1																		
AL DEKDEBRUN Allen Edward QB 5'10 182 Columbia; Cornell B: 5/11/1921 Buffalo, NY D: 3/29/2005 Cape Coral, FL Draft: 9-72 1946 BOS Pro: A																															
1949	HAM	10										5	1																		
1950	TOR	12										25	5					4													
1951	TOR	4																													
1953	MTL	14																													
1954	OTT	10							2	9				6	0	0.0	9	0													
5	Years	50							2	9		30	6	6	0	0.0	9	4													
PAUL DEKKER Paul Nelson OE 6'5 220 Michigan State B: 2/24/1931 Muskegon, MI D: 5/8/2001 Burlington, ON Draft: 3-27 1953 WAS Pro: N																															
1956	HAM	7										12	2						27	477	17.7	61	2								
1957	HAM	13										12	2						31	478	15.4	30	2								
1958	HAM+	14										30	5						38	638	16.8	46	5								
1959	HAM+	14										30	5						35	534	15.3	39	5								
1960	HAM+	14										36	6						50	790	15.8	60	6								
1961	HAM+	14										42	7						37	578	15.6	48	7								
1962	HAM	14																	16	223	13.9	24	0								
7	Years	90										162	27						234	3718	15.9	61	27								
GABRIEL DeLaGARZA Gabriel LB 6'2 240 Illinois B: 4/30/1965																															
1988	OTT	10	0		3	32																									
GREG DELAINE Greg DE 6'3 255 Southwest Minnesota State B: 3/24/1969 Fort Myers, FL																															
1992	BC	1																													
AKABA DELANEY Akaba DT-NT 6'1 290 Chabot JC; Portland State B: 3/20/1972 Oakland, CA																															
1995	BIR	12				24	3.0	22.0			1																	1	12	12.0	12
1996	EDM	4				0	1.0	9.0																							
2	Years	16				24	4.0	31.0			1																	1	12	12.0	12
DAVID DeLaPERRALLE David OT 6'7 320 Kentucky B: 5/2/1975 Montreal, QC Draft: 1-2 1999 TOR																															
1999	TOR	13				0																									
2002	OTT	8				1																									
2003	OTT	5				0																									
2005	CAL	18				0																									
4	Years	44				1																									
STEVE DEL COL Stephen DE-OT 6'4 245 Simon Fraser B: 12/6/1959 Toronto, ON Draft: TE 1982 TOR																															
1982	TOR	12					2.0																								
1983	TOR	15																													
1984	TOR	13					1.5		0	7																					
1985	TOR	16	0		1																										
1986	TOR	18																													
5	Years	74	0		1		3.5		0	7																					
GERRY DeLEEUW Gerry G-T 5'11 207 Winnipeg Grads Jrs.; St. Vital Ints. B: 1926 St. Vital, MB																															
1947	WPG	5																													
1948	WPG	11																													
1949	WPG	14																													
1950	WPG	14																													
1951	WPG	9																													
1952	WPG	14																													
6	Years	67																													
MARCEL deLEEUW Marcel FL-DB-P 6'1 195 Edmonton Wildcats Jrs. B: 11/6/1943 The Netherlands																															
1964	EDM	16																	3	41	13.7	19	0								
1965	EDM	3																						3	1	0.3	3				
1971	OTT	14	2		2							4	0																		
3	Years	33	2		2							4	0						3	41	13.7	19	0	3	1	0.3	3				
CURTIS DELGARDO Curtis RB 5'6 172 Portland State B: 10/19/1967 Seattle, WA																															
1992	SAS	4	1		0	2								12	16	1.3	9	0	4	23	5.8	7	0	18	164	9.1	35	5	89	17.8	35
SIR JAMES DELGARDO Sir James, Jr. DB 5'11 185 Western Washingon; Pima CC; Texas-El Paso B: 10/21/1982 Seattle, WA																															
2007	HAM	8				16			1	28	2																				
HOWARD DELL Howard DB 6'2 205 McMaster B: 4/14/1964 Toronto, ON																															
1990	TOR	5	1		0	2													3	48	16.0	32	0								
1991	TOR	2				0																									
1991	WPG	1				2																									
1991	Year	3				2																									
2	Years	7	1		0	4													3	48	16.0	32	0								
SPIRO DELLERBA Spiro HB-FW 5'11 200 Ohio State B: 1/25/1923 Ashtabula, OH D: 8/19/1968 Lake County, OH Pro: A																															
1946	HAM	7																													
JOE DeLUCA Joe G 5'10 215 Montana B: 1933																															
1955	BC	2										5	1	0	18		18	1													
SAM DeLUCA Samuel Frank T 6'2 247 South Carolina B: 5/2/1936 New York, NY D: 9/13/2011 Pelham, NY Draft: 2-23 1957 NYG Pro: N																															
1957	TOR	8																										2	15	7.5	12
1958	TOR	6																													
2	Years	14																										2	15	7.5	12
JERRY DeLUCCA Gerald Joseph T 6'2 249 Tennessee; Middle Tennessee State B: 7/17/1936 Peabody, MA Draft: 7-84 1957 CHIB Pro: N																															
1958	TOR	4																													
JACK DELVEAUX John LB-FB 6'1 215 Illinois B: 3/15/1937 Chicago, IL Draft: 9-107 1959 NYG																															
1959	WPG	5							1					4	10	2.5	4	0										2	43	21.5	23
1960	WPG	13	0		1				1			7	1											1	3	3.0	3				
1961	WPG	8							2	59		1	0															1	13	13.0	13
1962	WPG	16							4	44		11	0															10	214	21.4	61
1963	WPG	13							1			4	0															1	8	8.0	8
1964	WPG	10										14	2	30	117	3.9	24	2	4	74	18.5	37	0					4	70	17.5	21
6	Years	65	0		1				9	103		37	3	34	127	3.7	24	2	4	74	18.5	37	0	1	3	3.0	3	18	348	19.3	61
JOE DelVECCHIO Joe E 6'0 200 Manitoba; Fort Williams Redskins Ints. B: 3/15/1929 Fort William, ON																															
1951	CAL	1																													
1953	CAL	5																													
2	Years	6																													

Year	Team	GP	FM	FF	FR	TK	SK	YDS	IR	YDS	PD	PTS	TD	RA	YDS	AVG	LG	TD	REC	YDS	AVG	LG	TD	PR	YDS	AVG	LG	KOR	YDS	AVG	LG
BRYAN DeMARCHI Bryan DB 6'0 185 Eastern Michigan B: 1949																															
1970	HAM	8																						23	108	4.7	10	3	61	20.3	25
MARIO DeMARCO Mario G-T 5'11 200 Miami (Florida) B: 7/24/1924 Boonton, NJ D: 12/9/1956 Mount Slesse, BC Pro: N																															
1951	EDM+	14																													
1952	EDM+	13																													
1953	SAS	5																													
1954	SAS+	14																													
1955	SAS	9																													
1956	SAS	10																													
6	Years	65																													
FRANK DEMPSEY James Franklin LB 6'3 235 Florida B: 5/27/1925 Dothan, AL Draft: 13-166 1950 CHIB Pro: N																															
1954	HAM	13							1	5																					
1955	HAM	9							1	0																					
1955	OTT	3																													
1955	Year+	12																													
2	Years	22							2	5																					
WALLY DEMPSEY William Theodore LB 6'1 230 Glendale CC; Washington State B: 1/9/1944 Melrose Park, IL Pro: W																															
1965	SAS	12	0		2				1																						
1966	SAS	3																													
1967	SAS	16	0		4				2	32																					
1968	SAS*	16	0		3																							1	15	15.0	15
1969	SAS+	16	0		5				4	39																					
1970	BC	5							1	6																		1	19	19.0	19
1971	SAS	16	0		1				3	15																					
1972	SAS	4	0		1																										
8	Years	88	0		16				11	92																		2	34	17.0	19
DAVID DEN BRABER David QB 6'1 205 Ferris State B: 8/20/1966 Grand Rapids, MI																															
1989	CAL	1				0																									
JOHNNY DENGEL John Ernest (Duke) HB 5'11 195 Wayne State (Michigan) B: 8/11/1925																															
1949	OTT	12										20	4					3					1								
1950	OTT	4																													
2	Years	16										20	4					3					1								
PATRICE DENIS Patrice LB 6'2 230 Western Ontario B: 10/30/1972 Quebec City, QC Draft: 2-16 1997 EDM																															
1997	EDM	18				20																									
1998	EDM	18				25	1.0	10.0											1	26	26.0	26	0					1	3	3.0	3
1999	EDM	12	0	0	1	8																									
3	Years	48	0	0	1	53	1.0	10.0											1	26	26.0	26	0					1	3	3.0	3
TOM DENISON Tom QB 6'0 200 Queen's B: 10/7/1978																															
2004	CAL	1				0																									
CLARENCE DENMARK Clarence Traneil SB 5'11 185 Mississippi Delta CC; Troy; Arkansas-Monticello B: 9/29/1985 Jacksonville, FL																															
2011	WPG	17	2	0	1	1						30	5	7	81	11.6	26	0	65	818	12.6	82	5	7	85	12.1	46	5	52	10.4	18
JEROME DENNIS Jerome Lamar DH-CB-S 6'1 192 Utah State B: 12/6/1981 Los Angeles, CA																															
2007	BC	8	0	0	1	9					1	6	1																		
2008	BC	18	0	1	1	29	1.0	0.0			4																				
2009	BC	17	0	1	0	17																									
2010	HAM	18	0	0	1	58			2	17	5																				
2011	HAM	2				2																									
2011	BC	13	0	1	0	20	1.0	12.0																							
2011	Year	15	0	1	0	22	1.0	12.0																							
5	Years	63	0	3	3	135	2.0	12.0	2	17	10	6	1																		
LONNIE DENNIS Lonnie Morris OT-DT 6'1 230 Brigham Young B: 12/10/1937 Los Angeles County, CA D: 1/6/1997 Siskiyou County, CA Draft: FS 1960 DEN; 7B-78 1960 PIT																															
1960	BC	14																													
1961	BC	14																													
1962	BC+	16																										2	5	2.5	5
1963	BC*	15																													
1964	BC*	14	0		3														0	16		16	0								
1965	BC	2																													
1966	BC	14																													
1967	BC	1																													
1968	BC	3																													
9	Years	93	0		3														0	16		16	0					2	5	2.5	5
MARK DENNIS Mark LB 6'2 235 Central Michigan B: 10/25/1967 Windsor, ON Draft: 1-7 1990 HAM																															
1990	HAM	5				18																									
1991	HAM	17	0		1	26	1.0																								
1992	HAM	14	0		2	22	1.0	12.0																							
1993	HAM	1				2																									
4	Years	37	0		3	68	2.0	12.0																							
STEVE DENNIS Stephen CB 6'3 165 Grambling State B: 7/25/1951 Shreveport, LA Pro: W																															
1975	TOR	16	0		1				7	96		6	1											5	19	3.8	11				
1976	TOR+	16	0		2				5	119																					
1977	SAS	15							3	33														1	0	0.0	0	1	0	0.0	0
1978	SAS	7							1	9																					
1979	SAS	5							1	23																					
1979	OTT	6							2	53																					
1979	Year	11							3	76																					
1980	SAS	10							4	57																					
1981	SAS	16	0		1				6	58		6	1																		
1982	SAS	16	0		1		2.0		2	37																					
1983	SAS	16							4	64																					
1984	SAS	1																													
10	Years	118	0		5		2.0		35	549		12	2											6	19	3.2	11	1	0		0
TONY DENNIS Tony SB 5'11 185 Simon Fraser B: 7/24/1962 Windsor, ON Draft: 4A-28 1985 SAS																															
1985	SAS	6	1		2														5	85	17.0	23	0	2	13	6.5	9				
1986	SAS	16	1		2							18	3	2	7	3.5	7	0	53	806	15.2	85	3	1	7	7.0	7				
1987	SAS	18	1		1	0						8	1						34	401	11.8	43	1	5	30	6.0	18				
1988	CAL	14	1		1	0													7	106	15.1	28	0	15	120	8.0	17				
1990	BC	14				0						12	2						12	239	19.9	55	2								
5	Years	68	4		6	0						38	6	2	7	3.5	7	0	111	1637	14.7	85	6	23	170	7.4	18				
WAYNE DENNIS Wayne DT 6'1 240 Montana B: 7/23/1940																															
1964	BC	3																													
1964	WPG	5										1	0																		
1964	Year	8										1	0																		
1965	WPG	13																													
1966	WPG	14																													
1967	WPG	13	0		2																										
1968	BC	15	0		1																										
1969	BC	16																													
1970	BC	8	0		1																										
7	Years	82	0		4							1	0																		
DOUG DENNISON William Douglas RB 6'0 205 Kutztown B: 12/18/1951 Lancaster, PA Pro: NU																															
1980	TOR	2										6	1	14	22	1.6	10	1	5	19	3.8	7	0								
DAVE DENNY Dave TE-LB 6'3 225 Missouri Southern State B: 1949																															

Year	Team	GP	FM	FF	FR	TK	SK	YDS	IR	YDS	PD	PTS	TD	RA	YDS	AVG	LG	TD	REC	YDS	AVG	LG	TD	PR	YDS	AVG	LG	KOR	YDS	AVG	LG
1970	SAS	16	0		1							12	2						15	274	18.3	45	2								
1971	BC	12																	18	352	19.6	44	0					1	0	0.0	0
1972	BC	16	1		0														15	202	13.5	28	0					1	3	3.0	3
3	Years	44	1		1							12	2						48	828	17.3	45	2					2	3	1.5	3
GENO DeNOBILE Geno OG-OT 6'0 223 Hamilton Tiger-Cats B B: 1932																															
1956	HAM	4																													
1957	HAM	10																													
1958	HAM	13																													
1959	HAM	10																													
1960	HAM	12																													
1961	HAM	14												0	2		2	0													
1962	HAM	14																													
1963	HAM	14																													
1964	HAM	11	0		1																										
9	Years	102	0		1									0	2		2	0													
AUTRY DENSON Autry Lamont RB 5'10 200 Notre Dame B: 12/8/1976 Lauderhill, FL Draft: 7B-233 1999 TB Pro: EN																															
2004	MTL	16	1	1	0	4						72	12	159	772	4.9	41	9	31	454	14.6	60	3	3	19	6.3	17	7	118	16.9	26
BRANDON DENSON Brandon LB 5'11 230 Michigan State B: 7/22/1987																															
2011	HAM	4	0	0	1	12																									
MOSES DENSON Moses RB 6'1 215 Maryland-Eastern Shore B: 7/6/1944 Vredenburgh, AL Draft: 16-393(di) 1971 HOU; 8-203 1972 WAS Pro: N																															
1970	MTL+	14	5		0							12	2	116	820	7.1	69	1	25	327	13.1	39	1					16	451	28.2	63
1971	MTL	7	2		0							6	1	97	498	5.1	17	1	12	84	7.0	15	0					2	52	26.0	38
1972	MTL+	13	3		0							24	4	157	754	4.8	46	4	23	263	11.4	36	0					2	31	15.5	22
3	Years	34	10		0							42	7	370	2072	5.6	69	6	60	674	11.2	39	1					20	534	26.7	63
GEORGE DEPRES George B 5'10 150 Manitoba B: 10/28/1927 Winnipeg, MB D: 3/2/2008 Winnipeg, MB																															
1949	WPG	4																													
JIMMY DeRATT James Harold, Jr. DB-RB 6'0 203 North Carolina B: 1/19/1953 Wilson, NC Pro: N																															
1976	TOR	1												6	11	1.8	4	0													
1976	HAM	7							1	12				4	7	1.8	3	0													
1976	Year	8							1	12				10	18	1.8	4	0													
DWAYNE DERBAN Dwayne DL-LB 6'2 230 British Columbia B: 1/11/1965 Kamloops, BC Draft: 2B-12 1986 TOR																															
1987	BC	18				6	1.0																								
1988	BC	13				0																									
2	Years	31				6	1.0																								
MIKE DERKS Michael OT-C 6'5 285 Cincinnati B: 4/20/1962 Sudbury, ON Draft: 6-48 1984 HAM																															
1985	HAM	8																													
1986	HAM	1																													
1987	HAM	4				1																									
1988	HAM	14				0																									
1989	HAM	10	0		1	0																									
1990	HAM	18	0		1	0																									
1991	EDM	6																													
7	Years	61	0		2	1																									
HANK DERMER Henry C-LB 6'3 213 NDG Maple Leafs Jrs.; Montreal Navy Ints. B: 1928																															
1950	EDM	9																													
1951	EDM	14																													
1952	CAL	16																													
3	Years	39																													
BLAKE DERMOTT Blake OT-C-OG 6'3 255 Alberta B: 9/10/1961 Edmonton, AB Draft: TE 1983 EDM																															
1983	EDM	15	0		1																										
1984	EDM	16	0		1																										
1985	EDM	16	0		2																										
1986	EDM	18	0		1																										
1987	EDM	18				0																									
1988	EDM	18				2																									
1989	EDM+	18	0		1	0																									
1990	EDM	18	0		1	1																									
1991	EDM	18	0		1	2																									
1992	EDM	17				2																									
1993	EDM	18				0																									
1994	EDM+	18				6																									
1995	EDM	5				1																									
13	Years	213	0		8	14																									
BRIAN DeROO Brian Charles WR 6'3 193 Redlands B: 4/25/1956 Redlands, CA Draft: 5C-137 1978 NYG Pro: N																															
1982	MTL	6										36	6	1	3	3.0	3	0	34	650	19.1	50	6								
1983	MTL	8										30	5	3	-3	-1.0	3	0	32	469	14.7	34	5								
1984	MTL	10	2		0							14	2						25	362	14.5	34	2								
3	Years	24	2		0							80	13	4	0	0.0	3	0	91	1481	16.3	50	13								
DON DERRICK Don HB Oklahoma; Northwestern State (OK); Oklahoma State																															
1963	TOR	2												3	2	0.7	2	0						1	5	5.0	5				
1963	OTT	7							2	38				1	9	9.0	9	0													
1963	Year	9							2	38				4	11	2.8	9	0						1	5	5.0	5				
DANNY DERRICOTT Danny CB 5'9 170 Marshall B: 12/4/1976 Richmond, VA																															
2002	MTL	9				22	1.0		1	1	1																	2	31	15.5	21
2003	CAL	6	0	0	1	10					1													1	0	0.0	0				
2	Years	15	0	0	1	32	1.0		1	1	2													1	0	0.0	0	2	31	15.5	21
DOUG DERSCH Doug LB-OT 6'1 240 Calgary B: 4/18/1946 Innisfall, AB Draft: 1968 EDM																															
1968	EDM	14	0		1																										
1969	MTL	9																													
1970	EDM	16																													
1971	HAM	14	0		1																							1	13	13.0	13
1972	HAM	4																													
1972	TOR	8																													
1972	Year	12																													
5	Years	57	0		2																							1	13	13.0	13
DAN DeSANTIS Daniel Joseph HB-FW 6'0 180 Niagara B: 9/21/1918 Niagara Falls, NY D: 12/28/2004 Lockport, NY Pro: N																															
1946	HAM	10																													
JIM DeSILVA James Raymond C 6'1 250 Ottawa Sooners Jrs.; Carleton B: 10/3/1958 North Bay, ON D: 8/21/2007 Oshawa, ON Draft: TE 1984 OTT																															
1984	OTT	13	1		1																										
1985	OTT	2	0		1																										
2	Years	15	1		2																										
PAUL DESJARDINS Paul C 6'3 255 Ottawa B: 9/12/1943 Ottawa, ON Draft: 4-33 1963 MTL; 1-9 1964 HAM; 1-2 1965 WPG																															
1965	WPG	16	0		1																										
1966	WPG	16	1		0																										
1967	WPG	16	0		1																										
1968	WPG	16	1		2																										
1969	WPG	16																													
1970	WPG	16	0		1																										
1971	TOR+	14	2		3																							1	0	0.0	0
1972	TOR+	14																													
1973	TOR*	14	0		1																										
9	Years	138	4		9																							1	0	0.0	0

Year	Team	GP	FM	FF	FR	TK	SK	YDS	IR	YDS	PD	PTS	TD	RA	YDS	AVG	LG	TD	REC	YDS	AVG	LG	TD	PR	YDS	AVG	LG	KOR	YDS	AVG	LG
PIERRE DESJARDINS Pierre OT-OG 6'0 230 Wyoming B: 10/28/1941 Montreal, QC																														
1966	MTL	13	0		2																									
1967	MTL	13	0		1																									
1968	MTL	14																												
1969	MTL	14																								1	0	0.0	0
1970	MTL	14																												
1971	MTL	4																												
6	Years	72	0		3																						1	0	0.0	0
ERIC DESLAURIERS Eric Johnathan WR-SB 6'4 207 Eastern Michigan B: 3/21/1981 Gatineau, QC Draft: 1-7 2006 MTL																														
2007	MTL	15	1	0	0	1						6	1						23	325	14.1	44	1									
2008	MTL	18				1													12	89	7.4	13	0									
2009	MTL	4	0	0	1	0						6	1						1	5	5.0	5	0									
2010	MTL	5				5													6	49	8.2	12	0									
2011	MTL	18	1	0	0	6						12	2						6	98	16.3	31	2					1	0	0.0	0
5	Years	60	2	0	1	13						24	4						48	566	11.8	44	3					1	0	0.0	0
LAURENT DESLAURIERS Laurent S-WR 6'2 200 British Columbia B: 1/7/1962 Vancouver, BC Draft: TE 1984 BC																														
1984	EDM*	16	0		2				9	110															5	41	8.2	17	1	0	0.0	0
1985	EDM	16								9	183															2	7	3.5	7				
1986	EDM	9	1		0				4	104															1	12	12.0	12				
1988	TOR	17				41	1.0		5	65																					
4	Years	58	1		2	41	1.0		27	462															8	60	7.5	17	1	0	0.0	0
DICK DESMARAIS Richard R. HB 5'10 185 Boston University B: 6/19/1937																														
1961	OTT	7										24	4	53	345	6.5	41	3	9	143	15.9	33	1					8	265	33.1	56
DANNY DESRIVEAUX Danny SB-WR 5'9 194 Connecticut*; Richmond B: 11/20/1981 Montreal, QC Draft: 6-43 2006 MTL																														
2007	MTL	18	0	0	2	2						6	1						21	262	12.5	29	1									
2008	MTL	18	1	0	0	1						6	1						27	278	10.3	44	1									
2009	MTL	18				2													6	63	10.5	17	0									
2010	MTL	18				2													4	45	11.3	18	0									
2011	MTL	8				1													2	11	5.5	6	0									
5	Years	80	1	0	2	8						12	2						60	659	11.0	44	2									
ROBBY DESROSIERS Robby WR 6'2 210 Western Michigan; Laval B: 2/6/1972 Montreal, QC																														
1999	SAS	3				0																									
ROY DETLOR Roy Melvin T B: 1925 D: 2/4/1996																														
1946	SAS	7																												
1947	SAS	6																												
2	Years	13																												
DANNY DEVER Dan LB 6'0 180 Wake Forest B: 2/7/1946 Ottawa, ON																														
1968	OTT	3																												
1969	OTT	14																												
1970	OTT	14	0		1				3	105																			4	3	0.8	3
1971	OTT	14	1		3				1	0																			2	13	6.5	12
1972	OTT	14	0		1																								2	8	4.0	4
1973	OTT	14																										1	6	6.0	6
1974	BC	12	0		3																									
7	Years	85	1		8				4	105																			9	30	3.3	12
KEVIN DEVINE Kevin L. CB 5'9 182 California B: 12/11/1974 Jackson, MS Pro: EN																														
2002	OTT	1				1																									
ROY DEWALT Roy Lynn QB 6'1 210 Texas-Arlington B: 9/4/1956 Houston, TX Draft: 9-236 1980 CLE																														
1980	BC	16	6		2								12	2	42	253	6.0	40	2												
1981	BC	16	6		1										17	106	6.2	21	0												
1982	BC	15	9		0								30	5	49	415	8.5	52	5	1	-5	-5.0	-5	0								
1983	BC	15	8		1								12	2	58	352	6.1	40	2												
1984	BC	12	8		2								6	1	23	113	4.9	25	1												
1985	BC	16	9		1								30	5	48	161	3.4	22	5	1	1	1.0	1	0								
1986	BC	18	11		2								12	2	45	109	2.4	18	2	1	6	6.0	6	0								
1987	BC+	17	11		4	1						6	1	25	128	5.1	25	1												
1988	WPG	10	4		0	0								9	31	3.4	13	0												
1988	OTT	4	1		0	0						6	1	15	115	7.7	21	1												
1988	Year	14	5		0	0						6	1	24	146	6.1	21	1												
9	Years	135	73		13	1						114	19	331	1783	5.4	52	19	3	2	0.7	6	0								
MARK DEWIT Mark OG-C-TE-OT 6'2 288 Weber State; Calgary B: 11/3/1986 Calgary, AB Draft: 6A-42 2008 TOR																														
2008	TOR	18				0																									
2009	TOR	18				2																									
2011	HAM	9				0																									
3	Years	45				2																									
JOHN DeWITT John Donovan DL 6'4 277 Vanderbilt B: 11/13/1970 Fort Smith, AR Pro: EX																														
2001	MTL	3				4																									
WILLARD DEWVEALL Willard Charles (The Duke) E 6'4 224 Southern Methodist B: 4/29/1936 Springtown, TX D: 11/20/2006 Weatherford, TX Draft: 2-18 1958 CHIB Pro: N																														
1958	WPG	1																	1	9	9.0	9	0								
BENJY DIAL Benjamin Franklin QB 6'1 185 Eastern New Mexico B: 5/21/1943 Hall County, TX D: 4/5/2001 Dallas, TX Draft: 13-188 1966 PIT Pro: N																														
1970	WPG	7	3		0								6	1	14	15	1.1	5	1												
1971	WPG	7										1	0	8	11	1.4	9	0												
2	Years	14	3		0								7	1	22	26	1.2	9	1												
CHARLIE DIAMOND Charles John T 6'2 249 Miami (Florida) B: 7/19/1936 Miami, FL Pro: N																														
1959	BC	2																												
SKIP DIAZ Rance DT 5'9 262 Oregon State B: 2/17/1944 Honolulu, HI																														
1968	BC	9	0		3																									
DAVID DIAZ-INFANTE Gustavo David Mienez OG 6'3 296 San Jose State B: 3/31/1964 San Jose, CA Pro: ENX																														
1993	SAC	8				0																									
1994	SAC	18	0		1	5																									
2	Years	26	0		1	5																									
LARRY DIBBLES Larry James DE-DT 6'4 251 Texas Christian; New Mexico B: 3/30/1951 Dallas, TX Draft: 9-221 1973 MIN																														
1973	CAL	5																												
LARRY DICK Larry QB 6'2 195 Maryland B: 3/22/1955																														
1978	SAS	16												5	8	1.6	3	0												
1979	SAS	8												7	46	6.6	20	0												
2	Years	24												12	54	4.5	20	0												
BILLY DICKEN William C. QB 6'2 210 Purdue B: 12/28/1974 Bloomington, IL																														
2000	HAM	12	3	0	0	0						6	1	5	31	6.2	16	1												
DAVE DICKENSON Dave QB 5'11 185 Montana B: 1/11/1973 Great Falls, MT																														
1997	CAL	18	2	0	0	0								4	11	2.8	5	0												
1998	CAL	18	1	0	0	0						18	3	15	66	4.4	24	3												
1999	CAL	15	5	0	4	0						6	1	30	236	7.9	25	1												
2000	CAL*	18	8	0	2	0						36	6	56	309	5.5	36	5	1	25	25.0	25	1								
2003	BC+	18	7	0	5	0						12	2	44	311	7.1	21	2												
2004	BC	8	1	0	0	0								12	78	6.5	16	0												
2005	BC	14	1	0	0	1						18	3	49	299	6.1	24	3												
2006	BC	17	1	0	0	1								32	195	6.1	15	0												
2007	BC	8				0								9	44	4.9	13	0												
2008	CAL	9				0								2	11	5.5	6	0												
10	Years	143	26	0	11	2						90	15	253	1560	6.2	36	14	1	25	25.0	25	1								
ANTHONY DICKERSON Anthony Charles LB 6'2 222 Trinity Valley CC; Southern Methodist B: 6/9/1957 Texas City, TX Pro: N																														

Year	Team	GP	FM	FF	FR	TK	SK	YDS	IR	YDS	PD	PTS	TD	RA	YDS	AVG	LG	TD	REC	YDS	AVG	LG	TD	PR	YDS	AVG	LG	KOR	YDS	AVG	LG
1978	CAL	2							1	0																		1	0	0.0	0
1978	TOR	1	0		1																										
1978	Year	3	0		1				1	0																		1	0	0.0	0
CED DICKERSON Cedric DH 6'1 210 Valdosta State B: 10/31/1980 Selma, AL																															
2004	WPG	3				3			1	5	0																				
2005	WPG	2	0	0	1	11																									
2	Years	5	0	0	1	14			1	5	0																				
KORI DICKERSON Kori Markese TE-DE-FB 6'4 238 Southern California B: 12/6/1978 Pro: EN																															
2005	CAL	4				1													2	37	18.5	26	0								
2007	HAM	18	0	0	1	5						6	1	1	4	4.0	4	0	29	306	10.6	34	1					4	33	8.3	11
2008	HAM	5				3																									
3	Years	27	0	0	1	9						6	1	1	4	4.0	4	0	31	343	11.1	34	1					4	33	8.3	11
TOMMY DICKERSON Tom Lewis QB 5'10 185 Tulsa B: 3/31/1930 Chickasha, OK																															
1955	CAL	3										5	1	22	-1	-0.0	13	1													
TERRY DICKEY Terry SB-RB 5'7 170 DePauw B: 9/6/1970 Columbus, OH																															
1993	TOR	6	1		0	1								3	10	3.3	4	0	16	136	8.5	24	0	2	11	5.5	9	9	98	10.9	20
1994	TOR	4				0													11	200	18.2	58	0					1	24	24.0	24
2	Years	10	1		0	1								3	10	3.3	4	0	27	336	12.4	58	0	2	11	5.5	9	10	122	12.2	24
TROY DICKEY Troy WR 6'3 225 Coffeyville CC; Arizona B: 4/8/1971																															
1995	SAS	1				0																									
WALLACE DICKEY Wallace, Jr. OG 6'3 260 Victoria JC; Texas State B: 2/15/1941 San Antonio, TX Draft: 15-207 1965 DET Pro: N																															
1965	TOR	6	0		1																										
BOB DICKIE Bob QB 6'0 177 NDG Maple Leafs Jrs. B: 1937 Moose Jaw, SK																															
1957	BC	3																													
1958	MTL	14												3	5	1.7	5	0						16	40	2.5	10				
2	Years	17												3	5	1.7	5	0						16	40	2.5	10				
BO DICKINSON Richard Lee FB 6'2 218 Southern Mississippi B: 7/18/1935 Hattiesburg, MS Draft: 6-72 1957 CHIB Pro: N																															
1958	MTL	14										6	1	41	177	4.3	17	1	5	38	7.6	21	0					3	37	12.3	15
BRUCE DICKSON Bruce LB 6'2 225 Burlington Braves Jrs.; Simon Fraser B: 10/11/1967 Hamilton, ON Draft: 3A-18 1991 TOR																															
1991	TOR	3				2																									
1992	TOR	12	0		1	15																									
1993	EDM	15	1		2	26	1.0	6.0	1	22																		1	0	0.0	0
1994	EDM	18				27																									
1995	EDM	18	0		4	33	1.0	4.0																							
1996	EDM	18	0		1	25	1.0	3.0																							
1997	EDM	18	0	1	2	68	3.0	7.0																							
1998	BC	9	0	2	1	33																									
1998	MTL	7				6													1	11	11.0	11	0					1	0	0.0	0
1998	Year	16				39													1	11	11.0	11	0					1	0	0.0	0
8	Years	111	1	3	11	235	6.0	20.0	1	22									1	11	11.0	11	0					2	0	0.0	0
WAYNE DICKSON Elvis Wayne LB 6'3 253 Oklahoma B: 11/27/1967 Houston, TX Pro: E																															
1990	BC	4				5																									
1991	SAS	8				20	2.0																								
2	Years	12				25	2.0																								
DAHRRAN DIEDRICK Dahrran FB-RB 6'0 225 Nebraska B: 1/11/1979 Montego Bay, Jamaica Draft: 3-24 2002 EDM Pro: EN																															
2005	EDM	7				1								10	31	3.1	7	0										8	159	19.9	30
2006	EDM	3				0																									
2006	MTL	11				2								10	65	6.5	15	0	1	8	8.0	8	0					8	185	23.1	39
2006	Year	14				2								10	65	6.5	15	0	1	8	8.0	8	0					8	185	23.1	39
2007	MTL	16				9								10	46	4.6	11	0	1	3	3.0	3	0								
2008	MTL	16	0	0	1	3								42	263	6.3	39	0	3	18	6.0	8	0								
2009	MTL	14	0	1	0	16								19	106	5.6	45	0	1	8	8.0	8	0					1	6	6.0	6
2010	MTL	17	1	0	1	7						6	1	27	110	4.1	13	0	4	25	6.3	11	0					1	-8	-8.0	-8
2011	MTL	18	2	0	1	9						36	6	49	196	4.0	22	6	1	2	2.0	2	0								
7	Years	91	3	1	3	47						42	7	167	817	4.9	45	6	11	64	5.8	11	0					18	342	19.0	39
LOUIE DiFRANCESCO Louis OG-C 5'10 208 B: 2/21/1924																															
1947	HAM	10																													
1950	HAM	9																													
1951	HAM	12																													
1952	HAM	10																													
1953	HAM	1																													
5	Years	42																													
DANNY DiFRANCESCO Dante C-E B: 1926																															
1947	HAM	6																													
JOHN DIGGS John DB 5'10 190 Washington State B: 12/16/1968																															
1994	SAC	6				7																									
JIM DILLARD James A. FB-OHB 6'2 210 Oklahoma State B: 1939 Draft: 9-65 1962 OAK; 4-51 1962 BAL																															
1962	CAL	16	3									54	9	92	480	5.2	33	3	38	733	19.3	64	6					15	309	20.6	36
1963	CAL+	15	2		0							78	13	108	690	6.4	54	7	34	543	16.0	68	6					15	338	22.5	65
1964	CAL	5										18	3	30	179	6.0	18	0	16	224	14.0	39	3								
1965	OTT+	12	3		0							24	4	130	756	5.8	65	3	8	188	23.5	48	1					2	41	20.5	25
1966	OTT	14	1		0							42	7	129	627	4.9	41	7	22	250	11.4	33	0					1	9	9.0	9
1967	TOR+	12										54	9	124	670	5.4	60	7	19	242	12.7	44	2					12	318	26.5	41
1968	TOR	14	3		0							12	2	120	547	4.6	47	1	27	316	11.7	48	1								
7	Years	88	12		0							282	47	733	3949	5.4	65	28	164	2496	15.2	68	19					45	1015	22.6	65
JIM DILLARD James A. OT 6'4 255 Oklahoma State B: 2/19/1965																															
1989	CAL	4																													
MEL DILLARD Melvin Laurel FB 6'2 191 Purdue B: 2/27/1935 Draft: 11-124 1958 PHI																															
1958	CAL	2												2	15	7.5	12	0													
RAY DON DILLON Ray Dohn HB 6'2 195 Prairie View A&M B: 9/1929 Draft: 30-357 1952 DET																															
1952	HAM	8										20	4										2								
TODD DILLON Todd Matthew QB 6'0 195 San Joaquin Delta JC; Long Beach State B: 1/6/1962 Modesto, CA Draft: TD 1984 LA-USFL Pro: U																															
1986	OTT	12	1		0									4	6	1.5	3	0													
1987	OTT	14	4		3	0								29	228	7.9	19	0													
1988	OTT	7	3		0	2						18	3	16	109	6.8	37	3													
1989	HAM	18	4		1	0								22	106	4.8	32	0													
1990	HAM	18				0								14	59	4.2	18	0													
1991	HAM	17	1		0	2						12	2	39	243	6.2	25	2													
1992	HAM	18	2		2	3								7	47	6.7	23	0													
1993	HAM	1	1		0	0								5	23	4.6	11	0													
1994	HAM	18	2		0	1								12	32	2.7	14	0													
9	Years	123	18		6	8						30	5	148	853	5.8	37	5													
JOHN DILWORTH John DB 6'0 170 Northwestern State (Louisiana) B: 1/23/1953 Pine Bluff, AR Draft: 11-283 1975 MIA																															
1976	CAL	7																										4	69	17.3	25
FRANK DiMAGGIO Frank James QB 6'1 210 Temple B: 5/1/1950 New York, NY Pro: W																															
1973	OTT	1												3	18	6.0	13	0													
TOM DIMITROFF Thomas George QB-DB 5'11 200 Miami (Ohio) B: 6/6/1935 Akron, OH D: 1/20/1996 Strongsville, OH Draft: 25-294 1957 CLE Pro: N																															
1957	OTT	14										31	5	87	423	4.9	17	5													
1958	OTT	5										12	2	45	-31	-0.7	15	2													
2	Years	19										43	7	132	392	3.0	17	7													
TOM DIMMICK Thomas Evans G 6'6 253 Houston B: 5/1/1931 Opelousas, LA Draft: 10-113 1956 PHI Pro: N																															
1957	HAM	3																													

Year	Team	GP	FM	FF	FR	TK	SK	YDS	IR	YDS	PD	PTS	TD	RA	YDS	AVG	LG	TD	REC	YDS	AVG	LG	TD	PR	YDS	AVG	LG	KOR	YDS	AVG	LG
SHAUN DINER Shaun SB 6'2 199 New Hampshire B: 7/11/1980 Laval, QC																															
2005	MTL	7				4																						1	18	18.0	18
2006	MTL	14	0	0	1	13			1	5	0								3	18	6.0	8	0								
2007	MTL	9				3													1	6	6.0	6	0								
3	Years	30	0	0	1	20			1	5	0								4	24	6.0	8	0					1	18	18.0	18
MIKE DINGLE Miguel Bryce FB 6'2 240 South Carolina B: 1/30/1969 Moncks Corner, SC Draft: 8-211 1991 CIN Pro: N																															
1995	SA	6				3								5	4	0.8	4	0	1	44	44.0	44	0								
1995	MEM	4				1													4	36	9.0	12	0								
1995	Year	10				4								5	4	0.8	4	0	5	80	16.0	44	0								
DAVE DINNALL Dave RB 5'11 190 Burlington Braves Jrs. B: 9/4/1969 London, England																															
1992	HAM	3				4																						4	71	17.8	30
1993	HAM	15	1		1	15						12	2	12	117	9.8	63	1	2	23	11.5	14	0					1	16	16.0	16
1994	HAM	16	2		2	10						6	1	37	181	4.9	19	1	8	52	6.5	14	0	8	36	4.5	15	13	273	21.0	38
1995	OTT	6	2		1	2						6	1	20	79	4.0	16	1	11	96	8.7	18	0					1	8	8.0	8
1996	SAS	1				0								5	45	9.0	19	0	1	16	16.0	16	0								
1996	OTT	9	1		1	5						24	4	49	404	8.2	69	4	6	89	14.8	42	0	1	11	11.0	11	2	46	23.0	28
1996	Year	10	1		1	5						24	4	54	449	8.3	69	4	7	105	15.0	42	0	1	11	11.0	11	2	46	23.0	28
1997	SAS	4	1	0	0	0																		2	12	6.0	6	3	43	14.3	20
6	Years	45	7	0	5	36						48	8	123	826	6.7	69	7	28	276	9.9	42	0	11	59	5.4	15	24	457	19.0	38
RYAN DINWIDDIE Ryan Lee QB 6'1 190 Boise State B: 11/27/1980 Sacramento, CA Pro: E																															
2006	WPG	9				0								1	1	1.0	1	0													
2007	WPG	18				0								1	10	10.0	10	0													
2008	WPG	17	2	0	0	0						6	1	21	101	4.8	20	1													
2010	SAS	18				0																									
2011	SAS	18				0								13	65	5.0	18	0													
5	Years	80	2	0	0	0						6	1	36	177	4.9	20	1													
ROCKY DiPIETRO Rocky SB-TE-WR-RB 6'3 210 Ottawa B: 1/30/1956 Sault Ste. Marie, ON Draft: TE 1978 HAM																															
1978	HAM	16										14	2						29	463	16.0	42	2								
1979	HAM	4																													
1980	HAM	16	3		0							12	2						55	869	15.8	51	2	1	3	3.0	3				
1981	HAM+	16	3		2							36	6						59	868	14.7	42	6					3	12	4.0	6
1982	HAM+	16	1		2							30	5						85	1160	13.6	49	5								
1983	HAM	16	1		1							12	2	0	25		25	0	56	693	12.4	36	2					1	11	11.0	11
1984	HAM	16	1		0							32	5						71	1063	15.0	80	5					2	8	4.0	7
1985	HAM	14	2		0							24	4						52	593	11.4	45	4								
1986	HAM*	16	1		0							24	4						86	1087	12.6	47	4								
1987	HAM	12	2		0	5						24	4						54	654	12.1	52	4					1	0	0.0	0
1988	HAM	18	1		0	3						24	4						50	706	14.1	35	4								
1989	HAM*	18	1		0	2						12	2						58	883	15.2	44	2					3	-2	-0.7	-3
1990	HAM	8				1						6	1						13	197	15.2	32	1								
1991	HAM	18	1		0	6						24	4						38	525	13.8	43	4					1	0	0.0	0
14	Years	204	17		5	17						274	45	0	25		25	0	706	9761	13.8	80	45	1	3	3.0	3	11	29	2.6	11
MIKE DIRKS Marion Gearhart, Jr. DT-OG-OT 6'2 247 Wyoming B: 8/28/1946 Monticello, IA Draft: 5A-122 1968 PHI Pro: N																															
1972	WPG	3							1	5																					
1973	WPG	16	0		3																										
1974	WPG	9																													
1974	SAS	2																													
1974	Year	11																													
1975	SAS	16																													
1976	SAS	16																										1	15	15.0	15
1977	SAS	16																										2	20	10.0	12
1978	SAS	7																													
7	Years	83	0		3				1	5																		3	35	11.7	15
DOM DISIPIO Dominic																															
1946	OTT	1																													
CARLO DISIPIO Carlo RB 5'8 205 Ottawa B: 5/14/1970 Ottawa, ON																															
1996	OTT	5				1																									
DAN DISLEY Daniel SB 6'2 200 Western Ontario B: 10/27/1975 St. Catherines, ON Draft: 5-39 1999 CAL																															
1999	CAL	4				0																									
2000	CAL	12				6					1																				
2	Years	16				6					1																				
SETH DITTMAN Seth D. OT 6'7 300 Stanford B: 7/23/1972 Newberg, OR Pro: EX																															
1998	HAM	18				1																									
1999	HAM	18				0																									
2000	HAM	10				0																									
2001	HAM	18				0																									
2002	OTT	18				2																									
2003	OTT	18	0	0	1	1																									
2004	CAL+	18				4																									
7	Years	118	0	0	1	8																									
DE'AUDRA DIX De'Audra CB-DH 5'10 160 Johnson C. Smith B: 3/3/1984 Merritt Island, FL																															
2009	MTL	10				19			1	41	2																				
2010	MTL	18	0	1	0	34			2	4	6																	3	89	29.7	37
2011	MTL	17	0	0	3	30					7	6	1											1	15	15.0	15	4	73	18.3	23
3	Years	45	0	1	3	83			3	45	15	6	1											1	15	15.0	15	7	162	23.1	37
COREY DIXON Corey WR 5'7 155 Nebraska B: 2/16/1972																															
1995	SA	1	1		0	0																		2	9	4.5	5	3	51	17.0	21
DAVID DIXON David LB 6'2 235 Blinn JC; Hutchinson CC B: 2/14/1985																															
2006	HAM	5				9			1	32	0																				
GEORGE DIXON George OHB-DB-DB 6'1 195 Arnold; Bridgeport B: 10/19/1933 New Haven, CT D: 8/6/1990 Montreal, QC Draft: 9-97 1959 GB																															
1959	MTL	7										6	1	38	301	7.9	77	1	22	322	14.6	37	0	1	3	3.0	3	6	98	16.3	26
1960	MTL	12							1	5		108	18	161	976	6.1	70	9	33	455	13.8	47	9					14	284	20.3	29
1961	MTL	11										48	8	138	806	5.8	50	7	15	211	14.1	49	1	1	5	5.0	5	9	243	27.0	36
1962	MTL*	14										90	15	216	1520	7.0	75	11	24	393	16.4	67	4					12	296	24.7	43
1963	MTL*	14										66	11	189	1270	6.7	109	10	16	190	11.9	52	1					16	352	22.0	45
1964	MTL	12	2		2							30	5	107	594	5.6	76	4	18	155	8.6	49	1					12	329	27.4	41
1965	MTL	6										6	1	47	148	3.1	14	0	13	190	14.6	28	1								
7	Years	76	2		2				1	5		354	59	896	5615	6.3	109	42	141	1916	13.6	67	17	2	8	4.0	5	69	1602	23.2	45
GERALD DIXON Gerald CB 5'10 187 Alabama B: 10/7/1980 Jamaica Pro: E																															
2005	EDM	13				13					1																				
2006	EDM	16	0	2	1	48			2	72	1	6	1																		
2	Years	29	0	2	1	61			2	72	2	6	1																		
JOHNNIE DIXON Johnnie CB-LB-DH 5'11 194 Pearl River CC B: 12/11/1988 Belle Glade, FL																															
2010	CAL	3				4					1																				
2011	CAL	8				13					2																				
2	Years	11				17					3																				
JOHNNY DIXON Johnny DB 6'0 205 Mississippi B: 2/13/1971 New Orleans, LA Pro: E																															
1995	SHR	7				7																									
KEVIN DIXON Kevin FB 6'1 230 Richmond Raiders Jrs.; Walla Walla JC B: 12/14/1961 Montreal, QC																															
1987	BC	13	1		4	1						6	1	7	33	4.7	8	0										1	11	11.0	11
1988	BC	6				0																									
1989	SAS	9				1								1	1	1.0	1	0	1	24	24.0	24	0								

Year	Team	GP	FM	FF	FR	TK	SK	YDS	IR	YDS	PD	PTS	TD	RA	YDS	AVG	LG	TD	REC	YDS	AVG	LG	TD	PR	YDS	AVG	LG	KOR	YDS	AVG	LG
3	Years	28	1		4	2						6	1	8	34	4.3	8	0	1	24	24.0	24	0					1	11	11.0	11
KEVIN DIXON Kevin DE 6'2 260 Garden City CC; Nebraska; Troy B: 5/7/1987 Sebring, FL																															
2011	CAL	10	0	1	0	14	2.0	13.0																							
MARK DIXON Mark Keller OG-OT 6'4 299 Virginia B: 11/26/1970 Charlottesville, NC Pro: EN																															
1995	BAL	8				0																									
1996	MTL	18				1																									
1997	MTL	7				1																									
3	Years	33				2																									
ORVIL DIXON Orvil RB 5'11 195 Burlington Tiger-Cats Jrs. B: 1/16/1967 St. Mary's, Jamaica																															
1990	TOR	2				0																						1	0	0.0	0
RALPH DIXON Ralph CB 5'10 185 Arizona State B: 5/11/1958 Biloxi, MS																															
1982	EDM	4							1	24																					
1984	EDM	5																													
1984	TOR	4	1		0				2	36																					
1984	Year	9	1		0				2	36																					
1985	OTT	15	0		3		2.0		3	20		6	1											1	0	0.0	0				
3	Years	24	1		3		2.0		6	80		6	1											1	0	0.0	0				
TITUS DIXON Titus L. WR 5'6 152 Troy B: 6/15/1966 Clewiston, FL Draft: 6B-153 1989 NYJ Pro: EN																															
1993	SAC	15	3		1	2						30	5						61	1074	17.6	90	5	3	6	2.0	6	31	602	19.4	42
1994	TOR	4	2		0	2								2	11	5.5	14	0	9	83	9.2	20	0	4	25	6.3	16	12	262	21.8	44
1994	HAM	2				0													3	73	24.3	40	0	1	0	0.0	0	3	54	18.0	23
1994	Year	6				2								2	11	5.5	14	0	12	156	13.0	40	0	5	25	5.0	16	15	316	21.1	44
2	Years	19	5		1	4						30	5	2	11	5.5	14	0	73	1230	16.8	90	5	8	31	3.9	16	46	918	20.0	44
TOM DIXON Tom K-P 5'11 185 Richmond Raiders Jrs.; British Columbia B: 1/13/1960 Vancouver, BC																															
1985	EDM+	16	2		0							138	0																		
1986	EDM+	18	3		1							190	0																		
1987	EDM	5				0						48	0																		
1987	OTT	2	1		0	0						13	0																		
1987	Year	7	1		0	0						61	0																		
1988	OTT	18	3		0	0						121	0																		
4	Years	57	9		1	0						510	0																		
JOHN DLUGOS John T 6'0 202 Saskatoon Hilltops Jrs. B: 1928																															
1949	EDM	12																													
1950	EDM	12																													
1951	EDM	12																													
3	Years	36																													
DUANE DMYTRYSHYN Duane SB-FB 6'1 210 Saskatchewan B: 6/11/1971 Saskatoon, SK Draft: 3A-21 1993 CAL																															
1993	CAL	1				0																									
1994	CAL	17	1		0	14								1	4	4.0	4	0	1	5	5.0	5	0								
1995	TOR	5				3													1	7	7.0	7	0								
1996	TOR	18				5						12	2	2	5	2.5	5	0	13	218	16.8	28	2					1	0	0.0	0
1997	TOR	18				11						18	3						22	468	21.3	78	3								
1998	TOR	18	1	0	2	8						24	4	10	46	4.6	12	1	47	651	13.9	47	3								
1999	TOR	17	1	1	1	9								6	25	4.2	11	0	11	166	15.1	32	0								
2000	SAS	18				10						6	1						6	94	15.7	31	1								
8	Years	112	3	1	3	60						60	10	19	80	4.2	12	1	101	1609	15.9	78	9					1	0	0.0	0
RYAN DOAK Ryan DB 6'3 210 Northern Iowa B: 8/18/1978 Lincoln, NE																															
2001	BC	4	0	0	1	18																									
DAVE DOANE David QB 6'0 193 Missouri B: 1935																															
1957	TOR	2												8	30	3.8	14	0													
JACK DOANES Jack C																															
1948	WPG	9																													
JIM DOBBIN Jim HB 165 North Hill Blizzard Jrs.																															
1948	CAL	7																													
HERBIE DOBBINS Herbert OG 6'4 260 Mount San Antonio JC; San Diego State B: 6/22/1951 Pro: N																															
1977	EDM	16	0		3																										
GLENN DOBBS Glenn, Jr. QB 6'4 210 Tulsa B: 7/12/1920 McKinney, TX D: 11/12/2002 Tulsa, OK Draft: 1-3 1943 CHIC Pro: A																															
1951	SAS+	14										55	7	38	94	2.5		7													
1952	SAS	12												35	70	2.0	23	0	1	12	12.0	12	0								
1953	SAS	9										2	0	16	77	4.8		0													
1954	HAM	1										1	0																		
4	Years	36										58	7	89	241	2.7	23	7	1	12	12.0	12	0								
WALT DOBLER Walter QB 5'9 175 North Dakota B: 12/26/1919 ND D: 11/5/1995																															
1946	WPG+	6										12	0																		
JERRY DOBROVOLNY Jerry ot-og 6'5 255 British Columbia B: 7/24/1961 New Westminster, BC Draft: 1A-1 1983 CAL																															
1983	CAL	9	0		3																										
1984	CAL	16																													
1985	MTL	13																													
1986	MTL	6																													
1986	OTT	8																													
1986	Year	14																													
1987	OTT	6				0																									
5	Years	50	0		3	0																									
CLIFF DOBSON Cliff HB Regina Westend Gophers Jrs. D: 7/3/2009																															
1947	SAS	2																													
DUSTIN DOE Dustin LB 6'0 228 Florida B: 9/10/1987 Jasper, FL																															
2011	WPG	3				4																									
GEORGE DOEHLA George D. LB 6'3 227 Indiana B: 10/24/1956 Fort Wayne, IN																															
1979	HAM	2																													
HARRY DOERING Harry DE 6'4 240 Guelph B: 9/9/1959 Draft: 2A-10 1982 EDM																															
1983	EDM	3																													
1983	CAL	9																													
1983	Year	12																													
DERRICK DOGGETT Derrick Shawn LB 6'3 210 Oregon State B: 12/31/1984 San Diego, CA																															
2008	EDM	4				7																									
2009	WPG	15				36			1	0	0																				
2010	WPG	2				1																									
3	Years	21				44			1	0	0																				
GARRETT DOLL Garrett LB 6'2 220 Edmonton Huskies Jrs.; Alberta B: 1/9/1963 Fairview, AB Draft: 2A-11 1985 CAL																															
1985	CAL	11	0		1																										
1986	CAL	18					3.0		2	15																					
1987	CAL	2				0																									
3	Years	31	0		1	0	3.0		2	15																					
KEN DOMBROWSKI Kenneth DE-DT 6'4 260 Arizona Western JC; Cameron B: 6/25/1954 Buffalo, NY Pro: U																															
1977	HAM	3																													
1979	CAL	16																													
1980	CAL	13	0		1																										
1981	CAL	1					1.0																								
4	Years	33	0		1		1.0																								
MATT DOMINGUEZ Matthew Pilar WR-TE 6'2 219 Sam Houston State B: 6/27/1978 Georgetown, TX Pro: N																															
2003	SAS	18	0	0	1	3						18	3						75	1071	14.3	72	3								
2004	SAS	5				1						18	3						28	331	11.8	50	3								

Year	Team	GP	FM	FF	FR	TK	SK	YDS	IR	YDS	PD	PTS	TD	RA	YDS	AVG	LG	TD	REC	YDS	AVG	LG	TD	PR	YDS	AVG	LG	KOR	YDS	AVG	LG
2005	SAS	2				0						12	2						11	142	12.9	34	2								
2006	SAS*	17	1	0	0	1						32	5						72	1169	16.2	64	5								
2007	SAS	10				0						30	5						45	761	16.9	69	5								
2008	SAS	7	2	0	0	0						6	1						19	267	14.1	48	1								
6	Years	59	3	0	1	5						116	19						250	3741	15.0	72	19								
KEN DON Ken FB-HB 5'11 195 Regina Rams Jrs.; Arizona B: 1939																															
1960	SAS	5	0		2									6	17	2.8	13	0	2	28	14.0	15	0								
1961	SAS	14																						3	16	5.3	6	1	23	23.0	23
1963	SAS	3																													
3	Years	22	0		2									6	17	2.8	13	0	2	28	14.0	15	0	3	16	5.3	6	1	23	23.0	23
OSCAR DONAHUE Oscar OE-FL 6'3 195 San Francisco CC; San Jose State B: 6/7/1937 Draft: 12C-94 1962 OAK; 6B-84 1962 GB Pro: N																															
1963	TOR	2																	1	22	22.0	22	0								
BUD DONALD Bud T 6'0 200																															
1948	HAM	11																													
1949	HAM	9																													
2	Years	20																													
DAVE DONALDSON Dave S-CB-DH-WR 5'10 180 Manitoba B: 12/9/1972 Winnipeg, MB																															
1997	BC	12				2																						1	14	14.0	14
1998	BC	18	0	0	3	24			1	3	1								10	159	15.9	33	0					5	161	32.2	38
1999	BC	18				20																						3	57	19.0	25
2000	WPG	18	0	1	1	59			2	7	4								5	54	10.8	35	0	1	10	10.0	10	1	9	9.0	9
2001	WPG	18	0	3	2	36	3.0	22.0			2													1	1	1.0	1				
2002	WPG	18	0	1	1	38	1.0	6.0	1	10	5																				
2003	WPG	18	0	0	3	25			2	10	4	6	1																		
2004	OTT	16	0	1	3	34			1	9	2	6	1																		
2005	OTT	15	0	1	2	10					1																				
2006	TOR	13	0	1	0	11																						1	0	0.0	0
10	Years	164	0	8	15	259	4.0	28.0	7	39	19	12	2						15	213	14.2	35	0	2	11	5.5	10	11	241	21.9	38
GENE DONALDSON Eugene OT-DT 5'9 225 Kentucky B: 9/29/1930 Draft: 3B-37 1953 CLE Pro: N																															
1956	HAM	13																													
GENE DONALDSON Eugene Harold LB 6'2 225 Purdue B: 11/4/1942 Birmingham, AL D: 9/7/2002 Draft: 11-143 1964 WAS Pro: N																															
1966	TOR	11	0		1				1	13																					
1967	HAM	1																													
2	Years	12	0		1				1	13																					
CASSIDY DONEFF Cassidy WR 6'0 183 Calgary; Washburn B: 7/14/1986 Cochrane, AB Draft: 2009 HAM																															
2011	WPG	1				0																									
VENTSON DONELSON Ventson CB 5'11 180 Michigan State B: 2/2/1968 Rock Island, IL Draft: 12A-309 1990 NE																															
1991	SAS	3	1		0	10																						2	46	23.0	25
1992	SAS	18	0		1	72			3	7																		1	0	0.0	0
1993	SAS	14				43	1.0	4.0																							
1994	SAS	10				17			2	23	8																				
1995	SAS	18	0		1	57	1.0	16.0	2	5	4																				
1996	SAS	17				47			3	30	12																				
1997	SAS	11	0	1	2	32					5													1	0	0.0	0				
1998	SAS	9	0	1	1	26	2.0	18.0			1																				
1999	SAS	10	0	1	2	26	1.0	4.0	1	8	2																				
2000	SAS	5				26			1	0	0																				
10	Years	115	1	3	7	356	5.0	42.0	12	73	32													1	0	0.0	0	3	46	15.3	25
PAT DONLEY Patrick DE 6'4 255 Kentucky B: 7/6/1953 Toledo, OH																															
1977	HAM	5	0		1																										
DEE JAY DONLIN Dee Jay QB 6'1 188 Augustana (South Dakota) B: 7/19/1956 Merrill, IA																															
1978	WPG	4																													
DICK DONLIN Richard M. E-P 6'5 210 Hamline B: 6/19/1934 Draft: 2-21 1956 BAL																															
1957	WPG	1																													
BRIAN DONNELLY Brian DB 5'11 179 Simon Fraser B: 11/3/1948 Draft: 1A-1 1971 SAS																															
1971	BC	16			2				5	26														2	4	2.0	3				
1972	BC	16	0		1				5	62														4	20	5.0	9				
1973	BC	16							1	24														1	5	5.0	5				
1974	BC	4							2	42														4	9	2.3	5				
1974	HAM	7																						7	52	7.4	17				
1974	Year	11							2	42														11	61	5.5	17				
1975	SAS	1																													
5	Years	53	0		3				13	154														18	90	5.0	17				
RYAN DONNELLY Ryan C-OG 6'06 284 McMaster B: 12/13/1978 St. Catharines, ON Draft: 4-28 2001 HAM																															
2002	HAM	18	0	1	0	1																									
2003	HAM	17				2																									
2004	HAM	16				0																									
2005	HAM	18	0	0	1	0								1	3	3.0	3	0													
2006	HAM	18				0																									
2007	HAM	18				0																									
2008	WPG	15	0	0	1	3																									
2009	WPG	18				1																									
8	Years	138	0	1	2	7								1	3	3.0	3	0													
TOM DONNELLY Tom HB 5'11 185 Calgary Bronks Jrs. B: 1933																															
1955	SAS	10										5	1	9	1	0.1	8	0	2	81	40.5	52	1								
1956	SAS	3	1		0									6	13	2.2	5	0	2	55	27.5	51	0								
1957	SAS	9												2	9	4.5	5	0	1	2	2.0	2	0	1	0	0.0	0				
3	Years	22	1		0							5	1	17	23	1.4	8	0	5	138	27.6	52	1	1	0	0.0	0				
COR DORET Corradino DB-RB 6'0 190 Toronto B: 11/10/1950 Draft: 2B-18 1973 BC																															
1974	TOR	7																													
1975	TOR	5																													
2	Years	12																													
DAVID DORN David WR 6'1 195 Rutgers B: 7/25/1959 Elmer, NJ Draft: 8-206 1981 KC																															
1981	TOR	4										6	1						6	86	14.3	22	1					3	58	19.3	27
AL DOROW Albert Richard QB 6'0 193 Michigan State B: 11/15/1929 Imlay City, MI D: 12/7/2009 Okemos, MI Draft: 3-31 1952 WAS Pro: N																															
1958	SAS	2	2											6	-3	-0.5		0													
1958	BC	6										12	2	37	44	1.2		2													
1958	Year	8	2									12	2	43	41	1.0	17	2													
1959	TOR	7										12	2	27	173	6.4	24	2													
2	Years	9	2		0							24	4	70	214	3.1	24	4													
HENRY DORSCH Henry CB-FB-LB 5'11 197 Regina Rams Jrs.; Tulsa B: 1941 Weyburn, SK																															
1964	SAS	16	1		0									9	51	5.7	17	0													
1965	SAS	16												2	4	2.0	4	0													
1966	SAS	16	1		1							6	1	33	177	5.4	19	1										1	0	0.0	0
1967	SAS	16	0		2				1	15		6	1	8	31	3.9	15	1													
1968	SAS	16	1		1							12	2	9	45	5.0	11	2	2	20	10.0	23	0					1	12	12.0	12
1969	SAS	16	0		1				1	8				4	17	4.3	9	0										1	2	2.0	2
1970	SAS	16							4	44		12	2	1	1	1.0	1	1										1	24	24.0	24
1971	SAS	7																													
8	Years	119	3		5				6	67		36	6	66	326	4.9	19	5	2	20	10.0	23	0					4	38	9.5	24
DEAN DORSEY Dean K-P 5'11 190 Scarborough Rams Jrs.; Toronto B: 3/13/1957 Toronto, ON Pro: N																															
1982	TOR	7										55	0																		

Year	Team	GP	FM	FF	FR	TK	SK	YDS	IR	YDS	PD	PTS	TD	RA	YDS	AVG	LG	TD	REC	YDS	AVG	LG	TD	PR	YDS	AVG	LG	KOR	YDS	AVG	LG
1984	OTT	16										122	0																		
1985	OTT+	16										120	0																		
1986	OTT	18	1		0							134	0																		
1987	OTT+	16				0						141	0																		
1989	OTT	18	1		0	0						148	0																		
1990	OTT	18				0						176	0																		
1991	EDM	6	0		1	0						55	0																		
8	Years	115	2		1	0						951	0																		
DOMINIQUE DORSEY Dominique Ramone RB 5'7 170 Nevada-Las Vegas B: 5/7/1983 Victorville, CA																															
2005	SAS	5	1	0	0	0								1	8	8.0	8	0						21	247	11.8	65	13	267	20.5	34
2006	SAS	14	3	0	1	0						12	2	31	151	4.9	25	2	7	66	9.4	15	0	54	591	10.9	49	39	757	19.4	50
2007	TOR+	13	2	0	0	0						18	3	23	88	3.8	18	0	4	29	7.3	15	0	65	703	10.8	69	26	622	23.9	97
2008	TOR*	13	2	0	0	0						24	4	64	410	6.4	32	2	15	286	19.1	81	0	63	752	11.9	94	50	1257	25.1	92
2009	TOR	4				0																		10	73	7.3	17	17	336	19.8	34
2010	SAS	10	2	0	1	3																		46	286	6.2	20	24	500	20.8	31
6	Years	59	10	0	2	3						54	9	119	657	5.5	32	4	26	381	14.7	81	0	259	2652	10.2	94	169	3739	22.1	97
KEN DORSEY Kenneth Simon QB 6'4 215 Miami (Florida) B: 4/22/1981 Orinda, CA Draft: 7-241 2003 SF Pro: N																															
2010	TOR	17				0																									
LARRY DORSEY Larry Darnell DB 6'1 195 Tennessee State B: 8/15/1953 Corinth, MS Draft: 3-64 1976 SD Pro: N																															
1979	HAM	7	0		1				1	42														1	10	10.0	10				
PATRICK DORVELUS Patrick LB-S 6'1 199 Hofstra B: 6/28/1977 Montreal, QC Draft: 1-5 2002 MTL																															
2002	MTL	14	0	2	0	10																									
2003	MTL	5				7																									
2004	MTL	17	0	0	2	16																		1	0	0.0	0				
2005	MTL	18				23					1																	1	0	0.0	0
2006	MTL	17	0	0	1	9						6	1																		
2007	MTL	13				9			1	21	0																				
6	Years	84	0	2	3	74			1	21	1	6	1											1	0	0.0	0	1	0	0.0	0
AL DOSANT Alan CB 5'11 182 Windsor B: 8/29/1956 Draft: 2-15 1979 OTT																															
1979	OTT	2																													
1979	SAS	1																													
1979	HAM	6	0		1																			1	-4	-4.0	-4	6	101	16.8	23
1979	Year	9	0		1																			1	-4	-4.0	-4	6	101	16.8	23
1980	HAM	10																	1	18	18.0	18	0								
1980	TOR	1																													
1980	Year	11																	1	18	18.0	18	0								
1981	MTL	13	0		2				1	14																		2	23	11.5	15
1982	MTL	1																													
1982	OTT	5																													
1982	Year	6																													
4	Years	26	0		3				1	14									1	18	18.0	18	0	1	-4	-4.0	-4	8	124	15.5	23
BILLY JAMES DOSS Billy James DE-LB-OG 6'2 233 Southern University B: 1943																															
1966	MTL	5	0		2														2	47	23.5	37	0								
1967	MTL	5	0		1																										
1969	HAM	14																													
1970	HAM	2	0		1																										
4	Years	26	0		4														2	47	23.5	37	0								
YVES DOSSOUS Yves LB 6'1 220 Kent State B: 8/8/1976 Montreal, QC Draft: 6-41 2000 EDM																															
2001	EDM	17				20					2																				
AL DOTSON Alphonse Alan T 6'4 258 Grambling State B: 2/25/1943 Houston, TX Draft: RS-1- 1965 KC; 2-24 1965 GB Pro: NW																															
1971	WPG	6																													
FRED DOTY Fred (Scooter) QB 5'7 147 Toronto B: 1924 Toronto, ON																															
1946	TOR	3																													
1947	TOR	12										21	4					1					2								
1948	TOR	9										5	1										1								
1949	TOR	11																													
4	Years	35										26	5					1					3								
LARRY DOTY Larry SB 6'0 180 Linfield B: 11/12/1955																															
1980	SAS	3																	1	30	30.0	30	0	7	127	18.1	70				
GERRY DOUCETTE Gerry QB-HB 6'0 187 none B: 1934 D: 4//2001																															
1954	TOR	8										1	0	1	1	1.0	1	0													
1955	TOR	12												7	29	4.1	27	0													
1956	TOR	13										2	0	3	2	0.7	2	0													
1957	TOR	14										6	1	17	101	5.9	50	1	1	21	21.0	21	0	0	6		6				
1958	TOR	14												13	-47	-3.6	25	0													
1959	TOR	14										1	0	4	3	0.8	2	0													
1960	CAL	16																													
1961	MTL	11																													
8	Years	102										10	1	45	89	2.0	50	1	1	21	21.0	21	0	0	6		6				
ROBERT DOUGHERTY Robert D. QB 5'9 170 Boston University B: 12/18/1972 Visalia, CA Pro: E																															
1995	TOR	5	2		0	0								7	44	6.3	21	0													
1995	OTT	5				0								2	8	4.0	8	0													
1995	Year	10	2		0	0								9	52	5.8	21	0													
ANDRE DOUGLAS Andre OT 6'5 308 Rhode Island; Temple B: 9/14/1986 St. Elizabeth, Jamaica																															
2010	WPG	15				1																									
2011	WPG	18				3																									
2	Years	33				4																									
CURT DOUGLAS Curtis Michael DL 6'2 270 Georgia B: 12/24/1969																															
1995	SHR	1				0																									
DAVID DOUGLAS David DT-DE 6'1 240 Morgan State B: 1/8/1951 Washington, DC Pro: W																															
1975	HAM	1																													
GLEN DOUGLAS Glen E-HB 6'1 178 McGill B: 7/1/1928 Montreal, QC																															
1947	MTL	12										5	1										1								
1948	MTL	12										11	2										1								
1949	MTL	5										5	1										1								
1950	MTL	9																													
1951	MTL	8																													
1952	MTL	11																													
6	Years	57										21	4										3								
KARL DOUGLAS Karl Michael QB 6'2 215 Texas A&M-Kingsville B: 6/17/1949 Houston, TX Draft: 3-78 1971 BAL Pro: U																															
1973	BC	16	2		1							6	1	21	88	4.2	15	1													
1974	BC	13												3	11	3.7	8	0													
1974	CAL	3												2	8	4.0	6	0													
1974	Year	16												5	19	3.8	8	0													
1975	CAL	16										2	0	14	6	0.4	5	0													
3	Years	45	2		1							8	1	40	113	2.8	15	1													
LARRY DOUGLAS Larry WR 6'1 187 Southern University B: 4/26/1957 Independence, LA Pro: U																															
1980	WPG	2																	4	51	12.8	17	0								
SCOTT DOUGLAS Scott OT 6'3 265 Western Ontario B: 11/22/1967 Windsor, ON Draft: 5-39 1990 HAM																															
1991	HAM	18				2																									
1992	HAM	16				0																									
1993	HAM	18				0																									

Year	Team	GP	FM	FF	FR	TK	SK	YDS	IR	YDS	PD	PTS	TD	RA	YDS	AVG	LG	TD	REC	YDS	AVG	LG	TD	PR	YDS	AVG	LG	KOR	YDS	AVG	LG
1994	HAM	18	0		1	1																									
1995	OTT	6				1																									
1995	TOR	11				0																									
1995	Year	17				1																									
5	Years	76	0		1	4																									
MARCUS DOWDELL Marcus Llewellyn FB-WR 5'10 197 Tennessee State B: 5/22/1970 Birmingham, AL Draft: 10-276 1992 NO Pro: N																															
1994	SAC	7	1		0	1						6	1						19	268	14.1	55	1	10	60	6.0	12	6	198	33.0	76
1995	WPG	2	1		0	0																		3	15	5.0	7	3	35	11.7	24
1998	EDM	5	1	0	0	2						18	3						30	423	14.1	41	3	11	51	4.6	12	3	40	13.3	28
1999	CAL	16				2						8	1						45	683	15.2	64	1								
4	Years	30	3	0	0	5						32	5						94	1374	14.6	64	5	24	126	5.3	12	12	273	22.8	76
COREY DOWDEN Corey G. DB 5'11 190 Tulane B: 10/18/1968 New Orleans, LA Pro: N																															
1994	OTT	6				20					2																				
KENNY DOWNING Kenneth Ray S 5'10 185 Missouri B: 5/27/1954 Amarillo, TX Draft: 13-350 1976 NO																															
1978	OTT	16	1		4				7	63		6	1											2	44	22.0	36				
1979	OTT	7	1		1				2	46																					
1980	OTT	8							1	3																					
3	Years	31	2		5				10	112		6	1											2	44	22.0	36				
BOB DOWNS Robert LeRoy OG 5'10 210 Southern California B: 4/16/1927 Los Angeles, CA Pro: N																															
1952	EDM	4																													
MAURICE DOYLE Maurice FB 6'2 225 Toronto B: 10/13/1959 Draft: 1-3 1981 OTT																															
1982	OTT	4																													
1983	OTT	14										6	1	7	24	3.4	10	0	1	6	6.0	6	1					1	5	5.0	5
1984	OTT	3																	4	19	4.8	11	0	1	0	0.0	0				
3	Years	21										6	1	7	24	3.4	10	0	5	25	5.0	11	1	1	0	0.0	0	1	5	5.0	5
MICKEY DOYLE Michael Joseph LB 6'1 235 Kansas B: 3/18/1947 Topeka, KS																															
1970	WPG	16							2	27																					
1971	WPG	15							4	86																					
1972	WPG+	12	0		2				1	8																					
1973	WPG	16	0		1				1	1																					
1974	CAL	12																													
1974	BC	1																													
1974	Year	13																													
5	Years	71	0		3				8	122																					
CORNELIUS DOZIER Cornelius Leslie LB 6'2 190 Southern Methodist B: 2/5/1964 Ennis, TX Pro: N																															
1987	OTT	2	0		1	7																									
ERIC DRAGE Eric S. WR 6'1 180 Brigham Young B: 6/7/1971 Tucson, AZ																															
1994	TOR	9				6						30	5						20	332	16.6	87	5								
SEL DRAIN Selwyn Lamont DB 6'0 190 Ball State B: 9/23/1961 East St. Louis, IL Pro: U																															
1987	TOR	18	0		2	67	4.0		2	15														0	6		10				
1988	TOR*	18	1		1	47	5.0		6	70																					
2	Years	36	1		3	114	9.0		8	85														0	6		10				
VINNIE DRAKE Vincent Carl QB 6'2 210 Fordham B: 8/19/1930																															
1954	WPG	1																													
KEN DRAPER Ken HB Elmwood Roamers Jrs. B: 1919																															
1946	WPG	4																													
ANTHONY DRAWHORN Anthony DH 5'9 175 Cerritos JC; Nevada-Las Vegas B: 7/27/1965 Los Angeles, CA																															
1988	BC	18	0		3	61			5	93		6	1											8	60	7.5	23	31	691	22.3	57
1989	BC	5				10	1.0		1	10																		9	221	24.6	53
1990	BC	9	2		4	37	1.0		1	70														1	13	13.0	13	4	38	9.5	19
1991	OTT+	17	3		3	46	1.0		5	128		12	2											75	677	9.0	50	54	1095	20.3	70
1992	OTT*	18	1		1	56	1.0	9.0	8	77		6	1											38	166	4.4	16	13	233	17.9	25
1993	OTT	18	4		1	53			3	28														52	334	6.4	28	6	100	16.7	26
1994	SAS	17				64			3	6	10													1	9	9.0	9				
1995	BIR*	18				66			6	92	2													21	195	9.3	33	7	137	19.6	35
1996	SAS	7				11																		12	71	5.9	16				
1996	MTL	4				17			1	70	0	6	1																		
1996	Year	11				28			1	70	0	6	1											12	71	5.9	16				
1997	MTL	7				25			1	0	1																				
10	Years	134	10		12	446	4.0	9.0	34	574	13	30	5											208	1525	7.3	50	124	2515	20.3	70
BOB DRESSEL Robert OG-OT 6'4 270 Purdue B: 8/19/1969 Luke Air Force Base, AZ																															
1993	SAC	5				0																									
BERT DRESSLER Bert A. T 6'2 240 Marshall; North Carolina State B: 12/10/1923 Chilyon, WV																															
1947	OTT	10										10	0																		
WESTON DRESSLER Weston SB 5'8 169 North Dakota B: 10/6/1983 Bismarck, ND																															
2008	SAS	14	1	0	1	4						36	6	5	49	9.8	22	0	56	1128	20.1	67	6	39	411	10.5	31	29	603	20.8	47
2009	SAS+	14				1						30	5	11	63	5.7	13	1	62	941	15.2	52	4	11	85	7.7	24	1	14	14.0	14
2010	SAS	17				5						36	6	9	57	6.3	15	0	81	1189	14.7	77	6								
2011	SAS+	18	1	0	1	7						36	6	7	35	5.0	19	1	79	1061	13.4	75	5					1	17	17.0	17
4	Years	63	2	0	2	17						138	23	32	204	6.4	22	2	278	4319	15.5	77	21	50	496	9.9	31	31	634	20.5	47
DOUG DREW Douglas P. HB-G-C-QB-E Minot State B: 7/27/1920 Bowbells, ND D: 5/3/2005 Bowbells, ND																															
1947	SAS+	8										1	0																		
1948	SAS	12																													
2	Years	20										1	0																		
RANDEE DREW Randee Jordan DH 5'8 186 Northern Illinois B: 11/22/1981 Milwaukee, WI Pro: E																															
2007	MTL+	18	0	0	1	67	3.0	19.0	4	3	4																				
2008	MTL	8				19					2																				
2009	EDM	6				16					1																				
2010	EDM	9				12					3																				
4	Years	41	0	0	1	114	3.0	19.0	4	3	10																				
WAYNE DRINKWALTER Wayne DT 6'3 265 Thunder Bay Giants Jrs. B: 4/23/1966 Thunder Bay, ON Draft: 3-19 1989 HAM																															
1989	SAS	18	0		1	8																									
1990	SAS	18	0		1	4	2.0		1	9																					
1991	SAS	18	0		1	13	5.0																								
1992	SAS	18				9																									
1993	SAS	18				10	1.0	7.0																							
1994	SAS	17	1		0	11																									
1995	SAS	6				2																									
1996	CAL	17	0		1	7																									
1997	BC	10				5																									
9	Years	140	1		4	69	8.0	7.0	1	9																					
GEOFF DROVER Geoffrey WR-S 5'10 185 Calgary B: 6/7/1976 St. John's, NL																															
2001	WPG	2				0													1	4	4.0	4	0								
2002	WPG	17	0	1	1	5													18	250	13.9	39	0								
2003	WPG	18	0	0	1	9													10	170	17.0	39	0								
2004	WPG	17				19	1.0				1													1	0	0.0	0				
4	Years	54	0	1	2	33	1.0				1								29	424	14.6	39	0	1	0	0.0	0				
DARREN DROZDOV Darren A. DT 6'3 280 Maryland B: 4/7/1969 Wilmington, DE Pro: N																															
1996	MTL	1				0																									
MAX DRUEN Max E. G 6'2 230 Tulane B: 1928 Draft: 9-112 1950 PIT																															
1950	SAS+	14																													
ROBERT DRUMMOND Robert C. RB 6'1 205 Syracuse B: 6/21/1967 Apopka, FL Draft: 3A-76 1989 PHI Pro: N																															

Year	Team	GP	FM	FF	FR	TK	SK	YDS	IR	YDS	PD	PTS	TD	RA	YDS	AVG	LG	TD	REC	YDS	AVG	LG	TD	PR	YDS	AVG	LG	KOR	YDS	AVG	LG
1994	BAL	7	1		0	7						6	1						9	149	16.6	41	1					0	7		7
1995	BAL	18	1		3	13								45	228	5.1	18	0	27	270	10.0	40	0					4	44	11.0	18
1996	TOR*	18	6		5	8						102	17	160	935	5.8	79	11	72	798	11.1	45	6								
1997	TOR*	15	3	0	0	4						108	18	181	1134	6.3	78	12	85	840	9.9	75	6								
1998	BC	12	1	1	0	4						18	3	138	690	5.0	66	2	29	298	10.3	33	1								
1999	BC+	18	5	0	2	2						66	11	257	1309	5.1	52	8	54	417	7.7	25	3								
2000	BC	17	1	0	0	6						66	11	170	823	4.8	40	10	66	752	11.4	46	1								
2001	BC	18	3	0	4	7						60	10	178	809	4.5	28	10	34	383	11.3	54	0								
2002	TOR	13	1	0	0	3						24	4	151	778	5.2	63	4	15	126	8.4	46	0								
9	Years	136	22	1	14	54						450	75	1280	6706	5.2	79	57	391	4033	10.3	75	18					4	51	12.8	18
GEORGE DRUXMAN George Stanley C-LB 6'1 220 Portland B: 1929 Winnipeg, MB D: //1999																															
1955	WPG	2																													
1956	WPG+	14	0		2																										
1957	WPG	16	1																												
1958	WPG	9																													
1959	WPG	16																													
1960	WPG	15																													
1961	WPG	16																													
1962	WPG	15																													
1963	WPG	8																													
9	Years	111	1		2																										
MARC DUBE Marc LB 6'2 230 Maine B: 2/23/1968 Gloucester, ON Draft: 3-24 1992 TOR																															
1992	CAL	1				1																									
1993	CAL	10				14																									
1995	OTT	2				6																									
3	Years	13				21																									
GREG DUBINETZ Gregory George OG 6'4 260 Yale B: 4/15/1954 Chicago, IL Draft: 9A-220 1975 CIN Pro: NW																															
1976	TOR	1																													
1978	TOR	2																													
1980	HAM	1																													
3	Years	4																													
CURTIS DUBLANKO Chris LB 6'0 235 North Dakota B: 2/12/1988 Draft: 2B-15 2010 MTL																															
2011	MTL	4				0																									
TOM DUBLINSKI Thomas Eugene, Jr. QB 6'2 197 Utah B: 8/8/1930 Chicago, IL Draft: 8-93 1952 DET Pro: N																															
1955	TOR	12										5	1	38	140	3.7	18	1													
1957	TOR	4												4	3	0.8	1	0													
1959	HAM	4												4	27	6.8	15	0													
1961	HAM	11										6	1						2	44	22.0	28	1								
1962	TOR	5												0	0		0	0													
5	Years	36										11	2	46	170	3.7	18	1	2	44	22.0	28	1								
DEITAN DUBUC Deitan FB 6'4 248 Michigan B: 2/4/1977 Montreal, QC Draft: 2A-14 2002 CAL																															
2005	EDM	13				5													3	32	10.7	18	0								
2006	EDM	15				7																									
2	Years	28				12													3	32	10.7	18	0								
MATT DuBUC Matthew RB 5'7 175 Texas Tech B: 5/5/1973 Montreal, QC Draft: 1-9 1997 TOR																															
1997	TOR	16				1								2	4	2.0	5	0	2	5	2.5	4	0								
1998	WPG	18				9						6	1						25	280	11.2	32	1	4	31	7.8	10	1	0	0.0	0
1999	WPG	17	1	0	0	0													27	425	15.7	40	0								
3	Years	51	1	0	0	10						6	1	2	4	2.0	5	0	54	710	13.1	40	1	4	31	7.8	10	1	0	0.0	0
CHUCK DUBUQUE Charles HB 5'11 178 Vancouver Cubs Jrs.; Vancouver Blue Bombers Jrs. B: 1933 Edmonton, AB																															
1956	BC	2																													
1957	BC	16	2		0									10	28	2.8	9	0	4	14	3.5	10	0	3	10	3.3	5	16	276	17.3	25
1958	BC	3																						0	12		12				
1959	BC	3												1	-1	-1.0	-1	0	1	14	14.0	14	0								
4	Years	24	2		0									11	27	2.5	9	0	5	28	5.6	14	0	3	22	7.3	12	16	276	17.3	25
DAMANE DUCKETT Damane Jerrel OT 6'6 300 East Carolina B: 1/21/1981 Waterbury, CT Pro: N																															
2009	BC	1				0																									
2010	BC	6	0	0	2	1													1	2	2.0	2	0								
2	Years	7	0	0	2	1													1	2	2.0	2	0								
ELLIS DUCKETT Ellis HB 6'0 190 Michigan State B: 1932 Draft: 15-174 1955 PIT																															
1955	SAS	1							1	14				1	9	9.0	9	0													
FOREY DUCKETT William M. DB 6'3 195 Nevada-Reno B: 2/5/1970 Oakland, CA Draft: 5-117 1993 CIN Pro: EN																															
1996	WPG	1				4																									
FARRELL DUCLAIR Farrell FB 6'1 225 Concordia B: 5/10/1972 Port Au Prince, Haiti Draft: 1-8 1996 CAL																															
1996	CAL	18	1		0	16						12	2	7	20	2.9	9	2	1	5	5.0	5	0								
1997	CAL	17	0	0	1	8						12	2	12	61	5.1	9	1													
1998	CAL	11				4																									
1999	WPG	3	1	0	0	1								1	0	0.0	0	0													
4	Years	49	2	0	1	29						24	4	20	81	4.1	9	3	1	5	5.0	5	0								
PAUL DUDA Paul HB 5'11 196 Cortland State B: 1943																															
1965	HAM	1												6	24	4.0	6	0													
BRIAN DUDLEY Brian Christopher DB 6'1 180 Bethune-Cookman B: 8/30/1960 Los Angeles, CA Pro: N																															
1986	MTL	16	0		4		2.0		2	32														3	17	5.7	9				
PAUL DUDLEY Paul Eugene OHB 6'0 185 Arkansas B: 1/16/1939 Fort Smith, AR Draft: 4A-54(f) 1961 GB; 29-232(f) 1962 SD Pro: N																															
1964	CAL	5	2		1							6	1	34	139	4.1	13	1	6	67	11.2	30	0					6	167	27.8	57
1965	CAL	6										6	1	8	26	3.3	20	0	5	37	7.4	22	1					1	10	10.0	10
1966	SAS	16	10		2							18	3	120	584	4.9	36	1	32	442	13.8	59	2					23	543	23.6	41
3	Years	27	12		3							30	5	162	749	4.6	36	2	43	546	12.7	59	3					30	720	24.0	57
BOB DUGAN Bob DE 6'1 240 Mississippi State B: 1940 Buffalo, NY Draft: 20-157 1964 BUF																															
1965	TOR	13	0		1																										
GERRY DUGUID Gerry HB-FW 5'10 160 Weston Monarchs Jrs.; Winnipeg Rods Jrs. B: 1928																															
1950	WPG	14												15	27	1.8		0	2	34	17.0		0								
1951	WPG	4										5	1						1	19	19.0	19	1	6	54	9.0		7	84	12.0	
1952	CAL	15																	2	22	11.0	16	0	41	224	5.5	20	4	131	32.8	58
3	Years	33										5	1	15	27	1.8	0	0	5	75	15.0	19	1	47	278	5.9	20	11	215	19.5	58
HAROLD DUGUID Harold HB																															
1946	CAL	4																													
STEVE DUICH Stephen John OG 6'3 248 Mesa JC; San Diego State B: 2/28/1946 Long Beach, CA Draft: 5A-121 1968 GB Pro: N																															
1971	BC	4			1																										
JIM DUKE Jim DE-OT 6'3 250 Alabama B: 10/6/1948																															
1970	SAS	8																													
1971	BC	11																													
1972	WPG	16	0		3				1	0																					
1973	WPG	16							1	16				1	0	0.0	0	0										2	33	16.5	17
1974	WPG	16	0		1									1	1	1.0	1	0													
1975	WPG	16	0		1																										
6	Years	83	0		5				2	16				2	1	0.5	1	0										2	33	16.5	17
HAL DUKES Harold Carl DE 6'3 215 Hope; Michigan State B: 7/11/1935 Detroit, MI D: 4/25/1997 Draft: 13B-155 1958 SF																															
1960	TOR	2																													
1961	TOR	2																													
2	Years	4																													
GARY DULIN Gary Wayne DT-DE-NG 6'4 275 Ohio State B: 1/20/1957 Madisonville, KY Pro: N																															

Year	Team	GP	FM	FF	FR	TK	SK	YDS	IR	YDS	PD	PTS	TD	RA	YDS	AVG	LG	TD	REC	YDS	AVG	LG	TD	PR	YDS	AVG	LG	KOR	YDS	AVG	LG
1982	OTT+	13	0		1		3.0																								
1983	OTT*	16					11.5																								
1984	OTT	12					7.5																								
1985	SAS	8																													
1985	TOR	7					5.0																								
1985	Year	15					5.0																								
4	Years	49	0		1		27.0																								
DAN DULMAGE Dan DT 6'3 250 McGill; Western Ontario B: 3/1/1950 Draft: 2B-17 1971 CAL																															
1973	HAM	14	0		1																										
1974	HAM	16																													
2	Years	30	0		1																										
MIKE DuMARESQ Mike DT-OG 6'5 265 Western Ontario B: 9/4/1965 Toronto, ON																															
1990	EDM	6				0																									
1991	EDM	10				0																									
1992	EDM	18				2																									
1993	EDM	18				1																									
1994	EDM	18	0		2	1																									
1995	TOR	18				1																									
6	Years	88	0		2	5																									
DAVID DUMARS David Wayne DB 5'10 185 Louisiana-Monroe B: 1/21/1957 Natchitoches, LA Draft: 12-317 1980 NYJ Pro: U																															
1980	MTL	16	2		2				5	9														3	20	6.7	8	13	290	22.3	31
1981	MTL	16	1		2				1	13														9	119	13.2	41	1	12	12.0	12
2	Years	32	3		4				6	22														12	139	11.6	41	14	302	21.6	31
LARRY DUMELIE Larry CB-S 5'10 185 Regina Rams Jrs.; Arizona B: 1937																															
1960	SAS	11																										6	142	23.7	33
1961	SAS	14												3	8	2.7	5	0	2	20	10.0	22	0	1	7	7.0	7	5	102	20.4	29
1962	SAS	14							1															2	3	1.5	2	10	229	22.9	47
1963	SAS	16	0		3				1															3	27	9.0	12				
1964	SAS	16	0		2				6	62														1	0	0.0	0				
1965	SAS	16	0		1				3	0														4	11	2.8	4	2	32	16.0	24
1966	SAS	14							2	33														4	26	6.5	18				
1967	SAS	14	0		1																										
8	Years	115	0		7				13	95				3	8	2.7	5	0	2	20	10.0	22	0	15	74	4.9	18	23	505	22.0	47
PIERRE DUMONT Pierre LB 6'0 228 NDG Maple Leafs Jrs. B: 1945																															
1966	MTL	8							1	28																					
1967	MTL	14																													
1969	MTL	14							1	27		6	1											1	2	2.0	2				
3	Years	36							2	55		6	1											1	2	2.0	2				
KARL DUNBAR Karmichael MacKenzie NT 6'4 272 Louisiana State B: 5/18/1967 Opelousas, LA Draft: 8-209 1990 PIT Pro: EN																															
1996	MTL	1				2																									
ROGER DUNBRACK Roger DT 6'4 245 Western Ontario B: 10/8/1975 Hamilton, ON Draft: 2-12 1998 TOR																															
1998	TOR	13				5	1.0	1.0			1																				
1999	TOR	15	0	1	1	12	5.0	27.0																							
2000	TOR	18	0	2	0	24	9.0	74.0			1																				
2001	TOR	17	0	1	0	15	3.0	15.0																							
2002	TOR	18	0	0	2	26	2.0	13.0	1	0	2																				
2003	OTT	17	0	2	1	16	2.0	12.0			1																				
2004	OTT	14				13	5.0	42.0	1	2	2																				
2005	HAM	18				18																									
2006	HAM	11				7	3.0	16.0	1	0	0																				
2007	HAM	10	0	0	1	10	2.0	12.0																							
10	Years	151	0	6	5	146	32.0	212.0	3	2	7																				
DON DUNCALFE Donald T-LB 6'3 220 Edmonton Huskies Jrs. B: 1938																															
1959	EDM	15																													
1960	EDM	9																													
1961	EDM	16																													
1962	EDM	1																													
4	Years	41																													
DENNIS DUNCAN Dennis FB 6'2 230 Northwestern State (Louisiana) B: 1/24/1945 Pro: W																															
1968	MTL	11	1		0							30	5	87	429	4.9	69	2	21	235	11.2	28	3					7	103	14.7	22
1969	MTL+	14	10		0							60	10	199	1037	5.2	46	9	22	237	10.8	39	1					2	46	23.0	25
1970	MTL	14	6		0							49	8	175	823	4.7	85	6	26	399	15.3	46	2								
1971	OTT+	13	4		0							18	3	155	760	4.9	44	2	12	129	10.8	47	1					1	18	18.0	18
4	Years	52	21		0							157	26	616	3049	4.9	85	19	81	1000	12.3	47	7					10	167	16.7	25
GREG DUNCAN Greg K 5'10 175 Ottawa Sooners Jrs.; Murray State B: 11/16/1966																															
1993	OTT	1				0						1	0																		
JIM DUNCAN James RB 6'2 220 Queen's B: 1957 Draft: 6- 1977 EDM																															
1979	SAS	4	1		0									11	12	1.1	7	0	1	8	8.0	8	0								
JULIAN DUNCAN Julian Cornelius DB 6'3 240 Rice B: 10/31/1976 Humble, TX Pro: E																															
2002	SAS	1				0																									
MAURY DUNCAN Maurice Lialpierre QB 6'0 182 San Francisco State B: 7/18/1931 Oakland, CA Pro: N																															
1957	BC	15	5		2							9	0	33	-103	-3.1	11	0													
1958	CAL	9												10	-37	-3.7	6	0													
2	Years	24	5		2							9	0	43	-140	-3.3	11	0													
RANDY DUNCAN Hearst Randolph, Jr. QB 6'0 185 Iowa B: 3/15/1937 Osage, IA Draft: 1-1 1959 GB Pro: N																															
1959	BC	3												29	123	4.2	28	0													
1960	BC	7	3		0									10	50	5.0	18	0													
2	Years	10	3		0									39	173	4.4	28	0													
TED DUNCAN Ted QB-DB-P-K 5'11 180 Vancouver Blue Bombers Jrs.; British Columbia B: 1931																															
1955	BC	9							2	24		1	0	0	4		4	0						10	72	7.2	15				
1956	BC	7	1		0																			5	28	5.6	16				
1957	CAL	16	1		3				4	42		9	0	1	3	3.0	3	0						3	13	4.3	11	1	26	26.0	26
1958	CAL	14	1		1				1	10		4	0	2	-15	-7.5	0	0						7	30	4.3	16				
1961	CAL	3																													
5	Years	49	3		4				7	76		14	0	3	-8	-2.7	4	0						25	143	5.7	16	1	26	26.0	26
BOBBY DUNCUM Robert Eldon OT 6'3 250 West Texas A&M B: 8/14/1944 Austin, TX Draft: 13-331 1967 STL Pro: N																															
1969	BC	7																													
RICK DUNDAS Rick LB 6'1 220 Whitworth B: 12/26/1954 Draft: 1-8 1978 EDM																															
1978	SAS	4	0		2																							1	16	16.0	16
1979	SAS	2																													
2	Years	6	0		2																							1	16	16.0	16
RON DUNDAS Ron OE 6'3 212 Regina Rams Jrs. B: 1934																															
1956	SAS	7										6	1						7	180	25.7	50	1								
1957	SAS	16										6	1						38	625	16.4	52	1								
1958	SAS	15	2		2							6	1						22	362	16.5	36	1								
1959	SAS	16							1			18	3						24	506	21.1	52	3								
1960	SAS	16																	17	263	15.5	24	0								
1961	EDM	9										6	1						5	56	11.2	17	1								
6	Years	79	2		2				1	0		42	7						113	1992	17.6	52	7								
NOEL DUNFORD Noel OE-DB 6'3 213 St. James Rods Jrs.; St James Rams Ints. B: 12/24/1939 Kenora, ON																															
1963	WPG	15																	5	52	10.4	15	0								
1964	WPG	15										12	2						15	255	17.0	43	2								

Year	Team	GP	FM	FF	FR	TK	SK	YDS	IR	YDS	PD	PTS	TD	RA	YDS	AVG	LG	TD	REC	YDS	AVG	LG	TD	PR	YDS	AVG	LG	KOR	YDS	AVG	LG
1965	WPG	11																													
1966	WPG	16	1		0							12	2						15	174	11.6	28	2								
1967	WPG	13	0		1							12	2						9	162	18.0	58	2								
1968	WPG	16																	9	107	11.9	33	0								
6	Years	86	1		1							36	6						53	750	14.2	58	6								
MATT DUNIGAN Mathew A. QB 5'11 180 Louisiana Tech B: 12/6/1960 Lakewood, OH																															
1983	EDM	16	1		1									4	23	5.8	20	0													
1984	EDM	13	7		4							56	9	89	732	8.2	69	9													
1985	EDM*	14	9		2							54	9	113	737	6.5	55	9													
1986	EDM	18	11		1							24	4	118	594	5.0	24	4	1	0	0.0	0	0								
1987	EDM	13	4		0	0						24	4	51	287	5.6	33	4													
1988	BC*	17	11		3	1						36	6	97	501	5.2	31	6													
1989	BC	18	9		2	3						60	10	70	397	5.7	21	10													
1990	TOR	8	3		0	1						42	7	48	218	4.5	24	7													
1991	TOR	8	4		1	2						12	2	34	190	5.6	14	2													
1992	WPG	16	5		0	2						18	3	42	238	5.7	26	3													
1993	WPG+	16	7		1	5						66	11	84	517	6.2	37	11	1	28	28.0	28	0								
1994	WPG+	11	5		2	2						24	4	42	226	5.4	28	4													
1995	BIR*	18	7		3	1						44	7	38	213	5.6	29	7	1	-1	-1.0	-1	0								
1996	HAM	6	1		0	1						6	1	20	158	7.9	22	1													
14	Years	192	84		20	18						466	77	850	5031	5.9	69	77	3	27	9.0	28	0								
FRANK DUNLAP Frank FW-QB-DB 6'0 194 B: 8/10/1924 Ottawa, ON D: 10/26/1993 Ottawa, ON																															
1946	OTT+	12										10	2					1													
1947	OTT	12										5	1					1													
1948	TOR	12										20	4					4													
1949	TOR	12										10	2					1					1								
1950	OTT	12										5	1					1													
1951	OTT	9																													
6	Years	69										50	10					8					1								
JAKE DUNLAP John Gerard T-G-FW 6'1 215 St. Patrick Jrs. B: 8/18/1925 Ottawa, ON D: 10/17/2010 Ottawa, ON																															
1946	OTT	3																													
1947	OTT	12																													
1948	OTT	12																													
1949	TOR	10																													
1950	TOR	12										5	1																		
1951	OTT	10																													
1952	HAM	7																													
1953	OTT	7																													
1954	OTT	7																													
9	Years	80										5	1																		
JERRY DUNLAP Jerry DB 5'8 175 South Carolina; Youngstown State B: 2/4/1965 Lorain, OH																															
1990	OTT	8	0		2	30			2	73																					
CHRIS DUNN Chris LB 6'3 230 Army; Cal Poly (San Luis Obispo) B: 2/1/1966 Draft: 9-229 1989 ATL																															
1990	BC	1				3																									
FRED DUNN Fred DB 6'1 205 Edmonton Wildcats Jrs.; Drake B: 1944																															
1970	EDM	16																													
1971	EDM	10	1		0							1	0																		
2	Years	26	1		0							1	0																		
KASEY DUNN Kasey E. WR 6'2 200 Idaho B: 7/22/1969 San Diego, CA																															
1992	BC	4				0						12	2						15	222	14.8	31	2	1	2	2.0	2				
1992	EDM	2				1						6	1						5	91	18.2	31	1								
1992	Year	6				1						18	3						20	313	15.7	31	3	1	2	2.0	2				
1993	EDM	7				1						6	1						7	90	12.9	28	1								
2	Years	11				2						24	4						27	403	14.9	31	4	1	2	2.0	2				
BRIAN DUNSWORTH Brian (Doc) HB 5'9 173 Edmonton Ints. B: 1925																															
1949	EDM	14																													
1950	EDM	11																													
2	Years	25																													
DAMIR DUPIN Damir DL 6'2 255 Nevada-Las Vegas B: 5/31/1961 Edmonton, AB Draft: 3-22 1984 OTT																															
1984	OTT	14																													
1985	OTT	4																													
2	Years	18																													
MIKE DuPREE Michael Daniel DE 6'2 224 Florida B: 8/16/1957 Tallahassee, FL Draft: 10A-251 1979 KC																															
1979	WPG	2																													
DICK DUPUIS Dick DH-CB 5'10 180 Notre Dame B: 9/2/1942																															
1965	CAL	16	0		3				2	22														65	386	5.9	16	2	34	17.0	18
1966	CAL	16	4		3				2	25									1	6	6.0	6	0	69	380	5.5	17				
1967	CAL	16			1				5	46														42	335	8.0	25				
1968	EDM	16							1	0														51	449	8.8	26				
1969	EDM	16	0		2				7	68														51	476	9.3	32				
1970	EDM	16	1		2				5	93														48	412	8.6	18				
1971	EDM*	16			1				7	43														42	338	8.0	21				
1972	EDM+	16	1		2				2	7														8	50	6.3	16				
1973	EDM	9																						25	124	5.0	17				
1974	EDM	16			1				3	17		6	1											3	21	7.0	13				
1975	EDM	13							4	69														1	5	5.0	5				
1976	EDM	2																													
12	Years	168	6		15				38	390		6	1						1	6	6.0	6	0	405	2976	7.3	32	2	34	17.0	18
MICHEL DUPUIS Michel LB 6'0 225 Ottawa B: 3/9/1974 St. Jean-Sur Richelieu, QC																															
2001	TOR	17				14																									
2002	CAL	18				12																									
2003	CAL	17				4																									
3	Years	52				30																									
DARIAN DURANT Darian Bernard QB 5'11 221 North Carolina B: 8/19/1982 Florence, SC																															
2006	SAS	8				0								1	20	20.0	20	0													
2007	SAS	18				0																									
2008	SAS	15	1	0	1	0						6	1	27	204	7.6	25	1													
2009	SAS+	18	6	0	0	4						18	3	60	601	10.0	25	3	2	-11	-5.5	0	0								
2010	SAS	18	13	0	5	0						42	7	80	618	7.7	35	7													
2011	SAS	18	9	0	3	1						12	2	55	381	6.9	22	2													
6	Years	95	29	0	9	5						78	13	223	1824	8.2	35	13	2	-11	-5.5	0	0								
MIKE DURDEN Earnel Michael CB 6'1 185 UCLA B: 5/4/1959 Los Angeles, CA D: 11/26/2007 CA Draft: 14-167 1983 ARI-USFL																															
1983	EDM	1																													
1984	EDM	6	0		1																										
2	Years	7	0		1																										
REGGIE DURDEN Reginald Deon CB 5'7 163 Lincoln-Copiah JC; Texas A&M-Kingsville; Florida State B: 11/22/1976 Houston, TX Pro: X																															
2001	MTL	18	2	1	1	34						6	1											32	372	11.6	85	25	510	20.4	52
2002	MTL	18	0	1	1	62			2	55	9																				
2003	MTL	14				40	1.0	13.0			5																				
2004	MTL	16	0	0	1	27			3	19	5																				
2005	MTL	15	0	1	0	55			2	50	5	6	1																		
2006	EDM	6				14																									

Year	Team	GP	FM	FF	FR	TK	SK	YDS	IR	YDS	PD	PTS	TD	RA	YDS	AVG	LG	TD	REC	YDS	AVG	LG	TD	PR	YDS	AVG	LG	KOR	YDS	AVG	LG
6	Years	87	2	3	3	232	1.0	13.0	7	124	24	12	2											32	372	11.6	85	25	510	20.4	52
ANDRE DURIE Andre RB-SB 5'9 189 Mississauga Warriors Jrs.; York Lions Jrs.; York B: 7/27/1981 Mississauga, ON																															
2007	TOR	5				0						12	2	5	36	7.2	33	2													
2008	TOR	9				15								2	5	2.5	3	0										2	43	21.5	23
2009	TOR	18	0	0	1	11						6	1	1	1	1.0	1	0	2	25	12.5	16	0					43	1033	24.0	84
2010	TOR	18	0	1	0	5						6	1	11	70	6.4	15	0	54	632	11.7	57	1	7	33	4.7	11	7	101	14.4	24
2011	TOR	17	2	0	1	0						24	4	18	106	5.9	36	0	54	665	12.3	43	4					21	440	21.0	38
5	Years	67	2	1	2	31						48	8	37	218	5.9	36	2	110	1322	12.0	57	5	7	33	4.7	11	73	1617	22.2	84
DON DURNO Don T-G 6'3 233 none B: 10/31/1918 Thurso, Scotland D: 10/29/2011																															
1947	MTL	12										1	0																		
1948	TOR	12										4	0																		
1949	TOR	10										12	2																		
1950	EDM	14																													
1951	TOR	10																													
1952	HAM	1																													
6	Years	59										17	2																		
TED DUSHINSKI Ted CB-FL 6'0 195 Saskatoon Hilltops Jrs. B: 11/10/1943 Saskatoon, SK D: 10/24/2005 Vancouver, BC																															
1965	SAS	8																													
1966	SAS	14	0		1				2	11																					
1967	SAS	16	0		1				2	89		6	1											2	5	2.5	5				
1968	SAS	16							4	32														10	46	4.6	15				
1969	SAS	16	0		1				6	44														8	46	5.8	11				
1970	SAS+	16	0		1				5	79		6	1											4	23	5.8	12				
1971	SAS	16							4	110														11	84	7.6	19				
1972	SAS	14	0		2				1	27																					
1973	SAS	16	2		1				6	75														1	4	4.0	4				
1974	SAS	9							1	18																					
1975	SAS+	16	0		3				2	6		6	1											1	0	0.0	0				
1976	BC	15	0		1				2	55				1	4	4.0	4	0													
1977	BC	16	0		1																										
13	Years	188	2		12				35	546		18	3	1	4	4.0	4	0						37	208	5.6	19				
NORM DUTTON Norman QB B: 1925																															
1947	CAL	8																													
DAMON DUVAL Damon K-P 5'11 194 Auburn B: 4/13/1980 Morgan City, LA																															
2005	MTL	18	0	0	1	6						191	0	1	0	0.0	0	0													
2006	MTL+	18	1	0	0	3						201	0																		
2007	MTL*	18	2	0	1	3						146	0	1	-32	-32.0	-32	0													
2008	MTL+	17				6						206	0						1	0	0.0	0	0	4	46	11.5	19	1	14	14.0	14
2009	MTL*	18	3	0	0	10						242	0																		
2010	MTL+	15	0	1	0	3						156	0																		
2011	EDM	18	1	0	1	4						114	0																		
7	Years	122	7	1	3	35						1256	0	2	-32	-16.0	0	0	1	0	0.0	0	0	4	46	11.5	19	1	14	14.0	14
JACK DWYER John Joseph DB 5'11 175 Los Angeles CC; Loyola Marymount B: 1/15/1927 Los Angeles, CA Draft: 5-57 1951 PHI Pro: N																															
1956	MTL	14							7	50																					
BENNY DYACK Ben HB 5'11 185																															
1948	HAM	10										15	3					2					1								
1949	HAM	5										10	2					2													
2	Years	15										25	5					4					1								
PETER DYAKOWSKI Peter Stefan OG-OT 6'5 310 Louisiana State B: 4/19/1984 Vancouver, BC Draft: 2B-11 2006 HAM																															
2007	HAM	15				0																									
2008	HAM	18				0																									
2009	HAM	15				1																									
2010	HAM	18				0																									
2011	HAM	17				1																									
5	Years	83				2																									
JAMES DYE James L. WR 5'9 160 Utah Valley State JJC; Brigham Young B: 12/8/1973 Oakland, CA																															
1998	TOR	1				0																		8	59	7.4	13	4	66	16.5	34
JIMMY DYE Jim CB 5'10 163 Miami (Florida) B: 1/13/1945 Fulton, MO																															
1968	TOR	14							5	63																		12	296	24.7	32
1969	TOR	7							3	19																					
1972	TOR	14																						1	0	0.0	0				
1973	WPG	1																													
4	Years	36							8	82														1	0	0.0	0	12	296	24.7	32
NAT DYE Nathaniel Slaughter DE-DT-OG 6'3 220 Georgia B: 1938																															
1959	EDM	14																													
1960	EDM	11	0		1																										
1961	EDM	16										6	1																		
1962	EDM	16	0		2				1			6	1																		
1963	EDM	16							1																						
1964	EDM	4																													
1964	SAS	5	0		1																										
1964	Year	9	0		1																										
1965	SAS	8	0		1																										
7	Years	85	0		5				2	0		12	2																		
PAT DYE Patrick Fain G-E 5'11 210 Georgia B: 11/6/1939 Blythe, GA Draft: SS 1960 BOS; 24- 1961 DAL																															
1961	EDM	16			2														2	58	29.0	49	0								
1962	EDM	16	2		3				4	15		6	1																		
2	Years	32	2		5				4	15		6	1						2	58	29.0	49	0								
BRIAN DYET Brian E. DL 6'4 257 Colorado B: 12/12/1970																															
1994	SHR	1																													
SEAN DYKES Sean Rene DB 5'10 170 Eastern Arizona JC; Bowling Green State B: 8/8/1964 New Orleans, LA Pro: EN																															
1990	SAS	1				1																									
1991	SAS	7	0		1	24			1	56		6	1																		
2	Years	8	0		1	25			1	56		6	1																		
CHRIS DYKO Christopher Edward OT 6'6 305 Washington State B: 3/16/1966 Champaign, IL Draft: 8B-221 1989 CHIB Pro: EN																															
1993	SAC	16				0																									
1994	SAC	16				1																									
1995	BIR	15				1																									
3	Years	47				2																									
BRANDON DYSON Brandon Lee OG 6'4 290 Utah State B: 5/31/1976 Andrews, TX Pro: E																															
2001	WPG	14				1																									
JAYSON DZIKOWICZ Jayson S 5'11 190 Manitoba B: 4/11/1968 Winnipeg, MB Draft: 7-56 1991 WPG																															
1992	WPG	14	2		0	17	1.0	9.0	3	40														1	0	0.0	0	3	32	10.7	14
1993	WPG	16				36			2	20														1	1	1.0	1				
1994	WPG	16				16			3	4	4																				
1995	TOR	12				3																									
1996	OTT	15	0		1	60			2	20	3																				
5	Years	73	2		1	132	1.0	9.0	10	84	7													2	1	0.5	1	3	32	10.7	14
GREG EAGLIN Gregory O. CB 6'2 190 Texas; Arkansas-Pine Bluff B: 11/14/1967 Cleveland, TX Pro: E																															
1993	HAM	9	0		2	35						6	1																		
1993	CAL	6				16			1	14																					
1993	Year	15	0		2	51			1	14		6	1																		

Year	Team	GP	FM	FF	FR	TK	SK	YDS	IR	YDS	PD	PTS	TD	RA	YDS	AVG	LG	TD	REC	YDS	AVG	LG	TD	PR	YDS	AVG	LG	KOR	YDS	AVG	LG
1994	HAM	17	0		2	38			5	51	3	6	1																		
1995	TOR	12	0		1	30			3	14	5																				
1996	TOR	8				16						6	1																		
1996	HAM	5	0		2	13																									
1996	Year	13	0		2	29						6	1																		
4	Years	46	0		7	148			9	79	8	18	3																		
KEVIN EAKIN Kevin Lewis QB 6'0 219 Fordham B: 7/22/1981 St. Paul, MN Pro: E																															
2005	HAM	4	3	0	1	0								7	38	5.4	10	0													
2006	HAM	18	1	0	0	1								4	14	3.5	7	0													
2	Years	22	4	0	1	1								11	52	4.7	10	0													
CHUCK EALEY Chuck QB 6'0 195 Toledo B: 1/6/1950																															
1972	HAM+	14	6		1							24	4	87	515	5.9	47	4													
1973	HAM	14	1		0							24	4	129	687	5.3	69	4													
1974	HAM	7	2		0							6	1	58	238	4.1	37	1													
1974	WPG	10	2		0							6	1	55	300	5.5	25	1													
1974	Year	17	4		0							12	2	113	538	4.8	37	2													
1975	WPG	13	0		1							6	1	68	434	6.4	31	1													
1975	TOR	3	1		1							6	1	31	161	5.2	25	1													
1975	Year	16	1		2							12	2	99	595	6.0	34	2													
1976	TOR	16	3		1							12	2	85	613	7.2	86	2													
1977	TOR	16	7		0							26	4	99	663	6.7	30	4													
1978	TOR	12	2		1							6	1	52	373	7.2	37	1													
7	Years	92	24		5							116	19	664	3984	6.0	86	19													
KEITH EAMAN Keith (Skip) RB-WR 5'10 200 Queen's B: 8/14/1948 Montreal, QC Draft: 1A-3 1969 SAS																															
1971	OTT	14	2		0							6	1	19	75	3.9	22	1	11	158	14.4	27	0					2	44	22.0	25
1972	OTT	14												9	27	3.0	6	0	6	62	10.3	23	0								
1974	MTL	16	1		0							6	1	1	3	3.0	3	0	7	134	19.1	38	1	81	360	4.4	28				
1975	MTL	16										12	2	2	1	0.5	3	0	11	124	11.3	27	2	2	26	13.0	18				
4	Years	60	3		0							24	4	31	106	3.4	22	1	35	478	13.7	38	3	83	386	4.7	28	2	44	22.0	25
GUY EARLE Guy OG 6'4 290 Western Kentucky; Independence CC; Chadron State B: 4/1/1968 Red Bank, NJ																															
1994	BAL	11				1																									
1995	BAL	10				0																									
1995	MEM	8				0																									
1995	Year	18				0																									
1996	WPG	7				0																									
3	Years	28				1																									
JOHN EARLE John OG-C 6'5 284 Montclair State; Independence CC; Western Illinois B: 4/1/1968 Red Bank, NJ Draft: 11-283 1992 CIN																															
1994	BAL	11				1																									
1995	BAL	16				0																									
2	Years	27				1																									
BOB EARLY Bob HB 5'10 173 Saskatchewan; Saskatoon Hilltops Jrs. B: 1927																															
1948	SAS	11										5	1					1													
1949	SAS	13																													
1950	CAL	13												3	1	0.3		0													
3	Years	37										5	1	3	1	0.3	0	1													
DAVE EASLEY Dave DB 5'10 185 Vancouver Blue Bombers Jrs. B: 8/12/1947																															
1969	BC	16	2		2				4	70														50	359	7.2	25	3	89	29.7	46
1970	BC	15							1	9														12	82	6.8	21				
1971	BC	16			1				5	163		6	1											2	5	2.5	3				
1972	BC	16	0		2				4	58														2	5	2.5	3				
1973	HAM	10	0		1																			4	19	4.8	10				
1974	HAM	16	2		2																			34	162	4.8	17				
1975	HAM	11																													
1976	HAM	4																													
1976	EDM	11							1	0																					
1976	Year	15							1	0																					
8	Years	104	4		8				15	300		6	1											104	632	6.1	25	3	89	29.7	46
MEL EASLEY Melvin Artimus S 6'0 204 Oregon State B: 3/24/1947 San Francisco, CA Draft: 6-140 1970 NO																															
1973	SAS	5																													
1974	WPG	2																													
2	Years	7																													
JOHN EASON Arenouis John WR-K 6'2 220 Florida A&M B: 7/30/1945 Ocala, FL Draft: 9-244 1968 OAK Pro: N																															
1969	BC	1																													
1972	MTL	10	2		1							25	4						19	407	21.4	46	4					3	5	1.7	5
2	Years	11	2		1							25	4						19	407	21.4	46	4					3	5	1.7	5
BOBBY JOE EASTER Bobby Joe DB 5'10 200 Middle Tennessee State B: 7/29/1951 Lincolntown, NC Draft: 8B-226 1976 BUF																															
1977	CAL	7	3		0							6	1	80	334	4.2	24	1	17	197	11.6	39	0								
DICK EASTERLY Richard B. E-HB 5'11 185 Syracuse B: 1940 Draft: 14-190 1962 SF																															
1962	HAM	4										30	5						15	378	25.2	79	5								
1963	HAM	13										12	2						15	271	18.1	31	2	10	36	3.6	9	2	26	13.0	19
1964	HAM	1																	1	14	14.0	14	0								
3	Years	18										42	7						31	663	21.4	79	7	10	36	3.6	9	2	26	13.0	19
TYLER EBELL Tyler Jay RB 5'9 206 UCLA; Texas-El Paso B: 6/4/1983 Ventura, CA																															
2007	EDM	12	0	0	1	1						18	3	124	650	5.2	56	1	67	521	7.8	21	2	2	27	13.5	22	6	119	19.8	31
2009	BC	2	1	0	0	0								1	6	6.0	6	0	2	5	2.5	7	0	6	47	7.8	15	11	227	20.6	31
2	Years	14	1	0	1	1						18	3	125	656	5.2	56	1	69	526	7.6	21	2	8	74	9.3	22	17	346	20.4	31
MIKE EBEN Mike FL 6'1 185 Toronto B: 1/29/1946 Zatec, Czechoslovakia Draft: 1-1 1968 BC																															
1968	TOR	14																	1	7	7.0	7	0								
1969	TOR	14	2		1							12	2						11	141	12.8	25	2	74	487	6.6	33				
1970	EDM+	15	1		0							36	6	4	10	2.5	8	1	48	733	15.3	81	5	7	23	3.3	9				
1971	TOR+	12	1		0							18	3	3	7	2.3	9	0	36	572	15.9	77	3					1	-4	-4.0	-4
1972	TOR	14	1		0							24	4						46	551	12.0	41	4	3	9	3.0	5				
1973	TOR	14										24	4						39	637	16.3	49	4								
1974	TOR	16										6	1						42	579	13.8	50	1								
1975	TOR	16										6	1						63	729	11.6	41	1								
1976	TOR+	16										18	3						47	681	14.5	44	3								
1977	HAM	4																	3	55	18.3	28	0								
1977	TOR	4	0		1							6	1						3	42	14.0	20	1								
1977	OTT	4																	2	25	12.5	15	0								
1977	Year	12	0		1							6	1						8	122	15.3	28	1								
10	Years	135	5		2							150	25	7	17	2.4	9	1	341	4752	13.9	81	24	84	519	6.2	33	1	-4	-4.0	-4
RICK EBER Richard Lee WR 6'0 181 El Camino JC; Tulsa B: 4/17/1945 Torrance, CA Draft: 6C-162 1968 ATL Pro: NW																															
1973	SAS	16										42	7						46	730	15.9	67	7					1	44	44.0	23
MIKE ECHOLS Michael Kitome DB 5'10 190 Wisconsin B: 10/13/1978 Youngstown, OH Draft: 4A-110 2002 TEN Pro: N																															
2006	HAM	2				4			1	94	1	6	1																		
REUBEN ECKELS Reuben WR 5'9 155 Wichita State B: 11/2/1962 Wichita, KS Draft: TD 1984 OKL-USFL																															
1984	OTT	2																	2	26	13.0	13	0	13	110	8.5	18	2	40	20.0	37
ADAM ECKERT Adam WR-SB 5'11 183 Dickinson State B: 5/31/1978 Winnipeg, MB Draft: 6A-49 2005 MTL																															
2006	MTL	2				0																									
2006	WPG	9				0													9	97	10.8	20	0	2	5	2.5	5				
2006	Year	11				0													9	97	10.8	20	0	2	5	2.5	5				
2007	WPG	5				1													2	31	15.5	18	0								

Year	Team	GP	FM	FF	FR	TK	SK	YDS	IR	YDS	PD	PTS	TD	RA	YDS	AVG	LG	TD	REC	YDS	AVG	LG	TD	PR	YDS	AVG	LG	KOR	YDS	AVG	LG
2	Years	7				1													11	128	11.6	20	0	2	5	2.5	5				
JOHN ECKMAN John QB 6'0 195 Wichita State B: 1946																															
1969	HAM	14												32	187	5.8	19	0													
1970	HAM	14	0		1							12	2	12	37	3.1	10	2													
2	Years	28	0		1							12	2	44	224	5.1	19	2													
DAN ECKSTEIN Dan G. DB 5'10 180 Presbyterian B: 6/5/1947 Orangeburg, SC Draft: 15-376 1969 GB																															
1969	HAM	5	1		0																			7	68	9.7	22	3	48	16.0	38
AL ECUYER Allan LB-MG 5'10 210 Notre Dame B: 1938 Draft: 18-214 1959 NYG																															
1959	EDM+	12							1																						
1960	EDM	14	0		1																										
1961	EDM	16			4				3	14																					
1962	EDM	16																													
1963	EDM	16	0		4																										
1964	EDM	16	0		2				3	102																					
1965	EDM	16	0		3				1			1	0																		
1966	TOR	14	0		2				3	25															1	2	2.0	2				
1967	MTL	8	0		1				1	5																					
1968	MTL	13	0		3				1	8																					
10	Years	141	0		20				13	154		1	0											1	2	2.0	2				
JUNIOR EDGE Bias Milton Jr QB 6'2 220 North Carolina B: 10/16/1940 Pearces Mill, NC																															
1964	OTT	2																													
ART EDGSON Art DB 5'10 185 Idaho State B: 1/7/1950 Draft: 1-8 1973 SAS																															
1974	MTL	3																										3	80	26.7	34
1975	MTL	5																						1	0	0.0	0				
2	Years	8																						1	0	0.0	0	3	80	26.7	34
WES EDIGER Wesley T-G-E 6'2 220 Oregon State B: 9/17/1933 Dallas, OR																															
1957	CAL	1																													
DANNY EDWARDS Daniel Moody E 6'1 197 Georgia B: 7/18/1926 Osage, TX D: 8/7/2001 Gatesville, TX Draft: 3-13 1948 BKN-AAFC; 1-9 1948 PIT Pro: AN																															
1955	BC	16	1		0							15	3						41	681	16.6	50	3								
1956	BC+	16	1		0							18	3						41	672	16.4	41	3					2	6	3.0	6
1957	BC	11	1		0														23	357	15.5	34	0					1	9	9.0	9
3	Years	43	3		0							33	6						105	1710	16.3	50	6					3	15	5.0	9
DARNELL EDWARDS Darnell CB 6'3 200 Manitoba B: 10/8/1978 Winnipeg, MB Draft: 4-29 2002 SAS																															
2002	SAS	18	0	1	0	10																									
2003	SAS	11	0	0	1	24	2.0	13.0	1	29	3																				
2004	SAS	16	0	1	1	47			1	0	5																				
2005	SAS	12				13					3																				
2006	SAS	2				0																									
5	Years	59	0	2	2	94	2.0	13.0	2	29	11																				
DEMETRIUS EDWARDS Demetrius DL 6'3 287 Fresno State B: 3/25/1972 Pro: E																															
1995	SAS	1				0	4.0	29.0																							
DOVONTE EDWARDS Dovonte DH-CB 6'0 182 North Carolina State B: 10/17/1982 Pro: N																															
2009	TOR	18	2	0	0	39			0	0	2													17	83	4.9	18	13	197	15.2	27
DWIGHT EDWARDS Dwight FL 5'10 170 Mississauga Raiders Jrs. B: 6/16/1954 Manchester, Jamaica																															
1978	TOR	14										6	1	4	24	6.0	8	0	17	404	23.8	71	1					6	104	17.3	24
1979	TOR	16	3		1							6	1	7	57	8.1	36	0	43	738	17.2	50	1					5	103	20.6	27
1980	SAS	12	0		1							36	6	2	18	9.0	10	0	44	747	17.0	53	6	13	70	5.4	17	12	279	23.3	37
1981	SAS	16	1		0							30	5	2	28	14.0	25	0	42	614	14.6	53	5	5	75	15.0	60	26	537	20.7	58
1982	SAS	14	2		1							30	5						38	588	15.5	84	5	14	236	16.9	54	36	869	24.1	73
1983	SAS	15	1		0							24	4						37	544	14.7	84	4	14	139	9.9	42	28	640	22.9	38
1984	OTT	16	1		0							24	4	2	6	3.0	5	0	33	736	22.3	67	4	15	251	16.7	96	40	983	24.6	89
1985	CAL	6	2		1							12	2						12	250	20.8	51	2					11	200	18.2	53
1985	OTT	3																	2	81	40.5	60	0					4	92	23.0	33
1985	MTL	1	0		1																							1	13	13.0	13
1985	Year	10	4		2							12	2						14	331	23.6	60	2					16	305	19.1	53
1986	TOR	1												1	-7	-7.0	-7	0						4	26	6.5	11	4	103	25.8	59
1987	TOR	18	1		0	2								2	16	8.0	21	0	21	259	12.3	32	0					35	678	19.4	54
1988	TOR	18	1		0	1						6	1	1	-2	-2.0	-2	0	20	248	12.4	20	1	1	16	16.0	16	39	783	20.1	57
11	Years	146	12		5	3						174	29	21	140	6.7	36	0	309	5209	16.9	84	29	66	813	12.3	96	247	5384	21.8	89
EARL EDWARDS Earl OT 6'6 264 Wichita State B: 3/17/1946 Statesboro, GA Draft: 5-120 1969 SF Pro: N																															
1967	EDM	15																													
1968	EDM	16	0		2																										
2	Years	31	0		2																										
ERIC EDWARDS Corsemore Eric DB 6'0 184 Oregon B: 3/6/1975 Pasco, WA Pro: E																															
1999	EDM	9	0	0	1	14			2	13	1																				
2000	EDM	7				18					2																				
2	Years	16	0	0	1	32			2	13	3																				
GEORGE EDWARDS George Herman T 6'2 265 Kentucky State B: 1924																															
1946	MTL	1																													
HANK EDWARDS Hank SB-WR 6'3 181 Texas Southern B: 5/20/1983 Hollywood, FL																															
2009	TOR	2				1													2	17	8.5	13	0								
JIMMY EDWARDS Jimmy LaRoy RB 5'9 185 Oklahoma; Louisiana-Monroe B: 9/19/1952 Oklahoma City, OK Pro: NW																															
1976	HAM*	16	7		1							72	12	194	1046	5.4	87	7	57	457	8.0	36	4	53	690	13.0	103	13	372	28.6	59
1977	HAM*	16	12		1							40	6	250	1581	6.3	69	6	39	223	5.7	20	0	46	548	11.9	67	13	321	24.7	45
1978	HAM+	13	11		0							38	6	197	840	4.3	32	2	33	296	9.0	75	4	39	250	6.4	22	18	324	18.0	24
1981	WPG	1	2		0									18	67	3.7	13	0	1	10	10.0	10	0					1	14	14.0	14
1982	SAS	2	3		0							18	3	17	41	2.4	8	3	3	21	7.0	8	0	2	17	8.5	12	5	127	25.4	44
5	Years	48	35		2							168	27	676	3575	5.3	87	18	133	1007	7.6	75	8	140	1505	10.8	103	50	1158	23.2	59
ROBERT EDWARDS Robert Lee, III RB 5'11 219 Georgia B: 10/2/1974 Tennille, GA Draft: 1A-18 1998 NE Pro: N																															
2005	MTL+	14	4	0	0	0						48	8	187	1199	6.4	37	8	21	202	9.6	24	0					14	289	20.6	32
2006	MTL+	18	6	0	2	1						102	17	239	1155	4.8	14	14	27	211	7.8	26	3								
2007	MTL	3	2	0	0	0						6	1	27	72	2.7	7	1	4	38	9.5	13	0								
2007	TOR	9	1	0	0	0						12	2	123	596	4.8	57	2	3	10	3.3	7	0								
2007	Year	12	3	0	0	0						18	3	150	668	4.5	57	3	7	48	6.9	13	0								
3	Years	35	13	0	2	1						168	28	576	3022	5.2	57	25	55	461	8.4	26	3					14	289	20.6	32
TERRENCE EDWARDS Terrence WR-SB 6'0 176 Georgia B: 4/29/1979 Tennille, GA Pro: N																															
2005	MTL	2				0						6	1						6	44	7.3	12	0	6	8	1.3	4	3	84	28.0	49
2006	MTL	9	1	0	0	0						6	1	2	18	9.0	20	0	33	393	11.9	36	1								
2007	WPG*	18	2	1	1	4						54	9	2	24	12.0	17	0	80	1280	16.0	67	9								
2008	WPG	15	1	0	1	5						42	7	4	32	8.0	16	0	76	1010	13.3	64	7								
2009	WPG	16	1	0	0	1						30	5						52	816	15.7	57	5								
2010	WPG*	18	1	0	1	2						72	12	2	12	6.0	10	0	78	1372	17.6	90	12								
2011	WPG+	18	3	0	1	3						48	8						66	1124	17.0	68	8					1	0	0.0	0
7	Years	96	9	1	4	15						258	43	10	86	8.6	20	0	391	6039	15.4	90	42	6	8	1.3	4	4	84	21.0	49
TIM EDWARDS Timothy DT 6'1 270 Delta State B: 8/29/1968 Philadelphia, MS Draft: 12-307 1991 NE Pro: N																															
1995	SAS	11	0		1	23																									
1996	SAS	15	0		1	40	4.0	31.0			1																				
2	Years	26	0		2	63	4.0	31.0			1																				
TYRONE EDWARDS Tyrone E. RB 6'1 212 California B: 4/28/1973 Los Angeles, CA Pro: EX																															
1995	CAL	5				0						6	1	4	39	9.8	37	1										3	83	27.7	45
WALLY EDWARDS Walter W. T-C 6'1 220 Minnesota B: 1926 Minneapolis, MN																															
1949	WPG	14										12	0																		

Year	Team	GP	FM	FF	FR	TK	SK	YDS	IR	YDS	PD	PTS	TD	RA	YDS	AVG	LG	TD	REC	YDS	AVG	LG	TD	PR	YDS	AVG	LG	KOR	YDS	AVG	LG
TIM EGERTON Timothy Leon WR 5'11 165 Delaware State B: 9/1/1966 Plainfield, NJ Pro: E																															
1990	BC	3	2		0	1								1	18	18.0	18	0	4	54	13.5	28	0	6	27	4.5	9	16	383	23.9	45
RICK EGLOFF Richard Joseph CB 6'2 195 Wyoming B: 11/2/1944 Denver, CO Draft: 6-155 1967 OAK																															
1968	MTL	4																												
KEVIN EIBEN Kevin LB-DB 6'0 215 Bucknell B: 9/28/1979 Delta, BC Draft: 4-26 2001 TOR																															
2001	TOR	5				6																		1	8	8.0	8	1	11	11.0	11
2002	TOR	18	0	1	4	42																								
2003	TOR	18	0	1	0	54	1.0	8.0	2	19	2																			
2004	TOR*	18	1	1	1	114	2.0	12.0	1	1	2																			
2005	TOR*	18	0	2	2	118	2.0	7.0	1	19	2																			
2006	TOR+	17	0	0	1	86					1																			
2007	TOR*	18	0	1	3	94	6.0	50.0	1	22	5																			
2008	TOR	11	0	1	0	56	2.0	21.0			2																			
2009	TOR	18	0	1	1	90	1.0	7.0	3	9	7																			
2010	TOR+	18	0	1	2	105	1.0	2.0	2	15	2			1	-1	-1.0	0	0													
2011	TOR	6				18					1																			
11	Years	165	1	9	14	783	15.0	107.0	10	85	24			1	-1	-1.0	0	0						1	8	8.0	8	1	11	11.0	11
L.J. EIBEN Lawrence WR 5'10 180 Fresno CC; Humboldt State B: 8/17/1974 Draft: 3-20 1996 TOR																															
1996	BC	5				2																								
BUDDY JOE EILERS Joseph August DT-DE 6'1 235 Texas A&M B: 1/19/1939 Lavaca County, TX																															
1966	HAM	4																												
1966	SAS	7	0		2																									
1966	Year	11	0		2																									
LARRY EILMES Laurence D. FB 6'1 208 Washington State B: 5/30/1943 Spokane, WA																															
1966	BC	11	2		0							42	7	153	756	4.9	28	6	23	247	10.7	29	1					4	98	24.5	26
1967	BC	4	2		0							18	3	35	108	3.1	9	2	4	30	7.5	13	1					1	8	8.0	8
2	Years	15	4		0							60	10	188	864	4.6	28	8	27	277	10.3	29	2					5	106	21.2	26
TREVOR EKDAHL Trevor OG 6'2 240 Vancouver Meralomas Jrs.; Utah State B: 4/3/1942 SK D: 9/7/2005																															
1967	BC	16	0		1																									
1968	BC	16																												
1969	BC	16	0		2																									
1970	BC	16	0		1																									
1971	BC	10			1																									
1972	BC	16																												
1973	BC	16																												
1974	BC	9																												
1974	MTL	1																												
1974	Year	10																												
8	Years	115	0		5																									
EMIL EKIYOR Emil DL 6'3 270 Central Florida B: 12/25/1973 Lagos, Nigeria																															
1997	WPG	3				2																								
GARNER EKSTRAN Garner N. DE-LB-OE 6'0 225 Washington State B: 9/1/1941																															
1961	SAS	16			3													2	42	21.0	22	0								
1962	SAS*	16	0		3																									
1963	SAS*	15	0		1																									
1964	SAS	16	0		2				1																					
1965	SAS	15	0		2																									
1966	SAS+	16																												
1967	SAS*	16	0		2													3	33	11.0	19	0					2	8	4.0	8
1968	BC	8																												
8	Years	118	0		13				1									5	75	15.0	22	0					2	8	4.0	8
MAT ELAM Mat DT 6'2 272 Hawaii B: 1/7/1976 Honolulu, HI																															
2000	WPG	2				1																								
MIKE ELARMS Michael H. WR 5'8 170 Angelo State B: 10/9/1960 San Francisco, CA Draft: 23-266 1983 ARI-USFL																															
1985	SAS	15	0		1							20	3						51	811	15.9	65	3					13	274	21.1	66
1986	SAS	14										12	2	1	3	3.0	3	0	30	477	15.9	60	2					21	346	16.5	27
2	Years	29	0		1							32	5	1	3	3.0	3	0	81	1288	15.9	65	5					34	620	18.2	66
RYAN ELASCHUK Ryan P-K 5'10 215 Edmonton Wildcats Jrs,. B: 5/10/1986 Winnipeg, MB																															
2009	SAS	1				0																								
BRAD ELBERG Brad RB-S 5'11 210 Queen's B: 5/31/1971 Regina, SK Draft: 1-2 1993 SAS																															
1994	HAM	11	1		1	8								14	44	3.1	14	0	2	44	22.0	35	0					1	16	16.0	16
1995	HAM	7	1		1	8								2	12	6.0	8	0													
1997	WPG	11	0	0	1	26	1.0	11.0						1	1	1.0	1	0										8	196	24.5	49
1998	WPG	16				37	1.0	2.0	1	17	1																			
1999	TOR	5				6	1.0	11.0				6	1						2	17	8.5	12	1								
1999	WPG	4				2													1	17	17.0	17	0	1	10	10.0	10				
1999	Year	9				8	1.0	11.0				6	1						3	34	11.3	17	1	1	10	10.0	10				
2000	TOR	13	0	0	1	23					1																	1	10	10.0	10
2001	TOR	18	0	0	1	25			1	23																		1	0	0.0	0
2002	TOR	2				3																								
8	Years	83	2	0	5	138	3.0	24.0	2	40	2	6	1	17	57	3.4	14	0	5	78	15.6	35	1	1	10	10.0	10	11	222	20.2	49
JIM ELDER James, Jr. CB-OHB 5'10 185 Southern University B: 11/23/1947 Athens, GA Draft: 8A-194 1971 NO																															
1972	OTT	7	1		0				1	74																		7	127	18.1	28
1973	SAS	16	2		0				4	39				1	-1	-1.0	-1	0						15	203	13.5	78	14	352	25.1	39
1974	SAS	16							3	8														7	53	7.6	16	24	517	21.5	31
1975	SAS	11	1		0																			19	245	12.9	52	24	591	24.6	45
1976	TOR	11	2		0				1	0														19	159	8.4	25	4	105	26.3	35
1977	OTT	2							1	40																					
6	Years	63	6		0				10	161				1	-1	-1.0	-1	0						60	660	11.0	78	73	1692	23.2	45
DAVID ELDRIDGE David RB 6'1 215 Arizona B: 4/25/1966 Tucson, AZ																															
1990	BC	1				0								7	15	2.1	10	0	2	20	10.0	11	0					1	4	4.0	4
MO ELEWONIBI Mohammed Thomas David OT 6'4 298 Okanagan Sun Jrs.; Snow JC; Brigham Young B: 12/16/1965 Lagos, Nigeria Draft: 5-34 1990 BC; 3-76 1990 WAS Pro: EN																															
1997	BC	18				0																								
1998	BC*	18	0	0	1	1						6	1						1	4	4.0	4	1								
1999	BC	18	0	0	1	0																								
2000	WPG+	18	0	0	1	1																								
2001	WPG	11				0																								
2002	WPG	18	0	0	1	0																								
2003	WPG	18	1	0	0	0																								
2004	WPG	18				1																								
2005	BC	8				0																								
9	Years	145	1	0	4	3						6	1						1	4	4.0	4	1								
MONROE ELEY Monroe RB 6'2 210 Palo Verde CC; Arizona State B: 4/17/1949 Rocky Mount, NC Draft: 11-276(di) 1973 KC; 5B-128 1974 ATL; 13-146 1974 NY-WFL Pro: N																															
1972	BC	16	2		0							6	1	105	517	4.9	75	1	27	507	18.8	53	0					37	1033	27.9	56
1973	BC	13	2		0							18	3	72	373	5.2	40	1	26	388	14.9	51	2					12	327	27.3	46
1974	BC	16	7		1							48	8	191	1176	6.2	63	3	18	321	17.8	92	4					19	543	28.6	110
3	Years	45	11		1							72	12	368	2066	5.6	75	5	71	1216	17.1	92	6					68	1903	28.0	110
RAY ELGAARD Ray SB-TE-WR 6'3 220 Vancouver Meralomas Jrs.; Utah B: 8/29/1959 Edmonton, AB Draft: 2-12 1983 SAS																															
1983	SAS	15										8	1	2	7	3.5	6	0	7	41	5.9	17	1					3	50	16.7	25
1984	SAS	16	0		1							18	3						45	744	16.5	48	3					3	0	0.0	4
1985	SAS*	15	2		0							24	4	1	5	5.0	5	0	79	1193	15.1	44	4				

Year	Team	GP	FM	FF	FR	TK	SK	YDS	IR	YDS	PD	PTS	TD	RA	YDS	AVG	LG	TD	REC	YDS	AVG	LG	TD	PR	YDS	AVG	LG	KOR	YDS	AVG	LG
1986	SAS	16	0		2							24	4	1	-1	-1.0	-1	0	55	1003	18.2	59	4					0	1		1
1987	SAS+	18	2		1	0						24	4						63	865	13.7	51	4								
1988	SAS*	18				0						36	6						69	1290	18.7	75	6								
1989	SAS	13	1		0	1						36	6	2	32	16.0	34	0	40	717	17.9	44	6								
1990	SAS+	16	3		0	0						68	11	3	23	7.7	16	0	94	1494	15.9	81	11					1	6	6.0	6
1991	SAS	13	0		2	7						66	11						62	1069	17.2	59	11								
1992	SAS*	18	2		0	6						66	11	2	6	3.0	5	0	91	1444	15.9	51	11								
1993	SAS*	18	1		1	8						48	8	0	19		19	0	89	1393	15.7	64	8								
1994	SAS	18	2		0	7						42	7						71	1100	15.5	67	7								
1995	SAS	18	0		1	4						12	2						54	745	13.8	40	2								
1996	SAS	9				1													11	100	9.1	25	0								
14	Years	221	13		8	34						472	78	11	91	8.3	34	0	830	13198	15.9	81	78					7	57	8.1	25
LOUIE ELIAS Louis HB 5'8 173 UCLA B: 1936																															
1958	HAM	1																													
1958	TOR	10							2	36				1	12	12.0	12	0						23	129	5.6	15	1	21	21.0	21
1958	Year	11							2	36				1	12	12.0	12	0						23	129	5.6	15	1	21	21.0	21
SOLOMON ELIMINIAN Solomon LB 5'11 225 Hawaii B: 10/21/1986 Calabar, Nigeria																															
2010	BC	16	0	1	1	88	5.0	64.0			2																				
2011	BC*	16	0	2	1	100	4.0	18.0	2	17	1																				
2	Years	32	0	3	2	188	9.0	82.0	2	17	3																				
JIM ELIOPULOS Jim A. LB 6'2 231 Westminster; Wyoming B: 4/18/1959 Dearborn, MI Draft: 3-81 1982 DAL Pro: N																															
1987	TOR	3				5	2.0																								
JACK ELLENA Jack Duane G 6'1 226 Lassen JC; UCLA B: 10/27/1931 Susanville, CA Draft: 19-229(f) 1953 LARM Pro: N																															
1957	TOR	1																													
BILL ELLENBOGEN William A. OT 6'5 258 Buffalo; Virginia Tech B: 12/8/1950 Glen Cove, NY Pro: NW																															
1978	TOR	6																													
1979	WPG	3																													
2	Years	9																													
JAMES ELLINGSON James SB-WR 6'1 190 Richmond Raiders Jrs.; British Columbia B: 5/18/1963 Calgary, AB Draft: 2-11 1986 SAS																															
1986	SAS	4																	1	10	10.0	10	0								
1987	SAS	10	0		1	0													3	24	8.0	10	0								
1988	SAS	18				0						2	0						17	223	13.1	27	0								
1989	SAS	18	0		1	1						12	2						22	288	13.1	41	2					1	9	9.0	9
1990	SAS	6				0								1	10	10.0	10	0	18	244	13.6	34	0								
1990	OTT	12				0						6	1						31	391	12.6	25	1					1	0	0.0	0
1990	Year	18				0						6	1	1	10	10.0	10	0	49	635	13.0	34	1					1	0	0.0	0
1991	OTT	14	1		0	0													15	222	14.8	28	0								
1992	OTT	18	1		0	1						54	9						54	797	14.8	71	9								
1993	OTT	18				1						12	2						25	281	11.2	23	2								
1994	OTT	16	1		0	1						24	4						35	508	14.5	54	4								
1995	OTT	17	1		0	1													18	306	17.0	35	0					1	0	0.0	0
1996	OTT	16				1						6	1						16	208	13.0	35	1	1	5	5.0	5				
11	Years	155	4		2	6						116	19	1	10	10.0	10	0	255	3502	13.7	71	19	1	5	5.0	5	3	9	3.0	9
BILL ELLIOTT Bill G 6'0 190 Texas Christian B: 1930																															
1951	EDM	10																													
1952	EDM	1																													
2	Years	11																													
BRETT ELLIOTT Brett QB 6'3 210 Utah; Linfield B: 6/11/1982 Pro: E																															
2007	EDM	4				0																									
BRUCE ELLIOTT Bruce LB 6'3 220 Western Ontario B: 11/27/1964 Willowdale, ON Draft: 6-48 1986 TOR																															
1987	TOR	15	1		0	2																									
1988	TOR	18	0		1	6	1.0																								
1989	TOR	14	0		1	8	1.0																								
1990	TOR	18	0		3	26	2.0																	1	6	6.0	6				
1991	TOR	13	0		1	25																									
1992	TOR	8				13	2.0	13.0																							
1993	TOR	17	0		1	21	2.0	9.0																							
7	Years	103	1		7	101	8.0	22.0																1	6	6.0	6				
GEORGE ELLIOTT George HB-QB 6'0 180 Oklahoma; Northeastern State B: 7/3/1932 Muskogee, OK																															
1955	WPG	15	4						3	0		10	2	42	229	5.5	28	2	3	6	2.0	11	0	4	29	7.3	11	17	343	20.2	48
JOEY ELLIOTT Joseph Preston QB 6'2 216 Purdue B: 8/2/1986																															
2010	WPG	13				0								9	66	7.3	30	0													
2011	WPG	3				1								2	8	4.0	4	0													
2	Years	16				1								11	74	6.7	30	0													
CRAIG ELLIS Craig SB-RB-WR 5'11 180 Santa Barbara CC; San Diego State B: 1/26/1961 Los Angeles, CA Pro: N																															
1982	WPG	1																													
1983	CAL	9	7		1							20	3	82	413	5.0	29	1	30	451	15.0	86	2	10	119	11.9	40	4	102	25.5	39
1984	SAS+	16	11		1							72	12	141	690	4.9	65	8	91	871	9.6	37	4	1	14	14.0	14	42	1040	24.8	92
1985	SAS	16	6		2							102	17	149	569	3.8	45	14	102	977	9.6	36	3	4	29	7.3	11	12	223	18.6	25
1986	TOR	10	6		2							60	10	113	381	3.4	18	7	41	338	8.2	28	3					26	548	21.1	45
1989	EDM*	15				1						54	9	5	22	4.4	12	0	80	1264	15.8	59	9	1	7	7.0	7				
1990	EDM*	18	1		0	2						102	17	3	20	6.7	14	0	106	1654	15.6	63	17								
1991	EDM	18	1		0	2						60	10						66	1133	17.2	52	10					31	644	20.8	34
1992	EDM	17				4						60	10						62	1018	16.4	41	10					16	250	15.6	40
1993	TOR	1				0													2	51	25.5	38	0								
10	Years	121	32		6	9						530	88	493	2095	4.2	65	30	580	7757	13.4	86	58	16	169	10.6	40	131	2807	21.4	92
DUNC ELLIS Dunc T Toronto																															
1953	HAM	1																													
GODFREY ELLIS Godfrey C-OG-OT 6'2 297 Acadia B: 4/3/1982 Nassau, Bahamas Draft: 2-10 2005 CAL																															
2005	CAL	16	1	0	0	0																									
2006	CAL	18				0																									
2007	CAL	18	0	0	1	0																									
2008	CAL	2				0																									
2009	CAL	18				0																									
5	Years	72	1	0	1	0																									
KAI ELLIS Kai LB-DE 6'3 252 San Francisco CC; Washington B: 8/7/1989 Kent, WA																															
2003	CAL	5				10	2.0	9.0			1																				
2004	OTT	11	0	0	1	31	1.0	4.0																				1	8	8.0	8
2005	OTT	13	0	0	1	60	4.0	17.0			3																				
2006	MTL	16	0	1	0	75			2	8	1																				
2007	MTL	11	0	2	0	39	1.0	4.0			1																				
2008	MTL	5	0	1	1	10	1.0	6.0																							
2008	WPG	8	0	1	0	11	4.0	38.0	1	97	0	6	1																		
2008	Year	13	0	2	1	21	5.0	44.0	1	97	0	6	1																		
2009	EDM	18	0	1	1	73	6.0	26.0			4	6	1																		
2010	EDM	12	0	1	1	40	3.0	24.0			2																				
8	Years	91	0	7	5	349	22.0	128.0	3	105	12	12	2															1	8	8.0	8
RICKY ELLIS Richard Harold TE-WR 6'4 235 Los Angeles CC; Fullerton State B: 6/27/1955 Los Angeles, CA Pro: U																															
1978	BC	4										6	1						12	196	16.3	77	1								
1980	BC	9												1	3	3.0	3	0	17	176	10.4	30	0								
1981	BC	11	2		0							24	4	2	13	6.5	10	0	32	594	18.6	63	4								
1982	BC	12	1		1							12	2	4	61	15.3	38	0	30	516	17.2	41	2					1	0	0.0	0

Year	Team	GP	FM	FF	FR	TK	SK	YDS	IR	YDS	PD	PTS	TD	RA	YDS	AVG	LG	TD	REC	YDS	AVG	LG	TD	PR	YDS	AVG	LG	KOR	YDS	AVG	LG
4	Years	36	3		1							42	7	7	77	11.0	38	0	91	1482	16.3	77	7					1	0	0.0	0
ROGER ELLIS Roger Calvin LB-T 6'3 233 Maine B: 2/1/1938 Boston, MA D: 5/14/2008 Brewer, ME Draft: 14-166 1959 NYG Pro: N																															
1963	MTL	1																													
1964	SAS	3																													
2	Years	4																													
JERRY ELLISON Jerry DE 6'3 250 Ranger JC; North Texas B: 7/6/1950 Fort Worth, TX Pro: W																															
1975	BC	2																													
HICHAM EL-MASHTOUB Hicham C 6'2 305 Arizona B: 5/11/1972 Lebanon Draft: Bonus-5 1995 EDM; 6-174 1995 HOU Pro: N																															
1999	EDM	18	0	0	1	0																									
DOUG ELMORE James Douglas DB 6'0 188 Mississippi B: 12/15/1939 Reform, AL D: 9/28/2002 Jackson, MS Draft: 13-171(f) 1961 WAS; 31-248(f) 1962 SD Pro: N																															
1963	CAL	9																						25	227	9.1	22				
TED ELSBY Ted DT-OT 5'11 225 none B: 1/3/1932 Galt, ON D: 11/5/1985																															
1954	MTL	11																													
1955	MTL	12																													
1956	MTL	14																										1	0	0.0	0
1957	MTL	13																													
1958	MTL	14																													
1959	MTL	7																													
1960	MTL	9																													
1961	MTL	4																													
1962	MTL	14																													
1963	MTL	10																													
1964	MTL+	14	0		1							6	1																		
1965	MTL	13	0		1																										
12	Years	135	0		2							6	1															1	0	0.0	0
GORD ELSER Gordon LB 6'2 210 Calgary B: 12/11/1959 Draft: 2A-11 1981 TOR																															
1981	TOR	10																													
1982	TOR	9	0		2		0.5																								
1983	TOR	16																													
1984	HAM	5					2.0																								
4	Years	40	0		2		2.5																								
EARL ELSEY Earl D. HB-E 5'8 175 Santa Monica JC; Loyola Marymount B: 10/31/1917 AR D: 10/12/1972 Los Angeles County, CA Pro: A																															
1949	EDM	7																													
JACK ELWELL John Matthew OE 6'3 205 Purdue B: 8/1/1940 Cleveland, OH Draft: 3-20 1962 BUF; 6-75 1962 STL Pro: N																															
1963	TOR	5										12	2	0	3		3	0	9	190	21.1	46	2								
LARRY ELY Lawrence Orlo, Jr. LB 6'1 230 Iowa B: 12/19/1947 Iowa City, IA Draft: 16-397 1970 CIN Pro: NW																															
1972	BC	1																													
1973	BC	13																													
2	Years	14																													
KEITH EMBRAY Keith W. DT 6'4 265 Utah B: 11/29/1970 Pro: N																															
1994	LV	9				6	1.0	18.0																							
1995	HAM	9				24	3.0	13.0			2																				
1996	HAM	12				27	2.0	9.0			2																				
3	Years	30				57	6.0	40.0			4																				
JOHN EMBREE John William OE 6'4 201 Compton CC B: 7/13/1944 St. Louis, MO Pro: NW																															
1971	EDM	2										6	1						2	45	22.5	28	1								
MEL EMBREE Melvin Belton E 6'3 192 Los Angeles CC; Pepperdine B: 1/6/1927 D: 8/30/1996 Los Angeles, CA Pro: N																															
1951	CAL	1																	2	23	11.5		0								
1952	WPG	8										35	7						16	423	26.4	48	7								
2	Years	9										35	7						18	446	24.8	48	7								
DICK EMERICH Richard DE 6'2 240 West Chester B: 1939 Draft: 30-349 1959 GB																															
1959	OTT	1																													
TOM EMERSON Thomas E. T 6'4 220 Oklahoma B: 1935 Draft: 28-336 1957 CHIB																															
1958	EDM	16																													
1959	EDM	7																													
2	Years	23																													
ERIC EMERY Eric LB 6'3 215 Fullerton State B: 9/18/1963 Shreveport, LA																															
1985	BC	6					1.0																								
1986	CAL	6	0		2																										
1987	OTT	3				6	1.0																								
3	Years	15	0		2	6	2.0																								
MIKE EMERY Mike LB 6'0 220 British Columbia B: 3/29/1961 Steveston, BC Draft: 1-3 1983 SAS																															
1983	SAS	16																										1	15	15.0	15
1984	TOR	16							1	12																					
1985	TOR	8																													
1985	MTL	5	0		2																										
1985	Year	13	0		2																										
1986	CAL	7	0		1		1.0					6	1																		
1987	CAL	7				9																									
5	Years	54	0		3	9	1.0		1	12		6	1															1	15	15.0	15
SHEA EMRY Shea LB 6'1 230 Eastern Washington; British Columbia B: 4/23/1986 Richmond, BC Draft: 1-7 2008 MTL																															
2008	MTL	17	0	2	0	24																						3	9	3.0	7
2009	MTL	15				56	2.0	7.0			2																				
2010	MTL	18	0	4	0	67	1.0	14.0	1	10	3			1	7	7.0	7	0													
2011	MTL	8	0	0	1	16																									
4	Years	58	0	6	1	163	3.0	21.0	1	10	5			1	7	7.0	7	0										3	9	3.0	7
AL ENDRESS Albert Joseph E 6'2 200 St. Mary's (California); San Francisco State B: 2/18/1928 Oakland, CA Pro: N																															
1953	CAL	11							1	0		16	3	1	1	1.0	1	0	16	241	15.1	71	3								
ERIC ENGLAND Eric Jevon DE 6'2 283 Texas A&M B: 3/25/1971 Fort Wayne, IN Draft: 3B-89 1994 ARI Pro: NX																															
2000	BC	12				35	3.0	24.0																							
2003	TOR*	18	0	0	3	40	14.0	112.0			2																				
2004	TOR	15	0	6	2	45	4.0	28.0																							
2005	TOR	17	0	0	1	44	6.0	37.0	1	22	0																				
2006	TOR	16				43	5.0	48.0	1	80	1	6	1																		
5	Years	78	0	6	6	207	32.0	249.0	2	102	3	6	1																		
WAYNE ENGLAND Wayne LB 6'0 220 Guelph B: 4/3/1966 Hamilton, ON Draft: 6-47 1989 BC																															
1989	BC	11	0		1	3																									
RON ENGLESON Ronald DT-NG-NT 6'2 235 Simon Fraser B: 9/10/1958 Burnaby, BC Draft: 1C-8 1981 TOR																															
1981	TOR	5																													
1983	OTT	9																													
1984	OTT	16					6.0																								
1985	OTT	16					1.0																								
1986	OTT	18					2.0																								
1987	OTT	8				4	1.0																								
6	Years	72				4	10.0																								
ANDREW ENGLISH Andrew WR 5'10 180 British Columbia B: 2/10/1974 Vancouver, BC Draft: 2-15 1996 BC																															
1997	BC	16	0	1	0	4								1	4	4.0	4	0	12	125	10.4	21	0	3	8	2.7	10	2	27	13.5	15
1998	BC	4				0													3	15	5.0	5	0								
1998	TOR	13	2	0	2	2													38	443	11.7	45	0								
1998	Year	17	2	0	2	2													41	458	11.2	45	0								
1999	TOR	13				0						6	1						10	167	16.7	63	1								
2000	TOR	17				12													28	355	12.7	30	0								

Year	Team	GP	FM	FF	FR	TK	SK	YDS	IR	YDS	PD	PTS	TD	RA	YDS	AVG	LG	TD	REC	YDS	AVG	LG	TD	PR	YDS	AVG	LG	KOR	YDS	AVG	LG
2001	TOR	9				1													6	61	10.2	23	0								
2002	HAM	7				0																									
2003	HAM	6				0													7	65	9.3	13	0								
7	Years	72	2	1	2	19						6	1	1	4	4.0	4	0	104	1231	11.8	63	1	3	8	2.7	10	2	27	13.5	15
KEITH ENGLISH Keith E 5'11 161 none B: 2/13/1927 Montreal, QC																															
1948	MTL	12										12	2										1								
1949	MTL	11																													
1950	MTL	11										5	1										1								
1951	MTL	10																													
4	Years	44										17	3										2								
BRYAN ENGRAM Bryan E 6'1 200 Texas Christian B: 1934 Draft: 24-279 1956 PIT																															
1956	CAL	13										6	1	1	9	9.0	9	0	13	214	16.5	30	1								
1957	CAL	3	0		1																										
1958	CAL	1																													
3	Years	17	0		1							6	1	1	9	9.0	9	0	13	214	16.5	30	1								
ED ENOS Edmund DT 6'2 230 Connecticut B: 6/30/1934 Boston, MA D: 3/6/2007 Montreal, QC																															
1957	BC	10																													
1958	BC	13	1		2																			1	0	0.0	0				
2	Years	23	1		2																			1	0	0.0	0				
RAY ENRIGHT Ray HB-FW 6'0 177 Edmonton Jrs. B: 6/15/1929 Edmonton, AB																															
1951	EDM	9										25	5	32	173	5.4		5	2	56	28.0		0					7	122	17.4	
1952	EDM	16			1							20	4	28	112	4.0	10	2	13	164	12.6	40	2	2	24	12.0	13	6	164	27.3	60
1953	EDM	13												7	16	2.3		0	2	43	21.5		0	1	3	3.0	3				
1954	BC	14										5	1	18	63	3.5	11	0	4	49	12.3	21	1	4	35	8.8	15				
4	Years	52	0		1							50	10	85	364	4.3	11	7	21	312	14.9	40	3	7	62	8.9	15	13	286	22.0	60
JOE EPPELE Joseph OT-OG 6'7 309 Washington State B: 8/12/1987 Squamish, BC Draft: 1A-2 2010 TOR																															
2010	TOR	7				0																									
2011	TOR	18				3																									
2	Years	25				3																									
DWAN EPPS Dwan Resha LB 6'1 242 Texas Southern B: 1/18/1977 Harris County, TX Pro: E																															
2004	SAS	6	0	1	0	1	2.0	8.0																							
2006	SAS	8				16					1																				
2	Years	14	0	1	0	17	2.0	8.0			1																				
JAMES EPPS James Williard WR 6'2 188 Ranger JC; Texas A&M-Commerce B: 9/5/1973 Linden, TX																															
2000	SAS	4				0													4	104	26.0	54	0								
2001	SAS	5	1	0	1	1													11	142	12.9	61	0								
2	Years	9	1	0	1	1													15	246	16.4	61	0								
HAYDEN EPSTEIN Hayden Scott K-P 6'2 212 Michigan B: 11/16/1980 San Diego, CA Draft: 7C-247 2002 JAC Pro: EN																															
2005	EDM	4				1						38	0																		
JEROME ERDMAN Jerome WR-SB 5'10 165 Simon Fraser; Renfrew Trojans Jrs. B: 3/28/1961 Vancouver, BC Draft: 4-32 1983 BC																															
1983	SAS	7																													
1983	WPG	9																	7	111	15.9	46	0								
1983	Year	16																	7	111	15.9	46	0								
1984	WPG	14										6	1						14	165	11.8	32	1								
1985	WPG	16							1	2									33	538	16.3	41	0								
1986	WPG	11																	17	237	13.9	48	0								
1986	OTT	6	0		2																			3	18	6.0	13	2	37	18.5	23
1986	Year	17	0		2														17	237	13.9	48	0	3	18	6.0	13	2	37	18.5	23
1987	OTT	18	1		0	27			2	44		6	1						28	366	13.1	51	1								
1988	OTT	12	1		0	16													7	83	11.9	30	0								
1989	EDM	10				7																						1	0	0.0	0
7	Years	88	2		2	50			3	46		12	2						106	1500	14.2	51	2	3	18	6.0	13	3	37	12.3	23
JOHN ERICKSON John OG 6'3 240 Queen's B: 10/24/1941 Draft: 2-8 1962 TOR																															
1966	TOR	6																													
CORRIS ERVIN Corris D'Angelo CB 5'11 176 Central Florida B: 8/30/1966 Vineland, NJ Draft: 5-136 1988 DEN Pro: E																															
1991	HAM	18	0		3	66			3	34																					
1992	HAM	18	0		2	51			3	63																					
1993	TOR	6				25																									
1993	HAM	7				24			3	31																					
1993	Year	13				49			3	31																					
1994	HAM	4	0		1	18					2																				
1994	SHR	6	0		1	6					2																				
1994	Year	10	0		2	24					4																				
1995	BAL	5				5																									
1995	WPG	2				4			1	5	3																				
1995	Year	7				9			1	5	3																				
5	Years	51	0		7	199			10	133	7																				
PETER ESHENKO Peter WR-SB 6'0 179 Alberta B: 4/26/1960 Edmonton, AB Draft: TE 1982 EDM																															
1982	MTL	15																	8	130	16.3	44	0								
1983	EDM	4																													
1984	CAL	2																	2	15	7.5	11	0								
3	Years	21																	10	145	14.5	44	0								
JACK ESPENSHIP John M. LB-OHB 6'1 200 Florida State B: 3/9/1939 Miami, FL Draft: 19- 1961 SD																															
1961	MTL	13										10	1	8	20	2.5	6	0	10	181	18.1	51	1					1	13	13.0	13
1962	MTL	11							1	0		1	0	2	19	9.5	14	0	11	102	9.3	16	0					2	34	17.0	20
2	Years	24							1	0		11	1	10	39	3.9	14	0	21	283	13.5	51	1					3	47	15.7	20
RONNIE ESTAY Ronnie DE 6'1 240 Louisiana State B: 12/22/1948 New Orleans, LA Draft: 8-186 1972 DEN Pro: U																															
1972	BC	16	0		3																										
1973	BC	2																													
1973	EDM	13	0		1																										
1973	Year+	15	0		1																										
1974	EDM	16																										3	13	4.3	13
1975	EDM	13																										1	0	0.0	0
1976	EDM	8																													
1977	EDM*	16	0		2																										
1978	EDM+	16	0		2																										
1979	EDM	16																													
1980	EDM*	16	0		1																										
1981	EDM	16	0		1		10.0																								
1982	EDM	1					0.5																								
11	Years	136	0		10		10.5																					4	13	3.3	13
RICHARD ESTELL Richard Wayne WR-SB 6'2 210 Kansas B: 10/12/1963 Kansas City, KS Pro: N																															
1988	HAM	5				0						6	1						11	139	12.6	18	1								
1989	HAM	16	2		0	0						6	1						40	476	11.9	57	1								
1990	HAM	16	1		0	8						14	2						60	937	15.6	39	2								
3	Years	37	3		0	8						26	4						111	1552	14.0	57	4								
MARK ESTELLE Mark Anthony CB 5'9 183 Los Angeles Southwest JC; Utah State B: 7/29/1981 Compton, CA Pro: E																															
2006	MTL	1				3																									
2007	MTL	17	1	0	1	44			3	111	4	6	1																		
2008	MTL+	14	0	1	0	54			1	41	3																				
2009	MTL+	17	0	2	2	48			3	10	0																				
2010	MTL+	17				36			4	42	7																				

Year	Team	GP	FM	FF	FR	TK	SK	YDS	IR	YDS	PD	PTS	TD	RA	YDS	AVG	LG	TD	REC	YDS	AVG	LG	TD	PR	YDS	AVG	LG	KOR	YDS	AVG	LG
2011	MTL	8	0	1	1	32					1																				
6	Years	74	1	4	4	217			11	204	15	6	1																		
DON ESTES Donald Olarey OG-DE 6'2 250 Louisiana State B: 10/14/1938 Tomball, TX Draft: 2-15 1963 HOU; 4-45 1963 STL Pro: N																															
1963	OTT	2																													
1964	OTT	12																													
1965	MTL	14																													
3	Years	28	1		0																										
LARRY ESTES Lawrence G. DE 6'6 250 Alcorn State B: 12/9/1946 Louisville, MS Draft: 8-192 1970 NO Pro: NW																															
1973	TOR	1																													
CHUCK ESTY Charles OG-OT 6'5 300 St. Lawrence B: 12/30/1968 Boston, MA																															
1994	SAC	8				0																									
1995	SA	18	0		2	2																									
1996	OTT	12				1																									
3	Years	38	0		2	3																									
SAM ETCHEVERRY Samuel (The Rifle) QB 5'11 185 Denver B: 5/20/1930 Carlsbad, NM D: 8/29/2009 Montreal, QC Pro: N																															
1952	MTL	12										14	2					2													
1953	MTL+	14										11	2					2													
1954	MTL+	14										21	2	53	298	5.6	23	2													
1955	MTL+	12										13	2	79	371	4.7	24	2													
1956	MTL+	14										21	3	80	442	5.5	19	3													
1957	MTL+	14										16	2	54	209	3.9	15	2	1	5	5.0	5	0								
1958	MTL	14										21	3	107	-274	-2.6	15	3													
1959	MTL	14										18	2	64	190	3.0	15	2													
1960	MTL+	14										22	2	63	245	3.9	22	2						2	0	0.0	0				
9	Years	122										157	20	500	1481	3.0	24	20	1	5	5.0	5	0	2	0	0.0	0				
DAVE ETHERLY David L. CB 6'1 195 Oregon State; Portland State B: 12/22/1962 Alburgu, Mexico Pro: N																															
1987	WPG	1				5																									
RAY ETHRIDGE Raymond Arthur, Jr. WR 5'10 180 Pasadena CC B: 12/12/1968 Draft: 3-63 1992 SD Pro: N																															
1991	BC	6				0						12	2	1	-8	-8.0	-8	0	18	200	11.1	24	1	8	75	9.4	25	16	402	25.1	94
JADE ETIENNE Jade SB-WR 6'3 184 Saskatchewan B: 10/11/1989 Regina, SK Draft: 1-4 2011 WPG																															
2011	WPG	17				0																									
LeROY ETIENNE LeRoy Joseph LB 6'1 240 Nebraska B: 7/25/1966 Lafayette, LA Pro: N																															
1989	TOR	1																													
BILL ETTER William F. QB 6'2 195 Notre Dame B: 2/18/1950																															
1973	HAM	14										6	1	4	15	3.8	9	1													
1974	HAM	16	6		1									52	320	6.2	22	0													
1975	HAM	1												1	15	15.0	15	0													
3	Years	31	6		1							6	1	57	350	6.1	22	1													
DON ETTINGER Donald Nesbit (Red) LB-C 6'2 215 Kansas B: 11/20/1921 Independence, MO D: 2/13/1992 Cookeville, TN Draft: 11-59 1948 BAL-AAFC; 19-166 1948 NYG Pro: N																															
1951	SAS+	14										47	0											1	2	2.0	2				
1952	TOR+	12										18	0																		
1953	TOR+	14										2	0																		
1954	HAM+	12							5	32		5	1																		
4	Years	52							5	32		72	1											1	2	2.0	2				
JOHN EUBANKS John DH-LB 5'10 173 Southern Mississippi B: 7/13/1983 Mound Bayou, MS Pro: N																															
2009	CAL	11	0	1	1	36			1	9	5																	6	63	10.5	23
2011	SAS	2				4																									
2	Years	13	0	1	1	40			1	9	5																	6	63	10.5	23
TOM EUROPE Tom S 5'11 195 Bishop's B: 7/27/1970 Toronto, ON Draft: 2-7 1993 BC																															
1993	BC	18	0		1	54			2	35																					
1994	BC	18				59			3	16	7																				
1995	BC+	18	0		4	57	1.0	7.0	2	29	2																				
1996	BC	18				56	1.0	7.0	2	33	1																				
1997	MTL	9	0	0	2	26	1.0	7.0	3	24	3	6	1																		
1998	MTL	15	0	1	2	33			1	6	4																				
1999	WPG	18	0	1	1	67			1	19	3																				
2000	WPG	17	0	1	0	79			4	117	0																				
2001	WPG	18	0	1	1	50					1																				
2002	WPG+	18	0	1	0	39	2.0		3	32	0																				
2003	WPG	8	0	0	1	14					1	6	1																		
11	Years	175	0	5	12	534	5.0	21.0	21	311	22	12	2																		
JACK EVANOFF Jack G 6'0 180 St. John's Roamers Jrs.																															
1948	WPG	8																													
BART EVANS Bart OG 6'2 240 Manitoba B: 9/9/1952 Draft: 8-66 1973 WPG																															
1976	HAM	16	1		0																							2	17	8.5	17
1977	HAM	16																													
1978	HAM	16																													
1979	HAM	10																													
1979	WPG	6																													
1979	Year	16																													
4	Years	58	1		0																							2	17	8.5	17
BOBBY EVANS Bobby DH 6'2 195 Southern Arkansas B: 12/2/1967 Haynesville, LA																															
1990	WPG	3				7																									
1991	WPG	18	0		2	77	1.0		2	10																		1	11	11.0	11
1992	WPG	16	0		1	52	2.0	10.0	4	66		6	1																		
1993	WPG+	18	1		0	73	1.0	9.0	5	43																					
1994	WPG+	17	0		4	56	4.0	31.0	5	63	7	6	1															1	6	6.0	6
1995	SHR	9				26			1	9	2																				
1996	WPG	17	0		2	48			4	33	4	6	1						1	6	6.0	6	0								
7	Years	98	1		9	339	8.0	50.0	21	224	13	18	3						1	6	6.0	6	0					2	17	8.5	11
BRYAN EVANS Bryan CB 5'11 197 Georgia B: 12/12/1986 Orange Park, FL																															
2010	MTL	1	0	0	1	3																									
FERNANDO EVANS Fernando WR 6'1 188 Alcorn State B: 10/12/1969																															
1994	SHR	2																													
GORDON EVANS Gordon T																															
1947	CAL	5																													
JOHNNY EVANS John Albert QB-P 6'1 17 North Carolina State B: 2/18/1956 High Point, NC Draft: 2-39 1978 CLE Pro: N																															
1982	MTL	10	2		2							18	3	36	228	6.3	21	3													
1983	MTL	7	1		0							18	3	15	30	2.0	10	3													
1984	EDM	15	2		0							11	1	6	32	5.3	19	1													
3	Years	32	5		2							47	7	57	290	5.1	21	7													
McKINNEY EVANS McKinney DB 5'11 200 New Mexico Highlands B: 12/20/1948 Draft: 14-346 1971 PIT																															
1974	MTL	4							1	17																					
NEIL EVANS Neil DB-SB 6'0 205 Toronto B: 3/6/1958 Draft: 1-3 1982 CAL																															
1982	OTT	2																													
1983	HAM	6																													
2	Years	8																													
OMAR EVANS Omar CB 6'0 190 Howard B: 9/1/1976 Alexandria, VA																															
2001	SAS	18	1	1	2	35			1	6	9																				
2002	SAS	12	1	0	0	23			1	0	3																				
2003	MTL	15	0	1	0	42			2	0	7																				

Year	Team	GP	FM	FF	FR	TK	SK	YDS	IR	YDS	PD	PTS	TD	RA	YDS	AVG	LG	TD	REC	YDS	AVG	LG	TD	PR	YDS	AVG	LG	KOR	YDS	AVG	LG
2004	CAL	9	0	0	1	20	1.0	9.0	1	0	1																				
2005	WPG	17	0	0	1	44			5	74	8	12	2																		
2006	WPG	15	0	1	1	30			2	39	5																				
6	Years	86	2	3	5	194	1.0	9.0	12	119	33	12	2																		
SCOTT EVANS Scott OT-OG 6'7 280 Wilfrid Laurier B: 12/15/1983 Cambridge, ON																															
2009	TOR	3				0																									
STACY EVANS Stacy DE 6'3 270 South Carolina B: 7/28/1972 Laurens, SC Pro: E																															
1996	OTT	7	0		1	21	2.0	14.0	0	0	3																				
1997	CAL	2				3																									
2	Years	9	0		1	24	2.0	14.0																							
TERRY EVANSHEN Terry FL-SE 5'10 185 Utah State B: 6/13/1944 Montreal, QC																															
1965	MTL+	14	2		1							18	3	3	9	3.0	7	0	37	631	17.1	85	3	6	41	6.8	8	5	108	21.6	31
1966	CAL+	16										54	9						67	1200	17.9	109	9					2	29	14.5	21
1967	CAL*	16										102	17						96	1662	17.3	63	17								
1968	CAL+	16										54	9						63	1002	15.9	43	9								
1969	CAL+	16	1		0							48	8						65	951	14.6	45	8								
1970	MTL	14	1		0							42	7						37	625	16.9	48	7								
1971	MTL+	14										30	5	1	-7	-7.0	-7	0	50	852	17.0	65	5								
1972	MTL	14	0		1							18	3						33	407	12.3	35	3								
1973	MTL	14										6	1						18	278	15.4	64	1								
1974	HAM	14										6	1						29	431	14.9	33	1								
1975	HAM+	16										82	13						55	970	17.6	81	13								
1976	HAM	14										18	3						20	307	15.4	26	3								
1977	HAM	12																	19	245	12.9	39	0								
1978	TOR	8										6	1						11	136	12.4	30	1								
14	Years	198	4		2							484	80	4	2	0.5	7	0	600	9697	16.2	109	80	6	41	6.8	8	7	137	19.6	31
JIM EVENSON James Lee FB 6'2 220 Boise JC; Treasure Valley CC; Oregon B: 1/9/1947 Hillsboro, OR D: 1/30/2008 Draft: 4B-90 1970 PIT Pro: W																															
1968	BC+	16	7		1							30	5	248	1220	4.9	32	4	19	241	12.7	62	1					1	0	0.0	0
1969	BC+	16	1		0							30	5	255	1287	5.0	63	4	17	167	9.8	28	1					8	172	21.5	35
1970	BC*	14	5		1							66	11	204	1003	4.9	42	8	17	125	7.4	15	3					19	464	24.4	97
1971	BC*	15	8		0							48	8	260	1237	4.8	22	8	11	77	7.0	36	0					4	99	24.8	32
1972	BC	16	8		2							54	9	184	961	5.2	44	8	26	329	12.7	53	1								
1973	OTT+	16	6		0							24	4	211	909	4.3	25	4	17	124	7.3	30	0								
1974	OTT	9	2		1							6	1	98	443	4.5	68	1	9	84	9.3	18	0					1	26	26.0	26
7	Years	102	37		5							258	43	1460	7060	4.8	68	37	116	1147	9.9	62	6					33	761	23.1	97
RON EVERETT Ron DT-DE 6'2 240 North Dakota; Winnipeg Rods Jrs. B: 1944																															
1966	WPG	1																													
1966	MTL	6	0		1							6	1																		
1966	Year	7	0		1							6	1																		
1967	MTL	12																													
1968	MTL	13	0		1																										
1969	MTL	12																													
4	Years	38	0		2							6	1																		
TRE EVERETT Tre WR 5'9 170 Florida B: 12/10/1969 Washington, DC																															
1993	SAS	4	1		0	1						6	1						11	127	11.5	44	1	6	44	7.3	13	2	29	14.5	17
1993	SAC	4				2						6	1						2	10	5.0	13	1	0	0		0				
1993	Year	8	1		0	3						12	2						13	137	10.5	44	2	6	44	7.3	13	2	29	14.5	17
1994	SAC	14	1		0	1						6	1						20	336	16.8	43	1	2	-4	-2.0	0	11	214	19.5	26
2	Years	18	2		0	4						18	3						33	473	14.3	44	3	8	40	5.0	13	13	243	18.7	26
WILLIAM EVERS William T. DB 5'10 175 Florida A&M B: 9/24/1968 Cairo, GA Pro: N																															
1994	SHR	6				11			3	0																					
KEN EVRAIRE Ken SB-WR 6'1 205 Ottawa Sooners Jrs.; Wilfrid Laurier B: 7/17/1965 Toronto, ON Draft: 2A-9 1988 SAS																															
1988	OTT	11				1						6	1						8	74	9.3	16	1								
1989	OTT	15	0		1	5						26	4	1	9	9.0	9	0	26	427	16.4	44	4	1	12	12.0	12				
1990	OTT	7	0		1	0						12	2	1	5	5.0	5	0	22	315	14.3	30	2								
1990	HAM	4				0																									
1990	Year	11	0		1	0						12	2	1	5	5.0	5	0	22	315	14.3	30	2								
1991	HAM	15	1		0	11						24	4	1	-1	-1.0	-1	0	31	491	15.8	65	4								
1992	HAM+	18				4						18	3						61	1081	17.7	53	3								
1993	HAM	15	1		0	4													41	679	16.6	64	0					1	-2	-2.0	-2
1994	HAM	13				1						18	3						44	644	14.6	62	3								
1995	OTT	9	1		1	0						6	1						8	78	9.8	18	0	3	9	3.0	6				
1997	HAM	13				6													7	62	8.9	20	0								
9	Years	116	3		3	32						110	18	3	13	4.3	9	0	248	3851	15.5	65	17	4	21	5.3	12	1	-2	-2.0	-2
BILL EWING Bill DB 6'0 182 British Columbia																															
1953	CAL	16																	2	18	9.0		0								
CLARE EXELBY Clare CB-WB 5'11 185 Parkdale Lions Jrs. B: 11/5/1938																															
1958	TOR	14																						1	8	8.0	8	3	21	7.0	19
1959	TOR	2																													
1960	CAL+	16	2		2				8	142		12	2						1	13	13.0	13	0	39	225	5.8	22				
1961	TOR	14							4	88														31	172	5.5	14	1	22	22.0	22
1962	TOR	7																						6	16	2.7	8				
1963	TOR	14							1	59		6	1											43	231	5.4	18				
1964	MTL	14	0		3				3	26														3	1	0.3	1				
1965	MTL	5	1		0				2	40														8	47	5.9	11				
8	Years	86	3		5				18	355		18	3						1	13	13.0	13	0	131	700	5.3	22	4	43	10.8	22
KYLE EXUME Kyle RB 5'10 198 Bishop's B: 11/22/1987 Draft: 6-49 2011 SAS																															
2011	HAM	1				0																									
SCOTT EYSTER Scott QB 6'2 213 Delta State B: 4/2/1984 Hammond, LA																															
2007	EDM	1				0																									
LEO EZERINS Leo LB-TE 6'4 225 Winnipeg Hawkeyes Jrs.; Whitworth B: 8/10/1956 Winnipeg, MB Draft: TE 1978 WPG																															
1978	WPG	16																	23	252	11.0	30	0					1	13	13.0	13
1979	WPG	16	0		4				1	8																					
1980	WPG	16	1		0				3	53														2	3	1.5	3				
1981	WPG	16	0		2		3.0		5	57																					
1982	WPG	16	0		1		3.0		4	45																					
1983	HAM	15	0		3		3.0																					1	0	0.0	0
1984	HAM	13	1		0		1.0		3	17																		1	8	8.0	8
1985	HAM	16	0		1				3	55																					
1986	HAM+	18					1.0		3	8														1	0	0.0	0				
1987	HAM	15	0		1	46	2.0		3	18																					
10	Years	157	2		12	46	13.0		25	261									23	252	11.0	30	0	3	3	1.0	3	3	21	7.0	13
BLAKE EZOR Blake HB 5'9 183 Michigan State B: 10/11/1966 Las Vegas, NV Pro: N																															
1992	EDM	5				1								26	91	3.5	16	0	1	3	3.0	3	0					3	56	18.7	23
MARTIN FABI Martin TE-SE-P 6'5 235 St. Thomas Jrs. B: 11/1/1941 Durrbach, Romania																															
1962	MTL	3										1	0																		
1962	SAS	9																													
1962	Year	12										1	0																		
1963	SAS	16	1		1							15	0						5	77	15.4	21	0								
1964	SAS	15	0		1							8	0	1	-2	-2.0	-2	0	3	60	20.0	40	0								
1965	SAS	13										4	0						7	107	15.3	35	0								
4	Years	47	1		2							28	0	1	-2	-2.0	-2	0	15	244	16.3	40	0								

Year	Team	GP	FM	FF	FR	TK	SK	YDS	IR	YDS	PD	PTS	TD	RA	YDS	AVG	LG	TD	REC	YDS	AVG	LG	TD	PR	YDS	AVG	LG	KOR	YDS	AVG	LG
RANDY FABI Randy SB-RB-WR-DB 6'4 205 Western Ontario B: 3/8/1963 Regina, SK Draft: 8-72 1985 WPG																															
1985	WPG	9																	2	25	12.5	18	0								
1986	WPG	18										6	1						8	93	11.6	30	1								
1987	WPG	17	1		0	0													7	73	10.4	22	0					1	0	0.0	0
1988	WPG	15				0						6	1						40	459	11.5	36	1								
1989	WPG	17				2													33	338	10.2	24	0								
1990	HAM	2																													
6	Years	78	1		0	2						12	2						90	988	11.0	36	2					1	0	0.0	0
FRED FACCIOLLA Fred G. T 6'2 215 Menlo JC; Southern California B: 11/8/1919 Yugoslavia D: 9/26/1975 San Francisco, CA																															
1946	OTT	12										12	0																		
TOMMY FAGAN Tommy DE 6'5 280 Louisiana-Monroe B: 3/26/1971 Lamont, FL																															
1997	WPG	3	0	0	1	6			0	0	1																				
DEREK FAGGIANI Derek OG-OT 6'4 267 Simon Fraser B: 1/26/1959 Sanford, ON Draft: 2-15 1982 WPG																															
1982	WPG	2																													
1983	HAM	3																													
2	Years	5																													
DAVE FAHRNER Dave FB 6'0 230 Western Ontario B: 1948 Draft: 1A-2 1970 HAM																															
1970	EDM	16	1		0									22	57	2.6	8	0	5	52	10.4	20	0					1	13	13.0	13
LLOYD FAIRBANKS Lloyd OT-OG 6'4 240 Brigham Young B: 4/28/1953 Raymond, AB Draft: TE 1975 CAL																															
1975	CAL	14	0		1																			1	0	0.0	0	2	29	14.5	15
1976	CAL	16																													
1977	CAL	1																													
1978	CAL+	16																													
1979	CAL*	16																													
1980	CAL	16																													
1981	CAL	16	0		2																										
1982	CAL*	16																													
1983	MTL	13	0		1																										
1984	MTL+	16			2																										
1985	MTL+	16																													
1986	MTL+	18	0		1																										
1987	HAM	15				3																						1	3	3.0	3
1988	HAM	18				0																									
1989	CAL	14				0																									
1990	CAL+	18				0																									
1991	CAL	18	0		1	2								1	10	10.0	10	0													
17	Years	257	0		8	5								1	10	10.0	10	0						1	0	0.0	0	3	32	10.7	15
BEN FAIRBROTHER Ben OT 6'3 305 Calgary B: 6/23/1973 Coventry, England Draft: 1-2 1997 SAS																															
1997	SAS	18				0																									
1998	SAS	16	0	0	2	1																									
1999	SAS	18				1																									
2000	SAS	6	0	0	1	1																									
2001	BC	18	1	0	0	1																									
2002	BC	1				0																									
2003	BC	18				2																									
7	Years	95	1	0	3	6																									
GREG FAIRCHILD Gregory Thompson OG 6'4 257 Tulsa B: 3/10/1954 St. Louis, MO Draft: 4B-116 1976 CIN Pro: NU																															
1978	TOR	3	0		1																										
1979	TOR	3																													
2	Years	6	0		1																										
JEFF FAIRHOLM Jeffrey D. SB-WR 5'11 190 Arizona B: 11/7/1965 Montreal, QC Draft: 1A-2 1988 SAS																															
1988	SAS	18	1		1	3						60	10	4	32	8.0	15	0	45	833	18.5	79	10					0	6		6
1989	SAS+	15	0		1	6						66	11	5	43	8.6	14	0	45	893	19.8	73	11								
1990	SAS	8	0		1	1						24	4						34	471	13.9	107	4								
1991	SAS	18	1		1	1						78	13	11	102	9.3	26	0	70	1239	17.7	99	13					2	24	12.0	24
1992	SAS	17	0		3	3						36	6	3	10	3.3	8	0	74	1344	18.2	76	6								
1993	SAS	18	1		0	4						54	9	3	7	2.3	7	0	72	1391	19.3	78	9								
1994	TOR	11	0		1	2						24	4	2	-6	-3.0	-3	0	29	599	20.7	85	4								
1995	TOR	14	2		1	5						6	1						43	477	11.1	35	1								
1996	TOR	7				0						6	1						14	218	15.6	30	1								
9	Years	126	5		9	25						354	59	28	188	6.7	26	0	426	7465	17.5	107	59					2	30	15.0	24
LARRY FAIRHOLM Larry S-DH 6'0 195 Rosemount Bombers Jrs.; Arizona B: 12/15/1941 Montreal, QC																															
1965	MTL	14	1		1									1	1	1.0	1	0						21	161	7.7	16				
1966	MTL	14	0		1				3	14														46	289	6.3	19				
1967	MTL	14	3		1				2	51		6	1											69	358	5.2	23				
1968	MTL+	14							1	53														64	294	4.6	20				
1969	MTL*	14	0		4				5	46		6	1											59	296	5.0	19	3	75	25.0	26
1970	MTL	14	0		1				4	45														19	92	4.8	23				
1971	MTL	14							1	86		6	1																		
1972	MTL	14							3	2														3	20	6.7	18				
8	Years	112	4		8				19	297		18	3	1	1	1.0	1	0						281	1510	5.4	23	3	75	25.0	26
DOUG FALCONER Doug DB 5'11 181 Ottawa B: 1/30/1952 Calgary, AB Draft: 6-46 1976 TOR																															
1976	HAM	3																													
1976	TOR	2																													
1976	OTT	8	0		3				1	4														5	28	5.6	12	2	37	18.5	24
1976	Year	13	0		3				1	4														5	28	5.6	12	2	37	18.5	24
1977	CAL	16	0		2																										
1978	CAL	16							1	35		6	1																		
1979	SAS	2																													
1979	MTL	2																													
1979	Year	4																													
4	Years	37	0		5				2	39		6	1											5	28	5.6	12	2	37	18.5	24
GARY FALLON Gary R. HB 6'1 212 Syracuse B: 4/3/1939 Watertown, NY D: 4/29/1995 Lexington, VA Draft: 12-157 1962 MIN																															
1962	HAM	1												5	17	3.4	8	0	1	10	10.0	10	0								
MIKE FALLS Michael Lee G 6'1 240 Minnesota B: 3/3/1934 Bemidji, MN Draft: 20-237 1956 NYG Pro: N																															
1956	TOR	8										29	1																		
BERNIE FALONEY Bernie QB 6'0 195 Maryland B: 6/15/1932 Carnegie, PA D: 6/14/1999 Hamilton, ON Draft: 1-11 1954 SF																															
1954	EDM	11	6		0							30	6	53	59	1.1	12	6													
1957	HAM	14										12	2	61	295	4.8	23	2													
1958	HAM+	14										26	4	74	-26	-0.4	24	4													
1959	HAM+	14							1	3		23	3	61	300	4.9	51	3													
1960	HAM	14										25	4	64	465	7.3	47	4	1	2	2.0	2	0								
1961	HAM+	12										26	4	77	434	5.6	27	4													
1962	HAM	5												17	55	3.2	20	0													
1963	HAM	14										14	2	59	297	5.0	30	2													
1964	HAM+	14	4		0							37	6	64	331	5.2	20	6													
1965	MTL+	14	6		0							14	2	57	200	3.5	27	2													
1966	MTL	14	2		1							19	3	48	160	3.3	14	3													
1967	BC	16	7		1							12	2	59	236	4.0	25	2													
12	Years	156	25		2				1	3		238	38	694	2806	4.0	51	38	1	2	2.0	2	0								
CALVIN FANCE Calvin Cooledge RB 6'1 200 Rice B: 7/6/1959 Houston, TX Draft: 9-245 1981 ATL																															
1981	OTT	1										12	2	8	30	3.8	7	2										3	103	34.3	36

Year	Team	GP	FM	FF	FR	TK	SK	YDS	IR	YDS	PD	PTS	TD	RA	YDS	AVG	LG	TD	REC	YDS	AVG	LG	TD	PR	YDS	AVG	LG	KOR	YDS	AVG	LG
DONAVA FANN Donavan OG 6'4 280 Bethune-Cookman B: 12/27/1964 Jacksonville, FL																															
1987	CAL	3				3																									
1988	CAL	1				0																									
1988	BC	7				0																									
1988	Year	8				0																									
2	Years	4				3																									
ANDY FANTUZ Andrew SB 6'4 220 Western Ontario B: 12/18/1983 Chatham, ON Draft: 1-3 2006 SAS																															
2006	SAS	18	0	0	1	2						24	4	1	0	0.0	0	1	30	408	13.6	30	3								
2007	SAS	17	0	0	1	2						42	7						56	978	17.5	72	7								
2008	SAS	7				6						18	3						36	488	13.6	31	3								
2009	SAS	13	1	0	0	3						28	4						67	882	13.2	40	4								
2010	SAS*	18	2	0	2	2						36	6						87	1380	15.9	66	6								
2011	SAS	4				2													13	175	13.5	31	0								
6	Years	77	3	0	4	17						148	24	1	0	0.0	0	1	289	4311	14.9	72	23								
MIKE FANUCCI Michael Joseph DE 6'4 236 Arizona State B: 9/25/1949 Scranton, PA Draft: 9-219 1971 WAS Pro: N																															
1975	MTL	7	0		1				1	45																					
1976	MTL	5																										5	35	7.0	12
1976	CAL	5																													
1976	OTT	5	0		1																										
1976	Year	15																										5	35	7.0	12
1977	OTT	16	0		1																										
1978	OTT*	16	0		2				1	30		6	1																		
1979	OTT	12	0		1																										
5	Years	56	0		6				2	75		6	1															5	35	7.0	12
JOHN FARLER John FB 6'1 210 Colorado B: 1946 Draft: 14-380 1968 GB																															
1968	WPG	11	1		0									18	48	2.7	12	0	3	41	13.7	26	0					6	108	18.0	31
DALE FARLEY Dale Rice LB 6'4 235 West Virginia B: 5/27/1949 Sparta, TN Draft: 3-74 1971 MIA Pro: N																															
1974	TOR	2																													
TERRELL FARLEY Terrell Dwayne LB 5'11 200 Independence JC; Nebraska B: 8/16/1975 Columbus, GA																															
1998	SAS	1				2																									
1999	SAS	2				9																									
2	Years	3				11																									
JOHN FARLINGER John S 6'0 172 Edmonton Wildcats Jrs.; Calgary B: 3/4/1948 Draft: 7-51 1971 BC																															
1973	EDM	13	0		1				4	52														5	33	6.6	25				
1974	EDM	16			1				4	72																					
1975	EDM	10	0		1				3	75																					
1976	EDM	16			2				2	31														2	0	0.0	0				
1977	EDM	16	0		2				3	46														1	-1	-1.0	-1				
1978	EDM	16							2	15																					
6	Years	87	0		7				18	291														8	32	4.0	25				
JOHNNY FARMER Johnny HB-FW 5'11 170 B: 1925																															
1948	TOR	8																													
1949	TOR	6																													
1951	TOR	1																													
3	Years	15																													
AMARIAH FARROW Amariah OT 6'5 325 Garden City CC; Midwestern State B: 9/29/1980 Clanton, AL																															
2005	BC	2				0																									
2006	BC	1				0																									
2007	BC	1				0																									
3	Years	4				0																									
DAN FARTHING Dan SB 5'11 185 Saskatchewan B: 11/10/1969 Saskatoon, SK Draft: 1A-2 1991 SAS																															
1991	SAS	5				1						6	1						11	142	12.9	21	1					1	12	12.0	12
1992	SAS	16				3						6	1						17	182	10.7	31	1	5	28	5.6	10	4	35	8.8	19
1993	SAS	18	0		1	8													22	192	8.7	25	0	5	43	8.6	12	5	54	10.8	21
1994	SAS	17				3						6	1						35	458	13.1	43	1					4	32	8.0	21
1995	SAS	16				3						32	5						45	571	12.7	45	5	3	16	5.3	9				
1996	SAS	18				6													37	470	12.7	57	0					1	-1	-1.0	-1
1997	SAS	18	1	0	0	3						24	4						58	959	16.5	56	4	1	5	5.0	5				
1998	SAS	18				0													67	772	11.5	37	0								
1999	SAS	17				4						6	1						36	454	12.6	29	1	1	0	0.0	0				
2000	SAS	16				1						36	6						44	729	16.6	48	6	1	23	23.0	23				
2001	SAS	10				2													12	169	14.1	44	0								
11	Years	169	1	0	1	34						116	19						384	5098	13.3	57	19	16	115	7.2	23	15	132	8.8	21
GREG FASSITT Greg CB 5'11 186 Grambling State B: 4/4/1985 New Orleans, LA Pro: N																															
2011	CAL	15				38			1	0	2																				
MARIO FATAFEHI Mario P. DT 6'2 302 Snow JC; Kansas State B: 1/27/1979 Chicago, IL Draft: 5-133 2001 ARI Pro: N																															
2006	HAM	3				2																									
ADAM FAUL Adam T Regina Bombers Jrs. B: 4 18/18/1929 Regina, SK																															
1946	SAS	3																													
KYLE FAULKNER Kyle DE 6'1 230 Central State (Ohio) B: 6/15/1971 Longwood, FL																															
1995	BIR	18				22	1.0	3.0																							
SHAWN FAULKNER Shawn D. RB 6'0 195 Western Michigan B: 6/22/1962 Port Huron, MI Draft: TD 1984 MIC-USFL Pro: U																															
1986	MTL	6	2		1							18	3	85	356	4.2	24	1	16	211	13.2	49	2	4	13	3.3	5	5	95	19.0	33
1987	OTT	5	0		1	3						6	1	56	181	3.2	15	1	10	68	6.8	19	0					8	145	18.1	28
1988	CAL	12	3		1	0						6	1	42	184	4.4	20	1	8	86	10.8	33	0	38	439	11.6	49	13	297	22.8	36
1989	CAL	6	2		0									4	43	10.8	27	0						29	257	8.9	64	2	79	39.5	54
4	Years	29	7		3	3						30	5	187	764	4.1	27	3	34	365	10.7	49	2	71	709	10.0	64	28	616	22.0	54
JIM FAUVER Jim OHB 5'10 195 Texas Christian B: 1943																															
1965	EDM	6	0		1							24	4	26	108	4.2	10	2	3	26	8.7	7	2					6	129	21.5	36
HAL FAVERTY Harold Edward C 6'1 215 Wisconsin B: 9/26/1927 Hammond, IN Draft: 15-149 1949 CHIB Pro: N																															
1953	TOR	7										5	1										1								
BRAD FAWCETT Brad OT- 6'7 275 Saskatoon Hilltops Jrs. B: 6/30/1960 Saskatoon, SK																															
1982	SAS	1																													
1985	OTT	11																													
1986	OTT	11	0		1																										
1987	OTT	10				0																									
1988	OTT	18				2																									
1989	OTT	18				2																									
6	Years	69	0		1	4																									
WILLIE FEARS Willie Bert DT-DE 6'3 278 Holmes JC; Northwestern Louisiana B: 6/4/1964 Chicago, IL Pro: EN																															
1988	WPG	9	0		3	15	1.0																								
1989	OTT	6				19	3.0		1	0																					
1989	TOR	1				2																									
1989	Year	7				21	3.0		1	0																					
1994	SAC	18				29	6.0	51.0			1																				
1995	SA	18	0		1	21	1.0	7.0																							
4	Years	51	0		4	86	11.0	58.0	1	0	1																				
CLIFF FEATHERSTONE Clifford DB 5'11 183 Colorado State B: 4/6/1957 Draft: 7-180 1978 SD																															
1978	SAS	3	0		1																										
PAUL FEDOR Paul OE-DE 6'2 196 Queen's B: 1934 Draft: 1-2 1958 TOR																															
1958	TOR	13																	6	98	16.3	34	0								
1960	TOR	9										6	1						9	154	17.1	32	1								

Year	Team	GP	FM	FF	FR	TK	SK	YDS	IR	YDS	PD	PTS	TD	RA	YDS	AVG	LG	TD	REC	YDS	AVG	LG	TD	PR	YDS	AVG	LG	KOR	YDS	AVG	LG
1961	MTL	5																													
1962	MTL	6																						1	0	0.0	0				
4	Years	33										6	1						15	252	16.8	34	1	1	0	0.0	0				
JOHNNY FEDOSOFF John OHB-S 5'11 180 none B: 1933 Kenora, SK																															
1952	TOR	5										15	3					2					1								
1953	TOR	13										5	1																		
1954	TOR	14							1	0		5	1	22	93	4.2	16	0	4	117	29.3	55	1	73	605	8.3	47	11	200	18.2	55
1955	HAM+	12							3	23		20	4	44	241	5.5	81	4	5	75	15.0	38	0	43	501	11.7	46	3	24	8.0	18
1956	HAM	14							2	17		6	1	22	112	5.1	15	0	4	60	15.0	27	1	49	386	7.9	31	3	43	14.3	22
1957	HAM	14												6	13	2.2	5	0						50	211	4.2	11				
1958	MTL	2																						14	65	4.6	11				
1958	SAS	4	1											1	8	8.0	8	0	1	4	4.0	4	0	7	29	4.1	12				
1958	Year	6	1																					21	94	4.5	12				
7	Years	74	1		0				6	40		51	10	95	467	4.9	81	6	14	256	18.3	55	3	236	1797	7.6	47	17	267	15.7	55
WOLFGANG FELGEMACHER Wolfgang K 5'10 165 none B: 1941 Germany																															
1966	TOR	1										1	0																		
ART FELKER Arthur, Jr. E 6'3 200 Marquette B: 11/30/1927 Milwaukee, WI Draft: 22-258 1951 GB																															
1952	WPG	4																													
GERRY FELLNER Gerry WR-P 6'2 205 Regina Rams Jrs. B: 8/17/1954																															
1977	SAS	12																	1	20	20.0	20	0					1	2	2.0	2
1978	SAS	7																	3	40	13.3	19	0								
1979	SAS	16																	19	260	13.7	32	0								
1980	SAS	15										6	1						10	117	11.7	27	1								
4	Years	50										6	1						33	437	13.2	32	1					1	2	2.0	2
JACKIE FELLOWS Jack HB-QB 5'6 165 Fresno State B: 1922 Draft: 6-50 1944 WAS																															
1947	OTT	12																													
WILLIE FELLS Willie LB 6'1 225 Purdue B: 7/26/1976 Smithville, NC																															
2000	HAM	16	0	0	1	70	1.0	3.0	2	23	4																				
2001	CAL	14				45	2.0	9.0																							
2002	CAL	12	0	0	5	55	1.0	0.0			2																				
2003	CAL	17	0	3	3	50	1.0	10.0	1	12	2																				
2005	WPG	3	0	1	2	10						6	1																		
5	Years	62	0	4	11	230	5.0	22.0	3	35	8	6	1																		
BOBBY FELTS Bob HB 6'2 203 Florida A&M B: 6/26/1942 Miami, FL Draft: 13- 1965 HOU; 6B-71 1965 BAL Pro: N																															
1969	MTL	4	2		0							12	2	23	94	4.1	18	1	5	68	13.6	22	1					7	205	29.3	35
CHUCK FENENBOCK Charles Bernard HB-QB 5'9 174 UCLA B: 8/28/1918 Oakland, CA D: 7/27/1998 Santa Rosa, CA Pro: AN																															
1949	EDM	13										20	3					3													
1950	CAL	11										21	4	65	307	4.7	39	4	9	154	17.1	25	0								
2	Years	24										41	7	65	307	4.7	39	7	9	154	17.1	25	0								
GILL FENERTY Lawrence Gill RB 6'0 205 Holy Cross B: 8/24/1963 New Orleans, LA Draft: 7-173 1986 NO Pro: N																															
1987	TOR*	16	8		1	3						90	15	178	879	4.9	60	12	53	456	8.6	34	3					10	190	19.0	34
1988	TOR*	13	2		1	3						72	12	202	968	4.8	27	10	51	443	8.7	21	2								
1989	TOR+	16	5		2	0						72	12	245	1247	5.1	60	10	36	291	8.1	37	2					1	15	15.0	15
1994	SHR	2				3						6	1	6	4	0.7	4	1													
4	Years	47	15		4	9						240	40	631	3098	4.9	60	33	140	1190	8.5	37	7					11	205	18.6	34
DAVE FENNELL David A. DT 6'3 249 Edmonton Wildcats Jrs.; North Dakota B: 2/4/1953 Edmonton, AB Draft: TE 1974 EDM																															
1974	EDM	1			2																										
1975	EDM	16	0		2																										
1976	EDM	16			2																										
1977	EDM*	16	0		2																										
1978	EDM*	16	0		2																										
1979	EDM*	16	0		2																										
1980	EDM*	16	0		1				1	0																					
1981	EDM*	15	0		2		7.0		1	23		6	1																		
1982	EDM	16	0		2		7.0																								
1983	EDM	16					3.5																								
10	Years	144	0		17		17.5		2	23		6	1																		
DENNY FERDINAND Denis RB-FB 5'11 205 Montreal Alouettes Jrs. B: 3/22/1962 Port of Spain, Trinidad & Tobago D: 4/4/2002 Ottawa, ON																															
1982	MTL	15	5		0									52	231	4.4	18	0	3	7	2.3	14	0					31	757	24.4	47
1983	MTL	16	6		1							30	5	102	603	5.9	34	5	8	128	16.0	43	0					27	749	27.7	55
1984	MTL	8												42	157	3.7	11	0	8	68	8.5	26	0					2	59	29.5	33
1985	SAS	13	6		1							8	1	56	289	5.2	50	1	20	243	12.2	45	0	1	2	2.0	2	10	182	18.2	30
1986	SAS	17	3		0							12	2	112	572	5.1	33	2	29	277	9.6	28	0								
1987	SAS	3	1		0	0								12	55	4.6	16	0	4	17	4.3	7	0					7	195	27.9	59
1988	SAS	18	7		1	0						6	1	85	425	5.0	36	1	10	72	7.2	22	0					16	334	20.9	44
1989	OTT	6	1		0							12	2	12	14	1.2	4	2	10	26	2.6	10	0					2	37	18.5	21
8	Years	96	29		3	0						68	11	473	2346	5.0	50	11	92	838	9.1	45	0	1	2	2.0	2	95	2313	24.3	59
BILL FERGUSON William Michael LB 6'3 225 Washington; Grossmont JC; San Diego State B: 7/7/1951 San Diego, CA Draft: 4-90 1973 NYJ Pro: NW																															
1977	WPG	10	0		1																										
JOE FERGUSON Joseph Carlton, Jr. QB 6'1 190 Arkansas B: 4/23/1950 Alvin, TX Draft: 3A-57 1973 BUF Pro: N																															
1995	SA	2				0																									
KEN FERGUSON Kenneth LB-C 6'1 230 Utah State B: 3/21/1944 Saskatoon, SK																															
1967	BC	15	1		2																										
1968	BC	16	0		2									0	17		17	0													
1969	EDM	14	0		2																										
1970	EDM	10																													
1971	EDM	16																													
1972	EDM	3																													
1972	HAM	10																													
1972	Year	13																													
1973	HAM	14																													
1974	HAM	16																													
1975	HAM	12																													
9	Years	116	1		6									0	17		17	0													
LARRY FERGUSON Lawrence Pearly OHB 5'10 185 Iowa B: 3/19/1940 Madison, IL Draft: 17-129(f) 1962 OAK; 4B-52(f) 1962 DET Pro: N																															
1964	EDM	10	1		0							24	4	90	377	4.2	40	3	10	92	9.2	28	1					5	120	24.0	42
1965	EDM	1	1		0									4	33	8.3	18	0	1	2	2.0	2	0					3	38	12.7	19
1965	TOR	13	4		1							12	2	86	505	5.9	36	1	20	225	11.3	104	1					12	247	20.6	43
1965	Year	14	5		1							12	2	90	538	6.0	36	1	21	227	10.8	104	1					15	285	19.0	43
1966	TOR	5										18	3	36	204	5.7	75	1	9	112	12.4	45	2								
1967	TOR	4	1		0							6	1	32	108	3.4	13	1	7	55	7.9	20	0					4	81	20.3	36
4	Years	20	7		1							60	10	248	1227	4.9	75	6	47	486	10.3	104	4					24	486	20.3	43
NICK FERGUSON Nicholas A. CB 5'11 201 Morris Brown; Georgia Tech B: 11/27/1974 Miami, FL Pro: EN																															
1996	SAS	5				15					1																				
1997	WPG	15	0	0	1	55			2	35	2																				
1998	WPG	16	0	1	1	67			1	0	4																				
1999	WPG	3				12																									
4	Years	39	0	1	2	149			3	35	7																				
O.K. FERGUSON O.K. HB 6'0 202 Louisiana State B: 1934 Draft: 13-146 1956 DET																															
1956	TOR	13										42	7	154	802	5.2	21	6	21	194	9.2	19	1								
RUFUS FERGUSON Rufus Alexander (Roadrunner) HB 5'5 191 Wisconsin B: 4/28/1951 Perrine, FL Draft: 16-404 1973 ATL Pro: W																															
1973	WPG	1	1		0									6	7	1.2	8	0	4	32	8.0	13	0					1	23	23.0	23

Year	Team	GP	FM	FF	FR	TK	SK	YDS	IR	YDS	PD	PTS	TD	RA	YDS	AVG	LG	TD	REC	YDS	AVG	LG	TD	PR	YDS	AVG	LG	KOR	YDS	AVG	LG
MERVYN FERNANDEZ Mervyn L. WR 6'2 210 San Jose CC; DeAnza JC; San Jose State B: 12/29/1959 Merced, CA Draft: 10-277 1983 LARI Pro: N																															
1982	BC+	16	2		0							56	9	2	1	0.5	4	0	64	1046	16.3	84	8	20	179	9.0	74	1	32	32.0	32
1983	BC+	16	2		0							62	10						78	1284	16.5	74	10	2	19	9.5	12				
1984	BC*	15										102	17						89	1486	16.7	78	17								
1985	BC*	16	1		0							90	15	3	33	11.0	19	0	95	1727	18.2	90	15					1	3	3.0	3
1986	BC	11										30	5	7	69	9.9	22	0	48	865	18.0	72	5								
1994	BC	9										12	2						25	282	11.3	35	2	6	23	3.8	10	3	41	13.7	21
6	Years	83	5		0							352	58	12	103	8.6	22	0	399	6690	16.8	90	57	28	221	7.9	74	5	76	15.2	32
SAM FERNANDEZ Samuel David FB 5'11 205 Potomac State JC; Miami (Florida) B: 1941 Clarksburg, WV																															
1962	HAM	13							2	13				15	59	3.9	10	0													
TERRY FERNANDEZ Terry LB 6'1 225 Pearl River JC; Louisiana-Lafayette B: 9/10/1942 Miami, FL																															
1965	MTL	4																													
VINCE FERRAGAMO Vincent Anthony QB 6'3 209 California; Nebraska B: 4/24/1954 Torrance, CA Draft: 4A-91 1977 LARM Pro: N																															
1981	MTL	13	5		1									15	57	3.8	16	0													
FRANK FERRARA Frank, Jr. DT 6'3 275 Rhode Island B: 12/7/1975 New York, NY Pro: EN																															
2005	BC	18	0	1	0	28	3.0	28.0	1	21	1																	1	10	10.0	10
DIAMOND FERRI Diamond M. LB-DB 5'10 214 Syracuse B: 8/6/1981 Stoneham, MA Pro: EN																															
2007	MTL	13	0	1	0	57	2.0	16.0			1																				
2008	MTL	17	0	1	1	74	1.0	14.0	2	49	2																	1	12	12.0	12
2009	MTL	16	0	0	2	47			1	3	2																	1	21	21.0	21
2010	MTL	12	0	3	1	31	3.0	22.0	1	3	0	6	1															9	260	28.9	85
2011	MTL	17	2	3	3	56	3.0	26.0	1	0	1													4	22	5.5	12	28	573	20.5	54
5	Years	75	2	8	7	265	9.0	78.0	5	55	6	6	1											4	22	5.5	12	39	866	22.2	85
NEIL FERRIS Neil George DB 5'11 181 Loyola Marymount B: 10/31/1927 D: 1/30/1996 Lake Havasu City, AZ Pro: N																															
1954	CAL	1	1		2														2	16	8.0	9	0	4							
1954	BC	13							5	36														39				3	47	15.7	21
1954	Year	14	1		2														2	16	8.0	9	0	43	295	6.9	17	3	47	15.7	21
DAN FERRONE Dan OG-OT 6'2 255 Simon Fraser B: 4/3/1958 Oakville, ON Draft: TE 1981 TOR																															
1981	TOR	16																													
1982	TOR	14																													
1983	TOR+	16	0		1																							1	0	0.0	0
1984	TOR*	16																													
1985	TOR*	15	0		3									0	1		1	0													
1986	TOR+	18																													
1987	TOR*	15	0		1	0																									
1988	TOR	12	0		1	2																									
1989	CAL+	18				0																									
1990	TOR*	18	0		4	1																									
1991	TOR*	18	0		1	4																									
1992	TOR+	17	0		1	1																									
12	Years	193	0		12	8								0	1		1	0										1	0	0.0	0
STEVE FERRUGHELLI Steve FB 6'2 225 Rutgers B: 3/12/1949 Newark, NJ																															
1973	MTL	6												67	364	5.4	19	0	11	121	11.0	25	0								
1974	MTL+	16	4		1							18	3	228	1134	5.0	26	3	39	258	6.6	22	0					1	16	16.0	16
1975	MTL	16	2		0							48	8	209	893	4.3	17	8	29	368	12.7	34	0								
1976	MTL	5												45	195	4.3	16	0	8	47	5.9	16	0								
1976	EDM	5	1		0							18	3	55	186	3.4	14	2	25	168	6.7	20	1					2	17	8.5	14
1976	Year	10	1		0							18	3	100	381	3.8	16	2	33	215	6.5	20	1					2	17	8.5	14
4	Years	43	7		1							84	14	604	2772	4.6	26	13	112	962	8.6	34	1					3	33	11.0	16
GEORGE FESTERYGA George HB-QB 5'10 184 NDG Maple Leafs Jrs. B: 7/31/1926 Hamilton, ON D: 1/7/2010 Port Perry, ON																															
1947	HAM	8										5	1					1													
1949	MTL	9																													
1950	SAS	7										5	1	5	29	5.8		1													
1951	EDM	14										5	1	18	28	1.6		1										1	15	15.0	15
1952	EDM	16							1	5				1	1	1.0	1	0													
5	Years	54							1	5		15	3	24	58	2.4	1	3										1	15	15.0	15
KEVIN FETERIK Kevin M. QB 5'11 195 Brigham Young B: 9/14/1977 Westminster, CA																															
2001	CAL	13				0																									
2002	CAL	11				0																									
2003	CAL	15	3	0	1	0						6	1	36	153	4.3	18	0	1	12	12.0	12	1								
3	Years	39	3	0	1	0						6	1	36	153	4.3	18	0	1	12	12.0	12	1								
JOHN FEUGILL John Eark IOT 6'7 309 Maryland B: 12/20/1975 Lawrence, MA Pro: E																															
2003	TOR	17				1																									
2004	TOR	14				0																									
2005	WPG	12				0																									
3	Years	43				1																									
AARON FIACCONI Aaron C-OG-OT 6'4 298 Mansfield B: 11/12/1979 Sault Ste. Marie, ON Draft: 4A-32 2002 MTL																															
2002	MTL	2				0																									
2003	MTL	6				0																									
2004	MTL	5				0																									
2005	MTL	3				0																									
2005	WPG	14				2																									
2005	Year	17				2																									
2006	WPG	18				0																									
2007	WPG	8				0																									
2007	EDM	8				0																									
2007	Year	16				0																									
2008	EDM	4				0																									
2009	EDM	18	2	0	0	1																									
2010	EDM	17				0																									
2011	EDM	8	0	0	1	0																									
10	Years	89	2	0	1	3																									
ELETISE FIATOA Eletise DT 5'11 244 Long Beach State B: 7/31/1954																															
1978	MTL	6	0		1																										
BRAD FICHTEL Brad Alan C 6'2 285 Eastern Illinois B: 3/10/1970 Aurora, IL Draft: 7-179 1993 LARM Pro: N																															
1995	MEM	1				0																									
TONY FICKLIN Antonio FB 6'1 258 San Jose State B: 10/21/1981 Shreveport, LA																															
2006	CAL	3				1								1	3	3.0	3	0													
GREG FIEGER Greg FB-SB 5'10 185 Regina Rams Jrs. B: 10/30/1957 Beechy, SK																															
1980	SAS	12	1		1							12	2						16	256	16.0	37	2	1	2	2.0	2	2	24	12.0	22
1981	SAS	16	3		2							26	4	39	151	3.9	18	2	43	448	10.4	26	2								
1982	SAS	14	3		0							12	2	81	356	4.4	16	2	25	196	7.8	21	0								
1983	SAS	16	2		1							12	2	68	330	4.9	35	2	25	275	11.0	43	0								
1984	SAS	12	2		0									45	181	4.0	14	0	25	215	8.6	28	0					1	30	30.0	30
1985	CAL	16	1		3							12	2	23	81	3.5	12	0	44	347	7.9	30	2								
1986	CAL	13										6	1	9	36	4.0	10	1	8	53	6.6	9	0								
7	Years	99	12		7							80	13	265	1135	4.3	35	7	186	1790	9.6	43	6	1	2	2.0	2	3	54	18.0	30
AMOD FIELD Amod Lloyd WR 5'11 181 Montclair State B: 10/11/1967 Passaic, NJ Pro: N																															
1992	BC	9	1		0	12			2	11				1	0	0.0	0	0	3	55	18.3	28	0	5	25	5.0	14	33	672	20.4	49
JOHN FIELD John DB 5'10 200 Southern Illinois B: 5/24/1964																															
1990	TOR	7	1		0	19			1	29																		18	385	21.4	51
NORM FIELDGATE Norman LB-DE-S 6'2 210 Regina Dales Jrs.; British Columbia B: 6/12/1932 Regina, SK																															

Year	Team	GP	FM	FF	FR	TK	SK	YDS	IR	YDS	PD	PTS	TD	RA	YDS	AVG	LG	TD	REC	YDS	AVG	LG	TD	PR	YDS	AVG	LG	KOR	YDS	AVG	LG
1954	BC	16			4														16	201	12.6	26	0								
1955	BC	16	0		6							5	1						1	9	9.0	0	0	1	15	15.0	15				
1956	BC	15	0		0																										
1957	BC	16	0		3				0	10																					
1958	BC	16	1		3				2	9														2	19	9.5	19				
1959	BC+	16							4	53		6	1											2	9	4.5	5				
1960	BC+	16	0		1				4	36																					
1961	BC	16							5	70																					
1962	BC	16	1						4	38														2	5	2.5	5				
1963	BC*	16	0		4				2	11																					
1964	BC	16							2	27														2	4	2.0	4				
1965	BC	16							4	46		6	1											1	5	5.0	5				
1966	BC	16							6	59																					
1967	BC	16	0		2				4	36		6	1																		
14	Years	223	2		23				37	395		23	4						17	210	12.4	26	0	10	57	5.7	19				
CURLEY FIELDMAN Harold HB none B: 1925																															
1946	WPG	5																													
EARNEST FIELDS Earnest LB 5'11 236 Tennessee B: 10/15/1968 Milan, TN																															
1994	BAL	12	0		1	22			1	12	0	6	1																		
HAVEN FIELDS Haven Cornelius LB 6'0 219 Auburn B: 7/4/1978 Miami, FL Pro: X																															
2002	HAM	14	0	0	1	67	1.0																								
2003	BC	5				6																									
2	Years	19	0	0	1	73	1.0																								
HOWARD FIELDS Howard DB 5'10 190 Baylor B: 3/15/1958 Chickasha, OK Draft: 12-329 1980 PHI																															
1981	HAM	15	0		1				2	7														32	237	7.4	25	9	198	22.0	30
1982	HAM+	16	0		2		1.0		2	15														23	222	9.7	35	20	458	22.9	41
1983	HAM+	16	1		5				3	34														47	465	9.9	60	4	73	18.3	32
1984	HAM	16	2		5		1.0		4	11														15	117	7.8	20	9	257	28.6	46
1985	HAM*	16	1		1				3	46														4	36	9.0	24	23	535	23.3	54
1986	HAM	18							6	118														1	7	7.0	7	20	394	19.7	35
1987	HAM+	18	0		2	61			2	60		6	1											15	79	5.3	13	12	234	19.5	33
1988	HAM*	18	1		2	54			8	22														2	18	9.0	14	4	66	16.5	22
1989	CAL	16	1		3	35			3	34														11	50	4.5	16				
9	Years	149	6		21	150	2.0		33	347		6	1											150	1231	8.2	60	101	2215	21.9	54
JEFF FIELDS Jeffery D. NT-DT 6'3 320 Hinds CC; Arkansas State B: 7/3/1967 Jackson, MS Draft: 9-228 1991 LARM Pro: N																															
1991	HAM	5				15	2.0																								
1992	HAM+	18	0		1	52	7.0	44.0	1	10		6	1																		
1993	HAM	5	0		1	16	2.0	13.0																							
1994	HAM	7				18	3.0	19.0																							
1994	TOR	9				11	2.0	13.0																							
1994	Year	16				29	3.0	32.0																							
4	Years	35	0		2	112	16.0	89.0	1	10		6	1																		
JERRY FIELDS Jerry Eugene LB-QB 6'1 222 Ohio State B: 5/24/1938 Ironton, OH Draft: 13-179 1961 NYG Pro: N																															
1963	MTL	1																													
1964	MTL	13	0		1							6	1	18	78	4.3	17	0	3	26	8.7	12	1								
2	Years	14	0		1							6	1	18	78	4.3	17	0	3	26	8.7	12	1								
JITTER FIELDS Alfred Gene, Jr. CB 5'8 188 Texas B: 8/16/1962 Dallas, TX Draft: 5-123 1984 NO; TD 1984 SA-USFL Pro: N																															
1985	SAS	5							1	30		6	1											11	104	9.5	38	15	423	28.2	59
MIKE FIELDS Michael WR 5'7 160 Mississippi College B: 11/21/1964 Edwards, MO																															
1986	MTL	1																	3	25	8.3	11	0	2	7	3.5	5				
SHARAY FIELDS Sharay CB 5'9 165 New Mexico B: 9/16/1959																															
1981	OTT	3																													
WILLIAM FIELDS William CB-DH 5'8 175 Houston B: 6/21/1978 McKeesport, PA																															
2001	CAL	18	0	1	2	41			5	181	11	2	0																		
2002	CAL	18	1	3	0	48			2	69	8																				
2003	CAL	17	0	1	0	54	1.0	1.0	2	56	8																				
2004	CAL	12	0	0	1	28					4																				
2005	WPG	18	0	1	0	45			4	4	7																				
2006	WPG	4				7																									
6	Years	87	1	6	3	223	1.0	1.0	13	310	38	2	0																		
FRED FIGUEROA Fred FB 6'0 220 Fresno CC; Fresno State																															
1968	WPG	4	3		0									17	26	1.5	6	0	1	6	6.0	6	0					2	15	7.5	15
FRANK FILCHOCK Frank Joseph QB 5'10 193 Indiana B: 10/8/1916 Crucible, PA D: 6/20/1994 Washington County, OR Draft: 2-14 1938 PIT Pro: N																															
1947	HAM+	8																													
1949	MTL+	12										5	1																		
1950	MTL+	12																													
1951	EDM	13												3	-11	-3.7		0													
1952	EDM	12							1	15				4	-9	-2.3	4	0						1	0	0.0	0				
1953	SAS	16												9	-14	-1.6		0													
6	Years	73							1	15		5	1	16	-34	-2.1	4	0						1	0	0.0	0				
FABIO FILICE Fabio OG 6'2 285 McMaster B: 7/16/1981 Stoney Creek, ON Draft: 2-15 2005 HAM																															
2005	HAM	5				0																									
2006	HAM	18				1																									
2007	TOR	1				0																									
2008	CAL	15				0																									
4	Years	39				1																									
GENE FILIPSKI Eugene C. OHB 5'11 185 Army; Villanova B: 6/14/1931 Webster, MA D: 8/23/1994 Calgary, AB Draft: 7-84(f) 1953 CLE Pro: N																															
1958	CAL	9										30	5	52	296	5.7	20	1	24	399	16.6	40	4	8	41	5.1	16	6	135	22.5	33
1959	CAL+	16	4		0							55	9	155	967	6.2	41	4	46	572	12.4	62	5					10	226	22.6	51
1960	CAL	16	3		1							61	10	87	507	5.8	34	4	47	875	18.6	61	6	1	0	0.0	0	11	266	24.2	45
1961	CAL	13	3									42	6	65	306	4.7	23	4	30	380	12.7	41	2	38	240	6.3	14	1	11	11.0	11
4	Years	54	10		1							188	30	359	2076	5.8	41	13	147	2226	15.1	62	17	47	281	6.0	16	28	638	22.8	51
PASCAL FILS Pascal FB-RB 5'10 220 Sherbrooke B: 7/29/1984 Montreal, QC																															
2010	EDM	4	1	0	0	1								10	53	5.3	27	0	2	18	9.0	14	0								
2011	EDM	10				1								4	15	3.8	5	0													
2	Years	14	1	0	0	2								14	68	4.9	27	0	2	18	9.0	14	0								
LONNIE FINCH Lonnie, III DB 6'0 188 Oklahoma B: 10/12/1966 Longview, TX Pro: E																															
1990	BC	2	0		1	6			1	0																					
1991	BC	5				26			1	0																					
1993	HAM	8				18			2	0																					
3	Years	15	0		1	50			4	0																					
ANTHONY FINDLAY Anthony DB 5'10 190 British Columbia B: 11/15/1972																															
1994	SAS	1				0																									
BROOKS FINDLAY Brooks LB 6'4 235 Portland State B: 12/22/1970 Vancouver, BC Draft: 2-9 1993 SAS																															
1993	SAS	18				17																									
1994	SAS	18	0		2	31																									
1995	SAS	18				28																									
1996	SAS	16	0		3	25																									
1997	BC	11	0	0	1	24																									
2001	SAS	6				3																									
6	Years	87	0	0	6	128																									
CEC FINDLAY Cec HB-FB 5'11 180 McGill B: 1928 deceased																															

Year	Team	GP	FM	FF	FR	TK	SK	YDS	IR	YDS	PD	PTS	TD	RA	YDS	AVG	LG	TD	REC	YDS	AVG	LG	TD	PR	YDS	AVG	LG	KOR	YDS	AVG	LG
1952	MTL	9																												
1953	MTL	8																												
2	Years	17																												
DES FINDLAY Des G 5'9 210 Montreal Jrs. B: 7/1/1927 Montreal, QC																														
1951	SAS	14																												
1952	MTL	12																												
1953	MTL	10																												
1954	MTL	3																												
4	Years	39																												
GREG FINDLAY MacGregor LB-C-OE 6'3 240 Vancouver Meralomas Jrs.; Wenatchee Valley JC B: 8/24/1942																														
1962	BC	4																												
1963	BC	12																	2	19	9.5	11	0					1	7	7.0	7
1964	BC	16																												
1965	BC	16																												
1966	BC	16	0		2				1																1	1	1.0	1				
1967	BC	16	1		3				0	42		6	1																1	0	0.0	0
1968	BC+	16	0		1				2	20																					
1969	BC	16							3	39																					
1970	BC*	16	0		1				3	49																				2	10	5.0	10
1971	BC	16	1		3				3	43																					
1972	BC	16	0		1																								
1973	BC	16																												
12	Years	176	2		11				12	193		6	1						2	19	9.5	11	0	1	1	1.0	1	4	17	4.3	10
MIKE FINK Paul Michael DB 5'11 180 Missouri B: 12/24/1950 Kansas City, MO Draft: 9-210 1973 NO Pro: N																														
1975	EDM	7	1		0							12	2											28	347	12.4	80	12	280	23.3	81
1976	EDM	6			2				1	2														10	73	7.3	16	7	134	19.1	25
2	Years	13	1		2				1	2		12	2											38	420	11.1	80	19	414	21.8	81
JIM FINKS James Edward QB 5'11 175 Tulsa B: 8/31/1927 St. Louis, MO D: 5/8/1994 New Orleans, LA Draft: 4-22 1949 CHI-AAFC; 12-116 1949 PIT Pro: N																														
1957	CAL	7	2		0							6	1	20	-25	-1.3	13	1													
BARRY FINLAY Barry DB 6'2 185 McMaster B: 8/24/1950 Niagara Falls, ON Draft: 1-2 1973 TOR																														
1973	TOR	14							5	32																					
1974	TOR	16	0		1				2	33														2	-8	-4.0	0				
1975	TOR	16	0		1				5	50																					
1976	TOR	16							5	29																		1	24	24.0	24
1977	HAM	16	0		1																								
5	Years	78	0		3				17	144														2	-8	-4.0	0	1	24	24.0	24
MATT FINLAY Matt LB 6'2 225 Eastern Michigan B: 9/28/1962 Toronto, ON Draft: 1-5 1986 MTL																														
1986	MTL	18	0		1		1.0																						1	12	12.0	12
1987	CAL	15	0		1	31	1.0																						1	0	0.0	0
1987	TOR	1				6																								
1987	Year	16	0		1	37	1.0																									
1988	CAL	17			2	56	1.0		1	11																					
1989	CAL	18	0		1	57	2.0																						1	18	18.0	18
1990	CAL	18	0		1	80	3.0		2	65		6	1																1	32	32.0	32
1991	CAL	14	0		2	63	5.0		1	8																		1	0	0.0	0
1992	CAL+	18	0		2	100	2.0	22.0																							
1993	CAL	16	0		1	61			1	29																					
1994	CAL	17	0		2	65	3.0	26.0	1	17	1	6	1																	
1995	CAL	15	0		2	37			4	36	3																				
10	Years	166	0		15	556	18.0	48.0	10	166	4	12	2															5	62	12.4	32
PETE FINLAY Peter E-QB 5'11 175 McGill B: 1927																														
1946	MTL	7										5	1										1								
1947	OTT	11										5	1					1													
1948	OTT	2										5	1										1								
1949	OTT	12																												
4	Years	32										15	3					1					2								
DEVON FINN Devon Christopher DE 6'5 280 Illinois State B: 5/6/1978 Winfield, IL Pro: E																														
2004	HAM	6				3																									
REGGIE FISH Reggie WR 5'7 163 Arkansas B: 5/29/1987 Mesquite, TX																														
2010	HAM	2				0															5	41	8.2	13	0	1	2	2.0	2	3	38	12.7	14
OATTEN FISHER Oatten DE-T 6'3 215 North Carolina B: 4/1/1924 Salisbury, NC																														
1951	TOR	5																												
1954	TOR	11							1	92		7	1																1	8	8.0	8
1959	CAL	4																												
3	Years	20							1	92		7	1																1	8	8.0	8
RAY FISHER Raymond E. SB-WR 5'9 185 Indiana B: 9/12/1987 Cleveland, OH Draft: 7C-246 2010 IND																														
2011	EDM	2				0															2	21	10.5	11	0	3	25	8.3	10	3	71	23.7	31
ROD FISHER Roderick Renoir DB 5'10 190 Oklahoma State B: 11/23/1961 Dallas, TX Draft: 12A-309 1984 LARM; TD 1984 OKL-USFL																														
1987	SAS	13	0		2	39			2	39																					
STEVE FISHER Stephen Earl, Jr. CB 5'10 183 North Carolina B: 5/20/1976 New Bern, NC Pro: EX																														
2002	HAM	16	5	1	3	26			2	39	4													22	175	8.0	28	51	1208	23.7	50
2003	HAM	17	0	1	0	37			1	15	6													10	60	6.0	12	18	279	15.5	30
2004	WPG	8	1	0	0	19	1.0		2	59	1																	6	112	18.7	24
3	Years	41	6	2	3	82	1.0		5	113	11													32	235	7.3	28	75	1599	21.3	50
LOUIS FITE Louis J. RB 5'7 185 Texas A&M-Kingsville B: 9/24/1971 Los Angeles County, CA																														
1995	BAL	2	1		0	0							6	1	20	85	4.3	14	1	4	21	5.3	14	0	1	0	0.0	0	2	42	21.0	26
1996	MTL	2				1																					8	112	14.0	51	1	2	2.0	2
2	Years	4	1		0	1							6	1	20	85	4.3	14	1	4	21	5.3	14	0	9	112	12.4	51	3	44	14.7	26
ALEMA FITISEMANU Alema S., II LB 6'1 235 Brigham Young B: 5/29/1966																														
1991	SAS	2				1																									
F. FITZGERALD F. E 6'4 195 B: 1925																														
1949	HAM	1																												
GERRY FITZGERALD Gerry FB 6'0 190 Western Ontario B: 1930 Draft: 1952 HAM																														
1952	HAM	1																												
MARKESE FITZGERALD Markese Demetrius DB 5'10 184 Miami (Florida) B: 4/25/1979 St. Petersburg, FL																														
2004	WPG	5				12																									
NICK FitzGIBBON Nick RB 5'10 205 Guelph B: 4/25/1987 Psulinch, ON																														
2011	WPG	5				0																									
HARRY FITZGIBBONS Harris E-HB 5'11 192 none B: 11/9/1921																														
1946	WPG	8										5	1										1								
1948	WPG	12										5	1										1								
1949	WPG	11										5	1										1								
3	Years	31										15	3										3								
SHANNON FITZHUGH Shannon DB 5'11 200 Western Illinois B: 9/19/1981 Schaumburg, IL Pro: E																														
2007	HAM	1				1																									
SCOTT FITZKEE Scott Austin WR 6'0 187 Penn State B: 8/4/1957 York, PA Draft: 5-126 1979 PHI Pro: NU																														
1986	MTL	4										6	1						13	154	11.8	24	1								
D.J. FITZPATRICK Daniel Joseph K 6'1 208 Notre Dame B: 11/15/1982 Granger, IN Pro: E																														
2008	MTL	1				0						2	0																		
EUGENE FITZPATRICK Eugene C North Hill Blizzards Jrs.																														
1947	CAL	4																												
LARRY FITZPATRICK Larry Talye DT 6'4 275 Illinois State B: 8/17/1976 Detroit, MI Pro: EX																														

Year	Team	GP	FM	FF	FR	TK	SK	YDS	IR	YDS	PD	PTS	TD	RA	YDS	AVG	LG	TD	REC	YDS	AVG	LG	TD	PR	YDS	AVG	LG	KOR	YDS	AVG	LG
2001	HAM	5				7	1.0	5.0	0	0	1																				
2002	HAM	18	0	0	1	36	3.0	23.0	0	0	1																				
2	Years	23	0	0	1	43	4.0	28.0																							
TONY FITZPATRICK Anthony Gene DT 6'0 243 Miami (Florida) B: 4/10/1961 Clearwater, FL Draft: 7A-128 1984 HOU-USFL Pro: U																															
1986	OTT	3					2.0																								
BOBBY FIVEASH Bobby FB 5'11 185 Florida State B: 1933 Draft: 16-191 1954 SF																															
1954	TOR	1							1	3				3	12	4.0	7	0										1	9	9.0	9
SCOTT FLAGEL Scott S 6'2 190 Arizona Western JC B: 9/26/1961 Winnipeg, MB																															
1982	WPG	7																										1	13	13.0	13
1983	WPG	16																	1	5	5.0	5	0	1	8	8.0	8				
1984	WPG	16	0		3		1.0		4	152		6	1											7	69	9.9	24	2	0	0.0	0
1985	WPG+	16	0		2				4	62		6	1											3	18	6.0	8				
1986	WPG*	18	2		1		1.0		3	29				1	6	6.0	6	0						6	18	3.0	7	1	13	13.0	13
1987	WPG*	18			3	41			5	48																		1	15	15.0	15
1988	CAL	3				4			0	-3																					
1988	HAM	15	0		1	57			6	45														1	10	10.0	10	2	10	5.0	10
1988	Year	18	0		1	61			6	42														1	10	10.0	10	2	10	5.0	10
1989	HAM	11				35	1.0		3	48																					
1989	OTT	7	0		2	30	1.0		2	27																					
1989	Year*	18	0		2	65	2.0		5	75																					
1990	OTT+	18	2		6	41			8	95		12	2											3	14	4.7	7				
1991	OTT+	18	0		2	64	3.0		5	56																					
10	Years	141	4		20	337	7.0		40	562		24	4	1	6	6.0	6	0	1	5	5.0	5	0	21	137	6.5	24	7	51	7.3	15
ORLANDO FLANAGAN Orlando LB 6'2 225 Long Beach CC; Oklahoma B: 9/13/1960 Los Angeles, CA Pro: U																															
1984	MTL	4					1.5																								
ERIC FLEET Eric C Westmount Jrs. B: 1920																															
1946	MTL	10																													
1947	TOR	7																													
2	Years	17																													
MARQUEL FLEETWOOD Marquel QB 6'1 200 Minnesota B: 1/23/1970 Atlanta, GA Pro: E																															
1993	OTT	14				0								1	5	5.0	5	0													
1994	OTT	18	3		1	1						6	1	26	168	6.5	25	1													
1996	TOR	18				1						6	1	7	83	11.9	28	1													
1997	HAM	3	1	0	0	0						6	1	14	96	6.9	17	1													
4	Years	53	4	0	1	2						18	3	48	352	7.3	28	3													
LARRY FLEISHER Larry G-LB 5'8 215 Wake Forest B: 1935 Winnipeg, MB																															
1960	WPG	1																													
1960	EDM	4																													
1960	Year	5																													
1961	EDM	14																													
1962	EDM	16																													
1963	EDM	14																													
4	Years	45																													
TIM FLEISZER Timothy Marek DE 6'3 262 Harvard B: 8/14/1975 Montreal, QC Draft: 1-1 1998 HAM																															
1998	HAM	15				21	2.0	14.0																							
1999	HAM	1				0																									
2000	MTL	18				25	1.0	3.0			1																				
2001	MTL	17				30	2.0	3.0																							
2002	MTL	16				18																						1	0	0.0	0
2003	OTT	13				31																									
2004	OTT	18	0	0	4	31	4.0	27.0			2																				
2005	EDM	18	0	1	0	31	1.0	15.0																				4	4	1.0	4
2006	SAS	4				1																									
2007	SAS	6	0	1	0	4					2																				
10	Years	126	0	2	4	192	10.0	62.0			5																	5	4	0.8	4
DAVE FLEMING Dave OHB 6'0 205 none B: 3/9/1944																															
1965	HAM	3												17	78	4.6	11	0										2	46	23.0	28
1966	HAM	14	2		0				3	53		6	1	19	81	4.3	31	0	4	77	19.3	25	0					2	39	19.5	23
1967	HAM	13	4		3				2	8		18	3	59	303	5.1	47	2	18	311	17.3	44	1					10	220	22.0	33
1968	HAM	14	1		0							72	12	108	599	5.5	45	5	39	768	19.7	83	7								
1969	HAM	14	4		1							36	6	128	641	5.0	38	4	26	244	9.4	24	2	10	86	8.6	14	1	26	26.0	26
1970	HAM+	14	1		0							60	10	138	614	4.4	33	5	56	692	12.4	62	5	1	11	11.0	11	3	137	45.7	82
1971	HAM	14										18	3	88	287	3.3	26	1	24	400	16.7	108	2					5	131	26.2	29
1972	HAM	14	1		0							37	6	81	330	4.1	20	4	13	310	23.8	58	2								
1973	HAM	14										24	4	45	218	4.8	20	2	23	277	12.0	24	2	1	4	4.0	4				
1974	HAM	16										30	5	61	247	4.0	35	5	30	545	18.2	51	0	4	36	9.0	14	7	188	26.9	36
10	Years	130	13		4				5	61		301	50	744	3398	4.6	47	28	233	3624	15.6	108	21	16	137	8.6	14	30	787	26.2	82
FLINT FLEMING Flint E. DE 6'4 265 North Dakota State B: 3/17/1965 Madison, WI																															
1989	CAL	6				16	3.0																								
FRED FLEMING Fred MG 6'0 235 none B: 1940																															
1962	CAL	16							1																						
1963	CAL	4																													
1964	CAL	4																													
1964	WPG	7												25	78	3.1	14	0										7	175	25.0	40
1964	Year	11												25	78	3.1	14	0										7	175	25.0	40
1965	CAL	2																													
4	Years	26							1	0				25	78	3.1	14	0										7	175	25.0	40
GEORGE FLEMING George Tyree OHB 5'11 188 East Los Angeles JC; Washington B: 6/29/1938 Dallas, TX Draft: 2-13 1961 OAK; 6-76 1961 CHIB Pro: N																															
1963	WPG	14	2		0							135	9	61	227	3.7	21	3	21	566	27.0	70	5					16	496	31.0	93
1964	WPG	2										41	0						4	58	14.5	26	0								
2	Years	16	2		0							176	9	61	227	3.7	21	3	25	624	25.0	70	5					16	496	31.0	93
IAIN FLEMING Iain SB 6'3 203 Queen's B: 7/10/1982 Toronto, ON Draft: 5-41 2005 HAM																															
2005	HAM	4				1													1	3	3.0	3	0								
2006	HAM	4				0																									
2	Years	8				1													1	3	3.0	3	0								
JOE FLEMING Joe DT 6'3 290 New Hampshire B: 12/5/1971 Wellesley, MA																															
1996	BC	10				8	4.0	24.0																							
1997	BC+	18	0	1	1	52	9.0	48.0			1																				
1998	WPG*	18				48	15.0	115.0																				1	17	17.0	17
1999	WPG	9	0	2	0	15	3.0	11.0																							
2000	CAL*	18	0	0	1	26	7.0	55.0			1	6	1						2	16	8.0	13	1								
2001	CAL*	18	0	0	1	37	11.0	96.0	1	53	3	6	1																		
2003	CAL*	18				34	11.0	58.0			1																				
2004	CAL	14	0	1	2	21	4.0	28.0																							
2004	WPG	4				11	1.0	5.0			1																				
2004	Year+	18	0	1	2	32	5.0	33.0			1																				
2005	WPG	18	0	1	1	31	5.0	31.0																							
9	Years	141	0	5	6	283	70.0	471.0	1	53	7	12	2						2	16	8.0	13	1					1	17	17.0	17
MILLARD FLEMING Millard HB 6'1 197 Marshall B: 6/6/1940 Beckley, WV																															
1962	OTT	11										12	2	23	120	5.2	15	1	5	103	20.6	48	1					19	525	27.6	92
PAT FLEMING Pat P-K 6'2 190 Bowling Green State B: 6/30/1978 Ottawa, ON Draft: 2B-11 2002 OTT																															
2003	OTT	13				4					1	2	0	1	15	15.0	15	0													

Year	Team	GP	FM	FF	FR	TK	SK	YDS	IR	YDS	PD	PTS	TD	RA	YDS	AVG	LG	TD	REC	YDS	AVG	LG	TD	PR	YDS	AVG	LG	KOR	YDS	AVG	LG
2004	OTT	18	4	0	0	5						4	0	1	13	13.0	13	0													
2005	OTT	14	1	0	0	7						12	0	1	18	18.0	18	0													
2006	HAM	18	2	0	0	1						8	0																		
2007	WPG	3	1	0	0	1						3	0																		
5	Years	66	8	0	0	18						29	0	3	46	15.3	18	0													
SEAN FLEMING Sean Edan K-P 6'3 190 Wyoming B: 3/19/1970 Burnaby, BC Draft: 1A-6 1992 EDM																															
1992	EDM	18	1		1	6						164	0	1	0	0.0	0	0													
1993	EDM	18				8						166	0																		
1994	EDM	18				3						207	0																		
1995	EDM	18				6						207	0	1	6	6.0	6	0													
1996	EDM	13				1						132	0																		
1997	EDM	18	2	0	0	3						187	0	1	22	22.0	22	0	1	25	25.0	25	0								
1998	EDM	18	4	0	1	7						148	0																		
1999	EDM	7	3	0	0	2						60	0																		
2000	EDM	18	2	0	0	4						185	0	1	11	11.0	11	0						1	0	0.0	0				
2001	EDM+	17	3	0	0	4						183	0	1	20	20.0	20	0													
2002	EDM*	8	4	0	1	3						170	0																		
2003	EDM+	18	1	0	0	4						162	0																		
2004	EDM*	18	1	0	1	5						180	0																		
2005	EDM	16	3	0	2	3						121	0																		
2006	EDM	18	0	0	2	4						141	0																		
2007	EDM	18	4	0	0	2						159	0																		
16	Years	259	28	0	8	65						2572	0	5	59	11.8	22	0	1	25	25.0	25	0	1	0	0.0	0				
WILLIE FLEMING Willie, Jr. OHB 5'10 182 Iowa B: 2/2/1939 Detroit, MI Draft: 14-196 1961 PHI																															
1959	BC	16										48	8	110	774	7.0	52	3	26	517	19.9	53	5					21	545	26.0	52
1960	BC+	16	6		1							109	18	125	1051	8.4	98	10	20	399	20.0	56	8					15	494	32.9	81
1961	BC+	15										54	9	96	468	4.9	64	2	28	680	24.3	100	6	2	18	9.0	13	13	301	23.2	92
1962	BC	16	2									84	14	139	993	7.1	97	7	23	525	22.8	106	7					3	59	19.7	21
1963	BC*	16	2		0							72	12	127	1234	9.7	97	5	28	639	22.8	106	7					6	154	25.7	38
1964	BC	16	1		0							60	10	129	750	5.8	109	6	28	473	16.9	97	4					2	44	22.0	30
1965	BC	14	1									48	8	93	595	6.4	30	2	36	594	16.5	89	6					5	110	22.0	39
1966	BC	16										48	8	49	260	5.3	29	3	42	653	15.5	82	5					6	135	22.5	29
8	Years	125	12		1							523	87	868	6125	7.1	109	38	231	4480	19.4	106	48	2	18	9.0	13	71	1842	25.9	92
RONALD FLEMONS Ronald L. DE-DT-LB 6'5 270 Texas A&M B: 10/20/1979 Winslow, AZ Draft: 7C-226 2001 ATL Pro: N																															
2006	TOR	3				4	2.0	12.0																							
2007	TOR	18				12	1.0	1.0			2																				
2008	TOR	11	0	1	0	11	2.0	2.0			1																				
2009	TOR	18	0	1	0	42	6.0	40.0			1																				
2010	TOR	18	1	0	4	54	8.0	71.0			6																				
2011	TOR	18	0	1	1	43	3.0	10.0			10																				
6	Years	86	1	3	5	166	22.0	136.0			20																				
LANCE FLETCHER Lance OE-DB 6'3 215 British Columbia B: 1943 Draft: 1967 SAS																															
1967	SAS	1																													
1968	SAS	13							1	32									2	48	24.0	38	0								
1969	SAS	9																	1	19	19.0	19	0								
1970	WPG	16							1	21									2	41	20.5	25	0								
1971	WPG	16	0		1																										
1972	WPG	9																						25	127	5.1	15				
6	Years	64	0		1				2	53									5	108	21.6	38	0	25	127	5.1	15				
MICHAEL FLETCHER Michael E. LB-S 5'10 200 Oregon B: 2/17/1977 Gardena, CA																															
2000	BC	10	1	0	1	32	1.0	9.0	2	19	3													31	330	10.6	38	3	55	18.3	23
2001	BC	18	1	1	0	50	2.0	7.0	5	88	4	6	1											36	296	8.2	34	1	23	23.0	23
2002	TOR	15	0	1	0	60	1.0	3.0	3	132	3	6	1											4	36	9.0	12				
2003	TOR	18	0	0	2	84	1.0	3.0	1	3	2													4	31	7.8	12	2	28	14.0	28
2004	TOR	18	1	0	1	63	5.0	27.0	1	47	7	6	1											1	18	18.0	18	7	83	11.9	23
2005	TOR*	18	0	3	0	97	5.0	39.0	3	7	1																				
2006	TOR	14				57	1.0	6.0			4																	1	9	9.0	9
2007	TOR	18	0	0	1	68	7.0	44.0	3	102	5			1	26	26.0	26	0										1	0	0.0	0
2008	TOR	9				37	1.0	3.0			1																				
9	Years	138	3	5	5	548	24.0	141.0	18	398	30	18	3	1	26	26.0	26	0						76	711	9.4	38	15	198	13.2	28
D.J. FLICK David Julius WR-SB 5'10 175 Slippery Rock B: 4/27/1980 Eustis, FL																															
2002	OTT	3				3													4	83	20.8	37	0	4	35	8.8	14	2	35	17.5	18
2003	OTT+	18				3						42	7						60	917	15.3	75	7	16	111	6.9	18	1	11	11.0	11
2004	HAM*	18	0	0	1	5						48	8	1	1	1.0	1	0	68	1147	16.9	75	8	2	2	1.0	1	7	106	15.1	24
2005	HAM	18	2	0	1	7						38	6	1	7	7.0	7	0	80	1245	15.6	80	6								
2006	HAM	17	1	0	1	5						12	2						52	693	13.3	48	2					3	61	20.3	23
2007	SAS+	18	1	0	1	1						60	10	1	18	18.0	18	0	70	1020	14.6	53	10								
2008	SAS	3				0						6	1						5	65	13.0	33	1								
7	Years	95	4	0	4	24						206	34	3	26	8.7	18	0	339	5170	15.3	80	34	22	148	6.7	18	13	213	16.4	24
GEORGE FLINT George Howard OG 6'4 243 Arizona State B: 2/26/1937 Erie, PA Pro: N																															
1967	BC	8																													
BOBBY FLIPPIN Bobbie Ray HB 6'0 167 Midwestern B: 7/2/1928 Electra, TX																															
1952	EDM	3			1							10	2	6	18	3.0	9	1	6	116	19.3	59	1	8	69	8.6	20	3	67	22.3	24
1954	SAS	1							1	0				9	62	6.9	10	0	1	18	18.0	18	0	9	62	6.9	28				
1954	HAM	5												23	133	5.8	39	0	4	46	11.5	17	0	29	272	9.4	33	7	152	21.7	29
1954	Year	6												32	195	6.1	39	0	5	64	12.8	18	0	38	334	8.8	33	7	152	21.7	29
2	Years	4	0		1				1	0		10	2	38	213	5.6	39	1	11	180	16.4	59	1	46	403	8.8	33	10	219	21.9	29
BIFF FLISS Biff HB 6'2 235 Elmwood Ints. B: 1928																															
1948	WPG	10																													
1949	WPG	12																													
1950	WPG	10												12	68	5.7		0													
1951	WPG	13										5	1	61	181	3.0		1	2	32	16.0		0					1	10	10.0	10
4	Years	45										5	1	73	249	3.4	0	1	2	32	16.0		0					1	10	10.0	10
ANTHONY FLORENCE Anthony Wesly DB 6'0 185 Northeast Oklahoma JC; Bethune-Cookman B: 12/11/1966 Delray Beach, FL Draft: 4-90 1989 TB Pro: N																															
1993	WPG	3				3																									
ERIC FLORENCE Eric WR 5'10 170 Santa Clara B: 11/9/1964																															
1987	SAS	5				2													14	155	11.1	18	0	28	195	7.0	20	7	121	17.3	28
JON FLORENCE Jon HB 6'2 198 Manitoba; Weston Jrs. B: 1928																															
1949	WPG	3																													
RUDY FLORIO Rudy RB 5'10 195 Youngstown State B: 3/26/1950 Draft: 5-37 1973 BC																															
1973	MTL	14	1		0									6	36	6.0	13	0	2	-3	-1.5	0	0					3	62	20.7	37
1974	MTL	16	2		1									12	51	4.3	11	0	5	58	11.6	32	0	9	45	5.0	9	3	66	22.0	31
1975	MTL	16	0		1																							1	15	15.0	15
1976	MTL	15	1		0									17	60	3.5	11	0	4	18	4.5	22	0					1	4	4.0	4
1977	BC	16	0		1									4	14	3.5	4	0	1	11	11.0	11	0					4	54	13.5	23
1978	BC	9												5	23	4.6	7	0										3	49	16.3	21
6	Years	86	4		3									44	184	4.2	13	0	12	84	7.0	32	0	9	45	5.0	9	15	250	16.7	37
SCOTT FLORY Scott OG-OT 6'4 295 Saskatchewan B: 7/15/1976 Regina, SK Draft: 3A-15 1998 MTL																															
1999	MTL	5				0																									
2000	MTL	18				0																									
2001	MTL	18	0	0	1	1																									
2002	MTL*	18				0																									

Year	Team	GP	FM	FF	FR	TK	SK	YDS	IR	YDS	PD	PTS	TD	RA	YDS	AVG	LG	TD	REC	YDS	AVG	LG	TD	PR	YDS	AVG	LG	KOR	YDS	AVG	LG
2003	MTL*	18				3																									
2004	MTL+	18				1																									
2005	MTL*	18				1																									
2006	MTL*	18				1																									
2007	MTL*	18	1	0	0	1								1	-7	-7.0	-7	0													
2008	MTL*	18	0	0	1	0																									
2009	MTL*	18				2																									
2010	MTL*	17				1																									
2011	MTL+	18				0																									
13	Years	220	1	0	2	11								1	-7	-7.0	-7	0													
BERNIE FLOWERS Bernard Benjamin [born Kwiatkowski] OE 6'2 210 Purdue B: 2/14/1930 Erie, PA D: 4/14/2011 Bonita Springs, FL Draft: 2-14 1953 BAL Pro: N																															
1953	OTT+	13										45	9										9								
JASON FLOWERS Jason DB 6'0 187 Toledo B: 8/15/1983 Centerville, OH Pro: E																															
2007	EDM	12	0	1	1	36					1																				
ANTHONY FLOYD Anthony Franklin DB 5'10 202 Louisville B: 2/1/1981 Youngstown, OH Pro: EN																															
2006	EDM	2	0	1	0	9					2																				
GONZALO FLOYD Gonzalo DE 6'3 240 Texas-El Paso B: 9/2/1971 Green Cove Springs, FL																															
1995	CAL	6				9	1.0	1.0			1																				
1996	CAL	5				5																									
1996	HAM	7				21	2.0	6.0	1	0	5																				
1996	Year	12				26	2.0	6.0	1	0	5																				
1997	HAM	11	0	1	1	25	1.0	2.0	1	50	5	6	1						2	5	2.5	4	1								
1998	HAM	14	0	3	0	26	7.0	55.0	2	37	8																				
1999	HAM	13	0	0	2	41	2.0	14.0	2	10	4																				
2000	HAM	13	0	1	0	32	5.0	21.0			4																				
2001	HAM	9	0	0	1	25	5.0	37.0			5																				
7	Years	71	0	5	4	184	23.0	136.0	6	97	32	6	1						2	5	2.5	4	1								
HOMER FLOYD Homer HB 5'10 185 Kansas B: 5/16/1936 Wetempka, AL Draft: 26-311 1959 CLE																															
1959	EDM	6										12	2	24	128	5.3	12	1	7	85	12.1	19	1	20	118	5.9	18	4	106	26.5	53
LUCIUS FLOYD Lucius RB 6'0 195 Nevada-Reno B: 4/7/1966 Inglewood, CA																															
1990	SAS	13	4		0	2						30	5	91	421	4.6	37	0	73	811	11.1	78	5					1	19	19.0	19
1991	SAS	17	4		0	8						36	6	117	677	5.8	59	3	84	720	8.6	47	3					3	33	11.0	21
1992	SAS	14				7						36	6	92	373	4.1	38	4	74	645	8.7	33	2					3	61	20.3	22
1993	EDM	8	4		0	2						24	4	81	423	5.2	35	2	29	262	9.0	25	2					17	360	21.2	44
1994	EDM	18	8		0	1						42	7	151	669	4.4	35	3	64	875	13.7	77	4	3	105	35.0	57	39	845	21.7	56
1995	EDM	10				2						42	7	85	244	2.9	24	3	48	538	11.2	100	4					6	107	17.8	36
1995	MEM	6	0		2	7								11	21	1.9	6	0	6	85	14.2	35	0					10	209	20.9	36
1995	Year	16	0		2	9						42	7	96	365	3.8	24	3	54	623	11.5	100	4					16	316	19.8	36
6	Years	80	20		2	29						210	35	628	2828	4.5	59	15	378	3936	10.4	100	20	3	105	35.0	57	79	1634	20.7	56
OTIS FLOYD Otis LB 6'2 230 Louisville B: 6/13/1976 Detroit, MI Pro: X																															
2000	EDM	7				10																									
2001	CAL	17				53	1.0	2.0			2																				
2002	CAL	7	0	0	1	19	1.0	5.0																							
2003	CAL	15	0	3	1	40	3.0	20.0	1	0	2																				
2004	BC	15	0	1	2	55	5.0	27.0			3																				
2005	BC+	18	0	3	2	62	4.0	23.0																							
2006	BC*	18	0	5	2	73	8.0	31.0			1																				
2007	BC+	15	0	1	0	70	4.0	29.0			3																				
2008	BC	18	0	0	1	56	4.0	28.0			7																				
2009	HAM	15	0	2	0	67	5.0	16.0	1	28	2																				
2010	HAM	18	0	3	3	83	4.0	26.0			1																				
11	Years	163	0	18	12	588	39.0	207.0	2	28	21																				
PERRY FLOYD Perry WR-SB 5'8 168 Wingate B: 10/13/1988 Gastonia, NC																															
2011	WPG	5	3	0	2	0								2	7	3.5	11	0	2	28	14.0	25	0	6	66	11.0	41	19	346	18.2	56
2011	MTL	9	1	0	0	0																		31	209	6.7	40	26	525	20.2	41
2011	Year	14	4	0	2	0								2	7	3.5	11	0	2	28	14.0	25	0	37	275	7.4	41	45	871	19.4	56
DARREN FLUTIE Darren Paul WR 5'10 184 Boston College B: 11/18/1966 Manchester, MD Pro: N																															
1991	BC	8	3		1	1						36	6						52	860	16.5	51	6	1	5	5.0	5	14	292	20.9	30
1992	BC+	18	1		3	5						24	4						90	1336	14.8	76	4	15	104	6.9	24	4	65	16.3	24
1993	BC	17	0		1	2						30	5						78	1050	13.5	45	5	11	84	7.6	25	11	122	11.1	26
1994	BC+	18	4		1	6						48	8	2	2	1.0	5	0	111	1731	15.6	61	8	10	94	9.4	49				
1995	BC	12	2		2	1						12	2	1	7	7.0	7	0	59	893	15.1	58	2	1	13	13.0	13				
1996	EDM*	17	1		0	2						36	6	2	5	2.5	8	0	86	1362	15.8	42	6								
1997	EDM*	17	4	0	0	4						58	9	1	35	35.0	35	0	90	1313	14.6	51	9								
1998	HAM+	17	4	1	1	4						32	5	1	4	4.0	4	0	98	1386	14.1	73	5								
1999	HAM*	18	1	0	0	4						42	7	2	10	5.0	9	0	84	1155	13.8	37	7					1	0	0.0	0
2000	HAM	17	3	0	0	8						26	4						79	1120	14.2	58	4								
2001	HAM	18	1	0	0	1						36	6						80	1206	15.1	49	6								
2002	HAM	16	1	0	0	2						24	4	1	11	11.0	11	0	64	929	14.5	40	4								
12	Years	193	25	1	9	40						404	66	10	74	7.4	35	0	971	14341	14.8	76	66	38	300	7.9	49	30	479	16.0	30
DOUG FLUTIE Douglas Richard QB 5'10 178 Boston College B: 10/23/1962 Manchester, MD Draft: 11A-285 1985 LARM; TD 1985 NJ-USFL Pro: NU																															
1990	BC	16	6		1	0						18	3	79	662	8.4	32	3													
1991	BC*	18	7		3	0						86	14	120	610	5.1	32	14													
1992	CAL*	18	5		3	4						66	11	96	669	7.0	44	11													
1993	CAL*	18	5		1	1						66	11	74	373	5.0	50	11	1	-11	-11.0	-11	0								
1994	CAL*	18	7		3	0						48	8	96	760	7.9	57	8													
1995	CAL	11	2		0	0						30	5	46	288	6.3	38	5													
1996	TOR*	18	1		1	2						54	9	101	756	7.5	37	9													
1997	TOR*	18	3	0	0	4						30	5	92	542	5.9	34	5	1	0	0.0	0	0								
8	Years	135	36	0	12	11						398	66	704	4660	6.6	57	66	2	-11	-5.5	0	0								
CHRIS FLYNN Chris QB 6'1 190 St. Mary's (Nova Scotia) B: 11/17/1966 Ottawa, ON Draft: 5-35 1991 OTT Pro: E																															
1996	OTT	3				1																									
DON FLYNN Donald Max HB 6'0 203 Houston B: 9/14/1934 D: 4/14/2010 Tulsa, OK Pro: N																															
1957	EDM	1																													
1958	EDM	13	2		2							18	3	25	158	6.3	22	2	22	410	18.6	52	1	1	6	6.0	6	16	463	28.9	45
2	Years	14	2		2							18	3	25	158	6.3	22	2	22	410	18.6	52	1	1	6	6.0	6	16	463	28.9	45
LEE FOBBS LeAndrew, Jr. RB 5'11 197 Grambling State B: 7/20/1950 Monroe, LA Draft: 8-190 1973 BUF Pro: W																															
1973	OTT	1																	2	3	1.5	6	0								
1973	WPG	7	2		0							6	1	25	102	4.1	16	0	6	70	11.7	25	1								
1973	Year	8										6	1	25	102	4.1	16	0	8	73	9.1	25	1								
STEVE FOCHUK Steve HB-FB-LB 5'9 198 Hamilton Tigers Jrs.; Panther Ints. B: 1931																															
1953	OTT	4																													
1954	OTT	1																													
2	Years	5																													
CECE FODERINGHAM Cece T																															
1947	TOR	6																													
1948	TOR	8																													
2	Years	14																													
CARL FODOR Carl E., Jr. QB 6'2 190 Marshall B: 11/6/1963 Weirton, WV																															
1987	CAL	9	1		0	0						6	1	4	27	6.8	19	1													
1988	CAL	15	4		1	0								14	134	9.6	51	0													
2	Years	24	5		1	0						6	1	18	161	8.9	51	1													

Year	Team	GP	FM	FF	FR	TK	SK	YDS	IR	YDS	PD	PTS	TD	RA	YDS	AVG	LG	TD	REC	YDS	AVG	LG	TD	PR	YDS	AVG	LG	KOR	YDS	AVG	LG
RICKEY FOGGIE Rickey S. QB 6'1 185 Minnesota B: 7/15/1966 Laurens, SC																															
1988	BC	18	3		1	0						18	3	34	177	5.2	20	3													
1989	BC	18	1		0	0						2	0	10	89	8.9	16	0													
1990	BC	5	2		1	0								9	69	7.7	18	0	1	13	13.0	13	0								
1990	TOR	10	5		0	0						30	5	59	674	11.4	65	5													
1990	Year	15	7		0	0						30	5	68	743	10.9	65	5	1	13	13.0	13	0								
1991	TOR	18	8		1	0						48	8	95	644	6.8	61	8													
1992	TOR	18	8		2	2						48	8	67	444	6.6	25	8													
1993	EDM	18	1		0	0						12	2	12	32	2.7	14	2													
1994	EDM	18	2		0	0						6	1	21	79	3.8	12	1													
1995	MEM	18	4		0	0								26	159	6.1	23	0													
1997	HAM	9	8	0	4	0						18	3	32	138	4.3	22	3													
2002	BC	14	1	0	0	0								7	30	4.3	10	0													
10	Years	154	43	0	9	2						182	30	372	2535	6.8	65	30	1	13	13.0	13	0								
ANTHONY FOGLE Anthony Lee CB 6'0 195 Oklahoma B: 2/23/1975 New York, NY Pro: E																															
1999	EDM	16	1	0	0	47	1.0		4	71	3																	2	16	8.0	13
BRAD FOJTIK Bradley D. DT 6'5 270 Florida State B: 9/17/1961 Auburndale, FL																															
1986	TOR	7					1.0																								
JIM FOLEY James SB-WR-RB 5'11 189 St. Dunstan's; Prince Edward Island B: 10/27/1944 Ottawa, ON Draft: 1-9 1969 OTT; 5-38 1970 MTL																															
1971	MTL	14	3		0							12	2	8	18	2.3	5	0	20	252	12.6	28	2	42	353	8.4	27	12	324	27.0	39
1972	MTL	14	3		4							12	2						20	236	11.8	42	2	17	73	4.3	19				
1973	OTT	14										6	1	20	126	6.3	21	0	19	261	13.7	26	1	25	164	6.6	16	7	175	25.0	39
1974	OTT	15	1		0							18	3	14	43	3.1	15	0	27	459	17.0	49	3	20	90	4.5	10	1	21	21.0	21
1975	OTT	15	0		1							18	3	36	225	6.3	24	1	25	350	14.0	56	2								
1976	OTT	16	2		0							24	4	11	38	3.5	10	0	56	847	15.1	50	4								
1977	OTT	9	1		1							6	1	1	-1	-1.0	-1	0	15	244	16.3	41	1					1	12	12.0	12
7	Years	97	10		6							96	16	90	449	5.0	24	1	182	2649	14.6	56	15	104	680	6.5	27	21	532	25.3	39
MIKE FOLEY Mike DT 6'3 290 New Hampshire B: 11/12/1971 Worcester, MA Draft: 6-169 1996 ARI Pro: E																															
1998	MTL	1				1																									
RICKY FOLEY Ricky DE 6'2 258 York B: 6/9/1982 Coutrice, ON Draft: 1B-4 2006 BC																															
2006	BC	16	0	0	1	11																									
2007	BC	18	0	2	1	34	4.0	19.0				6	1						1	16	16.0	16	1								
2008	BC	18	0	4	1	23	4.0	23.0			1	6	1																		
2009	BC	18	0	0	1	53	12.0	73.0			2																				
2010	TOR	8	0	1	0	22	1.0	3.0			1																				
2011	TOR	18	0	0	3	69	6.0	26.0	1	0	2																				
6	Years	96	0	7	7	212	27.0	144.0	1	0	6	12	2						1	16	16.0	16	1								
BILL FOLK Bill E Regina Bombers Jrs.																															
1946	SAS	7																													
CHAD FOLK Chad C 6'1 280 Okanagan Sun Jrs.; Utah B: 10/28/1972 Kelowna, BC Draft: 1A-1 1997 TOR																															
1997	TOR	18				1																									
1998	TOR	18	4	0	0	3																									
1999	TOR	17	5	0	0	2																									
2000	TOR	6	2	0	0	1																									
2001	TOR	10				1																									
2002	TOR	18				2																									
2003	TOR	18	0	1	0	4																									
2004	TOR	18				4																									
2005	TOR	18				1																									
2006	TOR	18	0	0	2	3																									
2007	TOR	18	2	0	1	0																									
2008	TOR	18	1	0	1	1																									
12	Years	195	14	1	4	23																									
RYAN FOLK Ryan LB 5'10 195 Calgary B: 11/29/1978 Medicine Hat, AB Draft: 5-43 2004 WPG																															
2004	MTL	6	0	0	1	10																									
2005	MTL	10	0	0	1	7																									
2005	WPG	4				2																									
2005	Year	14	0	0	1	9																									
2006	MTL	7				7																									
3	Years	23	0	0	2	26																									
DWIGHT FOLLIN Dwight C. (Blackjack) C 6'1 195 Kent State B: 6/18/1922 Lakemore, OH D: 11/14/1997																															
1949	TOR	12																													
RAYMOND FONTAINE Raymond LB-DE 6'4 223 Kentucky B: 1/8/1980 Ottawa, ON Draft: 2A-11 2005 TOR																															
2006	TOR	18	0	0	1	25																									
2007	TOR	16	0	1	1	18					1																				
2008	TOR	15				16																									
2009	TOR	13	0	1	0	14																									
2010	TOR	6				4																									
2010	MTL	5				6																									
2010	Year	11				10																									
5	Years	68	0	2	2	83					1																				
STU FOORD Stuart RB 5'11 195 Regina Thunder Jrs. B: 9/23/1985 Regina, SK																															
2008	SAS	17	0	0	2	9						18	3	27	162	6.0	20	2	2	73	36.5	55	1								
2009	SAS	18	1	0	1	9						12	2	25	135	5.4	18	1	8	45	5.6	11	0					21	374	17.8	46
2010	SAS	18				10								1	6	6.0	6	0										9	141	15.7	24
2011	SAS	18				3								3	9	3.0	8	0	2	4	2.0	4	0					3	51	17.0	21
4	Years	71	1	0	3	31						30	5	56	312	5.6	20	3	12	122	10.2	55	1					33	566	17.2	46
MAURICE FORBES Maurice DT 6'3 300 Concordia (Quebec) B: 9/9/1987 Draft: 2-13 2011 HAM																															
2011	HAM	2				0																									
ROB FORBES Robert FB 6'1 221 Drake B: 9/17/1956 Toronto, ON Draft: TE 1979 CAL																															
1979	CAL	4												9	26	2.9	5	0													
1980	CAL	16										6	1	8	31	3.9	9	0	1	20	20.0	20	1								
1981	CAL	16	0		1									9	45	5.0	9	0	10	92	9.2	19	0								
1982	CAL	16	0		2							6	1	19	78	4.1	11	0	23	210	9.1	45	0								
1983	CAL	9												1	2	2.0	2	0													
1983	TOR	4												3	6	2.0	5	0													
1983	Year	13												4	8	2.0	5	0													
1984	TOR	16	1		1									2	0	0.0	1	0	6	35	5.8	11	0					1	0	0.0	0
6	Years	77	1		4							12	2	51	188	3.7	11	0	40	357	8.9	45	1					1	0	0.0	0
AL FORD Alan OHB-TE-LB-P 6'1 210 Pacific B: 1943 Regina, SK																															
1965	SAS	7	1		0									14	105	7.5	43	0	2	31	15.5	24	0					6	145	24.2	36
1966	SAS	16										7	1	26	114	4.4	18	0	13	188	14.5	45	1					13	267	20.5	30
1967	SAS	16	6		0							29	4	66	355	5.4	34	3	27	399	14.8	44	1					23	603	26.2	38
1968	SAS	16	6		1							34	5	68	288	4.2	36	2	39	626	16.1	66	3					16	425	26.6	43
1969	SAS	16	0		2							10	1	16	81	5.1	12	0	23	355	15.4	50	1					9	192	21.3	37
1970	SAS	16	1		1				4	49		1	0	11	60	5.5	31	0	9	162	18.0	39	0					5	112	22.4	30
1971	SAS	16	3		1							32	5	2	11	5.5	8	0	32	525	16.4	43	5								
1972	SAS	16	0		1							15	2						36	511	14.2	43	2					5	94	18.8	24
1973	SAS	16	3		2							8	1	1	1	1.0	1	1	23	391	17.0	45	0					2	21	10.5	21
1974	SAS	16	1		2							1	0	6	15	2.5	4	0	23	247	10.7	31	0								
1975	SAS	16										6	1						26	335	12.9	55	1					8	44	5.5	15
1976	SAS	15	1		0							12	2	20	56	2.8	8	2	8	80	10.0	23	0	1	5	5.0	5	3	32	10.7	20

Year	Team	GP	FM	FF	FR	TK	SK	YDS	IR	YDS	PD	PTS	TD	RA	YDS	AVG	LG	TD	REC	YDS	AVG	LG	TD	PR	YDS	AVG	LG	KOR	YDS	AVG	LG
12	Years	182	22		10				4	49		155	22	230	1086	4.7	43	8	261	3850	14.8	66	14	1	5	5.0	5	90	1935	21.5	43
BILL FORD Bill G 6'0 185 Western Ontario B: 1925																															
1951	TOR	4																												
DARRYL FORD Darryl Dewayne LB 6'1 225 New Mexico State B: 6/22/1966 Dallas, TX Pro: N																															
1990	TOR	17	0		1	78	1.0		2	1																				
1991	TOR*	18	0		2	117	3.0		3	45																				
1995	MEM	13	0		1	51					1																			
1996	SAS	3				6																								
4	Years	51	0		4	252	4.0		5	46	1																			
DERRICK FORD Derrick T. LB 6'1 240 Arizona State B: 2/28/1976 Long Beach, CA																															
2002	OTT	13	0	1	2	17	8.0																				2	25	12.5	16
2003	OTT	14	0	0	2	24	3.0																							
2004	CAL	3				5	1.0	2.0																						
3	Years	30	0	1	4	46	12.0	2.0																			2	25	12.5	16
DEVON FORD Devon DB 5'8 172 Appalachian State B: 5/31/1955																															
1978	BC	6	2		1																		13	96	7.4	23				
1979	BC	14	3		3				1	0													41	418	10.2	70	12	298	24.8	55
1980	BC	8	1		2				1	0		6	1											25	353	14.1	85	16	539	33.7	92
1981	BC	16	2		0				1	30													61	664	10.9	53	36	888	24.7	51
1982	BC	14	2		2				1	0													35	310	8.9	34	20	542	27.1	85
5	Years	58	10		8				4	30		6	1											175	1841	10.5	85	84	2267	27.0	92
HENRY FORD Henry DB 5'11 170 Pittsburgh B: 11/1/1931 Homestead, PA Draft: 9-109 1955 CLE Pro: N																															
1955	TOR	4							1	0		10	2	2	15	7.5	8	0	10	124	12.4	26	2	8	53	6.6	14	9	144	16.0	30
KENNY FORD Kenneth Wayne LB 6'2 215 Texas A&M B: 11/23/1962 Wharton, TX																															
1987	OTT	12	0		1	63	1.0		1	38		6	1															1	11	11.0	11
1988	HAM	3				14																						2	17	8.5	16
1988	CAL	14				77	2.0		3	18																				
1988	Year+	17				91	2.0		3	18																		2	17	8.5	16
1989	CAL	18	0		2	89	3.0		1	32													1	-11	-11.0	-11				
1990	CAL	12	0		1	53	1.0																							
4	Years	45	0		4	296	7.0		5	88		6	1											1	-11	-11.0	-11	3	28	9.3	16
MARIET FORD Mariet T. WR 5'8 160 Diablo JC; California B: 8/28/1961 San Francisco, CA Draft: TD 1983 OAK-USFL																															
1983	OTT	6	1		0							18	3	1	3	3.0	3	0	11	133	12.1	15	2	30	483	16.1	101	9	244	27.1	54
1984	SAS	1																	2	27	13.5	14	0	3	24	8.0		3	88	29.3	41
1984	TOR	2										6	1						3	90	30.0	63	1	6	91	15.2	46	2	39	19.5	24
1984	Year	3										6	1						5	117	23.4	63	1	9	115	12.8	46	5	127	25.4	41
2	Years	7	1		0							24	4	1	3	3.0	3	0	16	250	15.6	63	3	39	598	15.3	101	14	371	26.5	54
TOMMY FORD Tom HB-FW 5'10 175 none B: 1927																															
1949	TOR	2																												
1950	WPG	13										40	8	67	318	4.7		2	15	304	20.3		5								
1951	WPG	3																						10	100	10.0		5	61	12.2	
1952	WPG	15										25	5	28	214	7.6	95	1	16	460	28.8	76	3	13	197	15.2	60	2	43	21.5	25
1953	WPG	11										15	3	33	146	4.4		0	31	464	15.0		3	1	0	0.0	0	1	24	24.0	24
1954	WPG	3												3	11	3.7	7	0	1	9	9.0	9	0					1	0	0.0	0
1955	SAS	12	2		0							5	1	13	32	2.5	8	0	6	121	20.2	58	1	2	33	16.5	24				
7	Years	59	2		0							85	17	144	721	5.0	95	3	69	1358	19.7	76	12	26	330	12.7	60	9	128	14.2	25
BRIAN FORDE Brian Michael LB 6'2 255 Washington State B: 11/1/1963 Montreal, QC Draft: 1-8 1988 EDM; 7-190 1988 NO Pro: EN																															
1994	BC	18				45	2.0	2.0			2																	4	14	3.5	5
1995	BC	17	0		2	44	3.0	23.0			2																				
1996	MTL	4				4																								
3	Years	39	0		2	93	5.0	25.0			4																	4	14	3.5	5
DUANE FORDE Duane FB 6'0 230 Western Ontario B: 5/8/1969 Mississauga, ON Draft: 1-6 1991 CAL																															
1991	CAL	3				4																								
1992	CAL	18				2								9	26	2.9	10	0	9	86	9.6	18	0					1	4	4.0	4
1993	WPG	13				6								2	6	3.0	5	0													
1994	TOR	18	0		1	3								32	121	3.8	11	0	22	213	9.7	23	0					1	-1	-1.0	-1
1995	TOR	18	1		0	8						18	3	13	59	4.5	15	1	25	182	7.3	19	2					1	4	4.0	4
1996	CAL	18	1		1	10								11	29	2.6	7	0	6	90	15.0	28	0								
1997	CAL	18	1	0	0	3						6	1	2	8	4.0	5	0	20	239	12.0	27	1								
1998	CAL	18	2	0	1	1						24	4	5	6	1.2	3	3	6	106	17.7	25	1								
1999	CAL	18				4						18	3	6	10	1.7	4	3	4	29	7.3	12	0								
2000	CAL	18				4						18	3	11	18	1.6	3	3	6	72	12.0	21	0								
2001	HAM	11	2	0	1	2								13	24	1.8	9	0	11	99	9.0	15	0								
2002	HAM	18				2						12	2	6	14	2.3	7	2	8	65	8.1	13	0								
12	Years	189	7	0	4	49						96	16	110	321	2.9	15	12	117	1181	10.1	28	4					3	7	2.3	4
IAN FORDE Ian WR 5'9 178 Waterloo B: 7/15/1982 Cambridge, ON Draft: 6-53 2005 TOR																															
2005	TOR	1				0													1	5	5.0	5	0	1	24	24.0	24				
2006	TOR	1				0																								
2	Years	2				0													1	5	5.0	5	0	1	24	24.0	24				
GORD FORDYCE Gordon FL none																															
1946	WPG	1																												
BOB FOREST Robert LB 6'1 220 Carleton B: 8/17/1966 London, ON Draft: 8-57 1989 OTT																															
1989	OTT	11				4	1.0																							
TEDDY FORET Ted H. DE 5'11 250 Auburn B: 8/24/1936 Draft: 15-180 1959 BAL; SS 1960 DEN																															
1960	MTL	1																												
1960	CAL	8																												
1960	Year	9																												
AL FORKHEIM Al HB 5'11 168 Winnipeg Grads Jrs. B: 1930																															
1950	WPG	2																												
FRED FORSBERG Fred Carl G 6'1 233 Washington B: 7/4/1944 Tacoma, WA Draft: 14-121 1966 DEN Pro: N																															
1966	CAL	7																												
JAMIE FORSYTHE Jamie OT 6'4 310 Indianapolis B: 5/21/1976 Hamilton, ON Draft: 6-39 2000 SAS																															
2000	SAS	1				0																								
NEAL FORT Neal OT 6'5 279 Brigham Young B: 2/12/1968 Warner Robins, GA Draft: 6-143 1991 LARM																															
1994	BAL	18				2																								
1995	BAL*	18				1																								
1996	MTL+	18				0																								
1997	MTL*	18	1	0	0	0																								
1998	MTL	18				0																								
1999	MTL	18	0	0	2	1																								
2000	MTL	12				0																								
2001	MTL	18	0	0	1	1																								
2002	MTL	12				1																								
2003	MTL+	18				0																								
2004	MTL	2				0																								
11	Years	170	1	0	3	6																								
ELDON FORTIE Eldon HB 6'0 170 Brigham Young B: 1941																															
1963	EDM	7	0		1									11	36	3.3	12	0	3	40	13.3	21	0					16	427	26.7	40
STEPHANE FORTIN Stephane S 5'11 184 Indianapolis B: 6/21/1974 Laval, QC Draft: 2-10 1999 SAS																															
1999	SAS	18				10																								
2000	SAS	14				29																								
2001	SAS	18				9																								

Year	Team	GP	FM	FF	FR	TK	SK	YDS	IR	YDS	PD	PTS	TD	RA	YDS	AVG	LG	TD	REC	YDS	AVG	LG	TD	PR	YDS	AVG	LG	KOR	YDS	AVG	LG
2002	MTL	18	0	1	1	30						6	1																		
2003	MTL	17	1	0	1	14																						1	0	0.0	0
2004	MTL	15	0	0	1	8						6	1																		
2005	CAL	3				1																									
7	Years	103	1	1	3	101						12	2															1	0	0.0	0
DENNY FORTNEY Dennis Allen DT-DE 6'4 280 Miami (Florida) B: 12/27/1974 Hagerstown, MD																															
2001	WPG	18	0	1	3	35					4																				
2002	WPG*	18	0	0	1	22	7.0				4																				
2003	WPG	18	0	0	1	30	1.0		1	3	2																	1	15	15.0	15
2004	WPG	2	0	0	1	3																									
4	Years	56	0	1	6	90	8.0		1	3	10																	1	15	15.0	15
HOSEA FORTUNE Hosea Gerard WR 6'0 176 Rice B: 3/4/1959 New Orleans, LA Pro: N																															
1982	MTL	1																	1	7	7.0	7	0								
RON FORWICK Ron DE 6'3 245 Edmonton Huskies Jrs. B: 10/5/1943 D: 2001																															
1965	EDM	16																													
1966	EDM	16																													
1967	EDM	16	0		1																										
1968	EDM	8							1	34																					
1969	EDM	16	0		2																										
1970	EDM+	16	0		4				1	4																		1	0	0.0	0
1971	EDM	16			4																										
1972	EDM	4							1	45		6	1																		
1973	EDM	16																										1	0	0.0	0
1974	EDM	16			1																										
1975	HAM	16																													
11	Years	156	0		12				3	83		6	1															2	0	0.0	0
JOE FORZANI Joe LB-DE 6'2 233 Calgary Jrs.; Utah State B: 7/30/1945 Calgary, AB Draft: 17A-448 1968 PHI																															
1968	CAL	14																													
1969	CAL	16	0		3				1	3		1	0																		
1970	CAL	16	0		2				2	22																					
1971	CAL	16	1		3				4	36																					
1972	CAL	16							2	7																		1	10	10.0	10
1973	CAL	16	0		1				3	14																					
1974	CAL	12																													
1975	CAL+	16	0		1				1	40		6	1																		
8	Years	122	1		10				13	122		7	1															1	10	10.0	10
JOHN FORZANI John OG 6'2 245 Utah State B: 4/5/1947																															
1971	CAL	16																													
1972	CAL	16	0		2																										
1973	CAL	16																													
1974	CAL	16																													
1975	CAL	16																													
1976	CAL	16																													
6	Years	96	0		2																										
JOHNNY FORZANI Johnny WR 6'1 202 Calgary Colts Jrs.; Washington State B: 11/3/1988 Calgary, AB																															
2010	CAL	6				1													3	46	15.3	32	0					5	84	16.8	18
2011	CAL	18				4						30	5						45	761	16.9	46	5	3	24	8.0	12	1	8		8
2	Years	24				5						30	5						48	807	16.8	46	5	3	24	8.0	12	6	92	15.3	18
TOM FORZANI Tom WR 5'11 178 Utah State B: 6/15/1950 Draft: TE 1973 CAL																															
1973	CAL+	16										24	4						62	731	11.8	46	4	1	2	2.0	2				
1974	CAL+	16										36	6						61	841	13.8	37	6	2	2	1.0	2				
1975	CAL	16										54	9	1	-20	-20.0	-20	0	55	971	17.7	49	9								
1976	CAL	16	1		2							56	9						57	901	15.8	56	9								
1977	CAL*	16										32	5						51	894	17.5	74	5	50	406	8.1	35				
1978	CAL	16										30	5						43	731	17.0	67	5	37	230	6.2	23	4	39	9.8	27
1979	CAL	16	2		1							48	8						58	761	13.1	33	8	55	544	9.9	59	6	167	27.8	38
1980	CAL	16	1		0							30	5						50	792	15.8	86	5	30	206	6.9	18	1	14	14.0	14
1981	CAL	16	1		1							12	2						40	521	13.0	29	2	4	21	5.3	9				
1982	CAL	12										14	2						36	465	12.9	27	2	2	50	25.0	41				
1983	CAL	16	1		0							42	7						40	677	16.9	49	7								
11	Years	172	6		4							378	62	1	-20	-20.0	-20	0	553	8285	15.0	86	62	181	1461	8.1	59	11	220	20.0	38
MEL FOSS Melvin C. G 6'1 220 Colorado State B: 1940 Edmonton, AB																															
1963	EDM	13	0		1																										
1964	EDM	3																													
2	Years	16	0		1																										
AKEEM FOSTER Akeem WR-SB 6'4 212 St. Francis Xavier B: 3/20/1987 North York, ON Draft: 4B-25 2010 BC																															
2010	BC	8				1																									
2011	BC	16				1						36	6						33	593	18.0	56	6								
2	Years	24				2						36	6						33	593	18.0	56	6								
DICK FOSTER Dick T-G 6'2 220 Idaho B: 1935 Draft: 11-129 1957 WAS																															
1957	BC	14	1		0																			1	0	0.0	0				
GENE FOSTER Irving Eugene (Geno) OHB-FB 5'11 214 Arizona State B: 3/20/1942 Salem, NJ Draft: 10- 1965 SD; 15-201 1965 DAL Pro: N																															
1971	EDM	6	1		0							18	3						18	112	6.2	25	2					4	135	33.8	42
1972	EDM	9	4		2							18	3	118	581	4.9	25	2	15	183	12.2	34	1					7	199	28.4	36
1973	EDM	13	2		0							12	2	135	678	5.0	57	0	26	207	8.0	49	2					2	65	32.5	44
1974	OTT	1												5	15	3.0	9	0	3	43	14.3	25	0								
4	Years	29	7		2							48	8	324	1580	4.9	57	3	62	545	8.8	49	5					13	399	30.7	44
KEN FOSTER Kenneth FW-LB 5'10 199 McMaster B: 1929																															
1954	TOR	14																										4	35	8.8	13
1955	TOR	5							1	3																					
1956	HAM	2																													
3	Years	21							1	3																		4	35	8.8	13
PAT FOSTER Pat DL 6'5 255 Montana B: 12/2/1964 Draft: 9-231 1988 LARM																															
1988	OTT	3																													
WAYNE FOSTER Wayne F. DT-LB 6'2 250 Washington State B: 2/20/1944 Bremerton, WA Draft: 12-107 1966 OAK																															
1966	BC	11	0		1																										
1967	BC	6																													
1968	BC	1																													
3	Years	18	0		1																										
WILLIE FOSTER Willie WR 5'8 175 Rutgers B: 12/13/1984 Miami, FL																															
2007	WPG	1	1	0	0	1																		5	37	7.4	14	7	166	23.7	50
JOHN FOUBERT John OT-DT-OG-C 6'6 255 Ottawa Sooners Jrs. B: 9/29/1953																															
1978	TOR	14																													
1979	TOR	16																													
1980	TOR	16																													
1981	TOR	16																													
1982	MTL	11																													
5	Years	73																													
JIM FOUBISTER Jim FW-HB 5'11 200 none B: 10/4/1924 D: 12/30/2008																															
1946	WPG	8										10	2										2								
1948	WPG	12																													
1949	WPG	11										1	0																		

Year	Team	GP	FM	FF	FR	TK	SK	YDS	IR	YDS	PD	PTS	TD	RA	YDS	AVG	LG	TD	REC	YDS	AVG	LG	TD	PR	YDS	AVG	LG	KOR	YDS	AVG	LG
3	Years	31										11	2										2								
ED FOUCH Edward Vernon T 6'3 236 Southern California B: 5/17/1933 Santa Ana, CA Draft: 4B-43 1955 LARM																															
1955	TOR	1										2	0																		
1958	MTL	2																										1	0	0.0	0
2	Years	3										2	0															1	0	0.0	0
SEAN FOUDY Sean S 6'3 189 York B: 10/25/1966 Toronto, ON Draft: 3-17 1989 OTT																															
1989	OTT	6	0		1	10																									
1990	OTT	9				7																									
1991	OTT	18	0		1	24																									
1992	OTT	18	0		3	52	1.0	3.0	1	19																					
1993	BC	9	0		2	29																									
1994	BC	4	0		3	1																									
6	Years	64	0		10	123	1.0	3.0	1	19																					
JOHN FOURCADE John Charles, Jr. QB 6'1 211 Mississippi B: 10/11/1960 Gretna, LA Pro: N																															
1982	BC	4												2	37	18.5	28	0													
DAN FOURNIER Dan TE 6'3 210 Princeton B: 7/6/1954 Draft: TE 1977 OTT																															
1978	OTT	13	0		2							6	1						1	5	5.0	5	0								
GREG FOURNIER Greg OL 6'2 285 Rhode Island B: 10/12/1971																															
1995	SAS	2				0																									
RANDY FOURNIER Randy OT-DL 6'4 245 Cincinnati B: 12/31/1958 Sudbury, ON Draft: TE 1981 CAL																															
1981	OTT	1																													
1982	OTT	2																													
1983	OTT	6					0.5																								
1984	BC	6																													
4	Years	15					0.5																								
SAM FOURNIER Samuel FB 6'0 230 Laval B: 1/28/1986 Lacolle, QC Draft: 3A-19 2010 HAM																															
2010	HAM	7				2																						1	13	13.0	13
2010	EDM	3				1																									
2010	Year	10				3																						1	13	13.0	13
JOE FOURQUREAN Joe DB 6'0 190 Bluefield State B: 1/6/1950																															
1973	BC	11							2	-1																		2	35	17.5	33
1974	BC	16	0		1				2	0																					
1975	BC	16	0		1																										
1976	BC	16							2	7																					
1977	BC+	12							3	62																					
1978	BC	16	0		1				3	15																					
1979	BC	16	0		1																										
1980	BC	16	0		1				3	16																					
1981	BC	3																													
9	Years	122	0		5				15	99																		2	35	17.5	33
DICK FOUTS Richard Lee DE-OT-OG 6'6 233 Missouri B: 8/7/1934 Omaha, NE D: 8/5/2003 Monterey, CA Draft: 22-264 1956 LARM																															
1957	TOR	13							1	0																		6	67	11.2	15
1958	TOR+	14							1	12		6	1						1	9	9.0	9	0								
1959	TOR	14							1	0									7	90	12.9	19	0								
1960	TOR+	14																													
1961	TOR	13																													
1962	BC	16																													
1963	BC*	16	0		2							6	1											1	0	0.0	0				
1964	BC*	16	0		1																										
1965	BC*	13	0		2																										
1966	BC	15	0		1																										
1967	TOR	10																													
1968	BC	16																													
1969	BC	2																													
13	Years	172	0		6				3	12		12	2						8	99	12.4	19	0	1	0	0.0	0	6	67	11.2	15
BUD FOWLER Charles E-HB 6'0 192 none B: 1926																															
1950	TOR	12																													
1951	TOR	7																													
1952	TOR	4																													
1953	TOR	11										5	1																		
4	Years	34										5	1																		
CARLOS FOWLER Carlos DT 6'3 280 Wisconsin B: 8/30/1972 Cleveland, OH Pro: E																															
1994	TOR	5				6																									
1995	TOR	6				21	4.0	20.0																							
1995	HAM	1				0																									
1995	Year	7				21	4.0	20.0																							
2	Years	11				27	4.0	20.0																							
DeLAUN FOWLER DeLaun M. DT 6'0 215 Missouri State B: 12/27/1973																															
1996	OTT	1				1																									
DELBERT FOWLER Delbert LB 6'2 215 West Virginia B: 5/4/1958 Cleveland, OH Draft: 5-133 1981 HOU																															
1982	MTL	7	0		1		1.5																								
1983	MTL+	16	0		1		5.5																								
1984	WPG	15	0		1		6.0																								
1986	WPG	18	0		1		8.0		1	0																					
1987	WPG	18			1	33	8.0																					1	5	5.0	5
1988	WPG	2				1	2.0																								
6	Years	76	0		5	34	31.0		1	0																		1	5	5.0	5
DaVON FOWLKES DaVon LaMar WR 5'7 165 Appalachian State B: 2/8/1982 Fort Wayne, IN																															
2006	HAM	6				0						12	2						5	90	18.0	54	1	26	243	9.3	86	14	217	15.5	33
DION FOXX Dion Lamont LB 6'3 249 James Madison B: 6/11/1971 Richmond, VA Pro: NX																															
1998	SAS	9	0	0	1	31			1	41	1																				
RON FOXX Ronald E. LB 6'3 220 Alabama A&M B: 5/2/1951 Gainesville, FL Draft: 32-380 1974 BIR-WFL Pro: W																															
1976	TOR	13	0		2				2	143																					
1977	TOR	8	0		1																							2	29	14.5	15
1978	OTT	11																													
1979	OTT*	16	0		1				1	0																		1	-1	-1.0	-1
1980	OTT+	16	1		4				3	49																					
1981	OTT	10	0		2		0.5		1	10																					
1981	MTL	1																													
1981	TOR	3																													
1981	Year	14	0		2		0.5		1	10																					
6	Years	74	1		10		0.5		7	202																		3	28	9.3	15
GINO FRACAS Gino Mark FB-DG-LB 5'11 205 Western Ontario B: 4/28/1930 Windsor, ON D: 10/29/2009 London, ON Draft: 1-1 1955 OTT																															
1955	EDM	7	1		0				1	15		2	0	3	19	6.3	16	0													
1956	EDM	1																													
1957	EDM	11							1	0																					
1958	EDM	13																													
1959	EDM	10							4	16																					
1960	EDM	15	0		2																										
1961	EDM	11																													
1962	EDM	10	0		2																										
8	Years	78	1		4				6	31		2	0	3	19	6.3	16	0													

Year	Team	GP	FM	FF	FR	TK	SK	YDS	IR	YDS	PD	PTS	TD	RA	YDS	AVG	LG	TD	REC	YDS	AVG	LG	TD	PR	YDS	AVG	LG	KOR	YDS	AVG	LG
AUGUST FRACASSI August P. G-T none B: 8/29/1917 D: 8/11/1998																															
1946	HAM	7																													
EMILIO FRAIETTA Emilio DB 5'10 175 Edmonton Wildcats Jrs. B: 10/23/1955																															
1979	EDM	16	1		0																			34	361	10.6	51	11	226	20.5	30
1980	EDM	16	1		1																			58	468	8.1	44	18	425	23.6	96
1981	EDM	16	1		0		1.0																	52	395	7.6	51	4	62	15.5	17
1982	EDM	16	2		0				1	42		6	1											40	306	7.7	24	1	10	10.0	10
1983	EDM	16					1.0																	12	107	8.9	25	4	71	17.8	23
5	Years	80	5		1		2.0		1	42		6	1											196	1637	8.4	51	38	794	20.9	96
DANNY FRAME Danny OG 6'1 310 Acadia B: 6/19/1978 Halifax, NS																															
2003	TOR	5				0																									
2004	TOR	4				0																									
2	Years	9				0																									
TEDARO FRANCE Tedaro CB 6'0 196 Central Michigan B: 2/7/1978																															
2004	BC	1				1																									
JASON FRANCI Jason Arthur TE-SE 6'1 210 Santa Rosa JC; California-Santa Barbara B: 10/17/1943 Fort Bragg, CA Pro: N																															
1967	SAS	10																	24	383	16.0	33	0								
1968	SAS	16	1		2							12	2						28	434	15.5	38	1					1	28	28.0	28
2	Years	26	1		2							12	2						62	817	15.7	38	1					1	28	28.0	28
ANDRE FRANCIS Andre S. CB 5'9 170 New Mexico State B: 10/5/1960 Kingston, Jamaica Draft: TD 1983 ARI-USFL																															
1983	MTL	16							5	108																					
1984	MTL	16							3	84														0	34		20	7	143	20.4	30
1985	MTL	9																													
1985	SAS	1																													
1985	Year	10																													
1986	BC	10							2	23																		1	13	13.0	13
1987	BC	18	0		3	60			5	117		6	1											1	1	1.0	1				
1988	BC	18	1		1	39			7	101		6	1																		
1989	EDM+	18				42			5	101																					
1990	EDM+	18	0		1	45			7	137																					
1991	OTT	18	0		1	34			1	0																					
1992	BC	14	1		1	19			5	106		6	1																		
1993	BC	16	1		0	37			8	153		6	1																		
1994	OTT	18	2		0	42			3	21	8																				
12	Years	189	5		7	318			51	951	8	24	4											1	35	35.0	20	8	156	19.5	30
DANIEL FRANCIS Daniel James S-LB 5'11 185 Louisiana State B: 9/9/1984 Lafayette, LA																															
2009	SAS	11	0	1	0	10																									
2010	SAS	16	0	2	1	63	1.0	8.0			2																				
2011	HAM	6	0	1	0	20																									
3	Years	33	0	4	1	93	1.0	8.0			2																				
JOE FRANCIS Joseph Charles QB 6'1 195 Oregon State B: 4/21/1936 Honolulu, HI Draft: 5-51 1958 GB Pro: N																															
1961	MTL	3												1	1	1.0	1	0													
1962	MTL	6												7	24	3.4	10	0	1	7	7.0	7	0								
2	Years	9												8	25	3.1	10	0	1	7	7.0	7	0								
PETER FRANCIS Peter FL-S 6'0 178 Saskatchewan B: 2/17/1946																															
1968	WPG	16																						1	25	25.0	25				
1969	WPG	16			1				2	53														1	0	0.0	0				
1970	WPG	7							3	65																					
1970	BC	4																													
1970	Year	11							3	65																					
3	Years	39	0		1				5	118														2	25	12.5	25				
RON FRANCIS Ronald OE 6'5 226 North Carolina A&T State B: 8/13/1943 Burlington, NC																															
1969	SAS	1																	2	18	9.0	9	0								
RON FRANCIS Ronald Bernard DB 5'9 201 Baylor B: 4/7/1964 LaMarque, TX Draft: 2-39 1987 DAL Pro: N																															
1992	BC	9	0		2	20	1.0	9.0				6	1															6	95	15.8	31
1993	BC	2				8																									
2	Years	11	0		2	28	1.0	9.0				6	1															6	95	15.8	31
ROSS FRANCIS Ross OG 6'3 255 Queen's B: 5/7/1957 Oshawa, ON Draft: 1-9 1980 EDM																															
1981	HAM	16																													
1982	HAM	16																													
1983	HAM	16																													
1984	HAM	16	0		1																										
1985	HAM	3																													
1985	OTT	8																													
1985	Year	11																													
1986	OTT	7																													
6	Years	74	0		1																										
STEW FRANCIS Stewart OG-C-LB 6'1 231 Simon Fraser B: 6/14/1949 Southport, England Draft: 2A-12 1972 TOR																															
1972	TOR	14	0		1																										
1973	TOR	14	0		1																										
1974	TOR	16	0		2																										
1975	TOR	16																													
1976	TOR	16	0		1																										
1977	TOR	10	1		0																										
1978	TOR	14	0		1																										
7	Years	100	1		6																										
KENT FRANCISCO Kent OG-OT 6'2 255 UCLA B: 8/21/1942 Petaluma, CA Draft: 24-191(f) 1964 OAK; 14-196(f) 1964 CHIB																															
1966	EDM	2																													
1966	TOR	9																													
1966	Year	11																													
1967	TOR	14	0		1																										
2	Years	16	0		1																										
MIKE FRANCO Mike FW-HB																															
1946	OTT	9																													
BILL FRANK William B., Jr. OT 6'5 255 Colorado B: 4/13/1938 Denver, CO Draft: 24-186 1963 SD; 18-244 1963 DAL Pro: N																															
1962	BC	2																													
1963	BC	14																													
1964	BC	11																													
1965	TOR	8																													
1966	TOR*	13																	1	1	1.0	1	0								
1967	TOR*	14	0		2																										
1968	TOR*	14																													
1969	WPG	4																													
1970	WPG*	16																													
1971	WPG*	16	0		1																										
1972	WPG*	16																													
1973	WPG*	16												1	4	4.0	4	0													
1974	WPG	7																													
1975	WPG	16																													
1976	WPG	16	0		1																										
15	Years	183	0		4									1	4	4.0	4	0	1	1	1.0	1	0								
BOB FRANK Bob DE 6'0 200																															

Year	Team	GP	FM	FF	FR	TK	SK	YDS	IR	YDS	PD	PTS	TD	RA	YDS	AVG	LG	TD	REC	YDS	AVG	LG	TD	PR	YDS	AVG	LG	KOR	YDS	AVG	LG
1951	CAL	1																													
1953	CAL	15																													
2	Years	16																													
CHUCK FRANK Charles W. OG-OT 6'1 230 Michigan State B: 5/13/1932 Riverview, MI																															
1957	BC	14																													
1958	BC	15																										1	0	0.0	0
1960	TOR	2																													
3	Years	31																										1	0	0.0	0
GARRY FRANK Garry Van OT 6'2 310 Mississippi State B: 12/20/1964 Berlin, WI Draft: 7B-192 1988 DEN Pro: E																															
1993	SAC	4				0																									
JOHN FRANK John DE 6'4 280 Utah B: 7/1/1974 Salt Lake City, UT Draft: 6B-178 2000 PHI																															
2002	OTT	4				8	1.0	6.0																							
MALCOLM FRANK Baldwin Malcolm CB 5'8 182 Baylor B: 12/5/1968 Mamou, LA Pro: EN																															
1994	SAC	18	0		1	56			3	69	18																				
1995	SA	18	0		1	55			3	113	7	12	2																		
1996	EDM	18	0		2	44					8																				
1997	EDM	16	0	1	1	47			1	17	0																				
1998	EDM	18	0	0	1	64			3	61	4																				
2002	EDM	18	0	1	3	52			2	38	5	6	1																		
2003	EDM	17	0	1	1	62			1	17	7																				
2004	EDM*	17	0	2	0	68			7	263	4	30	5																		
2005	EDM+	17				55			1	0	3																				
2006	EDM	18				68					3																				
10	Years	175	0	5	10	571			21	578	59	48	8																		
J.T. FRANKENBERGER Jerome Thomas T 6'4 235 Kentucky B: 3/6/1935 Louisville, KY Draft: 6-69 1957 WAS																															
1959	EDM	8																										1	0	0.0	0
1960	SAS	15	0		1																										
2	Years	23	0		1																							1	0	0.0	0
ARJEI FRANKLIN Arjei WR-SB 5'9 186 Windsor B: 4/25/1982 Scarborough, ON Draft: 3A-19 2006 WPG																															
2006	WPG	16	0	0	1	3													16	161	10.1	24	0	3	25	8.3	12	1	3	3.0	3
2007	WPG	10				6								1	8	8.0	8	0	36	452	12.6	61	0								
2008	WPG	18	0	1	0	5						6	1						49	566	11.6	73	1								
2009	WPG	2				0													5	53	10.6	18	0	7	21	3.0	10				
2009	CAL	7				0													5	40	8.0	10	0								
2009	Year	9				0													10	93	9.3	18	0	7	21	3.0	10				
2010	CAL	18	1	0	0	3						18	1	2	5	2.5	4	1	42	523	12.5	39	2	2	24	12.0	21				
2011	CAL	9				5								2	5	2.5	7	0	6	68	11.3	25	0	4	33	8.3	11				
6	Years	73	1	1	1	22						24	2	5	18	3.6	8	1	159	1863	11.7	73	3	16	103	6.4	21	1	3	3.0	3
BRAD FRANKLIN Michael Bradford DH-CB 6'1 190 Louisiana-Lafayette B: 12/22/1979 Baton Rouge, LA Draft: 7B-258 2002 CAR Pro: EN																															
2005	WPG	16	0	1	0	59					3																				
DENNIS FRANKLIN Dennis E. QB-WR 6'1 185 Michigan B: 8/24/1953 Massillon, OH Draft: 6C-144 1975 DET Pro: N																															
1977	TOR	7	1		0									7	47	6.7	17	0	8	78	9.8	18	0								
1977	MTL	2												7	16	2.3	8	0													
1977	Year	9	1		0									14	63	4.5	17	0	8	78	9.8	18	0								
IAN FRANKLIN Ian CB 6'4 200 Weber State B: 4/16/1970 Morgan City, LA Draft: 1A-3 1997 EDM																															
1997	EDM	10				4			1	4	0																				
1998	EDM	5				10																									
2000	BC	5				9																									
3	Years	20				23			1	4	0																				
KEITH FRANKLIN Keith Lamont LB 6'2 230 Glendale JC; South Carolina B: 3/4/1970 Los Angeles, CA Pro: ENX																															
1999	BC	6	0	1	0	13	1.0	7.0	1	0	0																				
2000	BC	8	0	0	1	32	1.0	9.0			2																				
2	Years	14	0	1	1	45	2.0	16.0	1	0	2																				
PAUL FRANKLIN Paul DB 6'0 175 San Jose State B: 10/29/1968																															
1992	BC	2	0		1	6																									
CHARLES FRANKS Charles CB 5'10 185 Oklahoma B: 1/11/1970 Oklahoma City, OK																															
1993	SAC	10	1		0	29			3	93																					
1994	SHR	2				10																									
1994	SAC	4				5																									
1994	Year	6				15																									
1995	SA	15	0		1	31			3	86	2																				
3	Years	27	1		1	75			6	179	2																				
STANLEY FRANKS Stanley, Jr. DH 5'9 180 Long Beach CC; Idaho B: 7/7/1986 Long Beach, CA																															
2010	BC	18	0	3	3	71			3	5	5																				
2011	BC	1				3			1	7	0																				
2	Years	19	0	3	3	74			4	12	5																				
CAM FRASER Cam P-E-FW 6'2 215 Hamilton Tiger-Cats Jrs. B: 1932 Hamilton, ON D: 5/16/1999 Ancaster, ON																															
1951	HAM	1																													
1952	HAM	12										25	2										2								
1953	HAM	13										15	1																		
1954	HAM	13										15	0																		
1955	HAM	12										11	0						1	11	11.0	11	0								
1956	HAM	14										10	0																		
1957	HAM	14										13	0																		
1958	HAM	14										15	0																		
1959	HAM	14										9	0											1	3	3.0	3				
1960	HAM	8																													
1961	HAM	6										2	0											1	2	2.0	2				
1962	MTL	4										1	0											1	1	1.0	1				
1969	HAM	3																													
13	Years	128										116	3						1	11	11.0	11	2	3	6	2.0	3				
ERIC FRASER Eric S 6'1 205 Central Michigan B: 5/5/1987 Burnaby, BC Draft: 1-8 2009 CAL																															
2010	CAL	18				20																									
2011	CAL	18	0	0	2	37	1.0	7.0	2	9	1																				
2	Years	36	0	0	2	57	1.0	7.0	2	9	1																				
FRANK FRASER Frank OHB-DB 6'0 185 Tennessee State B: 1936																															
1956	OTT	10												1	8	8.0	8	0						2	11	5.5	7	1	21	21.0	21
1957	OTT	14							2	32		6	1	23	194	8.4	40	1	7	97	13.9	23	0	3	5	1.7	3				
1958	OTT	14							1	16		6	1	29	170	5.9	17	1	15	94	6.3	16	0	3	24	8.0	15	12	246	20.5	38
1959	SAS	16							2			6	1	18	64	3.6	12	0	7	27	3.9	23	0	22	139	6.3	16	20	419	21.0	50
1960	SAS	16	2		0									47	157	3.3	6	0	33	360	10.9	40	0	9	27	3.0	7	16	321	20.1	38
1961	WPG	1																													
1962	EDM	6																													
1963	WPG	5												3	-4	-1.3	3	0	1	14	14.0	14	0	25	137	5.5	12				
8	Years	82	2		0				5	48		18	3	121	589	4.9	40	2	63	592	9.4	40	0	64	343	5.4	16	49	1007	20.6	50
JIM FRASER James Gallagher OL-LB-P 6'3 236 Wisconsin B: 5/29/1936 Philadelphia, PA Draft: 21-250 1959 CLE Pro: N																															
1959	HAM	1																													
STEWART FRASER Stewart WR-TE 5'9 180 New Brunswick B: 3/7/1958 Chipman, NB Draft: 2-17 1980 SAS																															
1980	SAS	7	1		0																			28	234	8.4	16				
1981	SAS	16	5		0									3	20	6.7	18	0	3	86	28.7	36	0	77	529	6.9	32				
1982	SAS	16	1		0							6	1						11	181	16.5	44	0	83	722	8.7	78				
1983	SAS	16	1		1							8	1						38	511	13.4	44	1	13	128	9.8	34				

Year	Team	GP	FM	FF	FR	TK	SK	YDS	IR	YDS	PD	PTS	TD	RA	YDS	AVG	LG	TD	REC	YDS	AVG	LG	TD	PR	YDS	AVG	LG	KOR	YDS	AVG	LG
1984	SAS	16										12	2	1	1	1.0	1	0	22	248	11.3	28	2	14	138	9.9	34				
1985	SAS	13																	6	60	10.0	17	0	41	257	6.3	23	0	12		12
1985	OTT	1																	2	10	5.0	5	0								
1985	Year	14																	8	70	8.8	17	0	41	257	6.3	23	0	12		12
1986	OTT	1																													
7	Years	85	8		1							26	4	4	21	5.3	18	0	82	1096	13.4	44	3	256	2008	7.8	78	0	12		12
AL FRAZIER Adolphus Cornelius HB 5'11 180 Florida A&M B: 3/28/1935 Jacksonville, FL Draft: 20-240 1957 CHIB Pro: N																															
1957	TOR	1										6	1	11	84	7.6	50	1													
1960	OTT	1												4	8	2.0	4	0						1	2	2.0	2	4	81	20.3	30
2	Years	2										6	1	15	92	6.1	50	1						1	2	2.0	2	4	81	20.3	30
BOB FRAZIER Robert TE 6'5 225 Southern University B: 1951																															
1974	CAL	7	1		1							6	1						18	277	15.4	32	1								
DARYL FRAZIER Daryl WR 6'1 190 Florida B: 1/23/1971																															
1996	BC	4				1													9	123	13.7	39	0								
LANCE FRAZIER Elance Antonio DH-CB 5'10 183 West Virginia B: 5/23/1981 Boynton Beach, FL Pro: EN																															
2006	SAS	1				2																									
2007	SAS	9	0	0	1	24			1	3	1	6	1																		
2008	SAS	17	0	0	2	39			5	62	6																				
2009	SAS+	16	0	0	1	38			5	197	6	6	1																		
2010	SAS	18				35	1.0	8.0	4	151	1																				
2011	SAS	12	0	1	0	24					2																				
6	Years	73	0	1	4	162	1.0	8.0	15	413	16	12	2																		
TOMMIE FRAZIER Tommie QB 6'0 205 Nebraska B: 7/16/1974 Palmetto, FL																															
1996	MTL	3				0								1	0	0.0	0	0													
TED FRECHETTE Ted HB 5'9 190 Edmonton Huskies Jrs.; Alberta B: 1940																															
1962	EDM	14							1															13	110	8.5	21				
1963	EDM	16																						2	66	33.0	14				
2	Years	30							1															15	176	11.7	21				
PAUL FREDRICKSON Paul T 6'2 218 Manitoba B: 1925																															
1946	WPG	7																													
1947	WPG	6																													
1948	WPG	12																													
1949	WPG	14																													
4	Years	39																													
SOLOMON FREELON Solomon, Jr. OG 6'2 250 Grambling State B: 2/19/1951 Monroe, LA Draft: 3B-75 1972 HOU Pro: N																															
1975	EDM	2																													
1976	EDM	4																													
2	Years	6																													
CORIAN FREEMAN Corian LB 6'3 225 Florida State B: 8/16/1968 Jacksonville, FL Pro: E																															
1993	WPG	10	0		1	14	2.0	9.0	1	96		12	2																		
1993	SAC	5				7	1.0	5.0	1	15																					
1993	Year	15	0		1	21	3.0	14.0	2	111		12	2																		
1994	SAC	10	0		2	22	4.0	23.0	1	20	0																				
2	Years	20	0		3	43	7.0	37.0	3	131	0	12	2																		
EDDIE FREEMAN Eddie V. DT 6'5 307 Alabama-Birmingham B: 1/4/1978 Mobile, AL Draft: 2-43 2002 KC Pro: EN																															
2007	CAL	1	0	0	1	2	1.0	8.0																							
2008	CAL	18	0	0	1	24	3.0	21.0			1																				
2	Years	19	0	0	2	26	4.0	29.0			1																				
JERRELL FREEMAN Jerrell Alexander LB 6'0 220 Mary Hardin-Baylor B: 5/1/1986 Waco, TX																															
2009	SAS	17	0	2	2	40					1	6	1																		
2010	SAS	17	1	1	2	37	7.0	35.0			1																				
2011	SAS*	17	0	4	1	108	6.0	22.0	3	41	2																				
3	Years	51	1	7	5	185	13.0	57.0	3	41	4	6	1																		
KEN FREEMAN Ken E 5'11 183																															
1948	WPG	3																													
MACE FREEMAN Mace WR 5'9 180 Toledo B: 1/20/1976 Montreal, QC																															
1999	HAM	14				5																									
2000	HAM	4				1																									
2001	HAM	11				3													10	134	13.4	21	0	15	107	7.1	21				
2002	HAM	8	2	0	0	5													4	35	8.8	14	0	22	208	9.5	28	11	224	20.4	41
4	Years	37	2	0	0	14													14	169	12.1	21	0	37	315	8.5	28	11	224	20.4	41
TOM FREEMAN Tom DB 6'3 210 Eastern Kentucky B: 1946																															
1966	EDM	1																										6	119	19.8	30
BENJAMIN FRENCH Benjamin OT 6'4 310 Rutgers B: 2/27/1977 Takoma Park, MD																															
2000	HAM	8				2																									
FRANKIE FRENCH Audber HB 5'7 170 North Shore Lions Jrs. B: 1929 Strongfield, SK																															
1949	CAL	14										10	2					2													
1950	CAL	6																													
2	Years	20										10	2					2													
JASON FRENCH Jason WR 6'1 200 Murray State B: 4/7/1978 Montreal, QC Draft: 2-9 2001 SAS																															
2001	SAS	18	2	0	0	4								1	-12	-12.0	0	0	12	197	16.4	50	0								
2002	SAS	15				0													16	218	13.6	27	0								
2003	SAS	18				2						14	2						37	385	10.4	50	2					1	12	12.0	12
2004	SAS	18				1						26	4						52	869	16.7	70	4					1	1	1.0	1
2005	SAS	16	3	0	0	1						18	3						52	601	11.6	29	3								
2006	SAS	18				2						6	1						28	335	12.0	35	1								
2007	HAM	15	2	1	0	3						24	4						34	417	12.3	35	4								
2008	HAM	3				0																									
8	Years	121	7	1	0	13						88	14	1	-12	-12.0	0	0	231	3022	13.1	70	14					2	13	6.5	12
JOCELYN FRENETTE Jocelyn OG-C 6'3 280 Ottawa B: 1/11/1976 Montreal, QC Draft: 6-41 2001 SAS																															
2002	SAS	10				0																									
2003	SAS	18				4																									
2004	SAS	18				2																									
2005	SAS	6	2	0	0	0																									
2006	SAS	15				4																									
2007	SAS	16				1																									
2008	SAS	18				6																									
2009	SAS	18	0	0	1	4																									
2010	SAS	18				3																									
9	Years	137	2	0	1	24																									
GREG FRERS Greg S 5'11 185 Simon Fraser B: 8/4/1971 Mississauga, ON Draft: 2-14 1993 CAL																															
1993	CAL	16				21			2	10														1	4	4.0	4				
1994	CAL	18				31			1	0	1																				
1995	CAL	18	0		1	30																									
1996	WPG	16				33			1	18	1																				
1997	BC	18	0	0	1	46			3	79	0																	3	41	13.7	19
1998	CAL	11				19					1																				
1999	CAL+	18	0	1	4	71			3	53	6																				
2000	CAL*	18				54	1.0	11.0	7	146	6	12	2																		
2001	CAL+	18				54	1.0	2.0	4	91	4																				
2002	CAL	18	0	0	2	60			1	0	3	6	1																		
10	Years	169	0	1	8	419	2.0	13.0	22	397	22	18	3											1	4	4.0	4	3	41	13.7	19

Year	Team	GP	FM	FF	FR	TK	SK	YDS	IR	YDS	PD	PTS	TD	RA	YDS	AVG	LG	TD	REC	YDS	AVG	LG	TD	PR	YDS	AVG	LG	KOR	YDS	AVG	LG
BUDDY FRICK Fred WB 6'4 205 South Carolina B: 1935 Draft: 20-237 1957 WAS																															
1957	MTL	9							1	0									3	22	7.3	9	0								
LARRY FRIDAY Larry D. DB 6'4 215 Alcorn State; Mississippi State B: 1/23/1958 Jackson, MS Draft: 11-298 1981 CLE Pro: NU																															
1982	MTL	1																													
CHAD FRIEHAUF Chad QB 6'6 211 Colorado Mines B: 8/31/1982 Brush, CO																															
2008	SAS	3				0																									
BOB FRIEND Bob DB 5'11 185 Simon Fraser B: 4/4/1950 Draft: 3-21 1972 BC																															
1972	BC	16	3		0																			51	327	6.4	26				
1973	BC	16										0	0											46	252	5.5	25	1	15	15.0	15
1974	BC	7	2		0														1	4	4.0	4	0	33	95	2.9	10				
3	Years	39	5		0							0	0						1	4	4.0	4	0	130	674	5.2	26	1	15	15.0	15
JERRY FRIESEN Jerry LB 6'1 218 Saskatchewan B: 10/27/1955 Saskatoon, SK Draft: 2B-14 1978 MTL																															
1978	MTL	16																													
1979	MTL	16																													
1980	MTL	16							1	9																		2	22	11.0	16
1981	SAS	4					1.0																								
1982	SAS	16	0		1		1.5		1	1																					
1983	SAS	16					1.5																								
1984	SAS	16	0		2				1	0																		1	19	19.0	19
1985	SAS	9																													
8	Years	109	0		3		4.0		3	10																		3	41	13.7	19
JOHNNY FRIPP John FW Ottawa Jrs. B: 2/11/1921 Ottawa, ON																															
1946	OTT	11																													
PAUL FRISE Paul C 6'4 220 Peterborough Orfuns Jrs.																															
1953	CAL	2																													
KEN FRITH Kenneth DE 6'4 252 Louisiana-Monroe B: 12/1/1945 Lake Providence, LA Draft: 6-156 1971 BAL																															
1969	SAS	16	0		1				1	5																					
1970	SAS+	16	0		5																										
1971	SAS	5																													
3	Years	37	0		6				1	5																					
LUKE FRITZ Luke Terrence OT-OG 6'4 296 Eastern Washington B: 8/10/1978 Oliver, BC Draft: 1-7 2001 MTL Pro: E																															
2002	MTL	6				0																									
2003	MTL	18				1																									
2004	MTL	18				0																									
2005	MTL	17				0																									
2006	MTL	16	0	0	1	1																									
2007	MTL	10				0																									
2008	MTL	17				1																									
2009	WPG	18				0																									
2010	WPG	18				0																									
9	Years	138	0	0	1	3																									
RODNEY FRITZ Rodney, Jr. DT 6'1 260 Highland CC; Los Angeles Pierce JCC; Tennessee State B: 5/8/1987 Kansas City, MO																															
2011	WPG	3				4	1.0	7.0																							
PAUL FRLAN Paul LB 6'1 215 St. Francis Xavier B: 3/6/1972 Hamilton, ON Draft: 4A-29 1996 SAS																															
1997	SAS	13	0	0	1	13																									
1998	SAS	1				1																									
2	Years	14	0	0	1	14																									
ART FROESE Art HB 6'0 215 Western Ontario B: 1945 Czechoslovakia Draft: 3-19 1966 EDM; 1-3 1967 CAL																															
1967	CAL	16			1							6	1	2	-2	-1.0	1	0	1	8	8.0	8	0	1	0	0.0	0	3	56	18.7	27
1968	CAL	16												14	49	3.5	9	0	4	16	4.0	11	0								
2	Years	32	0		1							6	1	16	47	2.9	9	0	5	24	4.8	11	0	1	0	0.0	0	3	56	18.7	27
CHARLES FRYAR Charles James CB 5'10 175 Nebraska B: 11/28/1965 Mount Holly, NJ Pro: E																															
1993	SAC	1				3																									
BRIAN FRYER Brian WR-SB 6'1 185 Edmonton Wildcats Jrs.; Alberta B: 7/16/1953 Edmonton, AB Draft: TE 1976 EDM; 8-234(di) 1976 WAS Pro: N																															
1978	EDM	9										6	1						20	293	14.7	56	1								
1979	EDM	2																													
1980	EDM	15	0		3							12	2						23	408	17.7	42	2					1	0	0.0	0
1981	EDM	1																	1	11	11.0	11	0								
1982	EDM	15										12	2						55	812	14.8	38	2								
1983	EDM	14										6	1						46	639	13.9	39	1					1	0	0.0	0
1984	EDM	16																	31	464	15.0	31	0								
1985	OTT	3																	13	152	11.7		0								
1985	EDM	8										6	1						3	43	14.3		1								
1985	Year	11										6	1						16	195	12.2	26	1								
8	Years	75	0		3							42	7						192	2822	14.7	56	7					2	0	0.0	0
JAMAAL FUDGE Jamaal Jay DB 5'9 193 Clemson B: 5/17/1983 Jacksonville, FL Pro: N																															
2011	SAS	1				2																									
DON FUELL Donald Lee DB-QB 6'2 200 Auburn; Southern Mississippi B: 11/26/1938 Draft: 26-(f) 1961 HOU																															
1963	TOR	14							2	52		4	0	18	122	6.8	24	0	1	-4	-4.0	-4	0	2	4	2.0	4				
1964	TOR	7							3	29		6	1	24	174	7.3	26	0						1	4	4.0	4				
1965	TOR	3							1	0																					
1965	MTL	10	0		1				2	19																					
1965	Year	13	0		1				3	19																					
3	Years	24	0		1				8	100		10	1	42	296	7.0	26	0	1	-4	-4.0	-4	0	3	8	2.7	4				
DICK FUGLER Richard Guy T 6'2 242 Tulane B: 7/19/1931 Dallas, TX Draft: 5-51 1952 CHIC Pro: N																															
1952	HAM	2																													
TOM FUHLER Thomas J. DT 6'4 285 Harper JC; Tennessee B: 3/4/1969 Crystal Lake, IL																															
1994	BAL	7				3																									
GABRIEL FULBRIGHT Gabriel Paul CB 5'10 178 New Mexico B: 12/15/1982 Dallas, TX																															
2006	WPG	7				3																		5	13	2.6	6	1	21	21.0	21
2007	WPG	2				0																									
2	Years	9				3																		5	13	2.6	6	1	21	21.0	21
EDDIE FULLER Eddie Jerome RB 5'9 201 Louisiana State B: 6/22/1968 Leesville, LA Draft: 4-100 1990 BUF Pro: N																															
1995	SA	2				0								9	18	2.0	9	0													
JOE FULLER Joe Robert CB 5'10 180 Northern Iowa B: 9/25/1964 Milligan, FL Pro: N																															
1986	SAS	7																						6	34	5.7	11	5	106	21.2	26
1987	SAS	18	2		0	43	3.0		5	41														52	403	7.8	45	18	289	16.1	40
1988	SAS	18	3		1	40	2.0		7	131		6	1											54	426	7.9	89	4	55	13.8	25
1993	OTT	14	1		0	28			2	65		6	1															10	135	13.5	22
1994	SHR+	17				52			8	158	9																				
1995	SHR	8				11																									
1995	TOR	9	0		1	18			3	57	10																				
1995	Year	17	0		1	32			3	57	10																				
6	Years	82	6		2	192	5.0		25	452	19	12	2											112	863	7.7	89	37	585	15.8	40
EVERETT FULLWOOD Everett TE 6'2 209 Morgan State B: 1944 Baltimore, MD																															
1966	EDM	4																	2	24	12.0	15	0								
1967	EDM	5																	8	88	11.0	18	0								
2	Years	9																	10	112	11.2	18	0								
CHARLIE FULTON Charlie QB-OHB 5'11 180 Tennessee B: 1947 Draft: 16-413 1968 BOS																															
1968	EDM	16	3		0							12	2	66	297	4.5	36	2	5	48	9.6	15	0					2	37	18.5	28
1969	EDM	14	2		0									25	151	6.0	18	0	3	22	7.3	15	0								
2	Years	30	5		0							12	2	91	448	4.9	36	2	8	70	8.8	15	0					2	37	18.5	28

Year	Team	GP	FM	FF	FR	TK	SK	YDS	IR	YDS	PD	PTS	TD	RA	YDS	AVG	LG	TD	REC	YDS	AVG	LG	TD	PR	YDS	AVG	LG	KOR	YDS	AVG	LG
ED FULTON Edward Ulmer OT-OG 6'3 250 Maryland B: 1/27/1955 Abington, PA Draft: 3A-68 1977 LARM Pro: NU																															
1980	HAM	7	0		1																										
1981	HAM+	16																													
1982	HAM+	16	0		1																										
3	Years	39	0		2																										
LANCE FUNDERBURK Stephen Lance QB 6'5 220 Valdosta State B: 8/18/1974 Jacksonville, FL																															
1998	MTL	18				0						6	1	1	1	1.0	1	1													
FARRELL FUNSTON Farrell Wayne SE-TE-DB 6'2 217 Sacramento JC; Pacific B: 3/5/1936 Los Angeles, CA Draft: 5A-60 1958 CLE																															
1959	WPG	3										12	2						12	284	23.7	50	2								
1960	WPG	9										18	3						18	309	17.2	49	3					1	19	19.0	19
1961	WPG+	14										48	8						47	892	19.0	75	8								
1962	WPG	7	0		1							24	4						21	376	17.9	61	3								
1963	WPG+	16										54	9						60	835	13.9	36	9								
1964	WPG	4										12	2						14	299	21.4	67	2								
1965	WPG	16	1		0							30	5						37	549	14.8	32	5					1	-2	-2.0	-2
1966	WPG	5	1		0														11	205	18.6	40	0					1	0	0.0	0
8	Years	74	2		1							198	33						220	3749	17.0	75	32					3	17	5.7	19
TODD FURDYK Todd OT 6'7 305 Rocky Mountain B: 12/10/1969 Winnipeg, MB Draft: 1B-5 1992 BC																															
1994	BC	18	0		1	1																									
1995	BC	18	0		1	1																									
1996	BC	16	0		1	1																									
1997	BC	18	0	0	1	1																									
1998	WPG	18				2																									
5	Years	88	0	0	4	6																									
JIM FUREY James Andrew C-LB 6'0 230 Kansas State B: 9/22/1932 Newark, NJ Draft: 13-157 1956 CLE Pro: N																															
1958	CAL+	16	0		4				3	32																					
1959	BC	3							1																						
1960	BC	4	0		1																										
3	Years	23	0		5				4	32																					
JIM FURLONG Jim LB-DE-SE 6'2 225 Calgary Bronks Jrs.; Tulsa B: 3/24/1940 Winnipeg, MB																															
1962	CAL	16	1									6	0						8	162	20.3	54	0								
1963	CAL	16	0		1							7	0															1	7	7.0	7
1964	CAL	16	0		2							6	0																		
1965	CAL+	16	1		3				6	47		13	1	2	-11	-5.5	-5	0						1	0	0.0	0				
1966	CAL	6																													
1967	CAL	12							3	39		8	0																		
1968	CAL	16	1		1				3	38		2	0																		
1969	CAL	12																													
1970	CAL	16	1		1																										
1971	CAL	16							2	16																					
1972	CAL	16	0		2				1	11																					
1973	CAL	16	0		1							1	0																		
12	Years	174	4		11				15	151		43	1	2	-11	-5.5	-5	0	8	162	20.3	54	0	1	0	0.0	0	1	7	7.0	7
STEVE GABBARD Stephen Edward OT 6'4 297 Florida State B: 7/19/1966 Lexington, KY Pro: EN																															
1993	SAC	14				2																									
WALLY GABLER Wallace Frederick QB 6'2 195 New Mexico Military Institute; Michigan B: 6/9/1944 Royal Oak, MI																															
1966	TOR	14	7		2							6	1	67	373	5.6	27	1	1	4	4.0	4	0								
1967	TOR	14	4		1							13	2	88	494	5.6	34	2						1	0	0.0	0				
1968	TOR	14	3		1							24	4	72	458	6.4	28	4													
1969	TOR	3										6	1	3	31	10.3	24	1													
1969	WPG	13			1							6	1	44	209	4.8		1													
1969	Year	16										12	2	47	240	5.1	24	2													
1970	WPG	9	2		0							6	1	26	160	6.2	21	1	1	-2	-2.0	-2	0								
1970	HAM	5												17	29	1.7		0													
1970	Year	14	2		0							6	1	43	189	4.4	21	1													
1971	HAM	8												2	23	11.5	21	0													
1972	HAM	4										6	1					1													
1972	TOR	10	3		1													0													
1972	Year	14	3		1							6	1	27	100	3.7	15	1													
7	Years	66	19		6							67	11	319	1777	5.6	34	11	2	2	1.0	4	0	1	0	0.0	0				
FRED GABRIEL Fred C 5'11 215 Niagara B: 1/10/1920 D: 12//1971																															
1948	HAM	9																													
PETER GABRIEL Peter FL 6'1 187 McMaster B: 5/11/1954																															
1977	TOR	3																	3	47	15.7	21	0								
1979	TOR	3	0		1																										
2	Years	6	0		1														3	47	15.7	21	0								
TONY GABRIEL Anthony P. TE 6'4 209 Burlington Braves Jrs.; Syracuse B: 12/11/1948																															
1971	HAM	14										6	1						20	285	14.3	36	1					2	23	11.5	10
1972	HAM*	14	1		3							30	5						49	733	15.0	49	3					6	22	3.7	12
1973	HAM+	14	0		1							12	2	2	15	7.5	9	0	40	535	13.4	52	1					1	8	8.0	8
1974	HAM*	16	1		2							18	3						61	795	13.0	46	3					2	-2	-1.0	3
1975	OTT*	16	2		1							62	10						65	1115	17.2	46	10					2	1	0.5	1
1976	OTT*	16	1		0							84	14						72	1320	18.3	62	14								
1977	OTT*	16										48	8						65	1362	21.0	75	8								
1978	OTT*	16	1		0							66	11						67	1070	16.0	80	11								
1979	OTT*	16	1		0							48	8						48	761	15.9	44	8								
1980	OTT*	16										30	5						54	850	15.7	53	5								
1981	OTT+	14	2		2							30	5						73	1006	13.8	46	5								
11	Years	168	9		9							434	72	2	15	7.5	9	0	614	9832	16.0	80	69					13	52	4.0	12
JEFF GABRIELSON Jeffrey Louis LB 6'2 240 Ripon B: 8/11/1958 Milwaukee, WI Pro: U																															
1981	MTL	6	0		1		1.0																					4	69	17.3	27
1982	TOR	8	0		2		1.5		1	0																		2	30	15.0	17
1982	OTT	3																													
1982	Year	11	0		2		1.5		1	0																		2	30	15.0	17
2	Years	14	0		3		2.5		1	0																		6	99	16.5	27
BOB GADDIS Robert C. WR 5'11 178 Mississippi Valley State B: 1/20/1952 Jackson, MS Draft: 31-365 1974 BIR-WFL; 13-338 1975 PIT Pro: N																															
1977	MTL	4										6	1						3	120	40.0	89	1	5	30	6.0	17	1	19	19.0	19
1978	MTL*	16	2		1							18	3	1	15	15.0	15	0	45	814	18.1	64	3	1	16	16.0	16	4	44	11.0	23
1979	MTL+	16	1		0							12	2	3	24	8.0	14	0	46	578	12.6	30	2					3	64	21.3	26
1980	TOR+	16	1		0							18	3						68	1112	16.4	68	3								
1981	TOR	6																	14	219	15.6	26	0					2	54	27.0	29
1981	WPG	2										6	1						12	154	12.8	22	1					1	25	25.0	25
1981	Year	8										6	1						26	373	14.3	26	1					3	79	26.3	29
5	Years	58	4		1							60	10	4	39	9.8	15	0	188	2997	15.9	89	10	6	46	7.7	17	11	206	18.7	29
VERSIE GADDIS Versie WR 5'10 198 Indiana B: 5/1/1977 Prentiss, MS																															
2002	CAL	3				0													3	59	19.7	45	0	3	23	7.7	13				
ZEKE GADSON Ezekial I. LB 6'0 205 Pittsburgh B: 5/13/1966 Beaufort, SC Draft: 5A-123 1988 BUF Pro: E																															
1988	OTT	10	1		2	18	2.0																	1	-4	-4.0	-4				
JORDAN GAERTNER Jordan WR 5'10 185 Saskatchewan B: 2/12/1967 Moose Jaw, SK Draft: 5-38 1990 EDM																															
1990	EDM	18	1		2	2						6	1						3	41	13.7	17	1	1	-1	-1.0	-1				
1991	EDM	14	1		1	8								1	22	22.0	22	0	6	83	13.8	34	0					3	5	1.7	5
2	Years	32	2		3	10						6	1	1	22	22.0	22	0	9	124	13.8	34	1	1	-1	-1.0	-1	3	5	1.7	5

Year	Team	GP	FM	FF	FR	TK	SK	YDS	IR	YDS	PD	PTS	TD	RA	YDS	AVG	LG	TD	REC	YDS	AVG	LG	TD	PR	YDS	AVG	LG	KOR	YDS	AVG	LG
CEDRIC GAGNE-MARCOUX Cedric OG-OT 6'2 290 Central Florida B: 9/27/1982 Baie-Corneau, QC Draft: 1-8 2006 HAM																															
2007	HAM	18				3																									
2008	HAM	1				0																									
2009	HAM	4				0																									
2010	TOR	15				1																									
2011	TOR	17	0	0	1	2																									
5	Years	55	0	0	1	6																									
MARTIN GAGNON Martin LB 6'0 210 Laval B: 2/9/1980 Chicoutimi, QC Draft: 5-44 2004 EDM																															
2005	OTT	6				7																									
BOB GAIN Robert T 6'3 256 Kentucky B: 6/21/1929 Akron, OH Draft: 1-5 1951 GB Pro: N																															
1951	OTT+	10										37	1																		
BRUCE GAINER Bruce LB-C 6'0 223 Edmonton Huskies Jrs.; Alberta B: 1947 Draft: 1969 SAS																															
1969	SAS	16	1		0				1	31																					
1970	SAS	16																													
1971	SAS	8																													
1971	EDM	1																													
1971	Year	9																													
3	Years	40	1		0				1	31																					
BRAD GAINES Brad FB 5'11 226 Vanderbilt B: 8/25/1967 Nashville, TN																															
1994	SHR	5	1		0	2						6	1	11	40	3.6	16	0	10	110	11.0	30	1								
CHRIS GAINES Christopher Randall LB 6'0 238 Vanderbilt B: 2/3/1965 Nashville, TN Draft: 5A-120 1988 PHX Pro: N																															
1989	TOR	4	0		1	18			1	3																					
1990	TOR	17	0		2	117	2.0		6	123		6	1																		
1991	TOR	14	0		4	81	1.0		2	2																					
3	Years	35	0		7	216	3.0		9	128		6	1																		
DARRYL GAINES Darryl CB 6'0 195 Mississippi Valley State B: 11/9/1964 Mobile, AL																															
1988	EDM	1				3																									
GENE GAINES Eugene Carver S-CB-LB 5'11 185 UCLA B: 6/26/1938 Draft: 21- 1961 SD																															
1961	MTL	10							2	8														27	165	6.1	17				
1962	OTT	14							4	43				1	6	6.0	6	0						7	22	3.1	7	1	2	2.0	2
1963	OTT+	14							3	90		12	2	8	51	6.4	24	0	4	46	11.5	32	1	2	5	2.5	3	3	42	14.0	19
1964	OTT	14	2		0				3	14														3	10	3.3	7	12	258	21.5	41
1965	OTT*	14	1		2				2	17		6	1	9	36	4.0	7	0	3	60	20.0	28	1	5	27	5.4	12	20	357	17.9	30
1966	OTT*	14	2		2				6	114				8	39	4.9	8	0						8	26	3.3	10	7	167	23.9	30
1967	OTT*	14	0		1				1	0				2	4	2.0	5	0						2	21	10.5	20	13	286	22.0	33
1968	OTT	14	0		4				3	80																					
1969	OTT	14							2	58				2	7	3.5	6	0						1	0	0.0	0				
1970	MTL	14	0		2				4	23														1	7	7.0	7				
1971	MTL+	14							3	61														1	0	0.0	0				
1972	MTL	14							4	77																					
1973	MTL	5							3	70																					
1974	MTL	16							1	0																					
1975	MTL	16																													
1976	MTL	16	0		3				1	28																					
16	Years	217	5		14				42	683		18	3	30	143	4.8	24	0	7	106	15.1	32	2	57	283	5.0	20	56	1112	19.9	41
KEVIN GAINES Kevin DB 6'1 205 Louisville B: 8/7/1971 Pro: E																															
1996	HAM	4				9			0	0	1			1	3	3.0	3	0													
ROBERT GAINES Robert Wayne (Spider) WR 6'2 190 Washington B: 4/14/1957 Pittsburg, CA Draft: 6-140 1979 KC																															
1982	MTL	3																	7	85	12.1	22	0								
SHELDON GAINES Sheldon L. WR 5'9 155 Moorpark JC; Long Beach State B: 4/22/1964 Los Angeles, CA Pro: N																															
1987	WPG	2				0													4	57	14.3	20	0	5	35	7.0	19	1	20	20.0	20
MARTY GAINOR Martin Joseph (Butch) T 6'1 213 North Dakota B: 3/27/1915 Milnor, ND D: 12/30/1959 Milnor, ND																															
1946	WPG+	7										5	1																		
BRUCE GAIR Bruce WR 5'11 178 Bishop's B: 6/27/1957 Draft: TE 1980 MTL																															
1980	MTL	3																													
BOB GAITERS Robert James HB 5'10 210 Santa Ana JC; New Mexico State B: 2/26/1938 Zanesville, OH Draft: 1-5 1961 DEN; 2A-17 1961 NYG Pro: N																															
1964	HAM	8										12	2	57	203	3.6	12	1	2	48	24.0	36	1					8	180	22.5	28
MKE GALASSI Michael OG 6'4 315 Walsh B: 2/27/1985																															
2008	TOR	1				0																									
RICK GALBOS Richard FB 6'1 205 Ohio State B: 7/21/1951 Draft: 9A-218 1973 WAS																															
1973	CAL	10	2		2							12	2	30	163	5.4	50	1	28	451	16.1	42	1					12	342	28.5	57
1974	CAL	16	3		0							6	1	92	429	4.7	66	1	50	643	12.9	58	0					3	52	17.3	23
1975	CAL	16	2		2							30	5	47	194	4.1	13	1	37	426	11.5	40	4	4	28	7.0	10	4	35	8.8	22
1976	CAL	16	2		1							18	3	57	264	4.6	14	0	47	445	9.5	38	3					9	162	18.0	31
1977	CAL	1												4	13	3.3	4	0	2	8	4.0	6	0								
1977	MTL	6	1		0									47	181	3.9	12	0	8	43	5.4	24	0								
1977	Year	7	1		0									51	194	3.8	12	0	10	51	5.1	24	0								
5	Years	59	10		5							66	11	277	1244	4.5	66	3	172	2016	11.7	58	8	4	28	7.0	10	28	591	21.1	57
PETE GALES Peter QB 6'3 170 Iowa B: 11/6/1959 Paterson, NJ																															
1982	HAM	4																													
1983	HAM	6												6	16	2.7	14	0													
1984	HAM	8	1		1									4	-4	-1.0	7	0													
1985	HAM	1																													
4	Years	19	1		1									10	12	1.2	14	0													
CURTIS GALICK Curtis S 6'1 207 British Columbia B: 7/5/1974 Burnaby, BC Draft: 1-7 1998 SAS																															
1998	SAS	13	0	1	0	15																									
1999	SAS	18				46	1.0	8.0	1	0	2																				
2000	BC	2				1																									
2001	TOR	3	0	1	0	4																									
4	Years	36	0	2	0	66	1.0	8.0	1	0	2																				
ARNIE GALIFFA Arnold Anthony QB 6'2 193 Army B: 1/29/1927 Donora, PA D: 9/5/1978 Glenview, IL Draft: 18-225 1950 GB Pro: N																															
1955	BC	14	6		0									41	-52	-1.3	23	0													
1956	BC	1																													
1956	TOR	12										12	2	32	106	3.3	15	2													
1956	Year	13										12	2	32	106	3.3	15	2													
2	Years	15	6		0							12	2	73	54	0.7	23	2													
JULIUS GALL Julius HB																															
1946	HAM	1																													
ALLEN GALLAHER Allen Ross OG 6'3 255 Southern California B: 11/30/1950 San Fernando, CA D: 5/12/1977 Clovis, NM Draft: 4-82 1973 NE Pro: N																															
1975	BC	6																													
1976	BC	10																													
2	Years	16																													
SHAWN GALLANT Shawn S-LB 6'1 200 Eastern Kentucky B: 10/14/1976 Windsor, ON Draft: 2-8 2000 SAS																															
2000	SAS	14	0	0	1	16																									
2001	SAS	18	0	1	1	42	1.0	4.0	3	103	3	6	1																		
2002	OTT	15	0	0	1	34						6	1																		
2003	OTT	6	0	0	1	5																									
2004	OTT	9				9	1.0	7.0																							
2005	WPG	17	0	0	1	33			1	42	0																				
2006	WPG	18				30					1																				
2007	MTL	14				21																									
2008	MTL	15				19					2																				

Year	Team	GP	FM	FF	FR	TK	SK	YDS	IR	YDS	PD	PTS	TD	RA	YDS	AVG	LG	TD	REC	YDS	AVG	LG	TD	PR	YDS	AVG	LG	KOR	YDS	AVG	LG
2009	WPG	18	1	0	2	31						6	1																		
2010	WPG	4				3																									
11	Years	148	1	1	7	243	2.0	11.0	4	145	6	18	3																		
B.J. GALLIS B.J. LB 6'2 205 Lafayette B: 3/27/1975 Scranton, PA																															
1997	BC	12	0	3	0	54	4.0	20.0			2																				
1999	EDM	8	0	1	0	31	5.0				2																				
2	Years	20	0	4	0	85	9.0	20.0			4																				
MILLAR GALLOW Millar C-LB 6'3 205 Western Ontario B: 9/15/1929 Oakville, ON Draft: 4-13 1953 MTL																															
1953	MTL	13																													
DUANE GALLOWAY Duane Keith DB 5'8 181 Santa Monica CC; Arizona State B: 11/7/1961 Los Angeles, CA Draft: 19-217 1983 LA-USFL Pro: N																															
1983	SAS	6					1.0																								
KEN GALLOWAY Ken TE 6'1 212 NDG Maple Leafs Jrs.; St. Lamberts Saints Ints. B: 10/19/1943																															
1966	MTL	14																	5	84	16.8	26	0					1	4	4.0	4
1967	MTL	14																	1	3	3.0	3	0								
2	Years	28																	6	87	14.5	26	0					1	4	4.0	4
RALPH GALLOWAY Ralph William OG-OT-K 6'1 248 Southern Illinois B: 8/27/1946 Aurora, IL																															
1969	SAS	13	0		2																										
1970	SAS	16																													
1971	SAS	16	0		3																										
1972	SAS	16	0		1																										
1973	SAS+	16	0		1																										
1974	SAS+	16																													
1975	SAS+	16																										1	0	0.0	0
1976	SAS*	16			3																										
1977	SAS*	11																													
1978	SAS	15																													
1979	SAS	5																													
11	Years	156	0		10																							1	0	0.0	0
DAVID GAMBLE David Anthony WR 6'1 190 New Hampshire B: 6/14/1971 Albany, NY Pro: N																															
1994	SAC	6				2													1	11	11.0	11	0					1	22	22.0	22
1995	SA	12				7						24	4						17	381	22.4	49	4								
1998	WPG	3				2													4	39	9.8	14	0								
3	Years	21				11						24	4						22	431	19.6	49	4					1	22	22.0	22
DONTE GAMBLE Donte Kavon DB 5'7 165 San Diego State B: 7/14/1978 Los Angeles, CA																															
2002	OTT	8	0	0	1	13																		24	225	9.4	59	16	395	24.7	76
R.C. GAMBLE R.C., Jr. FB 6'3 220 South Carolina State B: 3/2/1943 Greensville, SC Draft: 4-88 1968 BOS Pro: N																															
1970	EDM	3										6	1	24	67	2.8		1	1		0.0		0								
1970	SAS	2										24	4	35	221	6.3		4	3		0.0		0								
1970	Year	5										30	5	59	288	4.9	23	5	4	20	5.0	11	0								
BILLY GAMBRELL William Edward FL 5'10 175 South Carolina B: 9/18/1941 Athens, GA Draft: 12A-92 1963 BOS Pro: N																															
1970	TOR	2																	9	194	21.6	69	0								
GEORGE GANAS George FB 6'0 215 York B: 5/22/1962 Toronto, ON Draft: 7-55 1985 OTT																															
1987	TOR	4				0								1	5	5.0	5	0	1	17	17.0	17	0					1	10	10.0	10
1988	TOR	10				0																						1	1	1.0	1
2	Years	14				0								1	5	5.0	5	0	1	17	17.0	17	0					2	11	5.5	10
DONOVAN GANS Donovan Loeb DE 6'2 235 Colorado State; Texas A&M-Kingsville B: 7/7/1971 Orange, TX																															
1995	BIR	18	0		2	44	3.0	26.0																							
JEROME GANTT Jerome Floyd OT-OG 6'4 266 North Carolina Central B: 10/20/1948 Greensboro, NC Draft: 4-82 1970 BUF Pro: NW																															
1972	HAM	14																										1	0	0.0	0
1973	HAM	12																													
1974	HAM	7																													
1974	SAS	4																													
1974	MTL	4																													
1974	Year	15																													
3	Years	33																										1	0	0.0	0
AL GARBARINO Alfred (Gabby) HB 5'9 160 none B: 7/13/1921 deceased																															
1947	MTL	1																													
JON GARBER Jon OT 6'3 305 Brigham Young; Western Washington B: 9/6/1967																															
1993	SAC	1				0																									
BOB GARBIG Robert QB 5'10 180 Toronto Balmy Beach Ints. B: 1936																															
1957	OTT	11												1	4	4.0	4	0													
JEFF GARCIA Jeffrey J. QB 6'1 199 Gavilan JC; San Jose State B: 2/24/1970 Gilroy, CA Pro: NU																															
1994	CAL	7				0								2	3	1.5	2	0													
1995	CAL+	18	4		1	1						30	5	61	396	6.5	25	5													
1996	CAL+	18	7		3	2						36	6	92	657	7.1	30	6													
1997	CAL+	17	5	0	4	2						44	7	135	727	5.4	28	7													
1998	CAL*	18	4	0	4	0						36	6	94	575	6.1	46	6													
5	Years	78	20	0	12	5						146	24	384	2358	6.1	46	24													
PETE GARDERE Peter Alexander QB-P 6'0 190 Texas B: 9/28/1969 Houston, TX																															
1993	SAC	10	1		0	3						5	0																		
1994	SAC	18	1		0	0						9	0	1	-1	-1.0	-1	0						1	26	26.0	26				
1995	MEM	12	1		1	4						4	0																		
3	Years	40	3		1	7						18	0	1	-1	-1.0	-1	0						1	26	26.0	26				
JOHNNY GARDINER Johnny QB 5'8 176 Minnesota; Purdue; Montana State B: 1922																															
1949	WPG	11																													
ROY GARDINER Roy QB-C-E 6'0 187 Concordia B: 1925																															
1947	WPG	4																													
1948	WPG	11																													
1949	WPG	11																													
1950	WPG	14																													
1951	CAL	9																													
5	Years	49																													
CHRIS GARDNER Chris K-P 6'1 190 Mississippi State B: 3/20/1971																															
1995	MEM	2				2						19	0																		
TALMAN GARDNER Talman J. WR 6'1 207 Florida State B: 3/10/1980 New Orleans, LA Draft: 7-231 2003 NO Pro: N																															
2007	HAM	7	1	0	0	1						6	1						18	276	15.3	67	1								
LEN GARGARELLO Len HB 5'11 180 Western Washington; McMaster																															
1961	HAM	1																													
ANTHONY GARGIULO Anthony DE 6'3 250 Dartmouth B: 10/20/1984 Hackensack, NJ																															
2007	CAL	10	0	1	1	21	5.0	35.0																							
KURT GARL Ralph C. LB 6'0 225 Santa Barbara CC; Humboldt State B: 10/13/1958 San Bernardino, CA																															
1982	MTL	9	0		2		3.0																								
1983	MTL	12	0		2		5.5																					1	11	11.0	11
1984	OTT	5					3.0																								
3	Years	26	0		4		11.5																					1	11	11.0	11
CHRIS GARRETT Chris RB 5'8 185 Ohio University B: 2/11/1987 New York, NY																															
2010	WPG	5				0								19	113	5.9	23	0	1	20	20.0	20	0					7	139	19.9	30
2011	WPG	6				1						24	4	92	576	6.3	32	4	20	91	4.6	15	0								
2	Years	11				1						24	4	111	689	6.2	32	4	21	111	5.3	20	0					7	139	19.9	30
JASON GARRETT Jason Calvin QB 6'2 197 Princeton; Columbia; Princeton B: 3/28/1966 Abington, PA Pro: EN																															
1991	OTT	13	1		0																										
JIM GARRETT James William HB 5'11 195 St. Mary's; Utah State B: 6/19/1930 Passaic, NJ																															

Year	Team	GP	FM	FF	FR	TK	SK	YDS	IR	YDS	PD	PTS	TD	RA	YDS	AVG	LG	TD	REC	YDS	AVG	LG	TD	PR	YDS	AVG	LG	KOR	YDS	AVG	LG
1955	BC	1												5	33	6.6	11	0	2	22	11.0	12	0								
JUDD GARRETT Judd Joseph SB-FB 6'2 220 Columbia; Princeton B: 6/25/1967 Abington, PA Draft: 12-327 1990 PHI Pro: E																															
1994	LV	8	1		0	3						18	3	50	232	4.6	24	3	9	105	11.7	32	0								
KEVIN GARRETT Kevin Rashard DB 5'10 194 Southern Methodist B: 7/29/1980 San Benito, TX Draft: 5C-172 2003 STL Pro: EN																															
2007	CAL	4				6			0	0	1																	2	33	16.5	19
SHANNON GARRETT Shannon D. DH-CB-LB 5'11 181 Mississippi College B: 1/24/1972 Bay St. Louis, MS																															
1995	WPG	17	1		1	55			4	35	2													1	4	4.0	4	5	101	20.2	38
1996	WPG	17	0		1	42			2	128	8	6	1																		
1997	WPG	16	0	1	2	46	1.0	19.0	4	115	5																				
1998	SAS	18				72			1	0	13																				
1999	SAS	18	0	1	0	55	1.0	4.0	3	20	9																				
2000	EDM	9				32					3																				
2001	EDM+	18	0	0	0	65	1.0	4.0	4	45	6	6	1																		
2002	EDM	13				23			4	70	2	6	1																		
2003	EDM+	18	0	1	0	49			3	28	5																				
2004	EDM	18				51			2	32	9																				
2005	EDM	18	0	1	0	53			3	0	5																	1	0	0.0	0
2006	EDM	18				46			2	12	6													1	0	0.0	0				
2007	EDM	17	0	1	0	64	5.0	23.0	2	33	2																				
2008	EDM	18	0	0	1	46	1.0	4.0	1	30	4	6	1																		
14	Years	233	1	5	5	699	9.0	54.0	35	548	79	24	4											2	4	2.0	4	6	101	16.8	38
CARL GARRIGUS Carl E. QB 5'10 192 Miami (Florida) B: 9/2/1931 D: 11/17/1975 Miami, FL																															
1955	HAM	11							1	19		10	2	35	226	6.5	38	2						1	4	4.0	4				
JEREMIAH GARRISON Jeremiah LB 6'1 233 South Carolina B: 8/1/1982 Anderson, SC																															
2005	MTL	4				18																									
BOB GARSIDE Bob LB 6'2 210 Toronto B: 1929 Draft: 1-1 1952 OTT																															
1952	OTT	11																													
1953	HAM	3																													
1954	HAM	14							1	8																					
3	Years	28							1	8																					
JOE GARTEN Joseph W. OG 6'2 286 Colorado B: 8/13/1968 Las Vegas, NV Draft: 6B-164 1991 GB Pro: E																															
1994	LV	12				1																									
1995	SA	4	1		0	1																									
2	Years	16	1		0	2																									
PATRICK GARTH Patrick DT-DE 6'3 282 Itawamba JC; South Carolina B: 12/25/1974 Aberdeen, MS																															
1998	WPG	1				0																									
2000	WPG	4				3																									
2	Years	5				3																									
GREG GARY Greg LB 6'1 221 Fullerton State B: 11/30/1958 Norwalk, IN																															
1983	HAM	5	0		1		2.5																								
1984	HAM	3					2.0																								
1985	HAM	8	0		2		3.0		2	24																					
1986	HAM	7	0		1																										
4	Years	23	0		4		7.5	0.0	2	24																					
KEITH GARY Keith Jerrold DE 6'3 269 Ferrum JC; Oklahoma B: 9/14/1959 Bethesda, MD Draft: 1-17 1981 PIT Pro: N																															
1981	MTL	13					5.5																								
1982	MTL	7	0		1		4.0																								
2	Years	20	0		1		9.5																								
SAMMY GARZA Samuel Mayorga, Jr. QB 6'1 184 Texas-El Paso B: 7/10/1965 Corpus Christi, TX Draft: 8-216 1987 SEA Pro: N																															
1989	WPG	5				0																									
1990	WPG	8				0																									
1991	WPG	18	1		0	0								3	14	4.7	8	0													
1992	WPG	18				0								11	46	4.2	12	0													
1993	WPG	13	1		0	0								4	25	6.3	12	0													
1994	WPG	8	1		0	1								1	18	18.0	18	0													
1995	WPG	5	6		1	0						12	2	13	22	1.7	3	2													
1995	OTT	13	2		0	0						12	2	11	48	4.4	18	2	1	-14	-14.0	-14	0								
1995	Year	18	8		0	0						24	4	24	70	2.9	18	4	1	-14	-14.0	-14	0								
7	Years	75	11		1	1						24	4	43	173	4.0	18	4	1	-14	-14.0	-14	0								
BILL GASKINS William T., Jr. CB 5'10 185 Washington State B: 11/23/1943																															
1966	CAL	5							1	0														23	74	3.2	11				
1967	CAL	5							2	36																					
2	Years	10							3	36														23	74	3.2	11				
A.J. GASS Anthony J. LB 6'3 205 Fresno State B: 11/29/1975 Bellflower, CA																															
1998	EDM	9	0	1	1	35	1.0	10.0																							
1999	EDM	14	0	2	3	69	1.0	1.0			1																				
2000	EDM	7	0	0	2	19																									
2001	EDM	11	0	0	1	66					2																				
2002	EDM	15	0	0	1	64	2.0	15.0			2																				
2003	EDM	13	0	0	1	56					1																				
2004	EDM	18				81	4.0	32.0	1	2	2																	1	10	10.0	10
2005	EDM	18	0	0	1	64	2.0	13.0	2	16	2																				
2006	EDM	10	0	2	0	29																									
2007	EDM	15	0	2	1	48	2.0	5.0			3																				
10	Years	130	0	7	11	531	12.0	76.0	3	18	13																	1	10	10.0	10
DAVE GASSER David LB 6'1 225 Bakersfield JC; West Texas A&M B: 1943																															
1967	EDM	15	0		1				1	0																					
1968	EDM	16							2	11																					
1969	EDM	16	0		1																										
1970	EDM+	16	0		3																							1	22	22.0	22
1971	EDM+	12							1	-1																					
1972	EDM*	16	0		2				2	22																					
6	Years	91	0		7				6	32																		1	22	22.0	22
MARK GASTINEAU Marcus Dell DE 6'5 270 Eastern Arizona JC; Arizona State; East Central B: 11/20/1956 Ardmore, OK Draft: 2-41 1979 NYJ Pro: N																															
1990	BC	2				6																									
ED GATAVECKAS Edward LB 6'0 215 Acadia B: 12/29/1957 Toronto, ON Draft: 3-27 1980 EDM																															
1981	HAM	16																													
1982	HAM	16																										2	24	12.0	13
1983	HAM	16	0		1																							1	8	8.0	8
1984	HAM	15	0		1		2.5		1	11																		0	3		3
1985	HAM	16	0		1				1	15																					
1986	HAM	18					1.0																								
1987	HAM	18	1		1	35	3.0		3	4																					
1988	HAM	17				18	1.0		1	0																		1	11	11.0	11
1989	HAM	18	0		1	5	1.0																					1	0	0.0	0
1990	HAM	7				10																						1	19	19.0	19
10	Years	157	1		5	68	8.5		6	30																		6	65	10.8	19
MARCUS GATES Marcus DB 5'8 170 Navarro JC; East Texas State B: 10/18/1972 Chicago, IL																															
1995	SA	17	1		2	18					1	12	2											25	171	6.8	81	15	373	24.9	93
TOM GATES Tom HB 6'1 205 San Bernardino Valley JC; Oregon State B: 1939 Draft: SS 1960 DAL; 18-206 1960 LARM																															
1963	TOR	1												2	8	4.0	8	0	1	10	10.0	10	0								
1963	MTL	4												7	25	3.6	6	0													

Year	Team	GP	FM	FF	FR	TK	SK	YDS	IR	YDS	PD	PTS	TD	RA	YDS	AVG	LG	TD	REC	YDS	AVG	LG	TD	PR	YDS	AVG	LG	KOR	YDS	AVG	LG
1963	Year	5												9	33	3.7	8	0	1	10	10.0	10	0								
JAKE GAUDAUR Jacob Gill C 6'2 220 B: 10/5/1920 Orillia, ON D: 12/4/2007 Burlington, ON																															
1947	MTL	12																													
1950	HAM	12																													
1951	HAM	9																													
1953	HAM	14																													
4	Years	47																													
GEORGE GAUSE George DE 6'4 275 South Carolina B: 6/20/1982 Conway, SC Pro: EU																															
2007	HAM	2				4	1.0	9.0																							
ALEXANDRE GAUTHIER Alexandre OT 6'6 326 Laval B: 12/8/1976 Maria, QC Draft: 1A-1 2002 OTT																															
2002	OTT	3				1																									
2003	OTT	7				1																									
2004	OTT	15				0																									
2005	CAL	16				1																									
2006	CAL	18				0																									
2007	WPG+	18				2																									
2008	WPG	18				1																									
2009	HAM	18				2																									
2010	HAM	18				1																									
2011	SAS	18				1																									
10	Years	149				10																									
DOUG GAUTHIER Doug HB-FB																															
1946	WPG	8										10	2										2								
PHILLIP GAUTHIER Phillip DB 6'0 214 Laval B: 7/10/1980 Gatineau, QC Draft: 2C-16 2005 MTL																															
2005	MTL	12	1	0	0	4																						1	5	5.0	5
2006	HAM	5				9																									
2007	HAM	16	0	0	2	18																									
3	Years	33	1	0	2	31																						1	5	5.0	5
JASON GAVADZA Jason FB 6'3 245 Kent State B: 1/31/1976 Toronto, ON Draft: 3B-19 2000 MTL; 6B-204 2000 PIT																															
2004	BC	16	0	0	1	5																									
2005	BC	18				5						6	1						1	4	4.0	4	1					1	0	0.0	0
2	Years	34	0	0	1	10						6	1						1	4	4.0	4	1					1	0	0.0	0
CHUCK GAVIN Charles E. OG-DE 6'0 243 Tennessee State B: 12/26/1933 Lake, MS Pro: N																															
1959	BC	11																													
TOMMY GAY Tommy Lee T 6'2 250 Wiley; Arkansas-Pine Bluff B: 5/15/1948 Shreveport, LA D: 3/14/2010 Benton, LA Draft: 12-291 1972 STL																															
1972	EDM	6																													
RASHID GAYLE Rashid Ali DH 5'8 174 Boise State B: 4/16/1974 New York NY Pro: N																															
1997	BC	6				18			3	50	1													4	57	14.3	20	8	128	16.0	26
1998	BC	10				39			3	72	2																				
1999	WPG	16	3	0	0	43			1	0	6								1	15	15.0	15	0	12	139	11.6	46	14	239	17.1	42
2000	WPG	3				14			1	9	0													2	2	1.0	6				
4	Years	35	3	0	0	114			8	131	9								1	15	15.0	15	0	18	198	11.0	46	22	367	16.7	42
TREVOR GAYLOR Trevor Alexander WR 6'3 195 Miami (Ohio) B: 11/3/1977 St. Louis, MO Draft: 4A-111 2000 SD Pro: N																															
2005	EDM	18	1	0	1	3						30	5						72	929	12.9	46	5								
2006	EDM	8				1						12	2						24	382	15.9	44	2								
2007	EDM	15	0	0	1	3						24	4						56	644	11.5	63	4					1	0	0.0	0
3	Years	41	1	0	2	7						66	11						152	1955	12.9	63	11					1	0	0.0	0
JEFF GAYLORD Jeffrey Scott DE 6'3 245 Missouri B: 10/15/1958 Des Moines, IA Draft: 4-88 1982 LARM Pro: U																															
1982	TOR	4					1.0																								
JACK GEARDING August John T 6'3 225 Xavier (Ohio) B: 11/19/1927 Draft: 4-42 1952 PIT																															
1952	OTT	8																													
1953	OTT	3																													
2	Years	11																													
BOB GEARY Bob OG-MG 5'9 223 Verdun Invictus Jrs. B: 10/6/1935 Montreal, QC D: 2/17/2001 SC																															
1955	CAL	14	0		1																										
1956	CAL	11	0		2																							1	18	18.0	18
1957	CAL	16																													
1958	MTL	14																													
1959	MTL	8																													
1960	MTL	3																													
1962	MTL	11																													
1963	MTL	14																													
8	Years	91	0		3																							1	18	18.0	18
JEREMY GEATHERS Jeremy James DE 6'2 265 Butler CC; Nevada-Las Vegas B: 6/19/1986 New Orleans, LA																															
2010	BC	1				0																									
ED GEDDES Ed QB Regina Dales Jrs.																															
1946	SAS	5																													
MARK GEFERT Mark Edward LB 6'2 210 Purdue B: 5/13/1952 Braddock, PA Draft: 8-204 1974 PIT; 16-191 1974 NY-WFL																															
1974	WPG	7																													
1975	WPG	9																													
2	Years	16																													
MARK GEHRING Mark TE 6'4 235 Olympic JC; Eastern Washington B: 4/16/1964 Burien, WA Pro: N																															
1987	CAL	2				0													1	12	12.0	12	0								
ALF GEISTHART Alf G-T 5'10 193 Regina Bombers Jrs. B: 1928																															
1949	SAS	14																													
1950	SAS	11																													
1951	SAS	2																													
3	Years	27																													
RON GEISTHART Ron 5'11 195 B: 1929																															
1950	EDM	6																													
STAN GELBAUGH Stanley Morris QB 6'3 207 Maryland B: 12/4/1962 Carlisle, PA Draft: 6B-150 1986 DAL Pro: EN																															
1986	SAS	5	1		0							1	0																		
NORM GELLER Norm HB 5'11 180 Winnipeg YMHA Jrs.																															
1946	WPG	4																													
1947	WPG	8																													
1948	WPG	11										3	0																		
1949	WPG	2																													
4	Years	25										3	0																		
STEVE GELLEY Steven S 6'1 185 Simon Fraser B: 4/10/1954 Draft: 1A-4 1976 OTT																															
1976	OTT	11			0				1	21																					
1976	HAM	4	1		0																										
1976	Year	15	1		0				1	21																					
1977	HAM	16	0		1				3	57														4	13	3.3	9				
1978	SAS	2							1	11																					
1979	MTL	3																													
1979	WPG	13																													
1979	Year	16																													
1980	MTL	16																													
1981	MTL	11							3	1																					
6	Years	59	1		1				8	90														4	13	3.3	9				
JERRY GENDRON Gerald DE-OE 6'3 260 Wisconsin-Eau Claire B: 1944 Draft: 16-239 1966 DET																															
1968	HAM	4																	5	80	16.0	26	0								

Year	Team	GP	FM	FF	FR	TK	SK	YDS	IR	YDS	PD	PTS	TD	RA	YDS	AVG	LG	TD	REC	YDS	AVG	LG	TD	PR	YDS	AVG	LG	KOR	YDS	AVG	LG
CHARLEY GENTHNER Charles W. T Texas Draft: 15-177 1953 SF																															
1953	EDM	2																													
CHRIS GEORGE Chris WR 6'0 190 Glenville State B: 11/27/1971																															
1995	EDM	3				0						6	1						10	109	10.9	17	1								
1998	HAM	2				0						6	1						7	71	10.1	19	1	3	26	8.7	17				
2	Years	5				0						12	2						17	180	10.6	19	2	3	26	8.7	17				
DON GEORGE Don T 6'3 220 Notre Dame B: 1934 Marianna, PA																															
1955	BC	16	1		0														1	25	25.0	25	0	1	0	0.0	0	2	37	18.5	20
1956	BC	1							1	0																					
2	Years	17	1		0				1	0									1	25	25.0	25	0	1	0	0.0	0	2	37	18.5	20
ED GEORGE Edward Gary OT 6'4 270 Ferrum JC; Wake Forest B: 8/10/1946 Norfolk, VA Draft: 4A-80 1970 PIT Pro: N																															
1970	MTL+	14																													
1971	MTL*	14																													
1972	MTL*	14																													
1973	MTL*	14																										1	0	0.0	0
1974	MTL*	13																													
1979	HAM	16																													
1980	HAM	16																													
7	Years	101																										1	0	0.0	0
JEFF GEORGE Jeffrey L. CB 6'1 185 Highland JC; Illinois State B: 12/24/1957 Atchison, KS Pro: NU																															
1982	MTL	3							1	0																					
1986	EDM	8	0		1				2	47																					
2	Years	11	0		1				3	47																					
TAMON GEORGE Tamon CB 6'0 181 Regina B: 11/21/1987 Regina, SK Draft: 2-9 2009 SAS																															
2009	SAS	8				2					1																				
2010	SAS	4				0																									
2011	SAS	9				0																									
3	Years	21				2					1																				
TEARRIUS GEORGE Tearrius Antwane DE 6'4 267 Los Angeles Valley CC; Kansas State B: 12/3/1982 Fayetteville, NC																															
2007	CAL	16	0	1	1	34	8.0	58.0																							
2009	CAL	8	0	0	1	19	1.0	2.0			1																				
2010	CAL	8	0	0	1	4	1.0	10.0																							
2011	SAS	12	0	1	0	21	5.0	31.0	0	10	0																				
4	Years	44	0	2	3	78	15.0	101.0	0	10	1																				
TRESTIN GEORGE Trestin Delorian CB 5'9 179 San Jose State B: 8/24/1983 Pasadena, CA																															
2009	BC	13	2	0	0	35					3													9	68	7.6	54	6	170	28.3	37
2010	BC	3				5																		6	68	11.3	23				
2	Years	16	2	0	0	40					3													15	136	9.1	54	6	170	28.3	37
METRO GERELA Metro K 5'10 180 none B: // Powell River, BC																															
1968	MTL	2																													
TED GERELA Ted K-OHB-FB-DB 5'10 205 Washington State B: 3/12/1944 Powell River, BC																															
1967	BC	16	4		1							77	0	9	15	1.7	4	0	3	21	7.0	13	0					5	87	17.4	27
1968	BC	16	1		0							115	0	5	56	11.2	46	0	7	72	10.3	21	0					4	40	10.0	14
1969	BC	16							2	51		98	0											3	21	7.0	15				
1970	BC	16	2		0							107	0																		
1971	BC	16										43	0	2	11	5.5	9	0										2	20	10.0	11
1972	BC	16	2		0							89	0						1	11	11.0	11	0					6	50	8.3	16
1973	BC	16	0		1							41	0						2	5	2.5	3	0					2	30	15.0	20
7	Years	112	9		2				2	51		570	0	16	82	5.1	46	0	13	109	8.4	21	0	3	21	7.0	15	19	227	11.9	27
BRUNO GEREMIA Bruno S 5'10 185 Calgary B: 12/31/1965 Calgary, AB Draft: 4-32 1987 CAL																															
1987	CAL	5	0		1	2																		1	0	0.0	0				
1988	CAL	9			2	2								1	3	3.0	3	0													
2	Years	14	0		3	4								1	3	3.0	3	0						1	0	0.0	0				
MASS GEREMIA Mass FB 5'11 230 British Columbia B: 9/12/1963 Calgary, AB																															
1987	CAL	4				0								4	35	8.8	22	0													
LARRY GERGLEY Larry G 6'1 232 Buffalo B: 1943 Chicago, IL																															
1964	EDM	1																													
DON GERHARDT Don DE 6'3 232 Concordia (Moorhead) B: 1944																															
1966	SAS	15																													
1967	SAS	16	0		1																										
1968	SAS	16	0		1																										
3	Years	47	0		2																										
TOMMY GERHART Thomas Edward S 6'1 195 Salem; Ohio University B: 6/4/1965 Lebanon, PA Pro: EN																															
1994	SAC	18	0		1	50			3	58	3																				
1995	SA	15	0		3	50	1.0	5.0	1	4	3																				
1996	HAM	18	0		1	84					1																				
1998	EDM	1				3																									
4	Years	52	0		5	187	1.0	5.0	4	62	7																				
JOE GERMAIN Joe WR 6'0 175 Simon Fraser B: 6/9/1965 Abbotsford, BC Draft: 1-9 1987 HAM																															
1987	BC	1				0																									
1988	BC	1																													
2	Years	2				0																									
RAE GERMAIN Rae FB-LB 6'0 218 Guelph B: 1942																															
1965	HAM	1	0		1																										
JIM GERMANY James Calvin HB 5'11 200 New Mexico State B: 2/20/1953 New York, NY Draft: 2-46 1975 STL																															
1977	EDM	16	5		0							60	10	211	1004	4.8	96	8	46	343	7.5	28	2					8	127	15.9	23
1978	EDM	15	6		1							60	10	179	885	4.9	34	10	33	280	8.5	31	0								
1979	EDM+	16	5		0							66	11	238	1324	5.6	40	9	18	261	14.5	47	2								
1980	EDM	16	4		0							60	10	181	1019	5.6	51	10	24	228	9.5	45	0								
1981	EDM*	16	3		1							114	19	157	861	5.5	44	18	31	286	9.2	19	1								
1982	EDM	8	3		0							42	7	83	480	5.8	39	7	11	142	12.9	28	0								
1983	EDM	5										24	4	33	157	4.8	18	3	9	102	11.3	27	1								
7	Years	92	26		2							426	71	1082	5730	5.3	96	65	172	1642	9.5	47	6					8	127	15.9	23
BRIAN GERVAIS Brian WR-SB-DB 6'0 192 Western Ontario B: 2/21/1951																															
1976	OTT	3																													
1977	CAL	16	0		1							18	3						36	484	13.4	24	3								
1978	WPG	12										6	1						5	109	21.8	50	1								
1979	WPG	16	1		0							6	1						35	413	11.8	38	1					1	17	17.0	17
4	Years	47	1		1							30	5						76	1006	13.2	50	5					1	17	17.0	17
JOASH GESSE Joash LB 5'11 221 Montreal B: 9/4/1986 Montreal, QC Draft: 3A-16 2010 BC																															
2010	BC	11				9																									
2011	BC	3				4																									
2	Years	14				13																									
JASON GESSER Jason John QB 6'1 204 Washington State B: 5/31/1979 Honolulu, HI																															
2005	CAL	14	1	0	0	0						6	1	7	33	4.7	21	1													
ERIC GETER Eric R. CB 5'11 195 Clemson B: 6/24/1970 Newnan, GA																															
1994	LV	11	0		1	18																									
1995	OTT	17				35			1	0	4																				
1996	OTT	3				11					1																				
3	Years	31	0		1	64			1	0	5																				
DALE GETTY Donald Dale, Jr. S 6'2 190 Weber State B: 10/29/1956 Draft: TE 1980 EDM																															
1982	OTT	10	0		1																										

Year	Team	GP	FM	FF	FR	TK	SK	YDS	IR	YDS	PD	PTS	TD	RA	YDS	AVG	LG	TD	REC	YDS	AVG	LG	TD	PR	YDS	AVG	LG	KOR	YDS	AVG	LG
DON GETTY Donald Ross QB-S 6'2 195 Western Ontario B: 6/20/1933 Westmount, QC Draft: 1-3 1955 HAM																																
1955	EDM	16	4		2									32	34	1.1	15	0													
1956	EDM	16												11	-24	-2.2	8	0													
1957	EDM	14	2		0									17	-15	-0.9	8	0													
1958	EDM	16	2									6	1	15	29	1.9	6	1													
1959	EDM	16												29	134	4.6	17	0													
1960	EDM	12	1									6	1	11	44	4.0	16	1													
1961	EDM	16										6	1	16	67	4.2	18	1													
1962	EDM	15	1											11	35	3.2	11	0													
1963	EDM	16	1		1							6	1	7	14	2.0	15	1													
1965	EDM	3																													
10	Years	140	11		3							24	4	149	318	2.1	18	4													
CHRIS GETZLAF Chris SB-WR 6'1 202 Regina B: 1/9/1983 Regina, SK Draft: 5A-33 2007 HAM																																
2007	HAM	2				0																									
2008	SAS	5				2						12	2						15	244	16.3	55	2								
2009	SAS	18	1	0	0	0						40	6						41	531	13.0	65	6								
2010	SAS	18	1	0	0	3						32	5						55	946	17.2	85	5								
2011	SAS	18				3						60	10						60	1071	17.9	70	10								
5	Years	61	2	0	0	8						144	23						171	2792	16.3	85	23								
KENDRICK GHOLSTON Kendrick D. DL 6'4 275 Louisville B: 4/30/1975 Chicago, IL Pro: E																																
2002	TOR	5	0	0	1	3																									
HAL GIANCANELLI Harold Arthur (Skippy) HB 5'10 177 Loyola Marymount B: 5/21/1929 Farr, CO Pro: N																																
1958	HAM	7							1	11				12	24	2.0	8	0	2	12	6.0	7	0								
DAN GIANCOLA Dan K 5'11 200 Niagara (Ontario)* B: 1/28/1970 St. Catherines, ON																																
1999	TOR	18				0						181	0																		
2000	BC	9				2						1	0																		
2001	TOR	13				1						112	0																		
2002	OTT	1				0						4	0																		
2004	TOR	1				0						8	0																		
5	Years	42				3						306	0																		
WAYNE GIARDINO Wayne LB-FB-DB 5'11 195 Florida State B: 11/7/1943 Peterborough, ON																																
1967	OTT	14							1	11				3	15	5.0	6	0										1	5	5.0	5
1968	OTT	14	0		2							6	1	3	18	6.0	11	0										1	7	7.0	7
1969	OTT	14	1		1				1	25		6	1	3	29	9.7	15	0													
1970	OTT	14							3	26		6	1	22	99	4.5	17	0	5	30	6.0	16	0					1	1	1.0	1
1971	OTT	14	2		0							1	0	54	201	3.7	18	0	20	127	6.4	20	0								
1972	OTT	14	0		3				2	36		18	3	3	13	4.3	13	0										2	9	4.5	6
1973	OTT	14	1		0							6	1	15	34	2.3	7	0	8	51	6.4	24	1								
1974	OTT	12	1		0									30	127	4.2	11	0	11	97	8.8	22	0					1	20	20.0	20
1975	OTT	3																													
9	Years	113	5		6				7	98		43	7	133	536	4.0	18	0	44	305	6.9	24	1					6	42	7.0	20
IAN GIBB Ian FW-HB 5'9 156 Norwood-St. Boniface Legion Ints. B: 1925																																
1949	WPG	14																													
1950	WPG	14																	13	197	15.2		0								
1951	WPG	14										5	1						2	17	8.5		1	2	3	1.5					
1952	WPG	15			2				1	16																					
4	Years	57	0		2				1	16		5	1						15	214	14.3		1	2	3	1.5	0				
WALTER GIBB Walter HB																																
1948	HAM	2																													
CHARLIE GIBBONS Charles E. G 5'10 237 Rhode Island B: 1935																																
1956	MTL	8																													
MIKE GIBBONS Mike FL 6'0 195 NDG Maple Leafs Jrs.; Tulsa B: 7/19/1941																																
1965	MTL	14	1		0														14	196	14.0	41	0								
1966	MTL	11																	11	139	12.6	24	0								
1967	MTL	13	1		0														10	152	15.2	24	0					1	-1	-1.0	-1
3	Years	38	2		0														35	487	13.9	41	0					1	-1	-1.0	-1
BEAU GIBBS Beau J. SB 6'4 254 Northern Iowa B: 6/22/1981 Waterloo, IA																																
2006	CAL	3				2													2	9	4.5	7	0								
DICK GIBBS Richard HB 6'1 190 Iowa B: 1945																																
1967	HAM	4	1		0							6	1	14	74	5.3	16	1	1	22	22.0	22	0	6	20	3.3	6	2	53	26.5	27
JEREMY GIBBS Jeremy DT-DE 6'3 283 Northeastern Oklahoma A&M JC; Oregon B: 7/3/1985 Stillwater, OK																																
2008	BC	1				0																									
2009	BC	14	0	1	1	23	2.0	3.0			1																				
2010	BC	2	0	0	1	3																									
2010	HAM	1	0	1	0	2																									
2010	Year	3	0	1	1	5																									
3	Years	17	0	2	2	28	2.0	3.0			1																				
NORMAN GIBBS Norman QB 6'1 185 Southern University B: 6/29/1960 Baton Rouge, LA																																
1983	WPG	6										6	1	10	10	1.0	7	1													
1985	WPG	1																													
1986	TOR	9	2		1									14	99	7.1	35	0													
3	Years	16	2		1							6	1	24	109	4.5	35	1													
NORRIS GIBBS Norris C. DB 6'1 180 Southern University B: 10/13/1963																																
1987	SAS	6	0		1	18																									
CRAIG GIBSON Craig C 6'2 270 Southern California B: 5/28/1971 Fort Leavenworth, KS																																
1994	LV	13				7																									
1995	BIR	18	1		0	4																									
2	Years	31	1		0	11																									
DEMOND GIBSON Demond Michael DL 6'3 205 Pittsburgh B: 5/25/1977 Pittsburgh, PA																																
2001	TOR	3	0	0	1	4					1																				
PAUL GIBSON Paul Edward (Spider) E-FW-T 6'0 195 North Carolina State B: 8/5/1924 D: 8/11/1999 Charleston, SC Draft: 9-66 1947 BUF-AAFC; 10-78 1947 PIT Pro: A																																
1950	OTT	11										20	4										3								
1951	HAM	12										30	6										4								
2	Years	23										50	10										7								
PHIL GIBSON Phil DT 6'2 295 Toledo B: 11/30/1978 Burlington, ON Draft: 3-18 2001 MTL																																
2002	MTL	1				0																									
2003	MTL	1				2	1.0																								
2003	SAS	11				8																									
2003	Year	12				10	1.0																								
2004	SAS	18				7																									
3	Years	20				17	1.0																								
RAHSAAN GIDDINGS Rahsaan LB 6'1 230 St. Hubert Rebels Jrs.; Rutgers B: 7/10/1972 Brossard, QC																																
1996	MTL	11	0		1	15																									
1997	MTL	18				27																									
1998	MTL	15	1	1	0	14			1	7	0																		2	9	4.5	5
1999	MTL	15	0	0	1	72	1.0	7.0			2																		3	30	10.0	17
4	Years	59	1	1	2	128	1.0	7.0	1	7	2																		5	39	7.8	17
SHERROD GIDEON Sherrod WR 5'11 171 Southern Mississippi B: 2/21/1977 Greenwood, MS Draft: 6C-200 2000 NO																																
2003	OTT	13				1						26	4	1	0	0.0	0	0	34	503	14.8	63	4								
2004	OTT	10				0													18	181	10.1	35	0								
2	Years	23				1						26	4	1	0	0.0	0	0	52	684	13.2	63	4								
WES GIDEON Wesley Alvin QB-DB 6'1 190 Trinity (Texas) B: 2/28/1937																																

Year	Team	GP	FM	FF	FR	TK	SK	YDS	IR	YDS	PD	PTS	TD	RA	YDS	AVG	LG	TD	REC	YDS	AVG	LG	TD	PR	YDS	AVG	LG	KOR	YDS	AVG	LG
1959	MTL	3							2	61				3	23	7.7	13	0						2	17	8.5	15				
1960	MTL	5							1	20																					
1961	TOR	8							3	46		8	0	6	14	2.3	5	0	4	53	13.3	21	0					1	9	9.0	9
3	Years	16							6	127		8	0	9	37	4.1	13	0	4	53	13.3	21	0	2	17	8.5	15	1	9	9.0	9
AL GIERUSCZAK Al G 5'8 170																															
1948	HAM	2																													
1949	HAM	1																													
2	Years	3																													
WAYNE GIESBRECHT Wayne J. DT-T 6'3 247 North Dakota B: 1945																															
1970	BC	5																													
1970	WPG	8																													
1970	Year	13																													
1971	WPG	6																													
2	Years	11																													
MIKE GIFFIN Michael FB 6'0 235 Queen's B: 1/24/1984 Kingston, ON Draft: 3-17 2008 HAM																															
2009	MTL	11	0	1	0	10						6	1						1	2	2.0	2	1								
2010	MTL	18	0	0	1	23																									
2011	MTL	7				9																									
3	Years	36	0	1	1	42						6	1						1	2	2.0	2	1								
SHAWN GIFFORD Shawn OT 6'5 285 Charleston Southern B: 5/6/1977 Ottawa, ON Draft: 4A-25 2001 MTL																															
2001	SAS	2				1																									
2002	SAS	18				1																									
2003	TOR	17				0																									
3	Years	37				2																									
PETE GIFTOPOULOS Peter LB-OG 6'3 240 Penn State B: 6/14/1965 Hamilton, ON Draft: 1B-6 1988 SAS																															
1988	HAM	8				1	1.0																	1	5	5.0	5				
1989	HAM	18	0		3	42	2.0		2	-1																		1	0	0.0	0
1990	HAM	16	0		2	77	3.0																								
1991	HAM	15				63	1.0		3	28																		1	0	0.0	0
1992	HAM	11	0		1	16																									
1993	HAM	18				17																									
1994	HAM	18				16																									
1995	HAM	16				15																									
8	Years	120	0	0	6	247	7.0		5	27														1	5	5.0	5	2	0	0.0	0
CHRIS GILBERT Chris OL 6'3 290 Arizona Western JC; Grand Valley State B: 7/4/1976 Port Huron, MI																															
2001	TOR	5				0																									
DAVE GILBERT Dave HB-QB Oshawa Ints.																															
1947	SAS	6																													
DON GILBERT Don DH-OHB-CB 5'10 196 Buffalo B: 10/6/1943																															
1965	OTT	13	1		0				4	179		12	2	1	12	12.0	12	0	1	19	19.0	19	0	13	88	6.8	21				
1966	OTT	14	4		0				3	39				1	1	1.0	1	0						49	201	4.1	16				
1967	OTT	14	2		1							12	2	40	137	3.4	15	1	16	195	12.2	30	1	40	263	6.6	16				
1968	WPG	16	0		2				6	45				8	29	3.6	11	0	4	19	4.8	19	0	1	2	2.0	2	8	121	15.1	25
4	Years	57	7		3				13	263		24	4	50	179	3.6	15	1	21	233	11.1	30	1	103	554	5.4	21	8	121	15.1	25
GEORGE GILBERT George William OG 6'3 265 Tulsa B: 3/11/1959 Elmira, NY Pro: U																															
1986	CAL	7																													
COOKIE GILCHRIST Carlton Chester FB-OHB-LB-K 6'3 249 none B: 5/25/1935 Brackenridge, PA D: 1/10/2011 Penn Hills, PA Pro: N																															
1956	HAM+	14							2	7		31	5	130	832	6.4	76	3	18	279	15.5	40	2					15	344	22.9	41
1957	HAM+	14							3	65		54	9	204	958	4.7	57	7	8	82	10.3	19	0					7	104	14.9	18
1958	SAS+	16	8		3							30	5	235	1254	5.3	73	5	15	144	9.6	41	0					17	436	25.6	83
1959	TOR+	14							4	66		75	5	87	496	5.7	69	4	5	70	14.0	38	1								
1960	TOR+	14							1	16		115	8	88	662	7.5	74	6	25	346	13.8	42	2								
1961	TOR	12							2	41		41	3	105	709	6.8	67	3	15	147	9.8	24	0					12	327	27.3	50
6	Years	84	8		3				12	195		346	35	849	4911	5.8	76	28	86	1068	12.4	42	5					51	1211	23.7	83
STACEY GILCREST Stacey L. DB 5'10 185 San Jose State B: 9/5/1963 San Jose, CA																															
1989	BC	2				3																									
DENNIS GILE Dennis QB 6'2 200 Central Missouri B: 2/17/1981																															
2004	SAS	17	1	0	0	1																									
LARRY GILES Larry WR 6'0 180 Saskatchewan B: 8/24/1950																															
1976	CAL	8																	5	103	20.6	58	0								
LAVARUS GILES Lavarus RB 6'2 215 Mississippi Delta JC; Jackson State B: 2/15/1986 Cleveland, MS																															
2009	WPG	4				0						12	2	14	54	3.9	15	2													
OSCAR GILES Oscar Riley, Jr. DL 6'2 250 Texas B: 9/27/1968 Dallas, TX																															
1995	SA	18				38	6.0	40.0			1																				
1996	TOR	7				18	3.0	30.0																							
1997	TOR	5				15					3																				
3	Years	30				71	9.0	70.0			4																				
GORDON GILKES Gordon (Gobbo) E 180 B: 1914																															
1946	CAL	7																													
JIMMY GILKES Jimmy HB-E 160 B: 1916																															
1946	CAL	6																													
RANDY GILL Arthur Randy LB 6'2 230 Mount Hood JC; San Jose State B: 8/1/1956 Ventura, CA D: 2/10/2002 Winnipeg, MB Draft: 10-265 1978 STL Pro: N																															
1979	TOR	2																													
TURNER GILL Turner Hillery, Jr. QB 6'0 190 Nebraska B: 8/13/1962 Fort Worth, TX Draft: 5-104 1984 HOU-USFL																															
1984	MTL	16	9		0							26	4	98	485	4.9	26	4													
1985	MTL	16	5		0							18	3	75	341	4.5	30	3													
2	Years	32	14		0							44	7	173	826	4.8	30	7													
BOB GILLAN Bob G 5'11 210 B: 1926																															
1948	OTT	7																													
MEL GILLETT Melvin Ronald HB-FB 6'0 195 Lewis & Clark B: 1935 Vernon, BC																															
1958	BC	16	0		2				1	0				2	13	6.5	9	0						3	31	10.3	15	3	59	19.7	23
1959	BC	2																													
2	Years	18	0		2				1	0				2	13	6.5	9	0						3	31	10.3	15	3	59	19.7	23
DONDRE GILLIAM Dondre A. WR 6'0 185 Cheyney; Millersville B: 2/9/1977 Baltimore, MD Pro: EN																															
2004	HAM	8	2	0	0	0													18	215	11.9	33	0					12	267	22.3	40
2005	HAM	16				14						12	2						27	241	8.9	31	2					1	12	12.0	12
2	Years	24	2	0	0	14						12	2						45	456	10.1	33	2					13	279	21.5	40
FRANK GILLIAM Franklin Delano OE-DE-DB-LB 6'2 190 Iowa B: 1/7/1934 Steubenville, OH Draft: 7-76 1957 GB																															
1957	WPG	10										6	1						13	220	16.9	31	1								
1958	WPG	16										12	2						15	233	15.5	30	2					1	10	10.0	10
1959	WPG	2										12	2						3	32	10.7	14	2								
1960	BC	8																	8	119	14.9	22	0								
4	Years	36										30	5						39	604	15.5	31	5					1	10	10.0	10
TIM GILLIGAN Tim WR 5'8 175 Boise State B: 2/17/1981 Elko, NV																															
2004	MTL	3				1																		20	174	8.7	32	13	252	19.4	28
2005	MTL	4				2													7	59	8.4	15	0					8	167	20.9	45
2	Years	7				3													7	59	8.4	15	0	20	174	8.7	32	21	419	20.0	45
MIKE GILLOCK Michael J. DB 5'10 175 Indianapolis B: 5/20/1972																															
1996	OTT	2				6					2																				
WILLIE GILLUS Willie Harden QB 6'4 215 Norfolk State B: 9/1/1963 Emporia, VA Pro: N																															
1988	BC	1				0																									
1989	OTT	2				0																									

Year	Team	GP	FM	FF	FR	TK	SK	YDS	IR	YDS	PD	PTS	TD	RA	YDS	AVG	LG	TD	REC	YDS	AVG	LG	TD	PR	YDS	AVG	LG	KOR	YDS	AVG	LG
1990	TOR	3				0						12	2	4	53	13.3	30	2													
1991	TOR	18				0						6	1	14	69	4.9	16	1													
4	Years	24				0						18	3	18	122	6.8	30	3													
WILL GILMORE Wilbert C. DB 6'0 208 Tulane B: 9/19/1972																															
1995	BIR	1				0																									
GEORGE GIOKAS George HB-T-E none																															
1947	SAS	8																													
1948	SAS	12																													
1949	SAS	14																													
3	Years	34																													
CHRIS GIOSKOS Chris OG 6'2 274 Ottawa B: 12/15/1967 Hamilton, ON Draft: 2B-15 1990 SAS																															
1990	SAS	14	0		1	0																									
1991	SAS	18				0																									
1992	SAS	18				2																									
1993	OTT	18				0																									
1994	OTT	17				1																									
1995	TOR	14				1																									
1996	TOR	18				0																									
1997	TOR	17				1																									
1998	TOR	18	0	1	0	2																									
1999	TOR	15				0																									
10	Years	167	0	1	1	7																									
PHILIPPE GIRARD Philippe DB-LB 6'2 215 Mount Allison B: 12/10/1973 Montreal, QC Draft: 1-5 1998 EDM																															
1998	EDM	18	0	0	1	24																									
1999	EDM	13				16																									
2000	EDM	7				7																		1	0	0.0	0				
2001	EDM	5	0	1	0	6																									
2003	MTL	14				0																									
2004	MTL	12				7																									
6	Years	69	0	1	1	60																		1	0	0.0	0				
SYLVAIN GIRARD Sylvain WR 6'1 198 Concordia (Canada) B: 10/3/1975 Chicoutimi, QC Draft: 1A-5 1999 MTL																															
1999	MTL	9				3													5	53	10.6	16	0					1	0	0.0	0
2000	MTL	18	0	0	1	10						6	1						4	34	8.5	14	0					1	0	0.0	0
2001	MTL	17	0	0	1	7						12	2						13	287	22.1	46	2					2	43	21.5	22
2002	MTL	18	0	1	1	9						12	2						11	202	18.4	42	2								
2003	MTL	14	0	1	0	8						18	3						29	477	16.4	67	3					0	13		13
2004	MTL	9	1	0	1	3						12	2						31	659	21.3	54	2								
2005	MTL	14	0	0	1	1						12	2	2	26	13.0	14	0	21	198	9.4	30	1								
2006	MTL	4				0													8	65	8.1	17	0								
8	Years	103	1	2	5	41						72	12	2	26	13.0	14	0	122	1975	16.2	67	10					4	56	14.0	22
RICHARD GIRAUD Richard (Butts) OG 6'0 240 Florida; Western Washington B: 1947																															
1970	WPG	12																													
PAUL GIRODAY Paul LB 6'2 225 California B: 3/20/1951 Draft: 2A-10 1973 BC																															
1975	BC	9	0		1																										
1976	BC	16							1	26																		3	22	7.3	22
1977	BC	16	0		3				1	13																		1	0	0.0	0
1978	BC	16	0		1																							2	10	5.0	10
1979	BC	9	0		1																										
5	Years	66	0		6				2	39																		6	32	5.3	22
PAUL GIRODO Paul LB 5'11 210 British Columbia B: 8/6/1973 Ottawa, ON																															
1998	WPG	6				2																									
1999	WPG	5				0																									
1999	SAS	10	0	1	0	7																									
1999	Year	15				7																									
2000	SAS	5	0	0	1	1																									
3	Years	16	0	1	1	10																									
PETER GISBORN Peter OT 6'2 275 Wilfrid Laurier B: 11/12/1969 Hamilton, ON																															
1994	HAM	7				4																									
LEE GISSENDANER Lee WR 5'9 175 Northwestern B: 10/25/1971 Akron, OH Draft: 6A-187 1994 HOU Pro: E																															
1995	TOR	1				0													1	5	5.0	5	0					2	16	8.0	10
REGGIE GIVENS Reginald Alonzo LB 6'0 234 Penn State B: 10/3/1971 Emporia, VA Draft: 8B-213 1993 DAL Pro: N																															
1994	WPG	4				16	2.0	12.0	1	0																					
1995	WPG	1				3																									
1995	BAL	4				7																									
1995	Year	5				10																									
1996	TOR+	18	1		4	68	8.0	58.0	1	0	3			1	1	1.0	1	0													
1997	TOR	18	0	3	2	59	6.0	57.0	1	6	6	12	2																		
2002	TOR	11	0	0	1	42	1.0																								
2004	OTT	8	0	1	1	49						6	1																		
6	Years	60	1	4	8	244	17.0	127.0	3	6	9	18	3	1	1	1.0	1	0													
CHET GLADCHUK Chester Stephen T 6'4 247 Boston College B: 4/4/1917 Bridgeport, CT D: 9/4/1967 Northampton, MA Draft: 2-12 1941 PIT Pro: N																															
1949	MTL	12																													
RONNIE GLANTON Ronnie L. DT 5'10 250 Livingston B: 4/17/1966 Dothan, AL																															
1989	HAM	8				25																									
1990	HAM	3	0		1	6	1.0																								
2	Years	11	0		1	31	1.0																								
DON GLANTZ Donald Robert T 6'0 215 Nebraska B: 7/8/1933 Central City, NE Draft: 5-52 1955 WAS																															
1955	EDM	15																													
JIM GLASGOW Jim R. DT 6'5 240 Jacksonville State B: 1935 Draft: SS 1960 HOU; 14-159 1960 DET																															
1960	MTL	1																													
RYAN GLASPER Ryan E. S 5'11 215 Boston College B: 6/15/1985 New Britain, CT Pro: U																															
2007	HAM	8	0	1	0	37					2																				
2008	HAM	10				35																									
2	Years	18	0	1	0	72					2																				
BILL GLASS William Sheppeard T 6'5 252 Baylor B: 8/16/1935 Texarkana, TX Draft: 1-12 1957 DET Pro: N																															
1957	SAS	11							3	21																					
SULLY GLASSER Sully HB-FB 5'10 180 none B: 1923 Regina, SK																															
1946	SAS+	8										11	2					1					1								
1947	SAS	8										10	2										2								
1948	SAS	12										20	4					1					2								
1949	SAS	8										5	1					1													
1950	SAS	14										10	2	17	51	3.0		1	3	46	15.3		1								
1951	SAS	13										5	1	35	177	5.1		1	2	36	18.0		0	6	30	5.0		2	41	20.5	
1952	SAS	16							2	48				58	267	4.6	22	0	1	20	20.0	20	0	4	6	1.5	4	3	67	22.3	31
1953	SAS	15										5	1	75	333	4.4		1	10	90	9.0		0					1	4	4.0	4
1954	SAS	16	2									10	2	96	395	4.1	15	2	6	60	10.0	24	0								
1955	SAS	16	3											102	500	4.9	17	0	9	118	13.1	19	0	1	5	5.0	5				
1956	SAS	16												40	177	4.4	33	0	14	42	3.0	16	0	1	0	0.0	0				
1957	SAS	13	1											25	111	4.4	12	0	1	14	14.0	14	0					2	31	15.5	15
12	Years	155	6		0				2	48		76	15	448	2011	4.5	33	8	46	426	9.3	24	6	12	41	3.4	5	8	143	17.9	31
JOHN GLASSFORD John LB 6'2 220 Wilfrid Laurier B: 6/5/1953 Draft: 3-25 1976 SAS																															
1977	OTT	16	0		1																										

Year	Team	GP	FM	FF	FR	TK	SK	YDS	IR	YDS	PD	PTS	TD	RA	YDS	AVG	LG	TD	REC	YDS	AVG	LG	TD	PR	YDS	AVG	LG	KOR	YDS	AVG	LG
1978	OTT	16																						1	2	2.0	2	1	17	17.0	17
1979	OTT	16	0		2																			1	0	0.0	0				
1980	OTT	16	0		2																										
1981	OTT	16	0		2		1.0		1	5		2	0						1	5	5.0	5	0								
1982	OTT	16	0		1				2	31																					
6	Years	96	0		8		1.0		3	36		2	0						1	5	5.0	5	0	2	2	1.0	2	1	17	17.0	17
JAVIER GLATT Javier LB 6'1 225 British Columbia B: 10/10/1981 Calgary, AB Draft: 2-15 2003 BC																															
2003	BC	18				26																									
2004	BC	12	0	1	0	23					1																				
2005	BC	18	0	0	1	55																									
2006	BC	18	0	1	1	91	6.0	45.0	4	93	4																				
2007	BC	15	0	1	0	56	4.0	14.0	1	56	2	6	1																		
2008	BC+	18	0	2	1	95	2.0	7.0	2	0	2																				
2009	BC	18	0	0	1	66	2.0	9.0	2	46	1																				
2010	EDM	18	0	1	0	32			2	15	0													1	10	10.0	10	3	17	5.7	18
8	Years	135	0	6	4	444	14.0	75.0	11	210	10	6	1											1	10	10.0	10	3	17	5.7	18
SASHA GLAVIC Sasha DB-LB 6'3 191 Windsor B: 5/9/1983 Pickering, ON																															
2007	HAM	9				3																									
2008	HAM	10	0	1	0	14																									
2009	HAM	8				3																									
3	Years	27	0	1	0	20																									
PATRICK GLEASON Patrick C 6'2 245 Western Ontario B: 3/3/1970																															
1995	TOR	4				0																									
HOWARD GLENN Howard Earl OT 6'0 225 Linfield B: 9/26/1934 Vancouver, WA D: 10/9/1960 Houston, TX Pro: N																															
1959	HAM	1																													
KEVIN GLENN Kevin QB 5'10 189 Illinois State B: 6/12/1979 Detroit, MI																															
2001	SAS	18	3	0	0	1						12	2	28	152	5.4	20	2													
2002	SAS	11	4	0	1	1						6	1	21	83	4.0	20	1													
2003	SAS	18	1	0	0	1								13	48	3.7	11	0													
2004	WPG	8	2	0	0	0						12	2	30	125	4.2	17	2													
2005	WPG	15	3	0	0	1						6	1	30	103	3.4	18	1	1	10	10.0	10	0								
2006	WPG	16	3	0	1	1						12	2	40	194	4.9	15	2													
2007	WPG+	18	5	0	1	2								41	132	3.2	14	0													
2008	WPG	18	3	0	1	2								29	102	3.5	13	0													
2009	HAM	18	3	0	0	0						12	2	21	134	6.4	22	2													
2010	HAM	18	4	0	1	2								27	185	6.9	22	0													
2011	HAM	18	2	0	1	0						6	1	21	112	5.3	15	1													
11	Years	176	33	0	6	11						66	11	301	1370	4.6	22	11	1	10	10.0	10	0								
O'NEIL GLENN O'Neil OG 6'2 290 Nassau CC; Maryland B: 1/27/1968 Hempstead, NY Draft: 9-224 1991 NE Pro: E																															
1994	BAL	5				0																									
STEVE GLENN Steve LB 6'3 230 Ottawa B: 5/4/1971 Ottawa, ON																															
1996	MTL	1				0																									
1996	BC	7				7																									
1996	Year	8				7																									
1997	BC	6				17																									
1998	BC	7				8																									
1999	WPG	18				11																									
2000	WPG	18				14																									
2001	WPG	18				12																									
2002	OTT	18				10																									
2003	OTT	18				4																									
2004	OTT	18	1	0	0	9																									
2005	SAS	12	2	0	0	2																									
10	Years	134	3	0	0	94																									
TOM GLENN Tom C-G 6'0 215																															
1946	TOR	11																													
1948	OTT	1																													
2	Years	12																													
BILL GLENNON William Patrick DE 6'3 240 Washington B: 12/12/1945 Billings, MT Draft: 7B-189 1968 PIT																															
1970	WPG	16																													
BERNIE GLIER Bernie DB-LB 6'1 195 British Columbia B: 6/9/1960 Vancouver, BC Draft: 1A-5 1982 BC																															
1983	BC	16	0		1		1.0		5	83																					
1984	BC	16	0		1				1	3									1	14	14.0	14	0								
1985	BC	16	0		1		1.0																								
1986	BC	11					1.0																								
1987	BC	17				41			1	2									1	8	8.0	8	0					1	1	1.0	1
1988	BC	14				2																									
1989	BC	12	0		1	20																									
7	Years	102	0		4	63	3.0		7	88									2	22	11.0	14	0					1	1	1.0	1
BILL GLOSSON William (Rock) OE-DB 6'0 185 Texas Southern B: 1937																															
1959	MTL	8							1	3		18	3						14	304	21.7	44	3					1	18	18.0	18
CLYDE GLOVER Clyde M. DL 6'6 280 Walla Walla CC; Fresno State B: 7/16/1960 New Orleans, LA Draft: TD 1984 OAK-USFL Pro: N																															
1985	TOR	5					2.0																								
LaVAR GLOVER LaVar A. CB 5'9 175 Cincinnati B: 12/17/1978 Dayton, OH Draft: 7A-212 2002 PIT Pro: N																															
2006	BC	18				32			2	13	5																				
2007	BC+	18				35			3	29	9																				
2008	BC	18	0	0	1	41			2	67	7	12	2																		
2009	BC	5				11					3																				
2010	WPG	12				34			2	39	4																				
5	Years	71	0	0	1	153			9	148	28	12	2																		
RICHARD GLOVER Richard L. DE 6'3 260 Michigan State B: 6/25/1971 Lima, OH																															
1994	SAS	2	0		1	4	2.0																								
1994	EDM	5				3																									
1994	Year	7	0		1	7	2.0																								
FRANK GNUP Frank Theodore QB-HB 5'10 180 Manhattan B: 1917 Aliquippa, PA D: 9/27/1976 Vancouver, BC																															
1948	HAM	6										5	1					1													
1950	TOR	6																													
2	Years	12										5	1					1													
PAUL GOAD Paul Ellis FB-HB 6'0 195 Tulane; Abilene Christian B: 9/7/1934 Cincinnati, OH D: 11/29/1978 Little Rock, AR Draft: 25-291 1956 SF Pro: N																															
1957	BC	1												9	44	4.9	9	0	1	4	4.0	4	0								
LARRY GOBLE Lawrence T-E 6'3 235 Western Ontario B: 1935																															
1958	BC	5																													
MARVIN GODBOLT Marvin T. LB 6'1 208 Texas Christian B: 6/5/1982																															
2005	TOR	1				0																									
KEITH GODDING Keith WR 5'11 193 Bishop's B: 1/28/1984 Ajax, ON																															
2010	TOR	4				0																									
WILF GODFREY Wilf HB-FW 5'9 175 Saskatoon Hilltops Jrs. B: 1928																															
1949	SAS	13										1	0																		
1950	CAL	13										6	0																		
1951	CAL	10																	1	27	27.0	27	0	1	9	9.0	9				
1952	CAL	14							1	14														2	24	12.0	17				
4	Years	50							1	14		7	0						1	27	27.0	27	0	3	33	11.0	17				

Year	Team	GP	FM	FF	FR	TK	SK	YDS	IR	YDS	PD	PTS	TD	RA	YDS	AVG	LG	TD	REC	YDS	AVG	LG	TD	PR	YDS	AVG	LG	KOR	YDS	AVG	LG
BRANDON GODSEY Brandon L. CB 6'0 200 Miami (Ohio) B: 9/10/1978 Springfield, OH Pro: E																															
2002	BC	4				8																									
2003	BC	1				3																									
2	Years	5				11																									
RON GOETZ Ronald William LB 6'3 236 Minnesota B: 2/8/1968 Waconia, MN Draft: 12-324 1990 MIN Pro: E																															
1993	OTT	17	0		1	78	8.0	54.0	1	-2																					
1994	SAS*	18	0		2	115	7.0	44.0	4	28	3																				
1995	SAS	17	0		3	69	6.0	57.0			7			1	7	7.0	7	0													
1996	SAS	6	0		1	20			1	0	1																				
1997	SAS	2	0	1	0	8																									
5	Years	60	0	1	7	290	21.0	155.0	6	26	11			1	7	7.0	7	0													
JEFF GOFF Jeff LB 6'1 215 Arkansas B: 12/27/1959 Fort Smith, AR Draft: 12B-322 1982 WAS																															
1983	EDM	1																													
PAUL GOHIER Paul OT 6'4 280 McGill B: 9/12/1957 Draft: 2-14 1980 BC																															
1983	HAM	7																													
RUSS GOINGS Russell L., Jr. G 6'2 226 Xavier (Ohio) B: 1932 Draft: 24-287 1959 CLE																															
1959	SAS	7																													
TONY GOLAB Tony HB-FW 6'2 210 none B: 1/17/1919 Windsor, ON																															
1946	OTT	12										13	2					2													
1947	OTT+	10										17	3					2													
1948	OTT+	11										46	9					7					1								
1949	OTT	6										17	3					3													
1950	OTT	11										5	1					1													
5	Years	50										98	18					15					1								
MIKE GOLD Mike OT 6'4 257 Utah State Draft: 8-193 1967 STL																															
1969	EDM	4																													
DOUG GOLDSBY Douglas Evan S 6'2 220 British Columbia B: 12/23/1986 Sacramento, CA																															
2009	MTL	4				3																									
VINCE GOLDSMITH Vincent P. DE-DT-LB 5'11 237 Oregon B: 7/20/1959 Fort Riley, KS																															
1981	SAS+	16					17.0																								
1982	SAS	16					12.5																								
1983	SAS+	15	0		2		20.0					6	1																		
1984	TOR	16	0		1		12.0		1	0																					
1985	CAL	10	0		1		6.0																								
1986	CAL	18	0		1		15.0					6	1																		
1987	CAL	18	0		5	31	12.0					12	2																		
1988	SAS+	18			2	31	15.0		0	5																					
1989	SAS	18	0		2	30	12.0																								
1990	SAS	18	0		3	37	9.0																								
10	Years	163	0		17	129	130.5		1	5		24	4																		
RALPH GOLDSTON Ralph Peter CB-OHB-OE 5'11 195 Indiana; Youngstown State B: 2/25/1929 Campbell, OH D: 7/9/2011 Columbus, OH Draft: 11-125 1952 PHI Pro: N																															
1956	HAM+	8							1	27		48	8	18	74	4.1	22	1	20	397	19.9	75	7					2	0	0.0	0
1957	HAM+	14							7	46				76	341	4.5	17	0	9	122	13.6	38	0					3	61	20.3	33
1958	HAM+	14							5	61				20	84	4.2	14	0	2	8	4.0	6	0	1	2	2.0	2				
1959	HAM+	14							9	131		6	1	6	35	5.8	14	0						2	3	1.5	3				
1960	HAM	11							3	7				9	32	3.6	6	0	2	13	6.5	15	0	1	0	0.0	0				
1961	HAM	13							2	9		18	3	10	43	4.3	7	1	25	414	16.6	72	2					2	19	9.5	14
1962	HAM	14							2	10				22	82	3.7	11	0	7	57	8.1	16	0	1	17	17.0	17	1	5	5.0	5
1963	HAM	14							1	43									1	10	10.0	10	0								
1964	HAM	14	0		2				1	16														1	4	4.0	4				
1965	MTL	14							1	66				8	25	3.1	6	0													
10	Years	130	0		2				32	416		72	12	169	716	4.2	22	2	66	1021	15.5	75	9	6	26	4.3	17	8	85	10.6	33
BOB GOLIC Robert OT-DT-DE 6'3 235 Indiana B: 1932 Willowick, OH																															
1956	MTL	6																													
1956	HAM	6																													
1956	Year	12																													
1957	HAM	5																													
1959	SAS	15										6	1																		
1960	SAS	15	0		1																										
1961	SAS	14																													
1962	SAS	3																													
6	Years	58	0		1							6	1																		
DAVE GOLINSKY David OG-OT 6'4 249 Washington State B: 1948																															
1969	BC	16																													
1970	BC	16	0		1																										
1971	BC	16																													
1972	BC	16																													
4	Years	64	0		1																										
DIMITRI GOLOUBEF Dimitri E 6'2 197 British Columbia B: 1924																															
1949	EDM	14										10	2										2								
1950	EDM	14																	2	40	20.0		0								
2	Years	28										10	2							2	40	20.0		2								
JUSTIN GOLTZ Justin QB 6'5 215 Occidental B: 8/23/1987 Walled Lake, MI																															
2010	WPG	2				0																									
2011	WPG	15				0																									
2	Years	17				0																									
RICK GOLTZ Ricardo Eugene DT 6'4 255 Simon Fraser B: 3/19/1955 Vancouver, BC Draft: 1-3 1978 BC Pro: N																															
1978	BC	15																													
1979	BC	8																													
1980	BC	16	0		1																										
1981	BC	9					6.0																								
1982	BC	16	0		1		3.0																								
1983	CAL	16					5.5																								
1984	SAS	16	0		2		9.0																								
1985	SAS	11					5.0																								
1986	SAS	18	0		1		6.0																								
1987	SAS	4				2																									
10	Years	129	0		5	2	34.5																								
DARWIN GONNERMAN Darwin Lynn FB-HB-SE 5'11 200 South Dakota State B: 1/3/1947 Rock County, MN																															
1969	OTT	6										6	1					0					1								
1969	WPG	3																0					0								
1969	Year	9										6	1	5	-2	-0.4	3	0	8	113	14.1	20	1					6	175	29.2	39
1970	EDM	2												7	31	4.4	10	0	3	37	12.3	17	0					6	175	29.2	39
2	Years	8										6	1	7	31	4.4	10	0	3	37	12.3	17	1					6	175	29.2	39
GUS GONZALES Gus E., Jr. G 6'2 230 Tulane B: 7/27/1940 Draft: 7-55 1962 HOU; 6A-77 1962 PHI																															
1963	TOR	4																													
1965	MTL	14	0		1																										
2	Years	18	0	0	1																										
DAN GONZALEZ Daniel QB 6'3 214 East Carolina B: 9/20/1974 Neptune, NJ Pro: E																															
2000	MTL	10				0																									
2001	MTL	18	1	0	0	1								9	7	0.8	3	0													
2	Years	28	1	0	0	1								9	7	0.8	3	0													

Year	Team	GP	FM	FF	FR	TK	SK	YDS	IR	YDS	PD	PTS	TD	RA	YDS	AVG	LG	TD	REC	YDS	AVG	LG	TD	PR	YDS	AVG	LG	KOR	YDS	AVG	LG
JOHN GONZALEZ Juan I. DE-DT 6'3 255 Oregon State B: 4/26/1963 Stockton, CA																														
1986	SAS	5																												
JOSE GONZALEZ Jose DT 6'4 260 Miami (Florida) B: 9/15/1952 Havana, Cuba Pro: W																														
1975	BC	1																												
PETE GONZALEZ Pete 1B 6'1 217 Pittsburgh B: 7/24/1974 Miami, FL Pro: N																														
2002	HAM	18				0								1	15	15.0	15	0													
2003	HAM	18	2	0	0	0						12	2	10	32	3.2	10	2													
2	Years	36	2	0	0	0						12	2	11	47	4.3	15	2													
KEITH GOOCH Keith N. CB 5'10 170 Fresno State B: 8/31/1959 Fort Ord, CA																														
1984	BC	5							2	42																					
1985	BC	16					1.0		2	40														1	12	12.0	12				
1986	BC	18	0		1				8	55														4	13	3.3	6				
1987	BC+	18	1		5	44	1.0		9	122		12	2											1	3	3.0	3				
1988	BC	18	0		1	60			7	71																					
1989	BC	17	1		3	41			6	167		18	3						1	21	21.0	21	0	1	5	5.0	5	0	31		31
1990	EDM+	18	0		1	49			7	160		6	1											1	6	6.0	6	1	0	0.0	0
7	Years	110	2		11	194	2.0		41	657		36	6						1	21	21.0	21	0	8	39	4.9	12	1	31	31.0	31
BOB GOOD Robert OHB 5'11 185 Oregon State; Queen's B: 1940																														
1962	SAS	16												1	9	9.0	9	0	1	11	11.0	11	0	1	2	2.0	2	2	34	17.0	22
1963	SAS	16												23	125	5.4	28	0	4	50	12.5	13	0					1	4	4.0	4
1964	SAS	15	1		1							12	2	33	169	5.1	29	1	9	99	11.0	33	1					5	96	19.2	40
1965	SAS	10	1		1									11	40	3.6	11	0	2	15	7.5	10	0	the							
1966	TOR	10	1		1									14	37	2.6	10	0	4	35	8.8	20	0					1	0	0.0	0
5	Years	67	3		3							12	2	82	380	4.6	29	1	20	210	10.5	33	1	1	2	2.0	2	9	134	14.9	40
DARRYL GOODEN Darryl LB 6'2 235 Carson-Newman B: 3/8/1971																														
1995	MEM	3				4																									
DARYL GOODLOW Daryl D. LB 6'2 235 Oklahoma B: 11/2/1960 St. Louis, MO Draft: TD 1984 OKL-USFL Pro: NU																														
1985	TOR	1																												
1986	TOR	4					2.0																							
2	Years	5					2.0																							
EUGENE GOODLOW Eugene WR 6'2 190 Kansas State B: 12/19/1958 St. Louis, MO Draft: 3B-66 1982 NO Pro: N																														
1980	WPG	5	1		0							6	1						17	206	12.1	43	1	3	22	7.3	11	2	38	19.0	22
1981	WPG+	16	0		2							84	14						100	1494	14.9	85	14					4	72	18.0	27
1982	WPG	6										48	8						30	515	17.2	58	8								
1989	OTT	2																	1	36	36.0	36	0								
4	Years	29	1		2							138	23						148	2251	15.2	85	23	3	22	7.3	11	6	110	18.3	27
NORM GOODMAN Norman DE-DT 6'3 228 Missouri B: 7/8/1956																														
1980	TOR	15	0		1																										
1981	TOR	1																												
2	Years	16	0		1																										
BENNIE GOODS Bennie DT-LB-DE 6'3 255 Alcorn State B: 2/20/1968 Pattison, MS																														
1990	EDM	2				1	1.0																								
1991	EDM	12	0		1	15	5.0																								
1992	EDM	18	0		1	32	10.0	70.0																							
1993	EDM+	18	0		3	27	14.0	135.0				6	1																			
1994	EDM*	18	0		1	24	9.0	65.0																							
1995	EDM*	17	0		1	31	14.0	117.0																							
1996	EDM*	18	0		1	25	12.0	83.0			1																				
1997	EDM+	14	0	0	1	29	4.0	38.0																				1	14	14.0	14
1998	EDM	18	0	2	1	29	6.0	47.0																				1	9	9.0	9
1999	WPG	16	0	2	3	31	5.0	23.0			1																				
2000	WPG	17	0	0	1	21	2.0	12.0	1	3	0																				
11	Years	168	0	4	14	265	82.0	590.0	1	3	2	6	1															2	23	11.5	14
BILL GOODS Bill FB-OHB-LB 6'0 206 Mount Royal College Jrs.; Tulsa B: 1942																														
1965	CAL	16												13	62	4.8	15	0										1	12	12.0	12
1966	CAL	16	1		0				1	0		12	2	48	211	4.4	30	1	4	48	12.0	20	1					4	59	14.8	15
1967	CAL	16	1		0							70	0	14	56	4.0	13	0										4	82	20.5	31
1968	SAS	16										78	0	22	98	4.5	25	0	7	76	10.9	15	0					1	0	0.0	0
1969	EDM	2										3	0																		
5	Years	66	2		0				1	0		163	2	97	427	4.4	30	1	11	124	11.3	20	1					10	153	15.3	31
DAN GOODSPEED Daniel Edward OT 6'6 300 Walsh; Kent State B: 5/20/1977 Cleveland, OH Pro: NX																														
2005	WPG	16				1																									
2006	WPG	5				0																									
2007	WPG*	18	0	0	2	1																									
2008	WPG*	18				0																									
2009	HAM*	18	0	0	1	3																									
2010	SAS	18				1																									
2011	SAS	18				1																									
7	Years	111	0	0	3	7																									
TIM GOODWELL Timothy Lawrence, II LB 6'0 243 Memphis B: 1/30/1984 Houston, TX Pro: E																														
2007	BC	4				7																									
2008	BC	1				2																									
2	Years	5				9																									
MALCOLM GOODWIN Malcolm DE-LB 6'2 230 Iowa State B: 7/15/1970 Philadelphia, PA																														
1994	BAL	17	0		2	41						18	3																		
1995	BAL	5				10			2	9	5																				
2	Years	22	0		2	51			2	9	5	18	3																		
MATT GOODWIN Matt CB-LB 6'2 205 Iowa State B: 7/15/1970 Philadelphia, PA																														
1994	BAL	17	0		8	72	3.0	38.0	3	54	5																				
1995	BAL	15	0		3	60	1.0	9.0																							
2	Years	32	0		11	132	4.0	47.0	3	54	5																				
TOM GOOSBY Tom Aaron OG 6'0 235 Baldwin-Wallace B: 5/24/1939 Alliance, OH Draft: 15-207(f) 1962 CLE Pro: N																														
1967	BC	4	0		1																										
ALEX GORDON Alex Groncier DE 6'5 245 Cincinnati B: 9/14/1964 Jacksonville, FL Draft: 2-42 1987 NYJ Pro: N																														
1995	MEM	16	0		2	61	7.0	53.0	0	0	3																				
1996	TOR	7				10	4.0	29.0	0	0	1																				
2	Years	23	0		2	71	11.0	82.0																							
ANDY GORDON Andrew J. QB 6'0 175 Pennsylvania; Villanova B: 1927																														
1949	OTT+	12										16	3					2					1								
1950	OTT	12										20	4					3													
2	Years	24										36	7					5					1								
BOB GORDON Robert WR 5'10 185 Nebraska-Omaha B: 7/9/1968 Detroit, MI																														
1991	OTT	8	2		0	2						6	1						25	410	16.4	56	1	10	94	9.4	40	20	365	18.3	30
1992	OTT	12	1		0	4						6	1						28	441	15.8	62	1	4	-15	-3.8	4	7	96	13.7	29
1993	TOR	7				1														20	266	13.3	24	0	13	104	8.0	27	11	289	26.3	48
1994	TOR	18	1		2	6						54	9	3	1	0.3	4	0	73	1002	13.7	46	9	8	79	9.9	40	31	588	19.0	41
1995	BC	16	1		0	4						24	4	1	15	15.0	15	0	48	824	17.2	44	4	32	249	7.8	43	1	13	13.0	13
1996	OTT	17	0		1	0						48	8						70	1049	15.0	55	8	15	55	3.7	12	4	67	16.8	25
1997	EDM	18	1	0	1	4						44	7	4	7	1.8	8	0	71	1073	15.1	39	7	2	13	6.5	11	1	18	18.0	18
1999	WPG+	15	1	0	0	0						24	4						59	863	14.6	44	4	18	161	8.9	22	15	291	19.4	36
2000	WPG+	18	1	0	0	4						44	7						89	1395	15.7	65	7	4	43	10.8	23	2	20	10.0	20
2001	WPG	12				3						24	4						54	857	15.9	46	4								

Year	Team	GP	FM	FF	FR	TK	SK	YDS	IR	YDS	PD	PTS	TD	RA	YDS	AVG	LG	TD	REC	YDS	AVG	LG	TD	PR	YDS	AVG	LG	KOR	YDS	AVG	LG
2002	WPG	2				1													7	82	11.7	20	0								
2003	WPG	16	1	0	0	1						24	4						47	896	19.1	51	4					1	21	21.0	21
2004	WPG	10				0						6	1						32	381	11.9	30	1					2	48	24.0	27
13	Years	169	9	0	4	30						304	50	8	23	2.9	15	0	623	9539	15.3	65	50	106	783	7.4	43	95	1816	19.1	48
CHARLES GORDON Charles DB 6'0 185 Eastern Michigan B: 7/30/1968 East Lansing, MI
1991	OTT	17				46			1	20									1	8	8.0	8	0								
1992	OTT	14	0		1	61			7	82																					
1993	OTT	9	0		1	30			3	51		6	1																		
1994	BC*	18				63			8	123	16	6	1																		
1995	BC	17	1		0	55			7	155	6	12	2																		
1996	MTL*	18	0		1	42	1.0	10.0	7	127	4	12	2						2	27	13.5	17	0								
1997	MTL	11	0	1	0	22			2	32	4	6	1																		
7	Years	104	1	1	3	319	1.0	10.0	35	590	30	42	7						3	35	11.7	17	0								
CURTIS GORDON Curtis WR 6'2 185 Greenville B: 8/18/1968 Chicago, IL
1995	HAM	4	1		0	0								1	4	4.0	4	0	9	141	15.7	35	0								
GREG GORDON Greg DB 6'2 192 Wisconsin B: 2/27/1957 Mobile, AL
1980	OTT	2							1	26																					
JERRY GORDON Jeremy Dale WR 5'10 175 Grambling State B: 9/10/1959 Huntsville, AL Pro: U
1987	CAL	2				0													3	44	14.7	27	0								
LAWRENCE GORDON Lawrence CB-DH 5'11 175 Florida Atlantic B: 3/30/1984 Hallandale, FL
2006	HAM	8				26			2	0	5																				
2007	HAM	18	0	1	0	61			2	0	6																				
2008	HAM	18	1	0	3	76					10																	1	18	18.0	18
2009	HAM	11	0	0	2	21					2																				
2010	EDM	16	0	1	0	62					4																				
5	Years	71	1	2	5	246			4	0	27																	1	18	18.0	18
SCOTT GORDON Scott S 5'11 200 Ottawa B: 2/21/1977 Kanata, ON Draft: 2B-18 2002 CAL
2002	SAS	8				5					1																				
2003	SAS	5				2																									
2004	SAS	17				26																									
2005	SAS	18	0	0	1	48	3.0	13.0			5																				
2006	HAM	4				4																									
2007	SAS	18	1	0	0	19	1.0	11.0	1	0	0																				
2008	SAS	16				33			1	9	1																				
2009	EDM	7				13			2	22	3																				
8	Years	93	1	0	1	150	4.0	24.0	4	31	10																				
SONNY GORDON Denman Preston S 5'11 182 Ohio State B: 7/30/1965 Lynn, MA Draft: 6-157 1987 CIN Pro: N
1989	HAM	18	2		3	68			3	133		12	2											7	57	8.1	18				
1990	HAM	15	0		1	54	1.0		1	57		6	1											4	25	6.3	10				
1991	SAS	5				21			1	9																					
3	Years	38	2		4	143	1.0		5	199		18	3											11	82	7.5	18				
SHAWN GORE Shawn SB-WR 6'0 198 Bishop's B: 4/12/1987 Toronto, ON Draft: 2-10 2010 BC
2010	BC	8				8																									
2011	BC	18	2	0	0	3						6	1	12	85	7.1	19	0	60	836	13.9	51	1					1	0	0.0	0
2	Years	26	2	0	0	11						6	1	12	85	7.1	19	0	60	836	13.9	51	1					1	0	0.0	0
ROGER GOREE Roger Neal LB 6'0 203 Baylor B: 11/4/1951 Draft: 15-365 1973 HOU
1973	CAL	16	0		1				2	12																					
1974	CAL	16	0		1				5	53		12	2															1	12	12.0	12
1975	SAS	16																													
1976	SAS	16							5	70																					
1977	SAS	16	0		3				1	0		6	1																		
1978	SAS	16	0		1																										
1979	SAS	9	0		1				1	54																					
1980	SAS	16	0		2				1	11																					
8	Years	121	0		9				15	200		18	3															1	12	12.0	12
MILES GORRELL Miles OT-DT 6'7 285 Calgary Mohawks Jrs.; Ottawa B: 10/16/1955 Calgary, AB Draft: TE 1978 CAL
1978	CAL	16							1	7																					
1979	CAL	16	0		1																										
1980	CAL	16	1		0																							1	0	0.0	0
1981	CAL	16					2.0																								
1982	CAL	8					2.0																								
1982	OTT	2																													
1982	MTL	7																													
1982	Year	17					2.0																								
1983	MTL+	16	0		2																										
1984	MTL+	16																													
1985	MTL	10																													
1985	HAM	1																													
1985	Year	11																													
1986	HAM+	18																													
1987	HAM	17				2																									
1988	HAM+	18				2																									
1989	HAM*	18	0		3	0																									
1990	HAM	18				2																									
1991	HAM	18				0																									
1992	WPG	18				3																									
1993	WPG	18	0		2	3																									
1994	WPG	18				1																									
1995	WPG	18				3																									
1996	HAM	18				0																									
19	Years	311	1		8	16	4.0		1	7																		1	0	0.0	0
PETE GOSICH Peter G-T 6'0 225
1951	OTT	2																													
1952	EDM	13																													
2	Years	15																													
JASON GOSS Jason Tamon C-DH-S 5'10 185 Texas Christian B: 10/4/1979 Fort Worth, TX Pro: N
2004	HAM	7	1	1	1	15					3													22	183	8.3	48	2	34	17.0	26
2005	HAM	18				55			7	187	7	12	2																		
2006	HAM	10				29	1.0	15.0	2	162	3	12	2																		
2007	EDM	18				45			5	164	6	12	2											11	84	7.6	15	0	5		5
2008	EDM*	18	3	0	4	52	1.0	10.0	5	182	6	12	2											1	5	5.0	5				
2009	EDM	18	0	1	0	60			3	23	7													7	42	6.0	15				
2010	EDM	15				43			3	72	1													1	4	4.0	4				
7	Years	104	4	2	5	299	2.0	25.0	25	790	33	48	8											42	318	7.6	48	2	39	19.5	26
GENE GOSSAGE Ezra Eugene OG-LB 6'3 239 Cincinnati; Northwestern B: 2/17/1935 Columbia, TN D: 5/1/2011 Old Saybrook, CT Draft: 28-328(f) 1958 PHI; FS 1960 DAL Pro: N
1963	HAM	8																													
1964	HAM	13																													
2	Years	21																													
JON GOTT Jon OG-C 6'2 294 Boise State B: 10/2/1985 Edmonton, AB Draft: 5-35 2008 CAL
2009	CAL	9				0																									
2010	CAL	3				0																									

Year	Team	GP	FM	FF	FR	TK	SK	YDS	IR	YDS	PD	PTS	TD	RA	YDS	AVG	LG	TD	REC	YDS	AVG	LG	TD	PR	YDS	AVG	LG	KOR	YDS	AVG	LG
2011	CAL	17				0																									
3	Years	29				0																									
JACK GOTTA John C. SE-DB 6'4 212 Minnesota State-Moorhead; Oregon State B: 11/14/1930 Bessemer, MI																															
1956	CAL	7	0		2							6	1						17	290	17.1	62	1								
1957	CAL+	16	1		1				5	60		12	2						39	652	16.7	47	2	1	10	10.0	10				
1958	CAL+	16	1		3				3	42		12	2						37	605	16.4	81	2					1	5	5.0	5
1959	CAL	7	0		1							6	1						6	96	16.0	27	1					1	0	0.0	0
1960	SAS	10	1		2				1			12	2						22	436	19.8	45	1					1	9	9.0	9
1961	SAS+	16			2							36	6						30	619	20.6	48	5					1	19	19.0	19
1962	SAS	16	1									18	3						39	779	20.0	73	3								
1963	SAS	16	1		0				1			30	5						34	478	14.1	38	4								
1964	SAS	5										6	1						7	100	14.3	17	1					1	3	3.0	3
1964	MTL	7										6	1						22	262	11.9	30	1								
1964	Year	12										12	2						29	362	12.5	30	2					1	3	3.0	3
9	Years	109	5		11				10	102		144	24						253	4317	17.1	81	21	1	10	10.0	10	5	36	7.2	19
JOHN GOUGH John E 6'5 210 Oklahoma B: NS																															
1952	EDM	1																													
1953	EDM	16																													
2	Years	17																													
CARL GOURGUES Carl OG 6'0 302 Rhode Island; Laval B: 7/8/1980 Cap-de-la-Madeleine, QC Draft: 3-24 2003 BC																															
2004	BC	12				0																									
2005	BC	12				0																									
2006	HAM	7				0																									
3	Years	31				0																									
VERN GOYER Vernon G-T 238 none																															
1946	TOR	1																													
JOHN GRACE John LB 5'10 215 Marshall B: 2/10/1977 Okeechobee, FL																															
2000	MTL	4				9																									
2001	MTL	3				3																									
2002	OTT*	16	0	8	5	82	4.0	23.0	3	37	1																				
2003	OTT	15	0	2	3	75	1.0	2.0	1	0	0																				
2004	CAL*	17	0	1	2	57	7.0	49.0	3	177	7	12	2																		
2005	CAL*	18	0	1	3	83	8.0	45.0	2	4	4	6	1																		
2006	CAL	12	0	2	0	54	4.0	18.0																							
2007	MTL	2				2																									
8	Years	87	0	14	13	365	24.0	137.0	9	218	14	18	3																		
FRANK GRAD Frank, Jr. T Regina Dales Jrs.																															
1946	SAS	7																													
DAVE GRAFFI David FB 6'0 220 Wilfird Laurier B: 6/10/1959 St. Catharines, ON																															
1981	HAM	16										6	1	21	89	4.2	14	1	9	68	7.6	32	0					1	0	0.0	0
1982	HAM	16										18	3	13	37	2.8	8	2	5	33	6.6	9	1								
1983	HAM	16	0		1									5	11	2.2	4	0	1	6	6.0	6	0					4	35	8.8	15
1984	HAM	16												17	50	2.9	13	0	6	54	9.0	13	0								
1985	HAM	16	1		1							6	1	17	60	3.5	9	0	18	115	6.4	13	1					3	18	6.0	10
1986	HAM	4												7	21	3.0	8	0	4	47	11.8	16	0								
6	Years	84	1		2							30	5	80	268	3.4	14	3	43	323	7.5	32	2					8	53	6.6	15
MIKE GRAFFI Michael LB 6'1 220 Wilfrid Laurier B: 5/4/1958																															
1982	OTT	14	0		2		1.0																								
1983	OTT	16																													
1984	HAM	1																										5	50	10.0	16
3	Years	31	0		2		1.0																					5	50	10.0	16
BILL GRAHAM Bill MG-OG-T 6'0 224 New Toronto Jrs.; Lakeshore Jrs.; East York Ints. B: 1938																															
1959	TOR	5																													
1960	TOR	4																													
1961	CAL	16																													
1962	BC	3																													
4	Years	28																													
BILLY GRAHAM Bill OHB 5'7 167 none B: 1936 Hamilton, ON																															
1953	HAM	4																													
1957	HAM	12										6	1	5	39	7.8	19	0	3	60	20.0	28	1	31	136	4.4	15	4	79	19.8	25
1958	HAM	10										7	0	1	2	2.0	2	0	1	24	24.0	14	0					2	39	19.5	21
1959	HAM	6												1	1	1.0	1	0	1	16	16.0	16	0					3	22	7.3	11
1960	HAM	2																													
5	Years	34										13	1	7	42	6.0	19	0	5	100	20.0	28	1	31	136	4.4	15	9	140	15.6	25
CHRIS GRAHAM Chris De'Monte LB 5'11 235 Michigan B: 9/30/1984 Indianapolis, IN																															
2011	SAS	4				18																									
DARNELL GRAHAM Darnell WR 5'11 185 Kent State B: 12/16/1963 Cleveland Heights, OH																															
1988	OTT	7				0																									
1989	TOR	2				0																						4	99	24.8	57
2	Years	9				0																						4	99	24.8	57
JAY GRAHAM Herman Jason RB 5'11 222 Tennessee B: 7/14/1975 Draft: 3-64 1997 BAL Pro: N																															
2003	MTL	4				1						24	4	37	135	3.6	19	4	6	67	11.2	28	0					1	5	5.0	5
JULIAN GRAHAM Julian DE 6'2 240 Pittsburgh B: 4/19/1977 Philadelphia, PA																															
2000	WPG	10				16	3.0	21.0			1																				
2001	WPG	8				0					1																				
2	Years	18				16	3.0	21.0			2																				
LORENZO GRAHAM Lorenzo RB 5'11 200 West Alabama B: 3/25/1965 Perdido, AL Pro: E																															
1988	TOR	10	3		1	1						30	5	82	432	5.3	31	4	16	134	8.4	24	1					8	237	29.6	86
1989	TOR	2				1								6	18	3.0	6	0	2	14	7.0	8	0					3	42	14.0	17
1989	CAL	12	5		0	0						54	9	136	650	4.8	38	6	19	328	17.3	35	3					17	372	21.9	48
1989	Year	14	5		0	1						54	9	142	668	4.7	38	6	21	342	16.3	35	3					20	414	20.7	48
1990	BC	13				2						44	7	96	476	5.0	22	6	45	441	9.8	41	1					33	830	25.2	52
1991	BC	13	1		0	10								25	191	7.6	64	0	2	25	12.5	19	0					49	1063	21.7	46
4	Years	38	9		1	14						128	21	345	1767	5.1	64	16	84	942	11.2	41	5					110	2544	23.1	86
MILT GRAHAM Milton Russell OT-DT-DE 6'6 235 Colgate B: 7/28/1934 Chatham, MA Draft: 14-167 1956 CHIB Pro: N																															
1956	OTT	7																													
1957	OTT	13																													
1958	OTT+	14							1	6		6	1						1	8	8.0	8	0								
1959	OTT	14																	2	28	14.0	19	0								
1960	OTT	14										6	1											1	0	0.0	0	1	0	0.0	0
1961	OTT	13																													
6	Years	75							1	6		12	2						3	36	12.0	19	0	1	0	0.0	0	1	0	0.0	0
NICK GRAHAM Nick Donnell CB 5'10 191 Tulsa B: 1/19/1984 Oklahoma City, OK Pro: N																															
2010	SAS	2				2																									
2011	SAS	17				57			2	8	5																				
2	Years	19				59			2	8	5																				
RANDY GRAHAM Randy CB 6'0 180 Simon Fraser B: 2/15/1954 Draft: 1A-2 1976 BC																															
1976	SAS	16																													
1977	SAS	16	0		1				3	47																					
1978	HAM	16							1	3																					
1979	HAM	16	0		1				1	9																					
1980	HAM	16	1		2				3	42																					

Year	Team	GP	FM	FF	FR	TK	SK	YDS	IR	YDS	PD	PTS	TD	RA	YDS	AVG	LG	TD	REC	YDS	AVG	LG	TD	PR	YDS	AVG	LG	KOR	YDS	AVG	LG
5	Years	80	1		4				8	101																					
SEAN GRAHAM Sean SB 6'3 220 British Columbia B: 7/26/1972 Richmond, BC Draft: Bonus-6 1995 WPG																															
1995	WPG	8				1													1	40	40.0	40	0								
1996	WPG	14	0		1	3													12	202	16.8	28	0								
1997	WPG	18				16													8	69	8.6	16	0								
1998	BC	3	1	0	1	12						12	2						12	147	12.3	20	1					1	0	0.0	0
1999	BC	13				4																									
2000	BC	15	1	1	0	2						6	1						25	364	14.6	41	1								
2001	BC	1				0																									
7	Years	72	2	1	2	38						18	3						58	822	14.2	41	2					1	0	0.0	0
VERN GRAHAM Vern FW-HB-K 6'0 182 B: 1924																															
1947	CAL	8																													
1949	CAL+	14										58	2										1								
1950	CAL	14										28	1	1	8	8.0	8	1	1	22	22.0	22	0								
1951	CAL	11																													
4	Years	47										86	3	1	8	8.0	8	1	1	22	22.0	22	1								
FRED GRAMBAU Frederick E. DE-DT 6'1 248 Michigan B: 8/30/1950 Detroit, MI Draft: 5-120 1973 KC																															
1973	HAM	6																													
1974	HAM	13																													
2	Years	19																													
JOHNNY GRAMLING John QB 6'0 175 South Carolina B: 1932 Draft: 24-288 1954 CLE																															
1954	OTT	6										5	1	24	117	4.9	19	1													
CHICK GRANING Charles H. QB-DB 6'1 197 Georgia Tech B: 1938 Draft: 18-(f) 1961 DEN; 9-120(f) 1961 STL																															
1966	BC	13							5	38																					
1967	BC	2																													
2	Years	15							5	38																					
ALAN GRANT Alan Hays DH 5'10 187 Stanford B: 10/1/1966 Draft: 4C-103 1990 IND Pro: N																															
1996	SAS	1				1																									
BAKARI GRANT Bakari Omotunde WR 6'4 195 UC Davis B: 6/24/1987 Oakland, CA																															
2011	HAM	13				7						12	2						42	507	12.1	43	2					2	16	8.0	9
BUD GRANT Harold Peter OE-DB 6'2 199 Minnesota B: 5/20/1927 Superior, WI Draft: 1-14 1950 PHI Pro: N																															
1953	WPG+	16							4	10		25	5	1	9	9.0	9	0	68	922	13.6		5	2	4	2.0					
1954	WPG+	16	3						1	5		25	5						49	752	15.3	62	5								
1955	WPG	16	1									10	2						36	556	15.4	62	2								
1956	WPG+	16	1						2	6		6	1						63	970	15.4	53	1	1	5	5.0	5	1	29	29.0	29
4	Years	64	5		0				7	21		66	13	1	9	9.0	9	0	216	3200	14.8	62	13	3	9	3.0	5	1	29	29.0	29
COREY GRANT Corey WR 5'11 179 Wilfrid Laurier B: 12/22/1976 Stoney Creek, ON Draft: 1-7 1999 HAM																															
1999	HAM	18	2	0	0	3						26	4						56	875	15.6	57	3	15	139	9.3	35	2	25	12.5	16
2000	HAM	18	1	0	0	4						12	2						32	499	15.6	55	2	21	165	7.9	27				
2001	HAM	18				3						18	3						38	544	14.3	65	3	7	26	3.7	12				
2002	MTL	13	2	0	1	3													25	385	15.4	43	0					3	60	20.0	28
2002	SAS	5				0																									
2002	Year	18	2	0	1	3													25	385	15.4	43	0					3	60	20.0	28
2003	SAS	18				5						18	3	1	17	17.0	17	0	39	511	13.1	53	3					13	279	21.5	29
2004	SAS	11				0								1	4	4.0	4	0	18	293	16.3	53	0					1	19	19.0	19
2005	SAS	17				3						6	1						20	197	9.9	29	1					2	28	14.0	16
2006	SAS	18	1	0	1	1						12	2	2	75	37.5	47	0	21	344	16.4	46	2	1	12	12.0	12	5	83	16.6	19
2007	SAS	18	1	0	0	1													38	458	12.1	30	0								
2008	SAS	16	1	0	0	1						6	1						30	284	9.5	31	1								
2009	HAM	17				1						6	1						9	89	9.9	17	1								
11	Years	182	8	0	2	25						104	17	4	96	24.0	47	0	326	4479	13.7	65	16	44	342	7.8	35	26	494	19.0	29
DONNOHUE GRANT Donnohue DB 5'11 185 Simon Fraser B: 9/28/1962 Kingston, Jamaica Draft: 2A-10 1986 TOR																															
1986	TOR	5																													
1987	WPG	5				1																		1	-3	-3.0	-3				
1988	HAM	15				12																									
1989	HAM	11				4			1	0																					
4	Years	36				17			1	0														1	-3	-3.0	-3				
FRED GRANT Fred W. HB 5'11 180 Wake Forrest; Alabama B: 1/20/1925 Christiansburg, VA D: 8/3/1993 Atlanta, GA Draft: B 1945 CHIC																															
1947	SAS	1																													
GEORGE GRANT George FL-FW																															
1946	WPG	6										5	1																		
1947	WPG	1																													
2	Years	7										5	1																		
GEORGE GRANT George Charles K 6'4 235 Colorado College B: 1/10/1932 Thunder Bay, ON D: 9/12/2004 Severna Park, MD																															
1960	BC	10										33	0																		
1961	BC	7										17	0																		
1962	BC	7										20	0																		
3	Years	24										70	0																		
KARIM GRANT Karim DE 6'4 235 Acadia B: 12/25/1976 Toronto, ON Draft: 2-12 2001 HAM																															
2002	HAM	6				5																									
2003	HAM	13				11																									
2004	MTL	4	0	0	1	5																									
3	Years	23	0	0	1	21																									
MARCUS GRANT Marcus Dwayne WR 5'9 176 Houston B: 9/12/1970 Dallas, TX																															
1995	BIR+	18				2						66	11						84	1559	18.6	86	11								
1996	HAM	9				4						6	1						18	409	22.7	51	1								
2	Years	27				6						72	12						102	1968	19.3	86	12								
MICHAEL GRANT Michael CB 5'11 186 Arkansas B: 3/30/1986 Stone Mountain, GA Pro: U																															
2010	TOR	6	0	1	1	15																									
REGGIE GRANT Reginald Leon DB 5'9 185 Oregon B: 9/2/1955 Atlanta, GA Draft: 9A-225 1978 NYJ Pro: N																															
1979	OTT	1																													
ROBERT GRANT Robert DB 6'0 200 Hawaii B: 8/26/1980																															
2003	EDM	16				53	4.0	36.0	5	300	2	12	2															4	72	18.0	24
2004	EDM	18	0	1	2	57	1.0	5.0	4	59	2	6	1						1	29	29.0	29	0								
2005	OTT	12	0	1	0	30	1.0	11.0			1																				
3	Years	46	0	2	2	140	6.0	52.0	9	359	5	18	3						1	29	29.0	29	0					4	72	18.0	24
STEVE GRANT Steve DT 6'3 245 Simon Fraser B: 10/3/1969 Delta, BC Draft: 3-24 1991 WPG																															
1991	WPG	16				17																									
1992	WPG	16				17																									
1995	HAM	9				14	2.0	18.0																							
3	Years	41				48	2.0	18.0																							
STEVE GRANT Steven Marshall QB 6'1 200 Chabot JC; Washington State B: 4/12/1957 Berkeley, CA Pro: U																															
1980	MTL	10	2		1									4	24	6.0	13	0													
TERRY GRANT Terry O'Neal RB 5'9 190 Alabama B: 3/3/1987																															
2011	HAM	4				1						18	3	20	151	7.6	89	2	6	87	14.5	31	1					9	200	22.2	53
TOMMY GRANT Thomas OHB-SE-DB 5'11 195 Windsor AKO Jrs. B: 1/9/1935 Windsor, ON D: 10/18/2011																															
1956	HAM	14										12	2	37	133	3.6	12	1	10	236	23.6	51	1	0	5		5	17	333	19.6	60
1957	HAM	13										6	1	3	2	0.7	3	0	16	332	20.8	70	1					7	206	29.4	66
1958	HAM	14										42	7	28	127	4.5	70	0	30	756	25.2	72	7					4	69	17.3	20
1959	HAM	12										18	3	15	70	4.7	16	0	29	453	15.6	45	3	2	3	1.5	3	1	0	0.0	0
1960	HAM	14										48	8	8	61	7.6	23	0	44	758	17.2	78	8	1	3	3.0	3	23	566	24.6	36
1961	HAM	3										6	1	1	4	4.0	4	0	7	78	11.1	16	1								

Year	Team	GP	FM	FF	FR	TK	SK	YDS	IR	YDS	PD	PTS	TD	RA	YDS	AVG	LG	TD	REC	YDS	AVG	LG	TD	PR	YDS	AVG	LG	KOR	YDS	AVG	LG
1962	HAM	14							2	36		24	4	31	139	4.5	15	1	28	292	10.4	42	2	27	179	6.6	20	20	615	30.8	105
1963	HAM+	14							2	46		42	7	2	5	2.5	5	0	40	834	20.9	57	7	36	271	7.5	32	8	209	26.1	63
1964	HAM*	14										42	7	2	18	9.0	9	0	44	1029	23.4	66	7								
1965	HAM	14										30	5						23	558	24.3	91	5	31	139	4.5	23				
1966	HAM	14	1		0							48	8						35	683	19.5	47	8	37	183	4.9	83				
1967	HAM	14	1		0														10	249	24.9	49	0	40	225	5.6	15				
1968	HAM	14										6	1						8	203	25.4	50	1	35	187	5.3	24				
1969	WPG	13																	5	81	16.2	28	0	3	3	1.0	2				
14	Years	181	2		0				4	82		324	54	127	559	4.4	70	2	329	6542	19.9	91	51	212	1198	5.7	83	80	1998	25.0	105
WARREN GRANT Warren WR 5'9 185 Ottawa B: 10/22/1970																															
1995	OTT	3				2																									
WES GRANT Wesley Louis DE 6'3 250 Santa Monica CC; UCLA B: 9/24/1946 Los Angeles, CA Draft: 4-97 1970 NYG Pro: NW																															
1972	MTL	2																													
RUDY GRASS Rudy G-E 6'2 210 Toronto B: 1921																															
1947	TOR	11																													
1948	TOR	11																													
1949	TOR	9																													
3	Years	31																													
MAURICE GRAVELY Maurice LB 6'4 210 Wake Forest B: 5/23/1971 Norton, VA																															
1995	BAL	6				13	1.0	10.0	1	4	5																	1	1	1.0	1
TRACY GRAVELY Tracy DB-LB 6'3 212 Concord B: 4/24/1968 Welch, WV																															
1991	OTT	5	0		1	13																									
1992	BC	8	0		1	35			3	10																					
1993	BC	5				15			1	0																					
1994	BAL	18				68			2	78	6																				
1995	BAL+	18	0		2	91						6	1																		
1996	MTL*	18	0		1	116			2	61	5			2	9	4.5	8	0						6	33	5.5	17	5	86	17.2	23
1997	MTL	17	0	2	2	83	1.0	6.0			3	6	1																		
1998	MTL	17	0	3	1	73			1	26	0																				
1999	MTL	14	0	0	3	46	3.0	19.0			1																				
2000	MTL	13				27	3.0	12.0			1																				
2001	MTL	18	0	1	1	24			1	14	0																				
11	Years	151	0	6	12	591	7.0	37.0	10	189	16	12	2	2	9	4.5	8	0						6	33	5.5	17	5	86	17.2	23
HOWARD GRAVES Howard HB 5'11 177 Michigan State B: 1930																															
1955	TOR	5							2	21				30	113	3.8	15	0	7	83	11.9	24	0	6	59	9.8	13	4	66	16.5	21
1956	CAL	1																													
2	Years	6							2	21				30	113	3.8	15	0	7	83	11.9	24	0	6	59	9.8	13	4	66	16.5	21
MARVIN GRAVES Marvin P. QB 6'1 195 Syracuse B: 2/7/1971 Washington, DC																															
1994	TOR	18	2		2	1						6	1	21	82	3.9	23	1													
1995	TOR	13	2		1	1						6	1	8	2	0.3	3	1													
1996	HAM	3	0		1	0								5	22	4.4	9	0													
1996	SAS	3				0								1	6	6.0	6	0													
1996	Year	6	0		1	0								6	28	4.7	9	0													
1997	MTL	13	2	0	1	0						6	1	9	24	2.7	7	1													
2000	SAS	14	3	0	0	1						6	1	10	44	4.4	17	1													
2001	SAS	8	7	0	0	1								24	50	2.1	9	0													
6	Years	69	16	0	5	4						24	4	78	230	2.9	23	4													
OBIE GRAVES Obie L. HB 5'9 170 Citrus JC; Fullerton State B: 4/21/1957 Collins, MS																															
1980	HAM	6	3		1									126	658	5.2	40	0	15	88	5.9	22	0	12	78	6.5	14	7	138	19.7	36
1981	WPG	11	3		0							54	9	132	661	5.0	36	8	48	361	7.5	25	1					4	101	25.3	33
1982	HAM	3	2		0							6	1	41	153	3.7	24	0	9	103	11.4	28	1								
3	Years	20	8		1							60	10	299	1472	4.9	40	8	72	552	7.7	28	2	12	78	6.5	14	11	239	21.7	36
ARCHIE GRAY Archie Eugene WR 6'0 180 Wyoming B: 3/13/1953 Omaha, NE Draft: 10B-260 1975 PIT																															
1977	MTL	5																	9	136	15.1	18	0					4	71	17.8	39
BILLY GRAY Bill DB-OHB-SE 5'11 195 Maryland-Eastern Shore B: 1939 Norfolk, VA																															
1961	SAS	6	3											54	312	5.8	60	0	8	44	5.5	17	0					12	311	25.9	44
1962	SAS	15	3									24	4	149	673	4.5	46	2	30	419	14.0	85	2					16	236	14.8	34
1963	SAS	7	1		0							12	2	59	316	5.4	75	1	20	268	13.4	45	1					3	75	25.0	29
1964	SAS	8	1		0							6	1	33	187	5.7	31	0	9	104	11.6	31	1					7	172	24.6	34
1965	SAS	12	5		1							18	3	99	494	5.0	44	2	14	164	11.7	19	1					9	184	20.4	38
5	Years	48	13		1							60	10	394	1982	5.0	75	5	81	999	12.3	85	5					47	978	20.8	44
DOUG GRAY Doug HB 5'9 158 Western Ontario B: 1928 D: 1999 North York, ON																															
1951	HAM	12																													
1952	HAM	10										10	2					2													
1954	TOR	12							2	22				2	16	8.0	12	0						7	36	5.1	16				
3	Years	34							2	22		10	2	2	16	8.0	12	2						7	36	5.1	16				
ED GRAY Edmon DE-OT-DT 6'2 220 Oklahoma B: 12/9/1934 D: 4/28/1976 Pecos County, TX Draft: 7-75 1957 LARM																															
1957	EDM	8																													
1958	EDM	16																													
1959	EDM+	16							1			6	1																		
1960	EDM+	16	1		3							6	1																		
1961	EDM	16																													
1962	EDM	13																													
6	Years	85	1		3				1	0		12	2																		
HERB GRAY Herbert William DE-OG-OT 6'1 218 Texas B: 6/22/1934 D: 1/21/2011 San Antonio, TX Draft: 5-55 1956 BAL																															
1956	WPG	16	0		3																										
1957	WPG+	14	0		3																										
1958	WPG+	16	0		2																										
1959	WPG+	16																													
1960	WPG+	15	0		2				1			6	1																		
1961	WPG+	16			2																										
1962	WPG*	16							1			6	1																		
1963	WPG	16	0		1																										
1964	WPG	16																													
1965	WPG+	15	0		1																										
10	Years	156	0		14				2	0		12	2																		
JACK GRAY Jack HB-E 5'10 167 Toronto B: 1927																															
1951	TOR	3																													
1952	TOR	11																													
1953	TOR	13										5	1																		
3	Years	27										5	1																		
KEVIN GRAY Kevin S 5'11 179 Kennedy-King JC; Eastern Illinois B: 9/11/1957 Chicago, IL Pro: NU																															
1985	OTT	8	0		1				1	1																		5	122	24.4	27
LEO GRAY Leonardo Bernard DB 5'11 175 Los Angeles Harbor JC; Los Angeles Southwest CC; Nevada-Las Vegas B: 1/8/1957 Los Angeles, CA																															
1982	TOR	9										6	1						3	67	22.3	32	1								
MIKE GRAY Michael DT 6'4 255 West Hills CC; Oregon B: 2/11/1960 Baltimore, MD																															
1985	BC*	16	0		3		13.0																								
1986	BC	17					8.0		2	6																					
1987	WPG	17			1	30	10.0																								
1988	WPG	18	0		2	41	11.0																								
1989	WPG+	18	0		2	44	11.0																								
1990	WPG	17	0		1	23	5.0																								

Year	Team	GP	FM	FF	FR	TK	SK	YDS	IR	YDS	PD	PTS	TD	RA	YDS	AVG	LG	TD	REC	YDS	AVG	LG	TD	PR	YDS	AVG	LG	KOR	YDS	AVG	LG
1991	WPG	16	0		2	38	2.0					6	1																		
1992	WPG	18	0		1	40	4.0	16.0																							
1993	WPG	3				8																									
9	Years	140	0		12	224	64.0	16.0	2	6		6	1																		
MIKE GRAY Mike FL-DB 5'11 185 Toronto B: 1943 Draft: 4-33 1966 CAL																															
1966	CAL	14																													
1967	MTL	11																													
1968	MTL	14										18	3						20	355	17.8	37	3								
1969	MTL	3	1		0																		0								
1969	BC	11																					0								
1969	Year	14	1		0														13	214	16.5	49	0								
4	Years	42	1		0							18	3						20	355	17.8	37	3								
PAUL GRAY Paul David LB 6'2 231 Western Kentucky B: 6/20/1962 Tulsa, OK Draft: 10-264 1984 NO; 6-116 1984 TB-USFL Pro: N																															
1984	MTL	9					1.0		1	12																					
1985	MTL	16	0		3		2.0																								
1986	MTL	2	0		1																										
3	Years	27	0		4		3.0		1	12																					
TY GRAY Tyrone WR-DB 6'2 203 Washington State B: 8/4/1955 New York, NY Draft: 12-309 1980 STL																															
1979	BC	8							2	13		6	1						22	356	16.2	38	1	1	11	11.0	11				
1980	BC	6										18	3						16	349	21.8	64	3	2	29	14.5	16				
1981	BC+	16	0		1							56	9	1	10	10.0	10	0	63	1428	22.7	91	9								
1982	BC	7	2		0							12	2						19	204	10.7	27	2								
1983	OTT	12										30	5						28	693	24.8	91	5								
1984	OTT	8										24	4						23	437	19.0		4								
1984	SAS	2	1		0														5	127	25.4	78	0					1	0	0.0	0
1984	Year	10	1		0							24	4						28	564	20.1	78	4					1	0	0.0	0
6	Years	57	3		1				2	13		146	24	1	10	10.0	10	0	176	3594	20.4	91	24	3	40	13.3	16	1	0	0.0	0
MIKE GRAYBILL Michael Alton OT 6'7 275 Boston University B: 10/14/1966 Washington, DC Draft: 7-187 1989 CLE Pro: EN																															
1993	OTT+	18	2		1	23																									
1994	OTT	18	0		1	19																									
2	Years	36	2		2	42																									
JEFFERY GRAYS Jeffery LB 6'2 225 Angelo State B: 1/21/1971																															
1994	WPG	1				1																									
DANNY GRAYSON Danny Ray LB 6'2 240 Washington State B: 7/27/1967 Paris, TX Draft: 7-182 1990 PIT																															
1992	SAS	7				23	1.0																								
CLINTON GREATHOUSE Clinton Beau P-K 5'10 221 Texas Tech B: 5/28/1980 Roswell, NM																															
2004	CAL	7	3	1	1	1						60	0																		
CHRIS GREAVES Christopher OG 6'8 297 Western Ontario B: 1/8/1987 Draft: 6-45 2010 WPG																															
2010	WPG	5				0																									
2011	WPG	18				0																						1	8	8.0	8
2	Years	23				0																						1	8	8.0	8
DICK GRECNI Richard E. LB 6'1 230 Ohio University B: 3/27/1938 Akron, OH Draft: SS-(f) 1960 BOS; 13-152(f) 1960 CLE Pro: N																															
1962	EDM	3																													
GARRETT GREEDY Garrett R. LB 6'3 250 UCLA B: 1/28/1971 Fullerton, CA																															
1994	LV	5				5	1.0																								
ART GREEN Arthur HB 5'11 198 Albany State B: 9/18/1949 Atlanta, GA Pro: N																															
1973	OTT	7										12	2	54	223	4.1	14	2	16	142	8.9	29	0					4	82	20.5	24
1974	OTT+	16	1		2							24	4	141	680	4.8	34	3	44	514	11.7	34	0					16	423	26.4	39
1975	OTT*	16	1		0							84	14	258	1188	4.6	47	11	47	537	11.4	39	3	28	285	10.2	29	6	157	26.2	35
1976	OTT*	16	6		0							90	15	234	1257	5.4	69	13	53	508	9.6	31	2	15	146	9.7	24				
1978	OTT+	16	3		2							54	9	58	238	4.1	64	3	40	580	14.5	47	6	13	113	8.7	31	21	500	23.8	46
5	Years	71	11		4							264	44	745	3586	4.8	69	32	200	2281	11.4	47	11	56	544	9.7	31	47	1162	24.7	46
BRUCE GREEN Bruce LB 6'2 230 Texas Southern B: 12/17/1962 St. Petersburg, FL Draft: 17-347 1984 LA-USFL; TD 1985 HOU-USFL																															
1986	EDM	4	0		1				1	0																					
1987	EDM	2				4	1.0																								
1987	CAL	12	0		1	33	0.0	0.0																							
1987	Year	14	0		1	37	1.0																								
1988	CAL	3				15	1.0																								
1988	OTT	1				2																									
1988	Year	4				17	1.0																								
3	Years	9	0		2	54	2.0		1	0																					
CAL GREEN Calvin DB 5'10 175 South Shore Combines Jrs.																															
1952	CAL	11			1				1	30														0	5		5				
1954	CAL	1																													
2	Years	12	0		1				1	30														0	5		5				
CHRIS GREEN Christopher OT 6'6 305 Ottawa Sooners Jrs.; Ottawa B: 3/30/1968 Kingston, ON Draft: 2B-13 1991 TOR																															
1992	TOR	14	0		1	1																									
1993	TOR	18				1																									
1995	EDM	16	0		1	2																									
1996	EDM	10				0																									
4	Years	58	0		2	4																									
DAVID GREEN David Fendell FB 5'10 200 Chowan JC; Edinboro B: 9/7/1953 Jacksonville, NC Pro: N																															
1978	MTL	5	3		0							18	3	62	309	5.0	45	2	7	36	5.1	11	1	1	8	8.0	8	5	127	25.4	33
1979	MTL*	16	7		1							66	11	287	1678	5.8	51	11	19	210	11.1	42	0					20	414	20.7	42
1980	MTL	14	7		1							54	9	205	873	4.3	33	7	31	435	14.0	46	2								
1981	HAM	6	1		0							12	2	66	208	3.2	16	2	8	66	8.3	18	0								
4	Years	41	18		2							150	25	620	3068	4.9	51	22	65	747	11.5	46	3	1	8	8.0	8	25	541	21.6	42
DAVID GREEN David J. RB 6'0 205 Carleton B: 9/26/1956 Draft: 4-33 1979 OTT																															
1979	TOR	2																													
DEXTER GREEN Dexter L. RB 5'9 172 Iowa State B: 5/20/1957 D: 5/11/2003																															
1979	HAM	2	2		0									23	64	2.8	15	0	3	25	8.3	17	0	7	51	7.3	19	3	62	20.7	24
JAMES GREEN James S-FB-LB 5'11 217 Calgary B: 6/22/1983 Vernon, BC Draft: 3-18 2009 TOR																															
2009	TOR	18				19																									
2010	WPG	8	0	1	0	12																									
2011	WPG	18	0	0	2	17																									
3	Years	44	0	1	2	48																									
JOHNNY GREEN John Edward QB 6'3 203 Tennessee-Chattanooga B: 10/12/1937 West Point, MS Draft: 21-247 1959 PIT Pro: N																															
1959	TOR	2												4	-2	-0.5	3	0													
LIONELL GREEN Lionell DB 6'0 180 Reedley CC; North Carolina B: 8/18/1983																															
2006	BC	1				9																									
LYLE GREEN Lyle FB 6'1 216 Toledo B: 2/4/1976 Kitchener, ON Draft: 1B-3 2001 BC																															
2001	BC	17	0	0	1	13								9	35	3.9	9	0	3	45	15.0	21	0								
2002	BC	18	2	0	1	12						18	3	60	343	5.7	29	3	9	86	9.6	20	0								
2003	BC	18	1	1	0	7						6	1	18	42	2.3	6	1	8	110	13.8	41	0								
2004	BC	18	0	1	1	2								11	43	3.9	12	0	22	248	11.3	47	0								
2005	BC	18	0	0	1	4						6	1	12	53	4.4	9	0	17	261	15.4	64	1								
2006	BC	18				0								2	31	15.5	16	0	6	35	5.8	10	0					3	9	3.0	6
2007	BC	18				5						6	1	3	18	6.0	13	0	4	32	8.0	22	1								
2008	BC	18	1	0	1	7						6	1						13	158	12.2	33	1					2	11	5.5	11
2009	BC	18	1	0	1	1								1	4	4.0	4	0	1	3	3.0	3	0								
2011	CAL	12				3																									
10	Years	173	5	2	6	54						42	7	116	569	4.9	29	4	83	978	11.8	64	3					5	20	4.0	11

Year	Team	GP	FM	FF	FR	TK	SK	YDS	IR	YDS	PD	PTS	TD	RA	YDS	AVG	LG	TD	REC	YDS	AVG	LG	TD	PR	YDS	AVG	LG	KOR	YDS	AVG	LG
S.J. GREEN Solomon Harold, II SB-WR 6'2 218 South Florida B: 6/20/1985 Fort Worth, TX																															
2007	MTL	3				1													6	73	12.2	23	0								
2008	MTL	2				0						6	1						5	41	8.2	12	1								
2009	MTL	8	1	0	0	1						12	2						15	239	15.9	48	2								
2010	MTL	18				1						64	10						58	875	15.1	67	10								
2011	MTL+	18	1	0	1	1						24	4						87	1147	13.2	51	4								
5	Years	49	2	0	1	4						106	17						171	2375	13.9	67	17								
SKYLER GREEN Skyler Levon SB-WR 5'9 190 Louisiana State B: 9/12/1984 Houma, LA Draft: 4-125 2006 DAL Pro: N																															
2009	EDM	1				0																		4	44	11.0	22	3	99	33.0	62
2010	EDM	3	1	0	0	0																		10	34	3.4	9	11	242	22.0	33
2	Years	4	1	0	0	0																		14	78	5.6	22	14	341	24.4	62
TRENT GREEN Trent Jason QB 6'3 214 Indiana B: 7/9/1970 Cedar Rapids, IA Draft: 8-222 1993 SD Pro: N																															
1994	BC	20																													
DAVE GREENBERG David QB-HB 6'0 184 Manitoba; McGill																															
1946	MTL	12										21	4					1					2								
1947	MTL	12										9	1										1								
1948	MTL	4																													
3	Years	28										30	5					1					3								
ANDREW GREENE Andrew Kirkpatrick OG-OT 6'4 304 Indiana B: 9/24/1969 Kingston, Jamaica Draft: 2-18 1994 SAS; 2-53 1995 MIA Pro: N																															
1997	SAS	5				1																									
1999	SAS	4	0	0	1	0																									
2000	SAS*	18				1																									
2001	SAS+	18				0																									
2002	SAS	6				0																									
2003	SAS*	18	1	0	2	1																									
2004	SAS*	17				2																									
2005	SAS*	15				1																									
2006	SAS	15				0													1	-21	-21.0	-21	0								
2007	WPG	18	0	0	2	0																									
2008	TOR	7				0																									
11	Years	141	1	0	5	6													1	-21	-21.0	-21	0								
DONTA GREENE Donta S. WR 5'7 166 Toledo B: 2/19/1980 Springfield, OH																															
2003	MTL	4	1	0	0	0								1	2	2.0	2	0	2	20	10.0	19	0	23	393	17.1	87	16	357	22.3	42
MARCELLUS GREENE Marcellus Lamont CB 6'0 185 Arizona B: 12/12/1957 Indianapolis, IN Draft: 11-296 1981 LARM Pro: N																															
1981	TOR	13							4	51														1	4	4.0	4	3	47	15.7	25
1982	SAS	16	0		1				2	0																					
1983	TOR	12	0		1				2	0														12	84	7.0	13	14	292	20.9	33
1985	TOR	6							1	0																					
1986	TOR	13	0		2				3	10																					
1987	TOR	2																													
6	Years	62	0		4				12	61														13	88	6.8	13	17	339	19.9	33
NEALON GREENE Nealon QB 6'0 195 Clemson B: 3/13/1976 Yonkers, NY																															
1998	TOR	18				0								7	41	5.9	14	0													
1999	EDM	15	7	0	3	0						24	4	97	878	9.1	68	4													
2000	EDM	18	9	0	2	1						12	2	101	765	7.6	36	2													
2001	EDM	18	4	0	0	2								45	280	6.2	30	0													
2002	SAS	18	12	0	4	1						18	3	94	548	5.8	48	3													
2003	SAS	18	8	0	0	0						30	5	121	723	6.0	43	5													
2004	SAS	1				0																									
2005	SAS	18	10	0	4	1						36	6	66	295	4.5	16	6													
2006	MTL	18	2	0	1	1								12	35	2.9	11	0													
9	Years	142	52	0	14	6						120	20	543	3565	6.6	68	20													
NELS GREENE Nelson HB-FB 5'10 185 Ottawa Combines Jrs. B: 1928																															
1947	OTT	12										10	2					1					1								
1948	OTT	11										6	1					1													
1950	SAS	11										21	4	75	415	5.5		4	4	72	18.0		0								
1951	SAS	12										5	1	45	177	3.9		1	1	17	17.0	17	0					1	13	13.0	13
1952	SAS	7										5	1	33	164	5.0	13	1	1	9	9.0	9	0					1	5	5.0	5
1953	SAS	9										5	1	13	38	2.9		0	4	36	9.0		1					1	32	32.0	32
6	Years	62										52	10	166	794	4.8	13	8	10	134	13.4	17	2					3	50	16.7	32
SAMMY GREENE Sam WR 6'1 190 Nevada-Las Vegas B: 1/28/1959 Draft: 4A-84 1981 MIA Pro: U																															
1983	BC	14	1		0							42	7	9	64	7.1	48	1	75	755	10.1	33	5					27	749	27.7	113
1984	SAS	5										18	3	1	-5	-5.0	-5	0	20	301	15.1	38	3					8	197	24.6	47
1984	CAL	3																	7	58	8.3		0					5	127	25.4	44
1984	Year	8										18	3	1	-5	-5.0	-5	0	27	359	13.3	38	3					13	324	24.9	47
2	Years	19	1		0							60	10	10	59	5.9	48	1	102	1114	10.9	38	8					40	1073	26.8	113
MIKE GREENFIELD Michael QB 6'1 195 Northwestern B: 4/30/1966 Elmwood Park, IL																															
1988	OTT	7	1		0	0								10	55	5.5	17	0													
1989	OTT	2																													
2	Years	9	1		0	0								10	55	5.5	17	0													
FRITZ GREENLEE William Frederick TE-OG 6'2 230 Air Force; Arizona B: 11/5/1943 Des Moines, IA Draft: RS-5-37 1966 MIA; 9-137(f) 1966 CHIB Pro: N																															
1968	MTL	7										6	1						7	96	13.7	30	1								
1970	EDM	11	1		0																							1	3	3.0	3
2	Years	18	1		0							6	1						7	96	13.7	30	1					1	3	3.0	3
DANIEL GREER Daniel Paul DL 6'2 285 Arizona B: 3/2/1976 Pro: E																															
2001	CAL	1				0	1.0	1.0																							
TERRY GREER Terry Lee WR 6'1 192 Alabama State B: 9/27/1957 Memphis, TN Draft: 11-304 1980 LARM Pro: N																															
1980	TOR	14										18	3	2	38	19.0	27	1	37	552	14.9	39	2					23	533	23.2	46
1981	TOR	6	1		0							24	4	1	22	22.0	22	0	21	284	13.5	45	3					11	418	38.0	109
1982	TOR*	15	1		0							74	12	7	52	7.4	28	1	85	1466	17.2	61	11					12	285	23.8	35
1983	TOR*	16	1		0							48	8	2	15	7.5	31	0	113	2003	17.7	12	8					1	0	0.0	0
1984	TOR+	15	1		0							84	14	2	13	6.5	11	0	70	1189	17.0	61	14					3	31	10.3	20
1985	TOR+	16	0		1							54	9	3	45	15.0	20	0	78	1323	17.0	65	9								
6	Years	82	4		1							302	50	17	185	10.9	31	2	404	6817	16.9	65	47					50	1267	25.3	109
GABRIEL GREGOIRE Gabriel DE-DT 6'3 230 Verdun Maple Leafs Jrs. B: 12/22/1953 Sainte-Martine, QC																															
1976	MTL	9																													
1977	MTL	14																													
1978	MTL	16																													
1979	MTL	13	0		1																										
1980	MTL	10	0		2																										
5	Years	62	0		3																										
DICK GREGORY Richard A. HB 5'10 175 Minnesota B: 4/15/1929 Billings, MT Draft: 22-260 1952 CHIB																															
1952	SAS	7												45	225	5.0	30	0	3	62	20.7	30	0	3	24	8.0	15	4	104	26.0	33
GEORGE GREGORY George E-HB-FW 5'7 156 Winnipeg Ints.																															
1947	WPG	5																													
1948	WPG	6																													
2	Years	11																													
BILL GREGUS William R. FB 5'11 210 Wake Forest B: 3/25/1928 oh D: 3/8/1982 Toledo, OH Draft: 9-108 1951 CHIB																															
1950	HAM+	12										50	10					10													
JOHN GREINER John TE 6'3 215 Purdue B: 4/2/1940 Brackenbridge, PA Draft: 13-175 1963 WAS																															
1965	EDM	3										6	1						3	61	20.3	31	1					1	3	3.0	3
HANK GRENDA Hendrik S. QB 6'3 215 Washington State B: 6/18/1947 D: 3/31/2006 Winfield, BC																															

Year	Team	GP	FM	FF	FR	TK	SK	YDS	IR	YDS	PD	PTS	TD	RA	YDS	AVG	LG	TD	REC	YDS	AVG	LG	TD	PR	YDS	AVG	LG	KOR	YDS	AVG	LG
1969	BC	16												3	8	2.7	6	0													
JIMMY GRETH James William FL 6'2 195 Arizona B: 4/11/1944 Covina, CA																															
1967	TOR	8										6	1	7	54	7.7		0	5	59	11.8		1								
1967	MTL	5												5	5	1.0		0	7	85	12.1		0								
1967	Year	13										6	1	12	59	4.9	21	0	12	144	12.0	28	1								
GEORGE GREVES George QB 6'2 197 Ithaca B: 12/3/1950																															
1974	HAM	10	1		0																			6	21	3.5	5				
ARNOLD GREVIOUS Arnold F. CB 6'2 195 James Madison B: 5/12/1965 Norfolk, VA																															
1988	HAM	14				25			1	11																					
HAL GRICE Hal G 5'9 201																															
1946	TOR	11																													
1947	MTL	8																													
1948	MTL	10																													
3	Years	29																													
RYAN GRICE-MULLEN Ryan Ashley WR-SB 5'11 180 Hawaii B: 9/12/1986 Rialto, CA																															
2008	BC	3				0						6	1						9	175	19.4	67	1								
2009	BC	15	3	0	0	4						18	3	8	42	5.3	24	2	20	210	10.5	27	1	43	411	9.6	54	47	1099	23.4	73
2010	SAS	6	4	0	1	1								1	9	9.0	9	0	4	39	9.8	23	0	22	177	8.0	35	24	498	20.8	43
2011	EDM	1				0													3	26	8.7	13	0								
4	Years	25	7	0	1	5						24	4	9	51	5.7	24	2	36	450	12.5	67	2	65	588	9.0	54	71	1597	22.5	73
DEREK GRIER Derek CB 6'0 185 Marshall B: 3/4/1970 Atlanta, GA																															
1993	BC	6	0		1	14			2	6									1	12	12.0	12	0								
1994	BC	2				6					3																				
1995	HAM	18	1		1	37			6	57	5													7	56	8.0	13	3	27	9.0	12
1996	HAM	18	0		1	44			4	43	5													4	34	8.5	13	2	51	25.5	34
1997	HAM	2				3					2																				
1998	HAM	18				29			4	47	6	6	1																		
6	Years	64	1		3	133			16	153	21	6	1						1	12	12.0	12	0	11	90	8.2	13	5	78	15.6	34
PROFAIL GRIER Profail RB 5'8 185 Utah State B: 3/1/1972 Atlanta, GA Pro: E																															
1996	OTT	5	1		0	4						12	2	53	255	4.8	38	1	7	57	8.1	23	1					6	53	8.8	17
1997	SAS	7	4	0	1	0								19	87	4.6	17	0	6	54	9.0	20	0	26	232	8.9	34	17	430	25.3	58
1998	SAS	4				0								2	7	3.5	4	0	1	6	6.0	6	0	14	95	6.8	12	17	388	22.8	45
3	Years	16	5	0	1	4						12	2	74	349	4.7	38	1	14	117	8.4	23	1	40	327	8.2	34	40	871	21.8	58
JIM GRIERSON Jim Toronto																															
1948	TOR	2																													
BOB GRIFFIN Robert Lloyd C 6'3 235 Arkansas B: 2/12/1929 Fort Worth, TX Draft: 2-25 1952 LARM Pro: N																															
1959	CAL	9	0		1																										
COURTNEY GRIFFIN Courtney F. DH 5'10 180 Fresno State B: 12/19/1966 Madera, CA Pro: N																															
1995	BAL	18	0		2	45			2	51	0																				
1996	TOR	7	0		1	19																									
1996	MTL	2				0					2																				
1996	Year	9	0		1	19					2																				
1997	WPG	4				11																									
3	Years	29	0		3	75			2	51	2																				
JERRY GRIFFIN Jerry Lynn LB 6'1 221 Southern Methodist B: 12/10/1944 Dallas, TX Draft: 8B-200 1967 CHIB																															
1967	EDM	16	0		3																										
1968	EDM	16	0		4				3	28														1	0	0.0	0				
1969	EDM	16	0		2				2	21																					
1970	EDM	16	0		1				3	35																					
1971	EDM	16			3				5	9		6	1															6	85	14.2	21
1972	EDM	7							1	0														1	0	0.0	0				
1973	EDM	5	0		1																										
1973	SAS	2																													
1973	Year	7	0		1																										
7	Years	92	0		14				14	93		6	1											2	0	0.0	0	6	85	14.2	21
JIM GRIFFIN James Bauman DT-E 6'3 258 Grambling State B: 12/18/1939 Lake Charles, LA Draft: 15-197 1964 SF Pro: N																															
1965	TOR	3																	6	72	12.0	21	0								
JOHN GRIFFIN John Watson CB-DH 6'1 190 Memphis B: 11/2/1939 Nashville, TN Draft: 8B-61 1963 DEN; 4-43 1963 LARM Pro: N																															
1967	BC	10	1		0				1	16														9	54	6.0	14				
1968	BC	16							4	46														7	12	1.7	3	4	96	24.0	30
2	Years	26	1		0				5	62														16	66	4.1	14	4	96	24.0	30
MALIKIA GRIFFIN Malikia D. DB 5'8 180 Mississippi B: 3/12/1975 Batesville, MS																															
1998	EDM	3	0	1	0	15																									
MURRAY GRIFFIN Murray HB 5'10 200 Queen's; Los Angeles JC; Loyola Marymount B: 1915																															
1949	TOR	1																													
THOMAS GRIFFIN Thomas LB 5'11 246 Grambling State B: 3/11/1968 Mobile, AL																															
1994	SHR	2																										1	1	1.0	1
DEAN GRIFFING Orrin Dean, Jr. C 195 Kansas State B: 5/17/1913 St. George, KS D: 2/9/1998 Sarasota County, FL																															
1946	CAL	6																													
1947	CAL	8																													
2	Years	14																													
RICH GRIFFITHS Richard A. LB 6'3 230 Miami (Florida) B: 12/8/1953 Hollis, NY Pro: W																															
1975	HAM	8	0		2				2	11																					
ANDREW GRIGG Andrew SB 6'2 190 Ottawa; Sault Ste. Marie Storm Jrs. B: 4/25/1971 Sault Ste. Marie, ON																															
1995	HAM	10	1		0	1													10	118	11.8	37	0	9	54	6.0	16	4	31	7.8	15
1996	HAM	9				6													2	17	8.5	11	0	2	5	2.5	5	5	58	11.6	23
1997	HAM	18	0	0	1	4						36	6	0	0		0	1	26	529	20.3	81	5	6	16	2.7	6	1	0	0.0	0
1998	HAM+	18				4						24	4						51	889	17.4	62	4	1	2	2.0	2				
1999	HAM	18	1	1	0	2						30	5						46	883	19.2	78	5								
2000	HAM	18	1	0	1	2						36	6						54	878	16.3	61	6								
2001	HAM+	18	3	1	1	6						23	3						77	1150	14.9	55	3								
2002	HAM	18				6						30	4						53	845	15.9	65	4								
8	Years	127	6	2	3	31						179	28					1	319	5309	16.6	81	27	18	77	4.3	16	10	89	8.9	23
LARRY GRIGG Larry HB 5'11 180 Oklahoma B: 1932 Draft: 2-16 1954 BAL																															
1954	MTL	8							2	26		20	4	60	300	5.0	25	4	6	37	6.2	15	0					3	57	19.0	23
PAT GRIGNON Pat DE 5'11 210 Idaho																															
1947	MTL	2																													
FRANCO GRILLA Franco K 6'1 195 Central Florida B: 7/21/1970 Fort Lauderdale, FL																															
1995	BIR	6				2						38	0																		
CLORINDO GRILLI Clorindo RB 5'10 180 McMaster B: 7/26/1962 Ascoli, Italy Draft: 4-32 1985 EDM																															
1986	OTT	15																	27	276	10.2	32	0	2	24	12.0	23				
BILLY JOE GRIMES William Joseph HB 6'1 195 Oklahoma State B: 7/27/1927 County Line, OK D: 3/26/2005 Oklahoma City, OK Draft: 5-34 1949 LA-AAFC; 2-20 1949 CHIB Pro: AN																															
1953	HAM	3										5	1					1													
DON GRIMES Donald J. G																															
1946	OTT	12																													
1947	OTT	1																													
2	Years	13																													
GREG GRIMES Gregory Charles DB 6'0 195 Washington B: 11/18/1957 Vernon, TX																															
1981	OTT	8							2	15																					
LLOYD GRIMSRUD Lloyd Alex DT-DE 6'2 255 Idaho B: 12/31/1951																															
1974	WPG	16	0		3																										

Year	Team	GP	FM	FF	FR	TK	SK	YDS	IR	YDS	PD	PTS	TD	RA	YDS	AVG	LG	TD	REC	YDS	AVG	LG	TD	PR	YDS	AVG	LG	KOR	YDS	AVG	LG
1975	WPG	13
1976	HAM	2
1977	EDM	1
1977	MTL	2
1977	Year	3
4	Years	32	0		3
LEO GROENEWEGEN Leo OG-OT-C 6'5 265 British Columbia B: 8/13/1965 Vancouver, BC Draft: 1-1 1987 OTT
1987	OTT	18	0		1	2
1988	OTT	18	0		1	0
1989	OTT	12				1
1989	BC	6				0
1989	Year	18				1
1990	BC	18	0		2	2
1991	BC*	18				2
1992	BC	18				0
1993	BC	18				0
1994	EDM	18				1
1995	EDM	18	0		1	1
1996	EDM*	18				0
1997	EDM+	18				2
1998	EDM	18	0	0	1	0
1999	EDM+	18	0	0	1	0
2000	EDM*	18				2
2001	EDM	8				0
2002	EDM	18				0
2003	EDM	10				0
17	Years	282	0	0	7	13
YORG GROMER Yorg RB 6'1 220 Montana Western B: 12/8/1960 Draft: 8-69 1983 CAL
1986	CAL	2
DICK GROOM Richard E 6'1 169 B: 1920 Hamilton, ON D: 6/17/2005 Brantford, ON
1946	HAM+	12										5	1
MATT GROOTEGOED Matthew Arthur LB 5'11 218 Southern California B: 5/6/1982 Huntington Beach, CA Pro: N
2007	CAL	13	0	2	0	20
2008	CAL	6				12
2009	CAL	4	0	1	1	9
3	Years	23	0	3	1	41
BYRON GROSS Byron LB 6'0 227 North Texas B: 7/31/1969
1995	BIR	6				8
LEE GROSSCUP Clyde Lee Edward QB 6'1 186 Washington; Santa Monica JC; Utah B: 12/27/1936 Santa Monica, CA Draft: 1-10 1959 NYG Pro: N
1963	SAS	1
DAVE GROSZ Dave QB 6'1 205 Oregon B: 1939 Draft: 12-139 1960 PHI; 28- 1961 OAK
1961	SAS	16	5		4							12	2	47	78	1.7	13	2	3	18	6.0	11	0
1962	MTL	10							1	28														1	1	1.0	1
2	Years	26	5		4				1	28		12	2	47	78	1.7	13	2	3	18	6.0	11	0	1	1	1.0	1
TYLER GROVESTEEN Tyler J. LB 6'1 225 Wisconsin-Whitewater B: 1/21/1977 Madison, WI
2001	TOR	3	0	0	1	10					1
BOB GRUPP Robert William P 5'11 193 Duke B: 5/8/1955 Philadelphia, PA Draft: 7B-171 1977 NYJ Pro: NU
1977	CAL	2	0		1
JIMMY GUARANTANO James SB 5'10 194 Rutgers B: 7/30/1969 New York, NY
1994	BAL	2				0
BILL GUDGEON Bill B Hamilton Jrs.
1947	HAM	1
BRIAN GUEBERT Brian DE 5'9 245 Saskatchewan B: 12/19/1981 Saskatoon, SK
2007	WPG	14	0	0	1	7																						1	12	12.0	12
2008	WPG	11				1
2	Years	25	0	0	1	8																						1	12	12.0	12
DULACK GUERRIER Dulack E. DE 6'3 235 Florida State B: 7/27/1971
1995	SHR	4	0		1	0
MIKE GUESS Michael A. DB 5'10 192 Ohio State B: 4/20/1958 Columbus, OH Draft: 6-156 1980 CHIB Pro: U
1980	BC	2																						4	60	15.0	35	1	26	26.0	26
TERRY GUESS Terry WR 6'0 200 Georgia Military JC; Gardner-Webb B: 9/22/1974 Orangeburg, SC Draft: 5C-165 1996 NO Pro: N
1997	HAM	2				1						6	1						3	65	21.7	50	1
DON GUEST Don FB 6'4 215 none B: 1935
1956	OTT	5												3	15	5.0	6	0
DENNIS GUEVIN Dennis OT 6'5 275 Simon Fraser B: 12/10/1959 Wainwright, AB Draft: TE 1982 BC
1982	BC	9	0		1
1983	BC	16	2		0
1984	BC	16
1985	BC	6
4	Years	47	2	0	1
DUDLEY GUICE Dudley, Jr. SB-WR 6'3 217 Northwestern State (Louisiana) B: 5/28/1986 Fayette, MS
2009	WPG	3				0													6	76	12.7	33	0
JOE GUIDO Joe HB 5'11 190 Youngstown State B: 10/17/1933 Leetonia, OH Draft: 14-162 1957 BAL
1955	OTT	4							2	25				6	15	2.5	5	0										1	23	23.0	23
GINO GUIDUGLI Gino QB 6'4 230 Cincinnati B: 3/13/1983 Cincinnati, OH
2007	BC	11	1	0	0	0								1	-3	-3.0	-3	0
BRANDON GUILLORY Brandon DE 6'4 253 Louisiana-Monroe B: 6/28/1983 New Orleans, LA
2006	EDM	3				5	3.0				1
2008	EDM	11				21	6.0	39.0			2
2	Years	14				26	9.0	39.0			3
TONY GUILLORY Anthony R. LB 6'4 232 Nebraska; Lamar B: 11/20/1942 Opelousas, LA Draft: 15- 1965 HOU; 7-93 1965 LARM Pro: N
1970	WPG	8							1	19
PIERRE GUINDON Joseph Antoine Pierre-Marie C 6'1 225 Ottawa B: 7/12/1947 Apple Hill, ON Draft: 1-3 1968 WPG
1968	WPG	16	1		0							68	0	1	0	0.0	0	0
1969	WPG	16										64	0
1970	MTL	3										0	0
3	Years	35	1		0							139	0	1	0	0.0	0	0
ERIC GULIFORD Eric Andre WR 5'8 170 Arizona State B: 10/25/1969 Kansas City, KS Pro: NX
1996	WPG	11	4		0	1						18	3	2	11	5.5	6	0	47	758	16.1	70	3	44	546	12.4	71	31	634	20.5	31
1999	SAS	14	1	0	0	6						24	4						50	675	13.5	48	4	45	342	7.6	25	3	53	17.7	22
2000	SAS	16	2	0	0	5						50	8						73	1084	14.8	81	8	52	651	12.5	71	1	28	28.0	28
2001	SAS	2				0													5	53	10.6	17	0	8	97	12.1	25
4	Years	43	7	0	0	12						92	15	2	11	5.5	6	0	175	2570	14.7	81	15	149	1636	11.0	71	35	715	20.4	31
CHUCK GULLICKSON Chuck OG-LB 5'11 210 Saskatoon Hilltops Jrs.; Western Michigan B: 1938
1963	SAS	1
MARK GUNN Mark Pierre DT 6'5 285 Merced JC; Pittsburgh B: 7/24/1968 Cleveland, OH Draft: 4-94 1991 NYJ Pro: N
1999	CAL	7	0	1	0	5					1
TOM GUNNARI Tom, Jr. T 6'2 220 Lower Columbia JC; Washington State B: 1933 Draft: 23-274(f) 1955 SF
1956	BC	8
JERRY GUSTAFSON Jerry F. QB 6'1 210 Stanford B: 1934 Draft: 27-315 1956 SF
1956	BC	10	9		0							18	3	56	43	0.8	16	3
ERIC GUTHRIE Eric QB-P 6'1 200 Vancouver Meralomas Jrs.; Boise State B: 4/27/1947 Vancouver, BC Draft: 14-356 1972 SF Pro: W

Year	Team	GP	FM	FF	FR	TK	SK	YDS	IR	YDS	PD	PTS	TD	RA	YDS	AVG	LG	TD	REC	YDS	AVG	LG	TD	PR	YDS	AVG	LG	KOR	YDS	AVG	LG
1972	BC	16										1	0	1	5	5.0	5	0													
1973	BC	16	1		2							3	0																		
1975	BC	16	4		0							32	1	6	5	0.8	11	1													
1976	BC	16	1		0							6	1	18	59	3.3	23	1													
1977	SAS	16												4	10	2.5	11	0													
5	Years	80	6		2							42	2	29	79	2.7	23	2													
MARK GUY Mark WR 5'9 170 Tennessee-Martin B: 1/28/1964 Olive Branch, MS																															
1989	SAS	7	1		1	0						6	1	1	-1	-1.0	-1	0	10	114	11.4	30	1	4	5	1.3	7	8	171	21.4	29
1990	SAS	12				1						12	2						29	328	11.3	27	2	5	13	2.6	6	3	45	15.0	17
1991	CAL	7	1		0	0						6	1						16	264	16.5	42	1	29	401	13.8	51	1	15	15.0	15
3	Years	26	2		1	1						24	4	1	-1	-1.0	-1	0	55	706	12.8	42	4	38	419	11.0	51	12	231	19.3	29
TIM GUY Timothy Mark DE 6'6 249 Oregon B: 8/16/1952 Compton, CA Draft: 5B-122 1974 BUF; 9-104 1974 PHI-WFL Pro: W																															
1977	SAS	2																													
RAMON GUZMAN Ramon L. LB 6'2 232 Buffalo B: 9/29/1982 New York, NY Pro: N																															
2009	MTL	16	0	0	1	44	2.0	9.0	1	25	3																				
2010	MTL	18	0	3	2	34	2.0	31.0	1	43	5	6	1																		
2011	MTL	18	0	1	1	59	1.0	4.0			4																				
3	Years	52	0	4	4	137	5.0	44.0	2	68	12	6	1																		
ROSS GWINN Charles Ross OG-OT 6'3 273 Northwestern State (Louisiana) B: 7/25/1944 Deport, TX Pro: N																															
1971	EDM	9																													
DAN GYETVAI Dan OG 6'7 280 Windsor B: 8/3/1978 Windsor, ON																															
2002	WPG	18				1																									
2003	WPG	18				2																									
2004	WPG	7				0																									
2005	WPG	17				0																									
4	Years	60				3																									
CED GYLES Cedric (Mickey) HB 6'0 178 Vancouver Blue Bombers Jrs. B: 1927																															
1948	CAL	10										5	1					1													
1950	CAL	13												8	31	3.9		0	2	26	13.0		0								
1951	CAL	14												16	40	2.5		0	4	50	12.5	12	0	29	163	5.6		7	95	13.6	
3	Years	37										5	1	24	71	3.0	0	1	6	76	12.7	12	0	29	163	5.6	0	7	95	13.6	
BOB HAAS Robert J. C 6'1 220 Army; Tulsa B: 1930 Dayton, OH																															
1956	WPG	11							1	0																					
NEIL HABIG Philip C-LB 6'0 225 Purdue B: 9/6/1936 Wheeling, WVDraft: 27-315 1958 GB																															
1958	SAS	10	0		3				1	14																					
1959	SAS+	15																													
1960	SAS+	14							1																						
1961	SAS+	15																													
1962	SAS*	16																													
1963	SAS+	16	0		1				7	63																					
1964	SAS+	12							1																						
7	Years	98	0		4				10	77																					
DAVE HACK David Michael OT 6'5 300 Maryland B: 4/22/1972 Holland, NY																															
1996	HAM	3				0																									
1998	HAM	18				1																									
1999	HAM+	18	0	0	1	1																									
2000	HAM+	18				4																									
2001	HAM+	18				0																									
2002	HAM+	17				1																									
2003	HAM	16				0																									
2004	HAM+	18				1																									
2005	HAM	12				1																									
9	Years	138	0	0	1	9																									
DALE HACKBART Dale Leonard DB 6'3 210 Wisconsin B: 7/21/1938 Madison, WI Draft: FS-1- 1960 OAK; 5-51 1960 GB Pro: N																															
1965	WPG	3							1																						
RICK HACKLEY Richard Matt OT 6'4 276 San Diego CC; New Mexico State B: 9/17/1946 Toledo, OH Draft: 7-162 1969 BOS																															
1969	SAS	2																													
CAM HACKNEY Campbell LB 6'2 210 Simon Fraser B: 12/6/1957 Draft: 2-16 1980 CAL																															
1980	HAM	8																													
1980	SAS	5																													
1980	Year	13																													
1981	SAS	16	0		1		2.0																								
1982	SAS	16	0		1		6.0																								
3	Years	40	0		2		8.0																								
DAVE HADDEN Dave WB-TE 5'11 209 Queen's B: 10/26/1952 Draft: 1A-8 1974 OTT																															
1975	TOR	16	0		1							18	3	14	53	3.8	16	1	16	149	9.3	24	2					1	10	10.0	10
1976	TOR	16										12	2	1	0	0.0	0	0	20	241	12.1	35	2					13	226	17.4	28
1977	SAS	7																	3	41	13.7	18	0								
1978	HAM	16																													
4	Years	55	0		1							30	5	15	53	3.5	16	1	39	431	11.1	35	4					14	236	16.9	28
BILLY HADDLETON Billy QB 5'4 145 Toronto Parkdale Jrs. B: 1926																															
1947	TOR	6																													
FRED HADLEY Fred WR 6'2 185 Mississippi State B: 3/18/1966 Tupelo, MS Draft: 8-213 1989 NO																															
1991	WPG	2	1		0	0													3	30	10.0	13	0	13	55	4.2	14	3	68	22.7	28
BUTCH HADNOT Derik O'Keith RB 6'0 220 Texas B: 3/31/1971 Kirbyville, TX																															
1993	TOR	1				1								1	4	4.0	4	0													
1994	SHR	7	1		0	4								11	29	2.6	10	0	6	71	11.8	32	0								
2	Years	8	1		0	5								12	33	2.8	10	0	6	71	11.8	32	0								
ART HAEGE Arthur T. LB 6'2 248 St. Ambrose B: 9/29/1937 D: 3/5/2007 Des Moines, IA																															
1963	SAS	1																													
DARIAN HAGAN Darian L. DB-QB 5'9 191 Colorado B: 2/1/1970 Lynwood, CA Draft: 9-242 1992 SF																															
1992	TOR	2												1	-6	-6.0	-6	0													
1994	LV	11	3		0	5								12	52	4.3	21	0	1	5	5.0	5	0	17	108	6.4	14	9	177	19.7	42
1995	EDM	14	0		2	41			3	36	7													1	3	3.0	3	5	133	26.6	41
1996	EDM	11	1		1	24	1.0	5.0	2	100	4													12	101	8.4	18	7	126	18.0	25
4	Years	38	4		3	70	1.0	5.0	5	136	11			13	46	3.5	21	0	1	5	5.0	5	0	30	212	7.1	18	21	436	20.8	42
ROGER HAGBERG Roger Wheeler FB-OHB-LB 6'2 216 Minnesota B: 2/28/1939 Winnebago, MN D: 4/15/1970 near Lafayette, CA Draft: 10A-128 1961 GB Pro: N																															
1961	WPG	9	3									36	6	79	432	5.5	19	6	1	18	18.0	18	0								
1962	WPG	16	4									36	6	157	856	5.5	64	4	29	373	12.9	38	2					2	35	17.5	25
1963	WPG	16	2		1							12	2	164	695	4.2	22	2	23	206	9.0	25	0					5	58	11.6	20
1964	WPG	4	1		0							6	1	43	154	3.6	11	1	2	13	6.5	10	0					2	7	3.5	6
4	Years	45	10		1							90	15	443	2137	4.8	64	13	55	610	11.1	38	2					9	100	11.1	25
MARWAN HAGE Marwan C 6'2 291 Colorado B: 9/14/1981 Beirut, Lebanon Draft: 2-14 2004 HAM																															
2004	HAM	3				1																									
2005	HAM	18	0	0	1	2																									
2006	HAM	17				2																									
2007	HAM+	18	1	0	0	1																									
2008	HAM	18	0	0	1	3																									
2009	HAM	18				0																									
2010	HAM*	18	1	0	0	0																									
2011	HAM	9				0																									
8	Years	119	2	0	2	9																									

Year	Team	GP	FM	FF	FR	TK	SK	YDS	IR	YDS	PD	PTS	TD	RA	YDS	AVG	LG	TD	REC	YDS	AVG	LG	TD	PR	YDS	AVG	LG	KOR	YDS	AVG	LG
IAN HAGEMOEN Ian DT-C-MG 6'2 235 Vancouver Meralomas Jrs. B: 1941 D: 10/9/2009																															
1962	BC	16																													
1963	BC	16	0		1																										
1964	BC	2																													
1964	EDM	10																							1	0	0.0	0				
1964	Year	12																							1	0	0.0	0				
1965	SAS	12																													
4	Years	46	0		1																				1	0	0.0	0				
JIM HAGERTY James HB 6'1 188 Pasadena CC; Washington State B: 12/5/1933 Blanchard, IA																															
1956	TOR	3																											5	65	13.0	24
MIKE HAGGARD Mike WR 6'3 181 South Carolina B: 7/4/1951 Alexander City, AL Draft: 7-169 1973 NYJ																															
1974	HAM	6										6	1	2	-5	-2.5		0	13	156	12.0	30	1								
JOE HAGINS Joe LB 6'0 215 Purdue B: 11/12/1973 Folkston, GA																															
1998	HAM	14	2	0	2	32					3													10	114	11.4	43	11	291	26.5	39
1999	HAM	16	0	1	5	57	4.0	26.0	1	34	2	24	4	3	0	0.0	3	2													
2	Years	30	2	1	7	89	4.0	26.0	1	34	5	24	4	3	0	0.0	3	2						10	114	11.4	43	11	291	26.5	39
MIKE HAGLER Collins OHB 5'10 180 Iowa B: 1935																															
1958	SAS	16	4		2							42	7	108	657	6.1	57	3	31	381	12.3	74	2	64	768	12.0	66	24	744	31.0	67
1959	SAS	5										6	1	19	147	7.7	36	0	5	39	7.8	20	1	7	72	10.3	29	10	223	22.3	38
1960	OTT	3												12	72	6.0	12	0	5	58	11.6	16	0	7	29	4.1	12	5	124	24.8	33
3	Years	24	4		2							48	8	139	876	6.3	57	3	41	478	11.7	74	3	78	869	11.1	66	39	1091	28.0	67
BERT HAIGH Herbert W. E 6'0 185 B: 1918																															
1946	OTT+	11										16	1										1								
1947	OTT+	11										8	1										1								
1948	OTT+	12										11	2										2								
1949	OTT	8										17	3										3								
4	Years	42										52	7										7								
KEN HAILEY Kenneth J. DB 5'10 174 San Francisco State B: 7/12/1961 Oceanside, CA																															
1983	WPG	5																										6	185	30.8	69
1984	WPG*	16	5		2		3.0		9	240		6	1											50	477	9.5	28	6	145	24.2	43
1985	WPG*	16	0		2				2	52														9	101	11.2	21	4	61	15.3	29
1986	WPG	18	0		1		3.0		2	42																		2	45	22.5	25
1987	WPG*	14			1	60			6	86		6	1											3	13	4.3	6				
1988	WPG	12				19	2.0		2	5																					
1989	WPG	13				39			3	11														1	-4	-4.0	-4				
1990	WPG	10	0		2	26			1	15		6	1															17	370	21.8	41
1991	WPG	6				26			2	32														4	32	8.0	9	7	126	18.0	23
1992	OTT	17	1		1	46	3.0		1	5														3	20	6.7	14	19	378	19.9	46
1993	BC	7	2		2	15																						11	201	18.3	36
11	Years	134	8		11	231	11.0		28	488		18	3											70	639	9.1	28	72	1511	21.0	69
KRIS HAINES David Kris WR 5'11 183 Notre Dame B: 7/23/1957 Akron, OH Draft: 9-233 1979 WAS Pro: NU																															
1985	MTL	10										12	2	4	29	7.3	18	0	16	223	13.9	53	2	0	-3		-3				
RUSS HAINES Russ T-G 6'1 237 Lakeshore Flyers Ints. B: 1935																															
1955	WPG	2																													
1958	SAS	6																													
1959	SAS	16																													
1960	SAS	2																													
1961	BC	6																													
5	Years	32																													
HENRY HAIR Henry R. E 6'4 218 Georgia Tech B: 8/17/1931 D: 7/17/2003 Atlanta, GA Draft: 3C-34 1954 LARM																															
1957	TOR	5							1	16									6	113	18.8	28	0								
1958	TOR	6																	2	19	9.5	11	0					2	27	13.5	14
2	Years	11							1	16									8	132	16.5	28	0					2	27	13.5	14
LARRY HAIRSTON Lawrence T 255 Nevada-Reno Draft: 12-144 1951 CHIB																															
1951	OTT	1																													
SAM HAIRSTON Samuel DE 6'4 260 North Carolina A&T State B: 11/9/1969 Winston-Salem, NC																															
1995	HAM	4				9	3.0	16.0	1	19	2																				
1996	HAM	7				0	5.0	32.0																							
1996	OTT	1				13					1																				
1996	Year	8				13	5.0	32.0			1																				
2	Years	11				22	8.0	48.0	1	19	3																				
STACEY HAIRSTON Stacey A. CB 5'9 180 Ohio Northern B: 8/16/1967 Columbus, OH Pro: N																															
1990	SAS	18	1		0	50	1.0												1	30	30.0	30	0	2	22	11.0	13	5	42	8.4	17
1991	SAS	18	0		2	63			3	0																		1	19	19.0	19
1992	SAS	13	0		1	50			5	42		6	1	0	11		8	0						3	19	6.3	12	1	14	14.0	11
3	Years	49	1		3	163	1.0		8	42		6	1	0	11		8	0	1	30	30.0	30	0	5	41	8.2	13	7	75	10.7	19
MICKEY HAJASH Grayson DB 6'0 195 Calgary North Hill Jrs.; Alberta B: 1925 Matramindszet, Hungary																															
1949	CAL	14																													
SHERKO HAJI-RASOULI Sherko OG-OT 6'6 326 Miami (Florida) B: 1/9/1980 Shiran, IranDraft: 2-12 2002 MTL																															
2003	MTL	1				0																									
2004	MTL	18				0																									
2005	BC	16	0	0	1	2													1	3	3.0	3	0								
2006	BC	18				0																									
2007	BC	17				1																									
2008	BC	15				2																									
2009	BC	18				0																									
2010	BC	8				1																									
8	Years	111	0	0	1	6													1	3	3.0	3	0								
DENNIS HALEY Dennis Sean LB 6'1 247 Virginia B: 2/18/1982 Roanoke, VA Pro: N																															
2009	HAM	4				19			1	0	0																				
JERMAINE HALEY Jermaine L. DT 6'4 315 Surrey Rams Jrs.; Okanagan Sun Jrs.; Butte JC B: 2/13/1973 Tulare County, CA Draft: 7A-232 1999 MIA Pro: N																															
1998	TOR	16	0	1	0	31	7.0	36.0			1																				
1999	TOR	18	0	1	0	37	2.0		1	0	1			3	15	5.0	6	0													
2	Years	34	0	2	0	68	9.0	36.0	1	0	2			3	15	5.0	6	0													
JIMMY HALEY Jimmy TE 6'3 250 Kentucky B: 11/14/1976 Lowell, MA																															
2000	TOR	6				2													1	7	7.0	7	0								
RONNIE HALIBURTON Ronnie Maurice DE-LB 6'4 230 Louisiana State B: 4/14/1968 New Orleans, LA Draft: 6-164 1990 DEN Pro: N																															
1994	SHR	3				6																									
AARON HALL Aaron LB 6'1 240 Purdue B: 9/29/1973 Circleville, OH																															
1996	CAL	1				1	3.0	31.0	3	1	4																				
ANTONIO HALL Antonio OT-OG 6'3 316 Kentucky B: 3/28/1982 Canton, OH																															
2006	SAS	3	0	0	1	0																									
2008	CAL	6				1																									
2009	CAL	1				1																									
2009	SAS	10				0																						1	0	0.0	0
2009	Year	11				1																						1	0	0.0	0
3	Years	10	0	0	1	2																						1	0	0.0	0
B.J. HALL Bakial James QB 6'3 217 Troy*; Solano CC; Webber International B: 1/27/1985 Tampa, FL																															
2011	TOR	18				0						6	1	12	25	2.1	11	1													
BOB HALL Robert F. CB 6'1 185 Brown B: 1944 Walpole, MA Draft: 14-120 1966 BOS; 5B-76 1966 MIN																															
1967	BC	10	0		1				4	22																					
CAM HALL Cam LB 6'1 220 Boise State B: 1/11/1982 Richland, WA																															

Year	Team	GP	FM	FF	FR	TK	SK	YDS	IR	YDS	PD	PTS	TD	RA	YDS	AVG	LG	TD	REC	YDS	AVG	LG	TD	PR	YDS	AVG	LG	KOR	YDS	AVG	LG
2007	WPG	18	0	1	2	78	2.0	8.0			4																				
2008	WPG	18	0	2	1	70	3.0	12.0	2	37	4	6	1																		
2	Years	36	0	3	3	148	5.0	20.0	2	37	8	6	1																		
DARRAN HALL Darran Lamont WR 5'8 170 Grossmont JC; Colorado State B: 9/8/1975 San Diego, CA Draft: 6-186 1999 TEN																																
2001	CAL	2	1	0	0	0						6	1						2	15	7.5	19	1	13	67	5.2	15	7	200	28.6	55
2001	EDM	6				1													9	166	18.4	44	0	8	131	16.4	55	11	250	22.7	48
2001	Year	8	1	0	0	1						6	1						11	181	16.5	44	1	21	198	9.4	55	18	450	25.0	55
2002	MTL	6	1	0	0	1						6	1						14	172	12.3	36	1					10	203	20.3	33
2	Years	8	2	0	0	2						12	2						25	353	14.1	44	2	21	198	9.4	55	28	653	23.3	55
DARRYL HALL Darryl Cavada CB 5'11 180 Long Beach CC; San Diego State B: 10/23/1959 Greensboro, NC Pro: N																																
1984	EDM	16	3		0				11	151		6	1											2	12	6.0	8	6	152	25.3	34
1985	EDM	11							2	28																					
1986	OTT	17							5	21																					
1987	OTT	3				6																									
4	Years	47	3		0	6			18	200		6	1											2	12	6.0	8	6	152	25.3	34
DARRYL HALL Darryl Edgar LB-DB 6'2 210 Washington B: 8/1/1966 Oscoda, MI Pro: N																																
1990	CAL	18	0		1	54			3	23																					
1991	CAL*	18	0		2	54			2	21																					
1992	CAL*	18				78			5	202		6	1																		
1996	CAL	18	0		3	61						6	1																		
1997	CAL	18	0	0	1	76	3.0	20.0	1	0	8																				
1998	CAL+	18	1	0	1	79	6.0	31.0	2	16	8																				
1999	CAL	17	0	0	1	74	4.0	29.0			4																				
2000	CAL	18	0	1	2	70	5.0	8.0			1																				
8	Years	143	1	1	11	546	18.0	88.0	13	262	21	12	2																		
GEORGE HALL George G 5'11 220 Ottawa Jrs. B: 1924																																
1946	OTT	9																													
1947	OTT	12										5	1																		
1948	OTT	8																													
1949	OTT	10																													
1950	OTT	6																													
5	Years	45										5	1																		
KALIN HALL Kalin RB 5'8 203 Brigham Young B: 1/12/1972 Las Vegas, NV																																
1994	LV	2				0						6	1	27	214	7.9	34	0	3	49	16.3	43	1								
1995	HAM	15	3		0	5						54	9	118	581	4.9	44	5	69	635	9.2	73	4								
2	Years	17	3		0	5						60	10	145	795	5.5	44	5	72	684	9.5	73	5								
KEN HALL Charles Kenneth HB 6'1 205 Texas A&M B: 12/13/1935 Madisonville, TX Draft: 14-165(f) 1958 BAL Pro: N																																
1957	EDM	12										28	4	48	376	7.8	34	1	15	370	24.7	85	3					9	292	32.4	34
KYLE HALL Kyle DB 6'2 190 Western Ontario B: 10/5/1965 Sarnia, ON Draft: 2A-10 1987 OTT																																
1987	OTT	10				28																									
1988	OTT	18	1		2	53			3	16														2	2	1.0	2				
1989	OTT	18				39																									
1990	OTT	18	0		2	5																									
1991	WPG	14				8			3	30																					
1992	WPG	12	0		2	29																									
6	Years	90	1		6	162			6	46														2	2	1.0	2				
MARK HALL Mark James DT 6'4 285 Louisiana State; Mississippi Gulf Coast JC; Louisiana-Lafayette B: 8/21/1965 Morgan City, LA Draft: 7-169 1989 GB Pro: N																																
1992	HAM	7	0		2	13	1.0																								
MARQUEZ HALL Marquez Vernett CB 5'9 175 Vanderbilt; Tennessee State B: 3/18/1988 Shorter, AL																																
2011	BC	1				2	1.0	10.0																							
NICKIE HALL Carl Nicholas QB 6'4 205 Tulane B: 8/1/1959 Lake Charles, LA Draft: 10-255 1981 GB																																
1983	WPG	12	3		1									27	193	7.1	22	0													
1983	SAS	1												1	4	4.0	4	0													
1983	Year	13	3		1									28	197	7.0	22	0													
1984	SAS	6	2		1									5	16	3.2	14	0													
2	Years	18	5		2									33	213	6.5	22	0													
PETE HALL Peter William QB 6'3 210 Marquette B: 2/28/1939 Sharon, PA Draft: SS 1960 BUF; 12-144 1960 NYG Pro: N																																
1962	TOR	4												14	42	3.0	13	0													
RANDY HALL Randy Lee DB 6'3 194 Idaho B: 2/8/1952 East Wenatchee, WA Draft: 13-317 1974 BAL; 34-401 1974 PHI-WFL Pro: N																																
1978	SAS	8							1	68		6	1																		
RICHIE HALL Richard Harold, Jr. DB 5'6 160 Colorado State B: 10/4/1960 San Antonio, TX																																
1983	CAL*	16	2		2				4	76		6	1											50	561	11.2	74	1	12	12.0	12
1984	CAL	16	2		2		2.5		2	83														37	316	8.5	23				
1985	CAL	15	2		0		1.0		3	74														54	442	8.2	43				
1986	CAL+	16	0		1		4.0		8	116														16	260	16.3	73				
1987	CAL	18	1		1	64	1.0		4	35														64	738	11.5	54	1	0	0.0	0
1988	SAS+	18	1		2	51	3.0		2	4														68	503	7.4	50				
1989	SAS	18	3		2	60	1.0		2	11														44	395	9.0	29				
1990	SAS+	18	0		2	62	3.0		6	132		6	1											1	0	0.0	0	1	0	0.0	0
1991	SAS	18	0		1	64	1.0		3	64																					
9	Years	153	11		13	301	16.5		34	595		12	2											334	3215	9.6	74	3	12	4.0	12
ROBERT HALL Robert QB 6'0 170 Texas Tech B: 12/30/1970 Atlanta, GA Pro: E																																
1994	SHR	11	4		2	0								7	47	6.7	20	0													
SANTINO HALL Santino DH-LB 6'0 190 Texas Southern B: 12/2/1981 West Palm Beach, FL																																
2004	SAS	15	0	1	0	51			3	8	14																				
2005	SAS	6	1	0	0	17																									
2005	WPG	2				1																									
2005	Year	8	1	0	0	18																									
2	Years	21	1	1	0	69			3	8	14																				
STEVE HALL Steven WR 6'2 191 Guelph B: 3/19/1960 Geelong, Australia Draft: 4-36 1983 EDM																																
1983	WPG	5																	2	22	11.0	15	0								
1983	TOR	1																													
1983	Year	6																	2	22	11.0	15	0								
1985	OTT	16	0		1														20	310	15.5	51	0					2	14	7.0	10
2	Years	21	0		1														22	332	15.1	51	0					2	14	7.0	10
HAROLD HALLMAN Harold E. DT 6'0 242 Auburn B: 12/10/1962 Macon, GA D: 12/23/2005 Macon, GA Draft: 10B-270 1986 SF																																
1986	CAL*	17	0		1		19.0																					1	8	8.0	8
1987	CAL+	16				34	15.0																								
1988	CAL	8				23	4.0																								
1988	TOR	7	0		1	16	7.0																								
1988	Year	15	0		1	39	11.0																								
1989	TOR*	18				57	15.0																								
1990	TOR*	18				43	9.0																								
1991	TOR*	17				48	7.0		1	29		6	1																		
1992	TOR	16				53	4.0	18.0																							
1993	TOR	13				33	2.0	17.0																							
8	Years	123	0		2	307	82.0	35.0	1	29		6	1															1	8	8.0	8
RANDY HALSALL Randel Kenneth OG-DL 6'3 255 Wake Forest B: 10/24/1949 Toronto, ON D: 8/21/2009 Gulf Breee, FL Draft: 1A-1 1974 TOR																																
1974	WPG	14																													
1975	WPG	16																													
1976	WPG	16																													
1977	WPG	16	0		1																									

Year	Team	GP	FM	FF	FR	TK	SK	YDS	IR	YDS	PD	PTS	TD	RA	YDS	AVG	LG	TD	REC	YDS	AVG	LG	TD	PR	YDS	AVG	LG	KOR	YDS	AVG	LG
1978	WPG	6																													
1978	MTL	5																													
1978	Year	11																													
1979	OTT	4																													
1979	HAM	5																													
1979	Year	9																													
6	Years	72	0		1																										
TRACY HAM Tracy D. QB 5'10 190 Georgia Southern B: 1/5/1964 High Springs, FL Draft: 9-240 1987 LARM																															
1987	EDM	5				0						6	1	9	56	6.2	20	1													
1988	EDM	14	9		2	0						30	5	86	628	7.3	44	5													
1989	EDM*	18	0		1	1						60	10	125	1005	8.0	55	10													
1990	EDM	18	9		0	4						30	5	136	1096	8.1	32	5													
1991	EDM	17	14		5	0						42	7	125	998	8.0	42	7													
1992	EDM	18	8		0	3						30	5	92	655	7.1	45	5													
1993	TOR	18	5		0	0						42	7	72	605	8.4	42	7	1	-7	-7.0	-7	0								
1994	BAL	18	8		2	1						24	4	76	613	8.1	80	4													
1995	BAL	18	4		0	2						24	4	83	610	7.3	45	4													
1996	MTL	17	3		0	2						24	4	74	604	8.2	57	4													
1997	MTL	18	8	0	2	2						36	6	82	584	7.1	41	6													
1998	MTL	18	2	0	0	1						6	1	55	378	6.9	22	1													
1999	MTL	18	5	0	0	2						18	3	44	211	4.8	16	3													
13	Years	215	80	0	12	18						372	62	1059	8043	7.6	80	62	1	-7	-7.0	-7	0								
JON HAMEISTER-RIES Jon OT-OG 6'6 308 Tulsa B: 1/26/1984 Edmonton, AB Draft: 2-15 2006 BC																															
2010	BC	17	1	0	1	1																									
2011	BC	9				1																									
2	Years	26	1	0	1	2																									
ROGER HAMELIN Roger DT-DE-OT 6'2 235 Weston Wildcats Jrs. B: 4/27/1941 Winnipeg, MB																															
1961	WPG	16																													
1962	WPG	16																													
1963	WPG	16																													
1964	WPG	16																													
1965	WPG	14																													
1966	WPG	16																													
1967	WPG	16										6	0																		
1968	WPG	2																													
1969	WPG	16																													
9	Years	128										6	0																		
MIKE HAMELUCK Michael C-OG-OT-DT 6'4 250 Ottawa Sooners Jrs. B: 8/27/1955 Ottawa, ON																															
1978	MTL	3																													
1979	MTL	12																													
1980	MTL	16	0		1																										
1981	MTL	15																													
1982	TOR	16	0		2									0	2		2	0										1	1	1.0	1
1983	TOR	16	1		1																										
1984	TOR	16																													
1985	OTT	7																													
1986	WPG	14																													
9	Years	115	1		4									0	2		2	0										1	1	1.0	1
MARSH HAMES Marshall G 5'10 217 Regina Dales Jrs.; Toronto Draft: 1- 1952 TOR																															
1949	SAS	5																													
1952	TOR	7																													
1953	TOR	13																													
3	Years	25																													
BOB HAMILTON Bob TE 6'2 220 Wilfrid Laurier B: 8/21/1947 Welland, ON Draft: 2-14 1971 TOR																															
1971	TOR	5																													
1973	HAM	7																													
2	Years	12																													
BRANDON HAMILTON Brandon CB 5'9 175 Tulane B: 3/5/1972 Baton Rouge, LA																															
1994	EDM	3				9																									
1995	SHR	11	0		1	23			1	14	5																				
1996	BC	17	0		1	63			5	82	7	12	2											1	18	18.0	18				
1997	WPG	18	0	3	0	53			5	105	4																				
1998	WPG	15	0	1	0	45			2	42	6																				
1999	WPG	13	0	1	0	34			1	0	4																				
2000	WPG	17	0	2	2	47			2	0	5																				
2001	HAM	18				48			1	31	8																				
2002	HAM	18				60			1	1	9																				
2003	HAM+	17	0	1	0	56			4	100	5	6	1																		
10	Years	147	0	8	4	438			22	375	53	18	3											1	18	18.0	18				
FREDDY HAMILTON Fred DB-FB-LB 5'11 188 Hamilton Wildcats Jrs.; Hamilton Ints. B: 1929																															
1952	SAS	14										15	3	40	161	4.0	18	1	2	25	12.5	21	2					2	17	8.5	12
1953	SAS	16												1	3	3.0	3	0	6	63	10.5		0								
1954	SAS	15												2	8	4.0	4	0						1	4	4.0	4	2	24	12.0	15
1955	SAS	15	1		0				1	0				6	23	3.8	7	0	1	5	5.0	5	0					7	92	13.1	26
1956	SAS	11							1	0				9	-12	-1.3	-6	0										10	167	16.7	37
1957	SAS	14	0		1							6	1															6	96	16.0	19
1958	SAS	5																													
7	Years	90	1		1				2	0		21	4	58	183	3.2	18	1	9	93	10.3	21	2	1	4	4.0	4	27	396	14.7	37
JAY HAMILTON Jay RB 6'0 200 Alberta B: 11/30/1973 Edmonton, AB Draft: 2-16 1996 EDM																															
1996	EDM	18				14					1			1	-3	-3.0	-3	0													
1997	EDM	11				7																									
1998	EDM	4				1													1	3	3.0	3	0								
3	Years	33				22					1			1	-3	-3.0	-3	0	1	3	3.0	3	0								
KELLY HAMILTON Kelly LB 6'2 215 Sequoias JC B: 8/20/1959																															
1983	HAM	1																										1	14	14.0	14
1984	HAM	3																													
2	Years	4																										1	14	14.0	14
MARSHALL HAMILTON Marshall S 5'10 170 Yale; Regina Rams Jrs. B: 10/5/1957																															
1981	SAS	16							1	4																					
1982	SAS	16							1	0																					
1983	SAS	16							5	44																					
1984	HAM	4																													
1984	CAL	2																													
1984	Year	6																													
4	Years	52							7	48																					
NORM HAMILTON Norman T-DE 5'11 215 Texas Christian B: 3/4/1935 Lolita, TX																															
1957	MTL	14																										1	0	0.0	0
SKIP HAMILTON Lenwood W. NT 6'2 265 North Carolina State; Southern University B: 5/14/1959 Philadelphia, PA Pro: N																															
1984	EDM	1																													
1985	EDM	4					1.0																								
2	Years	5					1.0																								
GEOFF HAMLIN Geoffrey FB 6'1 220 North Carolina; Queen's B: 9/29/1949 Ottawa, ON																															

Year	Team	GP	FM	FF	FR	TK	SK	YDS	IR	YDS	PD	PTS	TD	RA	YDS	AVG	LG	TD	REC	YDS	AVG	LG	TD	PR	YDS	AVG	LG	KOR	YDS	AVG	LG
1973	WPG	2																													
HORACE HAMM Horace A. WR 5'11 172 Lehigh B: 12/20/1969 Jamaica, WI																															
1993	SAC	2				0													4	60	15.0	25	0								
MATT HAMMER Matthew S 6'1 183 Guelph B: 12/4/1975 Inverary, ON Draft: 4-26 1999 SAS																															
1999	SAS	3				0																									
2000	SAS	1				0																									
2	Years	4				0																									
ALAN HAMMOND Alan HB 155 Calgary Jrs.																															
1947	CAL	6																													
JOHNNY HAMMOND John G 6'0 198 McGill B: 1923																															
1946	WPG	7																													
1947	MTL	10																													
1948	MTL	12																													
1949	MTL	10																													
1950	MTL	4																													
1951	MTL	4																													
6	Years	47																													
VANCE HAMMOND Vance G. DT-OT-OG 6'6 295 Clemson B: 12/4/1967 Spartanburg, SC Draft: 5-117 1991 PHX Pro: E																															
1993	SAC	18	0		1	37	4.0	25.0	1	28																					
1994	SAC	12				0																									
1995	MEM	18	1		0	3																									
3	Years	48	1		1	40	4.0	25.0	1	28																					
JUAN HAMMONDS Juan Decharles DL 6'3 260 Michigan State B: 3/5/1972																															
1996	MTL	6				15	1.0	2.0																							
ANDRE HAMPTON Andre LB 6'0 227 Valdosta State B: 6/4/1971																															
1995	SHR	1				1																									
BILL HAMPTON William Louis LB 6'1 220 Arkansas B: 6/13/1957 Chicago, IL																															
1979	MTL	5	0		1				1	15		6	1																		
1980	MTL	16	0		1																										
1981	MTL	16	0		2		3.0		3	14																					
1982	MTL+	14	0		1		2.0		1	7																					
1983	MTL	16	0		1		3.5		1	24																					
1984	MTL	7					3.0		1	10																					
6	Years	74	0		6		11.5		7	70		6	1																		
WILLIAM HAMPTON William Louis, Jr. CB 5'10 190 Murray State B: 3/7/1975 Little Rock, AR Pro: N																															
1997	CAL	12				30			4	80	9	6	1																		
1998	CAL	17	0	0	1	52			4	159	13	6	1											3	37	12.3	19				
1999	CAL*	18	0	0	2	53			8	193	12	18	3											16	93	5.8	13				
3	Years	47	0	0	3	135			16	432	34	30	5											19	130	6.8	19				
OMARI HAND Omari Sean DL 6'4 265 Tennessee B: 7/3/1980 Philadelphia, PA Pro: EN																															
2005	MTL	1				0																									
TED HAND Theodore Paul C 6'2 250 Eastern Michigan B: 7/10/1951 Hazel Park, NJ Pro: W																															
1975	HAM	11	1		0																										
GARRY HANDLEY Garry LB 6'3 235 Richmond Raiders Jrs. B: 7/27/1964																															
1988	BC	1																													
JIM HANIFAN James Martin Michael E 6'1 180 California B: 9/21/1933 Draft: 12-139 1955 LARM																															
1955	TOR	10																	25	325	13.0	25	0					2	22	11.0	14
JOHN HANKINSON John Herbert QB 6'2 185 Minnesota B: 2/6/1943 Edina, MN Draft: RS-7-55 1965 BOS; 8A-100(f) 1965 MIN																															
1968	EDM	2																													
TOM HANLON Thomas E 6'4 215 Pennsylvania B: 1930																															
1952	MTL	10										10	2										2								
JOCK HANNABACH Jock DB 5'10 165 Wyoming B: 1938																															
1961	MTL	1																													
1961	CAL	2																	1	12	12.0	12	0								
1961	Year	3																	1	12	12.0	12	0								
NICK HANNAH Nick James LB 6'1 220 Eastern Oregon B: 10/3/1981 East Wenatchee, WA Pro: E																															
2007	BC	5	0	0	1	5																									
TITO HANNAH Tito LB 6'3 230 South Carolina State B: 7/13/1976 Marion, SC																															
2000	MTL	12	0	1	0	23	5.0	16.0	0	0	1																				
2001	MTL	13	0	1	0	26	4.0	27.0																							
2002	EDM	1				0																									
3	Years	26	0	2	0	49	9.0	43.0																							
BARRIE HANSEN Barrie S 5'10 180 Los Angeles Pierce JC B: 1942 Winnipeg, MB																															
1961	MTL	14							2	41														1	3	3.0	3				
1962	MTL	14							1	0														3	20	6.7	13				
1963	MTL	13							1	1																					
1964	WPG	16	0		1				3	69																					
1965	WPG	13	0		1				2	10		6	1											3	33	11.0	15				
1966	WPG	16							2	0														1	8	8.0	8				
1967	HAM	14							1	0																					
1968	HAM	14							5	85																					
1969	HAM	14							1	30														1	0	0.0	0				
1970	BC	15							3	32														1	85	85.0	85				
10	Years	143	0		2				21	268		6	1											10	149	14.9	85				
GEORGE HANSEN George OT-OG 6'2 215 Calgary Bronks Jrs.; Georgia B: 4/22/1934 Calgary, AB																															
1959	CAL	16	0		4																										
1960	CAL	16																													
1961	CAL	11							1	0		59	0	1	-9	-9.0	-9	0													
1962	CAL	16										4	0																		
1963	CAL	16	0		1																										
1964	CAL	16																													
1965	CAL	16	0		2							6	1																		
1966	CAL	16																													
8	Years	123	0		7				1	0		69	1	1	-9	-9.0	-9	0													
HOWIE HANSEN E. Howard HB 6'0 177 Southern California*; UCLA B: 9/6/1925 Draft: 28-334 1951 PIT																															
1951	EDM	6										10	2						8	216	27.0		2	3	35	11.7					
JAYSON HANSEN Jayson OL 6'4 315 Butte CC; Texas Tech B: 7/25/1973 Kelowna, BC Draft: 4-33 1997 TOR																															
1998	TOR	10				0																									
FRITZ HANSON Melvin L. HB 5'8 160 North Dakota State B: 7/13/1914 Perham, MN D: 2/14/1996 Calgary, AB																															
1947	CAL	6										10	2					2													
1948	CAL	11										5	1										1								
2	Years	17										15	3					2					1								
RYAN HANSON Ryan RB 6'1 215 Slippery Rock B: 1/17/1964 London, England Draft: 1B-5 1988 WPG																															
1988	TOR	9	0		1	0						6	1	23	121	5.3	39	1	5	54	10.8	24	0								
1989	TOR	18	0		1	0						12	2	14	101	7.2	29	1	4	41	10.3	24	0					1	51	51.0	49
1990	TOR	10				0								1	1	1.0	1	0	2	16	8.0	10	0								
1990	BC	7	2		1	2						12	2	21	70	3.3	17	0	8	53	6.6	13	2								
1990	Year	17	2		1	2						12	2	22	71	3.2	17	0	10	69	6.9	13	2								
1991	BC	16	2		0	11						6	1	11	102	9.3	23	0	4	68	17.0	27	1								
1992	BC	15	1		1	12						18	3	32	203	6.3	48	2	15	216	14.4	57	1					1	21	21.0	21
1993	BC	18				11						6	1	15	143	9.5	45	1	1	9	9.0	9	0					6	113	18.8	48
1994	BC	18	1		0	16						12	2	17	57	3.4	10	1	4	27	6.8	13	1								

Year	Team	GP	FM	FF	FR	TK	SK	YDS	IR	YDS	PD	PTS	TD	RA	YDS	AVG	LG	TD	REC	YDS	AVG	LG	TD	PR	YDS	AVG	LG	KOR	YDS	AVG	LG
1995	BC	7	2		0	5								15	40	2.7	7	0	3	36	12.0	19	0								
8	Years	111	8		4	57						72	12	149	838	5.6	48	6	46	520	11.3	57	5					8	185	23.1	49
BOB HANTLA Robert Dean OT-DG-DT 6'1 220 Kansas B: 10/3/1931 St. John, KS Draft: 5A-55 1954 SF Pro: N																															
1956	BC	7																	1	12	12.0	12	0								
1957	BC	9																													
1959	WPG	1																													
3	Years	17																	1	12	12.0	12	0								
BERNIE HANULA Bernard S. T 6'1 225 Wake Forest B: 7/3/1923 D: 7/22/2004 Salter Path, NC Draft: 25-170 1949 BUF-AAFC; 6-60 1949 CHIC																															
1949	HAM	12																													
MERLE HAPES Merle Alison HB 5'10 190 Mississippi B: 5/9/1919 Garden Grove, CA D: 7/18/1994 Biloxi, MS Draft: 1-8 1942 NYG Pro: N																															
1953	HAM	14										5	0																		
1954	HAM	14										20	4	130	572	4.4	44	4	12	122	10.2	21	0								
2	Years	28										25	4	130	572	4.4	44	4	12	122	10.2	21	0								
ROBIN HARBER Robin DB 6'0 192 Ottawa B: 9/29/1953 Draft: 3A-19 1977 CAL																															
1977	CAL	14																						4	12	3.0	4				
1978	CAL	11																													
1979	OTT	4																													
3	Years	29																						4	12	3.0	4				
BILLY HARDEE Abraham William, Jr. DB 6'1 184 Virginia Tech B: 8/12/1954 Lakeland, FL D: 7/4/2011 Phoenix, AZ Pro: NU																															
1978	CAL	1																													
1978	TOR	6	1		0														1	27	27.0	27	0	5	25	5.0	10	2	18	9.0	10
1978	Year	7	1		0														1	27	27.0	27	0	5	25	5.0	10	2	18	9.0	10
1979	TOR+	16	0		1				8	55																		1	0	0.0	0
1980	TOR+	16	1		2				7	80		12	2											39	371	9.5	88				
1981	TOR	12							1	25														16	141	8.8	17				
1981	OTT	4							3	2																					
1981	Year	16							4	27														16	141	8.8	17				
1982	OTT	16	0		2				4	69		6	1											19	162	8.5	37				
5	Years	61	2		5				23	231		18	3						1	27	27.0	27	0	79	699	8.8	88	3	18	6.0	10
BUDDY HARDEMAN Willie Riley RB 6'0 196 Iowa State B: 10/21/1954 Auburn, NY Pro: NU																															
1978	TOR	3	1		0									7	13	1.9	4	0	4	37	9.3	22	0					3	85	28.3	42
BUD HARDEN Bud QB 6'0 180 Manitoba B: 6/24/1950																															
1978	WPG	2																													
CEDRIC HARDEN Cedric Bernard DE 6'6 260 Florida A&M B: 10/19/1974 Atlanta, GA Draft: 5-126 1998 SD Pro: ENX																															
2001	SAS	6				12	3.0	26.0																							
MICHAEL HARDEN Michael D. DB 5'11 190 Missouri B: 10/21/1981 Kansas City, MO Pro: EN																															
2007	HAM	7				18			1	7	1																				
STEVE HARDIN Steven John OT 6'7 334 Oregon B: 12/30/1971 Bellevue, WA Draft: 1-3 1998 BC Pro: EN																															
1998	BC	7				0																									
1999	BC	18				4																									
2000	BC	18				0																									
2001	BC	17				1																									
2002	BC+	18				0																									
5	Years	78				5																									
BOB HARDING Robert SB 6'6 235 York B: 6/3/1963 Agincourt, ON Draft: 2-13 1986 OTT																															
1986	OTT	4																	1	2	2.0	2	0								
CHUCK HARDING Charles QB-DB 6'1 192 Virginia B: 1932																															
1955	SAS	13	0		3				1	0				6	-11	-1.8	8	0						1	5	5.0	5	1	13	13.0	13
1956	OTT	14							7	52				20	176	8.8	35	0	1	14	14.0	14	0								
2	Years	27	0		3				8	52				26	165	6.3	35	0	1	14	14.0	14	0	1	5	5.0	5	1	13	13.0	13
GLEN HARDING Glen C 6'2 225 Toronto Draft: 1-2 1961 CAL																															
1961	CAL	3																													
GREG HARDING Gregory CB 6'2 202 Nicholls State B: 7/31/1960 New Orleans, LA Pro: N																															
1986	EDM	12							4	74		6	1																		
1987	EDM	1				2			1	0																					
2	Years	13				2			5	74		6	1																		
LARRY HARDING Lawrence F. DE 6'4 200 Michigan State B: 1936 Syracuse, NY Draft: 24-283 1958 LARM																															
1958	MTL	1																													
RODNEY HARDING Rodney DT-DE 6'2 250 Oklahoma State B: 8/1/1962 Oklahoma City, OK Draft: TD 1985 DEN-USFL																															
1985	TOR	14	0		2		8.0																								
1986	TOR+	18	0		1		10.0		1	13		6	1																		
1987	TOR+	17				26	13.0		1	70																		1	0	0.0	0
1988	TOR+	18				37	12.0																								
1989	TOR	17	0		2	29	9.0		1	16		6	1																		
1990	TOR	18	0		3	19	6.0		1	16		6	1																		
1991	TOR	11				16	3.0																								
1992	TOR*	17	0		3	31	12.0	72.0	1	11																					
1993	TOR	17	0		1	29	3.0	25.0																							
1994	TOR*	18	0		1	23	16.0	103.0																							
1995	MEM+	18				27	3.0	7.0			4																				
1996	CAL+	18	0		1	16	10.0	63.0			6																				
12	Years	201	0		14	253	105.0	270.0	5	126	10	18	3															1	0	0.0	0
DREW HARDVILLE Andrew Mason DB 6'1 190 Arizona B: 3/16/1958 Racine, WI																															
1981	TOR	6																													
CHRIS HARDY Chris S-P 5'11 180 Manitoba B: 6/6/1972 Portage La Prairie, MB Draft: 6-47 1997 EDM																															
1997	EDM	8				3													1	27	27.0	27	0								
1998	EDM	18				28			1	23	0																				
1999	EDM	17	0	0	2	55			2	55	0																				
2000	EDM	14				34			6	146	3																				
2001	EDM	16	0	0	1	23			1	0	1	1	0																		
2002	EDM	18				2																									
2003	TOR	14				10													1	16	16.0	16	0								
2004	TOR	18	0	0	1	5						9	0																		
2005	TOR	18				4						4	0																		
2006	TOR	18				10						1	0																		
2007	TOR	18				12						10	0						1	11	11.0	11	0								
2008	TOR	10				12																									
12	Years	187	0	0	4	198			10	224	4	25	0						3	54	18.0	27	0								
JOHN HARDY John Louis, Jr. CB 5'11 175 California B: 6/11/1968 Pasadena, CA Pro: EN																															
1993	OTT	1				1																									
1993	TOR	4				15			1	4																					
1993	Year	5				16			1	4																					
ROBERT HARDY Robert Kenneth RB 5'10 210 Lees-McRae JC; Carson-Newman B: 9/1/1967 Gaffney, SC Pro: N																															
1992	EDM	3	2		0	5								24	162	6.8	42	0													
1993	SAC	3				2						6	1	5	12	2.4	4	1	3	9	3.0	5	0								
2	Years	6	2		0	7						6	1	29	174	6.0	42	1	3	9	3.0	5	0								
TONY HARGAIN Anthony Michael WR 6'0 194 Oregon B: 12/26/1967 Palo Alto, CA Draft: 8-221 1991 SF Pro: N																															
1994	SAC	13				0													39	617	15.8	58	0								
AARON HARGREAVES Aaron WR-SB 6'1 215 Simon Fraser B: 1/26/1986 Ladner, BC Draft: 2-15 2008 WPG																															
2008	WPG	11	0	1	0	4													2	53	26.5	39	0								
2009	WPG	16				2													7	71	10.1	17	0					1	0	0.0	0
2010	WPG	18	1	0	0	1						6	1						14	115	8.2	17	1								

Year	Team	GP	FM	FF	FR	TK	SK	YDS	IR	YDS	PD	PTS	TD	RA	YDS	AVG	LG	TD	REC	YDS	AVG	LG	TD	PR	YDS	AVG	LG	KOR	YDS	AVG	LG
2011	WPG	17	1	0	2	0													30	292	9.7	21	0								
4	Years	62	2	1	2	7						6	1						53	531	10.0	39	1					1	0	0.0	0
DARRELL HARLE Darrell OT-OG 6'2 270 Eastern Michigan; Regina Rams Jrs. B: 3/4/1966 Regina, SK Draft: 6-42 1988 SAS																															
1989	HAM	16				0																									
1990	HAM	17				2																									
1991	HAM	18				4																									
1992	HAM	12	0		1	4																									
1993	TOR	8				0																									
1993	HAM	5				0																									
1993	Year	13				0																									
1994	HAM	18	1		0	2																									
6	Years	89	1		1	12																									
IDRIS HAROON Idris Mubarak DE 6'2 240 Arizona B: 9/16/1977 Houston, TX																															
2001	HAM	7	0	1	0	16	2.0	16.0	0	0	1																				
DAVID HARPER David Douglas LB-DE 6'1 220 Weber State; Humboldt State B: 5/5/1966 Eureka, CA Draft: 11-277 1990 DAL Pro: N																															
1994	SAC	10				15																									
1995	SA+	15				74	7.0	70.0	1	31	1																				
1996	OTT	2				3																									
3	Years	27				92	7.0	70.0	1	31	1																				
GLENN HARPER Glenn P-K 5'11 173 Washington State B: 9/12/1962 Edmonton, AB Draft: 5B-43 1986 SAS																															
1986	CAL	18	7		0							5	0																		
1987	CAL+	18	5		2	0						3	0	1	3	3.0	3	0													
1988	CAL	18	2		0	0						4	0																		
1989	TOR	8	1		0	0						3	0																		
1990	TOR	15	1		0	0						1	0																		
1991	EDM	4	1		0	0						3	0																		
1992	EDM	18	4		3	2						4	0	0	5		5	0													
1993	EDM+	18	1		0	0						7	0																		
1994	EDM	18	0		1	0						2	0																		
1995	EDM	18	2		1	1						6	0																		
1996	EDM	18	2		1	4						7	0																		
2002	OTT	16	2	0	0	0						3	0																		
2003	OTT	5				1						1	0																		
13	Years	192	28	0	8	8						49	0	1	8	8.0	5	0													
JACK HARPER John HB-LB-E 6'3 190 Montreal Ints. B: 1927																															
1949	MTL	12										15	3					1					2								
1950	MTL	7																													
1951	MTL	12										5	1										1								
1952	MTL	9																													
1953	SAS	15							1	2				4	17	4.3		0	5	58	11.6		0								
1954	SAS	15							1	0				7	19	2.7	4	0	1	9	9.0	9	0					3	37	12.3	20
1955	TOR	6																													
7	Years	76							2	2		20	4	11	36	3.3	4	1	6	67	11.2	9	3					3	37	12.3	20
JAMES HARPER James Terrell OG 6'2 285 Alcorn State B: 9/6/1966 Jackson, MS Pro: E																															
1993	SAC	8	0		1	1																									
JOHN HARPER John OT 6'3 250 Adams State B: 1946 Draft: 7-168 1968 OAK																															
1969	EDM	14																													
1970	EDM	6																													
2	Years	20																													
LESTER HARPER Lester LB 5'11 215 North Texas B: 10/29/1960																															
1984	CAL	3	0		1				1	15																			13	266	20.5	31
MICHAEL HARPER Michael WR-SB 5'10 180 Southern California B: 5/11/1961 Kansas City, KS Draft: 11A-293 1984 LARM; TD 1984 LA-USFL Pro: N																															
1984	CAL	4										12	2	1	-4	-4.0	-4	0	12	220	18.3	72	2	1	7	7.0	7				
1985	CAL	1												4	12	3.0	6	0	3	17	5.7	7	0	3	14	4.7	6				
2	Years	5										12	2	5	8	1.6	6	0	15	237	15.8	72	2	4	21	5.3	7				
NICK HARPER Nicholas Necosi CB 5'10 182 Fort Valley State B: 9/10/1974 Baldwin, GA Pro: N																															
2000	HAM	18	0	1	1	56			4	8	8																				
NOLAN HARPER Nolan LB 6'2 220 Idaho State B: 9/27/1964 Moscow, ID																															
1988	TOR	6				20	2.0																								
ROGER HARPER Roger Michael DB 6'2 223 Ohio State B: 10/26/1970 Columbus, OH Draft: 2-38 1993 ATL Pro: N																															
1999	BC	8				22			1	8	2																				
SCOTT HARPER Scott OT 6'4 302 Marshall B: 12/13/1977 Mobile, AL																															
2002	WPG	2				0																									
2003	WPG	2				0																									
2	Years	4				0																									
TOM HARPLEY Tom DE 6'0 197 Winnipeg Jrs. B: 1929																															
1951	TOR	10																													
1952	TOR	9																													
1953	WPG	16																													
1954	WPG	9																													
4	Years	44																													
FLOYD HARRAWOOD Floyd OT-DT-DG 6'2 245 Tulsa B: 9/8/1929 Kansas City, KS Draft: 9-104 1953 GB																															
1953	CAL	5																													
1954	CAL	4																	1	14	14.0	14	0								
1955	WPG+	16	1		3																										
1956	CAL	10																													
1957	CAL	15	0		1																										
5	Years	50	1		4														1	14	14.0	14	0								
CALVIN HARRELL Calvin F., Jr. FB-OHB 6'1 210 Arkansas State B: 9/7/1949 D: 6/26/1994 Little Rock, AR Draft: 7B-180 1972 MIA																															
1972	EDM	7	1		0							6	1	26	110	4.2	23	1	10	104	10.4	31	0								
1973	EDM	2										12	2	11	57	5.2	20	0	10	117	11.7	24	2								
1974	EDM	16	1		1							60	10	137	626	4.6	47	9	38	409	10.8	41	1								
1975	EDM	10	2		0							24	4	101	402	4.0	18	2	31	332	10.7	53	2					3	53	17.7	21
1976	EDM	10	1		1							30	5	71	224	3.2	12	3	27	241	8.9	36	2								
5	Years	45	5		2							132	22	346	1419	4.1	47	15	116	1203	10.4	53	7					3	53	17.7	21
GARY HARRELL Gary Lamar (The Flea) WR 5'7 170 Howard B: 1/23/1972 Miami, FL Pro: EN																															
1996	MTL	5	1		0	0						6	1						9	93	10.3	30	0	24	344	14.3	74	8	169	21.1	31
ED HARRINGTON Edison OG-DE 6'3 240 Minnesota; Langston B: 2/8/1941 Hugo, OK D: 11/27/2011 Field, ON																															
1963	TOR	12										6	1	1	-2	-2.0	-2	0													
1964	TOR+	14												0	-8		-8	0													
1965	TOR	3																													
1967	TOR	10	0		2							6	1																		
1968	TOR*	14	0		2																										
1969	TOR*	14			2							6	1																		
1970	TOR*	13																													
1971	TOR	6																													
1974	TOR	2																													
9	Years	88	0		6							18	3	1	-10	-10.0	-2	0													
CLAUDE HARRIOTT Claude Desmond DE 6'4 260 Pittsburgh B: 4/8/1981 West Moreland, Jamaica Draft: 5A-147 2004 CHIB Pro: EU																															
2008	TOR	7	0	1	0	20	2.0	7.0			1																				
2009	TOR	14				36	3.0	11.0			3																				
2	Years	21	0	1	0	56	5.0	18.0			4																				

Year	Team	GP	FM	FF	FR	TK	SK	YDS	IR	YDS	PD	PTS	TD	RA	YDS	AVG	LG	TD	REC	YDS	AVG	LG	TD	PR	YDS	AVG	LG	KOR	YDS	AVG	LG
A.J. HARRIS A.J. RB 6'0 225 Northern Illinois B: 8/8/1984 Downers Grove, IL Pro: E																															
2008	EDM	11	1	0	0	4						36	6	99	557	5.6	36	6	37	422	11.4	39	0								
2009	BC	3				0						12	2	33	141	4.3	16	1	7	128	18.3	32	1					1	18	18.0	18
2	Years	14	1	0	0	4						48	8	132	698	5.3	36	7	44	550	12.5	39	1					1	18	18.0	18
ANDREW HARRIS Andrew RB 5'11 195 Vancouver Island Raiders Jrs. B: 4/4/1987 Winnipeg, MB																															
2010	BC	18	2	1	2	3																		23	205	8.9	55	23	505	22.0	72
2011	BC	18	3	0	0	5						48	8	96	458	4.8	32	1	30	395	13.2	63	7	12	146	12.2	39	11	197	17.9	29
2	Years	36	5	1	2	8						48	8	96	458	4.8	32	1	30	395	13.2	63	7	35	351	10.0	55	34	702	20.6	72
AUNDRAE HARRIS Aundrae DB 5'10 177 Mesa CC; California B: 9/29/1977																															
2000	TOR	4				1					1																	1	7	7.0	7
BILLY HARRIS Bill HB 6'1 207 Colorado B: 5/30/1942 Hackensack, NJ Draft: 14-193 1964 NYG																															
1964	OTT	3	2		1									18	69	3.8	17	0	1	12	12.0	12	0					3	67	22.3	30
1964	CAL	2												12	42	3.5	10	0													
1964	Year	5	2		1									30	111	3.7	17	0	1	12	12.0	12	0					3	67	22.3	30
BOB HARRIS Robert OT 6'6 260 Bowling Green State B: 4/21/1958 Amherst, OH Draft: 9-245 1980 PHI																															
1980	HAM	2																													
BOBBY HARRIS Bobby Akeem OT 6'4 310 Mississippi B: 6/15/1983 Decatur, GA Pro: E																															
2009	SAS	8	0	0	1	0																									
CHUCK HARRIS Charlie DT 6'3 260 Tennessee State B: 1941																															
1964	MTL	1																													
COOPER HARRIS Cooper LB 6'1 225 Calgary Colts Jrs.; Pittsburg State B: 10/15/1970 Calgary, AB Draft: 6-48 1994 CAL																															
1996	TOR	18				22																						1	7	7.0	7
1997	HAM	16				20					1																				
1998	HAM	18				16																									
1999	HAM	11	0	1	0	19																									
2000	WPG	4				1																									
5	Years	67	0	1	0	78					1																	1	7	7.0	7
DAYRONI HARRIS Dayroni Deshawn DE 6'6 295 Los Angeles Southwest JC; Central Arkansas B: 7/15/1976 Los Angeles, CA																															
1999	WPG	3				4	1.0	2.0																							
2000	WPG	5				8	2.0	18.0	1	66	0	6	1																		
2000	BC	1				1			1	0	0																				
2000	Year	6				9	2.0	18.0	2	66	0																				
2	Years	8				13	3.0	20.0	2	66	0	6	1																		
DICKIE HARRIS Richard CB 5'11 178 South Carolina B: 5/24/1950 Draft: 5-114 1972 NYJ																															
1972	MTL	14	0		1				7	214		6	1						1	50	50.0	50	0					21	440	21.0	41
1973	MTL+	10	0		2				3	17		6	1											2	12	6.0	12	5	132	26.4	35
1974	MTL*	16	1		2				5	83		6	1															14	368	26.3	54
1975	MTL*	16	1		0				3	13														40	563	14.1	78	30	727	24.2	45
1976	MTL*	16	2		1				5	66														49	578	11.8	55	17	438	25.8	37
1977	MTL*	16	5		2				3	76														45	508	11.3	52				
1978	MTL*	11	1		1				3	96		6	1											19	163	8.6	78				
1979	MTL*	16	1		1				5	32		18	3											55	653	11.9	102	1	15	15.0	15
1980	MTL*	16	2		0				4	34														42	472	11.2	45	1	0	0.0	0
1982	MTL	3	1		0																			19	158	8.3	52				
10	Years	134	14		10				38	631		42	7						1	50	50.0	50	0	271	3107	11.5	102	89	2120	23.8	54
DONNIE HARRIS Don DB 6'2 185 Northland; Rutgers B: 2/8/1954 Elizabeth, NJ Draft: 11-300 1977 WAS Pro: NU																															
1981	MTL	1																													
DONNIE HARRIS Donald DB 6'1 185 Azusa Pacific B: 5/5/1963																															
1985	CAL	4																													
ERIC HARRIS Eric Wayne DB 6'3 202 Memphis B: 8/11/1955 Memphis, TN D: 2/19/2012 Little Rock, AR Draft: 4D-104 1977 KC Pro: N																															
1977	TOR+	16	1		4				7	166		6	1															3	0	0.0	0
1978	TOR+	16	1		2				3	27																		1	0	0.0	0
1979	TOR	16	0		2				3	12																					
3	Years	48	2		8				13	205		6	1															4	0	0.0	0
GERALD HARRIS Gerald RB 5'9 200 Georgia Southern B: 4/11/1964																															
1987	HAM	1				1								9	11	1.2	3	0	2	12	6.0	11	0								
GERALD HARRIS Gerald E. WR 5'11 186 Washington B: 9/23/1977 Stockton, CA Pro: E																															
2002	BC	5				0													1	7	7.0	7	0					1	14	14.0	14
2003	BC	2				0													1	25	25.0	25	0								
2004	BC	1				0													2	32	16.0	29	0								
2005	CAL	7	1	0	0	1													15	235	15.7	56	0								
2005	OTT	4	1	0	0	0						12	2						6	96	16.0	39	2								
2005	Year	11	2	0	0	1						12	2						21	331	15.8	56	2								
4	Years	15	2	0	0	1						12	2						25	395	15.8	56	2					1	14	14.0	14
GREG HARRIS Greg WR 5'7 170 Jackson State B: 9/17/1967 Greenwood, MS																															
1990	SAS	6	1		0	1													12	109	9.1	18	0	4	67	16.8	27	1	22	22.0	22
JAMIE HARRIS James Anthrum WR 5'8 170 Texas Tech; Oklahoma State B: 3/23/1962 McKinney, TX Draft: 7A-177 1985 WAS; TD 1985 DEN-USFL																															
1986	CAL	8	2		2							42	7	1	9	9.0	9	0	14	223	15.9	51	7	19	114	6.0	32	8	216	27.0	36
1990	HAM	1																	1	9	9.0	9	0	1	11	11.0	11	6	107	17.8	46
2	Years	9	2		2							42	7	1	9	9.0	9	0	15	232	15.5	51	7	20	125	6.3	32	14	323	23.1	46
JIM HARRIS Jim DB 5'10 171 Vancouver Blue Bombers Jrs. B: 11/8/1952																															
1975	BC	3																													
1977	CAL	4	0		1																			7	76	10.9	31	3	75	25.0	34
1977	WPG	1																													
1977	HAM	1																													
1977	Year	2	0		1																			7	76	10.9	31	3	75	25.0	34
2	Years	7	0		1																			7	76	10.9	31	3	75	25.0	34
JOE HARRIS Joe T 6'3 225 Toronto B: 1927 Draft: 1-2 1953 OTT																															
1954	OTT	14																													
JOE HARRIS Joseph Alexander LB 6'1 227 Georgia Tech B: 12/6/1952 Fayetteville, NC Draft: 8-197 1975 CHIB Pro: NU																															
1975	HAM	11																													
1976	HAM	16			5				1	0		6	1																		
2	Years	27	0		5				1	0		6	1																		
JOHN HARRIS John Hiram HB 6'1 195 Santa Monica CC B: 5/7/1933 San Antonio, TX Pro: N																															
1959	SAS	3										6	1	11	29	2.6	12	0	2	19	9.5	10	1	11	87	7.9	23	3	68	22.7	33
JOHNNIE HARRIS Johnnie DH 6'2 211 San Bernardino Valley JC; Mississippi State B: 8/21/1972 Chicago, IL Pro: N																															
1995	SA	2				0					1																				
1996	TOR	4				14					2																				
1997	TOR*	18	0	2	0	61			5	72	8																				
3	Years	24	0	2	0	75			5	72	11																				
JOSH HARRIS Joshua Eugene QB 6'1 238 Bowling Green State B: 9/9/1982 Westerville, OH Draft: 6A-187 2004 BAL																															
2005	CAL	6	1	0	1	0								5	40	8.0	36	0													
KELVIN HARRIS Kelvin Douglas C 6'2 285 Miami (Florida) B: 5/17/1969 Panama City, FL Draft: 12-312 1992 LARM Pro: E																															
1994	LV	4			1																										
1995	SA	4				0																									
2	Years	8	0		1	0																									
LOU HARRIS Lou RB 5'10 205 Sacramento CC; Southern California B: 1/1/1950 Jackson, MS Draft: 17-420 1972 DEN																															
1973	BC	15																													
1974	BC*	15																													
1975	BC+	13																													
1976	BC	13																													
1977	CAL	8																													

Year	Team	GP	FM	FF	FR	TK	SK	YDS	IR	YDS	PD	PTS	TD	RA	YDS	AVG	LG	TD	REC	YDS	AVG	LG	TD	PR	YDS	AVG	LG	KOR	YDS	AVG	LG
5	Years	64																													
MAJOR HARRIS Major C. QB 6'1 220 West Virginia B: 2/6/1968 Pittsburgh, PA Draft: 12A-317 1990 LARI																															
1990	BC	8	2		0	0						18	3	19	145	7.6	28	3													
MARK HARRIS Mark K 6'0 220 none B: 8/22/1948 Australia																															
1973	MTL	7										1	0																		
M.L. HARRIS Michael Lee RB-SB 6'5 238 Tampa; Kansas State B: 1/16/1954 Columbus, OH Pro: N																															
1976	HAM	11	2		1							24	4	5	-1	-0.2	0	1	24	550	22.9	76	3					3	51	17.0	19
1977	HAM	16	1		1							48	8	4	12	3.0	8	2	43	771	17.9	50	6								
1978	TOR	12										18	3	5	16	3.2	11	0	32	496	15.5	43	3					1	20	20.0	20
1979	TOR	12	1		0							6	1	3	13	4.3	7	0	46	530	11.5	35	1								
4	Years	51	4		2							96	16	17	40	2.4	11	3	145	2347	16.2	76	13					4	71	17.8	20
ODIE HARRIS Odie Lazar, Jr. DB 6'0 190 Sam Houston State B: 4/1/1966 Bryan, TX Pro: N																															
1998	EDM	11	0	1	0	49			1	6	4																				
ROD HARRIS Roderick World WR-SB 5'10 183 Texas A&M B: 11/14/1966 Dallas, TX Draft: 4-104 1989 HOU Pro: N																															
1993	SAC*	18	2		2	8						42	7						90	1379	15.3	56	7	1	24	24.0	24	1	0	0.0	0
1994	SAC*	18	5		0	3						66	11						86	1280	14.9	58	10	89	869	9.8	102	1	31	31.0	31
1995	SHR	6	2		0	3													8	95	11.9	24	0	11	81	7.4	19				
1996	SAS	18	3		2	1						6	1	2	4	2.0	6	0	58	655	11.3	31	0	41	595	14.5	77	21	417	19.9	42
1997	SAS	13	1	0	0	3						24	4	3	12	4.0	8	0	47	703	15.0	59	3	27	215	8.0	60	18	311	17.3	28
1998	BC	15	1	0	0	3						30	5						48	799	16.6	85	5	38	417	11.0	41	40	914	22.9	52
1999	BC	14	1	0	1	0						18	3						30	502	16.7	71	3	6	16	2.7	6	18	300	16.7	29
7	Years	102	15	0	5	21						186	31	5	16	3.2	8	0	367	5413	14.7	85	28	213	2217	10.4	102	99	1973	19.9	52
RON HARRIS Ronald RB 5'9 190 Colorado State B: 5/10/1955 Panama City, FL Draft: 11-299 1978 MIN																															
1979	OTT	1												8	10	1.3	7	0	1	11	11.0	11	0					5	139	27.8	29
SAMMIE HARRIS Sammy HB 6'0 190 Iowa B: 1939																															
1963	EDM	2	1		0							6	1	4	16	4.0	6	0	4	70	17.5	27	1	5	18	3.6	7				
1964	EDM	2																						2	10	5.0	10	9	193	21.4	31
2	Years	4	1		0							6	1	4	16	4.0	6	0	4	70	17.5	27	1	7	28	4.0	10	9	193	21.4	31
TUFF HARRIS Chester David CB 6'0 198 Montana B: 1/23/1983 St. Xavier, MT Pro: N																															
2011	EDM	1				0																									
WAYNE HARRIS Carrol Wayne LB 6'0 195 Arkansas B: 5/4/1938 Hampton, AR Draft: 12-91 1961 BOS																															
1961	CAL+	16																													
1962	CAL*	16	0		3																										
1963	CAL+	16	0		3				2	20																					
1964	CAL*	16							2	7																					
1965	CAL*	15	0		3				3	45																					
1966	CAL*	16	0		4				2	16																					
1967	CAL*	16			1				4	37																					
1968	CAL*	16	0		3				3	26																					
1969	CAL+	16	0		1				3	90																					
1970	CAL*	15	0		1				2	44																					
1971	CAL*	16	0		2				4	80																					
1972	CAL	6	1		0				3	24														1	19	19.0	19				
12	Years	180	1		21				28	389														1	19	19.0	19				
WAYNE HARRIS Wayne, Jr. LB 6'0 215 Calgary B: 10/30/1959 Draft: 7-60 1981 CAL																															
1982	CAL	16																										3	24	8.0	24
WILL HARRIS Will LB 6'1 210 Southern California B: 12/29/1986 Covina, CA																															
2010	EDM	8	0	0	1	5																									
BILL HARRISON Bill RB 6'0 198 Burlington Braves Jrs.; Ottawa B: 3/28/1953 Draft: TE 1976 HAM																															
1976	HAM	16												2	15	7.5	15	0										4	77	19.3	25
1977	HAM	16	1		0									35	150	4.3	23	0	19	183	9.6	45	0					11	203	18.5	28
1978	HAM	14	1		1									6	17	2.8	6	0	8	120	15.0	36	0	1	4	4.0	4	4	53	13.3	28
1979	HAM	16	0		1									5	19	3.8	7	0	2	31	15.5	24	0	1	8	8.0	8	2	35	17.5	20
1980	TOR	14	1		0							12	2	42	146	3.5	14	2	7	47	6.7	25	0					2	22	11.0	12
5	Years	76	3		2							12	2	90	347	3.9	23	2	36	381	10.6	45	0	2	12	6.0	8	23	390	17.0	28
BOB HARRISON Bob T 215 Calgary Altomahs Jrs. B: 1913																															
1946	CAL	6																													
CHUCK HARRISON Charles OT 6'3 245 Western Michigan B: 11/5/1942																															
1966	OTT	14																													
1967	OTT	14	0		1																										
1968	WPG	16	0		1																										
1969	WPG	16																													
1970	WPG	16	0		1																										
1971	WPG	16																													
1972	WPG	16																													
1973	WPG	16	0		1																										
1974	WPG	16																													
9	Years	140	0		4																										
CRAIG HARRISON Craig SB 6'3 220 Calgary B: 4/22/1968 Calgary, AB																															
1991	WPG	7	0		1	4						6	1																		
1992	WPG	6				3																									
2	Years	13	0		1	7						6	1																		
DICK HARRISON Richard E D: 5/24/2004 Toronto, ON																															
1947	TOR	7																													
EDWIN HARRISON Edwin Charles, II OT 6'4 308 Colorado B: 11/18/1984 Houston, TX																															
2010	CAL	15				0																									
2011	CAL	9				0																									
2	Years	24				0																									
HAL HARRISON Harold E. E 6'3 210 Washington State B: 1915																															
1946	CAL	6																													
1947	CAL	6																													
2	Years	12																													
HERM HARRISON Herman TE-LB 6'3 220 Arizona State B: 1939																															
1964	CAL	14	1		0				3	63									8	73	9.1	17	0								
1965	CAL+	16	1		1							24	4	0	2		2	0	53	826	15.6	43	4								
1966	CAL	6	1		0														15	202	13.5	23	0								
1967	CAL+	16	1		0							54	9						57	721	12.6	31	9								
1968	CAL*	16	1		1							42	7						67	1306	19.5	48	7					1	9	9.0	9
1969	CAL*	16	0		2							24	4						68	1043	15.3	43	4					1	3	3.0	3
1970	CAL*	16										72	12						70	1024	14.6	47	12								
1971	CAL+	16	1		3							24	4						70	980	14.0	44	4								
1972	CAL	16	1		1							18	3						35	518	14.8	46	3								
9	Years	132	7		8				3	63		258	43	0	2		2	0	443	6693	15.1	48	43					2	12	6.0	9
JIM HARRISON Hulet James, Jr. FB 6'4 236 Missouri B: 9/10/1948 San Antonio, TX Draft: 2A-28 1971 CHIB Pro: N																															
1977	BC	14	4		3							24	4	81	345	4.3	16	3	26	211	8.1	42	1								
MARCK HARRISON Marck A. RB 5'8 190 Wisconsin B: 4/20/1961 Columbus, OH Draft: TD 1985 JAC-USFL Pro: U																															
1987	OTT	1				0								6	10	1.7	4	0	1	3	3.0	3	0					4	72	18.0	25
RAY HARRISON Raymond DL 6'1 245 Seton Hall B: 11/23/1959 New Brunswick, NJ																															
1984	OTT	4	0		2		1.0					6	1																		
STEVE HARRISON Steve LB 6'2 225 Renfrew Trojans Jrs.; British Columbia B: 7/20/1960 Ashcroft, BC Draft: 1-2 1983 OTT																															
1983	OTT	13	0		1														1	14	14.0	14	0								
1984	OTT	13	1		1		1.5							1	0	0.0	0	0	5	40	8.0	17	0					1	12	12.0	12

Year	Team	GP	FM	FF	FR	TK	SK	YDS	IR	YDS	PD	PTS	TD	RA	YDS	AVG	LG	TD	REC	YDS	AVG	LG	TD	PR	YDS	AVG	LG	KOR	YDS	AVG	LG
1985	OTT	16																													
1986	OTT	16	0		1		2.0																								
1987	OTT	11					1.0																								
5	Years	69	1		3		4.5							1	0	0.0	0	0	6	54	9.0	17	0					1	12	12.0	12
ROB HARROD Robert WR 6'3 200 Ottawa B: 4/9/1976 Moose Jaw, SK Draft: 2A-9 2000 EDM																															
2000	EDM	5				0													2	30	15.0	20	0								
2001	EDM	12	0	0	1	10													4	57	14.3	24	0								
2002	EDM	1				0																						1	0	0.0	0
3	Years	18	0	0	1	10													6	87	14.5	24	0					1	0	0.0	0
CARL HARRY Carl David WR 5'9 169 Utah B: 10/26/1967 Inglewood, CA Pro: N																															
1994	LV	3												2	5	2.5	9	0	3	36	12.0	15	0								
BEN HART Benjamin Franklin, II OE 6'2 205 Oklahoma B: 8/19/1945 Oklahoma City, OK D: 8/27/2004 Garden City, KS Draft: 3B-80 1967 NO Pro: N																															
1968	EDM	2																										2	28	14.0	19
JEFF HART Jeffery Allen OT 6'5 263 Oregon State B: 9/10/1953 Portland, OR Draft: 3A-71 1975 SF Pro: NU																															
1977	WPG	3	0		1																										
1978	WPG	14																													
2	Years	17	0		1																										
ROY HART Roy, Jr. DT 6'1 280 South Carolina; Northwest Mississippi JC*; South Carolina B: 7/10/1965 Adel, GA Draft: 6-158 1988 SEA Pro: EN																															
1992	HAM	1				8																									
1993	HAM	9				27	2.0	15.0																							
1994	LV	5	0		1	12																									
3	Years	15	0		1	47	2.0	15.0																							
WILLIAM HART William C 5'11 185 Hamilton Panthers Ints. B: 1926 Hamilton, ON																															
1949	HAM	2																													
WALT HARTFIELD Walter, Jr. HB 6'2 220 Tillotson; Texas State B: 2/27/1950 Austin, TX Draft: 14-343 1975 CHIB																															
1974	OTT	4	1		0									13	43	3.3	11	0	2	8	4.0	6	0								
JACK HARTMAN Jack H. QB 5'10 175 Oklahoma State B: 10/7/1925 Dewey, OK D: 11/6/1998 Santa Fe, NM																															
1950	SAS	14										53	1	20	-28	-1.4		0	3	89	29.7		1								
DUNC HARVEY Dunc DB 5'11 190 Edmonton Huskies Jrs. B: 1939																															
1961	EDM	8																										1	28	28.0	28
1962	EDM	14	2									1	0	3	35	11.7	19	0						24	120	5.0	41	5	110	22.0	31
1963	EDM	4	0		1														1	16	16.0	16	0	1	1	1.0	1	1	10	10.0	10
3	Years	26	2		1							1	0	3	35	11.7	19	0	1	16	16.0	16	0	25	121	4.8	41	7	148	21.1	31
JOHN HARVEY John Wallace RB-QB 6'1 185 Texas-Arlington B: 1/26/1950 Austin, TX Draft: 7-158 1974 LARM; 22-261 1974 MEM-WFL Pro: W																															
1973	MTL*	14	10		0							18	3	137	1024	7.5	66	2	32	377	11.8	34	1					5	147	29.4	51
1976	TOR	10	3		0							42	7	16	61	3.8	13	1	26	459	17.7	89	6	34	329	9.7	35	12	274	22.8	28
1977	HAM	1	2		0									5	34	6.8	11	0	4	69	17.3	38	0	1	0	0.0	0	2	38	19.0	21
3	Years	25	15		0							60	10	158	1119	7.1	66	3	62	905	14.6	89	7	35	329	9.4	35	19	459	24.2	51
PETE HARVEY Peter WR 5'11 170 North Texas B: 12/22/1959 Buffalo, N																															
1982	MTL	8	1		0														19	272	14.3	31	0	5	52	10.4	19				
1983	EDM	3																		8	137	17.1	21	0								
2	Years	11	1		0														27	409	15.1	31	0	5	52	10.4	19				
WILLIE HARVEY Willie DE 6'5 285 Stephen F. Austin State B: 8/30/1977 New Orleans, LA																															
2002	CAL	5				7	3.0	12.0			4																				
THOMAS HASKINS Thomas, Jr. RB 5'8 175 Virginia Military Institute B: 8/11/1973 Richmond, VA																															
1997	MTL	2				0								18	134	7.4	30	0	2	15	7.5	10	0	3	17	5.7	8	4	94	23.5	32
1998	MTL	18	2	0	1	13						6	1	44	211	4.8	41	1	16	207	12.9	45	0	25	267	10.7	56	18	412	22.9	43
1999	MTL	15	2	0	0	1						36	6	52	271	5.2	19	2	30	545	18.2	67	4	12	68	5.7	21	39	815	20.9	45
2000	MTL	13	3	0	0	1						36	6	31	167	5.4	17	1	27	459	17.0	71	5	3	28	9.3	11	30	679	22.6	69
2001	MTL	16	3	0	0	3						24	4	71	344	4.8	33	1	50	472	9.4	39	3	20	243	12.2	27	28	556	19.9	37
2002	MTL	18				0						60	10	55	316	5.7	28	3	68	941	13.8	57	7								
6	Years	82	10	0	1	18						162	27	271	1443	5.3	41	8	193	2639	13.7	71	19	63	623	9.9	56	119	2556	21.5	69
HARALD HASSELBACH Harald DT 6'6 284 Washington B: 9/22/1967 Amsterdam, The Netherlands Draft: 5-34 1989 CAL Pro: N																															
1990	CAL	3	0		1	0																									
1991	CAL	11				14	3.0																								
1992	CAL	18	0		2	36	4.0	28.0																							
1993	CAL*	18	1		4	29	7.0	46.0	1	0																					
4	Years	50	1		7	79	14.0	74.0	1	0																					
BILL HATANAKA Bill WR 5'11 172 York B: 3/5/1954 Draft: 1B-6 1976 OTT																															
1976	OTT	5																						15	173	11.5	57	9	211	23.4	44
1977	OTT	15	1		0							12	2						20	318	15.9	41	2	42	441	10.5	46	23	576	25.0	39
1978	OTT	6	1		0														1	8	8.0	8	0	11	36	3.3	13	6	115	19.2	23
1979	HAM	4																						16	69	4.3	17	9	224	24.9	31
4	Years	30	2		0							12	2						21	326	15.5	41	2	84	719	8.6	57	47	1126	24.0	44
CHARLIE HATCH Charles E 6'1 210 Utah State B: 1931 Draft: 30-359 1955 DET																															
1957	SAS	7																										1	22	22.0	22
LAWRENCE HATCH Lawrence CB 5'11 194 Florida B: 5/22/1971 Tucker, GA Draft: 6-142 1993 NE																															
1994	WPG	6	1		2	13			6	3	3																				
RON HATCHER Ronald Allen FB 5'11 215 Michigan State B: 7/3/1939 Pittsburgh, PA Draft: 21-165 1962 NYT; 8-99 1962 WAS Pro: N																															
1963	TOR	3												16	95	5.9	22	0	1	-4	-4.0	-4	0					6	166	27.7	36
1964	TOR	6	1		0							12	2	31	134	4.3	14	1	6	40	6.7	12	1					1	3	3.0	3
2	Years	9	1		0							12	2	47	229	4.9	22	1	7	36	5.1	12	1					7	169	24.1	36
HAL HATFIELD Harold Knight E 6'2 210 Southern California B: 7/21/1927 Hermosa Beach, CA Draft: 16-188 1951 PHI																															
1951	EDM	1																		2	24	12.0		0								
1952	EDM	5			1														4	51	12.8	28	0								
2	Years	6	0		1														6	75	12.5	28	0								
MARK HATFIELD Mark OT-OG 6'6 305 Bishop's B: 8/21/1970 Ottawa, ON Draft: Bonus-8 1995 BC																															
1997	BC	7				1																									
1998	BC	2				0																									
1999	BC	9				1																									
3	Years	18				2																									
STEVE HATFIELD Steve DB 6'0 205 Shippensburg B: 1925 Draft: 17-215 1950 NYG																															
1951	OTT	12										10	1										1								
CORY HATHAWAY Cory FB 6'4 242 Tulsa B: 6/15/1983 Lethbridge, AB Draft: 4-28 2005 OTT																															
2005	OTT	17	0	0	1	8						18	3	3	10	3.3	6	1	17	239	14.1	36	2								
2006	SAS	13				1						6	1						4	76	19.0	38	1								
2	Years	30	0	0	1	9						24	4	3	10	3.3	6	1	21	315	15.0	38	3								
GREG HATTON Gregory Carroll DB 6'2 207 Pasadena CC; Westminster B: 6/16/1955 Chicago, IL																															
1980	TOR	9							2	44		6	1																			
1980	SAS	5																													
1980	Year	14							2	44		6	1																			
LEON HATZIIOANNOU Leon DT 6'1 255 Simon Fraser B: 3/28/1965 Toronto, ON Draft: 3-22 1988 OTT																															
1988	OTT	5	0		1	13																									
1988	WPG	9				3																									
1988	Year	14	0		1	16																									
1989	WPG	15				11																									
1990	WPG	18				7	1.0																								
1991	WPG	18				32	1.0																								
1992	WPG	13	0		1	20	2.0	8.0																							
1993	WPG	12	0		1	16																									
1994	TOR	14				9																									
1995	TOR	9	0		1	14	4.0	31.0																							

Year	Team	GP	FM	FF	FR	TK	SK	YDS	IR	YDS	PD	PTS	TD	RA	YDS	AVG	LG	TD	REC	YDS	AVG	LG	TD	PR	YDS	AVG	LG	KOR	YDS	AVG	LG
8	Years	104	0		4	125	8.0	39.0																							
SIDNEY HAUGABROOK Sidney Blair DB 5'10 190 Delaware B: 3/11/1982																															
2005	HAM	5	1	0	0	9																		8	35	4.4	8	5	123	24.6	40
BRANDON HAW Brandon Kue CB 6'0 200 Rutgers B: 9/24/1980 Cheverly, MD Pro: E																															
2006	CAL	1				0																									
2007	CAL	3				3																									
2	Years	4				3																									
JOE HAWCO Joe RB 5'10 188 Toronto B: 3/12/1957 Draft: 1-8 1980 MTL																															
1980	MTL	16	0		1									6	20	3.3	12	0	1	12	12.0	12	0					2	7	3.5	7
1981	MTL	6	0		1							6	1	9	44	4.9	18	1	6	31	5.2	12	0								
2	Years	22	0		2							6	1	15	64	4.3	18	1	7	43	6.1	12	0					2	7	3.5	7
ANDREW HAWKINS Andrew Austin Wyatt WR-SB 5'8 165 Toledo B: 3/10/1986 Johnstown, PA Pro: N																															
2009	MTL	7				6						18	3	1	5	5.0	5	0	13	131	10.1	19	3					9	163	18.1	29
2010	MTL	8	1	0	1	0						12	2	4	52	13.0	15	0	28	326	11.6	45	2	12	7	0.6	8	6	126	21.0	28
2	Years	15	1	0	1	6						30	5	5	57	11.4	15	0	41	457	11.1	45	5	12	7	0.6	8	15	289	19.3	29
BRENT HAWKINS Brent Lee DE 6'2 250 Purdue; Lewis & Clark CC*; Illinois State B: 9/1/1983 Godfrey, IL Draft: 5-160 2006 JAC Pro: N																															
2010	SAS	13	0	1	2	31	3.0	19.0				6	1																		
MIKE HAWKINS Michael RB 5'9 192 East Carolina B: 7/22/1958 Manson, NC																															
1981	CAL	2	1		0									6	17	2.8	8	0	1	13	13.0	13	0								
MEL HAWKRIGG Melvin M. HB 5'10 170 McMaster B: 1929 Draft: 1- 1952 HAM																															
1952	HAM	8																													
JACK HAWLEY Jack W. QB 6'2 215 San Diego State B: 5/21/1977 Harbor City, CA																															
2002	TOR	9				0								1	1	1.0	1	0													
JUNIOR HAWTHORNE Junior T 6'2 235 Kentucky B: 1941 Draft: 18-241(f) 1962 MIN																															
1964	EDM	1																													
J.T. HAY John T. K-P 6'0 175 Ottawa Sooners Jrs. B: 9/19/1954 Hawkesbury, ON																															
1978	OTT	16										136	0																		
1979	CAL	16										115	0																		
1980	CAL	16										100	0																		
1981	CAL	16	1		0							141	0																		
1982	CAL	16										131	0	1	2	2.0	2	0	1	8	8.0	8	0								
1983	CAL	16										134	0																		
1984	CAL	16	0		1							135	0																		
1985	CAL	16	1		0							120	0																		
1986	CAL+	18	1		0							181	0																		
1987	CAL	18				0						172	0																		
1988	CAL	8	0		1							46	0																		
11	Years	172	3		2	0						1411	0	1	2	2.0	2	0	1	8	8.0	8	0								
ED HAYES Edward Rogers CB 6'0 170 Morgan State B: 8/14/1946 Jacksonville, FL Draft: 4B-88 1969 DEN Pro: NW																															
1971	MTL	3							1	0																		1	15	15.0	15
1972	MTL	4	0		1				1	3																		2	28	14.0	20
2	Years	7	0		1				2	3																		3	43	14.3	20
GARY HAYES Gary L. CB-S 5'10 180 Fresno State B: 8/19/1957 Tucson, AZ Pro: N																															
1981	EDM	15	2		0		2.0		2	39														71	601	8.5	52	9	209	23.2	50
1982	EDM	16	2		0		1.0		2	27														100	818	8.2	45	5	95	19.0	27
1983	EDM	16	2		1		4.0		1	34														61	380	6.2	21	13	269	20.7	38
3	Years	47	6		1		7.0		5	100														232	1799	7.8	52	27	573	21.2	50
LARRY HAYES Larry Gene LB-OG-DG 6'3 230 Vanderbilt B: 7/21/1935 Nashville, TN Pro: N																															
1956	OTT+	14							1	0																					
1957	OTT+	14							2	11																					
1959	OTT+	14							1	7																					
1960	OTT	10																													
4	Years	52							4	18																					
MERCURY HAYES Mercury Wayne WR 5'11 195 Michigan B: 1/1/1973 Houston, TX Draft: 5A-136 1996 NO Pro: N																															
1999	MTL	1				0													4	43	10.8	14	0								
2000	MTL	7				1													13	234	18.0	33	0					8	142	17.8	30
2	Years	8				1													17	277	16.3	33	0					8	142	17.8	30
HARRY HAYNES Harry E																															
1946	CAL	2																													
HAYWARD HAYNES Hayward OG 6'2 285 Florida State B: 6/29/1967 Bartow, FL Draft: 7-182 1991 NO																															
1994	LV	9				0																									
BOB HAYTON Bob HB-FW Calgary Mustangs Jrs.																															
1953	EDM	1																													
1954	EDM	12																													
2	Years	13																													
JEROME HAYWOOD Jerome Randell DT 5'9 280 San Diego State B: 6/7/1978 Los Angeles, CA																															
2002	OTT	11	0	1	0	21	6.0	38.0			1																				
2003	OTT	17	0	2	0	38	5.0	33.0																							
2004	OTT	18	1	0	0	46	2.0	17.0			1			3	5	1.7	2	0													
2005	OTT	18	0	0	1	42	4.0	28.0																							
2006	MTL	11				9	4.0	33.0																				1	9	9.0	9
2007	WPG	14	0	1	1	27	5.0	48.0																							
2008	WPG	18	0	1	0	41	3.0	30.0			1																				
2009	EDM	5				7	2.0	18.0			1																				
8	Years	112	1	5	2	231	31.0	245.0			4			3	5	1.7	2	0										1	9	9.0	9
MANNY HAZARD Emmanuel J. SB-WR 5'8 177 San Francisco CC; Houston B: 7/22/1969 Providence, RI																															
1993	TOR	14				9						48	8						61	1033	16.9	61	8					2	39	19.5	24
1994	SHR	6				2													15	182	12.1	30	0					2	21	10.5	14
1995	HAM	13	1		0	5						18	3						43	531	12.3	45	3					5	100	20.0	28
1996	HAM	1				0																									
4	Years	34	1		0	16						66	11						119	1746	14.7	61	11					9	160	17.8	28
BOB HAZEL Robert E-HB-FW Guelph B: // Scotland																															
1946	HAM	12										5	1																		
1947	TOR	11										3	0																		
2	Years	23										8	1																		
CURTIS HEAD Curtis Ray K-P 5'10 180 Marshall B: 2/16/1981 Jefferson County, KY																															
2003	BC	18	1	0	0	3						191	0	1	8	8.0	8	0													
WIN HEADLEY Winthrop Sargent OG 6'3 250 Wake Forest B: 7/4/1949 Culver City, CA Draft: 8-193 1971 GB																															
1972	MTL	2																													
JIM HEALY James L. (Bubba) G 5'11 220 Holy Cross B: 7/31/1937 Worcester, MA D: 11/10/1980 Albany, NY Draft: 17-196 1959 WAS																															
1959	SAS	10							3	32																					
DENATAY HEARD Denatay L. CB 5'8 175 Stillman B: 3/18/1984 LaGrange, GA																															
2008	SAS	6				7			1	3	1													12	32	2.7	12	5	88	17.6	29
2009	SAS	3	1	0	0	2																		4	60	15.0	30	2	39	19.5	25
2	Years	9	1	0	0	9			1	3	1													16	92	5.8	30	7	127	18.1	29
HERMAN HEARD Herman Willie, Jr. RB 5'10 190 Fort Lewis; Southern Colorado B: 11/24/1961 Denver, CO Draft: 3-61 1984 KC Pro: N																															
1991	HAM	9	1		1	1						6	1	60	287	4.8	28	0	20	223	11.2	24	1								
DAVID HEASMAN David OT 6'5 335 Northern Arizona B: 3/14/1975 Calgary, AB Draft: 4-32 1997 EDM																															
1999	EDM	18				0																									
2000	CAL	18				0																									
2001	CAL	12				1																									
2002	CAL	18				0																									

Year	Team	GP	FM	FF	FR	TK	SK	YDS	IR	YDS	PD	PTS	TD	RA	YDS	AVG	LG	TD	REC	YDS	AVG	LG	TD	PR	YDS	AVG	LG	KOR	YDS	AVG	LG
2003	CAL	13				0																								
2004	BC	16				1																								
6	Years	95				2																								
JO JO HEATH Joseph Leroy, Jr. CB 5'10 182 Pittsburgh B: 3/9/1957 Monessen, PA D: 12/30/2002 Charleroi, PA Draft: 6A-141 1980 CIN Pro: NU																														
1982	TOR	15	0		1				6	33														7	58	8.3	18	23	512	22.3	38
1983	BC	14	3		5		1.0		5	108		12	2											34	305	9.0	25				
1985	OTT	7							3	25																					
3	Years	36	3		6		1.0		14	166		12	2											41	363	8.9	25	23	512	22.3	38
RODNEY HEATH Rodney Larece CB 5'10 174 Minnesota B: 10/29/1974 Cincinnati, OH Pro: N																														
2004	HAM	14				43			1	0	7																				
STAN HEATH Stanley R. QB 6'1 190 Wisconsin; Nevada-Reno B: 3/5/1927 Toledo, OH D: 9/26/2010 Jesup, GA Draft: 25-231 1948 GB; 1-1 1949 CHI-AAFC; 1-5 1949 GB Pro: N																														
1950	HAM	12										5	1										1								
1951	CAL	10														23	88	3.8	23	0													
1952	CAL	5														3	0	0.0	1	0													
1953	HAM	1																												
1954	CAL	15	1		2				1	19				4	-16	-4.0	-2	0													
5	Years	43	1		2				1	19		5	1	30	72	2.4	23	0					1								
KENNY HEATLY Kenneth Jai, Jr. CB 5'11 176 Bethune-Cookman B: 3/28/1982 St. Petersburg, FL																														
2008	TOR	14	0	0	1	38			0	0	3																				
DONALD HEAVEN Donald OT-OG 6'3 313 Florida State B: 4/7/1978 New York, NY																														
2002	SAS	14	0	0	1	1																								
2003	SAS	7				1																								
2004	SAS	11				0																								
3	Years	32	0	0	1	2																								
JEROME HEAVENS Jerome Kenneth HB 5'11 207 Notre Dame B: 8/1/1957 St. Louis, MO Draft: 9-230 1979 CHIB																														
1979	TOR	1												1	-1	-1.0	-1	0										2	46	23.0	24
NICK HEBELER Nick DE-DT 6'4 245 Renfrew Trojans Jrs.; Simon Fraser B: 7/18/1957 Vancouver, BC Draft: TE 1979 BC																														
1979	BC	1	0		2																									
1980	BC	14																												
1981	BC	16	0		2		12.0																				1	12	12.0	12
1982	BC*	15	0		3		14.0		1	27		6	1																		
1983	BC	5					2.0																							
1984	BC	9					10.5																							
1985	BC	16					8.0																							
1986	SAS	17	0		2		8.0																							
1987	SAS	10	0		2	12	2.0					6	1																		
9	Years	103	0		11	12	56.5		1	27		12	2															1	12	12.0	12
BILLY BOB HEBERT Billy Bob WR 6'2 215 Nicholls State B: 10/27/1966																														
1989	CAL	2																	3	10	3.3	5	0								
CHARLIE HEBERT Charles K-P 6'1 210 McNeese State B: 2/21/1978																														
2004	CAL	11	0	0	2	4						92	0																		
KYRIES HEBERT Kyries S-LB 6'3 220 Louisiana-Lafayette B: 10/9/1980 Lafayette, LA Pro: N																														
2004	OTT	18				83			2	0	1																				
2005	OTT	18	0	3	2	95	1.0	9.0	3	139	2	18	3																		
2006	WPG	14	0	5	1	57	2.0	17.0			2																				
2007	WPG	18	1	1	3	75	5.0	49.0	3	60	2																				
2010	HAM	2				4																								
5	Years	70	1	9	6	314	8.0	75.0	8	199	7	18	3																		
JEFF HECHT Jeff S-DH 5'10 202 St. Mary's (Nova Scotia) B: 9/24/1985 Edmonton, AB																														
2011	MTL	17	0	1	0	38			1	20	0																				
BOB HECK Robert Elgin E 6'3 207 Purdue B: 6/17/1925 South Bend, IN Draft: 22-150 1948 SF-AAFC; 13-110 1948 LARM Pro: A																														
1950	TOR	6										8	1										1								
1952	TOR	4										16	0																		
2	Years	10										24	1										1								
NORB HECKER Norbert Earl OE 6'2 193 Baldwin-Wallace B: 5/26/1927 Berea, OH D: 3/13/2004 Los Altos, CA Draft: 6-72 1951 LARM Pro: N																														
1954	TOR	14							1	27		48	2						44	652	14.8	59	2								
1958	HAM	2										5	0						1	9	9.0	9	0								
2	Years	16							1	27		53	2						45	661	14.7	59	2								
WILLIE HECTOR William, II OG-LB 6'2 220 Pacific B: 12/23/1939 New Iberia, LA Draft: 10-80 1961 SD; 5-60 1961 LARM Pro: N																														
1962	CAL	1																												
1963	CAL	5																												
2	Years	6																												
BRIAN HEDGES Brian DT 6'3 244 Carleton (Ontario) B: 8/2/1952 Draft: 3-21 1974 CAL																														
1976	OTT	14			2																									
1977	OTT	16	0		1																									
1978	OTT	16																												
1979	OTT	16																												
4	Years	62	0		3																									
DAREN HEERSPINK Daren John OT 6'6 315 Portland State B: 4/2/1984 Bellingham, WA																														
2009	BC	16				2																								
2005	TOR	1				0																								
2006	TOR	4				0																								
2	Years	5				0																								
JONATHAN HEFNEY Jonathan DH-LB 5'9 190 Tennessee B: 2/27/1985 Rock Hill, SC																														
2009	WPG*	18	1	0	0	71			4	2	10																	9	186	20.7	29
2010	WPG	6				27			2	0	2																	5	109	21.8	41
2011	WPG*	18	0	1	2	79	1.0	5.0	6	23	11																	1	20	20.0	20
3	Years	42	1	1	2	177	1.0	5.0	12	25	23																	15	315	21.0	41
JON HEIDENRICH Jon OT 6'6 295 Louisiana-Monroe B: 6/28/1969 New Orleans, LA Pro: E																														
1994	SHR	10				0																								
1995	SHR	18				1																								
2	Years	28				1																								
JIM HEIGHTON Jim DE-DT 6'3 252 none B: 9/22/1944																														
1969	BC	11																												
1970	WPG	14	0		1																									
1971	WPG	16	0		1																									
1972	WPG+	16	0		1																									
1973	WPG	16	0		1																									
1974	WPG+	15	0		2								6	1																		
1975	WPG	16	0		1																									
1976	WPG	16	0		2																									
1977	WPG	16	0		1				1	26																				
1978	WPG	16																												
1979	HAM	16	0		1																									
1981	MTL	3																												
12	Years	171	0		11				1	26		6	1																		
DENNIS HEIM Dennis James DT 6'4 248 Missouri State B: 4/16/1956 Monett, MO Draft: 11-286 1978 NYG																														
1978	TOR	2																												
1979	TOR	1																												
2	Years	3																												
DARIUS HELTON Darius Charles OT 6'2 260 North Carolina Central B: 10/2/1954 D: 10/3/2006 Charlotte, NC Draft: 4C-95 1977 KC Pro: N																														
1980	BC	2																												

Year	Team	GP	FM	FF	FR	TK	SK	YDS	IR	YDS	PD	PTS	TD	RA	YDS	AVG	LG	TD	REC	YDS	AVG	LG	TD	PR	YDS	AVG	LG	KOR	YDS	AVG	LG
JOHN HELTON John DT-DE 6'3 255 Arizona State B: 5/23/1947 Draft: 7-157 1969 BUF																															
1969	CAL+	16	0		3																										
1970	CAL+	16																										2	26	13.0	19
1971	CAL*	14	0		2																										
1972	CAL*	16	0		1																										
1973	CAL*	16																													
1974	CAL*	16																													
1975	CAL*	16	0		1																										
1976	CAL*	16																													
1977	CAL	14																													
1978	CAL*	16	0		1																										
1979	WPG*	16	0		2																										
1980	WPG	15	0		3																										
1981	WPG+	14					7.0																								
1982	WPG*	16	0		1		9.0																								
14	Years	217	0		14		16.0	0.0																				2	26	13.0	19
BYRON HEMINGWAY Byron Joseph LB 6'4 210 Boston College B: 6/16/1954 Newburgh, NY Draft: 9A-224 1977 TB																															
1977	HAM	5	1		1				1	23																					
1978	HAM	7	0		2																										
2	Years	12	1		3				1	23																					
ELTON HEMINGWAY Elton E-G-T 5'8 160 Queen's B: 1925																															
1948	HAM	10																													
1949	HAM	6										10	2					1					1								
2	Years	16										10	2					1					1								
ROSS HEMINGWAY Ross E 5'9 185 B: 1925																															
1948	HAM	3																													
1949	HAM	10																													
2	Years	13																													
DARRYL HEMPHILL Darryl Anthony DB 6'0 195 West Texas A&M B: 3/29/1960 San Antonio, TX Draft: 10-275 1982 NYJ Pro: NU																															
1987	BC	1				6	1.0		2	43		6	1																		
PAUL HENDERSHOT Paul DB 6'0 175 Wilfrid Laurier B: 1948 Draft: 3-21 1970 EDM																															
1971	BC	1																													
CURTIS HENDERSON Curtis Eugene WR 5'10 190 Morgan State B: 8/4/1958 Woonsocket, RI																															
1983	SAS	1																	3	33	11.0	15	0								
HAZEN HENDERSON Hazen DB 5'11 180 Simon Fraser B: 10/30/1957 Draft: 2-10 1981 SAS																															
1982	HAM	16	0		1				1	0																					
JIM HENDERSON James SE 6'4 215 Simpson B: 4/12/1943 Toronto, ON																															
1969	TOR	9			1														1	22	22.0	22	0								
1970	TOR	6	0		1							6	1						3	91	30.3	68	1					2	30	15.0	18
1971	TOR	7										12	2						18	273	15.2	41	2								
1972	TOR	3																													
4	Years	25	0		2							18	3						22	386	17.5	68	3					2	30	15.0	18
JOE HENDERSON Joe, Jr. LB 6'2 220 Alabama-Birmingham B: 3/6/1986 Birmingham, AL																															
2010	BC	11				41																									
2011	BC	5				10																									
2	Years	16				51																									
JON HENDERSON Jon Elliott WR 6'0 198 Colorado State B: 12/17/1944 Pittsburgh, PA Draft: 3A-61 1968 PIT Pro: NW																															
1971	CAL	5	1		0														2	37	18.5	23	0					4	95	23.8	50
REED HENDERSON Reed T 6'2 235 Utah State B: 1935 Draft: 15A-171 1956 SF																															
1956	EDM	16	0		1				1	0		6	1																		
1957	EDM	15																													
2	Years	31	0		1				1	0		6	1																		
ROBERT HENDERSON Robert DE 6'3 280 Southern Mississippi B: 11/9/1983 Ponchatoula, LA Draft: 6B-199 2008 NYG																															
2011	EDM	1				2																									
TRACY HENDERSON Tracy WR 6'0 185 Iowa State B: 6/7/1964 Melrose Park, IL Draft: 5-132 1985 NYG																															
1985	SAS	2																	3	57	19.0	33	0								
ZAC HENDERSON Zac Ryall DB 6'1 190 Oklahoma B: 10/14/1955 Jena, LA Pro: NU																															
1978	HAM	10							2	71		6	1																		
1979	HAM	16	1		1				3	3		2	0	1	8	8.0	8	0													
1982	TOR*	16	1		0		1.0		4	54														3	22	7.3	15	1	0	0.0	0
1983	TOR	1																													
4	Years	43	2		1		1.0		9	128		8	1	1	8	8.0	8	0						3	22	7.3	15	1	0		0
BART HENDRICKS Bart QB 6'0 212 Boise State B: 8/30/1978 Reno, NV Pro: E																															
2002	EDM	14				0								1	12	12.0	12	0													
2003	EDM	18	1	0	0	0						6	1	6	45	7.5	12	1	1	-1	-1.0	-1	0								
2004	EDM	18	1	0	0	0								5	23	4.6	7	0													
3	Years	50	2	0	0	0						6	1	12	80	6.7	12	1	1	-1	-1.0	-1	0								
MICHAEL HENDRICKS Michael CB 6'0 190 Texas A&M B: 2/24/1973																															
1995	SA	2				1																									
MICHAEL HENDRICKS Michael LB 6'3 235 Ottawa B: 1/23/1972 Middleton, NS Draft: 7-54 1996 OTT																															
1996	OTT	16				17																									
CRAIG HENDRICKSON Craig Steven OT 6'3 290 Arizona Western JC; Minnesota B: 5/5/1968 Tucson, AZ Draft: 3-21 1990 SAS																															
1991	SAS	8				1																									
1992	SAS	15				1																									
1993	SAS	18				0																									
1994	EDM	8				2													1	4	4.0	4	0								
1995	EDM	18	0		3	2																									
1996	BC	16				0																									
1997	WPG	18	0	0	2	1																									
1998	WPG	18				1																									
1999	WPG	9				3																									
1999	TOR	9				3																									
1999	Year	18				6																									
2000	BC	14				0						6	1						1	7	7.0	7	1								
2001	BC	18	0	0	1	1																									
11	Years	160	0	0	6	15						6	1						2	11	5.5	7	1								
LEFTY HENDRICKSON Lynn TE-LB 6'1 215 North Shore Cougars Jrs.; Oregon B: 4/27/1973																															
1968	BC	16																	1	9	9.0	9	0								
1969	BC	13										12	2						35	387	11.1	58	2					1	-3	-3.0	-3
1970	BC	16	3		4							6	1						31	431	13.9	26	1								
1971	BC	16			1							6	1						14	154	11.0	25	1					1	14	14.0	14
1973	BC+	16	1		1							18	3						39	631	16.2	73	3								
1974	BC	3																	3	57	19.0	29	0								
6	Years	80	4		6							42	7						123	1669	13.6	73	7					2	11	5.5	14
SCOTT HENDRICKSON Scott C-OG 6'3 275 Minnesota B: 1/25/1970 Tucson, AZ Draft: 2B-15 1992 SAS																															
1992	SAS	16				1																									
1993	SAS	18	0		1	2																									
1994	SAS	18	0		1	4																									
1995	SAS	17				0																									
1996	SAS	15	1		0	0																									
1997	SAS	13				2																									
1998	BC	18	1	0	0	2																									

Year	Team	GP	FM	FF	FR	TK	SK	YDS	IR	YDS	PD	PTS	TD	RA	YDS	AVG	LG	TD	REC	YDS	AVG	LG	TD	PR	YDS	AVG	LG	KOR	YDS	AVG	LG
1999	BC	2				0																									
2000	BC	12				0						6	1						1	1	1.0	1	1								
9	Years	129	2	0	2	11						6	1						1	1	1.0	1	1								
JESSE HENDRIX Jesse DB 5'9 170 Eastern Washington B: 8/19/1982 Lakewood, WA																															
2007	MTL	12				19					2																				
2008	MTL	3				2					1																				
2	Years	15				21					3																				
ED HENKE Edgar Edwin LB 6'3 227 Ventura JC; Southern California B: 12/13/1927 Ontario, CA Draft: 13-128 1949 WAS Pro: AN																															
1950	WPG	12																	6	87	14.5		0								
1954	CAL+	15	0		3				2	27																					
1955	CAL	10	0		2														1	12	12.0	12	0								
3	Years	37	0		5				2	27									7	99	14.1	12	0								
GARNEY HENLEY Garney DB-OHB-FL 6'0 180 South Dakota State*; Huron B: 12/21/1937 Elgin, SD Draft: SS 1960 NYT; 15-173 1960 GB																															
1960	HAM	10										18	3	3	13	4.3	7	0	9	306	34.0	96	3	1	0	0.0	0				
1961	HAM	10							3	44		12	2	7	69	9.9	52	1	9	114	12.7	27	0	31	186	6.0	20	4	97	24.3	43
1962	HAM	14										72	12	50	258	5.2	46	2	37	730	19.7	87	10	18	157	8.7	43	12	316	26.3	69
1963	HAM*	12							6	161		24	4	17	60	3.5	12	0	20	294	14.7	46	4	28	295	10.5	55	3	92	30.7	37
1964	HAM*	14	1		1				6	85		18	3	9	50	5.6	19	0	7	138	19.7	51	2	33	250	7.6	28	4	96	24.0	30
1965	HAM*	14	1						6	75		12	2						1	-5	-5.0	-5	0	67	657	9.8	54				
1966	HAM*	14	2		1				6	78									2	16	8.0	13	0	83	438	5.3	80				
1967	HAM*	13							4	20		6	1						5	213	42.6	92	1	8	80	10.0	27				
1968	HAM*	13	0		1				6	147		12	2	2	8	4.0	7	0	2	50	25.0	46	0	35	294	8.4	24	1	11	11.0	11
1969	HAM*	14	0		1				2	0		6	1	3	21	7.0	18	0	9	166	18.4	33	1	18	191	10.6	44	1	2	2.0	2
1970	HAM*	14	0		3				10	139		12	2	5	6	1.2	11	2	3	34	11.3	18	0	13	56	4.3	26	1	81	81.0	67
1971	HAM*	14	2		4				7	116		12	2						1	9	9.0	9	0	11	171	15.5	33	11	252	22.9	35
1972	HAM*	14										48	8	4	70	17.5	50	1	36	881	24.5	76	7	4	32	8.0	12				
1973	HAM	14										48	8	1	-15	-15.0	-15	0	40	639	16.0	68	8	5	41	8.2	18				
1974	HAM	16										24	4						41	714	17.4	46	4								
1975	HAM	16	1		2				4	51		12	2	1	12	12.0	12	0	21	358	17.0	45	2	6	96	16.0	50				
16	Years	216	7		13				60	916		336	56	102	552	5.4	52	6	243	4657	19.2	96	42	361	2944	8.2	80	37	947	25.6	69
JAHI HENLEY Jahi Joseph CB 5'9 192 Alabama*; Tennessee Tech B: 12/15/1978 Boston, MA																															
2002	CAL	2				5																									
STEVE HENLEY Stephen LB 6'0 230 Mankato State B: 8/30/1971 Ford Heights, IL																															
1995	BIR	10				30	1.0	13.0																							
ROGER HENNIG Roger S 6'0 190 British Columbia B: 10/3/1966 Penticton, BC Draft: 7-49 1991 HAM																															
1992	HAM	17	0		1	19	1.0	7.0																							
1993	HAM	18				19								1	6	6.0	6	0													
1994	HAM	14				16																									
1995	HAM	16				28			1	0	3																	1	0	0.0	0
1996	BC	5				6																									
5	Years	70	0		1	88	1.0	7.0	1	0	3			1	6	6.0	6	0										1	0	0.0	0
DAVID HENREY David K. S 6'5 240 UCLA B: 2/16/1973 Solvang, CA																															
2000	TOR	5				8																									
ALDI HENRY Aldi CB-S-DH 5'10 180 Michigan State B: 7/7/1972 Montreal, QC Draft: 3A-18 1997 TOR																															
1997	CAL	14	0	0	0	19																									
1998	CAL	18				25																									
1999	CAL	17	0	1	0	34					4																				
2000	CAL	18	0	0	1	36					2								1	20	20.0	20	0								
2001	CAL	18	0	1	0	38			1	41	0																				
2002	CAL	18				20																									
6	Years	103	0	2	1	172			1	41	6								1	20	20.0	20	0								
ANDREW HENRY Andrew S-LB 6'2 210 C.W. Post B: 8/23/1970 Kingston, Jamaica Draft: 1-4 1996 WPG																															
1996	WPG	13				18			2	69	0	6	1															1	0	0.0	0
1997	WPG	6				30					2																				
1997	SAS	5				4																									
1997	Year	11				34					2																				
1999	TOR	16				10																									
2000	TOR	2				5																									
2000	SAS	13	0	0	2	39	2.0	15.0			1																				
2000	Year	15	0	0	2	44	2.0	15.0			1																				
2001	EDM	10				2																									
5	Years	47	0	0	2	108	2.0	15.0	2	69	3	6	1															1	0	0.0	0
BILL HENRY William OG-C 6'0 267 British Columbia; Richmond Raiders Jrs. B: 8/30/1961 Draft: 5A-38 1986 SAS																															
1988	SAS	18				0																						1	0	0.0	0
1989	SAS	6				0																									
1989	HAM	12				1																									
1989	Year	18				1																									
1991	CAL	18	0		3	1																									
1992	BC	1				0																									
1993	TOR	2				0																									
1993	HAM	9				2																									
1993	Year	11				2																									
1994	EDM	7				0																									
6	Years	52	0		3	4																						1	0	0.0	0
DWIGHT HENRY Dwight Donovan CB 5'11 185 East Carolina B: 2/12/1974 St. Mary, Jamaica																															
1999	MTL	18	0	0	1	45			2	14	5	6	1																		
2000	MTL	1				1					1																				
2000	EDM	5	0	1	0	13					1																				
2000	Year	6	0	1	0	14					2																				
2	Years	19	0	1	1	59			2	14	7	6	1																		
JEFF HENRY Jeff DT 6'2 240 Louisville B: 12/22/1946																															
1980	WPG	4	0		1																										
LLOYD HENRY Lloyd, Jr. WR 6'3 208 Indian Hills CC; Truman State B: 12/7/1955 Waterloo, IA Draft: 7B-190 1978 MIA																															
1979	SAS	1																	1	18	18.0	18	0								
LLOYD HENRY Lloyd, III (Rocky) WR 6'0 185 Kemper Military JC; Utah B: 4/25/1975 Columbia, MO																															
1998	BC	4				1													11	175	15.9	34	0								
1999	BC	6				1						30	5						21	317	15.1	40	5								
2000	BC	5				1													10	104	10.4	21	0								
2000	WPG	1				0						6	1						2	15	7.5	11	1								
2000	Year	6				1						6	1						12	119	9.9	21	1								
2001	SAS	6				0						12	2						14	220	15.7	66	2								
2002	SAS	17	1	0	0	2						12	2						62	698	11.3	45	2								
2003	SAS	3				0													6	68	11.3	16	0								
6	Years	41	1	0	0	5						60	10						126	1597	12.7	66	10								
MARCUS HENRY Marcus WR-SB 6'4 212 Kansas B: 2/21/1986 Hinesville, GA Draft: 6-171 2008 NYJ																															
2011	EDM	11	0	1	0	0						6	1						33	384	11.6	22	1								
MARIO HENRY Mario WR 6'1 184 Rutgers B: 9/14/1971 Pro: E																															
1996	MTL	1				0																						1	20	20.0	20
MAURICE HENRY Maurice Eugene LB 5'11 220 Kansas State B: 3/12/1967 Starkville, MS Draft: 6-147 1990 DET Pro: N																															
1993	OTT	1				5																									
1994	OTT	2				9																									
2	Years	3				14																									

Year	Team	GP	FM	FF	FR	TK	SK	YDS	IR	YDS	PD	PTS	TD	RA	YDS	AVG	LG	TD	REC	YDS	AVG	LG	TD	PR	YDS	AVG	LG	KOR	YDS	AVG	LG
MIKE HENRY Michael LB 5'11 240 Sonoma State B: 10/19/1965																															
1990	BC	8	0		1	17	4.0																								
ROY HENRY Roy QB Notre Dame; Louisiana-Lafayette																															
1978	HAM	9										6	1	1	2	2.0	2	0													
TOMMY HENRY Tommy DH-CB 6'1 175 Florida State B: 11/4/1969 Acardia, FL																															
1993	SAC	9				15																									
1994	TOR	15	1		0	49			4	40	3																	0	27		27
1995	TOR	18	0		2	56			4	20	7																	5	106	21.2	29
1996	OTT	14				48			5	105	7	6	1											1	12	12.0	12	4	79	19.8	38
1997	EDM	18	0	2	0	55	2.0	4.0	5	100	8																				
1998	EDM	7				26																									
1998	SAS	3				15	1.0	10.0	1	0	1																				
1998	Year	10				41	1.0	10.0	1	0	1																				
1999	HAM	8				12					1																				
7	Years	89	1	2	2	276	3.0	14.0	19	265	27	6	1											1	12	12.0	12	9	212	23.6	38
URBAN HENRY Urban Andrew DT 6'4 265 Georgia Tech B: 6/7/1935 Berwick, LA D: 2/11/1979 Draft: 4A-38 1958 LARM Pro: N																															
1958	BC	16	0		2																										
1959	BC+	16										6	1						1	13	13.0	13	0								
1960	BC+	16	0		3																										
3	Years	48	0		5							6	1						1	13	13.0	13	0								
JIM HENSALL James DB 6'2 194 Western Ontario B: 4/6/1947 Draft: 2-12 1970 EDM																															
1970	EDM	16							2	13																					
1971	EDM	16							3	49														2	8	4.0	5				
1972	EDM	16							6	73														2	4	2.0	2				
1973	EDM	9																										1	19	19.0	19
4	Years	57							11	135														4	12	3.0	5	1	19	19.0	19
YORK HENTSCHEL York DT-DE 6'3 250 Red Deer Packers Jrs. B: 6/16/1953																															
1976	EDM	16																													
1977	EDM	16																						1	4	4.0	4				
1978	EDM	16																													
1979	EDM	16																													
1980	EDM	16	0		1																										
1981	HAM	2					1.0																								
1981	WPG	14					2.0																								
1981	Year	16					3.0																								
6	Years	82	0		1		3.0	0.0																1	4	4.0	4				
BRUNO HEPPELL Bruno RB 6'0 215 Western Michigan B: 2/14/1972 LaPrairie, QC Draft: 3-21 1997 MTL																															
1997	MTL	13	0	0	2	13						6	1															1	0	0.0	0
1998	MTL	14				7						6	1	9	43	4.8	8	1										2	44	22.0	23
1999	MTL	11				10																									
2000	MTL	17	1	0	1	5						12	2	23	83	3.6	21	1	10	161	16.1	38	1					1	10	10.0	10
2001	MTL	18	1	0	0	2						24	4	37	136	3.7	24	3	22	273	12.4	24	1					3	23	7.7	9
2002	MTL	18	1	0	2	14						12	2	20	109	5.5	40	1	9	196	21.8	58	0					1	11	11.0	11
2003	MTL	18				4						30	5	29	69	2.4	8	4	9	122	13.6	23	1								
2004	MTL	10	1	0	0	4						6	1	14	45	3.2	15	1	2	18	9.0	9	0								
8	Years	119	4	0	5	59						96	16	132	485	3.7	40	11	52	770	14.8	58	3					8	88	11.0	23
DAVE HERBERT Dave TE-OHB-LB 6'2 215 Edmonton Wildcats Jrs.; Drake B: 5/11/1946																															
1972	EDM	12	2		1														1	10	10.0	10	0	3	3	1.0	3				
1973	EDM	6																						11	67	6.1	14				
1973	CAL	1																													
1973	Year	7																						11	67	6.1	14				
2	Years	18	2		1														1	10	10.0	10	0	14	70	5.0	14				
DICK HERBERTSON Dick E 6'1 188 Weston Wildcats Jrs.; Winnipeg Rams Ints. B: 1933																															
1955	WPG	1																													
1957	SAS	3																													
2	Years	4																													
YVES HERCULE Yves LB 6'2 195 Laval B: 9/10/1981 Roxboro, QC																															
2007	TOR	4				3																									
CHUCK HERD Charles Ceaward WR 6'0 201 Penn State B: 12/20/1950 Meadowbrook, NY Draft: 10-256 1974 CIN																															
1974	TOR	9	0		1							24	4						19	532	28.0	74	4								
1975	TOR	4																	1	13	13.0	13	0								
2	Years	13	0		1							24	4						20	545	27.3	74	4								
JOE HERGERT Joseph Martin LB 6'1 216 Florida B: 6/7/1936 Wilkes-Barre, PA Draft: 24-277 1959 GB Pro: N																															
1960	MTL	1																													
TODD HERGET Todd D. LB 6'2 225 Brigham Young B: 8/9/1969 Williamsville, NY Draft: 7-55 1991 EDM																															
1994	EDM	8				5																									
MARK HERMAN Mark Lawrence TE 6'2 225 Yankton B: 3/5/1949 New York, NY Draft: 15-369 1972 STL																															
1973	CAL	6										6	1						10	111	11.1	24	1					1	11	11.0	11
BRIAN HERNANDEZ Brian Julio WR 6'0 183 Georgia Tech; Arizona State; Pima CC; Utah B: 4/13/1984 Phoenix, AZ Pro: U																															
2008	SAS	1				0													1	2	2.0	2	0								
JOE HERNANDEZ Jose M. CB-DH-FL 6'2 180 New Mexico Military Institute JC; Bakersfield JC; Arizona B: 2/9/1940 Bakersfield, CA Draft: 5-33 1962 OAK; 2-15 1962 WAS Pro: N																															
1962	TOR	12										18	3	33	146	4.4	19	0	24	328	13.7	75	3	20	125	6.3	21	21	594	28.3	75
1963	EDM	15	6		1							24	4	79	372	4.7	23	0	30	449	15.0	57	4	40	261	6.5	28	26	650	25.0	46
1966	EDM	7										12	2	9	29	3.2	16	0	9	223	24.8	43	1					4	117	29.3	38
1967	EDM+	16	1		1				6	28				2	5	2.5	7	0	4	59	14.8	21	0	49	222	4.5	23	20	485	24.3	39
1968	EDM	14	0		2				2	21									2	20	10.0	12	0	2	6	3.0	6	3	65	21.7	31
1969	EDM	16							4	37														2	3	1.5	3				
1970	EDM+	16	0		1				4	149		12	2											1	0	0.0	0	23	636	27.7	45
7		96	7		5				16	235		66	11	123	552	4.5	23	0	69	1079	15.6	75	8	114	617	5.4	28	97	2547	26.3	75
WARNER HERNDON Warner Jene, Jr. DB 6'2 211 Morgan State B: 2/9/1978 Sacramento, CA																															
2001	BC	16	0	1	2	41			3	40	1																				
DAVE HERNE David OE-DB 6'2 192 Benedictine (Kansas) B: 1941																															
1962	OTT	4																													
LACH HERON Lachlan Gordon SE-TE 6'1 195 Oregon B: 2/22/1944																															
1967	BC	13										6	1						21	336	16.0	46	1	1	2	2.0	2				
1968	BC	16										6	1						32	452	14.1	82	1	1	2	2.0	2				
1969	BC	12										6	1						20	300	15.0	40	1	6	36	6.0	11				
1970	BC	16	1		0														22	329	15.0	31	0	0	5		5				
1971	BC	16										6	1						13	155	11.9	18	1								
5	Years	73	1		0							24	4						108	1572	14.6	82	4	8	45	5.6	11				
BRIAN HEROSIAN Brian Berge DB 6'3 200 Connecticut B: 9/14/1950 Worcester, MA Pro: N																															
1975	WPG+	14							5	12														7	18	2.6	8				
1976	WPG*	16							5	96														5	36	7.2	10				
1977	WPG	16	0		5				3	24														11	36	3.3	16				
1978	WPG	15	0		2				4	51														1	10	10.0	10				
1979	WPG	4																													
5	Years	65	1		7				17	183														24	100	4.2	16				
DEAN HERRBOLDT Dean WR 6'0 190 South Dakota State B: 8/23/1971																															
1995	BC	2				0													2	54	27.0	40	0								
GEORGE HERRING George W. QB 6'2 200 Jones County JC; Southern Mississippi B: 6/18/1934 Gadsden, AL Draft: 16-184 1956 SF Pro: N																															
1958	BC	14	12									2	0	73	-111	-1.5	15	0													

Year	Team	GP	FM	FF	FR	TK	SK	YDS	IR	YDS	PD	PTS	TD	RA	YDS	AVG	LG	TD	REC	YDS	AVG	LG	TD	PR	YDS	AVG	LG	KOR	YDS	AVG	LG
1959	SAS	1										1	0	3	13	4.3	12	0													
2	Years	15	12		0							3	0	76	-98	-1.3	15	0													
BILL HERRON William OE 6'1 190 Fresno CC; Georgia B: 1937 Draft: SS 1960 OAK; 13-148 1960 WAS																															
1960	BC	6	0		1							12	2						7	158	22.6	78	2					1	33	33.0	33
GERRY HERRON Gerry CB-WR 6'1 195 Washington State B: 1948																															
1970	BC	10																													
LAMAR HERRON Lamar DH 6'0 207 Oregon State; Texas Southern B: 10/27/1984																															
2009	EDM	3				4			0	0	1																				
MACK HERRON Mack Willie RB 5'5 174 Hutchinson JC; Kansas State B: 7/24/1948 Biloxi, MS Draft: 6A-143 1970 ATL Pro: N																															
1971	WPG+	15	9		0							54	9	198	900	4.5	33	5	30	418	13.9	63	4					35	1019	29.1	62
1972	WPG*	16	9		1							96	16	258	1527	5.9	65	11	39	451	11.6	55	4					17	552	32.5	120
2	Years	31	18		1							150	25	456	2427	5.3	65	16	69	869	12.6	63	8					52	1571	30.2	120
GARY HERTZFELDT Gary Arthur QB 6'3 200 Utah B: 11/29/1940 Chico, CA																															
1964	EDM	4	1		1									7	22	3.1	8	0													
ED HERVEY Edward Lee WR 6'2 195 Pasadena CC; Southern California B: 5/4/1973 Houston, TX Draft: 5A-166 1995 DAL																															
1999	EDM	15	1	0	0	5						30	5						48	666	13.9	46	5								
2000	EDM	15				1						12	2						51	697	13.7	52	2								
2001	EDM*	18	3	0	0	3						72	12						77	1447	18.8	95	12								
2002	EDM	13				3						42	7	2	-6	-3.0	8	0	50	817	16.3	59	7								
2003	EDM*	17	2	0	1	5						48	8	1	23	23.0	23	0	72	1022	14.2	54	8								
2004	EDM	12				2						36	6						53	629	11.9	45	6								
2005	EDM	10	1	0	0	1													49	539	11.0	55	0								
2006	EDM	17	1	0	0	4						18	3						76	898	11.8	52	3								
8	Years	117	8	0	1	24						258	43	3	17	5.7	23	0	476	6715	14.1	95	43								
BILLY HESS William Edward WR-SB 5'8 175 West Chester B: 2/6/1966 Annapolis, MD Pro: E																															
1995	SA	18				6						24	4						55	736	13.4	40	4								
1996	OTT	8				1						6	1						22	327	14.9	35	1								
2	Years	26				7						30	5						77	1063	13.8	40	5								
BURDETTE HESS Burdette LB-OT 6'1 232 Idaho B: 1933 Draft: 15-178 1955 SF																															
1955	CAL	16							2	0																					
1956	CAL	16	0																												
1957	CAL	5																													
3	Years	37	0		0				2	0																					
GREG HETHERINGTON Greg WR-SB 6'4 220 McGill B: 5/10/1983 Toronto, ON Draft: 6-45 2007 CAL																															
2007	CAL	1				0																									
2009	BC	14				0													4	42	10.5	12	0								
2	Years	15				0													4	42	10.5	12	0								
CLIFF HEWITT Cliff DB 6'0 195 Eastern Utah JC B: 5/30/1961 Toronto, ON																															
1985	TOR	16	0		2		1.0		1	0		6	1															1	2	2.0	2
1986	TOR	18	0		1				1	3																					
1987	OTT	12				19																									
3	Years	46	0		3	19	1.0		2	3		6	1															1	2	2.0	2
DAVID HEWSON David LB 6'3 229 Manitoba B: 1/9/1982 Winnipeg, MB Draft: 5-36 2005 CAL																															
2006	TOR	12				11																									
2007	WPG	4				0																									
2	Years	16				11																									
BOB HEYDENFELDT Robert Marshall E-P 6'2 190 UCLA B: 9/17/1933 Canoga Park, CA																															
1955	EDM	16							1	0		24	3	1	-12	-12.0	-12	0	17	221	13.0	35	3								
KIRK HEYER Kirk Lane LB 6'5 260 Nebraska Southeast CC; Nebraska-Kearney B: 10/16/1953 Norfolk, NE Draft: 10A-247 1975 PIT Pro: W																															
1976	WPG	1																													
WILL HEYWARD William Murray CB-DH 5'9 190 Texas State B: 2/23/1984 Sequin, TX																															
2010	HAM	14	0	0	1	37																									
KEITH HEYWARD-JOHNSON Keith Maynard DB 5'11 185 Oregon State B: 2/2/1979 Washington, DC Pro: E																															
2001	BC	2				6			0	0	3																				
FRANK HICKEY Frank HB-FW-T 5'11 182 Toronto B: 1924																															
1947	TOR	5																													
1948	TOR	6																													
1949	EDM	14																													
1950	EDM	12										5	1						1	11	11.0	11	1								
1951	EDM	8																										1	21	21.0	21
5	Years	45										5	1						1	11	11.0	11	1					1	21	21.0	21
TOM HICKEY Tom HB																															
1946	HAM	4																													
PAUL HICKIE Paul P 6'2 220 Saskatchewan B: 4/8/1962 Toronto, ON Draft: 6-54 1983 EDM																															
1983	EDM	16	2		0							13	0	2	17	8.5	12	0						2	-1	-0.5	3				
1984	EDM	1																													
1984	SAS	13										4	0	1	1	1.0	1	0													
1984	Year	14										4	0	1	1	1.0	1	0													
2	Years	17	2		0							17	0	3	18	6.0	12	0						2	-1	-0.5	3				
DONNIE HICKMAN Donnie J. OG-OT 6'2 261 Southern California B: 6/11/1955 Flagstaff, AZ Draft: 5A-130 1977 LARM Pro: NU																															
1980	BC	12																													
1981	BC	14	0		2																										
1982	BC	13	0		2									0	2		2	0													
1983	BC	10																													
4	Years	49	0		4									0	2		2	0													
JUSTIN HICKMAN Justin Charles DE 6'2 263 Glendale CC; UCLA B: 7/20/1985 El Paso, TX																															
2009	HAM	18	0	3	2	51	7.0	55.0			1																				
2010	HAM	18	0	2	1	45	7.0	47.0			2																				
2011	HAM*	18	0	5	0	50	13.0	103.0			3																				
3	Years	54	0	10	3	146	27.0	205.0			6																				
LARRY HICKMAN Larry Dean FB-DB 6'1 230 Baylor B: 10/10/1935 Spring Hill, TX Draft: 3A-31 1959 LARM Pro: N																															
1961	HAM	5										6	1	69	447	6.5	67	1	2	5	2.5	6	0								
1962	HAM	1												11	59	5.4	12	0	1	7	7.0	7	0								
1962	MTL	7										6	1	59	354	6.0	39	1	2	17	8.5	13	0	1	0	0.0	0	5	54	10.8	16
1962	Year	8										6	1	70	413	5.9	39	1	3	24	8.0	13	0	1	0	0.0	0	5	54	10.8	16
1963	TOR	9										6	1	84	365	4.3	18	1	6	72	12.0	21	0								
3	Years	15										18	3	223	1225	5.5	67	3	11	101	9.2	21	0	1	0	0.0	0	5	54	10.8	16
ANTHONY HICKS Anthony O'Neil LB 6'1 243 Arkansas B: 3/31/1974 Strong, AR Draft: 5-160 1997 GB																															
1999	EDM	1																													
ARRINGTON HICKS Arrington Bernard DH 5'9 177 Eastern Michigan B: 10/3/1988 Orlando, FL																															
2011	WPG	1				1																									
BERNARD HICKS Bernard LB 5'11 207 California B: 10/17/1986																															
2010	WPG	3				15																									
DWIGHT HICKS Dwight H. DB 6'1 190 Michigan B: 4/5/1956 Mount Holly, NJ Draft: 6A-150 1978 DET Pro: N																															
1978	TOR	3							2	0														6	60	10.0	19				
EMERY HICKS Emery Lee LB 6'0 230 Kansas B: 8/10/1947 Bartlesville, OK D: 3/17/2005 Oklahoma City, OK Draft: 11-284 1970 OAK Pro: W																															
1971	WPG	7			0				1	18																					
1971	HAM	9			3							6	1																		
1971	Year	16	1		3				1	18		6	1																		
1972	HAM	2	0		1																										
2	Years	9	0		4				1	18		6	1																		
HAROLD HICKS Harold W. CB 6'0 200 San Diego State B: 12/7/1965 San Diego, CA Draft: 7-193 1988 WAS																															

Year	Team	GP	FM	FF	FR	TK	SK	YDS	IR	YDS	PD	PTS	TD	RA	YDS	AVG	LG	TD	REC	YDS	AVG	LG	TD	PR	YDS	AVG	LG	KOR	YDS	AVG	LG
1989	HAM	1				0																									
RICHARD HICKS Richard Winslow OT 6'4 250 Los Angeles Southwest JC; West Los Angeles JC; Humboldt State B: 1/4/1951 Cleveland, OH Pro: N																															
1976	HAM	5																													
SKIP HICKS Brian LaVell RB 6'0 230 UCLA B: 10/13/1974 Corsicana, TX Draft: 3-69 1998 WAS Pro: EN																															
2004	TOR	1				0						6	1	7	39	5.6	32	1	1	11	11.0	11	0								
TYRONE HICKS Tyrone WR 5'11 175 Ohio State B: 2/17/1957 Warren, OH																															
1980	SAS	1												2	0	0.0	2	0	3	52	17.3	23	0								
JIM HIGGINS James M. OG 6'1 255 Xavier (Ohio) B: 1/20/1942 Cincinnati, OH D: 9/28/2008 Cincinnati, OH Draft: 19-263 1964 CLE Pro: N																															
1964	EDM	10																													
1965	EDM	16	0		1																										
2	Years	26	0		1																										
MIKE HIGGINS Michael RB 6'1 200 Kansas B: 7/16/1957 Gretna, LA																															
1981	CAL	5	1		1									18	60	3.3	17	0	10	99	9.9	18	0					13	273	21.0	29
TOM HIGGINS Thomas Joseph John, Jr. LB 6'1 235 North Carolina State B: 7/13/1954 Newark, NJ Pro: N																															
1976	CAL	10	0		1																										
1980	SAS	7																													
2	Years	17	0		1																										
KEN HIGGS Kenneth Wilkinson FB-HB 5'11 192 Victoria Ints. B: 1/12/1931 Vancouver, BC D: 5//2006 Victoria, BC																															
1955	BC	7												11	26	2.4	6	0	2	23	11.5	12	0					3	65	21.7	27
1956	BC	8												7	31	4.4	8	0													
2	Years	15												18	57	3.2	8	0	2	23	11.5	12	0					3	65	21.7	27
LARRY HIGHBAUGH Larry E. CB-FL 5'9 179 Indiana B: 1/14/1950 Indianapolis, IN																															
1971	BC	12	1		0							30	5	48	327	6.8	45	2	27	488	18.1	51	3					9	332	36.9	67
1972	BC	10							2	0		12	2	4	13	3.3	20	0	18	278	15.4	54	2					14	445	31.8	
1972	EDM	3							4	17																		3	146	48.7	
1972	Year	13							6	17		12	2	4	13	3.3	20	0	18	278	15.4	54	2					17	591	34.8	83
1973	EDM*	16	0		2				6	99		6	1											8	161	20.1	22	22	873	39.7	102
1974	EDM*	16			1				2	0		24	4						17	234	13.8	42	4	10	99	9.9	21	14	606	43.3	90
1975	EDM+	16	1		0				3	62		24	4						3	40	13.3	29	2	42	705	16.8	116	23	775	33.7	109
1976	EDM	14			0				2	39		18	3						1	48	48.0	48	1	32	292	9.1	36	21	843	40.1	118
1977	EDM*	16	1		1				5	109		18	3	3	-3	-1.0	17	0	20	276	13.8	46	2	57	600	10.5	74	6	293	48.8	56
1978	EDM	16	0		1				7	100		6	1											28	218	7.8	53	9	230	25.6	31
1979	EDM	16	2		4				10	134		6	1											16	105	6.6	18	3	74	24.7	24
1980	EDM	16							9	115		6	1											5	33	6.6	9	11	239	21.7	45
1981	EDM	16							7	28														2	3	1.5	3	4	62	15.5	30
1982	EDM	14							4	27																		1	28	28.0	28
1983	EDM	15	1		0				5	40														4	-30	-7.5	-3	1	20	20.0	20
13	Years	193	6		9				66	770		150	25	55	337	6.1	45	2	86	1364	15.9	54	14	204	2186	10.7	116	141	4966	35.2	118
WALLY HIGHSMITH Walter OT-OG 6'4 238 Florida A&M B: 8/27/1943 Tampa, FL Pro: NW																															
1970	MTL	8	0		1																										
1971	MTL	14	0		1																										
1973	MTL	1	1		0																										
1976	TOR	16																										1	0	0.0	0
1977	TOR	5																													
5	Years	44	1		2																							1	0	0.0	0
MIKE HILDEBRAND Mike S 5'9 175 Calgary Colts Jrs.; Calgary B: 11/8/1965 Calgary, AB Draft: 7-53 1989 EDM																															
1989	EDM	18	1		1	20	1.0		1	0														2	0	0.0	0	1	0	0.0	0
1990	EDM	4				2																									
1990	TOR	4				3																									
1990	Year	8				5																									
2	Years	22	1		1	25	1.0		1	0														2	0	0.0	0	1	0	0.0	0
BRIAN HILK Brian Andrew LB 6'0 230 Akron B: 4/23/1969 Pittsburgh, PA																															
1991	HAM	7	0		1	42	1.0																					1	0	0.0	0
1993	TOR	1				7																									
1994	SHR	4				20	1.0	8.0																							
3	Years	12	0		1	69	2.0	8.0																				1	0	0.0	0
AARON HILL Aaron, Jr. DB 5'9 177 Lamar B: 6/6/1960 Dallas, TX																															
1983	MTL	1																													
1984	MTL	15			1				4	98		6	1																		
1985	MTL	16																										17	397	23.4	45
1986	OTT	1																													
4	Years	33	0		1				4	98		6	1															17	397	23.4	45
ANTHONEY HILL Anthoney QB 5'11 200 Colorado State B: 12/24/1971																															
1995	EDM	3				0								1	9	9.0	9	0													
BILL HILL Bill FB-E-DB 6'0 210 Presbyterian B: 1940 Draft: 19-253 1961 MIN																															
1961	EDM	3												6	19	3.2	12	0	4	40	10.0	14	0	5	24	4.8	8	4	84	21.0	32
1962	EDM	2												2	2	1.0	2	0	1	32	32.0	32	0								
1962	MTL	2																													
1962	Year	4												2	2	1.0	2	0	1	32	32.0	32	0								
2	Years	5												8	21	2.6	12	0	5	72	14.4	32	0	5	24	4.8	8	4	84	21.0	32
COREY HILL Corey DB 5'11 210 Stanford B: 2/5/1977 Tucson, AZ																															
2000	TOR	2	0	1	0	13			0	0	2																				
DEREK HILL Derek Keith WR 6'1 189 Arizona B: 11/4/1967 Detroit, MI Draft: 3-61 1989 PIT Pro: EN																															
1992	TOR	3				1													10	127	12.7	41	0								
1994	SHR	2	1		0	0													9	102	11.3	23	0								
2	Years	5	1		0	1													19	229	12.1	41	0								
DICK HILL Richard G 5'10 205 Michigan B: 1935																															
1957	MTL	1																													
EDDIE HILL Ed OG-LB 6'1 230 Miami (Ohio) B: 6/30/1936 Cincinnati, OH Draft: 18-215 1959 CLE																															
1959	MTL	6																													
EFREM HILL Efrem Dale WR-SB 6'0 179 Samford B: 7/23/1983 Fort Payne, AL																															
2009	EDM	3				0						6	1						12	167	13.9	39	1								
2010	EDM	2				0													9	64	7.1	15	0								
2011	SAS	18				1						6	1						66	812	12.3	49	1					2	-1	-0.5	0
3	Years	23				1						12	2						87	1043	12.0	49	2					2	-1	-0.5	0
GREG HILL Greg QB 5'11 170 Georgia Southern B: 10/26/1976 Sarasota, FL																															
2000	TOR	8				0								5	37	7.4	13	0													
2001	TOR	5				0													14	143	10.2	43	0					6	122	20.3	47
2	Years	13				0								5	37	7.4	13	0	14	143	10.2	43	0					6	122	20.3	47
HAKIM HILL Hakim Zellon RB 5'11 212 Arizona State B: 10/14/1982 Carmichael, CA Pro: U																															
2005	TOR	3	3	0	0	1						6	1	17	61	3.6	18	1	14	115	8.2	23	0								
JACK HILL Jack Flint OHB 6'1 185 Utah State B: 10/17/1932 Ogden, UT D: 9/26/2005 Farmington, UT Draft: 13-151 1956 BAL Pro: N																															
1957	SAS	14	2									24	4	111	542	4.9	76	4	10	125	12.5	43	0	8	78	9.8	20	2	21	10.5	15
1958	SAS+	16	3		3				2	0		145	16	14	33	2.4	12	2	60	1065	17.8	91	14	3	30	10.0	11	1	25	25.0	25
1959	SAS	8							3	53		7	1	32	131	4.1	12	0	16	160	10.0	28	0	1	0	0.0	0				
1960	SAS	13	0		2							40	4	6	15	2.5	6	0	36	510	14.2	62	4					18	403	22.4	36
4	Years	51	5		5				5	53		216	25	163	721	4.4	76	6	122	1860	15.2	91	18	12	108	9.0	20	21	449	21.4	36
JAMES HILL James RB 6'0 210 Colorado B: 2/20/1970																															
1994	LV	6				2						12	2	39	142	3.6	16	2	4	75	18.8	27	0	1	11	11.0	11	1	21	21.0	21
KAHLIL HILL Kahlil S. WR-SB 6'2 200 Iowa B: 3/18/1979 Richmond, MI Draft: 6-184 2002 ATL Pro: N																															
2005	HAM	6				0						12	2						16	208	13.0	34	1	13	204	15.7	80				
2006	HAM	2				0													1	11	11.0	11	0					4	131	32.8	78

Year	Team	GP	FM	FF	FR	TK	SK	YDS	IR	YDS	PD	PTS	TD	RA	YDS	AVG	LG	TD	REC	YDS	AVG	LG	TD	PR	YDS	AVG	LG	KOR	YDS	AVG	LG
2007	SAS	3				0													3	23	7.7	13	0	5	33	6.6	19	6	92	15.3	32
2008	BC	5				1						6	1						7	61	8.7	18	1					1	10	10.0	10
4	Years	16				1						18	3						27	303	11.2	34	2	18	237	13.2	80	11	233	21.2	78
LEN HILL Len E 185 Winnipeg Rods Jrs.																															
1948	CAL	1																													
LLOYD HILL Lloyd D. WR 6'1 189 Texas Tech B: 1/16/1972 Draft: 6-170 1994 CHIB																															
1994	SHR	9				1													4	42	10.5	26	0								
LONZELL HILL Lonzell Ramon WR 5'11 194 Washington B: 9/25/1965 Stockton, CA Draft: 2-40 1987 NO Pro: N																															
1992	HAM	7				2						12	2	1	-5	-5.0	-5	0	23	384	16.7	53	2	4	23	5.8	15				
1993	HAM	3				1						6	1						12	190	15.8	54	1	2	7	3.5	5				
1994	HAM	8	1		0	0						6	1						27	339	12.6	37	1								
3	Years	18	1		0	3						24	4	1	-5	-5.0	-5	0	62	913	14.7	54	4	6	30	5.0	15				
NORM HILL Norman OE-DE 6'2 192 Manitoba B: 11/8/1929																															
1948	CAL	11										10	2										2								
1949	CAL	14										5	1										1								
1950	CAL	13																													
1951	WPG	13																	8	77	9.6		0	1	15	15.0	15				
1952	WPG	16			1																										
1953	WPG	16							1	0																					
1954	CAL	16	0		1														1	8	8.0	8	0								
7	Years	99	0		2				1	0		15	3						9	85	9.4	8	3	1	15	15.0	15				
RALPH HILL Ralph Edward C 6'1 245 Florida A&M B: 11/10/1949 Chicago, IL Pro: NW																															
1978	TOR	11																													
ROD HILL Rodrick CB 6'0 184 Kentucky State B: 3/14/1959 Detroit, MI Draft: 1-25 1982 DAL Pro: N																															
1988	WPG	18				42			7	54																					
1989	WPG*	18	0		1	40			12	73																		1	0	0.0	0
1990	WPG*	18	0		1	31			12	138		6	1																		
1991	WPG	18	0		1	38			9	181		12	2											1	3	3.0	5				
1992	WPG+	18	0		2	39			7	36														1	2	2.0	2				
5	Years	90	0		5	190			47	482		18	3											2	5	2.5	5	1	0	0.0	0
STEWART HILL Stewart DE-LB 6'1 230 Washington B: 3/16/1962 Seattle, WA Draft: 4A-68 1984 DEN-USFL																															
1984	EDM*	16					18.0																								
1985	EDM	16	0		2		8.0		2	24																					
1986	EDM+	18	0		4		17.0		1	45		18	3						2	28	14.0	24	2								
1987	EDM	17				38	18.0					6	1						1	17	17.0	17	1								
1988	EDM	11			1	13	11.0		1	11		6	1																		
1989	EDM*	18	0		2	41	13.0																								
1990	EDM*	16	0		2	25	17.0		1	16																					
1991	BC+	18	0		2	48	8.0					6	1						1	5	5.0	5	1								
1992	BC	16				30	8.0	39.0																							
1993	SAS	18				36	8.0	59.0																							
10	Years	164	0		13	231	126.0	98.0	5	96		36	6						4	50	12.5	24	4								
T.J. HILL Tororris Jermal LB-DB 5'9 192 Northeastern B: 7/2/1980 Paterson, NJ																															
2007	MTL	18	0	0	1	80	2.0	8.0	1	0	6													1	0	0.0	0	1	0	0.0	0
2008	MTL+	18	0	0	1	87	4.0	15.0	1	23	1																				
2009	EDM	15				63	2.0	10.0	4	153	0	12	2																		
2010	EDM	18	0	1	2	100	3.0	23.0	3	36	2	6	1																		
2011	EDM	14	0	0	3	67			2	87	2																				
5	Years	83	0	1	7	397	11.0	56.0	11	299	11	18	3											1	0	0.0	0	1	0	0.0	0
TONY HILL Anthony RB 6'2 229 Stetson B: 11/15/1950																															
1977	TOR	8																	8	105	13.1	24	0								
TONY HILL Antonio LaVosia DE 6'6 252 Tennessee-Chattanooga B: 10/23/1968 Augusta, GA Draft: 4C-108 1991 DAL Pro: N																															
1994	WPG	2				7																									
1995	WPG	6	0		1	12	3.0	10.0																							
1996	WPG	12	0		2	16																									
3	Years	20	0		3	35	3.0	10.0																							
KARL HILZINGER Karl FB-S-P 5'10 190 NDG Maple Leafs Jrs.; Verdun Ints. B: 1933 Montreal, QC D: 12//1988																															
1952	MTL	1																													
1953	SAS	14										5	1	42	211	5.0		0	6	127	21.2		1					5	103	20.6	
1954	SAS	1												1	11	11.0	11	0													
1955	OTT	12												5	6	1.2	9	0	2	25	12.5	18	0	9	61	6.8	19	3	45	15.0	19
1956	OTT	10							1	0		12	2	39	218	5.6	18	2	3	27	9.0	15	0								
1957	OTT	3												8	11	1.4	5	0	1	8	8.0	8	0								
1958	OTT	12																													
7	Years	53							1	0		17	3	95	457	4.8	18	2	12	187	15.6	18	1	9	61	6.8	19	8	148	18.5	19
JONATHAN HIMEBAUCH Jonathan C 6'2 288 Southern California B: 8/13/1975 Greenwich, CT Pro: EX																															
1999	TOR	1	1	0	0	0																									
WILLIE HINCHCLIFF William John WR 5'11 195 Auckland Institute# B: 9/13/1969 Trenton, NJ Pro: E																															
1992	BC	2	1		1	0																						4	65	16.3	24
1993	BC	1				0																									
1995	SAS	2				1																									
1996	OTT	13	1		0	2						6	1	1	-10	-10.0	-10	0	17	368	21.6	46	1								
4	Years	18	2		1	3						6	1	1	-10	-10.0	-10	0	17	368	21.6	46	1					4	65	16.3	24
PAT HINDS Pat T 6'3 290 San Jose State B: 7/18/1966 Winnipeg, MB Draft: 3-18 1990 CAL																															
1991	CAL	15				0																									
RYAN HINDS Ryan CB-S 6'1 198 New Hampshire B: 6/19/1986 Georgetown, Guyana Draft: 2-13 2009 HAM																															
2010	HAM	9				26			1	9	3																				
2011	HAM	12				36					6																				
2	Years	21				62			1	9	9																				
STERLING HINDS Sterling RB 5'11 185 Washington B: 10/31/1961 Mississauga, ON Draft: TE 1984 TOR																															
1984	TOR	4												3	6	2.0	3	0	4	33	8.3	16	0					5	101	20.2	27
1985	TOR	3	0		2							6	1	5	19	3.8	13	0	1	33	33.0	33	0					4	114	28.5	51
2	Years	7	0		2							6	1	8	25	3.1	13	0	5	66	13.2	33	0					9	215	23.9	51
TYRONE HINES Tyrone LB 6'2 242 Tennessee B: 3/14/1973																															
1999	EDM	9	0	0	1	26	2.0					6	1																		
JIM HINESLY James E 6'0 200 Michigan State B: 12/11/1933 Titusville, FL Draft: 25-293 1957 PIT																															
1957	HAM	4							0	7		6	1						2	28	14.0	19	1								
DON HINEY Donald E. QB-HB 5'11 165 North Dakota																															
1946	WPG	8										11	0																		
1947	WPG	6										15	1					1													
1948	WPG+	11										18	0																		
3	Years	25										44	1					1													
GORD HINSE Gordon C-OT 6'4 305 Alberta B: 8/24/1987 Edmonton, AB Draft: 2-11 2009 EDM																															
2009	EDM	8				0																									
2010	EDM	18				1																									
2011	EDM	5				0																									
3	Years	31				1																									
AL HINTON Al G-DT 6'2 240 Iowa B: 11/27/1940 Columbus, GA Draft: 6-43 1962 DAL																															
1962	TOR	1																													
1963	TOR	14																													
2	Years	15																													
KEN HINTON Kenneth Leroy CB 5'9 170 San Diego State B: 7/2/1955 Los Angeles, CA																															

Year	Team	GP	FM	FF	FR	TK	SK	YDS	IR	YDS	PD	PTS	TD	RA	YDS	AVG	LG	TD	REC	YDS	AVG	LG	TD	PR	YDS	AVG	LG	KOR	YDS	AVG	LG
1977	BC	6	0		2				1	25		6	1											4	144	36.0	130	6	160	26.7	44
1978	BC	16	4		1				5	47														62	478	7.7	31	6	172	28.7	52
1979	BC	16	5		1				7	161														62	519	8.4	48	1	21	21.0	21
1980	BC	16							4	46									1	8	8.0	8	0	10	70	7.0	19				
1981	BC	16							6	119		6	1																		
1982	BC	16	0		1				2	15																					
1983	BC	1																													
1983	SAS	7																													
1983	Year	8																													
1984	SAS	13							2	71														1	4	4.0	4				
1985	SAS	4																													
9	Years	104	9		5				27	484		12	2						1	8	8.0	8	0	139	1215	8.7	130	13	353	27.2	52
PATRICK HINTON Patrick LB 6'2 230 South Carolina B: 11/2/1968 Atlanta, GA D: 6/13/2004 Atlanta, GA Pro: E																															
1993	WPG	4	0		1	13	1.0	4.0																							
TOM HINTON William Thomas OG 6'0 225 Louisiana Tech B: 1936 Draft: 12-135 1958 CHIC																															
1958	BC+	16	1																					1	0	0.0	0				
1959	BC+	16																													
1960	BC	15	0		1																										
1961	BC	9																													
1062	BC	10	0		2																										
1963	BC*	16	0		1																										
1964	BC+	16																													
1965	BC	16	0		1																										
1966	BC+	16																													
9	Years	136	1		5																			1	0	0.0	0				
TOM HIPSZ Tom DT 6'5 280 Toronto B: 3/5/1972 Toronto, ON Draft: 4-36 1996 MTL																															
1997	MTL	18	0	0	2	19	1.0	4.0	1	0	1																				
1998	MTL	16	0	0	2	21	3.0	21.0			1																				
1999	MTL	16				3																									
2000	BC	5				4																									
2000	TOR	3				2																									
2000	Year	8				6																									
2001	HAM	18	0	0	1	13	1.0	5.0																							
5	Years	73	0	0	5	62	5.0	30.0	1	0	2																				
JACK HIROSE Jack DB 6'0 181 British Columbia B: 1/3/1958 Draft: 1A-2 1980 SAS																															
1980	SAS	10																													
1981	TOR	2																													
2	Years	12																													
ED HIRSCH Edward Norman (Buckets) C-LB 5'10 210 Northwestern B: 3/26/1921 Clarence, NY D: 1/28/2000 Irving, NY Draft: 16-161 1944 CHIB Pro: A																															
1950	TOR+	10																													
1951	TOR+	12																													
1952	HAM	2																													
3	Years	24																													
STEVE HIRSCH Steven Wendell DB 6'0 195 Northern Illinois B: 5/18/1962 Pontiac, MI Pro: N																															
1985	OTT	1							1	0																					
ELGIN HIRST Elgin E-C-G 5'11 213 none B: 1929																															
1954	TOR	14																													
1955	TOR	12																													
1956	TOR	14																													
3	Years	40																													
KEITH HISCOX Keith OG-OT 6'2 270 Simon Fraser B: 4/29/1971 Ottawa, ON Draft: 3A-25 1995 OTT																															
1995	OTT	1				0																									
1996	SAS	15				1																									
2	Years	16				1																									
ROB HITCHCOCK Rob LB-S 6'2 203 Weber State B: 10/28/1970 Hamilton, ON Draft: 2-17 1995 HAM																															
1995	HAM	18	0		1	55					2																	1	13	13.0	13
1996	HAM	14				40	1.0	8.0	4	49	3																				
1997	HAM	18	0	1	1	42			5	43	5																	4	58	14.5	18
1998	HAM	18	0	0	1	59	1.0	9.0	4	74	1																				
1999	HAM*	18				63			5	25	2																				
2000	HAM	18	0	2	3	51			3	73	3	6	1																		
2001	HAM*	18	0	2	1	59	2.0	6.0	6	47	3																				
2002	HAM+	18	0	1	0	62			8	144	3																				
2003	HAM	8				20					2																				
2004	HAM	16	0	1	0	43			1	20	0																				
2005	HAM	18	0	2	0	69	6.0	54.0			2								1	19	19.0	19	0								
2006	HAM	18	0	0	1	43	1.0	5.0			1																				
2007	EDM	3				1																									
13	Years	203	0	9	8	607	11.0	82.0	36	475	27	6	1						1	19	19.0	19	0					5	71	14.2	18
CONRAD HITCHLER Conrad L. TE 6'3 217 Missouri B: 1/15/1939																															
1963	CAL	10																	8	77	9.6	15	0					1	0	0.0	0
KATO HITSON Donald RB 5'10 205 Georgia Military JC; Murray State B: 4/13/1974 Homerville, GA																															
1998	TOR	3				0						12	2											14	328	23.4	88	7	169	24.1	41
1999	TOR	1				2																						3	36	12.0	14
2	Years	4				2						12	2											14	328	23.4	88	10	205	20.5	41
STEVE HMIEL Steve DB-LB-OE 6'0 193 B: 1938																															
1960	HAM	3																													
1963	HAM	10							1	13																					
1964	HAM	7							1	0																					
1965	HAM	6																													
1966	HAM	10	0		1							6	1						1	12	12.0	12	0					1	28	28.0	28
5	Years	36	0		1				2	13		6	1						1	12	12.0	12	0					1	28	28.0	28
KEN HOBART Kenneth QB 6'0 210 Lewis & Clark; Idaho B: 1/27/1961 Cairo, GA Draft: 2-42 1984 JAC-USFL Pro: U																															
1985	HAM+	15	9		0							36	6	118	928	7.9	44	6													
1986	HAM	18	3		1							36	6	82	593	7.2	35	6													
1987	HAM	7				0						6	1	28	240	8.6	26	1													
1989	OTT	4				1						6	1	20	115	5.8	14	1													
1990	OTT	15	3		1	1						12	2	20	106	5.3	15	2													
5	Years	59	15		2	2						96	16	268	1982	7.4	44	16													
DARYL HOBBS Daryl Ray WR 6'2 180 Santa Monica CC; Pacific B: 5/23/1968 Victoria, TX Pro: NX																															
1999	MTL	1				0																									
2000	SAS	7				3						12	2						23	277	12.0	32	2	9	45	5.0	13				
2	Years	8				3						12	2						23	277	12.0	32	2	9	45	5.0	13				
HARRY HOBBS Harry HB-FW 5'8 170 Calgary West End Tornadoes Jrs.; Calgary Army Jrs.; Alberta B: 1925																															
1946	CAL	6										5	1					1													
1947	CAL	1																													
1949	EDM	14																													
1950	EDM	13												37	118	3.2		0													
4	Years	34										5	1	37	118	3.2	0	0													
BOB HOBERT Donald Robert OT-DT 6'0 240 Minnesota B: 6/25/1935 IA D: 11/2/1994 Minneapolis, MN Draft: 6-73 1957 NYG																															
1957	WPG	16	0		2				3	24																					
1958	WPG	15	0		3																										

Year	Team	GP	FM	FF	FR	TK	SK	YDS	IR	YDS	PD	PTS	TD	RA	YDS	AVG	LG	TD	REC	YDS	AVG	LG	TD	PR	YDS	AVG	LG	KOR	YDS	AVG	LG
2	Years	31	0		5				3	24																					
ELTON HOBSON Elton HB-FL-QB 5'9 187 B: 1925																															
1946	WPG	7																													
1947	WPG	6																													
1948	WPG	12										5	1										1								
3	Years	25										5	1										1								
SANDY HOCE Alexander E B: 3/30/1927 D: 1/11/2008 Regina, SK																															
1946	SAS	2																													
DOUG HOCKING Doug LB 6'1 230 Surrey Rams Jrs. B: 10/16/1969 Sarnia, ON																															
1991	BC	17	0		1	18																									
1992	BC	13				36																									
1993	BC	18				24																									
1994	BC	10	0		3	10																						1	0	0.0	0
1995	WPG	15	0		1	40					1																				
1996	WPG	17				19																									
1997	WPG	13	0	0	1	19	2.0	20.0																							
1998	WPG	6	0	1	0	10			1	2	1																				
1999	WPG	17				19	3.0	31.0																1	0	0.0	0				
2000	WPG	17	0	0	2	9																									
2001	WPG	18				16	1.0	6.0																							
2002	WPG	17	0	0	1	6																									
12	Years	178	0	1	9	226	6.0	57.0	1	2	2													1	0	0.0	0	1	0	0.0	0
ALPHONSO HODGE Alphonso J. S-CB 5'10 203 Miami (Ohio) B: 5/30/1982 Cleveland, OH Draft: 5B-147 2005 KC																															
2009	TOR	7	0	0	1	17			0	0	1																				
DAMON HODGE Damon WR 6'1 192 Alabama State B: 2/16/1977 Thomaston, AL Pro: N																															
2002	OTT	5	0	0	1	1						12	2						9	163	18.1	39	2					1	12	12.0	12
2003	HAM	5				0													16	278	17.4	49	0								
2	Years	10	0	0	1	1						12	2						25	441	17.6	49	2					1	12	12.0	12
HOWARD HODGES Howard Thomas, III DT-DE 6'2 255 Iowa B: 5/29/1981 Copperas Cove, TX Pro: E																															
2007	HAM	15	0	1	1	29	6.0	42.0																							
2008	CAL	15	0	0	1	11	2.0	12.0																				2	25	12.5	14
2	Years	30	0	1	2	40	8.0	54.0																				2	25	12.5	14
LAURIE HODGSON Laurie LB 6'0 210 Edmonton Rams Jrs. B: 1931																															
1953	EDM	15																						1	6	6.0	6				
1954	EDM	16																													
1955	EDM	10	1		0									0	-4		-4	0	1	23	23.0	23	0								
1956	BC	8	1		0				1	7														1	1	1.0	1				
1958	BC	16																													
5	Years	65	2		0				1	7				0	-4		-4	0	1	23	23.0	23	0	2	7	3.5	6				
ED HOERSTER Ed LB-DE-DT 6'2 230 Notre Dame B: 1941 Draft: 16-124 1963 BUF; 10-137 1963 CHIB																															
1963	TOR	10																													
1964	TOR	3																													
1964	HAM	10																													
1964	Year	13																													
1965	HAM	1							1	5																					
1965	SAS	8	0		2				1																						
1965	Year	9	0		2				2																						
3	Years	14	0		2				2	5																					
NATHAN HOFFART Nathan WR-SB 6'2 209 Saskatchewan B: 6/19/1982 Regina, SK Draft: 1C-7 2005 SAS																															
2005	SAS	3				0																									
2007	SAS	4				1													1	7	7.0	7	0	1	0	0.0	0				
2008	TOR	10				0													6	48	8.0	12	0								
3	Years	17				1													7	55	7.9	12	0	1	0	0.0	0				
DALTON HOFFMAN Johnnie Dalton FB 6'0 206 Baylor B: 12/23/1941 Ballinger, TX Pro: N																															
1965	EDM	2	1		0									5	10	2.0	5	0	1	7	7.0	7	0					4	49	12.3	22
JIM HOFFMAN James Warren DT 6'4 280 Arizona B: 12/14/1972 La Mesa, CA Pro: E																															
1997	TOR	1				0																									
JOHN HOFFMAN John DB 6'0 182 Saskatchewan B: 9/4/1966 Regina, SK Draft: 5-37 1988 SAS																															
1989	SAS	17	0		1	5																		1	6	6.0	6				
1990	SAS	18	1		1	6			2	8									1	17	17.0	17	0					1	-1	-1.0	-1
1991	SAS	8				7			1	22																					
1992	SAS	13				9																									
4	Years	56	1		2	27			3	30									1	17	17.0	17	0	1	6	6.0	6	1	-1	-1.0	-1
FRANK HOFFMANN Frank OG 6'4 281 York B: 1/9/1980 Draft: 4-30 2004 TOR																															
2004	TOR	1				0																									
BILL HOGAN Bill WR 5'9 175 Wilfrid Laurier B: 6/20/1949 Toronto, ON Draft: 2B-14 1972 CAL																															
1972	CAL	2																	1	7	7.0	7	0	10	50	5.0	13				
FLOYD HOGAN Floyd Gene DB 5'11 185 Arkansas B: 1/12/1953 Alvarado, TX Draft: 9B-215 1975 CLE																															
1975	BC	1																	1	18	18.0	18	0	3	30	10.0	12	2	107	53.5	92
JERRY HOGAN Jerry DE 5'11 201 McGill B: 6/17/1933 Montreal, QC																															
1954	MTL	11																													
1955	MTL	3																													
1956	MTL	1																													
1957	MTL	1																													
4	Years	16																													
JIM HOGAN James DE 6'3 230 Western Ontario B: 1941 Draft: 1-5 1963 SAS																															
1966	BC	1																													
GORD HOGARTH Gordon C 6'3 215 British Columbia B: 1927																															
1950	CAL	11																													
LARRY HOGUE Larry CB 5'9 175 Utah State B: 9/20/1960 Shelby, NC Draft: 10-278 1982 CIN																															
1983	CAL	12							1	5																		1	23	23.0	23
1984	CAL	16	0		1							6	1											1	13	13.0	13				
1985	CAL	16	0		3		1.0		3	28		6	1																		
1986	CAL	18	0		1		1.0		2	54																					
1987	CAL	16	0		2	56			2	38																					
1988	CAL	4			1	13			1	1																					
1989	OTT	3				9																									
1989	SAS	7				13																									
1989	Year	10				22																									
1990	SAS	18	0		2	43			4	37														1	6	6.0	6				
1991	SAS	4				17			1	0																					
9	Years	107	0		10	151	2.0		14	163		12	2											2	19	9.5	13	1	23	23.0	23
MIKE HOHENSEE Michael Louis QB 6'0 205 Mount San Antonio JC; Minnesota B: 2/22/1961 Draft: 5A-50 1983 WAS-USFL Pro: NU																															
1985	TOR	6	2		0							6	1	18	119	6.6	21	1													
1985	OTT	1	0		0																										
1985	Year	7	2		0							6	1	18	119	6.6	21	1													
JON HOHMAN Jon Carl OG 6'1 243 Wisconsin B: 10/23/1942 Antigo, WI Draft: 8- 1965 DEN Pro: N																															
1967	HAM	9																													
1968	HAM	14																													
1969	HAM	14																													
1970	HAM	14																													
1971	HAM	14	0		1																										

Year	Team	GP	FM	FF	FR	TK	SK	YDS	IR	YDS	PD	PTS	TD	RA	YDS	AVG	LG	TD	REC	YDS	AVG	LG	TD	PR	YDS	AVG	LG	KOR	YDS	AVG	LG
1972	HAM+	14																													
1973	HAM	14	0		1							6	1																		
7	Years	93	0		2							6	1																		
TREVOR HOILETT Trevor DB 6'1 200 Manitoba B: 4/20/1965 Draft: 6-52 1986 WPG																															
1988	WPG	1																													
BOB HOLBURN Bob HB 6'2 188 Vancouver Blue Bombers Jrs.																															
1954	BC	9																							1	0	0.0	0	2	18	9.0	12
1955	BC	10																	10	120	12.0	22	0								
2	Years	19																	10	120	12.0	22	0	1	0	0.0	0	2	18	9.0	12
SAM HOLDEN Samuel Lee, Jr. OT-OG 6'3 258 Southern Illinois; Grambling State B: 2/24/1947 Magnolia, MS Draft: 2-31 1971 NO Pro: NW																															
1976	SAS	16																													
1977	SAS	16	0		1																										
1978	SAS	11	0		1							6	1															1	15	15.0	15
3	Years	43	0		2							6	1															1	15	15.0	15
JACK HOLDSWORTH John QB-HB Calgary West End Tornadoes Jrs. deceased																															
1946	CAL	8																													
1947	CAL	8																													
2	Years	16																													
BRUCE HOLLAND Bruce DT 6'5 245 Wilfrid Laurier B: 6/26/1954 Draft: TE 1978 HAM																															
1978	HAM	5																													
JAMIE HOLLAND Jamie Lorenza WR 6'1 190 Butler County CC; Ohio State B: 2/1/1964 Raleigh, NC Draft: 7-173 1987 SD Pro: N																															
1994	WPG	12				2						12	2	1	7	7.0	7	0	35	485	13.9	47	2					8	164	20.5	26
1995	WPG	8				1						12	2						14	225	16.1	60	2								
1995	SAS	1				0													2	80	40.0	47	0								
1995	Year	9				1						12	2						16	305	19.1	60	2								
2	Years	20				3						24	4	1	7	7.0	7	0	51	790	15.5	60	4					8	164	20.5	26
JOHN HOLLAND John Calvin WR 6'1 190 Tennessee State B: 2/28/1952 Beckley, WV Draft: 2A-29 1974 MIN; 16-192 1974 HOU-WFL Pro: N																															
1979	HAM	9	1		0							12	2						37	582	15.7	53	2	17	61	3.6	12	6	89	14.8	27
1980	HAM	16										18	3						50	791	15.8	57	3	7	23	3.3	14	2	25	12.5	20
1981	CAL	13	1		0							24	4						56	1017	18.2	81	4								
1982	OTT	4	1		0							6	1						6	142	23.7	60	1								
4	Years	42	3		0							60	10						149	2532	17.0	81	10	24	84	3.5	14	8	114	14.3	27
JOHN HOLLAND John Robert CB 5'11 185 Monterey Peninsula JC; Sacramento State B: 7/18/1965 Monterey County, CA Pro: E																															
1990	BC	3	1		0	7			2	0														4	19	4.8	11	1	23	23.0	23
1993	EDM	9				31			5	56		6	1											5	41	8.2	13				
1994	EDM*	18	1		1	58			8	147	7	6	1											20	112	5.6	16	3	66	22.0	30
1995	EDM	13	0		2	37			1	0	5																	1	1	1.0	1
1996	SAS	4				6			1	0	1																				
1996	BC	4				7																									
1996	Year	8				13			1	0	1																				
1997	BC	15				38			2	41	5																				
6	Years	62	2		3	184			19	244	18	12	2											29	172	5.9	16	5	90	18.0	30
JUSTIN HOLLAND Justin Lee QB 6'2 219 Colorado State B: 4/16/1983 Denver, CO																															
2007	WPG	4				0																									
LOU HOLLAND Louis OHB 5'9 187 Wisconsin B: 1942																															
1964	BC	7	2		1							6	1	28	138	4.9	37	1	9	74	8.2	23	0					1	23	23.0	23
CHUCK HOLLAWAY Charles OHB-DB 5'9 175 UCLA B: 1932																															
1958	CAL	14	2		0				1	21		30	5	3	24	8.0	10	0	56	973	17.4	90	5					11	307	27.9	39
MARCUS HOLLIDAY Marcus Edward RB 5'11 222 Memphis B: 7/16/1973 Memphis, TN Pro: N																															
1997	HAM	1				0								2	7	3.5	9	0	2	7	3.5	6	0								
JOE HOLLIMON Joe CB 6'0 198 Arkansas State B: 11/5/1952 Trumann, AR Draft: 8-207 1975 MIN																															
1976	EDM+	14	4		3				1	0		12	2											50	568	11.4	58	26	794	30.5	82
1977	EDM	8	1		0				5	132														10	120	12.0	24	6	183	30.5	45
1978	EDM*	16	0		1				8	228		24	4											45	417	9.3	47	8	127	15.9	27
1979	EDM	16	2		0				2	25														15	85	5.7	17	23	609	26.5	55
1980	EDM	15							3	47		6	1											2	13	6.5	13	4	79	19.8	27
1981	EDM	16	1		2				5	27		6	1															8	167	20.9	29
1982	EDM+	16	1		3		1.5		9	178		6	1											4	29	7.3	15	12	271	22.6	39
1983	EDM	16	4		1				3	1														42	366	8.7	30	31	765	24.7	49
1984	EDM	15	1		0				3	51														32	250	7.8	55	7	176	25.1	36
1985	EDM	4	1		0				1	3														5	43	8.6	12	5	112	22.4	32
10	Years	136	15		10		1.5		40	692		54	9											205	1891	9.2	58	130	3283	25.3	82
DON HOLLINGWORTH Don HB-FW-FB 6'1 215 Ottawa Sooners Jrs. B: 1932																															
1952	OTT	7																													
1953	OTT	13																													
1954	BC	5																													
3	Years	25																													
ANDREW HOLLINGSWORTH Andrew DE 6'2 242 Towson State B: 2/12/1977 Brunswick, ME																															
2002	BC	1				0																									
DAVID HOLLIS David Lanier DB 5'11 175 Nevada-Las Vegas B: 7/4/1965 Harbor City, CA Pro: N																															
1994	LV	16	2		1	68			2	27	2			1	3	3.0	3	0						15	153	10.2	45	8	126	15.8	31
KENNETH HOLLIS Kenneth Jamal LB 6'0 225 East Mississippi JC; Louisiana State B: 10/29/1982 Fairfield, AL																															
2007	EDM	8	0	3	0	7																									
CONDREDGE HOLLOWAY Condredge, Jr. QB 5'10 185 Tennessee B: 1/25/1954 Huntsville, AL Draft: 12B-306 1975 NE																															
1975	OTT	16	4		1							12	2	58	465	8.0	51	1	2	28	14.0	25	1								
1976	OTT	16	3		1							8	1	43	340	7.9	32	1	1	19	19.0	19	0								
1977	OTT	16										1	0	38	235	6.2	16	0													
1978	OTT+	16	7		1							6	1	50	288	5.8	31	1													
1979	OTT	15	1		1							6	1	40	259	6.5	22	1													
1980	OTT	12	4		1									29	106	3.7	23	0													
1981	TOR	14	9		1							6	1	58	317	5.5	33	1													
1982	TOR*	16	3		0							12	2	62	448	7.2	32	2													
1983	TOR+	15	5		1							24	4	56	271	4.8	19	4													
1984	TOR	15	1		1									43	217	5.0	20	0													
1985	TOR	7	5		0							12	2	33	166	5.0	25	2	1	-2	-2.0	-2	0								
1986	TOR	18	3		2									23	53	2.3	12	0													
1987	BC	5	1		0	1								2	2	1.0	1	0													
13	Years	181	46		10	1						87	14	535	3167	5.9	51	13	4	45	11.3	25	1								
DEREK HOLLOWAY Derek Lance WR 5'7 166 Arkansas B: 1/17/1961 Riverside, NJ Draft: 23-274 1983 MIC-USFL Pro: ENU																															
1988	CAL	8										6	1	2	18	9.0	16	0	13	311	23.9	86	1	16	106	6.6	42	16	327	20.4	36
JOHNNY HOLLOWAY Johnny Owen CB 5'11 182 Northwestern; Butler County CC; Kansas B: 11/8/1963 Galveston, TX Draft: 7-185 1986 DAL Pro: N																															
1989	BC	5				23																									
WAYNE HOLM Wayne DB-QB 6'1 195 Simon Fraser B: 5/12/1949 Gander Bay, BC Draft: 8- 1969 BC; 1A-1 1970 CAL																															
1970	CAL	16												1	6	6.0	6	0													
1971	BC	16			1				1	0																					
1972	BC	16	0		1				2	16																					
1973	TOR	4	0		1																										
4	Years	52	0		3				3	16				1	6	6.0	6	0													
ALBERT HOLMES Albert Tommie, Jr. HB 6'1 175 Hawaii B: 2/3/1952 Travis County, TX Draft: 23-268 1974 MEM-WFL Pro: W																															
1974	TOR	2																													
BERNARD HOLMES Bernard WR 6'0 172 Sequoias JC; Texas A&M-Kingsville B: 5/13/1973																															
1996	CAL	2				1													2	12	6.0	9	0								

Year	Team	GP	FM	FF	FR	TK	SK	YDS	IR	YDS	PD	PTS	TD	RA	YDS	AVG	LG	TD	REC	YDS	AVG	LG	TD	PR	YDS	AVG	LG	KOR	YDS	AVG	LG
BRIAN HOLMES Brian K 5'11 195 Samford B: 10/9/1977 Pro: E																															
2004	OTT	2	0	0	1	0						12	0																		
BRUCE HOLMES Bruce Barton LB 6'2 220 Minnesota B: 10/24/1965 El Paso, TX Draft: 12-325 1987 KC Pro: N																															
1988	TOR	4				10			1	26																					
1989	TOR	13	1		3	67	1.0		5	41																					
1989	OTT	4	0		1	36																						1	9	9.0	9
1989	Year	17	1		4	103	1.0		5	41																		1	9	9.0	9
1990	OTT+	18	0		2	127	1.0		3	9																					
1991	BC	11	0		1	66			1	24																					
1992	TOR	2	0		2	5																									
5	Years	48	1		9	311	2.0		10	100																		1	9	9.0	9
CHUCK HOLMES Chuck HB 5'11 190 Los Angeles CC																															
1955	TOR	1							1	3		1	0	8	28	3.5	9	0	2	14	7.0	8	0								
COREY HOLMES Corey RB 5'8 189 Mississippi Valley State B: 11/19/1976 Greenville, MS																															
2001	SAS	3				0								1	3	3.0	3	0	1	8	8.0	8	0	4	42	10.5	16	2	48	24.0	29
2002	SAS*	17	1	0	1	0						42	7	45	334	7.4	56	5	24	285	11.9	47	1	82	1023	12.5	75	45	1035	23.0	42
2003	SAS	10	4	0	0	1						24	4	29	192	6.6	21	3	19	177	9.3	24	0	34	424	12.5	87	25	551	22.0	52
2004	SAS	18	2	0	0	3						18	3	100	635	6.4	35	2	51	536	10.5	39	0	74	705	9.5	66	37	702	19.0	45
2005	SAS*	18	6	0	1	1						30	5	139	899	6.5	56	1	56	523	9.3	32	1	55	835	15.2	89	43	1157	26.9	81
2006	HAM	10	5	0	1	2						6	1	64	369	5.8	25	1	33	263	8.0	28	0	25	125	5.0	20	22	472	21.5	35
2007	HAM	7				0								14	74	5.3	11	0	9	53	5.9	10	0	14	74	5.3	20	22	424	19.3	39
2007	SAS	9	3	0	0	0						24	4	14	73	5.2	17	2	10	135	13.5	36	2	35	411	11.7	31	33	584	17.7	34
2007	Year	16	3	0	0	0						24	4	28	147	5.3	17	2	19	188	9.9	36	2	49	485	9.9	31	55	1008	18.3	39
7	Years	83	21	0	3	7						144	24	406	2579	6.4	56	14	203	1980	9.8	47	4	323	3639	11.3	89	229	4973	21.7	81
GREG HOLMES Greg WR-SB-RB 5'11 180 Carroll (Wisconsin) B: 1/10/1959 Toronto, ON Draft: 1B-2 1982 TOR																															
1982	TOR	6																													
1983	TOR	13	1		0							8	1	1	5	5.0	5	0	2	87	43.5	87	1	20	129	6.5	22				
1984	TOR	16										2	0						28	328	11.7	30	0					8	174	21.8	40
1985	TOR	14	1		0							6	1						8	90	11.3	24	1								
1986	SAS	4																						9	71	7.9	16				
1986	MTL	7	2		0														4	43	10.8	17	0	13	74	5.7	16				
1986	Year	11	2		0														4	43	10.8	17	0	22	145	6.6	16				
5	Years	53	4		0							16	2	1	5	5.0	5	0	42	548	13.0	87	2	42	274	6.5	22	8	174	21.8	40
KEVIN HOLMES Kevin DT 6'2 298 Minnesota B: 10/5/1974 Lincoln Park, MI																															
2001	SAS	2				0																									
MIKE HOLMES Michael Raphael WR 6'2 195 Texas Southern B: 11/18/1950 Galveston, TX Draft: 1-18 1973 SF Pro: NU																															
1977	WPG	6										18	3						19	328	17.3	55	3					2	13	6.5	12
1978	WPG+	13										48	8	1	29	29.0	29	0	51	872	17.1	90	8	21	247	11.8	41	2	44	22.0	51
1979	WPG	16	1		1							60	10	1	-1	-1.0	-1	0	60	1034	17.2	75	10	43	300	7.0	41	15	401	26.7	47
1980	WPG*	16	1		1							62	10						79	1092	13.8	47	10	33	210	6.4	33	6	121	20.2	37
1981	WPG	1																													
1982	WPG	9										12	2						35	426	12.2	47	2								
6	Years	61	2		2							200	33	2	28	14.0	29	0	244	3752	15.4	90	33	97	757	7.8	41	25	579	23.2	51
PAT HOLMES James Patrick DT-DE 6'5 254 Texas Tech B: 8/3/1940 Durant, OK Draft: 3-40 1962 PHI Pro: N																															
1962	CAL	15																													
1963	CAL	16																													
1964	CAL	13	0		1																										
1965	CAL*	16																													
4	Years	60	0		1																										
REGGIE HOLMES Reggie DB 6'1 190 Wisconsin-Stout B: 9/13/1945 Macon, MS Draft: 12-310 1971 MIN Pro: W																															
1971	CAL	1																													
1972	CAL	12							1	38														32	175	5.5	23	4	81	20.3	29
2	Years	13							1	38														32	175	5.5	23	4	81	20.3	29
RICHARD HOLMES Richard RB 5'10 222 Edinboro B: 9/24/1952 Hope Mill, NC Pro: U																															
1977	TOR	3	2		0							6	1	31	151	4.9	28	1	8	46	5.8	13	0					2	48	24.0	31
1977	OTT	12	6		0							60	10	147	865	5.9	72	9	20	226	11.3	72	1					2	51	25.5	27
1977	Year+	15	8		0							66	11	178	1016	5.7	72	10	28	272	9.7	72	1					4	99	24.8	31
1978	OTT	16	4		1							24	4	142	607	4.3	54	3	30	313	10.4	53	1					3	79	26.3	30
1979	OTT	6										12	2	55	188	3.4	12	1	8	116	14.5	60	1					1	28	28.0	28
1979	WPG	4	1		0									29	130	4.5	18	0	5	26	5.2	11	0					3	88	29.3	50
1979	Year	10	1		0							12	2	84	318	3.8	18	1	13	142	10.9	60	1					4	116	29.0	50
3	Years	25	13		1							102	17	404	1941	4.8	72	14	71	727	10.2	72	3					11	294	26.7	50
ROBERT HOLMES Robert (Tank) FB 5'9 220 Southern University B: 10/5/1945 Draft: 14-375 1968 KC Pro: NW																															
1976	SAS	5	1		0									44	181	4.1	30	0	7	66	9.4	42	0								
SENECA HOLMES Seneca R. WR 5'9 170 Northwest Missouri State B: 6/24/1977 Denver, CO																															
2001	BC	8	2	0	2	2								1	3	3.0	3	0	12	169	14.1	34	0	19	218	11.5	37	13	237	18.2	31
MARK HOLMSTROM Mark LB 6'0 220 Manitoba B: 6/9/1973 Winnipeg, MB Draft: 6-48 1996 WPG																															
1996	WPG	3				2	1.0	1.0																							
1997	WPG	7				2																									
2	Years	10				4	1.0	1.0																							
STEVE HOLNESS Steven DH-S 5'11 194 Ottawa B: 7/20/1983 Montreal, QC																															
2008	WPG	18				12																									
2009	WPG	1				0																									
2010	MTL	4				2																									
3	Years	23				14																									
BERNARD HOLSEY Leonard Bernard DT 6'2 289 Duke B: 12/10/1973 Rome, GA Pro: N																															
2006	HAM	5				4																									
GLENN HOLT Glenn Clinton WR 5'11 185 Louisiana State; Western Kentucky B: 1/1/1965 Miami, FL																															
1989	TOR	3				1						6	1	1	-5	-5.0	-5	0	6	121	20.2	42	1					5	105	21.0	37
HARRY HOLT Harry Thompson, III RB-TE 6'4 240 Arizona B: 12/29/1957 Harlingen, TX Pro: N																															
1978	BC+	7	2		0							12	2	27	107	4.0	12	1	14	201	14.4	45	1	6	62	10.3	17	5	127	25.4	30
1979	BC	15	1		1							18	3	7	51	7.3	13	1	32	560	17.5	63	2								
1980	BC*	14	2		1							36	6	12	103	8.6	24	0	38	648	17.1	46	5	21	258	12.3	65	1	24	24.0	24
1981	BC	8										12	2	3	4	1.3	6	0	18	367	20.4	41	2								
1982	BC	10	0		1							25	4	4	21	5.3	22	0	35	588	16.8	80	4	1	5	5.0	5				
5	Years	54	5		3							103	17	53	286	5.4	24	2	137	2364	17.3	80	14	28	325	11.6	65	6	151	25.2	30
LINDSAY HOLT Lindsay E. FW Regina Dales Jrs. B: 1917 D: 4/11/2002																															
1946	SAS	8																													
RICHARD HOLT Richard H. DB 6'2 205 Arizona; El Camino JC; Arizona B: 9/10/1969 Carson, CA																															
1995	MEM	2				6																									
HARRY HOLTON Harold F. OG-OT 6'2 240 Texas-El Paso B: 10/1/1952 Draft: 9-220 1974 GB; 27-313 1974 HOU-WFL																															
1974	CAL	16																													
1975	CAL	13																										1	9	9.0	9
1976	CAL	16																													
1977	CAL	16	0		1																										
1978	CAL*	16	0		2																										
1979	OTT	6																													
1979	TOR	1																													
1979	Year	7																													
6	Years	83	0		3																							1	9	9.0	9
SONNY HOMER Lawrence FL-CB-OE 6'0 185 North Shore Cougars Jrs.; Grays Harbor JC B: 7/8/1936 Trail, BC D: 2/22/2006 Vancouver, BC																															
1958	BC	15										18	3	18	85	4.7	14	2	2	47	23.5	29	1					8	131	16.4	30

Year	Team	GP	FM	FF	FR	TK	SK	YDS	IR	YDS	PD	PTS	TD	RA	YDS	AVG	LG	TD	REC	YDS	AVG	LG	TD	PR	YDS	AVG	LG	KOR	YDS	AVG	LG
1959	BC	12							1			6	1	3	20	6.7	10	1						40	278	7.0	24	5	115	23.0	30
1960	BC	16	3		1				2	79				1	3	3.0	3	0						23	143	6.2	18				
1961	BC	15	2						3	36		6	1	3	16	5.3	14	0	1	9	9.0	9	1	5	54	10.8	18				
1962	BC	16							1			24	4						36	669	18.6	85	4								
1963	BC	11										18	3						33	608	18.4	54	3								
1964	BC	16	0		1							24	4						50	776	15.5	71	4								
1965	BC	16							1			6	1						12	295	24.6	46	1								
1966	BC	15										12	2						30	549	18.3	44	2								
1967	BC	15										6	1						26	397	15.3	40	1								
1968	BC	16	0		1							24	4						27	415	15.4	56	4								
11	Years	163	5		3				8	115		144	24	25	124	5.0	14	3	217	3765	17.4	85	21	68	475	7.0	24	13	246	18.9	30
MIKE HOMEWOOD Michael OG 6'5 295 Carleton (Ontario); Ottawa B: 12/10/1974 Toronto, ON																																
2002	SAS	1				0																										
2003	HAM	1				0																										
2004	OTT	3				1																										
3	Years	5				1																										
RAY HONEY Ray OT-OG-DT 6'4 255 Drake B: 3/5/1954 Draft: 1-4 1977 WPG																																
1977	WPG	12	0		4																											
1978	OTT	13																														
1979	OTT	12	0		1																											
1980	HAM	11																														
1981	MTL	5																														
5	Years	53	0		5																											
BOB HOOD Robert E 6'1 195 Alabama B: 1924 Draft: 24-164 1949 NY-AAFC; 10-96 1949 PIT																																
1949	HAM+	12										20	4										4								
HARRY HOOD Harry HB-QB-FB-FW 5'11 170 none B: 1926 Winnipeg, MB D: 5/18/1954 Calgary, AB																																
1946	WPG	7										10	2					2													
1947	WPG	6										5	1					1													
1948	CAL	12										21	4					1					2								
1949	CAL	14										20	4					2					2								
1950	CAL	14										5	1	87	359	4.1	18	1	23	407	17.7	55	0								
1951	CAL	13												25	90	3.6		0	8	104	13.0		0	21	220	10.5		4	56	14.0	
1952	CAL	16			1				1	7		10	2	4	13	3.3	10	0	1	10	10.0	10	1	21	112	5.3	12				
7	Years	82	0		1				1	7		71	14	116	462	4.0	18	7	32	521	16.3	55	5	42	332	7.9	12	4	56	14.0	
JAMES HOOD James H. WR 6'1 175 Arizona State B: 10/8/1961 Los Angeles, CA																																
1985	WPG	5	0		1														23	281	12.2	27	0								
1986	MTL*	18	0		1							12	2						95	1411	14.9	58	2								
1987	OTT	9	1		1	4						18	3	1	2	2.0	2	0	39	446	11.4	37	3								
1988	SAS	5				0						6	1						13	181	13.9	27	1								
4	Years	37	1		3	4						36	6	1	2	2.0	2	0	170	2319	13.6	58	6								
JOHN HOOD John M. RB 6'0 200 Central Michigan B: 1/7/1968 Pontiac, MI																																
1992	HAM	5	1		0	1						12	2	70	283	4.0	55	2	14	151	10.8	44	0	1	9	9.0	9	2	33	16.5	24
1993	HAM	4	1		0	5						6	1	41	146	3.6	14	1	3	21	7.0	13	0								
1994	HAM	9	2		0	4						18	3	103	415	4.0	24	3	16	128	8.0	33	0								
1995	SAS	2				0								33	121	3.7	17	0	5	49	9.8	14	0								
4	Years	20	4		0	10						36	6	247	965	3.9	55	6	38	349	9.2	44	0	1	9	9.0	9	2	33	16.5	24
JONATHAN HOOD Jonathan LB-DB 6'0 195 St. Francis Xavier; Western Ontario B: 12/23/1985 Mississauga, ON Draft: 4B-26 2008 EDM																																
2010	HAM	13				5																										
2011	HAM	17	0	0	1	11																										
2	Years	30	0	0	1	16																										
SHERM HOOD Sherman G 6'2 225 Queen's B: 1934																																
1957	BC	13																														
JIM HOOK James Edward HB-QB 5'10 182 Missouri B: 3/12/1930 Kansas City, MO																																
1955	CAL	1												5	17	3.4	6	0													
1956	SAS	1												2	20	10.0	12	0													
2	Years	2												7	37	5.3	12	0													
TIM HOOK Tim OG-C 6'2 246 Simon Fraser; Montana B: 9/27/1927 Draft: TE 1979 SAS																																
1979	SAS	11																														
1981	OTT	16																														
1982	OTT	16	0		1																											
1983	OTT	13																														
1984	OTT	3																														
1984	TOR	4																														
1984	Year	7																														
5	Years	59	0		1																											
BILLY HOOPER Horace Chilton, Jr. QB 6'0 185 Baylor B: 11/21/1931 Sweetwater, TX Draft: 26-302 1955 CHIC																																
1955	WPG	13	1		0				2	0		5	1	13	99	7.6	46	1													
CHRIS HOOPLE Chris LB-DB 6'3 240 Surrey Rams Jrs.; British Columbia B: 6/24/1973 Calgary, AB Draft: 2-12 1999 MTL																																
1999	MTL	16				11																										
2000	MTL	10				10																										
2001	MTL	10	0	0	1	11						6	1																			
2002	CAL	18				24																										
2003	SAS	16				13	1.0	10.0																								
2004	BC	18				25																										
2005	BC	7				4																										
7	Years	95	0	0	1	98	1.0	10.0				6	1																			
MEL HOOVER Melvin Charles WR 6'0 185 Arizona State B: 9/21/1959 Charlotte, NC Draft: 6A-145 1981 NYG Pro: N																																
1981	TOR	1																	1	13	13.0	13	0								
NORM HOPELY Norman OG 6'2 260 West Chester B: 3/5/1957 Philadelphia, PA																																
1981	CAL	16																														
1982	MTL	12	0		1																											
2	Years	28	0		1																											
ANDY HOPKINS Andrew Pochae HB 5'10 187 Stephen F. Austin State B: 10/19/1949 Crockett, TX Draft: 15-368 1971 HOU Pro: N																																
1973	HAM+	14	5		0							36	6	223	1223	5.5	97	5	33	277	8.4	45	1	2	33	16.5	17	4	76	19.0	25
1974	HAM+	16	2		1							24	4	232	943	4.1	36	4	42	325	7.7	19	0					1	0	0.0	0
1975	HAM	8	4		1							24	4	97	463	4.8	47	4	17	150	8.8	27	0	1	12	12.0	12				
1976	MTL+	14	8		1							18	3	219	1075	4.9	41	3	43	249	5.8	28	0					1	49	49.0	49
1977	MTL	5	2		0							12	2	52	218	4.2	20	2	11	120	10.9	33	0					2	60	30.0	45
5	Years	57	21		3							114	19	823	3922	4.8	97	18	146	1121	7.7	45	1	3	45	15.0	17	8	185	23.1	49
MARK HOPKINS Mark LB 6'2 230 York B: 8/3/1959 Toronto, ON Draft: 2-10 1983 MTL																																
1983	MTL	14	0		1		2.0																									
1984	MTL	2	2		1									2	13	6.5	7	0	4	31	7.8	11	0								
1985	MTL	16	0		1		1.0					6	1																			
1986	MTL	11					2.0																									
4	Years	43	2		3		5.0					6	1	2	13	6.5	7	0	4	31	7.8	11	0								
MOTON HOPKINS Moton DT 6'2 277 Tulsa B: 11/20/1986																																
2010	WPG	6	0	0	1	7	1.0	9.0	1	36	0	6	1																			
2011	MTL	10	0	1	1	17	4.0	25.0																								
2	Years	16	0	1	2	24	5.0	34.0	1	36	0	6	1																			
RON HOPKINS Ronald CB 5'10 180 Murray State B: 11/10/1960 Ridgely, TN Draft: 10-252 1983 BAL																																
1983	CAL	13	4		1		1.0		3	41														43	427	9.9	45	7	150	21.4	32
1984	CAL	7	1		0				2	12														17	166	9.8	42				

Year	Team	GP	FM	FF	FR	TK	SK	YDS	IR	YDS	PD	PTS	TD	RA	YDS	AVG	LG	TD	REC	YDS	AVG	LG	TD	PR	YDS	AVG	LG	KOR	YDS	AVG	LG
1985	CAL	15	2		1				2	51														9	43	4.8	9	15	294	19.6	50
1986	CAL	18	2		4				2	48																		30	633	21.1	93
1987	CAL	18	1		2	59			6	71																		47	1098	23.4	48
1988	CAL	16	2		5	53			3	19																		18	388	21.6	49
1989	CAL	18	0		1	48			5	131		6	1											1	0	0.0	0	37	904	24.4	100
1990	CAL	17	3		0	53			2	9		12	2											1	39	39.0	39	50	1287	25.7	95
1991	CAL	10	2		2	38			2	41														2	18	9.0	15	22	484	22.0	43
9	Years	132	17		16	251	1.0		27	423		18	3											73	693	9.5	45	226	5238	23.2	100
WADE HOPKINS Wade Alan WR 6'2 196 Southwest Baptist B: 8/23/1968 Bexar County, TX																															
1995	WPG	1				3													2	27	13.5	18	0								
DARREL HOPPER Darrel G. DB 6'1 196 El Camino JC; Southern California B: 3/14/1963 Los Angeles, CA Draft: TD 1985 LA-USFL Pro: N																															
1989	OTT	10	0		3	22			1	0		6	1																		
1990	OTT	6				12			1	25																					
2	Years	16	0		3	34			2	25		6	1																		
DAVE HOPPMANN David Peter FB 6'1 205 Iowa State B: 9/5/1940 Madison, WI D: 11/17/1975 Stuart, FL Draft: 7A-87 1963 NYG																															
1963	MTL	14										36	6	100	438	4.4	55	6	17	127	7.5	26	0					13	319	24.5	41
1964	MTL	6	1		0							6	1	45	162	3.6	22	1	6	39	6.5	13	0					10	202	20.2	29
2	Years	20	1		0							42	7	145	600	4.1	55	7	23	166	7.2	26	0					23	521	22.7	41
JIM HOPSON Jim OT-OG 6'2 237 Regina Rams Jrs. B: 3/1/1951																															
1973	SAS	5																													
1974	SAS	16																													
1975	SAS	10																													
1976	SAS	5																													
4	Years	36																													
JOE HORN Joseph WR 6'1 207 Itawamba CC B: 1/16/1972 New Haven, CT Draft: 5-135 1996 KC Pro: N																															
1995	MEM+	17	1		0	2						30	5						71	1415	19.9	90	5					2	17	8.5	16
BOB HORNES Bob DB 5'10 180 Idaho State B: 10/9/1949 Draft: 1-4 1974 BC																															
1974	BC	16	1		0				1	9														56	297	5.3	17				
1975	BC	5																													
1976	CAL	16	0		3				1	3																					
3	Years	37	1		3				2	12														56	297	5.3	17				
GERRY HORNETT Gerry OT 6'3 252 Simon Fraser B: 1/3/1956 Estevan, SK Draft: 1B-4 1979 SAS																															
1979	SAS	8																													
1980	SAS	16	2		0																							1	3	3.0	3
1981	SAS	16	0		2																										
1982	SAS	16	0		1																										
1984	SAS	16	0		1																										
1985	CAL	7																													
1985	OTT	5																													
1985	Year	12																													
1986	OTT	17																													
7	Years	96	2		4																							1	3	3.0	3
BILL HORTIE Bill HB-FB-FW-G 6'0 200 British Columbia B: 1931																															
1950	EDM	14												19	50	2.6		0													
1954	BC	14																						1	0	0.0	0				
1955	BC	13	0		3				1	0																					
1956	BC	2																													
4	Years	43	0		3				1	0				19	50	2.6	0	0						1	0	0.0	0				
BILL HORTON Bill G 6'1 200 Toronto Draft: 4-14 1955 TOR																															
1956	CAL	1																													
CHARLES HORTON Charles Edgar MG-OG 6'2 232 Baylor B: 11/30/1936 Waco, TX Draft: 2A-18 1959 DET																															
1959	BC	1																													
1959	TOR	6																										1	0	0.0	0
1959	Year	7																										1	0	0.0	0
CHARLEY HORTON Charles HB 6'0 190 Vanderbilt B: 1935 Draft: 15-172 1955 WAS; 1B-11 1956 LARM																															
1958	MTL	5							1	0				20	88	4.4	12	0	10	76	7.6	15	0					3	68	22.7	30
JASON HORTON Jason Dennard DB 6'0 191 North Carolina; North Carolina A&T B: 2/16/1980 Ahoskie, NC Pro: NU																															
2003	TOR	2				0																									
JEFF HORTON Jeff CB 6'0 200 East Tennessee State B: 4/30/1972 Rome, GA																															
1996	HAM	2				6																									
1997	WPG	3				15																									
2	Years	5				21																									
JON HORTON Jon WR 6'1 190 Arizona B: 12/26/1964 Tucson, AZ Pro: E																															
1987	BC	1				0								1	5	5.0	5	0	2	20	10.0	14	0								
LARRY HORTON Lawrence DE 6'2 248 Centerville JC; Iowa B: 4/29/1949 Gary, IN Draft: 9-219 1972 CHIB Pro: N																															
1974	MTL	2																													
MIKE HORTON Michael RB 5'10 206 Alabama A&M B: 7/19/1955 Pro: U																															
1982	OTT	1												16	67	4.2	14	0	2	17	8.5	14	0					5	86	17.2	19
MYKE HORTON Michael M. OT-OG 6'3 260 Gavilan JC; UCLA B: 7/17/1954 Portland, OR Draft: 17-428 1975 NE Pro: U																															
1975	TOR	6																													
1979	CAL	6																													
1980	CAL+	16																													
3	Years	28																													
MARK HORVATH Mark DB 6'1 185 McMaster B: 3/3/1962 Draft: 3A-23 1985 EDM																															
1986	OTT	2																													
BOBBY HOSEA Willie Samuel, Jr. DB 6'1 180 San Bernardino Valley JC; UCLA B: 12/5/1955 Murfreesboro, TN Pro: U																															
1979	MTL	13	0		1				2	24														2	10	5.0	6				
1980	SAS	15	1		0				2	18														3	22	7.3	14	2	32	16.0	19
1981	SAS	16	0		3				4	30														1	9	9.0	9	1	3	3.0	3
3	Years	44	1		4				8	72														6	41	6.8	14	3	35	11.7	19
ERIC HOSKINS Eric Lee WR-DB 5'11 170 Missouri Western State B: 12/30/1963 Kansas City, MO																															
1989	TOR	8				2						6	1						11	148	13.5	25	1					5	106	21.2	24
1995	TOR	1				0													2	45	22.5	36	0	2	4	2.0	4	1	28	28.0	28
2	Years	9				2						6	1						13	193	14.8	36	1	2	4	2.0	4	6	134	22.3	28
MARK HOUGHTON Mark WB-TE 6'1 218 California B: 1/11/1957 Draft: 1-3 1979 BC																															
1979	BC	16	1		3							6	1											1	3	3.0	3	1	10	10.0	10
1980	BC	16	0		1									7	24	3.4	10	0	3	31	10.3	30	0								
2	Years	32	1		4							6	1	7	24	3.4	10	0	3	31	10.3	30	0	1	3	3.0	3	1	10	10.0	10
MARK HOULDER Mark LB 6'1 230 York B: 8/22/1967 San Fernando, Trinidad & Tobago Draft: 6-47 1991 EDM																															
1993	TOR	1				0																									
BARRY HOULIHAN Barry HB 5'11 205 Washington; Simon Fraser B: 5/21/1953 Draft: TE 1975 BC																															
1975	BC	7												2	8	4.0	7	0													
1976	BC	15												6	32	5.3	14	0	9	94	10.4	23	0					4	80	20.0	26
2	Years	22												8	40	5.0	14	0	9	94	10.4	23	0					4	80	20.0	26
BOB HOUMARD Robert Alan FB 6'3 230 Ohio University B: 2/1/1947 Wooster, OH Draft: 14-342 1969 PIT Pro: W																															
1969	WPG	15	5		1							6	1	106	506	4.8	29	1	34	323	9.5	24	0					2	15	7.5	15
1970	WPG	16	4		0							48	8	194	810	4.2	32	8	23	259	11.3	25	0					2	10	5.0	10
1971	EDM	11			1							30	5	102	551	5.4	40	4	20	117	5.9	23	1								
1971	OTT	3			0							12	2	52	185	3.6		2	3	10	3.3		0								
1971	Year	14	8		1							42	7	154	736	4.8	40	6	23	127	5.5	23	1								
1972	OTT	7	2		0							12	2	61	226	3.7	20	2	5	31	6.2	13	0					3	49	16.3	22
4	Years	49	11		2							108	18	515	2278	4.4	40	17	85	740	8.7	25	1					7	74	10.6	22

Year	Team	GP	FM	FF	FR	TK	SK	YDS	IR	YDS	PD	PTS	TD	RA	YDS	AVG	LG	TD	REC	YDS	AVG	LG	TD	PR	YDS	AVG	LG	KOR	YDS	AVG	LG
CLEO HOUSE Cleo FB 5'10 228 Southern Arkansas B: 7/7/1950 DeKalb, TX Pro: W																														
1975	TOR	4	4		0							6	1	37	178	4.8	20	1	6	31	5.2	9	0					3	48	16.0	21
RAYMOND HOUSE Raymond I. DE 6'2 277 Arkansas B: 10/7/1980 Little Rock, AR																														
2004	OTT	4				3																								
RICK HOUSE Rick WR-SB-WB 5'10 180 Renfrew Trojans Jrs.; Simon Fraser B: 5/18/1957 New Westminster, BC Draft: 1-5 1979 WPG																														
1979	WPG	16										6	1	1	-1	-1.0	-1	0	15	261	17.4	48	1								
1980	WPG	16										42	7	3	1	0.3	4	0	40	757	18.9	68	7								
1981	WPG	16										60	10						61	1102	18.1	81	10								
1982	WPG	16										48	8	4	30	7.5	13	2	63	1020	16.2	49	6								
1983	WPG	14	1		0														28	545	19.5	54	0								
1984	WPG	13										24	4	4	13	3.3	8	1	38	494	13.0	30	3					2	39	19.5	21
1985	EDM	8	1		0							6	1	3	24	8.0	14	0	29	410	14.1	38	1								
1986	EDM	14	1		0							24	4						50	547	10.9	48	4					1	0	0.0	0
1987	EDM	11	1		0	3						24	4						31	534	17.2	46	4								
1988	EDM	15	1		0	2								1	3	3.0	3	0	27	382	14.1	27	0					1	5	5.0	5
1989	WPG	18	1		0	1						24	4	1	8	8.0	8	0	38	597	15.7	52	4								
1990	WPG+	18	3		0	6						48	8						63	883	14.0	41	8								
1991	WPG	14	1		2	4						42	7	2	6	3.0	5	0	39	607	15.6	42	7								
13	Years	189	10		2	16						348	58	19	84	4.4	14	3	522	8139	15.6	81	55					4	44	11.0	21
BRANDON HOUSTON Brandon Ashley OT 6'4 280 Oklahoma B: 4/2/1969 Lubbock, TX Draft: 12-326 1992 PHI																														
1994	LV	2																												
DANNY HOUSTON Danny RB 6'2 225 New Mexico Military Institute JC B: 1950																														
1969	MTL	1	1		0									4	4	1.0	4	0													
MARTAVIOUS HOUSTON Martavious DB 6'0 215 Auburn B: 3/8/1976 Lauderdale Lakes, FL																														
1999	TOR	18	0	3	1	93	2.0	23.0			1																				
2000	TOR	18	0	1	0	77	2.0	19.0	1	0	8																				
2002	TOR	18	0	1	0	88	1.0				4																				
2004	BC	7	0	1	0	18																								
4	Years	61	0	6	1	276	5.0	42.0	1	0	13																				
MELVIN HOUSTON Melvin WR 6'0 185 Central Michigan B: 8/10/1966 Flint, MI																														
1988	TOR	1				0													1	13	13.0	13	0								
DON HOVER Don R. LB 6'2 225 Washington State B: 12/13/1954 Seattle, WA Draft: 8B-219 1978 WAS Pro: N																														
1980	CAL	5																												
JIM HOVEY James Southerland LB 6'3 230 Kentucky B: 9/10/1952 St. Paul, MN Draft: 31-362 1974 NY-WFL																														
1975	HAM	1																												
BILL HOWARD William C 6'2 270 Western Ontario B: 5/15/1959 London, ON Draft: TE 1981 HAM																														
1983	HAM	9	0		1																									
1984	HAM	1																												
2	Years	10	0		1																									
BILLY HOWARD Billy DE-DT 6'4 255 Alcorn State B: 7/17/1950 Clarksdale, MS Draft: 2-39 1974 DET; 9-102 1974 POR-WFL Pro: N																														
1977	WPG	4																												
1978	WPG	12	0		2																									
1979	WPG	16	0		2														3	13	4.3	6	0								
3		32	0		4														3	13	4.3	6	0								
BOB HOWARD Bob SE 6'3 210 McMaster B: 9/23/1944 Toronto, ON Draft: 2B- 1967 WPG																														
1967	WPG	1																	1	20	20.0	20	0								
1968	WPG	16	1		0														6	146	24.3	41	0								
2	Years	17	1		0														7	166	23.7	41	0								
DAVE HOWARD David OE 6'1 200 Wisconsin B: 1935																														
1957	TOR	1																												
LUTHER HOWARD Luther CB 6'1 180 Delaware State B: 2/23/1951 New York, NY																														
1975	BC	1																										1	17	17.0	17
MARCUS HOWARD Marcus William DE 6'0 237 Georgia B: 10/10/1985 Huger, SC Draft: 5-161 2008 IND Pro: N																														
2011	EDM+	13	0	2	0	18	11.0	67.0																							
PETE HOWARD Peter OE 6'3 230 none B: 1941																														
1960	HAM	6																	1	19	19.0	19	0								
RON HOWARD Ronald DB 6'0 200 Tennessee State B: 9/20/1962 D: 3/17/2005 New Orleans, LA																														
1986	EDM	18	0		1		1.0		1	48									1	20	20.0	20	0	2	9	4.5	5	1	0	0.0	0
1987	EDM	18			3	70			6	38		6	1											2	9	4.5	6				
1988	EDM	12			1	39	1.0		4	41		12	2																		
1989	BC	15				65																		1	4	4.0	4				
4	Years	63	0		5	174	2.0		11	127		18	3						1	20	20.0	20	0	5	22	4.4	6	1	0	0.0	0
WALT HOWARD Walter TE 6'5 223 Wyoming B: 8/22/1955 Detroit, MI																														
1979	WPG	1																												
MARKUS HOWELL Markus WR-SB-CB 5'11 185 Texas Southern B: 4/21/1975 Winnipeg, MB Draft: 4-25 2000 WPG																														
2000	WPG	18	2	0	1	0						18	3						25	259	10.4	31	1	5	63	12.6	17	20	503	25.2	87
2001	WPG	18				3						6	1						19	307	16.2	38	1	8	83	10.4	24	4	80	20.0	32
2002	WPG	18	0	0	1	2						6	1						38	415	10.9	42	1	3	20	6.7	9				
2003	WPG	18				1						12	2	1	-1	-1.0	-1	0	20	282	14.1	47	2	1	4	4.0	4	9	238	26.4	47
2004	WPG	12				19			0	0	5								2	17	8.5	12	0								
2005	OTT	18	1	0	1	7						18	3	3	50	16.7	28	0	25	417	16.7	64	3					6	84	14.0	21
2006	CAL	18	0	1	0	7						6	1	2	9	4.5	9	0	20	340	17.0	81	1	35	384	11.0	57	1	27	27.0	27
2007	CAL	17	5	0	2	2						6	1	1	17	17.0	17	0	1	8	8.0	8	0	79	746	9.4	96	24	475	19.8	30
2008	CAL	16	2	0	0	3													1	31	31.0	31	0	67	591	8.8	55	9	194	21.6	33
2009	CAL	18	1	0	0	5													1	17	17.0	17	0	43	309	7.2	35	2	41	20.5	22
2010	WPG	5				0																		5	32	6.4	10	2	37	18.5	19
11	Years	176	11	1	5	49						72	12	7	75	10.7	28	0	152	2093	13.8	81	9	246	2232	9.1	96	77	1679	21.8	87
RON HOWELL Ron CB-FW-LB 6'0 185 none B: 12/4/1935 Hamilton, ON D: 3/16/1992																														
1954	HAM	10										5	1	5	58	11.6	21	1	6	92	15.3	51	0	2	13	6.5	12				
1955	HAM	12										20	4	17	135	7.9	50	1	6	162	27.0	41	2	53	580	10.9	90	3	59	19.7	26
1956	HAM	4										12	2						6	105	17.5	33	2	14	107	7.6	26	1	38	38.0	28
1957	HAM	12										6	1						4	97	24.3	37	0	65	391	6.0	83	2	20	10.0	10
1958	HAM+	14							2	51		48	8	1	6	6.0	6	0	34	756	22.2	66	6	81	553	6.8	69	14	391	27.9	56
1959	HAM+	14										60	10	1	7	7.0	5	0	25	624	25.0	82	8	60	478	8.0	82	9	199	22.1	36
1960	HAM	10										6	1	3	2	0.7	6	0	9	119	13.2	18	1	32	105	3.3	17	4	90	22.5	29
1961	HAM	13							3	41														56	174	3.1	26	2	46	23.0	24
1962	HAM	9							3	36														25	41	1.6	6				
1962	BC	5	1															1	14	14.0	14	0	15	46	3.1	13				
1962	Year	14	1						3	36									1	14	14.0	14	0	40	87	2.2	13				
1964	TOR	13	2		2				5	99		12	2						8	192	24.0	49	1	35	151	4.3	18				
1965	TOR	12	2		1				1	0														9	34	3.8	11				
1966	MTL	14	0		1				5	123		6	1											2	0	0.0	0				
12	Years	137	5		4				19	350		175	30	27	208	7.7	50	2	99	2161	21.8	82	20	449	2673	6.0	90	35	843	24.1	56
BOB HOWES Bob C 6'4 245 Queen's B: 1/4/1943 Draft: 3-24 1966 CAL																														
1968	BC	13																												
1969	BC	16																												
1970	BC	16	1		0																									
1971	BC	16			3							6	1																	
1972	EDM	16																												
1973	EDM+	16	1		0																									
1974	EDM	16																												
1975	EDM	16																												

Year	Team	GP	FM	FF	FR	TK	SK	YDS	IR	YDS	PD	PTS	TD	RA	YDS	AVG	LG	TD	REC	YDS	AVG	LG	TD	PR	YDS	AVG	LG	KOR	YDS	AVG	LG
1976	EDM	16			2																										
1977	EDM	16	1		0																										
1978	EDM	16																													
1979	EDM	16																													
1980	EDM	16																													
1981	EDM	10																													
14	Years	215	3		5							6	1																		
PETE HOWLETT Peter LB-FB 6'1 216 Loyola; McGill B: 1942 Draft: 1-6 1963 EDM; 6-50 1966 WPG																															
1967	MTL	14	0		2									2	13	6.5	10	0										3	42	14.0	24
1968	MTL	12							1	5				9	37	4.1	11	0													
1969	MTL	14	0		1							6	1	9	18	2.0	4	0	3	45	15.0	31	1					1	0	0.0	0
3	Years	40	0		3				1	5		6	1	20	68	3.4	11	0	3	45	15.0	31	1					4	42	10.5	24
STEVE HOWLETT Steve SB 5'11 180 Oshawa Hawkeyes Jrs.; Toronto B: 8/27/1962 Scarborough, ON																															
1985	EDM	10										6	1						14	153	10.9	33	1	5	29	5.8	11				
1986	EDM	16	1		0														5	91	18.2	27	0	8	92	11.5	36	1	0	0.0	0
1987	EDM	6				1						6	1						2	37	18.5	24	1	3	38	12.7	20	1	12	12.0	12
1987	OTT	5				0													3	43	14.3	23	0					2	23	11.5	13
1987	Year	11				1						6	1						5	80	16.0	24	1	3	38	12.7	20				
1989	OTT	11				0													3	80	26.7	56	0								
4	Years	43	1		0	1						12	2						27	404	15.0	56	2	16	159	9.9	36	4	35	8.8	13
JOHN HRUSKA John DE 6'1 207 Hamilton Panthers Ints. B: 1932																															
1955	HAM	3																													
1956	HAM	5																													
2	Years	8																													
JOHN HUARD John Roland LB 6'0 220 Maine B: 3/9/1944 Waterville, ME Draft: 5B-113 1967 DEN Pro: N																															
1972	MTL	4	1		0				1	7																					
1973	MTL	6							1	14																					
2	Years	10	1		0				2	21																					
CHARLEY HUBBARD Charles E 6'2 205 Charleston B: 1928 Draft: 27-326 1951 NYG																															
1952	MTL	2																													
DON HUBBARD Donald DT 6'0 250 New Mexico B: 11/29/1952 Pro: W																															
1976	WPG	10																													
1977	WPG	11	0		1																										
2	Years	21	0		1																										
FRED HUBBS Frederick L. OG 6'2 253 Miami (Florida) B: 12/29/1943																															
1968	BC	3																													
MAX HUBER Max Henry OT 6'3 252 Brigham Young B: 10/8/1945 Mesa, AZ Draft: 13-332 1968 BOS																															
1968	EDM	4	0		1																										
1968	BC	3																													
1968	Year	7	0		1																										
1969	BC	16	0		1																										
1970	BC	16																													
1971	BC	10																													
1971	HAM	5																													
1971	Year	15																													
1972	CAL	16																													
1973	CAL	16	0		1																										
1974	CAL	16																													
1975	CAL	16	0		2																										
1976	CAL	16																													
1977	MTL	10																													
10	Years	136	0		5																										
HENRY HUBERT Henry OG-OT 6'3 235 Southwestern Oklahoma State B: 1946																															
1968	EDM	8																													
1969	EDM	16																													
1970	EDM	16																													
1971	EDM	16	1		0																							1	2	2.0	2
4	Years	56	1		0																							1	2	2.0	2
HARLAN HUCKLEBY Harlan Charles RB 6'1 200 Michigan B: 12/30/1957 Detroit, MI Draft: 5-120 1979 NO Pro: N																															
1979	SAS	8	1		1							6	1	58	259	4.5	23	1	10	37	3.7	11	0					11	212	19.3	30
CORY HUCLACK Cory LB 6'0 216 Manitoba B: 2/29/1984 Winnipeg, MB																															
2007	MTL	14				7																									
2008	MTL	18				9																									
2009	MTL	16				12			1	38	8	6	1																		
2010	SAS	7	0	0	1	1																									
2011	SAS	18				12																		1	5	5.0	5				
5	Years	73	0	0	1	41			1	38	8	6	1											1	5	5.0	5				
DAN HUCLACK Dan FB-SB 6'2 205 Renfrew Trojans Jrs.; Simon Fraser B: 8/12/1957 Vancouver, BC Draft: 2-10 1979 TOR																															
1979	TOR	16	0		1							6	1						7	42	6.0	17	1								
1980	WPG	12										6	1	3	5	1.7	2	1	4	44	11.0	23	0					3	15	5.0	14
1981	WPG	15										12	2	20	64	3.2	7	2	26	209	8.0	18	0								
1982	WPG	16	1		1							18	3	5	10	2.0	5	2	26	229	8.8	21	1					2	23	11.5	12
1983	WPG	16	1		1							12	2	15	33	2.2	6	2	31	348	11.2	39	0								
1984	WPG	9										6	1	3	10	3.3	6	1	13	118	9.1	19	0								
1985	EDM	5	1		1									4	26	6.5	19	0	2	13	6.5	9	0								
1986	HAM	13										13	1	10	36	3.6	7	0	6	31	5.2	14	1								
1986	MTL	2												9	52	5.8	12	0	2	12	6.0	9	0								
1986	Year	15										13	1	19	88	4.6	12	0	8	43	5.4	14	1								
1987	HAM	17	3		0	0						18	3	73	310	4.2	23	2	35	258	7.4	16	1					1	12	12.0	12
9	Years	119	6		4	0						91	14	142	546	3.8	23	10	152	1304	8.6	39	4					6	50	8.3	14
BILLY HUDSON William Alex OT-DT 6'4 267 Clemson B: 7/9/1935 Lamar, SC Draft: 3-34 1957 CHIC Pro: N																															
1957	MTL	11																													
1958	MTL	12																													
1959	MTL	14										6	1																		
1960	MTL+	14																	1	13	13.0	13	0								
4	Years	51										6	1						1	13	13.0	13	0								
GEORGE HUDSON George C-OG-OT 6'4 310 New Mexico State B: 11/10/1976 St. Catherines, ON Draft: 3-17 2000 EDM																															
2000	EDM	5				1																									
2001	EDM	18				0																									
2002	OTT	15	0	0	1	0																									
2003	OTT	17	0	0	2	0																									
2004	OTT	17	0	0	1	0																									
2005	OTT	18	0	0	1	0								1	2	2.0	2	0													
2006	HAM	14	0	0	1	2																									
2007	HAM	9				0																									
2008	HAM	17				1																									
2009	HAM	17	0	0	1	1																									
2010	HAM	9				0																									
11	Years	156	0	0	7	5								1	2	2.0	2	0													
JESSE HUDSON Jesse E. LB 6'2 230 Oklahoma State B: 6/10/1952 Tawhuska, OK																															
1975	SAS	2																													
MIKE HUDSON Michael TE-SB 6'5 220 Guelph B: 6/25/1961 Almonte, ON Draft: TE 1983 OTT																															

Year	Team	GP	FM	FF	FR	TK	SK	YDS	IR	YDS	PD	PTS	TD	RA	YDS	AVG	LG	TD	REC	YDS	AVG	LG	TD	PR	YDS	AVG	LG	KOR	YDS	AVG	LG
1983	OTT	11																	1	21	21.0	21	0								
1984	OTT	12	0		1														10	95	9.5	17	0								
1985	OTT	15	1		1							6	1	1	1	1.0	1	0	26	278	10.7	30	1								
1986	OTT	16	0		1							2	0						20	222	11.1	44	0								
1987	OTT	8				2						6	1						14	199	14.2	24	1	1	2	2.0	2	1	2	2.0	2
1988	OTT	15																	31	432	13.9	50	0								
6	Years	77	1		3	2						14	2	1	1	1.0	1	0	102	1247	12.2	50	2	1	2	2.0	2	1	2	2.0	2
WARREN HUDSON Warren FB-LB 6'2 215 Oshawa Hawkeyes Jrs. B: 5/25/1962 Scarborough, ON D: 2/16/2012 Oakville, ON																															
1985	TOR	7																										2	20	10.0	20
1986	TOR	18	4		1									8	47	5.9	28	0	12	108	9.0	18	0					3	56	18.7	27
1987	TOR	15	2		0	3	1.0					6	1	18	74	4.1	11	1	7	66	9.4	21	0								
1988	TOR	18	3		1	4						18	3	37	164	4.4	21	1	31	283	9.1	41	2					1	17	17.0	17
1989	TOR	18	2		2	7								30	157	5.2	22	0	22	179	8.1	32	0					4	13	3.3	16
1990	WPG+	16	1		1	4						32	5	55	270	4.9	21	4	54	490	9.1	29	1					1	0	0.0	0
1991	WPG	18	2		1	8						12	2	35	178	5.1	18	0	47	537	11.4	66	2					1	19	19.0	19
1992	WPG+	16	0		1	1						48	8	60	397	6.6	38	6	14	109	7.8	17	2								
1993	TOR	18	4		4	2						24	4	53	220	4.2	28	3	17	179	10.5	24	1								
9	Years	144	18		11	29	1.0					140	23	296	1507	5.1	38	15	204	1951	9.6	66	8					12	125	10.4	27
BOBBY HUDSPETH Bob OT 6'3 275 Kansas; Southern Illinois B: 11/21/1945 Draft: 4B-102 1969 NO																															
1969	TOR	11			1																										
1970	TOR	14																													
1971	HAM	6																													
3	Years	34	0		1																										
CARLOS HUERTA Carlos Antonio K-P 5'7 185 Miami (Florida) B: 6/29/1969 Miami, FL Draft: 12-315 1992 SD Pro: EN																															
1994	LV	18	1		1	0						156	0						1	18	18.0	18	0								
1995	BAL	18	1		0	0						228	0																		
2	Years	36	2		1	0						384	0						1	18	18.0	18	0								
GENE HUEY Eugene Aaron DB 5'11 190 Wyoming B: 7/20/1947 Uniontown, PA Draft: 5B-123 1969 STL Pro: N																															
1969	MTL	2																													
BEN HUFF Benjamin John DT 6'4 297 Michigan B: 2/21/1975 D: 5/7/2006 Charlotte, NC Pro: X																															
2001	HAM	11				18	1.0	14.0			3																				
MARTY HUFF Ralph Martin LB 6'2 234 Michigan B: 12/19/1948 Houston, TX Draft: 5C-127 1971 SF Pro: NW																															
1973	EDM	6																													
1974	EDM	5																													
2	Years	11																													
DICK HUFFMAN Richard Maxwell OT-DT 6'1 255 Tennessee B: 3/27/1923 Charleston, WV D: 9/13/1992 Charleston, WV Draft: 9-81 1945 CLE Pro: N																															
1951	WPG	8										1	0											1	15	15.0	15				
1952	WPG+	14			1																							2	12	6.0	9
1953	WPG+	4																													
1954	WPG+	16	0		2							5	1						2	43	21.5	27	1								
1955	WPG+	16																													
1956	CAL+	16	0		3																										
1957	CAL+	16	0		1														1	18	18.0	18	0								
7	Years	90	0		7							6	1						3	61	20.3	27	1	1	15	15.0	15	2	12	6.0	9
JOHN HUFNAGEL John Coleman QB 6'1 194 Penn State B: 9/13/1951 Coraopolis, PA Draft: 14-348 1973 DEN Pro: N																															
1976	CAL	7	1		0							2	0	17	47	2.8	15	0													
1977	CAL	16	0		1							6	1	66	275	4.2	27	1													
1978	CAL	14	2		0							6	1	56	302	5.4	33	1													
1979	CAL	14	2		1							6	1	14	59	4.2	13	1													
1980	SAS	14	2		0							6	1	25	102	4.1	29	1													
1981	SAS	16	2		0									21	91	4.3	12	0													
1982	SAS	14	2		1							12	2	35	196	5.6	20	2													
1983	SAS	12												24	142	5.9	12	0													
1983	WPG	4	3		0									14	53	3.8	14	0													
1983	Year	16	3		0									38	195	5.1	14	0													
1984	WPG	16	2		0							12	2	14	76	5.4	18	2													
1985	WPG	16	3		0									11	36	3.3	7	0													
1986	WPG	18	5		0									22	88	4.0	16	0													
1987	SAS	1												3	28	9.3	15	0													
12	Years	158	24		3							50	8	322	1495	4.6	33	8													
FLOYD HUGGINS Floyd L. FB 6'0 210 Fort Scott CC; Florida B: 4/18/1928 Olathe, KS D: 3/26/2011 Olathe, KS																															
1954	WPG	14	4		0							20	4	84	331	3.9	13	4	5	48	9.6	18	0	1	8	8.0	8	1	8	8.0	8
LES HUGGINS Les WR 6'3 205 York B: 10/14/1954																															
1979	WPG	4																													
ALLEN HUGHES Allen Jeffries DT 6'3 250 Western Michigan B: 9/8/1959 Detroit, MI Draft: 12-320 1982 PIT Pro: U																															
1982	OTT	1																													
CHARLESTON HUGHES Charleston DE 6'1 244 Northwood B: 12/14/1983 Saginaw, MI																															
2008	CAL	16	0	1	2	65	5.0	43.0			5																				
2009	CAL	8	0	1	0	36	6.0	37.0			2																				
2010	CAL+	15	0	2	0	43	7.0	35.0			3																	1	13	13.0	13
2011	CAL	16	0	2	1	46	7.0	58.0	1	67	4	6	1																		
4	Years	55	0	6	3	190	25.0	173.0	1	67	14	6	1															1	13	13.0	13
DARREN HUGHES Darren L. DB 5'11 174 Carson-Newman B: 6/3/1967 Harbor City, TN Draft: 12-313 1991 MIN Pro: E																															
1993	TOR	11	0		1	48			3	19																					
DEREK HUGHES Derek P. RB 6'3 205 Michigan State B: 9/13/1959 Columbus, OH D: 7/18/2008 Columbus, OH Draft: TD 1983 MIC-USFL Pro: U																															
1987	HAM	1				0								4	13	3.3	7	0	3	32	10.7	16	0								
ED HUGHES Edward D. HB-E 6'1 184 Canisius; North Carolina State; Cameron JC; Tulsa B: 10/23/1927 Buffalo, NY D: 6/23/2000 Libertyville, IL Draft: 10A-117 1954 LARM Pro: N																															
1949	HAM	12										20	4					4													
GERRY HUGHES Gerald Arthur E 6'0 190 none B: 1935																															
1959	OTT	1																													
JIM HUGHES Jim C 6'4 225 Queen's B: 1936 Draft: 1A-1 1957 BC																															
1957	HAM	14										6	1																		
1958	HAM	12							1	0																					
2	Years	26							1	0		6	1																		
NEAL HUGHES Neal RB-FB 5'10 210 Regina Rams Jrs.; Regina B: 7/2/1980 Regina, SK																															
2004	SAS	14	0	1	0	10																		1	21	21.0	21	11	185	16.8	32
2005	SAS	5				3																									
2006	SAS	15	0	0	2	22																									
2007	SAS	18	0	0	1	22						6	1	4	18	4.5	6	1	2	20	10.0	12	0								
2008	SAS	12	1	0	0	8						42	7	35	130	3.7	13	4	16	187	11.7	34	3					1	12	12.0	12
2009	SAS	7				5													1	3	3.0	3	0					1	0	0.0	0
2010	SAS	18	0	0	1	15						6	1						1	8	8.0	8	1					4	35	8.8	16
2011	SAS	18				5						24	4	18	88	4.9	21	3	11	129	11.7	24	1					1	14	14.0	14
8	Years	107	1	1	4	90						78	13	57	236	4.1	21	8	31	347	11.2	34	5	1	21	21.0	21	18	246	13.7	32
RODNEY HUGHES Rodney WR 6'1 195 Delta State B: 2/24/1967 Memphis, TN																															
1990	WPG	1				0													4	48	12.0	33	0								
GEORGE HUGHLEY George Charles OHB 6'1 223 Santa Moncia CC; Central Oklahoma B: 6/26/1937 Los Angeles, CA D: 2/27/1999 Glendale, CA Pro: N																															
1963	TOR	3												18	108	6.0	14	0	7	106	15.1	27	0					4	173	43.3	94
1964	TOR	11										12	2	73	333	4.6	31	2	17	202	11.9	34	0					19	602	31.7	60
2	Years	14										12	2	91	441	4.8	31	2	24	308	12.8	34	0					23	775	33.7	94
TOM HUGO Thoma Kaluna, Jr. C-LB 5'10 211 Denver B: 8/25/1930 Nu'uanu, HI D: 11/15/2004 Honolulu, HI																															

Year	Team	GP	FM	FF	FR	TK	SK	YDS	IR	YDS	PD	PTS	TD	RA	YDS	AVG	LG	TD	REC	YDS	AVG	LG	TD	PR	YDS	AVG	LG	KOR	YDS	AVG	LG
1953	MTL+	13									5	1																	
1954	MTL+	13						6	81																				
1955	MTL+	12						2	25		5	1															3	56	18.7	22
1956	MTL+	14						3	71																		7	116	16.6	26
1957	MTL+	13						1	4																		2	37	18.5	21
1958	MTL+	14						9	106		6	1											1	0	0.0	0				
1959	MTL+	14						4	72																		2	38	19.0	24
7	Years	93						25	359		16	3											1	0	0.0	0	14	247	17.6	26
BART HULL Bart RB 5'11 210 Boise State B: 2/13/1969 Vancouver, BC Draft: 1A-4 1991 BC																														
1991	OTT	3	1		0	2																	2	10	5.0	6	1	11	11.0	11
1994	SAS	1			1																								
2	Years	4	1		0	3																	2	10	5.0	6	1	11	11.0	11
LEE HULL Leotha WR 6'0 185 Holy Cross B: 12/31/1965 Vineland, NJ																														
1990	WPG	12	4		0	2												33	464	14.1	40	0	33	275	8.3	64	14	237	16.9	28
1991	WPG	5				1												13	270	20.8	48	0	5	24	4.8	12	5	77	15.4	28
1992	WPG	1				0												2	22	11.0	11	0								
1992	TOR	1				0																								
1992	Year	2				0												2	22	11.0	11	0								
3	Years	18	4		0	3												48	756	15.8	48	0	38	299	7.9	64	19	314	16.5	28
TOM HULL Thomas Michael LB 6'3 230 Penn State B: 6/30/1952 Cumberland, MD Draft: 12-294 1974 SF; 14-161 1974 PHI-WFL Pro: N																														
1976	EDM	1																												
ED HULSE Walter Edward C 6'3 235 Lakeshore Bears Jrs.; East York Argos Ints. B: 8/29/1939																														
1966	TOR	9																												
1969	TOR	4																												
2	Years	13																												
ROD HUMENIUK Rod OG 6'1 234 Los Angeles Pierce JC; Southern California B: 6/17/1938 Detroit, MI																														
1960	WPG	6																												
1961	WPG	16																												
1962	WPG	16																												
3	Years	38																												
BEN HUMMEL Ben LB 6'4 234 UCLA B: 8/22/1966 Dayton, OH Draft: 12-317 1988 DAL																														
1988	OTT	8				14	8.0																							
GEORGE HUMMER George R. C 6'2 220 Arizona State B: 7/5/1946 Draft: 17-435 1969 STL																														
1969	EDM	4																												
BOBBY HUMPHERY Robert Charles CB-DH 5'10 180 New Mexico State B: 8/23/1961 Lubbock, TX Draft: 9-247 1983 NYJ Pro: EN																														
1993	SAC	18	0		2	39			5	54																				
1994	SAC	17				41					5																			
1995	SA	18	0		2	38			2	47	3																			
3	Years	53	0		4	118			7	101	8																			
JOHN HUMPHREY John A. RB 5'9 195 Texas A&M-Kingsville B: 12/30/1975																														
2003	TOR	6				2						12	2	25	48	1.9	12	0	10	164	16.4	102	2					5	107	21.4	27
TOMMY HUMPHREY Tommy Gale OT 6'6 260 Abilene Christian B: 3/24/1950 Comanche, TX Draft: 10-256 1973 CLE Pro: N																														
1978	CAL	16																												
1979	CAL	13	0		2																									
1980	BC	5																												
3	Years	34	0		2																									
LEONARD HUMPHRIES Leonard Deshawn CB 5'9 180 Penn State B: 6/19/1970 Akron, OH Draft: 8-223 1992 BUF Pro: N																														
1996	OTT	18				70			3	73	5	6	1																	
1997	BC	17	0	1	0	45			3	105	9	6	1																	
1999	TOR	1				3					1																			
3	Years	36	0	1	0	118			6	178	15	12	2																	
CHUCK HUNDEY Chuck E																														
1947	TOR	2																												
1948	TOR	3																												
2	Years	5																												
JAMES HUNDON James Henry WR 6'1 173 San Francisco CC; Portland State B: 4/9/1971 San Francisco, CA Pro: NX																														
2003	TOR	4				0						6	1						8	124	15.5	36	1	1	5	5.0	5	2	60	30.0	39
2003	CAL	9	0	0	1	2						6	1						17	271	15.9	55	0	22	136	6.2	36	19	411	21.6	103
2003	Year	13	0	0	1	2						12	2						25	395	15.8	55	1	23	141	6.1	36				
JOE HUNGLE Joseph G Regina Jrs.																														
1946	SAS	4																												
TONY HUNGLE Anthony E-G 5'11 201 Regina Bombers Jrs. B: 1926 D: 5/28/1997																														
1947	SAS	2																												
1948	SAS	11																												
1949	SAS	14																												
1950	SAS	14									5	1																	
1951	SAS	8																												
1952	SAS	10			1							5	1																	
1953	SAS	2																												
7	Years	61	0		1							10	2																	
CHUCK HUNSINGER Charles Ray HB 6'0 188 Florida B: 7/25/1925 Harrisburg, IL D: 3/23/1998 Harrisburg, IL Draft: 1A-3 1950 CHIB Pro: N																														
1953	MTL	14									55	11					6					4									
1954	MTL	10						5	72		40	8	86	516	6.0	55	6	22	421	19.1	77	2	2	6	3.0	6	10	178	17.8	22
1955	MTL	3									10	2	14	75	5.4	18	1	14	238	17.0	50	1	1	6	6.0	6				
3	Years	27						5	72		105	21	100	591	5.9	55	13	36	659	18.3	77	7	3	12	4.0	6	10	178	17.8	22
GARRETT HUNSPERGER Harold Garrett DT-DE 6'3 255 Central Missouri B: 10/8/1946 D: 2/26/2005 Kansas City, MO																														
1969	BC	16	0		4																									
1970	BC	9	0		1																									
1971	BC	14			3																									
1972	BC	11																												
1973	BC	12																												
1974	BC+	16																												
1975	TOR	13	0		1																									
7	Years	91	0		9																									
AARON HUNT Aaron Coffey DT-DE 6'3 270 Texas Tech B: 6/19/1980 Dallas, TX Draft: 6-194 2003 DEN Pro: E																														
2006	BC+	17	0	1	0	14	9.0	68.0			2																			
2007	BC+	18	0	1	1	38	8.0	63.0			10													1	0	0.0	0				
2008	BC*	18	0	2	2	39	11.0	83.0			5																			
2009	BC+	17	0	1	2	35	4.0	30.0			3																			
2010	BC	7				18	2.0	11.0	1	22	1																			
2011	BC*	17				29	7.0	41.0			4																			
6	Years	94	0	5	5	173	41.0	296.0	1	22	25													1	0	0.0	0				
PHILLIP HUNT Phillip Wayne, Jr. DE 6'2 260 Houston B: 1/10/1986 Fort Worth, TX Pro: N																														
2009	WPG	7	0	1	0	11	3.0				1																			
2010	WPG*	18	0	1	1	53	16.0	83.0			3																			
2	Years	25	0	2	1	64	19.0	83.0			4																			
REGGIE HUNT Reginald Lyn DB-LB 6'0 210 Texas Christian B: 10/14/1977 Denison, TX Pro: E																														
2002	SAS	18	0	0	3	103	3.0	34.0	1	2	4																			
2003	SAS*	18	0	5	0	99	7.0	52.0	3	63	0																			
2004	SAS+	18	0	0	1	79	6.0	50.0			3																			
2005	SAS	18	0	0	3	67	4.0	36.0			5																			
2006	SAS+	17	0	1	1	87	1.0	8.0			2																			

Year	Team	GP	FM	FF	FR	TK	SK	YDS	IR	YDS	PD	PTS	TD	RA	YDS	AVG	LG	TD	REC	YDS	AVG	LG	TD	PR	YDS	AVG	LG	KOR	YDS	AVG	LG
2007	SAS+	17	0	1	0	62	6.0	35.0	1	0	1																				
2008	MTL	14	0	1	1	61	1.0	9.0	3	35	2																				
2009	EDM	4				5																									
8	Years	124	0	8	9	563	28.0	224.0	8	100	17																				
TED HUNT Ted HB-FB-K 5'10 175 British Columbia B: 1933																															
1957	BC	16	4		0							38	2	4	9	2.3	5	0	3	93	31.0	38	2	69	407	5.9	14	5	114	22.8	32
1958	BC	16	2		2				0	14		27	0						2	41	20.5	23	0	71	478	6.7	20				
2	Years	32	6		2				0	14		65	2	4	9	2.3	5	0	5	134	26.8	38	2	140	885	6.3	20	5	114	22.8	32
ANTOINE HUNTER Antoine DH 6'0 180 Alabama B: 8/29/1977 Valdosta, GA																															
2000	SAS	17	0	2	1	33					10																				
DANIEL HUNTER Daniel Lewis CB 5'11 178 Henderson State B: 9/1/1962 Arkadelphia, PA Pro: N																															
1989	OTT	11	0		3	44			2	71																					
1990	OTT	9	0		1	31			6	13														1	3	3.0	3				
1991	OTT	18	1		0	71	3.0		3	47									1	28	28.0	28	0								
1992	OTT	17	1		1	51			3	8																		3	17	5.7	9
1993	OTT	1				4			1	0																					
1993	BC	4				14																									
1993	Year	5				18			1	0																					
1994	SHR	16	0		1	43			3	13																					
6	Years	72	2		6	258	3.0		18	152									1	28	28.0	28	0	1	3	3.0	3	3	17	5.7	9
DICK HUNTER Dick HB 5'7 167 North Carolina State B: 1936																															
1958	MTL	13							4	84		36	6	15	33	2.2	8	0	22	532	24.2	79	6	34	207	6.1	20	6	125	20.8	27
1959	OTT	1																													
2	Years	14							4	84		36	6	15	33	2.2	8	0	22	532	24.2	79	6	34	207	6.1	20	6	125	20.8	27
FUNTAINE HUNTER Funtaine LB 6'3 238 Vanderbilt B: 12/27/1983 Valdosta, GA																															
2008	CAL	2				9																									
JAMES HUNTER James Dale DT 6'5 251 Southern California B: 9/13/1957 Haskell, OK Draft: 9-239 1981 PIT Pro: N																															
1983	EDM	4					3.0																								
1984	EDM	12	0		2		5.0																								
2	Years	16	0		2		8.0																								
JEFF HUNTER Jeffrey Orlando DE 6'5 285 Albany State B: 4/12/1986 Hampton, VA Draft: 11-291 1989 PHX Pro: EN																															
1995	WPG	2				3																									
JIMMY HUNTER James L. LB 6'2 225 Indiana B: 4/10/1960 Birmingham, AL																															
1985	SAS	4					1.0																								
1986	SAS	3					1.0																								
2	Years	7					2.0																								
MALVIN HUNTER Malvin LB-DE 6'3 230 Wisconsin B: 11/20/1969 Harvey, IL Pro: E																															
1993	EDM	18	0		1	60	6.0	34.0	1	9																					
1994	EDM	18				79	7.0	60.0																							
1995	EDM	18	0		5	45	9.0	54.0			2	6	1	3	2	0.7	2	1													
1996	EDM*	18	0		2	30	14.0	124.0	1	3	3																				
1997	EDM+	18	0	2	2	41	9.0	49.0	1	0	0																	1	3	3.0	3
1998	EDM+	18	0	3	0	50	13.0	71.0	1	55	3																	1	11	11.0	11
1999	EDM	18	0	0	2	50	4.0	28.0			1																				
2000	EDM	7				15	4.0	26.0	1	10	1																				
8	Years	133	0	5	12	370	66.0	446.0	5	77	10	6	1	3	2	0.7	2	1										2	14	7.0	11
PETE HUNTER Ralph Everette DB 6'2 209 Virginia Union B: 5/25/1980 Atlantic City, NJ Draft: 5-168 2002 DAL Pro: N																															
2008	TOR	7	0	0	1	23			1	0	3																				
RALPH HUNTER Ralph HB-FW 188 Ricks JC B: 1932																															
1954	EDM	1																													
TONY HUNTER Anthony WR 5'8 160 Boise State B: 7/15/1963 Reno, NV																															
1989	EDM*	17	4		0	0						18	3						16	335	20.9	57	3	118	1181	10.0	63	20	441	22.1	49
1990	CAL	2				0													2	17	8.5	15	0	12	110	9.2	20	7	157	22.4	35
1990	BC	7	1		0	1						18	3						14	149	10.6	21	2	35	409	11.7	108	9	149	16.6	32
1990	Year	9	1		0	1						18	3						16	166	10.4	21	2	47	519	11.0	108	16	306	19.1	35
1991	BC	4	1		1	2						12	2						12	186	15.5	69	2	11	48	4.4	9	5	120	24.0	33
3	Years	23	6		1	3						48	8						44	687	15.6	69	7	176	1748	9.9	108	41	867	21.1	49
TOREY HUNTER Torey Hayward CB 5'9 176 Washington State B: 2/10/1972 Tacoma, WA Draft: 3C-95 1995 HOU Pro: EN																															
1997	MTL	17				65			3	14	7																				
1998	MTL	16	0	1	0	37			1	15	9																				
1999	EDM	15	0	1	2	37	1.0	12.0	4	46	3																				
2000	EDM	9	0	0	1	32			4	16	5																				
2001	EDM	5				16																									
2001	MTL	7				19					1																				
2001	Year	12				35					1																				
5	Years	62	0	3	3	206	1.0	12.0	12	91	25																				
KEVIN HUNTLEY Kevin DT 6'7 270 Valley Forge Military JC; Kansas State B: 4/9/1982 Washington, DC Pro: N																															
2009	TOR	17	0	0	2	36	9.0	45.0			2																				
2010	TOR*	14				41	9.0	63.0			2																				
2011	TOR+	15	0	1	0	25	6.0	34.0			3																				
3	Years	46	0	1	2	102	24.0	142.0			7																				
ROY HURD Roy WR 6'2 195 Phoenix JC; Arizona State B: 3/8/1966 Phoenix, AZ																															
1988	WPG	6	2		0	0								3	1	0.3	2	0	9	148	16.4	52	0	2	19	9.5	24	9	223	24.8	73
DAN HURLEY Dan Thomas OT 6'3 270 Nebraska B: 4/16/1959 Omaha, NE Pro: U																															
1987	BC	16	0		1	0																									
WILLIE HURST Willie Burnell RB 5'9 198 Washington B: 3/14/1980 Long Beach, CA																															
2002	BC	6	3	0	1	0						12	2	55	288	5.2	31	1	7	85	12.1	45	0	7	56	8.0	16	6	196	32.7	99
2003	BC	3	1	0	1	0								9	43	4.8	13	0	9	57	6.3	12	0	1	6	6.0	6	7	110	15.7	24
2	Years	9	4	0	2	0						12	2	64	331	5.2	31	1	16	142	8.9	45	0	8	62	7.8	16	13	306	23.5	99
ED HUSMANN Edward Earl DT 6'0 235 Nebraska B: 8/6/1931 Schuyler, NE Draft: 9A-100 1953 CHIC Pro: N																															
1966	EDM	13																													
BRIAN HUTCHINGS Brian OT 6'5 265 St. Mary's (Nova Scotia) B: 12/22/1965 Hamilton, ON																															
1989	HAM	9	0		1	0																									
1989	OTT	4				0																									
1989	Year	13	0		1	0																									
1990	CAL	9				1																									
1992	TOR	4				0																									
1993	TOR	2				0																									
4	Years	24	0		1	1																									
NICK HUTCHINS Nick C-OG 6'2 325 Regina B: 8/7/1987 Regina, SK Draft: 3-17 2009 SAS																															
2009	SAS	6				1																									
2010	SAS	9				0																									
2	Years	15				1																									
JACK HUTCHINSON Jack FB-HB 5'11 189 Saskatoon Hilltops Jrs.; British Columbia B: 1929 Toronto, ON																															
1952	SAS	15												24	74	3.1	18	0													
1954	BC	16	1		0							5	1	40	159	4.0	16	0	5	77	15.4	23	1	1	0	0.0	0	6	47	7.8	14
1955	BC	1																													
1956	WPG	16												9	63	7.0	12	0										1	16	16.0	16
1957	WPG	14	4									12	2	50	300	6.0	22	2	5	55	11.0	20	0					1	15	15.0	15
5	Years	62	5		0							17	3	123	596	4.8	22	2	10	132	13.2	23	1	1	0	0.0	0	8	78	9.8	16
HENRY HUTH Henry LB-DB 6'0 190 Vancouver Blue Bombers Jrs. B: 1939																															
1962	CAL	14	1																					27	143	5.3	16				

Year	Team	GP	FM	FF	FR	TK	SK	YDS	IR	YDS	PD	PTS	TD	RA	YDS	AVG	LG	TD	REC	YDS	AVG	LG	TD	PR	YDS	AVG	LG	KOR	YDS	AVG	LG
1963	CAL	16	2		0														1	4	4.0	4	0	19	46	2.4	5				
1964	CAL	14																						1	0	0.0	0				
1965	EDM	2																													
4	Years	46	3		0														1	4	4.0	4	0	47	189	4.0	16				
BILL HUTTON Bill C 6'3 207 Winnipeg Jrs. B: 1933
1955	WPG	3
ED HUYCKE Ed HB-FW 5'11 202 Toronto B: 1926
1949	TOR	5
1951	TOR	3
2	Years	8
DAVID HYLAND David S-CB-DH 6'0 198 Morehead State B: 5/30/1987 Woodstock, GA
2010	BC	6				19			1	22	2
2011	BC	3				4					2
2011	HAM	2				2
2011	Year	5				6					2
2	Years	9				25			1	22	4
MICHAEL HYMAN Michael WR 5'10 182 Tallahassee CC*; Long Beach CC B: 12/3/1984 Miami, FL
2009	WPG	1				0
CHARLES HYTHON Charles M. LB 6'2 255 Glenville State B: 1/25/1971 Steubenville, OH
2001	TOR	2				2
BERT IANNONE Albert N. G 5'10 195 Winnipeg Jrs. B: 1917 Winnipeg, MB
1946	WPG	5
1947	WPG+	7
1948	CAL+	10
1949	CAL	14										5	1
1950	SAS	14
1951	SAS+	14
1952	SAS	15
7	Years	79										5	1
MARCO IANNUZZI Marco WR 6'1 195 Harvard B: 5/21/1987 Calgary, AB Draft: 1-6 2011 BC
2011	BC	15	0	1	0	1			1	3	0								8	65	8.1	13	0	16	135	8.4	15	2	25	12.5	14
CURT IAUKEA Curtis Piehu, III T 6'3 265 Santa Rosa JC; California B: 1938
1958	BC	10
1959	BC	10
1959	MTL	3
1959	Year	13
2	Years	20
BENEDICT IBISI Benedict OG 6'0 288 Tennessee State B: 2/21/1979 Jos, Nigeria
2002	WPG	14				2
2003	WPG	1				0
2	Years	15				2
GERRY IFILL Gerry RB 5'7 185 McGill B: 3/26/1967 Ottawa, ON Draft: 6-44 1990 TOR
1990	TOR	9	0		1	1								4	31	7.8	22	0	3	24	8.0	9	0
DONALD IGWEBUIKE Donald Amechi K 5'9 187 Clemson B: 12/27/1960 Enugu, Nigeria Draft: 10-260 1985 TB Pro: N
1994	BAL	16	1		0	1						184	0
1995	MEM	4				0						17	0
2	Years	20	1		0	1						201	0
CHIMA IHEKWOABA Chima DE 6'4 255 Wilfrid Laurier B: 3/11/1988 Draft: 2A-14 2010 MTL
2010	MTL	6				0																						1	7	7.0	7
2011	MTL	17				3
2	Years	23				3																						1	7	7.0	7
VICTOR IKE Victor Chika S 5'11 200 Texas; Southern University B: 1/10/1980 Houston, TX
2004	CAL	12	1	0	1	1						12	2	73	245	3.4	30	2	38	239	6.3	21	0					1	15	15.0	15
HANK ILESIC Henry P-K 6'1 210 none B: 9/7/1959 Edmonton, AB Pro: N
1977	EDM	10	1		0							3	0
1978	EDM*	16										9	0
1979	EDM*	16										9	0											1	4	4.0	4
1980	EDM*	16										7	0	2	28	14.0	19	0						2	31	15.5	19
1981	EDM*	16	1		0							7	0											1	20	20.0	20	1	0	0.0	0
1982	EDM	14										7	0
1983	TOR	16	2		0							148	0	2	33	16.5	21	0
1984	TOR	16	1		0							159	0	2	19	9.5	14	0
1985	TOR	16										46	0
1986	TOR*	18										24	0
1987	TOR*	18	2		1	0						11	0	2	-5	-2.5	-8	0
1988	TOR	18	2		0	0						10	0
1989	TOR	10	1		0	0						6	0
1990	TOR	3				0
1991	TOR*	17				6						5	0
1992	TOR*	17	1		0	2						5	0
1993	TOR	11				1						2	0
1995	HAM	8	1		0	3						2	0
1998	BC	3				3
2001	EDM	2				0
20	Years	261	12		1	15						460	0	8	75	9.4	21	0						4	55	13.8	20	1	0	0.0	0
BRYAN ILLERBRUN Bryan OT-OG-DT 6'4 270 Regina Rams Jrs. B: 4/20/1957 Gainsborough, SK
1978	SAS	13																										1	6	6.0	6
1979	SAS	16
1980	SAS	15
1981	SAS	15
1982	SAS	16	0		2
1983	SAS	16
1984	BC	16
1985	BC	16	0		1									1	1	1.0	1	0
1986	BC	10	0		2
1986	SAS	5
1986	Year	15	0		2
1987	SAS	12	0		1	0
1988	SAS	18				1
1989	SAS	12	0		1	2
1990	OTT	18				1
1991	OTT	18	0		1	1
14	Years	211	0		8	5								1	1	1.0	1	0										1	6	6.0	6
MARTY IMHOF Martin Carl DE 6'6 256 Pasadena CC; San Diego State B: 10/9/1949 Seattle, WA Draft: 4B-84 1972 STL Pro: N
1980	BC	6
MIKE IMOH Michael U. RB 5'8 190 Virginia Tech B: 7/21/1984 Fairfax, VA
2007	MTL	5	2	0	0	0						6	1	26	96	3.7	18	0	6	55	9.2	24	1	3	9	3.0	9
2008	MTL	6				2						24	4	62	398	6.4	28	3	12	147	12.3	54	1
2	Years	11	2	0	0	2						30	5	88	494	5.6	28	3	18	202	11.2	54	2	3	9	3.0	9
B.C. INABINET Benjamin Claude, Jr. OT 6'6 265 Clemson B: 6/27/1934 SC D: 8/7/1983 Durham, NC Draft: 4-43 1956 BAL
1956	HAM	1
ERIC INCE Eric OL 6'4 296 Tri-City Bulldogs Jrs.; St. Mary's (Nova Scotia) B: 4/4/1981 Vancouver, BC Draft: 2B-13 2007 HAM

Year	Team	GP	FM	FF	FR	TK	SK	YDS	IR	YDS	PD	PTS	TD	RA	YDS	AVG	LG	TD	REC	YDS	AVG	LG	TD	PR	YDS	AVG	LG	KOR	YDS	AVG	LG
2007	HAM	4				0																									
LINDY INFANTE Gelindo, Jr. OHB Florida B: 5/27/1940 Miami, FL Draft: 11-81 1963 DAL; 12-163 1963 CLE																															
1963	HAM	1												3	12	4.0	6	0													
GERRY INGLIS Gerald C 6'0 232 Alberta B: 8/20/1954 Draft: 4-29 1976 BC																															
1977	BC	16																													
1978	BC	6																													
1978	WPG	10																													
1978	Year	16																													
1979	WPG	4																													
3	Years	26																													
JEFF INGLIS Jeffrey OT 6'5 252 Guelph B: 12/8/1956 Guelph, ON Draft: 3-25 1979 CAL																															
1981	CAL	16																	1	5	5.0	5	0								
1982	CAL	16																													
1983	CAL	16																													
1984	CAL	16												1	-2	-2.0	-2	0													
1985	TOR	15																													
1986	TOR	11																													
1986	SAS	3																													
1986	Year	14																													
6	Years	90												1	-2	-2.0	-2	0	1	5	5.0	5	0								
MALCOLM INGLIS Malcolm OT-DT-C-OG-DE 6'6 260 Carleton B: 11/10/1955 Draft: TE 1979 OTT																															
1979	OTT	16																													
1980	OTT	16	0		1																										
1981	OTT	16																													
3	Years	48	0		1																										
TAYLOR INGLIS Taylor C 6'3 247 Alberta; Edmonton Wildcats Jrs. B: 11/4/1983 Edmonton, AB																															
2005	EDM	18				4																									
2006	EDM	16	2	0	0	2																									
2007	EDM	17				5																									
2008	EDM	18				4																									
2009	EDM	18	1	0	0	3																									
2010	WPG	17				8																									
2011	EDM	18	1	0	0	5																									
7	Years	122	4	0	0	31																									
KEVIN INGRAM Kevin QB 6'0 178 East Carolina B: 4/26/1962 Philadelphia, PA Draft: 5-99 1984 NO-USFL Pro: N																															
1984	EDM	4	3		0							18	3	14	96	6.9	27	3													
LEPOLEON INGRAM Lepoleon, Jr. DB 5'9 174 Sacramento State B: 6/17/1956 Nashville, TN																															
1980	CAL	4	0		2				3	7														18	141	7.8	28	2	38	19.0	21
1981	CAL	15	2		0				5	96		6	1											57	488	8.6	95	13	230	17.7	29
1982	CAL	7																						5	22	4.4	9	6	125	20.8	32
1983	CAL	3																													
1984	SAS	1																													
5	Years	30	2		2				8	103		6	1											80	651	8.1	95	21	393	18.7	32
RON INGRAM Ronald Denard WR 5'10 168 Oklahoma State B: 10/27/1959 Dallas, TX Draft: 11-301 1982 PHI Pro: U																															
1985	HAM	4										18	3						14	265	18.9	52	3								
1986	HAM	5																	8	48	6.0	9	0								
1987	HAM	1	1		0	0													2	23	11.5	16	0								
1988	HAM	1										0	0						3	35	11.7	12	0								
1988	EDM	2										6	1						4	99	24.8	61	1	5	4	0.8	5	3	22	7.3	15
1988	Year	3										6	1						7	134	19.1	61	1	5	4	0.8	5	3	22	7.3	15
4	Years	11	1		0	0						24	4						31	470	15.2	61	4	5	4	0.8	5	3	22	7.3	15
GARY INSKEEP Gary Wayne DE-OT 6'4 265 Wisconsin-Stout B: 3/31/1947 Lonaconing, MD Draft: 13-325 1970 NYG																															
1970	TOR	6																													
1971	HAM	14	0		1																										
1972	HAM	14																													
1973	HAM	10																													
4	Years	44	0		1																										
SHANE IRELAND Shane LB 6'3 227 Ottawa Sooners Jrs. B: 12/18/1962 Ottawa, ON																															
1984	OTT	6																													
1985	OTT	5																													
1986	OTT	3																													
1986	MTL	2																													
1986	Year	5																													
1987	OTT	3				6																						1	11	11.0	11
4	Years	17				6																						1	11	11.0	11
TERRY IRELAND Terry DT-DE 6'2 240 Kent State B: 1946																															
1969	MTL	14	0		1																										
MARK IRVIN Mark K-P 5'9 215 Mount Allison B: 4/14/1978 Ottawa, ON																															
2005	OTT	5				0						25	0																		
TERRY IRVIN Terry CB 5'11 190 Jackson State B: 9/14/1954 Columbus, MS Draft: 12-322 1977 CHIB																															
1977	CAL	9	0		1				1	13																		10	201	20.1	36
1978	CAL+	15							7	159		6	1															2	48	24.0	26
1979	CAL+	16	0		2				7	147		6	1																		
1980	CAL	10	1		0				6	67														1	7	7.0	7				
1981	CAL	14	2		1				6	29																					
1982	CAL	16	0		1				3	56		6	1											1	4	4.0	4				
1983	CAL	9							4	2																					
1984	SAS+	15	0		2				11	79		6	1																		
1985	SAS	13	0		1				5	41		6	1																		
1986	MTL+	18	0		2				12	105														2	30	15.0	27				
1987	CAL	1																													
11	Years	136	3		10				62	698		30	5											4	41	10.3	27	12	249	20.8	36
DON IRVINE Don E 6'4																															
1946	HAM	2																													
JOHN IRVINE John C-LB 6'2 220 Maryland B: 3/9/1933 Evans City, PA Draft: 8-86 1955 CHIC																															
1956	HAM	14							2	14																					
BUD IRVING Harold K. G 5'11 178 none B: 5/2/1926																															
1946	WPG	8																													
1947	WPG	8																													
1948	WPG+	9										5	1																		
1949	WPG	14																													
1950	WPG	14																													
5	Years	53										5	1																		
HARRY IRVING Harry QB-HB 5'11 170 Calgary West End Tornadoes Jrs.; McGill B: 1927 D: 5//2006																															
1948	CAL	7																													
1949	EDM	3																													
2	Years	10																													
REGGIE IRVING Reginald Earl OT 6'2 260 Grambling State B: 12/22/1955 New Orleans, LA Pro: U																															
1988	CAL	2																													
AL IRWIN Alan TE 6'4 220 McMaster B: 3/16/1943 Toronto, ON Draft: 1-5 1964 MTL																															
1964	MTL	13	0		1							12	2						11	156	14.2	25	2								
1965	MTL	14																	2	25	12.5	14	0								

Year	Team	GP	FM	FF	FR	TK	SK	YDS	IR	YDS	PD	PTS	TD	RA	YDS	AVG	LG	TD	REC	YDS	AVG	LG	TD	PR	YDS	AVG	LG	KOR	YDS	AVG	LG
1966	TOR	14										24	4						12	399	33.3	75	4								
1967	TOR	14	1		0							6	1						12	222	18.5	61	1					1	-1	-1.0	-1
1968	TOR	14										18	3						30	541	18.0	73	3								
1969	EDM	16	1		0														26	445	17.1	47	0								
1970	HAM	10										6	1						5	87	17.4	21	1								
7	Years	95	2		1							66	11						98	1875	19.1	75	11					1	-1	-1.0	-1
DAVE IRWIN Dave SB 6'2 170 Guelph B: 9/12/1971 Belleville, ON Draft: 4-30 1994 TOR																															
1994	TOR	10				6													4	47	11.8	17	0								
BRANDON ISAAC Brandon J. DH 6'2 190 Georgia Military JC; South Carolina B: 12/11/1984 Blackville, SC																															
2010	CAL	16	0	2	2	31	3.0	18.0	1	2	1																				
2011	CAL	12				22					6																				
2	Years	28	0	2	2	53	3.0	18.0	1	2	7																				
CHRIS ISAAC Chris QB 5'11 160 Eastern Kentukcy B: 5/15/1959																															
1982	OTT	16	2		1							6	1	42	244	5.8	20	1													
1983	OTT	11	1		0									12	90	7.5	23	0													
2	Years	27	3		1							6	1	54	334	6.2	23	1													
LARRY ISBELL Larry Dale DB-QB-OE-OHB-P 6'1 190 Baylor B: 1/8/1930 Houston, TX D: 10/31/1978 Waco, TX Draft: 1-7 1952 WAS																															
1954	SAS	14	3		4				1	5		17	1	25	143	5.7	18	0	6	79	13.2	24	1	21	155	7.4	17				
1955	SAS	15							2	39		16	3						31	461	14.9	43	3								
1956	SAS+	15	2		4				4	37		55	6	17	98	5.8	23	1	28	533	19.0	41	5	4	30	7.5	14	1	0	0.0	0
1957	SAS+	16	0		3				3			19	2						27	361	13.4	46	2	1	0	0.0	0				
1958	SAS+	14							2	68		17	1						5	94	18.8	34	1								
5	Years	74	5		11				12	149		124	13	42	241	5.7	23	1	97	1528	15.8	46	12	26	185	7.1	17	1	0	0.0	0
ALLEN ISCHE Allen OG 6'2 235 Northern Michigan B: 1942 Stratford, ON																															
1967	EDM	14																													
1968	EDM	16																													
1969	EDM	16																													
1970	EDM	16																													
1971	EDM	16			1																										
5	Years	78	0		1																										
BEN ISHOLA Ben DE 6'3 248 Indiana B: 6/8/1980 Berlin, Germany Pro: E																															
2009	TOR	1				1																									
2010	TOR	3				4																									
2011	TOR	2				3																									
3	Years	6				8																									
ROCKET ISMAIL Raghib Ramadian WR 5'11 183 Notre Dame B: 11/18/1969 Elizabeth, NJ Draft: 4-100 1991 LARI Pro: N																															
1991	TOR*	17	8		2	9						80	13	36	271	7.5	42	3	64	1300	20.3	87	9	48	602	12.5	73	31	786	25.4	38
1992	TOR+	16	7		2	1						48	8	34	154	4.5	59	3	36	651	18.1	56	4	59	614	10.4	74	43	1139	26.5	55
2	Years	33	15		4	10						128	21	70	425	6.1	59	6	100	1951	19.5	87	13	107	1216	11.4	74	74	1925	26.0	55
JABARI ISSA Jabari DT 6'5 301 Washington B: 4/18/1978 San Francisco, CA Draft: 6-176 2000 ARI Pro: EN																															
2004	EDM	5	0	1	0	7																									
2005	EDM	9				8	1.0	1.0			2																				
2006	EDM	5				7					1																				
2007	WPG	4				4																									
4	Years	23	0	1	0	26	1.0	1.0			3																				
JEREMY ITO Jeremy Ray K-P 5'11 190 Rutgers B: 3/4/1986 Redlands, CA																															
2009	HAM	1				0						13	0																		
CLIFFORD IVORY Clifford Levyke CB 5'11 183 Troy B: 10/8/1975 Thomasville, GA Draft: 6-155 1998 SD Pro: E																															
2000	HAM	18	0	0	3	30	1.0	11.0				6	1																		
2001	HAM	18				34	1.0	4.0			4																				
2002	TOR*	18	0	1	2	52	2.0	14.0	8	124	6																				
2003	TOR*	17	1	1	2	46	1.0	13.0	3	148	6	24	4																		
2004	TOR*	17	1	2	1	51			4	71	5	12	2																	1	0	0.0	0
2005	TOR	18	1	1	1	34			3	53	6	6	1																		
2006	TOR	14	0	1	1	33			2	96	4																				
7	Years	120	3	6	10	280	5.0	42.0	20	492	31	48	8																	1	0	0.0	0
J.P. IZQUIERDO Jean-Paul RB-SB 5'11 195 Calgary B: 3/12/1969 Calgary, AB Draft: 2A-10 1991 TOR																															
1991	TOR	18	1		1	25						12	2	13	73	5.6	25	0	18	187	10.4	23	2					7	42	6.0	26
1992	TOR	18				25						6	1	4	11	2.8	6	0	3	38	12.7	19	1					2	35	17.5	20
1993	EDM	18	0		2	24						6	1	1	4	4.0	4	0	19	237	12.5	28	1					3	15	5.0	7
1994	EDM	11				12													10	163	16.3	40	0								
1995	EDM	17				18													3	49	16.3	23	0					2	21	10.5	17
1996	TOR	11				4													1	9	9.0	9	0					1	2	2.0	2
1997	CAL	15				4													3	40	13.3	22	0					1	9	9.0	9
7	Years	108	1		3	112						24	4	18	88	4.9	25	0	57	723	12.7	40	4					16	124	7.8	26
BRIAN JACK Brian TE 6'4 237 Lenoir-Rhyne B: 5/23/1948																															
1973	MTL	13										12	2						5	70	14.0	32	2					1	0	0.0	0
1974	WPG	16	0		1							12	2						25	413	16.5	45	2								
1975	WPG	16										6	1						22	348	15.8	53	1								
3	Years	45	0		1							30	5						52	831	16.0	53	5					1	0	0.0	0
KEITH JACK Keith WR 5'9 177 Houston B: 5/11/1971																															
1994	OTT	1				1													2	17	8.5	13	0	1	15	15.0	15	2	27	13.5	18
HAROLD JACKMANN Harold OG 6'2 235 Minnesota State-Moorhead B: 11/16/1961 Draft: 5-41 1983 BC																															
1983	WPG	3																													
ALFRED JACKSON Alfred Melvin, Jr. WR-CB 6'0 180 San Diego State B: 7/10/1967 Tulare, CA Draft: 5-135 1989 LARM Pro: N																															
1993	WPG	12	1		2	15						12	2						13	194	14.9	60	2	6	32	5.3	12				
1994	WPG	13	1		0	3						48	8	2	3	1.5	3	0	43	942	21.9	88	8	1	9	9.0	9	1	20	20.0	20
1997	BC*	18	3	0	0	2						60	10						79	1322	16.7	73	10								
1998	BC	8				0						8	1						33	400	12.1	47	1								
1999	BC	12	1	0	0	0													36	571	15.9	50	0								
2000	BC+	15				2						72	12	1	-4	-4.0	-4	0	59	1119	19.0	55	12								
2001	BC	12				1						56	9	2	-1	-0.5	0	0	38	661	17.4	67	9								
2002	BC	16				1						42	7						39	785	20.1	109	7					1	0	0.0	0
2003	TOR	10	1	0	0	0						12	2						29	413	14.2	53	2								
9	Years	116	7	0	2	24						310	51	5	-2	-0.4	3	0	369	6407	17.4	109	51	7	41	5.9	12	2	20	10.0	20
ARNOLD JACKSON Arnold WR 5'8 168 Louisville B: 4/9/1977 Jacksonville, FL Pro: N																															
2003	OTT	2				0																		4	9	2.3	7				
BILLY JACKSON Bill LB 6'0 232 Mississippi State B: 8/11/1962 Plant City, FL Draft: 9A-173 1984 HOU-USFL																															
1984	SAS	16	0		4		4.0		3	46		6	1																		
1985	SAS	15	0		3		2.0																								
1986	SAS+	18	0		1		2.0		2	53																					
1987	SAS	7	0		1	38	2.0																	1	11	11.0	11	1	15	15.0	15
1988	CAL	4				4																									
1989	OTT	7				42																									
6	Years	67	0		9	84	10.0		5	99		6	1											1	11	11.0	11	1	15	15.0	15
BYRON JACKSON Byron WR 5'7 160 Santa Monica JC; San Jose State B: 2/16/1968 Pittsburgh, PA																															
1993	SAC	3				0													2	12	6.0	8	0	1	-7	-7.0	0				
CHRIS JACKSON Chris WR 6'2 205 Millsaps B: 7/5/1984 Florence, AL																															
2007	CAL	1				0																									
2008	CAL	3				1						6	1						4	44	11.0	21	1								
2	Years	4				1						6	1						4	44	11.0	21	1								
CLIFF JACKSON Clifton HB 6'0 185 North Carolina Central B: 1937 Draft: 30-356 1959 CHIB																															

Year	Team	GP	FM	FF	FR	TK	SK	YDS	IR	YDS	PD	PTS	TD	RA	YDS	AVG	LG	TD	REC	YDS	AVG	LG	TD	PR	YDS	AVG	LG	KOR	YDS	AVG	LG
1959	EDM	1												1	4	4.0	4	0	2	18	9.0	13	0	6	29	4.8	16				
1960	EDM	1	2											2	12	6.0	7	0						2	11	5.5	8	1	14	14.0	14
2	Years	2	2		0									3	16	5.3	7	0	2	18	9.0	13	0	8	40	5.0	16	1	14	14.0	14
CURTIS JACKSON Curtis Ray WR 5'10 190 Texas B: 9/22/1973 Fort Worth, TX Pro: N																															
1999	HAM	9	1	0	0	0								1	6	6.0	6	0	5	95	19.0	37	0	28	246	8.8	26	11	193	17.5	26
2004	OTT	11	2	0	0	2						6	1						47	537	11.4	46	1								
2	Years	20	3	0	0	2						6	1	1	6	6.0	6	0	52	632	12.2	46	1	28	246	8.8	26	11	193	17.5	26
EARNEST JACKSON Earnest Lee WR 6'3 220 Cincinnati B: 2/18/1986 Southfield, MI																															
2008	HAM	3				0						6	1						5	97	19.4	38	1					1	0	0.0	0
ED JACKSON Edward LB 6'4 225 Louisiana Tech B: 2/5/1959 Shreveport, LA Draft: 5-123 1982 LARI Pro: U																															
1982	TOR	5	0		2																										
ENIS JACKSON Enis CB 5'9 180 Memphis B: 5/16/1963 Helena, AR Pro: N																															
1989	EDM*	14	0		2	36			6	99														1	0	0.0	0				
1990	EDM	18	0		1	43	1.0		2	38																		1	0	0.0	0
1991	EDM+	13				29			4	85																		1	52	52.0	26
1992	EDM+	18				54			3	43																					
1993	TOR	5				20	1.0	17.0																							
1994	BC	14	0		2	47			4	123	9																	1	0	0.0	0
1995	BC	13	0		1	26			6	76	4																				
7	Years	95	0		6	255	2.0	17.0	25	464	13													1	0	0.0	0	3	52	17.3	26
GLEN JACKSON Glen LB 6'3 206 Simon Fraser B: 4/5/1954 Vancouver, BC Draft: TE 1976 BC																															
1976	BC	16	0		4				2	1																					
1977	BC+	16	0		1				1	12																					
1978	BC+	16	0		1				2	12																					
1979	BC+	16	0		1				1	0																					
1980	BC	16	0		4				2	9														0	4		4				
1981	BC	16	0		2		5.0		5	41																					
1982	BC+	16	0		2		2.0		3	2																					
1983	BC	15	0		2		5.5																								
1984	BC	16	0		2		4.5		3	27		6	1																		
1985	BC+	16	0		2		5.0		2	22																					
1986	BC	17	0		3		8.0		1	3																					
1987	BC+	16	0		2	71	6.0		1	0																					
12	Years	192	0		26	71	36.0		23	129		6	1											0	4		4				
HOWARD JACKSON Howard Glenn, Jr. RB 5'10 160 Texas-El Paso B: 9/24/1982 Freeport, TX																															
2005	HAM	4	1	0	0	0								11	37	3.4	16	0						6	53	8.8	18	8	172	21.5	37
JACK JACKSON Elliot Cornelius, Jr. WR 5'8 174 Florida B: 11/11/1972 Moss Point, MS Draft: 4-116 1995 CHIB Pro: N																															
1997	TOR	3				0						12	2						12	130	10.8	35	2								
JAMAICA JACKSON Jamaica L. LB 6'1 225 South Carolina B: 9/16/1981 Sumter, SC D: 4/14/2008 Sumter, SC																															
2007	HAM	12	1	0	1	12																						2	22	11.0	16
JARIOUS JACKSON Jarious K. QB 6'0 228 Notre Dame B: 5/3/1977 Tupelo, MS Draft: 7A-214 2000 DEN Pro: EN																															
2005	BC	8				1								4	35	8.8	21	0													
2006	BC	18				0						6	1	46	137	3.0	15	1													
2007	BC	18	8	0	3	0						18	3	49	265	5.4	18	3													
2008	BC	18	4	0	1	0						12	2	63	362	5.7	25	2													
2009	BC	10	5	0	0	1						12	2	32	143	4.5	14	2													
2010	BC	18				0								11	26	2.4	7	0													
2011	BC	18	2	0	0	1								22	80	3.6	17	0													
7	Years	108	19	0	4	3						48	8	227	1048	4.6	25	8													
JEFF JACKSON Jeffery Paul LB 6'1 230 Auburn B: 10/9/1961 Shreveport, LA Draft: 8-206 1984 ATL; TD 1984 BIR-USFL Pro: N																															
1991	OTT	7				15			1	10																					
1992	OTT	3				7																									
1993	BC	7	0		1	17			1	0																					
3	Years	17	0		1	39			2	10																					
JERMAINE JACKSON Jermaine SB 6'2 208 Saginaw Valley State B: 5/22/1982 Detroit, MI																															
2009	CAL	7				0						6	1						12	122	10.2	17	1								
2010	CAL	1				0													4	32	8.0	11	0								
2	Years	8				0						6	1						16	154	9.6	17	1								
JOE JACKSON Joe LB 6'3 223 Penn State B: 7/27/1953 Chicopee, MA Draft: 10B-256 1975 MIA																															
1975	WPG	7																													
1976	WPG	5	0		1																										
2	Years	12	0		1																										
JOE JACKSON Joseph Loyd LB 6'1 225 San Francisco State B: 10/15/1962 Pro: N																															
1985	WPG	5	0		1		1.0		2	29																					
JOEY JACKSON Michael Joseph LB 6'4 263 New Mexico State B: 5/7/1949 Cincinnati, OH Draft: 6-139 1972 NYJ Pro: NW																															
1978	EDM	1																													
JOHN HENRY JACKSON John Henry QB-HB 6'2 205 Indiana B: 11/26/1938 Columbus, GA																															
1961	TOR	1																													
JOSEPH JACKSON Joseph LB 6'3 230 San Diego State B: 3/18/1976 Phoenix, AZ																															
2001	TOR	7				15																									
KEITH JACKSON Keith DL 6'4 307 Cheney State B: 4/16/1975 Philadelphia, PA																															
2000	BC	3	0	0	1	2	1.0	13.0																							
KEN JACKSON Kenneth Gene T 6'2 236 Texas B: 4/26/1929 Milam County, TX D: 1/28/1998 Houston, TX Draft: 2-22 1951 NYY Pro: N																															
1958	MTL	8																													
MALIK JACKSON Malik LB 6'2 245 Rutgers																															
1994	EDM	2																													
MALIK JACKSON Malik LB-DE 6'2 232 Louisville B: 6/10/1985 Dunwoody, GA																															
2009	CAL	15	0	2	0	73	3.0	22.0			1																				
2010	CAL	18	0	2	4	68	6.0	49.0	1	0	4	6	1																		
2011	CAL	12	0	0	1	33																									
3	Years	45	0	4	5	174	9.0	71.0	1	0	5	6	1																		
MARK JACKSON Mark QB 6'0 190 Baylor B: 6/12/1954 Carlsbad, NM																															
1977	MTL	8	5		0							6	1	38	134	3.5	16	1													
1979	TOR	16										12	2	9	39	4.3	10	2													
1980	TOR	16	3		1							12	2	62	393	6.3	31	2													
1981	WPG	16	2		0									13	35	2.7	12	0	1	-6	-6.0	-6	0								
1982	WPG	14												7	39	5.6	12	0													
1983	WPG	1	1		0									3	13	4.3	7	0													
6	Years	71	11		1							30	5	132	653	4.9	31	5	1	-6	-6.0	-6	0								
MARK JACKSON Mark Devalon DB 5'9 180 Abilene Christian B: 3/16/1962 Amarillo, TX Draft: 16-334 1984 SA-USFL Pro: N																															
1985	EDM	15	2		0																			5	11	2.2	6	9	178	19.8	30
1986	EDM	8	2		0				1	18														16	110	6.9	17	8	167	20.9	32
2	Years	23	4		0				1	18														21	121	5.8	17	17	345	20.3	32
MOODY JACKSON Moody WR 6'3 192 Phoenix JC; New Mexico State B: 3/7/1950																															
1974	CAL	12	1		0							30	5						39	718	18.4	97	5								
1975	OTT	15	2		0							26	4	10	106	10.6	57	1	29	429	14.8	49	3	6	84	14.0	23	16	422	26.4	35
1976	OTT	15	3		0							20	3	5	51	10.2	32	0	35	634	18.1	75	3	54	560	10.4	35	19	415	21.8	40
1977	SAS	3										6	1	1	-11	-11.0	-11	0	4	65	16.3	22	1	4	36	9.0	26	1	17	17.0	17
4	Years	45	6		0							82	13	16	146	9.1	57	1	107	1846	17.3	97	12	64	680	10.6	35	36	854	23.7	40
NOAH JACKSON Noah Dale OG-OT 6'2 268 Tampa B: 4/14/1951 Jacksonville Beach, FL Draft: 7A-161 1974 BAL; 26-302 1974 FLA-WFL Pro: N																															
1972	TOR	14																													
1973	TOR	14	0		2							6	1																		

Year	Team	GP	FM	FF	FR	TK	SK	YDS	IR	YDS	PD	PTS	TD	RA	YDS	AVG	LG	TD	REC	YDS	AVG	LG	TD	PR	YDS	AVG	LG	KOR	YDS	AVG	LG
1974	TOR+	16																													
3	Years	44	0		2							6	1																		
PARIS JACKSON Paris WR-SB 6'3 210 Butte JC; Utah B: 7/24/1980 Vancouver, BC Draft: 1-6 2003 BC																															
2003	BC	8				1													6	85	14.2	35	0								
2004	BC	18				0													10	138	13.8	28	0								
2005	BC	18				1						24	4						48	617	12.9	40	4								
2006	BC	18	2	0	0	1						24	4						51	634	12.4	49	4								
2007	BC	18	1	0	0	0						30	5						65	962	14.8	64	5					2	0	0.0	0
2008	BC+	18	1	0	0	2						50	8						76	1180	15.5	56	8					3	17	5.7	17
2009	BC	17				1						48	8						76	1042	13.7	57	8								
2010	BC	18	2	1	2	2						6	1						61	758	12.4	53	1					3	2	0.7	3
2011	BC	16				0						6	1						7	117	16.7	51	1								
9	Years	149	6	1	2	8						188	31						400	5533	13.8	64	31					8	19	2.4	17
PAT JACKSON Patrick Ryan WR 5'9 180 Waldorf JC; Kansas State B: 7/8/1969 Columbus, OH																															
1993	TOR	5	1		0	0						6	1	13	87	6.7	19	1	4	31	7.8	19	0	5	62	12.4	25	7	146	20.9	30
QUINCY JACKSON Quincy WR 6'2 194 East Mississippi JC; Alabama B: 4/2/1977 Brundidge, AL Pro: X																															
2001	EDM	13	1	0	0	0						24	4						46	777	16.9	85	4					7	137	19.6	24
2002	SAS	13				1						24	4						37	407	11.0	21	4								
2003	SAS	7	0	0	0	1													12	112	9.3	26	0								
2003	EDM	2				1													7	101	14.4	23	0								
2003	Year	9				2													19	213	11.2	26	0								
3	Years	33	1	0	0	3						48	8						102	1397	13.7	85	8					7	137	19.6	24
RENDELL JACKSON Rendell RB 5'11 205 West Georgia B: 4/10/1974 Macon, GA																															
1996	WPG	2				3						6	1	25	117	4.7	18	1	5	28	5.6	22	0					1	17	17.0	17
RUSS JACKSON Russ QB-HB 6'1 190 McMaster B: 7/28/1936 Hamilton, ON Draft: 1-4 1958 OTT																															
1958	OTT	14										30	5	66	357	5.4	51	5													
1959	OTT	14										18	3	69	385	5.6	30	3	1	8	8.0	8	0	2	22	11.0	11				
1960	OTT	12										36	6	52	381	7.3	25	6	1	10	10.0	10	0								
1961	OTT	14										36	6	67	472	7.0	24	6													
1962	OTT+	14										48	8	71	512	7.2	26	8													
1963	OTT+	14										30	5	64	384	6.0	42	5													
1964	OTT	14	4		0							24	4	81	588	7.3	33	3	2	25	12.5	30	1								
1965	OTT	14	1		0							12	2	24	129	5.4	26	2	1	28	28.0	28	0								
1966	OTT*	14	2		1							18	3	65	396	6.1	26	3	2	25	12.5	32	0								
1967	OTT+	14	5		0							24	4	61	329	5.4	23	4													
1968	OTT*	14	6		0							36	6	54	534	9.9	73	6													
1969	OTT*	14	3		2							18	3	64	578	9.0	49	3	1	13	13.0	13	0								
12	Years	166	21		3							330	55	738	5045	6.8	73	54	8	109	13.6	32	1	2	22	11.0	11				
SPENCER JACKSON Spencer, III WR 6'0 177 Florida B: 3/5/1961 Boynton Beach, FL Draft: TD 1983 TB-USFL Pro: U																															
1985	MTL	2										6	1						3	62	20.7		1								
1985	CAL	4																	8	128	16.0	39	0	2	20	10.0	10	2	47	23.5	24
1985	Year	6										6	1						11	190	17.3	39	1	2	20	10.0	10	2	47	23.5	24
STANLEY JACKSON Stanley QB 6'1 215 Ohio State B: 3/24/1975 Paterson, NJ																															
1999	MTL	3				0								2	5	2.5	5	0													
2000	MTL	18	3	0	0	1								23	136	5.9	26	0													
2001	TOR	15				7								1	2	2.0	2	0													
2002	TOR	2	1	0	0	1								4	31	7.8	10	0													
2004	WPG	18				0								2	19	9.5	12	0													
5	Years	56	4	0	0	9								32	193	6.0	26	0													
STEVE JACKSON Steve FB-WR-SB 6'3 230 London Beefeaters Jrs.; Guelph B: 3/30/1961 London, ON																															
1984	HAM	1																													
1985	HAM	16												2	3	1.5	2	0	2	14	7.0	12	0								
1986	HAM	18	0		1														8	65	8.1	18	0								
1987	HAM	14				1								3	2	0.7	3	0	6	53	8.8	14	0								
1988	HAM	18				1						6	1	13	34	2.6	7	0	8	40	5.0	10	1								
1989	HAM	12	0		1	0																									
6	Years	79	0		2	2						6	1	18	39	2.2	7	0	24	172	7.2	18	1								
TIM JACKSON Timothy Gerrard DB 5'11 192 Kansas State; Coffeyville JC; Nebraska B: 11/7/1965 Dallas, TX Draft: 9-224 1989 DAL Pro: EN																															
1991	HAM	15	0		4	66			3	47		6	1																		
1992	HAM	17	0		3	50																									
1993	HAM	12				46			2	3																		1	0	0.0	0
1994	TOR	2				6																									
4	Years	46	0		7	168			5	50		6	1															1	0	0.0	0
TONY JACKSON Tony RB 5'8 170 Vanderbilt B: 8/4/1971 Saginaw, MI																															
1994	BC	3				0						6	1	19	57	3.0	24	0	5	56	11.2	22	1	5	34	6.8	12	7	133	19.0	29
1995	SA	3				0								8	45	5.6	11	0	1	4	4.0	4	0	10	60	6.0	17	3	72	24.0	33
2	Years	6				0						6	1	27	102	3.8	24	0	6	60	10.0	22	1	15	94	6.3	17	10	205	20.5	33
TRISTAN JACKSON Tristan CB-DH 5'8 185 Central Arkansas B: 3/5/1986 Beaumont, MS																															
2008	EDM	17	3	1	0	12			2	123	4	24	4	2	18	9.0	13	0						79	809	10.2	67	35	839	24.0	94
2009	EDM	15	5	0	0	2						6	1	1	2	2.0	2	0						72	761	10.6	75	56	1167	20.8	56
2010	EDM	6	3	0	1	1																		27	130	4.8	21	18	355	19.7	34
2011	SAS	18	4	2	2	71			1	0	5													57	448	7.9	32	23	550	23.9	75
4	Years	56	15	3	3	86			3	123	9	30	5	3	20	6.7	13	0						235	2148	9.1	75	132	2911	22.1	94
XZAVIE JACKSON Xzavie Lee Heberon DL 6'4 285 Missouri B: 9/21/1984 Vacaville, CA																															
2009	EDM	5	0	1	0	9	1.0	3.0	0	0	2																				
AL JACOBS Al QB Toronto																															
1946	TOR	4																													
1947	TOR	2																													
2	Years	6																													
JACK JACOBS Jack (Indian Jack) QB-DB 6'1 186 Oklahoma B: 8/7/1919 Holdenville, OK D: 1/12/1974 Greensboro, NC Draft: 2-12 1942 CLE Pro: N																															
1950	WPG+	12										33	2	13	-17	-1.3		2													
1951	WPG	14										43	1	28	-97	-3.5		1													
1952	WPG+	16			1				3	15		27	0	15	-102	-6.8	6	0						3	17	5.7	10				
1953	WPG	16							1	0		6	0	14	-27	-1.9		0													
1954	WPG	16	4		1							18	2	28	-100	-3.6	10	1													
5	Years	74	4		2				4	15		127	5	98	-343	-3.5	10	4						3	17	5.7	10				
RAY JACOBS Ray Anthony DE 6'2 244 North Carolina B: 8/18/1972 Wilmington, NC Pro: N																															
1998	CAL	13	0	1	0	26	4.0	17.0			2																				
1999	CAL	14	0	0	1	26	3.0	7.0			1																				
2000	CAL	16	0	2	0	34	5.0	29.0			1																				
2001	CAL	18	0	3	0	42	9.0	55.0			3																				
2002	SAS	17	0	2	1	39	4.0	13.0			1																				
2003	BC*	13	0	1	1	30	10.0	64.0			1																				
2005	OTT	16	0	0	1	38	4.0	25.0																				1	11	11.0	11
7	Years	107	0	9	4	235	39.0	210.0			9																	1	11	11.0	11
ROMEO JACOBUCCI Romeo G 5'11 215 B: 8/16/1930 The Pas, MB																															
1952	CAL	3																													
WILLIS JACOX Willis Francis WR-SB 5'7 170 North Dakota B: 3/25/1965 Bloomington, MN																															
1987	SAS	3				0													7	73	10.4	17	0	15	114	7.6	33	10	243	24.3	66
1991	SAS	17	5		3	2						36	6	19	93	4.9	15	0	27	392	14.5	106	3	86	1063	12.4	108	58	1231	21.2	67
1992	SAS	8	4		0	10								16	100	6.3	26	0	7	58	8.3	10	0	45	369	8.2	72	18	397	22.1	43
1992	BC	7	4		1	0						6	1						0	0		0	0	40	416	10.4	78	28	473	16.9	38

Year	Team	GP	FM	FF	FR	TK	SK	YDS	IR	YDS	PD	PTS	TD	RA	YDS	AVG	LG	TD	REC	YDS	AVG	LG	TD	PR	YDS	AVG	LG	KOR	YDS	AVG	LG
1992	Year	15	8		1	10						6	1						7	58	8.3	10	0	86	785	9.1	78	46	870	18.9	43
3	Years	28	13		4	12						42	7	35	193	5.5	26	0	41	523	12.8	106	3	186	1962	10.5	108	114	2344	20.6	67
FRANK JAGAS Frank K 5'11 200 Western Ontario B: 1/8/1971 Kitchener, ON Draft: 6-40 1993 TOR																															
1996	EDM	5				0						50	0																		
1996	SAS	13				0						103	0																		
1996	Year	18				0						153	0																		
NICK JAMBROSIC Nikola K 5'10 165 Hamilton Hurricanes Jrs. B: 11/9/1956																															
1977	HAM	12										96	0						1	9	9.0	9	0								
1978	HAM	14	1		0							58	0																		
2	Years	26	1		0							154	0						1	9	9.0	9	0								
RON JAMERSON Ron RB 6'2 205 Canyons JC; Southern California B: 7/2/1952																															
1978	SAS	2												6	31	5.2	10	0	4	16	4.0	8	0	2	9	4.5	5				
BRANDON JAMES Brandon SB-WR 5'7 176 Florida B: 12/21/1987 St. Augustine, FL Pro: N																															
2011	EDM	5				0													2	9	4.5	10	0	15	97	6.5	15	6	105	17.5	29
DRISAN JAMES Drisan SB-WR 5'11 185 Boise State B: 1/1/1985 Phoenix, AZ																															
2009	HAM	9	1	0	0	0						6	1						21	313	14.9	32	1	10	61	6.1	15	6	90	15.0	25
2010	HAM	4				0								1	2	2.0	2	0	6	113	18.8	35	0								
2	Years	13	1	0	0	0						6	1	1	2	2.0	2	0	27	426	15.8	35	1	10	61	6.1	15	6	90	15.0	25
ELMER JAMES Elmer L. (Poncho) RB 5'10 198 Long Beach CC; San Francisco State B: 4/16/1961 Compton, CA Draft: 23-271 1983 OAK-USFL Pro: U																															
1985	HAM	6	2		0							18	3	62	241	3.9	25	3	12	62	5.2	21	0					6	129	21.5	27
FOB JAMES Fob, Jr. HB 5'9 170 Auburn B: 9/15/1934 Lanett, AL Draft: 11-125 1956 CHIC																															
1956	MTL	10										48	8	58	346	6.0	34	4	23	221	9.6	52	4	5	38	7.6	15	9	152	16.9	43
FRED JAMES Fred OT-C-DT-DE 6'5 250 Edmonton Wildcats Jrs.; Alberta B: 1944 Draft: 1A-3 1966 CAL																															
1967	CAL	3																													
1968	CAL	16																													
1969	CAL	16	0		1																										
1970	CAL	16	0		1																										
1971	CAL	16	0		2																										
1972	CAL	16	0		1							6	1																		
1973	CAL	16							1	30																					
1974	CAL	10																													
1975	CAL	3																													
1975	EDM	14																	1	28	28.0	28	0					3	26	8.7	13
1975	Year	17																	1	28	28.0	28	0					3	26	8.7	13
9	Years	112	0		5				1	30		6	1						1	28	28.0	28	0					3	26	8.7	13
GERRY JAMES Gerald Edwin FB-OHB-K 5'10 187 none B: 10/22/1934 Regina, SK																															
1952	WPG	11										20	4	10	93	9.3	25	2	5	63	12.6	31	2	52	517	9.9	27	4	94	23.5	29
1953	WPG	14										5	1	25	120	4.8		1	1	-2	-2.0	-2	0	38	357	9.4		4	78	19.5	
1954	WPG	15	3		0							25	5	106	576	5.4	71	4	11	136	12.4	23	1	4	18	4.5	7	17	403	23.7	55
1955	WPG+	16	10		0							35	7	189	1205	6.4	60	7	11	136	12.4	27	0	10	58	5.8	14	18	382	21.2	53
1957	WPG+	16	2									131	19	197	1192	6.1	74	18	12	190	15.8	32	1					12	279	23.3	40
1958	WPG	6										33	2	64	372	5.8	21	2	1	17	17.0	17	0					5	133	26.6	35
1959	WPG	10										43	6	49	261	5.3	44	6	2	21	10.5	15	0					1	14	14.0	14
1960	WPG	16	3									114	10	165	872	5.3	28	9	2	22	11.0	15	1								
1961	WPG	15	3									79	4	102	505	5.0	26	4	5	60	12.0	21	0								
1962	WPG	16	3									116	5	84	345	4.1	15	5	7	68	9.7	17	0								
1964	SAS	10										44	0	4	13	3.3	7	0	1	16	16.0	16	0								
11	Years	145	24		0							645	63	995	5554	5.6	74	58	58	727	12.5	32	5	104	950	9.1	27	61	1383	22.7	55
IAN JAMES Ian LB 6'0 225 Calgary B: 5/29/1966 Wetaskiwin, AB Draft: 8-60 1988 CAL																															
1989	CAL	1				1																									
JOHN JAMES John OT 6'3 300 Mississippi State B: 3/28/1970 Tuskegee, AL																															
1995	BAL	10				0																									
1996	SAS	17	0		1	0																									
2	Years	27	0		1	0																									
JUNE JAMES June, IV LB 6'1 218 Texas B: 12/2/1962 Jennings, LA D: 5/8/1990 Gonzales, LA Draft: 9-230 1985 DET; TD 1985 SA-USFL Pro: N																															
1988	SAS	4			1		1.0																								
LARRY JAMES Lawrence HB 6'2 215 Norfolk State B: 11/25/1948 Gainesville, FL Draft: 15-373 1971 DEN																															
1971	BC	1												4	24	6.0	14	0	1	8	8.0	8	0								
LARRY JAMES Larry Kent WR 6'2 195 Texas A&M-Kingsville B: 3/28/1960 Galveston, TX D: 1/2/2010 Galveston, TX Pro: U																															
1982	CAL	5	1		0														5	61	12.2	22	0								
1982	OTT	1																													
1982	Year	6	1		0														5	61	12.2	22	0								
LOLO JAMES Lahouri DB 5'9 170 New Mexico State B: 1/3/1969																															
1991	BC	3	0		2	15																									
LYNN JAMES Lynn Fitzpatrick WR 6'0 191 Southern Methodist; Arizona State B: 1/25/1965 Navasota, TX Draft: 5-122 1990 CIN Pro: N																															
1992	WPG	2	1		0	1																		6	27	4.5	8	6	115	19.2	30
MIKE JAMES Mike LB 6'0 215 Garden City CC; Mississippi State B: 11/8/1970 Belle Glade, FL																															
1995	BIR	18	1		4	95	1.0	10.0																							
NATE JAMES Nathaniel DB 6'1 195 Florida A&M B: 2/20/1944 Bartow, FL Draft: 6-152 1968 CLE Pro: N																															
1969	MTL	3																										1	14	14.0	14
SHANNON JAMES Shannon Clayton LB-S 5'9 193 Massachusetts B: 12/28/1983 Bridgeport, CT																															
2006	CAL	2				7																									
2007	CAL	18	0	1	0	67	4.0	21.0	2	51	5																				
2008	CAL	18	0	4	1	82	2.0	17.0	1	27	13	6	1																		
2009	CAL	18	0	1	0	67	1.0	13.0			3																				
2010	HAM	12				19																									
5	Years	68	0	6	1	242	7.0	51.0	3	78	21	6	1																		
WILLIAM JAMES William WR 5'10 165 Southern Utah B: 10/9/1960																															
1984	CAL	2																	5	64	12.8	33	0								
JOHN JANELLE John OG-DT 5'11 225 Kitchener-Waterloo Jrs. B: 4/16/1931 Kitchener, ON																															
1958	MTL	1																													
JERRY JANES Jerry OE 6'5 245 Louisiana State B: 1935 Draft: 21-252 1957 CHIB																															
1957	BC	13										36	6						25	503	20.1	68	6					1	8	8.0	8
1958	BC	13										32	5						47	868	18.5	85	5								
1959	BC	14										40	6						41	936	22.8	75	6								
1960	CAL	1																	2	29	14.5	15	0								
1960	HAM	1																	2	29	14.5	17	0								
1960	Year	2																	4	58	14.5	17	0								
1963	HAM	1																													
1963	BC	16										18	3	1	1	1.0	1	0	15	390	26.0	72	3					2	16	8.0	9
1963	Year	17										18	3	1	1	1.0	1	0	15	390	26.0	72	3					2	16	8.0	9
5	Years	42										126	20	1	1	1.0	1	0	132	2755	20.9	85	20					3	24	8.0	9
JOHN JANKANS John L. T-G 6'2 220 Arizona State B: 10/3/1932 Draft: 11-130 1956 CHIB																															
1956	BC	10	0		3				2	26																					
1957	BC	1																													
2	Years	11	0		3				2	26																					
GLENN JANUARY Glenn Arwin, Jr. OT 6'5 306 Texas Tech B: 5/25/1983 Houston, TX																															
2007	TOR	13				2																									
2008	SAS	16	0	0	2	1																									
2009	WPG	18				3																									
2011	WPG+	18	0	0	3	2						6	1	0	1		1	0													
4	Years	65	0	0	5	8						6	1	0	1		1	0													

Year	Team	GP	FM	FF	FR	TK	SK	YDS	IR	YDS	PD	PTS	TD	RA	YDS	AVG	LG	TD	REC	YDS	AVG	LG	TD	PR	YDS	AVG	LG	KOR	YDS	AVG	LG
TONY JANUARY Tony RB 5'9 190 Sam Houston State B: 11/7/1958 Orange, TX																															
1983	MTL	2	2		0									17	67	3.9	19	0	4	22	5.5	8	0								
1985	OTT	2																	6	57	9.5	19	0								
2	Years	4	2		0									17	67	3.9	19	0	10	79	7.9	19	0								
HENRY JANZEN Henry CB-OE-LB 5'10 185 Weston Wildcats Jrs. B: 6/7/1940																															
1959	WPG	16										6	1	7	56	8.0	23	0	6	90	15.0	27	1	67	499	7.4	25	1	28	28.0	28
1960	WPG	12	3		2							6	1	12	79	6.6	19	1	6	82	13.7	17	0	52	274	5.3	13	2	39	19.5	21
1961	WPG	16	3											4	13	3.3	9	0	2	37	18.5	16	0	54	394	7.3	53				
1962	WPG	16	3		2				4	73		18	3						5	85	17.0	41	1	39	244	6.3	21	20	494	24.7	39
1963	WPG	16	1		0				2	12				3	-2	-0.7	3	0						60	295	4.9	19				
1964	WPG	12	0		1				2	29														10	49	4.9	10				
1965	WPG+	15							7	139		6	1	2	7	3.5	6	0													
7	Years	103	10		5				15	253		36	6	28	153	5.5	23	1	19	294	15.5	41	2	282	1755	6.2	53	23	561	24.4	39
OLANZO JARRETT Olanzo LB 6'1 215 Toledo B: 12/19/1978 Kingston, Jamaica Draft: 5-42 2002 EDM																															
2003	EDM	11				5	1.0																								
2004	EDM	2				0																									
2	Years	13				5	1.0	0.0																							
BOB JARUS Robert FB-LB 6'1 210 Purdue B: 6/6/1938 Cleveland, OH Draft: 5-53 1960 CLE; FS 1960 OAK																															
1960	HAM	6										6	1	49	275	5.6	99	1	9	29	3.2	12	0								
1961	HAM	10												72	350	4.9	23	0	13	210	16.2	35	0					2	28	14.0	19
2	Years	16										6	1	121	625	5.2	99	1	22	239	10.9	35	0					2	28	14.0	19
RALPH JARVIS Ralph A. DE 6'4 255 Temple B: 6/1/1965 Philadelphia, PA Draft: 3-78 1988 CHIB Pro: N																															
1988	OTT	4																													
1989	CAL	1	0		1	1																									
2	Years	5	0		1	1																									
JIM JAUCH James Walter DB 6'1 180 North Carolina B: 6/25/1965 Iowa City, IA Draft: 3-18 1988 SAS																															
1989	CAL	17	1		0	1																									
1990	EDM	14				6			1	0																					
1992	HAM	11				10																						3	18	6.0	9
1993	HAM	11				16																						1	22	22.0	22
4	Years	53	1		0	33			1	0																		4	40	10.0	22
JOEY JAUCH Joey SB 6'1 195 North Carolina B: 4/25/1970 Edmonton, AB Draft: 2-9 1992 HAM																															
1992	HAM	4				6													2	31	15.5	22	0								
1993	HAM	18				12						6	1	1	25	25.0	25	0	31	512	16.5	41	1					0	39		39
1994	HAM	9	0		0	4						6	1						15	134	8.9	17	1								
1994	SAS	5	1		0	1													4	39	9.8	21	0								
1994	Year	14	1		0	5						6	1						19	173	9.1	21	1								
1995	SAS	16				12													3	50	16.7	22	0								
1996	MTL	17				5						6	1						12	153	12.8	21	1								
5	Years	64	1		0	40						18	3	1	25	25.0	25	0	67	919	13.7	41	3					0	39		39
RAY JAUCH Raymond Andrew OHB 5'11 175 Iowa B: 2/11/1938 Sublette, IL Draft: FS 1960 BUF																															
1960	WPG	9	2						1			36	6	52	298	5.7	49	2	13	181	13.9	34	3	1	9	9.0	9	9	270	30.0	47
1961	WPG	12	2									30	5	86	456	5.3	19	3	14	244	17.4	37	2					13	380	29.2	71
2	Years	21	4		0				1	0		66	11	138	754	5.5	49	5	27	425	15.7	37	5	1	9	9.0	9	22	650	29.5	71
HARRY JAVERNICK Harry J. T 6'3 230 Colorado B: 4/13/1936 Canon City, CO Draft: 12-145 1956 CLE																															
1958	SAS	1																													
1959	SAS	1																													
2	Years	2																													
MATT JAWORSKI Matthew Joseph LB 6'1 226 Colgate B: 10/23/1967 Blasdell, NY Pro: N																															
1994	SAC	2				2																									
TAREK JAYOUSSI Tarek SB 5'10 170 Calgary B: 5/13/1975 Calgary, AB Draft: 4-21 1998 HAM																															
1998	HAM	15				7																									
MICHAEL JEAN-LOUIS Michael DL 6'0 280 Laval B: 3/14/1982 Granby, QC Draft: 4A-26 2007 EDM																															
2007	EDM	17				3																						1	0	0.0	0
LEONARD JEAN-PIERRE Leonard SB 6'0 185 York B: 1/23/1971 North York, ON Draft: 4-31 1996 WPG																															
1996	WPG	18	0		1	15						6	1	25	131	5.2	13	1	8	71	8.9	12	0								
1997	WPG	5	1	0	1	6								10	34	3.4	13	0													
1997	CAL	1				1																									
1997	BC	3				4																									
1997	Year	9	1	0	1	11								10	34	3.4	13	0													
2	Years	23	1	0	2	26						6	1	35	165	4.7	13	1	8	71	8.9	12	0								
RASHAD JEANTY Rashad LB 6'3 242 Central Florida B: 4/17/1983 Miami, FL Pro: N																															
2003	EDM	5	0	1	0	6	1.0	5.0			1																				
2004	EDM	18	0	3	0	53	5.0	45.0			2																	3	28	9.3	13
2005	EDM	14	0	1	1	24	8.0	50.0			2																	2	13	6.5	8
3	Years	37	0	5	1	83	14.0	100.0			5																	5	41	8.2	13
LEMONT JEFFERS Lemont Holt LB 6'3 220 Tennessee B: 4/15/1960 Newport News, VA Draft: 6-153 1982 WAS Pro: U																															
1985	MTL	3																													
1986	MTL	16	0		1		7.0																								
1987	CAL	17	0		1	49	5.0					2	0						1	5	5.0	5	0								
1988	CAL	18				72	2.0		2	29																		1	0	0.0	0
1989	CAL	2				4			1	24																					
5	Years	56	0		2	125	14.0		3	53		2	0						1	5	5.0	5	0					1	0	0.0	0
TERENCE JEFFERS-HARRIS Terence SB 6'2 216 Connecticut; Vanderbilt B: 6/24/1988																															
2010	WPG	11	1	0	0	1						24	4	2	6	3.0	11	0	48	547	11.4	60	4					10	174	17.4	34
2011	WPG	8	2	0	0	0						12	2						29	347	12.0	84	2								
2	Years	19	3	0	0	1						36	6	2	6	3.0	11	0	77	894	11.6	84	6					10	174	17.4	34
BEN JEFFERSON William Benjamin OT 6'9 338 Maryland B: 1/15/1966 New Rochelle, NY Pro: EN																															
1994	LV	9				1																									
1995	SHR	6				0																									
2	Years	15				1																									
DAVID JEFFERSON David, Jr. LB 6'2 235 Miami (Florida) B: 11/24/1959 Winter Park, FL Draft: 9-228 1982 SEA Pro: U																															
1982	TOR	1																													
JAMES JEFFERSON James Andrew, III CB 6'1 195 Texas A&M-Kingsville B: 11/18/1963 Portsmouth, VA Pro: N																															
1986	WPG	14	1		1				2	38		6	1											44	415	9.4	76	4	91	22.8	37
1987	WPG*	17			3	51			8	99		24	4											4	73	18.3	58	0	26		26
1988	WPG+	18	5		1	54			2	56		12	2											71	650	9.2	75	28	666	23.8	94
1994	BC	14	2		0	32			1	21	6													19	148	7.8	18	8	136	17.0	36
1995	WPG	3				9			1	10	0																				
1995	BC	5	0		1	15			3	12	0																	1	13	13.0	13
1995	Year	8	0		1	24			4	22	7																	1	13	13.0	13
5	Years	66	8		6	161			17	236	6	42	7											138	1286	9.3	76	41	932	22.7	94
MIKE JEFFERSON Michael Wayne, Jr. OG 6'2 284 Nebraska B: 10/23/1971 Rowlett, TX																															
1994	SHR	2																													
NORM JEFFERSON Norman, Jr. CB 5'10 183 Louisiana State B: 8/7/1964 Marrero, LA Draft: 12-335 1987 GB Pro: N																															
1990	BC	15	2		0	46			2	59														23	166	7.2	25				
1991	BC	18	4		1	50			5	102														53	468	8.8	36	1	13	13.0	13
2	Years	33	6		1	96			7	161														76	634	8.3	36	1	13	13.0	13
JON JELACIC Jon Francis DE 6'3 250 Minnesota B: 12/19/1936 D: 9/17/1993 Beltrami County, MN Draft: 7-74 1958 CHIC Pro: N																															
1959	OTT	10																													
1960	OTT	13																													
2	Years	23																													

Year	Team	GP	FM	FF	FR	TK	SK	YDS	IR	YDS	PD	PTS	TD	RA	YDS	AVG	LG	TD	REC	YDS	AVG	LG	TD	PR	YDS	AVG	LG	KOR	YDS	AVG	LG
GENE JELKS Gene DB 5'10 185 Alabama B: 1/21/1966																															
1991	SAS	2				3																									
THAD JEMISON Thad WR 6'2 195 Ohio State B: 12/24/1961 Cincinnati, OH Draft: 12-310 1984 TB																															
1985	TOR	5	1		0									1	1	1.0	1	0	8	80	10.0	19	0					2	43	21.5	24
1985	OTT	1	0		0														5	59	11.8	19	0								
1985	Year	6	1		0									1	1	1.0	1	0	13	139	10.7	19	0					2	43	21.5	24
ALFRED JENKINS Alfred D. QB 6'4 215 Arizona B: 4/1/1964 Draft: 9-248 1987 WAS																															
1988	OTT	1																													
COREY JENKINS Corey LaVester LB 6'0 222 Garden City CC; South Carolina B: 8/25/1976 Columbia, SC Draft: 6A-181 2003 MIA Pro: N																															
2007	WPG	9	0	3	1	33			1	8	2																				
DeSHON JENKINS DeShon L. DB 6'1 198 Northwestern State (Louisiana) B: 12/19/1964																															
1988	OTT	2																													
JAMES JENKINS James FB 6'1 225 Clemson; Rhode Island																															
2000	TOR	3				0								7	18	2.6	6	0													
JASON JENKINS Jason DL 6'5 260 Dodge City CC; Nebraska B: 7/26/1973 Hammonton, NJ																															
2000	TOR	3				6					2																				
JEFF JENKINS Jeff WR 6'1 181 Utah B: 1966																															
1988	WPG	3	1		0							6	1						10	146	14.6	33	1	1	0	0.0	0				
JOE JENKINS Joe Prentiss LB 6'5 225 Alcorn State* B: 11/5/1957 Gulfport, MS																															
1984	EDM	8	0		2																										
JULIAN JENKINS Julian DL 6'3 277 Stanford B: 10/25/1983 Boston, MA Draft: 5-156 2006 TB Pro: N																															
2008	CAL	1				3																									
KEYVAN JENKINS Keyvan Lewis FB 5'10 190 Nevada-Las Vegas B: 1/6/1961 Stockton, CA Pro: N																															
1984	BC	3	3		0							12	2	30	170	5.7	19	2	7	56	8.0	18	0					6	173	28.8	43
1985	BC*	14	5		2							66	11	193	964	5.0	51	8	51	437	8.6	47	3					35	720	20.6	47
1986	BC	11	6		0							42	7	131	496	3.8	19	7	34	329	9.7	47	0					23	502	21.8	35
1990	CAL	5	1		0	1						18	3	53	238	4.5	29	3	8	107	13.4	20	0					7	146	20.9	55
1991	CAL	15	8		1	4						78	13	166	801	4.8	59	10	28	256	9.1	21	3					26	529	20.3	41
1992	CAL	10	2		0	4						42	7	97	535	5.5	34	5	28	376	13.4	45	2					3	69	23.0	26
1993	CAL	12	3		0	0						12	2	96	435	4.5	26	0	32	363	11.3	51	2					10	210	21.0	47
1994	SAC	7	2		0	10								12	80	6.7	25	0	3	35	11.7	17	0					1	26	26.0	26
8	Years	77	30		3	19						270	45	778	3719	4.8	59	35	191	1959	10.3	51	10					111	2375	21.4	55
MarTAY JENKINS Demar MarTay WR 6'0 200 North Iowa CC; Nebraska-Omaha B: 2/28/1975 Waterloo, IA Draft: 6-193 1999 DAL Pro: N																															
2005	CAL	15	1	0	1	11						24	4	2	0	0.0	1	0	25	382	15.3	50	4					19	382	20.1	41
MEL JENKINS Melvin CB 5'10 177 Hinds JC; Cincinnati B: 3/16/1962 Jackson, MS Pro: N																															
1984	CAL	13	4		3				3	50		6	1											41	349	8.5	43	15	312	20.8	42
1985	CAL	9	1		1				1	-5														7	74	10.6	25	6	110	18.3	31
1986	CAL+	18	0		1				7	139		6	1											1	10	10.0	10				
3	Years	40	5		5				11	184		12	2											49	433	8.8	43	21	422	20.1	42
MIKE JENKINS Michael Bernard RB 5'7 205 Coffeyville JC; Wyoming; Arkansas B: 8/27/1976 Bethesda, MD																															
2000	TOR	18	2	0	3	8						12	2	183	1050	5.7	30	2	37	400	10.8	25	0					5	108	21.6	26
2001	TOR	16	5	0	1	1						78	13	271	1484	5.5	59	8	43	361	8.4	55	5					8	149	18.6	25
2003	TOR	15	2	0	0	3						36	6	156	814	5.2	78	6	33	316	9.6	40	0								
2005	EDM	1				0								8	30	3.8	15	0	1	11	11.0	11	0								
4	Years	50	9	0	4	12						126	21	618	3378	5.5	78	16	114	1088	9.5	55	5					13	257	19.8	26
ORTEGE JENKINS Ortege Lamar QB 6'1 220 Arizona B: 2/1/1978 Santa Ana, CA																															
2001	BC	1				0																									
2002	BC	4				0								4	14	3.5	7	0													
2	Years	5				0								4	14	3.5	7	0													
RONNEY JENKINS Ronney Gene RB 5'11 188 Brigham Young; Northern Arizona B: 5/25/1977 Pro: N																															
2004	CAL	5	1	0	0	0								11	50	4.5	10	0	4	30	7.5	10	0					12	235	19.6	32
2005	CAL	6				2								11	84	7.6	18	0	3	13	4.3	6	0	1	15	15.0	15	26	487	18.7	30
2	Years	11	1	0	0	2								22	134	6.1	18	0	7	43	6.1	10	0	1	15	15.0	15	38	722	19.0	32
RUSS JENKINS Russell C-DT 6'3 240 Simon Fraser B: 1948																															
1971	BC	12																													
VENTRELL JENKINS Ventrell DT 6'2 285 Kentucky B: 11/16/1984 Orangeburg, SC																															
2011	HAM	1				2																									
WALT JENKINS Walter B. DE-OG 6'1 223 Wayne State (Michigan) B: 12/9/1930 Detroit, MI Draft: 9-108 1955 DET Pro: N																															
1956	HAM	2																													
BOBBY JENNINGS Francis Brown, Jr. C 6'1 195 Furman B: 5/24/1934 Columbia, SC Draft: 24-285 1957 WAS																															
1957	CAL	4																													
CHRIS JENNINGS Chris RB 5'10 210 Arizona Western JC; Arizona B: 12/12/1985 Yuma, AZ Pro: NU																															
2008	MTL	1				1																									
JIM JENNINGS James J. OT 6'4 295 San Diego State B: 4/4/1969 Bellflower, CA Draft: 8-213 1992 KC																															
1993	SAC	7				0																									
MIKE JENNINGS Michael A. WR 5'11 172 Grambling State*; Florida State* B: 9/7/1979 Jacksonville, FL Pro: EN																															
2008	CAL	2				0								1	-7	-7.0	-7	0						2	12	6.0	9	4	80	20.0	32
WILLIE JENNINGS Willie E., Jr. DT 6'5 290 Georgia; Savannah State B: 10/29/1971																															
1995	TOR	4				9																									
CRAIG JENSEN Craig DB 5'11 195 Brigham Young B: 9/19/1954																															
1977	HAM	4																													
ROY JENSON Roy Cameron OG-LB 6'2 210 UCLA B: 2/9/1927 Calgary, AB D: 4/24/2007 Los Angeles, CA																															
1951	CAL	13										5	1						1	13	13.0	13	1								
1952	CAL	15			1														1	9	9.0	9	0					1	14	14.0	14
1953	CAL	9																													
1954	CAL+	15																													
1955	CAL	16												2	13	6.5	11	0										1	2	2.0	2
1956	BC	13	2		0																										
1957	BC	14																													
7	Years	95	2		1							5	1	2	13	6.5	11	0	2	22	11.0	13	1					2	16	8.0	14
LUTHER JERALDS Luther Reginald DE 6'3 235 North Carolina Central B: 8/20/1938 D: 12/13/1992 Fayetteville, NC Pro: N																															
1963	EDM	2																													
ART JEROME Art HB 5'10 186 McMaster																															
1949	HAM	4																													
JIM JEROME James F. T 6'3 255 Cornell B: 1930																															
1954	OTT	13																													
CHARLES JESSAMY Charles RB 6'1 210 Kansas Wesleyan B: 10/6/1950 Yonkers, NY																															
1975	HAM	10	3		0									58	206	3.6	17	0	14	172	12.3	23	0								
DOUG JESSE Doug FW 6'0 200																															
1946	OTT	1																													
TIM JESSIE Timothy LaWayne RB 5'11 190 Auburn B: 3/1/1963 Opp, AL Draft: 11-305 1987 CHIB Pro: N																															
1988	WPG	7	6		2	0						18	3	93	359	3.9	26	1	13	196	15.1	54	2								
1989	WPG	12	3		0	2						66	11	160	808	5.1	67	9	18	165	9.2	32	2					1	17	17.0	17
1992	WPG	3	1		1	0													7	122	17.4	37	0								
3	Years	22	10		3	2						84	14	253	1167	4.6	67	10	38	483	12.7	54	4					1	17	17.0	17
BILLY JESSUP William Dean CB 6'1 195 Long Beach CC; Southern California B: 3/17/1929 Wray, CO Draft: 11-126 1951 SF Pro: N																															
1959	BC+	15							5	27		12	2						4	59	14.8	20	2	9	33	3.7	16				
BOB JETER Robert DeLafayette, Jr. DB-OHB 6'1 203 Iowa B: 5/9/1937 Union, SC D: 11/20/2008 Chicago, IL Draft: FS 1960 LAC; 2-17 1960 GB Pro: N																															
1960	BC	13	4		0							30	5	40	250	6.3	18	3	19	369	19.4	64	2	1	8	8.0	8	11	264	24.0	42
1961	BC	9	2									6	1	28	127	4.5	17	0	7	101	14.4	33	1	4	20	5.0	18	3	170	56.7	35
2	Years	22	6		0							36	6	68	377	5.5	18	3	26	470	18.1	64	3	5	28	5.6	18	14	434	31.0	42
DeWAYNE JETT DeWayne Edward WR 6'2 194 Hawaii B: 2/24/1958 Minneapolis, MN Draft: 9A-222 1980 DET																															

Year	Team	GP	FM	FF	FR	TK	SK	YDS	IR	YDS	PD	PTS	TD	RA	YDS	AVG	LG	TD	REC	YDS	AVG	LG	TD	PR	YDS	AVG	LG	KOR	YDS	AVG	LG
1984	HAM	6												3	-25	-8.3	1	0	16	149	9.3	13	0					1	0	0.0	0
BOB JEWETT Robert Gary OE 6'2 198 Michigan State B: 11/14/1934 Mason, MI Draft: 5-53 1958 CHIB Pro: N																															
1961	TOR	7										6	1						23	337	14.7	37	1								
1962	TOR	2																	2	19	9.5	11	0								
2	Years	9										6	1						25	356	14.2	37	1								
JASON JIMENEZ Jason OT 6'7 310 Southern Mississippi B: 5/1/1980 New York, NY Pro: E																															
2006	BC	18				0																									
2007	BC	18				0																									
2008	BC*	18				2																									
2009	BC	17				0																									
2010	HAM	9				0																									
2011	HAM	14				0																									
6	Years	94				2																									
STEVE JOACHIM William Steven QB 6'3 215 Penn State; Temple B: 3/27/1952 Newton Square, PA Draft: 32-381 1974 MEM-WFL; 7B-160 1975 BAL Pro: N																															
1975	TOR	5												8	36	4.5	15	0													
LEON JOE Leon Maurice LB 6'1 231 Maryland B: 10/26/1981 Xenia, OH Draft: 4B-112 2004 CHIB Pro: N																															
2009	MTL	1				0																									
2010	TOR	2				0																									
2	Years	3				0																									
GREG JOELSON Greg Gordon DT-DE 6'3 270 Willamette; Arizona State B: 8/22/1966 Roseburg, OR Pro: N																															
1990	BC	7	0		1	18	2.0																								
1993	SAC	11	0		2	13	3.0	19.0				6	1																		
1994	SAC	16	0		1	28	1.0	6.0			1																				
3	Years	34	0		4	59	6.0	25.0			1	6	1																		
TOM JOHANSEN Tom P-K 6'1 185 Colorado Mines B: 5/10/1944 Denmark																															
1969	TOR	6										32	0																		
AL JOHNS Alan DT-DE 6'4 242 Saskatoon Hilltops Jrs.; Pacific B: 3/11/1956 Viscount, SK Draft: TE 1979 SAS																															
1980	SAS	16	0		1																										
1981	SAS	16	0		1		2.0		1	4																					
1982	SAS	16					1.5																								
1983	SAS	16					3.5																								
1984	SAS	12	0		1		3.0																								
1985	SAS	11	0		1		1.0																								
1986	SAS	18	0		1		2.0																								
1987	SAS	16				11																									
8	Years	121	0		5	11	13.0		1	4																					
FREEMAN JOHNS Freeman, III WR 6'1 175 Southern Methodist B: 12/20/1953 Waco, TX Draft: 10-288 1976 LARM Pro: N																															
1978	SAS	5	1		0							18	3						22	317	14.4	36	3					0	10		10
1979	SAS	5										6	1						13	213	16.4	49	1								
2	Years	10	1		0							24	4						35	530	15.1	49	4					0	10		10
TONY JOHNS Tony RB 6'0 223 Henderson State B: 8/1/1960 Kingston, Jamaica Draft: 1-4 1985 MTL																															
1985	MTL	16	0		1							24	4	50	194	3.9	17	4	13	123	9.5	19	0								
1986	MTL	16	0		3							36	6	87	386	4.4	30	2	23	127	5.5	18	4								
1987	TOR	17	0		4	3						30	5	48	171	3.6	14	4	23	156	6.8	25	1					1	9	9.0	9
1988	WPG	15	2		3	1						24	4	88	294	3.3	24	4	21	229	10.9	26	0								
4	Years	64	2		11	4						114	19	273	1045	3.8	30	14	80	635	7.9	26	5					1	9	9.0	9
AHMANI JOHNSON Ahmani T. DL 6'3 245 Idaho; Oregon State B: 1/23/1973																															
1996	BC	2				2																									
ALBERT JOHNSON Albert Alphonso, III WR 5'9 190 Southern Methodist B: 11/11/1977 Houston, TX Pro: EN																															
1999	SAS	3				0								1	6	6.0	6	0	2	22	11.0	13	0	1	11	11.0	11	9	182	20.2	43
2000	WPG*	17	2	0	0	2						30	5	3	16	5.3	7	0	50	778	15.6	73	3	79	664	8.4	59	61	1506	24.7	96
2006	WPG*	17	4	0	1	1													6	51	8.5	13	0	85	810	9.5	41	50	1000	20.0	62
2007	WPG	15	2	0	1	4													5	49	9.8	25	0	69	448	6.5	27	39	776	19.9	37
4	Years	52	8	0	2	7						30	5	4	22	5.5	7	0	63	900	14.3	73	3	234	1933	8.3	59	159	3464	21.8	96
ALONDRA JOHNSON Alondra LB 5'11 225 El Camino JC; West Texas A&M B: 7/22/1965 Gardena, CA																															
1989	BC	18	0		1	115			2	10		2	0																		
1990	BC	14				62	3.0		1	82																					
1991	CAL+	16	1		4	94			4	127		12	2																		
1992	CAL+	18	0		2	105	5.0	45.0																							
1993	CAL	18	0		1	93	6.0	53.0				6	1																		
1994	CAL	18	0		2	90	4.0	29.0	1	27	8																				
1995	CAL*	18	0		1	75	7.0	66.0	1	12	7	6	1																		
1996	CAL	18	1		1	85	2.0	15.0	4	57	5																				
1997	CAL+	15	1	1	0	71	1.0	5.0	1	37	2													1	0	0.0	0				
1998	CAL*	18	0	1	0	87	3.0	29.0	1	7	5																				
1999	CAL	13	0	1	0	52	3.0	18.0			2																				
2000	CAL*	18	0	3	0	57	3.0	17.0			2																				
2001	CAL	18	0	0	3	78	3.0	14.0	1	2	1																	1	0	0.0	0
2002	CAL	18	0	2	0	82	6.0	42.0	1	6	1																				
2003	CAL	8	0	0	1	19					3																	1	8	8.0	8
2004	SAS	3				4					1																				
16	Years	249	3	8	16	1254	46.0	333.0	17	367	37	26	4											1	0	0.0	0	2	8	4.0	8
ANDRE JOHNSON Andre R. DB 5'10 180 Fisk B: 8/27/1952 Memphis, TN Pro: W																															
1977	TOR	2																													
1977	CAL	1	1		0																			4	40	10.0	20	2	42	21.0	25
1977	Year	3	1		0																			4	40	10.0	20	2	42	21.0	25
ART JOHNSON Arthur L. DH-CB 6'1 185 Michigan State B: 1938																															
1961	TOR	13							7	55		12	2	8	45	5.6	16	0	1	24	24.0	13	1	4	25	6.3	10	16	436	27.3	54
1962	TOR	14							5	60														4	13	3.3	7	12	233	19.4	37
1963	TOR	5												18	49	2.7	11	0	5	66	13.2	43	0					2	54	27.0	33
1963	CAL	2																										3	64	21.3	22
1963	Year	7												18	49	2.7	11	0	5	66	13.2	43	0					5	118	23.6	33
1964	CAL	16	0		1				1	41														2	5	2.5	5	1	2	2.0	2
1965	CAL	6																										1	20	20.0	20
1966	EDM	4																													
6	Years	58	0		1				13	156		12	2	26	94	3.6	16	0	6	90	15.0	43	1	10	43	4.3	10	35	809	23.1	54
BELTON JOHNSON Belton OT 6'6 303 Mississippi B: 7/23/1980 Coffeeville, MS																															
2006	WPG	1				0																									
2007	SAS	1				0																									
2008	SAS	9				0																									
2009	SAS	1				0																									
2010	HAM	5				0																									
2011	HAM	12				1																									
6	Years	29				1																									
BETHEL JOHNSON Bethel, Jr. WR 5'11 200 Texas A&M B: 2/11/1979 Dallas, TX Draft: 2B-45 2003 NE Pro: N																															
2008	TOR	7	1	0	0	0								1	0	0.0	0	0	16	189	11.8	37	0	1	2	2.0	2	5	109	21.8	28
BILL JOHNSON Bill C-T 6'4 240 Coalinga JC; Arizona State; Northeastern State B: 1938																															
1961	CAL	2																													
1963	OTT	14																													
1964	OTT	14																													
3	Years	30																													
BILL JOHNSON William James E 6'2 204 Florida A&M B: 8/11/1938																															

Year	Team	GP	FM	FF	FR	TK	SK	YDS	IR	YDS	PD	PTS	TD	RA	YDS	AVG	LG	TD	REC	YDS	AVG	LG	TD	PR	YDS	AVG	LG	KOR	YDS	AVG	LG
1965	TOR	1																													
BILLY JOHNSON William Arthur (White Shoes) WR 5'9 170 Widener B: 1/27/1952 Boothwyn, PA Draft: 15-365 1974 HOU; 15-177 1974 HAW-WFL Pro: N																															
1981	MTL	16	3		1							30	5	1	-9	-9.0	-9	0	65	1060	16.3	54	5	59	597	10.1	92				
BOB JOHNSON Robert OE 6'2 208 Michigan B: 1939 Draft: 22- 1961 BOS; 15-199 1961 WAS																															
1961	OTT	1																													
BOBBY JOHNSON Bob OE 6'4 203 Wisconsin B: 1941 Draft: 8B-108 1964 STL																															
1967	MTL	1																													
BOBBY JOHNSON Robert Lee RB 6'1 191 Monterey Peninsula JC; San Jose State B: 9/30/1962 Monterey, CA Draft: 11-285 1984 KC; TD 1984 OAK-USFL																															
1986	SAS*	13	4		0							78	13	182	869	4.8	36	12	43	373	8.7	29	1								
BRAD JOHNSON Brad FB 5'11 205 Georgia B: 1946																															
1969	BC	4												6	16	2.7	5	0	3	19	6.3	10	0								
BRENT JOHNSON Brent Kenneth DE-DT 6'3 265 Ohio State B: 12/7/1976 Kingston, ON Draft: 3-20 2000 BC																															
2001	BC	6				2																									
2002	BC	18	0	0	1	29	2.0	4.0																							
2003	BC	18	0	2	1	17	3.0	23.0	1	6	2																				
2004	BC+	18	0	3	1	39	10.0	59.0			5																				
2005	BC*	18	0	2	5	18	17.0	103.0			3																	1	0	0.0	0
2006	BC*	18	0	0	3	23	16.0	92.0	2	46	5	12	2						2	20	10.0	16	2								
2007	BC	18	0	4	4	34	12.0	40.0			4	6	1																		
2008	BC*	18	0	2	2	29	10.0	53.0	1	20	0																				
2009	BC	18	0	1	0	39	6.0	16.0			2																				
2010	BC+	18	0	3	0	29	7.0	53.0			2																				
2011	BC	17				18	6.0	45.0																							
11	Years	185	0	17	17	277	89.0	488.0	4	72	23	18	3						2	20	10.0	16	2					1	0	0.0	0
BRET JOHNSON Bret E. QB 6'0 200 Michigan State B: 2/6/1970 Newport Beach, CA																															
1993	TOR	18				0								2	25	12.5	14	0													
CARL JOHNSON Carl E																															
1946	WPG	1																													
CARLTON JOHNSON Carlton Elihjah CB 6'1 180 Nevada-Las Vegas B: 10/13/1969 Las Vegas, NV																															
1994	SHR	10	0		1	31					4																				
1995	SHR	7				25			1	17	2																				
2	Years	17	0		1	56			1	17	6																				
CEDRIC JOHNSON Cedric Romain WR 5'7 153 Texas-El Paso B: 10/7/1974 Houston, TX																															
1998	SAS	5				0								1	5	5.0	5	0	4	45	11.3	15	0	16	112	7.0	24	8	135	16.9	40
CHARLES JOHNSON Charles Adrian DB 5'11 181 Grambling State B: 5/5/1956 Mansfield, LA Draft: 4B-101 1979 ATL Pro: N																															
1982	OTT	6							4	30																					
1983	OTT	11							1	0																					
1984	OTT	14					1.0		2	40		6	1																		
3	Years	31					1.0		7	70		6	1																		
CHARLIE JOHNSON Charles OG 6'2 250 Villanova B: 1941 Draft: 17-131 1963 NYJ; 16-223 1963 DET																															
1965	WPG	1																													
CHRIS JOHNSON Christopher T'Maul S 6'0 205 San Diego State B: 8/7/1971 Dallas, TX Pro: N																															
1995	BAL	4				4			3	15	0																				
CURTIS JOHNSON Curtis LB 5'11 205 Texas A&M-Kingsville B: 6/7/1967																															
1991	CAL	3				16			1	12																					
DAMIAN JOHNSON Damian DB 6'1 208 Alabama State B: 7/18/1976 Vicksburg, MS																															
2001	TOR	2				9																									
DAN JOHNSON Dan HB 5'10 198 Lakeshore Flyers; Royal Military College Ints.																															
1953	MTL	1																													
DENNIS JOHNSON Dennis Leroy DT-DE 6'4 261 Delaware B: 10/22/1951 Passaic, NJ D: 3/15/1996 Draft: 13-337 1973 WAS Pro: N																															
1979	TOR	1																													
1980	TOR	2																													
2	Years	3																													
DICK JOHNSON Richard John OE-DE 6'4 220 Minnesota B: 1939 Pro: N																															
1960	BC	6																	1	18	18.0	18	0								
1961	BC	15			2							24	4						33	645	19.5	68	4					4	64	16.0	38
2	Years	21	0		2							24	4						34	663	19.5	68	4					4	64	16.0	38
D.J. JOHNSON Darrien Jermaine CB 5'11 215 Iowa B: 5/3/1980 Chicago, IL Pro: N																															
2003	MTL	14	0	1	2	18					1																				
2004	MTL	7				8	1.0	0.0	2	24	2																				
2	Years	21	0	1	2	26	1.0	0.0	2	24	3																				
DON JOHNSON Don G																															
1947	CAL	5																													
DONNELL JOHNSON Donnell Z. OL 6'7 310 Johnson C. Smith B: 12/24/1969 Las Vegas, NV Pro: N																															
1994	SHR	12				2																									
1995	SHR	18				0																									
2	Years	30				2																									
DUANE JOHNSON Duane CB 6'0 173 Johnson C. Smith B: 2/19/1971 New York, NY																															
1994	LV	1																													
ED JOHNSON Edward C. DT 6'3 258 Prairie View A&M B: 11/11/1944 Kaufman, TX																															
1967	TOR	1																													
EDDIE JOHNSON Eddie Lynn P-K 6'3 236 Orange Coast JC; Idaho State B: 3/2/1981 Costa Mesa, CA Draft: 6A-180 2003 MIN Pro: N																															
2009	TOR	2	1	0	0	1						7	0																		
2010	SAS	15	1	0	0	3						22	0											1	-8	-8.0	-8				
2011	SAS	6				1						46	0																		
3	Years	23	2	0	0	5						75	0											1	-8	-8.0	-8				
ELBERT JOHNSON Elbert OE 6'3 210 Texas Tech B: 1926 Draft: 27-343 1950 DET																															
1952	SAS	2										5	1						5	94	18.8	55	1								
ERIC JOHNSON Eric DL 6'2 280 Pittsburgh; Illinois State B: 2/4/1974 Chicago, IL Pro: X																															
1999	EDM	17				14	1.0	8.0																							
ERIC JOHNSON Eric Bernard DE 6'5 255 Stephen F. Austin State B: 3/11/1970 Nacogdoches, TX																															
1993	CAL	18				23	6.0	32.0																							
ERIC JOHNSON Eric LB-S 6'4 217 Holmes CC; Idaho State B: 6/28/1972 Gooding, MS Pro: X																															
1997	TOR	6	0	0	1	16																									
1998	TOR	18				26	2.0	21.0																							
1999	WPG	15				69	3.0	18.0			2																				
3	Years	39	0	0	1	111	5.0	39.0			2																				
GLENN JOHNSON Glenn Murry T 6'4 263 Arizona State B: 6/28/1922 Mesa, AZ D: 10/13/2001 Kirkland, WA Draft: 10-80 1948 LARM Pro: AN																															
1950	WPG+	11																													
GREG JOHNSON Gregory Devon DE 6'4 250 Florida State B: 12/3/1953 Leesburg, FL Draft: 5-135 1976 PHI Pro: N																															
1978	WPG	8																													
1979	WPG	2	0		1																										
2	Years	10	0		1																										
HERB JOHNSON Herbert Lorch HB-FW 5'10 172 Army; Washington B: 7/10/1928 Pro: N																															
1953	SAS	14							4	15		35	7	96	408	4.3		3	29	380	13.1		2	72	634	8.8	109	25	538	21.5	
HOLBERT JOHNSON Holbert Dwayne CB 5'9 180 Los Angeles Valley JC; New Mexico State B: 7/14/1960 Los Angeles, CA Pro: N																															
1984	WPG	3																													
JAMALL JOHNSON Jamall LB 6'1 210 Northwestern State (Louisiana) B: 10/12/1982 Norco, LA																															
2005	BC	6				7																									
2006	BC	7	0	0	1	12					1	6	1																		
2007	BC	12	0	0	1	44	1.0	10.0			1	6	1																		
2008	BC	17	0	1	0	59	5.0	51.0	1	59	0	6	1																		

Year	Team	GP	FM	FF	FR	TK	SK	YDS	IR	YDS	PD	PTS	TD	RA	YDS	AVG	LG	TD	REC	YDS	AVG	LG	TD	PR	YDS	AVG	LG	KOR	YDS	AVG	LG
2009	HAM*	17	0	2	0	117	2.0	7.0			1																				
2010	HAM	18	0	3	1	111	5.0	30.0	1	23	1																				
2011	HAM+	15	0	2	0	86	6.0	44.0			2													1	-8	-8.0	-8				
7	Years	92	0	8	3	436	19.0	142.0	2	82	6	18	3											1	-8	-8.0	-8				
JAMES JOHNSON James CB 5'7 180 West Los Angeles JC; Arkansas State B: 5/5/1980 Los Angeles, CA																															
2006	SAS	13	0	1	0	40			1	0	4													1	5	5.0	5				
2007	SAS+	16	0	2	2	52			5	121	12													24	179	7.5	15	5	118	23.6	65
2008	SAS	16	2	0	2	42			3	60	9													21	154	7.3	16	10	247	24.7	41
2009	WPG	7				0																									
4	Years	52	2	3	4	134			9	181	25													46	338	7.3	16	15	365	24.3	65
JASON JOHNSON Jason Ryan QB 6'2 205 Arizona B: 12/17/1979 Tacoma, WA																															
2004	EDM	18				0								1	9	9.0	9	0													
2005	EDM	18				0																									
2006	EDM	18	1	0	0	0								4	32	8.0	10	0													
3	Years	54	1	0	0	0								5	41	8.2	10	0													
JEFF JOHNSON Jeff FB 5'10 215 Cornell B: 3/7/1964 Burlington, ON Draft: 3-19 1987 WPG																															
1987	HAM	8	0		1	1								38	138	3.6	13	0	11	69	6.3	21	0					1	18	18.0	18
1988	CAL	7				0																						1	10	10.0	10
2	Years	15	0		1	1								38	138	3.6	13	0	11	69	6.3	21	0					2	28	14.0	18
JEFF JOHNSON Jeff RB-FB 5'8 205 York B: 2/28/1977 Toronto, ON																															
2000	HAM	18				4								6	23	3.8	9	0										10	190	19.0	28
2001	HAM	18	3	0	2	15						18	3	41	140	3.4	17	3	4	49	12.3	16	0					14	286	20.4	39
2002	TOR	17	1	1	1	9								11	30	2.7	12	0										6	106	17.7	26
2003	TOR	18				14								9	26	2.9	8	0	6	42	7.0	16	0					3	24	8.0	14
2004	TOR	18	0	1	0	19								9	41	4.6	8	0	5	36	7.2	12	0					1	11	11.0	11
2005	TOR	18				13						18	3	21	170	8.1	38	0	15	300	20.0	59	3					1	13	13.0	13
2006	TOR	17	5	0	3	4						18	3	54	227	4.2	33	2	36	264	7.3	18	1								
2007	TOR	11				8						12	2	14	36	2.6	6	1	8	96	12.0	30	1								
2008	TOR	18	2	0	0	7						6	1	8	31	3.9	8	1	11	46	4.2	12	0								
2009	TOR	15				5						18	3	15	52	3.5	16	1	14	80	5.7	16	2								
2010	TOR	17				9						18	3	26	141	5.4	19	2	15	83	5.5	13	1					2	17	8.5	9
2011	TOR	18	0	0	1	8						18	3	11	73	6.6	21	1	12	82	6.8	21	2					2	17	8.5	10
12		203	11	2	7	115						126	21	225	990	4.4	38	11	126	1078	8.6	59	10					39	664	17.0	39
J.J. JOHNSON J.J. LB 6'2 243 Kansas B: 5/25/1976 Los Angeles, CA																															
2001	WPG	3				2																									
JOE JOHNSON Joseph Pernell WR 5'9 165 Notre Dame B: 12/21/1962 Washington, DC Pro: EN																															
1993	SAC	7				0						36	6	1	16	16.0	16	0	22	421	19.1	39	5	22	205	9.3	63	1	17	17.0	17
1994	TOR	2				2					2																				
2	Years	9				2					2	36	6	1	16	16.0	16	0	22	421	19.1	39	5	22	205	9.3	63	1	17	17.0	17
JOHN HENRY JOHNSON John Henry HB 6'2 210 St. Mary's (California); Arizona State B: 11/24/1929 Waterproof, LA D: 6/3/2011 Tracy, CA Draft: 2-18 1953 PIT Pro: N																															
1953	CAL	15							5	20		45	9	107	648	6.1	51	5	33	365	11.1	40	3	47	386	8.2	25	20	578	28.9	104
JOHNNY JOHNSON Johnny QB 6'1 202 Illinois B: 1/21/1973																															
1997	HAM	1				0																									
JOVON JOHNSON Jovon CB-DH-S 5'9 177 Iowa B: 11/2/1983 Erie, PA Pro: N																															
2007	SAS	2				9					2																	1	7	7.0	7
2008	WPG	16	0	2	3	60			3	130	5	12	2											15	152	10.1	23	7	148	21.1	28
2009	WPG*	18	3	0	0	76			6	163	10	18	3											65	593	9.1	79	44	1049	23.8	54
2010	WPG+	18	2	2	0	62			4	59	7	18	3											90	957	10.6	83	5	54	10.8	21
2011	WPG*	18	0	0	1	56			8	104	5	12	2											67	594	8.9	51				
5	Years	72	5	4	4	263			21	456	29	60	10											237	2296	9.7	83	57	1258	22.1	54
JUAN JOHNSON Manwuan RB 6'1 215 Utah B: 1/28/1976 Columbus, GA Pro: EX																															
1998	BC+	15	2	0	0	3						54	9	156	973	6.2	54	8	33	235	7.1	26	1								
1999	BC	6				0								28	145	5.2	21	0	3	18	6.0	8	0								
2002	TOR	1				5								12	45	3.8	9	0										4	36	9.0	19
3	Years	22	2	0	0	8						54	9	196	1163	5.9	54	8	36	253	7.0	26	1					4	36	9.0	19
KELLEY JOHNSON Kelley Antonio WR 5'8 168 Los Angeles Valley JC; Colorado B: 6/3/1962 Carlsbad, NM Draft: TD 1985 DEN-USFL Pro: NU																															
1986	OTT	4										6	1	1	-8	-8.0	-8	0	5	158	31.6	45	1	13	29	2.2	10	1	10	10.0	10
KEN JOHNSON Kenneth Earl QB 6'2 205 Colorado B: 1/5/1951 Lansing, MI Draft: 34-403 1974 POR-WFL Pro: UW																															
1978	CAL	8												15	85	5.7	12	0													
1979	CAL	16	8		0									30	22	0.7	13	0													
1980	CAL	16	5		1							6	1	41	178	4.3	31	1													
1981	CAL	12	5		1									26	72	2.8	11	0													
1981	MTL	3	1		1									7	23	3.3	18	0													
1981	Year	15	6		2									33	95	2.9	18	0													
1982	MTL	2												5	9	1.8	7	0													
5	Years	54	19		3							6	1	124	389	3.1	31	1													
KERRY JOHNSON Kerry Cortez SB-WR 6'3 200 Mississippi B: 3/6/1982 Oxford, MS																															
2007	WPG	1				0													4	49	12.3	16	0								
2008	WPG	6				1													22	166	7.5	22	0								
2	Years	7				1													26	215	8.3	22	0								
KEVIN JOHNSON Kevin Nevereon LB 6'0 240 Northeastern Oklahoma A&M JC; Ohio State B: 12/27/1973 Winder, GA																															
1999	CAL	18	0	2	2	73	3.0	18.0	1	70	2																				
2000	CAL	7	0	1	0	15					1																	1	20	20.0	20
2001	CAL	3				11																									
2002	MTL+	18	0	2	3	72	5.0	21.0	2	37	2	6	1																		
2003	MTL+	18	0	2	3	82	4.0	44.0	1	25	3																				
2004	MTL+	18	1	1	4	71	4.0	24.0	2	38	4	6	1																		
2005	MTL	14	1	0	4	57	2.0	6.0			2																				
7	Years	96	2	8	16	381	18.0	113.0	6	170	14	12	2															1	20	20.0	20
KIERRIE JOHNSON Kierrie Terrell WR-SB 5'10 175 Blinn JC; Houston B: 8/4/1988 Houston, TX																															
2011	BC	8				1								7	53	7.6	16	0	20	235	11.8	29	0	10	73	7.3	26	4	82	20.5	34
LANCE JOHNSON Lance C 6'2 270 Notre Dame B: 11/27/1970																															
1994	LV	1																													
LEE JOHNSON Lee DT 6'1 275 Missouri B: 6/9/1967 Florissant, MO																															
1992	BC	16	0		1	37	3.0					6	1																		
1994	SHR	5																													
2	Years	21	0		1	37	3.0					6	1																		
LEONARD JOHNSON Leonard Taft DT 6'6 255 Georgia Military JC* B: 5/17/1963 Savannah, GA																															
1991	TOR	8	0		1	17	3.0																								
1992	TOR	5				6	2.0	18.0																							
1993	EDM	11	0		1	9	3.0	23.0																							
1994	OTT	7				14	1.0	1.0			1																				
1994	LV	3	0		2	8	1.0	5.0																							
1994	Year	10	0		2	22	2.0	6.0			1																				
1995	WPG	7	0		2	15					3																				
5	Years	38	0		6	69	10.0	47.0			4																				
LeROY JOHNSON LeRoy, Jr. LB 6'0 235 Navarro JC; Texas A&M-Commerce B: 9/26/1951 Corsicana, TX																															
1974	BC	3																													
MALCOLM JOHNSON Malcolm Alexander WR 6'5 215 Notre Dame B: 8/27/1977 Washington, DC Draft: 5B-166 1999 PIT Pro: N																															
2002	OTT	5				5													16	185	11.6	31	0								
MARCKARTHUR JOHNSON Marckarthur DE 6'3 255 Northwest Oklahoma State B: 7/5/1970 Chicago, IL																															
1995	MEM	3				1																									

Year	Team	GP	FM	FF	FR	TK	SK	YDS	IR	YDS	PD	PTS	TD	RA	YDS	AVG	LG	TD	REC	YDS	AVG	LG	TD	PR	YDS	AVG	LG	KOR	YDS	AVG	LG
1996	WPG	4				6	2.0	6.0																							
2	Years	7				7	2.0	6.0																							
MERRILL JOHNSON Merrill, Jr. LB 6'0 206 Auburn B: 11/22/1985																															
2010	WPG	11	0	0	1	19					1																				
2011	WPG	17	0	0	1	44	1.0	9.0			1																				
2	Years	28	0	0	2	63	1.0	9.0			2																				
MIKE JOHNSON Michael LB 6'0 255 North Alabama B: 9/8/1986 Panama City, FL																															
2010	BC	2				4																									
MIKE JOHNSON Michael J. QB 6'1 185 Arizona State; Mesa CC; Akron B: 5/2/1967 Los Angeles, CA Pro: E																															
1992	BC	15	3		1	0						2	0	29	176	6.1	20	0													
1994	SHR	8	5		0	1								18	81	4.5	21	0													
1995	SHR	6				0								4	14	3.5	8	0													
3	Years	29	8		1	1						2	0	51	271	5.3	21	0													
NATE JOHNSON Nathaniel WR 5'11 192 Mott CC; Hillsdale B: 5/12/1957 St. Petersburg, FL Draft: 7-193 1980 PIT Pro: N																															
1982	WPG	13	1		1				1	-8		24	4						24	368	15.3	46	4	17	171	10.1	40	22	587	26.7	56
1983	WPG	7										12	2						4	83	20.8	29	2	13	158	12.2	34	9	194	21.6	41
1983	SAS	4	2		0							6	1						15	282	18.8	56	1					7	265	37.9	11
1983	Year	11	2		0							18	3						19	365	19.2	56	3	13	158	12.2	34	16	459	28.7	11
1984	CAL	7	2		0							10	3	1	11	11.0	11	0	21	270	12.0	41	3	27	211	7.8	52	11	194	17.6	34
3	Years	27	5		1				1	-8		60	10	1	11	11.0	11	0	64	1003	15.7	56	10	57	540	9.5	52	49	1240	25.3	56
PAT JOHNSON Patrick Jevon WR 5'10 186 Oregon B: 8/10/1976 Gainesville, GA Draft: 2-42 1998 BAL Pro: N																															
2007	TOR	6				0						6	1	1	4	4.0	4	0	12	173	14.4	36	1								
PAUL JOHNSON Paul DB 6'0 188 Penn State B: 12/6/1947 Syracuse, NY Draft: 8-200 1970 WAS																															
1970	HAM	9	0		2				4	33																		1	24	24.0	24
1971	HAM	4	0		1																										
2	Years	13	0		3				4	33																		1	24	24.0	24
REGGIE JOHNSON Reggie A. DE 6'4 237 Arizona B: 12/11/1967 Chicago, IL Draft: 8-206 1991 MIN																															
1991	BC	6				9	2.0																								
1992	BC	4	0		1	6																									
2	Years	10	0		1	15	2.0																								
RIALL JOHNSON Riall S. LB-DE 6'3 243 Stanford B: 4/20/1978 White Rock, BC Draft: 6-168 2001 CIN Pro: EN																															
2005	TOR	17	0	0	1	13	2.0	19.0			1																				
2006	TOR	14	0	3	1	15	4.0	37.0																							
2007	TOR	14	0	1	0	31	10.0	63.0			2																				
2008	TOR	15	0	1	0	36	4.0	13.0																							
2009	WPG	7				6													1	8	8.0	8	0								
2009	MTL	3	1	0	0	2																						1	3	3.0	3
2009	Year	10	1	0	0	8													1	8	8.0	8	0					1	3	3.0	3
5	Years	67	1	5	2	103	20.0	132.0			3								1	8	8.0	8	0					1	3	3.0	3
RICH JOHNSON Richard Lavon RB 6'1 210 Illinois B: 5/13/1947 Canton, IL Draft: 3B-78 1969 HOU Pro: N																															
1970	WPG	1												4	12	3.0	6	0													
RICK JOHNSON Richard Allen QB 6'2 189 Southern Illinois B: 1/21/1961 Wheaton, IL Pro: U																															
1985	CAL	11	3		0									13	64	4.9	14	0													
1986	CAL*	18	1		1							24	4	38	200	5.3	26	4													
1987	CAL	10	6		0	1						18	3	25	182	7.3	21	3													
1988	CAL	3				0								2	8	4.0	6	0													
1989	TOR	6	5		1	0								13	42	3.2	21	0													
5	Years	48	15		2	1						42	7	91	496	5.5	26	7													
ROB JOHNSON Robert Allen WR 6'3 205 Northwestern; Western Illinois B: 4/20/1979																															
2002	CAL	14	1	0	1	3						12	2	2	5	2.5	5	0	34	595	17.5	60	2								
ROGER JOHNSON Roger OE 6'4 210 Oregon State B: 1940 Draft: 16-222 1962 NYG																															
1962	SAS	14	1																11	125	11.4	15	0					5	41	8.2	13
RON JOHNSON Ronald J. WR 6'3 188 Monterey Peninsula JC; Long Beach State B: 9/21/1958 Monterey, CA Draft: 7A-170 1981 SEA Pro: NU																															
1982	HAM	11	1		0							30	5	1	-3	-3.0	-3	0	37	505	13.6	55	5								
1983	HAM	16	1		0							36	6						53	914	17.2	86	6								
1984	HAM+	15										12	2						50	681	13.6	64	2								
3	Years	42	2		0							78	13	1	-3	-3.0	-3	0	140	2100	15.0	86	13								
RON JOHNSON Ronnie B. QB 6'1 190 Oklahoma State B: 1948																															
1969	WPG	2																													
1970	WPG	16	3		0							6	1	38	164	4.3	25	1													
2	Years	18	3		0							6	1	38	164	4.3	25	1													
RON JOHNSON Ron, Jr. WR 6'2 225 Minnesota B: 5/23/1980 Detroit, MI Draft: 4B-123 2002 BAL Pro: N																															
2006	CAL	4	0	1	0	3													2	66	33.0	51	0								
SAM JOHNSON Samuel Levi, III DB 6'1 195 Maryland B: 5/18/1959 Manchester, NC Draft: 6-155 1981 DET																															
1982	TOR	3	0		1		1.0		2	9																					
STAN JOHNSON Stanley WR 6'1 195 Wisconsin-LaCrosse B: 9/16/1963 Milwaukee, WI																															
1987	TOR	4				0								1	4	4.0	4	0	8	92	11.5	19	0								
STEVE JOHNSON Steve DB 5'9 187 Mississippi State B: 11/14/1961																															
1983	SAS	11	0		3																							3	79	26.3	36
1984	SAS	16	0		1		3.0		6	62		6	1																		
1985	TOR	8							1	0																					
3	Years	35	0		4		3.0		7	62		6	1															3	79	26.3	36
TEYO JOHNSON Teyo D. SB-FB 6'6 257 Stanford B: 11/29/1981 White Rock, BC Draft: 2-63 2003 OAK Pro: ENU																															
2008	CAL	12	0	0	1	1						12	2						15	248	16.5	52	2					1	0	0.0	0
2009	CAL	16				0						12	2						18	172	9.6	29	2					1	1	1.0	1
2	Years	28	0	0	1	1						24	4						33	420	12.7	52	4					2	1	0.5	1
TIM JOHNSON Tim Maurice LB 6'0 243 East Mississippi JC; Youngstown State B: 2/7/1978 Birmingham, AL Pro: EN																															
2009	CAL	11	0	1	0	60	1.0	8.0			1																				
TOM JOHNSON Tom DT 6'2 286 Mississippi Gulf Coast CC; Southern Mississippi B: 8/30/1984 Moss Point, MS Pro: EN																															
2009	CAL	6				13	3.0	18.0			2																				
2010	CAL+	17	0	0	1	43	4.0	17.0			1																				
2	Years	23	0	0	1	56	7.0	35.0			3																				
TROY JOHNSON Troy Dwan WR 6'1 175 Southeastern Louisiana; Southern University B: 10/20/1962 New Orleans, LA Pro: NU																															
1991	WPG	4	1		0	1						6	1						6	133	22.2	40	0	11	146	13.3	62	7	152	21.7	33
TRUMAINE JOHNSON Trumaine WR 6'1 196 Grambling State B: 1/16/1960 Bogaloosa, LA Draft: 6-141 1983 SD; 1B-11 1983 CHI-USFL Pro: NU																															
1990	TOR	4	1		0	0						6	1	2	-10	-5.0	-15	0	13	158	12.2	28	1								
1991	TOR	5				0						6	1						12	206	17.2	34	1								
2	Years	9	1		0	0						12	2	2	-10	-5.0	-15	0	25	364	14.6	34	2								
URIEL JOHNSON Uriel WR 5'11 175 Prairie View A&M B: 12/23/1945 Houston, TX Draft: 16-413 1969 KC																															
1970	CAL	6										6	1						11	232	21.1	52	1					3	65	21.7	30
WILL JOHNSON William Alexander DE 6'4 245 Louisiana-Monroe B: 12/4/1964 Monroe, LA Draft: 5B-138 1987 CHIB Pro: N																															
1989	CAL	9	0		1	22	9.0																								
1990	CAL+	17	0		2	40	16.0		1	18																					
1991	CAL*	18	0		3	59	15.0																								
1992	CAL*	17				45	10.0	47.0																							
1993	CAL*	18				27	12.0	50.0																				1	0	0.0	0
1994	CAL*	18	0		1	33	17.0	126.0			2																				
1995	CAL*	16				25	11.0	63.0			7																				
1996	CAL	16	0		1	37	9.0	69.0			5																				
1997	SAS	3				5					2																				
9	Years	132	0		8	293	99.0	355.0	1	18	16																	1	0	0.0	0
DAN JOHNSTON Dan SB-WR 6'0 195 Regina Rams Jrs. B: 4/11/1966 Regina, SK																															

Year	Team	GP	FM	FF	FR	TK	SK	YDS	IR	YDS	PD	PTS	TD	RA	YDS	AVG	LG	TD	REC	YDS	AVG	LG	TD	PR	YDS	AVG	LG	KOR	YDS	AVG	LG
1989	OTT	10				1						6	1						10	119	11.9	16	1								
1990	OTT	16				4						12	2						3	66	22.0	33	2					1	5	5.0	5
1991	OTT	7				8													1	13	13.0	13	0								
3	Years	33				13						18	3						14	198	14.1	33	3					1	5	5.0	5
DOUG JOHNSTON Douglas C 6'0 182 B: 2/7/1928																															
1949	WPG	11																													
HARRY JOHNSTON Harry QB none																															
1947	WPG	1																													
CHRIS JOHNSTONE Chris RB 6'3 215 Renfrew Trojans Jrs.; Bakersfield JC B: 12/12/1963 Kingston, Jamaica																															
1986	EDM	17	2		0							24	4	71	200	2.8	28	3	11	68	6.2	18	1								
1987	EDM	18	1		0	0						6	1	44	212	4.8	28	1	16	162	10.1	27	0					1	0	0.0	0
1988	EDM	13	4		0	1						18	3	84	346	4.1	17	2	16	124	7.8	24	1								
1989	EDM	14				2						48	8	63	253	4.0	13	7	10	103	10.3	23	1								
1990	EDM	17	3		0	2						12	2	32	119	3.7	11	2	2	23	11.5	13	0					2	29	14.5	18
1991	EDM	7	1		0	4								1	-1	-1.0	-1	0													
1992	EDM	16	1		0	22								2	4	2.0	2	0										4	80	20.0	41
1993	WPG+	18	2		1	4						30	5	45	196	4.4	24	4	18	259	14.4	33	1								
1994	WPG	18	2		0	3						18	3	42	203	4.8	24	3	21	218	10.4	25	0					1	10	10.0	10
1995	WPG	18	2		0	1						6	1	31	146	4.7	22	0	16	112	7.0	14	1								
10	Years	156	18		2	39						162	27	415	1678	4.0	28	22	110	1069	9.7	33	5					8	119	14.9	41
KEN JOINER Kenneth WR 5'9 175 Kentucky State B: 12/16/1962 Macon, MS																															
1986	TOR	11										12	2	2	6	3.0	16	0	45	603	13.4	52	2	9	46	5.1	10	7	156	22.3	34
1987	TOR	15	2		0	5						24	4	1	3	3.0	3	0	49	781	15.9	47	4	4	6	1.5	5				
2	Years	26	2		0	5						36	6	3	9	3.0	16	0	94	1384	14.7	52	6	13	52	4.0	10	7	156	22.3	34
ROY JOKANOVICH Roy OT-DT 6'1 235 British Columbia B: 1936 AB																															
1960	TOR	13																													
1961	TOR	13																													
1962	CAL	16																													
1963	CAL	15																										1	0	0.0	0
1964	CAL	16																													
5	Years	73																										1	0	0.0	0
EVAN JOLITZ Evan C. LB 6'2 225 Xavier (Ohio); Cincinnati B: 7/26/1951 Lincoln, NE Draft: 3B-73 1974 CIN; 27-323 1974 FLA-WFL Pro: N																															
1975	CAL	6																										1	14	14.0	14
1976	CAL	2	0		1																										
2	Years	8	0		1																							1	14	14.0	14
DON JONAS Donald Walter QB 5'11 195 Penn State B: 12/3/1938 Scranton, PA Draft: 13-182 1961 PHI; 32-253(f) 1962 NYT Pro: N																															
1970	TOR	14	4		0							100	3	30	142	4.7	19	3	1	5	5.0	5	0								
1971	WPG*	16	1		0							121	4	20	80	4.0	25	4													
1972	WPG*	16										97	1	18	81	4.5	21	1													
1973	WPG	16	5		2							54	2	27	73	2.7	11	2													
1974	WPG	6	2		2							1	0	8	11	1.4	9	0						1	0	0.0	0				
1974	HAM	9										12	2	18	39	2.2	15	2													
1974	Year	15	2		2							13	2	26	50	1.9	15	2						1	0	0.0	0				
5	Years	68	12		4							385	12	121	426	3.5	25	12	1	5	5.0	5	0	1	0	0.0	0				
ANDY JONASSEN Andy DE-C-DT 6'4 240 Calgary B: 9/25/1951 Draft: 3-22 1974 BC																															
1975	BC	16	0		1																										
1976	CAL	16																													
1977	CAL	16	0		1																										
1978	CAL	14	0		2																										
1979	CAL	16	0		2																										
1980	CAL	16																													
6	Years	94	0		6																										
JONES																															
1948	WPG	1																													
ANDRE JONES Andre V. DB 6'1 200 Nevada-Las Vegas B: 7/22/1956 Los Angeles, CA																															
1981	SAS	11	0		1				3	16		6	1																		
1982	SAS	3																													
1983	SAS	4							1	4																					
1983	BC	8	0		1							6	1																		
1983	Year	12	0		1				1	4		6	1																		
1984	BC	16	0		1		3.0		5	36																		3	46	15.3	20
1985	BC	12	0		2				2	106		6	1																		
1986	BC	6					1.0		2	45																					
6	Years	52	0		5		4.0		13	207		18	3															3	46	15.3	20
ANDRE JONES Andre Fitzgerald LB 6'2 245 Notre Dame B: 5/15/1969 Washington, DC D: 6/22/2011 Roswell, GA Draft: 7-185 1991 PIT Pro: N																															
1991	WPG	2				1																									
ANDREW JONES Andrew OG 6'4 305 McMaster B: 10/29/1982 Niagara Falls, ON Draft: 4-32 2007 BC																															
2009	BC	14				1																						1	6	6.0	6
2010	BC	3				0																									
2011	BC	18				0																									
3	Years	35				1																						1	6	6.0	6
BENNIE JONES Bennie DT-DE 6'3 247 Northeast Louisiana B: 7/27/1963																															
1985	BC	5					1.0																								
1986	BC	2					1.0																								
1987	BC	4				11	3.0																								
3	Years	11				11	5.0																								
BRIAN JONES Brian LB 6'2 215 Alberta B: 1950 Draft: 7-56 1973 EDM																															
1975	EDM	1																													
CAL JONES Calvin J. T 6'1 235 Iowa B: 2/7/1933 Steubenville, OH D: 12/9/1956 Mount Slesse, BC Draft: 9-98 1956 DET																															
1956	WPG	16	0		2																										
CARLOS JONES Carlos DB 5'11 190 Miami (Florida) B: 8/31/1973 New Orleans, LA Draft: 7-211 1997 SEA Pro: E																															
2000	WPG	2				5																									
CHRIS JONES Christopher WR 6'3 203 Jackson State B: 7/17/1982																															
2009	SAS	4				2													8	56	7.0	15	0								
CHRIS JONES Chris WR 6'3 202 Mississippi State B: 6/3/1972																															
1996	HAM	1				0																									
C.J. JONES Clinton WR 5'11 192 Garden City CC; Iowa B: 9/20/1980 Boynton Beach, FL Pro: E																															
2005	MTL	2				0																		6	55	9.2	21	9	236	26.2	43
CLAUDE JONES Claude OG 6'2 290 Miami (Florida) B: 9/12/1969 Fort Lauderdale, FL																															
1993	SAC	11				0																									
1994	LV	3																													
2	Years	14				0																									
CORBY JONES Corby Warren QB 6'0 222 Missouri B: 3/8/1976 Columbia, MO																															
1999	MTL	16	1	0	0	0								7	34	4.9	12	0													
DON JONES Donald Calvin DB 6'0 183 Los Angeles Harbor JC; Southern California B: 3/28/1958 San Francisco, CA Pro: U																															
1983	OTT	6							2	51																					
EARY JONES Eary DT 6'4 260 Memphis B: 7/5/1955 Memphis, TN Draft: 4B-107 1977 LARM																															
1978	SAS	16	1		1				1	8																					
1979	HAM	6	0		1																										
2	Years	22	1		2				1	8																					
ED JONES Ed (Too Small) DB 6'0 185 Rutgers B: 6/29/1952 Long Branch, NJ Draft: 9-226 1975 DAL Pro: N																															
1976	EDM	4																										1	20	20.0	20

Year	Team	GP	FM	FF	FR	TK	SK	YDS	IR	YDS	PD	PTS	TD	RA	YDS	AVG	LG	TD	REC	YDS	AVG	LG	TD	PR	YDS	AVG	LG	KOR	YDS	AVG	LG
1977	EDM	12	0		1				3	30														12	101	8.4	26	2	38	19.0	19
1978	EDM+	16	0		1				3	25																		1	22	22.0	22
1979	EDM*	16	0		1				4	38																		1	6	6.0	6
1980	EDM*	16							10	212		18	3											1	6	6.0	6				
1981	EDM*	16	1		3		2.5		7	28																					
1982	EDM	16	0		2		4.0		1	4																					
1983	EDM	14					1.0		3	18																					
1984	BC	9							1	7																					
9	Years	119	1		8		7.5		32	362		18	3											13	107	8.2	26	5	86	17.2	22
EDGAR JONES Edgar Francis (Special Delivery) HB 5'10 193 Pittsburgh B: 5/6/1918 Scranton, PA D: 5/18/2004 Scranton, PA Draft: 19-180 1942 CHIB Pro: AN																															
1950	HAM+	12										108	13					10					3								
GARRICK JONES Garrick DaJaun OT 6'5 315 Arkansas State B: 12/2/1978 Little Rock, AR																															
2002	WPG	5				0																									
2006	WPG	3				0																									
2007	CAL	16				3																									
2008	EDM	16				0																									
4	Years	40				3																									
GENE JONES Ray Gene OE 6'0 200 Rice B: 10/18/1936 D: 1/3/2008 Houston, TX Draft: 13-153 1959 CHIB Pro: N																															
1959	HAM	3										6	1						6	180	30.0	58	1								
1960	HAM	8							1	37									1	14	14.0	14	0								
2	Years	11							1	37		6	1						7	194	27.7	58	1								
GEORGE JONES George Dee RB 5'8 205 Bakersfield JC; San Diego State B: 12/31/1973 Greenville, SC Draft: 5-154 1997 PIT Pro: N																															
2000	WPG	10	1	0	0	0						42	7	105	407	3.9	98	7	18	111	6.2	21	0								
HARRY JONES Harry G 5'9 195																															
1946	MTL	10																													
JEFF JONES Jeffrey Raymond OT 6'6 310 Texas A&M B: 5/30/1972 Killeen, TX Pro: N																															
1998	BC	7				0																									
JERMAINE JONES Jermaine DB 5'8 183 Northwestern State (Louisiana) B: 7/25/1976 Morgan City, LA Draft: 5-162 1999 NYJ Pro: N																															
2001	EDM	8	0	0	2	22			1	5	5	6	1																		
JERMESE JONES Jermese Boyd OT 6'5 337 Virginia B: 12/11/1978 Durham, NC																															
2002	BC	2				0																									
2003	WPG	7	0	0	0	0																									
2004	WPG	13	0	0	2	0						6	1	0	0		0	1													
2005	WPG	6				0																									
2006	WPG	13	0	0	1	2																									
2007	SAS	18	0	0	1	1																									
6	Years	59	0	0	4	3						6	1					1													
JERRY JONES Gerald D. LB 6'1 200 Minnesota B: 1943																															
1963	WPG	8							2	37		6	1	3	10	3.3	4	0													
1964	WPG	4																										1	8	8.0	8
2	Years	12							2	37		6	1	3	10	3.3	4	0										1	8	8.0	8
JIM JONES James Ray FB-OHB-LB 6'1 205 Washington B: 5/6/1935 D: 10/5/1982 King County, WA Draft: 3-30 1958 LARM Pro: N																															
1960	BC	13	5		2							12	2	47	182	3.9	19	0	7	168	24.0	43	1					13	276	21.2	47
1961	BC	2												8	30	3.8	5	0	1	15	15.0	15	0					4	74	18.5	25
2	Years	15	5		2							12	2	55	212	3.9	19	0	8	183	22.9	43	1					17	350	20.6	47
JIMMIE LEE JONES Jimmie Lee RB 5'10 205 East Los Angeles JC; UCLA B: 6/15/1950 Los Angeles, CA Pro: NW																															
1976	HAM	1												6	20	3.3	8	0	4	53	13.3	21	0					2	52	26.0	26
JIMMY JONES Jimmy QB 6'1 196 Southern California B: 6/23/1950																															
1973	MTL	14	2		1							24	4	43	269	6.3	31	4													
1974	MTL+	16	3		1							30	5	90	577	6.4	25	5													
1975	MTL	16	3		0							6	1	59	301	5.1	32	1	2	31	15.5	16	0								
1976	HAM	14	4		1							6	1	44	96	2.2	16	1													
1977	HAM	16	6		3							30	5	58	342	5.9	39	5													
1978	HAM	16	4		1							8	1	43	204	4.7	28	1													
1979	OTT	16	4		0							6	1	27	112	4.1	19	1													
7	Years	108	26		7							110	18	364	1901	5.2	39	18	2	31	15.5	16	0								
J.J. JONES John Eddie QB 6'1 180 Fisk B: 4/16/1952 Memphis, TN D: 7/9/2009 University Place, WA Pro: EN																															
1976	CAL	4												1	-1	-1.0	-1	0													
1977	CAL	1																													
2	Years	5												1	-1	-1.0	-1	0													
JOCK JONES Jock Stacey LB 6'2 227 Virginia Tech B: 3/13/1968 Ashland, VA Draft: 8-212 1990 CLE Pro: N																															
1995	BAL	1	0		1	0																									
JOHNNIE JONES Johnnie RB 5'10 192 Tennessee B: 6/30/1962 Covington, TN Draft: 5C-137 1985 SEA; TD 1985 MEM-USFL																															
1987	HAM	6	2		0	1						6	1	77	408	5.3	41	1	27	210	7.8	30	0	1	16	16.0	16	18	336	18.7	34
1988	HAM	6	1		0							6	1	46	204	4.4	16	1	20	152	7.6	22	0					4	64	16.0	18
2	Years	12	3		0	1						12	2	123	612	5.0	41	2	47	362	7.7	30	0	1	16	16.0	16	22	400	18.2	34
JUNE JONES June Sheldon, III QB 6'4 200 Oregon; Hawaii; Portland State B: 2/19/1953 Portland, OR Pro: N																															
1982	TOR	1																													
KENDRICK JONES Kendrick WR 6'2 190 Illinois B: 11/30/1982 St. Louis, MO																															
2006	BC	12				2						12	2						21	308	14.7	45	2								
KENDRICK JONES Kendrick WR 5'8 185 Tennessee B: 12/1/1972																															
1995	MEM	5				0						6	1						4	67	16.8	30	1	5	35	7.0	14	2	100	50.0	73
KHARI JONES Khari O. QB 5'11 195 California-Davis B: 5/16/1971 Hammond, IN Pro: E																															
1998	BC	18				1								5	13	2.6	9	0													
1999	BC	18	2	0	1	0						6	1	12	55	4.6	15	1													
2000	WPG	18	4	0	1	0						12	2	64	424	6.6	24	2													
2001	WPG*	18	10	0	0	2						12	2	60	340	5.7	43	2													
2002	WPG+	18	12	0	2	0						6	1	50	235	4.7	19	1													
2003	WPG	18	6	0	2	1						18	3	56	350	6.3	20	3	1	-8	-8.0	0	0								
2004	WPG	11	1	0	0	2								30	152	5.1	16	0													
2004	CAL	3	4	0	2	0								8	54	6.8	13	0													
2004	Year	14	5	0	2	2								38	206	5.4	16	0													
2005	HAM	8	1	0	0	0						24	4	16	41	2.6	12	4													
8	Years	127	40	0	8	6						78	13	301	1664	5.5	43	13	1	-8	-8.0	0	0								
KITWANA JONES Kitwana Shaloyd DE-LB-DT 6'0 230 North Carolina; Hampton B: 7/7/1981 Wilmington, NC																															
2005	SAS	10				15	1.0	7.0																							
2006	SAS	18	0	1	0	31	8.0	56.0																							
2007	SAS	18	0	1	1	30	3.0	27.0				6	1																		
2008	SAS	18	0	2	4	66	5.0	50.0				12	2																		
2009	EDM	9	0	0	1	16	1.0	4.0																				1	4	4.0	4
2009	SAS	8				14																									
2009	Year	17	0	0	1	30	1.0	4.0																				1	4	4.0	4
2010	SAS	18	0	1	0	28	4.0	15.0																							
2011	MTL	17	0	2	1	25	2.0	11.0																							
7	Years	108	0	7	7	225	24.0	170.0				18	3															1	4	4.0	4
KYLE JONES Kyle LB 6'0 210 Bishop's B: 10/4/1986 Mississauga, ON																															
2009	TOR	8				8																						3	25	8.3	12
2010	TOR	1				0																									
2011	HAM	13	0	0	1	10																									
3	Years	22	0	0	1	18																						3	25	8.3	12
LaCURTIS JONES LaCurtis Burl LB 6'0 200 Baylor B: 6/23/1972 Waco, TX Draft: 4C-125 1996 MIA Pro: N																															
1998	MTL	1				2																									

Year	Team	GP	FM	FF	FR	TK	SK	YDS	IR	YDS	PD	PTS	TD	RA	YDS	AVG	LG	TD	REC	YDS	AVG	LG	TD	PR	YDS	AVG	LG	KOR	YDS	AVG	LG
LARRY JONES Larry W. RB 5'10 184 Colorado State B: 9/16/1959 Barstow, CA Draft: 10-270 1981 HOU
1983	BC	8	2		0							12	2	65	273	4.2	37	1	33	320	9.7	25	1					8	209	26.1	61
LEE JONES Lee DE 6'1 265 Nebraska B: 10/12/1964 Omaha, NE Pro: E
1990	HAM	1	0		1	1
LEROY JONES Leroy DE 6'8 261 Norfolk State B: 9/29/1950 Greenwood, MS Draft: 20-239 1974 NY-WFL; 2B-48 1975 LARM Pro: N
1974	EDM	14
1975	EDM	12
2	Years	26
LYNDELL JONES Anthony Lyndell CB 5'9 175 Columbia Basin JC; Hawaii B: 3/18/1959 Seattle, WA Pro: NU
1986	WPG	1
MARK JONES Mark LB 6'2 225 Washington B: 3/23/1968 Portland, OR
1991	BC	2				7
MARLON JONES Marlon Anthony DE 6'4 260 Central State (Ohio) B: 7/1/1964 Baltimore, MD Pro: N
1986	TOR	14	0		1		9.0		1	35
1987	TOR	10					3.0
2	Years	24	0		1		12.0	0.0	1	35
MIKE JONES Michael LB 6'2 214 Alcorn State B: 7/12/1954 Chicago, IL Pro: N
1975	SAS	3
MIKE JONES Michael DE-LB 6'4 224 Brockport State B: 8/14/1964 New York, NY Pro: N
1991	HAM	9				18	3.0
MILSON JONES Milson FB 6'0 215 North Dakota B: 8/14/1959 Linstead, Jamiaca Draft: TE 1982 WPG
1982	WPG	16										24	4	44	131	3.0	21	4	16	174	10.9	22	0					5	97	19.4	31
1983	WPG	4	1		1							6	1	34	180	5.3	69	1	2	31	15.5	16	0
1983	EDM	6	1		0							18	3	17	61	3.6	11	1	18	237	13.2	27	2
1983	Year	10	2		1							24	4	51	241	4.7	69	2	20	268	13.4	27	2
1984	EDM	16	3		1							12	2	50	331	6.6	28	1	20	250	12.5	25	1					23	460	20.0	37
1985	EDM	14	3		0							36	6	82	522	6.4	61	4	41	466	11.4	60	2					12	285	23.8	50
1986	EDM	18	2		2							18	3	94	448	4.8	40	0	55	535	9.7	32	3
1987	EDM	16	5		0	3						54	9	93	423	4.5	27	7	38	446	11.7	74	2
1988	SAS	17	4		1	0						72	12	141	730	5.2	49	11	26	253	9.7	28	1					5	107	21.4	36
1989	SAS	14	5		0	1						44	7	110	505	4.6	34	6	29	269	9.3	45	1					2	22	11.0	14
1990	SAS	18	2		0	3						72	12	136	765	5.6	41	11	40	459	11.5	33	1
1991	SAS	12	2		1	2						6	1	81	496	6.1	44	1	26	239	9.2	19	0
1992	SAS	16	7		2	3						18	3	91	338	3.7	16	1	48	514	10.7	64	2
11	Years	161	35		8	12						380	63	973	4930	5.1	69	48	359	3873	10.8	74	15					47	971	20.7	50
PHIL JONES Philip S 6'0 190 Simon Fraser B: 6/11/1956 Scarborough, ON Draft: TE 1980 TOR
1980	TOR	16							1	14														1	0	0.0	0
1981	TOR	16							4	46														1	7	7.0	7
1982	MTL	12	1		0				3	45		6	1											2	38	19.0	24	10	239	23.9	33
1983	MTL	9							2	30														27	247	9.1	30
1984	MTL+	14			2				4	2														22	200	9.1	36	8	185	23.1	43
1985	MTL	16	1		0		1.0		4	25														32	231	7.2	19	2	35	17.5	21
1986	OTT	7					2.0		1	0														26	211	8.1	31
1986	EDM	6	0		1				1	26														1	14	14.0	14
1986	Year	13	0		1		2.0		2	26														27	225	8.3	31
7	Years	90	2		3		3.0	0.0	20	188		6	1											112	948	8.5	36	20	459	23.0	43
PRESTON JONES Preston Wayne QB 6'3 223 Georgia B: 7/3/1970 Anderson, SC Pro: E
1994	LV	9												2	1	0.5	1	0
1995	SHR	1				0
2	Years	10				0								2	1	0.5	1	0
RAY JONES Ray E 5'10 192 Hamilton Panthers Ints. B: 1924
1949	HAM	12
1950	HAM	4
2	Years	16
RAY JONES Ray OHB 5'11 199 Los Angeles Harbor JC; Los Angeles State B: 1943 Draft: 12-108 1966 SD
1966	TOR	1												7	48	6.9	15	0
REGGIE JONES Reginald Lee WR 6'0 195 Butler County CC*; Louisiana State* B: 5/8/1971 Kansas City, MO Pro: EN
1999	SAS	8	3	0	0	1						20	3	3	-7	-2.3	5	0	38	625	16.4	69	3	3	33	11.0	19	8	116	14.5	30
2002	OTT	6				1						6	1	1	-10	-10.0	-10	0	18	226	12.6	28	1
2003	OTT	6	1	0	1	0													24	244	10.2	38	0
2003	WPG	4	1	0	0	0													6	169	28.2	71	0					3	73	24.3	30
2003	Year	10	2	0	1	0													30	413	13.8	71	0
2004	WPG	9	0	1	0	0													27	343	12.7	33	0
4	Years	29	5	1	1	2						26	4	4	-17	-4.3	5	0	113	1607	14.2	71	4	3	33	11.0	19	11	189	17.2	30
RICHARD JONES Richard Myron DT 6'1 281 Texas Tech B: 3/20/1987 Matagorda County, TX
2010	BC	3	0	0	1	1						6	1
RICKY JONES Rickey Lamond QB 6'0 185 Alabama State B: 2/12/1970 Jackson, MS Draft: 8-198 1992 LARM
1993	EDM	2	0		1	0
SHAWN JONES Shawn DB 5'10 185 Kutztown B: 7/19/1970
1993	BC	1				2
SHAWN JONES Andrew Shawn QB 6'1 200 Georgia Tech B: 6/16/1970 Thomasville, GA Pro: N
1994	BAL	18	1		0	1								5	50	10.0	24	0
1995	BAL	18	1		0	0								4	-1	-0.3	5	0
2	Years	36	2		0	1								9	49	5.4	24	0
STEPHAN JONES Stephan WR 6'0 180 Central Michigan B: 6/8/1960 Flint, MI
1985	SAS	8	1		0							6	1						18	311	17.3	46	1	7	25	3.6	9	3	99	33.0	48
1986	EDM	16	2		0							36	6						40	922	23.1	75	5	14	147	10.5	30	27	750	27.8	105
1987	EDM	18			2	0						48	8	3	34	11.3	20	0	55	1147	20.9	89	8					51	957	18.8	48
1988	EDM	17				2								2	22	11.0	18	0	26	389	15.0	32	0					31	635	20.5	88
1989	EDM	8				0						6	1						21	374	17.8	67	1					1	0	0.0	0
1990	OTT*	18	1		1	0						66	11						59	1182	20.0	66	11					11	175	15.9	28
1991	OTT	13	1		0	0						42	7	2	5	2.5	18	0	39	661	16.9	41	7					5	114	22.8	32
1992	OTT*	17				2						60	10	1	-14	-14.0	-14	0	75	1400	18.7	55	10
1993	OTT+	17	1		1	1						36	6						73	1274	17.5	76	6
1994	OTT	9				1													32	591	18.5	46	0
10	Years	141	7		4	6						300	50	8	47	5.9	20	0	438	8251	18.8	89	49	21	172	8.2	30	129	2730	21.2	105
TERRENCE JONES Terrence QB 6'1 210 Tulane B: 6/18/1966 New Orleans, LA Draft: 7B-195 1989 SD
1989	CAL	13	1		0	0						30	5	28	202	7.2	40	5
1990	CAL	17	5		1	1						12	2	29	202	7.0	44	2
1991	CAL	8	1		0	1								4	22	5.5	10	0
1991	OTT	5				0								1	7	7.0	7	0
1991	Year	13	1		0	1								5	29	5.8	10	0
1992	OTT	18	2		1	1						6	1	7	39	5.6	19	1
1993	OTT	18	2		1	1								8	47	5.9	24	0
1994	SHR	8	1		0	0						12	2	21	167	8.0	42	2
1995	SHR	5				0
7	Years	87	12		3	4						60	10	98	686	7.0	44	10
TODD JONES Todd A. OG 6'3 295 Arkansas; Henderson State B: 7/3/1967 Hope, AR Draft: 11-280 1991 CLE Pro: EN
1995	MEM	17				0
TOM JONES Thomas Lee OT-MG 6'5 250 Kentucky State; Miami (Ohio) B: 6/22/1931 Cincinnati, OH D: 8/28/1978 Muskoka District, ON Draft: 9-108(f) 1954 CLE Pro: N
1957	OTT	8
1958	OTT	14

Year	Team	GP	FM	FF	FR	TK	SK	YDS	IR	YDS	PD	PTS	TD	RA	YDS	AVG	LG	TD	REC	YDS	AVG	LG	TD	PR	YDS	AVG	LG	KOR	YDS	AVG	LG
1959	OTT	14																													
1960	OTT	14																													
1961	OTT+	14																										1	0	0.0	0
1962	TOR	2																													
6	Years	66																										1	0	0.0	0
TOMMY JONES Tommy QB 6'3 230 Indiana B: 8/3/1979																															
2004	CAL	18	5	0	0	0						12	2	18	147	8.2	35	2													
TOMMY JONES Tommy DB 6'0 190 Fresno State B: 1/25/1971 Pro: E																															
1994	SAS	1				0																									
TONY JONES Anthony Bernard WR 5'7 145 Angelina JC; Texas B: 12/30/1965 Grapeland, TX Draft: 6-153 1990 HOU Pro: EN																															
1994	SAC	7	0		2	1						6	1	1	1	1.0	1	0	9	167	18.6	63	1					5	58	11.6	17
TOYA JONES Toya Cardin DB 6'1 199 Texas A&M B: 10/28/1976 Victoria, TX Pro: X																															
2001	BC	17	0	1	1	64	1.0	7.0																1	0	0.0	0	6	82	13.7	17
2002	BC	7				17					1																				
2	Years	24	0	1	1	81	1.0	7.0			1													1	0	0.0	0	6	82	13.7	17
TYRONE JONES Tyrone LB 6'0 220 Southern University B: 8/3/1961 St. Marys, GA D: 6/10/2008 Jacksonville, FL Pro: N																															
1983	WPG	16					17.5		1	22																					
1984	WPG*	16					20.5		3	10														1	23	23.0	23				
1985	WPG*	16					11.0		1	5																					
1986	WPG*	16	0		2		10.0		1	2									1	7	7.0	7	0								
1987	WPG*	18			2	36	15.0		1	0		12	2						1	1	1.0	1	1								
1989	WPG	9	0		1	33	5.0		1	21		6	1																		
1990	WPG+	18	0		2	49	11.0		4	14																					
1991	WPG	9				20	8.0		1	14									1	17	17.0	17	0								
1992	SAS	18	0		1	72	4.0		2	1																					
1993	BC	15	0		1	25	8.0	71.0																							
10	Years	151	0		9	235	110.0	71.0	15	89		18	3						3	25	8.3	17	1	1	23	23.0	23				
VIC JONES Victor W. HB 6'0 197 Indiana B: 1938 Draft: SS 1960 DEN; 13-146 1960 STL																															
1960	EDM	1												3	-5	-1.7	0	0													
WARREN JONES Warren QB 6'2 200 Hawaii B: 9/23/1966																															
1990	EDM	14				0								1	2	2.0	2	0													
1991	EDM	18	5		0	0								15	51	3.4	22	0													
1992	SAS	18				0								8	60	7.5	13	0													
1993	SAS	18	1		0	0						6	1	24	62	2.6	10	1													
1994	SAS	16	1		0	1						12	2	25	137	5.5	18	2													
1995	SAS	18	3		1	1						18	3	49	286	5.8	20	3													
1996	SAS	8				3								12	59	4.9	14	0													
1996	EDM	1	1		0	1								2	0	0.0	0	0													
1996	Year	9	1		0	4								14	59	4.2	14	0													
7	Years	110	11		1	6						36	6	136	657	4.8	22	6													
WILLIE JONES Willie Lorenzo DE 6'4 244 Florida State B: 11/22/1957 Dublin, GA Draft: 2-42 1979 OAK Pro: N																															
1984	SAS	1					3.5																								
ZACK JONES Zachery CB 5'10 180 Louisiana Tech B: 10/4/1957																															
1980	SAS	13	0		1				4	62																		3	71	23.7	32
1981	SAS	5	0		1																										
1981	TOR	4	0		1																							3	57	19.0	22
1981	Year	9	0		2																							3	57	19.0	22
2	Years	18	0		3				4	62																		6	128	21.3	32
TERRY JONES-DUNCAN Terry LB 5'11 225 Louisiana-Monroe B: 2/13/1965 Shreveport, LA																															
1989	OTT	5				16																									
AL JORDAN Alfred CB 5'10 180 UCLA B: 2/25/1970 Washington, DC																															
1994	LV	18	0		2	39			1	23	10																				
1995	CAL	18				57	2.0	21.0	3	29	14																				
1996	CAL*	18				69			8	102	11													1	0	0.0	0				
1997	CAL	13				38					6																				
4	Years	67	0		2	203	2.0	21.0	12	154	41													1	0	0.0	0				
ANTHONY JORDAN Anthony RB 5'9 185 Samford B: 12/15/1972 Northport, AL																															
1995	MEM	12	6		3	10								2	10	5.0	6	0	12	149	12.4	45	0	52	487	9.4	24	23	533	23.2	48
HOMER JORDAN Homer QB 5'11 180 Clemson B: 3/21/1960 Atlanta, GA Draft: TD 1983 WAS-USFL																															
1983	SAS	10	1		0							12	2	30	150	5.0	23	2													
1984	SAS	11	3		1							8	1	31	140	4.5	21	1													
1985	SAS	15	2		0							6	1	35	160	4.6	21	1													
1986	WPG	8												3	14	4.7	12	0													
4	Years	44	6		1							26	4	99	464	4.7	23	4													
LARRY JORDAN Lawrence Gene OT 6'6 230 Youngstown State B: 4/18/1938 Youngstown, OH Pro: N																															
1966	MTL	14																													
MICHAEL JORDAN Michael CB 5'11 181 Tulane B: 1/8/1976 Baton Rouge, LA																															
1999	MTL	1				1																									
2000	BC	1				1																									
2	Years	2				2																									
ROBERT JORDAN Robert Darnell Demar WR 5'11 160 California B: 1/29/1986 Oakland, CA																															
2010	BC	4				0								4	22	5.5	13	0						15	141	9.4	25	16	295	18.4	33
STEPHEN JORDAN Stephen CB 5'10 195 Sacramento CC; Illinois B: 8/27/1967																															
1989	HAM+	18				54	1.0		5	127		6	1																		
1990	HAM	18	0		1	44			3	41																					
1991	EDM	2				9																									
1992	EDM	18	0		1	57	1.0		2	85																					
4	Years	56	0		2	164	2.0		10	253		6	1																		
TODD JORDAN Todd P-QB 6'2 240 Mississippi State B: 6/18/1970 Tupelo, MS																															
1995	SA	18	1		1	1						1	0																		
DALE JOSEPH Albert Dale CB-DH 6'0 175 Howard Payne B: 3/8/1967 Houston, TX Pro: E																															
1994	SAS	16	0		2	41	1.0	0.0			3	6	1															1	10	10.0	10
1995	SAS	17	0		1	44			4	51	3																				
1996	SAS	6				17					5																	1	0	0.0	0
1997	SAS+	18	0	1	3	47	1.0	1.0			6	6	1																		
1998	BC*	18	0	1	1	42			4	29	4																				
1999	BC+	18	0	0	1	41					5																				
6	Years	93	0	2	8	232	2.0	1.0	8	80	26	12	2															2	10	5.0	10
DARREN JOSEPH Darren RB 6'0 195 Ottawa Sooners Jrs. B: 8/29/1968 Ottawa, ON																															
1992	OTT	18	3		0	8						12	2	119	711	6.0	52	2	15	113	7.5	11	0					7	140	20.0	28
1993	OTT	14	3		1	4						6	1	108	398	3.7	23	1	33	403	12.2	54	0					2	21	10.5	15
1994	OTT	12	1		1	3						30	5	68	280	4.1	50	4	18	185	10.3	24	1					2	10	5.0	10
1995	SAS	12	5		0	9						44	7	137	590	4.3	50	5	16	276	17.3	76	2					1	0	0.0	0
1996	SAS	17	1		1	15								4	27	6.8	13	0	2	16	8.0	15	0								
1997	SAS	18				25								11	35	3.2	7	0	3	23	7.7	14	0								
1998	SAS	17	2	0	0	12								31	151	4.9	30	0	3	28	9.3	11	0								
1999	TOR	18	0	1	2	10						12	2	29	164	5.7	65	2	3	53	17.7	24	0					1	0	0.0	0
2000	TOR	4				6								8	29	3.6	5	0	1	3	3.0	3	0								
2000	MTL	9	1	0	1	11								2	2	1.0	4	0													
2000	Year	13	1	0	1	17								10	31	3.1	5	0	1	3	3.0	3	0								
2001	TOR	17				9						6	1	9	25	2.8	6	1	5	38	7.6	16	0					1	0	0.0	0
2002	OTT	11				12						6	1						4	37	9.3	12	1								

Year	Team	GP	FM	FF	FR	TK	SK	YDS	IR	YDS	PD	PTS	TD	RA	YDS	AVG	LG	TD	REC	YDS	AVG	LG	TD	PR	YDS	AVG	LG	KOR	YDS	AVG	LG
2003	OTT	6				13																									
2004	BC	5				6																									
13	Years	169	16	1	6	143						116	19	526	2412	4.6	65	15	103	1175	11.4	76	4					14	171	12.2	28
ELVIS JOSEPH Elvis RB 6'1 216 Louisiana-Lafayette; Southern University B: 8/30/1978 St. Michael's, Barbados Pro: N																															
2005	EDM	4				0								22	94	4.3	24	0	12	149	12.4	25	0								
JOHNSON JOSEPH Johnson WR 5'8 165 Texas Tech B: 11/22/1971 Montreal, QC																															
1996	OTT	5				1													4	48	12.0	17	0								
KERRY JOSEPH Kerry Tremaine QB 6'2 205 McNeese State B: 10/4/1973 New Iberia, LA Pro: EN																															
2003	OTT	18	11	0	2	5						36	6	82	616	7.5	63	6													
2004	OTT	12	4	0	0	2						24	4	57	418	7.3	46	4													
2005	OTT	18	14	0	5	1						54	9	153	1006	6.6	30	9													
2006	SAS	18	13	0	1	0						30	5	91	583	6.4	37	4	1	41	41.0	34	1								
2007	SAS*	18	5	0	0	1						78	13	90	737	8.2	37	13													
2008	TOR	18	8	0	4	0						24	4	78	493	6.3	24	4													
2009	TOR	18	6	0	0	1						12	2	52	302	5.8	26	2													
2010	EDM	1				0																									
2011	EDM	18				0						36	6	26	77	3.0	17	6													
9	Years	139	61	0	12	10						294	49	629	4232	6.7	63	48	1	41	41.0	34	1								
LLOYD JOSEPH Lloyd DL 6'0 270 Valley City State B: 8/3/1968 Grenada Draft: 6-42 1991 BC																															
1991	BC	5	0		1	1																									
SAMMY JOSEPH Samuel Louis CB-DH 5'11 190 Colorado; Louisiana State B: 5/10/1983 Marrero, LA																															
2009	TOR	6				13																									
2010	TOR	3				11					4																				
2	Years	9				24					4																				
BOB JOSLIN Robert V. E 6'1 200 Ohio State																															
1954	OTT	1																													
JEFF JOSLIN Jeff QB 6'0 175 Carson-Newman B: 5/22/1962																															
1986	TOR	3																													
STEVE JOSUE Steve DE 6'2 230 Carson-Newman B: 4/5/1980 Miami, FL Draft: 7D-257 2003 GB Pro: EN																															
2006	HAM	9	0	2	0	22	1.0	5.0																							
YONEL JOURDAIN Yonel RB 5'11 204 Southern Illinois B: 4/20/1971 New York, NY Pro: N																															
1997	HAM	6	2	0	1	1						6	1	13	56	4.3	14	0	14	113	8.1	33	1					12	250	20.8	41
MIKE JOVANOVICH Mike OT 6'4 278 Boston College B: 5/11/1967 Toronto, ON Draft: 2A-9 1991 HAM																															
1992	HAM	9	0		1	0																									
1993	HAM	18	0		1	10																									
1994	TOR	18				3																									
1995	TOR	6				1																									
1995	OTT	12	1		0	0																									
1995	Year	18	1		0	1																									
1996	OTT	10				0																									
1996	MTL	7				1																									
1996	Year	17				1																									
5	Years	61	1		2	15																									
JIM JOYCE Jim FB 6'0 210 Maryland B: 1937																															
1960	HAM	2												14	82	5.9	15	0	1	15	15.0	15	0								
PETE JOYCE Peter FB 6'1 220 Royal Military College; Toronto																															
1959	OTT	3												4	16	4.0	7	0													
ED JOYNER Edward M. OG 6'1 230 Lenoir-Rhyne B: 1945																															
1968	OTT	8	0		2				1	30																					
1969	OTT	10	0		4				1	5																					
1970	OTT	2																													
3	Years	20	0		6				2	35																					
BOBBY JUDD Bob OHB 5'9 185 Xavier (Ohio) B: 1932 deceased																															
1957	OTT	14							5	115		49	8	120	653	5.4	37	5	14	160	11.4	24	1	7	102	14.6	19	16	353	22.1	34
1958	OTT	14										30	5	125	596	4.8	40	5	25	272	10.9	30	0	1	11	11.0	11	20	439	22.0	35
2	Years	28							5	115		79	13	245	1249	5.1	40	10	39	432	11.1	30	1	8	113	14.1	19	36	792	22.0	35
GORD JUDGES Gordon DT-DE-OG 6'3 245 Scarborough Rams Jrs.; Bramalea Srs. B: 7/30/1947 Toronto, ON																															
1968	TOR	1																													
1968	MTL	4																													
1968	Year	5																													
1970	MTL	14																													
1971	MTL	14	0		1																										
1972	MTL	14																													
1973	MTL+	14	0		1																										
1974	MTL	13																													
1975	MTL	16	0		1																										
1976	MTL	6	0		2																										
1977	MTL	13																													
1978	MTL	16	0		2																										
1979	MTL	16	0		1																										
1980	MTL	6																													
1980	TOR	8	0		1																										
1980	Year	14	0		1																										
1981	TOR	7																													
1982	MTL	16																													
14	Years	166	0		9																										
GEORGE JUGUM George LB 6'0 232 Washington B: 6/5/1946 Seattle, WA Draft: 15-385 1969 LARM																															
1970	BC	7							2	27																					
MIKE JUHASZ Mike WR 6'2 202 North Dakota B: 7/23/1976 Calgary, AB Draft: 2-14 2000 HAM																															
2000	HAM	15				3						6	1						3	47	15.7	19	1								
2003	CAL	10				6													1	5	5.0	5	0								
2004	CAL	18	1	0	0	2						12	2						52	634	12.2	31	2					1	-1	-1.0	-1
2005	CAL	18	0	0	1	3													11	102	9.3	26	0								
4	Years	61	1	0	1	14						18	3						67	788	11.8	31	3					1	-1	-1.0	-1
KYLER JUKES Kyler OL 6'4 300 Regina B: 4/9/1979 Saltspring Island, BC Draft: 4-27 2005 CAL																															
2006	TOR	1				0																									
2006	HAM	1				0																									
2006	Year	2				0																									
JERRY-RALPH JULES Jerry-Ralph CB 5'10 181 Montreal B: 6/13/1981 Laval, QC																															
2010	WPG	4				2																									
2011	WPG	16				8																									
2	Years	20				10																									
CURRY JUNEAU Curry J., Jr. DE 6'2 220 Southern Mississippi B: 8/3/1934 Draft: 21-247 1957 CLE																															
1960	MTL	2												1	7	7.0	7	0	2	18	9.0	12	0								
1960	EDM	2																													
1960	Year	4												1	7	7.0	7	0	2	18	9.0	12	0								
1961	CAL	2										6	1																		
2	Years	4										6	1	1	7	7.0	7	0	2	18	9.0	12	0								
CRAIG JUNTUNEN Craig Mitchell QB 6'1 195 Idaho B: 12/12/1954 Los Angeles County, CA																															
1978	CAL	7												1	13	13.0	13	0													
1979	SAS	3	1		0									1	4	4.0	4	0													
2	Years	10	1		0									2	17	8.5	13	0													

Year	Team	GP	FM	FF	FR	TK	SK	YDS	IR	YDS	PD	PTS	TD	RA	YDS	AVG	LG	TD	REC	YDS	AVG	LG	TD	PR	YDS	AVG	LG	KOR	YDS	AVG	LG
BOBBY JURASIN Robert S. DE 6'1 250 Northern Michigan B: 8/26/1964 Wakefield, MI																															
1986	SAS	8	0		1		3.0																								
1987	SAS*	18	1		2	45	22.0		1	6														1	11	11.0	11				
1988	SAS*	18	0		3	39	16.0					6	1						2	27	13.5	24	1								
1989	SAS+	17				35	16.0					6	1						1	39	39.0	39	1								
1990	SAS	18	0		1	51	10.0																								
1991	SAS	16	0		4	34	10.0																								
1992	SAS*	14	0		3	24	10.0	78.0											1	13	13.0	13	0								
1993	SAS	17	0		1	25	14.0	70.0																							
1994	SAS+	18	0		8	36	10.0	68.0	1	32	0	6	1																		
1995	SAS	17	0		1	27	8.0	73.0																							
1996	SAS	18				44	11.0	69.0			1																				
1997	SAS*	18	0	0	2	55	10.0	59.0																							
1998	TOR	2				2																									
13	Years	199	1	0	26	417	140.0	417.0	2	38	1	18	3						4	79	19.8	39	2	1	11	11.0	11				
TERRELL JURINEACK Elliott Terrell DE 6'4 270 Coffeyville CC; Missouri B: 1/11/1977 Orlando, FL Pro: E																															
2003	HAM	6				11																									
2004	SAS	3				8	7.0	34.0																							
2005	SAS	7	0	3	1	16	3.0	24.0			2																				
2006	SAS	14				35	9.0	68.0			1																				
2007	SAS	1				2																									
5	Years	31	0	3	1	72	19.0	126.0			3																				
LARRY JUSDANIS Larry QB-SB 6'4 235 Central Florida; Acadia B: 12/3/1970 Hamilton, ON Draft: 5-47 1995 BC																															
1996	HAM	8	0		1	0								5	32	6.4	12	0													
1997	MTL	6				0																									
2	Years	14	0		1	0								5	32	6.4	12	0													
RUBE JUSTER Rubin J. T 6'2 230 Minnesota B: 9/9/1923 D: 1/14/1985 Chicago, IL Pro: N																															
1947	MTL	11																													
AIRABIN JUSTIN Airabin Jermaine CB 5'10 187 Utah; Northern Arizona B: 3/25/1980 Inglewood, CA																															
2004	HAM	5	0	2	0	12			2	21	1																				
2005	HAM	16	0	1	0	42			1	3	4																				
2006	HAM	9				21			1	7	0																				
2007	SAS	12				27			2	16	2																				
2008	EDM	2				0																									
5	Years	44	0	3	0	102			6	47	7																				
SID JUSTIN Sidney Arthur CB 5'10 170 Los Angeles Southwest JC; Long Beach State B: 8/14/1954 New Orleans, LA Pro: N																															
1980	WPG	2							1	2																					
STEVEN JYLES Steven QB 6'1 199 Louisiana-Monroe B: 9/25/1982 Independence, LA																															
2006	EDM	18				0						6	1	3	7	2.3	4	1													
2007	EDM	18				0						18	3	20	80	4.0	23	3													
2008	SAS	18	1	0	1	0								14	114	8.1	22	0													
2009	SAS	18	1	0	0	0						24	4	24	102	4.3	21	4													
2010	WPG	16	8	0	4	1						24	4	65	452	7.0	32	4													
2011	TOR	8	5	0	1	0						6	1	53	429	8.1	24	1													
6	Years	96	15	0	6	1						78	13	179	1184	6.6	32	13													
PATRICK KABONGO Watshdimba OG-OT 6'6 315 Nebraska B: 6/27/1979 Kinshasa, Zaire Draft: 3-19 2003 OTT																															
2004	EDM	1				0																									
2005	EDM	12				1																									
2006	EDM	18	0	0	1	0																									
2007	EDM	18	0	0	1	2																									
2008	EDM+	18	0	0	1	2																		2	9	4.5	5	3	24	8.0	15
2009	EDM	18				1																									
2010	EDM	18				0																									
2011	EDM	18				0																									
8	Years	121	0	0	3	6																		2	9	4.5	5	3	24	8.0	15
CLARENCE KACHMAN Clarence FL 5'7 155 Edmonton Huskies Jrs.; Alberta B: 1943 Draft: 1965 WPG																															
1965	EDM	3	1		0														3	10	3.3	7	0	12	54	4.5	11	4	76	19.0	25
CHAD KACKERT Charles Michael RB 5'9 199 New Hampshire B: 9/15/1986 Thousand Oaks, CA																															
2011	TOR	7	3	0	1	3						30	5	57	349	6.1	24	4	4	58	14.5	53	1	5	82	16.4	60	4	105	26.3	50
DAVE KADUHR Dave WR 6'1 180 Simon Fraser B: 5/14/1951 Draft: 4A-31 1974 BC																															
1974	BC	3	1		0																			13	57	4.4	18				
JASON KAISER Jason A. DH-CB 6'0 192 Culver-Stockton B: 11/9/1973 Denver, CO Pro: NX																															
1996	HAM	8				13			2	25	1													10	81	8.1	17	3	43	14.3	20
1997	HAM	2				3																						1	0	0.0	0
2	Years	10				16			2	25	1													10	81	8.1	17	4	43	10.8	20
JOHN KAISER John Frederick LB 6'3 227 Sequoias JC; Arizona B: 6/6/1962 Oconomowoc, WI Draft: 6-162 1984 SEA; TD 1984 ARI-USFL Pro: N																															
1989	WPG	1				1																									
JIM KALAFAT James William LB 6'0 235 Montana State B: 2/21/1962 Great Falls, MT Draft: 15B-315 1984 SA-USFL Pro: N																															
1985	TOR	1																													
MIKE KALAPOS Michael T 6'2 240 Purdue B: 1927																															
1951	OTT	1																													
JOHN KALIN John S 6'0 190 Calgary B: 7/18/1970 Calgary, AB Draft: 1A-8 1994 CAL																															
1994	EDM	10				5																									
1995	EDM	18	0		1	37			2	34	2																				
1996	MTL	18				9																									
1997	MTL	4				4																		1	-1	-1.0	-1				
1997	CAL	13				32			1	27	3																				
1997	Year	17				36			1	27	3													1	-1	-1.0	-1				
1998	WPG	14	0	1	3	16						12	2																		
5	Years	64	0	1	4	103			3	61	5	12	2											1	-1	-1.0	-1				
TOMMY KALMANIR Thomas J. HB 5'8 171 Pittsburgh; Nevada-Reno B: 3/30/1926 Jerome, PA D: 10/12/2004 Fresno, CA Draft: 25-229(f) 1947 PIT; 20-146 1949 NY-AAFC Pro: N																															
1955	EDM	1												2	6	3.0	3	0	1	16	16.0	16	0								
PETE KALUSKI Peter G 6'0 185 Ottawa Rough Riders Jrs. B: 1916																															
1946	OTT	1																													
STAN KALUZNICK Stan HB-FB 5'8 203 none B: 1931																															
1948	WPG	1																													
1950	CAL	14												17	72	4.2	11	0	1	0	0.0	0	0								
1951	CAL	14										10	2	67	341	5.1	20	2						1	20	20.0	20	7	143	20.4	
1952	CAL	15			1							5	1	27	126	4.7	17	1													
1953	CAL	16										1	0	20	64	3.2	20	0										1	1	1.0	1
1954	CAL	14	0		1									1	2	2.0	2	0										1	17	17.0	17
6	Years	74	0		2							16	3	132	605	4.6	20	3	1	0	0.0	0	0	1	20	20.0	20	9	161	17.9	17
RICK KALVAITIS Rick DE 6'4 235 Wilfrid Laurier B: 7/25/1958 Draft: 5-37 1980 TOR																															
1980	TOR	5																													
1981	HAM	15					1.0																								
2	Years	20					1.0	0.0																							
AMARA KAMARA Amara LB 6'0 240 Temple B: 2/2/1988 Liberia																															
2011	BC	2				2																									
IVAN KAMINSKI Ivan P. T 6'5 265 Nebraska-Kearney B: 8/23/1929 Ashton, NE D: 7/18/1986 Marietta, GA																															
1957	WPG	10																													
LES KAMINSKI Les RB 5'11 235 Montana State B: 12/26/1961 Draft: 4-30 1984 HAM																															

Year	Team	GP	FM	FF	FR	TK	SK	YDS	IR	YDS	PD	PTS	TD	RA	YDS	AVG	LG	TD	REC	YDS	AVG	LG	TD	PR	YDS	AVG	LG	KOR	YDS	AVG	LG
1984	CAL	12																										3	42	14.0	16
TOMMY KANE Thomas Henry WR 5'11 180 Syracuse B: 1/14/1964 Montreal, QC Draft: 3-23 1988 TOR; 3-75 1988 SEA Pro: N																															
1994	TOR	5				2						6	1						10	125	12.5	37	1								
ADAM KANIA Adam DE 6'4 266 St. Francis Xavier; Waterloo B: 8/3/1984 Toronto ON Draft: 6B-43 2007 HAM																															
2008	HAM	3				1																									
AARON KANNER Aaron P-K 6'2 215 Catawba B: 9/25/1970 Atlanta, GA																															
1994	SHR	18	7		0	3						5	0	2	5	2.5	5	0													
1995	MEM	6				0						2	0																		
2	Years	24	7		0	3						7	0	2	5	2.5	5	0													
NATHAN KANYA Nathan LB 6'2 210 British Columbia B: 10/16/1987 Congo																															
2011	HAM	18				13																									
STEVE KAPASKY Steve T 6'4 255 Toronto Balmy Beach Jrs. B: 1931 D: 8/17/2010 Burnaby, BC																															
1958	BC	1																													
JOE KAPP Joseph Robert QB 6'2 214 California B: 3/19/1939 Santa Fe, NM Draft: 18-209 1959 WAS Pro: N																															
1959	CAL	16	8		0							31	5	113	606	5.4	21	5						1	0	0.0	0				
1960	CAL	15	8		2							7	1	61	374	6.1	27	1													
1961	CAL	1																													
1961	BC	11												37	127	3.4	20	0													
1961	Year	12												37	127	3.4	20	0													
1962	BC	16	3									18	3	51	183	3.6	19	3													
1963	BC*	16	2		0							30	5	75	438	5.8	39	5													
1964	BC*	16	11		1							36	6	95	370	3.9	18	6													
1965	BC	16	3		1							24	4	64	345	5.4	21	4													
1966	BC	16	1		0							12	2	83	341	4.1	16	2													
8	Years	112	36		4							158	26	579	2784	4.8	39	26						1	0	0.0	0				
ZENO KARCZ Zeno LB-OHB-E 5'11 200 Michigan; Windsor AKO Jrs. B: 1936																															
1957	HAM	2																													
1958	HAM	3							1	29																					
1959	HAM	13							1	7		6	1						3	53	17.7	23	1								
1960	HAM	14										6	1						1	35	35.0	35	1	1	3	3.0	3				
1961	HAM	14							1	2																		1	4	4.0	4
1962	HAM+	14							2	2																					
1963	HAM	14							2	3		6	1																		
1964	HAM	14	0		2				1	0		6	1																		
1965	HAM*	14	0		3				2	0																					
1966	HAM	4																													
10	Years	106	0		5				10	43		24	4						4	88	22.0	35	2	1	3	3.0	3	1	4	4.0	4
JIM KARDASH Jim OT-OG 6'5 250 Western Ontario B: 5/17/1961 Brandon, MB Draft: 4-28 1983 MTL																															
1986	TOR	4																													
1987	TOR	18				2																									
1988	TOR	18				3																						1	0	0.0	0
1989	TOR	15	0		1	3								0	5		5	0													
1990	TOR	13				2																									
1991	TOR	18	0		1	6						6	1																		
1992	TOR	12	0		1	1																									
7	Years	98	0		3	17						6	1	0	5		5	0										1	0	0.0	0
TERRY KARG Terry W. QB 5'11 192 Yakima Valley JC; Mesa State; Central Washington B: 7/29/1969 Seattle, WA Pro: E																															
1998	WPG	4				0																									
RICHARD KARIKARI Richard S 5'11 205 St. Francis Xavier B: 7/23/1979 Accra, Ghana Draft: 2A-14 2003 MTL																															
2003	MTL	12				8																									
2004	MTL	18				21			1	10	0																				
2005	MTL*	18	0	3	0	47			9	188	1	6	1																		
2006	MTL	18	1	1	1	37	1.0	7.0	3	83	3																				
2007	HAM	18				27					2																				
2008	CAL	7	0	0	1	3					1																				
6	Years	91	1	4	2	143	1.0	7.0	13	281	7	6	1																		
PETE KARPUK Pete S-FW 5'9 160 none B: 1924 D: 3/4/1985																															
1948	OTT	8										10	2					1													
1949	OTT	9										20	4					1					2								
1950	OTT	4										5	1										1								
1951	OTT	12										10	2																		
1952	OTT	12										5	1																		
1953	OTT	5																													
1954	HAM	14							4	120		5	1											35	247	7.1	25				
1955	OTT	11							3	101														7	51	7.3	11				
1956	MTL	14							1	5														44	256	5.8	20				
1957	MTL	14										6	1						1	37	37.0	37	1	57	307	5.4	17				
10	Years	103							8	226		61	12					2	1	37	37.0	37	4	143	861	6.0	25				
BYRON KARRYS Byron HB-FW 6'0 175 none B: 1926																															
1946	TOR	10										10	2					1					1								
1947	TOR	12										11	2					2													
1948	TOR	9										10	2					2													
1949	TOR	8										5	1																		
1950	TOR	12										5	1																		
1951	TOR	2																													
6	Years	53										41	8					5					1								
STEVE KARRYS Steve HB-FW 6'0 180 Toronto B: 1924 D: //1997																															
1946	TOR	11										7	0																		
1948	OTT	11																													
1949	OTT	11										21	4					4													
1950	OTT	12																													
1951	TOR	11										1	0																		
1952	TOR	12																													
1953	TOR	14										9	0																		
7	Years	82										38	4					4													
GUS KASAPIS Constantinos DT 6'4 255 Iowa B: 3/18/1942 Detroit, MI Draft: 17-238 1964 CHIB																															
1964	BC	11	0		1																										
1965	BC	13	0		1																										
1966	CAL	5																													
1966	EDM	4																													
1966	Year	9																													
1967	EDM	1																													
4	Years	30	0		2																										
RICK KASER Richard DB-OE 6'0 175 Toledo B: 1933 Draft: 17-205 1954 DET																															
1957	BC	13	0		2				3	16		6	1						16	223	13.9	37	1	8	86	10.8	16	3	36	12.0	14
1958	BC	9							3	31		6	1						8	100	12.5	23	1	1	5	5.0	5				
1960	OTT	1																													
3	Years	23	0		2				6	47		12	2						24	323	13.5	37	2	9	91	10.1	16	3	36	12.0	14
ALAIN KASHAMA Alain Kaleta Olony T. DE-DT 6'4 259 Michigan B: 12/8/1979 Watsha, Zaire Draft: 1-8 2004 MTL Pro: EN																															
2006	MTL	3				2																									
2007	MTL	18	0	1	0	31	8.0	54.0			1																				
2008	MTL	4				4					1																				

Year	Team	GP	FM	FF	FR	TK	SK	YDS	IR	YDS	PD	PTS	TD	RA	YDS	AVG	LG	TD	REC	YDS	AVG	LG	TD	PR	YDS	AVG	LG	KOR	YDS	AVG	LG
2008	HAM	7				5	1.0	1.0																							
2008	Year	11				9	1.0	1.0			1																				
2009	CAL	6				13																									
4	Years	31	0	1	0	55	9.0	55.0			2																				
FERNAND KASHAMA Fernand LB-DE 6'3 221 Western Michigan B: 2/26/1985 Kinshasa, Zaire Draft: 2-16 2008 CAL																															
2009	CAL	17				9	1.0	10.0																							
2010	WPG	4				1																									
2011	WPG	18				18	2.0	4.0																							
3	Years	39				28	3.0	14.0																							
HAKEEM KASHAMA Nicolas Hakeem DL 6'4 279 Connecticut B: 2/22/1978 Zaire																															
2004	HAM	2				0																									
2005	HAM	8				4																									
2	Years	10				4																									
JIM KATES James Benjamin, Jr. LB 6'1 235 Penn State B: 6/20/1948 Charlottesville, VA Draft: 12-303 1970 WAS																															
1971	HAM	1																													
JERRY KAURIC Jerry K-P 6'0 210 Windsor AKO Jrs. B: 6/28/1963 Windsor, ON Pro: EN																															
1987	EDM	13	2		0	0						145	0																		
1988	EDM*	18	1		0	0						181	0	3	43	14.3	20	0	1	-15	-15.0	-15	0								
1989	EDM	18	1		0	0						224	0	1	16	16.0	16	0													
1991	EDM	2				0						27	0																		
1991	CAL	2				0																									
1991	Year	4				0						27	0																		
4	Years	51	4		0	0						577	0	4	59	14.8	20	0	1	-15	-15.0	-15	0								
WILSON KAUVAKA Wilson FB 6'0 265 Dixie JC B: 5/30/1971 Toneatapu, Tonga																															
1994	LV	2										6	1	5	18	3.6	6	1	1	5	5.0	5	0								
JESSE KAYE Jesse W, QB 6'0 190 Wisconsin; Tampa B: 3/7/1944																															
1967	SAS	5	1		0									2	8	4.0	6	0													
MUADIANVITA KAZADI Muadianvita Machaz LB 6'2 235 Tulsa B: 12/20/1973 Kinshasa, Zaire Draft: 6-179 1997 STL Pro: EN																															
1999	MTL	4				5																									
WARREN KEAN Warren K 6'1 200 Concordia (Canada) B: 6/21/1984 Toronto, ON Draft: 1-2 2007 EDM																															
2007	EDM	1				0						11	0																		
2010	SAS	2				0						15	0																		
2	Years	3				0						26	0																		
JIM KEANE James Patrick OE 6'4 217 Iowa B: 1/11/1924 Bellaire, OH D: 3/8/2011 McHenry, IL Draft: 18-182 1945 CHIB Pro: N																															
1952	SAS	2										5	1	2	24	12.0	18	0	6	77	12.8	17	1								
DAN KEARNS Dan DT-DE 6'2 240 Simon Fraser B: 11/23/1956 San Luis, Brazil Draft: 2-18 1980 EDM																															
1980	EDM	16																													
1981	EDM	16	0		1		2.0																								
1982	EDM	16	0		1		1.5		1	40		6	1																		
1983	EDM	12					2.0																								
1984	EDM	16	0		1		5.0																								
1985	EDM	16	0		2		3.0					6	1	1	29	29.0	29	0	2	44	22.0	39	1								
1986	EDM	18					2.0																								
1987	EDM	18			4	22	6.0																								
1988	EDM	18			2	4	2.0																								
1989	WPG	4				4																							1	0	0.0	0
10	Years	150	0		11	30	23.5		1	40		12	2	1	29	29.0	29	0	2	44	22.0	39	1					1	0	0.0	0
STEVE KEARNS Steve SB-WB-WR-TE 6'1 214 Liberty B: 11/23/1956 Sao Luis, Brazil Draft: TE 1980 CAL																															
1980	BC	5																	1	7	7.0	7	0								
1981	BC	13																	2	54	27.0	32	0								
1982	BC	7	0		1							12	2						2	42	21.0	27	2								
1982	HAM	9										12	2						16	213	13.3	39	2								
1982	Year	16	0		1							24	4						18	255	14.2	39	4								
1983	HAM	5										2	0						3	25	8.3	16	0								
1984	HAM	14																	3	34	11.3	12	0								
1985	HAM	2																										1	6	6.0	6
6	Years	46	0		1							26	4						27	375	13.9	39	4					1	6	6.0	6
TIM KEARSE Tim Allynn WR-SB 5'10 182 San Jose State B: 10/24/1959 York, PA Draft: 11A-303 1983 SD; TD 1983 OAK-USFL Pro: N																															
1983	BC	1																	2	23	11.5	12	0					1	24	24.0	24
1983	SAS	6										12	2						7	121	17.3	42	1	15	201	13.4	68				
1983	Year	7										12	2						9	144	16.0	42	1	15	201	13.4	68	1	24	24.0	24
1984	SAS	8	3		0							6	1	1	5	5.0	5	0	19	240	12.6	33	0	11	125	11.4	75	0	7		7
1988	SAS	6										6	1						8	148	18.5	3	1					1	11	11.0	11
3	Years	15	3		0							24	4	1	5	5.0	5	0	36	532	14.8	42	2	26	326	12.5	75	2	42	21.0	24
GLENN KEEBLE Glenn C 6'2 230 Verdun Maple Leafs Jrs. B: 10/31/1959 Montreal, QC																															
1981	MTL	14	1		2																										
1982	MTL	11	2		0														1	-3	-3.0	-3	0								
1983	MTL	15	0		1																										
1984	MTL	16			1																										
1985	MTL	16	0		1																										
1986	MTL	16																													
1987	TOR	2				0																									
7	Years	90	3		5	0													1	-3	-3.0	-3	0								
EARL KEELEY Clarence QB-P 6'0 180 Vancouver Meralomas Jrs.; Wenatchee JC; Montana B: 5/15/1936 deceased																															
1958	BC	2																													
1959	BC	16												6	5	0.8	12	0													
1960	BC	13	2		0									7	-57	-8.1	5	0													
1961	BC	8												2	6	3.0	8	0													
1962	BC	14												2	2	1.0	4	0													
1963	MTL	1																													
6	Years	54	2		0									17	-44	-2.6	12	0													
JERRY KEELING Jerry Ray QB-S 6'1 180 Tulsa B: 8/2/1939 Paris, TX																															
1961	CAL	16							5	6		6	1	19	116	6.1	14	1						1	0	0.0	0				
1962	CAL	16	1						3	57		18	3	32	211	6.6	39	3						1	26	26.0	26				
1963	CAL	16	0		1				4	28		6	1	16	88	5.5	19	1						1	1	1.0	1				
1964	CAL*	15	0		1				4	3		12	2	17	124	7.3	32	1													
1965	CAL*	16	3		0				2	32		24	4	23	95	4.1	20	4													
1966	CAL+	16	2		2				4	111		6	1	8	34	4.3	29	0													
1967	CAL*	16							5	40														7	37	5.3	12				
1968	CAL+	16							1	3		6	1	8	41	5.1	11	1						1	6	6.0	6				
1969	CAL	16	3		1							36	6	36	157	4.4	25	6													
1970	CAL	13	2		0							6	1	19	155	8.2	52	1													
1971	CAL	12	0		1							12	2	18	33	1.8	13	2													
1972	CAL	16										6	1	29	136	4.7	18	1													
1973	OTT	13	1		0									11	101	9.2	46	0													
1974	OTT	16	2		0									21	30	1.4	10	0													
1975	OTT	1																													
1975	HAM	15	2		3							6	1	37	72	1.9	18	1													
1975	Year	16	2		3							6	1	37	72	1.9	18	1													
15	Years	214	16		9				28	280		144	24	294	1393	4.7	52	22						11	70	6.4	26				
ROBBIE KEEN Robbie P-K 6'4 215 California B: 8/2/1968 Bremerton, WA Draft: 9-244 1991 KC Pro: E																															
1994	LV	18	2		2	6						3	0	1	-24	-24.0	-24	0													

Year	Team	GP	FM	FF	FR	TK	SK	YDS	IR	YDS	PD	PTS	TD	RA	YDS	AVG	LG	TD	REC	YDS	AVG	LG	TD	PR	YDS	AVG	LG	KOR	YDS	AVG	LG
1995	SHR	18	3		0	1						4	0																		
2	Years	36	5		2	7						7	0	1	-24	-24.0	-24	0													
JEFF KEEPING Jeff OG-NT-OT-FB-TE 6'5 282 Scarborough Thunder Jrs.; Western Ontario B: 7/19/1982 Uxbridge, ON Draft: 2C-18 2005 TOR																															
2005	TOR	17				10																									
2006	TOR	17	0	1	0	26	1.0	8.0			1																	1	10	10.0	10
2007	TOR	5				0						6	1						1	2	2.0	2	1								
2009	TOR	15				1																									
2010	TOR	13	0	0	1	0													1	5	5.0	5	0								
2011	TOR	18				0																									
6	Years	85	0	1	1	37	1.0	8.0			1	6	1						2	7	3.5	5	1					1	10	10.0	10
SEAN KEHOE Sean RB 6'0 180 Edmonton Wildcats Jrs.; Alberta B: 4/28/1958 Edmonton, AB Draft: TE 1981 EDM																															
1981	EDM	10												34	139	4.1	30	0	4	45	11.3	22	0					5	95	19.0	32
1982	EDM	13	2		0									28	142	5.1	31	0	15	162	10.8	31	0					18	451	25.1	55
1983	WPG	16	3		0							12	2	34	88	2.6	14	2	13	120	9.2	28	0								
1984	WPG	16	5		1							6	1	15	54	3.6	20	0	25	202	8.1	25	1	19	138	7.3	40	3	78	26.0	43
1985	WPG	16	1		2							24	4	29	80	2.8	13	1	54	513	9.5	62	2	15	51	3.4	13	7	106	15.1	21
1986	WPG	18	1		0							6	1	24	68	2.8	11	0	45	440	9.8	33	1	2	6	3.0	6	2	62	31.0	35
6	Years	89	12		3							48	8	164	571	3.5	31	3	156	1482	9.5	62	4	36	195	5.4	40	35	792	22.6	55
TONY KEHRER Tony FB-LB 5'8 190 Winnipeg Rods Jrs. B: 1/16/1937																															
1958	WPG	16	2									6	1	32	158	4.9	16	1	1	29	29.0	29	0								
1959	WPG	12										6	1	49	230	4.7	17	1	2	7	3.5	10	0	1	11	11.0	11	4	40	10.0	19
1960	WPG	2												4	29	7.3	13	0	1	10	10.0	10	0					1	26	26.0	26
1962	EDM	12										6	1	16	45	2.8	9	1										5	55	11.0	16
1963	EDM	11												16	86	5.4	13	0	4	26	6.5	10	0					6	44	7.3	14
5	Years	53	2		0							18	3	117	548	4.7	17	3	8	72	9.0	29	0	1	11	11.0	11	16	165	10.3	26
KEN KEIR Kenneth J. G-T-E 6'0 210 Calgary Jrs.; Washington State B: 1926																															
1949	CAL	14																													
1950	CAL	14																													
1951	CAL	14																													
1952	CAL	11																													
1953	CAL	16																													
5	Years	69																													
CHARLTON KEITH Charlton DE 6'5 225 Minnesota; Minnesota West CC; Kansas B: 5/4/1983 Canton, OH Pro: U																															
2007	HAM	8	0	0	2	24	4.0	19.0																							
2008	HAM	2				1																									
2	Years	10	0	0	2	25	4.0	19.0																							
KENTON KEITH Kenton Jermaine RB 5'11 198 New Mexico State B: 7/14/1980 Lincoln, NE Pro: N																															
2003	SAS	10	4	0	1	0						48	8	102	709	7.0	59	5	20	142	7.1	19	3								
2004	SAS+	14	3	0	0	3						66	11	190	1154	6.1	71	9	29	295	10.2	64	2								
2005	SAS	13	4	0	3	1						30	5	151	911	6.0	75	5	25	228	9.1	27	0					2	18	9.0	18
2006	SAS+	16	7	0	3	4						32	5	167	1037	6.2	38	2	52	513	9.9	80	3								
2008	HAM	4				0						6	1	29	102	3.5	19	0	9	74	8.2	21	1								
5	Years	57	18	0	7	8						182	30	639	3913	6.1	75	21	135	1252	9.3	80	9					2	18	9.0	18
GARY KEITHLEY Gary Tom QB 6'3 210 Texas; Texas-El Paso B: 1/11/1951 Alvin, TX Draft: 2-45 1973 STL Pro: N																															
1977	BC	16												9	92	10.2	32	0													
1978	BC	14	2		0							6	1	15	46	3.1	16	1													
2	Years	30	2		0							6	1	24	138	5.8	32	1													
JAKE KELCHNER Jake QB 6'2 215 Notre Dame; West Virginia B: 6/27/1970 Pro: E																															
1994	LV	1																													
GENE KELIIKULI Eugene (Buster) OG 6'1 260 Idaho State B: 6/24/1943 Lanai City, HI																															
1965	EDM	1																													
CHIP KELL Curtis OG 6'0 243 Tennessee B: 3/10/1949 Atlanta, GA Draft: 17-429 1971 SD																															
1971	EDM	5																													
1972	EDM	10																													
2	Years	15																													
KENNY KELLER Kenneth Kay HB 5'10 180 North Carolina B: 9/12/1934 Salina, PA D: 12/10/1997 Youngstown, OH Draft: 11-126 1956 PHI Pro: N																															
1959	SAS	1												6	31	5.2	24	0										3	53	17.7	19
MATT KELLETT Matt P-K 6'1 190 Regina Rams Jrs.; Saskatchewan B: 5/4/1973 Regina, SK Draft: 3-14 1998 BC																															
1999	EDM	12	2	0	1	2						44	0	1	2	2.0	2	0													
2001	BC	18	2	0	3	1						129	0																		
2002	BC	18	1	0	0	1						148	0																		
2003	MTL	18	0	0	1	5						191	0	1	6	6.0	6	0													
2004	MTL	15	1	0	1	2						174	0	1	-7	-7.0	-7	0													
2005	OTT	14	1	0	0	0						113	0																		
6	Years	95	7	0	6	11						799	0	3	1	0.3	6	0													
BILLIE KELLEY Billie R. E 6'2 195 Texas Tech B: 8/23/1926 Draft: 23-223 1949 GB Pro: N																															
1950	WPG	2																													
BOB KELLEY Robert C 6'2 232 West Texas A&M B: 5/8/1930 Draft: 25-293 1952 PHI Pro: N																															
1957	HAM	7																													
1958	HAM	14																										1	11	11.0	11
2	Years	21																										1	11	11.0	11
CHRIS KELLEY Chris WR 6'1 200 Northeast Mississippi JC; Memphis B: 1/11/1982 Huntington, WV																															
2005	EDM	7				1													6	61	10.2	18	0								
GORDEN KELLEY Gorden Bond LB 6'3 230 Georgia B: 6/11/1938 Atlanta, GA Draft: SS 1960 LAC Pro: N																															
1965	EDM	8							1																						
JEREMY KELLEY Jeremy SB 6'6 225 Maine B: 6/9/1988																															
2011	HAM	3				6													2	15	7.5	8	0								
MIKE KELLEY Michael Dennis QB 6'3 195 Georgia Tech B: 12/31/1959 Sonora, CA Draft: 6-149 1982 ATL Pro: NU																															
1986	SAS	5												2	5	2.5	7	0													
JACKIE KELLOGG Jack DH-S 6'2 195 Eastern Washington B: 3/29/1971 Tacoma, WA Pro: EX																															
1995	CAL	5	0		1	16					1																				
1996	CAL	16				33	3.0	15.0	3	32	0																				
1997	CAL	2				7					3																				
1998	CAL+	18				45			8	72	10	6	1																		
1999	CAL+	17	1	1	3	37	1.0	8.0	5	75	8			1	-9	-9.0	-9	0													
2000	CAL	17				31	2.0	17.0	5	151	6	12	2																		
2001	CAL	3	0	0	2	10																									
2001	EDM	7				28	1.0	6.0	5	128	6	12	2																		
2001	Year	10	0	0	2	38	1.0	6.0	5	128	6	12	2																		
2002	EDM	18				51	1.0		1	34	4	6	1																		
8	Years	96	1	1	6	258	8.0	46.0	27	492	38	36	6	1	-9	-9.0	-9	0													
AARON KELLY Aaron SB-WR 6'5 190 Clemson B: 4/2/1986																															
2011	HAM	9				5						12	2						27	383	14.2	34	2								
BEN KELLY Benjamin Oliver CB 5'9 185 Colorado B: 9/15/1978 Cleveland, OH Draft: 3-84 2000 MIA Pro: N																															
2005	CAL	13				27					7																	1	15	15.0	15
BRIAN KELLY Brian R. WR 5'9 170 Washington State B: 3/27/1956 San Francisco, CA																															
1979	EDM*	16										68	11						61	1098	18.0	80	11								
1980	EDM*	12	1		0							54	9						48	922	19.2	89	9								
1981	EDM*	16										66	11						74	1665	22.5	91	11								
1982	EDM	9	2		0							48	8						46	801	17.4	56	8								
1983	EDM*	16	0		1							68	11						104	1812	17.4	48	11								
1984	EDM*	16	1		0							108	18						66	1310	19.8	85	18								

Year	Team	GP	FM	FF	FR	TK	SK	YDS	IR	YDS	PD	PTS	TD	RA	YDS	AVG	LG	TD	REC	YDS	AVG	LG	TD	PR	YDS	AVG	LG	KOR	YDS	AVG	LG
1985	EDM	16										36	6						59	1034	17.5	54	6								
1986	EDM	18										60	10						49	901	18.4	65	10								
1987	EDM*	18										78	13						68	1626	23.9	97	13								
9	Years	137	4		1							586	97						575	11169	19.4	97	97								
CEDRIC KELLY Cedric LB 6'2 240 Jackson State B: 4/16/1963																															
1985	SAS	5					4.0																								
CON KELLY Con FB 6'0 190 Edmonton Wildcats Jrs. B: 1935																															
1955	EDM	16	0		2				1	15		10	2	5	8	1.6	6	0	2	26	13.0	15	1	3	7	2.3	3				
1956	EDM	15	1		2									12	22	1.8	7	0	1	16	16.0	16	0	1	0	0.0	0	1	11	11.0	11
2	Years	31	1		4				1	15		10	2	17	30	1.8	7	0	3	42	14.0	16	1	4	7	1.8	3	1	11	11.0	11
DOUG KELLY Doug G 5'8 178 Regina Dales Jrs. B: 1928 Regina, SK																															
1949	SAS	13																													
1950	SAS	10																													
1951	SAS	7																													
3	Years	30																													
ELLISON KELLY Ellison Lamar OT-OG-LB 6'1 231 Michigan State B: 5/17/1935 Butler, GA Draft: 5-59 1959 NYG Pro: N																															
1960	HAM	7							1	0																					
1961	HAM+	14																													
1962	HAM+	14																													
1963	HAM+	14																													
1964	HAM*	14																										1	0	0.0	0
1965	HAM	14																													
1966	HAM	14	0		1																										
1967	HAM	14																													
1968	HAM+	14																													
1969	HAM*	14																													
1970	HAM*	14																													
1971	TOR+	14																													
1972	TOR	14																													
13	Years	175	0		1				1	0																		1	0	0.0	0
JEFF KELLY Jeff Mitchell, III LB 5'11 251 Stephen F. Austin State; Garden City CC; Kansas State B: 12/13/1975 Fort Worth, TX Draft: 6A-198 1999 ATL Pro: N																															
2006	TOR	4	0	0	1	12	1.0	8.0																							
JOE KELLY Joe OHB-LB 5'11 203 New Mexico State B: 7/1/1937 Draft: 11-128 1959 LARM																															
1959	OTT	6										30	5	53	213	4.0	17	2	14	336	24.0	55	3					8	141	17.6	23
1960	OTT	13										54	9	75	441	5.9	31	6	27	459	17.0	68	3	1	5	5.0	5				
1961	OTT	3										18	3	36	191	5.3	22	3	6	119	19.8	31	0	1	0	0.0	0				
3	Years	22										102	17	164	845	5.2	31	11	47	914	19.4	68	6	2	5	2.5	5	8	141	17.6	23
KAREEM KELLY Kareem Rajai WR 5'11 186 Southern California B: 4/1/1981 Los Angeles, CA Draft: 6-203 2003 NO																															
2006	SAS	2	1	0	0	1													3	26	8.7	14	0	1	9	9.0	9				
KEITH KELLY Keith RB 5'11 205 Ottawa Sooners Jrs.; Bishop's B: 6/6/1964 St. Kitts Draft: 2B-12 1990 BC																															
1990	TOR	6				5								1	12	12.0	12	0										2	49	24.5	28
1991	TOR	8	1		1	1						6	1	30	137	4.6	27	1	6	38	6.3	17	0								
2	Years	14	1		1	6						6	1	31	149	4.8	27	1	6	38	6.3	17	0					2	49	24.5	28
KENNY KELLY Kenneth Charles, Jr. LB 6'0 207 East Central JC; Auburn B: 12/7/1977 Winston-Salem, NC																															
2002	TOR	3	0	1	0	6																									
MAURICE KELLY Maurice LB-S-CB-DH 6'0 199 East Tennessee State B: 10/9/1972 Orangeburg, SC Pro: N																															
1994	LV	18	0		1	99			4	35	15													1	21	21.0	21				
1995	TOR	15	1		2	58			1	21	4																				
1996	BC	18				58					5																				
1997	BC*	18	0	5	3	73	3.0	30.0	4	29	3	6	1																		
1998	WPG	18	1	4	4	84	1.0	10.0	5	121	4	12	2																		
1999	WPG*	18	0	3	8	94	5.0	17.0	2	2	2																				
2003	WPG	17	0	2	0	80			1	0	2																				
2004	WPG	18	0	1	2	85	1.0	3.0	1	25	0																	1	0	0.0	0
8	Years	140	2	15	20	631	10.0	60.0	18	233	35	18	3											1	21	21.0	21	1	0	0.0	0
RON KELLY Ronald FB-OHB-LB 6'1 208 Winnipeg Light Infantry Jrs. B: 10/5/1933																															
1953	WPG	7												21	97	4.6		0	1	17	17.0	17	0					1	4	4.0	4
1955	WPG	1																													
1956	WPG	11												1	0	0.0	0	0	1	15	15.0	15	0								
1957	CAL	15	0		1							1	0	1	5	5.0	5	0	1	16	16.0	16	0					7	158	22.6	34
1958	CAL	15												11	21	1.9	7	0	5	54	10.8	12	0					3	39	13.0	17
1959	CAL	16							5	32				2	4	2.0	4	0													
1960	SAS	11	0		1																							1	14	14.0	14
1961	SAS	2																													
8	Years	78	0		2				5	32		1	0	36	127	3.5	7	0	8	102	12.8	17	0					12	215	17.9	34
RON KELLY Ron SB 6'4 218 St. Mary's (Nova Scotia); Ottawa B: 11/18/1983																															
2010	CAL	3				0																									
TIM KELLY Timothy James LB 6'1 210 Notre Dame B: 12/25/1948 Dayton, OH D: 11/23/2010 Lake Wylie, SC Draft: 5-105 1971 NE																															
1971	EDM	4							2	6																		1	23	23.0	23
1972	EDM	3																													
2	Years	7							2	6																		1	23	23.0	23
BRIAN KELSEY Brian RB-WR 6'0 200 Colorado B: 1949																															
1971	MTL	5												1	-1	-1.0	-1	0	2		0.0		0	3	6	2.0	3				
1971	BC	9																	2		0.0		0								
1971	Year	14												1	-1	-1.0	-1	0	4	39	9.8	12	0	3	6	2.0	3				
DERRICK KELSON Derrick LaKeith CB 6'0 190 Purdue B: 5/14/1968 Warren, OH Draft: 11-279 1990 NYJ Pro: E																															
1992	HAM	1				1																									
1993	HAM	7	0		1	23			1	0																					
2	Years	8	0		1	24			1	0																					
DENNIS KEMP Dennis Garland OT 6'2 250 Tulsa B: 3/21/1946 Santa Monica, CA Pro: W																															
1971	CAL	15																													
JIMMY KEMP Jimmy QB 6'1 194 Wake Forest B: 6/27/1971 Potomac, MD																															
1994	SAC	7				0																									
1995	SA	18	7		2	1								17	54	3.2	23	0													
1996	MTL	8	1		0	0						6	1	10	61	6.1	17	1													
1996	SAS	10	5		1	2						6	1	20	37	1.9	10	1													
1996	Year	18	6		1	2						12	2	30	98	3.3	17	2													
1997	EDM	18	4	0	1	0								20	147	7.4	17	0													
1998	EDM	18	3	0	0	0						18	3	26	207	8.0	25	3													
1999	TOR	16	4	0	3	2						2	0	32	149	4.7	28	0													
2000	TOR	18	3	0	3	1								22	163	7.4	22	0													
2001	TOR	18	7	0	2	2						6	1	55	351	6.4	28	1													
8	Years	121	34	0	12	8						38	6	202	1169	5.8	28	6													
PETER KEMPF Peter K-FL-SE-FB -TE 6'2 200 Western Washington; British Columbia B: 1940																															
1963	BC	16	0		1							109	0						4	38	9.5	15	0								
1964	BC	16										81	0						3	48	16.0	27	0								
1965	BC	16							1			82	3						26	457	17.6	53	3								
1966	MTL	14										67	2						18	235	13.1	25	2								
1967	EDM	16	1		0							83	0						16	261	16.3	38	0								
1968	EDM	16	2		1							80	0						3	40	13.3	21	0								
6	Years	94	3		2				1	0		502	5						70	1079	15.4	53	5								
KEITH KENDALL Keith T 6'2 194 Weston Wildcats Jrs. B: 1929																															

Year	Team	GP	FM	FF	FR	TK	SK	YDS	IR	YDS	PD	PTS	TD	RA	YDS	AVG	LG	TD	REC	YDS	AVG	LG	TD	PR	YDS	AVG	LG	KOR	YDS	AVG	LG
1950	WPG	9																													
LELAND KENDALL Leland G. T 6'7 245 Oklahoma State B: 5/20/1933 D: 8/27/2008 Tulsa, OK Draft: 5-59 1955 CHIB																															
1955	SAS	15																													
1956	SAS	10																													
2	Years	25																													
MARV KENDRICKS Marvin RB 5'10 200 Riverside JC; UCLA B: 3/5/1949 Mount Vernon, IL Pro: W																															
1973	TOR	5	3		0									73	316	4.3	13	0	6	40	6.7	22	0					1	15	15.0	15
CHRIS KENEALLY Chris OT 6'6 290 Rhode Island B: 5/12/1972																															
1995	OTT	3				0																									
1996	OTT	4				0																									
2	Years	7				0																									
JOHN KENERSON John D. DE 6'3 255 Kentucky State B: 3/18/1938 Chicago, IL Pro: N																															
1963	OTT	9																													
1964	OTT	13																													
1965	MTL	4																													
1965	WPG	1																													
1965	Year	5																													
3	Years	26																													
ALEX KENESKY Alex C 6'1 215 B: 1925																															
1949	HAM	12																													
DARNELL KENNEDY Darnell QB 6'0 190 Alabama State B: 10/8/1979 Mobile, AL																															
2002	CAL	18	1	0	2	0								3	22	7.3	14	0													
2003	CAL	3	1	0	0	0								1	12	12.0	12	0													
2003	OTT	15	1	0	0	0								1	-7	-7.0	-7	0													
2003	Year	18	2	0	0	0								2	5	2.5	12	0													
2004	OTT	16	4	0	0	0						6	1	23	140	6.1	25	1													
2005	OTT	18				0								2	6	3.0	4	0													
2006	TOR	3				0																									
5	Years	58	7	0	2	0						6	1	30	173	5.8	25	1													
JOHN KENNEDY John OG-DT 6'1 240 Ottawa Sooners Jrs. B: 5/27/1952 Oshawa, ON																															
1972	OTT	6																													
1973	BC	1																													
1974	MTL	4																													
1975	TOR	16																													
1976	TOR	16	0		1																										
5	Years	43	0		1																										
STU KENNEDY Stu G-C 6'1 215 Carleton; Queen's B: 1931 Draft: 2-6 1953 OTT																															
1953	OTT	6																													
1954	OTT	14																													
2	Years	20																													
TREVOR KENNERD Trevor K-P 5'6 170 Alberta B: 12/23/1955 Calgary, AB																															
1980	WPG	16	0		1							142	0																		
1981	WPG*	16										185	0																		
1982	WPG	16										149	0	1	5	5.0	5	0													
1983	WPG+	16	0		1							166	0																		
1984	WPG	16										152	0											1	5	5.0	5				
1985	WPG*	16										198	0	1	5	5.0	5	0													
1986	WPG	9										105	0																		
1987	WPG	18	1		1	0						177	0																		
1988	WPG	18	2		0	0						149	0																		
1989	WPG	18	1		0	1						146	0																		
1990	WPG	18				0						182	0																		
1991	WPG	10	1		1	1						89	0	1	5	5.0	5	0													
12	Years	187	5		4	2						1840	0	3	15	5.0	5	0						1	5	5.0	5				
CLINT KENT Clinton LB-DH-CB 5'10 192 James Madison B: 10/14/1983 Macon, GA																															
2006	MTL	9	0	0	1	36	1.0				3																				
2010	WPG	17	0	2	1	90	2.0	22.0	1	0	4																				
2011	WPG	16	0	0	2	68	4.0	25.0			3																				
3	Years	42	0	2	4	194	7.0	47.0	1	0	10																				
PHILLIP KENT Phillip LB 6'0 240 Mississippi B: 9/19/1970 Jackson, MS																															
1994	TOR	4				8	1.0	9.0																							
ROBERT KENT Robert QB 6'4 222 Jackson State B: 10/6/1980 Greenville, MS																															
2007	TOR	2				0																									
DANNY KEPLEY Danny Ray LB 6'1 218 East Carolina B: 8/24/1953 Stanly County, NC																															
1975	EDM	4	0		1																										
1976	EDM	14			2																										
1977	EDM*	16	0		2				3	63		6	1															2	1	0.5	1
1978	EDM*	15	0		1				4	56																		1	11	11.0	11
1979	EDM*	16	0		1				3	17		6	1	1	37	37.0	37	0													
1980	EDM*	16	0		2				3	58																					
1981	EDM*	16	1		0		6.0		6	84																					
1982	EDM	16	0		1		5.0		3	16		6	1																		
1983	EDM	15	0		2		7.5		2	19																					
1984	EDM	10	0		2		4.0																								
10	Years	138	1		14		22.5	0.0	24	313		18	3	1	37	37.0	37	0										3	12	4.0	11
RANDY KERBOW Randall Morris FL-QB-SE 6'1 188 Rice B: 12/19/1940 Paris, TX Pro: N																															
1965	EDM	16	2		0							35	5	30	68	2.3	17	2	32	427	13.3	41	3								
1966	EDM	16	9		2							29	3	62	180	2.9	25	3	7	94	13.4	39	0								
1967	EDM	16	2		1							35	5	1	13	13.0	13	0	41	616	15.0	56	5								
1968	EDM	7										8	1	1	17	17.0	17	1	14	314	22.4	48	0								
4	Years	55	13		3							107	14	94	278	3.0	25	6	94	1451	15.4	56	8								
GARY KERL Gary Curtis LB 6'2 227 Laney JC; Utah B: 7/12/1947 Oakland, CA Draft: 11-279 1969 STL																															
1971	SAS	1																													
JOHN KERNS John Emery T 6'3 245 Ohio University; Duke; North Carolina; Ohio University B: 6/10/1923 Ashtabula, OH D: 6//1988 Draft: 15-137 1946 PHI Pro: A																															
1950	TOR	12										5	1																		
1951	TOR	12																													
2	Years	24										5	1																		
GARY KERR Gary Jim TE-WR 6'3 215 Cal Poly (San Luis Obispo) B: 4/3/1947 Hayward, CA																															
1972	CAL	16										18	3						38	721	19.0	73	3					1	18	18.0	18
MIKE KERR Mike A. LB 6'5 240 Florida B: 11/10/1969 Miami, FL Pro: E																															
1993	EDM	1																										1	4	4.0	4
1994	BAL	7				6																						1	4	4.0	4
2	Years	8				6																									
MIKE KERRIGAN Michael Joseph QB 6'3 205 Northwestern B: 4/27/1960 Chicago, IL Pro: N																															
1986	HAM+	18	5		0									25	81	3.2	16	0													
1987	HAM	14	3		2	1								9	22	2.4	6	0													
1988	HAM	13	5		1	1						6	1	20	59	3.0	12	1													
1989	HAM+	16	6		0	2								21	17	0.8	12	0													
1990	HAM	18	5		0	0						6	1	24	37	1.5	-22	1													
1991	HAM	18	3		2	0						6	1	16	28	1.8	5	1													
1992	TOR	13				0						6	1	2	4	2.0	2	1													
1993	TOR	7	1		0	1								4	11	2.8	4	0													

Year	Team	GP	FM	FF	FR	TK	SK	YDS	IR	YDS	PD	PTS	TD	RA	YDS	AVG	LG	TD	REC	YDS	AVG	LG	TD	PR	YDS	AVG	LG	KOR	YDS	AVG	LG
1994	TOR	10	1		1	0						6	1	8	29	3.6	11	1	1	18	18.0	18	0								
1995	HAM	18				1								2	3	1.5	3	0													
1996	HAM	9				2								4	14	3.5	7	0													
11	Years	154	29		6	8						30	5	135	305	2.3	16	5	1	18	18.0	18	0								
LARRY KERYCHUK Larry DB-FL-QB 6'1 190 Idaho State B: 1946																															
1969	EDM	12	1		0														1	5	5.0	5	0								
1970	EDM	14																													
1971	WPG	16	0		1				1	1																					
1972	WPG	6																						4	13	3.3	4				
4	Years	48	1		1				1	1									1	5	5.0	5	0	4	13	3.3	4				
PAT KESI Patrick OT 6'3 314 Washington B: 9/10/1973 American Samoa Pro: X																															
1999	TOR	7	0	0	1	1																									
1999	WPG	9	0	0	0	1																									
1999	Year	16	0	0	3	2																									
PHIL KESSEL Philip J. QB 6'2 197 Northern Michigan B: 4/28/1958 Ann Arbor, MI Draft: 10A-257 1981 WAS																															
1982	CAL	9	1		0									5	11	2.2	8	0													
ANTHONY KETCHUM Anthony Raye WR 5'8 160 Houston B: 11/20/1962 Needville, TX																															
1987	HAM	3				0													6	88	14.7	38	0	2	18	9.0	10	4	76	19.0	19
ROGER KETTLEWELL Roger DH-LB 6'2 205 Vancouver Blue Bombers Jrs.; Simon Fraser B: 1945																															
1966	BC	6																						1	0	0.0	0				
1967	BC	16							2	27														1	0	0.0	0	1	10	10.0	10
1968	BC	5	1		0																							1	9	9.0	9
1969	EDM	16							2	0		3	0											1	0	0.0	0				
4	Years	43	1		0				4	27		3	0											3	0	0.0	0	2	19	9.5	10
LARRY KEY Larry RB 5'9 185 Florida State B: 7/12/1956 Inverness, FL Draft: 10A-256 1978 GB Pro: U																															
1978	BC	16	2		0							60	10	215	1054	4.9	66	7	48	506	10.5	46	3					20	649	32.5	86
1979	BC+	16	5		0							54	9	204	1060	5.2	71	9	42	289	6.9	32	0					16	365	22.8	60
1980	BC	8	1		0							30	5	97	491	5.1	28	4	13	94	7.2	19	1					9	298	33.1	48
1981	BC+	16	2		4							114	19	204	1098	5.4	60	17	29	237	8.2	29	2					15	277	18.5	25
1982	BC	16	1		1							74	12	167	820	4.9	62	10	36	331	9.2	38	2					2	46	23.0	23
5	Years	72	11		5							332	55	887	4523	5.1	71	47	168	1457	8.7	46	8					62	1635	26.4	86
ADOLPH KEYES Adolph Leonard DB 5'9 180 Oregon; Georgia Southern B: 8/3/1981 Alameda County, CA																															
2004	SAS	3				5																									
BOBBY KEYES Bobby CB-DH 6'0 186 Jones County JC; Alabama-Birmingham B: 11/14/1982 Raleigh, MS																															
2009	EDM	13				43			1	67	3																				
EAGLE KEYS Eagle (Buddy) C-LB 6'3 217 Western Kentucky B: 12/4/1923																															
1949	MTL	12																													
1950	MTL	12																													
1951	MTL	11																													
1952	EDM	13			2				3	26																					
1953	EDM+	16																													
1954	EDM+	16	1		0																										
6	Years	80	1		2				3	26																					
ISAAC KEYS Van, II LB 6'3 247 North Alabama*; Morehouse B: 6/6/1978 St. Louis, MO Pro: EN																															
2007	EDM	8	0	0	1	6			0	0	2																				
TYRONE KEYS Tyrone Paree DE 6'7 268 Mississippi State B: 10/24/1960 Brookhaven, MS Draft: 5-113 1981 NYJ Pro: N																															
1981	BC	5					1.0																								
1982	BC	10					6.5																								
2	Years	15					7.5																								
OBBY KHAN Ibrahim C 6'3 306 Simon Fraser B: 10/8/1980 Ottawa, ON Draft: 1A-2 2004 OTT																															
2004	OTT	18				4																									
2005	OTT	15				0																									
2006	WPG	18				1																									
2007	WPG	8				0																									
2008	WPG	5				0																									
2009	WPG	18	0	0	1	2																									
2010	WPG	18	2	0	1	5																									
2011	WPG	18				1																									
8	Years	118	2	0	2	13																									
BILLY KIDD William Wayne, Jr. C 6'3 270 Houston B: 11/28/1959 Dallas, TX Pro: NU																															
1986	OTT	8																													
CARL KIDD Carl Edward LB-DB 6'1 205 Northeastern Oklahoma A&M JC; Arkansas B: 6/14/1973 Pine Bluff, AR Pro: N																															
2000	BC	5	0	0	1	21	4.0	32.0	1	0	3																				
2001	BC	4				9	1.0	7.0			1													3	32	10.7	14	10	227	22.7	34
2002	BC+	18	0	1	4	81	1.0	3.0	5	134	5	12	2															2	33	16.5	33
2003	BC	17	0	3	2	87	2.0	9.0	3	106	4	12	2															4	60	15.0	30
2004	BC	16	0	2	2	61	3.0	12.0	1	35	2	6	1																		
2005	BC	16				45	2.0	13.0																							
2006	BC+	18	0	1	2	63	4.0	22.0			2																				
7	Years	94	0	7	11	367	17.0	98.0	10	275	17	30	5											3	32	10.7	14	16	320	20.0	34
BLAIR KIEL Blair Armstrong QB 6'0 207 Notre Dame B: 11/29/1961 Columbus, IN D: 4/8/2012 Columbus, IN Draft: 11-281 1984 TB; TD 1984 CHI-USFL Pro: N																															
1992	TOR	6				0								2	14	7.0	11	0													
MONTE KIFFIN Monte G. OT 6'3 235 Nebraska B: 2/29/1940 Lexington, NE Draft: 15-202 1964 MIN																															
1965	WPG	3																													
FRED KIJEK Fred FW-HB 6'0 198 B: 1921																															
1947	MTL	12										6	0																		
1948	MTL	12										7	0																		
1949	MTL	12										7	0																		
1950	HAM	12										11	0																		
1951	HAM	12										7	0																		
5	Years	60										38	0																		
CHARLIE KILLETT Charles William HB 6'1 205 Mississippi; Memphis B: 11/8/1940 Helena, AR Draft: 29-228(f) 1963 BUF; 16-222(f) 1963 NYG Pro: N																															
1964	OTT	4												8	28	3.5	6	0	0	5		5	0					4	64	16.0	30
DOUG KILLOH Doug DE 6'0 187 Regina Bombers Jrs. B: 1932																															
1953	SAS	6																													
1954	SAS	14																						1	61	61.0	61				
1955	SAS	14	0		3							10	2	0	0		0	1										1	18	18.0	18
1956	SAS	15																													
1957	SAS	16																										1	3	3.0	3
1958	SAS	16																													
1959	SAS	16										6	1															4	31	7.8	18
1960	SAS	13																													
8	Years	110	0		3							16	3					1						1	61	61.0	61	6	52	8.7	18
KEN KILREA Ken LB 6'3 237 South Carolina B: 6/4/1940 D: 1/19/2008 Hamilton, ON																															
1960	HAM	2							1	0				5	22	4.4	9	0													
1961	HAM	11																													
1962	HAM	14										6	1						9	89	9.9	24	1								
1963	HAM	14																													
1964	HAM	4																													
1964	SAS	5																													
1964	Year	9																													
5	Years	45							1	0		6	1	5	22	4.4	9	0	9	89	9.9	24	1								

Year	Team	GP	FM	FF	FR	TK	SK	YDS	IR	YDS	PD	PTS	TD	RA	YDS	AVG	LG	TD	REC	YDS	AVG	LG	TD	PR	YDS	AVG	LG	KOR	YDS	AVG	LG
JUNG-YUL KIM Jung-Yul OT 6'4 250 Toronto B: 2/9/1973 Seoul, South Korea Draft: 5-44 1996 CAL
1996	CAL	1				0
1998	CAL	18				1
1999	CAL	17	0	0	1	2
2000	TOR	11				0
2001	TOR	3				0
5	Years	50	0	0	1	3
BRUCE KIMBALL Bruce Michael OG 6'2 260 Massachusetts B: 8/19/1956 Beverly, MA Draft: 7-192 1979 PIT Pro: N
1979	TOR	8
1980	TOR	11	0		2
2	Years	19	0		2
TONY KIMBROUGH Anthony QB 6'2 180 Grand Rapids JC; Western Michigan B: 1/20/1964 Detroit, MI
1989	OTT	15				1								13	93	7.2	14	0
1990	OTT	12	2		1	0								4	8	2.0	6	0
1991	BC	18				1						6	1	3	24	8.0	17	1
1992	BC	11	6		1	0								31	128	4.1	14	0
4	Years	56	8		2	2						6	1	51	253	5.0	17	1
BOB KIMOFF Bob FB-LB 6'0 190 Toronto B: 1932 Draft: 2-6 1955 TOR
1955	EDM	14	1		2							5	1	28	134	4.8	9	1	1	16	16.0	16	0	2	9	4.5	5
1956	EDM	9										12	2	27	115	4.3	13	2	1	11	11.0	11	0
1957	EDM	13							2	3				6	24	4.0	13	0	2	47	23.5	24	0	1	0	0.0	0
1958	EDM	9							1	0
4	Years	45	1		2				3	3		17	3	61	273	4.5	13	3	4	74	18.5	24	0	3	9	3.0	5
BLACKIE KINCAID James Davis DB 5'11 180 South Carolina B: 8/11/1930 Ansted, WV Draft: 3A-29 1954 LARM Pro: N
1955	HAM	2												2	15	7.5	12	0	1	20	20.0	20	0
1955	MTL	3												14	61	4.4	12	0	3	28	9.3	11	0	1	4	4.0	4	1	0	0.0	0
1955	Year	5												16	76	4.8	12	0	4	48	12.0	20	0	1	4	4.0	4	1	0	0.0	0
JOHN KINCH John FB 6'1 205 Youngstown State B: 12/20/1954 Draft: TE 1977 HAM
1977	HAM	15												1	0	0.0	0	0	1	11	11.0	11	0					1	18	18.0	18
1978	HAM	6	1		0							18	3	22	103	4.7	9	0	16	109	6.8	17	3
1978	TOR	8	1		0									21	82	3.9	13	0	8	14	1.8	12	0
1978	Year	14	2		0							18	3	43	185	4.3	13	0	24	123	5.1	17	3
1979	OTT	3										6	1						2	19	9.5	16	1					2	52	26.0	30
1979	SAS	12	1		1									23	92	4.0	21	0	6	69	11.5	21	0					1	9	9.0	9
1979	Year	15	1		1							6	1	23	92	4.0	21	0	8	88	11.0	21	1					3	61	20.3	30
1980	SAS	8	4		0							8	1	27	130	4.8	21	0	17	84	4.9	17	1					1	12	12.0	12
1981	TOR	8										6	1	5	9	1.8	5	0	3	32	10.7	18	1					1	10	10.0	10
5	Years	40	7		1							38	6	99	416	4.2	21	0	53	338	6.4	21	6					6	101	16.8	30
GREG KINDLE Gregory Lamarr OG 6'4 265 Tennessee State B: 9/16/1950 Houston, TX Draft: 2-33 1974 STL Pro: N
1978	WPG	13
1979	WPG	7
2	Years	20
BERNARD KING Bernard LB 6'1 228 Syracuse B: 7/5/1962 Griffin, GA Draft: TD 1984 NJ-USFL; 10-265 1985 CIN
1985	SAS	5	0		1
DAVE KING Dave WB-DB 5'11 180 Balmy Beach Marines Jrs. B: 10/25/1935 Toronto, ON
1958	MTL	13																						36	240	6.7	18	4	73	18.3	26
1959	MTL	7							1	15
1960	MTL	4																						3	13	4.3	8
3	Years	24							1	15														39	253	6.5	18	4	73	18.3	26
DON KING Don C Regina Dales Jrs. B: 3/23/1919 Regina, SK D: 6/28/1986
1946	SAS	2
DON KING Donald William T 6'3 260 Kentucky B: 3/11/1929 McBee, SC Pro: N
1955	OTT	7
ED KING Edward E'Dainia OT 6'4 303 Auburn B: 12/3/1969 Fort Benning, GA Draft: 2-29 1991 CLE Pro: ENX
1998	SAS	4				0
1999	MTL	2				0
2	Years	6				0
EMANUEL KING Emanuel DE 6'4 251 Alabama B: 8/15/1963 Leroy, AL Draft: 1B-25 1985 CIN; TD 1985 BIR-USFL Pro: EN
1993	SAC	5				4	2.0	17.0
EMMETT KING Emmett Lee RB 5'11 200 Houston B: 1/20/1956 Lufkin, TX Draft: 7A-179 1979 NYJ
1979	OTT	5	1		0							18	3	57	277	4.9	69	3	13	95	7.3	15	0
FRANKLIN KING Franklin NG-DT 6'0 255 Kansas B: 3/3/1957 Pocatello, ID
1980	BC	9																										2	16	8.0	11
1981	CAL	11					4.5
1982	CAL	9	0		1		5.5
1983	TOR+	16	0		1		4.0
1984	TOR	5					2.0																					1	-20	-20.0	-20
1985	HAM	2					1.0
6	Years	52	0		2		17.0																					3	-4	-1.3	11
HENRY KING Henry Louis CB-TE 6'4 205 San Francisco CC; Utah State B: 1/25/1945 Alameda County, CA Draft: 3B-74 1967 NYJ Pro: N
1970	EDM	16	2		1							6	1	10	17	1.7	5	0	51	638	12.5	46	1
1971	EDM	10																	26	259	10.0	32	0
2	Years	26	2		1							6	1	10	17	1.7	5	0	77	897	11.6	46	1
JAMES KING James Norris LB-DE 6'0 230 Trinity Valley JC; Texas A&M-Kingsville B: 2/9/1968 Dallas, TX
1990	SAS	7				5
1991	SAS	18	0		4	65	2.0		1	0
1992	SAS	5				25
1994	SAC	9				14	6.0	15.0
1995	SA	17	0		2	39	9.0	68.0			3
5	Years	56	0		6	148	17.0	83.0	1	0	3
KENNY KING Kenneth Leon RB 5'11 205 Oklahoma B: 3/7/1957 Clarendon, TX Draft: 3-72 1979 HOU Pro: N
1987	HAM	2	2		0	1						6	1	34	109	3.2	22	1	4	31	7.8	10	0
LENNIE KING Leonard J. OHB 6'0 205 Connecticut B: 1936 Waterbury, CT D: 7/10/1989 Cabin John, MD Draft: 18-210 1958 WAS
1960	SAS	5							2	10		1	0						1	23	23.0	23	0					2	41	20.5	25
LORNE KING Lorne RB 6'0 210 Toronto B: 4/12/1967 Scarborough, ON Draft: 1-4 1992 BC
1992	BC	18	1		1	22						18	3	27	125	4.6	57	3	6	44	7.3	13	0					1	9	9.0	9
1993	TOR	10				6								6	25	4.2	8	0
2	Years	28	1		1	28						18	3	33	150	4.5	57	3	6	44	7.3	13	0					1	9	9.0	9
MIKE KING Mike FB-DG-LB 6'0 210 B: 1925
1949	TOR	1
1950	EDM+	12										45	9	97	409	4.2		9
1951	EDM+	14										35	7	206	910	4.4		7										8	110	13.8
1952	EDM	16										20	4	100	562	5.6	36	4	3	63	21.0	34	0					3	53	17.7	23
1953	EDM	16							5	25				1	0	0.0	0	0
1954	EDM	12							1	7				5	26	5.2	13	0
1955	EDM	15
1956	EDM	1
1957	EDM	8	0		2
9	Years	95	0		2				6	32		100	20	409	1907	4.7	36	20	3	63	21.0	34	0					11	163	14.8	23
NORM KING Norman G-T 6'1 195 B: 1928
1949	WPG	2
PAT KING Pat E

Year	Team	GP	FM	FF	FR	TK	SK	YDS	IR	YDS	PD	PTS	TD	RA	YDS	AVG	LG	TD	REC	YDS	AVG	LG	TD	PR	YDS	AVG	LG	KOR	YDS	AVG	LG
1949	EDM	11																													
PETE KING Peter E 6'4 180 Queen's																															
1946	MTL	10										5	1										1								
1947	MTL	8										5	1																		
2	Years	18										10	2										1								
QUENTON KING Quenton DB 6'1 205 Appalachian State B: 8/9/1971 Chesapeake Beach, MD																															
1995	SHR	8				11																									
WILLIAM KING William LB 5'10 211 Marshall B: 10/30/1971 Cleveland, OH																															
1994	BAL	4				7																									
KLIFF KINGSBURY Kliff Timothy QB 6'4 210 Texas Tech B: 8/9/1979 San Antonio, TX Draft: 6-201 2003 NE Pro: EN																															
2007	WPG	14				0																									
GENE KINISKI Eugene N. T 6'3 225 Edmonton Jrs.; Arizona B: 11/23/1928 Edmonton, AB D: 4/14/2010 Blaine, WA																															
1949	EDM	10										5	1																		
1952	EDM	2																													
1953	EDM	13																													
3	Years	25										5	1																		
RODNEY KINLAW Rodney Eddrick RB 5'9 201 Penn State B: 4/6/1985																															
2009	EDM	1				0																						1	-2	-2.0	-2
GEORGE KINNEY George Raynard DE 6'4 250 Wiley B: 11/13/1942 Jackson, MS Draft: 9- 1965 HOU Pro: N																															
1966	MTL	9	0		2																										
KELVIN KINNEY Kelvin Lamonta DL 6'6 264 Virginia State B: 12/31/1972 Montgomery, WV Draft: 6-174 1996 WAS Pro: NX																															
2001	TOR	13	0	1	0	28	5.0	26.0			2																				
2002	EDM	12				16	3.0	30.0			1																				
2003	TOR	3				3	1.0	0.0																							
2003	EDM	10				11	8.0	63.0																							
2003	Year	13				14	9.0	63.0																							
2004	EDM	7				13	3.0	16.0																							
4	Years	35	0	1	0	71	20.0	135.0			3																				
DAVE KINZIE David DE 6'3 240 Bowling Green State B: 5/15/1965 Oakville, ON Draft: 3-22 1989 TOR																															
1989	TOR	11	0		1	1																									
MONTRESSA KIRBY Montressa Datone QB 6'0 198 Jacksonville State B: 12/1/1976 Anniston, AL																															
1999	HAM	18	1	0	0	1								5	45	9.0	18	0													
ROY KIRBYSON Roy HB 5'7 153																															
1946	MTL	5																													
1947	MTL	11																													
1948	MTL	4																													
3	Years	20																													
ERNIE KIRK Ernest T. DT-OG 6'2 265 Howard Payne B: 4/14/1952 Pro: N																															
1975	EDM	4																													
1976	EDM	11			3																										
2	Years	15	0		3																										
KELVIN KIRK Kelvin SE-SB 5'10 181 Dayton B: 12/31/1954 Mount Pleasant, FL D: 7/2/2003 Toronto, ON Draft: 17-487 1976 PIT																															
1977	TOR	16	4		1							18	3						32	577	18.0	62	3	30	213	7.1	36	12	265	22.1	34
1978	CAL	14	3		1									1	6	6.0	6	0	23	487	21.2	71	0	36	367	10.2	31	20	477	23.9	45
1979	SAS	3	3		0														9	85	9.4	16	0	14	205	14.6	26	2	39	19.5	29
1979	CAL	12	1		0							30	5						20	322	16.1	33	3	25	278	11.1	63	10	290	29.0	95
1979	Year	15	4		0							30	5						29	407	14.0	33	3	39	483	12.4	63	12	329	27.4	95
1980	CAL	11	1		0							8	1	2	11	5.5	9	0	10	206	20.6	52	1	14	145	10.4	36	10	217	21.7	32
1981	OTT	14										48	8	2	13	6.5	10	1	38	804	21.2	53	6	23	322	14.0	92	15	336	22.4	35
1982	OTT	5	2		0							18	3	3	-6	-2.0	9	0	15	344	22.9	88	3	14	81	5.8	16	10	239	23.9	30
1983	OTT	3																	6	117	19.5	59	0	7	67	9.6	16	3	59	19.7	21
7	Years	66	14		2							122	20	8	24	3.0	10	1	153	2942	19.2	88	16	163	1678	10.3	92	82	1922	23.4	95
MATT KIRK Matt DT 6'4 250 Queen's B: 6/30/1981 Kingston, ON Draft: 5-38 2004 OTT																															
2005	OTT	18				16																						1	9	9.0	9
2006	BC	18	0	1	0	5																									
2007	BC	18				5																									
2008	BC	18				7																						1	5	5.0	5
2009	HAM	18				24	4.0	21.0			1																				
2010	HAM	17	0	0	1	27	2.0	12.0																							
2011	HAM	7	0	1	0	7	1.0	9.0																							
7	Years	114	0	2	1	91	7.0	42.0			1																	2	14	7.0	9
JOE KIRKLAND Joseph Talmadge T-G 6'4 265 Ohio State; Virginia B: 12/18/1923 Jacksonville, FL D: 9/18/2004 West Palm Beach, FL Draft: 13-112 1946 BOS																															
1949	TOR	12																													
RON KIRKLAND Ron FB 6'3 213 Nebraska B: 10/12/1943 Dothan, AL Draft: 9-229 1967 BAL																															
1967	WPG	11	1		0							12	2	85	446	5.2	29	1	18	141	7.8	29	1					6	111	18.5	29
TREMAYNE KIRKLAND Tremayne Sy SB 5'11 165 Nevada-Las Vegas; Portland State B: 1/26/1984 Sacramento, CA																															
2010	EDM	3				1													2	2	1.0	3	0	2	29	14.5	24	5	113	22.6	30
MIKE KIRKLEY Michael FB 5'10 205 Western Ontario B: 10/10/1959 D: 9/9/2002 Byram Township, NJ Draft: 1A-1 1982 TOR																															
1982	TOR	5																										1	17	17.0	17
1982	CAL	11										6	1	6	11	1.8	7	1													
1982	Year	16										6	1	6	11	1.8	7	1										1	17	17.0	17
1983	BC	1																													
1983	SAS	2												1	0	0.0	0	0													
1983	Year	3												1	0	0.0	0	0													
2	Years	6										6	1	7	11	1.6	7	1										1	17	17.0	17
MIKE KIRKPATRICK Mike OT 6'3 255 South Carolina B: 1942																															
1964	TOR	6																													
WILLIAM KIRKSEY William W. LB 6'2 221 Southern Mississippi B: 1/29/1966 Birmingham, AL Pro: EN																															
1995	BIR	3				4																									
ANDRE KIRWAN Andre WR 6'1 180 Stanford B: 1/10/1974 Winnipeg, MB																															
1997	TOR	18				1						6	1						21	416	19.8	59	1								
1998	TOR	9				2						6	1						15	194	12.9	31	1								
1999	TOR	16	1	0	1	1						12	2						62	680	11.0	41	2								
2000	TOR	17	1	0	0	3						18	3						47	484	10.3	38	3								
2001	TOR	15				0						12	2						20	183	9.2	22	2					1	2	2.0	2
2003	OTT	10				0													12	109	9.1	15	0								
6	Years	85	2	0	1	7						54	9						177	2066	11.7	59	9					1	2		2
DAVE KIRZINGER Dave OT-OG 6'3 240 British Columbia B: 3/1/1956 Saskatoon, SK Draft: 1-1 1978 CAL																															
1978	CAL	16																													
1979	CAL	16																													
1980	CAL	16	0		1																										
1981	CAL	16	0		1																										
1982	CAL	16	0		1																										
1983	CAL+	16																													
1984	CAL	14	0		1																										
1985	CAL	16	0		1																										
1986	CAL	7																													
1986	TOR	6																													
1986	Year	13																													
9	Years	133	0		5																										
MIKE KISELAK Michael John C 6'3 300 Maryland B: 3/9/1967 North Tarrytown, NY Pro: ENX																															
1993	SAC	18																													

Year	Team	GP	FM	FF	FR	TK	SK	YDS	IR	YDS	PD	PTS	TD	RA	YDS	AVG	LG	TD	REC	YDS	AVG	LG	TD	PR	YDS	AVG	LG	KOR	YDS	AVG	LG
1994	SAC	18				3													1	2	2.0	2	0								
1995	SA*	18	0		1	3																									
1996	TOR*	18	1		1	0																									
1997	TOR*	18				2													1	-3	-3.0	-3	0								
5	Years	90	1		2	8													2	-1	-0.5	2	0								
RON KISSEL Ron T 6'2 235 Pittsburgh B: 5/5/1936 Draft: 9-105 1958 NYG																															
1959	TOR	1																														
JOHN KISSELL John Jay T 6'2 245 Boston College B: 5/14/1923 Nashua, NH D: 4/9/1992 Nashua, NH Draft: 14-123 1947 LARM Pro: AN																															
1953	OTT	14										5	1																		
MIKE KISSELL Michael Andrew G 5'11 205 Minnesota B: 2/4/1920 Minneapolis, MN D: 11/10/2009 Minneapolis, MN																															
1949	WPG+	12																														
TIM KIST Tim LB 6'1 215 Manitoba B: 4/17/1958 Winnipeg, MB Draft: TE 1980 MTL																															
1981	MTL	4																														
DOUG KITTS Doug DB 6'1 195 York B: 4/28/1952 Draft: 5-42 1976 OTT																															
1976	HAM	3																														
RAYSHAUN KIZER Rayshaun A. CB-DH 5'9 185 Walsh B: 2/3/1985 Euclid, OH																															
2008	MTL	10				29					1																				
DALE KLASSEN Doug DE 6'2 220 Shearwater Flyers Ints. B: 1935																															
1958	SAS	16																														
1959	HAM	3																														
1960	HAM	8																														
1960	TOR	2																														
1960	Year	10																														
1961	TOR	8																														
4	Years	35																														
RICK KLASSEN Rick DT-OG-DE 6'2 240 Simon Fraser B: 7/25/1959 Chilliwack, BC Draft: TE 1981 BC																															
1981	BC	16					1.0																							
1982	BC	16	0		1		8.5																							
1983	BC	16	0		2		7.0																							
1984	BC	16	0		2		11.5		1	0																				
1985	BC+	16	0		1		9.0																							
1986	BC	18	0		2		8.0																							
1987	BC	17				23	8.0																							
1988	SAS	18			2	21	2.0																							
1989	BC	18				35	10.0																							
1990	BC	9				9	1.0																							
10	Years	160	0		10	88	66.0		1	0																				
GEORGE KLEIN George HB 5'8 177 McGill B: 5/15/1932 Draft: 1-2 1954 OTT																															
1954	BC	16	1						1	25														41		0.0	20	1	10	10.0	10
1955	MTL	10												2	-4	-2.0		0						12	62	5.2	10				
2	Years	26	1		0				1	25				2	-4	-2.0	0	0						53	62	1.2	20	1	10	10.0	10
JOHN KLEIN John HB 5'10 175 Regina Rams Jrs.; Edmonton Rams Ints. B: 1939																															
1960	SAS	2																														
CLIFF KLIEWER Cliff HB 5'9 173 Fort Rouge Rods Jrs.; Winnipeg Rods Jrs. B: 1927 Winnipeg, MB																															
1948	CAL	12										15	3					1					2								
1949	CAL	14																														
1950	CAL	2																														
3	Years	28										15	3					1					2								
CHUCK KLINGBEIL Charles E. DT 6'1 263 Northern Michigan B: 11/2/1965 Houghton, MI Pro: N																															
1989	SAS	5				15	1.0																							
1990	SAS	18	0		1	34	7.0																							
2	Years	23	0		1	49	8.0																							
JIMMY KLINGLER Jimmy QB 6'3 215 Houston B: 2/17/1972 Lima, OH																															
1995	BIR	18	3		1	1								4	22	5.5	9	0													
MERT KLIPPERT Merton Louis HB 160 B: 4/27/1921																															
1946	CAL	3																														
DON KLOSTERMAN Donald Clement (Duke) QB 5'10 180 Loyola Marymount B: 1/18/1930 Le Mars, IA D: 6/7/2000 Los Angeles, CA Draft: 3A-26 1952 CLE Pro: N																															
1955	CAL	13	8		0							39	7	42	4	0.1	20	7													
1956	CAL	11	6		0							33	2	50	39	0.8	23	2													
2	Years	24	14		0							72	9	92	43	0.5	23	9													
BILL KLYM William G-T																															
1946	CAL	4																														
1947	CAL	4																														
2	Years	8																														
MIKE KMECH Mike OG-DG 5'11 204 Edmonton Jrs. B: 1935																															
1956	EDM	16																														
1957	EDM	16																														
1958	EDM	16																														
1959	EDM	16																														
1960	EDM	16																														
1961	EDM+	16																														
1962	EDM	9																														
7	Years	105																														
JEFF KNAPPLE Jeff Scott QB 6'2 200 UCLA; Colorado; Northern Colorado B: 8/27/1956 Wertzburg, Germany Pro: NU																															
1981	CAL	4	1		0								4	15	3.8	8	0													
DAVE KNECHTEL Dave DT-DE 6'3 247 Wilfrid Laurier B: 9/25/1945 Kitchener, ON Draft: 1967 SAS																															
1968	TOR	14																														
1969	TOR	1																														
1970	TOR	10	0		3																										
1971	TOR	14	0		2																										
1972	TOR	14	0		1																										
1973	EDM	16																														
1974	WPG	16																														
1975	WPG	16																														
1976	WPG	16																														
1977	WPG	4																														
1978	WPG	3																														
11	Years	124	0		6																										
GUS KNICKREHM Gustav Martin T 6'3 237 Oregon B: 3/11/1925 Hemet, CA																															
1951	CAL	2																														
1952	CAL	2																														
2	Years	4																														
DeWAYNE KNIGHT DeWayne LB 6'2 215 Virginia Tech B: 8/8/1970 Hampton, VA																															
1995	OTT	15	0		1	63	1.0	2.0	1	6	2																				
1996	OTT	18	0		1	0	2.0	5.0			6																				
1997	WPG	14	0	1	1	53	2.0	18.0																							
1998	BC	9	0	0	1	33			1	43	1																				
4	Years	56	0	1	4	149	5.0	25.0	2	49	9																				
HARRY KNIGHT Harry QB 6'3 208 Richmond B: 9/9/1953 Newport News, VA Draft: 9-232 1975 OAK																															
1975	WPG	3																														
1976	WPG	16	1		0								2	8	4.0	4	0													
1977	WPG	16	1		1								6	1	0.2	3	0													

Year	Team	GP	FM	FF	FR	TK	SK	YDS	IR	YDS	PD	PTS	TD	RA	YDS	AVG	LG	TD	REC	YDS	AVG	LG	TD	PR	YDS	AVG	LG	KOR	YDS	AVG	LG
1978	WPG	5	1		0									2	9	4.5	8	0													
4	Years	40	3		1									10	18	1.8	8	0													
LAL KNIGHT Lal T. WR 6'2 200 UCLA B: 10/8/1976 Los Angeles, CA																															
2002	TOR	4				3						6	1						2	34	17.0	31	1								
2003	TOR	18	1	0	1	3						18	3	1	0	0.0	0	0	27	580	21.5	78	3					17	275	16.2	40
2	Years	22	1	0	1	6						24	4	1	0	0.0	0	0	29	614	21.2	78	4					17	275	16.2	40
LEE KNIGHT Lee SB-FB 6'3 230 Burlington Tiger-Cats Jrs. B: 2/8/1965 Wallesey, England																															
1987	HAM	12	1		0	0						6	0						7	74	10.6	15	0	1	1	1.0	1	1	6	6.0	6
1988	HAM	17				1						12	2						17	261	15.4	37	2								
1989	HAM	18	1		0	2						6	1						17	238	14.0	28	1								
1990	HAM	18				6						6	1						41	635	15.5	32	1					2	13	6.5	13
1991	HAM	18	1		0	18						12	2	15	80	5.3	30	1	16	190	11.9	30	1								
1992	HAM	18	2		0	12						24	4	39	185	4.7	25	3	29	296	10.2	29	1								
1993	HAM	17	1		0	4						12	2	28	108	3.9	22	1	30	214	7.1	18	1	1	15	15.0	15	2	9	4.5	8
1994	HAM	14	0		2	8								3	4	1.3	4	0	17	134	7.9	28	0								
1995	HAM	18	3		2	3						28	4	1	4	4.0	4	0	43	484	11.3	47	4					1	16	16.0	16
1996	OTT	8				78						18	3	10	33	3.3	10	1	10	182	18.2	46	2								
1996	HAM	4				13																									
1996	Year	12				91						18	3					1	10	182	18.2	46	2								
1997	HAM	12				4						8	1	12	41	3.4	9	0	12	116	9.7	22	1					1	12	12.0	12
11	Years	170	9		4	149						132	20	108	455	4.2	30	6	239	2824	11.8	47	14	2	16	8.0	15	7	56	8.0	16
SHAWN KNIGHT Shawn QB 5'10 175 William & Mary B: 1/19/1972																															
1995	TOR	5				0								2	10	5.0	7	0													
PAUL KNILL Paul DB-K 6'1 190 Waterloo; Western Ontario B: 1951 Draft: 5-44 1972 CAL																															
1973	CAL	2																													
DON KNOWLES Don (Sleepy) DB 5'11 155 Point Edwards Jrs. B: 1927																															
1950	WPG	12										10	2	41	142	3.5		0	7	195	27.9		2								
1951	WPG	10																	1	15	15.0	15	0	2	23	11.5		1	10	10.0	10
1954	BC	2																													
3	Years	24										10	2	41	142	3.5	0	0	8	210	26.3	15	2	2	23	11.5	0	1	10	10.0	10
GORDIE KNOWLTON Gordon LB-RB 5'11 214 Jacksonville State B: 10/17/1949 Draft: TE 1974 MTL																															
1976	TOR	12												10	43	4.3	8	0										5	72	14.4	17
1977	TOR	14	1		2				2	21		6	1						3	55	18.3	22	0					1	8	8.0	8
1978	TOR	16	0		3																			2	9	4.5	7				
1979	TOR	8																													
1980	MTL	5																													
5	Years	55	1		5				2	21		6	1	10	43	4.3	8	0	3	55	18.3	22	0	2	9	4.5	7	6	80	13.3	17
MARKEITH KNOWLTON Markeith LB-DB 6'0 205 North Texas B: 6/4/1983 Elaine, AR																															
2006	BC	15	0	0	1	22			1	67	3	6	1																		
2007	BC	17	0	0	1	45	2.0	11.0			5																				
2008	HAM*	18	0	4	0	95	2.0	4.0	4	121	3	6	1																		
2009	HAM+	18	0	4	4	95	1.0	4.0	4	40	3	12	2																		
2010	HAM+	18	0	4	6	71	3.0	11.0	3	7	3	6	1																		
2011	HAM	18	0	1	2	64	3.0	14.0	1	1	4																				
6	Years	104	0	13	14	392	11.0	44.0	13	236	21	30	5																		
BILL KNOX William Robert DB 5'9 192 Purdue B: 6/19/1951 Elba, AL Pro: N																															
1978	HAM	4																													
GREG KNOX Greg S 6'0 180 Wilfried Laurier B: 12/6/1969 Toronto, ON Draft: 6-47 1992 CAL																															
1992	CAL	18	0		1	30			1	0																					
1993	CAL	18	1		2	38	1.0	10.0	3	15																					
1994	CAL*	18	0		2	66	2.0	17.0	10	151	6	6	1																		
1995	CAL	18	0		1	53	1.0	17.0	5	61	2																				
1996	CAL	18	0		2	44			3	58	8	6	1																		
1997	CAL	4				6																									
1998	CAL	4				5					1																				
7	Years	98	1		8	242	4.0	44.0	22	285	17	12	2																		
KEVIN KNOX Kevin DeVon WR 6'3 194 Florida State B: 1/30/1971 Niceville, FL Draft: 6B-192 1994 BUF Pro: EN																															
1997	HAM	3				1													3	30	10.0	12	0								
RONNIE KNOX Ronald QB 6'1 198 California; UCLA B: 2/14/1935 Chicago, IL D: 5/4/1992 San Francisco, CA Draft: 3-37 1957 CHIB Pro: N																															
1956	HAM	7												14	35	2.5	16	0													
1956	CAL	6	5		0							25	3	36	80	2.2	20	3													
1956	Year	13	5		0							25	3	50	115	2.3	20	3													
1958	TOR	8												32	-39	-1.2	12	0													
1959	TOR	5										1	0	14	49	3.5	15	0													
3	Years	20	5		0							26	3	96	125	1.3	20	3													
CARY KOCH Cary WR 6'0 198 Tulane; Virginia B: 8/28/1986 Baton Rouge, LA																															
2010	SAS	5				0						20	3						21	299	14.2	42	3								
2011	SAS	9				2								1	5	5.0	5	0	11	101	9.2	17	0					1	19	19.0	19
2	Years	14				2						20	3	1	5	5.0	5	0	32	400	12.5	42	3					1	19	19.0	19
KYLE KOCH Kyle OG-C 6'2 319 McMaster B: 12/10/1984 Kenora, ON																															
2007	WPG	4				0																									
2008	WPG	9				1																									
2009	EDM	18	0	0	1	2																									
2010	EDM	17				2																									
2011	EDM	13	0	0	2	0																									
5	Years	61	0	0	3	5																									
ROB KOCHEL Rob DB 5'11 176 Western Ontario B: 9/13/1955 Draft: 2-10 1978 CAL																															
1978	CAL	16	0		1																										
1979	CAL	16																													
1980	CAL	8																													
3	Years	40	0		1																										
DAVE KOCOUREK David Allen OE-DE 6'5 237 Wisconsin B: 8/20/1937 Chicago, IL Draft: 19-223 1959 PIT Pro: N																															
1959	WPG	8																	8	112	14.0	19	0								
RICH KOEPER Richard Manfred OT 6'4 245 Oregon State B: 7/23/1943 San Francisco, CA D: 3/10/2010 Corvallis, OR Draft: 6A-74 1965 GB Pro: N																															
1967	BC	4																													
RONNIE KOES Ron LB-OG 6'2 230 North Carolina B: 1938 Draft: 3A-30 1959 DET																															
1959	SAS	6										6	1																		
1960	SAS	1																													
1960	OTT	5							2	36																					
1960	Year	6							2	36																					
1961	OTT	8																													
3	Years	15							2	36		6	1																		
CRAIG KOINZAN Craig DE-LB 6'4 238 Doane B: 1948 Davenport, NE Draft: 13-324 1969 GB																															
1969	CAL	13	0		1																										
1970	CAL	16	1		5							6	1																		
1971	CAL*	16	0		1																										
1972	CAL	16	0		2																										
1973	CAL	8																													
1974	CAL	5																													
1974	EDM	2																													
1974	Year	7																													
6	Years	74	1		9							6	1																		

Year	Team	GP	FM	FF	FR	TK	SK	YDS	IR	YDS	PD	PTS	TD	RA	YDS	AVG	LG	TD	REC	YDS	AVG	LG	TD	PR	YDS	AVG	LG	KOR	YDS	AVG	LG
JEFF KOLBERG Jeff WR 5'11 190 Oregon State B: 1949																															
1974	WPG	16	1		2																			21	26	1.2	7	2	22	11.0	15
ART KOLISNYK Art G Manitoba B: 1922																															
1948	SAS	12																													
KEVIN KONAR Kevin LB 6'1 215 British Columbia B: 7/8/1958 Vancouver, BC Draft: 1-5 1980 BC																															
1980	BC	16																										1	0	0.0	0
1981	BC	16	0		1		3.0																								
1982	BC	16					1.5		2	52		6	1																		
1983	BC	16	1		1		3.0		2	8																					
1984	BC	16	0		1		2.0		1	0																					
1985	BC*	16					5.0		5	22																		1	0	0.0	0
1986	BC	17	0		1		5.0		2	7																					
1987	BC*	18	0		4	46	4.0		2	19		6	1																		
1988	BC	18	0		4	67	4.0		0	6																					
1989	BC	13	0		1	40	1.0																								
10	Years	162	1		13	153	28.5		14	114		12	2															2	0	0.0	0
WALT KONARSKI Walt T 6'2 212 Winnipeg Light Infantry Jrs. B: 1930																															
1950	WPG	14																													
1951	WPG	13																													
2	Years	27																													
TOMASI KONGAIKA Tomasi DL 6'1 295 Washington State B: 7/5/1980 Tonga																															
2003	TOR	1				2																									
JOHN KONIHOWSKI John FL 6'3 190 Saskatchewan B: 1/6/1950 Draft: 2A-13 1972 CAL																															
1974	EDM	4																													
1975	EDM	16										48	8						45	828	18.4	80	8								
1976	EDM	7																	13	170	13.1	43	0								
1977	EDM	10										12	2						21	368	17.5	47	2								
1978	EDM	7																	2	75	37.5	64	0								
1979	EDM	16										24	4						30	490	16.3	52	4					2	0	0.0	0
1980	EDM	5																	2	17	8.5	9	0								
1981	WPG	14																	20	254	12.7	24	0					1	2	2.0	2
1982	WPG	16																	3	30	10.0	22	0								
9	Years	95										84	14						136	2232	16.4	80	14					3	2	0.7	2
RICK KONOPKA Rick LB 6'2 218 Wilfrid Laurier B: 1/27/1950 Draft: 2-10 1974 TOR																															
1974	TOR	13	0		1				1	0																					
1975	CAL	16	0		1																							3	43	14.3	15
1976	CAL	4																													
1977	SAS	5																													
1977	HAM	3																													
1977	Year	8																													
4	Years	38	0		2				1	0																		3	43	14.3	15
CRAIG KOONTZ Craig Anthony David DE 6'5 260 Blinn JC; Central Missouri B: 1/15/1975 Harris County, TX																															
1999	BC	2				1																									
DARCY KOPP Darcy S 5'10 190 Calgary Colts Jrs.; Calgary B: 5/6/1963 Brooks, AB Draft: 6B-46 1984 SAS																															
1986	CAL	17	2		0							6	1						2	98	49.0	56	1	15	87	5.8	20	11	173	15.7	36
1987	CAL	18	0		1	22			2	81				1	11	11.0	11	0	1	15	15.0	15	0	8	60	7.5	14				
1988	CAL	18			1	17	1.0		2	58														4	20	5.0	9	2	9	4.5	7
1989	CAL	18	1		3	4			1	26														13	106	8.2	23				
1990	CAL	18	0		2	12																									
1991	CAL	18	0		1	17																						1	0	0.0	0
1992	CAL	6				4																									
7	Years	113	3		8	76	1.0		5	165		6	1	1	11	11.0	11	0	3	113	37.7	56	1	40	273	6.8	23	14	182	13.0	36
TROY KOPP Troy A. QB 6'2 210 Pacific B: 8/21/1971 Madison, WI																															
1998	WPG	11	6	0	0	0								9	28	3.1	19	0													
1999	WPG	18	3	0	0	1								2	-14	-7.0	0	0													
2000	CAL	11	3	0	0	0								8	14	1.8	6	0													
3	Years	40	12	0	0	1								19	28	1.5	19	0													
GEORGE KOPULOS George HB none																															
1948	HAM	6																													
JEFF KORADI Jeff FB 6'0 210 Ottawa Sooners Jrs. B: 1/20/1970																															
1995	OTT	5	1		0	3								3	8	2.7	6	0													
BUD KORCHAK Robert Borden FW-K 5'9 190 Winnipeg St. John's Grads Jrs.; Elmwood Ints. B: 8/15/1927																															
1949	WPG	12										10	2										2								
1950	WPG	13										12	2						11	249	22.6		2								
1951	WPG	14										35	7	2	-4	-2.0		0	34	491	14.4		7	1	8	8.0	8				
1952	WPG+	16							1	15		69	4	2	26	13.0	15	0	31	551	17.8	60	4								
1953	WPG+	16										66	1						18	281	15.6		1								
1954	WPG	11										28	0	1	14	14.0	14	0	1	6	6.0	6	0								
1955	MTL	10										60	0																		
1956	MTL	4										13	0						2	34	17.0	24	0								
1956	OTT	6										31	0																		
1956	Year	10										44	0						2	34	17.0	24	0								
1957	CAL	8										11	0						2	29	14.5	29	0								
9	Years	104							1	15		335	16	5	36	7.2	15	0	99	1641	16.6	60	16	1	8	8.0	8				
NICK KORDIC Nick DB-LB 6'0 210 Western Ontario B: 10/21/1983 Toronto, ON Draft: 5B-36 2007 HAM																															
2008	HAM	15	0	0	2	12																									
2009	WPG	8				10																									
2	Years	23	0	0	2	22																									
MARK KORFF Mark Curtis LB 6'1 230 Pasadena CC; Florida B: 4/5/1963 Canoga Park, CA D: 12/2/1998 CA Pro: N																															
1988	OTT	5	0		1		2.0																								
AL KORNBERG Allan G St. John's Jrs.																															
1950	WPG	1																													
TAD KORNEGAY Taddeus CB-DH-LB 5'10 183 Fordham B: 7/13/1982 Trenton, NJ																															
2005	HAM	18	0	0	2	33																									
2006	HAM	14	0	0	1	48	1.0	5.0	1	25	4																	8	192	24.0	36
2007	SAS	17				35					5																	3	87	29.0	52
2008	SAS	9	2	0	0	23	1.0	7.0			3													1	3	3.0	3	5	99	19.8	26
2009	SAS+	18	0	4	3	84			3	35	3																				
2010	SAS	17	0	4	0	50	1.0	2.0	1	18	6																				
2011	SAS	2				3																									
2011	BC	13	0	0	2	40			2	27	5																				
2011	Year	15	0	0		54			2	277	5																				
7	Years	95	2	8	8	316	3.0	14.0	7	105	26													1	3	3.0	3	16	378	23.6	52
FRANK KOSEC Mike LB 6'0 215 Waterloo B: 10/4/1958 Toronto, ON Draft: 1A-1 1981 CAL																															
1981	CAL	16	0		3		1.0																								
1982	MTL	10	0		1																										
1983	MTL	16	0		1				1	0																		7	98	14.0	11
1984	MTL	16			1							6	1											1	0	0.0	0	1	14	14.0	14
1985	MTL	12	1		1																							2	28	14.0	18
5	Years	70	1		7		1.0		1	0		6	1											1	0	0.0	0	10	140	14.0	18
BOB KOSID Robert DH-OHB 5'11 188 Kentucky B: 1942 Brandon, MB																															
1964	SAS	16												1	3	3.0	3	0	1	4	4.0	4	0	1	0	0.0	0	3	33	11.0	14

Year	Team	GP	FM	FF	FR	TK	SK	YDS	IR	YDS	PD	PTS	TD	RA	YDS	AVG	LG	TD	REC	YDS	AVG	LG	TD	PR	YDS	AVG	LG	KOR	YDS	AVG	LG
1965	SAS	16							2	1				2	3	1.5	3	0													
1966	SAS+	16							3	33														13	81	6.2	19				
1967	SAS	16	1		1				5	94														28	165	5.9	13	3	48	16.0	27
1968	SAS*	16	0		2				8	171		6	1											50	302	6.0	23				
1969	SAS	16	1		2				5	94		6	1											43	376	8.7	23				
1970	SAS	16	0		1				4	62														12	130	10.8	25				
1971	SAS	13							3	67		6	1											1	11	11.0	11				
1972	SAS	16	0		1				2	11														7	59	8.4	20				
9	Years	141	2		7				32	533		18	3	3	6	2.0	3	0	1	4	4.0	4	0	155	1124	7.3	25	6	81	13.5	27
MARK KOSMOS Mark LB 6'0 234 Oklahoma B: 10/28/1945 Baltimore, MD																															
1970	MTL	14	0		1				1	20																					
1971	MTL*	14	0		1				1	46		6	1																		
1972	HAM	12							2	0																					
1973	HAM	7	0		2				1	14																					
1973	OTT	6	0		1																										
1973	Year	13	0		3				1	14																					
1974	OTT	16							3	32		6	1																		
1975	OTT+	16	0		1				1	3																		1	11	11.0	11
1976	OTT*	16			6				1	23																		2	42	21.0	24
1977	OTT	4																													
8	Years	99	0		12				10	138		12	2															3	53	17.7	24
MIKE KOSTIN Mike QB-DB 6'1 195 Loyola Warriors Jrs.; Concordia (Canada) B: 1942 Draft: 3-20 1963 EDM																															
1964	EDM	16							4	28																					
RICK KOSWIN Rick WR 6'2 201 Manitoba B: 7/4/1954 Draft: TE 1976 WPG																															
1976	WPG	6																	1	10	10.0	10	0					1	-6	-6.0	-6
1977	WPG	16										6	1						6	83	13.8	32	1								
1978	TOR	2																													
3	Years	24										6	1						7	93	13.3	32	1					1	-6	-6.0	-6
BORIS KOTOFF Boris HB-FB 6'0 187 B: 1928																															
1954	OTT	14										5	1	13	39	3.0	10	1	1	15	15.0	15	0	25	146	5.8	13	5	72	14.4	22
1955	OTT	11												3	11	3.7	5	0						1	16	16.0	16	1	11	11.0	11
1956	OTT	14												14	78	5.6	12	0	6	91	15.2	25	0								
1957	OTT	10												1	4	4.0	4	0													
4	Years	49										5	1	31	132	4.3	12	1	7	106	15.1	25	0	26	162	6.2	16	6	83	13.8	22
ED KOTOWICH Edward Joseph OG 5'9 225 Winnipeg Rods Jrs. B: 1934 Winnipeg, MB																															
1955	WPG	13																													
1956	WPG	16																													
1957	WPG	16																													
1958	WPG	16	0		2									1	8	8.0	8	0													
1959	WPG+	16																													
1960	WPG	15	1																									1	0	0.0	0
1961	WPG	7																													
7	Years	99	1		2									1	8	8.0	8	0										1	0	0.0	0
DJEMIS KOUAME Djemis WR-SB 6'1 185 Montreal B: 4/5/1989 Montreal, QC Draft: 3-18 2011 TOR																															
2011	TOR	8				0																									
MIKE KOVAC Mike OG-DE 5'10 195 Western Ontario B: 6/7/1930 Hamilton, ON																															
1953	MTL	7																													
1954	MTL	14																													
1955	MTL	12																													
1956	MTL	14																													
1957	MTL	14																										1	0	0.0	0
1958	MTL	14																													
1959	MTL	10																													
1960	MTL	12																													
1961	MTL	13																													
9	Years	110																										1	0	0.0	0
ZOLLIE KOVACS Zolton G 6'0 225 Windsor AKO Jrs. B: 1935																															
1955	HAM	7																													
1957	HAM	2																													
2	Years	9																													
TIGER KOZAK Eddie 161 D: 1//1982 Arcadia, CA																															
1951	EDM	3																													
BOB KRAEMER Bob QB 5'11 175 Manitoba B: 5/31/1950 Draft: 1B-7 1971 WPG																															
1971	WPG	16	2		1							12	2	3	-10	-3.3	10	0	39	468	12.0	27	2								
1972	WPG	16	2		0									3	6	2.0	4	0	13	142	10.9	20	0	9	25	2.8	12				
1973	WPG	16	1		0							18	3	5	25	5.0	10	0	47	635	13.5	49	3	7	16	2.3	8				
1974	WPG	16												2	5	2.5	3	0	10	130	13.0	27	0								
4	Years	64	5		1							30	5	13	26	2.0	10	0	109	1375	12.6	49	5	16	41	2.6	12				
GARY KRAHN Gary DT-OG 6'2 242 North Dakota B: 5/12/1955 Draft: 9-76 1977 WPG																															
1977	WPG	3																													
1977	HAM	2																													
1977	Year	5																													
JOE KRALIK Joe WR 5'10 185 Washington B: 12/14/1970 DeKalb, IL																															
1995	SA	14	0		1	2						30	5						35	743	21.2	105	5								
1996	MTL	3				0													2	21	10.5	16	0								
1996	OTT	1				0													3	33	11.0	19	0								
1996	Year	4				0													5	54	10.8	19	0								
2	Years	17	0		1	2						30	5						40	797	19.9	105	5								
JASON KRALT Jason DB-LB 6'1 228 Carleton B: 2/8/1974 Ottawa, ON Draft: 3-19 1999 BC																															
1999	BC	18	0	1	0	22																									
2000	BC	18	0	0	2	56																									
2001	BC	18	3	0	1	17																									
2002	OTT	16				14								1	2	2.0	2	0													
2003	OTT	15				29					1			1	30	30.0	30	0										1	0	0.0	0
2004	OTT	18				24	1.0	10.0			1			1	15	15.0	15	0										2	13	6.5	8
2005	OTT	18				30			1	0	0																	3	37	12.3	22
7	Years	121	3	1	3	192	1.0	10.0	1	0	2			3	47	15.7	30	0										6	50	8.3	22
ERIK KRAMER William Erik QB 6'1 199 Los Angeles Pierce JC; North Carolina State B: 11/6/1964 Encino, CA Pro: N																															
1988	CAL	6	7		0	0						6	1	12	17	1.4	26	1													
MIKE KRAMER Michael T. DB 6'0 181 Alabama B: 10/13/1955																															
1979	TOR	14							4	51		6	1																		
ROGER KRAMER Roger OT 6'5 280 Kalamazoo B: 1939																															
1962	MTL	10																													
1963	OTT*	13																										1	0	0.0	0
1964	OTT*	14																													
1965	CAL	13																													
1966	CAL	11	0		1																										
1967	CAL+	16																													
1968	CAL	16	0		1																							1	2	2.0	2
1969	CAL	16																													
1970	CAL	16																													
9	Years	125	0		2																							2	2	1.0	2

Year	Team	GP	FM	FF	FR	TK	SK	YDS	IR	YDS	PD	PTS	TD	RA	YDS	AVG	LG	TD	REC	YDS	AVG	LG	TD	PR	YDS	AVG	LG	KOR	YDS	AVG	LG
JIM KRAPF James Paul G 6'0 240 Alabama B: 3/1/1950 Wilmington, DE Draft: 12-309 1973 OAK																															
1973	BC	1																													
GREG KRATZER Greg WR 5'9 195 Edmonton Wildcats Jrs.; Dickinson State B: 11/10/1962 Regina, SK Draft: 5-40 1988 EDM																															
1988	EDM	6	1		0	0																		6	41	6.8	17	4	85	21.3	33
JERRY KRAUSE Jerry G-T																															
1949	EDM	9																													
PAUL KRAUSE Paul OG-OT 6'4 245 Central Michigan B: 8/20/1951 Salzberg, Austria Draft: 3-72 1973 KC																															
1974	TOR	16	0		2									0	3		3	0													
SCOTT KRAUSE Scott QB 6'3 198 Wisconsin-Stevens Point B: 8/2/1980																															
2004	TOR	14				0								2	31	15.5	28	0													
ALEXANDER KRAUSNICK-GROH Alexander OG 6'3 290 Calgary B: 3/9/1989 Draft: 4-27 2011 SAS																															
2011	SAS	18				0																									
JOHN KRAWCZYK John DB 6'0 185 McMaster B: 1947 Draft: 1-5 1969 HAM																															
1969	HAM	1																						4	26	6.5	8				
TOM KRAWCZYK Tom OG-DE 6'1 220 McMaster B: 1947 Draft: 2- 1969 HAM																															
1969	HAM	10																													
HAL KREBS Harold OG-DE 6'0 225 none B: 1937 Edmonton, AB																															
1957	TOR	1																													
1957	HAM	2																													
1957	Year	3																													
1958	MTL	12																													
1959	MTL	14																													
1960	MTL	14																													
1961	MTL	14																													
1962	CAL	16																													
1963	CAL	16																										1	0	0.0	0
1964	CAL	12																													
1965	CAL	16	0		1																										
1966	CAL	16												1	-3	-3.0	-3	0													
1967	CAL	5																													
11	Years	136	0		1									1	-3	-3.0	-3	0										1	0	0.0	0
TOM KREBS Tom OG-C 6'3 248 Utah B: 10/17/1957 Draft: TE 1979 CAL																															
1979	CAL	11																													
1980	CAL	16																													
1981	CAL	15																													
1982	CAL	16																													
1983	CAL	3																													
1983	EDM	13																													
1983	Year	16																													
5	Years	61																													
TODD KRENBRINK Todd OL 6'7 327 Regina Rams Jrs.; Regina B: 2/22/1978 Draft: 3-22 2003 WPG																															
2004	WPG	3				0																									
ERIC KRESSER Eric Joel QB 6'2 223 Florida; Marshall B: 2/6/1973 Cincinnati, OH Pro: EN																															
2002	MTL	11	0	0	1	0																									
DEREK KRETE Derek LB 6'1 235 Western Ontario B: 11/18/1974 Peterborough, ON Draft: 4A-29 1997 MTL																															
1999	TOR	8				16																									
2000	SAS	15	0	0	1	15																									
2	Years	23	0	0	1	31																									
DOUG KRIEWALD Douglas Clark OL 6'4 245 West Texas A&M B: 8/30/1945 Seguin, TX Draft: 6B-143 1967 CHIB Pro: N																															
1971	BC	2																													
VIC KRISTOPAITIS Vic LB-FB-K 6'2 205 Dayton B: 1935 Draft: 16-188 1957 SF																															
1957	TOR	7							1	0		33	0																		
1958	TOR	14							5	49		57	0																		
1959	BC	13							4			65	0																		
1960	BC	7	1		2							16	0	1	-7	-7.0	-7	0													
1961	BC	9			2							33	0	1	-11	-11.0	-11	0													
1962	BC	7										29	0																		
6	Years	57	1		4				10	49		233	0	2	-18	-9.0	-7	0													
DARCY KROGH Darcy WR Calgary																															
1980	CAL	1																													
JIM KROHN James Marshall QB 6'3 195 Arizona B: 7/27/1957 Tucson, AZ Pro: U																															
1980	WPG	16										6	1	6	39	6.5	30	1													
CAS KROL Cas T 6'3 235 Detroit Mercy B: 1923 Draft: 16-187 1954 PIT																															
1954	TOR	10																													
JOE KROL Joseph (King) HB-QN-FB-K-P 6'0 200 Western Ontario B: 2/20/1919 Hamilton, ON D: 12/16/2008 Toronto, ON Pro: N																															
1946	TOR+	12										65	5					5													
1947	TOR+	11										41	3					1					2								
1948	TOR+	12										49	3					3													
1949	TOR	9										41	2					2													
1950	TOR	12										19	2																		
1951	TOR	11										48	0																		
1952	TOR	12										24	2					2													
1953	TOR	3																													
1955	TOR	3																													
9	Years	85										287	17					13					2								
BOB KRONENBERG Robert C 6'2 190 St. Cloud State B: 11/3/1971 Menomonee Falls, WI Pro: E																															
1994	LV	17	1		0	1																									
1995	TOR	3	1		0	0																									
2	Years	20	2		0	1																									
JOHN KROPKE John R. DT 6'4 271 Illinois State B: 1/3/1966 Chicago, IL																															
1989	OTT	2				2	1.0																								
1990	OTT	14	0		1	27	3.0																								
1991	OTT	18				46	2.0																								
1992	OTT+	17	0		1	40	7.0	43.0				6	1																		
1993	OTT+	18	0		1	31	6.0	31.0	2	38		6	1																		
1994	OTT+	18	0		3	41	5.0	36.0	1	4	1																				
1995	OTT+	18	0		3	57	1.0	7.0				6	1																		
1996	WPG	18	0		2	29	2.0	16.0	1	1	1																				
1997	SAS	18	0	0	1	43	4.0	26.0			3																				
9	Years	141	0	0	12	316	31.0	159.0	4	43	5	18	3																		
BOB KROUSE Bob LB-DB 6'1 193 none B: 2/21/1943																															
1963	HAM	14												2	-1	-0.5	3	0										3	23	7.7	13
1964	HAM	14	0		1									1	4	4.0	4	0										1	16	16.0	16
1965	HAM	14																										1	8	8.0	8
1966	HAM	6																													
1967	HAM+	14			3				2	6																		1	4	4.0	4
1968	HAM	14																						1	0	0.0	0				
1969	HAM	14							1	0																					
1970	HAM	14							2	21														1	0	0.0	0				
1971	HAM	14	1		1				1	11																					
1972	HAM	14	1		4				1	4																					
1973	HAM	14	0		3				1	25		6	1																		

Year	Team	GP	FM	FF	FR	TK	SK	YDS	IR	YDS	PD	PTS	TD	RA	YDS	AVG	LG	TD	REC	YDS	AVG	LG	TD	PR	YDS	AVG	LG	KOR	YDS	AVG	LG
1974	HAM	12	0		1																										
1975	HAM	16	0		1				1	9		6	1																		
13	Years	174	2		14				9	76		12	2	3	3	1.0	4	0						2	0	0.0	0	6	51	8.5	16
BLAINE KRUGER Blaine WR 6'4 210 Victoria Rebels Jrs.; British Columbia B: 8/23/1985 Cochrane, AB																															
2009	CAL	3				0																									
HARRY KRUGER Harry CB 5'10 175 Calgary Colts Jrs.; Calgary B: 3/11/1954 Draft: 5-44 1977 SAS																															
1979	OTT	11	0		1				3	18														2	11	5.5	10				
1979	WPG	3	0		1				1	14																					
1979	Year	14	0		2				4	32														2	11	5.5	10				
1980	WPG	11																													
1981	CAL	15	0		1																			6	25	4.2	11				
1982	CAL	16	1		0				1	0														47	306	6.5	23	1	-2	-2.0	-2
1983	CAL	16	0		1																			3	25	8.3	14				
5	Years	69	1		4				5	32														58	367	6.3	23	1	-2	-2.0	-2
OSCAR KRUGER Oskar S-OHB-CB 5'9 190 Edmonton Wildcats Jrs. B: 12/24/1932 Edmonton, AB D: 7/4/2010 Edmonton, AB																															
1954	EDM	15	1		0				2	18														44	317	7.2	20	2	38	19.0	21
1955	EDM	16	4		0							10	2	19	89	4.7	20	0	4	107	26.8	58	2	39	189	4.8	20	11	297	27.0	51
1956	EDM	16	2		7				7	28				1	3	3.0	3	0	1	23	23.0	23	0	25	140	5.6	16	4	86	21.5	34
1957	EDM+	16	1		3				7	76				9	43	4.8	18	0	2	60	30.0	39	0	12	123	10.3	24	6	151	25.2	38
1958	EDM+	13	0		3				7	53														10	50	5.0	20				
1959	EDM	16							4	3														8	56	7.0	15				
1960	EDM	10	0		2				3	66														6	42	7.0	18				
1961	EDM+	16							6	88														2	22	11.0	18				
1962	EDM+	16							4	52														7	28	4.0	16				
1963	EDM	16							6	33														5	21	4.2	7				
1964	EDM	3																													
1965	EDM	15																													
12	Years	168	8		15				46	417		10	2	29	135	4.7	20	0	7	190	27.1	58	2	158	988	6.3	24	23	572	24.9	51
STEVE KRUPEY Steve OG 6'3 265 Western Ontario B: 3/16/1965 Montreal, QC																															
1991	EDM	12				6																						1	13	13.0	13
1992	EDM	4				0																									
1993	EDM	18				2																									
1994	EDM	3				0																									
1994	OTT	5				0																									
1994	Year	8				0																									
1995	EDM	12				0													1	1	1.0	1	0								
5	Years	49				8													1	1	1.0	1	0					1	13	13.0	13
JOHN KRUSPE John DB 5'11 189 Wilfrid Laurier B: 7/5/1944 Clifford, ON Draft: 1969 MTL																															
1969	MTL	10																						1	0	0.0	0	3	59	19.7	22
1970	OTT	9							1	24																					
1971	OTT	14			2				3	65		6	1											1	0	0.0	0				
1972	OTT	14																													
1973	OTT	14							2	33														1	0	0.0	0				
1974	OTT	16							3	49																					
1975	HAM	16	0		2																										
7	Years	93	0		4				9	171		6	1											3	0	0.0	0	3	59	19.7	22
E.J. KUALE Ejiro DE-TE-LB 6'2 232 Georgia Tech; Dodge City CC; Louisiana State B: 6/22/1983 Daytona Beach, FL																															
2010	TOR	15	1	0	0	13						1	0						1	5	5.0	5	0					2	12	6.0	10
2011	TOR	15	0	1	0	58					1																				
2	Years	30	1	1	0	71					1	1	0						1	5	5.0	5	0					2	12	6.0	10
CHUCK KUBES Charles Joseph T 6'1 245 Minnesota B: 3/29/1931 Draft: 24-286(f) 1953 NYG																															
1955	HAM	3																													
DON KUBESH Don FB 6'1 195 Winnipeg Rods Jrs.; St. Vital Bulldogs Ints. B: 1940																															
1961	SAS	13																													
RICK KUCHMA Rick WB-WR 6'4 197 Hamilton Hurricanes Jrs. B: 1/28/1956																															
1979	HAM	2																													
1980	HAM	4																	1	12	12.0	12	0								
2	Years	6																	1	12	12.0	12	0								
ED KUCY Ed OT-OG 6'5 295 Arizona B: 10/19/1971 Edmonton, AB Draft: 4-35 1994 WPG																															
1994	WPG	5				0																									
1995	WPG	7				0																									
1996	EDM	18				1																									
3	Years	30				1																									
TOM KUDABA Thomas OG-C 6'0 252 Simon Fraser B: 12/4/1953 Draft: 1C-8 1976 EDM																															
1976	CAL	2																													
1976	HAM	5																													
1976	Year	7																													
1977	BC	16																													
1978	BC	16																													
1979	BC	4																													
1980	BC	16																													
1981	BC	16																													
6	Years	70																													
PETER KUDRYK Peter DT 6'4 255 none B: 1948																															
1972	HAM	14																													
MATT KUDU Matt DT 6'3 261 Mississauga Warriors Jrs.; Eastern Michigan B: 11/21/1981 Toronto, ON Draft: 3-21 2005 SAS																															
2006	TOR	7				5	2.0	7.0																							
MIKE KUHN Michael J. LB 6'3 220 Kansas State B: 1/13/1949 Manhattan, KS D: 11/29/2008 Manhattan, KS Pro: W																															
1972	WPG	12																										1	0	0.0	0
1973	WPG	5																										1	8	8.0	8
2	Years	17																										2	8	4.0	8
JASON KUIPERS Jason Francis OL 6'1 250 Florida State B: 2/26/1966 West Palm Beach, FL Pro: E																															
1994	SHR	1																													
JORMA KUISMA Jorma LB 6'0 222 Northridge State B: 1947																															
1970	MTL	14																													
1971	MTL	14																													
2	Years	28																													
JOE KUKLO Joseph S 6'2 175 Simon Fraser B: 6/22/1959 Draft: 3-22 1981 MTL																															
1981	MTL	13																													
1982	HAM	7							1	0																					
1983	BC	6																	1	8	8.0	8	0								
1984	BC	3																													
4	Years	29							1	0									1	8	8.0	8	0								
TED KUKOWSKI Theodore T. C 6'0 219 Navy; Syracuse B: 1930 Draft: 23-275 1953 NYG																															
1954	HAM	1																													
GLENN KULKA Glenn DE 6'3 255 Edmonton Huskies Jrs.; Bakersfield JC B: 5/3/1964 Edmonton AB																															
1986	MTL	6																													
1987	TOR	15	0		2	23	10.0																								
1988	TOR+	18	0		2	23	11.0																								
1989	TOR	16				32	8.0																								
1990	OTT	18				31	7.0																								
1991	OTT	15	0		1	20	3.0																								

Year	Team	GP	FM	FF	FR	TK	SK	YDS	IR	YDS	PD	PTS	TD	RA	YDS	AVG	LG	TD	REC	YDS	AVG	LG	TD	PR	YDS	AVG	LG	KOR	YDS	AVG	LG
1992	OTT	17				19	2.0	9.0																							
1993	OTT	16	0		1	12	2.0	21.0																							
1994	OTT	14				23	3.0	27.0																							
1995	SAS	16	0		2	20	2.0	4.0			2																				
1996	SAS	12				12																									
11	Years	163	0		8	215	48.0	61.0			2																				
BOBBY KUNTZ Robert John OHB-LB-DB 5'11 178 McMaster; Kitchener-Waterloo Jrs. B: 1932 Detroit, MI D: 1/7/2011 Waterloo, ON																															
1956	TOR	14							2	9		24	4	108	578	5.4	28	2	27	269	10.0	25	2					4	82	20.5	28
1957	TOR+	14							4	68		42	7	76	461	6.1	27	4	17	266	15.6	40	3					2	0	0.0	0
1958	TOR	14							1	25		18	3	40	117	2.9	23	2	24	292	12.2	31	1					1	18	18.0	18
1959	TOR	14												47	260	5.5	32	0	20	236	11.8	21	0								
1960	TOR	14												5	26	5.2	13	0	1	8	8.0	8	0					2	13	6.5	7
1961	TOR	14							1	0		18	3	69	475	6.9	59	3	8	109	13.6	62	0								
1962	HAM+	12										37	6	151	813	5.4	49	6	3	36	12.0	23	0					1	6	6.0	6
1963	HAM	14							1	3		30	5	87	323	3.7	13	5													
1964	HAM*	14	0		2				1	10		6	1	4	6	1.5	3	1						1	1	1.0	1				
1965	HAM	4																													
1966	HAM	14	4		0							36	6	115	504	4.4	17	5	7	102	14.6	38	1					2	26	13.0	14
11	Years	142	4		2				10	115		211	35	702	3563	5.1	59	28	107	1318	12.3	62	7	1	1	1.0	1	12	145	12.1	28
GERALD KUNYK Gerald K-P 6'1 185 Alberta B: 8/10/1953 Draft: 1A-3 1975 HAM																															
1975	CAL	16										7	0	1	-37	-37.0	-37	0													
1977	EDM	6																													
1977	OTT	7										1	0																		
1977	Year	13										1	0																		
1978	OTT	16	4		0							1	0																		
1980	WPG	1																													
4	Years	39	4		0							9	0	1	-37	-37.0	-37	0													
ANDY KUPP Andrew Charles OG 6'3 250 Idaho B: 5/25/1949 Sunnyside, WA Draft: 10-241 1972 NO Pro: W																															
1973	EDM	1																													
JOHNNY KUPSKAY John R. HB Winnipeg Grads Jrs.																															
1949	WPG	4																													
YORK KURINSKY York OL 6'4 290 Iowa Wesleyan; Valdosta State B: 11/11/1971 St. Charles, IL																															
1995	BIR	10				0																									
ROY KURTZ Roy K-P 5'11 184 Brantford Bisons Jrs.; Wilfrid Laurier B: 7/10/1962 Brantford, ON Draft: 2-17 1984 BC																															
1985	MTL	16										114	0																		
1986	MTL	12	2		0							101	0																		
1987	HAM	3				0						24	0																		
1988	BC	2	2		0							9	0																		
4	Years	33	4		0	0						248	0																		
BILL KUSHNIR Bill G 6'0 215 British Columbia																															
1954	CAL	8																													
LOU KUSSEROW Lou Joseph DB-OHB 6'1 200 Columbia B: 9/6/1927 Braddock, PA D: 6/30/2001 Rancho Mirage, CA Draft: 2A-SE 1949 NY-AAFC; 3-22 1949 DET Pro: AN																															
1953	HAM+	12										50	10					3					5								
1954	HAM+	14							5	108		50	10	90	338	3.8	17	4	49	702	14.3	73	5	1	0	0.0	0	6	116	19.3	26
1955	HAM+	12							1	12		40	8	127	743	5.9	68	7	14	195	13.9	27	1					5	98	19.6	28
1956	HAM	1												7	23	3.3	5	0	5	42	8.4	13	0								
4	Years	39							6	120		140	28	224	1104	4.9	68	14	68	939	13.8	73	11	1	0	0.0	0	11	214	19.5	28
ERNIE KUZYK Ernie HB 5'11 196 Weston Wildcats Jrs. B: 12/28/1942																															
1967	WPG	12	2		0							31	0	2	3	1.5	2	0													
GARY KUZYK Gary SE-SB 6'0 190 Otterbein B: 11/7/1946																															
1972	TOR	2																													
1973	HAM	14												1	6	6.0	6	0	18	292	16.2	31	0								
1974	HAM	16	0		2							6	1						11	137	12.5	19	1								
1975	OTT	16												1	2	2.0	2	0	14	242	17.3	33	0								
1976	OTT	14	1		0							6	1						3	21	7.0	10	1								
1977	OTT	6										12	2						2	34	17.0	21	2								
6	Years	68	1		2							24	4	2	8	4.0	6	0	48	726	15.1	33	4								
NORMIE KWONG Norman L. (The China Clipper) FB-HB-LB 5'9 190 North Hill Blizzard Jrs. B: 10/24/1929 Calgary, AB																															
1948	CAL	12										5	1					1													
1949	CAL	14										20	4					3					1								
1950	CAL	8										5	1	40	254	6.4	19	1	1	7	7.0	7	0								
1951	EDM+	14										40	8	178	933	5.2		7	3	46	15.3		0					2	27	13.5	
1952	EDM	15										55	11	84	480	5.7	38	8	14	227	16.2	42	3					1	16	16.0	16
1953	EDM+	15										10	2	117	802	6.9		2	6	42	7.0		0								
1954	EDM	12	1		0							5	1	120	572	4.8	21	1	1	1	1.0	1	0								
1955	EDM+	16	6		0							50	10	241	1250	5.2	39	10	6	36	6.0	17	0					1	20	20.0	20
1956	EDM+	15	9		0							36	6	232	1437	6.2	26	5	9	106	11.8	35	1								
1957	EDM	15	3		0							90	15	204	1050	5.1	22	15	14	172	12.3	19	0					1	5	5.0	5
1958	EDM	16	5									60	10	232	1033	4.5	23	9	9	106	11.8	24	1					2	24	12.0	18
1959	EDM	16										54	9	179	750	4.2	35	9	5	61	12.2	15	0					1	9	9.0	9
1960	EDM	16	2		1							30	5	118	461	3.9	22	5	7	99	14.1	23	0					3	42	14.0	23
13	Years	184	26		1							460	83	1745	9022	5.2	39	76	75	903	12.0	42	6					11	143	13.0	23
CHUCK KYLE Charles Douglas LB-G 6'2 225 Purdue B: 9/25/1947 Bellevue, KY Draft: 5-125 1969 DAL																															
1969	SAS	6																													
1970	SAS	12							2	11																					
2	Years	18							2	11																					
KEN KYLE Ken E																															
1947	HAM	1																													
ERNIE KYLIUK Ernie HB 6'1 190 Weston Wildcats Jrs.; St. James Ints. B: 1939 Winnipeg, MB																															
1962	SAS	3																													
JIMMY KYNES James Walter C 6'3 210 Florida B: 8/31/1928 D: 10/13/1988 St. Petersburg, FL Draft: 14-178 1950 PIT																															
1950	SAS	14																													
GALEN LAACK Galen William OG-LB 6'0 230 Pacific B: 4/3/1931 Abbotsford, WI D: 12/31/1958 Livermore, CA Draft: 9-105 1957 WAS Pro: N																															
1957	SAS	7							1	20																					
BRENDON LaBATTE Brendon OG-OT-C 6'4 316 Regina B: 9/12/1986 Weyburn, SK Draft: 1-6 2008 WPG																															
2008	WPG	17	0	0	1	0																									
2009	WPG+	18	0	0	1	1																									
2010	WPG+	16				1																									
2011	WPG*	18	0	1	2	4																									
4	Years	69	0	1	4	6																									
PIERRE-LUC LABBE Pierre-Luc LB 6'2 226 Sherbrooke B: 5/14/1984 Quebec City, QC Draft: 6-47 2008 WPG																															
2008	WPG	15	0	0	1	16																									
2009	WPG	16	0	0	1	20					1																				
2010	WPG	18	0	0	1	23						6	1																		
2011	WPG	18				29																									
4	Years	67	0	0	3	88					1	6	1																		
CRAIG LABBETT Craig TE 6'3 215 Western Ontario B: 5/15/1956 Draft: TE 1978 MTL																															
1978	MTL	6										6	1						1	12	12.0	12	1								
1979	TOR	1																													
1979	HAM	12										6	1						8	109	13.6	17	1								
1979	Year	13										6	1						8	109	13.6	17	1								
1980	TOR	10																													

Year	Team	GP	FM	FF	FR	TK	SK	YDS	IR	YDS	PD	PTS	TD	RA	YDS	AVG	LG	TD	REC	YDS	AVG	LG	TD	PR	YDS	AVG	LG	KOR	YDS	AVG	LG
1980	HAM	2	0		1							6	1																		
1980	Year	12	0		1							6	1																		
3	Years	17	0		1							18	3						9	121	13.4	17	2								
MIKE LABINJO Michael DE-DT-LB-FB 6'0 248 Michigan State B: 7/8/1980 Toronto, ON Draft: 3-25 2003 CAL Pro: N																															
2007	CAL	6				6																									
2008	CAL	15	0	2	1	34	5.0	32.0			3	6	1						1	1	1.0	1	1								
2009	CAL	10	0	0	1	16	1.0	2.0			1																				
2010	CAL	13	0	1	0	12																									
4	Years	44	0	3	2	68	6.0	34.0			4	6	1						1	1	1.0	1	1								
CLIFF LaBOY Clifford R. DE 6'4 240 Hawaii B: 8/1/1953 Honolulu, HI																															
1977	OTT	3	0		1				1	9																					
MARC LACELLE Marc RB 5'11 205 McGill B: 3/8/1958 Draft: TE 1981 MTL																															
1981	MTL	16	2		1							6	1	34	146	4.3	16	1	15	119	7.9	25	0					11	222	20.2	29
1982	MTL	12	0		1							24	4	35	108	3.1	9	1	11	111	10.1	42	3					1	14	14.0	14
2	Years	28	2		2							30	5	69	254	3.7	16	2	26	230	8.8	42	3					12	236	19.7	29
BRAD LaCOMBE Bradley David DL 5'11 230 St. Cloud State B: 3/19/1970 Minneapolis, MN																															
1994	LV	9				11	1.0	6.0																				1	7	7.0	7
PAUL LaCOSTE Paul Victor LB 6'2 242 Mississippi State B: 9/3/1974 Oxford, MS Pro: X																															
1999	BC+	18	0	1	2	87	1.0	2.0	1	28	2	6	1																		
2000	BC	5				25																									
2	Years	23	0	1	2	112	1.0	2.0	1	28	2	6	1																		
PETE LADYGO Peter Glenn OG 6'2 218 Potomac State JC; Maryland B: 6/23/1925 West Brownsville, PA Draft: 16-186 1952 PIT Pro: N																															
1955	OTT	12							2	12																					
BILL LaFLEUR William P 6'0 204 Nebraska B: 2/25/1976 Superior, NE Pro: EN																															
2001	MTL	3				0						1	0																		
JOHN LaGRONE John Wesley, III DT 5'10 235 Southern Methodist B: 11/4/1944 Borger, TX																															
1967	EDM+	16	0		4							6	1																		
1968	EDM*	16	0		1																										
1969	EDM*	16	0		6							6	1																		
1970	EDM	16	0		3							6	1																		
1971	EDM+	16	1		2																										
1972	EDM+	16	0		1																										
1973	EDM+	16	0		1																										
1974	EDM	13																													
8	Years	125	1		18							18	3																		
MIKE LaHOOD Michael James OG 6'3 249 Wyoming B: 12/11/1944 Peoria, IL Draft: 2B-51 1968 LARM Pro: N																															
1973	BC	8																													
1974	BC	13																													
2	Years	21																													
TRACE LAING Trace DT 6'4 275 Kings River CC; Cisco JC B: 9/3/1971 Mississauga, ON																															
1994	TOR	5				2																									
STU LAIRD Stuart DE-DT-LB 6'2 260 Calgary B: 7/8/1960 Assiniboia, SK																															
1985	CAL	16	0		1		2.0																								
1986	CAL	14	0		1		9.0																								
1987	CAL	18	0		1	27	7.0																								
1988	CAL	18			3	54	11.0																								
1989	CAL	5				3																									
1990	CAL	16	0		1	12	5.0																								
1991	CAL	14	0		3	34	5.0		1	0																					
1992	CAL	10	0		1	21	6.0	49.0																							
1993	CAL	14	0		1	18	8.0	67.0																							
1994	CAL+	17				26	9.0	92.0			2																				
1995	CAL	12	0		1	9	5.0	32.0			2																				
1996	CAL	16				15	5.0	43.0																							
12	Years	170	0		13	219	72.0	283.0	1	0	4																				
GENE LAKUSIAK Gene CB-FB 6'1 210 Tulsa B: 6/1/1943																															
1967	OTT	2																													
1968	WPG	16	2		0							6	1	34	155	4.6	22	1	6	71	11.8	36	0					4	47	11.8	16
1969	WPG	16	1		0				2	28														1	0	0.0	0				
1970	WPG	15										35	0											1	16	16.0	16				
1971	WPG	16							3	15														1	0	0.0	0	1	12	12.0	12
1972	WPG+	16							1	9														1	7	7.0	7				
1973	WPG+	16	0		2				1	25		1	0																		
1974	WPG	7	0		1									1	1	1.0	1	0													
8	Years	104	3		3				7	77		42	1	35	156	4.5	22	1	6	71	11.8	36	0	4	23	5.8	16	5	59	11.8	16
GEORGE LALICICH George G 5'11 220 Hamilton Tiger-Cats B B: 1939																															
1961	HAM	8																													
LALLY LALONDE Jean-Paul E 5'11 198 B: 1927																															
1948	OTT	11										10	2										1								
1950	OTT	2																													
1952	MTL	12																													
3	Years	25										10	2										1								
ROGER LaLONDE Roger Frederick DT 6'3 255 Muskingum B: 1/6/1942 Antwerp, NY Draft: 8B-61 1964 BOS; 15-201 1964 DET Pro: N																															
1966	MTL	14	0		1				1	4																					
1967	HAM	3																													
2	Years	17	0		1				1	4																					
JASON LAMAR Jason James LB 6'0 228 Toledo B: 11/10/1978 Detroit, MI Pro: N																															
2001	HAM+	18	0	0	1	108	5.0	36.0			5																				
2004	HAM	13	0	1	1	62	5.0		2	88	2	12	2																		
2004	MTL	2				9																									
2004	Year	15	0	1	1	71	5.0		2	88	2	12	2																		
2	Years	31	0	1	2	179	10.0	36.0	2	88	7	12	2																		
JACK LAMB Jack OT-DT 6'2 240 Calgary Jrs. B: 1934																															
1956	CAL	11																													
1957	CAL	7																													
1958	CAL	16																													
1959	CAL	3																													
1960	EDM	8																													
1961	EDM	10																													
1962	EDM	9																													
1964	EDM	4																													
8	Years	68																													
MACK LAMB Mack Edward DB 6'1 186 Tennessee State B: 5/9/1943 Miami, FL D: 10/28/2010 Miami, FL Pro: N																															
1970	BC	4	0		1																			1	10	10.0	10	8	202	25.3	
1970	HAM	10	0		2				1	19																		3	78	26.0	
1970	Year	14	0		3				1	19														1	10	10.0	10	11	280	25.5	29
PAUL LAMBERT Paul OG-C 6'4 300 Western Michigan B: 11/11/1975 Montreal, QC Draft: 3-22 2000 HAM																															
2001	HAM	18	1	0	0	4																									
2002	HAM	18	1	0	0	1																									
2003	MTL	16	0	0	1	1																									
2004	MTL*	18	1	0	0	1																									
2005	MTL	16				0																									

Year	Team	GP	FM	FF	FR	TK	SK	YDS	IR	YDS	PD	PTS	TD	RA	YDS	AVG	LG	TD	REC	YDS	AVG	LG	TD	PR	YDS	AVG	LG	KOR	YDS	AVG	LG
2006	MTL	18				0																								
2007	MTL	16	0	0	1	0																								
2008	MTL+	18				1																								
2009	MTL	13				0																								
2010	MTL	13				0																								
10	Years	164	3	0	2	8																								
WILLIE LAMBERT William John HB 5'10 170 McGill B: 3/23/1937 Wainfleet Township, ON D: 11/21/2009 Montreal, QC																														
1964	MTL	10										10	1						16	205	12.8	26	1	1	8	8.0	8				
AUBURN LAMBETH Auburn C. QB 6'1 200 Davidson B: 7/23/1930																														
1953	HAM	2										5	1					1													
MIKE LAMBRECHT Michael James DT 6'1 273 St. Cloud State B: 5/2/1963 Watertown, MN Pro: N																														
1990	OTT	6				3	1.0																								
MATT LAMBROS Matthew WR-SB 6'2 210 Liberty B: 2/8/1985 Calgary, AB Draft: 2-10 2009 TOR																														
2009	TOR	3				1						6	1						1	22	22.0	22	1								
2011	MTL	1				0																								
2	Years	4				1						6	1						1	22	22.0	22	1								
MIKE LAMBROS Mike LB 6'1 220 Queen's B: 1/31/1949 Wiarton, ON Draft: 1-2 1972 EDM																														
1972	EDM	10							1	0																			1	20	20.0	20
1973	EDM	5																												
1974	EDM	8																								3	0	0.0	0
1975	EDM	8																								2	25	12.5	16
4	Years	31							1	0																			6	45	7.5	20
WAYNE LAMMLE Wayne K-P 6'4 220 Utah B: 4/10/1969 Vancouver, BC Draft: SD-1-5 1991 TOR Pro: E																														
1992	BC	4				0						29	0											1	0	0.0	0				
1993	TOR	7	1		0	1						1	0																		
1994	TOR	18	4		1	6						180	0																		
1995	TOR	6	1		0	0						44	0																		
1995	OTT	12	3		0	6						89	0																		
1995	Year	18	4		0	6						133	0																		
1996	OTT	18	2		0	9						107	0	1	20	20.0	20	0													
1998	SAS	5	1	0	0	0						2	0																		
1999	SAS	1				0						5	0																		
7	Years	59	12	0	1	22						457	0	1	20	20.0	20	0						1	0	0.0	0				
BLAIN LAMOUREUX Blain LB 6'1 215 Washington State B: 1/13/1950 Draft: TE 1973 CAL																														
1973	CAL	16	0		1																							2	13	6.5	7
1974	CAL	16																								1	12	12.0	12
1975	CAL	10																												
1977	CAL	16	0		2																									
1978	CAL	16	0		1																									
1979	SAS	8	0		1																									
1980	TOR	3																												
1981	TOR	2																												
8	Years	87	0		5																							3	25	8.3	12
FRED LAMOUREUX Fred G-C-T 5'10 199																														
1946	OTT	8																												
1947	OTT	12																												
1948	MTL	6																												
3	Years	26																												
HARRY LAMPMAN Harry OE-DB 6'3 225 Hamilton Tigers Jrs.; Queen's B: 1929 Draft: 1-1 1952 MTL																														
1952	SAS	16			0							20	4						25	429	17.2	53	3								
1953	SAS	16							3	70		16	3						24	312	13.0		3	2	3	1.5					
1954	SAS	16							1	16		5	1						29	300	10.3	43	1	1	0	0.0	0				
1955	SAS	5	1		0															17	208	12.2	20	0								
1956	SAS	11	1		0							12	2						42	552	13.1	27	2								
1957	HAM	10							3	26										9	132	14.7	20	0								
1958	HAM	14										7	1						12	156	13.0	29	1	1	0	0.0	0				
1959	HAM	7										6	1						18	213	11.8	22	1								
1960	MTL	3																												
9	Years	98	2		0					7	112		66	12						176	2302	13.1	53	11	4	3	0.8	0				
MICHEL LAMY Michel OT-OG 6'2 280 Montreal Concorde Jrs.; Sequoias JC B: 6/25/1967 Tracy, QC																														
1989	OTT	10				2																								
1990	OTT	11	1		1	0																								
1991	OTT	15				0																								
1992	OTT	18				3																								
1993	OTT	18				0																								
1994	SAS	15				0																								
1995	SAS	16				0																								
1996	MTL	6				0																								
8	Years	109	1		1	5																								
RON LANCASTER Ronald QB-DB 5'10 190 Wittenberg B: 10/14/1938 Fairchance, PA D: 9/18/2008 Hamilton, ON																														
1960	OTT	14							3	51		6	1	19	134	7.1	40	0	1	17	17.0	17	0	2	13	6.5	8	1	5	5.0	5
1961	OTT	14										6	1	17	122	7.2	23	1													
1962	OTT	14												10	76	7.6	22	0													
1963	SAS	11	2		1							12	2	34	139	4.1	15	2													
1964	SAS	13	2		0							18	3	26	152	5.8	28	3													
1965	SAS	16	8		0							18	3	33	84	2.5	20	3													
1966	SAS+	15	3		0							6	1	29	91	3.1	24	1													
1967	SAS	16	1		0							12	2	29	131	4.5	21	2													
1968	SAS+	16	1		0							12	2	25	197	7.9	24	2													
1969	SAS+	16	4		0							18	3	22	115	5.2	48	3													
1970	SAS*	16	2		0							12	2	21	71	3.4	20	2	1	24	24.0	24	0								
1971	SAS	16	3		0									5	0	0.0	2	0	1	12	12.0	12	0								
1972	SAS	16	3		0									7	12	1.7	15	0													
1973	SAS*	16	2		0							6	1	8	17	2.1	13	1													
1974	SAS	16	0		2							6	1	8	15	1.9	12	1													
1975	SAS*	16	3		0									14	11	0.8	10	0													
1976	SAS*	16	1		0							12	2	5	5	1.0	2	2													
1977	SAS	14										18	3	14	48	3.4	9	3													
1978	SAS	16										18	3	10	8	0.8	2	3													
19	Years	287	35		3					3	51		180	30	336	1428	4.3	48	29	3	53	17.7	24	0	2	13	6.5	8	1	5	5.0	5
SACHA LANCASTER Sacha R. DE 6'2 262 Arkansas B: 3/29/1979 Pro: E																														
2008	HAM	1				1																								
CARLTON LANCE Carlton A. CB 6'0 195 Southwest State B: 10/3/1970 New York, NY Pro: E																														
1993	SAS	13	1		2	43	2.0	18.0	3	40		12	2															1	19	19.0	19
MEL LAND Melvin DE 6'3 242 Michigan State B: 11/30/1955 Youngstown, OH D: 4/27/1997 Campbell, OH Draft: 3B-63 1979 MIA Pro: NU																														
1982	TOR	1																												
LOWELL LANDER Lowell Ken HB 6'0 195 Westminster (Pennsylvania) B: 9/12/1932 Pittsburgh, PA D: 2/28/2001 Pittsburgh, PA Pro: N																														
1956	TOR	1							1	11															1	10	10.0	10	1	20	20.0	20
JONATHAN LANDON Jonathan OT 6'3 285 Queen's B: 7/22/1979 Kingston, ON Draft: 4B-33 2002 MTL																														
2004	TOR	17				0																								
2005	TOR	18				1																								
2006	TOR	18				0																								

Year	Team	GP	FM	FF	FR	TK	SK	YDS	IR	YDS	PD	PTS	TD	RA	YDS	AVG	LG	TD	REC	YDS	AVG	LG	TD	PR	YDS	AVG	LG	KOR	YDS	AVG	LG
3	Years	53				1																									
DOUG LANDRY Douglas James LB 6'2 225 Louisiana Tech B: 4/21/1964 New Orleans, LA Draft: 5A-118 1986 SD																															
1987	HAM	1				3																									
1987	TOR	9				47	3.0		3	73																					
1987	Year	10				50			3	73																					
1988	TOR	9				49			5	58																					
1988	CAL	6				33			1	19																					
1988	Year	15				82			6	77																					
1989	CAL	18				122	2.0		3	67																					
1990	BC	13	0		1	52	5.0		2	25																					
4	Years	41	0		1	306	10.0		14	242																					
EZRA LANDRY Ezra WR 5'4 160 Southern University B: 4/4/1982 New Orleans, LA																															
2004	MTL	13	1	0	2	0						18	3	1	0	0.0	0	0	3	27	9.0	28	0	67	728	10.9	89	29	584	20.1	41
2005	MTL	15	3	0	0	0						12	2	3	11	3.7	12	0	2	4	2.0	3	0	47	562	12.0	74	33	729	22.1	42
2	Years	28	4	0	2	0						30	5	4	11	2.8	12	0	5	31	6.2	28	0	114	1290	11.3	89	62	1313	21.2	42
MICHAEL LANDRY Michael Paul DT 6'3 267 Southern University B: 12/12/1978 Baton Rouge, LA Pro: E																															
2009	WPG	2				8																									
2010	CAL	2	0	1	1	3	1.0	0.0																							
2	Years	4	0	1	1	11	1.0	0.0																							
PIERRE LANDRY Pierre S 6'1 185 Ottawa B: 4/25/1976 La Prairie, QC Draft: 6-44 1999 MTL																															
1999	MTL	5				4																									
2000	MTL	1				0																									
2	Years	6				4																									
JOHN LANDS John OE 6'4 205 Wenatchee Valley CC; Montana B: 1936 Draft: 5-56 1959 LARM; FS 1960 HOU																															
1960	BC	4	0		1				1										1	11	11.0	11	0					1	6	6.0	6
FRANK LANDY Frank DT-DE 6'3 235 North Dakota B: 5/24/1950																															
1973	SAS	16	0		1																										
1974	SAS	6																													
1975	SAS	16																													
1976	SAS	16							1	9																					
1977	BC+	16	0		3																										
1978	BC	16	0		3																										
1979	BC	13																													
1980	BC	10																													
1980	TOR	3																													
1980	Year	13																													
8	Years	109	0		7				1	9																					
DAVE LANE David DB 5'11 180 Guelph B: 1950 Draft: 7A-56 1974 HAM																															
1975	HAM	1																						3	53	17.7	22				
GARY LANE Gary Owen QB 6'1 210 Missouri B: 12/21/1942 Alton, IL D: 6/27/2003 St. Louis, MO Draft: RS-2- 1965 BUF; 9-125(f) 1965 CLE Pro: N																															
1970	SAS	7										6	1	15	53	3.5	13	1													
GREG LANE Gregory Sean CB 5'9 180 Notre Dame B: 10/31/1971 Victoria, TX Pro: E																															
1995	HAM	5				2																									
SKIP LANE Paul John, Jr. DB 6'1 208 Mississippi B: 1/30/1960 Norwalk, CT Pro: N																															
1984	OTT	1																													
LE-LO LANG Le-Lo L. DB 5'11 185 Washington B: 1/23/1967 Los Angeles, CA Draft: 5B-136 1990 DEN Pro: N																															
1995	MEM	4				1																									
STU LANG Stuart SB-SE-FL 6'1 190 Queen's B: 1/26/1951 Draft: 6-53 1974 EDM																															
1974	EDM	16										12	2						22	280	12.7	52	2	2	7	3.5	5				
1975	EDM	16										8	1	2	8	4.0	12	0	20	211	10.6	39	1	15	51	3.4	14				
1976	EDM	16	1		0							18	3						40	590	14.8	50	3	12	78	6.5	32				
1977	EDM	16	0		1							6	1	1	5	5.0	5	0	37	540	14.6	62	1								
1978	EDM	16										24	4						48	618	12.9	47	4								
1979	EDM	16										12	2						29	479	16.5	37	2					1	0	0.0	0
1980	EDM	13																	23	321	14.0	38	0								
1981	EDM	13	1		0							6	1						12	164	13.7	34	1								
8	Years	122	2		1							86	14	3	13	4.3	12	0	231	3203	13.9	62	14	29	136	4.7	32	1	0	0.0	0
RAY LANGCASTER Ray DB-SB-RB 5'10 180 St. Francis Xavier B: 3/28/1947 Toronto, ON																															
1972	TOR	12												5	13	2.6	5	0	5	29	5.8	17	0								
1973	TOR	14	2		1							6	1	4	2	0.5	3	0	12	137	11.4	21	1								
1974	TOR	3																													
3	Years	29	2		1							6	1	9	15	1.7	5	0	17	166	9.8	21	1								
PAT LANGDON Patrick OL 6'4 258 Tennessee B: 10/24/1960 Burlington, ON Draft: 1A-6 1985 WPG																															
1985	WPG	3																													
HARRY LANGFORD Harry OG-DT 6'3 229 Weston Wildcats Jrs. B: 12/6/1929 Winnipeg, MB																															
1950	CAL	12																													
1951	CAL	14										5	1															1	0	0.0	0
1952	CAL	15																													
1953	CAL	15																													
1954	CAL	16	0		1																										
1955	CAL+	16	0		3																										
1956	CAL+	15																													
1957	CAL+	16																													
1958	CAL+	16																													
9	Years	135	0		4							5	1															1	0	0.0	0
JIM LANGFORD James T-C 6'3 198 Weston Wildcats Jrs. B: 1928																															
1949	CAL	14																													
1950	CAL	10																													
1951	CAL	6																													
3	Years	30																													
BILL LANGNER William OT 6'4 255 Scarborough Rams Jrs. B: 1951 D: 2/9/2011																															
1974	TOR	5																													
1974	HAM	11																													
1974	Year	16																													
ELLIS LANKSTER Ellis DB 5'9 190 Jones County JC; West Virginia B: 6/3/1987 Whistler, AL Draft: 7-220 2009 BUF Pro: N																															
2010	HAM	1				3																									
ERIC LaPOINTE Eric RB 6'0 205 Mount Allison B: 9/13/1974 Montreal, QC Draft: 3-20 1999 EDM																															
1999	HAM	15	2	0	1	11						30	5	105	691	6.6	91	5	9	70	7.8	12	0								
2000	TOR	11				7								11	29	2.6	8	0	2	11	5.5	6	0					1	0	0.0	0
2001	MTL	17	2	0	2	6								21	123	5.9	24	0	5	59	11.8	27	0								
2002	MTL	11	2	0	2	14								9	107	11.9	44	0	3	34	11.3	20	0								
2003	MTL	9	2	0	1	6						12	2	75	432	5.8	38	2	13	84	6.5	25	0								
2004	MTL	17	2	0	1	4						36	6	78	479	6.1	77	6	16	80	5.0	15	0								
2005	MTL	15				6						24	4	79	423	5.4	24	3	6	36	6.0	11	1								
2006	MTL	14	2	0	1	11								18	132	7.3	35	0	2	6	3.0	5	0								
8	Years	109	12	0	8	65						102	17	396	2416	6.1	91	16	56	380	6.8	27	1					1	0	0.0	0
MARTIN LAPOSTELLE Martin DL 6'1 283 Indiana B: 3/25/1980 Montreal, QC Draft: 5-38 2005 WPG																															
2005	WPG	11				1																									
2006	WPG	1				0																						1	0	0.0	0
2	Years	12				1																						1	0	0.0	0
TOM LAPUTKA Thomas W. DE-DT 6'3 255 Southern Illinois B: 12/30/1947 Philadelphia, PA Draft: 11-279 1972 SF Pro: W																															
1971	OTT+	14			2																										

Year	Team	GP	FM	FF	FR	TK	SK	YDS	IR	YDS	PD	PTS	TD	RA	YDS	AVG	LG	TD	REC	YDS	AVG	LG	TD	PR	YDS	AVG	LG	KOR	YDS	AVG	LG
1972	OTT	14	0		1																										
1973	OTT	14	0		2																										
1975	EDM	16																													
1976	EDM	4																													
5	Years	62	0		5																										
JOE LARKIN Joseph A. DB 5'11 195 Boise State B: 7/8/1951 Caldwell, ID Pro: W																															
1974	BC	2																													
BILL LaROCHELLE William D. HB-E 6'3 184 Western Ontario B: 1926 Calgary, AB																															
1949	OTT	10										15	3					1					2								
1950	OTT	12										30	6					4					2								
1951	OTT	8																													
1952	MTL	1																													
1953	WPG	4																													
1953	CAL	12																													
1953	Year	16																													
5	Years	35										45	9					5					4								
BOB LaROSE Bob DB-FL 6'3 213 Western Ontario B: 3/6/1946 Draft: 1-7 1970 WPG																															
1970	WPG	15	0		1				2	4																5	37	7.4	12	1	19	19.0	19
1971	WPG*	16	1		0							42	7						58	1080	18.6	70	7								
1972	WPG	16	4		1							30	5						49	929	19.0	73	5								
1973	WPG	16										42	7						44	855	19.4	69	7								
1974	WPG	16	1		0							24	4						24	356	14.8	28	4								
1975	WPG	16	0		1							30	4						29	587	20.2	44	4								
1976	WPG	16	0		1							12	2	0	6		6	0	23	402	17.5	51	2								
7	Years	111	6		4				2	4		180	29	0	6		6	0	227	4209	18.5	73	29	5	37	7.4	12	1	19	19.0	19
J.R. LaROSE Alozie S 6'0 200 Edmonton Huskies Jrs. B: 2/27/1984 Edmonton, AB																															
2005	EDM	1				0																									
2006	EDM	18	0	1	2	39					3																				
2007	EDM	18	0	0	2	42					5																				
2008	EDM	8				2					1																				
2010	BC	15	0	0	2	16																									
2011	BC	15	0	0	1	28	1.0	4.0			1																				
6	Years	75	0	1	7	127	1.0	4.0			10																				
BUTCH LaROUE Francis W. OG 6'1 232 Western Michigan B: 1/31/1942 D: 8/28/1998																															
1963	TOR	14							1	38		6	1																		
1964	TOR	12	0		1																										
1965	TOR	12																										1	0	0.0	0
3	Years	38	0		1				1	38		6	1															1	0	0.0	0
ADMIRAL DEWEY LARRY Admiral Dewey, Jr. DB 5'11 192 Southern University; Contra Costa JC; Nevada-Las Vegas B: 9/1/1958 New Orleans, LA Draft: 9-225 1981 NYJ Pro: U																															
1984	OTT	2																						3	13	4.3	8	3	52	17.3	21
TOM LARSCHEID Tom HB 5'8 170 Utah State B: 4/6/1940 Milwaukee, WI Draft: 18-251 1962 PHI																															
1962	BC	16	3		2							54	9	104	597	5.7	36	1	29	496	17.1	61	8					21	503	24.0	36
1963	BC	4												12	38	3.2	8	0	12	188	15.7	62	0					7	136	19.4	24
2	Years	20	3		2							54	9	116	635	5.5	36	1	41	684	16.7	62	8					28	639	22.8	36
BOB LARSEN Bob DE 6'5 230 Brigham Young B: 1952																															
1975	CAL	2																													
GEORGE LARSON George T																															
1947	HAM	10																													
LYNN LARSON Lyndon Arthur OG-OT 6'4 254 Phoenix JC; Kansas State B: 3/9/1948 Phoenix, AZ Draft: 4A-79 1970 CHIB Pro: N																															
1972	BC	5	0		1																										
RALPH LARUE Ralph FW 5'11 195 B: 1922																															
1948	HAM	8										4	0																		
1949	HAM	9																													
2	Years	17										4	0																		
MIKE LASHUK Mike FB-LB 6'0 190 Edmonton Huskies Jrs.; Alberta B: 1938																															
1957	EDM	15	3		0				2	15		12	2	27	164	6.1	32	1	6	83	13.8	22	1					3	21	7.0	13
1958	EDM	12							3	36				4	30	7.5	15	0													
1959	EDM	13							5	14				2	9	4.5	5	0						1	0	0.0	0				
1960	EDM	13	1		1				4	33		2	0	28	114	4.1	19	0	6	58	9.7	17	0					1	5	5.0	5
1961	EDM	13	6									25	4	123	757	6.2	50	4	10	133	13.3	18	0					1	22	22.0	22
1962	EDM	16	5									12	2	165	802	4.9	32	2	15	159	10.6	32	0	1	2	2.0	2	6	62	10.3	15
1963	EDM	13							2	37		12	2	20	70	3.5	16	1	9	107	11.9	23	1					3	33	11.0	19
7	Years	95	15		1				16	135		63	10	369	1946	5.3	50	8	46	540	11.7	32	2	2	2	1.0	2	14	143	10.2	22
FRANK LASKY Francis Joseph OG 6'2 265 Florida; Northeast Oklahoma A&M JC; Florida B: 10/4/1941 New York, NY Draft: 14A-106(f) 1963 SD; 2-26(f) 1963 NYG Pro: N																															
1969	MTL	7	0		1																										
DICK LASSE Richard Stephen G-LB 6'2 222 Syracuse B: 11/13/1935 Quincy, MA Draft: 6-68 1958 PIT Pro: N																															
1963	HAM	2																													
BILL LASSETER Bill OHB-DH-S 6'0 200 Vancouver Meralomas Jrs. B: 1941																															
1963	BC	16	1		0									28	110	3.9	14	0	8	105	13.1	27	0					6	80	13.3	26
1964	BC	16	1		0							6	1	28	111	4.0	12	0	6	50	8.3	24	1	10	21	2.1	6	7	152	21.7	47
1965	BC	15												10	15	1.5	6	0	7	44	6.3	15	0	29	132	4.6	13				
1966	BC	16	0		2				4	92														40	216	5.4	19	4	57	14.3	24
1967	BC	15	1		0				4	74				3	39	13.0	32	0	1	-1	-1.0	-1	0	57	265	4.6	19	2	38	19.0	28
1968	BC	16	1		1				2	17														22	114	5.2	14				
1969	BC	16	1		0				3	14									1	24	24.0	24	0	44	213	4.8	15	6	66	11.0	19
7	Years	110	5	0	3				13	197		6	1	69	275	4.0	32	0	23	222	9.7	27	1	202	961	4.8	19	25	393	15.7	47
ART LASTER Arthur L. DT 6'4 280 Maryland-Eastern Shore B: 3/2/1948 Gary, IN Draft: 5-128 1970 OAK Pro: N																															
1972	OTT	2																													
GREG LATHAN Gregory R. WR 6'1 195 Cincinnati B: 9/2/1964 San Diego, CA Pro: N																															
1988	OTT	4										6	1	1	-1	-1.0	-1	0	8	107	13.4	39	1								
MARION LATIMORE Marion I. OG-DE 6'0 235 Hutchinson CC; Kansas State B: 7/29/1949 Draft: 8-194 1972 NYJ																															
1972	CAL	6																													
1973	CAL	16																										1	23	23.0	23
1974	CAL	1																													
1974	SAS	11																										1	18	18.0	18
1974	HAM	1																													
1974	Year	13																										1	18	18.0	18
1975	HAM	16	0		1																										
4	Years	39	0		1																							2	41	20.5	23
RON LATOURELLE Ronald Guy (Pepe) OHB-DB-LB 5'8 175 Winnipeg Rods Jrs. B: 5/17/1934																															
1955	WPG	5																													
1956	WPG	16												5	18	3.6	5	0	4	30	7.5	22	0	47	254	5.4	18	10	201	20.1	34
1957	WPG	16	2		2							18	3	37	120	3.2	19	2	6	115	19.2	32	1	58	367	6.3	16	5	102	20.4	24
1958	WPG	16	3									18	3	26	54	2.1	13	3	9	162	18.0	24	0	80	467	5.8	17				
1959	WPG	15										12	2	9	40	4.4	15	0	3	60	20.0	25	1	46	191	4.2	15				
1960	WPG	9	1		1									4	22	5.5	6	0	1	31	31.0	23	0	38	170	4.5	17				
1961	WPG	16							2	35														46	178	3.9	14				
1962	WPG	16	1		4							6	1	13	63	4.8	20	0	3	97	32.3	66	1	68	384	5.6	20	1	31	31.0	31
1963	WPG	2												1	2	2.0	2	0	2	30	15.0	19	0	5	35	7.0	10				
1964	WPG	16	2		3							12	2	10	47	4.7	18	1	2	18	9.0	12	0	83	327	3.9	15				
10	Years	127	9		10				2	35		66	11	105	366	3.5	20	6	30	543	18.1	66	3	471	2373	5.0	20	16	334	20.9	34
LAWANN LATSON Lawann M. WR 5'7 180 Tyler Jc; Northwestern State (Louisiana) B: 11/3/1971																															

Year	Team	GP	FM	FF	FR	TK	SK	YDS	IR	YDS	PD	PTS	TD	RA	YDS	AVG	LG	TD	REC	YDS	AVG	LG	TD	PR	YDS	AVG	LG	KOR	YDS	AVG	LG
1994	OTT	2				2																									
WILLIE LATTA Willie Nathaniel RB 5'9 190 Winston-Salem State B: 4/5/1969 Oxford, NC																															
1996	SAS	1				0						6	1	9	10	1.1	7	1	1	13	13.0	13	0								
BUD LAUGHLIN Henry James FB 6'1 200 Kansas B: 1/15/1931 Kansas City, MO D: 3/20/1986 Shawnee Mission, KS Draft: 25-297(f) 1952 SF Pro: N																															
1957	BC	1												10	34	3.4	7	0													
MAL LAUGHTON Mal QB-LB-FB 5'11 195 Hamilton Tiger-Cats B Ints. B: 1939																															
1958	SAS	1																													
1959	HAM	2												1	4	4.0	4	0													
2	Years	3												1	4	4.0	4	0													
TED LAURENT Ted NT 6'1 303 Mississippi B: 1/1/1988 Montreal, QC Draft: SD-2nd 2011 EDM																															
2011	EDM	18	0	1	0	19	1.0	2.0			2																				
TIM LAVENS Tim OT 6'3 227 Idaho B: 1945 Draft: 9A-212 1967 NO																															
1967	EDM	5																										1	0	0.0	0
PETE LAVORATO Peter S 6'1 195 Edmonton Wildcats Jrs.; Utah State B: 8/26/1952 Edmonton, AB Draft: TE 1975 EDM																															
1975	EDM	16							3	38														6	29	4.8	16				
1976	EDM	14							2	7														1	0	0.0	0				
1977	EDM*	16	0		4							6	1																		
1978	EDM	16	0		1				2	31		6	1											1	2	2.0	2	6	85	14.2	25
1979	EDM	16							3	17														1	0	0.0	0				
1980	EDM	13							3	29																					
1981	EDM	12							3	63																					
1982	BC	16	0		1																										
1983	BC	6																						1	5	5.0	5				
1983	MTL	1																													
1983	Year	7																						1	5	5.0	5				
1984	MTL	6																										1	8	8.0	8
10	Years	131	0		6				16	185		12	2											10	36	3.6	16	7	93	13.3	25
MIKE LAW Mike CB-DH 5'11 177 Queen's; Waterloo B: 3/9/1942 Ottawa, ON																															
1967	HAM	2																						3	11	3.7					
1967	EDM	7	0		1				2	11														12	102	8.5		1	0	0.0	0
1967	Year	9	0		1				2	11														15	113	7.5	17	1	0	0.0	0
1968	EDM	14	0		2				1	1														11	79	7.2	11				
1969	EDM	16	0		2																			7	35	5.0	13				
1970	EDM	16	0		1				3	10		6	1											3	-3	-1.0	1				
1971	EDM	16							4	69		6	1											3	8	2.7	3				
1972	EDM	6																													
1972	WPG	3	0		3																			5	31	6.2	9				
1972	Year	9	0		3																			5	31	6.2	9				
1973	OTT	11																													
7	Years	81	0		9				10	91		12	2											44	263	6.0	13	1	0	0.0	0
JACK LAWRENCE Jack G 200 B: 1913																															
1946	CAL	4																													
JEREMY LAWRENCE Jeremy DE 6'3 248 Louisiana State B: 1/12/1979 Winnsboro, LA																															
2005	HAM	4				8																									
LARRY LAWRENCE Larry Robert QB 6'1 208 Miami (Florida); Iowa B: 4/11/1949 Mount Pleasant, IA Pro: N																															
1970	CAL	16	6		1									28	219	7.8	39	0													
1971	EDM	13	5		0							6	1	37	220	5.9	26	1	1	16	16.0	16	0								
1978	MTL	3																													
3	Years	32	11		1							6	1	65	439	6.8	39	1	1	16	16.0	16	0								
ALEX LAWSON Alex QB 6'3 185 Toronto B: 1930 Draft: 1952 OTT																															
1952	OTT	10																													
1953	OTT	1																													
2	Years	11																													
GORD LAWSON Gordon OE-DE 6'0 195 McMaster; Toronto B: 1924																															
1948	HAM	12																													
1950	HAM	12																													
2	Years	24																													
HUGH LAWSON Hugh DE 6'3 240 Wilfrid Laurier B: 1/23/1969 Draft: 8-64 1992 TOR																															
1993	TOR	2				0																									
JERRY LAWSON Jerome Lee DB 5'11 192 Santa Ana JC; Utah B: 9/30/1944 Bakersfield, CA Draft: 10-251 1968 BUF Pro: N																															
1969	HAM	4							1	9																					
MEL LAWSON Mel QB-HB 6'0 195 Toronto																															
1948	HAM	12																													
MICHAEL LAWSON Michael DT-NT 6'2 278 Miami (Florida) B: 2/22/1975 Kansas City, MO																															
1999	SAS	12	0	1	1	25	3.0		0	0	1																				
SHAWN LAWSON Shawn Miguiel DB 5'11 176 Prairie View A&M; Long Beach State; Baylor B: 9/27/1970 Gregg County, TX																															
1995	SHR	2				0																									
TONY LAWSON Anthony DE-LB 6'3 225 McGill B: 10/2/1960 Mandeville, Jamaica Draft: 1B-9 1983 EDM																															
1983	TOR	10																													
1984	TOR	8					0.5																								
1986	MTL	10					1.0																								
3	Years	28					1.5																								
GREG LAYBOURN Greg CB-S 5'10 201 Northern Arizona; Oregon State B: 12/30/1985 Portland, OR Pro: U																															
2011	MTL	9	0	0	1	22																									
DONNIE LAYTON Donnie O'Neal RB 6'0 200 South Carolina State B: 9/18/1951 Spartanburg, SC D: 6/28/2006 Spartanburg, SC Draft: 10-243 1975 SF																															
1975	EDM	2												12	63	5.3	14	0	1	17	17.0	17	0								
BOB LAZARK Robert W. CB 5'11 195 Oregon State; Sacramento State B: 1/21/1941 Dauphin, MB																															
1964	WPG	11	0		1																										
MIKE LAZECKI Michael P-K 6'2 200 Saskatchewan; Regina Rams Jrs. B: 2/8/1965 Regina, SK D: 1/30/2003																															
1990	SAS	18	1		0	0						2	0																		
1991	SAS	18	3		0	1						6	0	2	14	7.0	12	0													
1992	SAS	8				0								1	-2	-2.0	-2	0													
1993	OTT	1	0		1	0																									
4	Years	45	4		1	1						8	0	3	12	4.0	12	0													
ROB LAZEO Rob OG-C 6'5 305 Western Illinois B: 3/23/1973 Abbotsford, BC Draft: 1B-12 1995 SAS																															
1998	SAS	13				0																									
1999	SAS	11				0																									
2000	WPG	11				1																									
2001	WPG	12				0																									
2002	SAS	18				0																									
2003	SAS	18				1																									
2004	SAS	18	0	0	1	0																									
2005	SAS	18	1	0	0	0																									
2006	SAS	17				0						6	1						1	1	1.0	1	1								
2007	CAL	18				2																									
2008	CAL+	18	0	0	2	2																									
2009	CAL	12				0																									
2010	CAL	18				1																									
13	Years	202	1	0	3	7						6	1						1	1	1.0	1	1								
PETE LAZETICH Peter Gary DT 6'3 245 Stanford B: 2/4/1950 Billings, MT Draft: 2-36 1972 SD Pro: N																															
1975	CAL	4																													
PAUL LEA Paul Addison T 6'2 240 Tulane B: 2/19/1929 New Orleans, LA D: 5/19/2009 Raton, NM Draft: 7-84 1951 CHIB Pro: N																															

Year	Team	GP	FM	FF	FR	TK	SK	YDS	IR	YDS	PD	PTS	TD	RA	YDS	AVG	LG	TD	REC	YDS	AVG	LG	TD	PR	YDS	AVG	LG	KOR	YDS	AVG	LG
1952	CAL	4																													
ALLAN LEACH Allan E																															
1946	OTT	9																													
GLEN LEACH Glen DB 5'11 185 Wilfrid Laurier B: 6/21/1953 Draft: 4-35 1976 MTL																															
1976	MTL	6																													
1977	MTL	1																													
1977	BC	2																													
1977	Year	3																													
2	Years	7																													
JOHN LEACH John RB 5'9 215 Wake Forest B: 3/21/1972																															
1995	BC	3				2						6	1	23	88	3.8	34	1	8	55	6.9	12	0					1	54	54.0	54
SCOTT LEACH Scott Haywood LB 6'2 221 Ohio State B: 9/18/1963 Bridgeport, CT Draft: 9-234 1987 NO Pro: N																															
1989	BC	3				9	1.0																								
LAMAR LEACHMAN Lamar R. C 6'1 220 Tennessee B: 8/7/1934 Cartersville, GA Draft: 30-360 1955 CLE																															
1956	CAL	8	0		3				1	15																					
CHRIS LEAK Christopher Patrick QB 6'0 207 Florida B: 5/3/1985 Charlotte, NC																															
2009	MTL	18				0								2	9	4.5	7	0													
2010	MTL	17	1	0	0	0								5	32	6.4	14	0													
2	Years	35	1	0	0	0								7	41	5.9	14	0													
BUDDY LEAKE John Elgin, Jr. QB-HB 6'0 195 Oklahoma B: 5/25/1933 Draft: 3-29 1955 GB																															
1955	WPG	16	6		3							85	6	81	139	1.7	20	6													
1956	WPG	15	8		0				2	7		103	10	156	633	4.1	37	6	18	240	13.3	48	4					3	59	19.7	30
1957	WPG	8										14	0	31	174	5.6	16	0	1	11	11.0	11	0								
3	Years	39	14		3				2	7		202	16	268	946	3.5	37	12	19	251	13.2	48	4					3	59	19.7	30
LES LEAR Leslie (Butch) G 5'11 225 Winnipeg Victorias Jrs.; Manitoba B: 8/22/1918 Grafton, ND D: 1/5/1979 Dade County, FL Pro: N																															
1949	CAL	2																													
1950	CAL	5																													
2	Years	7																													
ED LEARN Harry Edward S-DH-OHB 6'0 175 none B: 9/30/1935 Welland, ON																															
1958	MTL	12																						33	216	6.5	18				
1959	MTL	14							6	112		6	1											11	41	3.7	13				
1960	MTL	14							5	30														26	96	3.7	12				
1961	MTL	12							2	27														47	348	7.4	20				
1962	MTL	14							3	25														72	379	5.3	19				
1963	MTL	14							3	29														42	255	6.1	28				
1964	MTL+	14	0		2				5	60														34	252	7.4	26	6	109	18.2	30
1965	MTL	14	1		1				4	27														69	379	5.5	21				
1966	MTL+	14	1		0				6	41														61	305	5.0	19				
1967	TOR	12	0		1				2	0														65	460	7.1	31				
1968	TOR*	14	1		1				7	79														36	255	7.1	23				
1969	TOR+	14			2				8	148		6	1																		
12	Years	162	3		7				51	578		12	2											496	2986	6.0	31	6	109	18.2	30
WESLEY LEASY Wesley LB 6'2 234 Mississippi State B: 9/7/1971 Vicksburg, MS Draft: 7B-224 1995 ARI Pro: N																															
1998	WPG	16				58	3.0	28.0	0	0	1																				
BOB LEATHEM Bob E 175																															
1946	CAL	8																													
1947	CAL	8																													
1948	CAL	11																													
3	Years	27																													
LARRY LEATHEM Larry WR 6'0 190 Calgary B: 3/30/1954 Draft: TE 1977 CAL																															
1977	CAL	13										12	2						11	163	14.8	31	2	5	61	12.2	20	1	17	17.0	17
EDDIE LeBARON Edward Wayne, Jr. QB-P 5'8 166 Pacific B: 1/7/1930 San Rafael, CA Draft: 10-123 1950 WAS Pro: N																															
1954	CAL	15	4		1				3	23		20	3	35	-33	-0.9	13	3													
BOB LeBLANC Robert OG-MG 6'1 225 Boston College B: 10/17/1936 Yarmouth, NS																															
1961	MTL	10																													
1962	MTL	11																													
1963	MTL	14																													
1964	MTL	8																													
4	Years	43																													
ROBERT LeBLANC Robert SB 6'1 191 McGill B: 9/28/1983 Vancouver, BC Draft: 5-40 2005 EDM																															
2005	EDM	5				0													2	28	14.0	17	0								
2006	EDM	17				3						1	0						1	21	21.0	21	0					3	4	1.3	4
2	Years	22				3						1	0						3	49	16.3	21	0					3	4	1.3	4
ANDY LECESSE Andy G 5'8 167 NDG Maple Leafs Jrs. B: 1928																															
1952	MTL	6																													
SCOTT LECKY Scott SB 6'1 195 Guelph B: 12/9/1964 New York, NY Draft: 4-36 1986 BC																															
1986	BC	17										12	2						16	222	13.9	31	2					1	0	0.0	0
1987	BC	4				0						6	1						8	80	10.0	25	1	0	9		9				
1988	BC	18	1		2	0						24	4						52	687	13.2	32	4					1	0	0.0	0
1989	BC	8				0						6	1						6	173	28.8	89	1	1	0	0.0	0				
4	Years	47	1		2	0						48	8						82	1162	14.2	89	8	1	9	9.0	9	2	0	0.0	0
JIM LeCLAIR James Michael QB 6'1 208 C.W. Post B: 3/23/1944 Mount Vernon, NY Draft: 16-241 1966 SF Pro: N																															
1971	MTL	1																													
CODY LEDBETTER Cody Wayne QB 6'1 205 New Mexico State B: 7/9/1973 Stephenville, TX																															
1996	EDM	18	3		1	0								10	81	8.1	26	0													
1998	HAM	18	2	0	1	0								8	45	5.6	19	0													
1999	HAM	18	2	0	0	1						6	1	15	105	7.0	16	1													
2000	HAM	7				0								5	20	4.0	10	0													
2001	HAM	18	1	0	1	0								8	26	3.3	7	0													
5	Years	79	8	0	3	1						6	1	46	277	6.0	26	1													
MARK LEDBETTER Mark D. LB-DE 6'4 235 Washington State B: 12/14/1966 Tacoma, WA Pro: E																															
1993	SAC	18	0		2	41	8.0	39.0																							
1994	SAC	18				36	4.0	19.0			2																				
1995	BIR	18	0		2	33	6.0	36.0			1	6	1																		
3	Years	54	0		4	110	18.0	94.0			3	6	1																		
COURTNEY LEDYARD Courtney M. LB 6'2 250 Michigan State B: 3/9/1977 Shaker Heights, OH Pro: EN																															
2004	MTL	3				4																						1	9	9.0	9
HAL LEDYARD Harold QB-DB 6'0 185 Tennessee-Chattanooga B: 7/7/1931 Montgomery, AL D: 4/21/1973 Big Sur, CA Draft: 9-105 1953 SF Pro: N																															
1956	OTT	14										6	1	51	353	6.9	25	1													
1957	OTT	8												20	103	5.2	10	0													
1958	OTT	9										1	0	30	-46	-1.5	33	0													
1961	WPG	13	2											37	80	2.2	11	0													
1962	WPG	16	2											13	40	3.1	12	0													
1963	WPG	16	1		0									4	38	9.5	19	0										1	6	6.0	6
1964	WPG	16	1		0									22	76	3.5	19	0													
1965	SAS	13																0													
1965	WPG	3																0													
1965	Year	16												6	34	5.7	18	0													
8	Years	105	6		0							7	1	177	644	3.6	33	1										1	6	6.0	6
BOB LEE Robert Edward T 6'1 245 Missouri B: 7/4/1935 Pro: N																															
1961	CAL	1																													
BUTCH LEE George D. E 6'1 210 Alabama B: 1924																															

Year	Team	GP	FM	FF	FR	TK	SK	YDS	IR	YDS	PD	PTS	TD	RA	YDS	AVG	LG	TD	REC	YDS	AVG	LG	TD	PR	YDS	AVG	LG	KOR	YDS	AVG	LG
1948	SAS	12										8	1										1								
DAVE LEE David DB 5'10 175 St. Catherines Rams Jrs. B: 1948																																
1973	BC	3																							6	22	3.7	6				
DWIGHT LEE Dwight Loniel RB 6'2 190 Michigan State B: 9/3/1945 Mount Clemens, MI Draft: 5-125 1968 SF Pro: N																																
1969	MTL	2	1		0									11	39	3.5	19	0	1	2	2.0	2	0					2	35	17.5	20
ERIC LEE Eric T. DB 5'11 180 Mississippi Gulf Coast JC; Wyoming B: 5/31/1979 Hattiesburg, MS																																
2003	OTT	11				32			1	0	4																				
HARRY LEE Harry C. OG-LB 6'2 210 Alabama B: 1/27/1932																																
1957	HAM	2																													
JAMALL LEE Jamall FB-RB 6'0 221 Bishop's B: 3/13/1987 Port Coquitlam, BC Draft: 1A-3 2009 BC																																
2009	BC	4				4												1	10	10.0	10	0								
2010	BC	14				7								3	16	5.3	10	0	8	99	12.4	24	0								
2011	BC	14	0	0	1	13								34	8	0.2	4	0	2	24	12.0	14	0								
3	Years	32	0	0	1	24								37	24	0.6	10	0	11	133	12.1	24	0								
JERMAINE LEE Jermaine DE 6'1 240 Albany B: 3/13/1984 New York, NY Draft: SD-6th 2006 EDM																																
2006	EDM	1				1																									
JIMMY LEE James Shannon WR 5'8 170 Rice B: 5/5/1972 San Antonio, TX																																
1995	SA	3				1								1	-8	-8.0	-8	0	3	47	15.7	29	0	4	50	12.5	38				
1997	TOR	2				0																						1	41	41.0	41
2	Years	5				1								1	-8	-8.0	-8	0	3	47	15.7	29	0	4	50	12.5	38	1	41	41.0	41
KEN LEE Kenneth Alan LB 6'4 220 Washington B: 9/3/1948 Honolulu, HI Draft: 8-204 1971 DET Pro: NW																																
1973	TOR	3	0		1																										
LAMAR LEE Lamar LB-DH 6'0 180 Arkansas State B: 8/19/1982 Boston, MA																																
2005	SAS	2				4			0	0	1																				
MARVIN LEE Marvin G 6'2 210 Luther B: 2/24/1940 Estevan, SK																																
1962	MTL	10																													
1963	MTL	5																													
1964	WPG	2																													
1964	EDM	1																													
1964	Year	3																													
3	Years	17																													
MIKE LEE Michael WR 5'11 175 Utah State B: 9/24/1972																																
1994	EDM	11	4		1	4						6	1	1	-13	-13.0	-13	0	28	476	17.0	75	1								
ORVILLE LEE Orville RB 5'10 190 Simon Fraser B: 4/4/1964 Ochos Rios, Jamaica Draft: 1-1 1988 OTT																																
1988	OTT*	18	4		0	2						12	2	232	1075	4.6	61	2	26	175	6.7	29	0	34	259	7.6	68	47	940	20.0	81
1989	OTT	16	5		0	3								137	398	2.9	22	0	32	319	10.0	40	0	5	22	4.4	20	22	403	18.3	29
1990	OTT	4				3								8	17	2.1	7	0	5	45	9.0	19	0								
1990	SAS	13	1		0	0						12	2	22	130	5.9	40	2	9	91	10.1	26	0	41	332	8.1	61	35	785	22.4	49
1990	Year	17	1		0	3						12	2	30	147	4.9	40	2	14	136	9.7	26	0	41	332	8.1	61	35	785	22.4	49
1991	SAS	5				6						6	1	25	68	2.7	12	1	18	109	6.1	15	0					2	40	20.0	25
1992	HAM	18	7		1	12						44	7	120	416	3.5	28	5	38	306	8.1	24	2					10	214	21.4	65
5	Years	61	17		1	26						74	12	544	2104	3.9	61	10	128	1045	8.2	40	2	80	613	7.7	68	116	2382	20.5	81
TERRANCE LEE Terrance DH 6-0 175 Arizona Western CC; Nevada-Las Vegas B: 5/30/1985																																
2011	HAM	3				7																									
TOMMY LEE Tommy QB 6'0 185 Willamette B: 9/11/1942 Honolulu, HI																																
1963	OTT	4												3	4	1.3	6	0													
WAYNE LEE Wayne SB-WR-DB 6'1 195 Ottawa B: 10/20/1959 Toronto, ON																																
1983	HAM	14																	1	12	12.0	12	0								
1984	HAM	16																	7	95	13.6	19	0								
1985	HAM	16	1		0														24	245	10.2	28	0	10	117	11.7	26	4	81	20.3	46
1986	HAM	18	3		1							12	2						46	564	12.3	36	2	40	351	8.8	76	4	63	15.8	22
1987	HAM	9	3		2	0													6	74	12.3	21	0	34	172	5.1	15	1	22	22.0	22
5	Years	73	7		3	0						12	2						84	990	11.8	36	2	84	640	7.6	76	9	166	18.4	46
WILLIE LEE Willie DT 6'4 250 Bethune-Cookman B: 7/13/1950 Daytona Beach, FL Draft: 5A-137 1976 KC Pro: N																																
1979	WPG	1																													
DWAYNE LeFALL Dwayne Joseph DE 6'3 270 Akron B: 4/21/1981 Oakland, CA Pro: U																																
2005	SAS	7				8	1.0	6.0	0	0	1																				
GARRY LeFEBVRE Garry FL-CB 6'0 185 Edmonton Wildcats Jrs. B: 11/12/1944																																
1966	EDM	16	1		0							18	3						9	228	25.3	55	3	21	82	3.9	11				
1967	EDM	16							2	91		24	4						13	336	25.8	74	2	1	11	11.0	11				
1968	EDM	15										20	3						19	319	16.8	59	3					4	132	33.0	50
1969	EDM	2																										1	26	26.0	26
1969	MTL	11	1		0							6	1										1								
1969	Year	13	1		0							6	1						18	357	19.8	58	1								
1970	MTL	2																	1	14	14.0	14	0								
1971	MTL	14										7	1						20	294	14.7	43	1								
1972	EDM	16	2		0				4	30									1	12	12.0	12	0	1	-3	-3.0	-3	2	13	6.5	13
1973	EDM	16	0		2				1	14		26	4						18	335	18.6	43	4	0	10		10				
1974	EDM	16	1		0							19	3						36	576	16.0	66	3								
1975	EDM	1										6	1						2	93	46.5	83	1								
1976	EDM	16										19	3						16	293	18.3	48	3								
11	Years	130	5		2				7	135		145	23						135	2500	18.5	83	21	23	100	4.3	11	7	171	24.4	50
GERRY LEFEBVRE Gerry G 5'11 222 B: 1925																																
1948	OTT	12																													
1949	OTT	12																													
1950	OTT	8																													
1951	OTT	5																													
1952	OTT	12																													
1953	OTT	14																													
6	Years	63																													
GREG LeFEVER Greg LB 5'11 215 Garden City CC; East Carolina B: 11/13/1978 Ocean City, NJ																																
2003	MTL	1				2																									
STEFAN LeFORS Stefan W. QB 6'0 201 Louisville B: 6/7/1981 Baton Rouge, LA Draft: 4-121 2005 CAR																																
2007	EDM	18	5	0	4	0						12	2	39	204	5.2	14	2													
2008	EDM	1				0								1	2	2.0	2	0													
2009	WPG	9	2	0	0	0								15	68	4.5	10	0													
3	Years	28	7	0	4	0						12	2	55	274	5.0	14	2													
KEVIN LEFSRUD Kevin C 6'3 305 Saskatchewan B: 1/28/1977 Edmonton, AB Draft: 5-37 1999 MTL																																
2000	MTL	15				0																									
2001	MTL	18				1																									
2002	MTL	18				1																									
2003	EDM	17	0	0	1	0																									
2004	EDM	18	1	0	1	3																									
2005	EDM	17	1	0	1	4																									
2007	EDM	6				1																									
7	Years	109	2	0	3	10																									
ETIENNE LEGARE Etienne DT-DE-NT 6'3 261 Laval B: 3/15/1983 Saint-Raymond, QC Draft: 1-2 2009 TOR																																
2009	TOR	17	1	0	0	6																									
2010	TOR	8				1																									
2010	EDM	4				2																									
2010	Year	12				3																									
2011	EDM	15	0	0	1	17	5.0	17.0																							

Year	Team	GP	FM	FF	FR	TK	SK	YDS	IR	YDS	PD	PTS	TD	RA	YDS	AVG	LG	TD	REC	YDS	AVG	LG	TD	PR	YDS	AVG	LG	KOR	YDS	AVG	LG
3	Years	40	1	0	1	26	5.0	17.0																							
CAMERON LEGAULT Cameron DT 6'3 255 Carleton B: 9/2/1974 Ottawa, ON Draft: 2-16 1999 CAL																															
1999	CAL	18	0	0	1	12																									
2000	BC	8				17	1.0	0.0			1																				
2001	BC	18	0	0	1	47	7.0	47.0			2																				
2002	BC	18				22	5.0	48.0																							
2003	BC	17				31	4.0	17.0																							
2004	BC	18	0	1	0	4																									
2005	OTT	18				22	2.0	21.0			1																				
2006	WPG	13				5	1.0																								
8	Years	128	0	1	2	160	20.0	133.0			4																				
LEN LeGAULT Leonard A. DT-OT-MG 6'4 232 Kansas State B: 1933																															
1957	SAS	16																													
1958	SAS	16	0		2																										
1959	SAS	16																													
1960	SAS	16	0		2																										
1961	SAS	12																													
1962	SAS	16	1		2																										
1963	SAS	16	0		1																										
1964	SAS	16	0		1																										
1965	SAS	15																													
9	Years	139	1		8																										
JOHN LeHEUP John Douglas OG-DL 6'2 250 South Carolina B: 10/13/1951 Tampa, FL Draft: 10B-259 1973 BUF Pro: W																															
1973	MTL	1																													
1973	TOR	1	0		1																										
1973	Year	2	0		1																										
1976	HAM	1																													
2	Years	2	0		1																										
KEN LEHMANN Kenneth Edward LB 5'11 222 Marquette; Xavier (Ohio) B: 1/16/1942																															
1964	OTT	14	0		2				2	25		6	1																		
1965	OTT*	14	0		2				4	134		6	1																		
1966	OTT*	14	0		1				4	63																					
1967	OTT+	14	0		1				2	64																		1	0	0.0	0
1968	OTT*	14							4	64																		3	21	7.0	10
1969	OTT*	14							1	3																		7	73	10.4	22
1970	OTT	9							1	4																					
1971	OTT	12																													
1972	BC	2																													
9	Years	107	0		6				18	357		12	2															11	94	8.5	22
TERRY LEHNE Terry DB 5'11 185 Saskatchewan B: 3/14/1959 Saskatoon, SK Draft: 2-17 1981 CAL																															
1983	HAM	6																													
1983	TOR	2																													
1983	MTL	3																													
1983	Year	12																													
1984	HAM	2																													
1985	HAM	16																													
1986	HAM	18	0		1																			2	3	1.5	3	2	25	12.5	15
1987	HAM	18				8																		1	9	9.0	9	5	65	13.0	21
1988	HAM	1																										1	0	0.0	0
1988	OTT	3																													
1988	Year	4																										1	0	0.0	0
6	Years	61	0		1	8																		3	12	4.0	9	8	90	11.3	21
CHARLIE LEIGH Charles Irving HB 5'11 203 none B: 10/30/1945 Fairfax, VA D: 10/26/2006 Albany, NY Pro: N																															
1970	OTT	5	2		0							6	1	48	100	2.1	12	1	4	40	10.0	21	0								
BRUCE LEMMERMAN Bruce B. QB 6'1 201 Northridge State B: 10/4/1945 Los Angeles, CA Pro: N																															
1971	EDM	7	1		0							12	2	26	87	3.3	21	2	1	8	8.0	8	0								
1972	EDM	3	5		0							18	3	12	39	3.3	15	3													
1973	EDM	16										6	1	36	95	2.6	13	1													
1974	EDM	16	1		0									9	26	2.9	7	0													
1975	EDM	16										8	1	19	61	3.2	11	1													
1976	EDM	16	1		0									24	137	5.7	18	0													
1977	EDM	16	1		0							6	1	18	5	0.3	14	1													
1978	EDM	1												5	-5	-1.0	2	0													
1980	HAM	8	1		1									6	26	4.3	16	0													
9	Years	99	10		1							50	8	155	471	3.0	21	8	1	8	8.0	8	0								
CLEO LEMON Cleotha, Jr. QB 6'2 215 Arkansas State B: 8/16/1979 Greenwood, MS Pro: N																															
2010	TOR	17	13	0	5	1						18	3	39	274	7.0	22	3	1	13	13.0	13	0								
2011	TOR	9	3	0	2	1						12	2	12	102	8.5	19	2													
2	Years	26	16	0	7	2						30	5	51	376	7.4	22	5	1	13	13.0	13	0								
SHAWN LEMON Shawn DE 6'1 238 Akron B: 8/25/1988 Charleston, SC																															
2011	SAS	1				0																									
WALLY LENCZ Anthony Walter FB-LB 6'0 212 NDG Maple Leafs Jrs. B: 4/12/1938 Montreal, QC D: 6/30/1971																															
1958	MTL	2												4	3	0.8	2	0													
1959	MTL	11												2	0	0.0	1	0						9	50	5.6	12				
2	Years	13												6	3	0.5	2	0						9	50	5.6	12				
JACK LENTZ Henry Edgar, Jr. DB 6'0 195 Holy Cross B: 2/22/1945 Baltimore, MD Draft: 16-399 1967 DEN Pro: N																															
1969	MTL	9	0		1				2	19																					
JIM LEO James Phillip LB-OHB-DB 6'1 222 Cincinnati B: 6/18/1937 Niagara Falls, NY Draft: FS 1960 BUF; 3-36 1960 NYG Pro: N																															
1963	TOR	8																													
1964	TOR	9																	10	132	13.2	19	0								
2	Years	17																	10	132	13.2	19	0								
ADAM LEONARD Adam LB 6'0 235 Hawaii B: 11/4/1986 Seattle, WA																															
2010	BC	12	0	2	0	32					2																				
2011	BC	4	0	1	0	10																									
2	Years	16	0	3	0	42					2																				
KENTON LEONARD Kenton CB 5'9 170 Nicholls State B: 5/2/1968 Point Coupee, LA																															
1991	CAL	17				62			2	33																					
1992	CAL	18	0		1	47			4	44		6	1																		
1993	CAL	15				45			1	26																					
1994	CAL	13	0		2	30			1	0	7																				
1995	CAL	15	0		1	26			1	0	3																				
1996	CAL	17	0		1	36	1.0	8.0	1	4	7																				
1997	CAL	15	0	1	1	42	1.0	10.0	2	14	12																				
7	Years	110	0	1	6	288	2.0	18.0	12	121	29	6	1																		
GLENN LEONHARD Glenn OG-OT-DT 6'4 255 Winnipeg Rods Jrs.; Manitoba B: 11/14/1954 Swan River, MB Draft: 4-30 1977 BC																															
1977	BC	5																													
1978	BC	16																													
1979	BC	12	0		1																										
1980	BC	16																													
1981	BC	16																													
1982	BC	16	0		1																										
1983	BC	16																										1	17	17.0	17

Year	Team	GP	FM	FF	FR	TK	SK	YDS	IR	YDS	PD	PTS	TD	RA	YDS	AVG	LG	TD	REC	YDS	AVG	LG	TD	PR	YDS	AVG	LG	KOR	YDS	AVG	LG
1984	BC	13																													
1985	BC	16																													
1986	BC	17	0		2																							2	17	8.5	17
10	Years	143	0		4																							3	34	11.3	17
TERRY LESCHUK Terry P-K 5'10 180 Simon Fraser; Calgary Cougars Jrs. B: 11/19/1961 Calgary, AB																															
1983	CAL	1																													
1985	SAS	6	1		0							5	0																		
2	Years	7	1		0							5	0																		
BRAD LESTER Brad RB 5'11 197 Auburn B: 10/24/1985 Lilburn, GA																															
2010	EDM	2	1	0	0	0								16	96	6.0	21	0													
GREG LESTER Gregory Jones WR 5'10 180 Georgia Tech B: 12/16/1970 Daytona Beach, FL																															
1994	SAS	2				0													3	44	14.7	20	0								
MARC LESTER Marc DB 6'4 200 Morgan State B: 11/5/1979 Harrisburg, PA Pro: E																															
2004	TOR	7				0													11	126	11.5	23	0					1	8	8.0	8
JIM LETCAVITS James L. OE 6'2 190 Kansas B: 12/1/1935																															
1958	EDM	8	1									12	2						23	413	18.0	85	2								
1959	EDM	16										12	2	1	1	1.0	1	0	28	497	17.8	54	2								
1960	EDM	16	0		1							12	2						28	474	16.9	42	2								
1961	EDM	15										24	4						21	405	19.3	57	4					1	2	2.0	2
1962	EDM	16	1									19	3						42	640	15.2	65	3					3	19	6.3	10
1963	MTL	2																													
6	Years	73	2		1							79	13	1	1	1.0	1	0	142	2429	17.1	85	13					4	21	5.3	10
JOHN LEVANTIS John (Babe) G-T B: 5/26/1925 D: 8/14/2010 Toronto, ON																															
1946	TOR	10																													
1947	TOR	3																													
2	Years	13																													
STEVE LEVANTIS Steve T 5'11 211 none B: 1915 D: //1993																															
1946	TOR	12																													
1947	TOR	12																													
1948	TOR	12										5	1																		
1949	TOR	7																													
1950	HAM	5																													
5	Years	48										5	1																		
MIKE LEVEILLE Michel FL 5'10 170 Ottawa B: 1948 Draft: 2A-12 1971 BC																															
1971	BC	16	2		0														5	84	16.8	21	0	78	442	5.7	19	3	77	25.7	30
1972	BC	11	1		1														13	177	13.6	38	0	37	184	5.0	23				
2	Years	27	3		1														18	261	14.5	38	0	115	626	5.4	23	3	77	25.7	30
BOB LEVENHAGEN Robert DG 6'0 215 Washington B: 10/2/1924 Tacoma, WA Draft: 17-109 1948 LA-AAFC; 25-230 1948 LARM																															
1953	CAL	1																													
1954	BC+	14	1		2				1	26														1	12	12.0	12				
1955	BC+	12	2		5							5	1											1	6	6.0	6				
3	Years	27	3		7				1	26		5	1											2	18	9.0	12				
MIKE LEVENSELLER Michael Thomas WR 6'1 180 Washington State B: 2/21/1956 Bremerton, WA Draft: 6B-164 1978 OAK Pro: N																															
1982	EDM	9										18	3						37	503	13.6	38	3								
1983	CAL	16	2		0							18	3						43	707	16.4	47	3								
1984	CAL	8	2		0							36	6						47	514	10.9	25	6								
3	Years	33	4		0							72	12						127	1724	13.6	47	12								
MOE LEVESQUE Maurice DT-OT 6'2 230 Rosemount Bombers Jrs.; HMCS Donnacona B: 7/12/1938 Ottawa, ON																															
1963	MTL	14																													
1964	MTL	14																													
1965	MTL	14	0		2																										
1966	SAS	15							1																						
1967	OTT	8																													
5	Years	65	0		2				1	0																					
BASHIR LEVINGSTON Bashir A. CB 5'9 180 Monterey Peninsula JC; Utah State; Eastern Washington B: 10/2/1976 Seaside, CA Pro: EN																															
2002	TOR	9	2	0	0	12			1	12	2	6	1											27	398	14.7	90	11	214	19.5	37
2003	TOR*	16	2	0	0	1						30	5	2	34	17.0	25	0	3	75	25.0	58	0	60	811	13.5	94	29	881	30.4	95
2004	TOR+	12	2	0	0	4						30	5											41	391	9.5	85	19	447	23.5	97
2005	TOR	17	2	0	1	1						12	2											59	604	10.2	109	42	855	20.4	44
2006	TOR	17	1	1	1	7						12	2	4	21	5.3	12	0	1	50	50.0	50	1	53	543	10.2	88	31	662	21.4	58
2007	TOR	7	2	0	0	4						6	1											31	174	5.6	21	16	297	18.6	42
6	Years	78	11	1	2	29			1	12	2	96	16	6	55	9.2	25	0	4	125	31.3	58	1	271	2921	10.8	109	148	3356	22.7	97
FRED LEVINSKY Fred OG 6'0 225 Villanova B: 1946																															
1968	WPG	4	0		1																										
CHUCK LEVY Charles RB 6'0 201 Arizona B: 1/7/1972 Torrance, CA Draft: 2-38 1994 ARI Pro: N																															
2000	BC	14	2	1	2	28	1.0	8.0				14	2	12	58	4.8	15	2	10	147	14.7	45	0	5	24	4.8	11	16	353	22.1	38
2001	TOR	12	1	0	0	30			1	13	5													24	290	12.1	70	20	438	21.9	39
2	Years	26	3	1	2	58	1.0	8.0	1	13	5	14	2	12	58	4.8	15	2	10	147	14.7	45	0	29	314	10.8	70	36	791	22.0	39
DARCEY LEVY Darcey D. WR 6'2 202 Notre Dame; Fort Range CC; Pittsburgh B: 7/5/1979 Aurora, CO Pro: E																															
2004	WPG	1				0													2	24	12.0	13	0								
2004	CAL	2				0													8	77	9.6	24	0								
2004	Year	3				0													10	101	10.1	24	0								
NIGEL LEVY Nigel WR 6'3 190 Western Ontario B: 2/16/1969 Scarborough, ON Draft: 3-18 1993 OTT																															
1993	OTT	1				0																									
BILL LEWIS William Glenn C 6'7 282 Nebraska B: 7/12/1963 Aurora, CO Draft: 7-191 1986 LARI Pro: N																															
1995	MEM	8				1																									
BRENT LEWIS Brent LB 6'0 222 Western Ontario B: 3/9/1965 Strathroy, ON Draft: 5-37 1987 OTT																															
1989	TOR	3				0																									
1990	OTT	15	0		1	3																									
1991	OTT	6				6																									
3	Years	24	0		1	9																									
CHRIS LEWIS Chris CB 5'11 205 Calgary B: 12/13/1974 Calgary, AB																															
1997	CAL	18				15													1	9	9.0	9	0								
1998	BC	2				2																									
2	Years	20				17													1	9	9.0	9	0								
DAVE LEWIS David Ray QB-OHB 6'2 216 Stanford B: 10/16/1945 Clovis, CA Draft: 5-109 1967 NYG Pro: N																															
1967	MTL	14	4		3				1	8		21	2	39	168	4.3	17	1						2	6	3.0	6	1	24	24.0	24
1968	MTL	14	3		0							13	2	20	114	5.7	37	0	41	794	19.4	75	2	4	6	1.5	7	3	69	23.0	24
1975	MTL	2	2		0														1	13	13.0	13	0								
3	Years	30	9		3				1	8		34	4	59	282	4.8	37	1	42	807	19.2	75	2	6	12	2.0	7	4	93	23.3	24
DERRICK LEWIS Derrick (Bo) CB 5'10 180 Jackson State B: 11/15/1974 Louisville, MS																															
1998	BC	6				19			2	16	4																				
1999	BC	18	0	1	1	29			3	61	7	6	1																		
2000	BC	17	0	2	0	42	1.0	9.0	4	99	4																				
2001	BC	18	0	1	0	51	1.0	8.0	4	5																					
2002	BC*	18	0	3	0	65			3	56	2																	1	0	0.0	0
2003	BC	12	0	1	1	34	1.0	8.0	1	0	4																				
2004	BC	18	1	1	2	42	2.0	8.0	1	0	2	6	1											1	0	0.0	0				
2005	TOR	11				18			2	8	2			1	7	7.0	7	0													
8	Years	118	1	9	4	300	5.0	33.0	20	245	25	12	2	1	7	7.0	7	0						1	0	0.0	0	1	0	0.0	0
DICK LEWIS Dick C 6'0 255																															
1947	MTL	12																													

Year	Team	GP	FM	FF	FR	TK	SK	YDS	IR	YDS	PD	PTS	TD	RA	YDS	AVG	LG	TD	REC	YDS	AVG	LG	TD	PR	YDS	AVG	LG	KOR	YDS	AVG	LG
DOMINIC LEWIS Dominic Xavier DT-DE 6'3 261 Kentucky B: 5/12/1985 Killeen, TX																															
2008	HAM	7				7	1.0				3																				
FRED LEWIS Fred CB 5'11 195 Louisiana Tech B: 11/14/1976 Iberia, LA																															
2001	EDM	7				12					2																				
GARRY LEWIS Garry, Jr. CB 5'11 185 Alcorn State B: 8/25/1967 New Orleans, LA Draft: 7-173 1990 LARI Pro: N																															
1994	OTT	14				50			1	0	4																				
1995	OTT	5				22			1	0	1																				
1995	HAM	10				31			5	38	1																				
1995	Year	15				53			6	39	2																				
1996	HAM	9				26			1	23	3																				
3	Years	28				129			8	61	9																				
GARY LEWIS Gary L. DT 6'3 260 Oklahoma State B: 1/14/1961 Oklahoma City, OK Draft: 4-98 1983 NO; 3-29 1983 BIR-USFL Pro: N																															
1985	OTT	2																													
1985	SAS	4	0		1		5.0																								
1985	Year	6	0		1		5.0																								
1986	SAS	18	0		1		9.0																								
1987	SAS	7				25	3.0																								
1988	SAS+	18			1	44	7.0					6	1																		
1989	SAS	18	0		1	31	10.0																								
1990	SAS	18				25	7.0																								
1991	SAS+	18				25	11.0																								
1992	SAS	18	0		2	30	6.0																								
1993	SAS	15				31	5.0	43.0																							
1994	SAS	18	0		4	31	5.0																								
10	Years	150	0		10	242	68.0	43.0				6	1																		
JAVES LEWIS Javes Ulysses, Jr. LB 6'1 190 Oregon B: 12/11/1989 Nuremburg, West Germany																															
2011	TOR	1	0	1	0	2																									
JOHNNY LEWIS Johnny Lee, Jr. DT 6'2 242 Oklahoma B: 5/17/1960 Pinehurst, GA Pro: U																															
1987	HAM	5	0		1	8	2.0																								
1988	HAM	1				0	1.0																								
1988	TOR	2				0																									
1988	OTT	4	0		1	0	1.0																								
1988	Year	7	0		1	0																									
2	Years	6	0		2	8	4.0																								
JONAS LEWIS Jonas W. Allen RB 5'9 210 San Diego State B: 12/27/1976 Riverside, CA Pro: EN																															
2004	MTL	4	0	1	0	5						12	2	20	123	6.2	40	2										1	28	28.0	28
2005	MTL	4	1	1	1	6								13	50	3.8	10	0	3	39	13.0	17	0								
2	Years	8	1	2	1	11						12	2	33	173	5.2	40	2	3	39	13.0	17	0					1	28	28.0	28
KIP LEWIS Sherman CB 5'10 170 Arizona B: 6/2/1967 East Elmhurst, NY Pro: E																															
1993	TOR	9				3						20	3						29	401	13.8	41	3								
LEO LEWIS Leo Everett, Jr. (Lincoln Locomotive) OHB-DB-FB 5'10 195 Lincoln (Missouri) B: 2/4/1933 Des Moines, IA Draft: 6-64 1955 BAL																															
1955	WPG+	16	8		0							30	6	135	834	6.2	41	5	11	345	31.4	59	1								
1957	WPG	16										48	8	119	817	6.9	69	5	13	261	20.1	54	3					26	854	32.8	76
1958	WPG+	16	4									66	11	167	1164	7.0	47	8	31	679	21.9	61	3					20	639	32.0	68
1959	WPG	16										54	9	112	730	6.5	37	2	43	695	16.2	50	7					15	397	26.5	65
1960	WPG+	14	3		1							36	6	106	923	8.7	85	5	18	374	20.8	78	1	3	21	7.0	12	16	417	26.1	82
1961	WPG+	16	3									49	8	146	1036	7.1	63	8	13	206	15.8	19	0					19	495	26.1	42
1962	WPG*	15	2									66	11	134	865	6.5	83	4	30	661	22.0	66	6					20	573	28.7	91
1963	WPG	16	3		0							30	5	133	691	5.2	92	3	27	390	14.4	40	2					29	796	27.4	50
1964	WPG*	15	4		0							41	6	114	845	7.4	87	3	26	314	12.1	55	3					24	768	32.0	84
1965	WPG	16	4		0							30	5	154	828	5.4	33	5	18	267	14.8	52	0					17	474	27.9	52
1966	WPG	5	0		2									31	128	4.1	10	0	4	59	14.8	28	0					1	30	30.0	30
11	Years	161	31		3							450	75	1351	8861	6.6	92	48	234	4251	18.2	78	26	3	21	7.0	12	187	5443	29.1	91
LEO LEWIS Leo Everett, III WR 5'8 169 Missouri B: 9/17/1956 Columbia, MO Pro: N																															
1980	CAL	5	1		0							12	2	1	62	62.0	62	1	7	82	11.7	18	1	18	133	7.4	14	13	309	23.8	36
1980	HAM	1	1		0														1	9	9.0	9	0	4	30	7.5	15	2	36	18.0	21
1980	Year	6	2		0							12	2	1	62	62.0	62	1	8	91	11.4	18	1	22	163	7.4	15	15	345	23.0	36
LOYD LEWIS Loyd Edward DT-DE 6'3 250 Texas A&M-Kingsville B: 2/23/1962 Dallas, TX Draft: 7B-196 1984 MIN; TD 1984 HOU-USFL Pro: U																															
1985	OTT+	15	0		1		7.0																								
1986	OTT	17	0		1		15.0																								
1987	OTT	16	0		1	33	13.0												1	17	17.0	17	0								
1988	OTT	4	0		1	11	1.0																								
1989	OTT	18				29	5.0																								
1990	OTT+	16	0		1	30	5.0																								
1991	OTT+	18	0		1	24	4.0																								
1992	EDM+	18	0		1	26	7.0	49.0																							
1993	WPG+	16	0		1	25	7.0	54.0	1	3		6	1																		
1994	WPG	18				27	12.0	82.0																							
1995	OTT	17				23	7.0	75.0																							
1996	OTT	7				17																									
12	Years	180	0		8	245	83.0	260.0	1	3		6	1						1	17	17.0	17	0								
MARC LEWIS Marc Allan WR 5'8 159 Missouri Western State B: 5/15/1960 Columbia, MO Pro: U																															
1986	OTT	18	1		0							24	4						71	1197	16.9	72	4	28	274	9.8	43	10	233	23.3	31
1987	OTT	18	4		1	1						18	3	3	23	7.7	11	0	94	1195	12.7	38	3	68	471	6.9	38	3	54	18.0	22
1988	OTT	7	1		0	1						6	1						30	327	10.9	22	1	17	124	7.3	33	6	140	23.3	26
1988	CAL	2	1		0	0													1	22	22.0	22	0	3	75	25.0	51	2	34	17.0	22
1988	Year	9	2		0	1						6	1						31	349	11.3	22	1	20	199	10.0	51	8	174	21.8	26
3	Years	43	7		1	2						48	8	3	23	7.7	11	0	196	2741	14.0	72	8	116	944	8.1	51	21	461	22.0	31
MILO LEWIS Milo Julius CB 5'11 183 San Francisco CC; Alabama B: 12/3/1977 San Diego, CA																															
2002	WPG	8				14	1.0		1	0	3																				
2003	WPG	13	0	1	1	39	1.0		2	0	3																				
2004	CAL	17	0	0	1	46			3	23	3	6	1																		
3	Years	38	0	1	2	99	2.0		6	23	9	6	1																		
NIK LEWIS Nikolas Burk SB-WR 5'10 212 Southern Arkansas B: 6/3/1982 Mineral Wells, TX																															
2004	CAL	18	2	0	0	5						48	8						72	1045	14.5	42	8	31	385	12.4	41	3	42	14.0	24
2005	CAL	18	1	1	3	6						66	11	2	30	15.0	19	0	80	1379	17.2	46	9	1	13	13.0	13				
2006	CAL+	18	3	0	2	5						30	5	2	12	6.0	12	0	77	1114	14.5	50	5	4	15	3.8	6	1	0	0.0	0
2007	CAL+	16	1	0	0	3						30	5	1	0	0.0	0	0	67	1101	16.4	85	5								
2008	CAL	18	1	0	1	4						60	10						87	1109	12.7	85	10								
2009	CAL	17	1	0	1	3						6	1						70	1013	14.5	52	1								
2010	CAL*	17	2	1	1	2						54	9	1	17	17.0	17	0	90	1262	14.0	74	9					2	0	0.0	0
2011	CAL*	18	1	0	1	5						30	5						93	1209	13.0	62	5								
8	Years	140	12	2	9	33						324	54	6	59	9.8	19	0	636	9232	14.5	85	52	36	413	11.5	41	6	42	7.0	24
PETE LEWIS Peter T 6'1 242 Oregon; British Columbia B: 4/24/1943 Draft: 6-45 1964 MTL																															
1964	MTL	4																													
1964	EDM	11	0		1																										
1964	Year	15	0		1																										
REGGIE LEWIS Reginald Anthony DE 6'2 260 Oregon; San Diego State B: 1/20/1954 New Orleans, LA D: 9/19/2008 Draft: 16-443 1976 SF Pro: N																															
1977	CAL	9																													
1978	CAL*	16	0		3																										
1979	CAL*	16	0		4							6	1																		
1980	CAL*	16	0		1																										

Year	Team	GP	FM	FF	FR	TK	SK	YDS	IR	YDS	PD	PTS	TD	RA	YDS	AVG	LG	TD	REC	YDS	AVG	LG	TD	PR	YDS	AVG	LG	KOR	YDS	AVG	LG
1981	CAL	8					4.5																								
1981	TOR	4					3.0																								
1981	Year	12					7.5																								
5	Years	65	0		8		7.5					6	1																		
RICH LEWIS Richard L. LB 6'2 223 Portland State B: 6/8/1950 Portland, OR Pro: N																															
1976	TOR	3																													
1977	TOR	1	0		1							6	1																		
1977	HAM	1																													
1977	Year	2	0		1							6	1																		
1978	TOR	5																													
1979	TOR	16	0		1																										
4	Years	25	0		2							6	1																		
SHERMAN LEWIS Sherman Paul OHB 5'9 159 Michigan State B: 6/29/1942 Louisville, KY Draft: 9-67 1964 NYJ; 18-250 1964 CLE Pro: N																															
1964	TOR	11	3		0							6	1	38	237	6.2	23	0	26	310	11.9	39	1					14	299	21.4	45
1965	TOR	1	1		0							6	1	6	10	1.7	6	1										1	33	33.0	33
1965	SAS	1												1	14	14.0	14	0	1	2	2.0	2	0								
1965	Year	2	1		0							6	1	7	14	2.0	14	1	1	2	2.0	2	0					1	33	33.0	33
2	Years	12	4		0							12	2	45	261	5.8	23	1	27	312	11.6	39	1					15	332	22.1	45
STAN LEWIS Stanley DE 6'4 240 Wayne State (Nebraska) B: 9/11/1953 Chicago, IL Draft: 10-238 1975 CLE Pro: N																															
1977	SAS	1																													
TAHAUN LEWIS Tahaun CN 5'10 175 Nebraska B: 9/29/1968 Draft: 9-247 1991 LARI Pro: N																															
1993	TOR	5				18																									
TOMMY LEWIS Tom FB 5'11 195 Alabama B: 1932 Draft: 10-110 1954 CHIC																															
1956	OTT	14							6	53		48	8	123	645	5.2	34	7	16	183	11.4	36	0					3	46	15.3	16
1957	OTT	10							3	48		49	8	92	437	4.8	36	6	11	105	9.5	20	1								
2	Years	24							9	101		97	16	215	1082	5.0	36	13	27	288	10.7	36	1					3	46	15.3	16
WALTER LEWIS Walter DeWayne QB 6'1 209 Alabama B: 4/26/1962 Brewton, AL Draft: TD 1984 BIR-USFL Pro: U																															
1986	MTL	11	7		0							6	1	46	281	6.1	36	1													
WILL LEWIS Will L. DB 5'9 185 Millersville B: 1/16/1958 Quakertown, PA Pro: NU																															
1986	MTL	2					1.0																								
1986	OTT	3							1	33																					
1986	Year	5					1.0		1	33																					
1987	OTT	17	1		2	43			2	78		6	1						1	35	35.0	35	0	59	544	9.2	53	23	480	20.9	58
1988	OTT	12	4		0	36			3	36														55	279	5.1	41	15	276	18.4	30
1989	WPG	3				0																		8	25	3.1	7	7	87	12.4	24
1989	HAM	13	0		1	32			3	78														7	29	4.1	11	1	19	19.0	19
1989	Year	16	0		1	32			3	78														15	54	3.6	11	8	106	13.3	24
4	Years	34	5		3	111	1.0		9	225		6	1						1	35	35.0	35	0	129	877	6.8	53	46	862	18.7	58
GILLES LEZI Gilles Patrick FB 6'0 245 Northwestern B: 2/13/1980 Kinshasa, Congo Draft: 2A-10 2004 EDM																															
2004	EDM	14				3								1	0	0.0	0	0	2	12	6.0	12	0					1	7	7.0	7
2005	OTT	17				15																						1	3	3.0	3
2006	CAL	10	0	0	1	1								2	10	5.0	9	0													
2007	WPG	18	1	1	0	10													4	40	10.0	14	0					1	5	5.0	5
4	Years	59	1	1	1	29								3	10	3.3	9	0	6	52	8.7	14	0					3	15	5.0	7
BILL LIDE William E. WR 5'11 190 Johnson C. Smith B: 2/14/1950 Darlington, SC																															
1974	CAL	3										6	1						9	114	12.7	27	1								
DENNIS LIEBRECHT Dennis FB 6'2 230 St. James Rams Ints. B: 8/14/1939																															
1965	WPG	4												1	5	5.0	5	0													
1966	WPG	16												6	41	6.8	18	0													
1967	WPG	3												3	4	1.3	3	0										2	53	26.5	40
3	Years	23												10	50	5.0	18	0										2	53	26.5	40
CHUCK LIEBROCK Charles OG 6'1 245 Windsor AKO Jrs.; St. Mary's (Nova Scotia) B: 5/24/1945 Windsor, ON Draft: 1-5 1968 TOR																															
1968	TOR	14																													
1969	TOR	14																													
1970	WPG	16	0		2							3	0	1	0	0.0	0	0													
1971	WPG	6																													
1972	WPG	16	0		1																										
1973	WPG	16	0		1																										
1974	WPG	16	0		1																										
1975	WPG	16																													
1976	WPG	16																													
1977	WPG	10																													
10	Years	140	0		5							3	0	1	0	0.0	0	0													
BOB LIGGETT Robert Ellsworth DT 6'2 255 Nebraska B: 12/8/1946 Aliquippa, PA Draft: 15-389 1970 KC Pro: N																															
1971	BC	2																													
GRANVILLE LIGGINS Granville DT-OG 6'0 225 Oklahoma B: 6/2/1946 Draft: 10-256 1968 DET																															
1968	CAL	15	0		2																										
1969	CAL	16	0		1																										
1970	CAL	7																													
1971	CAL*	16	0		1																										
1972	CAL+	16																													
1973	CAL	3																													
1973	TOR	1	0		1																										
1973	Year	4	0		1																										
1974	TOR	16																													
1975	TOR+	16																													
1976	TOR*	16	0		4																										
1977	TOR	7																													
1978	TOR	7																													
1978	HAM	3																													
1978	Year	10																													
11	Years	135	0		9																										
BOB LIGHT Bob QB-FL 6'3 200 Pacific (Oregon) B: 1941																															
1963	SAS	3																	1	11	11.0	11	0								
DEWEY LINCOLN Dewey Raymond DB 5'10 180 Michigan State B: 8/21/1942 Detroit, MI																															
1968	HAM	14	1		1									9	52	5.8	16	0	7	46	6.6	27	0	8	61	7.6	17	18	486	27.0	41
EARL LINDLEY Earl L. LB-OHB-FW 6'2 208 Utah State B: 3/13/1933 Wellsville, UT D: 2/14/2012 Smithfield, UT Draft: 16-186 1954 CHIB																															
1954	EDM	16							3	56		10	2						12	135	11.3	1	0	1	0	0.0	0	1	9	9.0	9
1955	EDM	12	4		0				3	32		15	3	82	542	6.6	73	1	12	290	24.2	55	1					4	58	14.5	22
1956	EDM+	14	2		3				3	88		48	8	57	357	6.3	24	2	17	312	18.4	51	4	1	13	13.0	13	14	284	20.3	43
1957	EDM	2							1	34		6	1																		
4	Years	44	6		3				10	210		79	14	139	899	6.5	73	3	41	737	18.0	55	5	2	13	6.5	13	19	351	18.5	43
A.J. LINDSAY Anton, Jr. DL 6'3 323 Joliet JC; Temple B: 7/10/1983 Indianapolis, IN																															
2007	CAL	1				0																									
TONY LINDSAY Tony RB 5'6 179 Utah B: 4/25/1958 Denver, CO																															
1981	TOR	1												8	31	3.9	8	0	1	-1	-1.0	1	0	2	16	8.0	10	6	161	26.8	35
JIM LINDSEY James Ellis QB 5'11 187 Abilene Christian B: 11/16/1948 Bay City, TX D: 9/9/1998 Colleyville, TX																															
1971	CAL	16	4		1							18	3	22	107	4.9	18	3													
1972	CAL	16	2		1							6	1	23	196	8.5	28	1													
1973	CAL	16	2		0									16	108	6.8	21	0													
1974	TOR	11	2		0									4	19	4.8	11	0													
4	Years	59	10		2							24	4	65	430	6.6	28	4													

Year	Team	GP	FM	FF	FR	TK	SK	YDS	IR	YDS	PD	PTS	TD	RA	YDS	AVG	LG	TD	REC	YDS	AVG	LG	TD	PR	YDS	AVG	LG	KOR	YDS	AVG	LG
KELVIN LINDSEY Kelvin A. RB 6'0 205 Ohio State B: 6/15/1960																															
1984	HAM	6	2		1							36	6	62	308	5.0	83	4	21	218	10.4	39	2					3	105	35.0	40
ERIC LINDSTROM Eric Karl LB 6'3 235 Boston College B: 5/27/1966 Weymouth, MA Draft: 7-178 1989 NE Pro: E																															
1992	TOR	1				2			1	86		6	1																		
MIKE LINDSTROM Mike WR 6'2 210 British Columbia B: 4/23/1981 Chilliwack, BC Draft: 5-40 2006 BC																															
2007	EDM	6				2																									
PAUL LINFORD Paul M. DT 6'6 265 Brigham Young B: 8/4/1953 Salt Lake City, UT Draft: 4B-93 1975 BAL																															
1975	HAM	1																													
AUBREY LINNE Aubrey Arthur, Jr. OE-P 6'7 235 Texas Christian B: 4/19/1939 Pro: N																															
1962	TOR	8										12	2						21	401	19.1	63	2								
1963	TOR	4																	6	86	14.3	19	0					1	5	5.0	5
1963	EDM	8	1		0							8	1	1	1	1.0	1	0	16	200	12.5	22	1								
1963	Year	12	1		0							8	1	1	1	1.0	1	0	22	286	13.0	22	1					1	5	5.0	5
2	Years	12	1		0							20	3	1	1	1.0	1	0	43	687	16.0	63	3					1	5	5.0	5
EDDIE LINSCOMB Eddie RB 5'9 190 Mount San Antonio JC; Missouri State B: 2/26/1979																															
2004	BC	6	3	0	1	0						12	2	40	220	5.5	37	2	2	12	6.0	8	0	3	11	3.7	9	12	196	16.3	33
RUDY LINTERMAN Rudy OHB-SB 5'11 205 Idaho B: 10/30/1947																															
1968	CAL	16	4		0									21	26	1.2	7	0	3	49	16.3	24	0	112	668	6.0	30	3	37	12.3	17
1969	CAL	16	9		1							24	4	101	609	6.0	69	2	42	500	11.9	70	2	23	126	5.5	22	19	505	26.6	35
1970	CAL	15	1		1							6	0	46	150	3.3	12	0	21	181	8.6	16	0					3	76	25.3	33
1971	CAL	16	5		0							24	4	41	146	3.6	17	0	36	394	10.9	33	4					5	135	27.0	48
1972	CAL	16	1		1							20	3	39	215	5.5	25	0	52	734	14.1	34	3	22	128	5.8	21	11	274	24.9	36
1973	CAL	16	3		2							22	3	41	150	3.7	14	0	60	719	12.0	53	3	2	22	11.0	12	19	417	21.9	43
1974	CAL+	16	3		0							6	1	3	33	11.0	24	0	64	951	14.9	62	1	5	31	6.2	12	12	269	22.4	42
1975	CAL	16	2		0							13	2	7	41	5.9	14	0	44	585	13.3	33	2	22	161	7.3	23	3	45	15.0	21
1976	CAL	16										12	2	3	12	4.0	7	0	37	574	15.5	45	2					3	72	24.0	29
1977	CAL	4										2	0						9	122	13.6	21	0								
1977	TOR	10										6	1	3	17	5.7	10	0	8	99	12.4	18	1	12	77	6.4	14				
1977	Year	14										8	1	3	17	5.7	10	0	17	221	13.0	21	1	12	77	6.4	14				
10	Years	147	28		5							135	20	305	1399	4.6	69	2	376	4908	13.1	70	18	198	1213	6.1	30	78	1830	23.5	48
JIM LIPINSKI James Victor T 6'4 238 Fairmont State B: 2/25/1927 Monongah, WV D: 5/28/2011 Sarasota, FL Draft: 22-281 1950 CHIC Pro: N																															
1951	CAL	13																						2	28	14.0					
JOEL LIPINSKI Joel CB 5'10 195 Regina; Vancouver Island Raiders Jrs.; St. Mary's (Nova Scotia) B: 7/29/1985 Regina, SK																															
2009	SAS	9				6																									
GLENN LIPPMAN Glenn Edward HB-S 5'8 168 Texas A&M B: 12/1/1929 Lavaca County, TX Draft: 22-256 1952 CHIC																															
1954	EDM	10	4									25	5	73	529	7.2	32	4	8	95	11.9	23	1					3	61	20.3	28
DON LISBON Donald OHB-FB 5'11 194 Bowling Green State B: 1/15/1941 Youngstown, OH Draft: 3-36 1963 SF Pro: N																															
1966	MTL+	14	9		1							30	5	199	1007	5.1	31	5	21	226	10.8	60	0					12	220	18.3	25
1967	MTL	7	2		0							6	1	83	385	4.6		1	16	185	11.6	32	0					6	146	24.3	29
1967	EDM	5	0		1									21	98	4.7		0	1	3	3.0	3	0					1	15	15.0	15
1967	Year	12	2		1							6	1	104	483	4.6	22	1	17	188	11.1	32	0					7	161	23.0	29
1968	EDM	7	1		0									23	87	3.8	13	0	4	32	8.0	15	0					4	67	16.8	23
3	Years	28	12		2							36	6	326	1577	4.8	31	6	42	446	10.6	60	0					23	448	19.5	29
PETE LISKE Peter Adrian QB 6'2 199 Penn State B: 5/24/1942 Plainfield, NJ Draft: 15-115(f) 1963 NYJ; 10-130(f) 1963 PHI Pro: N																															
1965	TOR	11	8		4							12	2	38	196	5.2	23	2													
1966	CAL	14	4		0				2	0		18	3	46	163	3.5	21	3	1	16	16.0	16	0								
1967	CAL*	16	2		1							6	1	50	206	4.1	19	1	1	4	4.0	4	0	1	-3	-3.0	-3				
1968	CAL	16	2		0							24	4	42	71	1.7	12	4													
1973	CAL	16	4		0							6	1	19	65	3.4	14	1													
1974	CAL	13										6	1	16	27	1.7	7	1													
1974	BC	3	1		0									4	9	2.3	5	0													
1974	Year	16	1		0							6	1	20	36	1.8	7	1													
1975	BC	16	5		1									24	31	1.3	9	0													
7	Years	102	26		6				2	0		72	12	239	768	3.2	23	12	2	20	10.0	16	0	1	-3	-3.0	-3				
DONNIE LITTLE Donald Keith WR 6'1 206 Texas B: 10/14/1959 Galveston, TX																															
1982	OTT	4												1	-1	-1.0	-1	0	17	301	17.7	36	0								
1983	OTT	8	3		0							6	1	2	18	9.0	15	0	29	452	15.6	31	1	26	211	8.1	27	4	107	26.8	32
2	Years	12	3		0							6	1	3	17	5.7	15	0	46	753	16.4	36	1	26	211	8.1	27	4	107	26.8	32
JOEY LITTLE Joey WR 6'3 200 Santa Ana JC; Fresno State B: 1/20/1962																															
1985	BC	3										6	1						3	89	29.7	77	1								
BILL LIVELY William James G-T 200 B: 1928 D: 7/16/2009																															
1948	TOR	4																													
IVAN LIVINGSTONE Lewis Ivan WB-DB 5'11 182 McGill; Dubuque B: 9/6/1930 Montreal, QC																															
1954	CAL	13	1		0							10	2	35	250	7.1	39	2	1	20	20.0	20	0	1	9	9.0	9	0	16		16
1955	CAL	5																													
1955	BC	4																	1	13	13.0	13	0	3	27	9.0	14	2	44	22.0	26
1955	Year	9																	1	13	13.0	13	0	3	27	9.0	14	2	44	22.0	26
1956	BC	1																													
1957	MTL	4												1	-5	-5.0	-5	0	2	29	14.5	20	0								
1958	MTL	14							2	0		12	2	7	16	2.3	11	0	22	478	21.7	79	2	1	0	0.0	0				
1959	MTL	10							1	15		12	2	2	4	2.0	6	0	10	241	24.1	80	2								
1960	MTL	1																										1	17	17.0	17
7	Years	48	1		0				3	15		34	6	45	265	5.9	39	2	36	781	21.7	80	4	5	36	7.2	14	3	77	25.7	26
JEFF LLOYD Jeffery John DT 6'6 255 West Texas A&M B: 3/14/1954 St. Mary's, PA Draft: 3A-62 1976 SEA Pro: N																															
1980	EDM	2																													
MAURICE LLOYD Maurice LB 5'11 230 Connecticut B: 2/15/1983 Daytona Beach, FL																															
2006	SAS	6				22																									
2007	SAS+	16	1	2	1	73	3.0	23.0	2	21	2																				
2008	SAS*	18	0	3	1	83	5.0	34.0																							
2009	EDM	15	0	1	0	59	4.0	24.0																							
2010	EDM	17				83	5.0	29.0	1	6	2																				
5	Years	72	1	6	2	320	17.0	110.0	3	27	4																				
RICKY LLOYD Ricky WR 5'11 170 West Los Angeles CC; Kansas State B: 12/2/1977																															
2003	CAL	3				0								1	6	6.0	6	0	1	3	3.0	3	0								
JOE LOBENDAHN Joe LB 5'10 236 Washington B: 2/15/1983 Honolulu, HI																															
2008	WPG	7	0	1	1	40	2.0	12.0			1																				
2009	WPG	11	0	3	1	61					1																				
2010	WPG	17	0	0	1	68	3.0	9.0			2	6	1																		
2011	WPG	9	0	1	3	32	2.0	9.0	1	0	1																				
4	Years	44	0	5	6	201	7.0	30.0	1	0	5	6	1																		
KELLY LOCHBAUM Kelly LB 6'2 240 Abbotsford Air Force Jrs.; Northern Arizona B: 4/3/1973 White Rock, BC Draft: 6-43 1997 BC																															
1997	BC	11				45																									
1998	BC	11	0	0	1	14																									
1999	BC	18				28																									
2000	BC	16	0	0	1	48																						1	10	10.0	10
2001	CAL	17				25	1.0	20.0																							
2002	BC	11	0	1	0	16																									
2003	BC	18				20																									
2004	BC	18				20																						1	0	0.0	0
2005	BC	9				4																						3	13	4.3	7
9	Years	129	0	1	2	220	1.0	20.0																				5	23	4.6	10
ROGER LOCKE Roger TE-DE 6'3 218 Arizona State B: 1942 Draft: 8-57 1963 OAK; 8-105(f) 1963 SF																															

Year	Team	GP	FM	FF	FR	TK	SK	YDS	IR	YDS	PD	PTS	TD	RA	YDS	AVG	LG	TD	REC	YDS	AVG	LG	TD	PR	YDS	AVG	LG	KOR	YDS	AVG	LG
1963	WPG	7																	12	178	14.8	30	0								
1964	WPG	10	0		2														6	82	13.7	20	0					1	3	3.0	3
2	Years	17	0		2														18	260	14.4	30	0					1	3	3.0	3
AARON LOCKETT Aaron DaRon WR 5'7 155 Kansas State B: 9/6/1978 Tulsa, OK Draft: 7C-254 2002 TB																															
2004	BC	11	3	0	2	0						12	2											46	504	11.0	105	24	555	23.1	90
2005	BC	17				0						12	2											62	808	13.0	90	61	1249	20.5	56
2006	BC	10	2	0	0	0																		51	386	7.6	43	29	483	16.7	30
3	Years	38	5	0	2	0						24	4											159	1698	10.7	105	114	2287	20.1	90
J.W. LOCKETT J.W. FB 6'2 229 Central Oklahoma B: 3/23/1937 Pro: N																															
1965	MTL	12	9		0							48	8	161	643	4.0	29	8	9	38	4.2	12	0								
1966	MTL	2	1		1									22	103	4.7	18	0	1	-3	-3.0	-3	0								
2	Years	14	10		1							48	8	183	746	4.1	29	8	10	35	3.5	12	0								
ALEC LOCKINGTON Alec QB-P 6'0 190 McMaster B: 3/10/1949 Draft: 6-53 1972 CAL																															
1973	HAM	14										2	0																		
BILLY RAY LOCKLIN William Ray DE-OG-MG 6'2 222 New Mexico State B: 8/9/1937 Draft: FS 1960 LAC Pro: N																															
1961	MTL+	11										6	1																		
1962	MTL+	14							1	1																					
1963	MTL	14																													
1964	MTL	14	0		1																										
1965	HAM*	14	0		2																										
1966	HAM*	14																													
1967	HAM	14			1																										
1968	HAM*	14	0		2																										
1969	HAM	11	0		2							6	1																		
1970	HAM	14																													
10	Years	134	0		8				1	1		12	2																		
VERN LOFSTROM Levern FB 5'8 185 Vancouver Meralomas Jrs. B: 1937																															
1957	BC	8												3	11	3.7	6	0										2	17	8.5	11
1959	BC	2										6	1	19	92	4.8	17	1	1	9	9.0	9	0								
1960	BC	5	1		0							6	1	17	73	4.3	9	1	2	10	5.0	13	0					1	11	11.0	11
1961	BC	13										6	1	9	35	3.9	10	0	4	66	16.5	22	1					3	25	8.3	17
4	Years	28	1		0							18	3	48	211	4.4	17	2	7	85	12.1	22	1					6	53	8.8	17
DAVID LOFTON David DB 6'4 215 Stanford B: 1/28/1984 Honolulu, HI Pro: U																															
2007	HAM	4				18	1.0	3.0			1																				
WILL LOFTUS William W 6'1 191 Surrey Rams Jrs.; Manitoba B: 6/3/1975 Vancouver, BC Draft: 3B-18 1998 MTL																															
1998	MTL	18	0	0	1	27																									
1999	MTL	14				13																									
2000	MTL	14				17					1																				
2001	MTL	18				47			3	32	2																				
2002	MTL	17	0	0	3	65			3	18	6																				
2003	MTL	17	0	1	1	61	1.0	7.0	2	2	3																				
2004	MTL	12	0	0	1	8																									
2005	EDM	17				13			1	0	0																				
2006	EDM	7				3																						1	0	0.0	0
2007	EDM	18	0	2	0	38			1	0	2																				
10	Years	152	0	3	6	292	1.0	7.0	10	52	14																	1	0	0.0	0
IAN LOGAN Ian S-CB 5'9 188 Wilfrid Laurier B: 8/19/1982 Waterloo, ON																															
2006	WPG	14				6																									
2007	WPG	15				19			2	16	2																				
2008	WPG	18				57	2.0	11.0																							
2009	WPG	18	0	1	0	57			4	18	1																				
2010	WPG	13				50	1.0	2.0	1	16	4																				
2011	WPG*	17	0	1	1	37			4	26	2																				
6	Years	95	0	2	1	226	3.0	13.0	11	76	9																				
MIKE LOGAN Mike QB-DB 6'2 198 Eastern Michigan B: 5/23/1950 Draft: 1-3 1973 CAL																															
1974	MTL	3																													
1975	CAL	6																													
1976	CAL	14							3	38																					
1977	TOR	5																													
4	Years	28							3	38																					
STEFAN LOGAN Stefan RB 5'7 183 South Dakota B: 6/2/1981 Tampa, FL Pro: N																															
2008	BC	12	4	0	1	1						20	3	122	889	7.3	66	0	52	477	9.2	31	3	13	138	10.6	29	9	266	29.6	51
TIP LOGAN John Robert E-K 6'1 194 Queen's B: 1927																															
1951	HAM	11										51	2										2								
1952	HAM	11										55	4										4								
1953	HAM	12										61	3										3								
1954	HAM	13										57	2						6	80	13.3	38	2								
1955	HAM	6										30	0						2	48	24.0	39	0								
5	Years	53										254	11						8	128	16.0	39	11								
TONY LOGAN Marvin WR 5'9 180 Nevada-Reno B: 3/22/1967 Las Vegas, NV																															
1991	HAM	3				2																		2	27	13.5	20	2	25	12.5	25
STEVE LOGOSZ Steve G-T																															
1946	CAL	8																													
JIM LOHMANN James Glen OT 6'5 265 Texas-El Paso B: 5/18/1955 Oakland, CA Pro: U																															
1978	BC	5																													
1979	BC	16	0		1																										
1980	BC	13	0		1																										
1981	BC	15																													
1982	BC	7																													
5	Years	56	0		2																										
PHIL LOHMANN Phil Jay TE 6'2 220 Oklahoma B: 1940 Draft: 14-195 1961 CLE; 34-272(f) 1962 SD																															
1962	CAL	16	1																20	257	12.9	25	0					1	5	5.0	5
MORRIS LOLAR Morris CB 5'11 190 Friends B: 2/18/1970 Lawrence, KS																															
1994	EDM	18	0		4	56			1	68	6	6	1																		
1995	EDM	8	0		1	43			4	126	4	12	2															1	18	18.0	18
1998	WPG	9	0	4	1	23			1	12	2																				
3	Years	35	0	4	6	122			6	206	12	18	3															1	18	18.0	18
BRANDON LONDON Brandon Jaime WR 6'4 210 Massachusetts B: 10/16/1984 Richmond, VA Pro: N																															
2010	MTL	1				1																									
2011	MTL	18	0	0	2	7						6	1						38	475	12.5	32	1					2	3	1.5	2
2	Years	19	0	0	2	8						6	1						38	475	12.5	32	1					2	3	1.5	2
DALE LONDON Dale, Jr. DL 6'5 315 Miami (Florida)*																															
1994	BAL	5				0																									
WALLY LONDON Wally Toronto																															
1950	TOR	2																													
DON LONEY Donald John C-G 6'1 199 none B: 11/16/1923 Ottawa, ON D: 6/19/2004 Sherbrooke, NS																															
1946	TOR+	10																													
1947	OTT+	12																													
1948	OTT+	12																													
1949	OTT+	11																													
1950	OTT	12																													
1951	OTT	12																													

Year	Team	GP	FM	FF	FR	TK	SK	YDS	IR	YDS	PD	PTS	TD	RA	YDS	AVG	LG	TD	REC	YDS	AVG	LG	TD	PR	YDS	AVG	LG	KOR	YDS	AVG	LG
1952	OTT	4																													
1954	CAL	13																													
8	Years	86																													
JIM LONG James DE-OT 6'1 230 Purdue B: 7/14/1944 Draft: 16-233 1966 PIT																															
1967	MTL	9	1		2							20	0																		
1968	MTL	2	0		1							4	0																		
2	Years	11	1		3							24	0																		
KHARI LONG Khari Ahmad DE 6'3 257 Baylor B: 5/23/1982 Wichita Falls, TX Draft: 6B-199 2005 KC Pro: N																															
2009	HAM	13	0	1	0	34	10.0	60.0	0	0	3																				
2010	HAM	7				11	1.0	0.0																							
2010	CAL	1				1																									
2010	Year	8				12	1.0	0.0																							
2	Years	20	0	1	0	46	*11.0	60.0																							
MEL LONG Melvin Alan, Jr. WR 6'1 190 Toledo B: 10/5/1977 Toledo, OH																															
2001	BC	4				1													7	111	15.9	40	0	7	81	11.6	25	4	107	26.8	40
ROCKY LONG Roderick J. CN-S 5'10 175 New Mexico B: 1/27/1950 Provo, UT Pro: W																															
1972	BC	15	0		2				3	79				5	12	2.4	8	0	2	3	1.5	5	0	5	48	9.6	21	5	146	29.2	38
1973	BC	7	0		2				1	2																					
1975	BC	16	1		1				8	88				1	-4	-4.0	-4	0						48	514	10.7	47	34	944	27.8	90
1976	BC	16	1		1				3	0		6	1	1	1	1.0	1	0						63	688	10.9	71	34	979	28.8	59
1977	BC+	14	2		0				2	9		6	1	1	10	10.0	10	1						81	774	9.6	68	27	690	25.6	63
5	Years	68	4		6				17	178		12	2	8	19	2.4	10	1	2	3	1.5	5	0	197	2024	10.3	71	100	2759	27.6	90
TED LONG Terrance LaMont WR-RB 5'10 185 Oklahoma B: 1/21/1969 Waco, TX																															
1995	BIR	18	3		0	2						6	1	2	1	0.5	3	0	65	620	9.5	35	1								
1996	HAM	16	2		1	3						30	5						68	775	11.4	46	5	5	36	7.2	13	16	298	18.6	35
1997	HAM	5	0	1	0	2						12	2	1	7	7.0	7	0	15	221	14.7	47	2								
1997	WPG	2				0						12	2						14	164	11.7	47	2					8	150	18.8	25
1997	Year	7				2						24	4	1	7	7.0	7	0	29	385	13.3	47	4					8	150	18.8	25
1998	WPG	7	2	0	0	2						12	2	3	4	1.3	7	0	18	184	10.2	65	2	14	111	7.9	22	19	329	17.3	40
4	Years	46	7	1	1	9						72	12	6	12	2.0	7	0	180	1964	10.9	65	12	19	147	7.7	22	43	777	18.1	40
CLINT LONGLEY Howard Clinton, Jr. QB 6'1 194 Abilene Christian B: 7/28/1952 Wichita Falls, TX Pro: N																															
1977	TOR	6	3		0									7	8	1.1	5	0													
KEVIN LOOMAN Kevin OT 6'4 248 Southern Mississippi B: 2/14/1953 Canton, OH																															
1974	CAL	4	0		1							6	1																		
HUGO LOPEZ Hugo CB-S-DH 6'3 205 Waterloo; Toronto B: 6/16/1987 Leon, Nicaragua Draft: 2-14 2011 EDM																															
2011	EDM	3				2																									
DON LORD Don DE-OE-FB-HB 6'2 192 Vancouver Meralomas Jrs.; British Columbia B: 10/13/1928 Vancouver, BC																															
1951	EDM	9										3	0	15	82	5.5		0										2	72	36.0	
1952	EDM	16			1				5	51		2	0	9	41	4.6	11	0	1	2	2.0	2	0	3	16	5.3	8	1	18	18.0	18
1953	EDM	16										1	0															1	11	11.0	11
1954	BC	9	2											1	-14	-14.0	-14	0	3	77	25.7	44	0								
1956	BC	14	1		0																			1	5	5.0	5				
1957	BC	14	0		4																										
1958	BC	9							1	10																					
1959	BC	16																													
8	Years	103	3		5				6	61		6	0	25	109	4.4	11	0	4	79	19.8	44	0	4	21	5.3	8	4	101	25.3	18
JIMMY LORENO Jim FB-HB 5'8 180 Oshawa Jrs. B: 1928																															
1949	HAM	11										5	1					1													
1950	HAM	6																													
2	Years	17										5	1					1													
TIM LORENZ Tim DE-DT 6'2 240 Santa Barbara State B: 2/12/1965 Vancouver, BC Draft: 2-11 1988 HAM																															
1988	HAM	18	0		2	13	2.0																								
1989	HAM	18	0		4	18	4.0																								
1990	HAM	8	0		1	11																									
1991	HAM	14				2	2.0																								
1992	BC	15				10	1.0	7.0																							
1993	BC	10				6	2.0	21.0																							
6	Years	83	0		7	60	11.0	28.0																							
FRANK LORIA Frank Paul DB 5'9 180 Virginia Tech B: 1/6/1947 Clarksburg, WV D: 11/14/1970 Huntington, WV																															
1969	HAM	2																						6	34	5.7	12				
1976	TOR	2																													
ROD LOSSOW Rodney Jay OG 6'3 275 Wisconsin B: 8/28/1965 Minneapolis, MN Draft: 10-267 1988 NE Pro: E																															
1988	CAL	8			1	1																									
GLENN LOTT Glenn Steven DB 6'2 200 Drake B: 6/27/1953 Alton, IL Draft: 2B-50 1975 BUF																															
1976	MTL	7	0		1				1	24																					
DON LOUCKS Don HB 6'2 185 Toronto; Edmonton Ints. B: 1926																															
1949	EDM	8										5	1																		
DON LOUCKS Donald HB-WB 5'11 185 Kitchener-Waterloo Dutchmen Jrs. B: 1936 Southampton, ON																															
1958	MTL	8																	1	10	10.0	10	0								
SAM LOUCKS Sam FB 6'2 215 McMaster B: 3/9/1965 St. Catharines, ON Draft: 6-43 1989 HAM																															
1989	HAM	18				0								12	51	4.3	11	0	4	40	10.0	15	0					3	13	4.3	8
1990	HAM	17	2		0	3						6	1	35	100	2.9	9	0	26	176	6.8	17	1					2	12	6.0	13
2	Years	35	2		0	3						6	1	47	151	3.2	11	0	30	216	7.2	17	1					5	25	5.0	13
KAMIL LOUD Kamil Kassan WR 6'0 190 Cal Poly (San Luis Obispo) B: 6/25/1976 Richmond, CA Draft: 7B-238 1998 BUF Pro: N																															
2001	CAL	5				1													5	66	13.2	26	0	4	22	5.5	8				
2002	CAL	6				1													11	191	17.4	39	0								
2	Years	11				2													16	257	16.1	39	0	4	22	5.5	8				
ROMMIE LOUDD Rommie Lee E 6'2 227 Los Angeles Valley JC; UCLA B: 6/8/1933 D: 5/9/1998 Miami, FL Draft: 26-304 1956 SF Pro: N																															
1956	BC	9	0		2							12	2						13	231	17.8	35	2								
TOM LOUDERBACK Thomas Franklin LB 6'2 235 Santa Rosa JC; San Jose State B: 3/5/1933 Petaluma, CA Draft: 10-111 1955 WAS Pro: N																															
1955	HAM	5							1	4																					
PETE LOUGHEED Peter HB 5'7 160 Calgary Tornadoes Jrs.; Alberta B: 7/26/1928 Calgary, AB																															
1949	EDM	13																													
1950	EDM	11																													
2	Years	24																													
MESENE LOUISDOR Mesene DB 5'10 180 Eastern Arizona JC; Central Michigan B: 12/3/1973 Nassau, Bahamas Pro: E																															
2003	OTT	7				12			1	4	1																				
JOHN LOVE John Louis WR 5'11 185 Cisco JC; North Texas B: 2/24/1944 Linden, TX Draft: 7B-172 1967 WAS Pro: N																															
1971	BC	4	1		0														12	193	16.1	41	0					4	135	33.8	50
REGGIE LOVE Reginald Jerel CB 5'11 185 North Carolina B: 10/4/1976 Clinton, NC																															
1998	HAM	11				21			1	4	1																				
1999	WPG	8				13																									
2	Years	19				34			1	4	1																				
CALVIN LOVEALL Calvin Earl CB 5'9 180 Idaho B: 7/23/1962 Kalispell MT Draft: 4-51 1985 DEN-USFL Pro: NU																															
1986	OTT	10							2	18																					
1987	OTT	18	0		1	71	1.0		5	45																					
2	Years	28	0		1	71	1.0		7	63																					
MATTHEW LOVELADY Matthew DE 6'3 235 Mississippi B: 8/7/1961																															
1984	TOR	1																													
EDDIE LOWE Eddie LB 5'11 205 Tennessee-Chattanooga; Alabama B: 2/1/1960 Columbus, GA Draft: TD 1983 BIR-USFL																															
1983	SAS	13	0		1		4.0																								
1984	SAS	16	0		2		5.0																								

Year	Team	GP	FM	FF	FR	TK	SK	YDS	IR	YDS	PD	PTS	TD	RA	YDS	AVG	LG	TD	REC	YDS	AVG	LG	TD	PR	YDS	AVG	LG	KOR	YDS	AVG	LG
1985	SAS	16					3.0																								
1986	SAS	18					4.0		4	73																					
1987	SAS	17	1		2	93	1.0		2	28														1	0	0.0	0				
1988	SAS	18				91	5.0																								
1989	SAS*	17	0		1	62	5.0		2	45																					
1990	SAS	18				87	1.0		6	130																					
1991	SAS	18	2		4	104	5.0		2	52																		1	0	0.0	0
9	Years	151	3		10	437	33.0		16	328														1	0	0.0	0	1	0	0.0	0
JOHN LOWE John RB-SB 5'11 195 Guelph B: 11/22/1957 Draft: 4-29 1981 TOR																															
1981	TOR	11	1		0									7	33	4.7	13	0	3	26	8.7	13	0					8	118	14.8	22
1982	TOR	7																										4	73	18.3	21
2	Years	18	1		0									7	33	4.7	13	0	3	26	8.7	13	0					12	191	15.9	22
KEVIN LOWE Kevin RB 6'0 195 Wyoming B: 3/3/1963																															
1985	TOR	3	3		0							6	1	33	125	3.8	12	1	7	58	8.3	23	0					4	71	17.8	32
REGGIE LOWE Reginald James DE 6'2 250 Troy B: 6/14/1975 Washington, DC Pro: ENX																															
2002	MTL	17	0	2	2	26	6.0																								
JOE LOWERY Joe RB 5'9 210 Jackson State B: 1/14/1953 McComb, MS Draft: 12-336 1976 BUF																															
1976	EDM	4												42	120	2.9	12	0	6	35	5.8	13	0					4	136	34.0	41
DAVID LOWRY David LB 6'3 239 Alberta B: 1/29/1981 Lethbridge, AB Draft: 3A-25 2005 BC																															
2007	WPG	7				5																									
TED LOZANSKI Ted QB 5'7 235 Winnipeg Grads Jrs.; Elmwood Bombers Ints. B: 1927																															
1949	WPG	14																													
BOB LUBIG Robert OG-OT-C 6'4 240 Montana State B: 9/17/1955 Rotterdam, The Netherlands Draft: TE 1978 CAL																															
1978	CAL	16	0		1																										
1979	CAL	10																													
1980	CAL	16	0		1																										
1981	CAL	3																													
1981	TOR	7																													
1981	Year	10																													
1982	CAL	16																													
1983	CAL	14	0		1																										
1984	CAL	16																													
1985	CAL	9																													
1986	MTL	8	0		1																										
9	Years	108	0		4																										
CHAD LUCAS Chad Dennard WR-SB 6'1 201 Troy; Alabama State B: 11/7/1981 Auburn, AL Pro: EN																															
2009	TOR	14	2	0	0	1						12	2						69	950	13.8	62	2								
2010	TOR	5	2	0	0	0													12	151	12.6	25	0								
2	Years	19	4	0	0	1						12	2						81	1101	13.6	62	2								
DAVID LUCAS David WR 5'10 165 Florida A&M B: 9/19/1969 Macon, GA																															
1992	HAM	13	3		0	1						6	1						22	364	16.5	55	1	36	301	8.4	39	28	489	17.5	40
1994	SHR	18	2		0	6						30	5						42	710	16.9	46	4	56	432	7.7	74	37	832	22.5	61
1995	SA	9	3		2	0						6	1	1	-7	-7.0	-7	0	7	97	13.9	26	0	36	347	9.6	105	27	607	22.5	72
3	Years	40	8		2	7						42	7	1	-7	-7.0	-7	0	71	1171	16.5	55	5	128	1080	8.4	105	92	1928	21.0	72
RYAN LUCAS Ryan DT 6'5 288 Simon Fraser; Western Washington B: 10/23/1984 Vancouver, BC																															
2007	MTL	1				0																									
2010	SAS	4	0	0	1	1																									
2011	MTL	3				1																									
3	Years	8	0	0	1	2																									
SEAN LUCAS Sean Christopher LB-DH 5'11 202 Tulane B: 12/8/1983 Atlanta, GA																															
2006	SAS	1				3																									
2007	SAS	17	0	2	1	67	2.0	29.0	1	0	2																				
2008	SAS	18	0	3	1	98			1	4	2																				
2009	SAS+	18	0	4	1	85	4.0	22.0	2	17	6																				
2010	SAS	17	0	0	0	79	1.0	4.0			4																				
2011	SAS	16				63			1	3	3																				
6	Years	87	0	9	3	395	7.0	55.0	5	24	17																				
DANTE LUCIANI Dante WR 6'0 203 Wilfrid Laurier B: 9/1/1985 Oakville, ON Draft: 5-34 2008 EDM																															
2009	WPG	1				0																									
TINY LUCID Sylvester T 6'2 230 B: 1912																															
1947	WPG	8																													
1948	WPG	11																													
2	Years	19																													
TERRY LUCK Terry Lee QB 6'3 205 Nebraska B: 12/14/1952 Fayetteville, NC Pro: N																															
1978	WPG	6												2	-2	-1.0	0	0													
DOCK LUCKIE Dock, Jr. DT 6'2 270 Florida B: 5/29/1959 Gainesville, FL Draft: 6-153 1981 KC																															
1981	WPG	1					1.0																								
BILL LUCKY William Henry, Jr. T 6'3 240 Baylor B: 8/24/1931 Temple, TX Draft: 19-224(di) 1953 GB; 5-60 1954 CLE Pro: N																															
1956	TOR	6																													
TREVOR LUDTKE Trevor LB 6'4 225 Saskatchewan B: 2/8/1976 Regina, SK																															
1999	WPG	4	0	0	1	1																						1	0	0.0	0
2000	WPG	12				10																									
2002	BC	2				0																									
3	Years	18	0	0	1	11																						1	0	0.0	0
RUBE LUDWIG Rube T 5'11 210 Winnipeg YMHA Jrs. B: 1919 Winnipeg, MB																															
1946	CAL	7																													
1947	CAL	7																													
1948	CAL	12																													
3	Years	26																													
BOB LUECK Bob OG 6'2 245 Arizona State B: 3/6/1943 Buckeye, AZ																															
1966	CAL	8																													
1967	CAL+	15			1																										
1968	CAL+	16																													
1969	CAL	16																													
1970	CAL	14																													
1971	WPG+	13	0		1																										
1972	WPG*	16																													
7	Years	98	0		2																										
DON LUFT Donald Richard E 6'5 220 Indiana B: 2/14/1930 Fisk, WI D: 6/19/2002 Indianapolis, IN Pro: N																															
1955	CAL	16	0		2							5	1						23	235	10.2	30	1								
1956	HAM	5										12	2						15	224	14.9	24	2								
2	Years	21	0		2							17	3						38	459	12.1	30	3								
CEC LUINING Cecil Roy DE-C 6'1 210 St. Boniface Jrs.; St. John's Jrs.; Winnipeg Rams Ints. B: 1931 Winnipeg, MB D: //1998																															
1954	WPG	1																													
1955	WPG	7																													
1956	WPG	16	0		1							6	1																		
1957	WPG	16	1		1							6	1											1	12	12.0	12				
1958	WPG	15	0		2																										
1959	WPG	14																													
1960	WPG	11	0		2																										
1961	WPG	14																													
1962	WPG	15																													

Year	Team	GP	FM	FF	FR	TK	SK	YDS	IR	YDS	PD	PTS	TD	RA	YDS	AVG	LG	TD	REC	YDS	AVG	LG	TD	PR	YDS	AVG	LG	KOR	YDS	AVG	LG
1963	WPG	1																													
10	Years	110	1		6							12	2											1	12	12.0	12				
JOE LUKASIK Joe DT 5'11 200 St. Joseph's (Indiana) B: 1933																															
1956	MTL	5																													
PHIL LUKE Phil DT-DE 6'5 230 Simon Fraser B: 2/4/1955 Draft: TE 1978 BC																															
1978	MTL	3																													
1979	MTL	8																													
2	Years	11																													
TRAVIS LULAY Travis Jacob QB 6'2 216 Montana State B: 9/27/1983 Aumsville, OR Pro: E																															
2009	BC	15				0								17	133	7.8	30	0													
2010	BC	18	8	0	2	1						18	3	62	396	6.4	20	3	1	14	14.0	14	0								
2011	BC*	18	1	0	2	1						18	3	47	391	8.3	53	5													
3	Years	51	9	0	4	2						36	6	126	920	7.3	53	8	1	14	14.0	14	0								
ROLLY LUMBALA Rolly FB 6'2 241 Idaho B: 1/30/1986 Libreville, Gabon Draft: 2-9 2008 BC																															
2008	BC	18	1	1	1	9						18	3	12	28	2.3	8	2	1	1	1.0	1	1								
2009	BC	18				23						6	1	6	10	1.7	4	1	5	45	9.0	22	0					3	22	7.3	12
2010	BC	9				8								1	2	2.0	2	0	4	27	6.8	11	0								
2011	BC	18				12						6	1	3	6	2.0	5	1	3	28	9.3	20	0					1	12	12.0	12
4	Years	63	1	1	1	52						30	5	22	46	2.1	8	4	13	101	7.8	22	1					4	34	8.5	12
CHUCK LUMSDEN Chuck DE-FB 6'1 196 Winnipeg Light Infantry Jrs. B: 1932																															
1952	WPG	1																													
1955	WPG	12																													
2	Years	13																													
JESSE LUMSDEN Jesse RB 6'2 224 McMaster B: 8/3/1982 Edmonton, AB Draft: 1-6 2005 HAM																															
2005	HAM	7	1	0	1	4						12	2	60	307	5.1	43	1	11	153	13.9	78	1					11	259	23.5	42
2006	HAM	4	0	0	1	0								40	163	4.1	25	0	5	51	10.2	35	0								
2007	HAM+	10	2	0	0	1						24	4	98	743	7.6	75	3	26	348	13.4	51	1								
2008	HAM	9	1	0	0	3						30	5	87	584	6.7	57	5	7	78	11.1	17	0								
2009	EDM	1				0								2	5	2.5	3	0	3	20	6.7	12	0								
2010	CAL	3				2						6	1	4	40	10.0	13	1										1	30	30.0	30
6	Years	34	4	0	2	10						72	12	291	1842	6.3	75	10	52	650	12.5	78	2					12	289	24.1	42
NEIL LUMSDEN Neil FB 6'1 225 Ottawa B: 12/19/1952 London, ON Draft: TE 1976 TOR																															
1976	TOR	15	6		0							24	4	85	412	4.8	36	3	8	98	12.3	28	1					4	73	18.3	23
1977	TOR	16	6		2							25	4	145	677	4.7	33	3	20	144	7.2	24	1					2	33	16.5	17
1978	TOR	6	1		0							6	1	12	48	4.0	9	1	3	7	2.3	8	0					1	29	29.0	29
1978	HAM	10	1		0							5	0	47	268	5.7	58	0	15	158	10.5	50	0								
1978	Year	16	2		0							11	1	59	316	5.4	58	1	18	165	9.2	50	0					1	29	29.0	29
1979	HAM	16	0		1							84	8	99	438	4.4	16	5	21	142	6.8	21	3								
1980	EDM	16	3		1							30	5	114	566	5.0	19	4	17	252	14.8	36	1	4	11	2.8	6				
1981	EDM	13	3		2							42	7	58	266	4.6	31	3	21	185	8.8	18	4								
1982	EDM	11	1		0							24	4	56	223	4.0	17	0	20	285	14.3	44	4								
1983	EDM	12										30	5	64	254	4.0	26	5	23	249	10.8	36	0								
1984	EDM	15	4		0							48	8	92	402	4.4	18	8	25	155	6.2	22	0								
1985	EDM	11	3		0							30	5	45	201	4.5	36	4	7	54	7.7	21	1								
10	Years	131	28		6							348	51	817	3755	4.6	58	36	180	1729	9.6	50	15	4	11	2.8	6	7	135	19.3	29
TOMMY LUMSDEN Thomas D. DE 6'3 223 Winnipeg Light Infantry Jrs. B: 1930 D: 6/24/1955 Winnipeg, MB																															
1951	WPG	13																													
1952	WPG	11																													
1953	WPG	16																													
1954	WPG	16	1		0																			2	41	20.5	27				
4	Years	56	1		0																			2	41	20.5	27				
GORD LUND Gordon HB 6'0 185 Edmonton Huskies Jrs. B: 1945																															
1967	EDM	13																	2	50	25.0	43	0					1	11	11.0	11
HAL LUND Harold DB 5'10 175 Richmond Raiders Jrs. B: 8/15/1957 D: 8/10/2002 Vancouver, BC																															
1977	BC	7																													
1978	BC	11																	1	9	9.0	9	0	1	0	0.0	0				
1979	BC	8																													
1980	BC	16	0		1				3	51																					
1981	BC	16	0		1		2.0																								
5	Years	58	0		2		2.0		3	51									1	9	9.0	9	0	1	0	0.0	0				
HARRY LUNN Harry OHB-S 6'0 185 Hamilton Panthers Ints. B: 1934																															
1955	SAS	16	4		0							5	1	28	175	6.3	21	1	2	32	16.0	12	0	61	486	8.0	22	17	557	32.8	53
1956	SAS	16	1		0				6	79				22	107	4.9	32	0	1	22	22.0	22	0	60	337	5.6	28	26	488	18.8	38
1957	SAS	16	2						1	6		18	3	54	326	6.0	77	2	11	163	14.8	31	1	63	327	5.2	26	28	699	25.0	54
1958	SAS	16	1						4	50		12	2	6	38	6.3	22	0						63	576	9.1	67	6	112	18.7	32
1959	OTT	12												2	11	5.5	10	0	3	18	6.0	8	0	30	198	6.6	15				
1960	HAM	1							1	3														51	262	5.1	19				
6	Years	77	8		0				12	138		35	6	112	657	5.9	77	3	17	235	13.8	31	1	328	2186	6.7	67	77	1856	24.1	54
EARL LUNSFORD Earl Monroe FB-LB 5'11 200 Oklahoma State B: 10/19/1933 Mehan, OK D: 9/3/2008 Fort Worth, TX Draft: 26-305 1956 PHI																															
1956	CAL	16	5		0				4	59		48	8	216	1283	5.9	57	7	13	108	8.3	19	0	1	0	0.0	0				
1959	CAL	16	6		3				2	4		60	10	183	1027	5.6	22	10	15	121	8.1	19	0					5	88	17.6	27
1960	CAL+	16	6		0							78	13	214	1343	6.3	85	13	6	56	9.3	20	0					3	55	18.3	23
1961	CAL+	16	8									60	10	296	1794	6.1	62	10	7	111	15.9	29	0	1	7	7.0	7	8	79	9.9	17
1962	CAL*	11										48	8	180	1016	5.6	64	8	6	67	11.2	22	0					1	6	6.0	6
1963	CAL	10	5		0							42	7	110	531	4.8	29	7	7	65	9.3	26	0					2	24	12.0	13
6	Years	85	30		3				6	63		336	56	1199	6994	5.8	85	55	54	528	9.8	29	0	2	7	3.5	7	19	252	13.3	27
MARV LUSTER Marvin E. S-OE-LB-DE-OHB 6'1 195 Los Angeles CC; UCLA B: 11/27/1937 Shreveport, LA Draft: SS-(f) 1960 BUF; 9-97 1960 LARM																															
1961	MTL+	14							1	10		12	2	4	-11	-2.8	5	0	31	539	17.4	84	2	3	6	2.0	4	12	221	18.4	36
1962	MTL+	14							1	17		30	5						36	725	20.1	64	5					3	58	19.3	25
1963	MTL	12							1	27		18	3						22	341	15.5	40	2					1	7	7.0	7
1964	MTL	6	1		0							6	1						13	206	15.8	81	1					3	40	13.3	19
1964	TOR	7	0		2				0	5									1	13	13.0	13	0								
1964	Year	13	1		2							6	1						14	219	15.6	81	1					3	40	13.3	19
1965	TOR	6							1	2		6	1						10	139	13.9	28	1								
1966	TOR*	14	0		3				7	24														5	18	3.6	9				
1967	TOR+	14	0		4							6	1															1	24	24.0	24
1968	TOR*	14	0		3				2	17																					
1969	TOR*	14			2				1	0														1	15	15.0	15				
1970	TOR*	14	0		2				3	56																					
1971	TOR*	14	0		1				4	53																					
1972	TOR*	14	0		1				5	106																					
1973	MTL	14	0		1																										
1974	MTL	11			1				2	10																					
14	Years	175	1		20				28	327		78	13	4	-11	-2.8	5	0	113	1963	17.4	84	11	9	39	4.3	15	20	350	17.5	36
DON LUZZI Donato, Jr. DT-DE-OT 6'0 245 Villanova B: 8/20/1935 CT D: 10/30/2005 Calgary, AB																															
1958	CAL+	13																													
1959	CAL	15	0		1																										
1960	CAL+	12	0		2							6	1																		
1961	CAL+	15			2																										
1962	CAL*	16							1																			2	-5	-2.5	-1
1963	CAL*	15	0		1																										
1964	CAL	13	0		1																										

Year	Team	GP	FM	FF	FR	TK	SK	YDS	IR	YDS	PD	PTS	TD	RA	YDS	AVG	LG	TD	REC	YDS	AVG	LG	TD	PR	YDS	AVG	LG	KOR	YDS	AVG	LG
1965	CAL	16	0		1				1	2																					
1966	CAL*	16	0		1																										
1967	CAL	16																													
1968	CAL	16																													
1969	CAL	4																													
12	Years	167	0		9				2	2		6	1															2	-5	-2.5	-1
RAY LYCHAK Ray OG 6'1 240 Foothill JC; San Jose State B: 6/30/1943 Prince Albert, SK																															
1966	MTL	14																													
1967	MTL	9																													
1968	MTL	14																													
1969	EDM	16	0		2																										
1970	BC	16																													
1971	BC	12																													
1972	WPG	16																													
1973	WPG	12																													
8	Years	109	0		2																										
DEL LYLES Delliere L. LB 6'1 220 Utah State B: 9/7/1970 Oakland, CA																															
1993	WPG	10				34	1.0	8.0																							
1994	WPG	15				32	6.0	29.0			1																				
1995	WPG	12	0		1	40	4.0	31.0			1																	1	20	20.0	20
3	Years	37	0		1	106	11.0	68.0			2																	1	20	20.0	20
TERRY LYMON Terry L. FB 5'10 195 Ball State B: 2/21/1962																															
1984	MTL	8										18	3	53	267	5.0	41	2	11	64	5.8	24	1					9	260	28.9	54
BRANDON LYNCH Brandon LB 5'11 192 Middle Tennessee State B: 1/31/1982 Augusta, GA																															
2007	SAS	6	0	0	1	8																									
2008	SAS	9	0	0	1	6																									
2	Years	15	0	0	2	14																									
BRIAN LYNCH Brian Thomas E 6'0 185 B: 1923 D: 12/10/2010																															
1946	OTT	3																													
1947	OTT	12																													
1948	OTT	12										10	2										1								
1949	OTT	11										6	1										1								
4	Years	38										16	3										2								
DICK LYNCH Dick E 6'0 184																															
1950	CAL	4																													
JOHN LYNCH John DB 6'0 175 Western Ontario B: 3/13/1960 Draft: 2-15 1983 CAL																															
1983	OTT	12	0		3				3	72																					
1984	OTT	13																	1	16	16.0	16	0								
2	Years	25	0		3				3	72									1	16	16.0	16	0								
TYLER LYNEM Tyler DT 6'6 280 Calgary B: 1/29/1981 Calgary, AB Draft: 2A-11 2004 CAL																															
2004	CAL	18				4																									
2005	CAL	4				0																									
2006	CAL	18				0																									
2007	CAL	4				0																									
4	Years	44				4																									
DAMION LYONS Damion E. CB 6'4 215 Laney JC; UCLA B: 4/28/1968 Berkeley, CA																															
1991	EDM	2				0																									
1992	EDM+	18				54			8	95																					
1993	EDM	18	0		2	39			3	70																					
1994	EDM	4	0		1	9																									
1995	MEM	18	1		1	43			5	76	5																				
1996	WPG	16				38			1	56	7	6	1																		
1997	BC	16	0	0	1	27			2	18	8																				
7	Years	92	1	0	5	210			19	315	20	6	1																		
DICKY LYONS Richard D. HB 6'0 190 Kentucky B: 8/11/1947 Louisville, KY Draft: 4B-103 1969 ATL Pro: NW																															
1971	BC	3	1		0									27	122	4.5	19	0	4	13	3.3	9	0					1	28	28.0	28
WES LYSACK Wes S 6'1 200 Rutgers; Manitoba B: 3/3/1978 Edmonton, AB Draft: 1C-5 2003 CAL																															
2003	CAL	10	0	0	1	18					1																				
2004	CAL	14	0	1	1	39			4	50	2																				
2004	WPG	3	0	0	1	8			1	0	1																				
2004	Year+	17	0	2	2	47			5	50	3																				
2005	WPG	14	0	1	1	71			1	61	4																				
2005	CAL	4				3																									
2005	Year	18	0	1	1	74			1	61	4																				
2006	CAL	18				48					2																				
2007	CAL	15				8																									
2008	CAL	16	0	0	2	26			4	101	6	6	1																		
2009	CAL	18	0	0	2	19	1.0	11.0	2	1	1			2	12	6.0	12	0													
2010	CAL	18	0	2	0	17	1.0	9.0			5																				
2011	TOR	14				5																									
9	Years	137	0	4	8	262	2.0	20.0	12	213	22	6	1	2	12	6.0	12	0													
LEON LYSZKIEWICZ Leon DT 6'4 240 Alberta B: 6/11/1955 Grand Prairie, AB Draft: TE 1977 EDM																															
1977	SAS	1																													
1978	WPG	13																													
1979	WPG	16	0		1																										
1980	TOR	16	0		1																										
1981	TOR	16					3.5																								
1982	TOR	16					6.0																								
1983	EDM	14					1.0																								
1984	HAM	14	0		2		5.5																								
1985	HAM	16																													
1986	HAM	5							1	0																					
10	Years	127	0		4		16.0		1	0																					
DEAN LYTLE Dean Lamont FB 6'3 240 Notre Dame B: 11/11/1971 Louisville, KY Pro: E																															
1996	WPG	15	3		0	8						12	2	43	187	4.3	26	1	30	271	9.0	23	1								
MATT LYTLE Matthew Robert QB 6'4 225 Pittsburgh B: 9/4/1975 Lancaster, PA Pro: EN																															
2002	MTL	7				0								1	-1	-1.0	-1	0													
JASON MAAS Jason Alan QB 6'2 210 Oregon B: 11/19/1975 Beaver Dam, WI																															
2000	EDM	18				0								1	1	1.0	1	0													
2001	EDM+	18	3	0	1	2						6	1	49	215	4.4	23	1													
2002	EDM	18	5	0	0	2								24	132	5.5	17	0													
2003	EDM	18				0						6	1	6	25	4.2	15	1													
2004	EDM	18	20	0	9	3						48	8	79	252	3.2	19	8													
2005	EDM	18				0																									
2006	HAM	18	10	0	1	4						18	3	52	290	5.6	24	3													
2007	HAM	9	6	0	1	2								28	165	5.9	20	0													
2007	MTL	9				1								3	5	1.7	3	0													
2007	Year	18	6	0	1	3								31	170	5.5	20	0													
2008	EDM	3	1	0	0	1								3	30	10.0	16	0													
2009	EDM	18	1	0	0	0								2	14	7.0	9	0													
2010	EDM	18				0						6	1	1	6	6.0	6	1													
11	Years	174	46	0	12	15						84	14	248	1135	4.6	24	14													

Year	Team	GP	FM	FF	FR	TK	SK	YDS	IR	YDS	PD	PTS	TD	RA	YDS	AVG	LG	TD	REC	YDS	AVG	LG	TD	PR	YDS	AVG	LG	KOR	YDS	AVG	LG
RON MABRA Ronald Edwin DB 5'10 169 Howard B: 6/4/1951 Talladega, AL Pro: NW
1979	WPG	1	0		0																			4	32	8.0	19
MARK MABRY Mark A. LB 6'0 235 Central State (Ohio) B: 3/7/1963
1987	TOR	7	0		2	34
SCOTT MacARTHUR Scott DE 6'6 245 Calgary B: 4/26/1959 Calgary, AB Draft: TE 1981 CAL
1981	CAL	7					2.5
1982	CAL	15					3.0
1983	CAL	16	0		1		1.5
3	Years	38	0		1		7.0
BOB MacAULEY Bob LB 6'1 215 Boise State B: 1/20/1957
1979	SAS	5
DEREK MacCREADY Derek DT-DE 6'5 265 Waldorf JC; Ohio State B: 5/4/1967 Montreal, QC Draft: 1-6 1989 BC; 9-226 1989 DET
1989	BC	2				0
1990	BC	17	0		1	32	4.0
1991	BC	18	0		1	35	7.0
1993	BC	16	0		2	22	5.0	20.0
1994	OTT	18				29	4.0	15.0
1995	OTT	16				32	5.0	30.0
1996	EDM	17				24	4.0	28.0			4
1997	EDM	18	0	1	0	39	5.0	32.0
1998	EDM	8	0	1	0	11	1.0	5.0
1999	HAM	13	0	0	1	9	3.0	12.0
10	Years	143	0	2	5	233	38.0	142.0			4
TOM MacCALLUM Tom, Jr. OT 6'3 270 Regina Rams Jrs. B: 12/22/1970 Regina, SK Draft: 6-42 1992 SAS
1993	SAS	18				0
1994	SAS	3				2
2	Years	21				2
ADAM MACDONALD Adam LB 5'11 215 St. Francis Xavier B: 10/22/1978 Lahr, West Germany
2003	HAM	4				6
BOB MacDONALD Bob G-DE 6'2 210 North Dakota State B: 1938 Winnipeg, MB
1960	WPG	1
BOB MacDONALD Robert OT 6'2 280 McMaster B: 10/15/1967 Hamilton, ON Draft: 2-14 1990 EDM
1991	CAL	2				0
1992	CAL	18				0
1993	HAM	12				0
3	Years	32				0
IAN MacDONALD Ian C-LB 6'5 235 Tulsa B: 1945 Montreal, QC
1967	TOR	8
1970	TOR	2
2	Years	10
JOHN MacDONALD John SB-DB 5'10 185 Simon Fraser B: 12/8/1965 Eston, SK
1989	BC	2				1													8	125	15.6	40	0
1990	BC	4				1													2	66	33.0	35	0
2	Years	6				2													10	191	19.1	40	0
JOHN MACDONALD John DT 6'2 275 McGill B: 8/30/1978 Simcoe, ON Draft: 1-7 2002 HAM
2002	HAM	18	0	1	0	9	1.0	6.0
2003	HAM	18	0	0	1	24	4.0	23.0	1	3	1
2004	HAM	6				6
3	Years	42	0	1	1	39	5.0	29.0	1	3	1
PAT MacDONALD Patrick DE 6'3 247 Calgary*; Alberta B: 2/20/1982 Oakville, ON Draft: 3-21 2007 CAL
2007	CAL	11	0	0	1	4	1.0	7.0
2008	CAL	3				0
2009	WPG	14	0	0	1	6																						2	16	8.0	11
2010	MTL	9				4	1.0	6.0
4	Years	37	0	0	2	14	2.0	13.0																				2	16	8.0	11
BENNY MacDONNELL Benny HB-FW 6'0 200 Quebec Swimmers Ints. B: 1930 D: 9/1/1969
1949	OTT	8
1950	OTT	12									5	1					1
1951	OTT	12									5	1					1
1952	OTT	11									5	1					1
1953	OTT	12
1954	OTT	14
1957	SAS	3
7	Years	72									15	3					3
BILL MacDOUGALL Bill G 6'1 220 Parkdale Lions Jrs. B: 1938
1959	HAM	3
1961	BC	5
2	Years	8
COREY MACE Corey DT-DE 6'3 287 Palomar CC; Wyoming B: 12/22/1985 Port Moody, BC Draft: 2-11 2007 WPG Pro: N
2010	CAL	8	0	0	1	6	1.0	5.0				6	1															1	14	14.0	14
2011	CAL	1				2	1.0	6.0
2	Years	9	0	0	1	8	2.0	11.0				6	1															1	14	14.0	14
DAVE MacGILLIVRAY David FL 5'9 170 El Camino JC; Weber State
1969	MTL	3	1		0														4	129	32.3	47	0					1	27	27.0	27
BLAKE MACHAN Blake SB 6'4 230 Calgary B: 5/10/1979 Rocky Mountain House, AB Draft: 5A-37 2003 CAL
2003	CAL	7	0	0	1	0													1	4	4.0	4	0
TOM MACHAN Tom DT 6'1 260 Edmonton Huskies Jrs. B: 1943
1964	EDM	8
1965	EDM	10
1966	EDM	2
3	Years	20
FRAN MACHINSKY Francis C. OG 6'0 215 Ohio State B: 1935 Draft: 4-41 1956 WAS
1956	TOR+	12							1	3
JAY MACIAS Jerome J. QB 6'2 195 Wisconsin B: 8/10/1973 Northridge, CA
1995	OTT	18				0								9	25	2.8	10	0
DOUG MacIVER Doug DT-DE 6'3 245 Manitoba B: 2/20/1953 Winnipeg, MB D: 1/26/2012 Winnipeg, MB Draft: TE 1975 WPG
1976	TOR	16	0		2							6	1
1977	TOR	16
1978	TOR	16
1979	SAS	16
1980	SAS	16
1981	SAS	16					3.5
1982	WPG	15					6.0
1983	WPG	16					1.0
1984	WPG	8
9	Years	135	0		2		10.5					6	1
GENE MACK Gene Arthur LB 6'2 240 Texas-El Paso B: 2/25/1949 Greenville, TX Draft: 7-180 1971 MIN
1971	TOR	14	0		1				2	52		6	1
1972	TOR+	14							1	6									1	17	17.0	17	0
1973	TOR+	13	0		1				2	4
1974	TOR	7
1975	TOR	16							2	34

Year	Team	GP	FM	FF	FR	TK	SK	YDS	IR	YDS	PD	PTS	TD	RA	YDS	AVG	LG	TD	REC	YDS	AVG	LG	TD	PR	YDS	AVG	LG	KOR	YDS	AVG	LG
1977	HAM	1																													
6	Years	65	0		2				7	96		6	1						1	17	17.0	17	0								
KIRBY MACK Kirby DE 6'0 235 Virginia; Columbia B: 7/5/1978 St. Louis, MO																															
2002	WPG	4				1																									
TRACEY MACK Tracey L. LB 6'1 229 Missouri B: 12/29/1961 St. Louis, MO Draft: 2- 1985 BIR-USFL																															
1986	WPG	2					3.0																								
1987	SAS	6	0		2	30			1	20														2	2	1.0	2	1	18	18.0	18
1987	OTT	4				17																									
1987	Year	10	0		2	47			1	20																					
2	Years	8	0		2	47	3.0		1	20														2	2	1.0	2	1	18	18.0	18
WILLIAM MacKALL William Benjamin WR 5'8 180 Tennessee-Martin B: 5/26/1967 Panama City, FL Draft: 9-239 1989 IND																															
1989	WPG	10				0													5	47	9.4	12	0	36	295	8.2	34	16	344	21.5	51
GLENN MacKAY Glenn WR 5'11 175 Windsor B: 8/27/1984 Burlington, ON																															
2009	MTL	4				0													3	17	5.7	7	0								
2010	HAM	2				2																									
2011	HAM	17				4													9	98	10.9	23	0	3	38	12.7	18				
3	Years	23				6													12	115	9.6	23	0	3	38	12.7	18				
DON MacKENZIE Don (Shanty) G-T 5'11 241 none B: 1922 D: 5//2001																															
1950	TOR	12																													
1951	TOR	11																													
1952	TOR	9																													
1953	TOR	8																													
4	Years	40																													
MICHAEL MacKENZIE Michael RB 5'11 210 Eastern Washington B: 1/5/1976 Vancouver, BC Draft: 5-38 1999 HAM																															
1999	HAM	3	0	0	1	0																									
EARL MACKEY Earl, Jr. LB 6'0 233 Southern University B: 5/25/1973																															
1997	CAL	2				2			1	2	0																				
1998	CAL	2																													
2	Years	4				2			1	2	0																				
LOUIS MACKEY Louis C. LB 6'1 225 Gavilan JC; Akron B: 12/29/1977 Richmond, CA Pro: N																															
2006	MTL	10				18	1.0	7.0																							
2007	MTL	6	0	2	0	19					2																				
2	Years	16	0	2	0	37	1.0	7.0			2																				
RON MACKEY Ronald E. DE 6'2 250 Central Oklahoma B: 6/9/1960																															
1983	SAS	1					0.5																								
BAZ MACKIE Clarence G 5'11 222 Toronto B: 1932 Draft: 3-10 1955 TOR																															
1955	TOR	11																													
1956	TOR	14																													
1957	TOR	12																													
3	Years	37																													
DUNCAN MacKINLAY Duncan LB 6'2 220 Western Ontario B: 1/3/1956 Draft: 3-22 1977 WPG																															
1978	WPG	14	0		1																										
1979	WPG	11																										2	39	19.5	39
1980	TOR	11	0		1																										
1981	TOR	8					1.0		1	0																					
1982	TOR	4					1.0																								
1982	MTL	3					0.5																	1	0	0.0	0				
1982	Year	7					1.5																	1	0	0.0	0				
5	Years	48	0		2		2.5		1	0														1	0	0.0	0	2	39	19.5	39
ALEX MACKLIN Alex DE-OT 6'0 225 Toronto B: 1932 Draft: 1-2 1955 TOR																															
1955	CAL	8																													
1956	CAL	15																										1	6	6.0	6
2	Years	23																										1	6	6.0	6
BILL MACKRIDES William Charles QB 5'11 182 Nevada-Reno B: 7/8/1925 Philadelphia, PA Draft: 17-130 1947 CHI-AAFC; 3-19 1947 PHI Pro: N																															
1952	HAM+	12										17	3					3													
ALAN MacLEAN Alan DE-C-OG-OT 6'2 245 Bishop's B: 2/14/1955 Draft: 3-20 1977 TOR																															
1977	TOR	15																													
1978	CAL	1																													
1979	TOR	14																													
1980	HAM	1																													
1980	TOR	12																													
1980	Year	13																													
4	Years	31																													
BOB MacLELLAN Robert Stanford C-LB 6'2 227 McGill B: 3/26/1930 Montreal, QC D: 4/1/2001 Burlington, VT																															
1955	MTL	12																													
1956	MTL	14							1	14																					
1957	MTL	14																										1	3	3.0	3
1958	MTL	8																													
1959	MTL	14																													
1960	MTL	4																													
6	Years	66							1	14																		1	3	3.0	3
DOUG MacLENNAN Doug G																															
1948	HAM	9																													
IAN MacLEOD Ian DH-CB 6'0 189 Edmonton Huskies Jrs. B: 1945																															
1966	EDM	16	1		1																			14	65	4.6	27				
1967	EDM	16	1		0				4	127		6	1																		
1968	EDM	16	0		1				4	76		6	1											1	2	2.0	2				
1969	EDM	16																													
4	Years	64	2		2				8	203		12	2											15	67	4.5	27				
RAY MacLEOD Ray T-G 6'0 213 Oregon B: 1931																															
1953	EDM	16																													
1954	EDM	13																													
1955	WPG	12																													
3	Years	41																													
IVAN MacMILLAN Ivan K 5'8 157 Ottawa Sooners Jrs. B: 2/8/1952 Alexandria, ON																															
1970	OTT	14	2		1							75	0																		
1971	TOR	13	0		1							66	0																		
1972	TOR	9										53	0																		
1973	BC	6										51	0																		
1974	BC	16										101	0																		
1975	SAS	1										10	0																		
1975	BC	2										6	0																		
1975	Year	3										16	0																		
6	Years	59	2		2							362	0																		
BRETT MacNEIL Brett OG 6'5 290 Ottawa Sooners Jrs.; Colgate; Boston University B: 11/27/1967 Nepean, ON Draft: 1-7 1991 OTT																															
1992	WPG	10				1																						1	0	0.0	0
1993	WPG	18				1																									
1994	WPG	18				1																									
1995	WPG	15				1																									
1996	WPG	16				3																									
1997	WPG	18				1																									
1999	WPG	18	0	0	1	1																									

Year	Team	GP	FM	FF	FR	TK	SK	YDS	IR	YDS	PD	PTS	TD	RA	YDS	AVG	LG	TD	REC	YDS	AVG	LG	TD	PR	YDS	AVG	LG	KOR	YDS	AVG	LG
2000	WPG	13				0																									
2001	WPG*	17				2																									
2002	WPG	8				2																									
10	Years	151	0	0	1	13																						1	0	0.0	0
JOHN MacNEILL John Arthur DT 6'4 260 New Hampshire; Michigan State B: 11/15/1968 Waukesha, WI Draft: 12B-320 1992 SEA																															
1992	BC	5				7	3.0	23.0																							
1993	BC	6				9	1.0	4.0																							
2	Years	11				16	4.0	27.0																							
EDDIE MACON Edwin Donald OHB-DB 6'0 177 Pacific B: 3/7/1927 Draft: 2-20 1952 CHIB Pro: N																															
1954	CAL+	15	7		3				7	84		35	7	126	803	6.4	59	5	16	258	16.1	50	1	15	81	5.4	16	10	302	30.2	85
1957	HAM	13							5	164		12	2	19	114	6.0	19	0	7	190	27.1	55	1	1	10	10.0	10	7	147	21.0	39
1958	HAM+	13							4	54		6	1	6	25	4.2	8	0						16	74	4.6	18	15	410	27.3	96
1959	HAM	1							1	13									1	16	16.0	16	0	2	12	6.0	12				
4	Years	42	7		3				17	315		53	10	151	942	6.2	59	5	24	464	19.3	55	2	34	177	5.2	18	32	859	26.8	96
BOB MACORITTI Robert K-P 6'0 190 Wooster B: 9/19/1950 Draft: TE 1973 HAM																															
1975	WPG	3										20	0																		
1976	SAS	16	2		1							133	0																		
1977	SAS	16										108	0																		
1978	SAS	16	1		2							132	0																		
1979	SAS	13										66	0																		
1980	SAS	16	2		4							117	0											1	3	3.0	3				
6	Years	80	5		7							576	0											1	3	3.0	3				
RAY MACORITTI Ray K-P 6'4 215 Western Ontario B: 1/10/1966 Hamilton, ON																															
1990	EDM	18	1		0	0						186	0																		
1991	EDM	12	2		0	4						124	0																		
1993	OTT	3	1		1	0						24	0																		
3	Years	33	4		1	4						334	0																		
IAN MacPHERSON Ian DT-C 6'3 245 Ottawa B: 11/6/1950 Draft: 1D-9 1976 EDM																															
1976	MTL	2																													
1976	HAM	8																													
1976	Year	10																													
BILL MacQUARRIE Bill G 5'11 210 B: 2/10/1924																															
1948	WPG	4																													
JIMMY MacRAE Jim E-HB 6'1 180 Alberta B: 1926																															
1949	EDM	10										5	1										1								
1950	EDM	13										10	2	30	53	1.8		0	4	85	21.3		1								
1951	EDM	12										5	1						4	92	23.0		1	26	218	8.4		2	30	15.0	
3	Years	35										20	4	30	53	1.8	0	0	8	177	22.1		3	26	218	8.4	0	2	30	15.0	
GERRY MacTAGGART Gerry E 6'3 187 McMaster B: 1931 Orillia, ON Draft: 4-16 1953 HAM																															
1953	HAM	12																													
RON MADDOCKS Ron QB 6'0 175 NDG Maple Leafs Jrs. B: 8/12/1941																															
1963	MTL	14												1	-2	-2.0	-2	0													
ANDRE MADDOX Andre LB 6'1 200 North Carolina State B: 10/8/1982 Miami, FL Draft: 5-161 2005 NYJ																															
2008	TOR	3				7																									
BOB MADDOX Robert Earl DE 6'5 245 Frostburg State B: 5/2/1949 Frederick, MD Draft: 15-383 1972 SF; 7-171 1973 CIN Pro: N																															
1978	HAM	1																													
LYNN MADSEN Lynn Thomas DE 6'4 260 Washington B: 8/8/1960 Blair, NE Draft: 3A-51 1984 NJ-USFL Pro: NU																															
1987	SAS	8				12	2.0		1	12																					
1988	OTT	5				9	2.0																								
2	Years	13				21	4.0		1	12																					
DAVID MAEVA David LB 6'0 210 Hawaii B: 3/23/1968 Honolulu, HI																															
1994	LV	5				16								1	33	33.0	33	0													
1996	BC	15	0		1	43	2.0	12.0			1																				
1997	BC	9	0	2	2	44	2.0	15.0	1	22	1	6	1																		
1998	WPG	15	0	1	1	86	4.0	22.0	1	20	1																				
4	Years	44	0	3	4	189	8.0	49.0	2	42	3	6	1	1	33	33.0	33	0													
ANTHONY MAGGIACCOMO Anthony LB 6'1 223 Wilfrid Laurier B: 4/25/1984 North York, ON																															
2008	WPG	17				7																						1	0	0.0	0
2009	MTL	4				1																									
2	Years	21				8																						1	0	0.0	0
KEN MAGLICIC Kenneth M. LB 5'11 220 Notre Dame B: 8/20/1943																															
1965	WPG	16	0		1				1																						
QUINN MAGNUSON Quinn OG 6'5 272 Washington State B: 3/3/1971 Saskatoon, SK Draft: 6-45 1993 WPG																															
1993	WPG	9				4																									
1994	SAS	1				0																									
1995	OTT	4				2																									
1996	MTL	10				6																									
4	Years	24				12																									
BUD MAGRUM Francis J. DT-DE 6'4 250 Colorado B: 7/2/1949 Sandusky, OH D: 11//1991																															
1973	BC	16	0		3																										
1974	BC	15																													
2	Years	31	0		3																										
MICKEY MAGUIRE Mickey FL 5'10 165 Montreal Ints. B: 1926																															
1949	MTL	3										5	1																		
1951	SAS	14												2	6	3.0		0						5	49	9.8		3	53	17.7	
1952	WPG	14							2	17		5	1	6	51	8.5	16	1	2	27	13.5	17	0	2	10	5.0	10	1	15	15.0	15
3	Years	31							2	17		10	2	8	57	7.1	16	1	2	27	13.5	17	0	7	59	8.4	10	4	68	17.0	15
DON MAHI Don RB 6'0 210 Idaho; Hawaii B: 1950																															
1973	MTL	2	2		0									8	19	2.4	7	0	4	34	8.5	24	0								
HAMID MAHMOUDI Hamid CB 5'9 177 Montreal B: 9/12/1985 Tehran, Iran Draft: 3B-20 2010 BC																															
2010	BC	2				0																									
2011	BC	7				4																									
2	Years	9				4																									
PAT MAHON Patrick C 6'3 252 Western Ontario B: 8/24/1968 Kingston, ON Draft: 8-59 1991 OTT																															
1993	CAL	6				0																									
1993	OTT	4				0																									
1993	Year	10				0																									
1994	HAM	7				2																									
1994	OTT	1				0																									
1994	Year	8				2																									
1995	OTT	5				0																									
3	Years	18				2																									
LIAM MAHONEY Liam WR 6-1 207 Concordia B: 12/13/1987 Lachine, QC Draft: 6-41																															
2011	HAM	7				1													5	80	16.0	32	0								
MIKE MAHONEY Mike LB 6'3 230 McGill B: 1/11/1981 Regina, SK Draft: 5-39 2004 TOR																															
2004	CAL	3				1																									
2005	SAS	5				2																									
2006	SAS	17				5																									
2007	WPG	9	0	0	1	5						6	1																		
4	Years	34	0	0	1	13						6	1																		
LONNIE MAICH Lonnie P. DE-G 6'2 240 Kent State B: 1945																															
1968	HAM	14																													

Year	Team	GP	FM	FF	FR	TK	SK	YDS	IR	YDS	PD	PTS	TD	RA	YDS	AVG	LG	TD	REC	YDS	AVG	LG	TD	PR	YDS	AVG	LG	KOR	YDS	AVG	LG
1969	HAM	14																													
1970	HAM	4																													
3	Years	32																													
PAUL MAINES Paul OT 6'5 275 Tulsa; Concordia (Canada) B: 5/16/1967 Draft: 3-20 1991 SAS																															
1992	HAM	1				0																									
KENNY MAINOR Kenny LB 6'4 221 Troy B: 10/30/1985 Atlanta, GA																															
2011	WPG	15	0	1	0	22	8.0	63.0																							
GIL MAINS Gilbert Lee T-E 6'2 243 Murray State B: 12/17/1929 Mount Carmel, IL D: 1/10/2009 West Branch, MI Draft: 20-237 1952 DET Pro: N																															
1955	TOR	3																													
DOUG MAITLAND Douglas HB 5'10 201 Montreal Pats Jrs. B: 6/25/1922 Laval, QC																															
1946	MTL	10										5	1										1								
1947	MTL	12																													
1948	MTL	9																													
1949	MTL	7										5	1										1								
4	Years	38										10	2										2								
CHRIS MAJOR Chris CB 5'8 180 South Carolina B: 4/8/1965 New York, NY																															
1987	CAL	2				9			2	52																		1	0	0.0	0
1988	CAL+	18			4	40			10	153		12	2																		
1989	CAL	7				22			2	14																					
1990	BC	12	0		2	52			3	18		6	1																		
1991	BC	13	0		1	45			5	58		6	1																		
1992	BC	6	0		2	32																		1	6	6.0	6				
6	Years	58	0		9	200			22	295		24	4											1	6	6.0	6	1	0	0.0	0
DORAN MAJOR Doran Oliver CB 5'10 175 Memphis B: 5/20/1961 Honolulu, HI Pro: U																															
1987	TOR	13	0		2	29																									
1988	TOR	18				32	1.0																	1	3	3.0	3				
1989	TOR	9	0		1	18																									
1990	TOR	1				2																									
4	Years	41	0		3	81	1.0																	1	3	3.0	3				
JOHNNY MAJORS John Terrill HB 5'11 175 Tennessee B: 5/21/1935 Lynchburg, TN																															
1957	MTL	4												18	22	1.2	20	0	12	108	9.0	16	0	7	21	3.0	6	2	18	9.0	23
LESLIE MAJORS Leslie John LB 5'10 180 Indiana B: 2/18/1986 South Holland, IL																															
2011	WPG	1				3																									
AL MAKOWIECKI Alexander M. DT-OG 6'2 230 Florida State B: 9/17/1932 Monaca, PA D: 6/2/2005 New Brighton, PA																															
1955	MTL	11																													
1957	MTL	11																													
2	Years	22																													
GENE MAKOWSKY Gene OG-OT-C 6'4 279 Saskatchewan B: 4/17/1973 Saskatoon, SK Draft: 2A-23 1995 SAS																															
1995	SAS	18				4																									
1996	SAS	5				0																									
1997	SAS	18				0																									
1998	SAS	17	0	0	1	0																									
1999	SAS	18	0	0	1	0													1	-3	-3.0	-3	0								
2000	SAS	16				3																									
2001	SAS	18				0																									
2002	SAS	18	0	0	1	2																									
2003	SAS	18				0																									
2004	SAS*	18	0	0	1	1																									
2005	SAS*	18				0																									
2006	SAS*	18				0																									
2007	SAS+	18	0	0	1	0																									
2008	SAS*	18				2																									
2009	SAS*	14				1																									
2010	SAS+	18				3																									
2011	SAS	18				0																									
17	Years	286	0	0	5	16													1	-3	-3.0	-3	0								
ANTHONY MALBROUGH Anthony Warrick DH 5'10 185 Texas Tech B: 12/9/1976 Beaumont, TX Draft: 5A-130 2000 CLE Pro: EN																															
2002	CAL	7	0	2	1	7					3	6	1																		
2003	CAL	12				27					3																				
2004	OTT	17	0	0	1	42			1	55	5	6	1																		
2005	CAL	9				19			2	44	2																				
2005	WPG	1				0																									
2005	Year	10				19			2	44	2																				
2006	WPG	17	0	2	3	40	1.0	9.0			6																				
2007	WPG	5				8					1																				
2008	WPG	15				35	2.0	15.0	2	34	2																				
2009	EDM	5				3																									
8	Years	87	0	4	5	181	3.0	24.0	5	133	22	12	2																		
JOHN MALINOSKY John M. OT-OG-DT 6'5 260 Michigan State B: 5/8/1955 Fernie, BC Draft: TE 1977 CAL																															
1978	CAL	9																													
1979	WPG	16																													
1980	TOR	14																													
1981	TOR	16																													
1982	TOR	16																													
1983	TOR	15	0		1																										
1984	TOR+	15																													
1985	HAM	14																													
1986	HAM	18																													
1987	HAM	15				0																									
10	Years	148	0		1	0																									
PAT MALLEN Pat DB Scarborough Rams Jrs.																															
1973	TOR	2																													
CRAIG MALLENDER Craig FB 6'0 207 Windsor B: 1/24/1958 Draft: 7-63 1981 EDM																															
1981	EDM	2												1	3	3.0	3	0	1	19	19.0	19	0								
1982	EDM	3																	1	9	9.0	9	0								
2	Years	5												1	3	3.0	3	0	2	28	14.0	19	0								
JASON MALLETT Jason S-CB 5'11 180 Carleton B: 4/14/1972 Orleans, ON Draft: 1-14 1995 WPG																															
1995	WPG	15	0		3	27					4	12	2																		
1996	WPG	18	0		1	31			1	20	3																				
1997	SAS	16	0	0	1	37	1.0	5.0	1	51	4																				
1998	HAM	6				1					2																				
2001	SAS	16				4																									
2002	SAS	17	0	0	2	39			1	29	4																				
2003	SAS	15	0	0	1	16			1	27	4	6	1																		
7	Years	103	0	0	8	155	1.0	5.0	4	127	21	18	3																		
MARTELL MALLETT Martell RB 6'0 195 Arkansas-Pine Bluff B: 5/13/1986 Pine Bluff, AR																															
2009	BC+	16	2	0	0	3						48	8	214	1240	5.8	54	6	43	342	8.0	26	2					10	225	22.5	49
CHRIS MALMGREN Christopher Paul DT 6'3 257 Kansas State; Boise State B: 2/15/1956 Cameron County, TX																															
1979	TOR	2																													
ART MALONE Arthur Lee CB 5'10 180 Washington B: 8/21/1966 Casa Grande, AZ Pro: E																															
1989	BC	7				32			2	84																					
1990	CAL	2				8																									

Year	Team	GP	FM	FF	FR	TK	SK	YDS	IR	YDS	PD	PTS	TD	RA	YDS	AVG	LG	TD	REC	YDS	AVG	LG	TD	PR	YDS	AVG	LG	KOR	YDS	AVG	LG
2	Years	9				40			2	84																					
MIKE MALONEY Mike OT-DT 6'4 245 Ottawa Sooners Jrs. B: 10/22/1948																															
1972	MTL	14	0		2																										
1973	MTL	14	1		0																										
2	Years	28	1		2																										
FELMAN MALVEAUX Felman, Jr. WR 6'0 179 Michigan B: 8/20/1973 Beaumont, TX																															
1997	TOR	3				1						6	1						9	88	9.8	30	1					3	65	21.7	30
KELLY MALVEAUX Kelly Thomas, II DH-LB 5'9 176 Arizona B: 5/11/1976 Bellflower, CA Pro: EUX																															
1999	SAS	2	0	0	1	5																									
2001	CAL	14				32			1	0	8																				
2002	CAL	17				48	1.0	9.0	3	5	9																				
2003	CAL	18				72	1.0	2.0			7													1	5	5.0	5				
2004	MTL+	18	0	1	0	43	1.0	4.0	4	80	2	6	1															3	18	6.0	10
2005	MTL	18				68	1.0	1.0	3	15	9																				
2006	WPG	18	1	1	0	53	1.0	4.0			6													2	4	2.0	4				
2007	WPG	18				51			2	0	4																				
2008	WPG+	17	0	1	0	65	1.0	2.0	2	39	6																				
2009	EDM	16	0	1	1	53			2	31	4																				
10	Years	156	1	4	2	490	6.0	22.0	17	170	55	6	1											3	9	3.0	5	3	18	6.0	10
TOMMY MANASTERSKY Tom HB 5'9 180 none B: 3/7/1929 Montreal, QC D: 3/11/2012 Toronto, ON																															
1946	MTL	10																													
1947	MTL	11																													
1949	MTL	11										17	3										2								
1950	MTL	12										35	7					4					3								
1951	MTL	11																													
1952	MTL	12																													
1953	MTL	12																													
1954	SAS	7																										6	92	15.3	20
8	Years	86										52	10					4					5					6	92	15.3	20
BILL MANCHUK Bill LB-DB 6'2 212 Edmonton Huskies Jrs.; Alberta B: 9/1/1947 Draft: 1B-6 1971 SAS																															
1971	SAS	16										6	1						7	85	12.1	29	1								
1972	SAS	16	0		1				3	53									1	23	23.0	23	0								
1973	SAS	16	2		1				2	15									3	28	9.3	11	0								
1974	SAS	16	0		1				2	11																					
1975	SAS	16	0		3																										
1976	SAS+	15			1				1	27		6	1																		
1977	SAS	9	0		1				1	6																					
1978	SAS	16	0		1				1	8																					
1979	SAS	16																													
1980	SAS	11	0		1				2	61		12	2																		
1981	EDM	14																										1	3	3.0	3
1982	EDM	16	0		1		2.0																					1	1	1.0	1
12	Years	177	2		11		2.0		12	181		24	4						11	136	12.4	29	1					2	4	2.0	3
JOHN MANDARICH John DT-OG 6'4 281 Kent State B: 8/1/1961 Thunder Bay, ON D: 2/8/1993 Burlington, ON Draft: 1C-8 1984 EDM																															
1984	EDM	15	0		2		1.0																								
1985	EDM	16					3.0																					2	3	1.5	3
1986	EDM	17	0		2		6.0																								
1987	EDM	12				13	1.0																								
1988	EDM	2				0	2.0																								
1989	EDM	18	0		1	19	1.0																								
1990	OTT	13	0		1	18	2.0																								
7	Years	93	0		6	50	16.0																					2	3	1.5	3
JOHN MANEL John QB 6'2 215 Kansas State B: 1947																															
1969	HAM	14	0		1									4	14	3.5	6	0										2	28	14.0	25
1970	HAM	13	0		1							7	1																		
1971	HAM	11	1		0									3	-1	-0.3	4	0													
3	Years	38	1		2							7	1	7	13	1.9	6	0										2	28	14.0	25
MARK MANGES Mark Roy QB 6'2 210 Maryland B: 1/10/1956 Cumberland, MD Draft: 4-105 1978 LARM Pro: N																															
1979	HAM	1												2	16	8.0	9	0													
PETER MANGOLD Peter FB 6'1 235 Western Kentucky B: 3/10/1965 Toronto, ON Draft: 2B-10 1988 SAS																															
1989	TOR	6	0		1	0																									
ROLAND MANGOLD Roland OG 6'1 225 Truman State B: 2/14/1956 Wels, Austria Draft: 4-35 1979 MTL																															
1979	MTL	160		2																											
1980	MTL	16	0		1																										
1981	MTL	16																													
1982	TOR	16																													
1983	TOR	8	0		2														0	2		2	0								
1983	MTL	7																													
1983	Year	15																	0	2		2	0								
1984	MTL	8																													
6	Years	80	0		5														0	2		2	0								
PETE MANGUM Ernest Glynde LB 6'0 219 Mississippi B: 1/17/1931 Forest, LA Draft: 23-268 1954 NYG Pro: N																															
1957	WPG	11	0		2				1	0																					
1958	WPG	2																													
2	Years	13	0		2				1	0																					
JIM MANKINS James Frank FB 6'1 235 Oklahoma; Hartnell JC; Florida State B: 6/23/1944 Los Angeles County, CA D: 4/1/2004 Anchorage, AK Draft: RS-4-28 1966 MIA; 12-184(f) 1966 GB Pro: N																															
1968	OTT	1	1		0									2	-1	-0.5	1	0													
1969	OTT	14	3		0							18	3	122	710	5.8	44	0	22	239	10.9	23	3					2	13	6.5	12
1970	OTT	9	1		0							12	2	98	456	4.7	31	2	14	134	9.6	24	0								
1970	EDM	1												3	8	2.7		0													
1970	Year	10	1		0							12	2	101	464	4.6	31	2	14	134	9.6	24	0								
3	Years	24	5		0							30	5	225	1173	5.2	44	2	36	373	10.4	24	3					2	13	6.5	12
DEXTER MANLEY Dexter Keith DE 6'3 257 Oklahoma State B: 2/2/1958 Houston, TX Draft: 5A-119 1981 WAS Pro: N																															
1992	OTT	3				0																									
1993	OTT	2	0		1	1																									
2	Years	5	0		1	1																									
WILLIE MANLEY William Leon OT 6'2 218 Oklahoma B: 5/20/1926 Hollis, OK D: 3/13/2010 Austin, TX Draft: 7-82 1950 GB Pro: N																															
1953	EDM+	14																													
1954	EDM	2																	1	7	7.0	7	0								
2	Years	16																	1	7	7.0	7	0								
WILTON MANLEY Wilton Eugene DE 6'4 247 West Texas A&M B: 12/24/1942																															
1965	SAS	2																													
DAVE MANN David Carl [born Wolferin, David] OHB-P-CB-FL-S-K 6'1 190 Oregon State B: 6/2/1932 Berkeley, CA Draft: 7-74 1954 CHIC Pro: N																															
1958	TOR	12							4	26		51	8	107	556	5.2	86	6	33	319	9.7	31	1	2	128	64.0	116	17	351	20.6	32
1960	TOR+	14										91	14	37	217	5.9	36	1	61	1380	22.6	103	13	1	0	0.0	0	4	117	29.3	32
1961	TOR+	14										46	6	32	121	3.8	31	0	53	659	12.4	45	5	2	27	13.5	25	7	164	23.4	29
1962	TOR	14										15	2	15	81	5.4	24	0	39	410	10.5	40	2	2	1	0.5	2	6	113	18.8	26
1963	TOR	9										13	2						11	190	17.3	33	2	1	0	0.0	0				
1964	TOR	14	0		2							7	0	1	10	10.0	10	0	2	10	5.0	12	0								
1965	TOR	14										12	1	2	1	0.5	4	0	5	57	11.4	17	1								
1966	TOR	14	1		0							11	0	8	67	8.4	40	0						1	0	0.0	0	1	10	10.0	10

Year	Team	GP	FM	FF	FR	TK	SK	YDS	IR	YDS	PD	PTS	TD	RA	YDS	AVG	LG	TD	REC	YDS	AVG	LG	TD	PR	YDS	AVG	LG	KOR	YDS	AVG	LG
1967	TOR	14	1		0							50	0	1	9	9.0	9	0						1	3	3.0	3	1	0	0.0	0
1968	TOR	14	2		0							72	0	1	9	9.0	9	0						1	0	0.0	0				
1969	TOR	8										54	0																		
1970	TOR	14										13	0															1	20	20.0	20
12	Years	155	4		2				4	26		435	33	204	1071	5.3	86	7	204	3025	14.8	103	24	11	159	14.5	116	37	775	20.9	32
MAURICE MANN Maurice William WR 6'1 190 Monterey Peninsula JC; Nevada-Reno B: 9/14/1982 Santa Clara, CA Draft: 5-149 2004 CIN Pro: N																															
2007	EDM	3				2													9	127	14.1	29	0								
2008	EDM	7				1						24	4						31	420	13.5	44	4								
2009	EDM	15	2	0	0	4						36	6						73	917	12.6	68	6								
2010	HAM	17	1	0	0	4						32	5						56	787	14.1	51	5								
2011	HAM	8	1	0	0	3						12	2						35	346	9.9	29	2					1	0	0.0	0
2011	TOR	2				0								1	14	14.0	14	0	2	12	6.0	7	0								
2011	Year	10				3								1	14	14.0	14	0	37	358	9.7	29	2					1	0	0.0	0
5	Years	50	4	0	0	14						104	17	1	14	14.0	14	0	206	2609	12.7	68	17					1	0	0.0	0
JACK MANNERS Jack D. T 5'9 205 B: 1915 Ottawa, ON D: 4/11/1986																															
1946	WPG	8																													
PETE MANNING Peter Jonathan TE-CB 6'3 208 Wake Forest B: 8/11/1937 Hudson, MA Draft: FS 1960 BOS; 8-93 1960 CHIB Pro: N																															
1962	CAL+	13										18	3	1	5	5.0	5	0	52	756	14.5	52	3								
1963	CAL*	16	1		0							18	3						63	988	15.7	46	3								
1964	CAL+	16																	47	663	14.1	45	0								
1965	CAL	16	0		1				2	33														1	0	0.0	0				
1966	TOR	14	0		1				2	38									13	154	11.8	18	0								
1967	TOR	1																	1	16	16.0	16	0								
6	Years	76	1		2				4	71		36	6	1	5	5.0	5	0	176	2577	14.6	52	6	1	0	0.0	0				
SEAN MANNING Sean DB 6'3 200 St. Francis Xavier B: 5/1/1984 Trail, BC																															
2007	CAL	6				2																									
2008	HAM	9	0	0	1	10			1	0	0																				
2	Years	15	0	0	1	12			1	0	0																				
ERIC MANNS Eric LB 6'2 214 Western Michigan; Wayne State (Michigan) B: 12/18/1958 South Bend, IN																															
1981	OTT	5					2.0																								
TEDDY MANOREK Ted C B: 1916 D: 1/9/2002 Milton, ON																															
1946	HAM	3																													
1947	HAM	10																													
2	Years	13																													
CORY MANTYKA Cory M. DE-OT-OG 6'5 275 Saskatoon Hilltops Jrs.; Jamestown B: 5/31/1970 Saskatoon, SK Draft: SD-4th 1993 BC																															
1994	BC	14				3																									
1995	BC	18				2																									
1996	BC	17				1																									
1997	BC	18	0	0	1	1						6	1	0	0		0	1													
1998	BC	15				1																									
1999	BC	15	0	0	1	2																									
2000	BC	18	0	0	1	2																									
2001	BC	18	0	0	1	4								1	8	8.0	8	0													
2002	BC	13				2																									
2003	BC+	18				6																									
2004	BC	17				1																									
2005	BC	18				1																									
12	Years	199	0	0	4	26						6	1	1	8	8.0	8	1													
DAN MANUCCI Daniel Joseph QB 6'2 194 Mesa CC; Kansas State B: 9/3/1957 Erie, PA Draft: 5B-116 1979 BUF Pro: NU																															
1981	TOR	6												8	18	2.3	12	0													
JIM MANZ Jim RB 5'11 217 Saskatchewan; Saskatoon Hilltops Jrs. B: 4/3/1959 Draft: TE 1980 SAS																															
1982	SAS	7												1	13	13.0	13	0													
1983	SAS	6	0		1									9	43	4.8	9	0													
2	Years	13	0		1									10	56	5.6	13	0													
DURELL MAPP Durell Desmond LB 6'1 240 North Carolina B: 12/1/1985 Burlington, NC																															
2011	TOR	2				5																									
REGGIE MARABLE Reginald H. LB 5'11 222 Morehouse B: 3/23/1973																															
1995	BIR	9				19	1.0	3.0																							
MIKE MARASCO Mike RB 5'11 200 British Columbia; Okanagan Sun Jrs. B: 5/16/1966 Kamloops, BC																															
1990	BC	9				0								11	53	4.8	10	0	3	13	4.3	6	0					1	3	3.0	3
1991	BC	15	0		2	13																						4	52	13.0	17
1992	BC	3				1								2	10	5.0	5	0	3	27	9.0	10	0					1	12	12.0	12
3	Years	27	0		2	14								13	63	4.8	10	0	6	40	6.7	10	0					6	67	11.2	17
KERRY MARBURY Kerry Lee RB 5'10 183 West Virginia B: 3/21/1952 Fairmont, WV Draft: 16-403 1975 NE Pro: W																															
1973	TOR	3										6	1	42	153	3.6	11	0	3	37	12.3	39	1								
1974	OTT	4	1		0							6	1	35	94	2.7	19	1	6	57	9.5	25	0					1	15	15.0	15
2	Years	7	1		0							12	2	77	247	3.2	19	1	9	94	10.4	39	1					1	15	15.0	15
AL MARCELIN Allen Jules DB-OHB 6'0 185 Arizona Western JC; Parsons B: 4/17/1945 New Orleans, LA Draft: 10-269 1968 LARM																															
1970	OTT*	14	3		1				9	176									0	2		2	0	25	223	8.9	22	21	659	31.4	85
1971	OTT	10	2		0				5	110		12	2	2	11	5.5	8	0						11	250	22.7	84	16	384	24.0	38
1972	OTT	9							2	21														2	19	9.5	16	12	327	27.3	63
1973	OTT*	14	1		0				8	81																		20	436	21.8	38
1974	OTT*	16							8	85																		8	199	24.9	35
1975	OTT	16	1		2				5	52														48	546	11.4	95	27	611	22.6	51
6	Years	79	7		3				37	525		12	2	2	11	5.5	8	0	0	2		2	0	86	1038	12.1	95	104	2616	25.2	85
JOE MARCH Joe DE 6'2 265 Murray State B: 6/18/1967 Ridgely, TN																															
1989	CAL	6	0		1	11	4.0		1	13																					
1989	TOR	1				0																									
1989	Year	7	0		1	11	4.0		1	13																					
BRIAN MARCIL Brian LB-DE-OT-DT-C 6'3 230 Loyola (Quebec) B: 4/6/1948 Richmond, QC																															
1970	CAL	12																													
1971	CAL	16	0		2																							1	15	15.0	15
1972	CAL	4																										1	16	16.0	16
1972	MTL	9	0		1																										
1972	Year	13	0		1																							1	16	16.0	16
1973	CAL	7	0		1																										
1974	CAL	7																													
1975	OTT	2																													
6	Years	48	0		4																							2	31	15.5	16
RON MARCINIAK Ronald Joseph G-LB 6'1 210 Kansas State B: 7/16/1932 Pittsburgh, PA Draft: 7B-80 1955 WAS Pro: N																															
1956	TOR	9							1	15																		1	11	11.0	11
ED MARCONTELL Edmon Dwight OT 6'0 250 Lamar B: 7/10/1945 Liberty, TX Draft: 11-279 1967 STL Pro: N																															
1968	EDM	6																													
ANDY MAREFOS Andrew Gust C-HB 6'0 223 St. Mary's (California) B: 7/16/1917 D: 2/18/1996 Sutter County, CA Draft: 12-107 1941 NYG Pro: AN																															
1949	EDM	12										7	1					1													
EDWARD MARENTETTE Edward QB-DB 6'0 190 B: 1938																															
1959	MTL	2																													
MARIO MARIANI Mario Natale DE 6'5 248 Contra Costa JC; New Mexico B: 6/5/1943 Alameda, CA																															
1965	WPG	10	0		5																										
1966	TOR	14	0		3																										
1967	TOR	2	0		1																										
3	Years	26	0		9																										

Year	Team	GP	FM	FF	FR	TK	SK	YDS	IR	YDS	PD	PTS	TD	RA	YDS	AVG	LG	TD	REC	YDS	AVG	LG	TD	PR	YDS	AVG	LG	KOR	YDS	AVG	LG
JACOB MARINI Jacob K-P 5'8 190 St. Francis Xavier B: 7/29/1977 Hamilton, ON																															
2000	TOR	18				0						123	0																		
2001	TOR	5	1	0	0	1						38	0																		
2	Years	23	1	0	0	1						161	0																		
TODD MARINOVICH Todd Marvin QB 6'4 215 Southern California B: 7/4/1969 San Leandro, CA Draft: 1-24 1991 LARI Pro: N																															
1999	BC	18				0																									
DAVE MARINUCCI David RB 6'0 200 Queen's B: 2/4/1957 Draft: 6-46 1980 TOR																															
1980	TOR	4																													
MARK MARISCAL Mark Joseph P 6'2 200 Colorado B: 9/10/1979 Tallahassee, FL																															
2004	MTL	6				2						23	0																		
RAY MARIUZ Ray LB 6'3 219 McMaster B: 12/25/1980 Hamilton, ON Draft: 4-28 2003 TOR																															
2003	TOR	15	1	0	0	17																						1	3	3.0	3
2004	TOR	18				33																									
2005	TOR	17				44	3.0	12.0																							
2006	HAM	18	0	0	1	48																									
2007	HAM	18				45																									
2008	HAM	18	0	1	1	80	2.0	18.0			1																				
2009	HAM	18	0	1	0	20					1																	1	0	0.0	0
2010	HAM	18	0	1	0	29	1.0	0.0																							
2011	HAM	6	0	0	2	14			1	21	1	6	1																		
9	Years	146	1	3	4	330	6.0	30.0	1	21	3	6	1															2	3	1.5	3
PAUL MARKLE Paul TE-LB 6'2 214 Wilfrid Laurier B: 10/23/1946 London, ON Draft: 1968 TOR																															
1968	TOR	14										6	1						2	30	15.0	21	1								
1969	TOR	14			1									0	6		6	0	3	55	18.3	33	0								
1970	TOR	14																	6	85	14.2	22	0								
1971	WPG	16	1		3							18	3						30	406	13.5	38	3								
1972	WPG	16												2	-19	-9.5	-4	0	31	266	8.6	20	0					1	0	0.0	0
1973	WPG	16	0		1														20	257	12.9	44	0								
1974	EDM	13																										2	23	11.5	14
7	Years	103	1		5							24	4	2	-13	-6.5	6	0	92	1099	11.9	44	4					3	23	7.7	14
VIC MARKS Vic FB-HB 5'10 200 Fort William Ints. B: 1935																															
1956	SAS	12												7	15	2.1	5	0	1	2	2.0	2	0								
1957	SAS	12	0		2							6	1	12	46	3.8	16	1										1	20	20.0	20
1958	SAS	16	0		0							12	2	5	27	5.4	10	1										2	29	14.5	16
1959	SAS	3												2	3	1.5	5	0													
1960	SAS	1																													
5	Years	44	0		2							18	3	26	91	3.5	16	2	1	2	2.0	2	0					3	49	16.3	20
DAVE MARLER David T. QB 6'1 195 Mississippi College; Mississippi State B: 12/20/1955 Draft: 10-253 1979 BUF																															
1979	HAM	5	3		2							13	1	12	85	7.1	27	1													
1980	HAM	13	8		1							12	2	43	245	5.7	22	2													
1981	HAM	16																													
1982	HAM	12												4	22	5.5	11	0													
1984	OTT	3												2	3	1.5	2	0													
5	Years	49	11		3							25	3	61	355	5.8	27	3													
ROHAN MARLEY Rohan Anthony LB 5'8 195 Miami (Florida) B: 5/19/1972 Kingston, Jamaica																															
1995	OTT	7	1		3	34			1	3	0																				
BOBBY MARLOW Robert R. FB-DB-LB 6'0 202 Alabama B: 2/8/1930 Athens, AL D: 6/5/1985 Houston, TX Draft: 1-8 1953 NYG																															
1953	SAS+	12							2	31		25	5	105	563	5.4		5	9	119	13.2		0					1	9	9.0	9
1954	SAS+	14	2		0							20	4	165	882	5.3	62	4	16	132	8.3	19	0								
1955	SAS+	16	2		2				1	12		30	6	121	690	5.7	34	6	13	97	7.5	20	0								
1956	SAS+	15	8		0				3	17		48	8	135	662	4.9	32	8	32	331	10.3	44	0								
1957	SAS+	13	1		2				3	38		60	10	144	749	5.2	42	8	11	133	12.1	33	0								
1958	SAS	13	8		2				1	14		6	1	157	710	4.5	17	0	12	54	4.5	17	0					1	2	2.0	2
1959	SAS	3							1					6	35	5.8	17	0	1	11	11.0	11	0								
7	Years	86	21		6				11	112		189	34	833	4291	5.2	62	31	94	877	9.3	44	0					2	11	5.5	9
FRANK MAROF Frank SB 6'0 190 Guelph B: 9/30/1968 Hamilton, ON Draft: 4A-27 1992 CAL																															
1992	CAL	18				6													2	23	11.5	17	0								
1993	CAL	18				14													6	49	8.2	13	0								
1994	OTT	5				7																						1	0	0.0	0
1994	HAM	5				5																						1	0	0.0	0
1994	Year	10				12																						2	0	0.0	0
1995	HAM	10	1		1	7						10	1						34	414	12.2	30	1								
1996	HAM	8				5													1	32	32.0	32	0					1	6	6.0	6
5	Years	59	1		1	44						10	1						43	518	12.0	32	1					3	6	2.0	6
NORM MARRATO Norm HB-FW 6'0 185																															
1948	HAM	7																													
FRANCIS MARRIOTT Francis (Bubba) QB 6'0 190 Troy B: 12/25/1938 Mobile, AL																															
1963	MTL	9												17	31	1.8	10	0													
RANDY MARRIOTT Randy DB 6'0 170 North Carolina B: 1/11/1965 Philadelphia, PA																															
1990	TOR	7	1	0	0							6	1	1	2	2.0	2	0	6	145	24.2	64	1								
SEAN MARRIOTT Sean LB 6'3 230 St. Mary's (Nova Scotia) B: 1/30/1971 Kingston, Jamaica Draft: 4C-39 1995 OTT																															
1995	OTT	10				11																						1	8	8.0	8
1996	BC	6				4																									
2	Years	16				15																						1	8	8.0	8
BRIAN MARROW Brian K. CB 5'11 190 Wisconsin B: 2/19/1962 Youngstown, OH																															
1985	TOR	3																													
CURTIS MARSH Curtis Joseph WR 6'2 206 Moorpark CC; Utah B: 11/24/1970 Los Angeles County, CA Draft: 7-219 1995 JAC Pro: N																															
2000	SAS*	17	5	0	3	4						66	11	0	1		1	1	102	1560	15.3	58	10								
2001	SAS	9				2						30	5	1	4	4.0	4	0	39	605	15.5	46	5								
2	Years	26	5	0	3	6						96	16	1	5	5.0	4	1	141	2165	15.4	58	15								
DANTE MARSH Dante Lamar CB 5'10 190 Fresno State B: 2/26/1979 Oakland, CA																															
2004	BC	18	0	1	0	65			3	28	3																	2	49	24.5	27
2005	BC	18	0	0	1	54			3	0	2																				
2006	BC+	18	0	0	2	55			4	63	5	6	1											1	9	9.0	9	2	36	18.0	21
2007	BC	9				27			1	3	5																				
2008	BC*	18	0	1	2	59			2	0	7													1	7	7.0	7				
2009	BC	18				71			2	35	1	6	1											2	15	7.5	8				
2010	BC	17	0	1	1	64			4	28	4													1	8	8.0	8				
2011	BC+	18	0	2	0	61	1.0	7.0	4	101	1																				
8	Years	134	0	5	6	456	1.0	7.0	23	258	28	12	2											5	39	7.8	9	4	85	21.3	27
STEVEN MARSH Steven DeCarlos LB-DB 6'0 180 Tennessee B: 10/3/1979 Wingate, NC																															
2004	EDM	11				33	1.0	8.0	0	0	3																				
2005	EDM	18	0	1	0	60	2.0	6.0	2	0	5																				
2	Years	29	0	1	0	93	3.0	14.0	2	0	8																				
BLAKE MARSHALL Blake FB 6'1 230 Western Ontario B: 5/17/1965 Guelph, ON Draft: 1A-2 1987 EDM																															
1987	EDM	7	1		0	0						6	1	21	87	4.1	12	1	5	58	11.6	15	0								
1988	EDM	12			1	1						30	5	69	315	4.6	38	5	10	58	5.8	15	0					4	34	8.5	16
1989	EDM	18	2		0	2						84	14	65	233	3.6	15	11	22	254	11.5	41	3					1	5	5.0	5
1990	EDM*	17	4		3	4						78	13	120	603	5.0	27	12	25	252	10.1	62	1								
1991	EDM*	16	2		1	8						120	20	125	615	4.9	34	16	50	619	12.4	40	4								
1992	EDM*	11	3		0	0						54	9	93	495	5.3	50	7	24	188	7.8	21	2								
1993	EDM	7	1		0	0						18	3	30	101	3.4	12	2	7	38	5.4	10	1								

Year	Team	GP	FM	FF	FR	TK	SK	YDS	IR	YDS	PD	PTS	TD	RA	YDS	AVG	LG	TD	REC	YDS	AVG	LG	TD	PR	YDS	AVG	LG	KOR	YDS	AVG	LG
7	Years	88	13		5	15						390	65	523	2449	4.7	50	54	143	1467	10.3	62	11					5	39	7.8	16
BOB MARSHALL Bob T-G-E 6'0 235 Michigan; McGill B: 1927																															
1951	TOR	8																													
1952	TOR	7																													
1953	TOR	3																													
3	Years	18																													
CHARLES MARSHALL Charles Lee (Tank) DT 6'4 245 Texas A&M B: 1/6/1955 Dallas, TX Draft: 3-72 1977 NYJ Pro: N																															
1978	WPG	3																													
DAVID MARSHALL David Mark LB 6'3 220 Eastern Michigan B: 1/31/1961 Cleveland, OH Draft: TD 1984 MIC-USFL Pro: N																															
1985	TOR	4	0		1				1	11																					
1986	TOR	18	0		5		3.0		3	23																					
2	Years	22	0		6		3.0		4	34																					
GREG MARSHALL Gregory Edward DT-DE 6'3 257 Oregon State B: 9/9/1956 Beverly, MA Draft: 7-186 1978 PHI Pro: N																															
1980	OTT	16	0		1																										
1981	OTT*	16	0		1		9.0					6	1																		
1982	OTT+	12					7.0																								
1983	OTT*	16	0		3		15.5																								
1984	OTT+	16	0		2		16.5																								
1985	OTT	15					6.0																								
1986	OTT	16	0		3		8.0																								
1987	OTT	13	0		3	23	9.0																								
8	Years	120	0		13	23	71.0					6	1																		
GREG MARSHALL Gregory D. RB 6'0 225 Western Ontario B: 4/16/1959 Guelph, ON Draft: TE 1982 EDM																															
1983	EDM	1																													
HERB MARSHALL Herbert Lenford DB-SE 6'3 204 Cameron B: 8/20/1949 Corpus Christi, TX Draft: 14-363 1973 WAS Pro: W																															
1973	OTT	3																													
JIM MARSHALL James Lawrence T 6'3 239 Ohio State B: 12/30/1937 Danville, KY Draft: SS 1960 HOU; 4B-44 1960 CLE Pro: N																															
1959	SAS	9										6	1						3	43	14.3	24	1								
JIM MARSHALL James Carl CB 6'0 187 Jackson State B: 9/8/1952 Magnolia, MS Pro: N																															
1975	SAS+	16	1		1				7	172		6	1											13	84	6.5	21	6	212	35.3	40
1976	SAS	13	1		0				3	40		6	1											2	14	7.0	10				
1977	TOR	13							3	42														1	0	0.0	0				
1978	TOR	16							2	0																		1	17	17.0	17
1979	TOR	6	0		1				2	0																					
1979	SAS	2																													
1979	MTL	3							1	0																					
1979	Year	8	0		1				3	0																					
1981	MTL	5	0		1				1	28		6	1																		
1982	MTL	3																													
7	Years	72	2		3				19	282		18	3											16	98	6.1	21	7	229	32.7	40
VINCENT MARSHALL Vincent Alexander WR-SB 5'8 176 Houston B: 11/12/1983 Ennis, TX																															
2007	SAS	3				0																									
2008	SAS	5	0	1	0	0						6	1						9	145	16.1	32	1	6	67	11.2	18	7	160	22.9	31
2	Years	8	0	1	0	0						6	1						9	145	16.1	32	1	6	67	11.2	18	7	160	22.9	31
WILLIS MARSHALL Willis Thurman, III WR 5'10 195 Youngstown State B: 8/12/1975 Detroit, MI																															
1998	CAL	8				2													17	154	9.1	18	0	3	25	8.3	9				
1999	CAL	2				0													1	7	7.0	7	0	3	87	29.0	59				
2	Years	10				2													18	161	8.9	18	0	6	112	18.7	59				
PETE MARTELL Peter LB-RB 6'1 215 St. Francis Xavier B: 4/23/1959 Draft: 7-61 1981 WPG																															
1981	WPG	3																													
1982	MTL	6																													
1983	MTL	5																													
3	Years	14																													
ANDREW MARTIN Andrew G. WR-DB 6'1 200 Cornell B: 3/31/1970 Toronto, ON Draft: 4-28 1992 WPG																															
1992	WPG	14	0		1	3													3	39	13.0	20	0					3	29	9.7	19
1993	WPG	5	0		1	1													2	11	5.5	6	0								
1994	OTT	3				2													2	15	7.5	8	0								
1995	OTT	2				2													2	14	7.0	8	0								
1995	HAM	10				10																									
1995	Year	12				12													2	14	7.0	8	0								
1996	HAM	4				1																									
5	Years	28	0		2	19													9	79	8.8	20	0					3	29	9.7	19
ANDY MARTIN Andy QB 175 none B: 1926																															
1946	TOR	5																													
BILLY MARTIN William Vance OHB 5'11 197 Minnesota B: 6/6/1938 Chicago, IL Draft: 4-43(f) 1960 CHIB; 30- 1961 BUF Pro: N																															
1965	EDM	8	1		0									46	155	3.4	38	0	19	240	12.6	37	0	5	21	4.2	7	10	243	24.3	31
1966	WPG	6	2		1									8	64	8.0	25	0						23	218	9.5	20	3	48	16.0	36
1966	TOR	6	2		1							6	1	47	184	3.9	21	1	9	108	12.0	33	0					9	205	22.8	37
1966	Year	12	4		2							6	1	55	248	4.5	25	1	9	108	12.0	33	0					12	253	21.1	37
2	Years	14	5		2							6	1	101	403	4.0	38	1	28	348	12.4	37	0	28	239	8.5	20	22	496	22.5	37
BOB MARTIN Robert S. DE 6'5 242 Washington B: 3/30/1953 Portland, OR Draft: 11-269 1975 GB																															
1976	CAL	8	0		1							6	1																		
1977	CAL	7																													
2	Years	15	0		1							6	1																		
CECIL MARTIN Cecil F. (Zeke) QB 6'1 185 North Texas B: 9/26/1924 Denton, TX D: 11/27/2006 Fort Worth, TX Draft: 23-268 1951 WAS																															
1951	HAM	2																													
CHRIS MARTIN Chris DB 5'11 190 Washington State B: 9/18/1976 New York, NY																															
2004	HAM	10	0	0	1	26	2.0	9.0	2	2	2																	9	178	19.8	45
2005	HAM	18	0	3	1	49	2.0	11.0	2	54	8																	18	323	17.9	27
2006	HAM	2				10																									
3	Years	30	0	3	2	85	4.0	20.0	4	56	10																	27	501	18.6	45
DAVID MARTIN David Earl DB 5'9 187 Villanova B: 3/15/1959 Philadelphia, PA Draft: 9B-240 1981 DET Pro: NU																															
1986	MTL	2																						10	92	9.2	18				
DERRICK MARTIN Derrick Roy DB 6'0 185 Arizona State; San Jose State B: 5/31/1957 Los Angeles, CA Pro: NU																															
1980	TOR	11							2	12														4	17	4.3	12	6	112	18.7	24
ERROL MARTIN Errol LB 6'2 210 Utah B: 3/25/1968 St. Vincent Draft: 2-14 1992 EDM																															
1993	EDM	18	0		1	39	6.0	53.0																							
1994	EDM	18	0		2	30	5.0	43.0																							
1995	EDM	18	0		2	29	7.0	54.0																				1	1	1.0	1
1996	EDM	17	0		2	23	4.0	21.0																							
1997	EDM	18	0	1	1	23	4.0	35.0																							
1998	EDM	18	0	0	2	29	2.0	12.0																							
2000	TOR	2				0																									
7	Years	109	0	1	10	173	28.0	218.0																				1	1	1.0	1
GEORGE MARTIN George LB 6'1 210 Bishop's B: 5/21/1962 Montreal, QC																															
1982	MTL	6																													
1983	MTL	1																													
2	Years	7																													
JACK MARTIN John E Regina Dales Jrs.																															
1946	SAS	1																													
JOHN MARTIN John (Tweet) RB 5'8 185 Sequoias JC; Memphis B: 8/31/1971 Homestead, FL																															
1995	MEM	5	3		0	2						6	1	34	160	4.7	15	1	4	27	6.8	8	0								

Year	Team	GP	FM	FF	FR	TK	SK	YDS	IR	YDS	PD	PTS	TD	RA	YDS	AVG	LG	TD	REC	YDS	AVG	LG	TD	PR	YDS	AVG	LG	KOR	YDS	AVG	LG
KENNARD MARTIN Kennard O. RB 5'11 205 North Carolina B: 6/10/1968																															
1989	CAL	5	2		1	2						6	1	28	139	5.0	13	0	5	40	8.0	18	1	12	113	9.4	25	8	175	21.9	50
1990	BC	9	2		1	0						18	3	45	207	4.6	18	2	19	168	8.8	16	1	4	8	2.0	8	19	362	19.1	35
2	Years	14	4		2	2						24	4	73	346	4.7	18	2	24	208	8.7	18	2	16	121	7.6	25	27	537	19.9	50
MANNY MARTIN Emanuel C. CB 5'11 184 Alabama State B: 7/31/1969 Miami, FL Pro: N																															
1994	OTT	3				15			1	0	2																				
1995	OTT	17	0		1	49	1.0	11.0	2	12	10	6	1											1	33	33.0	33				
2002	BC	10	0	0	1	16	1.0				2																				
3	Years	30	0	0	2	84	2.0	11.0	3	12	14	6	1											1	33	33.0	33				
MAURICE MARTIN Maurice DB 6'2 187 Toronto B: 10/3/1962 London, England Draft: 1-4 1984 OTT																															
1984	OTT	12	0		1				1	0																					
1985	OTT	5																													
2	Years	17	0		1				1	0																					
MEL MARTIN Melvin LB Ferrum JC; William & Mary																															
1979	SAS	3																													
MIKE MARTIN Edward DE-DT 6'3 240 Washington State B: 8/3/1940 Beaumont, TX Draft: 20-154 1962 DEN; 17-236 1962 PHI																															
1962	BC	16																													
1963	BC	13							1																						
1964	BC	16																													
1965	BC	16	0		3				1																						
1966	BC	16																													
1967	BC	16	0		1																										
1968	BC	16	1		2				1	26																					
7	Years	109	1		6				3	26																					
MIKE MARTIN Mike FL-QB 6'0 185 Akron B: 6/16/1944 Toronto, ON																															
1968	MTL	3																													
MOE MARTIN Moe FB-HB 6'1 190 NDG Maple Leafs Jrs.; Montreal Lakeshore Flyers Ints. B: 1932																															
1953	SAS	10												4	3	0.8		0													
1954	SAS	10												1	15	15.0	15	0													
1955	SAS	16												21	66	3.1	7	0	1	-1	-1.0	-1	0					1	25	25.0	25
1956	SAS	9							1	0				3	-1	-0.3	0	0										3	25	8.3	19
1957	SAS	10												4	25	6.3	16	0	2	31	15.5	20	0					2	20	10.0	16
5	Years	55							1	0				33	108	3.3	16	0	3	30	10.0	20	0					6	70	11.7	25
NELSON MARTIN Nelson, Jr. S-WR 6'0 185 Etobicoke Argos Jrs.; Simon Fraser; Seneca B: 8/24/1958 Toronto, ON Draft: 1-5 1981 BC																															
1981	BC	16	0		2		1.0		3	7														1	12	12.0	12				
1982	BC	16	0		1				1	19									1	12	12.0	12	0								
1983	BC	16	0		2				4	67																					
1984	BC	16	0		2				2	23														1	8	8.0	8				
1985	BC	16	1		2		3.0		2	9														1	4	4.0	4				
1986	BC	18	0		1		2.0		4	58														2	7	3.5	7				
1987	BC+	18	0		3	59	1.0		8	142		12	2																		
7	Years	116	1		13	59	7.0		24	325		12	2						1	12	12.0	12	0	5	31	6.2	12				
PAUL MARTIN Paul DT 6'3 245 South Carolina B: 10/6/1961 Miami, FL																															
1984	MTL	10			2		3.5																								
1985	MTL	5					2.0																								
2	Years	15	0		2		5.5																								
PETE MARTIN Peter LB 6'0 205 Western Ontario; East York Argos Srs. B: 10/10/1940 Toronto, ON Draft: 1-7 1964 OTT																															
1965	TOR	14	0		1				1	0																		2	15	7.5	12
1966	TOR	14	0		3																							1	0	0.0	0
1967	TOR	14	0		2				1	23																					
1968	TOR	14	0		1				1	0																					
1969	TOR	14							1	4																					
1970	TOR	14	0		1				1	7																					
1971	TOR	14							2	25																					
1972	TOR	6																													
8	Years	104	0		8				7	59																		3	15	5.0	12
PETE MARTIN Peter G 5'11 203 Regina Jrs. B: 1920																															
1946	SAS	8																													
1947	SAS	4																													
1948	SAS	11																													
1949	SAS	13																													
1950	SAS	14																													
1951	SAS	9																													
6	Years	59																													
P.J. MARTIN Peter J. FB 6'0 229 Wilfrid Laurier B: 5/1/1970 Mississauga, ON Draft: 2-12 1993 HAM																															
1993	HAM	16	0		1	3								3	21	7.0	14	0	1	11	11.0	11	0	1	8	8.0	8				
1994	HAM	9				7																									
1995	TOR	18				10								1	21	21.0	21	0													
3	Years	43	0		1	20								4	42	10.5	21	0	1	11	11.0	11	0	1	8	8.0	8				
RICKY MARTIN Roderick Darryl WR 6'2 205 New Mexico B: 10/26/1958 Los Angeles, CA Draft: 5-127 1981 PIT Pro: U																															
1982	WPG	3	1		2							6	1						10	141	14.1	30	1								
1983	WPG	2																	4	68	17.0	29	0								
2	Years	5	1		2							6	1						14	209	14.9	30	1								
RICKY MARTIN Ricky RB 5'10 185 Middle Tennessee State B: 8/1/1969 Rome, GA																															
1991	HAM	3	3		2	0								30	121	4.0	21	0	5	80	16.0	31	0					1	14	14.0	14
RIP MARTIN Ken C 6'0 190 B: 1919																															
1948	HAM	12																													
ROBERT MARTIN Robert																															
1969	MTL	4																													
RONALD MARTIN Ronald (Rusty) OT-C 6'1 240 Oklahoma State B: 1945																															
1966	EDM	16	0		3																										
TEE MARTIN Tamaurice Nigel QB 6'1 225 Tennessee B: 7/25/1978 Mobile, AL Draft: 5B-163 2000 PIT Pro: EN																															
2004	WPG	7				0																									
2005	WPG	18	2	0	1	0								13	64	4.9	15	0													
2	Years	25	2	0	1	0								13	64	4.9	15	0													
TRACY MARTIN Tracy Aaron WR 6'3 205 North Dakota B: 12/4/1964 Draft: 6-161 1987 NYJ Pro: N																															
1991	SAS	3				5													1	4	4.0	4	0								
WILLIE MARTIN Willie OG-OT 6'5 260 Northeastern State B: 4/27/1951 Draft: 13-313 1973 HOU																															
1973	EDM	16	0		1																										
1974	EDM	16			1																										
1975	EDM*	16	0		1																							2	0	0.0	0
1976	EDM	16																													
1977	EDM	16	0		1																										
1978	EDM	16																													
1979	HAM	13																													
1980	HAM+	15																													
1981	TOR	7																													
1982	WPG	4																													
10	Years	135	0		4																							2	0	0.0	0
MARTY MARTINELLO E.M. MG-OG 5'10 225 none B: 1/6/1931 Sydney, NS																															
1954	MTL	14																													
1955	MTL	12																													

Year	Team	GP	FM	FF	FR	TK	SK	YDS	IR	YDS	PD	PTS	TD	RA	YDS	AVG	LG	TD	REC	YDS	AVG	LG	TD	PR	YDS	AVG	LG	KOR	YDS	AVG	LG
1956	MTL	14																													
1957	MTL	14																													
1958	BC	14																													
1959	BC	11																													
1960	TOR+	13							1	6																					
1961	TOR+	14							1	39														1	0	0.0	0				
1962	TOR	14																													
1963	TOR	14																													
1964	TOR	14	0		1																										
1965	TOR	2																													
1965	HAM	7	0		1							6	1																		
1965	Year	9										6	1																		
1966	HAM	14	0		1																										
13	Years	164	0		3				2	45		6	1											1	0	0.0	0				
JOHN MARTINI John LB 6'2 220 Toronto B: 9/20/1954 Draft: 1-8 1977 HAM																															
1977	HAM	16	0		2				2	21																					
1978	HAM	16	0		1																										
1979	HAM	9																													
1979	WPG	5																													
1979	Year	14																													
1980	TOR	9							1	8																					
1981	TOR	7																										1	7	7.0	7
5	Years	57	0		3				3	29																		1	7	7.0	7
SANTO MARTINI Santo T-E 6'3 225 Toronto B: 1935 Draft: 1B-8 1957 CAL																															
1959	TOR	11																													
TONY MARTINO Anthony P-K 6'0 190 Renfrew Trojans Jrs.; Eastern Arizona JC; Kent State B: 6/9/1966 Kelowna, BC Draft: 1-7 1988 BC																															
1988	BC	4	2		0	0						14	0																		
1988	OTT	2				0						5	0																		
1988	Year	6	2		0	0						19	0																		
1990	BC	5				0						57	0																		
1992	CAL	18	1		0	2						7	0	3	49	16.3	22	0													
1993	CAL	18				2						3	0	2	29	14.5	16	0													
1994	CAL+	18				0						5	0	1	14	14.0	14	0													
1995	CAL	18	0		2	1						7	0																		
1996	CAL+	18				2						18	0																		
1997	CAL+	18				1						7	0	1	14	14.0	14	0													
1998	CAL*	18	1	0	0	1						10	0																		
1999	CAL	10	2	0	0	1						3	0	1	7	7.0	7	0													
2000	CAL+	18	2	0	0	0						7	0																		
2001	TOR	4	1	0	0	0						1	0																		
2001	BC	5				0						1	0																		
2001	Year	9	1	0	0	0						2	0																		
2002	BC	18	1	0	0	0						3	0	2	18	9.0	11	0													
13	Years	185	10	0	2	10						148	0	10	131	13.1	22	0													
GRANT MARTINSEN Grant DB 6'0 199 Utah State B: 1945 Draft: 15-389 1967 BUF																															
1967	BC	3																										1	27	27.0	27
MIKE MARUSKA Mike HB 5'10 184 Westmount Jrs.; NDG Maple Leafs Jrs. B: 1930 Regina, SK																															
1952	SAS	11										15	3	32	85	2.7	8	1	4	69	17.3	42	1	17	90	5.3	18	22	671	30.5	89
1953	SAS	6												9	22	2.4		0	3	18	6.0		0					2	55	27.5	
1954	SAS	6												3	12	4.0	10	0										2	30	15.0	24
1955	OTT	7																						4	36	9.0	10				
4	Years	30										15	3	44	119	2.7	10	1	7	87	12.4	42	1	21	126	6.0	18	26	756	29.1	89
ALEX MASH Alex DE 6'2 250 Georgia Southern B: 12/16/1970 Thomasville, GA Draft: 6-46 1995 OTT																															
1994	SHR	9	0		1	16	1.0	7.0				6	1																		
1995	SHR	11				31	1.0	7.0			1																				
2	Years	20	0		1	47	2.0	14.0			1	6	1																		
JOE MASNAGHETTI Joseph L., Jr. T 6'2 265 Marquette B: 10/26/1926 Bessemer, MI D: 9/30/2005 Grafton, WI Draft: 12-136 1952 CHIC																															
1952	SAS	3										1	0																		
KEVIN MASON Kevin M. QB 6'3 200 Syracuse B: 9/25/1972 Buffalo, NY																															
1996	SAS	5	1		1	0						12	2	28	163	5.8	25	2													
1997	SAS	18	8	0	0	3						18	3	53	387	7.3	40	3													
1998	WPG	8	3	0	1	0								20	125	6.3	20	0													
1999	EDM	8	1	0	1	0						6	1	37	282	7.6	31	1													
4	Years	39	13	0	3	3						36	6	138	957	6.9	40	6													
LARRY MASON Larry Darnell RB 5'11 205 Southern Mississippi; Troy B: 3/21/1961 Birmingham, AL Pro: NU																															
1985	CAL	5	1		1							12	2	51	247	4.8	39	1	18	152	8.4	23	1								
CHRISTIAN MASOTTI Christian SB 6'2 185 McGill B: 3/8/1968 Stoney Creek, ON Draft: 2-15 1991 EDM																															
1991	EDM	6				1													4	83	20.8	45	0								
PAUL MASOTTI Paul WR 6'0 185 Hamilton Hurricanes Jrs.; Acadia B: 3/10/1965 Hamilton, ON Draft: 2-15 1988 TOR																															
1988	TOR	7				1						6	1						2	50	25.0	33	1	18	127	7.1	39	1	25	25.0	25
1989	TOR	17	1		0	2						24	4						31	443	14.3	55	4								
1990	TOR	18				2						30	5						37	592	16.0	60	5					1	0	0.0	0
1991	TOR	17	2		3	11						12	2						23	360	15.7	36	2	1	5	5.0	5	1	4	4.0	6
1992	TOR	18	1		2	6						20	3						44	801	18.2	45	2					1	14	14.0	14
1993	TOR	12	1		1	4						18	3						36	606	16.8	72	3								
1994	TOR*	17				2						54	9						67	1280	19.1	67	9								
1995	TOR	16	4		0	4						18	3						70	1336	19.1	80	3	1	0	0.0	0				
1996	TOR+	16	1		0	0						42	7						73	1023	14.0	97	7								
1997	TOR+	18	2	0	0	2						30	5						77	1011	13.1	51	5								
1998	TOR+	18	4	0	0	4						12	2						66	897	13.6	66	2								
1999	TOR	16				1						6	1						30	373	12.4	31	1								
12	Years	190	16	0	6	39						272	45						556	8772	15.8	97	44	20	132	6.6	39	4	43	10.8	25
BILL MASSEY Bill RB 6'2 215 Hawaii B: 1949																															
1971	MTL	7	6		1							1	0	101	655	6.5	66	0	8	69	8.6	19	0					1	24	24.0	24
RICK MASSIE Richard Ray WR 6'1 190 Kentucky B: 1/16/1960 Paris, KY Pro: N																															
1984	CAL	9																	15	233	15.5	45	0								
CARL MASSIN Carl T 6'2 235 East York Argos B: 1935																															
1956	TOR	5																													
1957	TOR	12																													
2	Years	17																													
PASCAL MASSON Pascal DH-S 5'11 180 Laval B: 8/14/1979 Repentigny, QC Draft: 2B-16 2004 CAL																															
2004	CAL	17				14																									
2005	CAL	14				8					1																				
2006	CAL	18				1					1																				
2007	MTL	9				4																									
2008	MTL	4	0	1	1	9																									
5	Years	62	0	1	1	36					2																				
NORM MASTERS Norman Donald T 6'2 249 Michigan State B: 9/19/1933 Detroit, MI D: 4/19/2011 Bloomfield Hills, MI Draft: 2-18 1956 CHIC Pro: N																															
1956	BC	15	0		2														1	17	17.0	17	0								
JORDAN MATECHUK Jordan LB 5'10 238 Regina Thunder Jrs.; Winnipeg Rifles Jrs.; Victoria Rebels Jrs. B: 8/22/1985 Yorkton, SK																															
2008	HAM	5				3																									
2009	HAM	18				16																						2	2	1.0	5

Year	Team	GP	FM	FF	FR	TK	SK	YDS	IR	YDS	PD	PTS	TD	RA	YDS	AVG	LG	TD	REC	YDS	AVG	LG	TD	PR	YDS	AVG	LG	KOR	YDS	AVG	LG
2010	HAM	18	1	0	0	4																						1	2	2.0	2
3	Years	41	1	0	0	23																						3	4	1.3	5
JIM MATHENY James Charles C 6'1 228 UCLA B: 2/16/1936 Long Beach, CA Draft: 20-231 1958 CHIC																															
1957	TOR	12							1	10																					
WAYNE MATHERNE Wayne J. CB 6'1 190 Louisiana-Monroe B: 5/6/1949																															
1971	BC	16			1				7	119				3	-3	-1.0	2	0	1	9	9.0	9	0	1	4	4.0	4	13	316	24.3	35
1972	BC	16	0		2				2	64																					
1973	BC	9							2	31																					
1974	BC	16	0		2				4	32														1	0	0.0	0	1	17	17.0	17
1975	EDM	7							1	23														20	129	6.5	20	1	35	35.0	35
1976	EDM	12							2	18				2	8	4.0	5	0	1	12	12.0	12	0								
6	Years	76	0		5				18	287				5	5	1.0	5	0	2	21	10.5	12	0	22	133	6.0	20	15	368	24.5	35
FRANK MATHERS Frank Sydney HB-FW 6'1 182 B: 3/29/1924 Winnipeg, MB D: 2/9/2005 Hershey, PA																															
1946	OTT	12										10	2										2								
RILEY MATHESON Riley M. (Rattlesnake) G 6'2 207 Cameron*; Texas-El Paso B: 12/12/1914 D: 6//1987 Paraguay Pro: AN																															
1949	CAL+	13										2	0																		
1950	CAL+	11																													
2	Years	24										2	0																		
CLAUDE MATHEWS Claude DE-DT 6'2 254 Auburn B: 1/15/1958 Phenix City, AL Draft: 11-297 1981 HOU																															
1982	HAM	5	0		1																										
1983	HAM	6					3.5																								
2	Years	11	0		1		3.5																								
RAY MATHEWS Raymond Dyral HB 6'0 185 Clemson B: 2/26/1929 Dayton, PA Draft: 7-81 1951 PIT Pro: N																															
1961	CAL	3																	10	186	18.6	40	0								
DAVE MATHIESON David Michael QB 6'0 199 Washington State B: 4/20/1941 Los Angeles, CA Draft: 22-173(f) 1963 DEN; 6B-81(f) 1963 CHIB																															
1967	BC	1	1		0									2	7	3.5	7	0													
DEDRIC MATHIS Dedric Ronshell CB 5'10 188 Houston B: 9/26/1973 Cuero, TX Draft: 2-51 1996 IND Pro: N																															
2001	HAM	18	0	0	1	32			1	44	6	6	1																		
2002	HAM	16				31			4	7	11																				
2003	HAM	18	0	2	1	53			1	0	5																				
2004	HAM	16				35			1	0	4																				
2005	HAM	8	0	0	1	18					1																				
5	Years	76	0	2	3	169			7	51	27	6	1																		
JEROME MATHIS Jerome Alvon WR 5'11 189 Hampton B: 6/26/1983 Petersburg, VA Draft: 4-114 2005 HOU Pro: N																															
2009	TOR	2				0													3	22	7.3	10	0								
MARK MATHIS Mark E. CB 5'9 178 Liberty B: 8/23/1965 Mount Clemens, MI Pro: N																															
1989	EDM	4				14			3	12																					
1990	EDM	11				32	1.0		4	22														1	7	7.0	7				
1991	EDM	11	0		1	42			1	0														1	2	2.0	5				
1992	BC	4	0		2	12			1	25														6	95	15.8	61				
4	Years	30	0		3	100	1.0		9	59														8	104	13.0	61				
REGGIE MATHIS Reginald Levi LB 6'2 220 Navarro JC; Oklahoma B: 3/18/1956 Chattanooga, TN Draft: 2-38 1979 NO Pro: NU																															
1985	HAM	5	0		1																										
BRENT MATICH Brent P-K 6'1 200 Calgary B: 12/5/1966 Calgary, AB Draft: 6-41 1988 OTT																															
1989	CAL+	18	6		2	0						7	0	1	25	25.0	25	0													
1990	CAL+	18	4		1	0						5	0																		
1991	CAL+	16	1		0	2						6	0																		
1992	SAS	10	2		0	0						2	0																		
1993	SAS	16	1		0	0						7	0	1	16	16.0	16	0													
1994	SAS	18	4		2	2						8	0																		
1995	SAS	18	2		1	0						2	0																		
1996	SAS	18	5		0	1						5	0																		
8	Years	132	25		6	5						42	0	2	41	20.5	25	0													
TOM MATIJACIC Tom DE 6'1 255 Washington; Portland State B: 11/5/1976 Portland, OR																															
2002	HAM	1				0																									
MIKE MATOCHA Michael Allen DT 6'4 250 Texas-Arlington B: 2/15/1958 La Grange, TX Draft: 11-295 1980 WAS Pro: U																															
1980	SAS	3																													
JOHN MATSKO John L. C 5'10 205 Michigan State B: 12/20/1933 St. Michael, PA D: 12/24/2010 Johnstown, PA																															
1959	CAL	9																													
KRISTIAN MATTE Kristian OT 6'4 296 Concordia (Quebec) B: 9/3/1985 St. Hubert, QC Draft: 1-7 2010 MTL																															
2010	MTL	1				0																									
KEILAN MATTHEWS Keilan V. LB 6'2 220 Washington; Sacramento State B: 12/28/1965 Sacramento, CA																															
1993	SAC	12	1		6	60	1.0	10.0	1	12																		1	13	13.0	13
KEN MATTHEWS Kenneth WR 6'0 180 Rio Hondo JC; Long Beach State B: 3/27/1951 Pro: W																															
1973	TOR	1																													
DON MATTINGLEY Don C 6'1 233 none B: 1931																															
1951	WPG	14																													
RANDY MATTINGLY Randy Charles QB 6'4 206 Evansville B: 5/15/1951 Evansville, IN Draft: 4B-100 1973 CLE																															
1974	SAS	16	2		0									9	76	8.4	17	0													
1975	SAS	16												4	9	2.3	4	0													
1976	HAM	3												1	0	0.0	0	0													
3	Years	35	2		0									14	85	6.1	17	0													
STEVE MATTISON Steve FB 6'1 225 Illinois B: 12/28/1969 Kingston, Jamaica Draft: 1-15 1995 CAL																															
1995	CAL	1				1																									
TOM MAUDLIN Warren Thomas QB 6'2 185 Menlo JC; Southern California B: 7/28/1936 Los Angeles, CA																															
1962	TOR	7												1	2	2.0	2	0													
1963	EDM	2	1		0									8	36	4.5	17	0													
2	Years	9	1		0									9	38	4.2	17	0													
JOE MAULDIN Joseph QB 6'2 235 Los Angeles Valley JC; Missouri Western B: 11/26/1970																															
1994	HAM	2				0								1	3	3.0	3	0													
JACK MAULTSBY John Warren T 6'2 230 North Carolina B: 4/11/1931 Maysville, NC D: 5/2/2003 Clinton, NC Draft: 12-142 1954 LARM																															
1956	TOR	2																													
MIKE MAURER Mike FB 6'0 195 Regina Rams Jrs. B: 11/6/1975 Saskatoon, SK																															
1997	SAS	4				0																									
1998	SAS	13				14								4	28	7.0	15	0													
1999	SAS	18	0	0	1	20								1	4	4.0	4	0	1	6	6.0	6	0								
2000	SAS	5				3																						2	14	7.0	12
2000	BC	7				6								1	0	0.0	0	0													
2000	Year	12				9								1	0	0.0	0	0										2	14	7.0	12
2001	BC	17	2	2	0	35								1	0	0.0	0	0	1	8	8.0	8	0								
2002	OTT	10	0	0	1	12						6	1	1	3	3.0	3	1	7	72	10.3	20	0					1	0	0.0	0
2003	OTT	18				7						6	1	12	49	4.1	15	0	16	214	13.4	28	1					1	9	9.0	9
2004	OTT	16	1	0	0	9								4	5	1.3	6	0	8	91	11.4	22	0								
2005	EDM	17	0	1	0	20								5	15	3.0	4	0	12	76	6.3	10	0					1	10	10.0	10
2006	EDM	18	1	0	0	23						6	1	5	11	2.2	6	0	16	155	9.7	19	1								
2007	EDM	18				20						6	1						2	14	7.0	11	1					1	2	2.0	2
2008	EDM	4				3																									
2009	EDM	2				0													1	7	7.0	7	0								
13	Years	160	4	3	2	172						24	4	34	115	3.4	15	1	64	643	10.0	28	3					6	35	5.8	12
HAL MAUTHE Harold FW-HB 5'7 160 Winnipeg Light Infantry Jrs. B: 1929																															
1951	WPG	13												9	26	2.9		0	2	25	12.5		0	18	179	9.9		3	49	16.3	
1952	WPG	15												2	22	11.0	19	0	1	10	10.0	10	0								

Year	Team	GP	FM	FF	FR	TK	SK	YDS	IR	YDS	PD	PTS	TD	RA	YDS	AVG	LG	TD	REC	YDS	AVG	LG	TD	PR	YDS	AVG	LG	KOR	YDS	AVG	LG
2	Years	28												11	48	4.4	19	0	3	35	11.7	10	0	18	179	9.9	0	3	49	16.3	
ROB MAVER Rob K 6'0 214 Guelph B: 3/12/1986 Brampton, ON Draft: 1-5 2010 CAL																															
2010	CAL	18				2						185	0																		
2011	CAL	1				0						6	0																		
2	Years	19				2						191	0																		
DENNIS MAVRIN Dennis DB 5'10 204 York B: 8/21/1979 Toronto, ON																															
2003	SAS	18				18																									
2004	SAS	17				18																									
2	Years	35				36																									
DEMETRIOUS MAXIE Demetrious O. DE-FB 6'2 265 Long Beach CC; Texas-El Paso B: 10/18/1973 Florence, LA																															
1995	BAL	8				24	3.0	20.0			3																				
1996	MTL	10				19	1.0	8.0																							
1996	TOR	5				9	1.0	4.0			1																				
1996	Year	15				28	2.0	12.0																							
1997	TOR	18	0	2	0	29	7.0	53.0			1																				
1998	TOR	18	0	3	0	40	8.0	51.0						2	6	3.0	5	0													
1999	TOR*	18	0	2	2	29	11.0	72.0			1	6	1	3	34	11.3	30	1													
2000	SAS*	18				29	11.0	72.0	1	7	1																				
2001	SAS	8	0	2	0	15	1.0	3.0			1																				
2002	TOR	8				22	1.0	2.0			1																				
2003	CAL	18	0	1	3	28	8.0	49.0																							
2004	CAL	6				10	6.0	51.0																							
2005	CAL	12	0	1	0	14	5.0	29.0																							
2006	CAL	18	0	1	0	22	7.0	43.0			1																				
2007	CAL	2				1																									
13	Years	162	0	10	5	291	70.0	457.0	1	7	10	6	1	5	40	8.0	30	1													
VERNON MAXWELL Vernon Leroy LB 6'2 237 Arizona State B: 10/25/1961 Birmingham, AL Draft: 2-29 1983 BAL; TD 1983 ARI-USFL Pro: N																															
1991	HAM	9	1		1	25			1	4																					
1992	HAM	5				12			1	39		6	1																		
2	Years	14	1		1	37			2	43		6	1																		
ADRIAN MAYES Adrian Anthony LB-DB 6'1 215 Louisiana State B: 11/17/1980 Hattiesburg, MS Pro: N																															
2007	TOR	13				19	1.0	4.0																				1	12	12.0	12
2008	TOR	18				39					3																	1	8	8.0	8
2	Years	31				58	1.0	4.0			3																	2	20	10.0	12
WILLIAM MAYES William DL 6'3 265 Louisiana Tech B: 3/28/1976																															
1999	EDM	1				3																									
CURTIS MAYFIELD Curtis Edward WR 5'11 174 Oklahoma State B: 3/23/1968 Dallas, TX Draft: 10-253 1991 DEN Pro: E																															
1994	LV	17	1		0	1						74	12	1	1	1.0	1	0	61	1202	19.7	81	12								
1995	SHR	18	0		3	16						18	3						58	846	14.6	55	2					2	2	1.0	2
1996	SAS	18	1		0	2						36	6						51	963	18.9	95	6					9	152	16.9	28
1997	SAS	18				5						24	4						36	699	19.4	86	4	7	97	13.9	40	8	196	24.5	37
1998	SAS	14	3	0	2	2						42	7	1	4	4.0	4	0	42	703	16.7	73	6	17	132	7.8	32	10	293	29.3	93
1999	SAS	16	1	0	0	3						72	12	1	15	15.0	15	0	53	863	16.3	65	9	31	403	13.0	69	16	234	14.6	21
6	Years	101	6	0	5	29						266	44	3	20	6.7	15	0	301	5276	17.5	95	39	55	632	11.5	69	45	877	19.5	93
DON MAYNARD Donald Rogers HB 6'0 180 Rice; Texas-El Paso B: 1/25/1935 Crosbyton, TX Draft: 9-109(f) 1957 NYG Pro: NW																															
1959	HAM	1																	1	10	10.0	10	0								
SHAWN MAYNE Shawn A. DE-DT 6'3 247 Connecticut B: 5/5/1983 Montreal, QC Draft: 3-18 2006 HAM																															
2006	WPG	2				0																									
2007	WPG	5				4																									
2008	WPG	18				11	1.0	6.0																							
2009	WPG	7				6																									
2009	MTL	6	0	1	0	6	1.0	8.0																							
2009	Year	13	0	1	0	12	1.0	8.0																							
2011	CAL	3				1																									
5	Years	35	0	1	0	28	2.0	14.0																							
LYNEIL MAYO Lyneil W. LB 6'0 235 San Jose State B: 1/29/1968 Chicago, IL Pro: E																															
1991	BC	8	0		2	9	6.0																								
MIKE MAYOCK Michael Francis, Jr. DB 6'2 198 Boston College B: 8/14/1958 Philadelphia, PA Draft: 10-265 1981 PIT Pro: N																															
1981	TOR	1																													
TIM MAYPRAY Timothy Wayne, II WR 5'8 170 Virginia Military Institute B: 5/13/1988 Madisonville, KY																															
2010	MTL	14	0	0	1	1						12	2	1	2	2.0	2	0	2	30	15.0	23	0	43	337	7.8	25	44	1037	23.6	86
2011	MTL	8				0						6	1						1	55	55.0	55	1	23	207	9.0	22	15	329	21.9	45
2	Years	22	0	0	1	1						18	3	1	2	2.0	2	0	3	85	28.3	55	1	66	544	8.2	25	59	1366	23.2	86
JERMAINE MAYS Jermaine CB 5'11 198 Minnesota B: 7/13/1979 Miami, FL Pro: E																															
2006	TOR	8				17			2	59	1																				
2007	TOR	3				0																									
2008	TOR	3				4																						1	14	14.0	14
3	Years	14				21			2	59	1																	1	14	14.0	14
TOM MAYSON Tom HB 5'10 180 Alberta B: 2/21/1928 D: 10/18/2010 Edmonton, AB																															
1949	EDM	2																													
1950	EDM	1																													
2	Years	3																													
VIC MAYSON Victor FW-HB 5'10 172 Edmonton Maple Leafs Jrs.																															
1952	EDM	9										10	2	2	9	4.5	6	1	1	10	10.0	10	1								
1953	EDM	15							1	46																					
2	Years	24							1	46		10	2	2	9	4.5	6	1	1	10	10.0	10	1								
DON MAZUR Donald J. OT-C 6'1 230 Winnipeg Light Infantry Jrs. B: 1932																															
1953	WPG	15																													
JOHNNY MAZUR John Edward QB 6'2 216 Notre Dame B: 6/17/1930 Plymouth, PA																															
1954	BC	12	3									5	1	34	-53	-1.6	13	1													
WALT MAZUR Walter J. T 6'0 240 Penn State B: 1/23/1934 D: 6/27/1999 Salisbury Township, PA																															
1957	BC	4																													
STEVE MAZURAK Steve WR 6'2 195 Regina Rams Jrs. B: 5/25/1951																															
1973	SAS	16	3		0																			17	71	4.2	16				
1974	SAS	9										24	4						17	335	19.7	55	4	2	8	4.0	7				
1975	SAS	16										30	5						33	547	16.6	73	5	1	3	3.0	3				
1976	SAS	16										12	2						39	599	15.4	59	2	3	5	1.7	3	2	0	0.0	0
1977	SAS	16	2		0							12	2						52	978	18.8	63	2	5	39	7.8	13				
1978	SAS	8										12	2						21	360	17.1	63	2								
1979	SAS	11																	29	358	12.3	32	0								
1980	SAS	16	1		0							12	2						46	537	11.7	36	2								
8	Years	108	6		0							102	17						237	3714	15.7	73	17	28	126	4.5	16	2	0	0.0	0
VINCE MAZZA Vincent L. OT-DT-E 6'1 216 none B: 3/25/1925 Niagara Falls, NY D: 12/5/1993 Winona, ON Pro: AN																															
1950	HAM+	12										5	1										1								
1951	HAM+	11																													
1952	HAM+	12																													
1953	HAM+	14																													
1954	HAM+	12										6	0																		
5	Years	61										11	1										1								
GENO MAZZANTI Geno M., Jr. FW-HB 5'11 194 Arkansas B: 4/1/1929 Lake Village, AR Draft: 26-327 1950 BAL Pro: N																															
1952	OTT	4										5	1										1								
NICK MAZZOLI Nick WR 5'11 185 Simon Fraser B: 8/8/1968 Markham, ON Draft: 1-1 1991 HAM																															

Year	Team	GP	FM	FF	FR	TK	SK	YDS	IR	YDS	PD	PTS	TD	RA	YDS	AVG	LG	TD	REC	YDS	AVG	LG	TD	PR	YDS	AVG	LG	KOR	YDS	AVG	LG
1991	HAM	12	2		0	5						18	3	2	10	5.0	6	0	24	339	14.1	33	2	46	557	12.1	74	23	519	22.6	37
1992	HAM	14	1		0	3						30	5	1	8	8.0	8	0	41	757	18.5	82	5	17	152	8.9	29	11	168	15.3	55
1993	HAM	13				1													19	245	12.9	35	0	15	99	6.6	21	11	118	10.7	41
1994	OTT	18	4		1	4						12	2						40	648	16.2	48	2	52	327	6.3	21	4	79	19.8	27
1995	EDM	18				1						48	8	13	96	7.4	39	0	67	1044	15.6	67	8								
1996	EDM	8				4						6	1						23	351	15.3	34	1					1	18	18.0	18
1997	BC	6				2													14	136	9.7	16	0								
7	Years	89	7		1	20						114	19	16	114	7.1	39	0	228	3520	15.4	82	18	130	1135	8.7	74	50	902	18.0	55
DERRICK McADOO Derrick Mark RB 5'10 198 Baylor B: 4/2/1965 Pensacola, FL Pro: N
1989	HAM+	16	13		3	8						72	12	246	1039	4.2	45	11	57	699	12.3	48	1	12	72	6.0	18	18	402	22.3	46
1990	HAM	15	12		0	6						42	7	198	752	3.8	22	5	65	583	9.0	34	2	6	29	4.8	22	32	681	21.3	83
1991	HAM	3	2		0							6	1	21	107	5.1	20	1	4	27	6.8	12	0					5	69	13.8	22
1993	TOR	4	0		1	3						6	1	13	70	5.4	18	1	7	88	12.6	28	0					7	71	10.1	19
1995	HAM	8	2		0	8						6	1	50	218	4.4	32	1	13	133	10.2	40	0								
5	Years	46	29		5	25						132	22	528	2186	4.1	45	19	146	1530	10.5	48	3	18	101	5.6	22	62	1223	19.7	83
STEVE McADOO Stephen C. OT 6'3 297 Middle Tennessee State B: 11/6/1970
1994	SHR	7																													
ED McALENEY Edward P. DT 6'2 235 Massachusetts B: 9/21/1953 Portland, ME Draft: 8-237 1976 PIT Pro: NU
1977	CAL	9	0		1																										
1978	CAL	16	0		1				1	0																					
1979	CAL	16	0		1																										
1980	CAL+	16	0		2																										
1981	CAL	16					11.5																								
1982	CAL	16					14.0		1	10																					
1983	CAL	12	0		1		3.5																								
7	Years	101	0		6		29.0	0.0	2	10																					
BOBBY McALLISTER Robert QB 6'3 195 Michigan State B: 1/3/1966 Pompano Beach, FL Pro: E
1989	TOR	8	1		1	0								5	37	7.4	17	0													
RALPH McALLISTER Ralph D. HB-FB 6'1 200 Minnesota B: 1927 Draft: 8-96 1950 DET
1952	WPG	16							2	25		21	4	64	408	6.4	30	3	4	60	15.0	22	1	1	27	27.0	27	3	54	18.0	20
1953	WPG	10							2	24		5	1	37	208	5.6		1	5	52	10.4		0	1	0	0.0	0	7	105	15.0	
2	Years	26							4	49		26	5	101	616	6.1	30	4	9	112	12.4	22	1	2	27	13.5	27	10	159	15.9	20
DAN McALONAN Dan RB Hamilton Hurricanes Jrs.; Oakville Longhorns Jrs.; Hamilton Wildcats Jrs.; Oakville Longhorns Jrs.
1996	HAM	4				3																									
STEW McANDEWS Stewart LB 6'1 210 Alberta B: 5/19/1961 Draft: 2B-18 1983 EDM
1983	EDM	16																													
DANE McARTHUR Dane SB 6'0 195 Hawaii B: 8/15/1968 Prince Albert, SK Draft: 1B-8 1990 SAS
1991	SAS	10				6								1	3	3.0	3	0	5	47	9.4	13	0								
1993	SAS	2				0													1	15	15.0	15	0								
2	Years	12				6								1	3	3.0	3	0	6	62	10.3	15	0								
MIKE McARTHUR Michael G. RB 5'11 175 McNeese State B: 3/30/1955
1979	TOR	12	4		0							6	1	118	611	5.2	50	1	20	109	5.5	21	0	26	141	5.4	17	13	318	24.5	59
BILLY McBRIDE Billy CB-RB-WR 6'1 185 Tennessee State B: 7/31/1956 Syracuse, NY Draft: 11-276 1979 SF
1980	SAS	8										6	1						9	130	14.4	39	1	23	145	6.3	33	15	345	23.0	30
1981	SAS	16	1		2				4	19																		10	200	20.0	31
1982	SAS	16							5	32																		10	196	19.6	35
1983	SAS	5							1	0																					
1983	BC	2							1	0														3	26	8.7	18				
1983	Year	7							2	0																					
1984	BC	4	0		1				2	49																					
1984	OTT	7							3	47														1	35	35.0	35				
1984	Year	11	0		1				5	96														1	35	35.0	35				
5	Years	49	1		3				16	147		6	1						9	130	14.4	39	1	27	206	7.6	35	35	741	21.2	35
PAT McBRIDE Pat C 6'2 245 North Dakota State B: 3/21/1957 Draft: 1-6 1980 OTT
1980	OTT	10																													
MATT McCALL Matthew Clarence OT 6'6 315 Texas A&M B: 1/4/1969 Lufkin, TX Pro: E
1993	SAC	2				0																									
RON McCALL Ronald George LB 6'2 245 Utah State; Dixie JC; Weber State B: 7/11/1944 San Bernardino, CA Draft: 2A-40 1967 SD Pro: N
1969	SAS	5	0		1				1	12																					
LaDOUPHYOUS MaCALLA LaDouphyous Santez CB 5'8 190 Rice B: 1/1/1976 Tyler, TX
2000	SAS	18	0	0	1	53			1	56	4	12	2															0	33		33
2001	SAS	18	1	0	3	46			3	37	4													16	217	13.6	47				
2002	SAS	18				52					8													12	200	16.7	48	0	18		18
2003	SAS	16	1	0	2	47			1	0	4													13	166	12.8	61				
2004	SAS	5				13					2													5	25	5.0	10				
2005	SAS	16	0	1	1	40			4	31	6	6	1											7	62	8.9	23	1	9	9.0	9
6	Years	91	2	1	7	251			9	124	28	18	3											53	670	12.6	61	1	60	60.0	33
PAUL McCALLUM Paul K-P 5'11 185 Surrey Rams Jrs. B: 1/7/1970 Vancouver, BC Pro: EX
1993	BC	1	0		0	0						10	0																		
1993	OTT	3	0		1	2						24	0																		
1993	Year	4	0		1	2						34	0																		
1994	BC	4	0		1	1						43	0																		
1994	SAS	4				0						48	0																		
1994	Year	8	0		1	1						91	0																		
1995	SAS	2				0						26	0																		
1996	SAS	4				0						43	0																		
1997	SAS	18	2	1	1	3						165	0	3	17	5.7	7	0													
1998	SAS	18	1	0	0	9						137	0																		
1999	SAS	17	1	0	2	2						108	0	2	32	16.0	22	0													
2000	SAS	18	1	0	0	4						164	0	1	15	15.0	15	0													
2001	SAS	18	1	0	1	5						134	0	2	31	15.5	19	0													
2002	SAS	18	0	0	1	1						181	0	1	13	13.0	13	0						1	0	0.0	0				
2003	SAS+	18	1	0	1	1						181	0																		
2004	SAS	18	2	0	1	3						172	0	2	14	7.0	17	0													
2005	SAS	18	0	0	2	3						147	0																		
2006	BC	18				4						167	0																		
2007	BC+	18				0						166	0																		
2008	BC+	18				2						187	0	2	22	11.0	13	0													
2009	BC	7	1	0	0	1						63	0																		
2010	BC*	16				1						177	0	2	20	10.0	11	0													
2011	BC*	18	1	0	0	4						203	0																		
19	Years	267	11	1	11	46						2546	0	15	164	10.9	22	0						1	0	0.0	0				
ROSS McCALLUM Ross OT-DT 5'11 225 Montreal Army Ints.; NDG Maple Leafs Jrs. B: 1931
1952	CAL	1																													
1952	WPG	2																													
1952	Year	3																													
1953	WPG	15																													
1954	EDM	2																													
3	Years	18																													
JOHN McCAMBRIDGE John Raymond DE 6'4 245 Northwestern B: 8/30/1944 Klamath Falls, OR Draft: 6B-144 1967 DET Pro: N
1969	OTT	2																													
CHES McCANCE Chester FW-G 5'10 224 Winnipeg Deer Lodge Jrs. B: 2/19/1915 Winnipeg, MB D: 5/8/1956 Winnipeg, MB

Year	Team	GP	FM	FF	FR	TK	SK	YDS	IR	YDS	PD	PTS	TD	RA	YDS	AVG	LG	TD	REC	YDS	AVG	LG	TD	PR	YDS	AVG	LG	KOR	YDS	AVG	LG
1946	MTL	12										50	0																		
1947	MTL	12										31	0																		
1948	MTL	12										16	1																		
1949	MTL	12										61	3										1								
1950	MTL	12										7	1					1													
5	Years	60										165	5					1					1								
KEITHEN McCANT Keithen QB 6'2 205 Nebraska B: 3/8/1969 Draft: 12A-316 1992 CLE																															
1993	WPG	7				0																									
1994	WPG	18	1		0	0								21	121	5.8	30	0													
1995	BC	13	1		0	0								4	21	5.3	11	0													
3	Years	38	2		0	0								25	142	5.7	30	0													
DARNERIEN McCANTS Darnerien R. WR 6'3 214 Delaware State B: 8/1/1978 Odenton, MD Draft: 5-154 2001 WAS Pro: N																															
2007	HAM	3				0													1	7	7.0	7	0								
BOB McCARTHY Bob OHB-FL-SE 6'1 194 Ottawa Sooners Jrs. B: 1946																															
1965	OTT	14																	1	21	21.0	21	0	26	54	2.1	10				
1966	OTT	7																						6	22	3.7	7				
1967	CAL	15	1		1							6	1						21	322	15.3	46	1	74	325	4.4	16				
1968	CAL	16										36	6	3	10	3.3	4	0	58	959	16.5	73	6								
1969	CAL	16										12	2	4	29	7.3	22	0	14	175	12.5	31	2								
1970	CAL	4																	5	93	18.6		0								
1970	MTL	11										6	1						18	300	16.7		1	2	2	1.0	2				
1970	Year	15										6	1						23	393	17.1	59	1	2	2	1.0	2				
1971	EDM	2																						6	16	2.7	4				
7	Years	74	1		1							60	10	7	39	5.6	22	0	117	1870	16.0	73	10	114	419	3.7	16				
BRENDAN McCARTHY Brendan Barrett HB 6'3 220 Boston College B: 8/6/1945 Boston, MA D: 8/26/1997 Deep Creek Lake, MD Draft: 4A-92 1968 GB Pro: N																															
1969	EDM	2	1		0									11	21	1.9	9	0	5	62	12.4	15	0								
TONY McCARTHY Anthony E 5'11 180 none B: 1914																															
1946	OTT	12										5	1																		
1947	OTT	11										5	1										1								
2	Years	23										10	2										1								
KARL McCARTNEY Karl LB 6'0 231 Wilfrid Laurier; St. Mary's (Nova Scotia) B: 11/29/1987 Nassau, Bahamas Draft: 5-37 2010 CAL																															
2010	CAL	17				27	1.0	19.0																							
2011	CAL	8				15																									
2	Years	25				42	1.0	19.0																							
CALVIN McCARTY Calvin RB-FB 5'10 215 Boise State; Reedley JC; Western Washington B: 11/2/1984 Muskogee, OK Draft: 4B-27 2007 EDM																															
2007	EDM	18				6						6	1	6	13	2.2	11	0	7	99	14.1	44	1								
2008	EDM	18	4	0	1	14						30	5	88	490	5.6	34	4	70	583	8.3	27	1								
2009	EDM	11	0	0	1	8						42	7	67	348	5.2	37	5	20	124	6.2	17	2								
2010	EDM	15	3	0	0	9						30	5	62	287	4.6	46	3	36	278	7.7	22	2					1	5	5.0	5
2011	EDM	18				10						6	1	52	209	4.0	53	0	22	150	6.8	22	1								
5	Years	80	7	0	2	47						114	19	275	1347	4.9	53	12	155	1234	8.0	44	7					1	5	5.0	5
CHANCE McCARTY Chance Edwin DE-NT 6'3 248 Texas Christian B: 8/29/1975 Fort Worth, TX Draft: 7-212 1998 TB																															
2000	SAS	18				20	2.0	10.0	1	0	0																				
TANGO McCAULEY Tango OG 6'4 307 Texas A&M; Alabama State B: 10/27/1978																															
2003	SAS	11				0																									
2004	BC	1				0																									
2005	SAS	7				0																									
2006	MTL	5				0																									
4	Years	24				0																									
ANTHONY McCLANAHAN Anthony D. LB 6'2 220 Washington State B: 4/3/1971 Bakersfield, CA Pro: E																															
1995	CAL	13	0		1	47	7.0	66.0			3																				
1996	CAL	16				68	6.0	49.0	1	52	4	6	1																		
1997	CAL	15	0	1	2	66	3.0	15.0			4																				
1998	CAL	11	0	0	2	46	2.0	16.0			3																				
4	Years	55	0	1	5	227	18.0	146.0	1	52	14	6	1																		
BOB McCLELLAND Robert C 6'3 217 McGill Draft: 1952 MTL																															
1952	TOR	1																													
LES McCLELLAND Lester C. OT 6'0 227 Syracuse B: 9/5/1932 Masontown, PA D: 2/12/2007 Pittsburgh, PA Draft: 4A-43 1954 LARM																															
1954	HAM	12																													
CENTRAL McCLELLION Central Bernard DB 6'0 190 Ohio State B: 9/15/1975 Boynton Beach, FL Pro: EN																															
2000	BC	11	1	0	0	39			5	61	3																				
RON McCLENDON Ronald Dewayne RB 5'8 196 Butler County CC; Mississippi B: 4/2/1981 Ponchatoula, LA																															
2005	EDM	9	2	0	0	1						36	6	65	346	5.3	24	3	47	349	7.4	24	3					4	81	20.3	24
2006	EDM	2				0						12	2	38	243	6.4	26	2	7	45	6.4	10	0								
2007	EDM	6	1	0	0	0								40	170	4.3	47	0	29	219	7.6	17	0								
2008	EDM	2				0						6	1	13	64	4.9	19	1	8	67	8.4	14	0								
4	Years	19	3	0	0	1						54	9	156	823	5.3	47	6	91	680	7.5	24	3					4	81	20.3	24
WILLE McCLENDON William Alfred SB 6'1 225 Florida B: 6/11/1969 Jacksonville, FL																															
1995	BIR	1				1						6	1	6	43	7.2	20	1	4	55	13.8	19	0								
RUDY McCLINON Rudy DB 6'2 192 Xavier (Ohio) B: 9/21/1952 Cincinnati, OH Draft: 12-306 1974 CIN; 21-242 1974 NY-WFL																															
1976	CAL	6	0		1				2	29														0	3		3				
KIM McCLOUD Kimberly L. CB 6'0 185 Hawaii B: 5/8/1968 Los Angeles, CA																															
1991	SAS	9	0		1	17			1	0																		1	1	1.0	1
1992	SAS	15				30			1	0																					
2	Years	24	0		1	47			2	0																		1	1	1.0	1
WILLIE McCLUNG William Albert T 6'2 250 Florida A&M B: 5/9/1930 Marion, AR D: 7/28/2002 Pittsburgh, PA Pro: N																															
1962	HAM	5																													
JERRY McCLURG Jerry DE 6'4 250 Colorado B: 1942 Draft: 25-194(f) 1964 KC; 17-230(f) 1964 MIN																															
1965	CAL	8																													
1966	CAL	16	0		4																										
2	Years	24	0		4																										
GORD McCOLEMAN Gordon DT 6'4 245 Wilfrid Laurier B: 1/21/1948 Draft: 3-27 1973 HAM																															
1973	HAM	14	0		1																										
BILL McCOLLINS Bill DE 6'5 265 Northwest Mississippi CC B: 4/11/1970 Charleston, MS																															
1994	WPG	5	0		2	7	1.0	5.0																							
1995	WPG	4				7																									
2	Years	9	0		2	14	1.0	5.0																							
EVAN McCOLLOUGH Evan DH-CB 5'10 190 James Madison B: 9/2/1987																															
2010	TOR	17	0	0	2	70			1	0	6																				
2011	TOR	15	0	0	2	42			2	0	5	6	1						1	32	32.0	32	0					1	2	2.0	2
2	Years	32	0	0	4	112			3	0	11	6	1						1	32	32.0	32	0					1	2	2.0	2
JIM McCOLLUM James Henry (Bubba) DT 6'0 250 Kentucky B: 9/13/1952 Louisville, KY D: 9/5/2005 Lexington, KY Draft: 15-179 1974 FLA-WFL Pro: N																															
1975	OTT	1																													
McCOMISKEY G-T																															
1949	HAM	3																													
ANDREW McCONNELL Andrew OT-C 6'3 270 St. Francis Xavier B: 12/17/1964 Toronto, ON Draft: 1-6 1987 WPG																															
1988	EDM	5				1																									
1989	EDM	18				0																									
1990	EDM	16				2																									
3	Years	39				3																									
ARCHIE McCORD Archie OG-DE 6'1 230 Simon Fraser; North Dakota B: 1949 Draft: 1-3 1971 BC																															
1971	SAS	16																													

Year	Team	GP	FM	FF	FR	TK	SK	YDS	IR	YDS	PD	PTS	TD	RA	YDS	AVG	LG	TD	REC	YDS	AVG	LG	TD	PR	YDS	AVG	LG	KOR	YDS	AVG	LG
1972	SAS	16																													
1973	SAS	16																													
1974	SAS	13																													
4	Years	61																													
QUENTIN McCORD John Quentin WR 5'10 188 Kentucky B: 6/26/1978 LaGrange, GA Draft: 7D-236 2001 ATL Pro: N																															
2006	WPG	7				2													17	248	14.6	50	0					1	18	18.0	18
2007	EDM	3				2								1	4	4.0	4	0	6	48	8.0	13	0								
2	Years	10				4								1	4	4.0	4	0	23	296	12.9	50	0					1	18	18.0	18
GREG McCORMACK Greg DT-DE 6'3 255 Windsor AKO Jrs.; Simon Fraser B: 11/26/1963 Windsor, ON Draft: 3-24 1986 EDM																															
1987	EDM	1				0																									
1988	SAS	9				0																									
1990	SAS	18				0																									
3	Years	28				0																									
BILL McCORMICK Bill G-T 6'0 220 Miami (Ohio) B: 1928																															
1950	TOR	6																													
TOM McCORMICK Thomas Mike FB 5'11 185 Menlo; Pacific B: 5/16/1930 Waco, TX Draft: 8-97(f) 1952 LARM Pro: N																															
1957	TOR	2																													
JOHN McCORQUINDALE John RB 6'0 205 Brigham Young B: 12/26/1954 Draft: 5-40 1977 WPG																															
1978	WPG	16												4	15	3.8	6	0	1	20	20.0	20	0					2	31	15.5	18
1979	WPG	16												4	11	2.8	3	0	7	31	4.4	14	0					1	0	0.0	0
1980	WPG	4												1	2	2.0	2	0										1	9	9.0	9
1980	HAM	11	1		1							6	1	34	178	5.2	35	1	7	55	7.9	17	0								
1980	Year	15	1		1							6	1	35	180	5.1	35	1	7	55	7.9	17	0					1	9	9.0	9
1981	SAS	14	0		1							12	2	4	5	1.3	2	1						2	4	2.0	4				
1982	SAS	16	2		0							12	2	25	147	5.9	30	0	13	114	8.8	13	2					1	16	16.0	16
5	Years	66	3		2							30	5	72	358	5.0	35	2	28	220	7.9	20	2	2	4	2.0	4	5	56	11.2	18
KEZ McCORVEY Kezarrick Montines WR 6'0 190 Florida State B: 1/23/1972 Gautier, MS Draft: 5B-156 1995 DET Pro: EN																															
2000	EDM	18				4						90	15						73	962	13.2	40	15								
2001	EDM	6				0						6	1						19	249	13.1	42	1								
2	Years	24				4						96	16						92	1211	13.2	42	16								
BILL McCOURT Bill FB																															
1947	CAL	4																													
BILL McCOY Bill HB 6'0 185 Hamilton Jrs. B: 1936																															
1957	MTL	4																						5	26	5.2	11				
CHRIS McCOY Christopher Brandon DE 6'3 261 Middle Tennessee State B: 11/25/1986 Villa Rica, GA Draft: 7A-212 2010 MIA																															
2011	CAL	5				14	2.0	21.0			1																				
MIKE McCOY Michael Patrick QB 6'3 205 Long Beach State; Utah B: 4/1/1972 San Francisco, CA Pro: E																															
1999	CAL	14	2	0	0	1						6	1	35	110	3.1	11	1													
RICO McCOY Rico LB 6'0 224 Tennessee B: 11/6/1987 Washington, DC																															
2010	WPG	1	0	1	0	1																									
2011	EDM	1				0																									
2	Years	2	0	1	0	1																									
DAVID McCRARY David Lee CB-WR 5'10 170 Tennessee-Chattanooga B: 2/9/1963 Rockmart, GA																															
1987	CAL	13	0		3	51			3	76														1	8	8.0	8				
1988	CAL	17	1		0	60			4	62														37	432	11.7	59				
1989	CAL	17	2		1	44	4.0		5	48														35	348	9.9	36				
1990	CAL+	13				29	1.0		6	62		6	1											6	95	15.8	68				
1991	SAS	1				10																									
5	Years	61	3		4	194	5.0		18	248		6	1											79	883	11.2	68				
TIM McCRAY Tim RB 5'11 193 Independence JC; Tulane B: 8/20/1960 Waycross, GA																															
1984	OTT	10	3		1							36	6	137	701	5.1	81	6	30	288	9.6	32	0					15	295	19.7	40
1985	OTT	6	1		0							18	3	53	277	5.2	24	3	15	172	11.5	37	0								
1986	SAS	7	2		0							30	5	36	178	4.9	61	3	17	150	8.8	18	2					19	367	19.3	49
1987	SAS	6	3		0	0						6	1	86	457	5.3	34	1	11	58	5.3	15	0					6	201	33.5	78
1988	SAS	18	5		3	2						18	3	125	751	6.0	43	0	42	336	8.0	30	3					25	560	22.4	70
1989	SAS*	18	6		0	1						26	4	218	1285	5.9	44	2	75	749	10.0	40	2					29	650	22.4	45
1990	SAS	5				0								54	227	4.2	17	0	26	245	9.4	29	0					2	51	25.5	42
7	Years	70	20		4	3						134	22	709	3876	5.5	81	15	216	1998	9.3	40	7					96	2124	22.1	78
SCOTT McCUAIG Scott DE 6'3 229 South Fraser Rams Jrs.; British Columbia B: 6/5/1984 Surrey, BC Draft: 3-22 2009 HAM																															
2009	BC	7				1																									
JERAILL McCULLER Jeraill OT 607 325 North Carolina State B: 9/8/1987 Chesapeake, VA																															
2011	MTL	2				0																									
DAN McCULLOUGH Dan DE 6'3 242 Bishop's B: 4/17/1983 Fredericton, NB																															
2008	BC	18	1	0	0	5																									
2009	BC	18	1	0	0	5																									
2010	BC	18	0	0	2	7																									
2011	BC	18				9																									
4	Years	72	2	0	2	26																									
DELAND McCULLOUGH Deland RB 5'11 205 Miami (Ohio) B: 12/1/1972 Allegheny, PA																															
1998	WPG	9	2	0	2	4						24	4	94	429	4.6	26	4	14	112	8.0	38	0	1	0	0.0	0	9	205	22.8	32
1999	WPG	15	4	0	0	1						66	11	220	990	4.5	27	11	56	460	8.2	59	0					16	246	15.4	25
2	Years	24	6	0	2	5						90	15	314	1419	4.5	27	15	70	572	8.2	59	0	1	0	0.0	0	25	451	18.0	32
GEORGE McCULLOUGH George Wayne, Jr. DB 5'10 187 Baylor B: 2/18/1975 Galveston, TX Draft: 5-143 1997 TEN Pro: EN																															
2002	OTT	8				15			2	79	2	6	1											3	83	27.7	56	9	149	16.6	31
2003	OTT	12	0	0	1	32					3													1	5	5.0	5				
2004	OTT	11	0	0	1	37			1	62	2	6	1																		
3	Years	31	0	0	2	84			3	141	7	12	2											4	88	22.0	56	9	149	16.6	31
JASON McCULLOUGH Jason QB 6'1 215 Brown B: 4/24/1975																															
1997	HAM	1				0																									
MIKE McCULLOUGH Mike LB 6'3 225 St. Francis Xavier B: 3/17/1980 Oshawa, ON Draft: 3-23 2003 SAS																															
2003	SAS	18	0	1	0	19																									
2004	SAS	18				20																									
2005	SAS	18				20																									
2006	SAS	14				36	2.0	8.0			3																				
2007	SAS	18	0	1	0	31					1																				
2008	SAS	18				24	1.0	4.0																							
2009	SAS	18	0	1	1	43					3																				
2010	SAS	18	0	0	1	36	4.0	29.0			3																				
2011	SAS	18				20			1	5	0																				
9	Years	158	0	3	2	249	7.0	41.0	1	5	10																				
RUSS McCULLOUGH Russell Scott OL 6'9 313 Missouri B: 10/31/1969 Kansas City, MO Pro: E																															
1994	LV	4																													
SALADIN McCULLOUGH Saladin Rashed RB 5'9 195 El Camino JC; Oregon B: 7/17/1975 Monterey Park, CA Pro: X																															
1999	EDM	1				0								3	7	2.3	4	0										4	74	18.5	29
2003	CAL	13	3	0	0	1						18	3	129	734	5.7	27	3	32	298	9.3	34	0					4	86	21.5	25
2004	SAS	1				0																						5	116	23.2	33
3	Years	15	3	0	0	1						18	3	132	741	5.6	27	3	32	298	9.3	34	0					13	276	21.2	33
ROBERT McCUNE Robert LB-DE 6'0 245 Louisville B: 3/9/1979 Mobile, AL Draft: 5-154 2005 WAS Pro: N																															
2010	CAL	13	0	0	1	61	5.0	22.0			1																				
2011	CAL	14				57	3.0	17.0	1	52	1																				
2	Years	27	0	0	1	118	8.0	39.0	1	52	2																				
BRIAN McCURDY Brian DB 6'1 177 Northern Arizona B: 6/11/1967 Windsor, ON Draft: 2-8 1993 TOR																															

Year	Team	GP	FM	FF	FR	TK	SK	YDS	IR	YDS	PD	PTS	TD	RA	YDS	AVG	LG	TD	REC	YDS	AVG	LG	TD	PR	YDS	AVG	LG	KOR	YDS	AVG	LG
1993	TOR	12	0		1	18																							1	5	5.0	5
1994	TOR	10	1		3	27					3																				
1994	OTT	7	0		1	8	1.0	2.0																							
1994	Year	17	1		4	35	1.0	2.0			3																				
1995	HAM	13	0		1	21			1	20	2																				
3	Years	35	1		6	74	1.0	2.0	1	20	5																	1	5	5.0	5
GARY McCURTY Gary FB 5'7 202 Puget Sound B: 5/29/1971 Fort Hood, TX																																
1993	SAC	2				0																									
1994	SAC	5				1						6	1	7	34	4.9	13	1	3	26	8.7	9	0					3	36	12.0	18
2	Years	7				1						6	1	7	34	4.9	13	1	3	26	8.7	9	0					3	36	12.0	18
JOE McCUTCHEON Joseph Baker C-LB 6'1 215 Washington & Lee B: 6/10/1929 Webster Springs, WV D: 7/27/2004 Richmond, VA Draft: 11-129 1951 PIT																																
1953	MTL	1																													
MARQUAY McDANIEL McDaniel WR-SB 5'10 205 Hampton B: 4/20/1984 Virginia Beach, VA																																
2009	HAM	18	2	0	0	2						18	3						57	688	12.1	41	3	73	615	8.4	59	57	1153	20.2	56
2010	HAM	18	2	0	2	2						42	7	1	4	4.0	4	0	76	998	13.1	37	7	6	46	7.7	12	15	332	22.1	39
2011	HAM	1				0													4	60	15.0	24	0					1	16		16
3	Years	37	4	0	2	4						60	10	1	4	4.0	4	0	137	1746	12.7	41	10	79	661	8.4	59	73	1501	20.6	56
MARCUS McDAVID Marcus S-DH 5'10 170 New Mexico B: 7/23/1977 Colorado Springs, CO																																
2000	SAS	17	0	2	1	35	2.0	14.0	3	16	4																				
FRAN McDERMOTT Francis John DB 5'10 182 St. Mary's (California) B: 4/3/1960 Amarillo, TX																																
1982	SAS*	15	2		0				6	126		6	1											29	313	10.8	107	17	408	24.0	62
1983	SAS	16	2		0		1.0		3	43		6	1											49	397	8.1	30	16	360	22.5	30
1984	SAS	16	3		0				4	92		6	1											81	724	8.9	28				
1985	SAS	16	0		1				6	101														20	151	7.6	27				
1986	SAS	10					2.0		2	23														7	24	3.4	10				
5	Years	73	7		1		3.0		21	385		18	3											186	1609	8.7	107	33	768	23.3	62
JOHN McDERMOTT John OL 6'6 300 Clemson B: 9/18/1978 Babylon, NY																																
2002	TOR	1				0																									
LLOYD McDERMOTT Lloyd Ivan T 6'1 240 Kentucky B: 12/20/1925 Covington, KY D: 1/16/1964 Covington, KY Draft: 6-79 1950 PHI Pro: N																																
1952	OTT	11																													
BOB McDONALD Bob G 6'1 220 North Dakota State B: 1938																																
1961	SAS	14																													
BOB McDONALD Robert Matthew Turnbull DB-FW-HB 5'10 176 B: 9/26/1931 Hamilton, ON D: 6/9/2002																																
1950	HAM	9										5	1					1													
1951	HAM	11																													
1952	HAM	12										8	1																		
3	Years	32										13	2					1													
DARNELL McDONALD Darnell Ali WR 6'3 190 Garden City CC; Kansas State B: 5/26/1976 Chicago, IL Draft: 7C-240 1999 TB Pro: NX																																
2001	BC	10	1	0	0	0						12	2						31	558	18.0	65	2								
2003	CAL+	14	2	0	1	3						24	4						67	1002	15.0	47	4	2	40	20.0	32	15	327	21.8	36
2005	WPG	5				1						6	1						17	232	13.6	23	1	1	4	4.0	4	6	104	17.3	29
3	Years	29	3	0	1	4						42	7						115	1792	15.6	65	7	3	44	14.7	32	21	431	20.5	36
DON McDONALD Donald Gene (Flip) E 6'2 200 Oklahoma B: 2/12/1921 Webb City, MO D: 2/12/2002 Pro: AN																																
1949	OTT	9										25	5										5								
FRANK McDONALD Frank E 6'2 200 Miami (Florida) B: 1934 Draft: 7-75 1955 BAL																																
1955	HAM	9							1	2		15	3						12	202	16.8	53	2								
GORDIE McDONALD Gordon Edward C-LB 6'1 200 Wake Forest B: 1938																																
1958	BC	2																													
HAMISH McDONALD Hamish DE-OG 6'1 210 Vancouver Meralomas Jrs.; Vancouver Ints. B: 1931																																
1957	BC	5																													
MARK McDONALD Mark WR 5'10 170 Wenatchee JC; Washington B: 4/27/1951 Draft: TE 1975 BC																																
1975	WPG	16										12	2						28	577	20.6	72	2					5	81	16.2	39
1976	WPG	16										12	2	1	5	5.0	5	0	27	495	18.3	52	2					6	69	11.5	21
1977	WPG	10																	24	241	10.0	23	0								
1978	WPG	1																													
1978	CAL	5																	1	9	9.0	9	0								
1978	BC	1																													
1978	TOR	1																													
1978	Year	8																	1	9	9.0	9	0								
1979	TOR	2																													
1979	SAS	5																	3	36	12.0	18	0								
1979	Year	7																													
5	Years	45										24	4	1	5	5.0	5	0	83	1358	16.4	72	4					11	150	13.6	39
PETE McDONALD Pete E Dundas Bombers Ints.																																
1947	HAM	7										1	0																		
RAY McDONALD Raymondo WR 5'11 181 Florida B: 8/25/1964 Pahokee, FL Draft: 7A-187 1986 NE																																
1987	SAS	8				1								1	-1	-1.0	-1	0	16	295	18.4	49	0								
1988	SAS	15	0		2	1						26	4						45	725	16.1	44	4					0	33		33
1989	SAS	8				1						6	1						12	204	17.0	29	1								
1989	OTT	6				0						18	3						10	234	23.4	68	3								
1989	Year	14				1						24	4						22	438	19.9	68	4								
3	Years	31	0		2	3						50	8	1	-1	-1.0	-1	0	83	1458	17.6	68	8					0	33		33
ROD McDONALD Rod C Winnipeg Rods Jrs.																																
1946	WPG	8																													
DAN McDONOUGH Daniel F. LB 6'2 230 Missouri B: 6/7/1951 Belton, MO																																
1974	EDM	6			1				1	-6																					
1975	BC	11	0		1				1	12																					
1976	BC	8							1	10																					
3	Years	25	0		2				3	16																					
KEVIN McDOUGAL Kevin QB 6'2 195 Notre Dame B: 5/29/1972 Pompano Beach, FL Pro: EX																																
1995	WPG	8	1		1	0						6	1	16	115	7.2	42	1													
1996	WPG	6	2		0	1						6	1	5	6	1.2	2	1													
1997	WPG	13	1	0	2	0								34	308	9.1	33	0													
3	Years	27	4	0	3	1						12	2	55	429	7.8	42	2													
GERRY McDOUGALL Gerald Gordon OHB-FB 6'2 225 UCLA B: 3/21/1935 Long Beach, CA Pro: N																																
1957	HAM+	12										50	8	177	1053	5.9	44	8	12	131	10.9	29	0					4	72	18.0	25
1958	HAM+	14										53	8	212	1109	5.2	88	7	32	415	13.0	68	1					3	58	19.3	21
1959	HAM	14										54	8	230	1010	4.4	70	7	24	287	12.0	35	1					3	34	11.3	12
1960	HAM	14										79	7	125	557	4.5	19	3	30	531	17.7	65	4					7	140	20.0	26
1961	HAM	14										66	11	58	335	5.8	76	3	40	632	15.8	56	7					2	44	22.0	29
1962	TOR	13										42	7	146	811	5.6	59	7	32	300	9.4	37	0								
1965	HAM	13										6	1	28	131	4.7	15	1	9	183	20.3	58	0					3	66	22.0	23
1966	HAM	14										12	2	15	75	5.0	12	0	7	93	13.3	30	2					2	51	25.5	28
1967	EDM	1																													
9	Years	109										362	52	991	5081	5.1	88	36	186	2572	13.8	68	15					24	465	19.4	29
JOHN McDOWELL John Bernard OT-OG 6'3 260 St. John's (Minnesota) B: 2/12/1942 St. Paul, MN Draft: 9-125 1964 GB Pro: N																																
1967	BC	15																													
1968	BC	16																													
1969	BC	2																													
3	Years	33																													
LAYNE McDOWELL Layne Alan OT 6'3 255 Iowa B: 8/12/1949 Des Moines, IA Draft: 10-235 1971 NE																																
1972	BC	4																													

Year	Team	GP	FM	FF	FR	TK	SK	YDS	IR	YDS	PD	PTS	TD	RA	YDS	AVG	LG	TD	REC	YDS	AVG	LG	TD	PR	YDS	AVG	LG	KOR	YDS	AVG	LG
1973	BC	16																													
1974	BC	16	0		2																										
1975	BC+	16	0		1																										
1976	BC+	16	1		0									1	6	6.0	6	0													
1977	BC+	16																										1	0	0.0	0
6	Years	84	1		3									1	6	6.0	6	0										1	0	0.0	0
KEN McEACHERN Ken S 6'1 187 Weber State B: 1/14/1953 Draft: TE 1974 SAS																															
1974	SAS	16	1		1				4	43		6	1											3	-3	-1.0	3				
1975	SAS	3	0		2				1	26																					
1976	SAS+	16			1				6	128		6	1																		
1977	SAS	10	0		1				3	48		6	1																		
1978	SAS	16	0		1				4	100																					
1979	SAS	14							3	69														8	32	4.0	10				
1980	SAS*	16	0		2				10	190		6	1											2	27	13.5	22				
1981	SAS+	16	0		1				2	40														2	19	9.5	12				
1982	SAS	16					1.0		4	147		6	1																		
1983	TOR+	15	0		2		1.0		5	36														1	3	3.0	3				
1984	SAS	9	0		1		1.5		1	10																		1	0	0.0	0
11	Years	147	1		12		3.5		43	837		30	5											16	78	4.9	22	1	0	0.0	0
MIKE McMEACHERN Mike S 6'1 205 Western Illinois B: 6/8/1986 Calgary, AB Draft: 3-22 2008 BC																															
2009	BC	1				1																									
TED McEACHERN Ted LB 6'1 220 Guelph B: 9/30/1948																															
1974	TOR	3																													
1974	WPG	11	0		1				1	0																					
1974	Year	14	0		1				1	0																					
1975	WPG	1																													
1975	SAS	13							1	2																					
1975	Year	14																													
1976	BC	12																													
3	Years	16	0		1				2	2																					
NAKOA McELRATH Nakoa WR 6'2 195 Palomar JC; Washington State B: 4/18/1979 Chicago, IL																															
2002	BC	3				2																									
BUCKY McELROY William Murry, Jr. HB 5'11 195 Hinds CC; Southern Mississippi B: 1/23/1929 Monroe, LA Draft: 26-308(di) 1952 CHIB; 7A-76 1953 CHIB Pro: N																															
1955	HAM	8										30	6	121	632	5.2	37	6	8	85	10.6	20	0					6	130	21.7	34
JERMAINE McELVEEN Jermaine DT-DE 6'4 263 Alabama-Birmingham B: 8/19/1984 Chicago, IL																															
2008	MTL	8	0	3	2	18	6.0	29.0	1	-5	1																	1	13	13.0	13
2009	MTL	17				30	3.0	34.0																							
2010	MTL	18	0	2	4	23	8.0	44.0			2																				
2011	MTL	10				14	1.0	10.0	1	1	0																				
4	Years	53	0	5	6	85	18.0	117.0	2	-4	3																	1	13	13.0	13
TARRENCE McEVANS Tarrence CB 5'10 180 Western Michigan B: 12/20/1974 Detroit, MI																															
1998	CAL	7				7			1	0	2																				
CLAY McEVOY Clay RB 6'1 205 Simon Fraser B: 1947 Draft: 3-19 1971 WPG																															
1971	WPG	16												20	135	6.8	15	0	2	10	5.0	9	0					2	21	10.5	15
1972	WPG	16	1		1							6	1	10	34	3.4	6	1										2	12	6.0	12
1973	WPG	12												36	197	5.5	19	0	5	27	5.4	10	0								
3	Years	44	1		1							6	1	66	366	5.5	19	1	7	37	5.3	10	0					4	33	8.3	15
ART McEWAN Art G-T 5'10 207 Montreal Eastward Ints. B: 1925																															
1947	SAS	8																													
1948	SAS	12																													
1949	SAS	12																													
1950	SAS	14																													
1951	SAS	14																													
1952	SAS	13																													
1953	SAS	16																													
1954	SAS	5																													
8	Years	94																													
SCOTT McEWAN Scott QB 6'2 213 UCLA B: 9/30/1978 Portland, OR																															
2002	BC	12				0																									
KEN McFADDEN Ken E 6'2 185 Concordia (Minnesota) B: 1931																															
1952	CAL	12			1																										
MARQUES McFADDEN Marques Arthur OT 6'5 320 Arizona B: 9/12/1978 St. Louis, MO Pro: EN																															
2004	BC	15	0	0	1	0																									
CYRIL McFALL Cyril K-P 5'11 185 Winnipeg Rods Jrs.; Winnipeg Hawkeyes Jrs. B: 4/21/1953																															
1974	CAL	10	1		0							71	0																		
1975	CAL	16										111	0																		
1976	CAL	16										124	0																		
1977	CAL	16										109	0																		
1978	CAL	16										163	0																		
5	Years	74	1		0							578	0																		
MICKEY McFALL John Michael T 6'0 185 Montreal Comets Int. B: 4/16/1926 Toronto, ON D: 4/19/2011 Oakville, ON																															
1946	MTL	2																													
JACK McFARLAND Jack T none																															
1947	SAS	3																													
BILL McFARLANE Bill DB-OHB 6'0 178 Toronto B: 1930 Draft: 1954 TOR																															
1954	TOR+	11							10	209		5	1						2	20	10.0	10	0	31	192	6.2	19				
1955	TOR	6																						1	11	11.0	11				
1956	TOR	14							1	5									2	37	18.5	23	0	35	246	7.0	27	11	176	16.0	26
3	Years	31							11	214		5	1						4	57	14.3	23	0	67	449	6.7	27	11	176	16.0	26
BOB McFARLANE Bob HB 5'9 182 Western Ontario																															
1946	MTL	5																													
1947	MTL	2																													
2	Years	7																													
DAVE McFARLANE Dave T-C 6'3 210 British Columbia																															
1953	CAL	16																										2	18	9.0	
JIMMY McFAUL Jim T-HB 6'0 222 Burgh Rough Riders Jrs. B: 1917																															
1948	OTT	6																													
1949	SAS	12										1	0																		
1950	SAS	13																													
1951	SAS	14																													
1952	SAS	5																													
5	Years	50										1	0																		
DAARON McFIELD Daaron LB 6'3 280 British Columbia B: 8/15/1975 Vancouver, BC Draft: 1-2 2000 WPG																															
2000	WPG	18	0	0	1	15	1.0	12.0																							
2001	WPG	4				0																									
2001	BC	4				0																									
2001	EDM	4				0																									
2001	Year	8				0																									
2002	HAM	18	0	1	0	45	6.0																								
3	Years	40	0	1	1	60	7.0	12.0																							
CASEY McGAHEE Casey WR 5'9 155 Florida Atlantic B: 12/7/1983 Fort Myers, FL																															
2008	WPG	2	2	0	0	2						6	1						3	49	16.3	33	0	10	122	12.2	57	3	61	20.3	25

Year	Team	GP	FM	FF	FR	TK	SK	YDS	IR	YDS	PD	PTS	TD	RA	YDS	AVG	LG	TD	REC	YDS	AVG	LG	TD	PR	YDS	AVG	LG	KOR	YDS	AVG	LG
WANE McGARITY Wane Keith WR 5'8 195 Texas B: 9/30/1976 San Antonio, TX Draft: 4A-118 1999 DAL Pro: N																															
2002	CAL	5				0						12	2	2	-9	-4.5	0	0	15	205	13.7	37	2	12	66	5.5	12	9	212	23.6	41
2003	CAL+	14	2	0	0	1						54	9	7	51	7.3	17	0	55	799	14.5	51	6	52	663	12.8	70	16	399	24.9	51
2004	CAL	17	4	0	1	4						18	3	1	3	3.0	3	0	47	599	12.7	44	3	41	360	8.8	21	27	583	21.6	53
2005	WPG	6	2	0	0	0						2	0	2	3	1.5	6	0	14	123	8.8	31	0								
4	Years	42	8	0	1	5						86	14	12	48	4.0	17	0	131	1726	13.2	51	11	105	1089	10.4	70	52	1194	23.0	53
CLARENCE McGEARY Clarence Valentine, Jr. T 6'5 250 Minnesota; North Dakota State B: 8/8/1926 St. Paul, MN D: 4/6/1993 Salt Lake City, UT Draft: 30-212 1948 BKN-AAFC; 30-281 1948 GB Pro: N																															
1951	MTL	7																													
DON McGEE Don WR 5'11 203 North Texas B: 3/24/1981 Rockford, IL Pro: E																															
2005	CAL	5				5			0	0	1																				
DOUG McGEE Doug OG 6'1 248 Ottawa Sooners Jrs.; Richmond B: 9/6/1954 Draft: TE 1977 OTT																															
1977	OTT	12																													
1978	OTT	16	0		1																							3	50	16.7	18
1979	OTT	16	0		1																										
1980	OTT	1																													
4	Years	45	0		2																							3	50	16.7	18
JACK McGEE Jack G 5'11 210 Queen's B: 1932 Toronto, ON D: 8/16/2009 Peterborough, ON																															
1954	TOR	9																													
1955	HAM	2																													
2	Years	11																													
MOLLY McGEE McGee. Sylvester HB 5'10 184 Rhode Island B: 8/26/1952 Nyack, NY D: 7/18/1994 Draft: 16-408 1974 ATL; 31-368 1974 PHI-WFL Pro: NW																															
1975	OTT	1										6	1	13	32	2.5	7	1	3	13	4.3	5	0					1	34	34.0	34
1976	OTT	12			0							12	2	67	280	4.2	25	0	17	175	10.3	57	2					28	724	25.9	43
1976	SAS	2			1							6	1	34	162	4.8	16	1	7	150	21.4	59	0	1	0	0.0	0	3	43	14.3	27
1976	Year	14	6		0							18	3	101	442	4.4	25	1	24	325	13.5	59	2	1	0	0.0	0	31	767	24.7	43
1977	SAS	14	6		2							24	4	138	600	4.3	40	2	68	548	8.1	52	2					2	40	20.0	27
1978	SAS	8	1		0							12	2	32	110	3.4	16	0	22	205	9.3	33	2	3	37	12.3	16	4	80	20.0	27
1979	SAS	1																	3	5	1.7	5	0								
5	Years	36	7		3							60	10	284	1184	4.2	40	4	120	1096	9.1	59	6	4	37	9.3	16	38	921	24.2	43
SCOTT McGHEE Scott Allen WR 5'9 172 Eastern Illinois B: 3/15/1959 Evergreen Park, IL Pro: U																															
1982	TOR	7										18	3						14	221	15.8	42	3	4	19	4.8	6				
1983	TOR	3	0		1									0	4		4	0	5	44	8.8	13	0	7	55	7.9	10	5	116	23.2	33
2	Years	10	0		1							18	3	0	4		4	0	19	265	13.9	42	3	11	74	6.7	10	5	116	23.2	33
JIM McGILL Jim T 210 East End Arrows																															
1948	CAL	12																													
1949	CAL	1																													
2	Years	13																													
GEORGE McGOWAN George SE 6'2 187 Glendale JC; Kansas B: 3/10/1948 Bethesda, MD																															
1971	EDM	16										36	6	2	3	1.5	6	1	49	827	16.9	58	5					8	142	17.8	34
1972	EDM	16										66	11						54	1015	18.8	61	11					2	0	0.0	0
1973	EDM*	16	1		0							54	9						81	1123	13.9	44	9					1	5	5.0	5
1974	EDM	4			1							6	1						8	172	21.5	58	1								
1975	EDM*	16	1		1				1	10		50	8						98	1472	15.0	55	8								
1976	EDM*	16	1		0							26	4						60	833	13.9	50	4								
1977	EDM	10	0		1				1	0		18	3						40	412	10.3	33	3								
1978	EDM	10	1		0							6	1						34	402	11.8	29	1								
8	Years	104	4		3				2	10		262	43	2	3	1.5	6	1	424	6256	14.8	61	42					11	147	13.4	34
PAUL McGOWAN Paul Joseph LB 5'11 221 Florida State B: 1/13/1966 Raleigh, NC Draft: 9-237 1988 MIN Pro: E																															
1989	OTT	6	0		1	42																						2	25	12.5	13
1990	OTT	14	0		2	60			1	10																					
2	Years	20	0		3	102			1	10																		2	25	12.5	13
MEL McGOWEN Melvin Lawrence LB 6'1 210 Tulsa B: 8/5/1954 Houston, TX																															
1979	BC	3																													
GERRY McGRATH Gerald P-K 5'10 195 Verdun Maple Leafs Jrs. B: 6/14/1959 Montreal, QC																															
1980	MTL	10	2		0							76	0																		
1981	MTL	7	1		0							32	0																		
1983	MTL	9										2	0																		
1984	MTL	15	1		1							3	0	1	-18	-18.0	-18	0													
1985	SAS	10	0		2							1	0																		
1986	SAS	7	1		0							1	0																		
6	Years	58	5		3							115	0	1	-18	-18.0	-18	0													
JOE McGRATH Joe C 6'2 245 Idaho State B: 1947																															
1970	MTL	5																													
JOE McGRATH Joseph, Jr. OT-OG 6'5 315 Miami (Florida) B: 11/27/1980 Moose Jaw, SK Draft: 1B-2 2003 EDM																															
2004	EDM	15	0	0	1	1																									
2005	EDM	18	0	0	2	0																									
2006	EDM	18				1																									
2007	EDM	18				2																									
2008	EDM	13				0																									
2009	EDM	18				1																									
2010	EDM	5				1																									
2010	BC	11	0	0	1	1																									
2010	Year	16				2																									
7	Years	105	0	0	4	7																									
DONNIE McGRAW Donnie Hugh RB 5'10 176 Houston B: 2/24/1953 Dallas, TX Draft: 13-362 1976 DEN																															
1977	TOR	6	5		0							12	2	89	360	4.0	25	1	11	109	9.9	57	1					1	10	10.0	10
BOB McGREGOR Robert OHB-FB 5'11 205 Wilfrid Laurier; Alberta B: 2/8/1948 Draft: 8-64 1970 EDM																															
1972	EDM	16	1		1							6	1	16	59	3.7	7	0	11	77	7.0	12	1	38	208	5.5	25	2	44	22.0	23
1973	EDM	16	3		2									4	13	3.3	5	0						46	157	3.4	7				
1974	EDM	3												17	48	2.8	8	0						12	59	4.9	13				
3	Years	35	4		3							6	1	37	120	3.2	8	0	11	77	7.0	12	1	96	424	4.4	25	2	44	22.0	23
LAMAR McGRIGGS Clarence Lamar LB-DE 6'3 210 Ellsworth CC; Oklahoma State; Western Illinois B: 5/9/1968 Chicago, IL Draft: 8-223 1991 NYG Pro: N																															
1996	OTT+	10				61	1.0	9.0	1	2	1																				
1997	SAS	10	0	2	0	49	2.0	12.0	1	20	1	2	0						1	5	5.0	5	0								
1997	HAM	7	0	0	1	33	2.0	12.0	1	0	3																				
1997	Year	17	0	2	1	82	4.0	24.0	2	20	4	2	0						1	5	5.0	5	0								
1998	HAM	2				4	1.0	9.0																							
1999	HAM	18	0	1	1	65	4.0	27.0	1	3	3	6	1																		
2000	HAM	6				31					1																				
2000	WPG	3	0	0	1	7			1	0	0																				
2000	Year	9	0	0	1	38			1	0	1																				
2001	WPG	17				46	5.0	30.0	2	27	4																				
2002	WPG	18	0	1	1	51	5.0	27.0	3	55	3																				
2003	WPG	18	0	2	2	49	2.0	8.0			5																	3	41	13.7	15
2004	WPG	18	0	0	1	48			2	39	1	6	1																		
2005	WPG	16	0	0	2	54					1																				
10	Years	133	0	6	9	498	22.0	134.0	12	146	23	14	2						1	5	5.0	5	0					3	41	13.7	15
MIKE McGRUDER Michael J.P. (Scooter) CB 5'11 185 Kent State B: 5/6/1964 Cleveland, OH Pro: N																															
1986	SAS	14	0		1				5	35														0	-4		-4				
1987	SAS	14	0		4	46	1.0		5	26																					
1988	SAS	18			3	46			7	89		6	1																		

Year	Team	GP	FM	FF	FR	TK	SK	YDS	IR	YDS	PD	PTS	TD	RA	YDS	AVG	LG	TD	REC	YDS	AVG	LG	TD	PR	YDS	AVG	LG	KOR	YDS	AVG	LG
3	Years	46	0		8	92	1.0	0.0	17	150		6	1											0	-4		-4				
RICK McHALE Rick G 6'0 230 Washington B: 1947 London, ON																															
1968	BC	16																													
LAMAR McHAN Clarence Lamar QB 6'1 210 Arkansas B: 12/16/1932 Lake Village, AR D: 11/23/1998 Jefferson, LA Draft: 1-2 1954 CHIC Pro: N																															
1965	TOR	2	1		0									2	-1	-0.5	1	0													
SCOTT McHENRY Scott SB-WR-FB 6'2 217 Saskatchewan B: 5/25/1987 Saskatoon, SK Draft: 4C-32 2009 CAL																															
2010	WPG	10				2																									
2011	WPG	8				3																									
2011	SAS	8				1																									
2011	Year	16				4																									
2	Years	18				6																									
TOM McHUGH Thomas FB 5'11 195 Notre Dame B: 1926 Phoenixville, PA Draft: 6-62 1954 CHIC																															
1954	OTT	7										10	2	43	275	6.4	78	2	2	-3	-1.5	2	0					1	10	10.0	10
HUGH McINNIS Hugh Allen OE 6'3 219 Southern Mississippi B: 9/18/1938 Mobile, AL Draft: FS 1960 HOU; 3A-26 1960 STL Pro: N																															
1967	BC	1																	2	30	15.0	20	0								
TODDRICK McINTOSH Toddrick Poole DL 6'3 277 Florida State B: 1/22/1972 Tallahassee, FL Draft: 7-216 1994 DAL Pro: N																															
1998	TOR	18	0	1	0	24	5.0	40.0																							
GARRETT McINTYRE Garrett Robert DE-DT 6'3 262 Fresno State B: 11/26/1984 South Lake Tahoe, CA Pro: N																															
2009	HAM	9	0	0	1	19	1.0	0.0																							
2010	HAM	17	0	4	2	32	8.0	49.0			1																				
2	Years	26	0	4	3	51	9.0	49.0																							
MIKE McINTYRE Mike DB 5'11 185 New Brunswick B: 2/14/1958 Montreal, QC																															
1982	HAM	12	1		0				5	41									1	12	12.0	12	0								
1983	HAM	16	0		1				2	36																					
1984	HAM	16							2	9																					
1985	OTT	11																													
1986	OTT	17							2	-1														1	22	22.0	22	1	12	12.0	12
1987	OTT	4	1		0	0																						1	0	0.0	0
6	Years	76	2		1	0			11	85									1	12	12.0	12	0	1	22	22.0	22	2	12	6.0	12
PAUL McJULIEN Paul Dorien P 5'10 190 Jackson State B: 2/24/1965 Chicago, IL Pro: N																															
1993	SAC	4				0						1	0																		
PRINCE McJUNKINS Prince QB 6'1 170 Wichita State B: 12/16/1960 Draft: 13-153 1983 DEN-USFL																															
1983	OTT	7	4		0									37	328	8.9	31	0													
1984	OTT	7	1		0									14	91	6.5	19	0													
2	Years	14	5		0									51	419	8.2	31	0													
BOB McKAY Bob FW-QB-HB-E 5'11 190 B: 1923																															
1947	TOR	7																													
1948	HAM	7																													
1950	TOR	5																													
1951	CAL	13																													
1952	CAL	4																													
1955	OTT	1																													
6	Years	37																													
ORLANDO McKAY Orlando Rodriguez WR 5'10 175 Washington B: 10/2/1969 Indianapolis, IN Draft: 5B-130 1992 GB																															
1994	HAM	8				0						6	1	1	-1	-1.0	-1	0	14	226	16.1	69	1					1	16	16.0	16
1995	MEM	2	1		0	0													2	26	13.0	16	0								
2	Years	10	1		0	0						6	1	1	-1	-1.0	-1	0	16	252	15.8	69	1					1	16	16.0	16
PAUL McKAY Paul DB 6'0 195 Toronto B: 1947 Draft: 3A-23 1970 HAM																															
1970	HAM	6										1	0											17	122	7.2	15				
1971	HAM	14	1		0				3	14		1	0											38	235	6.2	26				
1972	HAM	2																													
1973	HAM	2																													
1974	CAL	15										1	0											23	62	2.7	12				
5	Years	39	1		0				3	14		3	0											78	419	5.4	26				
NAUTYN McKAY-LOESCHER Nautyn DE 6'3 260 Alabama B: 11/9/1981 Toronto, ON Draft: 2-13 2004 BC																															
2005	BC	18				2	3.0	21.0																							
2006	BC	18	0	4	1	9	5.0	22.0			2	6	1																		
2007	HAM	16	0	3	1	18	11.0	64.0			2																				
2008	HAM	17	0	0	1	13	2.0	9.0			2																				
2009	BC	12				7	4.0	14.0																							
5	Years	81	0	7	3	49	25.0	130.0			6	6	1																		
JIMMY McKEAN James Gilbert QB-P 6'1 204 NDG Maple Leafs Jrs. B: 5/26/1945 Montreal, QC																															
1964	MTL	11										1	0																		
1965	MTL	8	0		1							1	0																		
1966	SAS	6	1		0																										
3	Years	25	1		1							2	0																		
GRANT McKEE Robert Grant CB-LB 6'1 195 Michigan B: 9/14/1940																															
1961	HAM	14																						2	0	0.0	0				
1962	HAM	14										6	1											2	3	1.5	2				
1963	HAM	13																													
1964	EDM	15							1																						
1965	EDM	12	1		1				3	40																					
1965	TOR	3	0		1																										
1965	Year	15	1		2				3	40																					
1968	TOR	7																													
6	Years	75	1		2				4	40		6	1											4	3	0.8	2				
STEVE McKEE Steve LB 6'2 220 Guelph B: 11/13/1969 Toronto, ON																															
1994	HAM	18				23																									
1995	HAM	2				0																									
1995	OTT	2				3																									
1995	Year	4				3																									
2	Years	20				26																									
WALT McKEE Walter K 5'11 185 Manitoba B: 6/28/1949 Draft: 4-28 1971 WPG																															
1972	WPG	16	1		1							14	0																		
1973	WPG	16	0		1							52	0																		
1974	WPG	16	1		0							79	0						1	20	20.0	20	0	1	4	4.0	4				
1975	EDM	6										1	0																		
4	Years	54	2		2							146	0						1	20	20.0	20	0	1	4	4.0	4				
WILLIE McKELTON Willie James DB 5'11 185 Southern University B: 7/3/1949 Auburn, NY Draft: 11-284 1972 MIN Pro: W																															
1973	OTT	1							1	40																					
BILL McKENNA Bill OE-LB 6'3 215 Brandeis B: 1933 Draft: 7-81 1955 PHI																															
1955	CAL	16							2	5		25	5						34	665	19.6	104	5					1	15	15.0	15
1956	CAL	1																													
1959	CAL	16	1		0				1			12	2						30	422	14.1	45	2	1	4	4.0	4	2	9	4.5	9
1960	CAL	14	0		1							18	3						20	296	14.8	27	3					3	33	11.0	14
1961	CAL	12			2																			1	5	5.0	5				
1963	CAL	7																	4	53	13.3	21	0								
6	Years	66	1		3				3	5		55	10						88	1436	16.3	104	10	2	9	4.5	5	6	57	9.5	15
DICK McKENNA Dick CB 6'0 190 Mount Royal JC B: 1940																															
1964	WPG	1																													
BILL McKENNY Bill HB 5'11 185 Georgia B: 1941																															
1962	EDM	16	2		2							36	6	26	78	3.0	21	0	27	564	20.9	63	6	37	157	4.2	19	19	501	26.4	69

Year	Team	GP	FM	FF	FR	TK	SK	YDS	IR	YDS	PD	PTS	TD	RA	YDS	AVG	LG	TD	REC	YDS	AVG	LG	TD	PR	YDS	AVG	LG	KOR	YDS	AVG	LG
ANTON McKENZIE Anton Anthony LB 5'11 225 Massachusetts B: 1/4/1981 Stony Brook, NY																															
2006	SAS	7				18					1																				
2007	SAS	9				19					1																	1	0	0.0	0
2008	SAS*	15	0	3	0	75	1.0	14.0	2	4	1																				
2009	BC+	18	0	2	1	99	6.0	39.0			4																				
2010	BC	16	0	1	0	65	1.0	11.0			2																				
2011	BC	18	0	1	0	86	2.0	9.0			2																				
6	Years	83	0	7	1	362	10.0	73.0	2	4	11																	1	0	0.0	0
CHRIS McKENZIE Chris DH 5'8 182 Glendale CC; Arizona State B: 3/17/1982 New York, NY Pro: N																															
2009	SAS	8	0	1	0	20					2																				
2010	SAS	14	0	0	1	43					5																				
2011	SAS	16				53			2	76	7	12	2											1	17	17.0	17				
3	Years	38	0	1	1	116			2	76	14	12	2											1	17	17.0	17				
DOUG McKENZIE Doug FB 5'10 190 Western Ontario B: 1938 Draft: 1-6 1959 SAS																															
1959	SAS	15							1					14	58	4.1	7	0	4	57	14.3	17	0	5	5	1.0	2	5	74	14.8	18
1961	SAS	5																													
2	Years	20							1	0				14	58	4.1	7	0	4	57	14.3	17	0	5	5	1.0	2	5	74	14.8	18
SCOTT McKENZIE Scott P-K 6'2 215 Alberta B: 4/27/1971 Winnipeg, MB																															
1999	CAL	8				1						12	1	1	20	20.0	20	0													
2001	TOR	3				0																									
2	Years	11				1						12	1	1	20	20.0	20	0													
BOB McKEOWN Bob C-OG 6'2 225 Yale B: 10/10/1950 Ottawa, ON																															
1971	OTT	14																													
1972	OTT	14																													
1973	OTT	14																													
1974	OTT+	15	1		0																										
1975	OTT	13																													
5	Years	70	1		0																										
PETE McKEOWN Pete																															
1949	TOR	3																													
SEAN McKEOWN Sean Thomas OT-DL 6'5 273 Western Ontario B: 9/23/1962 London, ON Draft: 1-5 1984 CAL																															
1984	CAL	8																													
1985	CAL	11	0		1																										
1986	CAL	15	0		1																										
1988	CAL	10				0																									
1989	TOR	13				2																									
5	Years	57	0		2	2																									
DON McKETA Donald J. HB 5'11 185 Washington B: 11/11/1934 Draft: 20-277 1961 NYG																															
1961	SAS	5												7	20	2.9	6	0	3	55	18.3	33	0								
JOHN McKILLOP John DB 5'1 180 Western Ontario Draft: 1968 MTL																															
1968	EDM	3																													
KEN McKIM Ken G-T 6'0 190 none B: 1925																															
1946	TOR	4																													
1947	TOR	2																													
1948	TOR	1																													
1951	SAS	14																													
4	Years	21																													
NEIL McKINLAY Neil LB 5'11 218 Simon Fraser B: 4/25/1981 Langley, BC Draft: 4-33 2004 WPG																															
2004	WPG	18	0	0	1	24	1.0	7.0																							
2005	WPG	18				27																									
2006	WPG	16	0	1	1	34			1	0	0																				
2007	WPG	18				25	1.0	3.0																							
2008	WPG	17	0	0	1	23																						4	34	8.5	11
2009	WPG	17	0	1	1	17			1	6	0																				
2011	BC	2				0																									
7	Years	106	0	2	4	150	2.0	10.0	2	6	0																	4	34	8.5	11
BENNY McKINNEY Benny E																															
1946	SAS	2																													
SILAS McKINNIE Silas Anthony OHB SE-DB 6'2 208 Iowa B: 1/24/1946 Detroit, MI																															
1968	SAS	15	5		0							18	3	109	639	5.9	47	2	29	440	15.2	51	1					20	488	24.4	41
1969	SAS	10	1		0							12	2	65	336	5.2	24	1	33	407	12.3	39	1					9	269	29.9	39
1970	SAS+	16	1		1							48	8	109	612	5.6	21	3	39	682	17.5	91	5					21	530	25.2	45
1971	SAS	15	2		0							24	4	63	392	6.2	72	2	30	392	13.1	37	2					14	394	28.1	66
1973	CAL	2												4	5	1.3	4	0	4	43	10.8	20	0								
5	Years	58	9		1							102	17	350	1984	5.7	72	8	135	1964	14.5	91	9					64	1681	26.3	66
HUGH McKINNIS Hugh Lee, Jr. FB 6'1 210 Arizona State B: 6/9/1948 Sharon, PA Draft: 8-201 1972 CLE Pro: N																															
1970	CAL*	16	5		0							54	9	205	1135	5.5	37	9	20	296	14.8	39	0					1	11	11.0	11
1971	CAL	16	4		0							42	7	191	910	4.8	89	6	32	281	8.8	45	1					4	91	22.8	38
1972	CAL	6	1		0							12	2	64	312	4.9	28	1	12	109	9.1		1					11	266	24.2	
1972	OTT	4	1		0									28	80	2.9		0	2	18	9.0		0					4	79	19.8	
1972	Year	10	2		0							12	2	92	392	4.3	28	1	14	127	9.1	21	1					15	345	23.0	42
3	Years	38	11		0							108	18	488	2437	5.0	89	16	66	704	10.7	45	2					20	447	22.4	38
MATT McKNIGHT Matt LB-DB 6'0 193 Waterloo B: 12/14/1977 Thunder Bay, ON Draft: 6-42 2001 TOR																															
2002	TOR	18				7																									
2003	BC	10				1																									
2003	CAL	5				1																									
2003	Year	15				2																									
2004	CAL	14				14																		1	2	2.0	2				
3	Years	42				23																		1	2	2.0	2				
DAVE McKOY David WR 6'2 195 Guelph B: 7/5/1983 Mississauga, ON Draft: 2-9 2007 SAS																															
2007	SAS	9				0													2	13	6.5	8	0								
ROY McLACHLAN Roy																															
1947	WPG	5																													
RHETT McLANE Rhett OG 6'4 295 Saskatchewan B: 3/29/1978 Liberty, SK Draft: 2B-17 2004 EDM																															
2005	EDM	3				0																									
2006	EDM	18				0																									
2007	EDM	14				0																									
3	Years	35				0																									
ROB McLAREN Rob LB-TE 6'1 225 Simon Fraser B: 3/7/1947 Draft: 1B-2 1969 WPG																															
1969	WPG	16							1	0																					
1970	WPG	16	0		3																										
1971	WPG+	16	0		2				1	0																					
1972	WPG	16							1	3																					
1973	WPG	16																													
1974	EDM	14							1	0																					
1975	EDM	16	0		1				1	24																					
1976	EDM	4							1	2																					
1976	HAM	12																													
1976	Year	16							1	2																					
1977	BC	16	0		2																							1	0	0.0	0
9	Years	130	0		8				6	29																		1	0	0.0	0
TED McLARTY Ted DB 6'2 175 none B: 1925																															

Year	Team	GP	FM	FF	FR	TK	SK	YDS	IR	YDS	PD	PTS	TD	RA	YDS	AVG	LG	TD	REC	YDS	AVG	LG	TD	PR	YDS	AVG	LG	KOR	YDS	AVG	LG
1948	OTT	11										10	2										2								
1949	OTT	4										5	1					1													
1950	OTT	9																													
1951	OTT	12										5	1																		
1952	OTT	9																													
5	Years	45										20	4					1					2								
BRYAN McLAUGHLIN Bryan C 6'2 245 Simon Fraser B: 4/23/1954 Draft: TE 1977 OTT																															
1977	CAL	5																													
1977	TOR	1																													
1977	Year	6																													
MIKE McLEAN Michael LB 6'0 215 Alberta B: 7/7/1962 Red Deer, AB Draft: 9-77 1985 EDM																															
1986	EDM	6																													
1987	EDM	13			1	0																									
1988	EDM	18			2	0																									
1989	EDM	14	0		1	4			1	26																					
1990	EDM	17				12																									
1991	EDM	18				24																		1	0	0.0	0				
1992	EDM	12				23																									
7	Years	98	0		4	63			1	26														1	0	0.0	0				
DON McLELLAN Don LB 6'1 198 Simon Fraser B: 1/15/1953																															
1976	BC	1																													
SPENCER McLENNAN Spencer WR 5'10 190 Okanagan Sun Jrs.; Imperial Valley JC B: 10/10/1966 Kelowna, BC																															
1991	BC	14				9													2	22	11.0	16	0								
1992	BC	18	0		1	4													9	97	10.8	16	0								
1993	BC	18				24																						1	6	6.0	6
1994	BC	18	2		1	11						6	1						3	59	19.7	29	0	31	155	5.0	15	19	382	20.1	40
1995	BC	16	1		0	10													2	20	10.0	12	0	26	164	6.3	38	22	444	20.2	51
1996	MTL+	18	1		1	36			4	51	3								2	17	8.5	14	0	2	9	4.5	6	10	213	21.3	27
1997	MTL	7	1	1	1	11			1	63	0																				
1998	WPG	18	0	0	2	9													21	267	12.7	28	0								
1999	WPG	16				29													1	9	9.0	9	0								
2000	WPG	18	0	0	2	29																		1	4	4.0	4				
10	Years	161	5	1	8	172			5	114	3	6	1						40	491	12.3	29	0	60	332	5.5	38	52	1045	20.1	51
ANDY McLEOD Andy LB 5'11 190 Alberta B: 8/19/1951 Draft: TE 1973 SAS																															
1973	SAS	16																													
1974	SAS	16	0		1																										
1975	SAS	3																													
1975	OTT	3																													
1975	Year	6																													
3	Years	35	0		1																										
CRAIG McLEOD Craig LB 6'0 210 Calgary B: 1949 Draft: 7-58 1970 CAL																															
1971	CAL	4																													
1971	WPG	10	0		1																										
1971	Year	14	0		1																										
MIKE McLEOD Michael James S 6'0 180 Montana State B: 5/4/1958 Bozeman, MT Pro: N																															
1980	EDM	6							1	21														15	97	6.5	19				
1981	EDM	16	0		2				5	31																		1	25	25.0	25
1982	EDM	16					1.0		1	22														5	58	11.6	26	1	0	0.0	0
1983	EDM	16	0		1				4	52																					
1984	EDM	7	1		0				1	0														11	145	13.2	20				
5	Years	61	1		3		1.0		12	126														31	300	9.7	26	2	25	12.5	25
MARK McLOUGHLIN Mark L-P 6'1 205 South Dakota B: 10/26/1965 Liverpool, England Draft: 3-20 1988 CAL																															
1988	CAL	10				0						97	0																		
1989	CAL	18	1		0	0						202	0																		
1990	CAL	18	3		0	0						209	0											1	4	4.0	4				
1991	CAL	18				1						208	0																		
1992	CAL+	18	1		0	0						208	0																		
1993	CAL	18	0		1	0						215	0																		
1994	CAL*	18	2		1	1						199	0																		
1995	CAL+	18				1						220	0																		
1996	CAL*	18				2						221	0																		
1997	CAL+	18	1	0	0	2						174	0																		
1998	CAL	18				4						176	0																		
1999	CAL+	18	0	0	1	4						192	0																		
2000	CAL	18	1	0	0	2						199	0																		
2001	CAL	18				0						180	0																		
2002	CAL	18				0						151	0																		
2003	CAL	14				0						105	0																		
2005	BC	4				0						39	0																		
17	Years	280	9	0	3	17						2995	0											1	4	4.0	4				
BILL McMAHON Bill HB 5'10 185 B: 1931																															
1951	CAL	7												1	8	8.0	8	0	1	9	9.0	9	0								
MIKE McMAHON Michael Edward QB 6'2 212 Rutgers B: 2/8/1979 Pittsburgh, PA Draft: 5-149 2001 DET Pro: NU																															
2007	TOR	10				1								5	37	7.4	11	0													
CHUCK McMANN Charles TE-RB 6'0 200 Wilfrid Laurier B: 5/11/1951 Toronto, ON Draft: 3A-24 1976 MTL																															
1976	MTL	11	0		1									1	1	1.0	1	0	12	176	14.7	40	0								
1977	MTL	9																										1	15	15.0	15
1978	MTL	16	1		1							6	1	1	1	1.0	1	0	12	146	12.2	18	1								
1979	MTL	16										6	1	3	12	4.0	10	0	9	122	13.6	22	1					2	34	17.0	22
1980	MTL	16										6	1	13	57	4.4	9	1	28	423	15.1	35	0								
1981	MTL	16	1		1							6	1						13	192	14.8	33	1								
1982	MTL	16	0		1														4	75	18.8	24	0								
1983	MTL	10																	1	14	14.0	14	0								
1984	MTL	16			1							6	1	4	12	3.0	4	1						1	0	0.0	0	1	0	0.0	0
1985	MTL	4										6	1						1	2	2.0	2	1					1	14	14.0	14
10	Years	130	2		5							36	6	22	83	3.8	10	2	80	1150	14.4	40	4	1	0	0.0	0	5	63	12.6	22
DANNY McMANUS Danny QB 6'0 200 Florida State B: 6/17/1965 Dania, FL Draft: 11-282 1988 KC																															
1990	WPG	18	2		0	0								3	12	4.0	9	0													
1991	WPG	18				1																									
1992	WPG	18	2		1	1								4	7	1.8	8	0													
1993	BC	18	4		0	0								12	64	5.3	26	0													
1994	BC	18	1		0	3								1	-7	-7.0	-7	0													
1995	BC	17	10		2	0						12	2	11	-4	-0.4	7	2													
1996	EDM	17	4		1	1						18	3	10	41	4.1	11	3													
1997	EDM	15	2	0	2	1						6	1	12	24	2.0	12	1													
1998	HAM	18	4	0	4	3						24	4	24	72	3.0	19	4													
1999	HAM*	18	2	0	4	0						18	3	18	35	1.9	15	3													
2000	HAM	18	1	0	2	2								15	67	4.5	16	0													
2001	HAM	18	2	0	1	1						18	3	21	78	3.7	14	3													
2002	HAM	18	0	0	2	1						6	1	13	30	2.3	10	1													
2003	HAM	15	2	0	2	1						2	0	5	-9	-1.8	2	0													
2004	HAM	18	4	0	1	1								5	6	1.2	4	0													

Year	Team	GP	FM	FF	FR	TK	SK	YDS	IR	YDS	PD	PTS	TD	RA	YDS	AVG	LG	TD	REC	YDS	AVG	LG	TD	PR	YDS	AVG	LG	KOR	YDS	AVG	LG
2005	HAM	18	2	0	0	0						0	0	3	10	3.3	5	0													
2006	CAL	18				1																									
17	Years	298	42	0	22	17						104	17	157	426	2.7	26	17													
BOB McMILLAN Bob HB 5'10 175 Saskatoon Hilltops Jrs. B: 1932																															
1952	SAS	10							1	10														9	76	8.4	29	8	206	25.8	55
1953	SAS	13										5	1	17	39	2.3		0	3	20	6.7		1					7	93	13.3	
1954	SAS	5	1		0							5	1	5	14	2.8	19	1	2	60	30.0	4	0	1	0	0.0	0	5	116	23.2	40
3	Years	28	1		0				1	10		10	2	22	53	2.4	19	1	5	80	16.0	4	1	10	76	7.6	29	20	415	20.8	55
JIM McMILLAN Jim QB 6'1 175 Boise State B: 11/18/1952 Draft: 14-350 1975 DET																															
1975	HAM	16	5		1							4	0	47	297	6.3	52	0													
LEIGH McMILLAN Leigh FB-S 5'8 155 Edmonton Wildcats Jrs.; Alberta B: 1936																															
1956	EDM	16	4		2				1	0				1	-1	-1.0	-1	0						66	359	5.4	25				
1957	EDM	14	3		0																			61	388	6.4	20				
1958	EDM	16	5		2																			93	519	5.6	23				
3	Years	46	12		4				1	0				1	-1	-1.0	-1	0						220	1266	5.8	25				
ALFONZO McMILLIAN Alfonzo DB 6'2 200 Southwestern Oklahoma State B: 9/27/1956																															
1982	MTL	7																													
1983	HAM	2	0		1																										
2	Years	9	0		1																										
TODD McMILLON Todd M. CB 5'10 185 Northern Arizona B: 9/26/1973 Bellflower, CA Pro: EN																															
1997	SAS	12	0	0	1	37			1	8	5	6	1																			
1998	SAS	18				71			2	73	5	6	1												1	13	13.0	13				
1999	SAS	18	0	0	1	45			1	20	7																				
3	Years	48	0	0	2	153			4	101	17	12	2												1	13	13.0	13				
JOHN McMURTRY John LB-FB 6'0 206 Toronto B: 1939 Toronto, ON																															
1961	CAL	9												1	5	5.0	5	0													
FRED McNAIR Fred QB 6'1 220 Alcorn State B: 12/11/1968 Collins, MS Pro: E																															
1991	TOR	8				0																									
1992	SAS	14				0																									
2	Years	22				0																									
BOB McNAMARA John Robert OHB-S 6'0 189 Minnesota B: 8/12/1931 Hastings, MN Draft: 9-108 1953 CLE Pro: N																															
1955	WPG	2												9	51	5.7	10	0	1	20	20.0	20	0					2	68	34.0	36
1956	WPG+	16	4		0				2	0		102	17	178	1101	6.2	30	13	36	512	14.2	75	4					9	253	28.1	41
1957	WPG	6							1	74		12	2	18	90	5.0	19	1	3	19	6.3	15	0					1	29	29.0	29
1958	WPG	5										12	2	40	236	5.9	40	0	18	249	13.8	41	2								
4	Years	29	4		0				3	74		126	21	245	1478	6.0	40	14	58	800	13.8	75	6					12	350	29.2	41
JIM McNAUGHTON Jim TE 6'2 223 Utah State B: 1942 Draft: 17-129 1964 DEN; 12-165 1964 NYG																															
1964	BC	4																	1	15	15.0	15	0								
1964	SAS	1																													
1964	Year	5																	1	15	15.0	15	0								
GARY McNEAL Gary Tyrone DB 5'10 179 Virginia Military Institute B: 12/12/1956 Cincinnati, OH																															
1980	TOR	4	0		2				1	0																		1	21	21.0	21
REGGIE McNEAL Reginald Parrish WR-SB 6'2 205 Texas A&M B: 9/20/1983 Lufkin, TX Draft: 6-193 2006 CIN Pro: N																															
2008	TOR	12				0						12	2	1	4	4.0	4	0	43	606	14.1	91	2								
2009	TOR	9	1	0	0	1						18	3						24	309	12.9	52	3					13	273	21.0	27
2010	TOR	7	1	0	0	2													13	175	13.5	25	0								
2011	EDM	1				0																									
4	Years	29	2	0	0	3						30	5	1	4	4.0	4	0	80	1090	13.6	91	5					13	273	21.0	27
DAVE McNEEL David LB 6'1 220 Missouri B: 12/4/1959 Greenfield, MO																															
1983	BC	2																													
1984	BC	3					0.5																								
1985	EDM	5																													
3	Years	10					0.5																								
EMANUEL McNEIL Emanuel DT 6'3 285 Tennessee-Martin B: 6/9/1967 Richmond, VA Draft: 10-267 1989 NE Pro: N																															
1991	WPG	4	0		1	12	1.0																								
JAY McNEIL Jay OG 6'3 275 Kent State B: 8/20/1970 London, ON Draft: 4-34 1994 CAL																															
1994	CAL	4				0																									
1995	CAL	17				0																									
1996	CAL	18	0		1	1																									
1997	CAL	18				0																									
1998	CAL	18				1																									
1999	CAL	13				1																									
2000	CAL	18				0																									
2001	CAL*	18				3																									
2002	CAL*	18				3																									
2003	CAL	12				1																									
2004	CAL+	18				2																									
2005	CAL+	18	1	0	1	3																									
2006	CAL*	18	0	0	1	2																									
2007	CAL+	15				1																									
14	Years	223	1	0	3	18																									
PAT McNEIL Patrick Lamott FB 5'9 208 Baylor B: 2/28/1954 Pittsburg, CA Draft: 17-472 1976 KC Pro: N																															
1978	EDM	2	3		0									21	80	3.8	9	0	4	25	6.3	12	0								
SCOTT McNEILL Scott OG 6'3 280 Boise State B: 4/29/1971 Regina, SK																															
1995	EDM	5	1		0	2																									
PAT McNERNEY Pat DT-OT 6'4 265 Weber State B: 1/3/1971 St. Julian's, Malta Draft: 2-21 1994 EDM																															
1995	EDM	1				1																									
1996	EDM	2				0																									
1996	BC	13				7																									
1996	Year	15				7																									
1997	HAM	1				0																									
1998	WPG	7				3																									
4	Years	11				11																									
DOUG McNICHOL Douglas Stewart DE-DT-OE 6'4 226 Western Ontario B: 3/29/1930 Merritton, ON D: 2/15/2012 Mississauga, ON Draft: 1-1 1953 MTL																															
1953	MTL+	14																													
1954	MTL+	14																													
1955	MTL+	12																													
1956	MTL	14							1	0																					
1957	MTL	6																													
1958	MTL+	14							1	9																					
1959	MTL+	14																													
1960	MTL	13																													
1961	TOR	14																													
1962	TOR	12																													
1963	TOR	10																													
11	Years	137							2	9																					
PETER McPARTLAND Peter HB																															
1948	TOR	1																													
1949	MTL	2																													
2	Years	3																													
GEORGE McPHAIL George HB 5'9 165 none B: 1928																															
1948	OTT	5																													

Year	Team	GP	FM	FF	FR	TK	SK	YDS	IR	YDS	PD	PTS	TD	RA	YDS	AVG	LG	TD	REC	YDS	AVG	LG	TD	PR	YDS	AVG	LG	KOR	YDS	AVG	LG
1949	SAS	13																													
1950	WPG	10												36	86	2.4		0													
1951	WPG	12										10	2	28	146	5.2		0	6	69	11.5		2	21	127	6.0		28	454	16.2	
1952	WPG	10												10	15	1.5	14	0	1	16	16.0	16	0	5	23	4.6	9	2	33	16.5	18
1953	MTL	1																													
6	Years	51										10	2	74	247	3.3	14	0	7	85	12.1	16	2	26	150	5.8	9	30	487	16.2	18
ADRIAN McPHERSON Adrian Jamal QB 6'3 218 Florida State B: 5/8/1983 Bradenton, FL Draft: 5-152 2005 NO																															
2008	MTL	18	1	0	0	0						30	5	25	86	3.4	24	5													
2009	MTL	17				0						12	2	61	351	5.8	34	2													
2010	MTL	9				0								41	243	5.9	26	0													
2011	MTL	18	1	0	0	0						24	4	50	181	3.6	25	4													
4	Years	62	2	0	0	0						66	11	177	861	4.9	34	11													
DON McPHERSON Donald Glenn QB 6'1 193 Syracuse B: 4/2/1965 New York, NY Draft: 6A-149 1988 PHI																															
1991	HAM	11	1		0	0								12	75	6.3	23	0													
1992	HAM	18	2		1	0								5	25	5.0	21	0													
1993	HAM	18	11		5	1						12	2	55	299	5.4	30	2													
1994	OTT	18				0																									
4	Years	65	14		6	1						12	2	72	399	5.5	30	2													
JIM McPHERSON James Roy OG-C 6'2 207 Winnipeg Rods Jrs. B: 1928																															
1949	WPG	9																													
1950	WPG	14																													
1951	WPG	14																													
1952	WPG+	16			2																										
1953	WPG	12																													
5	Years	65	0		2																										
DICK McQUAID Dick HB																															
1946	SAS	8																													
1947	SAS	3																													
2	Years	11																													
ED McQUARTERS Eddie Lee DT 6'1 250 Oklahoma B: 4/16/1943 Tulsa, OK Draft: 18-250 1965 STL Pro: N																															
1966	SAS	8																													
1967	SAS*	16	0		2				1	68		6	1																		
1968	SAS*	16																													
1969	SAS*	16	0		3																										
1970	SAS	16	0		1																										
1971	SAS	10	0		1							6	1																		
1972	SAS	10																													
1973	SAS	7																													
1974	SAS	8	0		3																										
9	Years	107	0		10				1	68		12	2																		
EDDIE McQUARTERS Ed, Jr. OG 6'1 245 Minot State; Regina Rams Jrs. B: 5/17/1963 Tulsa, OK Draft: 4B-29 1984 SAS																															
1987	WPG	2				0																									
1988	WPG	4				0																									
2	Years	6				0																									
LEON McQUAY Leon HB 5'9 195 Tampa B: 3/19/1950 Tampa, FL D: 11/29/1995 Tampa, FL Draft: 5-119 1973 NYG Pro: N																															
1971	TOR*	12	2		0							54	9	138	977	7.1	81	5	26	429	16.5	81	4					3	80	26.7	40
1972	TOR	14	4		0							30	5	148	745	5.0	50	2	32	418	13.1	43	3								
1973	TOR	1	2		0									21	80	3.8	9	0	1	9	9.0	9	0								
1973	CAL	2	1		0									19	49	2.6	14	0	2	-13	-6.5	0	0								
1973	Year	3	3		0									40	129	3.2	14	0	3	-4	-1.3	9	0								
1977	TOR	7	2		0							6	1	76	307	4.0	16	0	13	139	10.7	35	1					5	114	22.8	33
4	Years	34	11		0							90	15	402	2158	5.4	81	7	74	982	13.3	81	8					8	194	24.3	40
BARRY McQUEEN Barry HB 5'10 190 Winnipeg Rods Jrs. B: 2/19/1935 Winnipeg, MB																															
1956	WPG	1																													
LARRY McSEED Larry S. LB 6'2 222 Delaware B: 9/27/1973 Philadelphia, PA Pro: E																															
1997	MTL	10	0	2	2	21	3.0	22.0			1																				
1998	MTL	5				7					1																				
1998	SAS	5				22																									
1998	Year	10				29					1																				
2	Years	15	0	2	2	50	3.0	22.0			3																				
GORD McTAGGART Gord QB 6'0 190 Lakeshore Bears Jrs.; East York Argonauts Ints. B: 1940																															
1965	TOR	6	1		1									3	6	2.0	4	0										1	5	5.0	5
MIKE McTAGUE Mike WR-P-SB-K 6'0 185 North Dakota State B: 5/31/1957 Ottawa, ON Draft: TE 1979 TOR																															
1979	CAL	16										11	0						1	9	9.0	9	0	1	2	2.0	2				
1980	CAL	16	1		0							43	0	1	22	22.0	22	0	11	126	11.5	20	0								
1981	CAL	16										17	2	3	94	31.3	44	0	43	519	12.1	39	2								
1982	CAL	16	1		0							16	2	1	15	15.0	15	0	32	483	15.1	36	2								
1983	CAL	15	2		1							19	1						19	272	14.3	42	1								
1984	CAL	16										29	3	2	15	7.5	15	0	34	517	15.2	34	3								
1985	MTL+	16	2		3							18	2	4	-24	-6.0	3	0	47	660	14.0	30	2								
1986	MTL	2	1		0														13	190	14.6	0.35	0								
1986	SAS	14	1		1							7	1						14	261	18.6	39	1								
1986	Year	16	2		0							7	1						27	451	16.7	39	1								
1987	SAS	3										8	0																		
9	Years	116	8		5							168	11	11	122	11.1	44	0	214	3037	14.2	42	11	1	2	2.0	2				
IAN McTAVISH Ian HB 6'1 220 Winnipeg St. Johns Grads Jrs. B: 6/5/1928																															
1948	WPG	7																													
1950	CAL	12																													
2	Years	19																													
JOHN McVEIGH John (Red) T 5'11 204 Edmonton Jrs.; Edmonton Ints. B: 1925																															
1949	EDM	13																													
1950	EDM	12																													
1951	EDM	5																													
3	Years	30																													
ANDY McVEY Andrew FB 6'1 210 Toronto B: 6/6/1963 Toronto, ON Draft: 2-14 1987 CAL																															
1987	CAL	18	3		4	3						6	1	36	209	5.8	16	1	5	28	5.6	19	0					26	534	20.5	82
1988	CAL	18	2		1	0						12	2	47	207	4.4	25	1	8	92	11.5	30	1					13	251	19.3	33
1989	CAL	18	1		0	0						6	1	39	218	5.6	37	1	11	103	9.4	21	0					2	12	6.0	8
1990	CAL	18	3		2	4						32	5	82	315	3.8	16	3	39	391	10.0	47	2					4	33	8.3	22
1991	CAL	17	4		1	5						12	2	36	158	4.4	19	1	26	266	10.2	25	1					3	30	10.0	15
1992	CAL	18	3		0	9						42	7	59	286	4.8	34	6	11	147	13.4	25	1					1	10	10.0	10
1993	CAL	18	6		2	7						12	2	41	185	4.5	17	2	35	293	8.4	22	0					2	20	10.0	20
7	Years	125	22		10	28						122	20	340	1578	4.6	37	15	135	1320	9.8	47	5					51	890	17.5	82
GLEN McWHINNEY Glen QB-WF-FW 5'10 170 Weston Wildcats Jrs.; St. Boniface Legionaires Ints. B: 1930																															
1952	EDM	16												4	-18	-4.5	0	0						23	145	6.3	22	8	73	9.1	20
1953	EDM	15												5	16	3.2		0	2	33	16.5		0	2	5	2.5					
1954	EDM	16	1		0							5	1						18	431	23.9	77	1								
1955	WPG	16	1		0														17	220	12.9	28	0	58	379	6.5	24				
1956	WPG	15	1		2														9	128	14.2	22	0	35	161	4.6	11	1	18	18.0	18
5	Years	78	3		2							5	1	9	-2	-0.2	0	0	46	812	17.7	77	1	118	690	5.8	24	9	91	10.1	20
JON McWILLIAMS Jon Blythe E 6'0 192 Nebraska B: 2/1/1934 Horton, KS D: 3/26/2011 Omaha, NE																															
1956	SAS	16	1		0							7	1						20	325	16.3	42	1								

Year	Team	GP	FM	FF	FR	TK	SK	YDS	IR	YDS	PD	PTS	TD	RA	YDS	AVG	LG	TD	REC	YDS	AVG	LG	TD	PR	YDS	AVG	LG	KOR	YDS	AVG	LG
LAMONT MEACHAM Lamont CB 6'0 170 Western Kentucky B: 1/20/1961 Clairton, PA Draft: 11-280 1982 BAL																														
1983	TOR	9							1	0																				
1984	TOR	14	1		0				3	90																				
1985	OTT	15	0		1				4	37																				
1986	OTT	8							1	36																				
4	Years	46	1		1				9	163																				
RON MEADMORE Ronald Hector DE-OG-OT 6'2 200 Weston Wildcats Jrs. B: 12/26/1933 Culross, MB																														
1957	WPG	4																												
1958	WPG	12																												
1959	WPG	9																												
1960	WPG	6	0		1																									
1961	WPG	15																												
1962	SAS	12																												
1963	SAS	14																												
1964	SAS	16	0		2																									
1965	SAS	3																												
9	Years	91	0		3																									
ED MEADOWS Edward Allen (Country) DE 6'2 221 Duke B: 2/19/1932 Oxford, NC D: 10/22/1974 Morehead City, NC Draft: 3-30 1954 CHIB Pro: N																														
1961	MTL	3																												
JACK MEAKIN Jack E 6'2 196 Edmonton Jrs.; Montana State B: 1933																														
1955	CAL	14	0		2							5	1																	
1956	CAL	1																												
2	Years	15	0		2							5	1																	
DAVE MEANS David Mitchell DE 6'4 235 Southeast Missouri State B: 1/23/1952 Hopkinsville, KY Draft: 12-303 1974 BUF; 31-361 1974 HOU-WFL Pro: N																														
1975	CAL	4																												
KELVIN MEANS Kelvin B. WR-RB 5'11 185 San Diego*; Fresno State B: 10/27/1969 Compton, CA																														
1994	HAM	12	3		0	3						18	3	1	-6	-6.0	-6	0	54	786	14.6	50	3	1	1	1.0	1	32	622	19.4	35
1995	HAM	4				1						6	1						15	159	10.6	28	1	2	12	6.0	9	7	196	28.0	46
1996	OTT	1				0													7	120	17.1	43	0					2	30	15.0	20
3	Years	17	3		0	4						24	4	1	-6	-6.0	-6	0	76	1065	14.0	50	4	3	13	4.3	9	41	848	20.7	46
LOYCE MEANS Loyce Carlton CB-DH 5'11 179 Houston B: 3/31/1989 Houston, TX																														
2011	HAM	6				14					1																			
GENE MEARS Gene C 6'4 200 Oklahoma																														
1955	WPG	2							1	17																				
JODY MEDFORD David Joe DT 6'2 265 Rice B: 7/30/1953 Draft: 14-352 1975 HOU																														
1976	HAM	1																												
1977	CAL	16	0		1																									
2	Years	17	0	0	1																									
JASON MEDLOCK Jason Duane DE 6'3 235 Navarro JC; Nevada-Las Vegas B: 1/24/1971 Dallas, TX																														
1994	LV	9				9	2.0	19.0																						
1995	CAL	1				1	1.0	1.0																						
2	Years	10				10	3.0	20.0																						
JUSTIN MEDLOCK Justin Charles K-P 5'11 201 UCLA B: 10/23/1983 Santa Clara, CA Draft: 5-160 2007 KC Pro: N																														
2009	TOR	17	2	0	0	1						147	0	1	19	19.0	19	0												
2010	TOR	4				0						27	0																	
2011	HAM+	18				0						197	0																	
3	Years	39	2	0	0	1						371	0	1	19	19.0	19	0												
RAMEL MEEKINS Ramel DT 5'11 284 Rutgers B: 8/6/1985 Westwood, NJ																														
2007	TOR	1				0																								
BOB MEEKS Robert Earl, Jr. OL 6'2 279 Auburn B: 5/28/1969 Andalusia, AL Draft: 10-278 1992 DEN Pro: EN																														
1995	BAL	2				0																								
RON MEEKS Ronald DB 5'9 180 Arkansas State B: 8/27/1954 Jacksonville, FL																														
1977	HAM	1																					6	48	8.0	30	3	87	29.0	38
1978	HAM	16	2		1																			13	85	6.5	16	23	471	20.5	46
1979	OTT	3	1		0				2	6														3	30	10.0	18				
1980	TOR	7							0	29																				
1981	TOR	6																												
5	Years	33	3		1				2	35														22	163	7.4	30	26	558	21.5	46
GEORGE MEEN George T-E Toronto																														
1947	TOR	12																												
1948	TOR	11																												
2	Years	23																												
MARC MEGNA Marc L. LB-DE 6'2 245 Richmond B: 7/30/1976 Fall River, MA Draft: 6A-183 1999 NYJ Pro: EN																														
2002	MTL+	18	0	2	1	51	7.0	50.0	1	0	2																			
2003	MTL	18	1	0	4	28	5.0	16.0	0	0	3																			
2004	MTL	10				36	2.0	15.0	1	0	3																			
2005	MTL	7	0	0	1	16																								
4	Years	53	1	2	6	131	14.0	81.0	2	0	8																			
DALE MEINERT Dale Herman OT-DT 6'2 220 Oklahoma State B: 12/18/1933 Lone Wolf, OK D: 5/10/2004 Clinton, OK Draft: 8-88(f) 1955 BAL Pro: N																														
1955	EDM+	15	2		5																			2	18	9.0	18				
MARV MEIROWITZ Marv T 6'1 205 Syracuse; McGill B: 1924																														
1952	MTL	11																												
1953	MTL	8																												
2	Years	19																												
MEL MELIN Melvin R. QB 6'1 194 Washington State B: 6/7/1940 Draft: 6-45 1962 NYT																														
1962	BC	2										4	0	3	13	4.3	7	0												
1963	BC	1																												
1964	BC	1																												
3	Years	4										4	0	3	13	4.3	7	0												
TERRENCE MELTON Terrence Lee DE 6'1 235 Rice B: 1/1/1977 Miami, FL Pro: NU																														
2002	SAS	18	0	0	1	42					2																			
2003	SAS	18	0	4	4	73	3.0				3	6	1																	
2	Years	36	0	4	5	115	3.0				5	6	1																	
LEN MELTZER Leonard OHB-E 6'0 189 Winnipeg St. John's Grads Jrs. B: 1931																														
1950	WPG	1												6	21	3.5		0												
1952	WPG	11										20	4	29	182	6.3	43	4	7	73	10.4	20	0	5	81	16.2	33	13	326	25.1	44
1953	WPG	10										15	3	40	203	5.1		3	7	49	7.0		0					8	172	21.5	
1954	WPG	4	2		0																		0							
1954	BC	11										15	3	9	-46	-5.1	3	0					2	7	157	22.4	115	14	328	23.4	37
1954	Year	15	2		0							15	3	9	-46	-5.1	3	0	8	130	16.3	38	2	7	157	22.4	115	14	328	23.4	37
4	Years	26	2		0							50	10	84	360	4.3	43	7	14	122	8.7	20	2	12	238	19.8	115	35	826	23.6	44
STEVE MENDRYK Steve DB-FW-E 6'1 187 Edmonton Jrs. B: 10/1/1928 Edmonton, AB																														
1949	EDM	13																												
1950	EDM	14												1	1	1.0	1	0									86				
1951	EDM	8										5	1											20	189	9.5		1	11	11.0	11
1952	EDM	16			3				3	55				4	2	0.5	4	0						33	243	7.4	30	9	211	23.4	35
1953	EDM	16							2	10		20	4	3	25	8.3		1	12	199	16.6		3	1	3	3.0	3				
1954	EDM	15			3				5	27														1	0	0.0	0				
1955	EDM	5							3	23														2	10	5.0	6				
1956	EDM	15							3	16																				
1958	EDM	9																												
9	Years	111	0		6				16	131		25	5	8	28	3.5	4	1	12	199	16.6		3	57	445	7.8	30	10	222	22.2	35

Year	Team	GP	FM	FF	FR	TK	SK	YDS	IR	YDS	PD	PTS	TD	RA	YDS	AVG	LG	TD	REC	YDS	AVG	LG	TD	PR	YDS	AVG	LG	KOR	YDS	AVG	LG
DENNIS MENDYK Dennis Arthur HB 6'0 190 Michigan State B: 1/16/1935 Draft: 3-35 1957 NYG																															
1957	WPG	4	1									12	2	19	109	5.7	20	2	2	47	23.5	38	0					2	37	18.5	19
SCOTT MENNIE Scott LB 6'1 228 Manitoba B: 9/25/1979 Lethbridge, AB Draft: 4-29 2005 WPG																															
2005	WPG	9				1																						1	0	0.0	0
2006	MTL	6				0																									
2	Years	15				1																						1	0	0.0	0
ED MERCHANT Edward F. HB 6'1 190 Miami (Ohio) B: 4/29/1932 Middletown, OH D: 1/3/1994 Warrensville Heights, OH Draft: 17-198 1955 PIT																															
1955	EDM	1												3	7	2.3	5	0													
RON MERKERSON Ronderick Devon LB 6'2 247 Colorado B: 8/30/1975 Clarksville, TN Draft: 5-145 1998 NE Pro: X																															
2002	HAM	1				2																									
JOE MERO Pershing CB 5'11 184 Louisiana State B: 2/8/1968 New Orleans, LA																															
1992	BC	9				18			1	0																					
1993	OTT	7				22			3	20																					
1994	SHR	11				36			1	2	2																				
1995	TOR	15				31			1	51	4																				
1996	OTT	18				46			4	26	6																				
5	Years	60				153			10	99	12																				
CHARLES MERRITT Charles LB 6'2 235 Carson-Newman B: 1/13/1963 Valdosta, GA																															
1989	OTT	6				22																									
JIM MERRITTS James Clystis NT 6'3 255 Connecticut; West Virginia B: 3/22/1961 Roaring Springs, PA Draft: TD 1984 PIT-USFL Pro: N																															
1985	TOR	1																													
CURT MERZ Curtis Carl DE 6'4 257 Iowa B: 4/17/1938 Newark, NJ Draft: FS 1960 NYT; 3-31 1960 PHI Pro: N																															
1960	WPG	3										6	1						6	145	24.2	41	1								
1960	OTT	5																	3	42	14.0	17	0					1	3	3.0	3
1960	Year	8										6	1						9	187	20.8	41	1					1	3	3.0	3
WALLY MERZ Wally T 6'4 220 Colorado B: 1935 Draft: 7-81 1957 WAS																															
1957	SAS	16																													
REG MESERVE Reginald P-FB 5'11 190 none B: 1935																															
1957	TOR	13										4	0											1	2	2.0	2				
1958	TOR	2																													
2	Years	15										4	0											1	2	2.0	2				
JEROME MESSAM Jerome FB-RB 6'3 245 North Dakota Science; Graceland B: 4/2/1985 Toronto, ON																															
2010	BC	17	2	0	1	8						12	2	23	92	4.0	16	2	5	57	11.4	20	0					5	91	18.2	23
2011	EDM*	18	4	0	0	1						38	6	195	1057	5.4	51	6	27	248	9.2	18	0					2	21	10.5	11
2	Years	35	6	0	1	9						50	8	218	1149	5.3	51	8	32	305	9.5	20	0					7	112	16.0	23
BO METCALF Isaac Scott CB 6'2 193 Baylor B: 4/18/1961 Waco, TX Draft: 4-106 1983 PIT Pro: N																															
1985	TOR	7							2	1																					
TERRY METCALF Terrance Randolph RB 5'10 185 Everett CC; Long Beach State B: 9/24/1951 Seattle, WA Draft: 3B-63 1973 STL Pro: N																															
1978	TOR	15	9		1							18	3	169	669	4.0	26	2	31	269	8.7	34	1	27	239	8.9	35	18	446	24.8	54
1979	TOR+	14	8		1							42	7	141	691	4.9	30	2	55	568	10.3	40	5	14	110	7.9	33	9	205	22.8	32
1980	TOR	15	7		0							30	5	140	554	4.0	25	4	51	417	8.2	39	1								
3	Years	44	24		2							90	15	450	1914	4.3	30	8	137	1254	9.2	40	7	41	349	8.5	35	27	651	24.1	54
JOHN METRAS John, Jr. C 6'2 235 Western Ontario B: 1941 Draft: 2-10 1963 TOR																															
1964	HAM	5																													
1965	HAM	14	1																												
2	Years	19	1		0																										
DENNIS MEYER John Dennis DB 5'11 186 Arkansas State B: 4/8/1950 Jefferson City, MO Draft: 6-143 1972 PIT Pro: NW																															
1975	CAL	9	0		1				3	55														31	246	7.9	24	7	152	21.7	32
1976	CAL	16	1		4				1	5														65	639	9.8	61	17	452	26.6	48
1977	CAL	2																						5	89	17.8	44	2	50	25.0	28
3	Years	27	1		5				4	60														101	974	9.6	61	26	654	25.2	48
ROHN MEYER Rohn OT 6'3 287 Calgary B: 1/17/1972 Rush Lake, SK																															
1996	CAL	18				0																									
1997	CAL	18				0						6	1						1	21	21.0	21	1								
1998	CAL	18				0																									
1999	CAL	18				1																									
2000	TOR	7				0																									
5	Years	79				1						6	1						1	21	21.0	21	1								
BOB MEYERS Robert Ellis, Jr. FB-P 6'2 185 Pasadena JC; Stanford B: 10/12/1930 Los Angeles, CA D: 4/19/1993 Morro Bay, CA Draft: 16-190 1952 SF Pro: N																															
1955	CAL	14	3		1				3	31		23	3	45	167	3.7	21	1	5	34	6.8	14	1								
FREDDIE MEYERS Fredric D. E-QB 6'2 205 Oklahoma State B: 1933 Draft: 8-93(f) 1955 SF																															
1958	EDM	3	2						1	2				1	4	4.0	4	0	3	44	14.7	23	0	3	7	2.3	12	3	51	17.0	27
1959	EDM	7										12	2	1	3	3.0	3	0	15	348	23.2	39	2								
2	Years	10	2		0				1	2		12	2	2	7	3.5	4	0	18	392	21.8	39	2	3	7	2.3	12	3	51	17.0	27
EDDIE MICHAELS Edward Joseph (Whitey) G 5'11 205 Villanova B: 6/11/1914 D: 1/21/1976 Wilmington, DE Draft: 2-14 1936 CHIB Pro: N																															
1948	OTT+	12																													
1949	OTT+	12																													
1950	OTT	11																													
3	Years	35																													
JOHN MICHALUK John C-LB 6'1 225 Kent State B: 1944																															
1966	HAM	14																													
1967	HAM	14																										1	12	12.0	12
1968	HAM	14	1		1																										
1969	HAM	14							1	25																					
4	Years	56	1		1				1	25																		1	12	12.0	12
JOHN MICHELS John Joseph G 5'11 200 Tennessee B: 2/15/1931 Philadelphia, PA Draft: 25-298 1953 PHI Pro: N																															
1957	WPG	13																										1	15	15.0	15
RUSS MICHNA Russell Walter QB 6'1 224 Western Illinois B: 2/3/1981 Elk Grove, IL Pro: U																															
2005	WPG	18	1	0	0	0								5	5	1.0	3	0													
2006	WPG	4	2	0	0	1																									
2	Years	22	3	0	0	1								5	5	1.0	3	0													
WILLIE MIDDLEBROOKS Willie Frank CB 6'1 200 Minnesota B: 2/12/1979 Miami, FL Draft: 1-24 2001 DEN Pro: N																															
2008	TOR	15				56			2	42	11																				
2009	TOR	11	0	1	0	36	1.0	5.0			1																				
2010	TOR	15				49			1	38	3																				
3	Years	41	0	1	0	141	1.0	5.0	3	80	15																				
MIKE MIDDLETON Michael LB 5'10 211 Indiana B: 12/4/1969 Cincinnati, OH Draft: 3-84 1993 DAL Pro: E																															
1993	SAS	5				13																									
ROBERT MIELE Robert DT 6'1 250 Concordia (Canada) B: 2/8/1950 Montreal, QC																															
1972	MTL	1																													
MIKE MIHELIC Michael OG 6'4 245 Indiana B: 3/11/1973 Brampton, ON Draft: 2B-14 1996 HAM																															
1997	WPG	14				0																									
1998	WPG	16				4																									
1999	WPG	18	0	0	1	8																									
2000	HAM	8				0																									
2001	HAM	9				1																									
2002	HAM	14				1																									
2003	HAM	18				2																									
2004	TOR	9				0																									
2005	TOR	13	0	0	2	3																									
2006	TOR	4				0																									
10	Years	123	0	0	3	19																									

Year	Team	GP	FM	FF	FR	TK	SK	YDS	IR	YDS	PD	PTS	TD	RA	YDS	AVG	LG	TD	REC	YDS	AVG	LG	TD	PR	YDS	AVG	LG	KOR	YDS	AVG	LG
STAN MIKAWOS Stan DT 6'4 245 North Dakota B: 5/11/1958 Gdansk, Poland Draft: TE 1982 WPG																														
1982	WPG	9					1.0																							
1983	WPG	6																												
1984	WPG	16	0		1		0.5																							
1985	WPG	16					4.0																							
1986	WPG	18	0		2		7.0																							
1987	WPG	13			1	23	3.0																							
1988	WPG	15	0		4	26	4.0																					4	2	0.5	2
1989	WPG	12	0		1	14	1.0																							
1990	WPG	18	0		1	26	2.0		1	28																				
1991	WPG	8				18																								
1992	WPG	18	0		1	30	2.0	5.0																						
1993	WPG+	18	0		2	35	3.0	35.0	1	0																				
1994	WPG	18	0		2	32	3.0	30.0			2													1	0	0.0	0				
1995	WPG	18				22	2.0	18.0			1																			
1996	WPG	17				2																								
15	Years	220	0		15	228	32.5	88.0	2	28	3													1	0	0.0	0	4	2	0.5	2
BOB MIKE Robert Melvin T 6'1 220 Florida A&M; UCLA B: 10/29/1923 GA Pro: A																														
1952	CAL	7																												
1953	CAL	14																									1	0	0.0	0
2	Years	21																									1	0	0.0	0
TED MIKLIECHUK Ted OG-LB 5'10 207 St. Vital Bulldogs Ints.; Winnipeg Rams Ints. B: 4/13/1935 Lac du Bonnet, MB																														
1958	WPG	5																												
1959	WPG	1																												
1960	WPG	3																												
1961	WPG	1																												
4	Years	10																												
RON MIKOLAJCZYK Ronald K. OT 6'3 280 Marshall; Tampa B: 6/2/1950 Passaic, NJ Draft: 5B-127 1973 OAK Pro: NUW																														
1972	TOR	14																												
1973	TOR	14																												
2	Years	28																												
DOUG MIKOLAS Douglas Adolph DL 6'1 270 Oregon Tech; Portland State B: 6/7/1961 Manteca, CA Draft: 7A-94 1985 DEN-USFL Pro: ENU																														
1986	TOR	3					3.0																							
CHET MIKSZA Chester C-T-E-FW-G-K 6'2 231 Hamilton Tiger-Cats Jrs. B: 1931 Hamilton, ON D: 10/29/1975 Welland, ON																														
1952	HAM	8																												
1953	HAM	8																												
1954	HAM	13										1	0																	
1955	HAM	8																												
1956	HAM	14										1	0																	
1957	HAM	14																									1	14	14.0	14
1958	HAM	14										1	0																	
1959	HAM	14										3	0	1	-9	-9.0	-9	0													
1960	HAM	14																												
1961	HAM	14																									2	27	13.5	19
1962	HAM	14																												
1963	HAM	14																												
1964	HAM*	14	0		2									0	28		28	0										1	5	5.0	5
1965	HAM	4																												
1966	MTL	14	0		1																									
1968	HAM	14																												
16	Years	195	0		3							6	0	1	19	19.0	28	0										4	46	11.5	19
SCOTT MILANOVICH Scott Stewart QB 6'3 227 Maryland B: 1/25/1973 Butler, PA Pro: ENX																														
2003	CAL	10	1	0	0	0								3	6	2.0	4	0													
MEL MILBRAITH Mel T 200																														
1947	CAL	8																												
DARRYL MILBURN Darryl Wayne DE 6'3 260 Grambling State B: 10/25/1968 Baton Rouge, LA Draft: 9-231 1991 DET Pro: N																														
1992	TOR	1				1																								
1993	TOR	4				8	1.0	1.0																						
2	Years	5				9	1.0	1.0																						
BARRON MILES Barron L. CB-S 5'8 165 Nebraska B: 1/1/1972 Roselle, NJ Draft: 6-199 1995 PIT Pro: E																														
1998	MTL	17	0	0	2	74			6	82	9																			
1999	MTL*	15	0	4	1	40			5	206	4	18	3																	
2000	MTL*	17	0	1	0	48	2.0	4.0	4	53	2	6	1																	
2002	MTL*	18	0	3	3	49	2.0	17.0	7	44	5																			
2003	MTL+	17	0	2	1	42	1.0	5.0	6	55	5	6	1											1	0	0.0	0				
2004	MTL	15	0	1	0	34	1.0	8.0	2	16	1																			
2005	BC+	17	0	0	3	42			6	35	3	6	1											1	0	0.0	0				
2006	BC*	18	0	3	1	39			10	206	4	6	1																	
2007	BC+	18				40			3	80	3																			
2008	BC*	18	1	1	0	46	1.0	8.0	9	119	2																			
2009	BC*	17	0	1	0	54			8	89	2	6	1																	
11	Years	187	1	16	11	508	7.0	42.0	66	985	40	48	8											2	0	0.0	0				
CHARLES MILES Charles RB 5'10 184 Ellsworth JC; East Carolina B: 10/12/1970 Indianapolis, IN																														
1994	SAC	15	3		0	4						24	4	80	403	5.0	23	3	19	229	12.1	32	1					22	410	18.6	33
1995	MEM	2				2						6	1	8	32	4.0	11	1													
2	Years	17	3		0	6						30	5	88	435	4.9	23	4	19	229	12.1	32	1					22	410	18.6	33
ELLARD MILES Ellard (Ed) T-G-C 6'1 202 none B: 1922																														
1946	MTL	11																												
1948	OTT	8																												
1949	OTT	11																												
1950	OTT	11																												
1951	OTT	1																												
5	Years	42																												
JERMAINE MILES Jermaine Lamont DE 6'4 265 Nassau CC; Georgia Tech B: 8/16/1974 New York, NY Pro: EX																														
1997	CAL	6	0	0	1	10	3.0	21.0																						
1998	CAL	17	0	1	1	27	5.0	28.0																						
1999	CAL	14	0	0	2	24	5.0	44.0	0	0	3																			
3	Years	37	0	1	4	61	13.0	93.0																						
LEE MILES Leonard Lee WR 5'6 156 Baylor B: 9/18/1969 Mart, TX Draft: 11A-294 1992 MIA																														
1993	EDM	2																									3	65	21.7	34
LEW MILES Lou HB 5'11 200																														
1946	WPG	7																												
1948	WPG	10																												
2	Years	17																												
ROLLIE MILES Roland E. OHB-S-LB 5'10 175 St. Augustine's B: 2/16/1927 Washington, DC D: 8/17/1995 Edmonton, AB																														
1951	EDM	10										20	4	52	416	8.0		3	3	41	13.7		1	33	269	8.2		7	103	14.7	
1952	EDM+	11			3				4	80		10	2	46	220	4.8	40	0	22	342	15.5	83	1	41	384	9.4	32	16	474	29.6	101
1953	EDM+	16							6	56		55	11	134	819	6.1	91	8	37	657	17.8		3	54	464	8.6		6	123	20.5	
1954	EDM+	16	5		3				4	71		30	6	148	834	5.6	27	4	16	283	17.7	44	2	18	124	6.9	25	17	406	23.9	52
1955	EDM+	14	4		3				3	60		15	3	50	224	4.5	15	0	16	235	14.7	47	3	1	13	13.0	13	5	117	23.4	63
1956	EDM+	15	6		2				4	145		36	6	38	226	5.9	30	2	29	410	14.1	37	3	1	15	15.0	15	15	403	26.9	52
1957	EDM	11	1		0							12	2	28	183	6.5	18	1	14	250	17.9	40	1					3	29	9.7	19

Year	Team	GP	FM	FF	FR	TK	SK	YDS	IR	YDS	PD	PTS	TD	RA	YDS	AVG	LG	TD	REC	YDS	AVG	LG	TD	PR	YDS	AVG	LG	KOR	YDS	AVG	LG
1958	EDM+	16	1		2				10	57				6	14	2.3	8	0	7	149	21.3	41	0	5	34	6.8	13	4	71	17.8	29
1959	EDM+	16							3	15		6	1	10	75	7.5	18	1	4	58	14.5	19	0	75	487	6.5	33	12	330	27.5	67
1960	EDM	16	1		1				2	24		6	1	3	21	7.0	9	0	1	23	23.0	23	1	33	208	6.3	22				
1961	EDM	16			2				2	39									1	8	8.0	8	0	18	87	4.8	16	3	75	25.0	32
11	Years	157	18		16				38	547		190	36	515	3032	5.9	91	19	150	2456	16.4	83	15	279	2085	7.5	33	88	2131	24.2	101
TONY MILES Antonio WR-SB 5'10 174 Northwest Missouri State B: 5/16/1978 Mart, TX																															
2002	HAM	12	4	0	2	8						18	3	1	13	13.0	13	0	48	670	14.0	51	3	26	502	19.3	96				
2003	TOR*	17	1	0	0	3						36	6	1	-4	-4.0	-4	0	67	1005	15.0	96	4	10	74	7.4	16	14	441	31.5	93
2004	TOR	13	1	0	1	3						12	2						62	741	12.0	58	2	10	127	12.7	64	9	172	19.1	25
2005	TOR	18				7						48	8	1	8	8.0	8	0	91	1275	14.0	67	8	1	4	4.0	4	1	36	36.0	36
2006	TOR	13	1	0	0	1						14	2						53	671	12.7	51	2								
2007	TOR	10				0						24	4						24	433	18.0	73	4								
2008	HAM	9	1	0	0	2													38	450	11.8	22	0								
7	Years	92	8	0	3	24						152	25	3	17	5.7	13	0	383	5245	13.7	96	23	47	707	15.0	96	24	649	27.0	93
WARNER MILES Warner OG-OT 6'2 235 Ottawa B: 7/16/1959 Ottawa, ON Draft: 2B-14 1981 TOR																															
1981	TOR	1																													
1982	TOR	8																													
1983	BC	12																												2	28	14.0	11
1984	HAM	9																													
1984	OTT	3																													
1984	Year	12																													
4	Years	30																												2	28	14.0	11
TED MILIAN Ted C-OT 6'1 250 Manitoba B: 2/18/1954 Draft: TE 1976 WPG																															
1978	EDM	16																													
1979	EDM	16	0		1																										
1980	EDM	16																													
1981	EDM	16																													
1982	EDM	16																													
1983	EDM	3																													
1983	CAL	13	1		0																										
1983	Year	16	1		0																										
6	Years	83	1		1																										
BILL MILLAR Bill FB 176 Hilltop Jrs. B: 1922																															
1946	CAL	8																													
1947	CAL	7																													
2	Years	15																													
CAM MILLAR Cam HB-FW 5'11 170 B: 1928																															
1949	WPG	14																													
1950	WPG	10												5	5	1.0		0													
2	Years	24												5	5	1.0	0	0													
NORM MILLEN Norman HB																															
1948	HAM	2																													
ALLEN MILLER Allen LB 6'0 224 Ohio University B: 4/18/1940 Fostoria, OH Draft: 17-133 1962 NYT; 17-225 1962 WAS Pro: N																															
1964	HAM	1																													
1965	WPG+	13							2	21																		2	21	10.5	16
1966	WPG	15	0		3				2	4																		1	19	19.0	19
1967	WPG	4	0		1																										
1968	SAS	4																													
1968	HAM	7							3	18																					
1968	Year	11							3	18																					
5	Years	37	0		4				7	43																		3	40	13.3	19
ARNOLD MILLER Arnold Thomas DE 6'3 239 Louisiana State B: 1/3/1975 New Orleans, LA Pro: N																															
2004	TOR	1				1																									
BILL MILLER W. DB 5'10 178 none B: 1939 Winnipeg, MB																															
1960	CAL	11																	1	8	8.0	8	0					6	107	17.8	31
1961	CAL	11							2	39									1	1	1.0	1	0	15	78	5.2	14				
1962	CAL	16							2	0									2	21	10.5	15	0	40	249	6.2	17				
1963	CAL	10	2		1				2	26														27	125	4.6	18				
1964	CAL	9	1		0																			48	225	4.7	16				
1964	WPG	6	0		1				2	0																					
1964	Year	15	1		1				2	0														48	225	4.7	16				
5	Years	57	3		2				8	65									4	30	7.5	15	0	130	677	5.2	18	6	107	17.8	31
BOB MILLER Robert OHB-DB 6'0 200 Western Ontario B: 1937 Draft: 1-3 1959 MTL																															
1959	MTL	14												2	0	0.0	3	0	2	15	7.5	8	0								
1960	SAS	11	0		1																							6	111	18.5	30
1961	SAS	14																	2	38	19.0	27	0	1	3	3.0	3	2	45	22.5	19
1962	SAS	12							2	43														1	0	0.0	0				
1963	MTL	1																													
5	Years	52	0		1				2	43				2	0	0.0	3	0	4	53	13.3	27	0	2	3	1.5	3	8	156	19.5	30
BRONZELL MILLER Bronzell LaJames DE 6'4 245 Eastern Arizona JC; Utah B: 10/12/1971 Federal Way, WA Draft: 7C-239 1995 STL Pro: ENX																															
1996	CAL	2	1		0	5																						1	5	5.0	5
1997	CAL	9	0	1	2	16	5.0	53.0			2																				
1998	CAL	17	0	2	3	22	7.0	44.0			2																				
1999	CAL	1				1					1																				
4	Years	29	1	3	5	44	12.0	97.0			5																	1	5	5.0	5
BRUCE MILLER Bruce CB 5'9 163 Southern Mississippi B: 9/25/1961 Ackerman, MS Draft: TD 1984 NO-USFL Pro: U																															
1985	SAS	3							3	20														1	11	11.0	11				
CALVIN MILLER Calvin DE 6'2 270 Mississippi Gulf Coast JC; Oklahoma State B: 8/31/1953 Gulfport, MS Pro: NW																															
1976	WPG	2	0		1																										
1976	EDM	8																													
1976	Year	10	0		1																										
CHARLES MILLER Charles DB 5'11 175 West Virginia B: 8/2/1953 Fairmont, WV Draft: 6A-150 1975 CLE																															
1975	EDM	1																													
DAN MILLER Dan Curtis G 5'10 215 Baylor B: 1933																															
1956	SAS	1																													
DON MILLER Donald LB 6'2 223 Eastern Utah JC; Utah State; Idaho State B: 4/6/1964 Chicago, IL Pro: N																															
1991	BC	4				14																									
1992	BC	2				9																									
2	Years	6				23																									
FRED MILLER Fred Louis OT 6'3 220 Santa Monica CC; Pacific B: 8/10/1931 Pro: N																															
1956	HAM	7																													
1957	BC	1																													
2	Years	8																													
GERALD MILLER Gerald G-T																															
1946	CAL	6																													
GORDON MILLER Gordon HB																															
1948	HAM	10										11	2					2													
GREG MILLER Gregory FB-LB 6'2 230 Concordia B: 8/26/1961 Toronto, ON Draft: 6-54 1985 WPG																															
1986	OTT	15	0		1									2	4	2.0	4	0													
1987	HAM	1				0																									
1988	EDM	2										6	1	4	7	1.8	4	1	1	0	0.0	0	0								
3	Years	18	0		1	0						6	1	6	11	1.8	4	1	1	0	0.0	0	0								

Year	Team	GP	FM	FF	FR	TK	SK	YDS	IR	YDS	PD	PTS	TD	RA	YDS	AVG	LG	TD	REC	YDS	AVG	LG	TD	PR	YDS	AVG	LG	KOR	YDS	AVG	LG
HENRY MILLER Henry DH 5'11 204 Northern Arizona B: 9/21/1964																															
1991	EDM	4				9																								
JIM MILLER Jim DE 5'11 221 McGill B: 2/20/1932 Draft: 3-9 1953 MTL																															
1953	MTL	12										7	1																		
1954	MTL	14																													
1955	MTL	12																		1	11	11.0	11	0								
1956	MTL+	14							1	17									3	25	8.3	12	0								
1957	MTL	14																		2	37	18.5	25	0								
1958	MTL	14																													
6	Years	80							1	17		7	1						6	73	12.2	25	0								
JOE MILLER Joseph OT 6'5 258 Villanova B: 2/6/1952 Baltimore, MD Draft: 11-282 1974 WAS; 12-135 1974 CHI-WFL Pro: W																															
1976	OTT	11																													
1976	SAS	1																													
1976	Year	12																													
1977	SAS	15																									1	0	0.0	0
1978	SAS	15																													
1979	SAS	11	0		3																									
1980	SAS	6																													
5	Years	58	0		3																						1	0	0.0	0
JOSH MILLER Joshua Harris P 6'3 224 Scottsdale CC; Arizona B: 7/14/1970 New York, NY Pro: N																															
1994	BAL*	18	1		0	1						6	0																		
1995	BAL*	18				2						5	0																		
2	Years	36	1		0	3						11	0																		
JOSH MILLER Josh DT 6'4 282 Saginaw Valley State B: 11/19/1986 Waterford, MI																															
2008	WPG	3				4	1.0	1.0																							
KEITH MILLER Keith LB 6'1 220 Northeastern State B: 8/30/1957 Valdosta, GA Draft: 8-212 1979 ATL																															
1979	SAS	7	0		3																									
KEN MILLER Kenneth Edward DB 5'11 180 Eastern Michigan B: 6/24/1958 Pine Bluff, AR Draft: 7B-191 1981 DAL																															
1981	MTL	3	1		0																						2	44	22.0	28
1982	MTL	12	0		2																									
1983	OTT	16							2	0																				
1984	OTT	15	0		2				4	35																				
1985	CAL	4																													
1986	CAL	2																													
6	Years	52	1		4				6	35																		2	44	22.0	28
KIRBY MILLER Donald Kirby E Texas B: 11/17/1933 Jefferson County, TX																															
1955	BC	1																													
LEE MILLER Lee P. DB 6'1 186 Fullerton State B: 1/25/1961 Los Angeles, CA Draft: 9A-239 1984 SF																															
1984	TOR	1																													
MARTIN MILLER Martin S 5'10 160 Manitoba B: 7/21/1972 Halifax, NS Draft: 4-27 1997 BC																															
1997	BC	1				0																								
MAURICE MILLER Maurice LB 6'3 230 Wake Forest B: 9/6/1969 Richmond, VA																															
1993	SAC	1				2																								
1994	SAC	18				99	4.0	14.0	5	73	4																				
1995	SA	9	0		3	46	3.0	21.0	2	28	3	18	3																		
1996	EDM	9				19	1.0	14.0			1																				
1997	EDM	11	0	1	0	28	2.0	19.0																							
1998	TOR	15				51	4.0	18.0	1	1	1																				
6	Years	63	0	1	3	245	14.0	86.0	8	102	9	18	3																		
MIKE MILLER Mike LB 6'0 208 Acadia B: 3/15/1989 Riverview, NB																															
2011	EDM	18				20																								
NICK MILLER Nick FB-CB-LB-FW 6'1 192 Winnipeg Light Infantry Jrs. B: 9/15/1931																															
1953	WPG	2																													
1955	WPG	2																													
1956	WPG	13							2	0																				
1957	WPG	12	3											23	146	6.3	36	0						1	0	0.0	0	3	55	18.3	20
1958	WPG	15	0		2				4	5				2	9	4.5	5	0													
1959	WPG	7																													
1960	WPG	16							3	44				1	3	3.0	3	0													
1961	WPG	16																						1	0	0.0	0	3	36	12.0	14
1962	WPG	15							2	14																				
1963	WPG	15	0		1																									
1964	WPG	16	0		1				1																					
11	Years	129	3		4				12	63				26	158	6.1	36	0						2	0	0.0	0	6	91	15.2	20
PAT MILLER Leon Patrick LB 6'1 220 Florida B: 6/24/1964 Panama City, FL Draft: 5-131 1986 SF Pro: N																															
1989	OTT	7				20	1.0																							
1990	OTT	6				23	1.0																							
2	Years	13				43	2.0																							
PETER MILLER Peter LB 6'2 215 Pacific B: 6/30/1973 Montreal, QC Draft: 7-50 1992 SAS; RS-5-41 1966 NYJ																															
1993	SAS	10				6	1.0	7.0																							
1994	SAS	11				9	2.0	28.0																							
1995	TOR	7				6																								
1997	BC	9	0	1	0	4																								
4	Years	37	0	1	0	25	3.0	35.0																							
RALPH MILLER Ralph OG 6'3 260 Alabama State; California Lutheran B: 8/13/1948 Hartford, AL Pro: N																															
1975	TOR	9																													
RAY MILLER Raymond Carlyle OT 6'5 250 Idaho B: 8/22/1943 Draft: 7-108(f) 1966 GB																															
1969	SAS	3																													
ROMARO MILLER Romaro QB 6'1 195 Mississippi B: 9/12/1978 Shannon, MS Pro: E																															
2003	OTT	18				0						6	1	7	66	9.4	23	0	1	10	10.0	10	1								
2004	TOR	10				0								1	2	2.0	2	0													
2	Years	28				0						6	1	8	68	8.5	23	0	1	10	10.0	10	1								
RON MILLER Ronald J, E 6'0 210 Indiana B: 1937																															
1960	HAM	1																													
1961	HAM	3																		1	8	8.0	8	0								
2	Years	4																		1	8	8.0	8	0								
RON MILLER Ronald Rudolph QB 6'0 190 Wisconsin B: 8/19/1939 Lyons, IL Draft: 21-(f) 1961 HOU; 3B-41(f) 1961 LARM Pro: N																															
1963	EDM	2											2	2	1.0	2	0													
SCOTT MILLER Scott DT-OG 6'4 285 Rutgers B: 4/22/1968 Paterson, NJ Pro: E																															
1994	BAL	18	1		0	11	2.0	27.0																							
1996	MTL	1				1																								
2	Years	19	1		0	12	2.0	27.0																							
SELVESTA MILLER Selvesta Norris DE 6'3 250 Lees-McRae JC; South Carolina B: 10/7/1975 Honolulu, HI																															
1999	MTL	4				4																								
2000	MTL	18	0	1	1	31	7.0	36.0			1																				
2	Years	22	0	1	1	35	7.0	36.0			1																				
SETH MILLER Seth Bane DB 6'4 207 Arizona State B: 3/20/1948 Carthage, AR Draft: 8B-195 1970 ATL Pro: W																															
1971	HAM	3	0		1				2	0																				
WADE MILLER Wade LB 5'9 210 Manitoba B: 6/10/1973 Winnipeg, MB Draft: 4-37 1995 WPG																															
1995	WPG	4				9																								
1996	WPG	16				27																								
1997	WPG	18				36																					1	0	0.0	0

Year	Team	GP	FM	FF	FR	TK	SK	YDS	IR	YDS	PD	PTS	TD	RA	YDS	AVG	LG	TD	REC	YDS	AVG	LG	TD	PR	YDS	AVG	LG	KOR	YDS	AVG	LG
1998	WPG	9	1	0	1	15																						1	0	0.0	0
1999	WPG+	18	1	0	1	38																						1	1	1.0	1
2000	WPG	6				2													2	23	11.5	20	0					1	10	10.0	10
2001	WPG	17				22								5	9	1.8	4	0	15	96	6.4	15	0								
2002	WPG	17	0	0	1	13								4	8	2.0	3	0													
2003	WPG	18	0	1	2	16								1	1	1.0	1	0													
2004	WPG	18				13								4	5	1.3	2	0	11	83	7.5	17	0					1	12	12.0	12
2005	WPG	18				3																						3	7	2.3	4
11	Years	159	2	1	5	194								14	23	1.6	4	0	28	202	7.2	20	0					8	30	3.8	12
WILLIAM MILLER William Edward RB 5'9 190 Ouachita Baptist B: 1/3/1957 Rison, AR Pro: U																															
1980	WPG*	14	2		0							42	7	218	1053	4.8	53	4	34	344	10.1	58	3					12	293	24.4	58
1981	WPG	10	1		0							36	6	132	684	5.2	39	4	24	236	9.8	60	2					5	195	39.0	53
1982	WPG*	14	3		1							48	8	202	1076	5.3	54	7	43	407	9.5	75	1					9	277	30.8	47
1986	TOR	4	1		0							6	1	49	171	3.5	14	1	21	126	6.0	22	0					1	13	13.0	13
4	Years	42	7		1							132	22	601	2984	5.0	54	16	122	1113	9.1	75	6					27	778	28.8	58
WILLIE MILLER Willie WR 5'10 180 Tampa B: 1/6/1950 Miami, FL Pro: W																															
1973	WPG	9										6	1						19	388	20.4	103	1					1	25	25.0	25
DAVID MILLER-JOHNSTON David K-P 6'0 180 Concordia (Canada) B: 10/27/1972 Vancouver, BC Draft: 1-2 1998 TOR																															
2002	OTT	6				0						23	0																		
BERNIE MILLHAM Bernard James E 6'3 185 Fordham* B: 6/12/1921 D: 5/25/2003 Draft: 18-168 1946 PHI																															
1946	OTT	12																													
KOJO MILLINGTON Kojo LB 6'2 210 Wilfrid Laurier B: 7/6/1976 Montreal, QC Draft: 4B-26 2000 TOR																															
2002	BC	2				0																									
SEAN MILLINGTON Sean RB 6'2 225 Simon Fraser B: 2/1/1968 Vancouver, BC Draft: 1A-1 1990 EDM																															
1991	EDM	2				5																									
1991	BC	4				7								2	12	6.0	7	0						1	5	5.0	5				
1991	Year	6				12								2	12	6.0	7	0						1	5	5.0	5				
1992	BC	17				17						6	1	8	52	6.5	12	1	6	60	10.0	20	0					1	0	0.0	0
1993	BC*	18	3		3	27						54	9	52	276	5.3	60	5	38	481	12.7	70	3								
1994	BC*	18				23						66	11	97	522	5.4	65	11	19	112	5.9	20	0					1	4	4.0	4
1995	BC	7	1		0	10						42	7	58	318	5.5	39	6	14	147	10.5	39	1								
1996	BC+	17	1		1	11						60	10	74	381	5.1	26	7	36	386	10.7	38	3					1	11	11.0	11
1997	BC+	16	4	0	0	24						30	5	153	865	5.7	54	5	49	469	9.6	29	0					1	0	0.0	0
1998	WPG	18	1	0	2	21						18	3	82	424	5.2	40	3	22	191	8.7	36	0								
1999	WPG	3				5								10	26	2.6	6	0	7	55	7.9	31	0								
1999	EDM	15	1	0	2	6						24	4	80	524	6.6	43	4	7	49	7.0	12	0								
1999	Year	18	1	0	2	11						24	4	90	550	6.1	43	4	14	104	7.4	31	0								
2000	BC*	17	2	0	1	17						42	7	156	1010	6.5	50	6	39	531	13.6	35	1								
2001	BC	18	4	0	1	11						72	12	163	804	4.9	32	11	34	313	9.2	41	1					3	65	21.7	27
2002	BC	16	2	0	0	15						96	16	170	740	4.4	37	14	36	372	10.3	32	2								
2005	TOR	8	2	0	0	2						12	2	24	128	5.3	18	2	5	70	14.0	23	0								
13	Years	175	21	0	10	201						522	87	1129	6082	5.4	65	75	312	3236	10.4	70	11	1	5	5.0	5	7	80	11.4	27
HAROLD MILLON Harold HB Southern University																															
1948	WPG	1																													
JIM MILLS James Anthony OT 6'9 281 Hawaii B: 9/23/1961 Vancouver, BC Draft: TE 1983 BC; 9A-225 1983 BAL; 6A-67 1983 LA-USFL Pro: N																															
1986	BC	9																													
1987	BC	18				1																									
1988	BC*	11				1																									
1989	BC	17				1																									
1990	BC*	18				4																									
1991	BC*	18				1																									
1992	BC+	18	0		1	1																									
1993	BC+	18	0		1	0																									
1994	OTT	15				1																									
1995	BC	2				0																									
10	Years	144	0		2	10																									
TOMMY MILLS Thomas DB 5'10 166 West Texas A&M B: 7/24/1955																															
1978	HAM	2							1	33																					
1978	SAS	1																													
1978	Year	3							1	33																					
TROY MILLS Troy A. FB 6'0 212 Los Medanos JC; Sacramento State B: 7/1/1966 Glendale, CA																															
1993	SAC	13	0		1	20						6	1	11	40	3.6	18	0	1	4	4.0	4	1					1	0	0.0	0
1994	SAC	15	5		0	8						72	12	178	1230	6.9	32	7	61	774	12.7	59	5					10	176	17.6	27
1995	SA	7	3		1	4						48	8	82	445	5.4	30	6	36	481	13.4	54	2								
1996	OTT	5				4						6	1	39	139	3.6	19	1	20	258	12.9	40	0					0	26		20
1998	EDM	15	4	0	0	5						12	2	177	813	4.6	23	2	50	648	13.0	38	0								
1999	EDM	11	3	0	0	1						36	6	172	1022	5.9	60	6	19	163	8.6	27	0								
2000	EDM	6	3	0	0	0						6	1	74	424	5.7	37	1	9	183	20.3	47	0					5	87	17.4	36
2001	WPG	13	1	0	0	1						48	8	91	430	4.7	38	8	27	214	7.9	20	0								
2003	EDM	13	0	0	1	9						48	8	38	150	3.9	22	4	21	333	15.9	69	4								
9	Years	98	19	0	3	52						282	47	862	4693	5.4	60	35	244	3058	12.5	69	12					16	289	18.1	36
CHRIS MILO Christopher K-P 5'11 205 Laval B: 11/2/1986 Montreal, QC Draft: 4-30 2011 SAS																															
2011	SAS	12				1						94	0																		
RAY MILO Raymond Wesley DB 5'11 178 New Mexico State B: 2/19/1954 Conroe, TX Draft: 11-280 1978 KC Pro: N																															
1978	SAS	1																													
1979	SAS	10																													
1980	SAS	1																													
3	Years	12																													
GEORGE MILOSEVIC George TE 6'2 220 Cornell B: 3/21/1950 Draft: TE 1973 HAM																															
1973	HAM	7																	5	71	14.2	19	0								
ROBERT MIMBS Robert RB 6'0 195 Kansas B: 8/6/1964 Kansas City, MO																															
1990	WPG*	18	12		1	0						48	8	285	1341	4.7	32	6	71	538	7.6	32	2					1	16	16.0	16
1991	WPG*	18	11		3	5						98	16	326	1769	5.4	47	15	39	438	11.2	33	1								
1992	WPG	7	3		0	3						24	4	76	392	5.2	36	4	24	202	8.4	28	0								
1992	BC	3	1		0	0								43	190	4.4	17	0	7	115	16.4	41	0								
1992	Year	10	4		0	3						24	4	119	582	4.9	36	4	31	317	10.2	41	0								
1993	BC	2	1		0	0						12	2	22	130	5.9	28	1	4	33	8.3	11	1								
1995	SAS	6	3		1	2						12	2	87	444	5.1	30	2	8	65	8.1	18	0								
1996	SAS*	17	8		2	0						48	8	292	1403	4.8	38	8	25	335	13.4	54	0								
1997	SAS	10	4	0	0	1						12	2	113	493	4.4	26	2	10	74	7.4	23	0								
7	Years	78	43	0	7	11						254	42	1244	6162	5.0	47	38	188	1800	9.6	54	4					1	16	16.0	16
JESSE MIMS Jesse Lee HB 5'11 203 Laney JC; New Mexico State B: 8/27/1948 Alameda, CA Pro: W																															
1971	CAL	16	8		0							30	5	146	834	5.7	75	2	37	454	12.3	47	3					8	215	26.9	35
1972	CAL	12	5		0							42	7	132	728	5.5	52	6	16	188	11.8	42	1					12	304	25.3	31
1973	CAL	2										6	1	19	54	2.8	16	0	9	110	12.2	21	1								
3	Years	30	13		0							78	13	297	1616	5.4	75	8	62	752	12.1	47	5					20	519	26.0	35
WALT MINCE Walter Ray HB 6'2 198 Bakersfield JC; Arizona B: 12/11/1938 Jackson County, AR Draft: 12-158 1961 LARM; 30-234(f) 1962 DEN																															
1962	SAS	2										6	1						1	44	44.0	44	1								
TOM MINER Thomas Earl E 6'3 235 Tulsa B: 5/14/1932 Checotah, OK D: 1/1/1988 Tucson, AZ Draft: 3-31 1954 PIT Pro: N																															
1954	CAL	15	0		2							84	1						24	298	12.4	29	1								
1955	CAL	16	1		3							40	1						10	108	10.8	19	1	2	31	15.5	29				
1956	WPG	16	0		6							34	1						5	67	13.4	28	0					1	6	6.0	6

Year	Team	GP	FM	FF	FR	TK	SK	YDS	IR	YDS	PD	PTS	TD	RA	YDS	AVG	LG	TD	REC	YDS	AVG	LG	TD	PR	YDS	AVG	LG	KOR	YDS	AVG	LG
3	Years	47	1		11							158	3						39	473	12.1	29	2	2	31	15.5	29	1	6	6.0	6
GINO MINGO Eugene DE 6'2 235 Oregon State B: 8/7/1965 Denver, CO																															
1988	BC	5				15	1.0																								
1989	BC	10	0		1	22	3.0																					2	27	13.5	20
2	Years	15	0		1	37	4.0																					2	27	13.5	20
BOB MINIHANE Bob DT 6'3 255 Boston University B: 3/9/1938 Draft: 25- 1961 BOS; 19-265 1961 CLE																															
1961	HAM	9																										1	0	0.0	0
1962	HAM	12																													
1963	HAM	5																													
1964	MTL	11	0		1																										
1965	MTL	12	0		2							6	1																		
1966	MTL	13																													
1967	MTL+	11							1	5																					
1968	MTL	14	0		1																										
8	Years	87	0		4				1	5		6	1															1	0	0.0	0
DAVE MINNICH Dave RB 5'10 215 Washington State B: 1/18/1974 Stonington, CT																															
2002	TOR	7				1								21	69	3.3	20	0	4	32	8.0	15	0					1	24	24.0	24
PHIL MINNICK Phil LB 6'2 225 Northern Iowa B: 12/28/1942																															
1965	WPG	14							1																						
1966	WPG*	14							1																						
1967	WPG	15	0		1				3	8																					
1968	WPG+	11	0		2				2	23																					
1969	WPG*	9			2				2	1		6	1																		
1970	WPG	1																													
1972	WPG	8	0		1				1	10																					
1973	WPG	15							1	8																					
8	Years	87	0		6				11	50		6	1																		
CEDRIC MINTER Cedric Alwyn HB 5'10 200 Boise State B: 11/13/1958 Charleston, SC Pro: N																															
1981	TOR+	15	2		2							22	3	182	815	4.5	54	3	28	371	13.3	55	0	3	41	13.7	35	12	266	22.2	36
1982	TOR+	16	1		0							76	12	120	563	4.7	73	7	61	828	13.6	79	5	3	42	14.0	30	12	227	18.9	24
1983	TOR	14	1		0							48	8	107	599	5.6	25	5	38	444	11.7	31	3								
1986	TOR	4										12	2	40	170	4.3	18	2	9	48	5.3	11	0					4	61	15.3	30
1987	OTT	13	5		1	1						42	7	150	627	4.2	24	7	37	327	8.8	57	0					30	611	20.4	38
5	Years	62	9		3	1						200	32	599	2774	4.6	73	24	173	2018	11.7	79	8	6	83	13.8	35	58	1165	20.1	38
BILL MINTSOULIS Bill WR 5'11 180 Toronto B: 1/1/1960 Toronto, On Draft: 3-24 1983 CAL																															
1983	CAL	2																										3	58	19.3	22
1984	CAL	8												1	-5	-5.0	-5	0	2	16	8.0	12	0					0	10		10
2	Years	10												1	-5	-5.0	-5	0	2	16	8.0	12	0					3	68	22.7	22
POLLY MIOCINOVICH Paul HB deceased																															
1946	HAM	12										23	4					4													
1947	HAM	12																													
2	Years	24										23	4					4													
GEORGE MIRA George Ignacio QB 5'1175 190 Miami (Florida) B: 1/11/1942 Key West, FL Draft: 18-137 1964 DEN; 2-15 1964 SF Pro: NW																															
1972	MTL	9	1		0									10	67	6.7	19	0													
1973	MTL	10	1		1									9	54	6.0	25	0													
1977	TOR	6	2		0									1	15	15.0	15	0													
3	Years	25	4		1									20	136	6.8	25	0													
KEIKI MISIPEKA Keiki RB 5'11 215 Palomar JC; Hawaii; Southeast Missouri State B: 6/12/1980																															
2003	EDM	1				0																									
ERIC MITCHEL Eric Von-Russell RB 6'0 210 Oklahoma B: 2/13/1967 Pine Bluff, AR Draft: 6-165 1989 NE Pro: E																															
1991	CAL	3	3		0	0						12	2	18	83	4.6	28	1	11	181	16.5	75	1					6	182	30.3	48
1992	CAL	8	5		1	0						30	5	73	310	4.2	62	5	24	258	10.8	49	0					15	352	23.5	62
1993	EDM	3				0																						8	232	29.0	51
1995	WPG	1				0								14	99	7.1	15	0	4	21	5.3	7	0								
4	Years	15	8		1	0						42	7	105	492	4.7	62	6	39	460	11.8	75	1					29	766	26.4	62
BILL MITCHELL Bill C-K-DE 6'1 225 Western Ontario B: 8/2/1935 London, England Draft: 1-1 1960 TOR																															
1960	TOR	11							2	6		0	0																		
1961	TOR	14										20	0																		
1962	TOR	14										60	0																		
1963	EDM	16	0		1							57	0																		
1964	EDM	16										57	0																		
1965	EDM	16	1		0							8	0	1	-8	-8.0	-8	0													
1966	BC	16	1		0							67	0																		
1967	BC	16																													
1968	BC	3																													
9	Years	122	2		1				2	6		269	0	1	-8	-8.0	-8	0													
DAVID MITCHELL Essex David DB 6'1 195 Ohio State B: 10/18/1979 Philadelphia, PA																															
2003	OTT	8	0	0	1	15			1	14	0	2	0																		
DENNIS MITCHELL Dennis CB 5'8 180 Western Kentucky B: 4/7/1983																															
2007	BC	5	0	0	1	22																									
DERRELL MITCHELL Derrell Lavoice SB 5'9 190 Joliet JC; Texas Tech B: 9/16/1971 Miami, FL Draft: 6-176 1994 NO Pro: EN																															
1997	TOR*	18				3						102	17	1	6	6.0	6	0	77	1457	18.9	71	17					1	17	17.0	17
1998	TOR*	18	1	0	0	3						60	10	3	19	6.3	15	0	160	2000	12.5	46	10					1	7	7.0	7
1999	TOR	10	1	0	0	0						42	7	3	8	2.7	3	0	39	682	17.5	74	7								
2000	TOR*	18	0	0	1	6						98	16	5	56	11.2	45	1	100	1398	14.0	76	14	2	28	14.0	20	6	211	35.2	101
2001	TOR+	16				1						36	6						78	1376	17.6	66	6					5	79	15.8	32
2002	TOR+	18				4						84	14	4	41	10.3	17	0	66	1027	15.6	86	13	1	18	18.0	18	1	31	31.0	31
2003	TOR	15				1						36	6						64	741	11.6	56	6					2	36	18.0	20
2004	EDM	18	2	0	2	4						72	12	1	12	12.0	12	1	48	868	18.1	73	10	1	10	10.0	10				
2005	EDM	18	1	0	0	3						30	5	1	13	13.0	13	0	94	1207	12.8	49	5								
2006	EDM	15				2						6	1	3	24	8.0	10	0	70	892	12.7	69	1	8	95	11.9	18				
2007	TOR	10	1	0	0	0						6	1						25	366	14.6	70	1								
11	Years	174	6	0	3	27						572	95	21	179	8.5	45	2	821	12014	14.6	86	90	12	151	12.6	20	16	381	23.8	101
DOUG MITCHELL Doug C 6'0 220 Colorado College; British Columbia B: 1940																															
1960	BC	3																													
DOUG MITCHELL Doug C-OT 6'2 240 Western Ontario B: 7/14/1942 Draft: 6-51 1966 HAM																															
1967	HAM	12																													
1968	HAM	14																													
1969	HAM	14										1	0																		
1970	HAM	14																													
1971	HAM	14	0		1							2	0											1	1	1.0	1				
1972	HAM	14	2		2																										
1973	HAM	14																													
1974	HAM	2																													
1974	MTL	8																													
1974	Year	10																													
8	Years	98	2		3							3	0											1	1	1.0	1				
ED MITCHELL Ed DB-OHB 5'10 175 Parkdale Lions Jrs. B: 11/15/1936 Toronto, ON																															
1959	MTL	14							3	35														59	409	6.9	22	1	13	13.0	13
1960	MTL	4																						2	4	2.0	3				
1960	CAL	3	0		1																			4	9	2.3	4				
1960	Year	7	0		1																			6	13	2.2	4				

Year	Team	GP	FM	FF	FR	TK	SK	YDS	IR	YDS	PD	PTS	TD	RA	YDS	AVG	LG	TD	REC	YDS	AVG	LG	TD	PR	YDS	AVG	LG	KOR	YDS	AVG	LG
2	Years	18	0		1				3	35														65	422	6.5	22	1	13	13.0	13
EDWARD MITCHELL Edward LB 6'0 215 Valdosta State B: 5/22/1973 Waycross, GA																															
1995	OTT	6	0		1	25					2																				
GORDIE MITCHELL Gordon OT-DT-C 6'3 230 Vancouver Meralomas Jrs. B: 1933 Edmonton, AB D: 1997																															
1955	BC	15	0		3																										
1956	BC	15	0		2																										
1957	BC	9																													
1958	BC	15																													
1959	BC	16																													
1960	BC	15	0		0																										
1961	BC	16			2																										
1962	BC	11	1																												
8	Years	112	1		7																										
JACKIE MITCHELL Jackie LB-S 6'1 185 Southern University B: 5/30/1976 Salisbury, NC																															
2000	SAS	12				49	1.0	9.0	1	13	2																				
2001	SAS	16	0	0	2	95	3.0	20.0	4	70	2	6	1																		
2002	SAS	15	1	2	2	61	2.0	15.0	2	26	4																				
2003	SAS*	18	0	0	1	74	3.0	25.0	7	107	3	12	2											1	3	3.0	3				
2004	SAS	11	0	0	1	50	2.0	18.0	2	37	3																				
2005	SAS	11	0	0	2	42			2	27	3	6	1																		
2006	SAS	13	0	2	1	45	1.0		1	22	2																				
7	Years	96	1	4	9	416	12.0	87.0	19	302	19	24	4											1	3	3.0	3				
JASON MITCHELL Jason Christopher WR 6'0 193 Los Angeles Harbor JC; Southern California B: 7/19/1981 Torrance, CA																															
2007	SAS	2				0													1	7	7.0	7	0								
JOE MITCHELL Joseph Rickey RB 6'2 210 Louisiana-Monroe B: 2/12/1953 Monroe, LA Pro: W																															
1978	MTL	2										6	1	14	32	2.3	8	1	1	0	0.0	0	0								
JOHNNY MITCHELL Johnnie, Jr. SB 6'3 263 Nebraska B: 1/20/1971 Chicago, IL Draft: 1-15 1992 NYJ Pro: N																															
2004	TOR	3				0													2	35	17.5	25	0								
KHALIF MITCHELL Khalif Quadree DT-NT 6'5 315 North Carolina; East Carolina B: 4/7/1985 Jersey City, NJ																															
2010	BC	7				6																									
2011	BC*	14				33	6.0	42.0			4																				
2	Years	21				39	6.0	42.0																							
KYLE MITCHELL Kyle DE 6'3 235 Indiana State B: 2/7/1983 East Chicago, IN																															
2006	SAS	1				3																									
2007	SAS	3	0	0	1	7			1	0	2	6	1																		
2	Years	4	0	0	1	10			1	0	2	6	1																		
LeRON MITCHELL LeRon CB 6'1 200 Western Ontario B: 11/24/1982 London, ON Draft: 2A-10 2006 TOR																															
2006	TOR	14				18																									
2007	TOR	15	0	0	3	13																									
2008	SAS	2				1																									
2009	SAS	4				4																									
2010	SAS	15	0	0	1	28																									
2011	SAS	9				4																									
6	Years	59	0	0	4	68																									
MARC MITCHELL Marc LB 6'3 220 Queen's B: 8/19/1981 Toronto, ON Draft: 5B-42 2004 CAL																															
2004	CAL	15	2	2	2	17					1																				
2005	CAL	16				12	1.0	8.0																							
2006	CAL	15				1																									
3	Years	46	2	2	2	30	1.0	8.0			1																				
MARK MITCHELL Mark CB 5'9 175 Georgia B: 12/21/1954 Augusta, GA																															
1977	OTT	6																						3	28	9.3	19				
1978	OTT	2																						8	52	6.5	23				
2	Years	8																						11	80	7.3	23				
MARKO MITCHELL Marko Terrill SB 6'4 218 Mesa CC; Nevada-Reno B: 3/11/1985 Port Huron, MI Draft: 7B-243 2009 WAS Pro: N																															
2010	EDM	2				1						6	1						2	77	38.5	69	1								
MARTIN MITCHELL Martin DB 6'1 180 Tulane B: 1/10/1954 Lake Charles, LA Draft: 6C-158 1977 PHI Pro: N																															
1978	WPG	1																													
1979	WPG	1																													
2	Years	2																													
MIKE MITCHELL Michael George CB 5'10 180 Howard Payne B: 10/18/1961 Waco, TX Pro: NU																															
1990	OTT	2				12																									
SCOTT MITCHELL Scott SB 6'3 222 Mount San Antonio JC; Kentucky B: 8/4/1984																															
2008	HAM	13	2	0	0	3						12	2						38	697	18.3	47	2					2	41	20.5	24
SCOTT MITCHELL Scott David Jackson OG 6'4 295 Rice B: 9/10/1989 Montreal, QC Draft: 1-2 2011 EDM																															
2011	EDM	4				0																									
VERNON MITCHELL Vernon DB 5'11 200 Florida A&M B: 4/21/1976 Miami, FL																															
2000	TOR	15	0	1	1	48			2	51	5	18	3																		
2001	TOR	2				10																									
2002	OTT	13				36			2	40	8																				
2003	OTT	4	0	0	1	4																		1	2	2.0	2				
4	Years	34	0	1	2	98			4	91	13	18	3											1	2	2.0	2				
WILLIAM MITCHELL William E. LB 6'0 213 Long Beach State B: 8/2/1959 Los Angeles, CA																															
1981	OTT	3	0		1																										
1982	OTT	13					1.5																								
1983	TOR+	12	0		2		1.0		2	12																					
1984	TOR+	15	0		1		2.5		3	37		6	1						1	2	2.0	2	1								
1985	TOR+	16					2.0																								
1986	MTL	15	0		1		2.0		1	25																					
1987	EDM	2				6	1.0																								
7	Years	76	0		5	6	10.0		6	74		6	1						1	2	2.0	2	1								
BARRY MITCHELSON Barry TE 6'5 230 Western Ontario B: 1942 Draft: 1-1 1964 EDM																															
1964	EDM	16																	10	109	10.9	23	0								
1965	EDM	16										0	0						20	235	11.8	19	0								
1966	EDM	5																	1	14	14.0	14	0								
1966	TOR	3																	1	9	9.0	9	0								
1966	Year	8																	2	23	11.5	14	0								
3	Years	37										0	0						32	367	11.5	23	0								
JIM MITCHENER Jim FW-HB-E 6'1 200 Vancouver Blue Bombers Jrs.; McGill B: 3/17/1929 Donavon, SK																															
1948	CAL	10										5	1																		
1952	MTL	12																													
1953	MTL	14																													
1954	MTL	13							1	10														1	4	4.0	4				
1956	BC	13	0		2				3	23																		1	1	1.0	1
5	Years	62	0		2				4	33		5	1											1	4	4.0	4	1	1	1.0	1
EDDIE MITTLESTEADT Edward HB 5'9 195 Buffalo B: 1924																															
1949	TOR	3																													
GORDIE MITTON Gordon E-HB Regina Dales Jrs.																															
1946	SAS	8																													
1948	SAS	3																													
2	Years	11																													
SINGOR MOBLEY Singor A. DB-LB 5'11 195 Washington State B: 10/12/1972 Tacoma, WA Pro: N																															
1995	EDM	17	0		3	62	1.0	3.0	1	4	3	6	1																		

Year	Team	GP	FM	FF	FR	TK	SK	YDS	IR	YDS	PD	PTS	TD	RA	YDS	AVG	LG	TD	REC	YDS	AVG	LG	TD	PR	YDS	AVG	LG	KOR	YDS	AVG	LG
1996	EDM	16	0		1	85	5.0	53.0			4																				
2000	EDM	18	1	0	3	82	3.0	25.0	3	128	1	12	2											4	57	14.3	46	15	367	24.5	75
2001	EDM	18	0	1	2	100	2.0	13.0	2	35	2																	6	117	19.5	29
2002	EDM	18	0	0	1	63	2.0	10.0	4	134	4	6	1															2	47	23.5	29
2003	EDM	18	1	0	4	63	1.0	2.0	3	50	6																				
2004	EDM	17	0	3	4	81	2.0	12.0	1	7	0													2	20	10.0	15				
2005	EDM	18	1	0	5	79	5.0	47.0			1	6	1											3	10	3.3	6	1	0	0.0	0
2006	EDM	18				65			1	2	3																				
9	Years	158	3	4	23	680	21.0	165.0	15	360	24	30	5											9	87	9.7	46	24	531	22.1	75
JOE MOBRA Joe E-K 6'2 210 Oklahoma B: 1934 Draft: 20-241 1956 CLE																																
1956	EDM	14	0		3				2	22		37	2						15	317	21.1	55	1					1	9	9.0	9
1957	EDM	16	2		0				1	26		99	2						25	366	14.6	29	2					1	5	5.0	5
1958	EDM	14	0		2				1	9		61	1						12	119	9.9	19	1					1	0	0.0	0
3	Years	44	2		5				4	57		197	5						52	802	15.4	55	4					3	14	4.7	9
CHAD MOCK Chad WR 5'11 171 Avila; Hawaii B: 3/23/1984 Long Beach, CA																																
2007	BC	3				0						6	1						5	51	10.2	15	1								
DON MOEN Donald LB 6'2 205 British Columbia B: 4/29/1960 Swift Current, SK Draft: 2-14 1982 BC																																
1982	TOR	16	0		3																			1	0	0.0	0				
1983	TOR	16	0		1		1.0																								
1984	TOR	16	0		1		5.5		1	0																					
1985	TOR	16					3.0		1	6																					
1986	TOR	18					4.0																								
1987	TOR	18	0		1	61	5.0		1	8																					
1988	TOR+	18	0		2	57	3.0		2	4		6	1																		
1989	TOR	18	0		2	65	2.0																								
1990	TOR	18	0		2	56	6.0		2	22		6	1																		
1991	TOR	18	0		2	75	3.0		2	0																					
1992	TOR	18				89	2.0		1	0																					
1993	TOR	17				72	1.0	9.0																						
1994	TOR	15	0		2	46			1	0																					
13	Years	222	0		16	521	35.5	9.0	11	40		12	2											1	0	0.0	0				
ALAN MOFFAT Alan DT-OG-OT 6'4 265 Ottawa B: 5/7/1952 Draft: 1B-3 1976 EDM																																
1976	HAM	16																													
1977	HAM	14	0		1				1	35		6	1																		
1978	HAM	12	1		0																							1	0	0.0	0
1979	HAM	16																													
1980	HAM+	14																													
1981	HAM	12																													
1982	HAM	7																													
7	Years	91	1		1				1	35		6	1															1	0	0.0	0
FRANK MOFFATT Frank DT 6'3 280 McMaster B: 11/4/1958																																
1978	HAM	4																													
DONALD MOFFETT Donald WR 5'9 176 Mississippi Gulf Coast CC; Houston B: 1/25/1972 Moss Point, MS																																
1995	BIR	11				2								10	91	9.1	53	0	17	131	7.7	23	0					7	154	22.0	41
IAN MOFFORD Ian RB-WR 5'9 180 Verdun Invictus Jrs. B: 8/12/1954 Verdun, QC																																
1974	MTL	16										12	2						8	134	16.8	31	2	1	3	3.0	3	2	40	20.0	21
1975	MTL	14												3	25	8.3	14	0	1	6	6.0	6	0					5	103	20.6	31
1976	MTL	16	1		1									13	60	4.6	8	0	5	38	7.6	18	0					4	38	9.5	24
1977	MTL	16	1		0									23	69	3.0	9	0	4	41	10.3	20	0	3	30	10.0	18	4	86	21.5	39
1978	MTL	16	2		0									4	17	4.3	6	0	8	76	9.5	24	0	4	36	9.0	16	27	579	21.4	40
1979	MTL	1																													
1979	OTT	14	1		0									6	26	4.3	9	0	7	99	14.1	29	0	11	53	4.8	11	29	701	24.2	99
1979	Year	15	1		0									6	26	4.3	9	0	7	99	14.1	29	0	11	53	4.8	11	29	701	24.2	99
1980	WPG	13	1		1							6	1						2	41	20.5	28	1	17	128	7.5	45	8	159	19.9	32
1981	WPG	11	3		0									3	11	3.7	5	0	2	35	17.5	18	0	20	127	6.4	15	1	27	27.0	27
1981	MTL	3																	1	12	12.0	12	0								
1981	Year	14	3		0									3	11	3.7	5	0	3	47	15.7	18	0	20	127	6.4	15	1	27	27.0	27
1982	MTL	4																													
9	Years	107	9		2							18	3	52	208	4.0	14	0	38	482	12.7	31	3	56	377	6.7	45	80	1733	21.7	99
LOU MOGUL Louis T 6'3 228 North Dakota State B: 1908 Winnipeg, MB D: 1/4/1966 Regina, SK																																
1946	MTL	10																													
1949	EDM	14																													
2	Years	24																													
LARRY MOHR Larry RB 6'0 214 Queen's B: 3/5/1961 New Hamburg, OH Draft: 5-42 1984 EDM																																
1986	EDM	8										6	1	10	41	4.1	17	1													
1987	OTT	16				2						26	4	18	148	8.2	46	1	13	90	6.9	14	3								
1988	OTT	18	0		3	0								13	47	3.6	11	0	11	80	7.3	21	0					7	119	17.0	23
3	Years	42	0		3	2						32	5	41	236	5.8	46	2	24	170	7.1	21	3					7	119	17.0	23
RICK MOHR Richard DE 6'3 255 California-Davis B: 7/27/1957 Pro: U																																
1982	TOR	9	0		1		6.5																								
1983	TOR*	16	0		2		15.5																								
1984	SAS	16	0		1		10.5					6	1																		
1985	SAS	14					10.0																								
4	Years	55	0		4		42.5					6	1																		
JOHN MOHRING John LB 6'1 217 Georgia Southern B: 8/31/1984																																
2009	MTL	1				4																									
DARRELL MOIR Darrell DB-WR 5'11 180 Calgary B: 8/15/1958 Saskatoon, SK Draft: 1-7 1979 CAL																																
1979	CAL	3																													
1980	CAL	16	0		1				1	35								3	66	22.0	26	0	2	7	3.5	5	1	5	5.0	5
1981	CAL	2																						3	16	5.3	10				
1982	CAL	16	2		1				6	118		6	1											25	210	8.4	42	1	22	22.0	22
1983	CAL	16	0		1		1.0		7	192		12	2											4	49	12.3	27				
1984	CAL	16	0		4				5	172		6	1											5	8	1.6	23				
1985	CAL	16	0		2				4	46		6	1											1	0	0.0	0				
1986	MTL	8							1	0																					
1986	TOR	8	0		1				1	17																					
1986	Year	16	0		1				2	17																					
8	Years	93	2		10		1.0		25	580		30	5						3	66	22.0	26	0	40	290	7.3	42	2	27	13.5	22
FILIPO MOKOFISI Filipo LB 6'1 230 Utah B: 10/22/1962 Salt Lake City, UT Draft: 8-200 1986 NO																																
1989	BC	1				0																									
BOBBY MOLDEN Bobby DE 6'5 248 Mississippi State B: 12/23/1955 Pascagoula, MS																																
1979	WPG	3																													
LARRY MOLINARI Larry OE 6'4 220 Virginia B: 1944																																
1966	HAM	3	0		1														4	57	14.3	21	0								
STAN MOLINSKI Stan HB																																
1947	OTT	3																													
BART MOLL Bart HB 6'0 187 Toronto Balmy Beach Marine Jrs. B: 1935																																
1956	TOR	14										11	0	6	11	1.8	7	0	1	22	22.0	22	0								
1957	TOR	13										26	1	9	46	5.1	15	1													
2	Years	27										37	1	15	57	3.8	15	1	1	22	22.0	22	0								
NAYLAND MOLL Nayland HB 5'10 177 Toronto Jrs. B: 1933																																
1955	TOR	12										5	1	44	221	5.0	19	1	6	90	15.0	36	0	2	19	9.5	10	6	105	17.5	21

Year	Team	GP	FM	FF	FR	TK	SK	YDS	IR	YDS	PD	PTS	TD	RA	YDS	AVG	LG	TD	REC	YDS	AVG	LG	TD	PR	YDS	AVG	LG	KOR	YDS	AVG	LG
1957	OTT	9										6	1	1	0	0.0	0	0	1	29	29.0	29	1	1	10	10.0	10				
2	Years	21										11	2	45	221	4.9	19	1	7	119	17.0	36	1	3	29	9.7	10	6	105	17.5	21
BOB MOLLE Bob OG 6'4 260 Saskatoon Hilltops Jrs.; Simon Fraser B: 9/23/1962 Vancouver, BC Draft: 1B-9 1985 WPG; 12C-173 1985 TB-USFL																															
1986	WPG	7					1.0																								
1987	WPG	18				0																									
1988	WPG	2				0																									
1989	WPG	18	0		1	0																									
1990	WPG	18				1																									
1991	WPG	18	0		1	3																									
1992	WPG	18				1																									
7	Years	99	0		2	5	1.0																								
KEVIN MOLLE Kevin OT 6'3 245 Saskatoon Hilltops Jrs.; Fresno State B: 9/14/1958 Saskatoon, SK Draft: TE 1982 CAL																															
1983	CAL	16	0		3																										
1984	CAL	16																													
1986	MTL	12																													
3	Years	44	0		3																										
STEVE MOLNAR Steve FB-OHB-DB 5'11 200 Regina Dales Jrs.; George Washington; Utah B: 2/28/1947																															
1969	SAS	16												10	47	4.7	30	0	2	34	17.0	22	0								
1970	SAS	16	3		0							18	3	62	272	4.4	34	3	8	68	8.5	20	0	43	342	8.0	18	1	25	25.0	25
1971	SAS	16	1		0							6	1	24	148	6.2	19	1	7	40	5.7	14	0	59	541	9.2	30	5	125	25.0	37
1972	SAS	16	5		3									27	88	3.3	10	0	7	106	15.1	33	0	51	385	7.5	26	1	14	14.0	14
1973	SAS	2										6	1	4	7	1.8	2	1						4	12	3.0	5				
1974	SAS	13	1		0							6	1	36	195	5.4	31	1	13	228	17.5	47	0	27	174	6.4	16				
1975	SAS	16	2		0							20	3	56	285	5.1	22	3	30	345	11.5	36	0					3	30	10.0	24
1976	SAS	14	5		1							36	6	180	822	4.6	23	5	33	260	7.9	31	1								
1977	SAS	16	3		0							42	7	115	470	4.1	23	6	26	279	10.7	63	1								
1978	SAS	16	3		0									56	215	3.8	17	0	16	192	12.0	29	0	1	-3	-3.0	-3	4	58	14.5	19
10	Years	141	23		4							134	22	570	2549	4.5	34	20	142	1552	10.9	63	2	185	1451	7.8	30	14	252	18.0	37
ED MOLSTAD Ed DE-DT-LB 6'6 250 Alberta B: 2/21/1947 Draft: 2A- 1967 WPG																															
1968	EDM	16																													
1969	EDM	16	0		1																										
1970	EDM	16	0		1																										
1971	EDM	16			1																										
1972	EDM	16	0		2																										
1973	EDM	16	0		2																										
6	Years	96	0		7																										
TONY MOMSEN Anton Henry, Jr. LB 6'1 215 Michigan B: 1/29/1928 Toledo, OH D: 3/6/1994 Columbus, OH Draft: 5-59 1951 LARM Pro: N																															
1953	CAL+	13																						1	20	20.0	20	1	6	6.0	6
MURRAY MONAGHAN Murray HB 5'8 160 Toronto Argonauts Jrs. B: 1929																															
1948	TOR	3																													
WONDERFUL MONDS Wonderful Terrific, Jr. CB 6'3 215 Indian Hills JC; Nebraska B: 5/3/1952 Fort Pierce, FL Draft: 4A-112 1976 PIT Pro: N																															
1976	OTT	9	2		2				4	58														1	3	3.0	3				
1977	OTT	15	0		3				1	-8																					
1979	OTT	6							1	5																					
3	Years	30	2		5				6	55														1	3	3.0	3				
TOM MONIOS Tom WR 5'11 188 Northeastern Draft: 2-12 1996 SAS																															
1996	SAS	3				0																									
ARIES MONROE Aries Laverne LB 6'2 233 Coffeyville JC; Alabama B: 1/23/1980 Tallahassee, FL																															
2002	MTL	1				3	1.0																								
2003	CAL	8	0	1	1	20	3.0	26.0	0	0	1																				
2	Years	9	0	1	1	23	4.0	26.0																							
FORBES MONROE Forbes G																															
1947	OTT	1																													
JAMES MONROE James C 6'2 270 Syracuse B: 9/16/1979 Montreal, QC Draft: 7-50 1993 OTT																															
1994	OTT	18				3																									
1995	OTT	18	0		1	1																									
1996	OTT	18	1		0	4																									
1997	SAS	13	0	0	1	1																									
1998	SAS	18				1																									
1999	SAS	14	0	0	2	0																									
2000	SAS	18				0																									
7	Years	117	1	0	4	10																									
DAVE MONTAGANO Dave S 5'11 185 Carleton (Ontario) B: 5/14/1958 Ottawa, ON																															
1974	WPG	7																						9	65	7.2	17				
1975	SAS	9	1		1																			8	3	0.4	7	2	40	20.0	22
1976	HAM	16							3	18																					
1977	EDM	9							1	0														1	1	1.0	1	1	10	10.0	10
1978	SAS	2																													
5	Years	43	1		1				4	18														18	69	3.8	17	3	50	16.7	22
DENIS MONTANA Denis WR 6'1 200 Concordia B: 1/6/1972 Montreal, QC Draft: 1-9 1996 MTL																															
1996	MTL	8				0													2	4	2.0	4	0								
1997	MTL	10				0						6	1						4	53	13.3	15	1								
1997	TOR	3				2																									
1997	Year	13				2						6	1						4	53	13.3	15	1								
1998	CAL	3				0								1	-9	-9.0	-9	0													
1999	TOR	2				0																									
2000	EDM	1				0																									
2000	BC	14				5													4	102	25.5	60	0					0	10		10
2000	Year	15				5													4	102	25.5	60	0					0	10		10
2001	BC	18	1	0	2	14						8	1						34	620	18.2	49	1								
2002	OTT	16	1	0	1	6						12	2						35	399	11.4	91	2					1	44	44.0	34
2003	OTT	18	0	0	1	5						18	3	1	6	6.0	6	0	39	595	15.3	48	3								
2004	CAL	17	1	0	0	5						6	1						37	461	12.5	45	1					1	0	0.0	0
9	Years	93	3	0	4	37						50	8	2	-3	-1.5	6	0	155	2234	14.4	91	8					2	54	27.0	34
IAN MONTEITH Ian FB-LB 6'1 200 McGill; East York Argonauts Ints. B: 1943 Draft: 1-9 1963 WPG																															
1963	WPG	9												5	9	1.8	4	0													
JOE MONTFORD Joe DE-LB 6'1 225 South Carolina State B: 7/30/1970 Columbia, SC																															
1995	SHR	4				11																									
1996	HAM	15	0		4	89	2.0	17.0			3																				
1997	HAM	18	0	1	1	54	8.0	86.0			3																				
1998	HAM*	18	0	6	3	65	21.0	164.0			2																				
1999	HAM*	18	0	5	5	37	26.0	158.0				18	3															1	0	0.0	0
2000	HAM*	18	0	8	0	52	20.0	131.0																							
2001	HAM*	18	0	4	4	65	19.0	115.0	1	1	2	6	1																		
2002	TOR*	18	0	3	0	72	9.0	48.0			1																				
2003	HAM	18	0	2	2	61	6.0	36.0			3																				
2004	HAM	18	0	1	0	37	13.0	107.0			2																				
2005	EDM	18	0	1	0	27	10.0	84.0			2																				
2006	EDM	4	0	1	0	7	1.0	3.0																							
12	Years	185	0	32	19	577	135.0	949.0	1	1	18	24	4															1	0	0.0	0
FRED MONTGOMERY Fred WR 5'10 195 New Mexico State B: 8/30/1971 Greenville, MS																															
1995	SHR	18	3		0	2						6	1						30	447	14.9	50	1					9	177	19.7	33

Year	Team	GP	FM	FF	FR	TK	SK	YDS	IR	YDS	PD	PTS	TD	RA	YDS	AVG	LG	TD	REC	YDS	AVG	LG	TD	PR	YDS	AVG	LG	KOR	YDS	AVG	LG
TYRONE MONTGOMERY Tyrone WR 5'11 185 Mississippi B: 8/3/1970 Greenville, MS Pro: N																															
1997	WPG	8	0	0	1	0						6	1	66	301	4.6	39	1	16	139	8.7	38	0					29	640	22.1	54
JOHN MOODY John C. (Big Train) FB 5'8 230 Morris Brown B: 1918																															
1946	MTL	12										14	1					1													
MIKE MOODY Michael K. OT 6'7 305 Southern California B: 5/9/1969 San Francisco, CA Pro: E																															
1996	WPG	1				1																									
DONN MOOMAW Donn Dement LB 6'4 220 UCLA B: 10/15/1931 Santa Ana, CA Draft: 1A-9 1953 LARM																															
1953	TOR	7										1	0																		
1955	OTT	2																													
2	Years	9										1	0																		
WARREN MOON Harold Warren QB 6'3 217 West Los Angeles JC; Washington B: 11/18/1956 Los Angeles, CA Pro: N																															
1978	EDM	15	1		0							6	1	30	114	3.8	17	1													
1979	EDM	16	1		0							12	2	56	150	2.7	17	2													
1980	EDM	16										18	3	55	352	6.4	29	3													
1981	EDM	15	1		0							18	3	50	298	6.0	27	3													
1982	EDM	16	1		1							24	4	54	259	4.8	33	4													
1983	EDM*	16	7		0							18	3	85	527	6.2	25	3	1	25	25.0	25	0								
6	Years	94	11		1							96	16	330	1700	5.2	33	16	1	25	25.0	25	0								
ANDREW MOORE Andrew N. C-OG 6'5 290 Mesa JC; Sonoma State B: 12/22/1972 San Diego, CA Pro: E																															
2001	SAS	18	0	0	1	63																									
2002	SAS	13	1	0	0	0																									
2003	TOR	1				0																									
3	Years	32	1	0	1	63																									
BILLY MOORE Bill OHB 6'1 195 Mississippi State B: 1943 Draft: RS-7-53 1965 KC																															
1966	BC	11	1		2									29	104	3.6	12	0	11	148	13.5	33	0					17	466	27.4	45
CURTIS MOORE Curtis LB 6'1 247 Kansas B: 11/2/1967 Lincoln, NE Draft: 10-267 1991 HOU Pro: E																															
1993	SAC	18	0		2	76	2.0	27.0	1	8																		1	0	0.0	0
1994	SAC	14	0		1	22	6.0	26.0	1	9	1																				
2	Years	32	0		3	98	8.0	53.0	2	17	1																	1	0	0.0	0
DICKIE MOORE Dickie HB 6'0 206 Western Kentucky B: 2/14/1947 D: 11/27/2001 Owensboro, KY																															
1969	TOR	2												18	113	6.3	28	0	2	14	7.0	15	0					1	17	17.0	17
FREDDIE MOORE Freddie Lee OT 6'6 304 Central Florida; Florida A&M B: 8/27/1977 Tallahassee, FL Pro: E																															
2003	BC	4				0																									
2004	BC	18				0																									
2005	OTT	9				0																									
3	Years	31				0																									
JOE MOORE Joseph Lee, Jr. RB 6'1 205 Missouri B: 6/29/1949 St. Louis, MO Draft: 1-11 1971 CHIB Pro: N																															
1974	EDM	1										6	1	17	67	3.9	11	1	1	1	1.0	1	0								
KEN MOORE W.K. G-T-E 6'0 214 Calgary Jrs.; Alberta B: 1926																															
1946	CAL	3																													
1949	EDM	13																													
1950	EDM	14										3	0																		
1951	CAL	11																													
4	Years	41										3	0																		
KEN MOORE Ken OT-RB-LB-TE 6'5 250 Hawaii B: 1/27/1961 Lethbridge, AB Draft: TE 1982 CAL																															
1983	CAL	2																	2	34	17.0	43	0								
1984	CAL	15	0		1		1.5												1	28	28.0	28	0								
1985	SAS	12																	8	61	7.6	15	0					1	4	4.0	4
1986	SAS	11																													
1987	SAS	18				1	2.0																								
1988	SAS	11				0																									
1989	SAS	18				1																									
1990	SAS	18				1																									
1991	CAL	18	0		2	2																									
1992	CAL	18				4																									
1993	CAL	18				0													0	0		0	0								
1994	CAL	16				0																									
12	Years	175	0		3	9	3.5												11	123	11.2	43	0					1	4	4.0	4
KENNY MOORE Ken LB-DE-DT 6'2 250 East Carolina B: 8/25/1952 Pro: W																															
1976	OTT	8																													
1977	OTT	11																										1	0	0.0	0
2	Years	19																										1	0	0.0	0
LARRY MOORE Larry Ray DE 6'3 235 Angelo State B: 6/11/1951 Gainesville, TX Draft: 17-437 1974 PIT																															
1974	CAL	7																													
1975	CAL	16																													
1976	CAL	4																													
3	Years	27																													
LeROY MOORE LeRoy Franklin DE 6'0 231 Fort Valley State B: 9/16/1935 Pontiac, MI Pro: N																															
1966	HAM	6	0		2																										
MACK MOORE Mack Henry DT 6'4 258 Texas A&M B: 3/4/1959 Monroe, LA Draft: 6A-152 1981 MIA Pro: N																															
1981	BC	16	0		2		5.5																								
1982	BC	12	0		1		9.5																								
1983	BC*	16	0		4		15.0																								
1984	BC*	16	0		1		9.0																								
1988	BC	14				25	11.0																								
1989	BC	18				24	6.0																								
6	Years	92	0		8	49	56.0																								
MARK MOORE Mark Quentin DB 6'0 194 Oklahoma State B: 9/3/1964 Nacogdoches, TX Draft: 4-104 1987 SEA Pro: EN																															
1991	CAL	1				1																									
NICK MOORE Nicholas A. WR 6'2 195 Toledo B: 6/25/1986 Columbus, OH																															
2011	BC	5				1								1	7	7.0	7	0	5	50	10.0	22	0								
PERNELL MOORE Pernell WR 5'9 160 Central State (Ohio) B: 9/7/1965 Perdido, AL																															
1988	TOR	13	2		1	1						24	4	2	21	10.5	13	0	38	610	16.1	75	2	74	764	10.3	109	11	206	18.7	27
RODNEY MOORE Rodney Branaird DB 6'1 200 North Texas B: 9/8/1960 Nacogdoches, TX																															
1986	OTT	1																													
RYAN MOORE Ryan WR 5'9 170 Hamilton Hurricanes Jrs. B: 2/16/1959																															
1983	HAM	4																													
SAM MOORE Sam WR 6'2 200 Sam Houston State B: 9/4/1962																															
1988	BC	4										6	1						8	172	21.5	68	1								
SHAWN MOORE Shawn Levique QB 6'2 213 Virginia B: 4/4/1968 Martinsville, VA Draft: 11-284 1991 DEN Pro: EN																															
1995	OTT	6	0		1	0						6	1	5	11	2.2	5	1													
1995	WPG	8	4		0	0						6	1	17	99	5.8	18	1													
1995	CAL	5				0								2	21	10.5	15	0													
1995	Year	19	4		0	0						12	2	24	131	5.5	18	2													
TERRENCE MOORE Terrence DB 6'3 205 Western Michigan B: 7/22/1979																															
2004	CAL	7	0	1	1	24			1	51	0																				
TRAVIS MOORE Travis D. WR 6'0 193 Ball State B: 8/5/1970 Santa Monica, CA Pro: X																															
1994	CAL	5				3						6	1						7	62	8.9	19	1								
1996	CAL	16	1		0	3						30	5	1	4	4.0	4	0	44	690	15.7	45	5	1	9	9.0	9				
1997	CAL	18	1	0	0	3						36	6	1	3	3.0	3	0	72	931	12.9	41	6								
1998	CAL	15	2	0	0	2						42	7						60	818	13.6	89	7								
1999	CAL*	18	1	0	1	2						44	7	1	8	8.0	8	0	70	1198	17.1	65	7	3	27	9.0	16				

Year	Team	GP	FM	FF	FR	TK	SK	YDS	IR	YDS	PD	PTS	TD	RA	YDS	AVG	LG	TD	REC	YDS	AVG	LG	TD	PR	YDS	AVG	LG	KOR	YDS	AVG	LG
2000	CAL*	16	1	0	0	2						90	15	1	3	3.0	3	0	71	1431	20.2	71	15	19	156	8.2	20				
2001	CAL*	13	1	0	0	2						38	6	3	22	7.3	11	0	76	1298	17.1	64	6	7	67	9.6	29				
2002	CAL	15	1	0	0	2						60	10	2	-1	-0.5	1	0	70	1108	15.8	80	10	2	23	11.5	15				
2003	SAS	15	1	0	0	2						54	9						70	942	13.5	53	9								
2004	SAS	18	2	0	1	2						54	9						72	1025	14.2	41	9								
2005	SAS	8				2						24	4						33	427	12.9	44	4								
11	Years	157	11	0	2	25						478	79	9	39	4.3	11	0	645	9930	15.4	89	79	32	282	8.8	29				
WILL MOORE Will Henry, III WR 6'1 189 Texas Southern B: 2/21/1970 Dallas, TX Pro: N																															
1992	CAL	1				0													3	38	12.7	16	0								
1993	CAL	18	2		0	6						72	12						73	1083	14.8	55	12								
1994	CAL	16				4						66	11						44	792	18.0	40	11					2	2	1.0	2
3	Years	35	2		0	10						138	23						120	1913	15.9	55	23					2	2	1.0	2
AL MOOREHOUSE Al (Bus) E																															
1947	TOR	1																													
BOBBY MOORHEAD Robert, Jr. DB 6'0 175 Georgia Tech B: 1932 Draft: 13-147 1953 BAL																															
1953	TOR	2																													
DON MOORHEAD Donald QB 6'3 210 Michigan B: 10/11/1948 Draft: 6-132 1971 NO																															
1971	BC	16	6		1							6	1	54	349	6.5	42	1	2	26	13.0	16	0								
1972	BC	16	8		2							6	1	70	330	4.7	17	1													
1973	BC	16	1		1									53	283	5.3	38	0													
1974	BC	16	1		0							18	3	63	204	3.2	23	3													
1975	BC	5										18	3	14	46	3.3	11	3													
5	Years	69	16		4							48	8	254	1212	4.8	42	8	2	26	13.0	16	0								
MARK MOORS Mark C-OG 6'2 240 Acadia B: 1/31/1957 Regina, SK Draft: 5-37 1978 CAL																															
1980	CAL	16																													
1981	CAL	16																													
1982	CAL	16	0		1																										
1983	WPG	16																													
1984	WPG	16																													
1985	WPG	16																													
1986	WPG	18	0		4																										
1988	OTT	6	0		1	0																									
1989	HAM	10																													
9	Years	130	0		6	0																									
MICHAEL MOOSBRUGGER Michael OL 6'7 296 Wake Forest B: 4/6/1979 Doylestown, PA																															
2002	WPG	1				0																									
TOM MORAN Tom OE-FW-LB-DE 6'1 193 Hamilton Panthers Ints. B: 8/16/1932 Hamilton, ON																															
1953	MTL	1																													
1954	MTL	13																						1	0	0.0	0				
1955	MTL	12							2	28		5	1						5	82	16.4	25	1								
1956	MTL	14							5	57									4	73	18.3	32	0	1	3	3.0	3				
1957	MTL	3							1	3									3	43	14.3	25	0								
1958	MTL	14										6	1	4	14	3.5	9	0	19	287	15.1	34	1								
1959	MTL	14							1	0		6	1						11	197	17.9	68	0								
1960	MTL	11										6	1						5	67	13.4	31	1								
1961	MTL	4																													
1961	HAM	10																													
1961	Year	14																													
9	Years	86							9	88		23	4	4	14	3.5	9	0	47	749	15.9	68	3	2	3	1.5	3				
JOHNNIE MORANT Johnnie E. WR 6'4 218 Syracuse B: 12/7/1981 Newark, NJ Draft: 5-134 2004 OAK Pro: N																															
2008	TOR	4				0						6	1						6	127	21.2	52	1								
JACQUES MOREAU Jacques OT 6'3 265 Concordia (Quebec) B: 6/9/1967 Hull, QC																															
1993	OTT	8				2																									
1995	OTT	2				0																									
1996	MTL	1				0																									
3	Years	11				2																									
RON MOREHOUSE Ron LB 5'11 215 Vancouver Meralomas Jrs.; San Diego State B: 12/10/1953 Draft: TE 1979 BC																															
1979	BC	16																										1	18	18.0	18
1980	BC	12	0		1																							2	28	14.0	14
1981	BC	16	0		1																							4	59	14.8	18
1982	BC	16							1	0																		4	80	20.0	26
1983	TOR	9					0.5		1	9																					
5	Years	69	0		2		0.5		2	9																		11	185	16.8	26
JOE MOREINO Joseph P., Jr. DT 6'6 246 Idaho State B: 4/4/1955 Providence, RI Pro: N																															
1979	SAS	6																													
ZEKE MORENO Ezekiel Aaron LB 6'2 242 Southern California B: 10/10/1978 Chula Vista, CA Draft: 5B-139 2001 SD Pro: NU																															
2007	HAM*	18	0	2	1	126	1.0	8.0	2	57	3	6	1																		
2008	HAM	10	0	1	0	53	2.0	15.0	1	19	0	6	1																		
2008	WPG	8				45	1.0	10.0			1																				
2008	Year*	18	0	1	0	98	3.0	25.0	1	19	1	6	1																		
2009	TOR	18	0	2	1	97	2.0	6.0	2	32	3																				
3	Years	46	0	5	2	321	6.0	39.0	5	108	7	12	2																		
ROB MORETTO Robert LB 6'0 200 British Columbia B: 11/14/1965 Burnaby, BC Draft: 7-61 1987 BC																															
1987	BC	14				0																									
1988	BC	4				0																									
1989	BC	18				15																									
3	Years	36				15																									
AINSWORTH MORGAN Ainsworth WR 5'9 175 Toledo B: 7/20/1969 Clarendon, Jamaica Draft: 3-24 1994 HAM																															
1994	TOR	1																										1	20	20.0	20
1995	TOR	6				4													1	15	15.0	15	0								
2	Years	7				4													1	15	15.0	15	0					1	20	20.0	20
BOB MORGAN Robert Francis OT-DE 6'0 235 Maryland B: 6/28/1930 Freeport, PA D: 10/10/1991 Westminster, CO Draft: 8-97(f) 1953 LARM Pro: N																															
1955	CAL	15	0		1																			0	19		19				
1956	CAL	8	0		1																										
2	Years	23	0		2																			0	19		19				
BOBBY MORGAN Robert Bernard DB 6'0 205 Independence CC; New Mexico B: 8/7/1940 Warnego, KS Pro: N																															
1969	TOR	7	1		1							6	1	19	72	3.8	16	0					1					3	53	17.7	18
1969	OTT	1	1		0									8	27	3.4		0					0					1	27	27.0	27
1969	Year	8	2		1							6	1	27	99	3.7	16	0	3	76	25.3	75	1					4	80	20.0	27
DWAYNE MORGAN Dwayne OT 6'4 300 Northeast Oklahoma JC; Clemson B: 5/3/1970 Griffin, GA Pro: N																															
1996	HAM	14				0																									
1998	TOR	16	0	0	1	1																									
1999	TOR	8				1																									
2000	MTL	12	0	0	2	1																									
2000	TOR	6				0																									
2000	Year	18				1																									
2001	TOR	14	0	0	1	5																									
2002	TOR	18				1																									
6	Years	82	0	0	4	9																									
JOSEPH MORGAN Joseph S 5'11 194 South Florida B: 8/9/1979 Etobicoke, ON																															
2003	WPG	18				23	1.0		1	20	0																				
2004	WPG	14	0	1	0	18			2	23	0																				

Year	Team	GP	FM	FF	FR	TK	SK	YDS	IR	YDS	PD	PTS	TD	RA	YDS	AVG	LG	TD	REC	YDS	AVG	LG	TD	PR	YDS	AVG	LG	KOR	YDS	AVG	LG
2	Years	32	0	1	0	41	1.0		3	43	0																				
KARL MORGAN Michael Karl NG 6'1 255 UCLA B: 2/23/1961 Houma, LA Draft: 21-242 1983 ARI-USFL Pro: N																															
1983	SAS	16	0		1		10.0																								
KENYATTE MORGAN Kenyatte E. WR 5'10 180 Montana State B: 7/3/1975 San Francisco, CA																															
2003	CAL	1				0													2	27	13.5	20	0	2	8	4.0	6				
OCTAVUS MORGAN Octavus LB 6'2 212 Illinois B: 9/11/1952 Atlanta, GA Draft: 16-412 1974 PIT; 15-178 1974 CHI-WFL																															
1974	CAL	4																													
OMARR MORGAN Omarr S. CB 5'9 176 Brigham Young B: 12/4/1976 Los Angeles, CA																															
2000	SAS	18	0	1	3	64			4	67	10																				
2001	SAS+	18	0	1	0	7			2	0	4																				
2002	SAS*	18	0	1	2	53			5	106	8	12	2																		
2003	SAS*	15	0	0	2	63			3	14	6	6	1																		
2004	SAS	18				57			3	26	9																				
2005	SAS*	17	0	1	1	44			4	92	2	6	1																		
2006	SAS	17				57					6																				
2007	EDM	16	0	0	1	52			2	0	7																				
2008	SAS	17	0	2	0	76					4																				
2009	SAS	18	0	0	2	52			4	94	3	6	1																		
2010	SAS	18	0	2	0	57					3																				
11	Years	190	0	8	11	582			27	399	62	30	5																		
NICKOLAS MORIN-SOUCY Nickolas DE 6'2 240 Montreal B: 6/25/1984 Gaspe, QC Draft: 3-23 2009 MTL																															
2010	MTL	7				2																									
DEMETRICE MORLEY Demetrice S 6'1 195 Tennessee B: 7/23/1987 Miami, FL																															
2011	CAL	16	1	4	1	41	4.0	23.0			2													4	4	1.0	3				
STEVE MORLEY Steven OG-OT 6'7 330 St. Mary's (Canada) B: 8/18/1981 Halifax, NS Draft: 1A-1 2003 CAL Pro: EN																															
2003	CAL	11				0																									
2007	TOR	8				1																									
2008	SAS	6				0																									
2009	WPG	18				2													1	8	8.0	8	0								
2010	WPG	18				0																									
2011	WPG	18				0																									
6	Years	79				3													1	8	8.0	8	0								
JACK MORNEAU Jack G 6'0 205 none B: 1926																															
1950	OTT	10										2	0																		
1951	OTT	9																													
2	Years	19										2	0																		
TONY MORO Tony TE-OHB 5'11 218 Dayton B: 12/4/1947 Udine, Italy Draft: 14-355 1970 WAS																															
1970	TOR	14	1		3							18	3	2	6	3.0	3	0	22	452	20.5	62	3					4	73	18.3	25
1971	TOR	14										12	2						5	76	15.2	32	2					1	0	0.0	0
1972	TOR	14										12	2						23	364	15.8	27	2								
1973	TOR	14										6	1	1	10	10.0	10	0	20	362	18.1	39	1								
1974	BC	16	1		0														17	341	20.1	65	0					2	6	3.0	3
1975	BC	16	0		1														21	285	13.6	29	0								
1977	TOR	7																	4	61	15.3	20	0								
7	Years	95	2		4							48	8	3	16	5.3	10	0	112	1941	17.3	65	8					7	79	11.3	25
FRANK MOROZ Frank QB 5'11 168 B: 1925																															
1948	HAM	12																													
1949	HAM	5																													
2	Years	17																													
MARK MOROZ Mark OG 6'4 305 Wake Forest B: 6/6/1981 Welland, ON Draft: 1-4 2004 TOR																															
2004	TOR	4				0																									
2005	HAM	1				0																									
2	Years	5				0																									
MIKE MORREALE Mike SB-WR 6'3 210 McMaster B: 8/10/1971 Hamilton, ON Draft: 2-17 1994 BC																															
1995	TOR	18	2		0	4													19	285	15.0	36	0					3	23	7.7	11
1996	TOR	18				12													19	378	19.9	47	0					2	2	1.0	2
1997	HAM	18	1	1	0	19						12	2						38	466	12.3	48	2								
1998	HAM	18	1	2	2	6						36	6						67	1076	16.1	92	6								
1999	HAM	18	4	0	1	4						6	1						46	573	12.5	43	1								
2000	HAM	18				2						12	2						49	778	15.9	50	2								
2001	HAM	18	2	0	0	2						12	2						43	464	10.8	41	2								
2002	TOR	18	1	0	0	7						6	1						32	345	10.8	57	1								
2003	TOR	18	0	0	2	6						24	4						37	462	12.5	51	4								
2004	HAM	18	3	0	1	1						30	5						75	876	11.7	42	5								
2005	HAM	18	3	0	1	4						6	1						58	624	10.8	42	1					2	8	4.0	8
2006	HAM	18	1	0	0	6													26	322	12.4	31	0	2	28	14.0	20	1	0	0.0	0
12	Years	216	18	3	7	73						144	24						509	6649	13.1	92	24	2	28	14.0	20	8	33	4.1	11
ALEX MORRIS Alex DB 6'0 186 Queen's B: 9/9/1952 Draft: 3B-27 1975 WPG																															
1975	WPG	3	1		0																			1	0	0.0	0				
1976	TOR	7							1	10																					
1977	TOR	2																	1	9	9.0	9	0								
1977	OTT	2																													
1977	CAL	11										2	0						2	19	9.5	14	0					8	156	19.5	26
1977	Year	15																	3	28	9.3	14	0					8	156	19.5	26
1978	CAL	3																	1	13	13.0	13	0								
4	Years	15	1		0				1	10		2	0						4	41	10.3	14	0	1	0	0.0	0	8	156	19.5	26
CHRIS MORRIS Chris OT 6'5 285 Toronto B: 9/13/1968 Scarborough, ON Draft: 1B-8 1992 EDM																															
1992	EDM	18				5																									
1993	EDM	18	0		1	0																									
1994	EDM	18	0		2	1																									
1995	EDM	9	0		1	0																									
1996	EDM	17				1																									
1997	EDM	18	0	0	1	0																									
1998	EDM	17				1																									
1999	EDM	17				0																									
2000	EDM	18				0																									
2001	EDM	17				1																									
2002	EDM	18	0	0	1	3																									
2003	EDM	18				1																									
2004	EDM	17				1																									
2005	EDM	16	0	0	1	2																									
14	Years	236	0	0	7	16																									
DELIUS MORRIS Delius WR 5'9 180 Phoenix JC; Central State (Ohio) B: 12/16/1970 Detroit, MI																															
1995	BIR	11	3		0	2						18	3						27	382	14.1	34	3	23	134	5.8	15	18	361	20.1	43
ERIC MORRIS Eric SB 5'8 174 Texas Tech B: 10/26/1985 Littlefield, TX																															
2009	SAS	4	0	0	1	0													1	17	17.0	17	0	16	87	5.4	20	22	392	17.8	25
FRANKIE MORRIS Frank OG-T 5'11 230 B: 5/14/1923 D: 4/10/2009 Edmonton, AB																															
1946	TOR	11										1	0																		
1947	TOR	12																													
1948	TOR	12																													
1949	TOR	7																													
1950	EDM	14																													

Year	Team	GP	FM	FF	FR	TK	SK	YDS	IR	YDS	PD	PTS	TD	RA	YDS	AVG	LG	TD	REC	YDS	AVG	LG	TD	PR	YDS	AVG	LG	KOR	YDS	AVG	LG
1951	EDM	14										5	1																		
1952	EDM	16			3							10	2																		
1953	EDM	9																													
1954	EDM	16																													
1955	EDM	13																													
1956	EDM	16																													
1957	EDM	12																													
1958	EDM	9																													
13	Years	161	0		3							16	3																		
GARY MORRIS Gary SB-WR 6'3 185 Norfolk State B: 6/26/1968 Norfolk, VA																															
1993	EDM	9				1						12	2						18	233	12.9	38	2					1	19	19.0	19
1994	HAM	1																	3	21	7.0	8	0								
1995	MEM	15				5													27	375	13.9	43	0								
3	Years	25				6						12	2						48	629	13.1	43	2					1	19	19.0	19
HORACE MORRIS Horace LB 6'2 230 Tennessee B: 5/29/1971 Miami, FL Draft: 5-152 1994 NYJ Pro: E																															
1995	OTT	12	0		1	22	6.0	51.0	0	0	1																				
JAMIE MORRIS James Walter RB 5'7 185 Michigan B: 6/6/1965 Southern Pines, NC Draft: 4-109 1988 WAS Pro: N																															
1991	HAM	12	3		2	2						18	3	139	591	4.3	32	2	28	263	9.4	58	1					19	435	22.9	52
LEE MORRIS Lee A., Jr. WR 5'11 180 Oklahoma B: 7/14/1964 Oklahoma City, OK Pro: EN																															
1988	TOR	2	1		0	0						6	1						8	127	15.9	31	1								
1989	TOR	8	2		1	2													11	99	9.0	28	0	8	73	9.1	16	18	411	22.8	37
1990	HAM	2																	5	122	24.4	55	0	7	13	1.9	7				
3	Years	12	3		1	2						6	1						24	348	14.5	55	1	15	86	5.7	16	18	411	22.8	37
LEONARD MORRIS Leonard RB 5'8 190 Hayward State B: 12/13/1968																															
1990	TOR	2	0		1	1								1	6	6.0	6	0						1	6	6.0	6	4	70	17.5	44
RON MORRIS Ron FL-DB-P 6'1 190 Arkansas; Tulsa B: 7/16/1936 Draft: 19-229 1957 NYG																															
1959	CAL	13	2		0				3	32		1	0	16	84	5.3	14	0	9	92	10.2	23	0	17	109	6.4	16	5	129	25.8	35
1960	CAL	15	4		1				7	128		23	3	14	50	3.6	15	0	19	215	11.3	35	2	9	14	1.6	7	3	55	18.3	22
1961	CAL	4	2						2	26		2	0	6	-2	-0.3	5	0						15	92	6.1	11	1	34	34.0	34
1961	TOR	7							3	47		12	2	2	1	0.5	1	0	23	459	20.0	60	2	1	3	3.0	3	2	41	20.5	30
1961	Year	11	2									14	2	8	-1	-0.1	5	0	23	459	20.0	60	2	16	95	5.9	11	3	75	25.0	34
1962	TOR	14							1	80		6	1	17	74	4.4	16	0	11	125	11.4	29	0	1	2	2.0	2	1	16	16.0	16
1963	TOR	5										4	0						10	198	19.8	56	0					1	18	18.0	18
1963	BC	6	1		0							12	2	25	110	4.4	16	1	15	242	16.1	43	1	24	120	5.0	14	3	53	17.7	25
1963	Year	11	1		0							16	2	25	110	4.4	16	1	25	440	17.6	56	1	24	120	5.0	14	4	71	17.8	25
1964	BC	16	4		1				2	9		14	2	40	168	4.2	12	1	17	173	10.2	39	1	68	407	6.0	28				
1965	BC	11	2		1							6	1	5	30	6.0	12	0	13	137	10.5	26	1	33	150	4.5	28				
7	Years	78	15		3				18	322		80	11	125	515	4.1	16	2	117	1641	14.0	60	7	168	897	5.3	28	16	346	21.6	35
RONNIE MORRIS Ronald QB 6'0 185 Tulsa B: 1931 Draft: 13B-149 1953 CHIC																															
1955	CAL	1												5	10	2.0	5	0													
TY MORRIS Ty WR 5'11 195 Puget Sound B: 9/21/1956 Draft: 2B-18 1978 MTL																															
1978	MTL	14	0		1																										
BERNIE MORRISON Bernie LB 6'0 215 Winnipeg Rods Jrs.; St. Vital Mustangs Jrs.; Manitoba B: 3/25/1955 Winnipeg, MB Draft: TE 1978 WPG																															
1978	CAL	12	0		2				2	8																		1	4	4.0	4
1979	CAL	16							2	5																		1	0	0.0	0
1980	CAL	16	0		1				3	45																					
1981	CAL	16					4.0		1	0																					
1982	CAL	16	0		1		1.0																					1	11	11.0	11
1983	CAL	15	0		1		3.0		3	51																					
1984	CAL	16	0		1		4.0		1	0																					
1985	CAL	16	0		2		3.0		1	4																					
1986	CAL	16	0		4		1.0		4	25																					
1987	CAL	18	0		1	99	1.0		3	22																		1	8	8.0	8
1988	CAL	2			1	2																									
11	Years	159	0		14	101	17.0		20	160																		4	23	5.8	11
DAVE MORRISON David DB 5'11 180 Texas State B: 1947 Draft: 16-433 1968 OAK Pro: N																															
1969	MTL	2																													
JIM MORSE James A. HB 6'0 185 Notre Dame B: 10/8/1935 Muskegon, MI Draft: 13-148 1957 GB																															
1957	CAL	15	1		0				3	23		30	5	61	273	4.5	24	1	14	327	23.4	79	4	1	4	4.0	4	4	106	26.5	42
1958	CAL	3										6	1	23	100	4.3	21	0	4	54	13.5	18	1					1	22	22.0	22
2	Years	18	1		0				3	23		36	6	84	373	4.4	24	1	18	381	21.2	79	5	1	4	4.0	4	5	128	25.6	42
TODD MORTENSEN Todd QB 6'4 225 Brigham Young; San Diego B: 7/12/1979 Mesa, AZ Pro: E																															
2006	BC	1				0																									
DICKEY MORTON Dickie Leville RB 5'10 176 Arkansas B: 10/29/1951 Bogota, TX Draft: 11-283 1974 PIT; 15-175 1974 SC-WFL																															
1975	TOR	7	2		1							24	4	35	158	4.5	40	2	19	272	14.3	63	2	4	27	6.8	14	9	240	26.7	36
JOHN MORTON John WR 6'0 185 Grand Rapids CC; Western Michigan B: 9/24/1969 Pontiac, MI Pro: E																															
1995	TOR	5	1		0	0						6	1						7	135	19.3	68	1					1	13	13.0	13
1996	TOR	2				0						6	1						8	86	10.8	21	1								
2	Years	7	1		0	0						12	2						15	221	14.7	68	2					1	13	13.0	13
ANGELO MOSCA Angelo DT 6'4 272 Notre Dame; Wyoming B: 3/13/1937 Waltham, MA Draft: 30-350 1959 PHI																															
1958	HAM	14																													
1959	HAM	13																													
1960	OTT+	14																													
1961	OTT	14																													
1962	MTL	5																													
1962	HAM	4																										2	12	6.0	11
1962	Year	9																										2	12	6.0	11
1963	HAM*	14																													
1964	HAM	12																													
1965	HAM+	13																													
1966	HAM+	14																													
1967	HAM	14																													
1968	HAM	14	0		1																										
1969	HAM	14	1		1																										
1970	HAM*	14	0		1																										
1971	HAM	14	0		2																										
1972	HAM	14	1		1																										
15	Years	197	2		6																							2	12	6.0	11
WAYNE MOSELEY Gerald Wayne RB 6'0 190 Alabama A&M B: 10/6/1952 Decatur, AL Pro: N																															
1975	BC	11	2		1							18	3	87	459	5.3	56	2	22	257	11.7	53	1	27	318	11.8	40	19	490	25.8	38
DOM MOSELLE Dominic Angelo HB 6'0 192 Wisconsin-Superior B: 6/3/1925 Hurley, WI D: 8/19/2010 Superior, WI Draft: 23-299 1950 CLE Pro: N																															
1955	CAL	16	1		0				1	7		15	3	65	264	4.1	19	2	24	410	17.1	49	1					9	192	21.3	30
CEDRIC MOSES Cedric DB 5'11 185 Jackson State B: 2/10/1964																															
1989	SAS	6				7			0	4																					
PAUL MOSES Paul TE 6'0 210 Ottawa Sooners Jrs. B: 11/12/1953																															
1976	OTT	1																													
GREG MOSS Gregory, Jr. CB 5'7 175 Virginia Union; Florida International B: 9/2/1982 Miami, FL																															
2005	OTT	18	0	0	3	51			1	30	5													2	21	10.5	15	6	151	25.2	48
2007	WPG	9				23					5																				
2	Years	27	0	0	3	74			1	30	10													2	21	10.5	15	6	151	25.2	48
JOE MOSS Joseph Charles T 6'1 220 Maryland B: 4/9/1930 Elkins, WV Draft: 14-169 1952 LARM Pro: N																															
1955	OTT	12																										1	0	0.0	0

Year	Team	GP	FM	FF	FR	TK	SK	YDS	IR	YDS	PD	PTS	TD	RA	YDS	AVG	LG	TD	REC	YDS	AVG	LG	TD	PR	YDS	AVG	LG	KOR	YDS	AVG	LG
LeROY MOSS LeRoy OHB-DB 5'8 193 Missouri B: 3/27/1951																															
1974	EDM	3												6	33	5.5	7	0	7	64	9.1	27	0					2	34	17.0	21
1975	EDM	3									6	1	25	118	4.7	23	1	3	35	11.7	18	0					0	5		5
1977	BC	2									6	1	10	34	3.4	7	1	8	70	8.8	19	0					2	38	19.0	21
3	Years	8									12	2	41	185	4.5	23	2	18	169	9.4	27	0					4	77	19.3	21
RICK MOSS Rick Louis CB 5'11 184 Purdue B: 11/3/1957 Mattoon, IL Draft: 8-203 1979 CHIB																															
1979	SAS	5							1	66																		3	59	19.7	28
TONY MOSS Tony WR 5'7 169 Louisiana State B: 6/6/1966 Bossier City, LA Draft: 4-88 1990 CHIB Pro: E																															
1994	SHR	15				3						12	2						22	322	14.6	45	2	4	55	13.8	27	1	3	3.0	3
TRISTAN MOSS Tristan Paul CB 5'10 180 Western Michigan B: 11/22/1972 Houston, TX Pro: E																															
1998	SAS	2				0																									
DAVE MOSSMAN David DB 6'0 195 Snow JC; Weber State; Hawaii B: 8/7/1964 Prince George, BC Draft: 6-42 1989 CAL																															
1990	HAM	2	0		1																										
GARY MOTEN Gary Kim LB 6'1 210 Southern Methodist B: 4/3/1961 Galveston, TX Draft: 7-175 1983 SF; 14-168 1983 LA-USFL Pro: NU																															
1985	WPG	9	0		1		4.0		2	52																					
1986	SAS	9					1.0		1	8																		1	14	14.0	14
1986	TOR	6	0		3																										
1986	Year	15	0		3		1.0		1	8																		1	14	14.0	14
1987	TOR	5	0		1	22	1.0																								
3	Years	23	0		5	22	6.0		3	60																		1	14	14.0	14
MIKE MOTEN Michael Edward DL 6'5 266 Florida B: 3/12/1974 Daytona Beach, FL Pro: N																															
2002	OTT	16	0	0	2	29	2.0				3																				
2003	OTT	8				8					1																				
2	Years	24	0	0	2	37	2.0				4																				
BARRY MOTON Barry DE 6'4 235 Illinois State B: 7/10/1962 Peoria, IL																															
1989	OTT	2				2																						1	6	6.0	6
DAVE MOTON David Oliver TE 6'1 225 Southern California B: 10/19/1944 Draft: 19-288 1966 GB																															
1966	BC	16	3		0							12	2	0	15		15	0	42	552	13.1	32	2								
JOHN MOTTON John LB 6'1 234 Arizona Western JC; Akron B: 6/20/1967 Columbus, OH																															
1991	HAM	17				76	4.0		4	137		12	2																		
1992	HAM*	18	1		6	98	1.0		4	67																					
1993	HAM*	18	0		4	89			1	15																					
1994	HAM	12				50			2	6	2																				
1995	BIR	2				11																									
1995	WPG	3				10					1																				
1995	Year	5				21					1																				
5	Years	67	1		10	334	5.0		11	225	3	12	2																		
DON MOULTON Don DB 6'3 180 Calgary B: 12/1/1949 Draft: 1-9 1972 CAL																															
1972	CAL	16	3		0				2	23		1	0																		
1973	CAL	11							2	19		2	0																		
1974	CAL	16	1		0				1	18																					
1975	CAL	13	0		2				2	24																					
4	Years	56	4		2				7	84		3	0																		
TOM MOULTON Tom FB-E 6'3 215 Detroit Mercy B: 1938 North Sydney, NS																															
1960	HAM	2																										1	5	5.0	5
1961	HAM	6																													
2	Years	8																										1	5	5.0	5
GEORGE MOUNTAIN George G-T																															
1946	HAM	12																													
1947	HAM	12																													
2	Years	24																													
CURLY MOYNAHAN Cyril C 6'1 180 Gladstone Jrs.; Strathcona Jrs.; Rangers Ints. B: 1914 deceased																															
1946	OTT	11																													
MARK MRAZ Mark David DE 6'4 260 Utah State B: 2/9/1965 San Gabriel, CA Draft: 5-125 1987 ATL Pro: EN																															
1991	HAM	3				10	1.0																								
1992	HAM	10	0		2	18	4.0																								
2	Years	13	0		2	28	5.0																								
GEORGE MRKONIC George Ralph T 6'2 225 Kansas B: 12/17/1929 McKeesport, PA D: 5/23/2011 Kansas City, KS Draft: 4-46 1953 PHI Pro: N																															
1956	BC	1																													
CAUCHY MUAMBA Cauchy CB-S 5'11 196 St. Francis Xavier B: 5/8/1987 Kinshasa, Congo Draft: 5-34 2010 BC																															
2010	BC	3				0																									
2011	BC	16	0	0	1	15			1	0	0																				
2	Years	19	0	0	1	15			1	0	0																				
HENOC MUAMBA Henoc LB 6'0 230 St. Francis Xavier B: 2/23/1989 Mississauga, ON Draft: 1-1 2011 WPG																															
2011	WPG	11	0	1	1	15						6	1																		
DAVE MUDGE David James OT 6'7 305 Michigan State B: 10/22/1974 Whitby, ON Draft: 3B-24 1997 TOR Pro: E																															
1999	TOR	8				1																									
2000	WPG	18	0	0	1	1																									
2001	WPG*	18	0	0	1	2																									
2002	WPG*	18				2																									
2003	WPG	14	0	0	1	0																									
2004	WPG	18				4																									
2005	WPG	3				1																									
2005	MTL	15				0																									
2005	Year	18				1																									
2006	MTL	5				1																									
2007	MTL	18	0	0	1	1																									
2008	MTL	3				0																									
10	Years	123	0	0	4	13																									
TOM MUECKE Thomas Warren, Jr. QB 6'1 195 Baylor B: 8/20/1963 Waco, TX																															
1986	WPG	10												1	0	0.0	0	0													
1987	WPG	18	2		0	0								2	0	0.0	-3	0													
1988	WPG	15	7		1	0						6	1	25	79	3.2	10	1													
1991	EDM	5	1		0	0								2	-8	-4.0	-10	0													
1992	EDM	18	2		1	0						6	1	12	48	4.0	22	1													
1993	EDM	18				0								3	15	5.0	12	0													
1994	SHR	7	1		0	1								6	10	1.7	9	0													
7	Years	91	13		2	1						12	2	51	144	2.8	22	2													
GARY MUELLER Gary LB 6'1 231 Wilfrid Laurier B: 3/19/1951 Draft: TE 1974 HAM																															
1976	CAL	13																													
CALVIN MUHAMMAD Calvin Saleem WR 5'11 190 Texas Southern B: 12/10/1958 Jacksonville, FL Draft: 12-322 1980 OAK Pro: N																															
1987	TOR	2				0													6	30	5.0	9	0								
MUSTAFAH MUHAMMAD Mustafah Asad [born Wilson, Stephen C.] DB 5'10 180 Shasta JC; Chaffey JC; Fresno State B: 10/19/1973 Orange County, CA Pro: N																															
1998	BC*	17	1	0	3	47			10	165	11	6	1											6	51	8.5	26	1	56	56.0	56
2002	WPG	7	0	1	0	15			1	0	1																				
2	Years	24	1	1	3	62			11	165	12	6	1											6	51	8.5	26	1	56	56.0	56
TAQIY MUHAMMAD Taqiy CB 5'11 180 Butler CC; South Carolina B: 7/18/1981 New York, NY																															
2005	MTL	1				5																									
DARRIN MUILENBURG Darrin OG 6'4 285 Colorado B: 3/29/1968 Lakewood, CO																															
1995	SA	18				0																									
PETE MUIR Peter Vary HB-FW-DB 5'11 182 Vancouver Blue Bombers Jrs.; St. Martin's; Western Washington B: 5/5/1930 Vancouver, BC D: 2/7/2011 Calgary, AB																															
1953	CAL	16							1	25		5	1	9	56	6.2	17	0	6	133	22.2	55	1	5	24	4.8	17	6	122	20.3	33

Year	Team	GP	FM	FF	FR	TK	SK	YDS	IR	YDS	PD	PTS	TD	RA	YDS	AVG	LG	TD	REC	YDS	AVG	LG	TD	PR	YDS	AVG	LG	KOR	YDS	AVG	LG
1954	CAL	12	2		0									2	36	18.0	28	0	1	5	5.0	5	0	21	104	5.0	16	4	69	17.3	24
1955	CAL	16	0		4				5	28		5	1	29	71	2.4	10	0	6	108	18.0	44	1	21	152	7.2	15	15	385	25.7	50
1956	CAL	10							2	13														6	31	5.2	10	1	0	0.0	0
1956	SAS	1																													
1956	Year	11							2	13														6	31	5.2	10	1	0	0.0	0
4	Years	54	6		4				8	66		10	2	40	163	4.1	28	0	13	246	18.9	55	2	53	311	5.9	17	26	576	22.2	50
SHAY MUIRBROOK Shay LB 6'0 230 Brigham Young B: 11/15/1976 Ogden, UT Pro: E																															
1999	WPG	3				11																									
1999	SAS	3	0	1	0	10																									
1999	Year	6				21																									
BOBBY MULGADO Robert C. OHB-DB 6'0 190 Arizona State B: 4/4/1936 Draft: 5-52 1958 PHI																															
1958	SAS	5										6	1	18	64	3.6	6	0	12	129	10.8	25	1	3	27	9.0	12	2	35	17.5	20
1959	SAS	7							2	23		15	2	32	167	5.2	35	2	14	131	9.4	31	0					8	179	22.4	44
2	Years	12							2	23		21	3	50	231	4.6	35	2	26	260	10.0	31	1	3	27	9.0	12	10	214	21.4	44
BRIAN MULHERN Brian HB-FW 5'10 182 Portland B: 1930																															
1951	CAL	10										15	3	18	119	6.6	11	3	6	43	7.2		0	5	31	6.2		3	56	18.7	
1952	CAL	15							1	14		5	1	25	131	5.2	14	0	4	55	13.8	25	1	3	18	6.0	10				
1953	CAL	12							3	49				19	48	2.5	9	0	11	120	10.9	17	0	3	0	0.0		3	48	16.0	22
1954	BC	8							1	0				1	6	6.0	6	0	6	83	13.8	18	0								
1955	WPG	11							2	7																					
1956	BC	13																													
6	Years	69							7	70		20	4	63	304	4.8	14	3	27	301	11.1	25	1	11	49	4.5	10	6	104	17.3	22
HERB MUL-KEY Herbert Felton RB 6'0 190 none B: 11/15/1949 Atlanta, GA Pro: N																															
1975	MTL	3	1		0									9	23	2.6	8	0	1	11	11.0	11	0	1	-2	-2.0	-2	11	221	20.1	32
ED MULLEN Ed C-T 6'4 235 B: 1925																															
1946	HAM	9																													
1947	HAM	7																													
1949	HAM	11																													
3	Years	27																													
JIM MULLER Jim DE-DT 6'3 215 Queen's B: 2/11/1957 Draft: 5-40 1980 HAM																															
1980	HAM	16	0		2																										
1981	HAM	16	0		2		3.5																								
1982	HAM	14	0		1		3.0																								
1983	HAM	1																													
4	Years	47	0		5		6.5																								
PETER MULLER Peter TE-WR-FB 6'4 230 Western Illinois B: 11/27/1951 Toronto, ON Draft: TE 1973 TOR																															
1973	TOR	13	1		0							12	2	2	9	4.5	10	0	24	421	17.5	58	2					2	0	0.0	0
1974	TOR	16	2		1							30	5						42	615	14.6	46	5	1	0	0.0	0				
1975	TOR	9	1		2							2	0						20	239	12.0	21	0								
1976	TOR	11																	27	348	12.9	32	0					3	0	0.0	0
1977	TOR	15																	43	475	11.0	35	0					2	0	0.0	0
1978	TOR	16	1		0							6	1	1	-4	-4.0	-4	0	45	585	13.0	42	1								
1979	TOR	16	1		1							26	4						52	542	10.4	42	4								
1980	TOR	16	2		0							6	1						30	374	12.5	40	1								
1981	TOR	14	0		1									4	8	2.0	4	0	25	227	9.1	25	0	1	6	6.0	6				
9	Years	126	8		5							82	13	7	13	1.9	10	0	308	3826	12.4	58	13	2	6	3.0	6	7	0	0.0	0
LUC MULLINDER Luc DE-NT-DT 6'4 284 Michigan State B: 9/25/1980 Auckland, New Zealand Draft: 4A-31 2004 SAS																															
2004	SAS	1				0																									
2005	SAS	18				8	1.0	6.0																							
2006	SAS	18				7	2.0	15.0			1																				
2007	SAS	15	0	0	1	10	3.0	15.0																							
2008	SAS	18				11	2.0	13.0			1																				
2009	SAS	18	0	1	1	20	2.0	17.0																				1	4	4.0	4
2010	SAS	18	0	1	0	24	4.0	21.0	1	21	0																				
2011	SAS	6				8	1.0	9.0																							
2011	MTL	1				0																									
2011	HAM	11				6																									
2011	Year	18				14	1.0	9.0																							
8	Years	112	0	2	2	94	15.0	96.0	1	21	2																	1	4	4.0	4
FRANK MULVEY Frank E 6'1 St. John's Roamers Jrs. B: 1918																															
1947	WPG	1																													
LLOYD MUMPHREY Lloyd Ellis DT-DE 6'3 260 Mississippi Valley State B: 2/14/1961 Memphis, TN Pro: N																															
1987	EDM	3			1	1																									
1988	EDM	5			1	5	1.0		1	3																					
1989	OTT	3				2																									
3	Years	11	0		2	8	1.0		1	3																					
CHRIS MUNFORD Chris DB 6'0 182 Simon Fraser B: 4/26/1960 Emekuku, Nigeria Draft: 5-39 1988 TOR																															
1989	HAM	7				1																									
1990	TOR	6				7	1.0		2	12																					
1991	TOR	15	1		2	25			5	59																					
1992	TOR	11				5																									
1993	SAS	12				6																									
5	Years	51	1		2	44	1.0		7	71																					
LEE MUNN Lee T 6'2 226 McMaster B: 1928 Draft: 2-7 1953 TOR																															
1953	SAS	15																													
1954	SAS	14																													
1955	SAS	16	0		3																										
1956	SAS	1																													
4	Years	46	0		3																										
DAMASO MUNOZ Damaso LB 5'11 210 Ruthgers B: 7/10/1975 Miami, FL																															
2011	EDM	18				81	1.0	4.0	1	0	3																				
JOSE MUNOZ Joe OL 6'4 300 Ball State B: 5/7/1971 Pro: E																															
1998	EDM	17				3																									
BILL MUNSEY William CB-FB-OHB 6'0 228 Minnesota B: 5/5/1941 Uniontown, PA D: 3/17/2002 Apple Valley, CA Draft: 18-139 1963 NYJ; 4-51 1963 CLE																															
1963	BC	16	0		2				5	82				1	0	0.0	0	0	1	14	14.0	14	0					4	109	27.3	39
1964	BC*	16							9	129														1	3	3.0	3	2	46	23.0	23
1965	BC	15	2		2				2	37		30	5	104	475	4.6	48	5	15	84	5.6	16	0	1	4	4.0	4	16	451	28.2	70
1966	BC	15	1		0							42	7	168	853	5.1	76	7	27	256	9.5	34	0					5	104	20.8	27
1967	BC	14	5		1									136	656	4.8	57	0	29	228	7.9	23	0					6	164	27.3	46
5	Years	76	8		5				16	248		72	12	409	1984	4.9	76	12	72	582	8.1	34	0	2	7	3.5	4	33	874	26.5	70
PHIL MUNTZ Philip FB-HB-LB 5'9 190 Toronto B: 1934 Draft: 1-2 1956 CAL																															
1956	CAL	9	2		0																			8	43	5.4	9	9	131	14.6	26
1958	TOR	13							1	0				15	83	5.5	11	0	2	0	0.0	4	0	33	214	6.5	24				
1959	TOR	13												28	99	3.5	15	0	3	26	8.7	20	0	34	188	5.5	22				
3	Years	35	2		0				1	0				43	182	4.2	15	0	5	26	5.2	20	0	75	445	5.9	24	9	131	14.6	26
GEARY MURDOCK Geary OT-OG 6'2 250 Iowa State B: 9/29/1952 Wichita, KS D: 3//2007 Draft: 11-274 1973 MIN																															
1974	CAL	16																													
1975	CAL	7																													
1975	BC	1																													
1975	Year	8																													
1977	CAL	16																													
3	Years	39																													

Year	Team	GP	FM	FF	FR	TK	SK	YDS	IR	YDS	PD	PTS	TD	RA	YDS	AVG	LG	TD	REC	YDS	AVG	LG	TD	PR	YDS	AVG	LG	KOR	YDS	AVG	LG
ARMANDO MURILLO Armando DH 5'10 193 Eastern Arizona CC; Nebraska B: 2/1/1986 Tampa, FL																															
2011	TOR	3				2																									
BILL MURMYLYK Bill FW 6'0 200 Hamilton Italo-Canadians Jrs. B: 1917 D: 5/16/1999 Ancaster, ON																															
1948	HAM	10										18	0																		
1949	HAM	11										11	0																		
2	Years	21										29	0																		
BRENT MURPHY Brent A. DL 6'2 265 none B: 6/23/1960 Fresno, CA																															
1985	EDM	6	0		1		1.0																								
BRIAN MURPHY Brian DT Toronto																															
1968	BC	1																													
CAL MURPHY Clarence DB 5'10 180 Vancouver CYO Red Raiders Jrs.; British Columbia B: 3/12/1932 Winnipeg, MB D: 2/18/2012																															
1956	BC	8												5	12	2.4	5	0	1	5	5.0	5	0	11	25	2.3	6				
DAN MURPHY Dan S 6'3 195 Acadia B: 8/28/1968 Ottawa, ON Draft: 1-3 1991 EDM																															
1991	EDM	16	0		1	23			2	28																					
1992	EDM	18	0		1	28			1	11																		1	0	0.0	0
1993	EDM	18				52			5	47																					
1994	EDM	18	0		4	34			2	5	5																				
1995	OTT	14				11					1																				
1995	TOR	2	0		1	8																									
1995	Year	16	0		1	19					1																				
1996	TOR	11				22			2	52	3																				
6	Years	95	0		7	178			12	143	9																	1	0	0.0	0
DEON MURPHY Deon WR 5'10 170 Coffeyville CC; Kansas State B: 4/15/1986 Houston, TX																															
2010	CAL	16	4	0	1	1						24	4	2	21	10.5	18	0	25	271	10.8	48	4	84	533	6.3	24	40	911	22.8	50
DON MURPHY Don DB 5'11 185 St. Mary's (Nova Scotia)																															
1968	MTL	10	0		1				1	5														1	8	8.0	8				
1969	MTL	14																	2	71	35.5	36	0					4	70	17.5	22
2	Years	24	0		1				1	5									2	71	35.5	36	0	1	8	8.0	8	4	70	17.5	22
FRANK MURPHY Frank WR 6'0 206 Itawamba CC; Garden City CC; Kansas State B: 2/11/1977 Jacksonville, FL Draft: 6A-170 2000 CHIB Pro: NU																															
2007	TOR	16				2						18	3	11	49	4.5	19	1	37	614	16.6	55	2					3	52	17.3	21
JAMES MURPHY James Jessie WR 5'10 177 Utah State B: 10/10/1959 Deland, FL Draft: 10-266 1981 MIN Pro: N																															
1983	WPG	14	1		0							24	4						61	1126	18.5	82	4					10	221	22.1	33
1984	WPG	16	0		1							78	13	1	2	2.0	2	0	70	1220	17.4	86	12	10	165	16.5	64				
1985	WPG	12	3		1							18	3	1	6	6.0	6	0	56	749	13.4	49	3	1	6	6.0	6	3	44	14.7	21
1986	WPG*	18	2		0							72	12	10	50	5.0	16	0	116	1746	15.1	82	12					19	462	24.3	57
1987	WPG+	16	1		1	3						60	10	2	14	7.0	13	0	84	1130	13.5	61	10					7	177	25.3	34
1988	WPG*	16	0		1	2						60	10						76	1409	18.5	72	10								
1989	WPG+	17	0		1	4						48	8	1	0	0.0	0	0	68	1150	16.9	58	8								
1990	WPG	12	2		0	3						12	2	1	15	15.0	15	0	42	506	12.0	28	2					1	17	17.0	17
8	Years	121	9		5	12						372	62	16	87	5.4	16	0	573	9036	15.8	86	61	11	171	15.5	64	40	921	23.0	57
MIKE MURPHY Mike FB 6'1 219 Ottawa B: 9/6/1954 Draft: TE 1977 OTT																															
1977	OTT	16	3		2							30	5	171	861	5.0	50	4	48	483	10.1	28	1					2	20	10.0	20
1978	OTT+	16	1		3							6	1	136	538	4.0	36	0	59	584	9.9	44	1					3	43	14.3	16
1979	OTT	11	1		0							12	2	88	345	3.9	16	2	24	204	8.5	22	0								
1980	OTT	16	1		1							16	2	48	239	5.0	30	0	32	363	11.3	48	2								
4	Years	59	6		6							64	10	443	1983	4.5	50	6	163	1634	10.0	48	4					5	63	12.6	20
MONTEZ MURPHY Montez Reeco DE-DT 6'6 256 Coffeyville CC*; Baylor B: 1/6/1982 Meridian, MS Pro: N																															
2008	EDM	12				24	3.0	27.0			4																				
2009	HAM	8	0	1	0	10	2.0	13.0			3																				
2010	SAS	5				14	3.0	9.0																							
2011	SAS	3				3					1																				
4	Years	28	0	1	0	51	8.0	49.0			8																				
ROB MURPHY Robert Donald OT 6'5 310 Ohio State B: 1/18/1977 Buffalo, NY Pro: ENX																															
2006	BC*	16				0																									
2007	BC*	17				1																									
2008	BC+	16	0	1	1	2																									
2009	TOR	18	0	0	1	3																									
2010	TOR*	16				1																									
2011	TOR	9				2																									
6	Years	92	0	1	2	9																									
ROGER MURPHY Roger T. FL-OE 6'3 185 Northwestern B: 1946 Draft: 8A-195 1967 CHIB																															
1967	MTL	14	1		0							30	5						31	701	22.6	64	5								
1968	MTL	8										6	1						33	535	16.2	44	1								
2	Years	22	1	0	0							36	6						64	1236	19.3	64	6								
RON MURPHY Ron OT-DT 6'2 215 McGill B: 1932 Hamilton, ON Draft: 1-6 1958 MTL																															
1958	MTL	12																													
1959	MTL	12																													
1960	MTL	14																													
1961	MTL	9																													
4	Years	47																													
VOLLEY MURPHY Volley James, III WR 5'10 180 Cisco JC; Texas-El Paso B: 10/4/1945 D: 11/25/2007 Lantana, TX Draft: 2B-43 1969 MIN																															
1971	EDM	4										12	2						14	351	25.1	97	2								
YO MURPHY Llewellyn P. WR 5'10 186 Idaho B: 5/11/1971 San Pedro, CA Pro: ENX																															
1993	BC	1				1																									
1994	BC	7	1		0	3													14	127	9.1	22	0								
1995	BC	10	1		0	1						12	2	1	15	15.0	15	0	31	510	16.5	78	2								
1996	BC	1				0																						1	20	20.0	20
2003	OTT	8				2													18	158	8.8	20	0	1	5	5.0	5	3	41	13.7	18
2004	OTT	18	1	0	0	2						36	6						61	1090	17.9	85	6								
2005	OTT	17				5						44	7						58	866	14.9	50	7					1	0	0.0	0
2006	SAS	6	1	0	0	0						6	1						19	251	13.2	26	1								
2007	SAS	6				0													12	173	14.4	34	0								
9	Years	74	4	0	0	14						98	16	1	15	15.0	15	0	213	3175	14.9	85	16	1	5	5.0	5	5	61	12.2	20
ANDREW MURRAY Andrew SB 6'3 200 Carleton B: 7/15/1954 Nepean, ON Draft: 4A-34 1987 BC																															
1988	BC	18				1													36	476	13.2	43	0								
1989	BC	3				0													5	52	10.4	18	0								
1990	TOR	16	0		1	0						18	3						37	629	17.0	47	3					2	16	8.0	11
1991	TOR	10				2						12	2						15	286	19.1	52	2					3	14	4.7	10
1992	TOR	18				3													21	342	16.3	89	0								
1993	TOR	18				4								1	-6	-6.0	-6	0	4	57	14.3	27	0								
1994	OTT	14				3						2	0						8	79	9.9	16	0								
7	Years	97	0		1	13						32	5	1	-6	-6.0	-6	0	126	1921	15.2	89	5					5	30	6.0	11
CRAIG MURRAY Craig CB-DH 5'10 197 Utah State B: 1940																															
1967	BC	11	0		3				5	88		12	2	30	123	4.1	13	0	10	125	12.5	24	1	22	148	6.7	14	5	92	18.4	24
1968	BC	16							2	44														0	5		5	1	18	18.0	18
1969	BC	14							4	37																					
3	Years	41	0		3				11	169		12	2	30	123	4.1	13	0	10	125	12.5	24	1	22	153	7.0	14	6	110	18.3	24
RICHARD MURRAY Richard Henry DE 6'2 260 Oklahoma B: 12/18/1954 Greenville, TX Draft: 11-289 1978 DET Pro: U																															
1979	BC	5	0		1																										
1980	BC	16	0		2																										
1981	BC	11	0		2		3.0																								
1982	BC	6					1.0																								

Year	Team	GP	FM	FF	FR	TK	SK	YDS	IR	YDS	PD	PTS	TD	RA	YDS	AVG	LG	TD	REC	YDS	AVG	LG	TD	PR	YDS	AVG	LG	KOR	YDS	AVG	LG
4	Years	38	0		5		4.0																								
STAN MURRAY Stan G																															
1946	OTT	4																													
WALTER MURRAY Walter Clyde WR 6'4 200 Hawaii B: 12/13/1962 Berkeley, CA Draft: 2B-45 1986 WAS Pro: N																															
1989	EDM	5				0						12	2	1	-7	-7.0	-7	0	8	121	15.1	44	2								
1990	HAM	2				2													4	74	18.5	28	0								
2	Years	7				2						12	2	1	-7	-7.0	-7	0	12	195	16.3	44	2								
DON MUSE Donald C. TE 6'2 225 Missouri B: 7/16/1952 St. Louis, MO																															
1975	EDM	4																	2	20	10.0	11	0					3	25	8.3	18
HAL MUSGROVE Harold HB																															
1947	CAL	5																													
GLEN MUSIC Glen DB 5'11 175 Calgary Colts Jrs.; Alberta B: 10/26/1957																															
1982	MTL	1																													
JOHNNY MUSSO John, Jr. RB 5'11 201 Alabama B: 3/6/1950 Birmingham, AL Draft: 3-62 1972 CHIB Pro: NW																															
1972	BC	15	1		0							18	3	88	405	4.6	21	1	39	556	14.3	41	2					1	0	0.0	0
1973	BC+	16	0		1							60	10	220	1029	4.7	25	10	46	475	10.3	27	0					1	17	17.0	17
1974	BC	3	1		0									12	59	4.9	15	0	5	36	7.2	13	0								
3	Years	34	2		1							78	13	320	1493	4.7	25	11	90	1067	11.9	41	2					2	17	8.5	17
WARREN MUZIKA Warren LB 6'0 212 Saskatoon Hilltops Jrs.; Saskatchewan B: 8/7/1973 Saskatoon, SK																															
1999	HAM	14	0	1	1	31																									
2000	HAM	18	0	0	1	16																									
2001	HAM	18	0	0	2	21																						3	23	7.7	9
2002	HAM	15	0	0	1	31					2																				
2003	HAM	10				8																						1	7	7.0	7
2003	WPG	8				2																						1	0	0.0	0
2003	Year	18				10																									
5	Years	75	0	1	5	109					2																	5	30	6.0	9
ALEX MUZYKA Alex T-G 5'11 208 Hamilton Tigers Jrs. B: 1929 D: 2//1993																															
1950	HAM	11																													
1951	HAM	5																													
1952	HAM	2																													
1953	HAM	13																													
1955	HAM	9																													
5	Years	40																													
STEVE MYDDLETON Steve OG 6'3 294 St. Francis Xavier B: 7/27/1986 Barrie, ON Draft: 4B-30 2009 CAL																															
2010	CAL	18				2																									
2011	CAL	14	0	0	1	1																									
2	Years	32	0	0	1	3																									
BILLY MYERS Billy HB-QB 136 Toronto B: 1925																															
1946	TOR	3										5	1										1								
1948	TOR	5																													
2	Years	8										5	1										1								
BOB MYERS Bob FB-HB 6'0 211 Saskatoon Hilltops Jrs. B: 1941																															
1962	SAS	10												1	2	2.0	2	0													
1963	SAS	15	0		1									1	2	2.0	2	0													
2	Years	25	0		1									2	4	2.0	2	0													
JEREL MYERS Erasmus Jerel WR 5'10 179 Louisiana State B: 7/18/1981 Houston, TX																															
2005	BC	15	3	0	1	2						12	2	1	-2	-2.0	-2	0	36	473	13.1	39	2	9	54	6.0	15	1	0	0.0	0
MARK MYERS Mark K 6'0 210 Florida Atlantic B: 7/13/1982 Rockledge, FL																															
2006	HAM	3				1						20	0																		
RUDY MYERS Rudolph DB 6'1 205 Southern University B: 1945																															
1967	MTL	6																													
SHANNON MYERS Shannon W. WR 6'0 171 Lenoir-Rhyne B: 6/16/1973 Draft: 7B-246 1995 MIA Pro: E																															
1997	EDM	5	1	0	0	1						12	2						15	298	19.9	69	2								
1998	EDM	13	1	0	1	1						18	3	1	11	11.0	11	0	30	482	16.1	40	3								
2	Years	18	2	0	1	2						30	5	1	11	11.0	11	0	45	780	17.3	69	5								
MARK MYHEDYN Mark WR Richmond Raiders Jrs.																															
1986	BC	1																													
STEVE MYHRA Stephen Murray LB-K 6'1 237 Minnesota; North Dakota B: 4/2/1934 Wahpeton, ND D: 8/4/1994 Detroit Lakes, MN Draft: 12-139(f) 1956 BAL Pro: N																															
1962	SAS	5	1						2	32		22	0																		
REGGIE MYLES Reginald L. DB 5'11 187 Alabama B: 10/10/1979 Pascagoula, MS Pro: N																															
2008	BC	14	0	1	1	38	1.0	0.0	2	6	2																				
NICK MYSTROM Nick K-P 6'3 205 Colorado College B: 7/16/1971																															
1995	MEM	13	1		1	1						137	0																		
RAFE NABORS Rafe Sims, Jr. (Moose) G-C 6'1 235 Texas Tech B: 11/13/1920 D: 10/7/2003																															
1946	MTL	12																													
BAZ NAGLE Douglas CB-S-OHB 5'11 188 Vancouver Meralomas Jrs. B: 1933 Vancouver, BC D: 4/11/1997																															
1954	CAL	3																	1	30	30.0	30	0	7	30	4.3	9	1	4	4.0	4
1955	CAL	15	8		2				3	106		10	2	54	277	5.1	45	0	4	70	17.5	39	1	56	414	7.4	22	8	142	17.8	28
1956	CAL	16	3		0							6	1	27	188	7.0	23	1	22	345	15.7	51	0	25	210	8.4	17	17	400	23.5	37
1957	CAL	16	1		0				1	9		6	1	9	32	3.6	9	1	2	7	3.5	5	0					1	15	15.0	15
1958	BC	16	2						1	32				1	3	3.0	3	0						5	20	4.0	10	1	15	15.0	15
1959	BC	16										6	1	9	33	3.7	13	0	2	27	13.5	20	0	36	187	5.2	14	1	16	16.0	16
1960	BC	16	1		2				2	0				9	25	2.8	5	0	2	28	14.0	15	0	18	96	5.3	13				
1961	BC	2																						1	5	5.0	5				
1961	WPG	12							2	20																					
1961	Year	14							2	20														1	5	5.0	5				
1962	BC	12							3	18				1	-1	-1.0	-1	0	1	11	11.0	11	0	18	41	2.3	8				
9	Years	112	15		4				12	185		28	5	110	557	5.1	45	2	34	518	15.2	51	1	166	1003	6.0	22	29	592	20.4	37
BRONKO NAGURSKI Bronko Kane OT 6'2 225 Notre Dame B: 12/25/1937 Hennepin County, MN D: 3/7/2011 International Falls, MN Draft: 10-114 1959 SF																															
1959	HAM	12																													
1960	HAM	11																													
1961	HAM	9																													
1962	HAM*	14																													
1963	HAM	14																													
1964	HAM+	14	0		1																										
1965	HAM*	14	0		1																										
1966	HAM	14																													
8	Years	102	0		2																										
ANDY NAGY Andy T 240 Regina Jrs.																															
1946	SAS+	8																													
PETE NAJARIAN Peter Michael LB 6'2 234 Minnesota B: 12/22/1963 San Francisco, CA Pro: EN																															
1988	TOR	1																													
AL NAMANNY Allan R. FB 6'1 218 San Mateo JC; Pacific B: 8/14/1948																															
1971	EDM	5												11	56	5.1	15	0	17	160	9.4	33	0					1	27	27.0	27
TERNA NANDE Terna LB 6'0 230 Miami (Ohio) B: 6/17/1983 Grand Rapids, MI Draft: 5A-137 2006 TEN Pro: N																															
2009	BC	7				15																									
SHELDON NAPASTUK Sheldon DE 6'4 270 Iowa State B: 8/15/1974 North Battleford, SK Draft: 3-25 1996 EDM																															
1999	SAS	4				0																									
2000	SAS	18				23	6.0	36.0																							
2001	SAS	16				11	1.0	6.0			1																				
2002	SAS	18				28					1																				

2003 CAL 18 0 0 1 25 2.0 10.0 2
2004 CAL 18 34 4.0 28.0 4
2005 CAL+ 18 0 1 0 26 8.0 54.0
2006 CAL 16 0 0 4 10 2.0 13.0
8 Years 126 0 1 5 157 23.0 147.0 8

MARK NAPIORKOWSKI Mark DE-DT 6'4 240 Richmond Raiders Jrs.; British Columbia B: 8/24/1962 Oshawa, ON
1985 BC 11 0 1
1986 BC 2
1986 HAM 16 0 3 6 1
1986 Year 18 0 3 6 1
1987 HAM 6 10 1.0
1988 HAM 15 13 3.0
1989 HAM 18 0 1 1
1990 HAM 18 25 3.0
1991 TOR 6 4 1.0
1992 TOR 5 3
8 Years 81 0 5 56 8.0 6 1

MARK NAPOLITAN Mark R. C 6'3 260 Michigan State B: 2/9/1962 Dearborn, MI Draft: 5A-123 1985 SEA; 8A- 1985 ARI-USFL
1986 TOR 1

JOHN NAPONICK John DT 6'10 300 Virginia B: 6/12/1946 Draft: 5-136 1968 OAK
1968 WPG 4

DON NARCISSE Donald Ray WR 5'9 169 Texas Southern B: 2/26/1965 Port Arthur, TX
1987 SAS 8 0 1 1 6 1 1 -2 -2.0 -2 0 25 319 12.8 43 1 2 45 22.5 24
1988 SAS 10 1 0 0 21 288 13.7 22 0
1989 SAS* 18 0 1 4 66 11 1 16 16.0 11 0 81 1419 17.5 74 11 3 30 10.0 14 5 63 12.6 18
1990 SAS* 18 3 56 9 1 -12 -12.0 -12 0 86 1129 13.1 47 9
1991 SAS 18 2 0 3 42 7 76 1043 13.7 59 7
1992 SAS 18 3 44 7 80 1034 12.9 65 7
1993 SAS+ 18 1 54 9 83 1171 14.1 44 9
1994 SAS* 18 2 36 6 72 1004 13.9 40 6
1995 SAS 18 2 0 2 50 8 1 10 10.0 10 0 123 1288 10.5 40 8
1996 SAS 18 2 24 4 66 906 13.7 77 4
1997 SAS 18 1 32 5 64 950 14.8 47 5
1998 SAS* 18 1 0 0 0 42 7 95 1215 12.8 44 7
1999 SAS 18 2 6 1 47 600 12.8 31 1
13 Years 216 6 0 2 24 458 75 4 12 3.0 11 0 919 12366 13.5 77 75 3 30 10.0 14 7 108 15.4 24

DON NARRELL Don T 6'5 245 Texas Christian B: 1929 Draft: 7-81 1950 NYB
1950 EDM 10

HAROLD NASH Harold, Jr. CB 5'8 180 Louisiana-Lafayette B: 5/5/1970 New Orleans, LA
1994 SHR 4 8
1995 SHR 18 48 3 18 6
1996 MTL 11 0 2 44 3 65 4 6 1 5 98 19.6 24
1997 MTL+ 15 0 1 1 26 4 95 2 12 2
1998 MTL 11 0 1 0 36 2 35 2
1999 MTL 2 3
1999 WPG 11 1 2 2 23 2 72 4 6 1
1999 Year 13 1 2 2 26 2 72 4 6 1
2000 WPG 17 0 1 4 59 2 57 8 12 2
2001 WPG* 17 0 0 1 51 4 47 5 6 1
2002 WPG+ 18 0 2 1 52 2 15 4
2003 WPG 14 0 0 1 46 2 48 7 4 53 13.3 30
2004 EDM 6 0 1 0 14 3
11 Years 133 1 8 12 410 24 452 45 42 7 9 151 16.8 30

JERRY NASH Jerome DB 6'1 190 Alberta B: 5/16/1962 Edmonton, AB Draft: 6-48 1985 SAS
1985 TOR 1
1986 TOR 11 1 1 1.0 1 1 0 0.0 0
2 Years 12 1 1 1.0 1 1 0 0.0 0

PAUL NASTASIUK Paul SB-RB-WR 6'0 195 Wilfrid Laurier B: 7/11/1963 Newmarket, ON Draft: 1-9 1986 BC
1986 BC 18 0 1 6 1 1 0 0.0 0 0 2 25 12.5 26 0
1987 BC 17 1 3 37 12.3 17 0
1988 OTT 7 0 6 1 5 84 16.8 33 1
1988 TOR 10 0 12 2 1 12 12.0 12 0 11 173 15.7 40 2
1988 Year 17 0 18 3 1 12 12.0 12 0 16 257 16.1 40 3
1989 BC 15 0 1 0 1 9 9.0 9 0
1990 TOR 7 0 1 4 12 2 6 50 8.3 28 1 4 50 12.5 19 0
1991 TOR 14 9 4 50 12.5 18 0
1992 TOR 18 1 2 3 4 0 45 219 4.9 40 0 19 217 11.4 26 0
7 Years 96 1 5 17 40 6 53 281 5.3 40 1 49 645 13.2 40 3

JEFF NEAL Jeffery Joseph OL 6'1 300 Howard Payne B: 4/10/1968 Pearland, TX
1995 BIR 18 0 1 1

KENNY NEAL Kenny WR 6'3 205 Texas B: 11/10/1971 Memphis, TN
1995 SA 6 17 1 25 25.0 25 0

KRIS NEAL Kristopher DL 6'3 205 Alabama-Birmingham B: 3/15/1976 Tucson, AZ
2001 TOR 11 0 2 0 43 4.0 11.0 1 50 7 6 1
2002 TOR 6 0 0 1 26 2
2 Years 17 0 2 1 69 4.0 11.0 1 50 9 6 1

BILL NEALE Bill QB
1946 TOR 3

MATTHEW NEALON Matthew WR 6'2 190 St. Mary's (Nova Scotia) B: 7/26/1966 Gatineau, QC Draft: 5B-40 1991 TOR
1991 TOR 2 1

BARRICK NEALY Barrick Dunya QB 6'5 230 Houston; Texas State B: 8/7/1983 Dallas, TX
2007 CAL 18 1 0 0 0 7 50 7.1 16 0
2008 CAL 18 1 0 1 0 18 3 9 112 12.4 30 3
2009 CAL 18 0 6 33 5.5 15 0
3 Years 54 2 0 1 0 18 3 22 195 8.9 30 3

TOMMY NECK Thomas Ulric DB 5'11 190 Louisiana State B: 1/10/1939 Marksville, LA Draft: 20-158 1962 BOS; 18-245 1962 CHIB Pro: N
1964 OTT 1

JASON NEDD Jason S 5'10 196 Akron B: 9/7/1981 Montreal, QC Draft: 2-10 2007 EDM
2007 EDM 4 0
2007 HAM 5 1 1
2007 Year 9 1 1
2008 HAM 18 12
2 Years 22 13 2

JOHN NEE John OL 6'5 301 Washington State; Elon B: 11/21/1967 Portland, ME
1994 LV 4

STEVE NEECE Stephen OT 6'2 253 Notre Dame B: 10/17/1952
1975 OTT 16

PETE NEFT Peter QB-FB 6'0 185 Pittsburgh B: 1934 Draft: 23-268 1956 PIT
1958 BC 1 2 5 2.5 3 0 2 21 10.5 11 0 1 2 2.0 2

KEVIN NEILES Kevin WR 5'10 180 Manitoba B: 6/25/1959 Winnipeg, MB
1984 WPG 16 2 2 12 2 6 135 22.5 34 1 27 295 10.9 64 15 345 23.0 42
1985 WPG 8 3 0 2 5 2.5 7 0 3 49 16.3 20 0 42 358 8.5 37 13 254 19.5 26
1986 WPG 10 1 0 6 1 2 28 14.0 20 0 39 343 8.8 81 18 415 23.1 60

Year	Team	GP	FM	FF	FR	TK	SK	YDS	IR	YDS	PD	PTS	TD	RA	YDS	AVG	LG	TD	REC	YDS	AVG	LG	TD	PR	YDS	AVG	LG	KOR	YDS	AVG	LG
1986	CAL	4																						6	52	8.7	14	7	174	24.9	38
1986	Year	14	1		0							6	1						2	28	14.0	20	0	45	395	8.8	81	25	589	23.6	60
3	Years	34	6		2							18	3	2	5	2.5	7	0	11	212	19.3	34	1	114	1048	9.2	81	53	1188	22.4	60
MIKE NELMS Michael Craig CB 6'1 185 Tarrant JC; Sam Houston State; Baylor B: 4/8/1955 Fort Worth, TX Draft: 7-170 1977 BUF Pro: N																															
1977	HAM	2							1	18														10	106	10.6	31	3	47	15.7	28
1977	OTT	3							2	68														7	82	11.7	20	2	53	26.5	27
1977	Year	5							3	86														17	188	11.1	31	5	100	20.0	28
1978	OTT	16	4		1				6	110		6	1											49	408	8.3	38	8	191	23.9	52
1979	OTT*	15	1		1				10	124		12	2											106	1155	10.9	71	3	71	23.7	30
3	Years	33	5		2				19	320		18	3											172	1751	10.2	71	16	362	22.6	52
LARRY NELS Lawrence Benjamin DT 6'1 235 Wyoming B: 6/6/1948 Ticonderoga, NY Draft: 12-297 1970 NYG																															
1971	BC	1																													
BOB NELSON Robert Cole C 6'1 214 Baylor B: 1/30/1920 D: 11/3/1986 Tarrant County, TX Draft: 5-35 1941 DET Pro: AN																															
1951	SAS	5																													
ERIC NELSON Eric DB 6'3 205 El Camino JC; Memphis B: 10/12/1969																															
1995	MEM	13	0		1	17			2	46	4																				
JOHN NELSON John FB 6'2 220 Manitoba B: 7/6/1955 Draft: 2A-13 1977 SAS																															
1978	SAS	7																													
LEONARD NELSON Leonard LB 6'1 220 American River JC; Sacramento State B: 11/21/1969																															
1993	SAC	10	0		1	22																									
1994	SAC	16				50	1.0	6.0			2																				
1995	SA	14				39																									
3	Years	40	0		1	111	1.0	6.0			2																				
MARK NELSON Mark LB 6'2 218 East Central B: 7/25/1957 Edmonton, AB Draft: TE 1980 CAL																															
1980	CAL	12																													
1981	CAL	11					1.0		0	1																		1	0	0.0	0
1982	CAL	7																													
1983	CAL	16																	1	25	25.0	25	0								
1984	CAL	16							2	2																					
1985	CAL	16	0		3		2.0																								
1986	SAS	4																										1	5	5.0	5
7	Years	82	0		3		3.0		2	3									1	25	25.0	25	0					2	5	2.5	5
PICASSO NELSON Picasso DB 6'0 205 Jackson State B: 5/1/1973 Hattiesburg, MS																															
1998	BC	10	0	0	1	34																									
1999	BC	1				4																									
1999	EDM	8				7																									
1999	Year	9				11																									
2	Years	11	0	0	1	45																									
REGGIE NELSON Reginald DeWayne OT 6'4 310 McNeese State B: 6/23/1976 Alexandria, LA Draft: 5B-141 1999 SD Pro: EN																															
2005	OTT	8				0																									
ROGER NELSON Roger Dean OT-DT 6'1 225 Oklahoma B: 5/8/1932 Memphis, TN D: 7/29/1996 Houston, TX Draft: 14-164 1954 WAS																															
1954	EDM	15							1	0																		1	0	0.0	0
1956	EDM	16																													
1957	EDM+	16																													
1958	EDM+	16							1	5																					
1959	EDM+	14																													
1960	EDM+	13	0		1																										
1961	EDM	10																													
1962	EDM	16																													
1963	EDM	16																													
1964	EDM	16																													
1965	EDM	16																													
1966	EDM	16																													
1967	EDM	16	0		1																										
13	Years	196	0		2				2	5																		1	0	0.0	0
RICHARD NEMETH Richard OT 6'6 245 Western Ontario B: 2/5/1962 Tillsonburg, ON Draft: 2-16 1984 WPG																															
1984	WPG	8																													
1985	WPG	16																													
1986	WPG	18	0		1																										
3	Years	42	0		1																										
STEVE NEMETH Steve Joseph QB 5'10 174 Notre Dame B: 12/10/1922 South Bend, IN D: 3/27/1998 South Bend, IN Pro: AN																															
1948	MTL	11										22	0																		
TEDDY NEPTUNE Teddy LB 6'1 218 Ottawa B: 5/23/1977 Ottawa, ON Draft: 3-17 2001 SAS																															
2001	SAS	16	0	1	0	8																									
2002	SAS	14				8																									
2002	EDM	3				0																									
2002	Year	17				8																									
2	Years	30	0	1	0	16																									
RON NERY Ronald Duane T 6'6 236 Kansas State B: 12/30/1934 New Kensington, PA D: 4/4/2002 Topeka, KS Draft: 7-81 1956 NYG Pro: N																															
1958	BC	1																													
GERRY NESBITT Gerald N. LB-FB-DB-P 5'10 200 Tyler JC*; Arkansas B: 6/8/1932 Draft: 27-321 1956 NYG																															
1958	OTT	13												48	264	5.5	22	0	2	33	16.5	23	0								
1959	OTT	14							3	32		7	1	14	83	5.9	18	0	5	21	4.2	13	0					1	15	15.0	15
1960	OTT+	10							2	10		15	2	28	179	6.4	25	2	3	18	6.0	13	0								
1961	OTT+	13							1	0		17	2	3	26	8.7	19	2										1	10	10.0	10
4	Years	50							6	42		39	5	93	552	5.9	25	4	10	72	7.2	23	0					2	25	12.5	15
CARL NESMITH Carl E. DB 6'2 212 Butler County CC; Kansas B: 3/19/1979 Jacksonville, FL																															
2001	TOR	1				4																									
JIM NETTLES James Arthur CB 5'9 177 Wisconsin B: 2/15/1942 Muncie, IN Pro: N																															
1973	MTL	9	0		1				2	35		6	1																		
RAY NETTLES Ernest Ray LB 6'2 220 Tennessee B: 8/1/1949 Jacksonville, FL D: 9/29/2009 Jacksonville, FL Draft: 6-155 1972 MIA																															
1972	BC*	16	0		1				3	23																					
1973	BC*	16	0		2				1	3																					
1974	BC+	16							1	0																					
1975	BC	16																													
1976	BC	15	0		2				1	10																					
1977	TOR+	16	0		3																										
1978	HAM	16	0		3				1	20																					
1979	OTT	14	0		2																										
1980	CAL	5																													
9	Years	130	0		13				7	56																					
TOM NETTLES Thomas Wayne SE 5'11 175 San Diego CC; San Diego State B: 7/11/1945 San Diego, CA Draft: 7-179 1969 KC																															
1969	EDM	8										12	2						25	288	11.5	41	2								
1970	EDM	7										6	1						24	354	14.8	68	1								
2	Years	15										18	3						49	642	13.1	68	3								
ALAN NEUFELD Alan C 6'1 265 Saskatchewan B: 11/15/1968 Saskatoon, SK Draft: 5-33 1990 OTT																															
1992	OTT	8				0																									
HAROLD NEUFELD Harold HB 5'8 172 Winnipeg Rods Jrs.; Norwood Legion Ints. B: 1928																															
1949	WPG	8																													
PATRICK NEUFELD Patrick OG-OT 6'5 291 Saskatchewan B: 12/26/1988 Regina, SK Draft: 5-33 2010 SAS																															
2011	SAS	17				0																									
PETE NEUMANN Peter DE 5'11 210 none B: 1930																															

Year	Team	GP	FM	FF	FR	TK	SK	YDS	IR	YDS	PD	PTS	TD	RA	YDS	AVG	LG	TD	REC	YDS	AVG	LG	TD	PR	YDS	AVG	LG	KOR	YDS	AVG	LG
1951	HAM	12										10	2																		
1952	HAM	12																													
1953	HAM+	14										2	0																		
1954	HAM+	11																													
1955	HAM+	12										5	1																		
1956	HAM+	14																													
1957	HAM+	13							1	2																					
1958	HAM+	14																													
1959	HAM+	14																													
1960	HAM	14										12	2																		
1961	HAM+	14										6	1																		
1962	HAM	14							1	13																					
1963	HAM	12																													
1964	HAM*	14																													
14	Years	184							2	15		35	6																		
SAM NEVILLS Samuel T 6'2 245 Purdue; Oregon B: 7/1925 Waterloo, IA Draft: 8-102 1950 CHIB																															
1952	WPG	3																										1	23	23.0	23
1953	WPG	3																													
2	Years	6																										1	23	23.0	23
HENRY NEWBY Henry LB 6'2 230 Fairmont State B: 6/21/1968 Farrell, PA																															
1994	BC	16	0		3	64	3.0	33.0			3																				
1995	BC	16	0		4	65	4.0	29.0			1																				
1996	BC	3				2	1.0	7.0																							
1997	SAS	9	0	0	0	41																									
1997	MTL	4				13					1																				
1997	Year	13	0	0	1	54					1																				
1998	CAL	3				13	1.0	2.0																							
1999	WPG	15	1	2	2	71	5.0	28.0	3	70	1																				
2000	WPG	2				1																									
7	Years	64	1	2	9	270	14.0	99.0	3	70	6																				
BOBBY NEWCOMBE Robert Wundu Sowa WR 5'10 195 Nebraska B: 8/8/1979 Sierra Leone Draft: 6-166 2001 ARI																															
2002	MTL	3				0													7	48	6.9	11	0								
PETE NEWELL Peter James DT 6'4 250 Michigan B: 3/9/1949 Milwaukee, WI Draft: 5-125 1971 DET																															
1971	BC	1																													
BRAD NEWMAN Brad LB 6'1 210 British Columbia B: 9/18/1981 New Westminster, BC																															
2007	WPG	4				1																									
DAVE NEWMAN David A. WR-SB 6'0 175 Missouri B: 6/27/1958 Kirksville, MO																															
1980	TOR+	16	4		1							62	10	6	26	4.3	12	0	50	823	16.5	87	10	40	355	8.9	80	18	436	24.2	63
1981	TOR	5										24	4	1	9	9.0	9	0	15	216	14.4	23	3	13	193	14.8	59	3	49	16.3	18
1982	TOR	10	1		1							20	3	4	28	7.0	12	0	34	513	15.1	40	3	13	123	9.5	28				
1983	OTT	14	1		1							48	8	3	31	10.3	12	0	34	662	19.5	56	8	52	484	9.3	45	3	63	21.0	24
1984	OTT	16	4		2							60	10	2	4	2.0	4	0	58	896	15.4	80	10	36	332	9.2	35	4	98	24.5	24
1985	OTT	1																	5	35	7.0	20	0								
6	Years	62	10		5							214	35	16	98	6.1	12	0	196	3145	16.0	87	34	154	1487	9.7	80	28	646	23.1	63
DON NEWMAN Donald David DB-SB-WR 6'1 190 Louisiana State; Grambling State; Idaho B: 11/22/1957 New Orleans, LA																															
1982	SAS	4																	1	-1	-1.0	-1	0								
1984	MTL	2																													
1985	OTT	3																	6	54	9.0	19	0								
1986	HAM	2																	1	3	3.0	3	0					1	19	19.0	19
4	Years	11																	8	56	7.0	19	0					1	19	19.0	19
JESSE NEWMAN Jesse OG-OT 6'4 305 Louisiana-Lafayette B: 9/23/1982 Vancouver, BC Draft: 1B-3 2008 CAL																															
2008	CAL	15				0																									
2009	CAL	15	0	0	1	2																									
2010	BC	9				0																									
2011	BC	18				0																									
4	Years	57	0	0	1	2																									
JOHN NEWMAN John S. G 6'2 211 McGill B: 12/11/1924\3 England D: 9/4/1985 Montreal, QC																															
1950	MTL	11																													
1951	MTL	9																													
2	Years	20																													
MYRON NEWSOME Myron Levelle LB 5'9 218 Butler County CC; Virginia Tech B: 5/13/1974 Hampton, VA Pro: E																															
2000	MTL	3				2			0	0	2																				
HAL NEWTON Harold B. DE 6'2 212 Windsor AKO Jrs. B: 1934 Windsor, ON																															
1957	HAM	9																													
1958	CAL	9																	1	13	13.0	13	0								
1959	CAL	12																										1	23	23.0	23
1959	TOR	2																													
1959	Year	14																										1	23	23.0	23
3	Years	30																	1	13	13.0	13	0					1	23	23.0	23
JOE NICELY Burel Joseph G 6'1 230 West Virginia B: 11/26/1934 Trout, WV D: 9/24/2010 Glendale, AZ Draft: 3-35 1958 BAL																															
1958	MTL	5																													
JEFF NICHOL Jefferson R. LB 6'2 226 Colgate B: 12/19/1972 Draft: 6-45 1994 HAM																															
1994	HAM	5				6																									
JOHN NICHOLS John J. FB-LB 5'11 190 Syracuse B: 1938																															
1963	OTT	10							1	8																					
CALVIN NICHOLSON Calvin T. DB 5'9 183 West Los Angeles JC; Oregon State B: 7/9/1967 Los Angeles, CA Draft: 11-300 1989 NO Pro: EN																															
1994	LV	12				38			1	0	5																				
DARRELL NICHOLSON Darrell LB 6'2 235 North Carolina B: 8/23/1959 Draft: 6-156 1982 NYG																															
1983	TOR+	16	0		2		2.0		1	5																					
1984	TOR	6	0		1		2.0		2	57																					
1985	CAL	4																													
1985	TOR	1							1	2																					
1985	Year	5							1	2																					
1986	OTT	6	0		1		1.0																								
4	Years	32	0		4		5.0	0.0	4	64																					
JIM NICHOLSON Jim HB 5'10 190 Willamette																															
1969	BC	1																													
KEVIN NICKERSON Kevin SB-WR 5'9 180 Central Missouri State B: 4/27/1980 Kansas City, MO																															
2003	SAS	9	2	0	1	0						6	1	5	59	11.8	26	0	8	103	12.9	34	0	24	178	7.4	22	17	402	23.6	96
2004	SAS	3				0								1	11	11.0	11	0	3	23	7.7	9	0	6	25	4.2	11	9	198	22.0	44
2	Years	12	2	0	1	0						6	1	6	70	11.7	26	0	11	126	11.5	34	0	30	203	6.8	22	26	600	23.1	96
ED NICKLA Edward Michael DT-LB 6'3 240 Tennessee; Maryland B: 8/11/1933 New York, NY Draft: 14-167 1955 CHIB Pro: N																															
1961	MTL	13							1	5																					
1962	MTL+	14							4	61																					
1963	MTL+	14																													
1964	MTL	2	0		1																										
1964	TOR	8																													
1964	Year	10	0		1																										
4	Years	43	0		1				5	66																					
CHRIS NICKSON Christopher Meltravis WR 6'1 212 Vanderbilt B: 12/11/1985																															
2009	MTL	1				0																									
NORM NICOLA Norman J. DE 6'0 236 Notre Dame B: 4/29/1943																															

Year	Team	GP	FM	FF	FR	TK	SK	YDS	IR	YDS	PD	PTS	TD	RA	YDS	AVG	LG	TD	REC	YDS	AVG	LG	TD	PR	YDS	AVG	LG	KOR	YDS	AVG	LG
1965	TOR	11																													
ADAM NICOLSON Adam SB-WR 6'4 223 Ottawa B: 8/13/1984 North Bay, ON Draft: 1-8 2007 BC																															
2007	BC	13	0	0	1	0																									
2008	BC	6				0													1	6	6.0	6	0								
2008	SAS	3				1						6	1						4	53	13.3	28	1								
2008	Year	9				1						6	1						5	59	11.8	28	1								
2009	SAS	13				0																									
2010	HAM	3				0													2	38	19.0	34	0								
4	Years	35	0	0	2	1						6	1						7	97	13.9	34	1								
EMIL NIELSEN Emil DB 5'10 179 Simon Fraser B: 8/19/1953 Draft: 1-3 1977 SAS																															
1977	SAS	16							2	0																					
1978	SAS	12																						1	22	22.0	22				
1979	SAS	16							3	14																					
1980	HAM	7																													
1981	HAM	16	0		1																			0	8		8				
5	Years	67	0		1				5	14														1	30	30.0	22				
JON NIELSEN Jon W . QB 6'1 280 Fresno State; Long Beach CC; Claremont-Mudd-Scripps B: 4/5/1973 Inglewood, CA																															
2001	TOR	3				0																									
KEN NIELSEN Ken FL-SE 6'1 182 Alberta B: 5/10/1942 Draft: 2-16 1963 CAL; 1A-3 1965 HAM																															
1965	HAM	2																													
1965	WPG	12										12	2						14	263	18.8	40	2								
1965	Year	14										12	2						14	263	18.8	40	2								
1966	WPG	16	0		1							66	11						44	719	16.3	72	11								
1967	WPG+	16										54	9						76	1121	14.8	49	9								
1968	WPG*	16	1		1							30	5						68	1031	15.2	72	5								
1969	WPG*	14										12	2						49	617	12.6	37	2								
1970	WPG	7										12	2						29	589	20.3	60	2								
6	Years	71	1		2							186	31						280	4340	15.5	72	31								
LAURIE NIEMI Laurie Jack T 6'1 251 Washington State B: 3/19/1925 Red Lodge, MT D: 2/19/1968 Spokane, WA Draft: 2-18 1949 WAS Pro: N																															
1954	BC	16																													
1955	BC	16	1		0																										
2	Years	32	1		0																										
RON NIETUPSKI Ronald S. T-G 6'2 225 Illinois B: 10/21/1937 Chicago, IL Draft: 29-346 1959 CLE																															
1960	EDM	1																													
1960	MTL	4																													
1960	Year	5																													
WALT NIKORAK Walter C 5'10 214 Hamilton Tigers Jrs. B: 1932																															
1954	HAM	14																													
1955	HAM	12																													
1956	HAM	11																													
3	Years	37																													
BLAKE NILL Blake DL-OT-C 6'6 275 Calgary B: 2/16/1962 Hannah, AB Draft: 3-19 1983 MTL																															
1983	MTL	11	0		1																										
1984	MTL	4																													
1985	MTL	11																													
1986	MTL	18																													
4	Years	44	0		1																										
GEORGE NIMAKO George S-RB 5'10 195 Liberty B: 3/9/1969 Nepean, ON Draft: 4-24 1993 TOR																															
1993	TOR	9				10													2	29	14.5	27	0								
1994	TOR	17	1		1	21	1.0				1	6	1	25	153	6.1	23	0										8	143	17.9	28
1995	TOR	5				4								1	3	3.0	3	0													
1996	TOR	18				24			1	6	0																				
1997	TOR	18	0	0	1	11																									
1998	TOR	18				17					1																				
2000	TOR	9	0	0	1	4																									
7	Years	94	1	0	3	91	1.0	0.0	1	6	2	6	1	26	156	6.0	23	0	2	29	14.5	27	0					8	143	17.9	28
BJORN NITTMO Bjorn Arne K-P 5'11 185 Appalachian State B: 7/26/1966 Lomma, Sweden Pro: EN																															
1994	SHR	18	0		2	1						127	0																		
1995	SHR	18				1						185	0																		
2	Years	36	0		2	2						312	0																		
CHUCK NIVEN Charles HB 5'9 188 B: 1932																															
1953	HAM	1																													
JACK NIX Jack Louis OE 6'2 205 Pasadena JC; Southern California B: 5/7/1928 Gary, IN Draft: 20-257 1950 SF Pro: N																															
1951	SAS	13										35	7						46	599	13.0		7								
JOHN NIX John G. DL 6'1 311 Southern Mississippi B: 11/24/1976 Lucedale, MS Draft: 7B-240 2001 DAL Pro: N																															
2005	MTL	14	0	1	1	13	2.0	16.0																							
RHOME NIXON Rhome Dennis TE-WR 6'3 209 Southern University B: 2/9/1944 Houston, TX Draft: RS-5-44 1966 SD; RS-1-6 1967 CHIB																															
1970	BC	6										6	1						11	271	24.6	52	1								
1972	OTT	10																	25	347	13.9	28	0								
1973	OTT	10										36	6						38	493	13.0	46	6								
1974	OTT*	16										42	7						54	950	17.6	68	7								
1975	OTT	15	1		0							18	3						27	452	16.7	64	3								
5	Years	57	1		0							102	17						155	2513	16.2	68	17								
KENNEDY NKEYASEN Kennedy S-FB 5'10 184 Idaho State B: 8/4/1974 Ghana Draft: 3-18 1999 SAS																															
1999	SAS	18	1	0	0	0								4	4	1.0	5	0	1	15	15.0	15	0					26	421	16.2	48
2000	SAS	18	1	0	0	4								3	12	4.0	7	0	1	15	15.0	15	0					20	374	18.7	34
2001	SAS	18				15													1	8	8.0	8	0					1	20	20.0	20
2002	SAS	18				15																						11	212	19.3	27
2003	SAS	18				21																									
2004	SAS	18				6																									
2005	SAS	18				6																									
2006	SAS	14				9																									
8	Years	140	2	0	0	76								7	16	2.3	7	0	3	38	12.7	15	0					58	1027	17.7	48
DEREK NOBLE Derek P-K 6'6 241 Burlington Tiger-Cats Jrs. B: 3/29/1965 Pro: E																															
1987	HAM	1	1		0	0						12	0																		
JAMES NOBLE James Brown, Jr. SB 6'0 193 Stephen F. Austin State B: 8/14/1963 Jacksonville, TX Pro: N																															
1988	TOR	5				1						12	2						16	232	14.5	39	2	9	40	4.4	16				
MORRIS NOBLE Morris CB 6'0 185 Compton CC; Washington State B: 5/2/1951 New Orleans, LA																															
1974	EDM	5																													
1975	HAM	7							1	0																					
2	Years	12							1	0																					
TERRY NOBLE Terry DB 5'10 170 Cincinnati B: 12/28/1965 Somerville, NJ																															
1988	TOR	3				11			1	0																					
ANDREW NOEL Andrew WR 6'4 233 Acadia B: 4/14/1979 Draft: 1-9 2003 MTL																															
2003	MTL	1				1																									
2004	TOR	5				0																									
2	Years	6				1																									
DEAN NOEL Dean FB-SB 5'11 200 Delaware State B: 2/21/1967 Ottawa, ON Draft: 4-26 1993 OTT																															
1993	OTT	8				12								2	4	2.0	3	0										3	35	11.7	17
1994	OTT	17	0		1	30						12	2	2	6	3.0	5	0	13	133	10.2	18	2					1	21	21.0	21
1995	HAM	13	1		0	19								12	38	3.2	19	0	8	59	7.4	17	0					1	13	13.0	13
1996	HAM	14				28								5	62	12.4	39	0	1	1	1.0	1	0								

Year	Team	GP	FM	FF	FR	TK	SK	YDS	IR	YDS	PD	PTS	TD	RA	YDS	AVG	LG	TD	REC	YDS	AVG	LG	TD	PR	YDS	AVG	LG	KOR	YDS	AVG	LG
1997	HAM	13	0	0	1	16								1	11	11.0	11	0	5	61	12.2	26	0					1	6	6.0	6
5	Years	65	1	0	2	105					1	12	2	22	121	5.5	39	0	27	254	9.4	26	2					6	75	12.5	21
ROBERT NOEL Robert (Red) G-E 6'2 208 Maine																															
1947	SAS+	7										5	1										1								
1948	MTL	12										5	1																		
2	Years	19										10	2										1								
CHRIS NOFOAIGA Chris LB 5'10 220 Idaho B: 6/28/1977 American Samoa																															
2001	BC	13				15																						1	9	9.0	9
GEORGE NOGA George LB 6'2 250 Hawaii B: 1/22/1973 Honolulu, HI																															
1997	WPG	8	0	0	1	11	3.0	25.0	0	0	2																				
MARK NOHRA Mark RB 5'11 228 British Columbia B: 10/23/1973 Toronto, ON Draft: 4-28 1997 BC																															
1998	BC	9				4																									
1999	BC	18	2	0	1	2						6	1	45	256	5.7	18	0	8	126	15.8	32	1					2	16	8.0	9
2000	EDM	15	2	0	1	0						36	6	150	760	5.1	35	5	12	120	10.0	26	1								
2001	EDM	17	3	0	1	1						18	3	152	666	4.4	32	3	19	108	5.7	35	0								
2002	OTT	18	1	0	0	7						16	2	47	188	4.0	9	2	15	154	10.3	21	0								
2003	BC	18	0	0	1	1								25	123	4.9	29	0													
2004	BC	2				0								2	4	2.0	4	0	3	56	18.7	46	0								
2006	BC	12				1								7	45	6.4	12	0	1	9	9.0	9	0								
8	Years	109	8	0	4	16						76	12	428	2042	4.8	35	10	58	573	9.9	46	2					2	16	8.0	9
KENDRICK NORD Kendrick QB 6'2 210 Grambling State B: 4/28/1972 Mobile, AL Pro: E																															
1997	HAM	2				0								1	2	2.0	2	0													
FRED NORDGREN Frederic Marvin DT 5'11 240 Portland State B: 12/11/1959 Hillsboro, OR Pro: NU																															
1982	TOR	5					3.5																								
BOB NORDOFF Bob HB 6'1 188 Michigan; Burlington Braves Jrs. B: 1938																															
1960	SAS	2																													
HAROLD NORFLEET Harold Jerome OT 6'6 275 Prairie View A&M B: 6/3/1957 Baytown, TX Pro: U																															
1981	TOR	3																													
BUTCH NORMAN Haywood Eugene OT-DE-OG 6'5 251 Marion Institute JC; Alabama B: 8/23/1952																															
1974	WPG	9																													
1975	WPG	16	0		1																										
1976	WPG*	16	0		1																										
1977	WPG	11																													
1978	WPG+	16																													
1979	WPG	13																													
1980	WPG*	16	0		1																										
7	Years	97	0		3																										
JIM NORMAN James Thomas G-T-C 6'2 248 none B: 1/2/1934 Fortress Monroe, VA Pro: N																															
1956	HAM	7																													
MARK NORMAN Mark S-CB 5'11 195 British Columbia B: 1/28/1965 Edinburgh, Scotland Draft: 3B-26 1987 EDM																															
1987	EDM	18			1	10			1	29																					
1988	EDM	9				9			1	29																					
1989	EDM	8				10			4	44																					
1990	EDM	18				31			4	10														1	7	7.0	7				
1991	EDM	3				6																									
5	Years	56	0		1	66			10	112														1	7	7.0	7				
TONY NORMAN Anthony Alexander DE 6'5 270 Iowa State B: 1/27/1955 Atlanta, GA Pro: N																															
1980	WPG	10	0		1																										
1981	WPG	16	0		4		12.0																								
1982	WPG	16					6.0																					1	12	12.0	12
1983	WPG+	16	0		1		8.5																								
1984	WPG+	16					14.5		1	3																		1	0	0.0	0
1985	WPG+	16	0		1		14.0																								
1986	WPG	5					4.0																								
7	Years	95	0		7		59.0		1	3																		2	12	6.0	12
BAYNE NORRIE Bayne CB-SE 5'10 190 Queen's B: 6/30/1944 Draft: 1-9 1965 BC; 2-14 1966 MTL																															
1968	EDM	13	0		1									1	3	3.0	3	0						17	129	7.6	18	16	386	24.1	36
1969	EDM	16	3		0				6	71				3	15	5.0	9	0						75	428	5.7	22	3	57	19.0	27
1970	EDM	16	3		0									7	20	2.9	10	0	12	194	16.2	42	0	76	402	5.3	20				
1971	EDM	16			1				2	39									10	164	16.4	36	0	49	190	3.9	11				
1972	EDM	16	0		1				4	68														46	196	4.3	19				
1973	EDM	2	0		1																			4	7	1.8	2				
1974	EDM	11	2		0									4	25	6.3	9	0						32	180	5.6	17	1	8	8.0	8
1975	EDM	8												3	3	1.0	2	0	2	7	3.5	4	0								
8	Years	98	8		4				12	178				18	66	3.7	10	0	24	365	15.2	42	0	299	1532	5.1	22	20	451	22.6	36
RON NORTH Ron DT 6'2 220 Purdue B: 7/23/1951 Chicago, IL																															
1973	TOR	1																													
BILL NORTON Bill OG-OT-DT 6'2 244 Weber State B: 1/16/1954 Draft: TE 1976 BC																															
1976	HAM	4																													
1976	CAL	1																													
1976	Year	5																													
1978	TOR	15																													
1979	TOR	15																													
1980	TOR	16																													
1981	MTL+	14																													
1982	MTL	6	0		1																										
1983	TOR	6																													
7	Years	76	0		1																										
ED NORVACK Edward T-G 6'1 225 B: 1924																															
1947	WPG	6																													
1948	WPG	12																													
1949	WPG	14																													
1950	WPG	13																													
1951	WPG	12																													
1954	WPG	2																													
6	Years	59																													
GORD NOSEWORTHY Gordon C 6'3 201 none B: 1/7/1919 Montreal, QC D: 11/18/1974																															
1946	MTL	9																													
1947	MTL	12																													
2	Years	21																													
MIKE NOTT Wesley Michael QB 6'3 203 Santa Clara B: 5/19/1952 Eureka, CA Pro: N																															
1977	SAS	3												1	-1	-1.0	-1	0													
1979	BC	8	1		0									1	6	6.0	6	0													
1980	BC	4	1		0									4	-1	-0.3	2	0													
3	Years	15	2		0									6	4	0.7	6	0													
DEXTER NOTTAGE Dexter Alexander DL 6'4 274 Florida A&M B: 11/14/1970 Nassau, Bahamas Draft: 6-163 1994 WAS Pro: N																															
1998	TOR	2				4																									
BERT NOVIS Bert T-G-FB 6'4 235 none B: 1931																															
1958	TOR	10																													
1959	CAL	1																													
2	Years	11																													
ART NOWACK Arthur T 6'0 225 Portland; Notre Dame B: 1930																															

Year	Team	GP	FM	FF	FR	TK	SK	YDS	IR	YDS	PD	PTS	TD	RA	YDS	AVG	LG	TD	REC	YDS	AVG	LG	TD	PR	YDS	AVG	LG	KOR	YDS	AVG	LG
1954	OTT	1																													
ANDREW NOWACKI Andrew WR-SB 6'0 198 Scottsdale CC; Murray State B: 10/10/1980 Stony Creek, ON Draft: 3-26 2004 EDM																															
2004	EDM	10				0													1	7	7.0	7	0								
2005	EDM	10				0													18	151	8.4	16	0								
2006	EDM	11				1													17	147	8.6	13	0								
2007	EDM	18				5						12	2						47	465	9.9	35	2								
2008	EDM	18	1	0	0	2						12	2						28	369	13.2	31	2								
2009	EDM	18	1	0	1	3						6	1						30	423	14.1	44	1								
2010	EDM	18				3													21	259	12.3	49	0								
2011	EDM	14				2						6	1						24	233	9.7	17	1								
8	Years	117	2	0	1	16						36	6						186	2054	11.0	49	6								
BOB NOWALKOSKI Bob C 6'1 234 St. Jean Ints. B: 7/23/1939																															
1963	MTL	2																													
RED NOWER Edward HB-FB 5'9 185 none B: 6/21/1921 Montreal, QC																															
1948	MTL	10																													
1949	MTL	2																													
2	Years	12																													
BRIAN NUGENT Brian WR 6'3 210 York B: 6/12/1979 Brampton, ON Draft: 1-9 2002 CAL																															
2002	CAL	18				16																									
2003	MTL	12	0	0	1	12																									
2004	MTL	8	0	0	1	5																									
3	Years	38	0	0	2	33																									
JASON NUGENT Jason S 6'1 212 Rutgers B: 5/18/1982 Scarborough, ON Draft: 2-17 2006 EDM																															
2006	EDM	1				0																									
2007	WPG	14	0	1	0	12																									
2008	WPG	15	0	0	1	24			1	0	1																				
2009	EDM	18	0	0	1	24																									
2010	EDM	16	0	0	1	31					2																				
2011	WPG	7				3																									
6	Years	71	0	1	3	94			1	0	3																				
TERRENCE NUNN Terrence Dwayne WR-SB 6'0 190 Nebraska B: 7/25/1986 Houston, TX																															
2011	SAS	8				0													13	171	13.2	28	0								
JACQUAY NUNNALLY Jacquay WR 5'10 200 Florida A&M B: 1/14/1978 Miami, FL																															
2001	TOR	1				0													1	9	9.0	9	0	1	4	4.0	4	1	13	13.0	13
RICHARD NURSE Richard WR-SB 5'11 185 Canisius B: 3/16/1967 Trinidad & Tobago Draft: 3-23 1990 HAM																															
1990	HAM	17				1						18	3						29	357	12.3	35	3	1	12	12.0	12	10	130	13.0	28
1991	HAM	16				10						6	1						11	142	12.9	34	1	1	1	1.0	1	5	139	27.8	44
1992	HAM	18				10			1	41		6	1						5	75	15.0	26	1					0	27		24
1993	HAM	18				15													2	27	13.5	16	0								
1994	HAM	18				21													2	20	10.0	13	0								
1995	HAM	14	0		1	8						6	1						10	120	12.0	26	1								
6	Years	101	0		1	65			1	41		36	6						59	741	12.6	35	6	2	13	6.5	12	15	296	19.7	44
DOUG NUSSMEIER Douglas Keith QB 6'3 211 Idaho B: 12/11/1970 Portland, OR Draft: 4-116 1994 NO Pro: EN																															
2000	BC	18				0						6	1	23	183	8.0	29	1													
TOM NUTTEN Thomas R. C 6'5 291 Western Michigan B: 6/8/1971 Toledo, OH Draft: Bonus-1 1995 HAM; 7A-221 1995 BUF Pro: EN																															
1997	HAM	13				1																									
NORM NYGAARD Norman G. FB 5'11 183 Mount San Antonio JC; San Diego State B: 12/23/1931 Oslo, Norway D: 9/15/2000 Reno, NV Draft: 4B-46 1954 LARM																															
1956	TOR	1																	1	8	8.0	8	0					2	53	26.5	30
DANNY NYKOLUK Dan OT-DT 6'3 248 none B: 6/16/1934 Toronto, ON																															
1955	TOR	12																													
1957	TOR	14																										1	0	0.0	0
1958	TOR	10																										1	3	3.0	3
1959	TOR	14																													
1960	TOR	14																	4	62	15.5	20	0								
1961	TOR	14																													
1962	TOR	14																													
1963	TOR	14																													
1964	TOR	14	0		1																										
1965	TOR	14																													
1966	TOR	14																													
1967	TOR+	14																													
1968	TOR	14																													
1969	TOR+	14																										1	0	0.0	0
1970	TOR	14																													
1971	TOR	1																													
16	Years	205	0		1														4	62	15.5	20	0					3	3	1.0	3
COREY OAKS Corey CB 5'10 203 Robert Morris B: 2/12/1979 Pittsburgh, P																															
2003	WPG	3	0	0	1	6																						1	16	16.0	16
TOMMY OATES Tommy DB 5'9 170 Union (Tennessee) B: 11/2/1971 Ocala, FL																															
1995	BIR	18	0		2	29			1	37	3																	1	37	37.0	37
TURHON O'BANNON Turhon R. WR 6'1 200 New Mexico B: 3/23/1970 Torrance, CA																															
1996	WPG	4	0		1	2								1	-19	-19.0	-19	0	10	144	14.4	28	0					3	50	16.7	18
1997	WPG	8				1						18	3						20	291	14.6	41	3								
2	Years	12	0		1	3						18	3	1	-19	-19.0	-19	0	30	435	14.5	41	3					3	50	16.7	18
TOM OBERG Thomas Harvey DB 6'0 185 Oregon State; Portland State B: 8/7/1945 Portland, OR Pro: NW																															
1971	WPG	16	0		2				1	0																					
1972	WPG	16	0		1				5	5														1	0	0.0	0				
1973	WPG	15							3	14		6	1											2	7	3.5	7	1	9	9.0	9
3	Years	47	0		3				9	19		6	1											3	7	2.3	7	1	9	9.0	9
BOB O'BILLOVICH Robert QB-S-DH 5'10 182 Montana B: 6/30/1940 Butte, MT Draft: 12-159 1962 STL																															
1963	OTT	13							2	25		6	1	8	35	4.4	11	1						16	83	5.2	9				
1964	OTT	14							6	191		13	2	3	7	2.3	4	0						7	46	6.6	13				
1965	OTT+	14	2		0				6	114		6	1											1	0	0.0	0				
1966	OTT	14	0		1				3	42																					
1967	OTT	14							7	38														4	27	6.8	13				
5	Years	69	2		1				24	410		25	4	11	42	3.8	11	1						28	156	5.6	13				
JACK O'BILLOVICH Melvin Jack LB 6'0 225 Oregon State B: 6/5/1942 Butte, MT D: 2/13/1995 Beaverton, OR Draft: 11-164 1966 DET																															
1967	HAM	1																													
TONY O'BILLOVICH Tony LB 6'1 210 Oregon State B: 8/30/1970 Eugene, OR																															
1994	TOR	4	1		0	4																						1	0	0.0	0
1995	TOR	2				9																									
2	Years	6	1		0	13																						1	0	0.0	0
ED O'BRADOVICH Edward DE 6'3 255 Illinois B: 5/21/1940 Melrose Park, IL Draft: 7-91 1962 CHIB Pro: N																															
1961	BC	3																													
1961	CAL	6																													
1961	Year	9																													
BILL O'BREZA Bill T-C-E																															
1946	HAM	12																													
1947	HAM	12																													
2	Years	24																													
JIM O'BRIEN James HB																															
1946	TOR	1																													

Year	Team	GP	FM	FF	FR	TK	SK	YDS	IR	YDS	PD	PTS	TD	RA	YDS	AVG	LG	TD	REC	YDS	AVG	LG	TD	PR	YDS	AVG	LG	KOR	YDS	AVG	LG
JOHN O'BRIEN John LB 6'2 215 York B: 10/27/1966 Hamilton, ON Draft: 1-8 1989 WPG																															
1990	HAM	3				0																									
KEVIN O'BRIEN Kevin LB 6'4 235 Bowling Green State B: 7/1/1970 Pro: E																															
1994	SAC	2				3																									
MIKE O'BRIEN Michael K-P 6'0 200 Western Ontario B: 7/27/1976 Hamilton, ON Draft: 4-23 2000 SAS																															
2001	SAS	1				0																									
2002	HAM	1	1	0	0	0																									
2	Years	2	1	0	0	0																									
TOM O'BRIEN Tom T 6'4 235 Notre Dame																															
1957	CAL	4																													
WAYNE O'BRIEN Wayne LB 6'1 228 St. Mary's (Nova Scotia); McMaster B: 1945 Draft: 2-18 1966 HAM																															
1968	MTL	14	0		1																							1	5	5.0	5
MIKE OBROVAC Michael Louis OG 6'6 275 Bowling Green State B: 10/11/1955 Canton, OH Pro: N																															
1979	TOR	16	0		1																										
1980	TOR	7																													
2	Years	23	0		1																										
ED OCHIENA Edward OE-DB 6'2 186 North York Knights Jrs.; Waterloo Lutheran B: 1/26/1938																															
1959	TOR	10																	4	49	12.3	18	0								
1960	TOR	14										24	4	12	75	6.3	27	0	30	495	16.5	59	4	1	2	2.0	2	5	67	13.4	25
1961	TOR	3																													
1962	HAM	9																										1	0	0.0	0
4	Years	36										24	4	12	75	6.3	27	0	34	544	16.0	59	4	1	2	2.0	2	6	67	11.2	25
RON OCKIMEY Ron LB 6'2 215 San Jose State B: 9/3/1978 Philadelphia, PA																															
2002	BC	8				19	1.0	13.0																							
2003	BC	18	0	1	0	69	1.0	12.0																							
2005	WPG	11	0	2	0	28	2.0	23.0																							
2006	WPG	13	1	1	2	17	2.0				1																	1	4	4.0	4
4	Years	50	1	4	2	133	6.0	48.0			1																	1	4	4.0	4
BILL O'CONNOR William Francis, Jr. (Zeke) E 6'4 220 Notre Dame B: 5/2/1926 New York, NY Draft: 4-24 1948 BUF-AAFC Pro: AN																															
1952	TOR	8										5	1										1								
1953	TOR	5																													
2	Years	13										5	1										1								
WINSTON OCTOBER Winston CB-WR 5'9 165 Richmond B: 7/12/1976 Guyana																															
1999	MTL	18	2	1	0	14			1	15	3													77	724	9.4	70	18	334	18.6	32
2000	MTL	14	3	0	0	14						18	3											79	898	11.4	76	23	435	18.9	38
2001	EDM	8	1	0	0	4						6	1											35	369	10.5	69	15	293	19.5	37
2002	EDM	16	3	0	0	4						6	1						1	14	14.0	14	0	87	833	9.6	95	37	789	21.3	43
2003	EDM	18	6	0	1	6						12	2	2	34	17.0	22	1	19	196	10.3	32	1	75	719	9.6	65	48	1018	21.2	39
2004	EDM	18	3	1	0	5						12	2						9	79	8.8	16	0	79	874	11.1	101	51	1073	21.0	43
6	Years	92	18	2	1	47			1	15	3	54	9	2	34	17.0	22	1	29	289	10.0	32	1	432	4417	10.2	101	192	3942	20.5	43
JEREMY O'DAY Jeremy C-OT-OG 6'3 223 Edinboro B: 8/31/1974 Buffalo, NY																															
1997	TOR	18				1						6	1						2	21	10.5	16	1								
1998	TOR	18				0													1	17	17.0	17	0					1	8	8.0	8
1999	SAS	18				1						6	1						1	7	7.0	7	1								
2000	SAS	18	0	0	1	0																									
2001	SAS	18				5																									
2002	SAS	13	0	0	1	2																									
2003	SAS+	18	0	0	1	1																									
2004	SAS	18	1	0	0	1																									
2005	SAS+	13	0	0	1	0																									
2006	SAS*	18				2																									
2007	SAS*	18	1	0	0	0																									
2008	SAS	14				0																									
2009	SAS*	18				1																									
2010	SAS+	18				0																									
14	Years	238	2	0	4	14						12	2						4	45	11.3	17	2					1	8	8.0	8
JOHN ODDONETTO John DB 6'0 187 Eastern Arizona CC; Kansas B: 11/17/1977 Globe, AZ																															
2002	BC	16				4																									
DON ODEGARD Donald Boyd CB 6'0 180 Oregon State; Nevada-Las Vegas B: 11/22/1966 Seattle, WA Draft: 6-150 1990 CIN Pro: N																															
1994	HAM	15	0		2	32			3	9	4													3	16	5.3	9				
1995	MEM	16				30			4	35	2																				
1996	TOR	11	0		1	19					3																				
3	Years	42	0		3	81			7	44	9													3	16	5.3	9				
BOB O'DOHERTY Bob WR-DB 6'0 185 Queen's B: 3/27/1956 Draft: 1-2 1978 HAM																															
1979	OTT	1																													
1979	WPG	12																	7	98	14.0	32	0								
1979	Year	13																	7	98	14.0	32	0								
1980	WPG	13																	2	58	29.0	39	0								
1981	WPG	12																	2	24	12.0	18	0								
3	Years	26																	11	180	16.4	39	0								
DeWAYNE ODOM Albert DeWayne LB 6'3 235 California B: 8/10/1968 Oceanside, CA																															
1992	EDM	18	1		0	54	3.0		2	10																		1	9	9.0	9
MARK ODOM Mark D. LB 5'11 215 Hawaii B: 4/7/1969 Carson, CA																															
1991	CAL	2				10																									
URBAN ODSON Urban Leroy T 6'3 251 Minnesota B: 11/17/1918 Clark, SD D: 6/22/1986 Rapid City, SD Draft: 1-9 1942 GB Pro: N																															
1950	MTL	10																													
RAY ODUMS Raymond CB 6'2 175 Alabama B: 10/30/1951 Pro: U																															
1975	WPG	8	0		1				1	70		6	1																		
1975	SAS	5	0		1				1	0																					
1975	Year	13	0		2				2	70		6	1																		
1976	SAS	5							2	0																					
1977	CAL	16							3	66		6	1																		
1978	CAL	16							3	62																					
1979	CAL+	16							3	51																					
1980	CAL*	16	0		1				3	63																					
1981	CAL*	16	0		1				4	122																					
1982	CAL*	16	0		1				4	68		6	1											1	-1	-1.0	-1				
1983	CAL	15	0		1				3	92		6	1	0	6		6	0						2	30	15.0	28				
1984	CAL	16	0		2				1	2																					
10	Years	140	0		8				28	596		24	4	0	6		6	0						3	29	9.7	28				
DEJI ODUWOLE Adeji Olanrewaju DE 6'3 250 St. Mary's (Nova Scotia); Calgary B: 8/23/1987 Coquitlam, BC																															
2010	WPG	17	0	0	1	7																									
2011	WPG	3				0																									
2	Years	20	0	0	1	7																									
TIM OESTERLING Tim OT 6'4 250 UCLA B: 5/5/1948 Bethesda, MD Draft: 10B-253 1971 OAK																															
1972	SAS	1																													
BOB OETTING Robert Lee OT 6'4 250 Concordia (Nebraska) B: 11/16/1942 Emma, MO																															
1965	BC	11																													
1966	TOR	4																													
2	Years	15																													
JERRY O'FLANAGAN Jerry E 6'2 215 McGill; British Columbia B: 1932 Draft: 3-23 1956 TOR																															
1956	TOR	9																													

Year	Team	GP	FM	FF	FR	TK	SK	YDS	IR	YDS	PD	PTS	TD	RA	YDS	AVG	LG	TD	REC	YDS	AVG	LG	TD	PR	YDS	AVG	LG	KOR	YDS	AVG	LG
1957	BC	1																													
2	Years	10																													
ED OGALSKI Ed C																															
1946	WPG	1																													
PETE O'GARRO Pete E 6'4 210 Riverside JC; UCLA B: 5/13/1931 Draft: 9-100 1954 NYG																															
1957	TOR	11										42	7						37	640	17.3	64	7								
1958	TOR	8										12	2						22	427	19.4	86	2					1	11	11.0	11
1959	TOR	1																													
1962	TOR	1										6	1						2	19	9.5	17	1								
4	Years	21										60	10						61	1086	17.8	86	10					1	11	11.0	11
WILF O'HAGAN Wilfred HB 5'10 165 Lakeshore Flyers Ints. B: 1928																															
1954	SAS	1																													
BRIAN O'HARA Brian WR-RB-WB 6'0 185 Whitworth B: 5/2/1954 Draft: TE 1976 SAS																															
1976	SAS	1																													
1977	SAS	16	1		0							12	2	2	-3	-1.5	2	0	21	311	14.8	53	2	2	-6	-3.0	2	1	19	19.0	19
1978	SAS	16	1		1							6	1	4	8	2.0	18	0	19	355	18.7	73	1	24	166	6.9	24	20	527	26.4	44
1979	SAS	16																	5	34	6.8	9	0					2	50	25.0	25
4	Years	49	2		1							18	3	6	5	0.8	18	0	45	700	15.6	73	3	26	160	6.2	24	23	596	25.9	44
FRANK O'HARA Frank T-G 5'11 200 B: 1924																															
1948	HAM	11																													
1949	HAM	10																													
2	Years	21																													
PETE OHLER Peter QB-DB 6'2 210 Wenatchee Valley JC; Washington B: 1941																															
1963	BC	16	1		0				1					10	11	1.1	14	0						20	73	3.7	10				
1964	BC	7												1	1	1.0	1	0													
1967	BC	13												1	-2	-2.0	-2	0													
1968	BC	15	2		0									11	32	2.9	9	0													
1969	BC	5																													
5	Years	56	3		0				1	0				23	42	1.8	14	0						20	73	3.7	10				
UZOOMA OKEKE Uzooma Emeka OT-OG 6'2 2310 Southern Methodist B: 9/3/1970 Beaumont, TX																															
1994	SHR	16	0		1	1																									
1995	SHR	18				0																									
1996	OTT	14				2																									
1997	MTL*	18				2																									
1998	MTL*	18				2																									
1999	MTL*	18				1																									
2000	MTL	8				0																									
2001	MTL	15				2																									
2002	MTL*	18				2																									
2003	MTL*	18	0	0	1	3																									
2004	MTL*	18	0	0	1	0																									
2005	MTL*	18	0	0	2	7																									
2006	MTL	14				0																									
13	Years	211	0	0	5	22																									
STEVE OKONIEWSKI John Stephen OT 6'3 257 Washington; Everett CC; Montana B: 8/22/1949 Bremerton, WA Draft: 2B-41 1972 ATL Pro: N																															
1978	WPG	4																													
SAMMY OKPRO Sammy DB 5'10 192 Concordia (Canada) B: 5/2/1984 Montreal, QC Draft: 4A-25 2008 EDM																															
2008	EDM	3				0																									
JOVAN OLAFIOYE Jovan OT-OG 6'6 325 Grand Rapids CC; North Carolina Central B: 12/16/1987 Detroit, MI																															
2010	BC+	18	0	0	1	3																									
2011	BC*	18				2																									
2	Years	36	0	0	1	5																									
CLIFF OLANDER Clifford Valmore QB 6'5 187 New Mexico State B: 4/22/1955 Hartford, CT Draft: 5B-128 1977 SD Pro: N																															
1982	EDM	16	2		0									2	4	2.0	3	0													
JIM OLDENBURG James G. HB 6'2 225 Canisius D: 8/20/1989 Buffalo, NY																															
1948	HAM	12										11	1					1													
HUGH OLDHAM Hugh Garsear FL 5'10 175 Oregon B: 3/18/1940 Caldwell, TX																															
1970	OTT	14	0		1							78	13	1	5	5.0	5	0	45	1043	23.2	73	13					13	340	26.2	36
1971	OTT	14			1							36	6	13	60	4.6	19	0	38	736	19.4	100	6					11	313	28.5	45
1972	OTT	14	2		0							42	7						36	719	20.0	60	7					2	67	33.5	34
1973	OTT	14										36	6						32	701	21.9	89	6								
1974	OTT	12										6	1						18	305	16.9	47	1								
5	Years	68	2		2							198	33	14	65	4.6	19	0	169	3504	20.7	100	33					26	720	27.7	45
JOHN O'LEARY John RB 6'1 210 Nebraska B: 7/10/1954 Mineola, NY Draft: 12-330 1976 CHIB																															
1977	MTL	16	5		0							24	4	199	859	4.3	25	1	35	235	6.7	23	3								
1978	MTL	15	5		0							30	5	146	584	4.0	15	4	24	445	18.5	57	1	1	3	3.0	3	4	80	20.0	27
1979	MTL	16	4		2							48	8	132	680	5.2	57	5	37	537	14.5	80	3					5	92	18.4	41
3	Years	47	14		2							102	17	477	2123	4.5	57	10	96	1217	12.7	80	7	1	3	3.0	3	9	172	19.1	41
PAT OLEKSIAK Roman HB 6'0 205 Tennessee B: 1933 Draft: 18-216 1955 DET																															
1955	WPG	2												11	7	0.6	13	0	3	30	10.0	16	0								
JASON OLFORD Jason Deon CB 5'10 183 Kilgore JC; Louisiana Tech B: 7/22/1978 Little Rock, AR Pro: E																															
2003	BC	2				2																									
MIKE OLIPHANT Michael Nathaniel RB 5'9 170 Puget Sound B: 5/19/1963 Jacksonville, FL Draft: 3-66 1988 WAS Pro: N																															
1993	SAC+	18	6		1	11						78	13	116	760	6.6	52	8	47	812	17.3	83	5	2	25	12.5	25	4	64	16.0	20
1994	SAC	3	2		0	0								11	27	2.5	12	0	6	75	12.5	23	0								
1995	WPG	4	0		1	0						12	2	25	54	2.2	23	1	14	140	10.0	40	1					2	29	14.5	18
3	Years	25	8		2	11						90	15	152	841	5.5	52	9	67	1027	15.3	83	6	2	25	12.5	25	6	93	15.5	20
BOBBY OLIVE Bobby Lee, Jr. WR 5'11 164 Ohio State B: 4/22/1969 Paris, TN Draft: 11-300 1991 KC Pro: EN																															
1998	HAM	16	1	0	0	4						18	3						46	663	14.4	41	3	65	496	7.6	38				
BOBBY JACK OLIVER Bobby Jack DT-OT-K 6'2 242 Baylor B: 1/9/1936 Abilene, TX Draft: 2B-21 1958 CHIC																															
1958	TOR	13							1	0																					
1959	TOR	14																													
1960	TOR	12							1	4																					
1961	MTL+	14										14	0																		
1962	MTL+	13										67	0																		
1963	MTL	7										22	0																		
1964	HAM	2																													
1964	EDM	11	0		3																										
1964	Year	13	0		3																										
7	Years	75	0		3				2	4		103	0																		
FRANK OLIVER Franklin Justice DB 6'0 194 Kentucky State B: 3/3/1952 Wetumpka, AL Draft: 4B-87 1975 SF Pro: N																															
1978	BC	16	1		1				2	4														1	4	4.0	4				
1979	BC	16							1	45														1	0	0.0	0				
1980	OTT	5																													
3	Years	37	1		1				3	49														2	4	2.0	4				
JIMMY OLIVER Jimmie Earl, Jr. WR 5'10 173 Texas Christian B: 1/30/1973 Dallas, TX Draft: 2C-61 1995 SD																															
1999	BC	4				0													13	200	15.4	45	0								
2000	BC	7	1	0	0	1						18	3						28	631	22.5	65	3					2	40	20.0	22
2001	BC	4	2	0	0	1						6	1	1	7	7.0	7	0	11	166	15.1	35	1								
2002	OTT+	18	2	0	0	4						36	6	2	-10	-5.0	3	0	82	1004	12.2	77	6	1	8	8.0	8				
2003	TOR	3				0													7	85	12.1	32	0								
5	Years	36	5	0	0	6						60	10	3	-3	-1.0	7	0	141	2086	14.8	77	10	1	8	8.0	8	2	40	20.0	22

Year	Team	GP	FM	FF	FR	TK	SK	YDS	IR	YDS	PD	PTS	TD	RA	YDS	AVG	LG	TD	REC	YDS	AVG	LG	TD	PR	YDS	AVG	LG	KOR	YDS	AVG	LG
TRAVIS OLIVER Travis Eugene CB 6'0 180 California B: 3/10/1968 Victoria, TX																															
1992	EDM	8				12																									
JERRY OLLINGER Jerry QB																															
1946	HAM	1																													
LOU OLSACHER Louis OT 6'2 270 Hamilton Hurricanes Jrs.; St. Mary's (Nova Scotia) B: 10/12/1965 Hamilton, ON Draft: 4-29 1989 EDM																															
1992	TOR	5				0																									
1993	TOR	3				1																									
2	Years	8				1																									
ALEX OLSEN Alex E 6'1 185 NDG Maple Leafs Jrs. B: 1930																															
1950	MTL	4																													
RUSTY OLSEN Richard F. DE-OT 6'2 255 Washington B: 6/18/1959 West Covina, CA Draft: 9-234 1981 DEN																															
1982	TOR	16	0		1		6.5		1	5																					
1983	SAS	7					2.5																								
1984	SAS	10	0		1		1.0																								
1985	SAS	1	0		1																										
4	Years	34	0		3		10.0		1	5																					
LANCE OLSSEN Lance Everett OT 6'5 262 Purdue B: 4/17/1947 Boston, MA Draft: 3A-65 1968 SF Pro: N																															
1971	EDM	12																										1	3	3.0	3
1972	EDM	8																													
2	Years	20																										1	3	3.0	3
ED OLSZEWSKI Edward S. G 5'10 195 Michigan State; Niagara B: 1/11/1921 Niagara Falls, NY D: 11/8/1992 Lewiston, NY																															
1948	HAM	12																													
HARRY OLSZEWSKI Harry Lee Thomas OG 5'11 245 Clemson B: 10/11/1946 Baltimore, MD D: 4/27/1998 Fort Lauderdale, FL Draft: 3A-64 1968 CLE																															
1969	MTL	14	0		2																										
1970	MTL	6																													
2	Years	20	0		2																										
CORY OLYNICK Cory FB 5'10 210 Regina Rams Jrs.; Regina B: 3/27/1977 Regina, SK Draft: 5-42 2003 WPG																															
2004	WPG	10				3																						1	5	5.0	5
JIM O'MAHONEY James John LB 6'1 231 Miami (Florida) B: 3/29/1941 Pittsburgh, PA Draft: 8-100 1963 MIN Pro: N																															
1967	MTL	5																													
DUNCAN O'MAHONY Duncan P-K 5'10 200 Abbotsford Air Force Jrs.; British Columbia B: 6/29/1976 Kilkenny, Ireland Draft: 2B-14 2001 CAL																															
2001	CAL	18	3	0	2	1						2	0																		
2002	CAL+	18	1	0	0	1						5	0																		
2003	CAL	18	2	0	0	4						22	0																		
2004	BC	18	1	0	0	2						172	0																		
2005	BC	18	0	0	1	4						134	0																		
2007	CAL	8	1	0	0	0						3	0	1	5	5.0	5	0													
6	Years	98	8	0	3	12						338	0	1	5	5.0	5	0													
TOM O'MALLEY Thomas Louis QB 5'11 185 Cincinnati B: 7/23/1925 Cincinnati, OH D: 6/11/2011 York, PA Draft: 6-45 1949 CLE-AAFC Pro: N																															
1951	OTT	12										8	1					1													
1952	OTT	12										3	0																		
1953	OTT	14										10	1					1													
3	Years	38										21	2					2													
MATT O'MEARA Matt OG-OT 6'4 294 McMaster B: 8/7/1982 Milton, ON Draft: 1A-3 2005 SAS																															
2005	SAS	6				0																									
2006	SAS	4				0																									
2007	WPG	2				0																									
2008	WPG	13				0																									
2009	SAS	2				1																									
5	Years	27				1																									
KENNY ONATOLU Olayiwola Kendae LB 6'2 225 Nebraska-Omaha B: 10/8/1982 Chicago, IL Pro: N																															
2007	EDM	10				12	1.0	4.0			1																				
2008	EDM	14	0	1	2	68	3.0	13.0			3																				
2	Years	24	0	1	2	80	4.0	17.0			4																				
CALVIN O'NEAL Calvin LB 6'1 235 Michigan B: 10/6/1954 Oceola, AR Draft: 6-163 1977 BAL Pro: N																															
1979	HAM	1																													
JESSE O'NEAL Jesse DE 6'4 255 Grambling State B: 7/11/1952 Crowley, LA Draft: 6-146 1975 HOU																															
1975	SAS	16	0		1																										
1976	SAS	16																													
1977	BC	14	0		1																										
1979	HAM	8	0		1				1	27		6	1																		
4	Years	54	0		3				1	27		6	1																		
BOB O'NEIL Robert Maioli DT-LB-DE 6'1 229 Duquesne; Notre Dame B: 2/21/1931 Draft: 15-174 1953 PIT Pro: N																															
1958	CAL	11																										1	7	7.0	7
1959	CAL	15																										1	0	0.0	0
1960	CAL	5																													
1960	MTL	5																													
1960	Year	10																													
3	Years	31																										2	7	3.5	7
TIM O'NEILL Timothy C-OG 6'3 304 Victoria Rebels Jrs.; Calgary B: 10/17/1979 Victoria, BC Draft: 3-22 2005 EDM																															
2008	CAL	14				0																									
2009	CAL	18				2																						2	8	4.0	7
2010	CAL	18				0																									
2011	CAL	18	1	0	0	0																									
4	Years	68	1	0	0	2																						2	8	4.0	7
STEVE ONESCHUK Steve DLB 5'10 177 Toronto B: 1931 Draft: 1-4 1954 HAM																															
1955	HAM	12							1	0		23	2	41	233	5.7	30	2	5	39	7.8	17	0								
1956	HAM	14							1	29		53	1	11	41	3.7	18	0	5	57	11.4	24	1					6	61	10.2	13
1957	HAM	14							2	24		61	1	22	102	4.6	17	1	2	4	2.0	7	0								
1958	HAM	9										12	0																		
1959	HAM	10							4	24		39	0	3	15	5.0	8	0						2	4	2.0	3				
1960	HAM	1										4	0																		
6	Years	60							8	77		192	4	77	391	5.1	30	3	12	100	8.3	24	1	2	4	2.0	3	6	61	10.2	13
CHIJIOKE ONYENEGECHA Chijioke Nwannnemdi DH 6'1 215 San Francisco CC; Oklahoma B: 3/15/1983 San Francisco, CA																															
2007	WPG	9				17			0	0	4																				
JON OOSTERHUIS Jon OL-DT-FB-DE 6'4 268 New Hampshire B: 6/13/1977 Fergus, ON Draft: 1-8 2002 CAL																															
2002	WPG	8				4																									
2003	WPG	18	0	1	1	8																									
2004	WPG	18				3																									
2005	WPG	18	0	0	1	16					1	6	1						1	1	1.0	1	1								
2006	WPG	18	1	0	2	3	2.0	15.0																							
2007	WPG	18				6						6	1						1	5	5.0	5	1								
2008	WPG	9				4													1	16	16.0	16	0								
2009	WPG	18	0	0	1	10								1	0	0.0	0	0	4	41	10.3	19	0					2	3	1.5	3
2010	WPG	18	0	0	1	1								0	12		12	0	1	0	0.0	0	0					1	1	1.0	1
9	Years	143	1	1	6	55	2.0	15.0			1	12	2	1	12	12.0	12	0	8	63	7.9	19	2					3	4	1.3	3
RED O'QUINN John William, Jr. OE-DE 6'2 195 Wake Forest B: 9/7/1925 Lilesville, NC D: 4/21/2002 Ottawa, ON Draft: 16-121 1949 BAL-AAFC; 3-31(f) 1949 CHIB Pro: N																															
1952	MTL+	12										10	2										2								
1953	MTL+	14										40	8										8								
1954	MTL+	14										30	6						62	1024	16.5	69	6					2	35	17.5	20
1955	MTL+	12										15	3						78	1097	14.1	38	3					5	46	9.2	16
1956	MTL	14										12	2						58	898	15.5	34	2					4	24	6.0	11

Year	Team	GP	FM	FF	FR	TK	SK	YDS	IR	YDS	PD	PTS	TD	RA	YDS	AVG	LG	TD	REC	YDS	AVG	LG	TD	PR	YDS	AVG	LG	KOR	YDS	AVG	LG
1957	MTL	14										24	4	1	2	2.0	2	0	61	1006	16.5	54	4	2	0	0.0	0	1	7	7.0	7
1958	MTL+	14										36	6						65	962	14.8	32	6					1	15	15.0	15
1959	MTL	14										18	3	1	3	3.0	3	0	53	692	13.1	34	3								
8	Years	108										185	34	2	5	2.5	3	0	377	5679	15.1	69	34	2	0	0.0	0	13	127	9.8	20
DON ORAMASIONWU Donald DT 6'3 272 Manitoba B: 6/4/1986 Winnipeg, MB Draft: 5-39 2008 WPG																															
2009	WPG	18	0	0	1	14	3.0	20.0			1																				
2010	WPG	18	0	1	1	9	3.0	21.0																				1	10	10.0	10
2011	WPG	18	0	1	1	16	3.0	22.0																							
3	Years	54	0	2	3	39	9.0	63.0			1																	1	10	10.0	10
DOYLE ORANGE Doyle RB 5'11 200 Southern Mississippi B: 8/6/1951 Waycross, GA Draft: 6-147 1974 ATL; 18-214 1974 JAC-WFL																															
1974	TOR	16	4		0							24	4	179	870	4.9	39	3	21	211	10.0	24	1					11	251	22.8	35
1975	TOR+	13	7		2							42	7	205	1055	5.1	56	5	22	219	10.0	35	2					3	41	13.7	20
1976	TOR	2	1		0							12	2	28	101	3.6	16	1	5	56	11.2	16	1								
1977	HAM	8	2		0							24	4	72	380	5.3	36	2	17	121	7.1	40	2								
4	Years	39	14		2							102	17	484	2406	5.0	56	11	65	607	9.3	40	6					14	292	20.9	35
BILL ORDWAY William O. (Bull) HB 6'0 204 North Dakota B: 1917																															
1946	WPG+	8																													
JONATHAN ORDWAY Jonathan DB 5'10 179 Boston College B: 10/19/1978 Tampa Bay, FL																															
2003	OTT	11				41					2																	5	114	22.8	60
2004	OTT	10	0	0	1	35			3	12	2																				
2	Years	21	0	0	1	76			3	12	4																	5	114	22.8	60
JOSEPH O'REILLY Joseph F. (Sefa) DE 6'2 240 Oregon State B: 12/29/1975 Los Angeles, CA																															
2001	WPG	17	0	3	1	28	4.0	28.0																							
GERRY ORGAN Gerry K-P-WR-TE 6'2 200 Guelph B: 12/4/1944 England																															
1971	OTT	14										92	1						3	86	28.7	48	1								
1972	OTT	14	0		1							131	1						1	2	2.0	2	1								
1973	OTT	14	1		0							123	0						2	27	13.5	16	0								
1974	OTT	16										134	0						3	69	23.0	45	0								
1975	OTT	16										124	0						4	125	31.3	55	0	1	8	8.0	8				
1976	OTT	16										113	0																		
1977	OTT	16										130	0						1	13	13.0	13	0								
1979	OTT	16	1		0							101	0	1	24	24.0	24	0													
1980	OTT	16	1		0							123	0																		
1981	OTT	16										122	0	1	15	15.0	15	0													
1982	OTT+	16	1		1							130	0	4	5	1.3	16	0													
1983	OTT	16										139	0	1	19	19.0	19	0													
12	Years	186	4		2							1462	2	7	63	9.0	24	0	14	322	23.0	55	2	1	8	8.0	8				
MIKE ORIARD Michael Vincent OT 6'4 223 Notre Dame B: 5/26/1948 Spokane, WA Draft: 5-130 1970 KC Pro: N																															
1974	HAM	6	0		1																										
MARK ORLANDO Mark WR 6'1 190 Towson State B: 10/23/1972 Baltimore, MD																															
1995	BAL	9	1		1	6						6	1						6	125	20.8	53	1					2	16	8.0	8
GUS ORNSTEIN Gus William QB 6'3 225 Notre Dame; Michigan State; Rowan B: 11/23/1974 New York, NY Pro: E																															
2002	BC	6				0																									
TOMMY ORR Thomas DB 5'10 197 West Virginia B: 8/14/1972 Elizabeth, NJ																															
1995	BIR	10				34	1.0	7.0	0	0	1																				
GLEN ORRIS Glen DB-WR 6'1 203 Simon Fraser B: 1949																															
1969	WPG	11																	1	5	5.0	5	0								
1970	WPG	16	0		1														4	29	7.3	11	0								
2	Years	27	0		1														5	34	6.8	11	0								
TRAVIS ORTEGA Travis LB 6'2 215 Rice B: 5/11/1977 San Antonio, TX																															
2003	WPG	9				9																									
2004	WPG	2				3																									
2	Years	11				12																									
CHASE ORTIZ Chase Patrick DE 6'2 255 Texas Christian B: 5/22/1985 League City, TX																															
2009	WPG	2				2																									
ROBERT ORTIZ Robert Joseph WR 6'1 195 San Diego State B: 5/30/1983 San Diego, CA Pro: E																															
2007	BC	1				0													1	12	12.0	12	0								
SEAN ORTIZ Sean DT-DE 6'2 239 Minot State; British Columbia B: 5/4/1985 White Rock, BC																															
2010	BC	6				2																									
2011	MTL	3				0																									
2011	HAM	4				1																									
2011	Year	7				1																									
2	Years	9				3																									
LEN ORTMAN Len C-G 5'11 208 Regina Collegiate Jrs. B: 1926																															
1946	SAS	7																													
1947	SAS	8																													
1948	SAS	12																													
1949	SAS	14																													
1950	SAS	13																													
1951	SAS	14																													
1952	SAS	12																													
7	Years	80																													
WOPAMO OSAISAI Wopamo Apere LB-CB 5'10 199 Stanford B: 9/13/1986 Alameda County, CA																															
2011	EDM	6				11			1	21	0																				
PAUL OSBALDISTON Paul K-P 6'3 210 Richmond Raiders Jrs.; Montana-Western B: 4/27/1964 Oldham, England Draft: 7-63 1986 BC																															
1986	HAM	9										92	0																		
1986	WPG	5										48	0																		
1986	BC	3										25	0																		
1986	Year	17										165	0																		
1987	HAM	3				0						18	0	1	7	7.0	7	0													
1988	HAM	18	1		0	0						178	0	1	-3	-3.0	-3	0													
1989	HAM+	18	2		0	1						233	0																		
1990	HAM+	18	2		0	2						212	0																		
1991	HAM	18	3		0	5						172	0	1	30	30.0	30	0													
1992	HAM	18	1		0	0						196	0																		
1993	HAM	18	5		0	1						136	0																		
1994	HAM	18	2		1	3						181	0	1	9	9.0	9	0													
1995	HAM	18	2		1	2						146	0																		
1996	HAM*	18	4		1	4						178	0	1	13	13.0	13	0													
1997	HAM	18	4	0	0	1						118	0																		
1998	HAM*	18	3	0	1	2						187	0																		
1999	HAM+	18	1	0	0	3						203	0																		
2000	HAM+	18				2						178	0																		
2001	HAM*	18	0	0	1	0						183	0																		
2002	HAM	17	2	0	0	1						160	0																		
2003	HAM	15	1	0	0	0						87	0																		
18	Years	296	33	0	5	27						2931	0	5	56	11.2	30	0													
DEE OSBORNE Dee LB 6'2 230 Miami (Ohio) B: 9/24/1975 Chicago, IL																															
1997	WPG	7	0	0	2	21					2																				
ELDONTA OSBORNE Eldonta R. LB 6'0 226 Louisiana Tech B: 8/12/1967 Jonesboro, LA Pro: N																															
1994	SHR	17				50																									
1995	SHR	15				27			1	24	1																				

Year	Team	GP	FM	FF	FR	TK	SK	YDS	IR	YDS	PD	PTS	TD	RA	YDS	AVG	LG	TD	REC	YDS	AVG	LG	TD	PR	YDS	AVG	LG	KOR	YDS	AVG	LG
2	Years	32				77			1	24	1																				
RAY OSBOURNE Ray T 6'6 235 Mississippi State B: 1940 Draft: 15-204 1962 SF																															
1963	BC	2																													
1964	WPG	4																													
2	Years	6																													
MIKE O'SHEA Michael LB 6'3 223 Guelph B: 9/21/1970 North Bay, ON Draft: 1-4 1993 EDM																															
1993	HAM	18	0		1	86	3.0	29.0																							
1994	HAM+	18				106			5	41	1																				
1995	HAM+	12				73			2	26	3																				
1996	TOR	8				34			2	24	1																	1	5	5.0	5
1997	TOR+	18	0	2	1	74	5.0	36.0	1	13	1																				
1998	TOR	18	0	1	0	83	6.0	58.0			1																				
1999	TOR*	18	0	5	0	97			3	8	3																	1	9	9.0	9
2000	HAM+	18	0	2	0	103	2.0	7.0			2																	1	1	1.0	1
2001	TOR	18	0	3	1	69	2.0	9.0			3																				
2002	TOR	18	0	2	1	95	1.0	10.0	3	70	1	6	1																		
2003	TOR	18	0	2	1	98	4.0	17.0	1	0	0																				
2004	TOR	18	0	4	2	98	2.0	11.0	3	81	5																				
2005	TOR	17	0	1	3	76					6																				
2006	TOR	18	0	1	1	73			2	26	0																				
2007	TOR	18	0	2	1	81	4.0	19.0			1																				
2008	TOR	18				74	1.0	9.0																							
16	Years	271	0	25	12	1320	30.0	205.0	22	289	29	6	1															3	15	5.0	9
JIM OSTENDARP James Elmore HB 5'8 178 Drexel; Bucknell B: 2/15/1923 Baltimore, MD D: 12/15/2005 Holyoke, MA Pro: N																															
1952	MTL	12										15	3					3													
ED OTTO Ed T																															
1948	HAM	5																													
VIC OTTO Vic T																															
1948	HAM	6																													
DAVID OUTLEY David DB 5'10 180 Louisiana-Monroe B: 3/15/1962																															
1985	OTT	1																													
DAVID OVERSTREET David Arthur RB 5'11 208 Oklahoma B: 9/20/1958 Big Sandy, TX D: 6/24/1984 Winona, TX Draft: 1-13 1981 MIA Pro: N																															
1981	MTL	15	15		1							54	9	203	952	4.7	37	8	48	356	7.4	26	1					9	185	20.6	29
1982	MTL	6	4		2									39	190	4.9	35	0	17	89	5.2	13	0								
2	Years	21	19		3							54	9	242	1142	4.7	37	8	65	445	6.8	26	1					9	185	20.6	29
BILL OVERTON William A. DB 6'2 226 McCook JC; Wake Forest B: 1947																															
1969	HAM	3							1	22																		1	0	0.0	0
KEN OWEN Kenneth Sam FB-HB-C 6'0 198 Georgia Tech B: 1935 Draft: 21-249 1957 WAS																															
1957	MTL	4										6	1	23	93	4.0	12	0	3	16	5.3	7	0					6	95	15.8	57
BUDDY OWENS Alton Leroy G 6'1 230 Michigan State B: 8/22/1944 Amherst, TX Draft: 16-138 1966 BOS																															
1967	BC	1																													
CHAD OWENS Chad Jas WR-SB 5'7 186 Hawaii B: 4/3/1982 Honolulu, HI Draft: 6A-185 2005 JAC Pro: N																															
2009	MTL	1				0													1	10	10.0	10	0	3	10	3.3	8	2	80	40.0	43
2010	TOR*	17	5	0	1	2						44	7	1	11	11.0	11	0	46	576	12.5	63	3	84	1060	12.6	90	53	1216	22.9	57
2011	TOR*	17	8	0	2	1						12	2	3	14	4.7	8	0	70	722	10.3	48	0	68	754	11.1	68	69	1750	25.4	91
3	Years	35	13	0	3	3						56	9	4	25	6.3	11	0	117	1308	11.2	63	3	155	1824	11.8	90	124	3046	24.6	91
DONDRE OWENS Dondre DB 5'9 170 Howard B: 7/10/1972 Baltimore, MD Pro: E																															
1994	CAL	4	0		1	4																									
1995	CAL	11				26			0	0	2																				
2	Years	15	0		1	30																									
JOHNNY OWENS John DE 6'5 255 Tennessee State B: 11/9/1953 Brownsville, TN Draft: 7B-200 1976 MIA																															
1976	CAL	4																													
ANTHONY OXLEY Anthony FB 5'11 195 St. Mary's (Nova Scotia) B: 7/24/1968 Halifax, NS Draft: SD- 1993 OTT																															
1994	OTT	4				2																									
MIKE OZARKO Mike T																															
1946	OTT	12										5	1																		
JIM PAAR Jim HB																															
1948	HAM	7										1	0																		
GAYLE PACE Gayle C 6'0 225 UCLA B: 12/30/1928 Salt Lake City, UT																															
1952	EDM	3							2	5																					
JIM PACE James Edward HB 6'0 200 Michigan B: 1/1/1936 Little Rock, AR D: 3/4/1983 Culver City, CA Draft: 1A-8 1958 SF Pro: N																															
1963	HAM	5										18	3	76	315	4.1	23	3	2	14	7.0	9	0					3	57	19.0	38
MARIO PACENTI Mario T-HB 6'2 240 Hamilton Jrs. B: 2/25/1930 Hamilton, ON																															
1951	MTL	11																													
1952	MTL	1																													
1952	HAM	1																													
1952	Year	2																													
1955	TOR	4																													
3	Years	16																													
BOB PAFFRATH Robert William FW-QB-HB-FB 5'8 190 Minnesota B: 7/3/1918 Mankato, MN D: 5/21/2005 Beaverton, OR Draft: 3-21 1941 GB Pro: A																															
1948	OTT+	12										40	8					7					1								
1949	OTT+	12																													
1950	EDM+	14										10	2	6	22	3.7		1	26	358	13.8		1								
1951	EDM+	14												1	1	1.0	1	0	26	407	15.7		0					7	90	12.9	
1952	EDM	9																													
5	Years	61										50	10	7	23	3.3	1	8	52	765	14.7		2					7	90	12.9	
FRED PAGAC Frederick TE 6'0 220 Ohio State B: 4/26/1952 Brownsville, PA Pro: NW																															
1977	OTT	1	0		1																							1	11	11.0	11
LEON PAGAC Leon OG 6'2 230 Tulsa B: 11/19/1940 Richeyville, PA																															
1964	WPG	10																													
LEFTY PAGE Lefty HB																															
1948	TOR	4																													
TED PAGE Ted DB 5'10 185 Compton JC B: 6/11/1942 North Bay, ON																															
1962	MTL	10																						6	46	7.7	13	1	13	13.0	13
1963	MTL	14																						53	307	5.8	20	5	36	7.2	10
1964	MTL	14	3		2				3	18		12	2						1	5	5.0	5	1	71	428	6.0	43	2	45	22.5	29
1965	HAM	14	0		2				4	108		6	1											24	164	6.8	24				
1966	HAM	14							2	12														3	14	4.7	6				
1967	HAM	14	2		3				2	28														74	370	5.0	19				
1968	HAM	14	0		1				2	0														22	117	5.3	15				
1969	HAM	13	1		1				4	75		6	1											18	87	4.8	23				
1970	HAM	14							2	15																					
1971	EDM	9			1				1	37														1	-2	-2.0	-2				
10	Years	130	6		10				20	293		24	4						1	5	5.0	5	1	272	1531	5.6	43	8	94	11.8	29
RONNIE PAGGETT Ron Carl DE 6'2 260 Louisiana Tech B: 1/1/1958 Jackson Parish, LA Pro: U																															
1980	CAL	14																													
1981	CAL	8					1.5																								
2	Years	22					1.5																								
JOE PAGLIEI Joseph Anthony HB 6'0 220 Clemson B: 4/12/1934 Clairton, PA Pro: N																															
1956	CAL	9	4		0				1	0		34	5	57	324	5.7	60	3	15	252	16.8	54	2					4	62	15.5	23
JOHN PAGLIO John Peter DT 6'2 235 Syracuse B: 8/27/1942 Cleveland, OH D: 5/5/1992 Euclid, OH Draft: 11-148 1964 BAL																															
1965	SAS	6																													

Year	Team	GP	FM	FF	FR	TK	SK	YDS	IR	YDS	PD	PTS	TD	RA	YDS	AVG	LG	TD	REC	YDS	AVG	LG	TD	PR	YDS	AVG	LG	KOR	YDS	AVG	LG
VERNON PAHL Vernon LB-FB 6'2 200 Prince Edward Island B: 2/19/1957 Montreal, QC Draft: 3B-21 1980 WPG																															
1980	WPG	13	0		1																							3	47	15.7	20
1981	WPG	15	0		1		4.0																					1	3	3.0	3
1982	WPG	16	0		1		5.5		1	15																					
1983	WPG	16	0		1		8.0																								
1984	WPG	16	1		1		2.5		4	41																					
1985	WPG	16	0		2																										
1986	WPG	18																													
1987	WPG	18			1	3						6	1	5	18	3.6	5	0	7	73	10.4	15	0								
1988	WPG	18				2								3	7	2.3	5	0	2	20	10.0	15	0					2	10	5.0	16
9	Years	146	1		8	5	20.0		5	56		6	1	8	25	3.1	5	0	9	93	10.3	15	0					6	60	10.0	20
ROY PAINTER Roy DB 6'1 185 Arkansas State B: 12/8/1953																															
1977	EDM	3							1	49																		1	9	9.0	9
NICK PAITHOUSKI Nick C 155 Queen's																															
1946	HAM	9																													
1947	HAM	5										5	1																		
2	Years	14										5	1																		
TONY PAJACZKOWSKI Tony OG-DE-DG-K 6'3 225 none B: 5/31/1936 Verdun, QC																															
1955	CAL	12	1		0																							1	0	0.0	0
1956	CAL	16																													
1957	CAL	16	1		1																							1	2	2.0	2
1958	CAL	16																													
1959	CAL	14																													
1960	CAL+	16	0		2																										
1961	CAL+	16			2																										
1962	CAL*	16	0		2																							1	0	0.0	0
1963	CAL*	16												1	2	2.0	2	0													
1964	CAL*	16	0		1																										
1965	CAL*	16	0		1																										
1966	MTL+	14	1		0																			1	0	0.0	0				
1967	MTL	14																													
13	Years	198	3		9									1	2	2.0	2	0						1	0	0.0	0	3	2	0.7	2
JOEY PAL Joey FW-S-WB 6'0 180 Concordia (Quebec) B: 8/2/1927 Hamilton, ON																															
1947	HAM	10										10	2					1													
1948	MTL	11																													
1950	MTL	11																													
1951	MTL	8										5	1										1								
1952	MTL	12										5	1										1								
1953	MTL	13										30	6										6								
1954	MTL+	14										30	6	2	28	14.0	24	0	36	681	18.9	63	6	66	488	7.4	23				
1955	MTL+	12							2	6		60	12						43	802	18.7	47	12	52	425	8.2	47	5	85	17.0	26
1956	MTL+	14										42	7						35	684	19.5	64	6	28	240	8.6	20	4	155	38.8	81
1957	MTL	11										12	2	1	6	6.0	6	0	13	281	21.6	43	2					2	30	15.0	18
10	Years	116							2	6		194	37	3	34	11.3	24	1	127	2448	19.3	64	34	146	1153	7.9	47	11	270	24.5	81
GREG PALAMOUNTAIN Gregory R. HB 5'11 195 California B: 5/20/1944 D: 7/21/2003 CA																															
1966	CAL	1																													
ERNIE PALANGO Ernie DB 6'2 190 Sheridan B: 12/18/1954																															
1975	HAM	12	1		0																			7	8	1.1	11				
JUSTIN PALARDY Justin K-P 5'11 200 St. Mary's (Nova Scotia) B: 5/24/1988 Truro, NS Draft: 5-36 2010 HAM																															
2010	HAM	5	3	0	0	1						2	0																		
2010	WPG	11				1						103	0																		
2010	Year	16	3	0	0	2						105	0																		
2011	WPG	18				1						165	0																		
2	Years	23	3	0	0	3						270	0																		
JOHN PALAZETI John LB-FB 6'1 215 Richmond B: 12/17/1952 Detroit, MI Draft: TE 1976 OTT																															
1976	OTT	16			1							12	2	15	57	3.8	14	1	4	32	8.0	19	1					1	7	7.0	7
1977	CAL	16	0		1														3	57	19.0	22	0					1	18	18.0	18
1978	CAL	16	0		1				3	31				13	54	4.2	25	0	6	58	9.7	18	0					4	72	18.0	30
1979	CAL	16												1	1	1.0	1	0										1	8	8.0	8
1980	CAL	16	0		3				1	56		6	1																		
1981	CAL	13							2	32																					
1982	MTL	16	0		2																							4	50	12.5	16
1983	CAL	3																													
1983	TOR	11												1	7	7.0	7	0	7	48	6.9	11	0					1	0	0.0	0
1983	Year	14												1	7	7.0	7	0	7	48	6.9	11	0					1	0	0.0	0
8	Years	112	0		8				6	119		18	3	30	119	4.0	25	1	20	195	9.8	22	1					12	155	12.9	30
MARTY PALAZETI Marty LB 6'1 215 Marshall B: 8/25/1962 Dearborn, MI Draft: 4-35 1985 OTT																															
1986	OTT	6																										1	14	14.0	14
1986	BC	1																													
1986	Year	7																										1	14	14.0	14
PETE PALIOTTI Peter WR 5'11 180 NDG Maple Leafs Jrs.; Concordia (Canada) B: 1950 Draft: 1B-5 1972 MTL																															
1972	MTL	1																													
PAUL PALMA Paul OT 6'3 273 Concordia (Canada) B: 5/1/1960 Toronto, ON Draft: 2-13 1983 HAM																															
1983	HAM	16																													
1984	HAM	10																													
1984	WPG	2																													
1984	Year	12																													
1985	CAL	6	0		1																										
3	Years	32	0		1																										
BILL PALMER Bill LB-DE-P 6'3 217 Bowling Green State B: 12/15/1952																															
1974	TOR	6																													
1974	OTT	4																													
1974	Year	10																													
1975	OTT	13																													
1976	CAL	16	0		1				1	0																		2	46	23.0	24
1977	CAL	16																										2	12	6.0	12
1978	WPG	6																													
1978	HAM	5	1		0																										
1978	Year	11	1		0																										
1979	TOR	9																													
6	Years	66	1		1				1	0																		4	58	14.5	24
BRIAN PALMER Brian LB-DB 5'10 182 Winnipeg Rods Jrs.; Kansas B: 1940 Winnipeg, MB																															
1963	WPG	16							1																						
1965	WPG	14							1					2	-4	-2.0	-2	0						1	8	8.0	8				
2	Years	30							2	0				2	-4	-2.0	-2	0						1	8	8.0	8				
GERRY PALMER Gerald B. DB 6'0 190 Toledo B: 1931 Toledo, OH																															
1952	WPG	13			2				3	56		30	6	35	154	4.4	29	1	16	330	20.6	71	5	7	80	11.4	21	5	110	22.0	27
1953	WPG	2																	2	15	7.5		0								
1954	BC	15	1						1	0														27	180	6.7	29	5	107	21.4	43
3	Years	30	1		2				4	56		30	6	35	154	4.4	29	1	18	345	19.2	71	5	34	260	7.6	29	10	217	21.7	43
KENSLEY PALMER Kensley RB 5'11 200 St. Vital Mustangs Jrs.; Manitoba B: 2/16/1967 St. Thomas, Jamaica																															
1991	OTT	14	0		1	12								10	53	5.3	9	0	6	53	8.8	15	0					1	2	2.0	2

Year	Team	GP	FM	FF	FR	TK	SK	YDS	IR	YDS	PD	PTS	TD	RA	YDS	AVG	LG	TD	REC	YDS	AVG	LG	TD	PR	YDS	AVG	LG	KOR	YDS	AVG	LG
1992	OTT	2	0		1	2																									
2	Years	16	0		2	14								10	53	5.3	9	0	6	53	8.8	15	0					1	2		2
MICHAEL PALMER Michael WR 5'10 190 Guelph B: 10/31/1980 Richmond, BC Draft: 6-48 2003 TOR																															
2003	TOR	18				5													6	68	11.3	20	0	2	11	5.5	7				
2004	TOR	16				2						6	1						15	166	11.1	29	1								
2005	TOR	18	0	0	1	3						6	1						17	179	10.5	31	1								
2006	TOR	9				0													13	129	9.9	17	0								
2007	TOR	8	2	0	1	2						6	1						6	76	12.7	16	1					1	0	0.0	0
2007	SAS	9				0													10	191	19.1	42	0								
2007	Year	17	2	0	1	2						6	1						16	267	16.7	42	1					1	0	0.0	0
2008	SAS	18	2	0	1	3													19	277	14.6	60	0								
6	Years	87	4	0	3	15						18	3						86	1086	12.6	60	3	2	11	5.5	7	1	0	0.0	0
PAUL PALMER Paul D. DB-QB 6'1 202 Michigan B: 1939																															
1960	HAM	12												1	7	7.0	7	0	1	6	6.0	6	0								
1961	HAM	14												1	0	0.0	0	0						9	52	5.8	13				
2	Years	26												2	7	3.5	7	0	1	6	6.0	6	0	9	52	5.8	13				
PAUL PALMER Paul Woodrow RB 5'9 181 Temple B: 10/14/1964 Bethesda, MD Draft: 1-19 1987 KC Pro: EN																															
1991	TOR	1												2	6	3.0	5	0										1	60	60.0	60
PETE PALMER Pete LB 6'0 212 Lenoir-Rhyne B: 9/26/1946 Toronto, ON																															
1970	WPG	1																													
1971	BC	16			2																							3	40	13.3	21
1972	BC	16	0		1				3	14									1	21	21.0	21	0					1	-1	-1.0	-1
1973	BC	15							1	4																					
1974	BC	16	0		4				1	0																					
1975	BC	14																													
6	Years	78	0		7				5	18									1	21	21.0	21	0					4	39	9.8	21
STEVE PALMER Stephen Lee C 6'3 220 UCLA B: 9/17/1934 Whittier, CA																															
1956	BC	13							1	27																					
GARY PALUMBIS Gary DT 6'1 275 Portland State B: 3/28/1963 Portland, OR																															
1987	EDM	6				2	2.0																								
1988	EDM	13			1	15	3.0																								
1989	OTT	15	0		1	28	5.0																								
3	Years	34	0		2	45	10.0																								
MIKE PALUMBO Mike OG-OT 6'2 270 Washington State B: 12/18/1961 Calgary, AB Draft: TE 1984 CAL																															
1985	CAL	7																													
1986	BC	6																													
1986	MTL	10	0		1																										
1986	Year	16	0		1																										
1987	CAL	7				0																									
1988	CAL	15			1	0																									
1989	CAL	18	1		2	0																									
1990	CAL	12	0		1	1																									
6	Years	65	1		5	1																									
TOM PALYGA Tom G 5'10 205 Regina Jrs. B: 1928																															
1949	SAS	5																													
CARLO PANARO Carlo OG-DL 6'2 280 Alberta B: 5/7/1977 Edmonton, AB Draft: 6-41 1999 SAS																															
2001	SAS	5				0																									
2003	EDM	18				1																									
2004	EDM	16				0																									
3	Years	39				1																									
MIKE PANASUK Michael P-K 5'11 215 Ferris State B: 12/1/1968 Southfield, MI Pro: X																															
2003	TOR	1				0						6	0																		
DON PANCIERA Donald Matthew QB 6'1 195 Boston College; San Francisco B: 6/23/1927 D: 2/9/2012 Westerly, RI Draft: 6-40 1949 NY-AAFC; 4-41 1949 PHI Pro: AN																															
1953	TOR	1																													
BOBBY PANDELIDIS Bobby OG 6'3 265 Eastern Michigan B: 5/4/1968 Laval, QC Draft: 3-23 1992 CAL																															
1994	CAL	18	0		1	3																									
1995	CAL	18				0																									
1996	WPG	18				1																									
3	Years	54	0		1	4																									
JOHN PANKRATZ John WR-SB 6'0 180 Vancouver Meralomas Jrs.; Simon Fraser B: 6/23/1957 Vancouver, BC Draft: TE 1980 BC																															
1980	BC	16	0		2							12	2						7	180	25.7	66	2								
1981	BC	14	0		1							30	0						19	279	14.7	36	5					1	0	0.0	0
1982	BC	16	1		0							38	6						40	683	17.1	66	6					2	0	0.0	0
1983	BC	16	1		1							42	7						63	961	15.3	79	7								
1984	BC	16	1		0							6	1						41	590	14.4	45	1								
1985	BC	16										24	4						58	632	10.9	29	4								
1986	BC	18										18	3						55	695	12.6	42	3								
1987	BC	18				0						12	2	1	10	10.0	10	0	61	720	11.8	43	2								
8	Years	130	3		4	0						182	25	1	10	10.0	10	0	344	4740	13.8	79	30					3	0	0.0	0
ROD PANTAGES Rod FB-HB-P-FW 5'11 200 Vancouver Blue Bombers Jrs. B: 1/24/1929 Vancouver, BC																															
1948	CAL	12										5	1																		
1949	CAL	14										26	5					3													
1950	MTL+	12										13	1					1													
1951	MTL	8										3	0																		
1952	EDM	16										23	3	52	277	5.3	50	3	4	91	22.8	34	0					1	20	20.0	20
1953	EDM	16										16	1	21	135	6.4		1	2	24	12.0		0								
1954	EDM	11	1		0							4	0	4	25	6.3	13	0													
1955	SAS	15	3		0							2	0	50	211	4.2	17	0	2	6	3.0	3	0								
1956	SAS	10										15	2	23	83	3.6	17	2	4	44	11.0	39	0								
9	Years	114	4		0							107	13	150	731	4.9	50	10	12	165	13.8	39	0					1	20	20.0	20
JOE PAOPAO Joseph QB 6'1 202 Mira Costa JC; Long Beach State B: 6/30/1955 Honolulu, HI																															
1978	BC	2																													
1979	BC	10	3		0									27	16	0.6	9	0													
1980	BC	10	3		0									22	57	2.6	13	0													
1981	BC	16	7		1									15	25	1.7	6	0													
1982	BC	14	1		0									5	7	1.4	2	0													
1983	BC	14	1		0									9	25	2.8	5	0													
1984	SAS	15	7		2							2	0	31	74	2.4	9	0													
1985	SAS	12	7		1							1	0	31	15	0.5	9	0													
1986	SAS	17	0		1									17	27	1.6	2	0	1	-11	-11.0	-11	0								
1987	OTT	13	2		0	1								17	81	4.8	15	0													
1990	BC	15	8		3	1						18	3	14	26	1.9	9	3													
11	Years	138	39		8	2						21	3	188	353	1.9	15	3	1	-11	-11.0	-11	0								
TYLER PAOPAO Tyler QB 6'0 200 Occidental B: 7/10/1980 Draft: 6-46 2002 OTT																															
2004	OTT	12				0																									
JIM PAPAI Jim OG 6'0 228 North Carolina B: 1949																															
1972	HAM	11																													
1972	EDM	1																													
1972	Year	12																													
STEVE PAPROSKI Steven Eugene G-T-C 6'0 245 North Dakota; Arizona B: 9/23/1928 Iwow, Poland D: 12/3/1993																															
1949	EDM	11																													
1951	EDM	14																													

Year	Team	GP	FM	FF	FR	TK	SK	YDS	IR	YDS	PD	PTS	TD	RA	YDS	AVG	LG	TD	REC	YDS	AVG	LG	TD	PR	YDS	AVG	LG	KOR	YDS	AVG	LG
1952	EDM	15																													
1953	EDM	9																													
1954	EDM	1																													
5	Years	50																													
DON PAQUETTE Don DE-OG 5'11 225 Hamilton Tiger-Cats B B: 1/23/1939																															
1958	HAM	4																													
1959	HAM	14																													
1960	HAM	6																											1	3	3.0	3
1961	MTL	14																													
1962	MTL	6																													
1963	MTL	14																													
1964	TOR	14	0		2				1	0																					
1965	CAL	4																													
1965	MTL	4																													
1965	Year	8																													
8	Years	76	0		2				1	0																			1	3	3.0	3
PETER PAQUETTE Peter DB 6'1 198 Iowa B: 6/26/1944 Iroquois Falls, ON																															
1968	MTL	14																											4	39	9.8	15
1969	MTL	14	0		1														1	17	17.0	17	0								
1971	TOR	14	2		0																			67	445	6.6	30				
1972	TOR	14	1		0				4	69														42	151	3.6	28	1	-2	-2.0	-2
1973	TOR	9																						10	50	5.0	8				
5	Years	65	3		1				4	69									1	17	17.0	17	0	119	646	5.4	30	5	37	7.4	15
RENE PAREDES Rene K 5'11 195 Concordia (Quebec) B: 5/15/1985 Caracas, Venezuela																															
2011	CAL	17	1	0	0	3						158	0																		
BOB PAREMORE Robert Cero OHB 5'11 190 Florida A&M B: 12/5/1939 Tallahassee, FL D: 7/22/2004 Tallahassee, FL Draft: 17-133 1963 DEN; 6-73 1963 STL Pro: N																															
1966	MTL	12	2		0							18	3	144	649	4.5	80	3	12	73	6.1	13	0					9	269	29.9	78
1967	CAL	10	2		0							18	3	26	84	3.2	18	0	14	341	24.4	68	3					5	95	19.0	31
1968	CAL	11	1		1							6	1	48	193	4.0	16	1	13	138	10.6	18	0					4	98	24.5	26
3	Years	33	5		1							42	7	218	926	4.2	80	4	39	552	14.2	68	3					18	462	25.7	78
MARC PARENTEAU Marc OG-C 6'5 300 Boston College B: 4/12/1980 Sherbrooke, ON Draft: 5-36 2003 OTT																															
2005	OTT	1				0																									
2005	WPG	1				0																									
2005	Year	2				0																									
2006	WPG	9				0																									
2007	SAS	18				0																									
2008	SAS	15	1	0	0	1																									
2009	SAS	18	0	0	2	2																									
2010	SAS	18	0	0	1	0													1	13	13.0	13	0								
2011	SAS	18	2	0	0	0																									
7	Years	97	3	0	3	3													1	13	13.0	13	0								
BABE PARILLI Vito QB 6'1 190 Kentucky B: 5/7/1929 Rochester, PA Draft: 1-4 1952 GB Pro: N																															
1959	OTT	6										7	0	4	20	5.0	15	0													
JOHN PARK John FB-TE 6'2 235 Bowling Green State B: 4/1/1958 Sarnia, ON Draft: TE 1981 OTT																															
1981	OTT	16	2		1									17	77	4.5	14	0	12	98	8.2	42	0					1	0	0.0	0
1982	OTT	14	1		1									5	8	1.6	8	0	1	15	15.0	15	0								
1983	OTT	4																													
1983	SAS	1										6	1	4	19	4.8	10	1													
1983	Year	5										6	1					1													
1984	SAS	4	0		1							6	1	4	31	7.8	14	0	1	-3	-3.0	-3	0								
1984	OTT	6												2	5	2.5	3	0	2	15	7.5	15	0					1	13	13.0	13
1984	Year	10	0		1							6	1	6	36	6.0	14	0	3	12	4.0	15	0					1	13	13.0	13
4	Years	38	3		3							12	2	32	140	4.4	14	1	16	125	7.8	42	0					2	13	6.5	13
ACE PARKER Ace HB 6'0 178 none																															
1948	SAS	3																													
ANTHONY PARKER Anthony Lawrence RB 6'0 207 Memphis B: 4/2/1961 Buffalo, NY Pro: U																															
1986	BC	5	2		1							12	2	76	340	4.5	23	2	16	110	6.9	19	0					2	26	13.0	15
1987	BC	14	5		1	1						12	2	157	635	4.0	27	1	29	356	12.3	77	1								
1988	BC+	18	6		6	0						36	6	142	851	6.0	56	5	39	429	11.0	43	1					3	35	11.7	19
1989	BC	15	6		0	0						36	6	104	595	5.7	23	4	45	454	10.1	56	2					4	61	15.3	22
1990	CAL	1	1		0	0								6	11	1.8	14	0	2	12	6.0	6	0								
5	Years	53	20		9	1						96	16	485	2432	5.0	56	12	131	1361	10.4	77	4					9	122	13.6	22
ANTHONY PARKER Anthony (Stoney) DT 6'3 214 Southern Mississippi B: 10/13/1955																															
1979	SAS	9	0		1																										
ANTHONY PARKER Anthony WR 6'0 210 Calgary B: 11/21/1989 Vancouver, BC Draft: 1-3 2011 CAL																															
2011	CAL	14				8			1	0	0			1	7	7.0	7	0	6	89	14.8	29	0	2	13	6.5	8	1	9	9.0	9
ARNOLD PARKER Arnold, Jr. DB 6'2 210 Utah B: 7/1/1981 Las Vegas, NV																															
2006	HAM	9				13																									
BILLY PARKER Billy DH-CB 6'0 195 William & Mary B: 5/17/1981 Mechanicsville, VA																															
2009	MTL	18	0	1	0	40			2	12	7																				
2010	MTL	18				53			2	15	13																				
2011	MTL	18	0	2	2	55			3	42	4																				
3	Years	54	0	3	2	148			7	69	24																				
BYRON PARKER Byron Wesley CB-DH 5'11 197 Tyler JC*; Tulane B: 3/7/1981 Madisonville, KY																															
2005	TOR	6				5						6	1						1	42	42.0	42	1	1	-8	-8.0	-8	5	116	23.2	40
2006	TOR	10				28			8	348	5	24	4																		
2007	TOR	18	0	0	1	34			6	143	10	24	4						1	27	27.0	27	1					2	31	15.5	17
2008	TOR	18				43			4	70	3													1	8	8.0	8	1	15	15.0	15
2009	TOR	2				1																		5	42	8.4	30				
2009	EDM	6				16			3	31	3													5	37	7.4	15	7	183	26.1	39
2009	Year	8				17			3	31	3													10	79	7.9	30	7	183	26.1	39
2010	TOR	15	0	2	1	35			2	50	5	6	1	1	9	9.0	9	0													
2011	TOR*	18	0	2	0	54			5	133	6	12	2											5	55	11.0	30	2	15	7.5	15
7	Years	87	0	4	2	216			28	775	32	72	12	1	9	9.0	9	0	2	69	34.5	42	2	17	134	7.9	30	17	360	21.2	40
CARL PARKER Carl Wayne SB-WR 6'2 201 Vanderbilt B: 2/5/1964 Columbus, GA Draft: 12-307 1988 CIN Pro: EN																															
1990	HAM	2	1		1	0						6	1						5	55	11.0	14	1	5	24	4.8	10	2	37	18.5	19
1993	SAC	17	0		1	6						30	5						46	684	14.9	43	5								
2	Years	19	1		2	6						36	6						51	739	14.5	43	6	5	24	4.8	10	2	37	18.5	19
CHARLIE PARKER Charlie Ruffing OG 6'0 246 Southern Mississippi B: 6/19/1941 Greenville, AL Draft: 13-97 1964 DEN; 13-176 1964 BAL Pro: N																															
1967	MTL	14	0		1																										
1968	MTL	14																													
1969	MTL	14	0		1																										
3	Years	42	0		2																										
ERVIN PARKER Ervin J. LB 6'5 236 South Carolina State B: 8/19/1958 Georgetown, SC Draft: 4-93 1980 BUF Pro: N																															
1987	HAM	1				3																									
EUROSIUS PARKER Eurosius CB 5'11 190 Jacksonville State B: 6/16/1976 Greenville, AL																															
1999	HAM	8				19																		26	335	12.9	47	10	193	19.3	36
JACKIE PARKER Jack Dickenson QB-OHB-S 6'0 185 Jones County JC; Mississippi State B: 8/3/1932 Knoxville, TN D: 11/7/2006 Edmonton, AB Draft: 27-326(di) 1953 DET; 17-196 1954 NYG																															
1954	EDM+	14	3		0				4	32		67	13	117	925	7.9	57	10	9	115	12.8	27	3	2	8	4.0	5	2	30	15.0	20
1955	EDM+	14										35	7	62	373	6.0	26	7													
1956	EDM+	16	7		2							66	10	92	583	6.3	39	10	2	21	10.5	12	0								

Year	Team	GP	FM	FF	FR	TK	SK	YDS	IR	YDS	PD	PTS	TD	RA	YDS	AVG	LG	TD	REC	YDS	AVG	LG	TD	PR	YDS	AVG	LG	KOR	YDS	AVG	LG
1957	EDM+	16	4		2				1	23		103	17	102	717	7.0	42	11	27	559	20.7	81	5					8	218	27.3	32
1958	EDM+	16	6						1	0		68	8	91	405	4.5	26	8	3	47	15.7	28	0					5	125	25.0	45
1959	EDM+	12							2	25		109	7	43	227	5.3	26	4	20	324	16.2	63	3	1	0	0.0	0				
1960	EDM+	16	5		3							107	10	109	668	6.1	29	8	10	216	21.6	50	2								
1961	EDM+	16	2									104	4	87	644	7.4	49	3	23	383	16.7	48	1	1	3	3.0	3				
1962	EDM	11	3									18	3	38	171	4.5	18	3	9	150	16.7	45	0								
1963	TOR	14										18	3	39	145	3.7	22	0	23	327	14.2	36	2								
1964	TOR	13	3		0							30	5	33	197	6.0	30	2	9	166	18.4	33	3								
1965	TOR	11	1		1				4	55		19	0	12	88	7.3	20	0						2	11	5.5	6				
1968	BC	8	1		0							6	1	29	67	2.3	11	1													
13	Years	177	35		8				12	135		750	88	854	5210	6.1	57	67	135	2308	17.1	81	19	6	22	3.7	6	15	373	24.9	45
JAMES PARKER James (Quick) DE-DT-LB 5'10 215 Wake Forest B: 1/1/1958 Philadelphia, PA																														
1980	EDM	7																												
1981	EDM*	16	0		1		18.5					6	1																	
1982	EDM*	16	1		1		17.5		1	5																				
1983	EDM*	16	0		1		15.0																							
1984	BC*	16	0		3		26.5																							
1985	BC*	16	0		2		12.0																							
1986	BC*	18	0		1		22.0																							
1987	BC	1					2	1.0																							
1988	BC	18	0		5	29	9.0					6	1																	
1989	BC	18					41	12.0																							
1990	TOR	18					33	6.0																							
1991	TOR	1					3																								
12	Years	161	1		14	108	139.5		1	5		12	2																	
KERRY PARKER Kerry Anthony CB 6'1 200 Grambling State B: 10/3/1955 New Orleans, LA Pro: N																														
1980	BC	1																												
1981	BC	12							2	0																				
1982	BC	16	0		2				3	37																				
1983	BC*	16	0		4				6	86		12	2											1	18	18.0	18				
1986	TOR	12	1		3				6	87		6	1																	
1987	TOR	2					10																								
1987	HAM	8	0		1	9			3	47														1	3	3.0	3				
1987	Year	10	0		1	19			3	47														1	3	3.0	3				
6	Years	59	1		10	19			20	257		18	3											2	21	10.5	18				
MARCUS PARKER Marcus Tabaris DT 6'2 273 New Mexico B: 5/18/1983 Dallas, TX																														
2007	CAL	1					2	1.0	6.0																						
2008	CAL	4					6																						1	14	14.0	14
2	Years	5					8	1.0	6.0																				1	14	14.0	14
RODNEY PARKER Rodney WR 6'1 190 Tennessee State B: 7/18/1953 Mobile, AL Draft: 6-152 1978 ATL Pro: NU																														
1978	SAS	5										12	2						15	349	23.3	52	2	12	119	9.9	24	8	218	27.3	55
1979	SAS	5	1		0														10	232	23.2	65	0	9	62	6.9	15	11	275	25.0	41
2	Years	10	1		0							12	2						25	581	23.2	65	2	21	181	8.6	24	19	493	25.9	55
SIRR PARKER Sirr Eluan RB 5'11 196 Texas A&M B: 10/31/1977 Los Angeles, CA Pro: N																														
2001	BC	2					0																		8	51	6.4	14	6	95	15.8	30
STEVE PARKER Steven Royce DE 6'4 250 Triton JC; Eastern Illinois B: 9/21/1958 Evanston, IL Pro: N																														
1981	HAM	4						0.5																							
1982	HAM	2						1.0																							
2	Years	6						1.5																							
LORNE PARKIN Lorne T-G 6'1 215 Oakwood Ints. B: 1920																														
1949	TOR	1																												
1950	TOR	9										5	1																	
1951	TOR	8																												
1952	TOR	11																												
1953	TOR	14																												
1954	TOR	10																												
1955	TOR	5																												
7	Years	58										5	1																	
JEREMY PARQUET Jeremy Michael OT 6'6 321 Southern Mississippi B: 4/11/1982 Norco, LA Draft: 7B-238 2005 KC Pro: ENU																														
2010	EDM	11	1	0	0	0																									
DOUG PARRISH Doug CB-SB 6'0 190 Taft JC; California; San Francisco State B: 2/25/1968 Tuscaloosa, AL Draft: 7-175 1991 NYJ																														
1991	EDM	5					12			2	27																		2	11	5.5	11
1992	EDM	10					23	1.0	2.0	1	0																				
1993	EDM	13	1		2	49	1.0	13.0	2	35		6	1											1	-1	-1.0	0	7	107	15.3	26
1994	SAC	3					5			1	10	0																			
4	Years	31	1		2	89	2.0	15.0	6	72	0	6	1											1	-1	-1.0	0	9	118	13.1	26
JERRY PARRISH Jerry WR 5'11 185 Eastern Kentucky B: 9/27/1959 Auburndale, FL Pro: U																														
1982	CAL	7	2		0									2	14	7.0	13	0	11	142	12.9	28	0					18	403	22.4	37
1983	MTL	6																	8	119	14.9	58	0								
2	Years	13	2		0									2	14	7.0	13	0	19	261	13.7	58	0					18	403	22.4	37
JOEL PARRISH Joel OG 6'3 256 Georgia B: 9/1/1955 Lowndes County, GA Draft: 11A-292 1977 CIN																														
1977	TOR	16	0		2																										
1978	TOR	6																												
2	Years	22	0		2																										
RONNIE PARSON Ron L. OE 6'4 230 Auburn; Austin Peay State B: 1944 Draft: RS-3-25 1966 OAK; 18-269(f) 1966 SF																														
1967	MTL	7	0		1							17	0																	
DALE PARSONS Dale C-LB 6'2 215 Regina Rams Jrs. B: 1934 Regina, SK																														
1957	SAS	14																												
1958	SAS	16																												
1959	SAS	5																												
1960	CAL	16	2		0																						1	0	0.0	0
1961	CAL	16			3							6	1																	
1962	CAL	16	0		2																										
1963	CAL	16	0		1																										
1964	CAL	15																												
1965	CAL	10																												
1966	CAL	16																									1	7	7.0	7
10	Years	140	2		6							6	1															2	7	3.5	7
PETER PARTCHENKO Peter OT 6'4 285 Michigan State B: 6/30/1970 Toronto, ON Draft: 6A-44 1992 TOR																														
1993	TOR	8					0																								
1994	OTT	2					0																								
2	Years	10					0																								
BOB PASCAL Robert HB 5'11 183 Duke B: 7/20/1934 Glen Ridge, NJ Draft: 3-33 1956 BAL																														
1956	MTL	14							4	58		48	8	57	278	4.9	18	4	13	222	17.1	66	3	1	3	3.0	3	4	66	16.5	19
DARRELL PASCO Darrell DH 6'0 170 Georgia Military JC; Georgia Southern B: 5/15/1987 Tampa, FL																														
2011	WPG	1	0	1	0	1																									
LUI PASSAGLIA Lui K-P 5'11 180 Simon Fraser B: 6/7/1954 Vancouver, BC Draft: 1B-5 1976 BC																														
1976	BC	16	1		0							130	1						1	10	10.0	10	1					1	44	44.0	44
1977	BC+	16	1		0							157	0																	
1978	BC	16	1		0							159	0																	
1979	BC*	16	1		0							144	0											1	2	2.0	2				
1980	BC+	16	2		0							147	0																	

Year	Team	GP	FM	FF	FR	TK	SK	YDS	IR	YDS	PD	PTS	TD	RA	YDS	AVG	LG	TD	REC	YDS	AVG	LG	TD	PR	YDS	AVG	LG	KOR	YDS	AVG	LG
1981	BC	16	1		0							144	0																			
1982	BC	16										134	0																			
1983	BC*	16	0		2							191	0																			
1984	BC*	16										167	0	1	1	1.0	1	0													
1985	BC	16										185	0	2	86	43.0	68	0													
1986	BC	15										166	0	2	18	9.0	15	0													
1987	BC	18	1		0	0						214	0																			
1988	BC	12				0						83	0	1	12	12.0	12	0													
1989	BC	18	2		0	0						175	0	2	38	19.0	25	0													
1990	BC	13	2		1	0						116	0	2	17	8.5	10	0													
1991	BC	18	1		0	3						210	0	1	-13	-13.0	-13	0													
1992	BC+	15	1		0	0						131	0	1	16	16.0	16	0													
1993	BC	17	1		0	1						176	0																			
1994	BC	14				2						137	0																			
1995	BC	18	2		0	0						194	0	2	33	16.5	18	0													
1996	BC	18	3		0	0						156	0	1	-2	-2.0	-2	0													
1997	BC	18				1						155	0																			
1998	BC+	18				3						197	0																			
1999	BC+	18	0	0	1	0						143	0																			
2000	BC*	18	3	0	0	0						180	1	1	1	1.0	1	1													
25	Years	408	23	0	5	10						3991	2	16	207	12.9	68	1	1	10	10.0	10	1	1	2	2.0	2	1	44	44.0	44
WALT PASSAGLIA Walter K-WR 5'11 183 Simon Fraser B: 1/11/1957 Vancouver, BC Draft: 3A-22 1979 WPG																																
1979	WPG	16										12	2						51	626	12.3	62	2								
1980	WPG	3																												
1981	MTL	3																												
3	Years	22										12	2						51	626	12.3	62	2								
TONY PASSANDER Tony QB 6'0 190 The Citadel B: 1949																																
1970	MTL	14	1		0							12	2	27	191	7.1	21	2													
AL PASSMAN Allan T-G 6'3 232 Manitoba B: 1923 D: 6//1984																																
1946	WPG	8																												
1947	WPG	8																												
1948	WPG	11																												
1949	WPG	7																												
1951	WPG	9																												
1952	WPG	14																												
1953	CAL	6																												
7	Years	63																												
DARIUS PASSMORE Darius WR 6'3 188 Sequoias JC; Marshall B: 4/7/1985 Florida City, FL																																
2010	BC	2				0														1	8	8.0	8	0								
DOUG PASSMORE Douglas G 5'10 170 B: 1924																																
1946	HAM	1																												
TOM PATE Tom LB 6'3 220 Nebraska B: 1952 D: 10/21/1975 Calgary, A																																
1975	HAM	12	0		1																									
HERB PATERRA Herbert E. LB 6'1 222 Michigan State B: 11/8/1940 Glassport, PA Draft: 18-140 1963 BUF Pro: N																																
1965	HAM	9								3	43																						
1966	HAM	14	0		1				1	18		6	1																			
1967	HAM	1																												
1968	HAM	2																												
4	Years	26	0		1				4	61		6	1																			
GORD PATERSON Gordon WR-TE-RB-DB 5'11 185 Manitoba B: 9/7/1950 Draft: 1-TE 1974 WPG																																
1974	WPG	13								1	21															49	365	7.4	32	2	31	15.5	19
1975	WPG	14	0		1				2	0		6	1	1	1	1.0	1	0	15	242	16.1	39	1	7	59	8.4	20	4	37	9.3	11
1976	WPG	16	1		0							32	5						41	541	13.2	31	5					4	23	5.8	14
1977	WPG+	16	1		1							30	5						67	882	13.2	58	5					2	19	9.5	19
1978	WPG	16	1		0							18	3						69	866	12.6	55	3								
1979	WPG	11	1		0							6	1						40	454	11.4	31	1								
1979	HAM	4										6	1						13	238	18.3	37	1								
1979	Year	15	1		0							12	2						53	692	13.1	37	2								
1980	HAM	1										12	2						6	88	14.7	33	2	1	2	2.0	2				
1981	HAM	16	1		0															20	283	14.2	29	0								
8	Years	103	5		2				3	21		110	18	1	1	1.0	1	0	271	3594	13.3	58	18	57	426	7.5	32	12	110	9.2	19
CHRIS PATRICK Chris OT 6'5 315 Nebraska B: 8/22/1984 Ashley, MI Pro: N																																
2011	EDM	11				1																									
GERRY PATRICK Gerald J. DE-OG 6'1 225 Illinois B: 1936																																
1961	TOR	13																												
1962	TOR*	11								1	0																						
1963	TOR	1																												
3	Years	25								1	0																						
GREG PATRICK Greg LB 6'0 215 Brown B: 6/12/1969 Canton, OH Pro: E																																
1994	HAM	4				5																									
1995	HAM	1	0		1	5																									
2	Years	5	0		1	10																									
JAMES PATRICK James S-CB-LB-DH 5'11 175 Stillman B: 6/4/1982 Tuskegee, AL																																
2008	SAS	17	0	0	2	16			2	47	1																		6	76	12.7	20
2009	SAS	18	0	1	1	76	1.0	2.0	2	11	6																				
2010	SAS*	18	0	0	1	75			9	195	0	6	1																			
2011	SAS	16	0	0	1	58	1.0	3.0	5	28	2																				
4	Years	69	0	1	5	225	2.0	5.0	18	281	9	6	1																6	76	12.7	20
STEVE PATRICK Stephen Clifford MG-OT-DT-OG 6'0 230 Winnipeg Light Infantry Jrs. B: 3/24/1932 Glenella, MB																																
1952	WPG	4																												
1953	WPG	16																										1	0	0.0	0
1954	WPG	14	0		2																									
1955	WPG	6																												
1956	WPG	16	0		2																									
1957	WPG	16	0		1							6	1																			
1958	WPG+	15																												
1959	WPG+	15																												
1960	WPG	16	0		3																									
1961	WPG	16																												
1962	WPG	16																												
1963	WPG	16	0		1																									
1964	WPG	6	0		1																									
13	Years	172	0		10							6	1																1	0	0.0	0
TERRANCE PATRICK Terrance DE-DT 6'5 262 Mercyhurst B: 7/7/1982 New York, NY																																
2005	CAL	13	0	1	0	23	2.0	11.0																							
2006	CAL	18	0	1	0	32	6.0	34.0			1																				
2007	CAL	18	0	1	2	41	5.0	47.0			1																		1	8	8.0	8
2008	HAM	17	0	0	1	37	3.0	20.0			4																				
4	Years	66	0	3	3	133	16.0	112.0			6																		1	8	8.0	8
BILL PATTEMORE Bill G-T																																
1948	CAL	1																												
ALONZO PATTERSON Alonzo RB 5'9 183 Wagner B: 4/30/1961																																

Year	Team	GP	FM	FF	FR	TK	SK	YDS	IR	YDS	PD	PTS	TD	RA	YDS	AVG	LG	TD	REC	YDS	AVG	LG	TD	PR	YDS	AVG	LG	KOR	YDS	AVG	LG
1983	TOR	2	2		1							6	1	12	47	3.9	11	1	3	26	8.7	10	0					2	23	11.5	23
DARRELL PATTERSON Darrell LB 6'3 230 Texas Christian B: 12/14/1961 Canonsburg, PA Draft: 6A-151 1983 NYG																															
1984	WPG	3	0		1		4.5																								
1985	WPG	16	0		4		7.0		2	68																					
1986	WPG	18					6.0		1	22																					
1987	WPG	12				47	8.0		1	41																					
1988	OTT	14				62	4.0																								
1988	HAM	4				29	1.0																								
1988	Year	18				91	5.0																								
1989	HAM	12	1		2	39	2.0																								
1990	HAM	13	0		1	82	1.0		1	5																					
7	Years	88	1		8	259	33.5	0.0	5	136																					
DeWAYNE PATTERSON DeWayne DE-DT-OT 6'1 250 Washington State B: 6/15/1972																															
1995	CAL	5	0		1	7						6	1																		
1996	CAL	2	0		1	1																									
1997	CAL	9	0	1	1	10	8.0	52.0			3																				
1998	SAS	17	0	0	1	37	11.0	69.0			1																				
4	Years	33	0	1	4	55	19.0	121.0			4	6	1																		
GABE PATTERSON Gabe HB-FB 190 Kentucky State																															
1947	SAS+	7										36	3					1					1								
1948	SAS+	10										32	2					1													
2	Years	17										68	5					2					1								
HAL PATTERSON Harold (Prince Hal) OE-DB 6'1 190 Garden City CC; Kansas B: 10/4/1932 Rozel, KS D: 11/21/2011 Kinsley, KS Draft: 14-165 1954 PHI																															
1954	MTL+	12							8	80		35	7	1	6	6.0	6	0	29	709	24.4	105	5	1	14	14.0	14	7	239	34.1	95
1955	MTL+	12							7	93		55	11						44	939	21.3	84	10	10	91	9.1	20	14	470	33.6	94
1956	MTL+	14							5	61		78	13	3	125	41.7	60	0	88	1914	21.8	109	12	2	48	24.0	20	28	771	27.5	105
1957	MTL+	13							4	45		78	13	31	268	8.6	22	4	45	919	20.4	88	7	0	35		16	24	648	27.0	54
1958	MTL+	8							2	36		6	1	17	237	13.9	42	1	18	252	14.0	63	0	1	47	47.0	36	11	291	26.5	37
1959	MTL	4							1	11		6	1	1	0	0.0	0	0	12	212	17.7	40	1	0	3		3				
1960	MTL+	14										42	7	6	23	3.8	9	0	61	1121	18.4	98	7					9	180	20.0	31
1961	HAM	8										18	3						20	452	22.6	65	3					12	272	22.7	38
1962	HAM*	12										36	6	1	4	4.0	4	0	39	881	22.6	95	6								
1963	HAM*	14										18	3						41	841	20.5	84	3								
1964	HAM*	14	0		1							36	6						31	657	21.2	86	6								
1965	HAM	4	1									6	1						3	75	25.0	50	1								
1966	HAM+	14										18	3						28	470	16.8	62	3								
1967	HAM	2																	1	31	31.0	31	0								
14	Years	145	1		1				27	326		432	75	60	663	11.1	60	5	460	9473	20.6	109	64	14	238	17.0	36	105	2871	27.3	105
IAN PATTERSON Ian DB 5'11 180 Central Florida B: 1/31/1965 Kingston, Jamaica																															
1990	OTT	5				12			1	0																					
JEFF PATTERSON Jeffery WR 5'11 170 Youngstown State B: 4/23/1961 Wheeling, WV																															
1983	MTL	16	1		0							30	5	1	5	5.0	5	0	43	531	12.3	41	5	37	503	13.6	49				
1984	MTL	11	1		0							6	1						16	215	13.4	41	1	51	437	8.6	67	1	21	21.0	21
1985	MTL	8										6	1	1	1	1.0	1	0	14	183	13.1	34	1	20	129	6.5	16				
1986	SAS	3																	3	48	16.0	20	0	7	45	6.4	10	3	56	18.7	20
4	Years	38	2		0							42	7	2	6	3.0	5	0	76	977	12.9	41	7	115	1114	9.7	67	4	77	19.3	21
LLOYD PATTERSON Lloyd QB 5'11 175 Memphis B: 5/26/1957																															
1979	SAS	9										6	1	21	109	5.2	15	1													
PAT PATTERSON Pat E Regina Jrs.																															
1946	SAS	5																													
PAUL PATTERSON Paul OT 6'5 255 Wilfrid Laurier B: 1947																															
1972	BC	14	0		1																										
ROOSEVELT PATTERSON Roosevelt OG 6'3 310 Alabama B: 7/12/1970 Mobile, AL Draft: 5-159 1994 LARI																															
1995	BIR	18				1																									
1996	HAM	8				0																									
1997	TOR	1				0																									
1997	MTL	2				1																									
1997	Year	3				1																									
3	Years	27				2																									
MARTIN PATTON Martin Baxter RB 6'1 205 Texas A&M-Kingsville B: 10/21/1970 Missouri City, TX																															
1994	SHR	14	3		1	5						54	9	143	659	4.6	39	8	24	210	8.8	21	1					3	33	11.0	16
1995	SHR	18	5		0	0						84	14	205	1040	5.1	53	12	25	280	11.2	61	2								
1996	WPG	1				0								6	35	5.8	7	0	6	54	9.0	14	0								
3	Years	33	8		1	5						138	23	354	1734	4.9	53	20	55	544	9.9	61	3					3	33	11.0	16
DOUG PAUL Doug T 5'10 195 B: 1917																															
1947	HAM	1																													
LEROY PAUL Leroy CB 5'10 185 Texas Southern B: 5/4/1957																															
1979	SAS	10	0		1				1	0														5	36	7.2	15				
1980	HAM	16	0		2				5	56																					
1981	HAM+	13	1		1				5	58		12	2															1	-10	-10.0	-10
1982	HAM	16	0		3				3	74																					
1983	TOR+	16	0		2				4	47		6	1																		
1984	TOR	2																													
1984	SAS	2																													
1984	OTT	2																													
1984	Year	4																													
6	Years	73	1		9				18	235		18	3											5	36	7.2	15	1	-10	-10.0	-10
SAM PAULESCU Samuel P 6'0 192 Fullerton JC; Oregon State B: 4/18/1984 Bell, CA Pro: N																															
2006	WPG	2				0																									
RICK PAULITSCH Rick FB 6'1 215 Alberta B: 10/7/1960 Draft: 6-54 1982 EDM																															
1983	WPG	1												1	15	15.0	15	0													
1984	OTT	2																													
2	Years	3												1	15	15.0	15	0													
SIG PAULSON Sigurdus (Ziggy) G 6'0 215 Weston Wildcats Jrs. B: 1933																															
1954	WPG	6																													
CORY PAUS Cory Robert QB 6'2 212 UCLA B: 4/4/1980 Hinsdale, IL																															
2003	CAL	4				0								2	4	2.0	2	0													
ROB PAVAN Rob LB 6'2 220 Guelph B: 12/18/1964 Guelph, ON Draft: 4-33 1987 WPG																															
1987	WPG	14				5																									
1988	OTT	8				1	1.0																								
2	Years	22				6	1.0	0.0																							
ROBERT PAVLOVIC Robert FB 6'4 255 South Carolina B: 11/1/1984 Mississauga, ON Draft: 4-25 2007 HAM																															
2008	HAM	18				3						12	2						3	21	7.0	16	2								
2009	HAM	16	0	0	1	0																									
2	Years	34	0	0	1	3						12	2						3	21	7.0	16	2								
MIKE PAWLAWSKI Michael Joseph QB 6'1 205 California B: 7/18/1969 Draft: 8B-222 1992 TB Pro: X																															
1995	SHR	10				0								5	24	4.8	15	0													
DAVE PAWLIK Dave LB 6'1 230 Memphis B: 9/29/1949 Buffalo, NY																															
1973	MTL	1																													
MARTIN PAWLIK Martin E																															
1946	SAS	6																													
RON PAWLOWSKI Ron C 6'2 215 Miami (Ohio) B: 1934																															

Year	Team	GP	FM	FF	FR	TK	SK	YDS	IR	YDS	PD	PTS	TD	RA	YDS	AVG	LG	TD	REC	YDS	AVG	LG	TD	PR	YDS	AVG	LG	KOR	YDS	AVG	LG
1957	OTT	14							1	6																					
BUDDY PAYNE Roland W., Jr. OE 6'3 210 North Carolina B: 3/16/1936 Elizabeth City, NC D: 11/19/2011 Dade City, FL Draft: 8-90 1958 WAS																															
1958	OTT	2										6	1						3	58	19.3	23	1								
DAN PAYNE Daniel OT-DT 6'7 290 Surrey Rams Jrs.; Simon Fraser B: 6/7/1966 Coquitlam, BC Draft: 2-9 1989 SAS																															
1989	SAS	7				0																									
1990	BC	3				0																									
1992	HAM	8				0																									
1993	SAS	18				3																									
1994	SAS	18	0		3	3																									
1995	SAS	18				1																									
1996	BC	4				0																									
1996	TOR	12	0		1	0																									
1996	Year	16				0																									
1997	TOR	18				1																									
1998	BC	18				1																									
1999	BC	18	0	0	1	2																									
2000	BC	18	0	0	1	2																									
2001	BC	17				0																									
2002	BC	18				1																									
2003	BC	18	0	0	1	1																									
14	Years	201	0	0	7	15																									
RODNEY PAYNE Rodney RB 6'0 195 Murray State B: 12/21/1965																															
1989	WPG	1	1		0									12	37	3.1	7	0	2	17	8.5	11	0					1	32	32.0	32
RONNY PAYNE Ron DE-OE-LB 6'2 220 Oklahoma B: 1940																															
1963	CAL	11	0		1				1										3	46	15.3	24	0								
1964	CAL	8	0		1																										
1965	CAL	3	0		1				1	0																					
1966	CAL	16	0		1				2	68		6	1						12	155	12.9	30	1								
1967	CAL	16			1																										
1968	CAL	16	0		3				1	15		12	2																		
1969	CAL	7																													
7	Years	77	0		8				5	83		18	3						15	201	13.4	30	1								
DOUG PAYTON Douglas Dwight OT-OG 6'4 255 Colorado B: 7/22/1952 Fort Knox, KY Draft: 6B-133 1975 ATL Pro: U																															
1978	MTL	15																													
1979	MTL	16																													
1980	MTL+	16																										1	0	0.0	0
1981	MTL+	15	0		1																										
1982	MTL+	13	0		1									0	8		8	0													
5	Years	75	0		2									0	8		8	0										1	0	0.0	0
EDDIE PAYTON Edward C. (Sweet P) RB 5'8 177 Jackson State B: 8/3/1951 Columbia, MS Pro: N																															
1979	TOR	2	1		0									15	51	3.4	12	0	3	24	8.0	9	0	3	27	9.0	11	3	84	28.0	32
ELFRID PAYTON Elfrid LB-DE 6'2 235 Grambling State B: 9/22/1967 Gretna, LA																															
1991	WPG	12	0		2	37	6.0		1	50																					
1992	WPG	9	0		1	27	6.0	43.0																							
1993	WPG*	18	0		2	29	22.0	150.0				6	1																		
1994	SHR	5				12																									
1994	BAL	11	0		4	27	4.0	30.0																							
1994	Year	16	0		4	39	4.0	30.0																							
1995	BAL+	18	0		4	40	18.0	144.0			7																				
1996	MTL	9				21	6.0	51.0			1																				
1997	MTL*	18	0	4	0	43	14.0	107.0			8																				
1998	MTL*	18	0	2	0	42	16.0	118.0			7																				
1999	MTL+	17	0	2	2	40	16.0	108.0			3	6	1																		
2000	WPG	16				41	8.0	36.0			5																				
2001	TOR*	18	0	2	4	41	15.0	96.0			3	6	1																		
2002	EDM*	18	0	4	3	48	16.0	87.0			3																				
2003	EDM	2				2	1.0	8.0																							
2004	WPG	16	0	4	3	35	5.0	38.0	1	18	0	6	1																		
14	Years	194	0	18	25	485	153.0	1016.0	2	68	37	24	4																		
JARRETT PAYTON Jarrett Walter RB 6'0 220 Miami (Florida) B: 12/26/1980 Arlington, IL Pro: EN																															
2007	MTL	13	4	0	1	0						54	9	163	852	5.2	35	8	17	118	6.9	15	1								
2009	TOR	8				0						1	0	3	10	3.3	7	0	7	37	5.3	8	0					1	13	13.0	13
2	Years	21	4	0	1	0						55	9	166	862	5.2	35	8	24	155	6.5	15	1					1	13	13.0	13
MICHAEL PAYTON Michael QB 6'1 220 Marshall B: 3/5/1970 Harrisburg, PA																															
1994	SAS	18				0																									
GREG PEACH Greg DE-LB 6'3 255 Eastern Washington B: 11/19/1986 Vancouver, WA																															
2009	EDM	16				46	6.0	39.0																							
2010	EDM	9	0	1	0	28	4.0	21.0			1																				
2011	EDM	12	0	1	1	25	3.0	7.0			1																				
3	Years	37	0	2	1	99	13.0	67.0			2																				
BOB PEARCE Robert Wayne WR-DB 5'10 186 Cisco JC; Texas-El Paso; Stephen F. Austin State B: 10/4/1946 Electra, TX Draft: 13-337 1970 MIN																															
1970	SAS	6	2		0							6	1	21	98	4.7	17	0	13	176	13.5	38	1					1	44	44.0	44
1971	SAS	8	0		1				2	33				8	36	4.5	10	0	2	15	7.5	9	0					6	187	31.2	33
1972	SAS	16	0		1							49	8	1	9	9.0	9	0	34	667	19.6	63	8								
1973	SAS	16										18	3	4	43	10.8	28	0	25	418	16.7	80	3					1	27	27.0	27
1974	SAS	10										12	2	1	1	1.0	1	0	8	174	21.8	57	2					5	212	42.4	63
1975	BC	7							1	11				1	3	3.0	3	0	5	75	15.0	27	0	8	49	6.1	14	5	128	25.6	38
1976	BC	1																						1	14	14.0	14				
7	Years	64	2		2				3	44		85	14	36	190	5.3	28	0	87	1525	17.5	80	14	9	63	7.0	14	18	598	33.2	63
KEITH PEARCE Keith Gordon DB-OE-FW-DE 6'2 185 Winnipeg Rods Jrs. B: 1928																															
1950	WPG	14										5	1						4	57	14.3		1								
1951	WPG	12										5	1						2	21	10.5		1								
1952	WPG	16										25	5	2	18	9.0	13	0	26	462	17.8	54	5								
1953	WPG	16																	5	63	12.6		0								
1954	WPG	14	0		2				5	54									2	2	1.0	2	0								
1955	WPG	15																													
1956	WPG	15	0		2				3	23														0	12		12				
1957	WPG	16							2	5									1	11	11.0	11	0					1	17	17.0	17
1958	WPG	10	1						2	17									3	50	16.7	19	0								
9	Years	128	1		4				12	99		35	7	2	18	9.0	13	0	43	666	15.5	54	7	0	12		12	1	17	17.0	17
MARK PEARCE Mark DL 6'7 285 Cape Breton B: 4/10/1967 Middlesex, England Draft: 1-6 1993 CAL Pro: E																															
1993	CAL	13				11	3.0	27.0																							
1994	CAL	9				6																									
1995	CAL	12				4																									
3	Years	34				21	3.0	27.0																							
MATT PEARCE Matt FB 6'2 205 British Columbia B: 4/22/1967 Cranbrook, BC Draft: 4-32 1989 WPG																															
1989	WPG	18	0		1	2								26	96	3.7	17	0	5	62	12.4	22	0	3	26	8.7	17	8	161	20.1	28
1990	WPG	18				1						6	1	10	38	3.8	7	0	10	137	13.7	57	1	9	56	6.2	13	8	94	11.8	22
1991	WPG	18	1		0	14								10	24	2.4	5	0	1	5	5.0	5	0	18	64	3.6	10	10	109	10.9	23
1992	WPG	18	3		0	10								1	8	8.0	8	0						15	60	4.0	13	3	15	5.0	10
1993	WPG	17				3						6	1	29	145	5.0	15	0	4	45	11.3	30	1	1	10	10.0	10	1	0	0.0	0
1994	WPG	18	1		0	2								6	38	6.3	21	0	2	16	8.0	12	0								

Year	Team	GP	FM	FF	FR	TK	SK	YDS	IR	YDS	PD	PTS	TD	RA	YDS	AVG	LG	TD	REC	YDS	AVG	LG	TD	PR	YDS	AVG	LG	KOR	YDS	AVG	LG
1995	WPG	15				3						6	1	4	56	14.0	44	1	4	11	2.8	9	0	3	8	2.7	8	1	14	14.0	14
7	Years	122	5		1	35						18	3	86	405	4.7	44	1	26	276	10.6	57	2	49	224	4.6	17	31	393	12.7	28
JEREMY PEARL Jeremy DB 6'3 210 North Texas B: 10/26/1980																															
2004	CAL	11				7					1																				
DAVID PEARSON David WR-SB 5'10 180 Toronto B: 10/22/1961 Mississauga, ON Draft: 5-45 1984 TOR																															
1986	TOR	5																													
DAVID PEARSON David LB 5'11 215 Western Ontario B: 11/12/1959 Draft: 4-28 1981 SAS																															
1982	WPG	16																													
MATT PEARSON Matthew DE 6'3 275 Baylor B: 9/11/1968 Baytown, TX																															
1994	BC	1				0																									
1995	SHR	4				5	1.0	8.0																							
2	Years	5				5	1.0	8.0																							
MIKE PEARSON Michael Wayne OT 6'7 305 Florida B: 8/22/1980 Tampa, FL Draft: 2-40 2002 JAC Pro: N																															
2007	TOR	9				0																									
PAUL PEARSON Paul WR-SB 6'0 180 British Columbia B: 6/15/1957 Campbell River, BC																															
1978	CAL	9																													
1979	SAS	2																													
1979	TOR	11										6	1						11	208	18.9	42	1								
1979	Year	13										6	1						11	208	18.9	42	1								
1980	TOR	16	2		1							6	1	16	86	5.4	21	0	19	267	14.1	34	1								
1981	TOR	16	1		1							12	2	2	1	0.5	2	0	55	796	14.5	38	2					1	18	18.0	18
1982	TOR	16	1		0							24	4	9	100	11.1	18	0	62	972	15.7	56	4								
1983	TOR	16	2		0							24	4	2	9	4.5	6	0	54	804	14.9	46	4								
1984	TOR+	16	1		1							30	5	6	32	5.3	11	0	71	910	12.8	42	5								
1985	TOR	14	0		1							18	3	4	29	7.3	21	0	58	649	11.2	71	3								
1986	TOR	18										36	6	2	10	5.0	7	0	49	693	14.1	37	6								
1987	TOR	13				0						12	2						45	568	12.6	29	2					1	0	0.0	0
10	Years	136	7		4	0						168	28	41	267	6.5	21	0	424	5867	13.8	71	28					2	18	9.0	18
TOMMY PEARSON Tom E 6'3 205 Oklahoma; Central Oklahoma B: 1936																															
1957	EDM	2	1		0														1	15	15.0	15	0								
DAVE PEAY Dave C North Carolina State																															
1947	OTT	11																													
TORCHY PECHET Harold B: 6/20/1929 Regina, SK D: 10/10/2010 Burnaby, BC																															
1948	WPG	1																													
ROY PECK Roy K. DT 6'2 240 East Central; Oklahoma State B: 1941																															
1965	SAS	1																													
JOE PEDICELLI Joe T 5'11 235 Montreal Lakeshore Alouette Flyers Ints. B: 2/7/1933 Montreal, QC																															
1954	MTL	3																													
DERREK PEELS Derrek J. RB 5'11 195 Santa Monica JC B: 9/5/1959 Los Angeles, CA																															
1981	OTT	1																										3	62	20.7	31
1985	HAM	3	3		0									26	37	1.4	9	0	8	33	4.1	8	0	3	21	7.0	13	4	86	21.5	25
2	Years	4	3		0									26	37	1.4	9	0	8	33	4.1	8	0	3	21	7.0	13	7	148	21.1	31
KEN PEEPLES Ken OG 6'2 245 Clemson B: 1/2/1952																															
1975	WPG	12																													
MIKE PEERMAN Mike LB-DT 6'2 237 Colorado B: 3/11/1957																															
1981	OTT	6					1.0																								
DAVE PEGG David K 5'11 179 Windsor B: 1/21/1951 Windsor, ON Draft: 1-SD1 1976 BC																															
1977	HAM	4										16	0																		
RAY PELFREY Raymond Harrison E 6'0 187 Auburn; Eastern Kentucky B: 1/11/1928 Sardinia, OH Draft: 17-197 1951 GB Pro: N																															
1954	WPG	11	2		0				1	0		1	0	3	23	7.7	16	0	11	113	10.3	25	0	1	15	15.0	15				
BOB PELLING Bob FL-FW 6'1 187 Regina Jrs. B: 1927																															
1947	SAS	7																													
1948	SAS	12																													
1949	SAS	14																													
1950	SAS	14										5	1						9	188	20.9		1								
1951	SAS	14										15	3	4	-2	-0.5		0	10	215	21.5		3								
1952	SAS	15			1				4	26		10	2	1	9	9.0	9	0	8	135	16.9	30	2	3	3	1.0	2				
1953	SAS	1																													
7	Years	77			1				4	26		30	6	5	7	1.4	9	0	27	538	19.9	30	6	3	3	1.0	2				
STEVE PELLUER Steven Carl QB 6'4 210 Washington B: 7/29/1962 Yakima, WA Draft: 5A-113 1984 DAL; 6A-111 1984 OAK-USFL Pro: EN																															
1995	WPG	7				0																									
J.C. PELUSI Jay Charles DE 6'1 245 Pittsburgh B: 12/16/1960 Youngstown, OH Draft: 16-185 1983 PHI-USFL																															
1983	SAS	8					1.0																								
NUYGEN PENDLETON Nuygen CB 5'8 160 Fullerton State B: 5/12/1967 Quincy, FL																															
1992	EDM	1				5																									
DARRELL PENNER Darrell DB 6'0 190 Queen's B: 8/27/1953 Draft: 3-27 1976 EDM																															
1978	TOR	2																													
1978	WPG	4	0		1																										
1978	Year	6	0		1																										
JOHNNY PENNOCK Johnny G none																															
1946	SAS	7																													
CARLOS PENNYWELL Carlos Jerome WR 6'2 180 Grambling State B: 3/18/1956 Crowley, LA Draft: 3-77 1978 NE Pro: N																															
1982	WPG	2																	5	79	15.8	20	0								
JOHN PENTECOST John Mathew OT-OG 6'2 250 Santa Ana JC; UCLA B: 12/23/1943 Lawndale, CA Pro: N																															
1965	OTT+	14																													
1968	WPG	11																													
1969	WPG	12																													
3	Years	37																													
SAM PEOPLES Sam CB 5'11 180 Portland State B: 1/14/1971																															
1995	BIR	8	0		3	13	15.0	90.0				6	1																		
SHONT'E PEOPLES Shont'e LB-DE 6'2 249 Michigan B: 8/30/1972 Saginaw, MI																															
1994	LV	16	0		5	29	14.0	105.0			3																				
1995	BIR	18	0		2	41					1	6	1																		
1997	WPG*	13	0	1	1	67	13.0	114.0			2																				
1998	WPG	1				3																									
1998	CAL	1				4	1.0	3.0																							
1998	Year	2				7	1.0	3.0																							
2000	CAL*	18	0	3	3	43	12.0	92.0	1	55	1	6	1																		
2001	SAS+	18	1	6	4	39	12.0	83.0			3																				
2002	SAS	14	0	2	1	26	2.0	19.0			10																				
2003	SAS	17	0	2	2	43	8.0	46.0			4																				
8	Years	115	1	14	18	295	62.0	462.0	1	55	24	12	2																		
BOB PEPE Bob E 6'2 225 North Carolina State B: 1937 Draft: 10-118 1959 NYG																															
1959	OTT	3																													
RENSO PERDONI Renso G. (Rock) DT 5'11 238 Ferrum JC; Georgia Tech B: 1948 Italy																															
1971	HAM	7																													
1971	WPG	4	0		1																										
1971	Year	11																													
1972	EDM	5																													
1972	SAS	5	0		1																										
1972	Year	10	0		1																										
1973	SAS	11	0		1																										

Year	Team	GP	FM	FF	FR	TK	SK	YDS	IR	YDS	PD	PTS	TD	RA	YDS	AVG	LG	TD	REC	YDS	AVG	LG	TD	PR	YDS	AVG	LG	KOR	YDS	AVG	LG
3	Years	23	0		3																										
ROGER PERDRIX Roger OG 6'1 225 Cincinnati B: 6/17/1943 Boston, MA																															
1966	OTT	14																													
1967	OTT*	14	0		1																										
1968	OTT	10																													
1969	OTT	14																													
1970	OTT	11																													
1971	OTT	14																													
1972	OTT	14																													
1973	OTT	13																													
1974	OTT	16	0		1																							2	33	16.5	18
9	Years	120	0		2																							2	33	16.5	18
TONY PEREA Tony LB 6'0 225 Texas-El Paso B: 4/15/1951																															
1975	HAM	5	0		2							6	1																		
CHRIS PEREZ Christopher James OT 6'5 285 Kansas B: 6/21/1969 Park Ridge, IL Draft: 5-124 1992 MIA Pro: EX																															
1995	MEM	18				1																									
1996	TOR*	18				0																									
1997	WPG	18				2																									
1998	WPG+	18	0	0	1	2																									
1999	WPG	18				2																									
2000	BC*	18				0																									
6	Years	108	0	0	1	7																									
GREG PEREZ Gregory (Gig) DB 5'11 185 Miami (Florida) B: 8/21/1948 Huntington Park, CA																															
1970	CAL	16							6	69														14	60	4.3	14	9	217	24.1	33
1971	HAM	6	0		2				1	31		6	1											1	-6	-6.0	-6				
1971	SAS	4																						1	9	9.0	9				
1971	Year	10	0		2				1	31		6	1											2	3	1.5	9				
1972	SAS	1																													
3	Years	23	0		2				7	100		6	1											16	63	3.9	14	9	217	24.1	33
ART PERKINS Arthur Ray FB 6'0 233 North Texas B: 5/1/1940 Fort Worth, TX Draft: 18-143 1962 HOU; 4-44 1962 LARM Pro: N																															
1964	WPG	9	3		0							36	6	81	287	3.5	10	5	8	72	9.0	19	1					2	17	8.5	11
1965	WPG	16	2		1							60	10	159	679	4.3	28	5	17	263	15.5	51	5								
1966	WPG	16	2		0							30	5	144	706	4.9	24	4	29	357	12.3	37	1					1	19	19.0	19
1967	EDM	16	1		0							24	4	137	602	4.4	21	4	29	317	10.9	66	0								
1968	EDM	10										24	4	110	500	4.5	23	3	18	153	8.5	47	1								
1969	EDM	7												50	187	3.7	19	0	23	224	9.7	24	0								
6	Years	74	8		1							174	29	681	2961	4.3	28	21	124	1386	11.2	66	8					3	36	12.0	19
BRUCE PERKINS Bruce Kerry FB 6'2 230 Butler CC; Arizona State B: 8/14/1967 Waterloo, IA Pro: N																															
1993	HAM	14	4		2	4						18	3	173	812	4.7	52	3	20	112	5.6	21	0					1	24	24.0	24
1994	HAM	4	1		0	2								26	89	3.4	12	0	9	19	2.1	5	0								
1995	MEM	18	3		1	12						12	2	76	271	3.6	23	2	47	443	9.4	20	0					1	27	27.0	27
3	Years	36	8		3	18						30	5	275	1172	4.3	52	5	76	574	7.6	21	0					2	51	25.5	27
HORACE PERKINS Horace Alonza, Jr. CB 5'11 180 Colorado B: 3/15/1954 El Campo, TX Draft: 8-207 1977 MIA Pro: N																															
1978	SAS	4																													
KEN PERKINS Kenneth DT 6'5 260 Texas A&M-Kingsville B: 1943																															
1966	EDM	4																													
NICO PERKINS Allen LB 6'0 208 Memphis B: 3/27/1967																															
1990	BC	2				4			1	2																					
1991	BC	3	0		1	9	1.0																								
2	Years	5	0		1	13	1.0		1	2																					
TOM PERKO Thomas Patrick LB 6'3 233 Pittsburgh B: 6/17/1954 Steubenville, OH D: 2/2/1980 Ambridge, PA Draft: 4-101 1976 GB Pro: N																															
1977	HAM	2																													
1978	HAM	4																													
2	Years	6																													
RON PEROWNE Ron WR-DB 5'10 180 Bishop's B: 2/5/1950 Montreal, QC Draft: 5-40 1972 OTT																															
1972	MTL	14	1		0														9	122	13.6	27	0	41	180	4.4	18	1	-3	-3.0	-3
1973	MTL	12	2		0				2	75														52	278	5.3	44				
1974	MTL	4																						25	100	4.0	19				
3	Years	30	3		0				2	75									9	122	13.6	27	0	118	558	4.7	44	1	-3	-3.0	-3
MARK PERRELLI Mark A. OT 6'4 255 Oklahoma State B: 1/24/1954																															
1977	HAM	1																													
1978	OTT	5																													
2	Years	6																													
JEFF PERRETT Jeff OT 6'7 320 Tulsa B: 3/23/1984 Taber, AB Draft: 3-24 2006 MTL																															
2007	MTL	8				0																									
2008	MTL	18	1	0	0	2								1	11	11.0	11	0													
2009	MTL	18	0	0	0	2																									
2010	MTL	17				3																									
2011	MTL	18				2																									
5	Years	79	1	0	0	9								1	11	11.0	11	0													
JOE PERRI Joe K 5'10 175 Concordia (Quebec) B: 5/8/1954 Draft: 1-SD2 1976 HAM																															
1976	HAM	3										6	0																		
KESLEY PERRIN Kesley S 5'10 190 Kent State B: 12/28/1975 Hamilton, ON																															
1997	WPG	11	0	0	1	12						6	1																		
BOBBY PERRY Bobby CB-LB 6'2 200 Prairie View A&M B: 4/4/1980 Miami, FL																															
2003	SAS	15	1	0	0	20					1																				
2004	SAS	2				3																									
2	Years	17	1	0	0	23					1																				
FRED PERRY Frederick Dewayne DE-LB 6'3 215 Northeast Oklahoma A&M JC; Southern Arkansas B: 1/5/1975 Fort Smith, AR Pro: X																															
1999	TOR	16	0	1	3	39	7.0	70.0																							
2000	TOR	15	0	5	2	48	4.0	17.0			4	6	1																		
2001	EDM	10	0	3	1	38	5.0	28.0			3																				
2003	OTT	15	0	1	0	34	7.0	54.0			3																				
2005	SAS	12	0	1	0	52	11.0	82.0			3																				
2006	SAS*	18	0	3	2	47	14.0	115.0	1	29	10	6	1																		
2007	SAS+	18	0	0	3	70	8.0	57.0			7																				
2008	EDM	7	0	1	1	17	1.0	9.0			1																				
2009	WPG	8	0	1	0	16	5.0	29.0			2																				
9	Years	119	0	16	12	361	62.0	461.0	1	29	33	12	2																		
GORD PERRY Gordon G-C-T-E 5'11 194 Regina Dales Jrs. B: 1921																															
1946	SAS	6																													
1947	WPG	8																													
1948	WPG	12																													
1949	WPG	14																													
1950	SAS	8																	2	33	16.5		0								
5	Years	48																	2	33	16.5		0								
JARVIS PERRY Jarvis RB 5'11 205 Rowan B: 2/3/1969 Camden, NJ																															
1995	MEM	4	1		0	7								8	19	2.4	6	0	1	5	5.0	5	0								
MARIO PERRY Mario LB 6'2 230 Massachusetts B: 7/28/1971 Albany, NY																															
1994	SHR	16	1		1	58	1.0	8.0	2	38																		1	3	3.0	3
1995	SHR	11	1		1	32	1.0	8.0	1	6	1	6	1																		
2	Years	27	2		2	90	2.0	16.0	3	44	1	6	1																		1	3	3.0	3

Year	Team	GP	FM	FF	FR	TK	SK	YDS	IR	YDS	PD	PTS	TD	RA	YDS	AVG	LG	TD	REC	YDS	AVG	LG	TD	PR	YDS	AVG	LG	KOR	YDS	AVG	LG
REGGIE PERRY Reginald Eugene FB-SB 6'2 205 Southern California B: 9/23/1970 Denison, TX																															
1994	BAL	5				4													7	155	22.1	79	0								
1995	BAL	14				4						12	2						25	402	16.1	35	2								
2	Years	19				8						12	2						32	557	17.4	79	2								
RON PERRY Ronald LB 6'1 226 Grambling State B: 2/28/1970 Columbus, OH																															
1994	SHR	10	0		1	40																									
1995	SHR	9	1		1	27																									
2	Years	19	1		2	67																									
VERNON PERRY Vernon, Jr. DB 6'2 211 Jackson State B: 9/22/1953 Jackson, MS Pro: N																															
1977	MTL	16							9	224		6	1																		
1978	MTL	4																													
2	Years	20							9	224		6	1																		
RAY PERRYMAN Raymond E. DB 5'11 198 Northern Arizona B: 11/27/1978 Phoenix, AZ Draft: 5-158 2001 OAK Pro: EN																															
2007	EDM	7				27	2.0	16.0	0	0	2																				
PETE PETCOFF Peter DE 6'0 208 Hamilton Jrs. B: 1932																															
1953	CAL	9																													
1955	OTT	12																										1	5	5.0	5
2	Years	21																										1	5	5.0	5
ANDY PETEK Andy LB 6'2 230 Montana B: 9/16/1978 Helena, MT																															
2005	HAM	1				2	1.0	1.0																							
DOUG PETERS Douglas Roy B 6'1 205 West Contra Costa JC; UCLA B: 10/23/1934 New Orleans, LA Draft: 29-338 1956 DET																															
1956	BC	5												20	78	3.9	15	0													
TERRY PETERS Terry DB 5'11 178 Independence JC; Oklahoma B: 4/26/1955 Pauls Valley, OK																															
1978	MTL	3																										1	26	26.0	26
DOUG PETERSEN Doug DE 6'5 290 Simon Fraser B: 11/28/1969 Charlie Lake, BC Draft: 2-13 1992 BC																															
1994	BC	7				3																									
1995	BC	18				16	6.0	50.0																				2	0	0.0	0
1996	MTL	18	0		2	51	7.0	44.0			1																				
1997	MTL*	18	0	1	2	44	4.0	22.0			3																				
1998	MTL+	18	0	1	0	55	6.0	52.0																							
1999	EDM+	15	0	1	2	51	5.0	39.0	1	61	2	6	1																		
2000	EDM	11	0	0	1	18	2.0	4.0																							
2001	EDM+	18	0	0	3	56	5.0	35.0			2																				
2002	EDM	11				6	1.0																								
9	Years	134	0	3	10	300	36.0	246.0	1	61	8	6	1															2	0	0.0	0
KEN PETERSEN Thornton Kenneth OT-DE 6'2 235 Utah B: 3/26/1939 Logan, UT Draft: 10-74 1961 OAK; 14-183 1961 MIN Pro: N																															
1963	EDM	16																													
1964	EDM	4																													
2	Years	20																													
BOB PETERSON Bob OG 6'1 235 Hastings B: 4/15/1942 Alma, NE																															
1968	TOR	5																													
CHARLIE PETERSON William Charles QB 6'2 194 Brigham Young B: 5/16/1977 San Jose, CA																															
2005	TOR	18	1	0	0	0								6	48	8.0	22	0													
DeVONTE PETERSON DeVonte Abdul DE 6'2 275 Catawba B: 4/1/1978 Fort Bragg, NC Pro: E																															
2004	HAM	6	0	1	0	8																									
2005	HAM	18	0	1	2	35	4.0	44.0			2																				
2006	HAM	12	0	0	1	18	3.0																								
3	Years	36	0	2	3	61	7.0	44.0			2																				
GREG PETERSON Gregory S 5'10 175 Brigham Young B: 2/18/1960 Calgary, AB Draft: TE 1982 CAL																															
1984	CAL	14	0		1																			9	63	7.0	19				
1985	CAL	16	0		1		1.0																								
1986	CAL	17	0		2		2.0		2	38														5	27	5.4	12				
1987	CAL	18	1		0	81	2.0		4	45																					
1988	CAL	17			2	50			2	36																					
1989	CAL	17	0		1	45			3	58																					
1990	CAL*	18	0		1	58			5	140		6	1											1	-1	-1.0	-1				
1991	CAL	17				48			4	101		6	1																		
1992	CAL	15				23	1.0		2	3																					
9	Years	149	1		8	305	6.0		22	421		12	2											15	89	5.9	19				
JEROME PETERSON Jerome J. CB 5'9 180 Northern Iowa B: 4/28/1976 Oakland, CA																															
2000	EDM	11				23			1	12	1													1	10	10.0	10	8	177	22.1	29
2001	EDM	1				0																									
2002	EDM	12				24			3	81	2	6	1																		
3	Years	24				47			4	93	3	6	1											1	10	10.0	10	8	177	22.1	29
KAMAU PETERSON Kamau Seitu WR-SB 6'0 192 New Hampshire B: 9/16/1978 Los Angeles, CA Draft: 1-6 2001 CAL																															
2001	CAL	18	2	0	0	8						6	1	3	-4	-1.3	-1	0	37	465	12.6	46	1								
2002	CAL	18	3	0	0	2						38	6	2	13	6.5	10	0	62	931	15.0	48	6					1	0	0.0	0
2003	CAL	8				0						6	1	1	1	1.0	1	0	28	354	12.6	42	1					6	100	16.7	26
2004	WPG	16	1	1	2	7						24	4	1	-2	-2.0	-2	0	50	637	12.7	45	4								
2005	WPG	7				4													15	218	14.5	61	0								
2005	HAM	12	1	0	0	0						18	3						27	332	12.3	44	3					1	2	2.0	2
2005	Year	19	1	0	0	4						18	3						42	550	13.1	61	3								
2006	HAM	16				2						6	1						51	567	11.1	41	1								
2007	EDM	18	2	0	0	2						42	7	1	-1	-1.0	-1	0	80	1068	13.4	64	7								
2008	EDM+	18	3	0	0	4						24	4	1	13	13.0	13	0	101	1317	13.0	66	4								
2009	EDM	18	2	0	0	2						8	1						63	788	12.5	63	1								
2010	EDM	4				0													8	66	8.3	11	0								
2011	BC	6				0						6	1						12	136	11.3	22	1								
11	Years	147	14	1	2	31						178	29	9	20	2.2	13	0	534	6879	12.9	66	29					8	102	12.8	26
PAUL PETERSON Paul HB-FW 5'8 180 B: 1922																															
1946	HAM	6																													
1948	HAM	12										5	1					1													
1949	HAM	5																													
3	Years	23										5	1					1													
PAUL PETERSON Paul QB 6'0 190 Boston College B: 7/29/1980 Allentown, PA																															
2005	OTT	7				0																									
GIL PETMANIS Elgis DH-OE-FL 6'0 179 Oakville Black Knights Srs. [OSFL] B: 4/2/1942 Riga, Latvia																															
1966	SAS	11	1		0																			13	63	4.8	17				
1968	TOR	14							1	-5														6	31	5.2	10				
1970	TOR	4																										1	21	21.0	21
3	Years	29	1		0				1	-5														19	94	4.9	17	1	21	21.0	21
BOB PETRICH Robert Mark DE 6'4 253 Los Angeles Valley JC; West Texas A&M B: 3/15/1941 Long Beach, CA Draft: 11-82 1963 SD; 6-82 1963 NYG Pro: N																															
1968	TOR	7																													
TIM PETROS Tim FB 5'10 180 Calgary B: 9/12/1961 Calgary, AB Draft: 5-42 1983 CAL																															
1984	CAL	16												22	71	3.2	10	0	10	83	8.3	19	0								
1985	CAL	16												1	2	2.0	2	0													
1986	CAL	16	2		2									74	348	4.7	35	0	23	172	7.5	14	0					1	6	6.0	6
1987	CAL	16	2		0	1						30	5	95	467	4.9	39	5	34	260	7.6	27	0								
1988	CAL	18	3		4	1						54	9	161	737	4.6	74	9	49	304	6.2	15	0								
1989	CAL	17	5		1	1						24	4	133	605	4.5	28	4	25	188	7.5	21	0								
1990	CAL	1				0								2	-2	-1.0	-1	0													
7	Years	100	12		7	3						108	18	488	2228	4.6	74	18	141	1007	7.1	27	0					1	6	6.0	6

Year	Team	GP	FM	FF	FR	TK	SK	YDS	IR	YDS	PD	PTS	TD	RA	YDS	AVG	LG	TD	REC	YDS	AVG	LG	TD	PR	YDS	AVG	LG	KOR	YDS	AVG	LG
GEORGE PETROVAS George LB 6'0 210 British Columbia B: 11/18/1966 Vancouver, BC																															
1990	BC	2				0																									
BILL PETROW Bill E 5'9 175 Norwood-St. Boniface Ints.; Ukrainian Vets B: 1927																															
1951	CAL	6																						1	4	4.0	4				
PETE PETROW Peter QB 5'9 165 Norwood-St. Boniface Ints.; Peterborough Ofuns Ints. B: 1926																															
1949	WPG	2																													
1950	WPG	14												10	26	2.6		0													
1951	WPG	14												11	-61	-5.5		0													
3	Years	30												21	-35	-1.7	0	0													
TONY PETRUCCIO Anthony Giacomo DE 6'4 245 Penn State B: 5/15/1957 Levittown, PA Draft: 10A-265 1979 SD																															
1979	MTL	6																													
1980	SAS	11																													
2	Years	17																													
STAN PETRY Stanley Edward CB 5'11 174 Texas Christian B: 8/14/1966 Alvin, TX Draft: 4-88 1989 KC Pro: N																															
1994	BAL	8				11	1.0	1.0																36	346	9.6	41	9	164	18.2	29
DAN PETSCHENIG Dan OT-OG 6'5 265 Carleton B: 8/19/1963 Ottawa, ON Draft: 5-42 1985 TOR																															
1985	TOR	5																													
1986	TOR	18	0		1																										
1987	TOR	4				0																									
3	Years	27	0		1	0																									
LEIF PETTERSEN Leif WR-P 6'2 183 Otterbein B: 12/23/1950 D: 7/30/2008 Draft: 2-15 1974 SAS																															
1974	SAS	16	4		0							18	3						15	237	15.8	31	3	51	269	5.3	21	1	0	0.0	0
1975	SAS	16							1	20		6	1						13	204	15.7	33	1	4	42	10.5	15				
1976	SAS	16										18	3						10	161	16.1	37	3	2	-5	-2.5	4	1	0	0.0	0
1977	SAS	4	1		1														12	134	11.2	17	0								
1978	HAM	16	0		1							3	0						41	557	13.6	38	0					1	0	0.0	0
1979	HAM+	16	1		1							26	4						56	838	15.0	52	4	4	48	12.0	18	1	13	13.0	13
1980	HAM	14										36	6						34	486	14.3	42	6								
1981	HAM	16	1		0							42	7						27	415	15.4	48	7					1	0	0.0	0
8	Years	114	7		3				1	20		149	24						208	3032	14.6	52	24	61	354	5.8	21	5	13	2.6	13
KEN PETTWAY Ken DB 5'10 180 California B: 6/25/1964 Selma, AL																															
1987	WPG	8			1	36			2	9														12	84	7.0	30				
1988	WPG	11	2		0	50			1	5														14	73	5.2	15	3	57	19.0	26
1989	WPG	17				66			3	16														1	7	7.0	7				
1990	WPG	11	0		3	26	1.0		3	0																		1	11	11.0	11
1991	BC	17	0		1	72			5	114														1	0	0.0	0				
1992	BC	5				10																									
6	Years	69	2		5	260	1.0		14	144														28	164	5.9	30	4	68	17.0	26
KENNY PETTWAY Kenneth Aaron DE 6'3 245 Southern Arkansas; Grambling State B: 11/13/1982 Houston, TX Draft: 7-227 2005 HOU Pro: N																															
2010	EDM	16	0	2	0	37	7.0	55.0	0	0	1																				
JOE PETTY Joseph Dock WR-DB 6'2 185 Arizona State B: 7/23/1951 Shelby, NC Draft: 16-397 1973 SD																															
1975	MTL	16	0		1							2	0						30	575	19.2	73	0								
1976	MTL	5																	5	126	25.2	51	0								
1977	MTL	6	0		1														6	101	16.8	24	0								
3	Years	27	0		2							2	0						41	802	19.6	73	0								
MAT PETZ Mat LB 6'3 250 Wake Forest B: 6/25/1977 Windsor, ON Draft: 2-12 2000 MTL																															
2000	MTL	10				12																									
2001	MTL	17	0	1	0	22																									
2002	MTL	13	0	2	1	9																						2	27	13.5	18
2003	MTL	11				9																						1	8	8.0	8
2004	HAM	18	0	2	2	20	1.0	9.0				6	1																		
2005	HAM	9				9																									
6	Years	78	0	5	3	81	1.0	9.0				6	1															3	35	11.7	18
BOB PEVIANI Robert Angelo G 6'1 210 Southern California B: 9/15/1931 Los Angeles, CA Draft: 6-70 1953 NYG Pro: N																															
1955	OTT	4																													
AL PFEIFER Albert OE 6'1 200 Fordham B: 1928 Draft: 16-194 1951 NYG																															
1951	TOR	6										40	8										8								
1953	TOR	5										10	2										2								
1954	TOR	14										30	6						68	1142	16.8	63	6								
1955	TOR+	12							1	0		98	15						75	1342	17.9	54	15								
1956	TOR	13							1	3		38	6						78	993	12.7	35	6	1	5	5.0	5	1	4	4.0	4
1957	OTT	14										18	3						44	700	15.9	57	3								
6	Years	64							2	3		234	40						265	4177	15.8	63	40	1	5	5.0	5	1	4	4.0	4
RALPH PFEIFER Ralph J. HB 6'0 210 Kansas State B: 1936 Draft: 7A-83 1958 DET																															
1958	EDM	5	3											8	36	4.5	24	0	5	89	17.8	43	0	11	106	9.6	28	3	70	23.3	27
LARRY PFOHL Lawrence Wendell OT 6'3 270 Penn State; Miami (Florida) B: 6/2/1958 Buffalo, NY Pro: U																															
1979	MTL	1																													
1980	MTL	11																													
1981	MTL	2																													
3	Years	14																													
AL PHANEUF Al S 6'0 190 Kentucky B: 2/4/1944 Almonte, ON																															
1969	MTL	14	0		3				4	31																					
1970	MTL*	14							9	65																					
1971	MTL	14							3	38																					
3	Years	42	0		3				16	134																					
CHARLIE PHARMS Charlie, III DB 5'11 185 Miami (Florida) B: 12/15/1969 Houston, TX																															
1994	TOR	6	0		2	16																									
TOMMY PHARR Tommy Lee QB 5'10 187 Gordon JC; Mississippi State B: 7/31/1947 Canton, GA Pro: N																															
1972	WPG	16	2		0				3	124		6	1	21	186	8.9	40	1													
1973	WPG	12	0		1									10	58	5.8	37	0	11	121	11.0	28	0								
1974	WPG	13	1		1				3	7														21	120	5.7	16				
3	Years	41	3		2				6	131		6	1	31	244	7.9	40	1	11	121	11.0	28	0	21	120	5.7	16				
VINCE PHASON Vincent James DB 5'10 190 Arizona B: 2/5/1953 Oakland, CA Draft: 11A-267 1975 SD																															
1975	EDM	3																													
1975	BC	1																													
1975	Year	4																													
1976	WPG	11	1		0				2	23														19	145	7.6	19				
1977	WPG	16	0		3				4	95														4	41	10.3	14				
1978	WPG	16	2		2				1	3														5	40	8.0	14	30	796	26.5	49
1979	WPG	16	1		0				1	26														10	153	15.3	48	18	434	24.1	44
1980	WPG	16	1		1				1	39														5	93	18.6	49	11	220	20.0	33
1981	WPG	16	0		2				6	98																		13	330	25.4	41
1982	WPG*	16	1		0				6	86		6	1											1	5	5.0	5				
1983	MTL	9	0		3				5	55		6	1											5	48	9.6	22	18	601	33.4	80
1984	MTL	16	1		2		1.0																					32	748	23.4	58
1985	MTL	16	0		4				2	69																		22	586	26.6	58
11	Years	151	7		17		1.0		28	494		12	2											49	525	10.7	49	144	3715	25.8	80
MIKE PHILBRICK Michael DT-DE 6'5 275 Carleton B: 10/23/1967 Hamilton, ON Draft: 4-25 1990 OTT																															
1990	OTT	1				0																									
1994	HAM	16	0		1	42	5.0	31.0																							
1995	HAM	17				28	2.0	11.0			1																				
1996	HAM+	18	0		3	52	5.0	37.0			1																				

Year	Team	GP	FM	FF	FR	TK	SK	YDS	IR	YDS	PD	PTS	TD	RA	YDS	AVG	LG	TD	REC	YDS	AVG	LG	TD	PR	YDS	AVG	LG	KOR	YDS	AVG	LG
1997	HAM	18	0	1	1	37	7.0	50.0			2																				
1998	HAM	18				40	4.0	33.0			1																				
1999	HAM	14				22	2.0	16.0																							
2000	HAM+	18	0	0	3	46	3.0	9.0			1																				
2001	HAM+	17	0	2	1	37	5.0	25.0			1																				
9	Years	137	0	3	9	304	33.0	212.0			7																				
WAYNE PHILBRICK Wayne DT 6'5 250 St. Catherines Rams Jrs. B: 1948																															
1971	HAM	2																													
ED PHILION Edmond Paul DT 6'3 285 Ferris State B: 3/27/1970 Windsor, ON Draft: 1B-11 1994 CAL Pro: EN																															
1999	MTL	17	0	1	2	37	6.0	43.0			2																				
2000	MTL	11				15	6.0	54.0																							
2001	MTL	12				16	2.0	17.0			1																				
2002	MTL	15				19	4.0	29.0																							
2003	MTL+	18	0	0	1	17	7.0	32.0	2	3	4																				
2004	MTL+	18	0	0	1	25	2.0	12.0			1																				
2005	MTL+	18				30	7.0	43.0			1																				
2006	MTL+	18	0	1	0	14	2.0				2																				
8	Years	127	0	2	4	173	36.0	230.0	2	3	11																				
JERRY PHILIP Jerry DB 5'8 165 York B: 8/17/1960 Draft: 5-45 1983 EDM																															
1983	EDM	7							1	17																					
AL PHILLIPS Al DT 6'1 190 UCLA B: 5/19/1950 Detroit, MI																															
1974	EDM	1																													
AUBREY PHILLIPS Aubrey (Red) C 6'1 215 Texas Tech B: 1930 Draft: 13-157 1952 LARM																															
1952	SAS	15			3																										
BOBBY PHILLIPS Bobby Eugene, II RB 5'9 194 Virginia Union B: 12/8/1969 Richmond, VA Pro: EN																															
1999	EDM	2				1						6	1	26	114	4.4	20	1	6	58	9.7	16	0								
EMMERSON PHILLIPS Emmerson DB 6'1 195 Boston College B: 4/18/1976 Toronto, ON																															
2003	HAM	6				1																									
HAL PHILLIPS Harold Bruce DB 6'1 190 Michigan State B: 5/19/1950 Detroit, MI Draft: 6-139 1971 DEN Pro: W																															
1971	BC	2																													
JASON PHILLIPS Jason Howell WR 5'7 166 Taft JC; Houston B: 10/11/1966 Crowley, LA Draft: 10-253 1989 DET Pro: N																															
1995	BIR*	16	2		1	4						48	8						76	1101	14.5	96	8								
1996	HAM	18	2		0	2						36	6						64	928	14.5	55	6								
2	Years	34	4		1	6						84	14						140	2029	14.5	96	14								
JEY PHILLIPS Jey DB 6'2 183 Arizona B: 12/21/1971 Pro: E																															
1996	HAM	3				8																									
JIM PHILLIPS James OG 5'11 245 Morgan State B: 1944																															
1968	WPG	16																													
JOE PHILLIPS Joe, Jr. WR 5'9 188 Kentucky B: 5/12/1963 Franklin, KY Pro: N																															
1986	TOR	1																	2	31	15.5	20	0					3	76	25.3	31
JUSTIN PHILLIPS Justin DE-LB 6'4 254 Wilfrid Laurier B: 4/24/1985 Ottawa, ON Draft: 1B-5 2007 CAL																															
2007	CAL	12				6					1																				
2008	CAL	18				20					1																				
2009	CAL	14	0	0	1	28	1.0	4.0																							
2010	CAL	15				19					1																				
2011	CAL	18	0	1	1	43	1.0	3.0			1																				
5	Years	77	0	1	2	116	2.0	7.0			4																				
KEN PHILLIPS Ken K-FB 6'0 210 Vancouver Meralomas Jrs. B: 1948 D: //1974																															
1969	BC	14										1	0																		
1970	BC	16	1		1							4	0																		
1971	BC	16	1		0							59	0																		
1972	BC	1																													
1972	EDM	1																													
1972	Year	2																													
4	Years	47	2		1							64	0																		
KIM PHILLIPS Kim Darnell CB 5'9 188 North Texas B: 10/28/1966 New Boston, TX Draft: 3-79 1989 NO Pro: N																															
1992	WPG	3	1		0	7																		4	37	9.3	17	2	19	9.5	11
1993	WPG+	13	0		1	35			5	26														1	16	16.0	16	2	19	9.5	19
1994	WPG	8				23			3	40	0																				
1995	CAL	4				10																									
1995	SHR	10				10					5																				
1995	Year	14				20					5																				
4	Years	28	1		1	85			8	66	5													5	53	10.6	17	4	38	9.5	19
LAWRENCE PHILLIPS Lawrence Lamond RB 6'0 222 Nebraska B: 5/12/1975 Little Rock, AR Draft: 1A-6 1996 STL Pro: EN																															
2002	MTL+	15	3	0	1	1						78	13	187	1022	5.5	51	13	33	292	8.8	30	0					1	24	24.0	24
2003	CAL	8	1	0	0	1						6	1	107	486	4.5	28	1	13	92	7.1	25	0								
2	Years	23	4	0	1	2						84	14	294	1508	5.1	51	14	46	384	8.3	30	0					1	24	24.0	24
MATT PHILLIPS Matt T 6'2 230 Pepperdine B: 1934 New Westminster, BC																															
1957	BC	2																													
MICAH PHILLIPS Micah Barron DH 6'0 195 Southern California B: 4/14/1973 Dallas, TX																															
1997	MTL	1				3																									
RUDY PHILLIPS Rudolph OG-OT 6'2 250 North Texas B: 2/25/1958 Dallas, TX																															
1981	OTT	6	0		1																										
1982	OTT*	13																													
1983	OTT*	16																													
1984	OTT	13																													
1986	EDM*	18	0		1																										
1987	EDM	10			1	0																									
1988	CAL	14				1																									
7	Years	90	0		3	1																									
RYAN PHILLIPS Ryan DH-CB 5'10 195 Mount San Antonio JC; Eastern Washington B: 11/15/1982 Seattle, WA																															
2005	BC	18				56			3	4	9																				
2006	BC	18	0	0	3	28	1.0	11.0	2	23	3	6	1																		
2007	BC*	18	0	0	1	68			12	299	11	6	1																		
2008	BC	18	0	1	1	45			1	1	9													1	0	0.0	0				
2009	BC	18	0	0	2	41			4	80	2	12	2																		
2010	BC*	18	1	1	0	51	4.0	18.0	5	109	1																				
2011	BC	18	0	1	1	49			4	112	7	6	1											1	0	0.0	0				
7	Years	126	1	3	8	338	5.0	29.0	31	628	42	30	5											2	0	0.0	0				
WES PHILLIPS Wesley Alan OT-OG 6'5 275 Savannah State; Lenoir-Rhyne B: 8/1/1953 Atlanta, GA Pro: NU																															
1979	OTT	1																													
1980	OTT	12																													
2	Years	13																													
GERRY PHILP Gerald FL-DB 6'0 195 Fullerton JC; Florida State B: 1932 ON																															
1958	TOR	14							1	0									3	58	19.3	30	0	27	245	9.1	26				
1959	TOR	14							3	18									8	127	15.9	47	0	36	282	7.8	17				
1960	TOR	13							1	1														31	202	6.5	37	7	159	22.7	30
1961	TOR	6										6	1						9	71	7.9	15	1	6	29	4.8	16	1	17	17.0	17
1962	TOR	14										12	2						15	190	12.7	27	2	1	1	1.0	1	2	17	8.5	11
1963	TOR	14										12	2	0	7		7	0	9	126	14.0	19	2								
1964	MTL	14										12	2						12	147	12.3	16	2								
7	Years	89							5	19		42	7	0	7		7	0	56	719	12.8	47	7	101	759	7.5	37	10	193	19.3	30

Year	Team	GP	FM	FF	FR	TK	SK	YDS	IR	YDS	PD	PTS	TD	RA	YDS	AVG	LG	TD	REC	YDS	AVG	LG	TD	PR	YDS	AVG	LG	KOR	YDS	AVG	LG
MARK PHILP Mark S-RB 5'9 170 Richmond B: 4/4/1957 Draft: 2A-11 1980 OTT																															
1980	OTT	16	0		1				1	34																				
1981	OTT	5	0		1																									
2	Years	21	0		2				1	34																				
CORY PHILPOT Cory RB 5'9 186 Itawamba CC; Mississippi B: 5/15/1970 Melbourne, FL																															
1993	BC	11	7		2	1						72	12	66	372	5.6	23	8	20	190	9.5	24	3	9	45	5.0	12	36	1008	28.0	91
1994	BC	15	7		0	3						84	14	201	1451	7.2	92	13	30	297	9.9	26	1					13	240	18.5	32
1995	BC+	15	8		2	4						134	22	229	1308	5.7	64	17	41	542	13.2	75	4					24	572	23.8	94
1996	BC	15	3		0	1						18	3	163	1024	6.3	77	1	16	260	16.3	45	2	1	9	9.0	9	30	586	19.5	47
1997	BC	14	2	0	2	3						24	4	68	304	4.5	48	3	36	294	8.2	23	1	1	5	5.0	5	12	224	18.7	28
1999	WPG	4	6	0	1	0								42	234	5.6	36	0	11	119	10.8	38	0					9	169	18.8	32
2000	WPG	11	4	0	2	0						24	4	113	520	4.6	23	4	19	168	8.8	30	0					9	207	23.0	32
7	Years	85	37	0	9	12						356	59	882	5213	5.9	92	46	173	1870	10.8	75	11	11	59	5.4	12	133	3006	22.6	94
RAYMOND PHILYAW Raymond QB 5'10 200 Louisiana-Monroe B: 7/31/1974 Shreveport, LA																															
1997	WPG	5				1								6	22	3.7	12	0													
JIM PIASKOSKI James DE-DT-OT 6'4 240 Eastern Michigan B: 10/8/1948 Levack, ON																															
1972	OTT	8																													
1973	OTT	14	0		2				1	3																				
1974	OTT	16																													
1975	OTT	16	0		1																									
1976	OTT	16			3																									
1977	OTT+	16	0		2																									
1978	OTT	16																													
1979	OTT	16	0		1																									
1980	OTT	9	0		2																									
1981	OTT	14	0		1		2.0																									
1982	OTT	14					2.5																									
11	Years	155	0		12		4.5		1	3																				
DOMINIC PICARD Dominic C 6'1 297 Laval B: 6/22/1982 Sainte-Foy, QC Draft: B3-23 2006 WPG																															
2006	WPG	1				0																									
2007	WPG	18				0																									
2008	WPG	12				3																									
2009	TOR	18	1	0	0	3																									
2010	TOR	18				2																									
2011	TOR+	18	1	0	0	1																									
6	Years	85	2	0	0	9																									
BOB PICKELL Bernard E 6'5 228 Portland B: 7/2/1927 Kaunas, Lithuania D: 8/8/1987 Toronto, ON																															
1951	EDM	8																													
BOB PICKENS Robert James OT-OG 6'4 258 Wisconsin; Nebraska B: 2/2/1943 Chicago, IL Draft: 3-44(f) 1966 CHIB; RS-2-15 1966 KC Pro: N																															
1969	EDM	3																													
1970	EDM	16	1		0																								1	2	2.0	2
2	Years	19	1		0																								1	2	2.0	2
CODY PICKETT Cody J. QB 6'3 227 Washington B: 6/30/1980 Caldwell, ID Draft: 7A-217 2004 SF Pro: EN																															
2007	TOR	4				0																									
2008	TOR	18	1	0	1	3								7	29	4.1	8	0													
2009	TOR	18	3	0	0	1								12	39	3.3	8	0													
2010	CAL	5				0																									
4	Years	45	4	0	1	4								19	68	3.6	8	0													
BUCK PIERCE Buck James QB 6'1 210 New Mexico State B: 11/15/1981 Hutchinson, KS																															
2005	BC	18				0						12	2	15	104	6.9	17	2													
2006	BC	18	2	0	2	1						18	3	31	294	9.5	39	3													
2007	BC	15				2						6	1	22	164	7.5	20	1													
2008	BC	18	2	0	0	1						12	2	29	177	6.1	16	2													
2009	BC	17	6	0	0	3						6	1	39	276	7.1	23	1													
2010	WPG	5	2	0	0	1						12	2	22	237	10.8	43	2													
2011	WPG	16	1	0	0	2						12	2	51	324	6.4	48	2													
7	Years	107	13	0	2	10						78	13	209	1576	7.5	48	13													
SAMMY PIERCE Sam HB-FB-FW 5'11 217 Baylor B: 1926 Draft: 21-204 1949 NYB																															
1949	SAS+	14										45	9					9													
1950	SAS	13										15	3	103	520	5.0		2													
2	Years	27										60	12	103	520	5.0	0	11													
TENNIE PIERCE Tennie E., Jr. TE 6'5 220 Northridge State B: 9/29/1955 Los Angeles, CA																															
1979	BC	1																	1	14	14.0	14	0								
1979	WPG	2										6	1						5	51	10.2	26	1								
1979	Year	3										6	1						6	65	10.8	26	1								
JEFF PIERCY Jeff FB 6'1 229 Saskatchewan B: 3/25/1983 Rosetown, SK Draft: 2A-12 2005 MTL																															
2005	MTL	18				10																									
2006	MTL	18				6						6	1	2	6	3.0	3	0	2	10	5.0	7	1	1	22	22.0	22				
2007	MTL	9				1								8	42	5.3	19	0	4	49	12.3	18	0								
2007	HAM	8				6								2	5	2.5	3	0													
2007	Year	17				7								10	47	4.7	19	0	4	49	12.3	18	0								
2008	HAM	18	0	0	1	5								14	48	3.4	11	0	3	46	15.3	16	0								
4	Years	63	0	0	1	28						6	1	26	101	3.9	19	0	9	105	11.7	18	1	1	22	22.0	22				
YOUSSY PIERRE Youssy WR 6'0 185 St. Leonard Cougars Jrs.; Montreal B: 8/8/1985 Montreal, QC Draft: 6-46 2011 EDM																															
2011	EDM	1				0			1	1	0																			
REGGIE PIERSON Reginald Lee CB 5'11 185 Arizona Western JC; Oklahoma State B: 12/13/1952 Pro: NW																															
1978	WPG	15								5	75													13	110	8.5	44	1	1	1.0	1
1979	WPG	16	0		1				3	24													1	10	10.0	10				
1980	WPG	16	0		3				6	114																				
1981	WPG	16	1		0				7	107													1	6	6.0	6				
1982	WPG	16	1		1				4	81																				
1983	WPG	12								2	38													1	0	0.0	0				
6	Years	91	2		5				27	439													16	126	7.9	44	1	1	1.0	1
TONY PIERSON Tony WR 5'11 175 Alberta B: 11/16/1952 Cardston, AB Draft: 6-50 1987 CAL																															
1987	CAL	9				1													2	57	28.5	38	0					1	18	18.0	18
JOE PIKULA Joe T 6'3 245 none B: 1944																															
1963	HAM	14																													
1964	HAM	13	0		1																									
2	Years	27	0		1																									
ROB PIKULA Rob P-K 5'9 175 Western Ontario B: 12/23/1981 Brantford, ON																															
2006	BC	3				0						24	0																		
2007	WPG	15				1						60	0																		
2	Years	18				1						84	0																		
WILLIE PILE Willie Marquis LB-S 6'2 206 Virginia Tech B: 5/25/1980 New York, NY Draft: 7B-252 2003 KC Pro: EN																															
2007	TOR	17	0	2	0	84	5.0	31.0			1																			
2008	TOR	17	0	0	1	83	2.0	11.0	3	34	3																			
2009	TOR	18	1	3	2	92	1.0	0.0	3	48	6																			
2010	TOR+	18	0	2	3	87	2.0	17.0	4	15	3																			
2011	TOR	18	0	6	0	95	2.0	9.0	2	2	2																			
5	Years	88	1	13	6	441	12.0	68.0	12	99	15																			
BRIAN PILLMAN Brian William LB 5'10 228 Miami (Ohio) B: 5/22/1962 Cincinnati, OH D: 10/5/1997 Bloomington, MN Draft: 10-204 1984 DEN-USFL Pro: N																															
1986	CAL	3					2.0																									

Year	Team	GP	FM	FF	FR	TK	SK	YDS	IR	YDS	PD	PTS	TD	RA	YDS	AVG	LG	TD	REC	YDS	AVG	LG	TD	PR	YDS	AVG	LG	KOR	YDS	AVG	LG
FRANK PILLOW William Frank, Jr. WR 5'10 170 Tennessee State B: 3/11/1965 Nashville, TN Draft: 11-279 1988 TB Pro: N																															
1992	WPG	10	0		1	1						6	1						13	306	23.5	67	1					3	55	18.3	24
CLAUDE PILON Claude DE-DT 6'4 265 Ottawa Sooners Jrs. B: 6/13/1950																															
1977	OTT	12																													
JEFF PILON Jeffrey Thomas OT-OG 6'6 300 Syracuse B: 3/21/1976 Ottawa, ON Draft: 3-17 1999 WPG Pro: X																															
2000	CAL	1				0																									
2001	CAL	13	0	0	1	2																									
2002	CAL	18				1																									
2003	CAL	18				2																									
2004	CAL	18	0	0	1	4																									
2005	CAL+	18	0	0	1	1																									
2006	CAL	11				0																									
2007	CAL	18	0	0	1	1																									
2008	CAL	15				0																									
2009	CAL	17	0	0	1	0																									
10	Years	147	0	0	5	11																									
MARC PILON Marc LB-DT 6'5 265 California (Pennsylvania); Syracuse B: 2/18/1975 Ottawa, ON Draft: 1-4 1998 CAL																															
1999	CAL	18				12	1.0	6.0																							
2000	CAL	18	0	2	1	25					1																				
2001	CAL	18	0	1	1	10	4.0	16.0																							
2002	EDM	2				4																									
2003	BC	17				0																									
2004	BC	18				8																									
2005	OTT	18				31	3.0	12.0																							
2006	TOR	2				2																									
2006	HAM	5				1																									
2006	Year	7				3																									
8	Years	111	0	3	2	101	8.0	34.0			1																				
FRANK PIMISKERN Frank S 5'9 186 British Columbia B: 12/18/1971 Vancouver, BC																															
1994	BC	2				2																									
1994	OTT	1				1																									
1994	Year	3				3																									
1995	BC	5				7																									
1996	BC	9				6																									
1997	BC	16				16					1																				
4	Years	32				32					1																				
MARK PIMISKERN Mark LB 6'3 230 Washington State B: 9/9/1974 Vancouver, BC Draft: 1-6 1996 BC																															
1996	BC	18				23					1								4	70	17.5	33	0								
ANDRE PINESETT Andrea T. DL 6'2 245 Fullerton State B: 7/25/1961 Los Angeles, CA Draft: 10-256 1985 IND; 14- 1985 POR-USFL																															
1985	EDM	7	0		1		2.0																							
1986	EDM	5					2.0																							
2	Years	12	0		1		4.0																							
DON PINHEY Donald C. OHB-S 5'10 177 Muskingum B: 12/1930																															
1954	OTT	10							1	10				11	65	5.9	28	0						20	156	7.8	25	13	274	21.1	34
1955	OTT	11							3	78		25	5	42	256	6.1	27	3	13	218	16.8	47	2	45	328	7.3	20	26	632	24.3	53
1956	OTT+	14							1	0		36	6	32	195	6.1	30	2	23	369	16.0	93	4	52	416	8.0	36	20	572	28.6	49
1957	OTT	14												48	181	3.8	19	0	8	71	8.9	16	0	57	430	7.5	21	12	268	22.3	29
1958	OTT	14										18	3	23	89	3.9	21	2	9	187	20.8	69	1	78	563	7.2	23				
5	Years	63							5	88		79	14	156	786	5.0	30	7	53	845	15.9	93	7	252	1893	7.5	36	71	1746	24.6	53
BOB PINKNEY Bob DB 6'0 178 Toronto B: 1934 Draft: 2-5 1955 OTT																															
1955	OTT	12							1	16																					
1957	OTT	2												3	12	4.0	8	0	1	13	13.0	13	0								
2	Years	14							1	16				3	12	4.0	8	0	1	13	13.0	13	0								
DICK PINKSTON Dick T Detroit Tech B: // 1924																															
1951	WPG	2																													
CORNEL PIPER Cornel OT-OG-DE-DG-DT 6'1 235 Winnipeg Rods Jrs. B: 4/2/1937 Ardmore, AB																															
1957	WPG	16																													
1958	WPG	16																													
1959	WPG	16																													
1960	WPG+	16	0		2							6	1																		
1961	WPG+	16																													
1962	WPG	16																													
1963	WPG	16																													
1964	WPG	16	0		1																										
1965	WPG	16	0		0																										
1966	WPG	5																													
1967	WPG	14																													
11	Years	163	0		3							6	1																		
GREG PIPES Gregory Mack DT 5'10 235 Baylor B: 8/4/1946 Fort Worth, TX Draft: 12-306 1968 BUF																															
1968	EDM	11																													
1969	EDM	16																													
1970	EDM*	16	0		2																										
1971	EDM	16			1																										
1972	EDM	11	0		1																										
5	Years	70	0		4																										
JERRELL PIPPENS Jerrell L. DB 6'3 200 Nebraska B: 6/30/1980 Philadelphia, PA Pro: N																															
2007	SAS	1				0																									
BRUCE PIRT Bruce H. E 6'1 187 Winnipeg Rods Jrs. B: 1928																															
1949	EDM	3																													
1951	OTT	5																													
2	Years	8																													
JOE PISARCIK Joseph Anthony QB 6'4 220 New Mexico State B: 7/2/1952 Kingston, PA Draft: 2-17 1974 PHI-WFL Pro: N																															
1974	CAL	16	1		0									16	63	3.9	22	0													
1975	CAL	16	1		0							18	3	30	92	3.1	12	3	1	0	0.0	0	0								
1976	CAL	11	2		0							6	1	22	56	2.5	11	1													
3	Years	43	4		0							24	4	68	211	3.1	22	4	1	0	0.0	0	0								
STEVE PISARKIEWICZ Stephen John QB 6'2 205 Missouri B: 11/10/1953 Florissant, MO Draft: 1-19 1977 STL Pro: NU																															
1982	WPG	2	1		0									1	-4	-4.0	-4	0													
ALAN PITCAITHLEY Alan Lewis HB-FB 6'2 215 Oregon B: 7/7/1948 Oakland, CA Draft: 11-273 1970 NYG																															
1970	EDM	8	1		0							6	1	74	278	3.8	37	1	9	93	10.3	26	0								
1971	EDM	1																0													
1971	OTT	1										6	1					1	2	41	20.5	24	0								
1971	Year	2										6	1	16	17	1.1	4	1	2	41	20.5	24	0								
2	Years	9	1		0							12	2	74	278	3.8	37	2	11	134	12.2	26	0								
DAVID PITCHER David SB-FB 6'2 240 Okanagan Sun Jrs. B: 1/29/1967 Port Alberni, BC																															
1990	SAS	10	0		1	1						6	1						6	77	12.8	24	1								
1991	SAS	16	0		1	13								1	0	0.0	0	0	1	9	9.0	9	0	0	2		2				
1992	SAS	18	0		2	15						6	1	2	26	13.0	19	0	10	84	8.4	16	0					2	33	16.5	19
1993	SAS	18				20								1	9	9.0	9	0	1	11	11.0	11	0								
1994	SAS	12	0		1	8													3	25	8.3	15	0	1	3	3.0	3				
1995	SAS	18				24													5	60	12.0	19	0	1	6	6.0	6	1	11	11.0	11
1996	MTL	8				10	1.0	8.0																							

Year	Team	GP	FM	FF	FR	TK	SK	YDS	IR	YDS	PD	PTS	TD	RA	YDS	AVG	LG	TD	REC	YDS	AVG	LG	TD	PR	YDS	AVG	LG	KOR	YDS	AVG	LG
1997	WPG	16				16													1	4	4.0	4	0					2	17	8.5	17
1998	EDM	10	0	0	1	10								1	4	4.0	4	0	1	22	22.0	22	0								
9	Years	126	0	0	6	117	1.0	8.0				12	2	5	39	7.8	19	0	28	292	10.4	24	1	2	11	5.5	6	5	61	12.2	19
DAVID PITTMAN David DH-S 5'11 182 Northwestern State (Louisiana) B: 10/14/1983 Gramercy, LA Draft: 3-87 2006 BAL Pro: NU																															
2011	EDM	12				25	2.0	11.0			2																				
DOMINIE PITTMAN Dominie DE 6'3 239 North Alabama B: 10/13/1986 Pensacola, FL																															
2010	BC	8	0	1	1	14	2.0	2.0																							
ALLEN PITTS Allen SN-WR 6'4 200 Fullerton State B: 6/28/1964 Tucson, AZ																															
1990	CAL	18	3		1	4						40	6	1	-5	-5.0	-5	0	65	1172	18.0	67	6								
1991	CAL*	18	3		0	5						90	15						118	1764	14.9	87	15					1	0	0.0	0
1992	CAL*	18	5		1	5						78	13						103	1591	15.4	53	13					1	0	0.0	0
1993	CAL	7	1		1	1						24	4						45	776	17.2	37	4					1	0	0.0	0
1994	CAL*	18	1		1	3						126	21						126	2036	16.2	54	21								
1995	CAL*	16	1		1	1						66	11						100	1492	14.9	63	11								
1996	CAL+	17	1		1	2						66	11						86	1309	15.2	41	11					1	-2	-2.0	-2
1997	CAL	11				2						58	9						53	885	16.7	43	9								
1998	CAL*	17	1	0	0	2						66	11						96	1372	14.3	62	11								
1999	CAL*	18				2						60	10						97	1449	14.9	63	10								
2000	CAL	18				1						36	6						77	1045	13.6	29	6					1	1	1.0	1
11	Years	176	16	0	6	28						710	117	1	-5	-5.0	-5	0	966	14891	15.4	87	117					5	-1	-0.2	1
ERNIE PITTS Ernest (Zazu) TE-SE-DH-S-CB 6'1 192 Denver B: 3/8/1935 Aliquppa, PA D: 9/24/1970 Thornton, CO Draft: 8-92 1957 SF																															
1957	WPG+	16							1	0		31	5						38	683	18.0	51	5					2	40	20.0	27
1958	WPG	11	2									36	6	1	6	6.0	6	0	26	552	21.2	107	6					1	68	68.0	68
1959	WPG+	16										96	16	1	3	3.0	3	0	68	1126	16.6	65	16					8	164	20.5	28
1960	WPG+	16	1									48	8						42	659	15.7	81	8					1	6	6.0	6
1961	WPG	16										36	6						45	762	16.9	62	6					4	40	10.0	29
1962	WPG	16	1		1							54	9						62	865	14.0	56	8					1	10	10.0	10
1963	WPG	9	2		0							12	2						22	387	17.6	44	2								
1964	WPG	15										18	3						32	459	14.3	34	3					2	23	11.5	18
1965	WPG	16	0		2																										
1966	WPG+	16	0		1				1										2	32	16.0	29	0								
1967	WPG	16	0		1				3	26																					
1968	WPG+	15	0		1				7	84																					
1969	WPG	16			1				5	53														1	0	0.0	0				
1970	BC	10																						0	5		5				
14	Years	204	6		7				17	163		331	55	2	9	4.5	6	0	337	5525	16.4	107	54	1	5	5.0	5	19	351	18.5	68
JOHN PITTS John LB 6'2 215 Western Ontario B: 8/2/1962 Southern Pines, NC Draft: 3-25 1983 WPG																															
1984	WPG	12																										1	7	7.0	7
MONTAVIS PITTS Montavis Demond DB 6'1 197 Auburn; Jacksonville State B: 3/3/1984 Loachapoka, AL																															
2007	HAM	1				0																									
REX PITTS Rex R. OT 6'4 255 Los Angeles State B: 8/7/1946 Pro: W																															
1971	WPG	3							1	25		6	1																		
WILEY PITTS Wiley, Jr. SE 6'1 175 Temple B: 4/4/1957 Asbury Park, NJ Draft: 12-328 1980 HOU																															
1981	OTT	6																	10	189	18.9	48	0								
DAVE PIVEC David John TE 6'3 240 Notre Dame B: 9/25/1943 Baltimore, MD Draft: 14-185 1965 CHIB Pro: N																															
1964	TOR	9	0		1									0	8		8	0	16	315	19.7	55	0								
1965	TOR	3																	3	24	8.0	10	0								
1970	OTT	5	1		0														15	155	10.3	26	0								
1971	OTT	14										24	4						27	362	13.4	42	4					1	12	12.0	12
4	Years	31	1		1							24	4	0	8		8	0	61	856	14.0	55	4					1	12	12.0	12
LARRY PLANCKE Larry OE-FL-OHB 6'2 217 Queen's B: 1947 Draft: 1-4 1968 EDM																															
1968	EDM	16	0		1							18	3						10	198	19.8	86	3								
1969	EDM	16										6	1	1	1	1.0	1	0	11	220	20.0	52	1					2	12	6.0	8
2	Years	32	0		1							24	4	1	1	1.0	1	0	21	418	19.9	86	4					2	12	6.0	8
LORNE PLANTE Lorne OG 6'7 305 Victoria Rebels Jrs.; Manitoba; Vancouver Island Raiders Jrs. B: 5/13/1984 Nanaimo, BC																															
2007	BC	1				0																									
2008	BC	12				0																									
2	Years	13				0																									
LEN PLATT Leonard SE 6'2 185 Tulsa B: 8/9/1953 Draft: 2A-10 1976 BC																															
1976	BC	7																	2	29	14.5	16	0								
1976	HAM	5										6	1						4	31	7.8	13	1								
1976	Year	12										6	1						6	60	10.0	16	1								
1977	OTT	1																	3	41	13.7	18	0								
2	Years	8										6	1						9	101	11.2	18	1								
SAM PLATT Sam L. FB 6'0 195 Florida State B: 8/19/1958 Jacksonville, FL Pro: U																															
1981	OTT	7	5		0							12	2	99	427	4.3	55	1	20	83	4.2	16	1					11	277	25.2	30
1982	OTT	1	2		0									9	41	4.6	21	0	3	59	19.7	26	0					2	45	22.5	24
2	Years	8	7		0							12	2	108	468	4.3	55	1	23	142	6.2	26	1					13	322	24.8	30
DON PLAXTON Don FW																															
1946	TOR	1																													
SCOTT PLAYER Scott Darwin P 6'1 215 Flagler#; Florida CC#; Florida State B: 12/17/1969 St. Augustine, FL Pro: ENU																															
1995	BIR	18	1		0	0						4	0																		
REGGIE PLEASANT Reginald Lecarno CB 5'10 175 Clemson B: 5/2/1962 Sumter, SC Draft: 6-152 1985 ATL; TD 1985 ORL-USFL Pro: N																															
1987	TOR	16	0		2	58			9	182																					
1988	TOR*	18				61			7	107		6	1											1	0	0.0	0				
1989	TOR+	17	0		4	52			9	124		12	2											2	0	0.0	0				
1990	TOR	18	0		2	57			9	171														0	0		0				
1991	TOR+	18	0		3	71			4	74																		1	12	12.0	12
1992	TOR	18	0		1	46			4	68																					
1993	TOR	18	1		0	52	1.0	9.0	3	27																		1	0	0.0	0
1994	TOR	16	0		2	57			2	28	6																				
1996	EDM	8				6			1	2	1																				
1997	EDM	7				17																									
10	Years	154	1		14	477	1.0	9.0	48	783	7	18	3											3	0	0.0	0	2	12	6.0	12
WILLIE PLESS Willie LB 5'10 215 Kansas B: 2/21/1964 Anniston, AL																															
1986	TOR*	12	0		3		3.0		3	8																					
1987	TOR	16	0		3	93	7.0		5	22																					
1988	TOR*	18	0		3	96	6.0		2	22																					
1989	TOR	5				30																									
1990	BC*	18	0		5	107	4.0		5	83																					
1991	EDM*	18	0		2	104	8.0		6	66																					
1992	EDM*	18	0		8	121	8.0	38.0	5	59		6	1															1	0	0.0	0
1993	EDM*	16	0		3	80	9.0	43.0	1	26		6	1																		
1994	EDM*	18	0		6	114	5.0	35.0	4	28	2													1	13	13.0	13				
1995	EDM*	18	1		5	101	4.0	22.0	1	7	1	6	1	8	18	2.3	4	0	3	69	23.0	62	1								
1996	EDM*	18	0		1	96	8.0	49.0	1	1	5	24	4	10	6	0.6	1	4													
1997	EDM*	18	1	3	2	116	7.0	20.0	3	55	1	12	2	4	2	0.5	1	1	1	12	12.0	12	1								
1998	EDM*	18				117	8.0	53.0																							
1999	SAS+	18				102	7.0	54.0	3	39	1																				
14	Years	229	2	3	41	1277	84.0	314.0	39	416	10	54	9	22	26	1.2	4	5	4	81	20.3	62	2	1	13	13.0	13	1	0	0.0	0
DOUG PLOEN Doug DB 5'10 180 North Dakota B: 8/31/1962 Draft: 6-52 1984 WPG																															
1985	CAL	1																													

Year	Team	GP	FM	FF	FR	TK	SK	YDS	IR	YDS	PD	PTS	TD	RA	YDS	AVG	LG	TD	REC	YDS	AVG	LG	TD	PR	YDS	AVG	LG	KOR	YDS	AVG	LG
KENNY PLOEN Kenneth Alan QB-S-CB 6'1 185 Iowa B: 6/3/1935 Lost Nation, IA Draft: 19-222 1957 CLE																															
1957	WPG+	16	5		2				3	39		55	5	100	319	3.2	30	4	3	58	19.3	27	1	2	28	14.0	17	1	43	43.0	43
1958	WPG	10	3						1	20		6	1	67	366	5.5	35	0	8	87	10.9	24	1								
1959	WPG+	16							10	104				14	83	5.9	15	0						9	61	6.8	32	3	71	23.7	25
1960	WPG	16	3						3	53		30	5	68	541	8.0	24	4	2	44	22.0	25	1								
1961	WPG	14	4									12	2	43	192	4.5	20	2	1	29	29.0	29	0	1	11	11.0	11				
1962	WPG	16	2									6	1	40	245	6.1	29	0	2	71	35.5	47	1								
1963	WPG	14	4		0									64	316	4.9	81	0	2	35	17.5	28	0								
1964	WPG	15	2		0							6	1	65	397	6.1	40	0	4	54	13.5	25	1								
1965	WPG*	13	4		0							18	3	59	230	3.9	16	2	2	30	15.0	19	1								
1966	WPG	15										6	1	35	163	4.7	20	0	1	13	13.0	13	1								
1967	WPG	11	2		0							6	1	33	149	4.5	42	1													
11	Years	156	29		2				17	216		145	20	588	3001	5.1	81	13	25	421	16.8	47	7	12	100	8.3	32	4	114	28.5	43
DAVE PLOUGHMAN David DB 5'11 180 Western Ontario B: 4/11/1960																															
1984	WPG	4																													
NEIL PLUMLEY Neil T 6'6 240 Oregon State B: 1940 Draft: 20- 1961 NYT; 8-108 1961 SF																															
1962	SAS	2																													
BRUCE PLUMMER Bruce Elliot DB 6'1 203 Mississippi State B: 9/1/1964 Bogalusa, LA Draft: 9-250 1987 DEN Pro: N																															
1992	WPG	5	1		2	18																		9	100	12.1	16	1	40	11.0	22
1993	BC	0				20			1	27																		1	6	6.0	6
2	Years	13	1		2	46			1	27														9	109	12.1	16	5	51	10.2	22
CHAD PLUMMER Chad J. WR 6'3 220 Cincinnati B: 11/30/1975 Delray Beach, FL Draft: 6B-204 1999 DEN Pro: N																															
2002	TOR	11				3						6	1	1	0	0.0	0	0	25	416	16.6	48	1								
2003	WPG	2				1													3	21	7.0	10	0								
2003	HAM	9				1						24	4	1	-3	-3.0	-3	0	24	465	19.4	81	4								
2003	Year	11				2						24	4	1	-3	-3.0	-3	0	27	486	18.0	81	4								
2	Years	13				5						30	5	2	-3	-1.5	0	0	52	902	17.3	81	5								
SCOTT PLUMMER Scott DB 5'11 197 Simon Fraser B: 11/30/1979 Burnaby, BC Draft: 3-22 2004 BC																															
2004	BC	6				0																									
2005	BC	4				0																									
2	Years	10				0																									
DAVE PLUMP Dave S 6'1 195 Vallejo JC; Fresno State B: 12/13/1942 Vicksburg, MS Draft: RS-10-78 1965 SD; 12-156(f) 1965 SF Pro: N																															
1967	BC	7							1	0														9	37	4.1	8	9	143	15.9	23
GARY POAGE Gary DB 6'1 195 Rice B: 1939																															
1962	CAL	1																													
KITO POBLAH Kito WR 6'2 213 Central Michigan B: 9/18/1987 Montreal, QC Draft: SD-1st 2011 WPG																															
2011	WPG	3				0													10	99	9.9	25	0								
TOM POE Thomas John LB 6'0 215 Washington State B: 11/29/1952 Vancouver, WA Pro: W																															
1978	TOR	5	0		2																										
1979	HAM	1																													
2	Years	6	0		2																										
DERON POINTER Deron WR 5'11 175 Washington State B: 9/9/1971 Pro: E																															
1995	TOR	1				1																						1	12	12.0	12
JOHN POINTER John Leslie LB 6'2 225 Vanderbilt B: 1/16/1958 Nashville, TN Pro: N																															
1981	EDM	1																													
1982	TOR+	14					1.0		1	12																					
1983	WPG	14	0		3		5.0		2	49		6	1																		
1984	MTL	7			1		1.0																								
1985	MTL	10	0		2		1.0																								
5	Years	46	0		6		8.0		3	61		6	1																		
JOE POIRIER Joe DH-CB 6'1 190 Loyola University Ints.; McGill B: 1938																															
1959	OTT	14																						2	10	5.0	10				
1960	OTT+	14							5	63														2	2	1.0	2				
1961	OTT	14							4	79														2	0	0.0	0				
1962	OTT+	14							5	85														3	-2	-0.7	-2				
1963	OTT+	14							1	18									3	55	18.3	22	0	1	0	0.0	0				
1964	OTT+	14	0		1				2	35														5	6	1.2	6				
1965	OTT	14							4	34																					
1966	OTT*	14							9	100		6	1																		
1967	OTT	14	0		1				3	33																					
1968	OTT	14	0		1				6	110		6	1																		
1969	OTT	14	0		1				6	86																					
1970	OTT	14	0		1				2	15														1	0	0.0	0				
12	Years	168	0		5				47	658		12	2						3	55	18.3	22	0	16	16	1.0	10				
PHIL POIRIER Phil DT 6'2 270 Cincinnati B: 7/28/1967 Sarnia, ON Draft: 7-50 1990 BC																															
1990	BC	2				1																									
DAVID POL David OG 6'4 300 British Columbia B: 8/31/1973 New Westminster, BC Draft: 2A-14 1999 BC																															
2001	CAL	8				0																									
GREENARD POLES Edgar Greenard LB-OG 5'11 225 Buffalo B: 8/16/1943																															
1966	EDM	15	0		1				2	34		6	1															2	4	2.0	4
1967	EDM	16	0		1																										
1968	EDM	16	0		2				2	10																					
1969	BC	11	0		2				3	43																					
1970	BC	10	0		2				3	59																					
5	Years	68	0		8				10	146		6	1															2	4	2.0	4
BOB POLEY Bob C-OG-DE 6'4 255 Regina Rams Jrs. B: 11/15/1955 Saskatoon, SK																															
1978	SAS	15																													
1979	SAS	16																													
1980	SAS	11																													
1981	SAS	16																													
1982	SAS	16																													
1983	SAS	16																										1	5	5.0	5
1984	SAS	16	1		1																										
1985	CAL	16	0		1																										
1986	CAL*	18																													
1987	CAL	15	0		1	1																									
1988	CAL	4				0																									
1988	SAS	8				0																									
1988	Year	12				0																									
1989	SAS	18				1																									
1990	SAS	18				0																									
1991	SAS	15				3																									
1992	SAS	18				5																									
15	Years	228	1		3	10																						1	5	5.0	5
MECO POLIZIANI Meco OHB-LB 6'0 187 Western Ontario B: 11/1/1937 Draft: 1-2 1960 MTL																															
1960	MTL	7										6	1	5	38	7.6	15	0	15	160	10.7	20	1					2	29	14.5	19
1961	MTL	11										6	1	4	23	5.8	18	1	15	122	8.1	15	0					4	54	13.5	23
1962	MTL	7																	7	56	8.0	14	0	10	50	5.0	12	2	29	14.5	18
1963	MTL	14										6	1						18	234	13.0	24	1					4	45	11.3	20
4	Years	39										18	3	9	61	6.8	18	1	55	572	10.4	24	2	10	50	5.0	12	12	157	13.1	23
AL POLLARD Alfred Lee FB-HB 6'0 196 Loyola Marymount; Army B: 9/7/1928 Glendale, CA D: 3/3/2002 Devon, PA Draft: 21-251 1951 NYY Pro: N																															
1954	BC	16	4									39	2	122	431	3.5	41	0	29	323	11.1	67	2	5	14	2.8	8	19	550	28.9	62

Year	Team	GP	FM	FF	FR	TK	SK	YDS	IR	YDS	PD	PTS	TD	RA	YDS	AVG	LG	TD	REC	YDS	AVG	LG	TD	PR	YDS	AVG	LG	KOR	YDS	AVG	LG
1955	BC	9	4		0							44	4	90	557	6.2	56	4	10	99	9.9	24	0	1	0	0.0	0	8	248	31.0	52
1956	BC	13	1		3							23	2	102	468	4.6	35	2	9	86	9.6	23	0	1	2	2.0	2				
1957	CAL	5										9	1	31	135	4.4	23	1	4	25	6.3	9	0					1	0	0.0	0
4	Years	43	9		3							115	9	345	1591	4.6	56	7	52	533	10.3	67	2	7	16	2.3	8	28	798	28.5	62
GREG POLLARD Gregory Tyronne DT 6'0 255 Colorado State B: 1/9/1978 Inglewood, CA																															
2001	BC	5				3																									
ZACHAEY POLLARI Zachary OT 6'6 277 Western Ontario B: 10/2/1986 Billings, MO Draft: 4-26 2009 TOR																															
2011	TOR	3				0																									
BRENT POLLOCK Brent OT 6'4 280 Fresno State B: 4/5/1966 Draft: 4B-28 1989 CAL																															
1991	SAS	3																													
FRANK POMARICO Frank OG-OT 6'1 242 Notre Dame B: 11/2/1952 New York, NY Draft: 14-353 1974 KC; 16-183 1974 CHI-WFL																															
1975	MTL	3																													
1976	MTL	6																													
1977	MTL	2																													
1977	OTT	14																													
1977	Year	17																													
1978	OTT	16																													
4	Years	27																													
DAVE PONDER David Earl DT 6'2 267 Florida State B: 6/27/1962 Cairo, GA Pro: N																															
1986	CAL	3					3.0																								
WILLIE PONDER Willie Columbus, Jr. WR 6'0 205 Tulsa; Coffeyville CC*; Southeast Missouri State B: 2/14/1980 Tulsa, OK Draft: 6A-199 2003 NYG Pro: N																															
2008	HAM	1				0																									
MICHEL-PIERRE PONTIBRAND Michel-Pierre FB 6'2 227 Laval B: 3/4/1983 St-Adele, QC																															
2011	WPG	9				0													2	45	22.5	41	0					1	2	2.0	2
ALEX PONTON Alex, Jr. FB-LB-K 6'1 205 Toronto Balmy Beach Jrs.; McMaster B: 1931																															
1952	OTT	12										1	0																		
1953	OTT	13																													
1954	TOR	14							1	0		6	0	5	17	3.4	7	0	1	12	12.0	12	0								
1955	TOR	11							1	3																					
1956	TOR	8																													
1957	TOR	9																													
1958	TOR	14							1	0																					
1959	TOR	13							1	0																		1	4	4.0	4
1960	TOR	1																													
1960	MTL	3							1	0																					
1960	Year	4							1	0																					
9	Years	95							5	3		7	0	5	17	3.4	7	0	1	12	12.0	12	0					1	4	4.0	4
DAVID POOL David Allen CB 5'9 182 Tennessee; Carson-Newman B: 12/20/1966 Cincinnati, OH Draft: 6C-145 1990 SD Pro: N																															
1995	WPG	6	0		1	12			0	0	3																				
1996	WPG	3				9																									
2	Years	9	0		1	21																									
LARRY POOLE Larry Eugene RB 6'0 195 Kent State B: 7/31/1952 Akron, OH Draft: 9A-213 1975 CLE Pro: N																															
1979	TOR	2												8	16	2.0	9	0	3	26	8.7	17	0								
NATHAN POOLE Nathan Lewis RB 5'9 210 Louisville B: 12/17/1956 Alexander City, AL Draft: 10-250 1979 CIN Pro: N																															
1981	TOR	1												6	33	5.5	13	0	1	4	4.0	4	0								
RAY POOLE Ray Smith OE 6'3 215 Mississippi; North Carolina; Mississippi B: 4/15/1921 Gloster, MS D: 4/2/2008 Oxford, MS Draft: 13-125 1944 NYG Pro: N																															
1953	MTL	14										81	2										2								
1954	MTL	12										58	0						18	225	12.5	38	0								
2	Years	26										139	2						18	225	12.5	38	2								
WILL POOLE William Starling S-DH-CB 5'10 193 Boston College; Ventura JC; Southern California B: 7/24/1981 Beckley, WV Draft: 4-102 2004 MIA Pro: NU																															
2008	TOR	5				16			1	15	2																				
2009	TOR	17	1	0	0	54	1.0	3.0	1	23	3													16	112	7.0	25				
2	Years	22	1	0	0	70	1.0	3.0	2	38	5													16	112	7.0	25				
JAMIE POPE Jamie FB 6'2 218 Gardner-Webb B: 11/16/1959 Draft: 17-196 1983 WAS-USFL																															
1983	MTL	2												3	1	0.3	1	0	2	11	5.5	9	0					1	20	20.0	20
JOHNNY POPE Johnny HB-FB none																															
1946	SAS	4																													
1947	SAS	8																													
2	Years	12																													
MARVIN POPE Marvin LB-DE 6'1 240 Central State (Ohio) B: 1/18/1969 Gainesville, FL																															
1992	CAL	6				24																									
1993	CAL+	18				73	1.0	8.0	1	25																		1	0	0.0	0
1994	CAL+	18				72	8.0	78.0	2	51	4																	1	9	9.0	9
1995	CAL	18				53	13.0	94.0			1	6	1	1	0	0.0	0	0	1	3	3.0	3	1					1	11	11.0	11
1996	CAL	12				1	2.0	16.0			1																	2	26	13.0	25
1997	CAL	18	0	0	1	38	3.0	28.0			1																	1	0	0.0	0
6	Years	90	0	0	1	261	27.0	224.0	3	76	7	6	1	1	0	0.0	0	0	1	3	3.0	3	1					6	46	7.7	25
O'LESTER POPE O'Lester OT 6'5 340 Southern Mississippi B: 8/24/1975 Jackson, MS Pro: E																															
2002	CAL	1				0																									
2003	CAL	2				1																									
2003	BC	1				0																									
2003	Year	3				1																									
2	Years	3				1																									
TYRONE POPE Tyrone CB 5'10 175 Colorado State; Fullerton State B: 3/15/1965 Welch, WV																															
1988	OTT	12	0		1	45			1	12																		1	22	22.0	22
1989	OTT	18	0		1	55																		1	6	6.0	6				
2	Years	30	0		2	100			1	12														1	6	6.0	6	1	22	22.0	22
JOE POPLAWSKI Joe WR 6'1 180 Alberta B: 8/2/1957 Edmonton, AB Draft: TE 1978 EDM																															
1978	WPG*	16										48	8						75	998	13.3	44	8								
1979	WPG	2																	3	35	11.7	17	0								
1980	WPG	14										30	5						56	897	16.0	68	5								
1981	WPG*	16	1		1							48	8						84	1271	15.1	55	8					2	0	0.0	0
1982	WPG	16	1		0							12	2						57	825	14.5	47	2								
1983	WPG	15	2		0							48	8						58	971	16.7	41	8					2	0	0.0	0
1984	WPG*	16										18	3						67	998	14.9	62	3								
1985	WPG*	16	2		2							36	6						75	1271	16.9	47	6					1	0	0.0	0
1986	WPG*	18	1		0							87	8						74	1075	14.5	65	8					1	0	0.0	0
9	Years	129	7		3							327	48						549	8341	15.2	68	48					6	0	0.0	0
JOHN POPLOWSKI John FB																															
1946	SAS	3																													
TOM PORRAS Tommy R. QB 6'2 200 Ventura JC; Washington B: 3/28/1958 Oxnard, CA																															
1985	HAM	8	1		0									12	27	2.3	11	0													
1986	HAM	18												1	0	0.0	0	0													
1987	HAM	15	2		0	3						8	1	57	247	4.3	30	1													
1988	HAM	18	2		0	0								45	169	3.8	15	0													
1989	CAL	11	1		0	0								8	66	8.3	27	0													
1990	TOR	5	5		1	2								24	74	3.1	15	0													
1990	CAL	3				0								2	13	6.5	13	0													
1990	Year	8	5		1	2								26	87	3.3	15	0													
1991	TOR	2				0																									
1993	WPG	18				0								1	-1	-1.0	-1	0													
1994	WPG	10				0								2	16	8.0	14	0													

Year	Team	GP	FM	FF	FR	TK	SK	YDS	IR	YDS	PD	PTS	TD	RA	YDS	AVG	LG	TD	REC	YDS	AVG	LG	TD	PR	YDS	AVG	LG	KOR	YDS	AVG	LG
9	Years	105	11		1	5						8	1	152	611	4.0	30	1													
DANIEL PORTER Daniel RB 5'9 197 Louisiana Tech B: 7/31/1987 Baton Rouge, LA																															
2010	EDM	6	0	0	1	0						12	2	86	603	7.0	34	2	6	50	8.3	11	0								
2011	EDM	5				0						18	3	28	89	3.2	12	2	3	21	7.0	5	1								
2011	HAM	1				0								8	24	3.0	5	0	2	23	11.5	13	0					4	89	22.3	31
2011	Year	6				0						18	3	36	113	3.1	12	2	5	44	8.8	13	1					4	89	22.3	31
2	Years	11	0	0	1	0						30	5	122	716	5.9	34	4	11	94	8.5	13	1					4	89	22.3	31
LEWIS PORTER Lewis DB 5'11 178 Southern University B: 3/7/1947 Clarksville, MS Draft: 8-208 1970 DEN Pro: N																															
1971	HAM	8	0		1							24	4	8	51	6.4	47	1	23	347	15.1	41	3					9	238	26.4	34
1972	HAM	14	0		2				2	50		12	2															18	614	34.1	98
1973	HAM*	14	0		1				4	167		6	1											3	14	4.7	10	20	539	27.0	62
1974	HAM	13	0		2				7	85																		14	345	24.6	35
1975	HAM	16	1		1				4	76									2	31	15.5	22	0	48	585	12.2	44	21	501	23.9	54
1976	HAM*	16	2		1				6	82		6	1						3	53	17.7	24	0	52	363	7.0	29	10	260	26.0	46
1977	HAM	16	0		3				1	19														10	70	7.0	25	11	267	24.3	44
7	Years	97	3		11				24	479		48	8	8	51	6.4	47	1	28	431	15.4	41	3	113	1032	9.1	44	103	2764	26.8	98
QUINTON PORTER Quinton George QB 6'5 233 Boston College B: 12/28/1982 Portland, ME Pro: E																															
2008	HAM	17	7	0	1	1						6	1	32	202	6.3	30	1													
2009	HAM	18	7	0	0	0						18	3	50	389	7.8	26	3													
2010	HAM	18	3	0	1	0						12	2	24	104	4.3	18	2													
2011	HAM	18	2	0	0	1						54	9	54	214	4.0	31	9													
4	Years	71	19	0	2	2						90	15	160	909	5.7	31	15													
RICKY PORTER Richard Anthony RB 5'10 195 Slippery Rock B: 1/14/1960 Sylacauga, AL Draft: 12A-319 1982 DET Pro: NU																															
1986	MTL	1												10	63	6.3	12	0	3	19	6.3	9	0					3	70	23.3	33
TERRY PORTER Terrence DB 5'11 179 Montclair State B: 10/21/1959 Gary, WV Pro: U																															
1982	MTL	3							1	18																					
GARRY PORTERFIELD Garry Mark LB 6'3 231 Tulsa B: 8/4/1943 Pawnee, OK Draft: 17- 1965 OAK; 14-187 1965 DAL Pro: N																															
1965	BC	5																													
1966	BC	16	0		1																										
2	Years	21	0		1																										
ODIE POSEY Odie Gordon DB 5'11 175 Southern University B: 4/23/1928 D: 2/26/2010 Zachary, LA Draft: 15-180 1951 LARM																															
1955	CAL	1							1	5																					
WILLIE POSTLER Willie C-OT 6'5 255 Montana B: 3/28/1949 Draft: 9-212 1972 HOU																															
1972	BC	16																													
1974	HAM	16																													
1975	EDM	2																													
3	Years	34																													
JEAN-VINCENT POSY-AUDETTE Jean-Vincent DB 6'1 205 Laval B: 2/15/1976 Port au Prince, Haiti Draft: 6-42 2000 TOR																															
2000	TOR	2				0																									
HECTOR POTHIER Hector OG-OT 6'3 254 McGill; St. Mary's (Nova Scotia) B: 6/13/1954 St. Catharines, ON Draft: 2-14 1977 MTL																															
1978	EDM	16																													
1979	EDM	11																													
1980	EDM	16																													
1981	EDM*	16																													
1982	EDM	15																													
1983	EDM	16	0		2																										
1984	EDM	16																													
1985	EDM	16	0		1																										
1986	EDM	16	0		2																										
1987	EDM+	18				1																									
1988	EDM+	18				0																									
1989	EDM+	18				0																									
12	Years	192	0		5	1																									
DALE POTTER Dale LB 6'2 225 Ottawa B: 9/11/1949 Draft: 2-15 1973 WPG																															
1973	WPG	16																										2	12	6.0	12
1974	EDM	16			1																										
1975	EDM	16	0		2				2	21																		3	52	17.3	24
1976	EDM	12							1	25																					
1977	EDM	16	0		1				2	14																					
1978	EDM	16	0		2																										
1979	EDM	16	0		2																										
1980	EDM*	16							2	21																					
1981	EDM	16	0		2		4.5		2	51		6	1																		
1982	EDM	16	0		2		3.0		1	8																					
1983	EDM	16					1.5																								
1984	TOR	5	0		2		2.0																								
12	Years	177	0		14		11.0		10	140		6	1															5	64	12.8	24
RICK POTTER Richard FB-LB 6'0 197 Parkdale Jrs. B: 3/10/1938 Milwaukee, WI																															
1957	TOR	9												12	58	4.8	10	0	2	-1	-0.5	5	0								
1958	WPG	2												5	55	11.0	22	0													
1959	WPG	10												6	12	2.0	5	0										1	9	9.0	9
1960	WPG	16	0		3				1			18	3	34	145	4.3	13	1	1	16	16.0	16	0					2	20	10.0	20
1961	WPG	14												22	104	4.7	12	0	5	67	13.4	20	0								
1962	WPG	16												11	44	4.0	7	0	1	6	6.0	6	0								
6	Years	67	0		3				1	0		18	3	90	418	4.6	22	1	9	88	9.8	20	0					3	29	9.7	20
RYAN POTTER Ryan FB 5'11 202 Western Ontario B: 12/25/1959 St. Boniface, MB Draft: 3A-23 1982 BC																															
1982	BC	6																													
1983	BC	16	0		2									4	19	4.8	13	0	4	53	13.3	20	0								
1984	BC	16	1		0									4	14	3.5	6	0	10	89	8.9	20	0								
1985	BC	16												10	40	4.0	10	0	4	40	10.0	13	0								
1986	CAL	9										6	1	11	39	3.5	10	1	1	6	6.0	6	0								
5	Years	63	1		2							6	1	29	112	3.9	13	1	19	188	9.9	20	0								
JASON POTTINGER Jason LB 6'2 232 McMaster B: 6/29/1983 Oshawa, ON Draft: 1A-2 2006 BC																															
2006	BC	18				25																									
2007	BC	18	0	1	0	46	1.0	3.0			1																				
2008	BC	18	0	0	1	44																									
2009	TOR	17	0	1	0	18	1.0	4.0																							
2010	TOR	18	0	1	1	72	2.0	20.0			3																				
2011	TOR	9	0	1	0	35	1.0	1.0			1																				
6	Years	98	0	4	2	240	5.0	28.0			5																				
CHARLIE POTTS Charles DB 6'3 210 Purdue B: 4/29/1949 Chicago, IL Draft: 6-145 1972 DET Pro: N																															
1974	WPG	1							1	53																					
ERNIE POUGH Ernest Leon WR 6'1 174 Texas Southern B: 5/17/1952 Jacksonville, FL Draft: 3B-88 1976 PIT Pro: N																															
1980	EDM	3																	6	113	18.8	65	0	3	17	5.7	6	2	49	24.5	15
JIMMY POULOS James RB 5'10 195 Georgia B: 3/14/1952 Decatur, GA Draft: 13-319 1974 STL; 15-173 1974 BIR-WFL Pro: W																															
1974	WPG	6	4		0									34	89	2.6	10	0	8	42	5.3	16	0								
PULU POUMELE Pulu Talo OT 6'3 315 Arizona B: 1/31/1972 American Samoa																															
1998	TOR	2				0																									
1999	TOR	9	0	0	1	0																									
2	Years	11	0	0	1	0																									
SHAR POURDANESH Shahriar OT 6'6 312 Nevada-Reno B: 7/19/1970 Tehran, Iran Pro: N																															
1994	BAL*	18				2																									

Year	Team	GP	FM	FF	FR	TK	SK	YDS	IR	YDS	PD	PTS	TD	RA	YDS	AVG	LG	TD	REC	YDS	AVG	LG	TD	PR	YDS	AVG	LG	KOR	YDS	AVG	LG
1995	BAL+	14				1																									
2	Years	32				3																									
KEITH POWE Keith Alonzo DL 6'3 251 Lamar; Texas-El Paso B: 6/5/1969 Biloxi, MS Pro: EN																															
1991	BC	9				16	1.0																								
1992	BC	14	0		1	28	8.0	63.0																							
1993	BC	4				4	1.0	6.0																							
1993	TOR	6	0		1	7	2.0	14.0																							
1993	Year	10	0		1	11	3.0	20.0																							
1997	WPG	2				1																									
4	Years	29	0		2	56	12.0	83.0																							
ACE POWELL Clayton Robert HB-FW 5'8 190 Ottawa Gladstones Jrs. B: 1921																															
1946	OTT	11										8	1																		
1947	OTT	12										10	2					1													
1948	OTT	12										6	1					1													
3	Years	35										24	4					2													
ART POWELL Arthur Louis OE 6'2 211 San Diego JC; San Jose State B: 2/25/1937 Draft: 11-123 1959 PHI Pro: N																															
1957	TOR	5										18	3						17	285	16.8	40	3					1	22	22.0	22
1957	MTL	5							2	19		6	1	7	71	10.1	40	0	16	362	22.6	39	0					3	51	17.0	18
1957	Year	10										24	4	7	71	10.1	40	0	33	647	19.6	40	3					4	73	18.3	22
CARL POWELL Carl L. WR 6'0 182 Jackson State B: 4/6/1958 Hazelhurst, MS Draft: 3-61 1982 WAS																															
1982	OTT	7	1		0							18	3	2	-11	-5.5	-6	0	25	444	17.8	76	3					1	0	0.0	0
1983	OTT	2																	5	55	11.0	18	0								
2	Years	9	1		0							18	3	2	-11	-5.5	-6	0	30	499	16.6	76	3					1	0	0.0	0
CLIFF POWELL Clifton M. LB 6'1 220 Arkansas B: 12/15/1948 Lake Village, AR Draft: 17-423 1970 STL																															
1971	BC	9			1																							3	52	17.3	26
CRAIG POWELL Craig Steven DE 6'4 235 Ohio State B: 11/13/1971 Youngstown, OH Draft: 1-30 1995 CLE Pro: NX																															
2002	BC	13	0	1	0	33			1	0	1																				
2003	BC	3				3																									
2	Years	16	0	1	0	36			1	0	1																				
DARIUS POWELL Darius DE 6'3 225 North Carolina; Fayetteville State B: 9/17/1988																															
2011	HAM	1				0																									
DARNELL POWELL Darnell RB 5'11 199 Tennessee-Chattanooga B: 5/31/1954 Atlanta, GA Draft: 6C-175 1976 BUF Pro: N																															
1977	MTL	2	2		0									19	74	3.9	12	0	2	6	3.0	5	0								
JAMAL POWELL Jamal W. OT 6'3 312 Texas Christian B: 4/10/1981 Houston, TX																															
2005	BC	12				0																									
2006	HAM	6				0																									
2	Years	18				0																									
JIM POWELL Jim FB																															
1947	CAL	6																													
1949	CAL	2																													
2	Years	8																													
KELVIN POWELL Kelvin LB 5'11 240 Tuskegee B: 7/11/1979 Tuskegee, AL																															
2002	EDM	10				43			1	2	1																				
2003	EDM	9	0	2	1	40	5.0																								
2004	EDM	3				14					1																				
2004	HAM	1				0																									
2004	Year	4				14					1																				
3	Years	22	0	2	1	97	5.0		1	2	2																				
KEVIN POWELL Kevin OT 6'4 255 Utah State B: 9/13/1955 Trail, BC Draft: 1-1 1979 TOR																															
1979	TOR	11	0		1																										
1980	TOR	16																													
1981	OTT	16																													
1982	OTT	16																													
1983	OTT*	16																													
1984	OTT	16	0		1																										
1985	OTT+	16	0		1																										
1986	OTT	18																													
1987	OTT	18	0		1	0																									
1988	EDM	17				0																									
1989	BC	11				0																									
1990	CAL	17				0																									
12	Years	188	0		4	0																									
PRESTON POWELL Preston FB 6'2 225 Grambling State B: 9/23/1936 Winnfield, LA Draft: 20- 1961 OAK; 7-97 1961 CLE Pro: N																															
1963	TOR	2												6	30	5.0	10	0													
STEVE POWELL Steven Orville RB 5'11 186 Truman State B: 1/2/1956 St. Louis, MO Draft: 7B-183 1978 BUF Pro: N																															
1980	HAM	1	1		0									11	15	1.4	8	0	1	2	2.0	2	0	4	48	12.0	28				
JOHN PRASSAS John Nicholas LB 6'1 225 Brown B: 9/7/1959 Los Angeles County, CA																															
1981	CAL	10	0		3																										
1982	MTL	12	0		2		1.0		2	14																					
2	Years	22	0		5		1.0		2	14																					
SHINO PRATER Shino L. CB 5'8 171 Penn State B: 4/16/1975 Cleveland, TN Pro: E																															
1999	HAM	7				14					1																				
ROLLIN PRATHER Rollin Wayne DE 6'5 232 Kansas State B: 1925 Draft: 18-115 1948 BAL-AAFC; 7-88 1950 CHIB; RS-4-35 1966 SD																															
1950	EDM	14										11	2						24	420	17.5		2								
1951	EDM	14										25	5						40	661	16.5		5					1	11	11.0	11
1952	EDM+	16			1							20	4	1	11	11.0	11	0	37	596	16.1	72	4					2	18	9.0	15
1953	EDM	1																													
1954	EDM	16	1		0							5	1						18	217	12.1	20	1								
5	Years	61	1		1							61	12	1	11	11.0	11	0	119	1894	15.9	72	12					3	29	9.7	15
GREG PRATOR Greg WR 6'1 220 Chaffey JC; Washington State B: 5/5/1984																															
2008	EDM	6				0													7	96	13.7	27	0								
KHEVIN PRATT Khevin R. WR 5'10 170 El Camino JC; Utah; Chico State B: 5/16/1970 Los Angeles, CA																															
1993	SAC	3				0													1	17	17.0	17	0								
LaVERLE PRATT LaVerle A. LB 6'2 235 Idaho B: 6/22/1943 Draft: 14-210(f) 1966 STL																															
1968	OTT	4																										1	5	5.0	5
1970	WPG	5																													
2	Years	9																										1	5	5.0	5
JOHN PRECHEK John T 6'3 235 Washington B: 1928																															
1952	SAS	15			1																										
1953	SAS	5																													
1954	SAS	1																													
1954	TOR	8																													
1954	Year	9																													
3	Years	21			1																										
NOEL PREFONTAINE Noel Michael P-K 6'0 195 Fullerton State; Arizona State; San Diego State B: 12/23/1973 Camp Pendleton, CA Pro: X																															
1998	TOR+	18				8						61	0	3	15	5.0	8	0													
1999	TOR*	18	1	0	1	8					2	13	0																		
2000	TOR*	18	5	0	2	6						10	0	1	17	17.0	17	0													
2001	TOR	11	2	1	0	3						5	0	2	4	2.0	10	0													
2002	TOR*	18	1	0	0	7						124	0																		
2003	TOR*	17	2	0	0	9						169	0	1	-9	-9.0	-9	0													
2004	TOR*	17	2	0	1	7						137	0	2	31	15.5	16	0													

Year	Team	GP	FM	FF	FR	TK	SK	YDS	IR	YDS	PD	PTS	TD	RA	YDS	AVG	LG	TD	REC	YDS	AVG	LG	TD	PR	YDS	AVG	LG	KOR	YDS	AVG	LG
2005	TOR+	18	1	2	1	8						160	0																		
2006	TOR*	18	1	0	1	9						136	0																		
2007	TOR	17	2	0	1	9						124	0																		
2008	EDM	17	3	0	1	5						171	0	1	10	10.0	10	0													
2009	EDM	17	1	0	0	5						135	0	2	38	19.0	31	0													
2010	EDM	13	2	0	3	1						96	0																		
2010	TOR	4	1	0	0	1						24	0																		
2010	Year	17	3	0	3	2						120	0																		
2011	TOR+	17				3						149	0																		
14	Years	234	24	3	11	89					2	1514	0	12	106	8.8	31	0													
ED PRELOCK Edward Patrick T 6'3 235 Kansas B: 9/1/1934 Cleveland, OH D: 3/11/2005 Draft: 16B-187 1957 BAL																															
1958	SAS	1																													
JOHN PRENDERGAST John C-E 6'1 217 Toronto B: 1930 Draft: 5-18 1955 TOR																															
1956	CAL	16	1		0																										
1957	CAL	16																										1	9	9.0	9
2	Years	32	1		0																							1	9	9.0	9
ROB PRESBURY Robert Lee, Jr. DT 6'3 260 Delaware State B: 7/18/1965 Aberdeen, MD Pro: E																															
1994	BAL	18	0		4	39	6.0	42.0																							
1995	BAL	11				19	4.0	28.0																							
1995	WPG	3	0		1	3																									
1995	Year	14	0		1	22																									
2	Years	29	0		5	61	10.0	70.0																							
BUTCH PRESSLEY William Neel FB-OHB-DB 5'11 205 Texas A&M-Kingsville B: 3/22/1941 San Patrico County, TX																															
1964	EDM	15	6		2				2	22		24	4	80	381	4.8	37	4	4	41	10.3	22	0	18	94	5.2	19	9	154	17.1	32
1965	EDM	16	2		1				1			24	4	112	563	5.0	52	4	7	48	6.9	17	0					4	43	10.8	24
1966	EDM	15	3		1							24	4	133	598	4.5	26	4	9	96	10.7	25	0								
1967	WPG	4	3		0									34	208	6.1	23	0	10	74	7.4	20	0					1	12	12.0	12
1968	WPG	7	1		0							6	1	19	123	6.5	26	0	5	68	13.6	30	1					3	113	37.7	47
1969	WPG	16	3		1							36	6	88	404	4.6	51	4	32	440	13.8	40	2					22	537	24.4	60
6	Years	73	18		5				3	22		114	19	466	2277	4.9	52	16	67	767	11.4	40	3	18	94	5.2	19	39	859	22.0	60
PRESTON C																															
1946	TOR	1																													
ED PRESTON Edward WR 6'1 173 Arkansas State* B: 12/12/1954 Pro: U																															
1979	WPG	6																													
KEN PRESTON Kenneth Joseph HB-QB 185 Queen's B: 10/19/1917 Portland, ON D: 8/2/1991																															
1946	SAS	8																													
1947	SAS	8																													
1948	SAS	12																													
3	Years	28																													
ROCK PRESTON Ricardo RB 5'8 180 Florida State B: 3/26/1975 Miami, FL																															
1999	CAL	16	0	0	1	2								37	197	5.3	23	0	5	40	8.0	28	0	3	24	8.0	13	25	543	21.7	80
2000	CAL	14	2	0	0	3						24	4	71	504	7.1	84	3	13	110	8.5	23	1	1	-1	-1.0	0	19	486	25.6	62
2001	SAS	17	2	0	1	1						6	1	41	152	3.7	15	1	12	136	11.3	22	0	24	146	6.1	26	31	639	20.6	46
3	Years	47	4	0	2	6						30	5	149	853	5.7	84	4	30	286	9.5	28	1	28	169	6.0	26	75	1668	22.2	80
ROELL PRESTON Roell WR 5'10 190 Northwest Mississippi CC; Mississippi B: 6/23/1972 Miami, FL Draft: 5-145 1995 ATL Pro: NX																															
2001	SAS	6	1	0	0	1						12	2						22	340	15.5	78	2	29	266	9.2	39				
MITCHELL PRICE Mitchell T. DE-DT 6'3 260 West Alabama B: 7/29/1961 Newberry, SC																															
1983	HAM	16	0		2		6.5		1	8																					
1984	HAM	12					5.0																								
1985	HAM	16	0		1		10.0																								
1986	HAM	15					7.0																								
1987	HAM	10	0		2	14	1.0																								
1988	CAL	6				14	4.0																								
1989	CAL	18	0		2	26	6.0																								
1990	CAL	18	0		1	36	3.0		1	3																					
1991	HAM	7				10																									
9	Years	118	0		8	100	42.5		2	11																					
PHIL PRICE Phillip Clinton CB 6'1 195 Idaho State B: 9/1/1949 Providence, RI Draft: 10-254 1972 OAK																															
1973	MTL	13							3	48																					
1974	MTL+	16			1				7	119		6	1											1	13	13.0	13				
1975	MTL	16	0		2				6	96		6	1																		
1976	MTL+	13	0		2				5	102																					
1977	SAS	6	0		1																										
1977	EDM	7	0		1				1	20																					
1977	Year	13	0		2				1	20																					
5	Years	64	0		7				22	385		12	2											1	13	13.0	13				
RAFAEL PRIEST Rafael Montre CB 5'10 180 Texas Christian B: 3/11/1987 Dallas, TX																															
2011	BC	1				1																									
FLOYD PRIESTER Floyd Wilmer, Jr. DB 6'1 195 Northeastern JC; Wyoming; Boston University B: 4/11/1949 Draft: 9-214 1972 DEN Pro: W																															
1972	CAL	9							1	2																					
1973	CAL	14							2	41																					
2	Years	23							3	43																					
JOHN PRIESTNER William John LB 6'2 230 Western Ontario B: 8/4/1958 Burlington, ON Draft: TE 1979 HAM; 11-280 1979 BAL																															
1980	HAM	7																													
1981	HAM+	16	0		3		0.5		2	31		2	0						1	5	5.0	5	0								
1982	HAM	11	0		1																										
1983	HAM	16	0		1		4.0		1	8														2	11	5.5	9	2	14	7.0	8
1984	HAM	12					4.0		1	0																					
1985	HAM	15	0		1																										
1986	HAM	3																													
7	Years	80	0		6		8.5		4	39		2	0						1	5	5.0	5	0	2	11	5.5	9	2	14	7.0	8
CAL PRINCE Calvin RB 5'9 195 Kansas; Louisville B: 5/5/1954 Americus, GA Draft: 11A-292 1978 CIN																															
1979	OTT	5	4		0							12	2	44	202	4.6	17	0	11	143	13.0	44	2								
MIKE PRINGLE Michael A. FB 5'8 186 Washington State; Fullerton State B: 10/1/1967 Los Angeles, CA Draft: 6-139 1990 ATL Pro: EN																															
1992	EDM	3				2								22	129	5.9	30	0	4	39	9.8	18	0					6	114	19.0	28
1993	SAC	18	4		1	36						30	5	60	366	6.1	44	4	56	523	9.3	24	1					27	549	20.3	36
1994	BAL*	18	9		2	10						96	16	308	1972	6.4	83	13	46	442	9.6	36	3					38	814	21.4	45
1995	BAL*	17	8		0	1						78	13	311	1791	5.8	86	13	33	276	8.4	39	0					13	320	24.6	67
1996	MTL+	8	2		0	3						42	7	127	825	6.5	65	5	12	160	13.3	41	2					26	573	22.0	41
1997	MTL*	17	2	0	1	1						80	13	306	1775	5.8	60	12	33	313	9.5	35	1					21	479	22.8	74
1998	MTL*	17	9	0	2	3						56	9	347	2065	6.0	56	9	26	349	13.4	56	0					5	78	15.6	25
1999	MTL*	16	9	0	0	2						84	14	322	1656	5.1	43	13	27	199	7.4	32	1					2	27	13.5	20
2000	MTL*	17	1	0	2	1						114	19	326	1778	5.5	62	19	34	333	9.8	35	0								
2001	MTL+	14	7	0	0	1						102	17	262	1323	5.0	47	16	28	285	10.2	32	1								
2002	MTL	6	2	0	0	0								39	227	5.8	40	0	3	47	15.7	18	0								
2003	EDM*	18	7	0	2	2						90	15	273	1376	5.0	61	13	46	419	9.1	35	2								
2004	EDM	18	6	0	1	2						54	9	259	1141	4.4	51	8	48	445	9.3	18	1								
13	Years	187	66	0	11	64						826	137	2962	16424	5.5	86	125	396	3830	9.7	56	12					138	2954	21.4	74
TIM PRINSEN Tim C 6'4 300 Edmonton Huskies Jrs.; North Dakota B: 3/1/1971 Edmonton, AB Draft: 1-4 1997 HAM																															
1997	HAM	16	0	0	1	0																									
1998	HAM	3	0	0	1	0																									
1999	HAM	17				0																									

Year	Team	GP	FM	FF	FR	TK	SK	YDS	IR	YDS	PD	PTS	TD	RA	YDS	AVG	LG	TD	REC	YDS	AVG	LG	TD	PR	YDS	AVG	LG	KOR	YDS	AVG	LG
2000	EDM	11				0																								
2001	EDM	18	1	0	0	0																								
2002	EDM	18				3																								
2003	EDM	18				1																								
2004	EDM	14				2																								
8	Years	115	1	0	2	6																								
BOB PRINT Robert Thomas LB 6'0 220 Dayton B: 1/16/1944 Cleveland, OH Pro: N																														
1969	EDM	1																												
CASEY PRINTERS Casey Jovan QB 6'2 216 Texas Christian; Florida A&M B: 5/16/1981 DeSoto, TX																														
2003	BC	18	2	0	2	0								2	44	22.0	34	0												
2004	BC*	18	10	0	3	3						54	9	82	469	5.7	40	9												
2005	BC	14	2	0	1	1						12	2	38	336	8.8	27	2												
2007	HAM	8	1	0	0	0						6	1	16	99	6.2	22	1												
2008	HAM	15	7	0	2	3						36	6	48	386	8.0	26	6												
2009	BC	5				0								10	58	5.8	25	0												
2010	BC	14	8	0	1	2						6	1	13	75	5.8	13	1												
7	Years	92	30	0	9	9						114	19	209	1467	7.0	40	19												
ANTHONY PRIOR Anthony Eugene CB 5'11 194 Washington State B: 3/27/1970 Lowell, MA Draft: 9-238 1992 NYG Pro: N																														
2000	CAL	18				76			4	135	14																		4	91	22.8	35
2001	CAL	18	0	1	0	42			1	49	14																			
2002	BC	13				38			1	0	4																			
2003	CAL	10				25					3																			
4	Years	59	0	1	0	181			6	184	35																		4	91	22.8	35
BOB PRITCHETT Robert Lewis LB-DE 6'4 235 Utah B: 6/25/1950 Palo Alto, CA																														
1974	WPG	9							2	20																				
1975	HAM	7							1	3																				
2	Years	16							3	23																				
HASSAN PROBHERBS Hassan A. DB 5'11 170 Desert JC; Portland State B: 5/28/1976 Draft: 4-29 2003 CAL																														
2003	CAL	7	0	0	3	13					1																			
2004	OTT	4				2																								
2	Years	11	0	0	3	15					1																			
BASIL PROCTOR Basil Ontario LB 6'4 245 Miami (Florida); West Virginia B: 10/6/1966 Miami, FL Draft: 7B-168 1990 NYJ Pro: E																														
1991	SAS	5				9	5.0																							
1993	SAC	3				4	1.0	7.0																						
2	Years	8				13	6.0	7.0																						
MICHAEL PROCTOR Michael QB 6'2 207 Murray State B: 7/14/1967 Sylvester, GA Pro: E																														
1993	SAS	3				0																								
WILL PROCTOR William Bartlett QB 6'2 210 Clemson B: 11/3/1983 Winter Park, FL																														
2007	MTL	4				0																								
2008	CAL	1				0								2	14	7.0	11	0												
2	Years	5				0								2	14	7.0	11	0												
ROB PRODANOVIC Rob DT 6'2 235 Calgary B: 6/1/1962 Calgary, AB Draft: 3-27 1985 WPG																														
1986	WPG	18	0		1		2.0																							
1987	WPG	18			1	17	5.0																							
1988	WPG	13	0		1	10	1.0																							
1989	WPG	9				5	2.0																							
1990	OTT	15				2																								
1991	OTT	18	1		1	12	1.0																							
1992	OTT	18	0		1	12																								
1995	BC	1				0																								
8	Years	110	1		5	58	11.0																							
MEL PROFIT Millan Earl, Jr. OE 6'5 226 UCLA B: 7/30/1941 New York, NY Draft: 16-128(f) 1963 KC; 9-113(f) 1963 LARM																														
1966	TOR	13																32	473	14.8	53	0				1	5	5.0	5
1967	TOR	14									6	1					30	432	14.4	5	1							
1968	TOR+	14	3		1						42	7	1	-9	-9.0	-9	0	40	805	20.1	66	7							
1969	TOR+	14			1						30	5					40	599	15.0	58	5							
1970	TOR+	14									12	2					39	649	16.6	47	2				1	3	3.0	3
1971	TOR*	14	0		1						30	5					39	725	18.6	75	5				1	9	9.0	9
6	Years	83	3		3						120	20	1	-9	-9.0	-9	0	220	3683	16.7	75	20				3	17	5.7	9
DAN PRONYK Dan RB 5'11 222 McGill B: 3/2/1975 Winnipeg, MB D: 12/17/2001 Thailand																														
1998	HAM	17	0	1	0	18								3	11	3.7	5	0	1	25	25.0	25	0							
TONY PROUDFOOT John Anthony S 6'1 195 New Brunswick B: 9/10/1949 Winnipeg, MB D: 12/29/2010 Montreal, QC Draft: 4-36 1971 MTL																														
1971	MTL	14	1		0				1	14														28	186	6.6	14				
1972	MTL	9							1	25																				
1973	MTL	14	0		1				1	5														51	250	4.9	21				
1974	MTL	11	1		0				1	0														17	61	3.6	9				
1975	MTL	16	0		1				1	0																				
1976	MTL	3																												
1977	MTL+	16	0		1																			1	0	0.0	0				
1978	MTL	8							1	3																		1	0	0.0	0
1979	MTL+	16	0		3				2	45																				
1980	BC	16	0		1				1	4																				
1981	BC	16	0		2		6.5		4	4																				
1982	BC	9					3.0																							
12	Years	148	2		9		9.5		13	100														97	497	5.1	21	1	0	0.0	0
MATTHIEU PROULX Matthieu S 6'1 205 Laval B: 4/16/1981 Plaster Rock, NB Draft: 1-5 2005 MTL																														
2005	MTL	18	0	3	0	23			1	56	1																			
2006	MTL	8				2																								
2007	MTL	13	0	1	0	23			2	30	3																			
2008	MTL	11	0	4	1	24	1.0	0.0	1	0	1																			
2009	MTL+	13	0	0	1	38			4	82	2																			
2010	MTL	13	0	0	2	34	1.0	3.0	1	4	3			1	22	22.0	22	0												
6	Years	76	0	8	4	144	2.0	3.0	9	172	10			1	22	22.0	22	0												
DWAYNE PROVO Dwayne Anthony CB 5'11 185 St. Mary's (Nova Scotia) B: 7/10/1970 Halifax, NS Draft: 1A-10 1995 SAS																														
1995	SAS	7				12																								
1996	SAS	8				16	1.0	8.0																						
1996	MTL	10				10					1																			
1996	Year	18				26	1.0	8.0			1																			
1998	MTL	5				6																								
1998	EDM	13				37			6	139	6	12	2																	
1998	Year	18				43			6	139	6	12	2																	
2000	EDM	18	0	1	0	37			1	2	8																			
2001	TOR	5	0	1	0	6																								
2002	OTT	2				5																								
2002	BC	2	0	1	0	1																								
2002	Year	4	0	1	0	6																								
6	Years	45	0	3	0	130	1.0	8.0	7	141	15	12	2																	
TED PROVOST Ted R. S 6'2 190 Ohio State B: 7/26/1948 Navarre, OH Draft: 7A-162 1970 LARM Pro: N																														
1973	SAS+	16	0		3				5	101		6	1																	
1974	SAS+	16	0		1				4	75																				
1975	SAS	1																												
1976	SAS	14							3	109																				

Year	Team	GP	FM	FF	FR	TK	SK	YDS	IR	YDS	PD	PTS	TD	RA	YDS	AVG	LG	TD	REC	YDS	AVG	LG	TD	PR	YDS	AVG	LG	KOR	YDS	AVG	LG
1977	SAS	14																						1	12	12.0	12				
5	Years	61	0		4				12	285		6	1											1	12	12.0	12				
KELVIN PRUENSTER Kelvin OT 6'6 265 Cal Poly (Pomona) B: 12/6/1960 Toronto, ON Draft: TE 1983 TOR																															
1983	TOR	11																													
1984	TOR	14																													
1985	TOR	16	0		1																										
1986	TOR	17																													
1987	TOR	18				1																									
1988	TOR	18				0																									
1989	TOR	18				0																									
1990	TOR	18				1																									
1991	TOR	16				2																									
9	Years	146	0		1	4																									
JAMES PRUITT James Bouvias WR-SB 6'3 200 Fullerton State B: 1/29/1964 Los Angeles, CA Draft: 4-107 1986 MIA Pro: N																															
1992	OTT	2				2													5	56	11.2	17	0								
1993	SAC	8				0						12	2						15	260	17.3	46	2								
1994	SAC	17	1		2	6						24	4						47	788	16.8	39	4					1	5	5.0	5
3	Years	27	1		2	8						36	6						67	1104	16.5	46	6					1	5	5.0	5
STEVE PRUSKI Steve G 6'0 195 B: 1925																															
1946	TOR	3																													
CECIL PRYOR Cecil Lemuel, Jr. DE 6'5 227 Michigan B: 10/7/1947 Corpus Christi, TX D: 9/13/2005 Ann Arbor, MI Draft: 5-120 1970 GB Pro: W																															
1973	MTL	5																													
GEORGE PsoFIMIS George DL 6'1 240 York B: 11/2/1972 Toronto, ON																															
2000	SAS	1				0																									
BOB PTACEK Robert J., Jr. CB-QB-LB 6'1 205 Michigan B: 4/23/1937 Cleveland, OH Draft: 8-87 1959 CLE Pro: N																															
1960	SAS	9	5		1							6	1	49	204	4.2	19	1													
1961	SAS+	16							3	94		6	1	23	88	3.8	17	0	6	112	18.7	47	0								
1962	SAS	16	4						1			12	2	34	149	4.4	18	2													
1963	SAS	15	0		1				3	71		6	1	7	0	0.0	3	0	2	31	15.5	22	0								
1964	SAS*	16	3		0				3	75		6	1	17	5	0.3	6	1						1	0	0.0	0				
1965	SAS	3	0		1																										
6	Years	75	12		3				10	240		36	6	130	446	3.4	19	4	8	143	17.9	47	0	1	0	0.0	0				
STEFAN PTASZEK Stefan WR 5'11 178 Wilfrid Laurier B: 4/15/1971 Burlington, ON Draft: 1B-9 1994 BC																															
1995	BC	3				0						6	1						4	52	13.0	20	1								
1996	BC	1				0													1	7	7.0	7	0								
1996	HAM	5				1																									
1996	Year	6				1													1	7	7.0	7	0								
1999	TOR	11				5													6	89	14.8	40	0								
2000	TOR	8				3						6	1						13	131	10.1	23	1								
4	Years	23				9						12	2						24	279	11.6	40	2								
NEIL PUFFER Neil C 6'4 230 Queen's B: 11/5/1985 Timmins, ON																															
2010	EDM	10				3																									
DAN PUGH Daniel C. RB 5'10 205 Mount Union B: 5/4/1980 Washington, DC																															
2003	MTL	7				8								9	68	7.6	46	0										5	93	18.6	22
CHARLES PULERI Charles C. QB 6'2 205 Westchester CC; Scottsdale CC; New Mexico State B: 3/1/1969 New York, NY Pro: EX																															
1993	SAC	8				0																									
BILL PULLAR William T-G-E 6'0 228 Westend Tornadoes Jrs.; McGill B: 1926																															
1946	CAL	7										5	1																		
1947	CAL+	8										5	1																		
1948	CAL	11										5	1																		
1952	CAL	13			5																										
1953	CAL	16										5	1															1	15	15.0	15
1954	CAL	15																													
1955	CAL	16	0		2				1	7																					
1956	CAL	14							1	0																		1	5	5.0	5
8	Years	100	0		7				2	7		20	4															2	20	10.0	15
TOM PULLEN Thomas TE-WR 6'3 210 Ottawa Sooners Jrs.; Michigan B: 1/31/1945 Ottawa, ON																															
1968	OTT	14	0		1														6	72	12.0	27	0					2	8	4.0	7
1969	OTT	14	2		0							6	1						17	220	12.9	60	1								
1970	MTL	14										6	1						9	104	11.6	17	1								
1971	MTL	14	0		1							18	3						34	487	14.3	74	3								
1972	OTT	14										12	2						26	353	13.6	28	2					1	0	0.0	0
1973	OTT	14																	24	375	15.6	42	0								
1974	OTT	16	1		0														32	386	12.1	26	0								
1975	TOR	7	0		1							2	0						9	101	11.2	22	0								
8	Years	107	3		3							44	7						157	2098	13.4	74	7					3	8	2.7	7
RAY PURDIN Raymond R. (Dutch) OHB 6'0 195 Northwestern B: 1939 Hillsboro, OH Draft: 7- 1961 OAK; 7-93 1961 SF																															
1961	SAS	11	3									30	5	95	473	5.0	69	3	27	281	10.4	27	2					13	343	26.4	60
1962	SAS*	15	7									84	14	131	809	6.2	93	8	34	771	22.7	104	6					17	437	25.7	35
1963	SAS	15	3		0							6	1	108	375	3.5	27	0	26	340	13.1	56	1					9	203	22.6	50
3	Years	41	13		0							120	20	334	1657	5.0	93	11	87	1392	16.0	104	9					39	983	25.2	60
DAVE PURVES David SB-TE 6'2 215 Simon Fraser B: 4/16/1961 Draft: 5-43 1982 HAM																															
1982	HAM	14																	8	66	8.3	19	0								
JOHNNY PYEATT John Joseph OE 6'3 204 none B: 9/16/1933 Florence, AZ Pro: N																															
1956	CAL	13	1		0														25	307	12.3	28	0								
1957	CAL	6	1		0							18	3						7	99	14.1	18	3					2	23	11.5	19
2	Years	19	2		0							18	3						32	406	12.7	28	3					2	23	11.5	19
FRAN PYNE Francis HB Regina Dales Jrs.																															
1947	SAS	1																													
ROB PYNE Rob DB 6'2 200 Tulsa; Regina Rams Jrs. B: 8/13/1950 Regina, SK																															
1972	SAS	8																	1	5	5.0	5	0								
1973	SAS	9	1		1																			18	65	3.6	9				
1973	WPG	2																													
1973	Year	11	1		1																			18	65	3.6	9				
1974	WPG	4																						2	0	0.0	0				
1974	CAL	9	1		1				1	12														30	73	2.4	8				
1974	Year	13	1		1				1	12														32	73	2.3	8				
3	Years	21	2		2				1	12									1	5	5.0	5	0	50	138	2.8	9				
WAYNE PYNE Wayne G-T 6'0 193 Regina Dales Jrs. B: 1918																															
1946	SAS	7																													
1947	SAS	8																													
1948	SAS	12										5	1																		
1949	SAS	13																													
1950	SAS	13																													
1951	SAS	14																													
1952	SAS	16			1																										
1953	SAS	2																													
8	Years	85			1							5	1																		
DOUG PYZER Doug HB-FW 5'9 175 B: 10/8/1923 Toronto, ON																															
1947	TOR	11										15	3					2					1								
1949	TOR	12										32	6					4					2								
1950	EDM	14										25	5	51	289	5.7		2	17	438	25.8	100	3								

Year	Team	GP	FM	FF	FR	TK	SK	YDS	IR	YDS	PD	PTS	TD	RA	YDS	AVG	LG	TD	REC	YDS	AVG	LG	TD	PR	YDS	AVG	LG	KOR	YDS	AVG	LG
1951	TOR	10										35	7					7													
1952	TOR	6										15	3					3													
1953	TOR	5										5	1										1								
6	Years	58										127	25	51	289	5.7	0	18	17	438	25.8	100	7								
AL QUALLS Albert Lawrence DE 6'3 222 Oklahoma B: 5/30/1949 Houston, TX Draft: 8A-191 1972 BAL																															
1974	SAS	1																													
BERNARD QUARLES Bernard Darwin QB 6'2 215 UCLA; Hawaii B: 1/4/1960 Los Angeles, CA Draft: 22-264 1983 LA-USFL Pro: N																															
1983	CAL	16	7		2							12	2	57	438	7.7	43	2													
1984	CAL	13	5		0							6	1	45	322	7.2	43	1													
1985	OTT	11	2		1									26	178	6.8	17	0													
1986	SAS	18	3		1									33	247	7.5	34	0													
4	Years	58	17		4							18	3	161	1185	7.4	43	3													
SHELTON QUARLES Shelton Eugene LB 6'1 228 Vanderbilt B: 9/11/1971 Nashville, TN Pro: N																															
1995	BC	16	0		2	72			1	0	1																				
1996	BC	16				55	10.0	64.0	1	22	1								1	21	21.0	21	0								
2	Years	32	0		2	127	10.0	64.0	2	22	2								1	21	21.0	21	0								
DICK QUAST Richard H. OG 6'2 238 Memphis B: 5/17/1941 Draft: 27-212(f) 1963 BUF; 16-215(f) 1963 BAL																															
1964	WPG	6																													
FRANK QUAYLE Frank Joseph, III HB 5'10 195 Virginia B: 1/15/1947 New York, NY Draft: 5-113 1969 DEN Pro: N																															
1971	HAM	2										6	1	14	12	0.9	8	1	1	22	22.0	22	0								
DAVE QUEEN Dave HB																															
1946	CAL	2																													
DAVE QUEHL David Keith WR 6'0 180 Holy Cross B: 10/4/1954 Cincinnati, OH Draft: 14-382 1976 NE																															
1978	HAM	5	2		0														13	120	9.2	22	0	2	17	8.5	15				
1979	OTT	1																	1	13	13.0	13	0	2	22	11.0	12				
1979	SAS	3																	10	126	12.6	21	0	1	8	8.0	8				
1979	Year	4																	11	139	12.6	21	0	3	30	10.0	12				
2	Years	6	2		0														24	259	10.8	22	0	5	47	9.4	15				
VERNON QUICK Everette Vernon G 6'1 220 Wofford B: 6/24/1929 Bennettsville, SC Draft: 25-295 1951 CHIC																															
1953	CAL	1																													
RONNIE QUILLIAN Ronald FB 6'2 210 Tulane B: 11/27/1933 Troy, AL Draft: 22-255 1957 GB																															
1957	OTT	5										3	0	77	317	4.1	15	0	3	5	1.7	7	0								
1958	OTT	12										9	1	95	547	5.8	23	1	9	79	8.8	25	0								
2	Years	17										12	1	172	864	5.0	23	1	12	84	7.0	25	0								
RONNIE QUILLEN Ronald E. HB 5'9 210 East Tennessee State B: 8/12/1939 Kingsport, TN																															
1961	EDM	8										24	4	11	64	5.8	11	0	12	252	21.0	65	4	28	112	4.0	24	3	96	32.0	59
CHUCK QUILTER Charles Rew DT 6'0 240 Tyler JC B: 5/8/1926 Shreveport, LA Pro: AN																															
1951	EDM	11																													
1953	EDM	4																													
1954	BC	12			2																										
1955	BC	16																													
1956	BC	6																													
1957	BC	12												0	4		4	0													
1958	BC	16												1	-3	-3.0	-3	0													
1959	BC	11																													
1960	CAL	16	0		2																										
9	Years	104	0		4									1	1	1.0	4	0													
NEIL QUILTER Neil OG 6'2 250 British Columbia B: 8/24/1956 Vancouver, BC Draft: 1A-6 1978 MTL																															
1979	SAS	14	0		1																										
1980	SAS	15																													
1981	SAS	16																													
1982	SAS	13																													
1983	SAS	16	0		1																										
1984	SAS	5																													
1985	SAS	16																													
1986	SAS	11																													
1987	WPG	1				0																									
9	Years	107	0		2	0																									
COLIN QUINEY Colin OT-OG 6'5 310 Grand Valley State B: 7/12/1972 Toronto, ON																															
1997	HAM	13				0																									
BILL QUINLAN William David DE 6'3 248 Michigan State B: 6/19/1932 Lawrence, MA Draft: 3B-37 1956 CLE Pro: N																															
1954	HAM	14										2	0															2	19	9.5	14
BRIAN QUINN Brian B none																															
1946	OTT	3																													
JOHNNY QUINN John M., Jr. WR 6'0 202 North Texas B: 11/6/1983 Harrisburg, PA																															
2009	SAS	18				1						6	1						13	218	16.8	38	1	2	4	2.0	6	5	84	16.8	26
MIKE QUINN Michael Patrick QB 6'4 218 Stephen F. Austin State B: 4/15/1974 Las Vegas, NV Pro: EN																															
2006	WPG	7	2	0	0	1								2	14	7.0	8	0													
PETER QUINN Peter FL 5'11 192 Queen's B: 1943 Draft: 1C-8 1963 OTT																															
1963	OTT	14							1	23														36	148	4.1	13				
1964	OTT	11	1		0														1	28	28.0	28	0	29	130	4.5	11				
2	Years	25	1		0				1	23									1	28	28.0	28	0	65	278	4.3	13				
VERNELL QUINN Vernell LB 6'1 230 Weber State B: 9/29/1964 Jackson, MS																															
1988	HAM	6	0		1	23	1.0		0	12																					
1989	CAL	14	0		1	28	2.0		1	0																					
2	Years	20	0		2	51	3.0		1	12																					
PETER QUINNEY Peter FB 6'1 220 Wilfrid Laurier B: 6/1/1986 Belleville, ON Draft: 5-35 2009 WPG																															
2010	TOR	10				1																									
WILLIE QUINNIE Willie WR 6'2 180 Alabama-Birmingham B: 10/2/1980 Birmingham, AL Pro: E																															
2006	HAM	8	3	0	0	0													2	38	19.0	34	0	12	59	4.9	12	25	464	18.6	35
BILL QUINTER William H. LB 6'1 215 Indiana B: 10/2/1939 Takoma Park, MD																															
1962	OTT	2																													
1963	OTT	14							1	6									1	7	7.0	7	0								
1964	OTT	9	0		1														1	16	16.0	16	0								
1965	OTT	13	0		1				1	-4																					
1966	OTT	3																													
5	Years	41	0		2				2	2									2	23	11.5	16	0								
ROBERT QUIROGA Robert Anthony WR 6'2 188 Baylor B: 2/7/1982 San Antonio, TX																															
2005	OTT	4				1													9	134	14.9	40	0								
MATTHIEU QUIVIGER Matthew OT 6'5 282 McGill B: 11/5/1970 Montreal, QC Draft: 1-10 1994 SAS																															
1996	MTL	4				0																									
JIM QUONDAMATTEO Jim OG 5'9 220 B: 10/7/1927 Hamilton, ON D: 11/16/2006 Burlington, ON																															
1949	MTL	12																													
1950	EDM	14																													
1951	EDM	14																													
1952	EDM	16			1																										
1953	EDM+	15																										1	0	0.0	0
1954	EDM	16																													
1955	EDM	16	0		4							5	1																		
7	Years	103	0		5							5	1															1	0	0.0	0
WARREN RABB Samuel Warren QB 6'1 202 Louisiana State B: 12/12/1937 Baton Rouge, LA Draft: FS 1960 DAL; 2-15 1960 DET Pro: N																															
1963	MTL	7										12	2	23	79	3.4	15	2													

Year	Team	GP	FM	FF	FR	TK	SK	YDS	IR	YDS	PD	PTS	TD	RA	YDS	AVG	LG	TD	REC	YDS	AVG	LG	TD	PR	YDS	AVG	LG	KOR	YDS	AVG	LG
MICHEL RABY Michel DT 6'1 260 Ottawa B: 12/17/1968 Hull, QC Draft: SD-1-3 1991 OTT																															
1991	OTT	4				4																									
1992	OTT	14	0		1	16	2.0	13.0																							
1993	OTT	16	0		1	20																									
1995	BC	3				0																									
1996	MTL	1				0																									
1996	SAS	2				2																									
1996	Year	3				2																									
5	Years	38	0		2	42	2.0	13.0																							
BRENT RACETTE Brent DE-DT 6'2 230 British Columbia B: 8/12/1955 Prince Albert, SK Draft: 4-28 1979 TOR																															
1980	TOR	16	0		1																										
1981	TOR	13																													
1982	BC	7					1.0																								
1983	BC	14	0		2		6.0																								
1984	SAS	1																													
1984	WPG	7					2.0																								
1984	Year	8					2.0																								
1985	WPG	16	0		3		1.0																								
6	Years	67	0		6		10.0																								
LATARIO RACHAL Latario Deshawn WR 5'11 183 El Camino JC; Fresno State B: 1/31/1973 Lynwood, CA Pro: ENX																															
2000	CAL	10	1	0	0	12						6	1						11	172	15.6	55	1	2	23	11.5	15	8	155	19.4	30
TRACO RACHAL Traco DB 6'1 195 Fresno CC; Texas A&M-Commerce B: 12/18/1975																															
2001	SAS	1				5																									
MOE RACINE Maurice OT-K 6'4 232 none B: 10/14/1937 Cornwall, ON																															
1959	OTT	4																													
1960	OTT	14																													
1961	OTT	14																													
1962	OTT+	14										79	0																		
1963	OTT	13										57	0																		
1964	OTT	14										68	0																		
1965	OTT+	14										75	0																		
1966	OTT+	14										71	0																		
1967	OTT	14										42	0																		
1968	OTT	14																													
1969	OTT	6																													
1970	OTT	14	1		1																										
1971	OTT	14																													
1972	OTT	14	0		1																										
1973	OTT	14	0		1									1	3	3.0	3	0													
1974	OTT	16																													
16	Years	207	1		3							392	0	1	3	3.0	3	0													
EMIL RADIK Emil J., Jr. HB 5'11 185 Nebraska-Omaha B: 8/1/1933 Draft: 11-123 1955 BAL																															
1955	MTL	3										5	1	20	88	4.4	12	1	3	46	15.3	34	0	3	11	3.7	10				
JULIAN RADLEIN Julian FB 6'2 245 British Columbia B: 2/6/1981 Kingston, Jamaica Draft: 1-3 2003 HAM																															
2003	HAM	18	2	0	0	9						42	7	59	167	2.8	22	7	24	204	8.5	23	0					3	22	7.3	11
2004	HAM	18	3	0	0	9						30	5	33	69	2.1	9	5	13	122	9.4	32	0								
2005	HAM	15	1	0	2	9						30	5	30	85	2.8	9	4	9	91	10.1	23	1								
2006	HAM	18	3	0	0	4						18	3	17	43	2.5	10	3	13	74	5.7	12	0					1	9	9.0	9
2007	HAM	15				1								5	22	4.4	6	0	7	60	8.6	23	0								
5	Years	84	9	0	2	32						120	20	144	386	2.7	22	19	66	551	8.3	32	1					4	31	7.8	11
CHUCK RADLEY Charles Justin T-G 6'0 205 Montreal Ints. B: 4/16/1925 Montreal, QC																															
1947	SAS	8																													
1948	SAS	3																													
1949	SAS	13																													
1950	SAS	11																													
1951	SAS	10																													
1952	SAS	10																													
6	Years	55																													
BILL RADOVICH William Alex T 5'9 238 Southern California B: 6/24/1915 Chicago, IL D: 3/7/2002 Newport Beach, CA Pro: AN																															
1949	EDM	14																													
WALT RADZICK Walter OT-MG 6'3 260 Toronto B: 5/25/1935																															
1958	CAL	16	0		2				1	8																					
1959	CAL	11																													
1960	TOR	11																													
1961	TOR	14																													
1962	TOR	14																													
1963	TOR	14																													
1964	TOR	13																													
1965	HAM	6																													
8	Years	99	0		2				1	8																					
MIKE RAE Michael John QB 6'0 200 Southern California B: 7/26/1951 Long Beach, CA Draft: 8-205 1973 OAK Pro: NU																															
1973	TOR	14	1		0									12	48	4.0	14	0													
1974	TOR	16	2		0									54	209	3.9	19	0													
1975	TOR	11	3		0									11	67	6.1	16	0													
3	Years	41	6		0									77	324	4.2	19	0													
PETE RAEFORD James Edward, Jr. CB 5'10 180 Northern Michigan B: 12/13/1959 Mooresville, NC Pro: U																															
1985	CAL	1																													
GENE RAESZ Eugene Ernest, Jr. FL 6'1 198 Rice B: 11/20/1940 Williamson County, TX Draft: 23-182 1963 HOU																															
1963	EDM	9										6	1	16	108	6.8	23	0	18	196	10.9	20	1								
ANGELO RAFFIN Angelo OG-OT 6'4 240 North Carolina B: 1946																															
1970	MTL	7																										1	0	0.0	0
1971	TOR	1																													
2	Years	8																										1	0	0.0	0
VITO RAGAZZO Vito E. OE 6'3 200 William & Mary B: 3/17/1927 Draft: 9-113 1950 CHIC																															
1953	HAM	13										5	1										1								
1954	HAM	14							4	31		10	2						22	263	12.0	37	2								
2	Years	27							4	31		15	3						22	263	12.0	37	3								
RANDY RAGON Randy FL 5'10 175 Calgary Jrs.; Oregon; Gavilan JC; U.S. International B: 1/5/1952 Calgary, AB Draft: 4-31 1975 BC																															
1975	CAL	12																						10	64	6.4	15				
1977	EDM	4																										1	16	16.0	16
1978	SAS	1																													
3	Years	17																						10	64	6.4	15	1	16		16
DAVE RAIMEY David E. OHB-DB 5'10 190 Michigan B: 11/18/1940 Dayton, OH Draft: 9-121 1963 CLE Pro: N																															
1965	WPG+	16	3		2							30	5	130	1052	8.1	45	4	20	218	10.9	30	0					22	635	28.9	105
1966	WPG*	16	2		0							24	4	188	1223	6.5	100	3	28	389	13.9	96	1					21	474	22.6	48
1967	WPG+	15	7		1							48	8	125	772	6.2	94	4	39	470	12.1	56	4					29	744	25.7	78
1968	WPG+	16	9		2							48	8	162	781	4.8	75	5	43	509	11.8	40	2					31	930	30.0	93
1969	WPG*	3	3		1									20	89	4.5		0					0								
1969	TOR	9	2		0							60	10	109	740	6.8	48	7					3					12	312	26.0	47
1969	Year	12	5		1							60	10	129	829	6.4		7	19	306	16.1	64	3					12	312	26.0	47
1970	TOR	14	0		1							24	4	142	839	5.9	39	2	19	297	15.6	60	2					3	69	23.0	28
1971	TOR	14							4	14		6	1															4	70	17.5	20

Year	Team	GP	FM	FF	FR	TK	SK	YDS	IR	YDS	PD	PTS	TD	RA	YDS	AVG	LG	TD	REC	YDS	AVG	LG	TD	PR	YDS	AVG	LG	KOR	YDS	AVG	LG
1972	TOR	13							3	5				7	32	4.6	15	0	2	0	0.0	9	0					4	85	21.3	27
1973	TOR	14	0		1				3	11														1	3	3.0	3				
1974	TOR	12							5	130		6	1															14	403	28.8	46
10	Years	133	26		8				15	160		246	41	883	5528	6.3	100	25	151	1883	12.5	96	12	1	3	3.0	3	140	3722	26.6	105
MIKE RAINES Vaughn Michael DT-DE 6'5 255 Alabama B: 2/14/1953 Montgomery, AL Draft: 6-138 1974 SF; 8-90 1974 SC-WFL Pro: NU																															
1975	MTL	5							1	11		6	1																		
1975	OTT	7	0		1				1	24																					
1975	Year	12	0		1				2	35		6	1																		
1976	OTT	9			1																										
1977	OTT	16	0		3																										
1978	OTT+	10	0		1																										
1979	OTT+	16	0		1																										
1980	OTT+	16	0		1																										
1981	OTT*	15					2.5																								
1982	OTT	7																													
1982	WPG	1																													
1982	Year	8																													
8	Years	94	0		8		2.5		2	35		6	1																		
BRETT RALPH Brett WR 5'10 178 Wyoming; Boise State; Alberta* B: 3/3/1982 Raymond, AB Draft: 6-45 2005 CAL																															
2005	CAL	18				2						18	3						34	609	17.9	61	3	1	2	2.0	2				
2006	CAL	18				0													7	76	10.9	24	0								
2007	CAL	18	1	0	0	8						18	3	5	30	6.0	24	0	53	695	13.1	39	3								
2008	CAL	18				3						30	5						49	683	13.9	65	5								
2009	CAL	18	1	0	0	3						6	1						29	403	13.9	62	1								
5	Years	90	2	0	0	16						72	12	5	30	6.0	24	0	172	2466	14.3	65	12	1	2	2.0	2				
BROCK RALPH Brock WR-SB 6'2 185 Wyoming B: 7/16/1980 Raymond, AB Draft: 2-13 2002 OTT																															
2003	EDM	7				2						6	1						2	20	10.0	13	1								
2004	EDM	16	1	0	1	2						6	1	1	-2	-2.0	-2	0	49	634	12.9	56	1					0	5		5
2005	EDM	5				0													4	40	10.0	17	0								
2005	HAM	5				1						6	1						5	56	11.2	36	1								
2005	Year	10				1						6	1						9	96	10.7	36	1								
2006	HAM	18	1	0	0	3						18	3						41	457	11.1	44	3	1	10	10.0	10	4	15	3.8	15
2007	HAM	14	1	0	0	4						18	3	7	43	6.1	13	0	50	721	14.4	88	3								
2008	EDM	10				2													13	164	12.6	46	0								
2009	WPG	17	2	0	0	2						12	2	22	135	6.1	24	0	43	559	13.0	32	2								
2010	WPG	16				1						8	1	2	24	12.0	22	0	31	394	12.7	49	1								
8	Years	103	5	0	1	17						74	12	32	200	6.3	24	0	238	3045	12.8	88	12	1	10	10.0	10	4	20	5.0	15
SEAN RALPH Sean FB Chateauguay Raiders Jrs.; Ottawa Draft: 3-26 1995 TOR																															
1995	OTT	4				1								1	3	3.0	3	0													
KEN-YON RAMBO Ken-Yon Cedric WR-SB 6'0 195 Ohio State B: 10/4/1978 Cerritos, CA Draft: 7B-229 2001 OAK Pro: N																															
2005	CAL	17	1	0	2	2						24	4	3	10	3.3	5	1	54	789	14.6	57	3	26	329	12.7	36	4	60	15.0	20
2006	CAL	17	2	0	2	2						30	5	12	113	9.4	36	0	50	704	14.1	60	5	15	100	6.7	18				
2007	CAL	17	1	0	0	2						60	10						62	983	15.9	57	10	7	19	2.7	10				
2008	CAL*	18	3	0	0	1						48	8	2	11	5.5	6	0	100	1473	14.7	81	8	1	15	15.0	15				
2009	CAL	3				0						2	0	1	0	0.0	0	0	17	179	10.5	36	0								
2010	CAL	14	2	0	0	7						48	8	2	6	3.0	3	0	72	1172	16.3	100	8								
2011	CAL	12				0						30	5						51	695	13.6	54	5								
7	Years	98	9	0	4	14						242	40	20	140	7.0	36	1	406	5995	14.8	100	39	49	463	9.4	36	4	60	15.0	20
JIM RAMEY James Edward, Jr. DE 6'4 247 Kentucky B: 3/9/1957 Louisville, KY Draft: 3-70 1979 CLE Pro: NU																															
1980	HAM	6																													
1981	HAM	12					5.0																								
1982	HAM	8					2.0																								
3	Years	26					7.0																								
BRIAN RAMSAY Brian OT-OG-TE 6'7 300 Rocky Mountain; Butte JC; New Mexico B: 2/24/1980 Victoria, BC Draft: 5-39 2006 TOR																															
2007	TOR	18				0																									
2008	TOR	18	0	0	1	1																									
2009	TOR	15				1																									
2010	HAM	13				1																									
2011	EDM	16				1																									
5	Years	80	0	0	1	4																									
RAY RAMSEY Raymond LeRoy OE 6'2 166 Bradley B: 7/18/1921 Springfield, IL D: 8/25/2009 Springfield, IL Draft: 10-82 1947 CHIC Pro: AN																															
1954	HAM+	12							4	54		40	8	3	8	2.7	14	0	42	770	18.3	88	8					1	37	37.0	37
1955	HAM	7							4	27									18	194	10.8	16	0					1	2	2.0	2
1956	HAM	1																													
3	Years	20							8	81		40	8	3	8	2.7	14	0	60	964	16.1	88	8					2	39	19.5	37
BARRY RANDALL Barry OT 6'3 245 Eastern Washington B: 3/25/1943 London, ON																															
1967	MTL	14																										1	0	0.0	0
1968	MTL	13																													
1969	MTL	14																													
1970	MTL	14																													
1971	MTL	14																													
1972	MTL	14	0		2																										
1973	MTL	14																													
1974	MTL	16																													
1975	MTL	16	0		1																										
1976	MTL	16																													
1977	MTL	16																													
11	Years	161	0		3																							1	0	0.0	0
BRIAN RANDALL Brian CB 5'11 185 Delaware State B: 1/28/1971 Salem, NJ																															
1994	OTT	5				10					2																				
1995	SAS	13	1		0	23			3	94	0	6	1											12	84	7.0	15				
2	Years	18	1		0	33			3	94	2	6	1											12	84	7.0	15				
BRYAN RANDALL Bryan Jemar QB 6'0 222 Virginia Tech B: 8/16/1983 Charleston, WV																															
2008	WPG	18				0								12	78	6.5	17	0													
2009	WPG	11				0								4	23	5.8	13	0													
2	Years	29				0								16	101	6.3	17	0													
GREG RANDALL Gregory Wayne OL 6'5 320 Coffeyville CC; Michigan State B: 6/23/1978 Galveston, TX Draft: 4-127 2000 NE Pro: N																															
2006	HAM	9				0																									
DANE RANDOLPH Dane OT 6'5 300 Maryland B: 9/4/1986 Pensacola, FL																															
2010	BC	7				0																									
HAROLD RANDOLPH James Harold LB 6'2 215 East Carolina B: 1/28/1956 Greenville, NC Draft: 6-166 1978 DAL Pro: U																															
1978	TOR	5																													
1981	MTL	3																													
2	Years	8																													
PAUL RANDOLPH Paul G. LB 6'0 235 Tennessee-Martin B: 6/22/1966 Gainesville, GA																															
1989	WPG	14	0		1	63	2.0																								
1990	WPG	13	0		1	52	3.0		1	0																					
1991	WPG	17	0		3	53	6.0		1	2									1	47	47.0	47	0					1	8	8.0	8
1992	WPG	18	0		1	80	7.0	39.0	1	27														2	4	2.0	4				
1993	WPG	18				59	3.0	24.0	4	74																					
1994	WPG	18				68	7.0	51.0	1	22	1																				
1995	WPG	12				33	4.0	34.0	1	16	0																	1	11	11.0	11

Year	Team	GP	FM	FF	FR	TK	SK	YDS	IR	YDS	PD	PTS	TD	RA	YDS	AVG	LG	TD	REC	YDS	AVG	LG	TD	PR	YDS	AVG	LG	KOR	YDS	AVG	LG
1996	MTL+	18	0		3	88	4.0	36.0	1	29	2	6	1						1	13	13.0	13	1								
1997	MTL	7				31																									
9	Years	135	0		9	527	36.0	184.0	10	170	3	6	1						2	60	30.0	47	1	2	4	2.0	4	2	19	9.5	11
JOSH RANEK Josh RB 5'8 205 South Dakota State B: 5/11/1978 Tyndall, SD																															
2002	OTT	13	6	0	0	4						30	5	128	689	5.4	28	3	49	456	9.3	25	2								
2003	OTT+	18	2	0	0	2						72	12	176	1122	6.4	38	8	41	373	9.1	32	4					28	554	19.8	36
2004	OTT+	18	2	0	3	5						60	10	219	1060	4.8	25	8	59	673	11.4	47	2					20	441	22.1	44
2005	OTT+	18	1	1	1	3						42	7	216	1157	5.4	71	5	76	750	9.9	51	2								
2006	HAM	10	2	0	0	2						18	3	85	343	4.0	22	0	26	254	9.8	37	3								
2007	SAS	1				0						6	1	2	6	3.0	4	1													
6	Years	78	13	1	4	16						228	38	826	4377	5.3	71	25	251	2506	10.0	51	13					48	995	20.7	44
AL RANKIN Al FL 6'0 202 Saskatoon Hilltops Jrs. B: 1947																															
1969	SAS	7																	1	27	27.0	27	0								
1970	SAS	16																	4	81	20.3	37	0								
1971	CAL	16	5		1														2	42	21.0	32	0	62	391	6.3	19	3	28	9.3	16
1972	BC	4																						13	55	4.2	11				
4	Years	43	5		1														7	150	21.4	37	0	75	446	5.9	19	3	28	9.3	16
CHRIS RANKIN Chris WR 5'8 185 McMaster B: 6/28/1980																															
2004	HAM	1				1																									
BRIAN RANSOM Brian Anthony QB 6'3 205 Tennessee State B: 7/9/1960 Omaha, NE																															
1986	MTL	18	9		0							12	2	37	141	3.8	24	2													
JOHN RAPOSO John DE 6'4 245 Toronto B: 8/8/1971 Toronto, ON Draft: 5-42 1995 TOR																															
1996	TOR	18				6																									
1997	TOR	18				14																									
1998	TOR	18	0	1	0	10					1																				
2000	TOR	18				18	1.0	2.0																				1	7	7.0	7
4	Years	72	0	1	0	48	1.0	2.0			1																	1	7	7.0	7
STEVE RAQUET Steve DE-TE 6'5 240 Holy Cross B: 2/1/1962 Buffalo, NY Draft: 12-316 1984 CIN; 8B-162 1984 OAK-USFL																															
1984	MTL*	12			3		15.0																					1	14	14.0	14
1985	MTL	15	0		3		6.0		1	22																					
1986	MTL	16	0		1		8.0																								
3	Years	43	0		7		29.0		1	22																		1	14	14.0	14
SALEEM RASHEED Saleem Abdul LB 6'2 229 Alabama B: 6/15/1981 Birmingham, AL Draft: 3-69 2002 SF Pro: N																															
2008	CAL	9				30																									
DAN RASHOVICH Dan LB 6'1 220 Simon Fraser B: 11/30/1960 Toronto, ON Draft: 2-13 1984 OTT																															
1984	OTT	16	0		2																										
1985	TOR	16																													
1986	TOR	18																										4	28	7.0	17
1987	SAS	15				2																									
1988	SAS	18				24	1.0																								
1989	SAS	10				22	1.0		1	3																		1	5	5.0	5
1990	SAS+	18	0		3	80	3.0		1	25																					
1991	SAS	18	0		2	84	3.0																								
1992	SAS	18	0		1	90	4.0	31.0																							
1993	SAS	11				19																									
1994	SAS	10	0		1	46	2.0	8.0	1	58	0	6	1																		
1995	SAS	18	0		5	40	1.0	6.0			1																				
1996	SAS	18	0		1	64	6.0	27.0																							
1997	SAS	16	0	0	2	27																									
1998	SAS	17	0	0	1	38	2.0	14.0			1																				
1999	SAS	18				31																									
16	Years	255	0	0	18	567	23.0	86.0	3	86	2	6	1															5	33	6.6	17
DON RATLIFF Donald Eugene DE 6'5 250 Maryland B: 7/17/1950 Baltimore, MD Pro: NW																															
1977	BC	1				1																									
GEORGE RATTERMAN George William QB 6'0 192 Notre Dame B: 11/12/1926 Cincinnati, OH D: 11/3/2007 Centennial, CO Draft: 16-139 1948 BOS Pro: AN																															
1951	MTL	11																													
NORM RAUHAUS Norm S-OE-CB 6'1 195 Weston Wildcats Jrs. B: 1935																															
1956	WPG	14							4	35									1	7	7.0	7	0								
1957	WPG	16	1		1				3	7		6	1						4	7	1.8	22	0								
1958	WPG	16	0		2				4	99									3	48	16.0	26	0	2	18	9.0	12				
1959	WPG	14							1										6	77	12.8	21	0	3	3	1.0	2				
1960	WPG	16	0		3				6	25									9	127	14.1	37	0	1	0	0.0	0				
1961	WPG+	15							3	46		6	1						5	62	12.4	26	0	2	3	1.5	8				
1962	WPG	16	1		3				1															2	3	1.5	3				
1963	WPG	16	0		1				2	25																					
1964	WPG	16	0		1				2	3		6	1						2	34	17.0	24	0	1	3	3.0	3				
1965	WPG	16	0		1				1										7	119	17.0	37	0					1	7	7.0	7
1966	WPG	15	0		1				4	58		6	1											1	0	0.0	0				
1967	WPG	15							3	19														1	27	27.0	27				
12	Years	185	2		13				34	317		24	4						37	481	13.0	37	0	13	57	4.4	27	1	7	7.0	7
JOHN RAULICK John OT-DT-OG 6'0 230 Eastern Michigan B: 1935 Gardenton, MB																															
1957	TOR	14																										2	18	9.0	18
1959	MTL	9																													
1960	MTL	14																													
1961	MTL	14																													
1962	MTL	3																													
1962	TOR	9																													
1962	Year	12																													
1963	TOR	14																													
1964	TOR	9																													
1966	TOR	8																													
8	Years	85																										2	18	9.0	18
JOE RAUSCH Joe E Regina Dales Jrs.																															
1946	SAS	3																													
MIKE RAWLUK Mike E Regina Dales Jrs.																															
1946	SAS	8																													
DARRYL RAY Darryl WR 6'3 207 Ottawa B: 10/5/1977 Thunder Bay, ON Draft: 6C-54 2002 TOR																															
2002	TOR	7				2													5	39	7.8	18	0								
2003	OTT	6				1													5	90	18.0	37	0								
2004	OTT	11				0													11	111	10.1	28	0					1	0	0.0	0
2005	OTT	6				0																						1	5	5.0	5
2006	WPG	5				1																									
5	Years	35				4													21	240	11.4	37	0					2	5	2.5	5
DAVID RAY David Eugene, Jr. K-P-S 6'0 192 Alabama B: 9/19/1944 Phenix, City, AL Draft: 16-243 1966 CLE Pro: N																															
1968	MTL	8							3	29		45	0																		
RICKY RAY Ricky Lee CB 5'11 185 Norfolk State B: 5/30/1957 Waynesboro, VA Draft: 6-146 1979 NO Pro: NU																															
1982	OTT	8	0		1																										
1983	OTT	2																													
2	Years	10	0		1																										
RICKY RAY Richard Junior QB 6'3 208 Shasta CC; Sacramento State B: 10/22/1979 Happy Camp, CA																															
2002	EDM	18	9	0	1	0						6	1	44	232	5.3	32	1	1	-4	-4.0	-4	0								
2003	EDM	18	9	0	2	1						12	2	62	352	5.7	35	2													

Year	Team	GP	FM	FF	FR	TK	SK	YDS	IR	YDS	PD	PTS	TD	RA	YDS	AVG	LG	TD	REC	YDS	AVG	LG	TD	PR	YDS	AVG	LG	KOR	YDS	AVG	LG
2005	EDM	18	13	4	6	0						54	9	83	353	4.3	26	9													
2006	EDM*	18	6	0	0	1						54	9	92	469	5.1	27	9													
2007	EDM	13	8	0	1	1								41	232	5.7	26	0													
2008	EDM	18	13	0	2	2						30	5	75	258	3.4	15	5													
2009	EDM	18	3	0	0	1						36	6	47	296	6.3	27	6													
2010	EDM	17	9	0	4	2						18	3	36	302	8.4	45	3													
2011	EDM	18	13	0	5	1						6	1	41	258	6.3	27	1													
9	Years	156	83	4	21	9						216	36	521	2752	5.3	45	36	1	-4	-4.0	-4	0								
RON RAY Ronald G. DT-DE-OG 6'4 245 Howard Payne B: 9/16/1933 Detroit, MI D: 4/25/2001 Draft: SS 1960 LAC; 11-125 1960 GB																															
1960	HAM	7																													
1961	HAM	14																													
1962	HAM	8																													
1963	HAM	12																													
4	Years	41																													
TERRY RAY Terry LB-S 6'1 187 Oklahoma B: 10/12/1969 Shape, Belgium Draft: 6-158 1992 ATL Pro: N																															
1999	EDM+	18	0	1	3	102	4.0	36.0	2	65	3	6	1																		
2000	EDM*	17	1	6	1	113	4.0	31.0	1	1	1																				
2001	EDM*	16	0	4	2	89	2.0	9.0	2	23	3																				
2002	EDM	14	0	2	1	77	4.0		2	18	4																	1	19	19.0	19
2003	WPG	13	0	3	1	36	1.0		1	1	0																				
2004	WPG	13	0	3	3	44			2	31	1			1	15	15.0	15	0													
6	Years	91	1	19	11	461	15.0	76.0	10	139	12	6	1	1	15	15.0	15	0										1	19	19.0	19
TOM RAYAM Thomas Leon OT 6'7 330 Alabama B: 1/3/1968 Orlando, FL Draft: 10B-270 1990 WAS Pro: N																															
1995	BIR	17	0		1	0																									
1996	EDM	18	0		2	1													1	1	1.0	1	0								
1997	EDM+	17				2																									
1998	EDM	18				1																									
1999	CAL	6				0																									
2000	CAL	18				3																									
2001	CAL	18	0	0	1	1																									
2002	TOR	14				0																									
8	Years	126	0	0	4	8													1	1	1.0	1	0								
JOHN RAYBORN John William QB 6'2 217 Texas-El Paso B: 8/21/1975 Arlington, TX																															
1999	SAS	18				0								3	8	2.7	4	0													
2000	SAS	18				0								2	14	7.0	8	0													
2	Years	36				0								5	22	4.4	8	0													
HAROLD RAYMOND Harold HB																															
1946	CAL	4																													
1947	CAL	5																													
2	Years	9																													
KEON RAYMOND Keon D. LB-DH-CB-S 5'9 192 Highland CC; Middle Tennessee State B: 11/27/1982 St. Louis, MO																															
2008	CAL	3	0	0	1	7						6	1																		
2009	CAL	18	0	0	1	58	1.0	13.0	1	6	4																				
2010	CAL	18	1	1	3	55	1.0	6.0	4	24	9	6	1																		
2011	CAL+	18	0	0	1	48			5	237	7	12	2											2	28	14.0	21	4	95	23.8	31
4	Years	57	1	1	6	168	2.0	19.0	10	267	20	24	4											2	28	14.0	21	4	95	23.8	31
FABIAN RAYNE Fabian RB 5'11 222 Western Ontario B: 3/31/1977 Antigua Draft: 6-44 2000 BC																															
2001	TOR	12	2	0	1	3								4	1	0.3	3	0	2	10	5.0	7	0								
CHASE RAYNOCK Chase A. OT 6'6 308 Montana B: 9/29/1977 Billings, MT Pro: EX																															
2003	BC	2				0																									
2003	HAM	14	0	0	1	2																									
2003	Year	16	0	0	1	2																									
RICK RAZZANO Richard Anthony LB 5'11 227 Virginia Tech B: 11/15/1955 New Castle, PA Pro: N																															
1978	TOR	8	0		1				1	0																					
1979	TOR	15	0		1				3	49																					
2	Years	23	0		2				4	49																					
SEAN READE Sean RB 5'11 210 Western Ontario B: 2/23/1974 Harrowsmith, ON Draft: 2B-13 1996 WPG																															
1996	TOR	1				1																						2	32	16.0	18
1996	OTT	15				2								3	11	3.7	10	0													
1996	Year	16				3																						2	32	16.0	18
RUSS READER Russell Burton, Jr. QB 6'0 185 Michigan State B: 6/26/1923 Ypsilanti, MI D: 8/11/1995 Milford, MI Draft: 21-195 1947 CHIB Pro: N																															
1949	TOR	4										11	2					2													
JOHNNY REAGAN John HB 6'1 190 Montana B: 1920 Draft: 4-28 1947 CHI-AAFC																															
1947	WPG	4										8	1										1								
TOMMY REAMON Thomas Waverly RB 5'10 192 Fort Scott CC; Missouri B: 3/12/1952 Virgilina, VA Draft: 9A-223 1974 PIT; 23-275 1974 FLA-WFL Pro: NW																															
1977	SAS	6	2		0							18	3	78	411	5.3	61	3	12	37	3.1	11	0	1	29	29.0	29	7	138	19.7	35
STEPHEN REAVES Stephen QB 6'1 204 Michigan State; Southern Mississippi B: 12/5/1984 Tampa, FL																															
2009	TOR	4	1	0	0	0								1	3	3.0	3	0													
WILLARD REAVES Willard Sheldon RB 5'11 200 Northern Arizona B: 8/17/1959 Flagstaff, AZ Pro: N																															
1983	WPG+	9	2		0							56	9	164	898	5.5	75	9	16	185	11.6	24	0					5	164	32.8	41
1984	WPG*	16	6		2							108	18	304	1733	5.7	68	14	40	407	10.2	27	4					6	143	23.8	34
1985	WPG*	16	6		2							60	10	267	1323	5.0	68	9	20	289	14.5	76	1					1	7	7.0	7
1986	WPG	6	2		0							18	3	104	498	4.8	27	3	10	68	6.8	16	0								
1987	WPG*	15	2		2	2						78	13	271	1471	5.4	69	9	27	253	9.4	19	4								
5	Years	62	18		6	2						320	53	1110	5923	5.3	75	44	113	1202	10.6	76	9					12	314	26.2	41
JON RECHNER Jon DB-FB-LB 6'0 200 Carroll (Wisconsin) B: 9/30/1937 Eau Claire, WI																															
1962	TOR	11																										3	43	14.3	23
1963	TOR	8												6	45	7.5	21	0	1	-2	-2.0	-2	0								
1964	TOR	14												5	25	5.0	7	0	2	37	18.5	30	0								
3	Years	33												11	70	6.4	21	0	3	35	11.7	30	0					3	43	14.3	23
JAMAICA RECTOR Jamaica Ray WR-SB 5'10 185 Northwest Missouri State B: 8/10/1981 Celeste, TX Pro: N																															
2009	EDM	14	4	0	0	3						6	1						48	532	11.1	43	1	6	43	7.2	12	3	56	18.7	20
2010	EDM	10				2													18	204	11.3	29	0	18	135	7.5	25	9	185	20.6	28
2	Years	24	4	0	0	5						6	1						66	736	11.2	43	1	24	178	7.4	25	12	241	20.1	28
ANTHONY REDDICK Anthony DH-LB 6'0 205 Miami (Florida) B: 12/26/1985 Fort Lauderdale, FL																															
2010	BC	18	0	1	1	38	5.0	55.0	3	26	2																				
2011	BC	13	0	1	0	63	3.0	22.0	1	3	2																				
2	Years	31	0	2	1	101	8.0	77.0	4	29	4																				
MIKE REDDICK Michael WR 5'8 165 Nevada-Las Vegas B: 7/11/1967																															
1992	BC	1	0	0	1									1	-15	-15.0	0	0	0	2		2	0	1	11	11.0	11				
BILL REDELL William Thome QB-DH 6'1 202 Southern California; Occidental B: 4/17/1941 Red Bluff, CA Draft: 28-221(f) 1963 DEN; 20-267(f) 1963 LARM																															
1964	EDM	11	2		0				1			24	4	46	117	2.5	16	4						6	30	5.0	10	14	387	27.6	73
1965	EDM	14	5		2							18	3	70	169	2.4	27	3						3	6	2.0	4	6	84	14.0	26
1966	EDM+	16	1		2				6	38		6	1	13	18	1.4	8	0													
1967	HAM	14			2				4	58		6	1																		
1968	HAM	14	1		0				6	35				5	34	6.8	11	0	1	-6	-6.0	-6	0	2	15	7.5	9				
1969	CAL	16	1		1				5	58		12	2	22	117	5.3	14	2						3	22	7.3	11				
6	Years	85	10		7				22	189		66	11	156	455	2.9	27	9	1	-6	-6.0	-6	0	14	73	5.2	11	20	471	23.6	73
CORNELIUS REDICK Cornelius T., Jr. WR-SB 5'11 185 Fullerton State B: 1/7/1964 Draft: 7A-169 1986 PHI Pro: N																															
1989	EDM	3				1													3	44	14.7	20	0	1	4	4.0	4	3	79	26.3	33
1989	OTT	7	2		0	3						18	3	1	-11	-11.0	-11	0	13	260	20.0	75	3	3	35	11.7	21	15	369	24.6	47
1989	Year	10	2		0	4						18	3	1	-11	-11.0	-11	0	16	304	19.0	75	3	4	39	9.8	21	18	448	24.9	47

Year	Team	GP	FM	FF	FR	TK	SK	YDS	IR	YDS	PD	PTS	TD	RA	YDS	AVG	LG	TD	REC	YDS	AVG	LG	TD	PR	YDS	AVG	LG	KOR	YDS	AVG	LG
1990	OTT	4	1		0	2													4	64	16.0	29	0	1	0	0.0	0	10	242	24.2	34
2	Years	7	3		0	6						18	3	1	-11	-11.0	-11	0	20	368	18.4	75	3	5	39	7.8	21	28	690	24.6	47
BOB REDKEY Bob FB-LB 5'10 210 Oregon State																															
1952	CAL	8			1				2	14		2	0	4	16	4.0	10	0	1	4	4.0	4	0	2	11	5.5	6				
DOUG REDL Doug C-OG 6'4 242 Saskatchewan B: 3/9/1956 Draft: TE 1978 SAS																															
1978	TOR	6																													
1979	TOR	13	0		1																										
1980	HAM	16																										1	7	7.0	7
1982	HAM	4	1		0																										
4	Years	39	1		1																							1	7	7.0	7
SCOTT REDL Scott DT-DE-OT-OG 6'4 245 Saskatchewan B: 7/19/1961 Saskatoon, SK Draft: TE 1983 SAS																															
1983	SAS	13																													
1984	SAS	4																													
1985	SAS	15	0		2		2.0																								
1986	SAS	11																													
1987	SAS	5				0																									
1989	WPG	18				0																									
1990	WPG	17	0		1	1																									
7	Years	83	0		3	1	2.0																								
JAMIE REDMOND Jamie DB 5'9 185 Middle Tennessee State B: 11/1/1060 Oak Ridge, TN																															
1994	SAC	8	0		1	15	2.0		2		2																				
1995	MEM	11				14					1																				
2	Years	19	0		1	29	2.0		2	0	3																				
ALONZO REED Alonzo OG 6'4 260 Nevada-Las Vegas B: 10/21/1970																															
1994	SHR	8				4																									
1995	SHR	17				0																									
2	Years	25				4																									
ANDRE REED Andre R. LB 6'3 250 Hinds CC; Jackson State B: 11/25/1976 Chicago, IL																															
2001	EDM	2	0	1	0	2																									
BOB REED Robert, Jr. OHB-K 5'11 187 Vallejo JC; Pacific B: 11/14/1939 New Orleans, LA Pro: N																															
1964	WPG	10	6		1							18	2	73	307	4.2	70	2	20	249	12.5	33	0					18	487	27.1	56
BOB REED Robert, Jr. OG-OT 6'1 258 Tennessee State B: 2/23/1943 Longview, TX Draft: 12- 1965 HOU; 16-217 1965 WAS Pro: N																															
1965	TOR	2												11	30	2.7	9	0	2	45	22.5	50	0					2	58	29.0	33
1966	WPG	7																													
1967	WPG	3																													
3	Years	12												11	30	2.7	9	0	2	45	22.5	50	0					2	58	29.0	33
GEORGE REED George Robert FB-LB-HB 6'0 205 Washington State B: 10/2/1939 Vicksburg, MS																															
1963	SAS	15	3		1							30	5	173	751	4.3	22	5	13	154	11.8	50	0					12	279	23.3	41
1964	SAS	16	5		0							60	10	185	1012	5.5	55	10	30	261	8.7	34	0					12	346	28.8	62
1965	SAS*	16	6		2							73	12	274	1768	6.5	46	12	18	229	12.7	37	0					10	225	22.5	38
1966	SAS*	16	7		0							42	7	266	1409	5.3	71	6	16	174	10.9	45	1					12	247	20.6	29
1967	SAS*	16	9		0							90	15	302	1471	4.9	50	15	9	70	7.8	23	0					2	42	21.0	25
1968	SAS*	16	5		0							96	16	268	1222	4.6	69	16	17	189	11.1	27	0								
1969	SAS*	16	5		0							72	12	273	1353	5.0	29	12	13	153	11.8	33	0					2	8	4.0	4
1970	SAS	12	3		2							30	5	193	821	4.3	21	5	21	198	9.4	36	0					1	8	8.0	8
1971	SAS*	16	5		1							72	12	218	1146	5.3	56	12	24	258	10.8	23	0								
1972	SAS*	16	5		0							78	13	224	1069	4.8	59	13	36	285	7.9	35	0								
1973	SAS*	16	5		0							84	14	256	1193	4.7	23	12	47	442	9.4	45	2								
1974	SAS*	16	5		0							30	5	288	1447	5.0	26	5	36	223	6.2	19	0								
1975	SAS+	16	7		0							66	11	323	1454	4.5	22	11	20	136	6.8	18	0					1	13	13.0	13
13	Years	203	70		6							823	137	3243	16116	5.0	71	134	300	2772	9.2	50	3					52	1168	22.5	62
JAMES REED James Curtis LB 6'2 230 San Jose CC; California B: 10/10/1955 Corpus Christi, TX Pro: NU																															
1979	WPG	12	0		2				1	20																					
1980	WPG	15							3	21																					
1981	WPG	16	0		1		3.0		1	48																					
1983	WPG	1																													
1983	MTL	1																													
1983	Year	2																													
1985	SAS	3																													
1985	TOR	4							2	16																					
1985	Year	7							2	16																					
5	Years	47	0		3		3.0		7	105																					
JIMMY REED Jimmy LB 5'8 205 Fort Valley State B: 9/7/1968 Fort Valley, GA																															
1995	BIR	17	0		4	70	4.0	14.0																							
KAVIS REED Kavis Darick CB 6'0 175 Furman B: 2/24/1973 Georgetown, SC																															
1995	EDM	13	0		1	52			5	80	7																				
1996	EDM	17	0		1	69			7	162	4	12	2																		
1997	EDM*	18				55			7	183	10	12	2						1	32	32.0	32	0								
1998	EDM	11				36			1	56	6	6	1																		
1999	EDM	8				11																									
5	Years	67	0		2	223			20	481	27	30	5						1	32	32.0	32	0								
KENNY REED Ken LB-DE-DT 6'0 230 Tulsa B: 1941 Draft: 17-232 1963 SF																															
1963	EDM	16	0		1																										
1964	EDM	14	0		2																										
1965	SAS	13	0		1																										
1966	SAS	16							1																						
1967	SAS	16	0		2				1	0																					
1968	SAS	16	0		2																										
1969	SAS+	16	0		1				1	19																		1	1	1.0	1
1970	SAS	12							1	3																					
8	Years	119	0		9				4	22																		1	1	1.0	1
LEO REED Leo Tautua G 6'3 260 Colorado State B: 1/3/1940 Kahuku, HI Draft: 20-274 1961 STL Pro: N																															
1963	TOR	6																													
MATTHEW REED Matthew QB 6'4 225 Grambling State B: 11/30/1951 Winnfeld, LA Draft: 10A-240 1973 BUF Pro: W																															
1976	TOR	16	5		0							7	1	43	402	9.3	39	1													
1977	TOR	2	1		0									5	46	9.2	18	0													
1977	CAL	12	2		0							8	1	24	283	11.8	35	1													
1977	Year	14	3		0							8	1	29	329	11.3	35	1													
1978	CAL	3												3	14	4.7	9	0													
3	Years	21	8		0							15	2	75	745	9.9	39	2													
ROBERT REED Robert E. SB 6'1 203 Arkansas; Hinds CC*; Mississippi; Lambuth B: 1/14/1975 Hinds County, MS Pro: N																															
2001	TOR	1				0													1	41	41.0	41	0					1	24	24.0	24
ALBERT REESE Albert A., Jr. LB-DT 6'6 275 Grambling State B: 4/29/1973 Mobile, AL Pro: N																															
2000	EDM	17				37	3.0	22.0			2																				
2001	EDM	18	0	1	1	36	1.0	6.0			2																				
2002	EDM	18				31	9.0				1																				
2003	EDM	16				25	2.0				3																				
2004	EDM	15				26	2.0																								
5	Years	84	0	1	1	155	17.0	28.0			8																				
LLOYD REESE Lloyd George (Bronko) FB-T 6'2 240 Tennessee* B: 6/17/1920 New Philadelphia, OH D: 10/28/1981 Dover, OH Pro: N																															
1948	MTL+	12										20	4					2													
1949	MTL	12										10	2					1													

Year	Team	GP	FM	FF	FR	TK	SK	YDS	IR	YDS	PD	PTS	TD	RA	YDS	AVG	LG	TD	REC	YDS	AVG	LG	TD	PR	YDS	AVG	LG	KOR	YDS	AVG	LG
2	Years	24									30	6					3													
HAL REEVE Hal E 6'2 220 Oregon B: 1933 Draft: 7-78 1955 PIT																															
1955	CAL	12	0		2																										
MARION REEVES Marion Francis DB 6'1 195 Clemson B: 2/23/1952 Lexington, SC Pro: NW																															
1975	WPG	2																												
1976	WPG	8							1	16																				
2	Years	10							1	16																				
RON REEVES Ron Garnet QB 6'2 215 Texas Tech B: 3/24/1960 Lubbock, TX Draft: 10-261 1982 HOU Pro: U																															
1983	MTL	7	1		1							12	2	30	174	5.8	47	2													
ROY REEVES Roy Don (Butch) WR-DB 5'11 182 South Carolina B: 2/8/1946 Americus, GA Draft: 14-352 1969 HOU Pro: N																															
1970	BC	2							1	16									1	4	4.0	4	0	1	2	2.0	2				
SCOTT REGIMBALD Scott SB-FB 6'3 245 Houston B: 11/23/1975 Montreal, QC Draft: 1B-7 2000 CAL																															
2000	CAL	18				11								4	21	5.3	8	0													
2001	CAL	18				4								1	2	2.0	2	0	6	85	14.2	24	0								
2002	CAL	18				3						12	2	3	18	6.0	13	2	13	198	15.2	44	0								
2003	CAL	18	0	0	1	2						6	1	6	9	1.5	4	0	20	167	8.4	22	1								
2004	CAL	14	2	0	0	0						18	3	19	49	2.6	8	3	11	94	8.5	27	0					2	8	4.0	7
2004	WPG	4	0	0	1	2						12	2	5	8	1.6	3	2	2	30	15.0	23	0								
2004	Year	18	2	0	1	2						30	5	24	57	2.4	8	5	13	124	9.5	27	0					2	8	4.0	7
2005	WPG	18	1	0	0	0						12	2	15	61	4.1	26	1	6	51	8.5	21	1					2	24	12.0	13
2006	WPG	18	1	0	0	1								10	21	2.1	4	0	7	84	12.0	18	0					2	2	1.0	1
7	Years	122	4	0	2	23						60	10	63	189	3.0	26	8	65	709	10.9	44	2					6	34	5.7	13
STEVE REHAGE Stephen Michael S 6'1 190 Louisiana State B: 11/6/1963 New Orleans, LA Pro: N																															
1988	OTT	7							1	18														1	0	0.0	0				
ALAN REID Alan DeWitt RB 5'8 197 Texas Christian; Los Angeles Pierce JC; Minnesota B: 9/6/1960 Wurzburg, Germany Draft: 19B-385 1984 MEM-USFL Pro: NU																															
1985	MTL	10	2		0							18	3	75	373	5.0	60	3	56	465	8.3	51	0	3	4	1.3	11				
1986	MTL	7	2		0							6	1	46	191	4.2	17	1	24	188	7.8	23	0								
2	Years	17	4		0							24	4	121	564	4.7	60	4	80	653	8.2	51	0	3	4	1.3	11				
ANGUS REID Angus C-DL 6'1 306 Simon Fraser B: 9/23/1976 Richmond, BC Draft: 1-4 2001 TOR																															
2001	MTL	2				2																										
2002	BC	18	0	0	1	5																										
2003	BC	18	3	0	0	1																										
2004	BC+	18	1	0	0	0																										
2005	BC	18	1	0	0	0																										
2006	BC	18				0																										
2007	BC	18				0																										
2008	BC	18	1	0	0	3																										
2009	BC	16	1	0	0	0																										
2010	BC	18	1	0	0	1																										
2011	BC*	18	2	0	0	0																										
11	Years	180	10	0	1	12																										
BRAD REID Bradley Steven WR 5'11 174 Iowa Lakes CC; Iowa B: 12/23/1957 Cedar Rapids, IA																															
1980	SAS	1																	2	24	12.0	13	0								
DOUG REID Doug HB-FB 5'10 182 British Columbia B: 1925 Vancouver, BC																															
1950	CAL	14												32	111	3.5	8	0													
1951	CAL	14																										1	18	18.0	18
1954	BC	11	2											12	43	3.6	12	0	1	10	10.0	10	0	7	47	6.7	12				
1955	BC	13												2	6	3.0	3	0										2	21	10.5	16
4	Years	52	2											46	160	3.5	12	0	1	10	10.0	10	0	7	47	6.7	12	3	39	13.0	18
FRANK REID Clifford Franklin OT-OG 6'2 235 Buffalo B: 2/11/1946 Belleville, ON																															
1970	OTT	10	0		1																										
1970	WPG	4																												
1970	Year	14	0		1																										
1971	WPG	16	0		3																										
1973	OTT	6	0		1																							1	0	0.0	0
1974	OTT	7																												
1975	OTT	16																												
5	Years	55	0		5																							1	0	0.0	0
FRED REID Fredrick T. RB 5'9 188 Mississippi State B: 3/16/1982 Tampa, FL																															
2007	WPG	18				14						12	2	40	270	6.8	44	2	8	120	15.0	41	0					9	213	23.7	63
2008	WPG+	17				8						18	3	101	709	7.0	49	3	13	96	7.4	22	0	8	47	5.9	11	24	447	18.6	33
2009	WPG+	18	2	0	0	6						48	8	238	1317	5.5	52	7	21	157	7.5	24	1					25	507	20.3	35
2010	WPG*	18	3	0	0	3						36	6	213	1396	6.6	61	6	35	255	7.3	18	0								
2011	WPG	12	1	0	0	1						24	4	181	759	4.2	47	4	22	182	8.3	44	0								
5	Years	83	6	0	0	32						138	23	773	4451	5.8	61	22	99	810	8.2	44	1	8	47	5.9	11	58	1167	20.1	63
JERMAINE REID Jermaine Andre DE-DT 6'4 275 Akron B: 4/19/1983 Pickering, ON Draft: 2A-9 2006 HAM																															
2007	HAM	14	0	1	0	11	1.0	5.0																						
2008	HAM	14	0	1	1	6																								
2009	HAM	8				2																								
2010	HAM	7	0	1	0	9	4.0	23.0																						
2011	EDM	18				14	1.0	4.0																						
5	Years	61	0	3	1	42	6.0	32.0																						
JIM REID James B. FB 6'3 230 Wilfrid Laurier B: 11/8/1957 Palmerston, ON Draft: TE 1979 HAM																															
1979	HAM	8	1		0									26	133	5.1	15	0	6	57	9.5	18	0								
1980	OTT	16	3		0							30	5	49	187	3.8	19	3	25	258	10.3	62	2					2	24	12.0	12
1981	OTT	16	1		2							6	1	30	183	6.1	19	0	26	258	9.9	19	1					5	82	16.4	22
1982	OTT	16	5		3							20	3	58	251	4.3	19	1	34	412	12.1	65	2								
1983	OTT	16	1		0									13	41	3.2	14	0	32	408	12.8	65	0					2	31	15.5	23
1984	OTT	5	1		0									17	75	4.4	12	0	7	34	4.9	8	0					1	11	11.0	11
1985	OTT	16	1		2									16	66	4.1	16	0	11	77	7.0	17	0								
1986	OTT+	18	3		2							12	2	69	395	5.7	22	1	30	325	10.8	26	1					2	44	22.0	23
1987	OTT	18				5						8	1	15	78	5.2	13	0	47	419	8.9	27	1					1	-10	-10.0	-10
1988	OTT	18	1		1							6	1	26	90	3.5	20	0	39	446	11.4	33	1								
10	Years	147	17		10	5						82	13	319	1499	4.7	22	5	257	2694	10.5	65	8					13	182	14.0	23
JOHN REID John C 6'4 255 Tulsa B: 1944																															
1968	HAM	14																												
1969	HAM	14																												
1970	HAM	14																												
1971	HAM	14																												
1972	SAS	16	1		0																										
5	Years	72	1		0																										
KEN REID Ken T 6'3 230 Western Washington; Vancouver Meralomas Jrs. B: 1938																															
1961	BC	2																												
KEVIN REID Kevin WR 5'10 180 Guelph B: 11/13/1975 Stoney Creek, ON Draft: Bonus-7 1995 CAL																															
1995	CAL	18				21																										
1996	CAL	18				17													3	30	10.0	16	0								
2	Years	36				38													3	30	10.0	16	0								
LAMONT REID Michael Lamont DB 5'11 187 North Carolina State B: 5/4/1982 Pro: EN																															
2009	HAM	8	0	0	1	13					1																				
LORNE REID Lorne OT-DT-DG 6'2 247 Vancouver Cubs Jrs. B: 1929 Saskatoon, SK																															
1954	BC	15																										2	10	5.0	10
1955	BC	16	1		0																			1	8	8.0	8				

Year	Team	GP	FM	FF	FR	TK	SK	YDS	IR	YDS	PD	PTS	TD	RA	YDS	AVG	LG	TD	REC	YDS	AVG	LG	TD	PR	YDS	AVG	LG	KOR	YDS	AVG	LG
1956	BC	16	0		3																										
1957	BC	11																													
1958	CAL	7	0		2																										
1959	CAL	16										6	1						1	18	18.0	18	1								
1960	CAL	16	0		1																										
1961	CAL	14																													
8	Years	111	1		6							6	1						1	18	18.0	18	1	1	8	8.0	8	2	10	5.0	10
MARK REID Mark OG 5'10 250 Simon Fraser B: 3/7/1965 Richmond, BC																															
1990	BC	8				0																									
PAT REID Pat E																															
1946	TOR	10																													
1947	TOR	7																													
2	Years	17																													
ROBERT REID Robert FB 5'11 185 Simon Fraser B: 11/29/1960 West Bromich, England Draft: 1-9 1984 SAS																															
1984	SAS	9												2	-1	-0.5	2	0										2	35	17.5	19
1985	SAS	6												7	34	4.9	16	0	2	17	8.5	12	0								
1985	OTT	2	0		1																										
1985	Year	8	0		1									7	34	4.9	16	0	2	17	8.5	12	0								
1986	OTT	18	4		1							24	4	70	314	4.5	24	2	27	341	12.6	65	2					20	382	19.1	20
1987	OTT	9				2																						0	-5		-5
1988	OTT	18	0		1	0						12	2	41	214	5.2	45	2	3	2	0.7		0								
1989	OTT	12	0		2	0								14	94	6.7	20	0	1	7	7.0	7	0					2	4	2.0	3
6	Years	72	4		5	2						36	6	134	655	4.9	45	4	33	367	11.1	65	2					24	416	17.3	29
STEFEN REID Stefen LB 6'2 220 Okanagan Sun Jrs.; Boise State B: 5/11/1972 Merritt, BC Draft: Bonus-2 1995 OTT																															
1995	OTT	16	0		1	47																									
1996	MTL	15				33	1.0	1.0																							
1997	MTL	14	0	1	1	34					1																				
1998	MTL	18	0	1	2	87	5.0	35.0	2	85	1	6	1																		
1999	MTL	16	0	1	1	57	2.0	9.0	2	0	0																				
2000	MTL	17	0	2	1	63					1																				
2001	MTL	17	0	1	1	53	3.0	10.0	1	0	1																				
2002	MTL+	18	0	2	1	65	6.0		2	3	5																				
8	Years	131	0	8	8	439	17.0	55.0	7	88	9	6	1																		
TIM REID Tim HB 5'10 180 University of Toronto Ints.; Toronto B: 1938 Draft: 1A-2 1959 HAM																															
1962	HAM	10										6	1	5	35	7.0	14	0	2	24	12.0	14	1					1	21	21.0	21
MIKE REILLY Michael QB 6'3 215 Washington State; Central Washington B: 1/25/1985 Richland, WA																															
2010	BC	4				0																									
2011	BC	18				0																									
2	Years	22				0																									
TOM REIMER Tom DH 6'0 190 British Columbia B: 2/24/1956 Draft: 6-46 1977 CAL																															
1978	CAL	13	0		1																			1	5	5.0	5				
1979	CAL	14	0		1																										
1980	CAL	12							2	1																		1	28	28.0	28
1981	CAL	12	1		1																			22	173	7.9	30				
4	Years	51	1		3				2	1														23	178	7.7	30	1	28	28.0	28
GLENN REINHARD Glenn B. T 6'3 255 Wake Forest B: 6/19/1925 Jacobus, PA D: 6/28/2010 Dover, PA																															
1951	MTL	1																													
ROGER REINSON Roger LB 6'0 215 Calgary B: 4/19/1968 Melville, SK Draft: 5-41 1994 CAL																															
1994	CAL	16	0		1	19																									
1995	CAL	4				3																									
1996	CAL	9	0		1	6																									
1997	CAL	18	0	0	1	31																									
1998	CAL	18	0	1	1	21																									
1999	CAL	18				27																									
2000	BC	18				24																									
2001	EDM	17	0	1	0	20																									
2002	EDM	18	0	0	1	18						6	1																		
2003	EDM	18	0	0	1	17																									
2004	EDM	18	1	0	0	7																									
11	Years	172	1	2	6	193						6	1																		
EDDIE REMEGIS Edward G 5'10 194																															
1946	HAM	7																													
1947	HAM+	12																													
1949	HAM	11																													
3	Years	30																													
CHAD REMPEL Chad WR-SB-RB 6'2 208 Saskatchewan B: 5/23/1981 Sherwood Park, AB Draft: 4-35 2004 EDM																															
2005	WPG	9	0	0	1	3																									
2006	TOR	8				7																									
2007	TOR	9	0	0	1	10													5	70	14.0	29	0								
2008	HAM	11				10													3	48	16.0	21	0								
2009	TOR	11				3													9	76	8.4	25	0					1	4	4.0	4
2010	TOR	18	1	0	0	10													1	1	1.0	1	0								
2011	TOR	18				9						12	2						3	73	24.3	43	2								
7	Years	84	1	0	2	52						12	2						21	268	12.8	43	2					1	4	4.0	4
JORDAN REMPEL Jordan OG 6'6 322 Saskatchewan B: 4/20/1985 Caronport, SK Draft: 2A-12 2007 HAM																															
2008	HAM	14				0																									
MIKE RENAUD Mike P 6'2 216 Concordia (Ontario) B: 5/25/1983 Ottawa, ON																															
2009	WPG	14	1	0	0	4						1	0	1	25	25.0	25	0													
2010	WPG+	17	2	0	2	1						9	0																		
2011	WPG	15	2	0	0	2						7	0																		
3	Years	46	5	0	2	7						17	0	1	25	25.0	25	0													
DEAN RENFRO Weldon Eugene HB 5'11 180 North Texas B: 6/15/1932 Draft: 2-25 1955 CLE Pro: N																															
1956	CAL	6										18	3	5	72	14.4	57	1	11	205	18.6	45	2					6	110	18.3	27
1957	CAL	12	2		0							30	5	14	9	0.6	17	0	23	556	24.2	82	5	1	5	5.0	5				
2	Years	18	2		0							48	8	19	81	4.3	57	1	34	761	22.4	82	7	1	5	5.0	5	6	110	18.3	27
GILBERT RENFROE Gilbert A. QB 6'1 195 Tennessee State B: 2/18/1963 Tuskegee, AL																															
1986	OTT	18	5		0							6	1	22	174	7.9	25	1													
1987	TOR	9	1		0	0						8	1	27	164	6.1	29	1													
1988	TOR+	18	9		1	1						6	1	36	95	2.6	12	1													
1989	TOR	8	1		0	1						6	1	19	78	4.1	12	1													
1991	CAL	9	5		1									7	29	4.1	14	0													
1992	BC	3	1		0									3	-4	-1.3	6	0													
1994	SHR	1																													
7	Years	66	22		2	2						26	4	114	536	4.7	29	4													
BOBBY RENN Robert Clifton OHB 6'0 180 Davidson; Florida State B: 5/25/1934 Henderson, NC D: 10/21/1971 Lakeland, FL Draft: 22-264 1958 CLE Pro: N																															
1959	SAS	10							4	20		6	1	21	101	4.8	47	0	10	212	21.2	40	1					6	160	26.7	31
1960	SAS	12							1			50	8	7	6	0.9	6	0	36	695	19.3	71	8					3	39	13.0	20
1961	SAS	2																	1	14	14.0	14	0								
3	Years	24							5	20		56	9	28	107	3.8	47	0	47	921	19.6	71	9					9	199	22.1	31
TARE RENNEBOHM Howard G-T Regina Jrs. B: 1924 D: 11/19/2009 Indian Head, SK																															
1946	SAS	2																													
1947	SAS	4																													

Year	Team	GP	FM	FF	FR	TK	SK	YDS	IR	YDS	PD	PTS	TD	RA	YDS	AVG	LG	TD	REC	YDS	AVG	LG	TD	PR	YDS	AVG	LG	KOR	YDS	AVG	LG
1948	SAS	12
3	Years	18
FRANK RENO Frank A. (Chief) E 6'0 195 West Virginia B: 7/31/1923 Greensburg, PA Draft: 16-161 1949 PHI
1949	TOR	12
GENE RENZI Eugene Carmen T 6'3 250 Brandeis; Northeastern B: 12/16/1933 Boston, MA D: 2/9/2008 North Springfield, VA Draft: 29-338 1955 CHIC
1956	WPG	1
RUDY RESCHKE Rudy LB-DE-C 6'2 234 British Columbia; Utah B: 1941 Germany
1966	BC	16
1967	BC	16	0		1
1968	MTL	12
3	Years	44	0		1
BILL RESTELLI William OG 6'2 240 Iowa B: 1944
1966	WPG	16
MARK RESTELLI Jonathan Mark LB 6'2 215 Cal Poly (San Luis Obispo) B: 3/4/1986 Houston, TX
2009	EDM	17	0	1	1	74					3
2010	EDM	6				21	4.0	41.0
2011	EDM	1				0
3	Years	24	0	1	1	95	4.0	41.0			3
DAVE RETHERFORD David G. WR 6'0 175 Purdue B: 4/19/1961 Glendale, AZ Draft: 18-378 1984 JAC-USFL
1984	CAL	2																3	31	10.3	17	0
GUS REVENBERG Gus DT-C 6'0 245 Windsor AKO Jrs. B: 1/26/1948
1970	OTT	11	0		1
1971	OTT	14
1972	OTT	14
1973	BC	3
4	Years	42	0		1
JOHN REYKDAL John C 6'1 230 British Columbia B: 12/12/1943 Draft: 6- 1965 BC
1966	TOR	1
1967	TOR	14	0		1
1968	EDM	16	1		1
1969	EDM	12
1970	CAL	1
5	Years	44	1		2
GREG REYNARD Greg DT 6'2 280 Montana-Western B: 12/18/1963 St. Jerome, QC Draft: 3-26 1986 HAM
1987	TOR	7				7
1988	CAL	9				5	1.0
1989	CAL	2				0
1990	HAM	4				2	1.0
4	Years	22				14	2.0
BILLY REYNOLDS William Dean OHB 5'11 195 Pittsburgh B: 7/20/1931 St. Marys, WV D: 12/2/2002 Bedford, OH Draft: 2-23 1953 CLE Pro: N
1959	HAM	8										12	2	72	287	4.0	12	2	20	216	10.8	36	0	6	26	4.3	10	2	53	26.5	28
JIM REYNOLDS Jim LB-DE-OE 6'2 212 Hillsdale B: 1/10/1938
1960	OTT	2							1	11
1961	OTT	13							1	5		12	2						1	8	8.0	8	0
1962	OTT	7										6	1						9	114	12.7	20	1
1962	MTL	4										6	1						3	40	13.3	23	1
1962	Year	11										12	2						12	154	12.8	23	2
1963	MTL+	12							1	26		12	2						1	22	22.0	22	0
1964	MTL	4							2	44
1965	MTL	4
1965	HAM	6																		1	16	16.0	16	0
1965	Year	10																		1	16	16.0	16	0
1966	HAM	14	0		1				1	14
1967	HAM	6							1	29		6	1
1967	TOR	4							1	0
1967	Year	10							2	29		6	1
1968	OTT	6
9	Years	68	0		1				8	129		42	7						15	200	13.3	23	2
JOFFREY REYNOLDS Joffrey Benjamin Roy HB 5'10 221 Houston B: 11/26/1979 Houston, TX Pro: EN
2004	CAL	5	2	0	1	1						12	2	90	497	5.5	55	2	6	58	9.7	20	0
2005	CAL*	18	4	0	1	1						54	9	247	1453	5.9	46	8	13	94	7.2	19	1
2006	CAL*	18	6	0	2	2						54	9	259	1541	5.9	53	9	27	401	14.9	62	0					1	29	29.0	29
2007	CAL+	17	5	0	1	1						30	5	214	1231	5.8	46	2	49	336	6.9	18	3					15	331	22.1	34
2008	CAL*	18	4	0	1	1						72	12	227	1310	5.8	50	10	41	288	7.0	21	2					16	405	25.3	51
2009	CAL*	18	3	0	0	1						80	13	235	1504	6.4	38	11	36	431	12.0	37	2					4	54	13.5	15
2010	CAL+	18	1	0	1	1						48	8	217	1200	5.5	32	8	37	286	7.7	23	0					2	30	15.0	21
2011	CAL	13	4	0	1	2						18	3	101	477	4.7	26	3	17	142	8.4	31	0
8	Years	125	29	0	8	10						368	61	1590	9213	5.8	55	53	226	2036	9.0	62	8					38	849	22.3	51
M.C. REYNOLDS Mack Charles QB 6'0 193 Louisiana State B: 2/11/1935 Mansfield, LA D: 9/8/1991 Shreveport, LA Pro: N
1963	SAS	2	1		0									2	-10	-5.0	-3	0
COBY RHINEHART Jacoby Marquie CB 5'10 192 Southern Methodist B: 2/7/1977 Dallas, TX Draft: 6A-190 1999 ARI Pro: N
2005	CAL	12	1	0	1	55			1	57	5	6	1
2006	CAL+	18	0	1	1	68	1.0	8.0	7	27	4
2007	MTL	17	0	2	1	21					2
3	Years	47	1	3	3	144	1.0	8.0	8	84	11	6	1
ED RHINELANDER Ed E 6'2 200 B: 1941
1962	HAM	1
RANDY RHINO Randall P. DB 5'9 185 Georgia Tech B: 12/2/1953 Atlanta, GA Draft: 14-344 1975 NO Pro: W
1976	MTL	16	0		2				2	61														9	59	6.6	26	10	217	21.7	35
1977	MTL*	16	0		1				7	229														49	595	12.1	43	14	360	25.7	49
1978	MTL*	16	0		1				2	36														76	868	11.4	49	2	53	26.5	27
1979	MTL	10	1		0				1	12														44	469	10.7	64	4	91	22.8	25
1980	MTL	16	3		0				6	66														45	458	10.2	42	1	4	4.0	4
1981	OTT*	15	1		1				2	24		6	1											73	918	12.6	56
6	Years	89	5		5				20	428		6	1											296	3367	11.4	64	31	725	23.4	49
ELTON RHOADES Elton DB 6'3 215 Central Oklahoma B: 5/22/1972
1995	HAM	1				0
BILL RHODES Bill FB 6'0 200 Western State (Colorado) B: 1935 Draft: 6A-62 1957 SF
1957	TOR	7							1	28				27	105	3.9	15	0
BILLY RHODES Bill OT 6'3 250 Florida State Draft: 4-97 1969 STL
1969	MTL	7
DANNY RHODES Danny Boyiet LB 6'2 220 Arkansas B: 3/18/1951 Texarkana, AR D: 7/22/2007 Lake Jackson, TX Draft: 6-140 1974 BAL; 10-118 1974 JAC-WFL Pro: N
1975	SAS	2	0		1
JERRY RHOME Jerry Byron QB 6'0 186 Southern Methodist; Tulsa B: 3/6/1942 Dallas, TX Draft: 13-172(f) 1964 DAL; 25-195(f) 1964 NYJ Pro: N
1972	MTL	1												1	6	6.0	6	0
BUSTER RHYMES George Buster WR 6'2 218 Oklahoma B: 1/27/1962 Miami, FL Draft: 4A-85 1985 MIN; TD 1985 SA-USFL Pro: N
1988	WPG	1				0						6	1	1	18	18.0	18	0	8	150	18.8	41	1	1	0	0.0	0	2	36	18.0	18
1989	WPG	8	2		0	2						12	2	2	27	13.5	16	0	16	239	14.9	32	2	9	47	5.2	18	8	149	18.6	28
2	Years	9	2		0	2						18	3	3	45	15.0	18	0	24	389	16.2	41	3	10	47	4.7	18	10	185	18.5	28
PETE RIBBINS Peter DB-WR 6'2 195 Burlington Braves Jrs.; Ottawa B: 8/31/1947 Belfast, Northern Ireland D: 12/12/2010 Grand Cayman, Grand Cayman Islands Draft: 1A-5 1971 WPG
1971	WPG	16																10	149	14.9	32	0

Year	Team	GP	FM	FF	FR	TK	SK	YDS	IR	YDS	PD	PTS	TD	RA	YDS	AVG	LG	TD	REC	YDS	AVG	LG	TD	PR	YDS	AVG	LG	KOR	YDS	AVG	LG
1972	WPG	16	1		1				9	85														55	309	5.6	41				
1973	WPG	11	1		0									3	19	6.3	15	0	3	31	10.3	15	0	8	61	7.6	13				
1973	HAM	4	0		1																										
1973	Year	15	1		1									3	19	6.3	15	0	3	31	10.3	15	0	8	61	7.6	13				
1974	WPG	3							1	33														4	36	9.0	17				
1975	WPG	15										6	1	2	-1	-0.5	6	0	5	97	19.4	40	1								
1976	WPG	16																	1	20	20.0	20	0					2	17	8.5	11
1977	EDM	5										6	1						2	38	19.0	32	1								
7	Years	82	2		2				10	118		12	2	5	18	3.6	15	0	21	335	16.0	40	2	67	406	6.1	41	2	17	8.5	11
TONY RICE Tony Eugene QB 6'1 200 Notre Dame B: 9/5/1967 Spartanburg, SC Pro: E																															
1990	SAS	8				0								3	7	2.3	5	0													
DWIGHT RICHARDS Dwight RB 5'10 200 Weber State B: 7/9/1969 Kingston, Jamaica Draft: 2-10 1993 OTT																															
1993	OTT	12	3		0	5								45	124	2.8	19	0	17	125	7.4	24	0	1	5	5.0	5	2	26	13.0	22
1993	TOR	3				3																									
1993	Year	15	3		0	8								45	124	2.8	19	0	17	125	7.4	24	0	1	5	5.0	5	2	26	13.0	22
JAMES RICHARDS James G. OT 6'4 290 Northridge State; Antelope Valley JC; California B: 11/7/1969 Lancaster, CA Draft: 3B-64 1991 DAL																															
1994	LV	3																													
JASON RICHARDS Jason DT 6'2 300 Toledo B: 11/17/1975 Ellwood City, PA																															
1999	MTL+	18	0	0	1	23	9.0	66.0			2																				
2000	MTL	15	0	0	1	36	2.0	9.0																							
2001	MTL	16	0	0	1	32					1																				
2002	MTL	18	0	1	1	15	2.0																								
4	Years	67	0	1	4	106	13.0	75.0			3																				
NICK RICHARDS Nicholas LB 6'2 240 Acadia B: 4/26/1967 Derby, England																															
1995	OTT	13				13																									
1996	OTT	9				8																						1	6	6.0	6
1997	BC	4				3																									
1998	BC	12				13																									
4	Years	38				37																						1	6	6.0	6
TOM RICHARDS Tom SB-RB 6'1 200 Alberta B: 8/10/1964 Brantford, ON Draft: 5-41 1985 EDM																															
1986	EDM	18	2		0							24	4						25	372	14.9	64	3	48	524	10.9	89	7	149	21.3	45
1987	EDM	18	3		0	3						24	4	2	25	12.5	15	0	26	473	18.2	72	3	26	236	9.1	88	1	57	57.0	46
1988	EDM	18				2						6	1	2	0	0.0	0	0	57	897	15.7	51	1	22	107	4.9	12				
1989	EDM	18	2		0	4						42	7						60	1239	20.7	63	7	5	45	9.0	13				
1990	EDM	2				0													4	52	13.0	19	0								
5	Years	74	7		0	9						96	16	4	25	6.3	15	0	172	3033	17.6	72	14	101	912	9.0	89	8	206	25.8	46
BOB RICHARDSON Robert George DB 6'0 185 UCLA B: 2/24/1944 Minneapolis, MN Pro: N																															
1967	HAM	10							1	3																					
1968	HAM	14	1		0				6	116														4	10	2.5	11	1	25	25.0	25
2	Years	24	1		0				7	119														4	10	2.5	11	1	25		25
BOB RICHARDSON Bob TE-OT 6'5 250 Iowa State B: 12/3/1948																															
1972	HAM	14	0		1							6	1						15	251	16.7	36	1					2	12	6.0	12
1973	HAM	14										6	1						9	72	8.0	19	1					2	32	16.0	21
1974	HAM	16																	3	61	20.3	37	0								
1975	SAS	16																	3	38	12.7	18	0	3	19	6.3	11				
1976	SAS+	16	1		1							18	3						41	527	12.9	29	3								
1977	SAS	11	2		0							2	0						28	334	11.9	42	0								
1978	SAS	11	2		0							6	1						22	237	10.8	37	1								
7	Years	98	5		2							38	6						121	1520	12.6	42	6	3	19	6.3	11	4	44	11.0	21
BRUCE RICHARDSON Bruce E 5'8 167 B: 1923 D: 8//2008 Canada																															
1946	TOR	4																													
1950	CAL	4																													
2	Years	8																													
DAVE RICHARDSON Dave OT 6'4 272 Edmonton Wildcats Jrs. B: 7/1/1967 Edmonton, AB																															
1988	EDM	15			1	0																									
1989	EDM	5				0																									
1990	HAM	7				0																									
1991	HAM	17	0		1	1																									
1992	HAM	14				1																									
1993	HAM	18	0		3	1								0	2		2	0													
1994	HAM	15	0		1	1																									
1995	HAM	17				0																									
1996	HAM	3				0																									
9	Years	111	0		6	4								0	2		2	0													
EDDIE RICHARDSON Edward, II WR 6'3 195 Merritt JC; Howard B: 7/23/1952 Monroe, LA Draft: 36-422 1974 FLA-WFL Pro: W																															
1977	CAL	2																													
ELLIOTT RICHARDSON Elliott S 5'9 190 Acadia B: 10/26/1985 Toronto, ON																															
2009	EDM	15				22																									
2010	EDM	8	0	1	0	21			2	100	0																				
2011	SAS	5				3																									
3	Years	28	0	1	0	46			2	100	0																				
JAMEL RICHARDSON Jamel SB-WR 6'3 211 Victor Valley CC B: 1/22/1982 Syracuse, NY																															
2003	SAS	6	1	0	0	2						6	1						22	328	14.9	35	1								
2004	SAS	6				2						6	1						20	210	10.5	35	1								
2005	SAS	14	1	0	3	2													55	663	12.1	42	0								
2006	SAS	4	1	0	1	0						12	2						16	270	16.9	49	2								
2008	MTL*	18	2	0	0	5						96	16						98	1287	13.1	81	16								
2009	MTL+	16	2	0	1	0						54	9						85	1055	12.4	63	9								
2010	MTL+	17	1	0	0	2						44	7	1	13	13.0	13	0	97	1271	13.1	61	7								
2011	MTL*	17	1	0	1	2						66	11						112	1777	15.9	59	11								
8	Years	98	9	0	6	15						284	47	1	13	13.0	13	0	505	6861	13.6	81	47								
JAMIE RICHARDSON Jamie WR 5'11 184 Florida B: 3/1/1976 Tallahassee, FL																															
1998	EDM	5				0						6	1						8	100	12.5	24	1					2	43	21.5	27
LORNE RICHARDSON Lorne CB 6'0 188 Colorado B: 3/9/1950																															
1973	SAS*	16	0		1				7	152														1	24	24.0	24				
1974	SAS*	16	0		4				3	36		12	2																		
1975	SAS*	16							4	77																					
1976	SAS*	16							7	144		6	1																		
1977	TOR	16	0		1				1	0																					
5	Years	80	0		6				22	409		18	3											1	24	24.0	24				
LOUIE RICHARDSON Louis DE 6'5 245 Western New Mexico; Florida State B: 9/16/1954 Draft: 10-254 1978 NYJ																															
1978	BC	16	0		4																										
1979	BC	12																													
2	Years	28	0		4																										
MIKE RICHARDSON Michael RB 6'0 195 Louisiana Tech B: 10/13/1969 Natchez, MS																															
1992	WPG*	11	12		2	3						36	6	211	1153	5.5	31	3	27	263	9.7	41	3					7	172	24.6	38
1993	WPG*	12	7		0	0						36	6	165	925	5.6	26	4	46	378	8.2	26	2								
1994	OTT	10	1		0	1						50	8	108	456	4.2	18	5	42	533	12.7	60	3					5	60	12.0	16
1995	OTT	11	6		0	4						18	3	117	555	4.7	33	1	37	396	10.7	59	2								
1996	WPG	10	5		1	4						48	8	91	378	4.2	18	5	27	237	8.8	39	3								
5	Years	54	31		3	12						188	31	692	3467	5.0	33	18	179	1807	10.1	60	13					12	232	19.3	38
MIKE RICHARDSON Michael Wayne RB 5'11 196 Southern Methodist B: 12/8/1946 Fort Worth, TX Draft: 7-171 1969 HOU Pro: NW																															

Year	Team	GP	FM	FF	FR	TK	SK	YDS	IR	YDS	PD	PTS	TD	RA	YDS	AVG	LG	TD	REC	YDS	AVG	LG	TD	PR	YDS	AVG	LG	KOR	YDS	AVG	LG
1972	WPG	5												24	109	4.5	16	0	1	13	13.0	13	0								
MIKE RICHARDSON Mike RB 5'10 190 Texas A&M-Commerce B: 6/23/1957																															
1980	WPG	1												11	47	4.3	9	0	1	16	16.0	16	0					2	55	27.5	34
ROSS RICHARDSON Ross OT-OG 6'1 230 Fort Garry Lions Jrs.; North Dakota B: 1946																															
1969	WPG	16																													
SHAUN RICHARDSON Shaun DE-LB 6'3 255 Joliet JC; Tennessee State B: 5/21/1985 St. Louis, MO																															
2009	EDM	3				7	1.0	1.0	0	0	1																				
JOEY RICHMAN Joey HB 5'6 150 B: 4/25/1915 Montreal, QC D: 12/2/2008																															
1946	MTL	10										10	2					1													
1947	MTL	12										5	1										1								
2	Years	22										15	3					1					1								
AKIM RICHMOND Akim A. WR 6'1 205 Mississippi Delta JC; Mississippi Valley State B: 10/22/1975 Inglewood, CA																															
1999	TOR	3				1													8	83	10.4	19	0								
CHRIS RICK Christopher LB 6'2 215 Queen's B: 1/21/1964 Draft: 5B-34 1988 OTT																															
1988	OTT	1																													
BOB RICKENBACH Robert Gene OG-TE 6'4 255 Penn State B: 10/31/1950 Philadelphia, PA Pro: W																															
1973	OTT	1																													
MARK RICKS Mark L. CB 5'9 160 Western Michigan B: 12/16/1970 Los Angeles, CA																															
1993	SAS	2				4																						2	31	15.5	19
1993	TOR	4	0		1	18			1	0																					
1993	Year	6	0		1	22			1	0																		2	31	15.5	19
1995	OTT	10	1		2	29			2	46	2	12	2											21	323	15.4	97	3	47	15.7	18
1995	WPG	2	1		2	0																		5	39	7.8	13	2	51	25.5	35
1995	Year	12	2		2	29			2	46	2	12	2											26	362	13.9	97	5	98	19.6	35
2	Years	12	2		5	51			3	46	2	12	2											26	362	13.9	97	7	129	18.4	35
ERIC RIDDICK Eric CB-LB 6'0 192 North Carolina State B: 4/17/1975 Norfolk, VA																															
2000	MTL	10				8			1	0	0																	1	0	0.0	0
2001	MTL	13				41			2	49	5																				
2002	CAL	1				2					1																				
2002	MTL	1				6																									
2002	Year	2				8					1																				
3	Years	24				57			3	49	6																	1	0	0.0	0
BRANDON RIDEAU Brandon Lee WR-SB 6'3 198 Kansas B: 10/18/1982 Beaumont, TX Pro: N																															
2010	TOR	12				0						6	1						24	443	18.5	55	1	1	13	13.0	13				
2011	TOR	14	1	0	0	6						30	5						43	551	12.8	69	5								
2	Years	26	1	0	0	6						36	6						67	994	14.8	69	6	1	13	13.0	13				
BRIAN RIDGEWAY Brian LB 6'3 210 Simon Fraser; St. Mary's (Nova Scotia) B: 4/26/1984 Grand Prairie, AB Draft: 5-39 2010 MTL																															
2011	MTL	17				6																									
DAVID RIDGWAY David K 6'0 190 Toledo B: 4/24/1959 Stockport, England Draft: 7-58 1981 MTL																															
1982	SAS*	16										163	0																		
1983	SAS	16										111	0																		
1984	SAS	16	1		0							127	0																		
1985	SAS	16	0		1							109	0																		
1986	SAS	18	1		1							153	0																		
1987	SAS*	17	1		0	0						174	0																		
1988	SAS*	18				0						215	0																		
1989	SAS*	18	1		0	0						216	0																		
1990	SAS*	18				0						233	0																		
1991	SAS+	18	2		0	1						216	0																		
1992	SAS	18	1		0	2						165	0																		
1993	SAS*	18	1		0	0						196	0																		
1994	SAS	13										128	0																		
1995	SAS	18				0						168	0																		
14	Years	238	8		2	3						2374	0																		
DICK RIGELHOF Dick LB 6'2 205 North Dakota B: 7/12/1956 Draft: 4-34 1981 WPG																															
1981	WPG	2																													
DAVE RIGG David DB 6'1 177 London Beefeaters Jrs.; Western Ontario B: 2/14/1954																															
1978	TOR	5	0		1				1	3														1	31	31.0	31				
1979	TOR	1																													
2	Years	6	0		1				1	3														1	31	31.0	31				
QUENTIN RIGGINS Quentin Patrick LB 5'11 210 Auburn B: 4/14/1966 Montgomery, AL Pro: E																															
1990	WPG	8	0		2	3																									
FRANK RIGNEY Frank Joseph OT-OG-DT 6'4 233 Iowa B: 4/9/1936 East St. Louis, IL D: 6/29/2010 North Vancouver, BC Draft: 4-43 1958 PHI																															
1958	WPG	15																													
1959	WPG+	15																	3	44	14.7	16	0								
1960	WPG+	16																	2	19	9.5	12	0								
1961	WPG+	16			0							6	1																		
1962	WPG*	11																													
1963	WPG	16																													
1964	WPG+	16																													
1965	WPG*	16	0		2							6	1																		
1966	WPG*	16																													
1967	WPG	16																													
10	Years	153	0		2							12	2						5	63	12.6	16	0								
NATE RILES Nate CB-DH 5'11 185 Akron; Ohio Northern B: 2/13/1974 Akron, OH																															
2001	WPG	6				9			1	0	1																				
BOB RILEY Bob WR																															
1978	HAM	4																	1	11	11.0	11	0								
JASON RILEY Jason OG-DT 6'3 260 Vancouver Meralomas Jrs.; British Columbia B: 10/4/1958 Scarborough, ON Draft: 1-7 1983 WPG																															
1983	WPG	3																													
1984	SAS	7	0		1																										
1984	HAM	6																													
1984	Year	13	0		1																										
1985	HAM	14	0		1																										
1986	HAM+	18																													
1987	HAM	18				0																									
1988	HAM+	17	0		1	0																									
1989	HAM*	18	0		1	2																									
1990	HAM	16	0		3	1																									
1991	HAM	18				3																									
1992	HAM*	18	0		2	2								1	-3	-3.0	-3	0													
1993	HAM	9				0																									
11	Years	156	0		9	8								1	-3	-3.0	-3	0													
KARON RILEY Karon J. DE 6'2 260 Southern Methodist; Minnesota B: 8/23/1978 Detroit, MI Draft: 4-103 2001 CHIB Pro: N																															
2005	TOR	2				6																									
LARRY RILEY Lawrence DB 5'10 192 Salem B: 11/21/1954 Eustis, FL Pro: N																															
1979	WPG	3																													
1980	BC	11							2	0																					
2	Years	14							2	0																					
MIKE RILEY Mike DT 6'4 255 Dalhousie B: 8/7/1954 Draft: 1A-1 1977 OTT																															
1977	OTT	16																													
1978	OTT	16																													

Year	Team	GP	FM	FF	FR	TK	SK	YDS	IR	YDS	PD	PTS	TD	RA	YDS	AVG	LG	TD	REC	YDS	AVG	LG	TD	PR	YDS	AVG	LG	KOR	YDS	AVG	LG
1979	HAM	10																													
1980	OTT	12																													
4	Years	54																													
PETE RILEY Pete DB 5'9 180 Livingston B: 4/8/1964 Draft: 8-69 1987 WPG																															
1987	WPG	1																													
JEROME RINEHART Jerome DT 6'4 245 Arizona Western JC; Tennessee-Martin B: 6/6/1965 Norristown, PA Draft: 11-299 1989 NYG																															
1990	WPG	4	0		1	7	2.0																								
1991	WPG	8	0		1	18	5.0																								
1992	WPG	1				2																									
3	Years	13	0		2	27	7.0																								
JUSTIN RING Justin LB 6'2 220 Simon Fraser B: 7/4/1973 Kamloops, BC Draft: 1-5 1996 HAM																															
1996	HAM	18	0		1	59	1.0	6.0	2	12	3																				
1997	HAM	18	0	1	2	52	1.0	2.0	2	3	1																				
1998	HAM	18	0	1	0	77	1.0	11.0			3																				
1999	EDM	18				33	1.0	7.0																	1	0	0.0	0	2	2	1.0	2
2000	EDM	18	0	1	0	17																									
2001	EDM	1				1																									
2002	EDM	18				15													1	8	8.0	8	0								
7	Years	109	0	3	3	254	4.0	26.0	4	15	7								1	8	8.0	8	0	1	0	0.0	0	2	2	1.0	2
KENT RING Kent LB 6'2 220 Simon Fraser B: 9/15/1977 Kamloops, BC Draft: 4-29 2000 CAL																															
2000	CAL	7	0	1	0	4																									
2001	CAL	13				8																									
2	Years	20	0	1	0	12																									
MIKE RINGER Mike DH 6'2 192 Oklahoma B: 11/8/1943 St. Louis, MO Draft: 15-130 1966 DEN; 10-149 1966 STL																															
1966	SAS	6												4	22	5.5	11	0						2	23	11.5	20				
ERIK RINGOEN Leif Erik LB 6'0 235 Hofstra B: 7/1/1968 Wilmington, DE Draft: 10-266 1991 SEA																															
1992	TOR	2				9																									
RENE RIOPELLE Rene FL-S 6'0 187 North Bay Ti-Cats B: 1943																															
1963	HAM	6												1	11	11.0	11	0						16	66	4.1	11				
1964	MTL	12	1		1									8	31	3.9	9	0	4	31	7.8	11	0								
1966	HAM	2																													
3	Years	20	1		1									9	42	4.7	11	0	4	31	7.8	11	0	16	66	4.1	11				
ANDRE RISON Andre Previn WR 6'0 191 Michigan State B: 3/18/1967 Flint, MI Draft: 1-22 1989 IND Pro: N																															
2004	TOR	6				0						6	1						14	174	12.4	35	1								
2005	TOR	1				1													1	4	4.0	4	0								
2	Years	7				1						6	1						15	178	11.9	35	1								
DOUG RITCHIE Doug FB																															
1950	WPG	2																													
ROBIN RITCHIE Robin DB 5'11 182 Parkdale Lions Jrs.; Queen's B: 1939																															
1961	OTT	2																													
CRAIG RITTER Craig W. OG 6'4 300 Arizona State B: 11/10/1970 Anaheim, CA Pro: E																															
1995	MEM	5				0																									
DAVID RIVERS David QB 6'3 220 Virginia; Western Carolina B: 9/1/1977 Greenville, SC Pro: E																															
2001	BC	18	1	0	0	0								2	5	2.5	4	0													
2002	TOR	4				0																									
2	Years	22	1	0	0	0								2	5	2.5	4	0													
LORENZO RIVERS Lorenzo RB-WR 5'9 160 Tennessee Tech B: 10/30/1964 Orlando, FL																															
1988	BC	8	4		1	0						6	1	9	30	3.3	10	1	2	18	9.0	13	0	36	205	5.7	36	23	389	16.9	32
1990	TOR	3	2		0	2						6	1	8	45	5.6	13	0	2	5	2.5	9	1	9	20	2.2	20	8	168	21.0	31
2	Years	11	6		1	2						12	2	17	75	4.4	13	1	4	23	5.8	13	1	45	225	5.0	36	31	557	18.0	32
JACK RIZZO John Ralph HB 5'10 200 Lehigh B: 6/15/1949 Westville, NH Pro: NW																															
1972	OTT	2	1		0									13	30	2.3	11	0	1	3	3.0	3	0					1	15	15.0	15
TRAVIS ROACH Travis Morgan, Jr. OG 6'2 260 Texas B: 3/18/1950 Hamilton, TX D: 5/30/1988 Austin, TX Draft: 6A-144 1973 NYJ Pro: N																															
1973	BC	1																													
CARL ROACHES Carl Edward WR 5'8 165 Texas A&M B: 10/2/1953 Houston, TX Draft: 14-377 1976 TB Pro: N																															
1977	SAS	3																						2	12	6.0	9				
DON ROBB Don E 6'0 190 Queen's Draft: 2-7 1961 CAL																															
1961	CAL	2																													
MIGUEL ROBEDE Miguel DT-DE 6'4 288 Miami (Florida); Laval B: 6/30/1981 Val d'Or, QC Draft: 1-1 2005 CAL																															
2006	CAL	9				0																									
2007	CAL	3				0																									
2008	CAL	18	0	0	1	19	5.0	38.0																							
2009	CAL	11				12					1																				
2010	CAL	12	0	1	0	11	2.0	17.0																							
5	Years	53	0	1	1	42	7.0	55.0			1																				
BRIAN ROBERSON Brian D. WR 5'9 168 Fresno State B: 1/8/1974 Panorama City, CA Pro: X																															
2002	SAS	5										6	1						11	163	14.8	35	1								
2003	SAS	4				0													6	50	8.3	12	0	5	27	5.4	10	2	49	24.5	28
2	Years	9				0						6	1						17	213	12.5	35	1	5	27	5.4	10	2	49	24.5	28
CLAY ROBERSON Johnny Clayton, Jr. LB 6'1 234 North Carolina B: 3/10/1981 Greenville, NC																															
2005	MTL	1				1																									
2005	CAL	3				2																									
2005	Year	4				3																									
ELI ROBERSON Eli, III QB 6'1 205 Kansas State B: 8/13/1980 Baytown, TX																															
2005	MTL	18				0																									
VERN ROBERSON Vernon Lee DB 6'2 195 Grambling State B: 8/3/1952 Natchitoches, MS Pro: N																															
1975	CAL*	16	0		1				10	145		12	2											18	98	5.4	20	5	107	21.4	29
1976	CAL	9	0		1				3	51																		3	77	25.7	34
1976	OTT	2																										5	123	24.6	31
1976	Year	11	0		1				3	51																		8	200	25.0	34
2	Years	25	0		2				13	196		12	2											18	98	5.4	20	13	307	23.6	34
BILL ROBERTS William J. HB 6'0 200 Dartmouth B: 9/11/1929 Dubuque, IA D: 8/15/2006 Edina, MN Pro: N																															
1957	BC	5	2		0				1	25		6	1	16	41	2.6	11	0	4	88	22.0	37	1					2	50	25.0	28
BUTCH ROBERTS Butch C																															
1947	CAL	5																													
CHARLES ROBERTS Charles Arthur RB 5'6 171 Sacramento State B: 4/3/1979 Montclair, CA																															
2001	WPG*	17	3	0	0	1						18	3	107	620	5.8	22	1	27	288	10.7	43	0	82	782	9.5	58	45	981	21.8	50
2002	WPG*	17	5	0	2	4						66	11	216	1162	5.4	70	5	55	613	11.1	59	6	44	476	10.8	75	27	539	20.0	42
2003	WPG*	18	2	0	2	1						60	10	264	1554	5.9	51	8	51	548	10.7	47	2	45	362	8.0	35	26	528	20.3	36
2004	WPG*	18	11	0	1	3						78	13	300	1522	5.1	49	8	53	398	7.5	26	5	3	28	9.3	26	4	84	21.0	41
2005	WPG*	18	5	0	1	7						72	12	290	1624	5.6	59	12	49	474	9.7	64	0	1	17	17.0	17	1	19	19.0	19
2006	WPG*	18	5	0	1	6						60	10	303	1609	5.3	33	10	42	411	9.8	32	0								
2007	WPG*	16	6	0	1	0						96	16	262	1379	5.3	56	16	47	358	7.6	35	0								
2008	WPG	9	3	0	3	1						24	4	111	517	4.7	33	4	38	251	6.6	14	0	7	70	10.0	26				
2008	BC	7	1	0	0	0						30	5	65	298	4.6	18	5	6	55	9.2	20	0	1	3	3.0	3	2	41	20.5	23
2008	Year	16	4	0	3	1						54	9	176	815	4.6	18	9	44	306	7.0	20	0	8	73	9.1	26	2	41	20.5	23
8	Years	131	41	0	11	23						504	84	1918	10285	5.4	70	69	368	3396	9.2	64	13	183	1738	9.5	75	105	2192	20.9	50
C.R. ROBERTS Cornelius R. HB-FB 6'3 202 Southern California B: 2/29/1936 Draft: 14-166 1958 NYG Pro: N																															
1957	TOR	2												23	117	5.1	17	0	0	10		10	0					2	49	24.5	20
1958	TOR	8										30	5	92	595	6.5	85	5	5	57	11.4	25	0					2	38	19.0	26
1962	HAM	2												8	23	2.9	8	0	1	7	7.0	7	0					1	17	17.0	17
3	Years	12										30	5	123	735	6.0	85	5	6	74	12.3	25	0					5	104	20.8	26

Year	Team	GP	FM	FF	FR	TK	SK	YDS	IR	YDS	PD	PTS	TD	RA	YDS	AVG	LG	TD	REC	YDS	AVG	LG	TD	PR	YDS	AVG	LG	KOR	YDS	AVG	LG
ELBERT ROBERTS Elbert DB 6'2 195 Savannah State B: 11/30/1959 New York, NY																															
1981	TOR	6							1	9																					
GENE ROBERTS Eugene O. (Choo-Choo) OHB 5'11 188 Kansas; Tennessee-Chattanooga B: 1/20/1923 D: 7/6/2009 Independence, MO Draft: 8-65 1946 NYG; SS 1947 BKN-AAFC Pro: N																															
1951	MTL	12										41	4					3					1								
1952	OTT+	12										45	9					6					3								
1953	OTT+	14										88	7					4					3								
1954	OTT	14										40	4	98	363	3.7	17	4	23	317	13.8	76	0	1	8	8.0	8	7	113	16.1	25
4	Years	52										214	24	98	363	3.7	17	17	23	317	13.8	76	7	1	8	8.0	8	7	113	16.1	25
GERRY ROBERTS Gerry DT 6'5 248 Desert JC; UCLA B: 4/3/1951 Draft: 11-286 1974 MIA; 22-264 1974 HOU-WFL																															
1976	WPG	3																													
JACK ROBERTS Jack G 5'10 207 Toronto Draft: 1952 TOR																															
1952	TOR	9																													
1953	TOR	6																													
2	Years	15																													
JAY ROBERTS Jay TE 6'4 222 Kansas B: 1942 Des Moines, IA D: 10/6/2010 Ottawa, ON																															
1964	OTT	13	1		0							6	1						9	138	15.3	28	1					2	2	1.0	2
1965	OTT	14	1		0														11	159	14.5	35	0								
1966	OTT	14	1		0							6	1						18	286	15.9	30	1					2	2	1.0	2
1967	OTT	14										6	1						21	309	14.7	37	1								
1968	OTT	14	1		1							6	1						32	566	17.7	38	1								
1969	OTT	14										18	3						8	148	18.5	29	3								
1970	OTT	5																	16	198	12.4	29	0								
7	Years	88	4		1							42	7						115	1804	15.7	38	7					4	4	1.0	2
JED ROBERTS Jed LB 6'2 230 Northern Colorado B: 11/10/1967																															
1990	EDM	2				0																									
1991	EDM	18				27																									
1992	EDM	18	0		3	30	2.0	16.0																							
1993	EDM	18				31	10.0	69.0																							
1994	EDM	18	0		1	22	3.0	26.0																							
1995	EDM	15	0		3	15	2.0	18.0																				2	14	7.0	10
1996	EDM	18	0		1	29																									
1997	EDM	18				25	3.0	9.0																				2	20	10.0	12
1998	EDM	7				6	1.0	5.0																				1	11	11.0	11
1999	EDM	9				10																						1	0	0.0	0
2000	EDM	16	0	0	1	23	1.0	8.0			1																				
2001	EDM	9	0	0	1	12																						2	16	8.0	9
2002	EDM	2				3																						1	13	13.0	13
13	Years	168	0	0	10	233	22.0	151.0			1																	9	74	8.2	13
JEFF ROBERTS Jeff LB 6'2 235 Tulane B: 12/23/1960 Miami, FL Draft: 7-168 1982 NE																															
1984	SAS	14	0		3		13.0																					1	0	0.0	0
1985	SAS	3																													
1985	OTT	3	0		1		4.0																								
1985	Year	6					4.0																								
1986	OTT	6					2.0																								
3	Years	23	0		4		19.0																					1	0	0.0	0
LANNY ROBERTS Laneair OE 6'3 212 Georgia B: 6/15/1934 Draft: 20-241 1957 NYG																															
1960	MTL	1												0	6		6	0	2	75	37.5	63	0								
MARSHALL ROBERTS Marshall CB 5'9 170 Rutgers B: 8/17/1969 Abington, PA																															
1993	SAC	5	0		1	7			1	0																					
MICHAEL ROBERTS Michael DB 5'11 185 Ohio State; Indiana State B: 9/16/1983 Toronto, ON Draft: 5-35 2006 HAM																															
2007	HAM	16				17					2																				
2008	HAM	1				0																									
2008	WPG	1				0																									
2008	Year	2				0																									
2	Years	17				17					2																				
R.J. ROBERTS Roosevelt, Jr. DE 6'3 240 Troy B: 8/24/1989 Enterprise, AL																															
2011	SAS	1				1																									
WILLIE ROBERTS Willie OE 6'2 190 Tulsa B: 3/8/1931 Chickasha, OK Draft: 4-49 1953 LARM																															
1955	CAL+	14	2		0							25	5	0	3		2	0	59	1091	18.5	76	5								
1957	CAL	11	1		0				1	14									5	83	16.6	48	0								
2	Years	25	3		0				1	14		25	5	0	3		2	0	64	1174	18.3	76	5								
JEFF ROBERTSHAW Jeff DE-DT 6'3 258 McMaster B: 3/27/1983 Hamilton, ON																															
2007	MTL	1				1																									
2008	MTL	11	0	1	0	5	1.0	4.0																							
2009	MTL	9				5																									
2010	MTL	10	0	1	0	7																						2	5	2.5	5
2011	MTL	1				0																									
5	Years	32	0	2	0	18	1.0	4.0																				2	5	2.5	5
DARRELL ROBERTSON Darrell Thomas DE 6'5 252 Georgia Tech B: 4/15/1986																															
2008	EDM	2				6			0	0	1																				
JAMAL ROBERTSON Jamal RB 5'10 211 Ohio Northern B: 1/10/1977 Washington, DC Pro: EN																															
2008	TOR	17	2	0	0	2						42	7	105	548	5.2	75	6	25	258	10.3	52	1					13	333	25.6	49
2009	TOR	18	4	0	0	3						54	9	209	1031	4.9	46	9	59	482	8.2	37	0					11	191	17.4	42
2010	BC	16	3	0	1	2						54	9	154	953	6.2	69	8	54	387	7.2	26	1								
2011	BC	9				0						24	4	63	296	4.7	19	3	19	170	8.9	35	1					3	69	23.0	27
4	Years	60	9	0	1	7						174	29	531	2828	5.3	75	26	157	1297	8.3	52	3					27	593	22.0	49
TAYLOR ROBERTSON John Taylor OG 6'6 325 Central Florida B: 9/8/1980 Brantford, ON Draft: 2A-11 2003 CAL																															
2003	CAL	2				0																									
2004	CAL	13	0	0	3	0																									
2005	CAL	18				0																									
2006	CAL	18				0																									
2007	TOR+	18	0	0	1	1																									
2008	TOR	18				2																									
2009	TOR	18				0																									
2010	TOR	18				3																									
2011	TOR	11				0																									
9	Years	134	0	0	4	6																									
VIRGIL ROBERTSON Virgil Terrell LB 6'2 230 Nicholls State B: 11/9/1966 New Orleans, LA Pro: E																															
1990	HAM	2				1																									
1991	HAM	2				10																									
1994	BC	17	0		3	40	3.0	31.0	1	0	2	6	1																		
1995	BC	15	0		4	33	8.0	60.0																							
1996	BC	15	0		1	31	3.0	25.0	1	41	2	6	1																		
1997	BC	18	0	0	3	30	9.0	71.0				12	2																		
1998	BC	2	0	0	1	9																									
7	Years	71	0	0	12	154	23.0	187.0	2	41	4	24	4																		
WES ROBERTSON Wesley J. LB 6'2 229 Benedict; Rutgers B: 11/19/1978 Camden, NJ																															
2004	CAL	10	0	1	0	18	1.0	10.0	0	0	1																				
MATT ROBICHAUD Matt LB 5'10 227 Bishop's B: 9/23/1975 Pointe Claire, ON																															
2001	HAM	12				7																									
2001	TOR	1				3																									

Year	Team	GP	FM	FF	FR	TK	SK	YDS	IR	YDS	PD	PTS	TD	RA	YDS	AVG	LG	TD	REC	YDS	AVG	LG	TD	PR	YDS	AVG	LG	KOR	YDS	AVG	LG
2001	Year	13				10																									
2002	OTT	2				3																									
2003	OTT	1				0																									
2004	HAM	18	0	0	2	8																									
2005	HAM	10				3																									
2006	HAM	18				0																									
2007	HAM	18				0																									
2008	HAM	15				2																									
2009	HAM	4				1																									
9	Years	98	0	0	2	27																									
MILT ROBICHAUX Milton J. E 6'6 215 Copiah-Lincoln CC; Trinity (Texas) B: 1932 Draft: 21-252 1956 LARM																															
1957	SAS	3																													
GENE ROBILLARD Eugene Thomas QB-HB 5'10 180 McGill B: 1/15/1929 D: 4/14/2007 Ottawa, ON Draft: 1952 MTL																															
1952	MTL	1																													
1954	BC	9	1											15	33	2.2	8	0													
2	Years	10	1		0									15	33	2.2	8	0													
MATT ROBILLARD Matt HB 6'0 200 none B: 1934 Ottawa, ON																															
1954	OTT	13												5	29	5.8	15	0										2	26	13.0	20
BILL ROBINSON William Andrew HB 5'11 195 Lincoln (Missouri) B: 9/29/1929 Pittsburgh, PA Draft: 25-294 1952 PIT Pro: N																															
1955	WPG	13	?		0				1	0				9	50	5.0	21	0										6	117	19.5	36
BILLY ROBINSON Bill QB-DB 5'11 177 St. Mary's (Nova Scotia) B: 4/23/1951 Toronto, ON Draft: 3-27 1974 OTT																															
1975	OTT	13							1	2				1	0	0.0	0	0													
1976	OTT	16			1									4	5	1.3	5	0													
2	Years	29	0		1				1	2				5	5	1.0	5	0													
BRADLEY ROBINSON Bradley Dale CB 5'8 180 Middle Tennessee State B: 1/24/1985 Duncan, SC																															
2008	EDM	8				15			3	52	2													6	33	5.5	9	4	59	14.8	24
2009	EDM	7	1	0	0	5			1	17	0													6	8	1.3	11	4	75	18.8	24
2	Years	15	1	0	0	20			4	69	2													12	41	3.4	11	8	134	16.8	24
DAVID ROBINSON David Lee, Jr. CB 5'9 185 East Carolina B: 2/3/1968 High Point, NC D: 9/30/1995 Winston-Salem, NC																															
1994	SAC	18	0		2	0			2	7	13																	1	18	18.0	18
1995	MEM	14				33			1	0	6																				
2	Years	32	0		2	33			3	7	19																	1	18	18.0	18
DON ROBINSON Don FW-G																															
1946	TOR	12																													
1947	TOR	4																													
1948	TOR	10																													
3	Years	26																													
DON ROBINSON Donald CB-DH 6'0 190 Kentucky B: 5/27/1972 Richmond, VA Pro: E																															
1994	LV	18			1	88	1.0	9.0	2	40	5								1	17	17.0	17	0								
1995	HAM	18	0		1	44			2	40	4																				
1996	HAM	18	0		3	31			5	73	9																				
1998	WPG	18	0	0	2	52			2	47	0																				
1999	WPG	6				21			3	9	2																				
5	Years	78	0	0	7	236	1.0	9.0	14	209	20								1	17	17.0	17	0								
DURELL ROBINSON Durell WR 6'3 217 Georgia; Northwest Mississippi CC B: 9/7/1981 Spartanburg, SC																															
2002	EDM	1				0																									
2003	EDM	4				0													7	81	11.6	20	0					1	27	27.0	27
2	Years	5				0													7	81	11.6	20	0					1	27	27.0	27
EMBRY ROBINSON Embry L. FB 5'9 200 Michigan State B: 1932 D: 3/23/1961 Pittsburgh, PA																															
1958	MTL	3																							1	-2	-2.0	-2				
FRANK ROBINSON Frank LB 6'0 204 Tulane B: 3/6/1959 Nassawadox, VA																															
1981	SAS	16	0		1		6.5		1	3																					
1982	SAS	16	0		1		3.0		1	20																					
1983	SAS	16	0		1				2	78									1	1	1.0	1	0								
1984	WPG	10	1		2		5.5																	1	0	0.0	0	1	5	5.0	5
1985	WPG	12	0		2		8.0		1	0																					
1985	TOR	2	0		4		3.0					6	1																		
1985	Year	14	0		0		11.0		1	0		6	1																		
1986	HAM	13					4.0		2	29																					
1987	HAM+	17	0		3	64	4.0		5	28																					
1988	HAM	18	1		2	74	2.0		3	60																					
1989	HAM+	18	0		3	72			4	73														1	2	2.0	2				
1990	HAM	13	0		2	66																									
10	Years	149	2		21	276	36.0		19	291		6	1						1	1	1.0	1	0	2	2	1.0	2	1	5	5.0	5
FRED ROBINSON Fred Lee DE 6'4 240 Miami (Florida) B: 10/22/1961 Miami, FL Draft: 8-198 1984 TB; 2A-25 1984 WAS-USFL Pro: N																															
1987	WPG	2				1	2.0																								
FRED ROBINSON Frederick Leroy, II OT-OG-DT 6'1 242 Washington B: 9/2/1930 West Haven, CT Draft: 14-169(f) 1955 CLE Pro: N																															
1956	BC	7																													
1958	TOR	9							1	1																					
1960	OTT	7																													
1961	OTT	2																													
1962	HAM	4																													
5	Years	29							1	1																					
GABE ROBINSON Gabe DE 6'3 252 Toronto B: 3/30/1976 Comox, BC																															
2003	TOR	8				5																									
2004	TOR	15				20	2.0																								
2	Years	23				25	2.0																								
GARY ROBINSON Gary DE-DT 6'4 255 Simon Fraser B: 7/7/1946 Draft: 1969 WPG																															
1969	BC	12	0		1																										
1970	BC	14																													
1971	BC	16			1																										
1972	BC	16																													
1973	BC	16																													
1974	BC	16																													
1975	BC	16							1	5																					
1976	BC	12																													
1977	BC	13	0		2																										
1978	BC	4																													
1978	HAM	12	0		1																										
1978	Year	16	0		1																										
10	Years	135	0		5				1	5																					
GLENN ROBINSON Glenn William DE 6'6 245 Navarro JC; Oklahoma State B: 10/20/1951 Killeen, TX Draft: 3A-57 1974 BAL; 9-87 1974 CHI-WFL Pro: N																															
1978	HAM	3																													
1979	HAM	11																													
2	Years	14																													
JACK ROBINSON John K-OE 6'1 211 St. James Rams Jrs. B: 4/1/1941																															
1964	WPG	2										10	0																		
JAMES ROBINSON James WR-SB 6'3 196 Butler County CC B: 12/6/1982 Fort Lauderdale, FL																															
2008	TOR	13	0	0	1	7						6	1						25	381	15.2	90	1								
2009	TOR	4				2													5	56	11.2	21	0								
2010	TOR	10	2	0	0	2						12	2						22	310	14.1	50	2								
2011	SAS	5				0						6	1						9	134	14.9	57	1								

Year	Team	GP	FM	FF	FR	TK	SK	YDS	IR	YDS	PD	PTS	TD	RA	YDS	AVG	LG	TD	REC	YDS	AVG	LG	TD	PR	YDS	AVG	LG	KOR	YDS	AVG	LG
4	Years	32	2	0	1	11						24	4						61	881	14.4	90	4								
JUNIOR ROBINSON Junior S-CB 6'0 186 West Island Broncos Jrs.; Guelph B: 8/11/1961 Kingston, Jamaica Draft: 2-11 1983 OTT																															
1983	OTT	16	0		1		1.0		4	41																					
1984	OTT	9																													
1985	SAS	4																													
1986	HAM	2																													
1986	BC	1																													
1986	Year	3																													
1987	EDM	18			3	41			1	0														1	3	3.0	3				
1988	EDM	17				1																		1	0	0.0	0				
1989	WPG	1				0																									
1989	SAS	11				9																									
1989	Year	12				9																									
1990	HAM	7				5																		1	2	2.0	2				
8	Years	74	0		4	56	1.0		5	41														3	5	1.7	3				
JUNIOR ROBINSON David Lee, Jr. CB 5'9 181 East Carolina B: 2/3/1968 High Point, NC D: 9/30/1995 Winston-Salem, NC Draft: 5A-110 1990 NE Pro: EN																															
1993	SAC	8				29			1	6																					
1994	SAC	18				2																									
2	Years	26				31			1	6																					
KELVIN ROBINSON Kelvin QB 6'2 215 Mississippi Gulf Coast CC; Alabama A&M B: 1/28/1978 Mobile, AL																															
2001	HAM	1				0																									
KEN ROBINSON Ken TE-LB 6'3 225 Arizona State B: 1/3/1951																															
1974	WPG	2																													
1974	CAL	2																	2	64	32.0	52	0								
1974	Year	4																	2	64	32.0	52	0								
KEVIN ROBINSON Kevin Lee WR 5'11 196 Utah State B: 12/19/1984 Fresno, CA Draft: 6B-182 2008 KC Pro: N																															
2009	HAM	1				0																		4	21	5.3	12	1	8	8.0	8
LARRY ROBINSON Larry DH-QB 6'0 190 Mount Royal College Cougars Jrs. B: 1942																															
1961	CAL	16										8	1						11	242	22.0	52	1								
1962	CAL	16										79	3						21	426	20.3	85	3								
1963	CAL	16							9	28		99	0						1	7	7.0	7	0	21	105	5.0	15				
1964	CAL	16	0		2				2	53		106	0											30	183	6.1	25	1	0	0.0	0
1965	CAL+	16	0		3				5	69		95	1											3	10	3.3	5				
1966	CAL	16	0		1				5	115		77	1											13	59	4.5	12	3	79	26.3	28
1967	CAL	16							4	70		6	0											16	60	3.8	11	3	59	19.7	24
1968	CAL	16	2		5				5	39		97	1											9	27	3.0	10	1	8	8.0	8
1969	CAL	16	1		2				6	64		95	0											10	52	5.2	14				
1970	CAL	16	0		1				1	12		74	0																		
1971	CAL+	16	1		2				6	158		81	1											1	11	11.0	11				
1972	CAL+	16	1		2				4	65		100	1																		
1973	CAL	16	0		1				2	36		80	0											1	0	0.0	0				
1974	CAL	16	1		0				1	8		33	0											3	11	3.7	5				
14	Years	224	6		19				50	717		1030	9						33	675	20.5	85	4	107	518	4.8	25	8	146	18.3	28
LEE ROBINSON Lee DE 6'2 256 Alcorn State B: 4/23/1987 Centreville, MS Pro: N																															
2011	EDM	1				0																									
LYBRANT ROBINSON Lybrant G. DE-DT 6'4 250 Delaware State B: 8/31/1964 Salisbury, MD Draft: 5B-139 1989 WAS Pro: N																															
1991	OTT	7	0		1	15	2.0																								
1992	OTT	15	0		1	39	3.0	7.0																							
1993	OTT	16				27	7.0	49.0																							
1994	OTT	2				3																									
1994	SAS	14	0		2	34	7.0	25.0																							
1994	Year	16	0		2	37	7.0	25.0																							
1995	SAS	18				36	8.0	74.0			1																				
1996	SAS	18	0		1	36	8.0	49.0			3																				
1997	SAS	8				11	2.0	9.0			2																				
7	Years	84	0		5	201	37.0	213.0			6																				
MIKE ROBINSON Michael LB 6'3 235 Utah State B: 10/29/1960 Hamilton, ON Draft: 1A-6 1984 EDM																															
1985	EDM	3																													
1985	WPG	8																													
1985	Year	11																													
1986	HAM	14																						1	9	9.0	9				
1987	HAM	15				6																									
1988	HAM	16	0		2	53						6	1																		
4	Years	48	0		2	59						6	1											1	9	9.0	9				
RAFAEL ROBINSON Eugene Rafael LB 5'11 200 Wisconsin B: 6/19/1969 Marshall, TX Pro: N																															
1998	BC	7				36	1.0	3.0	2	29	1																				
1999	BC	17	0	1	3	88			4	140	3	6	1																		
2000	BC	5				20																									
3	Years	29	0	1	3	144	1.0	3.0	6	169	4	6	1																		
RAY ROBINSON Ray DL 6'0 230 Illinois State B: 1/27/1981																															
2004	HAM	1				0																									
RICH ROBINSON Richard CB 5'10 175 Miami (Florida) B: 1946																															
1968	BC	12	0		1				3	83														6	42	7.0	13	9	207	23.0	27
1969	BC+	10							7	61																					
1970	BC	16	0		1				10	91														4	10	2.5	4				
3	Years	38	0		2				20	235														10	52	5.2	13	9	207	23.0	27
ROBERT ROBINSON Robert DL-OG 6'3 280 Cincinnati B: 12/11/1972 Toronto, ON Draft: 2-17 1996 CAL																															
1997	CAL	2				0																									
1997	WPG	10				5					1																				
1997	Year	12				5					1																				
1998	WPG	11				10	1.0	4.0																							
1999	CAL	5				1																									
1999	SAS	2				0																									
1999	Year	7				1																									
3	Years	18				16	1.0	4.0			2																				
RON ROBINSON Ronald WR-SB 6'4 192 Contra Costa JC; Utah State B: 1/31/1956																															
1980	CAL	5										24	4						10	216	21.6	95	4								
1981	CAL	1										6	1						1	8	8.0	8	1								
1982	SAS	16	2		1							54	9						54	723	13.4	41	9					1	8	8.0	8
1983	SAS	11										48	8						44	692	15.7	41	8					1	0	0.0	0
1983	MTL	6										36	6						29	687	23.7	60	6								
1983	Year*	17										84	14						13	1319	101.5	60	14					1	0	0.0	0
1984	MTL	4			0															10	242	24.2	55	0								
1984	BC	10	0		1							36	6						45	774	17.2	75	6								
1984	Year	14	2		0							36	6						55	1016	18.5	75	6								
1985	BC	12	3		0							18	3						28	471	16.8	46	3								
6	Years	49	5		2							222	37						221	3813	17.3	95	37					2	8	4.0	8
RONTARIUS ROBINSON Rontarius DH-CB-LB 5'11 185 Howard B: 4/8/1982 Tallahassee, FL																															
2005	SAS	3	0	0	1	6			1	0	2																				
2006	SAS	16	0	2	1	28			3	21	2																				
2007	SAS	14	0	1	0	49			1	0	2																				
2008	HAM	18	0	0	1	68	2.0	6.0	1	0	8																				

Year	Team	GP	FM	FF	FR	TK	SK	YDS	IR	YDS	PD	PTS	TD	RA	YDS	AVG	LG	TD	REC	YDS	AVG	LG	TD	PR	YDS	AVG	LG	KOR	YDS	AVG	LG
4	Years	51	0	3	3	151	2.0	6.0	6	21	14																				
ROY ROBINSON Roy DB 5'11 180 Montana B: 9/27/1946 Pasig, Philippines Draft: 9-220 1970 ATL																															
1972	SAS	14	0		3																							1	28	28.0	28
SCOTT ROBINSON Scott WR 6'2 200 Simon Fraser B: 2/8/1978 Maple Ridge, BC Draft: 3-24 2001 BC																															
2001	BC	2				1													5	62	12.4	33	0								
2001	EDM	2				0													1	13	13.0	13	0								
2001	Year	4				1													6	75	12.5	33	0								
2002	EDM	18	0	0	2	5						6	1						21	296	14.1	59	1								
2003	EDM	16				3						12	2						21	177	8.4	18	2	1	4	4.0	4				
2004	EDM	15				2													5	39	7.8	22	0								
2005	WPG	4				1													4	32	8.0	13	0								
5	Years	55	0	0	2	12						18	3						57	619	10.9	59	3	1	4	4.0	4				
TEX ROBINSON Theodore C. HB 6'2 205 Temple B: 12/22/1932 Bridgeton, NJ D: 4/3/2002 Vineland, NJ Draft: 29-349 1955 CLE																															
1956	HAM	13							3	79		42	7	100	577	5.8	52	3	18	242	13.4	82	3					3	44	14.7	22
WARREN ROBINSON Warren OT 6'4 260 York B: 3/18/1962 Mississauga, ON Draft: 4-30 1988 BC																															
1988	BC	2				0																									
ZANDER ROBINSON Alexander DE 6'5 255 Western Ontario B: 10/11/1989 Draft: 3-22 2011 TOR																															
2011	TOR	18	0	1	0	12																									
ZEDRICK ROBINSON Zedrick FB 6'1 197 Southern Utah B: 2/19/1971 Las Vegas, NV																															
1994	LV	8	1		1	7						12	2	58	271	4.7	35	2	9	112	12.4	23	0					5	96	19.2	41
1995	BC	3	2		0	0						18	3	33	161	4.9	19	3	2	7	3.5	7	0								
2	Years	11	3		1	7						30	5	91	432	4.7	35	5	11	119	10.8	23	0					5	96	19.2	41
RAE ROBIRTIS Rae C 6'4 256 Richmond Raiders Jrs.; British Columbia B: 4/5/1965 Vancouver, BC Draft: 4-28 1987 OTT																															
1987	OTT	12				1																									
1988	OTT	13				0																									
1989	OTT	11	0		1	2																									
1989	HAM	7	0		1	0																									
1989	Year	18	0		2	2																									
1990	HAM	18	0		1	3																									
1991	EDM	2																													
5	Years	56	0		3	6																									
GARY ROBSON Gary DE 6'1 204 St. James Rams Jrs. B: 1940																															
1962	WPG	7																													
KEVIN ROBSON Kevin C 6'3 270 North Dakota B: 3/26/1970 Winnipeg, MB Draft: 5-42 1994 WPG																															
1994	WPG	17				10																									
1995	WPG	18				12																									
1996	WPG	18	1		0	11																									
3	Years	53	1		0	33																									
PAUL ROBSON Paul LB-C 6'2 222 St. James Rods Jrs.; North Dakota B: 1/30/1941																															
1964	WPG	14																													
1965	WPG	16	1		0																										
1966	WPG	16	0		1																										
1967	WPG	16	1		2																										
1968	WPG	16																													
1969	WPG	16																													
1970	WPG	16																													
1971	WPG	16	1		0				2	34																		1	1	1.0	1
1972	WPG	16																													
9	Years	142	3		3				2	34																		1	1	1.0	1
SCOTT ROBSON Scott OG 6'2 265 North Dakota B: 9/9/1963 Grand Forks, ND Draft: 2-13 1985 MTL																															
1986	MTL	9	0		1																										
FRANK ROCCA Franco C-OT 6'4 295 Eastern Michigan B: 9/6/1972 Calabria, Italy Draft: 3-22 1997 CAL																															
1997	WPG	15				1																									
1998	HAM	18	1	0	2	4						6	1						1	6	6.0	6	1								
1999	HAM	15				0																									
2000	TOR	3				1																									
4	Years	51	1	0	2	6						6	1						1	6	6.0	6	1								
TOM ROCHE Tom DB 6'2 200 Ohio State B: 1956																															
1978	HAM	2																													
JIM ROCKFORD James Kyle DB 5'10 180 Oklahoma B: 9/5/1961 Bloomington, IL Draft: 12A-316 1985 TB; TD 1985 SA-USFL Pro: N																															
1987	HAM	14	0		1	34			1	2		6	1											1	0	0.0	0				
1988	HAM	14	0		2	35			4	22																					
1989	HAM	12	0		1	38			2	51																					
1990	HAM	13	0		1	41			3	59														1	-1	-1.0	-1				
1991	EDM	2	1		0	5			1	33																					
1991	TOR	2				9			1	0																					
1991	Year	4	1		0	16			2	33																					
1992	TOR	2				6																									
6	Years	57	1		5	168			12	167		6	1											2	-1	-0.5	0				
CHRIS RODAHAFFER Christopher David OL 6'5 295 San Diego State B: 4/30/1971 Jefferson County, KY																															
1995	BIR	2				0																									
STEVE RODEHUTSKORS Steven OT 6'6 265 Lethbridge*; Calgary B: 11/27/1963 Strathmore, AB D: 10/25/2007 Draft: 3B-22 1987 WPG																															
1987	WPG	18			1	0																									
1988	WPG	18				0																									
1989	WPG	18				1																									
1990	WPG	18				0																									
1991	WPG	18				1																									
1992	BC	18				2																									
1993	BC	2				1																									
1993	TOR	12				3																									
1993	Year	14				4																									
7	Years	110	0		1	8																									
DEVIN RODGER Devin OL 6'2 230 Manitoba B: 5/16/1997																															
2004	EDM	6				0																									
CORY RODGERS Dacor Temaine WR 6'0 187 Texas Christian B: 2/22/1983 Houston, TX Draft: 4A-104 2006 GB																															
2007	BC	17	1	0	0	2						20	3						27	336	12.4	51	3	3	8	2.7	8	14	246	17.6	36
2008	BC	4				1						12	2						8	111	13.9	37	2	1	10	10.0	10				
2009	TOR	3				2													12	130	10.8	35	0	10	68	6.8	18				
3	Years	24	1	0	0	5						32	5						47	577	12.3	51	5	14	86	6.1	18	14	246	17.6	36
JOHNNY RODGERS John Steve RB-WR 5'10 180 Nebraska B: 7/5/1951 Omaha, NE Draft: 1-25 1973 SD Pro: N																															
1973	MTL*	14	4		0							42	7	55	303	5.5	58	0	41	841	20.5	72	7					16	455	28.4	66
1974	MTL*	16	3		1							66	11	87	492	5.7	53	4	60	1024	17.1	70	7					10	291	29.1	66
1975	MTL*	15	3		0							74	12	54	293	5.4	38	2	40	849	21.2	70	8	60	912	15.2	101	13	380	29.2	50
1976	MTL+	14	3		1							44	7	20	50	2.5	41	1	45	749	16.6	56	6	75	931	12.4	53	17	444	26.1	43
4	Years	59	13		2							226	37	216	1138	5.3	58	7	186	3463	18.6	72	28	135	1843	13.7	101	56	1570	28.0	66
TOM RODGERS Tom QB-DB 6'0 185 Kentucky B: 1940 Draft: 18- 1961 BOS; 12-163 1961 DET																															
1961	OTT	5																													
1962	OTT	1																													
2	Years	6																													
TYRONE RODGERS Tyrone Dworin NT-DE-DT 6'3 266 Oklahoma; Washington B: 4/27/1969 Longview, TX Pro: N																															
1996	BC	18	0		1	25	4.0	25.0																							
1997	WPG	16	0	1	1	24	8.0	60.0			2																	1	3	3.0	3

Year	Team	GP	FM	FF	FR	TK	SK	YDS	IR	YDS	PD	PTS	TD	RA	YDS	AVG	LG	TD	REC	YDS	AVG	LG	TD	PR	YDS	AVG	LG	KOR	YDS	AVG	LG
1998	WPG	18	0	3	0	33	3.0	37.0																			1	0	0.0	0
1999	WPG	18	0	0	1	48	6.0	37.0			1																			
2000	TOR	13				30	4.0	14.0																						
2001	TOR	13	0	0	1	27	1.0	7.0			1																			
2002	CAL	16				35	3.0	13.0																						
7	Years	112	0	4	4	222	29.0	193.0			4																2	3	1.5	3
TED RODOSOVICH Theodore, Jr. OG 6'2 240 Army; Cincinnati B: 5/31/1942 Youngstown, OH Draft: 15- 1965 BOS; 12-168 1965 BAL																														
1965	WPG	5																												
MIKE RODRIGUE Michael Scott WR 6'0 184 Miami (Florida) B: 1/17/1960 Pensacola, FL Draft: 12-331 1982 MIA																														
1982	MTL	6	1		0							2	0						10	165	16.5	41	0								
PRECHAE RODRIGUEZ Prechae WR-SB 6'5 208 Coffeyville JC; Auburn B: 1/21/1985 Tampa, FL																														
2008	HAM	14	1	0	0	1						42	7						70	1099	15.7	86	7								
2009	HAM	12	1	0	0	2						18	3						45	495	11.0	38	3								
2010	SAS	10	3	0	1	2						12	2						30	376	12.5	43	2					2	0	0.0	0
2011	MTL	1				0																								
2011	EDM	3				1													8	98	12.3	49	0								
2011	TOR	2				0													5	30	6.0	17	0								
2011	Year	6				1													13	128	9.8	49	9								
4	Years	37	5	0	1	6						72	12						158	2098	13.3	86	12					2	0	0.0	0
ROBERT RODRIGUEZ Robert John LB 6'0 240 Texas-El Paso B: 12/25/1981 El Paso, TX Pro: E																														
2006	CAL	1	0	0	1	3																								
2007	CAL	1				1																								
2	Years	2	0	0	1	4																								
JOHN ROGAN John P. QB 6'1 200 Yale B: 1/30/1960 New York, NY																														
1982	MTL	1																												
1983	MTL	3	2		0									3	5	1.7	3	0													
2	Years	4	2		0									3	5	1.7	3	0													
FRAN ROGEL Francis Stephen FB 5'11 203 California (Pennsylvania); Penn State B: 12/12/1927 North Braddock, PA D: 6/2/2002 Gibsonia, PA Draft: 8-100 1950 PIT Pro: N																														
1958	HAM	1												10	39	3.9	9	0													
ADAM ROGERS Adam OG 6'5 310 Acadia B: 12/9/1985 Woodville, ON																														
2009	EDM	14				0																								
2010	EDM	3				0																								
2011	HAM	1				0																								
3	Years	18				0																								
AL ROGERS Allan (Butch) LB-HB 6'1 202 McMaster B: 1937 Hamilton, ON																														
1959	TOR	13							1	9																					
1960	HAM	5																												
1961	HAM	14										6	1																		
1962	HAM	1																												
4	Years	33							1	9		6	1																		
BRENDAN ROGERS Brendan LB 6'1 237 Vancouver Meralomas Jrs.; Eastern Washington B: 2/26/1968 Vancouver, BC Draft: 4-32 1991 WPG																														
1991	WPG	15				20	1.0																							
1992	WPG	16	0		1	21													1	-10	-10.0	-10	0	1	7	7.0	7	2	14	7.0	10
1993	WPG	18	0		1	36			1	0																					
1994	WPG	18				36																								
1995	WPG	18	0		1	27			1	11	1																			
1996	TOR	9				17																								
1997	TOR	18	0	0	1	20	1.0	7.0			1																			
1998	TOR	18	0	0	1	21																								
1999	SAS	4				5																								
9	Years	134	0	0	5	203	2.0	7.0	2	11	2								1	-10	-10.0	-10	0	1	7	7.0	7	2	14	7.0	10
BUCK ROGERS William C. OG-C-DG-T-HB 5'11 205 B: 5/6/1928 Ottawa, ON																														
1947	OTT	5										3	0																		
1948	OTT	12										13	2																		
1949	SAS	14										3	0																		
1950	OTT	11																												
1951	OTT	10																												
1952	OTT	12										36	0																		
1953	WPG	14																												
1954	WPG	16										9	0															2	2	1.0	2
1955	WPG	14																												
9	Years	108										64	2															2	2	1.0	2
ERNIE ROGERS Ernie O'Shea OT 6'6 260 Rice B: 2/28/1957 Cleveland, TX Pro: U																														
1980	SAS	3																												
ERNIE ROGERS Erald E. OT 6'5 290 California B: 1/3/1968 Santa Ana, CA Draft: 11-302 1991 MIA Pro: E																														
1993	SAC	2				0																								
FREDDIE ROGERS Freddie DT 6'2 265 Arkansas State B: 6/22/1962																														
1985	WPG	2																												
GARY ROGERS Gary Brian LB 6'3 225 Vanderbilt B: 9/18/1970 Pittsburgh, PA																														
1994	SAS	12				27	1.0	6.0			3																			
1995	SAS	18	0		2	41	3.0	15.0	1	1	4																			
1996	MTL	8				22	6.0	44.0	1	1	6																			
1996	SAS	8	0		1	18			1	0	6																			
1996	Year	16	0		1	40	6.0	44.0	2	1	12																			
1997	SAS	9	0	1	0	38	2.0	19.0			1																			
1998	SAS	6				20	1.0	3.0			4																			
1999	SAS	3				8					1																			
6	Years	56	0	1	3	174	13.0	87.0	3	2	25																			
GLENN ROGERS Glenn Edward, Jr. CB 6'0 185 Memphis B: 6/8/1969 Memphis, TN Pro: EN																														
1993	EDM*	18	0		2	65	1.0	12.0	5	7																				
1994	EDM	18	2		1	54	1.0	14.0	2	8	5																			
1995	EDM*	18				35	1.0	8.0	4	84	8	6	1																	
1996	EDM*	17	1		1	49	2.0	11.0	7	139	6																			
1997	EDM*	18				46			6	94	4																			
1998	BC+	18	0	1	1	38	1.0	13.0	6	82	5																1	0	0.0	0
1999	SAS	9				16	1.0		1	0	1																			
7	Years	116	3	1	5	303	7.0	58.0	31	414	29	6	1														1	0	0.0	0
JACK ROGERS Jack (Buddy) C 5'8 195 Hamilton Wildcats Jrs. B: 1929																														
1950	HAM	11																												
1951	HAM	12																												
1952	HAM	6																												
1953	MTL	1																												
4	Years	30																												
JOHNNY ROGERS John J. E 6'0 210 Temple B: 5/23/1922 D: 10/30/2002 Southampton, PA																														
1950	OTT	12										5	0																		
JOSEPH ROGERS Joseph WR-SB 5'8 165 Texas Southern B: 5/23/1971 Miami, FL																														
1996	OTT*	17	1		0	4						48	8						79	1253	15.9	90	8					2	59	29.5	36
1997	CAL	6				0								1	-1	-1.0	-1	0	23	282	12.3	44	0								
1997	WPG	7	2	0	0	0						8	1						29	294	10.1	41	1								
1997	Year	13	2	0	0	0						8	1	1	-1	-1.0	-1	0	52	576	11.1	44	1								
1998	EDM	7				0						12	2						21	324	15.4	34	2	2	30	15.0	19	6	127	21.2	30
1999	WPG	10				1						18	3						33	438	13.3	59	1	40	414	10.4	77	1	7	7.0	7

Year	Team	GP	FM	FF	FR	TK	SK	YDS	IR	YDS	PD	PTS	TD	RA	YDS	AVG	LG	TD	REC	YDS	AVG	LG	TD	PR	YDS	AVG	LG	KOR	YDS	AVG	LG
4	Years	40	3	0	0	5						86	14	1	-1	-1.0	-1	0	185	2591	14.0	90	12	42	444	10.6	77	9	193	21.4	36
PHIL ROGERS Phil RB 5'10 185 Virginia Tech B: 6/30/1954 Kingsport, TN Draft: 7-203 1976 STL																															
1978	TOR	4	1		0									25	105	4.2	15	0	13	86	6.6	13	0					1	21	21.0	21
REGGIE ROGERS Reginald O'Keith DE 6'6 280 Washington B: 1/21/1964 Sacramento, CA Draft: 1-7 1987 DET Pro: N																															
1993	HAM	4	0		1	6	4.0	21.0																							
1994	HAM	12				32	9.0	56.0			1																				
1994	SHR	4				12																									
1994	Year	16				44	9.0	56.0			1																				
1995	SHR	17	0		1	41	5.0	43.0			6																				
3	Years	33	0		2	91	18.0	120.0			8																				
RON ROGERS Ronald DB 5'10 180 Western Michigan B: 7/12/1978 Chicago, IL Pro: E																															
2004	OTT	5	0	1	0	19					3																				
2005	OTT	13	0	1	0	39			2	32	2																				
2	Years	18	0	2	0	58			2	32	5																				
SAM ROGERS Samuel, Jr. DH 5'11 190 Texas-El Paso B: 6/24/1973 Houston, TX																															
1995	HAM+	16	5		3	31			2	82	5	6	1											71	713	10.0	113	44	923	21.0	43
1996	HAM	14	5		0	40			2	0	7	6	1											35	346	9.9	72	28	547	19.5	50
1997	HAM	5	0	0	1	6			1	0	0													21	117	5.6	25	5	100	20.0	26
3	Years	35	10	0	4	77			5	82	12	12	2											127	1176	9.3	113	77	1570	20.4	50
BOBBY ROLAND Robert CB 5'11 185 Northeast Oklahoma A&M JC; Arizona B: 12/5/1969 Ponca City, OK																															
1995	BIR	10				36	2.0	10.0	0	0	2																				
MORLEY ROLHISER Morley F. G 6'3 226 Yakima JC; Washington B: 5/11/1942 ON																															
1965	EDM	6																													
1965	WPG	5	0		1																										
1965	Year	11	0		1																										
1966	WPG	16																													
1967	WPG	16	0		4																										
3	Years	38	0		5																										
TED ROMAN Ted OT 6'1 232 Western Ontario B: 1933 Draft: 2-11 1956 CAL																															
1959	BC	14																													
1960	BC	5	0		1																										
2	Years	19	0		1																										
ALEX ROMANIUK Alexander G-T Alberta																															
1949	EDM	5																													
AL ROMANO Albert (Butch) DT 6'3 225 Pittsburgh B: 4/4/1954 Schnectady, NY Draft: 11-289 1977 HOU																															
1977	HAM	8	0		1																										
1978	HAM	3																													
1978	TOR	6							1	3																					
1978	Year	9							1	3																					
2	Years	11	0		1				1	3																					
ROCCO ROMANO Rocco OG-OT 6'4 265 Concordia B: 1/23/1963 Hamilton, ON Draft: 1-5 1987 CAL																															
1987	CAL	15				0																									
1988	TOR	5				0																									
1989	OTT	17				0																									
1990	BC	18	0		1	0																									
1991	BC	17				2																									
1992	CAL*	18	0		1	2																									
1993	CAL+	18				2																									
1994	CAL*	18				0																									
1995	CAL*	18				0																									
1996	CAL*	18				1																									
1997	CAL*	18				1																									
1998	CAL	18	0	0	1	1																									
1999	CAL*	18				1																									
2000	CAL	16				1																									
14	Years	232	0	0	3	11																									
JERMAINE ROMANS Jermaine S 5'10 183 Acadia B: 12/7/1975 Jamaica Draft: 5B-39 2001 TOR																															
2002	HAM	2				0																									
TAG ROME Anthony Nicholas WR 5'9 175 Louisiana-Monroe B: 8/13/1961 Donalsonville, LA Pro: N																															
1984	EDM	2																	8	113	14.1	30	0								
1985	CAL	11																	25	410	16.4	43	0	30	214	7.1	40	5	102	20.4	26
1986	CAL	6																	15	253	16.9	43	0	16	103	6.4	15				
3	Years	19																	48	776	16.2	43	0	46	317	6.9	40	5	102	20.4	26
JEAN-FRANCOIS ROMEO Jean-Francois WR 6'0 196 Laval B: 8/21/1981 Montreal, QC																															
2006	EDM	8				0																									
2007	EDM	17				1													3	31	10.3	17	0								
2	Years	25				1													3	31	10.3	17	0								
DARIO ROMERO Dario A. DT 6'3 305 Eastern Washington B: 4/13/1978 Spokane, WA Pro: N																															
2001	EDM	12	0	2	0	20	3.0	26.0																							
2006	MTL	15				19					1																				
2007	MTL	16	0	0	1	28	4.0	18.0	1	0	2																				
2008	EDM+	16	0	1	1	30	6.0	42.0																							
2009	EDM+	12				25	6.0	42.0			2																				
2010	EDM	15	0	0	1	24	1.0	1.0																							
2011	SAS	18	0	0	2	34	2.0	15.0																							
7	Years	104	0	3	5	180	22.0	144.0	1	0	5																				
AL ROMINE Alton Rollon HB 6'2 191 North Alabama B: 3/10/1932 Florence, AL Pro: N																															
1956	TOR	7										30	5						29	538	18.6	72	5								
1959	OTT	10							4	71									2	26	13.0	16	0	1	4	4.0	4				
2	Years	17							4	71		30	5						31	564	18.2	72	5	1	4	4.0	4				
CLARE ROONEY Clare HB Calgary West End Tornadoes Jrs.																															
1947	CAL	7																													
JIM ROOT James Frederic QB 6'1 185 Miami (Ohio) B: 8/17/1931 Toledo, OH D: 5/26/2003 Orange Park, FL Draft: 23-269 1953 CHIC Pro: N																															
1954	OTT	8										5	1	21	79	3.8	15	1													
GERALD ROPER Gerald OG 6'4 255 Vancouver Meralomas Jrs.; Arizona B: 11/7/1959 Vancouver, BC Draft: TE 1982 BC																															
1982	BC	12	0		1																										
1983	BC	13	0		1														0	2		2	0								
1984	BC	16																													
1985	BC	16	0		1									0	13		13	0													
1986	BC	18																													
1987	BC+	14	0		1	0																									
1988	BC*	18				0																									
1989	BC	12				0																									
1989	OTT	6				0																									
1989	Year	18				0																									
1990	OTT+	18				2																									
1991	OTT+	18	0		1	1																									
1992	BC	3																													
11	Years	158	0		5	3								0	13		13	0	0	2		2	0								
JUAN ROQUE Juan Armando DL 6'8 332 Arizona State B: 2/6/1974 San Diego, CA Draft: 2A-35 1997 DET Pro: N																															
2001	TOR	18				1																									
2002	TOR	3				0																									

Year	Team	GP	FM	FF	FR	TK	SK	YDS	IR	YDS	PD	PTS	TD	RA	YDS	AVG	LG	TD	REC	YDS	AVG	LG	TD	PR	YDS	AVG	LG	KOR	YDS	AVG	LG
2	Years	21				1																									
CHAD RORABAUGH Chad A. DL 6'2 242 Western Washington B: 3/7/1975 Fontana, CA																															
1998	EDM	3				5	1.0	10.0																							
BARRY ROSE Barry Allan WR 6'0 185 Wisconsin-Stevens Point B: 7/28/1968 Hudson, WI Draft: 10-279 1992 BUF Pro: N																															
1995	HAM	9	1		0	3						6	1						33	365	11.1	42	1								
DONOVAN ROSE Donovan James CB 6'1 190 Hampton B: 3/9/1957 Norfolk, VA Pro: N																															
1981	TOR	8	0		2																			2	33	16.5	18	6	122	20.3	26
1982	TOR	9							1	34																					
1983	TOR	5	0		1				2	63		12	2																		
1983	WPG	3							2	35																					
1983	Year	8							4	98		12	2																		
1984	WPG	16	0		1				8	39																					
1985	HAM	13	0		1				6	151																					
5	Years	51	0		5				19	322		12	2											2	33	16.5	18	6	122	20.3	26
KEN ROSE Kenneth Frank LB 6'1 211 Nevada-Las Vegas B: 6/9/1962 Sacramento, CA Pro: N																															
1984	SAS	2					0.5																								
ROB ROSE Robert, Jr. DT 6'5 285 Ohio State B: 12/24/1987																															
2011	HAM	3				8	1.0	5.0			1																				
STAN ROSE Stan QB-HB Montreal Ints. B: 1924																															
1947	SAS	7										5	1																		
JIM ROSEBORO James Alexander HB 5'9 180 Ohio State B: 1/10/1935 OH D: 12/13/1997 Moreno Valley, CA Draft: 11-124 1957 GB																															
1957	OTT	1																													
BARRY ROSEBOROUGH Barry Wayne QB 6'0 205 North Dakota B: 1932																															
1956	WPG	12										2	0															1	7	7.0	7
1957	WPG	13												5	-19	-3.8	1	0													
1958	WPG	11	1											4	-7	-1.8	4	0													
3	Years	36	1		0							2	0	9	-26	-2.9	4	0										1	7	7.0	7
MARTY ROSEN Marty OHB 6'0 205 South Carolina B: 7/14/1943																															
1966	WPG	10	4		0				1					20	62	3.1	20	0	17	230	13.5	32	0	20	118	5.9	17	4	125	31.3	45
1967	WPG	9	1		1									17	63	3.7	12	0	8	62	7.8	14	0	6	21	3.5	10				
2	Years	19	5		1				1	0				37	125	3.4	20	0	25	292	11.7	32	0	26	139	5.3	17	4	125	31.3	45
TIMM ROSENBACH Timm Lane QB 6'1 210 Washington State B: 10/27/1966 Everett, WA Pro: N																															
1994	HAM	11	3		0	1						18	3	28	160	5.7	21	3													
TED ROSNAGLE Theodore J. CB 6'3 202 Fullerton JC; Portland State B: 9/29/1961 Pasadena, CA Draft: 7B-148 1984 MEM-USFL Pro: N																															
1984	TOR	1																													
GARY ROSOLOWICH Gary DB 5'10 185 Boise State B: 9/10/1955 Draft: TE 1977 WPG																															
1977	WPG	15	6		2																			60	590	9.8	46	13	286	22.0	29
1978	WPG	16	0		1				5	74														22	140	6.4	32				
1979	WPG	16	0		1				2	25				1	0	0.0	0	0						19	52	2.7	11				
1980	WPG	16	0		1				4	23																					
1981	WPG	16							1	20														8	37	4.6	12				
5	Years	79	6		5				12	142				1	0	0.0	0	0						109	819	7.5	46	13	286	22.0	29
DON ROSS Don E 6'3 190 British Columbia; Vancouver Cubs Jrs. B: 1933 Pontiac, MI D: 10/11/2007 Surrey, BC																															
1955	BC	8																	6	75	12.5	17	0								
1956	BC	1																													
1957	BC	6																													
3	Years	15																	6	75	12.5	17	0								
DON ROSS Don WR 6'5 200 Acadia B: 10/7/1956 Draft: TE 1980 HAM																															
1980	HAM	10																	1	18	18.0	18	0								
1981	TOR	2																	1	14	14.0	14	0								
2	Years	12																	2	32	16.0	18	0								
GORDIE ROSS Gordon C-G 6'3 215 Sherbrooke Ints. B: 9/13/1923 Sherbrooke, QC																															
1950	MTL	12																													
1951	MTL	12																													
1952	MTL	10																													
3	Years	34																													
RAE ROSS Rae OE-S-DE 6'1 185 Vancouver Blue Bombes Jrs.; British Columbia B: 1931 Winnipeg, MB D: 1993																															
1955	BC	15	1		2				1	30		5	1											17	111	6.5	25	2	17	8.5	12
1956	BC	14	0		4				6	165		12	2											12	48	4.0	15				
1957	BC	15																						21	127	6.0	24				
1958	CAL	16	0		2				9	127									1	7	7.0	7	0	2	6	3.0	4				
1959	WPG	15							7	64														3	17	5.7	8				
1960	WPG	16	0		1				3	19		6	1						1	58	58.0	58	1	1	5	5.0	5				
1961	BC	16							4	8																					
7	Years	107	1		9				30	413		23	4						2	65	32.5	58	1	56	314	5.6	25	2	17	8.5	12
WILLIE ROSS William James FB 5'10 200 Nebraska B: 6/6/1941 Helena, AR Draft: 12A-90 1964 BUF; 9-121 1964 STL Pro: N																															
1966	CAL	6	0		1									57	179	3.1	12	0	6	26	4.3	14	0					7	181	25.9	31
TOBIN ROTE Tobin Cornelius QB 6'3 211 Rice B: 1/18/1928 San Antonio, TX D: 6/27/2000 Saginaw, MI Draft: 2-17 1950 GB Pro: N																															
1960	TOR	14										6	1	23	42	1.8	12	1	1	-12	-12.0	-12	0								
1961	TOR	14										30	5	31	95	3.1	12	4													
1962	TOR	13												25	101	4.0	18	0													
3	Years	41										36	6	79	238	3.0	18	5	1	-12	-12.0	-12	0								
JAMIE ROTELLA Jamie LB 6'2 225 Tennessee B: 6/23/1951 Raleigh, NC Draft: 3B-62 1973 BAL																															
1973	HAM	7	0		1				1	14																					
1974	HAM	16	0		2				2	26																					
2	Years	23	0		3				3	40																					
TIM ROTH Timothy Roland DT-DE-OT 6'2 250 South Dakota State B: 8/14/1948 Madison, MN Draft: 16-414 1970 OAK																															
1971	SAS	16	0		1				1	23																					
1972	SAS	16	0		1																										
1973	SAS	16																													
1974	SAS	16	1		1							6	1																		
1975	SAS+	16	1		3																							1	10	10.0	10
1976	SAS+	16			2																										
1977	SAS	16	0		1																										
7	Years	112	2		9				1	23		6	1															1	10	10.0	10
HARRY ROTHWELL Harry HB 6'1 190 Calgary Bronks Jrs.																															
1954	CAL	13	1		1									9	80	8.9	25	0						3	9	3.0	4	6	117	19.5	26
1955	CAL	12																						6	47	7.8	21	2	27	13.5	22
2	Years	25	1		1									9	80	8.9	25	0						9	56	6.2	21	8	144	18.0	26
SIMEON ROTTIER Simeon OT-OG 6'6 295 Edmonton Huskies Jrs.; Alberta B: 1/21/1984 Westlock, AB Draft: 1A-1 2009 HAM																															
2009	HAM	18				1																									
2010	HAM	18	0	0	0	1																									
2011	HAM	18				1																									
3	Years	54	0	0	0	3																									
ALPHONSO ROUNDTREE Alphonso, Jr. DH-CB 6'0 190 Tulane B: 7/7/1977 Bradenton, FL Pro: E																															
2000	MTL	18				39			2	0	7																	1	13	13.0	13
2001	MTL	14	1	1	3	29			0	76	4	6	1											2	49	24.5	49				
2002	TOR	1	0	0	0	2																									
2002	OTT	12	2	1	0	25			4	63	9													7	64	9.1	18	3	40	13.3	20
2002	Year	13	2	1	2	27			4	63	9													7	64	9.1	18	3	40	13.3	20
2005	HAM	9	1	0	1	13			2	19	1																	1	7	7.0	7
4	Years	42	4	2	4	108			8	158	21	6	1											9	113	12.6	49	5	60	12.0	20

Year	Team	GP	FM	FF	FR	TK	SK	YDS	IR	YDS	PD	PTS	TD	RA	YDS	AVG	LG	TD	REC	YDS	AVG	LG	TD	PR	YDS	AVG	LG	KOR	YDS	AVG	LG
ANDRE ROUNDTREE Andre Church LB 6'3 225 Santa Ana JC; Iowa State B: 7/1/1953 Los Angeles, CA Draft: 12-300 1975 DET																															
1976	CAL	1																													
1977	HAM	1																													
2	Years	2																													
RALEIGH ROUNDTREE Raleigh Cito OG 6'4 295 South Carolina State B: 8/31/1975 Augusta, GA Draft: 4-109 1997 SD Pro: N																															
2006	EDM	9	0	0	1	0																									
2007	EDM	16				4																									
2	Years	25	0	0	1	4																									
JIM ROUNTREE James W. CB-S-OHB 5'10 193 Florida B: 4/21/1936 Miami, FL Draft: 25-298 1958 BAL																															
1958	TOR	7							3	50				25	200	8.0	25	0	8	87	10.9	21	0	1	4	4.0	4	6	159	26.5	46
1959	TOR+	13							4	8				4	17	4.3	11	0	1	7	7.0	7	0	13	159	12.2	26	16	433	27.1	40
1960	TOR+	14							10	80									1	8	8.0	8	0	24	104	4.3	16	11	253	23.0	33
1961	TOR+	14							5	0		12	2	3	15	5.0	7	0	26	427	16.4	108	2	2	3	1.5	3				
1962	TOR*	14							5	59									1	13	13.0	13	0								
1963	TOR+	14							3	33									1	2	2.0	2	0	1	2	2.0	2	10	174	17.4	48
1964	TOR+	14	1		2				3	31														4	11	2.8	10	7	106	15.1	24
1965	TOR	14	1		0				2	14		6	1						3	64	21.3	31	0	1	63	63.0	63	11	313	28.5	40
1966	TOR	13	0		1				4	127		6	1											1	6	6.0	6	7	177	25.3	32
1967	TOR+	14	0		1				2	62		6	1											2	8	4.0	6	1	7	7.0	7
10	Years	131	2		4				41	464		30	5	32	232	7.3	25	0	41	608	14.8	108	2	49	360	7.3	63	69	1622	23.5	48
KENNY ROWE Kenneth Lealand DE 6'2 244 Oregon B: 4/22/1989 Los Angeles, CA																															
2011	SAS	5				10	1.0	1.0			1																				
KENT ROWE Kent DE 6'7 245 Bishop's B: 7/16/1967 Draft: 6-41 1993 SAS																															
1994	TOR	2				2	1.0																								
1994	OTT	5				2	1.0																								
1994	Year	7				4																									
1995	OTT	1				2																									
2	Years	3				6	2.0																								
PAUL ROWE Paul Trimble FB-HB 6'0 202 Oregon B: 1/23/1917 Seattle, WA D: 8/27/1990 Calgary, AB																															
1946	CAL+	8										10	2					1													
1947	CAL+	7										5	1																		
1948	CAL+	12										35	7					7													
1949	CAL	14										30	6					6													
1950	CAL	10												33	152	4.6	18	0													
5	Years	51										80	16	33	152	4.6	18	13													
BILL ROWEKAMP William Henry E-HB-FW 6'1 200 Army; Missouri B: 1/1930 Marietta, OH Draft: 3-30 1953 CHIB																															
1953	EDM	1																										1	42	42.0	42
1956	EDM	16	1		3				4	29		12	2	8	15	1.9	4	0	15	262	17.5	44	2	2	8	4.0	4	2	39	19.5	24
2	Years	17	1		3				4	29		12	2	8	15	1.9	4	0	15	262	17.5	44	2	2	8	4.0	4	3	81	27.0	42
LEMARCUS ROWELL Lemarcus LB 6'2 218 Auburn; Jacksonville State B: 12/10/1982 Opelika, AL																															
2008	CAL	4				9			1	37	0																				
ED ROWLAND Edgar C. T 6'2 230 Oklahoma B: 2/25/1930 Ochelata, OK D: 6/1/2010 Lufkin, TX Draft: 16B-192 1952 CLE																															
1953	OTT	9																													
GORDIE ROWLAND Gordon LB-OHB-S-FW 5'9 172 Montreal Orfuns Ints. B: 9/1/1930 Montreal, QC																															
1954	WPG	16	2		3				2	72		5	1						3	38	12.7	17	0	51	435	8.5	25	13	257	19.8	30
1955	WPG	16	1		2				6	34														49	428	8.7	29	5	109	21.8	31
1956	WPG	16	1		2				5	54														44	265	6.0	25	5	125	25.0	32
1957	WPG+	16							3	15		6	1	1	3	3.0	3	0	1	15	15.0	15	1	54	428	7.9	52				
1958	WPG+	16	2						6	122		12	2	13	90	6.9	12	0	6	113	18.8	30	1	56	478	8.5	26	6	141	23.5	39
1959	WPG	13							3	42		6	1	1	9	9.0	9	0						2	8	4.0	7				
1960	WPG+	16	1		1				3	14		2	0						1	52	52.0	52	0	19	103	5.4	17	1	50	50.0	50
1961	WPG+	16			0							6	1											11	70	6.4	17				
1962	WPG*	14	0		2				3	42		6	1											1	2	2.0	2				
1963	WPG	16	0		1							4	0											37	178	4.8	20				
1964	WPG	8	0		1																										
11	Years	163	7		12				31	395		47	7	15	102	6.8	12	0	11	218	19.8	52	2	324	2395	7.4	52	30	682	22.7	50
RONNIE ROWLAND Ronnie Lewis RB 6'1 205 San Jose CC; Washington B: 1/30/1955 Muskegon, MI																															
1978	CAL	1												6	28	4.7	14	0	3	16	5.3	6	0								
1979	HAM	13	5		2							12	2	179	814	4.5	45	2	35	420	12.0	56	0					9	188	20.9	35
1980	HAM	6	1		1							24	4	50	175	3.5	15	4	7	57	8.1	18	0					2	72	36.0	58
3	Years	20	6		3							36	6	235	1017	4.3	45	6	45	493	11.0	56	0					11	260	23.6	58
BILLY ROY Billy OT-OG 6'0 240 Citrus JC B: 10/17/1942 Toronto, ON																															
1962	MTL	13																													
1963	MTL	14																										1	0	0.0	0
1964	MTL	14																													
1965	MTL	14																													
1966	EDM	16	0		2																										
1967	EDM	16																													
1968	CAL	16	0		1																										
1969	CAL	16																													
1970	CAL	16																										1	2	2.0	2
9	Years	135	0		3																							2	2	1.0	2
FRANK ROY Frank Edward DG 6'2 240 Long Beach JC; Utah B: 6/19/1942 Montgomery, WV Draft: 7-96 1965 STL Pro: N																															
1967	BC	5																													
JEAN-DANIEL ROY Jean-Daniel NT 6'3 255 Ottawa B: 3/12/1972 Gaspe, QC Draft: 4B-23 1998 WPG																															
1998	WPG	9	0	1	0	5	1.0	5.0																							
JEAN-FRANCOIS ROY Jean-Francois C 6'3 300 Bishop's B: 12/6/1977 Quebec City, QC																															
2005	OTT	6				0																									
NORB ROY Norbert Wayne G 6'0 220 Notre Dame B: 1940																															
1962	OTT	12							1	7																					
SEBASTIEN ROY Sebastien LB 6'0 223 Mount Allison B: 1/21/1978 Montreal, QC Draft: 4-32 2003 WPG																															
2003	WPG	17				6																									
2004	MTL	1				0																									
2005	CAL	1				0																									
3	Years	19				6																									
RICKEY ROYAL Ricky Bernard CB 5'9 187 Sam Houston State B: 7/26/1966 Gainesville, TX Draft: 7-177 1989 PHX Pro: EN																															
1991	HAM	8				19	1.0		2	0																					
1992	HAM	18				39																									
1993	HAM	18	0		1	48																									
1994	HAM	4				4																									
4	Years	48	0		1	110	1.0		2	0																					
TOM ROZANTZ Thomas Edward QB 6'1 194 William & Mary B: 4/17/1957 Greensburg, PA Pro: U																															
1980	SAS	5												2	-3	-1.5		0													
1980	HAM	7												3	14	4.7	11	0													
1980	Year	12												5	11	2.2	11	0													
1981	TOR	8	0		1							6	1	8	58	7.3	18	1													
2	Years	13	0		1							6	1	13	69	5.3	18	1													
BOB ROZIER Robert Earnest DE 6'3 240 Aberdeen JC; California B: 7/28/1955 Anchorage, AK Draft: 9-228 1979 STL Pro: N																															
1980	HAM	10	0		1				1	10																					
1980	SAS	2																													
1980	Year	12	0		1				1	10																					
AUBREY ROZZELL Aubrey Dale LB-C 6'2 215 Delta State B: 11/2/1932 Rome, MS Pro: N																															

Year	Team	GP	FM	FF	FR	TK	SK	YDS	IR	YDS	PD	PTS	TD	RA	YDS	AVG	LG	TD	REC	YDS	AVG	LG	TD	PR	YDS	AVG	LG	KOR	YDS	AVG	LG
1958	MTL	2																													
CLIFTON RUBIN Clifton DL 6'0 236 Baylor B: 2/5/1975 New Orleans, LA																															
2000	BC	1				1																									
T.J. RUBLEY Theron Joseph QB 6'3 205 Tulsa B: 11/29/1968 Davenport, IA Draft: 9-228 1992 LARM Pro: EN																															
1998	WPG	14	3	0	0	1								26	76	2.9	13	0													
1998	HAM	2				0								2	12	6.0	8	0													
1998	Year	16	3	0	0	1								28	88	3.1	13	0													
MARTIN RUBY Martin Owen OT-DT 6'3 249 Texas A&M B: 6/9/1920 D: 1/3/2002 Salmon Arm, BC Draft: 5-40 1942 CHIB Pro: AN																															
1951	SAS+	13																													
1952	SAS	15			1																										
1953	SAS+	13							1	1																					
1954	SAS+	15			2																			1	3	3.0	3				
1955	SAS	16																													
1956	SAS+	14	0		2																										
1957	SAS	2																													
7	Years	88	0		5				1	1														1	3	3.0	3				
MARCUS RUCKER Marcus Bernard LB 6'0 200 Rice B: 4/20/1985 El Dorado, AR																															
2007	SAS	1				0																									
JEREMI RUDOLPH Jeremi RB 5'8 169 Nevada-Las Vegas B: 1/27/1976 Orlando, FL																															
2001	MTL	1	2	0	0	0								5	24	4.8	17	0						2	14	7.0	8	7	161	23.0	51
AARON RUFFIN Aaron CB 5'10 175 Nicholls State B: 5/17/1969 Hammond, LA Pro: E																															
1992	CAL	2	0		1	7																									
1994	SAS	17	0		1	64			4	119	5	6	1											11	70	6.4	11	4	63	15.8	18
1995	SAS	18	2		1	43	2.0	15.0	2	85	7	6	1											57	553	9.7	55	48	989	20.6	66
1996	SAS	15	4		3	52			2	21	11	12	2											43	474	11.0	99	31	572	18.5	36
1997	HAM	9	1	0	1	21			1	43	1													13	57	4.4	11	31	664	21.4	38
5	Years	61	7	0	7	187	2.0	15.0	9	268	24	24	4											124	1154	9.3	99	114	2288	20.1	66
J.R. RUFFIN J.R. DH-CB 6'0 182 Citrus JC; Idaho B: 7/28/1982 Detroit, MI																															
2006	CAL	18	0	1	2	47			1	38	4	6	1											5	-3	-0.6	7	63	1461	23.2	90
2007	CAL	5				19					1																	10	211	21.1	32
2011	BC	4				6																									
3	Years	27	0	1	2	72			1	38	5	6	1											5	-3	-0.6	7	73	1672	22.9	90
FRED RUISH Fred HB 6'2 205 none B: 1934																															
1954	HAM	2																													
DONALD RUIZ Donald S 6'0 195 Bemidji State; Wilfrid Laurier B: 7/5/1976 Montreal, QC																															
2001	WPG	16	1	0	1	18			1	5	0																				
2002	OTT	17	0	0	1	31			1	0	0	6	1															3	51	17.0	23
2003	OTT	12				19			1	9	0																	1	0	0.0	0
2004	OTT	3				4					1																				
2005	OTT	13				13					2																	1	3	3.0	3
2006	SAS	14				13			1	38	0																				
6	Years	75	1	0	2	98			4	52	3	6	1															5	54	10.8	23
BOB RUMBALL Robert L. HB-FW 5'11 187 Toronto B: 1929 Draft: 5- 1952 OTT																															
1952	OTT	9										5	1										1								
1953	OTT	11																													
1954	OTT	12							1	0														44	263	6.0	18	8	198	24.8	58
1955	TOR	6																						5	22	4.4	9				
1956	OTT	3																													
5	Years	41							1	0		5	1										1	49	285	5.8	18	8	198	24.8	58
JOE RUMOLO Joe DT 6'4 219 Akron B: 6/23/1971 Scarborough, ON Draft: 2-12 1997 HAM																															
1997	HAM	18	0	2	1	12	1.0	4.0																							
1998	HAM	2				1																									
2000	TOR	1				0																									
2003	HAM	18	0	0	1	13	2.0																								
4	Years	39	0	2	2	26	3.0	4.0																							
DAN RUNGE Daniel SB-TE 6'9 250 Guelph B: 1/23/1961 Toronto, ON Draft: 4-33 1984 EDM																															
1984	EDM	16																	5	82	16.4	21	0					1	0	0.0	0
1985	EDM	7																	8	87	10.9	21	0								
1985	CAL	9	0		1														19	224	11.8	37	0								
1985	Year	16	0		1														24	306	12.8	37	0								
2	Years	23	0		1														32	393	12.3	37	0					1	0	0.0	0
MITCH RUNNING Mitchell Wayne SB 5'11 185 Kansas State B: 9/7/1972 Decorah, IA																															
1998	WPG	9	1	0	1	4						14	2	2	10	5.0	6	0	39	729	18.7	36	2								
1999	TOR	2				0													2	20	10.0	12	0								
2	Years	11	1	0	1	4						14	2	2	10	5.0	6	0	41	749	18.3	36	2								
BERNIE RUOFF Bernd A. P-K 6'0 185 Syracuse B: 10/12/1951 West Germany Draft: 1C-8 1975 WPG																															
1975	WPG	13	4		0							97	0	2	40	20.0	22	0													
1976	WPG	16	1		1							142	0											1	4	4.0	4				
1977	WPG	16	4		0							134	0																		
1978	WPG	16	1		0							149	0																		
1979	WPG	16	1		0							151	0																		
1980	HAM*	16	1		0							136	0	2	37	18.5	19	0													
1981	HAM+	16	1		0							152	0	2	20	10.0	10	0													
1982	HAM+	16	3		1							142	0																		
1983	HAM+	16	2		1							149	0	1	5	5.0	5	0													
1984	HAM*	16	1		0							145	0																		
1985	HAM+	14	1		1							154	0	2	-13	-6.5	6	0													
1986	HAM	9	1		1							76	0	1	5	5.0	5	0													
1987	HAM	11	1		0	0						115	0	1	9	9.0	9	0													
1988	BC	5	1		0							30	0																		
14	Years	196	23		5	0						1772	0	11	103	9.4	22	0						1	4	4.0	4				
KEILLY RUSH Keilly DE 6'7 255 Garden City JC; Tallahassee JC*; Florida State B: 6/18/1970 McKeesport, PA																															
1993	WPG	8	0		2	16	3.0	24.0																							
1994	WPG	11	0		8	21	6.0	36.0			2	6	1																		
1995	WPG	5	0		3	29	5.0	37.0			1																				
3	Years	24	0		13	66	14.0	97.0			3	6	1																		
TYRONE RUSH Tyrone Antonio RB 5'11 196 North Alabama B: 2/5/1971 Meridian, MS Pro: N																															
1996	HAM	3	4		0	0								31	104	3.4	16	0	11	89	8.1	30	0	2	5	2.5	4				
1996	MTL	4				0						12	2	35	210	6.0	36	1	5	55	11.0	24	1	9	41	4.6	18	11	257	23.4	42
1996	Year	7	4		0	0						12	2	66	314	4.8	36	1	16	144	9.0	30	1	11	46	4.2	18	11	257	23.4	42
MIKE RUSINEK John Michael DL 6'3 250 Scottsdale JC; California B: 5/1/1963 Scottsdale, AZ Pro: N																															
1988	EDM	1																													
TOM RUSK Thomas G. LB 6'2 230 Iowa B: 7/14/1957 Viroqua, WI Draft: 9-227 1979 NYG																															
1980	TOR	1																													
1981	TOR	7					1.0		4	79																					
2	Years	8					1.0		4	79																					
BERNARD RUSS Bernard Dion LB 6'1 238 Arizona Western JC; West Virginia B: 11/4/1973 Utica, NY Pro: ENX																															
2002	SAS	1	0	1	0	1																									
EDDIE RUSS Eddie, Jr, CB-DH 6'0 185 Antelope Valley JC; Harding B: 3/20/1987 Marianna, FL																															
2011	SAS	4				7																									
LEO RUSSAVAGE Leo T 6'4 249 North Carolina B: 2/20/1937 Duryea, PA Draft: 10-120 1958 CLE																															
1958	OTT	1																													

Year	Team	GP	FM	FF	FR	TK	SK	YDS	IR	YDS	PD	PTS	TD	RA	YDS	AVG	LG	TD	REC	YDS	AVG	LG	TD	PR	YDS	AVG	LG	KOR	YDS	AVG	LG
FRANK RUSSELL Frank WR 6'0 180 Maryland B: 9/3/1953 Wantagh, NY Draft: 17C-440 1975 BAL Pro: W																															
1978	SAS	10	0		2							14	2						22	379	17.2	46	2								
FRANK RUSSELL Frank A. DB 5'8 190 Southeast Missouri B: 6/22/1974 Compton, CA																															
1996	CAL	3				4																									
FRED RUSSELL Fred Robert RB 5'7 191 Iowa B: 9/14/1980 Wayne, MI Pro: E																															
2007	SAS	1				0																						1	10	10.0	10
JACK RUSSELL James Monroe E 6'1 215 Baylor B: 8/29/1919 Nemo, TX D: 1/16/2006 Cleburne, TX Draft: 3-22 1943 PIT Pro: AN																															
1951	SAS+	14										45	9						47	818	17.4		9								
ED RUTKOWSKI Edward John Anthony HB 6'1 204 Notre Dame B: 3/21/1941 Kingston, PA Pro: N																															
1969	MTL	7										6	1	2	10	5.0	7	1													
CHRIS RWABUKAMBA Chris CB 5'10 180 Duke B: 1/5/1987 Rwanda Draft: 4-27 2010 HAM																															
2011	HAM	6				1																									
JON RYAN Jonathan Robert P 6'0 213 Regina B: 11/26/1981 Regina, SK Draft: 3-24 2004 WPG Pro: N																															
2004	WPG	18	2	0	1	0						6	0	4	52	13.0	30	0													
2005	WPG*	17	5	0	1	4						12	0																		
2	Years	35	7	0	2	4						18	0	4	52	13.0	30	0													
RICK RYAN Rick S 5'10 195 Weber State B: 6/21/1962 Fort Erie, ON Draft: 1B-7 1985 BC																															
1985	MTL	5																													
1986	MTL+	18							8	92		8	0											4	3	0.8	6				
1987	TOR	16	0		2	20			2	19														1	3	3.0	3				
1988	BC	18	1		3	33			2	28																					
1989	BC	14				25			3	34																					
1990	BC	17	0		2	36			3	22		5	0						1	25	25.0	25	0								
6	Years	88	1		7	114			18	195		13	0						1	25	25.0	25	0	5	6	1.2	6				
TITUS RYAN Titus WR 6'0 193 East Central CC; Concordia (Alabama) B: 5/19/1984 Tuscaloosa, AL																															
2009	CAL	10	6	0	0	1						12	2						7	111	15.9	36	1	42	315	7.5	31	42	984	23.4	104
2009	WPG	4				0						18	3						8	285	35.6	65	3					10	214	21.4	37
2009	Year	14	6	0	0	1						30	5						15	396	26.4	65	4	42	315	7.5	31	52	1198	23.0	104
RANDY RYBANSKY Ryan FB 6'1 220 Wilfrid Laurier B: 9/2/1961 Chatham, ON																															
1985	TOR	5																													
HEATH RYLANCE Heath QB 6'1 205 Augustana (South Dakota) B: 6/21/1972 Mitchell, SD																															
1995	SAS	4				0																									
1996	SAS	9	2		0	0						6	1	15	96	6.4	16	1													
1998	SAS	18				0								5	20	4.0	7	0													
1999	CAL	2				0																									
4	Years	33	2		0	0						6	1	20	116	5.8	16	1													
DALLAS RYSAVY Dallas J. S 5'10 182 North Dakota B: 6/30/1971 Moose Jaw, SK																															
1994	SAS	17				17																									
1995	SAS	1				1																									
1995	OTT	5				4			1	17	0																				
1995	Year	6				5			1	17	0																				
1996	HAM	3				0																									
1996	OTT	4	1		0	1																									
1996	SAS	4				9																									
1996	Year	11	1		0	10																									
3	Years	21	1		0	32			1	17	0																				
BILL SABO Bill G Regina Dales Jrs.																															
1947	SAS	4																													
FRANK SACILOTTO Frank WR 5'9 175 Renfrew Trojans Jrs.; Simon Fraser B: 7/27/1954																															
1979	BC	1																													
ANDRE SADEGHIAN Andre FB 6'0 220 British Columbia; McMaster B: 10/25/1984 Beamsville, ON Draft: 3B-24 2007 BC																															
2007	BC	18				4								3	14	4.7	8	0													
2008	HAM	1				0																									
2009	HAM	15				7													1	12	12.0	12	0								
2010	WPG	18				1								1	0	0.0	0	0	2	12	6.0	9	0					2	36	18.0	19
4	Years	52				12								4	14	3.5	8	0	3	24	8.0	12	0					2	36	18.0	19
JASON SADLER Jason OT 6'5 296 Desert JC; Nevada-Reno B: 7/1/1975 Pro: X																															
1999	TOR	1				0																									
RICHARD SAENZ Richard Refugio OL 6'4 284 Vanderbilt B: 5/5/1973 Houston, TX Pro: E																															
1996	OTT	4	1		0	3																									
VAL ST. GERMAIN Val OG-OT 6'3 302 McGill B: 10/8/1971 Ottawa, ON Draft: Bonus-1 1994 HAM																															
1994	HAM	18				0																									
1995	HAM	18				1																									
1996	HAM	5				0																									
1997	HAM	18	0	0	1	3																									
1998	HAM+	17	0	0	1	2																									
1999	EDM+	15				0																									
2000	EDM	12	0	0	1	1													1	-5	-5.0	-5	0								
2001	EDM	18	0	0	1	0																									
2002	OTT	15				0																									
2003	OTT*	14	0	0	1	0																									
2004	OTT	16	0	0	2	2																									
2005	OTT	18				1																									
2006	WPG	16				0																									
2007	SAS	4				0																									
14	Years	204	0	0	7	10													1	-5	-5.0	-5	0								
TYSON ST. JAMES Tyson LB 6'0 240 British Columbia B: 6/5/1975 Nanaimo, BC Draft: 1-1 2000 SAS																															
2000	SAS	18	0	0	1	19																									
2001	SAS	18				22	2.0	15.0																							
2002	SAS	18				16																									
2003	WPG	15				15	1.0																					1	3	3.0	3
2004	WPG	18				17	1.0																								
5	Years	87	0	0	1	89	4.0	15.0																				1	3	3.0	3
DON ST. JOHN Don FB 5'11 205 Xavier (Ohio) B: 1935 Draft: 23-275 1956 WAS																															
1956	OTT	14							1	5		54	8	95	377	4.0	24	8	27	397	14.7	46	0								
1957	OTT	14												61	233	3.8	12	0	7	67	9.6	24	0								
2	Years	28							1	5		54	8	156	610	3.9	24	8	34	464	13.6	46	0								
JUDE ST. JOHN Jude OG 6'4 296 Western Ontario B: 12/4/1972 London, ON Draft: 2B-20 1995 HAM																															
1995	HAM	18				1																									
1996	HAM	18				1																									
1997	HAM	8				1																									
1998	TOR	18				1																									
1999	TOR	7				0																									
2000	TOR	18	0	0	1	0																									
2001	TOR+	18				2																									
2002	TOR	18	0	0	1	0																									
2003	TOR	18				1																									
2004	TOR	18	0	0	1	1																									
2005	TOR+	17				0																									
2006	TOR+	17				0																									
2007	TOR	18				0																									
2008	TOR	16				0																									

Year	Team	GP	FM	FF	FR	TK	SK	YDS	IR	YDS	PD	PTS	TD	RA	YDS	AVG	LG	TD	REC	YDS	AVG	LG	TD	PR	YDS	AVG	LG	KOR	YDS	AVG	LG
14	Years	227	0	0	3	8																									
MIKE ST. LOUIS Donald Michael OT 6'4 260 Northern Arizona; Central Missouri B: 7/31/1943 Kansas City, MO Draft: 13-338 1968 WAS																															
1968	BC	2																													
1969	BC	8																													
2	Years	10																													
JONATHAN ST. PIERRE Jonathan C-OT-TE 6'3 310 Miami (Florida); Illinois State B: 9/15/1983 Greenfield Park, QC Draft: 2-10 2008 SAS																															
2010	TOR	17				0																									
2011	TOR	7				0																									
2	Years	24				0																									
TIM ST. PIERRE Tim LB-FB 6'0 235 St. Mary's (Nova Scotia) B: 4/28/1986 Hamilton, ON Draft: 3A-19 2008 EDM																															
2008	EDM	18				3																									
2009	EDM	18	0	0	1	28																									
2010	EDM	17	1	0	0	14																									
2011	CAL	14				5													1	14	14.0	14	0					1	3	3.0	3
4	Years	67	1	0	1	50													1	14	14.0	14	0					1	3	3.0	3
JIMMY SAKEEL Jim HB-E 180 none B: 1928																															
1946	SAS	8																													
1947	TOR	3																													
2	Years	11																													
LOUIE SAKODA Louis Oliver P-K 5'9 177 Utah B: 10/28/1986 San Jose, CA																															
2009	SAS	3				0						2	0																		
2010	SAS	3				1						1	0																		
2010	WPG	1				0																									
2010	Year	4				1						1	0																		
2	Years	6				1						3	0																		
PAUL SALATA Paul Thomas (Slats) E 6'2 191 Southern California B: 10/17/1926 PA Draft: 10-118 1951 PIT Pro: AN																															
1951	CAL	6										15	3						29	441	15.2	48	3								
1952	CAL	15							1	0		55	11	4	32	8.0	16	0	65	1088	16.7	67	11								
1953	OTT	4										5	1										1								
3	Years	25							1	0		75	15	4	32	8.0	16	0	94	1529	16.3	67	15								
FLOYD SALAZAR Floyd DB 5'10 175 McGill B: 2/2/1965 Toronto, ON Draft: 4-31 1988 TOR																															
1988	TOR	1				0																									
1989	TOR	17	0		1	23			1	1																					
1990	TOR	1				0																									
1990	HAM	15				9																									
1990	Year	16				9																									
1991	TOR	3				4																									
4	Years	22	0		1	36			1	1																					
EDDIE SALEM Edward Joseph HB 5'11 190 Alabama B: 8/28/1928 Tucson, AZ D: 12/20/2001 Birmingham, AL Draft: 2A-15 1951 WAS Pro: N																															
1952	MTL	12										52	5					3					1								
ROLAND SALES Roland RB 6'1 203 Arkansas B: 12/5/1955 Draft: 11-294 1980 CLE																															
1980	MTL	3												14	54	3.9	6	0													
SEAN SALISBURY Richard Sean QB 6'5 217 Southern California B: 3/9/1963 Long Beach, CA Pro: N																															
1988	WPG	7	1		1	0								3	9	3.0	7	0													
1989	WPG	17	9		3	1								24	54	2.3	15	0	1	13	13.0	13	0								
2	Years	24	10		4	1								27	63	2.3	15	0	1	13	13.0	13	0								
STEVE SALTER Steven OG 6'4 300 Ottawa B: 6/9/1972 Sherbrooke, QC Draft: 2-17 1997 TOR																															
1997	TOR	1				0																									
1998	TOR	10				0																									
1999	TOR	17				1																									
2000	TOR	2				0																									
2001	HAM	3				0																									
5	Years	33				1																									
LEE SALTZ Lee QB 6'1 195 Temple B: 9/25/1963 Dover, NJ Pro: E																															
1988	WPG	3				0						6	1	4	46	11.5	27	1													
1989	WPG	14	1		0	0								17	45	2.6	11	0													
1993	HAM	1				0								2	6	3.0	5	0													
3	Years	18	1		0	0						6	1	23	97	4.2	27	1													
P.K. SAM Philip Kenwood, II WR-SB 6'3 210 Florida State B: 12/26/1983 Denver, CO Draft: 5-164 2004 NE Pro: EN																															
2008	TOR	6				0						18	3						36	499	13.9	59	3								
2009	TOR	9				1						12	2						27	385	14.3	39	2								
2010	CAL	3				1						6	1						13	129	9.9	16	1								
3	Years	18				2						36	6						76	1013	13.3	59	6								
MIKE SAMPLES Michael James DT-DE-NG 6'2 238 Missouri Southern State; Drake B: 6/27/1950 Bonne Terre, MO Draft: 12-298 1973 ATL																															
1973	BC	1																													
1974	HAM	14	0		1																										
1975	HAM	16	0		1																							1	18	18.0	18
1976	HAM+	16			2				1	4																					
1977	HAM	9																													
1978	HAM	6																													
1978	SAS	9																													
1978	Year	15																													
1979	SAS	16																													
1980	SAS	16	0		1																										
1981	SAS+	14	0		1		8.5																								
1982	SAS*	15					4.0																								
1983	SAS	3					1.0																								
11	Years	126	0		6		13.5		1	4																		1	18	18.0	18
DARRYL SAMPSON Darryl DB 6'2 175 York B: 9/21/1963 Scarborough, ON Draft: 2-16 1986 WPG																															
1986	WPG	18	1		2									1	21	21.0	21	0						40	428	10.7	28	16	348	21.8	35
1987	WPG	10	2		1	19			1	53		6	1											29	246	8.5	39	3	45	15.0	25
1988	WPG	17	0		3	58			1	21		6	1											1	0	0.0	0				
1989	WPG	17	0		2	48	2.0		1	8																					
1990	WPG	18	0		3	76			3	57																					
1991	WPG	15	0		2	57	2.0		1	38		6	1																		
1992	WPG	17				45	1.0		5	51																					
1993	WPG*	18				67			6	56																					
1994	WPG	16	0		1	47			2	14	4																				
1995	WPG	15				43			1	3	1																				
1996	HAM	9				31																									
11	Years	170	3		14	491	5.0		21	301	5	18	3	1	21	21.0	21	0						70	674	9.6	39	19	393	20.7	35
LEE SAMPSON Lee O. OE 6'3 225 New Mexico State B: 2/16/1939																															
1964	TOR	14	0		1							30	5						32	405	12.7	33	4					1	4	4.0	4
1965	HAM	1																													
2	Years	15	0		1							30	5						32	405	12.7	33	4					1	4	4.0	4
OTEMAN SAMPSON Oteman QB 6'0 195 Florida A&M B: 4/25/1975 Miami, FL Pro: X																															
1999	CAL	18				0								1	1	1.0	1	0													
2000	CAL	1				0																									
2000	TOR	8	1	0	1	0								7	43	6.1	24	0													
2000	Year	9	1	0	1	0								7	43	6.1	24	0													
2002	OTT	18	1	0	0	0								4	23	5.8	11	0													
3	Years	37	2	0	1	0								12	67	5.6	24	0													

Year	Team	GP	FM	FF	FR	TK	SK	YDS	IR	YDS	PD	PTS	TD	RA	YDS	AVG	LG	TD	REC	YDS	AVG	LG	TD	PR	YDS	AVG	LG	KOR	YDS	AVG	LG
TIERRE SAMS Tierre DB 5'9 169 Fresno State B: 9/30/1977 Fresno, CA Pro: E																															
2003	OTT	4				8			1	19	1																				
GERRY SAMUEL Gerry MG 6'4 245 Lakeshore Alouettes Jrs. B: 1936																															
1960	MTL	14																													
KHARI SAMUEL Khari Iman Mitchell LB 6'3 241 Massachusetts B: 10/14/1976 New York, NY Draft: 5B-144 1999 CHIB Pro: N																															
2004	MTL	11	0	1	1	20			0	0	2																				
BOBBY SAMUELS Robert DB 6'1 190 Penn State B: 1/3/1970																															
1992	SAS	2				4																									
STANFORD SAMUELS Stanford, Jr. CB-DH-LB 5'10 190 Florida State B: 7/27/1980 Miami, FL																															
2005	WPG	17	0	1	2	63	1.0	1.0	2	28	5	6	1																		
2006	WPG	12				28			3	33	5																				
2007	EDM	14				51			1	34	4																				
2008	WPG	11	0	3	2	32			2	16	4																				
2009	MTL	2				5					1																				
2010	MTL	1				3																				1	6	6.0	6				
6	Years	57	0	4	4	182	1.0	1.0	8	111	19	6	1													1	6	6.0	6				
DAVIS SANCHEZ Davis CB-S 5'10 190 Surrey Rams Jrs.; Capilano JC*; Butte JC; Oregon B: 8/7/1974 Vancouver, BC Draft: 1-6 1999 MTL Pro: N																															
1999	MTL	17				25			3	42	2																				
2000	MTL*	18	0	1	0	48			9	163	9	12	2													1	0	0.0	0				
2003	CAL	16				37			1	86	11	6	1																				
2004	MTL+	16				41			3	34	6															1	0	0.0	0				
2005	EDM	12				28	2.0	13.0	1	0	4																						
2006	MTL	13	0	1	1	35			3	52	6	6	1																				
2007	MTL	9	0	1	0	16			1	-1	8																				
2008	MTL+	18	0	0	2	35			3	53	6															1	9	9.0	9				
2009	MTL	16	0	0	1	24			2	24	4																				
2010	BC	15				37			2	66	6	6	1																				
2011	BC	5				7																									
11	Years	155	0	3	4	333	2.0	13.0	28	519	62	30	5													3	9	3.0	9				
EROS SANCHEZ Eros QB 6'0 201 Wayne State (Michigan); Santa Monica CC; New York U.; Virginia Tech B: 8/11/1967 New York, NY																															
1993	HAM	14				2								14	63	4.5	20	0													
1994	SHR	7	1		0									1	18	18.0	18	0													
2	Years	21	1		0	2								15	81	5.4	20	0													
JEFF SANCHEZ Jeffrey, Jr. CB 5'10 175 Tulane B: 1/21/1981 New Orleans, LA Pro: EN																															
2006	TOR	5				6																									
BOB SANDBERG Robert HB-FB-QB 6'1 209 Minnesota B: 1922 Draft: 6-44 1947 CHI-AAFC																															
1947	WPG+	8										35	5					4													
1948	WPG	12										25	4					4													
1949	WPG	11										20	3					1													
1951	SAS	11										6	1	42	136	3.2		0	4	76	19.0		1					6	98	16.3	
4	Years	42										86	13	42	136	3.2	0	9	4	76	19.0		1					6	98	16.3	
AL SANDERS Albert Taylor, Jr. C 6'5 230 Louisiana State; Southern Mississippi B: 11/10/1926 Fernwood, MS D: 6/17/1989 Baton Rouge, LA Draft: 18-135 1949 BAL-AAFC; 11-105 1949 PIT																															
1951	MTL	1																													
ANTWOINE SANDERS Antwoine DB 6'2 202 Arizona Western JC; Utah B: 9/22/1977 Fayetteville, NC Draft: 7C-258 2003 BAL																															
2005	HAM	7				14			1	0	1																				
DANNY SANDERS Danny Kay QB 6'4 203 Carson-Newman B: 5/14/1955 Oak Ridge, TN Draft: 11-288 1979 NYJ																															
1979	HAM	1																													
1979	SAS	5	1		1									5	6	1.2	5	0													
1979	Year	6	1		1									5	6	1.2	5	0													
1980	SAS	3																													
2	Years	4	1		1									5	6	1.2	5	0													
TYRONE SANDERS Yolande Tyrone, II DB 5'10 173 Texas Christian B: 2/22/1981 Dallas, TX																															
2005	BC	5				0			1	0	0																				
DALE SANDERSON Dale C-OT 6'3 260 Hamilton Hurricanes Jrs.; Tennessee B: 12/12/1961 Hamilton, ON Draft: 4-36 1985 HAM																															
1985	HAM	2																													
1986	HAM	18																													
1987	HAM	18				0																									
1988	HAM	18				4																									
1989	HAM+	18				3																									
1990	HAM	16	1		0	2																									
1991	HAM	18				1																									
1992	HAM	18	1		2	2																									
1993	HAM	7	1		0	0																									
1994	HAM	11				0																									
1995	HAM	17				1																									
1996	HAM	12	2		0	0													1	0	0.0	0	0								
1997	HAM	1				0																									
13	Years	174	5		2	13													1	0	0.0	0	0								
NORM SANDERSON Norm C 165 North Hill Jrs. B: 1925																															
1946	CAL	7																													
PAUL SANDOR Paul NT Toledo																															
1988	TOR	1																													
JON SANDSTROM Jon, Jr. LB 6'2 235 Oregon State B: 1947 Draft: 3B-67 1969 ATL																															
1970	WPG	2																													
JIM SANDUSKY Jim WR 5'9 180 Walla Walla CC; Nevada-Las Vegas; San Diego State B: 9/9/1961 Othello, WA Draft: 4-75 1984 PHI-USFL																															
1984	BC	9	1		0							12	2						27	406	15.0	62	2	13	137	10.5	42				
1985	BC	16	4		1							42	7	1	12	12.0	12	0	58	1073	18.5	68	7	21	210	10.0	33	2	41	20.5	25
1986	BC	15	0		1							6	1	1	1	1.0	1	0	60	858	14.3	50	1	42	459	10.9	62	1	23	23.0	23
1987	BC*	18	1		0	2						78	13						80	1437	18.0	75	12	58	492	8.5	55	9	125	13.9	29
1988	EDM	17	1		2	2						48	8						55	1089	19.8	59	8	9	82	9.1	38				
1991	EDM+	18	1		0	4						60	10						63	1063	16.9	65	10	3	19	6.3	16				
1992	EDM*	18	1		0	3						92	15						78	1243	15.9	68	15	1	0	0.0	0				
1993	EDM	8	1		0	1						18	3						24	482	20.1	64	3					1	20	20.0	20
1994	EDM	11				1						24	4						34	514	15.1	40	4								
1995	EDM	18	2		0	0						24	4	2	-3	-1.5	-1	0	58	888	15.3	78	4								
1996	EDM	6				2						6	1						14	216	15.4	37	1								
1998	BC	11	1	0	1	2						13	2						35	468	13.4	30	2	3	9	3.0	5				
12	Years	165	13	0	5	17						423	70	4	10	2.5	12	0	586	9737	16.6	78	69	150	1408	9.4	62	13	209	16.1	29
ROBERT SANFORD Robert RB 5'10 225 Western Michigan B: 4/17/1979 Miami, FL																															
2003	SAS	1				0								7	19	2.7	7	0	1	12	12.0	12	0								
SULECIO SANFORD Sulecio WR 5'10 190 Georgia Military JC; Middle Tennessee State B: 3/23/1976 Milledgeville, GA Draft: 7A-221 1999 CHIB Pro: E																															
2004	CAL	18	1	0	0	3						18	3						45	577	12.8	49	3					31	631	20.4	36
AMAR SANGHERA Amarpreet OL 6'5 315 British Columbia B: 7/19/1979 Draft: 1-9 2004 EDM																															
2004	EDM	1				0																									
DON SANGSTER Don HB 5'11 176 Parkdale Lions B: 1937																															
1955	TOR	2																													
BEN SANKEY Ben QB 6'2 220 Wake Forest B: 12/5/1976 Chicago, IL																															
2000	CAL	16	1	0	0	0								2	-2	-1.0	2	0													
2001	CAL	18	7	0	2	0						12	2	34	267	7.9	34	2													
2002	CAL	7	2	0	2	0								8	61	7.6	14	0													
2004	HAM	18	1	0	0	0																									

Year	Team	GP	FM	FF	FR	TK	SK	YDS	IR	YDS	PD	PTS	TD	RA	YDS	AVG	LG	TD	REC	YDS	AVG	LG	TD	PR	YDS	AVG	LG	KOR	YDS	AVG	LG
2007	BC	2				0																								
2007	CAL	6	3	0	0	0								6	34	5.7	21	0													
2007	Year	8	3	0	0	0								6	34	5.7	21	0													
2008	CAL	8				0						6	1	1	1	1.0	1	1													
6	Years	69	14	0	4	0						18	3	51	361	7.1	34	3													
ALEXIS SANSCHAGRIN Alex DB 6'2 203 Western Ontario B: 12/17/1976 Montreal, QC Draft: 4B-30 2002 TOR																															
2002	TOR	7				0																								
O.J. SANTIAGO Otis Jason SB 6'7 265 Kent State B: 3/4/1974 Whitby, ON Draft: 5-40 1997 EDM; 3-70 1997 ATL Pro: N																															
2010	MTL	4				2																								
RICKY SANTOS Ricky QB 6'1 210 New Hampshire B: 4/26/1984 Norwood, MA																															
2009	WPG	7				0						6	1	7	24	3.4	10	1													
2010	MTL	11	1	0	0	0						6	1	14	51	3.6	29	1													
2011	MTL	18				1								1	7	7.0	7	0													
3	Years	36	1	0	0	1						12	2	22	82	3.7	29	2													
AL SANTUCCI Al G Hamilton Jrs.																															
1947	HAM	2																												
ANGELO SANTUCCI Angelo HB-FB 5'11 190 St. Mary's (Nova Scotia) B: 2/2/1952 Draft: TE 1975 HAM																															
1975	HAM	16	3		1							6	1	101	452	4.5	24	1	22	87	4.0	16	0	23	254	11.0	31	11	251	22.8	41
1976	HAM	16	4		0							12	2	89	441	5.0	30	1	34	224	6.6	16	1								
1977	EDM	13	0		5							6	1	17	65	3.8	16	0	6	47	7.8	16	0	2	28	14.0	17	3	42	14.0	22
1978	EDM	16	1		2									36	117	3.3	9	0	8	52	6.5	16	0					5	68	13.6	16
1979	EDM	16	2		2							12	2	64	254	4.0	22	1	14	168	12.0	48	1								
1980	EDM	16	1		1									35	150	4.3	15	0	6	47	7.8	18	0					2	42	21.0	21
1981	EDM	14	1		0							6	1	29	127	4.4	23	1	6	56	9.3	13	0								
1982	EDM	11										6	1	25	79	3.2	0	1	4	33	8.3	16	0								
1983	EDM	8	1		1							6	1	18	98	5.4	20	1	11	72	6.5	14	0								
1984	OTT	1																												
10	Years	127	13		12							54	9	414	1783	4.3	30	6	111	786	7.1	48	2	25	282	11.3	31	21	403	19.2	41
PAT SANTUCCI Pat T-G 5'11 220 B: 1924 D: 10//1992 Burlington, ON																															
1946	TOR	11																												
1947	HAM	12										27	1																		
1949	SAS	12										28	0																		
1950	HAM	6										1	0																		
4	Years	41										56	1																		
SEKOU SANYIKA Sekou LB 6'3 243 California B: 3/17/1978 New Orleans, LA Draft: 7-215 2000 ARI Pro: N																															
2004	SAS	10				23	2.0																								
DAVE SAPUNJIS David SB 6'1 185 Western Ontario B: 9/7/1967 Toronto, ON Draft: 1-5 1990 CAL																															
1990	CAL	18	0		1	1						6	1						21	262	12.5	24	1								
1991	CAL	18				34						6	1	2	7	3.5	6	0	9	107	11.9	20	0	10	124	12.4	68				
1992	CAL	18				15						24	4	1	-7	-7.0	-7	0	77	1317	17.1	59	4					1	0	0.0	0
1993	CAL*	18	1		1	7						90	15	0	24		24	0	103	1484	14.4	75	15								
1994	CAL	12				4						36	6						57	686	12.0	28	6					1	0	0.0	0
1995	CAL*	18	1		0	3						72	12						111	1655	14.9	48	12								
1996	CAL	18				2						52	8						82	1075	13.1	61	8								
7	Years	120	2		2	66						286	47	3	24	8.0	24	0	460	6586	14.3	75	46	10	124	12.4	68	2	0	0.0	0
JOE SARDO Joe OE-DE 6'0 200 Brantford Tiger-Cats Ints. B: 1939																															
1958	HAM	13																												
1959	HAM	3																												
1960	TOR	1																	1	-8	-8.0	-8	0								
3	Years	17																	1	-8	-8.0	-8	0								
JOE SARDO Joe DB-LB 6'1 210 Hawaii B: 11/7/1969 Hamilton, ON Draft: 2B-16 1992 OTT																															
1992	OTT	18	0		1	19						6	1																		
1993	OTT	18	0		2	24																								
1994	OTT	3				3																								
1994	TOR	14	0		2	23	1.0	7.0	1	0	2																				
1994	Year	17	0		2	26	1.0	7.0	1	0	2																				
1995	TOR	18				60	3.0	21.0			3																				
4	Years	57	0		5	129	4.0	28.0	1	0	5	6	1																		
DAVE SARETTE David QB 6'0 193 Syracuse B: 1940																															
1962	SAS	13	1											9	62	6.9	23	0													
STEVE SARKISIAN Stephen A. QB 6'1 206 Brigham Young B: 3/8/1974 Torrance, CA																															
1997	SAS	3				0																								
1998	SAS	18	2	0	0	0								6	32	5.3	11	0													
1999	SAS	18	5	0	0	3						6	1	39	169	4.3	19	1													
3	Years	39	7	0	0	3						6	1	45	201	4.5	19	1													
MARTIN SARTIN Martin RB 5'10 202 Sequoias JC; Long Beach State B: 3/9/1963 Philadelphia, PA Pro: N																															
1988	HAM	9				4						48	8	123	460	3.7	18	5	35	248	7.1	32	3								
ALVIS SATELE Alvis LB 6'1 230 Hawaii B: 4/30/1963 Honolulu, HI																															
1986	CAL	6	0		2		7.0																								
1987	BC	9	0		1	17	2.0																					2	8	4.0	8
2	Years	15	0		3	17	9.0																					2	8	4.0	8
MAC SAULS Kirby McGee HB 6'0 185 Texas State B: 8/15/1945 Long Beach, CA Draft: 13-339 1968 STL Pro: N																															
1970	HAM	5	2		0				4	29																2	15	7.5	9				
ALEX SAUNDERS Alexander (Red) G 5'11 177 none B: 1929																															
1949	OTT	6																												
JOHN SAUNDERS John Wesley, III DB 6'3 198 Toledo B: 4/29/1950 Toledo, OH D: 2/11/2001 Draft: 4A-87 1972 LARM Pro: N																															
1973	EDM	2																										2	14	7.0	12
MIKE SAUNDERS Mike RB 5'11 205 Iowa B: 10/3/1969 Milton, WI Draft: 10-262 1992 PIT																															
1992	SAS	4	3		0	2						14	2	21	54	2.6	17	0	20	314	15.7	91	2	11	104	9.5	40	13	267	20.5	34
1993	SAS	13	10		1	3						30	5	135	683	5.1	52	4	58	612	10.6	43	1	24	194	8.1	35	17	341	20.1	58
1994	SAS+	17	8		0	4						90	15	234	1205	5.1	49	8	55	613	11.1	32	7	15	112	7.5	34	1	29	29.0	29
1995	SA*	18	5		4	0						96	16	206	1030	5.0	45	8	47	708	15.1	60	8					1	18	18.0	18
1996	MTL	4				0						6	1	33	154	4.7	15	1	8	75	9.4	16	0	4	12	3.0	4				
1996	HAM	6	3		0	3						24	4	48	198	4.1	20	2	24	274	11.4	50	2								
1996	Year	10	3		0	3						30	5	81	352	4.3	20	3	32	349	10.9	50	2	4	12	3.0	4				
1997	TOR	7				1						18	3	1	2	2.0	0	0	14	173	12.4	27	3	1	5	5.0	5	1	26	26.0	26
1997	SAS	8				4						30	5	131	586	4.5	36	5	11	121	11.0	24	0								
1997	Year	15				5						48	8	132	588	4.5	36	5	25	294	11.8	27	3					1	26	26.0	26
1998	SAS	17	2	0	2	3						66	11	160	897	5.6	46	5	59	670	11.4	57	6					3	53	17.7	26
1999	SAS	14	4	0	1	1						64	10	191	971	5.1	34	6	36	348	9.7	35	4	2	15	7.5	8	10	183	18.3	23
8	Years	94	35	0	8	21						438	72	1160	5780	5.0	52	39	332	3908	11.8	91	33	57	442	7.8	40	46	917	19.9	58
TROY SAUNDERS Troy CB 5'10 185 Florida State B: 4/25/1976 Bluefield, WV Pro: EX																															
2001	HAM	5				15			1	27	2																				
2002	HAM	16	0	0	1	52	1.0		1	2	1																				
2003	HAM	15	0	1	1	30			1	0	3																				
2004	HAM	16	0	1	0	32					1																				
4	Years	52	0	2	2	129	1.0		3	29	7																				
WALLY SAUNDERS Wally DB 6'3 200 Simon Fraser B: 9/8/1951																															
1975	BC	13																						4	8	2.0	6	1	0	0.0	0
DAVE SAUVE David DE-DT 6'4 260 Harvard B: 6/10/1959 Sudbury, ON Draft: 4-36 1982 EDM																															
1982	HAM	16																												
1983	HAM	16	0		1		3.5																								

Year	Team	GP	FM	FF	FR	TK	SK	YDS	IR	YDS	PD	PTS	TD	RA	YDS	AVG	LG	TD	REC	YDS	AVG	LG	TD	PR	YDS	AVG	LG	KOR	YDS	AVG	LG
1984	HAM	16					2.0																								
1985	HAM	15					2.0																								
1987	HAM	17				5																									
1988	HAM	12	0		1		3.0																								
6	Years	92	0		2	5	10.5																								
LARRY SAVAGE Lawrence Edward LB 6'2 225 Michigan State B: 6/18/1957 Connellsville, PA Draft: 8-216 1980 DAL																															
1981	TOR	1																													
RAY SAVAGE Raymond Lee, Jr. DE-LB 6'1 245 Virginia B: 3/1/1968 Hampton, VA Draft: 8A-198 1990 LARM Pro: E																															
1991	CAL	1				2																									
1994	SHR	14	0		1	27	7.0	46.0			1																				
1995	SHR	16	0		1	22	9.0	51.0			4																				
3	Years	31	0		2	51	16.0	97.0			5																				
ROGER SAVOIE Roger OT-DT-DE 6'0 240 Winnipeg Rods Jrs.; St. Boniface Ints. B: 7/29/1931 St. Boniface, MB D: 8/17/2009																															
1951	WPG	1																													
1952	WPG	13																													
1953	WPG	4																													
1954	WPG	13	0		2																										
1955	WPG	16																													
1956	WPG	16																													
1957	WPG	13																													
1958	WPG	14																													
1959	WPG	16																					1	0	0.0	0				
1960	WPG	16	0		3																										
1961	WPG	16			2																										
1962	WPG+	16																													
1963	WPG	16																													
1964	WPG	16	0		1																										
1965	WPG	5																													
15	Years	191	0		8																			1	0	0.0	0				
STEVE SAVOY Steven Sterling WR 5'11 191 Utah B: 2/27/1982 Washington, DC																															
2005	HAM	1				0																									
GARRY SAWATZKY Garry OG-OT 6'3 295 none B: 2/26/1962 Winnipeg, MB																															
1995	BC	11				0																									
1996	BC	16				0																									
1999	WPG	16				1																									
2000	WPG	18				2																									
2002	TOR	15	0	0	1	0																									
5	Years	76	0	0	1	3																									
BOB SAWYER Bob HB 6'1 208 Wake Forest; Wyoming B: 3/8/1937 Draft: 11-131 1959 NYG																															
1959	CAL	7												3	8	2.7	6	0	1	6	6.0	6	0								
1961	CAL	3																													
1961	MTL	1																													
1961	Year	4																													
2	Years	10												3	8	2.7	6	0	1	6	6.0	6	0								
JEFF SAWYER Jeff DE-LB-DT 6'3 235 Memphis B: 4/13/1970 Worcester, MA																															
1994	LV	16	0		1	19	7.0	43.0	1	6	7	6	1																		
1995	SA	6				8					3																				
1995	MEM	1				4																									
1995	Year	7				12					3																				
1996	BC	2				4					1																				
3	Years	24	0		1	35	7.0	43.0	1	6	11	6	1																		
JERRY SAZIO Jerry LB-T 5'10 226 William & Mary B: 1932 Draft: 19-218 1954 CHIC																															
1955	HAM	11							5	6		5	1																		
RALPH SAZIO Ralph Joseph T 6'1 220 William & Mary B: 7/22/1922 Avellino, Italy D: 9/26/2008 Burlington, ON Draft: 28-258 1947 PIT; 22-151 1948 BUF-AAFC Pro: A																															
1950	HAM+	12																													
1951	HAM	12																													
1953	HAM	1																													
3	Years	25																													
CHARLEY SCALES Charles Anderson HB 5'11 214 Indiana B: 1/11/1938 Pittsburgh, PA Pro: N																															
1967	MTL	13	6		0							12	2	101	370	3.7	25	2	13	109	8.4	23	0					24	541	22.5	51
ROGER SCALES Roger OG-C 6'0 235 Brigham Young B: 11/25/1944 Vernon, BC																															
1969	TOR	14																													
1970	TOR	14	0		1																										
1971	TOR	14																													
1972	TOR	4																													
1972	EDM	11																													
1972	Year	15																													
1973	EDM	16																													
1974	EDM	16																													
1975	EDM	16	0		1																										
1976	EDM	16																										2	12	6.0	7
1977	EDM	16	0		1																										
9	Years	126	0		3																							2	12	6.0	7
JACK SCARBATH John Carl QB 6'2 204 Maryland B: 8/12/1930 Baltimore, MD Draft: 1-3 1953 WAS Pro: N																															
1955	OTT	7										10	2	26	103	4.0	22	2													
SAM SCARBER Sam Willis FB 6'2 232 Northeastern JC; New Mexico B: 6/24/1949 St. Louis, MO Draft: 3A-69 1971 DAL Pro: NW																															
1971	EDM	5	1		1									75	301	4.0	19	0	4	9	2.3	9	0								
1972	EDM	9	2		2							18	3	65	339	5.2	18	3	8	39	4.9	8	0					15	373	24.9	40
1973	EDM	1												3	12	4.0	6	0	4	28	7.0	17	0								
3	Years	15	3		3							18	3	143	652	4.6	19	3	16	76	4.8	17	0					15	373	24.9	40
MIKE SCHAD Michael OG 6'5 290 Queen's B: 10/2/1963 Trenton, ON Draft: 1-4 1986 OTT; 1-23 1986 LARM Pro: N																															
1995	OTT	7				2																									
DON SCHAEFER Donald Thomas FB 5'11 195 Notre Dame B: 2/13/1934 Pittsburgh, PA Draft: 3-28 1956 PHI Pro: N																															
1959	HAM	1												7	12	1.7	5	0	1	10	10.0	10	0								
GREG SCHAEFER Greg OL 6'6 295 British Columbia B: 1/11/1978 Draft: 6-46 2003 CAL																															
2004	CAL	18				0																									
GLEN SCHAPANSKY Glen DT-DE 6'3 248 Weston Wildcats Jrs. B: 5/29/1946																															
1967	WPG	16																													
1968	WPG	16																													
1969	WPG	16			1																										
1970	WPG	16																													
1971	HAM	4																													
5	Years	68	0		1																										
GEORGE SCHECTERLY George OT 6'3 255 Penn State; South Carolina B: 7/11/1958																															
1981	TOR	15	0		1																										
CALVIN SCHEXNAYDER Calvin Paul WR 6'0 195 Fresno CC; Washington State B: 11/19/1969 Fresno, CA Pro: X																															
1993	SAC	2				0																									
DEREK SCHIAVONE Derek K-P 6'0 190 Western Ontario B: 5/9/1985 Fort Erie, ON																															
2008	EDM	1				0						13	0																		
2009	EDM	1				1						18	0																		
2010	EDM	5				1						58	0																		
2011	EDM	5				0						61	0																		

Year	Team	GP	FM	FF	FR	TK	SK	YDS	IR	YDS	PD	PTS	TD	RA	YDS	AVG	LG	TD	REC	YDS	AVG	LG	TD	PR	YDS	AVG	LG	KOR	YDS	AVG	LG
4	Years	12				2						150	0																		
HANK SCHICHTLE Henry Ernest QB 6'2 190 Wichita State B: 10/13/1941 Tulsa, OK Draft: 6-81 1964 NYG Pro: N																															
1967	BC	7												5	6	1.2	5	0													
TOM SCHIMMER Tom K 6'1 210 Boise State B: 11/27/1967 Vancouver, BC Draft: 4-25 1989 OTT																															
1989	OTT	18	5		0	1						6	0																		
MAURY SCHLEICHER Maurice Gene E-LB 6'3 238 Penn State B: 7/17/1937 Walnutport, PA D: 4/15/2004 Modesto, CA Draft: 5A-50 1959 CHIC Pro: N																															
1963	TOR	3																													
ART SCHLICHTER Arthur Ernest QB 6'2 210 Ohio State B: 4/25/1960 Washington Court House,OH Draft: 1B-4 1982 BAL Pro: N																															
1988	OTT	8	3		0									19	172	9.1	24	0													
BOB SCHLOREDT Bob QB-DB 6'0 195 Washington B: 10/2/1939 Deadwood, SD Draft: 27- 1961 DAL																															
1961	BC	11	3						3	42		1	0	26	48	1.8	42	0													
1962	BC	14							1			5	0											1	10	10.0	10				
2	Years	25	3		0				4	42		6	0	26	48	1.8	42	0						1	10	10.0	10				
ART SCHLOSSER Art E-HB 6'3 215 Hamilton Wildcats Jrs; East York Ints. B: 1938																															
1959	TOR	5										6	1						5	94	18.8	40	1								
1960	CAL	11																													
1961	CAL	16																	4	41	10.3	14	0					2	13	6.5	13
3	Years	32										6	1						9	135	15.0	40	1					2	13	6.5	13
PAUL SCHMIDLIN Paul R. DE 6'1 230 Ohio State B: 1949																															
1970	HAM	11	0		4							6	1																		
BLAINE SCHMIDT Blaine DE-C-OG 6'4 260 Guelph B: 8/23/1963 Sudbury, ON Draft: 2B-17 1986 EDM																															
1987	TOR	10				4																									
1988	TOR	18				2																									
1989	TOR	18	0		1	0																									
1990	TOR	18				4																									
1991	TOR	18	1		1	15								1	-1	-1.0	-1	0													
1992	TOR	18				22																									
1993	TOR	18	0		1	12																									
1994	TOR	18	1		0	9																									
1995	HAM	18	1		0	12																									
1996	HAM+	18				8																									
1997	HAM	18	0	0	1	7																									
11	Years	190	3	0	4	95								1	-1	-1.0	-1	0													
DAN SCHMIDT Dan OL Kansas B: 8/18/1970 Pro: E																															
1995	MEM	1				1																									
JIM SCHMIDT Jim LB 6'2 205 San Francisco State B: 1946 Draft: 17-437 1968 ATL																															
1969	BC	1																													
NEIL SCHMIDT Cornelius HB 6'0 168 Purdue B: 7/3/1927 Reinfeld, USSR D: 12/29/2005 Lake City, FL Draft: 9-102 1951 CHIC																															
1952	TOR	2																													
STEVE SCHMIDT Steve TE-FB 6'5 250 Butte JC; San Diego State B: 7/17/1984 Winnipeg, MB Draft: 4B-30 2007 TOR																															
2008	TOR	16	0	0	1	6													2	33	16.5	26	0					1	0	0.0	0
2009	TOR	15	2	0	0	5													4	25	6.3	11	0								
2010	HAM	9				1													1	1	1.0	1	0					1	1	1.0	1
3	Years	40	2	0	1	12													7	59	8.4	26	0					2	1	0.5	1
DICK SCHNAIBLE Richard George (Curly) QB-HB 6'1 187 Purdue B: 2/9/1929 Lafayette, IN																															
1954	OTT	9							3	76				22	104	4.7	16	0	12	106	8.8	24	0	7	35	5.0	13	6	121	20.2	31
JOHN SCHNEIDER John QB 6'1 185 Toledo B: 2/1/1945 Draft: 7-170 1968 BOS																															
1968	WPG	16	2		1							30	5	56	230	4.1	16	5													
1969	WPG	1																													
2	Years	17	2		1							30	5	56	230	4.1	16	5													
DICK SCHNELL Richard DT-DE-LB-C 6'3 225 Wyoming B: 1939 Draft: 19-260 1961 STL																															
1961	MTL	11																													
1962	MTL	11							1	29																					
1963	SAS	11	0		1				3	18																					
1964	SAS	11							1																						
1965	SAS	15	0		2																										
1966	SAS	3																													
6	Years	62	0		3				5	47																					
HOWARD SCHNELLENBERGER Howard Leslie E 6'1 222 Kentucky B: 3/16/1934 Louisville, KY Draft: 21-251 1956 WAS																															
1956	HAM	7										18	3						14	184	13.1	30	2								
1958	BC	3	1									6	1						10	172	17.2	41	1					1	0	0.0	0
2	Years	10	1		0							24	4						24	356	14.8	41	3					1	0	0.0	0
JIM SCHNIETZ James Michael OG-OT 6'3 253 Missouri B: 4/27/1951 St. Louis, MO Draft: 8-191 1974 SF																															
1975	BC	14	0		1																										
1976	BC	15	0		1																										
1977	BC	13	0		1																										
3	Years	42	0		3																										
RALPH SCHOENFELD Ralph QB 6'2 198 Saskatoon Hilltops Jrs. B: 5/10/1940																															
1967	WPG	12	1		0							1	0																		
RALPH SCHOLZ Ralph OG-DT-OT 6'5 270 Cornell B: 7/17/1961 Brantford, ON Draft: TE 1984 HAM																															
1984	HAM	9																													
1985	HAM	16	0		1																										
1986	HAM	10																													
1987	HAM	18				3																									
1988	HAM	18				2																									
1989	HAM	2				0																									
1990	HAM	9				0																									
7	Years	82	0		1	5																									
ERNIE SCHRAMAYR Ernie FB 5'10 215 Purdue B: 7/7/1966 Montreal, QC Draft: 2B-12 1989 HAM																															
1989	HAM	3	1		0	0													1	36	36.0	36	0					1	7	7.0	7
1990	HAM	18	2		0	4								26	143	5.5	43	0	7	76	10.9	30	0					5	52	10.4	16
1991	HAM	13				15						6	1	25	92	3.7	12	1	4	31	7.8	11	0								
1992	HAM	13	0		1	13								3	7	2.3	3	0													
1993	OTT	11				6													2	23	11.5	14	0								
5	Years	58	3		1	38						6	1	54	242	4.5	43	1	14	166	11.9	36	0					6	59	9.8	16
GARY SCHREIDER Gary E. K-OHB-LB-DB-FB-P 5'11 187 Queen's B: 1934 D: 1/22/2011 Ottawa, ON																															
1956	OTT	13							2	22		6	1	6	20	3.3	10	1	5	91	18.2	39	0	16	178	11.1	60	10	282	28.2	49
1957	OTT	14							3	16		68	2	50	197	3.9	11	2	2	25	12.5	19	0	44	325	7.4	18				
1958	OTT	14							1	41		15	1	33	156	4.7	15	0	2	24	12.0	17	0	36	240	6.7	16				
1959	OTT	14							1	18		43	2	1	1	1.0	1	1	3	20	6.7	11	1	5	24	4.8	19	1	20	20.0	20
1960	OTT+	14							5	62		71	2	3	18	6.0	9	0						3	7	2.3	5	2	26	13.0	16
1961	OTT	14							1	11		57	0	1	9	9.0	9	0	1	5	5.0	5	0								
1962	BC	7										12	1											3	23	7.7	16				
1962	HAM	5							1	32																		2	34	17.0	19
1962	Year	12							1	32		12	1											3	23	7.7	16	2	34	17.0	19
1963	OTT	3																						9	54	6.0	13				
1964	OTT	4																													
9	Years	97							14	202		272	9	94	401	4.3	15	4	13	165	12.7	39	1	116	851	7.3	60	15	362	24.1	49
TEX SCHRIEWER Menan Clyde OE-DE 6'4 220 Texas B: 9/20/1934 New Braunfels, TX Draft: 1-10 1956 CHIB																															
1956	TOR	13										18	3						24	386	16.1	68	3					1	16	16.0	16
1957	TOR+	14							1	22		12	2						43	691	16.1	73	1								
1958	TOR	14										6	1						6	71	11.8	21	1					2	40	20.0	22

Year	Team	GP	FM	FF	FR	TK	SK	YDS	IR	YDS	PD	PTS	TD	RA	YDS	AVG	LG	TD	REC	YDS	AVG	LG	TD	PR	YDS	AVG	LG	KOR	YDS	AVG	LG
1959	SAS	13							1			13	2						15	243	16.2	59	2								
1960	TOR	13																	7	104	14.9	20	0								
1961	TOR	8																	10	108	10.8	17	0					1	8	8.0	8
1962	TOR	11										6	1						3	43	14.3	21	1								
7	Years	86							2	22		55	9						108	1646	15.2	73	8					4	64	16.0	22
TOM SCHUETTE Thomas OG 6'1 238 Indiana B: 1/10/1945 East St. Louis, IL																															
1967	OTT	6																													
1968	OTT	14																													
1969	OTT	14	0		2																										
1970	OTT	14																													
1971	OTT	14																													
1972	OTT	14																													
1973	OTT	14																													
1974	OTT	16	0		1																							1	0	0.0	0
1975	OTT+	10	0		1							6	1																		
1976	OTT	9																													
1977	OTT	2																													
11	Years	127	0		4							6	1															1	0	0.0	0
CHRIS SCHULTZ Christopher OT 6'8 280 Arizona B: 2/16/1960 Hamilton, ON Draft: 1D-7 1982 TOR; 7-189 1983 DAL; TD 1983 ARI-USFL Pro: N																															
1986	TOR	7																													
1987	TOR*	18				1																									
1988	TOR*	14				0																									
1989	TOR	16				1																									
1990	TOR	18	0		2	2																									
1991	TOR+	18				1																									
1992	TOR	17				3																									
1993	TOR	1				0																									
1994	TOR	15				0																									
9	Years	124	0		2	8																									
SCOTT SCHULTZ Scott DT 6'2 297 North Dakota B: 4/19/1977 Moose Jaw, SK Draft: 1-1 2001 SAS																															
2001	SAS	8				19			0	0	1																				
2002	SAS	8	0	0	1	8																									
2003	SAS	18	0	1	0	32	6.0	34.0																							
2004	SAS	18	0	0	1	24	8.0	30.0																							
2005	SAS*	18	0	0	1	27	9.0	56.0																							
2006	SAS	17	0	1	0	18	6.0	52.0																							
2007	SAS	18	0	2	1	27	4.0	33.0																							
2008	SAS	18				20	2.0	11.0																							
2009	SAS	5				3																									
9	Years	128	0	4	4	178	35.0	216.0																							
TOM SCHULTZ Thomas OE-LB 6'3 222 North Carolina Central; Queen's; Ottawa B: 1/3/1947 Ottawa, ON Draft: 3-24 1970 CAL																															
1971	OTT	14																										1	13	13.0	13
1973	OTT	11																													
1974	OTT	16	0		1														1	19	19.0	19	0								
3	Years	41	0		1														1	19	19.0	19	0					1	13	13.0	13
TOM SCHULTZ Tom LB 6'2 210 Simon Fraser B: 7/16/1954 Draft: 2-15 1978 BC																															
1978	BC	5																													
1979	WPG	16	0		1																										
1980	WPG	5																													
1980	SAS	3																													
1980	Year	8																													
1981	SAS	15					4.5		2	4																					
1982	SAS	11					1.0																								
5	Years	52	0		1		5.5		2	4																					
DICK SCHULZ Dick OG 6'3 240 Ohio University B: 1940 Draft: 24-190 1963 BOS; 13-176 1963 SF																															
1964	SAS	2																													
HERB SCHUMM Herb OG-DT 6'1 240 Edmonton Wildcats Jrs. B: 1943 Spruce Grove, AB																															
1963	EDM	9																													
1964	EDM	11																													
1965	EDM	11																													
1967	CAL	16			1																							1	1	1.0	1
1968	CAL	16																													
1969	CAL	16																													
1970	CAL	16																													
1971	CAL	16																													
1972	CAL	16																										1	0	0.0	0
1973	CAL	11										1	0																		
10	Years	138			1							1	0															2	1	0.5	1
HOWIE SCHUMM Howard LB-DB-OHB-FB 6'2 200 Edmonton Wildcats Jrs. B: 1939																															
1959	EDM	16												12	57	4.8	14	0	7	152	21.7	47	0								
1960	EDM	16	2		2				3	83		6	1	1	5	5.0	5	0						1	1	1.0	1	1	5	5.0	5
1961	EDM	16										6	1	17	86	5.1	34	1						1	3	3.0	3				
1962	EDM	16	1		2				3	144		6	1	1	7	7.0	7	0	1	15	15.0	15	0	6	7	1.2	9	5	72	14.4	32
1963	EDM	16							1			6	1	1	2	2.0	2	0	2	23	11.5	12	0					3	44	14.7	21
1964	EDM	16												3	6	2.0	6	0	1	14	14.0	14	0	47	250	5.3	15	6	95	15.8	21
1965	EDM	16	0		2							6	1											50	199	4.0	15	4	62	15.5	20
1966	EDM	16	0		1																										
1967	EDM	15							2	18																		1	2	2.0	2
1968	EDM	16	1		0									8	36	4.5	9	0	1	-2	-2.0	-2	0	34	231	6.8	20	2	-2	-1.0	0
1969	EDM	4	1		0									2	16	8.0	13	0										1	4	4.0	4
1969	CAL	9																						2	9	4.5	9	1	0	0.0	0
1969	Year	13	1		0									2	16	8.0	13	0						2	9	4.5	9	2	4	2.0	4
1970	EDM	8																										1	0	0.0	0
1971	EDM	16							1	0				1	3	3.0	3	0													
1972	EDM	9							1	0																					
14	Years	196	5		7				11	245		30	5	46	218	4.7	34	1	12	202	16.8	47	0	141	700	5.0	20	25	282	11.3	32
DICK SCHWEIDLER Richard Matthew HB 6'0 182 none B: 8/18/1914 Culver, IN D: 3/18/2010 La Jolla, CA Pro: N																															
1947	MTL	6										5	1					1													
GARY SCHWERTFEGER Gary C-LB-OT 6'4 250 Montana B: 7/24/1940 Draft: 12B-92 1962 OAK																															
1962	BC	5																													
1963	BC	15	1		1																										
1964	BC	16	0		1																			1	4	4.0	4				
1965	BC	16	0		2																										
4	Years	52	1		4																			1	4	4.0	4				
JOHN SCIARRA John Michael QB-WR 5'11 185 UCLA B: 3/2/1954 Los Angeles, CA Draft: 4A-103 1976 CHIB Pro: N																															
1976	BC	16	2		1				1	4		6	1	30	92	3.1	27	1	34	563	16.6	53	0	46	598	13.0	66	8	169	21.1	34
1977	BC	1																	5	53	10.6	33	0					1	21	21.0	21
2	Years	17	2		1				1	4		6	1	30	92	3.1	27	1	39	616	15.8	53	0	46	598	13.0	66	9	190	21.1	34
SANDRO SCIORTINO Sandro K 5'9 220 Boston College B: 2/11/1979 Draft: 2B-12 2003 CAL																															
2004	OTT	14	0	0	1	5						90	0																		
SAM SCOCCIA Sam MG-DT 5'10 242 Hamilton Tiger-Cats Jrs.; Hamilton Panthers Ints. B: 1930 D: 5/12/1996 Hamilton, ON																															
1951	HAM	3																													

Year	Team	GP	FM	FF	FR	TK	SK	YDS	IR	YDS	PD	PTS	TD	RA	YDS	AVG	LG	TD	REC	YDS	AVG	LG	TD	PR	YDS	AVG	LG	KOR	YDS	AVG	LG
1952	SAS	12			1																										
1953	SAS	16																													
1954	SAS	14																													
1956	OTT	13																													
1957	OTT	14																													
1958	OTT	13																													
1959	OTT	14																													
1960	OTT	14							1	9																					
1961	OTT	14							1	0																					
1962	OTT	14																													
1963	OTT	14																													
1964	OTT	14	0		1																										
1965	OTT	14																													
14	Years	183	0		2				2	9																					
NICK SCOLLARD Nicholas M. E 6'4 217 St. Joseph's (Indiana) B: 4/3/1920 IN D: 1//1985 Draft: 2-12 1946 BOS Pro: N																															
1950	MTL	12										31	0																		
GLENN SCOLNIK Glenn H. WR 6'3 190 Indiana B: 6/16/1951 Hammond, IN Draft: 6B-154 1973 PIT Pro: N																															
1975	CAL	16										18	3						29	374	12.9	31	3								
1976	HAM	4										6	1						8	134	16.8	28	1								
2	Years	20										24	4						37	508	13.7	31	4								
VINCE SCORSONE Vincent OG-LB 6'1 220 Pittsburgh B: 1935 Draft: 4B-45 1957 WAS																															
1959	BC	5																													
BILL SCOTT William James DB 6'0 188 Idaho B: 5/18/1944 Washington, DC Draft: 16-144 1966 SD Pro: N																															
1966	TOR	1												4	13	3.3	9	0	2	29	14.5	21	0					3	64	21.3	24
BO SCOTT Robert Marilla OHB 6'3 213 Ohio State B: 3/30/1943 Connellsville, PA Draft: 20-155 1965 OAK; 3A-32 1965 CLE Pro: N																															
1964	OTT	1												2	71	35.5	57	0										0	18		18
1965	OTT*	14	6		0							36	6	126	672	5.3	87	3	21	226	10.8	27	2					13	361	27.8	98
1966	OTT+	14	2		0							30	5	140	648	4.6	33	2	17	166	9.8	39	3					16	434	27.1	58
1967	OTT*	13	5		0							60	10	136	762	5.6	49	6	24	351	14.6	80	4					4	100	25.0	48
1968	OTT+	11	2		0							48	8	137	911	6.6	60	7	16	115	7.2	20	1								
5	Years	53	15		0							174	29	541	3064	5.7	87	18	78	858	11.0	80	10					33	913	27.7	98
CEDRIC SCOTT Cedric A. DT 6'5 282 Southern Mississippi B: 10/19/1977 Gulfport, MS Draft: 4A-114 2001 NYG Pro: EN																															
2005	EDM	16	0	0	2	20	6.0	48.0	0	0	1																				
DON SCOTT Don E 6'0 171 Western Ontario B: 1925																															
1949	TOR	6																													
1950	TOR	5										5	1										1								
1951	TOR	5										5	1					1													
3	Years	16										10	2					1					1								
DOUG SCOTT Doug DT-DE 6'3 250 Verdun Maple Leafs Jrs.; Boise State B: 10/2/1956 Montreal, QC Draft: TE 1980 MTL																															
1980	MTL	16	0		2							6	1																		
1981	MTL	16	0		1		7.5																								
1982	MTL+	15	0		3		4.5		1	12		6	1																		
1984	MTL+	15			2		12.0																								
1985	MTL+	16					10.0																								
1986	MTL	15					10.0																								
6	Years	93	0		8		44.0		1	12		12	2																		
EARL SCOTT Earl C 6'2 316 Arkansas B: 8/31/1973 Little Rock, AR Pro: EX																															
2001	TOR	7	1	0	0	2													1	1	1.0	1	0								
EDGAR SCOTT Edgar J. HB 6'2 200 Bethune-Cookman B: 7/11/1949 Columbus, GA Pro: W																															
1972	SAS	1												1	1	1.0	1	0										1	35	35.0	35
FARRIS SCOTT Farris DE 6'3 247 Youngstown State B: 8/14/1952																															
1974	TOR	12	0		1				1	5																					
1975	TOR	5																													
2	Years	17	0		1				1	5																					
GEORGE SCOTT George Wendell, Jr. OHB-DB 6'1 180 Miami (Ohio) B: 7/14/1937 Bainbridge, OH D: 3/4/1995 Buffalo, NY Draft: 19-227 1959 NYG Pro: N																															
1960	HAM	6							1	14				2	9	4.5	6	0	3	20	6.7	12	0	4	16	4.0	8	14	343	24.5	79
1961	HAM	10										42	7	51	289	5.7	27	1	32	551	17.2	74	6	3	30	10.0	19	14	317	22.6	46
1962	HAM	4										6	1	24	75	3.1	19	1	5	55	11.0	26	0								
3	Years	20							1	14		48	8	77	373	4.8	27	2	40	626	15.7	74	6	7	46	6.6	19	28	660	23.6	79
HARVEY SCOTT Harvey G 6'2 225 Western Ontario B: 1940 Draft: 1A- 1962 CAL																															
1963	BC	15																													
JAKE SCOTT Jacob E., III FL-DB 6'0 188 Georgia B: 7/20/1945 Greenwood, SC Draft: 7-159 1970 MIA Pro: N																															
1969	BC	11										18	3	2	11	5.5	8	0	35	596	17.0	47	3					7	224	32.0	76
JAMES SCOTT Bernard James WR 6'1 190 Trinity Valley CC B: 3/28/1952 Longview, TX Draft: 8-193 1975 NYJ Pro: NW																															
1981	MTL*	15	3		2							40	6	2	1	0.5	3	0	81	1422	17.6	77	6								
JOE SCOTT Joseph Oscar, Jr. HB 6'1 198 Texas A&M; San Francisco B: 3/17/1926 Athens, TX Draft: 1-5 1948 SF-AAFC; 2-12 1948 NYG Pro: N																															
1953	MTL	2										5	1					1													
JOHNNY SCOTT Johnny Roy DT-DE-NT 6'2 265 none B: 7/15/1969 Austin, TX																															
1994	SHR	10				11	2.0	15.0																				1	3	3.0	3
1995	SHR	18	0		1	34	2.0	15.0			1	6	1																		
1996	BC	16				29	8.0	46.0																							
1997	BC	16	0	2	2	33	4.0	32.0			1																				
1998	BC*	18	0	1	1	42	13.0	108.0																							
1999	BC*	17	0	2	4	38	10.0	62.0			2																				
2000	TOR+	18	0	1	2	24	5.0	37.0			2																				
2001	TOR	5	0	2	0	8	2.0	9.0																							
2002	TOR+	16	0	2	1	35	4.0	35.0			1																				
2003	HAM	13	0	1	1	26	1.0	8.0																							
2004	HAM	16				33	4.0	28.0																							
2005	OTT	2				3																									
12	Years	165	0	11	12	316	55.0	395.0			5	6	1															1	3	3.0	3
KEVIN SCOTT Kevin Tommorse DB 5'9 175 Stanford B: 5/19/1969 Phoenix, AZ Draft: 4-91 1991 DET Pro: ENX																															
2003	TOR	7				22					1																				
KEVIN SCOTT Kevin DL 6'3 232 Queen's B: 7/17/1983 Ottawa, ON																															
2009	SAS	4				1																									
2011	HAM	18				5																									
2	Years	22				6																									
MARK SCOTT Mark LB 6'1 215 Virginia Tech B: 12/19/1968 Kingston, Jamaica Draft: 1-2 1992 SAS																															
1992	SAS	4				6																						1	0	0.0	0
1992	BC	11	0		1	11																									
1992	Year	15	0		1	17																						1	0	0.0	0
1993	HAM	16				18																									
1994	OTT	11				21																									
3	Years	31	0		1	56																						1	0	0.0	0
RANDY SCOTT Randy LB 5'11 220 Clemson B: 9/13/1957 Waycross, GA																															
1980	WPG	1																													
1980	CAL	3																													
1980	Year	4																													
SAM SCOTT Sam DE 6'5 235 West Chester B: 6/23/1987 Chester, PA																															
2011	CAL	2				7																									
TAYLOR SCOTT Taylor DT 6'4 265 Central Arkansas B: 7/16/1987 Little Rock, AR																															
2010	MTL	1				1																									

Year	Team	GP	FM	FF	FR	TK	SK	YDS	IR	YDS	PD	PTS	TD	RA	YDS	AVG	LG	TD	REC	YDS	AVG	LG	TD	PR	YDS	AVG	LG	KOR	YDS	AVG	LG
2011	TOR	1				2																									
2	Years	2				3																									
TERENCE SCOTT Terence Merez WR 5'11 170 Canyons JC; Oregon B: 9/25/1986 Macon, GA																															
2009	BC	1				0													1	1	1.0	1	0								
TOM SCOTT Thomas Cary WR-SB-WB 5'10 170 San Mateo JC; Washington B: 11/19/1951 Oakland, CA Draft: 12-304 1973 DET																															
1974	WPG	16	2		0							42	7	42	228	5.4	30	0	40	638	16.0	57	7					28	752	26.9	65
1975	WPG	11										30	5	34	160	4.7	16	1	16	303	18.9	43	4	22	148	6.7	29	17	443	26.1	60
1976	WPG	16	2		0							36	6	2	9	4.5	5	0	53	968	18.3	97	6	20	127	6.4	25	29	814	28.1	95
1977	WPG*	16										60	10	2	9	4.5	10	0	66	1079	16.3	98	10					19	395	20.8	47
1978	EDM*	16										60	10	2	-4	-2.0	4	0	67	1091	16.3	46	10	5	15	3.0	19	2	65	32.5	42
1979	EDM	16	1		0							36	6	1	5	5.0	5	1	42	832	19.8	54	5	1	4	4.0	4	1	22	22.0	22
1980	EDM*	16										84	14	1	4	4.0	4	1	73	1245	17.1	46	13					2	43	21.5	25
1981	EDM	16	0		1							48	8						73	1240	17.0	46	8								
1982	EDM*	16	0		1							78	13						91	1518	16.7	49	13								
1983	EDM*	16	0		1							54	9						80	1234	15.4	48	9					1	19	19.0	19
1984	CAL	14										18	3						48	689	14.4	40	3								
11	Years	169	5		3							546	91	84	411	4.9	30	3	649	10837	16.7	98	88	48	294	6.1	29	99	2553	25.8	95
TYLER SCOTT Tyler WR-SB 6'2 200 Saginaw Valley State; Western Ontario* B: 9/21/1985 Windsor, ON Draft: 6B-44 2008 TOR																															
2008	TOR	12				0													19	309	16.3	39	0								
2009	TOR	15	1	0	0	2						8	1						18	212	11.8	27	1								
2010	EDM	7				0													2	19	9.5	11	0								
2011	EDM	16				0						6	1						8	87	10.9	16	1								
4	Years	50	1	0	0	2						14	2						47	627	13.3	39	2								
VINCE SCOTT Vincent Joseph DG-MG-DT 5'8 215 Notre Dame B: 9/21/1922 Le Roy, NY D: 7/13/1992 Hamilton, ON Pro: A																															
1949	HAM+	12																													
1950	HAM+	11																													
1951	HAM	1																													
1952	HAM+	11										5	1																		
1953	HAM+	14																													
1954	HAM+	14																													
1955	HAM+	12																													
1956	HAM+	14																													
1957	HAM+	14																													
1958	HAM+	14																													
1959	HAM+	13																													
1960	HAM	12																													
1961	HAM	14																													
1962	HAM	14																													
14	Years	170										5	1																		
WILBERT SCOTT Wilbert James LB-DE-OT-OE 6'0 215 Indiana B: 3/13/1939 Connellsville, PA Draft: 16-215 1961 PIT Pro: N																															
1964	MTL	6																													
1965	MTL	14	0		1				3	0																		3	12	4.0	12
1966	MTL+	14							1	1																					
1967	MTL	13	0		2																										
1968	MTL	1																													
1968	HAM	12	0		2				2	31																					
1968	Year	13	0		2				2	31																					
5	Years	48	0		5				6	32																		3	12	4.0	12
WILLIAM SCOTT William C 6'4 260 Fresno State B: 4/22/1970																															
1994	SHR	1				11																									
YOHANCE SCOTT Yohance Abdullah-Hakuia CB 6'0 189 Eastern Arizona JC; Utah B: 1/29/1979 Los Angeles, CA																															
2003	TOR	1				1																									
DEMITRIS SCOURAS Demitris K 5'8 180 Manitoba B: 6/26/1973 Winnipeg, MB																															
2002	OTT	3	1	0	0	1						17	0																		
2004	OTT	2				0						9	0																		
2	Years	5	1	0	0	1						26	0																		
COLIN SCRIVENER Colin DT 6'5 285 Siskiyous JC; Oregon B: 1/4/1970 Winnipeg, MB																															
1995	WPG	18	0		1	17	1.0	7.0																							
1996	WPG	18				19	5.0	21.0	1	22	0																				
1997	WPG	18				12	1.0	4.0			2																				
1998	SAS	17	0	0	1	22	1.0	7.0																							
1999	SAS	18	0	1	0	28	5.0	30.0			1																				
2000	SAS	17	0	0	1	8	1.0	5.0			1																				
2001	SAS	12				11					2																				
2002	SAS	9				3																									
8	Years	127	0	1	3	120	14.0	74.0	1	22	6																				
GLEN SCRIVENER Glen DT 6'4 275 Fort Garry Lions Jrs.; William Jewell B: 7/14/1967 Winnipeg, MB Draft: 1A-3 1990 SAS																															
1991	SAS	18	0		3	20	3.0																								
1992	BC	17				41	5.0	39.0																							
1993	BC	18	0		1	24	10.0	79.0																							
1994	BC	15				22	6.0	51.0																							
1995	BC	17	0		3	21	6.0	39.0			3																				
1996	EDM	1				0																									
1997	WPG	11	0	1	1	9	2.0	10.0																							
1998	WPG	15				8	2.0	14.0																							
1999	WPG	18	0	2	0	25	3.0	18.0			2																				
2000	EDM	12	0	0	1	10	2.0	12.0																							
2001	TOR	1				1																									
11	Years	143	0	3	9	181	39.0	262.0			5																				
JOE SCUDERO Joseph Andrew (Scooter) OHB 5'10 173 San Francisco B: 7/2/1930 San Francisco, CA Pro: N																															
1953	TOR+	12										25	5										5								
ART SCULLION Art DE-C-LB-DT 6'2 217 B: 1920 deceased																															
1951	TOR	4																													
1952	TOR	12																													
1953	TOR	14																													
1954	TOR	14																													
1955	HAM	10																													
1957	CAL	14	0		2																										
1958	CAL	16	0		1																										
1959	CAL	15																													
1960	CAL	16	0		4																										
9	Years	115	0		7																										
STEVE SCULLY Stephen J. OT 6'2 270 Syracuse B: 8/28/1952 Draft: 1A-1 1975 WPG																															
1977	WPG	3																													
SKIP SEAGRAVES Albert Edward, IV OT-OG 6'5 300 North Carolina B: 4/27/1982 West Point, NY																															
2007	MTL	15				0																									
2009	MTL	5				2																									
2010	MTL	6				0																									
3	Years	26				2																									
J.T. SEAHOLM Julius Tilman T 6'4 230 Texas B: 4/30/1932 Austin, TX Draft: 13-150 1954 CHIB																															
1958	CAL	15	0		4																							1	0	0.0	0
MARK SEALE Mark DT-DE 6'3 250 Ottawa Sooners Jrs.; Richmond B: 3/10/1960 Halifax, NS Draft: TE 1982 OTT; 12-323 1982 NYG																															

Year	Team	GP	FM	FF	FR	TK	SK	YDS	IR	YDS	PD	PTS	TD	RA	YDS	AVG	LG	TD	REC	YDS	AVG	LG	TD	PR	YDS	AVG	LG	KOR	YDS	AVG	LG
1982	OTT	8					3.5																								
1983	OTT	16					8.5																								
1984	OTT	1																													
1985	OTT	1																													
1985	TOR	11																													
1985	Year	12																													
1986	TOR	18	0		2		2.0																								
1987	TOR	1				2																									
1987	WPG	13			2	18	4.0					6	1																		
1987	Year	14			2	20	4.0					6	1																		
1988	WPG	6					1.0																								
7	Years	51	0		4	20	19.0					6	1																		
PAUL SEALE Paul LB 6'3 223 Wenatchee Valley CC; Oregon State B: 1942																															
1963	BC	15							3	50																					
1964	BC	12																													
1965	BC	16	0		1														2	30	15.0	16	0								
3	Years	43	0		1				3	50									2	30	15.0	16	0								
DON SEAMAN Don LB-C 6'2 215 Saskatoon Hilltops Jrs. B: 1947																															
1969	SAS	16	0		1																										
1970	SAS	16	0		2							6	1																		
1971	SAS	16																										2	8	4.0	8
1972	SAS	7	0		1																										
4	Years	55	0		4							6	1															2	8	4.0	8
JERRY SEARIGHT Gerald C North Dakota																															
1946	CAL	7																													
1949	EDM	11																													
2	Years	18																													
JOHNNY SEARS Johnny Dewayne DH-CB 6'0 184 Michigan; Sequoias JC*; Eastern Michigan B: 3/16/1987 Fresno, CA																															
2010	WPG	1				4																									
2011	WPG	4				8			1	0	0																	1	14	14.0	14
2	Years	5				12			1	0	0																	1	14	14.0	14
BOB SEBRING Bob Donald LB-TE 6'2 238 Saddleback CC; Illinois B: 4/10/1963 Pittsburgh, PA Draft: 9-225 1986 HOU																															
1987	OTT	7				33			1	0																					
MOE SEGAL Moe G 5;8 185 none B: 2/2/1925 Quyon, QC																															
1946	OTT	4																													
NORM SEGALOWITZ Norm HB 5'10 216 Ottawa Gladstone Jrs.																															
1946	MTL	1																													
OLLIE SEGATORE Orlando G-HB 5'9 204 Rosemount Bombers Jrs. B: 7/28/1923 Montreal, QC																															
1946	MTL	5																													
1947	MTL	5																													
1948	MTL	10																													
1949	MTL	12																													
1951	MTL	8																													
5	Years	40																													
DANA SEGIN Dana K-P 6'1 210 St. Mary's (Nova Scotia) B: 11/13/1970 Edmonton, AB																															
2002	HAM	2	1	0	0	0						17	0																		
GONZALO SEGOVIA Gonzalo DT 6'1 280 Eastern Illinois B: 12/5/1977 Draft: 5-38 2002 SAS																															
2004	HAM	1				3																									
LEO SEGUIN Leo G 6'1 185 none B: 9/2/1917 D: 11/28/1981 Fort Lauderdale, FL																															
1946	OTT	12																													
1947	OTT	12																													
2	Years	24																													
RICHARD SEIGLER Richard Joseph LB-DE 6'2 238 Oregon State B: 10/19/1980 Las Vegas, NV Draft: 4B-127 2004 SF Pro: N																															
2008	TOR	14				16								12	97	8.1	39	0	2	13	6.5	12	0								
SERGE SEJOUR Serge DB 6'2 198 Howard B: 10/5/1980 Washington, DC																															
2003	OTT	9				27			3	29	0	6	1																		
2004	OTT	14	0	0	1	32	1.0		1	27	1	6	1																		
2	Years	23	0	0	1	59	1.0		4	56	1	12	2																		
LUTHER SELBO Luther QB 6'0 190 North Central B: 3/2/1946																															
1968	WPG	16	2		0									8	30	3.8	9	0													
JERRY SELINGER Jerry C 6'0 215 St. Joseph's (Indiana) B: 1935																															
1957	OTT	14							1	9																					
1958	OTT	2																													
1960	OTT	3																													
1961	OTT	14										6	1																		
1962	OTT	13																													
1963	OTT	14																													
1964	OTT	14																													
1965	OTT	14																													
1966	OTT	14																													
1967	OTT	14							1	4																					
1968	OTT	14																													
1969	OTT	14	1		0																										
12	Years	144	1		0				2	13		6	1																		
DAN SELLERS Daniel DL-LB 6'2 230 Cincinnati B: 6/12/1965 Morgantown, WV																															
1987	TOR	9	0		3	17	4.0					6	1																		
1988	TOR	4				7																									
1988	OTT	11	0		2	30	4.0																								
1988	Year	15	0		2	37	4.0																								
1990	HAM	12				22	3.0																								
3	Years	25	0		5	76	11.0					6	1																		
MIKE SELLERS Michael DE-RB-LB 6'3 270 Walla Walla CC B: 7/21/1975 Frankfurt, West Germany Pro: N																															
1996	EDM	17				23	3.0	11.0	0	0	3																				
1997	EDM	16	1	1	1	27	1.0	1.0	1	8	1	6	1	40	133	3.3	11	1	5	57	11.4	21	0					1	14	14.0	14
2002	WPG	18	4	2	1	25						24	4	77	377	4.9	20	2	63	643	10.2	46	2					7	102	14.6	19
2003	WPG	14	2	0	0	15						54	9	86	427	5.0	21	7	48	481	10.0	38	2					3	22	7.3	10
4	Years	65	7	3	2	90	4.0	12.0	1	8	4	84	14	203	937	4.6	21	10	116	1181	10.2	46	4					11	138	12.5	19
BILL SEMAN Bill G 6'2 225 Truman State B: 3/31/1944 Springfield, IL Draft: 16-395 1967 NYG																															
1967	HAM	5																													
YANNICK SEMANOU Yannick LB 6'4 295 Howard B: 7/26/1973 Togo Draft: 3-22 1999 MTL																															
1999	MTL	5				1																									
MEL SEMENKO Melvin R. DE 6'2 235 Wyoming; Colorado B: 11/62/1937 Draft: 27-318 1959 SF; FS-(f) 1960 DEN																															
1961	BC	15			2																										
1962	OTT+	11										6	1																		
1963	OTT	4																													
1963	MTL	5																													
1963	Year	9																													
3	Years	30			2							6	1																		
DAMIEN SEMIEN Damien M. WR 6'0 190 California B: 3/9/1971 San Francisco, CA																															
1994	SAC	5				0													1	0	0.0	0	0								
JOHN SENST John SE 6'1 185 Simon Fraser B: 1938 Draft: 2A-10 1970 WPG																															
1970	WPG	16										6	1						22	393	17.9	60	1								

Year	Team	GP	FM	FF	FR	TK	SK	YDS	IR	YDS	PD	PTS	TD	RA	YDS	AVG	LG	TD	REC	YDS	AVG	LG	TD	PR	YDS	AVG	LG	KOR	YDS	AVG	LG
1971	CAL	16										6	1						25	352	14.1	50	1	3	14	4.7	8				
1972	CAL	16	5		0														9	118	13.1	28	0	71	353	5.0	19				
1973	CAL	16	1		1														3	70	23.3	36	0	56	275	4.9	13				
4	Years	64	6		1							12	2						59	933	15.8	60	2	130	642	4.9	19				
ALEXIS SERNA Alexis K-P 5'7 170 Oregon State B: 2/8/1985 Upland, CA																															
2008	WPG	18	1	0	0	8						159	0																		
2009	WPG	18				6						161	0																		
2010	WPG	6	1	0	0	1						48	0																		
3	Years	42	2	0	0	15						368	0																		
NICK SETTA Nicholas K-P 5'11 202 Notre Dame B: 5/6/1981 Chicago, IL Pro: E																															
2007	HAM*	18				6						167	0	1	12	12.0	12	0													
2008	HAM*	18	2	0	0	4						143	0																		
2009	HAM	17	1	0	0	3						166	0																		
3	Years	53	3	0	0	13						476	0	1	12	12.0	12	0													
JOHN SETTLE John R. RB 5'9 209 Appalachian State B: 6/2/1965 Reidsville, NC Pro: N																															
1994	SHR	2												1	1	1.0	1	0										2	24	12.0	
TAWAMBI SETTLES Tawambi Jahmon LB 6'2 191 Duke B: 1/19/1976 Chattanooga, TN Pro: NX																															
2004	HAM	6				8																									
RUSTY SETZER Rusty RB 5'7 184 Notre Dame; Grand Valley State B: 12/16/1969																															
1994	LV	1	1		1									3	14	4.7	7	0						3	7	2.3		3	64	21.3	
JOE SEUMALO Joe DE 6'4 250 Hawaii B: 8/23/1966 Honolulu, HI Pro: E																															
1989	OTT	7	0		1	11	5.0																					1	0	0.0	0
1994	EDM	2																													
2	Years	9	0		1	11	5.0																					1	0	0.0	0
ALMONDO SEWELL Almondo NT 6'1 282 Akron B: 1/16/1987 Trenton, NJ																															
2011	EDM	3				1																									
FRITZ SEYFERTH John Frederick, Jr. HB-FB-TE 6'3 215 Michigan B: 5/18/1950 Muskegon, MI Draft: 17-419 1972 NYG																															
1972	CAL	9	1		0							12	2	67	283	4.2	20	1	17	216	12.7	21	1					2	19	9.5	16
1973	CAL	5	1		0														10	186	18.6	49	0					1	6	6.0	6
2	Years	14	2		0							12	2	67	283	4.2	20	1	27	402	14.9	49	1					3	25	8.3	16
DOUG SEYMOUR Doug DE-DT-NG 6'3 235 Missouri B: 10/16/1952 D: 4/10/2005 Orlando, FL Draft: 2B-12 1977 BC																															
1977	BC	16	0		1																							2	21	10.5	12
1978	BC	16	0		1																							2	24	12.0	19
1979	BC	13	0		1																							2	14	7.0	9
1980	BC	11	0		2																							4	48	12.0	19
1981	BC	5					1.0																								
1981	OTT	9	0		1		1.0																								
1981	Year	14	0		1		2.0																								
1982	OTT	12					1.5																								
1983	OTT	1																													
7	Years	74	0		6		3.5																					10	107	10.7	19
JIM SEYMOUR James E 6'1 180 Calgary Jrs. B: 1928																															
1949	CAL	10																													
1950	CAL	4																													
1951	CAL	5																													
3	Years	19																													
SIDDEEQ SHABAZZ Siddeeq Muneer LB-S 5'11 200 New Mexico State B: 2/5/1981 Frankfurt, West Germany Draft: 7A-246 2003 OAK Pro: EN																															
2007	EDM	18	0	1	3	95	4.0	22.0			2																				
2008	EDM	18	0	2	1	69	3.0	10.0	1	4	0																				
2009	WPG	16	0	1	2	85			4	66	0	12	2																		
2010	CAL	2				3																									
4	Years	54	0	4	6	252	7.0	32.0	5	70	2	12	2																		
LAMARK SHACKERFORD Leonard DT 6'0 255 Wisconsin B: 3/12/1972 Gary, IN																															
1994	LV	1																													
DAVID SHADRACH David DB 6'2 185 Simon Fraser B: 11/17/1962 Trinidad, Trinidad & Tobago Draft: 2-15 1984 EDM																															
1984	EDM	4																													
STEVE SHAFER Stephen Edward CB-DH-S 6'0 187 Sequoias JC; Utah State B: 12/8/1940 Glendale, CA Draft: 11-148 1963 SF																															
1963	BC	15	1		0																			17	26	1.5	8	4	76	19.0	24
1964	BC	8												3	35	11.7	33	0						1	9	9.0	9				
1965	BC	16	0		1				6	113				1	-1	-1.0	-1	0						3	4	1.3	2	4	70	17.5	20
1966	BC	3																													
1967	BC	5	0		1																										
5	Years	47	1		2				6	113				4	34	8.5	33	0						21	39	1.9	9	8	146	18.3	24
CRAIG SHAFFER Craig Alan LB 6'1 227 Indiana State B: 3/31/1959 Terre Haute, IN Draft: 6-150 1982 STL Pro: N																															
1985	EDM	8					2.0																								
1986	EDM	13	0		3		7.0		1	4																					
1987	OTT	5	0		2	19																									
1987	EDM	7				14	1.0		1	8																					
1987	Year	12	0		2	33	1.0		1	8																					
1988	EDM	7			2				1	7																					
4	Years	33	0		7	33	10.0		3	19																					
MUHAMMAD SHAMSID-DEEN Muhammad RB 5'11 200 Tennessee-Chattanooga B: 1/16/1969 Anderson, SC Draft: 8-207 1992 SEA																															
1994	TOR	6	1		1	0						48	8	75	333	4.4	29	8	6	38	6.3	16	0					3	66	22.0	29
DON SHANKLIN Donald Purcell HB 5'9 175 Kansas B: 11/3/1946 Amarillo, TX D: 8/30/2009 Amarillo, TX Draft: 10B-243 1969 PHI Pro: W																															
1969	BC	1	1		0									8	16	2.0	12	0													
ART SHANNON Art HB 5'9 175 Vancouver Meralomas Jrs.																															
1957	BC	11												3	14	4.7	9	0	1	14	14.0	14	0	15	89	5.9	13	3	46	15.3	22
CARVER SHANNON Carver Beauregard OHB-DB 6'1 201 Southern Illinois B: 4/28/1938 Corinth, MS Draft: 19-224 1959 LARM Pro: N																															
1959	WPG	14										44	7	88	512	5.8	53	1	31	517	16.7	90	6					14	355	25.4	46
1960	WPG	9	2		1							43	5	60	348	5.8	48	4	8	103	12.9	24	1					12	268	22.3	47
1961	WPG	4										22	1	20	81	4.1	26	0	7	79	11.3	26	1					6	125	20.8	29
1961	HAM	4										12	2	32	152	4.8	23	1	3	44	14.7	22	1					4	121	30.3	36
1961	Year	8										34	3	52	233	4.5	26	1	10	123	12.3	26	2					10	246	24.6	36
3	Years	27	2		1							121	15	200	1093	5.5	53	6	49	743	15.2	90	9					36	869	24.1	47
PAUL SHANNON Paul E 6'0 179 McMaster Draft: 6-23 1953 TOR																															
1953	TOR	2										2	0																		
ED SHARKEY Edward Joseph LB-OG 6'3 229 Duke; Nevada-Reno B: 7/6/1927 New York, NY Pro: AN																															
1957	BC+	14							1	7														1	5	5.0	5				
1958	BC	5																													
2	Years	19							1	7														1	5	5.0	5				
SHANE SHARPE Shane DB 6'0 187 Alberta B: 5/1/1975 Corner Brook, NL																															
2001	BC	1				1																									
CORBIN SHARUN Corbin LB-S 5'11 214 St. Francis Xavier; Edmonton Wildcats Jrs. B: 9/6/1988 Edmonton, AB Draft: 6-43 2010 EDM																															
2010	EDM	16				17																									
2011	EDM	18				26																									
2	Years	34				43																									
DICK SHATTO Richard D. OHB-QB-DB 6'2 196 Kentucky B: 6/23/1933 Springfield, OH D: 2/4/2003 St. Petersburg, FL Draft: 15-180 1956 LARM																															
1954	TOR	13							5	94		35	7	72	386	5.4	23	6	26	323	12.4	35	1					4	62	15.5	24
1955	TOR	7							2	5		5	1	87	423	4.9	17	0	13	195	15.0	34	1	2	2	1.0	2	1	18	18.0	18
1956	TOR+	14							3	72		54	9	118	575	4.9	67	3	41	553	13.5	45	5	1	25	25.0	25	25	636	25.4	54
1957	TOR+	14							3	22		24	4	179	875	4.9	32	4	28	240	8.6	26	0					6	171	28.5	35
1958	TOR+	14							2	66		54	9	154	969	6.3	41	5	35	536	15.3	59	4					10	221	22.1	31

Year	Team	GP	FM	FF	FR	TK	SK	YDS	IR	YDS	PD	PTS	TD	RA	YDS	AVG	LG	TD	REC	YDS	AVG	LG	TD	PR	YDS	AVG	LG	KOR	YDS	AVG	LG
1959	TOR+	14										30	5	174	950	5.5	45	3	46	518	11.3	72	2	1	8	8.0	8	3	40	13.3	20
1960	TOR	14										66	11	122	708	5.8	34	1	53	894	16.9	82	10					6	173	28.8	56
1961	TOR+	13										42	7	94	502	5.3	45	3	35	493	14.1	41	4					3	100	33.3	47
1962	TOR+	14										72	12	94	465	4.9	54	7	47	808	17.2	63	5					2	25	12.5	17
1963	TOR*	14										81	13	108	570	5.3	25	3	67	945	14.1	55	10					4	77	19.3	34
1964	TOR*	14										66	11	56	203	3.6	11	2	53	859	16.2	71	9					5	94	18.8	32
1965	TOR	14	5		0							13	2	64	332	5.2	22	1	22	320	14.5	38	1					14	374	26.7	50
12	Years	159	5		0				15	259		542	91	1322	6958	5.3	67	38	466	6684	14.3	82	52	4	35	8.8	25	83	1991	24.0	56
ROY SHATZKO Roy DE-DT 6'2 235 Vancouver Blue Bombers Jrs.; British Columbia B: 4/4/1940 D: 12/10/2009 Vancouver, BC Draft: 1-7 1963 CAL																														
1965	BC	16	0		1																									
1966	BC	16																												
1967	EDM	15	0		1																									
1968	EDM	16	0		1																							1	0	0.0	0
1969	EDM	16																												
1970	EDM	16																												
1971	EDM	16																												
1972	EDM	1																												
8	Years	112	0		3																							1	0	0.0	0
LUKE SHAVER Lukas DB 6'1 210 Ottawa B: 7/30/1977 Edmonton, AB Draft: 3B-23 2001 CAL																														
2001	CAL	1	0	0	1	1																								
2001	WPG	5				3																								
2001	Year	6	0	0	1	4																								
2002	WPG	6				1																								
2	Years	7	0	0	1	5																								
MICHAEL SHAVER Michael FB 6'2 230 Ottawa B: 7/19/1979 Cold Lake, AB Draft: 3-26 2002 WPG																														
2002	WPG	3				0																								
TYRONE SHAVERS Pernell Tyrone WR 6'3 210 Tyler JC; Lamar B: 2/9/1968 Texarkana, TX Draft: 6-142 1990 PHX Pro: N																														
1993	OTT	5				1													7	79	11.3	22	0							
ANDY SHAW Andy DT 6'4 250 Queen's B: 1943 Draft: 2-16 1964 OTT; 8- 1965 OTT																														
1965	OTT	13																												
1966	OTT	9																												
2	Years	22																												
BOB SHAW Robert E 6'4 226 Ohio State B: 5/22/1921 Richwood, OH D: 4/10/2011 Westerville, OH Draft: 10-97 1944 CLE Pro: N																														
1951	CAL	14										61	4						61	980	16.1	54	4							
1952	CAL+	16										110	9	1	-1	-1.0	-1	0	51	1094	21.5	82	9							
1953	CAL	2										1	0						4	73	18.3	22	0							
1953	TOR	8										14	0																	
1953	Year	9										15	0						4	73	18.3	22	0							
3	Years	32										186	13	1	-1	-1.0	-1	0	116	2147	18.5	82	13							
CLIFF SHAW Cliff LB-OG-DE 6'0 221 Saskatoon Hilltops Jrs. B: 1943																														
1966	SAS	16	0		2				1																					
1967	SAS	11																												
1968	SAS	16																												
1969	SAS	16																												
1970	SAS	16																												
5	Years	75	0		2				1	0																				
DAN SHAW Daniel John OT 6'6 270 Curry B: 8/5/1953 Brighton, MA																														
1977	CAL	2																												
DANNY SHAW Danny (Red) G-T 6'1 233 none B: 1934																														
1954	TOR	10																												
1955	TOR	11																												
1956	TOR	14																												
3	Years	35																												
DAVE SHAW Dave T 6'1 220 Saskatoon Hilltops Jrs. B: 1940																														
1960	SAS	16																												
1961	CAL	8																												
2	Years	24																												
DAVID SHAW David CB 6'0 180 Prairie View A&M B: 4/11/1953 Mountain Home, ID																														
1975	HAM	7							1	25														3	64	21.3	35	7	142	20.3	34
1976	HAM*	16	1		0				4	50														3	17	5.7	12	23	726	31.6	71
1977	HAM	13	0		2				2	42				1	2	2.0	2	0						21	207	9.9	49	11	185	16.8	25
1978	HAM	8	2		0				2	30														4	25	6.3	9				
1979	HAM	15	2		1				3	61														44	421	9.6	81				
1980	HAM*	16							4	63		6	1											24	341	14.2	102	1	6	6.0	6
1981	HAM*	16	0		1				3	73														24	271	11.3	101				
1982	HAM*	15	1		1				4	36														40	421	10.5	31				
1983	WPG+	14					1.0		2	22																				
1984	WPG*	16							2	61		6	1											9	101	11.2	22				
1985	WPG+	16							7	219		6	1																	
1986	WPG	6							2	58		6	1																	
12	Years	158	6		5		1.0		36	740		24	4	1	2	2.0	2	0						172	1868	10.9	102	42	1059	25.2	71
DENNIS SHAW Dennis OE 6'3 220 Trinity Valley CC; North Texas B: 1934 Draft: 11-127 1956 BAL																														
1957	WPG	6										6	1						5	68	13.6	29	1							
GARY SHAW Gary DB 5'11 187 Brigham Young B: 6/3/1954 Salt Lake City, UT Draft: 17-485 1976 LARM																														
1977	HAM	14	0		3																			1	6	6.0	6				
GERRY SHAW Gerry FL-CB-S 6'1 195 Mount Royal College Cougars Jrs.; Washington State B: 1943 Calgary, AB D: 3/18/1995 Calgary, AB																														
1965	CAL	16							2	22														2	5	2.5	5				
1966	CAL	10																	1	22	22.0	22	0							
1967	CAL	16			1							24	4						36	569	15.8	51	3							
1968	CAL	16	1		0							24	4						48	713	14.9	66	4							
1969	CAL	16	1		0							24	4						49	794	16.2	63	4							
1970	CAL	16	0		1							24	4						40	569	14.2	59	4							
1971	CAL	16	1		0							18	3						30	478	15.9	58	3							
1972	CAL+	16										72	12						65	1002	15.4	70	12							
1973	CAL	16										24	4						41	537	13.1	28	4							
1974	CAL	16	1		0														3	48	16.0	26	0	7	15	2.1	8				
10	Years	154	4		2				2	22		210	35						313	4732	15.1	70	34	9	20	2.2	8				
GRANT SHAW Grant LB-K-P 6'3 208 Edmonton Huskies Jrs.; Saskatchewan B: 8/3/1984 Edmonton, AB Draft: 2-11 2010 TOR																														
2010	TOR	18	2	0	0	3						93	0											1	9	9.0	9				
2011	TOR	18				3						18	0																	
2	Years	36	2	0	0	6						111	0											1	9	9.0	9				
JUSTIN SHAW Justin DE 6'4 235 Manitoba B: 9/23/1982 Victoria, BC Draft: 3A-18 2008 BC																														
2009	WPG	4				1																								
KEN SHAW Ken LB-DL 6'4 245 Sudbury Spartans Jrs.																														
1968	OTT	14																												
LEN SHAW Len E-HB-FW 5'11 185 McGill B: 1928 Draft: 2-6 1954 OTT																														
1947	OTT	6																												
1948	OTT	2																												
1954	OTT	14																	5	78	15.6	28	0					1	9	9.0	9
3	Years	22																	5	78	15.6	28	0					1	9	9.0	9
RICK SHAW Rick CB-SE 6'4 215 Arizona State B: 1946 Draft: 6-152 1969 DAL																														
1968	CAL	16	0		1				3	13		18	3						3	25	8.3	14	2	1	1	1.0	1				

Year	Team	GP	FM	FF	FR	TK	SK	YDS	IR	YDS	PD	PTS	TD	RA	YDS	AVG	LG	TD	REC	YDS	AVG	LG	TD	PR	YDS	AVG	LG	KOR	YDS	AVG	LG
1969	CAL	15							3	17																					
1970	WPG+	10	3		0							12	2						33	538	16.3	51	2					2	12	6.0	10
1972	HAM	14							3	36																					
4	Years	55	3		1				9	66		30	5						36	563	15.6	51	4	1	1	1.0	1	2	12	6.0	10
SEDRICK SHAW Sedrick Anton RB 6'0 214 Iowa B: 11/16/1973 Austin, TX Draft: 3A-61 1997 NE Pro: N																															
2002	SAS	18	3	0	0	2						24	4	204	950	4.7	32	4	25	209	8.4	35	0					1	0	0.0	0
2003	SAS	7	2	0	1	2						12	2	70	399	5.7	28	2	10	65	6.5	11	0					4	70	17.5	23
2	Years	25	5	0	1	4						36	6	274	1349	4.9	32	6	35	274	7.8	35	0					5	70	14.0	23
TREVOR SHAW Trevor WR 6'2 205 Weber State B: 11/12/1969 Hamilton, ON Draft: 1A-6 1994 BC																															
1995	BC	8				2													3	14	4.7	7	0								
1996	BC	6				7													1	5	5.0	5	0								
1997	BC	18				8													6	104	17.3	30	0								
1998	BC	4				3																									
1998	HAM	9				3						6	1						5	38	7.6	15	1								
1998	Year	13				6						6	1						5	38	7.6	15	1								
1999	HAM	18				10						18	3						25	346	13.8	54	3					1	0	0.0	0
2000	HAM	18				12						6	1						4	50	12.5	20	1								
2001	HAM	18	1	0	0	11													4	46	11.5	19	0					1	0	0.0	0
2002	HAM	18				9													20	177	8.9	23	0					3	19	6.3	12
2003	HAM	9	1	0	0	4						8	1						23	273	11.9	30	1					1	20	20.0	20
9	Years	117	2	0	0	69						38	6						91	1053	11.6	54	6					6	39	6.5	20
WAYNE SHAW Wayne LB-DE 6'0 215 Saskatoon Hilltops Jrs. B: 1939																															
1961	SAS	13																													
1962	SAS	16	0		2				2	36																					
1963	SAS+	16	0		6				1																						
1964	SAS+	15	0		3																										
1965	SAS	16	0		2				1																						
1966	SAS+	15	0		1				4	64		6	1																		
1967	SAS*	16	0		1																										
1968	SAS	16							3	10																					
1969	SAS+	16	0		1				2	12																					
1970	SAS	16	1		1				4	51																					
1971	SAS+	16	0		3				3	12																					
1972	SAS	16							1	25																					
12	Years	187	1		20				21	210		6	1																		
WAYNE SHAW Wayne CB 5'9 191 Kent State B: 2/14/1974 Winnipeg, MB Draft: 2-13 1999 TOR																															
1999	TOR	18	0	1	0	15					3																				
2000	TOR	18	0	0	1	46			2	97	10	12	2																		
2001	TOR*	15	0	0	1	43			6	162	9	12	2																		
2002	MTL+	18	0	1	0	36			6	98	9	12	2																		
2003	MTL	18				43			4	78	8																				
2004	HAM	18	0	1	1	33			4	38	9													1	5	5.0	5				
2005	HAM	18				34			3	21	7																				
2006	HAM	17	0	2	0	32	3.0	14.0			4																				
2007	HAM	2				4					1																				
2007	TOR	15	0	0	1	11																									
2007	Year	17	0	0	1	15					1																				
2008	TOR	3				6																									
10	Years	145	0	5	4	303	3.0	14.0	25	494	60	36	6											1	5	5.0	5				
JERRY SHAY Jerome Paul [born Dzedzeji] DE 6'3 244 Purdue B: 7/10/1944 Gary, IN Draft: 1-4 1966 DEN; 1-7 1966 MIN Pro: N																															
1972	EDM	3																													
LIN-J SHELL Lin-J DH-LB 5'11 175 Jacksonville B: 10/22/1981 Gainesville, FL Pro: E																															
2009	TOR	17	1	0	2	75	3.0	22.0	1	0	5																				
2010	TOR+	18	1	1	0	65			4	49	0																				
2011	TOR+	18	1	0	5	102	1.0	1.0	2	28	6																				
3	Years	53	3	1	7	242	4.0	23.0	7	77	11																				
CHRIS SHELLING Christopher A. DH-LB 5'10 180 Auburn B: 11/3/1972 Columbus, GA Pro: ENX																															
1998	HAM	2				11																									
1999	HAM	18				75					6																				
2000	HAM*	18				55			4	72	6	6	1																		
2001	HAM+	17	0	2	1	87	8.0	40.0	1	0	2																				
2002	HAM	18	0	1	2	64	1.0		4	39	2																				
2003	HAM	9				32	1.0				1																				
6	Years	82	0	3	3	324	10.0	40.0	9	111	17	6	1																		
TERRY SHELSTA Terry OG 6'3 250 Dakota Wesleyan B: 5/20/1949																															
1974	TOR	9																													
1975	TOR	16	0		1																										
1976	TOR	16	0		1																										
3	Years	41	0		2																										
ANTHONY SHELTON Anthony Levala S 6'1 195 Tennessee State*; Middle Tennessee State*; Tennessee State B: 9/4/1967 Fayetteville, TN Draft: 11-289 1990 SF Pro: N																															
1994	WPG	5				16			1	-1	1																				
1994	SHR	10				44			1	13	4																				
1994	Year	15				60			2	12	5																				
1995	SHR	17	1		2	74	2.0	20.0	2	22	2																				
2	Years	22	1		2	134	2.0	20.0	4	34	7																				
DAVE SHELTON David T. DB 5'11 200 Fresno State B: 1/29/1967 Los Angeles County, CA																															
1990	EDM	5				8	1.0																					4	55	13.8	22
1991	EDM	16	0		1	62			4	31																					
2	Years	21	0		1	70	1.0		4	31																		4	55	13.8	22
CHARLIE SHEPARD Charles Lafayette, Jr. FB-LB 6'2 215 North Texas B: 7/11/1933 Dallas, TX D: 6/23/2009 Plano, TX Draft: 18-208 1955 BAL Pro: N																															
1957	WPG	9	1									28	4	60	411	6.9	29	4													
1958	WPG	16	4									76	11	178	925	5.2	70	11	11	132	12.0	38	0					3	38	12.7	18
1959	WPG+	15										49	7	174	1076	6.2	45	6	6	150	25.0	36	1					3	37	12.3	23
1960	WPG	15	7		1							50	6	138	718	5.2	25	6	5	67	13.4	18	0					2	25	12.5	14
1961	WPG	10										21	1	86	435	5.1	21	1	7	54	7.7	25	0					3	38	12.7	18
1962	WPG	8	1									3	0	49	203	4.1	10	0	3	3	1.0	11	0								
6	Years	73	13		1							227	29	685	3768	5.5	70	28	32	406	12.7	38	1					11	138	12.5	23
JACOBY SHEPHERD Jacoby Lamar CB 6'1 198 Tyler JC; Cloud County CC*; Oklahoma State B: 8/31/1979 Lufkin, TX Draft: 2-62 2000 STL Pro: N																															
2005	CAL	2				3																									
JOHNNY SHEPHERD Johnny Ray RB 5'10 185 Liberty; West Alabama B: 4/24/1957 LaGrange, NC Pro: N																															
1983	HAM*	16	5		0							30	5	197	1069	5.4	62	1	58	583	10.1	66	4					28	738	26.4	61
1984	HAM	7	1		1							6	1	59	206	3.5	27	1	20	159	8.0	44	0					1	2	2.0	2
1985	HAM	5	2		1									65	189	2.9	15	0	19	139	7.3	19	0					3	46	15.3	18
1986	HAM	2												8	28	3.5	7	0	3	1	0.3	2	0								
4	Years	30	8		2							36	6	329	1492	4.5	62	2	100	882	8.8	66	4					32	786	24.6	61
LORNE SHERBINA Lorne DT 6'4 256 Idaho B: 5/6/1952 Draft: TE 1974 BC																															
1974	CAL	16																													
1975	CAL	16	0		1																										
1976	CAL	16																													
1977	CAL	16																													
4	Years	64	0		1																										
JUAN SHERIDAN Juan MG-LB 5'9 217 Toronto B: 2/2/1925 Havana, Cuba D: 10/7/1969 Howick, QC																															

Year	Team	GP	FM	FF	FR	TK	SK	YDS	IR	YDS	PD	PTS	TD	RA	YDS	AVG	LG	TD	REC	YDS	AVG	LG	TD	PR	YDS	AVG	LG	KOR	YDS	AVG	LG
1949	MTL	10																													
1950	MTL	9																													
1951	MTL	12																													
1952	MTL	12																													
1953	MTL	11										2	0																		
1954	MTL	14																													
1955	MTL	12										5	1																		
1956	MTL	11																													
1957	MTL	14																													
9	Years	105										7	1																		
MARK SHERIDAN Mark Francis Xavier WR 6'5 200 Holy Cross B: 12/3/1952 Washington, DC Draft: 9-219 1974 PHI; 31-371 1974 FLA-WFL																															
1974	OTT	1																													
MATT SHERIDAN Matthew OG-OT-C-DL 6'4 360 Manitoba B: 5/27/1977 Montreal, QC Draft: 6-40 2000 WPG																															
2001	WPG	4				1																									
2002	WPG	6				1																									
2003	WPG	18				1																									
2004	WPG	18	0	0	1	0																									
2005	WPG	18	0	0	1	1																									
2006	WPG	7	0	0	1	0																									
2007	WPG	15	0	1	0	2																									
7	Years	86	0	1	3	6																									
PAUL SHERIDAN Paul OG-DE 6'3 248 York B: 5/23/1954 Draft: 3-25 1977 HAM																															
1977	HAM	1																													
HEATH SHERMAN Heath B. RB 6'0 197 Texas A&M-Kingsville B: 3/27/1967 Wharton, TX Draft: 6-162 1989 PHI Pro: N																															
1995	SA	1				0						6	1	6	14	2.3	7	1													
TOM SHERMAN Thomas Joseph QB 6'0 190 Penn State B: 12/5/1945 Bellevue, PA Pro: NW																															
1976	CAL	7	2		0									7	38	5.4	14	0													
WILL SHERMAN Willard Arthur E-DB 6'2 197 St. Mary's (California) B: 10/20/1927 Weed, CA D: 10/11/1997 Draft: 26-311 1951 NYY Pro: N																															
1953	CAL	16							2	16		15	3						27	545	20.2	84	3								
LARRY SHERRER Larry RB 6'2 205 Hawaii B: 1/1/1950																															
1974	MTL	3										6	1	27	117	4.3	15	0	4	90	22.5	75	1								
1976	BC	2												13	89	6.8	22	0	1	4	4.0	4	0					4	94	23.5	38
2	Years	5										6	1	40	206	5.2	22	0	5	94	18.8	75	1					4	94	23.5	38
J.C. SHERRITT John Cody LB 5'10 215 Eastern Washington B: 5/2/1988 Truckee, CA																															
2011	EDM	16	0	3	0	85	3.0	13.0			3																				
CHUCK SHIELDS Chuck G-T 6'0 190 Guelph; Peterborough Ints. B: 1925																															
1949	TOR	1																													
LANCE SHIELDS Lance CB 6'0 178 Drake B: 4/1/1960 Buffalo, NY Pro: U																															
1986	HAM	13							8	37																					
1987	HAM	8	0		1	21			4	44																					
1988	HAM	18	0		2	53			9	137		18	3											1	5	5.0	5				
1989	HAM	18	0		2	49			7	35		6	1											2	28	14.0	24				
1990	HAM	7				20			3	13																					
1991	OTT	3	0		1	9																									
6	Years	67	0		6	152			31	266		24	4											3	33	11.0	24				
LeBRON SHIELDS LeBron B. T 6'4 245 Tennessee B: 7/23/1937 Walker County, GA Draft: 22-256(f) 1959 DET; FS 1960 DEN Pro: N																															
1962	TOR	5																													
GRAYSON SHILLINGFORD Grayson WR 5'9 192 British Columbia B: 3/25/1974 Toronto, ON Draft: 4-28 1996 OTT																															
1998	BC	3				1													4	45	11.3	18	0								
2000	TOR	6				1													3	21	7.0	11	0								
2001	TOR	17				5													14	162	11.6	20	0								
2002	OTT	11	1	0	0	11													6	70	11.7	22	0					10	196	19.6	31
2003	OTT	1				1																									
5	Years	38	1	0	0	19													27	298	11.0	22	0					10	196	19.6	31
WILLIE SHINE Willie FB-OE 6'3 235 Garden City JC; Buffalo B: 1945																															
1966	EDM	10												9	34	3.8	10	0	2	30	15.0	17	0								
JOE SHINN Joseph D. E 5'10 187 Tulane B: 1930 Draft: 30-359 1951 NYY																															
1951	HAM	6										15	3										2								
1952	HAM	12										20	4										4								
1953	HAM	1										5	1																		
3	Years	19										40	8										6								
JIM SHIPKA Jim FB 5'10 195 Edmonton Wildcats Jrs. B: 1935																															
1956	EDM	13	2		0							12	2	38	160	4.2	13	2	7	63	9.0	27	0								
1957	EDM	13										6	1	16	97	6.1	19	1													
1958	EDM	16	0		2									37	197	5.3	30	0	1	5	5.0	5	0					1	60	60.0	60
1959	EDM	16												32	121	3.8	12	0	5	28	5.6	16	0					5	47	9.4	15
1960	EDM	15												1	7	7.0	7	0	2	20	10.0	11	0					8	127	15.9	29
1961	EDM	5												4	11	2.8	6	0	1	14	14.0	14	0					2	25	12.5	15
6	Years	78	2		2							18	3	128	593	4.6	30	3	16	130	8.1	27	0					16	259	16.2	60
RON SHIPLEY Ronald H. C-OG 6'4 298 Chaffey CC; New Mexico B: 8/17/1968 Draft: 12-329 1991 KC Pro: E																															
1993	SAC	18	0		1	2																									
1994	SAC	3				0																									
1994	LV	12				1																						1	10	10.0	10
1994	Year	15				1																						1	10	10.0	10
2	Years	21	0		1	3																						1	10	10.0	10
STEPHEN SHIPLEY Stephen Frank WR 6'5 225 Texas Christian B: 5/17/1971 Burnet County, TX																															
1994	SHR	2																	1	8	8.0	8	0								
AL SHIPMAN Alfred SB-RB 5'8 175 Miami (Florida) B: 3/26/1974 Palm Beach, FL																															
1995	MEM	13	0		1	1						20	3	82	483	5.9	29	2	14	183	13.1	31	1					10	241	24.1	37
1996	OTT	1	1		0	0								3	10	3.3	6	0	1	6	6.0	6	0								
1997	BC	11	5	0	1	2						30	5	7	6	0.9	7	1	45	483	10.7	66	3	52	665	12.8	76	35	751	21.5	80
1998	BC	9	2	0	0	2						6	1	5	2	0.4	5	0	39	354	9.1	33	1	24	130	5.4	21	11	224	20.4	26
4	Years	34	10	0	3	5						56	9	97	501	5.2	29	3	99	1026	10.4	66	5	76	795	10.5	76	56	1216	21.7	80
BILLY SHIPP William Leonard DT-OT 6'5 275 Alabama B: 10/16/1930 Mobile, AL D: 6/9/2011 Mobile, AL Draft: 8-95(f) 1952 NYG Pro: N																															
1955	TOR+	12																													
1956	TOR	2																													
1956	MTL	5																													
1956	Year	7																													
1957	MTL	3																													
1958	MTL	14																													
1959	MTL+	14																													
1960	MTL	9																													
1961	TOR	14							1	3																					
1962	TOR	14																													
1963	TOR	12																													
1964	TOR+	13																													
1965	TOR	14	0		2																										
11	Years	121	0		2				1	3																					
CHARLIE SHIRA Charles N. T-G Texas A&M; Army																															
1953	EDM	2																													
MARSHALL SHIRK Chester Marshall DT 6'2 250 UCLA B: 8/3/1940 Los Angeles County, CA Draft: 9-67 1962 DAL; 9-114 1962 MIN																															
1965	OTT	14																													

Year	Team	GP	FM	FF	FR	TK	SK	YDS	IR	YDS	PD	PTS	TD	RA	YDS	AVG	LG	TD	REC	YDS	AVG	LG	TD	PR	YDS	AVG	LG	KOR	YDS	AVG	LG
1966	OTT	12																													
1967	OTT	13	0		2																										
1968	OTT+	14																													
1969	OTT+	14																													
1970	OTT+	13	0		4																										
1971	OTT	14			3																										
7	Years	94	0		9																										
JIM SHIRLEY Jim HB 6'0 200 Clemson B: 1932 Draft: 18-210 1953 CHIB																															
1955	TOR	1										5	1	17	84	4.9	11	1	3	30	10.0	13	0								
REX SHIVER Raymond Orville HB 6'0 189 Miami (Florida) B: 1/1/1932 Miami, FL Pro: N																															
1957	TOR	8							3	19									2	49	24.5	37	0	1	1	1.0	1				
JASON SHIVERS Jason DH-S 6'1 201 Arizona State B: 11/4/1982 Phoenix, AZ Draft: 5-158 2004 STL Pro: EN																															
2008	TOR	14	0	1	0	37			2	0	2																				
2009	TOR	17	0	3	2	68			1	4	5																				
2010	HAM	12	0	1	2	52			3	53	3																				
2011	HAM	14	0	2	1	36					3																				
4	Years	57	0	7	5	193			6	57	13																				
DEREK SHOLDICE Derek OG 6'4 290 Northern Illinois B: 10/5/1972 Brandon, MB Draft: 2-21 1995 EDM																															
1996	EDM	9				0																									
1997	EDM	15				2																									
1998	WPG	1				0																									
3	Years	25				2																									
KEITH SHOLOGAN Keith DT 6'1 285 Central Florida B: 11/26/1985 Spruce Groeb, AB Draft: 1-4 2008 SAS																															
2008	SAS	1				2																									
2009	SAS	18	0	2	2	27	3.0	11.0	0	0	1	6	1						1	1	1.0	1	1								
2010	SAS	18	0	1	0	30	3.0	25.0																							
2011	SAS	18				26	2.0	10.0																							
4	Years	55	0	3	2	85	8.0	46.0				6	1						1	1	1.0	1	1								
JOHNNY SHORE John C-G 6'0 206 Toronto B: 1924																															
1949	TOR	4																													
1950	TOR	9																													
1951	TOR	9																													
1952	TOR	11																													
1953	TOR	5																													
5	Years	38																													
NATE SHORE Nate E-G-C 5'10 198 Winnipeg Jrs.; Winnipeg YMHA B: 1920																															
1946	WPG+	8																													
1947	WPG	8																													
1949	EDM	12																													
3	Years	28																													
PAUL SHORTEN Paul WR 5'10 170 Toronto B: 1/23/1963 Toronto, ON Draft: 2C-18 1987 BC																															
1988	WPG	15				1													3	34	11.3	20	0	24	88	3.7	25	1	15	15.0	15
PETE SHORTS Peter John OT 6'8 278 Illinois State B: 7/12/1966 Clinton, WI Pro: EN																															
1994	SAC	18																													
1995	SA	7				0																									
1995	SAS	8				1																									
1995	Year	15				1																									
1996	SAS	2				0																									
1997	HAM	8				1																									
4	Years	35				2																									
JOHNNY SHOWALTER John QB 175 Oregon; Gonzaga																															
1946	SAS	8																													
MALCOLM SHOWELL Malcolm DE 6'6 264 Delaware State B: 1/10/1968 Pro: E																															
1994	BAL	2				3	1.0																								
GARY SHUGRUE Gary DE 6'5 240 Villanova B: 3/11/1954 Rockville Center, NY Draft: 11-307 1976 DET																															
1976	WPG	5							1	0																					
TOM SHUMAN Thomas Matthew QB 6'2 194 Penn State B: 11/9/1953 Pottstown, PA Draft: 6A-142 1975 CIN																															
1976	HAM	8	2		1																										
1977	HAM	16												1	2	2.0	2	0													
1978	HAM	7	3		0									5	30	6.0	8	0													
1978	MTL	3	1		1									5	4	0.8	7	0													
1978	Year	10	4		1									10	34	3.4	8	0													
3	Years	31	6		2									11	36	3.3	8	0													
MARK SHUMATE Mark Anthony DL 6'5 265 Wisconsin B: 3/30/1960 Poynette, WI Draft: 10-257 1983 KC Pro: N																															
1984	EDM	8					2.5																								
ED SHUTTLESWORTH Eugene Edward FB 6'2 235 Michigan B: 6/4/1952 Birmingham, AL Draft: 2B-37 1974 BAL; 4-37 1974 DET-WFL																															
1974	TOR	16	4		0							31	5	191	866	4.5	27	5	13	30	2.3	19	0					5	98	19.6	22
1975	TOR	5	1		1							6	1	21	101	4.8	14	0	8	53	6.6	11	1								
2	Years	21	5		1							37	6	212	967	4.6	27	5	21	83	4.0	19	1					5	98	19.6	22
JIM SIDES James FB 5'11 215 Texas Tech B: 1935 Draft: 13-150 1956 PHI																															
1956	CAL	3	1		0							1	0	6	35	5.8	20	0	3	16	5.3	9	0								
JIMMY SIDLE James Corbin TE 6'2 215 Auburn B: 2/7/1943 Birmingham, AL D: 11/14/1999 Montgomery, AL Draft: 9- 1965 NYJ; 4A-47 1965 DAL Pro: N																															
1967	BC	8	0		1							6	1						26	432	16.6	54	1					1	9	9.0	9
1968	BC	16	1		0														16	137	8.6	26	0								
2	Years	24	1		1							6	1						42	569	13.5	54	1					1	9	9.0	9
DAVE SIDOO David S 6'0 185 British Columbia B: 7/10/1959 New Westminster, BC Draft: 4-82 1982 BC																															
1983	SAS	16																						1	7	7.0	7				
1984	SAS	16							1	0														1	13	13.0	13				
1985	SAS	16	0		4		1.0																					1	0	0.0	0
1986	SAS	16																										1	0	0.0	0
1987	SAS	18				5			7	89																					
1988	BC	4				0																		1	0	0.0	0				
6	Years	86	0		4	5	1.0		8	89														3	20	6.7	13	2	0	0.0	0
BILL SIEKIERSKI William J. DT-OT 6'1 250 Missouri B: 1942 Draft: 10-131 1963 BAL																															
1963	OTT	14																													
1964	OTT	8																													
1965	OTT	4	0		1																										
3	Years	26	0		1																										
MIKE SIGANOS Mike DB 5'9 175 Kentucky B: 5/24/1955																															
1978	HAM	7	0		1				1	0														8	36	4.5	15	11	236	21.5	31
KEN SIGATY Ken FB-E 6'0 207 Edmonton Wildcats Jrs. B: 1944																															
1964	EDM	4																						1	2	2.0	2				
1966	EDM	3																													
2	Years	7																						1	2	2.0	2				
CHRIS SIGLER Christopher Lee DB 6'0 190 Indiana B: 11/19/1962 Owensboro, KY																															
1985	OTT	16	0		1				5	122														15	98	6.5	17	2	22	11.0	11
1986	OTT	9	0		1				6	107		6	1											6	58	9.7	16				
2	Years	25	0		2				11	229		6	1											21	156	7.4	17	2	22	11.0	11
BOB SIKORSKI Robert (Bobo) G 6'1 209 Vancouver Blue Bombers Jrs. B: 1930																															
1954	BC	9			2																										
1955	BC	9																													
2	Years	18	0		2																										

Year	Team	GP	FM	FF	FR	TK	SK	YDS	IR	YDS	PD	PTS	TD	RA	YDS	AVG	LG	TD	REC	YDS	AVG	LG	TD	PR	YDS	AVG	LG	KOR	YDS	AVG	LG
JOE SILIPO Joseph Martin OT 6'3 295 Tulane B: 12/31/1957 Glen Cove, NY Pro: NU																															
1981	MTL	2																													
CRAIG SILVERMAN Craig DT Nevada-Las Vegas																															
1980	SAS	7																													
GARY SILVESTRI Gary DE 6'5 233 Pittsburgh B: 6/20/1955 Oyster Bay, NY																															
1979	WPG	9																													
JIM SILYE Jim DB-FL 5'9 180 Ottawa B: 1946 Draft: 3B- 1969 CAL																															
1969	CAL	16	1		3																			89	566	6.4	22				
1970	CAL	16	2		0														7	135	19.3	49	0	120	729	6.1	22				
1971	CAL	16	1		0																			68	322	4.7	16				
1973	CAL	16	1		0				2	34														62	229	3.7	12				
1974	CAL	16	1		1				1	0														46	326	7.1	20				
1975	CAL	7	1		0				1	19														6	24	4.0	6				
6	Years	87	7		4				4	53									7	135	19.3	49	0	391	2196	5.6	22				
DENNIS SILZER Dennis OE 5'11 200 Regina Rams Jrs. B: 1938																															
1960	SAS	2																													
KEVIN SIMIEN Kevin WR 6'4 202 Oklahoma State; Fort Hays State B: 8/25/1966 Lafayette, LA																															
1992	WPG	1				0													1	11	11.0	11	0								
RAY SIMINSKI Raymond W. OE-DE 6'2 200 Furman B: 6/23/1937 Mount Carmel, PA																															
1959	MTL	11							1	6				2	8	4.0	6	0	17	254	14.9	24	0								
1960	MTL	2																	6	80	13.3	16	0								
2	Years	13							1	6				2	8	4.0	6	0	23	334	14.5	24	0								
CHRISTIAN SIMMERLING Christian DB 6'1 215 St. Mary's (Nova Scotia) B: 10/25/1981 Draft: 5A-37 2004 CAL																															
2004	CAL	8				5																									
BRIAN SIMMONS Brian OT 6'4 315 Oklahoma B: 3/16/1985																															
2011	HAM	10	0	0	1	0																									
CHARLIE SIMMONS Charlie WR 6'3 215 Georgia Tech B: 8/25/1972 Draft: 6-173 1995 GB																															
1997	HAM	1				0													1	0	0.0	0	0								
DWAYNE SIMMONS Dwayne LB 6'1 220 Northeastern Oklahoma A&M JC; Georgia B: 2/21/1970																															
1992	HAM	6	2		2	22	1.0		1	-2																					
JASON SIMMONS Jason DT-DE 6'5 265 Ohio State B: 12/20/1970 Akron, OH Pro: E																															
1994	HAM	6				10					1																				
1997	SAS	8	0	0	1	15	1.0	6.0			1																				
2	Years	14	0	0	1	25	1.0	6.0			2																				
JASPER SIMMONS Jasper LB 6'1 205 Hutchinson CC; Missouri B: 8/20/1989																															
2011	TOR	2				3			1	25	0																	1	6	6.0	6
JOHN SIMMONS John (J.B.) FL-TE 6'3 200 Nebraska-Omaha; Northeastern Oklahoma A&M JC; Tulsa B: 10/1/1939 Draft: 14-108(f) 1963 BUF; 6A-76(f) 1963 GB																															
1964	WPG	8										6	1						20	301	15.1	53	1								
KELVIN SIMMONS Kelvin QB 5'11 195 Northwest Mississippi CC; Troy B: 2/15/1970 Mobile, AL																															
1995	BIR	16	1		1	0						20	3	17	136	8.0	24	3													
1999	TOR	1				0																									
2	Years	17	1		1	0						20	3	17	136	8.0	24	3													
KING SIMMONS King David DB 6'2 199 Texas Tech B: 2/12/1963 Atlanta, GA Draft: 12-319 1986 CLE Pro: N																															
1988	HAM	1				3																									
MARCELLO SIMMONS Marcello Muhammad CB 6'1 180 Southern Methodist B: 8/8/1971 Tomball, TX Draft: 4-90 1993 CIN Pro: N																															
1995	TOR	5				16			1	4	3																				
1996	TOR	16				49			1	10	4																				
1997	TOR	18	0	0	1	52	4.0	25.0			2	6	1																		
1998	TOR	15	0	1	2	43	4.0	29.0			3	6	1											1	7	7.0	7				
1999	EDM	18	0	2	1	68	1.0	9.0			6																				
2000	BC	3				10					1																				
2000	TOR	12	0	1	2	33			1	14	3																				
2000	Year	15	0	1	2	43			1	14	4																				
2001	TOR	18				54			4	83	9	6	1																		
7	Years	93	0	4	6	325	9.0	63.0	7	111	31	18	3											1	7	7.0	7				
RAMSEY SIMMONS Ramsey LB 6'2 230 Arizona Western JC; Hawaii B: 1951																															
1976	CAL	1																													
RON SIMMONS Ronald K. LB 6'1 260 Florida State B: 5/15/1959 Perry, GA Draft: 6-160 1981 CLE Pro: U																															
1981	OTT	6	0		1		3.0																								
SHANE SIMMONS Shane LB 6'1 230 Idaho; Western Washington B: 8/9/1985																															
2009	BC	3				2																									
TERRANCE SIMMONS Terrance Demon OT 6'8 310 Alabama State B: 5/3/1976 Moss Point, MS Pro: EN																															
2000	TOR	1				0																									
TONY SIMMONS Anthony Earl DT 6'4 268 Tennessee B: 12/18/1962 Draft: 12A-318 1985 SD; TD 1985 MEM-USFL Pro: N																															
1989	BC	1				1																									
1990	BC	4				1	1.0																								
2	Years	5				2	1.0																								
TONY SIMMONS Tony De'Angelo WR 6'1 210 Wisconsin B: 12/8/1974 Chicago, IL Draft: 2A-52 1998 NE Pro: EN																															
2005	BC	5				1						6	1						15	218	14.5	54	1								
2006	BC	2				0						6	1						11	183	16.6	70	1					2	87	43.5	73
2007	BC	8	1	0	2	1						12	2						8	118	14.8	30	2								
3	Years	15	1	0	2	2						24	4						34	519	15.3	70	4					2	87	43.5	73
RANDY SIMMRIN Randall D. WR 6'0 170 Southern California B: 11/5/1956 Los Angeles, CA																															
1980	EDM	1	1		0														2	29	14.5	22	0								
EDDIE SIMMS Ed HB 5'11 190 none B: 1934																															
1956	CAL	11	1		1														5	52	10.4	21	0	13	55	4.2	10				
1958	SAS	2												1	9	9.0	9	0													
1959	TOR	1							1	17														2	15	7.5	13				
3	Years	14	1		1				1	17				1	9	9.0	9	0	5	52	10.4	21	0	15	70	4.7	13				
DON SIMON Donald HB 5'11 172 Edmonton Jrs. B: 1931																															
1949	EDM	14										5	1					1													
1950	EDM	9										10	2	34	214	6.3		2													
1951	EDM	8												20	52	2.6		0	1	56	56.0	56	0	3	28	9.3		4	37	9.3	
1952	EDM	16												13	60	4.6	14	0	2	17	8.5	13	0	2	16	8.0	9	5	117	23.4	41
1953	EDM	16										10	2	17	81	4.8		2	4	80	20.0		0					2	29	14.5	
1954	EDM	1																													
1955	EDM	10	3		0									9	57	6.3	15	0	2	30	15.0	20	0	36	214	5.9	19	3	45	15.0	18
1956	EDM	4	1		0									2	16	8.0	15	0						7	37	5.3	7	3	54	18.0	31
1957	EDM	10	2		0									6	27	4.5	9	0	1	26	26.0	26	0	13	80	6.2	16				
9	Years	88	6		0							25	5	101	507	5.0	15	5	10	209	20.9	56	0	61	375	6.1	19	17	282	16.6	41
GEROY SIMON Geroy Albert SB-WR 6'0 183 Maryland B: 9/11/1975 Johnstown, PA																															
1999	WPG	10				5													34	306	9.0	25	0	1	1	1.0	1				
2000	WPG	17	0	0	1	5						42	7	1	10	10.0	10	0	51	725	14.2	80	7								
2001	BC	6				1						6	1						14	182	13.0	33	1	19	107	5.6	21	9	169	18.8	44
2002	BC	17	2	0	0	4						12	2	4	25	6.3	12	0	50	754	15.1	42	2	51	464	9.1	47	19	385	20.3	46
2003	BC*	18	1	0	0	3						86	14	7	135	19.3	88	1	94	1687	17.9	103	13	16	86	5.4	38	10	256	25.6	51
2004	BC*	18	1	0	1	3						84	14	4	25	6.3	26	0	103	1750	17.0	89	14	1	5	5.0	5	7	123	17.6	30
2005	BC	18	1	0	0	3						62	10	1	-1	-1.0	-1	0	89	1322	14.9	83	10	4	33	8.3	21	1	0	0.0	0
2006	BC*	18				1						90	15	2	5	2.5	4	0	105	1856	17.7	92	15					1	0	0.0	0
2007	BC*	18	1	0	0	3						36	6	1	4	4.0	4	0	72	1308	18.2	96	6								
2008	BC*	16				4						60	10	1	3	3.0	3	0	82	1418	17.3	79	10								
2009	BC+	18				7						36	6						79	1239	15.7	62	6								

Year	Team	GP	FM	FF	FR	TK	SK	YDS	IR	YDS	PD	PTS	TD	RA	YDS	AVG	LG	TD	REC	YDS	AVG	LG	TD	PR	YDS	AVG	LG	KOR	YDS	AVG	LG
2010	BC	18	4	0	1	2						38	6	1	-8	-8.0	0	0	78	1190	15.3	98	6					1	3	3.0	3
2011	BC*	18	2	0	1	2						48	8	1	-4	-4.0	-4	0	84	1350	16.1	63	8								
13	Years	210	12	0	4	43						600	99	23	194	8.4	88	1	935	15087	16.1	103	98	92	696	7.6	47	48	936	19.5	51
WILFRED SIMON Wilffed DT 6'3 245 Tulane																															
1982	HAM	1																													
C.B. SIMONS Carlton B. C 6'2 230 Stanford B: 1942 Draft: 24-189 1963 DEN; 4B-56 1963 GB																															
1963	EDM	5																													
KEN SIMONTON Kenneth Paul RB 5'8 191 Oregon State B: 6/7/1979 Pittsburg, CA Pro: EN																															
2007	CAL	1				0						6	1	18	114	6.3	33	1	4	33	8.3	16	0					1	12	12.0	12
MOE SIMOVITCH Maurice Freedman C 6'0 210 Winnipeg YMHA Jrs. B: 1918 Elmwood, MB D: 2/8/1997 Deer Lodge, MB																															
1949	WPG	9																													
AL SIMPSON Allen Ralph, Jr. OT 6'5 255 McCook CC; Colorado State B: 7/27/1951 Pittsburgh, PA Draft: 2-27 1975 NYG Pro: N																															
1977	BC	1																													
1978	BC	11																													
2	Years	12																													
BARRIN SIMPSON Barrin LB 5'11 242 Mississippi State B: 10/1/1977 St. Louis, MO																															
2001	BC*	18	0	0	3	116	2.0	16.0	1	0																					
2002	BC*	18	0	0	1	92	6.0	61.0	2	4	3	6	1																		
2003	BC*	18	0	0	3	99	4.0	17.0	1	0	2																				
2004	BC*	18	0	4	3	91			2	9	3	6	1																		
2005	BC	18	0	2	1	77	6.0	35.0	1	17	1																	1	12	12.0	12
2006	WPG*	18	0	2	2	118	3.0	29.0	1	1	2																				
2007	WPG*	18	0	1	2	118	4.0	34.0	1	34	0																				
2008	WPG	3				29	2.0	12.0																							
2009	WPG	13	0	2	1	87	2.0	5.0	1	9	3																				
2010	SAS+	18	0	1	2	107	3.0	10.0			1																				
2011	SAS	16	0	1	0	72	5.0	35.0			1																				
11	Years	176	0	13	18	1006	37.0	254.0	10	74	16	12	2															1	12	12.0	12
BOB SIMPSON Bob OE-FW-S 6'0 200 Western Ontario* B: 4/20/1930 Windsor, ON D: 11/28/2007																															
1950	OTT	11										5	1										1								
1951	OTT+	12										35	7										6								
1952	OTT+	12										17	3										2								
1953	OTT+	13										15	3										3								
1954	OTT	11							1	0		30	6						37	767	20.7	85	6	1	6	6.0	6				
1955	OTT	12							5	135		60	12						23	676	29.4	74	9	6	83	13.8	55	5	57	11.4	18
1956	OTT+	14							4	27		42	7	1	-1	-1.0	-1	0	47	1030	21.9	58	7	25	162	6.5	23	4	49	12.3	21
1957	OTT+	14							6	31		42	7						31	703	22.7	65	7	21	125	6.0	21				
1958	OTT+	14							3	31		18	3						23	583	25.3	77	3	3	23	7.7	20				
1959	OTT+	14										48	8						36	787	21.9	59	8	5	24	4.8	10	2	41	20.5	31
1960	OTT	14							1	0		36	6						30	607	20.2	57	6	2	8	4.0	5	3	35	11.7	17
1961	OTT	14										18	3	0	4		4	0	20	428	21.4	63	3					2	22	11.0	12
1962	OTT	14										24	4						27	453	16.8	46	4					1	9	9.0	9
13	Years	169							20	224		390	70	1	3	3.0	4	0	274	6034	22.0	85	65	63	431	6.8	55	17	213	12.5	31
HUBERT SIMPSON Hubert RB 6'1 225 Tennessee B: 7/2/1958 Athens, TN Draft: 10-258 1981 CIN																															
1981	TOR	7	1		0							6	1	73	308	4.2	17	1	12	111	9.3	22	0	4	25	6.3	18	1	5	5.0	5
HUGH SIMPSON Hugh FB-HB 5'9 190 none B: 1939 Carleton Place, ON																															
1957	MTL	5												1	4	4.0	4	0													
1958	CAL	11	1		0									18	93	5.2	47	0										1	20	20.0	20
1959	CAL	1																													
3	Years	17	1		0									19	97	5.1	47	0										1	20	20.0	20
JACKI SIMPSON Jack Maylon OG-LB-DG-K 6'0 225 Mississippi B: 8/20/1936 Corinth, MS D: 6/2/1983 Pontiac, MI Draft: 21-246 1958 WAS Pro: N																															
1958	MTL+	14							1	0																					
1959	MTL	14																													
1960	MTL+	13							1	28																					
1961	MTL	1																													
1961	CAL	2																													
1961	Year	3																													
1965	WPG	8							1			22	0																		
1965	TOR	4	0		1							2	0																		
1965	Year	12							1			24	0																		
5	Years	50	0		1				3	28		48	0																		
JACKIE SIMPSON John S 5'10 183 Florida B: 4/2/1934 Miami, FL Draft: 4-44 1957 BAL Pro: N																															
1963	TOR	8							3	72				10	33	3.3	17	0	1	33	33.0	33	0	20	120	6.0	15	3	51	17.0	19
1964	HAM	13	1		2				5	78														19	117	6.2	16	3	61	20.3	34
1965	MTL	14	2		1				4	35		12	2	3	12	4.0	6	0	3	14	4.7	5	0	2	13	6.5	7	13	294	22.6	55
1966	MTL	12							2	24				1	2	2.0	2	0	2	23	11.5	15	0					7	167	23.9	33
4	Years	47	3		3				14	209		12	2	14	47	3.4	17	0	6	70	11.7	33	0	41	250	6.1	16	26	573	22.0	55
JUWAN SIMPSON Juwan LB-DE 6'2 231 Alabama B: 7/8/1984 Decatur, AL																															
2008	CAL	14	0	2	0	33	2.0	10.0																							
2009	CAL	5	0	1	0	14	1.0	8.0																							
2010	CAL*	17	1	1	3	88	7.0	28.0	1	23	4																				
2011	CAL	13	0	1	1	56	1.0	5.0			1																				
4	Years	49	1	5	4	191	11.0	51.0	1	23	5																				
LARRY SIMPSON Larry TE 6'4 225 Wilfrid Laurier B: 2/7/1950 Draft: 1B-5 1974 TOR																															
1974	TOR	16	1		1							6	1						22	246	11.2	24	1								
1975	TOR	16																	1	14	14.0	14	0					1	6	6.0	6
2	Years	32	1		1							6	1						23	260	11.3	24	1					1	6	6.0	6
TETO SIMPSON Teto DT 6'4 271 North Carolina B: 7/19/1976 Scranton, NC Pro: E																															
2003	MTL	3				5																									
2004	MTL	18	0	0	2	21	7.0		0	0	1																				
2	Years	21	0	0	2	26	7.0																								
E.A. SIMS E.A., Jr. TE-DE 6'2 215 New Mexico State B: 2/10/1937 Abilene, TX Draft: 24- 1961 DEN; 15-203 1961 BAL																															
1962	EDM	12	0		2							12	2						12	177	14.8	27	1								
1963	EDM	16	0		1							6	1						7	95	13.6	35	1					1	3	3.0	3
1964	EDM	12																	4	78	19.5	42	0								
1965	EDM+	16	0		1														5	85	17.0	31	0								
1966	EDM*	16	0		1							6	1						2	54	27.0	37	1								
1967	EDM*	14							1	0		6	1						3	66	22.0	38	1								
1968	EDM	11																	22	318	14.5		0								
1968	BC	5										6	1						8	124	15.5		1					1	1	1.0	1
1968	Year	16										6	1						30	442	14.7	29	1					1	1	1.0	1
1969	BC	4																													
1970	BC	1																										1	0	0.0	0
9	Years	102	0		5				1	0		36	6						63	997	15.8	42	5					3	4	1.3	3
FREDDIE SIMS Frederic W. RB 5'10 215 Oklahoma B: 1/4/1963 Sacramento, CA Draft: TD 1985 SA-USFL																															
1985	BC	2	3		0									30	166	5.5	27	0	4	24	6.0	13	0					2	43	21.5	25
1986	CAL	1												5	2	0.4	2	0	2	14	7.0	9	0								
1987	BC	2	2		0	1						12	2	40	182	4.6	16	1	6	78	13.0	25	1								
3	Years	5	5		0	1						12	2	75	350	4.7	27	1	12	116	9.7	25	1					2	43	21.5	25
KELLY SIMS Kelly CB 5'10 190 Cincinnati B: 11/10/1970 St. Petersburg, FL Pro: E																															
1993	BC	6				25																									
1994	BC	7				13			2	11	4																				

Year	Team	GP	FM	FF	FR	TK	SK	YDS	IR	YDS	PD	PTS	TD	RA	YDS	AVG	LG	TD	REC	YDS	AVG	LG	TD	PR	YDS	AVG	LG	KOR	YDS	AVG	LG
1995	BC	13	0		2	34			2	63	3																				
1996	BC	9				31			1	57	0																				
1998	BC	1				4																									
5	Years	36	0		2	107			5	131	7																				
RUDY SIMS Rudolph Edison DT-DE 6'0 255 Florida A&M B: 10/25/1948 Tampa, FL																															
1971	OTT+	14			2																										
1972	OTT+	14	0		3				1	26		6	1																		
1973	OTT*	14																													
1974	OTT+	16																													
1975	OTT	13	0		3																										
1976	OTT	16			1																										
1977	OTT	1																													
1977	TOR	3																													
1977	Year	4																													
1978	HAM	3																													
8	Years	91	0		9				1	26		6	1																		
DON SINCLAIR Don T-G 5'10 230																															
1948	HAM	10																													
IAN SINCLAIR Ian C-OG 6'4 260 London Beefeaters Jrs.; Miami (Florida) B: 7/22/1960 Toronto, ON Draft: 2-2 1984 MTL; TD 1985 ORL-USFL																															
1985	BC	5	0		2																							1	12	12.0	12
1986	BC	18																													
1987	BC	18				1																									
1988	BC	18				3																									
1989	BC	18	0		1	2																									
1990	BC	18				2																									
1991	BC	18				3																									
1992	BC	16	1		0	4																									
1993	BC	18	0		1	1																									
1994	BC	16				1																									
1995	BC	17				1																									
11	Years	180	1		4	18																						1	12	12.0	12
MARK SINGER Mark LB 5'11 230 Alberta B: 12/23/1967 Saskatoon, SK Draft: 2-13 1990 CAL																															
1990	CAL	18	0		1	12			1	20																					
1991	CAL	16	0		2	43			1	8																					
1992	CAL	4				2																									
3	Years	38	0		3	57			2	28																					
RUDY SINGER Rudy G 5'7 175 B: 1924 D: 8/18/2007 Calgary, AB																															
1947	CAL	1																													
1948	CAL	10																													
1949	CAL	5																													
3	Years	16																													
BOBBY SINGH Sandeep OG 6'3 315 Hawaii; Portland State B: 11/25/1975 Ba, Fiji Draft: 1-8 1999 CAL Pro: X																															
2002	CAL	17				2																									
2003	CAL	18				1																									
2004	BC	13	0	0	1	0																									
2005	BC	16				0																									
2006	BC	13				1																									
2007	CAL	17				0																									
2008	WPG	4				0																									
2009	BC	10				1																									
8	Years	108	0	0	1	5																									
HARVEY SINGLETON Harvey E 5'8 200 Kentucky State D: 12//2000																															
1952	TOR	1																													
JOHN SINGLETON John Steven DE 6'5 260 Texas-El Paso B: 12/22/1956 Houston, TX Draft: 11-303 1980 SD																															
1980	BC	2																													
RON SINGLETON Ronald Lee OT 6'7 245 Grambling State B: 4/15/1952 New Orleans, LA Draft: 4B-113 1976 SD Pro: N																															
1981	MTL	13																													
BRAD SINOPOLI Brad QB 6'4 210 Ottawa B: 4/14/1988 Peterborough, ON Draft: 4-29 2011 CAL																															
2011	CAL	18				1																									
MIKE SIROISHKA Mike WR 5'10 160 Calgary B: 12/27/1963 Calgary, AB Draft: 3-22 1986 TOR																															
1986	TOR	16										12	2						11	142	12.9	26	2								
1987	TOR	9				0													12	103	8.6	20	0								
1988	TOR	10				2													3	26	8.7	13	0								
1988	CAL	4				0						6	1						3	95	31.7	62	1					1	31	31.0	31
1988	Year	14				2						6	1						6	131	21.8	62	1					1	31	31.0	31
3	Years	35				2						18	3						29	366	12.6	62	3					1	31	31.0	31
JORDAN SISCO Jordan WR 6'0 212 Regina B: 2/24/1988 Draft: 2-8 2010 SAS																															
2011	SAS	8				0													2	13	6.5	8	0								
CAMERON SISKOWIC Cameron Carson LB 6'2 225 Washington State; Illinois State B: 4/10/1984 San Diego, CA																															
2008	HAM	6	0	1	1	28																									
ED SIUCIAK Ed LB 6'2 225 St. Mary's (Nova Scotia) B: 8/10/1952																															
1976	HAM	2																													
PAUL SKANSI Paul Anthony SB 5'11 185 Washington B: 1/11/1961 Tacoma, WA Draft: 5A-133 1983 PIT; 4-39 1983 MIC-USFL Pro: N																															
1992	OTT	2				1													2	25	12.5	23	0								
NEAL SKARIN Neal S. DT 6'4 250 Pasadena CC; Arizona State B: 9/13/1952 Elmhurst, IL Draft: 16-393 1974 SD; 12-138 1974 SC-WFL Pro: W																															
1976	BC	16																													
BOB SKEMP Robert OG-OT-DL 6'0 265 Richmond Raiders Jrs.; British Columbia B: 7/21/1963 La Crosse, WI Draft: 3B-27 1986 BC																															
1986	BC	8	0		1																							2	34	17.0	19
1987	TOR	16				0																									
1988	TOR	13				1																									
1989	TOR	11	0		1	1																									
1990	TOR	18				1																									
1991	TOR	14	0		2	2																									
1992	TOR	14				2																									
7	Years	94	0		4	7																						2	34	17.0	19
RAY SKERRETT Ray HB 5'9 165 Montreal New York Fashions Jrs. B: 1929																															
1949	OTT	2										5	1																		
1950	MTL	5																													
2	Years	7										5	1																		
ART SKIDMORE Art FW 6'0 none B: 1922																															
1946	TOR	9										8	1																		
1947	TOR	1																													
2	Years	10										8	1																		
RUFUS SKILLERN Rufus Earl WR 6'0 184 San Jose State B: 5/12/1982 Oakland, CA																															
2008	BC	5	0	1	0	0						6	1						19	188	9.9	20	1								
2009	BC	6				2													15	182	12.1	46	0								
2	Years	11	0	1	0	2						6	1						34	370	10.9	46	1								
VINCE SKILLINGS Vincent Scott DB 5'11 180 Ohio State B: 5/3/1959 Latrobe, PA Draft: 6-163 1981 DAL																															
1981	MTL	1																													
1982	MTL	1	0		1																										
1983	MTL	6	0		2		1.0		1	10																					
3	Years	8	0		3		1.0		1	10																					

Year	Team	GP	FM	FF	FR	TK	SK	YDS	IR	YDS	PD	PTS	TD	RA	YDS	AVG	LG	TD	REC	YDS	AVG	LG	TD	PR	YDS	AVG	LG	KOR	YDS	AVG	LG
ROD SKILLMAN Rodney DE 6'3 260 Missouri B: 4/23/1960 Mobley, MS Pro: U																															
1984	HAM	8	0		1		3.5		1	1																					
1985	HAM	8	0		1		2.0																								
1986	HAM	16					9.0																								
1987	HAM	16				31	8.0																								
1988	HAM	18				33	17.0																								
1989	HAM	16	0		3	34	4.0																								
1990	HAM	10	0		2	16	2.0																								
7	Years	92	0		7	114	45.5		1	1																					
CHRIS SKINNER Chris RB 5'11 212 Bishop's B: 12/18/1961 St. John, NB Draft: 1B-7 1984 EDM																															
1984	EDM	13	0		1									14	63	4.5	24	0	1	11	11.0	11	0					1	0	0.0	0
1985	EDM	16	2		1							12	2	39	248	6.4	40	1	13	146	11.2	31	1	1	11	11.0	11	14	255	18.2	25
1986	EDM	17	6		0							24	4	128	605	4.7	58	2	52	637	12.3	56	2					3	59	19.7	30
1987	EDM	18	5		1	4						24	4	84	369	4.4	43	0	52	518	10.0	43	4					1	15	15.0	15
1988	EDM	18	6		0	2						36	6	118	528	4.5	60	4	31	317	10.2	69	2								
1989	OTT	14	3		1	2						26	4	40	175	4.4	22	3	30	305	10.2	36	1					1	0	0.0	0
1990	BC	18	4		2	3						6	1	102	603	5.9	36	0	48	415	8.6	23	1								
1991	BC	18	2		0	3						18	3	45	269	6.0	49	2	51	525	10.3	48	1								
1993	BC	8				1						12	2	10	52	5.2	19	2	8	79	9.9	29	0								
9	Years	140	28		6	15						158	26	580	2912	5.0	60	14	286	2953	10.3	69	12	1	11	11.0	11	20	329	16.5	30
LEN SKINNER Len LB 6'2 220 none B: 1939																															
1959	CAL	13							1																						
1960	CAL	3	0		1																										
2	Years	16	0		1				1	0																					
HARRY SKIPPER Harry Gordon CB 5'11 175 South Carolina B: 2/4/1960 Baxley, GA Draft: TD 1983 WAS-USFL																															
1983	MTL*	15	1		3				10	198		6	1																		
1984	MTL*	16	1		2				8	253		18	3																		
1985	MTL	16	0		2		1.0		7	121		6	1											29	473	16.3	89				
1986	SAS	5							2	72		6	1											11	44	4.0	15				
1987	SAS+	18	2		0	48			8	198														15	44	2.9	29				
1988	SAS	18				40			8	185		6	1																		
1989	SAS	18	1		0	57			4	40														1	14	14.0	14				
7	Years	106	5		7	145	1.0		47	1067		42	7											56	575	10.3	89				
JOHN SKLOPAN John Joseph S 5'11 190 Southern Mississippi B: 9/12/1940 Pittsburgh, PA Draft: 8-64 1963 KC; 12-156 1963 MIN Pro: N																															
1965	EDM	12	0		1				3	34																		2	41	20.5	21
LAWRIE SKOLROOD Lawrence E. TE-OT-OG 6'4 240 North Dakota B: 4/2/1952 Saskatoon, SK Draft: TE 1974 SAS; 17-438 1974 DAL																															
1974	SAS	13																	10	109	10.9	24	0								
1975	HAM	16	2		1							6	1	0	1		1	0	32	400	12.5	31	1								
1976	HAM	14										12	2						15	226	15.1	43	2								
1977	HAM	16																	24	317	13.2	28	0								
1978	HAM	16	0		1							30	4	1	-14	-14.0	-14	0	40	661	16.5	57	4	1	1	1.0	1				
1979	HAM	8																	17	275	16.2	32	0								
1979	SAS	8																	14	189	13.5	42	0					1	0	0.0	0
1979	Year	16																	31	464	15.0	42	0					1	0	0.0	0
1980	SAS	12																	7	68	9.7	15	0					1	0	0.0	0
1981	SAS	12																													
1982	SAS	16	0		1																										
1983	SAS	16																													
1984	SAS	16	0		1																										
1985	SAS	16																	1	-1	-1.0	-1	0								
1986	SAS	18																													
1987	SAS	18				0																									
14	Years	207	2		4	0						48	7	1	-13	-13.0	1	0	160	2244	14.0	57	7	1	1	1.0	1	2	0	0.0	0
CHRIS SKOPELIANOS Chris DB 5'10 185 Western Ontario B: 8/9/1949 Florina, Greece Draft: 3-20 1973 TOR																															
1976	MTL	5																													
1976	HAM	4																													
1976	CAL	2																													
1976	Year	11																													
ANTE SKORPUT Ante OG 6'3 290 Michigan B: 12/24/1971 Draft: 2-22 1995 WPG																															
1996	OTT	1				0																									
DAVE SKRIEN David Albert LB-FB 6'1 208 Minnesota B: 4/4/1929 Brooten, MN D: 11/30/2010 Mound, MN																															
1953	WPG	9							1	45				2	1	0.5	2	0										1	15	15.0	15
ED SLABIKOWSKI Ed DB 6'2 205 Windsor B: 1/16/1960 Draft: 6-46 1983 MTL																															
1983	MTL	12																	2	38	19.0	21	0								
REGGIE SLACK Reginald Bernard QB 6'2 221 Auburn B: 5/2/1968 Milton, FL Draft: 12-321 1990 HOU Pro: E																															
1993	TOR	11	6		0	1						12	2	27	172	6.4	31	2													
1994	TOR	7	1		1	0								17	138	8.1	25	0													
1994	HAM	7	3		0	1						12	2	35	179	5.1	19	2													
1994	Year	14	4		1	1						12	2					2													
1995	BIR	2	1		1	0								8	53	6.6	14	0													
1995	WPG	15	7		2	1						24	4	52	356	6.8	48	4													
1995	Year	17	8		3	1						24	4	60	409	6.8	48	4													
1996	WPG	15	3		0	0						12	2	28	187	6.7	18	2													
1997	SAS	15	7	0	1	1						24	4	53	406	7.7	36	4													
1998	SAS	18	8	0	0	1						54	9	87	650	7.5	44	9													
1999	SAS	12	9	0	2	1						18	3	39	185	4.7	24	3													
2002	TOR	11	3	0	1	1						12	2	33	255	7.7	36	2													
2003	HAM	3	2	0	0	0								4	-3	-0.8	3	0													
9	Years	94	50	0	8	7						168	28	383	2578	6.7	48	28													
LAMAR SLADE Lamar WR 6'4 215 Pittsburgh B: 11/8/1980																															
2004	HAM	5	0	0	1	0													8	128	16.0	41	0								
JOHN SLAFKOSKY John T 6'4 250 Notre Dame B: 7/30/1941 Draft: 16-213 1963 STL																															
1964	SAS	1																													
LARRY SLAGLE Larry Michael OG 6'3 250 UCLA B: 7/19/1946 Okemah, OK Draft: 11-285 1968 STL																															
1968	WPG	13																													
1969	WPG	11			1																										
1970	WPG	16	0		1																										
1971	WPG	16												1	24	24.0	24	0													
4	Years	56	0		2									1	24	24.0	24	0													
DARRELL SLATER Darrell DB 5'9 170 Northeast Louisiana B: 2/26/1963 Shreveport, LA																															
1986	BC	8	0		1		1.0		1	7														1	8	8.0	8				
TONY SLATON Tony DB 6'0 190 Texas A&M B: 5/24/1963																															
1986	SAS	4																													
RASHAUD SLAUGHTER Rashaud 5'9 185 Alabama-Birmingham B: 11/1/1987 Birmingham, AL																															
2011	MTL	1			0																			3	22	7.3	10	5	90	18.0	22
LEROY SLEDGE Leroy James, Jr. FB-OHB-OE 6'2 230 Bakersfield JC B: 10/11/1946 Richmond, VA Pro: N																															
1967	BC	16	2		1							36	6	58	288	5.0	62	2	41	911	22.2	81	4					9	226	25.1	60
1968	BC	12	1		0									65	219	3.4	15	0	14	69	4.9	14	0					11	228	20.7	26
1969	BC	6	2		0							12	2	37	179	4.8	18	2	8	66	8.3	24	0					6	139	23.2	34
1970	EDM	1												5	7	1.4	9	0	1	5	5.0	5	0								
4	Years	35	5		1							48	8	165	693	4.2	62	4	64	1051	16.4	81	4					26	593	22.8	60
LEO SLOAN Leo RB 5'9 180 Linfield B: 6/18/1958																															

Year	Team	GP	FM	FF	FR	TK	SK	YDS	IR	YDS	PD	PTS	TD	RA	YDS	AVG	LG	TD	REC	YDS	AVG	LG	TD	PR	YDS	AVG	LG	KOR	YDS	AVG	LG
1980	BC	4	1		1									30	152	5.1	19	0	7	59	8.4	14	0	2	19	9.5	10	5	134	26.8	29
KEN SLUMAN Ken HB-E 6'2 194 B: 1924																															
1946	CAL	7																													
1947	CAL+	8										5	1																		
1949	EDM	8										8	1										1								
1950	EDM	1										1	0																		
4	Years	24										14	2										1								
JIGGY SMAHA Jiggy Ephram LB 6'2 235 Georgia B: 9/19/1946 Hazelton, PA Draft: 14-358 1969 CLE																															
1968	BC	8	0		1																										
TED SMALE Ted DE-OE 6'2 210 Toronto B: 1932 Draft: 1-5 1956 TOR																															
1956	OTT	14							1	5		6	1						1	19	19.0	19	0					1	13	13.0	13
1957	OTT	14										12	2															4	52	13.0	18
1958	OTT	14																	1	22	22.0	22	0					3	38	12.7	17
1959	OTT	14										12	2						24	490	20.4	49	2					1	11	11.0	11
1960	OTT	4																	1	23	23.0	23	0					1	5	5.0	5
1961	OTT	13										6	1						1	7	7.0	7	1								
1962	OTT	14																	6	88	14.7	20	0								
7	Years	87							1	5		36	6						34	649	19.1	49	3					10	119	11.9	18
DARNELL SMALL Darnell LB 6'0 230 Nicholls State B: 3/21/1974 New Orleans, LA																															
1996	WPG	4				17	1.0	4.0	1	34	1	6	1																		
1997	WPG	4	0	0	2	23	1.0	11.0																				2	4	2.0	4
1997	SAS	5				16																									
1997	Year	9	0	0	2	39	1.0	11.0																				2	4	2.0	4
1998	SAS	9	0	1	0	47	1.0	2.0			1																				
3	Years	17	0	1	2	103	3.0	17.0	1	34	2	6	1															2	4	2.0	4
ED SMALL Ed WR 6'1 185 Mississippi B: 9/12/1972 Jacksonville, FL																															
1995	OTT	6	1		0	5													9	118	13.1	27	0	16	108	6.8	20	16	318	19.9	36
GEORGE SMALL George Michael DT 6'2 260 Allegheny CC; North Carolina A&T State B: 11/18/1956 Shreveport, LA Pro: N																															
1981	CAL	6																													
1982	CAL	14					8.0																								
1983	CAL	2					3.5																								
3	Years	22					11.5																								
JESSIE SMALL Jessie Lee LB 6'3 239 Eastern Kentucky B: 11/30/1966 Boston, GA Draft: 2-49 1989 PHI Pro: N																															
1994	OTT	16	0		1	44	7.0	59.0	1	5	0	6	1																		
1995	HAM	17	1		1	44	11.0	107.0			1																				
1996	HAM	9	0		1	21	4.0	34.0			1																				
3	Years	42	1		3	109	22.0	200.0	1	5	2	6	1																		
SEAN SMALLS Sean Ramon CB 6'1 210 Massachusetts B: 4/20/1987 Richmond, VA																															
2010	TOR	1				4																									
2011	TOR	18	0	1	1	64			1	2	3																				
2	Years	19	0	1	1	68			1	2	3																				
IAN SMART Ian RB 5'8 192 C.W. Post B: 2/28/1980 Kingston, Jamaica Pro: EN																															
2006	MTL	1	1	0	0	0																		5	18	3.6	13				
2006	BC	6	1	0	0	0								10	39	3.9	10	0	1	5	5.0	5	0	27	263	9.7	27	14	324	23.1	44
2006	Year	7	2	0	0	0								10	39	3.9	10	0	1	5	5.0	5	0	32	281	8.8	27	14	324	23.1	44
2007	BC*	18	6	0	1	2						24	4	32	158	4.9	18	3	2	17	8.5	10	0	92	912	9.9	81	53	1228	23.2	88
2008	BC+	17	2	0	0	2						6	1	8	95	11.9	42	0	3	16	5.3	13	0	85	782	9.2	43	74	1805	24.4	91
2009	BC	7	1	0	0	1								5	26	5.2	13	0	1	21	21.0	21	0	16	119	7.4	16	20	399	20.0	27
4	Years	43	11	0	1	5						30	5	55	318	5.8	42	3	7	59	8.4	21	0	225	2094	9.3	81	161	3756	23.3	91
JOHN SMART John HB 5'10 185 Verdun Ints. B: 1937																															
1958	SAS	9												3	3	1.0	1	0													
ROD SMART Torrold D. (He Hate Me) RB 5'11 200 Western Kentucky B: 1/9/1977 Lakeland, FL Pro: NX																															
2001	EDM	1				0																		2	11	5.5	9	5	82	16.4	25
STEVE SMEAR Steve DE-LB 6'1 235 Penn State B: 5/18/1948 Johnstown, PA Draft: 4-95 1970 BAL																															
1970	MTL*	14																													
1971	MTL+	14	0		1																										
1972	MTL	14																													
1973	TOR	2																													
1974	SAS	13	0		1				1	1																					
5	Years	57	0		2				1	1																					
KEVIN SMELLIE Kevin RB 5'10 190 Massachusetts B: 7/27/1966 Battersey, England Draft: 1A-2 1989 SAS																															
1990	TOR	18	2		0	1						18	3	86	394	4.6	33	1	30	212	7.1	19	2					3	70	23.3	26
1991	TOR	18	3		2	15						12	2	48	252	5.3	21	2	7	57	8.1	17	0					3	27	9.0	19
1992	TOR	18	0		1	4						42	7	38	212	5.6	65	4	12	193	16.1	61	3								
1994	TOR	18				6						24	4	19	80	4.2	26	4	1	20	20.0	20	0								
4	Years	72	5		3	26						96	16	191	938	4.9	65	11	50	482	9.6	61	5					6	97	16.2	26
ADRION SMITH Adrion Carlos CB 5'10 185 Missouri State B: 9/29/1971 Kansas City, MO																															
1994	HAM	14	1		0	33	2.0	0.0	4	102	15													34	247	7.3	30	2	42	21.0	26
1995	MEM	15	5		1	19						6	1											47	519	11.0	94	14	261	18.6	58
1996	TOR+	15	1		0	42			5	71	18	6	1															0	11		11
1997	TOR+	18	0	1	2	70			5	73	13	12	2											7	51	7.3	25				
1998	TOR	8				32			2	0	8	6	1															2	47	23.5	32
1999	TOR*	18	3	0	1	27			6	149	8	6	1	6	25	4.2	11	0						52	430	8.3	45	2	13	6.5	8
2000	TOR	18	2	1	2	53			3	3	9													35	316	9.0	44	8	159	19.9	30
2001	TOR	18	3	1	3	34			3	26	15													44	402	9.1	51	4	92	23.0	31
2002	TOR+	18	1	1	1	47			7	48	6	8	1															1	0	0.0	0
2003	TOR*	18	1	0	0	51			8	238	5	6	1											7	123	17.6	48	1	0	0.0	0
2004	TOR	18				28			3	63	4													8	60	7.5	25	2	50	25.0	29
2005	TOR+	17				32			2	79	4	6	1																		
12	Years	195	17	4	10	468	2.0	0.0	48	852	105	56	9	6	25	4.2	11	0						234	2148	9.2	94	36	675	18.8	58
AKILI SMITH Kabisa Akili Maradufu QB 6'3 220 Grossmont JC; Oregon B: 8/21/1975 San Diego, CA Draft: 1-3 1999 CIN Pro: EN																															
2007	CAL	14	1	0	0	0								4	16	4.0	8	0													
ALBERT SMITH Albert, Jr. DT 6'0 301 Northwestern State (Louisiana) B: 12/5/1986 Matthews, LA																															
2010	HAM	1				1	1.0	4.0																							
2011	HAM	10				26	2.0	8.0																							
2	Years	11				27	3.0	12.0																							
ALFRED SMITH Alfred LB 6'3 240 Florida B: 2/21/1970 Lake City, FL																															
1994	OTT	13	0		2	34	1.0	2.0	0	0	2	6	1																		
1995	OTT	2				8																									
2	Years	15	0		2	42	1.0	2.0				6	1																		
ALLEN SMITH Allen Duncan HB 6'0 200 Fort Valley State B: 11/20/1942 Fort Valley, GA Draft: 15-136 1966 BUF Pro: N																															
1968	HAM	14	1		0							12	2	57	323	5.7	37	2	10	81	8.1	34	0					6	121	20.2	42
ASHAUNDAI SMITH Ashaundai J. WR 5'6 170 Kansas B: 6/3/1974																															
1997	HAM	15				2						12	2						35	452	12.9	49	2					10	217	21.7	31
BILL SMITH William Eugene (Nub) HB 6'0 185 Wake Forest B: 11/21/1927 D: 9/23/1999 AL																															
1953	MTL	5																													
BILL SMITH Bill CB-OE 6'1 185 Edmonton Wildcats Jrs. B: 12/11/1935																															
1956	EDM	3																													
1957	EDM	16							4	62														1	20	20.0	9				
1958	EDM	15							3	61														3	26	8.7	14				
1959	EDM	16							6	56														2	23	11.5	12				
1960	EDM+	16	2						6	65														2	1	0.5	1	1	27	27.0	27

Year	Team	GP	FM	FF	FR	TK	SK	YDS	IR	YDS	PD	PTS	TD	RA	YDS	AVG	LG	TD	REC	YDS	AVG	LG	TD	PR	YDS	AVG	LG	KOR	YDS	AVG	LG
1961	EDM	14							2	57														5	8	1.6	4				
1962	EDM	16	0		2				3	0														3	11	3.7	5				
1963	EDM	16							2	16									1	14	14.0	14	0								
8	Years	112	2		2				26	317									1	14	14.0	14	0	16	89	5.6	14	1	27	27.0	27
BO SMITH Tyler Bo'tez CB-DH 6'0 190 Kentucky; Weber State B: 6/8/1983 Owensboro, KY																															
2008	HAM	7				15								1	4	4.0	4	0													
2009	HAM	18				0																									
2010	HAM	6				28																									
2011	HAM	17	0	0	2	65			3	0	6																				
4	Years	48	0	0	2	108			3	0	6			1	4	4.0	4	0													
BOB SMITH Robert (Stonewall) T 220 Tuskegee																															
1947	WPG+	8																													
BRAD SMITH Brad WR-SB 6'0 192 Queen's B: 2/10/1983 Hudson, QC Draft: 6-45 2007 TOR																															
2007	TOR	1				0													1	8	8.0	8	0								
2007	MTL	7				0																									
2007	Year	8				0													1	8	8.0	8	0								
2009	TOR	8				1													14	142	10.1	21	0								
2010	EDM	9				0													2	18	9.0	11	0								
3	Years	18				1													17	168	9.9	21	0								
BRANDON SMITH Brandon DH 5'10 185 St. Mary's (California), Sacramento State B: 8/21/1984 Oakland, CA																															
2008	CAL	15	0	2	1	61	2.0	22.0	0	0	6																				
2010	CAL	17	1	0	0	43			4	60	0	6	1																		
2011	CAL	18	0	1	1	65			1	2	6																				
3	Years	50	1	3	2	169	2.0	22.0	5	62	12	6	1																		
BRIAN SMITH Brian DB 5'9 180 Central State (Ohio)*; Los Angeles Valley CC; Idaho B: 9/10/1966 Pittsburgh, PA																															
1991	TOR	3				12																						1	4	4.0	4
1992	BC	11	3		3	46			5	75																		16	251	15.7	29
2	Years	14	3		3	58			5	75																		17	255	15.0	29
BROCK SMITH Brock WR 6'0 175 Fresno State B: 10/2/1963 St. Louis, MO																															
1989	CAL	18				2						18	3	1	8	8.0	8	0	47	683	14.5	36	3								
1990	CAL	8				0						18	3						21	398	19.0	55	3								
1991	OTT	14	2		0	3						20	3						40	702	17.6	61	3					7	126	18.0	39
3	Years	40	2		0	5						56	9	1	8	8.0	8	0	108	1783	16.5	61	9					7	126	18.0	39
BRUCE SMITH Bruce DT-DE-OT 6'1 235 Colorado College B: 3/28/1949																															
1972	HAM	14	0		3				1	9		6	1															1	0	0.0	0
1973	HAM	14																													
1974	EDM	14			2																										
1975	OTT	1																													
1976	TOR	14	0		3																										
1977	TOR	3																													
1978	TOR	16	0		2																										
1979	TOR	11																													
8	Years	87	0		10				1	9		6	1															1	0	0.0	0
CHANDLER SMITH Chandler Marcelle DB 6'1 201 Southern Mississippi B: 3/29/1976 Vicksburg, MS Pro: E																															
2003	OTT	4				13					2																				
CHARLES SMITH Charles SB 5'8 180 Fresno State B: 3/26/1979 San Jose, CA																															
2003	OTT	2				0																		2	0	0.0	4	5	112	22.4	36
CHRIS SMITH Christopher LB 6'2 224 Queen's B: 1/31/1988 Toronto, ON Draft: 4A-28 2010 WPG																															
2010	WPG	15				4			1	40	0																				
2011	TOR	4				3																									
2	Years	19				7			1	40	0																				
CHRIS SMITH Chris S 5'10 207 Florida International B: 6/3/1985 Gainesville, FL																															
2008	MTL	9				22			0	0	2																				
COURTNEY SMITH Courtney LB 6'0 225 Texas State B: 10/26/1984 Millen, GA																															
2009	BC	4				5																									
2010	WPG	7				22					1																				
2	Years	11				27					1																				
DAMON SMITH Damon DB 5'10 170 Utah State B: 1/7/1971																															
1994	CAL	1				0																									
DARRELL SMITH Darrell RB 5'11 185 Santa Ana JC; Illinois B: 11/3/1960																															
1982	CAL	9	1		0							22	3	7	-5	-0.7	8	0	41	606	14.8	68	3	23	173	7.5	19	9	137	15.2	27
1983	CAL	9										18	3	3	10	3.3	8	0	30	331	11.0	45	3					17	467	27.5	49
1983	WPG	1												1	-7	-7.0	-7	0	1	7	7.0	7	0					4	94	23.5	29
1983	Year	10										18	3	4	3	0.8	8	0	31	338	10.9	45	3					21	561	26.7	48
2	Years	18	1		0							40	6	11	-2	-0.2	8	0	72	944	13.1	68	6	23	173	7.5	19	30	698	23.3	49
DARRELL SMITH Darrell K. SB-WR 6'2 192 Central State (Ohio) B: 11/5/1961 Youngstown, OH																															
1986	TOR	11	3		0							12	2	2	10	5.0	8	0	36	581	16.1	62	2	2	-7	-3.5	2	12	242	20.2	35
1987	TOR*	17				3						60	10	6	16	2.7	19	0	79	1392	17.6	54	10	6	36	6.0	12				
1988	TOR+	18	1		0	6						42	7	2	6	3.0	3	0	73	1306	17.9	67	7	8	108	13.5	51				
1989	TOR+	17	2		1	4						12	2	1	1	1.0	1	0	69	959	13.9	57	2	6	63	10.5	43	6	122	20.3	26
1990	TOR*	18	5		0	2						120	20	6	41	6.8	20	0	93	1826	19.6	88	20	13	119	9.2	26	11	191	17.4	27
1991	TOR+	18	2		0	4						60	10	7	33	4.7	16	1	73	1399	19.2	89	9	7	60	8.6	13	11	172	15.6	28
1992	TOR	13	1		0	3						12	2						42	681	16.2	43	2					2	23	11.5	23
1993	EDM	4				1													11	98	8.9	18	0					1	10	10.0	10
8	Years	116	14		1	23						318	53	24	107	4.5	20	1	476	8242	17.3	89	52	42	379	9.0	51	43	760	17.7	35
DARRYL SMITH Darryl Lloyd DVB 5'10 173 Lamar B: 6/13/1958 La Marque, TX																															
1982	CAL	9	2		1		3.0																								
1983	OTT	4	0		1				2	0																					
2	Years	13	2		2		3.0		2	0																					
DARYLE SMITH Daryle Ray OT 6'5 276 Tennessee B: 1/18/1964 Hawkins County, TN D: 2/11/2010 Knoxville, TN Pro: N																															
1993	TOR	4				1																									
1995	SA	14				5																									
2	Years	18				6																									
DEMETRIUS SMITH Demetrius (Pee-Wee) WR 6'1 180 Santa Monica JC; Miami (Florida) B: 1/3/1968																															
1990	CAL	6	2		0	0													5	107	21.4	53	0	16	194	12.1	47	4	72	18.0	32
1991	CAL	14	5		3	3						18	3	1	-6	-6.0	-6	0	36	467	13.0	48	0	48	713	14.9	87	29	700	24.1	89
1992	CAL	18	8		5	4						30	5	2	16	8.0	16	0	30	469	15.6	81	5	81	615	7.6	69	41	924	22.5	51
1993	CAL	16	1		0	10						12	2	1	2	2.0	2	0	33	417	12.6	31	1	21	281	13.4	67	7	161	23.0	41
1994	CAL	18	5		1	11						18	3						46	840	18.3	106	2	40	456	11.4	60	10	189	18.9	47
1995	CAL	18	1		1	5						18	3	2	9	4.5	12	0	57	836	14.7	45	3	25	192	7.7	26	24	412	17.2	38
6	Years	90	22		10	33						96	16	6	21	3.5	16	0	207	3136	15.1	106	11	231	2451	10.6	87	115	2458	21.4	89
DERRICK SMITH Derrick WR 6'0 190 Indiana (Pennsylvania) B: 8/22/1977																															
2004	WPG	11	1	0	1	0						6	1						35	556	15.9	49	1	3	13	4.3	9	2	43	21.5	25
DICK SMITH Richard Henry RB-DB 6'0 205 Northwestern B: 6/18/1944 Hamilton, OH Draft: 9- 1966 KC Pro: N																															
1969	MTL	7										42	7	89	491	5.5	87	5	22	333	15.1	49	2					5	129	25.8	46
1970	MTL	10	2		0							30	5	26	125	4.8		1	47	547	11.6		4								
1970	WPG	4												30	114	3.8		0	7	133	19.0		0					5	99	19.8	30
1970	Year	14	2		0							30	5	56	239	4.3	42	1	54	680	12.6	39	4					5	99	19.8	30
2	Years	17	2		0							72	12	145	730	5.0	87	6	76	1013	13.3	49	6					10	228	22.8	46
DON SMITH Don HB-FB 5'11 196 B: 1925																															
1946	WPG	3																													
1947	WPG	7										5	1										1								

Year	Team	GP	FM	FF	FR	TK	SK	YDS	IR	YDS	PD	PTS	TD	RA	YDS	AVG	LG	TD	REC	YDS	AVG	LG	TD	PR	YDS	AVG	LG	KOR	YDS	AVG	LG
1948	WPG	9										5	1					1													
1949	WPG	14										5	1					1													
4	Years	33										15	3					2					1								
DONALD SMITH Donald Ray CB 5'11 189 Liberty B: 2/21/1968 Danville, VA Draft: 10B-271 1990 MIN Pro: N																															
1992	WPG	17	1		1	91			3	0		6	1											23	208	9.0	71	11	165	15.0	40
1993	WPG+	18	0		3	61			5	24		6	1											6	50	8.3	25	5	142	28.4	73
1994	WPG+	18	0		2	56			6	77	3																	2	25	12.5	16
1995	MEM+	16	1		2	50			5	53	13													4	34	8.5	13				
1996	TOR	15	0		2	51			5	72	3																				
1997	TOR	14	0	0	2	56			4	36	6																				
1998	TOR+	18	0	2	2	69			3	31	12																				
1999	TOR	14	0	1	0	50			1	36	5																				
2000	HAM	9				22			1	41	3	6	1																		
9	Years	139	2	3	14	523			33	370	45	18	3											33	292	8.8	71	18	332	18.4	73
DONN SMITH Laton Donn Frederick C-OT 6'4 245 Purdue B: 9/3/1949 Rochester, MN Draft: TE 1973 OTT; 7-173 1973 KC																															
1973	OTT	14																													
1974	OTT	16																	1	13	13.0	13	0								
1975	OTT	16																													
1976	OTT+	16																													
1977	OTT+	16	2		1																										
1978	OTT+	16																													
1979	OTT	16																													
1980	OTT	11																													
8	Years	121	2		1														1	13	13.0	13	0								
DORIAN SMITH Dorian Miguel DT-DE-LB 6'3 273 Alabama A&M; Desert JC; Oregon State B: 8/19/1985 Van Nuys, CA																															
2009	WPG	16	0	1	1	47	8.0	30.0																							
2010	WPG	13	0	0	1	31	6.0	50.0			1																				
2011	WPG	7	0	0	2	13	2.0	17.0																							
3	Years	36	0	1	4	91	16.0	97.0			1																				
DOUG SMITH Doug HB-FW-QB 5'10 195 B: 1919																															
1946	HAM	12										12	1					1													
1947	HAM	12										5	0																		
1950	HAM	2																													
3	Years	26										17	1					1													
DOUG SMITH Doug C-OG 6'1 235 Wilfrid Laurier B: 6/16/1962 Galt, ON Draft: 4-34 1974 MTL																															
1974	MTL	12																													
1976	MTL	16	0		1																										
1977	MTL	16	0		1																										
1978	MTL	16																													
1979	MTL+	16	1		0									1	0	0.0	0	0													
1980	MTL	16																													
1981	TOR	16	1		0																										
1982	TOR	15																													
1983	MTL	16																	0	7		7	0								
1984	MTL	16	1		0																										
10	Years	155	3		2									1	0	0.0	0	0	0	7		7	0								
EARL SMITH Earl (Whipper) QB 5'9 168 NDG Maple Leafs Jrs.																															
1947	MTL	12																													
1948	MTL	4																													
2	Years	16																													
EARL SMITH Earl OE 6'0 200 San Francisco CC; Riverside CC; UCLA B: 1937																															
1961	SAS	1																	1	14	14.0	14	0								
EDDIE SMITH Eddie G-T 5'9 200 B: 1924																															
1950	OTT	2																													
EDDIE SMITH Eddie FB 5'9 200																															
1948	SAS	5																													
EDDIE SMITH Edward I. QB 6'0 170 Michigan State B: 1/13/1956																															
1979	HAM	16	2		0									13	58	4.5	19	0													
EDWARD SMITH Edward LB-DL 5'11 230 Mississippi State																															
1999	TOR	1				0																									
ERSKINE SMITH Erskine T																															
1946	HAM	3																													
FRANK SMITH Francis G-T 6'2 200 Olympic JC B: 1931																															
1953	CAL	16																													
1954	EDM	5																													
1955	WPG	6																													
1956	BC	3																													
4	Years	30																													
FRANKY SMITH Franky Lee OT 6'6 279 Alabama A&M B: 1/16/1956 Birmingham, AL Draft: 8-221 1978 DEN Pro: NU																															
1981	WPG	16																													
1982	WPG	10	0		1																										
1983	WPG	2																													
3	Years	28	0		1																										
GARRETT SMITH Garrett DL 6'3 300 Utah B: 2/18/1980 Tacoma, WA																															
2003	CAL	6				5	3.0	26.0																							
2004	CAL	15	0	2	0	25	3.0	16.0																							
2	Years	21	0	2	0	30	6.0	42.0																							
GEORGE SMITH George DE 6'3 250 Colorado B: 12/17/1960 Hilo, HI																															
1985	MTL	3																													
GERRY SMITH Gerry HB 5'7 165 B: 1929																															
1949	HAM	5																													
GORD SMITH Gordon (Red) E-FW 5'11 190 B: 1927 Winnipeg, MB																															
1946	WPG	5																													
1947	WPG	7																													
1948	SAS	1																													
3	Years	13																													
HAP SMITH Joe G-T 5'11 201 Maryland																															
1946	MTL	1																													
1947	MTL	4																													
2	Years	5																													
HAROLD SMITH Harold Jerone QB 6'3 210 Texas Southern B: 1/5/1962 Houston, TX																															
1985	SAS	5												5	14	2.8	3	0													
1986	SAS	8												1	0	0.0	0	0													
1988	EDM	1																													
3	Years	14												6	14	2.3	3	0													
HENRY SMITH Henry Glen LB 6'1 225 Texas A&M-Kingsville B: 12/22/1963 Houston, TX																															
1990	CAL	6	0		1	27																									
HERMAN SMITH Herman, III DE 6'5 277 Portland State B: 1/25/1971 Mound Bayou, MS Pro: EN																															
1994	HAM	3				6																									
1998	BC	9				20	7.0	34.0																							
1999	BC	18	0	0	2	56	7.0	40.0	1	0	0																				
2000	BC+	15	0	0	2	25	7.0	35.0			1																				

Year	Team	GP	FM	FF	FR	TK	SK	YDS	IR	YDS	PD	PTS	TD	RA	YDS	AVG	LG	TD	REC	YDS	AVG	LG	TD	PR	YDS	AVG	LG	KOR	YDS	AVG	LG
2001	BC+	18	0	1	0	47	9.0	48.0	1	1	3																				
2002	BC+	17	0	3	1	31	8.0				1																				
2003	BC	12				18	3.0				1																				
7	Years	92	0	4	5	203	41.0	157.0	2	1	6																				
HUGH SMITH Hugh Ben E 6'4 215 Nebraska; Kansas B: 8/27/1936 Henryetta, OK Pro: N																															
1963	EDM	1																													
HUGH SMITH Hugh Arthur WR 5'8 165 South Florida B: 5/8/1979 Coco Beach, FL																															
2005	HAM	8	3	0	0	2													6	79	13.2	27	0	23	91	4.0	11	21	449	21.4	49
IRVIN SMITH Irvin Martin CB 5'10 181 Maryland B: 3/12/1967 Poolesville, MD Pro: E																															
1994	BAL*	18				50			6	97	8													4	27	6.8	12				
1995	BAL*	16	1		2	25	1.0	10.0	1	18	8													2	17	8.5	19				
1996	MTL+	18	0		1	42			6	105	7	6	1											1	8	8.0	8				
1997	MTL	18	0	0	2	54			3	0	14																				
1998	MTL	17	0	2	3	40			3	9	5																				
1999	MTL+	18	0	1	2	33			7	51	9	6	1											1	2	2.0	2				
2000	MTL+	17				47			3	35	4																				
2001	MTL	16	0	0	2	38			2	37	5													1	7	7.0	7				
8	Years	138	1	3	12	329	1.0	10.0	31	352	60	12	2											9	61	6.8	19				
JAMAYEL SMITH Jamayel Ramir WR 6'0 186 Mississippi State B: 8/9/1984 Atlanta, GA Pro: U																															
2010	WPG	3				0													1	7	7.0	7	0					4	56	14.0	19
JARRETT SMITH Jarrett RB 5'11 210 Waterloo B: 5/22/1973 Hamilton, ON																															
1998	HAM	18				17								22	170	7.7	30	0	2	12	6.0	8	0								
1999	HAM	8	1	0	0	10								10	64	6.4	39	0	1	13	13.0	13	0								
2000	HAM	18	1	0	2	16						12	2	23	69	3.0	11	1	5	70	14.0	28	0								
2001	HAM	11	0	0	2	16						6	1																		
2002	HAM	18	3	0	2	6						24	4	59	221	3.7	23	3	13	104	8.0	17	0					11	207	18.8	35
2003	HAM	18	0	1	1	17								16	62	3.9	8	0	2	5	2.5	4	0					2	28	14.0	19
2005	TOR	1				2																									
7	Years	92	5	1	7	84						42	7	130	586	4.5	39	4	23	204	8.9	28	0					13	235	18.1	35
JEFF SMITH Jeffrey Jerome WR 6'4 180 Cal Poly (Pomona); Cal Poly (San Luis Obispo) B: 5/28/1962 Framingham, MA Pro: U																															
1984	TOR	1																													
1987	TOR	10	1		0	0						12	2						25	391	15.6	38	2					1	4	4.0	4
1988	WPG	9	1		0	0						6	1						39	436	11.2	21	1	8	32	4.0	9				
1989	WPG	9	2		0	1						12	2						30	358	11.9	51	2	15	97	6.5	20				
1990	OTT	10				1						18	3						28	342	12.2	22	3	6	18	3.0	11	3	46	15.3	28
5	Years	39	4		0	2						48	8						122	1527	12.5	51	8	29	147	5.1	20	4	50	12.5	28
JIMMY SMITH James Earl DB 6'3 190 San Joaquin JC; Utah State B: 7/12/1945 Stockton, CA Draft: 10-244 1969 DEN Pro: N																															
1970	OTT	1																													
JOE SMITH Joseph O'Brien RB 6'1 224 New Mexico Military JC; Louisiana Tech B: 8/26/1979 Monroe, LA Pro: E																															
2006	BC	14	2	0	0	1						60	10	166	887	5.3	66	9	51	420	8.2	26	1					2	34	17.0	27
2007	BC*	18	2	0	2	5						114	19	281	1510	5.4	38	18	23	180	7.8	24	1								
2008	BC	4				0						18	3	55	236	4.3	22	3	6	37	6.2	14	0								
2008	WPG	8				0						12	2	69	381	5.5	31	2	4	39	9.8	16	0					7	170	24.3	35
2008	Year	12				0						30	5	124	617	5.0	31	5	10	76	7.6	16	0					7	170	24.3	35
3	Years	36	4	0	2	6						204	34	571	3014	5.3	66	32	84	676	8.0	26	2					9	204	22.7	35
JOE BOB SMITH Joe Bob OHB 6'1 190 Houston B: 1936 Draft: 28-335 1957 DET																															
1958	EDM	11	3		2							22	3	22	90	4.1	35	0	31	457	14.7	38	3	15	98	6.5	15	9	224	24.9	56
1959	EDM	16										54	9	45	228	5.1	18	1	62	1108	17.9	80	8	27	161	6.0	15	14	367	26.2	50
1960	EDM	16	4		1							12	2	32	120	3.8	25	0	27	520	19.3	68	2	44	239	5.4	18	17	357	21.0	46
1961	EDM	8										18	3	16	66	4.1	24	0	17	314	18.5	48	3	20	115	5.8	18	13	332	25.5	76
4	Years	51	7		3							106	17	115	504	4.4	35	1	137	2399	17.5	80	16	106	613	5.8	18	53	1280	24.2	76
JUNIOR SMITH Junior RB 5'7 185 East Carolina B: 4/18/1973																															
1995	SHR	13	0		3	16						12	2	55	246	4.5	31	1	13	107	8.2	29	0								
KEITH SMITH Keith Alfred QB 5'11 210 Arizona B: 10/5/1976 Santa Barbara, CA																															
2001	SAS	16	1	0	0	2						12	2	31	172	5.5	24	2													
2003	CAL	5				0								1	3	3.0	3	0													
2	Years	21	1	0	0	2						12	2	32	175	5.5	24	2													
KELVIN SMITH Kelvin LB 6'1 235 Florida State B: 3/23/1969 Tallahassee, FL																															
1994	WPG	9	0		1	32	1.0		2	16	1																				
1995	WPG	4				7																									
2	Years	13	0		1	39	1.0		2	16	1																				
KENNY SMITH Kenneth DB 6'2 200 Southern Mississippi B: 8/16/1957 Atlanta, GA																															
1983	MTL	1																	1	20	20.0	20	0								
KENNY SMITH Kenneth DL 6'2 267 Benedict B: 6/6/1981 Detroit, MI																															
2006	MTL	1				2																									
KERRY SMITH Kerry WR 5'10 168 Scarborough Rams Jrs. B: 1/6/1954																															
1977	TOR	2																													
1977	HAM	5										12	2						9	144	16.0	31	2								
1977	Year	7										12	2						9	144	16.0	31	2								
1978	HAM	8	1		0							6	1	1	-14	-14.0	-14	0	12	256	21.3	50	1								
1979	HAM	11										6	1						12	171	14.3	32	1	6	36	6.0	13				
1980	SAS	12	1		0														11	121	11.0	25	0								
1981	HAM	14										6	1						4	62	15.5	28	1	1	9	9.0	9				
1982	HAM	14																													
6	Years	61	2		0							30	5	1	-14	-14.0	-14	0	48	754	15.7	50	5	7	45	6.4	13				
KHREEM SMITH Khreem DT-DE 6'3 270 Garden City CC; Oklahoma State B: 7/7/1979 St. James, Jamaica Pro: N																															
2011	BC	15	0	2	2	27	5.0	31.0																							
KIRK SMITH Kirk LB 6'0 218 Bishop's B: 7/18/1969																															
1997	MTL	1				0																									
KWAME SMITH Kwame CB 5'9 180 Coffeyville CC; West Virginia B: 1/1/1971																															
1994	BAL	1				2																									
1998	WPG	4				10																									
2	Years	5				12																									
LARRY SMITH Lawrence G 6'1 227 Virginia Tech; South Carolina B: 7/30/1929 Cadogan, PA Draft: 20-240 1951 CHIB																															
1952	MTL	1																													
LARRY SMITH Larry W. RB-TE 6'0 208 Bishop's B: 4/28/1951 Hudson, QC Draft: 1A-1 1972 MTL																															
1972	MTL	14	1		1							18	3	54	246	4.6	15	3	7	90	12.9	25	0					11	247	22.5	33
1973	MTL	14	4		1							36	6	104	422	4.1	21	2	22	196	8.9	20	4								
1974	MTL	16										18	3	48	232	4.8	22	0	29	420	14.5	55	3								
1975	MTL	16	1		0							30	5	92	385	4.2	24	0	52	560	10.8	47	5								
1976	MTL	16	1		0							2	0	85	312	3.7	21	0	36	268	7.4	40	0								
1977	MTL	16	0		1							18	3	9	33	3.7	12	3	28	314	11.2	27	0					3	56	18.7	19
1978	MTL	16										18	3	1	51	51.0	51	0	35	528	15.1	52	3								
1979	MTL	16	1		0							12	2	1	-1	-1.0	-1	0	21	317	15.1	40	2								
1980	MTL	16										6	1	3	16	5.3	8	0	8	79	9.9	20	1								
9	Years	140	8		3							158	26	397	1696	4.3	51	8	238	2772	11.6	55	18					14	303	21.6	33
LEROY SMITH Leroy DE 6'2 225 Iowa B: 1/6/1969 Pro: E																															
1993	TOR	1				1																									
LES SMITH Lester S 5'10 180 The Citadel B: 8/16/1970 Concord, NC																															
1994	BAL	11	2		1	17	1.0	10.0																51	582	11.4	53	9	183	20.3	34
1995	BAL	6	0		1	22					2													1	4	4.0	4	11	161	14.6	30
1996	TOR	2	0		1	3			1	40	0																				

Year	Team	GP	FM	FF	FR	TK	SK	YDS	IR	YDS	PD	PTS	TD	RA	YDS	AVG	LG	TD	REC	YDS	AVG	LG	TD	PR	YDS	AVG	LG	KOR	YDS	AVG	LG
1997	TOR*	18	0	1	1	47	5.0	34.0	6	104	3	6	1															5	94	18.8	31
1998	TOR+	18	0	1	1	55	1.0	5.0	6	57	3													14	179	12.8	48	4	89	22.3	35
1999	MTL	18	0	0	1	61			5	52	7																				
2000	MTL+	17				62			8	156	3																				
2001	MTL	6				19					2																				
8	Years	96	2	2	6	286	7.0	49.0	26	409	20	6	1											66	765	11.6	53	29	527	18.2	35
MARCEL SMITH Marcel CB 6'0 185 Northwest Missouri State B: 10/27/1979																															
2004	WPG	6	0	1	0	14					2																				
MARCUS SMITH Marcus Edward Blackwell DT 6'4 295 Arizona B: 2/7/1984 San Diego, CA Pro: U																															
2010	MTL	2				1																									
MARCUS SMITH Marcus CB 5'10 185 Memphis B: 8/17/1980 Pro: E																															
2004	WPG	6				29					3																				
MARIO SMITH Mario S-LB-DH 6'0 195 Kansas State B: 10/10/1974 Miami, FL																															
1998	HAM	1				51																									
1998	SAS	8	0	0	1	1			2	66	0																				
1998	Year	9	0	0	1	52			2	66	0																				
1999	SAS	5				25					2																				
1999	HAM	3				0																									
1999	Year	8				25					2																				
2	Years	6	0	0	1	77			2	66	2																				
MARK SMITH Mark LB 6'3 210 Langara B: 2/11/1966 London, England																															
1988	BC	3				0																									
MARTY SMITH Martin Joseph DT 6'3 250 Louisville B: 10/20/1953 Pattison, MS Draft: 15-390 1975 PIT Pro: NW																															
1977	WPG	1																													
1978	WPG	2																													
1978	TOR	2																													
1978	Year	4																													
2	Years	3																													
MAURICE SMITH Maurice DB 5'9 175 Texas A&M-Kingsville B: 10/4/1966 Detroit, MI																															
1991	BC	6	1		1	23			1	8														8	75	9.4	32	16	305	19.1	27
1992	BC	3	2		3	17																		5	24	4.8	13	10	302	30.2	59
2	Years	9	3		4	40			1	8														13	99	7.6	32	26	607	23.3	59
MEL SMITH Mel WR 6'2 205 Alberta B: 1949 Draft: 1-4 1971 EDM																															
1972	WPG	1																													
NEAL SMITH Neal DE-DT 6'5 250 Montana State B: 11/4/1974 Polson, MT																															
1999	SAS+	14	0	0	1	16	9.0	49.0																							
NEIL SMITH Neil OHB 6'0 195 Boston University B: 4/18/1946																															
1968	TOR	14										6	1	6	5	0.8	9	0	13	145	11.2	26	1					1	10	10.0	10
NICK SMITH Nick LB 6'2 230 Notre Dame B: 6/24/1971 Pro: E																															
1994	LV	11				11	1.0																								
PHIL SMITH Phillip Keith WR 6'3 188 San Diego State B: 4/28/1960 Draft: 4-85 1983 BAL; 11-122 1983 ARI-USFL Pro: N																															
1989	BC	5	1		0	1													7	114	16.3	32	0	1	9	9.0	9	6	91	15.2	23
RAY SMITH Ray FB-HB 5'11 200 UCLA B: 1938 Draft: FS 1960 OAK																															
1960	SAS	5										6	1	40	210	5.3	11	0	3	33	11.0	17	1					3	90	30.0	50
1961	SAS	15	2		2							30	5	128	557	4.4	25	3	13	112	8.6	14	1					14	343	24.5	41
1962	SAS	2												18	47	2.6	14	0	1	6	6.0	6	0					1	29	29.0	29
3	Years	22	2		2							36	6	186	814	4.4	25	3	17	151	8.9	17	2					18	462	25.7	50
ROB SMITH Robert J. OG-OT 6'4 245 Utah State B: 10/3/1958 New Westminster, BC Draft: TE 1981 BC																															
1981	BC	1																													
1982	TOR	1																													
1982	MTL	13																													
1982	Year	14																													
1983	MTL	16																													
1984	MTL	16			2																										
1985	MTL	16	0		1																										
1986	CAL	18	0		1																										
1987	CAL	18	0		1	1																									
1988	CAL	13				0																									
1988	BC	5				2																									
1988	Year	18				2																									
1989	BC	18	0		1	0																									
1990	OTT+	18	0		1	2																									
1991	OTT	18				1																									
1992	OTT*	18				4																									
1993	BC*	18	0		1	2																									
1994	BC+	18				2																						4	68	17.0	
14	Years	207	0		8	14																						4	68	17.0	
ROBERT SMITH Robert Benjamin DL 6'7 270 Grambling State B: 12/3/1962 Bogalusa, LA Draft: TD 1984 NO-USFL Pro: N																															
1990	TOR	5				8	2.0																								
ROD SMITH Rod T 6'2 250 Toronto B: 1925																															
1949	MTL	12																													
ROLLEN SMITH Rollen Toby DB 6'1 186 Garden City CC; Arkansas B: 10/12/1951 Greenville, MS Draft: 6B-145 1975 CIN Pro: W																															
1976	BC	1																													
ROY SMITH Roy Edward (Looney) G-FW-T-C 6'3 222 Tennessee B: 1/1/1928 D: 12/21/2008 Knoxville, TN																															
1953	OTT	8																													
1954	OTT	11							1	2																					
1955	OTT	6																													
3	Years	25							1	2																					
SHAWN SMITH Shawn LB 6'3 230 San Diego State B: 7/5/1971 Millville, NJ Pro: E																															
1995	HAM	9				38	1.0	7.0	0	0	1																				
SHERMAN SMITH Sherman WR 5'7 165 Houston B: 1971																															
1998	TOR	3	1	0	0	2													1	9	9.0	9	0	10	74	7.4	19	3	66	22.0	23
STAN SMITH Stan G 5'11 225 NDG Maple Leafs Jrs. B: 1945																															
1967	MTL	1																													
STEVE SMITH Stephen Brian QB 6'0 200 Michigan B: 12/19/1962 Flint, MI Draft: TD 1984 MIC-USFL																															
1984	MTL	16	1		0							6	1	15	104	6.9	46	0	3	45	15.0	37	1								
1985	OTT	2												5	45	9.0	31	0	3	18	6.0	17	0								
2	Years	18	1		0							6	1	20	149	7.5	46	0	6	63	10.5	37	1								
STEVE SMITH Steve Tyrone WR 5'8 170 Independence JC; Chaffey JC; Utah State B: 5/30/1974 Belle Glade, FL Pro: X																															
1998	TOR	4	3	0	0	2													3	36	12.0	25	0	19	180	9.5	39	12	249	20.8	37
TERRY SMITH Terry WR 5'9 170 Penn State B: 7/29/1969 Monroeville, PA Draft: 11-308 1992 WAS																															
1994	SHR	16	1		2	2													13	185	14.2	25	0	37	319	8.6	57	18	385	21.4	43
1995	SHR	12	0		1	3													15	242	16.1	71	0								
2	Years	28	1		3	5													28	427	15.3	71	0	37	319	8.6	57	18	385	21.4	43
TODD SMITH Todd WR 5'11 175 Morningside B: 2/11/1966 St. Petersburg, FL																															
1989	EDM	2				1																									
1990	EDM	4				1													6	81	13.5	31	0	8	45	5.6	16	8	110	13.8	27
2	Years	6				2													6	81	13.5	31	0	8	45	5.6	16	8	110	13.8	27
TOMMIE SMITH Tommie LB 6'2 225 Washington B: 8/7/1971 Bend, OR																															
1994	SAC	12	0		1	41			2	31	2																				
1995	SA	12				58	2.0	17.0	2	98	3	6	1																		
1996	WPG	1				1																									

Year	Team	GP	FM	FF	FR	TK	SK	YDS	IR	YDS	PD	PTS	TD	RA	YDS	AVG	LG	TD	REC	YDS	AVG	LG	TD	PR	YDS	AVG	LG	KOR	YDS	AVG	LG
1996	SAS	10	1		1	44	1.0	7.0	3	103	1	6	1																		
1996	Year	11	1		1	45	1.0	7.0	3	103	1	6	1																		
3	Years	25	1		2	144	3.0	24.0	7	232	6	12	2																		
TONY SMITH Tony Derrell RB 6'1 214 Southern Mississippi B: 6/29/1970 Chicago, IL Draft: 1B-19 1992 ATL Pro: N																															
1998	TOR	4				0						12	2	23	26	1.1	7	1	5	40	8.0	13	1	17	116	6.8	22	12	268	22.3	46
TRE SMITH Lyle C., III RB 5'11 195 Auburn B: 4/4/1984 Elkins, WV																															
2008	HAM	14	6	0	1	3						12	2	65	430	6.6	75	2	11	119	10.8	31	0	44	346	7.9	22	57	1172	20.6	38
2009	HAM	1				49			2	40	5								1	4	4.0	4	0					3	79	26.3	32
2	Years	15	6	0	1	52			2	40	5	12	2	65	430	6.6	75	2	12	123	10.3	31	0	44	346	7.9	22	60	1251	20.9	38
TREVIS SMITH Trevis LB 6'0 235 Alabama B: 9/8/1976 Montgomery, AL																															
1999	SAS	9	0	0	1	40																									
2000	SAS	12	0	0	2	34						6	1															1	11	11.0	11
2001	SAS	16	0	0	2	57	1.0	4.0			2																				
2002	SAS	18	0	1	0	63	1.0	8.0	2	43	0																	1	13	13.0	13
2003	SAS	5	0	0	2	17					1																				
2004	SAS	14	0	0	1	25	3.0	22.0	1	15	0																	2	0	0.0	0
2005	SAS	17	0	2	2	58	1.0	7.0	1	0	2																				
7	Years	91	0	3	10	294	6.0	41.0	4	58	5	6	1															4	24	6.0	13
TROY SMITH Troy WR 5'9 160 Texas Tech B: 9/9/1962																															
1987	OTT	4				1						6	1						9	187	20.8	67	1					9	158	17.6	26
WADDELL SMITH James Waddell SE 6'1 162 Los Angeles Southwest JC; Kansas B: 8/24/1955 New Orleans, LA Draft: 8B-215 1977 KC Pro: N																															
1977	EDM	6	1		0							12	2						19	253	13.3	48	2								
1978	EDM	16										54	9	1	19	19.0	19	0	58	875	15.1	50	9								
1979	EDM*	16	0		1							84	14	1	26	26.0	26	1	74	1214	16.4	77	13								
1980	EDM	12	3		1							24	4	2	-1	-0.5	6	0	30	482	16.1	58	4								
1981	EDM	16	2		1							56	9	3	84	28.0	54	0	65	1077	16.6	50	9					2	0	0.0	0
1982	EDM	14	0		1							42	7	4	40	10.0	28	0	41	729	17.8	58	7								
1983	EDM	13	0		1							42	7						55	887	16.1	51	7								
7	Years	93	6		5							314	52	11	168	15.3	54	1	342	5517	16.1	77	51					2	0	0.0	0
WARD SMITH Ward DB 5'10 186 Colorado State; Walla Walla CC B: 5/3/1947 Calgary, AB																															
1969	CAL	5	1		0									2	14	7.0		0													
1969	BC	9												3	23	7.7		0	1	9	9.0	9	0					4	116	29.0	44
1969	Year	14	1		0									5	37	7.4	23	0	1	9	9.0	9	0					4	116	29.0	44
1970	BC	1																										2	35	17.5	
1970	WPG	10	0		1																							5	115	23.0	
1970	Year	11	0		1																							7	150	21.4	36
1973	MTL	9							1	28		6	1											12	71	5.9	18				
1974	MTL	14	3		0																			14	81	5.8	19	9	174	19.3	38
1975	MTL	12	0		2				1	0																		1	32	32.0	32
1977	TOR	10	1		1				1	16														3	5	1.7	7	2	6	3.0	5
6	Years	51	5		4				3	44		6	1	5	37	7.4	0	0	1	9	9.0	9	0	29	157	5.4	19	23	478	20.8	44
WAYNE SMITH Wayne DE 6'4 230 Halifax Buccaneers Srs. B: 1/24/1950 Halifax, NS																															
1969	OTT	14																													
1970	OTT	14																													
1971	OTT	14			1																										
1972	OTT*	14	0		4				1	0																					
1973	OTT	7	0		1																										
1974	OTT*	16	0		1							6	1																		
1975	OTT	15	0		1																			1	0	0.0	0				
1976	BC	16																													
1977	TOR	16	0		3																										
1978	TOR	12	0		1																										
1979	TOR	7																													
1979	SAS	5																													
1979	Year	12																													
1980	SAS	2																													
1980	HAM	7																													
1980	Year	9																													
12	Years	147	0		12				1	0		6	1											1	0	0.0	0				
WAYNE SMITH Wayne Anthony OG-OT 6'3 305 Appalachian State B: 11/17/1979 Etobicoke, ON Draft: 1-1 2004 HAM																															
2004	HAM	18	0	0	1	3																									
2005	HAM	18				3																									
2006	HAM	13	0	0	1	1																									
2007	SAS	18	0	0	1	1																									
2008	SAS	14				3																									
2010	SAS	1				0																									
2011	HAM	18				0																									
7	Years	100	0	0	3	11																									
ZEKE SMITH Roger Duane G-LB 6'2 233 Auburn B: 9/29/1936 Walker Spring, AL Draft: 4-48(f) 1959 BAL; FS 1960 NYT Pro: N																															
1962	TOR	7							1	9																					
1963	EDM	4																													
2	Years	11							1	9																					
BILL SMITIUCH Bill OG 5'9 210 Winnipeg Rods Jrs. B: 5/17/1934																															
1955	WPG	15																													
1956	WPG	6																													
1957	WPG																														
3	Years	21																													
DOUG SMYLIE Douglas John HB-FW 6'1 197 none B: 6/3/1922 D: 3/19/1983																															
1946	MTL	8										5	1					1													
1948	OTT	11										21	4					2					2								
1949	TOR	8										7	1										1								
1950	TOR	12										5	1										1								
1951	TOR	11										30	6					4					2								
1952	TOR	12										5	1					1													
1953	TOR	13										15	3					3													
7	Years	75										88	17					11					6								
ROD SMYLIE Rodney David FW-HB-E 5'11 187 none B: 1924 D: 11//1991																															
1946	TOR	8																													
1948	TOR	12										5	1					1													
1949	TOR	7																													
1950	TOR	11										15	3					1					2								
1951	TOR	10										5	1										1								
1952	TOR	12										5	1										1								
1953	TOR	9																													
1954	TOR	11																	3	36	12.0	19	0								
1955	TOR	9																										1	11	11.0	11
9	Years	89										30	6					2	3	36	12.0	19	4					1	11	11.0	11
JIM SMYRL Jim OG-C 6'3 290 Winnipeg Jrs.; Manitoba B: 12/13/1969 Fort Garry, MB																															
1994	WPG	1																													
1995	WPG	10				0																									
1996	WPG	3				0																									
3	Years	14				0																									

Year	Team	GP	FM	FF	FR	TK	SK	YDS	IR	YDS	PD	PTS	TD	RA	YDS	AVG	LG	TD	REC	YDS	AVG	LG	TD	PR	YDS	AVG	LG	KOR	YDS	AVG	LG
MARK SMYTHE James M. DL 6'3 265 Indiana B: 12/12/1959 Bloomington, IN Draft: 10-269 1984 STL; 9-178 1984 NO-USFL																															
1985	OTT	2					1.0																								
WILLIE SNEAD Willis L. WR 5'11 193 Virginia; Florida B: 9/3/1966 Belle Glade, FL Draft: 12-321 1989 NYJ Pro: E																															
1989	TOR	3	0		1							6	1	1	1	1.0	1	0	4	65	16.3	40	1	2	6	3.0	6	1	28	28.0	28
KARL SNEIDER Karl Peter SE 6'2 200 Augsburg B: 6/13/1947																															
1969	EDM	7										6	1						13	206	15.8	38	1								
ANGELO SNIPES Angelo Bernard LB 6'0 228 West Georgia B: 1/11/1963 Atlanta, GA Draft: 14-196 1985 OAK-USFL Pro: NU																															
1991	OTT	15	0		1	56	5.0		1	89		6	1																		
1992	OTT*	18	0		1	46	20.0	146.0	1	10																					
1993	OTT+	18	0		1	33	14.0	128.0																							
1994	BC	18				62	11.0	73.0			2																				
1995	BIR	18				44	17.0	110.0			1																				
1996	WPG+	18	0		2	39	15.0	111.0			1	12	2																		
6	Years	105	0		5	280	82.0	568.0	2	99	4	18	3																		
GEORGE SNISCAK George V. T 235 Wake Forest B: 3/21/1928 D: 6/14/2005																															
1950	MTL	2																													
MIKE SNODGRASS Michael D. LB 6'2 218 Western Michigan B: 1941 Draft: 20-280 1962 GB																															
1962	OTT	14												1	-7	-7.0	-7	0													
BILL SNYDER Wilbur T 6'2 240 Utah B: 1930																															
1952	EDM	7			1							3	0						2	15	7.5	8	0								
1953	EDM	12										51	0	1	-18	-18.0	-18	0										1	4	4.0	4
2	Years	19			1							54	0	1	-18	-18.0	-18	0	2	15	7.5	8	0					1	4	4.0	4
DON SOBERDASH Donald FB 6'0 195 Maryland; Georgia B: 1936																															
1960	HAM	7										6	1	61	248	4.1	22	1	11	156	14.2	30	0					2	40	20.0	22
ED SOERGEL Edwin (Spider) QB 6'0 185 Eastern Illinois B: 4/3/1930 Glenview, IL																															
1952	TOR	10										5	1																		
ANDY SOKOL Andrew Cyril OHB-FW-G 5'11 200 none B: 1928																															
1946	HAM	9										2	0																		
1947	HAM	6																													
1950	WPG	13										5	1	42	191	4.5		1													
1951	WPG	14										35	7	69	290	4.2		2	31	435	14.0		4	4	42	10.5		2	10	5.0	
1952	WPG	14										10	2	31	125	4.0	9	0	15	153	10.2	37	2					2	12	6.0	8
1953	WPG	13										10	2	29	118	4.1		1	12	119	9.9		1					1	25	25.0	25
1954	WPG	11												11	48	4.4	15	0	2	12	6.0	6	0								
7	Years	80										62	12	182	772	4.2	15	4	60	719	12.0	37	7	4	42	10.5	0	5	47	9.4	25
STEVE SOLARI Steven Cornell LB 6'1 235 Purdue; Texas A&M B: 7/9/1971 Harris County, TX																															
1994	SHR	5			1	11																									
MICHAEL SOLES Michael FB 6'1 215 McGill B: 11/8/1966 Point Claire, QC Draft: 1A-5 1989 EDM																															
1989	EDM	18	0		3	3						12	2	33	215	6.5	31	2	3	17	5.7	9	0					2	20	10.0	14
1990	EDM	18	2		0	2						14	2	52	394	7.6	45	0	16	158	9.9	29	2					1	12	12.0	12
1991	EDM	16	1		1	19						18	3	45	302	6.7	49	1	16	135	8.4	16	2					2	3	1.5	3
1992	EDM	18	0		3	12						24	4	115	656	5.7	51	4	25	285	11.4	39	0					1	0	0.0	0
1993	EDM	18	1		2	9						18	3	79	334	4.2	18	3	26	263	10.1	25	0					1	0	0.0	0
1994	EDM	18	2		5	14						48	8	52	205	3.9	15	4	54	663	12.3	41	4	2	0	0.0		4	26	6.5	12
1995	EDM+	18	1		0	14						48	8	86	352	4.1	23	5	48	398	8.3	29	3					1	3	3.0	3
1996	MTL	17	2		1	8						48	8	64	340	5.3	28	0	42	506	12.0	44	8					4	67	16.8	29
1997	MTL	18	2	0	1	5						6	1	34	123	3.6	10	1	26	299	11.5	31	0								
1998	MTL	18	1	0	1	3						18	3	8	40	5.0	11	0	32	388	12.1	26	3					5	53	10.6	17
1999	MTL	18	1	0	1	8						18	3	11	46	4.2	11	0	38	388	10.2	31	3					1	10	10.0	10
11	Years	195	13	0	18	97						272	45	579	3007	5.2	51	20	326	3500	10.7	44	25	2	0	0.0	0	22	194	8.8	29
MERCED SOLIS Merced TE 6'2 223 West Texas A&M B: 5/10/1953 Pointe Claire, QC																															
1976	BC	13										6	1						17	329	19.4	55	1					3	15	5.0	13
ANDRE' SOMMERSELL Andre' Lawrence LB 6'2 230 Colorado State B: 6/26/1980 Guyana Draft: 7B-255 2004 OAK Pro: E																															
2006	EDM	8	0	1	0	9	3.0				1																				
BUTCH SONGIN Edward Frank QB 6'2 205 Boston College B: 5/11/1924 Walpole, MA D: 5/26/1976 Foxborough, MA Draft: 13-99(di) 1949 BUF-AAFC; 19-247 1950 CLE Pro: N																															
1953	HAM	9																													
1954	HAM	14												23	75	3.3	22	0													
2	Years	23												23	75	3.3	22	0													
TREG SONGY Treg Joseph DB 6'2 200 Tulane B: 6/15/1962 Houston, TX Draft: 12-320 1985 NO; TD 1985 POR-USFL Pro: N																															
1986	OTT	6							1	18																					
BRIAN SOPATYK Brian OG 6'2 235 Boise State B: 5/31/1947 Draft: 1A-1 1973 BC																															
1973	BC	7																													
1974	BC	16																													
1975	BC	16																													
1976	BC	16	0		1																										
4	Years	55	0		1																										
MERWIN SOPER Merwin T 6'3 244 Iowa State; Drake B: 1929																															
1951	EDM	3																													
JOHNNY SOPINKA John OHB-DB 5'11 170 Hamilton Tiger-Cats Jrs.; Toronto B: 3/19/1933 Broderick, SK D: 11/24/1997 Draft: 6-22 1955 TOR																															
1955	TOR	11							2	0		10	2						4	71	17.8	23	1								
1956	TOR	14							4	5									4	45	11.3	16	0	1	0	0.0	0				
1957	TOR	2																													
1957	MTL	8																						14	71	5.1	8				
1957	Year	10																						14	71	5.1	8				
3	Years	27							6	5		10	2						8	116	14.5	23	1	15	71	4.7	8				
JUSTIN SORENSEN Justin OT-OG 6'7 316 South Carolina B: 6/8/1986 Parksville, BC Draft: 1-5 2008 BC																															
2009	BC	18				0																									
2010	BC	18				0																									
2	Years	36				0																									
PETER SORENSON Peter OT 6'5 243 Bishop's B: 4/21/1951 Draft: 7B-56 1976 TOR																															
1977	TOR	13																													
DICK SORKORUM Richard DB 6'1 205 Paris# B: 10/30/1943 Detroit, MI																															
1967	BC	1																													
HENRY SORRELL Henry Thomas LB 6'2 225 Tennessee-Chattanooga B: 6/10/1943 Talladega, AL Draft: RS-8-66 1966 DEN; RS-1-5 1967 MIN Pro: N																															
1969	HAM+	14	0		2				1	4		6	1															2	67	33.5	56
1970	HAM	14	1		2				1	25																		1	28	28.0	28
1971	BC	1																													
3	Years	29	1		4				2	29		6	1															3	95	31.7	56
JERAME SOUTHERN Jerame DL 6'2 210 James Madison B: 11/25/1980 Lumberton, NC																															
2005	CAL	5	0	0	1	6					1																	2	17	8.5	10
RON SOUTHWICK Ron LB 6'2 220 McMaster B: 5/22/1951 Draft: 7-57 1974 CAL																															
1975	WPG	15	0		2																							5	29	5.8	9
1976	WPG	15	0		1																										
1977	WPG	16	0		1																										
1978	WPG	16							2	37		6	1																		
1979	TOR	16	1		1				3	56																					
1980	TOR	16																													
1981	TOR	16					4.0																								
7	Years	110	1		5		4.0		5	93		6	1															5	29	5.8	9
MIKE SOUZA Michael QB 6'0 185 Illinois State B: 1/16/1982																															
2004	CAL	18	1	0	1	0								9	40	4.4	8	0													
HENRY SOVIO Henry Peter TE 6'3 234 Hawaii B: 4/15/1949 Surrey, BC Draft: 13-327 1972 ATL																															

Year	Team	GP	FM	FF	FR	TK	SK	YDS	IR	YDS	PD	PTS	TD	RA	YDS	AVG	LG	TD	REC	YDS	AVG	LG	TD	PR	YDS	AVG	LG	KOR	YDS	AVG	LG
1974	BC	9																													
1975	CAL	10										12	2						7	87	12.4	17	2								
1976	CAL	12																	11	151	13.7	22	0								
1976	BC	3																	5	58	11.6	15	0								
1976	Year	15																	16	209	13.1	22	0								
1977	BC	3																													
1977	EDM	2																													
1977	Year	5																													
4	Years	34										12	2						23	296	12.9	22	2								
BILL SOWALSKI Bill OE-LB 5'11 200 Brantford Jrs. B: 1931 Fort Frances, ON																															
1954	OTT	12										10	2						8	175	21.9	45	2								
1955	OTT	10																	7	92	13.1	42	0					1	10	10.0	10
1956	OTT	13																													
1957	OTT	13							5	99		6	1																		
1958	OTT	14							4	80		12	2						4	76	19.0	26	0								
1959	OTT+	14																													
1960	OTT	12										6	1						5	78	15.6	21	1								
1961	OTT	14										12	2	1	4	4.0	4	0	16	298	18.6	45	2								
1962	OTT	7																	9	178	19.8	43	0								
9	Years	109							9	179		46	8	1	4	4.0	4	0	49	897	18.3	45	5					1	10	10.0	10
R. JAY SOWARD Rodney Jay WR 5'11 184 Southern California B: 1/16/1978 Pomona, CA Draft: 1-29 2000 JAC Pro: N																															
2004	TOR	12				2						30	5						15	336	22.4	67	5	1	0	0.0	0				
2005	TOR	11				1						24	4						20	206	10.3	44	4								
2006	TOR	12				2						12	2						13	243	18.7	75	2								
3	Years	35				5						66	11						48	785	16.4	75	11	1	0	0.0	0				
RICK SOWIETA Rick LB 6'3 215 Ottawa Sooners Jrs.; Richmond B: 1/16/1954 Heusden, Belgium Draft: 1-2 1977 TOR																															
1977	TOR	16	0		1																										
1978	TOR	12	0		6																										
1979	OTT	10																													
1980	OTT+	16	0		2				3	55		6	1						1	2	2.0	2	1								
1981	OTT	16	0		1		6.0																								
1982	OTT	14					1.0																								
1983	OTT+	16	0		1		4.0		2	0																					
1984	OTT	16	0		3		8.0		1	0																					
1985	OTT+	16					1.0		2	13																					
1986	OTT	14	0		1		1.0		1	58																					
10	Years	146	0		15		21.0		9	126		6	1						1	2	2.0	2	1								
JOEY SOYKA Joseph HB-FW 5'8 159 Hamilton Jrs. B: 1923																															
1946	MTL	1																													
1947	HAM	10										5	1					1													
2	Years	11										5	1					1													
KEITH SPAITH Robert Keith QB-HB 6'0 195 St. Mary's (California); Southern California B: 4/8/1923 Tulare County, CA D: 3/19/1977 Tulare County, CA																															
1948	CAL+	12										26	2					2													
1949	CAL+	14										13	1																		
1950	CAL	14										18	2	37	-145	-3.9		1	1	15	15.0	15	1								
1951	CAL	10												17	-67	-3.9		0						1	0	0.0	0				
1952	CAL	14										13	1	22	-114	-5.2	5	1													
1953	CAL	16										1	0	35	-188	-5.4		0						1	0	0.0	0				
1954	CAL	13	1		0							6	1	3	6	2.0	3	1						1	0	0.0	0				
7	Years	93	1		0							77	7	114	-508	-4.5	5	5	1	15	15.0	15	1	3	0	0.0	0				
GEORGE SPANACH George OT-DT 6'1 235 Edmonton Huskies Jrs. B: 1944																															
1966	EDM	12	0		1																										
1967	EDM	10																													
1967	MTL	4																													
1967	Year	14																													
2	Years	22	0		1																										
OBIE SPANIC Obrad DT 6'4 270 Weber State B: 1/2/1970 Hamilton, ON Draft: 4-31 1994 OTT																															
1995	OTT	5				1																									
1996	OTT	18	0		1	34	4.0	29.0																							
1997	HAM	3				2																									
1998	HAM	18	0	0	2	12	3.0	16.0																							
4	Years	44	0	0	3	49	7.0	45.0																							
DAVE SPARENBERG David OG 6'3 257 Western Ontario B: 5/28/1959 Talbotville, ON Draft: 4E-36 1984 SAS Pro: N																															
1985	EDM	2																													
1986	EDM	6																													
1987	HAM	2				0																									
3	Years	10				0																									
LEN SPARKS Leonard FL-DH-S-LB 6'2 207 Wyoming B: 1940																															
1963	OTT	9																													
1964	OTT	11																						3	9	3.0	6				
1965	TOR	14	0		2							18	3						16	306	19.1	79	2					1	1	1.0	1
1966	CAL	16	1		0									1	7	7.0	7	0	14	226	16.1	37	0					2	15	7.5	11
1967	CAL	4																													
1967	BC	6																										2	24	12.0	13
1967	Year	10																										2	24	12.0	13
1968	BC	16							1	26																					
1969	BC	16	0		1				1	18									6	93	15.5	25	0								
7	Years	86	1		3				2	44		18	3	1	7	7.0	7	0	36	625	17.4	79	2	3	9	3.0	6	3	16	5.3	11
NATE SPARKS Jonathon QB 6'2 215 Boise State B: 5/14/1976 Bakersfield, CA																															
2000	BC	18				0								2	7	3.5	5	0													
ROBERT SPARKS Robert C. DB 5'9 175 Monterey Peninsula JC; San Francisco State B: 1/23/1953 Tulsa, OK Draft: 12-345 1976 MIN Pro: U																															
1979	CAL	16	4		2				5	98														7	44	6.3	18	12	173	14.4	25
1980	SAS	1																													
1980	OTT	2	1		0																			3	-9	-3.0	10	2	31	15.5	25
1980	CAL	7							1	0																					
1980	Year	10	1		0				1	0														3	-9	-3.0	10	2	31	15.5	25
2	Years	17	5		2				6	98														10	35	3.5	18	14	204	14.6	25
BERT SPARROW Bert T																															
1946	CAL	1																													
HAL SPARROW Harold HB-FB-P 6'0 188 Vancouver Blue Bombers Jrs.; Wenatchee Valley JC B: 1936																															
1957	BC	11	1		0									4	13	3.3	11	0	1	11	11.0	11	0	1	13	13.0	13				
1959	BC	11										3	0	4	-14	-3.5	9	0													
1960	BC	7	1		0							2	0	2	-24	-12.0	0	0													
3	Years	29	2		0							5	0	10	-25	-2.5	11	0	1	11	11.0	11	0	1	13	13.0	13				
JIM SPAVITAL James J. FB 6'1 210 Oklahoma State B: 9/15/1926 Oklahoma City, OK D: 3/7/1993 Stillwater, OK Draft: 8-45 1948 LA-AAFC; 1-11 1948 CHIC; 1-13 1951 NYG Pro: AN																															
1951	WPG	9										10	2	50	285	5.7		2	4	68	17.0		0								
CRAIG SPEAR Craig WR 5'11 180 Queen's B: 7/28/1980																															
2004	CAL	1				0													1	6	6.0	6	0								
CALVIN SPEARS Calvin DB 6'0 195 Grambling State B: 8/8/1980 Baton Rouge, LA Pro: E																															
2002	MTL	1				1																									
DOUG SPECHT Doug LB 6'2 250 Brigham Young B: 2/7/1942																															

Year	Team	GP	FM	FF	FR	TK	SK	YDS	IR	YDS	PD	PTS	TD	RA	YDS	AVG	LG	TD	REC	YDS	AVG	LG	TD	PR	YDS	AVG	LG	KOR	YDS	AVG	LG
1965	OTT	14																													
1966	OTT+	14	1		1																										
1967	OTT	14																										1	0	0.0	0
1968	OTT	12																													
1969	OTT	14	1		0																										
1970	OTT	14																													
1971	OTT	14	1		0																										
7	Years	96	3		1																							1	0	0.0	0
MAC SPEEDIE Mac Curtis OE 6'3 203 Utah B: 1/12/1920 Odell, IL D: 3/12/1993 Laguna Hills, CA Draft: 15-135 1942 DET Pro: AN																															
1953	SAS+	15										35	7						57	817	14.3		7								
1954	SAS+	14	1		0							25	5						36	576	16.0	61	5								
1955	BC	1																	1	11	11.0	11	0								
3	Years	30	1		0							60	12						94	1404	14.9	61	12								
CHRIS SPENCE Chris RB 5'10 210 Simon Fraser B: 4/26/1963 Wembley, England Draft: 3B-26 1985 BC																															
1986	BC	1																													
SANDY SPENCE Sandy HB 5'9 162 McGill; Montreal Ints.																															
1952	SAS	3																						2	9	4.5	9				
MARCUS SPENCER Marcus Lamar DB 6'1 213 Alabama B: 2/15/1978 Demopolis, AL																															
2002	HAM	12	0	1	1	22	1.0				1																				
2003	HAM	17	0	3	2	78	1.0				2																				
2004	HAM	14	0	1	1	42	2.0		1	3	5																				
3	Years	43	0	5	4	142	4.0		1	3	8																				
RANDY SPENCER Randy DT 6'4 275 Weber State B: 3/3/1979 Ottawa, ON Draft: 1B-8 2003 EDM																															
2003	EDM	2																													
2004	EDM	17				22	6.0	30.0																							
2005	EDM	10				4	3.0	13.0																							
2006	EDM	10				6																									
2007	MTL	17				5																									
5	Years	56				37	9.0	43.0																							
WALLY SPENCER Wally HB 5'7 150 Tulsa																															
1946	MTL	12										16	3					1					2								
WALTER SPENCER Walter DB-LB 5'10 213 Indianapolis B: 11/11/1978 Detroit, MI Draft: 3-23 2004 SAS																															
2004	SAS	17				28																									
2005	SAS	17				30																									
2006	CAL	16	0	0	1	21																									
2007	MTL	17				35																									
2008	MTL	17				22																									
2009	MTL	8	0	0	1	10																									
2010	MTL	9				11																		1	3	3.0	3				
2011	MTL	18				23																		1	6	6.0	6	2	14	7.0	12
8	Years	119	0	0	2	180																		2	9	4.5	6	2	14	7.0	12
SEAN SPENDER Sean LB 6'2 225 Guelph B: 11/18/1978 Brantford, ON Draft: 6A-48 2002 TOR																															
2002	MTL	11	0	0	1	7																									
2003	MTL	1				2																									
2003	EDM	16				13																									
2003	Year	17				15																									
2004	EDM	16				17																									
3	Years	28	0	0	1	39																									
BUD SPICER Bud DH 6'0 200 Wyoming B: 1940																															
1966	BC	3							1																						
PAUL SPICER Paul M. DE 6'4 278 DuPage JC; Saginaw Valley State B: 8/18/1975 Indianapolis, IN Pro: EN																															
1998	SAS	6				16	4.0	24.0			1																				
MIKE SPITZER Michael Fred OG 6'4 250 West Valley JC; San Jose State B: 7/26/1945 Kenosha, WI Draft: 6-148 1968 DET																															
1968	CAL	8																													
LEE SPIVEY Lee David OT 6'2 275 Southern Methodist B: 12/7/1957 Houston, TX Draft: 7-182 1981 DET Pro: U																															
1987	CAL	9	0		1	0																									
1988	CAL	2																													
2	Years	11	0		1	0																									
TOM SPOLETINI Tom OG 6'1 270 Calgary B: 5/5/1963 Calgary, AB Draft: 2B-15 1985 CAL																															
1985	CAL	9																													
1986	CAL	18	0		1																										
1987	CAL	17				0																									
1988	CAL	18			1	0																									
1989	CAL	16				0																									
1990	CAL	18	0		1	0								13	46	3.5	7	0	6	55	9.2	14	0								
6	Years	96	0		3	0								13	46	3.5	7	0	6	55	9.2	14	0								
TONY SPOLETINI Tony RB 5'10 225 Calgary B: 10/14/1965 Calgary, AB Draft: 7-62 1987 EDM																															
1988	EDM	12	4		1	1						6	1	27	126	4.7	16	1	3	11	3.7	8	0					4	30	7.5	21
1989	CAL	12	0		1	0								2	8	4.0	6	0	2	28	14.0	16	0								
1991	CAL	18	1		1	8								10	39	3.9	11	0	7	72	10.3	20	0					1	16	16.0	16
3	Years	42	5		3	9						6	1	39	173	4.4	16	1	12	111	9.3	20	0					5	46	9.2	21
QUINTON SPOTWOOD Quinton Shar WR 5'11 190 Syracuse B: 12/13/1977 Newark, NJ																															
2002	HAM	2				0													3	44	14.7	23	0	5	40	8.0	18				
GEORGE SPRINGATE George P.G. K 6'1 200 St. Lambert Saints Ints.; McGill B: 5/12/1938 Montreal, QC Draft: 1968 HAM																															
1970	MTL	11	1		0							41	0																		
1971	MTL	4	1		0							10	0																		
1972	MTL	2										4	0																		
3	Years	17	2		0							55	0																		
TOAR SPRINGSTEIN Clarence T 6'2 262 Regina Dales Jrs.; Manitoba B: 1919																															
1946	SAS	4										5	0																		
1949	SAS	14										1	0																		
1950	SAS	14																													
1951	SAS	14																													
1952	SAS	10			1																										
5	Years	56			1							6	0																		
ELMER SPROGIS Elmars, Jr. DB 5'10 187 Trinity (Connecticut) B: 1/15/1947 Oldenburg, Germany																															
1972	TOR	14	3		1																			79	458	5.8	23				
SKIPPY SPRUILL Lafayette Lovell LB 6'2 230 Houston B: 2/8/1947 Tacoma, WA D: 1/29/2008																															
1967	CAL	1			1																										
1967	TOR	1																													
1967	Year	2			1																										
RANDY SROCHENSKI Randy LB 6'3 220 Regina Rams Jrs. B: 1/15/1973 Regina, SK																															
1994	SAS	5				0																									
1996	SAS	10				3																									
1997	SAS	18	1	0	0	15																									
1998	SAS	18				15																									
1999	SAS	16	0	1	1	15																									
2000	SAS	18				11																									
2001	SAS	17	1	0	1	24																									
2002	TOR	18				13																									
2003	TOR	15				0																									
2004	TOR	18				8																									

Year	Team	GP	FM	FF	FR	TK	SK	YDS	IR	YDS	PD	PTS	TD	RA	YDS	AVG	LG	TD	REC	YDS	AVG	LG	TD	PR	YDS	AVG	LG	KOR	YDS	AVG	LG
2005	TOR	18				7																									
2006	TOR	18				3																									
2007	TOR	18				5																									
2008	TOR	18				3																									
2009	TOR	2				0																									
15	Years	227	2	1	2	122																									
HARVEY STABLES Harvey SB 6'4 210 Wilfrid Laurier B: 6/24/1974 Belleville, ON Draft: 4-27 2000 MTL																															
2000	MTL	6				1																									
2001	MTL	10	0	1	0	9																									
2002	MTL	7				2																									
2003	BC	10				8																									
4	Years	33	0	1	0	20																									
MICHAEL STADNYK Michael DE 6'4 247 Montana B: 8/8/1986 Regina, SK Draft: 2-B14 2008 SAS																															
2009	SAS	6				4																									
ANTHONY STAFFORD Anthony RB 5'8 180 Oklahoma B: 11/20/1966 St. Louis, MO Draft: 6-152 1989 DEN																															
1989	OTT	3	2		0	0								36	73	2.0	-19	0	5	30	6.0	13	0					1	31	31.0	31
DAVE STALA Dave SB-WR 6'2 205 St. Mary's (Nova Scotia) B: 10/25/1979 Myslenice, Poland Draft: 6A-50 2003 MTL																															
2003	MTL	12				1						3	0						10	179	17.9	36	0								
2004	MTL	9	2	0	0							1	0						12	171	14.3	25	0								
2005	MTL	18	3	0	1	6						31	5	1	-3	-3.0	-3	0	83	1037	12.5	43	5								
2006	MTL	16				1						12	2						38	445	11.7	65	2								
2007	MTL	1				0													2	20	10.0	12	0								
2008	MTL	1				0																									
2009	HAM	18				1						12	2						67	751	11.2	69	2								
2010	HAM+	18	1	0	1	3						36	6						85	1015	11.9	41	6					1	2	2.0	2
2011	HAM	18				2						48	8						59	771	13.1	58	8								
9	Years	111	6	0	2	14						143	23	1	-3	-3.0	-3	0	356	4389	12.3	69	23					1	2	2.0	2
RAMONDO STALLINGS Ramondo Antonio DL 6'7 290 San Diego State B: 11/21/1971 Winston-Salem, NC Draft: 7-195 1994 CIN Pro: NX																															
2000	BC	3				2	3.0	18.0																							
2000	EDM	5				8	2.0	14.0																							
2000	Year	8				10	5.0	32.0																							
TONY STALLINGS Tony RB 5'11 200 Louisville B: 12/1/1977 Cleveland, OH																															
2005	CAL	3				0													2	11	5.5	10	0					5	78	15.6	25
BRIAN STALLWORTH Brian QB 6'1 218 Central Arkansas B: 10/5/1979 Baton Rouge, LA																															
2002	WPG	18				0																									
2003	WPG	18				0								2	9	4.5	8	0													
2	Years	36				0								2	9	4.5	8	0													
FRED STAMPS Fredrick Paul SB-WR 6'1 182 Louisiana-Lafayette B: 12/10/1980 New Orleans, LA																															
2007	EDM	9	0	0	1	0													28	289	10.3	21	0	1	-5	-5.0	0	4	72	18.0	30
2008	EDM	14	0	0	1	1						36	6						50	751	15.0	46	6					14	297	21.2	49
2009	EDM*	18	1	0	0	1						48	8	1	0	0.0	0	0	85	1402	16.5	63	8					1	-2	-2.0	-2
2010	EDM+	14	1	0	0	2						30	5	1	5	5.0	5	0	80	1223	15.3	51	5								
2011	EDM*	15	1	0	1	3						48	8	1	-2	-2.0	-2	0	82	1153	14.1	75	8					2	0	0.0	0
5	Years	70	3	0	3	7						162	27	3	3	1.0	5	0	325	4818	14.8	75	27	1	-5	-5.0	0	21	367	17.5	49
KEITH STANBERRY Keith DB 6'0 208 Oklahoma B: 9/3/1962																															
1987	HAM	1	0		1	1	1.0		1	33																					
T.J. STANCIL Thomas LB 6'2 215 Boston College B: 6/11/1982 Bensalem, PA																															
2005	SAS	10	0	0	1	39	1.0	10.0	1	13	3																				
2006	SAS	6				15					1																				
2007	SAS	6	0	1	0	36	1.0	4.0	1	2	3																				
3	Years	22	0	1	1	90	2.0	14.0	2	15	7																				
BOB STANDEN Robert T 5'10 180 B: 1928																															
1949	CAL	9																													
CHUCK STANLEY Charles HB 5'8 185 South Carolina State B: 1936																															
1961	OTT	5										6	1	34	334	9.8	62	1	1	-4	-4.0	-4	0	12	66	5.5	10	8	188	23.5	32
DAVID STANLEY David Wayne LB 6'1 225 Southern Methodist B: 4/10/1964 D: 6/5/2005 Angelton, TX																															
1988	WPG	3																													
DIMITRIOUS STANLEY Dimitrious W. WR 5'10 190 Ohio State B: 9/19/1974 Pahokee, FL																															
1998	WPG	3	1	0	0	0						6	1						16	134	8.4	26	1	1	8	8.0	8	5	91	18.2	23
KEN STANLEY Kenneth E 6'0 195 McMaster B: 1931 Toronto, ON D: 4/19/2008																															
1954	HAM	7																													
1955	HAM	8																													
2	Years	15																													
WALTER STANLEY Walter WR 5'9 180 Colorado; Mesa State* B: 11/5/1962 Chicago, IL Draft: 4-98 1985 GB; 4A-54 1985 MEM-USFL Pro: N																															
1993	OTT	8	1		0	0						6	1						11	302	27.5	57	1	32	175	5.5	44	8	110	13.8	21
1994	OTT	3				1													2	19	9.5	10	0	6	50	8.3	13				
2	Years	11	1		0	1						6	1						13	321	24.7	57	1	38	225	5.9	44	8	110	13.8	21
BILL STANTON William McKimmon DE-FW 6'2 210 North Carolina State B: 4/21/1924 Dillon, SC D: 5/9/2010 Garner, NC Draft: 27-252 1948 PHI Pro: A																															
1950	OTT+	12										10	2					1													
1951	OTT	11										5	1										1								
1952	OTT	6										10	2										2								
3	Years	29										25	5					1					3								
JEROME STANTON Jerome DB 6'0 187 Michigan State B: 6/7/1957 Detroit, MI Draft: 10A-258 1979 MIA																															
1981	OTT	13							3	61																					
STEVE STAPLER Steven G. WR-P 5'11 165 San Diego State B: 6/28/1958 Los Angeles, CA																															
1980	TOR	2																	5	59	11.8	21	0					3	59	19.7	25
1981	HAM	15	2		1							26	4	1	-13	-13.0	-13	0	48	903	18.8	74	4	40	383	9.6	36	18	450	25.0	59
1982	HAM	14										20	3	1	4	4.0	4	0	44	588	13.4	45	3	6	60	10.0	39	13	223	17.2	27
1984	HAM	5										12	2	1	14	14.0	14	0	21	361	17.2	83	2								
1985	HAM+	16	0		1							54	9						40	690	17.3	57	9								
1986	HAM	17	2		0							32	5	2	-15	-7.5	-10	0	62	861	13.9	51	5					4	64	16.0	20
1987	HAM+	18				2						81	13						85	1516	17.8	81	13					2	39	19.5	24
1988	HAM	14										24	4						48	870	18.1	75	4								
8	Years	101	4		2	2						249	40	5	-10	-2.0	14	0	353	5848	16.6	83	40	46	443	9.6	39	40	835	20.9	59
KEN STARCH Kenneth Earl RB 5'11 210 Wisconsin B: 3/5/1954 LaCrosse, WI Pro: N																															
1978	MTL	12	5		0							18	3	109	429	3.9	18	2	17	71	4.2	15	1								
KEVIN STARKEY Kevin James QB 6'1 185 El Camino JC; Long Beach State B: 7/9/1958 Santa Monica, CA Pro: U																															
1981	OTT	7	1		1									9	44	4.9	18	0													
1982	OTT	7												7	31	4.4	12	0													
1983	OTT	2												4	43	10.8	11	0													
1983	MTL	12	4		0									35	160	4.6	28	0													
1983	Year	12												39	203	5.2	28	0													
3	Years	16	5		1									55	278	5.1	28	0													
HOWARD STARKS Howard DB 6'1 185 Wichita State B: 1945																															
1966	MTL	2	1		0																			8	16	2.0	5				
1966	CAL	10	2		1							36	6	28	141	5.0	40	1	29	485	16.7	63	5	21	105	5.0	24	5	122	24.4	30
1966	Year	12	3		1							36	6	28	141	5.0	40	1	29	485	16.7	63	5	29	121	4.2	24	5	122	24.4	30
1969	CAL	16	1		0				2	80				7	34	4.9	19	0	4	46	11.5	15	0	10	91	9.1	30				
1970	CAL	16							6	70														9	119	13.2	23	6	166	27.7	48
1971	CAL+	16							5	111				3	5	1.7	5	0	2	43	21.5	23	0	12	187	15.6	26	5	125	25.0	30
1972	CAL	16							4	62		6	1	1	1	1.0	1	0	4	115	28.8	72	1	11	105	9.5	21				
1973	CAL	16																	1	14	14.0	14	0	4	36	9.0	19	2	46	23.0	27

Year	Team	GP	FM	FF	FR	TK	SK	YDS	IR	YDS	PD	PTS	TD	RA	YDS	AVG	LG	TD	REC	YDS	AVG	LG	TD	PR	YDS	AVG	LG	KOR	YDS	AVG	LG
1974	CAL+	16	0		1				5	101		12	2						1	27	27.0	27	0	5	37	7.4	15	1	17	17.0	17
1975	CAL	10							4	85														2	27	13.5	14				
8	Years	108	4		2				26	509		54	9	39	181	4.6	40	1	41	730	17.8	72	6	82	723	8.8	30	19	476	25.1	48
MARSHALL STARKS Marshall L. CB-DH 6'0 190 Illinois B: 3/6/1939 Draft: 8-106 1961 STL Pro: N																															
1966	EDM	16							1															1	4	4.0	4	2	52	26.0	30
KENDRICK STARLING Kendrick Ladell WR 6'0 193 Navarro JC; San Jose State B: 12/27/1979 Marshall, TX Pro: EN																															
2007	HAM	3				0													2	18	9.0	12	0								
BILL STARR William TE 6'3 225 John Carroll; Hofstra B: 5/5/1944																															
1969	MTL	14	0		1							7	1						51	686	13.5	66	1								
1970	HAM	4										6	1						7	134	19.1	38	1								
2	Years	18	0		1							13	2						58	820	14.1	66	2								
ERIC STARR Eric RB 5'9 195 North Carolina B: 2/2/1966 Ellenboro, NC																															
1990	BC	2	1		1	0								1	15	15.0	15	0	2	39	19.5	31	0					6	138	23.0	34
1992	BC	3				6																		2	4	2.0	4	5	102	20.4	28
2	Years	5	1		1	6								1	15	15.0	15	0	2	39	19.5	31	0	2	4	2.0	4	11	240	21.8	34
STAN STASICA Stanley Joseph QB-HB 5'10 175 Gordon Military JC; South Carolina; Illinois B: 6/24/1919 Rockford, IL Draft: 8-75 1944 CLE Pro: A																															
1947	SAS+	7										5	1					1													
RALPH STATEN Ralph Lahquan LB-DH 6'3 205 Alabama B: 12/3/1974 Mobile, AL Draft: 7C-236 1997 BAL Pro: N																															
2000	EDM+	17				44			4	7	12																				
2001	EDM	18	0	1	1	39	3.0	41.0	2	8	2																				
2002	OTT	8	0	0	1	16					4	6	1																		
3	Years	43	0	1	2	99	3.0	41.0	6	15	18	6	1																		
TONY STATEN Tony DB 5'9 178 Angelo State B: 2/6/1963 Washington, DC Draft: 7-174 1985 DET; TD 1985 SA-USFL																															
1986	SAS	1	1		0																			1	8	8.0	8	2	18	9.0	16
JIM STATON James Brooks, Jr. DT 6'4 240 Wake Forest B: 5/23/1927 Ansonville, NC D: 9/16/1993 Greensboro, NC Draft: 2B-21 1951 WAS Pro: N																															
1952	MTL+	11																													
1953	MTL	1																													
1954	MTL+	14																													
1955	MTL	9																													
1956	MTL	14																													
5	Years	49																													
PAT STAUB Patrick OT-OG 6'1 255 Temple B: 3/11/1955 Hanover, PA Pro: U																															
1980	OTT	16																													
1981	OTT	5																													
1982	OTT	12																													
3	Years	33																													
SCOTT STAUCH Scott Roy RB 5'11 204 UCLA B: 1/3/1959 Seattle, WA Pro: N																															
1983	EDM	10	1		1							12	2	55	330	6.0	34	2	21	178	8.5	20	0								
BENNY STECK Benny G-T 6'0 195 Montreal Rockland Jrs. B: 5/5/1921 Montreal, QC																															
1946	MTL+	11										5	1																		
1947	OTT	12																													
1948	OTT	8																													
1949	OTT	11																													
1950	OTT	11																													
1951	OTT	9																													
6	Years	62										5	1																		
DEREK STEELE Derek Lee NT 6'3 265 Maryland B: 12/27/1965 Newport News, VA Draft: 7-169 1992 IND																															
1993	TOR	2				1																									
EDDIE STEELE Eddie DT 6'0 273 Manitoba B: 7/4/1988 Winnipeg, MB Draft: 3B-22 2010 HAM																															
2011	HAM	18	0	0	1	28	1.0	1.0																							
GLENN STEELE Glenn WR-SB 5'8 180 Renfrew Trojans Jrs.; British Columbia B: 4/10/1963 Vancouver, BC Draft: 5-45 1985 WPG																															
1985	WPG	14	2		1							12	2						2	45	22.5	34	1	63	615	9.8	70	11	214	19.5	43
1986	OTT	6										2	0						4	73	18.3	29	0	11	76	6.9	14				
2	Years	20	2		1							14	2						6	118	19.7	34	1	74	691	9.3	70	11	214	19.5	43
JOHN STEELE John DB 6'1 202 Simon Fraser B: 11/12/1948 Draft: 2-15 1971 SAS																															
1971	SAS	16	0		1							9	0						1	12	12.0	12	0								
1972	SAS	9	0		1							0	0																		
1973	WPG	15	2		2				3	29				1	2	2.0	2	0	1	0	0.0	0	0	32	49	1.5	9				
3	Years	40	2		4				3	29		9	0	1	2	2.0	2	0	2	12	6.0	12	0	32	49	1.5	9				
GRANT STEEN Grant LB 6'2 242 Iowa B: 10/22/1980 Emmettsburg, IA Pro: E																															
2005	MTL	1				1																									
DYLAN STEENBERGEN Dylan OT-OG 6'5 285 Calgary B: 7/24/1987 Lethbridge, AB Draft: 1-7 2009 MTL																															
2010	MTL	1				0																									
2011	EDM	4				0																									
2	Years	5				0																									
GIL STEER Gil G-C-T 6'2 206 British Columbia B: 1929																															
1951	CAL	14																													
1952	CAL	14																													
1954	BC	12																													
3	Years	40																													
DICK STEERE Richard Edward T 6'4 240 Drake B: 3/2/1927 Chicago, IL Draft: 5A-53 1951 SF Pro: N																															
1952	EDM	2										1	0																		
JEREMY STEEVES Jeremy S 6'2 200 St. Francis Xavier B: 5/24/1983 Moncton, NB Draft: 4-32 2005 HAM																															
2007	EDM	4				0																									
GILL STEGALL Gill Anthony WR 5'9 170 Arkansas State; Harding B: 4/30/1961 Little Rock, AR D: 4/23/1988 Searcy, AR Draft: 11-152 1985 DEN-USFL Pro: U																															
1986	MTL	7										6	1						13	288	22.2	74	1								
MILT STEGALL Milt Eugene WR-SB 6'0 184 Miami (Ohio) B: 1/25/1970 Cincinnati, OH Pro: N																															
1995	WPG	6	1		1	3						24	4						25	469	18.8	51	4	2	85	42.5	80	10	172	17.2	42
1996	WPG	11	0		1	1						36	6						34	613	18.0	53	6	16	113	7.1	19				
1997	WPG*	18	1	0	0	1						84	14	5	21	4.2	9	0	61	1616	26.5	105	14	8	146	18.3	55	6	199	33.2	49
1998	WPG	7				0						42	7						32	403	12.6	62	6	2	91	45.5	80				
1999	WPG+	13	0	0	1	2						44	7	2	6	3.0	15	0	73	1193	16.3	99	6	1	4	4.0	4	1	-3	-3.0	-3
2000	WPG*	16	2	0	2	2						90	15	1	2	2.0	2	0	78	1499	19.2	86	15					1	1	1.0	1
2001	WPG*	16				3						86	14						81	1214	15.0	79	14					1	0	0.0	0
2002	WPG*	18	0	1	0	1						140	23						105	1862	17.7	83	23								
2003	WPG	18	1	0	0	4						90	15						68	1144	16.8	73	15								
2004	WPG	16	0	0	1	6						44	7	0	0		0	1	68	1121	16.5	67	6								
2005	WPG*	17	1	0	0	3						102	17						52	1184	22.8	101	17					1	0	0.0	0
2006	WPG*	14	1	0	0	3						42	7	2	34	17.0	20	0	79	1269	16.1	100	7								
2007	WPG+	17	1	0	0	2						48	8	2	-8	-4.0	-1	0	69	1108	16.1	49	8								
2008	WPG	12				1						18	3						29	458	15.8	92	3								
14	Years	199	8	1	6	32						890	147	12	55	4.6	20	1	854	15153	17.7	105	144	29	439	15.1	80	20	369	18.5	49
ORLANDO STEINAUER Orlando CB-S 5'10 180 Western Washington B: 6/9/1973 Seattle, WA																															
1996	OTT	2				2																									
1997	HAM+	18				67	1.0	1.0	7	184	0	6	1											27	137	5.1	12	6	97	16.2	23
1998	HAM*	15				53	1.0	5.0	8	138	2	6	1											12	95	7.9	20				
1999	HAM	18				55			3	146	7	12	2											1	35	35.0	35				
2001	TOR	16	0	0	2	89			5	138	2																				
2002	TOR*	18				94			4	132	6																				
2003	TOR*	18	0	0	2	42			6	132	6	6	1																		
2004	TOR*	17	0	3	2	62			4	53	5	6	1											1	9	9.0	9				
2005	TOR	18	0	1	3	45			3	99	4																				

Year	Team	GP	FM	FF	FR	TK	SK	YDS	IR	YDS	PD	PTS	TD	RA	YDS	AVG	LG	TD	REC	YDS	AVG	LG	TD	PR	YDS	AVG	LG	KOR	YDS	AVG	LG
2006	TOR+	18	0	1	0	62			1	0	1																				
2007	TOR*	18	0	0	1	41			7	143	5																				
2008	TOR	8	0	0	1	21			1	13	2																				
12	Years	184	0	5	11	633	2.0	6.0	49	1178	40	36	6											41	276	6.7	35	6	97	16.2	23
BOB STEINER Bob DT-DE-OT 6'4 245 Hamilton Hurricanes Jrs. B: 1945																															
1966	HAM	6																													
1967	HAM	8																													
1968	HAM	14																													
1969	HAM	14																										1	7	7.0	7
1970	HAM	14	0		1																										
1971	HAM	14	0		1																										
1972	EDM	13																													
7	Years	83	0		2																							1	7	7.0	7
PETER STENERSON Peter SB-DB-WR-WB 6'2 195 Carleton B: 8/6/1953 Draft: TE 1975 OTT																															
1975	OTT	10																	1	7	7.0	7	0					1	14	14.0	14
1976	OTT	16			2				5	97																					
1977	OTT	16	0		2				1	0																					
1978	OTT	16	0		1							30	5	3	10	3.3	5	0	20	278	13.9	35	5	1	0	0.0	0				
1979	OTT	10	2		0							12	2	3	3	1.0	6	0	20	312	15.6	40	2								
1980	OTT	16										6	1	8	52	6.5	18	0	31	477	15.4	56	1								
1981	OTT	7										6	1						2	19	9.5	10	1								
1982	OTT	10										12	2						25	367	14.7	37	2								
8	Years	101	2		5				6	97		66	11	14	65	4.6	18	0	99	1460	14.7	56	11	1	0	0.0	0	1	14	14.0	14
ANDY STENSRUD Andy OT 6'8 272 Iowa State B: 9/26/1978 Lake Mills, IA Pro: E																															
2002	BC	5				0																									
RICK STEPANEK Richard DT 6'6 244 Iowa B: 8/30/1948 Berwyn, IL Draft: 13-324 1970 ATL																															
1971	BC	2																													
JOHN STEPHANS John QB Holy Cross B: 1935 Draft: 18-207 1956 PIT																															
1956	TOR	2												2	3	1.5	3	0													
BOB STEPHEN George Robert C-OG 6'2 240 Ottawa Sooners Jrs. B: 2/23/1958 St. John, NB D: 2/8/2009 Ottawa, ON																															
1981	OTT	6																													
1982	OTT	16	3		0																										
1983	OTT	13	0		1																										
1984	OTT	15	1		2																										
1985	OTT	16																													
5	Years	66	4		3																										
BUS STEPHENS Buster FW-S 5'11 185 Tennessee B: 1923																															
1947	HAM	12										15	2					2													
FRANK STEPHENS Frank Lorenzo LB 6'2 197 UCLA B: 1/13/1956 San Diego, CA																															
1979	TOR	1																													
1980	TOR	9							2	2																					
2	Years	10							2	2																					
KEITH STEPHENS Keith RB Louisville																															
1990	BC	1	1		0																			2	16	8.0	10	2	41	20.5	28
MICHAEL STEPHENS Michael K. WR 6'2 195 Nevada-Reno B: 10/9/1972 Gardena, CA																															
1994	LV	10				0						18	3						18	330	18.3	68	3								
SANDY STEPHENS Sanford Emory, Jr. QB 6'1 225 Minnesota B: 9/21/1940 Pittsburgh, PA D: 6/6/2000 Bloomington, MN Draft: 1-5 1962 NYT; 2B-25 1962 CLE																															
1962	MTL	14										56	8	71	398	5.6	35	8	4	41	10.3	18	0								
1963	MTL	2										1	0	2	11	5.5	6	0													
1963	TOR	8										22	1	15	78	5.2	23	0	8	151	18.9	42	1								
1963	Year	10										23	1	17	89	5.2	23	0	8	151	18.9	42	1								
2	Years	16										79	9	88	487	5.5	35	8	12	192	16.0	42	1								
WALLY STEPHENS Wallace HB 185 Montana B: 1928																															
1947	CAL	7										15	3					3													
DARYL STEPHENSON Daryl RB 6'2 227 Windsor B: 10/8/1985 London, ON Draft: 3-24 2008 WPG																															
2008	WPG	2	1	0	0	0								9	19	2.1	5	0	2	12	6.0	8	0								
2009	WPG	18				0													1	1	1.0	1	0					2	18	9.0	17
2010	WPG	9				2								7	30	4.3	8	0										3	41	13.7	18
2011	HAM	9	0	0	1	5								6	17	2.8	8	0													
4	Years	38	1	0	1	7								22	66	3.0	8	0	3	13	4.3	8	0					5	59	11.8	18
DANA STEPHENSON Dana G. DB 6'2 190 Nebraska B: 4/19/1948 Lincoln, NE Draft: 8-183 1970 CHIB																															
1970	WPG	3	1		0																										
DON STEPHENSON Donald P. LB-C 6'0 205 Georgia Tech B: 1935 Draft: 19-222 1958 WAS																															
1958	EDM	16	0		3																										
1959	EDM	16							2	18																					
1960	EDM	16	0		3				6	98		6	1																		
1961	EDM	16	2		3				2	5																		2	3	1.5	3
1962	EDM	15																													
1963	EDM	10	0		2				1																						
1963	CAL	2																													
1963	Year	12	0		2				1																						
1964	CAL	16	0		3				2	26																					
1965	CAL	16	0		3				2	0																					
8	Years	121	2		17				15	147		6	1															2	3	1.5	3
GRANT STEPHENSON Grant LB 6'1 215 St. Mary's (Nova Scotia); St. Francis Xavier B: 12/30/1952 Draft: 4-34 1975 OTT																															
1976	HAM	1																													
JEFF STEPHENSON Jeffrey DL 6'4 240 St. Cloud State B: 12/14/1965 Forrest City, AR																															
1990	BC	1				1																									
DEE STERLING Dee DT 6'3 264 Queen's B: 2/3/1986 Kingston, ON Draft: 2B-12 2009 EDM																															
2009	EDM	17				5																									
2010	EDM	12				9	2.0	5.0																							
2	Years	29				14	2.0	5.0																							
JON STERLING Jon TE 6'3 235 Edmonton Huskies Jrs. B: 1945																															
1966	EDM	4																													
GERRY STERNBERG Gerald DB-FL 5'10 175 Toronto B: 3/18/1943 Orsk, Russia Draft: 1965 EDM																															
1966	MTL	10										6	1						11	181	16.5	48	1					1	17	17.0	17
1967	MTL	14	1		1							12	2						16	218	13.6	35	2								
1969	TOR	14	2		1				1	20														44	311	7.1	28	2	48	24.0	27
1970	TOR	14	1		0				3	36									1	36	36.0	36	0	65	307	4.7	25				
1971	TOR	7							1	7																					
1971	HAM	8	0		3				1	3																					
1971	Year	15							2	10																					
1972	HAM	14	1		1				4	30														44	299	6.8	34				
1973	TOR	14	1		2				4	102														41	243	5.9	18				
7	Years	87	6		8				14	198		18	3						28	435	15.5	48	3	194	1160	6.0	34	3	65	21.7	27
GEORGE STETTER George DB 5'11 180 Virginia B: 4/29/1945 Neptune, NJ Draft: 14B-367 1967 NO																															
1967	MTL	9							1	12														2	10	5.0	6				
1968	OTT	5																													
2	Years	14							1	12														2	10	5.0	6				
CORY STEVENS Cory P 6'3 245 Minot State B: 12/8/1968 Draft: 3B-26 1996 CAL																															
1999	SAS	2	1	0	0	2						1	0																		
KYLE STEVENS Kyle O. RB 5'8 180 Washington B: 7/13/1958 Loma Linda, CA																															

Year	Team	GP	FM	FF	FR	TK	SK	YDS	IR	YDS	PD	PTS	TD	RA	YDS	AVG	LG	TD	REC	YDS	AVG	LG	TD	PR	YDS	AVG	LG	KOR	YDS	AVG	LG
1982	HAM	5	3		0									42	174	4.1	17	0	25	232	9.3	34	0					10	234	23.4	33
MARK STEVENS Mark QB 6'1 190 Utah B: 2/19/1962 Passaic, NJ Pro: N																															
1985	MTL	12	2		0									25	96	3.8	9	0													
1986	MTL	8										6	1	4	25	6.3	11	1													
2	Years	20	2		0							6	1	29	121	4.2	11	1													
AL STEVENSON Al T-G 6'1 227 Montreal Pats Jrs. B: 12/23/1921 Montreal, QC D: 1/4/1958																															
1946	MTL	11																													
1947	MTL	11										5	1																		
1948	MTL	1																													
1949	MTL	12																													
1950	MTL	12																													
1951	MTL	2																													
6	Years	49										5	1																		
BILL STEVENSON Bill QB 6'0 190 Toronto B: 1933 Toronto, ON Draft: 3-12 1955 MTL																															
1955	CAL	16												11	37	3.4	27	0													
1956	CAL	15							1	5		1	0	5	31	6.2	47	0						3	23	7.7	9				
1957	CAL	8	0		1				1	17				1	2	2.0	2	0						1	8	8.0	8				
3	Years	39	0		1				2	22		1	0	17	70	4.1	47	0						4	31	7.8	9				
BILL STEVENSON William George OG-OT-DT-DE 6'4 270 Edmonton Huskies Jrs.; Drake B: 8/20/1950 High Prairie, AB D: 3/21/2007 Edmonton, AB Draft: TE 1974 EDM; 4-104 1974 MIA Pro: W																															
1975	EDM	3																													
1976	EDM	16																													
1977	EDM	16																													
1978	EDM*	16																													
1979	EDM+	16																													
1980	EDM	16																													
1981	EDM*	16																													
1982	EDM	16																													
1983	EDM	16																													
1984	EDM	16																													
1985	EDM	16																													
1987	EDM	18				0																									
1988	EDM	10				0																									
13	Years	191				0																									
NORRIS STEVENSON Norris HB 6'1 205 Missouri B: 1940 Draft: 12-93 1961 NYT; 11-142 1961 DAL																															
1963	BC	3	0		1									4	9	2.3	11	0													
ROBERT STEVENSON Robert OG 6'2 288 Florida State B: 12/20/1969 Pensacola, FL																															
1994	SAC	15				0																									
1995	SA	18	1		0	7																									
1996	OTT	15				0																									
3	Years	48	1		0	7																									
ROY STEVENSON Roy OG-OT-DE-DT 6'1 195 Toronto B: 1932																															
1955	EDM	3																													
1956	EDM	4																													
1957	EDM	14																													
1958	EDM	14							1	0																					
1959	EDM	16																													
1960	EDM	3																													
1961	EDM	14																													
7	Years	68							1	0																					
VIC STEVENSON Victor OT-OG-C 6'4 255 Calgary B: 9/22/1960 New Westminster, BC Draft: 5-37 1981 SAS																															
1983	SAS	10																													
1984	SAS	16	0		1																										
1985	SAS	16	0		1									0	2		2	0													
1986	SAS	12																													
1987	SAS	18	0		1	0																									
1988	SAS	18				1																									
1989	SAS	18				1																									
1990	SAS	18				0																									
1991	SAS+	18				1																									
1992	SAS*	18				0																									
1993	BC	18				0																									
1994	BC	14				0																									
1995	BC+	17				2																									
1996	TOR	18				0																									
1997	EDM	18				0																									
1998	SAS	10				0																									
1998	MTL	1				0																									
1998	Year	11				0																									
1999	MTL	1				0																									
17	Years	258	0		3	5								0	2		2	0													
ANDREW STEWART Andrew DE 6'5 265 Fresno CC; Cincinnati B: 11/20/1965 Kingston, Jamaica Draft: 4-107 1989 CLE Pro: N																															
1993	OTT	6	0		1	12																									
1994	BC	18	0		4	39	4.0	24.0																							
1995	BC+	18				20	5.0	42.0			2																				
1996	TOR	18				37	4.0	31.0																							
1997	TOR	18				19	8.0	45.0			1																				
1998	SAS	15	0	0	1	22	4.0	20.0			1																				
1999	WPG	8				6	1.0	3.0																							
7	Years	101	0	0	6	155	26.0	165.0			4																				
ANWAR STEWART Anwar DE 6'3 244 Kentucky B: 2/9/1976 Panama City, FL																															
2001	CAL	1				1																									
2002	MTL	14				19	1.0	8.0	2	46	1	6	1																		
2003	MTL+	18	1	1	2	38	7.0	40.0			1													2	22	11.0	16	4	20	5.0	12
2004	MTL*	18	1	3	0	25	9.0	79.0	4	64	11	12	2						2	44	22.0	35	0					2	7	3.5	5
2005	MTL	18	0	1	1	33	10.0	74.0			5								3	41	13.7	17	0					1	9	9.0	9
2006	MTL	18	0	0	1	30	9.0	63.0	1	35	5	6	1						1	52	52.0	52	0								
2007	MTL	18	0	2	0	35	4.0	21.0			2								4	51	12.8	21	0								
2008	MTL	18	0	0	1	31	4.0	11.0	1	19	5																	1	0	0.0	0
2009	MTL*	18	0	4	0	40	8.0	62.0	1	3	5																				
2010	MTL	17	0	2	2	26	6.0	34.0			5																				
2011	MTL	18	0	1	1	36	7.0	41.0	1	0	3																				
11	Years	176	2	14	8	314	65.0	433.0	10	167	43	24	4						10	188	18.8	52	0	2	22	11.0	16	8	36	4.5	12
ART STEWART Arthur O. HB 5'11 210 Southeastern Oklahoma State B: 11/21/1926 Wilson, OK Draft: 25-318 1950 WAS; 29-340 1951 WAS																															
1952	SAS	5			1									24	140	5.8	13	0													
BRANDON STEWART Brandon CB-DH 6'1 198 Eastern Arizona JC B: 5/16/1986 Seattle, WA																															
2007	CAL	1				2																									
2008	CAL	1				0																									
2009	WPG	4				3																									
2010	WPG	17	0	1	1	35			1	24	1								1	27	27.0	27	0								
2011	WPG	18	1	0	2	43			4	150	3	6	1											1	7	7.0	7				
5	Years	41	1	1	3	83			5	174	4	6	1						1	27	27.0	27	0	1	7	7.0	7				

Year	Team	GP	FM	FF	FR	TK	SK	YDS	IR	YDS	PD	PTS	TD	RA	YDS	AVG	LG	TD	REC	YDS	AVG	LG	TD	PR	YDS	AVG	LG	KOR	YDS	AVG	LG
BRODERICK STEWART Broderick William, II DE 6'5 230 Vanderbilt B: 8/31/1987																															
2010	TOR	4				5																									
DON STEWART Don DE 6'1 200 Western Ontario B: 1937																															
1959	SAS	14																													
DUANE STEWART Duane Anthony DB 6'3 200 Washington State B: 5/18/1975 Los Angeles, CA																															
1998	EDM	6	0	0	1	22																									
GORD STEWART Gordon DT-DE 6'4 248 Boise State B: 6/18/1945																															
1971	SAS	16																													
1972	SAS	8																													
1972	WPG	8																													
1972	Year	16																													
1973	WPG	16	0		1																										
1974	CAL	10																													
1976	HAM	1																													
5	Years	51	0		1																										
JACKIE STEWART Jack HB-FW 5'9 169 B: 1925																															
1946	HAM	12																													
1947	HAM	12										15	3					2					1								
1948	HAM	4										1	0																		
1950	HAM	12										10	2					2													
1951	HAM	11																													
1952	HAM	11										5	1										1								
6	Years	62										31	6					4					2								
KYE STEWART Kye LB 6'0 210 Illinois State B: 2/17/1985 Nashville, TN																															
2009	SAS	7	0	1	0	25			1	0	0																				
2010	SAS	10	0	1	1	24																									
2011	SAS	17	0	0	1	46	1.0	3.0			1																				
3	Years	34	0	2	2	95	1.0	3.0	1	0	1																				
MARK STEWART Mark Anthony LB 6'3 232 Washington B: 10/13/1959 Palo Alto, CA Draft: 5-127 1983 MIN; 2-22 1983 NJ-USFL Pro: N																															
1985	WPG	1																													
QUINCY STEWART Quincy Jermaine LB 6'1 227 Louisiana Tech B: 3/27/1978 Tyler, TX Pro: N																															
2005	EDM	1				0																									
2006	EDM	18				49	3.0																								
2	Years	19				49	3.0																								
ROB STEWART Rob DT 6'2 275 Manitoba B: 4/14/1977 Draft: 4A-28 2002 TOR																															
2003	SAS	7				1																									
RON STEWART Ron HB-FB British Columbia Draft: 2-11 1957 CAL																															
1957	CAL	1																													
1957	BC	3																													
1957	Year	4																													
RON STEWART Ron OHB 5'7 175 Queen's B: 9/25/1934 Toronto, ON																															
1958	OTT	8												3	1	0.3	3	0	2	32	16.0	20	0	22	117	5.3	12				
1959	OTT	13										18	3	82	425	5.2	31	2	15	150	10.0	28	1	40	271	6.8	28	13	265	20.4	38
1960	OTT+	14										96	16	139	1020	7.3	59	15	15	240	16.0	38	1	47	238	5.1	25	22	501	22.8	43
1961	OTT+	12										60	10	107	706	6.6	72	6	11	137	12.5	30	4					10	231	23.1	62
1962	OTT	14										30	5	96	555	5.8	68	2	19	347	18.3	37	3	8	27	3.4	11	4	88	22.0	31
1963	OTT	14										48	8	103	523	5.1	35	3	23	340	14.8	45	5	1	4	4.0	4	14	405	28.9	93
1964	OTT+	14	2		0							48	8	144	867	6.0	45	5	20	411	20.6	70	3					10	258	25.8	67
1965	OTT	14	1		0							24	4	68	314	4.6	16	2	16	162	10.1	36	2					3	32	10.7	19
1966	OTT	14	2		0							30	5	89	431	4.8	41	3	19	275	14.5	50	2					7	182	26.0	44
1967	OTT	14	1		2							30	5	64	488	7.6	70	4	25	316	12.6	51	1								
1968	OTT	14	1		0									31	114	3.7	16	0	14	129	9.2	23	0								
1969	OTT	14	1		1							18	3	29	151	5.2	26	1	14	148	10.6	29	1								
1970	OTT	8												28	95	3.4	12	0	9	40	4.4	10	0								
13	Years	167	8		3							402	67	983	5690	5.8	72	43	202	2727	13.5	70	23	118	657	5.6	28	83	1962	23.6	93
RON STEWART Ronald QB-DB-LB 6'3 200 Utah State B: 1943																															
1967	CAL	14	1		1				1	0																					
1968	CAL	16	0		1				5	57		3	0																		
1970	CAL	16	0		1				3	26		6	1																		
3	Years	46	1		3				9	83		9	1																		
SHAWN STEWART Shawn LB 6'0 215 Emporia State B: 2/16/1967 Montreal, QC																															
1990	BC	9																										1	12	12.0	12
TONY STEWART Tony RB 6'0 201 Iowa B: 1/30/1968 Chester, SC Draft: 11-297 1991 SEA																															
1993	CAL	6	3		1	2						6	1	53	196	3.7	17	1	8	87	10.9	20	0								
1994	CAL	18	6		1	3						114	19	208	1120	5.4	65	14	57	586	10.3	42	5					4	78	19.5	42
1995	CAL	17	8		1	2						36	6	153	735	4.8	18	3	56	504	9.0	36	3					3	57	19.0	26
1996	HAM	7	2		0	3						12	2	42	232	5.5	56	2	23	194	8.4	31	0								
4	Years	48	19		3	10						168	28	456	2283	5.0	65	20	144	1371	9.5	42	8					7	135	19.3	42
CHARLIE STICKA Charlie FB 5'11 195 Trinity (Connecticut) B: 9/13/1933 Draft: 10-120 1956 LARM																															
1957	TOR	3												22	70	3.2	13	0	3	-9	-3.0	5	0								
DAVE STILL David DT 6'3 250 Colorado State B: 12/2/1942																															
1965	TOR	12																													
1966	TOR	13	0		1																										
2	Years	25	0		1																										
DON STILLER Don T-E 6'3 210 Oklahoma B: 1937																															
1958	EDM	2										6	1						6	89	14.8	31	1					1	3	3.0	3
JIM STILLWAGON James R. DT 6'0 239 Ohio State B: 2/11/1949 Mount Vernon, OH Draft: 5B-124 1971 GB																															
1971	TOR*	14																													
1972	TOR*	14																													
1973	TOR	10	0		1							7	1																		
1974	TOR*	16																													
1975	TOR	3																													
5	Years	57	0		1							7	1																		
HARPO STILLWELL Harpo C Regina Dales Jrs.																															
1946	SAS	8																													
JIM STINNETTE James Edward (Buffalo) LB 6'1 230 Oregon State B: 12/3/1938 Corvallis, OR Draft: FS 1960 NYT Pro: N																															
1964	EDM	13	0		1				2	18																					
1965	EDM	11	0		1				1																						
1966	EDM	6							1																						
3	Years	30	0		2				4	18																					
DAVE STIPE David DB 6'0 205 Bishop's B: 9/23/1975 Mississauga, ON																															
2004	HAM	1				3																									
2005	HAM	2				0																									
2	Years	3				3																									
WALTER STITH Walter OT 6'9 320 North Carolina A&T State B: 1/2/1983 Atlanta, GA																															
2008	BC	2				1																									
MARK STOCK Mark Anthony WR 5'11 177 Virginia Military Institute B: 4/27/1966 Canton, OH Draft: 6-144 1989 PIT Pro: EN																															
1995	SA	18	1		1	5						36	6	1	15	15.0	15	0	60	949	15.8	45	6					1	14	14.0	14
BILL STOCKMAN Bill E 5'11 175 Toronto B: 1925																															
1949	OTT	6																													
ARNIE STOCKS Arnie HB 6'2 190 Toronto Argonauts Jrs. B: 1927																															
1949	TOR	6										10	2					1													

Year	Team	GP	FM	FF	FR	TK	SK	YDS	IR	YDS	PD	PTS	TD	RA	YDS	AVG	LG	TD	REC	YDS	AVG	LG	TD	PR	YDS	AVG	LG	KOR	YDS	AVG	LG
1950	TOR	7																													
1951	CAL	9																						1	6	6.0	6				
3	Years	22										10	2					1						1	6	6.0	6				
JAMIE STODDARD Jamie WR-SB 6'0 182 Alberta B: 12/29/1977 Richmond, BC																															
2000	WPG	12	1	0	1	0													6	81	13.5	28	0								
2001	WPG	18	2	0	2	4						24	4						34	526	15.5	68	4								
2002	WPG	18				5						6	1						27	387	14.3	35	1								
2003	WPG	18	0	0	1	3						6	1						27	401	14.9	40	1								
2004	WPG	16	2	0	0	2						12	2	1	-1	-1.0	-1	0	31	523	16.9	47	2								
2005	WPG	18	1	0	0	12						14	2						30	431	14.4	38	2								
2006	WPG	18				12						6	1						19	273	14.4	42	1					1	0	0.0	0
2007	WPG	16				8						2	0	1	9	9.0	9	0	11	110	10.0	20	0								
2008	WPG	18	1	0	0	12						2	0						6	76	12.7	21	0								
9	Years	152	7	0	4	58						72	11	2	8	4.0	9	0	191	2808	14.7	68	11					1	0	0.0	0
PAUL STOILEN Paul LB 6'0 223 Simon Fraser B: 8/18/1974 Draft: 3A-19 1997 BC																															
1998	BC	1																													
DON STOKES Don (Red) G 5'8 200 B: 1925																															
1949	EDM	12																													
KEITH STOKES Keith Lamont WR 5'8 180 Georgia Military JC; East Carolina B: 12/10/1978 South Toms River, NJ																															
2002	MTL+	18	6	0	1	2						36	6	4	-16	-4.0	5	0	43	572	13.3	45	3	76	896	11.8	88	25	527	21.1	40
2003	MTL	15	4	0	1	2						30	5	19	71	3.7	12	0	33	429	13.0	48	2	61	572	9.4	74	23	455	19.8	41
2004	WPG*	18	10	0	2	2						42	7	3	28	9.3	30	0	22	367	16.7	70	2	80	949	11.9	83	56	1112	19.9	108
2005	WPG	17	3	0	0	4						24	4	2	2	1.0	4	0	58	832	14.3	68	3	79	662	8.4	69	47	1022	21.7	62
2006	TOR	14	5	0	1	2													20	253	12.7	37	0	39	363	9.3	24	28	528	18.9	34
2007	WPG	2	1	0	0	0																		17	144	8.5	21	5	123	24.6	55
2008	TOR	4	1	0	0	0													2	64	32.0	62	0	15	148	9.9	55	19	365	19.2	35
7	Years	88	30	0	5	12						132	22	28	85	3.0	30	0	178	2517	14.1	70	10	367	3734	10.2	88	203	4132	20.4	108
TOMMY STOLHANDSKE Carl Thomas E 6'2 210 Texas B: 6/28/1931 Baytown, TX Draft: 1-10 1953 SF Pro: N																															
1953	EDM	14										20	4						19	382	20.1		4					1	8	8.0	8
AVATUS STONE Avatus Harry OHB-DB 6'1 195 Syracuse B: 4/21/1931 Washington, DC Draft: 9B-101 1953 CHIC Pro: N																															
1953	OTT+	13										65	11					4					6								
1954	OTT	14							6	112		18	3	82	404	4.9	31	2	18	193	10.7	32	0	1	19	19.0	19	8	158	19.8	28
1955	OTT+	12							4	14		14	2	102	505	5.0	50	2	12	232	19.3	46	0	2	10	5.0	5	8	201	25.1	40
1956	OTT	14							0	22		23	2	40	252	6.3	30	1	8	169	21.1	81	1					3	82	27.3	30
1957	MTL	9										11	1	62	305	4.9	25	1	15	152	10.1	20	0								
5	Years	62							10	148		131	19	286	1466	5.1	50	10	53	746	14.1	81	7	3	29	9.7	19	19	441	23.2	40
DAREN STONE Daren 6'3 217 LB Maine B: 8/21/1985 Jamaica Draft: 6D-203 ATL Pro: N																															
2011	CAL	8	0	0	1	27	1.0	6.0																							
DONNIE STONE Edward Donald OHB-DB 6'2 205 Arkansas B: 1/5/1937 Sioux City, IA Draft: 21-249 1959 CHIB Pro: N																															
1959	CAL	15	2		0							42	7	102	469	4.6	26	1	25	323	12.9	56	6					8	124	15.5	24
1960	CAL	13	5		1							42	7	115	638	5.5	45	5	19	254	13.4	28	2	2	0	0.0	0	12	290	24.2	65
1961	CAL	1												5	16	3.2	6	0	2	27	13.5	18	0								
3	Years	29	7		1							84	14	222	1123	5.1	45	6	46	604	13.1	56	8	2	0	0.0	0	20	414	20.7	65
NORM STONEBURGH Norm C-MG 6'2 245 Toronto Parkdale Jrs. B: 3/31/1935 Toronto, ON																															
1955	TOR	19																													
1956	TOR	11																													
1957	TOR	14										1	0																		
1958	TOR+	14												1	-13	-13.0	-13	0													
1960	TOR+	14																													
1961	TOR+	14																													
1962	TOR	10																													
1963	TOR	14																													
1964	TOR	14	3		0																										
1965	TOR+	14																													
1966	TOR	10	1		0																										
1967	TOR	14	0		1																										
12	Years	162	4		1							1	0	1	-13	-13.0	-13	0													
PAT STOQUA Pat SB-WB-DB 6'0 190 Carleton B: 4/29/1956 Ottawa, ON Draft: TE 1979 OTT																															
1979	OTT	1																													
1980	OTT	11																	1	13	13.0	13	0								
1981	OTT	10																	20	326	16.3	40	0								
1982	OTT	12	0		1							12	2						31	518	16.7	48	2	8	88	11.0	18				
1983	OTT	16										24	4						33	580	17.6	41	4	13	121	9.3	16	1	13	13.0	13
1984	OTT	8	2		1														7	109	15.6	34	0	7	40	5.7	12	1	0	0.0	0
6	Years	58	2		2							36	6						92	1546	16.8	48	6	28	249	8.9	18	2	13	6.5	13
BOB STOREY Bob DB-OE 6'1 198 Tulsa B: 1946																															
1967	HAM	14			1																										
1968	HAM	14																						6	42	7.0	12	2	26	13.0	16
1969	MTL	13	1		0									5	18	3.6	5	0	2	24	12.0	16	0	40	161	4.0	17	7	98	14.0	33
1970	MTL	14	1		0									1	4	4.0	4	0	1	9	9.0	9	0	49	219	4.5	15				
4	Years	55	2		1									6	22	3.7	5	0	3	33	11.0	16	0	95	422	4.4	17	9	124	13.8	33
TODD STORME Todd OT 6'5 275 Utah State B: 10/16/1964 Red Deer, AB Draft: 1B-3 1987 EDM																															
1989	EDM	2				0																									
1990	EDM	18	0		1	2																									
1991	EDM	4																													
1992	CAL	1																													
1993	CAL	18				1																									
1994	OTT	1																													
1995	BC	7				0																									
1996	SAS	16				1																									
8	Years	67	0		1	4																									
RON STOVER Ron OE 6'3 205 Oregon B: 1937 Draft: 30-352 1959 DET																															
1959	TOR	14										12	2						23	388	16.9	51	2								
1962	TOR	5										6	1						2	22	11.0	12	1								
2	Years	19										18	3						25	410	16.4	51	3								
SMOKEY STOVER Stewart Lynn LBB 6'0 229 Louisiana-Monroe B: 8/24/1938 McPherson, KS Pro: N																															
1967	HAM	10							2	14																					
ED STOWE Ed. G 5'11 210 Pittsburgh B: 1933																															
1958	SAS	5	0		2				1	4																					
MIKE STOWELL Mike T-C 6'2 292 Tennessee B: 3/24/1970 Knoxville, TN																															
1994	SHR	17				2																									
1995	SHR	17				0																									
2	Years	34				2																									
CURTIS STOWERS Curtis Hill LB 6'3 215 Mississippi State B: 7/3/1960 Jackson, MS Draft: 10-262 1982 ATL																															
1982	TOR	1																													
JOE STRACINA Joseph Stephen, Jr. C-LB 5'11 225 Montreal Lakeshore Flyers Ints. B: 7/18/1930 Montreal, QC D: 8/13/1996 Niagara Falls, ON																															
1952	SAS	7												3	5	1.7	5	0													
1955	OTT	10							1	3																					
1956	OTT	14																													
1957	OTT	14							1	0																					
1958	OTT	11																										1	13	13.0	13
1959	OTT	14																													

Year	Team	GP	FM	FF	FR	TK	SK	YDS	IR	YDS	PD	PTS	TD	RA	YDS	AVG	LG	TD	REC	YDS	AVG	LG	TD	PR	YDS	AVG	LG	KOR	YDS	AVG	LG
1960	OTT	14							1	6																					
1961	MTL	14																													
1962	MTL	11																													
1963	MTL	1																													
1964	MTL	14																										1	3	3.0	3
11	Years	124							3	9				3	5	1.7	5	0										2	16	8.0	13
ART STRAHAN Arthur Ray DT 6'5 265 Texas Southern B: 7/17/1943 Newton, TX Pro: N																															
1970	TOR	2																													
BOB STRANSKY Robert Joseph OHB-DB 6'1 190 Colorado B: 1/30/1936 Yankton, SD Draft: 2-24 1958 BAL Pro: N																															
1958	WPG	3										6	1	19	79	4.2	18	1	1	11	11.0	11	0	1	0	0.0	0				
LES STRAYHORN Leslie Dewey, Jr. RB 5'10 200 East Carolina B: 9/1/1951 Trenton, NC Draft: 17-438 1973 DAL Pro: N																															
1975	HAM	4	2		0									51	250	4.9	19	0	6	37	6.2	20	0								
1976	HAM	2										6	1	14	92	6.6	37	1	5	53	10.6	14	0								
1976	MTL	1	1		0									11	44	4.0	12	0													
1976	Year	3	1		0							6	1	25	136	5.4	37	1	5	53	10.6	14	0								
2	Years	6	3		0							6	1	76	386	5.1	37	1	11	90	8.2	20	0								
ERIC STREATER Eric Maurice WR 5'11 160 North Carolina B: 3/21/1964 Sylva, NC Pro: N																															
1988	BC	8	1		1	1						6	1	2	15	7.5	25	0	15	237	15.8	37	1								
1989	BC	18	0		1	2						36	6	4	8	2.0	12	0	76	1091	14.4	83	6								
1990	WPG	15	2		0	3						72	12						54	781	14.5	73	12	21	136	6.5	25	0	-2		-2
1991	WPG	15	1		1	2						24	4						44	707	16.1	58	4	12	94	7.8	17	12	199	16.6	40
1992	WPG	8	0		1	0						24	4						27	376	13.9	50	4					0	5		5
5	Years	64	4		4	8						162	27	6	23	3.8	25	0	216	3192	14.8	83	27	33	230	7.0	25	12	202	16.8	40
JIMMY STREATER Willis James, III QB 6'0 160 Tennessee B: 12/17/1957 Sylva, NC D: 2/20/2004 Asheville, NC																															
1980	TOR	12												9	38	4.2	20	0													
MARK STREETER Mark Alan DB 6'0 190 Youngstown State; North Iowa CC; Arizona B: 3/22/1957 Massillon, OH Draft: 5A-111 1980 DET																															
1982	WPG	9					1.0		1	17																					
1982	TOR	4							1	0																		6	121	20.2	26
1982	Year	13					1.0		2	17																		6	121	20.2	26
1983	HAM	15	0		1				3	45		6	1											4	25	6.3	9	1	14	14.0	14
1984	HAM	11					1.0		1	0																					
1985	HAM	16	0		2				2	34		6	1																		
1986	HAM*	18					2.0		9	207		12	2																		
1987	HAM	2				9																									
6	Years	71	0		3	9	4.0		17	303		24	4											4	25	6.3	9	7	135	19.3	26
BOB STREITER Bob DE 5'11 240 Miami (Florida) B: 6/26/1940																															
1964	TOR	14	0		1																										
BILL STRIBLING Majure Blanks OE-DE 6'1 206 Mississippi B: 11/5/1927 Edinburg, MS D: 8/22/2006 Rogers, AR Draft: 21-267(f) 1950 NYG Pro: N																															
1960	TOR	13										30	5						44	634	14.4	68	5								
CHUCK STRICKLAND Charles LB 6'2 225 Alabama B: 6/20/1952																															
1974	WPG	7																													
HOWARD STRICKLAND Elbert Howard HB 5'10 195 New Mexico Highlands; San Bernardino Valley JC; California B: 12/20/1952 Little Rock, AR D: 10/22/2010 Albuquerque, NM Draft: 11-281 1975 LARM Pro: W																															
1977	EDM	16	3		0							36	6	63	220	3.5	25	2	34	502	14.8	35	4	25	102	4.1	23	20	359	18.0	36
MIKE STRICKLAND Michael RB 5'8 180 Eastern Michigan B: 8/11/1951 Detroit, MI Draft: 14-363 1975 MIN																															
1975	BC	3												52	233	4.5	19	0	9	100	11.1	27	0					6	135	22.5	33
1976	BC+	16	5		0							66	11	223	1119	5.0	49	10	33	358	10.8	37	1					12	304	25.3	42
1977	BC	16	6		0							36	6	201	751	3.7	32	6	44	382	8.7	26	0								
1978	SAS*	16	2		0							42	7	284	1306	4.6	37	7	40	243	6.1	28	0	2	12	6.0	10	3	89	29.7	34
1979	SAS	16	2		0							36	6	176	770	4.4	28	4	43	406	9.4	30	2								
5	Years	67	15		0							180	30	936	4179	4.5	49	27	169	1489	8.8	37	3	2	12	6.0	10	21	528	25.1	42
TIM STRICKLAND Timothy CB-LB 5'9 183 Mississippi B: 1/13/1977 Memphis, TN Pro: E																															
2002	MTL	14	0	4	2	28	3.0	15.0	1	28	1	6	1																		
2003	MTL+	18	0	1	0	55	4.0	23.0	1	47	3	6	1																		
2004	MTL+	18	0	0	3	65	5.0	34.0	2	41	1																				
2005	MTL	15	0	1	0	56	2.0	7.0	2	17	4																				
2006	MTL*	17	0	1	1	56	7.0	49.0	1	4	6																				
2007	MTL	7				33			1	18	2																				
6	Years	89	0	7	6	293	21.0	128.0	8	155	17	12	2																		
GARY STRICKLER Gary T 6'3 220 Queen's B: 1939 Draft: 1-3 1962 TOR																															
1962	TOR	12																													
1963	TOR	8																													
2	Years	20																													
GEORGE STRINGER George G 6'2 230 East York Argos B: 5/30/1939																															
1965	TOR	3																													
ANDRE STRODE Andre DH 5'8 176 Colorado State B: 6/19/1972 Denver, CO																															
1995	BIR+	18	0		2	73			7	109	7	6	1																		
1996	BC+	18	0		1	65	2.0	15.0	3	81	5	6	1																		
1997	BC	1				1																									
1998	BC	17				54			2	72	4																				
1999	WPG	6				24					1																				
5	Years	60	0		3	217	2.0	15.0	12	262	17	12	2																		
WOODY STRODE Woodrow Wilson E 6'3 205 UCLA B: 7/25/1914 Los Angeles, CA D: 12/31/1994 Glendora, CA Pro: N																															
1948	CAL+	12										25	5										5								
1949	CAL+	14										30	6										4								
1950	CAL	12										20	4	1	0	0.0	0	0	22	377	17.1	44	4								
3	Years	38										75	15	1	0	0.0	0	0	22	377	17.1	44	13								
MIKE STROFOLINO Michael James LB 6'2 223 Villanova B: 2/6/1944 New York, NY Draft: 13- 1965 DEN; 4-50 1965 LARM Pro: N																															
1969	HAM	6	0		1																							1	6	6.0	6
1970	HAM	4																													
2	Years	10	0		1																							1	6	6.0	6
BRIAN STRONG Brian OT 6'5 260 Montana State B: 1/14/1961 Calgary, AB Draft: 4-33 1983 CAL																															
1984	CAL	1																													
1985	CAL	5																													
1986	HAM	4																													
3	Years	10																													
DOUG STRONG Douglas Reginald CB 6'0 192 Wilfrid Laurier B: 5/26/1946 D: 9/19/2009 Winnipeg, MB Draft: 1A-1 1969 WPG																															
1969	WPG	16	2		2				2	23		6	1	1	5	5.0	5	1						56	375	6.7	25	8	159	19.9	35
1970	WPG	16	2		2				4	21				1	3	3.0	3	0	4	4	1.0	8	0	56	410	7.3	20	12	232	19.3	29
1971	WPG	16	3		2				3	32														64	366	5.7	17				
1972	WPG	4							3	51		6	1											24	89	3.7	15				
1973	WPG	13	0		1				3	66		6	1											50	171	3.4	12				
1974	WPG	2	0		2																			7	19	2.7	9				
1974	SAS	3																						5	14	2.8	5				
1974	Year	5	0		2																			12	33	2.8	9				
6	Years	67	7		9				15	193		18	3	2	8	4.0	5	1	4	4	1.0	8	0	262	1444	5.5	25	20	391	19.6	35
RAY STRONG Raymond RB 5'9 184 Contra Costa JC; Nevada-Las Vegas B: 5/7/1956 Berkeley, CA Draft: 10B-263 1978 ATL Pro: N																															
1983	BC	4	3		0							12	2	34	173	5.1	21	2	16	141	8.8	33	0					7	187	26.7	58
JOHNNY STROPPA Johnny HB-FW 5'11 175 Elmwood Ints. B: 1/2/1926 Winnipeg, MB																															
1949	WPG	13																													
1950	WPG	14												36	95	2.6		0	1	29	29.0	29	0								
1951	WPG	7										5	1	2	4	2.0		0	5	48	9.6		1								

Year	Team	GP	FM	FF	FR	TK	SK	YDS	IR	YDS	PD	PTS	TD	RA	YDS	AVG	LG	TD	REC	YDS	AVG	LG	TD	PR	YDS	AVG	LG	KOR	YDS	AVG	LG
3	Years	34										5	1	38	99	2.6	0	0	6	77	12.8	29	1								
DEON STROTHER Deonshawn L. RB 5'11 213 Southern California B: 4/12/1972 Saginaw, MI Pro: N																															
1995	OTT	7	1		0	5						6	1	27	96	3.6	20	1	10	93	9.3	20	0								
BILL STUART William Charles HB 5'10 170 Vancouver Cubs Jrs. B: 6/14/1932 Vancouver, BC D: 4/6/2011 Kelowna, BC																															
1956	BC	13	3		0									4	12	3.0	7	0	1	15	15.0	15	0	40	152	3.8	12				
TAYLOR STUBBLEFIELD Taylor Evans WR 5'11 174 Purdue B: 1/21/1982 Yakima, WA																															
2005	HAM	3				0													1	7	7.0	7	0								
JOHN STUCKY John R. DT 6'0 230 Hutchinson CC; Kansas State B: 2/17/1949 Moundridge, KS D: 4/12/2007 Springdale, AR																															
1970	BC	16	0		2																										
ANNIS STUKUS Anicautus Paul K 6'1 207 Toronto Argos Jrs. B: 10/25/1914 Toronto, ON D: 5/20/2006 Canmore, AB																															
1950	EDM	14										38	0																		
1951	EDM	14										58	0																		
2	Years	28										96	0																		
BILL STUKUS William QB-HB 5'9 177 B: 1917 D: 7/1/2003																															
1947	TOR	10										10	2					2													
1949	EDM	14										10	2					1													
1950	EDM	14												8	14	1.8		0													
1951	EDM	13												2	-15	-7.5		0						13	59	4.5		4	-3	-0.8	
4	Years	51										20	4	10	-1	-0.1	0	3						13	59	4.5	0	4	-3	-0.8	
JIM STULL James Andrew OT 6'6 318 Delaware B: 1/19/1977 Westminster, MD Pro: EX																															
2000	TOR	3				0																									
GREGG STUMON Gregg LB-DE 6'0 225 Southern Arkansas B: 5/26/1963 Plain Dealing, LA																															
1986	BC	1	0		0																										
1987	BC*	17				34	23.0																								
1988	BC*	18	0		4	61	8.0		1	20		1	0																		
1989	EDM	18	0		2	25	8.0																								
1990	OTT*	18	0		2	59	13.0		1	21		6	1																		
1991	OTT	18	0		2	53	9.0																					1	0	0.0	0
1992	OTT+	17	1		3	39	11.0	74.0						1	5	5.0	5	0													
1993	OTT	18	0		2	41	8.0	58.0						1	3	3.0	3	0										1	0	0.0	0
1994	SHR	18				69	6.0	47.0			2																				
1995	SHR	1				0																									
10	Years	144	1		15	381	86.0	179.0	2	41	2	7	1	2	8	4.0	5	0										2	0	0.0	0
JOHN STURDIVANT John DE 6'4 265 Maryland; Ohio State* B: 5/25/1958 Newport News, VA																															
1983	WPG	2																													
1984	WPG	14					7.5																								
1985	WPG	12					2.0																								
1986	WPG	12					2.0																								
1987	WPG	1			1	2						6	1																		
5	Years	41			1	2	11.5					6	1																		
JERRY STURM Jerry Gordon C-OT 6'3 257 Illinois B: 12/31/1936 English, IN Pro: N																															
1959	CAL	12	0		2														1	39	39.0	39	0								
1960	CAL	9												1	-20	-20.0	-20	0													
2	Years	21	0		2									1	-20	-20.0	-20	0	1	39	39.0	39	0								
GORD STURTRIDGE Gordon DE 6'1 188 Winnipeg Rods Jrs.; Norwood-St. Boniface Legionaires Ints. B: 1928 D: 12/9/1956 Mount Slesse, BC																															
1953	SAS	15																	1	20	20.0	20	0					2	21	10.5	
1954	SAS	16																										1	0	0.0	0
1955	SAS+	15	1		6				2	10		5	1																		
1956	SAS+	16	0		2				1	5																					
4	Years	62	1		8				3	15		5	1						1	20	20.0	20	0					3	21	7.0	
CRAIG STUTZMANN Craig WR 5'10 189 Hawaii B: 7/14/1980 Hilo, HI																															
2002	BC	1				0																									
ALEX SUBER Alexander Paul DH 5'7 174 Middle Tennessee State B: 12/1/1985 Tampa, FL																															
2010	WPG	15	0	0	2	62					3																				
2011	WPG	18	0	0	2	68	1.0	6.0	1	66	2	6	1																		
2	Years	33	0	0	4	130	1.0	6.0	1	66	5	6	1																		
NICK SUBIS Nicholas Alexander C-OT 6'4 278 San Diego State B: 12/24/1967 Inglewood, CA Draft: 6-142 1991 DEN Pro: N																															
1993	SAC	4				0																									
1994	BAL+	17				0																									
1995	BAL	14	0		2	3																									
1996	MTL	10				1																									
4	Years	45	0		2	4																									
DICK SUDERMAN Dick DE 6'5 235 Western Ontario B: 1941 D: 10/16/1972 Edmonton, AB Draft: 3-22 1964 CAL																															
1964	CAL	7							1	4																					
1965	CAL	13																										1	17	17.0	17
1966	CAL	16																													
1967	CAL+	16																													
1968	CAL+	16	0		2																										
1970	CAL	16	1		3				1	0																					
1971	CAL+	16	0		3																										
1972	CAL	12																													
1972	EDM	1																													
1972	Year	13																													
8	Years	112	1		8				2	4																		1	17	17.0	17
KEN SUGARMAN Ken OT 6'3 250 Whitworth B: 6/16/1942 Draft: 7-92 1964 BAL																															
1964	BC	5																													
1965	BC	16																													
1966	BC	16	0		1																										
1967	BC	16	0		1									1	1	1.0	1	0													
1968	BC+	16	0		2																										
1969	BC+	16																													
1970	BC*	16	0		1																										
1971	BC+	16			1							6	1																		
1972	BC	16	0		1																										
9	Years	133	0		7							6	1	1	1	1.0	1	0													
SHAFER SUGGS Shafer L. DB 6'1 204 Ball State B: 4/28/1953 Elkhart, IN Draft: 2-33 1976 NYJ Pro: NU																															
1981	MTL	2																													
GLEN SUITOR Glen S 6'0 188 Simon Fraser B: 11/24/1962 Sidney, BC Draft: 2-10 1984 SAS																															
1984	SAS	16	1		1				4	67														5	25	5.0	8				
1985	SAS	16							5	50																					
1986	SAS	18	1		5				1	0				1	-1	-1.0	-1	0						1	0	0.0	0				
1987	SAS	18	0		2	50			7	112		18	3	1	12	12.0	12	1													
1988	SAS	18	2		1	28	1.0		2	80																					
1989	SAS+	18	1		2	38	2.0		5	49																					
1990	SAS	18	0		1	27	1.0		3	33				1	-7	-7.0	-7	0													
1991	SAS*	18	1		5	61			8	145																					
1992	SAS*	18	1		2	63			6	30														1	2	2.0	2				
1993	SAS*	18	0		1	44			5	72																					
1994	SAS	18	1		2	37	1.0	10.0	5	29	5																				
11	Years	194	8		22	348	5.0	10.0	51	667	5	18	3	3	4	1.3	12	1						7	27	3.9	8				
ED SULLIVAN Edward Allen C-LB 6'1 200 Notre Dame B: 1935 Draft: 12A-135 1957 GB																															
1959	BC	15							1																						

Year	Team	GP	FM	FF	FR	TK	SK	YDS	IR	YDS	PD	PTS	TD	RA	YDS	AVG	LG	TD	REC	YDS	AVG	LG	TD	PR	YDS	AVG	LG	KOR	YDS	AVG	LG
1960	BC	16	0		2				4	26
1961	BC	16
3	Years	47	0		2				5	26
JIM SULLIVAN James Edmund DE 6'4 243 Lincoln (Missouri) B: 8/29/1944 Detroit, MI Pro: NW
1972	WPG	13	0		2
JOE SULLIVAN Joseph Patrick OG 6'4 250 Boston College B: 5/16/1952 Medford, MA Draft: 7B-182 1974 MIA; 17-203 1974 FLA-WFL
1975	TOR	1
JOHN SULLIVAN John S 6'1 200 Waterloo B: 7/28/1981 Kitchener, ON Draft: 6-51 2004 WPG
2005	WPG	7				8
2006	WPG	10	0	0	1	8
2	Years	17	0	0	1	16
MARK SULLIVAN Mark DE 6'4 235 Ohio State B: 7/20/1957 New Bedford, MA
1979	HAM	1
MURRAY SULLIVAN Murray HB-E 6'0 190 none B: 1925
1946	TOR	3
1952	CAL	2
2	Years	5
RAY SULLIVAN Raymond L., Jr. DE 6'4 240 Maine B: 8/20/1961 Boston, MA
1983	WPG	3	0		1
SEAN SULLIVAN Sean RB 6'2 205 Simon Fraser B: 1953 Draft: 1B-5 1975 HAM
1975	EDM	1
DAVE SUMINSKI David Mitchell OG-OT-LB-DG 5'11 230 Wisconsin B: 6/18/1931 Ashland, WI D: 9/22/2005 Ashland, WI Draft: 15-172 1953 WAS Pro: N
1957	HAM+	14
1958	HAM	13
1959	HAM+	14
1960	HAM	12
4	Years	53
BRANDON SUMMERS Brandon QB 6'0 212 Toledo; Youngstown State B: 8/22/1986 Southfield, MI
2011	WPG	2				0
DEMETRIS SUMMERS Demetris RB 5'11 214 South Carolina B: 10/12/1983 Lexington, SC
2008	CAL	10	1	0	0	0						6	1	19	121	6.4	37	1	13	154	11.8	25	0	4	32	8.0	13	27	657	24.3	60
2009	CAL	8	3	0	0	0								8	67	8.4	24	0	2	33	16.5	21	0					29	716	24.7	75
2	Years	18	4	0	0	0						6	1	27	188	7.0	37	1	15	187	12.5	25	0	4	32	8.0	13	56	1373	24.5	75
TERRY SUMNER Terry HB-FW 5'11 190 B: 1932
1952	CAL	11			1
1953	SAS	2																										3	23	7.7	
2	Years	13			1																							3	23	7.7	
IAN SUNTER Ian James K-P 6'0 215 Burlington Braves Jrs. B: 12/21/1952 Dundee, Scotland Pro: N
1972	HAM	14	0		2							93	0
1973	HAM	14	1		0							102	0
1974	HAM	16	1		0							141	0
1975	HAM	16	1		0							109	0
1978	TOR	16										83	0
1979	TOR+	16	0		1							98	0
6	Years	92	3		3							626	0
JOHN SURLA John LB 5'10 225 Western Ontario B: 4/20/1988 Niagara Falls, ON
2011	MTL	6				1
TOM SURLAS Thomas J. LB 5'11 198 Alabama B: 7/19/1950 Mount Pleasant, PA Pro: W
1973	TOR	6
BILL SURPHLIS William C. QB 5'9 172 Pats Jrs.
1946	MTL	12
STEVE SUTER Steven WR 5'9 190 Maryland B: 6/26/1982 Port Jervis, NY
2005	HAM	2				0																		4	16	4.0	8	4	112	28.0	39
DON SUTHERIN Donald Paul CB-K 5'10 193 Ohio State B: 2/29/1936 Empire, OH Draft: 8-94 1958 NYG Pro: N
1958	HAM	7							1	3		13	1	23	62	2.7	13	1	3	22	7.3	13	0					2	9	4.5	8
1960	HAM	1							1	0		7	0
1961	HAM+	14							11	150		69	0	3	10	3.3	10	0	1	52	52.0	52	0	14	81	5.8	30	1	22	22.0	22
1962	HAM*	14							8	95		78	0	1	-2	-2.0	-2	0						44	203	4.6	29
1963	HAM	8										40	0											18	68	3.8	11
1964	HAM*	14	3		0				6	62		94	0											57	274	4.8	29
1965	HAM+	14	0		1				2	24		82	0	1	3	3.0	3	0						8	56	7.0	11
1966	HAM	14							6	35		67	0											15	56	3.7	24
1967	OTT	14	1		2				4	37		30	0	1	-3	-3.0	-3	0	1	14	14.0	14	0	6	41	6.8	22
1968	OTT+	14							5	64		112	1											2	2	1.0	2
1969	OTT*	14							10	98		116	1											3	12	4.0	12
1970	TOR	5							4	31		6	1
12	Years	133	4		3				58	599		714	4	29	70	2.4	13	1	5	88	17.6	52	0	167	793	4.7	30	3	31	10.3	22
GARRETT SUTHERLAND Garrett LB 6'1 230 Northern Illinois B: 4/30/1974 Mississauga, ON Draft: 4A-22 1998 WPG
1998	WPG	8				12
MIKE SUTHERLAND Mike C 6'5 285 Northern Illinois B: 6/25/1971 Ottawa, ON Draft: 1-3 1996 SAS
1996	SAS	1				0
1996	MTL	12				0
1996	Year	13				0
1997	MTL	18				0
1998	MTL	18				0
1999	MTL	18				0
2000	MTL	5				0
2001	WPG	16				1
2002	WPG	12	1	0	0	0
2003	OTT	16				1													1	13	13.0	13	0
2004	OTT	8				0
2005	OTT	8	0	0	1	0						6	1
10	Years	120	1	0	1	2						6	1						1	13	13.0	13	0
VINNY SUTHERLAND Vincent Joseph WR 5'8 191 Purdue B: 4/22/1978 West Palm Beach, FL Draft: 5-136 2001 ATL Pro: N
2005	WPG	5				2						6	1						8	121	15.1	37	1					9	148	16.4	33
DONALD SUTTON Donald Paul OT-OG 6'3 260 Pacific B: 12/22/1953 San Diego, CA
1977	CAL	4
ERIC SUTTON Eric D. CB-DH 5'10 169 San Diego State B: 10/24/1972 Los Angeles, CA Pro: N
1997	SAS	6	0	0	1	18			2	47	3
1998	SAS	18				54			1	13	9
1999	SAS	3				8					2
1999	CAL	11				18					4
1999	Year	14				26					6
2000	CAL	7				24					2
4	Years	34	0	0	1	122			3	60	20
JON SUTTON Jonathan E. CB 6'1 195 New Mexico B: 1/1/1957 New Orleans, LA Pro: NU
1979	OTT	5	1		0				2	45
1980	OTT	12	0		1				3	108
1981	TOR	3
1981	MTL	2	0		1
1981	OTT	8	1		0				5	109
1981	Year	13	1		1				5	109

Year	Team	GP	FM	FF	FR	TK	SK	YDS	IR	YDS	PD	PTS	TD	RA	YDS	AVG	LG	TD	REC	YDS	AVG	LG	TD	PR	YDS	AVG	LG	KOR	YDS	AVG	LG
1982	OTT	16							5	111														1	7	7.0	7				
4	Years	36	2		2				15	373														1	7	7.0	7				
MICKEY SUTTON Michael Thomas OHB-DB 6'0 190 Auburn B: 7/17/1943 Mobile, AL Draft: 6- 1965 KC; 7B-90 1965 CHIB Pro: N																															
1967	MTL	4	0		1							6	1	32	138	4.3	42	1	2	16	8.0	9	0					4	95	23.8	40
1968	MTL	14	0		0				1	18				17	58	3.4	15	0	4	47	11.8	24	0	13	78	6.0	13	3	61	20.3	24
2	Years	18	0		1				1	18		6	1	49	196	4.0	42	1	6	63	10.5	24	0	13	78	6.0	13	7	156	22.3	40
MICKEY SUTTON William Earl DB 5'8 168 Montana B: 8/28/1960 Greenville, MS Pro: NU																															
1983	HAM	1	0		1		1.0																								
MIKE SUTTON Michael Dewayne DL 6'4 263 Louisiana State B: 4/21/1975 Jacksonville, NC Pro: ENX																															
2003	BC	3				5			0	0	2																				
THEODORE SUTTON Theodore RB 5'9 209 East Carolina B: 1/21/1958 Kinston, NC																															
1982	WPG	1																													
STEVE SVITAK Stephen James LB-DT 6'1 232 Boise JC; Boise State B: 6/1/1945 Oakland, CA Draft: 7-180 1970 OAK																															
1972	SAS	12	0		2																										
1973	BC	2																													
1973	EDM	6	0		1																										
1973	Year	8	0		1																										
2	Years	14	0		3																										
DON SWAFFORD Donald L. OT 6'7 260 Florida B: 3/22/1957 Dayton, OH Draft: 7A-178 1979 PHI																															
1980	SAS	13																													
1981	SAS	16	0		1																										
1982	SAS	16	0		1																										
1983	SAS	2																													
1983	BC	6																												1	1	1.0	1
1983	Year	8																												1	1	1.0	1
4	Years	47	0		2																							1	1	1.0	1
DOUG SWAIL Doug HB-FB 5'10 177 Edmonton Jrs. B: 1930																															
1949	EDM	14																													
1950	EDM	1																													
2	Years	15																													
DAMIAN SWAIN Damian Antonio WR 6'1 175 Alabama State B: 7/23/1977																															
2002	BC	2				1																						1	15	15.0	15
KEN SWALWELL Ken DE 6'3 195 Western Washington B: 1930																															
1955	BC	13	1		3							5	1															4	53	13.3	20
1956	BC	3																													
2	Years	16	1		3							5	1															4	53	13.3	20
BILL SWAN Bill WB-DB 5'11 190 Lakeshore Flyers Ints. B: 5/26/1935 Montreal, QC																															
1959	MTL	6																													
TERRY SWARN Terry FL 6'3 205 Colorado State B: 5/25/1947 Mansfield, OH Draft: 6-147 1969 SD																															
1969	EDM	16										36	6	5	97	19.4	46	0	25	428	17.1	46	6					4	112	28.0	41
1970	EDM	16	1		0							48	8	40	244	6.1	45	2	61	739	12.1	50	5					4	210	52.5	99
1971	EDM	4			0														8	65	8.1	18	0					4	125	31.3	35
1971	OTT	3			0									12	53	4.4	30	0	10	87	8.7		0					3	93	31.0	49
1971	Year	7	3		0									12	53	4.4	30	0	18	152	8.4	18	0					7	218	31.1	49
3	Years	36	1		0							84	14	57	394	6.9	46	2	104	1319	12.7	50	11					15	540	36.0	99
HERB SWEDER Herb G-T 5'10 230 B: 1923																															
1949	CAL	10																													
FRANK SWEENEY Francis Edward G-T 5'11 215 Xavier (Ohio) B: 1/24/1934 Cuyahoga County, OH D: 4/10/2011 Lakewood, OH Draft: 26-303 1956 PIT																															
1956	OTT	14																													
JOE SWEENEY Joe HB																															
1946	CAL	5																													
LEO SWEENEY Leon LB 6'1 200 Vancouver CYO Red Raiders Jrs. B: 1930																															
1953	CAL	12																												1	0	0.0	0
1954	BC	14																													
1955	BC	16																													
3	Years	42																												1	0	0.0	0
DON SWEET Donald K-P 6'0 189 Washington State B: 7/13/1948 Vancouver, BC																															
1972	MTL	12	1		0							52	0																		
1973	MTL	14	0		1							87	0																		
1974	MTL	16										109	0																		
1975	MTL	16										107	0																		
1976	MTL	16										141	0																		
1977	MTL+	16										136	0																		
1978	MTL+	16										123	0																		
1979	MTL+	16										111	0																		
1980	MTL	6	1		0							34	0																		
1981	MTL	9										56	0																		
1982	MTL	16										109	0																		
1983	MTL	16	1		0							137	0																		
1984	MTL	16	1		0							131	0																		
1985	HAM	2										9	0																		
14	Years	187	4		1							1342	0																		
KARL SWEETAN Karl Robert QB 6'1 203 Texas A&M; Navarro JC; Wake Forest B: 10/2/1942 Dallas, TX D: 7/2/2000 Las Vegas, TX Draft: 18-249 1965 DET Pro: N																															
1964	TOR	13	1		0							32	0	8	43	5.4	11	0													
BOB SWIFT Bob C-FB-OG 6'1 233 Clemson B: 11/29/1943 Shawinigan Falls, QC																															
1964	BC	16	4		0							66	11	229	1054	4.6	24	11	12	93	7.8	20	0					1	21	21.0	21
1965	BC	16	5		1							48	8	122	501	4.1	16	8	5	37	7.4	8	0					2	9	4.5	10
1966	TOR	7										6	1	33	140	4.2	21	1	0	0		0	0					1	24	24.0	24
1967	TOR	14																													
1968	TOR	14																													
1969	TOR	14																													
1970	TOR	14	0		1																										
1971	WPG*	16																													
1972	WPG*	16																													
1973	WPG+	16																													
1974	WPG*	16																	1	1	1.0	1	0								
1975	WPG	16																													
1976	WPG	16																													
1977	WPG	16																													
14	Years	207	9		2							120	20	384	1695	4.4	24	20	18	131	7.3	20	0					4	54	13.5	24
REGGIE SWINTON Reginald Terrell WR 6'0 183 Murray State B: 7/24/1975 Live Oak, FL Pro: N																															
1999	WPG	4				2						12	2						11	162	14.7	28	1	5	18	3.6	8	7	235	33.6	96
1999	EDM	3				0													3	22	7.3	14	0	3	33	11.0	22	9	178	19.8	52
1999	Year	7				2						12	2										1	8	51	6.4	22	16	413	25.8	96
CAM SWITZER Cam HB																															
1947	OTT	1																													
VERYL SWITZER Veryl Allen FB-OHB-DB 5'11 190 Kansas State B: 8/6/1932 Nicodemus, KS Draft: 1B-4 1954 GB Pro: N																															
1958	CAL	7	4		0							36	6	56	269	4.8	55	6	15	125	8.3	31	0	9	43	4.8	15	4	84	21.0	24
1959	MTL	14										36	6	164	863	5.3	51	6	16	114	7.1	16	0					5	58	11.6	21
1960	MTL	12							1	0		12	2	16	105	6.6	22	0	12	148	12.3	24	2								
3	Years	33	4		0				1	0		84	14	236	1237	5.2	55	12	43	387	9.0	31	2	9	43	4.8	15	9	142	15.8	24
ROY SWOAPE Roy LB 6'2 220 Western Michigan B: 5/17/1963																															

Year	Team	GP	FM	FF	FR	TK	SK	YDS	IR	YDS	PD	PTS	TD	RA	YDS	AVG	LG	TD	REC	YDS	AVG	LG	TD	PR	YDS	AVG	LG	KOR	YDS	AVG	LG
1986	OTT	2																													
PAT SWOOPES Patrick Ramon DL 6'4 280 Mississippi State B: 3/4/1964 Florence, AL Draft: 11-284 1986 NO Pro: N																															
1988	HAM	4																													
STEVE SYBELDON Steven James OT 6'6 255 North Dakota B: 1/25/1956 Milwaukee, WI Draft: 10A-262 1979 NYJ																															
1980	BC	1																													
HARRY SYDNEY Harry Flanroy, III RB 6'0 217 Kansas B: 6/26/1959 Petersburg, VA Pro: NU																															
1986	MTL	4	1		1							14	2	38	115	3.0	16	2	18	162	9.0	23	0					5	134	26.8	33
JAMES SYKES James RB-SB-WR 5'11 185 Rice B: 11/7/1954 Draft: 10-273 1977 WAS																															
1978	CAL*	15	5		0							90	15	204	1020	5.0	31	13	50	614	12.3	62	1	21	241	11.5	67	20	496	24.8	36
1979	CAL	12	7		1							36	6	151	703	4.7	38	5	31	269	8.7	25	1	3	27	9.0	16	5	96	19.2	22
1980	CAL*	16	7		4							66	11	222	1263	5.7	75	10	57	582	10.2	72	1	18	217	12.1	33	30	715	23.8	61
1981	CAL	15	12		3							36	6	240	1107	4.6	68	6	51	495	9.7	65	0					25	594	23.8	45
1982	CAL+	15	9		3							66	11	193	1046	5.4	84	11	27	222	8.2	19	0					6	122	20.3	25
1983	CAL	4	1		0									37	222	6.0	24	0	9	42	4.7	18	0								
1983	WPG	1												12	62	5.2	15	0													
1983	Year	5	1		0									49	284	5.8	24	0	9	42	4.7	18	0								
1986	WPG	7	2		1							30	5	97	447	4.6	57	3	10	62	6.2	14	2								
7	Years	84	43		12							324	54	1156	5870	5.1	84	48	235	2286	9.7	72	5	42	485	11.5	67	86	2023	23.5	61
JOE SYKES Trumaine DE 6'2 266 Holmes CC; West Virginia; Southern University B: 10/22/1982 Grenada, MS Pro: N																															
2009	SAS	5				1					1																				
2011	EDM	4	0	0	1	3																									
2	Years	9	0	0	1	4					1																				
DAVE SYME David QB 6'1 191 Simon Fraser B: 7/18/1950 Draft: 6-46 1972 EDM																															
1972	EDM	13	3		0							6	1	9	50	5.6	14	1													
1973	EDM	16																													
1974	EDM	16																													
1976	SAS	16	2		0									5	-1	-0.2	9	0													
4	Years	61	5		0							6	1	14	49	3.5	14	1													
BILL SYMONS Bill OHB-DB 6'0 200 Colorado B: 6/14/1943 Nucla, CO Draft: 20-157 1965 KC; 6B-80 1965 GB																															
1966	BC	10	1		0				1					7	20	2.9	8	0	1	26	26.0	26	0					6	158	26.3	31
1967	TOR	9	3		0							12	2	63	349	5.5	22	2	11	205	18.6	65	0					8	263	32.9	75
1968	TOR*	14	5		0							66	11	164	1107	6.8	75	9	44	536	12.2	68	2					13	335	25.8	52
1969	TOR	14	3		1							54	9	165	905	5.5	36	6	23	319	13.9	41	3					5	165	33.0	54
1970	TOR*	14	2		0							48	8	170	908	5.3	98	6	26	329	12.7	75	2					14	342	24.4	50
1971	TOR	14	4		0							18	3	103	418	4.1	43	2	30	325	10.8	47	1					13	368	28.3	43
1972	TOR	14										24	4	58	235	4.1	29	3	28	317	11.3	27	1					19	405	21.3	46
1973	TOR	14	3		1							42	7	84	358	4.3	30	5	23	230	10.0	35	2								
8	Years	103	21		2				1	0		264	44	814	4300	5.3	98	33	186	2287	12.3	75	11					78	2036	26.1	75
JOHN SYPTAK John Ashley DL 6'1 253 Rice B: 3/16/1984 Houston, TX Pro: E																															
2007	CAL	5				5	1.0	7.0																							
RAY SYRNYK Ray N. G 5'11 212 Saskatoon Hilltops Jrs. B: 1933 D: 12/9/1956 Mount Slesse, BC																															
1954	SAS	1																													
1955	SAS	8																													
1956	SAS	12	0		2				2	14																					
3	Years	21	0		2				2	14																					
CHRIS SZARKA Chris FB 6'2 225 Eastern Illinois B: 2/12/1975 Vancouver, BC Draft: 2-13 1997 SAS																															
1997	SAS	17	0	2	2	13						6	1	1	0	0.0	0	0	7	78	11.1	21	1								
1998	SAS	17	0	1	2	12						6	1	5	14	2.8	6	0	12	168	14.0	45	0					1	8	8.0	8
1999	SAS	8	1	0	0	2								4	9	2.3	6	0	7	99	14.1	42	0					3	34	11.3	24
2000	SAS	16	0	0	2	1						8	1	24	149	6.2	24	0	13	174	13.4	35	1					2	16	8.0	16
2001	SAS	16				3						18	3	51	243	4.8	37	3	9	125	13.9	58	0					2	24	12.0	17
2002	SAS	18	2	0	0	5						30	5	104	424	4.1	25	5	9	145	16.1	33	0								
2003	SAS	18	0	0	1	9						72	12	87	324	3.7	30	11	5	88	17.6	31	1								
2004	SAS	13	1	0	0	4						24	4	36	115	3.2	12	3	5	86	17.2	53	1								
2005	SAS	18	3	0	0	4						18	3	43	165	3.8	16	3	1	6	6.0	6	0					1	10	10.0	10
2006	SAS	18	0	0	1	3						6	1	11	37	3.4	9	0	12	113	9.4	21	1					1	20	20.0	20
2007	SAS	15	1	1	0	6						6	1	25	104	4.2	14	1	11	158	14.4	29	0								
2008	SAS	14	0	0	1	2						6	1	7	20	2.9	5	0	3	35	11.7	16	0								
2009	SAS	18				2						36	6	15	78	5.2	36	6	3	20	6.7	10	0					3	13	4.3	8
2010	SAS	17				3						6	1	10	21	2.1	5	1	1	13	13.0	13	0					1	7	7.0	7
14	Years	223	8	4	9	69						242	40	423	1703	4.0	37	33	98	1308	13.3	58	5					14	132	9.4	24
ED SZPYTMA Ed DE-OT-OG 6'5 240 McMaster B: 11/17/1955 Hamilton, ON Draft: 3A-19 1979 MTL																															
1979	MTL	5																													
1980	MTL	13																										1	0	0.0	0
1981	HAM	1																													
3	Years	19																										1	0	0.0	0
DENNIS TABRON Dennis DB 5'9 182 Duke B: 3/19/1960 Bunn, NC Draft: 5B-134 1982 CHIB																															
1982	MTL	5	0		1																										
CHUCK TACK Chuck P 6'5 245 Nebraska B: 7/13/1979 Omaha, NE																															
2005	HAM	1				0																									
ADAM TAFRALIS Adam Gregory QB 6'1 221 San Jose State B: 8/30/1983 Daly City, CA																															
2008	HAM	3				0																									
2009	HAM	18				0						24	4	26	49	1.9	16	4													
2010	HAM	18	0	0	1	0								7	6	0.9	2	0													
3	Years	39	0	0	1	0						24	4	33	55	1.7	16	4													
JERRY TAGGE Jerry Lee QB 6'2 215 Nebraska B: 4/12/1950 Omaha, NE Draft: 1B-11 1972 GB Pro: NW																															
1977	BC*	16	3		0							8	1	46	48	1.0	12	1													
1978	BC	16	2		1									34	1	0.0	0	0													
1979	BC	8	1		0									11	38	3.5	10	0													
3	Years	40	6		1							8	1	91	87	1.0	12	1													
JUNIOR TAGOAI Leuea DE 6'0 295 Taft JC; Hawaii B: 4/29/1970 Honolulu, HI Pro: E																															
1996	OTT	2				6																									
1997	WPG	3	0	0	1	4	1.0	5.0			1																				
2	Years	5	0	0	1	10	1.0	5.0			1																				
GEORGE TAIT George FL-DB 6'1 195 Fort William Ints. B: 1933																															
1955	SAS	11							3	52									4	65	16.3	20	0	1	3	3.0	3				
1956	SAS	14	1		0														3	64	21.3	42	0								
1957	SAS	15							1	18		1	0						6	83	13.8	18	0					3	25	8.3	11
1959	CAL	11										12	2						18	401	22.3	55	2								
1960	CAL	6	1		0														8	163	20.4	54	0								
1962	CAL	1																	2	29	14.5	19	0								
6	Years	58	2		0				4	70		13	2						41	805	19.6	55	2	1	3	3.0	3	3	25	8.3	11
HERON TAIT Heron DB 6'0 190 Guelph B: 9/20/1970 Kingston, Jamaica Draft: 3A-27 1995 OTT																															
1995	TOR	6	0		2	6																									
PENE TALAMAIVAO Pene DT 6'4 310 Utah B: 6/14/1975 Fatuaia, Western Samoa Pro: EX																															
2002	OTT	8	0	1	0	8	1.0				2																				
2004	OTT	4				8																									
2	Years	12	0	1	0	16	1.0				2																				
ANDRE TALBOT Andre WR-SB 5'10 185 Wilfrid Laurier B: 5/3/1978 Toronto, ON Draft: 5A-34 2001 TOR																															
2001	TOR	10	0	1	0	8																									
2002	TOR	14				3													25	257	10.3	33	0								
2003	TOR	4				3																									

Year	Team	GP	FM	FF	FR	TK	SK	YDS	IR	YDS	PD	PTS	TD	RA	YDS	AVG	LG	TD	REC	YDS	AVG	LG	TD	PR	YDS	AVG	LG	KOR	YDS	AVG	LG
2004	TOR	18	1	0	1	7						18	3						34	464	13.6	44	3								
2005	TOR	18	1	0	0	2						12	2						48	679	14.1	39	2								
2006	TOR	14				2						12	2						24	280	11.7	66	2								
2007	TOR	17	1	0	0	3						36	6						53	803	15.2	70	6					1	1	1.0	1
2008	TOR	17	1	0	0	0						24	4						76	915	12.0	37	4								
2009	TOR	1				0													1	4	4.0	4	0								
2010	EDM	13				0						6	1						27	301	11.1	40	1								
10	Years	126	4	1	1	28						108	18						288	3703	12.9	70	18					1	1	1.0	1
JIM TALBOT James DT 6'0 235 Texas A&M-Commerce B: 11/21/1950 New York, NY																															
1973	TOR	4																													
DON TALCOTT Donald C. T 6'2 235 Nevada-Reno B: 5/21/1921 D: 4/22/1955 Reno, NV Draft: 26-272 1945 PHI Pro: N																															
1949	OTT	11																													
LANDAN TALLEY Landan SB-WR 6'0 178 Lambuth B: 2/21/1987 New Orleans, LA																															
2010	CAL	3				0						6	1						2	18	9.0	12	1	8	49	6.1	14	12	236	19.7	47
2011	CAL	7	1	0	0	2						20	3	3	43	14.3	18	0	19	317	16.7	81	3	4	3	0.8	6	8	239	29.9	44
2	Years	10	1	0	0	2						26	4	3	43	14.3	18	0	21	335	16.0	81	4	12	52	4.3	14	20	475	23.8	47
HANK TAMOWSKI Hank HB-E-FW 5'10 175 Toronto B: 1930 Draft: 4-14 1953 OTT																															
1953	OTT	5																													
1954	OTT	14							2	12														9	69	7.7	17				
2	Years	19							2	12														9	69	7.7	17				
JOHN TANNER John Vance DE 6'4 237 Brevard JC*; Tennessee Tech B: 3/8/1945 Orlando, FL D: 2/5/2009 Merritt Island, FL Draft: 9-221 1971 SD Pro: N																															
1972	TOR	9	0		1																										
1976	MTL	9	0		1																										
2	Years	18	0		2																										
MARTIN TANSIL Martin LB 6'2 222 Southern University B: 10/20/1942 Detroit, MI																															
1965	EDM	2																													
GREG TAPLIN Greg DE 6'4 266 Michigan State B: 1/18/1982 Hollywood, FL Pro: E																															
2005	HAM	7				15	2.0	10.0																							
JAMIE TARAS Jamie OG-RB 6'2 230 Western Ontario B: 1/31/1966 Acton, ON Draft: 3B-25 1987 BC																															
1987	BC	10	1		1	1								4	4	1.0	4	0	5	22	4.4	6	0								
1988	BC	13				2								2	8	4.0	4	0	2	25	12.5	13	0								
1989	BC	18				2								5	11	2.2	3	0	13	185	14.2	34	0								
1990	BC	16	0		2	0						6	1	1	0	0.0	0	0	3	15	5.0	8	0								
1991	BC	16	0		1	2																									
1992	BC	17				0																									
1993	BC	16				1																									
1994	BC	17				1																									
1995	BC*	18				1																									
1996	BC	18	1		0	1																									
1997	BC	18				0																									
1998	BC	18	0	0	1	1																									
1999	BC*	18	1	0	1	1																									
2000	BC	17				1																									
2001	BC+	18	1	0	0	0																									
2002	BC+	16	0	1	2	1																									
16	Years	264	4	1	8	15						6	1	12	23	1.9	4	0	23	247	10.7	34	0								
HURLEY TARVER Hurley James, Jr. CB 6'1 185 Central Oklahoma B: 11/30/1975 Mount Pleasant, TX Pro: EX																															
2004	TOR	1				4																									
LONNIE TARVES Lonnie E 160 East Calgary Jrs. B: 1920																															
1946	CAL	1																													
1947	CAL	8																													
2	Years	9																													
DAVANZO TATE Davanzo DH 5'10 185 West Virginia; Akron B: 1/15/1984																															
2009	CAL	7	0	1	1	22			1	5	2																				
DREW TATE Andrew Street QB 5'11 200 Iowa B: 10/8/1984 Baytown, TX																															
2009	CAL	18				0								2	20	10.0	20	0													
2010	CAL	18	1	0	0	0						30	5	36	189	5.3	40	5													
2011	CAL	13	1	0	1	1						24	4	44	149	3.4	16	4													
3	Years	49	2	0	1	1						54	9	82	358	4.4	40	9													
MARK TATE Mark Anthony CB 6'0 185 Penn State B: 3/20/1974 Erie, PA Pro: EX																															
1999	SAS	13				31					3																				
JOHNNY TATUM John P. C 6'0 205 Texas B: 1935 Draft: 24-286 1956 WAS																															
1956	EDM	16	0		3				2	6																					
1959	EDM	3																													
2	Years	19	0		3				2	6																					
BRUCE TAUPIER Bruce DT 6'4 265 Youngstown State B: 2/18/1949																															
1971	BC	6																													
BILLY TAYLOR William Lewis RB 5'10 205 Michigan B: 1/7/1949 Hoxie, AR Draft: 5A-109 1972 ATL Pro: W																															
1972	CAL	2	2		0									7	62	8.9	35	0	3	27	9.0	21	0					3	59	19.7	20
BLAKE TAYLOR Blake FB-FW 6'2 200 Western Ontario B: 4/15/1928 D: 11/27/2008																															
1951	HAM	12										5	1					1													
1952	HAM	10										5	1					1													
2	Years	22										10	2					2													
BOB TAYLOR Robert F. DE 6'3 238 Maryland-Eastern Shore B: 2/5/1940 Columbia, SC D: 6/4/2006 New York, NY Draft: 9-125 1963 NYG Pro: N																															
1965	WPG	8																													
1966	WPG	16																													
1967	WPG	16	0		1																										
1968	TOR	10												5	47	9.4	28	0										10	209	20.9	32
4	Years	50	0		1									5	47	9.4	28	0										10	209	20.9	32
BOBBY TAYLOR Bob FL-SE 5'10 190 Mount Royal College Cougars Jrs. B: 3/5/1941 Barrow-in-Furness, England																															
1961	CAL	6																													
1962	CAL	7	1																7	60	8.6	14	0								
1963	CAL	16	2		0							36	6						74	1057	14.3	60	6								
1964	CAL	16										54	9						66	917	13.9	50	9								
1965	CAL	16	1		1							36	6						42	685	16.3	74	6								
1966	TOR	14	1		0							36	6						56	827	14.8	46	6								
1967	TOR	14	1		0							30	5						53	965	18.2	55	5								
1968	TOR	14	1		0							24	4						56	985	17.6	35	4								
1969	TOR+	14	1		0							30	5						59	1183	20.1	79	5								
1970	TOR	4										12	2						10	159	15.9	23	2								
1971	HAM	6																	11	108	9.8		0								
1971	EDM	7										6	1						17	287	16.9	67	1								
1971	Year	13										6	1						28	395	14.1	67	1								
1972	EDM	16	1		0							24	4						51	800	15.7	82	4								
1973	EDM	6										12	2						17	169	9.9	17	2								
1974	TOR	6																	2	21	10.5	13	0								
14	Years	155	9		1							300	50						521	8223	15.8	82	50								
BRAD TAYLOR Brad QB 6'0 193 Arkansas B: 11/2/1962 Little Rock, AR																															
1985	EDM	2																													
1986	EDM	18												3	10	3.3	8	0													
1987	OTT	7				0								1	5	5.0	5	0													
3	Years	27				0								4	15	3.8	8	0													

Year	Team	GP	FM	FF	FR	TK	SK	YDS	IR	YDS	PD	PTS	TD	RA	YDS	AVG	LG	TD	REC	YDS	AVG	LG	TD	PR	YDS	AVG	LG	KOR	YDS	AVG	LG
CARL TAYLOR Carl DT-DE 6'3 260 Memphis B: 6/20/1950 Nashville, TN Draft: 17-437 1975 WAS																															
1974	OTT	15																													
1975	OTT	3																													
1975	SAS	1																													
1975	Year	4																													
2	Years	18																													
CHRIS TAYLOR Christopher Tremayne WR 5'10 187 Texas A&M B: 4/25/1979 Temple, TX Draft: 7-218 2001 PIT Pro: E																															
2003	BC	4	1	0	0	0													1	5	5.0	5	0	20	145	7.3	48	16	237	14.8	34
CORDELL TAYLOR Cordell Jerome CB 5'11 191 Hampton B: 12/22/1973 Norfolk, VA Draft: 2-57 1998 JAC Pro: EN																															
2001	EDM	12	0	2	0	25			1	0	4																				
2003	EDM	4				14																									
2	Years	16	0	2	0	39			1	0	4																				
DANNY TAYLOR Daniel Paul DB 5'9 177 Texas-El Paso B: 9/19/1964 Conroe, TX Draft: 9-238 1986 CLE																															
1988	EDM	9			1	26			1	41		6	1																		
DAVID TAYLOR David SB-TE 6'5 235 Simon Fraser B: 1/5/1963 Guelph, ON Draft: 4-34 1986 WPG																															
1986	WPG	5										6	1						2	32	16.0	19	1					1	7	7.0	7
1987	OTT	8				0													3	50	16.7	27	0					1	11	11.0	11
2	Years	13				0						6	1						5	82	16.4	27	1					2	18	9.0	11
DERRICK TAYLOR Derrick Howard DB 5'11 186 North Carolina State B: 3/15/1964 St. Louis, MO Pro: N																															
1988	CAL	16			2	34	3.0		3	80																					
1989	CAL	2				5																									
2	Years	18	0		2	39	3.0		3	80																					
DON TAYLOR Don RB 5'9 185 Central (Iowa) B: 8/29/1955 Edinburgh, Scotland Draft: 1-7 1978 OTT																															
1978	BC	9										12	2	15	137	9.1	70	2													
1979	BC	16	1		0									14	69	4.9	13	0	2	24	12.0	21	0					1	25	25.0	25
1980	BC	16	0		1							12	2	63	306	4.9	23	2	13	162	12.5	67	0					2	33	16.5	18
1981	BC	12										6	1	8	18	2.3	8	0	2	16	8.0	13	1								
1982	BC	15	0		2									13	65	5.0	12	0	5	39	7.8	16	0								
1983	BC	16										6	1	29	117	4.0	14	1	18	205	11.4	24	0								
1984	BC	16										6	1	42	196	4.7	38	1	11	80	7.3	26	0					1	2	2.0	2
7	Years	100	1		3							42	7	184	908	4.9	70	6	51	526	10.3	67	1					4	60	15.0	25
DREW TAYLOR Andrew DE 6'5 250 Long Beach CC; Golden West JC; San Jose State B: 9/8/1950 Pro: UW																															
1978	BC	8																													
1979	BC	15	0		1																							1	20	20.0	20
1980	HAM	16	0		2																							1	10	10.0	10
1981	TOR	3	0		1		0.5																								
1982	MTL	3																													
5	Years	45	0		4		0.5																					2	30	15.0	20
D'WAYNE TAYLOR D'Wayne DB-LB 6'0 215 New Mexico State B: 11/11/1978																															
2004	SAS	1				0																									
2005	OTT	17	0	1	2	69	2.0	12.0			2																				
2006	MTL	9				21	1.0	8.0	1	13	1																				
2008	MTL	6	0	0	1	28	1.0	8.0																							
4	Years	33	0	1	3	118	4.0	28.0	1	13	3																				
EDDIE TAYLOR Edward D. DB 5'9 175 San Jose State B: 10/12/1968 San Diego County, CA																															
1991	WPG	3				7																		2	1	0.5	4	3	65	21.7	32
1992	WPG	4				16			1	46														7	29	4.1	12	7	140	20.0	30
1993	BC	14	1		2	49			2	21														1	-6	-6.0	-6				
1995	WPG	1				0																									
4	Years	22	1		2	72			3	67														10	24	2.4	12	10	205	20.5	32
ELTON TAYLOR Elton DB-LB 5'11 187 Weston Wildcats Jrs. B: 1932																															
1954	WPG	3																													
1955	WPG	15	1		0				1	0		5	1	7	14	2.0	9	1													
1956	WPG	16	0		3				4	108		6	1	11	65	5.9	11	0	3	35	11.7	19	0					8	173	21.6	30
1957	WPG	9							1	19																					
4	Years	43	1		3				6	127		11	2	18	79	4.4	11	1	3	35	11.7	19	0					8	173	21.6	30
ERIC TAYLOR Eric DT 6'2 305 Memphis B: 12/14/1981 Winchester, TN Draft: 7-212 2004 PIT Pro: N																															
2008	EDM	6	0	0	2	17	1.0	4.0			1																				
2009	EDM	13				28	2.0	13.0			3																				
2010	TOR	13				17	3.0	17.0			2																				
2011	BC	7	0	1	0	21																									
4	Years	39	0	1	2	83	6.0	34.0			6																				
GENE TAYLOR Eugene Yarman WR 6'2 189 Contra Costa JC; Fresno State B: 11/12/1962 Berkeley, CA Draft: 6-163 1987 NE Pro: EN																															
1989	SAS	3	1		0	0						6	1						2	20	10.0	14	1					3	70	23.3	31
HENRY TAYLOR Henry LB 6'0 230 Florida State B: 9/24/1963 Niagara Falls, NY Draft: TD 1985 TB-USFL																															
1985	OTT	1																													
1986	OTT	11	0		1		2.0																								
2	Years	12	0		1		2.0																								
HUGH TAYLOR Hugh Wilson (Bones) E 6'4 194 Louisiana-Monroe; Tulane; Oklahoma City B: 7/6/1923 Wynne, AR D: 10/31/1992 Wynne, AR Pro: N																															
1955	OTT	12										10	2						31	636	20.5	80	2					1	28	28.0	28
JASON TAYLOR Jason DE 6'4 245 British Columbia B: 10/3/1979 Draft: 3-19 2004 CAL																															
2004	CAL	11				0																									
JIM TAYLOR Jimmie Glen LB 6'2 232 Baylor B: 6/27/1934 Rowden, TX D: 2/25/2005 Abilene, TX Draft: 3-29 1956 PIT Pro: N																															
1959	HAM	14							1	15																		1	11	11.0	11
1960	HAM	14							2	15		6	1																		
2	Years	28							3	30		6	1															1	11	11.0	11
JOE TAYLOR Joe WR-SB 6'1 190 Northern Arizona B: 6/28/1959																															
1981	MTL	1																	1	7	7.0	7	0								
JOHN TAYLOR John Allen OT 6'4 255 El Camino JC; Pacific B: 10/25/1953 Pro: W																															
1977	WPG	5																													
1978	MTL	6																													
2	Years	11																													
JOHNNY TAYLOR John Miles E-HB 5'10 174 McGill B: 1926 Montreal, QC D: 12/26/2005																															
1946	MTL	6																													
1948	MTL	11																													
1949	MTL	4																													
1950	MTL	9										5	1																		
1951	MTL	8										5	1										1								
5	Years	38										10	2										1								
KEN TAYLOR Kenneth WR 5'11 185 San Jose State B: 1960																															
1983	TOR	2																	1	8	8.0	8	0								
KERRY TAYLOR Kerry SB 5'11 184 Southern Connecticut State B: 10/23/1962 Yonkers, NY																															
1985	TOR	15	3		0							24	4	35	154	4.4	14	1	59	670	11.4	35	3	31	230	7.4	22	17	284	16.7	30
1986	MTL	7	1		0									3	-2	-0.7	0	0	32	338	10.6	41	0	25	247	9.9	27	16	371	23.2	32
2	Years	22	4		0							24	4	38	152	4.0	14	1	91	1008	11.1	41	3	56	477	8.5	27	33	655	19.8	32
KITRICK TAYLOR Kitrick Lavell WR 5'11 189 Washington State B: 7/22/1964 Draft: 5-128 1987 KC Pro: N																															
1995	SA	12				1						12	2						15	165	11.0	23	2								
LARRY TAYLOR Larry WR 5'6 177 Connecticut B: 5/30/1985 Fort Lauderdale, FL																															
2008	MTL	14				2						6	1	1	2	2.0	2	0						42	517	12.3	69	25	613	24.5	56
2009	MTL*	17	6	0	0	0						18	3	5	31	6.2	16	0	7	38	5.4	19	0	89	788	8.9	68	51	1059	20.8	56
2010	MTL	1				0																		1	4	4.0	4	1	16	16.0	16
2011	CAL+	17	2	0	0	0						18	3	11	59	5.4	17	0	19	147	7.7	25	2	67	538	8.0	48	43	1008	23.4	60

Year	Team	GP	FM	FF	FR	TK	SK	YDS	IR	YDS	PD	PTS	TD	RA	YDS	AVG	LG	TD	REC	YDS	AVG	LG	TD	PR	YDS	AVG	LG	KOR	YDS	AVG	LG
4	Years	49	8	0	0	2						42	7	17	92	5.4	17	0	26	185	7.1	25	2	199	1847	9.3	69	120	2696	22.5	60
LEO TAYLOR Leo OHB 5'10 185 North Texas B: 1949																															
1970	CAL	12	1		0									57	245	4.3	24	0	14	84	6.0	22	0	25	196	7.8	25	9	247	27.4	37
1971	CAL	2												7	16	2.3	4	0	4	32	8.0	15	0								
2	Years	14	1		0									64	261	4.1	24	0	18	116	6.4	22	0	25	196	7.8	25	9	247	27.4	37
REGGIE TAYLOR Reginald RB 5'8 175 Cincinnati B: 2/8/1964 Los Angeles, CA Draft: 11-280 1987 TB																															
1988	BC	7	4		0	0						12	2	72	428	5.9	30	2	12	86	7.2	18	0					5	149	29.8	58
1989	EDM*	18	6		1	1						36	6	237	1503	6.3	49	2	34	358	10.5	35	4	1	11	11.0	11				
1990	EDM+	12	4		0	1						42	7	102	662	6.5	81	2	23	348	15.1	67	5								
1991	EDM	18	6		0	4						30	5	198	1293	6.5	69	4	36	370	10.3	44	1								
4	Years	55	20		1	6						120	20	609	3886	6.4	81	10	105	1162	11.1	67	10	1	11	11.0	11	5	149	29.8	58
ROGER TAYLOR Roger Wayne OT 6'6 275 Oklahoma State B: 1/5/1958 Shawnee, OK Draft: 3B-75 1981 KC Pro: N																															
1982	WPG	4	0		1																										
ROSS TAYLOR Ross G 5'11 206 Parkdale Jrs. B: 1926																															
1951	CAL	5																													
SIMON TAYLOR Simon OT 6'6 270 Concordia B: 6/27/1969 Accrington, England Draft: 3-18 1992 EDM																															
1995	HAM	4				0																									
1996	HAM	1				0																									
2	Years	5				0																									
STEVE TAYLOR Steven L. QB 6'0 205 Nebraska B: 1/7/1967 Fresno, CA Draft: 12B-323 1989 IND																															
1989	EDM	2	2		0	0								4	21	5.3	11	0													
1990	EDM	12	1		0	0						6	1	17	169	9.9	26	1													
1991	CAL	18	2		0	0								38	263	6.9	22	0													
1992	CAL	18	1		1	1								10	88	8.8	22	0													
1993	CAL	18				0						12	2	23	155	6.7	32	2													
1994	CAL	18				1						6	1	10	69	6.9	15	1													
1995	HAM	16	6		2	0						6	1	53	386	7.3	29	1													
1996	OTT	18				2						12	2	25	196	7.8	24	2													
8	Years	120	12		3	4						42	7	180	1347	7.5	32	7													
SYNIKER TAYLOR Syniker O. DH 6'1 200 Mississippi B: 9/22/1979 Gulfport, MS																															
2004	OTT	13	0	3	1	36			1	53	2																				
2005	WPG	3	0	0	1	13					1																				
2	Years	16	0	3	2	49			1	53	3																				
TREAMELLE TAYLOR Treamelle WR 5'10 180 Nevada-Reno B: 11/8/1969 Draft: 9-233 1991 TB																															
1992	OTT	16	5		1	3						30	5	1	-6	-6.0	-6	0	30	487	16.2	45	3	79	936	11.8	96	21	395	18.8	37
TYRONE TAYLOR Tyrone Micah WR 5'10 170 Los Medanos JC; Sacramento State B: 9/29/1976 Detroit, MI Pro: E																															
2001	BC	5	1	0	0	0						12	2	1	34	34.0	34	0	2	103	51.5	78	2	19	232	12.2	49	18	363	20.2	30
2002	BC	2				0						6	1	1	7	7.0	7	0	1	5	5.0	5	0	4	27	6.8	19	6	127	21.2	32
2	Years	7	1	0	0	0						18	3	2	41	20.5	34	0	3	108	36.0	78	2	23	259	11.3	49	24	490	20.4	32
WILLIE TAYLOR Willie OG-C-LB 6'0 230 Florida A&M B: 12/17/1936 Tallahassee, FL																															
1961	HAM	10																													
1962	BC	8																													
1964	BC	3																													
1965	BC	1																													
4	Years	22																													
ZAC TAYLOR Zac QB 6'2 210 Wake Forest; Butler County CC; Nebraska B: 5/10/1983 Norman, OK																															
2007	WPG																														
MATTHEW TEAGUE Matthew Nathaniel DE 6'5 240 Prairie View A&M B: 10/22/1958 Cincinnati, OH Draft: 10-273(DI) 1980 DAL Pro: N																															
1982	OTT	2					1.0																								
1983	TOR	8	0		1		3.0																								
1984	SAS	4					4.0																								
3	Years	14	0		1		8.0																								
JIMMY TEAL James Franklin LB 6'3 225 Purdue B: 5/14/1950 Baltimore, MD Draft: 10-249 1972 DET Pro: NW																															
1977	OTT	5																													
JEFF TEDFORD Jeffery R. QB 6'0 187 Cerritos JC; Fresno State B: 11/2/1961 Lynwood, CA																															
1983	HAM	11							1	3				6	9	1.5	10	0													
1984	HAM	9												3	-6	-2.0	-3	0													
1985	HAM	8										6	1	12	28	2.3	9	1													
1986	CAL	18												2	10	5.0	9	0													
1987	SAS	3				0																									
1988	WPG	1																													
6	Years	50				0			1	3		6	1	23	41	1.8	10	1													
CRAIG TEFFT Craig HB 5'10 180 Central Michigan B: 12/7/1946 Honolulu, HI																															
1970	WPG	4	3		0									17	34	2.0	9	0	12	98	8.2	24	0					9	261	29.0	40
LANCE TEICHELMAN Lance Theodore DT 6'4 274 Texas A&M B: 10/21/1970 San Antonio, TX Draft: 7-196 1994 IND Pro: EN																															
1995	SA	3				4																									
TONY TELLA Tony Ferguson OG 6'4 308 Miami (Florida) B: 12/5/1982 Houston, TX																															
2007	EDM	2				0																									
TAWAN TEMPLE Tawan LB 6'1 235 East Mississippi JC B: 1/16/1969																															
1994	WPG	1				5					2																				
TIM TENNIGKEIT Tim M. DE-DT 6'5 240 UCLA B: 3/20/1955 Long Beach, CA																															
1979	SAS	3																													
TONY TERESA Anthony Michael HB-QB 5'9 185 Hartnell JC; San Jose State B: 12/8/1933 Pittsburg, CA D: 10/16/1984 Salinas, CA Pro: N																															
1956	BC	11	4		0				0	9		7	0	28	70	2.5	15	0	3	41	13.7	14	0	3	4	1.3	4				
1957	BC	2												3	12	4.0	6	0	1	18	18.0	18	0								
2	Years	13	4		0				0	9		7	0	31	82	2.6	15	0	4	59	14.8	18	0	3	4	1.3	4				
TOM TERHART Tom OT-OG 6'3 260 Lackawanna State B: 7/23/1949																															
1975	TOR	10																													
1976	TOR	5																													
2	Years	15																													
NEIL TERNOVATSKY Neil LB 6'2 230 Alberta B: 10/15/1984 Winnipeg, MB																															
2007	CAL	7				7																									
2008	CAL	9				6																									
2	Years	16				13																									
HAROLD TERRELL OG																															
1974	HAM	7																													
MARV TERRELL Marvin, Jr. OG 6'1 236 Mississippi B: 6/10/1938 West Memphis, AR Draft: FS 1960 DALT; 2B-24 1960 BAL Pro: N																															
1964	TOR	8																													
BUDDY TERRY William Everett, Jr. T 6'1 215 Houston B: 1934 Draft: 17-202 1957 CHIC																															
1957	WPG	1																													
COREY TERRY Corey TeWana LB 6'3 250 Garden City CC; Tennessee B: 3/6/1976 Warrenton, NC Draft: 7B-250 1999 IND Pro: N																															
2002	CAL	2				15																									
JOHN TERRY John Henry, III OT 6'4 292 Johnson C. Smith; Livingstone B: 8/30/1966 Greenwood, SC Draft: 10-275 1992 DAL																															
1995	TOR	15				0																									
1996	SAS	18				2																									
1997	SAS+	18	0	0	2	0																									
1998	SAS+	13				0																									
1999	SAS+	18				0																									
2000	SAS	14				1																									
2001	SAS	15	0	0	1	1																									
2002	TOR	4				0													1	-5	-5.0	-5	0								
8	Years	115	0	0	3	4													1	-5	-5.0	-5	0								

Year	Team	GP	FM	FF	FR	TK	SK	YDS	IR	YDS	PD	PTS	TD	RA	YDS	AVG	LG	TD	REC	YDS	AVG	LG	TD	PR	YDS	AVG	LG	KOR	YDS	AVG	LG
NATE TERRY Nate DH 6'2 185 West Virginia B: 10/5/1976 Homestead, FL Pro: E																															
2000	SAS	6				19	1.0	6.0			1																				
2004	CAL	14	0	0	1	37			3	62	8																				
2005	CAL	7				21			2	113	1																				
3	Years	27	0	0	1	77	1.0	6.0	5	175	10																				
RYAN TERRY Ryan Lamont RB 6'0 205 Iowa B: 9/20/1971 Fort Bragg, NC Pro: N																															
1999	TOR	13	4	0	0	2						18	3	135	762	5.6	54	3	15	131	8.7	29	0					15	406	27.1	47
2000	TOR	10	0	0	1	1						24	4	78	315	4.0	21	3	23	226	9.8	40	1					2	27	13.5	18
2001	EDM	3				0													2	53	26.5	47	0					6	142	23.7	43
2002	MTL	6	2	0	0	1						6	1	28	127	4.5	14	1	8	76	9.5	14	0					14	343	24.5	45
4	Years	32	6	0	1	4						48	8	241	1204	5.0	54	7	48	486	10.1	47	1					37	918	24.8	47
TIM TERRY Timothy L. DE 6'3 241 Temple B: 7/26/1974 Hempstead, NY Pro: N																															
1999	HAM	8	0	1	0	15	1.0																								
FRED TESONE Fred M. HB 5'9 169 Denver B: 9/1930																															
1955	CAL	1																						2	17	8.5	11	1	15	15.0	15
KIP TEXADA Kip Wagner CB 5'9 180 McNeese State B: 1/15/1968 Port Arthur, TX Pro: E																															
1993	SAC	17	0		2	41			5	61																					
1994	SHR	6	0		1	20					4																				
2	Years	23	0		3	61			5	61	4																				
DEL THACHUK Delmar E 5'10 185 Edmonton Wildcats Jrs. B: 1936																															
1959	EDM	2																													
CORKY THARP Thomas Allen OHB 5'10 180 Alabama B: 4/19/1931 Birmingham, AL Draft: 6-67 1955 LARM Pro: N																															
1955	TOR	7							1	0		20	4	130	798	6.1	61	4	15	257	17.1	40	0	6	33	5.5	14	16	370	23.1	48
1957	TOR	7										18	3	67	396	5.9	69	3	5	58	11.6	9	0					2	40	20.0	32
1958	TOR	6												6	7	1.2	7	0	3	64	21.3	44	0					5	130	26.0	30
1959	TOR	4										6	1	41	241	5.9	29	0	6	76	12.7	35	1					3	64	21.3	27
4	Years	24							1	0		44	8	244	1442	5.9	69	7	29	455	15.7	44	1	6	33	5.5	14	26	604	23.2	48
DAVE THEISEN David K-HB 6'2 205 Marquette; Nebraska B: 9/9/1941 Milwaukee, WI Draft: 26-207(f) 1963 HOU; 11-141(f) 1963 LARM																															
1964	TOR	3																													
1965	WPG	1										3	0																		
2	Years	4										3	0																		
JOE THEISMANN Joseph Robert QB 6'0 195 Notre Dame B: 9/9/1949 New Brunswick, NJ Draft: 4-99 1971 MIA Pro: N																															
1971	TOR+	14	5		0							8	1	81	564	7.0	84	1						1	7	7.0	7				
1972	TOR	6										6	1	21	147	7.0	16	1													
1973	TOR+	14	9		3							6	1	70	343	4.9	18	1													
3	Years	34	14		3							20	3	172	1054	6.1	84	3						1	7	7.0	7				
DAVE THELEN David FB-OHB 6'0 205 Miami (Ohio) B: 1937 Draft: 27-324 1958 CLE																															
1958	OTT+	14							2	14		12	2	100	696	7.0	77	2	12	175	14.6	41	0					6	140	23.3	28
1959	OTT+	14										66	11	228	1339	5.9	59	10	9	95	10.6	40	1					3	63	21.0	28
1960	OTT+	12										19	3	245	1407	5.7	52	3	10	91	9.1	19	0								
1961	OTT	12										30	5	180	1032	5.7	47	3	8	197	24.6	48	2								
1962	OTT	14										24	4	146	759	5.2	65	4	10	178	17.8	37	0								
1963	OTT+	14										66	11	151	907	6.0	62	9	12	213	17.8	47	2								
1964	OTT+	14	1		0							60	10	161	777	4.8	59	8	19	270	14.2	76	2								
1965	TOR+	14	3		1							30	5	152	801	5.3	38	3	22	297	13.5	38	2								
1966	TOR+	14	1		0							30	5	167	745	4.5	29	5	17	248	14.6	49	0								
9	Years	122	5		1				2	14		337	56	1530	8463	5.5	77	47	119	1764	14.8	76	9					9	203	22.6	28
RYAN THELWELL Ryan R. WR-SB 6'2 200 Minnesota B: 4/6/1973 Montego Bay, Jamaica Draft: 2-9 1998 BC; 7-215 1998 SF Pro: N																															
2001	BC	15				4						24	4						47	672	14.3	51	4								
2002	BC	17				2						30	5	1	43	43.0	43	0	48	815	17.0	53	5								
2003	BC	16	3	0	0	4						24	4						59	925	15.7	62	4					1	0	0.0	0
2004	BC+	18				1						36	6						54	909	16.8	46	6								
2005	BC+	18	0	0	1	0						46	7	1	19	19.0	19	0	74	1035	14.0	75	7					0	11		11
2006	BC	17	0	0	2	4						30	5						53	625	11.8	30	4					2	0	0.0	0
2007	CAL	11				3						24	4						40	733	18.3	70	4								
2008	CAL	17	1	1	1	1						18	3						23	385	16.7	35	3								
2009	CAL	10	0	0	1	1						6	1						31	492	15.9	45	1								
2010	CAL	13				0						6	1	1	7	7.0	7	0	12	125	10.4	18	1								
2011	BC	2				0																									
11	Years	154	4	1	5	20						244	40	3	69	23.0	43	0	441	6716	15.2	75	39					3	11	3.7	11
BARNEY THERRIEN Barney DT-OT 6'2 235 Washington B: 1940																															
1961	BC	16			2																										
1962	BC	16																													
1963	BC	16	0		2																										
1964	EDM	16	0		2																										
1965	EDM	16																													
1966	EDM	16																													
1967	EDM	16	0		1																										
7	Years	112	0		7																										
PATRICK THIBEAULT Patrick SB-WR 6'2 205 St. Mary's (Nova Scotia) B: 1/6/1977 Hauterive, QC Draft: 3-20 2002 SAS																															
2002	SAS	6				0																									
2003	SAS	17				0																									
2004	SAS	14				0													3	26	8.7	10	0								
3	Years	37				0													3	26	8.7	10	0								
JIM THIBERT James Gerald LB 6'3 230 Toledo B: 6/14/1940 Toledo, OH Draft: 22-176(f) 1962 SD Pro: N																															
1964	EDM	2																													
CHRIS THIENEMAN Christopher Allen DT 6'5 285 Louisville B: 6/6/1965 Louisville, KY Pro: E																															
1991	SAS	2	0		1	8																									
1993	SAC	7				3	1.0	7.0																							
1994	SAC	3				8	1.0	4.0			2																				
3	Years	12	0		1	19	2.0	11.0			2																				
MARCUS THIGPEN Marcus Arnette RB-SB 5'9 193 Indiana B: 5/15/1986 Detroit, MI																															
2010	HAM	18	4	0	2	1						42	7	28	234	8.4	31	2	20	234	11.7	41	1	63	554	8.8	93	39	784	20.1	93
2011	HAM	17	1	0	0	2						24	4	23	82	3.6	24	1	28	382	13.6	66	2	52	501	9.6	50	47	859	18.3	46
2	Years	35	5	0	2	3						66	11	51	316	6.2	31	3	48	616	12.8	66	3	115	1055	9.2	93	86	1643	19.1	93
PETE THODOS Peter HB-FW 5'8 182 Vancouver Meralomas Jrs. B: 11/11/1927 Vancouver, BC D: 12/25/2011 Vancouver, BC																															
1948	CAL	11										1	0																		
1949	CAL	13										20	4					3					1								
1950	MTL	8										10	2					1					1								
1951	MTL	12										10	2					2													
1952	CAL	16			1				1	10		20	4	61	222	3.6	24	2	33	524	15.9	54	2	8	128	16.0	48	32	816	25.5	94
1953	CAL	16										54	10	54	196	3.6	71	3	58	795	13.7	84	7	44	313	7.1	29	10	118	11.8	26
1954	BC	2	1		0													0					0	27	147	5.4	20				
1954	WPG	8										10	2					0					2					1	35	35.0	35
1954	Year	10	1		0							10	2	12	43	3.6	19	0	14	233	16.6	44	2	27	147	5.4	20	1	35	35.0	35
1955	SAS	12										10	2	41	189	4.6	26	1	8	199	24.9	63	1					9	119	13.2	36
1956	SAS	15	2		0							6	1	22	111	5.0	21	1	4	43	10.8	18	0	59	363	6.2	20	19	425	22.4	68
9	Years	105	3		1				1	10		141	27	178	718	4.0	71	13	103	1561	15.2	84	14	138	951	6.9	48	71	1513	21.3	94
RUSTY THOMAN Russ G 6'0 220 Queen's																															
1957	CAL	4																													
ALBERT THOMAS Albert CB 5'11 175 Tennessee State B: 3/25/1966 Atlanta, GA																															
1990	CAL	3				10			1	0																					

Year	Team	GP	FM	FF	FR	TK	SK	YDS	IR	YDS	PD	PTS	TD	RA	YDS	AVG	LG	TD	REC	YDS	AVG	LG	TD	PR	YDS	AVG	LG	KOR	YDS	AVG	LG
1990	HAM	5	0		1	12																									
1990	Year	8	0		1	22			1	0																					
ANDREW THOMAS Andrew CB 5'11 185 Massachusetts B: 10/5/1964 Kingston, Jamaica Draft: 1B-3 1989 SAS																															
1990	BC	3				8																									
1991	BC	13				39																									
1991	WPG	4				7																									
1991	Year	17				46																									
1992	WPG	14	0		2	29			2	27														0	3		3				
1993	TOR	16				31	1.0	7.0	1	9																					
1994	TOR	1				0																									
1994	OTT	12			1	45					3																				
1994	Year	13				45					3																				
5	Years	47	0		3	159	1.0	7.0	3	36	3													0	3		3				
BYRON THOMAS Byron OT 6'4 328 North Carolina B: 6/12/1976 Oxford, NC																															
1999	CAL	8				1																									
CARLOS THOMAS Carlos DH-S-CB 5'11 195 South Carolina B: 5/1/1987 College Park, GA																															
2009	SAS	1				0																									
2011	HAM	15				41			2	3	4																				
2	Years	16				41			2	3	4																				
CHARLES THOMAS Charles Phillip, Jr. OT 6'4 292 Troy B: 11/26/1978 Nashville, TN																															
2003	SAS	18				1																									
2004	SAS	18				0																									
2005	SAS	18				1																									
2006	SAS	18	1	0	3	0													1	0	0.0	0	0								
2008	HAM	15				1																									
5	Years	87	1	0	3	3													1	0	0.0	0	0								
CLYDE THOMAS Clyde A. HB 5'10 187 Ohio University B: 4/5/1939 Bellaire, OH D: 10/20/2006 Wheeling, WV																															
1961	BC	2												11	45	4.1	13	0	2	43	21.5	31	0								
CURT THOMAS Curtland Parrish WR 6'0 183 Missouri B: 2/19/1962 St. Louis, MO Draft: 12-335 1984 WAS; 18-371 1984 PHI-USFL Pro: N																															
1986	TOR	4																	9	139	15.4	27	0	23	149	6.5	18	4	90	22.5	27
DAVE THOMAS Dave LV 6'3 240 Austin Peay State; Eastern Illinois B: 1/12/1976 Summit, NJ Pro: EX																															
2002	OTT	9				43			1	4	1																				
2003	OTT	3				3																									
2003	HAM	11	0	0	1	37	2.0																								
2003	Year	14	0	0	1	40	2.0																								
2	Years	12	0	0	1	83	2.0	0.0	1	4	1																				
DAVID THOMAS David (Peanuts) DB 5'10 175 Texas Southern B: 9/11/1951 Newark, NJ Draft: 34-405 1974 MEM-WFL Pro: W																															
1977	TOR	2							2	27																					
1978	TOR	8	0		1														1	9	9.0	9	0	15	113	7.5	30	1	17	17.0	17
2	Years	10	0		1				2	27									1	9	9.0	9	0	15	113	7.5	30	1	17	17.0	17
DEE THOMAS Derward Heith DB 5'10 176 Nicholls State B: 11/7/1967 Morgan City, LA Draft: 10-264 1990 HOU Pro: EN																															
1994	TOR	3				13					2																				
DONNIE THOMAS Donald Maurice LB 6'2 245 Indiana B: 3/12/1953 Michigan City, IN Draft: 11-298 1976 NE Pro: N																															
1977	HAM	5							1	0																					
EDDIE LEE THOMAS Eddie Lee CB 5'9 180 San Jose State B: 7/9/1968 Chicago, IL																															
1991	EDM+	16	0		2	75			7	41		12	2															16	277	17.3	44
1992	EDM	17	1		1	66			4	17														10	81	8.1	18	5	86	17.2	22
1994	TOR	16	1		1	52			4	11	5	6	1																		
1995	BC	18	1		0	47			4	61	6	6	1											42	421	10.0	52	33	669	20.3	98
1997	BC	5				17			2	17	1																	2	13	6.5	8
1999	WPG	10	1	0	0	38			2	43	3													8	20	2.5	10	28	525	18.8	42
6	Years	82	4	0	4	295			23	190	15	24	4											60	522	8.7	52	84	1570	18.7	98
EDWARD THOMAS Edward Tervino LB 6'1 228 Georgia Southern B: 9/27/1975 Thomasville, GA Pro: EN																															
1997	MTL	7	0	0	3	19	1.0	11.0	1	0	0																				
1998	MTL	3				9																									
1999	MTL	12	0	1	0	34	2.0	8.0			1																				
3	Years	22	0	1	3	62	3.0	19.0	1	0	1																				
FERNANDO THOMAS Fernando CB 6'0 190 Southwestern Louisiana B: 10/30/1972 Shreveport, LA																															
1995	BIR	18				41			2	41	7	6	1																		
1996	BC	8	0		1	16																									
2	Years	26	0		1	57			2	41	7	6	1																		
FRED THOMAS Fred HB none																															
1949	TOR	1																													
GENE THOMAS Eugene Warren FB 6'1 210 Florida A&M B: 9/1/1942 Barberton, OH D: 8/27/1993 Independence, MO Pro: N																															
1974	CAL	6	3		0							24	4	53	251	4.7	43	4	10	42	4.2	15	0								
GENE THOMAS Gene WR 5'10 157 Pacific B: 6/7/1962 Draft: 11-304 1986 NE																															
1987	TOR	2				0													4	74	18.5	33	0								
IKE THOMAS Isaac DB 6'2 193 Bishop B: 11/4/1947 Newton, LA Draft: 2-51 1971 DAL Pro: NW																															
1977	TOR	11							2	44		6	1																		
1978	TOR	10	0		1																										
1978	HAM	5	0		1				2	45		6	1																		
1978	Year	15	0		2				2	45		6	1																		
1979	HAM	10							3	62																					
3	Years	31	0		2				7	151		12	2																		
JEFF THOMAS Jeff OT 6'8 305 Taft JC B: 1/31/1966 London, ON																															
1993	EDM	5				0																									
JESSE THOMAS Jesse LeRoy DB 5'10 180 Michigan State B: 5/23/1928 Guthrie, OK Draft: 10-119 1951 NYY Pro: N																															
1954	WPG	13	2		0				1	40		10	2	21	46	2.2	12	0	8	131	16.4	45	2	5	24	4.8	8	3	58	19.3	23
JIM THOMAS James (Long Gone) OHB 6'2 190 Mississippi Industrial B: 1939																															
1963	EDM	13	5		0							37	6	141	605	4.3	29	5	12	145	12.1	36	1					7	151	21.6	33
1964	EDM	12	5		0							25	4	74	429	5.8	97	2	20	366	18.3	88	2					20	530	26.5	63
1965	EDM+	16	7		0							54	9	115	981	8.5	104	7	19	277	14.6	70	2					16	446	27.9	47
1966	EDM*	12	3		0							54	9	156	989	6.3	100	6	26	298	11.5	67	3					10	254	25.4	38
1967	EDM*	15	4		0							48	8	172	1006	5.8	71	6	22	265	12.0	55	2								
1968	EDM	16	5		0							36	6	161	881	5.5	59	6	40	369	9.2	52	0					5	148	29.6	49
1969	EDM	16	1		0							30	5	190	849	4.5	64	4	46	505	11.0	41	1					12	300	25.0	34
1970	EDM	9	1		0							24	4	78	374	4.8	64	1	24	320	13.3	58	3					10	290	29.0	64
1971	EDM	4												24	47	2.0	16	0	12	97	8.1	20	0					8	171	21.4	34
9	Years	113	31		0							308	51	1111	6161	5.5	104	37	221	2642	12.0	88	14					88	2290	26.0	64
JOE THOMAS Joseph Earl WR 5'11 175 Mississippi Valley State B: 3/25/1963 Lafayette, LA Draft: 9-244 1986 DEN Pro: N																															
1987	HAM	1				1																									
JOEY THOMAS Joey Elleweyn DB 6'1 193 Washington*; Montana State B: 8/29/1980 Seattle, WA Draft: 3A-70 2004 GB Pro: N																															
2007	EDM	2				1																									
JUDGE THOMAS Judge RB 6'2 195 Virginia Union B: 4/24/1957 Martinsville, VA																															
1980	SAS	2	1		0									16	54	3.4	8	0	4	29	7.3	12	0								
KIWAUKEE THOMAS Kiwaukee Sanchez CB 5'11 190 Georgia Southern B: 6/19/1977 Warner Robins, GA Draft: 5-159 2000 JAC Pro: N																															
2008	MTL	3				2																									
MARCUS THOMAS Marcus DB 5'10 165 Wyoming B: 5/5/1965 San Diego, CA																															
1987	BC	2				5																						3	58	19.3	32
1988	BC	4				4			4	171		12	2															2	24	12.0	23
1989	BC	10				39			2	7																					
1990	TOR	2				3	1.0																								

Year	Team	GP	FM	FF	FR	TK	SK	YDS	IR	YDS	PD	PTS	TD	RA	YDS	AVG	LG	TD	REC	YDS	AVG	LG	TD	PR	YDS	AVG	LG	KOR	YDS	AVG	LG
1991	TOR	9	0		1	14																									
5	Years	27	0		1	65	1.0	0.0	6	178		12	2															5	82	16.4	32
MARKUS THOMAS Markus RB 5'10 192 Eastern Kentucky B: 7/12/1970 Cincinnati, OH Pro: E																															
1997	HAM	7				1						12	2	27	112	4.1	27	1	13	150	11.5	62	1								
MARVIN THOMAS Marvin A. DE 6'5 264 Memphis B: 10/19/1973 Bay Minette, AL Draft: 7B-233 1997 CHIB Pro: ENX																															
1999	BC	3				7																									
2000	BC	18	0	2	0	30	5.0	29.0			2																				
2002	OTT	6	0	1	0	10	3.0																								
2003	TOR	15	0	1	1	30	4.0				2																				
2004	TOR	7				11																									
5	Years	49	0	4	1	88	12.0	29.0			4																				
NEIL THOMAS Neil OT-DT 6'1 250 Hillsdale B: 1940 Draft: 24-186 1962 DEN																															
1962	WPG	10																													
1963	WPG	16	0		1																										
1964	WPG	1																													
3	Years	27	0		1																										
NORM THOMAS Norman E 5'11 185 British Columbia B: 1942 Draft: 10-58 1964 MTL																															
1965	EDM	13	2		0														3	65	21.7	35	0	28	122	4.4	13	2	26	13.0	24
NORRIS THOMAS Norris CB 5'11 190 Wisconsin-LaCrosse B: 1/16/1969 Inverness, MS																															
1994	WPG	8	3		2	8					1	6	1											12	66	5.5	15	17	448	26.4	97
1995	BAL	4				4			1	0	1																				
2	Years	12	3		2	12			1	0	2	6	1											12	66	5.5	15	17	448	26.4	97
RAY THOMAS Raymond Leslie FB 6'4 248 Wake Forest B: 3/25/1978																															
2003	HAM	7				0													2	12	6.0	8	0								
2004	HAM	18				15																						3	37	12.3	14
2	Years	25				15													2	12	6.0	8	0					3	37	12.3	14
RODNEY THOMAS Rodney Lamar CB 5'10 190 Brigham Young B: 12/21/1965 Los Angeles, CA Draft: 5-126 1988 MIA Pro: EN																															
1994	OTT	6				8			1	12	1																				
SAM THOMAS Sam OL 6'6 315 Jackson State B: 3/18/1976 Gulfport, MS																															
2000	EDM	1				0																									
SCOTT THOMAS Scott C. DB 6'2 205 Long Beach CC; Cerritos JC; Azusa Pacific B: 1/31/1975 Long Beach, CA																															
1999	BC	6				20					3																				
SPEEDY THOMAS Louis Timothy, III WR 6'1 174 Laney JC; Utah B: 4/13/1947 Alexandria, LA Draft: 3-57 1969 CIN Pro: N																															
1975	HAM	8										12	2	1	2	2.0	2	0	28	421	15.0	62	2								
WILLIE THOMAS William OG-C 6'1 227 Calgary Colts Jrs.; Calgary B: 8/14/1955 Winnipeg, MB																															
1977	CAL	16																													
1978	CAL	16																	1	-13	-13.0	-13	0								
1979	CAL	10	0		1																										
1980	WPG	16																													
1981	WPG	16																													
1982	WPG	1																													
1983	CAL	16																													
1984	CAL	16	1		1																										
1985	SAS	16	1		0																										
1986	TOR	16	0		1																										
10	Years	139	2		3														1	-13	-13.0	-13	0								
RICH THOMASELLI Richard J. RB 6'1 185 West Virginia Wesleyan B: 2/26/1957 Follansbee, WV Pro: N																															
1985	MTL	6	1		0							18	3	26	98	3.8	15	3	25	201	8.0	23	0								
JERRY THOMPKINS Jerry QB 6'2 207 Del Mar JC; Texas A&M-Kingsville B: 1937																															
1960	OTT	2																													
1961	MTL	8										12	2	72	361	5.0	19	2													
1962	MTL	2																													
3	Years	12										12	2	72	361	5.0	19	2													
ALAN THOMPSON Alan RB 6'0 205 Wisconsin B: 10/5/1949 Draft: 14-363 1972 DAL Pro: W																															
1972	OTT	2	1		0									18	94	5.2	44	0	3	25	8.3	13	0					1	22	22.0	22
ANDY THOMPSON Andy QB Toronto Argonauts Jrs.																															
1948	TOR	3																													
AUBREY THOMPSON Aubrey SB 6'1 230 Utah State B: 2/19/1971 Pro: E																															
1994	LV	9												11	56	5.1	13	0	8	50	6.3	14	0					1	22	22.0	22
BENNIE THOMPSON Bennie DB 6'0 214 Grambling State B: 2/10/1963 New Orleans, LA Pro: N																															
1986	WPG	9	0		2		2.0		2	49																					
1987	WPG	8			1	37			1	0																					
1988	WPG*	18	1		2	82	7.0		4	58														1	0	0.0	0				
3	Years	35	1		5	119	9.0		7	107														1	0	0.0	0				
BOBBY THOMPSON Bobby OHB 5'11 195 Arizona Western JC; Oklahoma B: 1/16/1947 Raleigh, NC Pro: N																															
1969	SAS	16	2		0							54	9	82	467	5.7	41	0	45	891	19.8	85	9					20	600	30.0	51
1970	SAS	8	1		0							24	4	45	336	7.5	65	2	18	379	21.1	94	2					4	87	21.8	30
1971	SAS	16	3		0							54	9	121	591	4.9	34	2	48	774	16.1	97	6					4	180	45.0	115
1972	SAS	16	2		0							42	7	97	461	4.8	69	0	51	821	16.1	91	7					4	117	29.3	42
1973	SAS	16	3		1							12	2	142	737	5.2	57	0	45	626	13.9	94	2					7	165	23.6	31
1974	SAS	16	2		0				1	24		36	6	68	305	4.5	32	1	56	711	12.7	66	5					12	266	22.2	34
1977	SAS	2	1		0									19	64	3.4	12	0	3	5	1.7	16	0					3	57	19.0	32
7	Years	90	14		1				1	24		222	37	574	2961	5.2	69	5	266	4207	15.8	97	31					54	1472	27.3	115
BOBBY THOMPSON Robert Lee CB 5'10 179 Compton JC; Arizona B: 3/30/1939 Minden, LA Draft: 12-91 1962 DAL; 3-38 1962 DET Pro: N																															
1962	MTL	14							4	38		12	2	27	126	4.7	19	1	13	151	11.6	45	0	7	30	4.3	6	14	396	28.3	106
1963	MTL	9							1	2		6	1	1	1	1.0	1	0	3	48	16.0	19	1	1	0	0.0	0				
1971	MTL	14							6	34																		7	200	28.6	38
3	Years	37							11	74		18	3	28	127	4.5	19	1	16	199	12.4	45	1	8	30	3.8	6	21	596	28.4	106
BOBBY THOMPSON Bobby OT 6'8 290 Kansas State B: 9/9/1959 D: 1/27/2005 Winnipeg, MB																															
1979	WPG	5																													
1980	WPG	15																													
1981	WPG	16	0		1																										
1982	WPG*	16																													
1983	WPG	13																													
1984	HAM	6																													
6	Years	71	0		1																										
CHARLES THOMPSON Charles RB 5'9 185 Oklahoma; Central State (Ohio) B: 5/28/1968 Lawton, OK Pro: E																															
1993	SAC	11	1		0	11								1	-15	-15.0	-15	0	12	143	11.9	27	0	14	120	8.6	22	20	425	21.3	62
1994	SHR	18	1		0	1						18	3	1	0	0.0	0	0	45	641	14.2	58	3	3	18	6.0	8	10	188	18.8	29
2	Years	29	2		0	12						18	3	2	-15	-7.5	0	0	57	784	13.8	58	3	17	138	8.1	22	30	613	20.4	62
CHRIS THOMPSON Christopher J. DH 6'0 187 Nicholls State B: 5/19/1982 New Orleans, LA Draft: 5B-150 2004 JAC Pro: EN																															
2007	EDM	9				12			1	40	1																				
2008	HAM*	18	0	0	1	62			9	99	10																				
2009	HAM	18				49			1	21	2	6	1																		
2010	EDM*	18	0	1	0	43			7	133	3	6	1																		
2011	EDM	18	0	4	0	49			3	94	4																	1	0	0.0	0
5	Years	81	0	5	1	215			21	387	20	12	2															1	0	0.0	0
DALE THOMPSON Dale G. DB 5'11 183 Fullerton State B: 3/20/1962 Los Angeles, CA																															
1984	EDM	2							1	7																					
1985	EDM	1																													
1986	OTT	1																													
3	Years	4							1	7																					

Year	Team	GP	FM	FF	FR	TK	SK	YDS	IR	YDS	PD	PTS	TD	RA	YDS	AVG	LG	TD	REC	YDS	AVG	LG	TD	PR	YDS	AVG	LG	KOR	YDS	AVG	LG
DOUG THOMPSON Doug HB 5'10 202 Clemson B: 1933																															
1956	TOR	14							2	0				3	35	11.7	20	0	1	10	10.0	10	0	18	127	7.1	22	6	130	21.7	30
DURFEY THOMPSON Durfey N. LB 6'0 228 Prairie View A&M B: 12/5/1951 Poteau, OK Pro: W																															
1976	HAM	1			1																										
GARY THOMPSON Gary DB 6'0 180 San Jose State*; Redwoods JC B: 2/23/1959 Castro Valley, CA Pro: N																															
1985	EDM	7							5	72		6	1											3	20	6.7	8	1	21	21.0	21
1986	EDM	10	0		1				3	21																					
2	Years	17	0		1				8	93		6	1											3	20	6.7	8	1	21	21.0	21
GREG THOMPSON Greg FB-HB 5'10 200 Ottawa Sooners Jrs. B: 1948																															
1969	OTT	8																													
1970	OTT	14												5	25	5.0	17	0	1	9	9.0	9	0	1	0	0.0	0				
1971	OTT	7																0													
1971	EDM	7										1	0					0	5	57	11.4	23	0								
1971	Year	14										1	0	6	13	2.2	6	0	5	57	11.4	23	0								
3	Years	29										1	0	5	25	5.0	17	0	6	66	11.0	23	0	1	0	0.0	0				
KEVIN THOMPSON Kevin WR 6'2 190 Surrey Rams Jrs.; Wenatchee Valley JC B: 7/1/1969 Vancouver, BC																															
1992	BC	7				1													3	54	18.0	26	0								
LANCE THOMPSON Lance LB 6'2 220 Carleton B: 1/25/1962 Hanover, Jamaica Draft: 2-17 1985 HAM																															
1985	HAM	3																													
1986	HAM	1																													
2	Years	4																													
LARRY THOMPSON Larry WR 5'11 171 Solano CC B: 5/25/1971 Fairfield, CA																															
1991	WPG	8	3		0	1						24	4						17	302	17.8	42	4	22	156	7.1	18	16	349	21.8	43
1992	WPG+	18	7		1	4						60	10	1	-6	-6.0	-6	0	61	1192	19.5	62	10	43	249	5.8	23	12	188	15.7	42
1994	SAS	14				1						18	3						58	907	15.6	55	3					31	500	16.1	31
1995	SAS	5				1													23	288	12.5	35	0	1	12	12.0	12	5	101	20.2	34
1995	HAM	12	2		1	1						36	6	3	3	1.0	14	0	53	907	17.1	82	6					7	91	13.0	24
1995	Year	17	2		1	2						36	6	3	3	1.0	14	0	76	1195	15.7	82	6	1	12	12.0	12	12	192	16.0	34
1996	BC	9				1						6	1	4	53	13.3	49	0	34	523	15.4	64	1	9	36	4.0	14	2	39	19.5	27
1997	BC	16	4	0	0	2						18	3						71	746	10.5	45	3	27	224	8.3	35	17	353	20.8	62
1998	WPG	7				2						6	1	1	-6	-6.0	-6	0	20	313	15.7	49	1								
1998	SAS	11				2						6	1	1	27	27.0	27	0	23	386	16.8	46	1	4	30	7.5	16	15	299	19.9	40
1998	Year	18				4						12	2	2	21	10.5	27	0	43	699	16.3	49	2	4	30	7.5	16	15	299	19.9	40
2002	BC	4				0						6	1	2	7	3.5	4	0	13	237	18.2	71	1								
8	Years	81	16	0	2	15						180	30	12	78	6.5	49	0	373	5801	15.6	82	30	106	707	6.7	35	105	1920	18.3	62
LAWRENCE THOMPSON Lawrence WR 5'11 170 Eastern Michigan B: 1/6/1961																															
1985	CAL	3	0		1														4	96	24.0	33	0								
LYNN THOMPSON Lynn HB Western Ontario																															
1946	TOR	1																													
MARK THOMPSON Mark LB 6'3 245 Richmond B: 7/21/1980 Fayetteville, NC																															
2003	MTL	16	0	0	2	25	5.0				1																				
PETE THOMPSON Peter OE 6'1 223 Queen's B: 5/14/1941 Port Arthur, ON																															
1965	OTT	7																													
1966	OTT	14																	2	25	12.5	14	0								
1967	OTT	14																										1	6	6.0	6
3	Years	35																	2	25	12.5	14	0					1	6	6.0	6
STEVE THOMPSON Stephen Marshall DT 6'5 245 Washington B: 2/12/1945 Seattle, WA Draft: 2-44 1968 NYJ Pro: NW																															
1975	BC	3							1	25																					
TOMMY THOMPSON Tommye Pryor QB 6'1 192 Tulsa B: 8/15/1916 Hutchinson, KS D: 4/21/1989 Calico Rock, AR Pro: N																															
1953	WPG	3												10	-116	-11.6		0													
CRAIG THOMSON Craig LB 6'0 210 Ottawa B: 5/6/1954 Draft: 1-5 1977 MTL																															
1977	MTL	6																													
1978	TOR	3																													
2	Years	9																													
TOM THOMSON Tom DH 6'1 190 British Columbia B: 1942 Draft: 2-10 1964 EDM																															
1964	EDM	16																													
1965	EDM	15																													
1966	EDM	15	0		2				3	17														1	5	5.0	5				
3	Years	46	0		2				3	17														1	5	5.0	5				
KEVIN THORNAL Kevin Royce WR 6'3 195 Southern Methodist B: 11/28/1973 Waco, TX																															
1999	TOR	4				1													2	13	6.5	11	0								
BURT THORNTON Burt Edward WR 6'2 210 Purdue B: 1/30/1972 Akron, OH																															
1996	HAM	13				2						18	3						42	672	16.0	39	3								
1997	HAM	10	0	0	1	4						24	4						34	586	17.2	47	4								
2	Years	23	0	0	1	6						42	7						76	1258	16.6	47	7								
DICK THORNTON Richard Brian CB-S-WR-QB 6'0 185 Northwestern B: 11/1/1939 Chicago, IL Draft: 21-(f) 1961 DAL; 6B-83(f) 1961 STL Pro: W																															
1961	WPG	4												3	26	8.7	26	0													
1962	WPG+	16	2						4	41		13	2	2	49	24.5	29	1													
1963	WPG*	16	0		3				6	200		25	4	10	72	7.2	14	0	2	55	27.5	30	0	2	12	6.0	11	1	26	26.0	26
1964	WPG	4	0		1																										
1965	WPG*	16	6		1				2	117		12	2	37	130	3.5	20	2	2	7	3.5	22	0	1	7	7.0	7	4	112	28.0	44
1966	WPG	13	1		1				1			6	1	9	51	5.7	15	0	1	16	16.0	16	1					4	104	26.0	40
1967	TOR	14	1		0				6	23		6	1	6	75	12.5	30	1										7	152	21.7	32
1968	TOR	14							2	71		6	1	5	57	11.4	38	1	1	6	6.0	6	0	1	18	18.0	18				
1969	TOR+	14			1				7	159		20	3	14	106	7.6	33	1	1	1	1.0	1	0								
1970	TOR	10							4	96		6	1	1	19	19.0	19	0	1	44	44.0	44	1					1	13	13.0	13
1971	TOR*	14							7	79		18	3						13	195	15.0	45	1	3	5	1.7	4	4	54	13.5	22
1972	TOR	4	0		2				3	61									2	14	7.0	8	0	1	8	8.0	8	6	64	10.7	24
12	Years	139	10		9				42	847		112	18	87	585	6.7	38	6	23	338	14.7	45	3	8	50	6.3	18	27	525	19.4	44
RANDY THORNTON Randy DE 6'3 220 Houston B: 12/23/1964 New Orleans, LA Pro: E																															
1993	SAC	7				4	1.0	24.0																							
WILLIE THORNTON Willie WR 5'10 180 Central Florida; Texas A&M-Commerce B: 2/15/1986 Belle Glade, FL																															
2010	HAM	1				0																									
CRAPHONSO THORPE Craphonso Ja'won WR 6'0 187 Florida State B: 6/27/1983 Tallahassee, FL Draft: 4-116 2005 KC Pro: NU																															
2009	WPG	2				0													2	27	13.5	14	0								
JIM THORPE James SE-FL-DB 6'1 185 Iowa; Hofstra B: 1/10/1946 Manhasset, NY Draft: 17-437 1969 LARM Pro: W																															
1969	TOR	14										48	8	21	47	2.2	14	0	26	724	27.8	87	8					12	279	23.3	37
1970	TOR*	12										36	6	4	20	5.0	10	0	43	671	15.6	75	6					8	185	23.1	38
1971	WPG*	16	1		1							54	9	1	0	0.0	0	0	70	1436	20.5	94	9								
1972	WPG+	16	1		0							66	11	1	15	15.0	15	0	70	1260	18.0	97	11					3	57	19.0	38
4	Years	58	2		1							204	34	27	82	3.0	15	0	209	4091	19.6	97	34					23	521	22.7	38
LEIF THORSEN Leif DL 6'5 285 Montana B: 2/28/1978 Prince George, BC Draft: 1-8 2001 BC																															
2001	BC	4				0																									
OSCAR THORSLAND Oscar A. DE 6'4 220 Clemson B: 4/30/1940 New York, NY																															
1963	OTT	4																													
SHERWYN THORSON Sherwyn OG-LB 6'1 228 Iowa B: 5/10/1940 Fort Dodge, IA Draft: 3-22 1962 BOS; 7A-87 1962 LARM																															
1962	WPG+	16												1	-12	-12.0	-12	0										1	0	0.0	0
1963	WPG	15	0		1																										
1964	WPG	16							1																						
1965	WPG	9																													
1966	WPG	16																													
1967	WPG	16																													

Year	Team	GP	FM	FF	FR	TK	SK	YDS	IR	YDS	PD	PTS	TD	RA	YDS	AVG	LG	TD	REC	YDS	AVG	LG	TD	PR	YDS	AVG	LG	KOR	YDS	AVG	LG
1968	WPG	3																													
7	Years	91	0		1				1	0				1	-12	-12.0	-12	0										1	0	0.0	0
FRANK THRASHER Frank C 6'2 215 West Texas A&M B: 1940																															
1963	CAL	6	0		1																										
BRUCE THREADGILL Bruce Craig QB 6'0 190 Mississippi State B: 5/7/1956 Nocona, TX Draft: 5B-133 1978 SF Pro: NU																															
1979	CAL	2												1	-2	-2.0	-2	0													
1980	CAL	13										6	1	12	131	10.9	58	1													
1981	CAL	16	5		0									38	158	4.2	26	0													
1982	CAL	6										12	2	19	217	11.4	55	2													
4	Years	37	5		0							18	3	70	504	7.2	58	3													
ANDRAE THURMAN D'Andrae Carnell WR 5'11 189 Arizona; Southern Oregon B: 10/25/1980 Houston, TX Pro: NU																															
2006	WPG	14	2	0	0	4						6	1	2	33	16.5	23	0	40	426	10.7	43	1	2	14	7.0	10	10	184	18.4	26
JUNIOR THURMAN Ulysses CB 6'0 180 West Los Angeles JC; Southern California B: 9/8/1964 Pro: N																															
1989	CAL	16	0		2	54			1	0		6	1																		
1990	CAL	18	0		1	51	1.0		2	4																					
1991	CAL*	18	0		2	61			5	13		12	2											1	7	7.0	7				
1992	CAL*	17	0		2	53			2	45														1	3	3.0	3				
1993	CAL	8				31			2	44																					
1994	CAL	18				54			2	54	12																				
1995	BIR	4				5			1	61	2	6	1						1	52	52.0	52	0								
7	Years	99	0		7	309	1.0		15	221	14	24	4						1	52	52.0	52	0	2	10	5.0	7				
MIKE THURMAN Mike Angelo DB 6'0 184 James Madison B: 6/27/1959 Roanoke, VA Draft: 19-220 1983 WAS-USFL Pro: U																															
1987	EDM	1				1																									
TYRONE THURMAN Tyrone Leonard WR 5'3 140 Texas Tech B: 12/31/1966 Odessa, TX																															
1989	OTT	10	1		0	0						12	2						3	54	18.0	36	1	51	678	13.3	91	23	386	16.8	36
1990	OTT	1																						7	33	4.7	14	7	110	15.7	21
2	Years	11	1		0	0						12	2						3	54	18.0	36	1	58	711	12.3	91	30	496	16.5	36
ELIJAH THURMON Elijah WR 6'3 206 Howard B: 8/2/1978 Heidelberg, Germany Pro: E																															
2004	SAS	13	0	0	1	2						12	2						50	620	12.4	50	2								
2005	SAS+	18	1	0	0	1						44	7						88	1048	11.9	60	7								
2006	CAL	18	1	0	0	3						30	5						57	728	12.8	73	5								
2007	MTL	16				1						18	3						67	926	13.8	44	3								
4	Years	65	2	0	1	7						104	17						262	3322	12.7	73	17								
SAM TIDMORE Samuel Edward LB 6'1 225 Ohio State B: 10/28/1938 Decatur, IL Draft: 20-156 1962 BUF; 6-81 1962 CLE Pro: N																															
1964	HAM	1																													
MATT TIEMANN Matthew C. DE-LB 6'1 234 Navarro JC; Cisco JC; North Texas B: 4/23/1963 San Diego, CA																															
1986	SAS	1																													
BRAD TIERNEY Brad OT-OG 6'4 265 Acadia B: 5/6/1965 Wolfville, NS Draft: 4A-25 1988 WPG																															
1988	WPG	14				0																						1	0	0.0	0
1989	WPG	1				0																									
1989	OTT	13	0		1	0																									
1989	Year	14	0		1	0																									
1990	OTT	15				0																									
1991	OTT	18				0																									
1992	OTT	17	0		1	1																									
1994	OTT	7				0																									
6	Years	72	0		2	1																						1	0	0.0	0
CALVIN TIGGLE Calvin Bernard LB 6'1 235 Lees-McRae JC; Georgia Tech B: 11/10/1968 Fort Washington, MD Draft: 7-174 1991 TB Pro: N																															
1994	TOR*	18	0		3	135	2.0	8.0	1	2	2	6	1																		
1995	TOR	13	0		1	69	2.0	13.0	1	4	3																				
1996	HAM	7				51																		1	55	55.0	55				
1997	HAM	18	0	0	1	85	1.0	11.0	1	20	3																				
1998	HAM*	18	0	1	0	99	1.0	2.0	3	60	4																				
1999	HAM*	18	0	3	0	108			2	32	3																				
2000	TOR+	18	0	1	2	80	3.0	12.0	1	7	6	6	1																		
2001	TOR	17	0	0	2	61	1.0	5.0			1	6	1																		
8	Years	127	0	5	9	688	10.0	51.0	9	125	22	18	3											1	55	55.0	55				
TONY TILLER Tony DB 5'11 180 East Tennessee State B: 12/20/1981 Atlanta, GA Pro: U																															
2005	BC	18	0	2	2	44	1.0	7.0	4	42	0																				
2006	CAL	13	0	1	0	30	1.0	3.0	4	45	2																				
2007	HAM	10				26			2	73	5																				
3	Years	41	0	3	2	100	2.0	10.0	10	160	7																				
DAWSON TILLEY Dawson FB 6'0 190 McGill B: 12/13/1930 Montreal, QC Draft: 1952 MTL																															
1952	MTL	9										5	1					1													
KEN TIMES Kenneth DT 6'2 248 Southern University B: 1/1/1956 Deerfield Beach, FL Draft: 5-112 1980 SF Pro: NU																															
1980	WPG	1																													
BRIAN TIMMIS Brian, Jr. HB 6'1 200 Hamilton Wildcats Jrs; McMaster; Queen's																															
1953	SAS	10										5	1	8	30	3.8		1										1	18	18.0	18
CARLOS TIMMONS Carlos WR 6'1 205 Montana B: 3/26/1968																															
1996	BC	4				3																									
KEVIN TIMOTHEE Kevin DB 5'11 191 Mississippi*; Florida International B: 11/30/1981 Spring Valley, NY Pro: E																															
2006	HAM	3				3																									
BUDDY TINSLEY Robert Porter, Jr. OT-DT 6'2 245 Baylor B: 8/16/1924 Damon, TX D: 9/14/2011 Winnipeg, MB Draft: 7-54 1948 PHI Pro: A																															
1950	WPG+	12																													
1951	WPG+	14										1	0						2	19	9.5		0	1	15	15.0	15				
1952	WPG+	15																						2	30	15.0	25				
1953	WPG	14																						1	0	0.0	0				
1954	WPG	14	1		2				1	21														1	18	18.0	18				
1955	WPG+	16																	2	35	17.5	24	0								
1956	WPG+	16																													
1957	WPG+	16																													
1958	WPG+	14	0		2																										
1959	WPG	15																													
1960	WPG	15	0		1				1			6	1	1	1	1.0	1	1													
11	Years	161	1		5				2	21		7	1	1	1	1.0	1	1	4	54	13.5	24	0	5	63	12.6	25				
BORIS TIPOFF Boris FB-HB 5'8 155 B: 1926 D: 9/26/2009																															
1946	TOR	11										5	1					1													
DAVE TIPTON David Joseph DT 6'2 255 Western Illinois B: 12/10/1953 Superior, WI Pro: NU																															
1977	HAM	4																													
GEOFF TISDALE Geoffrey Matthew DH-CB 6'1 185 Los Angeles Valley JC; Pittsburg State B: 2/21/1986 Los Angeles, CA																															
2008	HAM	11	0	1	1	41			4	74	4	6	1																		
2009	HAM	17	0	0	1	33			3	53	12	6	1																		
2010	HAM	18	0	0	1	58			4	59	8																				
2011	CAL	18				35			4	56	5																				
4	Years	64	0	1	3	167			15	242	29	12	2																		
PETE TITANIC Peter E 5'11 182 B: 1921 New Toronto, ON																															
1946	TOR	10										7	1										1								
1947	TOR	11										10	2										1								
1948	TOR	10										5	1										1								
1949	TOR	1																													
4	Years	32										22	4										3								
LARRY TITTLEY Laurent C 6'2 230 Concordia B: 5/15/1953 Montreal, QC Draft: 5-39 1976 CAL																															

Year	Team	GP	FM	FF	FR	TK	SK	YDS	IR	YDS	PD	PTS	TD	RA	YDS	AVG	LG	TD	REC	YDS	AVG	LG	TD	PR	YDS	AVG	LG	KOR	YDS	AVG	LG
1976	CAL	16	0		2																										
1977	CAL	16																													
1978	CAL	16																													
1979	CAL	16	0		2																										
1980	OTT	10																													
1981	OTT	16																													
1982	OTT	10																													
1983	OTT+	16	0		2																							1	0	0.0	0
1984	OTT	1																													
1985	MTL	3																													
10	Years	120	0		6																							1	0	0.0	0
MARC TOBERT Marc WR 5'11 190 Alberta B: 3/8/1971 Edmonton, AB Draft: 6-43 1993 EDM																															
1994	EDM	13				5						6	1						14	191	13.6	32	1								
1995	EDM	15	0		1	18						12	2	1	10	10.0	10	0	7	53	7.6	21	2	1	5	5.0	5				
1996	EDM	15				3						6	1						25	454	18.2	60	1								
1997	EDM	17				9													22	276	12.5	38	0								
1998	EDM	17				6						6	1						11	150	13.6	23	1								
1999	EDM	18				0													33	357	10.8	37	0								
2000	EDM	1	1	0	0	0													5	32	6.4	13	0								
7	Years	96	1	0	1	41						30	5	1	10	10.0	10	0	117	1513	12.9	60	5	1	5	5.0	5				
DAVE TOBEY David Morgan LB 6'3 230 Oregon B: 3/17/1943 Portland, OR Draft: RS-7-50 1965 DEN; 10-130(f) 1965 PIT Pro: N																															
1969	BC	16	0		1				2	21																					
1970	BC	12							2	16																		3	58	19.3	23
2	Years	28	0		1				4	37																		3	58	19.3	23
BILL TOBIN William Hugh OHB 5'11 210 Missouri B: 2/16/1941 Burlington Junction, MO Draft: 14-189 1963 SF Pro: N																															
1964	EDM	11	2		0							30	5	96	497	5.2	29	4	10	193	19.3	46	1								
1965	EDM	5	0		1							12	2	31	168	5.4	45	2	1	0	0.0	0	0					1	17	17.0	17
2	Years	16	2		1							42	7	127	665	5.2	45	6	11	193	17.5	46	1					1	17	17.0	17
BILL TODD Bill HB-QB 6'2 185 Winnipeg Light Infantry Jrs. B: 7/4/1930																															
1951	WPG	12												3	-18	-6.0		0													
1953	SAS	4										15	3	34	87	2.6		3	1	-2	-2.0	-2	0								
1954	SAS	14												8	43	5.4	15	0	1	9	9.0	9	0					1	16	16.0	16
1955	SAS	6	1		0									29	125	4.3	14	0	2	56	28.0	36	0								
1956	SAS	13							0	5				3	29	9.7	11	0													
5	Years	49	1		0				0	5		15	3	77	266	3.5	15	3	4	63	15.8	36	0					1	16	16.0	16
TOM TOFAUTE Tom C 6'2 220 North Carolina State B: 1928 Draft: 14-160 1952 CHIC																															
1952	MTL	12																													
EMANUEL TOLBERT Emanuel SB-WR 5'9 182 Southern Methodist B: 9/2/1958 North Little Rock, AR Draft: 7-183 1980 CHIB																															
1980	SAS	5										6	1	1	9	9.0	9	0	21	268	12.8	55	1					3	95	31.7	36
1981	SAS	16										44	7						46	619	13.5	57	7					19	430	22.6	58
1982	SAS	4																	15	165	11.0	21	0								
1983	TOR+	16	3		0							66	11	4	23	5.8	21	0	70	1225	17.5	80	11								
1984	TOR	7												3	8	2.7	6	0	21	396	18.9	56	0								
1985	CAL	16	1		0							36	6	1	10	10.0	10	0	67	1124	16.8	70	6								
1986	CAL+	18	0		1							66	11	4	68	17.0	54	0	69	1286	18.6	51	11								
1987	CAL+	17	3		1	3						36	6	11	44	4.0	24	0	57	1014	17.8	62	6								
1988	CAL*	18	1		1	2						42	7	2	41	20.5	24	0	67	1328	19.8	61	7								
1989	TOR	10				4						6	1	3	-4	-1.3	-17	0	32	358	11.2	42	1								
1990	BC	7				0						12	2						15	325	21.7	77	2								
11	Years	134	8		3	9						314	52	29	199	6.9	54	0	480	8108	16.9	80	52					22	525	23.9	58
ART TOLHURST Arthur DB 5'10 190 British Columbia B: 1/8/1976 Pittsburgh, PA																															
2003	BC	1				0																									
BILLY JOE TOLLIVER Billy Joe QB 6'1 217 Texas Tech B: 2/7/1966 Dallas, TX Draft: 2B-51 1989 SD Pro: N																															
1995	SHR	18	6		0	1						12	2	30	75	2.5	14	2													
DAVID TOLOUMU Arona David RB 5'11 190 Hawaii B: 3/3/1960 Oceanside, CA Draft: 7-176 1982 ATL																															
1984	BC	8	7		0							6	1	52	186	3.6	13	1	19	241	12.7	30	0	3	39	13.0	17	8	204	25.5	41
J.R. TOLVER Gregory Dale, Jr. WR 6'1 205 San Diego State B: 1/13/1980 Long Beach, CA Draft: 5B-169 2003 MIA																															
2007	CAL	1				0													1	47	47.0	47	0								
GEORGE TOMAN George Gerald E B: 3/7/1925 Esterhazy, SK D: 9/21/2008 Desert Hot Springs, CA																															
1946	WPG	4																													
1948	WPG	2																													
2	Years	6																													
TYLER TOMICH Tyler QB 6'0 190 Oregon State B: 11/8/1976 Long Beach, CA																															
2003	CAL	2				0																									
KERMIT TOMKINS Kermit G Regina Ints.																															
1946	SAS	8																													
ED TOMLIN Edward OHB 6'1 225 Hampton B: 6/7/1947 Ocala, FL D: 1/16/2012 Ocala, FL Draft: 10B-270 1968 BAL																															
1968	MTL	8	2		1							13	2	61	265	4.3	27	0	12	116	9.7	31	2					9	208	23.1	45
JIM TOMLIN Tim DB 5'11 186 Stephen F. Austin State B: 6/12/1946																															
1969	TOR	14							7	131																		12	317	26.4	80
1970	TOR+	14							1	0														10	61	6.1	13	14	319	22.8	40
1971	TOR	7							1	0																			126		
1971	BC	5							3	52																			82		
1971	Year	12							4	52																		8	208	26.0	34
3	Years	35							12	183														10	61	6.1	13	34	844	42.8	80
DAVE TOMLINSON Dave (Baldy) G-T 6'0 220 Calgary West End Tornadoes Jrs.; McGill B: 1926																															
1947	CAL	8										1	0																		
1948	CAL+	11																													
1952	MTL	12																													
1953	MTL	14																													
1954	CAL	4																													
5	Years	49										1	0																		
LARRY TOMLINSON Larry TE 6'1 207 Nebraska B: 5/24/1940 Pointe Claire, QC																															
1964	MTL	3							1	40		6	1																		
1965	MTL	14	0		1							6	1						28	476	17.0	49	1								
1966	MTL	1																	1	19	19.0	19	0								
1966	HAM	1																	1	6	6.0	6	0								
1966	Year	2																	2	25	12.5	19	0								
3	Years	18	0		1				1	40		12	2						30	501	16.7	49	1								
ANDY TOMMY Andy E 5'8 157 Mount Allison B: 12/14/1911 Hartland, NB D: 4/23/1972 Wakefield, QC																															
1946	OTT	2																													
JED TOMMY Jed FB 6'0 230 Guelph B: 1/29/1962 Ottawa, ON Draft: 1-8 1985 HAM																															
1986	HAM	17	1		1									42	139	3.3	8	0	12	57	4.8	10	0								
1987	HAM	2				0								4	4	1.0	4	0	4	56	14.0	27	0								
1988	HAM	17	2		1	3						18	3	91	342	3.8	18	3	35	276	7.9	24	0								
1989	HAM	18	2		1	5						6	1	53	211	4.0	19	0	28	184	6.6	18	1					1	1	1.0	1
1990	OTT	16				0						6	1	4	7	1.8	2	0	3	40	13.3	19	1					2	18	9.0	11
1995	OTT	6				2													4	31	7.8	12	0								
6	Years	76	5		3	10						30	5	194	703	3.6	19	3	86	644	7.5	27	2					3	19	6.3	11
TONY TOMPKINS Tony WR 5'8 165 Stephen F. Austin State B: 11/21/1982 Pineville, LA																															
2005	EDM	17	3	0	1	1						24	4						1	6	6.0	6	0	76	931	12.3	96	30	824	27.5	86
2006	EDM	17	1	0	0	0																		75	501	6.7	53	57	1145	20.1	39

Year	Team	GP	FM	FF	FR	TK	SK	YDS	IR	YDS	PD	PTS	TD	RA	YDS	AVG	LG	TD	REC	YDS	AVG	LG	TD	PR	YDS	AVG	LG	KOR	YDS	AVG	LG
2007	EDM	9				0																		48	376	7.8	33	28	520	18.6	38
3	Years	43	4	0	1	1						24	4						1	6	6.0	6	0	199	1808	9.1	96	115	2489	21.6	86
DON TOMS Don HB 5'11 197 none B: 1924 D: 1994																															
1948	HAM	11										10	2					1					1								
1949	HAM	11																													
1950	HAM	8										5	1					1													
3	Years	30										15	3					2					1								
BILL TONEGUSSO Bill OHB 5'10 185 Hamilton Jrs.; Brantford Jrs. B: 1936																															
1956	MTL	11										12	2	14	71	5.1	15	1	7	81	11.6	25	1	2	16	8.0	8				
MARSHALL TONER Marshall SB 6'2 195 Saskatchewan B: 5/22/1963 Saskatoon, SK																															
1986	CAL	17										12	2						41	403	9.8	36	2								
1987	CAL	15	1		0	3						6	1						18	217	12.1	27	1					4	46	11.5	15
1988	CAL	14			1	1						6	1						23	340	14.8	26	1					1	0	0.0	0
1989	CAL	17				1						6	1						36	766	21.3	55	1					1	0	0.0	0
1990	CAL	18				2						18	3						21	349	16.6	53	3	1	5	5.0	5				
1991	CAL	8				4													1	21	21.0	21	0								
6	Years	89	1		1	11						48	8						140	2096	15.0	55	8	1	5	5.0	5	6	46	7.7	15
CLIFF TONEY Clifford CB 6'0 185 Auburn B: 12/17/1958 Huntsville, AL Draft: 8-219 1981 ATL																															
1984	EDM	14	0		3		1.0		1	88		6	1																		
1985	EDM	14	0		1				1	50		6	1											1	2	2.0	2				
1986	EDM	11					1.0		5	35		6	1																		
1987	EDM	10			2	33			1	2																					
1988	EDM	15				44			4	160		12	2																		
5	Years	64	0		6	77	2.0		12	341		30	5											1	2	2.0	2				
DARREN TONEY Darren DH 5'11 185 Arkansas State B: 1/9/1984																															
2009	BC	18	0	1	0	55					7													4	17	4.3	7	4	54	13.5	20
EUDEAN TONEY Eudean DB 6'1 210 Grambling State B: 6/8/1968																															
1994	TOR	4				17					1																				
1995	TOR	1				0	1.0	8.0																							
2	Years	5				17	1.0	8.0			1																				
JIM TONN James Leonard QB 6'0 195 Weston Wildcats Jrs. B: 12/27/1935																															
1958	WPG	2												1	7	7.0	7	0	2	24	12.0	26	0								
BOB TOOGOOD Bob LB-DE 6'2 223 Weston Wildcats Jrs.; Manitoba B: 9/6/1948 Draft: 2-16 1972 SAS																															
1974	WPG	16	0		2				2	7																					
1975	WPG	16							1	3																		1	5	5.0	5
1976	WPG	16							1	25		6	1																		
1977	WPG	16	1		1				2	24		6	1																		
1978	WPG	13	0		1				1	11																					
1979	WPG	16							1	5																					
1980	WPG	16							1	9																					
7	Years	109	1		4				9	84		12	2															1	5	5.0	5
TED TOOGOOD Alexander Edgar S 5'9 164 Toronto B: 1925																															
1950	TOR	12										10	2																		
1951	TOR	10										5	1					1													
1952	TOR	11										5	1					1													
1953	TOR+	14																													
1954	TOR	6										5	1	25	138	5.5	39	1	2	3	1.5	4	0	1	8	8.0	8				
5	Years	53										25	5	25	138	5.5	39	3	2	3	1.5	4	0	1	8	8.0	8				
RALPH TOOHY Ralph LB-E-FW 6'0 197 none B: 1927 D: 7//1998 Sun City, AZ																															
1947	MTL	11										5	1										1								
1948	MTL+	12										25	5										4								
1949	MTL+	12										20	4										4								
1950	MTL	12										25	5										5								
1951	MTL	12										10	2										2								
1952	HAM	11										2	0																		
1953	HAM+	14										10	2										2								
1954	HAM	14												1	5	5.0	5	0	17	175	10.3	19	0	1	0	0.0	0	2	17	8.5	10
1955	HAM	12							1	0		5	1						2	48	24.0	31	0					4	32	8.0	15
1956	HAM	13										6	1	0	4		4	0	3	74	24.7	36	1								
1957	HAM	13																													
1958	HAM	10																													
12	Years	146							1	0		108	21	1	9	9.0	5	0	22	297	13.5	36	19	1	0	0.0	0	6	49	8.2	15
JIM TOON James Allen DE 6'2 240 North Carolina A&T State B: 10/12/1938 Dunn, NC																															
1960	EDM	9	0		3																										
MIKE TOPOLEVEC Mike DT-DE 6'3 245 Ottawa B: 11/23/1956 Draft: 7-57 1980 WPG																															
1980	WPG	4																													
BOB TORRANCE Bob QB 6'1 207 Calgary B: 6/4/1968 Calgary, AB D: 1/10/2012 NL Draft: 3-22 1991 CAL																															
1991	CAL	6				0																									
1992	CAL	18	1		1	0								2	-2	-1.0	2	0													
1993	HAM	11	0		1	0								12	71	5.9	32	0													
1995	CAL	3				0																									
4	Years	38	1		2	0								14	69	4.9	32	0													
WAYNE TOSH Wayne DB 5'11 180 Richmond B: 8/7/1947 Kitchener, ON																															
1971	OTT	14							3	60		6	1																		
1972	OTT	14	0		1				5	90																					
1973	OTT	14	0		1				2	17																					
1974	OTT	16	0		1				4	89																					
1975	OTT+	16	0		1				9	123																					
1976	OTT	16			2				3	47																					
1977	OTT	7	0		1																										
1978	OTT	16	0		1				2	7																					
8	Years	113	0		8				28	433		6	1																		
JOE TOTH Joseph John LB 6'1 210 North Dakota State B: 6/14/1972 Ramsey County, MN																															
1995	SAS	5	0		1	10																									
1996	SAS	4				5																									
2	Years	9	0		1	15																									
ZOLLIE TOTH Zollie Anthony FB 6'2 218 Louisiana State B: 1/26/1924 McKeesport, PA Draft: 4-42 1950 NYY Pro: N																															
1956	HAM	2										12	2	22	113	5.1	14	2	4	32	8.0	11	0					2	41	20.5	22
IBRAHIM TOUNKARA Ibrahim SB-WR 6'2 210 Ottawa B: 4/23/1976 Montreal, QC Draft: 1A-5 2000 CAL																															
2000	CAL	18	0	0	1	22																									
2001	CAL	18	1	0	0	13						12	2	2	11	5.5	9	0	20	234	11.7	33	2					1	0	0.0	0
2002	CAL	18	1	0	0	14						14	2						21	245	11.7	36	2								
2003	HAM	12				5						6	1						26	274	10.5	36	1								
2004	HAM	18	1	0	0	9						6	1						25	317	12.7	36	1					1	-4	-4.0	-4
2005	SAS	18	1	0	1	2													10	89	8.9	27	0								
2006	SAS	15				2						6	1						1	9	9.0	9	1								
7	Years	117	4	0	2	67						44	7	2	11	5.5	9	0	103	1168	11.3	36	7					2	-4	-2.0	0
OUSMANE TOUNKARA Ousmane WR 6'3 209 Ottawa B: 12/25/1973 Warsaw, Poland Draft: 2-8 1998 SAS																															
1998	SAS	6	1	0	0	1						6	1						1	22	22.0	22	1					1	-2	-2.0	-2
1999	SAS	18	0	0	1	4													3	36	12.0	14	0								
2000	SAS	5				0																									
3	Years	29	1		1	5						6	1						4	58	14.5	22	1					1	-2	-2.0	-2

Year	Team	GP	FM	FF	FR	TK	SK	YDS	IR	YDS	PD	PTS	TD	RA	YDS	AVG	LG	TD	REC	YDS	AVG	LG	TD	PR	YDS	AVG	LG	KOR	YDS	AVG	LG
LUC TOUSIGNANT Luc QB 6'4 205 Fairmont State B: 7/4/1958 Trois Rivieres, QC Draft: TE 1982 MTL; 8-218 1982 BUF																															
1982	MTL	16	4		1									39	200	5.1	49	0													
DARREL TOUSSAINT Darrel Lee DB 6'0 175 Tyler JC; Northwestern Louisiana B: 10/3/1958 Chicago, IL Pro: N																															
1982	CAL	15	0		2				2	31		6	1																		
1983	CAL	1																													
1985	SAS	6					1.0		2	7																					
1987	CAL	2	1		0	5			1	14																					
4	Years	24	1		2	5	1.0		5	52		6	1																		
TOM TOWNS Tom LB 6'0 220 Alberta B: 3/17/1953 Rosetown, SK Draft: TE 1975 EDM																															
1975	EDM	16																										1	2	2.0	2
1976	EDM	16																										3	1	0.3	1
1977	EDM	16	1		2							6	1															5	27	5.4	14
1978	EDM+	16	0		1																										
1979	EDM+	16							1	4		6	1																		
1980	EDM+	16	0		2																										
1981	EDM	16	0		2		4.0																								
1982	EDM	13					5.0																								
1983	EDM	16	0		2		1.5					6	1																		
1984	EDM	13					1.5		1	45																		1	12	12.0	12
1985	OTT	16	0		1		4.0		2	41																					
11	Years	170	1		10		16.0		4	90		18	3															10	42	4.2	14
BYRON TOWNSEND F. Byron FB 6'0 190 Texas B: 1930 Draft: 9-109 1952 LARM																															
1954	WPG	9	4		2							7	1	93	446	4.8	25	1	5	28	5.6	12	0								
DARYL TOWNSEND Daryl S 6'1 198 Windsor B: 9/25/1985 Windsor, ON																															
2011	WPG	1				0																									
GEOFF TOWNSEND Geoff SB-RB-WR 6'0 190 Boston College B: 11/17/1959 Mississauga, ON Draft: TE 1982 TOR																															
1982	TOR	16										6	1						1	35	35.0	35	1	1	6	6.0	6	8	211	26.4	50
1983	TOR	16												2	12	6.0	18	0	12	231	19.3	53	0	5	14	2.8	4	18	425	23.6	39
1984	TOR	13												2	2	1.0	1	0	7	73	10.4	19	0					7	220	31.4	70
1985	TOR	16	2		0							18	3	2	32	16.0	27	0	26	411	15.8	57	3	1	5	5.0	5	23	467	20.3	45
1986	TOR	7												1	0	0.0	0	0	1	57	57.0	57	0					3	57	19.0	22
5	Years	68	2		0							24	4	7	46	6.6	27	0	47	807	17.2	57	4	7	25	3.6	6	56	1323	23.6	70
JAMIE TOWNSEND James RB 5'10 185 Eastern Washington B: 8/7/1966 Kennewick, WA																															
1989	CAL	3				0								16	46	2.9	12	0	3	36	12.0	23	0	2	1	0.5	1	4	108	27.0	36
KEN TOWNSEND Ken HB 5'10 187 Regina Rams Jrs.; St. Francis Xavier B: 1937																															
1959	SAS	12												1	16	16.0	16	0						1	8	8.0	8				
TOM TRACY John Thomas (The Bomb) OHB 5'9 205 Tennessee B: 9/7/1934 Birmingham, MI D: 1/24/1996 Madison Heights, MI Draft: 5-50 1956 DET Pro: N																															
1955	OTT+	12										40	1	102	729	7.1	75	1	6	32	5.3	18	0	1	19	19.0	19	8	169	21.1	31
1956	OTT	3										12	0	11	51	4.6	19	0	5	85	17.0	34	0					1	31	31.0	31
2	Years	15										52	1	113	780	6.9	75	1	11	117	10.6	34	0	1	19	19.0	19	9	200	22.2	31
JOHN TRAINOR John OT-OG 6'2 238 Tennessee Tech B: 3/18/1947 Bangor, Northern Ireland																															
1971	TOR	10																													
1972	TOR	10																													
1973	TOR	14																													
1976	MTL	5																													
4	Years	39																													
SAMMY TRANKS Samuel SB-WR 6'0 186 Seton Hall B: 12/14/1986 Philadelphia, PA																															
2011	TOR	3				0						6	1						7	71	10.1	22	1					1	34	34.0	34
RANDY TRAUTMAN Randy NG-DT-DE 6'3 250 Boise State B: 5/27/1960 Caldwell, IN Draft: 9B-238 1982 WAS																															
1982	CAL	9					3.0																								
1983	CAL+	15					12.0																								
1984	CAL+	16					11.0																								
1985	CAL	10	0		2		5.0																								
4	Years	50	0		2		31.0																								
JEFF TRAVERSY Jeff DT 6'5 289 Arizona Western JC; Edinboro B: 4/18/1972 Ottawa, ON Draft: 2-15 1997 CAL																															
1997	CAL	18	0	0	1	7					2																				
1998	CAL	14	0	1	1	15	1.0	5.0			2																				
1999	CAL	18	0	1	0	24	3.0	13.0			3																				
2000	CAL	18	0	1	0	21	3.0	16.0			2																				
2001	CAL	13				17					1																				
2002	CAL	15				8					3																				
2003	BC	4				0																									
7	Years	100	0	3	2	92	7.0	34.0			13																				
PETE TRAVIS Peter C-OT 6'4 245 Louisville B: 11/11/1945																															
1968	BC	5																													
1970	EDM	16	0		2																										
1971	EDM	16			1																										
1972	EDM	16	0		1																										
1973	EDM	9	0		1																										
5	Years	62	0		5																										
HERB TRAWICK Herbert DG-OG-T 5'10 245 Kentucky State B: 2/22/1921 Elm Grove, PA D: 9/16/1985 Hawkesbury, ON																															
1946	MTL+	12																													
1947	MTL+	11										5	1																		
1948	MTL+	12										3	0																		
1949	MTL+	12																													
1950	MTL+	12										1	0																		
1951	MTL	10										3	0																		
1952	MTL	11																													
1953	MTL	14																													
1954	MTL+	14																													
1955	MTL+	12																													
1956	MTL	14																													
1957	MTL	13										6	1																		
12	Years	147										18	2																		
JEFF TREFTLIN Jeffrey DB 5'8 170 McMaster B: 8/11/1961 Fort Francis, ON Draft: 8-69 1984 EDM																															
1984	EDM	14	1		1							12	2											37	318	8.6	75	6	144	24.0	36
1985	EDM	16	2		0		1.0																	45	330	7.3	28				
1986	MTL+	18	2		0				1	5														72	491	6.8	62	46	984	21.4	42
1987	WPG	9	2		0	4																		35	202	5.8	17	11	199	18.1	38
1987	HAM	4				0																		10	30	3.0	8	11	279	25.4	32
1987	Year	13	2		0	4																		45	232	5.2	17				
1988	SAS	18	2		1	6																		8	53	6.6	26	6	45	7.5	17
1989	SAS	4	0		1	5																									
1990	SAS	10	1		0	1																		15	159	10.6	47	22	461	21.0	48
1991	SAS	10				11													1	36	36.0	36	0	1	3	3.0	5	2	34	17.0	32
8	Years	99	10		3	27	1.0		1	5		12	2						1	36	36.0	36	0	223	1586	7.1	75	104	2146	20.6	48
J.F. TREMBLAY Jean-Fredric WR 6'1 187 Laval B: 3/12/1980 Quebec City, QC Draft: 1-7 2004 TOR																															
2004	TOR	1				1													4	65	16.3	32	0								
2005	TOR	4				0													7	112	16.0	27	0								
2	Years	5				1													11	177	16.1	32	0								
WILF TREMBLAY Wilf FL-DB 5'7 140 Ottawa-New Edinburgh Jrs. B: 1917																															
1946	OTT	12										16	3										2								

Year	Team	GP	FM	FF	FR	TK	SK	YDS	IR	YDS	PD	PTS	TD	RA	YDS	AVG	LG	TD	REC	YDS	AVG	LG	TD	PR	YDS	AVG	LG	KOR	YDS	AVG	LG
1947	OTT	12										10	2										2								
1948	OTT	10										7	1										1								
1949	OTT	6																													
1950	OTT	3																													
1951	SAS	4										5	1	3	20	6.7		1	1	29	29.0	29	0	4	22	5.5					
6	Years	47										38	7	3	20	6.7	0	1	1	29	29.0	29	5	4	22	5.5	0				
MIKE TREVATHAN Michael R. WR-SB 6'1 205 Montana B: 3/26/1968 Los Angeles County, CA																															
1991	BC	14	2		1	4						6	1	2	14	7.0	8	0	45	579	12.9	51	1	10	69	6.9	23				
1992	BC	13	3		1	5						30	5	2	5	2.5	5	0	71	1004	14.1	50	5	3	26	8.7	13	1	0	0.0	0
1993	BC	17	0		3	4						72	12						64	965	15.1	44	12	11	64	5.8	11				
1994	BC	15	2		2	7						72	12						60	1069	17.8	67	12	8	70	8.8	19				
1995	BC	15	3		0	6						18	3	5	33	6.6	18	0	56	998	17.8	58	3	1	6	6.0	6				
1996	BC	18	0		1	7						62	10						65	1006	15.5	52	10	11	121	11.0	31	3	37	12.3	15
1997	BC	18				6						18	3						49	846	17.3	45	3	1	4	4.0	4				
1998	WPG	1				1													1	9	9.0	9	0								
8	Years	111	10		8	40						278	46	9	52	5.8	18	0	411	6476	15.8	67	46	45	360	8.0	31	4	37	9.3	15
TOM TRIFAUX Tom OG-OT 6'4 250 Calgary Colts Jrs.; Calgary B: 1/6/1959 Calgary, AB Draft: 1A-2 1981 TOR																															
1981	TOR	11																													
1982	TOR	16																													
1983	TOR	15	0		1									0	5		5	0													
1984	TOR	7																													
1984	SAS	10	1		0																							1	0	0.0	0
1984	Year	17	1		0																							1	0	0.0	0
1985	TOR	15																													
5	Years	64	1		1									0	5		5	0										1	0	0.0	0
MICKEY TRIMARKI Dominick Michael QB 6'1 195 West Virginia B: 2/21/1936 Draft: 13-148 1958 PHI																															
1958	HAM	1												1	-13	-13.0	-13	0													
PAUL TRIPOLI Paul Randall CB 6'0 197 Alabama B: 12/14/1961 Utica, NY Pro: N																															
1986	TOR	9							3	15																					
1987	TOR	2							2	33														4	36	9.0	15				
2	Years	11							5	48														4	36	9.0	15				
FRANK TRIPUCKA Francis Joseph QB 6'2 192 Notre Dame B: 12/8/1927 Bloomfield, NJ Draft: 2-Secret 1949 BUF-AAFC; 1-9 1949 PHI Pro: N																															
1953	SAS	4										3	0	5	-77	-15.4		0													
1954	SAS+	14	4		0							5	1	25	-125	-5.0	3	1													
1955	SAS	16	4		0									36	-155	-4.3	8	0													
1956	SAS	16	3		0							6	1	31	-138	-4.5	9	1													
1957	SAS	16										18	3	29	-95	-3.3	9	3													
1958	SAS	13	1									2	0	26	-58	-2.2	9	0													
1959	OTT	8										1	0	3	-3	-1.0		0													
1959	SAS	2												3	3	1.0	3	0													
1959	Year	10										1	0	6	0	0.0	3	0													
1963	SAS	7	2		1							6	0	4	-8	-2.0	2	0													
8	Years	94	14		1							41	5	162	-656	-4.0	9	5													
KELLY TRITHART Kelly LB 5'11 215 Saskatchewan; Regina Rams Jrs. B: 6/13/1967 Weyburn, SK Draft: 7-52 1989 SAS																															
1989	SAS	1				0																									
1990	SAS	4				0																									
1991	SAS	1				2																									
1992	SAS	4				5																									
1993	SAS	1				1																									
5	Years	11				8																									
JOE TRIVISONNO Joseph J. FB 5'11 214 Ohio State B: 1933																															
1958	TOR	4										6	1	3	13	4.3	8	0	1	-2	-2.0	-2	0	1	2	2.0	2				
ALEX TROOP Alex LB 6'2 225 Wilfrid Laurier B: 7/31/1963 Toronto, ON Draft: 6-51 1985 TOR																															
1986	OTT	2					1.0																								
1987	OTT	4				5																									
1988	OTT	16	0		1	6																									
3	Years	22	0		1	11	1.0																								
BILL TROUP Paul William, III QB 6'5 220 Virginia; South Carolina B: 4/2/1951 Pittsburgh, PA Pro: N																															
1979	WPG	16										6	1	16	32	2.0	8	1													
RAY TRUANT Ray DB 5'10 185 Western Ontario B: 1931 Draft: 1-4 1953 HAM																															
1953	HAM	14																													
1954	HAM	14							4	49		8	1	8	44	5.5	18	0	3	30	10.0	20	0	11	42	3.8	11	1	11	11.0	11
1955	HAM	12							3	19		18	0	3	17	5.7	9	0	19	332	17.5	47	0								
1956	HAM+	14							8	89		12	2	3	5	1.7	3	0	2	24	12.0	13	0	1	0	0.0	0				
1957	HAM	12												1	8	8.0	8	0													
5	Years	66							15	157		38	3	15	74	4.9	18	0	24	386	16.1	47	0	12	42	3.5	11	1	11	11.0	11
REMI TRUDEL Remi S 5'9 175 Simon Fraser B: 10/23/1968 Prince George, BC																															
1990	BC	9				17																		0	-3		-3	0	8		8
1991	BC	8				3																									
1992	BC	18	0		1	32			3	45																					
1993	OTT+	13	1		1	37			6	61														2	6	3.0	6				
1994	OTT	9	0		1	29					1																				
1995	OTT	18	0		3	90			3	42	0								1	23	23.0	23	0	1	4	4.0	4	5	114	22.8	36
6	Years	75	1		6	208			12	148	1								1	23	23.0	23	0	3	7	2.3	6	5	122	24.4	36
TONY TRUELOVE Tony RB 5'11 205 West Alabama B: 3/24/1964 Marion, AL																															
1989	HAM	6	1		0	1						18	3	45	196	4.4	31	3	13	133	10.2	26	0					16	297	18.6	36
LEROY TRUITT Leroy Lafayette, Jr. OL 6'3 308 Houston B: 5/23/1969 Galveston County, TX Pro: E																															
1995	SA	1				0																									
DON TRULL Donald Dean QB 6'1 189 Baylor B: 10/20/1941 Oklahoma City, OK Draft: 14-111(f) 1963 HOU; 9-117(f) 1963 BAL Pro: NW																															
1970	EDM	16	5		0							6	1	32	19	0.6	15	1													
1971	EDM	9	4		1									12	46	3.8	30	0													
2	Years	25	9		1							6	1	44	65	1.5	30	1													
R-KAL TRULUCK R-Kal K-Quan LB-DE 6'4 256 Cortland State B: 9/30/1974 New York, NY Pro: N																															
1998	SAS	3	0	0	1	13	3.0	15.0																							
1999	SAS	18	1	0	2	53	7.0	38.0			1																				
2000	SAS	17	0	2	2	40	1.0	5.0			1																				
2001	MTL	7	0	0	1	13	4.0	45.0																							
2006	MTL	9				19	5.0	30.0			2																				
2007	MTL	4				9																									
6	Years	58	1	2	6	147	20.0	133.0			4																				
LANCE TRUMBLE Lance FB-DE 6'2 237 McMaster B: 8/29/1967 Winnipeg, MB Draft: 3-22 1990 EDM																															
1990	HAM	5				2																									
1991	HAM	12	0		1	19																									
1992	HAM	6	0		2	11						6	1																		
1993	HAM	1				0																									
4	Years	24	0		3	32						6	1																		
JACK TRURAN Jack HB 5'11 180 Dixie JC B: 1/14/1942 Bassano, AB																															
1964	CAL	7																													
BOB TRYGSTAD Robert Kenneth DE-DT 6'3 230 Washington State B: 9/3/1945 Long Beach, CA Draft: 11-271 1967 MIN																															
1967	CAL	9																													
1968	MTL	14	0		5				1	5																					
1969	MTL	1																													

Year	Team	GP	FM	FF	FR	TK	SK	YDS	IR	YDS	PD	PTS	TD	RA	YDS	AVG	LG	TD	REC	YDS	AVG	LG	TD	PR	YDS	AVG	LG	KOR	YDS	AVG	LG
3	Years	24	0		5				1	5																					
CHRIS TSANGARIS Chris LB 6'2 240 Laval Scorpions Jrs.; Long Beach State B: 7/20/1968 Montreal, QC Draft: 2-12 1992 WPG																															
1992	WPG	10				22																									
1993	WPG	18	0		1	31																						2	11	5.5	9
1994	WPG	17	0		2	31	1.0	6.0																				1	0	0.0	0
1995	TOR	6				11																									
1995	OTT	10				22																									
1995	Year	16				33																									
1996	OTT	5				13																									
1996	MTL	6				6																									
1996	Year	11				19																									
5	Years	56	0		3	136	1.0	6.0																				3	11	3.7	9
GEORGE TSONOS George QB 5'11 195 Mount Allison Ints.; Lakeshore Alouette Flyers Ints. B: 3/19/1938 Montreal, QC																															
1959	MTL	11																													
1960	MTL	9																													
2	Years	20																													
DIMITRI TSOUMPAS Dimitri OG 6'3 313 Weber State B: 9/26/1985 Edmonton, AB Draft: 1A-2 2008 CAL																															
2008	CAL	18	0	0	1	0																									
2009	CAL+	18				3																									
2010	CAL*	12				1																									
2011	CAL*	16				2																									
4	Years	64	0	0	1	6																									
B.J. TUCKER Bagieh Joe DB 5'10 188 Wisconsin B: 10/12/1980 Sierra Leone Draft: 6A-178 2003 DAL Pro: EN																															
2008	BC	4				2																									
ERROLL TUCKER Erroll Roger CB 5'9 170 Long Beach CC; Utah B: 7/6/1964 Pittsburgh, PA Draft: 5A-122 1986 PIT Pro: EN																															
1991	CAL	3				3																				6	27	4.5	23	4	120	30.0	51
1992	CAL	16	1		0	55			1	11														14	135	9.6	62				
2	Years	19	1		0	58			1	11														20	162	8.1	62	4	120	30.0	51
GREG TUCKER Greg LB 6'2 230 Northern Colorado B: 12/23/1968 Colorado Springs, CO																															
1994	LV	10				21						2	0						1	5	5.0	5	0								
1995	BAL	6	0		1	13																									
2	Years	16	0		1	34						2	0						1	5	5.0	5	0								
JASON TUCKER Jason L. WR-SB 6'1 182 Texas Christian B: 6/24/1976 San Francisco, CA Draft: 6-167 1998 CIN Pro: EN																															
2002	EDM*	15	1	0	0	3						48	8	1	7	7.0	7	0	51	911	17.9	82	8	7	80	11.4	22	1	19	19.0	19
2003	EDM	13	1	0	1	2						62	10	1	14	14.0	14	1	41	744	18.1	65	9	2	7	3.5	7	1	13	13.0	13
2004	EDM*	18	2	0	0	5						66	11						67	1632	24.4	102	11					2	0	0.0	0
2005	EDM*	18	1	0	0	4						66	11						89	1411	15.9	105	11								
2006	EDM*	18	1	0	0	0						72	12						75	1321	17.6	47	12								
2007	EDM	13	1	0	0	0						36	6						51	792	15.5	62	6								
2008	EDM	5				1						12	2						14	235	16.8	36	2								
7	Years	100	7	0	1	15						362	60	2	21	10.5	14	1	388	7046	18.2	105	59	9	87	9.7	22	4	32	8.0	19
MARSHAUN TUCKER Marshaun Joseph WR 5'10 184 Southwestern JC; Oregon B: 10/6/1979 El Centro, CA																															
2002	CAL	3				0													3	39	13.0	17	0	9	68	7.6	20	9	221	24.6	42
PHIL TUCKER Phil OG 6'1 232 Texas Tech B: 1946																															
1968	EDM	7																													
WHIT TUCKER Whitman D. OHB-FL 5'11 175 Western Ontario B: 1941 Draft: 2-7 1962 OTT																															
1962	OTT	14							3	25		12	2						3	83	27.7	56	1	35	308	8.8	21				
1963	OTT	14										36	6	1	8	8.0	8	0	41	967	23.6	73	6					1	22	22.0	22
1964	OTT	13	3		0							30	5	1	-27	-27.0	-27	0	31	517	16.7	80	5								
1965	OTT	14										24	4						31	704	22.7	77	4								
1966	OTT+	14										42	7						35	804	23.0	69	7								
1967	OTT*	14										54	9						52	1171	22.5	94	9								
1968	OTT+	14	0		1							78	13						36	890	24.7	65	13								
1969	OTT	14	1		1							48	8						37	855	23.1	82	8								
1970	OTT	10																	6	101	16.8	28	0								
9	Years	121	4		2				3	25		324	54	2	-19	-9.5	8	0	272	6092	22.4	94	53	35	308	8.8	21	1	22	22.0	22
GARY TUFFORD Gary WR 5'9 160 Saskatoon Jrs. B: 8/26/1950																															
1976	TOR	5										12	2						7	162	23.1	55	2								
1977	HAM	11																	5	51	10.2	15	0								
2	Years	16										12	2						12	213	17.8	55	2								
MAWUKO TUGBENYOH Mawuko Kofidoe DE 6'1 245 California B: 4/9/1978 Hayward, CA Pro: E																															
2004	BC	18	0	0	2	18	6.0	31.0			1	6	1																		
2005	MTL	9	0	0	1	17	3.0	24.0			2																				
2	Years	27	0	0	3	35	9.0	55.0			3	6	1																		
MAC TUIAEA Mac Eti DL 6'6 295 Washington B: 5/29/1977 Ellensburg, WA Pro: X																															
2002	BC	1				1																									
TOM TUINEI Tumuauat DE-DT 6'4 250 Hawaii B: 2/21/1958 Oceanside, CA Draft: 9B-223 1980 DET Pro: N																															
1982	EDM	15	0		3		6.0																								
1983	EDM	12	0		2		6.0																								
1984	EDM	16	0		2		12.0					6	1																		
1985	EDM	16	0		3		9.0																								
1986	EDM	18					10.0																								
1987	EDM	14				12	5.0					6	1																		
6	Years	91	0		10	12	48.0					12	2																		
JOE TUIPALA Joseph Lafaele LB 6'1 244 San Diego State B: 9/13/1976 Honolulu, HI Pro: ENX																															
2005	WPG	2				3																									
PETER TUIPULOTU Peter Henry FB 5'10 205 Brigham Young B: 2/20/1969 Nu'ukalofa, Tonga Pro: N																															
1994	BAL+	18	4		1	5						12	2	13	42	3.2	10	0	53	657	12.4	36	2					3	27	9.0	19
1995	BAL	17				5						6	1	6	15	2.5	13	0	19	249	13.1	32	1					3	28	9.3	16
1996	SAS	9				3						18	3	11	35	3.2	6	3	31	297	9.6	36	0								
3	Years	44	4		1	13						36	6	30	92	3.1	13	3	103	1203	11.7	36	3					6	55	9.2	19
TED TULLY Ted LB-OG-FW 6'0 205 Vancouver Meralomas Jrs. B: 8/8/1929 Vancouver, BC D: 1/24/2003																															
1950	EDM	14																													
1951	EDM	13										5	1						3	40	13.3		0	1	5	5.0	5	1	19	19.0	19
1952	EDM	16							1	4				1	21	21.0	21	0						2	16	8.0	8				
1953	EDM	16										16	1											1	16	16.0	16				
1954	EDM	16							4	23		2	0											1	0	0.0	0				
1955	EDM+	16							3	34		5	1											1	8	8.0	8				
1956	EDM+	16	0		3				1	8																					
1957	EDM+	14	0		2				6	25																					
1958	EDM+	16	0		2				3	36																					
1959	BC	16							2	22																					
1960	EDM	12																													
1961	EDM	16										1	0											1	6	6.0	6				
1962	EDM	14							1			11	0																		
13	Years	195	0		7				21	152		40	3	1	21	21.0	21	0	3	40	13.3		0	7	51	7.3	16	1	19	19.0	19
JEFF TURCOTTE Jeff OT-OG-DT 6'5 255 Ottawa Sooners Jrs.; Colorado B: 1952 Draft: TE 1975 OTT; 17-435 1975 BUF																															
1975	OTT+	15	0		1																										
1976	OTT	16																													
1977	OTT*	14																													
1978	OTT	14																													
1980	OTT	6																													

Year	Team	GP	FM	FF	FR	TK	SK	YDS	IR	YDS	PD	PTS	TD	RA	YDS	AVG	LG	TD	REC	YDS	AVG	LG	TD	PR	YDS	AVG	LG	KOR	YDS	AVG	LG
5	Years	65	0		1																										
ED TUREK Erhard CB-OHB 5'11 195 Buffalo; Wilfrid Laurier B: 1945 Draft: 1-1 1966 EDM																															
1966	EDM	11																						2	9	4.5	6	7	128	18.3	24
1967	HAM	12												11	32	2.9	16	0	1	20	20.0	20	0					1	26	26.0	26
1968	HAM	14												15	120	8.0	66	0	6	86	14.3	38	0	2	12	6.0	9	13	345	26.5	50
1969	HAM	14	0		1									1	5	5.0	5	0						47	229	4.9	16	11	191	17.4	25
1970	HAM	14	0		1				1	0														51	339	6.6	20	3	69	23.0	25
1971	HAM	14	0		1									1	9	9.0	9	0						65	266	4.1	21				
6	Years	79	0		3				1	0				28	166	5.9	66	0	7	106	15.1	38	0	167	855	5.1	21	35	759	21.7	50
WOODNY TURENNE Woodny CB 6'0 184 Sequoias JC; Louisville B: 1/25/1987 Fort Lauderdale, FL Pro: N																															
2011	HAM	2				9					3																				
KEN TURNBULL Ken E B: 1921 D: 9//2008 Caledon, ON																															
1947	TOR	3																													
BRYANT TURNER Bryant, Jr. DT 6'2 260 Alabama-Birmingham B: 11/25/1987 Mobile, AL																															
2011	WPG	13	0	1	0	15	3.0	15.0			1																				
CHARLIE TURNER Charles OT 6'1 243 Ohio University B: 12/12/1943 Bellaire, OH																															
1967	HAM	10																													
1968	HAM	5																													
1970	HAM	11																													
1971	EDM	16			2																							2	26	13.0	14
1972	EDM+	16																													
1973	EDM*	15																													
1974	EDM*	15			1																										
1975	EDM*	16																													
1976	EDM	16												1	-11	-11.0	-11	0													
1977	EDM+	16	0		2																										
1978	EDM	16																													
1979	WPG	11	0		1																										
12	Years	163	0		6									1	-11	-11.0	-11	0										2	26	13.0	14
CLEM TURNER Clem FB-LB 6'2 230 Cincinnati B: 5/28/1945 Cincinnati, OH D: 12/20/2009 Cincinnati, OH Draft: 4-83 1969 CIN Pro: NW																															
1967	HAM	3										6	1	25	99	4.0	15	1	2	12	6.0	7	0								
DAVE TURNER Dave C-QB																															
1946	CAL	7																													
1949	CAL	8																													
2	Years	15																													
DERRICK TURNER Derrick OT 6'4 326 Florida A&M B: 8/27/1973 Pro: EX																															
2002	HAM	4				0																									
DOUG TURNER Douglas C 6'2 205 Toronto B: 1916 D: 9/26/1990 Toronto, ON																															
1947	TOR	12										5	1																		
1948	TOR	11																													
1949	CAL	8																													
3	Years	31										5	1																		
ELBERT TURNER Elbert Lamar, III WR 5'11 165 Illinois B: 3/19/1968 Winnfield, LA Draft: 7-189 1992 HOU																															
1992	BC	2				2													3	34	11.3	15	0								
1994	SAS	5										30	5						15	283	18.9	44	5								
1995	SAS	15	1		0	2						24	4	1	7	7.0	7	0	48	580	12.1	45	4					3	43	14.3	19
3	Years	22	1		0	4						54	9	1	7	7.0	7	0	66	897	13.6	45	9					3	43	14.3	19
HOWIE TURNER Howard DB 5'10 173 North Carolina State B: 1923 Draft: 8-57 1947 BAL-AAFC; 7-50 1947 CHIC																															
1947	OTT	9										17	3					1													
1948	OTT+	11										25	3					2					1								
1949	OTT+	11										57	10					7					3								
1950	OTT	9										13	2					1					1								
1951	OTT	12										50	10					2					7								
1952	OTT	12										25	5					2					3								
1953	OTT+	14										5	1																		
1954	OTT	13							1	0				10	15	1.5	6	0						25	105	4.2	13	10	223	22.3	40
8	Years	91							1	0		192	34	10	15	1.5	6	15					15	25	105	4.2	13	10	223	22.3	40
JOE TURNER Joe HB 195 B: 1919																															
1947	WPG	7										5	1										1								
1948	WPG	7										5	1					1													
1949	CAL	2																													
3	Years	16										10	2					1					1								
JUNIOR TURNER Junior DE-DT 6'3 257 Bishop's B: 9/2/1988 Toronto, ON Draft: 2-9 2011 CAL																															
2011	CAL	18	0	1	0	29	2.0	15.0																							
LONNIE TURNER Lonnie, Jr. WR 5'7 164 Los Angeles CC; Cal Poly (Pomona) B: 8/31/1959 Los Angeles, CA Pro: EU																															
1993	BC	10	3		0	3						12	2	4	25	6.3	16	0	27	420	15.6	50	2	38	270	7.1	43	11	196	17.8	45
MARCELOUS TURNER Marcelous RB 5'7 185 Alabama A&M B: 4/3/1970 Atlanta, GA																															
2002	TOR	6				0								3	0	0.0	4	0	2	45	22.5	23	0	21	197	9.4	43	19	460	24.2	46
2002	OTT	2	1	0	1	0						6	1	2	-2	-1.0	-1	0	2	74	37.0	40	0	26	381	14.7	85	7	122	17.4	48
2002	Year	8	1	0	1	0						6	1	5	-2	-0.4	4	0	4	119	29.8	40	0	47	578	12.3	85	26	582	22.4	48
MARK TURNER Mark DT 6'2 260 Miami (Ohio) B: 2/22/1963 Toronto, ON Draft: 2-18 1986 BC																															
1988	BC	17				5	1.0																								
1989	BC	12				0																									
1990	BC	4				0																									
3	Years	33				5	1.0																								
ODESSA TURNER Odessa WRWR 6'3 205 Northwestern State (Louisiana) B: 10/12/1964 Monroe, LA Draft: 4-112 1987 NYG Pro: N																															
1995	OTT	17				2						48	8						70	1054	15.1	66	8								
RICKY TURNER Ricky QB 5'10 168 Washington State B: 5/14/1962 Harbor City, CA Draft: 6-123 1984 SA-USFL Pro: N																															
1984	TOR	1																													
1985	TOR	8	2		0							6	1	38	284	7.5	31	1													
2	Years	9	2		0							6	1	38	284	7.5	31	1													
ROB TURNER Rob WR 6'3 202 Central Michigan B: 12/11/1980 Fort Lauderdale, FL																															
2003	BC	1				0													2	15	7.5	10	0								
ROBERT TURNER Robert CB 6'0 195 James Madison B: 2/12/1962 Draft: 15A-297 1984 MEM-USFL																															
1986	CAL	1																													
1987	CAL	1				0																									
2	Years	2				0																									
ROBERT TURNER Robert J. DB 6'3 200 Contra Costa CC; Washington State B: 9/5/1970 San Francisco, CA																															
1994	SAC	9				18																									
WYLIE TURNER Wylie Dewayne DB 5'10 182 Angelo State B: 4/19/1957 Dallas, TX Pro: N																															
1982	WPG	14	1		1				2	20														2	13	6.5	7	7	154	22.0	36
1983	WPG	12	0		2				3	22																					
1984	WPG	13	0		2																										
1985	WPG+	16					1.0		1	17																					
1986	WPG	7							2	28																					
1986	OTT	2	0		1																			1	9	9.0	9				
1986	Year	9	0		1				2	28														1	9	9.0	9				
5	Years	62	1		6		1.0		8	87														3	22	7.3	9	7	154	22.0	36
JOHN TURNTINE John O. DT 6'1 278 Texas Christian B: 5/6/1978 Greenwood, MS																															
2004	OTT	13	1	0	1	33	3.0	21.0	1	13	1																				
2005	MTL	1				2																									
2	Years	14	1	0	1	35	3.0	21.0	1	13	1																				

Year	Team	GP	FM	FF	FR	TK	SK	YDS	IR	YDS	PD	PTS	TD	RA	YDS	AVG	LG	TD	REC	YDS	AVG	LG	TD	PR	YDS	AVG	LG	KOR	YDS	AVG	LG
GERRY TUTTLE Gerry QB 5'11 190 Kent State B: 1926																															
1954	BC	11	5									5	1	20	-48	-2.4	7	1													
PERRY TUTTLE Perry Warren WR 6'0 178 Clemson B: 8/2/1959 Lexington, NC Draft: 1-19 1982 BUF Pro: N																															
1986	WPG	18	1		0							48	8	6	24	4.0	19	0	83	1373	16.5	85	8	6	27	4.5	13				
1987	WPG*	17	1		0	3						48	8	3	23	7.7	13	0	75	1310	17.5	72	8								
1988	WPG	17	1		0	2						48	8	1	-8	-8.0	-8	0	45	822	18.3	64	8								
1989	WPG	14	1		0	0						30	5						47	836	17.8	94	5								
1990	WPG	13				3						30	5						36	749	20.8	75	5								
1991	WPG	9				1						44	7						35	727	20.8	72	7								
6	Years	88	4		0	9						248	41	10	39	3.9	19	0	321	5817	18.1	94	41	6	27	4.5	13				
DEVIN TYLER Devin OT 6'7 300 Temple B: 7/2/1986 Washington, DC																															
2011	EDM	11				0																									
DIONE TYLER Dione L. RB 5'7 175 Cerritos JC; Southeast Missouri State B: 7/14/1974 Gardena, CA																															
1996	CAL	2				0								2	3	1.5	3	0						1	8	8.0	8	2	37	18.5	30
2000	SAS	7	1	0	0	0						12	2	65	390	6.0	61	2	7	32	4.6	9	0					15	307	20.5	53
2	Years	9	1	0	0	0						12	2	67	393	5.9	61	2	7	32	4.6	9	0	1	8	8.0	8	17	344	20.2	53
MAURICE TYLER Maurice Michael DB 6'0 186 Baltimore CC; Morgan State B: 7/19/1950 Baltimore, MD Draft: 10-235 1972 BUF Pro: NU																															
1980	OTT	8							2	22																					
SCOTT TYLER Scott DB 5'10 182 Miami (Ohio) B: 12/5/1939 Draft: 27-211(f) 1962 DAL; 11-149(f) 1962 BAL																															
1964	HAM	2																										1	18	18.0	18
LAWRENCE TYNES Lawrence James Henry K 6'1 202 Troy B: 5/3/1978 Greenock, Scotland Pro: EN																															
2002	OTT	8	1	0	0	1						79	0																		
2003	OTT*	18				0						198	0																		
2	Years	26	1	0	0	1						277	0																		
VERN UECKER Vernon G 5'11 215 Texas Christian																															
1957	WPG	4																										1	15	15.0	15
WILF UHREN Wilf G-T 6'3 195 Tulsa B: 1933																															
1956	SAS	1																													
HARRY ULINSKI Harry John C 6'4 229 Kentucky B: 4/4/1925 Pittsburgh, PA D: 4/20/2008 Louisville, KY Draft: 4-45 1950 WAS Pro: N																															
1952	OTT	11																													
ED ULMER Edward, Jr. DH-CB 6'2 184 Ohio State B: 7/21/1940 D: 1/28/2000																															
1963	OTT	2							2	26																		2	57	28.5	32
1964	OTT	13	0		1				4	121		4	0	1	3	3.0	3	0	1	7	7.0	7	0	24	167	7.0	41	2	37	18.5	27
1965	WPG	15	0		3				2	20		7	0	1	8	8.0	8	0						2	11	5.5	11	3	63	21.0	27
1966	WPG*	16	1		3				3	73		20	2	5	18	3.6	8	1	1	8	8.0	8	0	4	21	5.3	6				
1967	WPG	14	2		2				2	18		15	2											4	32	8.0	25				
1968	WPG	16	2		2				5	60		8	0											1	9	9.0	9	1	17	17.0	17
1969	WPG	16	3		0				3	15		5	0											4	34	8.5	25				
1970	WPG	16	1		1				9	152		3	0																		
1971	WPG	6							1	2		2	0																		
9	Years	114	9		12				31	487		64	4	7	29	4.1	8	1	2	15	7.5	8	0	39	274	7.0	41	8	174	21.8	32
JOHN ULMER John E. LB-DL 6'2 214 North Dakota B: 6/7/1963 Columbia, OH Draft: 1A-3 1985 BC																															
1985	BC	5																													
1986	BC	16																													
1987	BC	12	0		1	23	1.0		2	35		6	1																		
1988	BC	10				6	1.0																								
1989	OTT	9				16			1	18																					
5	Years	52	0		1	45	2.0		3	53		6	1																		
MIKE ULMER Michael Walter DB 6'0 189 Doane B: 12/28/1954 York, NE Pro: NU																															
1981	CAL	4	1		0				4	30				1	-5	-5.0	-5	0						14	184	13.1	43	4	127	31.8	49
TERRYL ULMER Terryl CB 5'10 170 Southern Mississippi B: 3/3/1971 Laurel, MS																															
1993	SAS	9	2		0	17																		22	118	5.4	13	12	230	19.2	47
1994	SAS	13	6		1	21			3	27	1			1	0	0.0	0	0	7	47	6.7	12	0	44	346	7.9	53	23	447	19.4	37
1995	SAS	18	2		4	44			3	71	10	6	1											42	462	11.0	79	10	149	14.9	31
1996	SAS	18	3		2	59			5	67	6													10	23	2.3	11	5	89	17.8	20
1997	SAS	16	1	1	0	56			1	5	5	6	1											33	330	10.0	68	4	67	16.8	27
1998	SAS	16	0	0	1	46			3	111	6	6	1											21	263	12.5	85	2	26	13.0	20
6	Years	90	14	1	8	243			15	281	28	18	3	1	0	0.0	0	0	7	47	6.7	12	0	172	1542	9.0	85	56	1008	18.0	47
P.W. UNDERWOOD P.W. OG-T 5'11 225 Southern Mississippi B: 1932 Draft: 28-330 1954 CHIB																															
1957	HAM	13																													
1958	HAM	11																													
2	Years	24																													
TERRY UNDERWOOD Terry RB 5'7 195 Wagner B: 6/28/1966 Perth Amboy, NJ																															
1989	TOR	2				1						6	1	29	135	4.7	14	1	5	42	8.4	13	0					3	66	22.0	30
JEREMY UNERTL Jeremy Dale LB-CB 6'1 210 Wisconsin-LaCrosse B: 9/15/1978 Hartford, WI Pro: EU																															
2010	TOR	12				23	1.0	11.0	2	98	0	6	1																		
2011	TOR	17	1	0	1	29													1	39	39.0	39	0								
2	Years	29	1	0	1	52	1.0	11.0	2	98	0	6	1						1	39	39.0	39	0								
MORRIS UNUTOA Braemer Taua OG 6'1 284 Brigham Young B: 3/10/1971 Torrance, CA Pro: N																															
2005	OTT	8				0																									
TUUFULI UPERESA Tuufuli OG 6'3 255 Montana B: 1/20/1948 American Samoa Draft: 16-396 1970 PHI Pro: N																															
1973	WPG	16	0		1																										
1974	WPG	16																													
1975	CAL	8																													
1975	OTT	4																										1	8	8.0	8
1975	Year	12																										1	8	8.0	8
1976	OTT	11																										1	16	16.0	16
1977	BC	2																													
5	Years	53	0		1																							2	24	12.0	16
BRAD UPSHAW Brad S-WR 6'0 180 Verdun Invictus Jrs. B: 1951																															
1971	MTL	14	3		2							6	1	1	2	2.0	2	0	4	41	10.3	29	1	70	483	6.9	22	4	72	18.0	26
1972	MTL	14	3		2				1	41		6	1											27	80	3.0	17	5	131	26.2	35
1973	MTL	2																													
3	Years	30	6		4				1	41		12	2	1	2	2.0	2	0	4	41	10.3	29	1	97	563	5.8	22	9	203	22.6	35
ERIC UPTON Eric OG-C 6'3 245 Ottawa B: 4/29/1953 Ottawa, ON Draft: 2B-18 1976 EDM																															
1976	EDM	7																													
1977	EDM	16																													
1978	EDM	16																													
1979	EDM+	16																													
1980	EDM	16	0		1																										
1981	EDM	16																													
1982	EDM	16																													
1984	EDM	13																													
8	Years	116	0		1																										
JOE UPTON Joseph C. T-G 6'2 248 Toronto B: 1925 D: 3/2/1967 Ottawa, ON																															
1953	OTT	11																													
1954	OTT	13																													
1955	OTT	11																													
1956	OTT	14																										1	1	1.0	1
1957	OTT	14										6	1																		
5	Years	63										6	1															1	1	1.0	1
JERRY URIAS Gerardo DH 5'10 192 Temple B: 10/23/1976 Los Angeles, CA																															

Year	Team	GP	FM	FF	FR	TK	SK	YDS	IR	YDS	PD	PTS	TD	RA	YDS	AVG	LG	TD	REC	YDS	AVG	LG	TD	PR	YDS	AVG	LG	KOR	YDS	AVG	LG
2000	HAM	8	1	0	1	23			1	16	1																				
JACK URNESS Jack FB-HB 6'2 195 Regina Rams Jrs. B: 1937																															
1959	SAS	10												4	0	0.0	3	0	1	4	4.0	4	0								
MARK URNESS Mark OG-C 6'1 230 Saskatoon Hilltops Jrs.; Boise State B: 8/22/1962 Regina, SK Draft: 7-57 1985 SAS																															
1985	SAS	10	2		0																										
1986	SAS	18	0		1																										
1987	SAS	18				0																									
1988	SAS	13				0																									
1989	SAS	12				0																									
5	Years	71	2		1	0																									
TED URNESS Harold Edward C-OG-DG 6'3 235 Regina Rams Jrs.; Arizona B: 1937																															
1961	SAS	15																													
1962	SAS	16																													
1963	SAS	15	0		1																										
1964	SAS	16																													
1965	SAS*	16																													
1966	SAS*	16																													
1967	SAS*	16																													
1968	SAS*	16	0		2																										
1969	SAS*	16																													
1970	SAS*	16	1		0																										
10	Years	158	1		3																										
ERIC URSIC Eric QB 6'2 215 Western Ontario B: 4/1/1970 Brampton, ON																															
1994	TOR	2				0																									
1995	HAM	2				0																									
2	Years	4				0																									
LARRY UTECK Larry DB 6'0 186 Colorado; Wilfrid Laurier B: 10/9/1952 Thornhill, ON D: 12/25/2002 Halifax, NS Draft: TE 1974 TOR																															
1974	TOR	15	0		1				4	6														35	234	6.7	25	3	30	10.0	21
1975	TOR+	16	1		0				3	46		6	1											33	259	7.8	37				
1976	TOR+	16	3		0				2	35														27	297	11.0	28				
1977	BC	7							1	20																		3	52	17.3	19
1978	MTL	16							2	48														1	6	6.0	6				
1979	MTL	16																													
1980	MTL	6																													
1980	OTT	2																													
1980	Year	8																													
7	Years	92	4		1				12	155		6	1											96	796	8.3	37	6	82	13.7	21
SONNY UTZ Silas OHB 6'0 210 Virginia Tech B: 5/21/1942 Draft: 13- 1965 NYJ; 6-75 1965 DAL																															
1967	WPG	12												12	16	1.3	8	0	15	145	9.7	32	0	2	21	10.5	21	12	272	22.7	42
RON VACCHER Ron DE-OE-DB 6'2 195 Winnipeg Rods Jrs. B: 1928																															
1948	WPG	12																													
1949	WPG	14																													
1950	WPG	13										10	2						11	142	12.9		2								
1951	WPG	14										25	5						33	547	16.6		5								
1952	WPG	16			4														5	111	22.2	31	0								
1953	WPG	6																													
1954	WPG	13	0		3																										
1955	WPG	16																													
8	Years	104	0		7							35	7						49	800	16.3	31	7								
PAUL VAJDA Paul OG 6'2 265 Concordia (Canada) B: 7/27/1966 Montreal, QC Draft: 1B-5 1991 SAS																															
1991	SAS	18				2																									
1992	SAS	5				0																									
1993	SAS	18	0		1	0																									
1994	SAS	14				1																									
1995	SAS	11				2																									
1996	SAS	18				10																									
6	Years	84	0		1	15																									
AL VALDES Alan HB 5'11 195 Calgary Bronks Jrs. B: 1935																															
1956	CAL	16	1		0							6	1	17	54	3.2	19	1	4	29	7.3	16	0								
1957	CAL	15	6		0							12	2	111	553	5.0	42	2	11	67	6.1	19	0								
1958	CAL	1																													
3	Years	32	7		0							18	3	128	607	4.7	42	3	15	96	6.4	19	0								
EARL VALIQUETTE Earl DT-G 5'11 205 B: 1922																															
1948	HAM	12																													
1949	HAM	12																													
1950	EDM	11																													
1951	HAM	12																													
1952	HAM	12																													
5	Years	59																													
DEAN VALLI Dean OG-C 6'5 300 Simon Fraser B: 10/5/1983 North Vancouver, BC Draft: 1C-6 2006 BC																															
2006	BC	12				0																									
2007	BC	18	0	0	1	0																									
2008	BC	18				1																									
2009	BC	18				1																									
2010	BC	9	0	0	1	0																									
2011	BC	18				1																									
6	Years	93	0	0	2	3																									
JOHN VAN John DL 6'4 243 Louisiana-Monroe B: 5/6/1976 Vancouver, BC																															
1999	SAS	3				0																									
DAVE VAN BELLEGHEM David S 5'10 185 Calgary B: 3/20/1967 Kingston, ON Draft: 4-28 1990 TOR																															
1990	TOR	17	0		2	21			2	42																		1	7	7.0	7
1991	TOR	12	0		1	18						6	1															1	0	0.0	0
1992	TOR	16	0		1	38			2	19																					
1993	TOR	17	0		1	53			3	38																					
1994	SAS	17	0		2	27			1	31	1																	0	3		3
1995	SAS	18	1		2	44	3.0	15.0	7	77	5																	1	33	33.0	33
1996	SAS	15	0		1	27	2.0	13.0	1	17	1																	1	5	5.0	5
1998	CAL	17	0	1	0	23	2.0	13.0	1	9	2																				
8	Years	129	1	1	10	251	7.0	41.0	17	233	9	6	1															4	48	12.0	33
BILL VAN BURKLEO Bill QB-CB-LB-P 5'11 185 Oklahoma; Tulsa B: 1943 Draft: 24-192(f) 1964 SD; 15-200(f) 1964 DAL																															
1966	TOR	4										1	0																		
1967	WPG	15	3		1				1	28		13	2	16	65	4.1	11	1													
1968	OTT	14	2		0				3	66		2	0	6	50	8.3	23	0						1	1	1.0	1				
1969	OTT	14	1		3				4	12		1	0	4	17	4.3	11	0						1	19	19.0	19				
1970	OTT	14	1		1				6	102		8	1	2	30	15.0	21	0						5	35	7.0	16				
1971	CAL	15							5	9		13	1	7	186	26.6	89	1						1	0	0.0	0				
1972	HAM	10										2	0	2	3	1.5	11	0						1	-2	-2.0	-2				
7	Years	86	7		5				19	217		40	4	37	351	9.5	89	2						9	53	5.9	19				
PIETER VANDEN BOS Pieter OG 6'1 250 British Columbia B: 11/5/1961 Toronto, ON Draft: 1A-4 1983 EDM																															
1983	WPG	6																													
1984	WPG	7																													
1984	OTT	3																													

Year	Team	GP	FM	FF	FR	TK	SK	YDS	IR	YDS	PD	PTS	TD	RA	YDS	AVG	LG	TD	REC	YDS	AVG	LG	TD	PR	YDS	AVG	LG	KOR	YDS	AVG	LG
1984	Year	10																												
1985	OTT	7	0		1																										
1986	OTT	13	0		1																										
1987	BC	17				0																									
1988	BC	12				0																									
1989	BC	7				0																									
7	Years	69	0		2	0																									
MIKE VANDERJAGT Michael John K-P 6'5 211 Allan Hancock JC; West Virginia B: 3/24/1970 Oakville, ON Draft: 8-58 1992 SAS Pro: N																														
1993	SAS	2	1		0	1								1	-8	-8.0	-8	0													
1996	TOR	18				3						198	0																		
1997	TOR*	18	1	0	0	4						190	0	2	25	12.5	13	0													
2008	TOR	18	2	0	0	3						161	0																		
4	Years	56	4	0	0	11						549	0	3	17	5.7	13	0													
RON VANDER KELEN Ronald QB 6'1 186 Wisconsin B: 11/6/1939 Green Bay, WI Draft: 21-163 1963 NYJ Pro: N																														
1968	CAL	5										12	2	5	10	2.0	4	2													
PHIL VANDERSEA Phillip John DE 6'3 228 Massachusetts B: 2/25/1943 Whitinsville, MA Draft: RS-9-66 1965 DEN; 16-220(f) 1965 GB Pro: N																														
1972	MTL	5	0		1																										
BOB VAN DUYNE Robert Scott OT 6'5 243 Idaho B: 5/15/1952 San Bernardino, CA Draft: 10A-240 1974 BAL; 30-360 1974 HOU-WFL Pro: NU																														
1981	HAM	16																												
1982	BC	2																												
2	Years	18																												
JASON VAN GEEL Jason LB 6'1 237 Waterloo B: 1/6/1975 Lambeth, ON Draft: 4-27 1998 SAS																														
1998	WPG	3				2																									
1999	HAM	15				9																						2	23	11.5	12
2	Years	18				11																						2	23	11.5	12
HARRY VAN HOFWEGEN Harry DT 6'2 246 Carleton B: 4/1/1966 Nepean, ON Draft: 2A-11 1996 WPG																														
1996	WPG	8				7																									
1997	WPG	7				2																									
1997	BC	10				20																									
1997	Year	17				22																									
1998	EDM	2				0																									
3	Years	17				29																									
DAVE VANKOUGHNETT Dave OG 6'4 255 Boise State B: 4/1/1966 Kamloops, BC Draft: 2-14 1988 BC																														
1989	WPG	1				0																									
1991	WPG	16				0																									
1992	WPG	18	1		2	1																		1	2	2.0	2				
1993	WPG+	18	0		1	0																									
1994	WPG	18	0		1	4																									
1995	WPG	18	0		1	4																									
1996	WPG	18	1		1	3																									
1997	WPG	18	1	0	1	1																									
1998	WPG	18	1	0	0	2																									
1999	WPG	18	2	0	0	2																									
2000	WPG	18	0	0	1	2																									
11	Years	179	6	0	8	19																		1	2	2.0	2				
CLEVELAND VANN Cleveland Leon LB 6'1 215 Oklahoma State B: 9/3/1951 Seguin, TX Draft: 5-130 1974 MIA; 10-114 1974 SC-WFL Pro: W																														
1976	SAS	16			1				1	20		12	2																		
1977	SAS	16	0		1				3	97									1	4	4.0	4	0								
1978	SAS	14	0		3				1	10																					
1979	SAS	3																												
1980	SAS	9																												
5	Years	58	0		5				5	127		12	2						1	4	4.0	4	0								
LaDARIS VANN LaDaris WR 5'11 210 Cincinnati B: 10/7/1980 Middle Bass, OH Pro: E																														
2003	WPG	10				2						12	2	1	9	9.0	9	0	21	324	15.4	65	2	15	147	9.8	35	16	307	19.2	39
LeROY VANN LeRoy CB 5'8 177 Florida A&M B: 11/18/1986 Tampa, FL																														
2010	MTL	4	1	0	1	6					1													8	52	6.5	13	15	297	19.8	35
RON VANN Ronald T. (Toppy) QB 5'11 190 Georgia Tech B: 1936																														
1957	BC	5										6	1	16	12	0.8	11	1													
BRUCE VAN NESS Bruce Roy RB 6'3 211 Rutgers B: 3/9/1946 Teaneck, NJ Draft: 5A-112 1970 ATL																														
1970	MTL	4												5	8	1.6	7	0	13	163	12.5	51	0					2	40	20.0	21
1971	MTL+	14	5		3							36	6	125	559	4.5	41	5	39	512	13.1	38	1					2	47	23.5	26
1972	MTL	6												6	5	0.8	4	0	2	15	7.5	14	0								
3	Years	24	5		3							36	6	136	572	4.2	41	5	54	690	12.8	51	1					4	87	21.8	26
CLINT VAN OSTRAND Clint OG 6'3 250 Whitworth B: 11/6/1960 Calgary, AB Draft: 2-11 1982 MTL																														
1982	MTL	3																												
TAMARICK VANOVER Tamarick T. WR 5'11 220 Florida State B: 2/25/1974 Tallahassee, FL Draft: 3A-81 1995 KC Pro: N																														
1994	LV	15	3		1	2						32	5	1	6	6.0	6	0	23	385	16.7	33	3	36	341	9.5	105	31	718	23.2	90
VERN VANOY Vernon Eugene DE 6'8 270 Kansas B: 12/31/1948 Kansas City, MO Draft: 3-60 1969 NYG Pro: NW																														
1969	TOR	14																												
AMOS VAN PELT Amos, Jr. OHB 6'2 215 Ball State B: 1948 Draft: 6-149 1969 STL																														
1969	WPG	16	4		1							18	3	121	504	4.2	41	3	24	245	10.2	33	0					13	341	26.2	45
1970	WPG	12	3		0							12	2	92	346	3.8	32	1	15	112	7.5	26	1								
2	Years	28	7		1							30	5	213	850	4.0	41	4	39	357	9.2	33	1					13	341	26.2	45
JIM VAN PELT James Sutton QB-S 5'11 183 Michigan B: 11/11/1935 Chicago, IL Draft: 5-54 1958 WAS																														
1958	WPG	12	1									65	2	38	171	4.5	24	2	1	5	5.0	5	0								
1959	WPG+	15										78	3	46	98	2.1	18	3	1	36	36.0	36	0								
2	Years	27	1		0							143	5	84	269	3.2	24	5	2	41	20.5	36	0								
STAN VAN SICHEM Stan LB 6'2 229 Regina B: 4/2/1987 Amsterdam, The Netherlands Draft: 4-25 2009 MTL																														
2009	MTL	2				0																									
PETE VAN VALKENBERG Pete HB 6'2 194 Brigham Young B: 5/19/1950 Sandy, UT Draft: 3-66 1973 NO Pro: N																														
1976	SAS	12	5		1							30	5	129	572	4.4	90	3	43	421	9.8	27	2					0	21		21
NELSON VAN WAES Nelson DT 6'5 275 Tulsa B: 10/14/1972 Calgary, AB Draft: 5-39 1996 SAS																														
1997	SAS	13				7																									
1998	SAS	17				13	1.0	14.0			1																				
1999	SAS	12	1	1	0	3																						1	-1	-1.0	-1
3	Years	42	1	1	0	23	1.0	14.0			1																	1	-1	-1.0	-1
CHRIS VAN ZEYL Chris OT-OG 6'6 292 McMaster B: 9/4/1983 Foothill, ON Draft: 3A-18 2007 MTL																														
2009	TOR	11				0																									
2010	TOR	14	0	0	2	2													1	10	10.0	10	0								
2011	TOR	15	0	0	1	3																									
3	Years	40	0	0	3	5													1	10	10.0	10	0								
CHRIS VARGAS Christopher E. QB 5'11 170 Nevada-Reno B: 1/29/1971 Hemet, CA																														
1994	EDM	18																												
1995	EDM	18				1						6	1	17	54	3.2	16	1													
1996	BC	16	1		0	0								1	3	3.0	3	0													
1997	WPG	18	7	0	0	2								22	108	4.9	17	0													
1998	WPG	5	1	0	0	0								1	2	2.0	2	0													
5	Years	75	9	0	0	3						6	1	41	167	4.1	17	1													
KEN VARGO Kenneth W. LB 6'1 200 Ohio State B: 1932 Draft: 9-106 1956 CHIB																														
1956	OTT+	14							1	1																					
1958	OTT	14																												
2	Years	28							1	1																					

Year	Team	GP	FM	FF	FR	TK	SK	YDS	IR	YDS	PD	PTS	TD	RA	YDS	AVG	LG	TD	REC	YDS	AVG	LG	TD	PR	YDS	AVG	LG	KOR	YDS	AVG	LG
JOHNNY VARNELL John DE 6'4 265 West Texas A&M B: 5/13/1941 Draft: 5A-33 1964 HOU; 7-91 1964 LARM																															
1966	TOR	3	0		1																										
JOHN VARONE John Patrick HB-FB-LB 5'11 194 Miami (Florida) B: 11/9/1936 Draft: 4-46 1958 SF																															
1958	WPG	15	2		3							12	2	65	250	3.8	14	0	9	160	17.8	55	2					3	30	10.0	13
1959	WPG	10							2	2				2	9	4.5	8	0	1	-2	-2.0	-2	0					1	8	8.0	8
2	Years	25	2		3				2	2		12	2	67	259	3.9	14	0	10	158	15.8	55	2					4	38	9.5	13
ARTO VARTANIAN Arto DT 6'6 285 Valdosta State B: 5/17/1977 Chicago, IL																															
1999	HAM	3				3																									
DON VASSOS Don DB-LB 5'10 180 Melville Jrs.; British Columbia B: 1938																															
1959	BC	13							3	20		6	1											2	17	8.5	17	4	57	14.3	25
1960	BC	6												6	21	3.5	8	0						3	12	4.0	8				
1961	SAS	16												2	8	4.0	7	0						3	2	0.7	6	1	30	30.0	30
1963	EDM	16	2		0				1															30	158	5.3	12	3	62	20.7	32
4	Years	51	2		0				4	20		6	1	8	29	3.6	8	0						38	189	5.0	17	8	149	18.6	32
JAKE VAUGHAN Jake DB 5'10 175 Bishop's B: 8/2/1963 Knowlton, QC Draft: 3-21 1987 TOR																															
1987	TOR	18	0		1	15			1	51		6	1															20	391	19.6	54
1988	TOR	18	0		2	11			1	27																					
2	Years	36	0		3	26			2	78		6	1															20	391	19.6	54
KAYE VAUGHAN Kaye OG-DT-OT-MG 6'2 225 Tulsa B: 1931 Draft: 12-135 1953 BAL																															
1953	OTT+	12																													
1954	OTT	14												1	9	9.0	9	0													
1956	OTT+	14																													
1957	OTT+	13																													
1958	OTT	14																													
1959	OTT+	14																										1	0	0.0	0
1960	OTT+	14																													
1961	OTT+	14																										1	3	3.0	3
1962	OTT*	14																													
1963	OTT	13																													
1964	OTT	10	0		1																										
1966	MTL	2																													
12	Years	148	0		1									1	9	9.0	9	0										2	3	1.5	3
RUBEN VAUGHAN Ruben Charles, Jr. DT 6'2 255 Colorado B: 8/5/1956 Draft: 6-138 1979 SF Pro: NU																															
1983	BC	4					1.5																								
GERALD VAUGHN Gerald Glenn DH 6'3 195 Mississippi B: 4/8/1970 Abbeville, MS																															
1993	CAL	18	0		3	52			4	24																					
1994	CAL	18	0		1	50			4	32	6																				
1995	CAL	18				35					4																	13	270	20.8	32
1996	WPG	18				52	1.0	6.0	2	25	11																				
1997	HAM	18	0	1	0	63			3	26	6																				
1998	HAM*	17				52			6	118	12	6	1																		
1999	HAM*	18	0	1	0	54			9	240	10	6	1															1	0	0.0	0
2000	HAM	8	0	0	2	18			1	3	5																				
2001	HAM	7	0	2	0	21			1	5	2																				
2002	OTT	16	1	1	0	50			3	109	10	6	1																		
2003	OTT	17	0	0	1	65	3.0	134.0	2	46	3	6	1																		
2004	OTT	17	1	3	5	63	1.0	11.0			4	6	1																		
2005	OTT	9				23	1.0	4.0																							
13	Years	199	2	8	12	598	6.0	155.0	35	628	73	30	5															14	270	19.3	32
LEE VAUGHN Lee DB 5'11 184 Wyoming B: 11/27/1974 Little Rock, AR Draft: 6-187 1997 DAL Pro: E																															
2001	BC	9	0	0	2	40			1	18	3																				
MICHAEL VAUGHN Michael RB 6'0 200 Mesa State B: 10/20/1966 Denver, CO																															
1990	HAM	1				0								7	28	4.0	8	0	1	3	3.0	3	0								
TERRY VAUGHN Terrance R. WR-SB 5'8 182 Arizona B: 12/25/1971 Sumter, SC																															
1995	CAL	18	3		1	3					3	32	5	5	12	2.4	7	0	72	1031	14.3	56	5	24	204	8.5	24				
1996	CAL+	17	2		1	2						30	5	2	16	8.0	12	0	74	1161	15.7	104	5	47	536	11.4	35	11	212	19.3	33
1997	CAL+	18	1	0	0	2						54	9	2	13	6.5	12	0	81	1020	12.6	37	9	36	326	9.1	20	8	157	19.6	25
1998	CAL*	17	1	0	0	0						30	5						81	1045	12.9	49	5	50	514	10.3	57	11	293	26.6	59
1999	EDM+	17	1	0	0	3						66	11						75	1057	14.1	60	11	3	19	6.3	9	5	83	16.6	22
2000	EDM+	17	2	0	0	1						36	6						94	1216	12.9	37	6	21	222	10.6	44	7	144	20.6	48
2001	EDM*	18	1	0	0	2						30	5						98	1497	15.3	52	5	9	89	9.9	23	2	29	14.5	16
2002	EDM*	18	1	0	0	2						54	9	3	12	4.0	9	0	94	1291	13.7	53	9	9	84	9.3	15	2	24	12.0	24
2003	EDM+	18	4	0	0	3						43	7						106	1558	14.7	72	7	1	10	10.0	10	2	31	15.5	25
2004	EDM	18	2	0	1	1						12	2	1	7	7.0	7	0	78	1062	13.6	50	2	1	19	19.0	19				
2005	MTL	17				1						48	8	3	6	2.0	5	0	93	1113	12.0	39	8					10	175	17.5	28
2006	HAM	18				1						6	1	1	4	4.0	4	0	60	695	11.6	45	1								
12	Years	211	18	0	3	21					3	441	73	17	70	4.1	12	0	1006	13746	13.7	104	73	201	2023	10.1	57	58	1148	19.8	59
VERNON VAUGHN Vernon OE 6'3 215 Maryland-Eastern Shore B: 1936 Draft: 7-81 1958 NYG																															
1958	SAS	10																	13	172	13.2	24	0								
1959	SAS	16							3	52									39	511	13.1	27	0	1	0	0.0	0				
1960	SAS	13	0		1							6	1						21	375	17.9	41	1								
3	Years	39	0		1				3	52		6	1						73	1058	14.5	41	1	1	0	0.0	0				
GREG VAVRA Greg QB 6'1 195 Calgary B: 2/19/1961 Red Deer, AB Draft: TE 1983 CAL																															
1984	CAL	11	5		1							6	1	31	153	4.9	25	1													
1985	CAL	10	2		0									13	28	2.2	11	0													
1986	BC	9												2	12	6.0	8	0													
1987	BC	14	3		1	0								3	-8	-2.7	4	0													
1988	EDM	11				0								2	9	4.5	8	0													
5	Years	55	10		2	0						6	1	51	194	3.8	25	1													
RONALD VEAL Ronald R. QB 5'10 190 Arizona B: 7/16/1968 Fernandina Beach, FL																															
1991	HAM	7				0								4	22	5.5	13	0													
JASON VEGA Jason LB-DT 6'5 265 Northeastern B: 5/30/1987 Brockton, MA																															
2011	WPG	11	1	1	0	26	7.0	43.0											1	19	19.0	19	0								
LEN VELLA Leonard T 6'3 250 Georgia B: 1940 Draft: 15-197 1962 WAS																															
1962	EDM	9																													
1963	EDM	5																													
2	Years	14																													
MARK VERBEEK Mark C 6'5 258 St. Francis Xavier B: 2/29/1972 Hamilton, ON Draft: 1B-8 1997 EDM																															
1997	EDM	18	0	0	1	21																									
2000	HAM	18				3													1	2	2.0	2	0								
2001	HAM	18	1	0	0	10																						1	14	14.0	14
2002	HAM	17				1																									
2003	HAM	18	1	1	1	9																						2	21	10.5	11
5	Years	89	2	1	2	44													1	2	2.0	2	0					3	35	11.7	14
PIERRE VERCHEVAL Pierre OG 6'1 275 Western Ontario B: 11/22/1964 Quebec City, QC Draft: 2-17 1987 EDM																															
1988	EDM	10				2																									
1989	EDM	18	0		2	1																									
1990	EDM	18	1		3	2																									
1991	EDM	14				4																									
1992	EDM*	17				3																									
1993	TOR	3				0																									
1994	TOR*	18				2																									

Year	Team	GP	FM	FF	FR	TK	SK	YDS	IR	YDS	PD	PTS	TD	RA	YDS	AVG	LG	TD	REC	YDS	AVG	LG	TD	PR	YDS	AVG	LG	KOR	YDS	AVG	LG
1995	TOR+	16				6																										
1996	TOR	8				0																										
1997	TOR*	18	0	0	1	2																										
1998	MTL*	18	0	0	0	0																										
1999	MTL*	18	0	0	0	1																										
2000	MTL*	18	0	0	2	0																										
2001	MTL	18				1																										
14	Years	212	1	0	8	24																										
CLARENCE VERDIN Clarence WR 5'8 164 Louisiana-Lafayette B: 6/14/1963 New Orleans, LA Draft: 17B-356 1984 HOU-USFL Pro: NU																																
1996	BC	4	1		0	0													10	67	6.7	17	0	25	133	5.3	21	19	415	21.8	43
JIMMY VERDON Jimmy Lee DT 6'3 280 Arizona State B: 11/4/1981 Pomona, CA Draft: 7-232 2005 NO Pro: EN																																
2008	SAS	8				12	1.0	11.0			1																				
JASON VERDUZCO Jason A. QB 5'9 190 Illinois B: 4/3/1970 Walnut Creek, CA																																
1993	BC	12				0																										
ED VEREB Edward John OHB-DB 6'0 190 Maryland B: 5/21/1934 Pittsburgh, PA Draft: 1-12 1956 WAS Pro: N																																
1956	BC+	15	6		2				4	60		84	14	95	514	5.4	52	6	17	178	10.5	41	7	12	90	7.5	16	15	281	18.7	44
1958	BC	12	7		2							30	5	80	424	5.3	24	2	19	174	9.2	29	3					10	250	25.0	49
1959	BC	16										24	4	129	648	5.0	40	1	31	544	17.5	91	3								
1961	BC	4												16	72	4.5	15	0	4	74	18.5	29	0								
4	Years	47	13		4				4	60		138	23	320	1658	5.2	52	9	71	970	13.7	91	13	12	90	7.5	16	25	531	21.2	49
HENRY VEREEN Henry Kiven SB 5'10 176 Nevada-Las Vegas B: 4/18/1957 Biloxi, MS Draft: 9-225 1979 TB																																
1984	BC	5												1	-12	-12.0	-12	0	5	28	5.6	11	0	21	271	12.9	79	7	168	24.0	30
EDDIE VERSPRILLE Ed DB 6'0 205 Alabama B: 8/18/1940 Norfolk, VA Draft: 11-151 1964 CLE																																
1964	HAM	2																													
BRIAN VERTEFEUILLE Brian Leonel OG-OT 6'3 252 Idaho State B: 4/4/1951 Willimantic, CT Draft: 13-314 1974 SD Pro: NW																																
1976	SAS	4	1		0																										
1976	TOR	3																													
1976	Year	7	1		0																										
BILLY VESSELS Billy Dale OHB 6'0 190 Oklahoma B: 3/22/1931 Cleveland, OK D: 11/17/2001 Coral Gables, FL Draft: 1-2 1953 BAL Pro: N																																
1953	EDM+	16							4	0		50	10	129	926	7.2		7	20	310	15.5		1	3	14	4.7		9	347	38.6	
DOM VETRO Dominic WR 5'10 180 Wilfrid Laurier B: 5/26/1958 St. Lawrence, NL Draft: 6-49 1981 MTL																																
1981	MTL	15	0		1														5	66	13.2	18	0					16	354	22.1	39
1982	MTL	9																	3	16	5.3	14	0	28	323	11.5	33	6	126	21.0	34
1983	MTL	3																													
1983	HAM	8																	2	47	23.5	39	0	1	14	14.0	14				
1983	Year	11																	2	47	23.5	39	0	1	14	14.0	14				
3	Years	27	0		1														10	129	12.9	39	0	29	337	11.6	33	22	480	21.8	39
ROB VIAN Robert A. OL 6'5 320 Boise State B: 11/8/1979 Dallas, OR																																
2004	SAS	2				0																										
BOB VICCARS Robert TE-LB 6'3 228 Calgary Mohawks Jrs. B: 6/4/1953 Calgary, AB																																
1975	CAL	8	1		0														1	13	13.0	13	0								
1976	CAL	16	1		1							6	1	1	-4	-4.0	-4	0	15	250	16.7	78	1								
1977	CAL	16	0		1														17	224	13.2	29	0								
1978	CAL	16										6	1						25	369	14.8	40	1								
1979	CAL	16	0		1							6	1						24	256	10.7	21	1								
1980	CAL	16										6	1						26	307	11.8	32	1					1	22	22.0	22
1981	CAL	16	0		1														22	294	13.4	46	0					1	19	19.0	19
7	Years	104	2		4							24	4	1	-4	-4.0	-4	0	130	1713	13.2	78	4					2	41	20.5	22
DON VICIC Donald J. (Magoo) FB-LB 6'1 215 Ohio State B: 1935 Draft: 27-320 1957 SF																																
1957	BC	11	2		2							18	3	77	399	5.2	19	3	7	44	6.3	17	0					1	17	17.0	17
1958	BC	15	2		2				2	5		6	1	61	205	3.4	14	1	4	64	16.0	24	0	1	0	0.0	0	3	53	17.7	37
1959	BC	16										36	6	165	802	4.9	23	6	9	93	10.3	22	0					4	47	11.8	17
1960	BC	14	1		1							12	2	58	246	4.2	16	1	4	54	13.5	20	1					2	18	9.0	18
1961	BC	9										6	1						1	7	7.0	7	1					2	24	12.0	16
1962	BC	15												4	20	5.0	11	0										2	32	16.0	22
1963	BC	5																													
1964	BC	4	0		1							6	1	8	24	3.0	5	1													
8	Years	89	5		6				2	5		84	14	373	1696	4.5	23	12	25	262	10.5	24	2	1	0	0.0	0	14	191	13.6	37
KAS VIDRUK Kas DG-C 5'9 216 none B: 10/5/1925 Slaule, Lithuania D: 10/21/1986																																
1946	WPG	8																													
1947	WPG	8																													
1948	MTL	12																													
1949	MTL	10																													
1950	MTL	8																													
1951	WPG	13																													
1952	WPG	16			2							5	1																		
1953	WPG	15																													
1954	WPG	16																													
1955	WPG	16																													
10	Years	122			2							5	1																		
JOE VIJUK Joe DE-DY 6'3 243 Hillsdale B: 11/17/1945 Belgrade, Yugoslavia																																
1970	OTT	14	0		2							6	1																		
1971	TOR	14	0		3																										
1972	TOR	2																													
3	Years	30	0		5							6	1																		
MIKE VILIMEK Mike RB 6'3 238 Simon Fraser B: 1/5/1979 North Vancouver, BC Draft: 1B-2 2002 OTT																																
2002	OTT	9				6								2	7	3.5	4	0													
2003	OTT	12				4								1	1	1.0	1	0	1	3	3.0	3	0								
2004	OTT	17	0	0	1	19								2	-1	-0.5	3	0													
2005	MTL	18				12						30	5	34	124	3.6	25	5	4	88	22.0	49	0					3	21	7.0	9
2006	MTL	16				6						6	1	15	40	2.7	6	1	3	34	11.3	18	0					2	18	9.0	12
2007	MTL	5				1								9	25	2.8	5	0	3	47	15.7	26	0					1	14	14.0	14
6	Years	77	0	0	1	48						36	6	63	196	3.1	25	6	11	172	15.6	49	0					6	53	8.8	14
PRIMO VILLANUEVA Primo HB-QB 5'10 175 UCLA B: 12/2/1931 Tucumcari, NM																																
1955	BC	14	4		0				5	87		20	4	63	317	5.0	26	2	16	234	14.6	37	2	14	103	7.4	20	3	42	14.0	15
1956	BC	10	2		1				1	13		1	0	25	97	3.9	20	0	1	12	12.0	12	0	2	0	0.0	0	3	72	24.0	40
1957	BC	10	2		0				1	0		18	3	40	247	6.2	58	1	9	175	19.4	44	2	1	0	0.0	0	5	94	18.8	28
1958	BC	3										6	1	11	72	6.5	16	1	3	34	11.3	17	0	1	7	7.0	7	4	71	17.8	20
4	Years	37	8		1				7	100		45	8	139	733	5.3	58	4	29	455	15.7	44	4	18	110	6.1	20	15	279	18.6	40
KEVIN VILLARS Kevin W. WR 6'4 205 Northwestern; Weber State B: 1963																																
1987	BC	4				0													16	172	10.8	28	0								
ZACH VILLE Zaccheus Ezekiel DT 6'1 291 West Hills JC; Missouri B: 4/24/1982 Miami, FL Pro: E																																
2007	SAS	1				1																										
JOHN VILUNAS John K-C-DT-LB 6'1 250 Lakeshore Bears Jrs.; East York Argos Ints. B: 2/21/1941																																
1964	TOR	14	0		1							6	1																		
1965	TOR	14										25	0																		
1966	TOR	14	0		2							37	0																		
1967	TOR	14	0		1							27	0																		
1968	SAS	16										0	0																		
1970	HAM	14	1		0														1	-19	-19.0	-19	0								
6	Years	86	1		4							95	1						1	-19	-19.0	-19	0								
GERRY VINCENT Gerry E-S-P 6'1 205 Winnipeg Rods Jrs. B: 1934																																

Year	Team	GP	FM	FF	FR	TK	SK	YDS	IR	YDS	PD	PTS	TD	RA	YDS	AVG	LG	TD	REC	YDS	AVG	LG	TD	PR	YDS	AVG	LG	KOR	YDS	AVG	LG
1955	WPG	4										1	0																		
1956	WPG	8										1	0																		
1957	WPG	16							1	14		9	0											1	10	10.0	6				
1958	WPG	11							2	22		1	0											1	0	0.0	0				
4	Years	39							3	36		12	0											2	10	5.0	6				
BRANKO VINCIC Branko DT 6'4 250 Eastern Michigan B: 11/1/1964 Fruitland, ON Draft: 2-16 1988 EDM																															
1989	TOR	7				2																									
1990	TOR	7	0		2	4																									
2	Years	14	0		2	6																									
SCOTT VIRKUS Scott DE 6'5 270 Purdue; San Francisco CC B: 9/7/1959 Pro: N																															
1986	SAS	8					6.0																								
TONY VISCO Anthony LB 6'4 235 Purdue B: 11/11/1963 Mississauga, ON Draft: 1A-4 1987 BC																															
1988	TOR	16	0		1	10			1	9		6	1																		
1989	TOR	18	0		1	43	2.0		1	0																					
1990	BC	12				36	1.0		1	0																		1	0	0.0	0
1990	SAS	5				0																									
1990	Year	17				36	1.0		1	0																		1	0	0.0	0
1991	HAM	6				10	5.0																					1	2	2.0	2
4	Years	52	0		2	99	8.0		3	9		6	1															2	2	1.0	2
MERV VISNESKIE Mervin E. FL 5'10 190 Ottawa Sooners Jrs. B: 6/5/1949 Cobden, ON																															
1971	EDM	11																	1	-1	-1.0	-1	0					2	45	22.5	28
1974	OTT	4																	1	4	4.0	4	0					2	46	23.0	29
2	Years	15																	2	3	1.5	4	0					4	91	22.8	29
LIONEL VITAL Lionel RB 5'9 195 Nicholls State B: 7/15/1963 New Iberia, LA Draft: 7B-185 1985 WAS; 13-187 1985 ARI-USFL Pro: N																															
1986	CAL	1	1		0									3	8	2.7	4	0						2	1	0.5	2				
1989	SAS	4				0						6	1	5	11	2.2	9	1	1	4	4.0	4	0	12	59	4.9	16	9	186	20.7	50
2	Years	5	1		0	0						6	1	8	19	2.4	9	1	1	4	4.0	4	0	14	60	4.3	16	9	186	20.7	50
DAVE VITI Dave DE-OE 6'2 235 Boston University B: 1940 Draft: 6-44 1962 BUF; 9-113 1962 WAS																															
1962	HAM	9										6	1						14	206	14.7	34	1								
1963	HAM	14										32	1						27	361	13.4	24	1								
1964	HAM	12																	1	13	13.0	13	0								
1965	HAM	14	1		1				1	0									2	30	15.0	21	0								
1966	HAM	14	1		1							6	1						10	186	18.6	41	1								
1967	HAM	14			4																										
1968	HAM	14										6	1						12	207	17.3	36	1								
1969	HAM	14																	18	234	13.0	28	0								
8	Years	105	2		6				1	0		50	4						84	1237	14.7	41	4								
GEORGE VOELK George DT 6'3 235 Saskatchewan B: 9/28/1962 Tisdale, SK Draft: 6-47 1984 MTL																															
1985	MTL	16	0		1																										
MIKE VOLCAN Mike DT-MG-OT 5'11 200 B: 1931																															
1955	EDM	6							1	5																					
1956	EDM	16																													
1957	EDM	16	0		2																										
1958	EDM	16	0		3																										
1959	EDM	15																													
1960	EDM	16	0		1																										
1961	EDM	16																													
1962	EDM	16																													
1963	EDM	16																													
1964	EDM	12																													
10	Years	145	0		6				1	5																					
JIM VOLLENWEIDER James Stephen FB 6'1 210 Miami (Florida) B: 9/2/1939 WI D: 6/1/1998 Ewa Beach, HI Draft: 18-137 1962 OAK; 8-106 1962 SF Pro: N																															
1964	TOR	8	4		0							18	3	93	464	5.0	18	2	11	30	2.7	9	1								
CARL VOLNY Carl, Jr. RB 5'10 195 Central Michigan B: 12/25/1987 Montreal, QC Draft: 5-32 2011 WPG																															
2011	WPG	12	2	0	1	2								9	71	7.9	17	0													
JEFF VOLPE Jeff S 6'2 200 Guelph B: 9/15/1964 Unionville, ON Draft: 2A-15 1986 EDM																															
1986	EDM	18							1	18		6	1											1	100	100.0	100				
JON VOLPE Jon RB 5'7 195 Stanford B: 4/17/1968 Kincheloe, MI																															
1991	BC+	17	11		2	4						120	20	239	1395	5.8	44	16	53	459	8.7	37	4					7	118	16.9	24
1992	BC+	14	5		1	0						92	15	184	941	5.1	27	13	36	303	8.4	28	2					2	32	16.0	21
1993	BC	5	1		0	1						24	4	45	136	3.0	13	4	10	117	11.7	25	0					4	134	33.5	45
1994	LV	4	2		0	0						18	3	43	182	4.2	17	3	1	17	17.0	17	0								
4	Years	40	19		3	5						254	42	511	2654	5.2	44	36	100	896	9.0	37	6					13	284	21.8	45
NICK VOLPE Nick QB 5'9 165 Toronto B: 1925																															
1949	TOR	10										38	5					4					1								
1950	TOR	12										44	0																		
1951	TOR	2										2	0																		
3	Years	24										84	5					4					1								
PETE VON HARTEN Carl Peter Constantine Lehman HB 5'10 180 Vancouver Cubs Jrs.; British Columbia B: 1/6/1932 Vancouver, BC D: 3/6/2002 Vernon, BC																															
1955	BC	12	2		0				1	0														25	210	8.4	32	10	190	19.0	26
CHRIS VRANTSIS Chris LB 6'2 215 McMaster B: 8/26/1981 Hamilton, ON																															
2005	MTL	18	1	0	0	1																									
2006	MTL	18				3																									
2007	MTL	15				11																									
2008	MTL	13				2																									
4	Years	64	1	0	0	17																									
LEW WACKER Louis A. DB-OHB 6'0 180 Richmond Draft: 11A-122 1956 DET																															
1956	CAL	1																													
JIMMY WADDELL Jim HB 5'11 187 Compton JC B: 1931 Draft: 21-250 1956 CHIB																															
1956	SAS	1	1		0							6	1	11	58	5.3	14	1													
JUDE WADDY Jude Michael LB 6'2 225 William & Mary B: 9/12/1975 Washington, DC Pro: EN																															
2005	CAL	1				0			0	0	1																				
RAY WADDY Raymond, Jr. DB 5'11 175 Wharton County JC; Texas A&M-Kingsville B: 8/21/1956 Freeport, TX Pro: NU																															
1983	BC	6																													
MICHAEL WADE Michael WR 5'9 195 Iowa State B: 2/4/1961 Waukegan, IL Draft: 19B-396 1984 MIC-USFL																															
1984	CAL	3	1		0									1	20	20.0	20	0	5	56	11.2	14	0					1	12	12.0	12
SONNY WADE Jesse QB 6'3 210 Emory & Henry B: 4/1/1947 Martinsville, VA Draft: 10A-236 1969 PHI																															
1969	MTL	14	4		0							27	3	31	144	4.6	16	3													
1970	MTL	14	5		1							28	4	37	220	5.9	28	3	1	8	8.0	8	1	1	26	26.0	26				
1971	MTL	14	6		0							1	0	20	142	7.1	18	0													
1972	MTL	13	6		0							9	1	17	104	6.1	19	1	1	9	9.0	9	0								
1973	MTL	1												1	9	9.0	9	0													
1974	MTL	13												2	23	11.5	16	0	1	16	16.0	16	0								
1975	MTL	16	1		0							4	0	10	14	1.4	18	0													
1976	MTL	16	4		0							0	0	20	117	5.9	41	0	1	8	8.0	8	0								
1977	MTL	13										3	0	6	13	2.2	9	0													
1978	MTL	4	0		1									4	16	4.0	8	0													
10	Years	118	26		2							72	8	148	802	5.4	41	7	4	41	10.3	16	1	1	26	26.0	26				
MIKE WADSWORTH Michael A. DT-DE 6'3 258 Notre Dame B: 6/4/1943 Ottawa, ON D: 4/28/2004 Rochester, MN																															
1966	TOR	14	0		3																										
1967	TOR	14	0		3																										
1968	TOR+	14																													

Year	Team	GP	FM	FF	FR	TK	SK	YDS	IR	YDS	PD	PTS	TD	RA	YDS	AVG	LG	TD	REC	YDS	AVG	LG	TD	PR	YDS	AVG	LG	KOR	YDS	AVG	LG
1969	TOR	14																												
1970	TOR	14	0		1																									
5	Years	70	0		7																									
HAL WAGGONER James H. OHB-DB 5'9 170 Little Rock JC; Tulane B: 1930 Draft: 17-202 1951 PHI																														
1951	HAM+	12									50	10					8					2							
1952	HAM+	11									50	10					7					3							
1953	HAM	3									5	1					1												
1954	HAM	1											4	18	4.5	11	0										2	40	20.0	27
1955	HAM	12						4	27		30	6	110	617	5.6	42	6	14	178	12.7	25	0					18	522	29.0	58
1956	HAM	14						3	11		36	6	37	132	3.6	23	1	26	585	22.5	80	5					10	238	23.8	52
1957	HAM	7						1	11				2	-1	-0.5	1	0	4	87	21.8	36	0								
1960	TOR	2																												
8	Years	62						8	49		171	33	153	766	5.0	42	23	44	850	19.3	80	10					30	800	26.7	58
AARON WAGNER Aaron LB-FB 6'2 247 Washington State; Brigham Young B: 7/5/1982 Cranbrook, BC Draft: 2B-14 2006 TOR																														
2007	TOR	9				4																								
2008	TOR	16				25																					2	12	6.0	7
2009	SAS	8	0	0	1	7																					1	12	12.0	12
3	Years	33	0	0	1	36																					3	24	8.0	12
BRAD WAGNER Brad DB 6'1 180 Kansas State B: 11/7/1955 Seneca, KS																														
1979	WPG	3																												
LOWELL WAGNER Lowell R. HB 6'0 194 Southern California B: 8/21/1923 Santa Monica, CA D: 9/26/2005 Kirkland, WA Pro: AN																														
1954	CAL	16	1		0				6	62		10	2	1	4	4.0	4	0	16	227	14.2	46	2	6	30	5.0	9				
VIRGIL WAGNER Virgil Edwin HB-FB-LB 6'0 185 Millikin B: 2/27/1922 Belleville, IL D: 8/22/1997 Belleville, IL Draft: 29-271 1943 DET																														
1946	MTL+	12									65	13					11												
1947	MTL+	12									71	14					10					3							
1948	MTL+	12									60	12					10					2							
1949	MTL+	12									77	15					12					2							
1950	MTL	10									60	12					7					5							
1951	MTL	12									30	6					6												
1952	MTL	12									20	4					1					3							
1953	MTL	14									5	1					1												
1954	MTL	14						2	27		10	2	68	329	4.8	21	2	5	63	12.6	21	0								
9	Years	110						2	27		398	79	68	329	4.8	21	60	5	63	12.6	21	15								
JOHN WAGONER John T-G-E 6'1 230 North Carolina State B: 6/7/1923 Lowe's Grove, NC																														
1948	OTT+	12																												
1949	OTT+	12																												
1950	OTT	11									5	1																	
1951	OTT	12																												
1952	OTT	12																												
1953	OTT	14																												
1954	BC	14			3							5	1	1	-1	-1.0	-1	0													
7	Years	87			3							10	2	1	-1	-1.0	-1	0													
TED WAHL Ted QB 6'1 210 South Dakota State B: 7/28/1965 Jamestown, ND																														
1991	SAS	18				0						8	1	6	57	9.5	27	1													
GALEN WAHLMEIER Galen C-LB 6'0 212 Dodge City JC; Kansas B: 1934																														
1957	SAS+	15	1		2				1	5																					
1959	SAS	6																												
1960	SAS	6	0		1				1																						
1961	SAS	2																												
1963	SAS	1																												
1965	SAS	16																										3	16	5.3	11
1966	SAS	16																												
1967	SAS	16																												
8	Years	78	1		3				2	5																		3	16	5.3	11
ROB WAITE Robert DT 6'1 251 Vancouver Meralomas Jrs.; British Columbia B: 3/5/1957 Draft: 2-12 1982 CAL																														
1982	CAL	2																												
1983	BC	3	0		1																									
1983	SAS	7																												
1983	Year	10	0		1																									
1984	SAS	1																												
3	Years	6	0		1																									
CAMERON WAKE Derek Cameron DE-LB 6'3 250 Penn State B: 1/30/1982 Beltsville, MD Pro: N																														
2007	BC*	18	0	3	0	72	16.0	94.0			4																			
2008	BC*	18	0	5	3	67	23.0	160.0			1	6	1																	
2	Years	36	0	8	3	139	39.0	254.0			5	6	1																	
CHRIS WALBY Chris OT-DT-OG 6'7 275 Winnipeg Rods Jrs.; Dickinson State B: 10/23/1956 Winnipeg, MB Draft: 1-4 1981 MTL																														
1981	MTL	5																												
1981	WPG	2	0		1							6	1																	
1981	Year	7	0		1																									
1982	WPG	16																												
1983	WPG	13	0		1																									
1984	WPG*	16	0		1																									
1985	WPG*	16																												
1986	WPG*	18	0		1																									
1987	WPG*	18				0																								
1988	WPG	18	0		2	0																								
1989	WPG*	17				3																								
1990	WPG*	14				1																								
1991	WPG*	18				1																								
1992	WPG+	14				0																								
1993	WPG*	18	0		1	1																								
1994	WPG*	18	0		2	5																								
1995	WPG	15				3																								
1996	WPG+	18				1																								
16	Years	252	0		9	15						6	1																	
KEN WALCOTT Ken DB 6'0 205 St. Mary's (Nova Scotia) B: 5/1/1969 Sydney, NS Draft: 2A-11 1992 OTT																														
1992	OTT	4	0		1	2																								
1993	OTT	15				16																					1	0	0.0	0
1994	TOR	7				6			1	71	1	6	1																	
1995	TOR	17				41			1	7	2																			
4	Years	43	0		1	65			2	78	3	6	1															1	0	0.0	0
MARK WALCZAK Mark Charles SB 6'6 246 Arizona B: 4/26/1962 Rochester, NY Pro: N																														
1995	MEM	15	1		0	4													1	10	10.0	10	0								
MARK WALD Mark DT 6'0 240 British Columbia B: 7/3/1954																														
1980	EDM	2																												
1981	EDM	6																												
2	Years	8																												
BOBBY WALDEN Robert Earl P-HB-DB Georgia B: 3/9/1938 Boston, GA Draft: 4-31 1961 HOU Pro: N																														
1961	EDM	14	4									43	6	45	185	4.1	24	0	36	513	14.3	29	6	40	280	7.0	19	16	487	30.4	57
1962	EDM	11	3						1			23	3	29	157	5.4	19	0	33	441	13.4	32	3					14	348	24.9	69
1963	EDM	2									1	0	3	8	2.7	4	0	3	43	14.3	37	0	9	28	3.1	12				
1963	HAM	1											5	14	2.8	5	0	2	-5	-2.5	2	0					2	54	27.0	28

Year	Team	GP	FM	FF	FR	TK	SK	YDS	IR	YDS	PD	PTS	TD	RA	YDS	AVG	LG	TD	REC	YDS	AVG	LG	TD	PR	YDS	AVG	LG	KOR	YDS	AVG	LG
1963	Year	3										1	0	8	22	2.8	5	0	5	38	7.6	37	0	9	28	3.1	12	2	54	27.0	28
3	Years	27	7		0				1	0		67	9	82	364	4.4	24	0	74	992	13.4	37	9	49	308	6.3	19	32	889	27.8	69
JIMMY WALDEN James C. QB-DB 6'2 185 Itawamba JC; Wyoming B: 4/10/1938 Aberdeeen, MS Draft: FS 1960 DEN; 16-188 1960 CLE																															
1960	BC	12	7		1							6	1	73	384	5.3	30	1						1	2	2.0	2				
1961	BC	3												12	69	5.8		0													
1961	CAL	3												7	14	2.0		0													
1961	Year	6												19	83	4.4	13	0													
1962	CAL	4																													
1962	EDM	8	1									6	1	3	10	3.3	7	1						25	172	6.9	22	3	71	23.7	59
1962	Year	12	1									6	1	3	10	3.3	7	1										3	71	23.7	59
3	Years	19	8		1							12	2	95	477	5.0	30	2						26	174	6.7	22	3	71	23.7	59
MIKE WALDERZAK Mike OG 6'2 250 Detroit Mercy B: 1943																															
1966	OTT	14																													
1967	OTT	13																													
2	Years	27																													
TOMMY WALDON Tom HB 5'8 165 Toronto B: 1923																															
1946	TOR	1																													
ROB WALDROP Robert F. DT 6'1 276 Arizona B: 12/1/1971 Atlanta, GA Draft: 5B-156 1994 KC Pro: N																															
1995	MEM	6				14	5.0	53.0																							
1996	TOR*	17	0		1	37	9.0	65.0			1																				
1997	TOR*	17				25	5.0	27.0																							
3	Years	40	0		1	76	19.0	145.0			1																				
BILLY WALIK William S. WR 5'11 180 Villanova B: 11/8/1947 New Haven, CT Draft: 11-268 1970 PHI Pro: NW																															
1973	WPG	2												1	4	4.0	4	0	1	23	23.0	23	0					2	46	23.0	23
ART WALKER Arthur D., Jr. DT-OG-DE-MG 5'11 230 Michigan B: 11/24/1933 D: 5/26/1973 Marquette, MI Draft: 12-137 1955 GB																															
1955	EDM+	16																													
1956	EDM	14	1		0																			1	3	3.0	3				
1957	EDM+	14																						2	12	6.0	12				
1958	EDM+	16							1	9									0	2		2	0								
1959	EDM+	16																													
1960	EDM	1	0		1																										
1961	EDM	15																													
7	Years	92	1		1				1	9									0	2		2	0	3	15	5.0	12				
BILL WALKER Bill OE-DE 6'0 185 Maryland B: 1935 Draft: 8B-96 1955 DET																															
1956	EDM	15	1		2							18	3						25	356	14.2	37	2								
1957	EDM	13	2									11	1						21	393	18.7	37	1								
1958	EDM	8	2		0							9	1	0	4		4	1	8	112	14.0	18	0								
3	Years	36	5		2							38	5	0	4		4	1	54	861	15.9	37	3								
BRUCE WALKER Bruce FL 6'0 170 Windsor B: 4/16/1955 Draft: TE 1978 OTT																															
1979	OTT	13	4		2							8	1	0	20		20	1	17	203	11.9	24	0	3	0	0.0	0				
1980	OTT	16	2		0							12	2						12	204	17.0	50	1	28	211	7.5	50				
1981	OTT	16										18	3						44	482	11.0	52	3	6	55	9.2	23				
1982	OTT	13	1		0							8	1	2	21	10.5	34	0	46	608	13.2	31	1	44	372	8.5	25	26	561	21.6	43
1984	OTT	8																	1	14	14.0	14	0	25	131	5.2	22				
5	Years	66	7		2							46	7	2	41	20.5	34	1	120	1511	12.6	52	5	106	769	7.3	50	26	561	21.6	43
CORNELIUS WALKER Cornelius James DT-DE 6'2 250 Rice B: 9/24/1953 Del Valle, TX Draft: 3-59 1975 KC																															
1976	TOR	7																													
1977	TOR	4																													
1978	OTT	6																													
3	Years	17																													
DANNY WALKER Danny Ranar WR 6'4 200 Scottsdale CC; Arizona B: 3/23/1956 Casa Grande, AZ																															
1979	CAL	3																	4	36	9.0	13	0								
DAVE WALKER David DB 6'0 195 Utah B: 5/4/1949 Royal, AB Pro: W																															
1971	EDM	7							3	0														10	41	4.1	8	3	88	29.3	30
1972	EDM	14	0		3				2	14		6	1											1	6	6.0	6	13	314	24.2	40
2	Years	21	0		3				5	14		6	1											11	47	4.3	8	16	402	25.1	40
DELL WALKER Dell RB 5'10 215 East Stroudsburg B: 1942																															
1984	CAL	2												6	16	2.7	5	0	3	10	3.3	6	0								
DEMETRIOS WALKER Demetrios C. DE 6'2 261 Fort Scott CC; Middle Tennessee State B: 4/21/1981 Kansas City, MO Pro: E																															
2005	HAM	6				5					1																				
2006	HAM	2				1																									
2	Years	8				6					1																				
EDDIE WALKER Ed E 5'10 200																															
1950	HAM	3																													
EDDIE RAY WALKER Eddie Ray CB 6'0 180 Southern Mississippi B: 1/2/1961 Pascagoula, MS Draft: 19-221 1983 BIR-USFL Pro: U																															
1985	SAS	16																													
1986	SAS	18	0		1		1.0		2	3																					
1988	SAS	2				2																									
1989	SAS	5				11	1.0		2	31																					
4	Years	41	0		1	13	2.0		4	34																					
ELBERT WALKER Elbert OT 6'3 282 Wisconsin B: 2/16/1948 Hamilton, OH Draft: 11-283 1972 KC																															
1974	SAS	3																													
ELLIOTT WALKER Elliott RB 5'11 193 Pittsburgh B: 9/10/1956 Indianola, MS Draft: 6-148 1978 SF Pro: N																															
1980	TOR	2												28	119	4.3	12	0	3	15	5.0	7	0								
GERRAN WALKER Gerran WR 5'9 188 Lehigh B: 10/2/1983 Atlanta, GA																															
2008	SAS	6				0													14	242	17.3	57	0					3	69	23.0	30
2009	SAS	13	1	0	0	2						14	2						36	401	11.1	43	2	6	7	1.2	7	10	147	14.7	23
2	Years	19	1	0	0	2						14	2						50	643	12.9	57	2	6	7	1.2	7	13	216	16.6	30
JABIR WALKER Jabir CB 5'11 180 Murray State B: 9/7/1977 Louisville, KY																															
2002	SAS	5				9					1																				
2003	SAS	6				18			1	34	1																				
2	Years	11				27			1	34	2																				
JAMES WALKER James Charles DE 6'1 250 Kansas State B: 12/9/1958 Muskogee, OK Pro: N																															
1985	CAL	16	0		2		7.0																								
1986	CAL	11																													
1986	SAS	3																													
1986	Year	14					8.0																								
2	Years	27	0		2		7.0																								
JAY WALKER Jewell Jay QB 6'3 229 Howard B: 1/24/1972 Draft: 7A-198 1994 NE Pro: EN																															
1998	WPG	5	1	0	0	0						6	1	5	16	3.2	10	1													
JIM WALKER James FL 6'1 180 Saskatchewan B: 1947 Draft: 1969 WPG																															
1969	WPG	5																													
1971	EDM	2																													
2	Years	7																													
JIMMY WALKER James Charles DE-DT 6'2 270 Arkansas B: 12/30/1956 Camden, AR Pro: NU																															
1979	EDM	14																													
1980	OTT	15	0		1																										
1981	OTT	2																													
3	Years	31	0		1																										
JOE WALKER Joseph DB 6'0 190 Northern Arizona B: 7/13/1957																															
1983	MTL	7							1	15																					
1984	MTL	1																													

Year	Team	GP	FM	FF	FR	TK	SK	YDS	IR	YDS	PD	PTS	TD	RA	YDS	AVG	LG	TD	REC	YDS	AVG	LG	TD	PR	YDS	AVG	LG	KOR	YDS	AVG	LG
2	Years	8							1	15																					
JOHN WALKER John Wayne DE 6'6 270 Nebraska-Omaha B: 9/12/1961 Omaha, NE Draft: 5-136 1983 NYJ; 13-152 1983 PHI-USFL Pro: NU																															
1987	SAS	2				1	1.0																								
1988	SAS	1																													
2	Years	3				1	1.0																								
JO JO WALKER Joseph Marvin Anthony WR-SB 5'9 178 Maryland B: 1/6/1983 Midland, TX																															
2007	HAM	18	2	0	0	4						18	3						29	288	9.9	22	2	35	292	8.3	71	7	109	15.6	20
2008	HAM	8				0													19	270	14.2	42	0	13	181	13.9	78	20	474	23.7	59
2	Years	26	2	0	0	4						18	3						48	558	11.6	42	2	48	473	9.9	78	27	583	21.6	59
KENNY WALKER Kenny Wayne DE 6'3 260 Nebraska B: 4/6/1967 Crane, TX Draft: 8-200 1991 DEN Pro: N																															
1994	CAL	18	0		3	28	9.0	43.0																							
1995	CAL	12	0		1	12	6.0	38.0			3																				
1995	WPG	3				7	2.0	21.0			2																				
1995	Year	15				19	8.0	59.0			5																				
1996	WPG	6	0		1	10	2.0	16.0			1																				
3	Years	36	0		5	57	19.0	118.0			11																				
KENYATTA WALKER Idrees Kenyatta OT-TE 6'5 302 Florida B: 2/1/1979 Meridian, MS Draft: 1-14 2001 TB Pro: N																															
2008	TOR	2				0																									
LEON WALKER Leon RB 5'8 180 Nevada-Las Vegas B: 1958																															
1980	SAS	3	1		0									14	40	2.9	11	0	5	29	5.8	8	0								
LEWIS WALKER Lewis T. RB 6'0 185 Antelope Valley JC; Utah B: 12/12/1958 Los Angeles, CA Draft: 10-268 1980 WAS																															
1984	CAL	13	4		1							18	3	139	732	5.3	87	2	55	595	10.8	86	1					7	147	21.0	26
1985	CAL	6	2		0							6	1	39	139	3.6	29	0	29	268	9.2	54	1	10	61	6.1	11	4	7	1.8	7
2	Years	19	6		1							24	4	178	871	4.9	87	2	84	863	10.3	86	2	10	61	6.1	11	11	154	14.0	26
MERV WALKER Mervin DB 6'0 180 Lakeshore Bears Jrs. B: 11/14/1952 Toronto, ON																															
1974	WPG	16							3	158		6	1											2	51	25.5	51	2	39	19.5	28
1975	WPG	13							1	2														11	57	5.2	30	3	43	14.3	22
1976	WPG	16	1		1				7	108														25	233	9.3	36	2	28	14.0	17
1977	WPG	16	1		1				6	110														9	112	12.4	34	1	0	0.0	0
1978	WPG	16							2	25														8	136	17.0	26				
1979	CAL	12																													
1980	CAL	16							2	33		6	1																		
1981	CAL	16	0		1				1	13														3	30	10.0	14				
1982	CAL	4																													
1982	TOR	7																													
1982	Year	11																													
1983	HAM	5																													
10	Years	130	2		3				22	449		12	2											58	619	10.7	51	8	110	13.8	28
MIKE WALKER Joseph Michael DE 6'4 235 Tulane B: 11/7/1949 Texarkana, AR Draft: 11-284 1971 MIN Pro: NW																															
1972	BC	10	0		1																										
1973	BC	16	0		1																										
1976	TOR	5																													
3	Years	31	0		2																										
MIKE WALKER Michael FB 6'0 195 Kitchener-Waterloo Thunderbirds B: 11/14/1950																															
1973	HAM	14	3		2									2	13	6.5	7	0	1	9	9.0	9	0	61	310	5.1	16				
1974	HAM	16	0		1									8	34	4.3	9	0	2	26	13.0	14	0	51	318	6.2	25				
1975	HAM	16	1		0									9	38	4.2	16	0	8	83	10.4	18	0	27	219	8.1	32	5	60	12.0	21
3	Years	46	4		3									19	85	4.5	16	0	11	118	10.7	18	0	139	847	6.1	32	5	60	12.0	21
MIKE WALKER Michael A. DT-DE 6'2 250 Washington State B: 4/7/1959 Indianapolis, IN																															
1982	HAM	12	0		1		6.5																								
1983	HAM	14					8.0																								
1984	HAM	6					3.0																								
1985	HAM	12	0		2		5.0					6	1																		
1986	HAM+	18	0		2		21.0																								
1987	HAM*	17	0		2	35	17.0		1	37		6	1																		
1988	HAM*	14				34	13.0																								
1989	HAM*	15				29	8.0		1	12																					
1990	EDM	18				37	9.0																								
1991	EDM	9				14	5.0																								
10	Years	135	0		7	149	95.5		2	49		12	2																		
PETE WALKER Peter OT 6'3 235 Royal Military College B: 7/19/1943 Draft: 1965 MTL																															
1965	MTL	10																													
SCOTT WALKER Scott WR 5'7 180 Lenoir-Rhyne B: 11/6/1967 Fayette County, AL																															
1992	HAM	2				0						6	1						6	92	15.3	34	0	5	102	20.4	62	2	67	33.5	55
1993	HAM	6	4		1	0						6	1						11	245	22.3	56	1	25	186	7.4	23	16	281	17.6	51
2	Years	8	4		1	0						12	2						17	337	19.8	56	1	30	288	9.6	62	18	348	19.3	55
SKIP WALKER Alvin Ray HB 5'9 191 Texas A&M B: 9/11/1954 Houston, TX Draft: 11-311 1976 HOU																															
1980	MTL+	13	4		0							60	10	114	692	6.1	64	9	34	511	15.0	75	1					17	434	25.5	54
1981	MTL	9	1		0									17	54	3.2	25	0	11	116	10.5	32	0					4	77	19.3	25
1982	OTT*	14	3		0							108	18	210	1141	5.4	35	13	28	536	19.1	96	5					13	288	22.2	42
1983	OTT*	16	7		1							74	12	238	1431	6.0	56	10	28	317	11.3	48	1					19	489	25.7	98
1984	OTT	6	3		0							6	1	69	256	3.7	18	1	13	145	11.2	34	0								
5	Years	58	18		1							248	41	648	3574	5.5	64	33	114	1625	14.3	96	7					53	1288	24.3	98
TOM WALKER Tom G 5'11 212 North Shore Cougars Jrs.; Iowa B: 1941																															
1962	BC	11																													
1963	BC	1																													
2	Years	12																													
TOM WALKER Tom FB 6'1 225 Simon Fraser; Wilfrid Laurier B: 10/5/1949 Draft: 1A-4 1972 HAM																															
1973	WPG	3	3		0									22	132	6.0	29	0													
1974	WPG	16												22	152	6.9	43	0	4	52	13.0	22	0								
1975	WPG	16										6	1	29	109	3.8	22	0	12	143	11.9	47	1	7	46	6.6	14	3	17	5.7	10
1976	WPG	16	1		0									8	35	4.4	11	0	1	3	3.0	3	0					2	10	5.0	10
1977	WPG	16										6	1	4	11	2.8	7	1										1	6	6.0	6
1978	WPG	16																	2	41	20.5	31	0					2	10	5.0	10
6	Years	83	4		0							12	2	85	439	5.2	43	1	19	239	12.6	47	1	7	46	6.6	14	8	43	5.4	10
TONY WALKER Anthony CB 5'11 185 Utah State B: 9/3/1978 Lancaster, CA																															
2002	BC	17	1	3	3	62	1.0		5	139	5																	1	14	14.0	14
2003	BC	16				37					3																				
2004	BC	2				1																									
3	Years	35	1	3	3	100	1.0		5	139	8																	1	14	14.0	14
WAYNE WALKER Ronald Wayne WR-SB 5'8 162 Texas Tech B: 12/27/1966 Waco, TX Pro: EN																															
1992	OTT	2	1		1	0													3	24	8.0	12	0					5	126	25.2	39
1993	OTT	13	2		0	2						54	9	2	30	15.0	22	0	38	830	21.8	98	9	21	187	8.9	37	20	268	13.4	24
1994	SHR	16	2		0	8						24	4	1	10	10.0	10	0	43	688	16.0	69	4	2	10	5.0	5				
1995	SHR	16	2		0	5						42	7	1	38	38.0	38	1	51	790	15.5	60	6					6	133	22.2	31
1996	OTT	4				1						18	3						13	240	18.5	49	3								
5	Years	51	7		1	16						138	23	4	78	19.5	38	1	148	2572	17.4	98	22	23	197	8.6	37	31	527	17.0	39
GENE WALL Gene RB 5'11 200 Saskatchewan B: 3/2/1958 Draft: TE 1980 SAS																															
1980	TOR	2																													
MARCUS WALL Marcus WR 5'9 165 North Carolina B: 12/10/1973 Fayetteville, NC																															
1997	MTL	1				1													3	64	21.3	34	0					3	92	30.7	46
MILAM WALL Milam HB 6'1 200 North Carolina B: 1939 Draft: 11-84 1961 BUF																															

Year	Team	GP	FM	FF	FR	TK	SK	YDS	IR	YDS	PD	PTS	TD	RA	YDS	AVG	LG	TD	REC	YDS	AVG	LG	TD	PR	YDS	AVG	LG	KOR	YDS	AVG	LG
1961	HAM	4										1	0	1	1	1.0	1	0	2	16	8.0	10	0								
1962	HAM	8							1	12																					
2	Years	12							1	12		1	0	1	1	1.0	1	0	2	16	8.0	10	0								
ALEX WALLACE Alfred Alexander DB 5'11 180 San Jose State B: 2/2/1979 Long Beach, CA																															
2002	BC	2				4			0	0	1																				
DARRELL WALLACE Darrell RB 5'9 180 Missouri B: 9/27/1965 St. Louis, MO																															
1989	BC	17	3		1	0						30	5	75	382	5.1	61	2	18	115	6.4	20	1	83	780	9.4	93	57	1225	21.5	91
1990	BC	5	1		1	0								5	13	2.6	5	0	5	19	3.8	12	0	16	59	3.7	27	10	163	16.3	29
1990	CAL	5	2		0	2						12	2	55	290	5.3	33	1	13	89	6.8	25	1	7	31	4.4	21	4	84	21.0	33
1990	Year	10	3		0	2						12	2	60	303	5.1	33	1	18	108	6.0	25	1	23	90	3.9	27	14	247	17.6	33
1993	SAS	3	2		0	0						18	3	36	156	4.3	26	3	15	181	12.1	35	0	11	55	5.0	16	7	122	17.4	25
1994	SAS	3				4								6	33	5.5	13	0	4	11	2.8	6	0	5	47	9.4	14	2	29	14.5	15
4	Years	28	8		2	6						60	10	177	874	4.9	61	6	55	415	7.5	35	2	122	972	8.0	93	80	1623	20.3	91
JASON WALLACE Jason K. DH-CB 5'10 170 Virginia B: 8/28/1969 Hampton, VA Pro: E																															
1993	SAC	11	0		1	40			1	26																					
1994	SAC	12				45			3	32	3	6	1																		
1995	SA	16				63			4	47	7																				
1996	OTT	1				0																									
4	Years	40	0		1	148			8	105	10	6	1																		
LARRY WALLACE Larry WR 6'1 178 Southern California B: 9/9/1970 Pro: E																															
1993	SAC	2				0																									
MARK WALLACE Mark LB 6'2 215 Winston-Salem State B: 12/12/1964 Wilmington, DE																															
1989	HAM	5				0																									
STAN WALLACE Stanley Howard S-OE 6'3 208 Illinois B: 11/15/1931 Hillsboro, IL D: 12/6/1999 Urbana, IL Draft: 1-6 1954 CHIB Pro: N																															
1960	TOR+	14							3	66									3	74	24.7	41	0								
1961	TOR	10												1	3	3.0	3	0	6	103	17.2	36	0	1	7	7.0	7				
2	Years	24							3	66				1	3	3.0	3	0	9	177	19.7	41	0	1	7	7.0	7				
VIC WALLACE Victor WR 5'11 165 Spokane Falls CC; Idaho B: 1960																															
1983	CAL	6										18	3						17	393	23.1	57	3					10	180	18.0	43
1984	SAS	4										6	1						10	160	16.0	59	1								
2	Years	10										24	4						27	553	20.5	59	4					10	180	18.0	43
TRAYVON WALLER Trayvon Ray DB 6'0 172 El Camino JC; Illinois B: 5/26/1979 Inglewood, CA																															
2002	TOR	2	0	0	1	3					1																				
2003	HAM	2				4																									
2	Years	4	0	0	1	7					1																				
BRIAN WALLING Brian FB 5'8 185 Acadia B: 9/16/1963 Toronto, ON																															
1987	TOR	4				0																						3	35	11.7	20
1988	EDM	12	1		1	0						12	2	29	148	5.1	22	1	3	7	2.3	6	1								
1989	EDM	10	1		1	0								14	49	3.5	16	0						1	11	11.0	11	1	9	9.0	9
1989	SAS	3				0								7	15	2.1	6	0	2	18	9.0	12	0	1	6	6.0	6				
1989	Year	13	1		1	0								21	64	3.0	16	0	2	18	9.0	12	0	2	17	8.5	11	1	9	9.0	9
1990	EDM	15	3		2	2						18	3	29	162	5.6	31	0	13	80	6.2	15	3								
1991	EDM	18	3		1	21								9	59	6.6	13	0	2	0	0.0	3	0								
1992	EDM	9	1		0	4								43	218	5.1	24	0													
1993	EDM	18	1		0	20								35	161	4.6	17	0	7	65	9.3	15	0	1	-1	-1.0	0				
1994	EDM	16				8								9	52	5.8	14	0	1	9	9.0	9	0								
1995	EDM	17				17						6	1	17	84	4.9	12	1													
1996	HAM	16				13								21	111	5.3	15	0	4	40	10.0	21	0								
10	Years	135	10		5	85						36	6	213	1059	5.0	31	2	32	219	6.8	21	4	3	16	5.3	11	4	44	11.0	20
ROB WALLOW Rob OG-OT 6'4 285 Itawamba CC; Northeast Louisiana B: 10/16/1962																															
1994	SHR	6			1																										
1995	MEM	10				0																									
2	Years	16	0		1	0																									
CRAIG WALLS Craig Stevens LB 6'1 215 Indiana B: 12/24/1958 Pittsburgh, PA Pro: NU																															
1986	OTT	5	0		1		3.0																								
GAVIN WALLS Gavin LB-DE 6'2 225 Coffeyville CC; Arkansas B: 1/29/1980 Ripley, MS Pro: E																															
2005	WPG+	17	0	2	1	43	12.0	68.0	1	10	4	12	2																		
2006	WPG+	18				32	11.0	90.0			1																				
2007	WPG	16	0	1	3	45	9.0	67.0			4	6	1																		
2008	WPG+	18	0	1	1	56	10.0	84.0			2			1	8	8.0	8	0													
2009	WPG	13				24	5.0	33.0			1			1	9	9.0	9	0													
5	Years	82	0	4	5	200	47.0	342.0	1	10	12	18	3	2	17	8.5	9	0													
GREG WALLS Greg DE 6'2 290 South Florida B: 12/24/1979																															
2004	HAM	1				1																									
LENNY WALLS Lenny Brad DH 6'4 194 St. Mary's (California); San Francisco CC; Boston College B: 9/26/1979 Sam Francisco, CA Pro: N																															
2008	CAL	4				24			1	9	0																				
2009	WPG+	18	0	2	1	48			7	93	3	12	2																		
2010	EDM	5	0	1	0	10					2																				
3	Years	27	0	3	1	82			8	102	5	12	2																		
TYRONE WALLS Tyrone TE 6'2 210 Missouri B: 12/31/1947 Chicago, IL Draft: 8B-185 1971 BUF																															
1972	EDM+	16	0		3							48	8	1	-2	-2.0	-2	0	50	811	16.2	67	6								
1973	EDM	16	3		1							24	4	1	-7	-7.0	-7	0	41	494	12.0	44	4								
1974	EDM+	16	1		0							12	2						50	623	12.5	42	2								
1975	EDM+	12	1		0							4	0						31	390	12.6	29	0								
1976	EDM	16	2		0							12	2						48	583	12.1	51	2					1	20	20.0	20
1977	BC	9																	18	153	8.5	20	0								
1978	BC	4																	5	56	11.2	32	0								
7	Years	89	7		4							100	16	2	-9	-4.5	-2	0	243	3110	12.8	67	14					1	20	20.0	20
CHUCK WALSH Chuck DL 6'4 238 Waterloo B: 2/9/1978 Windsor, ON Draft: 5B-45 2002 TOR																															
2002	TOR	15	0	0	1	14	1.0	9.0	1	0	0																				
2003	TOR	18				26	2.0	10.0																				1	11	11.0	11
2004	TOR	18				5																									
2005	TOR	6				6																									
4	Years	57	0	0	1	51	3.0	19.0	1	0	0																	1	11	11.0	11
DON WALSH Don (Nobby) OG-DG-DE 6'0 215 Denver; Montreal Ints. B: 1933 D: 4/1/2006																															
1953	CAL	15																													
1954	CAL	5																													
1955	CAL	3																													
1955	SAS	4																													
1955	Year	7																													
1956	SAS	11	0		2																										
1957	SAS	16	0		2																										
1958	SAS	15																													
1959	SAS	13																													
1960	SAS	16	0		2																										
1961	SAS	16																													
1962	SAS	16																													
1963	SAS	13	0		2							1	0															1	0	0.0	0
1964	SAS	15	0		1																										
12	Years	154	0		9							1	0															1	0	0.0	0
GERRY WALSH Gerry HB-E-T 6'2 210 B: 1921																															
1946	HAM	11																													

Year	Team	GP	FM	FF	FR	TK	SK	YDS	IR	YDS	PD	PTS	TD	RA	YDS	AVG	LG	TD	REC	YDS	AVG	LG	TD	PR	YDS	AVG	LG	KOR	YDS	AVG	LG
1947	HAM	10										15	3					3													
2	Years	21										15	3					3													
JIM WALTER Jim DB 5'11 195 St. Lambert Saints; Tulsa B: 1942																															
1965	TOR	4																						9	63	7.0	11				
1965	MTL	9	0		1																							2	21	10.5	10
1965	Year	13																										2	21	10.5	10
1966	MTL	12							1	23																		1	11	11.0	11
1967	MTL	14							1	17														6	33	5.5	13				
1968	MTL	14	0		2				2	54		6	1											7	73	10.4	16				
1969	MTL	4	2		0																			11	79	7.2	14				
1970	SAS	14							2	58														79	642	8.1	28				
1971	SAS	14	2		1				5	68														49	383	7.8	22	18	373	20.7	34
1972	SAS	16	3		1				1	0														59	406	6.9	19				
1973	SAS	16	1		1				1	47														69	451	6.5	30				
9	Years	108	8		6				13	267		6	1											289	2130	7.4	30	21	405	19.3	34
KEN WALTER Kenneth Gene OT 6'4 249 Texas Tech B: 3/2/1958 Corsicana, TX Draft: 8-195 1980 BAL																															
1982	EDM	1																													
1983	EDM	1																													
1983	WPG	1																													
1983	Year	2																													
2	Years	2																													
HARRY WALTERS Harry LB 6'1 220 Maryland B: 7/21/1952 Draft: 12-303 1975 DEN																															
1975	WPG+	16	0		4				1	22																					
1976	WPG*	14	0		1				4	73																					
1977	WPG	16	0		2				4	48																					
1978	WPG	16	0		3				3	47																		1	16	16.0	16
1979	HAM	4																													
1980	EDM	1							1	0																					
6	Years	67	0		10				13	190																		1	16	16.0	16
JOEY WALTERS Joey Laverne WR 5'11 175 Clemson B: 10/29/1954 Florence, SC Pro: NU																															
1977	WPG	4																	6	59	9.8	14	0	1	7	7.0	7	8	193	24.1	36
1977	SAS	10	1		1				1	0		30	5						23	404	17.6	45	4	20	223	11.2	50	0	59		38
1977	Year	14	1		1				1	0		30	5						29	463	16.0	45	4	21	230	11.0	50	8	252	31.5	38
1978	SAS	4	1		0							18	3	1	0	0.0	0	0	17	272	16.0	44	3	9	128	14.2	35				
1979	SAS	6	0		1							30	5						40	772	19.3	52	4	5	62	12.4	16	0	13		13
1980	SAS	7	1		0							6	1						17	326	19.2	32	1	13	190	14.6	44	3	84	28.0	39
1981	SAS*	16	2		0							84	14						91	1715	18.8	72	14	33	257	7.8	24	7	151	21.6	30
1982	SAS*	16	2		0							44	7						102	1692	16.6	12	7								
6	Years	53	7		2				1	0		212	35	1	0	0.0	0	0	296	5240	17.7	72	33	81	867	10.7	50	18	500	27.8	39
KYLE WALTERS Kyle S 5'10 175 Guelph B: 7/23/1973 St. Thomas, ON Draft: 2A-10 1996 HAM																															
1997	HAM	16				12			1	3																					
1998	HAM	18				21																									
1999	HAM	18				23			1	20																					
2000	HAM	18				17																		1	5	5.0	5				
2001	HAM	11	0	0	1	13																									
2002	HAM	17	0	1	0	14																									
2003	HAM	4	0	0	1	13																									
7	Years	102	0	1	2	113			2	23														1	5	5.0	5				
RICK WALTERS Rick SB 5'11 195 Simon Fraser B: 7/19/1971 Mandeville, Jamaica																															
1994	SAS	6	1		0	0						6	1	26	108	4.2	16	1	6	21	3.5	7	0					1	23	23.0	23
1995	SAS	12				7								17	84	4.9	12	0	9	57	6.3	14	0					1	1	1.0	1
1996	SAS	11	0		1	22													4	28	7.0	14	0								
1997	SAS	18	0	0	1	12													25	368	14.7	26	0					3	25	8.3	13
1998	SAS	7				5													5	48	9.6	15	0								
1999	EDM	18	0	0	2	12						18	3						27	256	9.5	19	2	3	11	3.7	7	3	78	26.0	36
2000	EDM	18	0	0	3	6						24	4	1	-5	-5.0	-5	0	47	696	14.8	86	3								
2001	EDM	17	3	0	0	4						8	1						41	396	9.7	18	1	15	173	11.5	68	4	59	14.8	22
2002	EDM	18	2	0	0	9						12	2						26	389	15.0	37	2	2	19	9.5	11				
2003	EDM	13	1	0	0	0						6	1						31	370	11.9	37	1								
10	Years	138	7	0	7	77						74	12	44	187	4.3	16	1	221	2629	11.9	86	9	20	203	10.2	68	12	186	15.5	36
TRENT WALTERS Trent OHB-DH-CB 5'10 187 Indiana B: 11/20/1943 Knoxville, TN																															
1966	EDM	14	5		1							30	5	87	500	5.7	43	4	7	34	4.9	18	0	56	346	6.2	53	19	557	29.3	90
1967	EDM	16	3		0				2	20		6	1	77	321	4.2	32	1	14	124	8.9	18	0	62	403	6.5	35	18	431	23.9	31
2	Years	30	8		1				2	20		36	6	164	821	5.0	43	5	21	158	7.5	18	0	118	749	6.3	53	37	988	26.7	90
ALVIN WALTON Alvin Earl LB 6'0 180 Mount San Jacinto JC; Kansas B: 3/14/1964 Riverside, CA Draft: 3-75 1986 WAS Pro: N																															
1994	BAL	14				44																									
1995	BAL	17				38																									
2	Years	31				82																									
ANDY WALTON Andrew OHB 5'8 180 Jackson State B: 1945																															
1968	MTL	8	2		0							24	4	71	227	3.2	15	0	21	307	14.6	69	4					20	380	19.0	35
1969	OTT	1												10	53	5.3	12	0													
2	Years	9	2		0							24	4	81	280	3.5	15	0	21	307	14.6	69	4					20	380	19.0	35
CHUCK WALTON Charles Richard (Dick) OG 6'3 253 Iowa State B: 7/7/1941 Shattuck, OK D: 10/6/1998 Shattuck, OK Draft: 13-98 1963 SD; 4-55 1963 DET Pro: N																															
1963	MTL+	13																										1	21	21.0	21
1964	MTL	11	0		3																										
1965	HAM+	14																													
1966	HAM*	14																													
4	Years	52	0		3																							1	21	21.0	21
SHANE WALTON Shane Scott DB 5'10 184 Notre Dame B: 10/9/1979 San Diego, CA Draft: 5B-170 2003 STL Pro: N																															
2005	CAL	9	0	0	1	25			1	0	4																				
TIM WALTON Timothy Lee LB 6'0 242 Ball State B: 7/1/1966 Detroit, MI Pro: E																															
1995	SA	2				5					1																				
DAVE WARD David Fontaine LB 6'2 231 Southern Arkansas B: 3/10/1964 Helena, AR Pro: N																															
1990	WPG	5				4	1.0																								
ERIC WARD Eric QB 6'2 220 Richmond B: 4/12/1987 Atlanta, GA																															
2011	EDM	18				1								2	15	7.5	13	0													
FRED WARD Fred WR 5'11 180 Mississippi State B: 8/26/1971 West Point, MS																															
1994	OTT	11	3		0	3						42	7	1	12	12.0	12	1	29	556	19.2	43	6	6	21	3.5	9	19	352	18.5	33
1995	WPG	5	2		0	1						6	1						17	298	17.5	51	1	3	15	5.0	9	5	147	29.4	69
2	Years	16	5		0	4						48	8	1	12	12.0	12	1	46	854	18.6	51	7	9	36	4.0	9	24	499	20.8	69
IAN WARD Ian DT 6'4 245 Western Ontario B: 1/11/1957 Draft: TE 1980 HAM																															
1980	HAM	5																													
1981	OTT	15																													
1982	OTT	5																													
3	Years	25																													
JIM WARD James DT 6'3 288 Slippery Rock B: 9/2/1971																															
1995	MEM	2				2																									
REGGIE WARD Reginald E. WR 5'10 185 Notre Dame B: 8/18/1966 Long Beach, CA																															
1988	OTT	8				2													7	73	10.4	23	0					1	22	22.0	22
1989	OTT	4	1		0							6	1						9	143	15.9	28	0	11	93	8.5	62	12	168	14.0	25
2	Years	12	1		0	2						6	1						16	216	13.5	28	0	11	93	8.5	62	13	190	14.6	25
DEL WARDIEN Darrell E. FL-DB 5'8 185 Montana B: 1/14/1924 MN D: 10/6/2007																															

Year	Team	GP	FM	FF	FR	TK	SK	YDS	IR	YDS	PD	PTS	TD	RA	YDS	AVG	LG	TD	REC	YDS	AVG	LG	TD	PR	YDS	AVG	LG	KOR	YDS	AVG	LG
1947	CAL+	7										17	3					3													
1948	SAS	7										25	5					4					1								
1949	SAS+	14										56	8					6					2								
1950	SAS	14										10	2	88	426	4.8		2	8	199	24.9		0								
1951	SAS	14										10	2	49	158	3.2		1	7	82	11.7		1	29	163	5.6		5	95	19.0	
1952	SAS	13			1							28	0	2	7	3.5	10	0	2	89	44.5	66	0	21	163	7.8	20	10	223	22.3	36
1953	SAS	16										47	1	5	19	3.8		0	3	51	17.0		1	1	0	0.0	0				
1954	SAS	15			2				3	27														1	17	17.0	17				
8	Years	100			3				3	27		193	21	144	610	4.2	10	16	20	421	21.1	66	5	52	343	6.6	20	15	318	21.2	36
BILL WARDLE Bill E 6'1 191 Western Ontario B: 1925																															
1949	TOR	7																													
1951	TOR	1																													
2	Years	8																													
ANDRE WARE Andre Trevor QB 6'2 205 Houston B: 7/31/1968 Galveston, TX Draft: 1-7 1990 DET Pro: EN																															
1995	OTT	7	3		0	1								20	148	7.4	23	0													
1996	BC	4	3		0	0								14	108	7.7	27	0													
1997	TOR	18	1	0	0	0						6	1	6	60	10.0	39	1													
3	Years	29	7	0	0	1						6	1	40	316	7.9	39	1													
SEAN WARE Sean LB 6'2 237 New Hampshire B: 1/31/1987 Bristol, CT																															
2011	CAL	3				5																									
TED WARKENTIN Ted SE-TE 6'4 203 Simon Fraser B: 1947 Draft: 1-7 1969 BC																															
1969	BC	6																	2	30	15.0	21	0								
1970	BC	16	0		2														4	80	20.0	22	0								
1971	EDM	6																	2	29	14.5	19	0								
3	Years	28	0		2														8	139	17.4	22	0								
ERNIE WARLICK Ernest (Big Hoss) OE-DE 6'4 234 North Carolina Central B: 7/21/1932 Washington, DC Pro: N																															
1957	CAL	11							1	0		12	2						24	378	15.8	32	2					2	23	11.5	13
1958	CAL+	16	2		0				3	48		30	5						47	739	15.7	65	4								
1959	CAL+	15	3		0							24	4						53	909	17.2	43	4					2	27	13.5	18
1960	CAL+	16	0		2							24	4						41	820	20.0	80	4					2	17	8.5	17
1961	CAL	15										12	2						37	486	13.1	31	2								
5	Years	73	5		2				4	48		102	17						202	3332	16.5	80	16					6	67	11.2	18
RON WARNER Ron DE 6'2 248 Independence CC; Kansas B: 9/26/1975 Independence, KS Draft: 7B-239 1998 NO Pro: EN																															
2000	WPG	9	0	2	0	20	6.0	53.0			1																				
2006	WPG	17				28	6.0	36.0																							
2007	EDM	15	0	2	0	35	4.0	25.0			1																				
3	Years	41	0	4	0	83	16.0	114.0			2																				
KENT WARNOCK Kent DE-DT 6'7 270 Calgary B: 6/3/1964 St. John, NB Draft: 1-1 1986 CAL																															
1987	CAL	8	0		1	10																									
1988	CAL	13				28																									
1989	CAL	17	0		3	31	14.0																								
1990	CAL*	18	0		4	55	16.0																								
1991	CAL	15				27	4.0																								
1992	CAL	14	0		1	17	4.0	31.0																							
1993	BC	17	0		2	23	4.0	32.0																							
1994	BC	6				5																									
8	Years	108	0		11	196	42.0	63.0																							
ANTONIO WARREN Antonio R. RB 5'10 212 Cal Poly (San Luis Obispo) B: 11/25/1975 San Francisco, CA																															
2001	CAL+	17	2	0	1	2						6	1	59	372	6.3	39	1	15	165	11.0	34	0	74	764	10.3	32	58	1501	25.9	90
2002	CAL	7	1	0	0	1						6	1	23	138	6.0	37	0	11	96	8.7	16	0	27	265	9.8	45	16	507	31.7	99
2004	BC	15	3	0	0	2						36	6	219	1136	5.2	37	5	34	278	8.2	24	1	3	32	10.7	16	38	809	21.3	64
2005	BC	18	7	0	1	4						96	16	205	983	4.8	50	13	68	718	10.6	42	3	1	10	10.0	10	20	468	23.4	68
2006	BC	5	1	0	0	0						8	1	41	169	4.1	16	0	17	169	9.9	32	1	5	15	3.0	7	8	168	21.0	28
5	Years	62	14	0	2	9						152	25	547	2798	5.1	50	19	145	1426	9.8	42	5	110	1086	9.9	45	140	3453	24.7	99
BRIAN WARREN Brian V. LB-DE 6'2 230 Arizona B: 7/25/1962 Phoenix, AZ																															
1987	EDM	13				33	4.0		1	22														1	1	1.0	1				
1988	EDM	18				43	4.0		1	14																					
1989	EDM	8	0		1	7	1.0																								
1990	BC	3				7																									
1990	OTT	2				7	1.0																								
1990	Year	5				14	1.0																								
1991	TOR+	18	1		2	40	10.0																								
1992	TOR	17	0		1	34	9.0	61.0											1	5	5.0	5	0								
1993	TOR	15				21	4.0	61.0																							
7	Years	92	1		4	192	33.0	122.0	2	36									1	5	5.0	5	0	1	1	1.0	1				
DAVID WARREN David DE 6'2 253 Florida State B: 10/14/1978 Tyler, TX																															
2003	BC	2				0																									
GARLAND WARREN Jimmy Garland LB-C-DE-OT 6'1 225 North Texas B: 5/19/1935 Bomarton, TX Draft: 28-335 1958 SF																															
1958	WPG	15	0		4				2	27																					
1959	WPG+	15							3	24																					
1960	WPG	16	0		5				5	55		6	1																		
1961	WPG	13																													
1962	WPG	16							1																						
1964	WPG	5	0		1				1																						
6	Years	80	0		10				12	106		6	1																		
KIRBY WARREN Kirby Chante RB 6'0 185 Pacific B: 3/1/1962 Dallas, TX Draft: TD 1984 LA-USFL Pro: U																															
1987	CAL	5	3		1	0						12	2	55	230	4.2	28	1	10	146	14.6	46	1					6	117	19.5	31
PETE WARREN Peter FL 5'10 180 East York Argos Ints. B: 1941																															
1965	TOR	10																	13	192	14.8	27	0								
1966	CAL	9																	3	39	13.0	14	0								
2	Years	19																	16	231	14.4	27	0								
TERRENCE WARREN Terrence Lee WR 6'1 200 Hampton B: 8/2/1969 Suffolk, VA Draft: 5-114 1993 SEA Pro: N																															
1998	TOR	2				0													4	26	6.5	14	0								
DON WARRINGTON Don OHB-TE 6'0 205 Simon Fraser B: 6/7/1948 Burnaby, BC D: 12/4/1980 Edmonton, AB Draft: 4-31 1970 BC																															
1971	EDM	10												1	14	14.0	14	0	7	109	15.6	20	0								
1972	EDM	15	0		3							12	2	3	18	6.0	9	0	35	458	13.1	39	2								
1973	EDM	16	3		0							6	1	6	36	6.0	16	0	30	358	11.9	33	1								
1974	EDM	16	2		0							24	4	7	29	4.1	7	0	44	509	11.6	42	4					1	0	0.0	0
1975	EDM	9	1		0							18	3	20	77	3.9	12	0	26	464	17.8	61	3								
1976	EDM	16	1		0							6	1	15	59	3.9	11	0	43	449	10.4	34	1					4	37	9.3	20
1977	EDM	16	2		0							12	2	1	3	3.0	3	0	35	527	15.1	78	2								
1978	EDM	16										6	1	32	152	4.8	17	0	7	27	3.9	9	1	3	16	5.3	8				
1979	EDM	14	1		0									22	124	5.6	25	0	3	17	5.7	10	0	1	1	1.0	1				
9	Years	128	10		3							84	14	107	512	4.8	25	0	230	2918	12.7	78	14	4	17	4.3	8	5	37	7.4	20
BRADY WASHBURN Brady OT 6'5 305 Clemson; Appalachian State B: 10/2/1979 Pro: E																															
2003	TOR	5				0																									
CLIFF WASHBURN Clifton OT 6'5 285 The Citadel B: 1/25/1980 Rutherfordton, NC Pro: EU																															
2006	TOR	5				1																									
2008	TOR	3				0																									
2011	EDM	5	0	0	2	0																									
3	Years	13	0	0	2	1																									
MIKE WASHBURN Michael WR-SB 6'0 190 New Brunswick B: 12/28/1958 Oromocto, NB Draft: 5-44 1980 MTL																															

Year	Team	GP	FM	FF	FR	TK	SK	YDS	IR	YDS	PD	PTS	TD	RA	YDS	AVG	LG	TD	REC	YDS	AVG	LG	TD	PR	YDS	AVG	LG	KOR	YDS	AVG	LG
1982	BC	1																													
1983	BC	2																													
1983	MTL	13	0		1														3	66	22.0	28	0					1	0	0.0	0
1983	Year	15	0		1														3	66	22.0	28	0					1	0	0.0	0
1984	MTL	9										6	1						5	153	30.6	39	1								
1985	MTL	9																	1	7	7.0	7	0								
4	Years	21	0		1							6	1						9	226	25.1	39	1					1	0	0.0	0
AL WASHINGTON Alvin Kent LB 6'3 255 Ohio State B: 9/25/1958 Erie, PA Draft: 4-86 1981 NYJ Pro: N																															
1983	OTT	16	1		1		1.5		2	8																					
1984	OTT+	16	0		3		8.5		1	-2		6	1																		
1985	OTT	16							1	12																					
1986	OTT	6																													
4	Years	54	1		4		10.0		4	18		6	1																		
BUTCHIE WASHINGTON James QB 6'0 210 Akron B: 11/5/1977 Columbus, OH																															
2001	HAM	17				0																									
2002	HAM	18	2	0	0	1																									
2	Years	35	2	0	0	1																									
CHARLES WASHINGTON Charles Edwin LB 6'1 212 Texas*; Cameron B: 10/8/1966 Shreveport, LA Draft: 7B-185 1989 IND Pro: N																															
1996	TOR	2				2																									
DAVE WASHINGTON David Eugene TE 6'4 228 Santa Monica CC; Southern California B: 12/28/1940 Pro: N																															
1963	SAS	3																	3	59	19.7	38	0								
1969	WPG	16	1		0							24	4						35	587	16.8	39	4					1	4	4.0	4
2	Years	19	1		0							24	4						38	646	17.0	39	4					1	4	4.0	4
DICK WASHINGTON Dick HB 6'1 210 Notre Dame B: 7/6/1933 Vanderbilt, PA																															
1957	CAL	5	0		1							6	1	12	50	4.2	19	0	5	71	14.2	27	0					1	36	36.0	36
1958	CAL	4	2		0				0	10		18	3	37	159	4.3	24	3	4	36	9.0	14	0								
2	Years	9	2		1				0	10		24	4	49	209	4.3	24	3	9	107	11.9	27	0					1	36	36.0	36
DUKE WASHINGTON Talmadge HB-FB 5'11 190 Washington State B: 10/11/1932 Forest, MS Draft: 10-118 1955 PHI																															
1958	BC	1												4	2	0.5	6	0	1	16	16.0	16	0								
JIM WASHINGTON Jim RB 6'1 205 Clemson B: 10/13/1951 Walterboro, SC Draft: 6-131 1974 KC																															
1974	WPG	7	0		1							24	4	117	582	5.0	41	3	2	11	5.5	8	0	1	5	5.0	5	1	26	26.0	26
1975	WPG	11	1		1							24	4	125	665	5.3	30	3	24	222	9.3	29	1					3	64	21.3	25
1976	WPG*	16	4		2							84	14	219	1277	5.8	68	12	47	428	9.1	33	2	1	4	4.0	4				
1977	WPG*	16	3		1							36	6	252	1262	5.0	54	5	33	263	8.0	61	1								
1978	WPG	16	2		0							42	7	200	1032	5.2	31	6	38	252	6.6	30	1								
1979	WPG	16	3		0							18	3	204	918	4.5	31	1	37	259	7.0	32	2								
1980	SAS	9	1		0							12	2	89	391	4.4	20	1	29	277	9.6	31	1								
7	Years	91	14		5							240	40	1206	6127	5.1	68	31	210	1712	8.2	61	8	2	9	4.5	5	4	90	22.5	26
JOE WASHINGTON Joe WR 6'3 202 Tuskegee B: 1/16/1970 Quincy, FL																															
1994	BAL	14				2						6	1						12	192	16.0	62	1								
JOHN WASHINGTON John Willie CB-S 6'1 202 Tulane B: 8/11/1953 Dallas, TX Draft: 8-204 1975 LARM																															
1976	SAS	3												6	28	4.7	13	0						1	5	5.0	5				
KEITH WASHINGTON Keith Anton WR 5'11 190 none B: 10/8/1959 Albany, NY																															
1985	EDM	1																													
LARRY WASHINGTON Larry HB 6'1 210 Tennessee-Martin B: 11/9/1954																															
1977	EDM	9	7		0									96	445	4.6	46	0	18	130	7.2	23	0								
1978	EDM	5	1		0							12	2	52	227	4.4	37	2	8	62	7.8	28	0								
1979	WPG	6										6	1	51	195	3.8	18	1	7	45	6.4	20	0								
1980	WPG	1												4	8	2.0	4	0	1	5	5.0	5	0								
4	Years	21	8		0							18	3	203	875	4.3	46	3	34	242	7.1	28	0								
MARCUS WASHINGTON Marcus Leon CB 6'1 217 Colorado B: 2/26/1975 Mobile, AL Draft: 6-180 1999 NE																															
2000	WPG	6				14			1	10	1																				
2001	WPG	1				0																									
2002	OTT	2				1	1.0																								
3	Years	9				15	1.0		1	10	1																				
MARK WASHINGTON Mark CB 5' 187 Rutgers B: 4/16/1973 Temple Hills, MD Pro: E																															
1997	MTL	2				13																									
1998	MTL	8	0	0	2	20					3																				
1999	MTL	18				61			2	0	2																				
2000	MTL	14	1	0	3	55			3	109	4	6	1																		
2001	MTL	17	0	2	1	63			3	69	8																				
2002	MTL	14	0	1	2	12			1	48	0	12	2																		
2003	BC+	18	0	1	1	78	1.0	1.0	1	0	4																				
2004	BC	17	0	0	2	60			3	21	9																				
2005	BC	12	0	0	1	58			1	39	5																				
2006	BC	18	0	1	1	70			3	95	6	6	1															1	0	0.0	0
2007	BC	18	0	1	1	41					1																				
11	Years	156	1	6	14	531	1.0	1.0	17	381	42	24	4															1	0	0.0	0
MIKE WASHINGTON Michael WR 6'2 179 Charleston Southern B: 3/13/1981 New Orleans, LA																															
2007	SAS	9				1						18	3						15	268	17.9	51	3					1	0	0.0	0
2008	SAS	3				0													5	46	9.2	11	0								
2	Years	12				1						18	3						20	314	15.7	51	3					1	0	0.0	0
MIKE WASHINGTON Mike WR 5'9 173 Texas Lutheran B: 6/10/1955																															
1977	WPG	5	2		0														8	107	13.4	39	0	13	127	9.8	19	4	108	27.0	41
MIKE WASHINGTON Michael R. RB 5'10 190 Washington State B: 10/29/1957 Memphis, TN																															
1982	SAS	10	1		0							30	5	103	614	6.0	33	5	14	105	7.5	14	0								
1983	SAS	15	2		2							12	2	155	639	4.1	28	1	45	447	9.9	44	1					2	42	21.0	21
1984	SAS	6												41	175	4.3	22	0	14	94	6.7	26	0					5	99	19.8	26
3	Years	31	3		2							42	7	299	1428	4.8	33	6	73	646	8.8	44	1					7	141	20.1	26
RICARDO WASHINGTON Ricardo LB 6'4 220 Louisiana State B: 4/28/1971 Bogalusa, LA																															
1994	BC	3				5																									
1995	BC	2				1																									
1995	OTT	5				7					1																				
1995	Year	7				8					1																				
2	Years	5				13					2																				
SHARRON WASHINGTON Sharron HB 6'0 195 Truman State B: 1/29/1943 Draft: 8B-201 1967 HOU																															
1967	HAM	1												2	3	1.5	3	0										1	19	19.0	19
STANLEY WASHINGTON Stanley Elliot WR 5'10 189 Texas Christian B: 1/2/1961 Dallas, TX Draft: 9-106 1983 MIC-USFL																															
1984	MTL	4										12	2						14	208	14.9	48	2								
1984	SAS	6										6	1						20	308	15.4	42	1								
1984	Year	10										20	3						34	516	15.2	48	3								
1985	TOR	1																	1	13	13.0	13	0								
2	Years	5										18	3						35	529	15.1	48	3								
TONY WASHINGTON Tony OT 6'7 295 Trinity Valley CC; Abilene Christian B: 2/17/1986 New Orleans, LA																															
2011	CAL	5				1																									
VIC WASHINGTON Victor Arnold FL 5'10 194 Wyoming B: 3/23/1946 Plainfield, NJ Draft: 4-87 1970 SF Pro: N																															
1968	OTT*	14	4		0				1	25		60	10	109	678	6.2	34	7	25	426	17.0	60	2	6	127	21.2	36	26	853	32.8	104
1969	OTT*	12	7		0							84	14	117	717	6.1	85	5	47	760	16.2	49	8	5	77	15.4	27	18	509	28.3	107
1970	BC	9	1		0							12	2	3	10	3.3	5	0	28	475	17.0	51	2					20	512	25.6	59
3	Years	35	12		0				1	25		156	26	229	1405	6.1	85	12	100	1661	16.6	60	12	11	204	18.5	36	64	1874	29.3	107
KONRAD WASIELA Konrad DB 5'9 180 British Columbia B: 6/14/1985 Vancouver, BC																															
2007	BC	3				0																									

Year	Team	GP	FM	FF	FR	TK	SK	YDS	IR	YDS	PD	PTS	TD	RA	YDS	AVG	LG	TD	REC	YDS	AVG	LG	TD	PR	YDS	AVG	LG	KOR	YDS	AVG	LG
2008	SAS	3				1																									
2009	MTL	1				1																									
3	Years	7				2																									
HENRY WASZCZUK Henry C-OG 6'0 230 Kent State B: 8/26/1950																															
1975	HAM	16	0		1																										
1976	HAM	16																													
1977	HAM	15	1		0																										
1978	HAM	16	0		3							6	1																		
1979	HAM	16	1		1																										
1980	HAM+	16																													
1981	HAM+	16	0		1														1	-5	-5.0	-5	0								
1982	HAM+	16	0		2																										
1983	HAM	13																													
1984	HAM+	16																													
10	Years	156	2		8							6	1						1	-5	-5.0	-5	0								
MIKE WASZCZUK Mike LB 5'11 234 Slippery Rock B: 8/27/1977 Hamilton, ON Draft: 5-36 2001 HAM																															
2001	SAS	1				0																									
2001	HAM	1				3																									
2001	Year	2				3																									
CHARLIE WATERMAN Charles C 5'8 185 B: 1919																															
1946	HAM	12																													
MARK WATERMAN Mark SB 6'1 190 Snow JC B: 2/14/1962 Red Deer, AB																															
1988	BC	2				0																									
1990	HAM	10	0		3	1																									
1991	HAM	11				8																									
1992	TOR	4	0		2	1						6	1																		
4	Years	27	0		5	10						6	1																		
KERRY WATKINS Kerry Junior WR 5'10 181 Georgia Tech B: 5/16/1979 LaPlace, LA																															
2004	MTL	4				1													4	36	9.0	19	0	12	117	9.8	31	3	43	14.3	28
2005	MTL*	17	2	0	0	4						56	9	3	62	20.7	42	0	97	1364	14.1	75	9								
2006	MTL+	17	2	0	1	2						30	5	7	57	8.1	30	0	86	1153	13.4	68	5								
2007	MTL	15				0						30	5	3	22	7.3	9	0	76	1092	14.4	70	5								
2008	MTL+	17				0						60	10	2	20	10.0	10	0	84	1178	14.0	36	10								
2009	MTL*	18	2	0	0	2						48	8						81	1243	15.3	71	8								
2010	MTL	13				0						48	8	4	23	5.8	20	0	56	970	17.3	54	8								
2011	MTL	12				1						18	3	2	-1	-0.5	1	0	31	395	12.7	22	3	1	4	4.0	4				
8	Years	113	6	0	1	10						290	48	21	183	8.7	42	0	515	7431	14.4	75	48	13	121	9.3	31	3	43	14.3	28
LARRY WATKINS Larry OG-OT 6'4 265 Western Kentucky B: 5/22/1948 Louisville, KY																															
1970	TOR	7																													
1971	HAM	8																													
1972	EDM+	16	0		1																										
1973	EDM	16	0		1																										
1974	EDM*	16																													
1975	EDM	16																													
1976	EDM	9																													
1976	TOR	4																													
1976	Year	13																													
1977	BC	16	0		1																										
1978	BC	16																													
1979	BC	16																													
10	Years	136	0		3																										
TED WATKINS Ted SE 6'3 200 Pacific; Stockton JC; Pacific B: 1941																															
1963	OTT+	14																	32	569	17.8	44	0								
1964	OTT+	13										42	7						29	743	25.6	107	7								
1965	OTT*	14	1		1							48	8						34	724	21.3	55	8					1	0	0.0	0
1966	OTT+	13	1		2							18	3						24	549	22.9	58	3					1	12	12.0	12
1967	HAM	14	1		0							18	3						35	550	15.7	56	3								
5	Years	68	3		3							126	21						154	3135	20.4	107	21					2	12	6.0	12
IRA WATLEY Ira Harry OT 6'6 267 San Diego State B: 11/1/1951 Sacramento, CA																															
1978	WPG	1																													
1978	TOR	1																													
1978	Year	2																													
RAY WATRIN Raymond OG-DT-DE 6'2 240 Utah State B: 2/1/1945																															
1969	CAL	11																													
1970	BC	6																													
1970	WPG	8																													
1970	Year	14																													
1971	WPG	9	0		2																										
1972	WPG	16																													
1973	WPG	3																													
1974	WPG	2																													
1974	MTL	5																													
1974	Year	7																													
1975	MTL	16																													
1977	MTL	16																													
1978	MTL	16																													
1979	MTL*	16	0		2																										
1980	MTL	5																													
1980	OTT	10	0		1																										
1980	Year	15	0		1																										
11	Years	116	0		5																										
ANTHONY WATSON Anthony DE 6'4 265 Eastern Kentucky B: 11/17/1976 Atlanta, GA																															
2002	CAL	2				5					1																				
BRENT WATSON Brent OT 6'4 256 Tennessee B: 12/16/1955 Twin Falls, ID Draft: 10-261 1978 CLE																															
1978	MTL	2																													
CORY WATSON Cory WR-SB 6'2 208 Concordia (Quebec) B: 3/27/1984 Dollard des Ormeaux, QC Draft: 2-9 2010 WPG																															
2010	WPG	15				6						6	1						17	277	16.3	55	1								
2011	WPG	18	3	0	1	12						6	1	2	4	2.0	3	0													
2	Years	33	3	0	1	18						12	2	2	4	2.0	3	0	17	277	16.3	55	1								
CRAIG WATSON Craig OG 6'2 250 Calgary B: 2/12/1963 Mississauga, ON Draft: 7-61 1986 WPG																															
1988	CAL	16				1																									
1989	CAL	17				1																									
2	Years	33				2																									
DARRIUS WATSON Darrius J. DH 6'0 195 Fullerton State; Louisville B: 6/11/1971 Harbor City, CA																															
1995	WPG	18				64	1.0	3.0	1	32	2													1	7	7.0	7	4	57	14.3	27
1996	WPG	9	1		0	26					1	6	1						4	76	19.0	40	1								
2	Years	27	1		0	90	1.0	3.0	1	32	3	6	1						4	76	19.0	40	1	1	7	7.0	7	4	57	14.3	27
DAVE WATSON Carl David OG 6'1 225 Georgia Tech B: 1/5/1941 Barbour County, AL Draft: 11B-87 1963 BOS; 9B-122 1963 CHIB Pro: N																															
1965	EDM	8	0		1																										
DEREK WATSON Derek RB 6'0 212 South Carolina; South Carolina State B: 5/1/1981 Anderson, SC																															
2009	CAL	2				0								5	10	2.0	5	0	1	6	6.0	6	0					3	55	18.3	40
GERALD WATSON Gerald FB 5'10 202 Utah State B: 1944																															

Year	Team	GP	FM	FF	FR	TK	SK	YDS	IR	YDS	PD	PTS	TD	RA	YDS	AVG	LG	TD	REC	YDS	AVG	LG	TD	PR	YDS	AVG	LG	KOR	YDS	AVG	LG
1968	CAL	6												19	47	2.5	6	0	2	11	5.5	9	0								
1969	CAL	16	0		2														1	7	7.0	7	0					1	12	12.0	12
2	Years	22	0		2									19	47	2.5	6	0	3	18	6.0	9	0					1	12	12.0	12
JEFF WATSON Jeff OG 6'3 270 St. Mary's (Canada) B: 12/31/1963 Halifax, NS Draft: 1-8 1986 HAM																															
1986	TOR	3																													
1987	TOR	3				0																									
2	Years	6				0																									
KARLTON WATSON Karlton QB 6'4 207 Winston-Salem State B: 10/26/1961 Detroit, MI																															
1985	BC	2																													
1986	BC	18	1		1									2	10	5.0	13	0													
2	Years	20	1		1									2	10	5.0	13	0													
KEN WATSON Kenneth DH-CB 6'1 190 Livingston B: 11/10/1966 Birmingham, AL Pro: E																															
1989	BC	8	0		1	31			4	72		6	1																		
1990	BC	17				56			3	17																					
1991	BC	9				35			1	19																					
1991	CAL	3				7																						1	6	6.0	6
1991	Year	12				42			1	19																		1	6	6.0	6
1992	CAL	10	0		2	30																									
1993	CAL	17	0		1	48			1	7																		3	14	4.7	10
1994	BAL	18				66			1	0	6	6	1																		
1995	BAL	18	0		2	49			1	0	5																				
1996	MTL	10	0		1	23			2	9	3																				
1997	MTL	3				12					1																				
1999	EDM	9	0	0	1	14					1																				
10	Years	119	0	0	8	371			13	124	16	12	2															4	20	5.0	10
LOUIS WATSON Louis WR 5'11 175 Mississippi Valley State B: 1/11/1963 Mobile, AL Pro: N																															
1988	OTT	6	1		0	1						12	2						15	274	18.3	72	2	1	0	0.0	0	3	71	23.7	31
PAT WATSON Pascal L., Jr. LB 6'1 215 Mississippi State B: 6/3/1943 D: 9/25/1999 Athens, GA																															
1965	TOR	14							1	0																					
PAUL WATSON Paul K 6'0 195 Washington State B: 8/13/1956 Draft: 3-26 1978 EDM																															
1981	SAS	16	1		0							126	0											1	0	0.0	0				
PETE WATSON Rodney Peter HB 6'1 210 Tufts B: 9/19/1950 New York, NY Pro: N																															
1973	TOR	4	2		0							12	2	52	295	5.7	29	1	7	154	22.0	80	1					6	149	24.8	34
1974	SAS	8	1		0							18	3	48	253	5.3	79	1	29	467	16.1	78	2								
2	Years	12	3		0							30	5	100	548	5.5	79	2	36	621	17.3	80	3					6	149	24.8	34
REMI WATSON Remi Fitzgerald WR 6'0 174 South Carolina State; Bethune-Cookman B: 8/8/1964 Plant City, FL Pro: N																															
1988	OTT	11	1		0	3						12	2						23	476	20.7	56	2	2	31	15.5	17	5	59	11.8	15
SPENCER WATT Spencer WR-SB 6'1 180 Minot State; Simon Fraser B: 12/15/1988 Draft: 3-18 2010 TOR																															
2010	TOR	11	0	0	1	2						12	2						14	201	14.4	50	2								
2011	TOR	17				4						6	1	1	2	2.0	2	0	29	345	11.9	48	1								
2	Years	28	0	0	1	6						18	3	1	2	2.0	2	0	43	546	12.7	50	3								
LORNE WATTERS Lorne LB 6'2 195 Calgary B: 1951 Draft: 7-55 1973 CAL																															
1974	BC	11																													
1975	BC	7																													
2	Years	18																													
RON WATTON Ron C-LB 6'1 219 Toronto Balmy Beach Jrs. B: 1932 Toronto, ON																															
1953	TOR	1																													
1954	TOR	12																										1	12	12.0	12
1956	BC	16							1	24																					
1957	BC	16							3	48																					
1958	BC	14																	0	1		1	0								
1959	BC	15																													
1960	BC	16	0		2																										
1961	BC	16																													
1962	HAM+	14																													
9	Years	120	0		2				4	72									0	1		1	0					1	12	12.0	12
J.C. WATTS Julius Caesar, Jr. QB 5'11 200 Oklahoma B: 11/18/1957 Eufaula, OK Draft: 8B-213 1981 NYJ																															
1981	OTT	9	3		1							6	1	37	260	7.0	26	1													
1983	OTT	12	6		0							30	5	76	552	7.3	29	5	1	14	14.0	14	0								
1984	OTT	15	5		2							6	1	61	357	5.9	26	1													
1985	OTT	16	10		3							6	1	106	710	6.7	38	1													
1986	TOR	11	8		1							26	4	35	227	6.5	32	4													
1986	OTT	6	3		0							6	1	31	206	6.6	22	1													
1986	Year	17	11		1							32	5	66	433	6.6	32	5													
5	Years	63	35		7							80	13	346	2312	6.7	38	13	1	14	14.0	14	0								
JON WAUFORD Jon DE 6'2 255 Miami (Ohio) B: 2/11/1970																															
1994	LV	2				6																									
HOWIE WAUGH Howard FB 6'0 200 Tulsa B: 1931 Draft: 6B-73 1953 LARM																															
1954	CAL	14	1		0							35	7	166	1043	6.3	43	7	6	86	14.3	20	0					8	113	14.1	27
1957	CAL	10	2		0							12	2	96	499	5.2	36	2	8	122	15.3	42	0					1	22	22.0	22
2	Years	24	3		0							47	9	262	1542	5.9	43	9	14	208	14.9	42	0					9	135	15.0	27
GUY WAY Guy T 6'0 220 UCLA																															
1952	CAL	1																													
CLINTON WAYNE Clinton DT 6'3 275 Ohio State B: 5/17/1977 Toronto, ON Draft: 3-21 2000 CAL																															
2001	CAL	10				7																						1	6	6.0	6
2002	OTT	18				25	2.0	10.0																				1	2	2.0	2
2003	OTT	17	0	0	1	30	2.0	24.0			1																				
2004	OTT	8	0	0	1	6	1.0	9.0																							
2004	EDM	8	0	1	1	15					1																				
2004	Year	16	0	1	2	21	1.0	9.0			1																				
2005	EDM	4				3	2.0	13.0																							
2005	MTL	11	0	0	1	10																									
2005	Year	15	0	0	1	13	2.0	13.0																							
2006	MTL	5				6					1																				
2006	HAM	7				12	5.0	33.0																							
2006	Year	12				18	5.0	33.0			1																				
2007	HAM	13	0	1	1	16																									
2008	HAM	5				3																									
2008	EDM	10				0																									
2008	Year	15				3																									
8	Years	80	0	2	5	133	12.0	89.0			5																	2	8	4.0	6
PATRICK WAYNE Patrick LB 6'3 225 Richmond Raiders Jrs.; Simon Fraser B: 2/22/1964 Guyana Draft: 2B-12 1987 OTT																															
1987	OTT	13	0		1	27	1.0												1	9	9.0	9	0					1	14	14.0	14
1988	OTT	18	0		2	26																						2	29	14.5	15
1989	OTT	18	0		2	64	3.0		1	14									0	-3		-3	0								
1990	OTT	18				57	8.0																								
1991	OTT	17	0		1	63	4.0																								
1992	OTT	17	1		5	65	4.0	36.0	1	4																		1	0	0.0	0
1993	BC	1				0																									
1993	TOR	5				0																									
1993	Year	6				6																									
1994	OTT	16				10	1.0																								

Year	Team	GP	FM	FF	FR	TK	SK	YDS	IR	YDS	PD	PTS	TD	RA	YDS	AVG	LG	TD	REC	YDS	AVG	LG	TD	PR	YDS	AVG	LG	KOR	YDS	AVG	LG
8	Years	118	1		11	312	21.0	36.0	2	18									1	6	6.0	9	0					4	43	10.8	15
BILLY WAYTE Bill DB 5'10 185 Fresno State B: 7/3/1938																														
1961	MTL	13							2	48														5	29	5.8	9				
1962	MTL	14							3	134		6	1																		
1963	MTL	14							5	77				1	1	1.0	1	0						1	0	0.0	0				
1964	MTL	14	1		0				1	27														1	4	4.0	4	3	100	33.3	44
1965	HAM*	14	1		1				9	142		12	2																		
1966	HAM	14	0		1				4	101																					
6	Years	83	2		2				24	529		18	3	1	1	1.0	1	0						7	33	4.7	9	3	100	33.3	44
JIM WEATHERALL James Preston, Jr. DT 6'4 245 Oklahoma B: 10/26/1929 Graham, OK D: 8/2/1992 Oklahoma City, OK Draft: 2-17 1952 PHI Pro: N																														
1954	EDM	13																													
CHARLIE WEATHERBIE Charles A. QB 6'2 192 Oklahoma State B: 1/17/1955 Sedan, KS																														
1979	HAM	1	1		0									3	9	3.0	13	0													
1979	OTT	1																													
1979	Year	2	1		0									3	9	3.0	13	0													
1980	OTT	6	3		1									8	35	4.4	11	0													
1980	HAM	4	1		0									4	21	5.3	10	0													
1980	Year	10	4		0									12	56	4.7	11	0													
2	Years	7	5		1									15	65	4.3	13	0													
CARL WEATHERS Carl LB 6'2 220 Long Beach CC; San Diego State B: 1/14/1948 New Orleans, LA Pro: N																														
1971	BC	5																													
1972	BC	7																													
1973	BC	6	0		1																										
3	Years	18	0		1																										
WAYNE WEATHERS Wayne LB-DE 6'4 235 Manitoba B: 6/4/1973 Toronto, ON Draft: 6-44 1997 WPG																														
1998	WPG	18	0	1	1	25	1.0	8.0																							
1999	WPG	18	0	1	0	26	1.0	6.0																							
2000	WPG	14				17																		1	10	10.0	10	1	2	2.0	2
2001	WPG	17	0	1	0	30	5.0	37.0			1																	1	15	15.0	15
2002	WPG	18	0	0	4	40	5.0	30.0				6	1																		
2003	TOR	18	0	0	1	57	3.0	11.0																							
2004	SAS	7				3																									
2005	SAS	18	0	1	0	3						2	0						1	5	5.0	5	0								
8	Years	128	0	4	6	201	15.0	92.0			1	8	1						1	5	5.0	5	0	1	10	10.0	10	2	17	8.5	15
ROSS WEAVER Ross OT-TE 6'6 304 Air Force B: 11/3/1982 Denver, CO																														
2008	TOR	6				1																									
WALT WEAVER Leroy DB-P 6'0 210 Adams State B: 1937 Draft: 10-133 1962 CHIB																														
1962	CAL	14							4	81		5	0											1	4	4.0	4				
CLOYD WEBB Cloyd William OE 6'4 210 Iowa B: 1941 D: 3/31/1991 Milwaukee County, WI Draft: 11B-85 1964 BUF; 13-182 1964 CHIB																														
1965	WPG	2																	1	20	20.0	20	0								
1965	HAM	6	1									6	1						8	111	13.9	29	1								
1965	Year	8	1									6	1						9	131	14.6	29	1								
DEE WEBB Demetrice A. DH-CB 5'11 186 Florida B: 12/8/1984 Jacksonville, FL Draft: 7B-236 2006 JAC Pro: N																														
2009	CAL	1	0	0	1	2																									
2011	TOR	11	1	0	0	22			1	0	2													1	-5	-5.0	-5				
2011	HAM	4				8					1																				
2011	Year	15				0																									
2	Years	12	1	0	1	32			1	0	3													1	-5	-5.0	-5				
JEFF WEBB Jeffrey Leon WR 6'2 211 San Diego State B: 1/31/1982 Pontiac, MI Draft: 6B-190 2006 KC Pro: N																														
2010	TOR	4				1													13	137	10.5	27	0								
RALPH WEBBER Ralph T 6'0 212 none B: 8/26/1926 Montreal, QC																														
1946	MTL	2																													
1948	MTL	11																													
2	Years	13																													
BOB WEBER Robert Wayne C 190 Colorado State B: 4/21/1933 Fort Collins, CO D: 11/1/2008 Tucson, AZ																														
1957	EDM	8																													
GORD WEBER Gordon LB 6'3 211 Ottawa B: 2/12/1965 Ottawa, ON Draft: 7-49 1989 OTT																														
1990	OTT	4				0																									
1991	OTT	18	0		1	17	1.0																							
1992	OTT	18	0		1	33	1.0	8.0	1	7																					
1993	OTT	10				21																									
4	Years	50	0		2	71	2.0	8.0	1	7																					
ALEX WEBSTER Alex I. OHB 6'3 218 North Carolina State B: 4/19/1931 Kearny, NJ D: 3/3/2012 Port St. Lucie, FL Draft: 11-124 1953 WAS Pro: N																														
1953	MTL	7										30	6					4					2								
1954	MTL+	14							2	0		80	16	176	984	5.6	23	10	23	376	16.3	44	6					18	393	21.8	41
2	Years	21							2	0		110	22	176	984	5.6	23	14	23	376	16.3	44	8					18	393	21.8	41
JIMMY WEBSTER Jim LB 5'11 204 Marquette B: 11/16/1936 Draft: SS 1960 BOS; 19-228 1960 NYG																														
1960	HAM	7											15	71	4.7	16	0	14	139	9.9	18	0								
KEITH WEBSTER Keith OHB-DB 5'7 170 Winnipeg Rods Jrs.; St. Vital Bulldogs Ints. B: 8/31/1937 Winnipeg, MB																														
1959	WPG	2											2	28	14.0	23	0						2	9	4.5	5				
1960	WPG	2	1																					4	4	1.0	2				
2	Years	4	1										2	28	14.0	23	0						6	13	2.2	5				
KEN WEBSTER Ken OG Saskatoon Hilltops Jrs.; Boise JC; Linfield B: // Yorkton																														
1963	SAS	3																													
MIKE WEBSTER Mike DT 6'4 256 Notre Dame B: 1944																														
1966	BC	16																													
1967	MTL	14																													
1968	MTL	14																													
1969	MTL	14	0		1																										
1970	MTL	14																													
5	Years	72	0		1																										
JACK WEDLEY Jack E 5'10 180 B: 1917 England D: 9/29/2003																														
1946	TOR	12										2	0																		
1947	TOR	10																													
1948	TOR	12										10	2										1								
1949	TOR	10																													
1950	TOR	12										5	1																		
1951	SAS	14																													
6	Years	70										17	3										1								
MARC WEEKLY Marc QB 5'11 190 Pacific Lutheran																														
1994	LV	3																													
CHUCK WEEKS Charles T 6'3 235 Southern California B: 1931 Draft: 7-82 1954 LARM																														
1957	TOR	2																													
JOE WEINBERG Joachim WR 6'1 190 Johnson C. Smith B: 10/17/1967 Washington, DC D: 12/15/2008 Los Angeles, CA Draft: 11-290 1991 SD																														
1991	EDM	3				1													10	118	11.8	24	0								
GARY WEINLEIN Gary John DB 5'10 180 Hudson Valley CC B: 6/22/1953 Albany, NY																														
1978	TOR	2	1		0																			2	2	1.0	3				
ARNIE WEINMEISTER Arnold George T 6'4 235 Washington B: 3/23/1923 Rhine, SK D: 6/28/2000 Seattle, WA Draft: 17-166 1945 BKN Pro: AN																														
1954	BC	5																													
1955	BC	10																													
2	Years	15																													
GLEN WEIR Glen DT 6'2 242 none B: 7/23/1951 London, ON																														

Year	Team	GP	FM	FF	FR	TK	SK	YDS	IR	YDS	PD	PTS	TD	RA	YDS	AVG	LG	TD	REC	YDS	AVG	LG	TD	PR	YDS	AVG	LG	KOR	YDS	AVG	LG
1972	MTL	14																												
1973	MTL	14	1		2																									
1974	MTL	16			2																									
1975	MTL*	16	0		3																									
1976	MTL+	15	0		2																									
1977	MTL*	16	0		3																									
1978	MTL+	15	0		4																									
1979	MTL+	16	0		1																									
1980	MTL	16	0		1																									
1981	MTL	16	0		1		6.0																							
1982	MTL+	16					7.0																							
1983	MTL	16					7.0																							
1984	MTL	16					2.0																							
13	Years	202	1		19		22.0																							
KEN WEIR Ken QB-E-T 5'11 177 Regina Bombers Jrs. B: 1928 Regina, SK																														
1949	SAS	14																												
1950	SAS	14																7	82	11.7		0								
1951	SAS	9																												
3	Years	37																7	82	11.7		0								
ROB WEIR Rob SB-DB 6'0 190 Queen's B: 2/10/1972																														
1996	EDM	7				4																								
1996	TOR	3	0		2	0																								
1996	Year	10	0		2	4																								
ROBERT WEIR Robert DT 6'3 270 Southern Methodist B: 2/4/1961 Birmingham, England																														
1987	OTT	12				3	1.0																							
1988	OTT	10				2	2.0																							
1989	OTT	18				4																								
1990	HAM	8				10	1.0																							
1992	TOR	2				0																								
5	Years	50				19	4.0																							
DON WEISS Don QB 6'1 200 Juniata B: 1947																														
1969	WPG	16	3		0							6	1	29	196	6.8	42	1													
1970	SAS	10										6	1	18	91	5.1	24	1													
2	Years	26	3		0							12	2	47	287	6.1	42	2													
MORGAN WELCH Morgan RB 5'8 205 Weber State B: 2/14/1976 Winnipeg, MB																														
2000	TOR	15				4								1	0	0.0	0	0										1	12	12.0	12
2001	EDM	2				0																								
2	Years	17				4								1	0	0.0	0	0										1	12	12.0	12
JIM WELLER Jim G 5'10 204 B: 1932																														
1954	TOR	2																												
TERRY WELLESLEY Terry OHB 6'0 205 Tennessee Tech B: 1/7/1948 Belleville, ON																														
1970	OTT	14	2		0							18	3	53	235	4.4	19	0	10	244	24.4	75	3								
1971	OTT	5												4	10	2.5	8	0	2	7	3.5	12	0								
1972	OTT	14										30	5	35	163	4.7	44	2	22	395	18.0	73	3								
1973	OTT	13	1		0							6	1	12	53	4.4	20	0	10	170	17.0	52	1								
1974	OTT	12												7	12	1.7	8	0	4	54	13.5	33	0								
1975	HAM	4																0	9		9	0								
1976	HAM	1																												
7	Years	63	3		0							54	9	111	473	4.3	44	2	48	879	18.3	75	7								
ANGELO WELLS Angelo DE 6'3 265 Morgan State B: 1/19/1954 Annapolis, MD Pro: U																														
1977	HAM	8																												
1978	HAM	4																												
1979	HAM	7																												
3	Years	19																												
GEORGE WELLS George Oliver DE 6'1 240 New Mexico State B: 10/31/1947 Oakland, CA Draft: 5B-122 1971 SF																														
1971	TOR	9	0		1																									
1972	TOR	1																												
1972	HAM	10	0		1				2	9																					
1972	Year+	11	0		1				2	9																					
1973	HAM	11																												
1974	SAS*	16																												
1975	SAS+	16																												
1976	SAS+	16			1																									
1977	SAS	13	0		1																									
1978	SAS	7																												
1978	HAM	9																												
1978	Year	16																												
8	Years	89	0		4				2	9																					
JAMES WELLS James DB 5'10 178 Missouri State B: 2/9/1979 Seattle, WA																														
2001	BC	1	0	0	1	1					1																			
JOEL WELLS Joel Whitlock OHB-DB 6'1 198 Clemson B: 11/26/1935 Columbia, SC Draft: 2-18 1957 GB Pro: N																														
1957	MTL	10							1	18		24	4	92	463	5.0	41	3	18	299	16.6	76	1					4	40	10.0	15
1958	MTL+	14							4	63		48	8	134	722	5.4	25	6	42	414	9.9	28	2	1	2	2.0	2	17	424	24.9	50
1959	MTL	11										24	4	105	461	4.4	63	3	35	390	11.1	53	1	2	2	1.0	2	23	395	17.2	33
3	Years	35							5	81		96	16	331	1646	5.0	63	12	95	1103	11.6	76	4	3	4	1.3	2	44	859	19.5	50
RIO WELLS Rio DH-CB 5'9 185 Fresno State B: 11/29/1973 Marrero, LA																														
1998	EDM	15	0	1	0	55			2	18	5													1	0	0.0	0				
1999	EDM	2				6																								
2000	WPG	15	0	1	0	44	1.0	9.0	2	52	5																				
2001	TOR	13	0	1	2	35	1.0	4.0	1	0	7																				
4	Years	45	0	3	2	140	2.0	13.0	5	70	17													1	0	0.0	0				
JOHN WELTON John DE 6'4 230 Queen's; Wake Forest B: 1930																														
1952	OTT	12																												
1953	OTT	14																												
1954	OTT	1																1	3	3.0	3	0								
1955	OTT	8							1	0																					
1955	TOR	3																												
1955	Year	11																												
1956	TOR	14																												
1957	TOR+	13																1	13	13.0	13	0					1	0	0.0	0
1958	TOR	14																												
7	Years	76							1	0									2	16	8.0	13	0					1	0	0.0	0
JOE WENDRYHOSKI Joseph Stanley DE 6'2 245 Illinois B: 3/1/1938 West Frankfort, IL D: 11/5/2008 Twin Lakes, WI Draft: 13-102 1961 NYT Pro: N																														
1961	BC	13																										1	2	2.0	2
SAM WESLEY Sam HB-DB 5'10 160 Oregon State B: 1935 Draft: 30-359 1957 CHIB																														
1957	SAS	15	4									24	4	49	157	3.2	15	0	15	451	30.1	92	4	21	98	4.7	30	20	356	17.8	35
DICK WESOLOWSKI Dick FB-TE 6'1 205 North Carolina B: 12/5/1945																														
1969	HAM	14												34	170	5.0	19	0	3	32	10.7	14	0					4	97	24.3	33
1970	HAM	14	2		0							12	2	90	464	5.2	24	2	6	82	13.7	26	0					4	53	13.3	18
1971	HAM	14	3		2							6	1	81	332	4.1	31	0	15	122	8.1	43	0					1	6	6.0	6
1972	HAM	14										6	1	4	9	2.3	8	1													
1973	CAL	16										12	2	52	244	4.7	20	2	17	241	14.2	37	0					3	41	13.7	20

Year	Team	GP	FM	FF	FR	TK	SK	YDS	IR	YDS	PD	PTS	TD	RA	YDS	AVG	LG	TD	REC	YDS	AVG	LG	TD	PR	YDS	AVG	LG	KOR	YDS	AVG	LG
1974	CAL	16												2	5	2.5	5	0	14	201	14.4	31	0					1	10	10.0	10
1975	CAL	16																	4	46	11.5	19	0								
1976	CAL	5																	5	78	15.6	32	0								
8	Years	109	5		2							36	6	263	1224	4.7	31	5	64	802	12.5	43	0					13	207	15.9	33
RICKY WESSON Ricky Charles DB 5'9 163 Southern Methodist B: 6/29/1955 Dallas, TX Pro: N																															
1979	WPG	10	1		0				4	18														25	205	8.2	40	9	200	22.2	39
1980	WPG	2																						1	38	38.0	38				
2	Years	12	1		0				4	18														26	243	9.3	40	9	200	22.2	39
ART WEST Art (Whippet) HB 5'11 185 none B: 1917																															
1946	TOR	1																													
1947	MTL	1																													
2	Years	2																													
BERNARD WEST Curtis Bernard LB 6'0 225 North Texas B: 3/13/1958 Conroe, TX Pro: U																															
1981	HAM	2	0		1																										
1981	SAS	2					1.0																								
1981	Year	4	0		1		1.0																								
1982	SAS	11					3.0																								
2	Years	13	0		1		4.0																								
BILL WEST Bill FB 6'3 215 Eastern Oregon B: 1934 Draft: 13-155 1957 DET																															
1957	SAS	8	1											23	68	3.0	11	0	6	28	4.7	11	0					1	11	11.0	11
BILL WEST William Henry DB 5'10 185 Tennessee State B: 3/3/1947 Steubenville, OH Draft: 10A-238 1971 OAK Pro: NW																															
1974	TOR	4																													
BRANDON WEST Brandon RB 5'10 193 Western Michigan B: 9/8/1987 Brunswick, GA																															
2011	SAS	13	1	0	0	0								45	233	5.2	22	0	7	55	7.9	18	0	9	104	11.6	48	44	985	22.4	42
DALE WEST Kenneth Dale S-CB-DH-FL-OHB 6'2 195 Arizona; Saskatchewan B: 1942																															
1962	SAS	15	1						1			18	3	3	-7	-2.3	1	0	13	306	23.5	79	3					1	0	0.0	0
1963	SAS+	16	0		1				10	226		24	4	1	3	3.0	3	0	5	174	34.8	86	3								
1964	SAS+	16							2	3														2	14	7.0	11	1	0	0.0	0
1965	SAS+	16	1		1				2	1														19	87	4.6	11	1	23	23.0	23
1966	SAS	12																						2	6	3.0	6				
1967	SAS	15							2	33														5	34	6.8	29				
1968	SAS	16																													
7	Years	106	2		2				17	263		42	7	4	-4	-1.0	3	0	18	480	26.7	86	6	28	141	5.0	29	3	23	7.7	23
DAVEY WEST Dave FL-FW-S 5'9 175 none B: 1925																															
1948	TOR	6																													
1951	CAL	14										40	8	48	136	2.8	21	2	17	403	23.7	33	5	32	345	10.8		7	230	32.9	90
1952	CAL	15			0							25	5	39	135	3.5	25	0	13	415	31.9	85	3	14	113	8.1	14	23	602	26.2	112
1953	WPG	9												5	-8	-1.6		0	6	57	9.5		0	20	129	6.5		4	120	30.0	
1954	EDM	16	2		0							5	1	11	24	2.2	8	1	2	78	39.0	69	0	49	265	5.4	28	8	130	16.3	33
1955	EDM	11	2		0							5	1	7	13	1.9	9	0	3	41	13.7	15	1	34	193	5.7	12	4	43	10.8	12
1956	HAM	14										30	5	1	1	1.0	1	0	10	205	20.5	34	5	35	300	8.6	37	7	124	17.7	28
1957	TOR	12							1	0		18	3	25	87	3.5	23	1	4	38	9.5	13	2	46	479	10.4	56	9	222	24.7	42
1959	OTT	14										1	0						19	355	18.7	31	0	58	315	5.4	20				
1960	OTT	13										36	6						14	418	29.9	91	6	23	130	5.7	13				
1961	OTT	4										6	1						5	157	31.4	61	1								
11	Years	128	4		0				1	0		166	30	136	388	2.9	25	4	93	2167	23.3	91	23	311	2269	7.3	56	62	1471	23.7	112
EDDIE WEST Ed QB 6'2 215 North Carolina State B: 1933 Draft: 17-205 1956 CLE																															
1956	CAL	2	0		1				1	3									4	59	14.8	37	0								
FRANK WEST Frank DH-CB-LB 5'11 175 Illinois State B: 3/21/1972 Magnolia, AR																															
1996	OTT	17	0		2	35					5	6	1																		
1997	HAM	17	0	0	1	54					7	6	1											1	9	9.0	9				
1998	HAM	13	0	1	1	46			4	39	2																				
1999	HAM	8				15			1	7	2																				
2000	HAM	3				8	2.0	24.0	1	0	2																				
5	Years	58	0	1	4	158	2.0	24.0	6	46	18	12	2											1	9	9.0	9				
JAMES WEST James Newcombe LB 6'2 220 Texas Southern B: 12/19/1956 Fort Worth, TX																															
1982	CAL	9	0		2		1.0																								
1983	CAL+	15	0		3		8.5		2	61																					
1984	CAL	13	0		1		4.0		2	31		6	1																		
1985	WPG	5					3.0																								
1986	WPG	18	0		2		4.0		2	3		6	1																		
1987	WPG*	18			1	75	7.0																								
1988	WPG+	17	0		4	76	8.0		3	63																					
1989	WPG*	12				69	5.0		3	64																					
1990	WPG	8	0		1	37	2.0		4	25																					
1991	WPG	16	0		1	81	3.0		2	0																					
1992	WPG	16	0		4	62	5.0	38.0	1	49		6	1																		
1993	BC	17	0		1	81	4.0	39.0	2	5																					
12	Years	164	0		20	481	54.5	77.0	21	301		18	3																		
JERRY WEST Jerry F. OG 5'11 235 Michigan State B: 8/16/1945 Durand, MI																															
1967	BC	5																													
MARCUS WEST Marcus Vern DL 6'3 268 Memphis B: 11/6/1983 Amory, MS Pro: E																															
2007	HAM	4				5																									
PAT WEST Patrick Michael HB 6'0 201 Pittsburgh; Southern California B: 2/21/1923 Florence, PA D: 2/7/1996 Winston-Salem, NC Draft: 28-290 1945 CLE Pro: N																															
1949	EDM	13										19	1					1													
BRIAN WESTELL Brian DE 6'3 235 British Columbia B: 1/23/1949 Montreal, QC																															
1973	TOR	14																													
CLEVE WESTER Cleve G 6'2 230 Auburn B: 8/22/1936 Lowndes County, GA D: 8/3/2009 Draft: 22-262 1958 NYG																															
1959	TOR	13																										7	74	10.6	23
CURTIS WESTER Curtis OG-OT 6'3 255 Texas A&M-Commerce B: 5/7/1951 Lawton, OK D: 5/8/1995 Las Vegas, NV Draft: 9-228 1973 CLE																															
1973	BC	7																													
1974	BC*	16	0		1																										
1975	BC	10																													
1976	TOR	8																													
1979	SAS	16																													
5	Years	57	0		1																										
DAVID WESTERBROOKS David DE 6'4 265 Howard B: 3/23/1968 Miami, FL																															
1993	SAC	9				3																									
BOB WESTLAKE Bob HB-FB 6'0 204 none B: 1927																															
1949	HAM	12										5	1					1													
1950	TOR	6										10	2					2													
1951	TOR	1																													
1952	CAL	8										15	3	23	270	11.7	75	3													
1953	CAL	15										5	1	15	113	7.5	75	1	2	24	12.0	16	0					2	24	12.0	
1955	MTL	8							1	0		5	1	5	23	4.6	8	1													
6	Years	50							1	0		40	8	43	406	9.4	75	8	2	24	12.0	16	0					2	24	12.0	
RON WESTON Ron E 6'3 187 B: 1928																															
1949	HAM	3																													
SEAN WESTON Pete Sean DB 5'9 185 Texas A&M B: 5/26/1981 Inglewood, CA																															
2005	OTT	8	0	2	1	15																									
JOHNNY WESTRUM John Howard E-T 6'4 235 Minnesota B: 3/6/1923 Minneapolis, MN D: 7/5/2000 St. Louis Park, MN																															
1947	WPG	8										5	1										1								

Year	Team	GP	FM	FF	FR	TK	SK	YDS	IR	YDS	PD	PTS	TD	RA	YDS	AVG	LG	TD	REC	YDS	AVG	LG	TD	PR	YDS	AVG	LG	KOR	YDS	AVG	LG
1948	WPG	12										5	1										1								
2	Years	20										10	2										2								
TROY WESTWOOD Troy K-P 5'10 165 Augustana (South Dakota) B: 3/21/1967 Dauphin, MB Draft: 6-48 1991 WPG																															
1991	WPG	8				0						75	0																		
1992	WPG*	18				1						199	0																		
1993	WPG+	18	2		0	1						209	0																		
1994	WPG+	18				2						213	0																		
1995	WPG	18				0						153	1	1	12	12.0	12	1													
1996	WPG	18	1		0	0						156	0	1	3	3.0	3	0													
1997	WPG	18				1						164	0						1	14	14.0	14	0								
1998	WPG	18				1						144	0																		
1999	WPG	18				1						141	0																		
2000	WPG	18	2	0	0	2						195	0	2	-3	-1.5	7	0													
2001	WPG	18				3						159	0																		
2002	WPG	18	2	0	0	0						203	0																		
2003	WPG	18	4	0	0	1						198	0																		
2004	WPG	18				0						166	0	1	8	8.0	8	0													
2005	WPG	18				1						138	0	1	6	6.0	6	0						1	6	6.0	6				
2006	WPG	18	1	0	0	2						137	0																		
2007	WPG	12	1	0	0	1						94	0																		
2009	WPG	3	0	0	0	0						4	0																		
18	Years	293	13	0	0	17						2748	1	6	26	4.3	12	1	1	14	14.0	14	0	1	6	6.0	6				
ALAN WETMORE Alan LB-FB 6'3 225 Acadia B: 5/17/1970 Halifax, NS Draft: 1-5 1993 WPG																															
1993	WPG	2				0																									
1994	WPG	7	0		1	7																									
1995	WPG	15				17								2	7	3.5	4	0	3	17	5.7	7	0								
1996	MTL	18	0		1	22								2	19	9.5	13	0										1	1	1.0	1
1997	MTL	18	3	1	3	29																									
1998	MTL	3				2																									
6	Years	63	3	1	5	77								4	26	6.5	13	0	3	17	5.7	7	0					1	1	1.0	1
PAUL WETMORE Paul LB 6'3 227 Acadia B: 10/10/1966 Halifax, NS Draft: 2-15 1989 BC																															
1989	BC	18				7																									
1990	BC	17				7	1.0																								
1991	BC	18	0		3	51	4.0																								
1992	BC	17	0		2	53	4.0	51.0																							
1993	SAS	3				5																									
1993	OTT	3				4																									
1993	Year	6				9																									
5	Years	73	0		5	127	9.0	51.0																							
JERRY WHALEN Gerald Cornelius T-G 6'1 240 Canisius B: 4/23/1928 Buffalo, NY D: 11//1973 Pro: A																															
1949	TOR	12																													
TEX WHALEN Raymond C-T 6'1 245 Buffalo																															
1949	TOR	4																													
MARV WHALEY Marvin E 6'4 205 Morgan State B: 1925																															
1950	TOR	12										20	4										3								
1951	TOR	12										10	2										2								
2	Years	24										30	6										5								
PAUL WHALEY Paul DB-RB 6'0 185 Guelph B: 8/8/1953 Draft: 3-22 1976 HAM																															
1976	HAM	4												1	2	2.0	2	0	2	30	15.0	18	0								
1977	HAM	9																	2	29	14.5	15	0								
2	Years	13												1	2	2.0	2	0	4	59	14.8	18	0								
KENNY WHEATON Kenneth Tyrone DH-S 5'10 193 Oregon B: 3/8/1975 Phoenix, AZ Draft: 3C-94 1997 DAL Pro: N																															
2003	TOR	18	0	4	1	80	1.0	5.0	2	31	5																				
2004	TOR	16	0	3	0	57	2.0	7.0	2	12	7																				
2005	TOR+	16	0	3	0	74			1	17	2																				
2006	TOR+	16	0	1	0	82			2	0	1																				
2007	TOR*	17	0	2	2	71	2.0	13.0	4	169	6	6	1																		
2008	TOR+	15	0	4	0	50	2.0	13.0	4	68	7																				
6	Years	98	0	17	3	414	7.0	38.0	15	297	28	6	1																		
RUSS WHEATON Russ G 5'11 177																															
1946	MTL	1																													
REG WHEELER Reg T B: 1920																															
1948	HAM	6																													
RON WHEELER Ronald Wayne TE 6'5 235 Merritt JC; Washington B: 9/5/1958 Oakland, CA Pro: NU																															
1987	CAL	7				2						6	1						22	340	15.5	43	1					1	12	12.0	12
TED WHEELER Theodore I., III OG-OT 6'3 240 West Texas A&M B: 9/16/1945 Detroit, MI Draft: 9-227 1967 STL Pro: NW																															
1971	BC	7			1																										
1972	BC	7																													
1973	BC	16	0		1																										
3	Years	30	0		2																										
ERNIE WHEELWRIGHT Ernest Lamour, IV WR 6'5 220 Minnesota B: 7/10/1984 Columbus, OH Pro: N																															
2011	SAS	2				0													2	18	9.0	11	0								
GREG WHELAN Greg LB 6'1 210 Edmonton Huskies Jrs.; Alberta B: 12/21/1983 Edmonton, AB																															
2009	EDM	5				2																									
BILL WHISLER Bill DE-OT-DT 6'3 221 Iowa B: 11/15/1940 Yankton, SD Draft: 13-169 1962 WAS																															
1962	WPG	9																	6	79	13.2	29	0								
1963	WPG	15																													
1964	WPG+	16	0		2				3	15		1	0																		
1965	WPG	5																													
1966	WPG	16	0		2																										
1967	WPG+	16																													
1968	WPG+	16	0		2																										
1969	WPG+	16	1		2				1	5																					
1970	BC	15	0		1																										
1971	MTL	14	0		1																										
10	Years	138	1		10				4	20		1	0						6	79	13.2	29	0								
BRANDON WHITAKER Brandon RB 5'10 198 Baylor B: 9/7/1985 Edmond, OK																															
2009	MTL	2				1						6	1	26	151	5.8	36	0	6	38	6.3	13	1								
2010	MTL	3				0						12	2	20	111	5.6	22	2	11	96	8.7	36	0								
2011	MTL*	18	2	0	0	4						60	10	226	1381	6.1	58	4	72	638	8.9	35	6								
3	Years	23	2	0	0	5						78	13	272	1643	6.0	58	6	89	772	8.7	36	7								
DENNY WHITAKER William Denis QB-E 148 Royal Military College B: 2/27/1915 Calgary, AB D: 5/30/2001 Oakville, ON																															
1946	HAM	2																													
DEONCE' WHITAKER Deonce' RB 5'6 180 San Jose State B: 10/25/1978 Las Vegas, NV																															
2002	BC	5				0						12	2	20	74	3.7	10	2	1	1	1.0	1	0	13	153	11.8	43	8	156	19.5	32
2003	WPG	1	1	0	0	0																		3	40	13.3	18				
2003	MTL	12	3	0	0	0						26	4	119	560	4.7	46	2	20	237	11.9	52	2	5	75	15.0	26	14	276	19.7	46
2003	Year	13	4	0	0	0						26	4	119	560	4.7	46	2					2	8	115	14.4	26				
2	Years	6	4	0	0	0						38	6	139	634	4.6	46	4	21	238	11.3	52	2	21	268	12.8	43	22	432	19.6	46
ALVIN WHITE Alvin George QB 6'3 219 Orange Coast JC; Oregon State B: 3/26/1953 Ontario, CA Draft: 15-385 1975 LARM Pro: UW																															
1978	TOR	5	2		0							18	3	15	47	3.1	15	3													
1980	CAL	3																													

Year	Team	GP	FM	FF	FR	TK	SK	YDS	IR	YDS	PD	PTS	TD	RA	YDS	AVG	LG	TD	REC	YDS	AVG	LG	TD	PR	YDS	AVG	LG	KOR	YDS	AVG	LG
1980	BC	1																										2	56	28.0	34
1980	Year	4																										2	56	28.0	34
2	Years	8	2		0							18	3	15	47	3.1	15	3										2	56	28.0	34
BILL WHITE Bill T 5'11 204 NDG Maple Leafs Jrs.																															
1948	MTL	8																													
BOB WHITE Bob OG-DE 6'0 214 St. James Rams Jrs. B: 1942																															
1963	WPG	16																													
1964	WPG	8	0		1																										
2	Years	24	0		1																										
BRENT WHITE Brent DeWayne DE 6'4 254 Michigan B: 2/28/1967 Wichita Falls, TX Draft: 11A-284 1990 CHIB Pro: E																															
1993	SAC	17	0		1	32																									
1994	BAL	1				0																									
2	Years	18	0		1	32																									
BRIAN WHITE Brian S 6'0 190 Dartmouth B: 4/21/1973																															
1995	BAL	3	0		1	6						6	1																		
CHRIS WHITE Christopher James DT 6'3 281 Nevada-Las Vegas; Southern University B: 9/28/1976 Shreveport, LA Draft: 7B-246 1999 JAC Pro: N																															
2002	SAS	3				5																									
CHUCK WHITE Charles L., III WR 6'1 185 Maryland B: 10/5/1955 Fort Knox, KY																															
1978	HAM	1																													
DARYL WHITE Robert Daryl OG-OT 6'3 250 Nebraska B: 10/12/1951 Newark, NJ Draft: 4B-98 1974 CIN; 4-43 1974 POR WFL Pro: N																															
1975	OTT	5																										1	0	0.0	0
1976	HAM	3																													
2	Years	8																										1	0	0.0	0
DERRICK WHITE Derrick Wayne DB 5'8 185 Oklahoma B: 11/11/1965 Lubbock, TX Draft: 6-164 1988 MIN Pro: E																															
1988	OTT	5				15																						8	190	23.8	33
1989	OTT	5				14																									
1990	OTT	8	0		1	41	1.0		1	16																					
3	Years	18	0		1	70	1.0		1	16																		8	190	23.8	33
ED WHITE Eddie Glynn RB 6'0 225 Tulsa B: 6/6/1951 Cason, TX Draft: 13B-321 1973 DEN Pro: W																															
1973	CAL	2												2	5	2.5	5	0	1	35	35.0	35	0					3	34	11.3	17
EMMETT WHITE Emmett RB 6'0 205 Utah State B: 10/6/1979 Ogden, UT																															
2002	BC	2				0								6	30	5.0	12	0						3	17	5.7	8	4	76	19.0	27
ERIK WHITE Erik QB 6'5 220 Bowling Green State B: 9/12/1970 Canton, OH Pro: E																															
1994	TOR	11	1		1	1								4	32	8.0	17	0													
1995	TOR	8				1								4	26	6.5	13	0													
1995	BC	4				0																									
1995	Year	12				1								4	26	6.5	13	0													
2	Years	19	1		1	2								8	58	7.3	17	0													
ERNIE WHITE Ernest Rudolph, II OHB 5'8 180 Dayton B: 1/26/1938																															
1960	HAM	4												3	13	4.3	7	0	1	3	3.0	3	0	6	149	24.8	108	3	55	18.3	23
1961	OTT	9							2	54		6	1	30	271	9.0	45	1	1	25	25.0	25	0	24	147	6.1	16	14	325	23.2	44
1962	OTT+	14										60	10	136	804	5.9	45	5	31	758	24.5	67	5					16	429	26.8	48
1963	OTT	12										42	7	62	395	6.4	47	4	20	468	23.4	68	3					19	665	35.0	85
1964	OTT	5	1		0									19	88	4.6	12	0	1	3	3.0	3	0					7	138	19.7	32
1965	MTL	5	2		1							6	1	29	109	3.8	9	1	5	150	30.0	74	0					2	41	20.5	30
6	Years	49	3		1				2	54		114	19	279	1680	6.0	47	11	59	1407	23.8	74	8	30	296	9.9	108	61	1653	27.1	85
FREEMAN WHITE Freeman, II OE 6'5 225 Nebraska B: 12/17/1943 Montgomery, AL Draft: 2-11 1966 DEN; 9-132 1966 NYG Pro: N																															
1970	OTT	7																	7	148	21.1	29	0								
GEORGE WHITE George Rodney, Jr. LB-DH 5'11 204 Boston College B: 11/17/1977 Detroit, MI																															
2000	SAS*	18	1	1	2	127	3.0	15.0			4																				
2001	SAS+	18	1	0	1	128	3.0	17.0	2	8	4																				
2002	SAS	5				10																									
2003	CAL	18	0	2	0	100	3.0	22.0			8																				
2004	CAL	18	0	1	1	99	5.0	36.0	2	97	2	6	1																		
2005	CAL+	17	0	4	3	136	3.0	16.0	2	54	5	6	1											1	-1	-1.0	-1	1	0	0.0	0
2006	CAL	7	0	2	1	39					1																				
2006	BC	3				7																									
2006	Year	10				46					1																				
7	Years	101	2	10	8	646	17.0	106.0	6	159	24	12	2											1	-1	-1.0	-1	1	0	0.0	0
JAFUS WHITE Jafus DB 6'3 215 Texas A&M-Kingsville B: 4/16/1957 Cameron, TX Draft: 10-253 1980 GB Pro: U																															
1981	TOR	2																													
JAMEL WHITE Jamel M. RB 5'9 215 Antelope Valley JC; South Dakota B: 2/11/1977 Los Angeles, CA Pro: N																															
2007	TOR	3	1	0	0	1								27	92	3.4	15	0	2	5	2.5	3	0								
2007	MTL	1	1	0	0	2								5	10	2.0	9	0										2	28	14.0	14
2007	Year	4	2	0	0	3								32	102	3.2	15	0	2	5	2.5	3	0					2	28	14.0	14
JERMAINE WHITE Jermaine WR 6'6 220 Kentucky B: 7/28/1978																															
2002	MTL	1				0																									
JIM WHITE James Charles TE 6'3 253 Northeastern JC; Colorado State B: 9/5/1948 Chicago, IL Draft: 3-73 1972 NE Pro: N																															
1971	BC	12			1														2	28	14.0	15	0								
JOHN WHITE John L. OE 6'3 230 Texas Southern B: 10/9/1935 Pro: N																															
1963	EDM	2																	4	31	7.8	11	0								
JOHN HENRY WHITE John Henry RB 5'9 190 Louisiana Tech B: 8/23/1955 Shreveport, LA Draft: 8-195 1978 KC																															
1978	BC	7	1		1							12	2	56	276	4.9	42	2	21	195	9.3	37	0					1	18	18.0	18
1979	BC	16	6		1							30	5	149	776	5.2	52	3	42	422	10.0	84	2								
1980	BC	16	4		1							30	5	148	834	5.6	38	4	43	283	6.6	35	1								
1981	BC	16	3		0							6	1	89	482	5.4	41	0	45	386	8.6	27	1								
1982	BC	16	2		1							36	6	111	624	5.6	24	5	38	290	7.6	25	1					3	52	17.3	23
1983	BC	14	1		1							48	8	84	441	5.3	30	7	31	404	13.0	57	1								
1984	BC	16	4		2							30	5	102	523	5.1	42	3	47	492	10.5	66	2								
1985	BC	16	4		2							6	1	75	265	3.5	17	1	44	391	8.9	30	0								
1986	BC	18	1		1							12	2	81	402	5.0	28	2	32	310	9.7	36	0								
1987	BC	3				0								19	92	4.8	15	0	13	134	10.3	48	0								
10	Years	138	26		10	0						210	35	914	4715	5.2	52	27	356	3307	9.3	84	8					4	70	17.5	23
REGGIE WHITE Reginald Andre RB 6'0 228 Oklahoma State B: 7/11/1979 Houston, TX Pro: N																															
2004	EDM	5				1													10	71	7.1	15	0								
RICHARD WHITE Richard LB 6'0 217 Simon Fraser B: 2/25/1960 Toronto, ON Draft: 3-21 1983 SAS																															
1984	SAS	6																													
1986	BC	1																													
2	Years	7																													
ROBB WHITE Robb Steven DT 6'4 270 South Dakota B: 5/26/1965 Aberdeen, SD Pro: EN																															
1993	SAC	18				33	2.0	12.0																							
TED WHITE Tederal Duralle QB 6'2 225 Howard B: 5/29/1976 Baton Rouge, LA Pro: E																															
2003	MTL	18				0								3	15	5.0	8	0													
2004	MTL	18				0						6	1	7	25	3.6	12	1													
2005	MTL	18	2	0	1	1								8	60	7.5	22	0													
3	Years	54	2	0	1	1						6	1	18	100	5.6	22	1													
TODD WHITE Todd WR 6'0 195 Fullerton State B: 9/15/1965 Draft: 7-176 1988 PHI																															
1989	BC	3																	9	115	12.8	42	0	5	37	7.4	13	2	27	13.5	14
TONY WHITE Tony LB 6'1 250 UCLA B: 3/22/1979 Key West, FL																															
2003	OTT	2				4																									
2004	OTT	11				37	2.0	11.0																							
2005	HAM	3				5																									

Year	Team	GP	FM	FF	FR	TK	SK	YDS	IR	YDS	PD	PTS	TD	RA	YDS	AVG	LG	TD	REC	YDS	AVG	LG	TD	PR	YDS	AVG	LG	KOR	YDS	AVG	LG
3	Years	16				46	2.0	11.0																							
VICTOR WHITE Victor CB 6'0 205 Winston-Salem State																															
2004	HAM	1				0																									
WES WHITE Wes DL 6'7 305 Duke B: 11/12/1977																															
2001	BC	14				1																									
WILFORD WHITE Wilford Parley (Whizzer) FW 5'9 171 Arizona State B: 9/26/1928 Mesa, AZ Draft: 3-36 1951 CHIB Pro: N																															
1955	TOR	3										23	3						11	213	19.4	79	3								
WILL WHITE Will D. DB 6'0 202 Florida B: 6/25/1970 Draft: 7- 1993 PHX																															
1995	SHR	16	0		2	34			2	8	3																				
WILLIE WHITEHEAD William DE 6'3 291 Auburn B: 1/26/1973 Tuskegee, AL Pro: EN																															
1995	BAL	1				0																									
1997	HAM+	15	0	0	1	43	13.0	104.0			1																				
1998	HAM	7				19	3.0	21.0																							
3	Years	23	0	0	1	62	16.0	125.0			1																				
DOUNIA WHITEHOUSE Dounia DB 6'1 205 Charleston Southern B: 3/29/1978 Bokobo, Chad Draft: 3A-20 2003 EDM																															
2003	EDM	3				1																									
2004	EDM	1				0																									
2005	CAL	4				1																									
3	Years	8				2																									
REG WHITEHOUSE Reg OT-OG-DT-LB 6'0 235 NDG Maple Leafs Jrs. B: 10/8/1932 D: 8/6/2008 Chilliwack, BC																															
1952	SAS	15										6	0	1	2	2.0	2	0													
1953	SAS	16										5	0															1	0	0.0	0
1954	SAS	16																													
1955	SAS	16										4	0																		
1956	SAS	15	0		2							74	0																		
1957	SAS	16	0		2				1	9		40	0																		
1958	SAS	16										12	0																		
1959	SAS	15										40	0																		
1960	SAS	16										27	0																		
1961	SAS	16										60	0															1	0	0.0	0
1962	SAS	16										41	0																		
1963	SAS	15										30	0																		
1964	SAS	16										16	0																		
1965	SAS	16																													
1966	SAS	16																													
15	Years	236	0		4				1	9		355	0	1	2	2.0	2	0										2	0	0.0	0
TOM WHITEHOUSE Tom G 5'11 210 Montreal Jrs. B: 1938																															
1958	SAS	8																													
1959	SAS	9																													
2	Years	17																													
DAVE WHITESIDE Dave OG-OT 6'3 244 Queen's B: 9/24/1949																															
1975	TOR	10																													
1976	TOR	13																													
2	Years	23																													
A.D. WHITFIELD A.D., Jr. RB 5'10 200 North Texas B: 9/2/1943 Rosebud, TX Pro: NW																															
1970	BC	16	8		1							18	3	155	754	4.9	28	1	27	295	10.9	71	2								
THOMAS WHITFIELD Thomas DB 5'9 190 Syracuse B: 11/2/1982 Detroit, MI Draft: 2B-13 2005 MTL																															
2006	MTL	9				5			1	12	0																				
AL WHITING Allen SB 6'0 186 East Carolina B: 1/27/1970 Tucson, AZ																															
1994	LV	12				2								1	-5	-5.0	-5	0	14	195	13.9	36	0	7	34	4.9	10				
HALL WHITLEY Hall Wood, III LB 6'2 225 Texas A&M-Kingsville B: 7/18/1935 Draft: 15-173 1957 BAL Pro: N																															
1957	WPG	16							1	15																					
1958	WPG	5																													
1958	BC	8	0		2																										
1958	Year	13	0		2																										
1959	BC	1																													
3	Years	22	0		2				1	15																					
JAMES WHITLEY James LaVell CB 5'11 190 Michigan B: 5/13/1979 Decatur, IL Pro: N																															
2001	MTL	14	0	1	0	31	1.0	3.0	2	18	4																				
2005	MTL	9	0	1	0	24			1	43	3																				
2005	BC	3	0	1	0	9																									
2005	Year	12	0	2	0	23			1	43	3																				
2	Years	23	0	3	0	64	1.0	3.0	3	61	7																				
KEVIN WHITLEY Kevin CB 5'10 190 Georgia Southern B: 2/26/1970 Greenville, NC																															
1993	TOR	13	0		2	37																						1	12	12.0	12
1994	TOR	10				33	1.0	10.0	2	57	6																				
2	Years	23	0		2	70	1.0	10.0	2	57	6																	1	12	12.0	12
ARKEE WHITLOCK Arkee RB 5'10 195 Coffeyville CC; Southern Illinois B: 5/10/1984 Rock Hill, SC																															
2009	EDM	17	5	0	0	1						78	13	211	1293	6.1	60	12	44	392	8.9	35	1					14	397	28.4	65
2010	EDM	9				1						30	5	118	689	5.8	40	4	12	78	6.5	16	1								
2011	EDM	2	1	0	0	0								17	92	5.4	18	0	2	9	4.5	6	0					5	93	18.6	22
3	Years	28	6	0	0	2						108	18	346	2074	6.0	60	16	58	479	8.3	35	2					19	490	25.8	65
KEN WHITLOCK Ken HB 175 Virginia State B: 1921																															
1948	TOR	4										7	1					1													
KEN WHITNEY Ken OT-OG 6'4 285 California Lutheran B: 7/1/1965 Montreal, QC Draft: 2A-10 1990 BC																															
1990	BC	11				0						6	1						1	5	5.0	5	1								
1991	BC	13				3																									
1992	CAL	1				0																									
1993	TOR	10				0																									
1994	SAS	4				0																									
1994	OTT	2				0																									
1994	Year	6				0																									
5	Years	39				3						6	1						1	5	5.0	5	1								
KEN WHITTEN Ken T-G 6'2 202 Vancouver Jrs. B: 1936																															
1957	BC	4																													
LEROY WHITTLE Leroy OHB 6'0 190 Santa Ana JC; Oregon State B: 3/21/1941 Fresno County, CA D: 12/12/2008 CA																															
1964	EDM	2	1		0									5	18	3.6	7	0						7	53	7.6	21	6	150	25.0	33
RICKY WHITTLE Ricky Jerome RB 5'9 200 Oregon B: 12/21/1971 Fresno, CA Draft: 4-103 1996 NO Pro: N																															
1999	SAS	4	3	0	0	1						12	2	45	135	3.0	16	2	6	84	14.0	22	0					3	57	19.0	31
SEAN WHYTE Sean K-P 5'9 175 South Surrey Big Kahuna Rams Jrs. B: 10/23/1985 Surrey, BC																															
2009	BC	11	1	0	0	1						90	0																		
2010	BC	3				0						27	0																		
2011	MTL	18	1	0	0	1						197	0																		
3	Years	32	2	0	0	2						314	0																		
JEFF WICKERSHAM Jeff QB 6'2 195 Louisiana State B: 12/5/1963 Merritt Island, FL Draft: 10-274 1986 MIA																															
1988	OTT	9	3		0	1						6	1	20	112	5.6	22	1													
DAN WICKLUM Dan LB 6'2 215 Ottawa Sooners Jrs.; Guelph B: 2/28/1965 Edmonton, AB Draft: 1A-3 1988 WPG																															
1988	WPG	17	0		3	34	4.0		1	3																		2	15	7.5	9
1989	CAL	14	0		1	0	1.0																					1	1	1.0	1
1990	CAL	18	0		2	22	1.0							1	12	12.0	12	0													
1991	CAL	14	0		3	31																									
4	Years	63	0		9	87	6.0		1	3				1	12	12.0	12	0										3	16	5.3	9

Year	Team	GP	FM	FF	FR	TK	SK	YDS	IR	YDS	PD	PTS	TD	RA	YDS	AVG	LG	TD	REC	YDS	AVG	LG	TD	PR	YDS	AVG	LG	KOR	YDS	AVG	LG
MIKE WICKLUM Mike DH 6'1 190 Queen's B: 5/18/1939 Draft: 1-4 1961 TOR																															
1962	TOR	14																						18	77	4.3	15	6	111	18.5	31
1963	EDM	13	0		1				2	40														9	97	10.8	17				
1964	EDM	16							4	74									2	25	12.5	13	0	16	48	3.0	20	4	88	22.0	29
1965	TOR	12																						10	51	5.1	23				
1966	TOR	14	0		1				6	45														2	45	22.5	32				
1967	TOR	10							1	38														0	10		10				
6	Years	79	0		2				13	197									2	25	12.5	13	0	55	328	6.0	32	10	199	19.9	31
RYLAND WICKMAN Ryland LB 5'10 225 Sacramento State B: 10/30/1975 Silver Spring, MD Pro: E																															
2000	WPG	18	0	0	3	89	2.0	8.0																							
2001	WPG	14				49	1.0	2.0	1	0	1																				
2002	WPG	18	0	1	2	74	5.0	31.0			3																				
2003	WPG	15	0	2	2	37			1	5	1																				
2004	WPG	14	0	3	0	48	2.0	20.0			1																				
2005	WPG	13				58	1.0	1.0	1	0	1																				
6	Years	92	0	6	7	355	11.0	62.0	3	5	7																				
MIKE WIDGER Mike LB 6'0 210 Virginia Tech B: 8/21/1948																															
1970	MTL+	14	0		2				1	9																					
1971	MTL	14	0		4							6	1																		
1972	MTL+	14	0		3				2	51																					
1973	MTL*	14	0		1																										
1974	MTL*	16			6				2	38																					
1975	MTL*	16	0		1				1	8																					
1976	MTL	16							2	11																					
1977	OTT*	16	0		3				2	5		6	1																		
1978	OTT	12	0		3																										
9	Years	132	0		23				10	122		12	2																		
JOHNNY WIDMAN John T																															
1947	TOR	1																													
RAY WIENS Raymond C 6'3 250 Saskatchewan B: 7/7/1968 Swift Current, SK Draft: 8-59 1990 WPG																															
1992	WPG	11				8																									
BRIAN WIFLEY Brian E																															
1946	WPG	3																													
BRIAN WIGGINS Brian Edward WR 5'11 185 Texas Southern B: 6/14/1968 New Rochelle, NY																															
1993	CAL	11	1		1	3						32	5						47	881	18.7	52	5	27	254	9.4	29	24	510	21.3	46
1994	CAL	18	4		0	3						36	6	5	7	1.4	5	0	64	859	13.4	42	5	25	226	9.0	50	28	640	22.9	79
1998	EDM	9				0													31	443	14.3	48	0	14	61	4.4	61	13	275	21.2	46
3	Years	38	5		1	6						68	11	5	7	1.4	5	0	142	2183	15.4	52	10	66	541	8.2	61	65	1425	21.9	79
STEVE WIGGINS Steve DB 6'0 180 Prairie View A&M B: 7/25/1963																															
1989	SAS	2	1		0	3																		2	8	4.0	6				
ERIC WILBUR Eric P 6'2 200 Florida B: 12/12/1984 Orlando, FL																															
2010	HAM	13				2						5	0	2	7	3.5	6	0													
BARRY WILBURN Barry Todd CB 6'3 186 Mississippi B: 12/9/1963 Memphis, TN Draft: 8-219 1985 WAS Pro: N																															
1993	SAS*	16	0		1	31			2	21																		1	0	0.0	0
1994	BC	5				16			1	21	6																				
1999	WPG	8				13					1																				
3	Years	29	0		1	60			3	42	7																	1	0	0.0	0
STEVE WILBURN Stephen T. DE-DT 6'4 266 Illinois State B: 2/25/1961 Chicago, IL D: 6/8/2005 Schaumburg, IL Draft: 8B-154 1984 DEN-USFL Pro: N																															
1983	CAL	11	0		1		2.0																								
1984	CAL	15	0		1		8.0		1	0																					
1985	CAL	5																													
1985	SAS	4					2.0																								
1985	Year	9					2.0																								
1986	SAS	2					1.0																								
1989	BC	1				1																									
1990	BC	3	0		2																										
1990	HAM	2																													
1990	Year	5	0		2	6																									
6	Years	37	0		4	1	13.0		1	0																					
GERALD WILCOX Gerald SB 6'2 225 Weber State B: 7/8/1966 London, England Draft: 1-1 1989 OTT																															
1989	OTT	15	1		0	1						18	3						24	331	13.8	36	3								
1990	OTT	3				2													6	71	11.8	33	0								
1991	OTT	18	0		2	8						18	3						26	455	17.5	61	3								
1992	WPG	4				1						6	1						20	352	17.6	48	1								
1993	WPG+	16				3						60	10						79	1340	17.0	75	10								
1994	WPG*	18	3		0	3						78	13						111	1624	14.6	46	13								
1995	WPG	15	0		1	2						30	5						69	1024	14.8	46	5								
1996	WPG	4				2						10	1						20	268	13.4	29	1								
1997	CAL	2				0													1	13	13.0	13	0								
9	Years	95	4		3	22						220	36						356	5478	15.4	75	36								
WILLIE WILDER Willie B. WR 6'1 195 Florida B: 9/19/1955 Loughman, FL Draft: 5B-128 1978 GB Pro: U																															
1979	SAS	8	1		0							12	2	2	-5	-2.5	11	0	14	397	28.4	96	2					8	185	23.1	36
AL WILEY Alan Scott OG 5'10 208 Western Ontario B: 1928																															
1950	WPG	14																													
1951	WPG	14																													
1952	WPG	16																													
1953	WPG	15																													
1954	WPG	16																													
5	Years	75																													
JOHN WILEY John DB 6'0 195 Auburn B: 8/8/1969 Tuskegee, AL																															
1993	SAC	18	0		1	82			4	46																					
KENNY WILHITE Kenny CB-DH 5'8 189 Dodge City CC; Nebraska B: 7/26/1970 St. Louis, MO																															
1994	SAC	10	0		2	9			1	26	1																	1	9	9.0	9
1995	SA	17	2		0	33			4	80	4													31	219	7.1	19	21	523	24.9	58
1996	OTT*	18	1		1	43			3	119	8	6	1											70	718	10.3	60	57	1167	20.5	55
1997	HAM	12	2	1	1	23			1	32	4	6	1											30	203	6.8	19	2	34	17.0	17
4	Years	57	5	1	4	108			9	257	17	12	2											131	1140	8.7	60	81	1733	21.4	58
GARY WILKERSON Gary Wayne CB 6'0 180 Penn State B: 10/11/1965 Sutherland, VA Draft: 6-160 1989 CLE																															
1990	HAM	18	0		2	51			7	111		12	2																		
1991	HAM	13				47			3	74		6	1																		
1992	HAM	11	0		2	38			1	51		6	1											0	3		3				
1993	HAM	11				43			3	73		12	2											1	29	29.0	29				
1994	HAM	15				41			1	20	5																				
1995	BAL	4				9			1	0	1																				
1995	EDM	7	0		2	28			3	89	4	6	1																		
1995	Year	11	0		2	37			4	89	5	6	1																		
6	Years	72	0		6	257			19	418	10	42	7											1	32	32.0	29				
BRUCE WILKINS Bruce FB 6'1 215 Bishop's; Concordia (Quebec) B: 6/29/1953 Draft: 8-68 1977 MTL																															
1980	SAS	16												13	31	2.4	6	0	9	81	9.0	18	0					5	76	15.2	18
1981	WPG	9	0		1									8	47	5.9	20	0	7	54	7.7	13	0					1	15	15.0	15
2	Years	25	0		1									21	78	3.7	20	0	16	135	8.4	18	0					6	91	15.2	18
DAVID WILKINS David DE 6'4 240 Eastern Kentucky B: 2/24/1969 Cincinnati, OH Pro: EN																															

Year	Team	GP	FM	FF	FR	TK	SK	YDS	IR	YDS	PD	PTS	TD	RA	YDS	AVG	LG	TD	REC	YDS	AVG	LG	TD	PR	YDS	AVG	LG	KOR	YDS	AVG	LG
1995	HAM	1				1																									
TERRENCE WILKINS Terrence Olondo WR 5'9 179 Virginia B: 7/29/1975 Washington, DC Pro: N																															
2005	CAL	6	2	0	0	0													3	12	4.0	8	0	31	302	9.7	29	12	275	22.9	33
RYAN WILKINSON Ryan S 6'2 210 Waterloo B: 9/14/1975 Scarborough, ON Draft: 6-40 1999 WPG																															
2001	HAM	7				1																									
TOM WILKINSON Thomas Edward QB 5'10 187 Wyoming B: 1/4/1943 Ottumwa, IA																															
1967	TOR	2												1	8	8.0	8	0													
1968	TOR	5												1	6	6.0	6	0													
1969	TOR	14	4		0							24	4	42	257	6.1	35	3	1	9	9.0	9	1								
1970	TOR	14	1		0							6	1	42	180	4.3	20	1													
1971	BC	1	1		0									3	10	3.3	9	0													
1972	EDM	16	2		1									48	260	5.4	23	0													
1973	EDM	16												25	78	3.1	20	0													
1974	EDM*	16										6	1	38	61	1.6	10	1													
1975	EDM	16	2		0							6	1	33	80	2.4	22	1													
1976	EDM	16	1		0									11	24	2.2	15	0													
1977	EDM	16	2		1									25	40	1.6	11	0													
1978	EDM*	16	3		0									23	42	1.8	16	0													
1979	EDM*	16	1		0									10	28	2.8	13	0													
1980	EDM	16	1		1									5	12	2.4	6	0													
1981	EDM	16	2		0							6	1	13	17	1.3	20	1													
15	Years	196	20		3							48	8	320	1103	3.4	35	7	1	9	9.0	9	1								
AARON WILLIAMS Aaron DT 6'5 275 Indiana B: 7/26/1974 Toronto, ON Draft: 2-9 1999 EDM																															
2000	HAM	18				8	1.0	8.0																							
2001	HAM	5				4	1.0	5.0																							
2002	CAL	2				1																									
3	Years	25				13	2.0	13.0																							
A.D. WILLIAMS A.D. E 6'2 210 Santa Monica JC; Pacific B: 11/21/1933 Little Rock, AR Draft: 3A-32 1956 LARM Pro: N																															
1962	TOR	1																	4	35	8.8	11	0								
1963	TOR	1																	2	36	18.0	25	0								
2	Years	2																	6	71	11.8	25	0								
AL WILLIAMS Alphonso WR 5'10 180 Nevada-Reno B: 2/4/1962 Vidalia, GA Draft: 8-364 1984 NJ-USFL Pro: NU																															
1989	HAM	3				1													9	144	16.0	28	0								
ALBERT WILLIAMS Albert Donnell LB 6'3 229 Texas-El Paso B: 9/7/1964 San Antonio, TX Pro: EN																															
1990	WPG	15	0		4	39	8.0					6	1																		
1991	WPG	11				13																									
2	Years	26	0		4	52	8.0					6	1																		
ANTHONY WILLIAMS Anthony LB 5'9 217 South Florida B: 9/8/1978																															
2002	WPG	4				1																									
ARNIE WILLIAMS Arnie LB 6'2 235 Southern Mississippi B: 8/14/1970 Bay Minette, AL																															
1993	TOR	7				30	1.0	12.0																							
BEN WILLIAMS Lewis Ben DE 6'2 282 Minnesota B: 5/28/1970 Belzoni, MS Pro: EN																															
1994	SHR+	16	0		1	46	7.0	53.0																							
1995	SHR	18	0		2	61	8.0	78.0																							
2000	EDM	6				7	2.0	20.0																							
3	Years	40	0		3	114	17.0	151.0																							
BERNARD WILLIAMS Bennie Bernard OT 6'8 317 Georgia B: 7/18/1972 Memphis, TN Draft: 1-14 1994 PHI Pro: NX																															
2000	BC	5				0													1	20	20.0	20	0								
2003	TOR	15	0	0	1	2																									
2004	TOR	14				0																									
2005	TOR+	18	0	0	1	2																									
2006	TOR+	16				0																									
5	Years	68	0	0	2	4													1	20	20.0	20	0								
BRANDON WILLIAMS Brandon CB 5'10 177 Mississippi Gulf Coast JC; Georgia B: 10/12/1980																															
2003	MTL	15				8																									
BRETT WILLIAMS Brett Joseph DE-DT 6'3 260 Memphis; Austin Peay State B: 5/23/1958 Norfolk, VA Pro: U																															
1985	MTL	10	0		1		3.0																								
1986	MTL*	18	0		2		21.0		1	16				2	1	0.5	1	0										4	41	10.3	18
1987	BC	14				28	10.0																								
1988	EDM*	18			1	40	12.0					6	1						1	7	7.0	7	1					5	28	5.6	15
1989	EDM+	17	0		3	27	9.0																					2	21	10.5	15
1990	EDM+	18	0		3	37	9.0																					2	22	11.0	12
1991	EDM*	17	0		1	30	11.0		1	0																					
1992	HAM	11				26	9.0																								
1993	HAM	10	0		1	20	5.0	26.0																							
1994	SHR	2				5																									
10	Years	135	0		12	213	89.0	26.0	2	16		6	1	2	1	0.5	1	0	1	7	7.0	7	1					13	112	8.6	18
BYRON WILLIAMS Byron Keith (B.K.) WR-SB 6'1 177 Texas-Arlington B: 10/31/1960 Texarkana, TX Draft: 10A-253 1983 GB; 21-249 1983 DEN-USFL Pro: EN																															
1987	BC	9	1		1	1						6	1	4	17	4.3	32	0	29	494	17.0	57	1								
1988	BC	4				0						6	1						10	187	18.7	57	1								
1989	OTT	10	1		1	3						12	2						37	666	18.0	64	2								
1991	SAS	7	1		0	1						18	3						24	463	19.3	85	3								
1992	SAS	10				1						26	4						32	596	18.6	83	4					8	123	15.4	31
1993	SAS	12	1		1	3						6	1	1	-4	-4.0	-4	0	37	545	14.7	59	1					1	0	0.0	0
1994	BAL	1				0																									
1995	BAL	2				1													2	54	27.0	38	0								
8	Years	55	4		3	10						74	12	5	13	2.6	32	0	171	3005	17.6	85	12					9	123	13.7	31
CALVIN WILLIAMS Calvin L., Jr. RB 6'1 205 Georgia Tech B: 8/29/1975 LaGrange, GA																															
1998	EDM	16	2	0	0	11						30	5	111	419	3.8	19	2	35	410	11.7	40	3					11	213	19.4	53
CARL WILLIAMS Carl A. LB 6'3 220 Michigan State B: 2/24/1961 Pro: U																															
1984	WPG	1																													
CARL WILLIAMS Carl WR 6'2 175 Louisville B: 1/21/1963 Atlanta, GA																															
1987	OTT	1				0						6	1						3	82	27.3	47	1								
CARROLL WILLIAMS Carroll QB 6'1 190 St. Francis Xavier B: 1945																															
1967	MTL	8	2		0							6	1	34	178	5.2	30	1	1	31	31.0	31	0								
1968	MTL	14	4		0							18	3	57	436	7.6	29	3													
1969	MTL	8	2		0									11	73	6.6	17	0													
1970	BC	7	1		0									8	34	4.3	17	0													
4	Years	37	9		0							24	4	110	721	6.6	30	4	1	31	31.0	31	0								
CHARLEY WILLIAMS Charles DB 6'1 180 Jackson State B: 9/14/1953 Magee, MS Draft: 9-230 1978 PHI Pro: N																															
1979	WPG	1																						1	1	1.0	1				
1980	WPG+	14							5	131																					
1981	WPG+	14							3	135		12	2																		
1982	WPG	5																													
4	Years	34							8	266		12	2											1	1	1.0	1				
CHRIS WILLIAMS Chris SB-WR 5'9 155 New Mexico State B: 9/16/1987 Fort Worth, TX																															
2011	HAM+	15	6	0	3	1						42	7	6	43	7.2	14	0	70	1064	15.2	71	6	12	81	6.8	30	13	252	19.4	93
CHRIS WILLIAMS Christopher Dorsey OG 6'5 319 Southern University B: 3/14/1976 Houston, TX																															
1999	CAL	2				0																									
CODY WILLIAMS Cody Andrew DB 5'9 190 Colgate B: 5/10/1986 Buffalo, NY																															
2009	HAM	1				0																									
DAVE WILLIAMS David Ray QB-HB 6'2 200 Colorado B: 3/10/1954 Minden, LA Draft: 7B-208 1976 DAL Pro: N																															

Year	Team	GP	FM	FF	FR	TK	SK	YDS	IR	YDS	PD	PTS	TD	RA	YDS	AVG	LG	TD	REC	YDS	AVG	LG	TD	PR	YDS	AVG	LG	KOR	YDS	AVG	LG
1976	CAL	3												3	9	3.0	9	0													
DAVID WILLIAMS David Lamar WR 6'3 189 Los Angeles Harbor JC; Illinois B: 6/10/1963 Los Angeles, CA Draft: 3-82 1986 CHIB Pro: N																															
1988	BC*	18	1		0	3						110	18	1	4	4.0	4	0	83	1468	17.7	77	18					1	20	20.0	20
1989	BC+	17	1		1	1						84	14						79	1446	18.3	71	14					1	21	21.0	21
1990	OTT	17	0		2	3						72	12						61	895	14.7	55	12								
1991	EDM	11				0						54	9						37	597	16.1	46	9								
1991	TOR	7	2		0	0						36	6						29	552	19.0	68	6								
1991	Year+	18	2		0	0						90	15						66	1149	17.4	68	15								
1992	TOR	9	2		0	4						6	1						30	444	14.8	39	1								
1993	WPG*	16	3		1	5						90	15	1	-14	-14.0	-14	0	84	1144	13.6	44	15								
1994	WPG	4	1		2	0						18	3						30	565	18.8	64	3								
1995	WPG	2				1													6	86	14.3	32	0								
8	Years	94	10		6	17						470	78	2	-10	-5.0	4	0	439	7197	16.4	77	78					2	41	20.5	21
ED WILLIAMS Ed WR 6'3 203 Iowa State B: 7/24/1976 Miami, FL																															
1998	CAL	1				0																									
EDDIE WILLIAMS Edward Lee RB 6'0 208 West Virginia B: 7/4/1949 Sandusky, OH Draft: 14-347 1973 BAL																															
1971	WPG	14	2		1							25	5	110	688	6.3	41	4	13	88	6.8	26	1					7	135	19.3	22
1972	WPG	11	1		1							24	4	98	494	5.0	47	3	2	51	25.5	33	1					1	9	9.0	9
2	Years	25	3		3							49	9	208	1182	5.7	47	7	15	139	9.3	33	2					8	144	18.0	22
ERNIE WILLIAMS Ernie FL 6'1 180 Winnipeg Roamers Jrs. B: 1921																															
1946	WPG	7																													
1947	WPG	8																													
1948	WPG	9																													
3	Years	24																													
FRANK WILLIAMS Frank Gordon, Jr. HB 6'2 215 Pepperdine B: 5/29/1932 Bowie County, TX Pro: N																															
1955	BC	2										10	2	8	24	3.0	11	1	2	71	35.5	51	1	2	16	8.0	10				
FRED WILLIAMS Fred HB 5'10 189 Arizona State B: 9/2/1955 St. Petersburg, FL Draft: 8B-221 1977 DAL																															
1977	SAS	2										12	2	13	87	6.7	30	2	1	-7	-7.0	-7	0								
GARY WILLIAMS Gary HB 5'10 180 Hamilton Panthers B: 1931																															
1956	OTT	1																													
GARY WILLIAMS Gary FW-HB Parkdale Lions Jrs.																															
1957	TOR	14										6	1	1	2	2.0	2	0	1	4	4.0	4	1	72	424	5.9	21				
1958	CAL	1																													
2	Years	15										6	1	1	2	2.0	2	0	1	4	4.0	4	1	72	424	5.9	21				
GEMARA WILLIAMS Gemara La'Juan CB 5'8 180 Buffalo B: 4/30/1983 Oak Park, MI																															
2008	MTL	1				1																									
2009	EDM	2				2																									
2	Years	3				3																									
HAL WILLIAMS Harold HB 6'2 195 Miami (Ohio) B: 6/13/1935 Dayton, OH Draft: 13-156 1958 CLE																															
1960	SAS	1										6	1	6	32	5.3	25	1	1	9	9.0	9	0								
HENRY WILLIAMS Henry James DB 5'11 182 Hartnell JC; San Diego State B: 12/2/1956 Greensboro, AL Draft: 6B-156 1979 OAK Pro: NU																															
1981	TOR	4																													
HENRY WILLIAMS Henry Lee (Gizmo) WR 5'6 181 Northwest Mississippi JC; East Carolina B: 5/31/1962 Memphis, TN Draft: 3-36 1985 MEM-USFL Pro: NU																															
1986	SAS	3																													
1986	EDM	8										12	2	2	49	24.5	36	1	3	79	26.3	56	0	37	423	11.4	74	9	210	23.3	35
1986	Year	11										12	2	2	49	24.5	36	1	3	79	26.3	56	0	37	423	11.4	74	9	210	23.3	35
1987	EDM*	16	2		1	0						30	5						4	48	12.0	21	0	80	951	11.9	91	26	623	24.0	43
1988	EDM+	17	4		1	3						42	7	3	-1	-0.3	-9	0	25	515	20.6	85	5	96	964	10.0	100	15	379	25.3	34
1990	EDM	16	6		1	2						24	4	2	-1	-0.5	-15	0	15	260	17.3	48	0	90	987	11.0	81	31	743	24.0	92
1991	EDM*	18	5		1	1						36	6	1	1	1.0	1	0	13	233	17.9	35	1	98	1440	14.7	88	32	593	18.5	51
1992	EDM*	18				1						54	9	6	57	9.5	26	0	41	948	23.1	81	6	92	1124	12.2	104	24	441	18.4	34
1993	EDM*	18	5		1	1						60	10	2	-3	-1.5	9	0	52	950	18.3	102	6	83	1157	13.9	104	21	381	18.1	28
1994	EDM*	14	3		0	0						24	4	3	-3	-1.0	4	0	30	375	12.5	36	1	67	683	10.2	74	18	451	25.1	53
1995	EDM	15	6		1	0													3	26	8.7	14	0	87	871	10.0	68	30	638	21.3	45
1996	EDM	7	1		0	1						6	1	1	-3	-3.0	-3	0						32	361	11.3	79	28	663	23.7	48
1997	EDM+	18	2	0	0	1						12	2	5	10	2.0	5	0	8	126	15.8	38	1	84	821	9.8	72	52	1105	21.3	42
1998	EDM	11	3	0	0	0						12	2						5	84	16.8	65	1	49	397	8.1	86	31	690	22.3	47
1999	EDM	11	1	0	0	0						6	1											53	499	9.4	48	13	314	24.2	100
2000	EDM	13	1	0	0	0																		55	549	10.0	59	5	123	24.6	32
14	Years	195	39	0	6	10						318	53	25	106	4.2	36	1	199	3644	18.3	102	21100311227			11.2	104	335	7354	22.0	100
IAN WILLIAMS Ian LB 6'3 227 Memphis B: 11/18/1976 Timmins, ON Draft: 1A-2 2001 BC																															
2001	BC	7				2																						1	27	27.0	27
JACK WILLIAMS Jack DE-LB 6'4 240 Bowling Green State B: 2/14/1957 Cleveland, OH Draft: 6-151 1978 STL																															
1982	OTT	4	0		1		4.0																								
1983	OTT	12	0		2		9.0																								
1984	OTT	13	0		3		4.5																								
1985	OTT	5																													
1985	EDM	1					3.0																								
1985	Year	6					3.0																								
4	Years	34	0		6		20.5	0.0																							
JAZZMEN WILLIAMS Jazzmen Juvar DB 5'8 181 Boston College B: 12/6/1982 Rochester, NY																															
2006	WPG	4				3																									
JOE WILLIAMS Joel OHB-FB 5'10 205 Iowa B: 3/16/1941 Savannah, GA Draft: 14-194 1963 NYG																															
1962	WPG	7										6	1	44	201	4.6	28	1	4	40	10.0	13	0								
1963	WPG	6	2		1							18	3	40	143	3.6	15	3	8	79	9.9	20	0					6	157	26.2	48
1963	OTT	2												13	32	2.5	8	0	7	99	14.1	19	0					0	20		20
1963	Year	8	2		1							18	3	53	175	3.3	15	3	15	178	11.9	20	0					6	177	29.5	48
1967	TOR	9										12	2	87	409	4.7	35	0	10	114	11.4	50	2					5	93	18.6	21
3	Years	22	2		1							36	6	184	785	4.3	35	4	29	332	11.4	50	2					11	270	24.5	48
JOE WILLIAMS Joe DE 6'3 263 Maryland-Eastern Shore B: 3/25/1946 Philadelphia, PA																															
1965	MTL	10	0		3																										
1966	MTL	3																													
1966	TOR	1																													
1966	Year	4																													
2	Years	13	0		3																										
JOEL WILLIAMS Joel Herschel C 6'1 220 Louisiana-Lafayette; Texas B: 3/18/1926 San Angelo, TX D: 3/10/1997 Ector County, TX Draft: 22-198 1948 WAS; 7-85 1951 NYG Pro: AN																															
1951	EDM	13																													
1952	HAM	2																													
2	Years	15																													
JOHN WILLIAMS John CB 6'1 190 New Mexico Highlands B: 9/19/1942																															
1967	CAL	10							1	10																					
1969	HAM	9	2		0				4	39														13	112	8.6	16	1	25	25.0	25
1970	HAM	14	2		3				4	82		6	1															6	136	22.7	33
1971	HAM+	14	0		1				5	110		6	1											0	53		30				
1972	HAM*	14							8	114		6	1											1	0	0.0	0				
1973	HAM	6																													
1974	HAM	9	1		1				2	4														1	2	2.0	2				
1974	EDM	3																													
1974	Year	12	1		1				2	4														1	2	2.0	2				
1975	TOR	7	0		1				2	3																					
8	Years	83	5		6				26	362		18	3											15	167	11.1	30	7	161	23.0	33

Year	Team	GP	FM	FF	FR	TK	SK	YDS	IR	YDS	PD	PTS	TD	RA	YDS	AVG	LG	TD	REC	YDS	AVG	LG	TD	PR	YDS	AVG	LG	KOR	YDS	AVG	LG
JOHN WILLIAMS John Alan RB 5'11 212 Wisconsin B: 10/26/1960 Muskegon, MI Draft: 14-159 1983 MIC-USFL Pro: NU																															
1988	CAL	6			1	0								44	130	3.0	18	0	7	50	7.1	19	0								
JOHN WILLIAMS John FB 6'1 204 Rhode Island; Edinboro B: 9/23/1977 Millgrove, ON Draft: 4-31 2002 BC																															
2002	BC	15	1	1	2	12								1	3	3.0	3	0						1	0	0.0	0	3	56	18.7	24
2004	TOR	18				14						6	1	3	37	12.3	22	1													
2005	TOR	13	0	2	0	9								4	13	3.3	5	0	2	13	6.5	14	0					1	14	14.0	14
2006	TOR	14	1	0	0	16								14	39	2.8	8	0	1	15	15.0	15	0								
2007	TOR	17				18								2	1	0.5	1	0	1	3	3.0	3	0								
2008	HAM	17				12								5	29	5.8	12	0	2	16	8.0	9	0								
2009	HAM	18	0	0	1	9								9	45	5.0	14	0	9	67	7.4	14	0								
7	Years	112	2	3	3	90						6	1	38	167	4.4	22	1	15	114	7.6	15	0	1	0	0.0	0	4	70	17.5	24
JOHNNY WILLIAMS John Elliott DB 5'11 177 Compton JC; Southern California B: 6/30/1927 Los Angeles, CA D: 2/26/2005 Dana Point, CA Draft: 26-304 1951 WAS Pro: N																															
1955	MTL	4							2	29				2	13	6.5	8	0						14	81	5.8	23				
JONATHAN WILLIAMS Jonathan DT 6'2 290 Mississippi Delta JC; South Carolina B: 11/22/1985 Augusta, GA																															
2009	BC	1				2																									
J.R. WILLIAMS Jesse Ross C-LB 6'4 230 Bakersfield JC; Fresno State B: 11/17/1940 Corcoran, CA Draft: 21-168(f) 1962 SD; 10-138(f) 1962 NYG																															
1964	BC	12																													
1965	BC	16							1																						
2	Years	28							1	0																					
JULIUS WILLIAMS Julius Earl DE 6'2 260 Connecticut B: 7/19/1986 Decatur, GA Pro: NU																															
2011	EDM	15				20	5.0	42.0																							
K.D. WILLIAMS Kevin Dewayne LB 6'0 240 Arizona Western JC; Henderson State B: 4/22/1973 Tampa, FL Pro: EN																															
1995	WPG	15	1		3	65	5.0	42.0	1	11	0																				
1996	WPG*	18	0		2	112	5.0	31.0	4	72	4	6	1																		
1997	SAS	10	0	1	0	64	3.0	19.0	2	38	4	6	1																		
1997	HAM	3				19	1.0	8.0	1	18	1																				
1997	Year	13	0	1	0	83	4.0	27.0	3	56	5	6	1																		
2002	SAS	2	0	1	1	4						6	1																		
2002	WPG	5				9	1.0																								
2002	Year	7	0	1	1	13	1.0					6	1																		
4	Years	45	1	2	6	273	15.0	100.0	8	139	9	18	3																		
KEITH WILLIAMS Keith DH 5'9 185 Florida A&M B: 12/12/1983 Mount Vernon, NY																															
2008	EDM	6	0	1	1	37			1	9	1																				
2008	MTL	1				2																									
2008	Year	7	0	1	1	39			1	9	1																				
KERON WILLIAMS Keron Donavan DT-DE 6'1 262 Massachusetts B: 9/3/1984 Manchester, Jamaica																															
2006	CAL	1				0																									
2007	CAL	15	0	2	2	28	6.0	60.0			1																	1	4	4.0	4
2008	MTL+	18	0	2	1	39	10.0	71.0																				2	24	12.0	15
2009	MTL*	18	0	1	3	32	9.0	52.0																							
2010	BC	16	0	0	1	40	5.0	40.0																							
2011	BC+	17	0	1	1	43	11.0	85.0			1																				
6	Years	85	0	6	8	182	41.0	308.0			2																	3	28	9.3	15
KHARY WILLIAMS Khary J. CB 6'0 200 Youngstown State B: 8/11/1973 Los Angeles, CA																															
1999	CAL	7				12					2																				
KYLE WILLIAMS Kyle Demon OT 6'2 330 Texas A&M-Kingsville B: 5/17/1972 Houston, TX																															
2000	TOR	1				0																									
LaFANN WILLIAMS LaFann DB 5'9 177 Pittsburgh; South Florida B: 7/3/1977 Warren City, MI																															
2000	CAL	4				4																						2	49	24.5	26
LEN WILLIAMS Len QB 6'0 220 Northwestern B: 10/29/1971 Rockford, IL																															
1994	LV	17	4		1							8	1	23	86	3.7	19	1													
1995	CAL	6				6								2	9	4.5	7	0													
2	Years	23	4		1	6						8	1	25	95	3.8	19	1													
LENNY WILLIAMS Lenny DH-CB 5'10 190 Southern University B: 12/16/1981 Lake Charles, LA Draft: 7C-252 2004 TB Pro: E																															
2007	EDM	7	1	0	1	17			1	0	1													15	130	8.7	22	4	105	26.3	32
2008	EDM	9	0	3	0	37			2	26	1																	4	99	24.8	39
2009	EDM	10				37					2																	3	45	15.0	17
3	Years	26	1	3	1	91			3	26	4													15	130	8.7	22	11	249	22.6	39
MAURICE WILLIAMS Maurice G Regina Jrs.																															
1948	SAS	6																													
MIKE WILLIAMS Michael Thomas DV 5'10 180 Texas A&M B: 12/21/1955 Houston, TX Draft: 11-297 1978 WAS Pro: U																															
1978	HAM	3										6	1											8	128	16.0	98				
1978	TOR	2	0		1																			6	40	6.7	15	2	33	16.5	17
1978	Year	5	0		1							6	1											14	168	12.0	98	2	33	16.5	17
1979	TOR	10	1		1				1	14														13	118	9.1	32	4	59	14.8	17
1980	TOR	16	2		0				6	90														14	90	6.4	18				
3	Years	29	3		2				7	104		6	1											41	376	9.2	98	6	92	15.3	17
MIKE WILLIAMS Michael J. (M.J.) QB 6'0 200 Grambling State B: 9/10/1958																															
1981	TOR	4												4	47	11.8	31	0													
1982	TOR	5																													
1984	BC	4												1	8	8.0	8	0													
3	Years	13												5	55	11.0	31	0													
MIKE WILLIAMS Mike SB 5'9 170 Drake B: 3/11/1960 Pro: U																															
1985	OTT	3	1		0														3	54	18.0	40	0	1	13	13.0	13	2	18	9.0	15
NIGEL WILLIAMS Nigel WR 6'4 206 Burlington Braves Jrs.; Hamilton Hurricanes Jrs. B: 8/16/1971 Montreal, QC																															
1995	OTT	15	3		0	3						12	2						20	309	15.5	76	2					23	447	19.4	45
1996	MTL	16				1						18	3						33	461	14.0	60	3					5	58	11.6	24
1997	MTL	14				3						12	2						25	336	13.4	45	2					3	44	14.7	20
1998	MTL	2				0													1	13	13.0	13	0								
1998	TOR	16	3	0	1	4						30	5						61	1057	17.3	65	5					6	117	19.5	29
1998	Year	18	3	0	1	4						30	5						62	1070	17.3	65	5					6	117	19.5	29
1999	WPG	9				0						8	1						22	311	14.1	94	1								
2000	EDM	18	0	0	1	1						24	4						40	414	10.4	36	4								
2001	TOR	13	2	0	0	1						24	4						24	381	15.9	88	4								
2002	TOR	6				0													7	89	12.7	19	0								
2002	OTT	9				0													9	155	17.2	78	0								
2002	Year	15				0													16	244	15.3	78	0								
8	Years	93	8	0	2	13						128	21						242	3526	14.6	94	21					37	666	18.0	45
NORD WILLIAMS Nord RB 5'10 200 York B: 11/21/1958 Draft: 3A-23 1984 CAL																															
1985	HAM	3												2	4	2.0	3	0													
NORM WILLIAMS Norm HB Toronto Draft: 1A-7 1957 CAL																															
1957	TOR	1																													
PAUL WILLIAMS Paul, Jr. CB-RB 5'11 180 Benedict; California B: 1/29/1947 Awendaw, SC Draft: 17-418 1969 ATL																															
1971	WPG	10							6	68		24	4	1	5	5.0	5	0	13	183	14.1	45	4					2	46	23.0	24
1972	WPG	16	1		0							54	9	8	72	9.0	68	1	60	817	13.6	69	8					23	492	21.4	44
1973	WPG	16	1		3				4	19		18	3						17	298	17.5	63	2	27	119	4.4	24	9	222	24.7	44
1974	WPG*	16	2		1				3	36		12	2											10	67	6.7	19	20	648	32.4	109
1975	WPG	8																						17	104	6.1	37	7	214	30.6	47
1976	SAS*	16	3		0				6	92		12	2											61	540	8.9	108	17	431	25.4	77
1977	SAS+	16	5		0				3	62		12	2						1	50	50.0	50	0	67	697	10.4	99	36	812	22.6	37
1978	SAS	13	2		0				3	98		12	2						4	139	34.8	57	1	19	61	3.2	22	12	269	22.4	53
8	Years	111	14		4				25	375		144	24	9	77	8.6	68	1	95	1487	15.7	69	15	201	1588	7.9	108	126	3134	24.9	109

Year	Team	GP	FM	FF	FR	TK	SK	YDS	IR	YDS	PD	PTS	TD	RA	YDS	AVG	LG	TD	REC	YDS	AVG	LG	TD	PR	YDS	AVG	LG	KOR	YDS	AVG	LG
PAYTON WILLIAMS Payton Mychal DB 5'7 170 Fresno State B: 11/19/1978 Riverside, CA Pro: EN																															
2002	CAL	2				5					1																				
QUENCY WILLIAMS Quency L. DE 6'4 230 Auburn B: 4/10/1961 Douglasville, GA Draft: TD 1984 BIR-USFL																															
1987	CAL	10				32	5.0																								
1988	CAL	18				59	9.0																								
1989	WPG	17				65	8.0																								
1990	WPG	15	0		2	46	6.0																								
1991	WPG	7				15	2.0																	1	0	0.0	0				
1992	WPG	1				4																									
6	Years	68	0		2	221	30.0																	1	0	0.0	0				
RENAULD WILLIAMS Renauld Duvall LB 6'0 229 Hofstra B: 2/23/1981 Stony Brook, NY Pro: N																															
2007	SAS	2				3																									
2008	SAS	16	0	2	1	57	3.0	31.0	1	42	2	6	1																		
2009	SAS	13	0	3	1	67	3.0	13.0	0	0	4	6	1																		
2011	HAM+	17	0	1	0	99	5.0	32.0	1	32	3																				
4	Years	48	0	6	2	226	11.0	76.0	2	74	9	12	2																		
RICHIE WILLIAMS Richie QB 6'2 190 Appalachian State B: 3/10/1983 Camden, SC																															
2006	HAM	18				0								4	55	13.8	20	0													
2007	HAM	18	3	0	1	1								32	169	5.3	20	0													
2008	HAM	18	2	0	1	2						12	2	43	307	7.1	19	2													
2009	WPG	4				0								2	9	4.5	8	0													
4	Years	58	5	0	2	3						12	2	81	540	6.7	20	2													
RICKY WILLIAMS Errick Lynne RB 5'10 230 Texas B: 5/21/1977 San Diego, CA Draft: 1-5 1999 NO Pro: N																															
2006	TOR	11	1	0	1	0						12	2	109	526	4.8	35	2	19	127	6.7	18	0								
ROBERT WILLIAMS Robert, III FB 6'1 215 Washington State B: 2/8/1961 Los Angeles, CA																															
1984	MTL	1												5	46	9.2	16	0													
RODERICK WILLIAMS Roderick CB 5'11 180 Alcorn State B: 5/27/1987 Monroe, LA																															
2010	EDM	12				23			1	10	3																				
2011	EDM+	15	0	1	0	44			6	70	4																				
2	Years	27	0	1	0	67			7	80	7																				
RODNEY WILLIAMS Rodney Colin P 6'0 178 Georgia Tech B: 4/25/1977 New York, NY Draft: 7-252 1999 STL Pro: EN																															
2006	EDM	1				0						1	0																		
ROE WILLIAMS Roosevelt, Jr. DB 6'0 202 Tuskegee B: 9/10/1978 Jacksonville, FL Draft: 3A-72 2002 CHIB Pro: N																															
2006	EDM	4	1	0	2	8			0	0	1																				
RONALD WILLIAMS Ronald RB 5'10 210 Clemson B: 5/19/1972 Marietta, GA Pro: E																															
1996	BC	12	1		0	1						12	2	92	535	5.8	38	2	15	195	13.0	57	0					1	16	16.0	16
1997	WPG	14	5	1	1	6						96	16	211	1120	5.3	52	16	30	258	8.6	23	0					3	54	18.0	20
1998	HAM+	16	3	0	0	2						78	13	154	807	5.2	66	13	21	250	11.9	36	0					12	235	19.6	31
1999	HAM+	18	3	0	2	2						90	15	207	1025	5.0	65	14	40	394	9.9	49	1								
2000	HAM+	18	3	0	1	3						90	15	267	1264	4.7	70	13	28	273	9.8	51	2					2	25	12.5	15
2001	HAM	7	3	0	0	1						18	3	120	607	5.1	34	3	11	91	8.3	22	0					1	28	28.0	28
2001	EDM	8	1	0	0	2						30	5	123	593	4.8	48	5	8	73	9.1	23	0								
2001	Year	15	4	0	0	3													19	164	8.6	23	0					1	28	28.0	28
2002	EDM	6				0						36	6	68	254	3.7	22	5	13	144	11.1	34	1								
7	Years	91	19	1	4	17						450	75	1242	6205	5.0	70	71	166	1678	10.1	57	4					19	358	18.8	31
SADRICK WILLIAMS Sadrick DB 5'9 175 Garden City CC; Kansas State B: 10/1/1979 Riveria Beach, FL																															
2006	CAL	17				31			1	0	4													3	19	6.3	9				
2007	CAL	11				16			1	0	1																				
2	Years	28				47			2	0	5													3	19	6.3	9				
SEANTE WILLIAMS Seante Teron DL 6'6 242 Coffeyville CC*; Southern Mississippi; Jacksonville State B: 9/16/1981 Newport News, VA Pro: E																															
2008	SAS	8				13	1.0	9.0			1																				
SETH WILLIAMS Seth CB 5'11 185 Richmond B: 10/24/1986																															
2011	MTL	10				51			1	20	6																				
SHOMARI WILLIAMS Shomari Gyasi DE 6'2 245 Houston; Queen's B: 3/8/1985 Toronto, ON Draft: 1-1 2010 SAS																															
2010	SAS	18	0	0	1	23																									
2011	SAS	18				32	3.0	20.0																							
2	Years	36	0	0	1	55	3.0	20.0																							
SID WILLIAMS Sidney QB 6'2 180 Wisconsin B: 12/31/1935 Little Rock, AR Draft: 11-129(f) 1958 NYG																															
1960	MTL	1							2	28																					
STAN WILLIAMS Stanley Neil OE-DB-OHB 6'2 195 Baylor B: 12/5/1929 Callahan County, TX Draft: 8A-86 1952 CLE Pro: N																															
1953	SAS	9							3	71		20	4						15	376	25.1		4								
1954	SAS+	16	2		2				8	94		20	4	61	217	3.6	21	1	27	378	14.0	49	3	23	205	8.9	40				
1955	SAS+	14	0		2				2	0		10	2						32	469	14.7	32	2	2	10	5.0	7	1	14	14.0	14
1956	SAS	8	1		0				1	0		6	1						21	448	21.3	54	1								
1957	SAS	15	2		1				1	5		12	2						29	384	13.2	32	1								
5	Years	62	5		5				15	170		68	13	61	217	3.6	21	1	124	2055	16.6	54	11	25	215	8.6	40	1	14	14.0	14
STEVE WILLIAMS Steven Ford DT 6'6 260 Western Carolina B: 1/12/1951 Columbia, SC Draft: 10-252 1972 SF Pro: N																															
1976	WPG	2																													
STEVE WILLIAMS Stephen Cabot DT 6'2 306 Indiana; Northern Illinois*; Northwest Missouri State B: 9/21/1981 Oak Park, IL Pro: N																															
2009	BC	7	0	1	1	19																						1	5	5.0	5
2010	BC	7				23	2.0	5.0																							
2	Years	14	0	1	1	42	2.0	5.0																				1	5	5.0	5
TALY WILLIAMS Taly DB 6'2 185 Waterloo B: 10/29/1970 Toronto, ON																															
1994	TOR	8				3								1	45	45.0	45	0													
1995	HAM	3				0																									
2	Years	11				3								1	45	45.0	45	0													
TOMMIE WILLIAMS Tommie CB 5'9 170 Texas A&M-Kingsville B: 5/9/1963																															
1987	OTT	18				55			2	33																					
1988	OTT	10				25																									
2	Years	28				80			2	33																					
TONY WILLIAMS Tony DB 5'10 185 Fullerton State B: 8/27/1966 Girardeau, MO																															
1989	OTT	7				18			1	4														10	58	5.8	11				
TONY WILLIAMS Anthony J. DB Massachusetts																															
1995	SHR	11				7					3																				
TRAVIS WILLIAMS Travis Craig CB 5'9 180 East Carolina B: 4/19/1985 Daytona Beach, FL																															
2011	BC	2				10					1																				
TREVOR WILLIAMS Trevor DB 5'10 185 York B: 9/24/1960 Draft: 1-3 1984 WPG																															
1984	WPG	2																													
TYRONE WILLIAMS Tyrone Robert WR 6'5 207 Western Ontario B: 3/26/1970 Halifax, NS Draft: 1B-7 1992 CAL; 9B-239 1992 PHX Pro: N																															
1995	CAL	7				0						6	1						6	81	13.5	32	1								
1996	TOR	18	2		1	3						42	7						60	895	14.9	45	7								
2	Years	25	2		1	3						48	8						66	976	14.8	45	8								
TYRONE WILLIAMS Tyrone M., Jr. DT 6'4 292 Wyoming B: 10/22/1972 Philadelphia, PA Pro: EN																															
2002	BC	12				27	4.0	25.0			1																				
2003	BC	18	0	1	0	42	6.0	27.0			2	12	2						2	23	11.5	22	2								
2004	BC	18	0	1	1	55	1.0	5.0	1	44	1																				
2005	BC	18	0	4	1	59	6.0	34.0			4																				
2006	BC*	18	0	2	0	43	4.0	16.0			5	6	1						1	1	1.0	1	1								
2007	BC*	18	0	2	2	68	5.0	21.0			4																				
2008	BC	18	0	2	1	50	1.0	10.0			2																				
2009	WPG	1				2					1																				
8	Years	121	0	12	5	346	27.0	138.0	1	44	20	18	3						3	24	8.0	22	3								

Year	Team	GP	FM	FF	FR	TK	SK	YDS	IR	YDS	PD	PTS	TD	RA	YDS	AVG	LG	TD	REC	YDS	AVG	LG	TD	PR	YDS	AVG	LG	KOR	YDS	AVG	LG
UNDRE WILLIAMS Undre WR 5'9 175 Clemson; Florida A&M B: 2/11/1975 Macon, GA																															
2000	TOR	4				1													2	14	7.0	9	0	14	32	2.3	11	9	183	20.3	39
WENDELL WILLIAMS Wendell DB 5'10 160 Fresno State B: 9/20/1958																															
1985	BC	2																													
WILLIE WILLIAMS Willie Lee, Jr. OT 6'6 300 Louisiana State B: 8/6/1967 Houston, TX Pro: EN																															
1997	TOR	17				1																									
1998	TOR	16				3																									
2	Years	33				4																									
DON WILLINGHAM Donald OHB 5'10 200 Wisconsin-Milwaukee B: 9/21/1950 De Pere, WI Draft: 14-357 1974 OAK; 29-346 1974 CHI-WFL Pro: W																															
1974	CAL	4	2		0							12	2	35	145	4.1	14	2	7	41	5.9	12	0					3	79	26.3	33
DARREN WILLIS Darren DB 5'11 180 Arizona State B: 12/19/1964 Pro: E																															
1990	BC	3				8																									
JAMAL WILLIS Jamalsikou Leirus RB 6'2 218 Brigham Young B: 12/12/1972 Altus, OK Pro: N																															
1998	BC	1				0								2	0	0.0	0	0	1	8	8.0	8	0								
LARRY WILLIS Larry Lee DB 5'11 170 Phoenix JC; Texas-El Paso B: 7/18/1948 Phoenix, AZ Pro: NW																															
1976	MTL	4	1		1				2	15																					
LARRY WILLIS Larry Ray WR 5'10 170 Taft JC; Fresno State B: 7/13/1963 Santa Monica, CA Draft: TD 1985 OAK-USFL																															
1986	CAL	1	1		0														6	72	12.0	20	0	4	25	6.3	23				
1987	CAL	18	4		3	3						60	10						74	1477	20.0	86	10	12	55	4.6	17	1	20	20.0	20
1988	CAL+	18	2		2	1						56	9						73	1328	18.2	72	9	3	17	5.7	10				
1989	CAL	18	2		1	3						60	10						73	1451	19.9	80	10								
1990	BC	12	1		0	1						36	6	4	15	3.8	13	0	49	837	17.1	48	6								
1990	EDM	4	3		0	1													14	193	13.8	45	0								
1990	Year	16	4		0	2						36	6	4	15	3.8	13	0	63	1030	16.3	48	6								
1991	WPG	11				7						18	3						36	741	20.6	104	3	3	8	2.7	5				
1992	WPG	4				3						6	1						22	291	13.2	56	1								
1993	TOR	3				1						6	1						11	195	17.7	54	1								
8	Years	85	13		6	20						242	40	4	15	3.8	13	0	358	6585	18.4	104	40	22	105	4.8	23	1	20	20.0	20
ODELL WILLIS Odell DE-LB-DT 6'2 265 West Georgia B: 12/28/1984 Meridian, MS																															
2009	CAL	9	0	0	2	11	6.0	48.0																							
2009	WPG	7	0	2	1	15	4.0	23.0			1																				
2009	Year	16	0	2	3	26	10.0	71.0			1																				
2010	WPG	18	0	4	0	25	11.0	87.0			6																				
2011	WPG*	18	0	4	0	27	13.0	59.0			2																				
3	Years	45	0	10	3	78	34.0	217.0			10																				
REMOND WILLIS Remond, III DE 6'1 253 Illinois; Tennessee State B: 8/28/1985 Dexter, MO																															
2010	WPG	1				1																									
2011	SAS	10				22	1.0	0.0																							
2	Years	11				23	1.0	0.0																							
SLADE WILLIS Slade FL-SE 6'1 180 Drake B: 5/1/1950 Draft: 1B-6 1973 BC																															
1973	BC	10																	15	197	13.1	24	0	15	97	6.5	21				
1974	BC	16	1		0							33	5						37	443	12.0	64	5	32	220	6.9	22				
1975	BC	16	1		0							2	0						23	294	12.8	62	0	6	29	4.8	16				
1976	BC	4	0		0							6	1						1	16	16.0	16	1	1	0	0.0	0				
1976	HAM	12			0														25	296	11.8	43	0								
1976	Year	16	1		0							6	1						26	312	12.0	43	1	1	0	0.0	0				
1977	WPG	10	1		0							6	1						6	124	20.7	45	1								
1977	TOR	6	1		2							6	1						7	98	14.0	29	1								
1977	Year	16	2		2							12	2						13	222	17.1	45	2								
1978	TOR	16	1		1							18	3						38	587	15.4	37	3								
1979	TOR	2																	1	5	5.0	5	0								
7	Years	74	5		3							71	11						153	2060	13.5	64	11	54	346	6.4	22				
CHUCK WILLS Charles Dale DB 6'3 195 Oregon B: 9/11/1953 Portland, OR Draft: 17-476 1976 WAS																															
1976	WPG	16							7	94														5	77	15.4	20				
1977	WPG+	16	0		1				4	7														1	0	0.0	0				
1978	WPG	2																													
1978	SAS	1							1	19																					
1978	Year	3							1	19																					
3	Years	34	0		1				12	120														6	77	12.8	20				
RAY WILLSEY Raymond L. DB-QB 5'10 180 California B: 9/30/1928 Regina, SK																															
1953	EDM+	16							7	61				10	76	7.6		0						42	378	9.0		9	130	14.4	
1954	EDM	8							4	43				1	0	0.0	0	0						2	5	2.5	5				
1955	EDM	13	1		3				4	48		0	0	1	7	7.0	7	0													
3	Years	37	1		3				15	152		0	0	12	83	6.9	7	0						44	383	8.7	5	9	130	14.4	
FRED WILMOT Fred HB-E-QB 175 West End Arrows; McGill B: 4/15/1927 Calgary, AB D: 10/27/2009 Calgary, AB Draft: 2-7 1954 MTL																															
1948	CAL	12										30	0																		
AL WILSON Alan C-OG 6'1 240 Montana State B: 4/6/1950 Duncan, BC																															
1972	BC	16	0		1																										
1973	BC	16	0		1																										
1974	BC	16	0		1																										
1975	BC*	16	1		2									1	3	3.0	3	0													
1976	BC*	16	0		1																										
1977	BC*	16																													
1978	BC*	16	0		1																										
1979	BC*	16																													
1980	BC*	16	0		1																										
1981	BC*	16	0		1																										
1982	BC	7																													
1983	BC	16	0		1																										
1984	BC	16	0		1																										
1985	BC	16	0		1																										
1986	BC	18	3		1																										
15	Years	233	4		13									1	3	3.0	3	0													
ANTONIO WILSON Antonio Demarcus LB 6'2 246 Texas A&M-Commerce B: 12/29/1977 Seagoville, TX Draft: 4A-106 2000 MIN Pro: EN																															
2004	EDM	2				2																									
CHRIS WILSON Chris DE 6'4 247 Northwood B: 7/10/1982 Flint, MI Pro: N																															
2005	BC	18	0	0	1	41	4.0	35.0			3	6	1																		
2006	BC	18	0	3	0	29	5.0	34.0	1	0	2																				
2	Years	36	0	3	1	70	9.0	69.0	1	0	5	6	1																		
DARRELL WILSON Darrell Kenton CB 5'11 180 Connecticut B: 7/28/1958 Camden, NJ Pro: N																															
1982	TOR	16							3	8														1	5	5.0	5				
1983	TOR+	16	0		1		1.0		4	115		6	1																		
1984	TOR	16	0		3				2	0		6	1															2	50	25.0	25
1985	TOR	16	1		2				4	46																					
1986	TOR	11	0		2				1	0		6	1											1	0	0.0	0				
5	Years	75	1		8		1.0		14	169		18	3											2	5	2.5	5	2	50	25.0	25
DON WILSON Donald Allen DB 6'2 190 Ellsworth JC; North Carolina State B: 7/21/1961 Washington, DC Pro: N																															
1987	EDM	15	1		2	69	1.0		7	127		6	1											10	83	8.3	16	1	9	9.0	9
1988	EDM+	18	0		2	54	1.0		7	68														4	5	1.3	4	2	44	22.0	23
1989	EDM*	18	0		2	57	4.0		4	35		6	1											8	124	15.5	37				
1990	TOR*	18	0		2	64			6	134		6	1						1	28	28.0	28	0								
1991	TOR*	18	0		1	66			7	184		6	1																		

Year	Team	GP	FM	FF	FR	TK	SK	YDS	IR	YDS	PD	PTS	TD	RA	YDS	AVG	LG	TD	REC	YDS	AVG	LG	TD	PR	YDS	AVG	LG	KOR	YDS	AVG	LG
1992	TOR+	18	2		1	55	2.0	9.0	6	162		12	2															3	39	13.0	25
1993	EDM*	18	0		1	72	2.0	15.0	7	68		6	1																		
1994	EDM	18				58	2.0	17.0	4	105	9																				
1995	TOR	17	1		0	63	1.0	9.0	6	46	7	6	1															1	9	9.0	9
1996	TOR	18	0		2	60	2.0	15.0	1	42	5																				
1997	BC	12	0	1	1	51			4	19	3																				
1998	EDM	9	0	0	1	28	3.0	18.0	2	56	1																				
12	Years	197	4	1	15	697	18.0	83.0	61	1046	25	48	8						1	28	28.0	28	0	22	212	9.6	37	7	101	14.4	25
DWAINE WILSON Dwaine RB 5'11 190 Long Beach JC; Idaho State B: 11/7/1959 D: 4/12/2008 Lake Elsinore, CA																															
1984	MTL*	16	8		1							30	5	226	1083	4.8	36	4	58	428	7.4	37	1					2	50	25.0	25
1985	MTL	13	2		1							12	2	110	435	4.0	43	1	45	381	8.5	75	1					6	106	17.7	24
2	Years	29	10		2							42	7	336	1518	4.5	43	5	103	809	7.9	75	2					8	156	19.5	25
EARL WILSON Earl DE-LB-DT 6'4 280 Kentucky B: 9/13/1958 Long Branch, NJ Pro: N																															
1982	TOR	11					4.5																								
1983	TOR	16	0		2		7.5																								
1984	TOR	14	0		2		5.0																								
3	Years	41	0		4		17.0																								
ERIC WILSON Eric DT-OG 6'3 287 Michigan B: 1/30/1978 Monroe, MI Pro: E																															
2002	WPG	15	0	0	1	12					1																				
2003	WPG	17	0	0	1	4																									
2006	WPG	6				0																									
2007	MTL	4	0	1	2	5																									
2008	MTL	18	0	0	1	12	1.0	5.0	1	0	1																	3	39	13.0	19
2009	MTL	15	0	0	1	13	1.0	3.0				6	1						1	1	1.0	1	1								
2010	MTL	18	0	0	1	12	2.0	7.0																							
2011	MTL	17	0	0	1	13	1.0	2.0			1																				
8	Years	110	0	1	8	83	5.0	17.0	1	0	3	6	1						1	1	1.0	1	1					3	39	13.0	19
GENE WILSON James Eugene OHB 6'0 183 South Carolina B: 11/10/1930 Barnwell, SC D: 4/26/2010 Tega Cay, SC Draft: 11-128 1954 WAS																															
1954	TOR+	13							4	73		35	7	108	702	6.5	55	5	34	379	11.1	37	2					14	282	20.1	39
1957	TOR	1												17	54	3.2	8	0	1	6	6.0	6	0								
1957	MTL	2												4	6	1.5	6	0	1	9	9.0	9	0								
1957	Year	3												21	60	2.9	8	0	2	15	7.5	9	0								
2	Years	14							4	73		35	7	129	762	5.9	55	5	36	394	10.9	37	2					14	282	20.1	39
JERRY WILSON Gerald Roscoe DE 6'2 238 Auburn B: 12/9/1936 Birmingham, AL Draft: 2-14 1959 CHIC Pro: N																															
1962	TOR	9																													
1963	TOR	10							1	-3		6	0						4	50	12.5	18	0					1	10	10.0	10
1964	TOR	2																	5	84	16.8	22	0								
3	Years	21							1	-3		6	0						9	134	14.9	22	0					1	10	10.0	10
JOHN WILSON John C 6'1 235 Alberta B: 1946 Draft: 1967 HAM; 2- 1968 OTT																															
1968	EDM	16	0		1																										
JONATHAN WILSON Jonathan DB 6'2 210 Hampton B: 12/20/1970 Hampton, VA																															
1992	TOR	11	4		1	18	2.0	21.0	1	0														9	29	3.2	14	9	183	20.3	40
1993	TOR	9	0		1	23	1.0	1.0	1	16																					
1994	SHR	3				4																									
1995	SHR	12	0		1	31			1	20	5																				
4	Years	35	4		3	76	3.0	22.0	3	36	5													9	29	3.2	14	9	183	20.3	40
JUSTIN WILSON Justin LB 5'10 194 Southern Mississippi B: 1/1/1988																															
2011	SAS	1				1																									
KIRBY WILSON Kirby DB 5'9 155 Pasadena CC; Illinois B: 8/24/1961																															
1983	WPG	13	1		2				2	5														16	186	11.6	44	13	294	22.6	42
LEN WILSON Leonard HB 6'1 192 Purdue B: 1938 Draft: FS 1960 LAC; 7A-76 1960 PIT																															
1960	SAS	7	0		1														2	26	13.0	17	0					4	87	21.8	27
MEL WILSON Melford C 6'2 230 Winnipeg St. John's Grads Jrs. B: 4/3/1917																															
1946	WPG+	8										1	0																		
1947	WPG+	8																													
1948	MTL	12																													
1949	CAL+	14																													
1950	CAL	10																													
1951	CAL	1																													
6	Years	53										1	0																		
MELVIN WILSON Melvin DB 6'1 193 Northridge State B: 12/10/1952 Draft: 5-136 1976 NYG																															
1976	CAL	5																													
MIKE WILSON Michael DeForest OT-OG 6'1 243 Dayton B: 10/20/1947 Wilmington, OH Draft: 14-343 1969 CIN Pro: NUW																															
1976	HAM	10																													
1977	HAM*	16	0		1																										
1978	HAM	16																													
1979	EDM*	15																													
1980	EDM*	15																													
5	Years	72	0		1																										
MIKE WILSON Michael S. DB 5'11 200 Western Illinois B: 11/19/1946 Washington, DC Pro: N																															
1971	BC	15			3				3	50														39	302	7.7	36	2	62	31.0	34
1972	BC	5							2	21														9	58	6.4	17	1	12	12.0	12
1973	BC	16	2		0				7	119		6	1											1	11	11.0	11				
1974	BC	6							3	57																					
4	Years	42	2		3				15	247		6	1											49	371	7.6	36	3	74	24.7	34
MIKE WILSON William Mike OT 6'5 280 Georgia B: 5/28/1955 Norfolk, VA Draft: 4B-103 1977 CIN Pro: N																															
1977	TOR	16	1		2														1	15	15.0	15	0								
MILT WILSON Milton DE 6'2 245 San Diego State B: 7/20/1964																															
1990	TOR	1																													
O'NEIL WILSON O'Neil SB-WR 6'2 191 Burlington Braves Jrs.; Connecticut B: 1/15/1978 Scarborough, ON Draft: 3B-25 2004 MTL																															
2004	MTL	14				3						6	1						20	263	13.2	37	1								
2005	MTL	10				2						6	1						3	6	2.0	7	1					1	6	6.0	6
2006	MTL	17	1	0	1	1													46	528	11.5	38	0								
2007	WPG	17				3													38	366	9.6	36	0								
2008	HAM	6	1	0	1	0													3	28	9.3	19	0								
2008	BC	7				2						12	2						17	175	10.3	21	2								
2008	Year	13	1	0	1	2						12	2						20	203	10.2	21	2								
2009	BC	18	1	0	0	3						6	1						35	405	11.6	33	1								
2010	BC	18	0	0	2	1													30	256	8.5	20	0								
7	Years	100	3	0	4	15						30	5						192	2027	10.6	38	5					1	6	6.0	6
PETER WILSON Peter C 6'2 235 Simon Fraser B: 9/6/1957 Draft: 6-50 1980 HAM																															
1981	BC	10																													
1982	BC	16	0		1																										
1983	SAS	6																													
3	Years	32	0		1																										
SAM WILSON Sammie DB 5'11 196 Fresno State B: 6/20/1976 Los Angeles, CA																															
1999	WPG	4				1																									
SPENCER WILSON Spencer OG 6'7 325 Okanagan Sun Jrs.; Saginaw Valley State; Calgary Colts Jrs. B: 4/7/1988 Toronto, ON																															
2011	CAL	3				0																									
TERRY WILSON Terry CB-DH 6'1 200 Stanford B: 1942																															
1964	EDM	16																	2	18	9.0	10	0								
1965	EDM	16	1		0																			2	4	2.0	4				

Year	Team	GP	FM	FF	FR	TK	SK	YDS	IR	YDS	PD	PTS	TD	RA	YDS	AVG	LG	TD	REC	YDS	AVG	LG	TD	PR	YDS	AVG	LG	KOR	YDS	AVG	LG
1966	EDM	16																										1	0	0.0	0
1967	EDM	16	0		1																										
1968	CAL	16	0		1				1	0																					
1969	CAL	16	0		1				5	119																					
1970	CAL	16	0		1				7	66																					
1971	CAL	16																													
1972	CAL	12							3	47																					
9	Years	140	1		4				16	232									2	18	9.0	10	0	2	4	2.0	4	1	0	0.0	0
TROY WILSON Troy Anthony CB 5'10 170 Notre Dame B: 9/19/1965 San Antonio, TX Pro: N																															
1987	OTT	2				1			2	41																					
1988	OTT	18	0		1	71	1.0		10	108		6	1																		
1989	OTT	13	0		2	54			4	64		6	1											4	35	8.8	25				
1990	OTT*	15	0		8	47			8	132		6	1											4	26	6.5	9				
4	Years	48	0		11	173	1.0		24	345		18	3											8	61	7.6	25				
WALTER WILSON Walter James WR 5'10 185 East Carolina B: 10/6/1966 Baltimore, MD Draft: 3C-67 1990 SD Pro: EN																															
1994	BAL	18				2						24	4						50	900	18.0	61	4								
1995	MEM	7				0						6	1						14	165	11.8	43	1								
2	Years	25				2						30	5						64	1065	16.6	61	5								
WOODROW WILSON Woodrow DB 5'10 182 North Carolina State B: 9/10/1956 Hampton, VA Draft: 10A-250 1980 PIT Pro: U																															
1980	MTL	13	0		3				2	47																					
1981	MTL	6	0		1				1	0																		2	56	28.0	37
2	Years	19	0		4				3	47																		2	56	28.0	37
KELLY WILTSHIRE Kelly LB-S 5'11 192 Hudson Valley CC; James Madison B: 6/28/1972 St. Laurent, QC Draft: 1-2 1996 TOR																															
1997	TOR	18	1	0	0	37	2.0	17.0	2	14	0																	3	27	9.0	14
1998	TOR+	18	0	2	4	80	4.0	29.0	3	48	5	12	2																		
1999	TOR	18	0	0	3	88	5.0	27.0	2	13	7																				
2000	MTL	18	0	0	2	74	5.0	32.0	1	5	4																				
2001	MTL	18	0	0	1	67	1.0	3.0	1	6	5	6	1																		
2002	OTT	18	0	0	2	92	3.0	27.0			4																				
2003	OTT+	18	0	2	0	91	3.0	25.0	2	15	6																				
2004	OTT	18	0	0	3	84	1.0	10.0	1	12	0																				
2005	EDM	17	0	1	0	51	1.0	5.0	3	13	4																				
2006	EDM	11				19					2																	3	17	5.7	11
10	Years	172	1	5	15	683	25.0	175.0	15	126	37	18	3															6	44	7.3	14
PRINCE WIMBLEY Prince, III SB-WR 5'9 178 Alabama B: 9/22/1970 Miami, FL																															
1994	LV	14	2		0	1						18	3						49	714	14.6	49	3								
1995	SAS	7				0													20	225	11.3	33	0					2	65	32.5	33
1995	BIR	1				0													4	54	13.5	36	0								
1995	Year	8				0													24	279	11.6	36	0					2	65	32.5	33
1997	HAM	13				2						8	1						42	637	15.2	69	1								
3	Years	34	2		0	3						26	4						115	1630	14.2	69	4					2	65	32.5	33
DANNY WIMPRINE Danny QB 6'1 222 Memphis B: 8/6/1981 New Orleans, LA																															
2005	CAL	18	1	0	0	0								3	22	7.3	14	0													
TYDUS WINANS Tydus Oran WR 5'11 185 Fresno State B: 7/26/1972 Draft: 3A-68 1994 WAS Pro: NX																															
1997	SAS	2				0													5	74	14.8	40	0					5	59	11.8	18
KEN WINEY Ken WR 5'11 180 Southern University B: 9/17/1962 Lake Charles, LA																															
1987	WPG	16	3		0	0						12	2						8	80	10.0	25	1	33	211	6.4	40	28	552	19.7	93
1988	WPG	8				0													2	36	18.0	18	0	1	8	8.0	8	4	36	9.0	15
1989	WPG	18	1		1	0						12	2						10	166	16.6	40	2	31	213	6.9	38	27	421	15.6	27
1990	WPG	8	2		0	0						6	1						11	173	15.7	34	1	26	246	9.5	43	11	170	15.5	29
1991	WPG	3				0													3	34	11.3	15	0	8	132	16.5	63	4	79	19.8	45
1992	EDM	10				1													9	180	20.0	38	0	3	2	0.7	3	1	7	7.0	7
1993	TOR	6	1		0	4													8	83	10.4	15	0	4	40	10.0	31	3	36	12.0	17
7	Years	69	7		1	5						30	5						51	752	14.7	40	4	106	852	8.0	63	78	1301	16.7	93
EARL WINFIELD Earl WR 5'11 185 North Carolina B: 8/6/1961 Petersburg, VA																															
1987	HAM	11	5		0	2						18	3						38	746	19.6	81	2	22	256	11.6	71	18	347	19.3	34
1988	HAM*	18	7		2	2						78	13	1	2	2.0	2	0	60	1213	20.2	73	8	74	865	11.7	101	20	532	26.6	100
1989	HAM	9	2		0	0						24	4	2	18	9.0	10	0	15	324	21.6	56	3	36	361	10.0	77	10	226	22.6	43
1990	HAM+	13	2		0	5						78	13						62	1054	17.0	75	13	24	102	4.3	19	8	164	20.5	34
1991	HAM	10	1		0	4						24	4	2	5	2.5	13	0	45	874	19.4	77	4	2	15	7.5	15	1	20	20.0	20
1992	HAM	12	3		0	5						66	11	1	7	7.0	7	0	52	880	16.9	80	9	22	291	13.2	77	1	20	20.0	20
1993	HAM	15	3		3	7						48	8	1	-8	-8.0	-8	0	61	1076	17.6	79	5	41	530	12.9	71	13	282	21.7	44
1994	HAM+	14	5		0	3						72	12	3	43	14.3	21	0	71	1211	17.1	79	12	37	267	7.2	43	3	56	18.7	28
1995	HAM*	18	1		0	4						78	13						92	1496	16.3	57	13	8	61	7.6	47				
1996	HAM	14	3		0	0						24	4						48	783	16.3	50	4	13	80	6.2	13	1	3	3.0	3
1997	HAM	6				0						12	2						29	462	15.9	59	2	2	6	3.0	3				
11	Years	140	32		5	32						522	87	10	67	6.7	21	0	573	10119	17.7	81	75	281	2834	10.1	101	75	1650	22.0	100
CARL WINFREY Carl LeNell (Chuck) LB 6'0 230 Wisconsin B: 3/27/1949 Chicago, IL Pro: N																															
1974	BC	3																													
1974	SAS	3																													
1974	Year	6																													
1975	MTL	6																													
2	Years	9																													
JARRED WINKEL Jarred RB 5'11 210 Alberta B: 10/28/1980 Edmonton, AB																															
2006	EDM	5	1	0	0	0								3	12	4.0	8	0													
2007	EDM	4				1																									
2	Years	9	1	0	0	1								3	12	4.0	8	0													
MARCUS WINN Marcus LB-DB 6'1 205 Alabama State B: 12/26/1981 Jackson, MS																															
2005	EDM	6	0	0	1	9																						1	0	0.0	0
2006	EDM	16				27																									
2007	WPG	3	0	2	0	3	1.0	0.0			1																				
2008	WPG	5				3																									
4	Years	30	0	2	1	42	1.0	0.0			1																	1	0	0.0	0
JOHN WINTERMEYER John RB-K 6'0 215 Queen's; Wilfrid Laurier B: 8/19/1951 Draft: 8-68 1974 TOR																															
1975	BC	8										37	0																		
BILL WINTERS William Randolph OT 6'5 270 Princeton B: 7/22/1954 New Shrewsbury, NJ Pro: U																															
1978	MTL	8																													
BOB WINTERS Bob QB 6'1 190 Yakima JC; Utah State B: 1936 Draft: 22-258 1957 CLE																															
1958	BC	1																													
CHARLES WINTERS Charles S-DH-LB 5'11 198 Michigan B: 2/7/1974 Detroit, MI																															
2003	TOR	17	0	1	2	38																						6	126	21.0	34
2004	TOR	14	0	1	2	31	1.0	4.0	1	5	2																	1	7	7.0	7
2005	TOR	14	0	2	0	38	2.0	7.0			3																				
2006	TOR	12	0	1	1	39	3.0	17.0			2																				
2007	TOR	16	0	3	0	38	1.0	7.0	1	8	7																				
2008	TOR	10	0	0	1	37					3																				
6	Years	83	0	8	6	221	7.0	35.0	2	13	17																	7	133	19.0	34
GEORGE WINTON George E none																															
1946	OTT	2																													
NORM WINTON Norm DT-K 6'3 246 Oregon State B: 4/7/1943 Vancouver, BC																															
1965	WPG	10										27	0																		
1966	WPG	16	0		3							70	1																		

Year	Team	GP	FM	FF	FR	TK	SK	YDS	IR	YDS	PD	PTS	TD	RA	YDS	AVG	LG	TD	REC	YDS	AVG	LG	TD	PR	YDS	AVG	LG	KOR	YDS	AVG	LG
1968	CAL	2																													
3	Years	28	0		3							97	1																		
NOBBY WIRKOWSKI Norbert QB-DB 5'10 175 Miami (Ohio) B: 8/20/1926 Chicago, IL																															
1951	TOR	9																													
1952	TOR	12										20	4					4													
1953	TOR	13																													
1954	TOR	13												21	72	3.4	13	0													
1955	HAM	12												8	12	1.5	5	0													
1956	HAM	8												10	58	5.8	14	0													
1957	CAL	11	4		0									33	-63	-1.9	12	0													
1958	CAL	16	5		2							30	5	45	-73	-1.6	10	5													
1959	CAL	16	1		0									2	9	4.5	9	0													
1960	TOR	14												3	13	4.3	7	0	1	-3	-3.0	-3	0								
10	Years	124	10		2							50	9	122	28	0.2	14	9	1	-3	-3.0	-3	0								
DEATRICH WISE Deatrich DE 6'5 260 Jackson State B: 6/5/1965 Rosedale, MS Draft: 9-242 1988 SEA																															
1990	BC	11	0		2	14	2.0																								
1991	BC	8	0		1	18	2.0																								
2	Years	19	0		3	32	4.0																								
MYRON WISE Myron Martinez SB-WR 6'1 170 Palomar CC B: 6/26/1972 Brenham, TX																															
1993	SAC	2				0																									
1994	SAC	10				10						18	3						20	340	17.0	28	3					3	62	20.7	21
1995	SA	15				12						18	3						27	606	22.4	75	3								
1996	WPG	8				5						12	2						32	502	15.7	50	2								
1998	EDM	6				2						18	3						13	215	16.5	31	3								
5	Years	41				29						66	11						92	1663	18.1	75	11					3	62	20.7	21
TODD WISEMAN Todd DB 5'11 185 Simon Fraser; San Diego State B: 5/26/1965 Dunnville, ON Draft: 2A-13 1987 BC																															
1987	BC	18	0		2	3			1	23		6	1											1	0	0.0	0				
1988	BC	17				6																		3	9	3.0	0				
1989	TOR	17	0		1	15	1.0		1	26																					
1991	HAM	18	1		2	79	1.0		3	87														7	46	6.6	10				
1992	HAM+	18	0		3	53			5	105																					
1993	HAM	18				30			2	46																					
1994	HAM	18	1		2	51			5	117	3	6	1																		
7	Years	124	2		10	237	2.0		17	404	3	12	2											11	55	5.0	10				
ALI WITHERSPOON Ali Hakim LB 6'1 225 Delaware B: 11/8/1962 Mount Holly, NJ Draft: TD 1985 BAL-USFL																															
1985	MTL	6	0		1																										
DERRICK WITHERSPOON Derrick Leon RB 5'10 196 Clemson B: 2/14/1971 Sumter, SC Pro: N																															
1994	SHR	1												3	1	0.3	1	0													
JIMMY WITHERSPOON Jim LB 6'0 230 Ouachita Baptist B: 3/14/1970																															
1994	SHR	6																													
MIKE WITHYCOMBE Mike W. OG-C 6'5 298 West Hills JC; Fresno State B: 11/18/1964 Meridian, MS Draft: 5-119 1988 NYJ Pro: EN																															
1995	BAL*	17	1		1	3																									
1996	MTL	11				0																									
1997	BC+	15	2	0	0	0																									
3	Years	43	3	0	1	3																									
STEVE WITKOWSKI Stephen G 6'1 240 Central Missouri B: 1943																															
1969	HAM	2																													
MEL WITT Hillery Melvin DE 6'3 261 Texas-Arlington B: 11/23/1945 Fort Worth, TX Draft: 5-128 1967 BOS Pro: N																															
1967	MTL	2																													
JOHN WITTE John August T 6'3 235 Oregon State B: 1/29/1933 D: 3/17/1993 Portland, OR Draft: 9-103 1955 LARM																															
1957	SAS	13																													
CAS WITUCKI Casimir Leo (Slug) OG 5'11 245 Indiana B: 5/26/1928 South Bend, IN Draft: 21-266 1950 WAS Pro: N																															
1955	TOR	6																													
RAY WLADICHUK Ray S 6'1 190 Simon Fraser B: 11/7/1987 Vernon, BC Draft: 5B-38 2009 HAM																															
2010	HAM	2				1																									
2011	HAM	14				6																									
2	Years	16				7																									
GENE WLASIUK Eugene OHB-DH-S 5'9 165 Winnipeg Rods Jrs. B: 2/24/1936 Winnipeg, MB																															
1957	WPG	4												2	5	2.5	4	0						2	13	6.5	11				
1958	WPG	7												3	14	4.7	8	0						4	37	9.3	19				
1959	WPG	1																													
1959	SAS	9										6	1	8	19	2.4	4	0	2	33	16.5	24	0	25	261	10.4	23	9	151	16.8	26
1959	Year	10										6	1	8	19	2.4	4	0	2	33	16.5	24	0	25	261	10.4	23	9	151	16.8	26
1960	SAS	16	0		2				3	10														47	322	6.9	18				
1961	SAS	16			3				4	30														50	334	6.7	27	2	34	17.0	21
1962	SAS	16	3						5	59		6	1											70	407	5.8	67	1	23	23.0	23
1963	SAS	14	2		1				4	73														55	325	5.9	24				
1964	SAS	16	0		2				5	80														51	307	6.0	23				
1965	SAS	16	3		2				1															78	528	6.8	33	2	39	19.5	22
1966	SAS	16	2		2				2	10														84	486	5.8	22	2	43	21.5	22
1967	SAS	16	3		0				3	25														79	326	4.1	16				
11	Years	138	13		12				27	287		12	2	13	38	2.9	8	0	2	33	16.5	24	0	545	3346	6.1	67	16	290	18.1	26
GREG WOJT Greg OG-OT 6'4 285 Central Michigan B: 11/22/1986 Warsaw, Poland Draft: 2-11 2008 EDM																															
2009	EDM	2				0																									
2010	EDM	17	0	0	1	1																									
2011	EDM+	14				0																									
3	Years	33	0	0	1	1																									
PAUL WOLDU Paul CB 6'0 168 Regina Thunder Jrs.; Saskatchewan B: 9/14/1984 Regina, SK Draft: 5-36 2008 MTL																															
2008	MTL	18				19			1	39	1																				
2009	MTL	16				25			1	72	1	6	1																		
2010	MTL	17				12																									
2011	MTL	14				22			1	0	2																				
4	Years	65				78			3	111	4	6	1																		
JIM WOLF James DE 6'3 250 Prairie View A&M B: 3/4/1952 Woodville, TX D: 12/17/2003 Beaumont, TX Draft: 6A-149 1974 PIT; 30-350 1974 FLA-WFL Pro: N																															
1975	TOR	2																													
1977	HAM	1																													
1978	SAS	1																													
3	Years	4																													
KEVIN WOLFOLK Kevin Jay LB 6'1 230 Portland State B: 6/2/1967 Cocoa Beach, FL Pro: E																															
1989	TOR	3				6																									
RICK WOLKENSPERG Rick WR-SB 6'3 190 Western Ontario B: 9/2/1965 Toronto, ON Draft: 7-55 1987 OTT																															
1987	OTT	18	1		0	0						6	1						31	467	15.1	37	1					1	4	4.0	4
STAN WOLKOWSKI Stan HB-QB 5'10 170 Hamilton Wildcats Jrs. B: 1925																															
1947	HAM	6																													
1950	HAM	11																													
2	Years	17																													
CASEY WOOD Casey T 6'5 245 Toronto B: 1940 Draft: 1A-1 1961 HAM																															
1961	TOR	14																													
CHUCK WOOD Chuck G 6'0 217 Lachine Lakers; Lakeshore Redskins; McGill B: 7/26/1940 Montreal, QC Draft: 1-2 1962 OTT																															
1962	OTT	13																													
1963	OTT	3																													
1964	MTL	11																													

Year	Team	GP	FM	FF	FR	TK	SK	YDS	IR	YDS	PD	PTS	TD	RA	YDS	AVG	LG	TD	REC	YDS	AVG	LG	TD	PR	YDS	AVG	LG	KOR	YDS	AVG	LG
3	Years	27																													
DUANE WOOD Duane Scott S-OHB-DH 6'1 196 Oklahoma State B: 9/20/1937 Wilburton, OK Pro: N																															
1959	HAM+	14							3	72		12	2	47	237	5.0	24	0	13	179	13.8	41	1	51	476	9.3	40	16	301	18.8	33
1960	HAM	6												8	49	6.1	18	0	7	123	17.6	43	0	6	25	4.2	14	2	61	30.5	37
1965	EDM	11							2	34																					
3	Years	31							5	106		12	2	55	286	5.2	24	0	20	302	15.1	43	1	57	501	8.8	40	18	362	20.1	37
GARY WOOD Gary Fay QB 5'11 188 Cornell B: 2/5/1942 Taylor, NY D: 3/2/1994 Melville, NY Draft: 17-132 1964 BOS; 8B-109 1964 NYG Pro: N																															
1970	OTT+	14	6		0							24	4	86	493	5.7	30	4													
1971	OTT	10	3		0							12	2	35	224	6.4	50	2													
2	Years	24	9		0							36	6	121	717	5.9	50	6													
JIM WOOD Jim D. E-P 6'1 225 Oklahoma State B: 1938 Draft: 4-40 1959 WAS																															
1959	BC	5												1	-2	-2.0	-2	0	5	124	24.8	60	0								
LARRY WOOD Lawrence A. DB 6'1 187 Northwestern B: 1939 Draft: 16- 1961 HOU; 6B-75 1961 LARM																															
1962	TOR	1							1	18																					
LIONEL WOOD Lionel G-E 6'0 210 B: 1925																															
1947	WPG	8																													
1949	WPG	13																													
2	Years	21																													
JONTA WOODARD Jonta Dewaine OT 6'5 341 San Joaquin Delta CC; Louisville B: 7/22/1978 Stockton, CA																															
2004	HAM	18	0	0	1	3																									
2005	HAM	17				1																									
2006	HAM	8				0																									
2007	HAM	18				2																									
2008	HAM	9				0																									
2008	TOR	3				0																									
2008	Year	12				0																									
2009	TOR	7				1																									
6	Years	77	0	0	1	7																									
PAT WOODCOCK Patrick I. WR-SB 5'9 166 Syracuse B: 4/27/1977 Ottawa, ON Draft: 2A-11 2001 MTL																															
2001	MTL	2				0																		2	16	8.0	12	6	113	18.8	21
2002	MTL+	15				1						30	5	1	13	13.0	13	0	35	838	23.9	95	5								
2003	MTL	7				2						6	1						22	222	10.1	30	1					1	17	17.0	17
2004	OTT	14	2	0	0	0						12	2	1	30	30.0	30	0	36	504	14.0	59	2								
2005	OTT	15				1						20	3	4	35	8.8	18	0	28	356	12.7	49	3								
2006	EDM	17				0						6	1	2	-22	-11.0	-9	0	32	419	13.1	47	1					7	157	22.4	61
2007	EDM	3				0													4	86	21.5	33	0	10	93	9.3	37	2	33	16.5	17
2008	HAM	18				0													21	353	16.8	50	0	6	57	9.5	20	5	77	15.4	20
8	Years	91	2	0	0	4						74	12	8	56	7.0	30	0	178	2778	15.6	95	12	18	166	9.2	37	21	397	18.9	61
DOUG WOODLIEF Douglas Eugene LB 6'3 231 Chipola JC; Memphis B: 9/4/1943 Marianna, FL Draft: RS-4- 1965 SD; 5B-65 1965 LARM Pro: N																															
1972	CAL	1																													
GERRY WOODLOCK Gerald G 6'1 185 Calgary West End Jrs. B: 1923																															
1946	CAL	7																													
1947	CAL	1																													
1949	EDM	13																													
3	Years	21																													
ANDREW WOODRUFF Andrew OG 6'3 320 Victoria Rebels Jrs.; Boise State B: 5/7/1985 Victoria, BC Draft: 2-12 2008 MTL																															
2009	MTL	7				0																									
2010	MTL	17				0																									
2011	MTL	18	0	0	1	1																									
3	Years	42	0	0	1	1																									
COWBOY WOODRUFF James Lee OHB 5'10 180 Mississippi																															
1960	EDM	12	5		1							10	1	32	134	4.2	18	0	10	134	13.4	40	1	36	158	4.4	15	10	201	20.1	33
TONY WOODRUFF Tony DeWayne WR 6'0 175 King's River CC; Los Angeles Harbor JC; Fresno State B: 11/12/1958 Hazen, AR Draft: 9-244 1982 PHI Pro: N																															
1986	CAL	5										24	4						14	283	20.2	51	4								
1987	CAL	9				2						6	1						13	306	23.5	69	1								
2	Years	14				2						30	5						27	589	21.8	69	5								
BILLY WOODS Billy Ray CB 6'1 200 Murray JC; North Texas B: 7/2/1946 Midland, TX Draft: 16-400 1969 DEN																															
1968	MTL	5	0		0																										
1969	HAM	1																													
2	Years	6	0		0																										
CHRIS WOODS Christopher Wyatt WR 5'10 195 Auburn B: 7/19/1962 Birmingham, AL Draft: TD 1984 BIR-USFL Pro: N																															
1984	EDM	15	3		1							42	7	3	60	20.0	24	0	38	837	22.0	81	6	31	303	9.8	90	18	442	24.6	62
1985	EDM	13	1		0							36	6	3	9	3.0	10	0	41	779	19.0	89	6	36	366	10.2	48	10	239	23.9	81
1986	TOR	17	1		1							36	6	2	10	5.0	7	0	61	1163	19.1	54	6	64	595	9.3	74	8	152	19.0	31
3	Years	45	5		2							114	19	8	79	9.9	24	0	140	2779	19.9	89	18	131	1264	9.6	90	36	833	23.1	81
GREG WOODS Greg RB 5'11 185 Kentucky B: 1/26/1955 Middletown, CT																															
1977	OTT	3										6	1	4	18	4.5	6	1										2	47	23.5	24
HAROLD WOODS Harold Lee CB 5'10 177 Potomac State; West Virginia B: 12/24/1955 Richmond, VA Pro: U																															
1978	SAS	5	0		1																			3	34	11.3	16	5	180	36.0	52
1979	HAM	16	1		1				5	39									1	19	19.0	19	0	9	54	6.0	12	18	416	23.1	50
1980	HAM*	16	0		1				2	12																		26	549	21.1	44
1981	HAM+	15	1		1				6	97		6	1															4	92	23.0	28
1982	HAM	2	1		0																							1	12	12.0	12
1982	TOR	5							1	1																		2	45	22.5	26
1982	Year	7	1		0				1	1																		3	57	19.0	26
1983	MTL	4	0		2																										
6	Years	58	3		6				14	149		6	1						1	19	19.0	19	0	12	88	7.3	16	56	1294	23.1	52
RASHAUN WOODS Rashaun Dorrell WR 6'2 202 Oklahoma State B: 10/17/1980 Oklahoma City, OK Draft: 1-31 2004 SF Pro: EN																															
2007	TOR	2				0													3	21	7.0	8	0								
2007	HAM	1				0																									
2007	Year	3				0													3	21	7.0	8	0								
ROBERT WOODS Robert Christopher WR 5'7 170 Grambling State B: 7/3/1955 New Orleans, LA Draft: 5C-134 1978 KC Pro: N																															
1980	WPG	8	1		1							20	3						35	500	14.3	64	2	8	136	17.0	62	3	50	16.7	22
SCOTT WOODS Scott DE-LB 6'0 240 Oregon State B: 1951																															
1973	SAS	3																													
SILAS WOODS Silas S. G 6'0 210 Marquette B: 6/30/1938 Draft: FS 1960 OAK; 4B-38 1960 STL																															
1960	HAM	1																										1	0	0.0	0
TED WOODS Ted FB-OHB 6'1 195 Colorado B: 1941 Draft: 5A-62 1962 SF																															
1964	CAL	13	1		0							12	2	82	426	5.2	41	2	4	39	9.8	22	0					7	92	13.1	26
1965	CAL	16	4		2							36	6	146	714	4.9	51	6	8	17	2.1	21	0					21	586	27.9	47
1966	CAL	2	1		0									17	99	5.8	28	0	1	-4	-4.0	-4	0					3	96	32.0	43
1968	CAL	15	2		1				1	9		24	4	53	289	5.5	54	1	11	82	7.5	23	3	1	1	1.0	1	15	361	24.1	53
1969	CAL	16	7		1							36	6	182	739	4.1	30	5	14	130	9.3	33	1					15	349	23.3	37
5	Years	62	15		4				1	9		108	18	480	2267	4.7	54	14	38	264	6.9	33	4	1	1	1.0	1	61	1484	24.3	53
TONY WOODS Clinton Anthony DT 6'4 274 Rose State*; Oklahoma B: 3/14/1966 Fort Lee, VA Draft: 8A-216 1989 CHIB Pro: EN																															
1993	EDM	16	0		2	25	8.0	45.0																							
1994	EDM	18				21	9.0	65.0																							
1995	EDM	14				25	2.0	27.0	0	0	1																				
3	Years	48	0		2	71	19.0	137.0																							
KEITH WOODSIDE Keith A. RB 5'11 213 Texas A&M B: 7/29/1964 Natchez, MS Draft: 3-61 1988 GB Pro: N																															
1994	WPG	2	1		0	1						6	1	20	120	6.0	27	1	13	101	7.8	21	0					5	98	19.6	23
1995	WPG	1				0								5	24	4.8	13	0	2	14	7.0	12	0								

Year	Team	GP	FM	FF	FR	TK	SK	YDS	IR	YDS	PD	PTS	TD	RA	YDS	AVG	LG	TD	REC	YDS	AVG	LG	TD	PR	YDS	AVG	LG	KOR	YDS	AVG	LG
1995	BIR	17	1		1	3						48	8	86	579	6.7	62	1	82	766	9.3	52	7					1	0	0.0	0
1995	Year	18	1		1	3								91	603	6.6	62	1	84	780	9.3	52	7					1	0	0.0	0
2	Years	3	2		1	4						54	9	111	723	6.5	62	2	97	881	9.1	52	7					6	98	16.3	23
ANTHONY WOODSON Anthony L. LB 6'2 225 Hawaii B: 7/12/1962 San Francisco, CA																															
1985	CAL	8					2.0																								
1986	CAL	15	0		1		5.0																								
1987	OTT	14				50	3.0																								
1988	OTT	1				0																									
4	Years	38	0		1	50	10.0																								
BEN WOODSON Robert B. OHB 5'11 190 Utah B: 1945 Draft: 15-384 1967 OAK																															
1967	CAL	14	5		1							6	1	85	401	4.7	41	0	24	200	8.3	54	1					13	268	20.6	30
SEAN WOODSON Sean Andre LB 6'1 214 Jackson State B: 8/27/1974 Jackson, MS Draft: 5-153 1997 BUF																															
2000	HAM	13	0	1	0	52			1	0	6																				
2001	HAM+	17	0	0	1	78	2.0	9.0	3	110	4	6	1																		
2002	HAM	18	0	1	2	75			1	30	3																	2	18	9.0	18
2003	HAM	14	0	0	1	67	3.0	8.0	1	20	1																				
2005	WPG	18	0	1	0	98	3.0	9.0			1																				
5	Years	80	0	3	4	370	8.0	26.0	6	160	15	6	1															2	18	9.0	18
SHAWN WOODSON Shawn Wilford LB 6'2 226 James Madison B: 8/12/1966 Charlottesville, VA Draft: 12A-331 1989 MIN Pro: E																															
1989	TOR	1				1																									
DOUG WOODWARD Douglas Philip QB 6'3 200 Pace B: 9/12/1958 Peekskill, NY Pro: U																															
1982	CAL	1																													
ROD WOODWARD Rodney William DB-FL 6'1 200 Renfrew Trojans Jrs.; Idaho B: 9/22/1944 Vancouver, BC																															
1967	MTL	13							1	10																					
1968	MTL	5																						5	37	7.4	12				
1969	MTL	14	0		2				5	98																					
1971	OTT	14	1		4				5	67														11	120	10.9	25				
1972	OTT+	14	2		1				7	116				1	8	8.0	8	0						13	114	8.8	21	4	99	24.8	30
1973	OTT	14	0		2				3	68		6	1											17	107	6.3	24	4	81	20.3	22
1974	OTT+	16							5	47		6	1	1	3	3.0	3	1						28	149	5.3	21				
1975	OTT*	12	2		2				8	189		12	2	2	10	5.0	7	1						21	59	2.8	20				
1976	OTT	16			1				3	56				2	12	6.0	24	0						4	52	13.0	19	1	24	24.0	24
1977	CAL	16							2	32																					
1978	HAM	4																													
11	Years	138	5		12				39	683		24	4	6	33	5.5	24	2						99	638	6.4	25	9	204	22.7	30
PETE WOOLLEY Pete G-T-HB 5'11 225 Hamilton Wildcats Jrs. B: 1930																															
1950	HAM	5																													
1951	HAM	12										5	1																		
1952	HAM	12																													
1953	HAM	12																													
1954	HAM	7																													
1956	HAM	12																													
6	Years	60										5	1																		
MARK WORD Mark Bernard DE 6'5 283 Hinds CC; Jacksonville State B: 11/23/1975 Miami, FL Pro: EN																															
2000	HAM	9				15	5.0	37.0			3																				
2001	HAM	1				3																									
2005	MTL	7	0	1	1	11	2.0	16.0			2																				
3	Years	17	0	1	1	29	7.0	53.0			5																				
JIM WORDEN James F. TE 6'1 230 Wittenberg B: 5/15/1942 D: 2/25/2007 Wellington, OH Draft: 14-185 1964 DAL																															
1964	SAS	16										12	2						11	228	20.7	75	2								
1965	SAS	16	1		0							18	3						26	433	16.7	52	3								
1966	SAS*	16	1		0							18	3						28	462	16.5	34	3					1	0	0.0	0
1967	SAS	13																	2	51	25.5	32	0								
1968	SAS	16	1		1							18	3						26	525	20.2	63	3								
1969	SAS	8																	4	90	22.5	43	0								
6	Years	85	3		1							66	11						97	1789	18.4	75	11					1	0	0.0	0
NEIL WORDEN Neil James (Bull) FB 5'10 193 Notre Dame B: 7/1/1931 Milwaukee, WI Draft: 1-9 1954 PHI Pro: N																															
1959	SAS	5												40	153	3.8	12	0	5	13	2.6	8	0					1	11	11.0	11
GEORGE WORKS George Kelly, Jr. RB 5'9 185 Northern Michigan B: 1/18/1960 Huntersville, NC Pro: U																															
1985	HAM	4	1		0									49	263	5.4	60	0	7	35	5.0	18	0								
RICK WORMAN Richard M. QB 6'2 200 Eastern Washington B: 10/21/1963 Mountain View, CA																															
1986	CAL	18																													
1987	CAL	17				0						30	5	29	180	6.2	16	5													
1988	CAL	13	4		1	0						14	2	19	148	7.8	25	2													
1988	EDM	4				0								2	6	3.0	4	0													
1988	Year	17	4		1	0						14	2	21	154	7.3	25	2													
1989	EDM	17				1								12	54	4.5	16	0													
1990	CAL	10	4		0	1						6	1	16	92	5.8	13	1													
1991	SAS	18	3		1	0						18	3	21	131	6.2	55	3													
6	Years	93	11		2	2						68	11	99	611	6.2	55	11													
ELWIN WOROBEC Elwin OT 6'3 250 Utah; Alberta B: 1958 Draft: 7-60 1980 OTT																															
1982	HAM	9																													
JOE WOROBEC Joe OG-OT 6'4 255 Drake B: 11/15/1951 Draft: TE 1973 EDM																															
1973	EDM	3																													
1974	EDM	16																													
1975	EDM	16																													
1976	EDM	16																													
1977	HAM	14																													
1978	SAS	8																													
6	Years	73																													
STEVE WORSTER Stephen Clark FB 6'2 218 Texas B: 7/8/1949 Draft: 4-90 1971 LARM																															
1971	HAM	3										6	1	23	72	3.1	9	0	5	83	16.6	55	1								
TOM WORTHINGTON Thomas John HB-FW 6'0 190 Northwestern B: 5/29/1925 Draft: 15-187 1950 DET																															
1951	HAM	6										1	0																		
ANTOINE WORTHMAN Antoine CB 5'10 193 Illinois State B: 6/20/1970 Gary, IN																															
1992	TOR	7				9	1.0	12.0																				3	6	2.0	3
1993	TOR	1	0		1	3																									
1994	SHR	14				33	1.0	11.0	2	11	3													1	11	11.0	11				
3	Years	22	0		1	45	2.0	23.0	2	11	3													1	11	11.0	11	3	6	2.0	3
FRED WORTHY Fred Lee DT 6'5 255 Clemson* B: 5/25/1959 Summerville, SC Pro: U																															
1985	CAL	1																													
JOHN WOYAT John HB 5'8 173 Vancouver Blue Bombers Jrs.; Oregon B: 1934																															
1955	EDM	3	1		0									1	2	2.0	2	0						4	15	3.8	15				
1956	EDM	9	2		0														0	26		26	0	24	128	5.3	13	1	3	3.0	3
1957	EDM	9	1																					47	200	4.3	19				
3	Years	21	4		0									1	2	2.0	2	0	0	26		26	0	75	343	4.6	19	1	3	3.0	3
LYALL WOZNESENSKY Lyall DE 6'7 240 St. Vital Mustangs Jrs.; Simon Fraser B: 4/4/1954 St. Boniface, MB Draft: TE 1977 WPG																															
1977	WPG	16	1		2																										
1978	WPG	16	0		1																										
1979	CAL	16	0		1																										
1980	HAM	16																													
1981	SAS+	16					14.0																								

Year	Team	GP	FM	FF	FR	TK	SK	YDS	IR	YDS	PD	PTS	TD	RA	YDS	AVG	LG	TD	REC	YDS	AVG	LG	TD	PR	YDS	AVG	LG	KOR	YDS	AVG	LG
1982	SAS	12					4.0																								
1983	TOR	6					1.0																								
1983	MTL	6	0		2		2.0																								
1983	Year	12	0		2		3.0																								
1984	CAL	16					15.0																								
8	Years	114	1		6		36.0																								
DICK WOZNEY Richard E. HB 5'8 180 North Dakota B: 4/17/1941 Brandon, MB																															
1965	WPG	16	1		0																			69	437	6.3	16	1	27	27.0	27
1966	WPG	11	2		1									4	18	4.5	6	0	1	13	13.0	13	0	39	201	5.2	17				
1967	WPG	15	2		2									8	31	3.9	13	0	2	16	8.0	14	0	44	257	5.8	15	2	44	22.0	22
1968	WPG	16	2		1																			77	512	6.6	31	2	48	24.0	30
4	Years	58	7		4									12	49	4.1	13	0	3	29	9.7	14	0	229	1407	6.1	31	5	119	23.8	30
JOHN WOZNIAK John Edward LB-C-OG 6'0 218 Alabama B: 8/2/1921 Arnold City, PA D: 8//1982 Tuscaloosa, AL Draft: 16-100 1948 BKN-AAFC; 5-34 1948 PIT Pro: AN																															
1953	SAS+	11							2	86														1	0	0.0	0				
1954	SAS+	14	1		0																										
1955	SAS	4							2	34																					
1956	SAS+	16	0		5				1	0																					
4	Years	45	1		5				5	120														1	0	0.0	0				
DAVE WRAY David LB 5'11 210 Alberta Draft: 1969 BC																															
1969	BC	16																													
GENE WREN Eugene RB 5'11 195 Southern Illinois; Jackson State B: 8/9/1945 Corinth, MS																															
1970	OTT	5	3		0							6	1	31	106	3.4	41	1	8	43	5.4	14	0					4	61	15.3	22
AL WRIGHT Al E																															
1948	SAS	7																													
CHARLIE WRIGHT Charles James CB 5'9 178 Highland CC; Fort Scott CC; Tulsa B: 4/5/1965 Carthage, MO Draft: 10-257 1987 STL Pro: N																															
1990	OTT	5	0		1	14			4	51																					
1991	OTT	9	0		1	16																									
1992	OTT	7				18			1	0														1	0	0.0	0				
1993	OTT	8				22			3	12														1	10	10.0	10				
1994	EDM	2				8	1.0																								
5	Years	31	0		2	78	1.0		8	63														2	10	5.0	10				
CHRIS WRIGHT Chris WR-RB 5'8 175 Georgia Southern B: 8/24/1972 Valdosta, GA D: 7/31/2005 Atlanta, GA																															
1995	BAL*	18	5		0	10						24	4	8	26	3.3	14	0	7	123	17.6	54	1	100	1236	12.4	89	41	897	21.9	62
1997	MTL	18	4	0	1	3						12	2						10	106	10.6	32	0	84	771	9.2	62	52	1088	20.9	87
1998	MTL	14	2	0	0	0													2	18	9.0	12	0	67	625	9.3	45	31	671	21.6	47
2002	BC	7	1	0	1	0								25	82	3.3	12	0	2	12	6.0	10	0	18	130	7.2	30	3	65	21.7	27
4	Years	57	12	0	2	13						36	6	33	108	3.3	14	0	21	259	12.3	54	1	269	2762	10.3	89	127	2721	21.4	87
DARRELL WRIGHT Darrell DE 6'4 285 Copiah-Lincoln JC; Reedley JC; Oregon B: 12/30/1979 Fort Pierce, FL Pro: E																															
2004	MTL	1				0																									
DONOVAN WRIGHT Donovan LB-CB 6'3 200 Slippery Rock B: 10/16/1966 Markham, ON Draft: 1C-4 1989 SAS																															
1989	SAS	12				7			1	5																		2	18	9.0	10
1991	TOR	6				7			1	34																		1	0	0.0	0
1992	BC	18	0		3	64	1.0	10.0	1	66		6	1																		
1993	BC	18	0		1	20																						1	0	0.0	0
1994	BC	18	0		1	23																									
1995	BC	17				22																						1	3	3.0	3
1996	HAM	18				24	1.0	4.0	1	0	1																				
1997	HAM	18				11																									
8	Years	125	0		5	178	2.0	14.0	4	105	1	6	1															5	21	4.2	10
DWAYNE WRIGHT Dwayne RB 5'11 228 West Hills JC; Fresno State B: 6/2/1983 Draft: 4-111 2007 BUF Pro: NU																															
2010	TOR	4				3						6	1	19	108	5.7	25	1													
FELIX WRIGHT Felix Carl DB 6'2 294 Drake B: 6/22/1959 Carthage, MO Pro: N																															
1982	HAM	2							2	32														1	3	3.0	3				
1983	HAM	12	2		3		1.5		6	140		6	1											7	36	5.1	11				
1984	HAM+	16	0		2				7	100		6	1																		
3	Years	30	2		5		1.5		15	272		12	2											8	39	4.9	11				
JAMES WRIGHT James Earl DB-QB 5'11 190 Memphis B: 3/27/1939 Columbus, MS Draft: 14-107(f) 1961 BOS; 3A-36(f) 1961 PHI Pro: N																															
1963	EDM	3	2		0									10	33	3.3	11	0													
JOEL WRIGHT Joel S-LB 5'11 190 Windsor AKO Fratmen Jrs.; Wilfrid Laurier B: 8/27/1980 Stoney Creek, ON Draft: 5-41 2006 MTL																															
2006	MTL	2				0																									
2007	MTL	2				1																									
2008	MTL	10	0	0	1	10																									
2009	MTL	8				9																									
4	Years	22	0	0	1	20																									
KEITH WRIGHT Keith WR 6'1 195 Northridge State B: 2/10/1964 New York, NY																															
1989	EDM	15	1		1	1						36	6						44	697	15.8	65	6	3	27	9.0	13	26	485	18.7	50
1990	EDM	17	1		0	3						54	9						54	900	16.7	53	9					2	27	13.5	24
2	Years	32	2		1	4						90	15						98	1597	16.3	65	15	3	27	9.0	13	28	512	18.3	50
LEN WRIGHT Len E 6'1 205 Hamilton Italo-Canadians Jrs. B: 1918																															
1947	HAM	12																													
MIKE WRIGHT Michael W. DT-OT 6'3 235 Minnesota B: 1938 Draft: FS 1960 OAK; 6-65 1960 MIN																															
1960	WPG	15																													
1961	WPG+	16			2																										
2	Years	31	0		2																										
PRENTISS WRIGHT Prentiss LB 5'11 220 Pittsburgh B: 7/4/1968 Orlando, FL																															
1991	TOR	2				3																									
RODRIQUE WRIGHT Rodrique Charles DT 6'5 300 Texas B: 7/31/1984 Houston, TX Draft: 7B-226 2006 MIA Pro: N																															
2010	SAS	1				2																									
ROY WRIGHT Roy QB-HB 5'11 177 none B: 1928																															
1946	SAS	8										17	3					1					2								
1947	SAS	8										12	2					1													
1948	SAS	10																													
1949	SAS	14										10	2					2													
1950	SAS	14										5	0	1	4	4.0	4	0													
1951	SAS	14												2	2	1.0		0						15	119	7.9					
1952	SAS	16			1				3	17									1	11	11.0	11	0	33	203	6.2	18				
7	Years	84			1				3	17		44	7	3	6	2.0	4	4	1	11	11.0	11	2	48	322	6.7	18				
SCOTTY WRIGHT George HB-WB B: 1912 D: 8/9/1995																															
1946	HAM	12										15	0																		
TERRY WRIGHT Terry Leon CB 6'0 195 Scottsdale CC; Temple B: 7/17/1965 Phoenix, AZ Pro: N																															
1991	HAM	12	2		4	40			3	53														1	5	5.0	5	5	76	15.2	23
1992	HAM	16	2		6	72	3.0	20.0	4	94		12	2															7	30	4.3	10
1993	HAM	18				84	3.0	25.0																				1	0	0.0	0
1994	HAM	8	1		2	25			1	2	1	6	1															3	20	6.7	14
4	Years	54	5		12	221	6.0	45.0	8	149	1	18	3											1	5	5.0	5	16	126	7.9	23
TORREY WRIGHT Torrey (T.C.) RB 5'10 192 Mesa CC; San Diego State B: 12/18/1969 Phoenix, AZ Pro: E																															
1994	LV	8										6	1	22	114	5.2	16	1													
WILL WRIGHT Will FB																															
1994	LV	2												2	8	4.0	5	0	15	127	8.5	31	0								
CLAUDE WROTEN Claude James DT 6'2 295 Mississippi Delta CC; Louisiana State B: 9/16/1983 Bastrop, LA Draft: 3A-68 2006 STL Pro: NU																															
2011	TOR	18	0	1	0	35	4.0	30.0			1																				
LARRY WRUCK Larry LB 6'0 220 Saskatoon Hilltops Jrs. B: 10/29/1962 Saskatoon, SK																															

Year	Team	GP	FM	FF	FR	TK	SK	YDS	IR	YDS	PD	PTS	TD	RA	YDS	AVG	LG	TD	REC	YDS	AVG	LG	TD	PR	YDS	AVG	LG	KOR	YDS	AVG	LG
1985	EDM	16	0		2		1.0					6	1																		
1986	EDM	18	0		3																										
1987	EDM	18				70			1	0																					
1988	EDM	18			1	44	3.0		1	0																					
1989	EDM+	18				51	8.0		2	3														1	-1	-1.0	-1				
1990	EDM	18	0		3	74	1.0																	2	6	3.0	6				
1991	EDM	18	0		1	59	5.0																								
1992	EDM	18				103	5.0		1	6																		1	11	11.0	11
1993	EDM	17				66			1	4																					
1994	EDM	18	0		1	92																									
1995	EDM	18	1		4	62	5.0	44.0	6	9	5																				
1996	EDM	18	0		1	52	2.0	8.0	0	0	2			1	7	7.0	7	0													
12	Years	213	1		16	673	30.0	52.0	12	22	7	6	1	1	7	7.0	7	0						3	5	1.7	6	1	11	11.0	11
DON WUNDERLY Don DT 6'3 235 Arkansas B: 7/26/1950 Fort Scott, KS Draft: 10-258 1973 PIT																															
1974	BC	2																													
1975	BC	10	0		1																										
1976	BC	16	0		2																										
1977	BC	16	0		3																										
4	Years	44	0		6																										
BILL WUSYK William HB-QB-WB 187 B: 4/18/1918 Calgary AB D: 12/8/1975 Calgary, AB																															
1946	CAL+	8										32	0																		
1947	CAL	8										21	0																		
1948	CAL	11										14	0																		
3	Years	27										67	0																		
FREDDY WYANT Frederick Mount, Jr. QB 6'0 200 West Virginia B: 4/26/1934 Weston, WV Draft: 3-36 1956 WAS Pro: N																															
1957	TOR	8										12	2	10	23	2.3	14	2													
BOB WYATT Robert Lee FB-HB 6'0 215 North Texas B: 9/21/1949 Victoria, TX Pro: W																															
1972	CAL	6	1		0							6	1	38	157	4.1	10	1	11	109	9.9	41	0					5	128	25.6	39
1973	CAL	13	2		0							6	1	94	335	3.6	25	1	28	273	9.8	23	0					7	109	15.6	41
2	Years	19	3		0							12	2	132	492	3.7	25	2	39	382	9.8	41	0					12	237	19.8	41
BUBBA WYCHE Joseph M. QB 6'0 190 Tennessee B: 4/4/1946 Pro: W																															
1969	SAS	16	1		1							6	1	12	62	5.2	30	1													
1971	SAS	16										6	1	5	23	4.6	8	1													
1972	SAS	16	2		0									5	23	4.6	8	0	4	28	7.0	9	0								
3	Years	48	3		1							12	2	22	108	4.9	30	2	4	28	7.0	9	0								
JOHN WYDARENY John S-OHB 6'0 180 Western Ontario B: 2/15/1941 Hearst, ON Draft: 1-1 1963 TOR																															
1963	TOR	14							2	37		6	1											10	60	6.0	11				
1964	TOR	14	0		3				3	4														5	22	4.4	7				
1965	TOR	9	1		0				3	42														12	76	6.3	16				
1966	EDM	16							3	33														3	23	7.7	15				
1967	EDM+	16	0		2				6	208		6	1											5	48	9.6	17				
1968	EDM	14	0		2				7	60																					
1969	EDM*	16							11	154														9	16	1.8	6				
1970	EDM*	16							11	151																					
1971	EDM	16			3				6	58																					
1972	EDM	3																													
10	Years	134	1		10				52	747		12	2											44	245	5.6	17				
HARVEY WYLIE Harvey S-OHB 5'9 178 Montana State B: 1934																															
1956	CAL	16	3		6				5	41		6	1	24	76	3.2	12	0	6	77	12.8	48	0	27	175	6.5	20	12	262	21.8	38
1957	CAL	15	2		0														2	23	11.5	14	0	8	47	5.9	14	20	559	28.0	50
1958	CAL	12	1		3				3	33		18	3	12	74	6.2	22	2	1	28	28.0	28	0	30	206	6.9	27	15	428	28.5	95
1959	CAL+	16	1		2				10	96		12	2	1	9	9.0	9	0	3	116	38.7	85	1	22	109	5.0	16	19	537	28.3	105
1960	CAL+	16	1		3				3	37		6	1						6	126	21.0	38	0	24	122	5.1	19	20	670	33.5	110
1961	CAL+	16	3		4				5	123		6	1	3	12	4.0	6	0	3	27	9.0	17	0	57	387	6.8	39	21	622	29.6	104
1962	CAL*	16	2						5	9		6	1	3	16	5.3	11	0	2	22	11.0	11	0	53	329	6.2	25	28	876	31.3	102
1963	CAL*	16	1		1				3	36				1	5	5.0	5	0	2	36	18.0	20	0	30	168	5.6	22	14	290	20.7	44
1964	CAL	16	0		1				1	33														6	12	2.0	6	2	49	24.5	26
9	Years	139	14		20				35	408		54	9	44	192	4.4	22	2	25	455	18.2	85	1	257	1555	6.1	39	151	4293	28.4	110
GEORGE WYNN George CB 5'9 165 Georgia B: 12/25/1970 Atlanta, GA																															
1992	SAS	8				27																									
SPERGON WYNN Spergon, III QB 6'3 226 Minnesota; Texas State B: 8/10/1978 Houston, TX Draft: 6A-183 2000 CLE Pro: EN																															
2003	BC	18	1	0	0	0						6	1	28	126	4.5	31	1													
2004	BC	15	1	0	0	0						6	1	8	19	2.4	9	1													
2005	WPG	3				0																									
2006	TOR	18	3	0	0	1						6	1	16	55	3.4	14	1													
4	Years	54	5	0	0	1						18	3	52	200	3.8	31	3													
PETE WYSOCKI Peter Joseph LB 6'2 225 Western Michigan B: 10/3/1948 Detroit, MI D: 6/14/2003 Vienna, VA Pro: N																															
1971	HAM	4																													
1972	TOR	1																													
1973	SAS	13	0		1				1	0																					
1974	SAS+	16	0		1				2	40																					
4	Years	34	0		2				3	40																					
ED YABLONSKI Ed FW-FB-HB 5'11 192 Hamilton Wildcats Jrs.; Detroit Mercy B: 1930 Hamilton, ON																															
1953	OTT	14																													
1955	OTT	7																	2	19	9.5	10	0								
2	Years	21																	2	19	9.5	10	0								
OREST YAKIMISCHAK Orest T 6'3 210 Winnipeg Jrs. B: 3/1/1928 D: 12/7/2008																															
1949	WPG	10																													
ALEX YAKUNIN Alex FB 5'11 185 Calgary Bronks Jrs. B: 1931																															
1954	CAL	5	1		0							5	1	8	56	7.0	19	1													
1955	CAL	12												2	9	4.5	6	0						0	3		3				
2	Years	17	1		0							5	1	10	65	6.5	19	1						0	3		3				
MIKE YAKYMYK Mike HB 5'8 164 Regina Bombers Jrs. B: 1924 Regina, SK																															
1946	SAS	8																													
1947	SAS	7																													
1948	SAS	12																													
1949	SAS	13																													
1950	SAS	14										10	2	2	15	7.5		1	1	4	4.0	4	1								
1951	SAS	7																													
6	Years	61										10	2	2	15	7.5	0	1	1	4	4.0	4	1								
BRAD YAMAOKA Brad RB 5'11 206 British Columbia B: 1/30/1973 Kamloops, BC Draft: 3-24 1996 BC																															
1997	BC	18	1	0	0	21								8	62	7.8	18	0	7	32	4.6	17	0								
1998	BC	13	0	1	0	7													1	17	17.0	17	0								
1999	WPG	17				10													1	3	3.0	3	0								
2000	WPG	18	0	0	1	12								1	0	0.0	0	0	3	20	6.7	10	0	1	5	5.0	5				
2001	WPG	5				1																									
2002	WPG	15	0	1	1	8								1	4	4.0	4	0													
2003	WPG	18				6																						1	0	0.0	0
7	Years	104	1	2	2	65								10	66	6.6	18	0	12	72	6.0	17	0	1	5	5.0	5	1	0	0.0	0
JOE YAMAUCHI Joe FB-OG 5'11 190 Calgary Jrs.; Eastern Washington; Edmonton Wildcats Jrs. B: 1933 Opal, AB																															
1955	CAL	14	4		3									49	223	4.6	21	0	16	102	6.4	13	0	3	14	4.7	7	3	51	17.0	19
1956	CAL	16	1		2									4	12	3.0	7	0	2	14	7.0	18	0					3	25	8.3	12

Year	Team	GP	FM	FF	FR	TK	SK	YDS	IR	YDS	PD	PTS	TD	RA	YDS	AVG	LG	TD	REC	YDS	AVG	LG	TD	PR	YDS	AVG	LG	KOR	YDS	AVG	LG
1957	BC	16	2		0							6	1	49	182	3.7	16	1	4	39	9.8	12	0					1	18	18.0	18
1958	BC	15	4											34	161	4.7	18	0	5	45	9.0	16	0	45	373	8.3	26	1	1	1.0	1
1959	BC	11												8	44	5.5	13	0	1	12	12.0	12	0	48	298	6.2	12				
1960	BC	4	0		1																										
6	Years	76	11		6							6	1	144	622	4.3	21	1	28	212	7.6	18	0	96	685	7.1	26	8	95	11.9	19
PIERRE-LUC YAO Pierre-Luc RB 5'10 205 Laval B: 11/4/1982 Quebec City, QC																															
2008	EDM	18				9																									
NELSON YARBROUGH A. Nelson QB 6'2 190 Virginia B: 1936																															
1961	MTL	4										12	2	26	107	4.1	17	2													
PAUL YATKOWSKI Paul DT 6'3 265 Tennessee B: 11/18/1970 Winnipeg, MB Draft: 1-3 1993 OTT																															
1994	OTT	4																													
1995	OTT	18	0		2	16	1.0	15.0			1																				
2	Years	22	0		2	16	1.0	15.0			1																				
JEFF YAUSIE Jeff DB 6'1 195 Saskatoon Hilltops Jrs.; Saskatchewan B: 7/25/1966 Saskatoon, SK Draft: 5-36 1988 CAL																															
1988	CAL	3				1																									
1989	OTT	2				1																						1	1	1.0	1
2	Years	5				2																						1	1	1.0	1
CRAIG YEAST Craig Nelson WR 5'7 164 Kentucky B: 11/20/1976 Danville, KY Draft: 4-98 1999 CIN Pro: N																															
2003	HAM	11	2	0	0	1						12	2						9	221	24.6	45	1	39	465	11.9	104	35	697	19.9	44
2004	HAM	18				3						54	9	6	44	7.3	16	0	59	1184	20.1	88	8	53	420	7.9	51	41	805	19.6	43
2005	HAM	17				6						24	4	2	-5	-2.5	4	0	65	1010	15.5	75	3	6	105	17.5	72	12	322	26.8	93
2006	HAM	7	1	0	1	1						8	1						25	298	11.9	39	1	16	148	9.3	47	4	70	17.5	20
2006	SAS	1				0													1	2	2.0	2	0								
2006	Year	8	1	0	1	1						8	1						26	300	11.5	39	1	16	148	9.3	47	4	70	17.5	20
4	Years	53	3	0	1	11						98	16	8	39	4.9	16	0	159	2715	17.1	88	13	114	1138	10.0	104	92	1894	20.6	93
FRANK YEBOAH-KODIE Frank CB 5'11 182 Penn State B: 9/6/1986 Ghana Draft: 4A-23 1993 HAM																															
1994	OTT	2				3																									
1995	TOR	5				6																									
2	Years	7				9																									
SCOTT YELDON Scott OT 6'6 264 Ottawa Sooners Jrs. B: 7/27/1962 Ottawa, ON																															
1985	OTT	3																													
BILLY YELVERTON William Grover DE 6'4 220 Mississippi B: 5/19/1933 Taylorsville, MS Draft: 18-208(f) 1956 SF Pro: N																															
1960	CAL	2																													
JEFF YEORGA Jeffrey OG 6'6 288 Regina B: 10/31/1981 Moose Jaw, SK																															
2006	TOR	13				0																									
CAM YEOW Cam LB 6'1 230 Akron B: 3/2/1979 Surrey, BC Draft: 1-2 2005 OTT																															
2005	OTT	15	0	0	1	10																									
2006	CAL	5				6																									
2	Years	20	0	0	1	16																									
DARREN YEWCHYN Darren SB-S 5'11 195 Siskiyous JC B: 9/15/1965 Windsor, ON																															
1987	WPG	6			1	0																						1	1	1.0	1
1988	WPG	14	0		1	1																									
2	Years	20	0		2	1																						1	1	1.0	1
KARI YLI-RENKO Kari Alan OT 6'5 270 Cincinnati B: 11/17/1959 Sudbury, ON Draft: TE 1982 HAM; 8-222 1982 CIN Pro: U																															
1985	HAM	10																													
1985	CAL	4																													
1985	Year	14																													
1986	CAL	18																													
1987	CAL	18				1																									
1988	OTT	18	0		1	0																									
1989	OTT	15				0																									
1990	OTT	18	0		1	0																									
1991	OTT	18				1																									
1992	OTT	14	0		1	0																									
1993	TOR	18				1																									
9	Years	147	0		3	3																									
DAN YOCHUM Daniel Lee OT 6'5 258 Syracuse B: 8/19/1950 Bethlehem, PA Draft: 2-37 1972 PHI																															
1972	MTL	11																													
1973	MTL+	14																													
1974	MTL+	10																													
1975	MTL*	13																													
1976	MTL*	16																													
1977	MTL*	14	0		1																										
1978	MTL*	16																													
1979	MTL+	16																													
1980	MTL	5																													
9	Years	115	0		1																										
MACK YOHO Mack J. K-OE-DE 6'2 239 Miami (Ohio) B: 6/14/1936 Reader, WV Pro: N																															
1958	OTT	14										34	1						6	112	18.7	33	1					3	32	10.7	14
1959	OTT	4										8	0																		
2	Years	18										42	1						6	112	18.7	33	1					3	32	10.7	14
JOHN YONAKOR John Joseph (Jumbo) E 6'5 222 Notre Dame B: 8/4/1921 Boston, MA D: 4/18/2001 Cleveland, OH Draft: 1-9 1945 PHI Pro: AN																															
1951	MTL	12										25	5										5								
ANDRE YOUNG Andre Curtis LB 6'1 220 Bowling Green State B: 4/16/1960 Akron, OH Draft: 12-332 1983 CIN; 24-280 1983 DEN-USFL																															
1983	CAL	1					1.0																								
ANTWONE YOUNG Antwone DE 6'2 270 San Diego State B: 1/28/1977 Pro: E																															
2002	CAL	13	0	2	0	16	4.0	20.0			3																	1	11	11.0	11
2003	CAL	18	0	3	2	20	5.0	35.0			1	6	1																		
2004	CAL	9	0	1	0	7	4.0	27.0			2																				
2005	WPG	3	0	1	0	3	2.0	33.0																							
4	Years	43	0	7	2	46	15.0	115.0			6	6	1															1	11	11.0	11
BOB YOUNG Robert H. QB-HB 6'1 195 Indiana B: 12/6/1921 Marion, OH																															
1948	OTT	11										5	1					1													
BRETT YOUNG Brett CB 5'9 180 Oregon B: 4/3/1967 Centralia, IL																															
1989	OTT	10	0		2	34			2	22		6	1																		
1990	OTT	14	0		1	44			5	28																					
1992	OTT	1				2																									
1992	BC	11	0		1	43			0	9																					
1992	Year	12	0		1	45			0	9																					
1993	OTT	13	0		1	37	1.0	10.0	1	0																					
1994	OTT	15	0		3	36	1.0	2.0	2	14	12																				
1995	OTT+	18	0		2	82			5	112	13	6	1																		
1996	HAM	12				34			2	0	4																				
7	Years	83	0		10	312	2.0	12.0	17	185	29	12	2																		
DICK YOUNG Richard A. LB 5'11 210 Tennessee-Chattanooga B: 8/25/1930 Trumbull, CT D: 3/31/2012 Milford, CT Draft: 18-206 1954 CHIC Pro: N																															
1960	HAM	3																													
FRED YOUNG Fred T-HB Regina Westend Gophers Jrs.																															
1947	SAS	8																													
1948	SAS	11																													
2	Years	19																													
GLEN YOUNG Glen H. LB 6'3 235 Syracuse B: 5/2/1969 Scarborough, ON Draft: 3B-22 1992 HAM Pro: N																															
1998	TOR	5	0	0	1	16																									

Year	Team	GP	FM	FF	FR	TK	SK	YDS	IR	YDS	PD	PTS	TD	RA	YDS	AVG	LG	TD	REC	YDS	AVG	LG	TD	PR	YDS	AVG	LG	KOR	YDS	AVG	LG
1999	TOR	11	0	0	3	33	2.0	19.0			1																				
2000	TOR	18	0	3	1	51	2.0	11.0	1	1	2																				
2001	MTL	18	0	0	1	60			2	33	0																				
2002	EDM	18	0	0	1	15																									
2003	EDM	16	0	0	1	25	2.0	10.0	1	24	3																	2	3	1.5	3
2004	EDM	18	0	0	2	43																									
2005	EDM	18	0	1	1	19	1.0	1.0																							
8	Years	122	0	4	11	262	7.0	41.0	4	58	6																	2	3	1.5	3
JIM YOUNG James Norman OHB-SE 6'0 205 Queen's B: 6/6/1943 Hamilton, ON Draft: 1-1 1965 TOR Pro: N																															
1967	BC	16	1		0							48	8	12	21	1.8	15	0	46	976	21.2	71	8					11	251	22.8	33
1968	BC	16	3		0							12	2	46	244	5.3	17	1	51	698	13.7	46	1					5	143	28.6	38
1969	BC+	15	1		0							42	7	18	82	4.6	13	0	50	773	15.5	65	7					4	112	28.0	39
1970	BC	16	0		1							42	7	30	171	5.7	24	1	54	1041	19.3	80	6								
1971	BC	16	1		1							42	7	36	220	6.1	39	0	55	793	14.4	60	7								
1972	BC*	16										66	11						63	1362	21.6	73	11								
1973	BC	16	0		1							18	3	11	49	4.5	9	1	45	719	16.0	49	2								
1974	BC	12										30	5	11	36	3.3	14	0	30	610	20.3	86	5								
1975	BC	16										54	9	7	27	3.9	7	0	43	935	21.7	72	9								
1976	BC	10										12	2						18	327	18.2	78	2								
1977	BC	16							1	12		20	3						37	537	14.5	54	3								
1978	BC	16	1		0							12	2						25	343	13.7	44	2								
1979	BC	16										12	2						5	134	26.8	87	2								
13	Years	197	7		3				1	12		410	68	171	850	5.0	39	3	522	9248	17.7	87	65					20	506	25.3	39
KOURTNEY YOUNG Kourtney CB 6'1 200 Eastern Illinois B: 8/9/1979 Chicago, IL																															
2003	HAM	9				14					4																				
MARCELL YOUNG Marcell CB-DH 6'2 200 Hinds CC; Jackson State B: 9/2/1987																															
2011	HAM	18	0	1	1	51			2	24	3																				
MARK YOUNG Mark DB 5'11 180 Morgan State B: 6/5/1960 Washington, DC																															
1982	MTL+	13	0		1				7	61																					
1983	MTL	7	0		2				1	18																					
1983	HAM	4							2	51														1	3	3.0	3	1	15	15.0	15
1983	Year	11	0		2				3	36														1	3	3.0	3				
1984	HAM	6	0		2				1	39														1	5	5.0	5				
3	Years	26	0		5				11	169														2	8	4.0	5	1	15	15.0	15
MITCH YOUNG Mitchell DL 6'3 253 Northwest Mississippi JC; Arkansas State B: 7/18/1961 Coldwater, MS Pro: N																															
1989	OTT	2				4																									
PRESTON YOUNG Preston S 6'0 180 Regina Rams Jrs.; Simon Fraser B: 7/15/1954 Regina, SK Draft: TE 1977 SAS																															
1978	SAS	16							1	40																					
1979	TOR	15							5	43																					
1980	TOR	16	0		2				6	47																					
1981	HAM	16	0		2				4	57																		1	0	0.0	0
1982	MTL	16	1		1				3	66		6	1											55	672	12.2	54				
1983	MTL	15	0		2				2	13														35	360	10.3	87				
1984	MTL	16	1		0				3	51														44	445	10.1	53	1	3	3.0	3
1985	MTL	11	0		0																			36	251	7.0	20				
1985	TOR	5	1		2							6	1											9	40	4.4	8				
1985	Year	16	1		2				2	28														45	291	6.5	20				
8	Years	121	3		9				24	317		12	2											179	1768	9.9	87	2	3	1.5	3
RICH YOUNG Rich LB 6'2 252 Glendale CC; Tulsa B: 5/12/1975 Chicago, IL Pro: X																															
1999	SAS	11				33																									
SAM YOUNG Sam CB 5'11 180 Trinity (Illinois); Illinois State B: 8/1/1978 Chicago, IL Pro: E																															
2003	CAL	8				14	2.0	7.0			2																				
2004	BC+	18	1	0	1	52			5	11	4																				
2005	BC	18	0	1	0	39			3	49	4	6	1																		
2006	BC	3				4					1																				
2006	HAM	10	1	0	1	26			2	57	4																				
2006	Year	13	1	0	1	30			2	57	5																				
2007	WPG	13				16					3																				
5	Years	60	2	1	2	151	2.0	7.0	10	117	18	6	1																		
STEPHEN YOUNG Stephen DE 6'5 250 McGill B: 6/11/1978 Oshawa, ON																															
2003	WPG	9				0																									
2004	MTL	1				1																									
2	Years	10				1																									
TODD YOUNG Michael Todd OG-OT 6'6 285 Penn State B: 2/2/1967 Columbus, OH Pro: E																															
1995	MEM	5				0																									
TREY YOUNG Trey DB-LB 6'0 210 Montana B: 2/4/1980 Chicago, IL Pro: U																															
2005	CAL	17	1	3	0	63	2.0	10.0	4	97	1																				
2006	CAL	15	0	1	2	45			2	0	3																				
2007	CAL	18	0	1	3	77			4	47	2	12	2						1	39	39.0	39	1								
2008	EDM	3	0	1	0	5			1	0	0																				
4	Years	53	1	6	5	190	2.0	10.0	11	144	6	12	2						1	39	39.0	39	1								
ULYSSES YOUNG Ulysses A. DB 6'2 190 Allen B: 12/19/1946 Clemson, SC																															
1972	OTT	5							1	-2																					
VIC YOUNG Vic FB 5'11 180 Weston Monarchs Jrs.; McGill B: 1927																															
1949	WPG	2																													
WENTY YOUNG Wentworth OT-DT-G 5'11 226 NDG Maple Leafs Jrs.; Montreal Lakeshore Flyers Ints. B: 1930 D: 2/16/2002																															
1953	WPG	15																													
1954	WPG	14																													
1955	WPG	2																													
1955	BC	7																													
1955	Year																														
3	Years	31																													
WILLIE YOUNG Willie Charles OT 6'4 270 Alcorn State B: 11/12/1947 Jefferson, MS D: 9/3/2008 Jackson, MS Pro: N																															
1970	EDM	2																													
JERMAINE YOUNGER Jermaine R. DE 6'0 240 Utah State B: 6/1/1971 San Francisco, CA																															
1995	TOR	5	0		1	26	2.0	20.0																							
1996	HAM	3				10																									
1996	OTT	9	0		1	39	2.0	4.0	0	3	4	6	1															1	3	3.0	3
1996	Year	12	0		1	49	2.0	4.0	0	3	4	6	1															1	3	3.0	3
1997	HAM	18				8																									
3	Years	26	0		2	83	4.0	24.0	0	3	4	6	1															1	3	3.0	3
JORDAN YOUNGER Jordan CB-LB 5'10 187 Connecticut B: 1/24/1978 Trenton, NJ Pro: E																															
2004	TOR	18				45			2	0	11																				
2005	TOR*	17				58			3	11	4																				
2006	TOR+	18				43	1.0	10.0	6	72	7	6	1																		
2007	TOR*	16				47					9																				
2008	EDM	15				52			1	5	8																				
2009	TOR	13	0	0	1	34					4	6	1																		
2010	TOR	17	0	1	3	52			2	39	2																				
2011	TOR	15	0	2	1	43	1.0	7.0			1																				
8	Years	129	0	3	5	374	2.0	17.0	14	127	46	12	2																		
JOHN YULE John LB 6'2 230 Manitoba B: 12/10/1967 Winnipeg, MB Draft: 3B-20 1990 TOR																															

Year	Team	GP	FM	FF	FR	TK	SK	YDS	IR	YDS	PD	PTS	TD	RA	YDS	AVG	LG	TD	REC	YDS	AVG	LG	TD	PR	YDS	AVG	LG	KOR	YDS	AVG	LG
1990	WPG	5				2																									
JAMES YURICHUK James LB 6'2 222 Bishop's B: 11/1/1986 Brampton, ON Draft: 1B-4 2009 BC																															
2009	BC	18	0	0	1	20			1	2	0	6	1																		
2010	BC	18				24																									
2011	BC	18	0	1	2	39					1																				
3	Years	54	0	1	3	83			1	2	1	6	1																		
JARED ZABRANSKY Jared QB 6'2 203 Boise State B: 12/4/1983 Hermiston, OR																															
2009	EDM	18				0																									
2010	EDM	18	4	0	2	0						6	1	28	209	7.5	22	1													
2	Years	36	4	0	2	0						6	1	28	209	7.5	22	1													
DAVE ZACHARKO Dave LB 6'0 215 Alberta B: 6/25/1956 Draft: 7-62 1978 EDM																															
1979	EDM	14																													
KENNY ZACHARY Ken R. RB 6'0 222 Oklahoma State B: 11/19/1963 Sapulpa, OK Pro: N																															
1986	HAM	4	2		0							12	2	59	275	4.7	34	2	12	116	9.7	24	0					2	38	19.0	21
1987	HAM	6	5		0	0						42	7	71	356	5.0	43	6	14	111	7.9	21	1					6	124	20.7	31
1988	HAM	4	2		1									37	183	4.9	20	0	9	64	7.1	15	0					1	11	11.0	11
3	Years	14	9		1	0						54	9	167	814	4.9	43	8	35	291	8.3	24	1					9	173	19.2	31
JAMES ZACHERY James Ray DT-DE-LB 6'2 245 Texas A&M B: 8/27/1958 Midland, TX Draft: 11-290 1980 NYJ																															
1980	MTL	7																													
1981	MTL	5	0		1		2.0																					1	15	15.0	15
1982	MTL	15					4.0		1	0																					
1983	MTL	16	0		2		9.5																								
1984	MTL	6					1.5		1	2																					
1985	EDM	9					8.0																								
1986	EDM+	17	0		2		9.0		1	0																		2	26	13.0	17
1987	EDM	18				23	3.0		1	4																					
8	Years	93	0		5	23	37.0		4	6																		3	41	13.7	17
FRANK ZAJACK Frank E 6'1 201																															
1948	WPG	12																													
JOHN ZAJDEL John LB 6'3 237 Vancouver Meralomas Jrs. B: 3/31/1967 Toronto, ON																															
1990	TOR	2				2			1	23																					
1990	HAM	7				3																									
1990	Year	9				5			1	23																					
1991	HAM	18	0		1	22																									
1992	HAM	18	0		2	29						6	1	0	1		1	1													
1993	TOR	2				1																									
4	Years	40	0		3	57			1	23		6	1	0	1		1	1													
GENE ZAKALA Eugene 5'10 180 Winnipeg Rods Jrs.																															
1948	WPG	1																													
JOE ZALESKI Joseph John QB-DB 6'0 194 Dayton B: 3/19/1930 New Kensington, PA																															
1952	WPG	13							3	9				6	22	3.7	18	0						2	10	5.0	6				
1953	WPG	10							2	0				4	-29	-7.3		0	1	6	6.0	6	0								
1954	WPG	15	3		0									7	-8	-1.1	55	0	1	-2	-2.0	-2	0								
1955	MTL	2																													
4	Years	40	3		0				5	9				17	-15	-0.9	55	0	2	4	2.0	6	0	2	10	5.0	6				
SLATER ZALESKI Slater WR-CB 5'11 180 Edmonton Huskies Jrs. B: 1/15/1966 Edmonton, AB																															
1988	EDM	3				0													3	43	14.3	19	0								
1989	TOR	5				0																									
1989	SAS	1				0																									
1989	Year	6				0																									
1990	SAS	6				0													3	29	9.7	16	0								
3	Years	14				0													6	72	12.0	19	0								
MITCH ZALNASKY Mitchell OE 6'3 220 Pittsburgh B: 6/14/1944 Tyre, PA Draft: 17-251 1966 WAS																															
1967	WPG	13																	24	334	13.9	30	0								
1968	WPG	11																	13	220	16.9	48	0								
2	Years	24																	37	554	15.0	48	0								
STEVE ZALUSKY Steve E Regina Jrs.																															
1946	SAS	2																													
BEN ZAMBIASI Ben LB 6'1 206 Georgia B: 9/19/1956 Valdosta, GA Draft: 10-271 1978 CHIB																															
1978	HAM*	10	0		1				1	44		6	1																		
1979	HAM*	16	0		4				1	42																					
1980	HAM*	14	0		1				3	32																					
1981	HAM*	14	0		2		4.0		3	59		6	1																		
1982	HAM*	16	0		1		4.0		4	77		6	1																		
1983	HAM*	11	0		2		2.0		2	42																					
1984	HAM+	15	0		1		7.0		1	8																					
1985	HAM*	15	0		3		2.0		3	32				1	-6	-6.0	-6	0													
1986	HAM+	16	0		2		4.0		2	48														1	7	7.0	7				
1987	HAM	15	0		4	51	3.0		3	31		6	1																		
1988	TOR	6				18			2	26																		1	9	9.0	9
11	Years	148	0		21	69	26.0		25	441		24	4	1	-6	-6.0	-6	0						1	7	7.0	7	1	9	9.0	9
SAM ZANDERS Sam RB 6'0 220 Illinois State B: 10/2/1976 Arlington, VA																															
2001	TOR	3	2	0	0	1						6	1	27	155	5.7	16	0	5	72	14.4	27	1								
2002	TOR	4	2	0	0	1								54	215	4.0	29	0													
2	Years	7	4	0	0	2						6	1	81	370	4.6	29	0	5	72	14.4	27	1								
CHUCK ZAPIEC Charles LB 6'2 218 Penn State B: 7/1/1949 Philadelphia, PA Draft: 4C-93 1972 DAL																															
1972	OTT	7	0		2				2	55																					
1973	OTT	7	0		1				2	16																					
1974	MTL+	16							3	43		6	1																		
1975	MTL	3																													
1976	MTL+	16	0		4							6	1																		
1977	MTL*	16	0		4																										
1978	MTL*	16	1		2				2	4																					
7	Years	81	1		13				9	118		12	2																		
GEORGE ZAREK George G-T 5'9 210 B: 1922																															
1946	HAM	12																													
1947	HAM	8																													
1950	HAM	4																													
3	Years	24																													
RAY ZASO Raymond C. T-G Canisius B: 1915 NY D: //1976																															
1946	HAM	10										1	0																		
1947	HAM	10																													
2	Years	20										1	0																		
STEVE ZATYLNY Steve WR 5'10 185 Montreal Concorde Jrs.; Bishop's B: 1/1/1966 Montreal, QC Draft: 6-43 1990 WPG																															
1990	WPG	15	1		0	2													2	15	7.5	9	0	14	103	7.4	16	25	491	19.6	38
1991	WPG	1				0																									
2	Years	16	1		0	2													2	15	7.5	9	0	14	103	7.4	16	25	491	19.6	38
WALLY ZATYLNY Walter WR-SB 5'9 180 Bishop's B: 3/25/1964 Montreal, QC Draft: 4-28 1988 CAL																															
1988	HAM	18	4		1	0						12	2						7	153	21.9	61	1	39	187	4.8	47	39	785	20.1	44
1989	HAM+	15	2		3	3						24	4	1	-4	-4.0	-4	0	16	279	17.4	67	2	58	523	9.0	66	40	793	19.8	56
1990	HAM	11	1		0	1						18	3	1	-2	-2.0	-2	0	15	325	21.7	57	2	47	445	9.5	42	33	687	20.8	93
1991	HAM	18	1		0	7						12	2						16	241	15.1	75	2	28	259	9.3	30	23	366	15.9	33

Year	Team	GP	FM	FF	FR	TK	SK	YDS	IR	YDS	PD	PTS	TD	RA	YDS	AVG	LG	TD	REC	YDS	AVG	LG	TD	PR	YDS	AVG	LG	KOR	YDS	AVG	LG
1992	HAM	17	2		0	13						12	2	1	-12	-12.0	0	0	11	153	13.9	29	2	20	201	10.1	46	8	156	19.5	48
1993	TOR	16	2		0	1						6	1						34	464	13.6	41	1	5	30	6.0	11	23	361	15.7	32
1994	HAM	17	2		1	11													3	103	34.3	43	0	16	86	5.4	16	10	173	17.3	32
1995	HAM	9	2		1	2													2	46	23.0	35	0	11	46	4.2	9	6	52	8.7	15
8	Years	121	16		6	38						84	14	3	-18	-6.0	0	0	104	1764	17.0	75	10	224	1777	7.9	66	182	3373	18.5	93
TOBY ZEIGLER Toby WR 6'0 198 Northwestern State (Louisiana) B: 10/14/1983 Monroe, LA																															
2006	EDM	1				0																		2	12	6.0	7	1	35	35.0	35
EMMETT ZELENKA Emmett K. T-G 6'1 230 Tulane B: 10/1935 Draft: 26-313 1957 NYG																															
1957	MTL	14																													
ALAN ZEMAITIS Alan Keith DH 6'1 193 Penn State B: 8/24/1982 Rochester, NY Draft: 4-122 2006 TB																															
2008	HAM	1				2																									
SAUL ZEMAITIS Saulis HB 5'10 205 North Carolina B: 1949																															
1971	HAM	14	0		1									1	5	5.0	5	0													
LUIS ZENDEJAS Luis Fernando K 5'9 180 Arizona State B: 10/22/1961 Mexico City, Mexico Draft: TD 1985 ARI-USFL Pro: NU																															
1995	BIR	12				0						144	0																		
DARIC ZENO Daric Daron WR 5'9 175 Central Oklahoma B: 7/1/1962 Dallas, TX Draft: 15A-296 1984 HOU-USFL																															
1985	OTT	11	5		0							24	4						35	323	9.2	29	2	52	590	11.3	74	25	507	20.3	57
1985	SAS	4	3		1							18	3	1	2	2.0	2	0	18	338	18.8	41	3	20	109	5.5	14	8	138	17.3	31
1985	Year	15	8		0							42	7	1	2	2.0	2	0	53	661	12.5	41	5	72	699	9.7	74	27	645	23.9	57
1986	SAS	14	2		0							18	3						49	624	12.7	32	3	69	442	6.4	21	17	339	19.9	32
2	Years	25	10		1							60	10	1	2	2.0	2	0	102	1285	12.6	41	8	141	1141	8.1	74	50	984	19.7	57
MARC ZENO Marc Anthony WR 6'3 205 Tulane B: 6/21/1965 New Orleans, LA Draft: 7-182 1988 PIT																															
1989	CAL	9				1						18	3						21	375	17.9	39	3								
1990	BC	2				0													2	30	15.0	15	0								
2	Years	11				1						18	3						23	405	17.6	39	3								
BLAIR ZERR Blair RB 6'0 200 Calgary Colts Jrs.; San Jose State B: 11/22/1966 Regina, SK Draft: 7-54 1991 CAL																															
1992	CAL	15				24																									
1993	CAL	18				16								2	3	1.5	2	0	3	38	12.7	19	0								
1994	CAL	18	2		2	9								10	28	2.8	7	0	6	58	9.7	19	0								
3	Years	51	2		2	49								12	31	2.6	7	0	9	96	10.7	19	0								
CHUCK ZICKEFOOSE Charles E. C-E 6'3 230 Kansas State B: 12/19/1934 Wichita, KS Draft: 26-306 1956 CHIC																															
1957	CAL	5	0		1				1	5		6	1											0	75		75				
1958	CAL	15	1		2				2	27																					
1965	CAL	13																													
1966	CAL	16	0		1																										
1967	CAL	16																													
1968	CAL	16																													
6	Years	81	1		4				3	32		6	1											0	75		75				
BILL ZIEGLER William J. HB 6'1 215 Missouri B: 3/25/1953																															
1976	CAL	5	1		0									16	67	4.2	20	0	5	37	7.4	14	0					6	179	29.8	38
CHRIS ZINGO Chris J. LB 5'11 210 Cornell B: 10/31/1972 Fairfield, CT																															
1995	SHR	10	0		1	62	2.0	18.0																							
LOU ZIVKOVICH Lou DT-OT-DE 6'3 230 Miami (Florida); New Mexico State B: 1939 Draft: 23-(f) 1961 DAL; 19-256 1961 LARM																															
1961	CAL	9																													
1962	CAL	16																													
1963	CAL	16																													
1964	CAL	16	0		1																										
1965	WPG	9																													
1965	EDM	5																													
1965	Year	14																													
5	Years	66	0		1																										
LUBO ZIZAKOVIC Lubo DT 6'8 280 Maryland B: 2/28/1968 Toronto, ON Draft: 3-17 1991 HAM																															
1992	HAM	8	0		1	11																									
1993	HAM	18				15	2.0	15.0																							
1994	CAL	17				22	4.0	29.0																							
1995	CAL	5				2																									
1995	SAS	2				0																									
1995	TOR	7				5																									
1995	Year	14				7																									
1996	OTT	18				22	4.0	30.0	1	4	1																				
5	Years	66	0		1	77	10.0	74.0	1	4	1																				
SRECKO ZIZAKOVIC Srecko DE-DT 6'5 255 Ohio State B: 8/13/1966 Weston, ON Draft: 4A-26 1989 CAL																															
1990	CAL	2				0																									
1991	CAL	15	0		3	34	5.0					6	1	0	0		0	1													
1992	CAL	15				19	6.0	22.0																				1	8	8.0	8
1993	CAL	13				22	3.0	17.0	1	21																					
1994	CAL	14				20	3.0	21.0																							
1995	CAL	18	2		0	31	5.0	29.0	1	36	1	6	1																		
6	Years	77	2		3	126	22.0	89.0	2	57	1	12	2					1										1	8	8.0	8
BILL ZOCK William MG 6'1 245 B: 1918 Toronto, ON D: 4/29/1988 Toronto, ON																															
1946	TOR+	12																													
1947	TOR+	10																													
1948	TOR	12																													
1949	TOR	10																													
1951	EDM	14																													
1952	EDM	16			3																										
1953	EDM	9																													
1954	EDM	14																													
8	Years	97			3																										
JIM ZORN James Arthur QB 6'2 200 Cerritos JC; Cal Poly (Pomona) B: 5/10/1953 Whittier, CA Pro: N																															
1986	WPG	9												5	11	2.2	5	0													
FARWAN ZUBEDI Farwan WR 5'10 170 Washington State B: 3/16/1978 Mengo, Uganda Draft: 3A-22 2001 CAL																															
2001	CAL	5				2																									
2002	BC	1				0																									
2003	HAM	3				0													4	65	16.3	29	0								
3	Years	9				2													4	65	16.3	29	0								
MORRIS ZUBKEWYCH Morris C 6'3 245 Simon Fraser B: 7/4/1951 Draft: TE 1974 TOR																															
1974	TOR	16																													
1976	TOR	9																													
1978	TOR	2																													
3	Years	27																													
JOE ZUGER Joe QB-DB-P 6'2 212 Arizona State B: 2/25/1940 Homestead, PA Draft: 18-248 1962 DET																															
1962	HAM	14							4	43		27	4	16	105	6.6	24	3													
1963	HAM	13							5	13		2	0	1	-5	-5.0	-5	0													
1964	HAM	8										2	0																		
1965	HAM	14	4		3							25	2	44	86	2.0	22	2													
1966	HAM	13	2		2							26	3	43	162	3.8	23	3													
1967	HAM	14	2		0							17	0	60	195	3.3	25	0													
1968	HAM	14	4		1							13	1	52	114	2.2	22	1						2	-5	-2.5	0				
1969	HAM	11	3		1							18	2	26	102	3.9	15	2	1	4	4.0	4	0								
1970	HAM	9	1		1							1	0	19	114	6.0	22	0													
1971	HAM	14	6		3							15	1	22	12	0.5	7	1													

Year	Team	GP	FM	FF	FR	TK	SK	YDS	IR	YDS	PD	PTS	TD	RA	YDS	AVG	LG	TD	REC	YDS	AVG	LG	TD	PR	YDS	AVG	LG	KOR	YDS	AVG	LG
10	Years	124	22		11				9	56		146	13	283	885	3.1	25	12	1	4	4.0	4	0	2	-5	-2.5	0				
JAKE ZUMBACH Jake DE 6'3 245 Nassau CC; Colorado B: 7/15/1950																															
1974	MTL	4																													

The Passing Register contains each player's passing record. These records were placed in this separate section because of space limitations in the overall player register.

Each entry is divided into two parts: The first is the player's name; the second is the player's year-by-year and career passing statistics.

The following column headings are used in this section:

ATT Attempts
AVG Average gain per pass attempt
COM Completions
COM% Completion percentage
INT Passes intercepted
INT% Interception percentage
LG Long gain
SK Sacks
TD Touchdowns
TD% Touchdown percentage
TEAM The following team abbreviations are used:

BAL	Baltimore (1994)
	Baltimore Stallions (1995)
BC	British Columbia Lions (1954-)
BIR	Birmingham Barracudas (1995)
CAL	Calgary Stampeders (1946-)
EDM	Edmonton Eskimos (1949-)
HAM	Hamilton Tigers (1946-1947)
	Hamilton Wildcats (1948-1949)
	Hamilton Tiger-Cats (1950-)
LV	Las Vegas Posse (1994)
MEM	Memphis Mad Dogs (1995)
MTL	Montreal Alouettes (1946-1981)
	Montreal Concordes (1982-1985)
	Montreal Alouettes (1986; 1996-)
OTT	Ottawa Rough Riders (1946-1996)
	Ottawa Renegades (2002-2005)
SA	San Antonio Texans (1995)
SAC	Sacramento Gold Miners (1993-1994)
SAS	Saskatchewan Roughriders (1946-)
SHR	Shreveport Pirates (1994-1995)
TOR	Toronto Argonauts (1946-)
WPG	Winnipeg Blue Bombers (1946-)
Totals	If a player has statistics for more than one season, his career totals will appear on this line.

YDS Yards
YEAR Year

Year	Team	ATT	COM	COM%	YDS	AVG	TD	TD%	INT	INT%	LG	SK
PAT ABBRUZZI												
1955	MTL	2	0	0.0	0	0.0	0	0.0	0	0.0		
1957	MTL	2	1	50.0	-6	-3.0	0	0.0	0	0.0	-6	
Totals		4	1	25.0	-6	-1.5	0	0.0	0	0.0	-6	
HARRY ABOFS												
1971	TOR	1	0	0.0	0	0.0	0	0.0	0	0.0		
1972	EDM	1	0	0.0	0	0.0	0	0.0	0	0.0		
1972	Year	1	0	0.0	0	0.0	0	0.0	0	0.0		
Totals		2	0	0.0	0	0.0	0	0.0	0	0.0		
RON ADAM												
1954	SAS	18	7	38.9	166	9.2	1	5.6	1	5.6		
1955	SAS	6	3	50.0	109	18.2	1	16.7	1	16.7	68	
1956	SAS	11	5	45.5	176	16.0	0	0.0	1	9.1	51	
1957	SAS	20	8	40.0	204	10.2	1	5.0	3	15.0	65	
1958	SAS	22	7	31.8	154	7.0	3	13.6	2	9.1	58	
1959	SAS	16	1	6.3	8	0.5	0	0.0	2	12.5	8	
1960	SAS	46	19	41.3	248	5.4	0	0.0	6	13.0	52	3
Totals		139	50	36.0	1065	7.7	6	4.3	16	11.5	68	3
DICKIE ADAMS												
1975	OTT	2	2	100.0	46	23.0	0	0.0	0	0.0	30	
JOE ADAMS												
1982	SAS	454	245	54.0	3312	7.3	19	4.2	16	3.5	84	
1983	SAS	208	104	50.0	1529	7.4	8	3.8	6	2.9	88	
1983	Year	208	104	50.0	1529	7.4	8	3.8	6	2.9	88	
1984	OTT	78	42	53.8	501	6.4	4	5.1	8	10.3	30	
Totals		740	391	52.8	5342	7.2	31	4.2	30	4.1	88	
TONY ADAMS												
1979	TOR	394	241	61.2	2692	6.8	13	3.3	18	4.6	50	
1980	TOR	72	39	54.2	539	7.5	0	0.0	6	8.3	68	
Totals		466	280	60.1	3231	6.9	13	2.8	24	5.2	68	
JOE AGUIRRE												
1952	EDM	1	0	0.0	0	0.0	0	0.0	0	0.0		
BRIAN AH YAT												
1999	WPG	2	0	0.0	0	0.0	0	0.0	0	0.0	0	45
2001	WPG	27	14	51.9	188	7.0	2	7.4	2	7.4	79	
Totals		29	14	48.3	188	6.5	2	6.9	2	6.9	79	45
STEVE ALATORRE												
1982	MTL	22	12	54.5	114	5.2	1	4.5	1	4.5	30	
FRANKIE ALBERT												
1953	CAL	225	104	46.2	1568	7.0	12	5.3	16	7.1	84	
RAY ALEXANDER												
1991	BC	1	1	100.0	26	26.0	0	0.0	0	0.0	26	
DON ALLARD												
1959	SAS	181	82	45.3	1170	6.5	6	3.3	21	11.6	59	
1960	SAS	178	82	46.1	1299	7.3	9	5.1	13	7.3	71	10
1961	MTL	42	16	38.1	196	4.7	2	4.8	3	7.1	36	2
Totals		401	180	44.9	2665	6.6	17	4.2	37	9.2	71	12
BARCLAY ALLEN												
1970	OTT	1	0	0.0	0	0.0	0	0.0	0	0.0		
1970	Year	1	0	0.0	0	0.0	0	0.0	0	0.0		
1971	OTT	1	1	100.0	10	10.0	0	0.0	0	0.0	10	
Totals		2	1	50.0	10	5.0	0	0.0	0	0.0	10	
DAMON ALLEN												
1985	EDM	98	48	49.0	661	6.7	3	3.1	3	3.1	54	
1986	EDM	87	49	56.3	878	10.1	8	9.2	3	3.4	75	
1987	EDM	287	150	52.3	2670	9.3	17	5.9	13	4.5	97	
1988	EDM	218	94	43.1	1309	6.0	4	1.8	12	5.5	44	
1989	OTT	434	209	48.2	3093	7.1	17	3.9	16	3.7	78	
1990	OTT	528	276	52.3	3883	7.4	34	6.4	23	4.4	74	
1991	OTT	546	282	51.6	4275	7.8	24	4.4	31	5.7	70	
1992	HAM	523	266	50.9	3858	7.4	19	3.6	14	2.7	82	
1993	EDM	400	214	53.5	3394	8.5	25	6.3	10	2.5	102	
1994	EDM	493	254	51.5	3554	7.2	19	3.9	15	3.0	83	
1995	MEM	390	228	58.5	3211	8.2	11	2.8	13	3.3	73	28
1996	BC	368	219	59.5	2772	7.5	13	3.5	10	2.7	64	36
1997	BC	583	378	64.8	4653	8.0	21	3.6	11	1.9	73	46
1998	BC	479	282	58.9	3519	7.3	16	3.3	16	3.3	85	42
1999	BC	521	315	60.5	4219	8.1	22	4.2	13	2.5	78	35
2000	BC	525	324	61.7	4840	9.2	24	4.6	11	2.1	67	30
2001	BC	471	251	53.3	3631	7.7	18	3.8	14	3.0	78	24
2002	BC	474	268	56.5	3987	8.4	22	4.6	10	2.1	109	35
2003	TOR	450	267	59.3	3395	7.5	17	3.8	10	2.2	102	27
2004	TOR	312	189	60.6	2438	7.8	12	3.8	4	1.3	63	33
2005	TOR	549	352	64.1	5082	9.3	33	6.0	15	2.7	90	43
2006	TOR	335	198	59.1	2567	7.7	12	3.6	11	3.3	83	22
2007	TOR	67	45	67.2	492	7.3	3	4.5	0	0.0	36	10
Totals		9138	5158	56.4	72381	7.9	394	4.3	278	3.0	109	411
ERNIE ALLEN												
1966	BC	9	2	22.2	82	9.1	0	0.0	1	11.1	63	1
GARY ALLEN												
1986	CAL	2	2	100.0	20	10.0	1	50.0	0	0.0	12	
RODNEY ALLISON												
1978	TOR	100	51	51.0	498	5.0	1	1.0	5	5.0	37	
WAYNE ALLISON												
1977	TOR	1	0	0.0	0	0.0	0	0.0	0	0.0		
1977	Year	1	0	0.0	0	0.0	0	0.0	0	0.0		
Totals		1	0	0.0	0	0.0	0	0.0	0			
GERALD ALPHIN												
1987	OTT	1	1	100.0	14	14.0	0	0.0	0	0.0	14	
1989	OTT	1	1	100.0	14	14.0	1	100.0	0	0.0	14	
1993	WPG	1	1	100.0	28	28.0	0	0.0	0	0.0	28	
Totals		3	3	100.0	56	18.7	1	33.3	0	0.0	28	
LYNN AMEDEE												
1963	EDM	211	99	46.9	1352	6.4	7	3.3	16	7.6	57	9
1964	EDM	68	29	42.6	436	6.4	1	1.5	2	2.9	72	7
Totals		279	128	45.9	1788	6.4	8	2.9	18	6.5	72	16
ARCHIE AMERSON												
1997	HAM	1	0	0.0	0	0.0	0	0.0	0	0.0		
1998	HAM	2	1	50.0	7	3.5	1	50.0	0	0.0	7	
Totals		3	1	33.3	7	2.3	1	33.3	0	0.0	7	
JON ANABO												
1964	EDM	98	48	49.0	621	6.3	4	4.1	7	7.1	46	10

Year	Team	ATT	COM	COM%	YDS	AVG	TD	TD%	INT	INT%	LG	SK
1965	EDM	47	17	36.2	182	3.9	1	2.1	1	2.1	39	
Totals		145	65	44.8	803	5.5	5	3.4	8	5.5	46	10
DAVE ANDERSON												
1952	CAL	143	64	44.8	1350	9.4	17	11.9	12	8.4	85	
MAX ANDERSON												
1971	HAM	1	0	0.0	0	0.0	0	0.0	0	0.0		
ZENON ANDRUSYSHYN												
1973	TOR	1	1	100.0	23	23.0	0	0.0	0	0.0	23	
1975	TOR	2	1	50.0	5	2.5	0	0.0	0	0.0	5	
1977	TOR	2	1	50.0	-4	-2.0	0	0.0	0	0.0	-4	
1979	HAM	1	1	100.0	19	19.0	0	0.0	0	0.0	19	
1980	TOR	1	1	100.0	-3	-3.0	0	0.0	0	0.0	3	
1981	TOR	1	0	0.0	0	0.0	0	0.0	0	0.0		
Totals		8	5	62.5	40	5.0	0	0.0	0	0.0	23	
TERRY ANDRYSIAK												
1988	HAM	8	4	50.0	33	4.1	0	0.0	1	12.5	12	
1989	HAM	3	1	33.3	13	4.3	0	0.0	0	0.0	13	
1990	HAM	30	15	50.0	191	6.4	0	0.0	2	6.7	21	
1991	OTT	2	0	0.0	0	0.0	0	0.0	0	0.0		
Totals		43	20	46.5	237	5.5	0	0.0	3	7.0	21	
DAVID ARCHER												
1993	SAC	701	403	57.5	6023	8.6	35	5.0	23	3.3	90	
1994	SAC	390	210	53.8	3340	8.6	21	5.4	15	3.8	79	
1995	SA	458	281	61.4	4471	9.8	30	6.6	8	1.7	105	
1996	OTT	523	292	55.8	3977	7.6	23	4.4	17	3.3	90	
1998	EDM	362	202	55.8	2860	7.9	11	3.0	8	2.2	48	
Totals		2434	1388	57.0	20671	8.5	120	4.9	71	2.9	105	
JASON ARMSTEAD												
2004	OTT	2	0	0.0	0	0.0	0	0.0	0	0.0		0
2005	OTT	1	0	0.0	0	0.0	0	0.0	0	0.0		0
2006	SAS	2	1	50.0	34	17.0	1	50.0	0	0.0	34	1
2009	SAS	1	1	100.0	34	34.0	1	100.0	0	0.0	34	1
Totals		6	2	33.3	68	11.3	2	33.3	0	0.0	34	2
WILLIE ARMSTEAD												
1982	CAL	1	1	100.0	33	33.0	1	100.0	0	0.0	33	
CLAUDE ARNOLD												
1952	EDM	254	137	53.9	2107	8.3	12	4.7	13	5.1	83	
1953	EDM	145	79	54.5	1171	8.1	7	4.8	12	8.3		
1954	EDM	15	9	60.0	191	12.7	0	0.0	1	6.7		
Totals		414	225	54.3	3469	8.4	19	4.6	26	6.3	83	
RICK ARRINGTON												
1974	TOR	7	3	42.9	47	6.7	0	0.0	0	0.0	38	
KENT AUSTIN												
1987	SAS	156	93	59.6	1172	7.5	3	1.9	10	6.4	51	
1988	SAS	277	162	58.5	2084	7.5	8	2.9	12	4.3	66	
1989	SAS	323	183	56.7	2650	8.2	16	5.0	12	3.7	74	
1990	SAS	618	360	58.3	4604	7.4	27	4.4	27	4.4	107	
1991	SAS	554	302	54.5	4137	7.5	32	5.8	18	3.2	99	
1992	SAS	770	459	59.6	6225	8.1	35	4.5	30	3.9	91	
1993	SAS	715	405	56.6	5754	8.0	31	4.3	25	3.5	78	
1994	BC	551	317	57.5	4193	7.6	24	4.4	22	4.0	88	
1995	TOR	422	252	59.7	3076	7.3	14	3.3	19	4.5	80	
1996	WPG	314	176	56.1	2135	6.8	8	2.5	16	5.1	70	
Totals		4700	2709	57.6	36030	7.7	198	4.2	191	4.1	107	
JEFF AVERY												
1978	OTT	1	1	100.0	22	22.0	0	0.0	0	0.0	22	
1980	OTT	1	1	100.0	20	20.0	0	0.0	0	0.0	20	
1981	OTT	1	1	100.0	5	5.0	0	0.0	0	0.0	5	
1982	OTT	1	1	100.0	5	5.0	0	0.0	0	0.0	5	
Totals		4	4	100.0	52	13.0	0	0.0	0	0.0	22	
JOHN AVERY												
2005	TOR	1	1	100.0	15	15.0	0	0.0	0	0.0	15	0
BUTCH AVINGER												
1952	SAS	15	5	33.3	124	8.3	0	0.0	0	0.0	45	
RICH BADAR												
1966	WPG	67	26	38.8	335	5.0	2	3.0	6	9.0	29	6
1967	WPG	7	2	28.6	29	4.1	0	0.0	1	14.3	21	
Totals		74	28	37.8	364	4.9	2	2.7	7	9.5	29	6
DON BAILEY												
1955	OTT	71	19	26.8	615	8.7	7	9.9	5	7.0	80	
1956	CAL	12	3	25.0	49	4.1	0	0.0	1	8.3	28	
Totals		83	22	26.5	664	8.0	7	8.4	6	7.2	80	
LU BAIN												
1964	CAL	2	0	0.0	0	0.0	0	0.0	1	50.0		0
1966	CAL	1	0	0.0	0	0.0	0	0.0	0	0.0		0
1966	Year	1	0	0.0	0	0.0	0	0.0	0	0.0		0
Totals		3	0	0.0	0	0.0	0	0.0	1	33.3		0
JOHN BAKER												
1968	MTL	1	1	100.0	10	10.0	0	0.0	0	0.0	10	
KEITH BAKER												
1979	MTL	1	0	0.0	0	0.0	0	0.0	0	0.0		
1981	HAM	1	0	0.0	0	0.0	0	0.0	0	0.0		
1982	HAM	2	1	50.0	15	7.5	1	50.0	0	0.0	15	
1983	HAM	1	0	0.0	0	0.0	0	0.0	1	100.0		
Totals		5	1	20.0	15	3.0	1	20.0	1	20.0	15	
TERRY BAKER												
1967	EDM	36	23	63.9	344	9.6	1	2.8	2	5.6	74	
TERRY BAKER												
1989	SAS	1	0	0.0	0	0.0	0	0.0	0	0.0		
1990	OTT	1	0	0.0	0	0.0	0	0.0	0	0.0		
1991	OTT	3	2	66.7	36	12.0	0	0.0	0	0.0	28	
1992	OTT	2	1	50.0	18	9.0	0	0.0	0	0.0	18	
1995	OTT	1	1	100.0	23	23.0	0	0.0	0	0.0	23	
1995	TOR	3	0	0.0	0	0.0	0	0.0	1	33.3		
1995	Year	4	1	25.0	23	5.8	0	0.0	1	25.0	23	
1998	MTL	1	1	100.0	11	11.0	0	0.0	0	0.0	11	
2001	MTL	2	1	50.0	27	13.5	0	0.0	0	0.0	27	
Totals		14	6	42.9	115	8.2	0	0.0	1	7.1	28	
JIM BALLARD												
1999	TOR	14	9	64.3	86	6.1	0	0.0	0	0.0	19	
2000	SAS	1	1	100.0	6	6.0	0	0.0	0	0.0	6	
2002	TOR	132	90	68.2	1083	8.2	4	3.0	4	3.0	74	2

Year	Team	ATT	COM	COM%	YDS	AVG	TD	TD%	INT	INT%	LG	SK
Totals		147	100	68.0	1175	8.0	4	2.7	4	2.7	74	2
TODD BANKHEAD												
2000	HAM	59	30	50.8	341	5.8	2	3.4	4	6.8	26	10
BRAD BANKS												
2004	OTT	106	67	63.2	849	8.0	7	6.6	2	1.9	85	12
2005	OTT	14	5	35.7	64	4.6	1	7.1	1	7.1	24	0
2006	WPG	52	22	42.3	219	4.2	1	1.9	3	5.8	19	4
2007	MTL	6	3	50.0	55	9.2	0	0.0	2	33.3	29	1
2008	MTL	1	1	100.0	8	8.0	0	0.0	0	0.0	8	
Totals		179	98	54.7	1195	6.7	9	5.0	8	4.5	85	17
JAY BARKER												
1998	TOR	174	104	59.8	1276	7.3	3	1.7	8	4.6	46	
1999	TOR	270	149	55.2	2023	7.5	8	3.0	8	3.0	68	
2000	TOR	26	16	61.5	134	5.2	0	0.0	3	11.5	22	5
Totals		470	269	57.2	3433	7.3	11	2.3	19	4.0	68	5
JOE BARNES												
1976	MTL	56	29	51.8	392	7.0	1	1.8	7	12.5	51	
1977	MTL	141	77	54.6	991	7.0	5	3.5	5	3.5	33	
1978	MTL	137	72	52.6	1177	8.6	10	7.3	9	6.6	82	
1979	MTL	305	163	53.4	2456	8.1	13	4.3	13	4.3	80	
1980	MTL	75	37	49.3	403	5.4	0	0.0	7	9.3	39	
1980	SAS	205	106	51.7	1322	6.4	8	3.9	13	6.3	55	
1980	Year	280	143	51.1	1725	6.2	8	2.9	20	7.1	55	
1981	SAS	290	151	52.1	2130	7.3	12	4.1	8	2.8	100	
1982	TOR	61	26	42.6	322	5.3	2	3.3	5	8.2	35	
1983	TOR	271	149	55.0	2274	8.4	11	4.1	8	3.0	87	
1984	TOR	378	231	61.1	3128	8.3	18	4.8	12	3.2	71	
1985	CAL	362	212	58.6	2864	7.9	11	3.0	19	5.2	67	
1985	MTL	91	53	58.2	568	6.2	2	2.2	4	4.4	24	
1985	Year	453	265	58.5	3432	7.6	13	2.9	23	5.1	67	
1986	MTL	82	44	53.7	464	5.7	1	1.2	7	8.5	44	14
Totals		2454	1350	55.0	18491	7.5	94	3.8	117	4.8	100	14
PAT BARNES												
2001	CAL	3	2	66.7	25	8.3	0	0.0	0	0.0	13	
2002	WPG	26	17	65.4	210	8.1	1	3.8	0	0.0	23	
2003	WPG	67	28	41.8	412	6.1	3	4.5	2	3.0	62	
Totals		96	47	49.0	647	6.7	4	4.2	2	2.1	62	
JAMIE BARNETTE												
2000	MTL	1	0	0.0	0	0.0	0	0.0	0	0.0		1
2001	MTL	32	13	40.6	158	4.9	1	3.1	2	6.3	24	4
Totals		33	13	39.4	158	4.8	1	3.0	2	6.1	24	5
DANNY BARRETT												
1983	CAL	23	8	34.8	213	9.3	1	4.3	1	4.3	56	
1984	CAL	79	34	43.0	319	4.0	2	2.5	8	10.1	31	
1985	CAL	1	1	100.0	15	15.0	0	0.0	0	0.0	15	
1985	TOR	30	18	60.0	193	6.4	2	6.7	0	0.0	20	
1985	Year	31	19	61.3	208	6.7	0	0.0	0	0.0	20	
1987	TOR	226	120	53.1	1453	6.4	7	3.1	3	1.3	49	
1988	TOR	23	10	43.5	154	6.7	1	4.3	2	8.7	34	
1989	CAL	333	160	48.0	2608	7.8	16	4.8	13	3.9	80	
1990	CAL	295	155	52.5	2677	9.1	19	6.4	13	4.4	67	
1991	CAL	438	249	56.8	3453	7.9	19	4.3	5	1.1	83	
1992	BC	306	172	56.2	2206	7.2	7	2.3	10	3.3	57	
1993	BC	513	293	57.1	4097	8.0	24	4.7	12	2.3	70	
1994	OTT	560	299	53.4	4173	7.5	22	3.9	16	2.9	60	
1995	OTT	82	41	50.0	511	6.2	3	3.7	6	7.3	40	
1996	CAL	120	71	59.2	1062	8.9	11	9.2	2	1.7	63	8
1998	BC	49	25	51.0	285	5.8	1	2.0	2	4.1	22	0
Totals		3078	1656	53.8	23419	7.6	135	4.4	93	3.0	83	8
GREG BARTON												
1971	TOR	92	55	59.8	682	7.4	4	4.3	6	6.5	49	
1972	TOR	82	32	39.0	335	4.1	0	0.0	9	11.0	40	
Totals		174	87	50.0	1017	5.8	4	2.3	15	8.6	49	
GIL BARTOSH												
1955	BC	9	3	33.3	53	5.9	0	0.0	0	0.0	24	
GORD BARWELL												
1966	SAS	1	1	100.0	27	27.0	0	0.0	0	0.0	27	0
1968	SAS	1	0	0.0	0	0.0	0	0.0	0	0.0		
Totals		2	1	50.0	27	13.5	0	0.0	0	0.0	27	0
BILLY BASS												
1948	MTL						1					
DAVID BATES												
1986	TOR	22	7	31.8	103	4.7	0	0.0	2	9.1	57	
PAT BATTEN												
1965	MTL	2	0	0.0	0	0.0	0	0.0	0	0.0		0
STEVE BEAIRD												
1975	WPG	1	0	0.0	0	0.0	0	0.0	1	100.0		
JONATHAN BEASLEY												
2001	SAS	2	0	0.0	0	0.0	0	0.0	0	0.0		
2002	SAS	18	3	16.7	28	1.6	0	0.0	1	5.6	10	
Totals		20	3	15.0	28	1.4	0	0.0	1	5.0	10	
DOUG BELDEN												
1949	SAS						4					
1952	SAS	78	30	38.5	470	6.0	5	6.4	5	6.4	58	
Totals		78	30	38.5	470	6.0	9	6.4	5	6.4	598	
DALTON BELL												
2010	TOR	63	37	58.7	461	7.3	1	1.6	3	4.8	34	3
2011	TOR	101	52	51.5	612	6.1	3	3.0	10	9.9	48	4
Totals		164	89	54.3	1073	6.5	4	2.4	13	7.9	48	7
KERWIN BELL												
1993	SAC	34	22	64.7	296	8.7	2	5.9	1	2.9	58	
1994	SAC	270	143	53.0	1812	6.7	6	2.2	9	3.3	69	
1995	EDM	396	246	62.1	3064	7.7	21	5.3	13	3.3	98	
1998	TOR	568	382	67.3	4991	8.8	27	4.8	14	2.5	66	
1999	WPG	630	375	59.5	4647	7.4	17	2.7	20	3.2	99	
2000	WPG	136	79	58.1	906	6.7	3	2.2	3	2.2	86	11
2000	TOR	293	175	59.7	2179	7.4	14	4.8	11	3.8	76	11
2000	Year	429	254	59.2	3085	7.2	17	4.0	14	3.3	86	10
2001	TOR	231	138	59.7	1641	7.1	11	4.8	9	3.9	88	22
Totals		2558	1560	61.0	19536	7.6	101	3.9	80	3.1	99	44
WALTER BENDER												
1987	SAS	1	0	0.0	0	0.0	0	0.0	0	0.0		

Year	Team	ATT	COM	COM%	YDS	AVG	TD	TD%	INT	INT%	LG	SK
BRUCE BENNETT												
1966	SAS	15	7	46.7	29	1.9	1	6.7	2	13.3	11	1
1967	SAS	2	1	50.0	10	5.0	0	0.0	0	0.0	10	
Totals		17	8	47.1	39	2.3	1	5.9	2	11.8	11	1
LORNE BENSON												
1953	WPG	1	0	0.0	0	0.0	0	0.0	0	0.0		
JEFF BENTRIM												
1987	SAS	182	80	44.0	905	5.0	2	1.1	10	5.5	49	
1988	SAS	4	1	25.0	13	3.3	1	25.0	1	25.0	13	
1990	SAS	167	86	51.5	1099	6.6	5	3.0	15	9.0	78	
Totals		353	167	47.3	2017	5.7	8	2.3	26	7.4	78	
COLE BERGQUIST												
2011	SAS	6	1	16.7	10	1.7	0	0.0	0	0.0	10	1
GINO BERRETTA												
1966	MTL	1	0	0.0	0	0.0	0	0.0	0	0.0		0
1969	MTL	1	1	100.0	10	10.0	0	0.0	0	0.0	10	
Totals		2	1	50.0	10	5.0	0	0.0	0	0.0	10	0
LINDY BERRY												
1950	EDM	254	129	50.8	2201	8.7	10	3.9	20	7.9	100	
Totals		254	129	50.8	2201	8.7	10	3.9	20	7.9	100	
WILLIE BETHEA												
1963	HAM	1	1	100.0	20	20.0	1	100.0	0	0.0	20	0
1964	HAM	1	1	100.0	60	60.0	0	0.0	0	0.0	60	0
1967	HAM	2	2	100.0	58	29.0	1	50.0	0	0.0	44	
1969	HAM	1	1	100.0	27	27.0	0	0.0	0	0.0	27	
Totals		5	5	100.0	165	33.0	2	40.0	0	0.0	60	0
BILL BEWLEY												
1956	MTL	1	1	100.0	12	12.0	0	0.0	0	0.0	12	
1957	MTL	1	0	0.0	0	0.0	0	0.0	0	0.0		
Totals		2	1	50.0	12	6.0	0	0.0	0	0.0	12	
MICHAEL BISHOP												
2002	TOR	148	63	42.6	1053	7.1	7	4.7	10	6.8	86	20
2003	TOR	20	8	40.0	215	10.8	1	5.0	2	10.0	58	4
2004	TOR	217	104	47.9	1508	6.9	6	2.8	15	6.9	67	17
2005	TOR	61	31	50.8	416	6.8	3	4.9	4	6.6	33	3
2006	TOR	12	5	41.7	75	6.3	2	16.7	1	8.3	24	0
2007	TOR	355	185	52.1	2920	8.2	22	6.2	11	3.1	73	16
2008	TOR	42	19	45.2	326	7.8	3	7.1	1	2.4	52	3
2008	SAS	232	141	60.8	2226	9.6	7	3.0	12	5.2	72	11
2008	Year	274	160	58.4	2552	9.3	10	3.6	13	4.7	72	14
2009	WPG	405	204	50.4	3035	7.5	15	3.7	20	4.9	65	18
Totals		1492	760	50.9	11774	7.9	66	4.4	76	5.1	86	92
RICK BLACK												
1963	OTT	0	0		0		0		0			2
DON BLAIR												
2002	CAL	2	1	50.0	6	3.0	0	0.0	0	0.0	6	
2003	CAL	2	0	0.0	0	0.0	0	0.0	0	0.0		
Totals		4	1	25.0	6	1.5	0	0.0	0	0.0	6	
EARL BLAIR												
1956	TOR	2	1	50.0	8	4.0	0	0.0	0	0.0	8	
ERIC BLOUNT												
1997	EDM	1	1	100.0	10	10.0	0	0.0	0	0.0	10	
AL BODINE												
1950	SAS	3	1	33.3	17	5.7	0	0.0	0	0.0	17	
TROY BODINE												
1985	OTT	12	6	50.0	47	3.9	0	0.0	2	16.7	22	
TAVARES BOLDEN												
2002	MTL	5	2	40.0	12	2.4	0	0.0	0	0.0	7	
2003	MTL	33	20	60.6	164	5.0	1	3.0	3	9.1	19	
Totals		38	22	57.9	176	4.6	1	2.6	3	7.9	19	
JASON BOLTUS												
2011	HAM	15	5	33.3	48	3.2	0	0.0	0	0.0	17	0
JAMIE BOREHAM												
2005	HAM	2	1	50.0	19	9.5	0	0.0	0	0.0	19	0
GEORGE BORK												
1964	MTL	179	87	48.6	906	5.1	6	3.4	10	5.6	44	15
1966	MTL	114	66	57.9	752	6.6	1	0.9	9	7.9	50	10
1967	MTL	131	66	50.4	935	7.1	5	3.8	8	6.1	64	
Totals		424	219	51.7	2593	6.1	12	2.8	27	6.4	64	25
LYNN BOTTOMS												
1954	CAL	1	0	0.0	0	0.0	0	0.0	0	0.0		
1955	CAL	28	15	53.6	210	7.5	0	0.0	1	3.6	29	
Totals		29	15	51.7	210	7.2	0	0.0	1	3.4	29	
CORY BOYD												
2010	TOR	1	1	100.0	13	13.0	0	0.0	0	0.0	13	0
MARCUS BRADY												
2002	TOR	3	2	66.7	24	8.0	0	0.0	0	0.0	20	0
2003	TOR	88	32	36.4	558	6.3	5	5.7	6	6.8	78	8
2004	HAM	87	48	55.2	482	5.5	0	0.0	2	2.3	28	2
2005	HAM	132	74	56.1	848	6.4	5	3.8	3	2.3	42	12
2006	MTL	7	4	57.1	49	7.0	0	0.0	0	0.0	18	1
2007	MTL	128	67	52.3	1161	9.1	3	2.3	4	3.1	59	15
2008	MTL	24	19	79.2	199	8.3	2	8.3	1	4.2	54	4
Totals		469	246	52.5	3321	7.1	15	3.2	16	3.4	78	42
CASEY BRAMLET												
2009	WPG	13	2	15.4	18	1.4	0	0.0	2	15.4	13	1
DANNY BRANNAGAN												
2010	TOR	4	2	50.0	32	8.0	0	0.0	0	0.0	17	0
JOHNNY BRIGHT												
1952	CAL	56	29	51.8	494	8.8	2	3.6	5	8.9	54	
1953	CAL	1	0	0.0	0	0.0	0	0.0	0	0.0		
1957	EDM	1	1	100.0	17	17.0	0	0.0	0	0.0	17	
1958	EDM	6	2	33.3	60	10.0	0	0.0	1	16.7	44	
1959	EDM	1	0	0.0	0	0.0	0	0.0	0	0.0		0
Totals		65	32	49.2	571	8.8	2	3.1	6	9.2	54	0
ALEX BRINK												
2010	WPG	40	15	37.5	130	3.3	0	0.0	1	2.5	45	3
2011	WPG	140	89	63.6	1023	7.3	5	3.6	4	2.9	52	6
Totals		180	104	57.8	1153	6.4	5	2.8	5	2.8	52	9
DIETER BROCK												
1974	WPG	27	12	44.4	176	6.5	0	0.0	2	7.4	42	
1975	WPG	244	116	47.5	1911	7.8	11	4.5	9	3.7	55	

Year	Team	ATT	COM	COM%	YDS	AVG	TD	TD%	INT	INT%	LG	SK
1976	WPG	402	223	55.5	3101	7.7	17	4.2	18	4.5	97	
1977	WPG	418	242	57.9	3063	7.3	23	5.5	19	4.5	98	
1978	WPG	486	294	60.5	3755	7.7	23	4.7	18	3.7	90	
1979	WPG	354	194	54.8	2383	6.7	15	4.2	12	3.4	75	
1980	WPG	514	304	59.1	4252	8.3	28	5.4	12	2.3	68	
1981	WPG	566	354	62.5	4796	8.5	32	5.7	15	2.7	85	
1982	WPG	543	314	57.8	4294	7.9	28	5.2	15	2.8	75	
1983	WPG	223	115	51.6	1892	8.5	10	4.5	9	4.0	82	
1983	HAM	197	114	57.9	1241	6.3	8	4.1	6	3.0	49	
1983	Year	420	229	54.5	3133	7.5	18	4.3	15	3.6	82	
1984	HAM	561	320	57.0	3966	7.1	15	2.7	23	4.1	83	
Totals		4535	2602	57.4	34830	7.7	210	4.6	158	3.5	98	
BOB BRODHEAD												
1959	SAS	129	62	48.1	762	5.9	4	3.1	15	11.6	47	
BRIAN BROOMELL												
1981	EDM	9	3	33.3	37	4.1	0	0.0	2	22.2	17	
PAUL BROTHERS												
1968	BC	153	77	50.3	1001	6.5	5	3.3	10	6.5	82	
1969	BC	406	200	49.3	2671	6.6	14	3.4	33	8.1	61	
1970	BC	322	169	52.5	2604	8.1	14	4.3	19	5.9	80	
1971	BC	119	60	50.4	885	7.4	2	1.7	9	7.6	47	
1971	OTT	3	0	0.0	0	0.0	0	0.0	2	66.7		
1971	Year	122	60	49.2	886	7.3	2	1.6	11	9.0	47	
1972	OTT	29	10	34.5	170	5.9	1	3.4	2	6.9	28	
Totals		1032	516	50.0	7331	7.1	36	3.5	75	7.3	82	
BOB BROWN												
1969	BC	3	1	33.3	5	1.7	0	0.0	0	0.0	5	
CARLOS BROWN												
1979	BC	20	6	30.0	75	3.8	0	0.0	1	5.0	21	
EDDIE BROWN												
1994	EDM	2	0	0.0	0	0.0	0	0.0	1	50.0		
1995	EDM	1	1	100.0	78	78.0	1	100.0	0	0.0	78	
1995	Year	1	1	100.0	78	78.0	1	100.0	0	0.0	78	
1999	BC	1	0	0.0	0	0.0	0	0.0	0	0.0		0
Totals		4	1	25.0	78	19.5	1	25.0	1	25.0	78	0
IKE BROWN												
1972	MTL	1	1	100.0	9	9.0	0	0.0	0	0.0	9	
STAN BROWN												
1973	WPG	1	0	0.0	0	0.0	0	0.0	0	0.0		
ARLAND BRUCE												
2005	TOR	1	1	100.0	31	31.0	0	0.0	0	0.0	31	0
2010	HAM	1	1	100.0	32	32.0	0	0.0	0	0.0	32	0
Totals		2	2	100.0	63	31.5	0	0.0	0	0.0	32	0
PAUL BRULE												
1968	WPG	1	0	0.0	0	0.0	0	0.0	0	0.0		
DAVE BUCHANAN												
1971	HAM	3	2	66.7	68	22.7	1	33.3	0	0.0	41	
1972	HAM	1	0	0.0	0	0.0	0	0.0	1	100.0		
Totals		4	2	50.0	68	17.0	1	25.0	1	25.0	41	
ED BUCHANAN												
1961	CAL	4	1	25.0	11	2.8	0	0.0	1	25.0	11	0
1962	CAL	4	0	0.0	0	0.0	0	0.0	0	0.0		0
1970	HAM	1	1	100.0	5	5.0	0	0.0	0	0.0	5	
Totals		9	2	22.2	16	1.8	0	0.0	1	11.1	11	0
DON BUNCE												
1972	BC	92	40	43.5	740	8.0	6	6.5	11	12.0	54	
WALLY BUONO												
1978	MTL	2	1	50.0	24	12.0	0	0.0	0	0.0	24	
1981	MTL	1	0	0.0	0	0.0	0	0.0	1	100.0		
Totals		3	1	33.3	24	8.0	0	0.0	1	33.3	24	
TOM BURGESS												
1986	OTT	199	95	47.7	1199	6.0	5	2.5	12	6.0	68	22
1987	SAS	243	127	52.3	1691	7.0	7	2.9	14	5.8	62	
1988	SAS	331	159	48.0	2575	7.8	19	5.7	14	4.2	79	
1989	SAS	342	162	47.4	2540	7.4	22	6.4	18	5.3	58	
1990	WPG	574	330	57.5	3958	6.9	25	4.4	27	4.7	75	
1991	WPG	525	261	49.7	4212	8.0	27	5.1	29	5.5	104	
1992	OTT	511	276	54.0	4026	7.9	29	5.7	24	4.7	71	
1993	OTT	591	329	55.7	5063	8.6	30	5.1	25	4.2	98	
1994	SAS	450	243	54.0	3442	7.6	19	4.2	14	3.1	81	
1995	SAS	268	136	50.7	1602	6.0	7	2.6	14	5.2	47	
Totals		4034	2118	52.5	30308	7.5	190	4.7	191	4.7	104	22
ORVILLE BURKE												
1946	OTT						3					
FERDIE BURKET												
1959	SAS	1	0	0.0	0	0.0	0	0.0	1	100.0		0
1961	SAS	1	0	0.0	0	0.0	0	0.0	1	100.0		0
1963	MTL	1	1	100.0	10	10.0	0	0.0	0	0.0	10	0
Totals		3	1	33.3	10	3.3	0	0.0	2	66.7	10	0
HENRY BURRIS												
1998	CAL	11	5	45.5	83	7.5	0	0.0	1	9.1	26	2
1999	CAL	60	36	60.0	529	8.8	4	6.7	4	6.7	63	5
2000	SAS	576	308	53.5	4647	8.1	30	5.2	25	4.3	81	26
2003	SAS	24	11	45.8	130	5.4	1	4.2	0	0.0	31	1
2004	SAS	544	322	59.2	4267	7.8	23	4.2	18	3.3	70	22
2005	CAL	435	265	60.9	4290	9.9	23	5.3	12	2.8	70	18
2006	CAL	537	305	56.8	4453	8.3	23	4.3	18	3.4	74	25
2007	CAL	471	285	60.5	4279	9.1	34	7.2	14	3.0	85	35
2008	CAL	591	381	64.5	5094	8.6	39	6.6	14	2.4	85	25
2009	CAL	571	339	59.4	4831	8.5	22	3.9	16	2.8	62	34
2010	CAL	559	370	66.2	4945	8.8	38	6.8	20	3.6	100	27
2011	CAL	442	281	63.6	3687	8.3	20	4.5	12	2.7	81	33
Totals		4821	2908	60.3	41235	8.6	257	5.3	154	3.2	100	226
IAN BUTLER												
2002	SAS	16	9	56.3	165	10.3	0	0.0	0	0.0	46	8
2003	SAS	1	1	100.0	18	18.0	0	0.0	0	0.0	18	0
2004	SAS	65	31	47.7	332	5.1	0	0.0	6	9.2	41	3
2005	SAS	1	1	100.0	5	5.0	0	0.0	0	0.0	5	0
2006	SAS	73	38	52.1	613	8.4	5	6.8	1	1.4	80	8
2007	TOR	86	50	58.1	699	8.1	3	3.5	6	7.0	40	10
Totals		242	130	53.7	1832	7.6	8	3.3	13	5.4	80	29
THERMUS BUTLER												
1969	EDM	1	0	0.0	0	0.0	0	0.0	0	0.0		
BILLY BYE												
1954	WPG	3	3	100.0	74	24.7	1	33.3	0	0.0		
BILL BYNUM												
1975	TOR	161	87	54.0	923	5.7	2	1.2	6	3.7	38	
BEN CAHOON												
2006	MTL	1	1	100.0	1	1.0	0	0.0	0	0.0	1	0
Totals		1	1	100.0	1	1.0	0	0.0	0		1	0
RON CALCAGNI												
1979	MTL	16	7	43.8	101	6.3	0	0.0	4	25.0	26	
1980	OTT	31	17	54.8	208	6.7	1	3.2	2	6.5	30	
1981	OTT	62	35	56.5	548	8.8	2	3.2	6	9.7	43	
Totals		109	59	54.1	857	7.9	3	2.8	12	11.0	43	
RON CALCAGNO												
1965	TOR	2	0	0.0	0	0.0	0	0.0	0	0.0		0
MIKE CALHOUN												
1983	MTL	2	0	0.0	0	0.0	0	0.0	0	0.0		
ANTHONY CALVILLO												
1994	LV	348	154	44.3	2582	7.4	13	3.7	15	4.3	77	
1995	HAM	385	211	54.8	2831	7.4	19	4.9	21	5.5	82	19
1996	HAM	265	157	59.2	2571	9.7	13	4.9	13	4.9	74	13
1997	HAM	278	160	57.6	2177	7.8	12	4.3	11	4.0	69	26
1998	MTL	172	98	57.0	1526	8.9	6	3.5	10	5.8	97	23
1999	MTL	249	166	66.7	2592	10.4	13	5.2	6	2.4	76	19
2000	MTL	435	272	62.5	4277	9.8	27	6.2	5	1.1	80	28
2001	MTL	412	250	60.7	3671	8.9	16	3.9	9	2.2	68	24
2002	MTL	569	338	59.4	5013	8.8	27	4.7	10	1.8	95	22
2003	MTL	675	408	60.4	5891	8.7	37	5.5	14	2.1	66	23
2004	MTL	690	431	62.5	6041	8.8	31	4.5	15	2.2	81	38
2005	MTL	661	437	66.1	5556	8.4	34	5.1	19	2.9	75	30
2006	MTL	640	402	62.8	4714	7.4	20	3.1	15	2.3	68	41
2007	MTL	459	308	67.1	3608	7.9	17	3.7	8	1.7	97	50
2008	MTL	682	472	69.2	5633	8.3	43	6.3	13	1.9	81	16
2009	MTL	550	396	72.0	4639	8.4	26	4.7	6	1.1	71	25
2010	MTL	562	380	67.6	4839	8.6	32	5.7	7	1.2	67	27
2011	MTL	654	404	61.8	5251	8.0	32	4.9	8	1.2	59	31
Totals		8686	5444	62.7	73412	8.5	418	4.8	205	2.4	97	455
BOB CAMERON												
1983	WPG	2	2	100.0	29	14.5	0	0.0	0	0.0	25	
1984	WPG	3	1	33.3	24	8.0	0	0.0	1	33.3	24	
1987	WPG	1	1	100.0	18	18.0	0	0.0	0	0.0	18	
1988	WPG	2	0	0.0	0	0.0	0	0.0	0	0.0		
1989	WPG	3	1	33.3	18	6.0	0	0.0	0	0.0	18	
1990	WPG	2	1	50.0	32	16.0	0	0.0	0	0.0	32	
1991	WPG	1	0	0.0	0	0.0	0	0.0	0	0.0		
1996	WPG	2	1	50.0	6	3.0	0	0.0	0	0.0	6	
1997	WPG	3	3	100.0	40	13.3	0	0.0	0	0.0	17	
1998	WPG	1	0	0.0	0	0.0	0	0.0	0	0.0		
1999	WPG	4	1	25.0	9	2.3	0	0.0	1	25.0	9	
Totals		24	11	45.8	176	7.3	0	0.0	2	8.3	32	
DeCHANE CAMERON												
1992	EDM	9	2	22.2	27	3.0	0	0.0	1	11.1	15	
PAUL CAMERON												
1956	BC	35	16	45.7	199	5.7	1	2.9	4	11.4	28	
1957	BC	10	2	20.0	57	5.7	1	10.0	0	0.0	44	
1958	BC	7	1	14.3	31	4.4	0	0.0	0	0.0	31	
Totals		52	19	36.5	287	5.5	2	3.8	4	7.7	44	
TOM CAMPANA												
1975	SAS	1	0	0.0	0	0.0	0	0.0	0	0.0		
HUGH CAMPBELL												
1965	SAS	1	0	0.0	0	0.0	0	0.0	1	100.0		0
SCOTT CAMPBELL												
1992	OTT	66	39	59.1	438	6.6	2	3.0	1	1.5	28	
GIULIO CARAVATTA												
1992	BC	8	3	37.5	27	3.4	0	0.0	0	0.0	13	
1994	BC	1	0	0.0	0	0.0	0	0.0	0	0.0		
1995	BC	49	26	53.1	302	6.2	1	2.0	1	2.0	39	
1996	BC	40	18	45.0	297	7.4	1	2.5	0	0.0	45	
1997	BC	13	7	53.8	64	4.9	0	0.0	1	7.7	16	
Totals		111	54	48.6	690	6.2	2	1.8	2	1.8	45	
VIDAL CARLIN												
1970	BC	45	22	48.9	306	6.8	0	0.0	4	8.9	33	
GIOVANNI CARMAZZI												
2004	BC	1	1	100.0	12	12.0	0	0.0	0	0.0	12	
ERNIE CARNEGIE												
1974	TOR	1	0	0.0	0	0.0	0	0.0	1	100.0		
KEN CARPENTER												
1954	SAS	1	0	0.0	0	0.0	0	0.0	0	0.0		
1955	SAS	2	0	0.0	0	0.0	0	0.0	0	0.0		
1956	SAS	5	3	60.0	50	10.0	0	0.0	1	20.0	26	
1957	SAS	1	1	100.0	18	18.0	0	0.0	0	0.0	18	
Totals		9	4	44.4	68	7.6	0	0.0	1	11.1	26	
KERRY CARTER												
2008	MTL	1	1	100.0	0	0.0	0	0.0	0	0.0	0	0
MARK CASALE												
1985	TOR	110	65	59.1	637	5.8	6	5.5	6	5.5	41	
JORDAN CASE												
1980	OTT	107	73	68.2	896	8.4	13	12.1	3	2.8	51	
1981	OTT	209	129	61.7	1521	7.3	10	4.8	7	3.3	52	
1982	OTT	65	36	55.4	526	8.1	2	3.1	3	4.6	60	
Totals		381	238	62.5	2943	7.7	25	6.6	13	3.4	60	
TOM CASEY												
1950	WPG	5	1	20.0	10	2.0	0	0.0	0	0.0	10	
1951	WPG	1	0	0.0	0	0.0	0	0.0	0	0.0		
1953	WPG	6	2	33.3	37	6.2	0	0.0	1	16.7		
1954	WPG	1	1	100.0	10	10.0	0	0.0	0	0.0	10	
1955	WPG	2	2	100.0	70	35.0	1	50.0	0	0.0	56	
Totals		15	6	40.0	127	8.5	1	6.7	1	6.7	56	
JIM CASON												
1953	SAS	6	1	16.7	28	4.7	1	16.7	1	16.7	28	
RICK CASSATA												
1968	SAS	41	9	22.0	206	5.0	0	0.0	0	0.0	40	

Year	Team	ATT	COM	COM%	YDS	AVG	TD	TD%	INT	INT%	LG	SK
1969	WPG	1	0	0.0	0	0.0	0	0.0	0	0.0		
1971	OTT	181	77	42.5	1100	6.1	7	3.9	14	7.7	100	
1972	OTT	357	179	50.1	2548	7.1	13	3.6	22	6.2	73	
1973	OTT	177	94	53.1	1255	7.1	4	2.3	6	3.4	52	
1974	OTT	210	88	41.9	1254	6.0	4	1.9	13	6.2	58	
1976	HAM	89	46	51.7	543	6.1	4	4.5	5	5.6	37	
1976	BC	169	78	46.2	954	5.6	1	0.6	7	4.1	53	
1976	Year	258	124	48.1	1497	5.8	5	1.9	12	4.7	53	
Totals		1225	571	46.6	7860	6.4	33	2.7	67	5.5	100	
LARRY CATES												
1976	CAL	1	0	0.0	0	0.0	0	0.0	0	0.0		
1977	OTT	2	1	50.0	33	16.5	0	0.0	0	0.0	33	
Totals		3	1	33.3	33	11.0	0	0.0	0	0.0	33	
TOMMY CATES												
1947	MTL						6					
MIKE CAWLEY												
1997	HAM	79	43	54.4	547	6.9	5	6.3	4	5.1	62	
1998	HAM	8	5	62.5	47	5.9	0	0.0	0	0.0	25	
1999	SAS	8	5	62.5	31	3.9	0	0.0	2	25.0	15	
2000	CAL	21	8	38.1	137	6.5	1	4.8	0	0.0	41	2
Totals		116	61	52.6	762	6.6	6	5.2	6	5.2	62	2
JIMMY CHAMBERS												
1951	EDM	2	0	0.0	0	0.0	0	0.0	0	0.0		
TONY CHAMPION												
1986	HAM	2	0	0.0	0	0.0	0	0.0	1	50.0		
ZAC CHAMPION												
2008	BC	3	2	66.7	111	37.0	1	33.3	0	0.0	6	0
2009	BC	14	4	28.6	35	2.5	0	0.0	2	14.3	17	0
Totals		17	6	35.3	146	8.6	1	5.9	2	11.8	17	0
TIMMY CHANG												
2007	HAM	89	42	47.2	467	5.2	1	1.1	7	7.9	71	5
2008	WPG	1	0	0.0	0	0.0	0	0.0	0	0.0	0	0
Totals		90	42	46.7	467	5.2	1	1.1	7	7.8	71	5
VIC CHAPMAN												
1954	BC	1	1	100.0	15	15.0	0	0.0	0	0.0	15	
1959	EDM	1	0	0.0	0	0.0	0	0.0	0	0.0		0
1960	EDM	1	1	100.0	5	5.0	0	0.0	0	0.0	5	0
Totals		3	2	66.7	20	6.7	0	0.0	0	0.0	15	0
KEN CHARLTON												
1949	SAS						1					
1950	SAS	10	3	30.0	80	8.0	1	10.0	2	20.0		
1951	SAS	2	1	50.0	20	10.0	0	0.0	0	0.0	20	
1952	SAS	1	0	0.0	0	0.0	0	0.0	0	0.0		
Totals		13	4	30.8	100	7.7	2	7.7	2	15.4	20	
JIM CHASEY												
1971	MTL	111	52	46.8	642	5.8	3	2.7	6	5.4	65	
1972	MTL	4	1	25.0	3	0.8	0	0.0	0	0.0	3	
1972	TOR	32	15	46.9	261	8.2	3	9.4	2	6.3	56	
1972	Year	36	16	44.4	264	7.3	3	8.3	2	5.6	56	
Totals		147	68	46.3	906	6.2	6	4.1	8	5.4	65	
LANCE CHOMYC												
1990	TOR	1	0	0.0	0	0.0	0	0.0	0	0.0		
JAY CHRISTENSEN												
1991	BC	1	0	0.0	0	0.0	0	0.0	0	0.0		
1995	OTT	1	0	0.0	0	0.0	0	0.0	0	0.0		
Totals		2	0	0.0	0	0.0	0	0.0	0	0.0		
JIM CHRISTOPHERSON												
1964	TOR	1	1	100.0	-2	-2.0	0	0.0	0	0.0	-2	0
GENE CICHOWSKI												
1960	CAL	16	7	43.8	93	5.8	0	0.0	1	6.3	38	4
1961	CAL	8	3	37.5	49	6.1	0	0.0	0	0.0	26	0
Totals		24	10	41.7	142	5.9	0	0.0	1	4.2	38	4
HOWIE CISSELL												
1961	MTL	1	0	0.0	0	0.0	0	0.0	0	0.0		0
BRIAN CLARK												
2006	CAL	1	1	100.0	11	11.0	0	0.0	0	0.0	11	
DON CLARK												
1961	MTL	2	0	0.0	0	0.0	0	0.0	2	100.0		0
HOWARD CLARK												
1970	EDM	125	61	48.8	850	6.8	3	2.4	18	14.4	81	
1971	EDM	3	2	66.7	20	6.7	0	0.0	0	0.0		
1971	BC	13	7	53.8	90	6.9	0	0.0	3	23.1		
1971	Year	16	9	56.3	110	6.9	0	0.0	3	18.8	18	
Totals		141	70	49.6	960	6.8	3	2.1	21	14.9	81	
KEN CLARK												
1977	HAM	1	1	100.0	14	14.0	0	0.0	0	0.0	14	
1978	TOR	1	1	100.0	27	27.0	0	0.0	0	0.0	27	
1981	SAS	1	1	100.0	15	15.0	0	0.0	0	0.0	15	
1982	SAS	1	1	100.0	-1	-1.0	0	0.0	0	0.0	-1	
1983	SAS	4	1	25.0	1	0.3	0	0.0	2	50.0	1	
1983	OTT	1	0	0.0	0	0.0	0	0.0	0	0.0		
1983	Year	5	1	20.0	1	0.2	0	0.0	2	40.0	1	
1984	OTT	2	1	50.0	16	8.0	0	0.0	1	50.0	16	
1987	OTT	2	2	100.0	44	22.0	0	0.0	0	0.0	35	
Totals		13	8	61.5	116	8.9	0	0.0	3	23.1	35	
STEVE CLARKSON												
1983	SAS	4	1	25.0	25	6.3	0	0.0	0	0.0	25	
CHUCK CLEMENTS												
2002	OTT	126	68	54.0	821	6.5	1	0.8	5	4.0	78	2
TOM CLEMENTS												
1975	OTT	252	144	57.1	2013	8.0	13	5.2	13	5.2	56	
1976	OTT	327	196	59.9	2856	8.7	20	6.1	13	4.0	75	
1977	OTT	298	182	61.1	2804	9.4	16	5.4	16	5.4	82	
1978	OTT	239	152	63.6	1990	8.3	17	7.1	12	5.0	80	
1979	SAS	159	81	50.9	994	6.3	2	1.3	11	6.9	49	
1979	HAM	211	130	61.6	1809	8.6	10	4.7	7	3.3	52	
1979	Year	370	211	57.0	2803	7.6	12	3.2	18	4.9	52	
1981	HAM	523	301	57.6	4536	8.7	27	5.2	23	4.4	81	
1982	HAM	546	356	65.2	4706	8.6	26	4.8	23	4.2	72	
1983	HAM	323	190	58.8	2416	7.5	19	5.9	15	4.6	86	
1983	WPG	60	30	50.0	424	7.1	2	3.3	1	1.7	46	
1983	Year	383	220	57.4	2840	7.4	21	5.5	16	4.2	86	

Year	Team	ATT	COM	COM%	YDS	AVG	TD	TD%	INT	INT%	LG	SK
1984	WPG	446	279	62.6	3845	8.6	29	6.5	22	4.9	86	
1985	WPG	425	257	60.5	3697	8.7	18	4.2	17	4.0	105	
1986	WPG	256	173	67.6	2265	8.8	18	7.0	11	4.3	49	
1987	WPG	592	336	56.8	4686	7.9	35	5.9	30	5.1	72	
Totals		4657	2807	60.3	39041	8.4	252	5.4	214	4.6	105	
MICHAEL CLEMONS												
1989	TOR	1	1	100.0	18	18.0	1	100.0	0	0.0	18	
1993	TOR	1	0	0.0	0	0.0	0	0.0	0	0.0		
1994	TOR	3	2	66.7	30	10.0	1	33.3	0	0.0	20	
1995	TOR	2	1	50.0	37	18.5	0	0.0	0	0.0	37	
1996	TOR	1	0	0.0	0	0.0	0	0.0	0	0.0		
1997	TOR	1	1	100.0	0	0.0	0	0.0	0	0.0	0	
Totals		9	5	55.6	85	9.4	2	22.2	0	0.0	37	
BILL CLINE												
1965	OTT	14	4	28.6	83	5.9	0	0.0	2	14.3	44	4
1966	OTT	11	3	27.3	30	2.7	0	0.0	1	9.1	11	1
1967	OTT	7	3	42.9	69	9.9	0	0.0	0	0.0	31	
Totals		32	10	31.3	182	5.7	0	0.0	3	9.4	44	5
RON CLINKSCALE												
1955	BC	00	30	45.5	402	7.0	2	3.0	0	13.0	30	
1956	CAL	10	4	40.0	41	4.1	0	0.0	1	10.0	19	
1956	Year	10	4	40.0	41	4.1	0	0.0	1	10.0	19	
1957	CAL	26	13	50.0	200	7.7	0	0.0	2	7.7	28	
1958	CAL	25	10	40.0	170	6.8	1	4.0	3	12.0	81	
Totals		127	57	44.9	873	6.9	3	2.4	15	11.8	81	
DeANDRA COBB												
2009	HAM	1	0	0.0	0	0.0	0	0.0	0	0.0		
ROBERT COBB												
1994	SHR	93	40	43.0	555	6.0	3	3.2	8	8.6	50	
1995	SHR	8	3	37.5	52	6.5	0	0.0	0	0.0	30	
Totals		101	43	42.6	607	6.0	3	3.0	8	7.9	50	
DICK COHEE												
1966	HAM	2	1	50.0	49	24.5	1	50.0	0	0.0	49	0
VERNON COLE												
1960	WPG	33	16	48.5	320	9.7	1	3.0	1	3.0	81	1
1964	MTL	69	32	46.4	454	6.6	3	4.3	5	7.2	81	11
Totals		102	48	47.1	774	7.6	4	3.9	6	5.9	81	12
COREY COLEHOUR												
1968	EDM	40	27	67.5	309	7.7	1	2.5	3	7.5	48	
1969	EDM	290	155	53.4	1947	6.7	9	3.1	17	5.9	47	
Totals		330	182	55.2	2256	6.8	10	3.0	20	6.1	48	
LOVELL COLEMAN												
1961	CAL	3	1	33.3	40	13.3	0	0.0	0	0.0	40	0
1963	CAL	1	0	0.0	0	0.0	0	0.0	0	0.0		0
1964	CAL	5	2	40.0	67	13.4	1	20.0	2	40.0	50	0
1965	CAL	5	2	40.0	47	9.4	2	40.0	0	0.0	26	
1966	CAL	1	0	0.0	0	0.0	0	0.0	0	0.0		0
1967	CAL	4	3	75.0	57	14.3	1	25.0	0	0.0	51	
Totals		19	8	42.1	211	11.1	4	21.1	2	10.5	51	0
REGGIE COLLIER												
1987	OTT	20	10	50.0	154	7.7	2	10.0	3	15.0	37	
SONNY COLVIN												
1948	TOR						1					
LOU CONFESSORI												
1967	WPG	8	3	37.5	23	2.9	0	0.0	2	25.0	9	
JOHN CONGEMI												
1987	TOR	187	104	55.6	1256	6.7	6	3.2	11	5.9	48	
1988	TOR	92	55	59.8	796	8.7	6	6.5	8	8.7	58	
1989	TOR	243	117	48.1	1472	6.1	6	2.5	12	4.9	57	
1990	TOR	152	84	55.3	1278	8.4	6	3.9	7	4.6	60	
1991	OTT	23	8	34.8	121	5.3	1	4.3	1	4.3	41	
1992	TOR	100	49	49.0	735	7.4	3	3.0	3	3.0	47	
1994	BAL	49	23	46.9	522	10.7	2	4.1	6	12.2	42	
Totals		846	440	52.0	6180	7.3	30	3.5	48	5.7	60	
JIM CONROY												
1961	OTT	1	0	0.0	0	0.0	0	0.0	0	0.0		0
JOHNNY COOK												
1948	SAS						3					
BILLY COOPER												
1965	WPG	1	0	0.0	0	0.0	0	0.0	0	0.0		0
JEREMAINE COPELAND												
2002	MTL	1	1	100.0	36	36.0	1	100.0	0	0.0	36	0
2003	MTL	2	1	50.0	36	18.0	0	0.0	0	0.0	36	0
2005	CAL	1	0	0.0	0	0.0	0	0.0	0	0.0		0
2007	CAL	2	0	0.0	0	0.0	0	0.0	0	0.0		0
2008	CAL	1	1	100.0	16	16.0	0	0.0	0	0.0	16	0
Totals		7	3	42.9	88	12.6	1	14.3	0	0.0	36	0
ROYAL COPELAND												
1946	TOR						1					
1947	TOR						2					
1949	TOR						1					
1950	CAL	4	2	50.0	13	3.3	1	25.0	0	0.0	12	
1951	CAL	3	0	0.0	0	0.0	0	0.0	1	33.3		
Totals		7	2	28.6	13	1.9	6	14.3	1	14.3	12	
TONY CORBIN												
2001	BC	95	51	53.7	762	8.0	4	4.2	6	6.3	67	0
DAVID CORLEY												
2003	HAM	32	19	59.4	212	6.6	1	3.1	1	3.1	29	1
FRANK COSENTINO												
1960	HAM	1	0	0.0	0	0.0	0	0.0	0	0.0		
1961	HAM	59	23	39.0	356	6.0	2	3.4	4	6.8	41	8
1962	HAM	145	68	46.9	1182	8.2	6	4.1	8	5.5	95	
1963	HAM	30	16	53.3	370	12.3	3	10.0	3	10.0	57	0
1964	HAM	28	16	57.1	387	13.8	4	14.3	2	7.1	65	2
1965	HAM	121	51	42.1	876	7.2	6	5.0	12	9.9	58	7
1966	HAM	123	57	46.3	913	7.4	9	7.3	13	10.6	62	5
1967	EDM	248	138	55.6	1936	7.8	9	3.6	15	6.0	66	
1968	EDM	139	68	48.9	858	6.2	5	3.6	5	3.6	59	
1969	TOR	102	45	44.1	800	7.8	9	8.8	4	3.9	74	
Totals		996	482	48.4	7678	7.7	53	5.3	66	6.6	95	22
BRUCE COULTER												
1948	MTL						8					

Year	Team	ATT	COM	COM%	YDS	AVG	TD	TD%	INT	INT%	LG	SK
1949	MTL						4					
1950	MTL						2					
1954	MTL	5	2	40.0	27	5.4	0	0.0	1	20.0	14	
1955	MTL	4	2	50.0	36	9.0	0	0.0	0	0.0	19	
1956	MTL	49	28	57.1	322	6.6	1	2.0	6	12.2	36	
1957	MTL	8	4	50.0	39	4.9	0	0.0	2	25.0	20	
Totals		66	36	54.5	424	6.4	15	1.5	9	13.6	36	
TEX COULTER												
1954	MTL	2	1	50.0	22	11.0	0	0.0	1	50.0	22	
1956	MTL	2	1	50.0	10	5.0	0	0.0	0	0.0	10	
Totals		4	2	50.0	32	8.0	0	0.0	1	25.0	22	
JOHNNY COUNTS												
1964	HAM	1	0	0.0	0	0.0	0	0.0	0	0.0		0
LARRY COWAN												
1984	EDM	1	1	100.0	19	19.0	0	0.0	0	0.0	19	
TIM COWAN												
1983	BC	21	5	23.8	53	2.5	0	0.0	0	0.0	20	
1984	BC	186	96	51.6	1434	7.7	13	7.0	10	5.4	57	
1985	BC	76	43	56.6	599	7.9	6	7.9	5	6.6	49	
1986	TOR	48	20	41.7	302	6.3	2	4.2	7	14.6		
1986	BC	47	20	42.6	271	5.8	0	0.0	4	8.5	46	
1986	Year	95	40	42.1	573	6.0	2	2.1	11	11.6	46	
Totals		378	184	48.7	2659	7.0	21	5.6	26	6.9	57	
GEOFF CRAIN												
1953	WPG	31	15	48.4	222	7.2	3	9.7	5	16.1		
1954	WPG	12	5	41.7	51	4.3	1	8.3	0	0.0		
1955	OTT	22	10	45.5	184	8.4	1	4.5	6	27.3	74	
Totals		65	30	46.2	457	7.0	5	7.7	11	16.9	74	
MARCUS CRANDELL												
1997	EDM	13	5	38.5	71	5.5	1	7.7	1	7.7	33	1
1998	EDM	9	4	44.4	100	11.1	1	11.1	2	22.2	65	0
1999	EDM	112	59	52.7	767	6.8	3	2.7	5	4.5	59	7
2001	CAL	386	239	61.9	3407	8.8	14	3.6	11	2.8	72	23
2002	CAL	516	268	51.9	4072	7.9	26	5.0	20	3.9	80	23
2003	CAL	291	147	50.5	2019	6.9	10	3.4	13	4.5	65	9
2004	CAL	372	211	56.7	2389	6.4	7	1.9	16	4.3	70	9
2005	SAS	351	200	57.0	2295	6.5	12	3.4	11	3.1	60	6
2006	SAS	30	19	63.3	201	6.7	0	0.0	1	3.3	30	1
2007	SAS	131	78	59.5	982	7.5	5	3.8	5	3.8	42	5
2008	SAS	128	67	52.3	924	7.2	7	5.5	3	2.3	73	3
Totals		2339	1297	55.5	17227	7.4	86	3.7	88	3.8	80	87
DAVE CRANMER												
1968	CAL	4	0	0.0	0	0.0	0	0.0	0	0.0		
1973	HAM	1	0	0.0	0	0.0	0	0.0	0	0.0		
1973	Year	1	0	0.0	0	0.0	0	0.0	0	0.0		
Totals		5	0	0.0	0	0.0	0	0.0	0	0.0		
RUFUS CRAWFORD												
1980	HAM	1	0	0.0	0	0.0	0	0.0	0	0.0		
ROB CRIFO												
1995	TOR	1	1	100.0	56	56.0	1	100.0	0	0.0	56	
ERIC CROUCH												
2006	TOR	13	6	46.2	127	9.8	0	0.0	1	7.7	94	
EDDIE CROWDER												
1953	EDM	28	12	42.9	234	8.4	1	3.6	3	10.7		
DAN CROWLEY												
1995	BAL	8	2	25.0	21	2.6	0	0.0	1	12.5	19	
1996	MTL	15	5	33.3	39	2.6	0	0.0	1	6.7	13	
1999	EDM	49	22	44.9	216	4.4	0	0.0	3	6.1	37	
2000	EDM	178	94	52.8	1313	7.4	10	5.6	13	7.3	45	11
2001	EDM	26	13	50.0	167	6.4	1	3.8	0	0.0	32	
2002	OTT	454	223	49.1	2697	5.9	16	3.5	19	4.2	91	
2003	OTT	86	43	50.0	480	5.6	2	2.3	3	3.5	42	
Totals		816	402	49.3	4933	6.0	29	3.6	40	4.9	91	11
JASON CRUMB												
2005	BC	1	0	0.0	0	0.0	0	0.0	0	0.0		0
RICHARD CRUMP												
1980	OTT	8	2	25.0	25	3.1	1	12.5	2	25.0	20	
1981	OTT	1	1	100.0	9	9.0	0	0.0	0	0.0	9	
Totals		9	3	33.3	34	3.8	1	11.1	2	22.2	20	
TONY CURCILLO												
1956	HAM	152	83	54.6	1726	11.4	18	11.8	20	13.2	80	
1957	HAM	14	4	28.6	84	6.0	0	0.0	3	21.4	37	
1958	HAM	6	2	33.3	29	4.8	0	0.0	1	16.7	21	
1960	HAM	1	0	0.0	0	0.0	0	0.0	1	100.0		
Totals		173	89	51.4	1839	10.6	18	10.4	25	14.5	80	
JASON CURRIE												
2003	HAM	1	0	0.0	0	0.0	0	0.0	1	100.0		
2004	HAM	1	0	0.0	0	0.0	0	0.0	0	0.0		0
Totals		2	0	0.0	0	0.0	0	0.0	1	50.0		0
CHUCK CURTIS												
1957	WPG	18	8	44.4	99	5.5	0	0.0	2	11.1	22	
ULYSSES CURTIS												
1954	TOR	1	0	0.0	0	0.0	0	0.0	0	0.0		
BERNIE CUSTIS												
1951	HAM						9					
1953	HAM						1					
1954	HAM	10	5	50.0	117	11.7	1	10.0	0	0.0	88	
1955	OTT	2	1	50.0	26	13.0	0	0.0	1	50.0	26	
Totals		12	6	50.0	143	11.9	11	8.3	1	8.3	88	
VINCE DANIELSEN												
1995	CAL	1	0	0.0	0	0.0	0	0.0	0	0.0		0
GERRY DATTILIO												
1976	MTL	3	1	33.3	14	4.7	0	0.0	0	0.0	14	
1977	MTL	2	1	50.0	20	10.0	1	50.0	0	0.0	20	
1978	MTL	142	78	54.9	1120	7.9	5	3.5	9	6.3	59	
1979	MTL	21	9	42.9	115	5.5	0	0.0	3	14.3	18	
1980	MTL	311	179	57.6	2892	9.3	19	6.1	20	6.4	75	
1981	MTL	122	69	56.6	1095	9.0	4	3.3	7	5.7	77	
1982	CAL	387	194	50.1	2788	7.2	11	2.8	22	5.7	68	
1983	CAL	183	104	56.8	1213	6.6	11	6.0	9	4.9	86	
1984	MTL	75	49	65.3	568	7.6	2	2.7	5	6.7	82	
1985	MTL	25	13	52.0	127	5.1	0	0.0	4	16.0	23	
Totals		1271	697	54.8	9952	7.8	53	4.2	79	6.2	86	
COTTON DAVIDSON												
1958	CAL	16	8	50.0	99	6.2	0	0.0	3	18.8	28	
MIKE DAVIES												
1958	BC	2	0	0.0	0	0.0	0	0.0	1	50.0		
1960	WPG	23	8	34.8	130	5.7	2	8.7	0	0.0	58	0
Totals		25	8	32.0	130	5.2	2	8.0	1	4.0	58	0
ANTHONY DAVIS												
1976	TOR	3	1	33.3	13	4.3	0	0.0	0	0.0	13	
DONNIE DAVIS												
1967	MTL	2	0	0.0	0	0.0	0	0.0	0	0.0		
JOSE DAVIS												
2000	WPG	17	7	41.2	75	4.4	0	0.0	1	5.9	15	1
2001	WPG	9	3	33.3	30	3.3	0	0.0	0	0.0	13	0
Totals		26	10	38.5	105	4.0	0	0.0	1	3.8	15	1
BOBBY DAWSON												
1956	HAM	15	7	46.7	95	6.3	1	6.7	0	0.0	23	
1959	HAM	9	2	22.2	16	1.8	0	0.0	2	22.2	16	1
Totals		24	9	37.5	111	4.6	1	4.2	2	8.3	23	1
DEXTER DAWSON												
1997	WPG	3	2	66.7	85	28.3	1	33.3	0	0.0	53	
GERRY DAWSON												
1948	OTT						2					
EAGLE DAY												
1956	WPG	254	137	53.9	1814	7.1	7	2.8	12	4.7	53	
1961	CAL	201	106	52.7	1800	9.0	10	5.0	10	5.0	100	
1962	CAL	262	156	59.5	2494	9.5	15	5.7	8	3.1	85	
1963	CAL	374	228	61.0	3126	8.4	13	3.5	10	2.7	61	25
1964	CAL	285	177	62.1	2197	7.7	11	3.9	14	4.9	46	38
1965	CAL	215	124	57.7	1892	8.8	12	5.6	8	3.7	90	
1966	CAL	55	27	49.1	301	5.5	0	0.0	6	10.9	35	11
1966	TOR	107	60	56.1	781	7.3	6	5.6	3	2.8	27	14
1966	Year	162	87	53.7	1082	6.7	6	3.7	9	5.6	35	25
Totals		1753	1015	57.9	14405	8.2	74	4.2	71	4.1	100	88
TERRY DEAN												
1995	WPG	30	10	33.3	109	3.6	0	0.0	3	10.0	31	
SCOTT DEIBERT												
2003	CAL	1	1	100.0	12	12.0	1	100.0	0	0.0	12	0
AL DEKDEBRUN												
1949	HAM						5					
1950	TOR						13					
1951	TOR						3					
1954	OTT	29	12	41.4	160	5.5	1	3.4	2	6.9	45	
Totals		29	12	41.4	160	5.5	22	3.4	2	6.9	45	
JACK DELVEAUX												
1964	WPG	1	0	0.0	0	0.0	0	0.0	0	0.0		0
AUTRY DENSON												
2004	MTL	1	0	0.0	0	0.0	0	0.0	1	100.0		
BRIAN DeROO												
1982	MTL	1	1	100.0	9	9.0	0	0.0	0	0.0	9	
DICK DESMARAIS												
1961	OTT	3	0	0.0	0	0.0	0	0.0	0	0.0		0
ROY DEWALT												
1980	BC	119	55	46.2	616	5.2	4	3.4	4	3.4	57	
1981	BC	55	27	49.1	343	6.2	1	1.8	1	1.8	41	
1982	BC	282	172	61.0	2505	8.9	18	6.4	6	2.1	85	
1983	BC	442	275	62.2	3637	8.2	22	5.0	16	3.6	79	
1984	BC	437	258	59.0	3613	8.3	21	4.8	15	3.4	78	
1985	BC	476	301	63.2	4237	8.9	27	5.7	12	2.5	90	
1986	BC	556	314	56.5	4057	7.3	17	3.1	16	2.9	72	
1987	BC	531	303	57.1	3855	7.3	19	3.6	14	2.6	77	
1988	WPG	131	58	44.3	719	5.5	2	1.5	6	4.6	48	
1988	OTT	101	40	39.6	565	5.6	1	1.0	6	5.9	61	
1988	Year	232	98	42.2	1284	5.5	3	1.3	12	5.2	61	
Totals		3130	1803	57.6	24147	7.7	132	4.2	96	3.1	90	
BENJY DIAL												
1970	WPG	89	45	50.6	597	6.7	1	1.1	7	7.9	51	
1971	WPG	41	15	36.6	252	6.1	2	4.9	3	7.3	63	
Totals		130	60	46.2	849	6.5	3	2.3	10	7.7	63	
LARRY DICK												
1978	SAS	113	56	49.6	918	8.1	4	3.5	4	3.5	57	
1979	SAS	68	39	57.4	523	7.7	1	1.5	5	7.4	65	
Totals		181	95	52.5	1441	8.0	5	2.8	9	5.0	65	
BILLY DICKEN												
2000	HAM	32	10	31.3	163	5.1	0	0.0	5	15.6	33	0
DAVE DICKENSON												
1997	CAL	49	36	73.5	407	8.3	2	4.1	1	2.0	31	10
1998	CAL	113	79	69.9	1170	10.4	10	8.8	4	3.5	89	14
1999	CAL	343	219	63.8	3048	8.9	16	4.7	10	2.9	76	27
2000	CAL	493	317	64.3	4636	9.4	36	7.3	6	1.2	71	47
2003	BC	549	370	67.4	5496	10.0	36	6.6	12	2.2	103	43
2004	BC	98	62	63.3	967	9.9	8	8.2	2	2.0	68	7
2005	BC	342	253	74.0	3338	9.8	21	6.1	5	1.5	83	46
2006	BC	338	238	70.4	3032	9.0	22	6.5	7	2.1	92	29
2007	BC	87	56	64.4	740	8.5	3	3.4	3	3.4	51	7
2008	CAL	9	5	55.6	79	8.8	0	0.0	0	0.0	39	0
Totals		2421	1635	67.5	22913	9.5	154	6.4	50	2.1	103	230
TOMMY DICKERSON												
1955	CAL	38	16	42.1	224	5.9	1	2.6	5	13.2	47	
TERRY DICKEY												
1994	TOR	1	1	100.0	33	33.0	0	0.0	0	0.0	30	
BOB DICKIE												
1957	BC	1	0	0.0	0	0.0	0	0.0	0	0.0		
1958	MTL	1	0	0.0	0	0.0	0	0.0	1	100.0		
Totals		2	0	0.0	0	0.0	0	0.0	1	50.0		
JIM DILLARD												
1963	CAL	1	0	0.0	0	0.0	0	0.0	1	100.0		0
1967	TOR	3	2	66.7	91	30.3	1	33.3	0	0.0	50	
1968	TOR	2	2	100.0	11	5.5	0	0.0	0	0.0	8	
Totals		6	4	66.7	102	17.0	1	16.7	1	16.7	50	0
TODD DILLON												
1986	OTT	186	102	54.8	1279	6.9	3	1.6	12	6.5	47	20

Year	Team	ATT	COM	COM%	YDS	AVG	TD	TD%	INT	INT%	LG	SK
1987	OTT	402	222	55.2	2901	7.2	14	3.5	18	4.5	57	
1988	OTT	185	97	52.4	1211	6.5	4	2.2	8	4.3	72	
1989	HAM	191	105	55.0	1368	7.2	5	2.6	3	1.6	53	
1990	HAM	193	113	58.5	1351	7.0	7	3.6	10	5.2	48	
1991	HAM	246	125	50.8	1551	6.3	8	3.3	10	4.1	75	
1992	HAM	46	20	43.5	371	8.1	2	4.3	2	4.3	53	
1993	HAM	22	14	63.6	192	8.7	1	4.5	1	4.5	46	
1994	HAM	188	91	48.4	1034	5.5	3	1.6	7	3.7	63	
Totals		1659	889	53.6	11258	6.8	47	2.8	71	4.3	75	20
FRANK DiMAGGIO												
1973	OTT	10	2	20.0	42	4.2	0	0.0	2	20.0	45	
TOM DIMITROFF												
1957	OTT	199	98	49.2	1750	8.8	12	6.0	16	8.0	84	
1958	OTT	47	25	53.2	391	8.3	2	4.3	1	2.1	45	
Totals		246	123	50.0	2141	8.7	14	5.7	17	6.9	84	
RYAN DINWIDDIE												
2006	WPG	24	11	45.8	107	4.5	1	4.2	3	12.5	20	
2007	WPG	24	17	70.8	175	7.3	0	0.0	0	0.0	41	0
2008	WPG	159	93	58.5	1299	8.2	5	3.1	6	3.8	85	7
2010	SAS	12	6	50.0	103	8.6	2	16.7	1	8.3	42	1
2011	SAS	111	56	50.5	847	7.6	3	2.7	4	3.6	72	12
Totals		330	183	55.5	2531	7.7	11	3.3	14	4.2	85	20
GEORGE DIXON												
1964	MTL	3	1	33.3	16	5.3	1	33.3	0	0.0	16	0
TOM DIXON												
1988	OTT	1	0	0.0	0	0.0	0	0.0	0	0.0		
DAVE DOANE												
1957	TOR	40	21	52.5	294	7.4	2	5.0	4	10.0	44	
GLENN DOBBS												
1951	SAS	274	145	52.9	2313	8.4	28	10.2	12	4.4		
1952	SAS	253	116	45.8	1977	7.8	14	5.5	12	4.7	79	
1953	SAS	128	67	52.3	906	7.1	9	7.0	7	5.5		
1954	HAM	2	0	0.0	0	0.0	0	0.0	0	0.0		
Totals		657	328	49.9	5196	7.9	51	7.8	31	4.7	79	
WALT DOBLER												
1946	WPG						4					
AL DOROW												
1958	SAS	23	7	30.4	58	2.5	0	0.0	4	17.4		
1958	BC	160	84	52.5	1212	7.6	9	5.6	14	8.8		
1958	Year	183	91	49.7	1270	6.9	9	4.9	18	9.8	67	
1959	TOR	151	74	49.0	1093	7.2	8	5.3	17	11.3	72	9
Totals		334	165	49.4	2363	7.1	17	5.1	35	10.5	72	9
DEAN DORSEY												
1989	OTT	1	1	100.0	-3	-3.0	0	0.0	0	0.0	-3	
GERRY DOUCETTE												
1954	TOR	7	4	57.1	31	4.4	0	0.0	0	0.0	13	
1955	TOR	20	8	40.0	126	6.3	0	0.0	2	10.0	29	
1956	TOR	36	19	52.8	350	9.7	1	2.8	5	13.9	40	
1957	TOR	137	61	44.5	822	6.0	8	5.8	14	10.2	64	
1958	TOR	93	46	49.5	606	6.5	2	2.2	7	7.5	59	
1959	TOR	54	27	50.0	371	6.9	2	3.7	3	5.6	32	1
1961	MTL	7	3	42.9	7	1.0	0	0.0	0	0.0	8	1
Totals		354	168	47.5	2313	6.5	13	3.7	31	8.8	64	2
ROBERT DOUGHERTY												
1995	TOR	18	11	61.1	80	4.4	0	0.0	0	0.0	14	
1995	OTT	3	3	100.0	36	12.0	0	0.0	0	0.0	15	
1995	Year	21	14	66.7	116	5.5	0	0.0	0	0.0	15	
KARL DOUGLAS												
1973	BC	128	61	47.7	1020	8.0	4	3.1	10	7.8	52	
1974	BC	18	5	27.8	97	5.4	0	0.0	2	11.1	46	
1974	CAL	12	6	50.0	95	7.9	0	0.0	1	8.3	37	
1974	Year	30	11	36.7	192	6.4	0	0.0	3	10.0	46	
1975	CAL	84	33	39.3	481	5.7	7	8.3	9	10.7	37	
Totals		242	105	43.4	1693	7.0	11	4.5	22	9.1	52	
WESTON DRESSLER												
2009	SAS	1	0	0.0	0	0.0	0	0.0	0	0.0		0
2010	SAS	2	0	0.0	0	0.0	0	0.0	0	0.0		0
2011	SAS	1	1	100.0	16	16.0	0	0.0	0	0.0	16	0
Totals		4	1	25.0	16	4.0	0	0.0	0	0.0	16	0
ROBERT DRUMMOND												
1996	TOR	1	0	0.0	0	0.0	0	0.0	0	0.0		
1997	TOR	1	0	0.0	0	0.0	0	0.0	0	0.0		
2000	BC	1	0	0.0	0	0.0	0	0.0	0	0.0		0
Totals		3	0	0.0	0	0.0	0	0.0	0	0.0		0
TOM DUBLINSKI												
1955	TOR	388	225	58.0	3561	9.2	30	7.7	34	8.8	79	
1957	TOR	122	64	52.5	863	7.1	4	3.3	10	8.2	43	
1959	HAM	56	34	60.7	540	9.6	5	8.9	3	5.4	45	4
1961	HAM	24	11	45.8	218	9.1	2	8.3	2	8.3	74	4
1962	TOR	29	17	58.6	172	5.9	2	6.9	3	10.3	27	
Totals		619	351	56.7	5354	8.6	43	6.9	52	8.4	79	8
FARRELL DUCLAIR												
1997	CAL	1	1	100.0	1	1.0	1	100.0	0	0.0	1	
PAUL DUDLEY												
1966	SAS	1	1	100.0	28	28.0	1	100.0	0	0.0	28	0
MAURY DUNCAN												
1957	BC	236	127	53.8	1827	7.7	12	5.1	18	7.6	70	
1958	CAL	90	55	61.1	720	8.0	5	5.6	4	4.4	49	
Totals		326	182	55.8	2547	7.8	17	5.2	22	6.7	70	
RANDY DUNCAN												
1959	BC	318	154	48.4	2746	8.6	18	5.7	30	9.4	91	
1960	BC	113	51	45.1	734	6.5	7	6.2	12	10.6	57	7
Totals		431	205	47.6	3480	8.1	25	5.8	42	9.7	91	7
TED DUNCAN												
1955	BC	1	0	0.0	0	0.0	0	0.0	0	0.0		
1957	CAL	1	1	100.0	16	16.0	0	0.0	0	0.0	16	
1958	CAL	1	1	100.0	12	12.0	0	0.0	0	0.0	12	
Totals		3	2	66.7	28	9.3	0	0.0	0	0.0	16	
MATT DUNIGAN												
1983	EDM	26	14	53.8	239	9.2	1	3.8	2	7.7	51	
1984	EDM	412	220	53.4	3273	7.9	21	5.1	19	4.6	81	
1985	EDM	405	242	59.8	3410	8.4	19	4.7	22	5.4	89	

Year	Team	ATT	COM	COM%	YDS	AVG	TD	TD%	INT	INT%	LG	SK
1986	EDM	485	275	56.7	3648	7.5	25	5.2	14	2.9	68	
1987	EDM	326	175	53.7	2823	8.7	21	6.4	19	5.8	89	
1988	BC	471	268	56.9	3776	8.0	26	5.5	22	4.7	76	
1989	BC	597	331	55.4	4509	7.6	27	4.5	20	3.4	83	
1990	TOR	262	144	55.0	2028	7.7	17	6.5	14	5.3	53	
1991	TOR	196	121	61.7	2011	10.3	16	8.2	10	5.1	87	
1992	WPG	411	205	49.9	2857	7.0	17	4.1	15	3.6	60	
1993	WPG	600	334	55.7	4682	7.8	36	6.0	18	3.0	75	
1994	WPG	431	252	58.5	3965	9.2	31	7.2	16	3.7	79	
1995	BIR*	643	362	56.3	4911	7.6	34	5.3	16	2.5	71	
1996	HAM	211	114	54.0	1725	8.2	12	5.7	4	1.9	51	
Totals		5476	3057	55.8	43857	8.0	303	5.5	211	3.9	89	
FRANK DUNLAP												
1946	OTT						7					
1947	OTT						6					
1948	TOR						1					
1950	OTT						1					
Totals							15					
DARIAN DURANT												
2006	SAS	1	1	100.0	14	14.0	0	0.0	0	0.0	14	0
2008	SAS	129	77	59.7	1122	8.7	7	5.4	6	4.7	67	14
2009	SAS	562	339	60.3	4348	7.7	24	4.3	21	3.7	65	34
2010	SAS	644	391	60.7	5542	8.6	25	3.9	22	3.4	87	41
2011	SAS	489	299	61.1	3653	7.5	18	3.7	14	2.9	75	28
Totals		1825	1107	60.7	14679	8.0	74	4.1	63	3.5	87	117
DAMON DUVAL												
2008	MTL	1	1	100.0	-12	-12.0	0	0.0	0	0.0	-12	
KEVIN EAKIN												
2005	HAM	74	44	59.5	666	9.0	4	5.4	2	2.7	80	4
2006	HAM	88	38	43.2	461	5.2	2	2.3	9	10.2	39	2
Totals		162	82	50.6	1127	7.0	6	3.7	11	6.8	80	6
CHUCK EALEY												
1972	HAM	253	148	58.5	2573	10.2	22	8.7	8	3.2	76	
1973	HAM	309	181	58.6	2312	7.5	14	4.5	14	4.5	68	
1974	HAM	130	71	54.6	1012	7.8	2	1.5	8	6.2	44	
1974	WPG	147	74	50.3	975	6.6	8	5.4	6	4.1	45	
1974	Year	277	145	52.3	1987	7.2	10	3.6	14	5.1	45	
1975	WPG	128	67	52.3	1028	8.0	6	4.7	4	3.1	72	
1975	TOR	68	35	51.5	507	7.5	2	2.9	2	2.9	63	
1975	Year	196	102	52.0	1535	7.8	8	4.1	6	3.1	72	
1976	TOR	245	132	53.9	1846	7.5	12	4.9	10	4.1	89	
1977	TOR	240	135	56.3	1653	6.9	8	3.3	11	4.6	62	
1978	TOR	206	112	54.4	1420	6.9	8	3.9	6	2.9	71	
Totals		1726	955	55.3	13326	7.7	82	4.8	69	4.0	89	
MIKE EBEN												
1968	TOR	1	1	100.0	13	13.0	0	0.0	0	0.0	13	
1970	EDM	3	1	33.3	11	3.7	1	33.3	2	66.7	11	
Totals		4	2	50.0	24	6.0	1	25.0	2	50.0	13	
JOHN ECKMAN												
1969	HAM	158	86	54.4	1291	8.2	6	3.8	19	12.0	83	
1970	HAM	80	38	47.5	617	7.7	4	5.0	7	8.8	44	
Totals		238	124	52.1	1908	8.0	10	4.2	26	10.9	83	
JUNIOR EDGE												
1964	OTT	1	1	100.0	4	4.0	0	0.0	0	0.0	4	1
JIMMY EDWARDS												
1977	HAM	2	1	50.0	9	4.5	1	50.0	0	0.0	9	
1978	HAM	3	0	0.0	0	0.0	0	0.0	0	0.0		
Totals		5	1	20.0	9	1.8	1	20.0	0	0.0	9	
TERRENCE EDWARDS												
2010	WPG	2	0	0.0	0	0.0	0	0.0	1	50.0		0
KEVIN EIBEN												
2003	TOR	1	1	100.0	-2	-2.0	0	0.0	0	0.0	-2	
LARRY EILMES												
1966	BC	1	0	0.0	0	0.0	0	0.0	1	100.0		0
RAY ELGAARD												
1988	SAS	1	0	0.0	0	0.0	0	0.0	0	0.0		
1989	SAS	1	0	0.0	0	0.0	0	0.0	0	0.0		
Totals		2	0	0.0	0	0.0	0	0.0	0	0.0		
GEORGE ELLIOTT												
1955	WPG	4	1	25.0	3	0.8	0	0.0	2	50.0	3	
JOEY ELLIOTT												
2010	WPG	74	36	48.6	446	6.0	2	2.7	3	4.1	55	5
2011	WPG	18	10	55.6	87	4.8	0	0.0	0	0.0	22	1
Totals		92	46	50.0	533	5.8	2	2.2	3	3.3	55	6
RAY ENRIGHT												
1953	EDM	1	1	100.0	15	15.0	0	0.0	0	0.0	15	
JEROME ERDMAN												
1988	OTT	1	1	100.0	-10	-10.0	0	0.0	0	0.0	-10	
JACK ESPENSHIP												
1961	MTL	1	1	100.0	20	20.0	0	0.0	0	0.0	20	0
SAM ETCHEVERRY												
1952	MTL						9					
1953	MTL						23					
1954	MTL	372	206	55.4	3610	9.7	25	6.7	29	7.8	105	
1955	MTL	400	227	56.8	3657	9.1	30	7.5	24	6.0	84	
1956	MTL	446	276	61.9	4723	10.6	32	7.2	23	5.2	109	
1957	MTL	408	215	52.7	3341	8.2	14	3.4	22	5.4	88	
1958	MTL	423	247	58.4	3548	8.4	18	4.3	25	5.9	87	
1959	MTL	402	231	57.5	3133	7.8	10	2.5	21	5.2	80	39
1960	MTL	378	229	60.6	3571	9.4	24	6.3	19	5.0	98	
Totals		2829	1631	57.7	25583	9.0	185	5.4	163	5.8	109	39
BILL ETTER												
1973	HAM	5	4	80.0	48	9.6	1	20.0	0	0.0	17	
1974	HAM	183	109	59.6	1446	7.9	4	2.2	9	4.9	46	
1975	HAM	1	1	100.0	7	7.0	0	0.0	0	0.0	7	
Totals		189	114	60.3	1501	7.9	5	2.6	9	4.8	46	
JOHNNY EVANS												
1982	MTL	312	163	52.2	2243	7.2	13	4.2	14	4.5	60	
1983	MTL	241	139	57.7	1864	7.7	9	3.7	12	5.0	60	
1984	EDM	78	41	52.6	613	7.9	4	5.1	7	9.0	85	
Totals		631	343	54.4	4720	7.5	26	4.1	33	5.2	85	
KEN EVRAIRE												

Year	Team	ATT	COM	COM%	YDS	AVG	TD	TD%	INT	INT%	LG	SK
1994	HAM	1	0	0.0	0	0.0	0	0.0	0	0.0		
MARTIN FABI												
1964	SAS	1	0	0.0	0	0.0	0	0.0	1	100.0		0
LARRY FAIRHOLM												
1965	MTL	2	0	0.0	0	0.0	0	0.0	0	0.0		0
1970	MTL	1	0	0.0	0	0.0	0	0.0	0	0.0		
Totals		3	0	0.0	0	0.0	0	0.0	0	0.0		0
BERNIE FALONEY												
1954	EDM	71	26	36.6	529	7.5	3	4.2	5	7.0		
1957	HAM	262	112	42.7	1759	6.7	6	2.3	16	6.1	70	
1958	HAM	309	167	54.0	2852	9.2	18	5.8	24	7.8	69	
1959	HAM	247	139	56.3	2187	8.9	15	6.1	12	4.9	86	19
1960	HAM	385	196	50.9	3075	8.0	24	6.2	31	8.1	96	
1961	HAM	274	156	56.9	2565	9.4	23	8.4	14	5.1	72	20
1962	HAM	89	46	51.7	743	8.3	5	5.6	6	6.7	87	
1963	HAM	273	143	52.4	2305	8.4	13	4.8	16	5.9	84	7
1964	HAM	221	106	48.0	1939	8.8	17	7.7	16	7.2	86	12
1965	MTL	275	148	53.8	2253	8.2	8	2.9	29	10.5	85	25
1966	MTL	116	54	46.6	754	6.5	2	1.7	11	9.5	60	14
1967	BC	354	200	56.5	3303	9.3	17	4.8	21	5.9	81	
Totals		2876	1493	51.9	24264	8.4	151	5.3	201	7.0	96	97
ANDY FANTUZ												
2007	SAS	1	0	0.0	0	0.0	0	0.0	0	0.0		0
2008	SAS	1	0	0.0	0	0.0	0	0.0	1	100.0		0
Totals		2	0	0.0	0	0.0	0	0.0	1	50.0		0
SHAWN FAULKNER												
1986	MTL	1	0	0.0	0	0.0	0	0.0	1	100.0		0
1988	CAL	1	0	0.0	0	0.0	0	0.0	0	0.0		
JACKIE FELLOWS												
1947	OTT					3						
CHUCK FENENBOCK												
1949	EDM						2					
1950	CAL	6	3	50.0	40	6.7	1	16.7	1	16.7	15	
Totals		6	3	50.0	40	6.7	3	16.7	1	16.7	15	
LARRY FERGUSON												
1964	EDM	3	0	0.0	0	0.0	0	0.0	0	0.0		0
1966	TOR	1	1	100.0	11	11.0	0	0.0	0	0.0	11	0
1967	TOR	1	1	100.0	28	28.0	0	0.0	0	0.0	28	
Totals		5	2	40.0	39	7.8	0	0.0	0	0.0	28	0
MERVYN FERNANDEZ												
1985	BC	1	1	100.0	55	55.0	0	0.0	0	0.0	55	
1986	BC	1	1	100.0	86	86.0	0	0.0	0	0.0	86	
Totals		2	2	100.0	141	70.5	0	0.0	0	0.0	86	0
VINCE FERRAGAMO												
1981	MTL	342	175	51.2	2182	6.4	7	2.0	25	7.3	67	
GEORGE FESTERYGA												
1947	HAM						1					
1951	EDM	6	2	33.3	58	9.7	1	16.7	1	16.7		
Totals		6	2	33.3	58	9.7	2	16.7	1	16.7		
KEVIN FETERIK												
2002	CAL	1	0	0.0	0	0.0	0	0.0	0	0.0		
2003	CAL	186	119	64.0	1497	8.0	6	3.2	7	3.8	55	
Totals		187	119	63.6	1497	8.0	6	3.2	7	3.7	55	
GREG FIEGER												
1984	SAS	1	0	0.0	0	0.0	0	0.0	0	0.0		
JERRY FIELDS												
1964	MTL	1	0	0.0	0	0.0	0	0.0	0	0.0		1
FRANK FILCHOCK												
1947	HAM						2					
1949	MTL						18					
1950	MTL						13					
1951	EDM	194	105	54.1	1826	9.4	12	6.2	10	5.2		
1952	EDM	74	41	55.4	560	7.6	7	9.5	3	4.1	69	
1953	SAS	106	62	58.5	925	8.7	5	4.7	7	6.6		
Totals		374	208	55.6	3311	8.9	57	6.4	20	5.3	69	
GENE FILIPSKI												
1959	CAL	3	1	33.3	16	5.3	1	33.3	1	33.3	16	0
1961	CAL	3	0	0.0	0	0.0	0	0.0	0	0.0		0
Totals		6	1	16.7	16	2.7	1	16.7	1	16.7	16	0
JIM FINKS												
1957	CAL	125	63	50.4	799	6.4	6	4.8	10	8.0	67	
MARQUEL FLEETWOOD												
1993	OTT	5	2	40.0	7	1.4	0	0.0	1	20.0	5	
1994	OTT	63	29	46.0	386	6.1	2	3.2	2	3.2	44	
1996	TOR	10	5	50.0	16	1.6	0	0.0	3	30.0	14	
1997	HAM	47	22	46.8	216	4.6	0	0.0	1	2.1	27	
Totals		125	58	46.4	625	5.0	2	1.6	7	5.6	44	
DAVE FLEMING												
1969	HAM	2	1	50.0	4	2.0	0	0.0	1	50.0	4	
GEORGE FLEMING												
1964	WPG	1	1	100.0	9	9.0	0	0.0	0	0.0	9	0
PAT FLEMING												
2006	HAM	2	0	0.0	0	0.0	0	0.0	2	100.0		
SEAN FLEMING												
1997	EDM	3	2	66.7	59	19.7	1	33.3	0	0.0	32	
1998	EDM	1	1	100.0	26	26.0	0	0.0	0	0.0	26	
1999	EDM	1	1	100.0	-11	-11.0	0	0.0	0	0.0	-11	
2000	EDM	1	1	100.0	86	86.0	1	100.0	0	0.0	86	0
2002	EDM	1	1	100.0	18	18.0	0	0.0	0	0.0	18	0
2003	EDM	1	1	100.0	7	7.0	0	0.0	0	0.0	7	0
2004	EDM	2	2	100.0	49	24.5	0	0.0	0	0.0	29	0
Totals		10	9	90.0	234	23.4	2	20.0	0	0.0	86	0
WILLIE FLEMING												
1959	BC	1	0	0.0	0	0.0	0	0.0	1	100.0		0
1960	BC	7	4	57.1	124	17.7	1	14.3	1	14.3	78	0
1961	BC	1	0	0.0	0	0.0	0	0.0	1	100.0		0
1963	BC	1	0	0.0	0	0.0	0	0.0	0	0.0		0
Totals		10	4	40.0	124	12.4	1	10.0	3	30.0	78	0
BOBBY FLIPPIN												
1952	EDM	1	0	0.0	0	0.0	0	0.0	0	0.0		
1954	SAS	2	1	50.0	14	7.0	0	0.0	0	0.0	14	
1954	HAM	2	2	100.0	21	10.5	0	0.0	0	0.0	12	
1954	Year	4	3	75.0	35	8.8	0	0.0	0	0.0	14	
Totals		5	3	60.0	35	7.0	0	0.0	0	0.0	14	
LUCIUS FLOYD												
1990	SAS	1	1	100.0	20	20.0	1	100.0	0	0.0	20	
1992	SAS	1	0	0.0	0	0.0	0	0.0	0	0.0		
Totals		2	1	50.0	20	10.0	1	50.0	0	0.0	20	
DARREN FLUTIE												
1991	BC	1	0	0.0	0	0.0	0	0.0	0	0.0		
1992	BC	1	0	0.0	0	0.0	0	0.0	1	100.0		
1993	BC	3	1	33.3	42	14.0	0	0.0	0	0.0	42	
1994	BC	1	1	100.0	29	29.0	0	0.0	0	0.0	29	
1996	EDM	1	0	0.0	0	0.0	0	0.0	0	0.0		
1998	HAM	1	0	0.0	0	0.0	0	0.0	0	0.0		
1999	HAM	5	2	40.0	38	7.6	0	0.0	1	20.0	28	
2000	HAM	1	0	0.0	0	0.0	0	0.0	0	0.0		0
Totals		14	4	28.6	109	7.8	0	0.0	2	14.3	42	0
DOUG FLUTIE												
1990	BC	392	207	52.8	2960	7.6	16	4.1	19	4.8	55	
1991	BC	730	466	63.8	6619	9.1	38	5.2	24	3.3	89	
1992	CAL	688	396	57.6	5945	8.6	32	4.7	30	4.4	81	
1993	CAL	703	416	59.2	6092	8.7	44	6.3	17	2.4	75	
1994	CAL	659	403	61.2	5726	8.7	48	7.3	19	2.9	106	
1995	CAL	332	223	67.2	2788	8.4	16	4.8	5	1.5	63	8
1996	TOR	677	434	64.1	5720	8.4	29	4.3	17	2.5	97	
1997	TOR	673	430	63.9	5505	8.2	47	7.0	24	3.6	78	
Totals		4854	2975	61.3	41355	8.5	270	5.6	155	3.2	106	8
CARL FODOR												
1987	CAL	16	3	18.8	58	3.6	0	0.0	1	6.3	21	
1988	CAL	127	53	41.7	751	5.9	1	0.8	11	8.7	46	
Totals		143	56	39.2	809	5.7	1	0.7	12	8.4	46	
RICKEY FOGGIE												
1988	BC	78	29	37.2	438	5.6	4	5.1	5	6.4	77	
1989	BC	53	26	49.1	419	7.9	5	9.4	3	5.7	62	
1990	BC	41	20	48.8	252	6.1	2	4.9	3	7.3	35	
1990	TOR	169	89	52.7	1676	9.9	21	12.4	5	3.0	76	
1990	Year	210	109	51.9	1928	9.2	23	11.0	8	3.8	76	
1991	TOR	352	171	48.6	3108	8.8	21	6.0	19	5.4	89	
1992	TOR	482	215	44.6	3507	7.3	18	3.7	25	5.2	89	
1993	EDM	96	42	43.8	738	7.7	4	4.2	4	4.2	64	
1994	EDM	156	81	51.9	1098	7.0	7	4.5	8	5.1	55	
1995	MEM	175	76	43.4	1193	6.8	3	1.7	7	4.0	90	
1997	HAM	179	99	55.3	1345	7.5	5	2.8	8	4.5	55	
2002	BC	36	13	36.1	235	6.5	1	2.8	3	8.3	42	
Totals		1817	861	47.4	14009	7.7	91	5.0	90	5.0	90	
JIM FOLEY												
1971	MTL	1	0	0.0	0	0.0	0	0.0	0	0.0		
1973	OTT	1	0	0.0	0	0.0	0	0.0	0	0.0		
1974	OTT	1	0	0.0	0	0.0	0	0.0	0	0.0		
1975	OTT	4	4	100.0	123	30.8	3	75.0	0	0.0	64	
1976	OTT	4	2	50.0	32	8.0	0	0.0	0	0.0	18	
Totals		11	6	54.5	155	14.1	3	27.3	0	0.0	64	
AL FORD												
1966	SAS	1	1	100.0	18	18.0	0	0.0	0	0.0	18	0
1968	SAS	1	1	100.0	6	6.0	0	0.0	0	0.0	6	
1970	SAS	1	1	100.0	31	31.0	0	0.0	0	0.0	31	
1971	SAS	1	0	0.0	0	0.0	0	0.0	0	0.0		
1973	SAS	1	0	0.0	0	0.0	0	0.0	0	0.0		
1975	SAS	1	0	0.0	0	0.0	0	0.0	0	0.0		
Totals		6	3	50.0	55	9.2	0	0.0	0	0.0	31	0
TOMMY FORD												
1953	WPG	1	0	0.0	0	0.0	0	0.0	0	0.0		
ELDON FORTIE												
1963	EDM	16	8	50.0	173	10.8	1	6.3	1	6.3	40	0
TOM FORZANI												
1976	CAL	1	1	100.0	45	45.0	0	0.0	0	0.0	45	
1980	CAL	1	0	0.0	0	0.0	0	0.0	1	100.0		
Totals		2	1	50.0	45	22.5	0	0.0	1	50.0	45	
GENE FOSTER												
1971	EDM	5	4	80.0	50	10.0	1	20.0	0	0.0	24	
1972	EDM	6	2	33.3	24	4.0	0	0.0	1	16.7	13	
1973	EDM	3	1	33.3	27	9.0	0	0.0	0	0.0	27	
Totals		14	7	50.0	101	7.2	1	7.1	1	7.1	27	
JOHN FOURCADE												
1982	BC	14	5	35.7	55	3.9	0	0.0	3	21.4	23	
JOE FRANCIS												
1961	MTL	11	3	27.3	28	2.5	0	0.0	0	0.0	13	3
1962	MTL	35	20	57.1	355	10.1	0	0.0	3	8.6	57	
Totals		46	23	50.0	383	8.3	0	0.0	3	6.5	57	3
DENNIS FRANKLIN												
1977	TOR	8	2	25.0	34	4.3	0	0.0	2	25.0	22	
1977	MTL	9	2	22.2	24	2.7	0	0.0	0	0.0	14	
1977	Year	17	4	23.5	58	3.4	0	0.0	2	11.8	22	
CAM FRASER												
1954	HAM	2	1	50.0	10	5.0	0	0.0	0	0.0	10	
1956	HAM	1	0	0.0	0	0.0	0	0.0	0	0.0		
1957	HAM	1	1	100.0	28	28.0	0	0.0	0	0.0	28	
Totals		4	2	50.0	38	9.5	0	0.0	0	0.0	28	
FRANK FRASER												
1957	OTT	2	1	50.0	21	10.5	0	0.0	0	0.0	21	
1958	OTT	2	1	50.0	43	21.5	0	0.0	0	0.0	43	
1959	SAS	2	0	0.0	0	0.0	0	0.0	1	50.0		
Totals		6	2	33.3	64	10.7	0	0.0	1	16.7	43	
STEWART FRASER												
1982	SAS	1	0	0.0	0	0.0	0	0.0	0	0.0		
1984	SAS	1	1	100.0	17	17.0	0	0.0	0	0.0	17	
Totals		2	1	50.0	17	8.5	0	0.0	0	0.0	17	
TOMMIE FRAZIER												
1996	MTL	17	6	35.3	55	3.2	0	0.0	1	5.9	26	
DON FUELL												
1963	TOR	41	11	26.8	122	3.0	1	2.4	2	4.9	28	3
1964	TOR	88	46	52.3	650	7.4	7	8.0	7	8.0	39	12
1965	MTL	3	0	0.0	0	0.0	0	0.0	0	0.0		0

Year	Team	ATT	COM	COM%	YDS	AVG	TD	TD%	INT	INT%	LG	SK
1965	Year	3	0	0.0	0	0.0	0	0.0	0	0.0		0
Totals		132	57	43.2	772	5.8	8	6.1	9	6.8	39	15
CHARLIE FULTON												
1968	EDM	119	52	43.7	729	6.1	1	0.8	7	5.9	86	
1969	EDM	104	47	45.2	611	5.9	1	1.0	12	11.5	52	
Totals		223	99	44.4	1340	6.0	2	0.9	19	8.5	86	
LANCE FUNDERBURK												
1998	MTL	4	2	50.0	57	14.3	0	0.0	1	25.0	31	
JIM FURLONG												
1965	CAL	1	1	100.0	46	46.0	1	100.0	0	0.0	46	
WALLY GABLER												
1966	TOR	219	99	45.2	1659	7.6	6	2.7	14	6.4	75	34
1967	TOR	273	137	50.2	2057	7.5	10	3.7	14	5.1	65	
1968	TOR	365	205	56.2	3242	8.9	18	4.9	22	6.0	73	
1969	TOR	7	4	57.1	94	13.4	0	0.0	1	14.3		
1969	WPG	338	168	49.7	2194	6.5	7	2.1	24	7.1		
1969	Year	345	172	49.9	2288	6.6	7	2.0	25	7.2	68	
1970	WPG	134	63	47.0	1077	8.0	4	3.0	13	9.7	68	
1970	HAM	100	59	59.0	831	8.3	6	6.0	7	7.0		
1970	Year	234	122	52.1	1908	8.2	10	4.3	20	8.5	68	
1971	HAM	38	16	42.1	237	6.2	2	5.3	4	10.5	55	
1972	HAM	34	16	47.1	341	10.0	1	2.9	3	8.8		
1972	TOR	182	87	47.8	1348	7.4	7	3.8	16	8.8		
1972	Year	216	103	47.7	1689	7.8	8	3.7	19	8.8	62	
Totals		1690	854	50.5	13080	7.7	61	3.6	118	7.0	75	34
BOB GADDIS												
1979	MTL	1	1	100.0	26	26.0	1	100.0	0	0.0	26	
PETE GALES												
1982	HAM	6	1	16.7	11	1.8	0	0.0	0	0.0	11	
1983	HAM	13	6	46.2	43	3.3	0	0.0	1	7.7	19	
1984	HAM	45	19	42.2	334	7.4	1	2.2	1	2.2	80	
1985	HAM	3	1	33.3	8	2.7	0	0.0	0	0.0	8	
Totals		67	27	40.3	396	5.9	1	1.5	2	3.0	80	
ARNIE GALIFFA												
1955	BC	271	155	57.2	2273	8.4	10	3.7	14	5.2	63	
1956	BC	3	1	33.3	13	4.3	0	0.0	1	33.3	13	
1956	TOR	441	256	58.0	3682	8.3	32	7.3	20	4.5	72	
Totals		715	412	57.6	5968	8.3	42	5.9	35	4.9	72	
JEFF GARCIA												
1994	CAL	3	2	66.7	17	5.7	0	0.0	0	0.0	9	
1995	CAL	364	230	63.2	3358	9.2	25	6.9	7	1.9	60	19
1996	CAL	537	315	58.7	4225	7.9	25	4.7	16	3.0	104	18
1997	CAL	566	354	62.5	4573	8.1	33	5.8	14	2.5	52	
1998	CAL	554	349	63.0	4276	7.7	28	5.1	15	2.7	62	
Totals		2024	1250	61.8	16449	8.1	111	5.5	52	2.6	104	37
JOHNNY GARDINER												
1949	WPG						3					
JASON GARRETT												
1991	OTT	3	2	66.7	28	9.3	0	0.0	0	0.0	18	
JUDD GARRETT												
1994	LV	1	1	100.0	20	20.0	0	0.0	0	0.0	20	
CARL GARRIGUS												
1955	HAM	37	23	62.2	308	8.3	0	0.0	3	8.1	53	
SAMMY GARZA												
1989	WPG	10	1	10.0	20	2.0	0	0.0	2	20.0	20	
1991	WPG	20	10	50.0	192	9.6	2	10.0	2	10.0	48	
1992	WPG	93	39	41.9	580	6.2	6	6.5	3	3.2	59	
1993	WPG	97	55	56.7	829	8.5	6	6.2	3	3.1	47	
1994	WPG	47	25	53.2	373	7.9	2	4.3	1	2.1	41	
1995	WPG	172	92	53.5	1168	6.8	3	1.7	9	5.2	60	
1995	OTT	239	132	55.2	1786	7.5	10	4.2	8	3.3	66	
1995	Year	411	224	54.5	2954	7.2	13	3.2	17	4.1	66	
Totals		678	354	52.2	4948	7.3	29	4.3	28	4.1	66	
JIM GERMANY												
1978	EDM	1	0	0.0	0	0.0	0	0.0	0	0.0		
JASON GESSER												
2005	CAL	42	23	54.8	356	8.5	4	9.5	5	11.9	43	2
DON GETTY												
1955	EDM	63	35	55.6	558	8.9	7	11.1	5	7.9	58	
1956	EDM	44	18	40.9	256	5.8	3	6.8	3	6.8	28	
1957	EDM	122	72	59.0	1359	11.1	11	9.0	8	6.6	81	
1958	EDM	60	23	38.3	334	5.6	1	1.7	2	3.3	43	
1959	EDM	198	116	58.6	2080	10.5	10	5.1	11	5.6	80	
1960	EDM	82	39	47.6	674	8.2	3	3.7	4	4.9	50	2
1961	EDM	126	69	54.8	1276	10.1	8	6.3	8	6.3	65	
1962	EDM	163	92	56.4	1463	9.0	8	4.9	9	5.5	63	
1963	EDM	125	64	51.2	913	7.3	6	4.8	8	6.4	79	11
1965	EDM	9	4	44.4	37	4.1	0	0.0	2	22.2	14	
Totals		992	532	53.6	8950	9.0	57	5.7	60	6.0	81	13
HAL GIANCANELLI												
1958	HAM	1	1	100.0	41	41.0	1	100.0	0	0.0	41	
WAYNE GIARDINO												
1970	OTT	1	0	0.0	0	0.0	0	0.0	0	0.0		
1971	OTT	1	0	0.0	0	0.0	0	0.0	0	0.0		
Totals		2	0	0.0	0	0.0	0	0.0	0	0.0		
NORMAN GIBBS												
1983	WPG	33	15	45.5	220	6.7	0	0.0	2	6.1	35	
1986	TOR	52	32	61.5	327	6.3	0	0.0	2	3.8	37	
Totals		85	47	55.3	547	6.4	0	0.0	4	4.7	37	
SHERROD GIDEON												
2003	OTT	1	1	100.0	10	10.0	1	100.0	0	0.0	10	
WES GIDEON												
1959	MTL	12	4	33.3	57	4.8	0	0.0	0	0.0	16	1
DON GILBERT												
1965	OTT	1	1	100.0	28	28.0	0	0.0	0	0.0	28	0
1967	OTT	2	1	50.0	51	25.5	1	50.0	1	50.0	51	
1968	WPG	2	0	0.0	0	0.0	0	0.0	0	0.0		
Totals		5	2	40.0	79	15.8	1	20.0	1	20.0	51	0
COOKIE GILCHRIST												
1957	HAM	1	0	0.0	0	0.0	0	0.0	1	100.0		
1961	TOR	2	0	0.0	0	0.0	0	0.0	1	50.0		0
Totals		3	0	0.0	0	0.0	0	0.0	2	66.7		0

Year	Team	ATT	COM	COM%	YDS	AVG	TD	TD%	INT	INT%	LG	SK
TURNER GILL												
1984	MTL	375	199	53.1	2673	7.1	16	4.3	17	4.5	77	
1985	MTL	352	212	60.2	2255	6.4	7	2.0	15	4.3	57	
Totals		727	411	56.5	4928	6.8	23	3.2	32	4.4	77	
WILLIE GILLUS												
1989	OTT	2	1	50.0	43	21.5	0	0.0	0	0.0	43	
1990	TOR	9	2	22.2	100	11.1	2	22.2	2	22.2	65	
1991	TOR	54	22	40.7	303	5.6	0	0.0	3	5.6	40	
Totals		65	25	38.5	446	6.9	2	3.1	5	7.7	65	
SULLY GLASSER												
1946	SAS						1					
1955	SAS	2	0	0.0	0	0.0	0	0.0	0	0.0		
1956	SAS	1	0	0.0	0	0.0	0	0.0	0	0.0		
Totals		3	0	0.0	0	0.0	1	0.0	0	0.0		
KEVIN GLENN												
2001	SAS	154	70	45.5	938	6.1	2	1.3	9	5.8	66	7
2002	SAS	95	60	63.2	777	8.2	3	3.2	3	3.2	78	4
2003	SAS	73	40	54.8	508	7.0	1	1.4	4	5.5	53	4
2004	WPG	274	166	60.6	2329	8.5	14	5.1	8	2.9	67	16
2005	WPG	403	231	57.3	3571	8.9	27	6.7	17	4.2	101	17
2006	WPG	430	249	57.9	3427	8.0	17	4.0	13	3.0	100	29
2007	WPG+	621	388	62.5	5117	8.2	25	4.0	13	2.1	67	27
2008	WPG	455	294	64.6	3675	8.1	20	4.4	20	4.4	92	22
2009	HAM	389	241	62.0	3077	7.9	18	4.6	7	1.8	69	12
2010	HAM	602	388	64.5	5106	8.5	33	5.5	17	2.8	58	21
2011	HAM	488	307	62.9	3963	8.1	19	3.9	17	3.5	71	25
Totals		3984	2434	61.1	32488	8.2	179	4.5	128	3.2	101	184
FRANK GNUP												
1948	HAM						1					
JUSTIN GOLTZ												
2011	WPG	6	3	50.0	36	6.0	1	16.7	0	0.0	18	2
DAN GONZALEZ												
2001	MTL	85	51	60.0	572	6.7	1	1.2	6	7.1	37	
PETE GONZALEZ												
2002	HAM	19	10	52.6	177	9.3	2	10.5	0	0.0	65	
2003	HAM	131	57	43.5	822	6.3	2	1.5	7	5.3	81	
Totals		150	67	44.7	999	6.7	4	2.7	7	4.7	81	
ANDY GORDON												
1949	OTT						2					
1950	OTT						8					
Totals							10					
LORENZO GRAHAM												
1991	BC	1	1	100.0	14	14.0	0	0.0	0	0.0	14	
JOHNNY GRAMLING												
1954	OTT	98	51	52.0	652	6.7	2	2.0	12	12.2	47	
ROBERT GRANT												
2005	OTT	1	0	0.0	0	0.0	0	0.0	0	0.0		
STEVE GRANT												
1980	MTL	22	10	45.5	145	6.6	0	0.0	3	13.6	29	
TOMMY GRANT												
1959	HAM	1	1	100.0	13	13.0	0	0.0	0	0.0	13	0
MARVIN GRAVES												
1994	TOR	230	119	51.7	1888	8.2	11	4.8	9	3.9	67	
1995	TOR	113	52	46.0	735	6.5	4	3.5	6	5.3	68	
1996	HAM	54	29	53.7	325	6.0	2	3.7	4	7.4	49	
1996	SAS	3	0	0.0	0	0.0	0	0.0	0	0.0		
1996	Year	57	29	50.9	325	5.7	2	3.5	4	7.0	49	
1997	MTL	72	43	59.7	568	7.9	3	4.2	5	6.9	45	
2000	SAS	77	43	55.8	667	8.7	6	7.8	2	2.6	48	1
2001	SAS	200	109	54.5	1534	7.7	8	4.0	9	4.5	78	
Totals		749	395	52.7	5717	7.6	34	4.5	35	4.7	78	1
BILLY GRAY												
1965	SAS	1	0	0.0	0	0.0	0	0.0	0	0.0		
TY GRAY												
1981	BC	2	0	0.0	0	0.0	0	0.0	0	0.0		
JOHNNY GREEN												
1959	TOR	20	8	40.0	62	3.1	0	0.0	3	15.0	27	3
DAVE GREENBERG												
1946	MTL						2					
1947	MTL						1					
Totals							3					
NEALON GREENE												
1998	TOR	15	10	66.7	123	8.2	0	0.0	0	0.0	40	7
1999	EDM	287	158	55.1	2046	7.1	14	4.9	12	4.2	60	26
2000	EDM	397	247	62.2	3059	7.7	22	5.5	6	1.5	58	46
2001	EDM	178	94	52.8	1241	7.0	2	1.1	7	3.9	52	19
2002	SAS	368	212	57.6	2621	7.1	13	3.5	9	2.4	100	39
2003	SAS	455	278	61.1	3398	7.5	20	4.4	9	2.0	72	14
2004	SAS	5	3	60.0	20	4.0	0	0.0	0	0.0	14	1
2005	SAS	298	182	61.1	1929	6.5	7	2.3	8	2.7	44	17
2006	MTL	15	8	53.3	81	5.4	0	0.0	5	33.3	14	
Totals		2018	1192	59.1	14518	7.2	78	3.9	56	2.8	100	169
MIKE GREENFIELD												
1988	OTT	25	9	36.0	123	4.9	1	4.0	2	8.0	44	
TERRY GREER												
1982	TOR	1	1	100.0	39	39.0	1	100.0	0	0.0	39	
1983	TOR	2	1	50.0	39	19.5	1	50.0	1	50.0	39	
1984	TOR	3	1	33.3	42	14.0	1	33.3	0	0.0	42	
1985	TOR	2	1	50.0	-1	-0.5	0	0.0	0	0.0	-1	
Totals		8	4	50.0	119	14.9	3	37.5	1	12.5	42	
HANK GRENDA												
1969	BC	9	3	33.3	57	6.3	0	0.0	2	22.2	24	
ANDREW GRIGG												
1997	HAM	2	1	50.0	30	15.0	1	50.0	0	0.0	30	
1998	HAM	1	0	0.0	0	0.0	0	0.0	0	0.0		
Totals		3	1	33.3	30	10.0	1	33.3	0	0.0	30	
LEE GROSSCUP												
1963	SAS	10	2	20.0	16	1.6	0	0.0	0	0.0	11	5
DAVE GROSZ												
1961	SAS	213	91	42.7	1341	6.3	8	3.8	20	9.4	52	
GINO GUIDUGLI												
2007	BC	11	6	54.5	138	12.5	1	9.1	1	9.1	96	1

Year	Team	ATT	COM	COM%	YDS	AVG	TD	TD%	INT	INT%	LG	SK
JERRY GUSTAFSON												
1956	BC	178	79	44.4	1214	6.8	11	6.2	17	9.6	72	
ERIC GUTHRIE												
1972	BC	13	6	46.2	100	7.7	0	0.0	2	15.4	33	
1973	BC	11	5	45.5	109	9.9	0	0.0	1	9.1	40	
1975	BC	84	39	46.4	624	7.4	5	6.0	7	8.3	70	
1976	BC	221	108	48.9	1399	6.3	6	2.7	11	5.0	78	
1977	SAS	81	32	39.5	458	5.7	1	1.2	6	7.4	62	
Totals		410	190	46.3	2690	6.6	12	2.9	27	6.6	78	
CED GYLES												
1950	CAL	1	0	0.0	0	0.0	0	0.0	0	0.0		
DARIAN HAGAN												
1994	LV	1	0	0.0	0	0.0	0	0.0	0	0.0		
MIKE HAGGARD												
1974	HAM	1	0	0.0	0	0.0	0	0.0	0	0.0		
B.J. HALL												
2011	TOR	3	0	0.0	0	0.0	0	0.0	0	0.0		1
KALIN HALL												
1995	HAM	1	0	0.0	0	0.0	0	0.0	0	0.0		
KEN HALL												
1957	EDM	7	5	71.4	96	13.7	0	0.0	1	14.3	39	
NICKIE HALL												
1983	WPG	145	66	45.5	1092	7.5	4	2.8	4	2.8	48	
1983	SAS	2	2	100.0	19	9.5	0	0.0	0	0.0	11	
1983	Year	147	68	46.3	1111	7.6	4	2.7	4	2.7	48	
1984	SAS	47	16	34.0	213	4.5	0	0.0	2	4.3	24	
Totals		194	84	43.3	1324	6.8	4	2.1	6	3.1	48	
PETE HALL												
1962	TOR	14	6	42.9	55	3.9	0	0.0	3	21.4	14	
ROBERT HALL												
1994	SHR	29	17	58.6	204	7.0	0	0.0	1	3.4	39	
TRACY HAM												
1987	EDM	36	15	41.7	231	6.4	1	2.8	3	8.3	38	
1988	EDM	339	185	54.6	2840	8.4	14	4.1	15	4.4	85	
1989	EDM	517	268	51.8	4366	8.4	30	5.8	18	3.5	67	
1990	EDM	559	285	51.0	4286	7.7	36	6.4	24	4.3	70	
1991	EDM	454	242	53.3	3862	8.5	31	6.8	16	3.5	66	
1992	EDM	428	221	51.6	3655	8.5	30	7.0	13	3.0	81	
1993	TOR	302	146	48.3	2147	7.1	8	2.6	11	3.6	64	
1994	BAL	519	280	53.9	4348	8.4	30	5.8	13	2.5	83	
1995	BAL	395	232	58.7	3357	8.5	21	5.3	14	3.5	54	
1996	MTL	396	229	57.8	3313	8.4	28	7.1	10	2.5	62	
1997	MTL	460	261	56.7	3687	8.0	23	5.0	12	2.6	65	
1998	MTL	326	178	54.6	2511	7.7	21	6.4	12	3.7	75	
1999	MTL	212	128	60.4	1931	9.1	11	5.2	3	1.4	67	
Totals		4943	2670	54.0	40534	8.2	284	5.7	164	3.3	85	
CHUCK HARDING												
1955	SAS	11	7	63.6	128	11.6	1	9.1	0	0.0	58	
1956	OTT	10	1	10.0	13	1.3	0	0.0	1	10.0	13	
Totals		21	8	38.1	141	6.7	1	4.8	1	4.8	58	
GLENN HARPER												
1986	CAL	2	2	100.0	98	49.0	1	50.0	0	0.0	56	
1987	CAL	4	3	75.0	43	10.8	0	0.0	0	0.0	23	
1988	CAL	1	0	0.0	0	0.0	0	0.0	0	0.0		
1990	TOR	2	1	50.0	14	7.0	0	0.0	0	0.0	14	
1991	EDM	1	1	100.0	16	16.0	0	0.0	0	0.0	16	
1992	EDM	1	0	0.0	0	0.0	0	0.0	0	0.0		
1993	EDM	2	2	100.0	2	1.0	1	50.0	0	0.0	6	
1995	EDM	3	3	100.0	26	8.7	1	33.3	0	0.0	17	
1996	EDM	1	0	0.0	0	0.0	0	0.0	0	0.0		
Totals		17	12	70.6	199	11.7	3	17.6	0	0.0	56	
CALVIN HARRELL												
1974	EDM	1	1	100.0	31	31.0	0	0.0	0	0.0	31	
1975	EDM	1	0	0.0	0	0.0	0	0.0	0	0.0		
1976	EDM	1	0	0.0	0	0.0	0	0.0	0	0.0		
Totals		3	1	33.3	31	10.3	0	0.0	0	0.0	31	
JOSH HARRIS												
2005	CAL	9	5	55.6	43	4.8	0	0.0	0	0.0	13	0
MAJOR HARRIS												
1990	BC	42	18	42.9	300	7.1	3	7.1	3	7.1	33	
JACK HARTMAN												
1950	SAS	162	78	48.1	1217	7.5	7	4.3	18	11.1		
JOHN HARVEY												
1976	TOR	1	1	100.0	22	22.0	0	0.0	0	0.0	22	
JACK HAWLEY												
2002	TOR	5	1	20.0	19	3.8	0	0.0	0	0.0	19	
J.T. HAY												
1985	CAL	1	1	100.0	22	22.0	0	0.0	0	0.0	22	
STAN HEATH												
1950	HAM						6					
1951	CAL	174	81	46.6	1167	6.7	7	4.0	13	7.5	76	
1952	CAL	51	25	49.0	386	7.6	4	7.8	2	3.9	38	
1954	CAL	52	25	48.1	471	9.1	1	1.9	4	7.7	95	
Totals		277	131	47.3	2024	7.3	18	4.3	19	6.9	95	
JIM HENDERSON												
1970	TOR	1	1	100.0	42	42.0	0	0.0	0	0.0	42	
BART HENDRICKS												
2003	EDM	35	21	60.0	331	9.5	0	0.0	2	5.7	69	
2004	EDM	24	12	50.0	164	6.8	0	0.0	1	4.2	39	
Totals		59	33	55.9	495	8.4	0	0.0	3	5.1	69	
GARNEY HENLEY												
1963	HAM	1	0	0.0	0	0.0	0	0.0	1	100.0		0
1970	HAM	1	1	100.0	7	7.0	1	100.0	0	0.0	7	
1972	HAM	1	1	100.0	15	15.0	0	0.0	0	0.0	15	
1973	HAM	1	0	0.0	0	0.0	0	0.0	0	0.0		
1975	HAM	2	1	50.0	10	5.0	0	0.0	0	0.0	10	
Totals		6	3	50.0	32	5.3	1	16.7	1	16.7	15	0
ROY HENRY												
1978	HAM	25	11	44.0	99	4.0	0	0.0	1	4.0	18	
JOE HERNANDEZ												
1963	EDM	3	2	66.7	43	14.3	0	0.0	0	0.0	25	0
1966	EDM	1	0	0.0	0	0.0	0	0.0	1	100.0		0
Totals		4	2	50.0	43	10.8	0	0.0	1	25.0	25	0
GEORGE HERRING												
1958	BC	232	113	48.7	1669	7.2	5	2.2	20	8.6	85	
1959	SAS	9	4	44.4	39	4.3	0	0.0	0	0.0	17	0
Totals		241	117	48.5	1708	7.1	5	2.1	20	8.3	85	0
MACK HERRON												
1972	WPG	1	1	100.0	31	31.0	0	0.0	0	0.0	31	
GARY HERTZFELDT												
1964	EDM	16	8	50.0	166	10.4	1	6.3	2	12.5	68	4
ED HERVEY												
2004	EDM	1	1	100.0	52	52.0	0	0.0	0	0.0	52	0
ANTHONEY HILL												
1995	EDM	3	1	33.3	9	3.0	0	0.0	0	0.0	9	
GREG HILL												
2000	TOR	3	1	33.3	5	1.7	0	0.0	0	0.0	5	1
JACK HILL												
1957	SAS	2	1	50.0	8	4.0	0	0.0	0	0.0	8	
1959	SAS	2	0	0.0	0	0.0	0	0.0	2	100.0		
Totals		4	1	25.0	8	2.0	0	0.0	2	50.0	8	
KARL HILZINGER												
1953	SAS	1	0	0.0	0	0.0	0	0.0	0	0.0		
DON HINEY												
1946	WPG						1					
1947	WPG						1					
Totals							2					
KEN HOBART												
1985	HAM	437	211	48.3	2522	5.8	19	4.3	14	3.2	67	
1986	HAM	217	104	47.9	1062	4.9	2	0.9	6	2.8	52	
1987	HAM	101	49	48.5	664	6.6	5	5.0	3	3.0	58	
1989	OTT	54	19	35.2	384	7.1	3	5.6	3	5.6	75	
1990	OTT	70	32	45.7	448	6.4	2	2.9	5	7.1	53	
Totals		879	415	47.2	5080	5.8	31	3.5	31	3.5	75	
MIKE HOHENSEE												
1985	TOR	84	37	44.0	571	6.8	3	3.6	7	8.3	71	
BOB HOLBURN												
1954	BC	2	1	50.0	26	13.0	0	0.0	0	0.0	26	
JOHN HOLLAND												
1979	HAM	1	0	0.0	0	0.0	0	0.0	0	0.0		
DAVID HOLLIS												
1994	LV	1	1	100.0	17	17.0	0	0.0	0	0.0	17	
CONDREDGE HOLLOWAY												
1975	OTT	148	60	40.5	984	6.6	6	4.1	9	6.1	44	
1976	OTT	106	59	55.7	973	9.2	9	8.5	6	5.7	59	
1977	OTT	102	62	60.8	972	9.5	5	4.9	5	4.9	75	
1978	OTT	214	132	61.7	1970	9.2	12	5.6	2	0.9	74	
1979	OTT	238	128	53.8	1965	8.3	17	7.1	8	3.4	66	
1980	OTT	189	106	56.1	1499	7.9	7	3.7	8	4.2	62	
1981	TOR	343	189	55.1	2578	7.5	12	3.5	11	3.2	58	
1982	TOR	507	299	59.0	4661	9.2	31	6.1	12	2.4	79	
1983	TOR	372	210	56.5	3184	8.6	18	4.8	5	1.3	80	
1984	TOR	254	146	57.5	2231	8.8	16	6.3	8	3.1	63	
1985	TOR	210	139	66.2	1735	8.3	7	3.3	4	1.9	65	
1986	TOR	302	166	55.0	2230	7.4	14	4.6	15	5.0	62	
1987	BC	28	14	50.0	211	7.5	1	3.6	1	3.6	43	
Totals		3013	1710	56.8	25193	8.4	155	5.1	94	3.1	80	0
WAYNE HOLM												
1970	CAL	1	0	0.0	0	0.0	0	0.0	0	0.0		
COREY HOLMES												
2002	SAS	1	1	100.0	9	9.0	0	0.0	0	0.0	9	0
2006	HAM	1	0	0.0	0	0.0	0	0.0	0	0.0		
Totals		2	1	50.0	9	4.5	0	0.0	0	0.0	9	0
HARRY HOLT												
1982	BC	1	0	0.0	0	0.0	0	0.0	0	0.0		
SONNY HOMER												
1958	BC	1	0	0.0	0	0.0	0	0.0	0	0.0		
HARRY HOOD												
1947	WPG						1					
1949	CAL						1					
1950	CAL	8	3	37.5	54	6.8	1	12.5	2	25.0		
Totals		8	3	37.5	54	6.8	3	12.5	2	25.0		
JOHN HOOD												
1992	HAM	1	0	0.0	0	0.0	0	0.0	1	100.0		
JIM HOOK												
1955	CAL	1	0	0.0	0	0.0	0	0.0	0	0.0		
1956	SAS	6	1	16.7	30	5.0	0	0.0	1	16.7	30	
Totals		7	1	14.3	30	4.3	0	0.0	1	14.3	30	
BILLY HOOPER												
1955	WPG	22	11	50.0	163	7.4	0	0.0	3	13.6	27	
ANDY HOPKINS												
1973	HAM	1	0	0.0	0	0.0	0	0.0	0	0.0		
DAVE HOPPMANN												
1963	MTL	3	1	33.3	8	2.7	1	33.3	0	0.0	8	2
1964	MTL	4	1	25.0	25	6.3	1	25.0	0	0.0	25	0
Totals		7	2	28.6	33	4.7	2	28.6	0	0.0	25	2
STEVE HOWLETT												
1989	OTT	1	0	0.0	0	0.0	0	0.0	0	0.0		
WARREN HUDSON												
1990	WPG	1	0	0.0	0	0.0	0	0.0	0	0.0		0
JOHN HUFNAGEL												
1976	CAL	156	86	55.1	1327	8.5	13	8.3	9	5.8	78	
1977	CAL	330	183	55.5	2276	6.9	9	2.7	13	3.9	60	
1978	CAL	315	169	53.7	2663	8.5	13	4.1	13	4.1	82	
1979	CAL	120	70	58.3	797	6.6	5	4.2	5	4.2	75	
1980	SAS	241	134	55.6	1576	6.5	5	2.1	12	5.0	50	
1981	SAS	300	169	56.3	2743	9.1	21	7.0	19	6.3	74	
1982	SAS	210	108	51.4	1535	7.3	6	2.9	10	4.8	72	
1983	SAS	229	116	50.7	1649	7.2	10	4.4	9	3.9	52	
1983	WPG	96	53	55.2	956	10.0	5	5.2	5	5.2	75	
1983	Year	325	169	52.0	2605	8.0	15	4.6	14	4.3	75	
1984	WPG	113	60	53.1	1026	9.1	7	6.2	7	6.2	75	
1985	WPG	162	95	58.6	1428	8.8	11	6.8	10	6.2	76	
1986	WPG	393	232	59.0	3394	8.6	21	5.3	16	4.1	85	

Year	Team	ATT	COM	COM%	YDS	AVG	TD	TD%	INT	INT%	LG	SK
1987	SAS	29	20	69.0	224	7.7	1	3.4	3	10.3	52	
Totals		2694	1495	55.5	21594	8.0	127	4.7	131	4.9	85	
HANK ILESIC												
1977	EDM	1	1	100.0	14	14.0	0	0.0	0	0.0	14	
1978	EDM	2	2	100.0	26	13.0	0	0.0	0	0.0	28	
1979	EDM	1	1	100.0	9	9.0	0	0.0	0	0.0	9	
1980	EDM	1	1	100.0	11	11.0	0	0.0	0	0.0	11	
1983	TOR	1	0	0.0	0	0.0	0	0.0	0	0.0		
1985	TOR	1	1	100.0	19	19.0	0	0.0	0	0.0	19	
1987	TOR	1	0	0.0	0	0.0	0	0.0	0	0.0		
1990	TOR	1	1	100.0	28	28.0	0	0.0	0	0.0	28	
Totals		9	7	77.8	107	11.9	0	0.0	0	0.0	28	
KEVIN INGRAM												
1984	EDM	32	15	46.9	295	9.2	1	3.1	1	3.1	48	
HARRY IRVING												
1948	CAL						1					
CHRIS ISAAC												
1982	OTT	402	204	50.7	3408	8.5	18	4.5	18	4.5	96	
1983	OTT	63	36	57.1	571	9.1	4	6.3	10	15.9	91	
Totals		465	240	51.6	3979	8.6	22	4.7	28	6.0	96	
LARRY ISBELL												
1954	SAS	10	5	50.0	82	8.2	1	10.0	3	30.0		
1956	SAS	7	5	71.4	89	12.7	0	0.0	0	0.0	32	
1958	SAS	1	1	100.0	3	3.0	0	0.0	0	0.0	3	
Totals		18	11	61.1	174	9.7	1	5.6	3	16.7	32	
ROCKET ISMAIL												
1991	TOR	1	0	0.0	0	0.0	0	0.0	0	0.0		
ALFRED JACKSON												
2000	BC	2	1	50.0	49	24.5	0	0.0	0	0.0	49	0
JARIOUS JACKSON												
2005	BC	6	3	50.0	30	5.0	0	0.0	0	0.0	16	0
2006	BC	79	37	46.8	477	6.0	3	3.8	2	2.5	43	8
2007	BC	304	167	54.9	2553	8.4	18	5.9	10	3.3	93	15
2008	BC	288	158	54.9	2164	7.5	17	5.9	10	3.5	76	18
2009	BC	155	90	58.1	1252	8.1	12	7.7	8	5.2	57	8
2010	BC	48	26	54.2	293	6.1	0	0.0	3	6.3	36	6
2011	BC	39	18	46.2	263	6.7	1	2.6	2	5.1	54	6
Totals		919	499	54.3	7032	7.7	51	5.5	35	3.8	93	61
JOHN HENRY JACKSON												
1961	TOR	4	2	50.0	8	2.0	0	0.0	0	0.0	9	1
MARK JACKSON												
1977	MTL	76	33	43.4	361	4.8	2	2.6	3	3.9	36	
1979	TOR	38	18	47.4	215	5.7	0	0.0	4	10.5	40	
1980	TOR	404	231	57.2	3041	7.5	16	4.0	17	4.2	87	
1981	WPG	52	37	71.2	435	8.4	4	7.7	0	0.0	35	
1982	WPG	40	22	55.0	266	6.7	0	0.0	1	2.5	28	
1983	WPG	11	4	36.4	55	5.0	0	0.0	0	0.0	39	
Totals		621	345	55.6	4373	7.0	22	3.5	25	4.0	87	
RUSS JACKSON												
1958	OTT	112	61	54.5	858	7.7	3	2.7	6	5.4	69	
1959	OTT	89	45	50.6	1009	11.3	7	7.9	7	7.9	59	21
1960	OTT	52	20	38.5	322	6.2	2	3.8	3	5.8	68	
1961	OTT	117	59	50.4	1048	9.0	8	6.8	7	6.0	61	17
1962	OTT	157	78	49.7	1427	9.1	10	6.4	13	8.3	63	
1963	OTT	259	152	58.7	2910	11.2	19	7.3	8	3.1	73	28
1964	OTT	230	116	50.4	2156	9.4	18	7.8	15	6.5	107	24
1965	OTT	252	130	51.6	2303	9.1	18	7.1	13	5.2	77	14
1966	OTT	276	142	51.4	2400	8.7	17	6.2	15	5.4	69	14
1967	OTT	323	189	58.5	3332	10.3	25	7.7	9	2.8	94	
1968	OTT	305	171	56.1	3187	10.4	25	8.2	16	5.2	65	
1969	OTT	358	193	53.9	3641	10.2	33	9.2	12	3.4	82	
Totals		2530	1356	53.6	24593	9.7	185	7.3	124	4.9	107	118
STANLEY JACKSON												
1999	MTL	4	2	50.0	23	5.8	0	0.0	0	0.0	14	
2000	MTL	86	48	55.8	656	7.6	1	1.2	3	3.5	49	8
2001	TOR	4	2	50.0	56	14.0	1	25.0	1	25.0	38	
2002	TOR	18	12	66.7	98	5.4	1	5.6	2	11.1	18	
2004	WPG	12	4	33.3	67	5.6	0	0.0	0	0.0	32	
Totals		124	68	54.8	900	7.3	3	2.4	6	4.8	49	8
JACK JACOBS												
1950	WPG	187	85	45.5	1604	8.6	14	7.5	8	4.3		
1951	WPG	355	204	57.5	3248	9.1	33	9.3	10	2.8	100	
1952	WPG	286	147	51.4	2586	9.0	34	11.9	12	4.2	76	
1953	WPG	252	146	57.9	1924	7.6	11	4.4	10	4.0		
1954	WPG	250	127	50.8	1732	6.9	12	4.8	13	5.2		
Totals		1330	709	53.3	11094	8.3	104	7.8	53	4.0	100	
FOB JAMES												
1956	MTL	1	0	0.0	0	0.0	0	0.0	1	100.0		
GERRY JAMES												
1954	WPG	1	0	0.0	0	0.0	0	0.0	0	0.0		
1955	WPG	1	0	0.0	0	0.0	0	0.0	1	100.0		
1961	WPG	1	0	0.0	0	0.0	0	0.0	0	0.0		
Totals		3	0	0.0	0	0.0	0	0.0	1	33.3		
JOEY JAUCH												
1993	HAM	1	0	0.0	0	0.0	0	0.0	0	0.0		
1995	SAS	1	0	0.0	0	0.0	0	0.0	0	0.0		
Totals		2	0	0.0	0	0.0	0	0.0	0	0.0		
MIKE JENKINS												
2003	TOR	1	0	0.0	0	0.0	0	0.0	0	0.0		0
ORTEGE JENKINS												
2002	BC	5	1	20.0	42	8.4	0	0.0	1	20.0	42	
BOB JETER												
1960	BC	1	1	100.0	14	14.0	0	0.0	0	0.0	14	0
1961	BC	1	0	0.0	0	0.0	0	0.0	0	0.0		
Totals		2	1	50.0	14	7.0	0	0.0	0	0.0	14	0
STEVE JOACHIM												
1975	TOR	41	20	48.8	228	5.6	2	4.9	4	9.8	51	
BILLY JOHNSON												
1981	MTL	1	1	100.0	12	12.0	1	100.0	0	0.0	12	
BRET JOHNSON												
1993	TOR	8	4	50.0	72	9.0	0	0.0	1	12.5	45	
JASON JOHNSON												

Year	Team	ATT	COM	COM%	YDS	AVG	TD	TD%	INT	INT%	LG	SK
2004	EDM	5	3	60.0	25	5.0	0	0.0	0	0.0	15	0
2006	EDM	17	11	64.7	135	7.9	0	0.0	0	0.0	26	
Totals		22	14	63.6	160	7.3	0	0.0	0	0.0	26	0
JOHN HENRY JOHNSON												
1953	CAL	11	5	45.5	62	5.6	0	0.0	1	9.1	9	
KEN JOHNSON												
1978	CAL	59	36	61.0	635	10.8	4	6.8	4	6.8	101	
1979	CAL	312	176	56.4	2344	7.5	19	6.1	8	2.6	105	
1980	CAL	389	218	56.0	3019	7.8	22	5.7	16	4.1	95	
1981	CAL	319	190	59.6	2429	7.6	18	5.6	10	3.1	81	
1981	MTL	109	64	58.7	935	8.6	5	4.6	3	2.8	54	
1981	Year	428	254	59.3	3364	7.9	18	4.2	13	3.0	81	
1982	MTL	59	34	57.6	275	4.7	0	0.0	2	3.4	22	
Totals		1247	718	57.6	9637	7.7	68	5.5	43	3.4	105	
MIKE JOHNSON												
1992	BC	146	66	45.2	1034	7.1	8	5.5	8	5.5	76	
1994	SHR	193	78	40.4	1259	6.5	4	2.1	12	6.2	64	
1995	SHR	61	28	45.9	322	5.3	1	1.6	0	0.0	31	
Totals		400	172	43.0	2615	6.5	13	3.3	20	5.0	76	
RICK JOHNSON												
1985	CAL	167	71	42.5	932	5.6	3	1.8	11	6.6	70	
1986	CAL	604	302	50.0	4379	7.3	31	5.1	27	4.5	59	
1987	CAL	234	112	47.9	1426	6.1	7	3.0	17	7.3	48	
1988	CAL	45	21	46.7	235	5.2	1	2.2	2	4.4	29	
1989	TOR	97	43	44.3	628	6.5	7	7.2	9	9.3	73	
Totals		1147	549	47.9	7600	6.6	49	4.3	66	5.8	73	
RON JOHNSON												
1970	WPG	154	73	47.4	805	5.2	5	3.2	9	5.8	30	
TRUMAINE JOHNSON												
1990	TOR	1	0	0.0	0	0.0	0	0.0	0	0.0		
DON JONAS												
1970	TOR	256	124	48.4	2041	8.0	17	6.6	25	9.8	69	
1971	WPG	485	253	52.2	4036	8.3	27	5.6	31	6.4	94	
1972	WPG	447	252	56.4	3583	8.0	27	6.0	26	5.8	97	
1973	WPG	452	226	50.0	3363	7.4	15	3.3	29	6.4	103	
1974	WPG	169	90	53.3	1309	7.7	8	4.7	9	5.3	57	
1974	HAM	121	52	43.0	732	6.0	4	3.3	10	8.3	51	
1974	Year	290	142	49.0	2041	7.0	12	4.1	19	6.6	47	
Totals		1930	997	51.7	15064	7.8	98	5.1	130	6.7	103	
CORBY JONES												
1999	MTL	16	7	43.8	58	3.6	0	0.0	0	0.0	12	
EDGAR JONES												
1950	HAM						1					
JIMMY JONES												
1973	MTL	117	72	61.5	912	7.8	6	5.1	5	4.3	56	
1974	MTL	311	163	52.4	2297	7.4	18	5.8	22	7.1	70	
1975	MTL	233	120	51.5	1865	8.0	10	4.3	11	4.7	73	
1976	HAM	290	144	49.7	1773	6.1	12	4.1	9	3.1	76	
1977	HAM	302	174	57.6	2156	7.1	9	3.0	14	4.6	71	
1978	HAM	269	159	59.1	2060	7.7	9	3.3	11	4.1	75	
1979	OTT	199	118	59.3	1342	6.7	8	4.0	12	6.0	53	
Totals		1721	950	55.2	12405	7.2	72	4.2	84	4.9	76	
JUNE JONES												
1982	TOR	5	2	40.0	17	3.4	0	0.0	0	0.0	12	
KHARI JONES												
1998	BC	18	11	61.1	89	4.9	0	0.0	2	11.1	19	1
1999	BC	25	12	48.0	140	5.6	0	0.0	0	0.0	26	0
2000	WPG	510	263	51.6	4142	8.1	31	6.1	23	4.5	82	24
2001	WPG	546	329	60.3	4545	8.3	30	5.5	23	4.2	68	39
2002	WPG	620	382	61.6	5334	8.6	46	7.4	29	4.7	83	27
2003	WPG	502	274	54.6	4016	8.0	25	5.0	15	3.0	73	37
2004	WPG	300	168	56.0	2138	7.1	7	2.3	8	2.7	70	23
2004	CAL	67	39	58.2	573	8.6	5	7.5	2	3.0	44	4
2004	Year	367	207	56.4	2711	7.4	12	3.3	10	2.7	70	27
2005	HAM	60	35	58.3	406	6.8	1	1.7	2	3.3	46	10
Totals		2648	1513	57.1	21383	8.1	145	5.5	104	3.9	83	165
MILSON JONES												
1982	WPG	1	0	0.0	0	0.0	0	0.0	1	100.0		
1992	SAS	1	0	0.0	0	0.0	0	0.0	0	0.0		
Totals		2	0	0.0	0	0.0	0	0.0	1	50.0		
PRESTON JONES												
1994	LV	53	23	43.4	361	6.8	1	1.9	3	5.7	43	
SHAWN JONES												
1994	BAL	35	13	37.1	230	6.6	1	2.9	3	8.6	39	
1995	BAL	67	37	55.2	470	7.0	3	4.5	3	4.5	39	
Totals		102	50	49.0	700	6.9	4	3.9	6	5.9	39	
STEPHAN JONES												
1986	EDM	1	0	0.0	0	0.0	0	0.0	0	0.0		
1987	EDM	1	1	100.0	52	52.0	0	0.0	0	0.0	52	
1988	EDM	1	0	0.0	0	0.0	0	0.0	0	0.0		
1993	OTT	2	2	100.0	92	46.0	1	50.0	0	0.0	46	
Totals		5	3	60.0	144	28.8	1	20.0	0	0.0	52	
TERRENCE JONES												
1989	CAL	92	43	46.7	816	8.9	2	2.2	6	6.5	55	
1990	CAL	130	64	49.2	958	7.4	3	2.3	10	7.7	56	
1991	CAL	17	6	35.3	123	7.2	1	5.9	3	17.6	54	
1991	OTT	3	2	66.7	21	7.0	0	0.0	1	33.3	17	
1991	Year	20	8	40.0	144	7.2	1	5.0	4	20.0	54	
1992	OTT	30	13	43.3	234	7.8	1	3.3	3	10.0	50	
1993	OTT	72	29	40.3	434	6.0	1	1.4	5	6.9	56	
1994	SHR	180	77	42.8	1046	5.8	4	2.2	9	5.0	61	
Totals		524	234	44.7	3632	6.9	12	2.3	37	7.1	61	
TOMMY JONES												
2004	CAL	182	94	51.6	1237	6.8	7	3.8	10	5.5	62	
WARREN JONES												
1990	EDM	55	33	60.0	390	7.1	3	5.5	2	3.6	43	
1991	EDM	149	83	55.7	1113	7.5	9	6.0	4	2.7	59	
1992	SAS	20	6	30.0	121	6.1	1	5.0	2	10.0	31	
1993	SAS	55	34	61.8	362	6.6	1	1.8	2	3.6	56	
1994	SAS	182	110	60.4	1313	7.2	11	6.0	7	3.8	60	
1995	SAS	432	253	58.6	2958	6.8	13	3.0	9	2.1	76	
1996	SAS	196	109	55.6	1372	7.0	2	1.0	8	4.1	77	

Year	Team	ATT	COM	COM%	YDS	AVG	TD	TD%	INT	INT%	LG	SK
1996	EDM	13	5	38.5	58	4.5	0	0.0	2	15.4	18	
1996	Year	209	114	54.5	1430	6.8	2	1.0	10	4.8	77	
Totals		1102	633	57.4	7687	7.0	40	3.6	36	3.3	77	
HOMER JORDAN												
1983	SAS	172	91	52.9	1310	7.6	10	5.8	5	2.9	71	
1984	SAS	146	80	54.8	1139	7.8	7	4.8	10	6.8	59	
1985	SAS	194	118	60.8	1610	8.3	4	2.1	8	4.1	65	
1986	WPG	22	8	36.4	110	5.0	0	0.0	3	13.6	31	
Totals		534	297	55.6	4169	7.8	21	3.9	26	4.9	71	
DARREN JOSEPH												
1992	OTT	1	1	100.0	10	10.0	1	100.0	0	0.0	10	
KERRY JOSEPH												
2003	OTT	475	269	56.6	3694	7.8	19	4.0	20	4.2	75	33
2004	OTT	317	197	62.1	2762	8.7	13	4.1	10	3.2	83	32
2005	OTT	537	337	62.8	4466	8.3	25	4.7	23	4.3	75	64
2006	SAS	463	267	57.7	3489	7.5	22	4.8	17	3.7	65	40
2007	SAS	459	267	58.2	4002	8.7	24	5.2	8	1.7	72	38
2008	TOR	536	307	57.3	4174	7.8	17	3.2	14	2.6	91	37
2009	TOR	337	185	54.9	2244	6.7	10	3.0	16	4.7	95	32
2011	EDM	31	18	58.1	226	7.3	0	0.0	1	3.2	49	5
Totals		3155	1847	58.5	25057	7.9	130	4.1	109	3.5	95	281
BOBBY JUDD												
1957	OTT	1	1	100.0	6	6.0	0	0.0	0	0.0	6	
1958	OTT	1	0	0.0	0	0.0	0	0.0	0	0.0		
Totals		2	1	50.0	6	3.0	0	0.0	0	0.0	6	
CRAIG JUNTUNEN												
1978	CAL	18	9	50.0	125	6.9	0	0.0	3	16.7	45	
1979	SAS	20	8	40.0	191	9.6	1	5.0	3	15.0	96	
Totals		38	17	44.7	316	8.3	1	2.6	6	15.8	96	
LARRY JUSDANIS												
1996	HAM	76	34	44.7	497	6.5	3	3.9	7	9.2	32	
STEVEN JYLES												
2006	EDM	11	6	54.5	48	4.4	0	0.0	0	0.0	13	0
2007	EDM	40	19	47.5	214	5.4	0	0.0	3	7.5	32	3
2008	SAS	61	42	68.9	533	8.7	4	6.6	6	9.8	55	7
2009	SAS	40	25	62.5	290	7.3	1	2.5	2	5.0	35	7
2010	WPG	318	196	61.6	2804	8.8	19	6.0	7	2.2	81	31
2011	TOR	218	124	56.9	1430	6.6	7	3.2	11	5.0	48	20
Totals		688	412	59.9	5319	7.7	31	4.5	29	4.2	81	68
AARON KANNER												
1995	MEM	1	0	0.0	0	0.0	0	0.0	0	0.0		
JOE KAPP												
1959	CAL	328	196	59.8	2990	9.1	21	6.4	14	4.3	85	
1960	CAL	337	182	54.0	3060	9.1	18	5.3	17	5.0	80	19
1961	CAL	22	9	40.9	139	6.3	0	0.0	0	0.0		
1961	BC	209	85	40.7	1580	7.6	9	4.3	15	7.2	100	
1961	Year	231	94	40.7	1719	7.4	9	3.9	15	6.5	100	
1962	BC	359	197	54.9	3279	9.1	28	7.8	18	5.0	106	
1963	BC	339	183	54.0	3011	8.9	20	5.9	15	4.4	106	24
1964	BC	329	194	59.0	2816	8.6	14	4.3	13	4.0	97	27
1965	BC	423	219	51.8	2961	7.0	15	3.5	19	4.5	89	
1966	BC	363	211	58.1	2889	8.0	11	3.0	18	5.0	82	23
Totals		2709	1476	54.5	22725	8.4	136	5.0	129	4.8	106	93
PETE KARPUK												
1949	OTT						1					
JERRY KAURIC												
1988	EDM	1	0	0.0	0	0.0	0	0.0	0	0.0		
JESSE KAYE												
1967	SAS	25	5	20.0	77	3.1	0	0.0	2	8.0	20	
DAN KEARNS												
1986	EDM	1	1	100.0	20	20.0	0	0.0	0	0.0	20	
EARL KEELEY												
1959	BC	26	16	61.5	232	8.9	2	7.7	4	15.4	53	
1960	BC	7	4	57.1	60	8.6	0	0.0	1	14.3	20	0
1961	BC	21	11	52.4	118	5.6	1	4.8	3	14.3	19	
1962	BC	4	2	50.0	13	3.3	0	0.0	0	0.0	11	
Totals		58	33	56.9	423	7.3	3	5.2	8	13.8	53	0
JERRY KEELING												
1961	CAL	74	33	44.6	399	5.4	3	4.1	3	4.1	36	
1962	CAL	79	32	40.5	498	6.3	1	1.3	9	11.4	64	
1963	CAL	41	25	61.0	486	11.9	6	14.6	0	0.0	68	0
1964	CAL	36	18	50.0	357	9.9	4	11.1	2	5.6	45	2
1965	CAL	105	48	45.7	581	5.5	4	3.8	5	4.8	23	
1966	CAL	87	38	43.7	677	7.8	5	5.7	13	14.9	109	4
1967	CAL	2	0	0.0	0	0.0	0	0.0	1	50.0		
1968	CAL	55	33	60.0	387	7.0	2	3.6	1	1.8	42	
1969	CAL	411	229	55.7	3179	7.7	20	4.9	28	6.8	70	
1970	CAL	327	161	49.2	2247	6.9	18	5.5	21	6.4	59	
1971	CAL	279	163	58.4	2038	7.3	8	2.9	17	6.1	58	
1972	CAL	292	157	53.8	2451	8.4	18	6.2	27	9.2	73	
1973	OTT	165	86	52.1	1175	7.1	11	6.7	4	2.4	89	
1974	OTT	250	130	52.0	1831	7.3	7	2.8	14	5.6	68	
1975	OTT	11	4	36.4	82	7.5	0	0.0	1	9.1	32	
1975	HAM	263	145	55.1	1851	7.0	12	4.6	12	4.6	81	
1975	Year	274	149	54.4	1933	7.1	12	4.4	13	4.7	81	
Totals		2477	1302	52.6	18239	7.4	119	4.8	158	6.4	109	6
ROBBIE KEEN												
1994	LV	3	3	100.0	62	20.7	1	33.3	0	0.0	25	
1995	SHR	2	2	100.0	36	18.0	0	0.0	0	0.0	24	
Totals		5	5	100.0	98	19.6	1	20.0	0	0.0	25	
GARY KEITHLEY												
1977	BC	81	39	48.1	478	5.9	3	3.7	6	7.4	78	
1978	BC	49	28	57.1	310	6.3	2	4.1	2	4.1	38	
Totals		130	67	51.5	788	6.1	5	3.8	8	6.2	78	
MATT KELLETT												
2001	BC	1	0	0.0	0	0.0	0	0.0	0	0.0		0
MIKE KELLEY												
1986	SAS	24	8	33.3	77	3.2	0	0.0	1	4.2	19	
JOE KELLY												
1960	OTT	2	1	50.0	24	12.0	0	0.0	0	0.0	24	
1961	OTT	0	0		0		0		0			1
Totals		2	1	50.0	24	12.0	0	0.0	0	0.0	24	1

Year	Team	ATT	COM	COM%	YDS	AVG	TD	TD%	INT	INT%	LG	SK
JIMMY KEMP												
1994	SAC	10	5	50.0	54	5.4	0	0.0	0	0.0	29	
1995	SA	100	53	53.0	769	7.7	4	4.0	9	9.0	50	
1996	MTL	74	43	58.1	560	7.6	4	5.4	2	2.7	44	
1996	SAS	173	94	54.3	1183	6.8	6	3.5	10	5.8	57	
1996	Year	247	137	55.5	1743	7.1	10	4.0	12	4.9	57	
1997	EDM	150	80	53.3	1175	7.8	3	2.0	9	6.0	69	
1998	EDM	199	107	53.8	1538	7.7	10	5.0	10	5.0	44	
1999	TOR	238	139	58.4	1771	7.4	8	3.4	12	5.0	74	
2000	TOR	226	122	54.0	1495	6.6	10	4.4	11	4.9	68	18
2001	TOR	320	188	58.8	2838	8.9	16	5.0	16	5.0	66	
Totals		1490	831	55.8	11383	7.6	61	4.1	79	5.3	74	18
PETER KEMPF												
1965	BC	1	1	100.0	10	10.0	0	0.0	0	0.0	10	
MARV KENDRICKS												
1973	TOR	1	1	100.0	10	10.0	1	100.0	0	0.0	10	
DARNELL KENNEDY												
2002	CAL	7	2	28.6	30	4.3	0	0.0	2	28.6	15	1
2003	CAL	1	1	100.0	4	4.0	1	100.0	0	0.0	4	0
2003	OTT	5	2	40.0	19	3.8	0	0.0	0	0.0	12	0
2003	Year	6	3	50.0	23	3.8	1	16.7	0	0.0	12	0
2004	OTT	131	69	52.7	893	6.8	5	3.8	3	2.3	71	13
2005	OTT	8	1	12.5	40	5.0	0	0.0	1	12.5	40	0
Totals		158	78	49.4	1009	6.4	7	4.4	6	3.8	71	14
TREVOR KENNERD												
1983	WPG	1	0	0.0	0	0.0	0	0.0	0	0.0		
RANDY KERBOW												
1965	EDM	119	66	55.5	963	8.1	1	0.8	10	8.4	62	
1966	EDM	222	100	45.0	1583	7.1	7	3.2	16	7.2	55	8
1967	EDM	2	0	0.0	0	0.0	0	0.0	1	50.0		
1968	EDM	1	0	0.0	0	0.0	0	0.0	1	100.0		
Totals		344	166	48.3	2546	7.4	8	2.3	28	8.1	62	8
MIKE KERRIGAN												
1986	HAM	424	242	57.1	3193	7.5	16	3.8	19	4.5	75	
1987	HAM	196	103	52.6	1339	6.8	5	2.6	15	7.7	75	
1988	HAM	342	188	55.0	2764	8.1	16	4.7	14	4.1	75	
1989	HAM	486	248	51.0	3635	7.5	20	4.1	28	5.8	67	
1990	HAM	479	249	52.0	3655	7.6	22	4.6	32	6.7	75	
1991	HAM	311	155	49.8	2242	7.2	13	4.2	19	6.1	77	
1992	TOR	59	31	52.5	406	6.9	3	5.1	5	8.5	43	
1993	TOR	153	86	56.2	1323	8.6	9	5.9	5	3.3	72	
1994	TOR	265	143	54.0	2224	8.4	17	6.4	14	5.3	68	
1995	HAM	50	32	64.0	308	6.2	2	4.0	6	12.0	30	
1996	HAM	105	57	54.3	625	6.0	3	2.9	6	5.7	53	
Totals		2870	1534	53.4	21714	7.6	126	4.4	163	5.7	77	
LARRY KERYCHUK												
1969	EDM	2	0	0.0	0	0.0	0	0.0	0	0.0		
PHIL KESSEL												
1982	CAL	56	30	53.6	399	7.1	4	7.1	4	7.1	74	
LARRY KEY												
1978	BC	2	1	50.0	89	44.5	1	50.0	0	0.0	89	
1979	BC	3	1	33.3	25	8.3	0	0.0	0	0.0	33	
1981	BC	1	0	0.0	0	0.0	0	0.0	0	0.0		
Totals		6	2	33.3	114	19.0	1	16.7	0	0.0	89	
BLAIR KIEL												
1992	TOR	28	6	21.4	108	3.9	0	0.0	3	10.7	72	
TONY KIMBROUGH												
1989	OTT	142	60	42.3	1079	7.6	10	7.0	7	4.9	56	
1990	OTT	9	2	22.2	62	6.9	0	0.0	3	33.3	48	
1991	BC	4	2	50.0	55	13.8	0	0.0	0	0.0	29	
1992	BC	255	128	50.2	1750	6.9	7	2.7	4	1.6	37	
Totals		410	192	46.8	2946	7.2	17	4.1	14	3.4	56	
JOHN KINCH												
1980	SAS	1	0	0.0	0	0.0	0	0.0	0	0.0		
MONTRESSA KIRBY												
1999	HAM	8	2	25.0	16	2.0	0	0.0	1	12.5	11	
JIMMY KLINGLER												
1995	BIR	98	47	48.0	645	6.6	4	4.1	7	7.1	96	
DON KLOSTERMAN												
1955	CAL	279	154	55.2	2405	8.6	13	4.7	20	7.2	104	
1956	CAL	177	97	54.8	1398	7.9	5	2.8	15	8.5	62	
Totals		456	251	55.0	3803	8.3	18	3.9	35	7.7	104	
JEFF KNAPPLE												
1981	CAL	42	20	47.6	340	8.1	0	0.0	4	9.5	41	
HARRY KNIGHT												
1976	WPG	28	15	53.6	191	6.8	1	3.6	2	7.1	21	
1977	WPG	80	41	51.3	489	6.1	1	1.3	5	6.3	39	
1978	WPG	30	16	53.3	227	7.6	1	3.3	0	0.0	30	
Totals		138	72	52.2	907	6.6	3	2.2	7	5.1	39	
LEE KNIGHT												
1993	HAM	1	0	0.0	0	0.0	0	0.0	0	0.0		
SHAWN KNIGHT												
1995	TOR	4	2	50.0	18	4.5	0	0.0	0	0.0	11	
RONNIE KNOX												
1956	HAM	66	39	59.1	609	9.2	5	7.6	4	6.1	60	
1956	CAL	130	61	46.9	782	6.0	2	1.5	5	3.8	32	
1956	Year	196	100	51.0	1391	7.1	7	3.6	9	4.6	60	
1958	TOR	193	116	60.1	1658	8.6	9	4.7	14	7.3	86	
1959	TOR	110	58	52.7	753	6.8	4	3.6	11	10.0	47	7
Totals		499	274	54.9	3802	7.6	20	4.0	34	6.8	86	7
DARCY KOPP												
1987	CAL	1	0	0.0	0	0.0	0	0.0	1	100.0		
TROY KOPP												
1998	WPG	187	95	50.8	1289	6.9	5	2.7	8	4.3	62	
1999	WPG	29	11	37.9	257	8.9	0	0.0	4	13.8	44	
2000	CAL	99	53	53.5	722	7.3	1	1.0	10	10.1	55	7
Totals		315	159	50.5	2268	7.2	6	1.9	22	7.0	62	7
BOB KRAEMER												
1971	WPG	4	1	25.0	10	2.5	1	25.0	0	0.0	10	
1972	WPG	2	1	50.0	33	16.5	1	50.0	0	0.0	33	
Totals		6	2	33.3	43	7.2	2	33.3	0	0.0	33	
ERIK KRAMER												

Year	Team	ATT	COM	COM%	YDS	AVG	TD	TD%	INT	INT%	LG	SK
1988	CAL	153	62	40.5	964	6.3	5	3.3	13	8.5	62	
SCOTT KRAUSE												
2004	TOR	5	3	60.0	19	3.8	0	0.0	0	0.0	12	
ERIC KRESSER												
2002	MTL	3	1	33.3	7	2.3	0	0.0	0	0.0	7	
JIM KROHN												
1980	WPG	17	10	58.8	140	8.2	1	5.9	4	23.5	28	
JOE KROL												
1946	TOR						2					
1947	TOR						5					
1948	TOR						2					
1949	TOR						5					
Totals							14					
OSCAR KRUGER												
1955	EDM	1	0	0.0	0	0.0	0	0.0	0	0.0		
1956	EDM	1	0	0.0	0	0.0	0	0.0	1	100.0		
1957	EDM+	1	0	0.0	0	0.0	0	0.0	0	0.0		
Totals		3	0	0.0	0	0.0	0	0.0	1	33.3		
GERALD KUNYK												
1975	CAL	1	0	0.0	0	0.0	0	0.0	1	100.0		
1977	EDM	2	2	100.0	47	23.5	0	0.0	0	0.0	31	
1977	Year	2	2	100.0	47	23.5	0	0.0	0	0.0	31	
Totals		3	2	66.7	47	15.7	0	0.0	1	33.3	31	
LOU KUSSEROW												
1953	HAM						1					
1954	HAM	2	1	50.0	1	0.5	0	0.0	0	0.0	1	
1955	HAM	1	1	100.0	15	15.0	0	0.0	0	0.0	15	
Totals		3	2	66.7	16	5.3	1	0.0	0	0.0	15	
GARY KUZYK												
1976	OTT	1	0	0.0	0	0.0	0	0.0	0	0.0		
Totals		1	0	0.0	0	0.0	0	0.0	0		0	0
AUBURN LAMBETH												
1953	HAM						1					
WAYNE LAMMLE												
1996	OTT	2	0	0.0	0	0.0	0	0.0	0	0.0		
RON LANCASTER												
1960	OTT	201	101	50.2	1843	9.2	16	8.0	18	9.0	91	
1961	OTT	100	49	49.0	966	9.7	9	9.0	8	8.0	63	5
1962	OTT	98	48	49.0	1016	10.4	9	9.2	12	12.2	67	
1963	SAS	226	106	46.9	1727	7.6	11	4.9	19	8.4	86	11
1964	SAS	263	144	54.8	2256	8.6	16	6.1	13	4.9	48	22
1965	SAS	305	160	52.5	2586	8.5	17	5.6	26	8.5	102	
1966	SAS	303	182	60.1	2976	9.8	28	9.2	20	6.6	80	13
1967	SAS	330	169	51.2	2809	8.5	16	4.8	24	7.3	88	
1968	SAS	358	181	50.6	2969	8.3	12	3.4	17	4.7	83	
1969	SAS	354	188	53.1	3104	8.8	25	7.1	28	7.9	83	
1970	SAS	330	175	53.0	2779	8.4	16	4.8	22	6.7	94	
1971	SAS	375	192	51.2	2759	7.4	16	4.3	23	6.1	97	
1972	SAS	357	208	58.3	2942	8.2	23	6.4	20	5.6	74	
1973	SAS	464	263	56.7	3767	8.1	22	4.7	27	5.8	94	
1974	SAS	395	222	56.2	2873	7.3	20	5.1	20	5.1	78	
1975	SAS	441	239	54.2	3545	8.0	23	5.2	27	6.1	85	
1976	SAS	494	297	60.1	3869	7.8	25	5.1	25	5.1	72	
1977	SAS	449	255	56.8	3072	6.8	14	3.1	20	4.5	63	
1978	SAS	390	205	52.6	2677	6.9	15	3.8	27	6.9	73	
Totals		6233	3384	54.3	50535	8.1	333	5.3	396	6.4	102	51
GARY LANE												
1970	SAS	26	11	42.3	165	6.3	0	0.0	3	11.5	31	
BOB LaROSE												
1972	WPG	1	0	0.0	0	0.0	0	0.0	1	100.0		
1973	WPG	1	0	0.0	0	0.0	0	0.0	0	0.0		
Totals		2	0	0.0	0	0.0	0	0.0	1	50.0		
TOM LARSCHEID												
1962	BC	2	1	50.0	33	16.5	0	0.0	0	0.0	33	0
1963	BC	1	0	0.0	0	0.0	0	0.0	0	0.0		0
Totals		3	1	33.3	33	11.0	0	0.0	0	0.0	33	0
MIKE LASHUK												
1961	EDM	1	0	0.0	0	0.0	0	0.0	0	0.0		0
RON LATOURELLE												
1964	WPG	1	1	100.0	-2	-2.0	0	0.0	0	0.0	-2	0
LARRY LAWRENCE												
1970	CAL	118	58	49.2	836	7.1	5	4.2	7	5.9	52	
1971	EDM	193	92	47.7	1247	6.5	3	1.6	18	9.3	58	
1978	MTL	3	2	66.7	31	10.3	0	0.0	0	0.0	24	
Totals		314	152	48.4	2114	6.7	8	2.5	25	8.0	58	
MEL LAWSON												
1948	HAM						1					
MIKE LAZECKI												
1990	SAS	2	1	50.0	30	15.0	0	0.0	1	50.0	30	
1991	SAS	1	1	100.0	36	36.0	0	0.0	0	0.0	36	
Totals		3	2	66.7	66	22.0	0	0.0	1	33.3	36	
CHRIS LEAK												
2009	MTL	11	8	72.7	46	4.2	1	9.1	0	0.0	11	0
2010	MTL	48	28	58.3	250	5.2	0	0.0	3	6.3	37	4
Totals		59	36	61.0	296	5.0	1	1.7	3	5.1	37	4
BUDDY LEAKE												
1955	WPG	210	91	43.3	1370	6.5	2	1.0	18	8.6	62	
1956	WPG	91	43	47.3	819	9.0	5	5.5	11	12.1	75	
1957	WPG	10	5	50.0	89	8.9	1	10.0	1	10.0	27	
Totals		311	139	44.7	2278	7.3	8	2.6	30	9.6	75	
EDDIE LeBARON												
1954	CAL	251	116	46.2	1815	7.2	8	3.2	24	9.6	79	
CODY LEDBETTER												
1996	EDM	67	25	37.3	364	5.4	3	4.5	1	1.5	42	
1998	HAM	33	18	54.5	189	5.7	1	3.0	3	9.1	37	
1999	HAM	20	8	40.0	105	5.3	1	5.0	0	0.0	30	
2000	HAM	40	20	50.0	284	7.1	1	2.5	3	7.5	43	2
2001	HAM	48	23	47.9	303	6.3	1	2.1	3	6.3	49	
Totals		208	94	45.2	1245	6.0	7	3.4	10	4.8	49	2
HAL LEDYARD												
1956	OTT	363	175	48.2	3151	8.7	17	4.7	28	7.7	93	
1957	OTT	105	55	52.4	982	9.4	6	5.7	6	5.7	68	

Year	Team	ATT	COM	COM%	YDS	AVG	TD	TD%	INT	INT%	LG	SK
1958	OTT	107	48	44.9	868	8.1	5	4.7	13	12.1	77	
1961	WPG	168	91	54.2	1398	8.3	10	6.0	9	5.4	62	
1962	WPG	84	41	48.8	633	7.5	5	6.0	5	6.0	63	
1963	WPG	90	45	50.0	707	7.9	4	4.4	4	4.4	44	6
1964	WPG	108	46	42.6	750	6.9	3	2.8	10	9.3	59	18
1965	SAS	32	11	34.4	136	4.3	0	0.0	2	6.3	17	
1965	Year	32	11	34.4	136	4.3	0	0.0	2	6.3	17	
Totals		1057	512	48.4	8625	8.2	50	4.7	77	7.3	93	24
ORVILLE LEE												
1988	OTT	1	0	0.0	0	0.0	0	0.0	1	100.0		
TOMMY LEE												
1963	OTT	2	1	50.0	7	3.5	0	0.0	1	50.0	7	0
GARRY LeFEBVRE												
1972	EDM	1	1	100.0	16	16.0	0	0.0	0	0.0	16	
1976	EDM	1	1	100.0	29	29.0	0	0.0	0	0.0	29	
Totals		2	2	100.0	45	22.5	0	0.0	0	0.0	29	
STEFAN LeFORS												
2007	EDM	181	110	60.8	1193	6.6	6	3.3	8	4.4	53	20
2008	EDM	4	1	25.0	9	2.3	0	0.0	1	25.0	9	0
2009	WPG	88	41	46.6	459	5.2	2	2.3	2	2.3	54	4
Totals		273	152	55.7	1661	6.1	8	2.9	11	4.0	54	24
BRUCE LEMMERMAN												
1971	EDM	145	73	50.3	1055	7.3	8	5.5	11	7.6	97	
1972	EDM	60	34	56.7	541	9.0	7	11.7	4	6.7	61	
1973	EDM	257	153	59.5	1851	7.2	14	5.4	16	6.2	44	
1974	EDM	140	68	48.6	858	6.1	4	2.9	10	7.1	66	
1975	EDM	170	97	57.1	1402	8.2	8	4.7	6	3.5	80	
1976	EDM	354	189	53.4	2271	6.4	13	3.7	18	5.1	50	
1977	EDM	219	117	53.4	1475	6.7	5	2.3	6	2.7	62	
1978	EDM	38	23	60.5	294	7.7	1	2.6	2	5.3	41	
1980	HAM	112	62	55.4	775	6.9	3	2.7	10	8.9	51	
Totals		1495	816	54.6	10522	7.0	63	4.2	83	5.6	97	
CLEO LEMON												
2010	TOR	462	285	61.7	3433	7.4	15	3.2	19	4.1	66	45
2011	TOR	218	145	66.5	1636	7.5	7	3.2	4	1.8	69	15
Totals		680	430	63.2	5069	7.5	22	3.2	23	3.4	69	60
MIKE LEVENSELLER												
1984	CAL	1	1	100.0	12	12.0	1	100.0	0	0.0	12	
CHUCK LEVY												
2000	BC	1	0	0.0	0	0.0	0	0.0	0	0.0		0
DAVE LEWIS												
1967	MTL	32	12	37.5	235	7.3	0	0.0	1	3.1	35	
1968	MTL	3	1	33.3	37	12.3	0	0.0	1	33.3	37	
Totals		35	13	37.1	272	7.8	0	0.0	2	5.7	37	
LEO LEWIS												
1955	WPG	9	4	44.4	102	11.3	2	22.2	0	0.0	37	
1957	WPG	3	2	66.7	60	20.0	0	0.0	0	0.0	38	
1958	WPG	13	10	76.9	217	16.7	2	15.4	0	0.0	55	
1959	WPG	17	7	41.2	109	6.4	2	11.8	2	11.8	36	0
1960	WPG	8	6	75.0	133	16.6	4	50.0	0	0.0	34	0
1961	WPG	7	4	57.1	98	14.0	1	14.3	1	14.3	37	0
1962	WPG	4	2	50.0	71	17.8	1	25.0	0	0.0	47	0
1963	WPG	6	4	66.7	58	9.7	0	0.0	1	16.7	28	0
1964	WPG	6	3	50.0	56	9.3	1	16.7	0	0.0	25	0
1965	WPG	7	3	42.9	15	2.1	1	14.3	3	42.9	19	0
Totals		80	45	56.3	919	11.5	14	17.5	7	8.8	55	0
NIK LEWIS												
2004	CAL	1	0	0.0	0	0.0	0	0.0	0	0.0		0
2005	CAL	1	0	0.0	0	0.0	0	0.0	0	0.0		0
Totals		2	0	0.0	0	0.0	0	0.0	0	0.0		0
WALTER LEWIS												
1986	MTL	134	65	48.5	833	6.2	3	2.2	8	6.0	47	26
EARL LINDLEY												
1955	EDM	2	1	50.0	27	13.5	0	0.0	1	50.0	27	
1956	EDM	4	1	25.0	17	4.3	0	0.0	0	0.0	17	
Totals		6	2	33.3	44	7.3	0	0.0	1	16.7	27	
JIM LINDSEY												
1971	CAL	168	79	47.0	1055	6.3	8	4.8	16	9.5	57	
1972	CAL	210	106	50.5	1413	6.7	7	3.3	17	8.1	51	
1973	CAL	107	49	45.8	644	6.0	2	1.9	12	11.2	49	
1974	TOR	15	8	53.3	66	4.4	0	0.0	2	13.3	15	
Totals		500	242	48.4	3178	6.4	17	3.4	47	9.4	57	
AUBREY LINNE												
1963	EDM	1	1	100.0	16	16.0	0	0.0	0	0.0	16	0
1963	Year	1	1	100.0	16	16.0	0	0.0	0	0.0	16	0
Totals		1	1	100.0	16	16.0	0	0.0	0		16	0
RUDY LINTERMAN												
1973	CAL	1	0	0.0	0	0.0	0	0.0	0	0.0		
GLENN LIPPMAN												
1954	EDM	5	2	40.0	20	4.0	0	0.0	1	20.0		
PETE LISKE												
1965	TOR	261	123	47.1	1847	7.1	10	3.8	17	6.5	104	37
1966	CAL	283	146	51.6	2177	7.7	14	4.9	15	5.3	63	26
1967	CAL	508	303	59.6	4479	8.8	40	7.9	25	4.9	84	
1968	CAL	438	271	61.9	4333	9.9	31	7.1	28	6.4	73	
1973	CAL	409	226	55.3	2861	7.0	12	2.9	21	5.1	53	
1974	CAL	333	199	59.8	2891	8.7	9	2.7	12	3.6	97	
1974	BC	59	29	49.2	368	6.2	1	1.7	6	10.2	39	
1974	Year	392	228	58.2	3259	8.3	10	2.6	18	4.6	97	
1975	BC	280	152	54.3	2310	8.3	13	4.6	9	3.2	72	
Totals		2571	1449	56.4	21266	8.3	130	5.1	133	5.2	104	63
DONNIE LITTLE												
1982	OTT	1	1	100.0	15	15.0	0	0.0	0	0.0	15	
1983	OTT	4	3	75.0	55	13.8	0	0.0	0	0.0	26	
Totals		5	4	80.0	70	14.0	0	0.0	0	0.0	26	
J.W. LOCKETT												
1965	MTL	3	0	0.0	0	0.0	0	0.0	1	33.3		0
STEFAN LOGAN												
2008	BC	1	0	0.0	0	0.0	0	0.0	0	0.0	0	0
TONY LOGAN												
1991	HAM	1	1	100.0	27	27.0	0	0.0	0	0.0	27	
ROCKY LONG												

Year	Team	ATT	COM	COM%	YDS	AVG	TD	TD%	INT	INT%	LG	SK
1972	BC	1	0	0.0	0	0.0	0	0.0	0	0.0		
1975	BC	1	0	0.0	0	0.0	0	0.0	0	0.0		
1976	BC	1	0	0.0	0	0.0	0	0.0	0	0.0		
1977	BC	1	0	0.0	0	0.0	0	0.0	0	0.0		
Totals		4	0	0.0	0	0.0	0	0.0	0	0.0		
CLINT LONGLEY												
1977	TOR	56	30	53.6	373	6.7	2	3.6	6	10.7	45	
TED LOZANSKI												
1949	WPG						1					
TERRY LUCK												
1978	WPG	18	7	38.9	70	3.9	0	0.0	0	0.0	17	
TRAVIS LULAY												
2009	BC	36	22	61.1	324	9.0	2	5.6	2	5.6	41	1
2010	BC	318	205	64.5	2602	8.2	9	2.8	11	3.5	98	34
2011	BC	583	242	41.5	4815	8.3	32	5.5	11	1.9	100	23
Totals		937	469	50.1	7741	8.3	43	4.6	24	2.6	100	58
NEIL LUMSDEN												
1977	TOR	2	1	50.0	10	5.0	0	0.0	0	0.0	10	
HARRY LUNN												
1957	SAS	1	0	0.0	0	0.0	0	0.0	0	0.0		
DICKY LYONS												
1971	BC	1	0	0.0	0	0.0	0	0.0	1	100.0		
MATT LYTLE												
2002	MTL	27	11	40.7	182	6.7	1	3.7	1	3.7	41	
JASON MAAS												
2000	EDM	26	17	65.4	177	6.8	1	3.8	1	3.8	35	2
2001	EDM	391	232	59.3	3646	9.3	21	5.4	12	3.1	95	29
2002	EDM	213	115	54.0	1872	8.8	9	4.2	6	2.8	101	16
2003	EDM	29	18	62.1	210	7.2	2	6.9	2	6.9	26	2
2004	EDM	549	361	65.8	5270	9.6	31	5.6	14	2.6	102	33
2005	EDM	3	3	100.0	75	25.0	1	33.3	0	0.0	37	0
2006	HAM	484	298	61.6	3204	6.6	8	1.7	17	3.5	45	19
2007	HAM	231	137	59.3	1749	7.6	7	3.0	6	2.6	88	20
2007	MTL	33	21	63.6	220	6.7	1	3.0	1	3.0	26	2
2007	Year	264	158	59.8	1969	7.5	8	3.0	7	2.7	88	2
2008	EDM	44	26	59.1	340	7.7	0	0.0	1	2.3	80	1
2009	EDM	29	18	62.1	235	8.1	0	0.0	2	6.9	38	2
2010	EDM	23	10	43.5	128	5.6	0	0.0	2	8.7	29	1
Totals		2055	1256	61.1	17126	8.3	81	3.9	64	3.1	102	127
JAY MACIAS												
1995	OTT	128	58	45.3	881	6.9	2	1.6	7	5.5	72	
BILL MACKRIDES												
1952	HAM						18					
EDDIE MACON												
1954	CAL	2	2	100.0	132	66.0	1	50.0	0	0.0	84	
BOB MACORITTI												
1976	SAS	2	1	50.0	31	15.5	0	0.0	0	0.0	31	
1977	SAS	1	0	0.0	0	0.0	0	0.0	0	0.0		
1978	SAS	1	0	0.0	0	0.0	0	0.0	0	0.0		
Totals		4	1	25.0	31	7.8	0	0.0	0	0.0	31	
RAY MACORITTI												
1993	OTT	1	0	0.0	0	0.0	0	0.0	1	100.0		
RON MADDOCKS												
1963	MTL	8	2	25.0	22	2.8	0	0.0	0	0.0	21	0
JOHNNY MAJORS												
1957	MTL	4	2	50.0	30	7.5	0	0.0	0	0.0	25	
JOHN MANEL												
1969	HAM	13	6	46.2	79	6.1	1	7.7	0	0.0	20	
1971	HAM	12	5	41.7	57	4.8	0	0.0	2	16.7	21	
Totals		25	11	44.0	136	5.4	1	4.0	2	8.0	21	
MARK MANGES												
1979	HAM	11	2	18.2	6	0.5	0	0.0	0	0.0	9	
JIM MANKINS												
1969	OTT	1	1	100.0	13	13.0	0	0.0	0	0.0	13	
DAVE MANN												
1958	TOR	5	4	80.0	54	10.8	1	20.0	0	0.0	21	
1960	TOR	2	0	0.0	0	0.0	0	0.0	0	0.0		
1961	TOR	1	1	100.0	36	36.0	0	0.0	0	0.0	36	3
1962	TOR	2	0	0.0	0	0.0	0	0.0	1	50.0		
1964	TOR	2	1	50.0	30	15.0	0	0.0	0	0.0	30	0
1965	TOR	1	0	0.0	0	0.0	0	0.0	1	100.0		0
1966	TOR	2	1	50.0	25	12.5	0	0.0	0	0.0	25	0
1967	TOR	1	1	100.0	39	39.0	1	100.0	0	0.0	39	
1968	TOR	2	2	100.0	58	29.0	1	50.0	0	0.0	39	
1969	TOR	1	0	0.0	0	0.0	0	0.0	0	0.0	87	
1970	TOR	1	0	0.0	0	0.0	0	0.0	1	100.0		
Totals		20	10	50.0	242	12.1	3	15.0	3	15.0	87	3
DAN MANUCCI												
1981	TOR	68	23	33.8	261	3.8	1	1.5	6	8.8	50	
VIC MARKS												
1958	SAS	1	0	0.0	0	0.0	0	0.0	0	0.0		
DAVE MARLER												
1979	HAM	89	39	43.8	549	6.2	2	2.2	9	10.1	32	
1980	HAM	265	139	52.5	1914	7.2	9	3.4	19	7.2	57	
1981	HAM	32	13	40.6	165	5.2	2	6.3	2	6.3	25	
1982	HAM	43	21	48.8	372	8.7	3	7.0	3	7.0	75	
1984	OTT	36	13	36.1	154	4.3	0	0.0	5	13.9	55	
Totals		465	225	48.4	3154	6.8	16	3.4	38	8.2	75	
BOBBY MARLOW												
1955	SAS	1	0	0.0	0	0.0	0	0.0	0	0.0		
1956	SAS	4	2	50.0	44	11.0	0	0.0	0	0.0	26	
Totals		5	2	40.0	44	8.8	0	0.0	0	0.0	26	
FRANCIS MARRIOTT												
1963	MTL	81	27	33.3	320	4.0	1	1.2	10	12.3	52	6
CECIL MARTIN												
1951	HAM						1					
TEE MARTIN												
2005	WPG	95	40	42.1	458	4.8	1	1.1	4	4.2	37	12
TONY MARTINO												
1988	BC	1	0	0.0	0	0.0	0	0.0	0	0.0		
1988	Year	1	0	0.0	0	0.0	0	0.0	0	0.0		
1990	BC	2	1	50.0	17	8.5	0	0.0	0	0.0	12	

Year	Team	ATT	COM	COM%	YDS	AVG	TD	TD%	INT	INT%	LG	SK
2000	CAL	3	1	33.3	20	6.7	0	0.0	1	33.3	20	0
2002	BC	1	1	100.0	10	10.0	0	0.0	0	0.0	10	
Totals		7	3	42.9	47	6.7	0	0.0	1	14.3	20	0
KEVIN MASON												
1996	SAS	106	63	59.4	835	7.9	3	2.8	3	2.8	95	
1997	SAS	228	115	50.4	1798	7.9	8	3.5	18	7.9	60	
1998	WPG	76	35	46.1	331	4.4	2	2.6	5	6.6	38	
1999	EDM	80	37	46.3	451	5.6	3	3.8	4	5.0	37	
Totals		490	250	51.0	3415	7.0	16	3.3	30	6.1	95	
PAUL MASOTTI												
1995	TOR	1	1	100.0	34	34.0	0	0.0	0	0.0	34	
DAVE MATHIESON												
1967	BC	11	6	54.5	82	7.5	0	0.0	0	0.0	23	
BRENT MATICH												
1989	CAL	2	0	0.0	0	0.0	0	0.0	0	0.0		
RANDY MATTINGLY												
1974	SAS	65	35	53.8	553	8.5	4	6.2	6	9.2	55	
1975	SAS	22	8	36.4	82	3.7	0	0.0	4	18.2	17	
1976	HAM	37	18	48.6	177	4.8	1	2.7	2	5.4	28	
Totals		124	61	49.2	812	6.5	5	4.0	12	9.7	55	
TOM MAUDLIN												
1962	TOR	1	1	100.0	12	12.0	0	0.0	0	0.0	12	
1963	EDM	40	18	45.0	261	6.5	1	2.5	8	20.0	37	1
Totals		41	19	46.3	273	6.7	1	2.4	8	19.5	37	1
JOE MAULDIN												
1994	HAM	3	0	0.0	0	0.0	0	0.0	1	33.3		
CURTIS MAYFIELD												
1999	SAS	1	0	0.0	0	0.0	0	0.0	0	0.0		
JOHNNY MAZUR												
1954	BC	128	54	42.2	645	5.0	2	1.6	10	7.8		
STEVE MAZURAK												
1977	SAS	1	0	0.0	0	0.0	0	0.0	0	0.0		
DERRICK McADOO												
1989	HAM	1	1	100.0	83	83.0	1	100.0	0	0.0	83	
1990	HAM	6	2	33.3	54	9.0	2	33.3	1	16.7	36	
Totals		7	3	42.9	137	19.6	3	42.9	1	14.3	83	
BOBBY McALLISTER												
1989	TOR	11	7	63.6	84	7.6	0	0.0	0	0.0	25	
PAUL McCALLUM												
1999	SAS	1	0	0.0	0	0.0	0	0.0	0	0.0		
2004	SAS	1	0	0.0	0	0.0	0	0.0	0	0.0		
2005	SAS	1	0	0.0	0	0.0	0	0.0	0	0.0		0
2008	BC	2	2	100.0	53	26.5	0	0.0	0	0.0	29	
2009	BC	1	0	0.0	0	0.0	0	0.0	0	0.0		0
Totals		6	2	33.3	53	8.8	0	0.0	0	0.0	29	0
KEITHEN McCANT												
1994	WPG	200	108	54.0	1425	7.1	12	6.0	13	6.5	67	
1995	BC	15	9	60.0	83	5.5	0	0.0	0	0.0	27	
Totals		215	117	54.4	1508	7.0	12	5.6	13	6.0	67	
BOB McCARTHY												
1969	CAL	1	1	100.0	28	28.0	0	0.0	0	0.0	28	
MIKE McCOY												
1999	CAL	183	117	63.9	1669	9.1	10	5.5	3	1.6	64	
TIM McCRAY												
1986	SAS	1	0	0.0	0	0.0	0	0.0	0	0.0		
JASON McCULLOUGH												
1997	HAM	9	6	66.7	127	14.1	0	0.0	2	22.2	30	
MARK McDONALD												
1976	WPG	1	0	0.0	0	0.0	0	0.0	0	0.0		
KEVIN McDOUGAL												
1995	WPG	65	40	61.5	515	7.9	1	1.5	3	4.6	40	
1996	WPG	100	47	47.0	567	5.7	1	1.0	5	5.0	52	
1997	WPG	162	98	60.5	1274	7.9	7	4.3	8	4.9	82	
Totals		327	185	56.6	2356	7.2	9	2.8	16	4.9	82	
GERRY McDOUGALL												
1957	HAM	1	1	100.0	8	8.0	0	0.0	0	0.0	8	
1958	HAM	5	2	40.0	97	19.4	2	40.0	2	40.0	72	
1959	HAM	7	3	42.9	61	8.7	1	14.3	0	0.0	31	1
1960	HAM	1	1	100.0	13	13.0	0	0.0	0	0.0	13	
1961	HAM	3	1	33.3	36	12.0	1	33.3	0	0.0	36	0
Totals		17	8	47.1	215	12.6	4	23.5	2	11.8	72	1
CYRIL McFALL												
1978	CAL	1	1	100.0	1	1.0	0	0.0	0	0.0	1	
WANE McGARITY												
2004	CAL	1	1	100.0	27	27.0	1	100.0	0	0.0	27	0
MOLLY McGEE												
1976	SAS	1	0	0.0	0	0.0	0	0.0	0	0.0		
GERRY McGRATH												
1985	SAS	1	0	0.0	0	0.0	0	0.0	0	0.0		
1986	SAS	1	0	0.0	0	0.0	0	0.0	0	0.0		
Totals		2	0	0.0	0	0.0	0	0.0	0	0.0		
LAMAR McHAN												
1965	TOR	34	12	35.3	200	5.9	1	2.9	0	0.0	50	4
PRINCE McJUNKINS												
1983	OTT	46	19	41.3	234	5.1	1	2.2	2	4.3	23	
1984	OTT	33	16	48.5	224	6.8	2	6.1	4	12.1	44	
Totals		79	35	44.3	458	5.8	3	3.8	6	7.6	44	
JIMMY McKEAN												
1964	MTL	33	10	30.3	139	4.2	1	3.0	3	9.1	26	1
HUGH McKINNIS												
1970	CAL	3	1	33.3	49	16.3	0	0.0	1	33.3	49	
1971	CAL	1	0	0.0	0	0.0	0	0.0	0	0.0		
1972	OTT	1	0	0.0	0	0.0	0	0.0	0	0.0		
1972	Year	1	0	0.0	0	0.0	0	0.0	0	0.0		
Totals		5	1	20.0	49	9.8	0	0.0	1	20.0	49	
MIKE McMAHON												
2007	TOR	38	15	39.5	177	4.7	1	2.6	3	7.9	32	4
DANNY McMANUS												
1990	WPG	130	55	42.3	946	7.3	7	5.4	4	3.1	73	
1991	WPG	119	54	45.4	985	8.3	3	2.5	8	6.7	47	
1992	WPG	122	56	45.9	1153	9.5	6	4.9	5	4.1	73	
1993	BC	223	114	51.1	1613	7.2	10	4.5	14	6.3	44	

Year	Team	ATT	COM	COM%	YDS	AVG	TD	TD%	INT	INT%	LG	SK
1994	BC	159	79	49.7	1258	7.9	8	5.0	9	5.7	67	
1995	BC	581	295	50.8	4655	8.0	19	3.3	26	4.5	78	13
1996	EDM	582	310	53.3	4425	7.6	19	3.3	27	4.6	60	17
1997	EDM	488	293	60.0	4099	8.4	22	4.5	19	3.9	71	13
1998	HAM	584	333	57.0	4864	8.3	24	4.1	19	3.3	92	13
1999	HAM	612	365	59.6	5334	8.7	28	4.6	16	2.6	78	5
2000	HAM	516	271	52.5	4200	8.1	21	4.1	29	5.6	75	3
2001	HAM	571	326	57.1	4465	7.8	19	3.3	9	1.6	65	10
2002	HAM	604	318	52.6	4531	7.5	23	3.8	30	5.0	84	9
2003	HAM	416	221	53.1	2869	6.9	9	2.2	15	3.6	61	5
2004	HAM	590	331	56.1	5034	8.5	29	4.9	30	5.1	88	8
2005	HAM	364	203	55.8	2544	7.0	11	3.0	18	4.9	75	9
2006	CAL	28	16	57.1	280	10.0	1	3.6	3	10.7	81	
Totals		6689	3640	54.4	53255	8.0	259	3.9	281	4.2	92	105
JIM McMILLAN												
1975	HAM	155	64	41.3	868	5.6	6	3.9	17	11.0	53	
FRED McNAIR												
1991	TOR	2	1	50.0	3	1.5	0	0.0	0	0.0	3	
BOB McNAMARA												
1956	WPG	1	1	100.0	6	6.0	0	0.0	0	0.0	6	
REGGIE McNEAL												
2008	TOR	2	0	0.0	0	0.0	0	0.0	0	0.0		0
2010	TOR	2	1	50.0	4	2.0	0	0.0	1	50.0	4	0
Totals		4	1	25.0	4	1.0	0	0.0	1	25.0	4	0
ADRIAN McPHERSON												
2008	MTL	3	1	33.3	1	0.3	1	33.3	1	33.3	1	1
2009	MTL	72	49	68.1	506	7.0	6	8.3	0	0.0	43	10
2010	MTL	94	48	51.1	492	5.2	1	1.1	3	3.2	35	2
2011	MTL	43	28	65.1	311	7.2	1	2.3	2	4.7	32	3
Totals		212	126	59.4	1310	6.2	9	4.2	6	2.8	43	16
DON McPHERSON												
1991	HAM	52	22	42.3	326	6.3	2	3.8	2	3.8	37	
1992	HAM	77	37	48.1	680	8.8	6	7.8	5	6.5	82	
1993	HAM	368	152	41.3	2242	6.1	6	1.6	21	5.7	79	
Totals		497	211	42.5	3248	6.5	14	2.8	28	5.6	82	
LEON McQUAY												
1971	TOR	2	0	0.0	0	0.0	0	0.0	0	0.0		
1972	TOR	1	0	0.0	0	0.0	0	0.0	0	0.0		
Totals		3	0	0.0	0	0.0	0	0.0	0	0.0		
GORD McTAGGART												
1965	TOR	6	1	16.7	14	2.3	0	0.0	2	33.3	14	1
MIKE McTAGUE												
1979	CAL	1	1	100.0	21	21.0	0	0.0	0	0.0	21	
1983	CAL	2	1	50.0	11	5.5	0	0.0	0	0.0	11	
1986	SAS	1	0	0.0	0	0.0	0	0.0	0	0.0		
1986	Year	1	0	0.0	0	0.0	0	0.0	0	0.0		
Totals		4	2	50.0	32	8.0	0	0.0	0	0.0	21	
ANDY McVEY												
1989	CAL	1	0	0.0	0	0.0	0	0.0	0	0.0		
GLEN McWHINNEY												
1952	EDM	8	5	62.5	80	10.0	1	12.5	1	12.5	36	
JUSTIN MEDLOCK												
2011	HAM	2	2	100.0	36	18.0	0	0.0	0	0.0	30	0
MEL MELIN												
1962	BC	11	5	45.5	106	9.6	0	0.0	0	0.0	47	
1963	BC	4	2	50.0	32	8.0	0	0.0	0	0.0	20	2
Totals		15	7	46.7	138	9.2	0	0.0	0	0.0	47	2
LEN MELTZER												
1953	WPG	2	1	50.0	17	8.5	0	0.0	1	50.0	17	
1954	BC	1	0	0.0	0	0.0	0	0.0	0	0.0		
1954	Year	1	0	0.0	0	0.0	0	0.0	0	0.0		
Totals		3	1	33.3	17	5.7	0	0.0	1	33.3	17	
DENNIS MENDYK												
1957	WPG	1	1	100.0	34	34.0	1	100.0	0	0.0	34	
REG MESERVE												
1957	TOR	1	1	100.0	8	8.0	0	0.0	0	0.0	8	
TERRY METCALF												
1978	TOR	4	1	25.0	16	4.0	0	0.0	0	0.0	16	
1979	TOR	2	0	0.0	0	0.0	0	0.0	0	0.0		
1980	TOR	2	0	0.0	0	0.0	0	0.0	0	0.0		
Totals		8	1	12.5	16	2.0	0	0.0	0	0.0	16	
FREDDIE MEYERS												
1958	EDM	1	1	100.0	12	12.0	0	0.0	0	0.0	12	
RUSS MICHNA												
2005	WPG	53	27	50.9	363	6.8	3	5.7	2	3.8	33	2
2006	WPG	3	1	33.3	4	1.3	0	0.0	0	0.0	4	0
Totals		56	28	50.0	367	6.6	3	5.4	2	3.6	33	2
SCOTT MILANOVICH												
2003	CAL	72	40	55.6	521	7.2	1	1.4	7	9.7	55	
ROLLIE MILES												
1951	EDM	9	3	33.3	162	18.0	1	11.1	0	0.0		
1952	EDM	14	6	42.9	183	13.1	2	14.3	0	0.0	79	
1953	EDM	27	12	44.4	287	10.6	2	7.4	1	3.7		
1954	EDM	64	31	48.4	410	6.4	3	4.7	4	6.3		
1955	EDM	6	1	16.7	38	6.3	0	0.0	0	0.0	38	
1956	EDM	6	2	33.3	30	5.0	1	16.7	0	0.0	17	
1957	EDM	4	1	25.0	8	2.0	0	0.0	1	25.0	8	
1958	EDM	3	3	100.0	47	15.7	0	0.0	0	0.0	28	
1960	EDM	5	1	20.0	9	1.8	0	0.0	2	40.0	9	0
Totals		138	60	43.5	1174	8.5	9	6.5	8	5.8	79	0
ROMARO MILLER												
2003	OTT	39	23	59.0	252	6.5	3	7.7	0	0.0	50	
2004	TOR	11	2	18.2	34	3.1	0	0.0	0	0.0	25	
Totals		50	25	50.0	286	5.7	3	6.0	0	0.0	50	
RON MILLER												
1963	EDM	20	9	45.0	85	4.3	1	5.0	0	0.0	23	0
TROY MILLS												
1994	SAC	1	0	0.0	0	0.0	0	0.0	0	0.0		
ROBERT MIMBS												
1991	WPG	1	0	0.0	0	0.0	0	0.0	1	100.0		
JESSE MIMS												
1971	CAL	1	0	0.0	0	0.0	0	0.0	0	0.0		

Year	Team	ATT	COM	COM%	YDS	AVG	TD	TD%	INT	INT%	LG	SK
1972	CAL	1	0	0.0	0	0.0	0	0.0	1	100.0		
Totals		2	0	0.0	0	0.0	0	0.0	1	50.0		
CEDRIC MINTER												
1981	TOR	1	1	100.0	22	22.0	1	100.0	0	0.0	22	
1982	TOR	1	0	0.0	0	0.0	0	0.0	0	0.0		
1986	TOR	1	1	100.0	15	15.0	1	100.0	0	0.0	15	
1987	OTT	1	0	0.0	0	0.0	0	0.0	0	0.0		
Totals		4	2	50.0	37	9.3	2	50.0	0	0.0	22	
GEORGE MIRA												
1972	MTL	146	61	41.8	887	6.1	8	5.5	14	9.6	44	
1973	MTL	168	92	54.8	1356	8.1	11	6.5	8	4.8	64	
1977	TOR	13	4	30.8	48	3.7	0	0.0	1	7.7	24	
Totals		327	157	48.0	2291	7.0	19	5.8	23	7.0	64	
LARRY MOHR												
1987	OTT	1	0	0.0	0	0.0	0	0.0	0	0.0		
DARRELL MOIR												
1986	MTL	1	0	0.0	0	0.0	0	0.0	0	0.0		0
NAYLAND MOLL												
1955	TOR	1	0	0.0	0	0.0	0	0.0	0	0.0		
JOHN MOODY												
1946	MTL						1					
WARREN MOON												
1978	EDM	173	89	51.4	1112	6.4	5	2.9	7	4.0	56	
1979	EDM	274	149	54.4	2382	8.7	20	7.3	12	4.4	77	
1980	EDM	331	181	54.7	3127	9.4	25	7.6	11	3.3	89	
1981	EDM	378	237	62.7	3959	10.5	27	7.1	12	3.2	91	
1982	EDM	562	333	59.3	5000	8.9	36	6.4	16	2.8	58	
1983	EDM	664	380	57.2	5648	8.5	31	4.7	19	2.9	48	
Totals		2382	1369	57.5	21228	8.9	144	6.0	77	3.2	91	
SHAWN MOORE												
1995	OTT	84	43	51.2	559	6.7	1	1.2	3	3.6	45	
1995	WPG	46	18	39.1	266	5.8	1	2.2	4	8.7	52	
1995	CAL	20	13	65.0	177	8.9	2	10.0	0	0.0	52	3
1995	Year	150	74	49.3	1002	6.7	4	2.7	7	4.7	52	
TRAVIS MOORE												
1997	CAL	1	0	0.0	0	0.0	0	0.0	1	100.0		
2001	CAL	1	0	0.0	0	0.0	0	0.0	0	0.0		0
Totals		2	0	0.0	0	0.0	0	0.0	1	50.0		0
WILL MOORE												
1994	CAL	2	2	100.0	52	26.0	0	0.0	0	0.0	52	
DON MOORHEAD												
1971	BC	182	98	53.8	1302	7.2	9	4.9	13	7.1	59	
1972	BC	326	159	48.8	2606	8.0	10	3.1	17	5.2	73	
1973	BC	278	160	57.6	2005	7.2	4	1.4	12	4.3	73	
1974	BC	306	160	52.3	2478	8.1	17	5.6	13	4.2	92	
1975	BC	42	25	59.5	298	7.1	2	4.8	3	7.1	29	
Totals		1134	602	53.1	8689	7.7	42	3.7	58	5.1	92	
RONNIE MORRIS												
1955	CAL	7	3	42.9	28	4.0	0	0.0	0	0.0	13	
JIM MORSE												
1957	CAL	2	1	50.0	14	7.0	1	50.0	1	50.0	14	
DOM MOSELLE												
1955	CAL	12	6	50.0	94	7.8	0	0.0	1	8.3	30	
TOM MUECKE												
1986	WPG	2	1	50.0	14	7.0	0	0.0	0	0.0	14	
1987	WPG	37	20	54.1	212	5.7	3	8.1	3	8.1	42	
1988	WPG	250	124	49.6	1892	7.6	11	4.4	11	4.4	52	
1991	EDM	27	15	55.6	185	6.9	2	7.4	1	3.7	40	
1992	EDM	157	80	51.0	1275	8.1	11	7.0	7	4.5	68	
1993	EDM	54	26	48.1	242	4.5	1	1.9	3	5.6	28	
1994	SHR	85	45	52.9	478	5.6	5	5.9	3	3.5	49	
Totals		612	311	50.8	4298	7.0	33	5.4	28	4.6	68	
PETE MUIR												
1955	CAL	1	0	0.0	0	0.0	0	0.0	0	0.0		
MIKE MURPHY												
1977	OTT	1	0	0.0	0	0.0	0	0.0	0	0.0		
JOHNNY MUSSO												
1973	BC	1	1	100.0	25	25.0	0	0.0	0	0.0	25	
BAZ NAGLE												
1955	CAL	1	0	0.0	0	0.0	0	0.0	0	0.0		
1956	CAL	1	0	0.0	0	0.0	0	0.0	0	0.0		
1960	BC	2	1	50.0	15	7.5	1	50.0	0	0.0	15	0
Totals		4	1	25.0	15	3.8	1	25.0	0	0.0	15	0
DON NARCISSE												
1995	SAS	2	2	100.0	78	39.0	1	50.0	0	0.0	45	
BILL NEALE												
1946	TOR						1					
BARRICK NEALY												
2007	CAL	17	5	29.4	91	5.4	0	0.0	0	0.0	34	1
2008	CAL	12	5	41.7	32	2.7	0	0.0	0	0.0	16	5
2009	CAL	10	6	60.0	72	7.2	2	20.0	0	0.0	25	1
Totals		39	16	41.0	195	5.0	2	5.1	0	0.0	34	7
PETE NEFT												
1958	BC	1	1	100.0	15	15.0	0	0.0	0	0.0	15	
STEVE NEMETH												
1948	MTL						4					
BJORN NITTMO												
1994	SHR	1	0	0.0	0	0.0	0	0.0	1	100.0		
KENDRICK NORD												
1997	HAM	5	0	0.0	0	0.0	0	0.0	0	0.0		
MIKE NOTT												
1977	SAS	15	4	26.7	70	4.7	0	0.0	2	13.3	32	
1979	BC	27	16	59.3	376	13.9	2	7.4	1	3.7	106	
1980	BC	43	20	46.5	383	8.9	3	7.0	3	7.0	64	
Totals		85	40	47.1	829	9.8	5	5.9	6	7.1	106	
DOUG NUSSMEIER												
2000	BC	94	54	57.4	768	8.2	6	6.4	2	2.1	41	7
BOB O'BILLOVICH												
1963	OTT	10	5	50.0	69	6.9	0	0.0	1	10.0	17	2
1964	OTT	5	1	20.0	3	0.6	0	0.0	1	20.0	3	0
1966	OTT	1	1	100.0	10	10.0	0	0.0	0	0.0	10	0
Totals		16	7	43.8	82	5.1	0	0.0	2	12.5	17	2

Year	Team	ATT	COM	COM%	YDS	AVG	TD	TD%	INT	INT%	LG	SK
PETE OHLER												
1963	BC	11	5	45.5	57	5.2	0	0.0	0	0.0	15	3
1964	BC	5	3	60.0	46	9.2	0	0.0	1	20.0	43	1
1967	BC	16	8	50.0	111	6.9	1	6.3	2	12.5	40	
1968	BC	153	93	60.8	1037	6.8	3	2.0	11	7.2	62	
1969	BC	13	6	46.2	56	4.3	0	0.0	2	15.4	20	
Totals		198	115	58.1	1307	6.6	4	2.0	16	8.1	62	4
CLIFF OLANDER												
1982	EDM	39	22	56.4	357	9.2	3	7.7	3	7.7	38	
HUGH OLDHAM												
1970	OTT	1	0	0.0	0	0.0	0	0.0	1	100.0		
JOHN O'LEARY												
1977	MTL	2	1	50.0	24	12.0	0	0.0	0	0.0	24	
TOM O'MALLEY												
1951	OTT						20					
1952	OTT						19					
1953	OTT						22					
Totals							61					
GERRY ORGAN												
1976	OTT	2	1	50.0	0	0.0	0	0.0	0	0.0	0	
1979	OTT	3	2	66.7	39	13.0	0	0.0	0	0.0	23	
1981	OTT	1	0	0.0	0	0.0	0	0.0	0	0.0		
1982	OTT	1	1	100.0	6	6.0	0	0.0	0	0.0	6	
Totals		7	4	57.1	45	6.4	0	0.0	0	0.0	23	
GUS ORNSTEIN												
2002	BC	2	1	50.0	12	6.0	0	0.0	0	0.0	12	
PAUL OSBALDISTON												
1986	HAM	1	1	100.0	-8	-8.0	0	0.0	0	0.0	-8	
1986	Year	1	1	100.0	-8	-8.0	0	0.0	0	0.0	-8	
1988	HAM	1	0	0.0	0	0.0	0	0.0	0	0.0		
2000	HAM	1	1	100.0	15	15.0	0	0.0	0	0.0	15	0
2001	HAM	1	0	0.0	0	0.0	0	0.0	0	0.0		
Totals		4	2	50.0	7	1.8	0	0.0	0	0.0	15	0
CHAD OWENS												
2010	TOR	1	1	100.0	37	37.0	0	0.0	0	0.0	37	0
JIM PACE												
1963	HAM	1	0	0.0	0	0.0	0	0.0	0	0.0		0
BOB PAFFRATH												
1948	OTT						8					
1949	OTT						13					
1950	EDM	4	3	75.0	40	10.0	2	50.0	0	0.0		
Totals		4	3	75.0	40	10.0	23	50.0	0	0.0		
BILL PALMER												
1977	CAL	2	2	100.0	30	15.0	0	0.0	0	0.0	16	
BRIAN PALMER												
1965	WPG	2	0	0.0	0	0.0	0	0.0	1	50.0		
PAUL PALMER												
1960	HAM	1	0	0.0	0	0.0	0	0.0	0	0.0		
DON PANCIERA												
1953	TOR						1					
ROD PANTAGES												
1956	SAS	1	0	0.0	0	0.0	0	0.0	0	0.0		
JOE PAOPAO												
1979	BC	223	126	56.5	1508	6.8	7	3.1	13	5.8	84	
1980	BC	231	145	62.8	2009	8.7	15	6.5	13	5.6	67	
1981	BC	421	229	54.4	3777	9.0	28	6.7	23	5.5	91	
1982	BC	214	115	53.7	1394	6.5	10	4.7	12	5.6	66	
1983	BC	147	85	57.8	968	6.6	2	1.4	11	7.5	34	
1984	SAS	453	260	57.4	3270	7.2	12	2.6	19	4.2	94	
1985	SAS	447	270	60.4	3420	7.7	9	2.0	20	4.5	54	
1986	SAS	363	207	57.0	2647	7.3	13	3.6	24	6.6	60	
1987	OTT	285	147	51.6	1629	5.7	7	2.5	15	5.3	51	
1990	BC	224	137	61.2	1852	8.3	14	6.3	7	3.1	77	
Totals		3008	1721	57.2	22474	7.5	117	3.9	157	5.2	94	
TYLER PAOPAO												
2004	OTT	1	1	100.0	1	1.0	0	0.0	0	0.0	1	0
BOB PAREMORE												
1966	MTL	1	0	0.0	0	0.0	0	0.0	1	100.0		0
BABE PARILLI												
1959	OTT	52	23	44.2	373	7.2	4	7.7	4	7.7	55	1
ANTHONY PARKER												
1988	BC	2	0	0.0	0	0.0	0	0.0	1	50.0		
JACKIE PARKER												
1954	EDM	55	36	65.5	558	10.1	2	3.6	3	5.5		
1955	EDM	120	48	40.0	775	6.5	6	5.0	6	5.0	55	
1956	EDM	226	117	51.8	1889	8.4	11	4.9	16	7.1	55	
1957	EDM	135	70	51.9	1250	9.3	3	2.2	11	8.1	85	
1958	EDM	241	124	51.5	1908	7.9	8	3.3	16	6.6	85	
1959	EDM	143	80	55.9	1207	8.4	8	5.6	9	6.3	57	
1960	EDM	179	92	51.4	1613	9.0	6	3.4	10	5.6	68	11
1961	EDM	184	92	50.0	1405	7.6	11	6.0	13	7.1	53	
1962	EDM	201	110	54.7	1532	7.6	15	7.5	9	4.5	57	
1963	TOR	219	115	52.5	1603	7.3	7	3.2	7	3.2	56	18
1964	TOR	233	137	58.8	1841	7.9	10	4.3	15	6.4	71	25
1965	TOR	34	14	41.2	169	5.0	1	2.9	3	8.8	31	6
1968	BC	91	54	59.3	726	8.0	0	0.0	5	5.5	54	
Totals		2061	1089	52.8	16476	8.0	88	4.3	123	6.0	85	60
LUI PASSAGLIA												
1976	BC	2	1	50.0	18	9.0	0	0.0	0	0.0	18	
1977	BC	2	1	50.0	11	5.5	0	0.0	0	0.0	11	
1978	BC	2	1	50.0	9	4.5	0	0.0	0	0.0	9	
1980	BC	2	1	50.0	8	4.0	0	0.0	0	0.0	8	
1982	BC	1	1	100.0	17	17.0	0	0.0	0	0.0	17	
1983	BC	2	0	0.0	0	0.0	0	0.0	1	50.0		
1984	BC	2	2	100.0	26	13.0	0	0.0	0	0.0	14	
1986	BC	2	1	50.0	26	13.0	0	0.0	1	50.0	26	
1987	BC	4	2	50.0	23	5.8	0	0.0	0	0.0	15	
1989	BC	4	3	75.0	130	32.5	1	25.0	0	0.0	89	
1990	BC	1	1	100.0	25	25.0	0	0.0	0	0.0	25	
1991	BC	1	0	0.0	0	0.0	0	0.0	1	100.0		
1992	BC	2	0	0.0	0	0.0	0	0.0	0	0.0		
1993	BC	1	1	100.0	12	12.0	0	0.0	0	0.0	12	

Year	Team	ATT	COM	COM%	YDS	AVG	TD	TD%	INT	INT%	LG	SK
1994	BC	1	1	100.0	4	4.0	0	0.0	0	0.0	4	
1996	BC	2	2	100.0	95	47.5	0	0.0	0	0.0	57	
1997	BC	2	1	50.0	-3	-1.5	0	0.0	1	50.0	-3	
1998	BC	1	1	100.0	17	17.0	0	0.0	0	0.0	17	0
1999	BC	1	1	100.0	20	20.0	0	0.0	0	0.0	20	0
2000	BC	4	3	75.0	40	10.0	0	0.0	0	0.0	23	0
Totals		39	24	61.5	478	12.3	1	2.6	4	10.3	89	0
TONY PASSANDER												
1970	MTL	102	49	48.0	664	6.5	3	2.9	5	4.9	59	
GABE PATTERSON												
1948	SAS						1					
HAL PATTERSON												
1957	MTL	10	5	50.0	154	15.4	1	10.0	2	20.0	76	
1958	MTL	1	0	0.0	0	0.0	0	0.0	0	0.0		
Totals		11	5	45.5	154	14.0	1	9.1	2	18.2	76	
LLOYD PATTERSON												
1979	SAS	113	40	35.4	533	4.7	1	0.9	12	10.6	70	
CORY PAUS												
2003	CAL	28	11	39.3	107	3.8	0	0.0	0	0.0	35	
MIKE PAWLAWSKI												
1995	SHR	4	1	25.0	12	3.0	0	0.0	0	0.0	12	
BOB PEARCE												
1970	SAS	2	2	100.0	43	21.5	0	0.0	0	0.0	25	
1971	SAS	3	1	33.3	12	4.0	0	0.0	0	0.0	12	
1972	SAS	4	2	50.0	114	28.5	1	25.0	0	0.0	91	
1973	SAS	7	1	14.3	11	1.6	0	0.0	0	0.0	11	
1974	SAS	2	1	50.0	42	21.0	0	0.0	0	0.0	42	
1975	BC	1	0	0.0	0	0.0	0	0.0	0	0.0		
Totals		19	7	36.8	222	11.7	1	5.3	0	0.0	91	
RAY PELFREY												
1954	WPG	1	0	0.0	0	0.0	0	0.0	1	100.0		
STEVE PELLUER												
1995	WPG	17	9	52.9	112	6.6	1	5.9	1	5.9	33	
BRUCE PERKINS												
1993	HAM	1	1	100.0	54	54.0	0	0.0	0	0.0	54	
CHARLIE PETERSON												
2005	TOR	21	11	52.4	106	5.0	1	4.8	3	14.3	25	1
PETE PETROW												
1950	WPG	53	18	34.0	290	5.5	3	5.7	7	13.2		
1951	WPG	51	17	33.3	272	5.3	3	5.9	4	7.8		
Totals		104	35	33.7	562	5.4	6	5.8	11	10.6		
LEIF PETTERSEN												
1981	HAM	2	2	100.0	31	15.5	0	0.0	0	0.0	26	
TOMMY PHARR												
1972	WPG	27	9	33.3	203	7.5	1	3.7	2	7.4	69	
1973	WPG	9	2	22.2	13	1.4	0	0.0	2	22.2	7	
Totals		36	11	30.6	216	6.0	1	2.8	4	11.1	69	
LAWRENCE PHILLIPS												
2002	MTL	1	0	0.0	0	0.0	0	0.0	0	0.0		
CORY PHILPOT												
1994	BC	1	1	100.0	5	5.0	1	100.0	0	0.0	5	
RAYMOND PHILYAW												
1997	WPG	17	10	58.8	81	4.8	1	5.9	1	5.9	26	
CODY PICKETT												
2008	TOR	104	63	60.6	610	5.9	1	1.0	2	1.9	27	7
2009	TOR	235	145	61.7	1553	6.6	3	1.3	3	1.3	62	19
Totals		339	208	61.4	2163	6.4	4	1.2	5	1.5	62	26
BUCK PIERCE												
2005	BC	71	43	60.6	679	9.6	3	4.2	1	1.4	54	9
2006	BC	186	137	73.7	1752	9.4	11	5.9	6	3.2	67	19
2007	BC	127	81	63.8	1013	8.0	5	3.9	3	2.4	35	9
2008	BC	362	232	64.1	3018	8.3	19	5.2	9	2.5	79	6
2009	BC	315	199	63.2	2272	7.2	10	3.2	12	3.8	62	27
2010	WPG	120	80	66.7	1080	9.0	6	5.0	4	3.3	90	8
2011	WPG	411	261	63.5	3348	8.1	14	3.4	16	3.9	92	37
Totals		1592	1033	64.9	13162	8.3	68	4.3	51	3.2	92	115
DON PINHEY												
1955	OTT	1	0	0.0	0	0.0	0	0.0	0	0.0		
1956	OTT	2	1	50.0	11	5.5	0	0.0	0	0.0	11	
Totals		3	1	33.3	11	3.7	0	0.0	0	0.0	11	
JOE PISARCIK												
1974	CAL	168	87	51.8	1087	6.5	5	3.0	3	1.8	62	
1975	CAL	320	181	56.6	2252	7.0	18	5.6	15	4.7	52	
1976	CAL	163	96	58.9	1128	6.9	2	1.2	9	5.5	36	
Totals		651	364	55.9	4467	6.9	25	3.8	27	4.1	62	
STEVE PISARKIEWICZ												
1982	WPG	3	0	0.0	0	0.0	0	0.0	0	0.0		
ALAN PITCAITHLE												
1970	EDM	1	0	0.0	0	0.0	0	0.0	0	0.0		
ALLEN PITTS												
2000	CAL	1	1	100.0	25	25.0	1	100.0	0	0.0	25	0
SCOTT PLAYER												
1995	BIR	2	1	50.0	53	26.5	0	0.0	0	0.0	53	
KENNY PLOEN												
1957	WPG	140	74	52.9	1284	9.2	10	7.1	8	5.7	71	
1958	WPG	77	33	42.9	626	8.1	4	5.2	5	6.5	61	
1959	WPG	56	30	53.6	467	8.3	3	5.4	4	7.1	65	
1960	WPG	201	103	51.2	1693	8.4	12	6.0	17	8.5	78	12
1961	WPG	96	50	52.1	905	9.4	5	5.2	4	4.2	75	
1962	WPG	208	137	65.9	2097	10.1	17	8.2	4	1.9	66	
1963	WPG	226	132	58.4	2026	9.0	14	6.2	15	6.6	70	26
1964	WPG	239	132	55.2	1878	7.9	12	5.0	13	5.4	67	30
1965	WPG	213	124	58.2	1789	8.4	15	7.0	14	6.6	53	
1966	WPG	257	153	59.5	2323	9.0	16	6.2	11	4.3	96	29
1967	WPG	203	116	57.1	1382	6.8	11	5.4	11	5.4	49	
Totals		1916	1084	56.6	16470	8.6	119	6.2	106	5.5	96	97
AL POLLARD												
1954	BC	11	4	36.4	95	8.6	0	0.0	2	18.2		
1955	BC	1	0	0.0	0	0.0	0	0.0	0	0.0		
Totals		12	4	33.3	95	7.9	0	0.0	2	16.7		
ALEX PONTON												
1954	TOR	2	2	100.0	28	14.0	0	0.0	0	0.0	19	

Year	Team	ATT	COM	COM%	YDS	AVG	TD	TD%	INT	INT%	LG	SK
JOE POPLAWSKI												
1978	WPG	1	0	0.0	0	0.0	0	0.0	1	100.0		
TOM PORRAS												
1985	HAM	17	12	70.6	134	7.9	0	0.0	1	5.9	28	
1986	HAM	1	1	100.0	16	16.0	0	0.0	0	0.0	16	
1987	HAM	406	242	59.6	3293	8.1	18	4.4	17	4.2	81	
1988	HAM	330	170	51.5	2172	6.6	13	3.9	16	4.8	62	
1989	CAL	151	69	45.7	1011	6.7	5	3.3	9	6.0	63	
1990	TOR	81	45	55.6	650	8.0	4	4.9	5	6.2	88	
1990	CAL	9	3	33.3	52	5.8	0	0.0	0	0.0	42	
1990	Year	90	48	53.3	702	7.8	4	4.4	5	5.6	88	
1993	WPG	10	6	60.0	127	12.7	1	10.0	0	0.0	54	
1994	WPG	21	9	42.9	90	4.3	2	9.5	2	9.5	36	
Totals		1026	557	54.3	7545	7.4	43	4.2	50	4.9	88	
QUINTON PORTER												
2008	HAM	177	118	66.7	1496	8.5	10	5.6	4	2.3	86	20
2009	HAM	261	167	64.0	1762	6.8	6	2.3	8	3.1	48	30
2010	HAM	21	10	47.6	148	7.0	1	4.8	2	9.5	31	5
2011	HAM	102	63	61.8	689	6.8	4	3.9	4	3.9	38	10
Totals		561	358	63.8	4095	7.3	21	3.7	18	3.2	86	65
ROLLIN PRATHER												
1950	EDM	1	1	100.0	13	13.0	0	0.0	0	0.0	13	
NOEL PREFONTAINE												
1999	TOR	2	1	50.0	29	14.5	0	0.0	0	0.0	29	0
2002	TOR	2	0	0.0	0	0.0	0	0.0	0	0.0		0
2003	TOR	2	1	50.0	16	8.0	0	0.0	0	0.0	16	0
2004	TOR	1	1	100.0	21	21.0	0	0.0	0	0.0	21	0
2005	TOR	3	1	33.3	28	9.3	0	0.0	0	0.0	28	0
2006	TOR	1	1	100.0	8	8.0	0	0.0	0	0.0	8	0
2007	TOR	1	1	100.0	11	11.0	0	0.0	0	0.0	11	0
2008	EDM	1	1	100.0	19	19.0	0	0.0	0	0.0	19	0
2009	EDM	1	0	0.0	0	0.0	0	0.0	1	100.0		0
2010	EDM	1	1	100.0	5	5.0	0	0.0	0	0.0	5	0
2011	TOR	5	3	60.0	92	18.4	0	0.0	2	40.0	39	0
Totals		20	11	55.0	229	11.5	0	0.0	3	15.0	39	0
KEN PRESTON												
1946	SAS						3					
CASEY PRINTERS												
2003	BC	2	1	50.0	4	2.0	1	50.0	0	0.0	4	1
2004	BC	494	325	65.8	5088	10.3	35	7.1	10	2.0	102	46
2005	BC	216	131	60.6	1671	7.7	9	4.2	6	2.8	75	19
2007	HAM	133	68	51.1	774	5.8	1	0.8	4	3.0	42	14
2008	HAM	223	124	55.6	1693	7.6	5	2.2	10	4.5	67	24
2009	BC	68	43	63.2	686	10.1	3	4.4	2	2.9	60	4
2010	BC	237	129	54.4	1731	7.3	10	4.2	6	2.5	58	24
Totals		1373	821	59.8	11647	8.5	64	4.7	38	2.8	102	132
WILL PROCTOR												
2008	CAL	1	1	100.0	49	49.0	0	0.0	0	0.0	49	0
MEL PROFIT												
1970	TOR	2	1	50.0	75	37.5	1	50.0	1	50.0	75	
1971	TOR	1	1	100.0	46	46.0	0	0.0	0	0.0	46	
Totals		3	2	66.7	121	40.3	1	33.3	1	33.3	75	
BOB PTACEK												
1960	SAS	178	99	55.6	1469	8.3	7	3.9	9	5.1	49	25
1961	SAS	52	29	55.8	317	6.1	0	0.0	5	9.6	35	
1962	SAS	206	125	60.7	2317	11.2	15	7.3	10	4.9	104	
1963	SAS	24	12	50.0	131	5.5	1	4.2	2	8.3	28	3
1964	SAS	65	34	52.3	413	6.4	2	3.1	8	12.3	75	7
Totals		525	299	57.0	4647	8.9	25	4.8	34	6.5	104	35
CHARLES PULERI												
1993	SAC	2	0	0.0	0	0.0	0	0.0	0	0.0		
DOUG PYZER												
1950	EDM	2	1	50.0	46	23.0	1	50.0	0	0.0	46	
BERNARD QUARLES												
1983	CAL	323	179	55.4	2841	8.8	17	5.3	19	5.9	57	
1984	CAL	177	92	52.0	1341	7.6	6	3.4	9	5.1	86	
1985	OTT	101	50	49.5	635	6.3	1	1.0	6	5.9	60	
1986	SAS	201	109	54.2	1672	8.3	6	3.0	6	3.0	85	
Totals		802	430	53.6	6489	8.1	30	3.7	40	5.0	86	
MIKE QUINN												
2006	WPG	62	33	53.2	355	5.7	3	4.8	5	8.1	34	
WARREN RABB												
1963	MTL	103	47	45.6	723	7.0	5	4.9	7	6.8	52	4
MIKE RAE												
1973	TOR	33	16	48.5	304	9.2	2	6.1	3	9.1	80	
1974	TOR	352	171	48.6	2501	7.1	15	4.3	19	5.4	74	
1975	TOR	112	64	57.1	770	6.9	4	3.6	8	7.1	46	
Totals		497	251	50.5	3575	7.2	21	4.2	30	6.0	80	
DAVE RAIMEY												
1966	WPG	2	0	0.0	0	0.0	0	0.0	1	50.0		0
1967	WPG	1	0	0.0	0	0.0	0	0.0	0	0.0		
1969	TOR	1	1	100.0	35	35.0	0	0.0	0	0.0	35	
1969	Year	1	1	100.0	35	35.0	0	0.0	0	0.0	35	
1970	TOR	2	0	0.0	0	0.0	0	0.0	1	50.0		
Totals		6	1	16.7	35	5.8	0	0.0	2	33.3	35	0
BRETT RALPH												
2007	CAL	2	1	50.0	39	19.5	1	50.0	0	0.0	39	0
BRYAN RANDALL												
2008	WPG	22	9	40.9	99	4.5	0	0.0	1	4.5	33	0
2009	WPG	20	6	30.0	58	2.9	0	0.0	4	20.0	16	1
Totals		42	15	35.7	157	3.7	0	0.0	5	11.9	33	1
JOSH RANEK												
2005	OTT	1	0	0.0	0	0.0	0	0.0	0	0.0		0
BRIAN RANSOM												
1986	MTL	494	247	50.0	3204	6.5	9	1.8	25	5.1	74	32
GEORGE RATTERMAN												
1951	MTL						11					
RICKY RAY												
2002	EDM	359	227	63.2	2991	8.3	24	6.7	9	2.5	70	17
2003	EDM	515	348	67.6	4640	9.0	35	6.8	13	2.5	72	18
2005	EDM	715	479	67.0	5510	7.7	25	3.5	24	3.4	105	37
2006	EDM	618	406	65.7	5000	8.1	21	3.4	18	2.9	69	40

Year	Team	ATT	COM	COM%	YDS	AVG	TD	TD%	INT	INT%	LG	SK
2007	EDM	445	311	69.9	3652	8.2	22	4.9	10	2.2	75	27
2008	EDM	605	422	69.8	5663	9.4	26	4.3	17	2.8	66	35
2009	EDM	596	401	67.3	4916	8.2	22	3.7	12	2.0	68	27
2010	EDM	448	288	64.3	3565	8.0	11	2.5	16	3.6	70	30
2011	EDM	526	343	65.2	4594	8.7	24	4.6	11	2.1	75	41
Totals		4827	3225	66.8	40531	8.4	210	4.4	130	2.7	105	272
JOHN RAYBORN												
1999	SAS	26	8	30.8	106	4.1	0	0.0	3	11.5	18	
2000	SAS	8	3	37.5	31	3.9	0	0.0	0	0.0	15	
Totals		34	11	32.4	137	4.0	0	0.0	3	8.8	18	
STEPHEN REAVES												
2009	TOR	56	33	58.9	331	5.9	1	1.8	6	10.7	46	
WILLARD REAVES												
1985	WPG	2	2	100.0	78	39.0	0	0.0	0	0.0	47	
BILL REDELL												
1964	EDM	120	67	55.8	920	7.7	4	3.3	5	4.2	88	4
1965	EDM	175	114	65.1	1633	9.3	8	4.6	12	6.9	75	
1966	EDM	69	37	53.6	426	6.2	2	2.9	6	8.7	40	8
1968	HAM	14	10	71.4	86	6.1	0	0.0	1	7.1	26	
1969	CAL	69	40	58.0	533	7.7	2	2.9	6	8.7	45	
Totals		447	268	60.0	3598	8.0	16	3.6	30	6.7	88	12
GEORGE REED												
1964	SAS	3	3	100.0	30	10.0	1	33.3	0	0.0	16	0
1965	SAS	5	0	0.0	0	0.0	0	0.0	0	0.0		
1966	SAS	3	1	33.3	26	8.7	0	0.0	0	0.0	26	1
1967	SAS	4	2	50.0	65	16.3	0	0.0	0	0.0	42	
1969	SAS	1	0	0.0	0	0.0	0	0.0	0	0.0		
Totals		16	6	37.5	121	7.6	1	6.3	0	0.0	42	1
MATTHEW REED												
1976	TOR	159	72	45.3	1096	6.9	8	5.0	10	6.3	82	
1977	TOR	18	4	22.2	48	2.7	0	0.0	2	11.1	20	
1977	CAL	112	48	42.9	708	6.3	3	2.7	6	5.4	74	
1977	Year	130	52	40.0	756	5.8	3	2.3	8	6.2	74	
1978	CAL	14	9	64.3	93	6.6	0	0.0	0	0.0	17	
Totals		303	133	43.9	1945	6.4	11	3.6	18	5.9	82	
RON REEVES												
1983	MTL	155	75	48.4	999	6.4	7	4.5	10	6.5	82	
FRED REID												
2008	WPG	1	0	0.0	0	0.0	0	0.0	1	100.0		0
MIKE REILLY												
2011	BC	2	1	50.0	12	6.0	0	0.0	0	0.0	12	0
MIKE RENAUD												
2010	WPG	2	1	50.0	27	13.5	0	0.0	0	0.0	27	0
GILBERT RENFROE												
1986	OTT	139	72	51.8	1051	7.6	7	5.0	9	6.5	65	16
1987	TOR	232	111	47.8	1686	7.3	9	3.9	4	1.7	54	
1988	TOR	527	290	55.0	4113	7.8	26	4.9	24	4.6	78	
1989	TOR	249	119	47.8	1335	5.4	1	0.4	13	5.2	48	
1991	CAL	125	61	48.8	897	7.2	5	4.0	2	1.6	56	
1992	BC	24	4	16.7	59	2.5	0	0.0	3	12.5	24	
Totals		1296	657	50.7	9141	7.1	48	3.7	55	4.2	78	16
BILLY REYNOLDS												
1959	HAM	1	0	0.0	0	0.0	0	0.0	1	100.0		0
M.C. REYNOLDS												
1963	SAS	12	4	33.3	53	4.4	0	0.0	1	8.3	21	3
BILL RHODES												
1957	TOR	1	1	100.0	21	21.0	0	0.0	0	0.0	21	
JERRY RHOME												
1972	MTL	11	3	27.3	40	3.6	0	0.0	1	9.1	20	
TONY RICE												
1990	SAS	5	2	40.0	40	8.0	0	0.0	0	0.0	23	
JAMEL RICHARDSON												
2010	MTL	1	0	0.0	0	0.0	0	0.0	0	0.0		0
MIKE RINGER												
1966	SAS	10	3	30.0	55	5.5	0	0.0	0	0.0	27	0
DAVID RIVERS												
2001	BC	5	3	60.0	37	7.4	0	0.0	1	20.0	20	0
2002	TOR	6	2	33.3	20	3.3	0	0.0	2	33.3	18	
Totals		11	5	45.5	57	5.2	0	0.0	3	27.3	20	0
CHARLES ROBERTS												
2005	WPG	2	1	50.0	35	17.5	0	0.0	1	50.0	35	0
2008	WPG	1	0	0.0	0	0.0	0	0.0	0	0.0		0
Totals		3	1	33.3	35	11.7	0	0.0	1	33.3	35	0
GENE ROBERTS												
1954	OTT	13	6	46.2	79	6.1	0	0.0	3	23.1	32	
GENE ROBILLARD												
1954	BC	42	16	38.1	161	3.8	0	0.0	6	14.3		
BILLY ROBINSON												
1975	OTT	15	6	40.0	78	5.2	1	6.7	1	6.7	20	
1976	OTT	9	4	44.4	33	3.7	0	0.0	2	22.2	14	
Totals		24	10	41.7	111	4.6	1	4.2	3	12.5	20	
LARRY ROBINSON												
1961	CAL	0	0		0		0		0			
1962	CAL	1	0	0.0	0	0.0	0	0.0	0	0.0		0
Totals		1	0	0.0	0	0.0	0	0.0	0	0.0		0
JOHNNY RODGERS												
1974	MTL	1	0	0.0	0	0.0	0	0.0	1	100.0		
1975	MTL	5	0	0.0	0	0.0	0	0.0	1	20.0		
Totals		6	0	0.0	0	0.0	0	0.0	2	33.3		
MIKE RODRIGUE												
1982	MTL	1	0	0.0	0	0.0	0	0.0	0	0.0		
JOHN ROGAN												
1983	MTL	25	12	48.0	108	4.3	0	0.0	2	8.0	25	
JIM ROOT												
1954	OTT	137	50	36.5	835	6.1	3	2.2	15	10.9	87	
BARRY ROSEBOROUGH												
1956	WPG	10	5	50.0	70	7.0	0	0.0	0	0.0	25	
1957	WPG	31	17	54.8	236	7.6	2	6.5	4	12.9	36	
1958	WPG	31	11	35.5	220	7.1	1	3.2	4	12.9	68	
Totals		72	33	45.8	526	7.3	3	4.2	8	11.1	68	
TIMM ROSENBACH												
1994	HAM	294	155	52.7	2083	7.1	10	3.4	10	3.4	69	

Year	Team	ATT	COM	COM%	YDS	AVG	TD	TD%	INT	INT%	LG	SK
TOBIN ROTE												
1960	TOR	450	256	56.9	4247	9.4	38	8.4	25	5.6	103	
1961	TOR	389	220	56.6	3093	8.0	16	4.1	16	4.1	108	17
1962	TOR	348	187	53.7	2532	7.3	12	3.4	17	4.9	75	
Totals		1187	663	55.9	9872	8.3	66	5.6	58	4.9	108	17
TOM ROZANTZ												
1980	SAS	40	19	47.5	236	5.9	2	5.0	0	0.0	31	
1980	HAM	40	19	47.5	286	7.2	2	5.0	4	10.0	29	
1980	Year	80	38	47.5	522	6.5	4	5.0	4	5.0	31	
1981	TOR	28	12	42.9	215	7.7	1	3.6	2	7.1	55	
Totals		108	50	46.3	737	6.8	5	4.6	6	5.6	55	
T.J. RUBLEY												
1998	WPG	240	141	58.8	1504	6.3	4	1.7	12	5.0	49	
1998	HAM	17	7	41.2	71	4.2	0	0.0	0	0.0	22	
1998	Year	257	148	57.6	1575	6.1	4	1.6	12	4.7	49	
BERNIE RUOFF												
1980	HAM	1	1	100.0	18	18.0	0	0.0	0	0.0	18	
1982	HAM	1	1	100.0	12	12.0	0	0.0	0	0.0	12	
1983	HAM	1	1	100.0	36	36.0	0	0.0	0	0.0	36	
Totals		3	3	100.0	66	22.0	0	0.0	0	0.0	36	
ED RUTKOWSKI												
1969	MTL	4	1	25.0	43	10.8	0	0.0	1	25.0	43	
JON RYAN												
2004	WPG	1	0	0.0	0	0.0	0	0.0	0	0.0		0
HEATH RYLANCE												
1996	SAS	72	37	51.4	614	8.5	0	0.0	3	4.2	79	
1998	SAS	49	21	42.9	305	6.2	1	2.0	2	4.1	46	
Totals		121	58	47.9	919	7.6	1	0.8	5	4.1	79	
SEAN SALISBURY												
1988	WPG	202	100	49.5	1566	7.8	11	5.4	5	2.5	72	
1989	WPG	595	293	49.2	4049	6.8	26	4.4	26	4.4	94	
Totals		797	393	49.3	5615	7.0	37	4.6	31	3.9	94	
LEE SALTZ												
1988	WPG	23	11	47.8	157	6.8	1	4.3	2	8.7	41	
1989	WPG	77	32	41.6	398	5.2	2	2.6	5	6.5	52	
1993	HAM	33	18	54.5	281	8.5	1	3.0	2	6.1	64	
Totals		133	61	45.9	836	6.3	4	3.0	9	6.8	64	
OTEMAN SAMPSON												
1999	CAL	2	1	50.0	10	5.0	0	0.0	0	0.0	10	0
2000	TOR	35	19	54.3	157	4.5	0	0.0	2	5.7	37	4
2000	Year	35	19	54.3	157	4.5	0	0.0	2	5.7	37	4
2002	OTT	72	43	59.7	426	5.9	1	1.4	1	1.4	25	
Totals		109	63	57.8	593	5.4	1	0.9	3	2.8	37	4
EROS SANCHEZ												
1993	HAM	42	18	42.9	251	6.0	1	2.4	1	2.4	33	
1994	SHR	4	1	25.0	12	3.0	0	0.0	1	25.0	12	
Totals		46	19	41.3	263	5.7	1	2.2	2	4.3	33	
BOB SANDBERG												
1947	WPG						1					
1948	WPG						3					
1949	WPG						1					
Totals							5					
DANNY SANDERS												
1979	SAS	133	65	48.9	1024	7.7	4	3.0	7	5.3	52	
1979	Year	133	65	48.9	1024	7.7	4	3.0	7	5.3	52	
1980	SAS	57	21	36.8	290	5.1	2	3.5	7	12.3	53	
Totals		190	86	45.3	1314	6.9	6	3.2	14	7.4	53	
JIM SANDUSKY												
1985	BC	2	2	100.0	42	21.0	0	0.0	0	0.0	41	
1986	BC	1	0	0.0	0	0.0	0	0.0	0	0.0		
1987	BC	4	2	50.0	65	16.3	0	0.0	0	0.0	49	
1992	EDM	2	1	50.0	18	9.0	0	0.0	0	0.0	18	
1995	EDM	1	0	0.0	0	0.0	0	0.0	0	0.0		
Totals		10	5	50.0	125	12.5	0	0.0	0	0.0	49	
BEN SANKEY												
2000	CAL	4	4	100.0	87	21.8	0	0.0	0	0.0	46	0
2001	CAL	156	93	59.6	1255	8.0	14	9.0	4	2.6	39	20
2002	CAL	78	49	62.8	658	8.4	3	3.8	3	3.8	41	9
2007	CAL	90	62	68.9	818	9.1	5	5.6	2	2.2	50	10
2007	Year	90	62	68.9	818	9.1	5	5.6	2	2.2	50	10
Totals		328	208	63.4	2818	8.6	22	6.7	9	2.7	50	39
RICKY SANTOS												
2010	MTL	13	11	84.6	94	7.2	3	23.1	0	0.0	27	1
DAVE SARETTE												
1962	SAS	50	18	36.0	250	5.0	1	2.0	5	10.0	34	
STEVE SARKISIAN												
1998	SAS	92	52	56.5	604	6.6	4	4.3	4	4.3	39	
1999	SAS	290	165	56.9	2290	7.9	16	5.5	21	7.2	69	
Totals		382	217	56.8	2894	7.6	20	5.2	25	6.5	69	
MIKE SAUNDERS												
1993	SAS	2	2	100.0	48	24.0	0	0.0	0	0.0	28	
1997	TOR	1	0	0.0	0	0.0	0	0.0	0	0.0		
1997	Year	1	0	0.0	0	0.0	0	0.0	0	0.0		
Totals		3	2	66.7	48	16.0	0	0.0	0	0.0	28	
JACK SCARBATH												
1955	OTT	156	74	47.4	1204	7.7	6	3.8	16	10.3	63	
HANK SCHICHTLE												
1967	BC	33	13	39.4	233	7.1	0	0.0	3	9.1	21	
ART SCHLICHTER												
1988	OTT	89	41	46.1	658	7.4	3	3.4	7	7.9	64	
BOB SCHLOREDT												
1961	BC	21	8	38.1	117	5.6	1	4.8	1	4.8	46	
DICK SCHNAIBLE												
1954	OTT	21	9	42.9	171	8.1	1	4.8	2	9.5	85	
JOHN SCHNEIDER												
1968	WPG	327	146	44.6	1949	6.0	8	2.4	28	8.6	48	
1969	WPG	10	3	30.0	13	1.3	0	0.0	0	0.0	13	
Totals		337	149	44.2	1962	5.8	8	2.4	28	8.3	48	
RALPH SCHOENFELD												
1967	WPG	2	0	0.0	0	0.0	0	0.0	0	0.0		
JOHN SCIARRA												
1976	BC	31	8	25.8	105	3.4	2	6.5	2	6.5	43	

Year	Team	ATT	COM	COM%	YDS	AVG	TD	TD%	INT	INT%	LG	SK
GEORGE SCOTT												
1961	HAM	1	1	100.0	8	8.0	0	0.0	0	0.0	8	0
JAMES SCOTT												
1981	MTL	1	0	0.0	0	0.0	0	0.0	0	0.0		
LUTHER SELBO												
1968	WPG	54	23	42.6	380	7.0	0	0.0	8	14.8	72	
NICK SETTA												
2008	HAM	2	2	100.0	33	16.5	0	0.0	0	0.0	21	0
2009	HAM	1	0	0.0	0	0.0	0	0.0	0	0.0		0
Totals		3	2	66.7	33	11.0	0	0.0	0	0.0	21	0
STEVE SHAFER												
1964	BC	8	5	62.5	79	9.9	0	0.0	1	12.5	39	1
1965	BC	14	7	50.0	99	7.1	0	0.0	0	0.0	21	0
Totals		22	12	54.5	178	8.1	0	0.0	1	4.5	39	1
DICK SHATTO												
1954	TOR	13	8	61.5	124	9.5	2	15.4	3	23.1	29	
1955	TOR	3	1	33.3	23	7.7	1	33.3	1	33.3	23	
1956	TOR	1	0	0.0	0	0.0	0	0.0	0	0.0		
1957	TOR	11	5	45.5	173	15.7	2	18.2	1	9.1	73	
1958	TOR	33	17	51.5	190	5.8	1	3.0	4	12.1	20	
1959	TOR	18	8	44.4	127	7.1	1	5.6	0	0.0	38	0
1960	TOR	6	3	50.0	125	20.8	0	0.0	1	16.7	50	
1961	TOR	6	0	0.0	0	0.0	0	0.0	2	33.3		2
1962	TOR	3	3	100.0	59	19.7	3	100.0	0	0.0	26	
1963	TOR	14	9	64.3	188	13.4	2	14.3	1	7.1	42	1
1964	TOR	15	7	46.7	188	12.5	3	20.0	0	0.0	49	2
1965	TOR	1	0	0.0	0	0.0	0	0.0	0	0.0		1
Totals		124	61	49.2	1197	9.7	15	12.1	13	10.5	73	6
BOB SHAW												
1952	CAL	2	1	50.0	10	5.0	1	50.0	0	0.0	10	
RICK SHAW												
1970	WPG	3	2	66.7	19	6.3	0	0.0	0	0.0	21	
1972	HAM	4	3	75.0	22	5.5	0	0.0	0	0.0	8	
Totals		7	5	71.4	41	5.9	0	0.0	0	0.0	21	
CHARLIE SHEPARD												
1958	WPG	3	2	66.7	52	17.3	1	33.3	0	0.0	41	
1959	WPG	1	0	0.0	0	0.0	0	0.0	1	100.0		0
1960	WPG	4	3	75.0	23	5.8	1	25.0	0	0.0	11	0
1961	WPG	1	1	100.0	26	26.0	0	0.0	0	0.0	26	0
Totals		9	6	66.7	101	11.2	2	22.2	1	11.1	41	0
TOM SHERMAN												
1976	CAL	116	59	50.9	596	5.1	3	2.6	4	3.4	58	
LARRY SHERRER												
1974	MTL	1	1	100.0	38	38.0	0	0.0	0	0.0	38	
1976	BC	1	0	0.0	0	0.0	0	0.0	0	0.0		
Totals		2	1	50.0	38	19.0	0	0.0	0	0.0	38	
JOHNNY SHOWALTER												
1946	SAS						1					
TOM SHUMAN												
1976	HAM	11	3	27.3	45	4.1	0	0.0	1	9.1	20	
1977	HAM	71	26	36.6	293	4.1	0	0.0	5	7.0	18	
1978	HAM	107	47	43.9	705	6.6	5	4.7	7	6.5	57	
1978	MTL	29	13	44.8	210	7.2	0	0.0	0	0.0	38	
1978	Year	136	60	44.1	915	6.7	5	3.7	7	5.1	57	
Totals		218	89	40.8	1253	5.7	5	2.3	13	6.0	57	
KELVIN SIMMONS												
1995	BIR	39	26	66.7	292	7.5	3	7.7	1	2.6	36	
GEROY SIMON												
2002	BC	1	1	100.0	71	71.0	1	100.0	0	0.0	71	0
2003	BC	2	1	50.0	52	26.0	1	50.0	0	0.0	52	0
2004	BC	1	0	0.0	0	0.0	0	0.0	0	0.0		0
2010	BC	1	1	100.0	14	14.0	0	0.0	0	0.0	14	0
Totals		5	3	60.0	137	27.4	2	40.0	0	0.0	71	0
BOB SIMPSON												
1957	OTT	1	0	0.0	0	0.0	0	0.0	1	100.0		
CHRIS SKINNER												
1990	BC	2	2	100.0	40	20.0	1	50.0	0	0.0	28	
REGGIE SLACK												
1993	TOR	184	104	56.5	1372	7.5	7	3.8	7	3.8	61	
1994	TOR	63	39	61.9	483	7.7	3	4.8	4	6.3	59	
1994	HAM	155	95	61.3	1313	8.5	8	5.2	7	4.5	102	
1994	Year	218	134	61.5	1796	8.2	11	5.0	11	5.0	102	
1995	BIR	32	18	56.3	184	5.8	0	0.0	1	3.1	41	
1995	WPG	302	159	52.6	2007	6.6	12	4.0	8	2.6	51	
1995	Year	334	177	53.0	2191	6.6	12	3.6	9	2.7	51	
1996	WPG	241	128	53.1	1863	7.7	10	4.1	7	2.9	60	
1997	SAS	326	172	52.8	2423	7.4	9	2.8	13	4.0	86	
1998	SAS	463	287	62.0	3721	8.0	19	4.1	16	3.5	73	
1999	SAS	226	126	55.8	1610	7.1	8	3.5	8	3.5	48	
2002	TOR	155	92	59.4	1055	6.8	7	4.5	3	1.9	46	
2003	HAM	41	21	51.2	142	3.5	1	2.4	1	2.4	18	
Totals		2188	1241	56.7	16173	7.4	84	3.8	75	3.4	102	
LEROY SLEDGE												
1967	BC	1	0	0.0	0	0.0	0	0.0	0	0.0		
IAN SMART												
2007	BC	1	0	0.0	0	0.0	0	0.0	0	0.0		0
ADRION SMITH												
1999	TOR	2	2	100.0	17	8.5	1	50.0	0	0.0	12	
AKILI SMITH												
2007	CAL	47	22	46.8	219	4.7	0	0.0	5	10.6	21	6
DARRELL SMITH												
1987	TOR	1	0	0.0	0	0.0	0	0.0	1	100.0		
DICK SMITH												
1970	MTL	2	1	50.0	8	4.0	1	50.0	1	50.0	8	
1970	WPG	1	1	100.0	31	31.0	0	0.0	0	0.0	31	
1970	Year	3	2	66.7	39	13.0	1	33.3	1	33.3	31	
Totals		3	2	66.7	39	13.0	1	33.3	1	33.3	31	
EDDIE SMITH												
1979	HAM	140	61	43.6	794	5.7	4	2.9	14	10.0	53	
HAROLD SMITH												
1985	SAS	42	18	42.9	208	5.0	1	2.4	4	9.5	26	
1986	SAS	24	9	37.5	127	5.3	0	0.0	2	8.3	40	

Year	Team	ATT	COM	COM%	YDS	AVG	TD	TD%	INT	INT%	LG	SK
Totals		66	27	40.9	335	5.1	1	1.5	6	9.1	40	
JOE BOB SMITH												
1958	EDM	3	2	66.7	48	16.0	0	0.0	0	0.0	29	
KEITH SMITH												
2001	SAS	154	75	48.7	1008	6.5	4	2.6	8	5.2	58	
2003	CAL	3	0	0.0	0	0.0	0	0.0	1	33.3		
Totals		157	75	47.8	1008	6.4	4	2.5	9	5.7	58	
LARRY SMITH												
1973	MTL	2	1	50.0	72	36.0	1	50.0	0	0.0	72	
1974	MTL	1	1	100.0	16	16.0	0	0.0	0	0.0	16	
1975	MTL	2	0	0.0	0	0.0	0	0.0	1	50.0		
1976	MTL	4	2	50.0	25	6.3	1	25.0	1	25.0	17	
Totals		9	4	44.4	113	12.6	2	22.2	2	22.2	72	
STEVE SMITH												
1984	MTL	45	19	42.2	263	5.8	3	6.7	7	15.6	39	
1985	OTT	1	0	0.0	0	0.0	0	0.0	0	0.0		
Totals		46	19	41.3	263	5.7	3	6.5	7	15.2	39	
TERRY SMITH												
1994	SHR	1	0	0.0	0	0.0	0	0.0	0	0.0		
WADDELL SMITH												
1979	EDM	2	1	50.0	36	18.0	1	50.0	0	0.0	36	
1982	EDM	1	1	100.0	27	27.0	1	100.0	0	0.0	27	
1983	EDM	1	0	0.0	0	0.0	0	0.0	0	0.0		
Totals		4	2	50.0	63	15.8	2	50.0	0	0.0	36	
ANDY SOKOL												
1950	WPG	1	0	0.0	0	0.0	0	0.0	1	100.0		
MICHAEL SOLES												
1992	EDM	1	0	0.0	0	0.0	0	0.0	1	100.0		
BUTCH SONGIN												
1953	HAM						10					
1954	HAM	340	187	55.0	2500	7.4	19	5.6	29	8.5	82	
Totals		340	187	55.0	2500	7.4	29	5.6	29	8.5	82	
MIKE SOUZA												
2004	CAL	66	33	50.0	425	6.4	0	0.0	3	4.5	44	
KEITH SPAITH												
1948	CAL						13					
1949	CAL						14					
1950	CAL	263	124	47.1	1920	7.3	6	2.3	13	4.9	55	
1951	CAL	216	116	53.7	1749	8.1	8	3.7	18	8.3	50	
1952	CAL	174	73	42.0	1213	7.0	4	2.3	12	6.9	57	
1953	CAL	151	76	50.3	1113	7.4	4	2.6	13	8.6	66	
1954	CAL	5	2	40.0	22	4.4	0	0.0	1	20.0	11	
Totals		809	391	48.3	6017	7.4	49	2.7	57	7.0	66	
WALLY SPENCER												
1946	MTL						1					
DAVE STALA												
2003	MTL	1	1	100.0	67	67.0	1	100.0	0	0.0	67	0
2004	MTL	1	1	100.0	35	35.0	0	0.0	0	0.0	35	0
2005	MTL	1	1	100.0	39	39.0	0	0.0	0	0.0	39	0
2006	MTL	2	1	50.0	8	4.0	0	0.0	0	0.0	8	0
2009	HAM	1	0	0.0	0	0.0	0	0.0	0	0.0		0
Totals		6	4	66.7	149	24.8	1	16.7	0	0.0	67	0
BRIAN STALLWORTH												
2003	WPG	2	0	0.0	0	0.0	0	0.0	0	0.0		
FRED STAMPS												
2010	EDM	1	0	0.0	0	0.0	0	0.0	0	0.0		0
CHUCK STANLEY												
1961	OTT	1	0	0.0	0	0.0	0	0.0	0	0.0		0
KEVIN STARKEY												
1981	OTT	82	40	48.8	573	7.0	3	3.7	9	11.0	49	
1982	OTT	26	17	65.4	209	8.0	1	3.8	2	7.7	31	
1983	OTT	21	8	38.1	65	3.1	0	0.0	3	14.3	19	
1983	MTL	113	56	49.6	789	7.0	4	3.5	6	5.3	58	
1983	Year	134	64	47.8	854	6.4	40	29.9	9	6.7	58	
Totals		242	121	50.0	1636	6.8	8	3.3	20	8.3	58	
STAN STASICA												
1947	SAS						3					
PETER STENERSON												
1978	OTT	2	2	100.0	57	28.5	1	50.0	0	0.0	48	
1979	OTT	1	0	0.0	0	0.0	0	0.0	0	0.0		
1980	OTT	3	1	33.3	27	9.0	0	0.0	1	33.3	27	
Totals		6	3	50.0	84	14.0	1	16.7	1	16.7	48	
JOHN STEPHANS												
1956	TOR	30	14	46.7	127	4.2	0	0.0	3	10.0	16	
SANDY STEPHENS												
1962	MTL	228	109	47.8	1542	6.8	11	4.8	22	9.6	67	
1963	MTL	54	24	44.4	293	5.4	2	3.7	3	5.6	39	
1963	TOR	126	65	51.6	988	7.8	9	7.1	13	10.3	55	
1963	Year	180	89	49.4	1281	7.1	11	6.1	16	8.9	55	3
Totals		408	198	48.5	2823	6.9	22	5.4	38	9.3	67	0
MARK STEVENS												
1985	MTL	56	28	50.0	377	6.7	2	3.6	4	7.1	75	
1986	MTL	23	11	47.8	107	4.7	0	0.0	1	4.3	41	2
Totals		79	39	49.4	484	6.1	2	2.5	5	6.3	75	2
BILL STEVENSON												
1955	CAL	18	7	38.9	186	10.3	3	16.7	2	11.1	57	
1956	CAL	7	2	28.6	13	1.9	0	0.0	3	42.9	12	
Totals		25	9	36.0	199	8.0	3	12.0	5	20.0	57	
RON STEWART												
1959	OTT	3	2	66.7	62	20.7	1	33.3	0	0.0	40	0
1960	OTT	5	1	20.0	17	3.4	0	0.0	2	40.0	17	
1962	OTT	3	2	66.7	2	0.7	0	0.0	0	0.0	3	
1963	OTT	1	1	100.0	16	16.0	0	0.0	0	0.0	16	0
1964	OTT	5	3	60.0	87	17.4	2	40.0	0	0.0	62	0
1965	OTT	2	0	0.0	0	0.0	0	0.0	0	0.0		0
1966	OTT	5	1	20.0	33	6.6	0	0.0	0	0.0	33	1
1967	OTT	1	0	0.0	0	0.0	0	0.0	1	100.0		
Totals		25	10	40.0	217	8.7	3	12.0	3	12.0	62	1
MARK STOCK												
1995	SA	1	1	100.0	44	44.0	0	0.0	0	0.0	44	
AVATUS STONE												
1953	OTT						1					

Year	Team	ATT	COM	COM%	YDS	AVG	TD	TD%	INT	INT%	LG	SK
1954	OTT	7	3	42.9	63	9.0	0	0.0	1	14.3	48	
1955	OTT	1	0	0.0	0	0.0	0	0.0	0	0.0		
1956	OTT	2	1	50.0	39	19.5	0	0.0	0	0.0	39	
1957	MTL	1	0	0.0	0	0.0	0	0.0	0	0.0		
Totals		11	4	36.4	102	9.3	1	0.0	1	9.1	48	
ERIC STREATER												
1988	BC	2	0	0.0	0	0.0	0	0.0	0	0.0		
1989	BC	1	1	100.0	36	36.0	0	0.0	0	0.0	36	
1991	WPG	1	0	0.0	0	0.0	0	0.0	0	0.0		
Totals		4	1	25.0	36	9.0	0	0.0	0	0.0	36	
JIMMY STREATER												
1980	TOR	24	9	37.5	141	5.9	2	8.3	2	8.3	37	
MIKE STRICKLAND												
1977	BC	2	1	50.0	57	28.5	1	50.0	0	0.0	57	
1978	SAS	1	0	0.0	0	0.0	0	0.0	0	0.0		
Totals		3	1	33.3	57	19.0	1	33.3	0	0.0	57	
BILL STUKUS												
1949	EDM						2					
1950	EDM	43	22	51.2	309	7.2	1	2.3	4	9.3		
1951	EDM	17	4	23.5	67	3.9	0	0.0	1	5.9		
Totals		60	26	43.3	376	6.3	3	1.7	5	8.3		
GLEN SUITOR												
1986	SAS	1	0	0.0	0	0.0	0	0.0	0	0.0		
IAN SUNTER												
1978	TOR	1	0	0.0	0	0.0	0	0.0	0	0.0		
1979	TOR	1	0	0.0	0	0.0	0	0.0	0	0.0		
Totals		2	0	0.0	0	0.0	0	0.0	0	0.0		
DON SUTHERIN												
1961	HAM	2	2	100.0	15	7.5	0	0.0	0	0.0	10	0
1962	HAM	1	0	0.0	0	0.0	0	0.0	0	0.0		
1963	HAM	1	0	0.0	0	0.0	0	0.0	0	0.0		0
1964	HAM	1	0	0.0	0	0.0	0	0.0	0	0.0		0
1965	HAM	1	0	0.0	0	0.0	0	0.0	1	100.0		0
Totals		6	2	33.3	15	2.5	0	0.0	1	16.7	10	0
KARL SWEETAN												
1964	TOR	39	15	38.5	197	5.1	0	0.0	2	5.1	18	4
VERYL SWITZER												
1958	CAL	1	0	0.0	0	0.0	0	0.0	0	0.0		
DAVE SYME												
1972	EDM	88	47	53.4	736	8.4	2	2.3	8	9.1	82	
1976	SAS	27	11	40.7	189	7.0	1	3.7	2	7.4	34	
Totals		115	58	50.4	925	8.0	3	2.6	10	8.7	82	
BILL SYMONS												
1967	TOR	1	1	100.0	38	38.0	1	100.0	0	0.0	38	
1968	TOR	5	0	0.0	0	0.0	0	0.0	0	0.0		
1969	TOR	6	3	50.0	124	20.7	0	0.0	0	0.0	79	
1970	TOR	4	3	75.0	28	7.0	0	0.0	0	0.0	16	
Totals		16	7	43.8	190	11.9	1	6.3	0	0.0	79	
ADAM TAFRALIS												
2008	HAM	39	20	51.3	268	6.9	3	7.7	1	2.6	37	3
2009	HAM	6	3	50.0	47	7.8	1	16.7	0	0.0	36	0
2010	HAM	12	7	58.3	43	3.6	0	0.0	0	0.0	17	0
Totals		57	30	52.6	358	6.3	4	7.0	1	1.8	37	3
JERRY TAGGE												
1977	BC	405	232	57.3	2787	6.9	14	3.5	13	3.2	76	
1978	BC	430	243	56.5	3134	7.3	13	3.0	20	4.7	77	
1979	BC	154	89	57.8	1131	7.3	5	3.2	5	3.2	44	
Totals		989	564	57.0	7052	7.1	32	3.2	38	3.8	77	
DREW TATE												
2009	CAL	11	9	81.8	78	7.1	0	0.0	0	0.0	22	0
2010	CAL	62	44	71.0	521	8.4	7	11.3	0	0.0	39	0
2011	CAL	158	101	63.9	1346	8.5	8	5.1	5	3.2	62	1
Totals		231	154	66.7	1945	8.4	15	6.5	5	2.2	62	0
BOB TAYLOR												
1968	TOR	1	0	0.0	0	0.0	0	0.0	0	0.0		
BRAD TAYLOR												
1985	EDM	6	3	50.0	26	4.3	0	0.0	0	0.0	12	
1986	EDM	13	8	61.5	201	15.5	0	0.0	1	7.7	52	
1987	OTT	54	20	37.0	290	5.4	0	0.0	3	5.6	67	
Totals		73	31	42.5	517	7.1	0	0.0	4	5.5	67	
LARRY TAYLOR												
2011	CAL	1	0	0.0	0	0.0	0	0.0	0			0
STEVE TAYLOR												
1989	EDM	10	3	30.0	35	3.5	0	0.0	0	0.0	14	
1990	EDM	49	29	59.2	367	7.5	4	8.2	4	8.2	49	
1991	CAL	127	69	54.3	980	7.7	7	5.5	8	6.3	87	
1992	CAL	36	23	63.9	285	7.9	2	5.6	0	0.0	29	
1993	CAL	56	28	50.0	402	7.2	5	8.9	1	1.8	54	
1994	CAL	39	23	59.0	409	10.5	4	10.3	1	2.6	40	
1995	HAM	335	191	57.0	2469	7.4	13	3.9	12	3.6	55	
1996	OTT	132	70	53.0	977	7.4	3	2.3	13	9.8	55	
Totals		784	436	55.6	5924	7.6	38	4.8	39	5.0	87	
JEFF TEDFORD												
1983	HAM	34	17	50.0	214	6.3	0	0.0	4	11.8	67	
1984	HAM	12	6	50.0	42	3.5	0	0.0	0	0.0	16	
1985	HAM	86	50	58.1	477	5.5	1	1.2	6	7.0	41	
1986	CAL	34	17	50.0	277	8.1	3	8.8	3	8.8	41	
1987	SAS	7	4	57.1	42	6.0	0	0.0	1	14.3	16	
Totals		173	94	54.3	1052	6.1	4	2.3	14	8.1	67	
TONY TERESA												
1956	BC	61	23	37.7	354	5.8	3	4.9	8	13.1	54	
1957	BC	6	1	16.7	17	2.8	0	0.0	0	0.0	17	
Totals		67	24	35.8	371	5.5	3	4.5	8	11.9	54	
JOE THEISMANN												
1971	TOR	278	148	53.2	2440	8.8	17	6.1	21	7.6	94	
1972	TOR	127	77	60.6	1157	9.1	10	7.9	13	10.2	62	
1973	TOR	274	157	57.3	2496	9.1	13	4.7	13	4.7	100	
Totals		679	382	56.3	6093	9.0	40	5.9	47	6.9	100	
PETE THODOS												
1953	CAL	4	2	50.0	43	10.8	1	25.0	0	0.0	27	
1955	SAS	1	1	100.0	52	52.0	1	100.0	0	0.0	52	
Totals		5	3	60.0	95	19.0	2	40.0	0	0.0	52	

Year	Team	ATT	COM	COM%	YDS	AVG	TD	TD%	INT	INT%	LG	SK
CHARLES THOMAS												
2006	SAS	1	1	100.0	-12	-12.0	0	0.0	0	0.0	-12	0
JIM THOMAS												
1966	EDM	1	0	0.0	0	0.0	0	0.0	0	0.0		0
1967	EDM	2	0	0.0	0	0.0	0	0.0	1	50.0		
1968	EDM	2	1	50.0	13	6.5	0	0.0	0	0.0	13	
1969	EDM	3	1	33.3	42	14.0	1	33.3	0	0.0	42	
Totals		8	2	25.0	55	6.9	1	12.5	1	12.5	42	0
JERRY THOMPKINS												
1960	OTT	1	1	100.0	36	36.0	1	100.0	0	0.0	36	
1961	MTL	113	55	48.7	1163	10.3	6	5.3	15	13.3	94	8
Totals		114	56	49.1	1199	10.5	7	6.1	15	13.2	94	8
BOBBY THOMPSON												
1973	SAS	1	0	0.0	0	0.0	0	0.0	0	0.0		
CHARLES THOMPSON												
1994	SHR	1	0	0.0	0	0.0	0	0.0	0	0.0		
TOMMY THOMPSON												
1953	WPG	68	43	63.2	511	7.5	4	5.9	3	4.4		
BURT THORNTON												
1997	HAM	1	1	100.0	81	81.0	1	100.0	0	0.0	81	
DICK THORNTON												
1961	WPG	12	6	50.0	83	6.9	1	8.3	0	0.0	33	
1962	WPG	5	3	60.0	44	8.8	0	0.0	0	0.0	20	
1963	WPG	9	4	44.4	57	6.3	0	0.0	0	0.0	19	3
1965	WPG	55	16	29.1	314	5.7	2	3.6	5	9.1	39	
1966	WPG	23	9	39.1	115	5.0	1	4.3	3	13.0	32	2
1967	TOR	9	3	33.3	38	4.2	0	0.0	2	22.2	15	
1968	TOR	2	1	50.0	19	9.5	0	0.0	0	0.0	19	
1969	TOR	1	1	100.0	9	9.0	0	0.0	0	0.0	9	
1971	TOR	1	0	0.0	0	0.0	0	0.0	1	100.0		
Totals		117	43	36.8	679	5.8	4	3.4	11	9.4	39	5
JIM THORPE												
1970	TOR	1	1	100.0	41	41.0	0	0.0	0	0.0	41	
1971	WPG	1	1	100.0	34	34.0	0	0.0	0	0.0	34	
1972	WPG	2	2	100.0	79	39.5	0	0.0	0	0.0	48	
Totals		4	4	100.0	154	38.5	0	0.0	0	0.0	48	
BRUCE THREADGILL												
1979	CAL	1	1	100.0	-1	-1.0	0	0.0	0	0.0	-1	
1980	CAL	99	41	41.4	585	5.9	4	4.0	10	10.1	78	
1981	CAL	204	109	53.4	1433	7.0	6	2.9	14	6.9	56	
1982	CAL	121	50	41.3	631	5.2	2	1.7	7	5.8	65	
Totals		425	201	47.3	2648	6.2	12	2.8	31	7.3	78	
BILL TODD												
1951	WPG	8	0	0.0	0	0.0	0	0.0	3	37.5		
1953	SAS	2	1	50.0	12	6.0	1	50.0	0	0.0	12	
1955	SAS	1	0	0.0	0	0.0	0	0.0	0	0.0		
1956	SAS	1	0	0.0	0	0.0	0	0.0	0	0.0		
Totals		12	1	8.3	12	1.0	1	8.3	3	25.0	12	
BILLY JOE TOLLIVER												
1995	SHR	461	273	59.2	3767	8.2	16	3.5	15	3.3	80	
TED TOOGOOD												
1950	TOR						2					
BOB TORRANCE												
1992	CAL	4	3	75.0	33	8.3	0	0.0	0	0.0	12	
1993	HAM	152	78	51.3	837	5.5	3	2.0	12	7.9	47	
Totals		156	81	51.9	870	5.6	3	1.9	12	7.7	47	
LUC TOUSIGNANT												
1982	MTL	174	75	43.1	989	5.7	4	2.3	11	6.3	46	
MICKEY TRIMARKI												
1958	HAM	1	0	0.0	0	0.0	0	0.0	1	100.0		
FRANK TRIPUCKA												
1953	SAS	94	59	62.8	703	7.5	4	4.3	5	5.3		
1954	SAS	259	152	58.7	2003	7.7	14	5.4	14	5.4		
1955	SAS	257	158	61.5	2306	9.0	11	4.3	17	6.6	53	
1956	SAS	383	216	56.4	3274	8.5	18	4.7	22	5.7	67	
1957	SAS	343	172	50.1	2589	7.5	12	3.5	29	8.5	92	
1958	SAS	338	189	55.9	2766	8.2	20	5.9	27	8.0	91	
1959	OTT	145	79	54.5	1119	7.7	4	2.8	14	9.7	57	12
1959	SAS	45	27	60.0	311	6.9	1	2.2	3	6.7	25	
1959	Year	190	106	55.8	1430	7.5	5	2.6	17	8.9	57	
1963	SAS	66	38	57.6	435	6.6	3	4.5	5	7.6	40	8
Totals		1930	1090	56.5	15506	8.0	87	4.5	136	7.0	92	20
BILL TROUP												
1979	WPG	148	81	54.7	963	6.5	3	2.0	8	5.4	53	
RAY TRUANT												
1954	HAM	1	1	100.0	10	10.0	1	100.0	0	0.0	10	
DON TRULL												
1970	EDM	364	185	50.8	2455	6.7	12	3.3	20	5.5	68	
1971	EDM	101	52	51.5	477	4.7	0	0.0	7	6.9	24	
Totals		465	237	51.0	2932	6.3	12	2.6	27	5.8	68	
WHIT TUCKER												
1965	OTT	1	0	0.0	0	0.0	0	0.0	0	0.0		0
ED TUREK												
1966	EDM	1	1	100.0	28	28.0	1	100.0	0	0.0	28	0
1968	HAM	1	0	0.0	0	0.0	0	0.0	0	0.0		
HOWIE TURNER												
1947	OTT						2					
1948	OTT						2					
1949	OTT						2					
1951	OTT						1					
1954	OTT	2	2	100.0	102	51.0	1	50.0	0	0.0	73	
Totals		2	2	100.0	102	51.0	8	50.0	0	0.0	73	
RICKY TURNER												
1985	TOR	155	81	52.3	1023	6.6	4	2.6	9	5.8	53	
GERRY TUTTLE												
1954	BC	148	70	47.3	991	6.7	4	2.7	15	10.1		
PERRY TUTTLE												
1986	WPG	1	0	0.0	0	0.0	0	0.0	0	0.0		
1988	WPG	1	0	0.0	0	0.0	0	0.0	0	0.0		
1989	WPG	2	1	50.0	13	6.5	0	0.0	0	0.0	13	
Totals		4	1	25.0	13	3.3	0	0.0	0	0.0	13	
ED ULMER												

Year	Team	ATT	COM	COM%	YDS	AVG	TD	TD%	INT	INT%	LG	SK
1970	WPG	1	1	100.0	25	25.0	0	0.0	0	0.0	25	
JACK URNESS												
1959	SAS	1	1	100.0	11	11.0	0	0.0	0	0.0	11	
BILL VAN BURKLEO												
1966	TOR	1	0	0.0	0	0.0	0	0.0	1	100.0		0
1967	WPG	175	92	52.6	1258	7.2	6	3.4	16	9.1	58	
1968	OTT	16	4	25.0	70	4.4	0	0.0	3	18.8	27	
1969	OTT	24	10	41.7	170	7.1	1	4.2	2	8.3	37	
1970	OTT	7	1	14.3	41	5.9	0	0.0	0	0.0	41	
1972	HAM	2	1	50.0	1	0.5	1	50.0	0	0.0	1	
Totals		225	108	48.0	1540	6.8	8	3.6	22	9.8	58	0
MIKE VANDERJAGT												
1993	SAS	1	0	0.0	0	0.0	0	0.0	0	0.0		
1996	TOR	2	1	50.0	28	14.0	0	0.0	0	0.0	28	
1997	TOR	1	0	0.0	0	0.0	0	0.0	0	0.0		
Totals		4	1	25.0	28	7.0	0	0.0	0	0.0	28	
RON VANDER KELEN												
1968	CAL	27	13	48.1	179	6.6	1	3.7	4	14.8	32	
RON VANN												
1957	BC	33	18	54.5	254	7.7	3	9.1	3	9.1	36	
BRUCE VAN NESS												
1970	MTL	1	1	100.0	22	22.0	0	0.0	0	0.0	22	
1971	MTL	10	5	50.0	153	15.3	2	20.0	1	10.0	43	
1972	MTL	1	0	0.0	0	0.0	0	0.0	0	0.0		
Totals		12	6	50.0	175	14.6	2	16.7	1	8.3	43	
AMOS VAN PELT												
1970	WPG	1	0	0.0	0	0.0	0	0.0	1	100.0		
JIM VAN PELT												
1958	WPG	160	90	56.3	1445	9.0	9	5.6	10	6.3	107	
1959	WPG+	300	160	53.3	2706	9.0	31	10.3	15	5.0	90	
Totals		460	250	54.3	4151	9.0	40	8.7	25	5.4	107	
CHRIS VARGAS												
1994	EDM	19	12	63.2	179	9.4	1	5.3	1	5.3	33	
1995	EDM	297	157	52.9	2302	7.8	13	4.4	11	3.7	100	
1996	BC	61	27	44.3	542	8.9	4	6.6	3	4.9	57	
1997	WPG	385	201	52.2	2618	6.8	15	3.9	20	5.2	105	
1998	WPG	30	12	40.0	180	6.0	1	3.3	2	6.7	65	
Totals		792	409	51.6	5821	7.3	34	4.3	37	4.7	105	
DON VASSOS												
1960	BC	1	0	0.0	0	0.0	0	0.0	1	100.0		0
TERRY VAUGHN												
1995	CAL	1	1	100.0	34	34.0	0	0.0	0	0.0	34	0
GREG VAVRA												
1984	CAL	324	161	49.7	1901	5.9	10	3.1	16	4.9	41	
1985	CAL	73	32	43.8	391	5.4	1	1.4	5	6.8	38	
1986	BC	9	4	44.4	75	8.3	0	0.0	1	11.1	49	
1987	BC	92	46	50.0	764	8.3	5	5.4	6	6.5	45	
1988	EDM	26	10	38.5	105	4.0	1	3.8	3	11.5	19	
Totals		524	253	48.3	3236	6.2	17	3.2	31	5.9	49	
RONALD VEAL												
1991	HAM	4	2	50.0	13	3.3	0	0.0	0	0.0	10	
ED VEREB												
1956	BC	11	5	45.5	125	11.4	0	0.0	1	9.1	46	
1958	BC	3	1	33.3	12	4.0	0	0.0	1	33.3	12	
1959	BC	15	4	26.7	94	6.3	0	0.0	0	0.0	48	0
1961	BC	1	0	0.0	0	0.0	0	0.0	0	0.0		0
Totals		30	10	33.3	231	7.7	0	0.0	2	6.7	48	0
BILLY VESSELS												
1953	EDM	30	18	60.0	393	13.1	4	13.3	1	3.3		
PRIMO VILLANUEVA												
1955	BC	8	4	50.0	62	7.8	1	12.5	1	12.5	23	
1956	BC	29	16	55.2	297	10.2	2	6.9	3	10.3	46	
1957	BC	46	21	45.7	406	8.8	4	8.7	3	6.5	64	
1958	BC	1	0	0.0	0	0.0	0	0.0	0	0.0		
Totals		84	41	48.8	765	9.1	7	8.3	7	8.3	64	
GERRY VINCENT												
1957	WPG	1	1	100.0	12	12.0	0	0.0	0	0.0	12	
DAVE VITI												
1963	HAM	1	0	0.0	0	0.0	0	0.0	0	0.0		0
JON VOLPE												
1992	BC	1	0	0.0	0	0.0	0	0.0	0	0.0		
1994	LV	1	0	0.0	0	0.0	0	0.0	0	0.0		
Totals		2	0	0.0	0	0.0	0	0.0	0	0.0		
SONNY WADE												
1969	MTL	348	164	47.1	2719	7.8	12	3.4	30	8.6	68	
1970	MTL	322	170	52.8	2411	7.5	14	4.3	31	9.6	56	
1971	MTL	338	155	45.9	2090	6.2	8	2.4	27	8.0	91	
1972	MTL	219	118	53.9	1537	7.0	9	4.1	26	11.9	50	
1973	MTL	5	3	60.0	27	5.4	0	0.0	2	40.0	10	
1974	MTL	64	35	54.7	551	8.6	5	7.8	5	7.8	75	
1975	MTL	196	103	52.6	1415	7.2	12	6.1	11	5.6	70	
1976	MTL	382	205	53.7	2504	6.6	17	4.5	27	7.1	62	
1977	MTL	136	91	66.9	1210	8.9	9	6.6	5	3.7	105	
1978	MTL	77	39	50.6	550	7.1	3	3.9	5	6.5	64	
Totals		2087	1083	51.9	15014	7.2	89	4.3	169	8.1	105	
HAL WAGGONER												
1956	HAM	1	1	100.0	22	22.0	0	0.0	0	0.0	22	
VIRGIL WAGNER												
1946	MTL						4					
TED WAHL												
1991	SAS	52	20	38.5	201	3.9	1	1.9	1	1.9	48	
BOBBY WALDEN												
1961	EDM	1	1	100.0	13	13.0	0	0.0	0	0.0	13	0
1962	EDM	1	0	0.0	0	0.0	0	0.0	1	100.0		0
Totals		2	1	50.0	13	6.5	0	0.0	1	50.0	13	0
JIMMY WALDEN												
1960	BC	110	42	38.2	828	7.5	8	7.3	11	10.0	64	14
1961	BC	61	33	54.1	514	8.4	3	4.9	2	3.3	40	0
1961	CAL	3	1	33.3	16	5.3	0	0.0	0	0.0	16	0
1961	Year	64	34	53.1	530	8.3	3	4.7	2	3.1	40	
1962	CAL	16	6	37.5	91	5.7	0	0.0	1	6.3	16	
1962	EDM	24	12	50.0	325	13.5	1	4.2	3	12.5	65	

Year	Team	ATT	COM	COM%	YDS	AVG	TD	TD%	INT	INT%	LG	SK
1962	Year	40	18	45.0	316	7.9	1	2.5	4	10.0	65	
Totals		214	94	43.9	1774	8.3	12	5.6	17	7.9	65	14
JAY WALKER												
1998	WPG	48	32	66.7	397	8.3	4	8.3	0	0.0	33	
LEWIS WALKER												
1984	CAL	1	1	100.0	22	22.0	0	0.0	0	0.0	22	
1985	CAL	1	0	0.0	0	0.0	0	0.0	0	0.0		
Totals		2	1	50.0	22	11.0	0	0.0	0	0.0	22	
SKIP WALKER												
1983	OTT	1	0	0.0	0	0.0	0	0.0	1	100.0		
TRENT WALTERS												
1966	EDM	2	0	0.0	0	0.0	0	0.0	0	0.0		0
1967	EDM	1	1	100.0	8	8.0	0	0.0	0	0.0	8	
Totals		3	1	33.3	8	2.7	0	0.0	0	0.0	8	0
ANDY WALTON												
1969	OTT	1	0	0.0	0	0.0	0	0.0	0	0.0		
ERIC WARD												
2011	EDM	1	1	100.0	1	1.0	0	0.0	0		1	0
DEL WARDIEN												
1949	SAS						4					
1950	SAS	15	9	60.0	236	15.7	2	13.3	1	6.7		
1953	SAS	2	2	100.0	30	15.0	0	0.0	0	0.0		
Totals		17	11	64.7	266	15.6	6	11.8	1	5.9		
ANDRE WARE												
1995	OTT	126	70	55.6	759	6.0	3	2.4	8	6.3	76	
1996	BC	97	49	50.5	590	6.1	5	5.2	2	2.1	39	
1997	TOR	26	15	57.7	193	7.4	2	7.7	0	0.0	71	
Totals		249	134	53.8	1542	6.2	10	4.0	10	4.0	76	
BUTCHIE WASHINGTON												
2001	HAM	2	1	50.0	5	2.5	0	0.0	0	0.0	5	
2002	HAM	26	10	38.5	99	3.8	0	0.0	1	3.8	19	
Totals		28	11	39.3	104	3.7	0	0.0	1	3.6	19	0
JIM WASHINGTON												
1978	WPG	1	0	0.0	0	0.0	0	0.0	0	0.0		
KERRY WATKINS												
2005	MTL	1	0	0.0	0	0.0	0	0.0	0	0.0		0
KARLTON WATSON												
1985	BC	5	1	20.0	11	2.2	0	0.0	1	20.0	11	
1986	BC	48	21	43.8	275	5.7	1	2.1	5	10.4	542	
Totals		53	22	41.5	286	5.4	1	1.9	6	11.3	542	
J.C. WATTS												
1981	OTT	142	77	54.2	957	6.7	3	2.1	11	7.7	53	
1983	OTT	358	175	48.9	3089	8.6	18	5.0	20	5.6	65	
1984	OTT	360	189	52.5	3052	8.5	21	5.8	23	6.4	90	
1985	OTT	439	236	53.8	2975	6.8	12	2.7	25	5.7	70	
1986	TOR	182	108	59.3	1477	8.1	5	2.7	5	2.7		
1986	OTT	127	66	52.0	864	6.8	7	5.5	9	7.1	72	11
1986	Year	309	174	56.3	2341	7.6	12	3.9	14	4.5	72	
Totals		1608	851	52.9	12414	7.7	66	4.1	93	5.8	90	11
CHARLIE WEATHERBIE												
1979	HAM	13	6	46.2	175	13.5	1	7.7	1	7.7	59	
1979	OTT	2	1	50.0	15	7.5	1	50.0	0	0.0	15	
1979	Year	15	7	46.7	190	12.7	2	13.3	1	6.7	59	
1980	OTT	60	29	48.3	331	5.5	1	1.7	6	10.0	56	
1980	HAM	25	13	52.0	203	8.1	2	8.0	4	16.0	44	
1980	Year	85	42	49.4	534	6.3	3	3.5	10	11.8	56	
Totals		100	49	49.0	724	7.2	5	5.0	11	11.0	59	
DON WEISS												
1969	WPG	62	32	51.6	419	6.8	1	1.6	5	8.1	50	
1970	SAS	15	9	60.0	140	9.3	1	6.7	3	20.0	26	
Totals		77	41	53.2	559	7.3	2	2.6	8	10.4	50	
JOEL WELLS												
1957	MTL	4	4	100.0	33	8.3	1	25.0	0	0.0	15	
1958	MTL	1	1	100.0	25	25.0	0	0.0	0	0.0	25	
1959	MTL	5	2	40.0	22	4.4	0	0.0	0	0.0	11	0
Totals		10	7	70.0	80	8.0	1	10.0	0	0.0	25	0
DAVEY WEST												
1953	WPG	2	0	0.0	0	0.0	0	0.0	0	0.0		
1954	EDM	1	0	0.0	0	0.0	0	0.0	0	0.0		
Totals		3	0	0.0	0	0.0	0	0.0	0	0.0		
TROY WESTWOOD												
1992	WPG	1	1	100.0	-10	-10.0	0	0.0	0	0.0	-10	
ALVIN WHITE												
1978	TOR	135	65	48.1	936	6.9	3	2.2	13	9.6	80	
1980	CAL	1	0	0.0	0	0.0	0	0.0	0	0.0		
1980	Year	1	0	0.0	0	0.0	0	0.0	0	0.0		
Totals		136	65	47.8	936	6.9	3	2.2	13	9.6	80	
ERIK WHITE												
1994	TOR	67	31	46.3	354	5.3	0	0.0	5	7.5	47	
1995	TOR	82	43	52.4	569	6.9	2	2.4	6	7.3	61	
1995	BC	5	2	40.0	18	3.6	0	0.0	0	0.0	13	
1995	Year	87	45	51.7	587	6.7	2	2.3	6	6.9	61	
Totals		154	76	49.4	941	6.1	2	1.3	11	7.1	61	
ERNIE WHITE												
1962	OTT	2	0	0.0	0	0.0	0	0.0	1	50.0		
JOHN HENRY WHITE												
1986	BC	1	**1**	**100.0**	**6**	**6.0**	**0**	**0.0**	**0**	**0.0**	**6**	
TED WHITE												
2003	MTL	13	3	23.1	33	2.5	0	0.0	1	7.7	15	0
2004	MTL	25	19	76.0	250	10.0	1	4.0	2	8.0	33	0
2005	MTL	50	22	44.0	229	4.6	1	2.0	4	8.0	39	3
Totals		88	44	50.0	512	5.8	2	2.3	7	8.0	39	3
JEFF WICKERSHAM												
1988	OTT	205	89	43.4	1393	6.8	5	2.4	12	5.9	57	
TOM WILKINSON												
1967	TOR	15	4	26.7	23	1.5	0	0.0	2	13.3	11	
1968	TOR	5	4	80.0	33	6.6	0	0.0	0	0.0	14	
1969	TOR	234	132	56.4	2331	10.0	18	7.7	19	8.1	87	
1970	TOR	137	80	58.4	1272	9.3	6	4.4	9	6.6	75	
1971	BC	19	11	57.9	236	12.4	1	5.3	0	0.0	60	
1972	EDM	268	177	66.0	2475	9.2	17	6.3	16	6.0	67	
1973	EDM	173	103	59.5	1159	6.7	10	5.8	7	4.0	49	

Year	Team	ATT	COM	COM%	YDS	AVG	TD	TD%	INT	INT%	LG	SK
1974	EDM*	262	173	66.0	2169	8.3	13	5.0	7	2.7	58	
1975	EDM	305	194	63.6	2859	9.4	19	6.2	12	3.9	83	
1976	EDM	184	109	59.2	1243	6.8	4	2.2	10	5.4	51	
1977	EDM	264	158	59.8	1900	7.2	14	5.3	11	4.2	78	
1978	EDM*	292	177	60.6	2394	8.2	20	6.8	9	3.1	64	
1979	EDM*	205	120	58.5	2132	10.4	17	8.3	11	5.4	80	
1980	EDM	147	83	56.5	1060	7.2	7	4.8	9	6.1	65	
1981	EDM	151	88	58.3	1293	8.6	8	5.3	4	2.6	43	
Totals		2661	1613	60.6	22579	8.5	154	5.8	126	4.7	87	
CALVIN WILLIAMS												
1998	EDM	2	1	50.0	51	25.5	1	50.0	1	50.0	51	
CARROLL WILLIAMS												
1967	MTL	139	61	43.9	1222	8.8	5	3.6	14	10.1	57	
1968	MTL	365	191	52.3	2968	8.1	20	5.5	33	9.0	73	
1969	MTL	53	30	56.6	480	9.1	4	7.5	1	1.9	66	
1970	BC	22	9	40.9	210	9.5	1	4.5	5	22.7	52	
Totals		579	291	50.3	4880	8.4	30	5.2	53	9.2	73	
DAVE WILLIAMS												
1976	CAL	20	7	35.0	119	6.0	1	5.0	1	5.0	28	
FRANK WILLIAMS												
1955	BC	1	0	0.0	0	0.0	0	0.0	0	0.0		
JOE WILLIAMS												
1967	TOR	2	0	0.0	0	0.0	0	0.0	0	0.0		
LEN WILLIAMS												
1994	LV	138	80	58.0	1222	8.9	10	7.2	8	5.8	51	
1995	CAL	6	2	33.3	41	6.8	0	0.0	0	0.0	22	3
Totals		144	82	56.9	1263	8.8	10	6.9	8	5.6	51	3
MIKE WILLIAMS												
1981	TOR	18	4	22.2	58	3.2	0	0.0	4	22.2	23	
1984	BC	5	3	60.0	45	9.0	0	0.0	1	20.0	20	
Totals		23	7	30.4	103	4.5	0	0.0	5	21.7	23	
RICHIE WILLIAMS												
2006	HAM	32	17	53.1	241	7.5	2	6.3	1	3.1	54	8
2007	HAM	130	80	61.5	852	6.6	6	4.6	3	2.3	48	10
2008	HAM	100	60	60.0	984	9.8	3	3.0	5	5.0	63	18
2009	WPG	10	3	30.0	30	3.0	0	0.0	0	0.0	15	2
Totals		272	160	58.8	2107	7.7	11	4.0	9	3.3	63	38
RONALD WILLIAMS												
1999	HAM	1	0	0.0	0	0.0	0	0.0	0	0.0		
LARRY WILLIS												
1991	WPG	1	0	0.0	0	0.0	0	0.0	0	0.0		
RAY WILLSEY												
1953	EDM	10	6	60.0	117	11.7	0	0.0	0	0.0		
DWAINE WILSON												
1984	MTL	1	0	0.0	0	0.0	0	0.0	0	0.0		
GENE WILSON												
1954	TOR	1	0	0.0	0	0.0	0	0.0	1	100.0		
DANNY WIMPRINE												
2005	CAL	46	19	41.3	270	5.9	2	4.3	3	6.5	28	5
EARL WINFIELD												
1990	HAM	1	0	0.0	0	0.0	0	0.0	0	0.0	0	
NOBBY WIRKOWSKI												
1951	TOR						12					
1952	TOR						21					
1953	TOR						15					
1954	TOR	355	198	55.8	2960	8.3	12	3.4	20	5.6	63	
1955	HAM	188	89	47.3	1329	7.1	6	3.2	9	4.8	47	
1956	HAM	133	73	54.9	999	7.5	11	8.3	8	6.0	82	
1957	CAL	181	94	51.9	1736	9.6	9	5.0	10	5.5	82	
1958	CAL	269	149	55.4	2300	8.6	13	4.8	12	4.5	90	
1959	CAL	40	17	42.5	201	5.0	1	2.5	6	15.0	34	
1960	TOR	16	10	62.5	176	11.0	1	6.3	0	0.0	46	
Totals		1182	630	53.3	9701	8.2	101	4.5	65	5.5	90	
DUANE WOOD												
1960	HAM	2	2	100.0	51	25.5	0	0.0	0	0.0	49	
GARY WOOD												
1970	OTT	340	174	51.2	2759	8.1	18	5.3	27	7.9	75	
1971	OTT	152	77	50.7	1057	7.0	10	6.6	8	5.3	62	
Totals		492	251	51.0	3816	7.8	28	5.7	35	7.1	75	
ROD WOODWARD												
1974	OTT	1	0	0.0	0	0.0	0	0.0	1	100.0		
1976	OTT	2	0	0.0	0	0.0	0	0.0	0	0.0		
Totals		3	0	0.0	0	0.0	0	0.0	1	33.3		
GEORGE WORKS												
1985	HAM	1	1	100.0	27	27.0	0	0.0	0	0.0	27	
RICK WORMAN												
1987	CAL	356	179	50.3	3021	8.5	16	4.5	19	5.3	86	
1988	CAL	302	151	50.0	2441	8.1	16	5.3	13	4.3	86	
1988	EDM	18	5	27.8	88	4.9	1	5.6	1	5.6	51	
1988	Year	320	156	48.8	2529	7.9	17	5.3	14	4.4	86	
1989	EDM	92	41	44.6	598	6.5	7	7.6	6	6.5	51	
1990	CAL	172	96	55.8	1226	7.1	7	4.1	7	4.1	58	
1991	SAS	175	91	52.0	1203	6.9	8	4.6	4	2.3	106	
Totals		1115	563	50.5	8577	7.7	55	4.9	50	4.5	106	
JAMES WRIGHT												
1963	EDM	15	5	33.3	89	5.9	1	6.7	4	26.7	36	2
ROY WRIGHT												
1947	SAS						1					
1949	SAS						1					
1950	SAS	38	11	28.9	192	5.1	0	0.0	2	5.3		
1951	SAS	15	6	40.0	100	6.7	0	0.0	3	20.0		
Totals		53	17	32.1	292	5.5	2	0.0	5	9.4		
FREDDY WYANT												
1957	TOR	72	28	38.9	440	6.1	2	2.8	8	11.1	43	
BOB WYATT												
1973	CAL	1	1	100.0	3	3.0	0	0.0	0	0.0	3	
BUBBA WYCHE												
1969	SAS	35	9	25.7	231	6.6	1	2.9	3	8.6	85	
1971	SAS	58	25	43.1	368	6.3	2	3.4	2	3.4	48	
1972	SAS	73	31	42.5	458	6.3	1	1.4	6	8.2	78	
Totals		166	65	39.2	1057	6.4	4	2.4	11	6.6	85	
HARVEY WYLIE												

Year	Team	ATT	COM	COM%	YDS	AVG	TD	TD%	INT	INT%	LG	SK
1956	CAL	2	0	0.0	0	0.0	0	0.0	0	0.0		
1963	CAL	1	0	0.0	0	0.0	0	0.0	0	0.0		0
Totals		3	0	0.0	0	0.0	0	0.0	0	0.0		0
SPERGON WYNN												
2003	BC	65	46	70.8	626	9.6	4	6.2	1	1.5	62	8
2004	BC	34	21	61.8	268	7.9	2	5.9	0	0.0	47	2
2006	TOR	147	93	63.3	1109	7.5	5	3.4	4	2.7	75	
Totals		246	160	65.0	2003	8.1	11	4.5	5	2.0	75	10
NELSON YARBROUGH												
1961	MTL	64	37	57.8	371	5.8	0	0.0	4	6.3	28	4
BOB YOUNG												
1948	OTT						3					
JARED ZABRANSKY												
2010	EDM	104	53	51.0	609	5.9	4	3.8	10	9.6	40	9
JOE ZALESKI												
1952	WPG	80	35	43.8	761	9.5	6	7.5	7	8.8	54	
1953	WPG	45	23	51.1	393	8.7	2	4.4	3	6.7		
1954	WPG	30	18	60.0	212	7.1	0	0.0	4	13.3		
1955	MTL	4	2	50.0	40	10.0	1	25.0	0	0.0	25	
Totals		159	78	49.1	1406	8.8	9	5.7	14	8.8	54	
JIM ZORN												
1986	WPG	25	13	52.0	175	7.0	0	0.0	1	4.0	55	
JOE ZUGER												
1962	HAM	115	64	55.7	1070	9.3	15	13.0	6	5.2	79	
1963	HAM	5	1	20.0	31	6.2	1	20.0	0	0.0	31	0
1965	HAM	108	41	38.0	669	6.2	2	1.9	7	6.5	91	21
1966	HAM	159	70	44.0	1252	7.9	7	4.4	11	6.9	48	14
1967	HAM	320	163	50.9	2771	8.7	11	3.4	17	5.3	92	
1968	HAM	316	160	50.6	2616	8.3	15	4.7	19	6.0	83	
1969	HAM	198	108	54.5	1562	7.9	14	7.1	6	3.0	68	
1970	HAM	132	78	59.1	1073	8.1	3	2.3	10	7.6	62	
1971	HAM	265	129	48.7	1632	6.2	8	3.0	19	7.2	108	
Totals		1618	814	50.3	12676	7.8	76	4.7	95	5.9	108	35

The Kicking Register contains each player's convert, field goal, punting and kickoff record. These records were placed in this separate section because of space limitations in the overall player register.

Each entry is divided into two parts: The first is the player's name; the second is the player's year-by-year and career kicking statistics.

The following column headings are used in this section:

AVG Average
CON One-point conversions made
CONA One-point conversions attempted
FG Field goals made
FGA Field goals attempted
KO Kickoffs
LG Long kick
PCT Percentage of attempts made
PUNT Punts
S Singles
TEAM The following team abbreviations are used:

BAL	Baltimore (1994)
	Baltimore Stallions (1995)
BC	British Columbia Lions (1954-)
BIR	Birmingham Barracudas (1995)
CAL	Calgary Stampeders (1946-)
EDM	Edmonton Eskimos (1949-)
HAM	Hamilton Tigers (1946-1947)
	Hamilton Wildcats (1948-1949)
	Hamilton Tiger-Cats (1950-)
LV	Las Vegas Posse (1994)
MEM	Memphis Mad Dogs (1995)
MTL	Montreal Alouettes (1946-1981)
	Montreal Concordes (1982-1985)
	Montreal Alouettes (1986; 1996-)
OTT	Ottawa Rough Riders (1946-1996)
	Ottawa Renegades (2002-2005)
SA	San Antonio Texans (1995)
SAC	Sacramento Gold Miners (1993-1994)
SAS	Saskatchewan Roughriders (1946-)
SHR	Shreveport Pirates (1994-1995)
TOR	Toronto Argonauts (1946-)
WPG	Winnipeg Blue Bombers (1946-)
Totals	If a player has statistics for more than one season, his career totals will appear on this line.

YDS Yards
YEAR Year

Year	Team	S	PUNT	YDS	AVG	LG	KO	YDS	AVG	LG	CON	CONA	PCT	FG	FGA	PCT
JACK ABENDSCHAN																
1965	SAS	4					39	2027	52.0	75	28	34	82.4	11	19	57.9
1966	SAS	10					55	2992	54.4	80	37	42	88.1	13	31	41.9
1967	SAS	5					50	2647	52.9	75	33	40	82.5	17	28	60.7
1968	SAS	7					22	1424	64.7	85	0	0		8	19	42.1
1969	SAS	11					60	3159	52.7	75	42	45	93.3	21	42	50.0
1970	SAS	8					54	2987	55.3	75	36	42	85.7	24	38	63.2
1971	SAS	14					31	1792	57.8	85	29	31	93.5	17	36	47.2
1972	SAS	6					57	3271	57.4	90	38	41	92.7	10	24	41.7
1973	SAS	7					58	3206	55.3	90	37	41	90.2	22	35	62.9
1975	SAS	2					61	2863	46.9	86	32	32	100.0	16	28	57.1
Totals		74					487	26368	54.1	90	312	348	89.7	159	300	53.0
DICKIE ADAMS																
1972	OTT	3	124	4845	39.1	71										
1973	OTT	0	112	4543	40.6	59										
1974	OTT	1	136	5480	40.3	58										
1975	OTT	2	122	4863	39.9	81										
Totals		6	494	19731	39.9	81										
BOB AGLER																
1951	CAL	1	37	1411	38.1											
JOE AGUIRRE																
1950	WPG	10									22	25	88.0	5	19	26.3
1951	WPG	1									19	23	82.6	1	7	14.3
1952	EDM	5	2	57	28.5	30	31	1789	57.7	70	24	26	92.3	1	10	10.0
1953	SAS	0					2	110	55.0		1	1	100.0	0	0	
1954	SAS	3					42	2223	52.9		25	28	89.3	19	30	63.3
1955	SAS	3					39	2136	54.8	80	28	33	84.8	14	23	60.9
Totals		22	2	57	28.5	30	114	6258	54.9	80	119	136	87.5	40	89	44.9
FRANKIE ALBERT																
1953	CAL	0	48	1926	40.1	70										
GEORGE ALEXANDER																
1946	CAL	1														
DON ALLARD																
1959	SAS	0	1	29	29.0	29										
BARCLAY ALLEN																
1970	MTL	0	3													
1970	OTT	0	6													
1970	Year	0	9	282	31.3	44										
1972	CAL	0	8	327	40.9	49										
Totals		0	17	609	35.8	49										
JOE ALLISON																
1995	MEM	2					6	340	56.7	70	0	0		1	3	33.3
BUDDY ALLISTON																
1956	WPG	0					3	147	49.0	58						
JIM AMBROSE																
1951	MTL	1									4			1		
BRET ANDERSON																
1997	BC	0	1	33	33.0	33	52	2728	52.5	67	0	0		0	0	
1998	BC	0					13	762	58.6	67	0	0		0	0	
1999	BC	2					73	4087	56.0	89	0	0		0	0	
2000	BC	0					13	698	53.7	67	0	0		0	0	
2001	BC	1					27	1540	57.0	85	0	0		0	0	
2002	BC	1	2	56	28.0	30	9	511	56.8	62	0	0		0	0	
2005	BC	1	1	40	40.0	40	57	165	2.9	91	0	0		0	0	
2006	BC	0	1	30	30.0	30	71	3995	56.3	71	0	0		0	0	
2007	BC	0					82	4695	57.3	67	4	4	100.0	2	2	100.0
2008	BC	0					30	1700	56.7	65	0	0		0	0	
Totals		5	5	159	31.8	40	427	20881	48.9	91	4	4	100.0	2	2	100.0
EZZRETT ANDERSON																
1953	CAL	0					2	117	58.5	62	2	2	100.0	0	0	
FRANKIE ANDERSON																
1952	EDM	1									7	10	70.0	0	1	0.0
ROMAN ANDERSON																
1994	SAC	14					75	4240	56.5	78	40	41	97.6	39	55	70.9
1995	SA	5					103	5753	55.9	80	62	63	98.4	56	65	86.2
Totals		19					178	9993	56.1	80	102	104	98.1	95	120	79.2
ZENON ANDRUSYSHYN																
1971	TOR	8	122	5346	43.8	68	48	2712	56.5	78	1	3	33.3	0	1	0.0
1972	TOR	14	125	5626	45.0	75	40	2276	56.9	65	3	4	75.0	6	16	37.5
1973	TOR	18	121	5521	45.6	67	40	2252	56.3	81	25	26	96.2	19	37	51.4
1974	TOR	16	142	6653	46.9	85	42	2312	55.0	81	22	24	91.7	32	54	59.3
1975	TOR	11	126	5432	43.1	69	59	3705	62.8	90	20	20	100.0	30	56	53.6
1976	TOR	7	132	5772	43.7	63	45	2463	54.7	75	29	29	100.0	22	38	57.9
1977	TOR	15	128	5788	45.2	108	43	2360	54.9	85	22	22	100.0	23	37	62.2
1979	HAM	10	51	2205	43.2	66	27	1686	62.4	90	15	16	93.8	10	20	50.0
1980	TOR	15	122	5524	45.3	83	55	3136	57.0	90	31	31	100.0	30	42	71.4
1981	TOR	16	149	7037	47.2	74	44	2406	54.7	85	21	21	100.0	18	25	72.0
1982	TOR	1	82	3759	45.8	70	30	2286	58.6	76	0	0		0	0	
1982	EDM	8	16	670	41.9	55	0	0			24	24	100.0	11	21	52.4
1982	Year	9	98	4429	45.2	70	39	2285	58.6	76	24	24	100.0	11	21	52.4
1986	MTL	4	51	2009	39.4	53	19	1110	58.4	69	9	9	100.0	14	18	77.8
Totals		143	1367	61342	44.9	108	501	28703	57.3	90	222	229	96.9	215	365	58.9
FRANK ASCHENBRENNER																
1951	MTL	1														
IMOKHAI ATOGWE																
2004	EDM	0	1	26	26.0	26										
KENT AUSTIN																
1990	SAS	0	1	39	39.0	39										
JEFF AVERY																
1977	OTT	0	54	2138	39.6	56										
1978	OTT	0	4	138	34.5	40										
Totals		0	58	2276	39.2	56										
BUTCH AVINGER																
1952	SAS	19	131	5855	44.7	82										
DAVE BADOWICH																
1983	SAS	1	42	1858	44.2	66										
1984	SAS	1	28	1200	42.9	60										
Totals		2	70	3058	43.7	66										
JIM BAFFICO																
1965	TOR	0					5	190	38.0	56						
DON BAILEY																
1956	CAL	0					1	39	39.0	39						

Year Team	S	PUNT	YDS	AVG	LG	KO	YDS	AVG	LG	CON	CONA	PCT	FG	FGA	PCT
CHARLIE BAILLIE															
1965 MTL	4									2	2	100.0	0	4	0.0
JOHN BAKER															
1964 MTL	1					23	1245	54.1	72	0	0		0	5	0.0
1965 MTL	1					40	2236	55.9	80	0	0		0	1	0.0
1966 MTL	0					29	1753	60.4	85	0	0		0	0	
1967 MTL	0					34	1928	56.7	67	0	0		0	0	
1968 MTL	5					35	2017	57.6	75	10	12	83.3	4	12	33.3
1969 MTL	2					46	2488	54.1	79	14	17	82.4	3	11	27.3
Totals	9					207	11667	56.4	85	24	29	82.8	7	29	24.1
JON BAKER															
1999 EDM	2					35	2119	60.5	72	21	21	100.0	20	28	71.4
2000 BC	1					16	948	59.3	70	0	0		3	6	50.0
2001 EDM	1									0	0		0	2	0.0
Totals	4					51	3067	60.1	72	21	21	100.0	23	36	63.9
RON BAKER															
1954 OTT	0									1	3	33.3	0	0	
1955 BC	2					28	1446	51.6	75	14	14	100.0	1	6	16.7
1956 BC	1					5	269	53.8	59	13	16	81.3	2	4	50.0
Totals	3					33	1715	52.0	75	28	33	84.8	3	10	30.0
STEVE BAKER															
2004 HAM	1	6	232	38.7	54	4	218	54.5	57	3	3	100.0	2	4	50.0
TERRY BAKER															
1987 SAS	6	137	5603	40.9	94					0	0		0	0	
1988 SAS	4	154	6118	39.7	75	4	173	43.3	61	0	0		0	0	
1989 SAS	7	142	5699	40.1	88					0	0		0	0	
1990 OTT	4	149	5935	39.8	81	3	139	46.3	53	0	0		0	0	
1991 OTT	19	126	5476	43.5	78	94	5339	56.8	82	45	46	97.8	46	60	76.7
1992 OTT	16	153	6526	42.7	75	82	4517	55.1	90	48	48	100.0	40	57	70.2
1993 OTT	11	91	4142	45.5	68	44	2491	56.6	86	24	24	100.0	18	30	60.0
1994 OTT	9	129	5373	41.7	67	73	4138	56.7	75	41	41	100.0	46	64	71.9
1995 OTT	7	53	2318	43.7	75	22	1298	59.0	70	9	9	100.0	9	15	60.0
1995 TOR	7	89	3663	41.2	65	48	2646	55.1	83	27	27	100.0	14	22	63.6
1995 Year	14	142	5981	42.1	75	70	3944	56.3	83	36	37	97.3	23	37	62.2
1996 MTL	12	133	5818	43.7	72	99	6021	60.8	77	55	55	100.0	37	46	80.4
1997 MTL	17	111	4932	44.4	80	80	4842	60.5	86	50	50	100.0	34	52	65.4
1998 MTL	16	125	5718	45.7	72	73	4598	63.0	83	43	43	100.0	47	66	71.2
1999 MTL	17	124	5878	47.4	90	86	5188	60.3	95	51	51	100.0	40	52	76.9
2000 MTL	22	119	5504	46.3	83	93	5657	60.8	86	60	60	100.0	46	60	76.7
2001 MTL	12	92	4236	46.0	78	70	4214	60.2	95	43	43	100.0	42	53	79.2
2002 MTL	16	104	4590	44.1	70	89	5525	62.1	94	61	61	100.0	36	54	66.7
Totals	202	2031	87529	43.1	94	960	56786	59.2	95	557	558	99.8	455	631	72.1
JIM BAKHTIAR															
1958 CAL	1					48	2742	57.1	88						
WALT BALASIUK															
1971 MTL	0					3	174	58.0	60						
RAPHAOL BALL															
2002 WPG	1	1	15	15.0	15										
DANNY BARRETT															
1993 BC	0	1	33	33.0	33										
JACK BARRY															
1953 TOR	0									3			1		
GORD BARWELL															
1967 SAS	0					2	106	53.0	56						
DANNY BASS															
1983 CAL	0	1	40	40.0	40										
PAT BATTEN															
1965 MTL	3									9	15	60.0	2	9	22.2
WALT BAUER															
1976 HAM	1									3	3	100.0	0	2	0.0
CHARLIE BAUMANN															
1994 BAL	3					13	765	58.8	73	8	8	100.0	6	10	60.0
JOHN BEATON															
1975 EDM	0	47	1790	38.1	57										
DON BEATTY															
1952 CAL	0	5	170	34.0	41										
NEAL BEAUMONT															
1961 BC	2	62	2686	43.3	57										
1962 BC	0	25	807	32.3	47										
1963 BC	6	114	4774	41.9	62										
1964 BC	3	90	3796	42.2	74										
1965 BC	3	128	5388	42.1	62										
1966 BC	3	88	3461	39.3	83										
1967 BC	0	117	4695	40.1	65										
Totals	17	624	25607	41.0	83										
BILLY BELL															
1947 TOR	0									1			0		
JOHN BELL															
1958 EDM	0									0	1	0.0	0	0	
JOHNNY BELL															
1946 SAS	1														
1497 SAS	3														
Totals	4														
GEORGE BELU															
1963 OTT	0					5	245	49.0	59	3	4	75.0	0	0	
BRUCE BENNETT															
1966 SAS	0					1	11	11.0	11						
1967 SAS	0					1	17	17.0	17						
1970 SAS	0					2	28	14.0	14						
1971 SAS	0					1	19	19.0	19						
1972 SAS	0					2	29	14.5	19						
Totals	0					7	104	14.9	19						
PAUL BENNETT															
1986 HAM	0	1	19	19.0	19										
LORNE BENSON															
1955 WPG	0	1	38	38.0	38										
BRIAN BERG															
1974 SAS	2					55	2799	50.9	77	35	37	94.6	15	27	55.6
1975 SAS	1					14	732	52.3	63	6	6	100.0	5	7	71.4
1975 BC	0									5	5	100.0	2	5	40.0
1975 Year	1					14	732	52.3	63	11	11	100.0	7	12	58.3
Totals	3					69	3531	51.2	77	46	48	95.8	22	39	56.4

Year Team	S	PUNT	YDS	AVG	LG	KO	YDS	AVG	LG	CON	CONA	PCT	FG	FGA	PCT
GINO BERRETTA															
1961 MTL	3	74	2982	40.3	60					0	0		0	0	
1963 MTL	8	110	4542	41.3	61	26	1502	57.8	76	18	20	90.0	5	8	62.5
1964 MTL	6	108	4584	42.4	76	17	876	51.5	70	15	21	71.4	1	9	11.1
1965 MTL	0	24	1001	41.7	53					1	1	100.0	0	0	
1966 MTL	4	123	4683	38.1	64					0	0		0	0	
1968 OTT	0	11	438	39.8	50					0	0		0	0	
1969 MTL	1					4	209	52.3	53	17	20	85.0	5	9	55.6
Totals	22	450	18230	40.5	76	47	2587	55.0	76	51	62	82.3	11	26	42.3
LINDY BERRY															
1950 EDM	0	2	102	51.0											
MARV BEVAN															
1958 OTT	0					1	48	48.0	48						
BILL BEWLEY															
1955 MTL	0									5	5	100.0	3	3	100.0
1956 MTL	3									45	54	83.3	1	4	25.0
1957 MTL	1									34	38	89.5	4	7	57.1
1958 MTL	4	7	250	35.7	52					28	35	80.0	6	13	46.2
1959 MTL	3					15	802	53.5	63	19	23	82.6	4	17	23.5
1960 MTL	7									41	44	93.2	4	15	26.7
1961 MTL	3					2	108	54.0	57	18	23	78.3	5	12	41.7
1965 MTL	0									3	6	50.0	1	4	25.0
Totals	21	7	250	35.7	52	17	910	53.5	63	193	228	84.6	28	75	37.3
AREK BIGOS															
1998 TOR	10					43	2485	57.8	77	32	32	100.0	23	36	63.9
RICK BLACK															
1963 OTT	6	79	2920	37.0	60	1	55	55.0	55	5	5	100.0	1	2	50.0
1964 OTT	0	8	272	34.0	41					0	0		0	0	
1965 OTT	0	2	58	29.0	37	1	52	52.0	52	0	0		0	0	
1966 OTT	0									1	1	100.0	0	0	
Totals	6	89	3250	36.5	60	2	107	53.5	55	6	6	100.0	1	2	50.0
TRISTAN BLACK															
2011 TOR	0	1	21	21.0	21										
JOHNNY BLAICHER															
1958 MTL						51	2627	51.5	73	0	0		0	0	
1959 MTL	0					10	431	43.1	53	1	2	50.0	0	0	
Totals	3					61	3058	50.1	73	1	2	50.0	0	0	
DON BLAIR															
1998 EDM	0	1	11	11.0	11										
2003 CAL	0	1	40	40.0	40										
Totals	0	2	51	25.5	40										
MIKE BLUM															
1965 OTT	0					1	12	12.0	12						
AL BODINE															
1950 SAS	1														
JAMIE BOREHAM															
2004 HAM	7	44	1712	38.9	65	52	3031	58.3	71	26	26	100.0	22	37	59.5
2005 HAM	9	116	4594	39.6	69	77	4490	58.3	95	39	39	100.0	23	32	71.9
2006 HAM	3					50	3056	61.1	75	19	19	100.0	26	36	72.2
2007 SAS	9	118	4954	42.0	66	86	5411	62.9	95	1	1	100.0	0	0	
2008 SAS	8	107	4451	41.6	71	78	5036	64.6	95	0	0		0	0	
2009 SAS	9	91	3839	42.2	67	76	4837	63.6	95	0	0		0	0	
2010 TOR	0	91	3680	40.4	62	46	3124	67.9	95	0	0		0	0	
2011 WPG	2	21	855	40.7	76	16	941	58.8	72	0	0		0	0	
Totals	47	588	24085	41.0	76	481	29926	62.2	95	85	85	100.0	71	105	67.6
GEORGE BORK															
1964 MTL	0	9	381	42.3	63										
LYNN BOTTOMS															
1956 CAL	1					11	596	54.2	69	2	3	66.7	0	2	0.0
1959 CAL	0	1	23	23.0	23					0	0		0	0	
Totals	1	1	23	23.0	23	11	596	54.2	69	2	3	66.7	0	2	0.0
REG BOUDREAU															
1979 SAS	0					28	1591	56.8	90	3	3	100.0	4	5	80.0
JERRY BRADLEY															
1968 BC	0	1	9	9.0	9										
MIKE BRADWELL															
2010 TOR	0	1	37	37.0	37										
MARCUS BRADY															
2007 MTL	0	5	196	39.2	47										
PAT BRADY															
1952 HAM	1														
BILL BRIGGS															
1947 TOR	1									0			0		
1950 EDM	3	80	2957	37.0						0	0		0	0	
1951 EDM	0	30	1130	37.7						0	0		0	0	
1952 EDM	0									1	4	25.0	0	0	
1954 EDM	0	1	20	20.0	20					0	0		0	0	
Totals	4	111	4107	37.0	20					1	4	25.0	0	0	
JOHNNY BRIGHT															
1952 CAL	0	1	52	52.0	52										
DICK BROWN															
1950 HAM	1														
1954 HAM	0	1	41	41.0	41										
Totals	1	1	41	41.0	41										
DOUG BROWN															
1958 CAL	3					11	574	52.2	61	36	43	83.7	4	10	40.0
1959 CAL	4					58	3054	52.7	65	37	42	88.1	14	25	56.0
1960 CAL	8					39	2120	54.4	75	40	47	85.1	11	24	45.8
Totals	15					108	5748	53.2	75	113	132	85.6	29	59	49.2
TOM BROWN															
1962 BC	0					9	354	39.3	51						
ED BUCHANAN															
1964 SAS	0	5	219	43.8	63										
AMOS BULLOCKS															
1965 BC	0									1	1	100.0	0	0	
TERRY BULYCH															
1973 SAS	0	1	46	46.0	46										
1975 SAS	1	66	2567	38.9	75										
Totals	1	67	2613	39.0	75										
WALLY BUONO															
1972 MTL	0	33	1156	35.0	48										
1973 MTL	3	102	3934	38.6	74										

Year	Team	S	PUNT	YDS	AVG	LG	KO	YDS	AVG	LG	CON	CONA	PCT	FG	FGA	PCT
1974	MTL	0	27	1025	38.0	50										
1977	MTL	0	43	1738	40.4	63										
1978	MTL	8	120	5241	43.7	90										
1979	MTL	4	132	5240	39.7	60										
1980	MTL	0	3	110	36.7	38										
1981	MTL	1	65	2626	40.4	65										
Totals		16	525	21070	40.1	90										
ORVILLE BURKE																
1946	OTT	0									1			1		
FERDIE BURKET																
1959	SAS	4	85	3420	40.2	66										
1960	SAS	5	84	3448	41.0	67										
1961	SAS	13	142	6361	44.8	75										
1962	SAS	13	136	6156	45.3	83										
1963	MTL	1	13	577	44.4	68										
Totals		36	460	19962	43.4	83										
PAUL BUSHEY																
1993	HAM	0	1	40	40.0	40										
BEN CAHOON																
2007	MTL	1									0	0		1	2	50.0
2010	MTL	0									2	2	100.0	0	0	
Totals		1									2	2	100.0	1	2	50.0
BOB CAMERON																
1980	WPG	2	104	4432	42.6	78					0	0		0	0	
1981	WPG	2	96	4249	44.3	69					0	0		0	0	
1982	WPG	5	130	5635	43.3	83					0	0		0	0	
1983	WPG	8	135	6337	46.9	75					0	0		0	0	
1984	WPG	5	113	5176	45.8	65					0	0		0	0	
1985	WPG	8	117	5256	44.9	95					0	0		0	0	
1986	WPG	11	133	5617	42.2	72					0	0		0	0	
1987	WPG	7	165	6904	41.8	77					0	0		0	0	
1988	WPG	6	188	8214	43.7	82					0	0		0	0	
1989	WPG	12	175	7425	42.4	77					0	0		0	0	
1990	WPG	10	160	6724	42.0	65					0	0		0	0	
1991	WPG	8	147	5902	40.1	65	6	291	48.5	52	4	4	100.0	0	0	
1992	WPG	6	161	6780	42.1	84					0	0		0	0	
1993	WPG	5	141	5916	42.0	70					0	0		0	0	
1994	WPG	4	129	5377	41.7	72					0	0		0	0	
1995	WPG	7	166	7070	42.6	81					0	0		0	0	
1996	WPG	7	163	6919	42.4	75					0	0		0	0	
1997	WPG	1	143	6192	43.3	67					0	0		0	0	
1998	WPG	5	139	6266	45.1	70	1	56	56.0	56	0	0		0	0	
1999	WPG	5	133	5690	42.8	66					0	0		0	0	
2000	WPG	2	65	2787	42.9	66					0	0		0	0	
2001	WPG	2	121	5121	42.3	73					0	0		0	0	
2002	WPG	2	105	4312	41.1	59					0	0		0	0	
Totals		130	3129	134301	42.9	95	7	347	49.6	56	4	4	100.0	0	0	
PAUL CAMERON																
1956	BC	2	20	926	46.3	64										
1957	BC	0	3	120	40.0	45										
1958	BC	0	1	40	40.0	40										
Totals		2	24	1086	45.3	64										
ROY CAMERON																
1963	SAS	0					20	831	41.6	54	0	2	0.0	1	1	100.0
TOM CAMPANA																
1973	SAS	0					1	20	20.0	20						
1974	SAS	0					1	23	23.0	23						
1975	SAS	0					1	11	11.0	11						
Totals		0					3	54	18.0	23						
JUSTIN CANALE																
1970	MTL	0					18	1068	59.3	90	0	0		1	5	20.0
1971	MTL	9					34	1829	53.8	75	11	14	78.6	19	39	48.7
Totals		9					52	2897	55.7	90	11	14	78.6	20	44	45.5
HERB CAPOZZI																
1953	MTL	1														
JOE CAPRIOTTI																
1947	HAM	1									1			0		
GIULIO CARAVATTA																
1991	BC	1					91	4841	53.2	90	0	0		0	0	
1992	BC	0	22	767	34.9	52	10	518	51.8	62	0	0		0	0	
1993	BC	0	8	331	41.4	49					0	0		0	0	
1994	BC	3	55	2013	36.6	59					2	3	66.7	3	3	100.0
1995	BC	3					79	4491	56.8	80	0	0		0	0	
1996	BC	0					76	4132	54.4	67	0	0		0	0	
1997	BC	0	31	1214	39.2	54	24	1266	52.8	67	0	0		0	0	
Totals		7	116	4325	37.3	59	280	15248	54.5	90	2	3	66.7	3	3	100.0
DONNIE CARAWAY																
1957	CAL	0					10	520	52.0	69	3	3	100.0	1	2	50.0
1958	TOR	2	25	981	39.2	89	2	100	50.0	52	0	0		0		
Totals		2	25	981	39.2	89	12	620	51.7	69	3	3	100.0	1	2	50.0
JAN CARINCI																
1982	TOR	1	2	86	43.0	49	6	312	52.0	61	2	2	100.0	1	1	100.0
1983	TOR	0	2	83	41.5	44	2	114	57.0	66	2	2	100.0	0	0	
1984	TOR	0	1	39	39.0	39					0	0		0	0	
1985	TOR	0	1	35	35.0	35					0	0		0	0	
1986	BC	0					55	3080	56.0	71	0	0		0	0	
1987	BC	0					4	251	62.8	70	0	0		0	0	
1990	BC	0	2	47	23.5	24	2	104	52.0	53	0	0		0	0	
Totals		1	8	290	36.3	49	69	3861	56.0	71	4	4	100.0	1	1	100.0
KEN CARPENTER																
1954	SAS	0	5	195	39.0	46					0	0		0	0	
1955	SAS	0	2	72	36.0	37	6	362	60.3	68	0	0		0	0	
1956	SAS	0					21	1147	54.6	70	0	0		0	0	
1957	SAS	0					14	709	50.6	65	0	0		0	0	
1958	SAS	0	25	953	38.1	69	2	111	55.5	56	0	0		0	0	
1959	SAS	0	3	90	30.0	40	11	517	47.0	70	0	0		0	1	0.0
Totals		0	35	1310	37.4	69	54	2846	52.7	70	0	0		0	1	0.0
TOM CASEY																
1949	HAM	10									6			0		
1950	WPG	1	18	746	41.4						0	0		0	0	
1951	WPG	1	23	814	35.4						0	0		0	0	
1952	WPG	0	1	67	67.0	67					0	0		0	0	

Year	Team	S	PUNT	YDS	AVG	LG	KO	YDS	AVG	LG	CON	CONA	PCT	FG	FGA	PCT
1954	WPG	0	5	195	39.0	47					0	0		0	0	
1955	WPG	4	92	3932	42.7	78					0	0		0	0	
Totals		16	139	5754	41.4	78					6	0		0	0	
RICK CASSATA																
1969	WPG	1									1	1	100.0	0	0	
TOMMY CATES																
1947	MTL	0									1			0		
WALT CHAHLEY																
1949	CAL	1									5			0		
1950	CAL	1									3	4	75.0	0	3	0.0
Totals		2									8	4	75.0	0	3	0.0
JIMMY CHAMBERS																
1951	EDM	0	1	19	19.0											
VIC CHAPMAN																
1952	CAL	1	1	35	35.0	35										
1954	BC	1	100	3804	38.0	77										
1955	BC	7	95	4022	42.3	91										
1956	BC	6	112	4766	42.6	64										
1957	BC	7	130	5514	42.4	65										
1958	BC	1	36	1393	38.7	72										
1959	EDM	5	132	5371	40.7	79										
1960	EDM	6	108	4393	40.7	73										
1961	EDM	5	45	1892	42.0	60										
1962	EDM	7	73	3102	42.5	60										
1962	MTL	2	6	277	46.2	71										
1962	Year	9	79	3179	40.2	71										
Totals		48	838	34569	41.3	91										
KEN CHARLTON																
1946	OTT	3									1			0		
1948	SAS	13									0			0		
1949	SAS	8									0			0		
1950	SAS	7	100	3756	37.6						0	0		0	0	
1951	SAS	2	31	1139	36.7						0	0		0	0	
1953	SAS	4	51	2155	42.3						0	0		0	0	
Totals		37	182	7050	38.7						1	0		0	0	
RANDY CHEVRIER																
2010	CAL	0	1	52	52.0	52										
ERIC CHIPPER																
1946	OTT	0									7			0		
1947	OTT	1									6			6		
1948	OTT	0									23			3		
1949	OTT	0									34			1		
1950	OTT	0									14			4		
Totals		1									84			14		
PAUL CHOLAKIS																
1949	WPG	1														
LANCE CHOMYC																
1985	TOR	9	1	37	37.0	37	9	457	50.8	61	21	21	100.0	14	26	53.8
1986	TOR	8					19	1059	55.7	83	38	38	100.0	37	48	77.1
1987	TOR	8	1	45	45.0	45	65	3807	58.6	95	44	44	100.0	47	64	73.4
1988	TOR	5									58	58	100.0	48	59	81.4
1989	TOR	10	17	691	40.6	54	48	2688	56.0	90	35	35	100.0	33	50	66.0
1990	TOR	10					110	5688	51.7	68	76	77	98.7	38	52	73.1
1991	TOR	7	13	434	33.4	48	50	2574	51.5	73	64	64	100.0	55	65	84.6
1992	TOR	8	17	618	36.4	43	22	993	45.1	71	41	42	97.6	35	49	71.4
1993	TOR	10	3	77	25.7	34	24	1311	54.6	80	35	35	100.0	30	44	68.2
Totals		75	52	1902	36.6	54	347	18577	53.5	95	412	414	99.5	337	457	73.7
AL CHORNEY																
1979	SAS	3	18	606	33.7	50	9	500	55.6	72	1	1	100.0	1	4	25.0
1980	SAS	0					26	1470	56.5	71	0	0		0	0	
Totals		3	18	606	33.7	50	35	1970	56.3	72	1	1	100.0	1	4	25.0
JAY CHRISTENSEN																
1991	BC	0	1	23	23.0	23										
GLEN CHRISTIAN																
1953	CAL	1					7	332	47.4	60	14	15	93.3	1	4	25.0
1954	CAL	1	1	32	32.0	32					1	1	100.0	0	0	
1957	CAL	0									5	8	62.5	0	0	
Totals		2	1	32	32.0	32	7	332	47.4	60	20	24	83.3	1	4	25.0
STEVE CHRISTIE																
2007	TOR	1					6	330	55.0	62	3	3	100.0	2	4	50.0
JIM CHRISTOPHERSON																
1964	TOR	0					4	192	48.0	62	4	5	80.0	0	2	0.0
GENE CICHOWSKI																
1960	CAL		6	220	36.7	55										
KEN CLARK																
1975	HAM	3	134	5873	43.8	84					0	0		0	0	
1976	HAM	24	139	6531	47.0	94	44	2514	57.1	79	22	23	95.7	9	22	40.9
1977	HAM	11	136	6359	46.8	70					0	0		0	0	
1978	HAM	1	40	1885	47.1	71					0	0		0	0	
1978	TOR	5	98	4337	44.3	76					0	0		0	0	
1978	Year	6	138	6222	45.1	76					0	0		0	0	
1980	SAS	1	26	1048	40.3	80					0	0		0	0	
1981	SAS	5	133	5917	44.5	64					0	0		0	0	
1982	SAS	6	124	5867	47.3	85					0	0		0	0	
1983	SAS	10	110	5210	47.4	101	1	68	68.0	68	1	1	100.0	1	1	100.0
1983	OTT	1	36	1557	43.3	58					0	0		0	0	
1983	Year	11	146	6767	46.3	101	1	68	68.0	68	1	1	100.0	1	1	100.0
1984	OTT	4	150	7023	46.8	80					0	0		0	0	
1985	OTT	8	140	6573	47.0	78					0	0		0	0	
1986	OTT	8	158	7307	46.2	80					0	0		0	0	
1987	OTT	11	168	7033	41.9	80					0	0		0	0	
Totals		98	1592	72520	45.6	101	45	2582	57.4	79	23	24	95.8	10	23	43.5
REG CLARKSON																
1951	CAL	1	8	291	36.4											
BRIAN CLAYBOURN																
2006	WPG	0	18	691	38.4	57										
MICHAEL CLEMONS																
1993	TOR	0	1	28	28.0	28										
JOCK CLIMIE																
1992	OTT	0	1	16	16.0	16										
1993	OTT	1	15	506	33.7	55										
Totals		1	16	522	32.6	55										

Year	Team	S	PUNT	YDS	AVG	LG	KO	YDS	AVG	LG	CON	CONA	PCT	FG	FGA	PCT
BILL CLINE																
1965	OTT	7	114	4643	40.7	71										
1966	OTT	0	119	4435	37.3	58										
1967	OTT	3	101	3951	39.1	62										
Totals		10	334	13029	39.0	71										
TOMMY JOE COFFEY																
1959	EDM	3					26	1417	54.5	85	3	8	37.5	4	11	36.4
1960	EDM	0					58	2988	51.5	74	4	6	66.7	3	6	50.0
1962	EDM	4					36	1886	52.4	80	26	31	83.9	9	16	56.3
1963	EDM	2	15	490	32.7	41	40	2054	51.4	75	2	5	40.0	1	4	25.0
1965	EDM	3	3	142	47.3	56	6	143	23.8	30	17	23	73.9	11	19	57.9
1966	EDM	7					39	2134	54.7	73	24	30	80.0	5	15	33.3
1967	HAM	3									20	26	76.9	18	27	66.7
1968	HAM	10	1	12	12.0	12	17	871	51.2	70	23	28	82.1	18	33	54.5
1969	HAM	7					1	57	57.0	57	30	33	90.9	13	31	41.9
1970	HAM	9									29	34	85.3	15	30	50.0
1971	HAM	5									26	27	96.3	11	27	40.7
Totals		53	19	644	33.9	56	223	11550	51.8	85	204	251	81.3	108	219	49.3
VERNON COLE																
1960	WPG	1	12	518	43.2	48										
Totals		1	12	518	43.2	48										
MERV COLLINS																
1959	OTT	0					36	1794	49.8	69						
1963	OTT	0					5	204	40.8	52						
1965	OTT	0					1	40	40.0	40						
Totals		0					42	2038	48.5	69						
SONNY COLVIN																
1948	TOR	1									1			0		
LUCA CONGI																
2006	SAS	7	136	5167	38.0	80	83	4089	49.3	74	42	42	100.0	38	44	86.4
2007	SAS	6									57	57	100.0	31	45	68.9
2008	SAS	2	9	343	38.1	50	6	307	51.2	66	50	50	100.0	38	44	86.4
2009	SAS	5	20	788	39.4	71	17	931	54.8	69	47	48	97.9	33	43	76.7
2010	SAS	2	2	69	34.5	42	1	21	21.0	21	41	41	100.0	26	34	76.5
Totals		22	167	6367	38.1	80	107	5348	50.0	74	237	238	99.6	166	210	79.0
JIM CONROY																
1960	OTT	5	80	2960	37.0	55										
1961	OTT	3	71	3092	43.5	86										
1962	OTT	2	105	3783	36.0	55										
Totals		10	256	9835	38.4	86										
DOUG COOK																
1947	SAS	1														
BILLY COOPER																
1964	WPG	0					14	733	52.4	62						
1965	WPG	0					1	40	40.0	40						
1967	WPG	0					3	88	29.3	56						
Totals		0					18	861	47.8	62						
ROYAL COPELAND																
1948	TOR	1														
TEX COULTER																
1953	MTL	3														
1954	MTL	7	138	5764	41.8	65										
1955	MTL	8	90	3613	40.1	60										
1956	MTL	5	47	1945	41.4	64										
Totals		23	275	11322	41.2	65										
DAVE CRANMER																
1969	CAL	1	45	1714	38.1	63										
1970	CAL	1	8	318	39.8	59										
Totals		2	53	2032	38.3	63										
LARRY CRAWFORD																
1986	BC	0					1	62	62.0	62						
TAD CRAWFORD																
2009	BC	0					2	108	54.0	59	2	2	100.0	0	0	
Totals		0					2	108	54.0	59	2	2	100.0	0	0	
MARC CROMBEEN																
1996	HAM						2	125	62.5	69						
JIM CROUCH																
1993	SAC	16	34	1220	35.9	58	78	4441	56.9	95	56	56	100.0	28	45	62.2
DON CROWE																
1949	TOR	3														
BRUCE CIUMMINGS																
1950	OTT	11														
1951	OTT	13														
1952	OTT	8														
1953	OTT	1														
Totals		33														
BOB CUNNINGHAM																
1949	MTL	3														
JASON CURRIE																
2003	HAM	7	94	3756	40.0	73	48	2490	51.9	86	4	4	100.0	1	2	50.0
2004	HAM	4	61	2393	39.2	55	23	1226	53.3	69	16	16	100.0	4	12	33.3
Totals		11	155	6149	39.7	73	71	3716	52.3	86	20	20	100.0	5	14	35.7
DAVE CUTLER																
1969	EDM	12					35	1866	53.3	80	14	21	66.7	17	36	47.2
1970	EDM	12					45	2718	60.4	90	28	29	96.6	22	42	52.4
1971	EDM	14	1	14	14.0	14	39	2413	61.9	90	23	25	92.0	16	47	34.0
1972	EDM	13					55	3207	58.3	89	38	42	90.5	25	48	52.1
1973	EDM	8					48	2675	55.7	90	29	31	93.5	32	54	59.3
1974	EDM	10					49	2836	57.9	90	32	33	97.0	34	53	64.2
1975	EDM	13					86	4655	54.1	95	36	36	100.0	40	69	58.0
1976	EDM	14					58	3376	58.2	90	28	28	100.0	28	48	58.3
1977	EDM	11					76	4462	58.7	90	34	34	100.0	50	73	68.5
1978	EDM	14					71	4283	60.3	90	45	46	97.8	36	49	73.5
1979	EDM	12					73	4316	59.1	90	53	54	98.1	25	46	54.3
1980	EDM	19					79	4688	59.3	90	55	56	98.2	28	49	57.1
1981	EDM	14					89	5120	57.5	90	62	63	98.4	33	48	68.8
1982	EDM	18					86	5347	62.2	90	59	60	98.3	31	48	64.6
1983	EDM	18					63	3935	62.5	90	44	45	97.8	27	45	60.0
1984	EDM	16					78	4541	58.2	90	47	47	100.0	20	35	57.1
Totals		218	1	14	14.0	14	1030	60438	58.7	95	627	650	96.5	464	790	58.7
MARCO CYNCAR																
1980	HAM	0	2	54	27.0	28	3	169	56.3	59	2	3	66.7	0	0	

Year	Team	S	PUNT	YDS	AVG	LG	KO	YDS	AVG	LG	CON	CONA	PCT	FG	FGA	PCT
1989	EDM	0					71	3744	52.7	73	0	0		0	0	
1990	EDM	0					26	1329	51.1	65	0	0		0	0	
Totals		0	2	54	27.0	28	100	5242	52.4	73	2	3	66.7	0	0	
WALT CYZ																
1952	SAS						6	254	42.3	51						
DARCY DAHLEM																
1994	SAS	1					4	221	55.3	63	3	3	100.0	0	1	0.0
1996	SAS	0					3	168	56.0	60	1	1	100.0	2	2	100.0
Totals		1					7	389	55.6	63	4	4	100.0	2	3	66.7
DOUG DAIGNEAULT																
1961	OTT	0					1	23	23.0	23						
BURKE DALES																
2005	CAL	4	115	5094	44.3	86										
2006	CAL	5	109	4902	45.0	74										
2007	CAL	4	72	3218	44.7	80										
2008	CAL	6	110	5076	46.1	68										
2009	CAL	10	122	5609	46.0	71										
2010	CAL	5	118	5366	45.5	68										
2011	CAL	11	111	5243	47.2	82	1	58	58.0	58						
Totals		45	757	34508	45.6	86	1	58	58.0	58						
PETER DALLA RIVA																
1969	MTL	0	5	169	33.8	37										
1970	MTL	0					15	759	50.6	63						
1971	MTL	0	4	119	29.8	37										
Totals		0	9	288	32.0	37	15	759	50.6	63						
KEN DANCHUK																
1966	WPG	0					4	186	46.5	55	0	0		0	1	0.0
COLT DAVID																
2010	MTL	2	14	528	37.7	52	14	796	56.9	74	6	6	100.0	9	12	75.0
MARVIN DAVIS																
1976	MTL						31	1707	55.1	68						
DEXTER DAWSON																
1996	MTL	0	1	29	29.0	29										
EAGLE DAY																
1956	WPG	1	47	1795	38.2	59										
1961	CAL	1	54	2191	40.6	67										
1963	CAL	1	9	331	36.8	70										
1966	CAL		16	653	40.8	56										
1966	Year		16	653	40.8	56										
Totals		3	126	4970	39.4	70										
TOM DEACON																
1970	WPG	0					3	151	50.3	57	1	4	25.0	0	1	0.0
1970	Year	0					3	151	50.3	57	1	4	25.0	0	1	0.0
BOB DEAN																
1954	EDM	3					48	2551	53.1	80	35	35	100.0	8	18	44.4
1955	EDM	2					45	2331	51.8	65	34	36	94.4	14	28	50.0
1956	EDM	5					26	1404	54.0	80	14	21	66.7	6	13	46.2
1957	MTL	0									0	0		1	3	33.3
Totals		10					119	6286	52.8	80	83	92	90.2	29	62	46.8
SANDRO DeANGELIS																
2005	CAL	5					84	4947	58.9	95	54	54	100.0	40	52	76.9
2006	CAL	4					84	4762	56.7	78	42	42	100.0	56	65	86.2
2007	CAL	3					76	4586	60.3	86	51	51	100.0	30	35	85.7
2008	CAL	6					97	5830	60.1	82	61	61	100.0	50	58	86.2
2009	CAL	2	1	34	34.0	34	109	6615	60.7	95	48	48	100.0	42	49	85.7
2010	HAM	3					67	3796	56.7	93	45	46	97.8	32	42	76.2
Totals		23	1	34	34.0	34	517	30536	59.1	95	301	302	99.7	250	301	83.1
ALLEN DeGRAFFENREID																
1996	WPG						1	61	61.0	61						
MARCEL deLEEUW																
1964	EDM	0	101	3836	38.0	73										
1971	OTT	4	136	5785	42.5	67										
Totals		4	237	9621	40.6	73										
JACK DELVEAUX																
1960	WPG	1	9	310	34.4	62										
1961	WPG	1	21	764	36.4	47										
1962	WPG	11	62	2668	43.0	84										
1963	WPG	4	68	3047	44.8	72										
1964	WPG	2	67	2763	41.2	68	3	144	48.0	53						
Totals		19	227	9552	42.1	84	3	144	48.0	53						
WAYNE DENNIS																
1964	WPG	1	12	429	35.8	43										
1964	Year	1	12	429	35.8	43										
Totals		1	12	429	35.8	43										
BENJY DIAL																
1971	WPG	1	1	90	90.0	90	1	50	50.0	50						
TOM DIMITROFF																
1957	OTT	1	18	616	34.2	49										
TOM DIXON																
1985	EDM	14	134	6096	45.5	76	69	4072	59.0	88	49	49	100.0	25	36	69.4
1986	EDM	33	144	6523	45.3	74	87	5255	60.4	95	55	56	98.2	34	60	56.7
1987	EDM	5	36	1501	41.7	57	30	1726	57.5	71	22	22	100.0	7	11	63.6
1987	OTT	1					7	372	53.1	61	3	3	100.0	3	6	50.0
1987	Year	6	36	1501	41.7	57	37	2098	56.7	71	25	25	100.0	10	17	58.8
1988	OTT	24	168	6726	40.0	59	58	3352	57.8	91	22	22	100.0	25	49	51.0
Totals		77	482	20846	43.2	76	251	14777	58.9	95	151	152	99.3	94	162	58.0
GLENN DOBBS																
1951	SAS	20	90	3974	44.2											
1952	SAS	0	1	43	43.0	43										
1953	SAS	2	50	2291	45.8											
1954	HAM	1	12	529	44.1	60										
Totals		23	153	6837	44.7	60										
WALT DOBLER																
1946	WPG	2									4	5	80.0	2		
AL DOROW																
1959	TOR	0	59	2181	37.0	51										
DEAN DORSEY																
1982	TOR	4	57	2309	40.5	101	24	1198	49.9	63	15	15	100.0	12	17	70.6
1984	OTT	7					63	3524	55.9	90	37	37	100.0	26	31	83.9
1985	OTT	12					50	2803	56.1	90	24	24	100.0	28	38	73.7
1986	OTT	7					67	3715	55.4	76	28	28	100.0	33	42	78.6
1987	OTT	5					62	3277	52.9	68	28	28	100.0	36	44	81.8

Year Team	S	PUNT	YDS	AVG	LG	KO	YDS	AVG	LG	CON	CONA	PCT	FG	FGA	PCT
1989 OTT	7					87	4530	52.1	79	36	36	100.0	35	50	70.0
1990 OTT	7					103	5620	54.6	80	55	55	100.0	38	53	71.7
1991 EDM	1					36	1814	50.4	62	21	21	100.0	11	15	73.3
Totals	50	57	2309	40.5	101	492	26481	53.8	90	244	244	100.0	219	290	75.5
FRED DOTY															
1947 TOR	0									1			0		
GERRY DOUCETTE															
1954 TOR	1	31	1137	36.7	56										
1955 TOR	0	34	1295	38.1	56										
1956 TOR	2	106	3919	37.0	64										
1959 TOR	1	9	343	38.1	49										
1961 MTL	0	2	45	22.5	29										
Totals	4	182	6739	37.0	64										
GLEN DOUGLAS															
1948 MTL	0									1			0		
BERT DRESSLER															
1947 OTT	0									10			0		
DOUG DREW															
1947 SAS	1														
GERRY DUGUID															
1950 WPG	0	1	35	35.0	35										
GREG DUNCAN															
1993 OTT	1					1	49	49.0	49	0	0		0	1	0.0
MAURY DUNCAN															
1957 BC	0					12	651	54.3	70	9	15	60.0	0	1	0.0
TED DUNCAN															
1955 BC	1	23	937	40.7	57										
1957 CAL	9	119	5008	42.1	72										
1958 CAL	4	148	6180	41.8	66									0	
1961 CAL	0	34	1271	37.4	57										
Totals	14	324	13396	41.3	72										
FRED DUNN															
1970 EDM	0	128	5326	41.6	60										
1971 EDM	1	76	3041	40.0	87										
Totals	1	204	8367	41.0	87										
DICK DUPUIS															
1969 EDM	0	1	37	37.0	37										
DON DURNO															
1947 MTL	0									1			0		
1948 TOR	0									1			1		
1949 TOR	1									1			0		
Totals	1									3			1		
DAMON DUVAL															
2005 MTL	17	96	4283	44.6	78	101	6445	63.8	95	60	60	100.0	38	52	73.1
2006 MTL	8	110	4999	45.4	75	71	4332	61.0	75	40	40	100.0	51	59	86.4
2007 MTL	15	127	5966	47.0	90	68	4359	64.1	95	35	35	100.0	32	45	71.1
2008 MTL	14	81	3741	46.2	77	92	5697	61.9	91	60	61	98.4	44	53	83.0
2009 MTL	21	109	4884	44.8	70	130	8279	63.7	95	56	56	100.0	55	63	87.3
2010 MTL	13	94	4227	45.0	69	70	4398	62.8	95	41	41	100.0	34	47	72.3
2011 EDM	20	137	6434	47.0	77	80	4877	61.0	85	27	27	100.0	23	34	67.6
Totals	108	754	34534	45.8	90	612	38387	62.7	95	319	320	99.7	277	353	78.5
KEITH EAMAN															
1972 OTT	0	1	60	60.0	60										
1974 MTL	0	1	51	51.0	51										
Totals	0	2	111	55.5	60										
JOHN EASON															
1972 MTL	1					22	1215	55.2	90						
WALLY EDWARDS															
1949 WPG	1									8	11	72.7	1		
RAY ELGAARD															
1995 SAS	0	1	16	16.0	16										
JAMES ELLINGSON															
1992 OTT	0	1	5	5.0	5										
SHEA EMRY															
2010 MTL	0	5	194	38.8	46	4	255	63.8	75						
AL ENDRESS															
1953 CAL	0									1	1	100.0	0	0	
ANDREW ENGLISH															
2002 HAM	0					4	193	48.3	55						
2003 HAM	0					2	118	59.0	65						
Totals	0					6	311	51.8	65						
HAYDEN EPSTEIN															
2005 EDM	3	16	656	41.0	63	12	657	54.8	68	11	11	100.0	8	12	66.7
JACK ESPENSHIP															
1961 MTL	4	54	2160	40.0	70										
1962 MTL	1	21	806	38.4	60										
Totals	5	75	2966	39.5	70										
RONNIE ESTAY															
1972 BC	0	3	91	30.3	33										
1975 EDM	0	12	481	40.1	49										
Totals	0	15	572	38.1	49										
SAM ETCHEVERRY															
1952 MTL	3									1			0		
1954 MTL	0	3	131	43.7	60					11	12	91.7	0	0	
1955 MTL	1	19	733	38.6	51					2	2	100.0	0	0	
1956 MTL	3	48	1968	41.0	56					0	0		0	0	
1957 MTL	4	66	2634	39.9	55					0	0		0	0	
1958 MTL	3	145	5668	39.1	80					0	0		0	0	
1959 MTL	6	131	4937	37.7	60					0	0		0	0	
1960 MTL	10	102	4196	41.1	61					0	0		0	0	
Totals	31	514	20267	39.4	80					14	14	92.9	0	0	
DON ETTINGER															
1951 SAS	1									34	40	85.0	4	11	36.4
1952 TOR	1									17			0		
1953 TOR	0									2			0		
Totals	2									53	40	85.0	4	11	36.4
JOHNNY EVANS															
1982 MTL	0	12	455	37.9	51					0	0		0	0	
1983 MTL	0	1	29	29.0	29					0	0		0	0	
1984 EDM	5	123	5404	43.9	65					0	0		0	0	
Totals	5	136	5888	43.3	65					0	0		0	0	
CLARE EXELBY															

Year	Team	S	PUNT	YDS	AVG	LG	KO	YDS	AVG	LG	CON	CONA	PCT	FG	FGA	PCT
1964	MTL						2	36	18.0	19						
MARTIN FABI																
1962	MTL	1	24	937	39.0	60					0	0		0	0	
1962	Year	1	24	937	39.0	60					0	0		0	0	
1963	SAS	15	149	6556	44.0	76	4	195	48.8	60	0	0		0	0	
1964	SAS	7	106	4282	40.4	69	42	2340	55.7	72	1	1	100.0	0	3	0.0
1965	SAS	4	84	3566	42.5	71	3	177	59.0	62	0	0		0	0	
Totals		27	363	15341	42.3	76	49	2712	55.3	72	1	1	100.0	0	3	0.0
RANDY FABI																
1986	WPG	0					25	1350	54.0	67						
FRED FACCIOLLA																
1946	OTT	1									8			1		
JEFF FAIRHOLM																
1991	SAS	0	1	28	28.0	28										
LARRY FAIRHOLM																
1969	MTL	0					1	42	42.0	42						
MIKE FALLS																
1956	TOR	0									23	28	82.1	0	0	
BERNIE FALONEY																
1954	EDM	0	21	864	41.1	54										
1957	HAM	0	3	132	44.0	46										
1958	HAM	2	1	85	85.0	85										
1959	HAM	5	12	755	62.9	84										
1960	HAM	1	49	2092	42.7	65										
1961	HAM	2	50	2287	45.7	58										
1963	HAM	2	18	861	47.8	73										
1964	HAM	1	44	1944	44.2	85										
1965	MTL	2	14	542	38.7	54										
1966	MTL	1	5	200	40.0	81										
1967	BC	0	1	47	47.0	47										
Totals		16	218	9809	45.0	85										
ANDY FANTUZ																
2010	SAS	0					1	11	11.0	11						
PAUL FEDOR																
1962	MTL	0	1	34	34.0	34										
WOLFGANG FELGEMACHER																
1966	TOR	0					2	118	59.0	60	1	1	100.0	0	2	0.0
GERRY FELLNER																
1980	SAS	0	6	195	32.5	51										
CHUCK FENENBOCK																
1949	EDM	4														
1950	CAL	1	4	167	41.8	55										
Totals		5	4	167	41.8	55										
MERVYN FERNANDEZ																
1986	BC	0	14	476	34.0	45										
NORM FIELDGATE																
1958	BC	0					5	199	39.8	57						
1962	BC	0					1	40	40.0	40						
Totals		0					6	239	39.8	57						
GENE FILIPSKI																
1959	CAL	0									1	2	50.0	0	0	
1961	CAL	1					2	39	19.5	25	5	6	83.3	0	1	0.0
Totals		2					2	39	19.5	25	6	8	75.0	0	1	0.0
D.J. FITZPATRICK																
2008	MTL	0	6	239	39.8	44	3	147	49.0	54	2	2	100.0	0	0	
GEORGE FLEMIN																
1963	WPG	11					19	1117	58.8	77	25	30	83.3	15	30	50.0%
1964	WPG	6					15	840	56.0	72	14	16	87.5	7	17	41.2
Totals		17					34	1957	57.6	77	39	46	84.8	22	47	46.8
PAT FLEMING																
2003	OTT	2	85	3558	41.9	65					0	0		0	0	
2004	OTT	4	135	5359	39.7	64					0	0		0	0	
2005	OTT	6	97	4025	41.5	61	11	563	51.2	65	3	3	100.0	1	3	33.3
2006	HAM	8	130	5625	43.3	78					0	0		0	0	
2007	WPG	3	29	1266	43.7	69					0	0		0	0	
Totals		23	476	19833	41.7	78	11	563	51.2	65	3	3	100.0	1	3	33.3
SEAN FLEMING																
1992	EDM	14					102	5732	56.2	70	60	61	98.4	30	49	61.2
1993	EDM	10					82	4908	59.9	74	54	54	100.0	34	48	70.8
1994	EDM	15	1	30	30.0	30	78	4619	59.2	82	48	49	98.0	48	62	77.4
1995	EDM	15	3	154	51.3	67	95	5611	59.1	83	60	61	98.4	44	63	69.8
1996	EDM	3	1	50	50.0	50	51	3134	61.5	80	33	33	100.0	32	39	82.1
1997	EDM	23	115	4667	40.6	91	78	4751	60.9	87	41	41	100.0	41	56	73.2
1998	EDM	9	146	5993	41.0	69	72	4300	59.7	95	37	37	100.0	34	40	85.0
1999	EDM	6	36	1545	42.9	71	26	1504	57.8	71	12	12	100.0	14	26	53.8
2000	EDM	21	126	5334	42.3	74	72	4539	63.0	88	53	53	100.0	37	55	67.3
2001	EDM	11	123	5291	43.0	75	67	3903	58.3	73	37	37	100.0	45	57	78.9
2002	EDM	14	126	5362	42.6	73	74	4920	66.5	80	54	56	96.4	34	42	81.0
2003	EDM	5	124	5173	41.7	86	98	5640	57.6	80	61	61	100.0	32	39	82.1
2004	EDM	12	118	5043	42.7	72	86	4751	55.2	75	57	57	100.0	37	47	78.7
2005	EDM	10	110	4420	40.2	65	68	3828	56.3	69	36	36	100.0	25	37	67.6
2006	EDM	7	113	4575	40.5	63	70	3903	55.8	72	35	36	97.2	33	43	76.7
2007	EDM	22	122	5330	43.7	72	67	3948	58.9	95	35	35	100.0	34	50	68.0
Totals		197	1264	52967	41.9	91	1186	69991	59.0	95	713	719	99.2	554	753	73.6
WILLIE FLEMING																
1960	BC	0									1	1	100.0	0	0	
DARREN FLUTIE																
1998	HAM	0	1	36	36.0	36										
2000	HAM	0	1	40	40.0	40										
Totals		0	2	76	38.0	40										
JIM FOLE																
1973	OTT	0	1	48	48.0	48										
AL FORD																
1966	SAS	1	75	2971	39.6	74										
1967	SAS	5	116	4492	38.7	89										
1968	SAS	4	133	5532	41.6	68										
1969	SAS	4	123	4731	38.5	84										
1970	SAS	1	133	5424	40.8	69										
1971	SAS	2	123	5014	40.8	81										
1972	SAS	3	73	3070	42.1	76										
1973	SAS	2	111	4478	40.3	75										
1974	SAS	1	117	4754	40.6	55										

Year Team	S	PUNT	YDS	AVG	LG	KO	YDS	AVG	LG	CON	CONA	PCT	FG	FGA	PCT
1975 SAS	0	37	1414	38.2	57										
Totals	23	1041	41880	40.2	89										
TOMMY FORD															
1950 WPG	0	1	30	30.0	30										
JOE FORZANI															
1969 CAL	1	32	1109	34.7	64										
JIM FOUBISTER															
1949 WPG	1														
ED FOUCH															
1955 TOR	0									2	2	100.0	0	0	
GINO FRACAS															
1955 EDM	0					10	482	48.2	57	2	2	100.0	0	0	
CAM FRASER															
1952 HAM	15														
1953 HAM	10														
1954 HAM	15	138	5944	43.1	73										
1955 HAM	11	125	5920	47.4	84										
1956 HAM	10	121	5566	46.0	77										
1957 HAM	13	157	7222	46.0	73										
1958 HAM	15	156	7108	45.6	73										
1959 HAM	9	125	5643	45.1	71										
1960 HAM	0	58	2509	43.3	62										
1961 HAM	2	51	2210	43.3	67										
1962 MTL	1	36	1418	39.4	55										
1969 HAM	0	20	747	37.4	48										
Totals	101	987	44287	44.9	84										
STEWART FRASE															
1982 SAS	0	1	25	25.0	25										
1983 SAS	0	1	77	77.0	77										
1984 SAS	0	1	47	47.0	47										
Totals	0	3	149	49.7	77										
BOB FRIEND															
1973 BC	0									0	2	0.0	0	0	
DON FUEL															
1963 TOR	1									3	6	50.0	0	1	0.0
JIM FURLONG															
1962 CAL	6	43	1706	39.7	73										
1963 CAL	7	125	5233	41.9	87										
1964 CAL	6	125	5110	40.9	86										
1965 CAL	7	137	5578	40.7	68										
1966 CAL	0	46	1753	38.1	57										
1967 CAL	8	84	3741	44.5	87										
1968 CAL	2	43	1728	40.2	40										
1969 CAL	0	24	923	38.5	58										
1970 CAL	0	13	466	35.8	51										
1971 CAL	0	10	399	39.9	50										
1972 CAL	0	4	123	30.8	36										
1973 CAL	1	53	2138	40.3	72										
Totals	37	707	28898	40.9	87										
WALLY GABLER															
1967 TOR	1	1	38	38.0	38										
1968 TOR	0	1	46	46.0	46										
1970 WPG	0	1	59	59.0	59										
1970 HAM	0	1	47	47.0	47										
1970 Year	0	2	106	53.0	59										
1972 TOR	0	1	30	30.0	30										
Totals	1	5	220	44.0	59										
BOB GAIN															
1951 OTT	3									23			2		
GENE GAINES															
1961 MTL	0	1	47	47.0	47										
1972 MTL	0	1	20	20.0	20										
Totals	0	2	67	33.5	47										
RALPH GALLOWAY															
1970 SAS	0					1	42	42.0	42						
PETE GARDERE															
1993 SAC	5	77	3246	42.2	63										
1994 SAC	9	136	5793	42.6	77										
1995 MEM	4	86	3730	43.4	72										
Totals	18	299	12769	42.7	77										
CHRIS GARDNER															
1995 MEM	5	5	215	43.0	49	5	316	63.2	69	2	2	100.0	4	10	40.0
STAN GELBAUGH															
1986 SAS	1	45	1811	40.2	60										
NORM GELLER															
1948 WPG	0									0			1		
TED GERELA															
1967 BC	8	1	4	4.0	4	44	2504	56.9	78	21	27	77.8	16	35	45.7
1968 BC	9	109	4226	38.8	60	32	1836	57.4	81	16	16	100.0	30	59	50.8
1969 BC	15					38	2341	61.6	85	17	22	77.3	22	54	40.7
1970 BC	11					46	2767	60.2	90	30	30	100.0	22	43	51.2
1971 BC	12					46	2758	60.0	75	7	8	87.5	8	26	30.8
1972 BC	7					40	2291	57.3	80	25	27	92.6	19	33	57.6
1973 BC	7					33	1820	55.2	85	16	18	88.9	6	21	28.6
Totals	69	110	4230	38.5	60	279	16317	58.5	90	132	148	89.2	123	271	45.4
DAN GIANCOLA															
1999 TOR	9									28	28	100.0	48	61	78.7
2000 BC	0					48	2659	55.4	63	1	1	100.0	0	0	
2001 TOR	9					12	619	51.6	60	28	28	100.0	25	39	64.1
2002 OTT	1									0	0		1	2	50.0
2004 TOR	0					5	272	54.4	60	2	2	100.0	2	3	66.7
Totals	19					65	3550	54.6	63	59	59	100.0	76	105	72.4
WAYNE GIARDINO															
1970 OTT	0									0	0		0	2	0.0
1971 OTT	0									1	1	100.0	0	0	
Totals	0									1	1	100.0	0	2	0.0
WES GIDEON															
1961 TOR	0									5	6	83.3	1	1	100.0
COOKIE GILCHRIST															
1957 HAM	0									0	0		0	1	0.0
1958 SAS	0					47	2466	52.5	74	0	0		0	0	
1959 TOR	2					40	2105	52.6	69	16	24	66.7	9	14	64.3

Year	Team	S	PUNT	YDS	AVG	LG	KO	YDS	AVG	LG	CON	CONA	PCT	FG	FGA	PCT
1960	TOR	9									43	48	89.6	5	18	27.8
1961	TOR	3					18	1093	60.7	70	5	11	45.5	5	9	55.6
Totals		15					105	5664	53.9	74	64	83	77.1	19	42	45.2
BILL GLASS																
1957	SAS	0					5	244	48.8	70						
SULLY GLASSER																
1946	SAS	1														
1955	SAS	0	2	92	46.0	56										
Totals		1	2	92	46.0	56										
WILF GODFREY																
1949	SAS	0									1			0		
1950	CAL	0									6	8	75.0	0	0	
Totals		0									7	8	75.0	0	0	
TONY GOLAB																
1946	OTT	3									0			0		
1947	OTT	2									0			0		
1948	OTT	0									1			0		
1949	OTT	2									0			-		
Totals		7									1			0		
PETE GONZALEZ																
2003	HAM	0	1	36	36.0	36										
BILL GOODS																
1967	CAL	9					1	20	20.0	20	37	42	88.1	8	22	36.4
1968	SAS	9					28	1525	54.5	71	36	38	94.7	11	28	39.3
1969	EDM	2					7	367	52.4	63	1	5	20.0	0	5	0.0
Totals		20					36	1912	53.1	71	74	85	87.1	19	55	34.5
ANDY GORDON																
1949	OTT	1														
BOB GORDON																
2004	WPG	0	1	54	54.0	54										
BILLY GRAHAM																
1957	HAM	0									0	2	0.0	0	0	
1958	HAM	0									7	9	77.8	0	0	
Totals		0									7	11	63.6	0	0	
VERN GRAHAM																
1949	CAL	0									27			7		
1950	CAL	0									8	10	80.0	5	9	55.6
Totals		0									35	10	80.0	12	9	55.6
CHICK GRANING																
1966	BC		31	1160	37.4	73										
COREY GRANT																
2000	HAM	0	1	27	27.0	27										
2006	SAS	0	1	46	46.0	46										
Totals		0	2	73	36.5	46										
GEORGE GRANT																
1960	BC	1					35	2005	57.3	80	23	25	92.0	3	7	42.9
1961	BC	0					21	1060	50.5	70	8	13	61.5	3	9	33.3
1962	BC	3					24	1254	52.3	70	14	18	77.8	1	6	16.7
Totals		4					80	4319	54.0	80	45	56	80.4	7	22	31.8
MARVIN GRAVES																
1994	TOR	0	1	29	29.0	29					0	0		0	0	
CLINTON GREATHOUSE																
2004	CAL	6	52	2097	40.3	77	28	1367	48.8	72	12	12	100.0	14	17	82.4
JOHNNY GREEN																
1959	TOR	0	12	460	38.3	43										
DAVE GREENBERG																
1946	MTL	1														
1947	MTL	0									4			0		
Totals		1									4			0		
NELS GREENE																
1948	OTT	1									1			0		
1950	SAS	1	24	874	36.4						0	0		0	0	
Totals		2	24	874	36.4						1	0		0	0	
HANK GRENDA																
1969	BC	0	11	366	33.3	44										
ANDREW GRIGG																
2001	HAM	0									1	1	100.0	0	0	
2002	HAM	1	5	163	32.6	51					3	3	100.0	0	2	0.0
Totals		1	5	163	32.6	51					4	4	100.0	0	2	0.0
FRANCO GRILLA																
1995	BIR	3					26	1595	61.3	95	17	17	100.0	6	12	50.0
DAVE GROSZ																
1962	MTL	0	16	549	34.3	51										
PIERRE GUINDON																
1968	WPG	4	1	21	21.0	21	34	1889	55.6	73	19	27	70.4	15	34	44.1
1969	WPG	3					26	1426	54.8	73	16	19	84.2	15	34	44.1
1970	MTL	1					12	649	54.1	65	6	8	75.0	0	2	0.0
Totals		8	1	21	21.0	21	72	3964	55.1	73	41	54	75.9	30	70	42.9
ERIC GUTHRIE																
1972	BC	1	119	5017	42.2	64					0	0		0	0	
1973	BC	3	117	4926	42.1	70	9	500	55.6	62	0	0		0	2	0.0
1975	BC	8	123	5048	41.0	56	27	1255	46.5	70	6	7	85.7	4	10	40.0
1976	BC	0					10	480	48.0	60	0	0		0	0	
Totals		12	359	14991	41.8	70	46	2235	48.6	70	6	7	85.7	4	12	33.3
CED GYLES																
1950	CAL	0	1	38	38.0	38										
ROGER HAGBERG																
1963	WPG	0	2	100	50.0	54										
BERT HAIGH																
1946	OTT	10									1			0		
1947	OTT	3									0			0		
1948	OTT	1									0			0		
1949	OTT	2									0			0		
Totals		16									1			0		
KEN HALL																
1957	EDM	3	22	908	41.3	82					1	1	100.0	0		
ROGER HAMELIN																
1967	WPG	1					13	619	47.6	59	5	11	45.5	0	2	0.0
MIKE HAMELUCK																
1986	WPG						1	44	44.0	44						
FREDDY HAMILTON																
1955	SAS	0	1	36	36.0	36										

Year	Team	S	PUNT	YDS	AVG	LG	KO	YDS	AVG	LG	CON	CONA	PCT	FG	FGA	PCT
GEORGE HANSEN																
1961	CAL	5									27	32	84.4	9	17	52.9
1962	CAL	0									4	5	80.0	0	0	
Totals		5									31	37	83.8	9	17	52.9
MERLE HAPES																
1953	HAM	5														
1954	HAM	0	1	32	32.0	32										
Totals		5	1	32	32.0	32										
ROBIN HARBER																
1978	CAL	0	2	72	36.0	39										
CHRIS HARDY																
2001	EDM	1									0	0		0	1	0.0
2002	EDM	0					1	6	6.0	6	0	0		0	0	
2003	TOR	0					1	43	43.0	43	0	0		0	0	
2004	TOR	0	14	488	34.9	45	2	64	32.0	49	0	0		3	3	100.0
2005	TOR	0	2	75	37.5	39					1	1	100.0	1	1	100.0
2006	TOR	0					3	167	55.7	60	1	1	100.0	0	0	
2007	TOR	0	18	664	36.9	56	8	405	50.6	58	7	7	100.0	1	1	100.0
2008	TOR	0	1	21	21.0	21					0	0		0	0	
Totals		1	36	1248	35.7	50	15	685	45.7	60	9	9	100.0	5	6	83.3
GLENN HARPER																
1986	CAL	5	156	6487	41.6	83					0	0		0	0	
1987	CAL	3	140	5986	42.8	69					0	0		0	0	
1988	CAL	4	165	6684	40.5	81					0	0		0	0	
1989	TOR	3	85	3343	39.3	63					0	0		0	0	
1990	TOR	1	103	4133	40.1	61					0	0		0	0	
1991	EDM	3	33	1258	38.1	62					0	0		0	0	
1992	EDM	2	130	5261	40.5	74					0	0		0	0	
1993	EDM	7	154	6385	41.5	71					0	0		0	0	
1994	EDM	2	138	5598	40.6	65					0	0		0	0	
1995	EDM	5	144	5962	41.4	65					1	1	100.0	0	0	
1996	EDM	7	156	6544	41.9	72	1	35	35.0	35	0	0		0	0	
2002	OTT	3	127	5145	40.5	61	1	39	39.0	39	0	0		0	0	
2003	OTT	1	38	1533	40.3	64					0	0		0	0	
Totals		46	1569	64319	41.0	83	2	74	37.0	39	1	1	100.0	0	0	
MARK HARRIS																
1973	MTL	1					24	1471	61.3	90						
JACK HARTMAN																
1950	SAS	5									22	23	95.7	7	15	46.7
DUNC HARVEY																
1962	EDM	1	13	486	37.4	83										
1963	EDM	0	17	590	34.7	44										
Totals		1	30	1076	35.9	83										
STEVE HATFIELD																
1951	OTT	0									5			0		
J.T. HAY																
1978	OTT	15					73	3826	52.4	68	43	43	100.0	26	43	60.5
1979	CAL	14	1	52	52.0	52	63	3728	59.2	90	38	38	100.0	21	32	65.6
1980	CAL	6					34	2068	60.8	90	28	28	100.0	22	28	78.6
1981	CAL	11	4	103	25.8	37	50	2813	56.3	90	22	22	100.0	36	48	75.0
1982	CAL	7					61	3727	61.1	90	37	37	100.0	29	39	74.4
1983	CAL	12	15	623	41.5	51	65	3923	60.4	90	41	41	100.0	27	41	65.9
1984	CAL	11					53	3094	58.4	90	25	25	100.0	33	45	73.3
1985	CAL	18	163	6682	41.0	77	48	2738	57.0	90	21	21	100.0	27	42	64.3
1986	CAL	14					84	4524	53.9	72	47	47	100.0	40	57	70.2
1987	CAL	13					79	3999	50.6	70	42	42	100.0	39	55	70.9
1988	CAL	3					40	2141	53.5	63	19	19	100.0	8	15	53.3
Totals		124	183	7460	40.8	77	650	36581	56.3	90	363	363	100.0	308	445	69.2
GARY HAYES																
1981	EDM	0	1	30	30.0	30										
CURTIS HEAD																
2003	BC	5	103	4015	39.0	67	92	5178	56.3	75	54	55	98.2	44	56	78.6
CHARLIE HEBERT																
2004	CAL	11	81	3584	44.2	89	47	2653	56.4	72	24	25	96.0	19	27	70.4
BOB HECK																
1950	TOR	0									0			1		
1952	TOR	0									13			1		
Totals		0									13			2		
NORB HECKER																
1954	TOR	1									31	33	93.9	2	3	66.7
1958	HAM	0	1	40	40.0	40					5	6	83.3	0		
Totals		1	1	40	40.0	40					36	39	92.3	2	3	66.7
JIM HEIGHTON																
1971	WPG	0					3	150	50.0	57						
ZAC HENDERSON																
1978	HAM	0	11	503	45.7	51										
1979	HAM	2	58	2259	38.9	80										
1982	TOR	0	4	116	29.0	44										
Totals		2	73	2878	39.4	80										
GARNEY HENLEY																
1970	HAM	0	1	46	46.0	46	1	21	21.0	21						
1975	HAM	0	1	27	27.0	27										
Totals		0	2	73	36.5	46	1	21	21.0	21						
URBAN HENRY																
1958	BC	0					7	271	38.7	48						
1959	BC	0					1	45	45.0	45						
Totals		0					8	316	39.5	48						
GEORGE HERRING																
1958	BC	2	107	4570	42.7	77										
1959	SAS	1	10	443	44.3	59										
Totals		3	117	5013	42.8	77										
GARY HERTZFELDT																
1964	EDM		20	715	35.8	58										
BURDETTE HESS																
1956	CAL	0					5	250	50.0	55						
BOB HEYDENFELDT																
1955	EDM	9	107	4635	43.3	68										
PAUL HICKIE																
1983	EDM	13	123	5512	44.8	79										
1984	EDM	0	8	370	46.3	59										
1984	SAS	4	102	4427	43.4	63										
Totals		17	233	10309	44.2	79										

Year Team	S	PUNT	YDS	AVG	LG	KO	YDS	AVG	LG	CON	CONA	PCT	FG	FGA	PCT
LARRY HICKMAN															
1962 MTL	0	2	96	48.0	50										
JACK HILL															
1957 SAS	0	11	372	33.8	63	15	873	58.2	80	0	0		0	0	
1958 SAS	1									36	41	87.8	4	7	57.1
1959 SAS	1					14	818	58.4	80	0	0		0	0	
1960 SAS	1					14	810	57.9	75	6	6	100.0	3	7	42.9
Totals	3	11	372	33.8	63	43	2501	58.2	80	42	47	89.4	7	14	50.0
KARL HILZINGER															
1953 SAS	0	2	80	40.0											
DON HINEY															
1946 WPG	0									2	3	66.7	3		
1947 WPG	1									9			0		
1948 WPG	3									3			4		
Totals	4									14	3	66.7	7		
KEN HOBART															
1986 HAM	0					1	35	35.0	35						
BOB HOLBURN															
1954 BC	0	12	438	36.5	64										
CONDREDGE HOLLOWAY															
1977 OTT	1	1	43	43.0	43										
BRIAN HOLMES															
2004 OTT	1					6	325	54.2	65	5	5	100.0	2	4	50.0
CHUCK HOLMES															
1955 TOR	1	11	399	36.3	48										
HARRY HOLT															
1982 BC	1					48	2687	56.0	80						
HARRY HOOD															
1948 CAL	0									1			0		
ANDY HOPKINS															
1973 HAM	0					3	136	45.3	63						
BOB HORNES															
1974 BC		1	55	55.0	55										
BOB HOUMARD															
1972 OTT	0	1	25	25.0	25										
RON HOWELL															
1959 HAM	0	1	25	25.0	25										
1962 HAM	0	2	83	41.5	43										
Totals	0	3	108	36.0	43										
DAN HUCLACK															
1986 HAM	2					1	39	39.0	39	2	3	66.7	1	3	33.3
CARLOS HUERTA															
1994 LV	5	3	112	37.3	52					37	37	100.0	38	46	82.6
1995 BAL	7					35	1933	55.2	67	50	50	100.0	57	72	79.2
Totals	12	3	112	37.3	52	35	1933	55.2	67	87	87	100.0	95	118	80.5
DICK HUFFMAN															
1951 WPG	1														
NEAL HUGHES															
2004 SAS	0	2	70	35.0	36										
TED HUNT															
1957 BC	0	1	37	37.0	37					20	25	80.0	2	4	50.0
1958 BC	2	4	140	35.0	65	3	87	29.0	45	19	27	70.4	2	6	33.3
Totals	2	5	177	35.4	65	3	87	29.0	45	39	52	75.0	4	10	40.0
DONALD IGWEBUIKE															
1994 BAL	8					71	4062	57.2	73	47	48	97.9	43	53	81.1
1995 MEM	4									4	4	100.0	3	7	42.9
Totals	12					71	4062	57.2	73	51	52	98.1	46	60	76.7
HANK ILESIC															
1977 EDM	3	77	3469	45.1	87					0	0		0	0	
1978 EDM	9	132	6240	47.3	87	1	55	55.0	55	0	0		0	0	
1979 EDM	8	119	5610	47.1	76	2	129	64.5	67	1	2	50.0	0	0	
1980 EDM	7	120	5466	45.6	71					0	0		0	0	
1981 EDM	7	115	5252	45.7	88					0	0		0	0	
1982 EDM	7	115	5297	46.1	81					0	0		0	0	
1983 TOR	30	137	6094	44.5	90	68	4269	62.8	90	40	41	97.6	26	39	66.7
1984 TOR	25	140	6192	44.2	71	69	4602	66.7	90	44	46	95.7	30	43	69.8
1985 TOR	24	164	7181	43.8	83	45	2705	60.1	90	13	14	92.9	3	8	37.5
1986 TOR	24	165	8004	48.5	88	47	3106	66.1	95	0	0		0	0	
1987 TOR	11	147	6268	42.6	71	14	853	60.9	74	0	0		0	0	
1988 TOR	10	142	6246	44.0	77	87	5216	60.0	95	0	0		0	0	
1989 TOR	6	68	2894	42.6	62	19	1163	61.2	75	0	0		0	0	
1990 TOR	0	20	784	39.2	52	14	925	66.1	80	0	0		0	0	
1991 TOR	5	109	4844	44.4	77	64	3891	60.8	78	0	0		0	0	
1992 TOR	5	131	5891	45.0	81	61	3655	59.9	70	0	0		0	0	
1993 TOR	2	89	3672	41.3	66	23	1401	60.9	95	0	0		0	0	
1995 HAM	2	59	2349	39.8	78	25	1450	58.0	83	0	0		0	0	
1998 BC	0					12	635	52.9	62	0	0		0	0	
2001 EDM	0	13	528	40.6	56	2	118	59.0	65	0	0		0	0	
Totals	185	2062	92281	44.8	90	553	34173	61.8	95	98	103	95.1	59	90	65.6
MARK IRVIN															
2005 OTT	1	8	244	30.5	39	12	583	48.6	60	6	6	100.0	6	9	66.7
LARRY ISBELL															
1954 SAS	12	106	4909	46.3	83										
1955 SAS	1	69	2849	41.3	82										
1956 SAS	19	128	5667	44.3	75										
1957 SAS	7	125	5089	40.7	74										
1958 SAS	11	111	4548	41.0	78										
Totals	50	539	23062	42.8	83										
ROCKET ISMAIL															
1992 TOR	0	1	15	15.0	15										
JEREMY ITO															
2009 HAM	0	10	403	40.3	61	8	456	57.0	70	4	4	100.0	3	3	100.0
PARIS JACKSON															
2009 BC	0	2	89	44.5	50										
2010 BC	0	1	34	34.0	34										
Totals	0	3	123	41.0	50										
RUSS JACKSON															
1962 OTT	0	1	45	45.0	45										
STEVE JACKSON															
1986 HAM						1	43	43.0	43						
JACK JACOBS															
1950 WPG	18	94	3772	40.1						2	4	50.0	1	2	50.0

Year Team	S	PUNT	YDS	AVG	LG	KO	YDS	AVG	LG	CON	CONA	PCT	FG	FGA	PCT
1951 WPG	12	95	3900	41.1						20	23	87.0	2	3	66.7
1952 WPG	13	103	4522	43.9	88					14	17	82.4	0	0	
1953 WPG	6	112	4440	39.6						0	0		0	0	
1954 WPG	8	114	4614	40.5	82					0	0		0	0	
Totals	57	518	21248	41.0	88					36	44	81.8	3	5	60.0
FRANK JAGAS															
1996 EDM	4					16	828	51.8	64	10	11	90.9	12	17	70.6
1996 SAS	5					54	2929	54.2	68	23	23	100.0	25	36	69.4
1996 Year	9					70	3757	53.7	68	33	34	97.1	37	53	69.8
NICK JAMBROSIC															
1977 HAM	6					47	2407	51.2	69	21	21	100.0	23	30	76.7
1978 HAM	13	54	2353	43.6	68	38	2013	53.0	70	12	13	92.3	11	23	47.8
Totals	19	54	2353	43.6	68	85	4420	52.0	70	33	34	97.1	34	53	64.2
GERRY JAMES															
1955 WPG	0					1	55	55.0	55	0	0		0	0	
1957 WPG	2	1	40	40.0	40	69	3719	53.9	77	3	4	75.0	4	5	80.0
1958 WPG	0					19	978	51.5	64	9	13	69.2	4	6	66.7
1959 WPG	0					40	2258	56.5	85	4	5	80.0	1	1	100.0
1960 WPG	4					4	198	49.5	58	32	40	80.0	6	10	60.0
1961 WPG	4					6	300	51.0	50	27	37	73.0	8	16	50.0
1962 WPG	9	1	41	41.0	41	13	785	60.4	80	41	47	87.2	12	27	44.4
1964 SAS	2					18	926	51.4	80	27	33	81.8	5	11	45.5
Totals	21	2	81	40.5	41	170	9227	54.3	85	143	179	79.9	40	76	52.6
JERRY JANES															
1957 BC	0					44	2195	49.9	70	0	0		0	0	
1958 BC	1					30	1541	51.4	68	1	1	100.0	0	2	0.0
1959 BC	0					9	431	47.9	60	4	7	57.1	0	1	0.0
Totals	1					83	4167	50.2	70	5	8	62.5	0	3	0.0
BILLY JESSUP															
1959 BC	0	1	21	21.0	21										
TOM JOHANSEN															
1969 TOR	2					26	1607	61.8	82	21	22	95.5	3	9	33.3
EDDIE JOHNSON															
2009 TOR	1	16	742	46.4	61	5	298	59.6	65	3	3	100.0	1	1	100.0
2010 SAS	12	101	4400	43.6	69	62	4096	66.1	95	4	4	100.0	2	3	66.7
2011 SAS	5	41	1706	41.6	64	23	1380	60.0	95	11	11	100.0	10	14	71.4
Totals	18	158	6848	43.3	69	90	5774	64.2	95	18	18	100.0	13	18	72.2
RON JOHNSON															
1969 WPG	0	13	512	39.4	54										
1970 WPG	0	6	212	35.3	50										
Totals	0	19	724	38.1	54										
DON JONAS															
1970 TOR	4									33	38	86.8	15	26	57.7
1971 WPG	12	1	29	29.0	29	9	521	57.9	90	40	44	90.9	15	36	41.7
1972 WPG	4									45	48	93.8	14	21	66.7
1973 WPG	3	1	42	42.0	42					12	14	85.7	9	17	52.9
Totals	24	2	71	35.5	42	9	521	57.9	90	130	144	90.3	53	100	53.0
EDGAR JONES															
1950 HAM	6									25			4		
PHIL JONES															
1984 MTL	0	1	46	46.0	46										
TODD JORDAN															
1995 SA	1	107	4459	41.7	68										
KERRY JOSEPH															
2004 OTT	0	1	38	38.0	38										
BOBBY JUDD															
1957 OTT	1	84	2986	35.5	58										
1958 OTT	0	13	482	37.1	45										
Totals	1	97	3468	35.8	58										
MIKE JUHASZ															
2004 CAL	0	2	65	32.5	45										
STAN KALUZNICK															
1953 CAL	0									1	4	25.0	0	0	
AARON KANNER															
1994 SHR	5	148	6287	42.5	75										
1995 MEM	2	44	1811	41.2	65	8	491	61.4	70						
Totals	7	192	8098	42.2	75	8	491	61.4	70					0	
JOE KAPP															
1959 CAL	1	69	2735	39.6	80										
BYRON KARRYS															
1947 TOR	1														
STEVE KARRYS															
1946 TOR	1									0			2		
1949 TOR	1									0			0		
1951 TOR	1									0			0		
1953 TOR	9									0			0		
Totals	12									0			2		
JERRY KAURIC															
1987 EDM	14	99	3826	38.6	70	75	4239	56.5	78	47	47	100.0	28	41	68.3
1988 EDM	18	154	6718	43.6	75	81	4378	54.0	74	46	46	100.0	39	56	69.6
1989 EDM	19	141	5623	39.9	83	42	2371	56.5	72	70	70	100.0	45	66	68.2
1991 EDM	2	17	606	35.6	55	11	546	49.6	72	7	7	100.0	6	10	60.0
1991 CAL	0	20	680	34.0	48					0	0		0	0	
1991 Year	2	37	1286	34.8	55	11	546	49.6	72	7	7	100.0	6	10	60.0
Totals	53	431	17453	40.5	83	209	11534	55.2	78	170	170	100.0	118	173	68.2
WARREN KEAN															
2007 EDM	1					2	81	40.5	62	1	1	100.0	3	4	75.0
2010 SAS	1									5	5	100.0	3	5	60.0
Totals	2					2	81	40.5	62	6	6	100.0	6	9	66.7
EARL KEELEY															
1960 BC	0	35	1383	39.5	50										
1961 BC	0	9	334	37.1	44										
1962 BC	0	4	148	37.0	48										
Totals	0	48	1865	38.9	50										
ROBBIE KEEN															
1994 LV	3	138	5760	41.7	75	56	3265	58.3	79						
1995 SHR	4	129	5645	43.8	84										
Totals	7	267	11405	42.7	84	56	3265	58.3	79						
KENTON KEITH															
2005 SAS	0	1	34	34.0	34										
MATT KELLETT															
1999 EDM	3	81	3324	41.0	68	11	593	53.9	65	8	10	80.0	11	14	78.6

Year	Team	S	PUNT	YDS	AVG	LG	KO	YDS	AVG	LG	CON	CONA	PCT	FG	FGA	PCT
2001	BC	11	97	3923	40.4	84	52	2736	52.6	78	43	43	100.0	25	38	65.8
2002	BC	6					73	4073	55.8	72	49	49	100.0	31	47	66.0
2003	MTL	6	102	4238	41.5	83	101	5469	54.1	73	56	56	100.0	43	55	78.2
2004	MTL	12	74	3032	41.0	68	55	3150	57.3	78	51	51	100.0	37	49	75.5
2005	OTT	5	22	881	40.0	59	63	3452	54.8	82	33	33	100.0	25	36	69.4
Totals		43	376	15398	41.0	84	355	19473	54.9	82	240	242	99.2	172	239	72.0
RON KELLY																
1957	CAL	0									1	1	100.0	0	0	
PETER KEMPF																
1963	BC	4					62	3316	53.5	72	39	45	86.7	22	33	66.7
1964	BC	4					57	3056	53.6	70	32	40	80.0	15	25	60.0
1965	BC	3					52	2885	55.5	70	31	34	91.2	10	24	41.7
1966	MTL	4									15	16	93.8	12	24	50.0
1967	EDM	3					42	2402	57.2	89	29	29	100.0	17	30	56.7
1968	EDM	11					40	2283	57.1	75	21	24	87.5	16	31	51.6
Totals		29					253	13942	55.1	89	167	188	88.8	92	167	55.1
TREVOR KENNERD																
1980	WPG	11					68	3910	57.5	90	38	38	100.0	31	47	66.0
1981	WPG	13					85	4874	57.3	90	55	55	100.0	39	58	67.2
1982	WPG	22					74	4320	58.4	90	46	46	100.0	27	52	51.9
1983	WPG	12					60	3489	58.2	73	34	35	97.1	40	50	80.0
1984	WPG	13	1	57	57.0	57	82	4497	54.8	75	61	61	100.0	26	44	59.1
1985	WPG	22					79	4464	56.5	90	47	47	100.0	43	64	67.2
1986	WPG	10					44	2411	54.8	80	23	23	100.0	24	40	60.0
1987	WPG	13					91	4848	53.3	95	59	59	100.0	35	57	61.4
1988	WPG	8					74	4092	55.3	80	39	40	97.5	34	47	72.3
1989	WPG	12					79	4317	54.6	72	41	41	100.0	31	47	66.0
1990	WPG	10					81	4622	57.1	95	43	43	100.0	43	58	74.1
1991	WPG	3					50	2813	56.3	74	23	23	100.0	21	28	75.0
Totals		149	1	57	57.0	57	867	48657	56.1	95	509	511	99.6	394	592	66.6
RANDY KERBOW																
1965	EDM	5	114	4835	42.4	79										
1966	EDM	11	136	5832	42.9	78										
1967	EDM	5	130	5422	41.7	74										
1968	EDM	2	58	2425	41.8	59										
Totals		23	438	18514	42.3	79										
LARRY KERYCHUK																
1971	WPG	0	19	660	34.7	52										
ROGER KETTLEWELL																
1969	EDM	3	121	4627	38.2	69										
FRED KIJEK																
1947	MTL	6														
1948	MTL	7														
1949	MTL	7														
1950	HAM	11														
1951	HAM	7														
Totals		38														
KEN KILREA																
1962	HAM	0	1	47	47.0	47								0		
LENNIE KING																
1960	SAS	1	17	663	39.0	50										
DON KLOSTERMAN																
1955	CAL	0									1	1	100.0	1	4	25.0
1956	CAL	1									17	20	85.0	1	4	25.0
Totals		1									18	21	85.7	2	8	25.0
LEE KNIGHT																
1987	HAM	2					3	131	43.7	48	1	1	100.0	1	3	33.3
1994	HAM	0	1	35	35.0	35					0	0		0	0	
1995	HAM	0	1	47	47.0	47					0	0		0	0	
1996	OTT	0					1	9	9.0	9	0	0		0	0	
Totals		2	2	82	41.0	47	4	140	35.0	48	1	1	100.0	1	3	33.3
PAUL KNILL																
1973	CAL	0	18	677	37.6	53										
RONNIE KNOX																
1956	HAM	0	2	78	39.0	46										
1956	CAL	4	30	1152	38.4	66	2	78	39.0	41	3	8	37.5	0	3	0.0
1956	Year	4	32	1230	38.4	66	2	78	39.0	41	3	8	37.5	0	3	0.0
1959	TOR	1	45	1826	40.6	58					0	0		0	0	
Totals		5	77	3056	39.7	66	2	78	39.0	41	3	8	37.5	0	3	0.0
BUD KORCHAK																
1950	WPG	1									1	1	100.0	0	0	
1952	WPG	3					77	4034	52.4	65	34	46	73.9	4	6	66.7
1953	WPG	5					51	2659	52.1	80	29	31	93.5	9	19	47.4
1954	WPG	4					27	1378	51.0	70	12	18	66.7	4	10	40.0
1955	MTL	2									49	52	94.2	3	7	42.9
1956	MTL	1									9	12	75.0	1	2	50.0
1956	OTT	1									21	26	80.8	3	6	50.0
1956	Year	2									30	38	78.9	4	8	50.0
1957	CAL	0					24	1266	52.8	66	8	15	53.3	1	2	50.0
Totals		17					179	9337	52.2	80	163	201	81.1	25	52	48.1
VIC KRISTOPAITIS																
1957	TOR	1									14	19	73.7	6	12	50.0
1958	TOR	1	14	484	34.6	47	45	2507	55.7	69	32	34	94.1	8	22	36.4
1959	BC	2	9	365	40.6	51	45	2415	53.7	66	27	32	84.4	12	25	48.0
1960	BC	2	37	1537	41.5	55	19	1074	56.5	77	8	14	57.1	2	5	40.0
1961	BC	4	22	907	41.2	76	24	1253	52.2	71	14	14	100.0	5	12	41.7
1962	BC	1					26	1398	53.8	70	13	19	68.4	5	9	55.6
Totals		11	82	3293	40.2	76	159	8647	54.4	77	108	132	81.8	38	85	44.7
JOE KROL																
1946	TOR	10									12			6		
1947	TOR	5									15			2		
1948	TOR	9									13			4		
1949	TOR	11									14			2		
1950	TOR	7									0			0		
1951	TOR	12									24			4		
1952	TOR	7									7			0		
1955	TOR	0	22	659	30.0	45					0			0		
Totals		61	22	659	30.0	45					85			18		
HARRY KRUGER																
1983	CAL	0	1	39	39.0	39										
E.J. KUALE																
2010	TOR	1	1	64	64.0	64										

Year Team	S	PUNT	YDS	AVG	LG	KO	YDS	AVG	LG	CON	CONA	PCT	FG	FGA	PCT
BOBBY KUNTZ															
1962 HAM	1														
1964 HAM	0					1	21	21.0	21						
Totals	1					1	21	21.0	21						
GERALD KUNYK															
1975 CAL	7	101	4636	45.9	76										
1977 EDM	0	41	1714	41.8	59										
1977 OTT	1	49	2025	41.3	73										
1977 Year	1	90	3739	41.5	73										
1978 OTT	1	106	4265	40.2	60										
1980 WPG	0	8	279	34.9	51										
Totals	9	305	12919	42.4	76										
ROY KURT															
1985 MTL	4					16	841	52.6	61	26	26	100.0	28	39	71.8
1986 MTL	11	91	3833	42.1	73	39	2131	54.6	69	12	12	100.0	26	37	70.3
1987 HAM	4	16	508	31.8	39	14	679	48.5	55	8	8	100.0	4	9	44.4
1988 BC	1	9	295	32.8	48	6	354	59.0	66	2	2	100.0	2	5	40.0
Totals	20	116	4636	40.0	73	75	4005	53.4	69	48	48	100.0	60	90	66.7
ERNIE KUZYK															
1967 WPG	5					28	1534	54.8	87	11	16	68.8	5	14	35.7
BILL LaFLEUR															
2001 MTL	1	18	774	43.0	59					0	0		0	0	
GENE LAKUSIAK															
1968 WPG	0					3	32	10.7	19	0	0		0	0	
1969 WPG	0					9	449	49.9	63	0	0		0	0	
1970 WPG	9					35	1749	50.0	73	14	18	77.8	4	26	15.4
1971 WPG	0					41	2119	51.7	70	0	0		0	0	
1973 WPG	1					11	620	56.4	77	0	0		0	0	
Totals	10					99	4969	50.2	77	14	18	77.8	4	26	15.4
WILLIE LAMBERT															
1964 MTL	0									4	5	80.0	0	0	
WAYNE LAMMLE															
1992 BC	3	1	8	8.0	8	17	871	51.2	69	8	8	100.0	6	11	54.5
1993 TOR	1	49	1901	38.8	61	24	1356	56.5	69	0	0		0	0	
1994 TOR	18	132	4887	37.0	62	90	5118	56.9	74	51	51	100.0	37	57	64.9
1995 TOR	5	56	2236	39.9	58	27	1612	59.7	85	12	12	100.0	9	13	69.2
1995 OTT	4	100	3993	39.9	70	44	2231	50.7	71	19	19	100.0	22	29	75.9
1995 Year	9	156	6229	39.9	70	71	3843	54.1	85	31	31	100.0	31	43	72.1
1996 OTT	18	154	6484	42.1	89	68	3872	56.9	95	35	35	100.0	18	31	58.1
1998 SAS	2	39	1610	41.3	68	18	1023	56.8	78	0	0		0	0	
1999 SAS	0					3	164	54.7	61	2	2	100.0	1	2	50.0
Totals	51	531	21119	39.8	89	247	14016	56.7	95	127	127	100.0	93	143	65.0
HARRY LAMPMAN															
1953 SAS	0									1	1	100.0	0	0	
1958 HAM	0									1	1	100.0	0	0	
Totals	0									2	2	100.0	0	0	
TOM LARSCHEID															
1962 BC	0	3	129	43.0	71					0	2	0.0	0	0	
RALPH LARUE															
1948 HAM	4														
MIKE LASHUK															
1959 EDM	0	1	40	40.0	40										
1960 EDM	2	18	650	36.1	61										
1961 EDM	1														
1963 EDM	0	41	1595	38.9	65										
Totals	3	60	2285	38.1	65										
RON LATOURELLE															
1959 WPG	0	1	23	23.0	23										
1964 WPG	0	1	27	27.0	27										
Totals	0	2	50	25.0	27										
MIKE LAZECKI															
1990 SAS	2	111	4174	37.6	65										
1991 SAS	6	140	5471	39.1	78										
1992 SAS	0	67	2557	38.2	54										
1993 OTT	0	8	265	33.1	43	4	228	57.0	65						
Totals	8	326	12467	38.2	78	4	228	57.0	65						
BUDDY LEAKE															
1955 WPG	6									28	30	93.3	7	19	36.8
1956 WPG	1	2	59	29.5	59					30	32	93.8	4	5	80.0
1957 WPG	0									14	18	77.8	0	2	0.0
Totals	7	2	59	29.5	59					72	80	90.0	11	26	42.3
ED LEARN															
1965 MTL	0	7	231	33.0	50										
1966 MTL	0	1	26	26.0	26	1	25	25.0	25						
Totals	0	8	257	32.1	50	1	25	25.0	25						
EDDIE LeBARON															
1954 CAL	5	109	4264	39.1	80										
ROBERT LeBLANC															
2006 EDM	1	1	51	51.0	51										
CODY LEDBETTER															
1999 HAM	0					10	508	50.8	57						
2001 HAM	0					3	112	37.3	54						
Totals	0					13	620	47.7	57						
HAL LEDYARD															
1956 OTT	1														
1957 OTT	0	1	48	48.0	48										
1961 WPG	0	4	175	43.8	51										
Totals	1	5	223	44.6	51										
BUTCH LEE															
1948 SAS	1									2			0		
GARRY LeFEBVRE															
1966 EDM	0					5	229	45.8	60						
1967 EDM	0	4	130	32.5	38										
1968 EDM	2	83	3239	39.0	69										
1969 EDM	0	19	716	37.7											
1969 MTL	0	5	157	31.4											
1969 Year	0	24	783	32.6	66										
1971 MTL	1	30	1149	38.3	59										
1972 EDM	0	103	3984	38.7	61										
1973 EDM	2	102	4239	41.6	74										
1974 EDM	1	103	4211	40.9	69										
1975 EDM	0	4	153	38.3	50										

Year	Team	S	PUNT	YDS	AVG	LG	KO	YDS	AVG	LG	CON	CONA	PCT	FG	FGA	PCT
1976	EDM	1	127	5005	39.4	84										
Totals		7	580	22983	39.6	84	5	229	45.8	60						
STEFAN LeFORS																
2007	EDM	0	1	21	21.0	21										
TERRY LESCHUK																
1983	CAL	0					5	254	50.8	65	0	0		0	0	
1985	SAS	1	44	1753	39.8	71	1	60	60.0	60	1	1	100.0	1	1	100.0
Totals		1	44	1753	39.8	71	6	314	52.3	65	1	1	100.0	1	1	100.0
JIM LETCAVITS																
1958	EDM	0	25	851	34.0	63					0	1	0.0	0	0	
1962	EDM	1									0	0		0	0	
Totals		1	25	851	34.0	63					0	1	0.0	0	0	
DAVE LEWIS																
1967	MTL	9	121	5197	43.0	79										
1968	MTL	1	109	5100	46.8	73										
1975	MTL	0	7	287	41.0	50										
Totals		10	237	10584	44.7	79										
LEO LEWIS																
1961	WPG	0									1	2	50.0	0	0	
1964	WPG	1									4	5	80.0	0	2	0.0
Totals		1									5	7	71.4	0	2	0.0
WALTER LEWIS																
1986	MTL	0	10	380	38.0	48										
CHUCK LIEBROCK																
1970	WPG	0					1	25	25.0	25	0	0		1	1	100.0
AUBREY LINNE																
1963	TOR	0	1	52	52.0	52										
1963	EDM	2	43	1750	40.7	73										
1963	Year	2	44	1802	41.0	73										
Totals		2	44	1802	41.0	73										
RUDY LINTERMAN																
1969	CAL	0					1	22	22.0	22	0	0		0	0	
1970	CAL	3					10	644	64.4	80	3	5	60.0	0	4	0.0
1971	CAL	0					1	65	65.0	65	0	0		0	0	
1972	CAL	1					47	2683	57.1	86	1	3	33.3	0	0	
1973	CAL	4					34	2197	64.6	90	0	0		0	0	
1974	CAL	0					39	2548	65.3	90	0	0		0	2	0.0
1975	CAL	1					45	2582	57.4	90	0	0		0	0	
1976	CAL	0					10	565	56.5	75	0	0		0	0	
1977	CAL	0					3	201	67.0	73	0	0		0	0	
Totals		9					190	11507	60.6	90	4	8	50.0	0	6	0.0
GLENN LIPPMAN																
1954	EDM	0	3	107	35.7	38										
PETE LISKE																
1965	TOR	0	1	54	54.0	54										
1966	CAL	0	6	243	40.5	51										
Totals		0	7	297	42.4	54										
ALEC LOCKINGTON																
1973	HAM	2	112	4391	39.2	56	35	1778	50.8	64						
TIP LOGAN																
1951	HAM	0									26			5		
1952	HAM	1									34			0		
1953	HAM	2									32	32	100.0	4		
1954	HAM	3									35	36	97.2	3	8	37.5
1955	HAM	0									21	22	95.5	3	5	60.0
Totals		6									148	90	97.8	15	13	46.2
JIM LONG																
1967	MTL	2									6	9	66.7	4	7	57.1
1968	MTL	0									1	1	100.0	1	1	100.0
Totals		2									7	10	70.0	5	8	62.5
DON LORD																
1951	EDM	3	64	2447	38.2											
1952	EDM	2	6	252	42.0	52	6	298	49.7	60						
1953	EDM	1														
1954	BC	0	35	1265	36.1	58										
Totals		6	105	3964	37.8	58	6	298	49.7	60						
DON LUFT																
1955	CAL	0	17	597	35.1	47										
TRAVIS LULAY																
2009	BC	0	1	52	52.0	52										
NEIL LUMSDEN																
1976	TOR	0	7	290	41.4	66	18	1049	58.3	71	0	0		0	0	
1977	TOR	1	8	465	58.1	86					0	0		0	0	
1978	TOR	0	3	115	38.3	54					0	0		0	0	
1978	HAM	2	13	464	35.7	57	8	507	63.4	75	3	3	100.0	0	2	0.0
1978	Year	2	16	579	36.2	57					3	3	100.0	0	0	
1979	HAM	5					15	846	56.4	75	7	7	100.0	8	12	66.7
1980	EDM	0	1	39	39.0	39					0	0		0	0	
1983	EDM	0	1	55	55.0	55					0	0		0	0	
Totals		8	33	1428	43.3	86	41	2402	58.6	75	10	10	100.0	8	14	57.1
HARRY LUNN																
1960	HAM	0	2	98	49.0	50										
EARL LUNSFORD																
1956	CAL	0	7	324	46.3	60	2	87	43.5	45						
BRIAN LYNCH																
1949	OTT	1														
BILL MACKRIDES																
1952	HAM	1									1			0		
IVAN MacMILLAN																
1970	OTT	8					43	2489	57.9	75	25	28	89.3	14	29	48.3
1971	TOR	4					1	46	46.0	46	26	30	86.7	12	20	60.0
1972	TOR	7									22	23	95.7	8	17	47.1
1973	BC	2									7	7	100.0	14	23	60.9
1974	BC	19					48	2629	54.8	72	28	32	87.5	18	42	42.9
1975	SAS	0					4	212	53.0	68	1	1	100.0	3	3	100.0
1975	BC	2									1	1	100.0	1	5	20.0
1975	Year	2					4	212	53.0	68	2	2	100.0	4	8	50.0
Totals		42					96	5376	56.0	75	110	122	90.2	70	139	50.4
BOB MACORITTI																
1975	WPG	3	29	1278	44.1	72	13	657	50.5	75	5	5	100.0	4	5	80.0
1976	SAS	16	127	5307	41.8	76	83	4341	52.3	78	48	49	98.0	23	35	65.7
1977	SAS	11	144	6095	42.3	86	60	2962	49.4	73	31	31	100.0	22	36	61.1

Year	Team	S	PUNT	YDS	AVG	LG	KO	YDS	AVG	LG	CON	CONA	PCT	FG	FGA	PCT
1978	SAS	9	124	5533	44.6	82	68	3554	52.3	83	27	27	100.0	32	41	78.0
1979	SAS	14	112	4999	44.6	82	6	291	48.5	67	10	10	100.0	14	26	53.8
1980	SAS	12	90	3605	40.1	71	32	1607	50.2	75	24	24	100.0	27	47	57.4
Totals		65	626	26817	42.8	86	262	13412	51.2	83	145	146	99.3	122	190	64.2
RAY MACORITTI																
1990	EDM	14	134	5765	43.0	87	95	5037	53.0	66	64	64	100.0	36	53	67.9
1991	EDM	8	72	2775	38.5	65	70	3780	54.0	68	47	47	100.0	23	37	62.2
1993	OTT	0	36	1256	34.9	47	16	836	52.3	59	9	9	100.0	5	5	100.0
Totals		22	242	9796	40.5	87	181	9653	53.3	68	120	120	100.0	64	95	67.4
TOMMY MANASTERSKY																
1949	MTL	0									2			0		
JOHN MANEL																
1970	HAM	1	10	355	35.5	45						0		0	0	
DAVE MANN																
1958	TOR	3	103	4324	42.0	70					0	0		0	0	
1960	TOR	7	98	4305	43.9	90					0	0		0	0	
1961	TOR	10	107	5140	48.0	81	1	13	13.0	13	0	0		0	0	
1962	TOR	3	105	4592	43.7	86					0	0		0	0	
1963	TOR	1	64	2671	41.7	67	4	208	52.0	55	0	0		0	0	
1964	TOR	7	111	4582	41.3	69					0	0		0	0	
1965	TOR	6	123	5196	42.2	64					0	0		0	0	
1966	TOR	11	127	5482	43.2	102					0	0		0	0	
1967	TOR	10	131	6136	46.8	86	1	24	24.0	24	13	15	86.7	9	14	64.3
1968	TOR	18	115	5274	45.9	69	50	2971	59.4	87	33	35	94.3	7	22	31.8
1969	TOR	9	58	2706	46.7	64	40	2171	54.3	75	27	31	87.1	6	14	42.9
1970	TOR	13	119	5337	44.8	77	43	2472	57.5	80	0	0		0	0	
Totals		98	1261	55745	44.2	102	139	7859	56.5	87	73	81	90.1	22	50	44.0
ANDY MAREFOS																
1949	EDM	0									2			0		
JACOB MARINI																
2000	TOR	6	2	65	32.5	40	23	1315	57.2	70	36	37	97.3	27	40	67.5
2001	TOR	3					20	1163	58.2	75	14	14	100.0	7	11	63.6
Totals		9	2	65	32.5	40	43	2478	57.6	75	50	51	98.0	34	51	66.7
MARK MARISCAL																
2004	MTL	4	34	1479	43.5	67	26	1601	61.6	73	10	10	100.0	3	7	42.9
DAVE MARLER																
1979	HAM	4	19	812	42.7	65	5	268	53.6	73	3	3	100.0	0	4	0.0
1980	HAM	0	5	107	21.4	36					0	0		0	0	
Totals		4	24	919	38.3	65	5	268	53.6	73	3	3	100.0	0	4	0.0
BOBBY MARLOW																
1957	SAS	0	1	14	14.0	14										
BLAKE MARSHALL																
1992	EDM	0	1	25	25.0	25										
TONY MARTINO																
1988	BC	3	28	1047	37.4	54	13	695	53.5	60	11	11	100.0	0	2	0.0
1988	OTT	0									2	2	100.0	1	2	50.0
1988	Year	3	28	1047	37.4	54	13	695	53.5	60	13	13	100.0	1	4	25.0
1990	BC	4	37	1315	35.5	55	30	1513	50.4	68	14	14	100.0	13	18	72.2
1992	CAL	7	111	4347	39.2	82					0	0		0	0	
1993	CAL	3	121	4939	40.8	76	22	1291	58.7	81	0	0		0	0	
1994	CAL	5	104	4432	42.6	75					0	0		0	0	
1995	CAL	7	108	4531	42.0	72					0	0		0	0	
1996	CAL	6	120	5221	43.5	73	5	299	59.8	69	3	3	100.0	1	1	100.0
1997	CAL	7	121	5396	44.6	79					0	0		0	0	
1998	CAL	9	113	5451	48.2	81	1	61	61.0	61	1	1	100.0	0	0	
1999	CAL	3	65	2783	42.8	78					0	0		0	0	
2000	CAL	7	138	5952	43.1	74	4	217	54.3	58	0	0		0	0	
2001	TOR	1	25	1084	43.4	88					0	0		0	0	
2001	BC	1	45	1827	40.6	60					0	0		0	0	
2001	Year	2	70	2911	41.6	88					0	0		0	0	
2002	BC	3	137	5640	41.2	74					0	0		0	0	
Totals		66	1273	53965	42.4	88	75	4076	54.3	81	31	31	100.0	15	23	65.2
JOE MASNAGHETTI																
1952	SAS	1					9	476	52.9	75				0		
PAUL MASOTTI																
1991	TOR	0	1	36	36.0	36										
1995	TOR	0	1	7	7.0	7										
Totals		0	2	43	21.5	36									0	
BILL MASSE																
1971	MTL	0	5	126	25.2	34	1	37	37.0	37	1	1	100.0	0	0	
BRENT MATICH																
1989	CAL	7	144	6116	42.5	72					0	0		0	0	
1990	CAL	5	133	5728	43.1	71					0	0		0	0	
1991	CAL	6	120	5124	42.7	69					0	0		0	0	
1992	SAS	2	78	3116	39.9	61					0	0		0	0	
1993	SAS	7	123	5052	41.1	84					0	0		0	0	
1994	SAS	8	132	5510	41.7	77	3	147	49.0	53	0	0		0	0	
1995	SAS	2	147	6111	41.6	68					0	0		0	0	
1996	SAS	3	155	6441	41.6	68	2	105	52.5	54	2	2	100.0	0	0	
Totals		40	1032	43198	41.9	84	5	252	50.4	54	2	2	100.0	0	0	
RANDY MATTINGLY																
1975	SAS	0	10	349	34.9	45										
ROB MAVER																
2010	CAL	4					110	6510	59.2	79	70	70	100.0	37	47	78.7
2011	CAL	2					2	111	55.5	61	1	1	100.0	1	4	25.0
Totals		6					112	6621	59.1	79	71	71	100.0	38	51	74.5
RALPH McALLISTER																
1952	WPG	1	8	303	37.9	52										
Totals		1	8	303	37.9	52										
PAUL McCALLUM																
1993	BC	0					2	84	42.0	51	1	1	100.0	3	4	75.0
1993	OTT	1	15	511	34.1	70	7	341	48.7	61	5	5	100.0	6	8	75.0
1993	Year	1	15	511	34.1	70	9	425	47.2	61	6	6	100.0	9	12	75.0
1994	BC	5					19	966	50.8	100	14	14	100.0	8	13	61.5
1994	SAS	2					20	1078	53.9	72	13	13	100.0	11	13	84.6
1994	Year	7					39	2044	52.4	100	27	27	100.0	19	26	73.1
1995	SAS	1					7	411	58.7	67	1	1	100.0	8	9	88.9
1996	SAS	4					12	771	64.3	79	6	6	100.0	11	15	73.3
1997	SAS	11	135	5568	41.2	79	69	3870	56.1	86	34	34	100.0	40	57	70.2
1998	SAS	11	100	4073	40.7	59	53	3067	57.9	95	42	42	100.0	28	39	71.8
1999	SAS	8	135	5363	39.7	73	56	3100	55.4	95	34	34	100.0	22	27	81.5
2000	SAS	8	114	4596	40.3	63	85	4977	58.6	81	54	54	100.0	34	45	75.6

Year	Team	S	PUNT	YDS	AVG	LG	KO	YDS	AVG	LG	CON	CONA	PCT	FG	FGA	PCT
2001	SAS	9	140	5830	41.6	72	61	3793	62.2	95	26	26	100.0	33	47	70.2
2002	SAS	19	137	5853	42.7	81	62	3894	62.8	95	39	39	100.0	41	54	75.9
2003	SAS	5	124	5119	41.3	77	92	5271	57.3	95	53	53	100.0	41	48	85.4
2004	SAS	8	120	4785	39.9	78	78	4601	59.0	95	47	47	100.0	39	53	73.6
2005	SAS	13	111	4483	40.4	74	84	4531	53.9	95	41	41	100.0	31	42	73.8
2006	BC	4	119	4903	41.2	66	38	2110	55.5	95	52	52	100.0	37	44	84.1
2007	BC	9	116	5138	44.3	86	2	127	63.5	67	52	52	100.0	35	43	81.4
2008	BC	12	127	5621	44.3	64	62	3753	60.5	95	55	55	100.0	40	48	83.3
2009	BC	3	53	2217	41.8	66	38	2201	57.9	71	15	15	100.0	15	17	88.2
2010	BC	6	123	5132	41.7	77	82	4714	57.5	85	33	33	100.0	46	52	88.5
2011	BC	5	123	5183	42.1	63	102	5877	57.6	74	48	48	100.0	50	53	94.3
Totals		144	1792	74375	41.5	86	1031	59537	57.7	100	665	665	100.0	579	731	79.2
CHES McCANCE																
1946	MTL	2									21			9		
1947	MTL	4									9			6		
1948	MTL	1									10			0		
1949	MTL	4									33			3		
1950	MTL	0									2			0		
Totals		11									75			18		
BOB McDONALD																
1952	HAM	0									3			0		
PETE McDONALD																
1947	HAM	0									1			0		
GERRY McDOUGALL																
1958	HAM	1	1	30	30.0	30					1	3	33.3	1		
1959	HAM	1	1	23	23.0	23					2	5	40.0	1	4	25.0
1960	HAM	0	2	53	26.5	30					28	35	80.0	3	7	42.9
1961	HAM	0	3	182	60.7	72					0	0		0	0	
Totals		4	7	288	41.1	72					31	43	72.1	5	11	36.4
CYRIL McFALL																
1974	CAL	3	5	182	36.4	42	10	581	58.1	67	17	19	89.5	17	29	58.6
1975	CAL	7	13	503	38.7	49	27	1518	56.2	90	41	41	100.0	21	41	51.2
1976	CAL	11	89	3687	41.4	65	62	3356	54.1	78	26	26	100.0	29	46	63.0
1977	CAL	8					49	2670	54.5	88	11	11	100.0	30	51	58.8
1978	CAL	16	128	5769	45.1	95	66	3898	59.1	90	36	36	100.0	37	53	69.8
Totals		45	235	10141	43.2	95	214	12023	56.2	90	131	133	98.5	134	220	60.9
JIMMY McFAUL																
1949	SAS	1														
GERRY McGRATH																
1980	MTL	7	69	2757	40.0	58	45	2621	58.2	67	33	33	100.0	12	20	60.0
1981	MTL	8	59	2546	43.2	60	22	1136	51.6	65	9	10	90.0	5	11	45.5
1983	MTL	2	70	3017	43.1	62	37	2183	59.0	90	0	0		0	0	
1984	MTL	3	120	5289	44.1	64	53	3084	58.2	85	0	0		0	0	
1985	SAS	1	80	3235	40.4	57					0	0		0	0	
1986	SAS	1	62	2526	40.7	63					0	0		0	0	
Totals		22	460	19370	42.1	64	157	9024	57.5	90	42	43	97.7	17	31	54.8
LAMAR McHAN																
1965	TOR	0	1	70	70.0	70										
PAUL McJULIEN																
1993	SAC	1	27	983	36.4	54										
PAUL McKAY																
1970	HAM	1	40	1764	44.1	73										
1971	HAM	1	7	316	45.1	70										
1972	HAM	0	8	319	39.9	71										
1974	CAL	1	81	3332	41.1	58										
Totals		3	136	5731	42.1	73										
JIMMY McKEAN																
1964	MTL	1	15	597	39.8	52										
1965	MTL	1	66	2564	38.8	57										
1966	SAS	0	35	1309	37.4	58										
Totals		2	116	4470	38.5	58										
WALT McKEE																
1972	WPG	5	108	4486	41.5	68	66	3721	56.4	90	0	1	0.0	3	12	25.0
1973	WPG	14	129	5696	44.2	83	34	1942	57.1	90	11	14	78.6	9	22	40.9
1974	WPG	14	142	5929	41.8	75	44	2290	52.0	70	20	28	71.4	15	35	42.9
1975	EDM	1	36	1506	41.8	60					0	0		0	0	
Totals		34	415	17617	42.5	83	144	7953	55.2	90	31	43	72.1	27	69	39.1
SCOTT McKENZIE																
1999	CAL	6	51	2157	42.3	72										
2001	TOR	0	21	804	38.3	51	4	215	53.8	60						
Totals		6	72	2961	41.1	72	4	215	53.8	60						
JOHN McKILLOP																
1968	EDM		14	547	39.1	50										
MARK McLOUGHLIN																
1988	CAL	8					39	2217	56.8	87	17	18	94.4	24	36	66.7
1989	CAL	15	1	39	39.0	39	91	5469	60.1	95	43	46	93.5	48	67	71.6
1990	CAL	18					112	6746	60.2	91	56	57	98.2	45	69	65.2
1991	CAL	13	9	318	35.3	48	111	6391	57.6	95	57	57	100.0	46	64	71.9
1992	CAL	13					102	5754	56.4	95	63	63	100.0	44	64	68.8
1993	CAL	11					87	5089	58.5	93	63	63	100.0	47	62	75.8
1994	CAL	8	3	118	39.3	52	108	6502	60.2	83	80	80	100.0	37	44	84.1
1995	CAL	7					105	6126	58.3	87	63	64	98.4	50	60	83.3
1996	CAL	3					90	5397	60.0	74	56	56	100.0	54	67	80.6
1997	CAL	7					88	5286	60.1	82	50	50	100.0	39	51	76.5
1998	CAL	15					96	5843	60.9	95	56	58	96.6	35	54	64.8
1999	CAL	4	1	18	18.0	18	94	5431	57.8	80	44	44	100.0	48	59	81.4
2000	CAL	7					90	5313	59.0	75	63	63	100.0	43	55	78.2
2001	CAL	10					87	4906	56.4	93	44	44	100.0	42	57	73.7
2002	CAL	7					69	3867	56.0	72	42	42	100.0	34	52	65.4
2003	CAL	2									19	19	100.0	28	36	77.8
2005	BC	1					1	57	57.0	57	11	11	100.0	9	12	75.0
Totals		149	14	493	35.2	52	1370	80394	58.7	95	827	835	99.0	673	909	74.0
LEIGH McMILLAN																
1957	EDM	0	2	74	37.0	41										
BOB McNAMARA																
1956	WPG	0									0	1	0.0	0	0	
MIKE McTAGUE																
1979	CAL	11	146	6331	43.4	81					0	0		0	0	
1980	CAL	16	125	5485	43.9	73	31	1869	60.3	90	12	12	100.0	5	8	62.5
1981	CAL	5	120	5171	43.1	74					0	0		0	0	
1982	CAL	4	148	6316	42.7	67					0	0		0	0	
1983	CAL	13	112	5371	48.0	89					0	0		0	0	

Year	Team	S	PUNT	YDS	AVG	LG	KO	YDS	AVG	LG	CON	CONA	PCT	FG	FGA	PCT
1984	CAL	11	153	6796	44.4	92					0	0		0	0	
1985	MTL	6	141	5896	41.8	65	42	2303	54.8	90	0	0		0	0	
1986	MTL	0	15	544	36.3	47					0	0		0	0	
1986	SAS	1	47	1816	38.6	69					0	0		0	0	
1986	Year	1	62	2360	38.1	69					0	0		0	0	
1987	SAS	0	33	1159	35.1	51	5	297	59.4	73	2	3	66.7	2	3	66.7
Totals		67	1040	44885	43.2	92	78	4469	57.3	90	14	15	93.3	7	11	63.6
JUSTIN MEDLOCK																
2009	TOR	5	120	5076	42.3	67	79	4764	60.3	95	22	22	100.0	40	46	87.0
2010	TOR	1	1	39	39.0	39					5	6	83.3	7	10	70.0
2011	HAM	4	119	4948	41.6	73	93	5602	60.2	95	46	46	100.0	49	55	89.1
Totals		10	240	10063	41.9	73	172	10366	60.3	95	73	74	98.6	96	111	86.5
MEL MELIN																
1962	BC	0									1	2	50.0	1	1	100.0
LEN MELTZER																
1950	WPG	0	8	301	37.6											
REG MESERVE																
1957	TOR	4	144	5688	39.5	70										
BOB MEYERS																
1955	CAL	8	100	4280	42.8	83	13	369	28.4	63						
FREDDIE MEYERS																
1959	EDM	0					36	1803	50.1	65						
CHET MIKSZA																
1954	HAM	1									0	0		0	1	0.0
1956	HAM	1									0	0		0	1	0.0
1958	HAM	1	3	66	22.0	42	31	1595	51.5	62	0	1	0.0	0	0	
1959	HAM	0					51	2477	48.6	71	0	2	0.0	1	1	100.0
1960	HAM	0	1	17	17.0	17					0	0		0	0	
1963	HAM	0					21	1099	52.3	65	0	0		0	0	
Totals		3	4	83	20.8	42	103	5171	50.2	71	0	3	0.0	1	3	33.3
ROLLIE MILES																
1951	EDM	0	24	925	38.5											
1954	EDM	0	4	104	26.0	40										
1955	EDM	0					3	68	22.7	33						
1957	EDM	0	1	42	42.0	42										
1959	EDM	0	1	48	48.0	48	1	18	18.0	18						
1961	EDM	0					1	12	12.0	12						
Totals		0	30	1119	37.3	48	5	98	19.6	33						
GORDON MILLER																
1948	HAM	1														
JOSH MILLER																
1994	BAL	6	117	5024	42.9	64	7	378	54.0	64						
1995	BAL	5	118	5629	47.7	80	57	3311	58.1	69						
Totals		11	235	10653	45.3	80	64	3689	57.6	69						
NICK MILLER																
1956	WPG	0					51	2716	53.3	66						
DAVID MILLER-JOHNSTON																
2002	OTT	1	19	705	37.1	54	20	1132	56.6	67	10	10	100.0	4	8	50.0
CHRIS MILO																
2011	SAS	5	79	3410	43.2	108	57	2518	44.2	70	23	23	100.0	22	26	84.6
TOM MINER																
1954	CAL	4					40	2146	53.7		33	36	91.7	14	30	46.7
1955	CAL	4					35	1818	51.9	77	28	31	90.3	1	9	11.1
1956	WPG	2									2	6	33.3	8	15	53.3
Totals		10					75	3964	52.9	77	63	73	86.3	23	54	42.6
POLLY MIOCINOVICH																
1946	HAM	0									0			1		
BILL MITCHELL																
1960	TOR	0									0	1	0.0	0	0	
1961	TOR	1					25	1426	57.0	73	10	15	66.7	3	6	50.0
1962	TOR	5									28	32	87.5	9	19	47.4
1963	EDM	3					2	77	38.5	52	18	20	90.0	12	16	75.0
1964	EDM	10					43	2648	61.6	85	17	27	63.0	10	29	34.5
1965	EDM	2					40	2485	62.1	80	3	5	60.0	1	5	20.0
1966	BC	10					45	2572	57.2	75	24	30	80.0	11	25	44.0
Totals		31					155	9208	59.4	85	100	130	76.9	46	100	46.0
DOUG MITCHELL																
1967	HAM	0					32	1822	56.9	68						
1968	HAM	0					13	685	52.7	73						
1969	HAM	1					34	2109	62.0	89						
1970	HAM	0					48	2838	59.1	83						
1971	HAM	2					40	2303	57.6	86						
1972	HAM	0					9	479	53.2	85						
1974	MTL	0					31	1634	52.7	73						
Totals		3					207	11870	57.3	89						
BARRY MITCHELSON																
1965	EDM	0									0	2	0.0	0	0	
JOE MOBRA																
1956	EDM	0					40	2166	54.2	75	22	27	81.5	1	4	25.0
1957	EDM	8	1	67	67.0	67	72	3899	54.2	85	49	62	79.0	10	18	55.6
1958	EDM	9					44	2452	55.7	85	16	23	69.6	10	23	43.5
Totals		17	1	67	67.0	67	156	8517	54.6	85	87	112	77.7	21	45	46.7
DON MOEN																
1994	TOR	0	1	12	12.0	12										
BART MOLL																
1956	TOR	0									8	15	53.3	1	3	33.3
1957	TOR	1									13	17	76.5	2	6	33.3
Totals		1									21	32	65.6	3	9	33.3
TONY MOMSEN																
1953	CAL	0					2	59	29.5	39						
JOHN MOODY																
1946	MTL	4									2			1		
DONN MOOMAW																
1953	TOR	0									1			0		
KEN MOORE																
1950	EDM	3	13	506	38.9											
MIKE MORREALE																
2001	HAM	0	1	31	31.0	31										
2006	HAM	1	40	40.0	40											
Totals		0	2	71	35.5	40										
FRANKIE MORRIS																
1946	TOR	1														

Year	Team	S	PUNT	YDS	AVG	LG	KO	YDS	AVG	LG	CON	CONA	PCT	FG	FGA	PCT
RON MORRIS																
1959	CAL	1	56	2032	36.3	55										
1960	CAL	5	98	3982	40.6	73										
1961	CAL	2	33	1477	44.8	67										
1961	Year	2	33	1477	44.8	67										
1963	TOR	4	50	1991	39.8	66										
1963	BC	0	2	86	43.0	65										
1963	Year	4	52	2077	39.9	66										
1964	BC	2	33	1301	39.4	60										
1965	BC	0	10	385	38.5	53										
Totals		14	282	11254	39.9	73										
DON MOULTON																
1972	CAL	1	120	4745	39.5	71										
1973	CAL	2	81	3075	38.0	61										
1974	CAL	0	35	1333	38.1	54										
Totals		3	236	9153	38.8	71										
BOBBY MULGADO																
1959	SAS	1	48	1784	37.2	59	1	54	54.0	54	2	2	100.0	0	1	0.0
PETER MULLER																
1979	TOR	0	1	12	12.0	12										
BILL MURMYLYK																
1948	HAM	4									8			2		
1949	HAM	1									7			1		
Totals		5									15			3		
ANDREW MURRAY																
1993	TOR	0	1	39	39.0	39										
MARK MYERS																
2006	HAM	0					12	692	57.7	70	5	5	100.0	5	6	83.3
STEVE MYHRA																
1962	SAS	4					19	1055	55.5	65	12	14	85.7	2	7	28.6
NICK MYSTROM																
1995	MEM	8	2	56	28.0	30	49	2836	57.9	71	18	18	100.0	37	47	78.7
STEVE NEMETH																
1948	MTL	1									15			2		
GERRY NESBITT																
1958	OTT	0	51	1811	35.5	57										
1959	OTT	1	24	923	38.5	48										
1960	OTT	3	49	2016	41.1	63										
1961	OTT	5	45	1778	39.5	64										
Totals		9	169	6528	38.6	64										
EMIL NIELSEN																
1979	SAS	0	1	40	40.0	40										
BJORN NITTMO																
1994	SHR	8	1	44	44.0	44	63	3634	57.7	64	29	31	93.5	30	38	78.9
1995	SHR	4					76	4370	57.5	95	43	43	100.0	46	53	86.8
Totals		12	1	44	44.0	44	139	8004	57.6	95	72	74	97.3	76	91	83.5
DEREK NOBLE																
1987	HAM	2	2	89	44.5	45	6	350	58.3	67	4	4	100.0	2	4	50.0
BAYNE NORRIE																
1971	EDM	0	1	34	34.0	34										
BOB O'BILLOVICH																
1964	OTT	0									1	1	100.0	0	0	
MIKE O'BRIEN																
2001	SAS	0					1	56	56.0	56						
2002	HAM	0	7	210	30.0	40										
Totals		0	7	210	30.0	40	1	56	56.0	56						
JIM OLDENBURG																
1948	HAM	0									0			2		
BOBBY JACK OLIVER																
1961	MTL	0					39	2061	52.8	66	2	3	66.7	4	4	100.0
1962	MTL	6	9	333	37.0	49					34	36	94.4	9	16	56.3
1963	MTL	3					20	1110	55.5	76	10	13	76.9	3	6	50.0
Totals		9	9	333	37.0	49	59	3171	53.7	76	46	52	88.5	16	26	61.5
TOM O'MALLEY																
1951	OTT	3														
1952	OTT	3														
1953	OTT	5														
Totals		11														
DUNCAN O'MAHONY																
2001	CAL	2	122	5169	42.4	63					0	0		0	0	
2002	CAL	5	126	5732	45.5	68					0	0		0	0	
2003	CAL	9	152	6290	41.4	84	64	3619	56.5	76	7	8	87.5	2	9	22.2
2004	BC	9	117	4854	41.5	66	109	5825	53.4	78	64	65	98.5	33	45	73.3
2005	BC	16	116	4935	42.5	69	38	2117	55.7	76	40	42	95.2	26	42	61.9
2007	CAL	3	51	2158	42.3	65					0	0		0	1	0.0
Totals		44	684	29138	42.6	84	211	11561	54.8	78	111	115	96.5	61	97	62.9
STEVE ONESCHUK																
1955	HAM	1									0	0		4	5	80.0
1956	HAM	2									42	51	82.4	1	4	25.0
1957	HAM	5									23	28	82.1	9	17	52.9
1958	HAM	0	1	17	17.0	17					12	16	75.0	0	1	0.0
1959	HAM	4									26	31	83.9	3	8	37.5
1960	HAM	0									1	1	100.0	1	1	100.0
Totals		12	1	17	17.0	17					104	127	81.9	18	36	50.0
GERRY ORGAN																
1971	OTT	4					45	2526	56.1	75	31	32	96.9	17	26	65.4
1972	OTT	10	1	28	28.0	28	38	1520	40.0	65	28	28	100.0	29	50	58.0
1973	OTT	5	10	387	38.7	58	37	1970	53.2	70	25	25	100.0	31	48	64.6
1974	OTT	7					36	2008	55.8	70	19	20	95.0	36	56	64.3
1975	OTT	5					86	4386	51.0	75	38	38	100.0	27	44	61.4
1976	OTT	11	97	3863	39.8	63	83	4043	48.7	70	45	45	100.0	19	38	50.0
1977	OTT	4	5	222	44.4	51	64	2947	46.0	90	36	36	100.0	30	45	66.7
1979	OTT	12	144	5710	39.7	59	62	3319	53.5	70	38	39	97.4	17	38	44.7
1980	OTT	13	124	5293	42.7	88	61	3158	51.8	74	32	33	97.0	26	41	63.4
1981	OTT	10	123	5167	42.0	64	55	2972	54.0	88	28	28	100.0	28	38	73.7
1982	OTT	9	129	5165	40.0	72	70	3904	55.8	72	37	37	100.0	28	33	84.8
1983	OTT	15	95	4066	42.8	59	64	3577	55.9	69	34	34	100.0	30	45	66.7
Totals		105	728	29901	41.1	88	701	36330	51.8	90	391	395	99.0	318	502	63.3
PAUL OSBALDISTON																
1986	HAM	7	27	1056	39.1	59	39	2095	53.7	66	16	16	100.0	23	30	76.7
1986	WPG	4					17	907	53.4	61	17	17	100.0	9	15	60.0
1986	BC	4	15	641	42.7	56	13	739	56.8	65	6	6	100.0	5	9	55.6

Year	Team	S	PUNT	YDS	AVG	LG	KO	YDS	AVG	LG	CON	CONA	PCT	FG	FGA	PCT
1986	Year	15	42	1697	40.4	59	69	3741	54.2	66	39	39	100.0	37	54	68.5
1987	HAM	5	19	675	35.5	68	7	326	46.6	66	1	1	100.0	4	8	50.0
1988	HAM	21	158	5976	37.8	83	87	5130	59.0	95	49	49	100.0	36	56	64.3
1989	HAM	24	151	6056	40.1	73	96	5622	58.6	94	47	47	100.0	54	74	73.0
1990	HAM	15	128	4983	38.9	74	91	5319	58.5	90	41	41	100.0	52	62	83.9
1991	HAM	19	146	6105	41.8	77	83	4814	58.0	100	33	33	100.0	40	61	65.6
1992	HAM	21	149	6032	40.5	79	91	5041	55.4	75	52	53	98.1	41	64	64.1
1993	HAM	15	164	6648	40.5	84	57	3094	54.3	79	28	28	100.0	31	48	64.6
1994	HAM	12	166	6681	40.2	66	68	3845	56.5	95	40	40	100.0	43	55	78.2
1995	HAM	16	85	3772	44.4	73	48	2633	54.9	85	37	37	100.0	31	49	63.3
1996	HAM	12	124	5446	43.9	72	75	4421	58.9	83	37	38	97.4	43	57	75.4
1997	HAM	15	147	6411	43.6	82	79	4499	56.9	74	31	31	100.0	24	42	57.1
1998	HAM	14	140	6055	43.3	73	92	5263	57.2	90	50	50	100.0	41	50	82.0
1999	HAM	11	125	5334	42.7	74	90	5299	58.9	91	63	63	100.0	43	53	81.1
2000	HAM	7	123	5387	43.8	88	76	4343	57.1	81	42	42	100.0	43	53	81.1
2001	HAM	8	125	5376	43.0	81	76	4269	56.2	82	34	34	100.0	47	58	81.0
2002	HAM	16	109	4918	45.1	97	56	3172	56.6	83	30	30	100.0	38	47	80.9
2003	HAM	3	42	1551	36.9	54	12	592	49.3	68	21	22	95.5	21	36	58.3
Totals		249	2143	89103	41.6	97	1253	71423	57.0	100	675	678	99.6	669	927	72.2
JIM PAAR																
1948	HAM	1														
MARIO PACENTI																
1955	TOR	0	12	367	30.6	41										
BOB PAFFRATH																
1951	EDM	0	2	67	33.5											
JOE PAGLIEI																
1956	CAL	4	64	2415	37.7	58										
TONY PAJACZKOWSKI																
1955	CAL	0					3	170	56.7	63						
1956	CAL	0					3	118	39.3	44						
1957	CAL	0					8	391	48.9	58						
1959	CAL	0					3	135	45.0	60						
1960	CAL	0					27	1495	55.4	75						
1961	CAL	0					51	2845	55.8	85						
1962	CAL	0					38	1955	51.4	70						
1963	CAL	0					1	50	50.0	50						
Totals		0					134	7159	53.4	85						
JUSTIN PALARDY																
2010	HAM	2	27	1138	42.1	79					0	0		0	0	
2010	WPG	5					47	2533	53.9	88	20	20	100.0	26	30	86.7
2010	Year	7									20	20	100.0	26	30	86.7
2011	WPG	6					70	3999	57.1	76	39	39	100.0	40	52	76.9
Totals		13	27	1138	42.1	79	117	6532	55.8	88	59	59	100.0	66	82	80.5
BILL PALMER																
1976	CAL	0	46	1904	41.4	63										
1977	CAL	0	128	5152	40.3	61										
1978	HAM	0	11	417	37.9	61										
Totals		0	185	7473	40.4	63										
GERRY PALMER																
1954	BC	0	1	19	19.0	19										
MIKE PANASUK																
2003	TOR	1	9	344	38.2	52	3	140	46.7	58	2	2	100.0	1	2	50.0
ROD PANTAGES																
1949	CAL	0									1			0		
1950	MTL	7									1			0		
1951	MTL	3									0			0		
1952	EDM	8	109	4718	43.3	65					0	0		0	0	
1953	EDM	11	118	5247	44.5	82					0	0		0	0	
1954	EDM	4	48	2065	43.0	66					0	0		0	0	
1955	SAS	2	56	2260	40.4	71					0	0		0	0	
1956	SAS	3	8	544	68.0	77					0	0		0	0	
Totals		38	339	14834	43.8	82					2	0		0	0	
JOE PAOPAO																
1985	SAS	1	2	109	54.5	62										
RENE PAREDES																
2011	CAL	5					88	5289	60.1	80	48	48	100.0	35	45	77.8
BABE PARILLI																
1959	OTT	7	65	2497	38.4	58										
JACKIE PARKER																
1954	EDM	2	49	2013	41.1	78					0	0		0	0	
1955	EDM	0	17	673	39.6	51					0	0		0	0	
1956	EDM	6	86	3575	41.6	66					0	0		0	0	
1957	EDM	1	4	212	53.0	68					0	0		0	0	
1958	EDM	3	51	1963	38.5	67					5	8	62.5	4	6	66.7
1959	EDM	0	1	45	45.0	45					31	38	81.6	12	15	80.0
1960	EDM	3	2	94	47.0	52					17	31	54.8	9	17	52.9
1961	EDM	4	4	215	53.8	71	1	41	41.0	41	34	39	87.2	14	21	66.7
1962	EDM	0	1	54	54.0	54					0	0		0	0	
1965	TOR	0					1	36	36.0	36	16	16	100.0	1	3	33.3
Totals		19	215	8844	41.1	78	2	77	38.5	41	103	132	78.0	40	62	64.5
RONNIE PARSON																
1967	MTL	3					3	165	55.0	62	8	11	72.7	2	11	18.2
LUI PASSAGLIA																
1976	BC	12	143	5913	41.3	67	53	2531	47.8	75	28	28	100.0	28	49	57.1
1977	BC	7	123	5456	44.4	78	70	4229	60.4	76	30	30	100.0	40	53	75.5
1978	BC	18	128	5966	46.6	82	68	4148	61.0	88	30	30	100.0	37	44	84.1
1979	BC	21	133	6287	47.3	73	52	3066	59.0	70	27	27	100.0	32	45	71.1
1980	BC	16	128	5544	43.3	81	58	3436	59.2	79	38	38	100.0	31	46	67.4
1981	BC	21	141	6487	46.0	76	66	3994	60.5	90	42	42	100.0	27	40	67.5
1982	BC	11	142	5813	40.9	59	27	1299	48.1	63	45	45	100.0	26	35	74.3
1983	BC	17	117	5868	50.2	93	69	3815	55.3	82	45	46	97.8	43	59	72.9
1984	BC	16	125	5803	46.4	89	70	3834	54.8	70	46	46	100.0	35	48	72.9
1985	BC	25	140	6287	44.9	76	76	4381	57.6	90	49	49	100.0	37	55	67.3
1986	BC	15	138	5686	41.2	68	5	253	50.6	57	34	34	100.0	39	56	69.6
1987	BC	11	161	6631	41.2	97	91	4876	53.6	93	47	47	100.0	52	66	78.8
1988	BC	13	101	4049	40.1	71	50	2456	49.1	62	31	31	100.0	13	20	65.0
1989	BC	12	154	6345	41.2	67	100	5202	52.0	81	52	52	100.0	37	51	72.5
1990	BC	8	81	3169	39.1	60	44	2179	49.5	67	33	33	100.0	25	39	64.1
1991	BC	11	111	4608	41.5	71	35	1663	47.5	60	67	67	100.0	44	59	74.6
1992	BC	9	119	4799	40.3	62	58	2790	48.1	72	38	38	100.0	28	38	73.7
1993	BC	9	116	4616	39.8	71	88	3941	44.8	64	62	62	100.0	35	47	74.5
1994	BC	4	69	2756	39.9	79	42	2247	53.5	67	49	49	100.0	28	36	77.8

Year	Team	S	PUNT	YDS	AVG	LG	KO	YDS	AVG	LG	CON	CONA	PCT	FG	FGA	PCT
1995	BC	9	133	5129	38.6	58	11	529	48.1	58	50	51	98.0	45	62	72.6
1996	BC	8	131	5492	41.9	65	3	104	34.7	53	40	40	100.0	36	53	67.9
1997	BC	7	114	4703	41.3	76	3	41	13.7	18	43	43	100.0	35	45	77.8
1998	BC	11	130	5736	44.1	75	51	2843	55.7	92	30	30	100.0	52	66	78.8
1999	BC	14	140	5882	42.0	75	2	29	14.5	15	39	40	97.5	30	47	63.8
2000	BC	4	124	4807	38.8	57	7	245	35.0	73	50	50	100.0	40	44	90.9
Totals		309	3142	133832	42.6	97	1199	64131	53.5	93	1045	1048	99.7	875	1203	72.7
GABE PATTERSON																
1947	SAS	3									3			5		
1948	SAS	2									14			2		
Totals		5									17			7		
SAM PAULESCU																
2006	WPG	0	12	464	38.7	60										
JARRETT PAYTON																
2009	TOR	0					1	55	55.0	55	0	1	0.0	0	0	
BOB PEARCE																
1972	SAS	1	43	1769	41.1	66										
1973	SAS	0	1	36	36.0	36										
1974	SAS	0					1	7	7.0	7						
Totals		1	44	1805	41.0	66	1	7	7.0	7						
DAVE PEGG																
1977	HAM	1					9	542	60.2	78	3	3	100.0	4	7	57.1
RAY PELFREY																
1954	WPG	1	20	793	39.7	57										
JOE PERRI																
1976	HAM	2					8	338	42.3	85	4	4	100.0	0	1	0.0
GIL PETMANIS																
1966	SAS	0	2	71	35.5	39										
LEIF PETTERSEN																
1978	HAM	1									0	0		0	1	0.0
AL PFEIFER																
1955	TOR	0									23	30	76.7	0	2	0.0
1956	TOR	0									2	5	40.0	0	0	
Totals		0									25	35	71.4	0	2	0.0
KEN PHILLIPS																
1969	BC	1	118	4786	40.6	64					0	0		0	0	
1970	BC	4	128	5704	44.6	72					0	0		0	0	
1971	BC	8	117	4988	42.6	68					18	22	81.8	11	20	55.0
1972	BC	0	6	215	35.8	43					0	0		0	0	
Totals		13	369	15693	42.5	72					18	22	81.8	11	20	55.0
CORY PHILPOT																
1996	BC	0	1	49	49.0	49										
ROB PIKULA																
2006	BC	3	6	289	48.2	60					3	3	100.0	6	7	85.7
2007	WPG	14	94	3924	41.7	78	29	1633	56.3	74	16	16	100.0	10	16	62.5
Totals		17	100	4213	42.1	78	29	1633	56.3	74	19	19	100.0	16	23	69.6
DON PINHEY																
1954	OTT	0	1	35	35.0	35					0	0		0	0	
1955	OTT	0									0	1	0.0	0	0	
Totals		0	1	35	35.0	35					0	1	0.0	0	0	
ERNIE PITTS																
1957	WPG	0									1	1	100.0	0	0	
SCOTT PLAYER																
1995	BIR	4	143	6247	43.7	78										
KENNY PLOEN																
1957	WPG	0					2	45	22.5	35	25	32	78.1	0	0	
AL POLLARD																
1954	BC	0	9	389	43.2	61	31	1681	54.2	69	11	14	78.6	6	11	54.5
1955	BC	1					22	1254	57.0	77	17	18	94.4	2	2	100.0
1956	BC	3					43	2430	56.5	85	5	11	45.5	1	2	50.0
1957	CAL	1					5	249	49.8	70	2	4	50.0	0	2	0.0
Totals		5	9	389	43.2	61	101	5614	55.6	85	35	47	74.5	9	17	52.9
ALEX PONTON																
1952	OTT	1														
1954	TOR	6	112	4188	37.4	60										
1955	TOR	0	26	868	33.4	50										
1956	TOR	0	12	496	41.3	64										
Totals		7	150	5552	37.0	64										
RAY POOLE																
1953	MTL	0									38			11		
1954	MTL	3									37	40	92.5	6	14	42.9
Totals		3									75	40	92.5	17	14	42.9
JOE POPLAWSKI																
1978	WPG	0					1	14	14.0	14	0	0		0	0	
1980	WPG	0					2	26	13.0	13	0	0		0	0	
1981	WPG	0					1	14	14.0	14	0	0		0	0	
1986	WPG	1	3	154	51.3	75	3	162	54.0	68	14	14	100.0	8	10	80.0
Totals		1	3	154	51.3	75	7	216	30.9	68	14	14	100.0	8	10	80.0
ACE POWELL																
1946	OTT	0									0			1		
ROLLIN PRATHER																
1950	EDM	1														
NOEL PREFONTAINE																
1998	TOR	19	132	6169	46.7	86	36	1923	53.4	70	12	12	100.0	10	23	43.5
1999	TOR	13	142	6775	47.7	88	62	3553	57.3	87	0	0		0	5	0.0
2000	TOR	10	134	6369	47.5	84	52	2894	55.7	80	0	0		0	3	0.0
2001	TOR	5	70	3132	44.7	66	44	2646	60.1	69	0	0		0	0	
2002	TOR	11	156	7197	46.1	72	64	3941	61.6	78	32	32	100.0	27	32	84.4
2003	TOR	9	117	5484	46.9	81	77	4541	59.0	70	43	44	97.7	39	54	72.2%
2004	TOR	10	125	5740	45.9	84	66	3790	57.4	80	40	40	100.0	29	40	72.5
2005	TOR	12	100	4524	45.2	69	82	5007	61.1	75	49	49	100.0	33	44	75.0
2006	TOR	12	137	6345	46.3	69	66	3989	60.4	73	31	31	100.0	31	42	73.8
2007	TOR	10	119	5484	46.1	70	65	3981	61.2	71	36	37	97.3	26	39	66.7
2008	EDM	18	103	4831	46.9	75	77	4636	60.2	73	48	48	100.0	35	46	76.1
2009	EDM	7	114	5054	44.3	81	98	5555	56.7	72	44	44	100.0	28	37	75.7
2010	EDM	8	87	3747	43.1	81	52	3011	57.9	86	25	25	100.0	21	25	84.0
2010	TOR	0	21	888	42.3	56	14	826	59.0	65	6	6	100.0	6	7	85.7
2010	Year	8	108	4635	42.9	81	66	3837	58.1	86	31	31	100.0	27	32	84.4
2011	TOR	5	105	4545	43.3	75	4	159	39.8	63	33	33	100.0	37	45	82.2
Totals		149	1662	76284	45.9	88	859	50452	58.7	87	399	401	99.5	322	442	72.9
BUTCH PRESSLEY																
1964	EDM	0	8	269	33.6	48										

Year	Team	S	PUNT	YDS	AVG	LG	KO	YDS	AVG	LG	CON	CONA	PCT	FG	FGA	PCT
RONNIE QUILLIAN																
1957	OTT	3	51	1913	37.5	73										
1958	OTT	3	86	3255	37.8	62										
Totals		6	137	5168	37.7	73										
MOE RACINE																
1961	OTT	0					62	3077	49.6	80	0	0		0	0	
1962	OTT	7									36	43	83.7	12	24	50.0
1963	OTT	6					44	2416	54.9	85	24	33	72.7	9	19	47.4
1964	OTT	3					54	3073	56.9	73	32	39	82.1	11	21	52.4
1965	OTT	5					48	2601	54.2	75	34	36	94.4	12	21	57.1
1966	OTT	7					49	2760	56.3	73	28	33	84.8	12	27	44.4
1967	OTT	2					14	798	57.0	65	22	27	81.5	6	13	46.2
1972	OTT	0					3	164	54.7	66	0	0		0	0	
Totals		30					274	14889	54.3	85	176	211	83.4	62	125	49.6
EMIL RADIK																
1955	MTL	0									0	0		0	1	0.0
DAVID RAY																
1968	MTL	1	1	37	37.0	37	4	217	54.3	60	11	12	91.7	11	18	61.1
RUSS READER																
1949	TOR	0									1			0		
JOHNNY REAGAN																
1947	WPG	0									0			1		
BILL REDELL																
1966	EDM	0					1	42	42.0	42						
1969	CAL	0	2	61	30.5	35										
Totals		0	2	61	30.5	35	1	42	42.0	42						
BOB REDKEY																
1952	CAL	2	7	256	36.6	52	1	33	33.0	33						
BOB REED																
1964	WPG	2									4	5	80.0	0	3	0.0
DOUG REID																
1950	CAL	0	2	92	46.0											
MIKE RENAUD																
2009	WPG	1	115	4717	41.0	59					0	0		0	0	
2010	WPG	5	131	5623	42.9	79					4	4	100.0	0	0	
2011	WPG	7	122	5136	42.1	72					0	0		0	0	
Totals		13	368	15476	42.1	79					4	4	100.0	0	0	
BOBBY RENN																
1959	SAS	0	1	34	34.0	34										
1960	SAS	2	39	1594	40.9	68										
Totals		2	40	1628	40.7	68										
JIM REYNOLDS																
1962	OTT	0	1	42	42.0	42										
1962	Year	0	1	42	42.0	42										
Totals		0	1	42	42.0	42										
BILL RHODES																
1957	TOR	0	2	129	64.5	71										
DAVID RIDGWAY																
1982	SAS	15					65	3810	58.6	90	34	34	100.0	38	51	74.5
1983	SAS	14					60	3400	56.7	90	31	32	96.9	22	35	62.9
1984	SAS	13	10	411	41.1	57	60	3412	56.9	90	30	30	100.0	28	42	66.7
1985	SAS	15					53	3146	59.4	89	25	25	100.0	23	38	60.5
1986	SAS	8					77	4629	60.1	72	34	35	97.1	37	50	74.0
1987	SAS	4					67	3489	52.1	83	23	23	100.0	49	57	86.0
1988	SAS	5					83	4449	53.6	95	45	45	100.0	55	66	83.3
1989	SAS	5					90	4737	52.6	95	49	49	100.0	54	68	79.4
1990	SAS	9					99	5219	52.7	72	47	48	97.9	59	72	81.9
1991	SAS	4					108	5600	51.9	75	56	56	100.0	52	61	85.2
1992	SAS	7					97	4959	51.1	71	50	50	100.0	36	47	76.6
1993	SAS	1					86	4450	51.7	76	51	51	100.0	48	53	90.6
1994	SAS	3					59	3306	56.0	73	35	35	100.0	30	39	76.9
1995	SAS	8					64	3414	53.3	67	31	31	100.0	43	57	75.4
Totals		111	10	411	41.1	57	1068	58020	54.3	95	541	544	99.4	574	736	78.0
CHARLES ROBERTS																
2004	WPG	0	1	20	20.0	20										
GENE ROBERTS																
1951	MTL	1									14			2		
1953	OTT	2									36			5		
1954	OTT	1									13	18	72.2	2	5	40.0
Totals		4									63	18	72.2	9	5	40.0
GENE ROBILLARD																
1954	BC	0	1	32	32.0	32										
JACK ROBINSON																
1964	WPG	2	10	285	28.5	50	9	510	56.7	80	5	7	71.4	1	4	25.0
LARRY ROBINSON																
1961	CAL	2	20	764	38.2	56	1	58	58.0	58	0	0		0	1	0.0
1962	CAL	2					24	949	39.5	55	35	41	85.4	8	13	61.5
1963	CAL	9					66	3593	54.4	87	45	52	86.5	15	25	60.0
1964	CAL	9					54	2991	55.4	89	31	40	77.5	22	37	59.5
1965	CAL	8					58	3509	60.5	77	36	40	90.0	15	28	53.6
1966	CAL	13	56	2046	36.5	58	44	2659	60.4	75	19	24	79.2	13	42	31.0
1967	CAL	1					68	4189	61.6	80	5	7	71.4	0	11	0.0
1968	CAL	10					71	4396	61.9	85	45	52	86.5	12	28	42.9
1969	CAL	11	20	637	31.9	53	53	3143	59.3	89	30	37	81.1	18	37	48.6
1970	CAL	10					41	2401	58.6	80	28	30	93.3	12	32	37.5
1971	CAL	12					48	2805	58.4	90	30	31	96.8	11	26	42.3
1972	CAL	5					16	984	61.5	90	32	36	88.9	19	29	65.5
1973	CAL	5									18	20	90.0	19	30	63.3
1974	CAL	4									8	11	72.7	7	15	46.7
Totals		101	96	3447	35.9	58	544	31677	58.2	90	362	421	86.0	171	354	48.3
BUCK ROGERS																
1947	OTT	1									2			0		
1948	OTT	0									3			0		
1949	SAS	0									3			0		
1952	OTT	3									24			3		
1953	WPG	0					1	45	45.0		0			0		
1954	WPG	0					18	836	46.4		9	12	75.0	0	2	0.0
1955	WPG	0					32	1625	50.8	73	0	0		0	0	
Totals		4					51	2506	49.1	73	41	12	75.0	3	2	0.0
JOHNNY ROGERS																
1950	OTT	1									4			0		
BARRY ROSEBOROUGH																

Year	Team	S	PUNT	YDS	AVG	LG	KO	YDS	AVG	LG	CON	CONA	PCT	FG	FGA	PCT
1956	WPG	2	27	980	36.3	49										
1957	WPG	0	1	35	35.0	35										
Totals		2	28	1015	36.3	49										
JIM ROUNTREE																
1961	TOR	0	2	66	33.0	33										
GORDIE ROWLAND																
1955	WPG	0					7	365	52.1	61	0	0		0	0	
1956	WPG	0					3	73	24.3	47	0	0		0	0	
1958	WPG	0	1	47	47.0	47					0	0		0	0	
1960	WPG	2					71	3702	52.1	90	0	0		0	0	
1961	WPG	0					49	2047	41.8	69	0	0		0	0	
1962	WPG	0					47	1869	39.8	65	0	0		0	0	
1963	WPG	1					30	1273	42.4	85	3	5	60.0	0	1	0.0
1964	WPG	0					8	217	27.1	46	0	0		0	0	
Totals		3	1	47	47.0	47	215	9546	44.4	90	3	5	60.0	0	1	0.0
BOB RUMBALL																
1954	OTT	0	1	39	39.0	39										
1955	TOR	0	6	242	40.3	47										
Totals		0	7	281	40.1	47										
BERNIE RUOFF																
1975	WPG	9	94	4138	44.0	73	58	3107	53.6	90	22	23	95.7	22	43	51.2
1976	WPG	12	131	5904	45.1	79	79	4970	62.9	90	37	38	97.4	31	50	62.0
1977	WPG	21	131	5695	43.5	81	69	3776	54.7	95	38	39	97.4	25	57	43.9
1978	WPG	23	132	6190	46.9	76	68	4132	60.8	90	33	34	97.1	31	43	72.1
1979	WPG	16	133	5999	45.1	68	50	2976	59.5	90	18	22	81.8	39	52	75.0
1980	HAM	14	121	5118	42.3	75	55	3163	57.5	76	26	26	100.0	32	46	69.6
1981	HAM	25	131	5947	45.4	71	69	4226	61.2	90	40	40	100.0	29	46	63.0
1982	HAM	18	116	5256	45.3	79	62	3561	57.4	90	34	36	94.4	30	51	58.8
1983	HAM	21	150	7108	47.4	96	64	3687	57.6	90	35	35	100.0	31	42	73.8
1984	HAM	14	156	7302	46.8	77	55	3363	61.1	92	29	29	100.0	34	44	77.3
1985	HAM	25	130	5886	45.3	77	54	3231	59.8	90	33	33	100.0	32	48	66.7
1986	HAM	9	82	3506	42.8	68	35	2043	58.4	70	19	19	100.0	16	25	64.0
1987	HAM	8	93	3752	40.3	58	56	2934	52.4	95	29	29	100.0	26	34	76.5
1988	BC	4					17	973	57.2	68	8	9	88.9	6	14	42.9
Totals		219	1600	71801	44.9	96	791	46142	58.3	95	401	412	97.3	384	595	64.5
JON RYAN																
2004	WPG	6	118	5095	43.2	92										
2005	WPG	12	118	5967	50.6	80										
Totals		18	236	11062	46.9	92										
RICK RYAN																
1986	MTL	1					3	151	50.3	55	1	1	100.0	2	3	66.7
1990	BC	1					27	1414	52.4	67	1	1	100.0	1	4	25.0
Totals		2					30	1565	52.2	67	2	2	100.0	3	7	42.9
DON ST. JOHN																
1956	OTT	1	24	928	38.7	53					5	8	62.5	0	0	
LOUIE SAKODA																
2009	SAS	2	13	578	44.5	57	12	801	66.8	90						
2010	SAS	1	15	508	33.9	63	20	1196	59.8	80						
2010	Year	1	15	508	33.9	63	20	1196	59.8	80						
Totals		3	28	1086	38.8	63	32	1997	62.4	90					0	
EDDIE SALE																
1952	MTL	1									17			3		
BOB SANDBERG																
1947	WPG	9									1			0		
1948	WPG	5									0			0		
1949	WPG	5									0			0		
1951	SAS	1	17	673	39.6	90					0	0		0	0	
Totals		20	17	673	39.6	90					1	0		0	0	
JIM SANDUSKY																
1995	EDM	0	1	46	46.0	46										
1998	BC	1	1	57	57.0	57										
Totals		1	2	103	51.5	57										
PAT SANTUCCI																
1947	HAM	1									9			4		
1949	SAS	2									20			2		
1950	HAM	1														
Totals		4									29			6		
DEREK SCHIAVONE																
2008	EDM	0	3	109	36.3	41	5	258	51.6	53	4	4	100.0	3	3	100.0
2009	EDM	0	5	184	36.8	45	9	475	52.8	61	3	3	100.0	5	5	100.0
2010	EDM	3	25	1008	40.3	72	20	969	48.5	65	10	10	100.0	15	18	83.3
2011	EDM	2									11	11	100.0	16	19	84.2
Totals		5	33	1301	39.4	72	34	1702	50.1	65	28	28	100.0	39	45	86.7
TOM SCHIMMER																
1989	OTT	6	155	5903	38.1	73										
BOB SCHLOREDT																
1961	BC	1	42	1720	41.0	58										
1962	BC	5	81	3424	42.3	63										
Totals		6	123	5144	41.8	63										
RALPH SCHOENFELD																
1967	WPG	1	23	879	38.2	63										
ERNIE SCHRAMAYR																
1990	HAM	0	2	75	37.5	49										
1991	HAM	0	1	36	36.0	36										
Totals		0	3	111	37.0	49										
GARY SCHREIDER																
1957	OTT	2									33	44	75.0	7	12	58.3
1958	OTT	2	3	78	26.0	40					7	13	53.8	0	3	0.0
1959	OTT	0					4	179	44.8	58	22	30	73.3	3	5	60.0
1960	OTT	2									42	55	76.4	5	10	50.0
1961	OTT	1									44	49	89.8	4	10	40.0
1962	BC	0									3	5	60.0	1	2	50.0
1962	Year	0									3	5	60.0	1	2	50.0
Totals		7	3	78	26.0	40	4	179	44.8	58	151	196	77.0	20	42	47.6
HERB SCHUMM																
1973	CAL	1	1	40	40.0	40										
SANDRO SCIORTINO																
2004	OTT	4					54	2866	53.1	85	35	36	97.2	17	30	56.7
NICK SCOLLARD																
1950	MTL	2									20			3		
GEORGE SCOTT																
1962	HAM	0									1	1	100.0	0	0	

Year	Team	S	PUNT	YDS	AVG	LG	KO	YDS	AVG	LG	CON	CONA	PCT	FG	FGA	PCT
WILBERT SCOTT																
1968	HAM	0					1	43	43.0	43						
DEMITRIS SCOURAS																
2002	OTT	1					12	694	57.8	66	7	7	100.0	3	5	60.0
2004	OTT	1					7	360	51.4	65	5	5	100.0	1	4	25.0
Totals		2					19	1054	55.5	66	12	12	100.0	4	9	44.4
DANA SEGIN																
2002	HAM	0	4	98	24.5	35	6	266	44.3	60	2	2	100.0	5	6	83.3
ALEXIS SERNA																
2008	WPG	17	124	5215	42.1	59	73	4291	58.8	95	40	40	100.0	34	51	66.7
2009	WPG	7	12	477	39.8	68	101	5795	57.4	82	34	34	100.0	40	49	81.6
2010	WPG	4	9	406	45.1	66					20	20	100.0	8	14	57.1
Totals		28	145	6098	42.1	68	174	10086	58.0	95	94	94	100.0	82	114	71.9
NICK SETTA																
2007	HAM	13	130	5725	44.0	97	53	3166	59.7	90	19	19	100.0	45	53	84.9
2008	HAM	14	114	5401	47.4	97	78	4715	60.4	95	45	45	100.0	28	36	77.8
2009	HAM	13	121	5196	42.9	73	96	5448	56.8	73	39	40	97.5	38	50	76.0
Totals		40	365	16322	44.7	97	227	13329	58.7	95	103	104	99.0	111	139	79.9
CARVER SHANNON																
1959	WPG	0									2	6	33.3	0	0	
1960	WPG	1									12	21	57.1	0	1	0.0
1961	WPG	2									5	6	83.3	3	6	50.0
1961	Year	2									5	6	83.3	3	6	50.0
Totals		3									19	33	57.6	3	7	42.9
DICK SHATTO																
1959	TOR	0	1	43	43.0	43					0	0		0	0	
1963	TOR	0									3	3	100.0	0	0	
Totals		1	1	43	43.0	43					3	3	100.0	0	0	
ROY SHATZKO																
1967	EDM	0					2	109	54.5	56						
BOB SHAW																
1951	CAL	2									30	32	93.8	3	10	30.0
1952	CAL	3	1	40	40.0	40	50	2455	49.1	63	38	43	88.4	8	15	53.3
1953	CAL	0									1	3	33.3	0	1	0.0
1953	TOR	0									11			1		
1953	Year	0									12			1		
Totals		5	1	40	40.0	40	50	2455	49.1	63	80	78	88.5	12	26	42.3
GRANT SHAW																
2010	TOR	6	5	245	49.0	63	6	370	61.7	68	21	22	95.5	22	33	66.7
2011	TOR	1	12	450	37.5	53	74	4603	62.2	80	5	5	100.0	4	5	80.0
Totals		7	17	695	40.9	63	80	4973	62.2	80	26	27	96.3	26	38	68.4
CHARLIE SHEPARD																
1957	WPG	4	28	1152	41.1	92										
1958	WPG	10	143	6324	44.2	79										
1959	WPG	7	121	5224	43.2	61										
1960	WPG	14	98	4386	44.8	95										
1961	WPG	15	85	3855	45.4	89										
1962	WPG	3	46	2054	44.7	85										
Totals		53	521	22995	44.1	95										
JIM SHIPKA																
1956	EDM	0	4	119	29.8	40	1	47	47.0	47						
1957	EDM	0					3	162	54.0	58						
Totals		0	4	119	29.8	40	4	209	52.3	58						
JIM SIDES																
1956	CAL	0					7	378	54.0	59	1	1	100.0%	0	1	0.0%
JACKI SIMPSON																
1959	MTL	0					16	833	52.1	61						
1965	WPG	4					18	976	54.2	65	6	11	54.5	4	10	40.0
1965	TOR	2									0	0		0	3	0.0
1965	Year	6					18	976	54.2	65	6	11	54.5	4	13	30.8
Totals		12					34	1809	53.2	65	12	22	54.5	8	26	30.8
E.A. SIMS																
1962	EDM	0					5	205	41.0	53						
ART SKIDMORE																
1946	TOR	3														
CHRIS SKINNER																
1989	OTT	0	1	5	5.0	5										
KEN SLUMAN																
1949	EDM	3														
1950	EDM	1	7	267	38.1											
Totals		4	7	267	38.1											
BRAD SMITH																
2007	MTL	0					1	4	4.0	4						
DOUG SMITH																
1946	HAM	7														
1947	HAM	5														
Totals		12														
JOE BOB SMITH																
1958	EDM	0									4	5	80.0	0	0	
1961	EDM	0					1	8	8.0	8	0	0		0	0	
Totals		0					1	8	8.0	8	4	5	80.0	0	0	
DOUG SMYLIE																
1948	OTT	0									1			0		
1949	TOR	0									2			0		
Totals		0									3			0		
BILL SNYDER																
1952	EDM	0									3	4	75.0	0	0	
1953	EDM	5	1	33	33.0		43	2221	51.7	88	31	31	100.0	5	14	35.7
Totals		5	1	33	33.0		43	2221	51.7	88	34	35	97.1	5	14	35.7
ANDY SOKOL																
1946	HAM	0									2			0		
1950	WPG	0	1	35	35.0	35					0	0		0	0	
Totals		0	1	35	35.0	35					2	0		0	0	
BUTCH SONGIN																
1954	HAM	0	1	50	50.0	50										
HENRY SOVIO																
1976	BC	0					7	427	61.0	64						
KEITH SPAITH																
1948	CAL	16														
1949	CAL	8														
1950	CAL	8	109	4519	41.5	74										
1951	CAL	0	77	2899	37.6											

Year	Team	S	PUNT	YDS	AVG	LG	KO	YDS	AVG	LG	CON	CONA	PCT	FG	FGA	PCT
1952	CAL	8	95	3622	38.1	58										
1953	CAL	1	102	3946	38.7	65	22	876	39.8	62						
1954	CAL	0	14	576	41.1	55										
Totals		41	397	15562	39.2	74	22	876	39.8	62						
HAL SPARROW																
1957	BC	0	2	64	32.0	33										
1959	BC	3	77	2940	38.2	53										
1960	BC	2	44	1668	37.9	73										
Totals		5	123	4672	38.0	73										
WALLY SPENCER																
1946	MTL	1														
GEORGE SPRINGATE																
1970	MTL	2					2	95	47.5	50	15	21	71.4	8	14	57.1
1971	MTL	2									5	7	71.4	1	4	25.0
1972	MTL	0									1	1	100.0	1	1	100.0
Totals		4					2	95	47.5	50	21	29	72.4	10	19	52.6
TOAR SPRINGSTEIN																
1946	SAS	0									2			1		
1949	SAS	0									1			0		
Totals		0									3			1		
DAVE STALA																
2003	MTL	1	2	96	48.0	64	3	139	46.3	58	2	2	100.0	0	0	
2004	MTL	1	15	537	35.8	50	22	1250	56.8	78	0	0		0	0	
2005	MTL	1	3	134	44.7	54					0	0		0	0	
2006	MTL	0	4	165	41.3	50					0	0		0	0	
2009	HAM	0					3	154	51.3	55	0	0		0	0	
2010	HAM	0	2	78	39.0	44					0	0		0	0	
Totals		3	26	1010	38.8	64	28	1543	55.1	78	2	2	100.0	0	0	
STEVE STAPLER																
1986	HAM	2	64	2606	40.7	78										
1987	HAM	1	23	755	32.8	75										
1988	HAM	0	1	41	41.0	41										
Totals		3	88	3402	38.7	78										
BILL STARR																
1969	MTL	0									1			0	0	
JOHN STEELE																
1971	SAS	0					22	1182	53.7	68	9	9	100.0	0	1	0.0
1972	SAS	0									0	0		0	1	0.0
Totals		0					22	1182	53.7	68	9	9	100.0	0	2	0.0
DICK STEERE																
1952	EDM	0					2	93	46.5	50	1	2	50.0	0	0	
BUS STEPHENS																
1947	HAM	4									1			0		
SANDY STEPHENS																
1962	MTL	0	1	6	6.0	6					2	2	100.0	2	2	100.0
1963	MTL	0					1	55	55.0	55	1	1	100.0	0	0	
1963	TOR	1	1	34	34.0	34					9	16	56.3	2	6	33.3
1963	Year	1	1	34	34.0	34	1	55	55.0	55	10	17	58.8	2	6	33.3
Totals		1	2	40	20.0	34	1	55	55.0	55	12	19	63.2	4	8	50.0
CORY STEVENS																
1999	SAS	1	17	681	40.1	63										
BILL STEVENSON																
1956	CAL	1	22	818	37.2	57	8	361	45.1	56						
1957	CAL	0	2	26	13.0	25										
Totals		1	24	844	35.2	57	8	361	45.1	56						
ART STEWART																
1952	SAS	0					6	279	46.5	55						
JACKIE STEWART																
1948	HAM	1														
RON STEWART																
1959	OTT	0	1	33	33.0	33										
RON STEWART																
1967	CAL	0	30	1121	37.4	55										
1968	CAL	3	84	3551	42.3	75										
1970	CAL	0	131	5336	40.7	63										
Totals		3	245	10008	40.8	75										
AVATUS STONE																
1953	OTT	10														
1954	OTT	3	163	6913	42.4	79										
1955	OTT	4	118	5179	43.9	71										
1956	OTT	11	100	4499	45.0	71										
1957	MTL	5	76	3123	41.1	61										
Totals		33	457	19714	43.1	79										
GARY STRICKLER																
1963	TOR	0					18	822	45.7	55						
DOUG STRONG																
1970	WPG	0	1	40	40.0	40										
1971	WPG	0					1	13	13.0	13						
1973	WPG	0	1	25	25.0	25										
Totals		0	2	65	32.5	40	1	13	13.0	13						
ANNIS STUKUS																
1950	EDM	1	1	38	38.0	38					28	31	90.3	3	10	30.0
1951	EDM	7									42	49	85.7	3	14	21.4
Totals		8	1	38	38.0	38					70	80	87.5	6	24	25.0
GREGG STUMON																
1988	BC	1	1	20	20.0	20										
GLEN SUITOR																
1991	SAS	0	1	41	41.0	41										
IAN SUNTER																
1972	HAM	7	20	676	33.8	47	49	2573	52.5	80	44	45	97.8	14	38	36.8
1973	HAM	7					8	414	51.8	57	32	33	97.0	21	35	60.0
1974	HAM	14	151	5840	38.7	74	38	2084	54.8	80	22	23	95.7	35	53	66.0
1975	HAM	8					61	3476	57.0	87	17	17	100.0	28	43	65.1
1978	TOR	13	41	1599	39.0	89	43	2316	53.9	90	22	22	100.0	16	33	48.5
1979	TOR	17	147	6123	41.7	66	44	2530	57.5	83	18	18	100.0	21	32	65.6
Totals		66	359	14238	39.7	89	243	13393	55.1	90	155	158	98.1	135	234	57.7
DON SUTHERIN																
1958	HAM	3	4	142	35.5	47	22	1223	55.6	83	1	2	50.0	1	5	20.0
1960	HAM	0									1	1	100.0	2	4	50.0
1961	HAM	4	15	639	42.6	84	58	3414	58.9	79	35	43	81.4	10	25	40.0
1962	HAM	5									37	44	84.1	12	27	44.4
1963	HAM	4					35	2067	59.1	75	15	22	68.2	7	14	50.0

Year	Team	S	PUNT	YDS	AVG	LG	KO	YDS	AVG	LG	CON	CONA	PCT	FG	FGA	PCT
1964	HAM	15	2	81	40.5	44	47	2722	57.9	80	34	37	91.9	15	35	42.9
1965	HAM	6					39	2242	57.5	85	19	25	76.0	19	36	52.8
1966	HAM	12	13	502	38.6	50	43	2574	59.9	77	25	31	80.6	10	25	40.0
1967	OTT	5					41	2343	57.1	90	16	16	100.0	3	7	42.9
1968	OTT	11					63	3749	59.5	85	44	51	86.3	17	37	45.9
1969	OTT	13					63	3686	58.5	80	43	47	91.5	18	42	42.9
1970	TOR	0					7	341	48.7	65	0	0		0	1	0.0
Totals		78	34	1364	40.1	84	418	24361	58.3	90	270	319	84.6	114	258	44.2
DON SWEET																
1972	MTL	7					22	1105	50.2	73	21	30	70.0	8	20	40.0
1973	MTL	1					21	1054	50.2	61	29	29	100.0	19	29	65.5
1974	MTL	5					23	1259	54.7	71	32	38	84.2	24	41	58.5
1975	MTL	7					75	4129	55.1	76	25	25	100.0	25	38	65.8
1976	MTL	4					46	2394	52.0	87	23	23	100.0	38	50	76.0
1977	MTL	4					64	3433	53.6	70	27	27	100.0	35	46	76.1
1978	MTL	2					56	3154	56.3	71	31	31	100.0	30	35	85.7
1979	MTL	7	6	245	40.8	52	63	3669	58.2	71	38	38	100.0	22	32	68.8
1980	MTL	6	52	2104	40.5	54	15	907	60.5	80	7	7	100.0	7	11	63.6
1981	MTL	4	11	434	39.5	52	23	1239	53.9	71	13	13	100.0	13	20	65.0
1982	MTL	12	133	5437	40.9	61	50	2662	53.2	85	16	18	88.9	27	38	71.1
1983	MTL	8	69	2981	43.2	57	22	1235	56.1	64	36	36	100.0	31	46	67.4
1984	MTL	5	8	309	38.6	51	14	530	37.9	67	27	27	100.0	33	43	76.7
1985	HAM	1	21	843	40.1	53	5	234	46.8	59	2	2	100.0	2	8	25.0
Totals		73	300	12353	41.2	61	499	27004	54.1	87	327	344	95.1	314	457	68.7
KARL SWEETAN																
1964	TOR	1	1	44	44.0	44	29	1611	55.6	68	22	28	78.6	3	6	50.0
CHUCK TACK																
2005	HAM	0	2	52	26.0	36										
GEORGE TAIT																
1957	SAS	0									1	1	100.0	0	0	
1959	CAL	0	1	41	41.0	41					0	0		0	0	
Totals		0	1	41	41.0	41					1	1	100.0	0	0	
TONY TERESA																
1956	BC	0									4	6	66.7	1	2	50.0
DAVE THEISEN																
1965	WPG	1					4	210	52.5	58	2	3	66.7	0	1	0.0
JOE THEISMANN																
1971	TOR	1	3	182	60.7	69					1	1	100.0	0	0	
PETE THODOS																
1948	CAL	0									1			0		
1952	CAL	0	2	69	34.5						0	0		0	0	
1953	CAL	0									4	7	57.1	0	0	
Totals		0	2	69	34.5						5	7	57.1	0	0	
GREG THOMPSON																
1969	OTT	0	14	493	35.2	52										
1970	OTT	0	1	35	35.0	35										
1971	EDM	1	47	1886	40.1	74										
1971	Year	1	47	1886	40.1	74										
Totals		1	62	2414	38.9	74										
DICK THORNTON																
1961	WPG	0	13	461	35.5	54										
1962	WPG	1	15	424	28.3	54										
1963	WPG	1	62	2358	38.0	62										
1964	WPG	0	5	178	35.6	46										
1965	WPG	0	9	313	34.8	45										
1966	WPG	0	6	222	37.0	43										
1967	TOR	0	1	42	42.0	42										
1969	TOR	2	52	2012	38.7	68										
1972	TOR		1	3	3.0	3										
Totals		4	164	6013	36.7	68										
JIM THORPE																
1971	WPG	0	49	1802	36.8	54	2	109	54.5	57						
BRIAN TIMMIS																
1953	SAS	0	1	37	37.0											
BUDDY TINSLEY																
1951	WPG	1	13	387	29.8											
ED TOMLIN																
1968	MTL	0									1	1	100.0%	0	0	
DAVE TOMLINSON																
1947	CAL	1														
BOB TORRANCE																
1993	HAM	0	1	57	57.0	57										
TOM TRACY																
1955	OTT	0	1	24	24.0	24					23	26	88.5	4	7	57.1
1956	OTT	0									9	9	100.0	1	1	100.0
Totals		0	1	24	24.0	24					32	35	91.4	5	8	62.5
HERB TRAWICK																
1948	MTL	1														
1950	MTL	1														
1951	MTL	1														
Totals		3														
WILF TREMBLAY																
1946	OTT	0									1			0		
1948	OTT	0									2			0		
Totals		0									3			0		
MIKE TREVATHAN																
1994	BC	0	2	86	43.0	46										
1996	BC	0	1	33	33.0	33										
Totals		0	3	119	39.7	46										
FRANK TRIPUCKA																
1953	SAS	3	31	1463	47.2						0	0		0	0	
1954	SAS	0	16	686	42.9	55					0	0		0	0	
1955	SAS	0	7	242	34.6	58					0	0		0	0	
1956	SAS	0									0	1	0.0	0	0	
1958	SAS	2	19	936	49.3	80					0	0		0	0	
1959	OTT	1	52	2057	39.6	58					0	0		0	0	
1959	Year	1	52	2057	39.6	58					0	0		0	0	
1963	SAS	1	4	185	46.3	65					5	5	100.0	0	1	0.0
Totals		7	129	5569	43.2	80					5	6	83.3	0	1	0.0
RAY TRUANT																
1954	HAM	0									3	4	75.0	0	0	
1955	HAM	0									15	17	88.2	1	1	100.0

Year	Team	S	PUNT	YDS	AVG	LG	KO	YDS	AVG	LG	CON	CONA	PCT	FG	FGA	PCT
Totals		0									18	21	85.7	1	1	100.0
TED TULLY																
1952	EDM	0					14	693	49.5	62	0			0		
1953	EDM	1					15	768	51.2		7	8	87.5	1	3	33.3
1954	EDM	0					3	86	28.7		2	2	100.0	0	0	
1958	EDM	0					10	503	50.3	64	0	0		0	0	
1961	EDM	0					52	2525	48.6	68	1	1	100.0	0	0	
1962	EDM	0					13	615	47.3	62	5	7	71.4	2	3	66.7
Totals		1					107	5190	48.5	68	15	18	83.3	3	6	50.0
ED TUREK																
1968	HAM	0					7	386	55.1	64						
1969	HAM	0					2	79	39.5	40						
Totals		0					9	465	51.7	64						
CHARLIE TURNER																
1967	HAM	0					8	457	57.1	63						
HOWIE TURNER																
1947	OTT	2									0			0		
1948	OTT	9									1			0		
1949	OTT	7									0			0		
1950	OTT	1									0			0		
Totals		19									1			0		
GERRY TUTTLE																
1954	BC	0	2	91	45.5	59										
LAWRENCE TYNES																
2002	OTT	4					32	1923	60.1	95	15	16	93.8	20	25	80.0
2003	OTT	9					83	4937	59.5	95	36	36	100.0	51	62	82.3
Totals		13					115	6860	59.7	95	51	52	98.1	71	87	81.6
ED ULMER																
1963	OTT	0	7	289	41.3	52										
1964	OTT	4	98	4095	41.8	64										
1965	WPG	7	127	5265	41.5	68										
1966	WPG	8	126	5396	42.8	86										
1967	WPG	3	65	2616	40.2	76										
1968	WPG	8	138	5931	43.0	80										
1969	WPG	5	115	4690	40.8	91										
1970	WPG	3	134	5604	41.8	69										
1971	WPG	2	53	2166	40.9	60										
Totals		40	863	36052	41.8	91										
RON VACCHER																
1952	WPG	0					1	37	37.0	37						
BILL VAN BURKLEO																
1966	TOR	1	3	185	61.7	82										
1967	WPG	1	40	1756	43.9	57										
1968	OTT	2	84	3538	42.1	65										
1969	OTT	1	86	3514	40.9	64										
1970	OTT	2	112	4609	41.2	71										
1971	CAL	7	140	5855	41.8	61										
1972	HAM	2	88	3484	39.6	53										
Totals		16	553	22941	41.5	82										
MIKE VANDERJAGT																
1993	SAS	0	17	672	39.5	59	2	109	54.5	57						
1996	TOR	19	103	4459	43.3	70	85	4933	58.0	83	59	59	100.0	40	56	71.4
1997	TOR	14	118	5303	44.9	80	113	6650	58.8	88	77	77	100.0	33	43	76.7
2008	TOR	9	131	5818	44.4	71	81	4504	55.6	83	35	35	100.0	39	51	76.5
Totals		42	369	16252	44.0	80	281	16196	57.6	88	171	171	100.0	112	150	74.7
BRUCE VAN NESS																
1971	MTL	0	4	135	33.8	40										
JIM VAN PELT																
1958	WPG	3					42	2221	52.9	66	26	32	81.3	8	13	61.5
1959	WPG	2	14	538	38.4	50	30	1534	51.1	64	34	46	73.9	8	15	53.3
Totals		5	14	538	38.4	50	72	3755	52.2	66	60	78	76.9	16	28	57.1
TERRY VAUGHN																
2003	EDM	1	1	56	56.0	56										
GREG VAVRA																
1984	CAL	0	1	43	43.0	43										
1986	BC	0	1	6	6.0	6	7	359	51.3	58						
1987	BC	0	1	18	18.0	18										
Totals		0	3	67	22.3	43	7	359	51.3	58						
MIKE VILIMEK																
2006	MTL	0					1	27	27.0	27						
PRIMO VILLANUEVA																
1955	BC	0	4	124	31.0	40					0	0		0	0	
1956	BC	0									1	1	100.0	0	0	
Totals		0	4	124	31.0	40					1	1	100.0	0	0	
JOHN VILUNAS																
1964	TOR	0					15	714	47.6	65	0	0		0	0	
1965	TOR	2					31	1579	50.9	67	5	6	83.3	6	10	60.0
1966	TOR	5					34	1751	51.5	70	14	20	70.0	6	14	42.9
1967	TOR	8					40	2074	51.9	67	10	13	76.9	3	17	17.6
1968	SAS	0									0	0		0	1	0.0
Totals		15					120	6118	51.0	70	29	39	74.4	15	42	35.7
GERRY VINCENT																
1955	WPG	1	24	956	39.8	54										
1956	WPG	1	56	2131	38.1	63										
1957	WPG	9	101	4025	39.9	65										
1958	WPG	1	4	186	46.5	55										
Totals		12	185	7298	39.4	65										
DAVE VITI																
1963	HAM	1					2	91	45.5	53	13	17	76.5	4	8	50.0
1965	HAM	0					2	99	49.5	59	0	0		0	0	
1968	HAM	0					4	162	40.5	65	0	0		0	0	
1969	HAM	0					10	466	46.6	62	0	0		0	0	
Totals		1					18	818	45.4	65	13	17	76.5	4	8	50.0
NICK VOLPE																
1949	TOR	0									7			2		
1950	TOR	0									41			1		
1951	TOR	0									2			0		
Totals		0									50			3		
SONNY WADE																
1969	MTL	9	114	4721	41.4	87										
1970	MTL	4	102	4157	40.8	73										
1971	MTL	1	79	3073	38.9	64										

Year	Team	S	PUNT	YDS	AVG	LG	KO	YDS	AVG	LG	CON	CONA	PCT	FG	FGA	PCT
1972	MTL	3	86	3402	39.6	69										
1973	MTL	0	4	198	49.5	63										
1974	MTL	0	105	4179	39.8	80										
1975	MTL	4	124	5139	41.4	63										
1976	MTL	2	137	5846	42.7	63										
1977	MTL	3	95	4141	43.6	60										
1978	MTL	0	6	274	45.7	50										
Totals		26	852	35130	41.2	87										
VIRGIL WAGNER																
1947	MTL	0									1			0		
1949	MTL	0									2			0		
Totals		0									3			0		
BOBBY WALDEN																
1961	EDM	7	63	2953	46.9	79										
1962	EDM	5	40	1946	48.7	74										
1963	EDM	1	13	543	41.8	59										
1963	HAM	0	9	398	44.2	55										
1963	Year	1	22	941	42.8	59										
Totals		13	125	5840	46.7	79										
BILL WALKER																
1956	EDM	0	27	1034	38.3	51										
1957	EDM	5	71	2891	40.7	70										
1958	EDM	3	62	2259	36.4	63										
Totals		8	160	6184	38.7	70										
MIKE WALKER																
1974	HAM		1	15	15.0	15										
MILAM WALL																
1961	HAM	0									1	1	100.0	0	0	
DON WALSH																
1953	CAL	0					13	679	52.2	60	0	0		0	0	
1954	CAL	0					12	658	54.8		0	0		0	0	
1955	SAS	0					6	333	55.5	63	0	0		0	0	
1955	Year	0					6	333	55.5	63	0	0		0	0	
1956	SAS	0					18	943	52.4	75	0	0		0	0	
1957	SAS	0					16	741	46.3	60	0	0		0	0	
1958	SAS	0					3	151	50.3	53	0	0		0	0	
1959	SAS	0					1	60	60.0	60	0	0		0	0	
1963	SAS	1									0	0		0	1	0.0
Totals		1					69	3565	51.7	75	0	0		0	1	0.0
JIM WALTER																
1965	MTL	0	3	93	31.0	35										
1968	MTL	0	2	64	32.0	33								0		
Totals		0	5	157	31.4	35								0		
RICK WALTERS																
1999	EDM	0					7	346	49.4	57						
2000	EDM	0					1	54	54.0	54						
2001	EDM	0					1	49	49.0	49						
Totals		0					9	449	49.9	57						
DEL WARDIEN																
1947	CAL	1									1	1	100.0	0		
1949	SAS	5									5			2		
1950	SAS	0	2	45	22.5						0	0		0	0	
1952	SAS	1					18	930	51.7	65	24	27	88.9	1	3	33.3
1953	SAS	4	2	75	37.5		42	1744	41.5		23	27	85.2	5	14	35.7
Totals		11	4	120	30.0		60	2674	44.6	65	53	55	87.3	8	17	35.3
PAUL WATSON																
1981	SAS	19					64	3864	60.4	90	41	41	100.0	22	41	53.7
RON WATTON																
1957	BC	0					1	11	11.0	11						
JIM WEATHERALL																
1954	EDM	0					5	190	38.0							
WALT WEAVER																
1962	CAL	5	97	3739	38.5	71										
ALEX WEBSTER																
1954	MTL	0	12	377	31.4	43										
DALE WEST																
1963	SAS	0	2	63	31.5	33										
1965	SAS	0	1	67	67.0	67										
1966	SAS	0	5	188	37.6	48										
1967	SAS	0	3	125	41.7	44	1	55	55.0	55						
Totals		0	11	443	40.3	67	1	55	55.0	55						
DAVEY WEST																
1959	OTT	0									1	1	100.0	0	0	
EDDIE WEST																
1956	CAL	0	4	151	37.8	42	3	130	43.3	54						
PAT WEST																
1949	EDM	2									6			2		
TROY WESTWOOD																
1991	WPG	6					42	2266	54.0	76	21	21	100.0	16	22	72.7
1992	WPG	11					89	5176	58.2	86	47	48	97.9	47	62	75.8
1993	WPG	6					105	5990	57.0	95	68	69	98.6	45	56	80.4
1994	WPG	15					104	5971	57.4	86	72	72	100.0	42	58	72.4
1995	WPG	5					75	4135	55.1	95	34	34	100.0	36	49	73.5
1996	WPG	9					69	4314	62.5	95	36	36	100.0	37	51	72.5
1997	WPG	7					79	4707	59.6	91	40	40	100.0	39	54	72.2
1998	WPG	6					60	3360	56.0	85	30	30	100.0	36	54	66.7
1999	WPG	12					60	3073	51.2	70	27	27	100.0	34	49	69.4
2000	WPG	8	66	2830	42.9	70	85	5071	59.7	95	52	52	100.0	45	58	77.6
2001	WPG	12					79	4804	60.8	95	54	54	100.0	31	51	60.8
2002	WPG	12	1	52	52.0	52	93	5626	60.5	95	56	56	100.0	45	62	72.6
2003	WPG	9	136	5661	41.6	73	84	4471	53.2	90	48	48	100.0	47	61	77.0
2004	WPG	8					78	4232	54.3	95	41	41	100.0	39	50	78.0
2005	WPG	8	5	199	39.8	49	82	4454	54.3	94	46	49	93.9	28	40	70.0
2006	WPG	15	113	4844	42.9	76	64	3739	58.4	80	32	32	100.0	30	43	69.8
2007	WPG	6	7	397	56.7	85	43	2704	62.9	95	28	28	100.0	20	33	60.6
2009	WPG	4	30	1319	44.0	74					0	0		0	0	
Totals		159	358	15302	42.7	85	1291	74093	57.4	95	732	737	99.3	617	853	72.3
BILL WHISLER																
1964	WPG	1	32	1082	33.8	63										
WILFORD WHITE																
1955	TOR	0									8	9	88.9	0	0	
REG WHITEHOUSE																

Year	Team	S	PUNT	YDS	AVG	LG	KO	YDS	AVG	LG	CON	CONA	PCT	FG	FGA	PCT
1952	SAS	1					11	543	49.4	57	5	5	100.0	0	1	0.0
1953	SAS	0									5	6	83.3	0	0	
1955	SAS	0					1	50	50.0	50	4	5	80.0	0	1	0.0
1956	SAS	0					2	92	46.0	47	35	41	85.4	13	17	76.5
1957	SAS	0									28	36	77.8	4	7	57.1
1958	SAS	3									0	0		3	9	33.3
1959	SAS	0	1	42	42.0	42	16	807	50.4	70	22	25	88.0	6	8	75.0
1960	SAS	1					26	1322	50.8	65	17	19	89.5	3	7	42.9
1961	SAS	4					39	1837	47.1	70	20	23	87.0	12	27	44.4
1962	SAS	5					30	1330	44.3	64	15	18	83.3	7	17	41.2
1963	SAS	2					20	898	44.9	62	10	19	52.6	6	11	54.5
1964	SAS	1									6	9	66.7	3	5	60.0
1965	SAS	0					8	328	41.0	55						
Totals		17	1	42	42.0	42	153	7207	47.1	70	167	206	81.1	57	110	51.8
KEN WHITLOCK																
1948	TOR	2														
SEAN WHYTE																
2009	BC	3	71	2947	41.5	68	57	3402	59.7	71	24	24	100.0	21	29	72.4%
2010	BC	3	15	601	40.1	59	9	540	60.0	79	6	6	100.0	6	6	100.0%
2011	MTL	12	115	4746	41.3	68	91	5129	56.4	94	50	50	100.0	45	52	86.5%
Totals		18	201	8294	41.3	68	157	9071	57.8	94	80	80	100.0	72	87	82.8%
ERIC WILBUR																
2010	HAM	5	85	3651	43.0	69	25	1437	57.5	70						
TOM WILKINSON																
1974	EDM	0	9	218	24.2	36					0	0		0	1	0.0
1979	EDM	0	1	40	40.0	40					0	0		0	0	
Totals		0	10	258	25.8	40					0	0		0	1	0.0
PAUL WILLIAMS																
1971	WPG	0					4	130	32.5	63						
RODNEY WILLIAMS																
2006	EDM	1	7	284	40.6	56										
STAN WILLIAMS																
1956	SAS	0					11	581	52.8	88						
SLADE WILLIS																
1974	BC	3	132	5258	39.8	71								0		
1975	BC	0	5	161	32.2	46								0		
Totals		3	137	5419	39.6	71								0		
RAY WILLSEY																
1955	EDM	0									0	1	0.0	0	0	
FRED WILMOT																
1948	CAL	0									15			5		
JERRY WILSON																
1963	TOR	2					17	851	50.1	75	1	3	33.3	1	4	25.0
JONATHAN WILSON																
1992	TOR	0	1	51	51.0	51										
MEL WILSON																
1946	WPG	0									1	1	100.0	0		
JOHN WINTERMEYER																
1975	BC	5					31	1667	53.8	70	17	17	100.0	5	14	35.7
NORM WINTON																
1965	WPG	3					31	1459	47.1	70	18	25	72.0	2	7	28.6
1966	WPG	5					43	2278	53.0	68	26	31	83.9	11	20	55.0
Totals		8					74	3737	50.5	70	44	56	78.6	13	27	48.1
TODD WISEMAN																
1992	HAM	0	1	48	48.0	48					0	0		0	0	
1994	HAM	0									0	0		0	1	0.0
Totals		0	1	48	48.0	48					0	0		0	1	0.0
GENE WLASIUK																
1965	SAS	0	33	1180	35.8	54										
1966	SAS	0	4	131	32.8	36										
1967	SAS	0	2	118	59.0	90										
Totals		0	39	1429	36.6	90										
DUANE WOOD																
1959	HAM	0	2	96	48.0	52										
JIM WOOD																
1959	BC	0	26	1076	41.4	57										
COWBOY WOODRUFF																
1960	EDM	0									4	4	100.0	0	0	
BILLY WOODS																
1968	MTL	0					2	56	28.0	32						
ROD WOODWARD																
1972	OTT	0	1	25	25.0	25										
1974	OTT	0	1	14	14.0	14										
Totals		0	2	39	19.5	25										
TOM WORTHINGTON																
1951	HAM	1														
ROY WRIGHT																
1946	SAS	0									2			0		
1947	SAS	0									2			0		
1950	SAS	0									5	6	83.3	0	0	
Totals		0									9	6	83.3	0	0	
SCOTTY WRIGHT																
1946	HAM	4									5			2		
BILL WUSYK																
1946	CAL	4									4			8		
1947	CAL	1									9	10	90.0	4		
1948	CAL	0									11			1		
Totals		5									24	10	90.0	13	0	
BUBBA WYCHE																
1971	SAS	0	1	36	36.0	36										
HARVEY WYLIE																
1956	CAL	0					6	257	42.8	62						
1959	CAL	0	1	25	25.0	25										
1961	CAL	0	3	127	42.3	72	1	14	14.0	14						
1962	CAL	0	1	58	58.0	54										
Totals		0	5	210	42.0	72	7	271	38.7	62						
MACK YOHO																
1958	OTT	5	9	230	25.6	53	44	2420	55.0	64	11	19	57.9	4		
1959	OTT	0					10	554	55.4	66	5	6	83.3	1	3	33.3
Totals		5	9	230	25.6	53	54	2974	55.1	66	16	25	64.0	5	3	33.3
CHUCK ZAPIEC																
1978	MTL	0	1	35	35.0	35										

Year	Team	S	PUNT	YDS	AVG	LG	KO	YDS	AVG	LG	CON	CONA	PCT	FG	FGA	PCT
RAY ZASO																
1946	HAM	1														
LUIS ZENDEJAS																
1995	BIR	4					70	3867	55.2	65	38	38	100.0	34	43	79.1
JOE ZUGER																
1962	HAM	3	120	5197	43.3	60										
1963	HAM	2	86	3462	40.3	65										
1964	HAM	2	63	2695	42.8	69										
1965	HAM	13	134	5990	44.7	81										
1966	HAM	8	118	5195	44.0	81										
1967	HAM	17	125	5726	45.8	81										
1968	HAM	7	129	6249	48.4	85										
1969	HAM	6	97	4676	48.2	73										
1970	HAM	1	62	2900	46.8	65										
1971	HAM	9	141	6840	48.5	76										
Totals		68	1075	48930	45.5	85										

CPSIA information can be obtained at www.ICGtesting.com
Printed in the USA
LVOW031658030712

288738LV00019B/1/P